ISBN 978-0-260-06314-4
PIBN 10925419

FB &c Ltd, Dalton House, 60 Windsor Avenue, London, SW19 2RR.
Company number 08720141. Registered in England and Wales.

For support please visit www.forgottenbooks.com

REPORTS OF CASES

ADJUDGED AND DETERMINED

IN THE

Supreme Court of Judicature

AND

COURT FOR THE TRIAL OF IMPEACHMENTS

AND

CORRECTION OF ERRORS

OF

THE STATE OF NEW YORK.

WITH COPIOUS NOTES AND REFERENCES, TABLES OF CITATIONS, &c.

BY

EDWIN BURRITT SMITH

AND

ERNEST HITCHCOCK,

COUNSELORS AT LAW.

BOOK VIII.

CONTAINING COWEN'S REPORTS, VOLUMES 3–6.

THE LAWYERS' CO-OPERATIVE PUBLISHING COMPANY,

NEWARK, WAYNE COUNTY, NEW YORK.

1884.

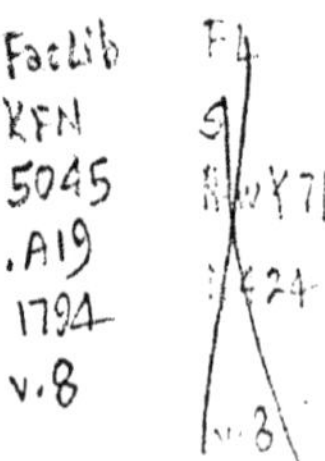

E. R. Andrews, Printer, Rochester, N. Y.

JUDGES

OF THE

SUPREME COURT

OF THE

STATE OF NEW YORK,

DURING THE PERIOD OF THESE REPORTS.

JOHN SAVAGE, *Chief Justice.*

JACOB SUTHERLAND, } *Justices.*
JOHN WOODWORTH, }

CIRCUIT JUDGES.

FIRST CIRCUIT.

OGDEN EDWARDS.

SECOND CIRCUIT.

SAMUEL R. BETTS.*

THIRD CIRCUIT.

WILLIAM A. DUER.

FOURTH CIRCUIT.

R. HYDE WALWORTH.

FIFTH CIRCUIT.

NATHAN WILLIAMS.

SIXTH CIRCUIT.

SAMUEL NELSON.

SEVENTH CIRCUIT

ENOS T. THROOP.

EIGHTH CIRCUIT

WM. B. ROCHESTER.†

SAMUEL A. TALCOTT, *Attorney-General.*

*Succeeded Feb'y 21, 1827, by Hon. James Emott.
†Succeeded April 18, 1826, by Hon. John Birdsall.

JUDGES

OF THE

COURT FOR THE TRIAL OF IMPEACHMENTS

AND THE

CORRECTION OF ERRORS,

DURING THE TIME OF THE FOLLOWING REPORTS.

ERASTUS ROOT,* Lieutenant-Governor, *President.*
JAMES TALLMADGE,† Lieutenant-Governer, *President.*
NATHAN SANFORD, *Chancellor.*
JOHN SAVAGE, *Ch. J.*
JACOB SUTHERLAND, } *Justices of the Supreme Court.*
JOHN WOODWORTH,

SENATORS.

FIRST DISTRICT.

WALTER BOWNE,* JASPER WARD, JOHN LEFFERTS, DAVID GARDINER, CADWALLADER D. COLDEN.†

SECOND DISTRICT.

JOHN SUDAM,* STEPHEN THORN, JAMES BURT, WILLIAM NELSON, WELLS LAKE.†

THIRD DISTRICT.

CHARLES E. DUDLEY,* EDWARD P. LIVINGSTON, JAMES MALLORY, JACOB HAIGHT, RICHARD MCMICHAEL.†

FOURTH DISTRICT.

MELANCTON WHEELER,* ARCHIBALD M'INTYRE, JOHN CRAMER, SILAS WRIGHT, JR., JOHN CRARY.†

FIFTH DISTRICT.

ALVIN BRONSON,* SHERMAN WOOSTER, PERLEY KEYES, THOMAS GREENLY, GEORGE BRAYTON.†

SIXTH DISTRICT.

FARRAND STRANAHAN,* TILLY LINDE, ISAAC OGDEN, LATHAM A. BURROWS, STUKELY ELLSWORTH.†

SEVENTH DISTRICT.

BYRAM GREEN,* JONAS EARLL, JR., JESSE CLARK, JEDIAH MORGAN, JOHN C. SPENCER.†

EIGHTH DISTRICT.

DAVID EASON,* JAMES M'CALL, HEMAN J. REDFIELD, JOHN BOWMAN, SAMUEL WILKINSON.†

SAMUEL A. TALCOTT, *Attorney-General.*

*For 1824 sessions only. †For 1825 sessions only.

GENERAL TABLE OF CASES REPORTED

IN THIS BOOK.

CASES REPORTED IN COWEN, VOL. III.

CASES REPORTED IN COWEN, VOL. IV.

CASES REPORTED IN COWEN, VOL. V.

CASES REPORTED IN COWEN, VOL. VI.

CITATIONS

IN OPINIONS OF THE JUDGES CONTAINED IN THIS BOOK—COWEN, VOLUMES 3-6.

CASES CITED.

A

Abeel *v.* Radcliff, 15 Johns. 505, 507 .... 4 Cow. 350, 351
Abingdon's case, 2 Anst. 381.... 5 Cow. 568
Ackley *v.* Hoskins, 14 Johns. 374 5 Cow. 172
Adam *v.* Kers, 1 B. & P. 360 ... 5 Cow. 386
Adams *v.* Pease, 2 Com. 483.... 6 Cow. 376
Adams *v.* Supervisors, &c., 8 Johns. 323, 326... 4 Cow. 141 ; 5 Cow. 649
Adams *v.* Weare, 1 Bro. Ch. 567 .... 3 Cow. 511, 514
Alcott *v.* Phelps, 1 Cow. 170.... 4 Cow. 143
Alendorf *v.* Stickle, 2 Cow. 412 .... 5 Cow. 425 ; 6 Cow. 58
Alexander *v.* Gibson, 2 Camp. 555 6 Cow. 100
Alfred *v.* Fitz James, 3 Esp. 4... 5 Cow. 533
Alsop *v.* Caines, 10 Johns. 396, 399 .... 5 Cow. 235, 369
Amory *v.* Fairbanks, 3 Mass. 562 5 Cow. 382
Ancaster *v.* Mayer, 1 Bro. Ch. 462 3 Cow. 145
Anderson *v.* Coxeter, 1 Str. 301.. 5 Cow. 425
Anderson *v.* Fox, 2 Hen. & M. 245 4 Cow. 744
Anderson *v.* Hayman, 1 H. Bl. 120 4 Cow. 435
Anderson *v.* Pitcher, 2 B. & P. 164 6 Cow. 268
Andrews *v.* Hesiat, 4 Cow. 529, 530 *n.*.... 6 Cow. 47
Andrews *v.* Montgomery, 19 Johns. 162 .... 4 Cow. 295
Andrews *v.* Vanduzer, 11 Johns. 38 6 Cow. 122
Andrews *v.* Waring, 20 Johns. 153 .... 3 Cow. 332, 333
Angel *v.* Felton, 8 Johns. 115... 3 Cow. 150
Ann Davis' case, 4 Co. 17....... 5 Cow. 359
Anonymous, 1 Johns. 315, 350 ....3 Cow. 435 ; 5 Cow. 596, 612, 617
Anonymous, 2 Salk. 588........ 6 Cow. 300
Anonymous, 3 Salk. 3.......... 5 Cow. 454
Anonymous, Hard. 420.......... 5 Cow. 608
Anonymous, 2 Cow. 579........ 4 Cow. 54
Anonymous, 1 Str. 423.......... 6 Cow. 738
Anonymous, Dyer 179.......... 5 Cow. 59
Apsey, *Ex parte*, 3 Bro. Ch. Cas. 265 .... 6 Cow. 502
Argal, Lady, *v.* Cheney, Palm. 403 6 Cow. 749
Arnold *v.* Bell, 1 Hayw. 397, *note* 3 Cow. 622
Arnold *v.* Crane, 8 Johns., 79–82 5 Cow. 668
Arnold *v.* U.S., 9 Cranch, 104–120 3 Cow. 158
Armroyd *v.* Union Ins. Co., 2 Binn. 394 .... 3 Cow. 118
Armroyd *v.* Union Ins. Co., 3 Binn. 448 .... 6 Cow. 510
Armstrong *v.* Pierse, 3 Burr. 1901 4 Cow. 598
Aslin *v.* Parkin, 2 Burr. 667, 668 4 Cow. 339
Atkinson *v.* Baker, 4 D. & E. 229 5 Cow. 389
Atkinson *v.* Braybrooke, 4 Camp. 380 .... 3 Cow. 421
Atkins *v.* Barnwell, 2 East, 505.. 5 Cow. 664
Atkins *v.* Hill, Cowp. 284....... 3 Cow. 144
Attersol *v.* Bryant, 1 Camp. 410. 6 Cow. 655
Atty-Gen. *v.* Bowman, 2 B. & P. 532, *n.* (*a*).... 6 Cow. 675
Atty-Gen. *v.* Brewers Co., 1 P. Wms. 376...3 Cow. 430 ; 5 Cow. 612, 617
Atty-Gen. *v.* Day, 1 Ves. 220.... 3 Cow. 508
Atty-Gen. *v.* Grote, 3 Met. 316.. 6 Cow. 341
Atty-Gen. *v.* Moses, &c., 2 Madd. Ch. 294 .... 4 Cow. 700
Atty-Gen. *v.* Parish, 4 B. & P. 104 5 Cow. 196
Augusta *v.* Paris, 16 Johns. 281. 3 Cow. 301
Austin *v.* Bell, 20 Johns. 442–447 .... 5 Cow. 560, 561, 570
Austen *v.* Willward, Cro. Eliz. 860 6 Cow. 315
Aylet *v* Hill, 2 Dick. 551........ 5 Cow. 381

B

Bach *v.* Owen, 5 T. R. 409...... 5 Cow. 518
Bachtlinck *v.* Schneider, 3 Esp. 58 6 Cow. 429
Backwell's case, 1 Vern. 152.... 5 Cow. 194
Bailey *v.* Caldwell, 3 Johns. 451. 5 Cow. 439
Bain *v.* Clark, 10 Johns. 432.... 6 Cow. 708
Bailey *v.* Devereux, 1 Vern. 269. 6 Cow. 464
Bainbridge *v.* Neilson, 10 East, 341 4 Cow. 242
Baker's case, 3 Coke, 25........ 6 Cow. 622
Baker *v.* Phoenix Ins. Co., 8 Johns. 319 .... 6 Cow. 676
Baldwin *v.* Cole, 6 Mod. 212.... 5 Cow. 326
Ball *v.* Herbert, 3 T. R. 262 .... 3 Cow. 219
Ballard *v.* Walker, 3 Johns. Cas. 60 6 Cow. 448
Ballou *v.* Kip, 7 Johns. 177..... 6 Cow. 745
Bancker Lawrence *v.* Ash, 9 Johns. 250 .... 4 Cow. 420
Bancroft *v.* White, 1 Cai. 190... 5 Cow. 301
Banerman *v.* Radenius, 7 T. R. 665 .... 6 Cow. 100
Bank of Auburn *v.* Throop, 18 Johns. 505 .... 5 Cow. 444
Bank of Columbia *v.* Newcomb, 6 Johns. 98 .... 6 Cow. 696
Bank of Orange *v.* Wakeman, 1 Cow. 46.........4 Cow. 553 ; 6 Cow. 468
Bank of Utica *v.* Smith, 18 Johns. 239, 240 .... 5 Cow. 305, 309
Bantleon *v.* Smith, 2 Binn. 146.. 4 Cow. 575
Barker, Matter of, 2 Johns. Ch. 332 .... 4 Cow. 217
Barker *v.* Phoenix Ins. Co., 8 Johns. 307 .... 6 Cow. 415
Barnard *v.* Gostling, 2 East, 570. 5 Cow. 685
Barnardiston *v.* Lingwood, 2 Atk. 133 .... 3 Cow. 507
Barnes *v.* Greenwel, Cro. Eliz. 858 5 Cow. 199
Barnes *v.* Hollaway, 8 T. R. 150. 5 Cow. 515
Barney *v.* Dewey, 13 Johns. 224, 325, 395 .... 6 Cow. 354
Barrie *v.* Dana, 20 Johns. 307... 3 Cow. 57
Barrington *v.* Turner, 3 Lev. 28. 4 Cow. 352

D

E

F

G

I

J

Johnson v. Nott, 1 Vern. 271, 272 3 Cow. 514
Johnson v. Stagg, 2 Johns. 250.. 3 Cow. 80
Jones v. Barkley, Doug. 690.... 6 Cow. 297
Jones v. Caswell, 3 Johns. Cas. 32 4 Cow. 732
Jones v. Cook, 1 Cow. 349...... 5 Cow. 181
Jones v. Cooper, Cowp. 227..... 4 Cow. 435
Jones v. Fales, 4 Mass. 245...... 5 Cow. 187
Jones v. Gardner, 10 Johns. 266. 5 Cow. 405
Jordaine v. Lashbrooke, 7 T. R. 597–601 .... 5 Cow. 159
Joynes v. Stratham, 3 Atk. 388 3 Cow. 507
Judah v. Harris, 19 Johns. 144.. 5 Cow. 187
Judson v. Wass, 11 Johns. 525.. 3 Cow. 520
Juhel v. Church, 2 Johns. Cas. 333...................... 6 Cow. 331
Jumel v. Mar. Ins. Co., 1 Johns. 425...................... 6 Cow. 431

K

Kahl v. Jansen, 4 Taunt. 565.... 6 Cow. 100
Kane v. Com. Ins. Co., N. Y., 8 Johns. 234................ 3 Cow. 219
Kane v. Sanger, 14 Johns. 89 ....5 Cow. 139, 140
Kanes v. Smith, 12 Johns. 156 ....3 Cow. 423, 435, 437, 599, 613
Keath's case, 1 Salk. 103........ 5 Cow. 52
Keating v. Price, 1 Johns. Cas. 22 5 Cow. 498
Keble v. Thompson, 3 Bro. Ch. Cas. 112.................. 6 Cow. 503
Keen v. Stuckely, Gilb. 155, 156. 3 Cow. 521
Keith v. Jones, 9 Johns. 120.... 5 Cow. 187
Kellett v. Kellett, 1 Ball. & B. 543 .... 6 Cow. 341
Kellogg v. Griffin, 17 Johns. 274 5 Cow. 395
Kelsey v. Deyo, 3 Cow. 133..... 6 Cow. 340
Kendell v. John, 2 Salk. 505; Fortes, 125................ 6 Cow. 294
Kenebel v. Scrafton, 13 Ves. 370 5 Cow. 565
Kennedy v. Strong, 14 Johns. 128 5 Cow. 614
Kent v. Dodge, 8 Johns. 447.... 4 Cow. 554
Kent v. Welch, 7 Johns. 258.... 6 Cow. 126
Ketchum v. Clark, 6 Johns. 144 ....5 Cow. 536; 6 Cow. 704
Ketchum v. Evertson, 13 Johns. 363...................... 6 Cow. 22
Ketchum v. Ketchum, 4 Cow. 87 ....4 Cow. 551, 552; 5 Cow. 268
Kerrison v. Cooke, 3 Camp. 362. 6 Cow. 492
Ketletas v. Fleet, 7 Johns. 324.. 5 Cow. 483
Keyes v. Stone, 5 Mass. 391 .... 4 Cow. 289
Kien v. Stukely, 1 Bro. P. C. 191 ....3 Cow. 513, 520
Kies v. Tifft, 1 Cow. 98......4 Cow. 184, 188
Kilham v. Ward, 2 Mass. 343... 6 Cow. 280
Killmer v. Crary, 13 Johns. 229. 6 Cow. 260
King v. Baldwin, 17 Johns. 388. 4 Cow. 728
King v. Berry, 4 T. R. 218 ..... 5 Cow. 515
King v. Bp. of Ely, 1 W. Bl. 187 4 Cow. 381
King v. Boston, 4 East, 582...... 6 Cow. 31
King v. Butler, 15 Johns. 281... ....5 Cow. 312, 664; 6 Cow. 280
King (The) v. Eltham, 5 East, 113 6 Cow. 763
King v. Emonds, 4 Barn. & A. 470...................... 6 Cow. 563
King v. Hardwick, 11 East, 578. 3 Cow. 623
King v. Inhab. of Aickles, 12 Mod. 554.................. 5 Cow. 367
King v. Inhab. of Eriswell, 3 T. R. 723................... 5 Cow. 239
King v. Inhab. of Holy Trin., &c., 3 D. & E. 607......... 5 Cow. 367
King v. Inhab. of Martley, 5 East. 41 .... 6 Cow. 717
King v. Jolliffe, 4 T. R. 290..6 Cow. 164, 165
King v. Judd, 2 T. R. 267...... 5 Cow. 58
King v. Lenox, 19 Johns. 236... 6 Cow. 177
King v. City of London, 3 Harg. St. Tr. 545................ 6 Cow. 209
King v. Marks, 3 East, 157–165.5 Cow. 52–58
King v. Martyr, 13 East, 58, n.. 6 Cow. 260
King v. Peppard, Carth. 280; Comb. 227.............5 Cow. 185, 186
King v. Poynes, 3 Bulst. 113...5 Cow. 58, 60
King v. Stow, 6 Johns. Ch. 323. 3 Cow. 250
King v. Sir Henry Vane, 1 Keb. 324...................... 6 Cow. 561
King v. Wilson, 2 Str., 873..... 4 Cow. 436
King v. Woolf, 1 Chit. 401...... 4 Cow. 33
King v. City of Worcester, Skin. 101...................... 6 Cow. 560
King v. Wyer, 2 T. R. 77....... 5 Cow. 52
Kingston's (Duchess of) case, 11 St. Tri. 11 (fol.) 261, 20 (8 vo.) 261.............3 Cow. 126; 4 Cow. 562
Kingston v. M'Intosh, 1 Camp. 518...................... 3 Cow. 421
Kinnion v. Davies, Cro. Car. 487 4 Cow. 353
Kip v. Brigham, 6 Johns. 158.4 Cow. 258, 345
Kip v. Brigham, 7 Johns. 168.4 Cow. 258, 345
Kirby v. Cogswell, 1 Cai. 484, 485 5 Cow. 439
Knight v. Crockford, 1 Esp. 190 6 Cow. 18
Knight v. Maclean, 3 Bro. Ch. 496 3 Cow. 157
Korts v. Carpenter, 5 Johns. 120 4 Cow. 343

L

Lacon v. Briggs, 3 Atk. 105..... 4 Cow. 641
Lacy's case, 6 Ves. 625, 631..... ....4 Cow. 735, 738, 744
Ladd v. Blunt, 4 Mass. 403...... 4 Cow. 418
Lamb v. Bunce, 4 M. & S. 275.. 5 Cow. 668
Lambert v. Paulding, 18 Johns. 311...................4 Cow. 411, 469
Langdale v. Trimmer, 15 East, 291 5 Cow. 308
Langferd v. Pitt, 2 P. Wms. 630 3 Cow. 519
Langfert v. Tiler, 1 Salk. 113... 3 Cow. 85
Langthom v. Allnutt, 4 Taunt. 511 6 Cow. 100
Lansing v. Gaine, 2 Johns. 304.. ....5 Cow. 536; 6 Cow. 704
Lansing v. Lansing, 18 Johns. 503 4 Cow. 447
Lansing v. Prendergast, 9 Johns. 127...................... 5 Cow. 278
Law v. Hollingsworth, 1 T. R. 160 6 Cow. 273
Lawler v. Keaquick, 1 Johns. Cas. 178, 179............... 6 Cow. 134
Lawrence v. Dale, 3 Johns. Ch. 23 4 Cow. 567
Lawrence v. Dickinson, 1 Cow. 580...................... 3 Cow. 381
Lawrence v. Grose, 20 Johns. 382 5 Cow. 308
Lawrence v. Ocean Ins. Co., 11 Johns. 245, note............ 4 Cow. 401
Lawrence v. Van Horne, 1 Cow. 286...................... 6 Cow. 680
Lawton v. Lawton, 3 Atk. 12... ....5 Cow. 327; 6 Cow. 668
Lawton v. Salmon, 1 H. Bl. 259. 6 Cow. 668
Laxton v. Peat, 2 Camp. 185.... 6 Cow. 492
Lazarus v. Bryson, 3 Binn. 64... 4 Cow. 744
Le Baron v. Crombie, 14 Mass. 234, 236...................6 Cow. 164, 165
Le Guen v. Gouverneur, 1 Johns. Cas. 493.................. 5 Cow. 735
Lee v. Clark, 2 East, 333........ 6 Cow. 294
Lee v. Lee, 2 Vern. 548......... 5 Cow. 733

M

N

S

28

U

V

W

STATUTES CITED.

REPORTS OF CASES

ARGUED AND DETERMINED

IN THE

SUPREME COURT,

AND IN THE

COURT FOR THE TRIAL OF IMPEACHMENTS

AND

THE CORRECTION OF ERRORS,

IN THE

STATE OF NEW YORK.

BY ESEK COWEN,

COUNSELOR AT LAW.

VOL. III.

3

1835.

JUDGES

OF THE

SUPREME COURT

OF THE

STATE OF NEW YORK,

DURING THE PERIOD OF THESE REPORTS.

JOHN SAVAGE, *Chief Justice.*
JACOB SUTHERLAND, *Associate Justice.*
JOHN WOODWORTH, *Associate Justice.*

CIRCUIT JUDGES.

FIRST CIRCUIT.
OGDEN EDWARDS.

SECOND CIRCUIT.
SAMUEL R. BETTS.

THIRD CIRCUIT.
WILLIAM A. DUER.

FOURTH CIRCUIT.
R. HYDE WALWORTH.

FIFTH CIRCUIT.
NATHAN WILLIAMS.

SIXTH CIRCUIT.
SAMUEL NELSON.

SEVENTH CIRCUIT.
ENOS T. THROOP.

EIGHTH CIRCUIT.
WM. B. ROCHESTER.

SAMUEL A. TALCOTT, *Attorney-General.*

CASES

ARGUED AND DETERMINED

IN THE

SUPREME COURT

OF THE

STATE OF NEW YORK,

IN

AUGUST TERM, 1824, IN THE FORTY-NINTH YEAR OF OUR INDEPENDENCE.

ROBERTSON
v.
CROWELL, Impleaded with PADD and SNOWDON.

Discharge from Imprisonment—How Defendant may Avail Himself of it.

To avail himself of a discharge of the person from imprisonment, the defendant should plead such discharge; or he may give it in evidence on the trial, and if found valid, this finding should make a part of the *postea*, on which a modified judgment may be entered.

But where this course was overruled by the circuit judge, and the plaintiff did not express a desire to contest the discharge at the Circuit, nor impeached it by affidavit, on motion, in the Supreme Court, to have the judgment qualified, the motion was granted.

ASSUMPSIT. The defendant, Crowell, pleaded the general issue, and gave notice, with that plea, that he should, on the trial, give in evidence his discharge under the Act for Abolishing Imprisonment for Debt in Certain Cases; and at the last Circuit Court in the City of N. Y., the cause coming on to be tried, the discharge was accordingly offered in evidence; but the circuit judge, supposing this to be the subject of a special application to this court, overruled the evidence, and directed a general verdict for the plaintiff; and now,

Mr. W. Thompson, for Crowell, moved that the judgment to be rendered be qualified and confined to the property of Crowell, so that no execution issue against his body.

14*] **Mr. W. King*, contra, said that by allowing the discharge to be introduced on a summary application, the plaintiff was deprived of all opportunity to contest its validity before the jury. Crowell had a chance to prove, and have it tried at the circuit, and it is now too late. *Palmer* v. *Hutchins*, 1 Cow., 42. If the judge erred, the proper course was to make a case, and bring up the question in that form.

WOODWORTH, *J.* You did not dispute the validity of the discharge at the circuit.

SAVAGE, *Ch. J.* Do you now deny this by affidavit?

Mr. King. We do not deny it, because we supposed this to be the wrong time for doing so.

Curia. The judge should have received evidence of the discharge, and on the jury finding in favor of its validity, this should have been indorsed as a part of the *postea*, and returned; upon which the plaintiff should have taken his judgment so modified as not to reach the defendant's person. But the discharge was not contested at the circuit, nor is it now questioned. We, therefore, grant the application, under the special circumstances of this case.

Motion granted.

Cited in—3 Barb. Ch., 363.

JOHNSON *v.* ROGERS AND ROGERS.

Change of Venue—Affidavit.

The affidavit to change the venue must state the advice of counsel as to the materiality of the witnesses.

MR. E. COWEN moved to change the venue, in this cause, from the County of Warren to the County of Saratoga, on an affidavit, in which one of the defendants swore that he had upwards of 20 material witnesses residing in the latter county, and in counties south of this. He also swore that he had a good and substantial defense on the merits, as he was advised by counsel and verily believed; but the affidavit did not state that he was advised by counsel that his witnesses were material; and, for this omission,

**Mr. R. Weston* opposed the motion. [*15

Curia. We require the same strictness, in this respect, as in showing the defense on the merits generally. The party must, in both cases, swear to the advice of counsel.

Motion denied, with costs.

JACKSON, ex dem. GORMAN, v. HOOKER.

Default of Plaintiff—Offer to Stipulate and Pay Costs of Circuit—Motion by Defendant for Judgment as in Case of Nonsuit—Costs.

After first default in trying cause, plaintiff offers, if defendant will make out his bill, to stipulate and pay costs of Circuit.

Defendant does not make his bill, but moves for judgment as in case of nonsuit; and rule that plaintiff stipulate and pay costs of Circuit, but that defendant pay costs of motion.

Applications to this court, in cases where a party may have the effect of his motion without coming here, are to be discountenanced.

THE plaintiff having made default in trying this cause, pursuant to notice for that purpose, at the first circuit after issue joined, the plaintiff's attorney told the defendant's attorney that if he would make out his bill of costs he would pay it, and stipulate to try at the next circuit. This he did not do, but now moved for judgment as in case of nonsuit.

Mr. S. Forman, for the motion.

Mr. D. Woods, contra.

Curia. The plaintiff's attorney must now stipulate, and pay the costs of the Circuit, but the defendant must pay the costs of this motion. Applications to this court should certainly be discountenanced, where we cannot but see that the party might have taken the full effect of his application without coming here. A formal tender of the money or stipulation was not necessary till the defendant had made out his bill of costs. There is no pretense that the offer of the plaintiff's attorney was not in perfect good faith, and we consider the proceeding on his part as equivalent to a tender.

Rule accordingly.

16*] *THE PEOPLE
v.
JAMES L. THURMAN.

Nonsuit—People not Subject to.

The people cannot be nonsuited.

In this respect, as well as in many others, they enjoy the prerogatives of the British Crown.

MR. D. RUSSELL, for the defendant, moved for judgment as in case of nonsuit.

Mr. W. H. Maynard, contra, objected that judgment of nonsuit cannot be rendered against the people.

Mr. Russell said the suit was prosecuted for the benefit of one V. B., and he wished the court to make such an order in this matter as finally to dispose of it, even if they could not render a technical judgment of nonsuit; but it not sufficiently appearing, by the affidavits which he produced, that this was the case, and these affidavits not having been served on V. B., and he having no notice of this motion,

The Court declined interfering. They said the prerogatives of the people were in this, and many other respects, similar to those of the British Crown. In this point of view they cannot be nonsuited.

Motion denied.

Cited in—8 Barb., 193; 7 How. Pr., 250.

GRISWOLD v. STEWART ET AL.

Issues Joined at Different Times in Same Cause—Place on Calendar.

Where there are several issues in law joined at different times, in the same cause, its order on the calendar is determined by the date of the first issue.

THE defendant pleaded four pleas, and in Oct., 1821, there was a demurrer to the first, and joinder, and issue on the others. Afterwards the defendants amended the first plea, but the plaintiff again demurred, and there was a joinder in demurrer Feb. 5, 1822. Afterwards a further plea was interposed, by leave of the court, on special application, to which the plaintiff demurred, and there was a joinder in demurrer thereon in May last; and the plaintiff's attorney had noticed the cause for argument at this term, and placed it on the calendar according to the date of the first issue in law; and on the first day of this term,

**Mr. D. Kellogg*, for the defendants, [*17 moved to correct the calendar by placing it according to the date of the last issue.

Mr. J. Lynch, contra.

Curia. The cause is correctly placed at the date of the first issue.

Motion denied.

Cited in—6 Cow., 32.

CLUTE v. VAN SLYCK.

Action against Sheriff—Costs on Certiorari.

The Statute (1 R. L., 155, sec. 1) giving the sheriff, &c., double costs, on verdict, &c., in his favor, does not apply to a proceeding upon *certiorari*.

Citation—Sess. 24, ch. 47, sec. 1.

ON *certiorari*. The defendant, being sheriff of the County of Schenectady, was sued before a justice of the peace, for an escape of a prisoner upon execution; and the justice gave judgment in his favor. On *certiorari* to this court the judgment was affirmed; and now,

Mr. N. F. Beck moved for double costs, upon the Statute (sess. 24, ch. 47, sec. 1; 1 R. L., 155).

Mr. S. A. Foot, contra, said the Statute did not apply to a proceeding on *certiorari*; that it contemplated an action in which there could be a verdict or discontinuance, or a nonsuit.

Curia. We do not think the Statute applies to this case.

Motion denied.

JACKSON, ex dem. TITUS. v. JONES.

Deeds Relied on by Defendant in Ejectment—Ordered Placed in Clerk's Office, for Plaintiff's Inspection.

Rule made that the defendant deposit deeds, which he relied on in defense of an ejectment brought against him, in the clerk's office of M., to the end that the plaintiff might, with witnesses, inspect the same.

This rule made on affidavit of the lessor of the plaintiff that he expected thus to be enabled to prove the deeds forgeries.

MR. A. CONKLING, for the plaintiff, moved for a rule that the defendant cause two certain deeds, described in the affidavits 18*] *whereon he moved, to be deposited in the clerk's office of the County of Monroe, or in such other place as the court should direct, to the end that the lessor of the plaintiff and his witnesses might have access thereto. This motion was founded on various affidavits, by which it appeared that the defendant relied on these deeds for his defense in this action, and on an affidavit of the lessor of the plaintiff, that he expected to be able to prove, with proper opportunity for that purpose, that both the deeds were forgeries.

Mr. A. Sampson, contra, opposed the motion as unprecedented. It might go to convict the defendant of forgery, and the court will never require a party to furnish his adversary with the means for this purpose. He also read an affidavit of the defendant, that he had control of but one of these deeds, and that the other would be necessary, as he was advised by his counsel and believed, in the execution of a commission which had been issued in this cause; but he did not swear that he would not use both deeds on the trial.

The Court granted a rule that the deeds should be deposited with the Monroe Co. clerk, for the purpose mentioned on the motion, 8 days before the next circuit in Monroe. They said this would give time for first using the deeds on the execution of the commission.

RULE. On, &c., ordered, that the said defendant, Samuel Jones, cause the deeds from Nathan Wood to David Wood, and from the said Nathan Wood to Seth Jones, in the affidavit of the lessor of the plaintiff mentioned, to be deposited, at least 8 days before the next Circuit Court to be held in and for the County of Monroe, with the clerk of the said county.[1]

Cited in—4 Cow., 401; 20 Hun, 536; 25 How. Pr., 528; 19 Abb. Pr., 393; 1 Rob., 665, 686.

1.—Mr. C. Graham (in whose behalf Mr. Conkling moved) furnished him with a note of the following case: M. S. "John Brush v. Thomas Gibbon. In Aug. Term, 1811. Mr. Graham, upon an affidavit of the defendant, stating that the suit was upon a note of $5,000, alleged to have been made by him, but that he never signed the same, and believed it to be a forgery, and that he could prove it to be so, the 19*] court would direct *it to be deposited in some place where his witnesses could have reasonable access to it, moved for an order upon the plaintiff to deposit the note with one of the officers of the court, or the Recorder of N. Y. The motion was opposed; but,

The court granted it, and ordered the note to be deposited with the clerk of the Supreme Court; and that the defendant's witnesses should have access to it, for the purpose of examining it."

See 2 Cow., 590, *note a* to Denslow v. Fowler, where the cases to this point are collected; and see, also, People v. Com. of Newcastle, *Id.*, 623. For a summary of the English practice as to compelling the production and inspection of papers in the hands of the adverse party, whether they be public or private papers, see 1 Archb. Pr., 144, 145; 2 *Id.*, 196, 197.

SMALL v. M'CHESNEY.

When Fractions of Day, Noticed.

The law will not notice the fractions of a day, as between the parties, in order to determine whether the judgment record was filed before execution issued, unless to prevent actual injustice.

MR. M. HOFFMAN moved to set aside the execution and subsequent proceedings in this cause. He showed, by affidavit, that the execution had issued against the defendant and been levied before the record of judgment, which was by bond and warrant of attorney, had been filed; that is to say, the execution was issued and levied between 2 and 4 o'clock in the morning of July 13, 1824, whereas the judgment was not signed till about 11 o'clock of the same morning, and the record was not filed till 4 P. M. of the same day.

He relied upon *Barrie* v. *Dana*, 20 Johns., 307, and *Leman* v. *Heirs of Staats*, 1 Cow., 592. The court said, in the latter case, they would examine the fractions of a day when necessary for the purposes of justice; and it is surely so here. Had the defendant been allowed time to pay the money till the record was filed, perhaps no execution would have been necessary.

Mr. L. Ford, contra, said that *Barrie* v. *Dana* was the case of an execution issued several days after the record filed. Fractions of a day were not in question.

Curia. The party who moves has sustained no injury by this proceeding. He does not show that the money would *have been [*20 paid, and farther costs prevented, had execution been delayed till after the filing of the record. The whole proceeding is on the same day, which the law will not divide into fractions, unless this be necessary for the purpose of guarding against injustice. Here has been none. The objection is merely technical, and the technical answer is enough where there has been no injury from the proceeding.

Motion denied.

Cited in—18 Wend., 533; 3 Den., 264; 4 Den., 243; 4 N. Y., 418; 5 How. Pr., 200; 6 How., Pr., 287.

FOX v. JOHNSON.

Return to Certiorari—*Set Aside, when drawn by Attorney.*

A return to a *certiorari* will be set aside, if it be drawn by the attorney for the plaintiff in error.

ON *certiorari* from a justice's court.

Mr. I. Seelye moved to set aside the return to the *certiorari* in this cause, with all subsequent proceedings, upon an affidavit of the defendant's attorney, that the justice who tried the cause in the court below informed him that one of the attorneys for the plaintiff in error drew his return. He cited *Rudd* v. *Baker*, 7 Johns., 548.

Mr. S. A. Foot, contra, read an affidavit of the justice, stating that he delivered the *certiorari*, and a copy of the affidavit upon which it was founded, to the attorneys for the plaintiff in error, and requested them to draw the return; that this was without any previous request or solicitation, for that purpose, by them or either of them; that one of them did draw the return, which he read over to the justice, and the same being correct, he signed it. He also read an affidavit of one of the attorneys for the plaintiff in error, who drew the return, confirming the justice's affidavit.

He said that *Rudd* v. *Baker* was the case of an officious intermeddling on the part of the attorney; but the present is a case of plain, honest dealing. The justice may employ such agent as he pleases to draw up his return. If it be false he is accountable.

21*] *WOODWORTH, *J.* He should have employed some one other than the attorney for the plaintiff. The practice of resorting to the attorney for the plaintiff in error is a dangerous one. It is liable to great abuse, being in the hands of one who is interested to reverse the judgment. The rights of the defendant in error are concluded by the return, who must submit, or be put to the expense and delay of an action, if the return be false.

SUTHERLAND, *J.* It is our duty to reject this return, on the same principle that we refuse to hear an affidavit, taken before the attorney in the cause. It might be different, if the attorney simply wrote what the justice dictated, acting the part of a mere amanuensis.

Mr. Foot. The present case is little, if anything, beyond that.

WOODWORTH, *J.* If the justice dictated the return, it was very easy to say so in the affidavits.

Mr. Foot. The rule which the court appear inclined to establish, would hardly allow the attorney to correct a clerical or grammatical inaccuracy, or to make a copy of the return.

SAVAGE, *Ch. J.* That would, perhaps, be a different case, but the attorney here draws the whole return, upon the general request of the justice. We are all clearly in favor of the motion.

Motion granted.

Cited in—4 Cow., 505, 537; 18 Wend., 552.

22*] *COLT *v.* GREGORY.

Irregular Proceedings against an Attorney—Affidavit to Set Aside.

On moving to set aside proceedings against an attorney, for irregularity, because they were as against a common person, the attorney need not state in his affidavit that he was a practicing attorney, &c.

But it is enough that he swear he was an attorney, which throws it upon the other party to show that he had not practiced within the year.

MR. E. GRIFFIN, moved to set aside the judgment against the defendant, and all subsequent proceedings, and he read an affidavit of the defendant, stating that "at the time of issuing the *capias ad respondendum* in this cause, and for a long time before, and ever since, he has been and still is an attorney and counselor of this court." The affidavit then set forth that a *capias* had been served on the defendant, but without serving any other papers, either on him or his agent; that the plaintiff's attorney had treated him as a common person, and proceeded to judgment.

Mr. Ostram objected that the affidavit did not state that he was a practicing attorney at the time of the suit brought.

Curia. This was not necessary. He swears that he was an attorney and counselor, and this is sufficient, *prima facie*, to show that he had practiced within the year. If otherwise, it lay with the plaintiff to show it.

Motion granted.

JACKSON, ex dem. ALLEN ET AL.,
v.
CARPENTER.

Ejectment—Costs in Former Action, in Federal Court, for Same Premises—Stay of Proceedings.

Proceedings stayed till the costs paid, in a suit for the same cause in the Circuit Court of the U. S.

MR. J. LYNCH, for the defendant, moved to stay proceedings in this cause, until the lessors of the plaintiff had paid certain costs incurred by the one under whom the defendant is in possession, in prosecuting an action of ejectment against the tenant of the lessors, for the same premises, in the U. S. District Court of the Northern District of N. Y., wherein the title of the present lessors was in question through their tenant, and wherein the plaintiff succeeded. He insisted that this came within the case of *Jackson* v. *Edwards*, 1 Cow., 138.

Mr. B. F. Butler*, among other grounds [*23** of opposition to the motion, mentioned that the first suit was in a court proceeding under the Constitution and laws of the U. S., and submitted whether, being under another government than that under which this court acts, they would so far notice the proceeding there as to interfere in this manner; but he did not much insist upon that ground.

Mr. Lynch, in reply, cited *Perkins* v. *Hinman*, 19 Johns., 237, where this court stayed the proceedings in a suit here for the same cause as one which had before been brought in the C. P., till the costs of the first were paid.

The Court, without assigning their reasons on this point, granted the motion.

Motion granted.

Cited in—27 How. Pr., 156; 8 W. Dig., 21.

FOX *v.* SMITH.

Practice—Polling Jury.

The jury may be polled at any time before the verdict is recorded, at the instance of either party, whether it be a sealed or oral verdict.

MR. E. GRIFFIN, for the defendant, moved to set aside the verdict in this cause, which was rendered for the plaintiff at the last Jefferson Circuit, under the following circumstances: The trial not being closed till evening, it was agreed by the counsel for the parties, that the jury might bring in their verdict sealed the next morning, which was accordingly done. On the jury coming into the box the next morning, and presenting their verdict sealed, the defendant's counsel requested of the judge to have the jury polled, which he denied, and the verdict was recorded.

Mr. C. P. Kirkland, contra, said he found nothing in the English cases which authorized the polling of a jury under any circumstances. If the right arises from the nature and construction of juries, and because the party has a right to see that it is the separate verdict of each as well as that of the whole, here he has the proper evidence of that by an arrangement to which he was a party, by which the jurors each affix their hand. In the case of 24*] *Root* v. *Sherwood*, 6 Johns., *68, the only question was, whether the circuit judge has the power to poll the jury. His power was established by that case, but it is a matter of discretion with him. An unqualified right to poll the jury, by a party who has had every chance to tamper with them, might lead to the greatest abuse. In *Blackley* v. *Sheldon*, 7 Johns 32, it is said the jury may be examined by the poll, if the court please; and again; "if the verdict be delivered in writing, as it was here, the justice has a right to permit the verdict to be taken by the poll."

WOODWORTH, *J.* Conceding that the judge may order the jury polled, seems to give the party a sight to insist on it. I think this cannot be a matter of mere discretion. It has been the uniform practice at the Circuit, as far as I have been acquainted with it, to allow the jury to be polled, whether the verdict be sealed, as here, by consent, or delivered *ore tenus* by the foreman.

Curia. We think the jury may be polled, at the instance of either party, at any time before the verdict is recorded, whether it be sealed, by consent, or is oral.

Motion granted.

Cited in—4 N. Y., 550; 52 N. Y., 440; 12 How. Pr., 431.

JACKSON, ex dem. PORTER ET AL., *v.* GALE.

Costs in Ejectment—Retaxation.

On retaxation of costs in ejectment, and case made for argument, the following items allowed: Serving *narr*. Rule for *remanet*—attorney's fee on argument for each term at which noticed—drawing judgment record, fol. 4, and same in *N. P.* record—*fi. fa.* for costs—fee on serving writ of possession. Motion and rule for argument disallowed.

THE plaintiff having recovered in ejectment, on verdict and a case made and argued, the commissioner had taxed the following, among other items, in the bill of costs:

Serving *narr*, - - - - - - - - - -	$1.00
Mo. and rule for argument, - - -	68¼
Rule for *remanet*, - - - - - - -	72¼
Att's fee on argument (several terms),	3.75
Drawing judgment record, fol. 4, at 19,	76
25*] *Sheriff's fees on serving writ of possession, with aid, &c., - - -	3.75
Fi. fa. for costs, - - - - - - -	1.32

Mr. J. C. Spencer, for the defendant, moved for a retaxation. He did this, he said, principally with a view to the attorney's fee on argument, which here amounted to a large sum, as the cause had been noticed for argument a great number of times, and an attorney's fee charged for each term. He insisted that the attorney would be entitled to but one fee on argument, and this for the term at which the cause was, in fact, argued. The phrase providing for the allowance of this fee, differs from the one which allows a fee to counsel. The latter is, attending prepared for argument—the former is, arguing, &c. (2 R. L., 15, 16.)

Mr. A. Samson, contra.

Curia. It is reasonable that this fee should be allowed for each term at which the cause is noticed for argument. The attorney attends, whether he succeed in reaching the cause on the calendar or not. The other items are correct, with the exception of that for serving writ of possession, which must be reduced to $1.25, and motion and rule for argument, which must be stricken out. The only objection against the *fi. fa.* for costs, is that it might have been incorporated into the writ of possession. This is true, but the party may also elect to proceed with it separately. Though the 4 folios are drawn for the *N. P.* record, yet it is necessary to make another draft when the judgment roll comes to be framed. It is no objection that a similar charge was allowed in the *N. P.* record. They are distinct instruments.

Mr. Samson. The $3.75 were taxed by anticipation, on the ground that aid might be necessary in executing the writ of possession. It was thought that this should be placed at its highest, and a deduction made in the event of execution being executed in the ordinary way.

SAVAGE, *Ch. J.* We cannot anticipate resistance to the officer, so that aid will be necessary.

Rule accordingly.

---

*THE PEOPLE [*26
v.
HONSENFRATTS.

Practice in Ejectment—What Necessary, before Attachment.

Ejectment and judgment for costs against the plaintiff. Presenting the lessor of the plaintiff with the *ca. sa.* and serving him with the consent rule, and demanding the costs, is not enough to warrant an attachment, but the taxed bill should be served by showing him the original and delivering a copy.

THE defendant was lessor of the plaintiff in ejectment, entered into the consent rule, and the verdict and judgment were against James Jackson, the nominal plaintiff. Hereupon the defendant's attorney issued a *ca. sa.* against James Jackson, for the costs, which was shown to Honsenfratts, the lessor, who was shown at the same time, the original consent rule, and served with a copy thereof by one who had a written authority from the defendant's attorney to receive the costs. He demanded the costs of Honsenfratts upon these papers, and they not being paid, an attachment was issued, which, being served and returned at this term,

Mr. Noxon, for the defendant, objected that the attachment had improvidently issued, inasmuch as no taxed bill of costs had been shown and demanded, nor was any copy served.

Mr. S. Wood, for the plaintiffs, said the *ca. sa.* is, in this case, conclusive evidence as to the amount. The English practice is, to demand the amount contained in the *ca. sa.* and, on non-payment, move for an attachment, as was done in this case. He cited Runn. on Eject., 416, and 2 Sell., 116, where this is laid down as the rule of the K. B. which governs this court.

Curia. The defendant must be discharged. The plaintiffs have proceeded irregularly. The lessor of the plaintiff should also have been served with a taxed bill of the costs, by showing him the original and delivering a copy, before moving for the attachment.

Rule accordingly.

27*] *IN THE MATTER OF LEMUEL SMITH *v.* THE JUDGES OF THE COURT OF COMMON PLEAS OF THE COUNTY OF PUTNAM.

Removal of Cause by Habeas Corpus—*Lower Court no Jurisdiction, until* Procedendo *Filed.*

A cause being removed by *habeas corpus* from the C. P. to this court, the former have no jurisdiction till a *procedendo* filed; and till this be done, any proceeding in the cause in the court below is irregular.

A CAUSE between Fitzpatrick, plaintiff, and Smith, defendant, had been commenced and carried to issue in the Putnam C. P.; and then the defendant removed it by *habeas corpus* into this court, but putting in no bail, a *procedendo* issued and was filed in the C. P. in Feb. Term last, and on the last day of that term the plaintiff's attorney moved to bring the cause on to trial. This was resisted by the defendant's counsel, on the ground that the cause had but the day before, as appeared by the *procedendo* on file, been brought into that court; and therefore no notice of trial could regularly have been given. The court decided that they would hear the cause, and it was tried accordingly; and a verdict found for the plaintiff, the counsel for the defendant declining to appear. At the next term, in June last, a motion was made to the C. P. to set aside the verdict, &c., as irreguar, but they denied the motion.

A motion was now made for a *mandamus*, requiring the Court of C. P. to vacate and set aside this verdict and the subsequent proceedings.

Mr. W. Nelson, for the motion.

Mr. J. Oppie, contra.

Curia. The court had no jurisdiction of the cause, and could not proceed till after the *procedendo* filed. Of course, there could have been no regular notice of trial. The proceedings of the court below were, for this reason, irregular, and the motion must be granted.

Rule for a mandamus.

*ROSE *v.* BATES, Sheriff of ONTARIO. [*28

Practice—Stay of Proceedings by Circuit Judge after Verdict.

A circuit judge may grant an order for a stay of proceedings till the further order of this court, upon a verdict, &c., though before a case settled.

A TRIAL being had and a verdict rendered for the defendant, in June last, at the Ontario Circuit, the plaintiff's attorney made and served the case for the purposes of a new trial, to which amendments had been proposed and notice of settling the case given; but before settled, the circuit judge granted a general order that "all proceedings on the part of the defendant in this cause, upon the verdict rendered in the same, be stayed until the further order of this court;" and now,

Mr. J. C. Spencer, for the defendant, moved to set aside the order as irregular. He said the judge had power to enlarge the time for making a case, proposing amendments, &c., but he cannot grant an indefinite order to stay proceedings "until the further order of the court." It may deprive the party of an appeal to this court, from an order on the case settled, where the opposite party has ample time to settle the case before the term.

Mr. W. Hubbell, contra.

Curia. We think the judge had a right to grant this order. He understands the case; it is tried and finally settled before him; and he will not grant the order unless satisfied that, when settled, there will be probable cause for setting aside the verdict. We see no reason for requiring the party to wait till after the case settled, before he obtains this general order.

Motion denied.

---

*GAY *v.* PATTERSON. [*29

Costs on Reference—What Allowed, under Statute.

The Statute of Apr. 5, 1813 (sess. 36, ch. 56, sec. 6), providing that, in case of reference, "a reasonable allowance shall be made to the prevailing party for such services and expenses as may accrue upon or attend the reference of, the cause" does not extend to the fees of counsel, &c., but is confined to the incidental expenses of the referees.

THIS cause had been referred, and the report being in favor of the plaintiff, the taxing officer had allowed in the taxation of costs $40, as a counsel fee for 5 days' attendance of counsel before the referees.

Mr. E. Williams, for the defendant, appealed from this taxation. He said he was aware that this charge had been allowed under the clause of the Act of Apr. 5, 1813 (1 R. L., 517, sec. 4), which declares that on taxation of costs upon a reference, "a reasonable allowance shall be made to the prevailing party, for such services and expenses as may accrue upon, or attend the reference of the cause." With deference, he considered the practice incorrect. The fee bill was passed Apr. 9, of the same year (2 R. L., 3), fixing the allowance to attorneys, counsel, witnesses, &c., and if the former Act contemplated an extra allowance, it was repealed by the latter. But the Statute authorizing this reasonable allowance, may be satisfied, entirely independent of attorney and counsel fees. It means no more than that the allowance shall be made for those expenses not embraced by the fee bill, owing to the peculiar course of proceeding; such as the expenses of the referees, as house room, board, &c. In all other respects the *quantum* should be graduated by the fee bill. If you give an extra allowance to counsel, there is nothing to prevent your enlarging the fees of the attorney, witnesses, the magistrate for swearing the referees, &c. This may certainly be done upon the same principle.

Messrs. W. H. Maynard and *G. C. Bronson*, contra, relied upon the practice as settled, and mentioned a manuscript case decided several years ago, upon the authority of which this allowance had been repeatedly made.

Curia. This counsel fee has been allowed in practice; but, on examining the subject, we 30*] think the allowance was *erroneous. The words of the Statute may be satisfied by taxing the incidental expenses of the referees; and we think this is all the Legislature intended. We direct a retaxation accordingly.

Rule accordingly.

CUTLER v. COLVER.

Fi.Fa.—*Cannot be withdrawn, after Levy—Issue of* Ca. Sa., *Irregular.*

After a *fi. fa.* has been levied, the plaintiff cannot withdraw it, and issue a *ca. sa.*

JUDGMENT being against the defendant, who had not put in special bail, the plaintiff issued a *fi. fa.* returnable at the present term, with which the sheriff called on the defendant, who said that he had no personal property to satisfy it, but he had real estate, which he pointed out to the sheriff. This real estate being heavily incumbered by previous judgments, &c., the plaintiff took back the *fi. fa.* and gave the sheriff a *ca. sa.*, which he executed. The defendant being in prison, a motion was now made for his discharge, and the only question was, whether taking back the *fi. fa.* and issuing a *ca. sa.* was, under the circumstances, regular.

Curia. Had there been no effort on the part of the sheriff to execute this *fi. fa.*, it would be, at least, questionable whether the plaintiff might not have withdrawn it and taken his *ca. sa.* But here was a virtual levy of the *fi. fa.*, after which it could not be withdrawn. Its execution should have been completed. The *ca. sa.* must be set aside, on the defendant's stipulating not to bring false imprisonment.

Rule accordingly.

31*] *IN THE MATTER OF UPDEGROFF ET AL.

v.

THE JUDGES OF THE COURT OF COMMON PLEAS OF THE COUNTY OF NIAGARA.

Action on Bond—Informality of Verdict—Effect of.

In action on a bond for the performance of covenants, and an assignment of breaches, the execution will not be set aside for a mere informality of the verdict in not assessing damages for the breach, but referring the damages to the detention of the debt.

DEBT, in the court below, by Potter, assignee of a jail bond, against Updegroff and two others, the obligors. The declaration set forth a *ca. sa.* in favor of Potter against Updegroff, the arrest of Updegroff, the execution of the bond, with the condition, which was, that Updegroff should remain a true and faithful prisoner, and should not, at any time, or in anywise, escape or go without the limits, &c. The declaration then averred an escape, whereby the bond became forfeited, &c. Plea, *nil debent.* Verdict, "that the defendants do owe, &c., and they assess the damages of the said plaintiff on occasion of the detention of the within debt, over and above, &c., to $830.05." On this verdict, the plaintiff entered up judgment and took out execution for the whole damages. A motion was made in the court below to set it aside, which was denied; and now,

Mr. J. C. Spencer moved for a *mandamus* requiring them to grant the motion, on the ground that there was no assignment of breaches, nor writ of inquiry of damages; or at any rate, if the declaration did assign breaches, the verdict did not assess damages upon the breaches. He cited *Van Benthuysen* v. *De Witt*, 4 Johns., 213; *Caverley* v. *Nichols*, *Id.*, 189; *Hardy* v. *Bern*, 5 T. R., 636; *Welch* v. *Ireland*, 6 East, 613, and 2 Saund., 187, *n.* 2.

Mr. J. Platt, contra, said that the objection to the proceedings below, if well founded, was mere matter of error, not irregularity, and could not be corrected summarily. We have a right to be heard in a more solemn form; the party should have brought his writ of error, upon which, if the decision of this court should be against us, we might go to the Court of Errors. But the assignment of breaches was sufficient. The parties went to trial upon that assignment, and the verdict *was rendered upon it. The cases cited [*32 e those where no assessment of damages was had.

Mr. Spencer, in reply. The verdict has no relation to the breach assigned. That was for the escape. The verdict is for the detention of the debt. It is the same, then, as if no assessment of damages had been made in the cause.

Curia. The assignment of breaches was sufficient; but it is said the verdict does not pursue the assignment. The parties went to trial upon the breach assigned, and we cannot help seeing that the omission in the verdict to refer to the breach in assessing damages, must have arisen from a mere clerical mistake in the entry, which is amendable by the court below. The case differs altogether from those cited. In those cases there was no attempt to assign breaches. Even on error brought, the least we could do would be to send this verdict back to be amended, or amend it ourselves.

Motion denied.

SHIPHERD AND STORRS v. WHITE,

and

CAMPBELL v. SCHULT.

Practice—Exceptions Should be Noted at Trial—Notice of Settling Bill of Exceptions—Execution of Bill—When Set Aside—Mandamus.

Exceptions to a judge's or court's opinion should be noted down upon the trial, or they cannot be used in a bill of exceptions.
On settling the bill, notice of time and place when and where this is to be done, should be given to the defendant in error:
Otherwise, the judge or court will not be compelled, by *mandamus*, to execute the bill.
And if executed, it will be set aside.
Whenever a bill of exception is signed, under circumstances wherein the Supreme Court would not compel its execution by *mandamus*, it will be set aside on motion.

Citations—9 Johns., 345.

THESE causes had been tried in the C. P. of Washington Co.—the first in Dec. Term, 1819; the second in Aug. Term, 1820; and immediately removed, by writ of error, to this court. In the first cause, the decision was so late in term that the attorney for Shipherd and Storrs had no time to reduce a bill of exceptions to writing, though they mentioned their exceptions on the trial; but on the intimation of one or more of the judges, that this 33*] would be *sufficient, he drew and took the bill with him at the next term, and gave it to White's attorney for inspection, with a request that he would amend it, so that the draft and amendments might be submitted together. He requested time to look at his minutes, which he said he had not with him, promised to amend the bill the first opportunity, and retained it for that purpose. He was repeatedly solicited to propose amendments, which he omitted to do, and ruled the plaintiffs to assign errors while he had possession of the draft.

In neither of the causes were the exceptions reduced to writing on the trial, and both bills were finally settled and signed by three of the judges, after they had gone out of office, and without giving any notice of the time and place of their being so settled to the attorneys of White and Schult respectively. An issue of *in nulla est erratum* having been joined, and the causes noticed for argument at this term,

Mr. R. Weston moved to strike them out from the calendar, or that the bill of exceptions be set aside.

Mr. J. L. Wendell, contra.

Curia. If the plaintiffs were pressed for time to assign errors, they should have obtained a judge's order to extend it, till the bills could have been fairly settled. The defendants in error should, at least, have had notice of the time and place when and where the bills would have been submitted to the judges for their sanction. This should always be so—more especially at such a distance of time from the trial. We would not have compelled the judges, by *mandamus*, to seal the bills, without such notice; and when bills of exceptions are signed under such circumstances as would not call for our interference by *mandamus*, we will on application, set them aside, as improvidently executed. (*a*) *This rule [*34 is applicable here upon another ground. In neither of these causes were the exceptions reduced to writing upon the trial, or during the term. *Midberry* v. *Collins*, 9 Johns., 345.

Mr. D. Russell, for the plaintiffs in error, submitted whether the court would not refer the bills to the judges of the court below, for revision.

Curia. The plaintiffs in error were irregular in the outset. The exceptions should have been noted down upon the trial. Their remedy by bill of exceptions is gone.

Mr. Russell. Will not the court allow the plaintiffs to discontinue without costs? They have gone on in perfect good faith.

Curia. We see no reason for this. It was palpably irregular to proceed and settle the bills without the least notice of the time and place at which this was to have been done.

Motion granted.

Cited in—3 Wend., 313; 5 Park., 15; 3 Wood & M., 537; 36 N. J. L., 64.

(*a*) When the court will compel the judges to sign by *mandamus*; *vide* Sikes v. Ransom, 6 Johns., 279; Midberry v. Collins, 9 Johns., 345; Lanuse v. Barker, 10 *Id.*, 312; Pratt v. Malcolm, 13 *Id.*, 320.

JANSEN, Administrator of JANSEN,

v.

TAPPEN.

Reference—Affidavit for.

An affidavit for a reference should state that issue is joined.

MR. E. WILLIAMS, for the defendant, moved for a reference in this cause.

Mr. E. Cowen, contra, objected that it did not appear from the affidavit on which the motion was founded, that issue had been joined in the cause; and for this reason,

Motion denied.

Cited in—2 Abb. N. S., 307; 4 Rob., 688.

---

*IN THE MATTER OF THE APPLICATION [*35 OF TIMOTHY HURD

v.

MAGEE, Sheriff of STEUBEN.

Right of Judgment Creditor to Redeem Land—Judgment must be Lien—Question of Fraud in Sale—Not Tried on Motion.

A judgment creditor has no right to redeem under the 3d section of the Act of Apr. 12, 1820 (sess. 43, ch. 184), unless his judgment be a lien on the land which he seeks to redeem.
It cannot be a lien where the land of the debtor is sold and conveyed, either by the debtor or by the sheriff, before the judgment of the creditor claiming to redeem is docketed.
And though it be insisted that the sale was fraudulent and void as to creditors, the court will not try this question on motion.

NOV. 21, 1818, a judgment was docketed in this court, in favor of Reeve against Smith, for $192.09, on which execution issued, tested Oct. 9 of the same year, returnable at the ensuing Jan. Term, directed to the sheriff of Steuben; who, Jan. 19, 1819, sold the farm on which Smith then resided, to Hurd, and executed a deed for the same to him. This was before the Act, which allows the redemption of lands sold upon execution, had passed. Oct. 18, 1814, a judgment for $103.88 was docketed in this court, in favor of one Peterson, against the same Smith. On this judgment execution issued, by virtue whereof Magee, sheriff of Steuben, Nov. 30, 1822, sold the same farm to Hurd, for $159.06, and gave a certificate of this sale, &c. Apr. 6, 1823, a judgment was docketed in this court, in favor of Henry Welles, against Smith, for $210; and Oct. 3, 1820, a judgment was docketed in this court, in favor of Baker and another, defendants, at the suit of Smith, for $33.55 costs. After the expiration of fifteen months from the sale by Magee, Hurd demanded his deed of Magee, which he declined giving, having previously executed a deed to Welles, who had redeemed as creditor by judgment, and as assignee of the judgment in favor of Baker. On affidavits of these facts,

Mr. J. C. Spencer moved for a *mandamus* requiring the sheriff to execute a deed to Hurd.

Mr. J. A. Collier, contra, read an affidavit, stating that the judgment in favor of Peterson was in the Steuben C. P.; and that on the sale in 1822, Hurd and one Tuthill became joint purchasers; that Welles redeemed after a year, and before fifteen months from this sale; that Smith continued in possession of the farm in question till after Welles' judgment was obtained; and that there was a material variance

36*] *between the judgment and execution under which Hurd originally purchased.

He argued, that though Hurd had a right to insist on his first purchase, he cannot do so at this stage of the proceeding. He should have confined himself solely to the right which he thus acquired. But he has waived his former right, and must now be confined to that which he acquired under the sale of 1822. After thus making his election, it is in the power of any judgment creditor to come in and redeem, if his judgment is of a date anterior to the expiration of fifteen months after that sale. He submits to the elder and better title. This he had a right to do, and might have redeemed as between us and Peterson. He admits that he acquired no right upon his first purchase; and indeed, this is true, independent of his second, as it respects the creditors of Smith, who continued in possession of the farm long after the first, which was evidently fraudulent. We were right in disregarding it, and redeeming. Hurd a right to redeem from us, as assignee or grantee of the land, but the time for this has gone by. The year—the fifteen months have expired. Had he redeemed as grantee, the second sale would have been void. (Sess. 43, ch. 184. sec. 2.) What right has he to lie by, and compel us to suffer his taking a title under the elder judgment? Can Hurd, having waived his title to redeem, say, after the year and his rights are gone, "I am grantee, and yet have a right to a deed under the senior judgment, in virtue of my second purchase?" His remedy would have been complete without this. If evicted, either by a stranger or any other person, the Statute (1 R. L., 504) declares that the money which he has paid shall be refunded. He waives all right to that remedy, by his second purchase, because actual eviction is the sole foundation upon which it would rest. This court have decided that the judgment is a lien, though obtained more than a year after the sale. Thus our right is complete, as it respects the second sale; and will the court suffer Hurd to lie by till his right is gone as grantee, and then come forward in the character of a purchaser? Will such a course accord with the spirit of the Act to which this court have given a construction? "This *Statute, says the *Chief Justice*, [***37** in *Van Rensselaer* v. *Sheriff of Albany*, 1 Cow., 510, " is evidently remedial; and in its exposition, it is our duty to bear in mind the evil intended to be prevented and the remedy proposed, and so to construe the Act as to suppress the evil and advance the remedy." Are we not within the intention of the Legislature? Will not the object of the Statute, as avowed by all the court, which is to keep up a perpetual auction, be in this manner the most effectually promoted? Other judgment creditors ought not to stand peaceably by and see Hurd invested with this additional title, which fortifies his first, and renders him secure in a purchase which was evidently fraudulent.

SUTHERLAND, *J.* But it is necessary that you should show your judgment to be a lien on this land. How can this be, when the title of Smith was sold before the passage of the Act, and a deed given which passed the title?

Mr. Collier. Smith was still suffered to continue in possession. Our judgment found him there; and at any rate it attached upon his possessory interest, or whatever interest he had. He could not set up an outstanding title in Hurd, or anyone else, to defeat an ejectment founded on a purchase under our judgment against him. It would be no more than fair to iufer that he had acquired a title since the first sale. We cannot be conusant of what his right is, and at any rate should not be concluded by this summary application. We say Hurd's purchase was fraudulent, and that the sale was upon an irregular execution. The whole was void; and the court would not order an amendment so as to conclude us. They will rather incline to keep the right of redemption open to all the creditors. They should leave Hurd to his elder title. He has no right to his double character. It is enough that he claims under a fraudulent sale, or doubtful title. The court should not deprive us of our right to contest it. I agree that the language of some of the court, in *Dickinson* v. *Gilliland*, is against the idea of our having a lien. But the sale, in that case, to Prindle, was absolute and *honest. Here, we [***38** say, the sale was not only fraudulent, but it was subject to an elder judgment, under which a subsequent sale takes place. Besides, in that case, the grantee was in possession.

Mr. Spencer, in reply. Welles has no right to appear here at all; or, if otherwise, we have a prior right to redeem. The sale under the first judgment was absolute and binding upon Smith, as if he had executed the deed himself, subject, to be sure, like every other sale, to be defeated by a paramount title, either by judgment or otherwise. How can Hurd's acts be made to operate as a waiver of rights which he had acquired by deed? This is the first time, I believe, it was ever contended that a man forfeited his right to land by the purchase of a judgment, or bidding in under a judgment with the view to fortify and sustain his title. The course of Welles was plain. He should have attended the sale, and become a purchaser himself.

It is said that Smith was in possession, but this was no evidence of title. Admit that he could not controvert Welles' title in an action of ejectment: a recovery in that action is not conclusive evidence of title. It relates merely to the right of possession. It is not enough for Welles to say that he will contest the right acquired under Reeve's judgment, without showing a single fact to impeach it; for I presume the variance between the judgment and execution is not seriously insisted on. A subsequent judgment creditor cannot object this. If anything serious was intended on the head of fraud, why was not the proper remedy resorted to? Why was not a bill in equity filed in order to sift the fraud? The variance is plainly amendable. Fraud is the only ground of opposition at law or in equity, and the right to relief, in either case, is gone by our purchase.

It is said that a perpetual auction is to be kept up. Between whom? Those creditors, only, whose judgments are a lien upon the land. It has been twice decided, that where there is no lien there is no right to redeem. (*Erwin* v. *Schriver*, 19 Johns., 379; *Dickinson* v. *Gilliland*, 1 Cow., 481.) And a sale under Hurd's judgment, before the Redemption Act, **39***] *devested Smith's title, so that there was nothing upon which Welles' or Baker's judgment could operate.

Curia. This motion must be granted. The sheriff's sale and conveyance under Reeve's judgment devested the title of Smith, the judgment debtor. He then had no interest upon which the subsequent judgment, either of Baker or Welles, could become a lien. Having no lien, it is well settled by the authorities cited, that Welles had no right to redeem.

Then it is said that the judgment of Reeve, and the purchase of Hurd, were fraudulent as to the other creditors of Smith; but the suggestion is almost entirely gratuitous. There is nothing in the affidavits showing anything like fraud; yet suppose a case of fraud made out, we could not try it in this summary form. Welles should have caused the proceedings to be stayed, or filed his bill in equity, and prevented the second sale, till the question had been settled whether his judgment could be let in, on account of the fraud, or not.

The sheriff must execute the deed to Hurd, as it is applied for; but we do not interfere with the conveyance to Welles. It can do no harm, if, as we hold, it passed nothing.

Motion granted.

Cited in—4 Cow., 418; 9 Barb., 24.

CHICHESTER & VAN WYCK,
v.
CANDE, Impleaded with LASHER.

Judgment and Execution—Omission to File Record—Second Judgment and Execution, with Knowledge of Former Judgment—Levy under both Executions, on Same Property—Relative Rights of Creditors.

Judgment and execution by A against B, but by accident the record was not filed; then judgment and execution in favor of C against B. Both executions being levied on the same personal property which was sold and the avails paid over, by order of this court, in certain portions, to A and C, before the latter discovered that A's judgment was imperfect. Then C, on discovering this, applies for a preference as to the whole of the money. This was denied, and on A's application he was allowed to file his record *nunc pro tunc*, it appearing that his execution was first levied, and C having full notice of A's judgment, before his (C's) judgment was obtained.

Citations—3 Johns., 526; 2 Johns., 307.

SEVEN judgments had been obtained in the Onondaga C. P. against Lasher alone, to the amount of *$2,725.19, a *fi. fa.* on each [***40** of which was delivered to the sheriff of Onondaga Sept. 24, 1821. The following judgments were obtained in this court, viz.: one in favor of Chichester & Van Wyck, for $959.28, against Lasher & Cande, partners, on which a *fi. fa.* was delivered to the sheriff of Onondaga, Sept. 27, 1821—a judgment in favor of Tredwell *et al.*, against Cande, impleaded with Lasher, for $784.09—and another judgment in favor of Humphrey against Cande, impleaded with Lasher, for $942.53. The last two judgments were also against the defendants as partners, and the *fi. fa.* in each was delivered to the sheriff of Onondaga, Oct. 29, 1821. On these executions the sheriff levied on partnership property, and on his application to this court for direction, in Jan. Term, 1822, he was ordered to sell the goods and bring the money into court, which he did, to the amount of $1,764.50. At May Term, 1822, this court directed that the execution in favor of Chichester & Van Wyck, be first satisfied, secondly, the other two judgments in this court, which had been assigned to Russ, and that the C. P. executions be postponed to these. The sheriff accordingly paid to Chichester & Van Wyck, $986.34, and $776.78 to Russ. Russ, on the last application to the Supreme Court, sought to obtain preference over C. & V. on the ground that their execution was returnable at the wrong place, had issued contrary to stipulation, and was sealed with an old seal, before used; but he failed in all these grounds. The *fi. fa.* was amended as to the place of return, and the stipulation and seal, being before used, were denied.

In Nov. last, Russ discovered, for the first time, that no record of any judgment in favor of C. & V. had ever been filed. Application was accordingly made by Russ, at the last Feb. Term, to vacate the former proceedings, set aside the execution of C. & V., as having issued without any judgment to support it, and that the moneys paid to them be paid over to Russ, on his judgments. On account of a mistake in the title of the papers, the motion

was then denied, but renewed again at the
41*] last May Term, whence it *was postponed to the present term, for the purpose of producing additional affidavits.

The attorney of C. & V. swore that he had inclosed a record in their cause, duly signed, with the warrant of attorney to confess judgment and directed them, by mail, to the clerk's office of this court, at Utica, in season for their arrival, in the ordinary course of the mail, so as to warrant the *fi. fa.* which he issued; and he supposed that they had been regularly filed till Jan., 1823, when they were returned to him from the general postoffice, as a dead letter; which fact he concealed till the present motion was noticed.

A motion was also made and continued as above, on the part of C. & V., to amend, by filing the warrant of attorney and record *nunc pro tunc.*

Messrs. S. L. Edwards and *H. Bleecker*, in support of the motion to vacate the former proceedings, and set aside the execution of Chichester & Van Wyck, &c., and against the motion to amend.

The money was ordered to C. & V., on the ground that they were judgment creditors. It turns out, in fact, that there was no such ground. The whole was a mere fabrication; and we believe the court have never gone so far as to give the party a judgment *nunc pro tunc*, where he never had one, and not a paper ever reached the proper office. Russ, the assignee of the other judgment, would have received the money, if the truth had been known, Saying the least, the whole proceeding was founded in mistake. Russ was always legally entitled to this money, and shall C. & V. profit by the concealment? An execution issued before the judgment record is filed, is a nullity. *Barrie* v. *Dana*, 20 Johns., 307; Vin. Abr., Judgment, A, 1, K, *a*. There can be no doubt that the court has power to order what we ask under these circumstances. They may order the money refunded, as if the judgment had been reversed by them on error. (2 Salk., 587, 588.)

Mr. A. Spencer, contra. It is said here was no judgment. That we deny. True there was no judgment docketed, but the record was signed upon a regular bond and warrant
42*] of *attorney. Filing and docketing does not give the record its validity. This is derived from the act of signing. Full notice of this judgment is not denied on the part of Russ. I do not question the physical power of the court to vacate all these proceedings but I do deny that it would be a discreet exercise of power, and there is little doubt of the court's power to amend. The cases I cite to this point are, *Jackson* v. *Hammond*, 1 Cai., 496; *Seaman* v. *Drake, Id.*, 9; *People* v. *Burdock*, 3 *Id.*, 104; *White* v. *Lovejoy*, 3 Johns., 448; *Close* v. *Gillespey, Id.*, 526. The language of the court in *Barrie* v. *Dana*, to be sure, is pretty strong in relation to that case; but it should be confined to the case, which was a *ca. sa.* issued before the record filed, on which the defendant had been imprisoned. There is a difference in this respect, between execution against the body and the mere goods and chattels. Courts will go very far in amending proceedings which are defective through mistake. In *Hart* v. *Reynolds* (not reported), the defendant's real name, in the bond and warrant of attorney, was John Reynolds, but all the proceedings, from the *cognovit* to the docket, inclusive, were in the name of Elisha Reynolds. There was, then, no judgment against John Reynolds upon the docket, or even in the record, yet a subsequent judgment obtained by Doe was denied a preference, on the ground that when he obtained his judgment he had notice of Hart's as a judgment against the real defendant; and Hart's judgment was amended throughout, saving the rights of purchasers who had not notice. This, too, was a proceeding in relation to real estate.(a)

(a) R. P. HART v. JOHN REYNOLDS—August Term, 1817.

In this cause the facts were, briefly, that John Reynolds, of Moreau, in Saratoga Co., had executed to Richard P. Hart a bond and warrant of attorney to confess judgment for $10,000, but, by mistake, all the proceedings, including the docket of the judgment, were in the name of Elisha Reynolds, defendant. The papers were filed and the judgment docketed, June 6, 1811. Afterwards two judgments were obtained in this court, and regularly docketed —one in favor of Walter Doe, and another in favor of James Taylor—previous to which last judgment, and before Doe's execution issued, all the personal property of Reynolds had been sold upon a *fi. fa.* in favor of Hart, leaving a considerable balance yet due, which was claimed by Hart to be a lien on Reynolds' real estate. Doe and Taylor had actual notice of Hart's judgment, and supposed it had been regularly docketed, till after their judgments were perfected. On discovering Hart's mistake they moved to set aside his execution, which was opposed, and a cross-motion made to amend, upon the papers introduced for and against the first motion. J. Reynolds gave a written consent to the amendment.

The motion was argued by *Mr. J. Tallmadge*, for Doe and Taylor, and *Mr. L. Mitchell*, for Hart.

Mr. Tallmadge reasoned, with great ingenuity, against the court's going the length of creating a judgment in the name of amending it.

Mr. Mitchell answered, and his researches extended to the whole law of amendment in relation to this subject. As the result of his argument was adopted by the court, I think it will be found highly useful and acceptable to the profession.

1. He objected to the motion for setting aside the execution because made by persons having no right to make it. The personal property of Reynolds was exhausted by Hart's execution, before it could be affected either by Doe's or Taylor's; and, as to the realty, there is no necessity for setting aside the first execution to secure Taylor and Doe: for they contend that they have the oldest judgments. If so, they are safe, whether we sell or not. Ejectment is their remedy, and not this motion.

The motion, then, must be rejected, as being officiously made by strangers, without Reynolds' consent, and against his wishes.

2. The defects in our judgment, &c., are amendable, and this we may avail ourselves of, on this motion, as it was held in Seaman v. Drake, 1 Cai., 9, where a motion was made by bail to set aside proceedings, and denied, because the defect was amendable. We move to amend the judgment and proceedings, and that the judgment be docketed against John Reynolds, *nunc pro tunc*, absolutely as to Taylor and Doe, who make the present motion, and that the docket shall contain a saving of the right of prior purchasers. If the court think it necessary, we wish that they should reserve the power of modifying the rule as to the other judgment creditors, on their showing that a particular injury will result to them within (say) three months as they did in the case of Wardell v. Eden, 2 Johns. Cas., 126, the rule to be otherwise made absolute as to them. No such qualification is necessary or proper, if it be true that none but purchasers can avail themselves of the docket. At all events, Taylor's and Doe's judgments should be postponed without any reservation.

This motion for amendment is made by Hart, with the cognizance and consent of Reynolds; and the

43*] *Mr. *Bleecker*, in reply. None of the cases cited obviate the objection against an amendment here. The rights of a creditor are in question, who had a regular judgment. None of the cases cited present the question as
44*] to creditors, except *that of *Hart* v. *Reynolds*, and there the rights of creditors were saved. The question between these parties depends on their respective diligence. There is no natural equity in the case. There is no difference between the case of real and personal estate, which can affect this question. The *judgment is a lien on the realty, [*45
and the execution on the personalty; but neither can operate if they are void. No execution can issue without a judgment, and the

first question which presents, relates to the extent of the power of the court on applications for amendments.

Where an appeal is made to the equitable side of the court, the Statutes of Amendments and Jeofails are thrown out of view, although they control in all cases of amendment after writ of error brought. On such applications as the present, the broad rule has been adopted by the Court of B. R. that the court will amend whenever the ends of justice requires it. In Mara v. Quin, 6 T. R., 8, Lord Kenyon, *Ch. J.*, says: "The forms of the court are always best used when they are made subservient to the justice of the case;" and Ashurst, *J.*, observes: "It is admitted that amendments have been made, at all times, in order to forward the justice of the case." In that case the court put the judgment, *forti manu*, two years back, to prevent injustice, because it could not injure third persons. In The King v. The Mayor of Grampond, 7 T. R., 699, Ld. Kenyon says: "I wish that that could be attained, that Ld. Hardwicke, in the case before him, lamented could not be done, namely: that these amendments were reduced to some certain rules: but there being no such rule, each particular case must be left to the sound judgment of the court. And the best principle seems to be that on which Lord Hardwicke relied, in the same case, that an amendment shall or shall not be permitted to be made, as it will best tend to the furtherance of justice. Amendments of this kind are not made under the Statutes of Jeofails. but under the general authority of the court." In Seaman v. Drake, 1 Cai., 9, the court allowed the judgment to be signed *nunc pro tunc*, because they said the omission was a neglect of one of their officers, which ought not to prejudice any one. It is to be observed, that by 1 R. L., 501, sec. 2, it is enacted, that no judgment shall affect land, &c., as to purchasers, &c., but from the actual filing of the roll, after the same shall have been signed. Of course, by this Statute, subsequent purchasers had acquired a priority of lien; yet the court destroyed that priority by an amendment, *nunc pro tunc*, without calling even purchasers before them. And the reason was, that they had notice, and supposed there was a valid judgment, to which they expected their lien would be postponed. The amendment could not, therefore, disappoint them, nor work injustice; but the second incumbrance might well be supposed to have been taken, subject to such amendments in their prior record as the court should think fit and proper to direct. In Close v. Gillespie, 3 Johns., 526, the attorney's name was allowed to be signed to the plea, *nunc pro tunc*, and per Spencer, *J.*: "I cannot discover any difference, as to the allowing of an amendment, whether the mistake has happened through the omission of an attorney, or by mistake of the clerk. Both are equally officers of the court. In the present case, the judgment having been docketed, Mancius had, in legal intendment, notice of it. Had error been brought, there might have been more doubt. I cannot perceive that Mancius (the judgment creditor) has any right to avail himself of the irregularity which has intervened; nor can I perceive that our right to amend, in case of mistake of one of our officers, is to be controlled by the effect which may be produced in another case. All amendments affect more or less third persons." This opinion adopts, in their fullest extent, the liberal and humane principles, towards officers of the court, which prevail in the Court of B. R. and is full to the point, that a judgment creditor, with notice, shall not control the power of the court to amend in cases of mistake of its officers, whether clerks or attorneys. The judgment, in that case, was as radically defective and irregular, till amended, as is the judgment in the principal case; and the court, by the amendment, created a preference which before did not exist. These cases furnish a conclusive answer to the objection, that the subsequent creditors' supposing there was a valid and legal judgment did not make it so; and they could not know of the existence of a valid judgment when none such, in fact, did exist. In neither of the two last cases was the judgment a valid one.

But the truth is, the notice destroyed the equity of the subsequent incumbrancers, and with it the right of objection to an amendment. In Seaman v. Drake, there was no judgment as to the real estate, so far as purchasers were concerned, until the amendment was made. In the case of Close v. Gillespie, there was no regular or valid judgment, until the plea was signed, because a void judgment is as none; but the court, in the former case, created a lien; in other words, a judgment as to the realty, by relation, because the furtherance of justice made it necessary. In the latter case, a proceeding was validated, which before was nugatory, upon the same principle of equity. In the case of Mara v. Quin, the court, by a most extraordinary exertion of its equitable powers, with strong hand, allowed the judgment to be signed, filed and docketed, as of a day two years before it was, in fact, obtained, because it advanced the purposes of justice, and the want of notice could not injure third persons. Here we propose that the rights of third persons, purchasers without notice, be expressly saved. In Mackay v. Rhinelander, 1 Johns. Cas., 410, a judgment was entered *nunc pro tunc*, several months before it was, in fact, signed, or filed, or rendered.

One objection is, that there is nothing to amend by. To this we answer, it is impertinent. It could be proper only on a writ of error—not where an appeal is made to the general authority of the court, with consent of the defendant. Nothing can prevent the success of such an application, except the immoral tendency of the amendment, the only inquiry being, whether the amendment would contribute to the advancement of justice. On this principle the court proceeded, in Mara v. Quin, in placing the judgment two years earlier on the docket than it was recovered. Yet, I ask, what was there in that case to amend by?

But there is something to amend by, viz.: the warrant of attorney—the foundation of all the proceedings. This, according to 1 R. L., 416, must be filed with the record; and was, in this case, attached to the proceedings. It, therefore, identified the defendant, and a judgment may as well be rendered against John, by the name of Elisha, as he might be arrested by that name, or execute a bond by that name. A mistake of the name in the judgment may be corrected, provided the real defendant be ascertained in the previous part of the roll, even without the defendant's consent. Cro. Car., 594; Bac. Abr., tit. Amendment, F. The warrant is a part of one entire security, the nature of which is ascertained by the warrant. Thus, the consideration of a judgment, entered by virtue of a warrant, is the subject of inquiry, on which the court may award a feigned issue; but not on a judgment in a contested suit. This judgment by confession is *sui generis*, the nature of which is ascertained by the warrant. It is a judgment by contract, as contradistinguished from a judgment by operation of law, and will be amended to fulfill the intent of the parties, *ut res magis valeat quam pereat*. Puleston v. Warburton, 1 Salk., 48, was "Ejectment. Verdict, *pro quer.*, wherein he had counted of a demise, the 10th Apr., 1697, instead of 1696, for 97 was not come at the time of the trial; and the court agreed that in a judgment by confession on warrant of attorney, it had and might be amended in ejectment, because without such amendment, the agreement and intent of the parties could not be fulfilled, but denied it in the principal case, because it altered the issue, and made another title." In this case from Salkeld there was nothing by which to amend the declaration, and the judgment roll, and the *consideratum est*, except the warrant; yet the court say all might be amended; for the judgment being for the said term, refers to the declaration, and thus, by altering one, the other would necessarily be altered. That amendment, too, would have been made against the will of the defendant

decision in *Barrie* v. *Dana* would have been the same in relation to a *fi. fa.* as it was in relation to the *ca. sa.* The latter may or may **46*]** *not affect the party more severely than a *fi. fa.* and is the judgment of the court to be controlled by such a consideration? The gentlemen opposed to me (then *Ch. J.*) lays down the rule generally and unqualifiedly in *Barrie* v. *Dana*, that the record must be filed before execution can go, *and declares that such **[*47** has been the practice for 30 years. There is no difference between the different kinds of execution, either in law or common sense.

Suppose a *cap ad. resp.* sent to a sheriff, who never receives it, or a letter directing a rule for judgment, to be entered, *which mis- **[48**

But, in the principal case, Hart has the consent of Reynolds to every amendment. Of course, every amendment must be made down to the entry of the judgment. The case from Salkeld shows that the declaration may be amended. No third person has a right to object, till we arrive at the *consideratum est*, &c., and if the previous proceedings be considered as amended, the objection that there is nothing to amend by falls to the ground.

The question, then, arises, whether if the other proceedings be right, the *consideratum, est, &c.*, may be altered, so as to become conformable to the previous proceedings, and this question is answered in the affirmative, by numberless authorities. In Pelham v. Henning, Cro. Car., 594, the marginal note is thus: "If the name of a party be right in the record, but wrong in the judgment, the judgment may be amended by the record. 'Tis a misprision of the clerk." In affirmance of the judgment, the judgment itself may be set right, and amended by another part of the record, in a fact which appears to be the misprision of the clerk, as in the mistake of names of parties. *Vide* Bac. Abr., Amendment, F, which cites 1 Roll. Abr., 357, and gives, as an example, "*Prædictus* A," instead of "B," and "Charles" instead of "Robert." There is a strong analogy between a security created by common recovery, and one given by warrant of attorney. Both are a kind of judicial lien; and there are many instances of amendments in the names of the parties in these common recoveries, as well as in fines. Recovery, entered by A, B and C, but the name of W totally omitted, ordered by the court to be amended. For example; warrant by W. R. and Hester—recovery, W. R. and Margaret, his wife, amended. Vin. Abr., Amendment, L. On an application for such an amendment, it was objected that the heirs at law would be prejudiced, if the fine was amended. The court said they could not take notice, whether it would be a prejudice to the heirs at law or not; but it was the duty of the court to make the fine agreeable to the deed and intention of the parties. *Ib.*

It will again be objected that the docket cannot, by law, be amended, for that might be injurious to purchasers and judgment creditors. We answer, the court have the same power over the docket as over other proceedings, that of making it subserve the ends of justice. The rights of purchasers we wish to have saved, either by a conditional docket, expressly reserving the rights of prior purchasers and mortgagees, or by enjoining it on Hart to release them.

We shall here be told that judgment creditors are entitled to the benefit of the Statute Relative to Docketing Judgments. The Statute (1 R. L., 531) enacts, that no judgment not docketed and entered in the books, &c., shall affect any lands or tenements, as to purchasers or mortgagees, or have preference against heirs, executors or administrators. *Expressio unius exclusio alterius*; by making the docket necessary as to purchasers and mortgagees, it is made so only as to them. This consideration is the more forcible, when it is recollected that, in the 1st section of the same Act, the Legislature have enacted, that no judgment shall continue, for more than ten years, a lien as against *bona fide* purchasers, or subsequent incumbrancers, by mortgage, judgment, or otherwise.

The question, then, again recurs, is a judgment creditor a purchaser, within the meaning of this Statute? A purchaser is one who acquires title otherwise than by descent (2 Bl. Com., 241); but a judgment creditor has no title to the defendant's real estate. For aught that appears, he may go against the person or personal property. Indeed, it has been settled in this State that a judgment gives no title *per se*. Of course the judgment creditor can never insist on the docketing clause of the Statute. The court, in considering him as a purchaser, would usurp legislative power. They would assume *jus dare—non jus exponere*.

It will be said that he may sell the defendant's real estate, and if his judgment be the oldest one docketed, may apply the avails to satisfy it, and vest the title in the purchaser. I answer, in that case the Statute would apply, but until a sale no purchaser can intervene; and, of course, the Statute, by the terms of it, can have no application.

The question, then, arises, whether this possibility of availing himself of this clause of the Statute is not sufficient to constitute him a purchaser; and this question is emphatically answered in the negative, by the decision in Jackson v. Dubois, 4 Johns., 216. It was there decided that a mortgage not registered has a preference over a subsequent judgment docketed. The clause in 1 R. L., 373, respecting mortgages, coincides with that on the subject of docketing judgments. It is this: "No mortgage, nor any deed, conveyance or writing, in the nature of a mortgage, shall defeat or prejudice the title or interest of any *bona fide* purchaser of any lands, tenements or hereditaments, unless the same shall have been duly registered as aforesaid." The language in the two statutes is so nearly the same, that the decision last cited may be considered in point to show, that until a sale under the judgment first docketed, the prior docketing creates no preference, and the Statute has no application. His Honor, *Judge* Spencer, in delivering the opinion of the court, says: "Before this Statute, there was no necessity of registering mortgages. They would have stood upon the same footing as any other lien on real property. Since the Statute, they must be registered, or lose their priority as to junior mortgages, and be liable to be defeated in case of a *bona fide* purchase prior to the registry. There is nothing in the Statute which gives a preference to a judgment docketed over an unregistered mortgage. Should the mortgagee permit a sale to take place prior to the registry, then, in my opinion, the vendee of the sheriff would be protected from the mortgage, and it would lose its priority.

After this decision, it may be said, with the utmost confidence, that the present case stands on the same footing as it would before the Statute Relative to Dockets; and there cannot be a doubt that before the Statute this judgment of Hart would have been a lien on John Reynolds' estate; and the court, to give effect to the intent and agreement of the parties, would have ordered an amendment, precisely as a court of equity would have ordered a mistake in a mortgage to be corrected, as against a mortgagor, and all persons who bought with notice of the defective mortgage.

Here it appeared from the records of the court, so that the fact could not be misunderstood, that by the agreement of John Reynolds, Hart's debt was to be secured by a judgment against his real estate, and such judgment was actually given, though informally. To say that the judgment is not against John, is puerile sophistry. It is a judgment against him, though not by his right name. This objection would, on the principle of our opponents, always prevent an alteration in the name of a party, in a conveyance, or fine, or a recovery, or a judgment. But the books teem with amendments in every one of these cases. Of the records of the court all persons were bound, before the Statute, to take notice, even executors and administrators, to determine the priority of debts. 6 T. R., 1. So it is said, in Tidd, 860, that before the Statute the defendant's lands were held from the time of the judgment, but since, the docketing is necessary as to purchasers and mortgagees. If this court can direct the signing of a judgment *nunc pro tunc*, so as to perfect the oldest judgment, though radically defective, they certainly may supply any other deficiency; for a judgment not signed is, as to the real estate, a nullity so far forth as purchasers are concerned. To supply the signing *nunc pro tunc*, makes the judgment, as to all, different from what it was before signing. Thus, if the Christian name of either party were altered, it renders that operative which before was void. As to the lien upon real property, the court create a new judgment, as much in one case as in the other.

The truth is, that every alteration makes the judgment a new one; *i. e.*, it makes it different from

carries, and a thousand other cases arising in our complex system of practice, by which another obtains preference; will the court relieve against such mistakes? Will they take away a preference, because accident was against the party who moved first? Is it enough that a judgment is planned without being perfected? **49]** Where is the *discretion of this court, arising upon questions of diligence, to end? We have gained a legal preference, and are entitled to retain it.

WOODWORTH, *J.*, delivered the opinion of the court. He went much at large into the **50*]** facts of the case, which were *scattered through a great variety of papers, and gave the opinion of the court on several minor points, which I have not deemed it material to notice. He then spoke to the principal points nearly as follows:

We have considered this case as deliberately and fully as we think its importance and novelty require; and we are *satisfied that **[*51** the respective applications of these parties are addressed to the sound discretion of the court. We do not forget that we are bound by decisions, as far as they can be made to apply to such a case; but we do not find ourselves tied down by these to any particular course of proceeding. The whole tenor and scope of the cases appear to call for a *very exten- **[*52** sive exercise of discretion in the amendment of proceedings conducted in good faith, by filling the chasms which may have intervened through accident or mistake; especially in a case where the person whose rights are to be affected has had full information that the proceedings are perfect, and has gone on under the idea that they were so. *We feel less delicacy in **[*53**

what it was before the alteration; and the futile argument, that "if the party knew of Hart's judgment, yet that the *scienter* did not make it a valid one, and that he must be supposed to have known it to be defective," would prevent every amendment. It might have been urged, with the same force, in the case of Seaman v. Drake, where the judgment was not signed, as in this case. If the judgment had been perfect, no amendment would have been necessary. Every application for an amendment supposes the judgment to be defective. The distinction between a judgment creditor and a purchaser, is not only founded on the language of the Statute, but in good sense; for the lien of a purchaser is specific. The money is advanced upon the title and credit of the estate, but that of a judgment creditor is general. He may go against the person. So in Tidd., 851: "If one article to buy an estate, and pay the purchase money, and afterwards a judgment is recovered against the vendor by a third person, who had no notice, yet this judgment shall not, in equity, affect the estate. But a mortgagee, &c., shall hold place against the covenantee; for in this case the money is lent upon the title and credit of the estate, and attaches upon the land; but a judgment is only a general security—not a specific lien upon the land." So, in 2 Ves., 662, per *Ld. Chancellor:* "A prior mortgagee, having a subsequent judgment, may tack the judgment to the mortgage, but a prior judgment creditor, getting a subsequent mortgage, cannot do it, because the judgment is not a specific lien upon the land; that is, he does not go on the security—he has not trusted to the credit of the estate."

It is again to be observed in this case, that the creditors had notice of Hart's judgment, when they took their own. The object of a docket is to give notice to purchasers, as much as it is the object of registering a mortgage. There is not the least shade of distinction. Actual notice, then, supersedes the necessity of a docket, certainly as respects judgment creditors, who are not named in the Docketing Statute, and it is sufficient, in case of a mortgagee, that he had notice at the time of taking his mortgage. By the notice the object of the Act is answered, and taking the deed or lien, under such circumstances, is a fraud. This doctrine is fully canvassed in Jackson v. Burgott, 10 Johns., 461, where the late *Ch.* J. Kent says: "It may be assumed, as a settled principle in the English law, that where a subsequent purchaser, whose deed is registered, had notice, at the time of his purchase, of a prior unregistered deed, the prior deed shall have preference. The purchase, under such circumstances, is a fraud. It is considered as done *mala fide*, by assisting the original vendor to defraud the prior vendee; and the courts will not suffer a statute, made to prevent fraud, to be a protection to fraud. The foundation of the English doctrine is, the fraud of the second purchase, under a knowledge of the first. An unregistered deed is in no case void. It is always good as against the grantor and his heirs." He continues: "When the Statute says that every deed not recorded shall be adjudged fraudulent and void, against a subsequent purchaser for valuable consideration, whose deed shall be recorded, it undoubtedly meant a subsequent purchaser in good faith. A subsequent purchaser *mala fide* was not within the purview of the Act. Consequently, in the case of a second purchaser, with notice, no estate passes to him by the deed." The whole of this opinion is worthy of particular attention, and "*mutatis mutandis*," applies with peculiar force to a subsequent judgment creditor with notice of a former lien.

The moment such a creditor attempts to wrest from the older incumbrancer his security, he himself becomes an incumbrancer *mala fide*. In such case, no lien passes to him by the second judgment. It is urged by the opposite counsel, that when the credit was given, the subsequent judgment creditors had received no notice: and therefore they are purchasers within the Docketing Statute. This notion is too absurd to require refutation. The credit was not given on the defendant's land. The creditors do not pretend to have examined the records before credit given, "*qui tacet consentire videtur.*" Taylor admitted that he did not examine them. It appears from Reynolds' affidavit that he told both Taylor and Doe, at the time of executing their bonds and warrant, of the existence of Hart's judgment. Taylor admitted to Mitchell that he knew of Hart's judgment and execution when he took his own. Doe, in his affidavit, admits that he knew of Hart's judgment when Hart's execution issued, viz.: the 28th of July, whereas the judgment in favor of Doe was filed the 5th of Aug., and Doe stated that he knew of no irregularity in Hart's judgment until Sept. Suppose A takes a mortgage, but does not have it registered, and B lends money on a note of the mortgagor, without notice of the mortgage, and afterwards, after A's mortgage is registered, B takes another mortgage, it would be ludicrous for him to claim priority, as a purchaser, because when he advanced the money on a note he knew not of A's mortgage. Suppose in the case now before the court, on an application for an amendment, there appeared to be no judgment creditors, nor any one to oppose, except a grocer, who had credited Reynolds a few shillings; and suppose he should allege, that he would not have trusted him if he had known of Hart's jugment; would such opposition avail anything? Or could he be considered, in any sense, as a purchaser? It is sufficient, in the case of a deed or mortgage, that the subsequent grantee or mortgagee had notice when he took his deed or mortgage. By taking it he does an act against conscience; *i. e.*, if it is ever applied to destroy an older lien. 9 Johns., 168.

The present is an appeal to the equitable powers of the court. Of course they ought to give such relief as a court of equity would give in this or similar cases. Suppose A contracts to sell to B, and he afterwards sells to C—B files a bill to compel specific p rf m nc , charging C with collusion—C must, inhisanswer, not only make out that he is a fair *bona fide* purchaser, for a valuable consideration, but also that this was without notice of B's interest. Here Hart applies for the specific lien intended, and agreed to be given. No one can prevent the equitable interference of the court but a purchaser, and that without notice. Doe and Taylor are neither of them purchasers, and they both had notice.

Again; a defective security will be enforced in equity, against creditors who have only a general —not a specific lien, as judgment creditors. In Taylor v. Wheeler, 2 Salk., 449, a copyholder in fee surrendered to the use of the mortgagee in fee, and became bankrupt before presentment, and there

going for this purpose to the utmost limit of our power, when it is plain that no one can suffer from its exercise. The amendment of proceedings must, in a great measure, rest upon this consideration.

Here is not a struggle in relation to the avails of a freehold estate, the disposition of **54***] which might be controlled by *the priority of the judgments, which are in themselves liens upon that kind of property; but it relates to the personalty, which is bound by an execution alone. A knowledge that there was or was not a judgment in existence, could in no way be material to Russ, or the creditor who assigned to him, for the reason that a judgment, *per se*, could not affect their rights. The important facts in relation to this case were perfectly understood by all the parties in interest, as early as May Term, 1822, when the subject was before this court upon a disclosure of those facts. The money now in question was *awarded to Chichester & Van [***55** Wyck, and the rights of the parties fully settled. Now here is nothing *in fieri*. The various executions were levied—a sale made under the direction of the court—the avails paid into court, to abide our order, which awarded the money to Chichester & Van Wyck—and that money has been actually paid. The order of the court has been executed. It is, at least, doubtful, on this ground alone, whether we have power to disturb the dispositions which have been made—whether this money has not passed beyond the bounds of our summary jurisdiction. It is true that a matter once passed upon, in this way, is not deemed technically *res judicata*. It may be opened. We will hear it again, upon good cause being

never was any presentment made, and the question was, whether the assignees of the Commissioners of Bankruptcy, or the mortgagee, should be preferred; and per *Ld. Chancellor*: "Though the surrender was void in law, for want of a presentment, and that might be the laches of the mortgagee, in not procuring it, yet the surrender was a lien, and bound the land in equity, and the assignee ought not to be in a better case than the bankrupt, who was plainly bound, in equity, by this defective conveyance. It was amended, as appears by 2 Vern., 564, S. C. On the same principle, there cannot be a doubt but a court of equity would order this judgment docketed *nunc pro tunc*, as against all but *bona fide* purchasers. The opposition of a judgment creditor could not prevent it. More especially, when it appeared that he took his incumbrance with notice of the defective one, a Court of Chancery would refuse to listen to his objection for a moment. If chancery would give the relief sought, will this court drive us to the enormous expense of applying to that court for relief, which this court has equal power to give? It appears from the cases cited (6 T. R., 8, and 7 T. R., 699) that this court can do whatever the ends of justice require, in regard to amending their records.

That the second judgment creditor knew of the older judgment at the time of obtaining his own—that he has equal equity with the first, while attempting to defeat the prior one, and wrest from the oldest creditor his security, is a doctrine which would be scouted from a court of equity.

As to the case of Sale v. Crompton, 1 Wils., 61, and Wentworth v. Staford, Ld. Raym., 68, cited on the other side, against an amendment, they both proceed on the ground that an amendment would be injurious to p c sers. The judgments, in both cases, were old ones; the purchasers could not be ascertained; nor was any offer made to release them, or have their rights saved. In the case now before the court, Reynolds swears there are but three purchasers, and those Hart offers to release, or to have their rights and those of all other possible purchasers, saved by a conditional docket. In Bac. Abr., Amendment, F, also cited on the other side, it is conceded, that if the rights of purchasers did not come in question, the judgment might be amended to any extent.

Neither can it be said that a judgment not docketed is not a lien; for the case of Seaman v. Drake, shows the incorrectness of such a position. In that case the judgment was not signed, and therefore, had no lien as to purchasers; yet the court allowed it to be amended, as well as to purchasers as judgment creditors. The truth is, a judgment not docketed is a lien. It was so at common law, and in Seaman v. Drake the court created a lien where none before existed. In the case cited from 2 Vern., 564, chancery made good a totally void surrender, stating that though void, yet it was a lien as between the parties, and the assignees were only general creditors, and had not a specific lien, as mortgages have. So, in this case, our judgment was a lien; equity would compel the defendant to comply with his agreement, and the resistance of those creditors who knew of Hart's judgment is unconscientious, dishonest and fraudulent. In asking that the judgment be amended, as to Taylor and Doe, we request nothing unreasonable or improper. As to the other judgment creditors, not now before the court, we are not very anxious that the court should interfere.

The Court directed the following

RULE: August 22d, 1817.

(After the title of the cause.)

A motion having been made on behalf of Walter Doe and James Taylor, judgment creditors of John Reynolds, to set aside the execution issued to the sheriff of Saratoga Co., in the above cause, on the grounds specified in the notice of said motion, and a cross-motion having been made by Richard P. Hart, to amend the record of judgment and proceedings connected with such record, filed the 6th day of June, one thousand eight hundred and eleven, in favor of Richard P. Hart, against Elisha Reynolds, entered and filed by virtue of a warrant of attorney attached to said record, executed by John Reynolds, and also the docket of said judgment and the entry of the time of signing said record *nunc pro tunc*, on the grounds set forth in the affidavits on which said cross-motion is founded; on reading and filing the affidavits read in this cause, ordered, on motion of *Mr. Mitchel*, counsel for Richard P. Hart, that the motion to set aside said execution be denied, upon the payment of the costs of the motion to set the same aside, by the said Richard P. Hart. It is further ordered, by and with the consent of John Reynolds, that the judgment record and proceedings connected with such record, filed June 6, one thousand eight hundred and eleven, in favor of Richard P. Hart against Elisha Reynolds, entered and filed by virtue of a warrant of attorney attached to said record, executed by John Reynolds, for ten thousand dollars, be amended by inserting the name of John Reynolds instead of Elisha Reynolds, as often as the latter occurs in said record of judgment and such proceedings, and that the book of dockets, as far as it relates to said judgment, be altered, so as to conform to the amended judgment as to the defendant's name and the amount of the judgment, and that the day of signing said judgment be altered to the day when it was docketed; and that said amendments be made *nunc pro tunc*, so that the said judgment shall be, in all respects, a perfect judgment for ten thousand dollars, against John Reynolds, entered, signed, filed, docketed and inserted in the book of dockets, the said June 6, one thousand eight hundred and eleven; provided, that the clerk shall express in the said book of dockets, opposite said defendant's name, where said judgment is docketed therein, that the rights of *bona fide* purchasers from, and mortgagees of said John Reynolds, between the 6th of June, one thousand eight hundred and eleven, and the day of entering this rule, shall not be prejudiced by such alteration of said books of dockets, and provided a copy of this rule be attached to the said record. It is further ordered, that a copy of this rule be served on each of the judgment creditors of John Reynolds, whose lien accrued before this day, within six weeks from this time. It is understood, however, that this court will make such order the next term of this court as shall be just, in relation to the judgment in this cause, as to all judgment creditors of the said John Reynolds, whose lien accrued before the day of entering this rule, except Walter Doe and James Taylor, provided application be duly made theretor, the next term of this court, and not afterwards.

shown; but where the order made has been carried into full execution, and the party has gone off with the avails in his pocket, it is deserving of great consideration, at least, whether we can bring him back into court upon motion, and dictate the course he shall take, whatever additional light may be thrown around the subject; and this, in a special manner, where all has gone forward in good faith. Take the case of a motion to enter satisfaction upon the judgment roll, on the ground that the money has been paid: the defendant swears to the payment, which the plaintiff as solemnly denies: the case being balanced, the motion is denied. At another term, the defendant renews his application, upon the ground that he has since discovered a release, or receipt of the plaintiff, acknowledging that he had received the money. We might hear the application, and grant the necessary relief, provided the judgment yet remained *in fieri*; but suppose, in the meantime, that the money had been paid to, and pocketed by the plaintiff, I should doubt the power of the court to afford redress in this manner. The suit is at an end, and the whole becomes a matter *in pais*. So of a motion for a new trial, on the ground that undiscovered evidence was behind, which is refused; and the judgment perfected and execution had; a second application would hardly be received, under such circumstances, however strong the appeal. There is a point at which these summary applications should cease, like every other litigation, for the sake of certainty and social quiet.

56*] *But there is a precedent which is very direct to bear us out in amending this proceeding on the part of Chichester & Van Wyck, even were the money now in the hands of the clerk. I allude to the case of *Close v. Gillespey*, 3 Johns., 526. A judgment had been signed and docketed upon a warrant of attorney; but, through mistake, the name of the defendant's attorney was neither subscribed to the *cognovit* nor inserted in the roll. Mancius having obtained a subsequent judgment against the defendant, a motion was made by the plaintiff to amend the proceedings *nunc pro tunc*. Now that record was invalid. Both parties considered it so; and the application was opposed because the rights of Mancins were to be affected by the amendment. Executions on both judgments had been delivered to the sheriff, the execution of Close being first delivered, and both he and Mancius claimed a preference; yet Close was allowed to amend, though both executions were levied on the same property. The judge who gave the opinion of the court declares broadly (and in this he is sustained by all the authorities): "I cannot perceive that our right to amend, in case of the mistake of one of our officers, is to be controlled by the effect which is to be produced in another case. All amendments affect, more or less third persons." That case is much in point, and, indeed, appears to me precisely parallel in principle with the one before us, the application for an amendment in which comes strongly commended to us by the principles of justice. Chichester & Van Wyck had a judgment and execution, perfect in every particular, as it respects personal property, except in the mere formality of filing in the clerk's office. Instead of being answered by a constructive docket-notice, which was deemed sufficient for the junior creditor in *Close* v. *Gillespey*, Russ had actual notice, in the most explicit manner, by an execution and levy. We leave him in possession of all the rights upon which he could ever calculate, in legal propriety, without granting his motion. This must be denied; and Chichester & Van Wyck must take the effect of their motion to amend.

SUTHERLAND, *J.* It is, perhaps, proper to add, that in forming the opinion which has been delivered, we must not *be under- [***57** stood as questioning the case of *Barrie* v. *Dana*, or as doubting that, in all cases, the roll should be filed before execution can issue. We have been governed much by the peculiar circumstances attending this particular case. The subsequent creditor knew of the judgment, and relied solely on technical ground to defeat it. We hear no complaints from the party defendant.

Rule accordingly.

Distinguished—21 Hun, 511.
Cited in—10 Wend., 543; 18 Wend., 677; 19 Wend., 92; 4 Den., 243; 10 Paige, 361; 2 Sand. Ch., 165; 1 N. Y., 172; 17 N. Y., 449; 34 N. Y., 333; 36 N. Y., 636; 55 N. Y., 166; 67 N. Y., 202; 3 Trans. App., 239; 1 Lans., 192; 6 Barb., 313; 3 How. Pr., 215; 4 How. Pr., 18; 5 How. Pr., 383; 6 How. Pr., 289; 7 How. Pr., 267; 52 How. Pr., 161; 56 How. Pr., 10; 43 Super., 529; 2 Daly, 205; Co. N. S., 49; 9 Bank. Reg., 164; 25 Hun, 535; 36 Mich., 103; 44 Mo., 342; 21 Minn., 55.

JACKSON, ex dem. WILLIAMS and WASHBURN,
v.
MILLER.

Ejectment—Motion to Stay Proceedings until Costs in Former Suit are Paid—When may be Made.

A motion to stay proceedings in a second suit, till the costs of a former suit for the same cause are paid, is in season, if made at any time while the latter is in a course of litigation.

Thus, the court will hear it after verdict for the plaintiff in the second cause, subject to the opinion of the court, and a case made and noticed for argument by the defendant.

MR. R. WESTON, for the defendant, moved that proceedings be stayed, on the part of the plaintiff, till the costs of a former ejectment, brought by Jackson (the now defendant), against Washburn, one of the lessors of the plaintiff for the same premises now in question, in which a verdict and judgment were rendered for the then plaintiff, and a writ of possession executed, in virtue whereof the (now) defendant was put in possession, be paid. It appeared, by affidavit, that on the trial of the first ejectment, Washburn, the defendant, made title, by a lease from Williams, the other lessor in this suit, and that Williams claimed as heir of his father. On the trial of this cause, the same title came in question, on nearly the same evidence as in the first; that a verdict was taken therein for the (now) plaintiff subject to the opinion of the court, upon which a case had been made, but not yet argued, though it had been noticed for argument by the defendant's attorney. Washburn had absconded shortly after the trial of the first action, the costs of which had never been paid.

This motion was made on the authority of *Jackson* v. *Edwards*, 1 Cow., 138.

Mr. D. Russell, contra, said the application was too late. The court might as well be called on to stay a writ of possession, after judgment docketed. Where the defendant has **58***] thought *proper to meet the question of title upon its merits, and that has been decided against him, the court should not listen to an application of this kind. There is no case to be found where such an application has been sustained, at this stage of the proceedings. It would be unjust to permit a party to lie by, until the costs of the plaintiff have accumulated by a trial and verdict; and after nearly all the expense has been incurred which could arise in the whole course of the suit, then obtain a stay of proceedings. The application might, and should have been made at an earlier stage of the cause; and has been waived by delay.

Curia. We think otherwise; and that the application comes before us in season, if made at any time while the cause is in a course of litigation.

Motion granted.

Cited in—10 Wend., 544; 18 Wend., 653; 27 How. Pr. 156.

MARSH *v.* EASTMAN.

Certiorari—*Course of Defendant, when Justice Fails to Make Return.*

On *certiorari*, the defendant cannot compel a return.

His course is to *non pros.* the plaintiff in error, if he does not cause a return to be made.

ON *certiorari* to a justice's court. The parties had proceeded to an issue of *in nullo est erratum*, without the justice's having made any return; and now,

A motion was made, on the part of the defendant, for a rule requiring the justice to make a return.

Curia. He should *non pros.* the plaintiff, if he does not cause a return to be made. The defendant has no right to call upon a justice to make a return. This is the business of the plaintiff.

Motion denied.

59*] *IN THE MATTER OF GILBERT

v.

THE JUDGES OF THE COURT OF COMMON PLEAS OF THE COUNTY OF NIAGARA.

Mandamus—*Will not Issue to Control Discretion of Common Pleas.*

On setting aside a *ca. sa.* for irregularity, the Court of C. P. required the party against whom it issued to stipulate that he would not bring false imprisonment; and on motion to this court for a *mandamus* requiring them to vacate the condition, held, that this was matter of discretion in the court below with which this court would not interfere.

A VERDICT in the C. P of Niagara had been rendered against Gilbert in favor of one Tuttle. Gilbert brought error, and put in bail, after which Tuttle sued out a *ca. sa.*, on which Gilbert was arrested. The C. P. afterwards set this writ aside, on the ground that the writ of error was a *supersedeas* of execution, but imposed the condition that Gilbert should stipulate not to bring false imprisonment. And now,

A motion was made for a *mandamus* commanding the judges below to strike out this condition; but,

The Court were clear against the motion, and denied a rule to show cause. They said that requiring this condition was a mere matter of discretion with the court below, and this court would not interfere.

Motion denied.

Cited in—5 Wend. 123; 3 Abb. Pr., 63.

IN THE MATTER OF UNDERWOOD, an Insolvent Debtor,

v.

THE HON. J. T. IRVING, First Judge of the Court of Common Pleas of the City of NEW YORK.

Application for Discharge, under Act to Abolish Imprisonment for Debt—Order for Ten Weeks' Advertisement—Affidavit of Six Weeks' Advertisement—Order on, for Assignment, Void.

On an application for a discharge, under the Act to Abolish Imprisonment for Debt in Certain Cases (sess. 42, ch. 101), and order for ten weeks' advertisement to creditors, and a publication of only six weeks, and then an order, by mistake, for assignment, which is made, the second order is a nullity, being made without jurisdiction, and the commissioner may refuse to sign the discharge.

MAR. 6, 1824, the insolvent presented his petition to the Hon. J. T. Irving, First Judge of the Court of C. P. of the City of N. Y., for a discharge under the "Act to Abolish Imprisonment for Debt in Certain Cases," passed Apr. 7, 1819. His Honor made the usual order for the creditors to appear May 24 following, and directed by this order that the same should be published for *ten weeks. [***60** May 24 affidavits of publication were produced, and no person appearing to oppose, the usual order for an assignment was made, the assignment executed, and on the next day a certificate was produced from the assignees appointed by the judge that the insolvent had executed the assignment. But, on application for a discharge, the judge stated that since making the order for assignment he had discovered that two of the affidavits of publication stated the same to have been made six weeks instead of ten. The attorney of the insolvent was ignorant, till then, that the affidavits were defective, and he insisted that the judge was bound to sign the discharge, it being too late after making the order and executing the assignment, there being no objection on the score of want of good faith in the insolvent to inquire into the regularity of notice. But the judge was of a different opinion, and refused to sign the discharge. The omission to advertise the ten weeks was through inadvertence.

A motion was now made for a *mandamus* commanding *Judge* Irving to proceed and grant the discharge, and,

Mr. R. Sedgwick, for the motion, cited 5 L. N. Y., 116 *a*, sess. 42, ch. 101, sec. 2, and insisted that it was intended by the law that the whole investigation to be made by the judge, the whole trial, &c., should be made before the order for assignment. When that order is made, all prior questions are *res judicata.* It is certain that there can be but one trial by jury; and it is well understood that all questions of fraud are to be settled, if heard by the judge, before granting the order. *A fortiori,* questions of form, notice, &c., ought to be adjudged before that time.

The 3d section of the Act is imperative that upon the insolvent's producing a certificate, &c., the judge shall declare under his hand and seal, &c.

He cited the case of *Bradstreet,* 13 Johns., 385, as in point. The ground on which the court held, in that case, that the Recorder could vacate the order was collusion to prevent the creditors from opposing. Besides, the whole matter was there *in fieri* when the
61*] Recorder was applied *to to vacate the order. The assignment had not been made and certified. How can the assigned property in this case be got back? The assignees hold it in trust for the creditors. The judge had executed his powers, and the assignment vested the property in the assignee.

Curia. We do not view the matter in this light. The first order made pursuant to the Statute had been disregarded. The ten weeks' advertisement was necessary to give the commissioner jurisdiction. Till this was done, he had no authority, and the second order was a nullity. The assignment must probably share the same fate, though it is not necessary to pass upon the effect of this, and we must not be understood as doing so. We are not to be guided by a consideration of the embarrassment which may arise from that act.

Motion denied.

Cited in—1 Hill, 140; 3 Barb., 346; 16 Barb., 350; 19 How. Pr., 240; 2 Abb. Pr., 179; 10 Abb. Pr., 471; 8 Abb. N. S., 204; 2 Abb. N. C., 375; 4 E. D. S., 309.

MANN *v.* SWIFT.

Return to Certiorari.

The return to a *certiorari* must contain a complete history of the proceedings in itself—not by reference to the affidavit on which it is founded.

ON *certiorari* to a justice's court. The return of the justice merely referred to the copy of the affidavits on which the *certiorari* was founded, and stated that "the same were substantially true, except such parts as relate to the separation and drinking of spirituous liquors by the jurors who tried said cause, which may be true, but the following is what came to my observation," &c.

Mr. M. Hoffman moved to set this return aside as irregular.

Mr. J. Lynch, contra.

Curia. This practice of referring to, and adopting the affidavit on which the *certiorari* is founded, is irregular. The return should contain a complete history of the proceedings in itself. Not doing so, it must be set aside.

Rule accordingly.

---

*ROGERS *v.* COLEMAN. [*62

Action on Bond—Verdict for Plaintiff, without Assignment of Breaches or Assessment of Damages—Subsequent Assignment and Assessment, by writ of Inquiry, Proper.

Debt on bond to perform covenants—issue and verdict for plaintiff but no assignment of breaches nor assessment of damages by the jury; the plaintiff may afterwards assign breaches and have his damages assessed upon a writ of inquiry, under the Statute (sess. 36, ch. 56, sec. 7, 1 R. L., 518).

DEBT on bond for the performance of covenants. Plea, *non est factum.* Upon this plea the plaintiff proceeded to trial, and took a verdict for the plaintiff, without having yet assigned breaches, at the Monroe Circuit, in Mar. last. Apr. 22, the plaintiff's attorney served the defendant's attorney with a copy of the assignment of breaches, and with notice of executing a writ of inquiry, for May 4, before the sheriff of Monroe Co., on which day it was accordingly executed.

Mr. A. Sampson moved to set aside the proceedings as irregular. He said there should have been an assignment of breaches, and an assessment of damages by the jury who tried the cause. He cited *Tuxbury* v. *Miller,* 19 Johns., 311.

Mr. S. M. Hopkins, contra.

Curia. The ordinary practice is to assign breaches, and have the damages assessed by the jury who try the cause, yet, where this is omitted, we are clear that the plaintiff is not foreclosed, but may proceed as he has done in this case.

Motion denied.(a)

(a) *Vide* 1 Saund. 58, *n.* 1, and the cases there cited, and forms given by Sergeant Williams. Also, 2 Saund., 187 *a*, 187 *b*, *n.* 2, where this practice of assigning breaches and assessing damages, after verdict, and before judgment, is mentioned and approved of by him. And he says that the form of entering theysuggestion may be the same as in case of judgment on demurrer, which he gave in 1 Saund., 58, *n.* 1. The proceeding in England is founded on the 8 & 9 Wm. III., ch. 11, of which our Statute (sess. 36, ch. 56, sec. 7; 1 R. L., 518) is nearly a copy. One difference, however, is, that the writ of inquiry may here run to to the sheriff, to summon a jury before the circuit judge, or himself, to inquire, &c., but in England it is confined to the Assizes. The form (which is on judgment upon demurrer) given by Sergeant Williams is now well established, having undergone the revision and been approved both by Ld. Alvanley, *Ch. J.*, in Hankin v. Broomhead, 3 Bos. & P., 607, 611, and by the House of Lords, on error, in *Johnes v. [*63 Johnes, 3 Dow's Parl. Cas., 1 to 23, in which the *Ld. Chancellor* read the form from the record, said it was copied from Mr. Williams' note, and iterated the compliment bestowed upon that learned practitioner by Ld. Alvanley, in Hankin v. Broomhead. Johnes v. Johnes traveled through the Court of Exchequer Chamber, silently, into the House of Lords, where it was argued for the first time, which accounts for some expressions of the *Lord Chancellor*, in the opinion which he gives in that cause.

67*] *STEWART v. ATKINS.

Neglect to Plead—Default on, Set Aside.

H. & W., attorneys, being partners, issued a *cap. ad. resp.*, on which the defendant indorsed his appearance, in the name of W., as attorney, filed a declaration, and entered a rule to plead as on the motion of H. & W., and gave notice thereof in the name of W. The defendant's attorney searched the common rule book (W), found no rule entered, and neglected to plead, the rule being entered in rule book (H), and a default was, therefore, entered, for want of a plea; and because the defendant was misled, the court set aside the default, without costs.

THE *capias ad respondendum*, on which the defendant indorsed his appearance, was signed by O. M. Willey, attorney; and the notice of the rule to plead, indorsed upon the declaration, was signed by the same attorney, and served personally on the defendant, who retained an attorney, who wrote and inquired of his agent whether any rule to plead had been actually entered, and received for answer that there had not. He, therefore, omitted to plead, and the plaintiff took judgment by default. On further search, it turned out that the rule to plead was entered in the name of Hastings & Willey, who were partners, but whose business was done in the name of Willey, as attorney. The mistake, therefore, arose from the search being made in the common rule book (W) instead of (H).

Mr. A. Samson moved to set aside the proceedings for irregularity.

Mr. C. P. Kirkland, contra.

Curia. For the reason, alone that the defendant has been misled by this proceeding, we set aside the default, without costs.

Rule accordingly.

68*] *BENNETT
v.
N. DAVIS AND W. M. DAVIS.

Bond and Warrant of Attorney, Executed by Two Parties—Death of one before Entry of Judgment—Entry of, as of Preceding Term, Irregular.

The judgment and proceedings in entering up a judgment in one term cannot be made to relate to, and be entitled as of a term preceding.

And where a bond and warrant of attorney to confess judgment, were executed by two, Apr. 10, 1824, and one of them died Apr. 14, a judgment entered thereon during the subsequent May Term, as of the preceding Feb. Term, was set aside as irregular.

JUDGMENT for the plaintiff on bond and warrant of attorney. The proper papers were filed, and the judgment perfected, May 6, last, being after the commencement of May Term. The bond and warrant were executed Apr. 10, last, the latter containing the usual clause authorizing any attorney, &c., in term or vacation, &c., to confess judgment for the obligors, and to release all errors, &c. The declaration was entitled of Feb. Term, 1824, and the *placita* was of the same term. N. Davis, one of the defendants, died Apr. 14, last.

Mr. J. A. Spencer moved to set aside the judgment as irregular, on the ground that N. Davis, one of the defendants, died before the term at which the judgment was entered. He said the judgment being entered in May Term could not be made to relate to the previous term. If this should be deemed an error, and, as such, capable of being released, within the provision in the warrant of attorney, the power conferred by that instrument was gone, being revoked by the death of N. Davis. He referred to 1 Dunl. Pr., 364, and the cases there cited, and *Gee* v. *Lane*, 15 East, 592.

Mr. G. C. Bronson, contra, cited *King* v. *Shaw*, 3 Johns., 142; *Mackay* v. *Rhinelander*, 1 Johns. Cas., 410; 2 Archb. Pr., 15; Tidd, 495; *Gladwin* v. *Scott*, Barn., 53; *Odes* v. *Woodward*, 2 Ld. Raym., 766; *Id.*, 849, S. C.; 1 Salk., 87, S. C.; 3 Salk., 116, S. C.; 1 Saund., 219 *e*.

The Court set aside the proceedings as irregular, upon the grounds taken by *Mr. Spencer*.

Rule accordingly.

Cited in—4 Cow., 460, n.; 6 Hill, 242; 10 N. Y., 169; 13 How. Pr., 122; 8 Abb. N. S., 466; 57 Barb., 175; 21 Wall., 386.

---

*IN THE MATTER OF MARSH [*69
v.
WENDOVER, Sheriff of the City and County of NEW YORK.

Assignment, under Insolvent Act—Passes Land—Creditor, whose Judgment Perfected, after Assignment, cannot Redeem.

Land passes by a general assignment under the Insolvent Act, and a creditor, whose judgment against the insolvent is perfected after the assignment, has no lien; and therefore cannot redeem within the Act (sess. 43, ch. 184, sec. 3).

JAN. 25, 1823, Gibbons recovered judgment in this court, against W. Messerve, for $1,514.10. Stamler, on the same day, recovered a judgment, in this court, against Messerve, for $1,789.10. Feb. 22, 1823, writs of *fi. fa.* issued on these judgments; and Apr. 29, 1823, Gibbons & Stamler became joint purchasers for $600 of the real estate of Messerve. They received the sheriff's certificate, by which they were entitled to a sheriff's deed, July 29, 1824.

Apr. 24, 1823, Stevens recovered a judgment in the N. Y. C. P. against Messerve, for $218.04, which was assigned in Aug. of the same year to Reed.

May 13, 1823, Messerve was discharged under the Act to Abolish Imprisonment for Debt in Certain Cases (sess. 42, ch. 101), and Stamler became his assignee.

July 25, 1823, Stevens & Rindge recovered judgment in the N. Y. C. P., against Messerve, for $405.76, which, Feb. 16, 1824, they assigned to Marsh. The judgment was upon a *relicta* and *cognovit*, reserving the exemption of Messerve's body.

July 28, 1824, Reed, as the assignee of Stevens, redeemed from Gibbons & Stamler, and on the same day Marsh redeemed from Reed.

Messrs. J. Leveridge and *S. M. Hopkins* moved for a *mandamus*, commanding the sheriff to convey to Marsh. They contended that the conveyance of the land, by the assignment under the Insolvent Act, or by operation of law, from Messerve to his assignees, would not prevent the judgment of Stevens & Rindge operating as a lien, though not recovered till after the assignment. The discharge was under the Body Act and left the previous and future acquisition of the insolvent liable to the judgment and execution of creditors. Stamler, being an assignee for all the creditors, was 70*] their trustee, and *could do no act to prejudice the rights of his *cestuis que trust*, Cas. Eq. Abr., 384.

Mr. J. Platt, contra.

Curia. We think the assignment placed the property beyond the reach of the judgment, which was not a lien. Marsh, therefore, had no right to redeem, and the motion must be denied.

Motion denied.

BROWN *v.* HANKERSON.

Arbitration Bonds—Construction of Recital—Award, Void for Uncertainty—When Whole Award, Bad for Uncertainty of Part.

The arbitration bonds were dated Aug. 21, 1813, and the award was dated Aug. 23, 1813, and recited bonds dated Aug. 21, last past; held, that if a correct recital were necessary, it should be construed, in support of the award, to refer to the day; *i. e.*, the 21st last past, instead of the month; *i. e.*, Aug. last past.

Where the award was that H. should deliver the said farm to B. &c., and that B. should pay H. certain moneys; held, that the delivery of the farm was a consideration for the money, and the award being uncertain, in not describing the farm by reference or otherwise, the award of the money was also void.

If that part of the award, which is void, is so connected with the rest as to affect the justice of the case, the award is for the whole.

Citations—Dy., 376 *c*; Ord Us., 61, *n.*; Cro., Jac., 314, 646; 1 Ld. Raym., 123; 5 Str., 1024; Kyd. Aw., 259, 260, 246; Lutw., 169.

ERROR from the Court of C. P. of Schoharie Co. The action below was debt on a general arbitration bond, executed by Brown and payable to Hankerson, dated Aug. 21, 1813, and conditioned that the award should be made, &c. on or before Aug. 23, thereafter.

Plea, no award.

Replication—that the arbitrators mentioned in the condition of the bond, within the time limited, &c., made their award of and concerning the premises in the said condition mentioned, by which they awarded that all actions, &c., arisen before the day of the date of the bond, should cease, &c., that each party should pay his own costs, &c., and that Hankerson should deliver, or cause to be delivered, to Brown his right and claim of the said farm, reserving the privilege of taking off the summer crops when ripe, and of leaving the house by the first of Sept. then next; that Brown should, on or before Jan. 1, then next, pay $17.50, and should further pay unto Hankerson $17.50, on or before Aug. 1, then next; and that, on the payment of the $35, the parties should execute mutual general releases, of all demands, &c., from the beginning of the world to Aug. 21, then last past, and assigning a breach in the non-payment of the money.

*Rejoinder—denying that any such [*71 award was made, and issue.

On the trial, the plaintiff offered in evidence an award, dated Aug. 23, 1813, reciting mutual arbitration bonds between the parties, bearing date Aug. 21, now last past, the award being in other respects as set forth in the replication. The award was objected to, as not pursuing the authorit conferred by the bonds. The court overruled the objection, and the jury, under their direction, found a verdict for the plaintiff, and assessed his damages to $40.32. The defendants excepted to this opinion, and there being judgment for the plaintiff below, brought error to this court.

Mr. T. Lawyer, for the plaintiff in error. To support the objection taken upon the trial, he cited *Allen* v. *Watson*, 16 Johns., 205, *Fisher* v. *Pimbly*, 11 East, 187; *Macomb* v. *Wilber*, 16 Johns., 227, and *Foreland* v. *Manygold*, 1 Salk. 72. And he insisted, 2d, that the award was void for uncertainty, in support of which he relied upon *Schuyler* v. *Van Der Veer*, 2 Cai., 235; *Cockson* v. *Ogle*, Lutw., 500; Kyd on Aw., 194, 258, 259; 2 Saund., 293 *a*, *note* 1, and the cases there cited.

Mr. J. Coming, contra, said the words "last past" might well refer to the day, viz.: the 21st, and not the month; but if there was a clear misrecital, this will not vitiate the award. 11 Johns., 103; 2 Mod., 169; 1 Salk., 72; 1 Ld. Raym., 715; 12 Mod., 534.

Curia, per SUTHERLAND, *J.* The objection taken to the award, below, was, that it bore date the 23d Aug. 1813, and purported to be made by virtue of a bond of submission, which bore date "August 21st, now last past," whereas the bond declared on and prodneed in evidence bore date Aug. 21, 1813, being Aug. instant, instead of past. The arbitrators also awarded general releases between the parties, from the beginning of the world until the "21st day of August last past, being the day of the date of the arbitration bond," thus showing that the award was made under a bond of submission, of Aug. 21, 1812, whereas the bond declared *on was dated Aug. [*72 21, 1813; and consequently no authority was shown to make the award.

The strict grammatical construction of the award is, perhaps, as contended for by the plaintiff in error. But the intention of the arbitrators is perfectly clear. They run into a mere inaccuracy of expression. To avoid

NOTE.—*Arbitration and award.* That an award must be within the submission, certain to a common intent and final. See Purdy v. Delavan, 1 Cai., 304, *note.*

When an award is bad in part, if the objeetionable part can be separated from the rest the good part will be sustained. Barrows v. Capon, 11 Cush., 37; Wynn v. Bellas, 34 Pa. St., 160; Dake v. James, 4 N. Y., 567; Rixford v. Nye, 20, Vt., 132; Rogers v. Tatum, 25 N. J. L., 281; Banks v. Adams, 28 Me., 259; Tracy v. Herrick, 25 N. H., 381; Orcutt v. Butler, 42 Me., 83.

Compare Jackson v. Ambler, 14 Johns., 96, *note.*

Presumption in favor of an award. Karthaus v. Ferrer, 1 Pet., 222; Ott v. Schroeppel, 5 N. Y., 482; Haywood v. Harmon, 17 Ill., 477; Kendrick v. Tarbell, 26 Vt., 416; Fryeberg Canal v. Frye, 5 Me., 38; Tomlinson v. Hammond, 8 Ia., 40; Strong v. Strong, 9 Cush., 560.

such an objection we may, without any great violence, suppose that the words "last past" were intended by the arbitrators to refer to the day, and not to the month. (*Vide* Dy., 376 *c*; Ord on Usury, 61, *n.*; Cro. Jac., 646.) These awards are frequently made and drawn up by illiterate men, and it will not do to test them by the strict rules of grammar. If there had, in truth, been another bond of submission in 1812, it was competent for the defendant to show it.

But the award is bad for uncertainty. It directs "that the said James Hankerson should deliver, or cause to be delivered, to the said George Brown, his right and claim of the said farm, reserving the right of taking off the summer crops, when ripe, &c., and that the said George Brown shall, on or before 1st day of Jan. next, pay, &c. No farm was mentioned either in the bond of submission or in any previous part of the award; nor is there any averment in the pleadings of the plaintiff in relation to it, if, indeed, it could be helped by averment. What farm the arbitrators intended is, therefore, altogether uncertain, and incapable of being ascertained.

In *Bedam* v. *Clerkson*, 1 Ld. Raym., 123, an award "that one of the parties shall deliver up to the other a certain writing obligatory, or a certain bill obligatory, which he had before," was held to be bad for uncertainty, no description either of the date, the maker, or the amount of the bond, being stated. So in *Cockson* v. *Ogle*, Lutw., 169, an award "that the defendant shall deliver several books,"&c., was held bad, the award not specifying what books. So in *Thinne* v. *Rigby*, Cro. Jac., 314, an award that "the defendant should give security to the plaintiff, for the payment of £16, at two days," was held bad for uncertainty, not showing what security he should give, whether by bond or otherwise. So, also, in **73*]** **Tipping* v. *Smith*, 2 Str., 1024, that the defendants shall give security, without specifying what, was held bad.

The award, being void in this particular, is void throughout, because the delivering of the farm by the plaintiff to the defendant, was the only act or thing which he was directed to do, and was the consideration intended by the arbitrators for the money which they directed the defendant to pay to him, and for the recovery of which this action was brought. (Kyd on Aw., 259, 260, and the cases there cited.) If that part of the award which is void is so connected with the rest as to affect the justice of the case between the parties, the award is void for the whole. (Kyd on Aw., 246.) The judgment below must, therefore, be reversed.

Judgment reversed.

Cit d in—5 Wend., 270; 12 Wend., 380; 1 E. D. S., 442. e

JACKSON, ex dem. Dox, *v.* JACKSON.

Order to Stay Proceedings by Commissioner—Not a Nullity.

An order to stay proceedings upon a case made for the purpose of obtaining a new trial, granted by a commissioner to perform the chamber duties of a Judge of the Supreme Court, is not a nullity; but is valid till revoked by the commissioner or set aside by the court.

EJECTMENT. The cause was tried at the last Ontario Circuit, before His Honor, E. T. Throop, Circuit Judge, and a verdict found for the plaintiff. Afterwards, a case being made and settled on the part of the defendant, for the purpose of moving for a new trial, he obtained of a commissioner to do the chamber duties of a judge of the Supreme Court, an order that all further proceedings on the part of the plaintiff be stayed until the further order of this court, though it appeared that *Judge* Throop was at home, and might have been applied to for the order.

The plaintiff's attorney treated this order as a nullity, and proceeded to sign judgment.

Mr. E. Williams moved to set aside all the proceedings subsequent to the order. He said the Acts (sess. 36, ch. 16, 1 R. L., 322, and sess. 41, ch. 195, sec. 1) give these commissioners the same chamber powers with a judge of this court. To declare this order a nullity, would be to repeal the Act.

Mr. J. C. Spencer*, contra. The Stat- **[*74 ute must be taken in reference to the settled practice, which has been understood for 20 years, to confine the power of making this order to the judge who tried the cause. Even this court will not hear the question whether such an order shall be granted until it has been denied by the circuit judge. *Bach* v. *Coles*, 3 Cai., 83. I do not mean to contend that there may not be cases of necessity in which a temporary stay may be granted by a commissioner; but to interfere in this way, as a matter of course, is a palpable excess of jurisdiction. The statute is, in terms, broad enough to embrace orders for the allowance of classical studies to a clerk, yet the court have reserved this exclusively to themselves, as a matter not fit to be delegated to commissioners. To say that any one of the 200 commissioners in the State may grant the order in question, and, which is the same thing, if one refuses, you may appeal from him to another, will, in effect, be saying that no man shall have judgment in any case till the calendar of arguments is cleared.

Mr. Williams, in reply. If the order was improperly granted, the court will strike the cause off the calender, or set the order aside; and with costs, too; but it is one thing to say that it shall be set aside, and another that it shall be disregarded and treated as a nullity. Here has been no application to the court for any such purpose. Suppose one of your Honors had granted the order, could counsel say "it is void, because you did not try the cause?" The gentleman concedes all we ask, when he says a commissioner may grant the order from necessity. If the commissioner mistake the existence of this necessity, as if the judge be at home when he was supposed to be absent, he should be asked to revoke his order, upon which it should come by way of appeal to this court in the event of his refusal. As to orders of clerkship, this pertains to the admission of attorneys, which is the act of the court; not a mere chamber duty.

Curia. The chamber powers of a commissioner are, by the Statute, made equal to those of a judge of this court. *The expe- **[*75** diency of granting such a power is not in question. The commissioner may have acted indiscreetly; but whether this be so or not, the party has mistaken his remedy. Should the commissioner refuse to revoke an order granted upon insufficient grounds, we might, on appeal, summarily review the matter, and revoke it ourselves. But the order cannot be treated as a nullity.

Motion granted.

Cited in—4 Hill, 556; 3 Paige, 198; 8 Daly, 109.

JACKSON, ex dem. DE FOREST and M'MICHAEL,
v.
RAMSAY.

Matter of Defense Arising after Issue Joined—Must be Pleaded Puis Darrein Continuance—*Sheriff's Deed Relates Back to Sale—Relation in General.*

Matter of defense arising after issue joined, must be pleaded *puis darrein continuance.*

This rule applies as well to ejectment as to other actions; as where the defendant acquires title by deed after issue.

But where R. purchased the premises at sheriff's sale on a judgment and execution against M. and took no deed; and then M.'s devisee brought ejectment, after issue joined, in which, R. obtained a sheriff's deed; held, that this need not be pleaded; but might be given in evidence upon the general issue.

A deed given by a sheriff upon a previous sale on execution relates back to, and, in judgment of law, is executed at the time of sale.

Where there are diverse acts concurrent to make a conveyance, estate or other thing, the original act shall be preferred; and to this the other act shall have relation.

Cases supporting this rule considered; and applied to a deed executed more than four years after the sheriff's sale.

Citations—7 Johns., 194; 9 Johns., 60; 11 Johns., 424; 9 Johns., 168; Vin. Abr., tit. Relation, 290; 1 Johns. Cas., 81, 85, n.; 3 Cai., 262; 4 Johns., 234; 12 Johns., 140; 15 Johns., 309; 2 Johns., 250; 8 Johns., 552, 3.

EJECTMENT for premises in Rotterdam, County of Schenectady, tried before Duer, Circuit Judge, at the Schenectady Circuit, Oct., 1823.

On the trial, it was shown that the declaration was served on the defendant, who was in possession, in the vacation after Jan. Term, 1823, and that it was returnable at the May Term thereafter. Issue was joined in the vacation after May Term.

The plaintiff claimed as devisee of the premises in the will of A. M. M'Michael, which was proved, dated Apr. 17, 1718, shortly after which the testator died seized.

The defendant then introduced in evidence the exemplification of the record of the judgment recovered in the Court of C. P. of the County of Schenectady, by William M'Martin against A. M'Michael, the testator, for $338.44, and also the exemplification of the record of a judgment recovered in the same court by Daniel Martin, against the testator, for $60.21, both which records were filed Sept. 13, 1817. **76***] The defendant *then introduced in evidence a *fi. fa.* against goods and lands issued upon the judgment of Wm. M'Martin, tested Jan. 3, in the 44th year of our Independence, and returnable on the 2d Tuesday of May then next, indorsed for $217.90, &c., and to which the following return was attached: "There being no goods and chattels to be found whereof I could levy the amount of debt and the costs due on the annexed execution, and another in favor of Daniel Martin, I have seized, and exposed to sale at public auction, all the right and title of A. M'Michael, deceased, of, in and to the following described lands, &c. (part of the premises in question), to Philip Ramsay, for the sum of $15, being the highest sum bid for the same when sold, being, on the 2d day of October, 1818.

JOHN CORL, Under-Sheriff."

The defendant also introduced in evidence a *fi. fa.* against goods and lands upon the judgment of Martin, tested Jan. 3, in the 42d year of our Independence, and returnable on the 2d Tuesday of May then next, to which was attached the following return: "There being no goods and chattels to be found whereof I could levy the amount of the damages and costs due on the annexed execution, and another in favor of Wm. M'Martin, I have seized and exposed to sale at public auction, all the right and title of Alexander M'Michael, deceased, of and to all the following described property, situate, &c. (part of the premises in question), to Philip Ramsay, for the sum of $300, being the highest sum bid for the same when sold, being the 2d October, 1818. JOHN COLE, Under-Sheriff."

The defendant then offered in evidence two sheriff's deeds, purporting to have been given by Gideon Holiday, Esq., former sheriff of the County of Schenectady, to Philip Ramsay, the defendant, as a purchaser of the premises in question, at a sale of the same premises by the sheriff, Oct. 2, 1818, by virtue of the two writs of *fi. fa.* before described. These deeds bore date *Aug. 12, 1823. To their introduc- [***77** tion in evidence, the plaintiff's counsel objected, upon the ground that they were given since issue was joined; and such have been pleaded *puis darrein continuance* at the last Aug. Term, or, at all events, at the (then) Circuit Court before the trial of the cause; and it was agreed by the counsel that issue was joined June 4, 1823. The consent rule was in the usual form. It was also objected that the deeds were void, being in violation of the 1st section of the Act to Prevent and Punish Champerty and Maintenance; and also because they were not given within a reasonable time after the sale. The judge rejected the deeds on the ground that they should have been pleaded *puis darrein continuance.*

A motion was now made for a new trial.

Mr. E. Yates, in support of the motion, denied that a plea *puis darrein continuance* was applicable to an action of ejectment. At any rate, it is confined to the case of an alien enemy. But if otherwise, the sheriff's deeds were not new matter within the rule which requires such matter to be interposed by plea. This court have often decided that a sheriff's deed relates back to the time of the sale, although executed afterwards. *Jackson* v. *Dickenson*, 15 Johns., 309. The delay is the fault of the officer, and should not prejudice the purchaser.

NOTE.—*Relation—When separate acts construed as one.* See Jackson v. Davenport, 20 Johns., 537; Jackson v. Dunsbaugh, 1 Johns. Cas., 91, *notes.*

Indeed it is a general rule that a conveyance executed in pursuance of a previous contract relates back to the time of the contract. *Jackson* v. *Bull*, 1 Johns. Cas., 81; *Jackson* v. *Raymond*, *Id.*, 85, *n. a.; Johnson* v. *Stagg*, 2 Johns., 510.

It is not maintenance for a defendant to perfect a title *pendente lite*. *Jackson* v. *Ketchum*, 8 Johns., 479.

Mr. A. C. Paige, contra. The rule is peremptory, that where matter of defense arises after issue joined, it must be pleaded *puis darrein continuance*. This must be done the first opportunity, and before a term intervenes. Bull. *N. P.*, 309; 1 Seiw. *N. P.*, 147; 1 Chit. Pl., 635, 532; Tidd, 773; 5 Bac. Abr., 477, 6th ed.; 3 Bl. Com., 317; *Jackson* v. *M'Connell*, 11 Johns., 424. If the matter of defense
78*] arise intermediate *the term and the next circuit, it must be pleaded at the circuit, to prevent a trial. 13 Johns., 157; 3 Cai., 173; Tidd, 773; 2 Chit. Pl., 577, *n.;* 2 Dunl., 622. These rules extend to actions of ejectment. *Jackson* v. *Rich*, 7 Johns., 194; *Jackson* v. *Demont*, 9 Johns., 55, per Kent, *Ch. J.; Jackson* v. *M'Connell*, 11 Johns., 424, per Spencer, *J.; Jackson* v. *Bell*, 19 Johns., 168.

In this case, before issue joined, the defendant had no title. It was acquired by the deeds only. Without this, the levy sale and return, even if accompanied with payment of the money, carried no title. They did not devest the estate of the debtor. *Jackson* v. *Catlin*, 2 Johns., 248; 8 Johns., 520, S. C., affirmed on error; *Simonds* v. *Catlin*, 2 Cai., 61.

The doctrine of relation takes place only where it becomes necessary for the preservation of the estate, or to promote the ends of justice; as to avoid the effect of an adverse possession, intermediate the conclusion of the contract, and the giving of the deed (1 Johns. Cas., 85); or to render an intermediate sale by the grantee valid (*Id.*, 81; 2 Johns., 510); or to enable a grantee to sustain an action of trespass for cutting timber after the contract but before the deed (12 Johns., 140); or to prevent a purchaser at a sheriff's sale being foreclosed from contesting the validity of a mortgage in an action of ejectment at law, a bill of foreclosure having been filed in chancery before the execution of the sheriff's deed, but subsequent to the sale. 15 Johns., 309. The general rule is otherwise. The deed does not, if there be no special circumstances to require it, relate to the time of the contract. *Doe* v. *Telling*, 2 East, 256.

But the deed was void within the Statute of Champerty and Maintenance (1 R. L., 172), being a purchase of lands pending the suit. 1 Hawk. P. C., ch. 84, sec. 9; *Jackson* v. *Ketchum*, 8 Johns., 479; *Same* v. *Demont*, 9 *Id.*, 55.

Again; the deed should have been executed within a reasonable time. Is it competent to wait several years? Can the deed be executed at any distance of time? The delay must not be unreasonable. *Catlin* v. *Jackson*, 8 Johns., 552, per Lansing, *Chancellor*.
79*] *The doctrine of relation is held only as between the parties to the grant. It is never adopted when third persons, not parties or privies, will be prejudiced. 12 Johns., 140; 4 *Id.*, 234; Cai., 263; Jac. L. D., Relation.

Curia, per SUTHERLAND, *J.* The principal question in this case is, whether a sheriff's deed, executed after issue joined in the cause, the sale having been made before the commencement of the suit, can be given in evidence by the defendant under the general issue, or should be pleaded *puis darrein continuance*.

The declaration was returnable May Term, 1823. The consent rule bore date May 28, and issue was joined June 4 in the same year. The sheriff's sale of the premises in question was made Oct. 2, 1818, but the deeds which were offered in evidence, and which were made in pursuance of that sale, were dated Aug. 12, 1823.

That the general rule, requiring matter of defense which has arisen after issue joined, to be pleaded *puis darrein continuance*, is applicable to this as well as other actions, is abundantly settled in this court. *Jackson* v. *Rich*, 7 Johns., 194; *Jackson* v. *Demont*, 9 Johns., 60, per Kent. *Ch. J.; Jackson* v. *M'Connell*, 11 Johns., 424; *Jackson* v. *Bell*, 19 Johns., 168.

But it is contended on the part of the defendant that the deeds relate back to the day of sale by the sheriff; and in judgment of law are considered as having been then given. The lessors of the plaintiff derived their title under the will of Alexander M'Michael; and the sheriff's sale was under judgments obtained against M'Michael in his lifetime. When the defendant entered into possession does not appear; but it is to be presumed that he entered under the title acquired by him at the sheriff's sale. The lessors of the plaintiff stand in the same relation to the defendant that Alexander M'Michael would, had he been living and made a lessor. This, therefore, is a case to which the doctrine of relation is peculiarly applicable, there being no strangers or third persons, whose interest can be affected by it. That doctrine *is this: where [***80**
there are divers acts concurrent to make a conveyance, estate or other thing, the original act shall be preferred; and to this the other act shall have relation. *Harper* v. *The Bailiffs of Derby*, Vin. Abr., tit. Relation, 290. This principle has been repeatedly recognized. In *Jackson* v. *Bull*, 1 Johns. Cas., 81, it was held "that a deed executed in pursuance of a previous contract for the same premises, is good by relation, from the time of making a contract, so as to render valid every intermediate sale or disposition of the land by the grantees. *Jackson* v. *Raymond*, *Id.*, 85, *note; Case* v. *De Goes*. 3 Cai., 262, per Thompson, *J.*, *Jackson* v. *Bard*, 4 Johns., 234. In *Heath* v. *Ross*, 12 Johns., 140, a patent for land, dated Dec. 4, but which did not pass the great seal until the 28th, was held to relate back as between the parties, so as to vest the title in the patentee from the date. *Jackson* v. *Dickinson*, 15 Johns., 309, was the case of a sheriff's sale made on the 1st of March, and the deed not delivered until the 9th. On the 10th of the same month, a mortgagee of the same land filed a bill of foreclosure, without making the purchaser at the sheriff's sale a party. It was held that the deed related back to the time of the sale; that the purchaser's title was acquired previous to the filing of the bill, and he was not precluded from contesting the validity of the mortgage in an action of ejectment. The

court say "the subsequent delivery of the deed, being mere matter of form, must have relation back to the time of purchase at the sheriff's sale." *Johnson* v. *Stagg*, 2 Johns., 520, per Kent, *Ch. J.*, S. P.

But the lapse of time between the sale and the giving of the deeds is objected to their validity, or, at all events, to their relation back to the time of sale; and the observations of *Chancellor* Lansing in *Catlin* v. *Jackson*, 8 Johns., 552-3, are supposed to countenance the objection. But in that case, the purchaser at the sheriff's sale had never paid his bid; and the deed was delivered to a third person as an escrow to take effect, when the consideration money should be paid, without any time being limited for the purpose. The remarks of the *Chancellor* are applicable to that state **81***] *of facts. But in this case the consideration money was paid by the purchaser. He had done everything to entitle him to a deed. The money must be presumed to have been paid over by the sheriff to the plaintiff in the execution, in satisfaction of the debt, and, of course, for the benefit of the estate of A. M'Michael, whom the lessors of the plaintiff represent. The essential and important part of the sheriff's duty had then been performed; and nothing remained to be done but the formal act of delivering the deed—the purchaser having been in possession, as we have right to presume, from the day of the sale. The lapse of time, under such circumstances, and between these parties, can afford no objection either to the validity of the deed or to its relation back to the time of the sale.

But admitting that by relation it is to be considered as having been given at the time of the sale, does that dispense with the necessity of pleading the fact of delivery, according to its truth, *puis darrein continuance?* I am of opinion that it does. The defense relied on was the title acquired under the sheriff's sale. When did that title vest in the defendant, is the point of inquiry. If before the commencement of the suit, it was available under the general issue. If after issue joined, it should have been pleaded *puis darrein continuance;* and the date or time of delivery of one of the evidences of the title, is perfectly immaterial. The legal effect and operation of such delivery is the matter of defense, and not the instrument itself. The legal effect of the delivery, then, in this case, having been to vest the title in the defendant by relation, as of Oct. 2, 1818, the matter of defense did not arise subsequent to the joining of the issue, and need not be pleaded *puis darrein continuance.* I am of opinion, therefore, that the judge erred in rejecting the sheriff's deeds on that ground; and that a new trial must be granted.

New trial granted.

Pleading—Matter of defense arising after issue joined. Cited in—41 Super., 379; 30 Cal., 474; 23 Mich., 250; 24 Mich., 149.

Sheriff's deed relates back to time of sale. Cited in—5 Cow., 462; 8 Cow., 56; 22 Wend., 125; 4 Hill, 174; 3 Denio, 80; 2 N. Y., 377; 4 Barb., 183; 7 Barb., 52; 21 Barb., 591; 66 Barb., 220, 31 Cal., 304; 79 Ill., 467; 28 Mich., 296.

Doctrine of relation. Cited in—23 Wend., 24; 24 Wend., 168; 5 Hill, 587; 2 N. Y., 256; 45 N. Y., 100; 10 How. (U. S.), 328, 372.

Also cited in—78 Ind., 120.

*WEST [*82

v.

WENTWORTH & BEACH.

Note Payable in Specific Articles—Action on—Measure of Damages.

In *assumpsit* on a note payable in specific articles, the measure of damages is the highest market price of those articles at any time between the notes falling due and the time of the trial.

So in trover, the damages are measured by the highest pric intermediate the time of conversion and trial. e

Citations—2 Cai. Cas., 216; 2 East, 211; 3 Burr., 1363; 2 Bl., 902.

ASSUMPSIT, tried at the Onondaga Circuit July 11, 1823, before Throop, Circuit Judge.

On the trial, the counsel for the plaintiff introduced two notes, or memorandums in writing (the execution of which was admitted by defendant's counsel), in the following words: First note. "In the month of June next, we, jointly and severally, promise to pay Simeon West eighty-eight barrels good salt, in good barrels, well nailed, delivered at Liverpool, value received, November 1st, 1819, subject to duties." Signed "Wm. Wentworth, Wm. H. Beach." Second note. "In the month of October next, we, jointly and severally, promise to pay Simeon West eighty seven barrels good salt, in good barrels, well nailed, delivered at Liverpool, subject to duties, value received, November 1st, 1819," Signed "Wm. Wentworth, Wm. H. Beach."

The counsel for the plaintiff then offered to prove the maximum price of salt between the times the notes became due and the time he demanded payment, to which the counsel for the defendants objected, contending that the plaintiff should be confined to the times the notes fell due, in proving the value.

The judge decided that the plaintiff was entitled to recover the maximum price of salt, between the times when the notes fell due, and the demand of payment by the plaintiff. The defendants, by their counsel, admitted that the salt was demanded Oct. 26, 1822, and that the price on that day was $1.50 per barrel; that being the highest price between the times the notes fell due, and the time of the demand. The jury, under the charge of the judge, found a verdict for the plaintiff for $262.50 damages, being the value of the salt, at $1.50 per barrel.

Messrs. J. G. Forbes and *B. D. Noxon* moved for a new trial on the ground of misdirection as to the measure of damages; *and [*83 cited *Davis* v. *Exrs. of Richardson*, 1 Bay, 105, and *Dutch* v. *Warren*, cited, and a short note of it given in Burr., 1010.

Mr. D. Kellogg, contra.

Curia, per SUTHERLAND, *J.* The measure of damages adopted at the circuit was the true one. The case of *Cortelyou* v. *Lansing*, 2 Cai. Cas., 216, and of *Shepherd* v. *Johnson*, 2 East, 211, are precisely in point. The latter was an action upon a contract to replace a quantity of stock by a given day; and it was held that the

NOTE.—*Contract for future delivery of chattels—Breach—Measure of damages.* See Clark v. Pinney, 7 Cow., 681, *note.*

plaintiff was entitled to recover the highest value of the stock as it stood at the time of the trial; and not its value on the day when it should have been delivered. Grose, *J.*, says: "The true measure of damages, in all these cases, is that which will completely indemnify the plaintiff for the breach of the engagement. If the defendant neglect to replace the stock at the day appointed, and the stock afterwards rise in value, the plaintiff can only be indemnified by giving him the price of it at the time of trial; and it is no answer to say that the defendant may be prejudiced by the plaintiff's delaying to bring his action; for it is his own fault that he does not perform his engagement at the time." *Cortelyou* v. *Lansing* was an action of *assumpsit* brought by the representatives of a pawnor against the pawnee of a depreciation note, which the pawnee had sold before application was made to redeem; and it was held that the plaintiffs were entitled to recover the value of the note at the time of the application, and not at the time of the pledge. So in trover, if the chattel be not of a fixed and determinate value, its worth at the time of conversion is not the rule of damages; but they may be enhanced according to the increased value of the chattel subsequent to that time. *Fisher* v. *Prince*, 3 Burr., 1363; *Whitten* v. *Fuller*, 2 Bl., 902.

New trial refused.

Criticised—7 Cow., 687; 3 Sand., 629.

Cited in—3 Hill, 337; 26 N. Y., 312; 53 N. Y., 223; 56 N. Y., 28; 4 Abb. App. Dec. 162 *n.*; 4 Barb., 368; 22 Barb., 291; 24 Barb., 296; 7 Bos., 538; 5 Daly, 90; 33 Cal., 120; 39 Cal., 421-2; 13 Am. Rep., 517; 2 Am. Rep., 468, 469 (39 Cal., 412).

84*] *CLARKSON *v.* CARTER.

Parties—Dormant Partner—Competency of Witnesses—Sale of Chattels—When Vendee Entitled to Possession.

A dormant partner need not be named as plaintiff in *assumpsit* for goods sold, founded on a contract at the time of making which his interest was unknown to the defendant.

On releasing or selling his interest to his copartner, he is a competent witness for the latter.

On a cash sale of goods, the vendee is not entitled to possession till he pays the price.

Rights of vendor and vendee in this respect, considered, where earnest has or has not been paid.

Citations—1 Chit. Pl., 7, 8; 2 Esp., 468; 2 Taunt., 324, 326; 1 Salk., 113; 5 Johns., 410, 11.

ASSUMPSIT brought for a refusal by the defendant to receive and pay for 300 barrels of flour sold to him by the plaintiff. The cause was heard before three referees, Sept. 24, 1823, who reported for the plaintiff $512.29 damages.

It was proved before the referees that one Blood, a broker, Oct. 25, 1821, sold to the defendant, at N. Y., 300 barrels of Petersburgh flour, for the account of the plaintiff, at $8 per barrel, of which he made a memorandum. The flour had not arrived at the time of the sale, but was daily expected; $8 was then the fair market price.

Henry Ogden was offered and admitted as a witness, on the part of the plaintiff. Being objected to on account of his interest, he stated upon his *voir dire*, that when the flour was sold, he was jointly interested with the plaintiff in it; but sold out to him before this suit was brought, and had no interest whatever at the time of the hearing. He testified that he was absent at the time of the sale; but, on his return called upon the defendant, and offered him the flour. The defendant at first declined receiving it; but afterwards said he would take it, and pay the price agreed on, and directed that it should be sent to his store. The flour was placed on the dock, and was ready to be delivered, and the defendant told the plaintiff to send it to his store, and he would give him his (the defendant's) check for the price; but the plaintiff refused to have it removed till paid for. Not being paid for, it was not delivered; and was afterwards sold by Crassons, another broker, for $6.50 per barrel, flour having declined to this price in the market. The report was for the difference between the price of the flour at $8 and $6.50, with the interest on that difference.

A motion was made to set aside the report.

Mr. P. A. Jay, for the plaintiff. [*85

Messrs. C. W. Sandford and *C. Livingston*, for the defendant.

Curia, per SAVAGE, *Ch. J.* There are two questions arising in this cause.

1. Was Ogden a competent witness; or ought he not to have been joined with the plaintiff?

2. Was the plaintiff bound to deliver the flour before he was paid for it?

Ogden seems to have been a dormant partner with the plaintiff; but that fact was not known by the defendant at the time of the sale by Blood, the broker; and the rule is well settled that a dormant partner need not be joined in an action on a contract with a defendant who did not deal with him or know him in the transaction. 1 Chit. Pl., 7, 8; 2 Esp., 468; 2 Taunt., 324, 326. Ogden was a competent witness, having no interest, and not being a party to the suit.

The next question is whether the plaintiff was bound to deliver the flour, without first receiving pay for it. This was a cash sale. The delivery and payment should be simultaneous acts. A person's check is no more payment than his note. He may have no funds in the bank on which he draws; or, if he has, the bank may be justified in withholding payment.

In *Langfort* v. *Tiler*, 1 Salk., 113, the defendant bought 81 tubs of tea, paid for and took away one, and paid £50 earnest. Holt, *Ch. J.*, ruled that, notwithstanding the earnest, the money must be paid upon fetching away the goods, no other time for payment being appointed; that a demand without payment is void; and that after earnest, the vendor cannot sell the goods to another without default in the vendee; and if the vendee does not come and pay and take away the goods, the vendor ought to go and request him; and then if the vendee does not come in convenient time, and pay and take away the goods, the agreement is dissolved, and he is at liberty to sell them to any other person. *In [*86 *Sands* v. *Taylor*, 5 Johns., 410, 11, Kent, *Ch. J.*, lays down a rule nearly similar, and adds: "It would be unreasonable to oblige him (the vendor) to let the article perish on his hands, and run the risk of the solvency of the buyer."

I am of opinion, therefore, that the motion must be denied, and that the plaintiff have judgment.

Motion denied.

Cited in—4 Wend., 629; 15 Wend., 225; 21 Wend., 188; 22 Wend., 366; 23 Wend., 457; 8 N. Y., 446; 30 N. Y., 380; 52 N. Y., 272; 87 N. Y., 465; 54 How. Pr., 196; 1 Bos., 36; 4 Duer, 419; 6 Duer, 336.

WILLIAMS ET AL. v. HOUGHTALING & BEVIER.

Bond Payable in Installments—How Interest Cast—Partial Payment.

Rule for casting interest where bond is payable by installment, and the interest, though it runs from the date, is not demandable till the installment falls due, and a payment is made on an installment not due and payable.

Citation—3 Johns., 229.

COVENANT on the assignment of a bond executed by Whigton & Thompson, to the defendants, and by the latter assigned to the plaintiffs, with a covenant that $1,308.18 principal and interest, besides costs, were due at the time of the assignment, which was dated Nov. 2, 1816. The bond assigned was dated Mar. 31, 1803. The condition was, that if the obligors should pay to the obligees $4,250, viz.: "$750 on or before the 1st day of May, 1804; $875 on or before the 1st day of May, 1805; $875 on or before the 1st day of May, 1806; $875 on or before the 1st day of May, 1807; and $875 on or before the 1st day of May, 1808, with interest, at 7 *per cent. per annum*, from the date on each and every payment of the above sum as they become due, then," &c.

On this bond were indorsements as follows: "Received January 5th, 1804, of Mahar Whigton and Robert Thompson, Jr., the sum of $750, being the first payment on the obligation; and the interest due thereon. Received at the same time, $20, on the second payment on the within obligation. Received, June 1st, 1805, of Robert Thompson, Jr., the sum of £369 18*s*. 7*d*. in full for principal and interest on the 2d payment on this obligation; and also received, the same day, £100 on the 3d payment in part thereof; Received, July 26, 1806, $350. January 8, 1807' $854. June 22d, 1811, $300; May 23d, 1812, $500. January 27, *1814, $500. January 28, 1815, [*87 $450. February 24, 1815, $100.50."

Upon a case containing these facts, it was submitted upon what principle the interest should be calculated; and how the payments should be applied; and agreed that the clerk should compute the interest according to the rule which the court might direct; and that a *cognovit* should be given for the sum thus ascertained to be due.

Curia. When, according to the terms of a bond payable by installments, interest cannot be demanded till the principal is payable (as in this case), payments made on an installment not due and payable should be applied to the extinguishment of principal, and such proportion of interest as has accrued on the principal so extinguished. For instance, an installment on a bond of $500 is due Jan. 1, 1825, with interest from Jan. 1, 1824; July 1, 1824, the obligor pays $207; the $7 should be applied to pay the 6 months' interest accrued on $200, and the $200 extinguishes so much principal. If the whole be applied to the extinguishment of principal, no interest could be recovered upon the principal money extinguished; for interest ceases and is not due after its principal is paid. *Tillotson* v. *Preston*, 3 Johns., 229.

Rule accordingly.(a)

Cited in—15 Wend., 24, 80; 11 Paige, 625; 2 Hun, 529; 7 Barb., 456, 562; 5 T. & C., 138; 5 How. Pr., 42; 5 Daly 364; 13 Pet., 371; 35 Cal., 694; 50 Am. Dec., 286 (2 Fla., 445).

NOTE.—*Interest—Partial payments—Rule for computation.*

Parsons (Contracts, Vol. II., p. 635) says there are three methods. 1. Casting on the whole sum to the day of making up the account, and also upon each payment from the time when made to the same day, the difference between these sums being the amount due. 2. Casting on the whole sum to the time when the first payment is made adding to the original debt, and the payment being deducted on the remainder until the next payment, and so on. 3. The method given in the N. Y. cases. See Reporter's note at end of the principal case. The latter is the mode usually adopted.

In addition to the cases cited in the reporter's note, see French v. Kennedy, 7 Barb., 452; U. S. v. McLemore, 4 How., 286; Story v. Livingston, 13 Pet., 359; Russell v. Russell, 31 N. H., 386; Den's Estate, 35 Cal., 692; Smith v. Coopers, 9 Ia., 376; Commonwealth v. Miller, 8 S. & R., 452; Riney v. Hill, 14 Mo., 500; Pierce v. Tanner, 53 Me., 351; Markel v. Spilter, 28 Ind., 488; Whitacre v. Fuller, 5 Minn., 508; Hearit v. Rhodes, 66 Ill., 351; Brooks v. Robinson, 54 Miss., 272.

(a) Rule for calculating interest where partial payments have been made:

The judges of the Supreme Court, in answer to the question put to them as the mode of calculating interest when sundry payments have made, state that they do not know that the question has been judicially settled; but, according to their understanding, the rule of practice is, to calculate interest on the principal up to the time when the payment has been made; add this interest to the principal, and then deduct the payment without regard to the time when made, whether before or after the expiration of the year. This rule, however, is to be adopted only in cases where the payment exceeds the interest due; otherwise it will be taking interest upon interest. When the payment falls short of the interest due, interest must be calculated on the principal up to the time when the payments will overrun the interest due on the principal debt; and the deduction then be made. S. THOMPSON.

*The above is taken from a written entry [*88 on a blank leaf in the printed book containing the general rules of this court, kept by Mr. Breese, the clerk at Utica. Mr. Breese does not remember when the entry was made, except that it was some time while the Hon. Smith Thompson was *Chief Justice* of this court.

The principle adopted by the late *Chancellor* Kent, is laid down by him in nearly the same words. "The rule (says he) for casting interest, when partial payments have been made, is to apply the payment, in the first place, to the discharge of the interest then due. If the payment exceeds the interest, the surplus goes towards discharging the principal, and the subsequent interest is to be computed on the balance of principal remaining due. If the payment be less than the interest, the surplus of interest must not be taken to augment the principal; but interest continues on the former principal until the period when the payments taken together exceed the interest due, and then the surplus is to be applied towards discharging the principal; and interest is to be computed on the balance of the principal as aforesaid. Connecticut v. Jackson, 1 Johns. Ch., 17, 18; Stoughton v. Lynch, 2 *Id.*, 209, S. P.

The same rule prevails in Mass., Edes v. Goodridge, 4 Tyng, 103; Dean v. Williams, 17 Tyng, 417, 418; Fay v. Bradley, 1 Pick., 194. In Va., Lightfoot v. Price, 4 Hen. & Munf., 431. N. C., Bunn v. Moore's Executors, 1 Hayw., 278; Anonymous, 2 *Id.*, 17; North & Prescott v. Mattell, *Id.*, 151. Md., Chapline v. Scott, 4 Harr. & M'H., 94. Ky., 4 Hall's Law Jour., 122. S. C., Administrators of Norwood, ads. Manning, 2 Nott & M'Cord, 395, 397.

In Conn., the rule is the same, with the qualification that the first payment shall not be applied to the extinguishment of the interest, unless it be made at least one year from the time the interest began to run, nor as to subsequent payments, unless there be at least one year between them. General Rule, Kirby 49; Kissam v. Burrall, *Id.*, 326. This is upon the ground that interest cannot be due except from year to year.

In N. J. the rule is the same as in this State, with the difference that it disregards the amount of the payment which is applied to the extinguishment of the interest whenever paid, and whether less or more than the interest accrued. At least no distinction is made between these two cases, in Meredith v. Banks. 1 Halstead, 408, where the rule is laid down.

In Tracy v. Wikoff, 1 Dall., 124, Pa., M'Kean, *Ch. J.*, said: "The rule of computing interest must be such, that the interest of money paid in before the time must be deducted from the interest of the whole sum due at the time appointed by the instrument for making the payments. For instance, a bond to pay £100, with annual interest at 6 *per cent.*, and at the end of 6 months, £50 is paid in. This payment shall not be apportioned, £3 to the discharge of the half year's interest, and £47 to the diminution of the principal, so as to calculate the remaining interest at 6 *per cent.* on £53 for 6 months; but the interest shall be charged at the end of the year upon £100; the payment of £50 shall then be deducted from the aggregate sum of £106, and the
89*] obligor receive a credit *for £1 10s. as the interest of £50 for 6 months." In Penrose v. Hart, *Id.*, 378, Shippen, President, said he remembered to have heard of an old decison, when Logan was *Chief Justice*, in which it was expressly settled, that money paid on account of a bond, should first be applied to discharge the interest due at the time of the payment; and the residue, if any, credited towards satisfaction of the principal; and this rule had been adopted as the uniform practice.

In Lewis' Exr. v. Bacon's Legatee, 3 Hen. & Munf., Va., 89, where a creditor kept an account current with his debtor, and also an interest account, in which he charged interest on the several items of debit to a particular period, and gave credit by interest on the several payments to the same period, and charged in the account current the balance appearing on the interest account, and a balance being then struck, interest was again charged on the balance thus consisting of principal and interest, the court held it to be compound interest, and not allowable.

JACKSON, ex dem. SCOFIELD, v. COLLINS.

Ejectment—Objection that Plaintiff Failed to Make out Title—Must be First Made at Trial —Adverse Possession, to avoid Conveyance—Sale by Deputy, after Sheriff out of Office—When Valid—Deputy, as Assignee of Judgment, may Purchase under Execution Directed to Sheriff—Construction of Statute—Intent of Legislature.

In ejectment, an objection cannot be made at the bar that the plaintiff failed at the trial to make out a title, unless such objection was previously made at the trial.

One claiming under a deed from a judgment debtor has not such an adverse possession as will avoid a conveyance executed by a purchaser under an execution upon a judgment.

A deputy-sheriff may complete an execution by sale and conveyance, after the sheriff goes out of office, provided the execution was levied before.

A deputy-sheriff who is plaintiff in, or assignee of, a judgment, may purchase under an execution thereon directed to his principal.

In construing a statute, wherever the intention of the Legislature can be discover, it should be followed with reason and discretion, though such construction seem contrary to the letter of the statute.

Cases illustrating this proposition referred to by the plaintiff's counsel.

Citations—1 Ld. Raym., 659; 1 Salk., 95; 20 Johns., 64; Bac. Abr., tit. Statutes; 15 Johns., 380.

EJECTMENT, tried at the Monroe Circuit, before the late *Mr. Justice* Platt, July 4, 1822, for lots number 61, 62, and the north half of 63, situate in the village of Rochester.

The demise in the declaration was laid Mar. 14, 1822. On the trial, the lessors of the plaintiff showed the following title: 1. A deed duly acknowledged and proved, dated Jan. 2, 1818, from N. Rochester, C. Carroll and William Fitzhugh, to William Robb, for lots number 61, 62, and 63, in the village of Rochester. The deed was executed by N. Rochester, for himself, and for Carroll and Fitzhugh, by N. Rochester, their attorney. 2. An exemplification of a judgment in the Supreme Court, in favor of Jonathan R. Hale, against Robb, for $483.62, *filed Aug. 30, 1819, and an [*90
alius testatum fi. fa. on this judgment, directed to the sheriff of the County of Genesee, tested Aug. and returnable Oct. Term, 1820. It was then proved on the part of the plaintiff, that the above lots 61, 62, and the north half of 63, were sold by virtue of the execution, by Oliver Lee, a deputy-sheriff, Oct. 4, 1820, to Ralph Wadhams, for $535.50, being the full amount of the execution and sheriff's costs, and it was further proved, that, at the time of the sale, Lee gave to Wadham a certificate that, at the expiration of 15 months, he would be entitled to a deed. The plaintiff then produced a deed duly proved, dated Feb. 9, 1822, of the above premises, from Parmenio Adams, late sheriff of the County of Genesee, by Oliver Lee, deputy to Ralph Wadhams, the purchaser, for the consideration of $535.50; and a quitclaim deed, duly proved, from Wadhams to Scofield, the lessor, dated Feb. 18, 1822, for the con-

---

NOTE.—*Construction of statute—Intent of legislature—When it will control the letter of a statute.*

Where the intent of the Legislature can be ascertained with reasonable certainty, the statute will be construed in accordance therewith, although such construction may conflict with the ordinary meaning of the letter. See Tonnele v. Hall, 4 N. Y., 140; Simonds v. Powers, 28 Vt., 354; Staniels v. Raymond, 4 Cush., 314; Brown v. Wright, 13 N. J., 240; Ryegate v. Wardsboro, 30 Vt., 746; Minor v. Mechanic's Bank, 1 Pet., 64; Sprowl v. Lawrence, 33 Ala., 674; Crocker v. Crane, 21 Wend., 211.

Compare Swift v. Luce, 27 Me., 285; Whitney v. Whitney, 14 Mass., 88; Maxwell v. Collins, 8 Ind., 38; Bradbury v. Wagenhorst, 54 Pa. St., 180.

What is termed the policy of the government with reference to any particular legislation, is too unstable a ground upon which to rest the judgment of the court in the interpretation of statutes. Hadden v. Collector, 5 Wall., 107. See 7 Mass., 524.

In general, the intent of the Legislature must be found in the statute itself. Tyman v. Walker, 35 Cal., 634. But see State v. Nicholls, 30 La. Ann., Pt. II., 980; Edger v. Randolph Co. Commr's., 70 Ind., 331, and others upon the same subject. Ezekiel v. Dixon, 3 Ga., 146.

The mischief existing at the time of the enactment, and the remedy intended, are to be considered in construing the statute. Winslow v. Kimball, 25 Me., 493; Sibley v. Smith, 2 Mich., 486; Alexander v. Worthington, 5 Md., 471. See also, Catlin v. Hull, 21 Vt., 152; Doane v. Phillips, 12 Pick., 223; Farrell Foundry v. Dart, 26 Conn., 376; State v. Brewster, 42 N. J. L., 125; United States v. Bowen, 100 U. S., 508; State v. Liedtke, 9 Neb., 468; Baxter v. Tripp, 12 R. I., 810.

sideration of $600. It was also proved by the plaintiff that the defendant, at the time of the demise in the declaration, and at the time of trial, was in possession of the premises, and that he confessed that he rented the premises of one Harvey Montgomery; and that Montgomery, four or five years since, said that he had the premises in question, of Robb, from whom the lessor of the plaintiff claimed title.

It appeared that the defendant was in possession of the premises under Montgomery, at the date of the deed from Wadhams, to the lessor of the plaintiff; that Lee, at the time he sold the premises, was a deputy-sheriff; that Adams, the sheriff, went out of office in the winter of 1821, about a year previous to the date of the deed given by Lee, in the name of the sheriff to Wadhams.

Lee, the deputy-sheriff, was then called as a witness by the defendant. He stated that Scofield, the lessor, handed him the execution in favor of Hale, against Robb, and directed him to sell the premises in question, stating, at the same time, that he had bought the judgment of Hale; that at the time he sold the premises, he 91*] informed the bystanders *the amount of the execution, and the sum he wished to raise, and that there were several bids from different persons; that Wadhams, to whom it was sold, overbid the rest. The witness further stated, that the purchase money was not paid by Wadhams, at the time of the sale; that in a conversation between the lessor of the plaintiff and Wadhams, after the sale, Scofield, the lessor, offered to take Wadhams' note; witness saw Scofield and Wadhams sit down at a table to write, but did not see Wadhams deliver the note to Scofield; that at the time they were writing the note, the witness left the room. Soon after, Scofield, the lessor, as assignee of Hale receipted the execution in full. It appeared that Scofield, at the time the premises were sold, was a deputy-sheriff of the County of Genesee.

From the above facts, it was contended by the defendant, 1. That Wadhams was the trustee of Scofield, and purchased the land for his benefit. 2. That the purchase was void, Scofield being a deputy at the time. 3. That the deed given by Lee, the deputy, after Adams, the sheriff, went out of office, was void; and 4. That if Wadhams was not the trustee of Scofield, there was an adverse possession on the 18th day of Feb., 1822, at the date of Wadhams' deed to Scofield, the lessor.

A verdict was taken for the plaintiff, subject to the opinion of the court on the above case.

Messrs. H. D. Mason and *J. C. Spencer*, for the plaintiff. The 16th section of the Act Concerning Judgments and Executions (1 R. L., 506) is general, and forbids a sheriff to whom an execution is directed, and his deputies, from purchasing; but this must mean the officer acting in the sale, or to whom the process is delivered. If not so, then a deputy having a judgment, cannot adopt the only effectual means of getting his money, that of bidding under the execution; for, in such a case, the execution cannot go to the coroner. It goes to him only when the sheriff is interested. *Done* v. *Smethier*, Cro. Car., 416. "Such a construction ought to be put on a statute as may best answer the intention which the makers had in view; and this intention is sometimes to be collected from the case or necessity of making *the statute, and sometimes from [*92 other circumstances; and whenever such intention can be discovered, it ought to be followed with reason and discretion in the construction of the statute, although such construction seem contrary to the letter of the statute; and a thing which is within the letter of a statute, is not within the statute, unless it be within the intention of the makers." These propositions are sustained and illustrated by various English cases of construction upon statutes where the courts have departed from the letter in order to reach the spirit and intent of the Act. *Reniger* v. *Foggassa*, Plowd., 18; *Straunge* v. *Croker*, *Id.*, 88; 2 Inst., 64; *The King* v. *Younger*, 5 T. R., 449; *Margate Pier Co.* v. *Hannani*, 3 B. & A., 266; *Edwards* v. *Deck*, 4 *Id.*, 212, per Holroyd, *J.*

Here was not an adverse possession in the defendant at the time of Wadham's conveyance to Scofield. If the former was the trustee of the latter, as insisted by one of the defendant's points, and which we concede, of course, adverse possession is out of the question. But, proceeding upon the ground that Wadhams purchased for his own benefit, we deny that there was such an adverse possession as prevented his conveying to Scofield. The defendant, Collins, held under Montgomery, who purchased of Robb, the defendant in the judgment and execution. Both Montgomery and Collins were *quasi* the tenants of the purchaser. *Jackson* v. *Sternburgh*, 1 Johns. Cas., 155; *Same* v *Graham*, 3 Cai., 188.

Lee had a right to convey, though his principal had gone out of office. The sale was complete Oct. 14, 1820. The sheriff had obeyed the execution; and all that remained was to give the evidence of the sale, if the property should not be redeemed. In *Jackson* v. *Bush*, 10 Johns., 223, the court say: "A sale and the consummation of that sale by a deed, are acts which the sheriff may do by deputy. The law does not require them to be done by the sheriff in person." Here no distinction is made between the deputy of a sheriff out of office, or one in. The case, indeed, did not call for it; but as far as it goes, it shows that the deputy may do whatever the sheriff can. Lee was proved to be a general deputy. *Jackson* v. *Davis*, 18 Johns., 10. Execution being an entire thing, he *who [*93 begins must end it, and therefore, if a sheriff seize goods, and is removed, yet he is to proceed in the sale. Dalt. Shff., 19; Salk., 323; Cro. Jac., 73; *Devoe* v. *Elliot*, 2 Cai., 243. The authority of the principal, therefore, continued (Bac. Abr., Sheriff, J; *Hempstead* v. *Weed*, 20 Johns., 64); and an authority from him to the deputy being indefinite in time is not revoked unless it be countermanded, or cease by the death of the principal or agent. Co. Litt., 52 *b*; Bac. Abr., Authority, E. The appointment of a deputy is so long as the principal shall be sheriff, or have anything to do as sheriff; and if he may execute process after he is out of office, he does this as sheriff. So far has this doctrine been carried that on the renewal of a sheriff's commission under the old Constitution, no new appointment of an under-sheriff was necessary; neither need his bond be renewed; but he continued under-sheriff, and his bond continued in full force. *Hughes* v. *Smith*, 5 Johns., 168. Dalton, in his treatise on the office of sheriff (456), calls the under-sheriff (who answers to our deputy) the attorney of the sheriff; and that he may be appointed at will, and revoked as an attorney may be. Why may not a removed sheriff appoint an attorney to do that which the principal is authorized to perform? And what is the difference whether the appointment be before or after his removal?

No objection to Robb's title was taken at the trial. It is too late to raise it now. But it is unfounded in point of fact. Rochester's authority to execute the deed was not questioned at the trial. Besides, Montgomery claimed under Robb. *Jackson* v. *Scott*, 18 Johns., 94.

Messrs. W. C. Van Ness and *J. A. Collier*, for the defendant. No title is shown in the lessor of the plaintiff. Even a *prima facie* case was not made; and this is not one of that class of objections from which we are precluded by having omitted to make it at the trial. The objection goes to the merits; there is a defect in the title; and the defendant shall not be precluded from urging it merely because other objections were made at the trial. *Palmer* v. *Lorillard*, 16 Johns., 348, 353, per Woodworth, *J.*, in 18 Johns., 564–5.

The deputy-sheriff had no power to execute a deed after the sheriff, his principal, was removed from office. We can find no adjudged case upon this subject, but contend that after **94***] *the sheriff is removed from office, the power of his deputy is, *ipso facto*, at an end; and that, at all events, no one can thereafter act without new and special authority from the sheriff. He and his sureties would not be bound for the misconduct of his deputy after the expiration of his term of office. Suppose the deputy should sell the goods of a stranger, after the sheriff's term of office had expired; would he be liable for this act of his late deputy? Previous to the Redemption Act (as it is called), suppose the late deputy of a late sheriff should have given a deed, without any previous levy or sale—nothing more need be shown than the judgment, execution and sheriff's deed to entitle the plaintiff to recover. Would such a deed from the late deputy be sufficient, then, to authorize a judgment against the defendant in possession? There is no responsibility resting upon the late deputy. He acts under no oath of office. His own sureties would not be bound beyond the period of the sheriff's term, and neither the sheriff nor his sureties for any act after this period. The authority of an agent or attorney ceases upon the death of his principal. Does not the power and authority of a deputy also cease, upon the political death of the sheriff?

The defendant (or Montgomery) was in possession, claiming adversely, at the date of the deed to the lessor of the plaintiff. The defendant had rented the premises of Montgomery, and neither of them acknowledged any subsisting interest in Robb. The defendant claimed to hold under his lease, and Montgomery, who said he had the premises of Robb, claimed and exercised the right of leasing the premises to the defendant, without the privity or consent of Robb or any other person; and the defendant was in possession under the lease.

Curia, per SAVAGE, *Ch. J.* It is objected:

1. That no title was shown in Robb subsequent to the judgment. Title was in Robb Jan. 2, 1818, and judgment Aug, 30, 1819. The presumption is, therefore, in the absence of all proof to the contrary, that it continued in him during the intermediate time. Besides, had the objection been taken at the trial, that fact might have been shown.

*2. It is objected that Lee, as deputy [***95** to Adams, had no right to execute a deed after Adams was out of office, Lee being no longer deputy. It is not denied that during Adams' continuance in office, the deputy had authority to do any act which his principal could do in his official capacity, except the appointment of deputies. And *vide Parker* v. *Kett*, 1 Ld. Raym., 659, and S. C., 1 Salk., 95. But it is contended that the authority of the deputy ceased when the new sheriff had taken the office upon him. In my opinion, the authority of the deputy is limited by the duration of the authority of his principal. An execution against the property of a defendant, partly executed by the old sheriff, shall be completed by him, and in relation to any such execution in the sheriff's hands, when he goes out of office, he continues sheriff, and may act by deputy, as if he was still in office. He is in office *quoad hoc*, and the acts of a deputy in relation to such an execution are the acts of the sheriff himself. Even in the case of a *ca. sa.* upon which the defendant has been arrested, and is imprisoned, it is optional with the old sheriff whether he will transfer the prisoner to the new sheriff. The old sheriff has a right to retain the custody of the prisoner, and complete the execution of the writ. *Hempstead* v. *Weed*, 20 Johns., 64.

3. There was no adverse possession shown, to defeat the operation of the deed, either from the sheriff to Wadhams, or from Wadhams to the lessor of the plaintiff.

4. It is made a point that Wadhams was a mere trustee for Scofield, and that he, being a deputy of the sheriff at the time of the sale, was prohibited by statute from purchasing. The Statute is, "that it shall not be lawful for any sheriff, or other officer, to whom any such execution shall be directed, or any of their deputies, or any person for them or either of them, to purchase any goods or chattels, lands or tenements, at any sale, by virtue of any execution, and all purchases so made by them, or any of them, or for the use of them, or any of them, shall be void." Admitting, as the plaintiff does, that Wadhams purchased for the use of Scofield, the purchase comes within the letter of the Act, but it could never have been the intention of the Legislature to have prevented a deputy-sheriff, when plaintiff in an execution, from bidding, in *order [***96** to secure his money. The object was to prevent abuse—that the sheriff or his deputies should not be allowed to become purchasers at their own sales, and thereby be induced to conduct corruptly in relation to them. But surely it was never intened to place those persons in a worse situation than others, as to the

collection of their own demands. "Whenever the intention of the makers of a statute can be discovered, it ought to be followed with reason and discretion in the construction of the statute, although such construction seem contrary to the letter of the statute." Bac. Abr., tit. Statute, I, 15 Johns., 380, per *Ch. J.* Thompson. A thing which is within the letter of a statute is not within the statute, unless it be within the intention of the makers. This proposition is fully established and illustrated by the cases cited on the part of the plaintiff.

I am, therefore, of opinion that Scofield had a right to bid and purchase, *bona fide*, as we are to presume he did in this case; for fraud, of any kind, is not imputed. The plaintiff is accordingly entitled to judgment.

Judgment for the plaintiff.

Criticised—48 Ill., 24.

Statutes—Construction of. Cited in—1 Edw., 312; 59 N. Y., 199; 15 Barb., 470; 16 Barb., 12; 21 Barb., 438; 24 Barb., 135; 25 Barb., 201; 42 Barb., 642; 45 Barb., 206; 1 T. & C., 201; 12 How. Pr., 91; 13 How. Pr., 127, 444; 22 How. Pr., 449; 2 Park., 418; 1 Sweeny, 440; 1 Hilt., 274; 1 Daly, 240; 7 Bank Reg., 208; 3 Biss., 235; 29 Ind., 109; 10 Minn., 118; 67 Mo., 408; 66 Mo., 423.

De[illegible] may complete execution, after sheriff's term of o[illegible] has expired. Cited in—9 Cow., 239; 7 Wend., 221; 20 Wend., 605; 68 N. Y., 478.

Also cited in—4 Barb., 183.

GRISWOLD AND GRISWOLD
v.
THE NATIONAL INSURANCE COMPANY OF THE CITY OF NEW YORK.

Action on Policy of Insurance—Pleading—Effect of Demurrer—Contract, Sufficiently Stated in First Count, need not be Repeated—Pleading Survey—Averment of Unseaworthiness, by Reason of Rottenness—What Survey should State—Departure in Pleading.

On demurrer, the party who commits the first substantial fault in pleading, shall have judgment against him.

A plea which is bad in substance is not aided by a replication.

In declaring upon a contract, which is sufficiently stated in the first count, it need not be repeated in the subsequent counts of the same declaration; but it is enough to declare that it is the same as is set forth in the first count; and per Woodworth, *J.*, interrupting Wells, counsel, S. P.

Thus, where the plaintiff declared upon a policy of insurance, setting it out in the first count, and in the subsequent counts declared as upon another policy, "for the same voyage, and upon the same subject-matter, and upon the same terms and stipulations, and containing therein to the same effect as in the said policy of insurance in the said first count mentioned, &c.," held, that the subsequent counts were good.

Form of pleading a survey upon a vessel, according to the rotten clause in a policy of insurance. *Note a.*

Such a survey is properly made within a reasonable time after the vessel's arrival at her port of destination—it need not be made before.

In pleading such a survey, the defendant need not state the particular manner and circumstances of the survey, but merely that it was regular—circumstances of impeachment come more properly from the assured, if he have a right to impeach the the survey at all, as to which, *quære*.

An averment that the ship was by such survey declared unseaworthy, by reason of being rotten, is sufficient, within the rotten clause:

But an averment that the ship was found by the survey to be in a very bad and rotten condition, is not good. It implies a mixed cause of unseaworthiness; whereas, to make a survey a flat bar, within the rotten clause, it should appear plainly that the unseaworthiness arose from rottenness solely.

Matter which comes more properly from the plaintiff, need not be stated in the plea.

A survey is always made at the instance, and for the benefit of the owner or master of the vessel, and goes, of course, into his hands. The assurers are not parties to the survey.

It is proper, but not indispensable, for a survey to state the particulars of the decay.

The plea stated a survey made at Cadiz, and the replication traversed that the survey was made at Cadiz or elsewhere; held bad, on special demurrer.

The issue must be as broad as the traverse, and a rejoinder to such a replication would be a departure.

Declaration, averring a physical total loss of a ship; plea, a survey at Cadiz, the port of destination; replication, a different survey at Cadiz, and traversing the survey in the plea; held, a departure: for the ship arriving at her port of destination, there could not be a physical total loss.

Citations—20 Johns., 328; 4 Johns., 135; 7 Wh., 612, 581; 2 Serg. & R., 298, 297; 1 Binn., 595, 598; 2 Binn., 394; 8 Johns., 167; Com. Dig. Pl., E, 37, M, 1, 2; 8 Co., 120 *b*; 2 Salk., 519; 15 Johns., 191.

ASSUMPSIT. The first count of the declaration was upon a policy of insurance on the ship William, dated Aug. *21, 1819, [*97 at and from N. Y. to Cadiz, averring that the ship sailed on the voyage insured, and alleging her physical total loss, and that the ship became of no use or value, by perils of the sea. The second count set forth another policy upon the same vessel and voyage, in the same terms as the policy described in the first count, and averred the loss to be a technical total one, as amounting to more than a moiety of the ship. The third count was the same as the second, superadding a general average loss by a jettison. The fourth was the usual money counts, consolidated in one. The policy, as set forth in each count, contained the usual rotten clause, "that if the above vessel, upon a regular survey, should be thereby declared unseaworthy, by reason of her being unsound, or rotten, or incapable of prosecuting her voyage on account of her being unsound or rotten, then the assurers should not be bound to pay their subscription on that policy." The policy in the second and third counts was set forth thus: "For the same voyage, and upon the same subject-matter of insurance, and upon the same terms and stipulations, and containing therein to the same effect as in the said policy of insurance in the said first count of this declaration is above mentioned," &c.

*Pleas: to the 1st, 2d and 4th counts, [*98 the general issue—to the 1st and 2d counts, a regular survey on the vessel, upon and immediately after her arrival at Cadiz, to wit: Oct. 15, 1819, on which she was declared unseaworthy, by reason of her being rotten; to the 1st count, alone, a regular survey on the vessel, upon and immediately after her arrival at Cadiz, to wit: Oct. 15, 1819, by which she was found to be in a very bad and rotten condition, and that to make her seaworthy would amount to $5,000 or upwards, according to the report of Thomas Hill, one of the surveyors, a ship carpenter of that port, and in which the surveyors coincide, and that it was their firm opinion it would be best for all parties concerned in the ship, that she should be condemned; to the 2d count, alone, the same, omitting the report of the ship carpenter; to the 3d count *non assumpsit*, as to the general average, and as to the residue a survey in the same form as the last mentioned plea to the 2d count.

99*] *Replication, to the 2d plea, which covered the 1st and 2d counts, that the ship arrived at Cadiz, Sept. 25, 1819; and after the expiration of at least 15 days, to wit: Oct. 11, 1819, a survey on the vessel, by which it was found that the stern frame had apparently worked, the wooding ends under the counter open, and the ship making a great deal of water; that after the expiration of at least 19 days, and not sooner, to wit: Oct. 15, 1819, a second survey, supplemental to the first, to ascertain the expense of the repairs reported by the first survey, by which survey it was found as stated in the 3d plea, with an averment that the second survey is the same as the one mentioned in the 2d plea; that this survey was not ordered by a court of admiralty, or other competent jurisdiction; that the surveyors were not sworn according to maritime law and usage; that it was not a regular survey within the policy; and concluded with a formal traverse, that this survey, or any other had upon the ship at Cadiz, or elsewhere, found the vessel unseaworthy by reason of her being rotten in manner and form, &c.; to the 3d plea the same, omitting the traverse; to the 4th plea the same, except concluding with a traverse that the survey mentioned in the 4th plea was of any other tenor and effect than in the replication set out; to the residue of the 5th plea, the same as to the 4th.

Special demurrer to each of the replications, assigning the following causes:

I. To the replication to the 2d plea:

1. The traverse seeks to put in issue matters not in the plea.

2. It is double and multifarious.

3. No apt and proper issue can be taken upon the traverse.

4. The traverse tenders an issue upon matters contained in the inducement.

5. In other respects, double, uncertain, &c.

II. To the replication to the 3d plea:

1. It does not traverse or avoid the matters contained in the plea, except by inference and legal construction.

2. It is evasive, uncertain, not issuable, and argumentative, in alleging that the surveys

100*] were made, one at *least 15, and the other at least 19 days after the arrival of the ship.

3. It is double and multifarious, seeking to put in issue distinct and independent facts, thus: 1. That the second survey was not had by the order of a court of admiralty, or other competent authority. 2. Surveyors not sworn. 3. Not a regular survey, within the meaning of the policy. 4. That there was another survey of Oct. 11. 5. That the one of the 15th was supplemental to the other.

4. In other respects double, uncertain, &c.

III. To the replication to the 4th plea:

1. The traverse seeks to put in issue the matters contained in the inducement.

2. It contains only matter of legal inference and construction, arising out of the inducement.

3. No apt or proper issue can be taken on it.

4. It is in other respects uncertain, &c.

IV. To the replication to the residue of the 5th plea, the same causes as to the replication to the 4th plea.

Joinder in demurrer to each separately.

The cause was argued at May Term, 1823, by the late *Mr. J. Wells*, for the defendants, in support of the demurrers, and *Messrs. G. Griffin* and *T. A. Emmet*, for the plaintiffs.

Mr. J. Wells, in support of the demurrers. The pleadings in question all turn upon the rotten clause in the policy. The second plea sets forth the survey according to its legal effect, and the traverse is to a matter not alleged in the plea. The averment is of a survey at Cadiz, on the 15th of Oct. The traverse does not deny this, but says merely that neither by that, nor any other survey, was it found, &c. This is traveling out of the plea, which speaks of but one survey. A traverse of matter not in the plea is bad. *Killigrew* v. *Sawyer*, 2 Vent., 79; *Gwinne* v. *Poole*, 2 Lutw., 1065; *Talbot* v. *Woodhouse*, *Id.*, 1480; *Humphreys* v. *Churchman*, Cas. *t.* Hardw., 275. This traverse is, moreover, double. It speaks not only of the survey set forth, but of any other survey. *The rule is that the issue must [*101 be as broad as the traverse; and what kind of an issue would this give us? It would be an affirmative on our part, that there was such a survey Oct. 15, or some other survey. We had no choice but to rejoin in this manner. Going down to the circuit, upon such an issue, would be a mistrial. 1 Chit. Pl., 519, 520.

The replication to the third plea omits the traverse, and is, therefore, the more defective. It contains mere matter of inducement, which cannot be traversed. 1 Chit. Pl., 596. Again; the object is to impeach our survey. The replication attempts to do this by setting out another survey, and showing the defects which exist in ours Thus it contains, in itself, several distinct and independent matters, not all leading to a single point; and is defective in this particular. You may state as many matters as you please, by way of inducement, if you make them all converge to one point; but you cannot set up a variety of matters independent of each other, and leave them there. They must be connected, and made to constitute a single whole. 1 Chit. Pl., 512, 577, and the cases there cited; *Patcher* v. *Sprague*, 2 Johns., 462; *Cooper* v. *Heermance*, 3 *Id.*, 315. The last case is in point. In replying *per fraudem* to a plea of an insolvent discharge, the plaintiff set up distinctly every species of fraud recognized by the Insolvent Act, constituting as many distinct points of defense. This was holden ill. The replication is also defective, in averring that the second survey was supplemental to the first. *Brandegee* v. *Nat. Ins. Co.*, 20 Johns., 328, makes the survey conclusive. It must be judged of by itself, and the pleadings should relate directly to it. It is uncertain and argumentative in its attack upon the survey. The effect of similar language is considered in *Pullen* v. *Benson*, 2 Salk., 628. The same objection applies to the part which speaks of time, viz.: after the expiration of 19 days, and not sooner, in reply to our plea that he survey took place immediately. Besides, it tenders, in this respect, an issue on time, which is immaterial. *Rogers* v. *Burk*, 10 Johns., 400.

*The traverse in the replication to the [*102 4th, and the residue of the 5th plea, seeks to put in issue matter contained in the inducement, which is not traversable. It concludes the survey mentioned in our pleas was not of any other tenor or effect than as in the replication set forth, which draws into inquiry the whole matter stated by way of inducement. 1 Chit. Pl., 596; Com. Dig. Pleader, G, 18, 20.

All these replications are bad, as containing a negative pregnant (2 Saund., 314, 319, *n.* 6), besides being argumentative. Instances of bad traverses, for this latter reason, will be found in *Goddard* v. *Thorlton*, Yelv., 170; *Roy* v. *Kilderley*, Sid., 427. The same subject is also considered in *Fanshaw* v. *Morrison*, 2 Salk., 520, and *Snider* v. *Croy*, 2 Johns., 227.

Again; the qualifications of this survey, insisted on by the plea, are mere matters of legal inference; and the replication is, therefore, bad. 1 Saund., 23, *n.* 5; 2 *Id.*, 159 *a*, *n.*; 10 *Id.*, 161, *n.* 11. The replications should be confined to mere matters of fact.

Nor are we to be prejudiced by our admissions. A demurrer does not make a replication good, because its truth is admitted by this form of taking advantage of its defects; no facts are admitted by a demurrer, except such as are well and sufficiently pleaded. Co. Litt., 72, *a*.

The idea of these replications is probably taken from *Condy's Marshall*, 159 *a*, *note* 15; but it is no objection to the survey that it was not taken under the order of a court of admiralty. It is not the practice to procure such an order, and there cannot be a more dangerous principle than the one contended for. It is upon surveys of this description that vessels are to be sold, the assured entitled to abandon, or the assurer to defend under the rotten clause. In many cases, the sanction of a court of admiralty cannot possibly be procured. Suppose, as is every day the case, a vessel is driven into a port where there is no court of admiralty; must you then seek out the next nearest court? It is, perhaps, well enough, and may be necessary, where there is a court of admiralty, that its sanction should be procured; but the pleader who wishes to avoid
103*] the survey, because this *formalty is omitted, should, at least, show that there is a court of admiralty at the port where the survey takes place. The replication here assumes the broad ground that a survey is void, in all cases, unless done under the authority of that court. The practice is otherwise. This business is generally done under the order of our consuls; if there be no consul, under that of the magistrates of the place; and if there be no magistrates, then by discreet men. Not a single survey was ever made in this city, under the orders of a court of admiralty, though that court is always open here. It is usually made through the wardens of the port. According to the replication, we have been in an error on this head ever since the establishment of the government. But this question was considered in *Dorr* v. *Pacific Ins. Co.*, 7 Wh., 581, and it was said by *Judge* Johnson, that "every commercial country has its own regulations on the subject of surveys. It is properly a subject of admiralty jurisdiction; since mariners and freighters have to claim the aid of the admiralty to release them from their contract, in cases of a defect of seaworthiness. A regular survey must, therefore, in every instance, be such as is known to the laws and customs of the port in which a vessel happens to be." This survey, then, like every other, must be presumed regular, until the contrary is shown. Allow that it must be made according to the usage and custom of the port where it is taken, still the plea, which would impeach it, should show that it was not taken in conformity to the custom.

But the replications defeat themselves. They show that the second survey was supplemental to the first, and was made by the same persons who made the first. Hence, as the survey first set out is regular, it follows that the second was so. The first must be considered regular, because every pleading is to be taken most strongly against the pleader. 1 Saund., 259, *n.* 8; *De Symonds* v. *Shedden*, 2 Bos & P., 155. In point of practice, nothing is more usual than two or three surveys, before the operation is complete. In the case of *Dorr* v. *Pacific Ins. Co.*, the survey acted upon and recognized was a second one. Again; what issue could we *take upon this part of [***104** the replication, which says that it is not a survey, within the true intent and meaning of the policy. Matter of law is pleaded, instead of fact, and the case of *Kidder* v. *West*, 3 Lev., 167, is in point.

What is the effect of the survey of Oct. 11? It states that the stern frame had apparently worked the wooding ends under the counter open, and the ship making a great deal of water. The language shows that it was merely an incipient survey, to be completed at another day. Accordingly, a few days after, a further survey is made. There is nothing inconsistent between the two; but both constitute one only. The looseness of the stern frame, &c., are merely stated as the effects of the rottenness, so that the vessel is condemned for this cause, the *casus fœderis* between the parties. It matters not what was the result of the first survey, if the final condemnation was for rottenness. *Garrigues* v. *Coxe*, 1 Binn., 592; *Armroyd* v. *Union Ins. Co.*, 2 *Id.*, 394; *Steinmets* v. *U. S. Ins. Co.*, 2 Serg. & R., 293; *Haff* v. *Mar. Ins. Co.*, 8 Johns., 163; *Dorr* v. *Pacific Ins. Co.*, 7 Wh., 581. A mixed cause of condemnation is quite another thing.

The effect of a survey is given in *Brandegee* v. *Nat. Ins. Co.*, 20 Johns., 328, and the cases there cited. When the loss arises from rottenness, and this fact appears by the survey, this survey is in itself a bar to the action. It is, therefore, the proper subject of a plea, and not of evidence merely. It may better be put to the court by way of plea, which is a shorter and more direct mode of determining the question.

The replication to the 2d plea is bad even on general demurrer. The first count of the declaration avers a physical total loss. We plead the arrival of the vessel and the survey. The replication then varies from that count. It admits that the vessel arrived and sets forth a technical total loss. The replication should support or enlarge upon the declaration. 2 Saund., 84 *a*; Co. Litt., 304 *a*; *Allen* v. *Watson*, 16 Johns., 205; *Andrus* v. *Waring*, 20 Johns., 163; *Archb., 247. It is un- [***105** necessary to quote authorities to show that a departure is bad on general demurrer.

The declaration is also defective. The 2d and 3d counts set forth the policy by reference merely to the 1st. This may have the authority of Chitty, but is not warranted by any direction adjudication. *Phillips* v. *Fielding*, 2 H. Bl., 131, supports this objection.

WOODWORTH, *J.* I think you will find this form of declaring supported by *Crookshank* v. *Gray*, 20 Jobus., 344.

Messrs. G. Griffin and *T. A. Emmet*, contra. The party committing the first fault in pleading must have judgment against him. *Woodward* v. *Robinson*, 1 Str., 302, 303; Com. Dig., Pleader, M, 2. The 2d and 3d counts are good by way of reference. Why should a long policy be reiterated in each count? This would be against the policy of our jurisprudence, which abridges pleadings and other proceedings as far as possible, with a view to a saving of expense. This form is according to the practice of the best pleaders among the profession.

This survey is set up as a flat bar—thus shutting out all inquiry as to its merits, and making it conclusive. It is then incumbent on the defendant to show clearly that it is within the rotten clause. There are but three cases extant in which this survey is holden a bar.

1. The survey is alleged to have been made after the voyage had ended. This voyage was at and from N. Y. to Cadiz. The averments as to time are the same in all the pleas. This differs, therefore, from the cases of *Brandegee* v. *Nat. Ins. Co.*, 20 Johns., 328; *Steinmets* v. *U. S. Ins. Co.*, 2 Serg. & R., 293, and *Dorr* v. *Pacific Ins. Co.*, 7 Wh., 581. To be a bar, the survey must be within the clause, which contemplates one pending the voyage. Without this clause, the survey would have been mere preliminary proof. [The counsel read the usual rotten clause from a printed policy.] It means a survey while the ship is sailing, or **106*]** *in some port of necessity; not that the underwriter shall be discharged because the vessel is unseaworthy as to some other voyage, but as to the very voyage. "The vessel may be condemned for a variety of reasons, which imply nothing against her seaworthiness when the risk commenced; but if she be condemned as being unsound or rotten, this can so seldom occur unless she was so when she started, that the parties are willing to consider this circumstance, if established by regular survey and condemnation, as evidence of the fact of want of seaworthiness, when she sailed, without going into other proof which it is always difficult to procure. Cond. Marsh., 159 *b*, *n.* 15. In construing a clause which is to bar us, the court will not extend it by implication.

The object, as between the assurers and the assured, is always the state of the vessel, not at the end, but during the voyage. The word "immediately" has no legal meaning, and the pleas may be read upon and after the vessel's arrival. Every vessel has a point of time at which it passes from a sperate to a desperate state, or arrives at a situation of unseaworthiness. Who shall undertake to say that the unseaworthiness did not attach after the arrival? Can a court of justice judicially say so? If you depart from the construction for which we contend, that it must be during the voyage, where will you stop as to the time of survey? At one day or one year after the arrival of the ship? To strengthen this construction still further, look at other parts of the policy. The Company takes upon itself to bear certain perils in this voyage, which may, by construction, be extended to and reiterated in every clause. The reason for its insertion is evident. To make a policy attach, the ship must be seaworthy at the point of starting. It being difficult to determine this, the policy adds another precaution, viz.: that a future survey finding unseaworthiness shall be evidence of original rottenness. When a ship arrives at her port of destination, the precaution ceases to be necessary. The voyage is finished. It does not appear how long after the arrival the survey was had.

2. The manner of the survey is not set forth. The words of the rotten clause are, that if, on a regular survey, &c. To *say that a **[*107** survey was made, is not enough; but the party should set forth the manner and circumstances under which it was made. In this particular the pleas vary from those in the cases cited to support them. Facts should be shown to enable the court to judge whether the survey be regular or not. Instead of finding fault with the manner in which we deny the necessary circumstances, and impeach the survey at Cadiz as disagreeing with usage, the *onus* lies upon the defendants, who must show affirmatively that it is agreeable to usage. The survey is a judicial act, and should be performed under the direction of a court of admiralty, unless this is excused by the absence of such a court from the port of survey. If not done through the instrumentality of such a court, it lies with the defendant to show the reason, in order to give a survey the effect of a pleaded bar. It was decided in *Robinson* v. *Clifford*, Cond. Marsh., 159 *a*, *note*, that a warrant of survey and report is a judicial proceeding. Now a party relying on a judicial proceeding, is bound to set it out particularly. The words "regularly" and "truly," &c., will not do. Com. Dig., Pl., E, 18; *Cruger* v. *Cropsey*, 3 Johns., 242; *Currie* v. *Henry*, 2 Johns., 433; *Slade* v. *Drade*, Hob., 296; *Morgan* v. *Dyer*, 10 Johns., 161; *Evans* v. *Munkley*, 4 Taunt., 48. If there be no court, and no usage at the port, this should be shown by way of excuse. If there be usage, this should be shown in order to establish the regularity. It involves a question of law, and should be put upon the record, that we may have a writ of error, if determined erroneously. The regularity is the important and turning point of the controversy. Bac. Abr., Pleas and Pleading, I, 3; 1 Saund., 298, *n.* 1; *Walker* v. *Maxwell*, 1 Mass., 104; *Hill* v. *Montague*, 2 Maule & S., 377. The contents of the survey are important, because it is agreed that if there be a mixed cause of condemnation, it will not operate as a bar. "Where a man avers that he has done a thing which involves in it a question of law, whether it is done as the law directs, the *quo modo* must be averred." Per Reeve, *J.*, in *Wright* v. *Tuttle*, 4 Day Cas., 322, 323. Suppose the pleas had said merely that a survey was held, leaving out the word "regular," *this would have **[*108** been defective; and if so, the epithet will not

help it, because it has no legal meaning any more than the word "immediately." No issue could be joined upon either of these words. The law has no ear which listens to such general words. 1 Chit. Pl., 240; *Mure* v. *Kaye*, 4 Taunt., 34. It is like the word "sufficient." Where a man was bound to show a sufficient discharge, it was held not enough to aver generally in pleading that a sufficient discharge was offered to be shown; but the party must show the particulars, in order that its sufficieney may be judicially seen. The case of *The Abbot of Strata Mercella*, 9 Co., 25 *a*. Suppose the policy had provided, as is sometimes done, for leaving the adjustment of a loss to arbitrators; would it be good pleading to say that it had been adjusted by a regular award? Was an award ever pleaded in this way? No. You must allege that the matter was submitted, and give a history of the steps taken.

The 1st plea does not set forth the survey at all, but only its legal effect. Now, though this may answer in declaring, it will not do in a plea. 1 Chit. Pl., 236, 237; 1 Saund., 276 *a*, *n*. 2; *Clements* v. *Lambert*, 1 Taunt., 207, Shepherd, Sergt., *arguendo; Wright* v. *Clements*, 3 B. & A., 509, per Holroyd, *J.; Bender* v. *Sampson*, 11 Mass., 44, 45. In the last case it is said, of pleading a discharge under a sealed power of attorney, that "it is in all cases to be pleaded specially, how and in what manner the discharge was made: as the sufficiency of such an instrument, the purport and effect of it, is a question of law, which the party whose deed or contract it is alleged to be, has the privilege of referring to the court."

The court will not conclude that the survey in the 2d plea is different from the one set out in the 3d and 4th. Now, do these surveys bring the case within the rotten clause? We wish to argue from both connectedly; but they have not referred to the first; and we will take the 3d plea for the present. It alleges that the ship was bad and rotten, &c., and the firm opinion of the surveyors that it would be best for all parties concerned that she should be condemned; but she is not declared incapable of prosecuting the voyage on account of rottenness. It may mean a mixed cause; and should
109*] not be *so construed as to exclude any other. The survey does not say, as in *Steinmets* v. *U. S. Ins. Co.*, 2 Serg. & R., 293, that the vessel was decayed, and stop there; but it finds her "bad" and rotten; and how are the court to say that the badness is all rottenness? If badness can mean anything else besides rottenness, it destroys the flat bar, and lets us in to try the question. The plea should have averred, at least, that rottenness was the sole cause.

Again; the surveyors do not say that she was so rotten as to be unseaworthy, or as to be incapable of prosecuting a voyage. This was requisite, though it might have been enough to find that $5,000 were necessary in repairs, had the survey been pending the voyage.

This plea also omits to state previous examination; on whose application the survey was made; how the surveyors came to a knowledge of the rottenness; and in what single particular the ship was rotten. In the cases relied upon to support this plea, there is, at least, an examination stated, and some particulars.

In *Dorr* v. *Pacific Ins. Co.*, 7 Wh., 581, at page 611, Johnson, *J.*, says: "The words of the contract expressly look forward to a future event, if the vessel, upon a regular survey, should be thereby declared unseaworthy; obviously contemplating two objects: first, that a state of rottenness, ascertained at any period of the voyage insured, shall be conclusive evidence of original unsoundness." This shows his understanding that the survey should be made during the voyage.

But we shall probably be met by saying that the voyage was not at an end. Now the end of a voyage is an arrival and remaining in safe moorings for twenty-four hours; not if the ship be ordered off for quarantine, it is true; but if she is there uninjured by any previous mal-accident for twenty-four hours, she is at the risk of the assured. The voyage in question was ended within this rule. If made within twenty-four hours the survey might have been good; but it cannot be so within the rotten clause, if made after that time. Great strictness should be observed throughout. In *Armroyd* v. *Union Ins. Co.*, cited from the 2d of Binn., therefore, Tilghman, **Ch. J.*, says: "I am called on to give [***110**
my opinion on the construction of the memorandum, and of the survey and condemnation in this case. It is a contract which bears hard upon the assured, especially in long voyages; but being the agreement of the parties, and not being contrary to law, no court has a right to say that it is void. It is to receive a fair construction; but not to be extended beyond the plain meaning of the words. If there is a regular survey and condemnation for unsoundness or rottenness, the assurers are discharged. When I say unsoundness, I mean as the law was decided in *Garrigues* v. *Coxe*, an unsoundness arising from decay, and not from accidental injury. But then the unsoundness or rottenness must be the sole cause of condemnation. If the condemnation is grounded partly on rottenness and partly on damages sustained by violence of storms, &c., the case is not within the contract. In the present case the survey and condemnation are regular in point of form. There was a petition to the judge by the captain, a warrant of survey, a report of the surveyors, and a decree founded thereon. It is not necessary that the judge should make use of the word "condemn," in cases of this kind. It is enough if, upon the whole matter, he orders a sale of the vessel. There is no occasion to decide whether, in all cases, there must be a decree of a judge. Surveys may sometimes be made in places where there is no court. But on this I give no opinion." The opinion of the learned judge shows also that the survey must be sanctioned by a court of admiralty, or something done which is equivalent to this. In the case of *Steinmets* v. *U. S. Ins. Co.*, cited from 2 Serg. & R., the same judge says: "If this be not a condemnation within the meaning of the policy, the clause will be nugatory, because, upon a survey, the particular parts which are found in a decayed state are always mentioned; and indeed it would not be proper to say, in general, that the vessel was rotten," evincing the *Chief Justice's* idea of the strict regularity which should attend these surveys.

It may be said we have cured all defect by replying to these pleas. But a replication does 111*] not cure any defect which is *the subject of a general demurrer. *Comly* v. *Lockwood*, 15 Johns., 191, per Thompson, *Ch. J.*; *Anonymous*, 2 Salk., 519; Com. Dig., Pleader, M, 1, 2. The objections that the survey was not made during the voyage; that the sole ground of rottenness is not stated; that the surveyors have not detailed their steps in proceeding to the survey; that the manner and circumstances are not detailed, &c., are objectionable by general demurrer, if so in any shape. At common law a general demurrer reached every defect except duplicity. Then came the Statute of 27 Elizabeth, ch. 5, and 4 Ann., ch. 16; and *vide* 1 R. L., 120, sec. 7, by which a special demurrer is required for everything but substance involving the merits of the cause, and the right of the case, which these objections do. There is not, in the language of the Statute, enough appearing upon the face of these pleas, to enable the court, according to the right of the case, to give judgment for the defendant. In *Mure* v. *Kaye*, 4 Taunt., 34, a general demurrer was allowed, because facts and circumstances were not set forth. In *Beake* v. *Tyrrell*, 1 Show., 6; Carth., 1, S. C., a capture and condemnation as prize, were pleaded as a justification, and held bad on general demurrer, because not shown how the vessel was prize, nor by whom condemned. Com. Dig., Pleader, M, 2, states that want of certainty is not cured by replying, and cites Poph., 209. True, there are exceptions to this rule of Comyn; but these are where the want of certainty is merely formal; as if the circumstances going to the regularity had here been informally set out, instead of being omitted altogether. Other cases, where replying has been holden not to cure a bad plea, may be found in *Grocer's Co.* v. *Archbishop of Canterbury*, 3 Wils., 221, 234; *Burdick* v. *Green*, 18 Johns., 14, and *Boardman* v. *Ives*, 10 *Id.*, 164, *n. a.* In the last case the question was much the same as here. It related to the form of giving jurisdiction to the court in pleading, like the present, which is a question of jurisdiction as to the surveyors.

The replications are the same substantially, except that to the 3d plea. They deny the 112*] existence of circumstances *which the defendant ought to have stated. In pleading, if the party do not set out an entire instrument, the opposite party may do it. *Fisher* v. *Pimbley*, 11 East, 188. We have done nothing more. So much was necessary in order to spread the whole merits before the court. We were led to it by a want of fullness in the pleas. It is said the replications set out too much, but this will not vitiate. *Duffield* v. *Scott*, 3 T. R., 374; Bac. Abr., tit. Pleas and Pleadings, I, 4; *U. S.* v. *Burnham*, 1 Mas., 67.

Here is no departure. We aver, in the first count, that the vessel was so much injured as to be useless to us—not merely a physical total loss as is supposed. There is then no departure or inconsistency in saying that the vessel arrived at Cadiz in a disabled state.

As to multifariousness of matter, you may state what number of facts you please, if they all go to make only one point. 1 Chit. Pl., 512, 576; *Patcher* v. *Sprague*, 2 Johns., 462; *Currie* v. *Henry*, *Id.*, 433; *Thomas* v. *Rumsey*, 6 *Id.*, 26. Accordingly, all the matters shown by us tend to the same point, which is an irregular survey.

As to the traverse, that there is any other survey, it is, at most, surplusage. But this traverse applies to the second plea only, which is bad, as professing to set out a survey according to its legal effect, merely. You may sometimes traverse matter of law, as simony, seisin in fee, or in tail; thus denying not only the facts, but the law arising from them.

Mr. Wells, in reply. The question in relation to this survey, are mere questions of law; and it is desirable that they should be determined by the court upon the special pleas. It is said that these are bad, because we have not set out the authority of, and circumstances attending the survey. But by alleging a survey, all the necessary authority and circumstances to render it perfect are involved equally as if we had mentioned them specifically. It is said that rottenness does not appear to be the sole ground of unseaworthiness; that the word "bad" may signify something else; but "bad" and "rotten" are evidently used as convertible terms. The former *is [*113 spoken of as the consequence of the latter, according to the natural import of the phrase.

Again; it is objected that the survey should be pending the voyage; that a survey is not conclusive after the perils of the voyage have ceased, the underwriters then having no interest in it. But the underwriters have an interest in determining whether the vessel was a proper subject of insurance, as being or not being within the rotten clause. The plea says that the survey was made upon and immediately after the arrival; and the court will presume, if necessary, that this was before the voyage terminated, or the twenty-four hours' mooring. But the time is immaterial. The survey is in reference to the contract between the parties; and is not to affect their rights of recovery or defense. The plaintiffs would make the curious distinction, that it is valid for their purposes to enable them to recover; but nor for our's as a matter of defense. The clause relating to the perils of the sea, doubtless means during the voyage, but cannot be carried forward to the time of the survey. The survey may be made after the voyage in reference either to a total or partial loss, or the right of recovery within the rotten clause. Two things are contemplated. If the vessel be unsound or rotten, and therefore unseaworthy, the underwriters are not to pay if the loss happened from rottenness, whether the vessel arrived or not at the port of destination. The object was not to have the vessel thrown upon the hands of the underwriters as a total loss, when it arose from perils not insured against. It is enough that the survey is made within a reasonable time; and this was so even by the replication.

The form of pleading the survey is proper. It is stated to be a regular survey held at the port of Cadiz; and the 1st plea says that the vessel was found, within the policy, unsound and rotten. Each plea must stand upon itself. Per Spencer, *J.*, in *Currie* v. *Henry*, 2 Johns., 433, 437. One plea cannot be invoked in aid

of another. These are, therefore, to be considered as distinct surveys in each plea. The law presumes the survey to be regular. A judgment means, *ex vi termini*, a regular judg-
114*] ment. So of a survey; *and in all the cases cited to show that we must be particular, the party was defending his conduct in a proceeding to which he was a party, if we except the case of the sequestration mentioned *arguendo* in Hobart, 296, referred to the year books, 5 ed. 4, 29, where I presume even this will be found attended with the same circumstance.(*a*) One is not bound to defend himself by the regularity of a proceeding to which he is not a party. A familiar case is that of a sheriff sued for the execution of process. It is enough if it appear to be regular upon its face. So of this survey. We are not a party to it. Surveys are made on the part of the assured. The court will notice, judicially, that this is so. It is the duty of the assured to have the survey made as a matter of preliminary proof; and when presented as such, this is the first knowledge of the underwriters upon the subject. *Haff* v. *Mar. Ins. Co.*, 4 Johns., 132; 1 Chit. Pl., 220; *Chandler* v. *Grieves*, 2 H. Bl., 606, *n. a.* These cases show that the court will take judicial notice of marine customs. We are not bound to, nor can we do more than introduce the simple survey, which the captain is bound to take officially in behalf of the assured. What is one's duty shall be presumed to have been done. Bull. *N. P.*, 298; *Hilts* v. *Colvin*, 14 Johns., 182. The plaintiffs, then, are here attempting to impeach a proceeding of their own, carried on for their benefit, of which they claim to avail themselves in preliminary proof, but would impeach the moment it is attempted to use it against them. It was certainly enough for us to state the survey as they themselves furnished it to us.

Matters which come more properly from the other side need not be stated by us. Com. Dig., Pleader, C, 81; 2 Saund., 62 *b*, *n.* 5; *Casseres* v. *Bell*, general principle, per Ld. Kenyon, *Ch. J.*; 8 T. R., 167; *Chapman* v. *Pickersgill*, 2 Wils., 147, per *Ld. Ch. J.*; *The King* v. *Holland*, per Buller, *J.*, 5 T. R., 615. Now the underwriter could not know the *quo modo* in which the survey is done. The plaintiffs require him here to set out what he
115*] is no party to, and *matter of which he is entirely ignorant. We state enough to constitute a defense; and the plaintiffs may spread the whole matter before the court. In *Hill* v. *Montagu*, 2 Maule & S., 377, 378, Bayley, *J.*, says: "I have always understood that the party who pleads a contract must set it out if he be a party to the contract. It lies as much within the knowledge of the defendant as of the plaintiff." In *Wright* v. *Tuttle*, 4 Day Cas., 422, Reeve, *J.*, says: "If the *quo modo* had been averred, it would not have rendered the averment ill, but it would have been a needless surplusage."

Now, suppose the pleas to be bad in substance, you cannot always go back to a defect, because it may be reached by a general demurrer. True, in the language of *Ch. J.* Thompson, quoted on the other side, it must be bad on general demurrer; but though it be so, if the replication be such as to waive the substantial defect, it cures the plea. Here, had the plaintiffs demurred directly for lack of going into particulars as to the survey, it would have brought up the question; but by answering over, they have waived the right to except for this cause. *Stutfield* v. *Somerset*, Cro. Eliz., 825, was the case of a palpably bad plea, yet it was cured by a special replication. Com. Dig., Pleader, E, 37; *Knighton* v. *Morton*, 3 Lev., 311, S. P.

Curia, per SUTHERLAND, *J.* This case comes before the court upon several special demurrers to the plaintiffs' replications to the defendants' pleas in bar; and the first question for consideration is whether those pleas are substantially good; for if not, although the demurrers may be well taken, still the plaintiffs will be entitled to judgment, unless the defects of the pleas are cured by the replications.

The pleadings turn upon the rotten clause in the policy of insurance, which provides "that if the vessel, upon a regular survey, should be thereby declared unseaworthy by reason of her being unsound or rotten, or incapable of prosecuting her voyage on account of her being unsound or rotten, then the assurers should not be bound to pay their subscription on that policy."

*The special plea to the 1st and 2d [***116**
counts of the declaration set forth "that upon and immediately after the arrival of the ship at Cadiz, in the course of the said voyage, and in reference to the said voyage, and to any damage which the said ship had sustained in the prosecution thereof, a regular survey was had, &c., on the 15th day of October, 1819, upon which survey the said ship was thereby declared unseaworthy by reason of her being rotten," with a verification; and for further plea to the first count a regular survey as before, whereby it was declared that the said ship was in a very bad and rotten condition, and that she was not worth repairing, and that it was best for all parties that she should be condemned, &c.

The same plea as the last was also pleaded separately to the 2d and 3d counts.

These pleas are said to be substantially bad on three grounds.

1. Because the survey is alleged to have been made after the arrival of the ship at the port of destination, and, of course, after the termination of the voyage insured; and,

2. Because the pleas do not state the manner and circumstances of the survey, but merely state it to have been regular.

3. Because the survey itself, as set out, is bad, and does not amount to a bar.

1. There is no validity in the first objection. The survey was made by the assured as a foundation for an abandonment of the ship as for a total loss, in order to charge the underwriters; and they certainly have a right to avail themselves of it, for the purpose of showing that the injury sustained (and which caused the abandonment) was not owing to any of the perils insured against, but to the rottenness of the ship. The terms of the rotten clause do not render it necessary that

(*a*) The case is stated with about the same brevity in 5 ed. 4, 29, as in Hob., 296.

the survey should be made before the termination of the voyage, or before the ship arrives at her port of destination. Nor is it exclusively intended to guard the underwriters against the contingency of her being unable to prosecute her voyage on account of her being unsound or rotten; but also against all claims **117***] of the assured *for any loss or injury which can be traced to the unsoundness or rottenness of the ship. A regular survey, whereby the ship is declared unseaworthy by reason of her being unsound or rotten, is, by the agreement of the parties, made conclusive evidence of the fact; and if the survey is made with reference to the voyage and perils to which the policy relates, within a reasonable time after the termination of the voyage, it is sufficient.

In many cases no survey could be made except at the port of destination; and in most cases it would be impossible to make it before the termination of the voyage (that is within 24 hours after the ship has come to her moorings, and cast her anchor); because it cannot be satisfactorily and thoroughly made until the vessel is unladen. But the plea in this case alleges the survey to have been made upon and immediately after her arrival, which, if it were necessary, would be intended to be before the termination of the voyage.

2. It was not necessary to set forth in the plea the manner and circumstances of the survey. It was not done in the case of *Brandegee* v. *Nat. Ins. Co.*, 20 Johns., 328. The pleas there are, in this respect, precisely like those in this case. They simply state that a regular survey was had, and no objection was made to them on that ground. The survey is the act of the assured, in order to charge the underwriters. The latter are not parties to it. In *Haff* v. *Mar. Ins. Co.*, 4 Johns., 135, Thompson, *J.*, says: "It (the survey) is to be presumed *prima facie*, to be in the possession of the plaintiff, the assured. It is always made at the instance, and for the benefit of the owner or master of the vessel, and it goes of course into his hands."

Whether they would be permitted to impeach the regularity of their own survey, may well be questioned. But it certainly is not incumbent upon the defendants to set forth in their plea all the facts and circumstances which show it to be regular. Not being parties to the survey, they may not know those facts and circumstances. They must be **118***] known *to the plaintiffs, and if they afford any ground for impeaching the regularity of the survey, the statement would come more properly from them, provided it is competent for them to impeach it. It falls within the general rule of pleading, that matter which comes more properly from the other side need not be stated. 1 Chit. Pl., 228, and cases there cited; and *vide* the opinion of Johnson, *J.*, in *Dorr* v. *Pacific Ins. Co.*, 7 Wh., 612.

3. The survey, as set out in the second plea to the first and second counts of the declaration, is undoubtedly a good bar to the action. After stating the arrival of the vessel at Cadiz, and that a regular survey was had upon her, it states the survey itself, and its result, in the following terms: "Upon which survey the said ship was thereby declared unseaworthy, by reason of her being rotten." The test is, does it appear from the survey that rottenness was the sole cause of condemnation. If it does, the survey is a good bar. But if the condemnation is in part for decay, and in part for damage occasioned by the perils of the sea, then it is no defense for the underwriters. *Steinmets* v. *U. S. Ins Co.*, 2 Serg. & R., 293; *Garrigues* v. *Coxe*, 1 Binn., 598; *Armroyd* v. *Union Ins. Co.*, 2 *Id.*, 394; *Brandegee* v. *Nat. Ins. Co.*, 20 Johns., 328; *Dorr* v. *Pacific Ins. Co.*, 7 Wh., 581; *Haff* v. *Mar. Ins. Co.*, 8 Johns., 167. In all these cases, the survey stated, with more or less particularity, the circumstances of the ship's conditions; and the principal inquiry in each of them was, whether all the particulars stated, made out of the fact of rottenness to be the sole ground of condemnation.

It seems to be taken for granted, in all the cases, that if the survey states the condemnation to be for rottenness alone, without stating the particulars which are affected, it is conclusive. *Tilghman, Ch. J.*, in *Garrigues* v. *Coxe*, 1 Binn., 595, says; "If the survey should say she was unsound, and no more, the plaintiff would be barred." It is true that the same learned, judge, in *Steinmets* v. *U. S. Ins. Co.*, 2 Serg. & R., 297, remarks, "that, upon a survey, the particular parts which are found in a decayed *state are always mentioned; [***119** and, indeed, it would not be proper to say, in general, that the vessel was rotten." He was reasoning against the position which had been urged by the plaintiff's counsel, that the survey ought to be in the very words of the policy. He thought, instead of confining themselves to the expressions used in the policy, it was proper for the surveyors to state the particulars of the decay. It is undoubtedly proper, but not indispensable.

The 3d plea, which is to the first count alone, states that a survey was had upon the vessel, &c., by which she was found to be in a very bad and rotten condition. This plea is bad. Rottenness does not appear to be the sole cause of condemnation. A vessel may be in a very bad condition, without being rotten. She may be rotten in some of her timbers, without being unseaworthy. The cause of her condemnation, then, upon this survey, is left doubtful; and that is a fatal objection to it in a plea in bar.

The 4th plea, which is to the second count, is the same as the third, and is bad for the same reasons.

The 5th plea is to the third count, and is the same as the last two (except that part which relates to the general average), and is bad for the same reasons.

These pleas being bad in substance, are not cured by the replication: for a bar which wants substance cannot be aided by a replication. Com. Dig., Pleader, E, 37; 8 Col., 120 *b*, Com. Dig., Pleader, M, 1, 2; 2 Salk., 519; 15 Johns., 191, per Thompson, *Ch. J.* It is unnecessary, therefore, to consider whether the demurrers to the replications to these pleas are well taken or not; for the pleas being bad, the plaintiff must have judgment.

It remains, then, only to consider the causes of demurrer to the replication to the 2d plea.

The first cause of demurrer assigned is, that the traverse seeks to put in issue matters not in the plea. The plea states a survey made at Cadiz. The replication traverses a survey at Cadiz or elsewhere. The issue must be as broad as the traverse; but a rejoinder as broad as the replication would have been a departure from the plea, and have subjected the defendant to a demurrer. That cause is well taken. It is also a departure from the
120*] *declaration. It alleges the survey to have been at Cadiz, after the arrival, whereas the declaration avers a physical total loss.

The defendants are, therefore, entitled to judgment upon their demurrers to the replication of the 2d plea; with leave to the plaintiffs to amend, on payment of costs; and the plaintiff must have judgment upon the replications to the other pleas.

Judgment accordingly.

Cited in—1 Den., 570, *n.*; 2 Hall, 100; 1 Sand., 319; 2 Binn., 249.

GARDNER *v.* BUCKBEE.

Judgment of a Court of Concurrent Jurisdiction —When Conclusive of the Same Matter in Another Suit.

The judgment of a court of concurrent jurisdiction, directly upon a point, is conclusive between the same parties, upon the same matter coming directly in question in another suit;

And this, whether it be pleaded, or given in evidence under the general issue.

It is conclusive, whether it appear upon the face of the record in the former suit that the same matter was tried and passed upon or not.

If it was, in fact, so tried, without this fact appearing of record, the proper course is to give the record in evidence, and then prove, by parol, that the matter did arise, and was tried upon the pleadings in the record.

Where B. sued G. upon a promissory note, in the Marine Court, and G. pleaded the general issue, with notice that the note was given upon the fraudulent sale of a vessel by B. to G., which was the question upon the trial, and the verdict was for the defendant; and afterwards B, sued G. in the C. P., upon another note given upon the same purchase; held, that upon the trial of the second cause, the record and proceedings in the first were conclusive evidence of the fraud, and were a conclusive bar to the second action; that the proper course was to give the record of the Marine Court in evidence, and then show by parol evidence (e. g., by the justice who tried the first cause), that the same question had been tried before him.

Whether, in *assumpsit*, a former trial for the same cause may be given in evidence under the general issue, *quære.*

Citations—11 State Tri., 261; 1 Phil. Ev., 223; 1 Pet., 202; 1 Chit., 472.

ON ERROR to the Court of C. P. of the City of N. Y., the case was this: The defendant in error sold to the plaintiff in error and others, the schooner Tiger, and for the consideration money took two promissory notes, signed by the plaintiff in error, and the other purchasers. The Tiger, upon examination, proving utterly unseaworthy, the plaintiff in error refused to pay the notes, on the ground of fraudulent misrepresentations in the sale by the defendant in error. Hereupon the defendant in error prosecuted the plaintiff in error, on one of the notes, in the Marine Court of the City of N. Y., who contested the payment upon the general *issue, accom- [***121** panied with notice of a total failure of consideration, on the ground of fraud in the sale of the schooner, and a trial being there had, on this very point, judgment passed in favor of the plaintiff in error. The defendant in error then brought this action on the remaining note against the plaintiff in error, in the Court of C. P. for the City of N. Y., and at the trial, the plaintiff in error offered in evidence, in bar of the suit, the record of the judgment in his favor, on the other note, in the Marine Court, contending that it was conclusive; the defense, by the notice in this case, being fraud, and the judgment offered in evidence being directly on the point in issue, and between the same parties. The Court of C. P. decided that the judgment was no bar, but admitted it in evidence to the jury, in connection with other proof of fraud; to which opinion the plaintiff in error excepted. The case will also be found stated at large in the opinion of the court, to which I refer for the manner in which the proceedings on the first trial were made out.

Mr. J. Anthon, for the plaintiff in error.

1. This case falls so fully within the rule laid down by *Ch. J.* De Grey, in *The Duchess of Kingston's* case, as to preclude all argument. *Vide* 11 State Tr., 261; 1 Phil. Ev., 223. He says, "relative to judgments being given in evidence in civil suits, it seems to follow as generally true, that the judgment of a court of concurrent jurisdiction directly on the point, is, as a plea, a bar, or, as evidence, conclusive

---

NOTE.—*Former adjudication—When a bar—Parol evidence—When admissible to show what was decided in former suit.*

The judgment of a court of concurrent jurisdiction directly upon the point is, as a plea in bar, or evidence, conclusive upon the same parties upon the same matter directly in question in another court. Wood v. Jackson, 8 Wend., 9; Burt v. Sternbergh, 4 Cow., 559; Lawrence v. Hunt, 10 Wend., 81; Baker v. Rand, 13 Barb., 152; Birckhead v. Brown, 5 Sand., 134; Demarest v. Darg, 32 N. Y., 281; Stowell v. Chamberlain, 60 N. Y., 272.

Such a judgment is conclusive as to all matters coming within the legitimate purview of the action, whether actually determined or not. Le Guen v. Gouverneur, 1 Johns. Cas., 436; Southgate v. Montgomery, 1 Paige, 41; Bruen v. Howe, 2 Barb., 586; Clemens v. Clemens, 37 N. Y., 59; Embury v. Conner, 3 N. Y., 511; Jordan v. Van Epps, 85 N. Y., 427; Barrett v. Failing, 8 Or., 152; Smith v. Smith, 79 N. Y., 634; Tuska v. O'Brien, 68 N. Y., 446.

Compare Smith v. Weeks, 26 Barb., 463; Burwell v. Knight, 51 Barb., 267; Barth v. Burt, 17 Abb. Pr., 349; 43 Barb., 628; Campbell v. Consalus, 25 N. Y., 613; Sweet v. Tuttle, 14 N. Y., 465; Perry v. Dickerson, 85 N. Y., 345; Emery v. Wilson, 79 N. Y., 78; Masten v. Olcott, 24 Hun, 587; Remington Paper Co. v. O'Dougherty, 81 N. Y., 474.

Where several securities arise from one transaction, and a defense which applies equally to all is interposed in an action on one, the judgment is conclusive as to all. Gardner v. Buckbee, *supra*; Bouchand v. Dias, 3 Den., 238; Birckhead v. Brown, 5 Sand., 134. See also, Hoff v. Meyers, 42 Barb., 270; Foster v. Konkright, 70 Ind., 123; Guernsey v. Carver, 8 Wend., 492; Guest v. City of Brooklyn, 79 N. Y., 624; Geiser Threshing Machine Co. v. Farmer, 27 Minn., 428; Danziger v. Williams, 91 Pa. St., 234.

See, generally, Russell v. Farquhar, 55 Tex., 355; Morrison v. Clark, 55 Tex., 437; Hanna v. Read, 102 Ill., 596; Drea v. Cariveau, 28 Minn., 280; Hardin v. Palmerlee, 28 Minn., 450; Meredith v. Santa Clara Mining Ass., 56 Cal., 178; Harryman v. Roberts, 52 Md., 64; Krutzinger v. Brown, 72 Ind., 466; Hudson v. Detroit Sup. Ct. Judge, 42 Mich., 239.

Admissibility of parol evidence, to show what was in issue in former suit. See Manny v. Harris, 2 Johns., 24 *note.*

between the same parties, upon the same matter directly in question in another cause." "Where several courts have each an original, direct and concurrent jurisdiction, the same question may arise in each of them, either directly or indirectly, and either court may decide the cause. But if the matter be directly decided by either court, before the decision of the same question is brought forward in the other court, such decision would be final." *Graham* v. *Maingay*, 1 Irish T. R., 54. "The decision of a court of competent jurisdiction, directly upon the same point, is conclusive, when the same point comes again in controversy between the same parties, directly or **122***] *collaterally." 1 Pet., 202; *Wright* v. *Deklyn*, C. C. U. S., per *Judge* Washington. "It is a well established rule, in England, that the judgment, sentence or decree of a court of exclusive jurisdiction upon the point, may be given in evidence as conclusive between the same parties, upon the same matter coming incidentally in question in another court." *Croudson* v. *Leonard*, per Johnson, *J.*, 4 Cr., 436. The same rule applies when the courts have a concurrent jurisdiction. 1 Irish T. R., 54. "A person is, in all cases, concluded by a decree, sentence or judgment of a court of competent jurisdiction, in a suit in which he was a party, in all future trials of the same question, and whether that question arises directly or collaterally. And such judgment is conclusive, not only of the right it establishes, but of the fact which it decides." *Outram* v. *Morewood*, 3 East, 345; 6 Mass. T. R., 277; 8 *Id.*, 536; 11 *Id.*, 445; 12 *Id.*, 268.

2. This record was admissible in evidence under the plea of *non assumpsit*, and did not require to be specially pleaded. "In an action of *assumpsit*, the defendant may either plead a judgment recovered, or give it in evidence under the general issue. *Bird* v. *Randall*, per Ld. Mansfield, 3 Burr., 1353; 1 Chit., 473; 1 Phil. Ev., 224; 16 Johns., 136.

Mr. J. Wyckoff, contra. Whatever was the former law upon the subject, the latest adjudications require that a former judgment should be pleaded specially, and refuse to receive a record in evidence, under the plea of *non assumpsit*. *Vooght* v. *Winch*, 2 B. & A., 669. In this case the doctrine as laid down by Ld. Mansfield, "that a former recovery need not be pleaded in bar, but may be given in evidence under the general issue," is overruled by Abbott, *Ch. J.*, and Bayley and Holroyd, *JJ.* 1 Phil. Ev., 225, *note*.

2. The former judgment should have been pleaded by way of estoppel; but the plaint- **123***] iff in error has elected to *submit all the facts in evidence to the jury, by pleading the general issue. *Ib.*, and 2 B. & A., 662.

3. The record of the Marine Court neither negated nor affirmed any particular fact in issue, but the judgment was general and indefinite; and as the actions in the Marine Court and the Court of C. P. were upon distinct obligations, payable at different times, the defenses were founded upon the same or a different state of facts, neither inferable from the language of the record; for the record must be taken by itself unconnected with the parol explanations of the justice who rendered judgment. 1 Phil. Ev., 218.

By the record of the Marine Court, therefore, no single fact in issue appears to have been decided, which would necessarily arise under the pleadings in the cause in the Court of C. P. The record, therefore, would be no bar, even if pleaded specially, for it must be upon the same point in issue in both causes. 1 Phil. Ev., 223, and the authorities there cited.

Mr. Anthon, in reply. The case of *Vooght* v. *Winch*, 2 B. & A., 662, on which, alone, the defendant in error relies, is not law. The argument of Marryat, Lawes and Comyn, in that case, sets forth the law truly, and consistently with the opinion of the twelve judges *The Duchess of Kingston's* case, which, from the time it was decided, down to the year 1819, when *Vooght* v. *Winch* was decided, has been the unquestioned law of England.

The conclusiveness of records, when given in evidence, underwent a very full discussion in the Exchequer Chamber in Ireland, upon a writ of error, in the case of *Maingay* v. *Gahan*, Irish T. R., 1 to 80, and was fully sustained on the authority of *The Duchess of Kingston's* case.

It is absurd, and against sound reason, that a record which imports perfect verity, should be conclusive when offered to the court, and of no positive avail when left to a jury. In the language of Marryatt, in *Vooght* v. *Winch*, 2 B. & A., 66, its effect surely cannot be varied by the mode in which it is brought before the court.

The doctrine of *The Duchess of Kingston's* case, independent of the other authorities cited for the plaintiff in error, is supported in *the case of *Shelton* v. *Barbour*, 2 [***124** Wash. 64. Mr. Phillips, also (1 Phil. Ev., ch. 2, sec. 1, p. 223), at the very place cited by the defendant in error, rejects this doctrine, and that of the judges in *Vooght* v. *Winch*, and says: "In an action of *assumpsit* the defendant may either plead a judgment recovered or g[illegible] it in evidence under the general issue, and it is difficult to assign a reason why the judgment should not have the same conclusive operation, if given in evidence without pleading, as it would be admitted to have if pleaded in bar." He also notices the doctrine of estoppel, relied upon by the defendant in error, and confines it to its legitimate subject —" title in the realty."

As to the third point made by the defendant in error, which relates to the generality of the record in the Marine Court, the fact is misstated. The plea was *non assumpsit*, with special notice of failure of consideration, which is tantamount to a special plea. In the case of *Manny* v. *Harris*, 2 Johns., 28, Spencer, *J.*, lays down the true rule as to auxiliary testimony in aid of a record. In commenting on the record offered in evidence in that case, and the auxiliary proof received by the judge who tried the cause, he observes: "It is, therefore, only necessary to inquire whether that issue warranted the giving the present bond in evidence, so that the jury might allow it to the plaintiff; for if the issue did not embrace the present cause of action, evidence ought not to have been received that the jury did decide upon it. This language, as applied to this case, would be: "It is, therefore, only necessary to inquire whether the issue in the Marine Court warranted the giving in evidence the matters offered by the defendant in his defense in the C. P.; for if the issue did not warrant it, the evidence ought not to have been received that the jury did then decide upon it." Now the issue below was expressly on the point: the testimony of the justice, showing that the court had decided the very point, was admissible (and indeed, was received without opposition), and made the record conclusive, leaving to the opposite party the right to contradict him, if this could be done.

125*] *It is true, that from the form of the pleadings, the whole case necessarily went to the jury. But the judge was bound to charge them as to the effect of documentary evidence in the law. He ought, therefore, to have charged them, that if, from all the evidence, they should find that the matters between the parties had been passed upon in the Marine Court, then the record was final. Instead of so doing, he totally neutralized that evidence, by charging that it was entitled to their serious consideration, to which indefinite charge we excepted.

Curia, per WOODWORTH, *J.* This is a writ of error to the C. P. of the City of N. Y. Buckbee, plaintiff in the court below, commenced an action against Gardner, on a promissory note. The defendant pleaded the general issue, and gave notice of special matter, that the note was given in part payment for a vessel called The Tiger, sold to the defendant and others, and alleged fraud by the plaintiff in the sale; the vessel being at the time rotten and unseaworthy, and that known to the plaintiff. At the trial the plaintiff admitted that the note was one of two promissory notes, for the same amount, given by the defendant and two others, as the consideration upon the sale of the vessel.

The defendant offered to prove, in bar of the plaintiff's demand, that the plaintiff impleaded the defendant, in the Marine Court of the City of N. Y., upon a promissory note, bearing even date, and for the same amount as the one now in question, signed by the same parties, and given for the consideration money; that, upon the trial in the Marine Court, the fraud of the plaintiff in the sale was the only point in question; and that judgment had been rendered in that court in favor of the defendant, on the ground that the sale was fraudulent. The plaintiff objected to the testimony, because the judgment had not been pleaded, or notice given; and that the note on which the present suit was brought, is a different instrument from that declared on in the Marine Court. The judge declared the evidence was not admissible, in that stage of the **126*]** cause, but might be *offered, after proof to the jury of the fraud, and in support thereof, to which the defendant excepted.

The defendant, then, in proof of the fraud, offered in evidence the record of the judgment in the Marine Court, in favor of the defendant, on the other note. By the record it appeared that the defendant pleaded the general issue, and gave notice of a total failure of the consideration. I. B. Scott, one of the justices of that court, testified that the matters directly in question before the Marine Court were, the unseaworthiness of the vessel at the time of sale, and the knowledge of that fact by the plaintiff—it not being disclosed at the time of sale to the defendant.

The counsel for the defendant then insisted that the record was a judgment of a court of concurrent jurisdiction, upon the same matters in question in the court below, and was conclusive evidence in favor of the defendant to entitle him to a verdict. The judge decided, and charged the jury, that the matters given in evidence by the defendant were not, in themselves, sufficient to bar the plaintiff's action, but were entitled to the serious consideration of the jury, and were to be taken by them in conjunction with the other evidence of fraud offered in proof. The jury found a verdict for the plaintiff. The defendant excepted to the opinion.

It appears clearly that the question of fraud was tried between the parties, in the Marine Court, on one of the notes given in part payment of the vessel. That court had concurrent jurisdiction. The question is, whether the judgment thus obtained is not a conclusive bar to a recovery in this cause. The law is well settled, that the judgment of a court of concurrent jurisdiction, directly upon the point, is, as a plea in bar, or evidence, conclusive between the same parties, upon the same matter directly in question in another court. This was the rule laid down by De Gray, *Ch. J.*, in delivering judgment in *The Duchess of Kingston's* case, 11 St. Tr., 261; 1 Phil. Ev., 223; 1 Pet., 202, C. C. U. S. I am not aware that it has been departed from by our courts. The general principle does not appear to be controverted by the counsel for the defendant *in error; but it is urged **[*127** that the judgement in the Marine Court does not affirm any particular fact in issue in this cause, but is general and indefinite; and that from the language of the record, it cannot be inferred whether the the two cases were founded on the same or a different state of facts. It is true, the record merely proves the pleadings, and that judgment was rendered for the defendant. Without other proof it would not make out the defense. The record shows that it was competent, on the trial, to establish the fraud of the plaintiff. Whether fraud was made out, and whether that was the point upon which the decision was founded, must necessarily be proved by evidence extrinsic to the record. To do so is not inconsistent with the record, nor does it impugn its verity. The jury must have passed on the fraud. It was directly in question. Scott testifies that the unseaworthiness was not disclosed at the time of sale to the defendant. The inquiry, then, was solely directed to the question, was the vessel unseaworthy, and had the plaintiff knowledge of that fact when he sold? By the finding of the jury, both propositions are affirmed. The judgment became conclusive between these parties, on these points, and is an effectual bar to the action to recover the residue of the consideration money. It is unnecessary to consider whether the record was admissible in evidence under the general issue, without notice. It was admitted, and no exception was taken on that ground. The effect ascribed to it seems to be the material question in the case. It is in general true, that, under *non-*

assumpsit, most matters in discharge of the action, which show that at the time of the commencement of the suit the plaintiff had no cause of action, may be taken advantage of. 1 Chit., 472. This rule may appear somewhat arbitrary, as the object of pleading is to apprise the adverse party of the grounds of defense. It is, however, peculiar to this action, although, as Chitty observes, not according with the logical precision which usually prevails in pleadings. The judge ought to have charged the jury, that if, from the evidence, they are satisfied that the matters in question had been passed upon in the Marine Court, the record was conclusive against the plaintiff's right to recover.

128*] *I am of opinion that the exceptions are well taken, and that the judgment ought to be reversed.

Judgment reversed.

Cited in—4 Cow., 562; 6 Cow., 691; 6 Wend., 289; 8 Wend., 23, 44; 12 Wend., 403; 18 Wend., 122; 25 Wend., 100; 2 Hill., 480; 6 Hill., 132; 3 Den., 243, 361; 3 N. Y., 522; 4 N. Y., 74; 6 N. Y., 143; 37 N. Y., 299; 62 N. Y., 374; 71 N. Y., 601; 4 Trans. App., 251; 5 Lans., 226; 3 Barb., 173, 184; 7 Barb., 497; 13 Barb., 161; 14 Barb., 620; 34 Barb., 221; 36 Barb., 94; 42 Barb., 663; 44 Barb., 324; 10 How. Pr., 306; 11 Abb. Pr., 16; 5 Sand., 142; 6 Bos., 547; 3 Daly, 461; 2 Leg. Obs., 258; 24 How. U. S., 342; 7 Wall., 97, 622; 2 Paine, 219; 1 Wood. & M., 182; 26 Cal., 505, 494; 34 Cal., 327; 36 Cal., 37; 58 Mo., 330; 48 Ind., 408; 50 Ind., 420; 29 Wis., 624; 46 Sup. Ct., 302; 56 Mo., 414; 41 Mich., 95; 15 Am. Dec., 403; 21 Am. Dec., 323; 22 Am. Dec., 619; 35 Am. Dec., 662; 36 Am. Dec., 373 (12 Vt., 692); 40 Am. Rep., 612 (101 Ill., 569).

BRADFORD, Impleaded with QUACKENBUSH, v. CONSAULUS, Assignee of the Sheriff of the County of SCHENECTADY.

Bond for Prisoner on Limits—Subsequent Arrest for Felony—Close Confinement—Escape—Surety on Bond, not Liable.

A prisoner enjoying the jail limits under a bond of surety, conditioned that he shall remain a true and lawful prisoner, was arrested on a charge of felony and committed to close confinement; and while so confined, broke the jail and escaped: held that the surety was not liable.

Citation—1 R. L., 429.

ERROR from the Court of C. P. of the County of Schenectady. The action in the court below was debt on a jail bond, by Consaulus, as assignee, under the Statute (1 R. L., 429, sec. 6, 7). The bond was dated May 19, 1819, executed by the defendants below, and after reciting that Quackenbush was confined in the jail of Schenectady, by virtue of an execution in favor of the plaintiff below, for $131.27, the condition was, that if Quackenbush should remain a true and faithful prisoner, within the jail liberties, and should not escape, &c., then the bond to be void.

It appeared upon the trial that Quackenbush, while within the liberties by virtue of this bond, Aug. 29, 1819, was, by virtue of criminal process, on a charge of felony, committed to close confinement in the Schenectady jail, from which he escaped Mar. 27, 1820, by breaking the jail. It was for this escape that the action was brought. The counsel for the defendant below, on this ground, moved for a nonsuit, which was overruled; and a bill of exceptions taken to this point. Verdict and judgment for the plaintiff below.

Mr. A. C. Paige, for the plaintiff in error. The sheriff cannot hold a double security against the escape of a prisoner in custody on civil process. If he have the common law security of the prison doors, he cannot have the statute security of a bond. By a commitment for felony, the sheriff acquired his common law security, and his statute security ceased. It is, in law, equivalent to a surrender of the *prisoner by the surety to [***129** the sheriff, and operates as a discharge of the bond. Besides, to bring the escape within the bond, it should be from the jail limits, while the prisoner is in their enjoyment. The escape was owing to the negligence of the sheriff. After he had the prisoner in close confinement, he should have kept him at his peril; he cannot make his own neglect a cause of action against the surety; and the assignee has no greater rights than his assignor. 10 Johns., 583, 4. Again; the liberty of the debtor is the consideration of the bond, which fails as soon as he is committed to close confinement. To hold the bail after this would be unreasonable. It is true the bail have no right to make a formal surrender; but they are discharged by operation of law. It is like the case of special bail where the principal is confined in the State Prison. An *exoneretur* will be entered even after the time for a regular surrender has expired. *Cathcart* v. *Cannon*, 1 Johns. Cas., 28. At least, the bond was suspended in its operation during the imprisonment; and a personal obligation once suspended is destroyed. A limit bond is one of indemnity merely. *Barry* v. *Mandell*, 10 Johns., 583. The right to grant the limits to a prisoner is confined by the Statute (1 R. L., 429, sec. 6) to civil process only; and it is absurd to say that a bond could not be taken after the confinement for felony, and yet should be operative. Had Quackenbush been committed to close custody on another execution, it would equally have rendered this bond inoperative; for the Statute was not intended to enlarge the sheriff's security, but only to substitute one security for another. A commitment imposes the common law duty upon the sheriff of keeping the prisoner at his peril. The custody of the body is a complete and perfect security in itself. Like every other agreement, the bond should be construed according to the intention of the parties. This was to give liberty to the prisoner; and shall the surety be liable, when the object of his bond is not attained? If the surety is insufficient, the sheriff may commit for that reason alone (1 R. L., 429, sec. 6), while the surety has no control over his principal; and *he would be remediless [***130** unless discharged by this act of the law; whereas, to hold him released would be doing justice both to the sheriff and surety. The bond is intended for the indemnity of the sheriff only. It must pursue the statute strictly, or it is void; and to make it good, the case should come precisely within the statute. The condition of the bond was complied with. It is, that he should remain a true and faithful prisoner on the limits. This must be construed according to the subject-matter. It presupposes a volition on the part of the prisoner to stay or to escape. While he had this, he did remain a true prisoner.

Mr. S. A. Foot, contra. The records of English jurisprudence afford no example of this defense. That it is the first in this country, is also proved by the fact that no authority in point is produced.

Here was neither an actual nor constructive surrender of Quackenbush. To constitute the former, the sureties must deliver the prisoner to the sheriff, and give him notice that they will no longer be holden. Can there be a constructive surrender? No adjudged case for this is produced. If we admit the operation of the bond to be commensurate only with the allowance of the jail liberties, there is nothing here to show that the sheriff denied these to the prisoner. To deprive the sheriff of all security from the bond, it should be shown that he was in default. The commitment here was for a distinct cause and by operation of law. After the cause of imprisonment is removed, or the prisoner removes it himself, he returns to the limits. A case might be supposed in which it would be very hard upon the sheriff to be bound to a detention of the prisoner, at all events. Suppose the latter committed for a trifling cause, in consequence of which the sheriff relaxes his vigilance, and even suffers the prisoner to go at large, as he may do, perhaps, with safety, so far as the second cause of commitment is concerned; shall such a commitment (it may be) for a moment work a discharge? The cases of *exoneretur* do not apply. No doubt the surety might have given notice to the sheriff, that he would no longer **131***] be liable, *which would operate as a surrender. If transferred to the State Prison by process of law, this would not be an escape. It would confer no right of action against the sheriff, and none by him against the sureties; for we agree that the bond is one of indemnity merely. It is said, too, that a second commitmitment on execution, would work a discharge; but a case is stated by the court, in *Hemstead* v. *Weed*, 20 Johns., 72, which negatives this idea. *Westby* v. *Skinner*, 3 Rep., 71, and Cro. Eliz., 365, is there cited, where the debtor was in the sheriff's custody, on two executions; and was delivered over by the sheriffs on their going out of office, to their successors, on one of the executions only, omitting that of the plaintiff; and after this assignment, the debtor escaped. It was held that the debtor was out of the custody of the old sheriffs, and could not be in custody of the new on the plaintiff's execution. This shows that each execution stands on separate and independent grounds. The sheriff would not be bound to hold upon the second execution, because he has no notice but that the surety is still willing to be bound. Would it be fair to make him accountable without notice? Such a doctrine would lead to great confusion, and produce very serious difficulties. Suppose the first execution only $25, upon which a jail bond is taken, and the debtor is afterwards committed on one for $10,000, but discharged from the latter—must the sheriff take a new bond, or does the prisoner return to the limits and with him the liability of the surety upon the first execution? The criticism upon the terms of this bond begs the question. The prisoner returns to the limits as soon as he is out of close confinement.

Mr. Paige, in reply. That no precedent for this defense is to be found, can be no objection to it; at least, in England, where they have no such statute as the one under which this bond was given. A contract cannot be dissolved by the act of one party only. Mere notice from the sureties, therefore, would not discharge them. It would be without effect. The act and operation of law is what we rely *upon; and it is enough for our pur- [***132** pose to show that the bond was inoperative while Quackenbush was in close confinement. Whether the bond was canceled or suspended, the result is the same.

Curia, per SAVAGE, *Ch. J.* By the Statute (1 R. L., 429), it is the duty of the sheriff to permit any prisoner who shall be in his custody on civil process only, to go at large within the limits, &c., on giving a bond with sureties. It follows that if a prisoner be confined on civil and criminal process both, the sheriff cannot take such a bond. If the imprisonment be inconsistent with the liberties of the limits, and a bond should be taken, it would be void.

The enjoyment of the liberties of the limits by the prisoner is, then, the consideration of the bond; and when the consideration fails, the obligation must be at an end. The bond is taken for the indemnity of the sheriff only; but when the prisoner is in close confinement, the sheriff wants no indemnity. If he should desire it, he cannot take it. The bond, in this case, was valid when taken; but, by subsequent circumstances, the consideration failed. Shall the obligation, then, continue? The prisoner was placed in a situation which rendered the taking a bond from him unlawful. Shall the sheriff then be permitted to retain a security which it would be unlawful for him to take? Or shall the previous obligation be suspended? If so, it must remain suspended till the prisoner is discharged from the criminal accusation. The sheriff is authorized to commit any prisoner upon the limits on a bond, if he shall discover that his bail is insufficient. Suppose the sheriff, in this case, had committed Quackenbush for that cause, would the bail be holden for an escape? Clearly not. It seems to me, therefore, that the enjoyment of the limits by the prisoner, is not only the consideration, but the condition of the bail's liability. This seems to follow from the language of the bond itself. The condition is "that the prisoner shall remain a true and faithful prisoner within the liberties of the said jail; and shall not, at any time, or in anywise, escape or go *without the limits of the said liber- [***133** ties, until, &c. But if, after taking the bond, the sheriff does not choose to permit the prisoner the use of such limits, surely neither law nor justice should permit him to hold the sureties liable for an escape from the walls of the prison. In my opinion the court below erred, and their judgment should be reversed.

Judgment of reversal.

Cited in—10 Wend., 435; 39 Barb., 77.

KELSEY *v.* DEYO ET UX.

Action againt Devisee for Legacy—When it Lies—Part Payment as Evidence of Promise.

An action at law lies for a legacy directed by will to be paid by a devisee of lands, and expressly charged on the lands; if the devisee has entered upon the lands, and promised to pay it.

Part payment is conclusive evidence of such a promise.

So where, from the whole will, it appears to have been the intention of the testator that the legacy should be a charge on the lands devised; although the land was not expressly charged with its payment.

Where a testator bequeathed his personal estate to his wife for life; and what should remain of this at her decease, over, to be equally divided between all his children; and then devised his real estate to one of his sons; and bequeathed certain legacies in money to his other children, to be paid by his son, the one half to be paid in two years after his (the testator's) decease, and made his son the devisee, with others, executors; and his son entered into possession, and paid part of one of the legacies; held, that an action lay for the residue of this legacy.

Citations—Cowp., 284, 289; 3 East, 120; 5 T. R., 690; 10 Johns., 30; 7 Johns., 99; 3 Johns. Ch., 312; 1 Bro. Ch., 462.

ERROR from the Court of C. P. of the County of Ulster. The action in the court below was *assumpsit* by Deyo and wife against Kelsey, for a legacy bequeathed to them by the will of Nathaniel Kelsey, deceased, and alleged in the declaration to have been charged on his real estate devised to the defendant below. The declaration averred that the defendant entered into possession of the premises devised to him by the will, thereby became liable to pay, and, in consideration thereof, promised to pay the plaintiffs, the legacy so charged. Plea, *non assumpsit.*

On the trial, the will of Nathaniel Kelsey, dated Apr. 9, 1803, duly executed to pass real estate, was given in evidence by the plaintiff, containing, among others, the following devises and bequests: 1st. That all his debts be paid out of his personal estate; 2d. He gave to his wife, Lucretia Kelsey, all his personal estate, after paying his debts, except what he thereinafter granted to his daughter Sarah **134***] Kelsey. He *also gave to his wife the use, profit and benefit of his homestead farm; also the right and privilege of cutting timber for firewood and other uses as she might want; also pasture for cattle and horses, as usual, in and on his farm adjoining the mountain; the above rights and privileges bequeathed to his wife to continue undisturbed during the term of her natural life; and at her decease, what remained of his personal property, to be equally divided between all his children or their heirs. He then bequeathed to his son Nathaniel Kelsey (the defendant below) all his real estate to him and his heirs forever, excepting such rights and privileges as had theretofore or should thereafter be granted by him respecting the premises. The will then proceeded as follows: "And I do hereby order and direct that my son Nathaniel Kelsey (the defendant below), or his heirs, pay the following legacies, that is to say: to my daughter Abigail Woolsey, the sum of £100; to my daughter Lucretia Verhooy £100; to my daughter Julia Deyo (who, and her husband, were plaintiffs below) £100; the one half of each of the above legacies to be paid within two years after my decease; and the other half to be paid in two years after the decease of my wife, without interest." He then gave to his daughter, Sarah Kelsey, the use of his bed room with a fire place up stairs; and a proportionable right in the kitchen, cellar and chamber in his dwelling-house; the privilege of firewood and apples; hay and pasture for two cows; and the use of the barn and other outhouses; to continue to her so long as she remained unmarried, but no longer; that if there should be any money to be paid at the decease of his (the testator's) father and Hannah his wife, to the heirs of his father, as specified in an agreement between him and his father, it be paid by his son Nathaniel Kelsey (the defendant below) as soon after his father's decease as his (N. K's) circumstances would admit, to be paid out of the real estate, without interest. The will then appointed Kelsey (the defendant below), Woolsey, the testator's son-in-law, executors, and the testator's wife executrix.

It was admitted by the defendant below that he had entered upon the lands and premises described in the will in pursuance of the devise to him; and occupied and possessed them *from the year 1803 until the time of [***135** the trial, Apr., 1821; and that during that period, and before the commencement of the suit, he had, at different times, made payments to the plaintiff on the legacy to them, reducing the same to $191.28. Upon this, the plaintiffs below rested their cause.

The defendant below moved for a nonsuit: 1. because the will in evidence did not support the plaintiffs' action; 2. because the legacy bequeathed to Deyo's wife was payable out of the personal estate of Nathaniel Kelsey, and was not a charge upon the real estate. The court below overruled the motion; and charged the jury to find for the plaintiffs the above sum of $191.28, which they found accordingly. The defendant below excepted upon the above two points, and the questions came here upon a bill of exceptions.

Mr. J. Sudam, for the plaintiff in error. If the devise had been declared upon in the words of the will, the defendant might have demurred generally. No consideration for the promise is expressed in the will. It is merely directory. There is, therefore, a variance between the declaration and the proof. The declaration states a consideration; but none is made out in evidence. The testator says, "I do hereby order and direct" that my son Nathaniel Kelsey pay the legacy. The devise of the real estate to him was absolute; the order to pay the legacy was directory merely.

NOTE.—*Effect of part payment as a promise.* See Shoemaker v. Benedict, 11 N. Y., 176; Van Orden v. Van Orden, 10 Johns., 30; Huntington v. Ballou, 2 Lans., 120.

So evidence of payment on an altered contract is relevant to show consent to the alteration. Abb. Tr. Ev., 408.

As to evidence of part payment to bar statute of limitations, see Roseboom v. Billington, 17 Johns., 186, *note.*

As to when legacy is a personal charge on devisee, compare Jackson v. Martin, 8 Johns., 31, *note*; Kelsey v. Western, 2 N. Y., 500; Dodge v. Manning, 11 Paige, 334; Beecker v. Beeker, 7 Johns., 99; Pelletreau v. Rathbone, 18 Johns., 428; Livingston v. Livingston, 3 Johns., 189; Brown v. Knapp, 79 N. Y., 136.

Is the real estate charged with the payment of these legacies, in exclusion of the personal property ?. Unless it be so, the latter must be called in. Unless the legacy is expressly charged on lands specifically devised; or the sale of real estate is directed for the payment, the personal property is never exonerated, if we except specific bequests. This is an unerring rule, whenever it appears by the will that the testator understood the difference between an express and an implied charge. The legacy in question being general, and there being a debt specifically devised to be paid out of the land, show that he did understand the difference perfectly. I allude to the debt that may be due upon the agreement between the testator and his father, which is made payable **136*]** *out of the real estate expressly. The testator gives real estate absolutely; he gives several legacies, without expressly designating any fund from which they are to be paid; and then, at the close of the will, he expressly charges the real estate with the payment of a single legacy. It is enough for us to show that the personal estate should come in aid of the real; for if so, this clause belongs exclusively to the Court of Chancery; and a court of common law has no jurisdiction. This question was examined in *Livingston* v. *Newkirk*, 3 Johns. Ch., 319. That was certainly a stronger case in favor of charging the real estate, than the present; but the *Chancellor* refused to charge the real estate; and sums up the doctrine in these words: "It is too well settled to be questioned, that the personal estate is to be first applied to the payment of debts and legacies, and that a mere charge on the land will not exonerate the personal estate, nor anything short of express words, or a plain intent in the will of the testator." If the legacy was a condition to the enjoyment of the real estate, the legatee should enter as for a condition broken. The remedy is not by action. The general principles of the common law were all in favor of charging the personalty; and the question, when the real estate might be resorted to, was in an unsettled state till the case of *Ancaster* v. *Mayer*, 1 Bro. Ch., 454. The subject was there very fully considered. It was found obscured and involved in a labyrinth of loose and careless *dicta*. But that case places it upon its proper footing; the intent of the testator; and gives the rules for arriving at his intention. The *Chancellor* goes back to first principles; and concludes that to warrant a resort to real estate, it must be expressly charged.

It is true that this court have, in several instances, taken cognizance of actions for legacies of this description; but it will be found that, in all those cases, the charge on land was specific. In *Beecker* v. *Beecker*, 7 Johns., 99, the real estate was devised, subject to the legacy, in terms; and Kent, *Ch. J.*, who delivered the opinion of the court, places the case on the ground of its being an express charge on the land. There is also a distinction between the effect of a charge on the person and on land. In the former case the will carries a fee without words of perpetuity. *Van Orden* **137*]** *v. *Van Orden*, 10 Johns., 30. To work this consequence, the person must be expressly, not impliedly charged. In *Pelletreau* v. *Rathbone*, 18 Johns., 428, both the real and personal estate were expressly charged; and it was holden that the action would not lie. The party is driven into chancery even in such a case, where the assets may be marshaled, and the personal assets are liable in the first instance. Debts and legacies are on the same footing in this respect. Had Kelsey been directed to pay debts, the personal estate must have been applied in the same manner. Toll. L. E., 240; p. 332 of the Phil. ed., 1803; 2 Bl. Com., 512. There is a class of cases in which legacies were given in various ways by words pointing more directly to the real estate than here, and which yet were holden not to charge it. *Manning* v. *Spooner*, 3 Ves., Jr., 114. In *Milnes* v. *Slater*, 8 *Id.*, 295, Ld. Eldon agrees that, to exonerate the personal estate from the payment of debts, it must be exempted by declaration plain, or inference as plain. And in *Ancaster* v. *Mayer*, 1 Bro. Ch., 459, 460, Ld. Thurlow said, "one step has been taken towards a settled rule, by its being laid down that charging the estate in any way is not, of itself, an exemption of the personal estate; that the personal estate being the fund first liable, where it is to be aided by either a legal or equitable fund, it must be itself in the first place applied." He then states the very case under consideration: "The question that next arises is, whether a real estate being charged and the personal given away, a presumption arises that this shall be exempted from the debts. I never heard, till the arguments in this case, that such a rule had been extracted from the authorities on the subject; on the contrary, I have always understood, that in order to exempt the personal estate, the testator must express an intention so to do." That case was one of a general charge, as here. The personal estate was given over to one distinct from the person charged with the legacies; but the bequest of the personal property was holden subject to the payment of the legacies. "I therefore," says the *Chancellor*, "take the rule *in primis* to be, that neither the charge of the debts upon the real estate, or the gift of the personal, is sufficient of itself to exempt it." *In *Ld. Inchiquin* v. **[*138** *French*, Ambl., 33, 37, decided in 1744, it was holden that personal estate was not exempt from debts and legacies by devise of a competent part of real estate to be sold to pay them; that the intention to exempt the personal property must be manifested by a specific bequest of that property. Thus early was this doctrine established by Ld. Hardwicke. *Watson* v. *Brickwood*, 9 Ves., 447, S. P. In *Ancaster* v. *Mayer* it was held to be immaterial what words were used, unless the legacy was expressly, definitely and exclusively charged upon the real estate. Otherwise the personal must first be exhausted. The case depends upon authority. No matter what may be thought as to expediency. The law has been settled against this action for ages. The case of *Watson* v. *Brickwood*, 9 Ves., 447, considers the question as put at rest by *Ancaster* v. *Mayer*. It is true there is some confusion in the cases upon the question, if the same rule shall apply, whether the bequest over be general or specific; but *Webb* v. *Jones*, 2 Bro. Ch., 60, decides that the testator cannot exonerate the personal estate without expressly providing another fund. Suppose there had been no words of inheritance in relation to this devise; though the legacy had been expressly charged on the land, it would not have carried a fee; otherwise, if a personal charge on the devisee. In the first case it would be for life only. *Jackson* v. *Martin*, 18 Johns., 31. In either case, the personal property would not be exonerated; because the will creates no fund. *Lupton* v. *Lupton*, 2 Johns. Ch., 614, 623, and the cases there cited. In the last case the *Chancellor* says: "When the real estate is charged, and not in the most explicit and direct terms, it is usually done in terms that indicate a pretty clear intention that the legacies were, at all events, to be paid. Thus, where the testator devises the real estate, after payment of debts and legacies, as in *Tompkins* v. *Tompkins*, Prec. in Ch., 397, and in *Shallcross* v. *Finder*, 3 Ves., 738, or where he devises the real estate, after a direction that debts and legacies be first paid, as in *Holt* v. *Vernon*, Prec. in Ch., 430, and in *Williams* v. *Chitty*, 3 Ves., 545, the real estate has been held to be discharged. It **139***] is not sufficient that debts *or legacies are directed to be paid. That alone does not create the charge; but they must be directed to be first or previously paid, or the devise declared to be after they are paid." He gives it as the result of all the cases, that a bequest of several legacies by a testator, and then devising the residue of his real and personal property to one, after payment of debts and legacies, does not create an exclusive charge on the real estate. Courts of equity will never marshal assets in favor of a legatee, unless there be a trust in the executors for that purpose expressly in respect to the real estate. *Keeling* v. *Brown*, 5 Ves., 359.

But, admitting a trust in this case, clearly the remedy is not at law, but only in equity. *Gorton* v. *Dyson*, 1 Neil Gow, 78; *Webb* v. *Jiggs*, 4 M. &. S., 113. The importance of confining the remedy to a court of equity, in all cases of a general legacy, was ably vindicated in *Deeks* v. *Strutt*, 5 T. R., 690.

It may be said that Kelsey has paid a part of this claim; but he was one of the executors; and it will be intended that he paid in that capacity. If not so, a payment in ignorance of his rights should not conclude him.

Mr. C. H. Ruggles, contra. It is well settled that *assumpsit* lies against a devisee of land, upon his express promise to pay a legacy chargeable on the land, or on the devisee in respect to the land. *Livingston* v. *The Exrs. of Livingston*, 3 Johns., 189; *Beecker* v. *Beecker*, 7 *Id.*, 99; *Van Orden* v. *Van Orden*, 10 *Id.*, 30.

1. The legacy to Deyo's wife was intended by the testator to be paid by the defendant, in consideration of the devise made to him of the whole real estate; and he became chargeable with it by entering on the lands devised. The testator directs that his debts be paid out of his personal estate, but does not direct the payment of his legacies out of that fund. He bequeaths to his wife all his personal estate, after payment of his debts, except what was bequeathed to his daughter Sarah. The rights and privileges bequeathed to his wife are to continue undisturbed during the term of her natural life; and thus the personal fund is locked up till *her death; and yet one [***140**
half the legacies are payable within two years after the testator's death. He further declares that after the decease of his wife, what remains of his personal estate shall be equally divided among all his children; thus disposing of the whole, and leaving nothing in the hands of his executors by which legacies could be paid. Upon the bequest of the personal property to the wife, there are several restrictions—the previous payment of debts; the limitation of interest to her natural life; and the exception in favor of Sarah—but the payment of legacies is not mentioned or provided for; though the first payment would, in all probability, fall due during her life. He directs this legacy to be paid by the defendant, individually, and his heirs—not by the executors, or by the defendant as one of them; and the direction to pay the legacy follows immediately upon the devise of the real estate. It is connected with it, not only in the same clause, but in the same sentence. The devise to the defendant excepts such rights and privileges as have theretofore or shall thereafter be g by the testator. This language is broad enough to embrace the legacies. The executors had no interest in the personal property, except for the payment of debts.

But it is said the testator understood himself: that when he meant the real estate should be charged, he said so; that, therefore, nothing is left for implication; and the provision for the money due to the heirs of the testator's father is appealed to in proof of this. This was the last disposing clause in the will. It related to a debt doubtful as to its ever being demanded, its amount, and the time when it would become due; and having already provided as to his debts in general, that they should be paid out of his personal estate, it required an express order to make the exception. This demand might lie dormant till after the wife's death; and it was very proper to guard against the implication that it was payable out of the personal property for this reason. That was not the case with the legacy in question, and no such distinction was necessary.

True, it is a general rule of law, that legacies are payable first out of the personal estate, and that a general charge of *real es- [***141**
tate does not exempt the personal. Toll. L. E., 410. But, we answer, the personal estate was never charged for the payment of these legacies; and a distinguishing characteristic of the cases cited to this point on the other side is, that in all of them the legacies were left, or ordered to be paid by the executors, or by trustees. No case is cited of a devise directing the devisee to pay, or making the legacy depend either expressly or by construction upon the acceptance of the devise, where the real estate was holden exempt, or postponed to the personalty. In the case so much relied on, of *Ancaster* v. *Mayer*, 1 Bro. Ch., 462, 3, a term was raised to two executors to pay debts and legacies; the personal estate was given to him who should take the freehold: and the executors were ordered to pay debts and legacies by such methods, ways and means, as they should be advised, &c.

It then becomes a question, what is the mode

of expression to give the personal estate exempt from the payment of debts (or legacies) when the rule of law is, that such estate is first liable. "Therefore, if there be a declaration plain, or manifestation clear, so that it is apparent on the face of the whole will that there is such a plain intention, the rule then is not to disappoint, but to carry such intention into effect." *Ib.* In *Watson* v. *Brickwood*, 19 Ves., 454, it was held "now too late to say that it is not open to the court to collect from the whole will an intention to exonerate the personal estate, though that intention is not expressed in any positive or conclusive words." In *Webb* v. *Jones*, 2 Bro. Ch., 60 it is said, "the general rule is very clear, that the personal estate is the fund first liable, and that the testator cannot exonerate it without first substituting another fund. But there is no magic in words. No peculiar form of expression is necessary, in order to exonerate the personal estate. If the intention of the testator be evident to exonerate the personal estate, it must be exonerated." *Livingston* v. *Newkirk*, 3 Johns. Ch., 312; *Lupton* v. *Lupton*, 2 *Id.*, 614, S. P.

It is said that where the personal estate is not expressly exempted, the testator's intention must be manifested by a specific bequest of the personal property, in order to exempt it.
142*] *For this, *Ld. Inchiquin* v. *French*, Ambl., 33, 37, is cited. This case is not law. The position is found nowhere else, and it is in contradiction to the other cases. Where such a specific bequest exists, it is, to be sure, a very satisfactory g of exception; but not the only ground. But take the rule as laid down in Ambler. What is meant by a specific devise of personal property? Anything which indicates the testator's intent to give away the whole of it, without subjecting it to the payment of legacies. *Wainright* v. *Bendlowes*, 2 Vern., 718. In this case, I. Bendlowes devised his fee farm rents to be sold for the payment of his debts and the surplus to his brothers, John and Philip, and his brother-in-law, Wainright; and willed that his household goods should go along with his house; and then bequeathed the rest and residue of his personal estate to his sister, Wainright, and made her his executrix; and the personal property was retained by his sister, although executrix, and exempted from the payment of debts. This was held a specific bequest of all the personal property except the household goods. The bequest under consideration is specific, within the rules of law, according to the case cited, and other authorities. 2 Fonbl., 294, B. 3, ch. 2, sec. 5; *Id.* 285, B. 3, ch. 2, sec. 1, *note a.*; *Adams* v. *Meyricle*, 1 Eq. Cas. Abr., 271, case 13. Then Kelsey's personal property being specifically bequeathed, the intention to exempt it is clearly manifest, within the rule laid down on the other side.

2. Part payment of the legacy is conclusive evidence of a promise to pay the whole. *Van Orden* v. *Van Orden*, 10 Johns., 30.

3. But if the real and personal assets should be marshaled, part payment is evidence of the exhaustion of the latter, and binds Kelsey, whether there be personal estate or not. In *Pelletreau* v. *Rathbone*, 18 Johns., 31, there was no promise, no part payment, nor any other thing equivalent to a promise.

Mr. Sudam, in reply. Both courts of law and equity profess to follow the intention of the testator in the construction of wills. If this question were now raised for the first time, or rested *on inference and conjecture, the **[*143** other side might be right. But there are certain settled rules to which the court will adhere, because the authorities are a safer guide than individual opinion, and better answer another object of the law, which is certainty. Now it is perfectly well settled, that the personalty is never exempt, unless expressly declared so by the will, or by something which is plainly equivalent to an express declaration. This was settled as long ago as Ld. Thurlow's time. If so settled, the court cannot get by this doctrine here. The giving real estate and legacies generally, and making a single legacy a charge upon the real estate at the close of the will, render the authorities directly applicable. It is said that one half of the legacies were to be paid within one year after the testator's death—possibly before the widow's decease—and an implied charge upon the real estate is deduced from this circumstance. But no matter when the general legacies are payable. They will not take preference of the specific bequest of the personal property. They must wait till there is enough of the personal estate to satisfy them, and if this is never the case, they must fail; for they are considered as a debt created and charged upon the personalty. This brings us back to the terms of the will, and an examination of the cases. I refer particularly to those cited by the *Chancellor*, in *Lupton* v. *Lupton*, 2 Johns. Ch., 623. The charge must precede the devise, in order to subject the real estate. This is the conclusion to which he comes, from all the cases. Could a legatee have pursued this real property, in the hands of a *bona fide* purchaser? Was this legacy an incumbrance which attached and adhered to the land? I think no lawyer would go to that extent. Yet if the argument on the other side be right, here is a lien upon this land, which equity would follow, and enforce, in whose hands soever it might come. *Caveat emptor* must be applied to a purchaser. After satisfaction of the specific legacy to Sarah, the bequest over is general to the wife. This is improperly called a specific legacy. It is not of specific things, though it may have sometimes been so considered, when another fund has been created for the payment of debts, and widows are *con- **[*144** cerned. The whole doctrine of English equity is against its being so considered in this case.

Curia, per SAVAGE, *Ch. J.* Two questions are presented to the court, for their decision:

1. Whether an action at law lies for a legacy charged upon land.

2. Whether from the whole will, it was clearly the intention of the testator to discharge his personal estate from the payment of the legacy in question, and charge it upon the realty.

The first question was not directly raised on the argument, though we were referred to several English cases, which question the plaintiff's right to a remedy at law. It has been settled, that without a promise to pay a legacy charged upon the realty, an action does not lie; and that it will lie for any general legacy, even when there has been a promise, the English authorities are not uniform. The first case appearing in our own reports, is *Beecker* v. *Beecker*, 7 Johns., 99. That was an action for an annuity charged on land devised to the defendant, in which there was an express promise to pay. Kent, *Ch. J.*, reviewed the English cases, and decided in favor of the legatee, on the authority of *Atkins* v. *Hill*, Cowp., 284; *Hawkes* v. *Saunders*, *Id.*, 289; *Doe* v. *Guy*, 3 East, 120, and distinguished the case from that of *Deeks* v. *Strutt*, 5 T. R., 690. The next case is *Van Orden* v. *Van Orden*, 10 Johns., 30. In this case there was no express promise to pay, but the defendants had paid part, the estate left by the testator being sufficient to pay all the debts and legacies. The case was admitted not to be within that of *Beecker* v. *Beecker*, but it was precisely within the case of *Deeks* v. *Strutt*. The court considered the payments made by the defendants to the plaintiff as conclusive evidence of an express promise to pay, so as to entitle the plaintiff to recover. The case of *Deeks* v. *Strutt* is, therefore, overruled, and with it all the corresponding class of cases.

In the present case there was no direct evidence of an express promise to pay, but payments have been made from time to time, from which, according to the case last quoted, an **145***] *express promise may be inferred. The plaintiffs in the court below were, therefore, entitled to recover, unless, from an examination of the will, it appears that the legacy in question was to have been paid out of the personal estate. The rule for marshaling assets towards the payment of debts is correctly laid down by *Chancellor* Kent, in *Livingston* v. *Newkirk*, 3 Johns. Ch., 312. He there says: "It is too well settled to be questioned, that the personal estate is to be first applied to the payment of debts and legacies, and that a mere charge on the land will not exonerate the personal estate, nor anything short of express words, or a plain intent in the will of the testator."

In *Ancaster* v. *Mayer*, 1 Bro. Ch., 462, Lord Thurlow says: "Where there is a declaration plain, that shall stand in lieu of express words." Again; "If there be a declaration plain, or manifestation clear, so that it is apparent upon the face of the will that there is such a plain intention, the rule then is, not to disappoint, but to carry such intent into execution." What, then, was the intention of the testator?

1. He first directs his debts to be paid out of his personal estate.

2. He gives his wife Lucretia all his personal estate, after payment of his debts, and a legacy to one of his daughters, and goes on to make other provision for his wife upon his homestead farm.

3. After his wife's death, what remains of the personal property is to be divided equally among his children.

4. The following clause: "I also will, devise and bequeath, to my son, Nathaniel Kelsey, all my real estate, to him and his heirs forever, excepting such rights and privileges as have heretofore or shall hereafter be granted by me respecting the premises; and my will and desire is, and I do hereby order and direct that my son, Nathaniel Kelsey, or his heirs, pay the following legacies." Then follow the legacies, of £100 each, to his three daughters, one of whom (Julia) was a plaintiff in this cause below. He adds, "one half of each of the above legacies to be paid within two years after *my decease, and the other half [***146** to be paid in two years after the decease of my wife, without interest." He next directs a certain sum, if to be paid at all, after the death of Daniel Kelsey, to be paid out of the real estate; and makes his wife executrix, and Nathaniel Kelsey, and his son-in-law, Moses Woolsey, his executors. Did the testator intend that these legacies should be paid from his personal estate? Or was it his intention that Nathaniel Kelsey should pay to each of his sisters £100, as their right in the farm which was devised to him? It is to be observed that the personal estate was all given to the widow during her life. She might have lived 20 years; and yet one half the legacies was to be paid in two years after the testator's death. Out of what fund? The personal property? That was in the hands of the widow. What other fund had Nathaniel? The farm. Again; by whom were these legacies to be paid? By the executors? No; by Nathaniel Kelsey—not as executor. If the legacies were to be paid out of the personalty, we must suppose that the testator, in his last moments, was mocking his wife with the appearance of making provision for her, by giving her all his personal property, when, in fact, he intended to give her none of it. It has been well remarked by Lord Thurlow, I think, that such a construction should be given to wills as will make the testator's intentions honest. Would it be honest for a husband thus to deceive his wife? Again; one legacy is given to the wife of one of the executors. Why is the legacy to be paid by N. Kelsey? If the legacy were good, and to be paid out of the personal estate, the husband of Abigail Woolsey might retain the money in his own hands, as executor, to pay his wife's legacy. The only part of the will calculated to create any doubt is the last clause; and even that may admit of a construction, that all the payments by Nathaniel Kelsey are to be made out of the real estate. But admitting it to apply to the sum contingently spoken of, it is not sufficient, in my judgment, to change the whole complexion of the will.

I am, therefore, of opinion that the legacy to the plaintiff Julia was a charge on the real estate devised to the plaintiff in error; and that by paying part he gave conclusive evidence *of a promise to pay the whole; [***147** and, consequently, that the judgment of the Common Pleas should be affirmed.

Judgment affirmed.

Cited in—6 Cow., 340; 1 Barb. Ch., 401; 4 Edw., 739; 1 N. Y., 122; 2 N. Y., 508; 7 N. Y., 168; 5 Barb., 411; 26 Barb., 361; 33 Barb., 253; 1 T. & C., 270; 55 Wis., 644.

RAYMOND *v.* MERCHANT.

Discharge in Insolvency—Bar to what Actions—Promissory Note, not Extinguishment of Preceding Debt—Contract, in this State, after Enactment of Statute—Effect of Note Subsequently Given in Vermont.

A discharge under the Act for Giving Relief in Cases of Insolvency (1 R. L., 464-5, sec. 9), passed Apr. 12, 1813, is a bar to an action on a contract made in this State subsequent to that day.

A promissory negotiable note, given for an antecedent debt is not absolutely an extinguishment of that debt; but an action may still be maintained for the original consideration, provided the note be lost, or produced and canceled at the trial.

Where such antecedent debt was contracted in this State, subsequent to the Act for Giving Relief in Cases of Insolvency; and a negotiable note was afterwards given for that debt in the State of Vt.; held, that a discharge under that Act was a bar to an action on the note, the original consideration of which might be inquired into, in reference to the discharge.

Citations—16 Johns., 233; 19 Johns., 153; 1 Johns., 36-7; 1 Johns., 34; 8 Johns., 115; 1 Cow., 316.

ASSUMPSIT. Declaration on a negotiable promissory note, made by the defendant and payable to the plaintiff, dated Nov. 3, 1814; for $130. Plea: 1st, *non assumpsit.* 2, That after making the note, &c., to wit: Dec. 26, 1816, at the City of Albany, Stephen Merchant was the defendant's creditor; that the defendant was then and there imprisoned and had been imprisoned for sixty days and upwards, upon execution, in a civil action; that Stephen Merchant, being then and there apprehensive that the estate or effects of the defendant would be wasted or embezzled, did apply to Philip S. Parker, who then was, and from thence hitherto hath been, &c., Recorder of the City of Albany, for relief according to the "Act for Giving Relief in Cases of Insolvency," passed Apr. 12, 1813 (going on and setting forth a regular discharge of the defendant, under the 9th section of that Act, 1 R. L., 464-5, Feb. 28, 1817, by Mr. Parker, Recorder, from all debts, &c.)

Replication, that the note declared on, was, at the day it bore date, executed at Bennington, in the State of Vt.; and that, at its date, and ever since, the plaintiff was and yet is an actual resident of that State.

Rejoinder, admitting the truth of the replication; and averring that after the passage of 148*] the Act under which the *discharge was granted, to wit: Oct. 29, 1814, the defendant was indebted to certain merchants then residing in the City of N. Y., partners, by the name of Little & White, in $232.70, for goods, &c., sold him by them; that he paid them $100, and requested the plaintiff, who was then at N. Y., to pay the residue; that it was agreed there, between the plaintiff and defendant, that the former should pay or secure $132.70; and that the defendant should secure or pay the same sum to the plaintiff; that the plaintiff, accordingly, at N. Y., did pay or secure the $132.70; and that afterwards, at Bennington, in Vt., the defendant executed the note declared on, for and on account of that sum; that this was the sole ground and consideration of his note.

General demurrer and joinder.

Mr. S. A. Foot, in support of the demurrer. We conceive it to be immaterial, whether the debt in question arose in or out of this State. If there is anything in such a distinction, the note is evidence that it arose out of the State. Being a negotiable note, it extinguished the debt for the purposes of this question. The original consideration cannot be set up and sued for, till the note is produced and canceled. Though it may not be a technical extinguishment, yet it is a suspension (*Holmes* v. *D'Camp,* 1 Johns., 34), which is the same thing for the purposes of this question. It may be said that we had an option to go upon the note or not; for we might have given it up. This is true; but it is equally so that we may elect and have elected otherwise. By taking the note, the nature of the original transaction is changed, and we ought to have the benefit of our security as we have drawn it. There is an attempt in the rejoinder to make the act of giving the note the fulfillment of a previous agreement. This can make no difference. The rejoinder shows that the true consideration of the note was the N. Y. debt for goods sold.

Mr. I. Hamilton, contra, relied upon the case of *Wyman* v. *Mitchell,* 1 Cow., 316, where, to a plea of an insolvent's *discharge in [*149 bar of a judgment obtained in this State since the Insolvent Act was passed. The court allowed the plaintiff to show in reply that the consideration of the judgment arose in Mass. before the Act; and held that the consideration was not merged in the judgment. *A fortiori,* he said, the note is not a merger. It is only in equal degree with the debt it was given to secure. He also referred to *Mather* v. *Bush,* 16 Johns., 243, and several of the cases there cited. He said the defendant resided in this State, and the contract and ground of the debt wholly arose here. This is enough. The consideration is an essential part of the contract. Without this the note would be a nullity; and it is perfectly well settled that where a promissory note is given for a precedent debt, it is no extinguishment. The payee may sue upon the original debt; waiving the note altogether.

Mr. Foot, in reply, said it is true the consideration of a judgment may be inquired into. It is a judicial act, an act of the court which should not preclude the party from going back and availing himself of the ground of the judgment. The present is an attempt to invalidate the party's own act, by which the nature of the original contract was changed. What is the contract upon which we sue? A promissory note founded on good consideration. Is not the note a contract? It is said a consideration is essential to a contract. This is conceded; but are the consideration and contract identical? Suppose the consideration had been before the Act—the note afterwards—the whole in this State; could we go back to the consideration, and say the note is not discharged? A breach of a marriage promise forms a good consideration for a note; though

NOTE.—*Discharge under state insolvent law—Bar to actions on what contract.* Hicks v. Brown, 12 Johns., 142, *note.*

Promissory note—Not, in general, extinguishment of precedent debt. Compare Murray v. Gouverneur, 2 Johns. Cas., 438, *note;* Herring v. Sanger, 3 Johns. Cas., 71, *note.*

it is not the subject of an insolvent discharge. So a moral obligation is a valid consideration for a promise, but it is not, therefore, the contract itself. Had we sued on the implied promise arising from the payment, it might have been different. But the action is on the special agreement, and this alone should be looked to.

150*] **Curia*, per SAVAGE, *Ch. J.* Under the pleadings in this case, and the previous decisions in this court (*Mather* v. *Bush*, 16 Johns., 243; *Matter of Wendell*, 19 Johns., 153), the question raised is whether the note executed in Vt. be an extinguishment of the previous contract or indebtedness on which the note was predicated. The principle adopted by this court, in *Holmes* v. *D'Camp*, 1 Jobus., 36–7, is that a negotiable note is not absolutely an extinguishment of an antecedent, simple contract debt; but that the plaintiff may recover upon the original consideration, provided he shows the note to be lost, or produces and cancels it at the trial. Had the plaintiff declared on the original consideration, a plea that a note had been given for it would have been bad on demurrer. The giving the note must be taken advantage of on the trial.

I think, therefore, that as the contract was made in the State of N. Y., and is not extinguished by the note given in Vt., the discharge is a good defense. The defendant must have judgment.

SUTHERLAND, *J.*, dissenting. The demurrer in this case appears to me to be well taken. The contract between the parties is the note on which the suit is brought. All previous contracts or agreements in relation to the subject-matter of the note were merged in it. The plaintiff could not have recovered upon the original consideration of this note, as long as the note was in being. He would have been obliged, either to have shown that it was lost, or to have produced and canceled it at the trial. *Holmes* v. *D'Camp*, 1 Johns., 34; *Angel* v. *Felton*, 8 *Id.*, 149. The final agreement between the parties is the contract; and the law of the place where that agreement is made is to govern its construction, unless it appear upon its face to have been made with reference to the laws of some other place, and with a view of being executed there. It may be that the note was not given in N. Y., for the very purpose of avoiding the operation of our Insolvent Laws, and that by the express agreement of the parties.

151*] *The case of *Wyman* v. *Mitchell*, cited by the counsel for the defendant, is very distinguishable from this. That was an action of debt upon a judgment obtained in this State. The defendant pleaded his discharge under one of our Insolvent Acts. The plaintiff replied, stating the contract upon which the judgment was obtained, to have been made in Mass., before the passing of the Act under which the defendant was discharged. To this the defendant demurred, and we overruled the demurrer, on the ground that the judgment upon which the suit was brought was not a contract between the parties, but only evidence of a pre-existing contract; and that it was proper to show when and where that contract was made. A judgment is not a voluntary agreement between the parties. It can never, therefore, be said that a judgment is a contract entered into with reference to the laws of the place where it is obtained, and that those laws are to be presumed to have been within the contemplation and intent of the parties. We, therefore, permitted the plaintiff to go back until he came to an agreement or contract, and no farther. We held, expressly, that the consideration of such agreement or contract was not to be inquired into, with a view of showing that it arose at a different time or place from the contract itself.

I am accordingly of opinion that the plaintiff should have judgment.

Judgment for the defendant.

Cited in—21 Wend., 452; 3 N. Y., 220; 13 Hun, 181; 3 Barb., 317, 434, 449; 12 Barb., 470; 2 Hilt, 116.

CLARK AND TUBBS, Executors of BARNEY,

v.

BUSH, Impleaded with M'CRACKEN.

Promissory Note by Two Partners—Bond by Payee and one Partner, to Indemnify Second Partner against Partnership Liabilities—Payment for this Purpose, by Payee of Note up to amount of Bond—Second Partner, Liable on the Note—Surety, not Liable beyond Penalty of Bond.

A bond or covenant by the creditor to save harmless and indemnify the debtor against the debt, operates as a release of the debt.

A and B gave a note to C, of $2,000; and then B and C became bound in the penalty of $3000, to indemnify A against all the partnership debts due from A and B, the $2,000 debt due to C being one of them; and C paid under this bond to the amount of the penalty by way of indemnifying A against other debts due from the firm of A and B, and then brought his action against A upon the note to C. Held, that he should recover; for he shall not be holden to pay beyond the penalty of his bond; more especially as he was a mere surety; and the bond shall not operate as a release of a debt which he could not be called upon to pay.

A surety is not liable beyond the penalty of his bond.

The rule seems to be the same as to the principal.

The English and American cases upon these two heads considered.

Citations—2 Johns., 186; 8 Johns., 58, 59; 4 Burr., 22, 28; 2 Esp. *N. P.*, 279; 2 Bl., 1190; Doug., 49; 2 T. R., 388; Bunb., 23; 2 Burr., 820; 2 Saund., 106; 3 Bro. Ch., 596, 490; 6 T. R., 303; 8 & 9 W. 3, ch. 11, sec. 8; 1 East, 436; 1 Taunt., 218; South, 498; 4 Dall., 149; 4 Yeates, 32; 1 Mass., 308; 2 Wash., 143; 1 Gall., 348, 360; 9 Cr., 104, 120; 1 Bl., 395; 11 Mass., 83.

ASSUMPSIT upon a note given by the defendants to the testator of the plaintiffs, dated Nov. 2, 1815, for $2,000, payable Oct. 9, 1820, with interest, to be paid annually. Bush, one of the defendants, pleaded the general issue, *payment and a release; to **[*152** which pleas was also subjoined a notice that there would be given in evidence on the trial, a release of the testator of all debts, dues, claims and demands, of what name or nature soever existing against the firm of Bush &

NOTE.—*Principal and surety—Surety not liable beyond penalty of bond.* See Walsh v. Bailee, 10 Johns., 180, *note.*

M'Cracken, with the necessary and proper averments, &c.; also that the testator, in his lifetime, together with M'Cracken, the defendant executed to Bush a bond bearing date Oct. 1, 1816, in the penal sum of $3,000, with condition that if Barney (the testator of the plaintiffs) and M'Cracken, their heirs, &c., should well and truly, at all times, indemnify and save harmless, Bush, his heirs, &c., from and against all debts, dues, claims and demands, of what name or nature soever existing against the firm of Bush & M'Cracken (the same before named), including as well all debts and demands then due by and from the firm, as all contracts theretofore made by them in and about the firm of Bush & M'Cracken, by means of which contracts Bush might, in any manner thereafter, be made liable; then, &c., else, &c

On the plea of payment, the plaintiffs took issue; and to the plea of a release they replied *non est factum.*

The cause was tried before the late *Mr. Justice* Yates, at the Washington Circuit, June 14, 1822. The plaintiffs proved the note declared on, upon which was indorsed $140, Nov. 2, 1816, for interest. The balance due being $2,807.33.

The defendant, Bush, then produced and proved the bond set forth in his notice.

The counsel for the plaintiffs then produced and proved the two following receipts or instruments in writing, signed by Bush, and insisted that the penalty of the bond being satisfied, it did not operate as a release of the **153***] plaintiffs' demand, *or in any manner bar their right to recover. The receipts were as follows: "Whereas, judgment was obtained in the Court of Common Pleas, of the County of Washington, in favor of William A. Moore, against Amos T. Bush, in May Term, 1818, which judgment was obtained on a demand against the late firm of Bush & M'Cracken; damages, $1,417.16, and costs $28.36, making in all, as specified in the execution issued thereon, $1,445.52, the interest thereon up to this 21st June, 1819, $106.80—whole amount $1,552.32, the above judgment having been obtained on demands against which the said Amos T. was indemnified by a certain bond given by one James Barney (deceased), and said Charles M'Cracken, to said Amos T., bearing date the 1st October, 1816, as by reference to said bond will fully appear; and such proceedings being had whereby the executors of the said James Barney, deceased, have agreed to settle the above sum of $1,552.32. And I, the said Amos T. Bush, do hereby certify that I have this day received of George Clark of Fort Ann, one of the executors of the said James Barney, deceased, the above sum of one thousand five hundred and fifty-two dollars and thirty-two cents, on the account of the said bond, and which said bond is so far canceled as may relate to said demand above in part specified. Dated 21st June, 1819. Amos T. Bush." "Received, Fort Ann, 19th May, 1820, of George Clark, one of the executors of the within named James Barney, deceased, on the within mentioned bond, the further sum of one thousand four hundred forty-eight dollars and thirty-nine cents, making in all paid to me by said George Clark, as one of the executors as aforesaid, in virtue of said bond, the sum of three thousand dollars, and $\frac{71}{100}$.

AMOS T. BUSH."

The counsel for the defendant, Bush, insisted that he had shown enough to defeat the right of action, and that, therefore, the plaintiffs ought not to recover. His Honor, without deciding the question, directed that a verdict should be *found for the plaintiffs [***154** for $2,807, with leave for the defendant to make a case, and to turn the same into a bill of exceptions if he pleased; and the jury found accordingly.

Mr. R. Weston, for the defendant, made the following points:

1. The bond was in the nature of a release to Bush, of all demands due from Bush & M'Cracken to Barney the testator. *Cuyler* v. *Cuyler*, 2 Johns., 186; *Lacy* v. *Kynaston*, 2 Salk., 574; *Phelps* v. *Johnson*, 8 Johns., 58.

2. The bond being for indemnity against all these demands, was not satisfied by payment of the penalty, especially after the death of Barney.

3. The demand of the testator, having been once released by the operation of the bond, could never be revived by payment of the penalty after the death of Barney.

Mr. Z. R. Shipherd, contra. It is a well settled rule, that paying the penalty of a bond discharges the condition. If this had been a mere covenant to save Bush harmless, it would be different; but the obligors' liability is limited by a penalty. How then can it operate as a release of sums beyond the amount of the penalty? Here is no circuity of action to be guarded against; and the construction contended for would be grossly inequitable. No action could be maintained upon this bond by Bush, for any debts which he might pay to third persons, and the note in question stands on the same footing. The court should look at the intent of the parties in every contract. Is there a doubt that they intended to limit the liability of Barney to the penalty? If this be not so, there are no terms by which the parties can limit themselves. Upon what principle can this defendant say to the payees, "you shall take up the note which I owe to you?"

Mr. Weston, in reply. If this writing had been a covenant, secured by a penalty, there is no doubt the covenantee might have disregarded the penalty and proceeded for all his damages upon the covenant. The difficulty, then, is one of form merely. There is no real difference whether the defeasance be underwritten in a bond or included in a covenant. *The equity is the same; the remedy [***155** of the obligor is suspended; and if the bond operates as a release for a moment, it is not denied (indeed it will not admit of discussion) that it will always continue so. Perhaps we could not maintain an action of debt. The forms of law would be against us; but the question is not whether we are to have an action—it is whether we are to retain what we already have in our hands. This is like a sum paid by an infant on his promise or an insolvent upon a debt barred by his discharge, or by a debtor, the demand against whom is barred by the Statute of Limitations. The forms of law are against the remedy to compel either; but the money, when once paid, cannot be recovered back.

Curia, per SAVAGE, *Ch. J.*, after stating the facts. It is contended by the counsel for the defendant Bush: 1. That the bond operated by way of release. 2. That its operation is not changed by the payment of the penalty. 3. That payment of the penalty was not a discharge of the liability of Barney.

If the condition of the bond was not discharged by payment of the penalty, then the bond must operate by way of release to prevent circuity of action; for it would be useless for the plaintiffs to recover on the note if the defendant Bush might turn round and recover the whole amount back on the bond. 2 Johns., 186; 8 *Id.*, 58, 59.

On the question whether the obligor in a bond can be compelled to pay more than the penalty, the decisions have not been uniform. In *Lowe* v. *Peers*, 4 Burr., 2228, the questions were: 1. Whether the £1,000 mentioned were stipulated damages. 2. Whether the contract was lawful. Lord Mansfield, in giving his opinion, says: "There is a difference between covenants in general and covenants secured by a penalty or forfeiture. In the latter case the obligee has his election. He may either bring an action of debt for the penalty and recover the penalty (after which recovery of the penalty he cannot resort to the covenant; because the penalty is to be a satisfaction for the whole); or if he does not choose to go for the penalty, **156***] he may proceed upon the *covenant and recover more or less than the penalty *toties quoties*." This *dictum* of Lord Mansfield was not called for by the case, nor is any adjudged case cited. It is, however, considered good law by Epinasse in his law of *nisi prius*. 2 Esp. *N. P.*, 279. In *Branguin* v. *Perrot*, in the C. P., 2 Bl., 1190, the defendant moved to pay into court the penalty of the bond, the condition being to indemnify a parish against the maintenance of a bastard child. This was opposed on the ground that the action was for a single breach; after which the penalty should remain to answer subsequent breaches, *in infinitum*. But De Gray, *Ch. J.*, said: "This is really so plain a case that one knows not what to say to make it clearer. The bond ascertains the damage by consent of parties. If, therefore, the defendant pays the plaintiff the whole stated damages what can he desire more?" The other judges, Gould, Blackstone and Nares, concurred. In *White* v. *Sealy*, Doug., 49, the defendants gave a bond in a penalty of £600, conditioned for the payment of a yearly rent by another person of £570. Two judgments had been recovered on the bond; and to the third action the defendants pleaded the first judgment in bar. The question was whether the bond was a standing security for the rent for the whole term of 22 years, or only to the amount of the penalty. Buller, *J.*, at first, thought that the plaintiff might assign breaches under the Statute and recover more than the penalty; but finally concurred with Lords Mansfield and Ashhurst, that the defendants were liable only for the penalty. Ashhurst, *J.*, thought that though a recovery beyond the penalty might be right as to the principal, it would be inequitable as against the sureties. Afterwards, in *Lonsdale* v. *Church*, 2 T. R., 388, the question arose on a bond executed by the defendant and others. The defendant, as receiver of the harbor dues of Whitehaven, entered into three bonds of £2,000 each, conditioned to account for all sums received by him. He moved for a stay of proceedings on the payment of the penalty of two of the bonds. Buller, *J.*, declared that he was not satisfied with the decision in *White* v. *Sealy*; and cited *Elliot* v. *Davis*, Buuh., 23; *Collins* v. *Collins*, Burr., 820, and *Holdip* v. *Otway*, 2 Saund., 106, where the plaintiff had been allowed to recover more *than the pen- [***157** alty by way of damages, being the interest due by the condition of the bond, or costs. And the court refused a stay of proceedings. Another case (*Knight* v. *McLean*, 3 Bro. Ch., 596) came before Buller, *J.*, sitting for the *Lord Chancellor*, and exceptions were taken to the report of the master, because in calculating interest on a bond for the payment of money he had only computed interest to the amount of the penalty; and Buller allowed the exception, deciding that the master should have gone on with the interest, notwithstanding it might exceed the penalty; and he said that *White* v. *Sealy* went upon the defendants' being sureties. But Ld. Thurlow, the *Chancellor*, on a reargument, overruled the exception, on the ground that the penalty was the extent of the obligor's liability. He had just before decided the same thing in *Tew* v. *The Earl of Winterton*, 3 Bro. Ch., 490. The question came again before the K. B. in *Wilde* v. *Clarkson*, 6 T. R., 303, on a bond to indemnify the parish against the maintenance of a bastard child. The motion was, that satisfaction should be entered on payment of the penalty; and the case of *Lonsdale* v. *Church* was cited against it. But Ld. Kenyon said: "I cannot accede to the authority of that case. According to that, an obligor who became bound in a penalty of £1,000, conditioned to indemnify the obligee, may be called upon to pay £10,000, or any larger sum however enormous. In actions on bonds, or any penal sums for performance of covenants, the Act (8 and 9 W. III., ch. 11, sec. 8) says there shall be judgment for the penalty; and that the judgment shall stand for further breaches: but the obligor is not answerable in the whole beyond the amount of the penalty." The authority of this last case and the corresponding class of cases, was expressly recognized by the Court of K. B. in *M'Clure* v. *Dunkin*, 1 East, 436, and by the C. B. in *Hefford* v. *Alger*, 1 Taunt., 218.

The few American decisions that are to be found are also at variance. In *Tunison* v. *Cramer*, South., 498, an intimation is given, that there are cases in which a recovery may be had beyond the penalty; but it was held, in terms, that this could not be against a surety. In *Graham* v. *Bickham*, *4 Dall., 149; [***158** 4 Yeates, 32, S. C., it was decided that where the penalty is not in the nature of stated and ascertained damages, the injured party may recover beyond the penalty. That case was on a contract not under seal for the transfer of stock. In *Harris* v. *Clapp*, 1 Mass., 308, the same thing was holden of a bond, and against a surety, Sedgwick, *J.*, dissenting. But in

Payne v. *Ellzey*, 5 Wash., 143, in debt, on a prison bounds bond, against the surety, the Court of Appeals in Va. decided, that though the plaintiff may recover less, he cannot recover more than the penalty; and they lay this down as a general rule, without distinguishing between a surety and principal. In *U. S.* v. *Arnold*, 1 Gall., 348, 360, Story, *J.*, remarks: "Noticing some contrariety in the books, I think the true principle supported by the better authorities is, that the court cannot go beyond the penalty and interest thereon, from the time it becomes due by the breach." On error, the judgment in that cause was affirmed by the Supreme Court. S. C., 9 Cr. 104, 120. But the amount to be recovered was not drawn in question.

The weight of these authorities is, I think, in favor of the doctrine, that in debt on bond nothing more than the penalty can be recovered; at any rate, nothing beyond that and interest, after a forfeiture, even against the principal obligor.

But, admitting the doctrine to apply as laid down by Ld. Mansfield in *Lowe* v. *Peers*, and that an action of covenant would lie on the bond in question, in which form Bush might recover the whole amount necessary to a complete indemnity (see, also, *Winter* v. *Trimmer*, 1 Bl., 395, and *Perkins* v. *Lyman*, 11 Mass., 83); still it is clear that this can hold only as to M'Cracken, the principal; but not against Barney, who was a surety, and the extent of whose liability is the penalty of the bond. All the cases agree in this, with the single exception of *Harris* v. *Clapp;* and this was against the opinion of Sedgwick, *J.*

The plaintiffs are, therefore, entitled to judgment.

Judgment for the plaintiffs.

Reviewed—16 W. Va., 484.

Cited in—5 Cow., 425; 6 Cow., 64; 21 Wend., 266; 6 Paige, 93; 2 Edw., 172; 8 N. Y., 154; 18 N. Y., 37, 582; 2 Hun, 464; 7 Barb., 582; 23 Barb., 604; 24 Barb., 57; 3 Rob., 713; 1 E. D. S., 252; 3 Co. R., 231; 4 How. U. S., 278; 2 McLean, 587; 13 Mich., 202; 46 Mo., 381; 40 Am. Rep., 363 (73 Me., 384).

159*] *BRYAR *v.* WILLCOCKS.

Statute of Limitations—Inventory and Affidavit of Insolvent as a Bar—Note, Given before Repeal of Act of 1811, Barred by Discharge under Act of 1813.

An inventory and affidavit of a debt made by an insolvent before a commissioner, in order to obtain his discharge (which is granted) under the Insolvent Act, is a sufficient acknowledgment to take the debt out of the Statute of Limitations.

An action on a note given Feb. 6, 1812, just before the repeal of the Insolvent Act of 1811, which was repealed Feb. 14, 1812, is barred by a discharge under the Insolvent Act of Apr. 12, 1813.

Citations—15 Johns., 511; 16 Johns., 246, 251; Act, April 3, 1811; Act, April 12, 1813; Act, April 3, 1801; 19 Johns., 153.

ASSUMPSIT, on a promissory note, *Payee* v. *Baker*. Plea, *non assumpsit, et non accrevit infra sex annos.*

On the trial, at the Apr. sittings in N. Y. (1822), before *Mr. Justice* Woodworth, the plaintiff gave in evidence the note, dated Feb. 6, 1812, for $772.04, payable four months after date; and proved that the *cap. ad. resp.* was issued Dec. 2, 1819, and served on the same day.

Then to take the note without the operation of the Statute of Limitations, the plaintiff produced the petition and proceedings of the defendant, under the "Act for Giving Relief in Cases of Insolvency," passed Apr. 12, 1813 (1 R. L., 460), including a sworn inventory of the debt due upon the note at $853.25, principal and interest.

The plaintiff then gave credit for $134.79, received Aug. 19, 1817, and rested.

The defendant's counsel moved for a nonsuit, on the ground that no promise had been proved within six years before the suit was commenced; but the judge denied the motion.

The defendant then offered in evidence his discharge under the above Act, the reading of which was objected to by the plaintiff's counsel, on the ground that it was under an Act passed after the note was given; but the judge overruled the objection, and the discharge was read in evidence.

This was followed by proof that the above sum of $134.79 was received by the plaintiff of the defendant's assignee, as a dividend under the Insolvent Act.

Other evidence was given in the cause by the plaintiff, which is not deemed material to the questions raised by counsel and determined by the court.

Verdict for the plaintiff for $1,221.38, subject to the opinion of the Supreme Court upon a case, with leave to either party to turn it into a bill of exceptions or special verdict.

**Mr T. A. Emmet*, for the plaintiff. [*160

To show that the defendant's inventory and oath took the case out of the Statute of Limitations, he cited *Smith* v. *Ludlow*, 6 Johns., 267, 269; *Bryan* v. *Horseman*, 4 East, 559; *Rucker* v. *Hanny*, *Id.*, 604, *note a; Truman* v. *Fenton*, Cowp., 548, per Ld. Mansfield; *Johnson* v. *Beardsley*, 15 Johns., 3; *King* v. *Riddle*, 7 Cr., 168, which last case he said was in point, as well as the case of *Mountstephen* v. *Brooke*, 3 B. & A., 141.

That the receipt of the dividend could not operate as an accord and satisfaction, he cited what the court said in *Johnson* v. *Brannan*, 5 Johns., 271; and *Watkinson* v. *Inglesby*, *Id.*, 386; *Fitch* v. *Sutton*, 5 East, 230; *Peyton's* case, 9 Rep., 79 *b.*

That the insolvent discharge was inoperative, he relied on *Roosevelt* v. *Cebra*, 17 Johns., 108.

Messrs. J. Anthon and *J. O. Hoffman*, for the defendant, said the main question arises upon the insolvent discharge. The "Act for the Benefit of Insolvent Debtors and their Creditors" (sess. 34, ch. 123), of Apr. 3, 1811, was in force at the date of the note. This Act authorized the defendant to apply for and obtain a discharge of equal efficacy with the one under consideration, on his own petition merely; and according to the doctrine laid down in *Mather* v. *Bush*, 16 Johns., 233, the Statute of 1811 was a part of the contract. The qualification of the defendant's promise

NOTE.—*What acknowledgment will bar statute of limitations.* See Sands v. Gelston, 15 Johns., 511; Danforth v. Culver, 11 Johns., 146, *notes.*

Discharge under insolvent act—Bar to actions on what contracts. See Hicks v. Brown, 12 Johns., 142, *note.*

was, then, that he should pay the debt unless he should become insolvent, and be duly discharged upon a surrender of his property for the benefit of his creditors. Then came the Act of Apr. 12, 1813, by which a new condition was imposed, the assent of creditors, two-thirds in amount. The defendant complied with this added condition, and was discharged. Now the single question is, whether such a law can be said to impair the obligation of the original contract; and surely this cannot be pretended. The demand of the plaintiff was rather fortified by this farther condition. The case of *Wendell*, 19 Johns., 153, in effect disposes of this question. It was there held that a contract made in Oct., 1812, being after the **161***] repeal of *the Act of 1811; and therefore, in reference to the Act of Apr. 3, 1801 (1 K. & R., 428), was not discharged by the Act of Apr. 12, 1813; and this upon the express ground that when the contract was made, the Three Fourths Act was in force; and the Two Third Act narrowed the rights of the creditor and impaired his contract. The converse of the proposition follows, in this case, throughout, and we ask the corresponding conclusion. This court have repeatedly declared that they will not go beyond the spirit of the U. S. decisions, which are founded upon the idea of impairing contracts.

Again; the plaintiff is concluded by receiving the dividend. He has himself taken the benefit of the Statute by a very deliberate act. Notice is given; he proves his debt and is paid. This is an acquiescence in the proceedings by which the creditor should be concluded. He stands in the light of an ordinary petitioning creditor. The only difference is, that the plaintiff consented after the discharge; whereas the petitioning creditor does the same thing before. This case is certainly much stronger than that of *Field* v. *Howland*, 17 Johns., 85. The plaintiff's acts of acquiescence are much less equivocal here than in that case. The ground of a discharge under the English Bankrupt Law, is similar to that which we take here. The receiving a dividend, and signing a certificate, are deemed an election of the creditor by which he is concluded. *Ex parte Freeman*, 4 Ves., 836; *Grosvener, Ex parte*, 14 Ves., 587. After the creditor has proved his debt and received a dividend, he is never permitted to proceed, until he first refunds what he has received (1 Cooke's Bl., 127, and the cases there cited); not a case can be found to the contrary; and it is a fatal objection to this action, that the plaintiff has not refunded.

The Statute of Limitations has been so nearly explained away, that courts feel a disinclination to multiply exceptions to it beyond what has been done already. *Clementson* v. *Williams*, 8 Cr., 72. It is now well settled by the decisions of this court, that the admission **162***] of *what will constitute a debt, but at the same time claiming a discharge from it, will not prevent its being barred. *Sands* v. *Gelston*, 15 Johns., 511. The admission insisted on here, depends upon the same principle. It was for the purpose of obtaining a discharge.

Mr. Emmet, in reply. The objection that the dividend should be refunded, was not made at the trial; and it is, therefore, to late to raise that point here. But the English doctrine relied upon does not apply. It is for the benefit of the creditor, who may, by the act of refunding, avoid the discharge, and proceed at law; but will not be permitted to do this till he places everything *in statu quo*. Accordingly, if he elect to withhold his sanction to the proceedings under the commission, he must refund his dividend for the benefit of the other creditors. His remedy depends upon his own choice. The law there has full power to discharge: and the doctrine goes upon that ground. With us, the discharge does not effect the contract. The election which the plaintiff sets up against us as conclusive, is merely an election to give the discharge its true operation, which does not affect the contract beyond the amount of the dividend. *Sturges* v. *Crowninshield*, 4 Wh., 122, gives us a right to proceed against the property acquired after the assignment, for the balance beyond the dividend; though it protects the person of the debtor; a case very different from the English bankrupt discharge, whose clear operation is to take away all liability, both from property and person. We are bound so far as the law is valid, but no farther. The case of *Field* v. *Howland*, does not apply. All the court say in that case is, that where they would have granted a discontinuance at a previous stage of the action, they will stay execution perpetually, if the application to discontinue is delayed and lost by suffering final judgment. The appeal comes, in such a case, to the equitable powers of the court. The doctrine of election was not, perhaps, sufficiently considered in that case; for, surely, nothing is plainer than that election should never bind any farther than the Statute can legally operate; and the withdrawing all opposition *to the discharge in that [***163** case was, in law, and, probably, in fact, merely saying, "I will suffer the law to take its course, and discharge the person." It could operate in that way only; and why should an abandonment of opposition, and even the receiving a dividend, or taking that which the creditor cannot have in any other way, bind him to all intents?

As to the question whether the discharge affects the contract, what are the circumstances? The note was given Feb. 6, 1812. It may more properly be said to have been made in reference to the law which had then probably passed both houses of the Legislature; and was merely awaiting the sanction of the Council of Revision, the Act of Feb. 14, 1812, which finally passed only 8 days after the date of the note, repealing the Act of 1811, and leaving the contract to the operation of the Act of 1801. Yet we are told that the law of 1811 interweaves itself in the contract. This should be qualified with the provision that the law continues. Taking the reasoning of the other party, without this qualification, the defendant may say, "I will still have the benefit of the Act of 1811, though repealed. It was part of my contract; and the repeal impairs the obligation of the contract on my side, and for my benefit." But this will not be contended. The Act of 1811 is put out of the way by the repeal. It is as if it had never been; and the note stood subject to be discharged by the Three Fourths Act only. Then the Act of 1813 attempts to impair the contract by granting greater facilities of discharge. If the Act of 1813 had repealed the Act of 1811, so that the one system had passed smoothly and unbroken into the other, there might be plausibility in the opposite argument.

WOODWORTH, *J.* The length you go would make it out that the new Insolvent Act, though it recognize the principle of the old one existing at the time of the contract, and narrow the facility of discharge, would be inoperative, because a new and distinct Act.

164*] **Mr. Emmet.* Certainly. Upon any other principle, the debtor could never be deprived of the benefit of the Insolvent Law, as it existed at the time at the time of the contract.

Curia, per SAVAGE, *Ch. J.*, after stating the case. The first question is, whether the inventory and affidavit of the defendant is a sufficient acknowledgment to take the debt out of the Statute of Limitations. It is certainly an admission that the note was due and unpaid, and that will authorize us to presume a promise, unless the acknowledgment is accompanied with expressions which negative that idea. *Sands* v. *Gelston*, 15 Johns., 511.

2. Was the defendant's discharge a bar? The note was given before the repeal of the Act of 1811; and according to the decision of this court in *Mather* v. *Bush*, 16 Johns., 246, 251, the contract between the parties was, that the note should be paid, unless the defendant became an insolvent debtor within the meaning of the Act of 1811, and was duly discharged from his debts according to its provisions. By that Act, he was entitled to his discharge on his own petition, and on surrendering his property for the benefit of his creditors. By the repeal of the Law of 1811, which took place a few days after the date of the note, the law of 1801 was revived, which requires the assent of three fourths of the creditors of the insolvent, before he can be discharged. The repeal of the law, therefore, was favorable to the plaintiff. The Act of 1813 materially varied the principle of the Law of 1801, inasmuch as it removed some of the difficulties in the way of obtaining a discharge by substituting the assent of two thirds instead of three fourths of the creditors.

It cannot be denied, that according to the decisions of this court, a discharge under the Act of 1811, which did not require the assent of any one creditor of the defendant, would, had that Act continued in force, have discharged the defendant from the payment of the note in question. Had the Law of 1811 been immediately followed by that of 1813, the provisions of which are so much more unfavorable for the defendant, the validity of the discharge would not be disputed; for it is distinctly admitted by the reasoning of **165***] *the court, in the Matter of *Wendell*, 19 Johns., 153, that had the provisions of 1801 been continued in force, the Law of 1813 would have been valid as to contracts entered into under the Law of 1801, notwithstanding any revision or re-enactment of those provisions. Does, then, the fact that the Law of 1801 was in force for about one year after the date of the note, alter the rights of the parties? The Act of 1801 was not in the contemplation of the parties when they entered into this contract. It is true, that while that Act was in force the defendant could not have obtained his discharge without the assent of three fourths of his creditors. But had the Legislature, on the 12th Apr. 1813, re-enacted the Act of 1811, instead of the Two Thirds Act, would not a discharge under the former be valid, as being the precise terms on which it was originally agreed, that the defendant should be absolved from his contract? Most certainly. If, then, the defendant has done all which his contract required, to absolve him from it, and something more, shall the additional difficulties, the assent of two thirds of his creditors, imposed on him by the Act of 1813, operate to his prejudice, and invalidate a discharge which, without such assent, would have been valid between these parties? I think not; and am, accordingly, of opinion that the defendant is entitled to judgment.

Judgment for the defendant.

Overruled—6 Abb. Pr., 147.
Cit d in—6 Hun, 82; 12 Hun, 388; 12 Bank. Reg., 542. e

---

*BISSELL *v.* HOPKINS. [*166

Sale of Chattels—Possession of Vendor, not Conclusive Evidence of Fraud—Explanation—Mortgage of Chattels—Bill of Sale.

The possession of goods continuing in the vendor after sale, is not conclusive, but only, *prima facie*, evidence of fraud as to creditors, and may be explained.

It is a sufficient explanation that the sale was *bona fide*, and for a valuable consideration, and that the possession of the vendor was in pursuance of some agreement not inconsistent with honesty in the transaction: as where a tenant sells oxen to his landlord, in payment of rent, upon an agreement that the former should retain them to work his farm.

So where D. mortgaged a mare, and various other personal chattels, to H., to secure an honest debt, but retained possession of the mare, with H.'s consent, in order to settle and close D.'s business as constable, he having no other horse, and also retained possession of the other articles to carry on his business; held, a sufficient explanation, and that this was not fraudulent as to creditors.

A bill of sale of chattels, declaring that it is to secure a debt, and providing that, on payment of the debt by the articles or otherwise, the surplus and remaining articles shall be released to the vendor, is a mortgage; and possession of the chattels continuing in the mortgagor, is not evidence of fraud.

Citations—3 Co., 80; 9 Johns., 338; 5 Johns., 261; Cowp., 435; 15 Mass., 244; 7 Taunt., 149.

ON error from the Court of C. P., of the County of Livingston. The action in the court below was trover, for a bay mare, by Hopkins against Bissell, in which the jury found a special verdict, as follows:

That, before the conversion of the mare, one Jesse Dryer was the owner, and had the pos-

NOTE.—*Sale of chattels—Possession remaining in vendor—How far evidence of fraud.* See Sturtevant v. Ballard, 9 Johns., 337, *note.*

Mortgage of chattels—Possession of mortgagor. See Barrow v. Paxton, 5 Johns., 258, *note.*

Chattel mortgages—Validity of. See Barrow v. Paxton, 5 Johns., 258, *note.*

session of her; and Oct. 1, 1819, executed and delivered to Hopkins a cèrtian instrument in writing as follows: "$274.84½. Whereas, I, Jesse Dryer, am indebted to Samuel M. Hopkins in the sum of two hundred and seventy-four dollars and eighty-four and a half cents, being the balance of our accounts this day adjusted; therefore, to provide for the payment and security thereof, I have sold and delivered to the said Samuel M. Hopkins the following goods and chattels, to wit: one bay mare, one cow, three yearling heifers, four grown hogs and five shoats, one stack of hay, a quantity of hay in the barn, four and a half acres of corn on the Talmadge flats, three acres of corn on the upland in the Stimson lot, one acre of potatoes, one half the garden vegetables, one bed and bedding, one bedstead, two sets of chairs, two tables, one cupboard and three pair of fire-dogs, one five-pail kettle, part of a set of blacksmith tools. And whereas part of the above articles are growing crops, and cannot now be justly estimated, therefore it is agreed that the other above articles shall be appraised by Jerome Curtiss, and the corn and other crops, shall be estimated at fair value, according to the quantity when harvested; and thereupon, the condition of this conveyance is, that upon payment being made in the above articles, or otherwise, to the above amount, the surplus and remaining articles, if any, shall be released to the said Jesse Dryer. Leicester, 1st October, 1819. Jesse Dryer." Upon the back of which instrument there was, Oct. 2, 1819, an indorsement made by Jerome Curtiss, as follows:

167*] *"*Appraisal of the within goods and chattels.*

The bay mare,		$ 60 00
Cow,		15 00
3 yearling heifers, at $6,		18 00
4 grown hogs, at $4,		16 00
5 shoats, at $1		5 00
1 stack hay, about 2 tons,		10 00
4 tons hay in the barn, $6 ton,		24 00
1 bed and bedding,		26 00
1 bedstead (walnut),		2 00
2 sets chairs—one at 36*s.* and one 60*s.*,		12 00
2 pine tables, $3,		6 00
1 pine cupboard,		5 00
2 pr. fire-dogs (cast),		6 00
1 five-pail kettle,		5 00
Blacksmith's tools, viz.: 1 bellows (old),	$15 00	
1 stake or beak horn,	2 00	
4 pr. tongs,	3 00	
1 small sledge-hammer, and 3 hand hammers,	6 00	
1 buttress, 4*s.*; shoeing iron, 4*s.*; clenching iron, 2*s.*,	1 25	
3 punches,	50	
		27 75
		$237 75

2d October, 1819. Jerome Curtiss."

That Jan. 1, 1821, Dryer executed to Hopkins a certain other instrument in writing, which was written on the same paper containing the first in these words: "1821. Jan. 1. Settled the account of the above to this time, and adjusted the balance at one hundred and forty-six 61-100 dollars, for which so much of the above property as remains on hand is to remain liable. The bay mare above mentioned is to be delivered to Malcom M'Naughton, on demand, but she is intended to remain in said Dryer's use for the present, and he is to pay into Elihu Scofield's hands, for said Hopkins, in g judgments or securities, or to said M'Naughton's hands in grain, *the [*168 amount of fifty dollars, within one month, and on continuing his payments in proportion, the mare is intended to remain with him. Jesse Dryer." That, in the month of Apr., 1817, a book account commenced between the plaintiff and Dryer; that settlements were made at different times between them, beside those already mentioned in writing; and that, at the time of the several settlements, including the above written ones, Dryer was justly indebted to the plaintiff to the amount of the several sums in the intruments in writing mentioned; that, from the time the plaintiff's account commenced, Dryer continued considerably indebted to him, and is now justly indebted to him to the amount of more than $100; that in Sept., 1817, Dryer rented of the plaintiff a tavern stand and small farm, at $120 *per annum*, and continued therein (but subsequently at reduced rents), till the time the mare in question was sold by direction of the defendant, as hereinafter mentioned; that a large part of the plaintiff's account was for rent, and that, at the time of the sale of the mare by the defendant, more than one year's rent was due from Dryer to the plaintiff. That in the month of Nov., 1817, an account commenced between Dryer and the defendant, and in Mar., 1820, a considerable balance being due the defendant, he commenced an action against Dryer, in the Court of C. P., of the County of Genesee, and in Sept. Term thereafter recovered a judgment against Dryer, in that court, for $91.58, and Jan. 4, 1821, the defendant caused execution to be issued on his judgment, and delivered to the sheriff of Genesee; that the defendant directed the sheriff to levy on the mare in question, by virtue of his execution, if possible, while the mare was off the premises rented by Dryer of the plaintiff; that, pursuant to such directions, the sheriff did levy and seize upon the mare, while off the premises, but in the possession of the said Dryer, and sold the same at public auction or vendue, in the month of Feb., 1821, at which sale the defendant became the purchaser, and took and led away the mare; and that no rent was tendered or offered to be paid to the plaintiff; that before the sale, the defendant had notice of the plaintiff's claim to the mare, that Dryer had been a constable, *and had considerable unsettled busi- [*169 ness, and the special object of leaving the mare in his possession was (as he had no other horse) to close such business, by which means as he stated at the time, he hoped to make his payments; that applications were afterwards made to Dryer to sell the mare (being a well known animal, and considered valuable), to which he always, after the pledge, answered that she was not his, and that the plaintiff had a claim on her, or owned her, and the fact of the plaintiff's claim was publicly known; that the appraisal by Curtiss was meant to be a fair one, according to his best judgment; that

Curtiss and also M'Naughton (being the only persons who were present at, and conversant with the transaction between the plaintiff and Dryer), both supposed that no secrecy or concealment was intended, and never themselves had the least reserve upon the subject, or knew of any; that, at the time the bill of sale was executed, Dryer was indebted to the plaintiff, and to the defendant and to others, but no judgment or execution existed against him, unless for some trivial amount, till subsequently to the assignment; that the mare remained in Dryer's possession from the time when the instrument in writing first above mentioned was executed, till the seizure by the sheriff; that part of the articles mentioned in the appraisal hereinbefore mentioned, had, from time to time, been delivered and credited to Dryer in account, but that Dryer made no payment after the settlement of Jan. 1, 1821, except the sum of $1.50, till the time of sale. And if, &c., then the jurors say, &c., and then they assess the damages of the plaintiff, &c., to $62.62, &c. And hereupon, &c.

Judgment was for the plaintiff below.

Mr. Talcott, Atty-Gen., for the plaintiff in error, submitted the following written points or propositions to the court.

1. The first bill of sale does not show on its face that the possession of the horse should be in the vendor; and therefore it is fraudulent in law against creditors. Whether there was fraud, in fact, is not material.

170*] *2. This bill of sale is not a mortgage. There was no time for the payment of the debt secured by it—no means pointed out of obtaining payment out of the property. It was an everlasting pledge, without delivery of the thing pledged, and therefore void. If a creditor can keep other creditors at bay by such a contrivance for one day, he may for ten years. Leaving the horse in the debtor's possession was, therefore, fraudulent against creditors.

3. Payment of the debt was not the creditor's object in taking the bill of sale. It was to prevent other creditors from taking the property. The memorandum at the foot of the bill of sale, dated in Jan., 1821, was an attempt, four days before the levy, to account for the possession of the property continuing in the vendor, and thus change the nature of the sale. The excuse for leaving the horse in the vendor's possession, was not sufficient. A year and a half is an unreasonable time to settle his accounts as constable, &c. Both plaintiff and defendant were creditors, and the one obtaining the possession ought to have the property.

4. The defendant's knowing of the plaintiff's claim cannot affect the case; for if the sale was void, as against him, his knowledge of such void claim is nothing.

5. As landlord, the defendant in error might have distrained, if any rent was due, and the property having been seized off the premises, he cannot maintain trover for it. Besides, it does not appear that the rent due was that of the last preceding year.

6. At the time of the taking and sale, the defendant in error had no right of possession.

He added that in examining these propositions, it becomes necessary to look back to the Statute of Elizabeth. 13 Eliz., ch. 5, enacted almost *verbatim;* 1 R. L., 75. Upon the question, whether leaving property in the hands of the vendor is fraudulent as to creditors, a variety of principles are scattered through the books. Sometimes we are told the court are to take the question into their own hands; sometimes that it is to be left to the jury; sometimes that such a possession is fraud, *per se;* sometimes that it is so, *prima facie*, only; sometimes that possession is not fraudulent where the sale is conditional; sometimes that it is so, whether the *sale be absolute [***171** or conditional. I take this to be the general principle, that the whole depends upon the intention of the parties. That intention in this, as in all other cases, is sometimes to be found by the jury, and sometimes it is matter of law, referable to the court, and to be presumed not only with, but even against evidence. Thus, Lord Mansfield, in *Worseley* v. *De Mattos*, 1 Burr., 474: "Whether a transaction be fair or fraudulent, is often a question of law: it is the judgment of law, upon facts and intents." Intent is either in fact or in law. There is a variety of circumstances from which the law will infer an intent; in others it must be found by a jury, and is then a question of fact. An inference of law is not to be resisted, and this proposition is well illustrated by the criminal code. One sends a child to a drawer, who takes thence a poisoned apple, eats it and is killed. It is a question of fact for the jury whether the child was sent on purpose. If he was, they should find the sender guilty of murder. On the other hand, if one gives a poisoned apple to A, with intent to murder A by his eating, and it should accidentally come to the hands of the child, and the donor should even interfere to prevent the child's eating it, yet the child being killed by eating the poisoned apple, the donor is guilty of murder; for the law will infer an intention to kill the child, even against the fact. It is the same thing as to fraud. Where it depends on the actual intent, it is for the jury—if upon the constructive intent, the whole is a matter of legal inference for the court.

We shall doubtless be told that this is the case of a mere mortgage, and that therefore possession need not follow. This position is not maintainable; and the only case which looks that way is *Barrow* v. *Paxton*, 5 Johns., 258. The acknowledged distinction between a mortgage of goods and a pledge, will be found in 1 Pow. on Morts., 3, 4, and in the 2d chapter, p. 29, the subject is taken up, and almost the whole of that chapter is devoted to the inquiry, in what cases possession of the mortgagor and vendor is fraudulent as to creditors and purchasers; and mortgages and absolute sales are placed by him on the same footing, in which he is abundantly sustained by the cases which he cites. He begins the chapter *by saying that "A mortgage being a [***172** contract of sale executed, with power to redeem, must have all the properties and qualities incidental to the validity of an absolute dispositiou." He then proceeds directly to apply the Statute of Elizabeth to fraudulent mortgages of chattels; and considers the mortgagor who continues in full possession, as within its purview. We do not deny the doctrine that when there is such a conditional sale, that possession in the vendor is consistent with it, the possession is no evidence of fraud; but a mortgage is not that case. There the property passes presently, defeasible by condition subsequent; but it is only where the condition is precedent that the vendor's possession may be said to be consistent with the deed. The bill of sale should be such as to vest a future interest; as where it is to become absolute on the payment of a sum of money at another day. What the court say, in *Barrow* v. *Paxton*, is, that "delivery always accompanies a pledge, but a mortgage of goods is often valid without delivery." These words "often valid," are very cautious and qualified. They are no more than may be said of an absolute sale without change of possession, which, in common with a mortgage, may, under peculiar circumstances, often be valid. *Barrow* v. *Paxton* presented one of those circumstances. The bill of sale retained a right of distress. The goods continued on the demised premises, and the rights of creditors were not at all in question. The defendant was a purchaser, with full notice of the plaintiff's claim—a mere fraudulent volunteer, who had no right to protection. The remark of the court that a mortgage may be often valid, unaccompanied with delivery, is sustained by various other acknowledged exceptions to be found in the 2d chapter of Powell, before quoted. Why should there be any distinction between an absolute sale and a mortgage? Why is it that continuance of possession in the vendor is holden fraudulent? Because it gives him credit. Where is the difference in fact, whether the vendor has given a mortgage or bill of sale? How much better off is the creditor on account of the proviso in the bill of sale than if he had been deprived of the property without a proviso? The principle contended for on the **173***] other *side, leads to all the evils of allowing an absolute sale, without a transfer of possession. All the parties need do, in order to give it complete effect, is to attach a proviso.

In *Clayborn* v. *Hill*, 1 Wash., 177, a mortgage of personal property, the possession continuing in the mortgagor, was declared valid upon the sole ground that such mortgages were recognized by a Statute of Virginia, which guarded against fraud, by providing that the mortgage should be recorded, like our mortgages of land. But, even in that case, the question did not necessarily arise; and the conveyance was pronounced void, on the ground that the equity of redemption had been released, and the possession of the vendor continued notwithstanding. This was the only point directly before the court. The remarks in regard to the mortgage, as such (*Id.*, 184, S. C.), are mere *obiter dicta* of the President.

The case of *Clow* v. *Woods*, decided by the Supreme Court of Pa., at Pittsburgh, Sept., 1819, MS. (17 Ves., Jr., Phil. ed. of 1822, 196 *n.* 1), drew in question the validity of an unrecorded mortgage of goods, which continued in possession of the mortgagor. It was adjudged fraudulent as to creditors, from the mere circumstance of the continued possession; and, per Gibson, *J.*, in delivering the opinion of the court: "The Statute 13 Eliz., does not in words declare a conveyance of goods fraudulent, where the vendor retains possession; but, in general terms, renders void all conveyances made to the end, purpose and intent of defrauding creditors. Hence it becomes incumbent on the courts to determine, from all circumstances of the case, whether the conveyance be or be not made with a fraudulent intention; and in judging of that, it is held that any neglect in leaving the vendor in possession, is fraudulent within the Statute. The general rule is that the possession must be transferred to the purchaser. But, it has been said, the rule does not apply to conditional sales: that is altogether without foundation; for neither this Statute nor 27 Eliz., which provides for the securing of purchasers, makes any difference between absolute and conditional sales. The only question is, whether the sale be fraudulent; *and if it be, is it within the [***174** Statute? Delivery of the subject-matter of the contract is as requisite in the case of a mortgage of goods as it is in the case of an absolute sale.

In *Ryall* v. *Rolle*, 1 Atk., 165, 185, this question was much considered and the doctrine laid down is, in terms, the same as that in *Clow* v. *Woods*. The questions of fraud are held to depend on the same circumstances, whether they arise under 13 Eliz. or the Statute of Bankrupts, 21 Jac., 1. The very question here under consideration underwent the direct examination of Lord Hardwicke, C; Lee, *Ch. J.*, of the K. B; Parker, *Ch. B.*, of the Exchequer, and Burnet, *J.*, of the C. P., and they all agreed, in terms, 1. That the possession continuing in the mortgagor was not consistent with the deed, and that it was fraudulent in relation to creditors, considered either under the Statute of Fraudulent Conveyances or of Bankrupts; and the cases before that decision (A. D., 1749) to this point, are all summed up, in the course of the discussion, by the different judges. Burnet, *J.* says (1 Atk., 167, S. C.): "The next question to be considered will be in relation to the condition of creditors, where the debtor continues in possession of the goods mortgaged. This was fraudulent at the common law, and the 13 Eliz., ch. 5, secs. 1, 2, provides against it, that it shall be void. There is no distinction whether the sale be absolute or conditional." Again (*Id.*, 170): "the only thing contended for is, whether the mortgagee shall be considered as the true owner, or the mortgagor; and there is no doubt the conditional vendee is the true owner, or proprietary; and there is no reason to make a distinction between an absolute and conditional vendee, but by confounding the difference betwixt pawns and mortgages. There might some doubt arise, if this was the case of a pawn, as in the case (3 Bulstr., 17), but it cannot be doubted in the case of a mortgage, for it is an immediate sale to the mortgagee, and though the mortgagor may buy it again, or redeem by favor of a court of equity, till then the vendee is the absolute proprietor. A pawn is complete by a delivery, but on a conditional or absolute sale, the sale is complete by the contract, and the party is entitled to a delivery of the goods, as soon as he has paid the price. Salk., 113; Dyer, 20, 203." *Again; [***175** "as there is no authority to warrant a distinction between absolute and conditional sales, so there is a case that destroys it. *Stevens* v. *Sole*, in Ch. Trin., 1736, 1 Ves., 352."

This, as I before remarked, should be understood of a sale defeasible upon condition subsequent, not precedent, as in the case put by Burnet, *J.*, of a sale of goods which remain because the money is not paid; but, he adds (*Ib.*): "If a conditional vendee pay the money, and does not insist upon a delivery of the goods, he confides in the credit of the vendor, and not in any real or particular security; and ought to come in under the commission, as much as any other person that places a confidence in the bankrupt, and not in any other security." It is only, therefore, in case of a precedent condition, that the vendor may hold possession; and this distinction was taken by Lee, *Ch. J.* (*Id.*, 179), on referring to 2 Bulst., 226; and, on recurring to what Coke, *J.*, says, in *Stone* v. *Grubham*, 2 Bulst., 226, it will be seen that he makes the same distinction, in terms.

The bill of sale in question, in *Manton* v. *Moore*, 7 T. R., 63, was but a mortgage; and yet it is evident the court consider it resting on the same footing as an absolute bill of sale; or why should they advert to the various particular circumstances of the case to find a warrant for the goods continuing with the mortgagor?

Worseley v. *De Mattos*, 1 Burr., 467, arose under the Statute of 1 Jac., 1, ch. 15. It was a mortgage of goods, and it was agreed that possession was material. Ld. Mansfield remarks upon, and distinguishes three cases cited to show that a change of possession was not necessary (*Id.*, 482, &c.), and says the first was against, and the other two could not be considered as deciding the proposition; and proceeds: "If he mortgages and parts with the possession of goods, the world has notice; but to give priority from mortgaging goods, of which the trader is allowed to act and appear as the owner, would be enabling him to impose upon mankind, and draw them in by false appearances. No injustice is done to such mortgagee; because he really trusts only to the general credit of the trader. The conveyance is not a fraud against him, but against his other creditors." In *Wilson* v. *Day*, 2 Burr., 827, which was also the case of a per-
176*] sonal *mortgage, he says the same thing (*Id.*, 830), and per Foster, *J.* (*Id.*, 831), a trader, before bankruptcy, may pay a particular creditor; or he may mortgage his effects to a particular creditor, with possession delivered; and here it is a mortgage, it is true, with a resulting trust to Lawson; but there is no alteration of possession; no delivery, which is the badge of ownership. *Twine's* case, 3 Co., 81, *a*, Wilmot, *J.*, concurred, in the same terms. *Ladbroke* v. *Crickett*, 2 T. R., 649, was a question between an execution creditor who had levied upon a vessel, and a creditor by bottomry (in nature of a mortgage) on the same vessel; and because the latter had reduced the ship into his own possession before the levy, he recovered; but, per Lord Kenyon, *Ch. J.*: "If no possession had been taken under this instrument, it would have been fraudulent, and any other creditor might have taken her in execution; but here the title of the first purchaser was consummated by taking possession of the ship."

In *Mace* v. *Cadell*, Cowp., 232, Ld. Mansfield takes up and considers what is the true distinction between questions arising under the 13 Eliz. and 21 Jac. The latter, he held, subjects goods to the commission of bankruptcy, though they were not originally the bankrupt's, but were merely leased to him, if he used and possessed them as owner; and he says if this latter Statute "meant to comprehend nothing more than is contained in the preamble, it means nothing at all; because even before the statute, if a man had conveyed his own goods to a third person, and had kept the possession, such possession would have been void, as being fraudulent, according to the doctrine in *Twine's* case, 3 Rep., 81." In all other points the doctrine is the same, whether upon the Statute of Eliz. or James.

Thus the court will perceive, by adverting to the cases, that they all concur in the general rule, whether the bill of sale be absolute or conditional, that possession must follow the sale. Cases where it may be retained are mere exceptions to the rule arising from special circumstances. Whether the sale be absolute or conditional, a continuing possession in the vendor may be explained, but not in one case any more than in the other. What reasons are available, then, *in case the sale is ab- [***177**
solute? Property not capable of delivery is one, as a ship at sea. Where the vendor refuses to deliver, though the money be paid, holds the vendee at arm's length, and puts him to his action of trover, is another. It is true that it may become material to inquire into the conditions of the sale, to see whether the reasons for retaining possession be good. If the sale be absolute, necessity alone is an excuse. If left even from the most humane motives, fraud is a presumption *de juris et de jure*, which nothing can resist. By classifying the cases, it will be seen that there is no difference of principle, though there may be in the expressions used. By some cases, we are told that where one makes a bill of sale to secure a debt and the bill is absolute on its face, and there is a continuance of possession in the vendor, it will be deemed fraudulent unless such conduct be fully accounted for. We say necessity alone will account for it under this rule. The same rule and same explanation holds where the owner sells for cash advanced, or an antecedent debt, though otherwise of money lent to buy the goods with. Where it is necessary that the vendor should do something about the goods for the benefit of the vendee, the former may retain possession for this purpose; and circumstances may render it imperiously necessary that he should retain the goods for the purpose of selling them for the vendee's benefit. In such a case the sale was holden not to be fraudulent. For these distinctions see the cases cited by Kent, *Ch. J.*, in *Sturtevant* v. *Ballard*, 9 Johns., 337. Another exception may perhaps be considered as established; and that is, where the goods are disposed of by a public judicial sale to one, other than the creditor, and are left with the debtor; there it may be necessary to show actual fraud. *Cole* v. *Davies*, 1 Ld. Raym., 754, 725. Accordingly, in *Guthrie* v. *Wood*, 1 Stark., 367, 369, Ld.

Ellenborough said: "The doctrine of possession applies to cases of conveyance from the party himself. The Statute of Eliz. does not apply to a case like this, where the property is sold not by the party, but under a distress for rent." Goods conveyed by a marriage settlement, by a husband to trustees, in trust for the wife, are also an exception, from the peculiar nature of the transaction and the relation of the parties. *Cadogan* v. *Kennet*, Cowp., 432.

It cannot be pretended that the present case comes within any of the exceptions to the gen-
178*] eral rule. The doctrine *is universal that there must be a satisfactory explanation why the possession continues with the vendor. Here is none. The possession was not even confined to a reasonable time for the vendor to arrange his affairs as a constable. It was left for the debtor's own use, for a long and unreasonable time. No case can be found justifying this. The money was due from the moment of the sale, but no time specified for its payment. The doctrine of the other side will enable any man to defeat his creditors of their just debts, and yet enjoy his property during his whole life.

Mr. S. M. Hopkins, defendant, *in pro. per.*, submitted to the court the following propositions, points and references in writing:

1. It is admitted to be the general rule that a sale of chattels, unaccompanied by possession, is, by presumption of law, *prima facie*, fraudulent.

2. But this rule is subject to exceptions in all cases where the vendor's possession is for a fair and lawful reason; and where that possession accompanies and follows the deed or bill of sale. Cowp., 432; 2 Bulst., 225; Prec. in Ch., 285; 1 Ld. Raym., 724; 2 T. R., 579, per Buller, *J.*; 1 Cr., 309; 9 Johns., 201, and 9 Johns., 337, in which most of the above are cited.

3. And our decisions have fully recognized the doctrine that sales, subject to a general presumption of legal fraud, may still be valid in special cases, to be approved by judgment of law, such, as, where the intent is fair—not calculated to work a wrong, &c., &c. 9 Johns., 33, per Kent, Ch. *J.*, "unless in special cases to be approved by the court." 5 Johns., per Spencer, *J.*

4. And on those grounds a *bona fide* mortgage of goods is universally allowed.

5. In this case, the first instrument was a plain mortgage, payable on demand. It has all the qualities of a mortgage: 1. A debt acknowledged. 2. A property conveyed to secure payment. 3. A clause of redemption.

6. The second instrument was plainly a mortgage also—or rather a continuation of the first, occasioned by a second adjustment of the ac-
179*] counts, *made at the close of the year; and it is upon the effect of the second instrument that the question turns.

7. This transaction was perfectly fair, reasonable, public, and well known to the defendant below.

8. In such a case as this, it would be no objection that the property might be kept from the other creditors a long time or even forever, if that had been the intent; for the other creditors can never have any just claim upon it.

He added, the conveyance here is of definite property, which is made the subject of a definite appraisal; and the *bona fides* admitted. There is nothing to intend. Everything necessary to sustain the transaction is found by a special verdict, upon which, it should be remembered, the question arises. That verdict finds the *bona fides*. It is enough that it does not find *mala fides*; and the only question for the court to decide is, whether fraud arises from such a case by necessary legal intendment. The value of the property is short of the debt. The bill of sale provides that, on payment, the surplus shall be released. Bissell did not obtain judgment nor even prosecute for his debt till after the pledge; and the seizure and conversion upon his execution was before default of paying the debt upon the second mortgage.

Much has been said about legal fraud and fraud in fact; and I agree that the understanding to be derived from the books is not very clear, as to what these phrases mean, and the distinction between them. One sells goods which, from motives of humanity merely, the vendee still suffers to remain in the possession of the vendor. The rules of law say this is liable to the imputation of fraud. The reason, says the Atty-Gen., is, because it gives a false credit. On this I take issue. The reason is totally different. It is that the parties have power to hatch up a fictitious debt, give it the appearance of fairness, and made it a colorable lien on property. The law, therefore, comes with a general rule to supply the defect of human testimony, and reach the truth. It seizes upon *indicia* as a standard of proof, and by a *presumption *de jure*, pronounces the [***180**
continuance of possession fraudulent. Then, I say, though *prima facie* fraudulent, this presumption may, in all cases, be repelled. It is always subject to be rebutted by proof that the sale is not fraudulent.

Two positions are taken on the other side, not exactly consistent. It is first said that possession continuing in the vendor is always an indication of fraud; and then again, that in certain cases it may be accounted for: and that the goods, being the subject of a mortgage, is one way of giving such an account. The moment you admit it may be accounted for, the rule is gone as to there being a presumption *de juris et de jure;* for it depends upon and is a question of fact. If a question of fact, may not human affairs be so modified as to present facts beyond those which have ever before entered into any case? Is necessity alone an answer? Shall it be said that a *bona fide* possession and nobody injured, is not equally an excuse? One gives property with fair appraisement, to an amount less than the debt, and passes it by mortgages. Is not this one of the answers which may be given? Suppose it mortgaged at seven years or seventy years: the debtor has a right to mete it out to creditors as he chooses; and why not seventy years, if no one is injured? But "we cannot levy upon it." No matter. You gave no credit on the faith of it, and are not injured. Then we come back to the inquiry; wherefore does the law object? Why does it interpose presumption? I answer because, for aught we know, there may be fraud, and it being so liable, we will presume, and deny the truth and reality of the business, and call it a fictitious sale until explained and answered. Here it is explained. The record says it is fair; and the plaintiff in error is driven to the length of saying that, in the face of a record, the court must find bad faith.

Although the line of distinction which I advance, may not be well drawn, yet it has been constantly recognized by the courts. It is not necessary to extend our inquiries beyond the 13 Eliz. and the cases upon that Statute. Nor will I say that where third persons are
181*] injured by giving *credit or purchasing on the faith of the possession, courts will not presume fraud in order to protect them. I was going on to cite cases to establish the distinction I last advanced; but I will first examine *Edwards* v. *Harben*, 2 T. R., 597, Buller, *J.*, speaks of non-delivery as a circumstance, *per se*, which makes the sale void in point of law; and adds, "we are all of opinion, that if there be nothing but the absolute conveyance without the possession, in point of law it is fraudulent." It is upon such propositions as this, scattered through the books, that legal intendment is insisted on. In that case the vendor sold, but retained possesson; and I admit the legal intendment of fraud followed; but what becomes of the presumption, if there be something else in the case besides conveyance and possession? How does this differ from cases of presumption *de jure* upon facts found by special verdict, or admitted by a demurrer? Not one case can be found in which *bona fides* was made out, where fraud was ever presumed; and the whole course of the authorities go on this ground. The late case of *Benton* v. *Thornhill*, 7 Taunt., 149; 2 Marsh., 427, S. C., I shall not largely insist on, because I agree that it was of a mixed character upon the question of possession, which was left to the jury, to say whether fraudulent or not; but contending for delivery upon a mortgage, is in the face of *Barrow* v. *Paxton*, 5 Johns., 258, decided by this court, which is a leading case, and which has guided the profession in transactions of this kind ever since. In *Craig* v. *Ward*, 9 Johns., 197, 201, the court say: "There must be a fraudulent or deceptive purpose in view, or implied, under the special circumstances of the case. In *Sturtevant* v. *Ballard*, *Id.*, 337, 339, the court again recognize fraud as matter of actual intent. There must, say they (*Id.*, 339). "be some sufficient motive, and of which the court is to judge, for the non-delivery of the goods, or the law will still presume the sale to have been made with a view to "delay, hinder or defraud creditors." Again: "In such cases, it has been frequently said not to be absolutely fraudulent; or not so in point of law, to permit the donor to continue in possession. The only inquiry would be as to matter of fact, whether the transaction was really
182*] and *intrinsically fair and honest." And after a full review of the cases, the whole are summed up in these words: "We may, therefore, safely conclude, that a voluntary sale of chattels, with an agreement, either in or out of the deed, that the vendor may keep possession, is, except in special cases, and for special reasons, to be shown to, and approved of by the court, fraudulent and void as against creditors." In *Manton* v. *Moore*, 7 T. R., 68, Grose, *J.*, says: "I am of opinion that the question of fraud was for the consideration of the jury, and the duty of the jury, in this case, has devolved on the arbitrator, who has determined that there was no fraud." *Kidd* v. *Rawlinson*, 2 Bos. & P., 59, was a purchase of goods at sheriff's sale, but not by the judgment creditor, and the goods were left with the debtor; and Ld. Eldon relied upon this to take it out of the general rule; yet he treated it as a question of fact, and left it to the jury to pronounce upon the intent. In *Worseley* v. *DeMattos*, 1 Burr., 484, per Ld. Mansfield: "Nay, the not taking possession, being only evidence of fraud, may be explained." In *Ryall* v. *Rolle*, 1 Atk., 167-8, per Burnet, *J.*: "Courts of equity and juries are to consider upon the whole evidence, whether the conveyance was made with a view to defraud or not." In *Heselinton* v. *Gill*, 3 T. R., 620, 621, *n. a*, per Buller, *J.*: "It has been frequently determined, that possession alone is not evidence of fraud; the transaction must be shown to be fraudulent from other circumstances." In *Edwards* v. *Harben*, 2 T. R., 597, per Buller, *J.*: "On the other hand, there are cases, where the vendor has continued in possession, and the bill of sale has not been adjudged fraudulent, if the want of immediate possession be consistent with the deed." The 21 Jac. has a different scope and object from the 13 Eliz. and the cases of *Worseley* v. *DeMattos* and *Ryall* v. *Rolle*, and other cases arising under that Act, do not apply; yet it will be seen by these cases, that fraud may be disproved even under the 21 Jac. This is apparent from the authorities cited by Ld. Mansfield, in the latter case. 1 Burr., 478, &c. Powell has been cited. He, too, proceeds throughout upon the idea that no delivery may be made, and yet the transaction not fraudulent; and he sums up the law in this manner: *1 Pow. [***183**
on Mort., 43, 44, 1 Am. from 4 Lond. ed. "Another ground upon which cases have been considered as not within the purview of the Statute of Eliz. is that, by the specific words of the contract, possession was not meant to follow immediately thereupon; for the circumstance which stains the transaction with fraud, is the false appearance held out, when one thing is done and an appearance permitted, which imports the contrary; an absolute, unqualified transfer of the right to the vendee, but the possession and use retained by the vendor, with no other object but to defraud. But there can be no fraud where the appearances agree with the real state of things. And what was the intrinsic nature of the contract, as to the retaining or parting with the possession, may be made out from the deeds where the transaction is in writing, and where the transaction is *en pais*, by such parol evidence as can be adduced for the purpose of proving it." Then, after illustrating this proposition by the case of *Bucknal* v. *Royston*, Prec. Ch., 285, he adopts (*Id.*, 45, 46), the words of Ld. Mansfield, in *Cadogan* v. *Kennet*, Cowp., 432. "Therefore the Statute did not militate against any transaction *bona fide*, and where there was no imagination of fraud; and so was the common law. The question, therefore, in every case was, whether the act done was a *bona fide*

transaction, or whether it was a trick and contrivance to defeat creditors." In *Cortelyou* v. *Lansing*, 2 Cai. Cas., 202, per Kent, *J.*, speaking of a pledge: "It is, therefore, to be distinguished from a mortgage of goods, for that is an absolute pledge, to become an absolute interest if not redeemed at a fixed time. Besides, delivery is essential to a pledge; but a mortgage of goods is, in certain cases, valid without delivery." *Bucknal* v. *Royston*, Prec. Ch., 285, case 227, is a leading case upon these questions as to the validity of a mortgage without delivery, as between the parties, and as to creditors, under the Statute of Eliz. Brewer there mortgaged a ship in port, with the cargo and the profits of the voyage, but retained possession, and sold the cargo and invested the proceeds in other goods in the course of the voyage. A judgment creditor claimed the goods upon the return of the ship; but the **184***]claim was overruled. *Was the delivery in that case impossible? Could not the adventure have been taken into the lender's own hands, and the money lent at simple interest, instead of *respondentia*? Certainly no physical or moral imposibility intervened. What, then, becomes of the doctrine of necessity? It is admitted that a condition precedent shall excuse, according to what Coke, *J.*, says, in 2 Bulst., 226. But this is only one exception among many; and the same effect has, again and again, been given to a condition subsequent. In *Cole* v. *Davies*, 1 Ld. Raym., 724–5, it was resolved that if goods of A are seized upon a *fieri facias*, and sold to B, *bona fide*, upon valuable consideration; though B permits A to have the goods in his possession, upon condition that A shall pay to B the money, as he shall raise it by the sale of the goods, this will not make the execution fraudulent;" though it was agreed that actual fraud might be shown. If a mortgage require delivery, wherein does it differ from a pledge? Yet a distinction is constantly kept up.

Mr. Talcott, in reply. It is true that the books often say possession continuing in the vendor is only *prima facie* evidence of fraud, and may be explained. This proposition I admit; but I deny its application to the present case. It should be taken in the same sense in which it was advanced by Buller, *J.*, in *Edwards* v. *Harben*, 2 T. R., 587, but the ulterior inquiry must be, is the explanation such as satisfies the law. This depends on the nature of the agreement between the parties and the circumstances attending the sale. I do not contend for a physical or moral necessity as the only explanation which can be given. There are, I admit, other cases, among which *Bucknall* v. *Royston* is the strongest. Ld. Mansfield says (1 Burr., 482–3) that was a case "upon the course of administration of assets, where secret liens give priority. Besides, the possession there was a trust under an authority to negotiate and sell; and could not be meant to give any false credit." As to the distinction between a mortgage and pledge, in the latter there must be a delivery as between the pawnor and pawnee; the former **185***] may be good as between *mortgagor and mortgagee without delivery, but not as to creditors; and so is the passage from *Cortelyou* v. *Lansing*, as read by the gentleman; "a mortgage of goods is, in certain cases, valid without delivery." Such language recognizes the doctrine that, as a general rule, delivery is necessary in the case of a mortgage. *Barrow* v. *Paxton*, I have shown, maintains the same doctrine. "Often valid," as used in that case, is certainly not "always." In *Bucknal* v. *Royston* it was part of the trust that the goods should remain. Why give this reason, if possession is always consistent with the mortgage? Would it not have been enough to say, "here is a mortgage," and stop there?

It is said the jury have found no fraud. This is a mistake. They have, in the language of the cases, found certain facts and intents, and referred the question of law arising upon these to the court, and it is a proper question for the court to determine. "Fraud is a question of law, and especially when there is no dispute about the facts. It is the judgment of the law on facts and intents, as has been frequently observed by judges of the greatest eminence." 9 Johns., 342, per Kent, *Ch. J.* The jury find that a year and a half before the sale, a large variety of personal property, including the horse, was conveyed by a bill of sale to secure a debt, the whole continuing in possession of the debtor during all the time, from the date of the bill of sale to the time when the horse was taken in execution at the suit of the defendant below. These circumstances, standing alone, render the sale void as to creditors, within all the English cases. It lies with the vendee to explain them, and the court are to say whether the explanation be sufficient, as to sales conveying a present interest. Something more than mere convenience is necessary. *Benton* v. *Thornhill*, 7 Taunt., 149, cited for the defendant in error, is against him. That was a bill of sale for securing a debt, and yet it was left to the jury to say whether the vendee's possession was honest. The jury were not called upon to say whether the vendor's possession was evidence of fraud, but whether the vendee's possession being colorable, was *not, in truth, the vendor's possession; [***186** and if the latter, it was agreed that the sale must be adjudged fraudulent. The jury found possession in the vendee. The case was put upon the question of possession alone; and the jury were correctly told, that though the debt was honest, yet the sale was fraudulent unless possession passed; this, too, in the case of a mere mortgage or bill of sale, to secure a debt. So the jury here have not, as supposed, found against any fraudulent intent. They found possession continued, and for what purpose, expressly; but it is for the court to pronounce the conclusion of law, as was held in *Benton* v. *Thornhill*. *Maggot* v. *Mills*, Ld. Raym., 286, is relied on. In answer to this, I will barely refer to 1 Atk., 176, where it is said: "If the sale there had been to any other person than the landlord, it would have been fraudulent." Thus that case is considered as proceeding on a very narrow doctrine, which was equally applicable to *Barrow* v. *Paxton*. Indeed, in the latter case, the language of the court rather seems to put it upon the doctrine of landlord and tenant.

Curia, per SAVAGE, *Ch. J.* The facts in

this case are shortly these : In Sept., 1817, one Jesse Dryer rented of Hopkins a tavern stand and small farm, at an annual rent of $120 ; which, however, was subsequently reduced. A book account had commenced between them in Apr., preceding. Settlements were made at differeut times. At one of them, on Oct. 1, 1819, Dryer was found in arrear $274.84¼ ; and to provide for the payment and security of this sum, he executed a bill of sale of a variety of articles of personal property, including the mare now in controversy. It was agreed that the articles should be appraised by Jerome Curtiss ; and, upon payment being made, in the articles or otherwise, the surplus and remaining articles, if any, should be released. On the next day the articles were appraised by Curtiss at $237.75, and the appraisement indorsed on the bill of sale.

Jan. 1, 1821, another settlement took place, at which a balance of $146.61 was found due **187*]** from Dryer, *and another agreement was written on the same paper with the first, as follows: "1821, January 1. Settled the amount of the above to this time, and adjusted the balance at $146.61, for which so much of the above property as remains on hand is to remain liable. The mare above mentioned is to be delivered to Malcolm M'Naughton, on demand, but she is intended to remain in said Dryer's use for the present, and he is to pay into Elihu Scofield's hands, for said Hopkins, in good judgments or securities, or to said M'Naughton's hands, in grain, the amount of $50, within one month, and on continuing his payments in proportion, the mare is intended to remain with him." Dryer continued indebted to Hopkins, and at the time of the trial in the court below (May, 1821) was still indebted more than $100. A large portion of his debt was for rent. More than one year's rent was due at the time of the sale.

In the month of Nov., 1817, an account commenced between Dryer and Bissell, and in Mar., 1820, a considerable balance being due, a suit was commenced against Dryer, and a judgment recovered in Sept. for $91.58. Execution was issued Jan. 4, 1821, and delivered to the sheriff, who was directed by Bissell to levy on the mare while she was off the premises rented by Dryer of Hopkins. This was done while the mare was in Dryer's possession, and in Feb. she was sold at auction. Bissell became the purchaser. No rent was tendered or offered to be paid, and Bissell had notice of Hopkins' claim on the mare before the sale.

The object of leaving the mare with Dryer was to enable him to settle and close his business as constable, he having no other horse. Applications were make to him for the purchase of the mare, to which he always answered she was not his, and that Hopkins had a claim on her, or owned her. Hopkins' claim was publicly known. There was no secrecy about the transaction. When the bill of sale was executed, Dryer was indebted to both plaintiff and defendant, and to others, but no judgment or execution of consequence was obtained against him till after the assignment. The mare remained in Dryer's possession from **188*]** the date of *the first instrument, till seized by the sheriff Part of the articles had been delivered and credited on account.

The bill of sale of Oct. 1, 1819, was clearly a mortgage payable on demand, and I can see no grounds for the imputation of fraud in fact ; nor do I conceive the facts such as to constitute legal fraud. It is very distinguishable from *Twine's* case, 3 Rep., 80. The property was received at a fair valuation. The donor continued in possession ; but no person was deceived or defrauded. There was no secrecy—no concealment—no suit pending till several months afterwards.

I do not think it necessary to enter upon a minute review of the cases. Kent, *Ch. J.*, has examined many of them, in *Sturtevant* v. *Ballard*, 9 Johns., 338, and comes to the conclusion that a voluntary sale of chattels, with an agreement, either in or out of the deed, that the vendor may keep possession, is, except in special cases, and for special reasons, to be shown to and approved of by the court, fraudulent and void as against creditors. The learned judge, no doubt, intended to stay here, as in *Barrow* v. *Paxton*, 5 Johns., 261, that possession continuing in the vendor is only, *prima facie*, evidence of fraud, and may be explained. The question in every case is, whether the act done is a *bona fide* transaction, or whether it is a trick and contrivance to defeat creditors. *Cadogan* v. *Kennet*, Cowp., 435. The possession, by the vendor, of personal chattels after the sale, is not conclusive evidence of fraud. The vendee may, notwithstanding, upon proof that the sale was *bona fide*, and for a valuable consideration, and that the possession of the vendor, after such sale, was in pursuance of some agreement not inconsistent with honesty in the transaction, hold under his purchase, against creditors. These points were directly resolved in *Brooks* v. *Powers*, 15 Mass., 244. It appeared in that case, that one Witt, in the years 1816 and 1817, lived on a farm of the plaintiff, under distinct leases for each year, dated the 1st Apr. Apr. 14, 1817, a few days before the defendant's attachment issued, Witt gave the plaintiff a bill of sale of the oxen in controversy, and delivered them on the farm in payment of the rent of part of the preceding *year and **[*189** the whole of the ensuing year. The plaintiff then agreed that Witt should have the oxen to carry on the farm, and they remained in his possession when the defendant caused them to be seized under his attachment. The court held the sale valid, and expressed themselves generally as to the effect of the vendor's continuing in possession in the manner I have already stated. *Benton* v. *Thornhill*, 7 Taunt., 149, is a case somewhat similar.

The reason why the continuance of the vendor in possession will be accounted fraudulent is, that it gives him a false credit, by which third persons are deceived. That reason fails in this instance. When the bill of sale was executed, Dryer was known to be indebted to several persons, but whether he was reputed to be insolvent does not appear. His landlord had an undoubted right to secure himself for his rent. Dryer had a right to prefer one creditor, provided it were fairly and honestly done. In this case, the *bona fides* of the transaction is not questioned. A good reason is given, in my judgment, why the tenant was not at once stripped of his property, as thereby his power of acquiring the means to pay his debts would have been taken from him. No deception was practiced. The transaction was public. Dryer himself always, after the mortgage, stated the property of the mare to be in Hopkins. Bissell knew it before the sale, and probably before he prosecuted Dryer.

In my opinion the Common Pleas decided correctly, and their judgment should be affirmed.

Judgment affirmed.[1]

Cited in—8 Cow., 453; 2 Wend., 449, 600; 3 Wend., 349; 4 Wend., 518; 5 Wend., 275; 8 Wend., 391; 9 Wend., 200; 16 Wend., 527; 20 Wend., 519, 548; 24 Wend., 136; 4 Hill, 290; 2 Edw., 320; 15 N. Y., 120; 44 N. Y., 248; 19 Hun, 173; 3 T. & C., 414; 20 How. Pr., 71; 1 Pet., 449; 4 Mason, 535; Olcott, 202; 2 Wood & M., 117, 387; 37 Am. Dee., 142 (3 Met., 332); 28 Am. Dec., 40 (4 Blackf., 26); 46 Am. Dec., 374; 29 Cal., 477; 37 Am. Dec., 142 (3 Met., 332); 28 Am. Dee., 40 (4 Blackf., 26); 46 Am. Dec., 374 (2 Ga., 1); 24 Am. Dec., 589 (3 Yerg., 475); 20 Am. Dee., 637; 37 Am. Dec., 91 (2 Met., 258).

1.—Perhaps nothing farther, upon the much litigated question, how far possession by the vendor, after a sale of goods, shall be evidence of fraud as to creditors, ever can be reached by way of legal rule, than what is advanced by the court in this case, to wit: that such possession is, *prima facie*, evidence of fraud, but may be explained. *Vide* Dickenson v. Cook, 17 Johns., 332. It seems to be a mere rule of evidence calculated to shift the *onus probandi* from the creditor to the vendee. The details or circumstances which shall constitute fraud, like those of usury, or the degree of neglect which shall render a man liable in an action on the case, seem to mock the efforts of a general rule, and **190***] must be ranged forever without the *line which divides the province of the court from that of the jury. The law may declare that fraud shall vitiate the sale; but as the devices by which that fraud is to be compassed and disguised may be various, so the evidence by which it is to be established or repelled must frequently vary with the cases as they arise.

Some judges have started, with a high-toned rule, that unless a change of possession follows immediately, it is not only evidence of fraud, but, *per se*, makes the sale fraudulent and void. Edwards v. Harben, 2 T. R., 596-7, per Buller, *J.*; Hamilton v. Russell, 1 Cr., 317, 318, per Marshall, *Ch. J.*; Dawes v. Cope, 4 Binn., per Tilghman, *Ch. J.* But these learned judges were embarrassed with numerous exceptions in the outset; and when the late *Ch. J.* Kent made an effort, in Sturtevant v. Ballard, 9 Johns., 337, to introduce the same rule, as far as possible, into the jurisprudence of this State, he found it incumbered with the following exceptions, which he enumerates: 1. Where a creditor is knowing and assenting to the sale. Steel v. Brown, 1 Taunt., 381. 2. Where the sale is conditional (per Coke, *J.*, in Stone v. Grubham, 2 Bulst., 225: and per Buller, *J.*, in Edwards v. Harben, 2 T. R., 596), *i. e.*, in the last case, a condition precedent to be performed by the vendee. 3. Where the goods remain with the vendor, to be sold for the benefit of the vendee, the vendor being a borrower on bottomry (*i. e.*, a mortgagor), the trust being declared by the deed. Bucknal v. Royston, Prec. in Ch., 285. 4. Where A purchases the goods on a *fi. fa.* in in favor of B, and leaves them with the judgment debtor, to the intent that he pay for and redeem them. Cole v. Davies, 1 Ld. Raym., 724. 5. Where the goods purchased in this manner are left, from benevolence, or for a temporary and honest purpose. Kidd v. Rawlinson, 2 Bos. & P., 59. 6. Where money is lent to buy furniture, and a bill of sale honestly taken to secure the repayment of the money. 7. Where the purchase was a fair one, at public sale, and the goods are left with a relation or friend. Per Shippen, *Ch. J.*, in Waters v. M'Clellan, 4 Dall., 208. 8. Where the vendor is an intended husband, and sells to trustees to make a marriage settlement upon his future wife. Haselinton v. Gill, 3 T. R., 620, in notes; Cadogan v. Kennet, Cowp., 432. And he concludes that, except in special cases, and for special reasons, to be shown to and approved of by the court, continuance of possession is fraudulent.

To these may be added, from our own reports, 9 Barrow v. Paxton, 5 Johns., 258, where stress was laid almost exclusively on the circumstance that the bill of sale was a mortgage. U. S. v. Hooe, 3 Cr., 88, 89, per Marshall, *Ch. J.*, S. P. 10. Where the non-delivery arises from the sickness of the vendor's depositary. Beals v. Guernsey, 8 Johns., 451. To these exceptions may be added: 11. Where the assignment is of a cargo in a ship lying at the port where the assignment is executed, but bound to a foreign port, the assignment providing that remittances shall be made to liquidate the debt due to the vendee, in consideration of which debt the assignment is made, &c. Dawes v. Cope, 4 Binn., 258. 12. Where the conveyance was late on Saturday night, and the possession remained unchanged till Monday. Wilt v. Franklin, 1 Binn., 517. 13. The Supreme Court, in M'Instry v. Tanner, 9 Johns., 135, seem to question the right of the creditor in an *execution, to purchase goods under his exe- [***191** cution and leave them with his debtor, but in England even this distinction is done away by the case of Watkins v. Birch, 4 Taunt., 822.

See Reed v. Blades, 5 Taunt., 216, S. P., per Gibbs, *J.*; Guthrie v. Wood, 1 Stark. *N. P.*, 367.

*15. A ship abroad may, of course, be sold, [***192** and possession retained by the vendor till her return. Putnam v. Dutch, 8 Mass., 287.

16. A *bona fide* sale of bricks in a brickyard, accompanied with a lease of the yard to the vendee, until the bricks should be sold and removed, was held valid against the creditors of the vendor, without actual removal. Allen v. Smith, 10 Mass., 308. See Benton v. Thornhill, 7 Taunt., 149.

*The case of Dewey v. Baynton, 6 East, 257, [***194** presents another exception, viz.: that a wife may, after marriage, buy her husband's personal property in exchange for her separate estate, and leave it in his possession as before; and yet this shall not be deemed fraudulent as to creditors, provided it be proved fair in all other respects.

*A motion was afterwards made in Dewey [***195** v. Baynton, for a new trial, which was granted; the cause tried a second time, when a verdict was again obtained for the plaintiff, upon which a motion was again made for a new trial upon the circumstances as above detailed from the report of the case in 6 East, 257; but in the meantime, the question was again up before the *Ld. Chancellor* in Lady Arundell v. Phipps, 10 Ves., 146, 7, &c., and his opinion shows the great variety of considerations which may enter into a question of fraud.

*19. The modern English decisions seem to [***198** maintain a determined conflict with the strong rule in Edwards v. Harben, 2 T. R., 596. See Steward v. Lombe, 1 Brod. & Bingh., 506; Kidd v. Rawlinson, 2 Bos. & P., 59.

*In Steel v. Brown, 1 Taunt., 381, Law- [***200** rence, *J.*, said: "Edwards v. Harben is good law, though not applicable here."

20. Exceptions to Edwards v. Harden are multiplying in this country. In Bartlett v. Williams, 1 Pick., 288, A gave a bill of sale of a vessel to B., and B promised in writing to reconvey upon the payment of a promissory note due from A. B, however, did not take possession until 8 months after the delivery of the bill of sale. Held, nevertheless, that B's title was good against an attachment made by a creditor of A. after such possession taken. Putnam, *J.*, who delivered the opinion of the court, recognizes Edwards v. Harben as sound law; "but there," he says, "the vendee did not obtain possession under the bill of sale, before the right of the creditors of the vendor accrued;" and he relies for the distinction upon Robinson v. Donnell, 2 B. & A., 134. See, also, Bedlam v. Tucker, 1 Pick., 389.

*A mortgage of goods, as to the possession [***202** continuing in the mortgagor, has been considered by several of the State Legislatures, on the same footing with a mortgage of lands; and provision by statute accordingly made for recording the mortgage in both cases. Such was the law of Virginia, as appears by Clayborn v. Hill, 1 Wash., 177. There it is valid, if recorded; otherwise not, where the possession continues with the mortgagor. **Id.* [***203** But in relation the absolute unconditional sales, the doctrine in Edwards v. Harben, and Hamilton v. Russell, is maintained in its highest tone, *i. e.*, that retaining possession is, *per se*, fraudulent in law, not merely evidence of fraud. Fitzburgh v. Anderson, 2 Hen. & Munf., 302, 3, per Roane, *J.*; Alexander v. Denealo, 2 Munf., 341; Williams v. Farley, Gilmer's Va., 15. On the other hand, where a statute provides that bills of sale shall be registered, the mere circumstance of recording will not be conclusive evidence of good faith; but the sale may be impeached for fraud notwithstanding. Such is the law of Md., where, it seems, the Statute requires even an absolute bill of sale to be recorded; yet the vendor's continuing in possession, is evidence of fraud. Garrett v. Hughlett, 1 Harr. & J., 3. In N. C., where, it seems, the same statute regulation prevails (Hodges v. Haywood, 414, 415, per *Cur.*), the authority of Edwards v. Harben, is denied and possession declared *prima facie* evidence of fraud merely (*Id.*, Vick v. Kegs, 2 Haywood, 126; Falkner v. Perkins, *Id.*, 224); while that case has been adopted in its greatest extent by the judges of Tennessee. Raygrau v. Kennedy, 1 Tenn., 97. So in S. C., Kennedy v. Ross, 2 Rep. Const. Court, S. C., 125. See, also, Vredenburgh v. White, 1 Johns. Cas., 156; Butts v. Swartwood, 2 Cow., 431; Brooks v. Powers, 15 Mass., 244.

206*] *ADKINS

v.

BREWER AND HARVEY.

Issue of Attachment, without Proper Proof—Goods of Defendant Sold—Justice and Plaintiff, Liable for Trespass.

To give a justice jurisdiction of a cause upon attachment, proof must be made that the defendant is concealed, or has departed, &c. And if the attachment issue without such proof, and be executed, the whole proceeding being void, the justice and the plaintiff are trespassers.

So, *come semble*, if security by bond be not given, or mere blank bonds executed by the surety.

In trespass against a justice for issuing attachments and executions, &c., which were void, it appeared that the constable, who levied and sold under these, had several other executions, older than the void ones, upon which he levied and sold at the same time, and the sale was under all the executions indiscriminately; but the void executions, as well as the others, were satisfied by the sale, and the money paid to the plaintiff; held, that trespass lay against the justice and party.

When the justice wants jurisdiction, he is liable as a trespasser; otherwise, where he has jurisdiction, and errs in the exercise of it.

In trespass against an officer, for issuing process, by virtue of which the plaintiff's goods are taken, to justify the taking, the officer must show affirmatively, on his part, that he had jurisdiction; especially where, from the plaintiff's proof, there is reason to presume that the proper steps were not taken to confer jurisdiction.

Citations—10 Johns., 169; 11 Johns., 175; 17 Johns., 146; 2 Johns. Cas., 27; 14 Johns., 246; 19 Johns., 39.

ON error from the Otsego C. P. The action in the court below was trespass by Adkins against Brewer and Harvey, for taking and carrying away, and converting the goods and chattels of Adkins. Plea, not guilty. The cause came on to be tried in Feb. Term, 1822, when the plaintiff called one White as a witness, who testified that he went, at the request of Harvey, to the office of Brewer, who was a justice of the peace, in order to become bail for Harvey, to procure certain attachments against Adkins, which Harvey contemplated taking out; that the witness, in conjunction with Harvey, signed, sealed and delivered printed blank bonds for that purpose; that one of them was either partially or totally filled up before its execution; that three others were signed, sealed and executed in blank (these were then produced, and appeared still to be blanks); that the witness was in a hurry, as well as Harvey; that the witness delivered the bonds to Brewer, the justice, with directions to fill them up; *that Brewer was [*207 then filling up an attachment. The counsel for the defendant, on notice, produced but one attachment. The counsel for the plaintiff then gave in evidence three several executions, issued upon three several judgments, by Brewer against Adkins, in favor of Harvey, and also proved that the property in question was sold by one Holden, a constable, by virtue of an execution in favor of one Aaron Bigelow, and seven executions in favor of Selah Havens, all older than Harvey's, as well as by virtue of the several executions issued by Brewer; that about $102 of the money raised by the sale was paid to Harvey, upon his executions, which were issued on judgments rendered upon attachments where no bonds had been filled up, or executed, otherwise than as above stated.

The counsel for the defendant thereupon moved for a nonsuit, which was opposed, on the ground that there was no evidence of any proof of the absence or concealment of the plaintiff having been taken at the time the attachments issued; and that no bonds were taken pursuant to the 23d section of the Twenty-five Dollar Act; that the defendants were, therefore, trespassers; but the motion was granted by the court below, on the ground that the judgments were voidable only; and that inasmuch as it appeared that the constable's sale was made on a variety of other executions, as well as Harvey's, without discrimination, trespass would not lie. To this opinion the plaintiff excepted.

Mr. S. M. Hopkins, for the plaintiff in error, cited 1 R. L., 398, sec. 23; *Vosburgh* v. *Welch*, 11 Johns., 175; *Curry* v. *Pringle*, *Id.*, 444; *Percival* v. *Jones*, 2 Johns. Cas., 49; *Case* v. *Shepherd*, *Id.*, 27; *Bigelow* v. *Stearns*, 19 Johns., 39; *Collins* v. *Ferris*, 14 Johns., 246; *Cable* v. *Cooper*, 15 Johns., 152; 1 Phil. Ev., 150.

Mr. I. Seelye, contra, to show that the law would presume the proper proof to have been taken before the attachments issued, cited *Van Dyck* v. *Van Buren*, 1 Cai., 84; *England* v. *Slade*, 4 T. R., 682; *Jackson* v. *Woolsey*, 11 Johns., 456; per Yates, *J.*; *Gray* v. *Gardner*, 3 Mass., 399; *Coleman* v. *Anderson*, 10 *Id.*, 105; 1 Phil. Ev., 150, 151, 2d *Am. [*208 from 3d Lond. ed.; *The King* v. *Hawkins*, 11 East, 216, per Ld. Ellenborough, *Ch. J.*; *Powell* v. *Milbanke*, 3 Wils., 362, 366; 2 Bl., 852, S. C.; *Williams* v. *The E. I. Co.*, 3 East, 192; *Monk* v. *Butler*, 1 Rol., 83; *Dr. Harscot's* case, Comb, 202; Bull. *N. P.*, 298; *Evans* v. *Birch*, 3 Camph., 10, 12; Peak. Ev., 5; *Hartwell* v. *Root*, 19 Johns., 345.

He said that all the executions, except three, were admitted to be regular; and the sale being upon them all, indiscriminately, trespass would not lie. The action should have been case. The proceeding is like taking an excessive distress for which trespass will not lie. A party having two authorities may justify under one, though the other be void. *Crother* v. *Ramsbottom*, 7 T. R., 654, per Lawrence, *J.*; *Greenville* v. *Coll. of Physicians*, 12 Mod., 386, per Holt, *Ch. J.* And as to the remedy by

---

NOTE.—*Personal liability of judicial officers—Of other officers—When process protection to an officer.* See Yates v. Lansing, 9 Johns., 395; Wallsworth v. McCullough, 10 Johns., 93; Warner v. Shed, 10 Johns., 138; Henderson v. Brown, 1 Cai., 92, *notes*.

trespass, he cited *Hutchins* v. *Chambers*, 1 Burr., 579; *Lynne* v. *Moody*, 2 Str., 851.

Though there were no bonds, this was error merely; and the attachments, therefore, not void for this reason, but voidable only. *Butler* v. *Potter*, 17 Johns., 145; *Prig* v. *Adams*, 2 Salk., 674.

Though the attachment had been on the oath of the party, it would have been error merely. *Van Steenbergh* v. *Kortz*, 10 Johns., 167. So, if without oath.

Curia, per SAVAGE, *Ch. J.* The defendants are called on directly, not collaterally, to show why they have undertaken to dispose of the plaintiffs property. They must then show a lawful authority. A power to act is the first thing to be shown by a court of limited special jurisdiction. To give the justice jurisdiction, it must appear that the person against whose property an attachment is sought, is either concealed within the county, with the intent mentioned in the Act, or has departed, or is about to depart the country, with the like intent.

In *Van Steenbergh* v. *Kortz*, 10 Johns., 169, the court seem to consider the proof of this necessary to confer jurisdiction; and Spencer, *J.*, takes the distinction between proof before **209***] *a court which is to give it jurisdiction, and before a court that already has jurisdiction.

In *Vosburgh* v. *Welch*, 11 Johns., 175, the court says the justice must be considered as having issued the attachment without any proof whatever of the departure or concealment required by the act; and, of course, without authority. The rule as to the justice's liability, is, that when he has no jurisdiction whatever, and undertakes to act, his acts are *coram non judice*, and void—equally so if he was not a justice. If he has jurisdiction, but errs in exercising it, then his acts are not void, but voidably only. In the former case he is personally liable—in the latter not. 17 Johns., 146; 2 Johns. Cas., 27; 14 Johns., 246; 19 Johns., 39.

I do not consider this case as coming within the rule that an officer is presumed to have done an act, the omission of which would render him liable for negligence. There is presumptive proof, at least, that no evidence was taken by the justice, and positive proof, that no security was taken, except in one cause out of four. The sale by the constable, after the other executions were satisfied, could not be justified, except upon the authority of these executions; and as they were void, there was no authority whatever: all persons concerned were trespassers.

The judgment of the court below must be reversed.

Judgment reversed.

Cited in—8 Cow., 187; 3 Wend., 248; 4 Wend., 441. 7 Wend., 203; 8 Wend., 466; 10 Wend., 199; 13 Wend., 48; 16 Wend., 44, 365; 4 N. Y., 256, 383; 55 N. Y., 4; 3 Lans., 48; 3 Barb., 188; 4 Barb., 16; 6 Barb., 610, 623; 14 Barb., 98; 62 Barb., 442; 3 How. Pr., 349; 4 How. Pr., 430; 6 How. Pr., 74; 1 Co. R. N. S., 269; Abb. Ad., 467; 37 Wis., 545; 47 Am. Dec. 60 (2 Doug., 433).

*WHITNEY v. THE AMERICAN INSURANCE COMPANY. [*210

Marine Insurance—When Valuation Conclusive—Insurance on Goods and Return of those Goods "Out and Home."

The contract in a valued policy is to pay the assured the whole valuation, if the subject of the policy be lost; and the valuation in the policy is conclusive as to the amount of recovery, if the subject be lost by the perils insured against, unless there be fraud or imposition in fixing the value.

Where the insurance was of goods, valued at $14,000, on board a ship, and the returns of those goods on a voyage out and home; and the goods in the course of the voyage round were delivered to L. upon his advance of $7,000, and his receipt, promising to answer drafts of the assured to $3,000 more; the goods to be sold by L. for his reimbursement and the proceeds remitted to the assured; and the $7,000 were vested in a return cargo, together with $1,621, for which he drew on L., making in the whole an investment to $8,469.85; and L. paid the draft as he had agreed; and the return cargo was lost by the perils insured against; and the outward cargo, on actual sale, did not bring enough to reimburse L. by $4,680.26, for which he drew on the assured; held, that the assured was entitled to recover, as for a total loss, the $14,000, and interest.

But it would be otherwise, if part only of the value of the goods had been invested in the return cargo.

Citations—2 Burr., 1172; Phil. Ins., 307; 3 Taunt., 506; 6 Cr., 220, 221; 3 Cai., 20; 3 T. R., 362; 8 Johns., 234; 2 East, 109; 2 Campb., 69; 13 East, 323; 12 Mass., 76.

ASSUMPSIT on a policy of insurance, tried Apr. 13, 1822, at the N. Y. sittings, before *Mr. Justice* Woodworth; when a verdict was taken, by consent, for the plaintiff for $20,000, subject to the opinion of the court, and to adjustment, upon the following case, with liberty to either party to turn it into a special verdict or bill of exceptions.

The policy was dated July 7, 1818, and was effected by the plaintiff in his own name, and upon his own account, and underwritten by the defendants, upon all kinds of lawful goods and merchandises, laden or to be laden on board the ship America, Vibberts, master, on a voyage at and from N. Y. to Bourbon, with liberty to use the Isle of France, and two ports in Java, and back to a port of discharge in the U. S., and with liberty to use either port first, being upon 137 whole, and 48 half pipes of wine out, and return home, valued at $14,000, being the sum insured, at a premium of 6 *per cent.* to return one half *per cent.* for each port not used, and the risk ending safely. By a memorandum indorsed on the policy, signed by the defendants, and dated July 21, in the same year, in consideration of an additional premium of one *per cent.* permission was given by the defendants to use Calcutta, without prejudice to the policy, the one *per cent.* to be returned, if the permission should not be used.

The policy, in all other respects, was in the usual printed *form of policies com- [*211

NOTE.—*Insurance—Valuation in policy—How far conclusive.* See Davy v. Hallett, 3 Cai., 16; Kenny v. Clarkson, 1 Johns., 385; Minturn v. Columbian Ins. Co., 10 Johns., 75; Harris v. Eagle Fire Ins. Co., 5 Johns., 368, *notes.*

mouly used in the City of N. Y., and either party had permission to refer to it upon the argument.

July 3, in the same year, the plaintiff shipped, and laded on board The America, in the port of N. Y., for his own account, the wine specified in the policy, the invoice cost of which was $14,028.87, and took from Capt. Vibberts a bill of lading under that date, for the wine thus shipped, deliverable at the Isle of France to Elmslie Garrigues and William A. Field or their assigns, as the consignees, who went out in the The America as supercargoes upon the voyage insured.

The ship sailed from the port of N. Y. with the wine on board upon the voyage insured, on or about July 7 in the same year, and arrived in safety at Bourbon on or about Oct. 21, following, where she remained a short time, and proceeded thence to Batavia, being a port in Java, at which latter place she arrived in safety, having the insured wine still on board, on or about Dec. 25 in the same year.

At Batavia the supercargoes, owing to the depressed state of the market at that time, being unable to dispose of the wine there, unless at a very great sacrifice, made an arrangement with Abraham E. Loesman, of that place, by which he was to receive the wine for sale, and make an advance upon it of $7,000, and permit the supercargoes to draw upon him from Calcutta to any amount not exceeding $3,000 more, the whole of which was supposed to be less than what the proceeds of the wine would be, he holding the wine for his reimbursement, and accounting to the plaintiff for the proceeds when sold. The wine was, pursuant to this arrangement, landed at Batavia, and by the consignees and supercargoes delivered to Loesman, who thereupon gave them a receipt in the following words: "Batavia, January 15, 1819. Received from Elmslie Garrigues and William A. Field, supercargoes of the ship America, of New York, one hundred and thirty-six pipes, and forty-seven half pipes of Catalonia wine, to be sold by me for account of Mr. Stephen Whitney, merchant, New York, and proceeds to be remitted to him. (Triplicate.) A. E. Loesman."

212*] *Loesman accordingly advanced in Batavia, and upon the receipt of the wine, 6,930 Spanish dollars and 69 cents to the supercargoes, for the use and benefit of the plaintiff, which sum, allowing one *per cent.* premium for Spanish dollars, made the sum of $7,000. The supercargoes thereupon gave Loesman a receipt for the advance in these words: "Batavia, January 18, 1819. Received of Mr. A. E. Loesman six thousand nine hundred and thirty Spanish dollars, and sixty-nine cents, which with one *per cent* for Spanish dollars, will make seven thousand dollars.

$6,930 69
69 31

$7,000 00

ELMSLIE GARRIGUES, for self and WM. A. FIELD."

The supercargoes, on the same day, shipped and laded the dollars on board The America, in Batavia, and took a bill of lading therefor, signed by Capt. Vibberts, deliverable to themselves at Calcutta. The ship, with the dollars on board, sailed from Batavia on or about Feb. 1, 1819, and proceeded direct for Calcutta, at which latter place she arrived in safety with the specie, on or about Mar. 28 following.

While The America lay at Calcutta, the supercargoes received the specie from Capt. Vibberts, and with it, and the amount for which they drew on Loesman, purchased there goods for the account of the plaintiff, the invoice cost of which was $8,469.85; for the difference between which and the advance made by Loesman, they drew on him to the amount of $1,621, pursuant to the arrangement between them, and he paid that sum accordingly.

The goods so purchased in Calcutta were there, by the supercargoes, shipped and laded on board The America, for which they took Capt. Vibbert's bill of lading, dated in Calcutta June 20, 1819, deliverable to the plaintiff, or his assigns, in Philadelphia, that being understood and intended as the ship's port of discharge in the U. S., upon her return. The America, with a valuable cargo, including these goods, left Calcutta on or about July 1, *following, for Philadelphia; and was [***213** afterwards, on or about Dec. 19 following, and before the termination and in the due prosecution of the voyage, cast away and totally lost near Sandy Hook by means of the perils insured against.

Loesman subsequently sold the wines deposited with him, which, after debiting the plaintiff with the $7,000 advanced, and the $1,621 drawn for by the supercargoes, and crediting the plaintiff with the net proceeds of the wine, left a balance due from the plaintiff to Loesman of $4,680.26, for which amount he drew upon the plaintiff.

Mr. G. Griffin, for the plaintiff, took two grounds: 1. That the policy being a valued one, and on the voyage round, the valuation is to regulate the amount of the recovery. 2. It makes no difference that the return cargo was purchased with moneys advanced in anticipation of the sales of the outward cargo, as the whole of its proceeds, and even a greater amount, were, in fact, invested in the return cargo.

1. Insurances, he said, are of two kinds, open and valued. In the latter, the valuation always controls unless there be fraud; *Lewis* v. *Rucker*, 2 Burr., 1171; *Feise* v. *Aguilar*, 3 Taunt., 506; *Miner* v. *Tagert*, 3 Binn., 204; *Hodgson* v. *Mar. Ins. Co.*, 5 Cr., 110, 111, per Cushing, *J.*; *Mar. Ins. Co.* v. *Hodgson*, 6 Cr., 206; *Davy* v. *Hallett*, 3 Cai., 16; *Kane* v. *Com. Ins. Co.*, 8 Johns., 229; and the fraud must be gross and palpable, like the case put by Ld. Mansfield in *Lewis* v. *Rucker*; an insurance of £2,000, when the insured had no interest beyond a cable. In *Mar. Ins. Co. of Alexandria* v. *Hodgson*, the difference in value was $2,000; that is, the valuation at $10,000, and the real value at $8,000; yet this striking difference was not admitted in evidence, because there was no fraud. Here goods were shipped beyond the value in the policy. A valued policy upon goods will not be opened where there is no fraud, except in the single instance of leaving part of the goods on shore, upon the same principle that a valued policy

214*] *upon freight was opened in *Forbes* v. *Aspinall*, 13 East, 323.

2. The return cargo was the returns of the wines within the language of the policy, and indeed upon the most rigid technical construction of the term. It makes no difference whether the wines were hypothecated or sold, to procure the return cargo. It was not only the same in its legal, but in its actual effect; for the wines were finally sold to pay the money actually invested in the proceeds. *Haven* v. *Gray*, 12 Mass., 71, is a case precisely in point for the plaintiff, except in a single particular that the word "proceeds" is used there instead of "returns" as here.

Nor let it be said that this is a hard case. There must be some fixed and uniform rule applicable to both parties. Suppose the case had been the other way, the goods lost far above the value insured, would the court open the policy for the benefit of the assured? This never would be thought of. *Shawe* v. *Felton*, 2 East, 109, shows the inflexibility of the rule. The assurers were holden to the value, though the property was deteriorated before the loss, by the act of the assured himself. I appeal particularly to the strong language of Ld. Kenyon in that case, pp. 114, 115.

Messrs. J. Duer and *D. B. Ogden*, for the defendants, made the following points: 1. That the policy never attached upon the goods lost, they not being the returns of the outward cargo. 2. If the defendants are liable, it is only for a partial loss. 3. If the policy be construed to attach upon the goods lost, although not the returns of the outward cargo, the loss should be adjusted as upon an open policy.

They said the plaintiff claims $14,000, when, by his own showing, he has lost but about $8,000. The general presumption of law is, that an insurance is for the mere purpose of indemnity; and where a party sets up an agreement controlling the general intendment of law, he must, as in all cases of a special agreement, bring himself precisely within its terms. What did the parties understand by wines out, and returns home? It is said the latter words mean any returns. This we deny.
215*] It must be returns of *the wines. To constitute this, the wines should be exchanged for, or sold and invested in the return cargo. If anything else had been meant, would not the parties have said so in their contract? The plaintiff understood the sense of the clause as we do, at the trial; and the struggle was to show the return cargo purchased on the credit of the outward cargo.

The parties also intended that, to make the policy attach on the return cargo, there should be a total shipment of the whole proceeds—not a partial one. The contrary course would give rise to frauds innumerable. One fourth in value may be reshipped—lost; and the whole original value recovered; and by and by the residue sold in a foreign country. The underwriters have nothing to do with the market. It was Whitney's duty to sell the wine and invest it in a return cargo, for which alone the defendants were liable. An advance of $10,000 might have been had, for it was offered; but only $8,000 were received. The truth is, the whole was no more than a loan by Whitney, and an after purchase entirely distinct from, and independent of the avails of the outward cargo. The wine was pledged merely as a collateral security; and the receipt concludes with a promise to remit the proceeds. When? Why, when sold; and yet it is now contended that, even before the wines were sold, their proceeds had been shipped and were on their return voyage. The supercargoes then gave a receipt for the money, without saying on what account, and whether on the credit of Whitney or the wines. Loesman has since drawn upon Whitney for the balance over and above the avails. Whitney's personal credit was evidently pledged. Then the money was not the proceeds of the wine, but of Whitney's credit. The rights of the parties are to be tested by the state of things at the time the cargo was shipped—not by anything which transpired afterwards.

It never should be the interest of the assured that a loss should happen. In *Forbes* v. *Aspinall*, cited for the plaintiff, a case of valued policy on freight, exactly analogous in principle, the reasoning of Ld. Ellenborough, *Ch.* *J., meets the present case precisely. [*216
"And so (says he), if, by the perils insured against, the freight of part only of the goods to be carried be lost, the assured can only recover in respect to that loss, according to the proportion which that part bears to the whole sum at which the entire freight was estimated in the valuation. If, for instance, the insurance be generally upon goods, and the goods intended to be protected be 500 hogsheads of sugar, and a valuation be made accordingly, but the ship, by accident, takes on board 100 only and sails, and is afterwards lost, by one of the perils insured against, with those 100 on board—can it be contended that the assured shall recover to the full amount of the valuation; that is, for the whole 500, when he has lost only 100? So in the case of freight; if the ship would carry 500 tons, and in fixing the valuation the assured calculate his freight upon 500 tons, but when he reaches the loading port he can get 10 tons only upon freight, and sails upon the voyage insured with those 10 tons only; is it to be allowed that if the ship be lost by any of the perils insured against, and he thereby lose freight upon 10 tons, he shall be entitled to the valuation, which includes the freight upon 500 tons? And yet to this extent the plaintiff's argument in this case is carried. The proposition is monstrous. Instead of confining the policy, as it ought to be confined, to a contract, as nearly as may be, of indemnity against what may be lost in respect of freight by the perils insured against, it converts it into a contract of indemnity against a different class of accidents, which may operate to prevent the assured from being able to procure a full cargo upon freight, and may make it the interest of the assured, which it never ought to be, that a loss should happen." So here, the plaintiff asks the court to convert this contract into the risk of a market in India, or the circumstance which prevented his getting the full proceeds on board as a return cargo.

Rather than admit this consequence, the court will divide the policy, making it a valued one on the outward, but an open one on the return cargo. If the construction contended for by the plaintiff be correct, we 217*] should be liable to *the extent of the valuation, though the return cargo should contain but a single bale of goods. Of the value of the outward cargo the parties always have the means of judging. In this case all the articles were enumerated. The parties presumed they would continue at the value fixed, throughout the voyage. As to this, they ran a mutual risk. After the avails of the outward are once fairly invested in a return cargo which is shipped, the policy is not to be opened merely because the latter may be worth less than the former. It was upon this principle that *Havens* v. *Gray*, cited for the plaintiff, was decided. Phil. on Ins., 311. We admit that *Havens* v. *Gray* appears to be against us as to the return cargo being really the proceeds of the outward; yet, however respectable the court by whom the case was decided, it is not binding upon this tribunal. This court will not yield to it as an authority, but only so far as the arguments by which it is supported shall be found convincing.

Mr. J. O. Hoffman, in reply. It is very easy to cite and establish the general principle that insurance is for idemnity merely; but to what extent is the saying applicable? This must depend on the nature of the contract; and, accordingly, the rule never extends to a valued policy. The valuation is for the very purpose of avoiding the question of indemnity according to the value. In an open policy the two items of proof are the loss and the value. Upon a valued policy you stop at the first, for the agreed valuation is the measure of damages. In this valuation it is right to include certain charges which would not be reached by an open policy, and you may anticipate port charges, extraordinary duties, commissions, and even freight. The whole may be covered by the valuation. Hence the principle that nothing shall avoid the valuation short of fraud. Phil. on Ins., 306. Even gaming policies are allowable in this State, for the Statute 19 Geo. II. has not been enacted here. All the laws on this question will be found collected in Philips on Ins., 307.

I admit, as a general principle, that the 218*] underwriter is *not to be affected by the fall of the market. But I deny that the rule extends to a valued policy. Here, even the market may be insured.

I admit that the valuation was on the outward cargo, and I agree that if only part of the returns were on board at the time of the loss, the plaintiff is entitled to no more than a *pro rata* allowance. But the entire proceeds were on board. I am at a loss to discover how, when the advance is on the credit of the fund, you can distinguish it from the proceeds of the fund. There can be no doubt that the credit of the wines was employed. They were deposited as security. If the advance had been on Whitney's personal credit solely, I agree that it could not be considered the returns or proceeds of the wines. But the outward cargo was applied in payment. Loesman received it for sale, made an advance of $7,000, and authorized a draft for the whole; and a partial draft was answered, conformably to the arrangement. So says the case in terms. It might as well be said that money is advanced on the personal credit of a mortgagor, or by a factor who holds the goods of his principal, or by a consignee of goods under the usual agreement to answer drafts for two thirds of the value. Were we bound to take the market as we found it, and make an absolute sale at a sacrifice, or lie by and wait for a market till the vessel rotted? No. The object was a speedy sale and investment, if to be had. According to gentlemen, we could even recover back the premium, because no risk on the return cargo ever commenced. The ground taken certainly leads to this extravagant consequence. No. The object of all was that a home investment should be as large as possible. Had we sold for a trifling sum, the defense would have been fraud in the sale.

But the question is with us upon authority. *Havens* v. *Gray* has been questioned, and to this has been opposed the authority of Ld. Ellenborough in *Forbes* v. *Aspinall*. If there be any difference in the two cases, *Havens* v. *Gray* is as binding here as *Forbes* v. *Aspinall*. The former was decided at *nisi prius* by that great master of commercial law, the late *Ch. J.*, Parsons; and his decision was sanctioned *by the learned judges of the Supreme [*219 Court of Mass., after full deliberation, in the time of his successor, *Ch. J.* Parker. And the opinion will be found fully sustained by the reasons assigned for it.

Curia, per SAVAGE, *Ch. J.* The contract in this valued policy is, "that the goods shall come safe to the port of delivery; or, if they do not, to indemnify the plaintiff to the amount of the prime cost or value of the policy." 2 Burr., 1172, per Ld. Mansfield. The valuation is admitted in the policy; it is the amount to be recovered if the property insured is lost by the perils insured against. Phil. on Ins., 307; 3 Taunt., 506; 6 Cr., 220–1; 3 Cai., 20; 3 T. R., 362. And this value is conclusive upon the underwriters, when there is no suggestion of fraud or imposition. *Id.*; 8 Johns., 234; 2 East, 109; 2 Camph., 69. There is no question, in this case, that the whole quantity of wine insured was on board during the outward voyage; and an amount beyond its avails was invested in the return cargo. The exception, therefore, established by *Forbes* v. *Aspinall*, 13 East, 323, where part, only, of the goods insured are on board at the time of the loss, does not apply.

Had the wines themselves been lost on the outward voyage, there could be no doubt as to the amount of the recovery; but the loss was of the return cargo. The insurance being upon the wine out, and returns home, valued at $14,000, the remaining question and the principal one made at the bar is, whether the goods lost were the returns of the wine. Had the wine been sold for $7,000 and the return cargo purchased with the avails, there is no doubt the defendants would have been liable under the authorities cited for the whole $14,000. Now, whether the money was paid by Loesman on a sale of the wines, or advanced on a pledge of them, makes no sort of difference to the defendants; though it would be otherwise if the advance had been less than the value of the wine—one half, for instance. In such a case, if the plaintiff were permitted to recover to the extent of the valuation, he would compel the defendants to pay for the whole of his wine and yet have the one half safe at Batavia. **220***] It should appear, therefore, that *the whole proceeds of the wine were invested in the goods lost. The policy then attaches for the whole, though it may be more than a mere indemnity. *Havens* v. *Gray*, 12 Mass., 76.

Although when the $7,000 were advanced, the wine was supposed to be worth more than $10,000, yet the actual sales were subsequently made for less than $4,000. The whole proceeds, therefore, or returns of the wine, and more, were invested in the goods lost. I cannot consider the $8,621 advanced by Loesman as loaned upon the plaintiff's personal credit. Loesman advanced the money upon the deposit of the wine, and that was all the security he took —no doubt supposing it amply sufficient to indemnify him and something beyond, as we find provision made in the receipt for a remittance of the balance. Subsequent events have shown, however, that the advance exceeded the whole proceeds.

I am, therefore, of opinion that the plaintiff is entitled to recover the $14,000 and interest.

Judgment accordingly.

Affirmed—5 Cow., 712.
Cited in—8 Wend., 167; 1 Hall, 172; 38 Super, 304.

JACKSON, ex dem. BLANCHARD, v. ALLEN.

Lease, with Reservation of Right of Way—Construction of—Estate, Conditional without Express Clause of Re-entry—Receipt of Rent, as Waiver of Forfeiture.

B. owned an alley 24 feet wide, between two lots, one owned by A. and the other by H. A. built a large brick house on his lot, which extended 12 feet across the alley at one end, and B. built a fence lengthwise of the alley on a line corresponding with A.'s house, so as to narrow the whole alley one half or more, which alley, thus narrowed, B. used as a way. Then B. gave a lease in fee to A. of the whole 24 feet, describing it as a lot on which A.'s house partly stood at a rent of $15, reserving a way through the alley for himself, his teams, carts, &c.; and the lease was declared to be upon condition that A. should leave B. in the unobstructed enjoyment of the way. Held, that a continuance of the fence, as B. had himself made it, was not an obstruction of the way within the words of the condition; that a reasonable way for the purposes expressed, was all that B. could exact; and that his acts in making the fence, and leasing with the house partly across the alley, were facts from which a jury would be bound to consider the alley, as it was narrowed by the house and fence, the full extent of the way intended by the parties to be reserved; the lessee having a right to reduce all the residue of the alley to his exclusive possession.

The words, "and these presents are upon this condition," viz.: that the lessee shall suffer the lessor to enjoy a way reserved through the demised premises without obstruction, are sufficient, in a durable lease, to make the estate a conditional one, without an express clause of re-entry; and if the way be obstructed, ejectment lies.

To make a receipt for rent operate as a waiver of a forfeiture of the estate demised, the rent must not only be received after the forfeiture is incurred, but such rent so received must have accrued after that time.

And this validates the lease only to the time when the rent so received accrued; but will not operate as a waiver of a forfeiture incurred by continuing the original cause of the forfeiture after the day on which the rent received fell due.

Citations—Woodf. L. & T., 203, 204; Cowp., 246, 482, 803; 2 T. R., 425; 1 Saund., 287 c, n. (16); 3 Co., 64; 4 Taunt., 735; 4 B. & A., 401; Co. Litt., sec. 203, 211, b., 328, 9, 30, 31.

EJECTMENT for a small lot or alley, in the village of Salem, Washington Co., tried before the late *Mr. Justice* Yates, at the Washington Circuit, June 10, 1822.

*The declaration was entitled of [***221** Thursday, May 4, in May Term, 1820, and the ouster laid May 3, 1820.

On the trial James Rowan testified that the alley was laid out by John Williams, the proprietor of that and the adjoining lands, as early as 1796. In that year he sold the lot adjoining the alley on the north to Becker, who then took possession of and sold it to Crookshank, who sold it to the defendant, who occupied it ever since. The alley runs from the road east to the rear of the lots. Several years ago the defendant built a barn on the rear of his lot. In 1806 he built a large brick house on the west end of his lot adjoining the highway. The lot adjoining the alley on the south was sold by Williams to Peebles, who built upon it, and in 1800 Hawley built a barn in the rear of that lot, he then owning it.

The plaintiff then gave in evidence a lease in fee from Blanchard (the lessor of the plaintiff), to Allen (the defendant), dated Dec. 13, 1809, by which Blanchard granted, bargained, sold, aliened, remised, released and confirmed to Allen, his heirs, &c., the alley by the description of "all that lot, &c., situate, &c., beginning at the N. W. corner of the lot lately belonging to Hawley, &c.; then northerly to the S. W. corner of the lot heretofore granted to Allen (the lessee), by Crookshank, 24 feet; thence easterly along the S. side of the same lot to the S. E. corner thereof; thence S. to the N. E. corner of the barn now in the occupation of Robert M'Murray, Jr., and standing on the land of Blanchard (the lessor); thence westerly along the N. side of the said barn, to the north corner thereof; thence southerly to the said lot formerly of the said Hawley; thence westerly along the N. side of the same lot to the place of beginning, part of the dwelling-house of the said Allen (the lessee), standing on part of the west end of said lot hereby granted—excepting and reserving in and out of the said *granted lot, &c., to the [***222** said Blanchard, his heirs and assigns, a right of way, as well a footway as a horseway, and a way for his and their carts, carriages and servants, in, out and through the granted lot, at all times;" and reserving a yearly rent of $15, payable Dec. 30, in every year, forever, &c., with the usual clause of distress and re-entry, if the rent should be in arrear for 20 days. Then came this clause: "And these presents are upon this condition: that the said Allen, his heirs, &c., shall and do at all times, forever hereafter, permit and suffer the said Blanchard, his heirs, &c., to have, use and enjoy the right of way above mentioned, without any obstruction or let whatsoever; but nothing herein contained shall extend to prevent the said Allen, his heirs, &c., erecting a gate or gates on the west part of said granted lot, subject to be opened by the said Blanchard, his heirs, &c., at their discretion." Then followed the usual covenant for quiet enjoyment he, the lessee, fulfilling the covenants on his part, &c.

The lessor then admitted that in Sept. 1820, the defendant paid the rent, which fell due Dec. 30, 1819.

Johnathan Morey then testified that he surveyed the alley; that it was originally 24 feet wide, and extended from the road to the lessor's land on the east; that about 12 feet of the south end of the defendant's brick house stands on the alley; that the defendant has inclosed in his garden, by a permanent fence, all the alley, except a strip 9¼ feet wide, on the north side of the alley, and the part so inclosed is occupied by the defendant as a garden; that there is a gate near the west end of the alley, on the south side of the defendant's house. On the south side, the alley is 181½ feet long. Joseph Cooper testified that the garden fence now stands where it did in Apr., 1820. Thaddeus Smith testified that a part of the alley was inclosed and occupied as a garden in 1807, and so continued to the present time; that the part of the alley left open is of sufficient width to allow a wagon or carriage to pass with safety, but not wide enough for two wagons to pass each other, if they should meet. Archibald M'Athelie testified that in the 223*] autumn of 1819 *the refuse of the alley was piled up at the east end of it, with the manure which was thrown from the shed adjoining the alley. This manure continued there till the spring of 1820, when it was drawn away by the defendant. That part of the alley next to and adjoining the defendant's barn, was usually occupied by the defendant's cows in the winter, and his cows were g fed there.. In one instance there hadebeeallywood thrown into the alley by the defendant, but it did not obstruct the passage to the back part of the alley, and it was soon cut up and piled away. George Coggswell testified that in Apr., 1820, he was sent by the lessor to ask the defendant to remove the manure which was there piled up at the east end of the alley; that there was a rack standing on the manure, from which the cattle ate their fodder; that the rack was lengthwise the alley. The defendant said the manure was so frozen he could not then remove it. The lessor's barn stands on the south side, and at the east end of the alley, where a gate opens to the lessor's land. The door of the lessor's barn opens on the north side of his barn, into the alley; the rack stood within four feet of the door of the lessor's barn; and the manure was piled up two or three feet high against the lessor's barn door, so that the witness could not open it during the month of Apr., 1820. At another time this witness went with a team of horses to go through the alley, when the defendant told him he could not get through, which he found to be true, the rack being frozen down on a pile of manure; and if the rack had been removed, it would have been impossible to drive a loaded cart or wagon over the manure, without upsetting; that the alley, at the east end, is only about 12 feet wide. Lyman Gleason testified that in the latter part of Apr., 1820, he was employed by the defendant to clear out the manure and filth from the alley; that cattle appeared to have been fed there, the manure being scattered pretty much over that part of the alley which was occupied as a pass way to the rear of the lot. There was also a pile of manure near the gate, at the east end of the alley, over which they passed with the wagons when drawing the manure. The rack which stood upon it was removed; by one man's taking hold of one end* [*224 of it, and one other hold of the other end, and setting it against the side of the barn, out of the way. The pile of manure was about in the center of the alley, but did not extend south to the barn of the lessor; that the snow had drifted against the barn door, which prevented its opening, but the manure formed no impediment, and was not within eight feet of the door. The witness scraped up the manure, and found that it did not extend either to the gate or the barn upon the south. The manure from the defendant's stable was thrown into the garden, and not into the alley. The pile appeared to have been scraped up the fall before, from what had accumulated in the alley the previous summer. John Smart testified that he assisted Gleason in removing the manure, but did not come till the second day. He could not drive a loaded wagon over the manure, through the alley, into the lessor's lot, but thinks an empty wagon might have been driven over it. When he drove in his wagon to get out the manure, he was obliged to take his horses from the wagon and turn it round by hand. Isaac Powers testified that he saw the pile of manure, drove his wagon with a load of hay to the defendant's barn, and unloaded it, but could not turn round in the alley. He opened the gate at the east end, drove through on to the lessor's land, turned round, and then drove his wagon empty, back through the alley. A loaded wagon could not have been driven over it with safety. Russell Bassett testified that he saw the pile of manure, about half way between the defendant's barn and the lessor's. He went in with a load of hay, and drove round the pile of manure with ease. He saw the rack, and thinks it formed no obstruction. Thinks there might have been three or four loads of manure in the pile.

The defendant then moved for a nonsuit:

1. Because, if there was any obstruction, the lessor's only remedy was by a personal action. The lease was not forfeited.

2. That if the defendant left unobstructed a straight way from one end of the alley to the other, of the same width as that part which adjoined to, and was not covered by the house, it was all the lessor had a right to claim.

*3. That the defendant had a right [*225 to inclose and cultivate all the alley, except a convenient and sufficient way over it for the lessor's use.

4. That the obstruction formed by the house and fence, including a part of the alley in the garden, being upon the alley at the time the lease was given, was to be received as evidence of the acquiescence and consent of the lessor to their continuance, and that for them no forfeiture could exist.

5. That the obstruction having existed pre-

visions to the rent's becoming due, in 1819, the lessor's receiving that rent was a waiver of the forfeiture, if any had accrued.

The judge decided that an obstruction of the lessor's right of way over any part of the demised premises, would be a forfeiture of the estate; that this was a question of law, which, however, depended upon the fact of such obstruction; and he charged the jury, that if they believed, from the testimony, that a part of the alley, as described by the witnesses, was, between Dec. 30, 1819, and May 3, 1820, inclosed by a fence in the defendant's garden, and appropriated to his exclusive use, and the obstruction in the remaining part of the alley rendered the passage, with loaded teams, unsafe and hazardous, the plaintiff would be entitled to recover on the ground of forfeiture; but that the house, having been mentioned in the lease as standing on the premises, could not constitute an obstruction, within the terms of the lease. The recognition of this fact by the lease, clearly showed that it was not so considered at the time the lease was executed. The jury gave a verdict for the plaintiff for the alley.

Mr. S. Stevens, for the defendant, now moved for a new trial, on the grounds taken at the circuit.

He added, in relation to the first point, that the words of the lease, "these presents are upon this condition, &c.," did not import a forfeiture for the obstruction. To have this effect, the words should be express and explicit; but the lease contains no plain words of forfeiture, except for the non-payment of rent. The **226***] plaintiff had a complete remedy *by a personal action against the lessee or his assigns. The words which are claimed to warrant a forfeiture are, at least, of doubtful import; and the court will lean against a harsh construction. Courts always lean against the forfeiture of leases. In *Jackson* v. *Brownson*, 7 Johns., 235, Spencer, *J.*, says: "It is an established principle, that in construing a covenant which is to work a forfeiture, courts adhere strictly to the precise words of the condition. This rule, for its equity and reasonableness, deserves constantly to be kept in view. It is, in most cases, rigorous and harsh, to break up a lease, for the violation of covenants which may be compensated in damages; and the present case appears to be one of that description." In that case, the lessee had agreed, expressly, that if the covenants in the lease should be violated, it should operate as a forfeiture.

As to the other points, he remarked that Allen had done no act to work a forfeiture. When he took the lease, at this rent, he certainly had a right to expect some benefit from it, beyond the mere right of way. No casualty should be allowed to work a forfeiture. Some affirmative act should be shown, tending directly to deprive Blanchard of a right of way. The condition should be violated in its precise language, before the law will allow the act to operate as a forfeiture. *Jackson* v. *Brownson*, 7 Johns., 227, 232, 235; *Jackson* v. *Harrison*, 17 *Id.*, 66, 70, 71; Woodf. L. & T., 203; Bull. *N. P.*, 96.

Here was a waiver of the forfeiture, by receiving rent. Woodf. L. & T., 519; Cowp., 247; *Roe* v. *Harrison*, 2 T. R., 425; *Doe* v. *Bancks*, 4 B. & A., 401. The last was a strong case to this point. It may be objected that the receipt here was of rent due before the forfeiture; but this is true as to only a part of it.

Messrs. J. Willard and *J. Crary*, contra. The lease having mentioned the fact that part of the alley was covered by the house, we did not insist on a forfeiture for that reason; but a part was also inclosed by the defendant for the purposes of a garden. This we do insist on as a forfeiture; and the very circumstance that the lease provides for the house and gate, implies that no other obstruction was admissible. All *others are excluded by this [***227** provision. The argument that the garden fence may be continued, because it was there when the lease was given, proves too much. It might as well be said that had all the premises been permanently inclosed at that time, therefore, no way whatever should be allowed to the lessor. The reservation of the way is in strong technical terms, and clearly manifests an intention to reserve all not covered by the house. But suppose its extent was, in some measure, at the discretion of the defendant; here has been a total obstruction. If the testimony was contradictory, it was fairly submitted to the jury, who have found the obstruction.

A clause of re-entry was not necessary to provide for the forfeiture. The lease rested expressly upon the condition that there should be no obstruction; and the condition is well expressed. 2 Cruise Dig., 1, 2; Co. Litt., 201 *a; Id.*, 203 *a.* It is a reasonable condition. The remedy for condition broken is by ejectment. Even an actual entry is not necessary. The confession of lease, entry and ouster, by the consent rule, is enough. 2 Cruise Dig. 49; Adams' Eject., Am. ed., 90; *Jackson* v. *Crysler*, 1 Johns. Cas., 125; *Langendyck* v. *Burhans*, 11 Johns., 461.

The acceptance of rent was no waiver of the forfeiture. We received no rent which fell due after Dec. 30, 1819. Our act supposed the lease good to that time, and has no further effect. The acts of forfeiture complained of were all subsequent. We were restrained in our evidence to the time which intervened between that day and May 3, 1820, when the ouster was laid in the declaration. Though the receipt of rent may operate as a confirmation of the estate, it does not discharge the condition. The lessee had the estate free of the forfeiture to the time up to which we received the rent; not after.

The argument that we should have taken our remedy by personal action, we presume, means that we should have brought covenant or case. But there is no covenant against the obstruction. It is guarded against by condition only; and conceding that we might bring case, the same circumstances which would warrant this action, will authorize an ejectment *for the forfeiture. The whole [***228** extent of this alley is less than the statute would allow for a private way; yet, after being narrowed to nine feet by permanent erections, it is totally obstructed by the filth, manure and rack. Only one witness says he could pass around it; and he mentions no time when this was done. All the other witnesses concur in saying there was a total obstruction.

Mr. D. Russell, in reply. I ask again, was it intended by the parties that Blanchard should enjoy a way over this whole alley, and yet receive the $15 rent? The testimony shows abundantly that the way left was enough for all ordinary use; and the occupation and acts of the lessor, before the lease was executed, defined the extent which was necessary. The way has not been altered since the lease. It is now as broad as the lessor himself made it when he had the whole control. The house was then built, and the fence made. Here is a covenant on the part of the lessor, that on the defendant's fulfilling the covenants on his part, he shall enjoy the premises. It is said here is no covenant against obstruction. Be it so. There is then a fulfillment of all our covenants, and, in the very terms of the lease, can be no forfeiture. The lessor can have a remedy by an action on the case alone.

The judge did not, as supposed on the other side, put the case fairly to the jury. It was decided by him that any, the least obstruction, would be a forfeiture, and taking this for the rule, the verdict was inevitable.

But, in reality, there was no obstruction; nothing to prejudice the lessor. The whole was temporary and casual; and on being apprised of the lessor's wishes to that effect, every effort was promptly made to remove it; and it was removed before suit commenced. The reasoning of the judges in *Senhouse* v. *Christian*, 1 T. R., 560, will be found in point upon the question of obstruction.

For the effect of an acceptance of rent, the court are referred to what Ld. Mansfield says in *Jenkins* v. *Church*, Cowp., 482, and *Goodright* v. *Davids*, *Id.*, 803. Also, to what was said in *Fox* v. *Swann*, Styles, 482-3.

229*] *The receipt was of rent accrued after the pretended forfeiture, viz.: of rent due Dec. 30, 1819; whereas the obstruction was in piling refuse, &c., the fall before.

Curia, per SUTHERLAND, *J.* I think the judge erred in charging the jury, that if they believed a part of the alley, as described in the lease, was, between Dec. 30, 1819, and May 3, 1820, inclosed by a fence, in the defendant's garden and appropriated to his exclusive use, and the obstruction in the remaining part of the alley rendered the passage with loaded teams unsafe and hazardous, the plaintiff would be entitled to recover on the ground of forfeiture. These two causes of forfeiture should have been separately and distinctly presented to the jury.

The exceptions and condition in the lease did not bind the defendant to leave the whole of the demised premises unoccupied and unimproved; unless the whole was necessary for a convenient way or passage for the horses, carriages, carts and servants of the lessor. Suppose the premises conveyed had been one hundred, instead of four and twenty feet in width, would it be contended that the reservation of a right of way extended to each and every part of them, and prohibited the defendant from inclosing any portion? It should have been submitted to the jury, as a matter of fact, whether enough of the alley was left uninclosed to afford a convenient passage for the lessor, and if they were of opinion that there was, then, clearly, the plaintiff would not be entitled to recover on that ground. If the construction contended for by the plaintiff's counsel be correct, the effect of the conveyance was merely to give to the defendant a right of way through the alley; for if he could not inclose any portion of it, he could not use it permanently in any other way, without encroaching on the lessor's rights. Now if this had been the understanding and intention of the parties, they would most naturally have carried it directly into effect, by a simple conveyance of a right of way to the defendant.

But again; the fence complained of was on the premises at the time of giving the lease, and had been there several *years be- [*230 fore. It took no more in width from the alley than was covered by the defendant's house. These are strong circumstances which a jury would be authorized, and, I think, bound to consider equivalent to an admission on the part of the lessor, that neither the house nor the fence encroached upon the right of way intended to be reserved by him. But, at all events, the question of fact should have been submitted to the jury.

As to the obstruction occasioned by the manure, the evidence was contradictory. It appears to have been about the centre of the alley. Bassett testified "that he took a load of hay to the defendant's barn and drove round the pile of manure with ease; and thinks that it formed no obstruction;" that there might have been three or four loads of it. Powers also drove a load of hay to the defendant's barn, and he thought a loaded wagon could not have been driven over the manure with safety; but he does not say that there was not room to pass round it, and from the diagram it would appear that he must have gone round it with his load, in order to get at the defendant's barn. Other witnesses stated that loaded teams could not be driven over the manure with safety; but there is not one who swears that after the rack was removed, a loaded wagon could not have passed round the manure without danger or inconvenience. The jury might well have come to the conclusion that the manure did not so obstruct the alley as to deprive the lessor of a convenient passage through it.

If the obstruction did amount to a forfeiture, the receipt of rent by the lessor in Sep., 1820, was not a waiver of it. The manure was not removed, until the last of Apr., 1820. The rent which was received, fell due in Dec., 1819. In order to render the receipt of rent a waiver, it is necessary that the rent should have accrued as well as have been received subsequent to the forfeiture. It proceeds upon the principle that the lessor, by receiving the rent, affirms the lease to have continuance as Ld. Coke expresses it; but that can only relate to the time when the rent fell due, and not to the time of its payment; and so are all the authorities. Co. Litt., 211 *b*; Woodf. L. & T., 203-4; *Doe* *v. *Batten*, Cowp., 246, [*231 Ashton, *J.*; *Jenkins* v. *Church*, *Id.*, 482; *Goodright* v. *Davids*, *Id.*, 803; *Roe* v. *Harri-*

son, 2 T. R., 425; 1 Saund., 287 *c*, *n*. 16; *Pennant's* case, 3 Rep., 64. The receipt of rent was an affirmance of the lease on the 30th of Dec., 1819; but the obstruction still continuing, the subsequent forfeiture has not been waived. The case of *Doe* v. *Bliss*, 4 Taunt., 735, is precisely analogous on this point; and the same doctrine is fully sustained by the subseqnent case of *Doe* v. *Bancks*, 4 B. & A., 401. The lease was not absolutely void, but voidable at the option of the lessor upon a breach of the condition. *Doe* v. *Bancks*, 4 B. & A., 401. If the lessor, therefore, with a full knowledge of the forfeiture, had accepted rent, which fell due after that event, the cases already cited show that it would have been a waiver.

The lessee had but an estate upon condition, on breach of which, the lessor undoubtedly had a right to re-enter. Co. Litt., 203 *a*, *et seq.*, secs. 328-9, 30, 31.

But a new trial must be granted, for the misdirection of the judge, the costs to abide the event.

New trial granted.

Cited in—12 Wend., 675; 13 Wend., 535; 46 N. Y., 416; 1 Abb. App. Dec., 320; 11 Barb., 35; 10 Abb. N. S., 172; 2 Sweeny, 295; 3 Wood. & M., 85; 24 Hun, 619; 40 Mo., 460; 53 Mo., 412; 18 Am. Rep., 148; 31 Md., 43; 25 Cal., 394.

GOODRICH *v.* WOOLCOTT.

Action for Slander—Charge of Crime against Nature—Allegation of—Innuendo—*Meaning of Words, when for Jury.*

A count in slander, charging that the defendant uttered and published these words: "He (meaning the said I., the plaintiff) has been with a sow; and I (meaning the said C., the defendant) can prove it," preceded and followed by a recital and averment, that the words were intended to charge the plaintiff with the crime against nature, &c., held sufficient.

Where words are of doubtful import, the jury are to find their meaning.

The office of an *inuendo* is merely explanatory. It cannot enlarge the meaning of words, beyond their natural signification.

Citations—9 East, 96; 1 Cowp., 272, 273, 278; 2 Bl., 961, 962; 12 Johns., 260; 5 East, 463.

MOTION in arrest of judgment, for the insufficiency of the declaration. This contained four counts, in slander, upon which a general verdict had been found for the plaintiff; and the motion was founded upon the insufficiency of the last count only, the goodness of the others being conceded by the counsel for the defendant. The declaration contained a general recital, that "the said Charles 232*] (the defendant) *contriving and wickedly and maliciously intending to injure the said Issachar (the plaintiff) in his good name, fame and credit, and to bring him into public scandal, infamy and disgrace with and among all his neighbors, and other good and worthy citizens of this State, and to cause it to be suspected and believed that he, the said Issachar, was a person of unnatural passions and appetites, and was guilty of the abominable and detestable crime against nature; and to cause him to be abhorred and shunned as a person unfit for, and unworthy of all society; and to subject him to the pains and penalties by the laws of this State made and provided, and inflicted upon persons guilty thereof; and to vex, harass, oppress, impoverish and wholly ruin the said Issachar, on, &c., at, &c.," spoke the words in the 1st count. The 4th count was as follows: "That on, &c., at, &c., the said Charles, farther contriving, and intending as aforesaid, in a certain other discourse, which he, the said Charles, then and there had, of and concerning the said Issachar, in the presence and hearing of divers other good and worthy citizens of the State aforesaid, then and there, in the presence and hearing of the said last mentioned citizens, falsely and maliciously spoke and published of and concerning the said Issachar, these other false, scandalous, malicious and defamatory words, following, that is to say: He (meaning the said Issachar) has been with a sow; and I (meaning the said Charles) can prove it." And the said Issachar, in fact, saith, that the words last aforesaid were so uttered and published by the said Charles, with intent and meaning to convey, and that the same were by the said last mentioned citizens, in whose presence they were so uttered and published, understood and believed to convey a charge against the said Issachar, that he was a person of unnatural passions and appetites, and capable of committing, and had committed, the detestable and abominable crime against nature, and that he the said Charles could prove it; and was thereby rendered infamous and unfit for, and unworthy of all society; and was subject to the pains and penalties by the laws of this State made and provided and inflicted upon persons guilty thereof. By means, &c."

Mr. Z. A. Leland for the defendant. [*233

It is well settled that an *inuendo* does not enlarge the sense of the words; and we have, therefore, a right to consider the words charged to have been spoken, entirely independent of any averment in this count as to their meaning.

[The counsel was about to cite authorities to this point, but *the Court* told him it was too plain to require any reference to authorities.]

Mr. Leland. The modern doctrine is well established, that the words charged must, of themselves, clearly convey the idea of a crime; and, indeed, neither the ancient nor modern cases will support this count. In *Miller* v. *Buckdon*, 2 Bulst., 10, the defendant and another, having some speech about the death of a child of one Dowland, the defendant said that the plaintiff was the cause of the death of the child, and that he (the defendant) would swear it upon a book. On verdict for the plaintiff, a motion was made in arrest; and the court held the words not actionable for want of a *colloquium*, pointing them to a case of poisoning, murdering, or some other untimely death. Without this, they were pronounced too general; that the plaintiff caused the death, was not enough; and the court put a case by way of illustration, that one may be the cause of another's death, and yet be perfectly innocent; as where it is caused by lawful imprisonment. In *Harrison* v. *King*, 7

NOTE.—*Action for slander—Where words charged are of doubtful import their meaning should be left to the jury.* See *Ex parte* Bailey, 2 Cow., 479, *note.*

Taunt., 431, on error to the Exchequer Chamber, the words in one count were, "I will take him to Bow St. on a charge of forgery;" *inuendo*, that the plaintiff had been guilty of forgery. On verdict and judgment for the plaintiff, generally, upon all the counts, the error assigned was, "that the words did not import any express or precise imputation of the plaintiff below having committed forgery; but only an intention of the defendant below to take the plaintiff to Bow St. (without showing where, in that street, or for what purpose, upon a charge of forgery, without stating by or against whom made, or of what forgery), and which words of themselves constituted no cause of action, although they were laid in a separate count, as a separate cause of action, without any special damage." And for these causes, the judgment was reversed.

234*] **Peake* v. *Oldham*, Cowp., 275, will probably be relied on for the plaintiff; and is undoubtedly the strongest case against us. There the defendant told the plaintiff he was guilty of the death of a person. This was charged in the 4th count, the others being sufficient. Ld. Mansfield lays much stress upon the word "guilty," which is wanting here, as showing from the whole frame of the words, that they imported a charge of murder. Upon the same principle, in *Carpenter* v. *Tarrant*, Rep. *t.* Hardw., 325, these words were holden actionable: "Robert Carpenter was in Winchester jail and tried for his life, and would have been hanged had it not been for Leggat, for breaking open the granary of farmer A., and stealing his bacon." So in *Roberts* v. *Camden*, 9 East, 93. "He was under a charge of prosecution for perjury, and G. W., an attorney, had the Attorney-General's directions to prosecute him for perjury," were holden actionable. Ld. Ellenborough says, "the words must mean that he was ordered by the Attorney-General to be prosecuted, either for a perjury which he had committed, or which he had not committed; or which he was supposed only to have committed. In the first sense, they are clearly actionable. In the second, they cannot possibly be understood consistently with the context. He concludes upon the whole matter, that these words must fairly be understood in the first of the three senses, and refers to *Carpenter* v. *Tarrant*. The words should convey a charge directly; not merely by way of inference. *Onslow* v. *Horne*, 3 Wils., 177. They should not be doubtful or equivocal. *Harrison* v. *Stratton*, 4 Esp., 218. Within this rule, saying of the plaintiff he is forsworn, is not slanderous, unless it be said of some judicial proceeding in which he had been sworn. *Holt* v. *Scholfield*, 6 T. R., 690; *Hopkins* v. *Beadle*, 1 Cai., 347. The rule, as laid down by Ld. Kenyon, is, that "either the words themselves must be such as can only be understood in a criminal sense, or it must be shown by a *colloquium* in the introductory part, that they have that meaning, otherwise they are not actionable." 6 T. R., 694. "You swore to a lie, for which you stand indicted," were holden actionable by this court, on the ground that the concluding words, "you stand indicted," imply that the false oath could **235***] have been none other than *perjury; otherwise an indictment would not lie. *Pelton* v. *Ward*, 3 Cai., 73. Independent of such an explanation, most clearly the words would not have been actionable. *Ward* v. *Clark*, 2 Johns., 10; *Stafford* v. *Green*, 1 *Id.*, 505. *Brooker* v. *Coffin*, 5 *Id.*, 188, was strikingly analogous to the present case. The frame of the words imported perjury, much more directly than those in the present case import the crime against nature or any other crime; yet they were holden not actionable.

Suppose it asserted of a man that he was with a woman, would it imply an illicit connexion? A charge of hooking, or of being a cow-boy, have been holden not actionable. There should be a fixed legal sense to words, by which their quality can be certainly determined. General understanding would pronounce a charge of swearing false to import perjury; yet, in themselves, these words are clearly not so. It is, therefore, no argument for sustaining this count, that bystanders may have understood the words charged to import the crime of bestiality.

Mr. S. M. Hopkins, contra. Is it true that in order to maintain an action of slander, the crime imputed must be charged in legal terms? Is it true that the slanderer shall escape, if he evades the use of technical or legal terms, although he utter those which all mankind understand to import an abominable crime? Take the words "hooking," or "cow-boy," put by the gentleman; is there no way in which a pleader may so frame a declaration as to reach the real intent of the speaker, and make them a slander upon record? How the declaration should be drawn, in such cases, I do not undertake to say; but it would be a libel upon the law, and a still greater one upon counsel, to say that it could not be done. Take the case put, of "being with a woman;" might not such a charge be preceded or followed by such explanations, as to make it convey a charge of adultery? The law says that a man may be libeled by paintings or pictures; and yet is there no mode of declaring by which he can reach the offense? Certainly he may do this, no matter how equivocal the slander.

As to cases; we rely principally upon *Peake* v. *Oldham*, already cited from Cowper, and two cases in East—*Woolnoth* *v. *Meadows*, 5 East, 463; and *Roberts* v. *Camden*, 9 *Id.*, [*236 93, the latter also cited on the other side. *Woolnoth* v. *Meadows* will be found a precedent for most of the count in question. The same introductory matter, and the same concluding averments and *inuendoes*, almost word for word, will be found there; and the words charged were certainly not more definite than here, in fixing the crime. They were these: "His character is infamous. He would be disgraceful to any society. Whoever proposed him must have intended it as an insult. I will pursue him and hunt him from all society. If his name is enrolled in the Royal Academy, I will cause it to be erased, and will not leave a stone unturned, to publish his shame and infamy; delicacy forbids me from bringing a direct charge; but it was a male child of nine years old, who complained to me." Such words, accompanied with our averments, were held actionable. This is after verdict. The jury have passed upon the case; and where words are equivocal, it is the province of the jury to determine their import. Cowp., 277, per Ld. Mansfield. They have declared that the words intended to convey the imputation averred. If it be said that the declaration here varies from that in *Woolnoth* v. *Meadows*, in not naming the crime, we answer, that it is enough to follow the Statute, which also forbears to name it (1 R. L., 408, sec. 3); whereas the Statute of Hen. VIII. does give the crime a name. This accounts for its being named by the English pleader. That it was not named in this instance, arose from a delicate and accurate distinction between the English Act and ours; and the court will the more readily countenance this general form to avoid offensiveness.

In the language of Ld. Mansfield, then, in *Peake* v. *Oldham*, will the court, after the jury have found the fact, "be guessing and inventing a mode in which it may be barely possible for these words to be spoken by the defendant, without meaning to charge a crime? That case is full to our purpose. "The jury," says he, "have found the fact, namely: that such was the meaning of the defendant." And he also cites and comments upon the manuscript
237*] *case of *Ward* v. *Reynolds*, which is still more strongly in point. The defendant said to the plaintiff: "I know you very well; how did your husband die?" The plaintiff answered: "As you may, if it please God." The defendant replied: "No; he died of a wound you gave him." On not guilty, there was a verdict for the plaintiff; and on motion in arrest of judgment, the court held the words actionable; because, from the whole frame of them, they were spoken by way of imputation." And *Ld. Ch. J.* Parker, said; "It is very odd that, after verdict, a court of justice should be trying whether there may not be a possible case, in which words spoken by way of scandal might not be innocently said. Whereas, if that were, in truth, the case, the defendant might have justified, or the verdict would have been otherwise." After citing that case, Ld. Mansfield remarks: "So here, if found to be innocently spoken, the jury might have found a verdict for the defendant; but they have put a contrary construction, &c." *Poturite* v. *Barrel*, Sid., 220, was not stronger against the defendant than the present; and Comyn, in his Digest, Action upon the Case for Defamation, E, &c., refers to scores of cases, which are less so, and yet the action was held to lie. But *Peake* v. *Oldham* is a sufficient authority and cannot be shaken. That case begun in the C. P., where the question first came up on a motion in arrest, which was denied (W. Bl., 959); whence it was carried to the K. B.; and the report in Cowper is on error. It was a case strongly litigated, and underwent very great examination by the ablest judges.

Roberts v. *Cambden*, 9 East, 93, is our last case. There the charge was, that the plaintiff was under a prosecution for perjury. Now this may be consistent with the plaintiff's perfect innocence; yet the court were unanimous that the action lay.

Mr. Leland, in reply. The case of *Woolnoth* v. *Meadows* bears no analogy to the one under consideration. The words there alleged to have been spoken, conveyed a clear charge of the *crime to the understanding of every- [*238 body. Taking the whole together, there was no room to suppose any other intent than to charge the plaintiff directly with a crime. It is evident that nothing could have been made out of the words in *Peake* v. *Oldham*, had it not been for the word "guilty," used by the defendant, which was the only word the court could find to support the record. As Ld. Mansfield objects, after verdict, to guessing out innocence, may we not, at least, with equal propriety, respond by asking, will the court set themselves about guessing or hunting out guilt? What is called an averment in this case, and is relied on to help the defect in the naked words, is no more than a mere *inuendo*, and if not warranted by the words, it goes for nothing. This is now the settled doctrine, and was applied by Spencer, *J.*, in *Brooker* v. *Coffin*, 5 Johns., 192, to a case in principle precisely like the present. He says the averment is not warranted by the words. So here, there must be premises to warrant the *inuendo*, which is no more than a necessary conclusion, following the words themselves. This is not the case of a *colloquium* about the offense set forth in the declaration, and the words applied to it. That would have been a different thing. The apology is, that the words are offensive. Had counsel thought of this when pleading, it was easy to have helped it by a *colloquium*, which should have been as modest as the *inuendo*.

There is no ambiguity in this case to be helped by a verdict. The full force of the expression comes out in the declaration: and must be tortured to make out an imputation of guilt. They are simply, "he has been with the animal." This is the whole; and there is nothing on the record, which can be legally called in as controlling the import. In the eye of the law, it is the same as if the recital and *inuendo* were stricken out; and it is hardly possible to conceive that they could impute a crime. Delicacy, either in the Statute or counsel, would not forbid his pursuing the words of the Act, by alleging that the defendant asserted, in substance, that the plaintiff had committed the crime against nature; and then it would have been for the *jury to say [*239 whether the words proved were tantamount to those complained of by the plaintiff.

Curia, per SUTHERLAND, *J.* The first three counts in the declaration are unquestionably good. They contain a clear and explicit charge of the abominable crime against nature, in language which none of the hearers could misunderstand. The only question is as to the 4th count. If that is bad, the judgment must be arrested, the verdict being general.

The words in the fourth court are: "He (meaning the said Issachar) has been with a sow, and I (meaning the said Charles) can prove it." What is the plain and natural import of these words, and what idea are they calculated to convey to the bystanders? Can it admit of a doubt that ninety-nine persons out of a hundred would understand them as conveying a charge against the plaintiff, of having had a criminal and unnatural connexion with a sow? The inquiry is not whether the words could have been understood in any other terms, but whether that is the construe-tion which common persons would naturally put upon them. *Roberts* v. *Cambden*, 9 East, 96, per Ld. Ellenborough, *Ch. J.*

In *Peake* v. *Oldham*, 1 Cowp., 272-3, Ld. Mansfield says, "where words, from their general import, appear to have been spoken with a view to defame a party, the court ought not to be industrious in putting a construction upon them different from what they bear in the common acceptaion and meaning of them." But this count goes on and avers, "that the words last aforesaid were so uttered and published by the said Charles, with intent and meaning to convey, and that the same were by the last mentioned citizens, in whose presence they were so uttered and published, understood and believed to convey a charge against the said Issachar, that he was a person of unnatural passions and appetites, and capable of committing, and had committed the detestable and abominable crime against nature, and that he, the said Charles, could prove it."

240*] *If the words were of doubtful signification, it was the province of the jury to determine in what sense they were used. *Oldham* v. *Peake*, 2 Bl., 961-2; *Dexter* v. *Taber*, 12 Johns., 260. In *Woolhnoth* v. *Meadows*, 5 East, 463, the declaration contained an averment similar to this; and Ld. Ellenborough, in his opinion, page 470, speaking of the averment, says: "Upon a count so framed, the plaintiff must have gone into other proof than the mere speaking of the words; and he must have not only shown that the defendant's meaning was to impute a crime of that nature to the plaintiff, but that the words were so understood by the hearers." So in *Peake* v. *Oldham*, Cowp., 278, Ld. Mansfield says: "If the words had been shown to have been innocently spoken, the jury might have found a verdict for the defendant. But they have put a contrary construction upon the words as laid, and have found that the defendant meant a charge of murder: and he quotes, with approbation, the language of *Lord Ch. J.* Parker, who says: "It is very odd, that after verdict, a court of justice should be trying whether there may not be a possible case, in which words spoken by way of scandal, might be innocently said. Whereas, if that were in truth the case, the defendant might have justified, or the verdict would have been otherwise." In this case, therefore, the jury, by their general verdict, have found the words to have been spoken and understood in the sense set forth in the averment. The motion must be denied.

Judgment for the plaintiff.

Affirmed—5 Cow., 714.
Cited in—5 Cow., 505, 515; 6 Cow., 87; 15 Wend., 329; 19 Wend., 298; 21 Wend., 71; 25 Wend., 201; 3 Hill, 24; 1 Den., 361; 16 N. Y., 376; 3 Barb., 633; 4 Barb., 514; 6 Barb., 47, 59; 5 How. Pr., 176; Edm., 229; 5 Sand., 266; 34 Cal., 60; 38 Wis., 273.

241*] *JACKSON, ex. dem. WORDEN,
v.
HARRIS.

Advertisement of Mortgage Sale—What Sufficient Description of Premises—Posting up Advertisements—Power of Commissioners to Sell on Credit.

An advertisement of mortgaged premises for sale, under the "Authorizing a Loan of Moneys to the Citizens of this State," passed Apr. 11, 1808 (sess. 31, ch. 216, 5 W. & S., 392), is sufficiently particular in its description of the premises, if it contain the name of the mortgagor, and date and number of the mortgage, the number of the lot in which the premises lie, the town in which it was situated when the mortgage was given, and the quantity of acres mortgaged, without describing the premises by metes and bounds.

A proper form of an advertisement for sale of several lots by Commissioners, under the 17th section of that Act.

The 17th section, directing the Commissioners to put up advertisements of sale at three of the most public places in the county, is sufficiently complied with, by fixing them in three of the most public places, though they are all remote from the premises in question.

Whether the Commissioners have a right to sell on credit, *quære*.

But the objection that the Commissioners gave a credit for the surplus money, beyond the principal and interest due, can only be made by the mortgagor.

It seems that it is no objection to the validity of the sale, that the Commissioners do not proceed and sell on the first default; but wait till several years' interest accumulates.

Citations—Act April 11, 1808; 3 Johns. Ch., 332; 9 Johns. Ch., 323.

EJECTMENT, for part of lot No. 4, in the old township of Brutus, in Cayuga County; tried at the Cayuga Circuit, before the late *Mr. Justice* Platt, May 27, 1822.

After the defendant had confessed lease, entry and ouster, at the trial, the plaintiff produced a deed from Daniel Avery and William Satterlee, Commissioners for Loaning Money of the County of Cayuga, to Allen Worden, the lessor of the plaintiff, dated Sep. 15, 1820, expressed to be for the consideration of $115, to them in hand paid, by Worden; and declaring that, pursuant to "an Act Authorizing the Loan of Moneys to Citizens of this State," (*a*) they granted, bargained, &c., to Worden, in fee, "all that certain tract of land, situate in the town of Cato, formerly Brutus, County of Cayuga, and State of N. Y., being a part of lot number 4, in the original township of Brutus, beginning, &c." (by metes and bounds), "containing 100 acres of land, being the same land mortgaged to the Commissioners for Loaning Money aforesaid, by Peter Wolverton, on the 15th day of July, 1808." The deed was executed by Daniel Avery and William Satterlee, and witnessed by Glen Cuyler and Jedediah Morgan.

*The plaintiff then read in evidence, a mortgage, for the consideration of $76, executed by Wolverton to the Commissioners, dated July 15, 1808, for the premises in question, being the same described in the deed, *habendum*, &c.; "unto the said Commissioners, and their successors and assigns forever, and for the uses and purposes mentioned in an Act, &c., entitled an Act Appointing a Loan of Moneys to the Citizens of this State;" providing that if Wolverton, &c., should pay, or cause to be paid to the Commissioners, the interest of $76, at 7 *per cent. per annum*, on the first Tuesday of May, yearly and every year, and should also pay them the principal sum, &c., when the same [***242**

(*a*) This is entitled "An Act Authorizing a Loan of Moneys to the Citizens of this State, and was passed Apr. 11, 1808." It will be found at large in the Acts (sess. 31, ch. 216) printed by W. & S., Vol. V., p. 392, amended sess. 32, ch. 152, *Id.*, p. 510, sess. 38, ch. 56; sess. 42, ch. 36, sess. 44, ch. 189, sess. 45, ch. 249.

should by them be demanded, at any time after the first Tuesday of May, 1815, then the mortgage to be void, &c.

It was admitted, on the part of the defendant, that he derived title from Wolverton, the mortgagor, subsequent to the time when the mortgage was executed.

The plaintiff's counsel then called William Satterlee, one of the Commissioners, who testified that the interest due on the mortgage remaining unpaid for three years, the Commissioners, May 26, 1820, advertised the mortgaged premises for sale, in pursuance of the Statute on that subject, to be sold at the court house, in the County of Cayuga, on the 3d Tuesday of Sep., at 10 o'clock in the forenoon of that day; and that the same were exposed to sale in conformity with the advertisement, and struck off to the lessor of the plaintiff, who was the highest bidder therefor; that he immediately paid what was due on the mortgage to the witness; that some time in Oct. next succeeding the sale, the witness executed a deed to the lessor of the plaintiff, and sent it by one of the witnesses to the deed, to Daniel Avery, the other Commissioner, for his signature. The plaintiff's counsel then called Daniel Avery, the other Commissioner, who testified that he received the deed from Glen Cuyler, one of the witnesses to it, and executed and returned it to the lessor of the plaintiff by Cuyler's hands. He further testified that no person had caused his name to be entered on the books of the Commissioners, as **243***] *assignee of the mortgagor. The counsel for the plaintiff here rested the cause.

The counsel for the defendant then produced a printed copy of the advertisement of the Commissioners of Loans, referred to by William Satterlee, which was admitted by the plaintiff's counsel, to be a correct copy of the original, and was in the words and figures following, to wit: "Default having been made in the payment of the interest due upon moneys secured to be paid to the Commissioners for Loaning Moneys for the County or Cayuga, on the following pieces or parcels of lands, described in the following list or schedule; and for a more particular description thereof, reference to their several mortgages and minutes will appear:

Names of Mortgagors.	No. of Mortgage.	Date of Mortgage.	Lying in what town at the date of the mortgage.	On what lot.	No. of acres.	Townships.
Henry Burgess,	9	13th July, 1808	Sempronius,	No. 47	87	
Thomas Lacy,	51	14th July, 1808	Dryden,	" 58	150	
James Savage,	57	15th July, 1808	Lock,	" 29	100	
Peter Wolverton,	28	15th July, 1808	Cato,	" 4	100	Brutus.
Nehemiah Webb,	230	1st May, 1815	Scipio,	" 94	25	
W. C. Wilson,	243	1st May, 1815	Brutus,	" 29	50	Aurelius.

Now, therefore, in pursuance of the Act, entitled "An Act Authorizing a Loan of Moneys to the Citizens of this State," and its subsequent amendments; notice is hereby given, that on the 3d Tuesday in September next, the said several mortgaged premises will be sold, at 10 o'clock in the forenoon of said day, at the court house, in said county, at public vendue, to the highest bidder. Dated at Auburn, this twenty-sixth day of May, 1820. DANIEL AVERY, } Commissioners." WM. SATTERLEE, }

The defendant's counsel then called William Satterlee, one of the Commissioners, who testified, that he put an advertisement on the court house door, at Auburn, in Cayuga Co.; one at Strong's tavern, in Owasco, 8 miles southeast *of Auburn; one at Keeler's [***244** tavern, in Sempronius, 16 miles southeast of the court house; and sent one to Aurora, which is 16 miles southwest of the court house; and that the premises in question lie 15 miles north of the court house; that James B. Clark tendered him the amount of interest and principal, after the premises were sold to Worden, the lessor of the plaintiff, and after he executed the deed to Worden; that the offer of Clark was made sometime in the winter after the sale. The sum of about $15, being the surplus for which the land sold to Worden, over and above what was due on the mortgage, and which was due to Wolverton, remained some time in the hands of Worden, after sale; the Commissioners of Loans not wishing to receive it until it could be paid to Wolverton, who had removed from the State. The defendant's counsel then called Daniel Avery, the other Commissioner of Loans, who testified that no particular arrangement was made with Worden as to the overplus money going to Wolverton, and that there was no condition that the deed was given to be held by the Commissioners until the overplus was paid. He further testified that he thought he saw the notice of sale posted up in a public house in Aurora. The plaintiff, by consent, took a verdict, subject to the opinion of the Supreme Court on a case to be made.

Mr. J. L. Richardson, for the plaintiff, contended that he derived a perfect title under the deed of the Commissioners; that they acted within their authority, and in conformity with the directions of the Statute.

The objection will probably be made, that the description of the premises, in the advertisement of sale, was not so full as the act requires. The regularity of the proceedings depends upon the construction of the various sections in relation to this subject. The 11th section (sess. 31, ch. 216, sec. 11) fixes the time for paying the interest of the loan annually on the 1st Tuesday of May. By the 15th section, if not paid within 22 days after, the borrower is forever foreclosed; and the Commissioners are to advertise and sell as directed in the 17th section. The provisions of this section have been complied with, in terms, as to time. As to description, they are to 245*] *"cause advertisements to be fixed up at not less than three of the most public places in the county where the premises are situate, describing the quantity and situation of the lands mentioned in the several mortgages foreclosed as aforesaid, and giving notice, &c." They are also to advertise in one of the public papers of the county. In this case, advertisements were fixed up in four or five different places, beside being published in the newspaper.

The counsel here read the advertisement, and insisted that it was a substantial compliance with the Act, in point of description. He said the Act evidently contemplated a very brief notice, for section 20, which determines the expense of proceeding, allows but $3 for all the services and expenses of the sale.

The tender of the money by Clark, being after the sale, was too late; besides, he established no right to make the tender. He assumes to be an assignee of the mortgagor, but, by the 20th section, the Commissioners were not bound to recognize him in this character, unless he had been recorded as such in their books.

Mr. D. Cady, contra, submitted the following points or propositions, in writing:

I. The sale by the loan officers was void, and no title passed to the lessor of the plaintiff.

1. Because the advertisement did not contain a sufficient description of the situation of the land.
2. Because the advertisements were not put up and continued in the proper places.
3. Because the sale was, in part, at least, upon credit, and the deed not executed in the presence of two witnesses.
4. Because the sale was not on the day prescribed by law; and,
5. Because the loan officers had no power, by law, to sell the premises.

II. There having been no regular sale of the premises, and the person under whom the 246*] defendant holds having *tendered to the loan officers the whole sum due upon the mortgage, he is entitled to retain the possession.

He added, that it is for the court to say what degree of particularity in the description is required by the Statute. There certainly may be a description which is insufficient; and we think the Legislature intended it should be enough, at all events, to put the possessor of the land on his guard, as well as to enable those who attend the sale to find the land, acquaint themselves with its value, and be prepared to bid. "Lot No. 1, in Brutus," would enable any one to examine; but an advertisement by the Commissioners, that they would sell "one of the lots in Brutus," would not enable a purchaser to bid understandingly, without examining every lot in the town. It is a matter of public law that Brutus was divided into lots of 600 acres. Now, the Commissioners say that they will sell 100 acres of a certain lot. Who, from this, could say what part of the 600 acres were to be sold? It may be said that the name of the mortgagor was mentioned, and that an examination of the Commissioners' files would be a guide; but this is not enough. One cannot know through whose hands the land may have passed. Neither name nor record would, therefore, guide him, and he must examine 600 acres instead of one.

Again; the premises lie 14 or 15 miles north of the court house; yet all the advertisements are fixed up from 8 to 16 miles south of that place.

$15 yet remain unpaid by the purchaser. The law is express that money must be paid, on a sale of this description. The Commissioners have no power to sell on credit, and they must exact and receive the whole money. If they may give day for the $15, they may do the same with $15,000. The rule is, in its nature, inflexible, and cannot accommodate itself to the amount. There is no title in the purchaser, till the money is, in fact, paid to the utmost farthing.

It is conceded that the Commissioners acted under a limited authority. Then, we say again, the sale was void, as not being made on the day required by the Statute. Previous to *the day of sale, three years' interest [*247 had been suffered to accumulate. By the 18th section, the Commissioners are directed to sell on the third Tuesday of Sep., annually, all the lands mortgaged, in respect to which there shall have been a default in not paying the interest; and by the 19th section, if no person will bid to the principal and interest, they are to enter upon, and lease the lands for the benefit of the State. They are then to offer the land for sale, again, at the next Apr.; and if there is then no purchaser for an adequate sum, the State become seised of the lands, subject to a right of redemption in the mortgagor. Now it is fairly to be presumed that all these steps were taken. It was the duty of the Commissioners to set about them immediately on the mortgagor's default. Whether they did so or not, their powers of sale, in the ordinary way, ceased; and a tender was made before they had regularly sold. The proceeding was void —it was as no sale—and the tender in season.

It is said, that on default of payment, the Commissioners were, by the 15th section, seised of an absolute estate in the lands; but though this be so, they held it for certain specified purposes. They cannot sit down and dispose of the land in any manner they choose, but must be guided by the Statute. *Denning* v. *Smith*, 3 Johns. Ch., 332.

Mr. Richardson, in reply, cited *King* v. *Stow*, 6 Johns. Ch., 323, as in point, to show that any irregularity in the proceedings of the Commissioners in relation to fixing up advertisements, or making entries, &c., could not be objected against a *bona fide* purchaser at the sale. The description was sufficient——

WOODWORTH, *J.* As far as I remember the practice under this Act, the advertisements of sale have always been in the form which was used here.

Mr. Richardson. And the practice is correct in principle. No one could be deceived who lived on Wolverton's land. This is a declaration to the possessor, and to purchasers, that Wolverton's land, to the extent of 100 acres, would be sold. Nor does it lie in the mouth **248***] of the defendant to say *that because the Commissioners have indulged him three years, they must, therefore, relinquish the whole amount. This was a matter which lay exclusively between them and the public. The same answer applies to the objection that the whole purchase money was not paid. The Commissioners had a right to make the purchaser a depositary of the $15, or any larger amount, if they chose. They have done no more. The money remained with him, waiting a chance to be sent to the mortgagor.

Beside, though the Commissioners gave credit for the whole, it is not for the defendant to object. They may assume the whole, and it will operate as a payment, although nothing be, in fact, paid.

Curia, per SUTHERLAND, *J.* The lessor of the plaintiff claims his title to the premises in question, by virtue of a deed from the Commissioners for Loaning Money in the County of Cayuga, under the Act "Authorizing a Loan of Moneys to the Citizens of this State," passed Apr. 11, 1808. Vol. V., Laws by W. & S., 392. The premises were mortgaged to the Commissioners by one Peter Wolverton, July 15, 1808; and default having been made by him in the payment of the interest, the Commissioners, in pursuance of the directions of the Act, sold them at public auction, and the lessor of the plaintiff became the purchaser. The defendant derives title, also, from Peter Wolverton, by a conveyance subsequent to the mortgage; and after the sale to the lessor of the plaintiff, he offered, by the hand of Clark, to redeem, by paying the amount due.

The only question in the case is, whether the sale by the Commissioners was in conformity to the provisions of the Act.

The principal objections are:

1. That the advertisements did not contain a sufficiently minute description of the situation of the land.

2. That they were not put up in the proper places.

3. That the purchase money was not all paid on the day of sale.

There is no pretense of fraud on the part of the Commissioners. They are admitted to have **249***] acted in good *faith, and the lessor of the plaintiff is a *bona fide* purchaser for a valuable consideration.

1. The 17th section of the Act directs "that the Commissioners shall cause advertisements to be fixed up at not less than three of the most public places in the county where the premises are situate, describing the quantity and situation of the land, &c., and shall also cause such notice to be given in, at least, one of the public newspapers in the county, if any such there be." The advertisement, in this case, contained the name of the mortgagor, the date and number of the mortgage, the number of the lot, the town in which it was situated when the mortgage was given, and the quantity of acres mortgaged. It could not have been more particular, without giving a description of the premises by metes and bounds, as contained in the mortgage. The Act does not require such particularity. It contemplates only a general description, sufficient to apprise the mortgagor that his land is to be sold, and to enable any persons who may wish to purchase, or who may be interested in the premises by subsequent liens, to locate and identify them.

In *Denning* v. *Smith*, 3 Johns. Ch., 332, one of the advertisements neither contained the name of the mortgagor, nor the number of one of the lots; and these omissions were held to be fatal. But the *Chancellor* seems to admit that if the name of the mortgagor, and the number of the lot, had been inserted, the advertisement would have been good. He says the "omission of the mortgagor's name and of the number of the lot in the advertisement in Cattskill, where the agent of the owner resided, was a most unfortunate circumstance, &c. It was also an omission fatal, in any view, to the legality of the notice." The other notices, the sufficiency of which, in point of form, was not questioned, were not as particular in their description as the advertisement in this case. They described the premises as being in the town of Cairo, and as being "lot No. 11, and part of lot No. 14, near Perce's mill, containing 125 acres, mortgaged by Henry Persen;" without designating what part or portion of the mortgaged premises was in each or either of the lots. The first objection, therefore, is unfounded.

*2. The second objection appears to [***250** be founded on the fact that the advertisements were put up in places remote from the mortgaged premises; for there is nothing in the case to show that the places where they were put up were not three of the most public places in the county. This is all that the Act requires. It is not necessary that one of the advertisements should be upon or near the premises; and unless one of the three most public places in the county was near the premises, an advertisement there would not be a compliance with the Act. In *Denning* v. *Smith* the omission to put up an advertisement in Cairo, which was in the neighborhood of the premises, and was one of the most public and central places in the county, was held by the *Chancellor* to be a circumstance which, in conjunction with other facts, tended to show a fraudulent intent on the part of the Commissioners. But, in this case, it does not appear that there was any public place near the mortgaged premises.

In *King* v. *Stow*, 6 Johns. Ch., 323, all the advertisements were put up in the village of Elizabethtown, twenty miles distant from the mortgaged premises; and although it appeared that a public road passed through the premises, and that two public ferries were maintained within two miles and a half of them, the notices were held to be good; there being no evidence of a fraudulent intent, and Elizabethtown being, in fact, the most public place in the county. The notices in this case were, therefore, regular.

3. The reason why the surplus, beyond the amount due to the State, was not immediately exacted from the purchaser, is stated by the Commissioners to have been because the mortgagor, to whom it was to be paid, had left the State, and the Commissioners did not want the

money until they could pay it over. They state expressly, in their testimony, that there was no agreement for a credit. The surplus was only $15, and there is nothing to show that it was not paid on demand. But this is an objection which, if it can be raised at all, can be urged only by the mortgagor.

Judgment for the plaintiff.

Cited in—8 Wend., 660; 3 Sandf. Ch., 52.

251*] *TOMPKINS v. CURTIS.

Surety on Appeal—Discharged for Purpose of Being Witness.

The Court of C. P., on motion, at the trial, are bound to discharge a surety for the prosecution of an appeal, and substitute other competent security; so that the first may be a witness for the appellant.

Citation—8 Johns., 407.

ERROR from the C. P. of Onondaga Co. Curtis sued Tompkins before a justice of that county and recovered judgment. Tompkins thereupon appealed to the C. P., and Nathaniel Tompkins, one of the witnesses before the justice, became security for the appellant, and signed the bond to prosecute the appeal, &c. On the trial in the C. P., the appellant, wishing to have Nathaniel Tompkins sworn for him, moved the court to have him discharged from his bond, which had been duly returned by the justice and filed with the clerk, that other security might be substituted; and that N. T. might then be sworn as a witness; but the court overruled the motion, and gave judgment for the appellee; and this point, among several others, came here upon a bill of exceptions.

Mr. G. Lawrence, for the plaintiff in error, cited *Irwin* v. *Caryell*, 8 Johns., 407.

Mr. J. R. Lawrence, contra.

Curia, per SUTHERLAND, *J.* The court erred in refusing to permit another surety to be substituted. There cannot be a doubt that the person so substituted would be liable upon the bond, so that no possible injury could result from the change. The power of the court to grant the application is clear. They were fully possessed of the cause. The bond, with the other papers and proceedings, had been returned and filed with the clerk. The surety was in the nature of bail, whom it is the established practice of the courts to discharge upon other bail being substituted, when the first is a material witness for his principal. The case cited of *Irwin* v. *Caryell* is in point. The judgment must be reversed, and a *venire de novo* go from the C. P.

Judgment reversed.

252*] *WILLIAMS v. MATTHEWS.

Competency of Witness—Examination on Voir Dire—*Transferee of Note Indorsed in Blank as Witness—Transfer of Paper, after Dishonor—Rights of Transferee—Filling up Blank Indorsement at Trial—Act Forbidding Attorneys to Buy Chose in Action—Demand and Notice—Pleading and Evidence—Third Day of Grace, Saturday—Notice on Monday, Sufficient.*

Where a witness is called, and on objection to his competency is put on his *voir dire*, and answers, generally, that he is interested, he should be rejected. If the party calling him wishes to show the nature of the interest, as that it is ideal, or such as will not exclude the witness, he should follow up the examination with particular questions.

One who held a note indorsed in blank and sold it to another, without indorsing it, is, after the execution of the note is proved, a competent witness for the holder, in an action by him against the indorser.

W. purchased a note of M., who indorsed it in blank before due; W. sold it to another before due, who charged the indorser by demand and notice, &c.; and after it was due, W. repurchased it, and sold it to I.; held, that I. might maintain an action on the note against the indorser in his (I.'s) own name.

A note is indorsed and dishonored, and the indorser charged by demand and notice; this is no objection to further negotiation of the note, and any subsequent holder may sue in his own name, either the maker or the indorser who has been so charged; and the original demand of the maker, and notice to the indorser, inures to the benefit of all subsequent holders.

The only difference between negotiable paper which has been dishonored and that which is not yet due, is, that the former must be taken subject to all the equities existing between those who were parties before the paper became due.

The holder of a note indorsed in blank may fill it up before, or at the trial, with what name he pleases. Other parties to the note (*e. g.*, a prior indorser) have no concern with this question.

Construction of the Act (1 R. L., 417) prohibiting an attorney to buy a chose in action for prosecution. To bring an attorney within the Act, there must have been an intent to prosecute.

A count by indorsee against indorser, averring a demand of payment, and notice of non-payment, in the usual form, is satisfied by proving a state of facts which dispenses with actual demand, &c., and showing due diligence, &c. The facts need not be specially stated in pleading.

A demand of payment, and notice of non-payment, should be made and given by the holder of a note or his agent.

Where the third day of grace is Saturday, notice of non-payment need not be given till Monday.

Citations—Chit. Bills, 141, 142, ed. 1817; 7 T. R., 430; 3 T. R., 80; 1 Campb., 383; 11 Johns., 53; Act, April 21, 1818; 2 Johns. Cas., 76; 2 Cai., 344, 127, 343; 2 H. Bl., 510; 2 Johns., 274; 8 Johns., 428.

ERROR from the Court of C. P. of the County of Washington. Williams, the plaintiff below, declared as indorsee against Matthews, the defendant below, as indorser of a promissory note, made by Abner & Hugh Harsha, dated Apr. 9, 1815, for $73 with interest from the date, payable to the defendant, or order, on or before Nov. 1, then next. The first count of the declaration set forth a demand of the makers, and notice thereof, and of non-payment, in the usual form, upon Nov. 4, 1815. The 2d count averred that before the note fell due, H. Harsha absconded, &c., and then set forth the demand upon A. Harsha, in the usual form, on the 4th, and notice on Nov. 6, 1815. Plea, *non assumpsit.* On the trial, the plaintiff proved the execution of the note by the makers, and the *indorsement [*253 of the defendant's name on the note in blank. He then offered to prove that A. Harsha, one of the makers, was an infant at the date of the note, but this being objected to, the court overruled the evidence. He then called A. Har-

NOTE.—*Negotiable paper—When payment is extinguishment of.* Havens v. Huntington, 1 Cow., 387.

Rights of holder of paper transferred after maturity—Equities. See Johnson v. Bloodgood, 1 Johns. Cas., 51, *note.*

sha, one of the makers of the note, who was sworn on his *voir dire*. He said that he was interested, and objected to testifying. The defendant also objected to his admissibility on the gronnd of interest. The plaintiff then offered to confine the inquiry to the fact that a demand of payment was made; but the defendant persisted in his objection, and the court sustained it, and would not permit the witness to be sworn. The plaintiff then called the attorney for the plaintiff, who was sworn on his *voir dire*, and said that he bought the note of the defendant before it fell due, and paid him $73 for it; and that, also before it fell due he sold and transferred it to a third person, who is not the plaintiff; that after it fell due, it came again into his hands, and he commenced a suit upon it, in the name of one Seth White, against the defendant; that the witness had the sole control of the note at the time the suit was commenced in the name of White, and that White had nothing to do with it. That suit was discontinued, and in Sept., 1817, the note became the property of the plaintiff, who had no interest in it before that time. The note was then sold to the plaintiff by the witness; that the plaintiff is, and was then an attorney both in the C. P. of Washington Co. and the Supreme Court. The witness was then sworn in chief; and the plaintiff offered to prove by him that the note was indorsed to him, the witness, before it fell due; that, on the 3d day of grace, payment was demanded of A. Harsha by him, H. Harsha, the other maker, having absconded before the note fell due; and that on the succeeding day, after demand had been made, he, the witness, gave notice to the defendant of the demand and non-payment; and that, before the commencement of this suit, the money was again demanded of the defendant, by the plaintiff's direction. The witness then stated, on his examination in chief, that the relation given by him upon his *voir dire* was true; whereupon the defendants counsel objected to the evi-
254*] dence *offered; and the court sustained the objection, and nonsuited the plaintiff. The plaintiff's counsel excepted to these several decisions of the court below and the cause came here upon a bill of exceptions.

Mr. I. Williams, for the plaintiff in error:

1. Proof of A. Harsha's infancy was improperly rejected. A promissory note made by an infant is void; and demand of payment in such a case is not necessary to charge an indorser. Chit. on Bills, 20; 10 Johns., 33. This proof followed, as it was intended to be, by the fact of H. Harsha's absconding would render a demand of payment wholly unnecessary. The declaration is special and warrants this proof.

2. A. Harsha was improperly rejected as a witness. No interest is shown other than that growing out of his relation to the parties as maker, which left him indifferent between them. 8 Johns., 428; 15 *Id.*, 270; 16 *Id.*, 70; 17 *Id.*, 176, 188. If the plaintiff will waive the interest of a witness against him, the latter cannot object on account of his own interest. Peake Ev., 192, 194. Harsha could have no interest in favor of the plaintiff, nor against himself, in the fact which he was called to prove. 2 Esp. *N. P.*, 348; 4 Cr., 69; 2 Root, 132; 3 T. R., 35, per Buller, *J.* The court should have ascertained that there was an interest; and that it was not merely ideal, before they rejected the witness. If it were mere fancy (as it must have been in this case) he should have been sworn. Peake Ev., 164; 8 Johns., 428.

3. The attorney for the plaintiff was competent to prove the facts offered to be shown in evidence by him, and his testimony was improperly overruled. Even an indorser may be admitted as a witness, and that too in behalf of the maker, to impeach the note, by facts arising subsequent to the time of its execution. 15 Johns., 240; 10 *Id.*, 231; Peake *N. P.*, C. 6; 3 Johns. Cas., 195, per Thompson, *J.* A payee of a note payable to bearer or a third person, who has sold or transferred such a note, are not incompetent to show any other fact beside the execution of the note. He is shut out from this solely on the ground that he has, impliedly, warranted the note to be genuine, not forged. 15 Johns., 204; 16 *Id.*, 201. There being no other objection, when the execution of the note is proved, he is competent. But the witness offered in this case was not an indorser, and the objection was not even made to his competency, but related solely to the sufficiency of the matter proposed *to be proved by him. The [***255** court decided that this would not sustain the action. Had the decision related to the competency, on the ground of interest, the objection might have been removed by a release. In any point of view, however, interest cannot be objected here; for, taking the examination upon the *voir dire*, in connection with the offer of evidence, it is perfectly clear that the witness was not interested.

But the prominent point which the defendant in error probably intends to rely upon is, that the note could not be negotiated after the indorser was charged. In answer to this, we say, there is no legal objection to it, if it in fact remained unpaid to the time of the transfer. Chit. on Bills, ed. 1809, p. 104; 1 Show., 163; 1 T. R., 430; Bayl., 38, *n. d;* Doug., 633; Kyd on Bills, 89; 3 T. R., 80; 1 Bos. & P., 398. An indorser of a note for the accommodation of the maker, and without consideration, that fact being known to the indorser when he took the bill, is notwithstanding, liable to the indorsee; and that too even if the indorsee took the bill after it was due. 7 Johns., 361; 3 Esp., 46; 1 Taunt., 224. In *Lovell* v. *Evertson*, 11 Johns., 52, the note was indorsed after it became due. In that case, this court decided that when a note has been indorsed in blank, the owner had a right to fill it up with whose name he please, the defendant having nothing to do with the interest of the plaintiff. This point was also decided in 1800 by the Court of Errors, in *Cooper* v. *Kerr*, cited by Kent, *J.*, 3 Johns., Cas., 264. The only objection to the transfer of a note after it becomes due is, that it subjects the holder to all equities in favor of the preceding parties.

Should the objection be made that the indorsment was not filled up in fact, we answer, that the objection was not made in the court below, and being merely formal, should not be listened to here.

If it should be said that the plaintiff purchased the note *mala fide*, with intention to sue, we answer, that a party is not to be charged with a crime on mere presumption; but if otherwise, every presumption is repelled by the fact that a third person is employed as the attorney to prosecute the suit, the plaintiff deriving no benefit to himself by way of costs; and the money being demanded before this suit was brought. Again; if he intended to violate the Statue, still he has a remedy to recover the note, the transaction being before the Act of 1818. Indeed, the Act of 1813, which alone 256*] *can be objected here, was repealed by the Act of 1818. The suit in favor of White is not brought to the plaintiff's knowledge.

Messrs. D. Russell and *J. L Viele*, contra. To dispense with a demand upon the maker, when he was accessible, it was not enough to show that he was an infant. The note was not absolutely void for that reason, but continued good till the infant chose to void it. The law regards his interest alone in saying that it is void. As to all the other parties, it is good. To show infancy was, therefore, no benefit to the plaintiff. An indorsement like this always creates a mere contingent liability, resting upon the condition that a demand shall be made of the maker. It does not follow that he would have availed himself of his infancy, or that he had not ample funds to pay the note.

A. Harsha was not a competent witness. On being asked the question, he answered generally, that he was interested. The court are blamed for not pursuing the inquiry, and ascertaining whether the interest was fancied or real; but it is the counsel who was to blame. From the general answer, the court will intend that it was an actual, legal interest, until the contrary is shown by a particular explanation, which the witness should have been called on by the counsel to make. It does not follow that he could be interested merely as a party to the note. It might have arisen from some other transaction like the interest by which the witness was excluded in *Cowles* v. *Wilcox*, 4 Day Cas., 108.

The attorney was not a competent witness. In the first place he had transferred the note to the plaintiff, and was responsible to him if it should prove inoperative, or the claim upon it should fail in any way.

But if he was competent, his testimony was not so, to sustain the action. He swears that he transferred the note before it was due—took it up, and then transferred it to the plaintiff after it fell due. To this testimony an objection was made in gross, and the court rejected it, for what reason does not appear. Indeed, the bill is so general, in this respect, that it is unavailable to the party. It presents 257*] *no single point, and draws in question the whole merits of the case. 2 Cai., 168; 5 Johns., 467; 8 *Id.*, 495; 1 Bac. Abr., 528. But suppose all the points now made, to be reached by it, the plaintiff could not recover. In one count, the notice of non-payment is averred to be on the 4th; in the other, the 6th of Nov., either of which is too late; and the indorser was discharged.

Again; after the note had been taken up by Williams, supposing the notice to have been regular, it could not be transferred again. The rights of the indorsee, who fixed the indorser by notice, were personal. To make a demand and notice inure to the benefit of any indorsee, he should hold the note, or his name should appear upon it previous to or at the time the notice is given. A demand and notice cannot inure to the benefit of any one who is not a party when those steps are taken. The indorser engages that the maker shall honor the note; but no case goes so far as to make the liability of an indorser negotiable, after the note has been dishonored. The object of making a note negotiable at all, is to improve the facilities of commerce, by the circulation of commercial paper. Is this object to be answered by dishonored paper, the abhorrence of commercial policy? Under such circumstances, the transfer creates a new contract, unknown to the commercial law, and operative between the immediate parties only, as in the transfer of a chose in action at the common law. The law says that in all cases, to charge the indorser, the holder or his agent, must make the demand. Kyd on Bills, 125, 126; Chit. on Bills, 145, and cases there cited. Here the necessity and the right of a demand by the plaintiff had ceased. He did not hold in a commercial character. The right of action as between holder and indorser depends upon the privity of contract, and this contract is always that a demand shall be made and notice of non-payment given by the holder. Thus, where there are three indorsers, a demand of payment and notice by the second will not inure to the benefit of the third. Kyd on Bills, 117; Chit. on Bills, 240, 241. But a notice from a fifth indorsee to the first indorser, will inure to the benefit of all the intermediate indorsers. *Id, Ibid.* Yet, in the latter case, it could avail nothing, if notice was already given before the indorsement, for it was no longer a benefit to the indorser.

*Again; this note has been paid and [*258 taken up by the indorser. This is plainly inferable from the case, where we find it coming back into his hands; and the negotiability of the note was at an end within the cases of *Blake* v. *Sewall*, 3 Mass., 556, and *Boylston* v. *Green*, 8 *Id.*, 465.

That the note had been purchased by an attorney, was alone a sufficient objection to the recovery, unless he shows that he bought it in a manner consistent with the Act of 1813. 1 R. L., 417, sec. 7. No contract can avail, if it be in violation of a public Statute. 2 Cai., 147; 1 Com. on Cont., 30; Cowp., 343; 3 T. R., 23, 454; 5 *Id.*, 600; 5 Johns., 333.

Nor does it appear that the notice of non-payment, given in this case, was sufficient. A simple notice that the money had been demanded, and not paid, was not enough. It should not only be given by the holder, or one authorized by him; but apprise the indorser that he is to be looked to for payment.

Again; the indorsement was originally in blank, and remained so—and remains so still. The plaintiff could not recover upon it until it was filled up. Whoever might hold the note would have the same right to an action as the plaintiff. His name should have been inserted, either at or before the trial. This not being done, his case was not made out, and he was rightly nonsuited.

Mr. Williams, in reply, said the demand and notice were rightly stated in the declaration. The note being nominally payable Nov. 1, the 3d day of grace was the 4th. But the notice was in truth given on the 6th, because the 3d day of grace was on Saturday, a circumstance which entitled the holder to delay notice till Monday, which brought the time to the 6th. The second count was drawn with a view to this state of facts.

Curia, per WOODWORTH, *J.* The plaintiff declared against the defendant as indorser of a promissory note, made by Abner Harsha and Hugh Harsha, payable Nov. 1, 1815. The first count avers a demand of payment Nov. 4, and notice to the indorser. The second count avers that before the note fell due Hugh **259***] *Harsha absconded to places unknown, and afterwards, Nov. 4, payment was demanded of Abner Harsha, and notice given to the defendant, Nov. 6. At the trial, the plaintiff offered to prove that Abner Harsha, at the time of making the note, was an infant, which was overruled. Abner Harsha was then offered as a witness, who being sworn on his *voire dire*, testified that he was interested in the event of the suit. The plaintiff proposed to confine the inquiry to the fact of demanding payment; but the testimony was rejected.

William Williams, attorney for the plaintiff, sworn on his *voire dire*, testified that he bought the note in question of the defendant and paid $73; before it fell due, he sold it to a third person, who was not the plaintiff; that after it fell due it came into his hands again. He commenced a suit in the name of Seth White, who had nothing to do with the suit, the witness having the sole control of the note. The suit was discontinued. In Sept., 1817, the note became the property of the plaintiff, for whom the witness commenced this action. The witness was then sworn in chief. The plaintiff offered to prove that payment was demanded by him on the third day of grace of Abner Harsha; that Hugh Harsha had absconded before the note fell due; that on the day after the demand, the witness gave notice of the non-payment to the defendant. The witness then stated that the plaintiff first acquired an interest in the note in Sept., 1817, and that the relation given by him on his *voire dire* was true. The defendant objected to the evidence. The court sustained the objection, and the plaintiff offering no other testimony, directed him to be nonsuited. The plaintiff excepted to the opinion of the court on all the preceding points.

The court decided correctly in rejecting the testimony of Abner Harsha—whether he had an interest favorable to the plaintiff or defendant, does not appear; and without further explanation, the court had no means of judging. The plaintiff might have pursued the inquiry and ascertained the nature of the interest, and if it had then appeared that the interest was merely ideal, or against the party calling him, **260***] *he ought to have been admitted. 8 Johns., 428. Without doubt, the court were authorized to require from the witness a statement of the nature of his interest; but this was discretionary, and does not seem to have been called for. The plaintiff acquiesced in the general answer.

The evidence of Williams ought to have been received. He passed the note to the plaintiff on the original indorsement; but the execution by the makers being established, it does not appear that he had any interest in favor of the plaintiff's recovery. The evidence to prove a demand on one of the makers, and the absconding of the other, was relevant and material.

But it is urged, by the defendant's counsel, that the note was transferred to the plaintiff after it became due, and after it had been paid by the witness, Williams, and taken back by him; and therefore the plaintiff could not recover against the indorser, as upon a promissory note obtained before it became due; the right acquired by an indorsee, after having charged the indorser, not being transferable. It is a mistake to say that Williams had paid the note, and taken it back, whereby it lost its negotiability. The course of the transaction was this: Williams sold and transferred the note to a third person before it became due. After it became due, it came back to his hands; which does not imply a payment and taking up the note, but rather that he repurchased it of the holder. He afterwards sold it to the plaintiff. There is no legal objection to the validity of the transfer of a note after due, provided it remain unpaid, by any of the parties, whether the transfer is made by indorsement or mere delivery. When the indorsee takes a note after due, it is presumed he was acquainted with, or had notice of the circumstances, which would affect the validity of the note, had it been in the hands of the person who was holder at the time it became due, and consequently must stand in the character of the person who was the holder at that time. Chit. on Bills, 141, 142, ed. 1817; 7 T. R., 430; 3 T. R., 80; 1 Camph., 383.

The note being indorsed in blank, the owner had a right to fill it up with what name he pleased; the defendant had *no con-[***261** cern with that question. 11 Johns, 53. It was competent to fill up the blank on the trial, but as the court excluded the testimony, there was no necessity of doing so. A further answer is, that no objection was made on that ground.

It is also contended that Williams, being an attorney, could not purchase the note so as to maintain an action upon it, without showing that his purchase was consistent with the provisions of the Act on that subject. The Act of Apr. 21, 1818, has no connection with this case, which must be governed by the 7th section of the Act (1 R. L., 417). The former Act was passed subsequent to the trial of this cause, and does not affect it. The latter declares, that if an attorney shall purchase a note with intent to commence a suit thereon, and shall commence such suit, he shall be deemed guilty of a misdemeanor. This Statute puts the purchase upon the intent. The mere purchase cannot, I apprehend, warrant the conclusion that it was for the purpose of prosecution. It might equally well have been for other lawful cause. But admitting that the mere purchase of the note was, *prima facie*, sufficient, it was not conclusive as to the intent. Had the cause progressed, and that point been raised afterwards, it would have been competent for the plaintiff to have rebutted the presumption, and shown the fairness of the transaction, and submitted the question of intent to the jury. But the conclusive answer to this objection is, that it cannot now be alleged to support the opinion of the court below, in rejecting the testimony of Williams. The plaintiff was bound to prove a demand and notice. Without this he could not proceed a step. When he offers to prove it, it is premature to say, this evidence will answer no purpose, because the purchase was in violation of the Statute. It could not, in that stage of the cause, be known what would be the result of the trial, on that point. It was open to proof that might be subsequently introduced. It would, therefore, be both absurd and unjust not to permit the party to make out one part of this case, because, perchance, the plaintiff might not be able to remove another difficulty lying in his way.

262*] *The only remaining inquiry is, whether the proof offered would support the declaration. The first count alleges a demand of payment, and notice to the defendant Nov. 4, 1815. On that day it became due and payable. The general principle is, that the holder must use due diligence; for the indorser is only responsible after a default on the part of the maker. 2 Johns. Cas., 76; 2 Cai., 344. In *Stewart* v. *Eden*, 2 Cai., 127, the declaration was in the common form, stating a demand on the maker, a refusal to pay, and notice to the indorser. It appeared that the makers could not be found at their store, and a demand was made on their clerk. The court considered the precise question raised here; that is to say, if the maker, when a note falls due, cannot be found, nor payment demanded of him personally, should not the declaration state this fact specially, instead of averring generally, that the note was presented and payment refused? It was held that evidence of due diligence in the holder to obtain payment, without an actual demand, will support the averment; and under such a count the plaintiff may give evidence of any diligence which is deemed equivalent to an actual presentation of it to the maker. The same principle is recognized in *Saunderson* v. *Judge*, 2 H. Bl., 510, and *Ogden* v. *Cowley*, 2 Johns., 274.

But if the first count was objectionable, the second is special. It was, that Hugh Harsha had absconded; that a demand on the maker was made on the 4th, and notice given to the indorser Nov. 6. This was not too late; for Nov. 4 fell on Saturday in that year, so that the next legal day for serving notice was Monday, the 6th. 2 Cai., 343. When the plaintiff offers to prove notice given the next day after the demand, it must be understood as intending the next day proper for the transaction of secular business. At least, it ought so to have been considered by the court, until the plaintiff had been called on to answer whether, by the evidence, it was intended to prove notice on Sunday.

It is also objected that a demand made by Williams could be of no avail, on the ground, it is presumed, that he was not the holder when the note fell due. Notice must, undoubtedly, *be given by the holder or [*263 his agent. Williams sold the note before due; but it is to be inferred that he had the possession of it when he demanded payment, and must be considered the agent of the holder for that purpose, until it is shown he acted as a stranger, and without authority. We cannot prejudge this question, previous to an inquiry in what character and by what authority Williams acted. Had the evidence been admitted, the defendant might then have pursued the examination, and had it appeared, subsequently, that he did not stand in a situation to make a legal demand, the defendant would be entitled to the benefit of the objection. On the whole, I am of opinion that the judgment ought to be reversed, and a *venire de novo* issued by the Washington C. P.

Judgment reversed.

Cited in—6 Cow., 492; 19 Wend., 562; 23 Wend., 384; 7 Hill, 369; 1 Den., 612; 21 N. Y., 487; 31 N. Y., 445; 2 Keyes, 116; 3 Abb. App. Dec., 160; 6 Barb., 554; 29 How. Pr., 151; 6 Duer, 591; 1 Hilt., 530; 99 Mass., 621; 42 Am. Dec., 69; 26 Am. Dec., 733; 7 N. H., 202.

BURR v. VAN BUSKIRK.

Landlord and Tenant—Construction of Act Concerning Distresses—Distress, after Goods Removed—Filing Affidavit—Avowry.

The 13th section of the Act Concerning Distresses, &c., giving a right to distrain goods within a certain time after they are removed, is confined to the continuance of the lease, or the continuance of the landlord's right and the tenant's possession. Though the landlord's right continue, if the tenant's possession has ceased, there cannot be a distress, within that section, of the tenant's goods removed off the demised premises, though such distress be made within thirty days after the rent fell due.

An avowry of taking goods off the demised premises, for rent arrear, should show affirmatively that such possession continued, if the lease have expired, or it will be bad on general demurrer.

The 13th section of the Act Concerning Distresses, &c. (1 R. L., 437), as amended by the Act (sess. 43, ch. 194, sec. 7), authorizes the taking of goods which are removed off the demised premises, within thirty days after the rent for which they are distrained falls due; but they cannot be distrained for rent which fell due more than thirty days previous to the distress.

The common law did not allow a distress off the premises.

Previous to a distress for rent in the City of N. Y., the landlord must file an affidavit with the clerk of the city and county, that the rent distrained for is due, according to the Act (sess. 38, ch. 153).

The avowry must aver that this was done, or it will be bad on demurrer.

An avowry substantially bad in part is bad for the whole. *E. g.*, in an avowry for rent, arrear of taking goods off the demised premises, if only a part of the rent avowed for is the subject of distress, the avowry is bad for the whole.

Citations—Act, April 5, 1813; 4 Johns., 306; Act, April 13, 1820; Act, April 11, 1815.

REPLEVIN, for certain goods and chattels of the plaintiff, alleged in the declaration to have been taken May 8, 1821, at house No. 280, Broadway, City of N. Y.

*Avowry, substantially as follows: [*264 And the said defendant defends the wrong and injury, when, &c., and well avows, &c., because he says that at the time of making the demise unto the said plaintiff, hereinafter next mentioned, and from thence, &c., and at the said time when, &c., he, the said defendant, was and still is lawfully possessed of a certain unexpired term of thirty years from Mar. 25, A. D. 1804, of and in all that certain lot, &c. (describing certain premises in the City of N. Y.), and whereof the Rector and inhabitants of the Protestant Episcopal Church in the State of N. Y., on the said Mar. 25, were, &c., seised, &c., in fee; and which, on, &c., they demised to the said defendant for the term aforesaid, to wit: at, &c.; and being so possessed, &c., before the said time when, &c., to wit: Nov. 7, A. D. 1816, at, &c., the said defendant, by a certain note or memorandum in writing, bearing date the same day and year last aforesaid, and signed as well by the said defendant as by the said plaintiff, demised to the said plaintiff; and he, the said plaintiff, then and there rented of the said defendant all that certain dwelling-house and premises, known as house No. 61, Vesey St., in the City of N. Y., with its appurtenances, being part and parcel of the said lot, piece or parcel of land hereinbefore mentioned and described, and which the said Rector, &c., had heretofore demised to the said defendant, and whereof he was possessed as aforesaid, to have and to hold, &c., to him, the said plaintiff, for and during the term of five years, from May 1 then last past, &c., at and for the yearly rent of $250, &c., payable quarterly, &c., on the 1st days of Aug., Nov., Feb. and May, in each and every year of the said term, &c., in and by even and equal portions of $87.50, on each, &c. By virtue of which said demise, &c., he, the said plaintiff, entered, &c., and because the sum of $350, for the rent aforesaid, for a part of the 2d quarter and the whole of the two last quarters of the last year of the said term of five years, ending May 1, A. D. 1821, and from thence until, and at the said time when, &c., was due and in arrear from the said plaintiff to the said defendant, the residue of the said rent and sum of $350, **265***] for *the said last year, to wit: the sum of $87.50 for the 1st quarter, and $12.50 in part and on account of the 2d quarter of the said last year of the said term of five years, with all the previous rents having been paid and satisfied; and because the said plaintiff, within thirty days next before the taking of the said goods, &c., or any part thereof, to wit: on the same day and year in the said declaration mentioned, had conveyed and carried off from the aforesaid premises, so as aforesaid demised to him, the said goods and chattels in the said declaration mentioned, being the proper goods and chattels of the said plaintiff, leaving the aforesaid sum of $250, above mentioned, as parcel of the said rent as aforesaid due and unpaid; and had conveyed and carried the said goods and chattels into the said dwelling-house in the said declaration mentioned, in which, &c., he, the said defendant, well avows the taking the said goods and chattels in the aforesaid dwelling-house, in which, &c., at the said time when, &c., after the aforesaid sum of $250, &c., was so in arrear and unpaid as aforesaid; and being within thirty days next after the said goods and chattels were and had been so conveyed and carried off and from the aforesaid premises demised to the said plaintiff as aforesaid, and justly, &c., as and for a distress for the said sum of $250, &c., and which said sum of $250 still remains due and in arrear to the said defendant, &c., to wit: at, &c., and this, &c., wherefore, &c.

A second and third avowry followed this, being substantially the same as the first, for the purpose of the questions raised by the counsel or determined by the court.

Demurrer and joinder to each avowry, assigning, for causes of demurrer: 1. That, upon the facts set forth, the defendant would not have been entitled to a distress at common law; and the avowries showed no custom and referred to no statute authorizing the distress. 2. That the avowries were introduced by the words, "comes and defends the wrong and injury," &c., whereas they should have been "force and injury," &c. 3. That it did not appear by the avowries that the defendant, previous to making the distress, complied with the requisitions of the "Act Concerning Distressess for Rent in the City of N. Y." passed Apr. 11, 1815, by making *an affidavit [***266** of the amount of rent due, and filing it as required by that Act. *Vide* 3 Laws, sess. 38, ch. 153. Nor did the avowries in any way refer to the Act.

Mr. A. Burr, in support of the demurrers:

1. The defendant avows upon the 13th section of the Act of 1813, commonly called the Landlord and Tenant Act (1 R. L., 437), which allows the landlord to follow the goods for thirty days after their removal, and after the rent becomes due. This section does not authorize a distress, after the determination of the lease. The 17th section of this Act gives that power, under several restrictions, one of which is that the distress, after the determination of the lease, must be made during the continuance of the tenant's possession. But this section does not allow the distress to be made off the premises. That is done by the 13th section, but then the distress must be made during the continuance of the lease. By common law, a distress could not be made off the premises. We have no statute authorizing a distress, after the determination of the lease, off the premises; nor have the English. Such a distress would be illegal.

In his avowries, the defendant shows that he distrained the goods after the lease was determined, and off from the premises, bringing himself within the provisions of the 13th section: and, *mutatis mutandis*, he follows the English precedents under 8 Anne, ch. 14, secs. 1, 2, from which the 13th section of our Statute is taken. The 6th and 7th sections of this Statute of Anne give the power of distress after the determination of the lease. The 17th section of our Statute is, in all essential parts, a transcript of the 6th and 7th sections of Anne.

2. The 13th section of the Act of 1813, upon which the defendant avows, is repealed by the 7th section of the Act of 1820 (sess. 43, ch. 194). He has, therefore, shown no authority for making the distress; for a distress at common law was not allowed off the premises. This is good cause of general demurrer.

3. The avowries do not show a conformity to the requisitions of the Statute of Apr. 11, 1815 (sess. 38, ch. 153), which requires an affidavit to be made and filed previously *to [***267** a distress, in the City of N. Y. This is a

public Act, though not declared to be so expressly; for it is, in effect, only an amendment to the general Act relating to the City, of 1813, which is public; and it creates a penalty which is equivalent to a forfeiture; and it concerns the people, for they must sue for the penalty.

4. The defendant confesses a distress off the premises, for rent which had been due longer than 30 days. This is not authorized by any statute, and if the defendant had avowed upon the right statute (Statute of 1820), he would be a wrong-doer by his own showing; for the Statute of 1820 extends the power of distress off the premises, to 30 days only, after the rent became due; so that he had only a right to distrain for the last quarter; what remained upon the previous quarter having been due more than 30 days before the distress. The avowries are entire, and being bad for part, are bad for the whole.

5. The fee in all the avowries, is laid in the Corporation of Trinity Church. Corporations cannot hold real estate without authority by statute, and no statute is set out or referred to, giving that authority.

Mr. E. Williams, contra. The answer to the first cause of demurrer is, that the right of distress, in all cases, is incident to the lease, and herein the Act is a public one. The court will take notice of it, without its being pleaded or referred to.

The formal objection, that wrong is used instead of force, is contradicted by all the precedents of avowries, to be found in the books of practice. The word "force" is not substituted for "wrong" in all actions of tort. It is only used in such actions of tort as are accompanied by force, such as trespass *vi et armis*, either to the person, or to property real or personal. But no force is presumed in replevin. The gist of his action consists not in the wrongful taking, but in the wrongful detaining of the goods, &c., which negatives the idea of force.

If no affidavit was made or filed, the plaintiff should have availed himself of the omission by plea. It is in the nature of a proviso in the Statute, and the party pleading need not 268*] *negative or aver it in the first instance, but may leave it himself, if the opposite party should take advantage of it by plea, to reply as the facts and nature of the case may require.

The old Statute, giving a right to distrain goods off the premises, was an enlargement of the common law right of distress; an extension of that right to goods removed off the demised premises, if exercised within 30 days after the goods are removed, for any rent which would reach them on the premises, provided they had continued there during that time. But the provisions of the 13th section of that Act (1 R. L., 437) were defective. If the tenant removed his goods more than 30 days before the rent fell due, he evaded the distress. The rent not being due at the time of the removal, the landlord could not then distrain; and when the rent accrued, his right was no better, because the 30 days had expired. It being found that the 13th section of the old Act thus defeated its own object, it was amended by the 7th section of the Statute (sess 43, ch. 194), which extends the right conferred by the old law to 30 days after the rent falls due, leaving it in full force as to all the rent which had fallen due at any time previous to a removal of the goods. The last repeals only the repugnant parts of the previous section. Standing together, they read thus: "the landlord may distrain the goods for any rent due at the time of, or within 30 days after their removal, and for any rent which may afterwards accrue, within 30 days after it becomes due and payable." The old was repugnant to the new section in the single particular only, that it confined the taking, in all cases, to 30 days from the act of removal. The entire rent became due May 1, and the landlord had a right, within these Statutes, to an entire distress for the whole, within 30 days after the removal. The opposite construction would drive the landlord to different remedies, for different quarters of the same rent.

Curia, per WOODWORTH, *J.* It appears from the avowries that the defendant demised to the plaintiff certain premises in N. Y., for the term of five years, ending May 1, 1821, at the yearly rent of $350, payable quarterly. The defendant avows the taking of the goods off the premises, May 8, 1821, for $250 rent in arrear, being for *the rent of the two [*269 last quarters, and a part of the second quarter of the last year; the plaintiff having removed the goods from the demised premises within 30 days previous to the time of making the distress. The lease having terminated May 1, 1821, the first question is, whether the remedy by distress is applicable to this case.

The 13th section of the Act Concerning Distresses (1 R. L., 437) declares, that if the lessee shall convey his goods or chattels from the demised premises, leaving the rent unpaid, it shall be lawful for the lessor, within 30 days, to seize the goods as a distress. The remedy thus given is operative, during the continuance of the lease only. After the term has expired, the lessor, by this section, had no other than the common law remedy, which did not allow a distress off the premises. That this is the construction to be given, is apparent by adverting to the 16th and 17th sections of the same Act, which, after reciting that lessees for years frequently hold over the tenements demised, after the determination of the lease, and that after the determination of such lease, no distress by law can be made for arrears of rent that grew due previous to such determination, gives the right to distrain in such cases, in the same manner the lessor might have done, if the lease had not been determined; provided the distress be made within six months, and during the continuance of the landlord's title, and during the possession of the tenant, from whom the rent became due. In this case, the distress was made within the time limited; the landlord's title continued; but there is no averment that the plaintiff's possession continued. The question, then, arises, is the avowry good on general demurrer, without alleging that the plaintiff continued in possession of the demised premises when the distress was made. It is a general rule that matter which should come more properly from the other side, need not be stated. Unless the plaintiff's possession continued, there was no right of distress; it was, therefore, matter of substance to allege the fact, in order to support the avowry. The proviso forms no part of the plaintiff's title; he declares for unlawfully taking his goods. The defendant **270*]** *must rely on the right given by the 17th section to support his avowries. That right is not general, but qualified. Without bringing himself within the proviso, the court cannot say that any right to distrain existed. The proviso may be said to furnish matter of excuse or justification for the defendant, and need not be negatived in the declaration. *Teel* v. *Fonda*, 4 Johns., 306. I think the avowries bad on this ground.

There is another objection which seems to be conclusive. Apr. 13, 1820 (Vol. V., L., 178 *b*), an Act passed to amend the Act of Apr. 5, 1813, Concerning Distresses. This was prior to the distress made, and so far as it applies must govern. It has made some material alterations, as to the right of the landlord to distrain. The 7th section declares that the landlord, within 30 days after the rent shall became due, may seize, as a distress, the goods or chattels of the lessee, which may have been conveyed away, or carried from the demised premises, and that so much of the 13th section of the Act of 1813, as is repugnant thereto, be repealed. Here, then, it is manifest, that even if the defendant had brought himself within the proviso of the 17th section of the preceding Act, his right must be governed by the 13th section as amended by the 7th section of the Act of 1820. The effect of the amendment is to take away the right to seize the goods within 30 days after they were carried away, and, instead thereof, to authorize a seizure within 30 days after the rent became due. In this respect, the 13th section is repugnant to the 7th section. Before the passing of this Act, the landlord, by virtue of the 17th section, could, if within its proviso, distrain in the same manner he might have done if the lease had not been determined; that is, he might take the goods without reference to the time the rent became due, but within a certain time after they were conveyed away. After the Act of 1820, there was no right to distrain goods off the premises in any case, but from the time the rent was payable. Although the general right to distrain, after the termination of the lease, is six months, by the 7th section, that right cannot be exercised, where more than 30 days have elapsed after the rent became due.

271*] *This alteration materially affects the security of the landlord; it is thereby lessened. Before Apr. 13, 1820, if, at the end of the third quarter, the tenant removed his goods, the landlord might distrain within 30 days, for three quarters' rent; but now, on the same state of facts, he can only distrain for the rent of the third quarter; because no more than that became due within thirty days. The landlord's right is, in like manner, restricted, where the term has ended—he would only be authorized to distrain for the last quarter of the term, because all the preceding quarters had been due more than 30 days; and as to the last quarter, the right is lost unless exercised within that period.

In the avowries pleaded, the defendant claims rent for the third, fourth and part of the second quarter, amounting to $250, and has distrained for that sum. All but the last quarter had been due more than 30 days, and the second quarter more than 6 months. The defendant had no right to distrain for more than the last quarter, and consequently the avowry is bad for all beyond that amount. Being materially defective in part, it is bad for the whole on general demurrer.

There is another defect in the avowry, which I incline to think material. The Act of Apr. 11, 1815 (Vol. III. L., 156 *c*), declares that no landlord shall distrain in the City of N. Y. before making an affidavit, stating the amount due for rent, and filing the affidavit in the clerk's office. There is no averment that this step has been taken. Without it, the distress was illegal. This being matter within the knowledge of the defendant, and necessary for his defense, the fact ought to have been alleged in the avowry.

Judgment for plaintff on the demurrer, with leave to the defendant to amend.

Rule accordingly.

Explained—6 Hill, 30.
Overruled—5 Cow., 408.
Cited in—5 Cow., 329; 1 Wend., 309.

---

*REW *v.* BARBER. [*272

(*Vide* S. C., by the title of Rew v. Barker, 2 Cow., 508, where the record was amended as to the time of sale.)

Levy, under Execution—Whether Leaving Property with Debtor, Renders Execution Fraudulent—Taking Note of Third Party, in Payment of Debt—Warranty of Title.

Where a sheriff levied on a horse under a *fi. fa.* and conveyed him to the plaintiff in the *fi. fa.*, who directed him to return the horse to the defendant, which he did and left him there in the defendant's possession—who sold the horse to R., who sold him him to B., who purchased *bona fide*, without notice of the levy, from whom the sheriff took him, and sold him at auction under the execution: the first sale to R. was also *bona fide* and without notice of the levy; in an action by B. against R. upon a breach of the implied warranty of title, held, that B. was entitled to recover.

Merely leaving property levied upon in the possession of the defendant in the execution, though with the plaintiff's consent, is not, *per se*, fraudulent, either as against subsequent creditors or purchasers.

Otherwise, where the sheriff is directed to delay the execution or sale.

The acceptance of the note of a third person on the sale of a chattel, for the consideration money, is payment.

It is equivalent to the payment of money, and on a failure of title, an action lies for money had and received, to recover the amount of the consideration money and interest.

Assumpsit is the proper form of action, where there is a warranty of title express or implied in the sale of a chattel.

A warranty of title is implied on the sale of a chattel.

Citations—2 Johns., 416; 2 T. R., 596; 7 Mod., 37; 11 Johns., 110, 409; 8 Johns., 20; 2 Esp., 517; 6 Johns., 168; 1 Johns., 274.

NOTE.—*Execution—Leaving property levied on, in hands of debtor—When it renders execution void.* The result of the authorities is, that it is sufficient to constitute a valid levy even against a subsequent *bona fide* purchaser from the debtor; that 1. The

ERROR from the Court of C. P. of the County of Onondaga. Barber sued Rew in the court below, and declared against him for money lent and money had and received. Plea, the general issue. The cause was tried at Nov. Term, 1819, when the jury found a special verdict as follows: "that on the 19th Nov., 1818, Rew (the defendant below) sold a certain brown horse to Barber (the plaintiff below) for $111; and the plaintiff paid him in a note against one Shankland for $130, the defendant giving his note to the plaintiff for the balance; that in the month of Oct., next previous to the sale, Jabish Castle, one of the deputies of the sheriff of Onondaga, having a *fi. fa.* for $59, in favor of Elijah Rust against Peter W. Yates, who then owned the horse in question, came to the house of Yates and levied on the horse; that at the time of the levy there were two other horses, two cows and his library and farming utensils in the deputy's sight and power. He did not take an inventory of them as levied on; but, considering the horse as sufficient, took him away, and carried him to Aaron Benedict, who then bought the execution, and requested him to keep the horse; but directed him to take the horse back and leave him in Yates' custody—which he accordingly did. Yates soon after sold the horse to the defendant, who purchased him in good faith, without knowledge of the levy. That in the month of Nov., next thereafter, Castle received another *fi. fa.* in favor of Benedict against Yates, which he **273***] levied upon all the property of *Yates, taking an inventory of it under the second execution. The horse, having been previously sold by Yates, was not in his possession at the time of the second levy. Castle then advertised for sale all the property levied on by the two executions, generally, without discrimination, and having taken the horse from the plaintiff previous to the day of sale, proceeded to sell the other property first, without reference to any specific execution, until it was exhausted. The sales amounted to several hundred dollars, being enough to satisfy the second execution and $4 over. He then set up the horse on the first execution, sold him for $54, to one Daniel Wood, who bid in behalf of Benedict, and delivered him to Wood. Both executions were returnable at Nov. Term, 1818, and the second levy was prior to the return day of the first. But whether, &c., and pray, &c., and if, &c., they assess the damages of the plaintiff to $118.77, &c. But if, &c." Judgment for the plaintiff below on the special verdict, whence the defendant below brought error to this court.

Mr. Talcott, Atty-Gen., for the plaintiff in error.

1. Leaving the horse in Yates' possession rendered the levy fraudulent and void against purchasers as well as creditors. Sending the horse back to Yates discharged the lien, and his sale to a *bona fide* purchaser conveyed a good title. No doubt there was a valid levy originally (2 Johns., 422); but it was discontinued. Suffering property levied upon to remain with the debtor is fraudulent and void as against subsequent executions. This is the general rule as recognized in *Whipple* v. *Foot Id.*, 418; though the removal of a growing crop was excused as being an exception to the rule, founded in necessity. And in *Storm* v. *Woods*, 11 Johns., 112, the general rule is laid down and enforced in terms, "that if a creditor seize the goods of his debtor, on an execution, and suffer them to remain in his hands, the execution is deemed fraudulent and void against a subsequent execution." This rule, say the judges, has been long established in the English courts (1 Wils., 44; 1 Salk., 720, 721; 1 Ld. Raym., 251; 5 Mod., 377; 7 Mod., 37; 2 T. R., 287, 596; 1 Tidd. Pr., 919, 920; 1 Esp., 205; 1 Campb., 333), and is founded upon reasons best calculated to prevent fraud." Yet it is not necessary, in this case, to contend that an actual removal *is necessary. [***274** The creditor does more to indicate fraud than a mere neglect to remove. After having the property removed, and in the actual custody of the deputy, he relinquishes all control over it, and sends it back to the debtor, as if the execution had been discharged. It was giving Yates a false credit, and exciting a confidence, upon the strength of which Rew became a purchaser. As such, it comes directly within the language of the court in *Knox* v. *Summers*, 4 Yeates, 477, 478-9; and in the previous case of *Guardians of the Poor* v. *Lawrence, Id.*, 194, the court decided that where the plaintiff, or his attorney, deems it necessary to put an officer in the defendant's house, to preserve the lien of an execution, the withdrawing him, and suffering the defendant to go on as usual with his business, is a relinquishment of the execution. The court admit that, by the practice of Pennsylvania, the plaintiff does not lose his lien on a *fi. fa.* by the sheriff's not removing the goods levied upon, unless their continuance in the defendant's possession led to a false credit, and injured third persons. They say that the practice, however, is different in England, which had been adopted by the U. S. Circuit Court for that district; that it is held, in England, that the goods of the defendant must be removed to a place of safe custody, within a reasonable time, otherwise the officer who was placed in the house would become a trespasser; and that the late practice in the City of Philadelphia was the same;

---

property is in the view and under the control of the officer. 2. That he takes possession of it either by removing it or by an oral declaration that a levy is intended and that he claims to hold the goods under such levy. 3. That an inventory or at least a memorandum of the levy is made at the time. 4. Leaving the goods in the possession of the debtor, until the sale, is at the risk of the officer, but does not invalidate the levy. Bond v. Willett, 1 Abb. Ct. App. Dec., 165; 1 Keyes, 377; 29 How. Pr., 47. See, also, Dean v. Campbell, 19 Hun, 534; Farrington v. Sinclair, 15 Johns., 428; Farrington v. Caswell, 15 Johns., 430; Dickenson v. Cook, 17 Johns., 332; Russell v. Gibbs, 5 Cow., 390; Roth v. Wells, 29 N. Y., 471; Ray v. Harcourt, 19 Wend., 495; Dunderdale v. Sanvestre, 13 Abb. Pr., 116; Camp v. Chamberlain, 5 Den., 198.

To constitute a valid levy the property must be within the power and control of the officer when it is made, and he must take it into his possession in a reasonable time thereafter, and in such an open unequivocal manner as to apprise everybody that it has been taken in execution. Davidson v. Waldron, 31 Ill., 130. See Quackenbush v. Henry, 42 Mich., 75; Wunderlich v. Roberts, 67 Ind., 421; Murphy v. Swadener, 33 Ohio St., 85.

Acceptance of note, of third person, as payment. See Whitbeck v. Van Ness, 11 Johns., 409, *note*.

that the plaintiff's attorney having proceeded according to that practice, but withdrawn the officer, this must be deemed a relinquishment of the effect of the execution. In the *U. S.* v. *Conyngham*, 4 Dall., 358, the naked point was decided by the Circuit Court of the U. S., that leaving goods with the defendant in the execution is fraudulent as to subsequent executions. In *Chancellor* v. *Philips*, *Id.*, 213, the Supreme Court of Pa. decided the very point in question here, admitting it to depend upon a mere neglect to remove the goods. The sheriff had levied on a kiln of unburnt bricks, and other property, in June, 1798, but suffered them to remain in the defendant's possession till Apr., 1799, when, on putting them up for sale, it was found that one of the defendants had sold **275***] the bricks to *a *bona fide* purchaser without notice of the levy. The sheriff, at the time of the levy, employed a man to call at the brick yard occasionally, but did not keep any person constantly there. On this state of facts, it was decided that the purchaser should hold the bricks, although the court agreed that a different practice had prevailed and been established in cases of a levy upon household furniture, which might be left with the defendant without prejudice to the levy. The present is certainly a stronger case for the purchaser, as the acts of abandonment are much less equivocal.

2. But if we are wrong in supposing that all lien was lost, we then say that the evidence does not support the declaration. The action was for money lent, and money had and received; whereas, in fact, no money passed between the parties. But, if otherwise, it is, at least, questionable whether such an action will lie to try the title upon a breach of warranty.

Mr. S. A. Foot, contra. I am not aware that it can make any difference in principle, whether the horse was returned to Yates with or without the consent of the plaintiff in the execution, or his assignee. This is not a litigation between him and the purchaser, or between the sheriff and the purchaser; but it is an action by a purchaser, two removes from Yates, the defendant in the execution, against the first purchaser, upon the implied warranty of title. The second purchaser, deriving title from Yates, buys and takes possession, which possession is devested by the sheriff, who claims a prior title under Yates. We must, then, look to the source whence these two derive their title. Had Yates a title, and a right to sell and pass the property to the defendant below? As between Yates and the sheriff, had the former a title? This is the true inquiry; because the purchaser must always take care as to what right passes by the sale; and if it fails, he must look to his vendor. If Yates had no title, how could he give one to Rew, and Rew to Barber? The cases cited are all, I presume, where the question raised was directly between the plaintiff in the execution levied, and some third person claiming, **276***] as against him, the priority either as *a creditor or purchaser. I agree that where the plaintiff either levies or purchases, and leaves the property remaining in possession of the debtor, he cannot enforce his claim directly against third persons.

It is conceded that this was a good levy; and if so, Yates had no right to sell. Whatever the judges of Pa., or the U. S. Circuit Court of that State, may say upon this question, we have our own settled law as to what shall constitute a levy. It is not material, even at the beginning, that the sheriff should take the property into his actual possession. If he sees it, and has it within his reach, and under his control, it is enough. This constitutes a levy; and does the law require that the acts of possession should be more distinct and open, in order to continue a levy, than to constitute the levy itself? The mere taking an inventory, without any further act, would clearly amount to a levy, the sheriff having the property within his power; or any other act manifesting a mere intention to take. *Haggerty* v. *Wilber*, 16 Johns., 287. If the levy was good, it follows, as a necessary consequence, that the sheriff may afterwards take the property, wherever he can find it. If a levy is good, and good even without actual possession, how can it come to nothing, from the mere want of actual possession? If the levy was good, the argument of the other side fails entirely. At any rate, it is not inquirable between these parties, whether the sheriff took or retained the property in his actual possession, or not. Is it to be endured that Barber, a purchaser, shall be made accountable for the irregularity of the sheriff's proceedings? It is enough that these were regular on their face. Is a purchaser bound to examine all the sheriff's acts in detail? The horse was taken from our possession, and sold for Yates' benefit, who was the first vendor. The burden of the litigation is thrown upon us, and we had the right, on an authority being presented which is regular on its face, or apparently good, to surrender the property, without further inquiry. The vendor is bound to afford the vendee a full indemnity against every claim of title *prima facie*, good; and all he can exact is, that the vendee should keep the property till a claim is presented apparently fair.

*The case of *Witherby* v. *Mann*, 11 [***277** Johns., 518, and *Barclay* v. *Goock*, 2 Esp., 571, decide that we had a right to treat the note given in consideration, as money. It was received in payment. *Id. Ibid. Whitbeck* v. *Van Ness*, 11 Johns., 409. The consideration having totally failed, it is well settled that we may disaffirm the contract, and bring our action for the consideration money paid.

The Atty-Gen., in reply. The gentleman is certainly mistaken in his doctrine as to the extent of indemnity which the vendor is bound to yield. It is true, that if the vendee gives notice to the vendor, of a suit pending against the former, in which the title is involved, a recovery against him, upon whatever foundation, will render the vendor liable: but this court have established no rule by which he is entitled to indemnity for vexatious claims, however plausible. It is a strange doctrine, that the vendee shall be paid the value of the article by the vendor, merely because the claim upon which he surrenders the property is, *prima facie*, good. Suppose it had appeared that the judgment had been released, a fact which the vendee might not know, but yet he thinks proper to surrender the article sold; how do we stand, within the rule contended for on the other side? We cannot bring an action for the horse, because we have sold, and have no title. The vendee, alone, can vindicate the true claim; and if he is protected, in the surrender, by a *prima facie* case, and can recover over against us, we are left without remedy.

The question between these parties must be the same as between any others. If the sheriff had been sued by Barber for his wrongful act in taking the property, he could not have set up his execution and levy as a defense. The question would be, in that case, as it is here, whether the levy had not been waived. Suppose the horse had passed through 500 hands, by as many sales; the derivative title of the last vendee must depend upon the very same inquiry as would be pertinent between the plaintiff in the execution and third persons, or between him and the sheriff in reference to the rights of third persons. Is the title of a remote 278*] vendee to *be assailed, in this manner, by a dormant execution, merely because an ultimate remedy by suit may be had against, perhaps, an insolvent vendor? The very man who seeks to avoid the sale, is the one who put it in the power of the defendant, the original insolvent vendor, to make the sale. The plaintiff in the execution was a party to the fraud, and comes to avoid the sale in his own wrong.

Curia, per WOODWORTH, *J.* It is found, by the special verdict, that on the 19th Nov., 1818, the defendant in the court below sold a horse to the plaintiff, and received in payment a note against a third person.

In Oct., previous to the sale, the sheriff levied on the horse, under an execution, in favor of A. Rust, against Peter W. Yates, the horse then being his, and brought the horse to Benedict, who purchased the execution, and directed the sheriff to return and leave the horse in the custody of Yates. Yates soon after sold to Rew, the plaintiff, who purchased in good faith, without knowledge of the levy. In Nov. the sheriff received another execution, in favor of Benedict against Yates, and levied on all his property. The sheriff took the horse from Barber, and sold under both executions. Benedict became the purchaser of the horse.

If the plaintiff's title has failed, he has good cause of action against the defendant. That will depend on the question, whether leaving the horse in the possession of Yates, rendered the execution fraudulent. There was no direction to suspend or delay the execution, or permission to Yates to use the property. The case of *Whipple* v. *Foot*, 2 Johns., 416, is relied on, by the plaintiff in error, to show that the execution was fraudulent. In that case, the sheriff levied on wheat growing, and several months afterwards, when the wheat was ripe for harvest, cut and carried it away, and sold it at auction. A subsequent execution was issued, and levied on the same wheat in the sheaf. It was held that the first execution was not dormant, the sheriff having taken all the possession of which the nature of the chattel was susceptible; that it could not be considered as coming within the operation of *the rule, that if a creditor seize the [*279 goods of his debtor on execution, and suffer them to remain in his hands, the execution is deemed fraudulent and void against a subsequent execution. As the chattel, in that case, could not be removed before harvest, the execution could not be affected by the omission, admitting that the single fact of directing property levied on to remain with the debtor, until sale, would, in general, render it fraudulent. It was not necessary to decide this last point, for the cause did not depend on it. But mere possession by the defendant will not affect the creditor's claim, or give a second execution priority. The cases cited do not support the doctrine to that extent. In *Edwards* v. *Harben*, 2 T. R., 596, it was held that where an absolute bill of sale was given, and the creditor agrees to leave the goods in possession of the debtor, it is fraudulent against creditors. But this, I apprehend, has no connection with the question of permitting the goods to remain with the defendant in the execution, after levy, until the day of sale. The case in 7 Mod., 37, referred to by the court, was this: the creditor caused a levy to be made, but would not let the sheriff proceed further, and suffered the goods to remain in the custody of the debtor. This was held to be a fraudulent execution, and that a second execution might seize the same goods. The ground here evidently was, making use of the execution as a cover, by directing the sheriff not to proceed; and is in accordance with the cases in our courts, where executions have been held dormant, in consequence of directions given by the creditor, to delay, and not proceed; but it is no authority to prove that the mere possession by the debtor will produce the same result, although the sale takes place as early as the return day of the writ, or within a few days after. The broad principle laid down in *Whipple* v. *Foot* is recognized in *Storm* v. *Woods*, 11 Johns., 110, and would seem to sanction the doctrine contended for; but it must be understood, that when the court say "suffering the goods to remain in the hands of the debtor, the possession is deemed fraudulent," that the debtor retains such execution in consequence of instructions by the creditor to delay, or not to proceed on the execution. The subsequent cases show that *the [*280 latter is the ground upon which this doctrine rests. Thus, in *Doty* v. *Turner*, 8 Johns., 20, the plaintiff, by his agent, directed the sheriff to levy on the property, and informed him that if it remained in the possession of the defendant, after the levy, the plaintiff would not hold the sheriff responsible if it was squandered, and that he need not take a receipt for it. After the levy he did nothing further until after the return day, and a second execution delivered, when he sold on both. It was held that as there was no instruction to delay the execution after the seizure, or to let it sleep in the sheriff's hands, the first execution did not lose its preference. The decision is founded on this, that there was no direction for delay. The court put it upon this ground, and observe, "therefore, the case does not come within the rule of the common law recognized in *Whipple* v. *Foot*." All the cases I have met with proceed on the principle that the creditor had interfered and directed a delay of sale, and left the goods with the debtor. In every such case a second execution would have the preference. The sheriff, then, rightfully took possession of the horse and sold him, whereby the title of Barber failed.

The only remaining question is, whether he has selected the proper form of action. The acceptance of the note of a third person, was payment and satisfaction for the consideration money. *Whitbeck* v. *Van Ness*, 11 Johns., 409; 2 Esp., 517. *Assumpsit* is the proper form of action, where there is warranty, express or implied, in the sale of a chattel. 6 Johns., 168. A warranty of a title is implied. 1 Johns., 274. The consideration upon which money was paid having failed, it may be recovered back under the count for money had and received.

I am of opinion that the judgment of the court below be affirmed.

Judgment affirmed.

S. C.—2 Cow., 408.

Cited in—5 Cow., 395; 5 Wend., 275; 15 Wend., 629; 16 Wend., 350; 21 Wend., 452; 2 Den., 142; 13 N. Y., 171; 40 N. Y., 285; 45 N. Y., 496; 1 Lans., 145; 3 Barb., 329; 18 Barb., 323; 2 T. & C., 343; 33 How. Pr., 191; 36 How. Pr., 526; 1 Sand., 87; 2 Duer, 381; 12 Leg. Obs., 10; 5 Biss., 42; 27 Am. Dec., 653 (2 Porter, 280).

281*] *VIANNA ET AL.

v.

BARCLAY AND BARCLAY.

Factors—Instructions of Principal—Expressing Belief, as to Price, does not Constitute Instructions — Principal's Assent Presumed from Silence.

Letters of instruction from a merchant to his consignee and factor, not expressly mentioning a price below which goods consigned for sale shall not be sold, but merely communicating a belief that the excellent qualities of the goods will command a certain price, and expressing it as the sum confidently expected to be realized on a sale, will not be construed as fixing the minimum price at which the goods shall be sold; and a sale for a less sum by the factor, in good faith and withour negligence, will not be deemed a breach of instructions, nor render the factor liable in damages.

Though a factor disregard his instructions, the principal, after advice of this fact, ought to dissent, and give notice of his dissent in a reasonable time; otherwise, his assent to his factor's acts will be presumed.

Citation—12 Johns., 300.

CASE by the plaintiffs, merchants in Portugal, against the defendants, commission merchants in N. Y., for selling a quantity of port wine, consigned by the former to the latter, at a less price than directed, tried at the N. Y. sittings, Nov. 4, 1821.

At the trial the consignment and delivery of the wine were proved; and the only dispute was whether the defendants had acted fraudulently or negligently, or had violated the plaintiffs' instructions by selling below the price to which they were limited; or, if they had done the latter, whether the plaintiffs had not waived the instructions which they gave, limiting the price, by certain acts of recognition subsequent to the sale. These questions depended on a voluminous mass of evidence, including a tedious correspondence between the parties, the whole of which was spread upon the case, and very fully examined by the learned counsel who argued the cause, the only difference between whom related to the result of the evidence. This result, and all the evidence material to a report, being given in the opinion of the court, I omit a statement of the case here. Verdict for the plaintiff for $1,500, subject to the opinion of the court.

Mr. A. L. M'Donald, for the plaintiff.

Mr. J. Duer, contra.

Mr. D. B. Ogden, in reply.

Curia, per WOODWORTH, *J.* From a review of the testimony it appears, very satisfactorily, that the defendants used reasonable diligence to make sale of the wine to the best advantage. I have not discovered any ground for the *imputation of fraud while acting [*282 as agents and factors of the plaintiffs; and if the defendants are liable, it must be on the ground of a departure from instructions given as to the terms of sale. This is a question of fact, the decision of which must depend upon the construction of the correspondence between the parties. There is nothing explicit on this point. The letter of June 18, 1816, accompanying the consignment of the wine, says "its price is £52 per pipe," expressing a hope that it may be sold readily, being of superior quality. The defendants, in reply, stated that the market was overstocked; that saving sales could not then be effected; and that the plaintiffs might be assured of their best exertions when it could be without a sacrifice.

I incline to think the plaintiffs did not intend, by the instructions, to fix the minimum price at £52. The expressions seem rather to have proceeded from a belief that the excellent quality of the wine would command that sum; and, therefore, instead of directing generally to sell for the best price that could be obtained, they specify the sum confidently expected to be realized, probably to prevent precipitancy in the disposition of the property and induce greater exertions, if, unfortunately, they had consigned to an unfavorable market. The fact that the instructions are somewhat ambiguous supports this construction; for if an express limitation was in view at the time, it is reasonable to expect it would have been explicitly given. What was the state of the market was unknown. If unfavorable, it must have occurred to the plaintiffs, how are the defendants to act? Such a state of things would seem to call for explicit directions as to the minimum price. The

NOTE.—*Principal and agent — Unauthorized acts of agent—Silence of principal after notice, a ratification.* See Cairnes v. Bleecker, 12 Johns., 300, *note.*

Instructions, how construed. "It is the duty of a principal to give his instructions in clear and direct language, for it is but a reasonable principle of interpretation, as well as a requirement of justice, that instructions should not be construed as intended to be obligatory, unless they are distinct, positive, and express, and that an agent should not be made liable for a departure from the will of his principal where his orders are ambiguous, doubtful, or are not explicit." 1 Wait's Actions and Defenses, 212, citing Jervis v. Hoyt, 2 Hun, 637; 5 T. & C., 199; De Tastet v. Crousillat, 2 Wash. C. C., 132, 137; Bessent v. Harris, 63 N. C., 542; Foster v. Rockwell, 104 Mass., 167; Long v. Pool, 68 N. C., 479; Marsh v. Whitmore, 21 Wall., 178. See, also, Russell v. Wetmore, 3 N. Y. Leg. Obs., 318; Bell v. Palmer, 6 Cow., 128; La Farge v. Kneeland, 7 Cow., 456.

omission, I apprehend, was not accidental; the plaintiffs intending not to interfere with the sound discretion of their agents.

The answer of the defendants appears to be in accordance with this construction. "They would close the sales when it could be done without a sacrifice." Such was, undoubtedly, their intention, as faithful agents anxious not to disappoint the expectations of their principal. Had they considered themselves expressly restricted, it is more probable they would have suggested the improbability of 283*] effecting a sale *on the terms required, and the propriety of vesting in them a discretion to act as circumstances might require. The market was such as to warrant this course. But admitting that the words of the letter will bear a stricter construction, or that the defendants at the time may have supposed they were limited, this is not conclusive upon them. If, on further reflection and inquiry, they found that the plaintiffs' instructions would justify the course they pursued, they were at liberty to act upon them. The question is not whether the defendants, in the first instance, considered themselves limited, but were they so by the plaintiffs' instructions?

The plaintiffs, in their letter of Feb. 3, 1818, to S. Weaver, drew for the net proceeds of the wine, which had been remitted to London. They express surprise that it brought so small a price, and suspect fraud on the part of the sellers. Violation of orders are not intimated, when it might be expected if reliance for redress was placed on this ground. The remedy was, in such case, perfect. It cannot be credited, that if the plaintiffs considered the consignment limited to £52 per pipe, they would have resorted to the question of fraud, instead of pursuing the plain path before them.

June 2, 1818, the plaintiffs write to the defendants, acknowledging the receipt of the net proceeds. There is no complaint or intimation of dissatisfaction, but a proposition for a joint speculation in corn, which the defendants declined. Nov. 24, 1818, the plaintiffs wrote to the defendants, expressing, for the first time, dissatisfaction, and claiming to hold the defendants responsible. This notice to the defendants was nearly a year after the plaintiffs had received the net proceeds. If the defendants had disregarded their instructions, the plaintiffs, after advice, ought to have dissented, and given notice in a reasonable time; otherwise, their assent to their agents' acts will be presumed. 12 Johns., 300. After the letter of Nov. 2, 1818, the defendants had reason to conclude that the authority of the plaintiffs to sell was not questioned. I do not, however, place my opinion on the ground of acquiescence, being satisfied, from an attentive examination of the testi- 284*] mony, that *the defendants were not restricted as to price, and that the manner of effecting the sale was not, under the circumstances, objectionable. The defendants are entitled to judgment.

Judgment for the defendants.

Cited in—7 Cow., 459; 6 Wend., 155; 2 Hun, 641; 5 T. & C., 202; 32 How. Pr., 350; 2 Daly, 109; 3 Leg. Obs., 323; 96 U. S., 645; 44 Am. Dec., 513 (10 Ala., 755); 21 Am. Dec., 306.

ARCHIBALD

v.

THOMAS, Impleaded with VARNUM.

Usury—Bond for Payment, of Principal in Installments, with Interest—Susceptible of Two Significations, one Usurious, the other not—Held not Usurious—Contract Usurious on its Face—Prima Facie *Evidence of Corrupt Agreement—Open to Explanation—Mistake—Question of Construction for Court—Interest means at Legal Rate.*

Bond, dated July 26, 1815, with condition to pay $3,000, with interest, as follows: $500, with interest, on the whole sum unpaid, from Oct. 1, 1815, on or before Oct. 1, 1816; and $500 more thereof, with interest, on the whole sum unpaid, from Oct. 1, next, on or before Oct. 1, 1817; the residue expressed to be payable in installments of $500 yearly in like manner; held, not usurious on the face of the condition, though, upon one construction, every installment would draw interest from Oct. 1, 1815, notwithstanding it might have been previously paid; and thus the 2d installment might draw 14 *per cent.* interest, the 3d, 21 *per cent.*, and so in that progression to the last; but to avoid this consequence, held that the words "with interest on the whole sum unpaid" should rather be deemed to refer to the interest as well as the principal, and to mean that $500 was payable Oct. 1, 1817, together with the interest that accrued on the balance of principal subsequent to Oct. 1, 1815, and remained unpaid.

Where a contract admits of two significations, that should be adopted which renders it operative, rather than that which renders it void.

If a contract is susceptible of two constructions, one of which will bring it within and the other without the Statute of Usury, the latter construction should be adopted.

A contract reserving more than legal interest, on its face, is, *prima facie*, evidence of a corrupt agreement, which is the foundation of usury; but this may be repelled by showing that more than legal interest was reserved by mistake; *e. g.*, a mistake of the scrivener in wording the bond, whether such mistake be of the fact or of the law.

The court have the exclusive power of deciding whether a contract be usurious on its face.

A contract to pay interest generally means the legal standard of interest.

Citations—Cro. Car., 501; 2 Vent., 83; Cro. Jac., 677; 3 Cr., 180; Poth. on Obl., pt. 1, ch. 1, sec. 1, art. 7; 2 Com. Con., 532.

DEBT on bond. The defense was usury, apparent on the face of the condition. The usury was pleaded in due form. The cause was tried at the Warren Circuit, June 17, 1822, before His Honor, the late *Mr. Justice* Yates.

On the trial the execution of the bond was proved by one of the subscribing witnesses. It was executed by the defendants, payable to the plaintiff, dated July 26, 1815, and in the penalty of $6,000. The condition was as follows: "That if the above bounden Joshua Thomas and Aaron Varnum, their heirs, &c., shall well and truly pay or cause to be paid to the above named James Archibald, his executors, &c., $3,000, with interest, as follows, to wit: $500, part thereof, with interest on the whole sum, from the 1st day of October next, on or before the 1st day of October, 1816; and $500 more thereof, with interest on the whole

NOTE.—*Construction of contracts—Usury.*

The rule, that the construction of a contract which will render it legal, is preferred to one which will have the opposite effect, is fully established. "Thus, if parties agreed that one should pay the other, for a certain consideration, sums of money at various times 'with interest,' and it was clear either from

285*] *sum unpaid from the first day of October next, on or before the 1st day of October, 1817; and $500 more thereof, with interest on the whole sum unpaid from the 1st day of October next, on or before the 1st day of October, 1818; and $500 more thereof, with interest from the 1st day of October next on the whole sum unpaid, on or before the 1st day of October, 1819; and $500 more thereof, with interest on the whole sum unpaid from the 1st day of October next, on or before the 1st day of October, 1820; and $500, the residue thereof, with interest from the 1st day of October next on the whole sum unpaid, on or before the 1st day of October which will be in the year of our Lord 1821, without any fraud, &c., then, &c., otherwise, &c."

The counsel for the defendant then submitted whether the defense was not made out by the reading of the bond, as the plea, alleging usury, adopted the very words of the condition, and the plaintiff, by his general replication, admitted that the plea was competent; and thereby putting in issue the facts only which were proved by the bond and condition underwritten; that if the plaintiff had intended to take issue on the inferential averment, that the agreement was corrupt and usurious, he should have answered by demurrer; but the judge decided that the replication put in issue not only the facts pleaded as constituting the usury, but the averment of the plea that the agreement was usurious. The counsel for the defendant then proposed going to the jury upon the evidence of usury afforded by the bond. This the judge refused to permit, deciding that, as the bond was the sole evidence upon the point, the question was one of law—not of fact; and belonged to the court—not the jury. He thereupon gave his opinion, that the word "unpaid" in the condition of the bond qualified the words which immediately preceded it; and that the interest was intended by the parties to be computed, after the payment of one of the installments, on the whole sum unpaid only, and not on the whole sum of $3,000; and the jury, pursuant to his direction, found a verdict for the plaintiff.

286*] **Mr. H. B. Davis*, for the defendants, now moved for a new trial. He repeated the arguments used before the judge at the circuit; and added, that the objection did not rest upon the bond, carrying usury for too large a sum, but for too long a time. The condition is palpably usurious on its face, if the words used are to be taken in their ordinary import. The excess reserved is enormous; and, on a calculation, the court will perceive that it will exceed $1,200. The court have nothing to do with any supposed mistake of these parties. They are confined to the face of the contract; or, if going out of it upon evidence *aliunde*, would be tolerated, there is here no such evidence, from which the usurious intent can be explained away. It will not be pretended that the court can take judicial notice of a mistake, whether of the law or of the fact, in the scrivener who drew the bond. If there was any such mistake, the burden of showing it lay with the plaintiff; and the judge erred in not requiring this. In either view of the case, the jury should have been permitted to pass upon the issue. The question whether there was a corrupt agreement within the Statute of Usury was one fact—not of law, as decided by His Honor. If it appear, on the face of the contract, that more than legal interest was reserved, this is *prima facie* evidence, at least, that the contract was usurious; and the jury should have been directed so to consider it.

If we are correct in supposing that the parties are concluded by the face of the contract, then the plaintiff should be nonsuited. There can be no use in going back to a new trial; because no other evidence can be given, and no other view taken of the subject than what is already before the court.

Mr. R. Weston, contra. The judge was right at the trial, in not suffering the jury to pass upon the question; because the proof of usury was the written contract only. This was susceptible of construction; and the construction of contracts belongs to the court, and not to the jury. The contract, upon the face of it, is not usurious. The Statute declares all contracts to be void, on which more than 7 *per cent.* *shall be reserved, &c. In [*287 this case there is no specific sum agreed upon as interest, exceeding the rate of 7 *per cent.* nor is there any rate or percentage agreed on: one of which is necessary, to bring the contract within the Statute. The *quantum* of interest is thus left by the parties to be fixed by the court; and it would be absurd to say, when, by the agreement, the parties thereby intended to violate the law. The intent of the parties is to govern, and not the words used. Bac. Abr., tit. Usury, D, 4, *Ib.*, C, 23; Cro. Eliz., 642; Cowp., 770. The parties meant annual interest. The blunder arose from the fact that interest commenced three months after the date of the bond. The innocence of the intent is also inferable from that circumstance. The debt is honestly due; and courts incline to such a construction as will take the contract out of the Statute of Usury. Bac. Abr., tit. Usury, C, *note* to pl. 4, *Ib.*, K, 12.

In construing the bond, the word "unpaid" may be understood to relate to the interest as unpaid, and not to the principal. Thus: "interest on the whole sum whereon interest shall remain unpaid." Or the words "from the first day of October next," may be construed to relate to the last antecedent, viz.:

---

the whole contract or from independent evidence that the parties meant by this 'compound interest' it may be presumed (assuming that a contract for compound interest is unlawful) that no court would admit this interpretation; because, if the bargain were expressly for compound interest, it would be invalid." 2 Parsons on Cont., 497. See, also, in support of the rule, Shore v. Wilson, 9 Clark & F., 397; Riley v. Van Houten, 4 How. (Miss.), 428; Many v. Beekman Iron Co., 9 Paige, 188.

As to the general rule, that the construction of a contract is for the court. See Neilson v. Harford, 8 M. & W., 806; Eaton v. Smith, 20 Pick., 150; Wason v. Rowe, 16 Vt., 525: Brown v. Orland, 36 Me., 376.

As to province of jury, in case new, unusual or technical words are, used. See Burnham v. Allen, 1 Gray, 496; Brown v. Orland, and Eaton v. Smith, above cited.

As to what constitutes usury in general, see Bank of Utica v. Wager, 2 Cow. 712, *note*.

Reserving usury by mistake, compare N. Y. F. Ins. Co. v. Ely, 2 Cow., 678, *note*.

"whole sum," and not to the interest; or these words may be rejected as unmeaning.

The plea of usury always sets up a previous agreement to pay a particular sum; and that, in pursuance of such corrupt agreement, the contract in question was entered into, &c.; and this agreement must be proved precisely as pleaded. But, here, the defendant produces no proof of a corrupt agreement, and relies on the bond, which is indefinite. This cannot support the plea. If the usury is apparent on the face of the instrument itself, the defendant ought to demur. If not apparent, he must plead the usurious agreement, and prove it on the trial by evidence *dehors* the contract. Cro. Car., 501; Bac. Abr., Usury, K, pl. 14.

If the opinion of the court should be against the plaintiff, then a new trial must be awarded for the misdirection of the judge, to give the **288***] plaintiff an opportunity of proving *the mistake of the scrivener. This he may do on the trial. *Vide* Cro. Car., 501; Bac. Abr., Usury, K, 4, already cited, and Cro. Jac., 678.

Curia, per WOODWORTH, *J.* This is an application for a new trial. The plaintiff commenced an action of debt on bond, dated Jan. 27, 1815, conditioned to pay $3,000, with interest, as follows: $500, with interest on the whole sum, from Oct. 1, 1815, on or before Oct. 1, 1816; and $500 more thereof, with interest on the whole sum unpaid, from Oct. 1, next, on or before Oct. 1, 1817. The residue is payable in installments of $500 yearly in like manner. The case states that the pleas alleging the usury adopted the language of the condition of the bond, to which the plaintiff filed a general replication. The counsel for the defendant contended that the facts pleaded were proven by reading the bond. No other evidence was introduced. The judge directed the jury to find a verdict for the plaintiff.

Several questions were raised on the trial, not necessary to be stated. The question is, whether, on the preceding facts, the plaintiff was entitled to recover. The plea is not set out; but it is presumed to be in due form, averring a corrupt agreement to lend money, payable at the times, and with the interest specified in the condition of the bond; and that in pursuance of such corrupt agreement the bond was executed. The replication is not before us. It is stated to be general, and must be considered as putting in issue the allegation of usury.

If, by a sound construction of the bond, it reserves more than legal interest, then the usury is made out *prima facie*. For, without further proof, the reservation of unlawful interest will be considered as evidence of a corrupt agreement, which is the foundation of usurious contracts. But it was competent for the plaintiff, at the trial, to repel the *prima facie* evidence of a corrupt agreement, arising from the face of the bond, by showing, if in his power, that more than the rate of interest was reserved by mistake, and contrary to the intent of the party. This was done in *Nevison* **289***] v. *Whitby*, *Cro. Car., 501. So, also, in *Bush* v. *Buckingham*, 2 Vent., 83, the agreement was to lend £50; and the scrivener, by mistake, drew a bond for more than legal interest, against the will and without the knowledge of the lender; yet he was held entitled to recover. In such case, it makes no difference whether the scrivener be in an error in fact or of law, as the security bears a different construction in point of law from what the parties intended, such mistake will not prejudiee the lender, where his intention was incorrupt. *Buckley* v. *Guildbank*, Cro. Jac., 677.

The remaining inquiry then, is, what is the legal construction of the words used in the condition? The principal is payable in six yearly installments of $500 each, from Oct. 1, 1815. It is contended that in all the installments payable after the first, interest is reserved from Oct. 1, 1815. If the words of the bond require this construction, then more than legal interest is reserved. Thus, Oct. 1, 1817, the defendants were bound to pay $500 principal, and interest on $2,000, the residue of the principal for two years, although the interest for one of those years had been paid Oct. 1, 1816. A covenant to pay interest, generally, means the legal standard of interest, which is 7 *per cent.* and consequently, on this construction, more than legal interest was reserved. If the condition is susceptible of a fair construction not at variance with the Statute, it is the duty of the court so to construe it. They have the exclusive power of deciding whether a written contract be usurious. *Levy* v. *Gadsby*, 3 Cr., 180. There is some obscurity in the words used. I think it highly probable the parties merely intended to secure the payment of interest annually on such parts of the principal as remained unpaid at the time each installment became due. If interest is to be calculated from Oct. 1, 1815, the consequence is, that at the end of the second year, the plaintiff is entitled to interest at the rate of 14 *per cent.* for one year; at the end of the third year, 21 *per cent.*, and thus increasing annually until the end of the last year, when for the last $500, 35 *per cent.* interest for one year might be demanded. However oppressive may be this premium for forbearance, *or great the diffi- [***290** culty in assigning a cause for increasing the rate of interest each successive year, the court cannot, on this ground, depart from the construction which the words of the condition import.

It is a well settled rule, in the interpretation of contracts, that when a clause is capable of two significations, it should be understood in that which will have some operation, rather than in that in which it will have none. Poth. on Obl., pt. 1, ch. 1, sec. 1, art. 7; 2 Com. on Cont., 532.

If the word "unpaid" relates only to the principal money, then it is clear that interest is to be calculated at the end of every year from Oct. 1, 1815. But if, in the expression, "with interest on the whole sum unpaid," it has also reference to the interest as well as the principal, no more than legal interest would be reserved. The meaning of the sentence would, in that case be, that $500 was payable Oct. 1, 1817, together with the interest that accrued on the balance of principle subsequent to Oct. 1, 1815, and remained unpaid. I think the words will admit, and ought to receive this construction, rather than that urged by the defendants. I have little doubt it is conformable to the intention of the parties. But my opinion is placed on the ground that where a contract admits of two significations, that ought to be adopted which renders it operative, rather than that which renders it null and void. If this conclusion be correct, the plaintiff was entitled to a verdict; if not, then the verdict ought to be set aside and a new trial granted.

I am of opinion that the motion for a new trial be denied.

Motion denied.

Cited in—7 Wend., 610; 8 Wend., 534; 11 Wend., 209; 1 Edw., 198; 3 N. Y., 30; 1 Barb., 235; 11 Barb., 85; 22 Barb., 561; 32 Barb., 560; 7 Wall., 506; 15 Am. Rep., 160 (27 Mich., 15); 41 Am. Dec., 137 (16 Conn., 192); 25 Am. Dec., 639.

291*] *JACKSON, ex dem. EDEN ET AL.,
v.
RATHBONE, Landlord, AND GOULD, Tenant, *Joint Defendants.*

Ejectment—Of What Plaintiff may Take Possession, under Hab. Fac. Possessionem *where Judgment and Verdict General—Where Judgment on Special Verdict.*

In ejectment, where the declaration, verdict and judgment are general, the plaintiff may take possession, at his peril, to any extent which he chooses under the writ of *hab. fac. possessionem*, subject to be put right by the court, if he takes too much.

But where the judgment is upon a special verdict, describing the premises, the plaintiff is confined to such location in the first instance, and the sheriff may refuse to give him possession beyond it.

IN ejectment, the plaintiff recovered certain premises situate in the City of N. Y., particularly described in a special verdict found by the jury. The declaration was in the usual general form, for five acres, &c., in a certain ward of the city. Judgment having been entered for the plaintiff, an *habere facias possessionem* thereupon issued to the sheriff of the City and County of N. Y., who declined executing it on account of the doubt which existed, whether any land in possession of Gould, the tenant, with whom Rathbone had been admitted to defend, as landlord, was included in the description in the special verdict, he holding himself bound by this description.

Mr. L. Mitchell, for the plaintiff, moved for a rule upon the sheriff, requiring him to execute the *hab. fa. pos.*, either according to the direction of the plaintiff's attorney, or to the extent of the description in the special verdict which, as he contended, covered the premises of which the plaintiff sought to obtain possession. He produced an affidavit showing that the plaintiff's attorney had pointed out certain premises to the sheriff, lying in the ward mentioned, which were in the tenant's possession when the suit was commenced, and of which the plaintiff claimed possession under the writ, and that an indemnity was offered to the sheriff, &c. He also produced various affidavits, maps, &c., and a bill in chancery, filed by one of the defendants, from which he contended that, upon a true location under the special verdict, the premises pointed out were included in it. But whether this were so or not, he contended that the sheriff should have gone on according to the direction of the plaintiffs attorney. It is too late for the defendants to come in, after having pleaded and gone to trial, and say that the recovery is a nullity, because the tenant was not in possession of the subject matter of the ejectment. The proceedings in *this action are always general and in- [*292 definite. The particular premises in dispute are never designated in the declaration; and where the defendant goes on without demanding a bill of particulars, there is no mode of reaching them, besides the one we have pursued. The general form gives notice to the tenant that we go for all the land he possesses in the ward referred to by the declaration. And where the landlord comes in, as here, he is bound to take notice, at his peril, of what his tenant defends for. The extent of his claim is measured by that of the tenant under whom he comes in; and we have a right to take, under our execution, according to the possession of the tenant. It may be said the special verdict controls and limits the generality of the count; or, if it describes lands which are not in existence, that the plaintiff can take nothing under his judgment. Is this so? If the verdict does not, in fact, embrace the premises, this must have arisen from mistake; and in this fictitious action of ejectment, the court will rectify or overlook the mistake and bring back the proceedings to the real point in dispute. They will mold them according to the truth of the case. The action of ejectment is a creature of the court, and entirely under their control for all the purposes of justice. The premises in question are understood, universally, to be those in possession of the defendant when the suit is commenced. In case of a judgment by default, they are identified by an affidavit of serving the declaration, and occupancy by the tenant. If he comes to defend, as here, he must plead not guilty—of what? Of trespassing on the premises in question; that is to say, all the lands in his possession. These are the very words of the consent rule in the English C. P., as will appear from *Goodright* v. *Rich*, 7 T. R., 323. It will be seen from the opinions of Ld. Kenyon, *Ch. J.*, and Ashhurst, *J.*, *Id.*, 329, 330, which he read, that under the more general consent rule of the K. B., and in this court, the actual possession of the tenant in the town or ward mentioned by the declaration, is the guide upon executing the writ of possession.

*The extent of the defendant's pos- [*293 session cannot be controlled by the verdict, though we admit that it may be by other considerations. The judgment is for the term yet to come, of and in the premises aforesaid—not the lands described by the verdict, but the declaration. The sheriff must depend on the information of the plaintiff. We admit that he is entitled to an indemnity against any liability which he may incur by reason of the information being mistaken or false. This has been offered and declined. We do not wish the sheriff to act without indemnity, either by a bond with sureties, or the advice and protection of the court. "In this fictitious action," says Ld. Mansfield, in *Cottingham* v. *King*, 1 Burr., 629, "the plaintiff is to show the sheriff, and is to take possession at his peril of only what he has title to. If he takes more than he has recovered or shown title to, the court will, in a summary way, set it right."

Again; in *Connor* v. *West*, 5 Burr., 2673, the same judge remarks, that, "in truth and in fact, the sheriff delivers possession at the showing of the plaintiff, and at the peril of the plaintiff, who is at his peril, to take possession of no more than he was entitled to. I remember an issue directed, to try whether the sheriff had delivered possession properly, according to the recovery." In *Roe* v. *Dawson*, 3 Wils., 49, the ejectment was for five eighths of a cottage, and the sheriff having delivered possession of the whole, the court made a rule upon him to redeliver possession of the three eighths to the defendant. In *Denn* v. *Purvis*, 1 Burr., 326, it was held that the plaintiff must take according to his title, though the declaration demand more. The judgment is, that the plaintiff recover his term in the whole premises, not merely a moiety, though the ejectment be against two defendants, and one of them die, after issue joined, but before trial. *Farr* v. *Denn*, *Id.*, 362, and *vide* 2 Sell, Pr., 121. The case of *Jackson* v. *Van Bergen*, 1 Johns. Cas., 101, shows how little the verdict is to be regarded, in determining the extent of the possession to be taken. The verdict for the plaintiff was general for the whole premises, but the evidence on the **294***] trial related *only to an undivided moiety; and the court, on motion, restrained the execution to the latter.

Mr. G. Griffin and *W. Slosson*, contra, would not dispute the proposition that, in general, the sheriff is bound to deliver possession to the plaintiff according to his directions; but this is a prerogative of the plaintiff which the court will watch with jealousy. Suppose a recovery, in fact, for but 300 feet in this city, but the plaintiff claims 10 acres; would not the court restrain him? Has he a right to take possession, and put the defendant to a summary application to reclaim it? One mode of restricting this right is, by proof at the trial. *Brookes* v. *Baldwyn*, Barnes, 468. And such is the doctrine of *Jackson* v. *Van Bergen*, cited on the other side. There being a general verdict, the court went to the evidence upon the trial to determine its application. When the verdict is special, there is no need of this. The result of all the proof on the trial is given by the verdict; and where the premises are specifically described, as here, you cannot travel out of it. It is the finding of the jury, under the direction of the court, and must be taken as undeniably true, between the parties, not only in the immediate suit, but in all others. It is, in itself, an estoppel upon both parties. Will it admit of question, that such a verdict cannot be overthrown by affidavit? In *Roe* v. *Dawson*, cited for the plaintiff, the court say, in terms, "the writ ought to have pursued the verdict;" and because it did not, the possession was restored. The verdict there was for five eighths only, and, *quoad hoc*, it was special. *Denn* v. *Purvis*, also cited for the plaintiff, maintains the same doctrine. It is denied that this judgment is on the special verdict, and insisted that it refers to the declaration. Is it meant by this, that the plaintiff will be entitled to take the whole five acres? It is not pretended that the tenant was ever in possession to that extent. Then the declaration can be no guide. The jury say, they try the title to certain property marked upon the map which makes a part of their verdict; and the court are asked to execute that verdict upon other land, on the same map, which was not in the defendant's possession; because the verdict is alleged to be inaccurate, *by *ex parte* affidavits. Are we to be [***295** ousted of our freehold in this manner? It has been long settled, that the rights of parties are not thus to be trifled with. *Ex parte Reynolds*, 1 Cai., 500. If the verdict cover nothing, the plaintiff cannot have execution at all. It is conceded that the generality of the declaration may be restrained by the proof at the trial, and the extent of the defendant's possession—*a fortiori*, may it by the description in the special verdict? What is the object of the writ? It is to carry into effect the judgment of the court alone. This judgment is rendered upon the description of the special verdict. You cannot go beyond this, even though the defendant may have admitted, in the clearest terms, that it was too narrow. You might as well send out execution for double the amount of a judgment in debt, because the defendant had admitted that, by mistake, the judgment was too small by one half. It is not enough to say that the court will correct the plaintiff if he grasps too much. They ought not to sit still and see an injury committed, because they have the power to redress it. Preventive justice is, in these cases, the most useful and important, and it accords with the course of the court. Such was the case of *Jackson* v. *Van Bergen*, 1 Johns. Cas., 101; 7 T. R., 118, *note*, S. P. The counsel examined the affidavits, maps, and other proofs before the court upon the motion, as to the location of the special verdict, and contended that it covered nothing of which the tenant was in possession; and that, therefore, the writ of possession could have no effect whatever. They concluded by citing the following additional authorities, as to the conclusive nature of a record and special verdict; *Witman* v. *Earl of Derby*, 1 Wils., 55; *Jenks* v. *Hallet*, 1 Cai., 64; *Taylor* v. *Horde*, 1 Burr., 114; *Crosswell* v. *Byrnes*, 9 Johns., 287, *Dunscombe* v. *Wingfield*, Hob., 262; Phil. Ev., 2d Am. ed., 218; *Bradish* v. *Gee*, Ambl., 229; *French* v. *Shotwell*, 5 Johns. Ch., 564—and as to the extent of the plaintiff's right in taking possession upon the writ, 2 Dunl., Pr., 1048.

Mr. E. Williams*, in reply, confined [*296** himself to the question, whether the location, according to the description in the special verdict, would include the premises of which the plaintiff sought to obtain possession. He examined the proofs before the court, and contended that the plaintiff had attempted to take possession of no more than was covered by the special verdict.

The cause was argued in May Term last, and remained under advisement to the present term, when,

WOODWORTH, *J.*, delivered the opinion of the court. He said *the Court* were with the counsel for the defendant, that although upon a general declaration, and a verdict and judgment equally general, the plaintiff might take possession at his peril, subject to be put right by *the Court* if he took more than the premises in question upon the trial; yet, where there is a special verdict, as in this case, locating those premises, the parties and sheriff should be guided by this. He then went at large into the facts, and added, that *the Court* had very carefully examined the questions which had been raised upon them, as to the location, and were satisfied that the directions by the attorney of the plaintiff, to the sheriff, did not go beyond the description contained in the verdict; and that a rule must, therefore, be made upon the sheriff, that he deliver possession pursuant to those directions.

Rule accordingly.

Cited in—39 Am. Dec., 310 (4 Ala., 592).

THE SAME v. THE SAME.

Execution of Writ of Inquiry—Error of Sheriff—Sheriff and Coroner, Interested—Whether Elisors Appointed—Nominal Damages.

The sheriff having erred upon the merits, in executing a writ of inquiry, under the 3d section of the Act to Prevent Delays of Execution, &c. (1 R. L., 143), the inquisition was set aside on motion.

But the court refused to appoint elisors to execute the writ; though it appeared that both the sheriff and coroner were members of a corporation which was interested in, and had defended another cause, at the suit of the plaintiff in the writ of inquiry, that depended upon the same questions as those upon which the suit in which the writ issued were determined.

It seems that upon such a writ of inquiry, the plaintiff is entitled to recover nominal damages, at all events; and that an inquest which finds for the defendant, will be set aside on that ground alone.

THE last cause having been removed by the defendant on a writ of error to the Court **297***] of Errors, where the judgment *was affirmed, and the record remitted, &c., a writ of inquiry issued, and an inquisition was taken under the 3d section of the Act (1 R. L., 143) Concerning Writs of Error, and to prevent delays of execution, before the under-sheriff of the City and County of N. Y., Apr. 28, 1824. On the hearing, before the under-sheriff and jury, all parol evidence of location was overruled and disregarded, except what related to the special verdict; and, on the ground that the description in the special verdict did not comprise any land in possession of Gould, at the commencement of the suit, the jury found for the defendant; and that the plaintiff had sustained no damages for *mesne* profits. The sheriff and coroner of N. Y. are members of the Mechanics' Society; and a suit brought by the same plaintiff, on the demises of the same lessors, against Robert Chew, at the time of the commencement of the suit, and now a tenant of the Society, and an actual occupant under them, of the premises claimed in that action, had been defended at the expense of the Society. This suit, together with several suits against the Bank of N. Y. and their tenants, depend upon the same title, and were commenced at the same time.

Upon affidavits of these facts *Messrs. L. Mitchell* and *E. Williams* moved to set aside the inquisition, and that elisors be appointed to execute the writ. They made this motion before the court had passed upon the motion in the last cause.

WOODWORTH, *J.*, suggested that the material question here would be disposed of by the decision upon that motion. If for the plaintiff, he must have his damages upon the writ of inquiry: otherwise, if for the defendant.

Mr. Williams. Yes. But whatever be the fate of that motion, the inquest must be set aside. The plaintiff recovered something in the Court of Errors. Of this the record was conclusive evidence. The sheriff and jury could not overrule or reverse the decision of that court, and deny us all damages.

WOODWORTH, *J.* True; this was an informality. You are entitled to nominal damages in any event.

Mr. Mitchell* said the authorities [*298** were plain for the appointment of elisors on account of the sheriff's and coroner's interest. And,

Mr. Williams said, there is a difference between jury and executive process. Here the sheriff or coroner must act judicially, and a remote interest disqualifies him.

Mr. Clisbe, contra, insisted that the mere circumstance that the officer is a member of a corporation which is interested in opposing the plaintiff in another cause, though the question be the same, is too remote an interest, of itself, to disqualify him. No evidence of corruption or partiality is furnished. A sheriff may execute his own process, if it be ministerial.

At another day, and when *the Court* came to decide the motion in the last cause, they said that it disposed of this motion to set aside the inquisition, which must be granted. But as to the motion for appointing elisors, they denied it; saying, that though the sheriff had acted erroneously, he had not acted partially; that the objection of interest was so remote as not, of itself, to be a disqualification. It went merely to the favor of the officer; and the court were to determine from the facts, whether it would so far influence him as to render the execution of the writ of inquiry by him unsafe for the plaintiff. They did not think so. Upon the evidence before them, they were satisfied that the error was one of judgment merely.

Rule accordingly.

THE SAME v. ROBERT CHEW.

Ejectment—Writ of Possession—Sheriff and Coroner, Interested—Elisors Appointed.

On judgment for plaintiff in ejectment, the sheriff and coroner being members of a corporation which claimed to own the premises in question, and had demised them to the defendant, and defended the action, at their own expense, through their tenant, the court appointed elisors to execute the writ of possession.

ELISORS were appointed to execute the writ of possession in this cause, on affidavit of the facts detailed in the last *cause, [***299** touching the interest of the sheriff and coroner of N. Y.

Mr. A. Burr, for the motion, cited Co. Litt., 156, 157; Bac. Abr., Sheriff, M.

Mr. M. Ulshoeffer, contra.

The Court said the sheriff and coroner had a direct interest(a) in the execution of this process, and the motion must, therefore, be granted without regard to the probable influence which it might have upon them.

Rule accordingly.

THE OVERSEERS OF BRIDGEWATER
v.
THE OVERSEERS OF BROOKFIELD.

Pauper—Purchase of Equitable Interest in Land —When Confers Settlement—Administrator —No Control over Intestate's Land.

The purchase of an equitable interest in lands, and paying $75, constitute a settlement; but this must be an indefeasible interest, derived from a grantor having title.

A contract, by an administratrix, to convey lands of her intestate, when a surrogate's order for that purpose shall be obtained, does not vest such an interest, though an order be afterwards obtained.

Such a contract is void, and incapable of being enforced either at law or in equity, both because the administratrix has no interest, and as being contrary to the policy of the Act authorizing administrators to sell the real estate of their intestate.

An administrator has no interest in, or control over the real estate of his intestate; and though after a contract to sell land when a surrogate's order shall be obtained for that purpose, an order be actually obtained, the administrator takes no beneficial interest, which can inure to make the contract binding, even if it were not contrary to the policy of the law.

The cases which hold that where one conveys without title, and afterwards becomes owner, this shall inure to the benefit of the grantee, mean that the grantor must acquire a beneficial interest in the premises sold, not a mere naked authority to sell.

Citations—14 Johns., 469; 16 Johns., 281; 11 Johns., 7; 13 Johns., 316; 1 R. L., 280.

ON *certiorari* to the General Sessions of Madison Co., Zilpha Ward, a pauper, was removed, by an order of two justices, from the town of Brookfield to the town of Bridgewater, in Madison Co.; and on appeal to the Sessions, they affirmed the order. Brookfield claimed **300***] that the pauper *had acquired a derivative settlement in Bridgewater from her father, J. B. Ward; and the single question before the Sessions was, whether he was settled there by virtue of an equitable estate, which Brookfield alleged he had acquired under a contract to purchase a farm of Betsey Converse. She had, as administratrix of W. Converse, deceased, executed a bond to F. Stratton, the condition of which, after reciting that her intestate was seised of the farm, that she, as administratrix, had sold it to Stewart Bennet, and received $60, as a full compensation, and that Bennet had sold to Stratton, was, that after she had obtained the requisite order from the surrogate, she should sell and convey to Stratton in fee. This contract was assigned by Stratton to J. B. Ward; and afterwards by him to Stewart Bennet. Ward paid $100 as the consideration of the assignment to him. The surrogate afterwards made an order of sale; and the land was sold under it at public auction, to Stewart Bennet, the highest bidder, at $60.

Mr. F. C. White, for the plaintiffs in error, contended that the father of the pauper did not acquire such an indefeasible equitable interest as was necessary, within the cases, to confer a settlement; and he cited and examined, *O. of Blenheim* v. *O. of Windham*, 11 Johns., 7; *O. of Schaghticoke* v. *O. of Brunswick*, 14 Johns., 199; *O. of Whitestown* v. *O. of Constable*, *Id.*, 469; *O. of Augusta* v. *O. of Paris*, 16 Johns., 279; *O. of Pompey* v. *O. of Laurens*, 19 Johns., 238. No specific execution of such a contract as this would ever have been decreed by a court of equity. The obligor had no interest but a mere naked contingent authority. Besides, the contract was contrary to the policy of the statute authorizing sales under an order of surrogates. To say that the administratrix may bind herself to sell in this manner, would put down all competition at the auction required by law. The bond is void for this reason. *Jones* v. *Caswell*, 3 Johns. Cas., 29; *Doolin* v. *Ward*, 6 Johns., 194; *Wilbur* v. *How*, 8 Johns., 444.

Messrs. J. A. Spencer and *J. G. Stower*, contra, cited *Jackson* v. *Stevens*, 13 Johns., 316.

Curia*, per SUTHERLAND, *J.* In *O. of* [*301** *Whitestown* v. *O. of Constable*, 14 Johns., 469, it was held "that an indefeasible equitable interest in land was a purchase of an estate or interest, within the meaning of the 4th section of the Act for the Relief and Settlement to the Poor." (1 R. L., 280), and gave a settlement to the owner of it, in the town where the land lay, provided he actually paid for it the sum of $75; and in *Augusta* v. *Paris*, 16 Johns., 281, Spencer, *J.*, in delivering the opinion of the court, says, "the Statute contemplates two things—the ability of the purchaser to pay, and his actually paying $75, in order that the payment shall acquire to the purchaser an estate or interest in lands." The money must not only be paid, but an indefeasible interest in land, either legal or equitable, must be actually acquired. If the vendor, therefore, has no title or interest in the land which he undertakes to sell, the vendee is not a purchaser, within the meaning of the Statute, although he may have paid a full consideration for a good title. *Blenheim* v. *Windham*, 11 Johns., 7.

In this case, Betsey Converse, the administratrix of W. Converse, had no authority to sell the lands of her intestate, until the surrogate made an order for that purpose. An administrator has no control over the lands of the intestate. His authority extends only to the personalty. If that is insufficient to pay the debts of the intestate, the Statute directs the manner in which an order for the sale of a sufficient quantity of the real estate to pay the debts may be obtained. But, until such order is made, any contract which the administrator may make for the sale of the land, is utterly void, and incapable of being enforced, either at law or in equity.

The doctrine, that where a person, having no title to land, conveys to another, and afterwards acquires a title to the same land, the subsequently acquired title shall inure to the benefit of his grantee, and the confirmation of his title, as established in *Jackson* v. *Stevens*, 13

(a) Substantially they were parties to the cause. Wash. Ins. Co. v. Price, 1 Hopkins' Ch., 1.

302*] Johns., 316, and the cases *there cited, is not applicable to a case like this. The administratrix never did acquire a beneficial interest in the land of her intestate. The surrogate's order gave her merely a naked authority to sell; and it would be against the policy of the law to permit the exercise of that authority to be influenced or controlled by any previous contract which she may have made. The sale, as finally made, gives the title, and can have no relation to any previous agreement. The bond of Betsey Converse to Stratton, by which she bound herself to give him a deed for the land, being absolutely void, the assignment of it to Ward passed no estate or interest in land, by which he acquired a settlement in the town of Bridgewater.

Order of Sessions reversed.

Cited in—5 Wend., 579; 20 Wend., 29; 1 Hill, 115; 4 N. Y., 457; 21 Wall., 449; 3 Wood & M., 499.

[END OF AUGUST TERM, 1824.]

CASES

ARGUED AND DETERMINED

IN THE

SUPREME COURT

OF THE

STATE OF NEW YORK,

IN

OCTOBER TERM, 1824, IN THE FORTY-NINTH YEAR OF OUR INDEPENDENCE.

ROWLEY *v.* BALL.

Negotiable Paper—Note Payable to Bearer, Lost—When Holder Can Recover in Court of Law.

An action at law cannot be sustained on a negotiable promissory note payable to bearer, by the holder, on his proving that the note was lost, though he show that he lost it after it became due.

His only remedy is in a court of equity, which alone can afford the defendant adequate protection against future liability.

But if he show that the note was, in fact, destroyed, he may recover in a court of law.

So, if the note be not negotiable, or if negotiable, and it appear not to have been negotiated.

What is sufficient proof of the execution of a lost note.

Citations—16 Johns., 201; 10 Johns., 104; 2 Campb., 211; 6 Ves., 812; Chit. Bills, 173, ed. of 1817.

ERROR from the C. P. of the County of Monroe. The cause was originally commenced by Rowley against Ball, before a justice of that county, who gave judgment against Ball, who appealed to the C. P., where the cause was tried Jan. 10, 1822.

Rowley declared against Ball upon a promissory note given by the latter to one William Huxley, payable to him or bearer, for $30, dated on or about the middle of June, 1819; and transferred to the plaintiff; and the declaration averred that the note had since been stolen, lost or destroyed, or taken from the plaintiff without his consent or knowledge.

Plea, the general issue.

Upon the trial, J. D. Bailis testified that he had seen a note in Rowley's possession, purporting to have been given by Ball, for $30, dated some time in June, 1819. The precise time when it was payable he could not tell; but recollected *that it was payable to [*304 William Huxley or bearer, and when he saw the note, which was in Apr., 1821, it was due. It was admitted by Rowley's counsel, that Ball could neither read nor write, but signed by his mark; and that there was no subscribing witness to the note. Rowley, the appellee, swore, that he put the note into his pocketbook, and some time after made diligent search for it, both in his pocketbook, and desk, but could not find it; that the note was either lost, stolen, or destroyed; that he had reason to believe that the note had been taken from his pocketbook, and given to Ball; for the story of his having lost the note came to him from Ball's, before he knew or suspected the loss. On being cross-examined, he stated that it was first suggested to him that the note was lost by Samuel Darling, his own brother-in-law. Hiram Huxley swore that he came to Ball's in company with his brother, John Huxley, who told Ball that he had a note against him, which was given to Wm. Huxley. Ball replied that whoever held the notes must pay for keeping Wm. Huxley's wife; but requested John Huxley to take a gun of him, and apply it on the notes; and it was agreed between them, that J. Huxley should take the gun upon trial, and

---

NOTE.—*Negotiable paper—Last note—Suit on.* In England, courts of equity have exclusive jurisdiction of actions on lost bills and notes. Housard v. Robinson, 7 Barn. & C., 90.

In the States of the Union where the distinction between law and chancery courts is clearly maintained, the same doctrine usually prevails. See Thayer v. King, 15 Ohio, 242; Wofford v. Board of Police, 44 Miss., 579; Hinsdale v. Bank of Orange, 6 Wend., 378; Swift v. Stevens, 8 Conn., 431; Moses v. Price, 21 Gratt., 556; Aborn v. Bosworth, 1 R. I., 401. See, however, Fales v. Russell, 16 Pick., 315; Hinckley v. Union Pacific R. R. Co., 129 Mass., 52; Willis v. Cresey, 17 Me., 9; Conn. Bank v. Benedict, 18 B. Mon., 307; Bridgeford v. Masonville Co., 34 Conn., 546.

Some American authorities support the distinction taken between paper lost before and after maturity, holding that suit at law can be maintained on the latter, but the weight of authority is against this. Lazell v. Lazell, 12 Vt., 443; Chewning v. Singleton, 2 Hill, 371; Moses v. Price, 21 Gratt., 556; Hopkins v. Adams., 20 Vt., 407.

As to tender of indemnity, see Smith v. Rockwell, 2 Hill, 482; N. Y. Code Civil Procedure, secs. 1917, 1918.

As to actions on destroyed instruments, see Hinsdale v. Bank of Orange, 6 Wend., 378.

That bond is not required unless lost instrument was negotiable, see Blade v. Noland, 12 Wend., 173.

For full discussion of general subject, see 2 Daniels Neg. Ins'st. Ch., 46, secs. 2, 1475–1485.

if he liked it, he should allow $14 on the notes. If he did not like it, he was to return it. John Huxley testified that he received of Wm. Huxley two notes against Ball, in the State of Ohio, one for $30 and one for $20, as they were read to him; that he could neither read nor write; that he went to Ball's, as stated by H. Huxley, in company with him, and told Ball that he had notes against him, which were given to Wm. Huxley, one for $30 and one for $20, and he answered, that whoever held the notes must pay him for keeping Wm. Huxley's wife. The witness requested Ball to pay him some money; but Ball said he could not. He then requested him to let the witness have some leather; but Ball answered that he had none to spare. The conversation then followed about the gun, as stated by H. Huxley. The witness took the gun, but afterwards returned it, and sold the $30 note to one Clark.

The counsel for Ball insisted that he ought not to be put upon his defense, till Rowley had **305***] proved the actual destruction *of the note. The counsel for Rowley insisted that there was already sufficient evidence of the destruction of the note, or at least, sufficient to entitle him to go to the jury, upon the ground that he had proved the loss of the note after it fell due. This was opposed by Ball's counsel; and,

The judges gave their opinion that the several matters proved and given in evidence, were not sufficient to entitle Rowley's counsel to go to the jury, inasmuch as an actual destruction of the note had not been proved; that Rowley could not recover on a negotiable note, although it was lost after it became due, unless this was followed by proof of its destruction; and gave judgment of nonsuit. To this opinion Rowley's counsel excepted, and the cause came to this court upon a bill of exceptions, containing the above matters.

Mr. A. Samson, for the plaintiff in error, briefly stated the case, and cited *Pintard* v. *Tackington*, 10 Johns., 104; Chit. on Bills, Phil. ed., 202; Marius on Bills, 19; Maxwell on Bills, 136; *Meeker* v. *Jackson*, 3 Yeates, 442; 2 Campb., 214, *note* to *Pierson* v. *Hutchinson; Freeman* v. *Boynton*, 7 Mass., 483, 486, per Parker, *J.; Brown* v. *Messiter*, 3 Maule & S., 281; *Anderson* v. *Robson*; 2 Bay, 495. These authorities, he said, supported the position that an action may be sustained on a lost note, though negotiable, if lost when overdue.

At any rate, the court below erred in not suffering the plaintiff below to go to the jury, upon the presumption afforded by the circumstances that the note had been, in fact, destroyed.

Mr. J. Dickson, contra. The only real question in the Court of C. P. was, whether the appellee had a right to go to the jury; though the court may have given reasons which are not strictly confined to that point. Nor does it appear that the grounds taken by the court were the only foundation of the nonsuit. There might have been other objections; and, if they appear upon the case, we certainly **306***] *have a right to insist upon them, though the court may have stopped short, and deemed the reasons actually given sufficient. In truth, the court will perceive that there were other and important reasons. In the first place, the evidence of the execution of the note was altogether insufficient. So was the proof that it had ever been transfered to the plaintiff. *Shaver* v. *Ehle*, 16 Johns., 201. And more than this, J. Huxley, who transferred the note to Clarke, was interested. *Ib.* Both these considerations might have entered into the decision given by the C. P.; and, at any rate, we have a right to the benefit of them here.

No action, however, will lie on a promissory negotiable note, lost, but not destroyed. If the note were lost before it fell due, there could be no question on the subject; and we contend that its being due can make no difference. True, in an old edition of Chitty, it is said that an action will lie in the latter case; and the same remark is repeated in the Phila. edition; but that author refers to cases in its support, which have been overruled. Chit. on Bills, 195 to 205, Phil. ed. He is overruled by *Pierson* v. *Hutchinson*, 2 Campb., 211; 6 Esp., 126, S. C.; *Mayor* v. *Johnson*, 3 Camph., 324; and *vide* Bayley, 169; Chit. on Bills, Phil. ed., 484–5. The case of *Davis* v. *Dodd*, 4 Taunt., 602, is also against this action; and *Poole* v. *Smith*, Holt *N. P.*, 144, is in point. The bill there was lost after it was due, from the pocket of the attorney's clerk, a few days only before the trial; and the action was fully sustained by all the requisite proof; yet, as the bill was negotiable, and did not appear to have been destroyed, the plaintiff was nonsuited. This case is also sustained by several authorities cited in a note. *Id.*, 145.

But suppose the action will lie, it cannot be sustained without a previous offer of an indemnity against the note. That the note was due, and therefore subject to all the equities between the original parties, or that an action upon it is defeasible by the defendant's proving the loss, are neither of them sufficient answers to this objection. Chitty (*vide* Phila. ed., 197, 200) lays down his doctrine with this qualification, in relation to a note transferable by delivery, though it be lost when over due.

*But, in any event, we say the rem- [***307** edy is in equity alone; and should, from the very nature of the subject, be confined exclusively to the Court of Chancery. It is upon authority; for, most obviously, equity would not relieve if a remedy could be had at law. This is the distinction upon which a court of chancery rests its jurisdiction. The following authorities sustain both these positions *Walmsley* v. *Child*, 1 Ves. Sr., 341; 1 Fonbl. Eq., 17; *Ex parte Greenway*, 6 Ves., Jr., 812. In the last case, speaking of the very point under consideration, the *Ld. Chancellor* says "There must be a complete indemnity going to all the consequences against the holder, if the bill has not been paid; and against any demand that may be made by future possible holders, if it should have been paid. When I was *Chief Justice*, I tried an action in the C. P., upon a bill alleged to be lost, which had been previously lost by the payee. An indemnity was offered by bond, but I nonsuited the plaintiff. The counsel objected strongly upon the offer of indemnity; and it came before the court upon a motion for a new trial; and there was a long discussion upon the nature of these indemnities in a court of law. The court had not come to a decision upon it when I left them; and I do not know the result. But I could never understand by what authority courts of law compelled parties to take the indemnity." The course of practice, on trials at law, will demonstrate the importance of the *Ld. Chancellor's* remark, that a most full and complete indemnity should be given; which can be effected under the direction of a court of equity only. Although the note were negotiated never so long after it is due, all the plaintiff is bound to prove at the trial, is the existence and loss of the note, and that he was the holder. The burden of showing when the note was transferred, in order to let in the defence, lies with the defendant. Till the contrary is shown, the legal intendment would be that the note was transferred before it fell due, in the fair course of trade; and that the plaintiff is a *bona fide* holder. Both the hazard and expense of such testimony should fall on the one who is in fault, the loser of the note. This is one of the consequences of the **308***] loss against which, in the language *of the *Ld. Chancellor*, the party should be indemnified. A court of law is not so constituted as to be able to afford such a protection. Their course of proceeding is opposed to it. Chancery alone is a competent forum. The powers of that court are more ample, and alone can give full and adequate relief. But, at any rate, whether the question belongs to this or the other side of the hall, indemnity must, in all cases, be given. In the principal case, it has not been even offered or intimated.

It is said this court have already settled the question against us; but no case goes so far. In *Pintard* v. *Tackington*, 10 Johns., 104, it did not appear that the note was negotiable; and the court expressly recognize the authority of *Pierson* v. *Hutchinson*, and *Ex parte Greenway*, upon which we rely; and by which the action was denied upon lost negotiable paper. *Meeker* v. *Jackson*, 3 Yeates, 442, was not the case of a negotiable note. But, if otherwise, it has no application here. The State of Pa. has properly no court of chancery, and the Supreme Court of law has been driven to the necessity of exercising equitable powers. This is sanctioned by a law of that State; and the decision cited was the offspring of this mixed authority. *Brown* v. *Messiter*, 3 Maule & S., 281, passed *ex parte*, on a rule to show cause, which was made absolute before a single judge, without looking into the authorities. All that *Freeman* v. *Boynton*, 7 Mass., 486, contains on this head, is a *dictum* of *Mr. Justice* Parker, remarking that a lost note may be made good by indemnity; without saying that it would be so of a negotiable note, or whether the indemnity is to be taken by a court of law or equity. In *Anderson* v. *Robson*, 2 Bay, 495, also, it did not appear that the bill was negotiable, nor was any question made as to the jurisdiction of the court. The only question was, whether the proof of loss was sufficient.

Mr. Sampson, in reply. The gentleman has no right to examine questions here, which were not made in the court below. The discussion should be confined to the points distinctly made upon the face of the bill of exceptions; and cannot be *extended to [***309** the whole merits of the case, either as it appears from the facts in the bill, or might possibly have existed in the C. P. The case was there put upon the ground, alone, that an action is not maintainable upon a lost note, but that this must be followed by evidence that the note was, in fact, destroyed. Such were the points embraced by the application for a nonsuit; and such the points decided by the court. We hear not a syllable of indemnity. No objection was made on account of its absence. And if such a difficulty had been started, *non constat*, but it would have been immediately obviated by the proof; or the requisite indemnity produced and given upon the spot. It is sufficient, if it be tendered or given upon the trial.

All the elementary writers agree that an action is maintainable upon a lost promissory note, though it be negotiable; and it is using too broad a language, to say that the English decisions are opposed to this. In all the cases (with the exception of *Poole* v. *Smith*), where the action has been denied, the note was lost before it fell due, though perhaps that fact does not expressly appear in the report. In *Pierson* v. *Hutchinson* the plaintiff was nonsuited because the destruction of the note did not appear in proof; and the reason assigned by Ld. Ellenborough, in conclusion, is, that the defendant might be compelled to pay the bill a second time. This remark implies that the bill was, in fact, lost before it fell due; otherwise there would have been no possible obligation to pay. *Poole* v. *Smith*, decided at *N. P.*, I venture to say, is the only case where a recovery was ever denied upon a bill or note lost when over due. In that case, the bill had been drawn more than six years before the trial; and the proof was wretchedly defective that there was a subsisting debt upon the bill. All the proof of the demand upon the trial, was that it had been shown to the acceptor after the action was brought, who admitted the acceptance to be his handwriting, but said he was under no obligation to pay, inasmuch as between him and the drawer, it had been satisfied by other bills. The *Ch. J.*, upon this proof coming out, remarked, generally, that this evidence was not *enough with- [***310** out producing the bill; but upon the matter being pressed by the plaintiff's counsel, he concludes: "Upon the ground of the non-production of the bill, I think I am called upon to nonsuit the plaintiff. The rule is an extremely salutary one, and ought not to be relaxed." It is evident that this case depended on its own special circumstances. The demand was a stale one; which fortified the defendant's declaration on its being presented, that it had been paid. There was enough, independent of the loss, to show that the plaintiff should be nonsuited. In *Powell* v. *Roche*, 6 Esp., 76, it was held enough, either to produce the note or show it to be lost. In *Davis* v. *Dodd*, the prominent question was as to the form of the action; and whether the plaintiff should not have gone upon the promise to give a new bill. The court, to be sure, intimate that no action will lie; but the remark, as to this, deserves no greater weight than the merest *obiter dictum*.

It is true, as remarked, that courts of equity give relief; and on compelling the payment of a lost bill or note, they require an indemnity from the complainant; but this power to take an indemnity is not, as supposed, the source of their jurisdiction. A paper has been lost through accident, which is a very usual and broad ground of going into a court of chancery; but it was never denied that a court of law have a concurrent jurisdiction in such cases, provided the truth can be reached without the aid of the defendant's oath. This generally becomes necessary in case of loss; and when the cause is once in a court of chancery, it requires an indemnity as an incidental means of making all parties secure. The question of indemnity is one of form merely; and depends upon the different manner in which the courts are organized, and their different course of proceeding. In the case before the court, no indemnity has ever been required. A recovery would forever conclude against any future action upon this note. The possibility that the maker may not be able to make out a defense on the ground of that recovery, would be equally an objection to maintaining any action for any cause, and especially upon negotiable paper. In all cases, the defendant runs the 311*] hazard that the plaintiff *may not be an honest holder; and if so, the first recovery will not avail him against a second. The loss merely varies the mode of getting this link into the chain of proof. *Pierson* v. *Hutchinson* is in point, that a court of law have no power to exact an indemnity. If the defendant insists upon one, he must go into chancery himself, provided the plaintiff refuses to give it.

WOODWORTH, *J.* It certainly cannot be necessary to pursue the question of indemnity. The defendant should have put himself upon this defect in the court below.

SUTHERLAND, *J.* It strikes me that the only objection made below, and, of course, the only one which the defendant can properly take here, is that the action was not sustainable, because the actual destruction of the note was not proved.

Mr. Samson. I would then only add, that to turn the party out of court, upon the ground that he should have gone to a court of equity, would be to deny him all remedy. On filing his bill, he would be told, in the uniform and settled language of the Court of Chancery, that it is beneath the dignity of that court to interfere in a matter of $30. Such has been the decision of that court, and such it will of course be again, unless an exception arises, and our reception is to be more favorable on the other side of the hall, from the circumstance of our being sent there by this court. *Vide Mitchell* v. *Tighe*, 1 Hopkins' Ch., 119. *Vredenberg* v. *Johnson*, *Id.*, 112.

Curia, per WOODWORTH, *J.* No exception was taken to the proof given as to the execution of the note. Were it necessary, however, to express an opinion, I should consider the evidence, *prima facie*, sufficient. The witness stated to the defendant that he held two notes against him given to William Huxley—one for $30, the other for $20. The defendant in repy, admitted the notes, and offered to make part payment. The identity of the note to which the confession related, is established with reasonable certainty. *The case of *Shaver* [*312 v. *Ehle*, 16 Johns., 201, is clearly distinguishable from the present.

The remaining question is, whether an action at law can be sustained on a negotiable promissory note, payable to bearer, by a person who was the holder, on his proving that the note was lost.

If the note had not been negotiable, or if negotiable, had not, in fact, been negotiated, the plaintiff would be entitled to recover. *Pintard* v. *Tackington*, 10 Johns., 104. The cases which have not permitted a recovery at law upon negotiable paper lost, but not destroyed, were those in which the paper had been indorsed before it was lost. *Pierson* v. *Hutchinson*, 2 Campb., 211; *Ex parte Greenway*, 6 Ves., 812. In this case, the note being payable to bearer, the holder could make out, *prima facie*, a cause of action, and although the note was due at the time it was lost, the maker would be exposed to the hazard of showing that fact by legal evidence. It would, therefore, seem to be a hard doctrine, which should place the maker in this situation, without requiring an indemnity. In such cases it is better to leave the party to his remedy in equity, where a suitable indemnity will be provided against any subsequent recovery. This subject peculiarly belongs to equity jurisdiction. In *Ex parte Greenway*, Ld. Eldon observes: "I never could understand by what authority courts of law compelled parties to take the indemnity." In *Pierson* v. *Hutchinson*, Ld. Ellenborough held that whether an indemnity be sufficient or insufficient, is a question of which a court of law cannot judge; and although there are *dicta*, that upon the offer of an indemnity, the indorsee of a lost bill may recover at law, they are so contrary to the principles upon which the judicial system rests, he could not venture to proceed upon them. Chitty, in his Treatise on Bills, p. 173, ed. of 1817, is of opinion that where the bill has been lost after it became due, there is no reason why the person who lost it should not be permitted to proceed at law, without offering an indemnity, inasmuch as the law would, in such case, secure all the parties to the bill against future liability to a person who becomes the holder of it after it fails due, This is undoubtedly *correct, provided the maker of the [*313 note, or acceptor of the bill, could prove that it came to the hands of the holder after due. If, in the present case, the plaintiff recovers against the defendant, and subsequently a suit is commenced on the note by another, claiming to be a *bona fide* holder, the recovery had would not alone be a sufficient defense. The defendant must also prove the fact, that it was due when it was lost by the present plaintiff. If he could not, then the subsequent holder would recover, on the ground that it did not appear he received the note after it became due.

It is not necessary that the plaintiff should have a remedy at law in such a case. His redress is ample in equity, where the defendant can be protected against subsequent liability. I have not found any adjudged case on this precise point; but from the reason of the thing, and the analogy to cases where notes have been lost after they were indorsed, I think the action cannot be sustained, without proving that the note was destroyed.

Judgment affirmed.

Cited in—2 Wend., 552; 3 Wend., 347; 11 Wend., 364; 12 Wend., 175; 2 Hill. 483; 2 Edw., 487; 16 N. Y., 588; 8 Barb., 409; 1 Abb. Pr., 149; 5 Duer, 161; 3 E. D. S., 550; 1 Daly, 157; 4 McLean, 130; 3 Allen, 389; 27 Am. Dec., 127; 28 Am. Dec., 380 (7 N. H., 549); 38 Am. Dec., 353 (12 Vt., 443).

M'CLURE, late Sheriff of STEUBEN,

v.

ERWIN ET AL.

Bond, Given by Jailer to Sheriff—Action on, for Escape—Pleading—Failure of Sheriff, in Action against Him for the Escape, to set up Statute of Limitations, no Defense to Jailer or his Sureties—Whether Jailer Entitled to Notice of Suit against Sheriff.

First count of *narr.* on bond from jailer, and his sureties, defts., to the sheriff, plaintiff stating condition, that if the former executed his trust, and would not suffer any prisoners to escape, then, &c., averring that O. S. T. was committed to jail on *ca. sa.* at the suit of O. H. and jailer negligently suffered him to escape, whereby the plaintiff sustained damages to $5,000.

Second count the same; averring also a suit against the sheriff for the escape, and judgment against him; and notice to the defendants of the pendency of that suit, whereby the plaintiff had sustained damages to $5,000.

Pleas to first count:

1. That jailer did not permit O. S. T. to escape.

2. That O. S. T. was not committed, and issue to the country on both pleas.

3. That O. H., plaintiff in the *ca. sa.*, p[illegible] d O. S. T. to escape, concluding with a verification.

4. That O. H. did not sue the sheriff within one year after escape; and that the sheriff sustained no damage from the escape within the year, concluding with a verification.

Pleas to the second count:

1. No escape; and that defendants had no notice of suit pending, concluding with a verification.

2. No commitment; and no notice of suit pending, with the like conclusion.

3. That O. H. permitted the escape; and no notice of suit pending, with the like conclusion.

4. That O. H. did not sue sheriff in one year from time of escape, no notice of suit pending; and that sheriff neglected to avail himself of Statute of Limitation, with the like conclusion.

Replications to the 3d plea to 1st count, and issue to the country.

To 4th plea to 1st count, judgment against the sheriff for the escape, and notice to defendants of the suit pending, concluding with a verification.

To 3d plea to 2d count, and issue to the country.

Rejoinder to replication to 4th plea to 1st count, denying notice of the suit pending; and averring that it was defended without defendant's knowledge; that sheriff neglected to avail himself of Statute of Limitation.

On special demurrers to the 1st, 2d and 4th pleas to the 2d count, and to the rejoinder to the replication to the 4th plea to the 1st count; held, that the rejoinder was not double, within the rule which denies the right to include two distinct and independent matters, requiring two separate answers, in the same pleading; that the several facts contained in it were connected and dependent, all tending to the point of defense sought to be introduced, viz.: that judgment against the plaintiff was recovered through his default, in not availing himself of the Statute of Limitation (1 R. L., 427, sec. 26).

Held, also, that the rejoinder properly concluded with a verification; inasmuch as it introduced new matter, viz.: the neglect of the plaintiff in not setting up a proper defense to the action for the escape, which matter was not set up in the plea.

But held, also, that the plea, being properly one *non damnificatus*, was bad, as being inapplicable to the condition of the bond, and the breach assigned;

Also, that the matter of substance set up in the rejoinder, viz: want of notice, neglect, &c., were no bar even when taken in connection with the plea which it followed.

Held, also, that the 4th plea to the 2d count was bad for the same reasons; and,

That the 1st and 2d pleas to the 2d count were defective in form; inasmuch as they were a mere denial of the substance of the declaration, and should, therefore, have concluded to the country.

The plea of *non damnificatus* is applicable to an action on a bond to save harmless and indemnify the obligee, but to an action on no other bond.

A jailer, who has given a bond to his principal, the sheriff, not to permit an escape, cannot defend himself against an action for the breach of that condition, upon the ground that in an action against the sheriff, for an escape which the jailer had permitted, the former neglected to plead the Statute of Limitation, which had run against the action.

A plea, &c., which introduces several facts, all of which are necessary to constitute but one point of defense, is not bad for duplicity.

A plea, &c., which introduces new matter, should conclude with a verification.

But where it denies the whole substance of the plaintiff's declaration, it should conclude to the country.

Citations—1 R. L., 427, sec. 26; 1 Chit. Pl., 512, 535, 537; 1 Burr., 316; 2 Johns., 433, 462; 1 Saund., 103, *n.* (1) & 117, *n.* (1); Cro. Jac., 363, 634; 2 Wils., 126; 2 Co., 4; 5 Johns., 42; 20 Johns., 153; 2 T. R., 439.

PLACITA of Oct. Term, 1822. Memorandum of Jan. Term, 1822. Steuben Co., *ss.* George M'Clure, late Sheriff of the County of Steuben, plaintiff in this suit, complains of Francis Erwin, John Knox and Eldad Mead, defendants in this suit, in custody, &c., of a plea that they render to him $5,000 of debt, which they owe to and unjustly detain from him, for this, to wit: that whereas the said Francis, John and Eldad, and one Benjamin Parker, in his lifetime, now deceased, and whom the said Francis, John and Eldad have survived, heretofore, to wit: on the 26th day of March, A. D. 1816, at, &c., by their certain writing, obligatory, sealed, &c., and to the court, &c., the date whereof, &c., acknowledged themselves to be held and firmly bound unto *the said plaintiff, Sheriff of the [*314 County of Steuben, in the sum above demanded, to be paid, &c., when they, the said Benjamin, &c., should be thereunto afterwards requested; which said writing obligatory was and is subject to a certain condition, thereunder written, to the effect following, to wit: Whereas the above bound Benjamin Parker was appointed to the office of jailer, or jail-keeper, of the said County of Steuben, on the said day of March, in the year aforesaid; therefore, the condition of the said above obligation was such, that if the said Benjamin should well and faithfully, in all things, perform and execute the trust reposed in him as jailer of the county aforesaid, during his continuance in the said office by virtue of the said appointment, faithfully, without fraud, deceit, or oppression, and would not, at any time, suffer any prisoners, committed to his charge to escape from said prison, through his neglect, until legally discharged, then the said obligation to be void, else to remain in full force and virtue. And the said plaintiff avers, that one

---

NOTE.—*Principal and surety—Defense of principal to an action by security after having paid the creditor—Failure of surety to interpose defense of Statute of Limitations in action by creditor.* Compare above case with Shaw v. Loud, 12 Mass., 447; Reynolds v. Harral, 2 Strobh., 87; Wade v. Green, 3 Humph., 547; Germain v. Wing, 1 Buff. Super., Ct., 441.

Olney S. Thatcher, afterwards, to wit: on the 24th day of March, A. D. 1817, at, &c., was committed to the jail of the said County of Steuben, he, the said Benjamin, then being jailer as aforesaid, under and by virtue of the said appointment, in the said writing obligatory mentioned, on a *capias ad satisfaciendum*, directed to the Sheriff of the said County of Steuben, and delivered to the said George M'Clure, then being Sheriff of the said County of Steuben, issued out of the Supreme Court of Judicature of the State of N. Y., at the suit of one Olney Hines, tested on the 1st Monday of Jan., A. D. 1817, and returnable on the 1st Monday of May, in the year last aforesaid, for the sum of $84.07, with directions indorsed thereon, to receive the said sum of $84.07, with interest from the 20th of August, 1815, besides sheriff's fees. And the said plaintiff further avers, that after the said Olney S. Thatcher, otherwise called Samuel O. Thatcher, was committed to the jail of the said County of Steuben, as aforesaid, he the said Benjamin being such jailer as aforesaid, the said Benjamin, in his lifetime, afterwards, to wit: on the 1st day of June, A. D. 1817, at, &c., negligently suffered and permitted the said Olney S. Thatcher, 315*] otherwise *called Samuel O. Thatcher, he, the said, &c., then not being legally discharged, to escape and go at large wheresoever he would, out of the jail of the said county, he the said Benjamin being such jailer as aforesaid, under and by virtue of the said appointment in the said writing obligatory mentioned, he the said plaintiff baving been, during all the time aforesaid, Sheriff of the said County of Steuben; by means of which said premises, the said plaintiff hath sustained damages to a large amount, to wit: to the amount of $5,000, whereby an action hath accrued, &c.

Second count, setting forth another bond, commitment and escape as in the first count, and adding—"by means of which said last mentioned negligence of the said Benjamin, as such jailer as aforesaid, in suffering and permitting the said Olney S. Thatcher, otherwise, &c., to escape and go at large out of the said last mentioned jail, and out of the charge and custody of him, the said Benjamin, as such jailer as last aforesaid, the said Olney Hines, afterwards, to wit: in the Term of January, A. D. 1819, in the Court of C. P. in the said County of Steuben, before the judges of the same court, then and now being held at, &c., levied his certain plaint in a plea of debt against the said plaintiff, as such Sheriff as aforesaid, for the same identical escape last mentioned, of the said Olney S. Thatcher, otherwise, &c., from the jail of the said County of Steuben, and from and out of the charge and custody of the said Benjamin, as such jailer as aforesaid; and such proceedings were thereupon had, in the said Court of C. P., before the aforesaid judges thereof, that afterwards, to wit: in the Term of February, of the said Court of C. P., A. D. 1820, it was considered and adjudged by the said court, before the aforesaid judges thereof, that the said Olney Hines should recover against the said plaintiff $84.07, of debt, and also $25.49, for the damages which the said Olney Hines had sustained, on occasion of the detaining that debt, over and above his cost and charges, by him, the said Olney Hines, about his suit in that behalf expended, and for those costs and charges $27.85, whereof the said plaintiff is convicted, as by the record and proceedings, &c. (averring the escape from the jail of *Steuben, [*316 and the escape for which the recovery was had, to be the same). And the said plaintiff further avers, that after the commencement of the aforesaid suit against him the said plaintiff, by the said Olney Hines, for the said last mentioned escape of the said Olney S. Thatcher, otherwise, &c., from the said jail as aforesaid, and before the giving of the said judgment by the said Court of C. P., in favor of the said Olney Hines, against the said plaintiff, for the said last mentioned escape of the said Olney S. Thatcher, otherwise, &c., as aforesaid, to wit: on the 1st day of January, A. D. 1820, at, &c., the said Francis, John and Eldad, survivors as aforesaid, there had notice of the said suit which was so commenced as aforesaid, by the said Olney Hines against the said plaintiff, for the said last mentioned escape of the said Olney S. Thatcher, otherwise, &c., from the said jail as aforesaid. By means of all which said last mentioned premises, in this count mentioned, the said plaintiff hath sustained damages to a large amount, to wit: the amount of $5,000, whereby an action hath accrued, &c."

Imparlance to Oct. Term, 1822.

Pleas to the first count:

1. That the said Benjamin Parker did not suffer and permit the said Olney S. Thatcher to escape, and go at large wheresoever he would, out of the said jail of the said County of Steuben (concluding to the country).

2. That the said Olney S. Thatcher was not committed to the said jail, whilst he the said Benjamin was the jailer thereof (concluding to the country).

3. That, at the said time, when the said Benjamin is supposed to have suffered and permitted the said Olney S. Thatcher to escape, and go at large out of the said jail, the said Olney Hines did permit and suffer the said Olney S. Thatcher to escape, and go at large out of said jail wheresoever he would; and which is the same going at large out of the said jail in the said first count mentioned (concluding with a verification and prayer of judgment, &c.)

*4. That the said Olney Hines did [*317 not, at any time within one year from the time of the said escape of the said Olney S. Thatcher, in the said first count mentioned, bring or commence any action against him, the said George, for the said escape; and that the said George did not, at any time within the said year, sustain any damage by reason, or on account of the said escape (concluding with a verification and prayer of judgment, &c.)

Pleas to the second count:

1. That the said Benjamin did not suffer and permit the said Olney S. Thatcher to escape, and go at large, as in that count is alleged; and further, that the said Francis, John and Eldad had not, nor bad either of them, at any time after the commencement of the said suit by the said Olney Hines against the said George, and before the giving of the said judgment therein, notice of the pendency

of the said suit (concluding with a verification and prayer of judgment, &c.)

2. That the said Olney S. Thatcher was not committed to the said jail whilst he, the said Benjamin, was jailer thereof; and that the said Francis, John and Eldad had not, nor had either of them, at any time after the commencement of the said suit by the said Olney Hines against the said George, and before the giving of the said judgment therein, notice of the pendency of the said suit (concluding with a verification and prayer of judgment, &c.)

3. That at the said time when the said Benjamin in the said second count is supposed to have suffered the said Olney S. Thatcher to escape and go at large out of the said jail, the said Olney Hines did permit and suffer the said Olney S. Thatcher to go at large out of the said jail wheresoever he would, and which is the same going at large out of the said jail in the said second count mentioned; that the said Francis, John and Eldad had not, nor had either of them, at any time after the commencement of the said suit, by the said Olney Hines, against the said George, and before the giving the said judgment therein, notice of the pendency of the said suit (concluding with a verification and prayer of judgment,&c.)

318*] *4. That the said Olney Hines did not, at any time within one year from the time of the said escape of the said Olney S. Thatcher, in the said second count mentioned, bring or commence any action against the said George, for the said escape last mentioned; and that the said Francis, John and Eldad had not, nor had either of them, at any time after the commencement of the suit by the said Olney Hines against the said George, and before the giving of the said judgment therein, notice of the pendency of the said suit; that the said George did not plead to the said suit, or give in evidence at the trial thereof that the same was not commenced in one year from the said escape in the second count mentioned as aforesaid; but wholly neglected so to do, and so the said Francis, &c., say that the said recovery was had by the said Olney Hines against the said George in his own wrong, and by his own default (concluding with a verification and prayer of judgment, &c.)

Replications relative to the first count:

1. To the 3d plea to the 1st count: that the said Olney Hines did not permit and suffer the said Olney S. Thatcher to escape and go at large out of the said jail, in the said 1st count mentioned, wheresoever he would, in manner and form as the said Francis, John and Eldad, survivors as aforesaid, have, in their said plea to the said 1st count of the said declaration of him, the said George, alleged (concluding to the country).

2. To the 4th plea to the 1st count; that after the said escape of the said Olney S. Thatcher, in the said 1st count mentioned, to wit: in the Term of Jan., A. D. 1819, of the Court of C. P., in the said County of Steuben, before the judges of the same court, then, and now being held at, &c., the said Olney Hines levied his certain plaint, in a plea of debt, against the said George, as such sheriff as aforesaid, for the same identical escape of the said Olney S. Thatcher, from the jail of the said County of Steuben, and from and out of the charge and custody of the said Benjamin, as such jailer as aforesaid in the said 1st count mentioned; and such proceedings were thereupon had in the said Court of C. P., before the aforesaid judges thereof; that afterwards, to wit: in the term of Feb., in the said Court *of C. P., A. D. 1820, it was consid- [***319** ered and adjudged by the said court before the aforesaid judges thereof, that the said Olney Hines should recover against the said George, in the said plea, $84.07 of debt, and also $25.49 for the damages which he the said Olney Hines had sustained on occasion of the detaining that debt, over and above his costs and charges by him, the said Olney Hines, about his suit in that behalf expended, and for those costs and charges, $27.85, &c., whereof the said George is convicted, &c., as by the record and proceedings, &c.; and the said George further says that he was obliged to pay, lay out and expend, and necessarily did pay, lay out and expend, a large sum of money, to wit: the sum of $50, in and about his defense in the said suit so prosecuted against him by the said Olney Hines for the said escape of the said Olney S. Thatcher, to wit: on, &c., at, &c. (averring the escape from jail, and the escape for which the recovery was had, were the same). That after the commencement of the last aforesaid suit against him, the said George, by the said Olney Hines, for the said escape of the said Olney S. Thatcher from the said jail as aforesaid, in the said 1st count mentioned, and before the giving of the said last mentioned judgment by the said Court of C. P. in favor of the said Olney Hines against the said George for the said escape in the said 1st count mentioned as aforesaid, to wit: Jan. 1, A. D. 1820, at, &c., the said Francis, &c., survivors, &c., there had notice of the said suit, &c., which said suit was then depending in the said court of C. P., and undetermined as aforesaid (concluding with a verification and prayer of judgment, &c.)

Replication concerning the 2d count, to the 3d plea to that count; that they the said Francis, &c., survivors as aforesaid, after the commencement of the said suit by the said Olney Hines against the said George for the escape of the said Olney S. Thatcher, in the said 2d count of the said declaration of him the said George mentioned, and before the giving of the said judgment therein, had notice of the pendency of the said suit, in manner and form as he, the said George hath in the said 2d count of the said declaration of him, *the said George, in that behalf alleged [***320** (concluding to the country).

Demurrers concerning the 2d count: to the 1st, 2d and 4th pleas to that count, assigning for causes, as to the 1st and 2d pleas, that they deny the matters contained in that count, making complete issues, without setting forth any new matter whatever, and yet conclude with a verification; whereas they should have concluded to the country; and assigning for cause, as to the 4th plea, that it is double in alleging that no suit was commenced within the year, &c.; and also that the plaintiff neglected to plead that fact on the trial in the C. P., and also that the defendants had no notice of the suit, &c. Joinder in demurrer.

Rejoinder concerning the 1st count to the replication to the 4th plea. That the defendants had not, nor had either of them, at any time after the commencement of the said suit by the said Olney Hines against the said George, in the said replication mentioned, and before the said judgment therein, any notice of the said suit; and that the said George defended the said suit without the privity or knowledge of them, the said defendants, or either of them; also that the said George in so as aforesaid defending the said suit, wholly omitted and neglected to plead thereto, or to give in evidence, or insist, upon the trial thereof, that the said suit was not brought or commenced against him, the said George, within one year from the time of the said escape in the said 1st count mentioned; and so the said Francis, &c., say that the said judgment against the said George, in the said replication mentioned, was recovered against him, the said George, by his own neglect and default (concluding with a verification and prayer of judgment, &c.)

Demurrer to this rejoinder, assigning for cause, that it is double in denying notice of the suit, also in alleging that it was defended without the privity, &c., of the defendants; also in alleging that the plaintiff omitted to plead or give in evidence the Statute of Limitation; that the rejoinder concludes with a verification, though it only denies matters alleged in the replication, and should, therefore, have concluded to the country. Joinder in demurrer.

321]* *Mr. J. C. Spencer*, in support of the demurrers, insisted:

1. That the 4th plea to the 1st count of the declaration was bad, because it set up matter in defense which was no bar to the action. It is a plea of *non damnificatus*, and hardly that; for the conclusion is not, in the general language of such a plea, that the plaintiff had sustained no damages, but merely that he had sustained none within a year after the escape. The plea of *non damnificatus*, in its broadest and most general language, would not be applicable. It is confined to a mere bond of indemnity. This is not so. The condition is, that the jailer shall well and faithfully, in all things, perform and execute the trust reposed in him, &c., and will not, at any time, suffer any prisoners, committed to his charge, to escape from the prison, through his neglect, until legally discharged, &c. The declaration avers that he permitted an escape, an act which, *per se*, subjected him to a forfeiture of the bond; and, whether the plaintiff had sustained damages or not, he must recover. This very point was decided in *Andrus* v. *Waring*, 20 Johns., 153, and still more distinctly in the previous case of *Woods* v. *Rowan*, 5 Johns., 42.

The rejoinder to the replication to that plea is also bad, for the same reason. It not only seeks to support the plea, which is a qualified *non damnificatus*, but the matter which it **322*]** *contains, is, in itself, no bar. It is also bad for the special causes assigned—duplicity (1 Ch. Pl., 512), and a wrong conclusion, being to the court instead of the country. It is also a departure from the plea. It admits that the plaintiff has sustained damages; but endeavors to throw the fault upon him, in not pleading the Statute of Limitation. The plea which it was to support, denies the damages. The departure in *Andrus* v. *Waring* was much like this.

The 1st and 2d pleas to the 2d count of the declaration, are bad for the special cause assigned, viz.: a wrong conclusion. Each should have concluded to the country; because they advance no new matter, but take issue upon facts which are fully and distinctly set forth in declaring, and upon which direct issues should have been taken.

The 4th plea to the 2d count is still more objectionable. It is not only double or triple, but the 3d averment is objectionable upon the same ground which we take in relation to the 4th plea to the 1st count. It sets up matter which is substantially bad, and forms no defense. The bond was forfeited *eo instanti* with Thatcher's escape, and it cannot be material whether the Statute of Limitations had run against the escape or not. An objection of this kind, can, at most, go only to the damages. If each fact set up in this plea would constitute a valid defense, they cannot be joined.

Mr. J. Platt, contra. To determine the sufficiency of the 4th plea to the 1st count, it is necessary to advert not only to the condition of the bond, as set forth in the declaration, but to the breaches assigned. The condition was correctly stated by the opening counsel; but the only breach assigned is, that the jailer permitted Thatcher to escape. To this, alone, the plea was intended as an answer; and if it is, in truth, a legal answer to the allegation of an escape, the plaintiff's action must fail. Being thus narrowed down to an escape, the case is altogether distinguishable from that of *Andrus* v. *Waring*, relied upon by the plaintiff's counsel. There were, in that case, a great variety of breaches insisted upon; but no escape from a *ca. sa.* was alleged. The latter is the only one insisted upon here, which the plea attempts *to answer, by saying that the sheriff **[*323** was not sued for the escape till all actions were barred by the Statute of Limitation of one year; and that, within the year, the sheriff had sustained no damages. The plea has all the constituent requisites of a plea of *non damnificatus;* and the success of the sheriff's action must depend upon the same ground as if the bond had been one of mere indemnity. If the two allegations of the plea be true, there is no damage to the Sheriff. He should have given notice to the bail, thrown the *onus* on them, and pleaded the Statute of Limitations. Having omitted these things, the whole is in his own wrong, and no damages are sustained, within the meaning of the condition. His Honor, *Judge* Woodworth, who delivered the opinion of the court in *Andrus* v. *Waring*, remarks, that a bond like the one there in question, was not to be regarded as a bond of indemnity merely. If it had been given for indemnity, he admits that *non damnificatus* would be a good plea. It was not necessary to express an opinion upon this point, because the rejoinders were clearly bad, as being a departure from the plea; so that the demurrers must have prevailed, whether the plea was good for anything or not. Even as to that bond, therefore, the question may not be considered as fully and finally settled by this court. Is it the less so, because His Honors' opinion was founded on the case of *Woods* v. *Rowan*, also cited for the plaintiff. That case does decide, that a bond conditioned against an escape is not technically a bond of indemnity, and that a plea of *non damnificatus* is, therefore, inapplicable; but it has been repeatedly questioned, and finally overruled. It followed the case of *Tillman* v. *Lansing*, 4 Johns., 45, by which the community were so much agitated, that the Legislature interfered by a declaratory Act, in 1809 and 1810 (sess. 32, ch. 148; sess. 33, ch. 187; and *vide* 1 R. L., 429, sec. 6), confining an escape bond to the purposes of indemnity merely, and finally declaring, in terms, that the bond shall be for indemnity only. About the same time, the case of *Jansen* v. *Hilton*, 10 Johns., 549, and *Barry* v. *Mandell*, 10 Johns., 563, in the Court of Errors, overruled two former decisions; and the court declared that, independent of the 324*] *statute, and upon common law principles, the bond was a mere indemnity. If so, according to the doctrine of all the cases, it is enough for us to plead *non damnificatus*. This is admitted in *Andrus* v. *Waring*. The declaration here assigns the escape alone for breach, and, *quoad hoc*, the question is precisely like that in relation to a bond for the jail liberties. In *Andrus* v. *Waring* the plaintiff proceeded upon much broader grounds. The declaration was in debt on bond, generally, without noticing the condition. Upon oyer the condition was, that one of the defendants should well and duly perform the office of deputy-sheriff, in all things according to law, and should render a just and true account of all business that should come into his hands, as a deputy-sheriff ought to do, &c. His Honor, *Judge* Woodworth, may very properly have said, that *non damnificatus* was a bad plea at this stage of the pleadings, because the matter was left open, and it was not seen to what point it might come. It was not narrowed down, as here, to an escape only. It did not appear what the plaintiff would go for; whether for moneys not accounted for, or neglect in the not serving process, or for an escape. A plea or averment may be good in one stage of the record, though it would be bad in another. No matter what followed that plea. Being bad at the point where it was put in, nothing which succeeded could make it good, even though the matter might have been so narrowed as to render the plea afterwards applicable, provided it had been reserved for a future purpose. That case is, therefore, not applicable here.

But whatever be the merits of the plea, it is said we have departed from it in the rejoinder to which the demurrer is taken. If we have done so, as the act consists merely in following where the plaintiff led us, it cannot be imputed to us as a fault. The departure will be found in the replication. This sets up a recovery against M'Clure, and notice of the suit in which the recovery was had. Not a word of this in the 1st count of the declaration. And is the plaintiff warranted in urging against us, as a departure, the introduction of facts which form an answer to his replication? He shifts his ground, and, by the replication, attempts 325*] *to ingraft into the 1st count the closing averments of the 2d. He enlarges the 1st count, by setting forth facts entirely independent of, and disconnected with it; calls upon us for an answer, and then censures us because we have complied with the necessity which he imposed.

There is but a single demurrer to the 1st, 2d and 4th pleas to the 2d count; and if we maintain any one plea included in the joint demurrer, we must prevail. The 2d count sets forth the bond, condition, commitment and escape, an action brought for that escape, notice to the defendants during the pendency of the suit, and finally, a recovery for the escape against the sheriff. The 1st plea denies the escape and notice of the suit; the 2d denies the commitment and notice of the suit; and the third denies the commencement of a suit within the year, notice of its pendency, and that the sheriff availed himself of the Statute of Limitation; and all these pleas conclude with a verification.

To determine the manner in which these pleas should conclude, it is necessary to consult three classes of cases. One relates to a plea containing a simple negative of a naked fact, in which case it should conclude to the country; a second class is, where it sets forth a new fact, or a new set of facts, by way of avoidance, when it should conclude to the court; and there is yet a third class of cases, where the conclusion is good either way. *Hedges* v. *Sandon*, 2 T. R., 459, belongs to the latter class. To a declaration upon bond, the defendant pleaded that it was given for a gaming debt; to which the plaintiff replied, that it was given for money justly due, and not for a gaming debt; and it was held that the replication might conclude either to the country, or with an averment; and per Buller, *J.*, "the general rule is that which has been stated by my brother Ashhurst. If the replication put the whole substance of the defendant's plea in issue, he may conclude to the country. At the same time, there are exceptions to that rule, and there many cases in which the conclusion is good either way." And he illustrates the proposition by the case of *Sandford* v. *Rogers*, 2 Wils., *113. "That was (says he) [*326 an action for goods sold. Plea, judgment recovered in the K. B. for the same promises. Replication, *nul tiel record, et hoc paratus est verificare*. Demurrer, and special causes shown, that, by the replication, the issue upon the plea in bar is complete, and the plaintiff ought not to have concluded by a general averment only. After argument, judgment was given for the plaintiff. The court thought that the issue was completely joined; and therefore the conclusion might have been otherwise; but, inasmuch as the precedents were of conclusions with an averment, they were for supporting it. They said there was no general rule to be laid down as to these things. Practice had, in many instances, allowed special pleas, which amount to the general issue; so conclusions with an averment, where they may be to the country. And they said, that in *Gardiner* v. *Fisher*, Mich., 1 Geo. I., the defendant pleaded another action pending; the plaintiff replied, that the cause of action was different, *absque hoc*, that the cause of action in this and the former were the same as alleged in the plea, *et hoc paratus est*, &c.

Special demurrer, because the replication should have concluded to the country; but judgment was given to answer over, because the traverse makes the point more certain. Sir Raym., 199; 1 Vent., 101; 2 Keb., 692, S. P. F. But they concluded with saying it might be either way. So are all the cases, except that of *Mulliner* v. *Wilkes*, which was passed over without much notice. Therefore, I am of opinion that, in such cases, the conclusion may be either way." *Mr. Justice* Ashurst said: "I thought that this case had been so well settled by a variety of modern determinations, that it was not even intended to be argued. The general rule is this: where the replication denies the whole substance of the defendant's plea, there the plaintiff may tender issue, and conclude to the country. But where he selects one out of several facts, he may traverse that one, and conclude with a verification." The rule laid down by Ashurst, *J.*, extends, in terms, to this very case; viz.: the 1st and 2d pleas demurred to. Certain facts are selected from the declaration, by each plea, and denied. **327***] This warrants the *conclusion of *et hoc paratus*, &c. And *vide* 1 Saund., 103 *a*, *n.* 1.

As to duplicity in the rejoinder to the replication to the 4th plea to the 1st count and in answer to the objection of duplicity to any of the pleadings, it is true, the general position will be found in Co. Litt., 304 *a*, that a plea, containing a multiplicity of distinct matters to one and the same thing, whereunto several answers (admitting each of them to be good) are required, is not allowable in law. But this case does not come within that rule. The averments are not of distinct matters, or independent facts, requiring separate answers, but all the facts go to the same point of defense. All the facts averred are necessary to the defense. Abundant authority illustrating this distinction is to be found in the books. *Robinson* v. *Bayley*, 1 Burr., 316; *Patcher* v. *Sprague*, 2 Johns., 462; 1 Chit. Pl., 512; Plowd., 193, 194; *Currie* v. *Henry*, 2 Johns., 433. Courts are liberal in allowing these pleas, where there is the remotest tendency, in the several matters, to a single point; though there is good sense in the rule which denies plain and palpable duplicity. After laying down the premises in the plea, that the Statute of Limitation had run, and following it, in the rejoinder, with the fact that no notice of the suit pending was given, and no limitation pleaded, the concluding clause is mere matter of inference, and may be rejected as surplusage. It was necessary to say, the Sheriff neither pleaded, gave notice or otherwise availed himself of the defense, after saying that the suit was barred. The whole is a mere allegation that he did not use due and legal means of defense. Yet we might have been liable on another contingency, although the suit was barred; as if the Sheriff had given us notice, and troubled his head no further about it, and we had suffered judgment to go against him. It was, therefore, necessary, in order to exclude all cause of action, to show that we had no notice of the suit. The rejoinder embodies the whole merits of the defense.

The same remarks, so far as duplicity is concerned, apply both to the 4th plea to the 2d **328***] count, and the rejoinder to *the replication to the 4th plea to the 1st count, when taken in connection with the plea which it follows.

Mr. Spencer, in reply, did not deem it necessary, indeed it would hardly be decorous, to enter into a systematic vindication, of the late judgment of this court, in *Andrus* v. *Waring*, against the criticisms of the gentlemen. But he would ask the indulgence of the court in remarking, that the history given, of conflicting decisions, and legislative declarations, relate entirely to another species of bond—a bond given by the sureties of a prisoner on execution, to secure him the jail liberties. Without much regard to the wording of that contract, it is finally settled, that it is one of mere indemnity. By the force of legislative Acts, and the decisions of our tribunals, it forms an exception to the rule which applies to all other bonds similarly worded. It is sufficient to reply, that neither *Andrus* v. *Waring* nor this case are actions upon such a bond. The former was on a bond from a deputy-sheriff, and the present on a bond from a jailer, conditioned against defaults in the execution of their respective offices, against suffering escapes, &c. The reasoning of the judge, therefore, in *Andrus* v. *Waring*, is sound, and accords with the rule which governs in these cases. *Holmes* v. *Rhodes*, 1 Bos. & P., 638, referred to in *Andrus* v. *Waring*, is a case as strongly to our purpose as *Woods* v. *Rowan*, 5 Johns., 42. The reasoning of the court in *Andrus* v. *Waring* was pertinent and necessary, and moreover directly applicable to the plea of *non damnificatus* in this case. The question was the same as here, upon the 4th plea to the 1st count; although the plaintiff might not have specifically pleaded his damages in the same stage of the record. It is said, we have narrowed down our claim to the escape. So, in *Andrus* v. *Waring*, the demand was narrowed to a point, which would as much warrant a plea of *non damnificatus* as the present declaration. It was seen, from the nature of the bond, on oyer, what breaches alone the plaintiff could insist upon, and *non damnificatus* would reach either of them as effectually as the present. One branch of the condition was, that the deputy should pay *over moneys, which, from its nature, [***329** must have been, and was followed by an averment that he had neglected this, and thrown the duty upon the plaintiff, by which the latter had received damage. The same remark is applicable to all the breaches.

The duplicity in the rejoinder is almost too plain to admit of demonstration. It sets up three distinct matters, relating to as many distinct allegations in the assignment of breaches; and how is it possible to dispose of the several issues to be joined upon these matters, by a single finding in the *postea?*

Several cases were cited by the gentleman, as to the manner in which pleas are to conclude; the general rule upon which we insist is not denied, and the cases cited merely go to show a well established and admitted exception in the plea or replication of *nul tiel* record. Some elementary writers, it is true, have confounded the conclusion of this plea with a conclusion upon matter *in pais*. In relation to this, disconnected with matter of record, Chitty (1 Chit. Pl., 535 to 539) reconciles all the cases to the distinction that, where new matter is introduced, a verification is proper; but where denial is interposed, either to the whole substance of the declaration or plea, or to any insulated fact which they contain, the proper and only conclusion is to the country. The single anomaly which he allows is, where the traverse relates to a matter of record. Then suppose the matters do all tend to one point, in the 4th plea to the second count, and the rejoinder in support of the 4th plea to the 1st count, being no more than simple denials of matter *in pais*, they should not conclude with the verification. What is the pleader to do? Carry on a perpetual negative, at the will of the defendant? In this way, the plaintiff can never command an issue, and prepare his cause for trial.

It is said the rejoinder contains all the merits of the former pleas. If so, it may be added, that it contains all their faults. Neither the plea principally in question, nor the rejoinder, contain matter which will constitute a bar, if the substance alone is to be regarded. That the action was not brought against the sheriff within one year is no bar.

330*] *The Statute of Limitation was a privilege personal to the sheriff. It is confined to him. The statute has not extended it to the bail. They are not embraced, either in its terms, or its policy. Notice of the suit pending was not necessary. Denying this was a mere anticipation of what the plaintiff might possibly have replied, to sustain his action upon some point not yet arisen. You might as well anticipate the defense of infancy, by averring in your declaration that goods were necessaries.

Again; having shown that if the rejoinder is a mere negative, the conclusion is wrong, we say, if it puts in new matter, it is, therefore, a departure, and no matter how it concludes. Let the defendant choose either horn of the dilemma, it is alike fatal to his rejoinder.

Curia, per SUTHERLAND, *J.* The first point made by the plaintiff is, that the 4th plea to the 1st count of the declaration is bad, as it sets up matter of defense which is no bar.

The action is brought by the plaintiff, as late Sheriff of the County of Steuben, upon a bond given by Benjamin Parker, the jailer, and the defendants as his sureties, conditioned that he should well and faithfully, in all things, perform and execute the trust reposed in him as jailer, during his continuance in office, without fraud, deceit or oppression; and that he would not, at any time, suffer any prisoner committed to his charge to escape from the prison, through his neglect until legally discharged. The 1st count of the declaration, after stating the bond and condition, avers, that after giving the bond, and while Parker was jailer, one Thatcher was committed to the jail under a *ca. sa.* at the suit of one Hines; and that after he was so committed, Parker, being jailer, negligently suffered and permitted him to escape; by means whereof the plaintiff sustained damage, &c. To this count the defendant pleaded four separate pleas, the last only of which is in question. It is, that Hines (the plaintiff in the execution) did not, within one year from the time of the escape, prosecute an action for it against the plaintiff; and further, that the plaintiff did not, at any time, within the year, *sustain any damage by reason of the [***331** escape. *Vide* 1 R. L., 427, sec. 26. To this plea the plaintiff replied, that after the escape of Thatcher, Hines prosecuted an action of debt against the plaintiff for the escape, and recovered judgment; and that while the suit was pending, and before judgment, the defendants had notice of it. To this replication, the defendants rejoin that they had not notice of the suit before judgment; that the defense was conducted without their privity or knowledge, and the plaintiff wholly omitted to plead or otherwise avail himself of the fact that the Statute of Limitation had run against the escape; and so, they say, the judgment recovered against the plaintiff was so recovered by his own neglect and default. This rejoinder the defendants concluded with a verification; and the plaintiff demurs to it for two special causes, viz.: duplicity and a wrong conclusion.

Neither of the two formal exceptions are well taken. The rejoinder is not double within the sense of the rule relied upon. The several matters which it contains all tend to the same conclusion. The point or main proposition which it seeks to establish is, that the judgment which Hines recovered against the plaintiff, was recovered against him through his own neglect or default, in not availing himself in his defense of the fact that the suit was not commenced within a year after the escape. In order to maintain that proposition, the defendants aver, first, that they had no notice of the suit; and that the plaintiff defended it without their privity or knowledge. But this, of itself, is no ground of defense; for if the plaintiff had set up every matter of defense within the power of the defendants, they were not injured by the omission. This became important, therefore, only when connected with the subsequent averment, that the plaintiff omitted to avail himself of a legal defense. Nor would the latter averment, alone, have been sufficient. The plaintiff, in his replication, had distinctly charged the defendants with notice of the suit. If that averment is material, and the defendants had omitted all answer, the notice would have stood confessed upon the record; and been a complete answer to the allegation that the plaintiff had not availed himself of every legal matter of defense. The two averments, *therefore, form one connected propo- [***332** sition; and are constituent parts of the same entire defense. 1 Chit. Pl., 512; 1 Burr., 316; 2 Johns., 433; *Id.*, 462.

The rejoinder properly concluded with a verification. The averment that the plaintiff neglected to avail himself of the fact that the suit of Hines was not commenced within a year after the escape, was new matter. The plea alleges merely, that the suit was not commenced within the year. The replication answers that allegation, by averring that the defendants had notice of the suit. The rejoinder denies the notice; and then adds that the plaintiff neglected to avail himself of that defense. Whether this be a departure from the plea or not is a distinct question; but it is clearly new matter; and brings the rejoinder within the established rule of pleading, that whenever new matter is introduced on either side, the conclusion must be with a verification. 1 Chit. Pl., 537; 1 Saund., 103, *n.* 1.

But the material inquiry is, whether the plea and rejoinder are good in substance. The plea is substantially one of *non damnificatus.* This is a good plea in all cases where the condition is to indemnify and save harmless; because it answers the condition in terms. But it is good in that case only. 1 Saund., 117, *n.* 1; *Codner* v. *Dalby*, Cro. Jac., 363; *Horseman* v. *Obbins*, *Id.*, 634; *Hulland* v. *Malken*, 2 Wils., 126; *Manser's* case, 2 Rep., 4; *Woods* v. *Rowan*, 5 Johns., 42; *Andrus* v. *Waring*, 20 Johns., 153. The plea should go to the right of action—not to the question of damages. The plaintiff, so far as it depends upon the pleadings, shows his right to recover, by setting forth the bond and its condition, and alleging a breach of that condition, either general or special, as the case may require. If the defendant, by his plea, admit that the condition has been broken, he concedes the plaintiff's right to recover; and by not denying the breach assigned, but instead of doing this, interposing the general plea of *non damnificatus*, he, in effect, admits the breach. In this case, the part of the condition alleged to be broken is, that Parker would not, at any time, suffer any prisoner to escape. The plea is, that the plaintiff did not suffer any damage **333***] by the escape. *The escape, and consequently, the breach of the condition, are thus admitted; and the right of action follows. *Andrus* v. *Waring*, 20 Johns., 153, is in point. That was an action upon a bond given by a deputy-sheriff to his principal. The condition, so far as it related to the question raised upon the pleadings, was substantially the same as in this case. It was held not to be a bond of indemnity; and the plea of *non damnificatus* was overruled as inapplicable. The rejoinder is bad for the same reasons, and must follow the fate of the plea. It admits the breach of the condition, alleging that the plaintiff might have avoided the consequence only of that breach.

The second count of the declaration differs from the first only in this, that it sets forth the suit and recovery by Hines against the plaintiff for the escape of Thatcher, and avers notice of that suit to the defendants. The first plea to this count denies the escape of Thatcher, and notice of Hines' suit against the plaintiff; and concludes with a verification. The second plea denies that Thatcher was committed to jail while Parker was jailer, with notice of Hines' suit; and also concludes with a verification. As to the third plea, there is no question, the plaintiff having replied and taken issue upon it, The fourth plea alleges that the suit of Hines against the plaintiff was not commenced within a year after the escape; that the defendants had no notice of the suit; and that the plaintiff did not avail himself, in his defense, of the fact that it was barred by the Statute of Limitation. The plaintiff demurred to the first, second and fourth pleas specially; and one cause of demurrer assigned both to the first and second pleas is, that they should have concluded to the country, and not to the court. The exception is well taken. Those pleas deny the whole substance of the declaration. In such case the plea should conclude to the country. 1 Chit. Pl., 535; 2 T. R., 439. The fourth plea is good in form, but bad in substance, for the reasons which have already been given in relation to the fourth plea to the first count.

Judgment for the plaintiff upon all the demurrers.

Cited in—4 Cow., 259; 7 Cow., 452; 43 Barb., 101; 15 Minn., 468.

---

*THE PEOPLE [*334
v.
MARSH, Sheriff of ONONDAGA.

Plaintiff Non-resident—Liability of Attorney for Costs.

Where the original plaintiff is a non-resident of this State, his attorney is liable to pay the costs of setting aside an attachment for irregularity, granted against the sheriff for not bringing in the body.

The people are merely a nominal party and the case is within the spirit of the 13th rule of Jan. Term, 1799.

IN Oct. Term, 1823, an attachment was granted against the defendant for not bringing in the bodies of Wallace and Baker, in a cause at the suit of Butterfield, which, at the last Feb. Term, was set aside as irregular, with costs. The plaintiff, Butterfield, being a non-resident of the State.

Mr. John Porter now moved for a rule requiring his attorneys to pay the costs, within the 13th general rule of Jan. Term, 1799.

Mr. J. Platt, contra, said the application certainly does not come within the terms of that rule. The plaintiffs in this suit are not non-residents.

Curia. True, but the people are a nominal party. The suit is really in favor of Butterfield; and the defendant comes within the spirit of the rule.

Motion granted.

IN THE MATTER OF MASCRAFT
v.
VAN ANTWERP, Sheriff of Albany.

Advertisement of Sale on Execution—Certificate of Sale, Should not State Another Execution Subsequently Received by Sheriff—Statement of Purchase Money.

A sheriff who advertises for sale on but one execution, cannot sell under that and another execution, coming subsequently to his hands, by virtue of the same advertisement.

On a sale of lands, the whole purchase money should be inserted in the certificate of sale.

MAY 11, 1824, a *fi. fa.* was issued, and delivered to the sheriff of Albany, in favor of Stephen P. Schuyler, against Benjamin Covell, for $60.09, on a judgment obtained in a justice's court, a transcript whereof had been filed in the clerk's office, May 6, 1824. On this execution, the sheriff advertised for

sale two small lots in Watervliet, to be sold June 23, 1824. The execution upon Schuyler's judgment was delivered to the sheriff May 11, 1824, and on the same day another *fi. fa.* was delivered to a deputy of the same sheriff against Covell, in favor of John V. Fassett and William I. Seldon for $113.72 on a judgment in this court, docketed Mar. 18, 1824; but the advertisement of sale did not include this execution, which was delivered at a
335*] later *hour in the day than that of Schuyler. At the time and place appointed in the advertisement, the two lots were sold, both executions being then in the sheriff's hands, which was known to the purchaser at the sale. William Mascraft purchased, at a bid of $175.

The question was now submitted by *Mr. J. V. N. Yates*, in behalf of Mascraft, and Cornelius Van Antwerp, the sheriff, in person, whether in the certificate of sale he ought to state both executions, so as to entitle the purchaser to all the benefits of a sale under both.

It was insisted, in behalf of Mascraft, that when a sheriff advertises on one execution, and subsequently receives another, the sale proceeds on both, without requiring a second advertisement. A debtor's property might never be sold, if every execution, as it came to hand, required another advertisement.

The sheriff submitted, that, as the advertisement specified but one execution, the certificate of sale should be confined to that alone.

Curia. As the sheriff advertised on one execution only, he can state no other in the certificate or deed of sale; but the whole sum bid by Mascraft should be inserted, that the debtor or a creditor, coming to redeem, may know the amount of principal and interest he is to pay, and the purchaser, on the other hand, be secure of receiving the amount which he has paid.

Rule accordingly.

Cited in—4 How. Pr., 220; 17 Abb. Pr., 150.

BEARD *v.* VAN WICKLE.

Declaration on Promissory Notes—Joinder of Money Counts—Judgment by Default—Assessment of Damages.

Where the general money counts are joined with one on a promissory note in the same declaration, it is erroneous for the clerk to assess the damages without first entering a *nolle prosequi* as to the money counts.

In such a case, the defendant cannot compel the plaintiff to enter a *nolle prosequi*, and it is at his option, to assess damages by a jury, though his claim be founded on the note alone.

Citations—2 Cow., 36 to 39, *n.* (*f*).

THE plaintiff declared upon a promissory note of about $103, and joined the money
336*] counts in the same declaration. *Judgment having passed against the defendant by default, the plaintiff assessed his damages upon a writ of inquiry, which the defendant now moved to set aside, on the ground that the damages should have been assessed by the clerk, inasmuch as the plaintiff's demand was confined to the promissory note, upon which alone he claimed damages before the jury; that the defendant ought not to be subjected to the additional costs of a writ of inquiry; and Laws, sess. 41, ch. 259, sec. 10; and 1 Dunl. Pr., 384, were cited in support of the motion.

Mr. R. S. Church, for the motion.

Mr. W. Sisson, contra.

Curia. The plaintiff cannot have his damages assessed by the clerk, where the declaration includes the money counts, with a count upon a promissory note, without first entering a *nolle prosequi* upon the former. *Burr* v. *Waterman*, 2 Cow., 36 to 39, *note f.* The defendant cannot compel the plaintiff to enter a *nolle prosequi*. This is at his option; and, of course, he must choose whether he will proceed by assessment before the clerk, or a writ of inquiry.

Motion denied, with costs.

THE PRESIDENT, DIRECTORS AND COMPANY OF THE BANK OF COLUMBIA, *v.* SOUTHERLAND, Impleaded with SOUTHERLAND.

Paying Money into Court—Practice.

Forms and practice, on paying money into court.

The sum paid is to deemed stricken out of the declaration, and unless a larger sum is proved by the plaintiff, at the trial, verdict should be for the defendant.

But where, in such a case, a verdict is taken for the plaintiff, subject to the question of practice, to be settled by this court, that question must be determined on a case made—not as a non-enumerated motion.

THE declaration was in *assumpsit*, on a promissory note, dated July, 2, 1820, for $320.02, with interest from date, including, also, the usual money counts. Pleas, the general issue, *and payment, with notice [*337 of special matter. Before pleading, Mar. 9, 1824, the defendant paid $60 into court.

The cause was tried at the last Columbia Circuit, before Walworth, Circuit Judge, when the plaintiff sought to recover upon another note, given by one Harris, under the money counts, and evidence was given on both sides touching this claim.

The defendant then gave in evidence the following rule:

"DAVID SOUTHERLAND, impleaded with EBENEZER SOUTHERLAND,
ads.
THE PRESIDENT, DIRECTORS & COMPANY OF THE BANK OF COLUMBIA.

In Supreme Court, March 9th, 1824. On motion of *M'Kinstry & Tallmadge*, attorneys for defendant, ordered, that the defendant have leave to bring into court $60; and thereupon, unless the plaintiffs shall accept thereof, with costs to be taxed, in full discharge of this action, the said sum of $60 shall be struck out of the declaration, and the said sum shall be paid out of the court, to the plaintiff or his attorney; and on the trial of the issue in this cause, the plaintiff shall not be permitted to give evidence for the sum brought into court.

(A copy) JOHN KEYS PAIGE, Clk."

Also the following receipt:

"Received from *M'Kinstry & Tallmadge*, Esqrs., the defendants' attorneys in the above cause, $60, referred to in the above rule, and to be applied or paid agreeable to said rule. March 9th, 1824.

JOHN KEYS PAIGE, Clk."

It was admitted by the counsel for the plaintiff, that the amount paid into court exceeded the amount due upon the note declared on, at the date of the rule; and that the rule and receipt for the moneys had been served on the plaintiffs' attorney.

The judge, having some doubt about the practice of paying money into court, said he would direct the jury to find their verdict, without regarding the money paid into court, and reserve all questions of practice for the **338***] Supreme Court. *He accordingly directed the jury, that if they were of opinion that the defendants were liable for the amount of the Harris note, they would find a verdict for the plaintiff for this, together wit the defendant's note, both being $182.22; bht if they were of opinion that the defendants were not liable for the amount of the Harris note, that they would then find a verdict for the plaintiff, for the sum due upon the note the defendants, amounting to $62.10. The jury found for the plaintiff, to the amount of the latter sum.

Mr. D. B. Tallmadge, now moved that a judgment be entered for the defendant, upon an affidavit stating the above facts. The motion was noticed as a non-enumerated motion. He cited 1 Saund., 33, *n.* 2; *Griffeths* v. *Williams*, 1 T. R., 710.

Mr. E. Williams, contra, objected that the motion should be brought on as an enumerated motion upon a case made.

Curia. It is irregular to come in this form. Like all other questions arising on the trial, which relate to the direction of the judge, or points reserved there, it should be brought here upon a case made. But the practice is well settled, upon the facts before us, that, in in a case like this, where money may be properly paid into court, the sum paid in must be considered as stricken out of the declaration. It is a defense, *pro tanto*, and unless the plaintiff proves a sum beyond what is paid, there should be a verdict for the defendant. We deny this motion, with costs; but as the form of bringing it forward has been misapprehended, we give the defendants ten days, within which to make a case, and bring the question properly before us.

Rule accordingly.

Cited in—1 Wend., 539; 7 Hill, 31; 14 Abb. Pr., 52; 9 Bos., 593; 1 E. D. S., 400; 42 Am. Dec., 34.

339*] *M'KINSTRY *v.* DAVIS ET UX.

Feme Covert—*Imprisonment on* Ca. Sa.

A *feme covert* may be imprisoned on a *ca. sa.*, with or without her husband; though otherwise as to *mesne* process.

BOTH the defendants had been sued, and judgment obtained against them in *assumpsit;* but Davis, having been discharged under the Act to Abolish Imprisonment for Debt in Certain Cases, he was not liable to the imprisonment of his body, and the plaintiff stipulated to allow him the benefit of this discharge, without plea. Having proceeded regularly to judgment against him and his wife, the plaintiff issued a *ca. sa.*, upon which, by his direction, the wife alone was imprisoned.

Mr. C. Miller moved that she be discharged.

Mr. F. Williams, contra.

Curia. Clearly, this motion cannot be granted. A *feme covert* is liable to be imprisoned on a *ca. sa.*, with or without her husband; and so are all the cases; though it is otherwise as to *mesne* process.

Motion denied.

Cited in—42 Barb., 438.

JANSEN AND JANSEN, Administrator, *v.* TAPPEN.

Demurrer—Reference.

A reference will not be granted, if there be a demurrer in the cause, which relates to the whole action, and is undetermined.

MOTION for a reference, in behalf of the plaintiff; but it appeared that, besides other pleas upon which issues of fact were joined, the defendant had pleaded *non assumpsit infra sex annos*, to which the plaintiff had replied, and the defendant had demurred to the replication, upon which the plaintiff had joined in demurrer; which issue in law was not yet determined; and the motion was opposed for this reason.

Messrs. Myer* and *Van Buren*, for [*340** the motion.

Mr. H. M. Romeyn, contra.

Curia. The motion must be denied. Here is a demurrer pending upon a replication to a plea which goes to the whole cause of action. The motion is premature; for, should the report be for the plaintiff, still the decision upon the demurrer may be for the defendant, which would render this proceeding nugatory.

Motion denied.

THE PEOPLE *v.* TEFFT.

Rule for Further Return to Certiorari—*Arrest of Justice for Contempt—Costs—Practice.*

Practice as to taking bail on recognizance, upon arrest by attachment for contempt.

A defendant being arrested by attachment, for a contempt merely technical, and offering to give bail for his appearance, but the sheriff declining to go with him before a judge for this purpose, and having appeared and answered interrogatories, was discharged, on payment of costs, not including the sheriff's fees for attendance upon the attachment.

When, how, before whom, bail on attachment should be taken; and the duty of the officer taking it.

What the sheriff should do on arrest.
Party's own recognizance to be taken, or plaintiff may demand bail.

THE defendant, a justice of the peace, being brought up on an attachment, at the present term, for a contempt in disobeying a rule to make a further return to a *certiorari*, had answered interrogatories, explaining the reason of his neglect, and now returned fully, and to the satisfaction of the plaintiff's counsel; but it was agreed that he must pay the costs; and the only question was, how much these should be. The defendant had been arrested upon the attachment, by the sheriff of the County of Erie, where he resided; and after being so arrested, the sheriff suffered him to go at large, which he did till the return day of the attachment, when he voluntarily appeared. Shortly after the arrest, however, the sheriff told him that he was advised by the attorney for the plaintiff that he must attend this court personally, to return the attachment, upon which the defendant offered to give bail, or a sufficient recognizance to appear, which the sheriff told him he could not accept; and at-
341*] tended this *court accordingly. The sheriff made an affidavit that he acted in good faith, and as he supposed his duty to be.

Mr. J. Platt, for the plaintiffs.
Mr. S. M. Hopkins, contra.

Curia. The usual practice is, when the defendant is arrested upon the attachment, either to take his recognizance, or the recognizance of him and his bail, conditioned that he shall appear at the return day, &c. There is, in general, no need of committing him to close confinement. But the plaintiffs, or rather the party who prosecutes in their name, may exact not only the defendant's recognizance, but that of a surety; and in either event, the books of practice say, the sheriff should, in all cases of contempt, indiscriminately, take the defendant before a judge, who will exercise a sound discretion, under the circumstances of the case, whether the defendant shall be let out on bail at all, and upon what terms, whether upon his own recognizance alone, or with a surety or sureties, and in what amount. This is highly reasonable and necessary. It would be extremely rigorous, in the case of a trifling contempt, to commit a party to close custody, and finally conduct him (as in this case) a distance of 300 miles, at enormous expense, for a contempt which is, perhaps, merely technical, and unattended with a single circumstance of aggravation. We think, therefore, that when the party requires it, the sheriff should take him before a judge or commissioner authorized by the statute to take bail in these cases, who will determine what shall be the proper course, on being instructed as to the nature of the case. If not aggravated, and nothing beyond costs appears to be involved in the issue, a recognizance, in the usual sum of $100, will be taken, or a larger sum, if the aggravation of the offense or the amount in controversy shall demand more. In ordinary cases, too, when the defendant comes in upon the attachment, his recognizance is taken in the usual sum, to appear, *de die in diem*, and answer interrogatories. In the present case, it could not be necessary for the sheriff to incur *the loss of time, and the heavy dis- [*342 bursements incident to a personal attendance. Let the defendant be discharged, on payment of costs to be taxed, exclusive of those for the attendance of the sheriff upon the attachment, for the purpose of bringing the defendant into court.

Rule accordingly.

JACKSON, ex dem. LIVINGSTON ET AL.,
v.
THURSTON.

Verdict Set Aside—Costs.

Where a verdict is set aside, on the ground that it was against the weight of evidence, this should be on payment of costs by the party against whom the jury found.

AT the Sullivan Circuit, the jury found a verdict for the defendant, which was afterwards set aside by this court, and a new trial granted, with costs to abide the event. The sole ground of setting aside this verdict was, that the jury had found against evidence, and on deciding upon the case, the court did not advert to this in reference to the costs of the trial. And it now being mentioned to the court, that the rule was wrong in this respect—

Per Curiam. It is so. The jury having decided contrary to evidence, the rule should have been, on payment of costs by the plaintiff. Such is the uniform practice. Let the rule be modified accordingly.

Rule modified.

NOTE. The order for setting aside the verdict, and that the costs abide the event, was entered at a previous term.

Cited in—4 Hill, 106 (*n.*); 8 How. Pr., 2; 28 How. Pr., 152; 2 Abb., N. S., 476; 4 Rob., 610.

---

*COWEN *v.* BUSH. [*343

Appeal from Justice Court—Trial by Common Pleas Without Jury—Error.

It is erroneous for a court of C. P. to proceed as a Court of Error, on appeal from a justice, and try the cause without jury, even though both parties elect this form of trial.

ON error from the Washington C. P. The cause was brought into that court by appeal from a justice's court, wherein Cowen recovered a verdict and judgment of $50, against Bush. The latter appealed to the C. P., and, according to the rules of practice in that court, assigned errors generally, upon the coming in of the return, and Cowen pleaded *in nullo est erratum*. The cause was, thereupon, continued by *Curia advisare vult*, to Dec. Term of that court, 1820; and then the record proceeded as follows: "Whereupon the said parties elected to have the said cause tried by the said court, and not by a jury; and thereupon the said court caused the said parties to proceed to the hearing of the said cause, on the examination, in open court, of the witnesses named in the said return, that were sworn and testified before the said justice; whereupon all and singular the said premises being seen, and by the court, &c., fully understood," &c. Judgment of reversal, as upon a writ of error.

Mr. L. Wait, for the plaintiff in error. The court below erected themselves into a Court of Error, and all the proceedings went on upon this idea. They profess to give judgment of reversal as to the proceedings of the justice, whereas they have no power even to reverse their own judgments. At most, this was an arbitration—a reference by consent, without any agreement that the court should give judgment, which is void, within the cases of *Camp* v. *Root*, 18 Johns., 22, and *Yates* v. *Russell*, 17 *Id.*, 461. The court were bound to proceed upon this appeal, according to the course of the common law, which ties them to a trial by jury.

[Here *Mr. Wait* was stopped by *the Court*, who desired to hear the other side.]

Mr. R. Weston, for the defendant in error. It appears of record, that the parties elected the court to stand in the place of a jury, and perform their office.

344*] *WOODWORTH, *J.* So far it was very well; but where is the consent that they should go farther, and give judgment?

Mr. Weston. Numerous cases are cited in *Yates* v. *Russell*, where the parties substituted a less number of jurors than 12 to try the cause, upon which judgment was rendered, and holden well.——

WOODWORTH, *J.* But had the court any other rights than what were conferred by the agreement of the parties? Is it anything more than the selection of three bystanders, to arbitrate this matter?

Mr. Weston. It is like a trial by three jurors.

SUTHERLAND, *J.* But in the cases to which you allude, all the forms of the trial are preserved—a *venire*, return and a formal verdict entered. The record was perfect.

Mr. Weston. Certainly the same thing was intended here. The election spoken of in the record, implies an agreement that the act of the court should be equivalent to the finding of the jury. A party for whose benefit the trial by jury is intended, may waive it.

Mr. Wait, in reply, was again stopped by *the Court*, who all agreed that the case was too plain for argument.

Judgment reversed.

BACKUS *v.* SMITH.

Motion for Reference—Selection of Referees.

The party against whom a reference is moved, may nominate one of the referees, instead of any one named in the notice; but he cannot, by showing cause, entitle himself to a further nomination. If a name is rejected for cause, it lies with the mover to nominate a substitute. So the mover is always entitled to nominate two referees.

MR. E. LIVINGSTON moved to refer this cause.

Mr. J. Platt, contra, read an affidavit, showing that one of the referees named in the notice **345***] of the motion was not indifferent *between the parties; and then claimed the right allowed the party against whom the motion is made to substitute one referee, as of course, instead of one named by the mover, and also to nominate one instead of the referee struck out for cause.

SAVAGE, *Ch. J.* The settled practice is otherwise. You substitute one referee for any one named in the notice; and the mover may substitute some other person for the one against whom cause is shown. The mover is always entitled to the nomination of two referees.

Mr. Livingston then nominated; and

Per totam Curiam—

Rule accordingly.

NICHOLS *v.* COWLES.

Affidavit for Certiorari—*Title.*

An affidavit for a *certiorari* must not be entitled in this court.

MR. J. A. SPENCER, moved to set aside the writ of *certiorari* to a justice's court, because the affidavit upon which it was founded was entitled in this court; and cited *Haight* v. *Turner*, 2 Johns., 371, and *Whitney* v. *Warner*, 2 Cow., 499.

Mr. D. Cady, contra.

Curia. The motion must be granted.

Rule Accordingly.

Cited in—3 Den., 56.

---

*CROMWELL [*346

v.

VAN RENSSELAER, Gentleman, one, &c.

Recovery in Trespass—Costs.

A defendant who is a counselor of this court, making an affidavit to change the venue, need not swear to the advice of counsel that his witnesses are material.

For the purposes of the motion, the court will take notice that he is of the degree of counsel.

MR. J. S. VAN RENSSELAER, the defendant in person, moved to change the venue in this cause, but his affidavit did not state that his witnesses were material, as advised by counsel; nor did it state that he is a counselor of this court.

Mr. A. Conkling, contra, objected, that, for this reason, it was insufficient.

Curia. We will take notice, for the purposes of this motion, that the defendant is himself a counselor of this court, and requires no advice upon that question *aliunde*.

Mr. Conkling then showing by affidavit, that a balance of witnesses for the plaintiff resided in the county where the venue was laid, the motion, for this reason, was denied, without costs.

Rule Accordingly.

Cited in—4 Hill, 64 (*n*).

HASBROUCK ET AL. v. SCHOONMAKER.

Change of Venue—Affidavits of Merits When Party is a Counselor.

A plaintiff recovering at the circuit for a trespass under the Statute (1 R. L., 525-6, sec. 29), a sum which when trebled amounts to less than $50, is not entitled to recover treble costs.

A justice has jurisdiction of such an action.

Semble, therefore, that it does not necessarily involve a question of title to land.

IN trespass for cutting timber, contrary to the Statute (1 R. L., 525, 526, sec. 29), the plaintiffs had recovered damages to $6; and

Mr. C. H. Ruggles, for the plaintiff, moved for treble damages and treble costs. He said this did not depend upon the general Statute of Costs. Treble costs result from the statute which inflicts treble damages. This means treble the Supreme Court costs. *Beekman* v. *Chalmers*, 1 Cow., 584, must have gone upon this ground. It denies any effect to the general Statute (sess. 41, ch. 94, sec. 5), providing that in actions cognizable before a justice, the plaintiff shall not recover costs, unless his damages exceed $50.

Another ground of the application is, that a justice has no cognizance of this action. It is 347*] true that the Statute gives *him, in terms, jurisdiction of trespass on lands; but not of trespasses committed under this Statute. Again; he has no power to try an action, where the title comes in question. In this action, is it not necessarily in question? It has been holden at the circuit that, in an action for a statute trespass, it is not enough for the plaintiff to show himself in possession, as he might in trespass *quare*, &c., at the common law. The penalty is for cutting timber, treble the value of which is to be recovered; and possession must be followed by proof of title. A reversioner or remainder-man might maintain this action, even against the tenant in possession. *Vide Wickham* v. *Freeman*, 12 Johns., 183.

SUTHERLAND, *J.* We have frequently had the question before us, and never entertained a doubt that this action may be brought before a justice; and

Per totam Curiam (without hearing *Mr. J. Sudam*, who was to have argued against the motion), the motion for trebling the damages was granted, but denied as to the costs.

Rule Accordingly.

THE PEOPLE v. BUTLER.

Petit Larceny—Second Offense—What Constitutes, Within Statute.

The true construction of the Statute (sess. 42, ch. 246, sec. 4), providing that every person who shall be a second time convicted of petit larceny, shall be adjudged to imprisonment in the State Prison, is, that the second offense must be committed after a conviction for the first, in order to warrant the enhanced penalty.

It is not enough that there be two successive petit larcenies by the same person, which are severally and successively prosecuted to conviction; though the second indictment charge the first conviction as a part of the crime.

Citations—Act, March 26, 1796, 3 Greenl., 160, sec. 2, 4; Act, March 21, 1801: Act, March 19, 1013; Hawk. P. C., ch. 40, sec. 3, and Jac. L. D., tit. Convict, 1.

AT the last Oyer and Terminer of Oneida the defendant was convicted on an indictment, which set forth, that Mar. 9, 1824, at, &c., a certain indictment was found and presented, in due form of law, in the Court of General Sessions of the Peace, then and there held before Truman Enos and Samuel Jones, Esqs., Judges of the County Court in and for said county, and Uriah Stephens, Esq., one of the justices of the peace of said county, and others their associates, all justices assigned to keep the peace, and also to hear and determine, &c., by the first count of which said indictment, &c., it was charged and alleged that Edmund Butler, *late, &c., on Mar. 1, A. D. [*348 1824, with, &c., at, &c., one bag of the value of $1, the goods and chattels of, &c., then and there being, feloniously did steal, take and carry away, to the great damage, &c.; that by the 2d count of the said indictment, &c., it was charged and alleged, &c., that he received a bag and two bushels of corn, knowing them to be stolen Mar. 1, 1824; that process issued, by which he was arrested and brought before the court, Mar. 9, 1824, pleaded not guilty, and at the following Court of Sessions in May, 1824, was convicted, on his *relicta and cognovit*, of the 1st count; that a *nolle prosequi* was entered as to the 2d count, and that Butler was fined $10; that the said Butler, Mar. 1, A. D. 1824, with, &c., at, &c., one blanket of the value of $5, &c., the goods and chattels of, &c., then and there being, feloniously did steal, take and carry away, to the great damage, &c.

The record of the conviction upon this indictment being now brought here upon *certiorari*, the question was, whether the offense, as charged, was within the Statute of 1819, sess. 42, ch. 246, sec. 4.

Mr. Talcott, Atty-Gen. The Statute under which this conviction took place provides, "that every person who shall, hereafter, be a second time, or oftener, convicted of petit larceny, shall be adjudged by the court who may give judgment thereon to imprisonment in the State Prison, &c., for any time not exceeding three years;" and we contend that there is nothing in its phraseology which requires the second crime to have been committed after the first conviction. By recurring to other statutes, inflicting an increased punishment for a second offense, it will be seen that this was the sense of the Legislature. In cases where they intended that a conviction should precede the second offense they have said so. 1 R. L., 409, sec. 5. The 9th section of the same Statute contains a provision worded like the one under consideration. Why should the Legislature express themselves in these two different ways in the same Statute, unless they intended that the two phrases should have a different effect? When they intend that the conviction shall be a part of the crime, they say so.

**Messrs. C. P. Kirkland and J. A.* [*349 *Spencer*, for the prisoner. The Act should be constructed according to its spirit and intent, which undoubtedly was, that the conviction should precede the second offense. The mischief was a want of reformation by the first punishment. The conviction was intended as evidence that the mild corrective for one offense had failed of its effect. The object can be attained in no other way than by waiting for the effect of the first punishment. Had the Legislature intended otherwise, it would have been easy to say, in terms, that a conviction for two offenses shall subject to the punishment. Construe the Act as contended for, by Mr. Attorney-General, and a first and second indictment and conviction of the same day for two successive offenses before committed, would make out the State Prison offense. Two petit larcenies are to be punished in the State Prison, or county jail, at the election of the public prosecutor. The fate of the prisoner will depend upon the question whether both offenses are charged in the same, or separate indictments. We are without any direct authority upon this question; but it will be perceived that the revisors, in the marginal abstract of the two sections quoted by Mr. Attorney-General, have put the same construction upon both. Though the prisoner comes within the general language of the Statute, yet it is well established that this is to be controlled by the intent of the Legislature. It is the same as if they had declared that he should be punished in the State Prison, for a second offense of the same kind. The same construction may be given to both cases. The latter has received the construction for which we contend. Jac. L. D., Convict, 1, 1 Hawk., ch. 40, sec. 3. The first conviction should be, accordingly, stated in the indictment, and show to have preceded the second offense. *Id.* Dy., 323 *b*, states a case much like the present. The language of the Statute in that case was, "for a second offense, or second conviction," as it appears from the reasoning of the court.

Both these convictions are for a similar offense. The moral turpitude is the same in both. Yet one, it is said, must be punished in the county, the other in the State Prison. **350*]** *The provision, under consideration, was omitted in the revisal of 1813; but was made in 1819 to supply the deficiency. This, probably, arose from observing that petit larcenies were increasing in community, in consequence of the trifling punishment which followed. Can there be a doubt that the Legislature intended that the culprit should first hear the monitory voice of the law, before the heavier doom should be announced? The Statute goes upon the sound maxim, that if gentle means will not avail, the more severe punishment shall be applied.

WOODWORTH, *J.* Another consequence of the construction contended for by Mr. Attorney would be, that of two crimes, one committed now, and one six months hence, the punishment might be the greater for the first offense. To effect this, all you have to do is to indict and convict first for the second offense, and connect this with the first by a subsequent indictment and conviction. The offense which argues the greatest depravity receives in such a case the slightest punishment.

Mr. Talcott, Atty-Gen., in reply. It is conceded that the Legislature have power to punish, in a manner called for by a literal construction of this Act; or that they may disregard the relative depravity of crimes in the manner stated by His Honor. So they may, at their pleasure, require a conviction to precede the second offense, before they demand the enhanced punishment. The case has been argued for the prisoner, as if conviction was the measure of guilt. Not so. It is only the evidence of it. No matter, then, whether the conviction be for the first or the second offense. The enhanced punishment is not for a single offense, in the case stated from the bench; but in all the cases supposed, it is for a series of offenses, betraying a hardness and depravity in guilt, whether the second conviction be for the first or second offense. My construction, then, is not to be impugned because it works an unequal distribution of retributive justice. The Act goes upon a disposition to repeat offenses, which is the same whether before or after a conviction. The argument, that the punishment is at the *option of the **[*351** prosecutor, proves too much. It would go against all punishments for a second offense, whether before or after conviction for the first; for, in both cases, is the prosecutor to choose whether he will avail himself of the first conviction. In either case he may omit it in the indictment; and a punishment as for the single offense, follows: so that, to follow up the argument, this court must legislate all the like statutes out of existence.

This Statute does not give room to apply the authorities cited upon the other side. I agree that where there is a doubt whether the Legislature may not have intended that the offense should be committed after a conviction, the benign construction shall prevail. When it speaks of a second offense, it shall accordingly be held to mean an offense after a conviction. But here the Statute is a second time, not a second offense. The offenses are no otherwise named than to designate the crime; not a succession of trial and conviction. Your Honors are asked to insert a clause to this effect, because it is done in some other Acts. But there is no more to require this than there is for putting in any reasonable clause in any other Act. If absurd consequences follow its omission, the court will lean against them. But, upon what principle can it be maintained that the Legislature have left the Act to be departed from in respect to its plain provisions?

Curia, per SAVAGE, *Ch. J.* The language of this Statute, upon which we are asked to put a construction, has prevailed in various Acts, through a series of revisals, and in relation to different offenses. The Statutes providing for the punishment of second offenses are worded differently; some of them declaring, "that every person who shall be a second time duly convicted or attainted of any of the said felonies comitted after the said first conviction" (Act of Mar. 26, 1796, 3 Greenl., 160, sec. 2); sometimes, "shall be a second time, or oftener, duly convicted, or attainted," &c. *Id.* sec. 4.

Similar provisions passed into the Act of Mar. 21, 1801 (1 K. & R. 254, sec. 4, 5), and the Act of Mar. 19, 1813, 1 R. L. 409, 410, sec. 5, 13.

*A second offense of petit larceny **[*352** not being provided for in the revision of 1813, the Legislature, in 1819, adopted the phraseology which had provided for this case in the old revisions. This Act of 1819 is the one under consideration.

We think the difference of phraseology in these several statutes was entirely accidental; that the Legislature meant the same thing in each, which is, that a conviction shall precede the second offense. The reasonable construction is given by Hawkins (P. C. ch, 40, sec. 3, and Jac. L. D., tit. Convict, 1), to which we were referred by the prisoner's counsel, where the rule is thus laid down—"When a statute makes a second offense felony, or subject to a heavier punishment than the first, it is always implied that such second offense ought to be committed after a conviction for the first; for the gentler method shall first be tried, which, perhaps, may prove effectual."

The prisoner was sentenced to the county jail of Oneida for six months.

Rule accordingly.

Cited in—42 Barb., 643, 6 Kan., 883.

NICHOLS v. DOTY.

Witness from Foreign State—Fees.

The fees of a witness attending from a foreign State are 50 cents a day.

MR. D. RUSSELL, moved for a retaxation of costs. A town clerk, from the State of Vt., attended the trial; and the only question was whether he should be allowed 25 or 50 cents a day. *Mr. Russell* said that he was not a witness attending from a foreign county, within the Act (2 R. L., 29), and was, therefore, entitled to but 25 cents.

Mr. J. Crary, contra.

Curia. The witness is entitled to 50 cents per day, to be computed from the time he left home.

Rule accordingly,

Cited in—7 How. Pr., 143.

353*] *CHAMBERLIN v. DAY.

Rights of Assignee of Chose in Action—Set off of Judgment.

An assignee of a chose in action takes it subject to all equities existing against it at the time of the assignment, though he have no notice of such equity.

Where W. purchased a judgment of C., against D., without notice that D. had previously purchased a judgment against C., h ld, that D. might, notwithstanding set off his judgment so purchased, against the judgment in favor of C.

Assignee of a judgment against the plaintiff, allowed, on motion, to set it off against the judgment in favor of the plaintiff against the assignee.

CHAMBERLIN obtained judgment in this court against Day, for $103.61, at Aug. Term, 1824, which was assigned by Chamberlin to Wiley, for a valuable consideration paid, without any notice or information that Day had purchased a judgment against Chamberlin nor had Chamberlin any notice or information to this effect at the time of the assignment. A *fi. fa.* had issued upon the judgment in favor of Chamberlin, upon which the sheriff had levied $30. On the other hand, one Gold had recovered a judgment in this court against Chamberlin, in Oct. Term, 1823, for $172.72, which Gold, for a valuable consideration, paid, sold and assigned to Day, June 14, 1824.

It was now moved that the deputy be ordered to pay back the $30 to Day, and that the residue of Chamberlin's judgment be set off against the judgment assigned to Day.

Mr. E. S. Lee, for the motion.

Mr. W. W. Brown, contra.

Curia. Wiley took the assignment subject to all the equities actually existing against Chamberlin's judgment at the time of the assignment. Want of notice will not protect against these. Day had purchased and took an assignment of Gold's judgment, before Chamberlin's was assigned; and having a right to this set-off prior to that assignment, it did not devest that right. The motion must be granted.

Rule accordingly.

Cited in—13 Wend., 653; 2 Barb., 261; 3 How. Pr., 389; 2 Abb. N. C., 259; 2 Co. R., 6; 6 Wall., 336; 5 Mason, 217; 39 N. J. L., 243; 28 Am. Dec., 497.

---

*GRANT v. ROOT AND HOBBLE. [*354

Judgment—When Perfected—Power of Commissioner to Stay Proceedings.

A judgment of this court is perfect after four days from the time of entering a rule for judgment, though the record be not filed.

After this, a commissioner has not the power to order a stay of proceedings, with a view to a motion for a new trial;

But where the practice, on this head, was mistaken by the attorney, the court set aside the proceedings, and granted liberty to move for a new trial, on payment of costs.

THE defendants having obtained a verdict, entered their rule for judgment, and after the lapse of four days thereafter taxed their costs; and then, before the record was filed, the plaintiff obtained an order to stay proceedings, from the Recorder of Albany, with a view to move for a new trial, on account of newly discovered evidence; and on a motion by *Mr. C. H. Ruggles*, which was opposed by *Mr. J. Sudam*, one question was, whether this order was regular; and,

SUTHERLAND, *J.*, said the judgment was perfect after four days, though the record was not filed, so that no order could be granted by a single judge or commissioner—to which the other justices agreed; but,

Per Curiam. As here has been a misapprehension of the practice by the plaintiff's attorney, and he has proceeded in good faith, and as there is probable cause for a new trial, we set aside the defendants proceedings, on payment of costs, and let the plaintiff in to move for a new trial, in the same manner as if he had proceeded regularly, for that purpose in the first instance.

Rule accordingly.

Cit d in—10 How. Pr., 219; 4 Rob., 640; 1 Bradf., 489. e

BLUE v. STOUT AND FISHER.

Special bail cannot object to an amendment of the ac etiam.

A MOTION was made, in this cause, to amend the *ac etiam* of the *capias ad respondendum*, which the attorney for the plaintiff, by mistake, issued in covenant, when it should have been in *assumpsit*.

This was opposed, because special bail had been put in.

Mr. S. M. Perkins, for the motion.

Messrs. Dayton and *Woods*, contra.

355*] **Curia*. The bail have no right to object to the amendment. *Christie* v. *Walker*, 1 Bing., 68. The motion must be granted, on payment of costs.

Rule accordingly.

Cited in—19 Barb., 52; 1 Abb. Pr., 66; 5 Abb. Pr., 70.

Ex Parte HILL.

Irregularity of Juror.

If a juror leave his seat for a short time, without the knowledge of the court or parties, but no testimony is given during his absence, and he holds communication with no one on the subject of the cause; though this be a contempt of court, yet it does not avoid the verdict.

Citation—1 Cow., 221.

MR. J. A. SPENCER, moved for a *mandamus* to the judges of the Court of Common Pleas of Madison Co., commanding them to vacate a rule setting aside a verdict for irregularity, in an action between Hill, plaintiff, and one Clark, defendant. The verdict was for Hill, and the court set it aside, on Clark's motion, because one of the jurors, during the trial, left the box, without permission of the parties or the court, went out of doors, and was absent some minutes, returned and took his seat, and joined in the verdict against the defendant. Neither of the parties knew of his absence till he had gone some time, but no testimony was given to the jury while he was gone; and he spoke with no one, except to tell the constable, who came after him and brought him back, that he was one of the jury.

Mr. J. Platt, contra.

Curia. It is the settled doctrine, that though such conduct as this is a contempt of the court, yet it is not a ground for avoiding the verdict. The cases on this subject are all collected by the reporter, in a note to *Smith* v. *Thompson*, 1 Cow., 221. Let an alternate *mandamus* issue.

Rule accordingly.

Cited in—7 Wend., 423; 1 Hill, 211; 4 How. Pr., 255; 9 How. Pr., 12; 44 How. Pr., 363; 1 Park., 260; 3 Park., 42; 4 Bos., 518; 21 Am. Dec., 714 (9 Conn., 47).

356*] *JACKSON, *ex dem.* SMITH,
v.
STILES, COMBS & GARRISON, *Tenants.*

Ejectment—Joint Defendants—Consent Rule.

Where two defendants are sued jointly in ejectment, they have no right to enter into separate consent rules in the name of each alone.

A DECLARATION having been served on Combs & Garrison, the notice from the casual ejector being directed to them jointly, they separately retained an attorney to appear, and he tendered separate consent rules to the attorney for the plaintiff, which mentioned one defendant only as being made defendant, without stating that he was impleaded with the other. The plaintiff's attorney refused to accept such a consent rule, and took a default, which,

Mr. J. Maynard now moved to set aside for irregularity.

Mr. A. Gibbs, contra.

Curia. The plaintiff is regular. The consent rule should have been in the name of both defendants.

Motion denied.

Cited in—5 Wend., 97.

JACKSON, ex dem. PALMER ET AL.,
v.
TRAVIS.

Ejectment—Adding Demises—Costs.

Several demises added in ejectment on payment of costs, it appearing that the lessors sought to be added had a subsisting legal title.

MR. L. H. PALMER, for the plaintiff, moved to amend the declaration, by adding demises from several lessors. The attorney for the plaintiff made an affidavit, on which the motion was founded, "that he is informed and believes, that the title to one third of the premises in question has been vested in the lessor sought to be added, for the recovery of which premises it became necessary to add demises from them."

This was opposed by an affidavit on the part of the defendant, that the plaintiff's attorney had acknowledged that the claim of the lessors (who were sought to be added) was merely under a deed of trust, for the benefit of the present lessors, and that he believed that, as to all of them except one, they had not assented to the use of their names as lessors; that from conversations with the plaintiff's attorney, he entertained *no doubt that the benefi- [*357 cial interest was now vested in the present lessors; and that granting the motion would impose very great additional difficulty in making out the defense.

Mr. H. A. Oothout, contra.

Curia. The motion must be granted. We will always allow an amendment, by adding new demises, where it appears that the lessors sought to be added have a subsisting legal title to the premises in question, on payment of costs.

Rule accordingly.

THE PEOPLE
v.
RICHARDSON, Clerk of WAYNE COUNTY.

Quo Warranto—*Practice.*

On filing an information in nature of a *quo warranto*, the court granted a rule that defendant appear and plead in 20 days after service of a copy of the information, and notice of the rule, or that the Attorney-General have leave to enter an appearance for him, and take judgment by *nihil dicit*.

MR. TALCOTT, Atty-Gen., having obtained leave of the court, at a former term, to file an information, in the nature of a *quo warranto*, against the defendant, to try his right to the clerkship of the County of Wayne, and having filed such information, now moved for a rule that the defendant enter an appearance, and plead in 20 days after service of a copy of the information, and the rule to be made, or that the Attorney-General have leave to enter an appearance for him, and take judgment by *nil dicit*.

Curia. This not coming within the rules which apply to ordinary cases, and warrant proceedings of course, we think a special application proper, and grant the rule as applied for.

Rule accordingly.

Overruled—4 Cow., 97.

358*] *WOOLSEY *v.* CAMP.

Case Turned into Special Verdict, only by Stipulation.

A case cannot be turned into a special verdict, unless there be a stipulation to this effect at the trial.

THE verdict being for the defendant, and a case being made presenting several questions of law, as to the decisions of the judge at *Nisi Prius*;

Mr. S. A. Foot, on an affidavit that the defendant's counsel omitted, by mistake, at the trial, either to take a bill of exceptions upon the points of law arising and decided there, or to request the circuit judge that the case might be turned into a bill of exceptions, or a special verdict, and that he was desirous to bring error, if the judgment should be against him, moved for leave to turn the case into a bill of exceptions.

Mr. J. Platt, contra.

Curia. This is never done, unless there is a stipulation to that effect at the trial. It is almost a matter of course for a circuit judge to grant leave to turn a contemplated case into a special verdict or bill of exceptions, if requested by either party, at the trial; but this should appear, by stipulation, in the case, or in some other way. A bill of exceptions, or special verdict, is a part of the business of the trial, and if not sought for in any way there, it cannot be obtained afterwards.

Motion denied.

Cited in—4 How. Pr., 287; 2 Hill, 251.

EX PARTE THE COMMON COUNCIL OF ALBANY.

Duty of Supervisors, to Raise Money Pursuant to Resolution of Common Council of Albany—Mandamus.

A resolution of the Common Council of the City of Albany, that certain sums should be raised for the support of the poor, and for the city nightwatch and lamps, and to pay the interest of the city funded debt, &c., is imperative upon the Board of Supervisors of the City and County of Albany, who are bound to raise such sums upon the city.

They have no right to refuse, on the ground that large sums of money, heretofore raised for these purposes, have been misapplied.

The duties of the Board of Supervisors, in raising moneys on vote of towns to destroy noxious animals, &c. (2 R. L., 132, sec. 15), and on the certificate of Commissioners of Highways, to improve roads (2 R. L., 280, sec. 31) placed on the same footing by *Mr. A. Spencer, arg.*, and adverted to by the court, in delivering their opinion, as illustrating the main question.

It seems, therefore, that in these and the like cases, the duties of the Board of Supervisors, in raising money, are merely ministerial.

MR. A. SPENCER moved for a *mandamus* to the Board of Supervisors of the City and County of Albany, commanding them to *assess certain taxes on the City of [*359 Albany, pursuant to a resolution of the Common Council of that city.

It appeared by the papers presented to the court, that Oct. 4, 1824, the Common Council resolved that there be raised, by tax upon the citizens of that city, $8,000, to pay the interest on the city funded debt; $8,000 for the payment of the nightwatch and city lamps, and $10,000 for the support of the poor the ensuing year. A certified copy of this resolution was furnished to the Board of Supervisors of the County of Albany, at their ensuing meeting, Oct. 20, 1824.

The Supervisors referred this resolution to a committee of their body, who examined the books of the city chamberlain, and reported that, as it appeared from these, more than $26,000 had been raised, beyond what had been expended in the object specified in the resolution, from 1817 to 1823; and they recommend a resolution, which was adopted by the Board, that $8,000 be raised, to pay the interest on the funded debt; $6,000 for the payment of the night watch, and city lamps, and $8,000 for the support of the poor.

He said the Board of Supervisors refused to comply with the full extent of the resolution, upon the ground that they were invested with a sound discretion, and were interposed, by the general Act under which they convened, between the Common Council and the citizens, for the protection of the latter against the abuse of trust by the former. The Act Concerning the City of Albany (2 R. L., 465, sec. 5), after conferring other powers upon the Common Council, enacts, "that the Common Council shall yearly determine the sum necessary to be raised by tax for the support and maintenance of the poor of the said city for the ensuing year, and the Supervisors of the City and County of Albany being served with a copy of the resolution of the said Common Council directing such sum, shall cause the same to be raised, assessed and collected, according to law; and such moneys, when collected by tax, shall be paid to the chamberlain of the said city, and shall be drawn for and applied under the direction of the Common Council." The 21st section of the same Act (2 R. L., 475), enacts, "that the Common Council shall and may, from *year to [*360 year, cause a tax, not exceeding $15,000, to be assessed, collected and paid, in the same manner as the other contingent expenses of the said county are assessed, collected and

paid, for defraying the expenses of supporting the night watch, and lighting the lamps within the said city; and the chamberlain shall annually publish a statement of the moneys received and expended by virtue of this section, in one or more of the public papers printed in the said city." As we read these provisions, the Board of Supervisors have no discretion. The City of Albany (containing five wards), is, by law, to elect a supervisor for each ward. The several towns of the county (eight in number), are required to elect a supervisor for each. Of these, forming the county Board, a majority, being non-residents of the city, claim the right to protect the citizens of Albany, who have no voice in their election, against the Common Council, who are the immediate representatives of the citizens, and may be deposed by them for abusing their trust. To suppose that the Legislature ever meant to vest a discretionary power, such as is claimed here by the Board of Supervisors, would be absurd. The power of refusing is as injurious as the right of imposing taxes, by persons who, or whose constituents, have no manner of interest in them, when raised. What becomes of the city interests, while this conflict is going forward? The object in convening the whole Supervisors of the county, to provide for levying taxes, is, that the State, county, city and town taxes, may all be levied by a single operation. Their powers, in relation to the city, are no more than are conferred relative to the towns, by the 2d section of the Act for Defraying the Public and Necessary Charges in the Respective Counties of the State (2 R. L., 137), where they are enjoined to allow certain accounts against the county; or (which more nearly resembles the present case), by section 15 of the Act Relative to the Duties and Privileges of Towns (2 R. L., 132), where they are required to raise certain sums voted by the towns, to be levied upon themselves, and expended in the destruction of wolves or other noxious animals. Though left to the towns exclusively to fix the amount, a return is to be made to the general Board,
361*] who are to levy the tax voted. *The words of the various Acts, on these and the like subjects, are mandatory. The Board have nothing to do with the propriety or impropriety of the levy. The tax is to be collected in the same manner as the contingent charges of the county. Here is no charge of misapplication. It is not pretended that one cent of the $26,000 has been devoted to any other than city purposes.

Mr. A. Van Vechten, contra. The question is, whether the Board of Supervisors have a right to see that the moneys already raised by the Common Council, for certain specified objects, have been properly appropriated, before they are compellable to raise more. They had already raised more than enough to make up the difference between the sum now asked for, and the sum levied by the Board. When the Statute says that moneys shall be raised for a specific object, and they have been raised and not applied, does it mean that further moneys shall be raised for the same object, when there is enough for this purpose in the treasury? Shall this be tolerated? The interposition of the court is sought upon the supposition that the Board have neglected their duty, in refusing to Act; and I grant that, if it appeared necessary to raise these moneys, a refusal would be such neglect. But when it appears there is enough on hand, the object cannot be to meet the wants of the city. It is said, to be sure, that "with this the Board have nothing to do. The money is gone. There is none in the treasury. No matter what the purpose to which it has been applied, if for city purposes. It is enough that we are to be turned out of office, if we conduct ourselves improperly. It is enough that it has not been applied to the proper objects for which it was intended." Is it so? The Legislature have limited the Corporation to a certain sum, for several of these objects. Here, at least, their power is not unlimited. But the law implies a discretion, when it orders money to be raised for a specific purpose. It is plain that if the Common Council raise a surplus, one year for one object, it should be added to the corresponding fund for the next year. Otherwise the limitation would be none at all. It might be evaded at pleasure. When it is plainly *seen that the moneys have been ap- [***362**
plied to the wrong object, the Supervisors have a right to interfere, upon the same principle. The expenditure from the respective funds, after 1817, falls much short of the moneys raised; and the balance should have been carried over to the next year, to the credit of those funds. After raising nearly the sum required, the Supervisors find a large amount yet unexpended. "No," say the Common Council, "we are to command, and you are to obey." This depends on the question whether the law sanctions the demand. Shall the Board raise $20,000 when only $10,000 are requisite? Suppose a demand of $15,000 for the night-watch, and the Board find that $10,000 only are necessary; and the parties come here; would this court sanction and enforce the demand? The refusal to grant would be no breach of duty, and consequently, no violation of the law. It is said the moneys have not been misapplied; but they have. If raised for a specific object, and not used to answer it, but for another purpose, this is the very definition of the term misapplication. The Corporation have power, because they have the means to ascertain what sums are necessary to be raised; but does this authorize them to require twice that sum? It is asked, what have the town Supervisors to do with the city? I ask in turn, what have the city Supervisors to do with the towns? Are they all here as mere puppets, to dance as the Common Council shall play the wires? They have power to inquire, and ascertain if the levy is necessary; and when they find it not to be so, can they conscientiously raise it? Suppose the Common Council corrupt, and ordering large sums to be raised, when they have plenty of money already; are the Supervisors bound to obey the *sic volo* of such a body? Are they not intended as a check? They are the general guardians of the county. Where is the evidence that this $26,000 has been duly expended, or expended at all? If it has been wrongfully expended, are not the court bound to notice the misapplication? Or, if on hand, to say, "you ask for money, when you have plenty already?"

Every application for a *mandamus* is addressed to the sound discretion of this court; 363*] and when right and wrong *are so mixed as to render the right doubtful, they will refuse to interfere. We protest against raising this money, when there is enough on hand. Whose fault is it that inconveniences are to arise for the want of it, if it has been misapplied? That of the Common Council. They are to answer for it. Does it lie with them to ask, "what is to become of the city unless you raise the whole sum demanded?" They should apply to the Legislature for leave to raise money for other objects. The law should be the only measure of expenditure; otherwise, you give an unlimited discretion.

Mr. Spencer, in reply. On the principle claimed here, the Supervisors may refuse anything, imposed upon them as a duty by any of the statutes. Indeed, to have been consistent, they should have adjudged that we wanted nothing, and refused wholly to comply with our resolution. We lie completely at their mercy. We cannot tax our own constituents without their consent. This would result from their having a discretion. This court, according to *People* v. *Supervisors of Albany*, 12 Johns., 414, can exercise no control over them. When once passed upon, the question is *res judicata*.

The amount of the argument on the other side is, that we have abused our power—not that the Board have any power to refuse the levy requested. But we say again, the office of the Supervisors is merely ministerial. There is no restraint upon us as to the amount of moneys to be raised for the support of the poor, though we are confined to $15,000 for the night-watch, &c. Had we gone beyond the latter sum, we should have exceeded our power; and the Act would not have been binding. There is no pretense that we have not acted within the limits of our jurisdiction. But it is said that this $26,000 should have been applied to the specific object of the resolution upon which it is raised. That I deny. Any money in the treasury may be applied to any other demands against the Corporation. The means of raising money for certain objects are specified; and none other can be resorted to; but it is not material to the city how the moneys raised are applied if it be for their purposes. It will be 364*] *intended that the moneys have been so applied; that the officers of the city have done their duty. But suppose it otherwise; suppose a previous violation of duty; is this a reason why the city should not be lighted or the poor maintained for the time to come? Nor will the court intend that we can borrow the money which is wanted.

No authority is cited to support the powers of the Board to rejudge this question. The language of every Act imposing the duty to raise money upon the Board of Supervisors is at war with this construction. Such are the provisions, already adverted to, and such the language of the whole Act to which I before referred the court (2 R. L., 127), touching the general and special powers of the Board. It requires them to assess, levy, &c. There is also a provision in the Act to Regulate Highways (2 R. L., 280, sec. 31), much like the one under consideration. The Board are required to raise such sum, not exceeding $250, as shall be ordered by the Commissioners of Highways of a town.

SUTHERLAND, *J.*, delivered the opinion of the court, to the following effect. The Act under which the Common Council made this order so far as form is concerned, has been strictly complied with, and the only question submitted to us relates to their power. This law gives, in terms, full authority to do precisely what they have done; to order the levying of these moneys by the Board of Supervisors. Then have the latter any discretion, whether they shall comply with the order? The provision as to raising money for the support of the poor is couched in very positive language. It is that the Common Council shall yearly determine the sum necessary to be raised for this purpose; and the Supervisors being served with a copy of the corporate resolution "shall cause the same to be raised, assessed and collected according to law." Here a power is given without limitation or control, to direct such sums to be raised as the Council may think proper; and it is imperiously made the duty of the Supervisors to raise that sum. The provision as to the city watch confers the power in the same terms, limiting it to the compass of $15,000 *per annum*. This, by the 21st section,*is to be raised in the same [*365 manner. Both provisions are equally imperative, in terms, upon the Supervisors. They, however, contend that they have a discretion in this business; that they are not mere ministerial officers; that they are authorized to judge whether the sums heretofore raised for specific objects have been properly expended; that otherwise they might be made the instruments of oppression; and they show by extracts from the books of the Common Council, that large sums heretofore raised for specific objects have not been expended for these purposes. From the statement made by the committee, in their report, this would seem to be so to the amount of 20 or $30,000. They insist on a power, implied by law, to guard against such excesses; and demanded that this sum should be carried to the credit of the city in account with their officers. This may all be very proper; but I am satisfied that no such discretion is conferred by the law, either in its terms or the general provisions and policy of the Act under which the Board of Supervisors proceed. The contrary is rather to be implied from various provisions similar to those under consideration, to which we were referred at the bar. The Council, like the Legislature, are responsible to their constituents only for the manner in which they discharge these duties, so long as they act within the scope of their authority. The course is for the former to take the remedy into their own hands; and remove their public agents, if they have abused their authority, which we do not pretend to say is the case. The Statute is imperative upon the Supervisors. They cannot exercise the least control in determining the amount to be raised. The sums sought to be levied are for the use of the citizens of Albany, to be paid by them. We grant an alternative *mandamus*.

Rule accordingly.

366*] *THE PEOPLE, ex rel. GLANDER & PERSON,

v.

THE JUSTICES OF THE MARINE COURT OF THE CITY OF NEW YORK.

Act to Relieve Debtors from Imprisonment—Construction of.

The Act for the Relief of Debtors with Respect to the Imprisonment of their Persons (1 R. L., 348, sec. 4), extends to debtors in execution on judgments founded on wrongs as well as on contracts; *e. g.*, on an assault and battery.

ON showing cause why a *mandamus* should not issue, it appeared that the relators were sued in the Marine Court for an assault and battery, to which they severally pleaded not guilty; judgment passed against them, and they were committed to jail on a *capias ad satisfaciendum* for $160 damages and costs; that Sept. 23, 1824, they respectively petitioned the Marine Court for a discharge under the "Act for the Relief of Debtors with Respect to the Imprisonment of their Persons," passed Apr. 9th, 1813 (1 R. L., 348); which was opposed, because the judgment was founded on a wrong—not on contract. Upon this ground, the prisoners were remanded; and the hearing of the application adjourned.

Mr. J. E. Lovett, for the defendants, said the word "debt," used in the Statute, applies to a judgment founded upon contract. The Statute was passed for the benefit of the unfortunate debtor, not for the relief of the guilty. The cases of *Jackson* v. *Smith*, 5 Johns., 115; *The King* v. *Wakefield*, 13 East, 189, and *Ex parte Benj. Lawrence*, 1 Bos. &. P., 477, do not apply to the present question.

Mr. J. M'Kown, for the relators. The words of the Act are too broad to be misunderstood. To warrant the interference of the court, it is only necessary that the applicant should be charged in execution for a sum of money. *Strong* v. *White*, 9 Johns., 161, has no application for the Act of 1811 was expressly limited to the case of judgments upon contract. In *Jackson* v. *Smith*, 5 Johns., 117, the court leave it strongly to be implied that if the defendant had been in actual custody upon a conviction for the contempt, the C. P. would have been right in discharging.

367*] **Curia*. The question now is the same as it was upon the motion for a rule to show cause; and we see no reason to change the opinion we then expressed.

Rule absolute.

Cited in—31 How. Pr., 127.

MIRWAN *v.* INGERSOL.

Practice.

The defendant may appear at the circuit, after the jury are impaneled for an inquest by default.

A special verdict, finding that the defendant does not appear, nor offer any evidence in support of his plea, is a nullity.

The plaintiff cannot take judgment, of course, upon a special verdict, but it should be on motion in court.

ON *certiorari* to a justice's court; the plaintiff assigned errors; and the defendant pleaded a special plea in bar, of accord and satisfaction, to which the plaintiff replied, taking issue. At the last Monroe Circuit, the cause coming on to be tried, the circuit judge decided that the defendant held the affirmative. And, he not being ready with his proof, his counsel declined appearing, and the cause was called, and the jury impaneled as upon an inquest by default. While the counsel for the plaintiff was engaged in drawing a special verdict, the defendant's witness appeared, and his counsel then asked leave to appear and try the cause, stating that he could prove the truth of his plea. This was denied by the judge; and the plaintiff's counsel hastily drew a special verdict in these words: "And the jury find that Thomas Ingersol does not appear nor offer any evidence to prove the allegations contained in his plea." This was received and entered as the verdict of the jury; and the plaintiff afterwards proceeded, without submitting the verdict to this court, to tax his costs, perfect his judgment, and issue his execution.

A motion was now made in behalf of the defendant, to set aside the verdict and all subsequent proceedings for irregularity, on these grounds, among others, viz.: 1. That the defendant should have been suffered to appear. 2. That the verdict was void. 3. That, at any rate, judgment could not be taken upon the verdict, without a special motion to this court. And Com. Dig., Pleader, S., 21, 22, was cited to show the verdict void.

Mr. D. D. Barnard, for the motion.

**Mr. R. Beach*, contra. [*368

Curia. The objections are all well taken, and the motion must be granted.

Rule accordingly.

MACAULEY *v.* STERNBURGH.

Reversal of Judgment—Costs.

On reversing a judgment upon error, the plaintiff is entitled to costs.

And he may perfect his judgment and issue execution for them immediately, without waiting for the final event upon a *venire de novo* awarded.

IN the Herkimer C. P. the judgment was for the defendant. And on error to this court, it was reversed, and at the last Oct. Term a *venire de novo* was awarded to the circuit; but the plaintiff, without waiting for the event of the cause upon the trial, taxed his costs and perfected his judgment of reversal, which it was now moved to set aside as premature and irregular.

Mr. O. G. Otis, for the motion.

Mr. A. Conkling, contra.

Curia. The plaintiff in error was not bound to wait the event of the suit upon the *venire de novo*. When a judgment is reversed on error, the plaintiff is entitled to recover his costs, and may perfect his judgment immediately and issue execution as in other cases.

Motion denied.

GAY v. ROGERS AND WAIT.

Action Against Attorney and Layman—Liability of Attorney to Arrest.

An attorney, or other officer of the court, is never privileged from arrest, when sued with another, though during the actual sitting of the court, and during his attendance at court.

Citations—13 Johns., 252; 1 R. L., 387, 418, sec. 12.

THE defendant, Wait, an attorney and counselor of this court, attending at this term, was arrested on a bailable *capias* against him and Rogers, a common person.

Mr. S. A. Foot moved that Wait be discharged.

Mr. S. Stevens, contra, said he could not have his privilege, being sued with another. He cited *Tiffany* v. *Driggs*, 13 Johns., 252.

369*] **Mr. Foot.* That case was decided on common law grounds. But the Statute (1 R. L., 418, sec. 12) exempts the profession from arrest, generally, during term.

Curia. That Statute circumscribes the common law privilege to actual term time, during which it is no greater than it was before the Statute. Officers of the court were never privileged, when sued with others. The reasoning of the court in *Tiffany* v. *Driggs*, as to the Statute (1 R. L., 387), applies, therefore, to the Act (1 R. L., 418, sec. 12) upon which the defendant moves.

Motion denied.

AVERY AND AVERY
v.
CURTISS AND WEED.

Recovery against One of Two Defendants—Costs.

In an action arising *ex contractu*, against several defendants, some of whom succeed, and others have a verdict against them, the former are not entitled to costs.

Citations—1 Cow., 417; 1 R. L., 343, 345.

ACTION on a joint and several promissory note, made by the defendants, who pleaded separately the general issue. On the trial, the verdict was for the plaintiff against Curtiss, and for Weed, against the plaintiff, upon which Weed's attorney entered a rule for judgment, in his favor, with costs, which it was now moved to set aside, on the authority of the case, *Ex parte E. Nelson*, 1 Cow., 422.

Mr. J. Maynard, for the motion.

Mr. A. Gibbs, contra.

Curia. This case comes within the 2d section of the general Statute Concerning Costs (1 R. L., 343), the construction of which, in reference to this question, was considered in the case *Ex parte Nelson*, 1 Cow., 417. Though the question was not directly decided, the reasoning of that case applies. The course upon the English Statute, which is worded like our 2d section, has always been to deny costs to one whose co-defendants are convicted, though a verdict pass for him. The 10th section (1 R. L., 345) applies to certain actions arising *ex delicto* only. The motion must be granted.

Motion granted.

*LENT v. BUTLER. [*370

Slander—Notice, with Plea that Defendant would Prove Words True—When Plea may be Withdrawn.

In slander the defendant gave notice with his plea, that he would prove the words true; which plea he afterwards moved to withdraw, on an affidavit that the notice was given in good faith: motion refused, unless he would swear to the falsity of the notice.

SLANDER, for charging the plaintiff with stealing goods. Plea, the general issue, with notice that the defendant, on the trial, would prove the truth of the words spoken, in his justification. And now,

Mr. C. H. Ruggles moved to withdraw this notice and to substitute another, which he produced, and which set up the Statute of Limitations, with certain matters which went to mitigate the damages. He read the defendant's affidavit, stating that the first notice was interposed in good faith, and under the advice of counsel; that when it was delivered, he verily believed he should be able to prove the material facts stated in it; that W. N. Palmer, formerly of Poughkeepsie, was the witness upon whom he placed the principal reliance for this purpose; but that he had left the State, with his family, without the defendant's knowledge; and, as he was informed by the witness' friends, had gone to reside in some part of South America, and would not return to this country.

He supposed the gentleman opposed to him (*Mr. J. Tallmadge*) would take the same ground here as he did in *Clinton* v. *Mitchell*, 3 Johns., 144, and insist that the notice should not be withdrawn till its falsity was acknowledged by the defendant. The case, however, was distinguishable. It did not, in that case, as in this, appear that the notice was given in good faith; which is the reason assigned by the court for refusing the rule.

Mr. J. Tallmadge, contra, did rely upon that case, and should contend for its doctrine, without the qualification alluded to. The defendant has followed up his slander by a gross libel upon the record, and which the plaintiff is entitled to have falsified in the same way. This must be either by the defendant's affidavit of its falsity, or the verdict of a jury, giving those aggravated damages which such a notice called for.

**The Court* were clear with the coun- [*371 sel for the plaintiff, that, for these reasons, the motion must be denied; and Woodworth, *J.*, said, that this application was even a still farther aggravation of the slander; for the defendant says, in his affidavit, "the charge which I advanced against the plaintiff is true; but by reason of Palmer's absence, alone, I am, unfortunately, not able to prove it.

Motion denied.

Cited in—21 Wend., 334; 8 Minn., 293; 34 Am. Dec., 247.

EX PARTE JOHNSON.

Common Pleas—Discretion as to Hearing Charge against Justice of Peace.

Under the 7th section of the 4th article of the Constitution, the judge of the C. P. have a discretion whether they will hear a charge, preferred against a justice of the peace; and the Supreme Court will not interfere with its exercise.

Citation—N. Y. Const., art. 4, sec. 7.

PHEBE JOHNSON petitioned the judges of the Court of C. P. of Montgomery Co., that such proceedings might be had against ——— ———, a justice of the peace, of that county, as the Constitution and laws of this State require, for a false return to a writ of *certiorari*, and for keeping his office in a grog or dram shop, setting forth the particulars, and verifying the petition by her affidavit. The petition was presented to the judges Oct. 12, 1824, at which time they made a rule, that the prayer of the petitioner be denied, without hearing the merits.

Mr. P. Brooks now moved for a *mandamus*, commanding the judges to take cognizance of this matter; but,

Per Curiam. The whole was a mere matter of discretion with the C. P. Under the Constitution (art. 4, sec. 7), they are the sole judges whether they will notice the charges preferred or not. They hold a constitutional power, with which we will not interfere. Besides, it is a sufficient answer to that part of the case which complains of a false return, that it is more properly triable in another form.

Motion denied.

Cited in—19 How. Pr., 178; 11 Abb. Pr., 21.

372*] *EX PARTE KELLOGG.

Appeal from Justice Court—Filing Return of Justice in Common Pleas—Practice—Costs.

Though on appeal, pursuant to the Statute (sess. 47, ch. 238, sec. 36, 37), the justice do not file his return till after the first day of the term of the C. P. next after the appeal; they ought not to quash the return, but proceed thereon when the return comes in.

The fact that the costs were paid to the justice, need not be indorsed on the appeal bond.

KELLOGG sued Griffin before a justice of the peace of Herkimer Co., and Aug, 25, 1824, the justice rendered judgment for the plaintiff, of $7.59, from which the defendant appealed, Sept. 4, pursuant to the Act of Apr. 12, 1824 (sess. 47, ch. 238, sec. 36, 37), to the next Court of C. P. of Herkimer; but it was not indorsed upon the bond given on such appeal, that the costs of the proceedings in the court below had been paid by the appellant; and the justice, moreover, omitted to file the return, till after the first day of the then next term of the C. P.; for which reasons a motion was made there to quash the return, but denied; and now,

Mr. B. D. Noxon moved for a *mandamus* commanding them to do this; but,

Per Curiam. The Statute is merely directory. True, if the justice does not return on or before the first day of the next term after the appeal, it is an omission of duty; but the party is not to suffer by this. If filed at any time afterwards, he may proceed in his appeal. The Statute does not require that the payment of costs should be indorsed upon the bond. If, in fact, paid, this is enough; and the contrary is not pretended.

Motion denied.

---

*JACKSON, ex dem. EDEN, [*373
v.
RATHBONE.

Judgment Affirmed on Error—Executive Writ of Inquiry—Continuing Record—Costs.

On executing a writ of inquiry under the Statute (1 R. L., 343, sec. 3), judgment being affirmed on error, and the record being remitted, a new judgment record is not necessary; but the proceedings may be continued at the foot of the original roll.

How this is to be done. May be on separate paper and attached to record as in assigning breaches, *toties quoties*, &c., after judgment bond to perform covenants, or court, on motion, would allow record on file to be continued, &c.

FOR the facts out of which the present question grew, see 2 Cow., 602, S. C. On referring the costs for taxation, as there mentioned (page 604), *Judge* Irving refused to tax a new record of judgment upon the return of the writ of inquiry, and the services about entering and perfecting a new judgment; but he allowed the appropriate services for continuing down the original record remitted from the Court of Errors, with a history of the proceedings.

Mr. A. Burr, moved for are taxation, on this ground, among others. He said the Statute (1 R. L., 144, sec. 3) speaks of inquiry, judgment and award of execution, for damages, with costs of suit. If no rule for judgment, and no record, there is no authority to "award execution for the damages and costs of suit."

Mr. C. H. Ruggles, contra, insisted that there was no need of a new record. It was sufficient to continue the proceedings upon the old one.

Mr. Burr said the Statute evidently contemplated a new judgment, independent of, and distinct from the first, and therefore authorized a new record. This might as well be denied of a *scire facias*, or debt on judgment. The original record, when filed, is beyond the control of the attorney. It can be altered by the clerk, only, under the direction of the court. The new judgment should be docketed. There is no authority for this, unless there be a new record signed and filed.

Curia. A new record was unnecessary. The proceeding by inquiry might have been continued upon the record remitted from the Court of Errors; and Woodworth, *J.*, said this did not mean taking the record from the clerk, and continuing the history upon that. All that is necessary is, *to make the [*374 proper suggestion, and give a history of the subsequent proceedings upon separate paper, and attach this to the original roll, as is done when you assign new breaches, *toties quoties*, on the record of judgment upon a bond for the performance of covenants. And Sutherland, *J.*, said that if it were otherwise, that would be no argument in favor of a new record; for this court, on application, would grant leave, of course, to continue the original record in the hands of the clerk, provided it were necessary.

Motion denied.

HALL v. ROCHESTER, ATKINSON AND CAMPBELL.

Action Ex Contractu *against Several Defendants—Effect of Discontinuance as to Part.*

In *assumpsit* against three, on a joint and several promissory note, two pleaded that the note was fraudulently and oppressively obtained, upon which the plaintiff entered a *nolle prosequi* as to them, and took judgment by default against the third: held, that the action was discontinued as to all.

In actions *ex contractu*, against several, unless the defense as to one go merely to his personal discharge, a *nolle prosequi* cannot be entered as to him, and the suit be continued as to another.

ASSUMPSIT, on a joint and several promissory note—payee against the makers. The first count was on the note, and the second and third were the common money counts, and an account stated. Rochester and Atkinson pleaded *non assumpsit;* and to the first count, that the note was fraudulently and oppressively obtained, setting forth the particulars. Upon the receipt of this plea, the plaintiff entered a *nolle prosequi* as to them, and took a judgment by default against Atkinson, which it was now moved to set aside as irregular.

Mr. E. Pomroy, for the motion, said the *nolle prosequi* was a discontinuance as to all the defendants. *Noke* v. *Ingham*, 1 Wils., 89; *Hartness* v. *Thompson*, 5 Johns., 160; *Morton* v. *Croghan*, 20 Johns., 122, per Spencer, *Ch. J.*; 1 Chit. Plead., 546 Tidd, 632. The result of these authorities is, that in actions in form *ex delicto*, the plaintiff may enter a *nolle prosequi* as to one of several defendants; but in actions *ex contractu*, unless the defense go merely to the personal discharge of one, a *nolle prosequi* cannot be entered as to one and the suit be continued as to the other, but the *nolle prosequi* discontinues the suit as to the whole. Actions *ex contractu*, against several, are joint. The plaintiff, to sustain his action, must show a **375***] joint contract made by *all; and a plea, by one, to the action of the writ, inures to the benefit of all the defendants. 1 Chit. Pl., 31, 32; *Boulter* v. *Ford*, 1 Sid., 76; *Sheriff* v. *Wilkes*, 1 East, 52; *Gray* v. *Palmer*, 1 Esp., 135. That the note is joint and several, makes no difference. The plaintiff has elected to proceed against the defendants jointly; and, for the purposes of this question, the demand must be treated as a joint one.

Mr. F. M. Haight, contra, said there was no direct authority for this application. In *Morton* v. *Croghan*, cited by the defendant's counsel, the decision is put on the ground that the defendants were all necessarily parties. Accordingly, per Spencer, *J.*: "Where all the defendants are necessarily parties, and the plaintiff was obliged to make them parties, as in a proceeding against terre-tenants, a discontinuance as to some is a discontinuance as to all." Here the action was not necessarily joint. It might have been several; and it is the same thing to the defendant (Atkinson) as if he, alone, had been sued.

Curia. The distinction contended for, by the defendant's counsel, is fully borne out by the cases to which he refers.

Motion granted.

Cited in—5 Wend., 229; 14 N. Y., 491; 15 Barb., 183; 46 Am. Dec., 478 (4 Gilm., 536).

VAN LEW ET AL. v. KING.

Common Pleas—Costs.

In the Court of C. P. of the City of N. Y., the plaintiff has costs, though he recover less than $50, if his recovery exceed $25. And this, though the action might have been brought before a justice of the peace.

MAY 8, 1824, the plaintiffs brought *assumpsit* for money had and received, against the defendant, in the N. Y C. P., and laid their damages at $250. The cause was tried Sept. 25th, and the jury found for the plaintiff, $38.33. The total amount of the accounts in controversy between the parties, was $394. The plaintiff *procured his costs to be [***376** taxed at $51.59, for which he took judgment; and on submitting the question to this court, whether the plaintiff was entitled to costs in the court below, he having recovered less than $50, the Act of Apr. 12, 1824 (sess. 47, ch. 238, sec. 33), was relied upon, as denying costs.

It was said that the suit was cognizable before a justice, the amount recovered less than $50, and the accounts less than $400. The words, in the 1st section of the Act, "the City and County of N. Y. excepted," do not extend to the provisions of the 33d section. Several new regulations, introduced by the Act, were intended to be general; such as extending the remedy to executors (sec. 1), transferring judgments to the county clerk's office, so as to become a lien on land. Sec. 20, 21. So of sections 29, 41, 45, &c. The 10th, 11th, and 16th sections, expressly mention city or town. Section 27, in giving the precedent of a conviction, begins, "City of New York," or, "Westchester County." Sections 37 and 38 say, Cts. of C. P. or Mayor's Courts, and clerk's office of city or county; and section 40 expressly authorizes the several Courts of C. P. and Mayor's Courts in this State, to make rules to regulate the practice on appeals. The 41st section speaks the same language.

The words "City and County of N. Y.," in the 1st section, apply to the jurisdiction of the magistrate only. The 106th section of the Act to Reduce the Several Laws Relating Particularly to the City of N. Y. into One Statute, passed Apr. 9, 1813 (2 R. L., 342), gives jurisdiction of $50 to the justice's court of that city; and it was not necessary to repeat it again in the Act of 1824. The Act of 1818 (sess. 41, ch. 94, sec. 5) contains the same proviso as to costs on recoveries under $50, as is contained in the 33d section of the Act of 1824; but as the former is repealed by the latter (sec. 43), it can have no application to the present question.

Against the motion, it was said that the 85th section of the Act to Reduce the Several Laws Relating Particularly to the City of N. Y., into One Act, passed Apr. 9, 1813, establishes 377*] *Assistant Justices' Courts in the several wards in the City of N. Y., and gives them jurisdiction over certain actions, where the damages, or thing in demand, shall not exceed $25. The 105th and 106th sections establish the Justice's Court with jurisdiction to $50. The jurisdiction of the Marine Court is extended to $100 by the Act of Apr. 15, 1817 (sess. 40, ch. 249; 4 L. N. Y., 288 b). The Court of Assistant Justices is established in the several wards, excepting the 9th, with jurisdiction to $50, by the Act of Jan. 4, 1820 (sess. 43, ch. 1; 5 L. N. Y., 3 b).

The general Act to Extend the Jurisdiction of Justices, passed Apr. 10, 1818 (4 L. N. Y., 89 c), extends their jurisdiction to $50; and provides (sec. 5) that if, in any action brought in any court of record, the plaintiff shall fail to recover over $50, he shall not recover any costs, if the suit might have been commenced before a justice by virtue of this Act. The Act modifying this last mentioned Act, passed Apr. 21, 1818 (sess. 41, ch. 265; 4 L. N. Y., 287 c), gives the assistant justices in the City of N. Y. the like jurisdiction and power as justices of the peace under the Act of Apr. 10, of the same year.

The Act of 1824 for the Better and More Speedy Recovery of Debts to the Value of $50, is intended to supersede all the other Acts relating to the proceedings of justice's courts, excepting in the City of N. Y. Act of 1824, *supra*, 47th sess., L. N. Y., 279. The 43d section of this Act repeals the old Justice's Act for the country, of 1813 (1 R. L., 387), and the Act to Extend the Jurisdiction of Justices of the Peace (4 L. N. Y., 79 c), which applied to the City of N. Y. The 33d section of the Act of 1824 provides, "that if the plaintiff, in any suit which may be brought in any court of record in this State, after the 1st day of May next, shall fail to recover a sum exceeding $50, he shall not recover any costs of the defendant, provided the suit so brought might have been commenced before a justice of the peace by virtue of this Act." The first section expressly excepts the City and County of N. Y.; for it specifies the particular actions which shall be cognizable before any justice of the peace, with the exception of the City and 378*] County of N. *Y.; so that the justices' courts of that city must depend for their jurisdiction upon the local Acts provided for them; and in none of these local Acts is there any provision that restrains a party from recovering costs, where he fails to recover a sum over $50.

The only restriction is that of the 5th section of the Act Concerning Costs (1 R. L., 344), which provides, "that if any action, not concerning any freehold or title of land, nor for any assault, battery or imprisonment, nor slander, nor malicious prosecution, nor by or against executors or administrators, be brought in any Court of C. P., and the plaintiff shall not recover over $25, he shall not recover, but pay costs."

The reason why the Act of 1824 mentions city or town, will be seen by looking at the 46th section, by which the provisions of that Act are extended to all the cities in the State by name, except N. Y.

The counsel for the plaintiff remarked that his argument against the motion was little more than a copy of the opinion given by His Honor, J. T. Irving, the first judge of N. Y., who taxed the costs under review.

Mr. C. Graham, for the defendant.

Mr. R. I. Wells, contra.

This Court adopted the reasoning of *Judge* Irving in the court below, and gave their opinion that he was right in allowing the plaintiffs their costs; that as to all actions in which the plaintiff recovers upwards of 25 and less than $50, though they be cognizable before a justice, the Common Pleas of the City of N. Y. has concurrent jurisdiction, not only of the subject-matter, but of the costs.

Cited in—5 Daly, 176.

---

*STONE *v.* BURT. [*379

Affirmance of Judgment on Error—Costs.

Double costs are not allowed of course to the defendant in error on affirming the judgment; but it should be shown that execution was actually delayed by the writ of error; and this should be proved to the taxing officer before he is warranted in doubling the costs, within the Statute (1 R. L., 346, sec. 14).

ON ERROR from the C. P. and judgment affirmed, double costs were taxed, without proof to the taxing officer that the plaintiff in error had delayed the execution below by putting in bail.

Mr. C. P. Kirkland moved for a retaxation on this ground, and cited 1 R. L., 346, sec. 14; 2 Sayer on Costs, 200; *Peters* v. *Henry*, 6 Johns., 278.

Curia. The Statute cited gives double costs in those cases only where execution is actually delayed by the writ of error. Such delay should be proved to the officer before he is warranted in taxing double costs.

Motion granted.

Cited in—4 Cow., 54.

EX PARTE JOHN H. CLARKE.

Notice of Appeal from Justice Court.

The notice of appeal served on the justice pursuant to the Act (sess. 47, ch. 238, sec. 36), did not state that the party appealed to the Court of C. P. of, &c., but the appeal bond recited that the appeal was to that court; and the justice made a return; held, regular.

Semb., the party cannot object that the notice of appeal is defective, but this lies with the justice only. If he deem himself sufficiently informed, and return accordingly, it is enough.

ON AN appeal from a justices' court to the Onondaga C. P., between Clarke, appellant, and Pratt, appellee, the notice of appeal served on the justice did not state that he appealed to the Court of C. P. of the County of Onondaga. The appeal bond recited that the appeal was to that court, and the justice duly made and filed his return; but the court, on motion, quashed it on the ground of the above defect in the notice.

Mr. V. Birdseye moved for a *mandamus* commanding the C. P. to proceed with the appeal.

Curia. The C. P. have nothing to do with the question whether the notice was good or **380***] bad. If it contained *such information as satisfied the justice, and instructed him as to the place of return, it does not lie with the party to object that it is defective. Here was nothing to mislead or injure him. The bond was in the proper form; and the intention of the appellant could not be mistaken.

Rule for an alternative mandamus.

CLARKE *v.* RATHBUN.

Reversal of Judgment in Common Pleas—Costs.

Where a judgment is reversed on error to the C. P. upon a bill of exceptions taken there, costs should be taxed for the bill at the C. P. rate only.

ON ERROR from the Court of C. P. upon a bill of exceptions, the judgment being reversed, the taxing officer allowed Supreme Court costs for drawing and copying the bill of exceptions. A motion was now made to retax the bill in this particular.

Mr. D. Tillinghast, for the motion.

Mr. C. E. Clarke, contra.

Curia. This is a service performed in the court below; and the costs should be allowed at the C. P. rate, only.

Motion granted.

EX PARTE STONE.

Removal of Suit from Common Pleas, by Habeas Corpus—*New Suit in Common Pleas—Stay of Proceedings till Costs of First Suit Paid.*

Where a suit was brought in the C. P. and removed by the defendant into the Supreme Court by *habeas corpus*, and the plaintiff neglected to follow the suit here; but brought another action for the same cause in the C. P.: held, that the court below might stay the proceedings of the plaintiff in the second suit till the costs of the first were paid.

Citations—2 Bl., 904; 19 Johns., 238; Tidd, 478; 1 Dunl. Pr., 337; 3 Bos. & P., 23, *n.* (*a*); 4 Mod., 379; 2 Cow., 580.

IN A cause in the C. P. of Jefferson, between Stone, plaintiff, and Hooker, defendant, the court made a rule that all proceedings on the part of the plaintiff be stayed till the costs of a previous action for the same cause against the same defendant brought in the same court, and removed, by the defendant, into this court by *habeas corpus*, be first paid. The suit upon **381***] the *habeas corpus*, not *being pursued by the plaintiff, was at an end. A motion was now made for a *mandamus* commanding the court below to proceed to the trial of the cause notwithstanding the rule.

Mr. N. Rathbun, for the motion.

Mr. J. Butterfield, contra.

Curia. The power exercised by the courts to stay proceedings, till the costs of a former suit for the same cause are paid, does not depend exclusively upon the question whether their collection can be enforced by execution. It is an equitable jurisdiction; and intended to prevent the vexatious multiplication of suits. *Ginger* v. *Barnardiston,* 2 Bl., 904. Here the plaintiff has voluntarily, and without showing any excuse, forborne to pursue his action upon the *habeas corpus.* The C. P. were right in staying the proceedings. *Perkins* v. *Hinman,* 19 Johns., 238; Tidd, 478; 1 Duul. Pr., 337; 3 Bos. & P., 23, *n. a;* 4 Mod., 379. In *Lawrence* v. *Dickenson,* 2 Cow., 580, the plaintiff offered to proceed upon the *habeas corpus;* but the defendant refused to receive a declaration.

Motion denied.

Cited in—27 How. Pr., 156.

SANFORD *v.* CHASE.

Privilege of Witness.

One attending as a witness from a foreign State, before arbitrators, being arrested by virtue of a *capias ad respondendum,* was discharged absolutely; without being required to file common bail.

Citations—2 Johns., 294; 7 Johns., 538.

THE defendant was arrested and holden to bail, while he was attending as a witness before arbitrators. The defendant then resided in the State of Mass., but being in the County of Columbia, was subpœnaed to attend.

A motion was now made, that he be discharged from the arrest, and that the bail-bond be delivered up to be canceled.

Mr. U. Cole, for the motion.

Mr. A. P. Holdridge,* contra. [*382**

Curia. The only question is, whether the defendant is to be discharged on filing common bail, or absolutely, from the suit. In *Norris* v. *Beach,* 2 Johns., 294, this court discharged the defendant from the arrest, entirely and absolutely. In a subsequent case (*Bours* v. *Tuckerman,* 7 Johns., 538), he was discharged on filing common bail. We adopt the first case. The privilege of a witness should be absolute. An arrest should not be valid even for the purpose of giving jurisdiction to the court out of which the process issues; more especially where the witness is attending from a foreign State.

Motion granted.

Cited in—66 N. Y., 126; 73 N. Y., 135; 23 How. Pr., 332; 27 How. Pr., 157; 8 Abb. Pr., 417; 7 Abb. N. S., 71; 3 Duer, 624; 40 Mich., 732; 23 Am. Rep., 36 (66 N. Y., 124); 38 Am. Rep., 714 (53 Vt., 694).

TUNNICLIFF *v.* LAWYER.

Action for Obstructing, Stream—Prescription, as Defense—Costs.

Case, for obstructing a stream, and flowing the plaintiff's land. Plea, the general issue. The defendant, on the trial, gave evidence to show that he and those under whom he claimed, had so obstructed the stream for twenty years. Verdict for the plaintiff, $90. Held, that he was entitled to Supreme Court costs, as the title to the freehold was drawn in question, within the Statute (1 R. L., 344, sec. 4).

CASE, for obstructing the waters in the outlet of a lake, by which the plaintiff's lands were flowed and injured, tried at the Otsego Circuit, and a verdict found for the plaintiff, of $90. The plea was the general issue. On the trial, the defendant contended for a right to make the obstruction complained of, on the ground that he, and those under whom he claimed, had exercised this right for more than twenty years before the commencement of the suit; and this was the principal question, upon the trial, to which witnesses were examined. The plaintiff's costs being taxed as Supreme Court costs, a motion was now made to have them retaxed as C. P. costs.

Mr. T. Lawyer, for the motion, cited 1 Bos. & P., 400; 2 Saund., 175 *a*, *n*. 2; 1 R. L., 344, sec. 4; 2 Dunl. Pr., 714, and the authorities there cited.

Mr. I. Seelye, contra.

Curia. It is not stated with what view the evidence of twenty years' enjoyment of the **383***] right to obstruct was offered; but *we may fairly intend, from the papers submitted, that it was to establish a prescription. The evidence tended to this, though it came short of making it out. It is not necessary, to give the plaintiff costs, that the defendant should set up an attempt to establish a title by deed. An attempt to make out his right by adverse possession, or prescription to have an incorporeal right in the land of another, equally draws the title to freehold in question, and satisfies the words of the Statute. It is enough that the defendant offers evidence pertinent to the question of title, which he has done in this instance. The principle of taxation was, therefore, right; but as some of the items are exceptionable, let them be retaxed, as Supreme Court costs, at the expense of the plaintiff.

Rule accordingly.

Cited in—10 Wend., 565; 21 N. Y., 469 10 How. Pr., 409; 25 Am. Dec., 579.

KNICKERBACKER *v.* SHIPHERD.

Sale of Land on Execution—Sheriff's Right to Retain Fees, out of Proceeds for other Executions against Same Defendant.

The sheriff sells lands on execution, in favor of K., against S., having, at the same time, some executions on older, and some on younger judgments; against the same defendant, which are paid, excepting the fees. He may retain his fees upon those executions which are on judgments older than K.'s, but not so as to those which are younger.

A *fi. fa.* was issued, in this cause, to John Doty, Esq., late sheriff of the County of Washington, about Sept. 1, 1820, directing him to collect $1,273.64, with interest from May 7, 1819. Doty then had in his hands several writs of *fi. fa.* against the defendant, in favor of different plaintiffs, which were arranged and paid; but the sheriff claimed fees upon them to $31.51. The defendant had personal property to the value of $2 .0 or $300, which was levied upon about June 1, 1822, by virtue of several justice's executions, and sold about July 27 following. In Aug. 1821, preceding, and at two different times afterwards, before Apr. 1, 1822, the plaintiff in this cause directed the sheriff to stay proceedings on the *fi. fa.* on condition that the defendant paid the interest, which, however, was not done; but the sheriff contended that the plaintiff had lost his lien by these several delays. In 1822, the plaintiff directed the defendant's property to be advertised and sold on his execution, in consequence of which the sheriff *ad- [***384** vertised the real estate of the defendant for sale, on several executions, being the plaintiff's and the several executions first above referred to. The real estate was sold about Sept. 15, 1822, and purchased by the plaintiff, for less than the amount due on his *fi. fa.*, from which the sheriff claimed to deduct $22, for fees on this, and $31.51, for fees on the other executions, which were satisfied when this was delivered. $7.24 of the $31.51 were thus claimed on two judgments docketed subsequent to this, as the parties supposed, though it was agreed that this might be corrected by the docket.

Mr. J. Bloore, for the plaintiff.

Messrs. J. Billings and *J. Willard*, for the sheriff, cited *Hildreth* v. *Ellice*, 1 Cai., 192.

Curia. The sheriff may retain on the elder judgments, but not on those which are younger than the plaintiff's. Payment of the debts did not pay the fees; and unless the sheriff is allowed to retain upon the elder, the consequence would be that the plaintiffs in those executions must pay the fees out of their own pockets; while sufficient property remains for that purpose.

The sheriff is liable to refund $7.24, unless the two judgments supposed to be docketed subsequent to Knickerbacker's shall appear, by the docket, to be earlier.

Rule accordingly.

Cited in—1 Edw., 637; 8 How. Pr., 110.

---

*JACKSON, ex dem. PIONEER ET AL., [***385** *v.* GARNSEY.

(Eight other several causes, on the same demise against different defendants.)

Motion, by Several Defendants in Different Causes, on one set of Affidavits—Costs.

Motion, by several different defendants, on one set of affidavits, in divers causes, at the suit of the same lessors of the plaintiff; opposed on one set of affidavits entitled in all the causes, and the motion denied with costs.

Held, that there should be only one taxation in all; the services of the attorney and counsel for the plaintiff to to be taxed as if there were only one cause, but clerk's fees to be allowed in the several causes, according to Boyce v. Thompson, 20 Johns., 274.

Citations—20 Johns., 274; 18 Johns., 310.

AT the last Aug. Term, application was made, in these causes, for judgment as in case of nonsuit, which was founded on one notice and affidavit, embracing all the causes; and but one motion was made for the whole. This motion was resisted by one set of affidavits, embracing all the causes, and containing the same facts as to all. The motion was denied, with costs, and only one rule entered. These costs were taxed at $14.18 in the first, and $8.43 in each of the other causes.

Mr. A. Van Vechten, for the defendants, moved an appeal from this taxation, on the authority of *Jackson* v. *Keller*, 18 Johns., 310.

Mr. L. H. Palmer, contra, cited *Boyce* v. *Thompson*, 20 Johns., 274. He said *Jackson* v. *Keller*, was the case of a motion granted. Here it was denied, with costs; and the grounds of opposition might be different in each cause.

Curia. Let the costs be retaxed; the whole to be included in one bill, and but one taxation to be charged; the clerk's fees to be allowed and included in the bill, according to the rule in *Boyce* v. *Thompson*, 20 Johns., 274. We allow but one fee to the attorney, one fee to counsel, and on brief, one copy of costs, one notice of taxation, and one attendance, one service of rule, and one power to demand costs. It is true that *Jackson* v. *Keller* was the case of a motion granted; but the principle is the same, whether the costs be on granting or denying the motion. If it be plain, in either case, that one set of affidavits is sufficient, no more should be allowed.

Rule accordingly.

Cited in—4 Cow., 533 (n); 2 Wend., 211; 11 Wend., 173; 1 Den., 683; 8 Paige, 623; 50 N. Y., 181.

386*] *WARNER, q. t. THE PEOPLE,
v.
TOOKER.

Practice—Form of Verdict.

In debt upon the 4th section of the Act for the Prevention of Frauds (1 R. L., 76), whether the jury should find the value of the goods, *quære*. If they omit this, and find for the plaintiff generally, the verdict is not void; and a judgment thereon will not be set aside for irregularity.

If the defendant have any remedy, it is by writ of error.

If a verdict be irregular, the party should move to set it aside the next term after it is rendered.

DEBT upon the 4th section of the Act for the Prevention of Frauds (1 R. L., 76). The declaration commenced by demanding $1,000 of debt; and the 1st and 2d counts, respectively, stated the value of the goods at $325, and demanded that sum. The 3d count stated the value of the goods at $350, and demanded that sum; the sums in the three counts making $1,000. Plea the general issue. Verdict for the plaintiff at the Oneido Circuit, Dec. 26, 1823. The verdict was sealed, and in these words: "In the above cause we find for the plaintiff." The circuit judge certified that the amount to be recovered was not contested on the trial; but the amount claimed by the plaintiff's counsel was $391.23, being the amount which the defendant confessed he gave for the property in question. Upon this verdict a judgment was perfected in Mar., 1824, for $391.23, with a *remittitur* of $608.77, of which the defendant's attorney was not informed till after last May Term.

At the last Aug. Term, a motion was made to set aside the verdict for irregularity, because all the jury were not present when the verdict was delivered; but the court were of opinion, that admitting the verdict to be irregular for that reason, the motion came too late. The party should have moved at the next term after the verdict.

A motion was also made at the last Aug. Term to set aside the judgment, on the ground that it was entered upon a verdict void on its face.

Mr. G. C. Bronson, for the defendant, adverted to the Statute (1 R. L., 76), and insisted that one material part of the issue was upon the value of the goods; and the jury omitting to pass upon this, the verdict was a mere nullity; and the judgment, therefore, irregular. He cited to this point, Bac. Abr., Verdict, M, pl. 1, Q, pl. 1, Z, pl. 3; 3 Salk., 372, 374; *Brockway* v. *Kinney*, 2 Johns., 210; *Brown* v. *Smith*, 3 *Cai., 81; Bac. Abr., Action [***387** *qui tam*, B; 2 Hawk. P. C., 380, Dub. ed., 1 *Id.*, 480, sec. 6, 484, sec. 21; Com. Dig., Pleader, S., 19, 20, 21.

The jury do not pronounce upon which count they give their verdict.

Mr. S. Beardsley, contra. The verdict was not void. It was in the usual form, and would, in strictness, perhaps, have warranted an entry upon the *postea* of a finding for the whole sum claimed of $1,000; but as it was doubtless the intention of the jury to find the amount proved, we have remitted all except this. The verdict may be thus amended either by the judge's minutes, or by a *remittitur*, as was done here. 2 Archb. Pr., 241, 242; 1 Wils., 33. Verdicts should be construed favorably (Burr., 699; 700; 2 Salk., 664), and it appearing that no injustice has been done, is a reason against setting a verdict aside. Burr., 1255–6; Dunl. Pr., 679, and cases there cited.

Curia. It is an answer to this application that the verdict is not void, so as to make the judgment irregular. Without saying whether the verdict be voidable or not, we are clear that the defendant cannot try that question in this form. The verdict appears upon the record, and the party must be put to his writ of error.

Motion denied.

REID, Admx. of REID,
v.
THE PRESIDENT, &c., OF THE RENSSELAER GLASS FACTORY.

Reference—Practice—What Incorporated in Record.

The facts which appeared before referees appointed pursuant to the Statute (1 R. L., 516, sec. 2), ordered to be entered upon the judgment record, so that the party might review the case on error.

THIS cause having been referred pursuant to the Statute (1 R. L., 516, sec. 2), the referees had reported generally for the plaintiff, upon which the attorneys for the respective parties agreed upon a case containing the facts as they appeared in evidence before the referees, and thereupon submitted a question of law to this court, in form of a motion to set aside the report. This court having decided

the question and given judgment, the defendant's attorney, being desirous to have the same question considered by the Court of Errors,
388*] **Mr. B. F. Butler* moved for a rule requiring the plaintiff to incorporate the facts contained in the case in the record of judgment.

Mr. S. A. Foot, contra, could hardly suppose the motion to be urged seriously. It is unprecedented; and the record sought for would differ from any which had ever before been made. There are but three ways of getting the facts upon record. These are by demurrer to evidence, bill of exceptions, or special verdict. He supposed some authority would be shown for the anomaly now sought to be introduced into our forms. As well, and indeed better, might a case be turned into a special verdict or bill of exceptions, without any stipulation for the purpose. Yet this was never allowed, and has been repeatedly denied. It may be said that if this motion be denied, we never can go from a reference into a court of error upon the facts appearing before the referees. That is true. If there be a question of law in the cause, the course is for the party against whom the application is made, to show this in answer to the application for a reference; and thus drive the party moving, to a jury where he can take a bill of exceptions. By not doing this, he waives his right to bring error, as fully as if he suffers a trial to pass without demurring to the evidence, or taking a bill of exceptions, or asking for a special verdict. He cited Tidd, 788; and said that *Sikes* v. *Ransom*, 6 Johns., 279; *Medberry* v. *Collins*, 9 *Id.*, 345, and *Lanuse* v. *Barker*, 10 *Id.*, 312, all go upon this ground; and depend on a familiar principle in the English practice.

Mr. Butler, in reply, said the analogy to a trial and omission to demur, &c., which was insisted upon, did not hold. In that case, the party has power to demur or except; but it is not pretended that any such form could be resorted to before referees. This motion rests upon the principle of *Shotwell's* case, 10 Johns., 304; 12 *Id.*, 31. There being no other mode to get before a court of error than that of bringing up the facts by affidavit or case agreed upon, necessity dictates the course to be taken. The motion rests on the same ground as if the cause had been brought before the court in the usual way by affidavit and counter affidavit.
389*] *A writ of error cannot be denied to the parties. It is a writ of right. The referees are made judges by act of law, which will give the remedy. A case in point from England is not to be expected. They have no such form of proceeding. References there are at common law, by the act of the court, being a mere matter of discretion. Our Statute is imperative. A question of law may or may not arise before the referees. The party is not put to determine at his peril, what no human being can do, whether a question of law is to arise before them or not. The most important question may come up there, without either party being able to anticipate it. The whole cause may turn upon the improper rejection or admission of testimony; and indeed, it is not always an objection to a reference, that questions of law will arise, where it appears that they are mixed up with accounts.

The judgment is always entered as upon the report. Granting this motion is only changing a general into a special report. It is introducing nothing new on the record, but merely changing the form of that which is uniformly entered there, and in the same place, with a view to further the right of the case.

The Court, after having the cause several days under advisement, directed the following,

RULE: "That a statement of the facts in this cause be drawn up under the direction of the *Chief Justice*, to be incorporated in the record, in this cause, in order that the defendants may be enabled to prosecute their writ of error, if they shall be advised so to do."

WOODWORTH, *J.*, being interested in the cause, gave no opinion.

Affirmed—5 Cow., 587.
Cited in—6 Cow., 53; 20 Wend., 665; 3 N. Y., 504; 8 N. Y., 157; 10 N. Y., 197; 15 N. Y., 399; 19 Hun, 598.

---

*JACKSON, ex dem. HADLEY ET AL., [*390
v.
CHAPMAN ET AL.

Settler on Military Tract—When may be Ejected without Pay for Improvements.

A defendant in ejectment, though he settled under color of a *bona fide* purchase on a military lot, may be turned out of possession without pay for his improvements, within the Statute (1 R. L., 303, sec. 2, 4; 3 W. & S., 399; sess. 26, ch. 78, sec. 2), unless he show that he settled there before Apr. 8, 1813, when the last Act Concerning Lands in the Military Tract, passed.

EJECTMENT for lot No. 90, in Hector, in the County of Tompkins. Verdict for the plaintiff, at a circuit in Tompkins, in 1823, before Nelson, *Ch. J.*, who certified that it appeared, at the trial, that this lot had been patented to Bishop Hadley, a soldier of the Revolutionary War, in the line of the State of N. Y., in the Army of the U. S., who died before Mar. 27, 1783; and that the lessors of the plaintiff were his heirs at law, upon which title the plaintiff recovered; that it farther appeared, on the trial, that the defendants respectively were actual settlers on this lot, and had entered and settled on the same under color of a *bona fide* purchase, about the year 1818, and before the commencement of the suit; and had made improvements on the several parts of the lot occupied by them respectively; and that the lessors of the plaintiff, before the commencement of the suit, offered to have these improvements appraised, and to pay for them, which the tenants refused.

Two other causes were similarly situated. Upon these facts,

Mr. J. A. Collier moved for rules staying all proceedings on the part of the plaintiffs respectively, till their lessors should pay to the several defendants the value of their respective improvements, which they had made at the time the suits were brought, according to the Statutes of 1803 and 1813 (1 R. L., 303, sec. 2, 4; 3 W. & S., 399, sess. 26, ch. 78, sec. 2), which provide that where "any person or persons shall have" actually settled on any of these military lands, under color of a *bona fide* purchase, and, in any action to be instituted for the recovery of the lands, a judgment or decree shall pass for the plaintiff against the tenant, the former shall not be permitted to take possession, till he shall have paid the tenant the value of the improvements made by him, or those under whom he claims, &c.

391*] *He was aware that the motion would be opposed, on the ground that the words of the Statute, "where any person or persons shall have settled," &c., are retrospective, and relate merely to such defendants as settled on these lands previous to the passage of the Act; but there are several statutes couched in similar language, which are daily construed to operate prospectively, and under which important rights have arisen. Thus the Statute Relative to the Court of Probates and Surrogates (1 N. R. L., 450, sec. 23) provides that when any executor or administrator, whose testator or intestate shall have died seised, &c., shall discover that the personal estate is insufficient to pay debts, it shall be lawful for him to sell the real estate, &c. So the Statute authorizing the general issue and double costs, in certain cases, to be awarded to defendants (1 R. L., 155, sec. 1), gives the double costs which they shall have sustained by reason of the suit. So, by the Statute (1 R. L., 468, sec. 19) as to distributing the moneys of insolvent debtors, the assignees are to distribute the moneys which shall have come to their hands. So, in the Poor Act (1 R. L., 278), every person who shall have come to inhabit, &c., shall be deemed settled, &c. So, in the Act for the Relief of Cities and Towns Against the Maintenance of Bastard Children (1 R. L., 309, sec. 6), the putative father is to be discharged, unless an order of filiation shall be made in eight weeks after the mother shall have been delivered. Similar words are found in other statutes, which are constantly construed to have a prospective effect.

The words in question are, "shall have settled." The Legislature never meant to confine this to a period between 1783 and 1813. If so, the words would have been, "shall have heretofore settled," &c.

Mr. S. Stevens, contra. The Acts referred to by the counsel for the defendants, to illustrate the propriety of his construction, were all passed for the purpose of providing a remedy in cases thereafter arising. They were prospective, from the nature of the subject-matter. The Act in question relates to past tenants—to facts which already existed at the time when it passed. The words are not,

392*] "persons who *may hereafter settle." The case of *Jackson* v. *Bush*, 3 Johns., 512, virtually disposes of this question. It was there taken for granted that, in order to constitute a right to improvements, the defendant must show that he entered before Apr. 5, 1803; and the court treat the finding of this fact as very material.

Mr. D. Cady (*ut amicus Curiæ*) referred to a MS. case, *Jackson* v. *Williams*, lately decided by this court, in which they recognized the construction contended for by *Mr. Stevens*.

Cur. adv. vult.

At another day,

SAVAGE, *Ch. J.*, said, that taking up this question as undecided, the court had differed in the construction to be given to the Act, and they had accordingly availed themselves of the case to which they had been referred by *Mr. Cady*. That case not being distinctly within the recollection of either of the present members of the bench, it struck the court, at first, that it might have turned on some point different from that supposed by *Mr. Cady*. He (the *Ch. J.*) had therefore inquired of the late *Ch. J.* Spencer, who was on the bench when the question arose, and took part in the decision; and he agrees, in his recollection, with *Mr. Cady*. The court deem it their duty to yield to the authority of this case, and are unanimous that the Act must be deemed retrospective in its operation; and consequently, that the defendants can take nothing by their motion.

Motion denied.

Cited in—1 Wend., 293; 7 Wend., 247.

---

*REID, Admx. of REID, [*393

v.

THE PRESIDENT AND DIRECTORS OF THE RENSSELAER GLASS FACTORY.

Interest—When Allowed on Accounts—Cash Balances—Unliquidated Account for Work and Labor—General Doctrines.

On May 1, 1812, the President, &c., of the Rensselaer Glass Factory, a Company engaged extensively in the manufacture of glass, entered into copartnership for a year with R. and A., two stockholders, in conducting the concern, R. and A. to make the necessary advances in money, and receive interest. On May 1, 1813, the Company appointed R. their general agent, large advances being necessary to carry on their business. No salary was agreed on, but a previous agent had received a salary of $1,250 *per annum*, and this was no more than a reasonable compensation for R.'s services while agent, until the factory was destroyed by fire May 3, 1815. R. continued agent from May 1, 1813, till his death, in Aug., 1821; residing in the vicinity of his principals, who occasionally met at his house. During the period of his agency, he made necessary cash advances in and about carrying on the concerns of the Company to more than $100,000, which he had charged in an account of more than 500 items; and had received in cash nearly the same amount, which he credited in the same book in upwards of 700 items. He never rendered any account to the Company; nor did he apprise them that they were in arrear until Jan. 2, 1819, when he was requested by one or more of the Directors to present his account; which request was afterwards repeated by one or more of the Directors, but never complied with. On his death, his personal representative claimed interest on the advances, as well as on the salary or compensation for his services; held, that she should recover interest upon the advances to Jan. 2, 1819, when he was requested to make out his account, but not after; held, also, that she should not recover interest on the salary.

As a general rule, interest is allowable on cash advances, though they rest in the form of a mutual, current, unliquidated account.

Whether such charges come strictly within the definition of an account, *quære*.

Interest is not allowable on an unliquidated account for work and labor.

The English and American cases examined at large by the court and counsel in reference to the following heads:

1. Interest on money lent.
2. On money paid, &c., or advanced.
3. On money had and received.
4. On money due for work, labor and services.

NOTE.—*Interest—When allowable on running account.* See Newell v. Griswold, 6 Johns., 45, note.

5. For goods, &c., sold and delivered.
6. On open, current, unliquidated accounts.
7. On an account stated, or balance struck.
8. The general principles upon which interest is chargeable.

Citations—1 Campb., 50, 128, 129, 518; 2 Campb., 426; 15 East, 223; 1 Bos. & P., 306-7, S. P.; 4 Campb., 380; 3 Wils., 205; 2 Bl., 761; Bull. *N. P.*, 2745, S. P.; 1 H. Bl., 304, 305; 2 Bos. & P., 337, 471, 472; 1 Campb., 149; 3 Cai., 226, 234, 266; 6 Johns., 24, 45; 8 Johns., 446; 9 Johns., 71; 12 Johns., 156; 7 Mass., 24; 11 Mass., 504; 13 Mass., 218; 1 Dall., 349; 3 Binn., 123; 1 Binn., 488, 494; 2 Salk., 623; 1 P. Wms., 376; 2 Str., 910; 2 Burr, 1005, 1085; 1 Dick., 428; 6 Br. P. C., 364; 2 Liv. Agency, 17; 1 Ves., Jr., 63; 4 Dall., 289; 1 Serg. & R., 179; 12 Mass., 4; 1 Conn., 32, 35; 3 Conn., 171, 185; 2 Wall., 45; 1 Johns., 315; 7 Johns., 213; 14 Johns., 255; 15 Johns., 424.

ASSUMPSIT to recover the balance of an unsettled account. The declaration was for money paid, laid out and expended, and lent and advanced by the intestate for and to the use of the defendants, money had and received by the defendants for the use of the intestate, goods, wares and merchandises sold and delivered, work, labor and services rendered, and materials furnished by the intestate for and to the defendants, for pay and salary as their agent, and on an account stated. The defendants pleaded the general issue, with a notice of set-off, of moneys paid, laid out and expended, moneys lent and advanced, moneys had and received, goods sold, work and labor, &c.

394*] *The cause requiring the examination of long accounts, it was referred at Jan. Term, 1822, heard by the referees Feb. 18 of the same year. and at various subsequent days, and submitted to them on Mar. 21, 1822; two of whom reported for the plaintiff $14,913.40, after deducting $2,317.53, being the amount agreed between the parties to be due from John Reid, the intestate, to the defendants, on an account current between him and a joint concern, in which the defendants and John Reid and Robert Alsop were interested.

It appeared in evidence before the referees that the defendants' factory was situated in the town of Sandlake, in the County of Rensselaer, about ten miles from the City of Albany. John Reid, the intestate, was agent for the defendants from June 2, 1812, to the time of his death in Aug., 1821, and during the time of his agency resided in the City of Albany. The factory of the defendants was in actual operation from May 1, 1813, to May 3, 1815, when it was destroyed by fire, and after this no glass was manufactured by the defendants. The plaintiff produced an account current, showing a large balance due to her for principal and interest. The debit side of the account contained 527 items, each of which was for cash advanced, or paid out by the intestate, for the purpose of keeping the factory of the defendants in operation. The credit side of the account contained 787 items, each of which was for cash received by the intestate, for glass made at the factory, and for other property of the defendants, sold by the intestate on their account. The whole amount of cash advanced and paid by the intestate, for the defendants, between May 1, 1813, and the time of his death, and charged to them, was $107,579.74. The amount received by him during the same time, and credited to the defendants, was $100,099.88.

The plaintiff proved an actual advance, or payment of cash, in every instance, as charged in the debit side of her account, with the exception of four items, amounting in the whole, without interest, to $288.99.

*The referees charged the plaintiff, [*395 in making up their report, with $105.11, being the amount, exclusive of interest, of two debts due the defendants; on the ground that she had not sworn that the intestate used due diligence in collecting them.

The defendants were charged with the sum of $3,125, for the intestate's salary as agent, from May 1, 1813, to Nov. 1, 1815, at the rate of $1,250.

They were also charged with the necessary disbursements of the intestate in and about the business. An interest account was also stated, in a general account current, in which the defendants were charged with interest from the time of the advance, or payment of each sum of money, to the 4th day of May Term, 1823, and credited with interest on each sum of money received, from the time of its receipt till the same 4th day of May Term. Interest was also calculated on the items of salary, from the end of the year when the salary became due, to the same time. The balance of interest thus found on all the debits proved and receipts admitted before the referees was $10,348.08.

The balance of principal which the referees found due at the date of their report was $6,882.91.

In March, 1806, the factory of the defendants went into operation. In that month the defendants appointed James Kane, of the City of Albany, their agent, by a resolution in the following words: "Resolved, that James Kane be, and he is hereby appointed agent." Kane continued to be the agent of the defendants from the time of his appointment till the intestate's appointment. In the month of Apr., 1809, the defendants leased their factory, together with all things in, and attached to it, for three years, from May 1, 1809, to five stockholders. Kane, one of the lessees, was their agent, and resided in the City of Albany during the time of his agency. At the expiration of this lease, namely: May 1, 1812, the intestate, Robert Alsop, and the defendants entered into a copartnership under the name of John Reid & Co., for the purpose of manufacturing glass at the defendant's factory, which was to continue for one year. Robert Alsop superintended the business at the factory, and *resided there. The intestate resided [*396 in the City of Albany, and made the necessary advances of money for the concern, and received the proceeds of the sales of glass, and other property, in the same way as he advanced and received money while agent of the defendants. By the articles of this copartnership, the stock and materials of the defendants on hand May 1, 1812, and which amounted as per inventory then made, to $13,997.87, was deemed, by the parties, an advance to the partnership fund, and an equal quantity of materials was to be returned to the defendants May 1, 1813; or the deficiency charged to the intestate and Alsop. When this copartnership ended, viz.: May 1, 1813, an inventory was taken of all the materials and stock then owned by the defendants. They were found to amount to $13,186.58. The accounts of the business of this copartnership where rendered by the plaintiff to the defendants and Alsop, during the reference, and adjusted by mutual consent, and the balance sheet produced on the hearing. A balance of this concern was struck as of Jan. 1, 1815. In the liquidation of the account of this concern with the intestate, interest was debited and credited, and allowed by the defendants in the same manner as it was debited and credited in the general account current of the plaintiff before mentioned, and there was a balance of interest thus allowed to the intestate of $1,393.10. By the articles of copartnership, it was agreed that interest should be allowed on the amount of the inventory, and on all moneys advanced by Reid & Alsop, who, by the articles of copartnership, were to make all necessary advances of cash to carry on the business; and it was also expressly reserved by the defendants, at the time of the adjustment of the partnership concern, that the question of interest in this cause should not be affected by that adjustment, any further than the articles of copartnership and the account made in pursuance of them affect that question. A balance of principal and interest was found due to the defendants from the intestate Jan. 1, 1815, of $1,531.38, and, by agreement of the parties, this sum, together with the interest to the 4th day of May Term, 1822, being $786.15, was to be deducted from **397***] *the amount found due from the defendants to the plaintiff; but the interest on that balance, from Jan. 1, 1815, was not to be deducted, unless interest was allowed on the accounts between the parties in this suit.

When the intestate was first appointed agent, it was by a resolution in the following words: "Resolved, that John Reid be, and he is hereby appointed agent for this Corporation"—and every subsequent appointment was in the same words, or words of like import. When the intestate took the active agency of the factory, in May, 1813, the stock, materials and funds of the defendants, were insufficient to keep the factory in operation, and large advances were required for that purpose.

No specific agreement, between the intestate and the defendants, relative to his salary, was proved. It was, however, fully proved, that $1,250 per year, exclusive of disbursements, was a reasonable compensation for his services as agent; that Kane, who proceded him as agent for the defendants, was allowed by them, on the settlement of his accounts, the same sum per year, for salary, besides expenses, although there had been no agreement between him and the defendants on the subject; and that Kane had been allowed the same compensation by the lessees, some of whom were directors of the Company when the intestate was appointed their agent, and while he continued to be so. The proceeds of all the glass manufactured by the defendants, after May 1, 1813, were received exclusively by the intestate. All the accounts of the Corporation, and book of minutes, were kept by the intestate. The general account current produced by the plaintiff, was rendered to the defendants Oct. 12, 1821. An account of the sales of glass received and sold by the intestate, on account of the defendants, was rendered to them at the same time, and no account current, or account of sales, was ever before rendered to them.

The whole of the accounts were not made out until after the death of the intestate, owing to his habits, though several attempts were made to complete them.

*It was admitted, that on Jan. 2, [*398 1819, when there was a meeting of the Directors at his house, the intestate stated to the Directors that there was a balance due to him from the defendants. Then one or more of the Directors asked him to make out his account, and present it to the Directors; and since that time he has been asked for the account by one or more of the Directors. These requests were made by the Directors, individually, but no resolution or entry was made, concerning the intestate's accounts, on the minutes. At a meeting of the Directors, on Dec. 27, 1817, the subject of the accounts of James Kane was agitated before the Board, and the following entry was made in the book of minutes: "John Reid brought the subject of James Kane's demand against the Company before the Directors, and, after various views of the same, it was agreed that Mr. James and John Reid be appointed a committee to liquidate and adjust the same." Nov. 27, 1806, a resolution was passed, appointing a committee to audit the accounts of Kane: also, on Apr. 14th, 1807; also, on Sept. 23d, 1807; and also, on Feb. 23d, 1809.

The referees were unanimous in opinion, that there was due to the plaintiff, at the date of their report, for principal, the sum of $6,-882.91; but they differed in their opinion on the subject of interest, the referee dissenting from the report, being of opinion that interest ought to be calculated only to Jan. 1, 1816, and the two referees making the report being of opinion that it should be calculated to the 4th of May Term, 1822.

The question of interest was the only one raised upon the case; and it was agreed, by the parties, that this court should settle the principles on which it should be calculated, and to what time, and refer it again to the referees, to report the amount in addition to the principal due; that their reports be deemed as one, and considered as made of May Term, 1822; but no judgment to be entered, until four days in term shall have elapsed, after the making of such additional report.

**Mr. B. F. Butler*, for the defendants: [*399

1. Whatever may be the plaintiff's rights as to interest, upon other parts of this account, it is impossible that she should be entitled to it on the charges for the salary of the intestate. The general rule is, that interest is not recoverable on uncertain demands, where damages are recoverable, and where the amount is unliquidated; and if there is any case in which the rule should be applied, it is in an action for work and labor where the amount is unliquidated, especially when that amount is to be settled on a *quantum meruit*, in the same action where the interest is sought to be recovered. Here the amount due to the intestate, for his services, was wholly undetermined by the parties. There was no agreement between them on the subject. The referees heard the

evidence, and fixed the amount of compensation.

Reid never demanded payment for his services; and not doing this, the defendants had a right to infer that he had paid himself out of the moneys which he had received. At most, therefore, interest should be allowed only from the commencement of the suit.

That the referees erred, in allowing interest on the salary, he cited *Sweatland* v. *Squire*, 2 Salk., 623; *Trelawney* v. *Thomas*, 1 H. Bl., 303; *Walker* v. *Bayley*, 2 Bos. & P., 219; *Skirving* v. *Stobo*, 2 Bay., 233; *Gammell* v. *Skinner*, 2 Gall., 45; Chit. on Bills, 538, Phil. ed. In *Gammell* v. *Skinner*, which was a libel for mariner's wages, on the instance side of the admiralty, *Judge* Story says: "There is no difference, in this respect, between the practice of our courts of common law and that of the admiralty. In the latter, interest is generally allowed from the time of a demand made for the wages; and if no special demand is proved, from the time of the commencement of the suit."

2. The referees erred in allowing interest on the general account. This was wholly unliquidated. On May 1, 1813, Reid took charge of the factory, as agent, and from that time to May 1815, when the factory was destroyed, made advances of money, carried on the establishment, and received all the avails of glass manufactured. There is no evidence of any agreement, between the parties, as to the **400***] *allowance of interest, nor any circumstances from which such an agreement can be inferred. Reid advanced to the amount of $104,000. He received about $100,000; and the balance due him on advances was short of $4,000; which, with $3,125, for salary, made the sum of $6,882, the balance of principal found by the referees. The whole balance found by them is $17,230, viz.: $6,882 for principal—$10,348 for interest; the interest on the salary being $1,600, and on the cash account $10,300. The balance of interest due on the cash account is more than twice the amount of the principal. This account was not stated, nor the balance demanded, till Oct. 12, 1821; and until that demand, at any rate, the plaintiff was not entitled to interest on this part of the account.

A recovery of interest must, to be sure, depend very much on the circumstances of the case; but the general rule is, that it is not allowable on a running, unliquidated, open and mutual account, until such account is stated by the parties, or, at least, rendered by one party to the other, which is considered a liquidation if assented to, or if not objected to within a reasonable time. The only exceptions are, 1. Where an express agreement to pay interest has been made and proved; 2. Where an intent to pay interest can be inferred, from the course of dealing between the parties, or the particular custom of the trade or place; or, 3. Where there has been fraudulent conduct, or a vexatious detention of the debt. *Borret* v. *Goodere*, 1 Dick., 428; *Liotard* v. *Graves*, 3 Cai., 226; *Anonymous*, 1 Johns., 315; *Newell* v. *Griswold*, 6 Johns., 45; *Holliday* v. *Marshall*, 7 *Id.*, 211; *Kane* v. *Smith*, 12 *Id.*, 156; *Walden* v. *Sherburne*, 15 *Id.*, 409; *Consequa* v. *Fanning*, 3 Johns. Ch., 601; *Selleck* v. *French*, 1 Con., N. S., 32., *Williams* v. *Craig*, 1 Dall., 313; *M'Connico* v. *Curzen*, 1 Call., 358, with the cases already cited to the first point.

The principle of the rule, that where no agreement to allow interest has been made, nor can be inferred, the parties are not to be charged with it, applies with peculiar force here. Interest is in the nature of damages, for not paying the balance due; and is it fair that the party should be called *on for [***401** such damages, when it is seen that he was ignorant of the amount of the balance; or, indeed, that any balance whatever was due? It was impossible for the defendants to know, until the settlement, whether Reid had advanced his own money or theirs. He had the custody of the books, could alone state them, and it was impossible for the defendants to know the situation of the accounts until Reid presented them. If the rule is right between merchants, *a fortiori*, it is so here. Among merchants, each party keeps the accounts, and each may know their state with reasonable accuracy.

But it was insisted, before the referees, and will, doubtless, be contended here, that the rule denying interest on unliquidated accounts is confined to those for goods sold, and other mercantile dealings between merchants and their customers; and that interest should be allowed here, on the ground that the debits were made up of moneys advanced for the use of the defendants. In support of this, *Liotard* v. *Graves*, 3 Cai., 226, was cited. In that case, the Supreme Court departed from the rule previously established by adjudged cases in England; for, though there was a loose *dictum* in Bunbury, and one or two adjudged cases in other books, in which it was said that interest was allowable on money lent or advanced, without any agreement, express or implied, yet the general current of the authorities was otherwise; and when *Liotard* v *Graves* was decided (August, 1805), the law was settled, in England, against the allowance, as was afterwards declared in *Calton* v. *Bragg*, 15 East, 223, where all the authorities are cited. The court there held that interest is not allowable on money lent or advanced, even where the whole advance is of one sum, unless there is a contract for its allowance expressed, or to be inferred from the circumstances. The propriety of allowing interest in *Liotard* v. *Graves*, under the circumstances of that case, is not disputed. Its application to the present case is, however, denied. The court did not decide, nor did they mean to decide, that, in all cases of money advanced, interest should be allowed. They only meant to say that where a person requests another to lend him money, or advance it for his use, having no funds in his hands, it is so *much out of the [***402** ordinary course of mercantile business, that an agreement to pay interest is to be presumed. They did not intend to lay down a rule of universal application, without regard to circumstances. Accordingly, in *Pease* v. *Barber*, 3 Cai., 266, afterwards determined, *Ch. J.* Kent admitted that, allowing that interest must depend much upon particular circumstances, even in that case, which was an action for money had and received. The advances in *Liotard* v. *Graves* were specific, when the defendant had no funds in the plaintiff's hands. They were for prosecuting an appeal, and out of the ordinary course of business between the parties—not like this, which is the case of an agent making advances at his own discretion, on the strength of receipts either actual or expected, under his general authority, and without specific request. No settlement was necessary, to enable Graves to ascertain whether he was indebted for those advances. Being specific, and for a special purpose, they stood precisely on the same ground, so far as the question of interest was concerned, as if there had been no other dealings between the parties. Besides, Livingston *J.*, mentions, that there had been previous accounts rendered, on which interest had been charged and allowed by mutual consent. In this case, besides the distinguishing circumstances already noticed, there are a series of advances on one side, and receipts on the other, the whole accounts consisting of moneys debited and credited, constituting a running cash account, at the same time that it was utterly impossible for either party, and particularly for the defendants, to ascertain how the balance stood, until the account was stated.

This court has itself departed from the broad rule in *Liotard* v, *Graves*. It did so in *Kane* v. *Smith*, 12 Johns., 156, which cannot be distinguished from this case. The Kanes at N. Y., were to advance moneys in purchasing cargoes; while the Smiths, at Maderia, were to send wines to the East Indies, to be sold there, the Kanes to receive the moneys, and reimburse themselves. They advanced more than they received, and claimed interest. The moneyed transactions between the parties were precisely like those in this case. But interest **403***] on the advances was denied. *This was followed by other decisions of this court and the Court of Chancery, to the same affect. *Waldon* v. *Sherburne*, 15 Johns., 409 ; *Consequa* v. *Fanning*, 3 Johns. Ch., 601 ; *Campbell* v. *Mesier*, 6 Johns. Ch., 21.

So, too, in the other States, although I admit there has been a general inclination to depart from the English rules so far as to allow interest on money lent or money had and received, still the courts which have gone farthest on the subject have always confined the allowance to cases where the amount was certain, and the peculiar equity of the particular case. They have never given interest on an unliquidated cash account, where the defendant's conduct was fair. The Supreme Court of Mass. allowed interest in *Fowler* v. *Shearer*, 7 Mass., 24; *Wood* v. *Robbins*, 11 *Id.*, 504; *Weeks* v. *Hasty*, 13 *Id.*, 218; but refused it in *Porter* v. *Bussey*, 1 *Id.*, 438, and *Storer* v. *Storer*, 9 *Id.*, 37. In *Winthrop* v. *Carleton*, 12 *Id.*, 4, it was allowed only from the commencement of the suit; and in *Wyman* v. *Hubbard*, 13 *Id.*, 232, it was denied altogether. These are cases of money paid or money had and received ; and it will be seen by an examination of them that if the present case was to be determined in Mass., there could be no question that interest would be denied.

The Superior Court of Conn. allowed interest in *Selleck* v. *French*, 1 Conn. N. S., 32 ; but Swift, *Ch. J.*, limits the rule in that very case so as to exclude this ; and in *Thompson* v. *Stewart*, 3 *Id.*, 171, the court denied interest on principles which apply here.

Pennsylvania has gone farther than any other State in allowing interest for moneys. *Rapelie* v. *Emory*, 1 Dall., 349, and *note* to that case ; *Lessee of Dilworth* v. *Sinderling*, 1 Binn., 494; *Commonwealth* v. *Crevor*, 3 *Id.*, 121. But the Supreme Court of that State denied interest in *Jacobs* v. *Adams*, 1 Dall., 52; and limited its allowance in *Brown* v. *Campbell*, 1 Serg. & R., 179, on the very principles we contend for here.

In South Carolina the judges find fault with the English rule, and allowed interest in *Goddard* ads. *Bulow*, 1 Nott & M'Cord, 45, and *Thompson* v. *Stevens*, 2 *Id.*, 493; but in *deciding the last case the court lay [***404** down the rule in terms and for reasons which would deny interest here; and they accordingly denied interest in *Moore* v. *Treasurer*, 1 *Id.*, 214.

It may safely be said that none of the American cases are in favor of allowing interest in this case, but that when all the cases of each court are considered in connection, they lay down principles fatal to the present plaintiff's claim, if we except, perhaps, *Lessee of Dilworth* v. *Sinderling*, 1 Binn., 494.

Whether, therefore, the case be decided by our own decisions, by those of the English courts, or a majority of American courts, the result is the same. In England interest is not allowed on moneys advanced or received, in any case, unless there is a contract expressed or to be inferred. In most of the U. S. interest is allowed on moneys paid, advanced or received, though there be no contract expressed or to be inferred, where either, 1. The advance is of a single sum, or all the advances are on one side, and there are no mutual accounts to be settled ; or 2. Where the money has been obtained by fraud or unreasonably withheld, thereby placing an account for moneys, when running and unliquidated, on precisely the same grounds with other running accounts.

We never had the accounts till Oct., 1821. The whole business remained in the dark for years, though there was no excuse for the delay. As agent, it was Reid's duty to have accounted annually; at all events, when the factory was destroyed, and the business suspended ; yet he continued to keep back the accounts, notwithstanding the request to make them out (in Jan., 1819), until Oct., 1821, six years after the business was at an end. The excuse attempted (his habits), instead of extenuating, aggravates the neglect. It is not to be tolerated that an agent shall withhold his accounts for such a length of time, leave his principal without information, and then set up an enormous claim for interest. Still more unjust is it to give the intestate a reward for his neglect, and visit upon the defendants the effect of his misconduct or misfortunes.

*The default is all on Reid's part ; [***405** yet, by the report, the defendants suffer, and he gains by his laches. A rule so manifestly unjust cannot be supported. The rules of courts of equity, as applied by them to agents, may properly be resorted to in this case. These are: 1. That where an agent has received moneys, and has promptly exhibited his accounts, and there is no delay on his part, the court never charge him with interest on moneys in his hands. 2. But where he has delayed rendering his accounts, and is guilty of laches or other misconduct, the Court of Chancery will charge him with interest on the balance in his hands. 3. And though a balance may be due him, if he has been guilty of laches, and has not made out his accounts seasonably, he will be deprived, not only of interest, but of commissions, poundage, &c. *White* v. *Lincoln*, 8 Ves., 363; *Lady Ormond* v. *Hutchinson*, 13 Ves., 53; *Pearse* v. *Green*, 1 Jac. & Walk., 135. Had we filed our bill against Reid in 1821, for an account, and the balance had been found as here, a court of chancery would not have given him interest.

For these reasons the defendants claim that the plaintiff was not entitled to interest until Oct., 1821, when they first became acquainted with their indebtedness.

3. If, however, it should be thought that the intestate was entitled to state an interest account from the commencement of his advances, the question then arises—for how long shall the plaintiff be entitled to claim interest? For the whole period, as the referees have decided, or for a stated period?

We contend that it should be stopped at a reasonable time after the closing of the agency. The factory was destroyed in May, 1815; and the business was essentially, and to all practical purposes, closed in Nov. of that year. Reid charges his salary only to that time; and should have stated an account Jan. 1st, 1816. Not having done so, interest should cease from that time. At all events, it must be stopped on Jan. 2d, 1819, when the intestate was called upon for his accounts. The authorities and course of argument on the second point apply to this; and *Dent* v. *Dunn*, 3 Campb., 296, is in point.

406*] **Mr. S. A. Foot*, contra. The intestate stood in the relation of a trustee or steward, managing all the concerns of the defendants, who were a Corporation extensively engaged in the manufacture and sale of glass. The plaintiff's account consists of more than 500 items, involving an amount of upwards of $100,000. Both the ability and fidelity of this agent were most manifest throughout the whole term of his engagement; and were not impeached as to any particular in any material degree. It is now said that no account of his agency could be procured from him on account of his bad habits. This is an entirely gratuitous assertion. The case says that no account could be procured on account of his habits, without distinguishing whether they were those of piety or inebriety. It is also said that interest ought not, at any rate, to be allowed after Jan. 2d, 1819, because an account was then demanded. True, but this was by an individual director or directors, after a corporate meeting had broken up without adopting any resolution on the subject. It was not a request, then, because not a corporate act. It was no more than if the request had been made by a stranger. Nor is it surprising that the interest should exceed the principal due, when we look at the enormous amount of the whole account.

The law of interest has undergone very great changes. The Stat. 3 Hen., VII. allowed interets on a judgment affirmed upon a writ of error; and yet the judges were so conscientious as to refuse carrying it into effect. Till 37 Hen. VIII., it was unlawful to demand interest; but after the simplicity of barter went off with the middle ages, it began to be allowed on certain demands, and has been gradually extending to others ever since. The Stat. 37 Hen. VIII. was the first which tolerated the demand; and from that year till 1812, the decisions of the English courts were strangely contradictory as to the cases in which it might be demanded. If we compare the English and American cases, it will be found that there is no branch of jurisprudence involved in greater obscurity and contradiction. There are but two judges who have undertaken to lay down any general rule on the subject. These are Ld. Ellenborough, and *Mr. Justice* Spencer. *The rule of the latter will [*407 be found in *Liotard* v. *Graves*, 3 Cai., 226. He there says (p. 234): "For goods sold and delivered, unless there be evidence of an agreement to pay interest, none is recoverable until a liquidation of the account takes place. If an account be transmitted by a creditor, and acquiesced in, or assented to by his debtor, it becomes thereby liquidated, and interest is allowable. On money advanced, interest is legally demandable. By the usage of a particular trade, interest may be allowed." *De Haviland* v. *Bowerbank*, 1 Campb., 50, contains Lord Ellenborough's rule. He says: "Interest ought to be allowed only in cases where there is a contract for the payment of money on a certain day, as on bills of exchange, promissory notes, &c.; or where there has been an express promise to pay interest; or where, from the course of dealing between the parties, it may be inferred that this was their intention; or where it can be proved that the money has been used and interest actually made."

This rule does not embrace money advanced, or money lent, as such. The case is quoted in *Newell* v. *Griswold*, 6 Johns., 45, to show merely that interest is not allowable on an unliquidated account for goods sold. Campbell, the reporter, appends as many as 20 cases to *De Haviland* v. *Bowerbank*, as supporting the rule, that interest is not allowable for money had and received; and it is remarkable that they will just as well support any other rule. Another case decided by Ld. Ellenborough is *Crockford* v. *Winter*, 1 Campb., 128, which was an action for money had and received, grounded on the fact that the money was obtained by fraud, which was plainly made out in evidence; yet interest was denied. But this court say, in *Amory* v. *M'Gregor*, 15 Johns., 38, that if there be any fraud or gross misconduct on the part of the defendant, interest should be allowed; and that too in a case where interest would, by no means, be allowed without fraud; a position directly at war with the case of *Crockford* v. *Winter*. In *Kingston* v. *M'Intosh*, 1 Campb., 518, the court deny interest on a policy of insurance; and overrule the practice of Buller *J.*, mentioned in *De Bernales* v. *Fuller*, 2 Campb., 427; whereas a case in *1 Johns., 315, de- [*408 cides directly the reverse. In *Gordon* v. *Swan*

2 Camph., 429, in *note*, and *Atkinson* v. *Braybroke*, 4 *Id.*, 380, Ld. Ellenborough refused interest in an action for goods sold to be paid for at a particular day; and in an action on a foreign judgment; though in *Mountford* v. *Willes*, 2 Bos. & P., 337, it was decided that a debt for goods sold does draw interest after the credit has expired. Yet that case must, it seems, yield to Ld. Ellenborough's rule, which is now in daily practice in this State, as to goods sold. In *Thomas* v. *Weed*, 14 Johns., 255, what this court say, in delivering their opinion, is in direct hostility again to Ld. Ellenborough's rule in relation to allowing interest upon money had and received. In *Harris* v. *Benson*, in 5 Geo. II., Str., 910, the K. B. decided that interest was not allowable on money lent; but in *Trelawney* v. *Thomas*, 1 H. Bl. 303, the C. B. overruled the K. B. on that very point. In *Calton* v. *Bragg*, 15 East, 223, in 1812, the decision denied interest on money lent, whereas both money lent and money had and received, are now put on the same footing by our cases, and both carry interest. In *Trelawney* v. *Thomas* there was a discussion of considerable length. The demand was for money laid out, and for day wages; and the court allowed interest on the former, but denied it as to the latter. In *Walker* v. *Constable*, 1 Bos. & P., 307, and *Tappenden* v. *Randall*, 2 *Id.*, 467, the C. B. refused interest for money had and received; but in *Pease* v. *Barber*, 3 Cai., 266, this court decided directly the reverse. Which is the most reasonable?

We can turn with pride from the English decisions to those of this court. It will be found that our own judges have decided consistently, and entertained enlightened views of the policy and nature of a circulating medium. The principal objection against our recovery of interest is, that our account is open, and that no demand was made till after the intestate's death. In other words the defendants claim an exemption from the general rule, which is against them on the ground that the advances of money rest in open account. This is mainly a question of principle. *Liotard* v. *Graves* is certainly much in point. That, also, was a **409***] case *in which no account was rendered. It has been assailed, and its application denied in very strong terms. In reply, I shall merely take the words of the several judges who delivered opinions. That case came before the court with a view to the settlement of abstract principles, as a guide to referees who had the subject before them. Kent, *Ch. J.*, said (p. 245) the account was not liquidated, but a naked account current; and interest was allowable only on such items in it as were made for moneys advanced.

The decision of that case, then, was in reference to an account exhibited just before the suit was brought, as here. Spencer, *J.* (p. 234), said he should content himself by laying down principles, and leave the arbitrators to make the application, and then advances the general rule which I have mentioned. Thompson, *J.*, says: "With respect to interest on the plaintiff's account, it appears to me they had a right to charge it on the money advanced. The account cannot be considered as settled, and on that ground carrying interest. It is merely an account current between the parties, and unless some usage or practice is shown to warrant the allowance, I should think interest ought not to be calculated except on the money advanced." Livingston, *J.*, says: "If there be no special agreement between the parties, or usage of trade between Amsterdam and N. Y., to the contrary, it ought to be allowed on all moneys advanced from their respective payments, and on the goods supplied after such time as is conformable to the course of trade between the two countries."

What then, is the rule established? Why, that interest is not allowable on an unliquidated account, without an agreement, express or implied, excepting, however, an account for money advanced, whether liquidated or unliquidated. Within this exception, interest is due here. Livingston, *J.*, was mistaken, in supposing an account previously rendered. The court do not place themselves on this ground. Had an account been rendered, interest would have been allowed on the whole, as a liquidated account, even for the goods sold, after three months, had there been no objection. So material a circumstance could not have escaped *both court and coun- [***410** sel. Then we come exactly within the principle of that case, when we prove actual advances as charged in our account. Is not this authority conclusive? If fully respected, it certainly is so.

But it is said that in *Pease* v. *Barber*, 3 Cai., 266, this court overrule *Liotard* v. *Graves*. That case decides, merely, that no objection can be made to interest, from the form of the action, and that case must depend on circumstances.

Mr. Butler. I cited that case to establish the latter position only.

Mr. Foot. Before considering *Kane* v. *Smith*, 12 Johns., 156, I would ask, what are the general grounds upon which the allowance of interest depends. There are, we conceive, three great principles upon which it may be claimed. 1. An agreement, either expressed or inferrible from the circumstances. Among other examples, under this head, is that of an account sent to the debtor, and not objected to within a reasonable time. Another is, the the custom of a particular store at which he trades. 2. A second general ground of the allowance is, the default of the party in omitting what he is bound to do, either by express contract or legal obligation, as upon an express agreement to pay money, at a particular day for goods, or other consideration, at the expiration of the term of credit, or an implied agreement to pay money, which is received to another's use, as in *Slingerland* v. *Swart*, 13 Johns., 255, and *Linch* v. *De Viar*, 3 Johns. Cas., 310, or the legal obligation to pay the price of goods, wrongfully converted, to the right owner, which is recovered in an action of trover. Neither of these principles reach the case of interest for money lent or advanced; and yet the books are full of cases where it has been allowed, not merely from the time of default to pay, on demand. This was never made a criterion in any case. What is the reason of this? When a note is given, or money lent or advanced, generally, without time of payment, it is legally due from the date of the note, loan, or advance. In other 411*] *words, it is due presently; and a suit may be immediately brought. *Thompson* v. *Ketcham*, 8 Johns., 189. 3. The third principle, then, is, that interest is allowed in these two cases, upon the nature of money, and in reference to its use. It is the circulating medium, having a fixed value by law, and when out of one's possession, he loses 7 *per cent.*, the legal interest. Hence it should bear interest from the time of the loan or advance. It commands everything a man has. It gives profit, and may be used in a thousand ways, to make it yield the legal interest. Not so as to merchandise. This lies, for a time, as a dead weight upon the hands of the merchant. Its conversion into money is a work of delay, and depends upon circumstances. In every one of these cases where interest is allowed, on the ground of an account liquidated, it was for things other than money. What is an account? Not a list of cash advances; but regular entries in relation to dealings of another nature. The books of entry constitute an item of proof in establishing the account before a jury or referees. Not so as to cash advances; because entries, in relation to these, are not an account, in any sense of the word. *Vosburgh* v. *Thayer*, 12 Johns., 461; *Case* v. *Potter*, 8 *Id.*, 212. You cannot prove them as an account, but only one by one, in the ordinary modes of proof.

It is stated that interest is not due upon an account unliquidated; and we agree to this, as a general rule. The gentleman cites a great variety of cases to establish and illustrate it, and said that in *Consequa* v. *Fanning*, 3 Johns. Ch., 601, the late *Chancellor* denied interest on cash advances. This is a mistake. There were no cash advances in the case. *Weeks* v. *Hasty*, 13 Mass., 218, is a fair specimen of the rule which allows interest for money paid. The demand was for money paid to J. B. for account of the defendants; and interest was allowed from the time of the payment. No special circumstances are considered; but the marginal note is, simply, that "interest was allowed on money paid, where the defendant suffered judgment to go by default."

412*] **Thompson* v. *Stewart*, 3 Conn. N. S., is said to be against us; but that was a question whether interest should be allowed on the avails of goods sold by one having a lien, which lien continued; and interest was denied during its continuance. *Borret* v. *Goodere*, 1 Dick., 428, was the case of an open mutual account. The rule laid down in *Anonymous*, 1 Johns., 315, relates to unliquidated damages. *Newell* v. *Griswold*, 6 Johns., 45, was an unliquidated account for goods sold; and *Holliday* v. *Marshall*, 7 *Id.*, 211, the case of unliquidated damages. The rule in relation to unliquidated accounts is too limited to reach the point in controversy here. Numerous cases may be supposed where it cannot apply. Take a single loan or a single advance, and the lapse of a year; ought not interest to be allowed for the whole time? Would not this make an account equally as an hundred advances, or how many items must an account consist of? Would this court ever refuse interest even for goods sold, after a day of payment fixed by the parties? The gentleman admits that there is an inclination in the American cases to depart from the English rule, by multiplying the instances in which interest shall be allowed. Whether this be so or not, it may be difficult to determine; but we take the admission.

The case of *Kane* v. *Smith*, 12 Johns., 156, will be found, on a full examination, not to oppose *Liotard* v. *Graves*, 3 Cai., 226. It is true there was a claim of interest on advances, which was denied; but this was by reason of a special agreement in the case, upon which a question of construction arose; and the decision is founded on the circumstances of the case growing out of that agreement. The court thought the whole case negatived any intention to allow interest. The defendant was found not at all in default as to fulfilling his agreement. One item on the debit side of the Kanes was the amount of the goods. Another was for moneys advanced, though it will be seen by the case that none was, in fact, advanced. Other charges were for freight and commissions on sale. The plaintiffs were to be reimbursed for all their expenses by the proceeds of wines in the East Indies, over which they had the entire control, which they sold and kept an account of; and upon the whole, it was thought unfair *to allow [*413 interest on more than the balance, and that only from the time when they had rendered an account, and ascertained the balance. From that time only could it be deemed fairly due. The operation was on a very broad scale, and of an uncertain nature. The accounts were like those in *Walden* v. *Sherburne*, 15 Johns., 409; *Consequa* v. *Fanning*, 3 Johns. Ch., 601; and *Campbell* v. *Mesier*, 6 *Id.*, 24. I can find no charge of cash advanced in *Walden* v. *Sherburne*. In *Campbell* v. *Mesier* interest was allowed, and the remark of the *Chancellor*, that money paid carries interest after demand and default in payment, is true, but it does not go far enough. It is allowable from the time of the advance, for the money is then due.

It is said, among other things, that the intestate should have presented his account in Jan., 1816, in order to claim interest. What rule required this? The gentleman admits there is none, but refers this, with several of his arguments, to the special circumstances of the case. With deference, the doctrine of peculiar circumstances is, in most cases, little better than legal quackery. Philosophy requires us to take a higher and broader view of human transactions; to look at them on a large scale, and govern them by general rules. The contrary was the rock on which the celebrated Jeffries foundered. It goes to the root of all legal science, and admonishes us to burn our libraries.

All the moneys received were promptly applied; and what benefit could the defendants derive from an exhibition of the account? Have they lost anything by withholding it? It may be said, perhaps, that they would have paid, but they had, by a formal resolution, abandoned the concern. The cases cited from chancery are those of receivers or trustees, where the *Chancellor* denied interest because they were not in default.

It is said that both parties expected the

agent would be paid out of the receipts, and even that he had no authority to make advances; but Reid was a general agent confined by no limitation; large advances were required. The Company understood, or, which is the
414*] same thing, were bound to *understand this perfectly. It was known by them that the intestate was making advances; the books were theirs, and, beyond all doubt, they examined and understood nearly the amount of the arrears. If they omitted this, it was their own fault, for which the agent should not suffer. If knowledge were necessary, the court will imply that it existed. Could the Company have expected that our advances should be gratuitous? This would be extravagant; and the strongest expectation of the kind could make no difference. A man sends produce to market; puts it in deposit; and takes up money upon it. No doubt he expects it will sell and meet the advance. This is the expectation of both parties; but was it ever heard that interest should be denied upon the advance, because the avails of the sale happened to fall short of the loan.

The *Lessee of Dilworth* v. *Sinderling*, 1 Binn., 488, settles this case upon authority. The precise questions here. arose in that case. It was there objected that the account of advances remained open. All the decisions upon the subject were canvassed; the case was decided on full argument, and with very great deliberation.

Mr. Butler, in reply. I do not rely upon the English authorities in relation to money lent or advanced. I merely adverted to them in order to show how matters stood in England, and for this purpose cited *Calton* v. *Bragg*, 15 East, 224. That case definitely settles the question, and stops two removes short of allowing interest on moneys advanced, and charged in an open account. It is useful as introductory matter to the history of American decisions, and I am content to submit this case entirely on these. Has any American case gone the length contended for here? *Lessee of Dilworth* v. *Sinderling*, 1 Binn., 494, goes the farthest; and even that case is distinguishable in several particulars. Ld. Ellenborough speaks for himself in *Calton* v. *Bragg*, to which I refer, in reply to the attack which has been made upon him; but I agree that our courts have departed from his rules. This court did so in *Liotard* v. *Graves*, which is principally relied upon against us. I will merely add, in relation to this case, that it was not one of a
415*] running cash *account. Unless the gentleman finds a case of this kind, he does not reach the present. That was placed on the ordinary ground of money received on one side only; not as here, a long history of payment and reimbursement. *Pease* v. *Barber*, 3 Cai., 266, was referred to in order to show that the rule in *Liotard* v. *Graves* was not intended to be universal, but may be qualified by circumstances. This doctrine there advanced by Kent, *J.*, is pronounced by the gentleman mere legal quackery; but the same has been often affirmed before, in relation to this subject, by the most distinguished jurists. It will be seen by the American State Papers (Vol. I., 198, 199, 250, Boston ed., A. D. 1792) that Mr. Hammond, the British Minister, complained to the General Government that interest was not allowed by our courts on claims of the British merchants for debts contracted before the Revolutionary War; although, in the spirit of the Treaty and usage between the two countries, it should be allowed after a year from the time of the contract. Mr. Jefferson, then Secretary of State, replied in these words: "Even in England, the allowance of interest is not given by express law, but rests in the discretion of judges and jurors as arbiters of damages. Sometimes the judge has enlarged the interest to 20 *per cent. per annum.* 1 Ch., 57. In other cases he fixes it habitually one *per cent.* lower than the legal rate (2 Atk., 343); and in a multitude of cases he refuses it altogether. As for instance, no interest is allowed, 1. On arrears of rents, profits or annuities. 1 Ch., 184; 2 P. W., 163; Cast. Talb., 2. 2. For maintenance. Vin. Abr., Interest, C., 10. 3. For moneys advanced by executors. 2 Eq. Abr., 431, 15. 4. For goods sold and delivered. 3 Wils., 206. 5. On books debts, open accounts or simple contracts. 3 Ch., 64; Freem. Ch., 133; Doug., 376. 6. For money lent without a note. 2 Str., 910. 7. On inland bills of exchange, if no protest is taken. 2 Str., 910. 8. On a bond after 20 years. 2 Vern., 448, or after a tender. 9. On a decree in certain cases. Freem. Ch., 181. 10. On judgments in certain cases, as battery and slander. Freem. Ch., 37. 11. On any decrees or judgments in certain courts, as the Exchequer Chamber. *Doug., 753. 12. [*416
On costs. 2 Eq. Abr., 530, 7. And we may add, once for all, that there is no instrument or title to debt so formal or sacred as to give a right to interest on it under all possible circumstances. The words of Ld. Mansfield (Doug., 753), where he says, 'that the question was, what was to be the rule of assessing the damage, and that, in this case, the interest ought to be the measure of the damage, the action being for a debt, but in a case of another sort the rule might be different;' his words (Doug., 376): 'that interest might be payable in cases of delay, if a jury, in their discretion, shall think fit to allow it;' and the doctrine in *Giles* v. *Hart*, 2 Salk., 622, that damages, or interest, are but an accessary to the debt, which may be barred by circumstances, which do not touch the debt itself, suffice to prove that interest is not a part of the debt; neither comprehended in the thing nor in the term; that words which pass the debt do not give interest necessarily; that the interest depends altogether on the discretion of the judges and jurors, who will govern themselves by all existing circumstances; will take the legal interest for the measure of their damages, or more, or less, as they think right; will give it from the date of the contract or a year after, or deny it altogether, according as the fault or the sufferings of the one or the other party shall dictate."

One distinction taken on the other side, between the ground of allowing interest on money and goods, is, that the former is the circulating medium of the country, and produces a profit, whereas the contrary is the case with goods. The gentleman takes the precise reverse of the ancient proposition. Aristotle's reason for denying interest on money is, that it is barren and unproductive, and therefore interest should be denied. *Vide* Ord on Usury, 3. I admit the opposite ground is entitled to about the same weight.

The reason why books of account are not evidence of money lent or advanced is, that they are more rarely made matter of account in the course of business; but surely interest cannot follow from the greater or less degree of strictness in relation to the proof. Nor is the gentleman right in supposing that in all the cases of denying interest on an open ac-
417*] count, *it was for goods sold—not for money The case of *Campbell* v. *Mesier*, 6 Johns. Ch., 21, was of money advanced, but interest was denied till demand. *Potter* v. *Bussey*, 1 Mass., 438; *Storer* v. *Storer*, 9 *Id.*, 37; *Winthrop* v *Carleton*, 12 *Id.*, 4, and *Wyman* v. *Hubbard*, 13 *Id.*, 232, are of the same character. So of *Thompson* v. *Stewart*, 3 Conn. N. S., 171. *Selleck* v. *French*, 1 *Id.*, 32, amounts to the same thing. *Jacobs* v. *Adams*, 1 Dall., 52, and *Williams* v. *Craig*, *Id.*, 313, speak the same language. *Moore's Ex'rs* ads. *Treasurer*, 1 Nott & M'Cord, 214, to the same point. These were all cases of money advanced; and yet interest was denied, either totally, or allowed from a certain time subsequent to the money falling due. *Kane* v. *Smith*, 12 Johns., 156, was also such a case. Nothing, as supposed, rested upon the agreement of the parties. That provided nothing in relation to interest. The Kanes advanced money to buy goods. What else is meant by the term "advances," as used there? The word itself imports money or its equivalent—not goods. The concern was not so extensive or important as the one involved in the present case; and though the Kanes expected a handsome profit, they were not allowed even interest. In truth, that case is on all fours with the present one.

I have challenged the production of a single case in which interest was ever allowed on a mutual running cash account; and the gentleman has resorted to *Lessee of Dilworth* v. *Sinderling*, 1 Binn., 494, in answer. This is the only case which he produces; and I have admitted that the language and reasoning of the court is against me. That was ejectment for lands held in trust by the defendant; and the recovery was subject to the payment of his advances as trustee, to be settled by the court; and the question was, whether he should be allowed interest upon those advances, of which he had kept an account. The court held that he should; and Tilghman, *Ch. J.*, considered this interfering with the old rule that interest was not allowable on money advanced. Now that question might have been decided, without inquiring whether interest be allowable on an account for money lent or advanced. It was the cause of a
418*] *charity; the defendant had no expectation of profit. He could not before account to the children, who were infants. In truth, the case depended upon the principle that a trustee shall neither make gain, nor be accountable for, nor suffer loss in the management of the trust fund. The present is the case of an agent acting under a very liberal compensation. But if *Lessee of Dilworth* v. *Sinderling* be, as supposed, against us, it does not overrule the various cases in this State, Mass., S. C., &c., which stand directly opposed to it. It is but one decision in a court in this country against all the other courts; and *Ch. J.* Tilghman himself, afterwards, in *Brown* v. *Campbell*, 1 Serg. & R., 179, laid down the rule with some qualification. This shows that he did not intend, in the previous case of *Lessee of Dilworth* v. *Sinderling*, to advance a general rule, but leave the matter to depend on circumstances.

The rule we contend for may be applied with ease. The term "open account" has a meaning sufficiently certain, legal and fixed. It is well understood by the law, and the gentleman admits that it is known in the case of goods sold, where interest is denied. It may as easily be known in the case of money advanced; and is recognized in both cases by the Court of Chancery; where you cannot go for an account or *ne exeat*, in certain cases resting properly in *assumpsit*, unless there be an open running account. The term, therefore, is well understood, and, at any rate, there can be no mistake here. An account of 500 items would, by all the world, be emphatically called an open running one.

Lastly, it is said that the court may, nay, will infer an agreement to allow interest, from the circumstances of this case. Perhaps this is the real question in the cause, and it may be necessary to inquire, with a little more particularity, into the state of facts from which courts will make the inference contended for. What, then, is meant by inferring or implying an intent to pay interest, from the circumstances of the case? 1. If the parties have been previously engaged in the same business, and interest has been charged and paid, without objection, as where accounts have been stated *and settled, with an- [***419**
nual rests, &c., even in the case of goods sold, &c. 2. If it be proved that the custom of trade, in a particular place, is to allow interest, either generally or after a particular time of credit; 3. Or the custom of a particular trade, as the American trade with England; 4. Or the practice of a particular merchant, as in every days' practice among us. When these usages are shown, with the fact that the party had, or might have had, knowledge of them, the contract is presumed to have been made with reference to such usage, and an agreement is inferred accordingly. Neither of the cases supposed, exist here. The parties never dealt before, and this is a special business—not of such a nature that any general usage could exist. However fit it might have been for Reid to have exacted interest, in the event of his being in advance, it is a sufficient answer to say that he did not do it. This omission is itself the strongest of all possible reasons against inferring an agreement. The nature of the transaction was not such as to warrant the inference. Both parties expected that the receipts would cover the expenditures; otherwise, they would not have embarked in the business. If this had not been so, there would have been a special contract with Reid to advance. If, then, they did not contemplate Reid's advancing, how could they contemplate the payment of interest on advances? At all events, under this strong expectation, that the receipts would cover the advances, it

was proper, as in *Kane* v. *Smith*, that the defendants should have had notice of the deficiency, before interest began to run. Till this was done, they had every reason to believe that the advances were out of their own funds.

SUTHERLAND, *J.* It is admitted that on Mar. 22, 1822, when the report of the referees was made, the defendants were justly indebted to the plaintiff in the principal sum of $6,882.91; and the only error complained of in the report of the referees, is in the interest allowed to the plaintiff. The principle upon which the interest is to be calculated, and the time to which, are the only questions for the determination of the court.

420*] *It was justly remarked, at the bar, that there is no subject, in the whole range of the English law, on which the authorities are so little in harmony with each other, as on that of interest: and the American authorities are scarcely less contradictory. It may now, however, be considered as settled, in England, that no interest is recoverable upon money lent, money had and received, or paid, laid out and expended, without an express contract for its payment, or proof that the money has actually been used by the defendant, or of special circumstances, from which an agreement to pay interest may be inferred. Where money is lent upon a written security, fixing the day of payment, interest is also recoverable from that day. But where goods are sold upon a credit, no interest is recoverable from the time when the credit expires, without an agreement, either express or implied, to pay it.

In *De Haviland* v. *Bowerbank*, 1 Camph., 50, the question was, whether an agent was responsible for interest upon money had and received, to the use of his principal; and if liable at all, whether interest should run from the time when the money was received, or from the time when payment was demanded. It was held, by Ld. Ellenborough, *Ch. J.*, that no interest could be recovered; and he stated the rule to be, that where money of the plaintiff had come to the hands of the defendant, to establish a right to interest upon it, there should either be a specific agreement to that effect, or something should appear from which a promise to pay interest might be inferred, or proofs should be given of the money being used. *De Bernales* v. *Fuller*, 2 Campb., 426, was also a case of money had and received. Interest was refused; the rule laid down in *De Haviland* v. *Bowerbank* was reiterated, and was also stated to have been confirmed by the Court of K. B. In a note to this case, *Gordon* v. *Swan* is stated, in which the Court of K. B. determined, that interest is not recoverable in an action for goods sold and delivered, to be paid for at a certain day. Bayley, *J.*, observed, that the six months credit was for the **421***] benefit of the purchaser *and meant merely that he should not be arrested or sued till the expiration of that time.

In *Calton* v. *Bragg*, 15 East, 223., the question was, as to a right to recover interest upon money lent. It was argued that there is a difference between the case of money had and received and money actually lent; but the distinction was repelled by the court; and after a consideration of all the authorities, the rule, as laid down by Ld. Ellenborough, in the cases already cited, was fully sactioned and established. *Walker* v. *Constable*, 1, Bos. & P., 306; *Tappenden* v. *Randall*, 2 *Id.*, 472, S. P. His Lordship has been uniform and consistent in the application of this rule; for in *Kingston* v. *M'Intosh*, 1 Camph., 518, he refused interest upon the sum insured in an action upon the policy; in *Atkinson* v. *Lord Braybrooke*, 4 *Id.*, 380, he decided that no interest was recoverable in an action upon a foreign judgment; and in *Crockford* v. *Winter*, 1 *Id.*, 129, he refused interest in an action for money had and received, although the money had been obtained by fraud.

Before the time of Ld. Ellenborough, it had been held, in the case of *Blaney* v *Hendrick*, 3 Wils., 205; 2 Bl., 761, S. C., that interest was recoverable upon an account stated, and upon money lent (*Robinson* v. *Bland*, Bull. *N. P.*, 274–5, S. P.); and in *Trelawney* v. *Thomas*, 1 H. Bl., 305, that it was also recoverable upon money laid out for the use of another, and for money lent, and that the two cases stood upon the same ground of reason, justice and equity; and in *Mountford* v. *Willes*, 2 Bos. & P., 337, interest was allowed in an action for goods sold, from the expiration of the credit given.

Numerous as have been the cases in England, in which this question has been raised and discussed, very little has been said by any of the judges as to the reason or principle upon which the allowance or refusal of interest depends. Ld. Ellenborough, and the other judges who have gone with him upon the subject, seem to consider interest as a demand altogether distinct from, and independent of, the original debt; and not as growing out of, or necessarily connected *with it.(a) [***422** They have, therefore, held that, like every other original demand, it must rest either upon an express or implied promise; and that such promise can never be implied from the circumstances under which the original indebtedness accrued. Thus, Grose, *J.*, in *Calton* v. *Bragg*, 15 East, 223, says: "It is the lender's own fault, if he do not contract for interest when he advances his money. Why should interest be paid at all, without a contract for it? If there be no proof of a contract, it might be given against the intention of the parties at the time of the loan. If they do not then contract for interest, it shows that they did not mean to receive it." In *Crockford* v. *Winter*, 1 Campb., 149, therefore, the court held, as they were bound in consistency to do, that although the money had been obtained by fraud, no interest could be recovered for it; because interest is not given by way of damages, but on the ground of contract only.

Why a promise to pay interest should be implied, from a written instrument to pay money by a day certain, and not from a parol promise, as was held by Ld. Ellenborough, in *Gordon* v. *Swan*, I must confess I cannot understand. The nature of the undertaking is not altered by its being reduced to writing. A parol promise to repay a sum of money bor-

(a) The same view is taken of the subject, in Mr. Jefferson's letter, edited by Butler, *arg.*, in reply, *supra*.

rowed, by a given day, is as obligatory, between the original parties, as though it had been put into the form of a promissory note; and I can perceive no reason why the breach of the one should not be followed by the same legal consequences as the breach of the other.

The strictness of the English courts, upon this subject, has never been adopted by this court, or, I may say, generally by the courts of this country. Thus, in *Pease* v. *Barber*, 3 Cai., 266, it was held that interest may be recovered under a count for money had and received, against the express decision of the English C. B., in *Walker* v. *Constable*, 1 Bos. & P., 307, and *Tappenden* v. *Randall*, 2 *Id.*, 472. The Supreme Court there say: "The **423***] action for money *had and received, is an equitable action, and the party must show that he has equity and conscience on his side. The rule, in equity, is, to allow interest, in many cases, for money had and received.

In *Liotard* v. *Graves*, 3 Cai., 234, it was held, by all the judges, that interest is recoverable upon money paid or advanced, from the date of its advancement; but that, upon an account for goods sold, no interest is recoverable, unless there be evidence of an agreement to pay it, until a liquidation of the account takes place. *Newell* v. *Griswold*, 6 Johns., 45, also decides the latter point.

In *Beals* v. *Guernsey*, 8 Johns., 446, which was an action of trespass against a sheriff, for illegally taking the plaintiff's personal property, interest was allowed by way of damages. The court say: "The plaintiff ought not to be deprived of his property, for years, without compensation for the loss of the use of it; and the jury had a discretion to allow interest in this case, as damages. It has been allowed in actions of trover, and the same rule applies in trespass, when brought for the recovery of property."

In *The People* v. *Gasherie*, 9 Johns., 71, interest was allowed on money which had been collected and applied, by the testator of the defendant, to his own use, from the time when it ought to have been paid over. The court advert to the (then) late English decisions, in which interest had been refused on liquidated sums, and on money obtained by fraud, and express their dissatisfaction with them. They say: "If the defendant retains and converts to his own use the plaintiff's money, he ought to pay interest. It is allowable in actions for money had and received. In trover, for a specific chattel, the jury may, and in many cases ought, to allow interest for the detention, by way of damages."

The case of *Kane* v. *Smith*, 12 Johns., 156, falls within the principle of unliquidated accounts for goods, &c. The advances made by the plaintiffs were not in money, but in cargoes; that is in merchandise. The defendant furnished a cargo of wine, which the plaintiff's ship took to the East Indies, under a special agreement as the manner in which the proceeds should be disposed of. One part of **424***] the agreement *was, that the plaintiffs should be reimbursed out of the net proceeds of the wines, for their advances; and for the surplus of such proceeds, to furnish cargoes to the defendants, or bills on London, allowing interest from the time of the sale in India on the overplus; and should the wines not net sufficient to pay the advances, the defendants were to make up the deficiency. Here, then, was a special agreement, on the part of the plaintiffs, to pay interest on the overplus, if the wines should produce more than their advances; but if they should produce less, the defendants were to make up the deficiency. Nothing was said about interest, from which the inference is very strong that it was the understanding of the parties that they were not to pay interest. It was, therefore, properly disallowed to the plaintiffs, either upon the ground that it was an unliquidated account, in relation to goods, wares and merchandises, or upon the ground of the special agreement.

The same general principles have been established in Mass. and Pa. *Fowler* v. *Shearer*, 7 Mass., 24; *Wood* v. *Robins*, 11 Mass., 504; *Weeks* v. *Hasty*, 13 Mass., 218. These were actions for money paid, and money had and received, and interest was recovered from the time the money was paid or received.

So in *Rapelie* v. *Emory*, 1 Dall., 349, interest was allowed on money had and received. It was put upon the same ground as money lent, and held to be clearly distinguishable from the case of goods sold and delivered, where no money passes between the parties. In *Commonwealth* v. *Crevor*, 3 Binn., 123, Tilghman, *Ch. J.*, says, it is considered as settled, that interest shall be recovered against a man who has received the money of another, and holds it against his consent. *The Lessee of Dilworth* v. *Sinderling*, 1 Binn., 488, is very analogous, so far as the question of interest was concerned, to the one now under consideration. There a trustee was allowed interest upon advances made by him for the use of the *cestui que trust*. Those advances were part of a general unsettled account with the trust estate, composed of charges for expenses and advances in erecting buildings, &c., on the one side, and of credits for *rent received [***425** on the other. The account was of thirty years standing; and the principal advances on which interest was allowed, were made eighteen years before the trial. The *cestuis que trust* were not consulted upon the propriety of making the advances; nor was any account ever rendered by the trustee. It was admitted that the advances made were judicious and proper; and that the trustee had discharged his trust with fidelity. Tilghman, *Ch. J.*, in delivering the opinion of the court, says: "It seems to have been formerly held, that interest was not allowable on an account for money lent and advanced. That opinion gradually declined, upon more mature reflection, and it may now be affirmed to be the settled law, that interest is recoverable for money lent and advanced. Is there anything peculiar in this case to distinguish it from the general rule? If the trustee had borrowed money, he must have paid interest, which would have fallen on the trust estate. Now where is the difference to to the *cestui que trust*, whether interest is paid to the trustee or to a stranger? There is no just cause of complaint, because the jury have allowed interest."

These cases appear to me to put the claim of interest upon its true principle. They consider it as a necessary incident to the principal debt; and imply a promise to pay it from the day the debt becomes due, if it is not paid. This promise is supported by the universal obligation which rests upon every man to render a just equivalent for the use or detention of that which does not belong to him. The value of money is the legal rate of interest. That, then, shall be paid.

In actions sounding in tort, where no contract can be supposed to exist, the same rule of compensation may be adopted for the improper detention of specific articles of personal property; but it shall be given by way of damages, and not as interest.

No interest shall be allowed upon an unliquidated account for goods, wares, and merchandise, without an agreement to allow it either expressed or implied; because the balance of the account, only, constitutes the debt, and until that is ascertained, there is, strictly speaking, no debt due. This appears from the manner in which an account may be proved. **426***] *It is not necessary to show the delivery of each article; but proof that some were delivered, and that the plaintiff keeps honest and fair books of account, &c., is evidence of the delivery of all the articles charged in the book. Thus, the whole account is considered as one transaction. But an unliquidated account for money paid, laid out and expended, stands upon a different footing. Each advance of money is a loan, distinct and independent of any other advance. It is not, strictly speaking, matter of account. Each charge must be specifically proved. The proof of several advances, together with the keeping of correct books of account, would not be evidence of the other advances charged in the same account. Each sum paid, or laid out, must, therefore, be considered a debt, due from the time it is advanced, and, of course, carrying interest, unless there be some agreement to the contrary.

The reason sometimes given, why an unliquidated account should not carry interest, viz.: "that the defendant does not know how much he has to pay," can not be the true one. It would be a sufficient answer to it, to say that he can always ascertain the balance by application to the plaintiff. But again; an agreement, either expressed or implied, to pay interest on the different items of an account, either from the day of their delivery, or after a given credit, will be effectual. But, notwithstanding such agreement, the defendant is as ignorant of the balance of the account as though it had not been made. If such ignorance, therefore, was the ground for refusing interest, it would not and ought not to be allowed, notwithstanding the agreement. But such agreement breaks up and destroys the individuality of the account, and renders each item a distinct independent debt, due at the time agreed upon, and, of course, carrying interest from that time.

But whether this reasoning be sound or not is of very little importance. For I conceive the principle which it is intended to illustrate to be fully established in the case of *Liotard* v. *Graves*, and of *The Lessees of Dilworth* v. *Sinderling*, already cited, viz.: that an unliquidated account for money paid, or lent, does carry interest. Whenever *it is said, [***427** therefore, that no interest is recoverable upon an unliquidated account, an account other than for money lent, or advanced, or had and received, must be understood.

To apply these principles to the case before us. In May, 1813, Reid entered upon the duties of active agent for the defendants. The case states, "that, at that time, the stock, materials and funds of the defendants were insufficient to keep the factory in operation; and large advances were required for that purpose. No express authority or direction was given to Reid to make the advances; but if they were necessary to keep the factory in operation, and no provision was made by the Company for them, an authority to the agent to procure them was necessarily implied. It must be understood that the defendants were well informed of the state of their affairs when Reid entered upon the agency. Knowing, then, that advances were necessary to keep the works in operation, and it being the business and duty of the agent to keep them in operation, the fact of his appointment as agent, under such circumstances, implied an authority to make advances, or borrow money for the purpose. His skill and fidelity in the management of the concerns of the Company have not been called in question. It is not pretended that the advances exceeded the agencies of the concern, or that they have not been proved and established with the most scrupulous exactness.

The case states that the debtor side of the plaintiff's account consisted of more than 500 charges, for distinct advances, each of which was clearly proved. The particular purposes to which the money thus advanced was applied is not stated in the case. That they were such as came within the scope of the authority of a general agent, there can be no doubt, or the plaintiff's demand would have been resisted on that ground. But the only ground of complaint is, that the intestate did not render his account, and apprise the defendants that it was a losing concern. No reluctance was ever manifested by him to account. His account was never asked for until 1819, when he stated to some of the Directors that the Company were in his debt; *but no [***428** formal demand of his account was then made. He appears to have exerted himself faithfully and successfully in collecting the funds of the Company, and applying them to the discharge of their debt; and there is nothing in the case from which the slightest impression can be derived that the Company could or would have made other or more advantageous arrangements, if they had been fully apprised of the state of the account. All the Directors, and most of the stockholders of the Company, resided in the same city with the plaintiff, where the business was conducted; and it is hardly to be supposed that they were not individually informed of the true state of their affairs, although no formal report was ever made to a board of directors. It appears to me, therefore, that upon every principle of justice and equity, Reid's representatives are entitled to interest upon the moneys advanced by him for the use of the Company, at least until 1819, when some of the individual Directors asked him for his account.

I think he is not entitled to interest upon his compensation as agent. No agreement was ever made as to the amount which he was to receive. His predecessor, it is true, had received $1,250; but the Company were not concluded by that circumstance from lessening the compensation to him, if, either from the diminished duties of the station, or the state of their funds, they thought it expedient. There was nothing by which either party was concluded as to the amount of compensation. It could be recovered only upon a *quantum meruit;* and must be considered as an uncertain and unliquidated demand; and therefore cannot carry interest until demand made. *Trelawney* v. *Thomas*, 1 H. Bl., 305, per Gould, *J.* With these modifications, I am of opinion that the report of the referees should be confirmed.

SAVAGE, *Ch. J.* The questions for the decision of the court are, whether the plaintiff is entitled to interest on any part of her demand; and if any, on what part, and for what time.

To decide these questions correctly, it seems to me important to understand what was the
429*] agreement between the *parties; and if nothing was expressed as to the mode of carrying on the business, what they must have understood to be the contract between them in this respect. Reid was a stockholder from the organization of the Company. He knew, and so did the defendants, how the business had been carried on. Whether it had been profitable while Kane was agent, does not appear; nor whether he made the necessary advances during that time. In 1809 five stockholders took a lease of the works for three years. In May, 1812, a partnership was formed between the defendants and Reid & Alsop, in which it was stipulated that Reid & Alsop should make the necessary advances of money, and receive interest for it. They did so; but whether the copartnership was profitable or otherwise, does not appear, except that, on settlement, a balance was due to the defendants.

It is stated in the case, that when Reid was appointed agent in 1813, "the stock, materials and funds of the defendants were insufficient to keep the factory in operation, and large advances were required for that purpose." What, then, was the understanding of the parties as to the manner of carrying on the business? How were those advances to be made, and by whom? And on what terms? Without funds the business could not be prosecuted. Had the defendants intended to furnish the necessary funds themselves, they would have made a further call upon the stockholders. Not having done so, they must have intended that the advances should be procured in some other way; and, of course, by the agent, as he was the only active person engaged in the business, and had, the preceding year, made the advances in the same business. It was certainly no part of his duty, as agent, to make advances from his own funds. Suppose it had not been in his power to do this: the defendants did not furnish them; and suppose that, under these circumstances, he had borrowed the necessary amount. Would it be contended that he should pay the interest himself? Why should he do this? Was he to be benefited by the use of the money? Or was it the defendants, the principals for whom the agent acted, who were to receive the contemplated profits *from the use of the money borrowed? [***430**
The agent had no further interest in the profits than as a stockholder. It was the same thing to the defendants, whether they had advanced the funds themselves, or had borrowed them. In the first case, they would have diverted so much money, which was producing them, at least, the interest; in the second, they were taking the interest of their own money to pay the interest of that which was borrowed to carry on the factory—so that whether the agent borrowed the money of others, or advanced his own, was precisely the same thing to the defendants. The interest of the capital employed, is certainly a proper item to charge in ascertaining the profit or loss in the prosecution of any business; and had the business, in this instance, been profitable, I apprehend the objection would not have been thought of. On the other hand, is there any principle of law or justice, which requires an agent to carry on the business of his principal at his own expense?

It was contended on the argument, that interest is not recoverable on an unliquidated account for moneys, unless there be an agreement to pay interest, express or implied, or a fraudulent detention or vexatious delay; and that the case under consideration comes within that principle. A review of some of the cases on this subject may be of use.

The oldest case cited is that of *Sweatland* v. *Squire*, 2 Salk., 623, A. D. 1699, where it is said by Powell, *J.*, that interest is recovered by way of damages, when damages are recovered *ratione detentionis debiti*; but not when damages only are recovered: for interest is not recovered *occasione dampnorum*. In the *Attorney-General* v. *The Brewer's Co.*, 1 P. Wms., 376, A. D. 1717, the defendants were trustees of a charity; and, by improving the trust estate, had brought the charity in debt. On rendering an account, Ld. Cowper refused to allow interest before the confirmation of the master's report; for, until then, it was not a liquidated sum. In *Harris* v. *Benson*, 2 Str., 910, A. D. 1732, the *Chief Justice* said interest had never been allowed for money lent, without a note. In *Robinson* v. *Bland*, 2 Burr., 1085, A. D. 1760, it was decided that interest was recoverable *on money lent, from [***431**
the time when it was agreed to be paid. In *Borret* v. *Goodere*, 1 Dick., 428, A. D. 1769, Ld. Camden said there is no instance where interest is given on an open mutual account, without some particular circumstances. That was a case of cash advances, as appears from a full report of it in 6 Bro. P. C., 364. *Blaney* v. *Hendricks*, 2 Bl. 761, A. D., 1770, allowed interest on an account stated; and the judges remarked, that it was properly allowable on money lent. In *Trelawney* v. *Thomas*, 1 H. Bl., 304, A. D. 1789, Gould, *J.*, said interest was recoverable on money lent; and that money laid out for the use of another, and money lent, stood on the same ground in respect to reason, justice and equity, but that no interest should be allowed for work and labor, or goods sold and delivered. Upon the authority of this case, Livermore, in his Treatise on Agency (Vol. II., p. 17), lays down the rule that an agent who has

advanced money for his principal, will be entitled to interest from the time of the advance. In *Craven* v. *Tickell*, 1 Ves., Jr., 63, A. D. 1789, Ld. Thurlow said, money paid to workmen, who were to have been paid by the defendant, was money advanced for him; and that it was the constant practice at Guildhall, either by the contract or in damages, to give interest upon every debt detained. In *Walker* v. *Constable*, 1 Bos. & P., 307, A. D. 1798, the court were of opinion that, in an action for money had and received, no interest could be recovered. In *Mountford* v. *Willes*, 2 Bos. & P., 337, A. D. 1800, interest was allowed on goods sold, after the term of credit agreed on had expired. In *Tappenden* v. *Randall*, 2 Bos. & P., 471, A. D. 1801, the rule, as previously laid down in *Walker* v. *Constable*, was adhered to; and *Moses* v. *M'Farlan*, 2 Burr., 1005, was cited, where it is incidentally said, that the plaintiff can recover no more than the money retained by the defendant, against conscience. In *De Haviland* v. *Bowerbank*, 1 Campb., 50, A. D. 1807, Ld. Ellenborough said, where money of the plaintiff had come to the hands of the defendant, interest ought not to be recovered, without an agreement, or something from which an agreement might be inferred, or proof that the money had been 432*] used. In *De *Bernales* v. *Fuller*, 2 Campb., 426, A. D. 1810, he adhered to the same rule; and the whole Court of K. B. concurred, that the money should not draw interest even after a demand of payment; and afterwards, in *Calton* v. *Bragg*, 15 East, 223, A. D. 1812, the same judge said that Ld. Mansfield had sat in the K. B. for upwards of 30 years, and Ld. Kenyon for more than 13 years; that he had been there above 9 years; and during all that time no case had occurred where interest had been allowed upon money lent without an agreement for it, or for the payment of the principal, at a certain time, or under special circumstances, from which a contract might be inferred.

In *Rapelie* v. *Emory*, 1 Dall., 349, A. D. 1788, it was ruled by Shippen, *President*, that when one man has received the money of another, and retains it without his consent, it is to be considered in the same light as money lent, and should carry interest. In *Crawford* v. *Willing*, 4 Dall., 289, A. D. 1803, Smith, *J.*, said: "Whatever may have been the doctrine in former times, we have traced, with pleasure, the progress of improvement, upon the subject of interest, to the honest and rational rule, that wherever one man retains the money of another, against his declared will, the legal compensation for the use of money shall be charged and allowed; and that, in the case of goods sold, interest should be allowed after the time of credit had elapsed, and demand of payment was made. In *Lessee of Dilworth* v. *Sinderling*, 1 Binn., 494, A. D. 1808, Tilghman, *Ch. J.*, declared the law to be settled, that interest is recoverable on an account for money lent and advanced; and it was allowed to a trustee, upon advances laid out in improvements upon the trust estate, it appearing that the improvements were necessary and proper. In *The Commonwealth* v. *Crevor*, 3 Binn., 123, A. D. 1810, he says it is settled, that interest shall be recovered against a man who receives the money of another and holds it against his consent. In *Brown* v. *Campbell*, 1 Serg. & R., 179, A. D. 1814, he again says, the rule is, to allow interest where the defendant has retained the money of the plaintiff unlawfully, and against his consent; that, until the defendant was informed that the plaintiff's money was applied to his *use, he was in no default, and [*433 therefore ought not to pay interest; but being informed, he became a wrong-doer in withholding payment, and therefore should pay interest.

In *Wood* v. *Robbins*, 11 Mass., 504, A. D. 1814, the defendant had fraudulently obtained possession of the plaintiff's money; and Putnam, *J.*, after reviewing most of the authorities, says there may be cases where interest should not be allowed, as where the defendant was a mere stockholder, ready to pay the money to the party entitled; but when the defendant has fraudulently obtained the money, or wrongfully detained it, he must be charged with interest. In *Winthrop* v. *Carleton*, 12 Mass., 4, A. D. 1815, the plaintiff, as consignee, made necessary advances, and recovered interest on them after suit brought.

In Connecticut, as appears by *Selleck* v. *French*, 1 Conn. N. S., 32, 35, per Swift, *J.*, A. D. 1814, interest is allowed on the ground of a contract expressed or implied, or as damages for the breach of a contract, or the violation of some duty, *e. g.*: 1. Upon an express contract. 2. Upon an implied contract, arising from the usage of trade, or former dealings between the parties. 3. Upon a written contract to pay at a day certain, as on bills and notes, and on a policy after the money becomes due. 4. For goods sold, after the time of credit has expired. 5. For money received to the use of another, and retained contrary to duty. 6. For money obtained fraudulently, if the tort is waived, and *assumpsit* brought. 7. On a liquidated account. 8. On book account for services performed or articles sold, when, from the nature of the transaction, it appears not to be the intention of the parties that the services or articles were to rest on the footing of a mutual account on book. 9. But where there are mutual accounts, founded on mutual dealings, unless there be some promise or usage to pay interest, it will not be allowed. In such cases, no time of payment is stipulated; each party is making payment; the balance is constantly changing; and the presumption is, that no interest is to be charged. In the case then before the court, interest was allowed; there were no mutual dealings; the advances were all on the part of the plaintiff; there was no liquidated account, nor promise, nor usage; but the debt was *due, and payment [*434 unreasonably delayed. The particular circumstances of the case are not stated. See, also, *Thompson* v. *Stewart*, 3 Conn. N. S., 171, 185, A. D. 1819.

In *Gammell* v. *Skinner*, 2 Gall., 45, A. D. 1814, interest was denied on seamen's wages, until after demand made; and where there had been no actual demand, it was held to run from the commencement of the suit.

In this State there have been several decisions on the subject of interest, which apply to most of the questions under consideration. *Liotard* v. *Graves*, 3 Cai., 226, A. D. 1805, is a leading case. There, an account current had been rendered in 1797, containing a charge of interest, which was not objected to in the succeeding correspondence between the parties. Spencer, *J.*, says, that for goods sold and delivered, unless there be evidence of an agreement to pay interest, none is recoverable until liquidation; that an account transmitted to a debtor, and acquiesced in, becomes liquidated, and interest is allowable; that on money advanced interest is legally demandable; and so by the usage of a particular trade. Thompson, *J.*, said the plaintiffs had a right to charge interest on the money advanced; that the account could not be considered settled, and on that ground carrying interest; that it was merely an account current between the parties; and unless some usage or practice was shown to warrant the allowance, he should think interest ought not to be calculated except on the money advanced. Livingston, *J.*, said: "If there be no special agreement between the parties, or usage of trade to the contrary, it ought to be allowed on all moneys advanced from their respective payments. One account is rendered as early as 1797, in which interest is calculated, and yet no objection is made to it in the succeeding correspondence, from which I conclude such charge consisted with the understanding of the parties." Kent, *Ch. J.*, said, "the account exhibited is not an account liquidated, but a naked account current; and interest is allowable only on such items in it as are for moneys advanced, except the usage of trade has provided some particular rules on the subject." At the next term, the case of *Pease* v. *Barber*, 3 **435***] Cai., 266, A. D. *1805, was decided. It did not state any facts, but the question was submitted, whether interest could, in any case, be recovered under a count for money had and received. Kent, *Ch. J.*, delivered the opinion of the court, that interest may be recovered in such an action. He says there may be cases in which the defendant ought to refund the principal merely; and there may be other cases in which he ought, *ex equo et bono*, to refund the principal with interest. Each case will depend upon the justice and equity arising out of its peculiar circumstances, to be disclosed at the trial. In an anonymous case (1 Johns., 315, A. D. 1806), the court said the general rule is, that interest is not to be recovered on unliquidated damages, or for an uncertain demand. The question arose in an action upon a policy of insurance, and they said it was a case for the discretion of a jury. *Newell* v. *Griswold*, 6 Johns., 45, A. D. 1810, was *assumpsit* for goods sold; and there were mutual accounts; but no account stated, or balance struck. The court said, "there is nothing in the course of dealing between the parties from which an intent or agreement to allow interest can be inferred. It is, therefore, not a case of interest." In *Holliday* v. *Marshall*, 7 Johns., 213, A. D. 1810, the plaintiff had procured an appraisement of certain buildings under a covenant in a lease, of which the defendant had notice. The plaintiff claimed interest on the appraisement; but the court said it was not conclusive; that the value of the buildings was open for inquiry at the trial; and the damages were, therefore, unliquidated; and no interest was recoverable. In *The People* v. *Gasherie*, 9 Johns., 71, A. D. 1812, a recovery was had for money retained by a loan officer, with interest from the time when he ought to have paid it into the treasury. The court said: "It is just and reasonable, in itself, that the defendant, who retains and converts the money of another to his own use, should pay interest for that use." And they declared *Crockford* v. *Winter*, 1 Campb., 128, and *De Bernales* v. *Fuller*, 2 Camph., 426, not to be law here. In *Kane* v. *Smith*, 12 Johns., 156, A. D. 1815, the plaintiffs, at N. Y., sent to the defendants at Madeira, pursuant to an agreement, certain *vessels, which were to be employed [***436** in carrying wines to the East Indies. The plaintiffs were to advance two thirds of the invoice price of the wines, to be reimbursed out of their net proceeds; and should these be insufficient to pay the advances, then the defendants were to make up the deficiency. The wines, contrary to the expectation of the parties, did not prove sufficient to reimburse the plaintiffs for their advances; and on the question whether the interest should be allowed upon these, the court said the plaintiffs were not entitled to interest, till the deficiency was ascertained and notified to the defendants; that the wines went in the plaintiffs' vessel; that they alone could ascertain the proceeds, and furnish the accounts of sales to show the balance; that the defendants were not in default, till the balance was ascertained and notified to them. *Thomas* v. *Weed*, 14 Johns., 255, A. D. 1817, was an action of debt upon the statute, against a constable, for not returning an execution. The court recognize the law that interest is recoverable for money received by the defendant for the plaintiff, or lost by negligence; but the form of the action precluded its allowance in that case. In *Walden* v. *Sherburne*, 15 Johns., 424, A. D. 1818, Spencer, *J.*, says: "We have uniformly decided, that after an account has been liquidated it carries interest; and that an account is to be considered liquidated after it is rendered, if objections are not made to it."

In *Campbell* v. *Mesier*, 6 Johns. Ch., 24, A. D. 1822, *Chancellor* Kent says, "it is the settled rule in the law of this State, that money received or advanced for the use of another carries interest after a default in payment; and it is a very reasonable and just rule."

From an examination of these cases, it seems that interest is allowed: 1. Upon a special agreement. 2. Upon an implied promise to pay it; and this may arise from usage between the parties, or usage of a particular trade. 3. Where money is withheld against the will of the owner. 4. By way of punishment for any illegal conversion or use of another's property. 5. Upon advances of cash, on the authority of *Liotard* v. *Graves*.

*Among all the cases examined, [***437** however, I do not find any one precisely parallel to the present. Here, both parties were upon the spot when the business was transacted. The agent acted almost constantly under the eye of his principals. The reason why the court would not give interest in *Kane* v. *Smith*, 12 Johns., 156, till rendering the account, was, that the plaintiffs alone knew the fact that the proceeds of the wine did not reimburse the advances. In this case, it may be said, that Reid alone knew he had not been reimbursed for his advances by the proceeds of the glass. He alone kept the books; but it is equally certain that the defendants knew of his advances, and they might have known the state of the accounts by inspecting the books. They often held their meetings at Reid's store, where the books were undoubtedly kept.

But was it not his duty, as agent, to have rendered accounts regularly to his principals, and to have kept them advised of the true state of their affairs? There certainly appears to have been a culpable negligence on both sides. The defendants do not seem to have appointed any committee, to examine Reid's accounts, as they did Kane's, when he was their agent.

The defendants, having agreed to pay interest upon the advances made by Reid & Alsop, admitted, in that instance, at least, the propriety of such a charge against them. And on the whole, I am of opinion, that from the manner in which the business had been done, the year next previous to the appointment of Reid as agent, from this being done, with a full knowledge on both sides that large advances were necessary, if the defendants did not mean to pay interest, they ought so to have informed Reid, in order that he might not be using a large capital in their service when it was to be totally unproductive to him. Although Reid had the means of ascertaining the true state of the accounts, yet he had not the sole means. The defendants were equally able to determine by an inspection of the books whether he had been reimbursed for his advances. The case does not inform us that
438*] *any intimation was given by Reid of a balance due to him till the 1st of Jan., 1819, though the factory was burnt May 3, 1815. Nor does it appear, that before the 1st of Jan., 1819, any step whatever was taken by the defendants to ascertain their standing with Reid. After that time Reid alone was in fault, as he neglected to furnish an account, and none was rendered till after his death. I think, therefore, that interest is properly chargeable on the moneys advanced from the time of such advances respectively to the time when there was an attempt by the defendants to liquidate and settle the account.

As to the compensation for Reid's services, no sum was ever agreed upon between the parties; and his claim for these was never liquidated till it was done by the referees. Interest ought not, therefore, be allowed on his salary.

WOODWORTH, *J.*, being a stockholder in the Company, gave no opinion.

RULE: That the report of the referees, made in this cause, be set aside, so far as it allows interest to the plaintiff, after Jan. 2, 1819; and on the charges for the salary due the intestate; and that in pursuance of the stipulation of the parties, the cause be again referred to the referees appointed therein; and that they calculate and report the amount due to the plaintiff for interest up to Jan. 2, 1819: and in addition to the sum reported to be due to her; and that the calculation be made by allowing interest on the receipts and advances of cash, from the time of making or receiving the same, to the said Jan. 2; and that neither party be allowed, as against the other, costs of the motion to set aside the report.

Affirmed—5 Cow., 587.
Cited in—4 Cow., 498; 5 Cow., 334; 6 Cow., 195; 10 Wend., 97; 5 Den., 137; 8 N. Y., 157; 10 N. Y., 197; 15 N. Y., 403; 3 Hun, 218; 10 Hun, 526; 2 Barb., 666; 4 Barb., 47; 17 Barb., 456; 41 Barb., 22; 5 T. & C., 677; 26 How. Pr., 237; 58 How. Pr., 324; 12 Abb. N. S., 242; 1 Bradf., 234; 63 How. Pr., 337; 37 Wis., 152.

---

*GENERAL RULE. [*439

IN SUPREME COURT, October Term, November, 13, 1824.

ORDERED, that when a bill of exceptions is taken at the Circuit, the party obtaining a verdict may notice the bill of exceptions for argument as frivolous, and the same shall have a preference, as in case of a frivolous demurrer, unless the party taking such exception shall, within four days after the trial, or before the same is noticed for argument, obtain, and serve on the opposite party, a certificate of the circuit judge, that there is probable cause to stay the proceedings, until the cause is reached in its regular order on the calendar.

[END OF OCTOBER TERM, 1824.]

CASES ARGUED AND DETERMINED

IN THE

Court for the Trial of Impeachments

AND THE

CORRECTION OF ERRORS

OF THE

STATE OF NEW YORK,

IN APRIL, 1824.

WILLIAM SEYMOUR, *Appellant*,

v.

THOMAS J. DELANCY ET AL., *Respondents.*

Contract for Exchange of Lands—Bill, in Chancery, for Specific Performance—Discretion of the Court—What Party Claiming Performance, Must Show—Inadequacy of Price, as Defense to Bill for Specific Performance—When Agreement Ordered Delivered up to be Canceled—Effect of Possession, Under Contract—Title of Vendor—Loss of Vendor's Remedy at Law.

Whether a Court of Chancery shall decree the specific performance of an agreement or not, is a matter resting in its discretion; but this is a sound legal discretion.

The party claiming performance must present a case fair, just and reasonable; the contract to be performed must have been entered into upon adequate consideration; and must be free from fraud, misrepresentation or surprise; and it must not be hard, unconscionable, or unequal.

Where the inadequacy of price, in a contract to sell or convey, is so inadequate as to be conclusive evidence of fraud, as where it would shock the moral sense of an indifferent man, a Court of Chancery should not carry it into effect.

But inadequacy of price, merely, without being such as to prove fraud conclusively, the contract being entered into deliberately, and fair in all its parts, is not an objection to its being executed.

The cases upon this point of mere inadequacy cited, and the substance of them stated in chronological order, per Savage, *Ch. J.*

A Court of Chancery requires stronger reasons for setting aside an agreement, or delivering it up to be canceled, than would be sufficient to warrant denying a specific performance.

446*] *So a Court of Chancery will, in many cases, not disturb an agreement executed, though it might have denied a specific performance.

It will order an agreement to be delivered up to be canceled for fraud, circumvention or misrepresentation.

Drunkenness. Cases cited by counsel, upon the question, how far this shall operate as a defense against a bill for the specific performance of a contract.

On a bill filed by the vendor, to compel a specific performance, it is sufficient, if he can make a good title at the time of the decree, unless he has been quickened by the vendee, or time be of the essence of the contract; as where it relates to stocks or personal chattels.

It is, in general, no objection, that the vendor's remedy is gone at law, by reason of there being a mortgage on the estate, &c., so that he could not convey a good title at the day fixed upon by the contract.

Cases to this point cited in their chronological order, per Savage, *Ch. J.*

It is the peculiar province of courts of equity to interfere, where the remedy is defective at law, if such interference be not against conscience.

Citations—Reeve Dom. Rel., 386; Newland Cont., 89, 223, 224; 2 Sch. & L., 347, 352; Cas. t. Talb., 236: 12 Ves., 331; 1 Ves., Jr., 566; 7 Ves., 30, 35, 202; 9 Ves., 246, 603, 608; 2 Bro. P. C., 396, 398, 415; 3 Atk., 383, 412; 2 Atk., 133; 1 Ves., 12, 220; 2 Ves., 279, 307: 13 Ves., 37, 238; 2 Cox, 77: 1 Cox, 428; 10 Ves., 292, 301, 315, 470; 16 Ves., 33, 83; 3 Ves. & B., 187, 193; 2 Bro. Ch., 118, 179, 605, *n*; 2 Vern., 423; 1 Bro. Ch., 556, 567, 156; 8 Ves., 518; 18 Ves., 10; 1 Vern., 271, 272: 3 Bro. Ch., 228; 5 Vin., 539 to 549; 1 Dess., 257, 263, 382, 398; 1 Wash., 279; 2 Binn., 133; 2 Johns. Ch., 23; 2 P. Wms., 630: 6 Wh., 528; 5 Cr., 262; 1 Wh., 195, 196; 11 Johns., 525: 9 Johns., 466; Gilb., 155, 156; Sug. Vend., 281: 2 Pow. Cont., 266, 267; 3 Eq. Abr., 690; 6 Ves., 646; 2 Johns., 595, 614.

ON appeal from the Court of Chancery. On Mar., 14, 1821, the appellant filed his bill in the Court of Chancery, against the respondents, the real and personal representatives of

---

NOTE.—*Specific performance—When decreed by court of equity.* See, generally, Pratt v. Carroll, 8 Cranch, 471; Hepburn v. Dunlop, 1 Wh., 180; Colson v. Thompson, 2 Wh., 336; Brashier v. Grats, 6 Wh., 528, *notes* Law. ed.

Inadequacy of price—Not sufficient ground for setting aside contract, unless such as to shock the conscience and amount in itself to satisfactory evidence of fraud. 1 Story Eq. Jur., sec. 241.

Some cases seem to support the doctrine that mere inadequacy of price is sufficient to defeat an action for specific performance. See Falcke v. Gray, 4 Drew & Sm., 651; 5 Jur. N. S., 645; Lear v. Chouteau, 23 Ill., 42; Andrews v. Andrew, 28 Ala., 432; Gasque v. Small, 2 Strobh. Eq., 72. Compare, also, Conrad v. Schwamb, 53 Wis., 372.

But the weight of authority is the other way. See Shaddle v. Disborough, 30 N. J. Eq., 370; Ready v. Noakes, 29 N. J. Eq., 497; Haywood v. Cope, 25 Beaw., 140; Harrison v. Town, 17 Mo., 237; Powers v. Hale, 25 N. H., 145; Lee v. Kirby, 104 Mass., —; Western R. R. Co. v. Babcock, 6 Met., 346; Erwin v. Parham, 12 How., 197; Galloway v. Barr, 12 Ohio, 354; Park v. Johnson, 4 Allen, 259. See, also, cases referred to in table of citations at end of principal case.

As to exercise of judicial discretion as to decreeing specific performance, see Quinn v. Roath, 37 Conn., 16; McComas v. Easley, 21 Gratt., 23; Sherman v. Wright, 49 N. Y., 227; Burling v. King, 2 T. & C., 545; Kelso v. Lorillard, 85 N. Y., 177.

Thomas Ellison, deceased, to compel the specific performance of articles of agreement made between the appellant and Thomas Ellison, in his lifetime, dated Jan. 14, 1820, by which Ellison covenanted that he would, on or before June 1, 1820, convey to the appellant, in fee, a certain lot, situate in the Town of Montgomery, and another lot situate in the Town of Walkill, both in the County of Orange, with covenants for quiet enjoyment, and against incumbrances, also, with covenants of seisin and warranty; and for further assurance—in consideration of which premises, the appellant covenanted that he would, on or before June 1, 1820, convey to Ellison, in fee, the one equal undivided third part of two lots in the village of Newburgh, in Orange Co., with a stipulation that each might enter into immediate possession of the premises so to be conveyed to him, and have and receive the profits to his own use. The parties, shortly after, took possession accordingly, which had continued to the time of filing the bill.

The bill stated that the appellant had always been ready to execute a conveyance, according to his covenant; but set up, as an excuse for not having done it in Ellison's life-

447*] *time, that he was, for several months previous to his death, which happened Aug. 3, 1820, incapable of business; that some of his heirs were infants, and therefore incapable of executing the contract.

The grounds of defense insisted upon by the answer were: 1. That, before the articles were executed, the appellant had conveyed some part, or the whole of his right in the Newburgh lots, to his sister, Esther Seymour, and that his title was very questionable. 2. That the bargain or agreement, as contained in the articles, was a most unconscionable one on the part of the appellant, inasmuch as the lots in Montgomery and Walkill exceeded the value of the Newburgh lots several thousand dollars. 3. That the appellant could not, during the lifetime of Ellison, have made a good title to the Newburgh lots; for that, independent of the questions which existed in relation to the title when the articles were executed, and which remained at the time of the answer, the appellant and his wife had mortgaged these premises to Thomas Buckley and John B. Lawrence, to secure $5,000, with interest, which remained unpaid till after Ellison's death, and until a short time previous to filing the bill. 4. That the appellant had never offered to execute a deed, pursuant to the articles, nor required a deed of Ellison, though he was, from the time of executing the articles to the 1st day of June, thereafter, when the conveyances were, by the articles, to have been executed, perfectly capable of transacting business.

To this answer, the appellant filed a general replication, and testimony was taken, in the cause, to the above points stated in the answer.

The inadequacy of price insisted on by the answer was established—to what degree the judges who passed upon the evidence differed, as will be seen by their opinions. The mortgage upon the Newburgh lots was also proved to have existed, as insisted by the answer. Proof was likewise taken as to the mental capacity of Ellison to make the bargain in question, the respondents insisting that he was disqualified by habits of intoxication, and the appellant denying this. The evidence upon the point was contradictory. For this I also refer to the opinions delivered, as well as for *the proof in relation to Ellison's ca- [*448 pacity to have fulfilled the articles. The testimony in the cause was very voluminous, occupying, in the abstract printed for the use of the court, more than 100 pages. I forbear stating it, because all that may be material to the questions raised by the counsel or determined by the court, will be found in the opinions of the *Chancellor* and judges.

Aug. 7th, 1822, the Court of Chancery declared, that from the great inadequacy in value of the Newburgh lots, compared with the two farms in Montgomery and Walkill; also from the habits of intoxication in which Ellison had indulged in the last years of his life, and the mental debility produced thereby; also from the want of readiness and ability in the complainant, to convey a good and unincumbered title, at the time fixed for the performance of the contract, or at any time after, during the life of Ellison, the articles ought not, in equity and good conscience, to be decreed to be carried into effect; and dismissed the bill, with costs.

The late *Chancellor* Kent assigned the reasons for this decree, as in 6 Johns. Ch., 223 to 235, S. C.

Mr. J. Duer, for the appellant, submitted the following points:

1. That there was, in fact, no material inadequacy of consideration.

2. That it was a speculation on the part of Ellison, and any trifling inadequacy of value that may appear arises from subsequent circumstances.

3. That, in addition to the evidence offered by the manner in which the bargain was negotiated, the direct testimony in the cause, as to Ellison's competency, is conclusive in favor of the appellant.

4. That the negotiation between the parties was honorably conducted, and the agreement just, fair and equal in all its parts.

After examining the case very fully, in relation to these questions of fact, an outline of which is given in the opinions of the *Chief Justice* and Sudam, *Senator*, he proceeded to the discussion of the following legal points:

*1. That inadequacy of considera- [*449 tion is not, of itself, a sufficient ground to deny a specific performance.

2. That occasional intoxication is no ground of defense in any case, or under any circumstances.

3. The existence of a mortgage upon property agreed to be sold or conveyed is no reason for refusing a decree of specific performance; and the appellant was not otherwise in fault.

4. That the appellant is without remedy at law.

He said there are two classes of cases, in which a Court of Chancery will enforce the specific performance of a contract: 1. Where the party seeking the performance has lost his remedy at law by accident, or not by his own culpable neglect or omission. In such case a specific execution of the contract ought not to be refused except upon such grounds as would justify the court in setting it aside. 2. Inadequacy of price, unless so gross as to be in itself evidence of fraud, or unless accompanied by circumstances of fraud or misrepresentation in the party seeking performance, or surprise, ignorance, mistake, delusion or incapacity of mind on the other side, is no ground for refusing a specific performance.

At law, where a party would recover damages, he must show a literal compliance with a condition precedent; but, as an omission of this does not affect the equity of the claim, chancery will will yet relieve. *Davis* v. *Hone*, 2 Sch. & L., 347, lays down the general doctrine on the subject, and partially illustrates it. Ld. Redesdale says: "a court of equity frequently decrees specific performance where the action at law has been lost by the default of the very party seeking the performance, if it be, notwithstanding, conscientious that the agreement should be performed; as in case where the terms of the agreement have not been strictly performed on the part of the person seeking specific performance; and, to sustain an action at law, performance must be averred according to the very terms of the contract. Nothing but specific execution of the contract, so far as it can be executed, will do justice in such a case." His Lordship refers **450***] to a loss *of the remedy by neglect. The interposition of the court may be still more imperiously called for where it is gone by the sickness, absence or death of the party. In case of his death, the obligation descends upon the heir. *Holtham* v. *Ryland*, Nels., 205.

There is a well grounded distinction between cases where the party is wholly without remedy at law, and where, though he has a remedy there, it may be inadequate. In the latter case if a specific performance be denied, yet, by recurring to his action, he may obtain damages; but in the former, the reasons for denying a specific performance should be stronger; for if a remedy is denied in that shape, he must go wholly unredressed. The *Chancellor* omits to notice this distinction. He takes it for granted that our remedy at law still exists in full force, and speaks of leaving the appellant to seek his compensation in damages there. "If (says he) the party be sent to law to submit his case to a jury, relief can be afforded in damages, with a moderation agreeable to equity and good conscience." Thus he, in terms, denies what we think cannot be questioned, that the effect of his decree was to deprive us of all remedy whatever; because it is not pretended that the articles were so far literally complied with as to save our legal remedy. Ld. Hardwicke says, in *Attorney-General* v. *Day*, 1 Ves., Sr., 222, "the general rule certainly is, that this (carrying a contract into execution) is discretionary in the court, but will not hold in the present; for that is generally in cases where there may be an election of two remedies, by coming here for a specific performance, or by action at law; whereas here there can be no remedy at law." He does indeed say, that on a strong objection, the court may refuse a decree even in that case; but this is not at all inconsistent with what he had before said; or with what we contend for. On a strong objection, a contract would not only be denied the aid of equity, but would be set aside, even after it was executed. If we are entitled to the benefit of his doctrine, in its full and unqualified extent; if it be true that where the remedy at law is gone, not by neglect but by accident, as in this case, the reasons for refusing to decree must be of a very strong and *imperative character, and, at least, [***451** as strong as will warrant the setting aside a contract, the present cause is disposed of. The only ground upon which the *Chancellor* proceeds is inadequacy; and nothing is clearer than that this is no cause for setting a contract aside, unless it be so gross as to warrant the inference of fraud. This the *Chancellor* admits was not the case. Here was no refusal of performance at the day. The non-performance arose from the sickness of Ellison, who, if he had recovered, would doubtless have accepted the conveyance. Under such circumstances, we were not bound to put ourselves in a capacity to tender the deed. [The counsel contended, from the evidence, that the *Chancellor* was mistaken in supposing Ellison capable of business on June 1, 1820.]

But suppose we are mistaken in this view of the subject; at any rate the *Chancellor* had a discretion to grant or refuse the performance; and we proceed to inquire into the manner in which this has been and should be exercised. The *Chancellor* says, "it is not a case requiring the aid of the court *ex debito justitiæ.*" If not, then we are subjected to the mere arbitrary discretion, the caprice and humor of the judge. We had supposed the remedy for a specific performance was to be viewed in a very favorable light; and to be upheld if possible. It is a remedy alone adequate to the injury received, and good faith mainly depends upon its enforcement. There is an obvious distinction between the case of real and personal property. For the latter a satisfaction in money may generally be obtained. But purchases of real estate are, many times, the most important transactions of a man's life. They are generally made with a view to settle himself or family. There are a thousand circumstances which a jury cannot reach; and when the contract is violated, we claim the same right to a specific performance as to damages from a jury. The *Chancellor* may deny a specific performance, but he cannot do so unless according to established rules. In *Hall* v. *Warren*, 9 Ves., 608, the Master of the Rolls says: "It is as much of course, in this court, to decree a specific performance as it is to give damages at law." And in *Halsey* v. *Grant*, 13 Ves., 76, *Ld. Erskine said: "This jurisdiction [***452** had its origin upon the foundation of a legal right, the law giving the title; but a court of law from the modes in which justice is there administered, not being capable of giving a complete remedy and all the relief to which the party was entitled." How is this reconcilable with the language of Ld. Elden, as quoted by the *Chancellor* from *Mortlock* v. *Buller*, 10 Ves., 292, and *Willan* v. *Willan*, 16 *Id.*, 83? There is, in truth, no difficulty or inconsistency in these cases, when understood. No doubt specific performance may be refused and the party put to his remedy at law; but there are also cases governed by fixed rules. The discretion to be exercised is not arbitrary. It was said in *White* v. *Damon*, 7 Ves., 30, 35, "that giving specific performance is matter of discretion; but that is not an arbitrary capricious discretion. It must be regulated upon grounds that will make it judicial."

Why is it that specific performance is ever denied? We answer, because there are circumstances which should influence a jury in their estimate of the damages. Unless this is so the reason fails, and the party has a perfect legal right to a performance. He should not gain an advantage by the choice of his forum; and the only inquiry should be, are there circumstances upon which the case should go to a jury?

To mere inadequacy of price, unless so gross as to be evidence of fraud or attended with actual fraud, surprise, ignorance, mistake, delusion or imbecility of mind, *caveat emptor* applies, both in courts of law and equity. If the party agree to take real property at a given day and is not ready to receive it, the vendor may set it up at auction the very next day, and, in an action, recover the difference between the prices of the two sales; or he may enforce the contract, specifically, in chancery. But what does the doctrine amount to, that mere inadequacy shall be a defense? Do gentlemen mean to say there must be an exact equality; and abolish at one blow, the entire equity jurisdiction upon this head? If not, what is to be the degree of inequality? Shall it be one fourth, one fifth or one tenth? This, it is said, must **453***] be referred to *the doctrine of discretion. We ask, is not such a system dangerous, as being arbitrary and dependent on rules, of which the party is unapprised till the moment they are promulgated, a doctrine which converts the bench of a judge into the throne of a tyrant? It is perfectly easy to see whether a contract is such as should be performed. To deny this is to say we have no moral sense. There is, then, no uncertainty in the rule for which we contend; nor does it place the matter beyond the exercise of a legal and sound discretion, such as may be reduced to practice. There is, on the other hand, an uncertainty in the value of land, and other articles of sale. This must be so, from the nature of things. It is a subject on which witnesses may differ and always do. If this be the case in England, where the value of real property is very nearly fixed, how much more so in this country, where it depends on speculation and contingency.

We also admit that equity is not bound to decree performance, where the bargain is hard and unconscionable; but this does not follow from the price being inadequate. All the cases which went on this ground (perhaps with a a single exception), besides mere inadequacy, involved moral considerations. *The Marquis of Normanby* v. *Ld. Beckley*, cited in 5 Vin., 539, as stated by the *Chancellor*, is that the contract must be reasonably fair in every particular. This is not a reported case. It is taken from the statement of counsel, unaccompanied with the facts upon which it proceeded. The *Chancellor* says it was sanctioned in *Young* v. *Clerk*, Prec. in Ch., 538, but, in truth, that was a case of actual fraud. Ld. Macclesfield says it was "a shameful contract," which marks his sense of the moral turpitude of the transaction. The case in 5th Vin., 549, pl. 12 (*Squire* v. *Baker*), does not tell us what constitutes an unreasonable contract. It purports to have come from Ld. Harcourt, though it was not found among his manuscripts, but among those of his secretary. 2 Ves., 159, 627. Cases coming from this source have been frequently treated as wanting all authority. This will be seen in *Creuze* v. *Hunter*, 2 Ves., 159; *Connolly* v. *Parsons*, 3 *Id.*, 627, and *Mortlock* v. *Buller*, *10 *Id.*, 306, Sol. Gen., *arguendo*. *Savage* v. *Taylor*, Cas. *t.* Talb., 234, is next relied [***454** on by the *Chancellor*; but, according to his own statement, fraud was the ground there expressly taken. The articles were unfairly obtained. I do not find, in that case, the words quoted by the *Chancellor*, that it would not alter the case, even if possession had been given under the articles, which may be owing to a difference in the editions which we have examined.

The *Chancellor* next relies upon *Thompson* v. *Harcourt*, 2 Bro. Parl. Cas., 415, and he says the bill was dismissed, and the decree affirmed in Parliament, on the ground of inequality. Now, strange as it may seem, the bill was in that case sustained, and a specific performance decreed, as appears by the case itself, both in the old ed. of Bro. P. C., Vol. II., p. 415, and in 1 *Id.*, Tomlin's ed., 193. In that case the parties agreed, on the day of performance, to a postponement; and an Act of Parliament passed, declaring the contract void, unless the vendor had the whole stock, which he contracted to sell, at the day. The amount sold was £1,000, for the consideration of £9,200. Two objections were taken. 1. Great inadequacy of price. 2. Want of the whole amount at the day, the vendor having on hand only £290 at that time. For the residue he relied on his being the owner of certain stock, as trustee, to make up the amount; but this was held not to be within the Statute. Yet the court decreed a specific execution as to the £290, thus overruling the objection of inadequacy, and leaving the case, so far from being against us, a decisive one in our favor.

Barnardiston v. *Lingwood*, 2 Atk., 133, was a bill, not to execute but set aside a contract, upon a familiar principle, that it had been obtained from a necessitous remainder-man. In *Buxton* v. *Lister*, 3 Atk., 385, the remarks of Ld. Hardwicke, as quoted by the *Chancellor*, will be seen, on an examination of the whole case, to apply solely to contracts concerning personal property. He uses the general words relied on by the *Chancellor*, as to certainty, fairness and justness, but they have no relation whatever to inadeqnacy of consideration, as will be seen by adverting to the questions raised in that cause. Yet he gives them the same *force, and quotes them nearly in [***455** the same language as did the counsel in *Mortlock* v. *Buller*, 10 Ves., 301-2. Nor did the question arise in *Joynes* v. *Statham*, 3 Atk., 388. *London* v. *Nash*, 1 Ves., Sr., 12; 3 Atk., 512, S. C., was a case of peculiar hardship. The defendant agreed to rebuild houses under what is called a building lease; but, instead of doing this literally, he made extensive and valuable repairs. The effect of the bill would have compelled him to pull down the repaired houses; which, the *Lord Chancellor* said, might be equal to new ones; and, if not, adequate damages might be given at law. This view of the case shows that it had nothing to do with inadequacy of consideration. In *Underwood* v. *Hitchcox*, 1 Ves., Sr., 279, I admit that Ld. Hardwicke lays stress upon inadequacy of consideration; but that was by no means the sole ground. The defendant articled with his uncle for the purchase of a copyhold in fee; and the plaintiff soon after agreed with the defendant to purchase of him. The uncle surrendered to the nephew and his wife, and to the heirs of their bodies, remainder to the nephew in fee; but, notwithstanding the formal title, as derived from the surrender, the plaintiff insisted that the defendant should execute, the uncle being, in fact, a mere trustee for the nephew. Unless the surrender was first set aside, the defendant could not make a good title. The material inquiry was as to the legality of the surrender, therefore, which, as contended, was fraudulent. Ld. Hardwicke said the uncle intended it as a bounty to the family of the nephew, and therefore he would not set it aside in favor of a purchaser who should take it away from the family. I agree that he does afterwards advert to inadequacy, as a distinct ground, and I am willing the case should be considered an authority against us; but it is the only one. *Faine* v. *Brown*, cited in *Ramsden* v. *Hylton*, is also relied upon, and stated at large by the *Chancellor;* but this is not a reported decision. It was merely cited by counsel, in the course of the argument, and was not recognized as an authority, nor even mentioned by Ld. Hardwicke in the course of **456***] the argument, or examination *of the principal case. No inadequacy is mentioned, as the ground of decision; and for aught that appears, a full price was given. Would the court have refused a decree, on the naked ground of inconvenience, which is the only one stated in the case? It is not a good authority.

Day v. *Newman*, 2 Cox, 77, is, perhaps, the most formidable case with which we have to contend. This was cited by counsel in *Mortlock* v. *Buller*, 10 Ves., 292, 300. The *Chancellor* says of it that it "came before Ld. Alvanley in 1788, and there was an agreement, in writing, for the purchase of an estate of £20,000, which was proved not to be worth above £10,000. There was no circumstance of fraud or surprise in the case, and he thought the inadequacy of price alone was sufficient not to induce him to decree a specific performance." I admit the Master of the Rolls does appear to have rested his decree on the inadequacy; but, on referring to the case, the court will perceive that if there was not fraud, the vendor's conduct had been such as to deprive him of all countenance. The sale was to a young man, the son, for £20,000, of an estate, which had before been offered to the father for £9,000. The young man was at the vendor's house and inveigled into the purchase. Though these circumstances were not mentioned by the Master of the Rolls, they must have influenced his opinion. He says: "If I had any doubt about the inadequacy of the price, I would put it in some mode of inquiry; but, as the case stands, the value is £9,000. And then the question is, whether a young man shall, in this court, be holden to a bargain like this." Why mention the vendee's youth, if he intended to rely solely on inadequacy? Clearly, because he had been misled by his inexperience. Again; he had such strong suspicion of fraud, that on the question coming up as to costs, he proposed to the plaintiff that he should give up his contract, and his bill should be dismissed without, and the defendant's with costs." Why should he doubt about the costs, if the conduct of the party had been fair? The quotation of this case by counsel, in *Mortlock* v. *Buller*, 10 Ves., 292, shows the danger of trusting to their statement alone. As cited by them, it went on the *mere [***457** ground of inadequacy. This remark will enable us to judge of the weight due to *Tilly* v. *Peers*, 10 Ves., 301, which is the next case relied upon by the *Chancellor*, from the mere statement of Sir Samuel Romilly, counsel in the cause. Eyre, *Ch. B.*, is there stated to have relied solely on the hardness of the bargain. What degree of inadequacy constituted the hardness of the bargain does not appear. It might have been so great as, *per se*, to have evinced fraud. But this case rests on the mere authority of Sir Samuel Romilly, who afterwords, in *Western* v. *Russell*, 3 Ves. & B., 187, 190, took directly the opposite ground, declaring, in terms, that "mere inadequacy of price, if it had been proved, is no ground for refusing a specific performance. It was much pressed, certainly, in *Mortlock* v. *Buller*, but the argument received no countenance from the *Lord Chancellor*.

Of *White* v. *Damon*, 7 Ves., 30, *Chancellor* Kent declares, "Ld. Eldon was inclined to say, that the sale by auction could not be set aside for mere inadequacy of price. This was an auction case, which undoubtedly rests on peculiar grounds, and the *Chancellor* spoke of setting aside the sale. So far the case has no application." The inference, from this statement of the case, is, that the bill was filed to set aside the sale. It was, in fact, to compel a specific performance; and it was held that inadequacy was no ground for refusing. Ld. Eldon says: "I am inclined to say, that a sale by auction, no fraud, surprise, &c., cannot be set aside for mere inadequacy of price. It will be very difficult to sustain sales by auction, if this court shall not sustain the agreement." This is a very material addition. *Chancellor* Kent admits that the execution of the contract was rightly denied on other grounds, but relies upon Ld. Rosslyn's doctrine, as evidence of the general rule, that the execution of a sale will be denied merely for inadequacy. I read from this opinion, to show that this is not so. Ld. Rosslyn says: "This bill is filed for a specific performance of an agreement for the sale of a freehold estate, &c. The facts *are very short. [***458** This lot was put up, together with other lots, part of the same estate, at Gosport. There was no bidding for that lot. There were bidders for all the other lots. After the sale, Smith, the auctioneer, advanced £1,000 to the vendor with great security, for he had all the deposits, and the money was to be paid into his hands for all the other lots; so that, except the temporary accommodation, the vendor, whom Smith knew to be a distressed man, forced to sell, had no other benefit of that advance. The auctioneer, however, chose to take a better security than he would have had as auctioneer; and he chose to take, as an additional security, a conveyance of this lot, with a power to sell, and his receipt to be a discharge for the price. The manner in which he proceeded was, after having received a considerable part of the money upon the other lots, in 1797, exactly a year, he puts up this wharf and premises, situated at Gosport, to sale at Garroway's, certainly not without the knowledge, but certainly without the consent of the owner. The place of sale was not very proper, and the time was very rapid. The premises were bought for £1,120, and the bill is filed by the purchaser. It appears in proof, and very distinctly, that the value of the premises is upwards of £2,000 a year. I have nothing to do with this case in a court of equity." What then, is that case? Is it not the misconduct of the auctioneer, in taking advantage of a distressed man, which is almost solely relied upon as the ground of the decree? Similar ground was taken by Ld. Eldon, in *Mortlock* v. *Buller*, 10 Ves., 292.

Such are the authorities on which the *Chancellor* has founded his opinion. They amount to this, and no more, that chancery is not bound to decree the performance of a hard and unconscionable bargain. What weight there is in the conclusion which the *Chancellor* has drawn from them, I shall not, at present, stop to inquire further; but proceed to the cases upon which we rely, the greater part of which have also been passed upon by the *Chancellor*.

In *Parker* v. *Palmer*, 1 Ch. Cas., 41, inadequacy was the sole defense; but relief was **459***] denied. I do not rely much *on this case. The report of it is obscure; nor does it appear whether the inadequacy existed at the sale, or arose afterwards. In *City of London* v. *Richmond*, 2 Vern., 421, 423, the bill was to enforce the specific performance of a contract to take a lease at a rent of £750, the real annual value being only £300. The *Chancellor* said, "as a beneficial bargain will be decreed in equity, so if it happens to be a losing bargain, for the same reason it ought to be decreed." In the case (cited in *Mortimer* v. *Capper*, 1 Bro. Ch. Cas., 158) by Ld. Thurlow, in giving his opinion, the defense was, that the contract was to inclose for £20; whereas it was worth £200. This was on a bill for a specific performance, and the inadequacy was admitted; yet it was held no defense. In the argument of *Mortlock* v. *Buller*, 10 Ves., 298, it is true that Sir Samuel Romilly, and other counsel, denied the authority of this case; but the decision of that cause shows that court approved of it.

Adams v. *Weare*, 1 Bro. Ch. Cas., 567, is not merely analogous, but exactly similar, in all its material circumstances, to the present case, except that it was vastly stronger in the extent of inadequacy, which was the sole defense. The Master of the Rolls decreed a performance, and the decree was affirmed by the *Lord Chancellor*, who says (pp. 568–9): "I am not very anxious to discuss the point, what bargains the court will execute or not; but when the court has laid it down as an article of equity which men shall obtain here, and which they cannot obtain at law, that, instead of damages, they shall have a specific performance, and that every agreement must be performed, unless something, at the time of making the bargain, or something done since, is to amount to a waiver of it at the time of carrying it into execution; if you do not confine yourself within that limit, there are no bounds whatsoever; for rules ought to be fixed, and it would be calamitous that the matter should rest upon such loose expressions as hard and unconscionable; which expressions, unless they are properly to be applied, mean nothing." Again (p. 570): "It does not appear what the value of the premises would be, if applied to the purpose of working the mill. What the advantage of it might be is not stated. Therefore, I think that without entering *into the partic- [***460** ulars of the case, the Master of the Rolls has done right; for no case can be cited, where parties have made a bargain with their eyes perfectly open, and no surprise whatever, as in this case, on which the court has refused to decree a specific performance. Here is no mistake of the object, as in *Hick* v. *Phillips*; and as to the greatness of the price, Adams had a right to ask a large sum, and the other had agreed to give it." How strikingly does this observation appeal to the common sense of every man. Has not any one a right, not merely legal and civil, but moral, to ask what he pleases? And if another, with his eyes open, and on full deliberation, consents to give it, on what ground can a court of equity gainsay the deed, and deny performance?

Collier v. *Brown*, 1 Cox, 428, cited by the *Chancellor*, was the case of an agreement to sell at £275. But the seller repented of his bargain, on an offer, a short time after, of £400. The parties bargained with their eyes open. It was contended, on a bill filed by the purchaser for a specific execution, that it was the constant course, in courts of equity, to refuse their assistance in enforcing a contract, where the price was grossly below the real value; but the court said "the parties bargained with their eyes open, and that no imposition or surprise was proved in the case; that Mary Turner was very well satisfied with her bargain, until she found she could get more for the premises; that under these circumstances, mere inadequacy of price (where it cannot be used as evidence of fraud) is not, of itself, sufficient to prevent the court from administering its usual equity." Here was a direct and solemn decision on the very point we are discussing. The *Chancellor* supposes that the case went upon its special circumstances. Does he mean to say, that in order to be relieved, one must express his dissatisfaction with the bargain immediately? Is such a doctrine rational, or consistent with his own view of the case? Will not the injury be the same, at whatever period the error or delusion is made known? How is this case? Ellison was satisfied to the time of his death, and this controversy would, in all probability, never have arisen, had he not died.

*Specific performance, on the ground [***461** of inadequacy, was resisted in *Emery* v. *Wase*,

8 Ves., 517, combined with the fact that the lands sold belonged to the defendant's wife; but Ld. Eldon said: "I do not deny that mere difference in value, though considerable, is not of itself a sufficient ground for refusing a specific performance of a contract; thus laying down our position in terms; and in *Coles* v. *Trecothick*, 9 Ves., 246, he says: "Inadequacy of price does not depend upon a person giving *pretium affectionis*, from any particular motive, beyond what any other man would give, the reasonable price. But further, unless the inadequacy of price is such as shocks the conscience, and amounts, of itself, to conclusive and decisive evidence of fraud in the transaction, it is not itself a sufficient ground for refusing a specific performance. The *Chancellor* thinks this declaration not entitled to much weight, because it was said of a sale at auction; but the observation was general, and not intended to be confined to sales at auction. The *Lord Chancellor* speaks of such inadequacy as will shock the conscience; but sales at auction, at whatever undervalue, cannot, with any propriety, be treated as having such an effect. This is plain from the manner in which the same *Chancellor* treated the same subject in the previous case of *White* v. *Damon*, 7 Ves., 30, where he considers auction sales as standing on peculiar grounds, not to be governed by inadequacy. The rule was also laid down by him in *Coles* v. *Trecothick*, as one applicable to all cases.

In *Burrows* v. *Lock*, 10 Ves., 470, the defendant, by will, had a ninth share of the residue of a testator's estate in the hands of a trustee, worth £288; and being indebted to the plaintiff, agreed to assign his interest at £132, being apprised before the agreement of the amount due to him. On a bill filed to enforce an assignment, this was resisted on the ground of inadequacy; but the Master of the Rolls said: "I do not know, if fraud is out of the case, that I can set aside this contract, or refuse to act upon it, merely on the ground of inadequacy of price;" and he overruled the objection, and decreed according to the prayer of the bill. It may be objected that the Master **462***] of the Rolls speaks of *setting aside contracts; but from the nature of the controversy, this must have been a mere mistake of words. He could mean no other than denying a decree of performance. This is a very strong case. The plaintiff had obtained a contract for the assignment, from the *cestui que trust*, and was under the necessity of going to a court of equity to enforce a specific performance; but his remedy would have been nearly the same at law, so far as the amount of the recovery was concerned; and he would have been left to law, had he not come plainly within the rules upon which chancery decrees performance. The price was palpably inadequate; yet he was compelled to perform. Nor let it be objected that the subject was personal property. This is a still stronger feature in our favor; for specific performance, is, in such a case, much less favored than in cases of real property.

We also rely upon *Cadman* v. *Horner*, 18 Ves., 10. This also involved the question of inadequacy. The value of the property agreed to be conveyed was £1,200, and the price to be given £600. The Master of the Rolls would, however, evidently have decreed performance, notwithstanding the inadequacy, had it not been that the vendee had been guilty of misrepresentation.

The last case relied upon by the *Chancellor*, is *Western* v. *Russell*, 3 Ves. & B., 187, before Sir Wm. Grant, Master of the Rolls, who declares that "it is unnecessary to determine, as a general question, whether inadequacy of price might or might not be a ground for refusing performance; the case before the court being that of the proprietor of an estate not alleged to have been under any incapacity, or deficiency of judgment, or to have been led, by accident or design, into a misrepresentation of the value." The general question there, then, was not passed upon; and to make it an authority for the decree, in this case, it must be taken for granted that the question of inadequacy could never arise, without being blended with others.

Are this court, then, prepared to say, with the *Chancellor*, there is a very great weight of authority against us? Take a summary of the cases upon which he relies. *Young* v. *Clerk* *was a case of fraud *London* v. *Nash*, [***463** does not present the question, and in *Faine* v. *Brown* the question of inadequacy did not arise, for the price was not unequal. *Day* v. *Newman* contained other circumstances. *Tilly* v. *Peers* rests upon the quotation of counsel, and in *White* v. *Damon* the ground was oppression and injustice; so that he is reduced to the single case of *Underwood* v. *Hitchcox*, 1 Ves., 279, which, alone, is a direct authority in support of his opinion.

On the other hand, we present to the court, not authorities extracted from the statements of counsel, or loose *dicta* of judges, but eight cases, in which the objection of inadequacy was distinctly taken, and overruled, viz.: *Parker* v. *Palmer*, 1 Ch. Cas., 41; *London* v. *Richmond*, 2 Vern., 421, 3; the case cited in *Mortimer* v. *Capper*, 1 Bro. Ch. Cas., 158; *Thompson* v. *Harcourt*, 2 Bro. P. C., 415; *Collier* v. *Brown*, 1 Cox, 428; *Emery* v. *Wase*, 8 Ves., 517; *Coles* v. *Trecothick*, 9 Ves., 246, and *Burrowes* v. *Lock*, 10 Ves., 470.

This is not all. Numerous other cases are not susceptible of explanation, if the ideas of the *Chancellor* be correct. He takes the naked position that inadequacy, alone, is enough to stamp the case with the character of hardship, &c. Now take the numerous class of cases which relate to sales at auction, and inadequacy arising from subsequent circumstances, with cases in which *pretium affectionis* is given. All these are anomalous, if the *Chancellor's* reasoning be correct. He admits, however, that it does not apply to sales at auction; but on what ground do courts refuse to set these aside for inadequacy? Not of public p c; because they may be set aside, if fraud intervene; but because the sale, being open and public, and the parties having a full chance to inform themselves, fraud is not to be presumed from inadequacy, whatever it may be. The same reasons apply to every fair sale, where parties act understandingly. Again; where the property is deteriorated in value, from subsequent circumstances, as in *Pope* v. *Roots*, 7 Bro. P. C., 118; *Mortimer* v. *Capper*,

1 Bro. Ch. Cas., 156, and *Jackson* v. *Lever*, 3 Bro. Ch. Cas., 604, be the inadequacy what it **464*]** *may, yet the contract will be enforced; and the reason is, because, from the nature of the transaction, every presumption of fraud is repelled. So, where the property is purchased with the view to a speculation, as in *Adams* v. *Weare*, 1 Bro. Ch. Cas., 569, cited to this point, 1 Madd. Ch., 324. Inadequacy can never be a mere abstract question, but must always depend upon the motives and circumstances. Whenever these are peculiar, they are placed on the ground of *pretium affectionis*, where inadequacy, to any degree, is no reason for denying performance.

In the civil law, as stated by the *Chancellor*, a contract for the sale of land was rescinded by judicial authority, though made in good faith, if the price was below half the value. But it will be seen, by 1 Evans Poth., 22, that, even by that law, *pretium affectionis* is excepted. Why such an exception, if the *Chancellor* be correct? If inadequacy is enough, there is no propriety in the exception. Is it not obvious that the reason of the civil law and our own is the same, viz.: the presumption of fraud, which may be repelled by showing the motive, and, in our own law, any other circumstances?

[Here the counsel examined the facts relied upon to show that the case was within two of the exceptions to the rule which makes even gross inadequacy evidence of fraud, viz.: that the purchase was viewed by Ellison as a speculation, from the general belief, prevailing at the time of the bargain, that the U. S. Navy Yard would be established at Newburgh; and also that it came within the exception of the *pretium affectionis*, Ellison having previously bought the other two thirds of the property, and having ample means for improving the whole, and rendering it valuable to him far beyond the price which he gave. See opinion of Sudam, *Senator*, *post.*]

It is not competent for the respondents to insist on artifice or misrepresentation. No such defense was set up by the answer; nor is it there pretended that Ellison was incapable of contracting. All the answer says is, that he was occasionally incapable of business; but this was with a view to answer our excuse for not tendering the deed at the day. The *Chancellor* is not correct in supposing this to **465*]** have been set *up as matter of defense. Independently of the purpose for which it was introduced, what do the words import? Do they not imply that Ellison was, generally, capable of business? Suppose we should say that his His Honor, the *Chancellor*, was occasionally incorrect; that he occasionally quoted cases, omitting the material circumstances; that he occasionally did this without examining the original cases, but relied on the quotations of counsel; that he occasionally cited cases as being against, when they were for us; would this be to deny his general accuracy, or that he was usually laborious and successful?

Drunkenness can certainly constitute no defense, unless the party, on becoming sober, disavows the contract. This is not proved or pretended. So far from it, there is no doubt that Ellison displayed, through the business, more than ordinary prudence and capacity.

The *Chancellor* relies upon the mortgage as another circumstance in the defense, which ought to be taken into consideration. I do not know whether he means that this alone would form a bar; or that it is to be connected with inability and inadequacy, and that the whole, conjunctly, are to preclude the relief sought, or any two of them are to have this effect. But if neither, separately, would do this, how could their union do it? There may be circumstances connected with inadequacy which would require the court to deny a specific execution; but they are all moral considerations. If inability to make a title at the day, alone, is relied on, I have only to express my astonishment; for there is no doctrine better settled than that this is no bar; and, in nine instances out of ten, the only inquiry is, whether a title can be made at the time of the decree. I admit that neglect without excuse, followed by great delay, may grow into a waiver. So Ellison might have rescinded the bargain, by dissent, if there had been a default in tendering the deed without a proper excuse. But so far from dissenting, he left us in quiet possession. In relation to this part of the case, the *Chancellor* says he should have tendered the deed; for Ellison was competent to do business, though he *had **[*466** just declared that, for two years before his death, he was incompetent. This was while incompetency was necessary for another head of the defense. When our failure depends upon his competency, the fact is changed, and by the magic power of the *Chancellor* he is suddenly healed. If competency was important at any point of the transaction, it was so at the period when the deed was to have been executed.

In *Langford* v. *Pitt*, 2 P. Wms., 631, the Master of the Rolls says: "It is sufficient if the party entering into the articles to sell has a good title at the time of the decree, the direction of the court being, in all these cases, to inquire whether the seller can, not whether he could make a title at the time of executing the agreement." He refers to the case of *Lord Stourton* v. *Sir Thomas Meers*, in which the Ld. Stourton, at the time of the articles for a sale, or even when the decree was pronounced, could not make a title, the reversion in fee being in the Crown; and yet the court indulged him with time more than once for the getting in this title from the Crown, which could not be effected without an Act of Parliament to be obtained in the following Sessions. However, it was at length procured, and Sir Thomas Meers decreed to be the purchaser. The same point was resolved in *Wynn* v. *Morgan*, 7 Ves., 202.

SUDAM, *Senator*. His Honor, the *Chancellor*, appears to admit this to be the practice at the close of his opinion. He says he heard no evidence upon the title; because it is the course of the court to refer the inquiry on that head to a master.

Mr. Duer. True. This is only another inconsistency. Notwithstanding this admission of the *Chancellor*, I see the want of title is inserted among the printed points upon the other side. No position is better settled than that a good title in the grantor at the time of the decree is sufficient. No point of practice is more familiar. In *Wynn* v. *Morgan*, 7 Ves., 208, it was said by the Master of the Rolls that the defendant did not allege that the execution at the day was material to him, or that he considered it so; but merely that at the day a good title could not be made. He 467*] would not *say that a plaintiff could come into court with a title at any distance of time, though he had none when the contract was made, or should have been executed; but he said he was called on to say, that if he could not make a title at the time fixed on, he never could come for an execution. That, he said, would contradict the whole current of authorities, and would oppose the uniform practice; there was not a single instance of the objection having prevailed, when so nakedly stated. *The Marquis of Hertford* v. *Boore*, 5 Ves., 720, S. P. And in *Mortlock* v. *Buller*, 10 Ves., 292, one of the cases cited by the *Chancellor*, Ld. Eldon, at p.315, lays down the same doctrines as perfectly unquestionable.

Mr. J. V. Henry, same side, said he would apprise the counsel for the respondents that he should, in his reply, rely upon the following authorities in addition to those cited by his associate counsel:

To show that the mortgage was no impediment to a specific execution, *Jenkins* v. *Hiles*, 6 Ves., 646; *Clute* v. *Robison*, 2 Johns., 595; *Hepburn* v. *Auld*, 5 Cr., 262.

That the want of a remedy at law is a reason for granting relief in equity, Newl. on Cont., 89; *Flint* v. *Brandon*, 8 Ves., 163, per Master of the Rolls.

As to the objection on the ground of incapacity by reason of intoxication, 1 Pow. on Cont., 29, 30, and 1 Madd. Ch., 239, Am. ed. 1817; *Cook* v. *Clayworth*, 18 Ves., 12.

That incapacity is not in issue, *James* v. *M'Kernon*, 6 Johns., 543.

Mr. Talcott, Atty-Gen., for the respondents; *Mr. S. Jones*, same side. It will be important to remember, that the bill was filed in the court below, not to set aside, but enforce the specific execution of the contract. In this character, it invoked the extraordinary powers of the court, and conferred the right and duty of taking into consideration every circumstance, which might render the interposition of the court unconscientious or inequitable. Though, perhaps, not intoxicated at the time, Ellison had, for several years, been in habits of intoxication; the price was grossly inade- 468*] quate, *and the *Chancellor* was of opinion that it was not right, upon the facts, to decree a specific execution against these infant heirs. Does this refusal deserve the epithets bestowed upon it? Does it deserve to be called the exercise of a power dangerous and tremendous in its consequences, as referring everything to discretion, and erecting the seat of a judge into the throne of a tyrant? What does the language of the *Chancellor* amount to? Merely that one going into this court has not a right *ex debito justitiæ* to demand the execution of a contract, because, according the doctrines of a court of law, it might be made the subject of an action; but that he has a right to examine the circumstances under which it was made, and be guided by these. This is by no means a novel doctrine, nor is it without the most direct and ample authority in its support. In *Howorth* v. *Deem*, 1 Eden, 355, the enforcing specific execution is treated as mere matter of discretion. So in *Atty-Gen.* v. *Day*, 1 Ves., Sr., 221, 222, even where there is no remedy at law; and *Underwood* v. *Hitchcox*, 1 Ves., 769, S. P. So in *Bromley* v. *Jeffereys*, Prec. in Ch., 138; and *Carberry* v. *Tannehill*, 1 Harr. & J., 224.

In *Perkins* v. *Wright*, 3 Harr. & M'H., 326, it is recited in the decree as an established principle in chancery, that a decree for a specific performance of any contract whatever is not a matter of course, but rests entirely in the discretion of the court, upon a consideration of all the circumstances; that the *Chancellor* was acquainted with no precedent of a decree for such a performance, where either the contract appeared hard or unreasonable in itself, or where, from a material change of circumstances since the contract, the performance would be attended with peculiar hardship on the defendant, it being the invariable practice of the court, in such case, to refer the complainant to his remedy at law." *Simmons* v. *Hill*, 4 Harr. & M'H., 258, contains this remark: "How often is it necessary to repeat, that when a contract is established, even by admission, it is still a matter of sound discretion, whether or not, under all circumstances, a performance shall be decreed." The [*469 doctrine represented as being fraught with such direful consequences, thus comes, on examination, to be a rule so well established, and so equitable, that no one can mistake it; and none can deny its excellence.

It is said the *Chancellor* has inverted cases; that peculiar circumstances, essential to their decision, are not mentioned by him. On examination, it will be found he can be defended from these imputations. But before I proceed to examine the cases cited by him, I call upon the court to view some of the leading features of the transaction it becomes necessary to investigate. [The counsel here considered the evidence, as to the circumstances from which the contract arose, the inadequacy of value, and the incumbrance upon the Newburgh lots, and asked]: Ought such a contract to be carried into execution, unless some imperious rule of the court demands it?

It becomes necessary to examine the principles upon which courts of equity proceed, in decreeing a specific performance. They operate in a two-fold way, according to the justice and equity of the case. They either rescind the contract, and deprive the party of all remedy, or simply deny all interference. Circumstances which authorize the latter course need not be so strong as those which warrant the former. In the former cases, courts, both of law and equity, have concurrent jurisdiction, as in cases of fraud, against which either may relieve; and the only difference is in the remedy—a court of equity canceling the instrument, and destroying all remedy, and a court of law merely refusing to enforce it. A court of equity sets aside and annuls the instrument, therefore; and upon slighter circumstances of impeachment, it may merely refuse to carry it into execution; or, as is often done, modify the relief sought. In the latter case, it merely refuses the cumulative relief of a court of equity, but leaves the party to his remedy at law, if he has any. It follows, from the nature of the subject, that the grounds of relief are different in the two given cases, of enforcing or setting aside. It is absurd to say that a court of equity will require the same evidence, to turn a party round to his legal remedy, on **470*]** the one hand, *or cancel all remedy on the other, by going a step farther, rescinding the instrument, and declaring that it ought not to be enforced anywhere. This distinction has always been recognized, from the origin of chancery jurisdiction over contracts. *Savage* v. *Taylor*, Cas. *t.* Talb., 234; *Day* v. *Newman*, 2 Cox, 77; *Mortlock* v. *Buller*, 10 Ves., 292; *Davis* v. *Symonds*, 2 Cox, 406. So of all the cases wherever the question has arisen. The different degrees of evidence are regulated by the different effect and operation of the decree in the two given cases. A decree to set aside a contract may be bottomed on fraud, proved in a variety of ways. One is inadequacy, so gross as to warrant the inference of fraud, according to the cases cited on the other side. It must, then, be such as to shock the judgment of rational men. Where the object is not to annul the contract, but induce the court to say it shall not be specifically performed, the inadequacy need not be so striking; and when the court require the same evidence in both cases, they confound and destroy a well settled and ancient distinction. Why should that strong proof be required, to secure the neutrality of the court, which is necessary to set aside the contract? The very reason why chancery sends the party back to a court of law, presupposes that the contract is valid, and not to be set aside; and to call for the proof of fraud, in such a case, is absurd. It is calling for what destroys the instrument, in order to warrant the sending it to another forum, with a view that it may be enforced, though to a less rigorous extent. It may be difficult to lay down any general rule, by which this class of cases are to be governed; but thus much may be said, that before the Court of Chancery will lend its gratuitous aid to compel the execution of a contract, it will be satisfied that the contract is, beyond all doubt, just and fair. The matter must, then, as the *Chancellor* says, rest in sound judicial discretion. That such is the rule, is established by a multitude of adjudged cases, some of which have been cited by the *Chancellor*, and some of which he did not think it important to cite. In *Johnson* v. *Nott*, 1 Vern, 271, decided in 1684, Hill purchased of Nott a reversion, at an under value. At first the contract **471*]** was set aside, but the Lord *Keeper reversed that decree. Then a bill was filed to enforce it; but this was denied by the Lord Keeper, who said: "Upon the first hearing, on Nott's bill, he thought it a hard case, though he did not see sufficient reason to set aside the contract;" but, as to the plaintiff's bill, he said, "a contract which carries an equity, to have it decreed in specie, ought to be above all objection." As to purchases made of heirs, the subject in relation to which he speaks, I admit the courts are more strict than where the party is in an independent situation; but the case shows that there may exist such inadequacy as, though not evidence of fraud, and calling upon the courts to set aside the contract, yet they will be sufficient to warrant them in refusing to give it effect.

It is said, that the expressions "hard" and "unreasonable" could not be applied to simple inadequacy; but the import is perfectly applicable, not only in common sense, but upon authority. What do courts, and everybody else understand, when it is said that a neighbor has made a hard bargain? Is it not, simply, "that he has given too much for the whistle?" *Johnson* v. *Nott*, 1 Vern, 271, is an authority to show its legal meaning. In *The Marquis of Normanby* v. *Beckley*, 5 Vin., 539, Ld. Somers, C., had said, long before, that "the court would not carry agreements into execution, unless the contract was reasonable and fair in every particular" Nor is this case answered, by saying it was a quotation of counsel, or questioning the manner in which it found its way before the public. The same distinction was sanctioned by *Green* v. *Green*, 5 Vin., 538, in the House of Lords, A. D. 1710; and the same point is advanced in the Grounds and Rudiments of Law and Equity, 76. Whether *Young* v. *Clerk*, Prec. in Ch., 538, involved actual fraud and corruption or not, these were not at all relied upon in the decision. Ld. Macclesfield said he was "clear of opinion that this court was not bound to decree a specific execution of articles, where they appeared to be unreasonable, or founded on fraud, or where it would be unjust or unconscionable to assist them; that, from the circumstances of this case, these articles were plainly of that sort; that though there was no direct fraud proved, yet, from the great undervalue of the *land, and that, too, without any ex- **[*472** pense whatsoever on the plaintiff's part, it appeared to him to be an unreasonable and shameful contract;" thus putting it distinctly on the value of the land. Are the counsel correct, in saying the inadequacy was so gross as to evince fraud? The court said not—that there was no actual fraud—and is it fair, in determining the weight of a case, to imagine circumstances which might have been, but were not taken into consideration? The *Chancellor* is not alone in this exposition of *Young* v. *Clerk*. The same case is cited in *Hick* v. *Phillips*, Prec. in Ch., 575, and the reason of it given. The defendant, in that case, articled to purchase of the plaintiff an estate, at 35 years, paying £50, the whole estate being represented to be freehold; whereas a part was copyhold. The plaintiff covenanted to convey, on payment of the purchase money; but because a part was copyhold, the defendant refused to go on, and the *Lord Chancellor* refused to decree an execution. He said "courts of equity were not bound to assist contracts which were harsh and unequitable, or were attended with such circumstances as would be a hardship on the defendant; that the case was proper for a jury at law, who could mitigate the damages, according to the circumstances, which a court of equity could not; and he left the plaintiff to make the most of it at law. It is added, that the plaintiff, in strictness, could not perform. This, by-the-by, also shows that the rule of standing or leaving a party to his chance at law does not depend upon the question, whether, from what appears, he has a remedy there or not. The case goes on, and the case of *Young* v. *Clerk* was cited, wherein the overvalue of the land was the reason the court would not decree an execution of leases; and for the same reason, ought not, for the overvalue of the money in this case; and therefore dismissed the bill." This was within two years after the decision in *Young* v. *Clerk*. The court not only declare that case to have gone on the value of the land, but they take the same ground themselves.

We are told that the *Chancellor* has exactly inverted the case of *Thompson* v. *Harcourt;* that a specific execution was decreed *pro tanto;* but it is the counsel who are mistaken. There **473***] *were two agreements for the transfer of the stock. The last, which was made Oct. 5, 1720, provided that the appellant should, at the next opening the books after Christmas, 1720, upon payment of £9,200, transfer to the respondent £1,000 South Sea stock; and the respondent covenanted to pay the £9,200 on that day, and bound himself to this in a penalty of £6,000. This was the contract in question. The appellant not having the stock on hand at the time of the contract, except £290, afterwards procured and tendered it at the opening of the books. Being refused, he sued the respondent at law in the Exchequer; and the respondent filed his bill in the same court for relief against the contract and the penalty. It went through several stages; and, in the meantime, the Act of Parliament passed, as mentioned on the other side. In Mich. Term, 1721, the vendor filed a cross-bill to compel the specific execution, and the case then stood thus: the vendee's bill was to have the agreement canceled in consequence of the bursting of the bubble, while the vendor's bill was to have a specific performance; but the decree was in favor of the vendee, who sought the rescission of the contract, on the ground that it was void, except as to the £290. The court did not set aside the contract, but merely relieved against the penalty, and ordered it to be delivered up; dismissing the bill for a specific execution, and granting a perpetual injunction against proceedings at law. The result, then, was that the vendee was relieved against the penalty on the usual grounds; and the vendor denied the specific performance which he sought. The court did not find sufficient inadequacy to set aside the contract; but they did find it enough to warrant them in a refusal to decree its specific execution, within the distinction for which we have contended. Another ground was that the fall in the value of the property, subsequent to the contract, was not a foundation for setting it aside. On appeal, it was argued that a specific execution should be denied: 1st, upon the statute which had passed; and 2d, upon the extreme hardship of the case. The decree being no more than a simple affirmance, we **474***] cannot see the grounds taken *by the court, except as we guess from the arguments of the counsel. It is cited in 5 Vin., 548, as having gone on the grounds supposed by the *Chancellor*. The grounds and rudiments of Law and Equity, p. 76, supposes it to have gone on that ground. That it did go on this ground is fairly to be supposed from the repeated declarations of those who lived near the time when the decision took place. The case is stated in Viner, as coming from the MS. of Ld. Harcourt. If we are incorrect in our ground, at any rate, it decides either that when one goes to be relieved against a penalty, he shall first be required to pay what is really due, or that there was not hardship enough to annul the agreement, entirely on the ground that the stock had subsequently fallen. One of these consequences must follow, from the vendee being held to pay what was secured, and the case cannot possibly be used as an authority against us.

To the case of *Squire* v. *Baker*, 5 Vin., 549, pl. 12, A. D. 1726, cited by the *Chancellor*, may be added several cases, to the same point, also cited in the same volume of Viner, 523. These cases, it is true, in common with *Squire* v. *Baker*, are collected from Ld. Harcourt's manuscript tables. To diminish their authority, they are called by counsel the tables of his secretary. Whether so or not, they must have been made under his direction, and for his use. Would he employ a man, for this purpose, so inaccurate that his labors could not be relied upon? If so, would he have not corrected them? But, it is most surprising, that he should have fallen into the same inaccuracy, in five or six cases given to us from the same source. Rudiments of Law and Equity, p. 76, supports the same doctrine. So does *Barnardiston* v. *Lingwood*, 2 Atk., 133. It is there said: "In the case of a hard bargain, where it is not absolutely executed, but executory only, the constant rule of the court is, not to carry it into execution." Whether this case related to the question of inadequacy or not, here is an important *dictum* in favor of the ground taken by the *Chancellor*. It was insinuated that he must have taken his view of *Buxton* v. *Lister*, 3 Atk., 385, from the quotation of counsel in *Mortlock* v. *Buller*, 10 Ves., 301-2. He says, Ld. Hardwicke remarked, in *that case, "that nothing was better [***475** established in chancery, than that every agreement or contract of sale ought to be certain, fair, and just, in all its parts; and if any of these ingredients were wanting in the case, the court would not decree a specific performance. It was in the discretion of the court, whether they would decree a specific performance; otherwise, a decree might be made which would tend to the ruin of one party." In this, he pursues the sense of Ld. Hardwicke, 3 Atk., 385-6, most strictly and fairly; and uses words which are not found in the quotation of counsel in *Mortlock* v. *Buller*. He does not profess to quote his Lordship literally; and yet stands perfectly clear of the imputation that he took the case at second hand through the counsel. Whether the *Chancellor* mistook the case itself, is another question. He is said to have done it, because a previous part of Ld. Hardwicke's opinion relates to the specific execution of contracts for goods and chattels; and it is insisted that the part relied on by the *Chancellor* relates to the same subject, and should not have been quoted as general, or applicable to contracts for the sale of lands. Ld. Hardwicke does, indeed, speak of goods and chattels in one part of his opinion; and reasons against a specific execution of contracts, in relation to them, on the ground of their frequent fluctuation in value—(the very reason, by-the-by, which counsel here give for enforcing contracts concerning lands), and he then thinks that the party may come, in that case, within the rule as to lands; and states what the general rule in relation to these is; declaring also that, with one exception, it is the same as to both lands and chattels. The amount of that case is, then, as stated by the *Chancellor*. In *London* v. *Nash*, 1 Ves., 12, Ld. Hardwicke said, in so many words, "the most material objection for the defendant, and which has weight with me, is, that the court is not obliged to decree a specific performance, and will not, where it would be a hardship.

Underwood v. *Hitchcox*, 1 Ves., 279, is admitted to be a case in point for the *Chancellor's* opinion. There the uncle articled to sell a **476***] copyhold estate to his nephew, the *defendant, who articled to sell to the plaintiff. The estate was then surrendered by the uncle to the nephew, his wife and family; and it was contended that the nephew's taking a conveyance in this form was a breach of trust, and that he should convey notwithstanding; and that the purchaser might go back to the uncle as trustee. Ld. Hardwicke said: "The rule of equity in carrying agreements into specific execution is well known; and the court is not obliged to decree every agreement entered into, though for valuable consideration in strictness of law, it depending on the circumstances. And undoubtedly every agreement, of which there should be a specific performance, ought to be in writing, certain and fair in all its parts, and for adequate consideration." Again: "Nor was the consideration adequate between the uncle and nephew;" and he expressly declared, that for this inadequacy, both between the uncle and nephew, and the nephew and the plaintiff, a specific performance should not be decreed. Ld. Hardwicke, then, considers a bargain for an inadequate consideration a hard bargain, within the rule which makes hardship a cause for denying a specific performance. Counsel will certainly not complain, that treating inadequacy and hardship as synonymous in this case, is novel or extraordinary, after seeing that such a judge as Ld. Hardwicke has done the same thing, of whom it is said, he sat 30 years in the Court of Chancery, and never had a decision reversed by the House of Lords. Ld. Erskine cites, and relies upon this case, in *Mason* v. *Armitage*, 13 Ves., 37. *Faine* v. *Brown*, cited in *Ramsden* v. *Hytton*, 2 Ves., 304, also relied upon by the *Chancellor*, went upon the same kind of hardship. It is true this case depends upon the citation of counsel, and a reliance upon it is said to be dangerous, for that reason; but this is by no means the first instance in which it has been relied upon. The same case was quoted in *Howell* v. *George*, 1 Madd., 1, and *Revell* v. *Hussey*, 2 Ball & B., 287; and the same doctrine will be found in Gilb. Lex. Pret., and in *Franks* v. *Martin*, 1 Eden, 323. In *Vaughan* v. *Thomas*, 1 Bro. Ch., 556, specific performance was denied by the *Chancellor*, because, as he said, it would **477***] be giving *aid to a very unconscientious bargain, the question turning upon the value of the annuity, which was the subject of purchase; and in *Collet* v. *Wollaston*, 3 Bro. Ch., 228, an inquiry into value was directed, before the Master of the Rolls would decree a performance, the reversion appearing to have been sold for a very low price.

Day v. *Newman*, 2 Cox, 77, it is said, depended on other circumstances besides inadequacy; but none such are relied upon in the decision. Indeed, they are expressly excluded by Ld. Alvanley, Master of the Rolls, who decided that cause. At page 80 he makes the general distinction for which we contend, between a bill to set aside, and one to enforce a contract. He asks: "Is, then, this such an inadequacy of price as will induce the court to set aside the contract, or, at least, not to enforce it? These are the two questions. The inadequacy of price is certainly great, but I am not prepared to say, that it is sufficient to induce the court to make the party deliver up the contract; but, I am satisfied, it is a sufficient reason to induce the court not to decree a specific performance;" thus relying on inadequacy expressly. At page 81 he denies that there was any hardship, independent of this; and at page 82: "I am, therefore, bound to look into that second cause; and there I find that a bargain was made for buying an estate, at a very inadequate price—so enormous that all mankind must, at the first mention of it, concur in thinking it so. If I had any doubt about the inadequacy of price, I would put it in some mode of inquiry; but, as the ease stands, the value is £9,000; and then the question is, whether a young man, in this court, shall be holden to a bargain like this. *Howell* v. *George*, 1 Madd., 1, again recognizes hardship as a defense. In Madd. Ch., last ed., 405, it is said, "a defendant will not be compelled to perform an unreasonable contract;" which is a correction; for the word was omitted in the corresponding passage of the first edition, though the author inserted it in page 336 of that edition, relative to the same subject.

In *Clitherall* v. *Ogilvie*, 1 Des. Eq., 257, the principles for which we contend are explicitly asserted. *The case is stated [***478** to be clear of all fraud, imposition, or misrepresentation, and the question was, whether, under all the circumstances of the case, the court would decree a specific execution, or leave the party to his remedy at law. The power of the court was declared to be discretionary; not arbitrary, but governed by the rules of equity; that though there was no fraud charged, yet, in order to entitle the party to a specific performance, it ought to be fair, certain, just, equal in all its parts, and for adequate consideration; that if any of these ingredients were wanting, the court would not decree performance; and at pages 258-9, it is said, "though an inadequate consideration may not alone be sufficient to set aside a contract, yet it is a material ingredient, and will go a great way, where the property has been sold for a sum grossly inadequate to its real value. The court, although it may not go so far as to set aside the agreement, will not, however, lend its aid in compelling a specific performance, but leave the party to his remedy at law, to recover damages for the non-performance." At page 260: "But there is a distinction to be made, between the court's setting aside an unreasonable contract, after it is executed, and compelling a specific performance of such an one. In the latter case, they will use their discretion with greater liberality than in the former." Again (261): "Being altogether an executory contract, and the complainant coming here for a specific execution, this court will not depart from the constant rule in the case of a hard bargain, where it is not absolutely executed but executory only, of refusing to carry it into execution." *Perkins* v. *Wright*, 3 Harr. & M'H., 324, contains the same general doctrine; and in *Campbell* v. *Spencer*, 2 Binn., 129, the remarks of Tilghman, *Ch. J.*, are to the same effect. (*Vide Id.*, p. 133.)

In answer to our authorities and arguments, we are told that the doctrine of inadequacy is too vague to be practicable; that the estimate of men as to the value of property is different; and so long as their opinions and habits of life differ, the rule cannot be safely enforced. But the same difficulty exists in other cases, and must exist in many from the nature of **479***] *things? In an action, how can the jury assess damages, except upon the opinion of witnesses? So, upon questions of fraud or surprise, when sent to a jury for trial, they must labor under the same uncertainty; and indeed, saying that this contract might go to, and be passed upon, by a jury in reference to the damages, gives up the objection. No matter whether we begin with inadequacy or mistake. Gross inadequacy, too, when relied on as evidence of fraud, must be ascertained in some way. If this cannot be done, when it is small, how is it to be reached when large? Such questions must rest upon the opinions of men till courts are more enlightened that they ever can be. The opposite doctrine would preclude all inquiry into value. We must not expect to arrive at demonstrative certainty, but take the best lights we can obtain.

It is asked, why send the party to law, when, if there be a legal remedy at all it must embrace as the measure of damages the value of the property of which a conveyance was refused pursuant to the contract. I need not remark, that even this admits there must be an inquiry into its value. But we deny that the contract price is the only one by which the jury are to be regulated. The cases cited as to hard bargains show that the jury may give mitigated damages, according to the reason of the case. If the jury had nothing more to do than look at the contract price, all the *Chancellors* who had made these decisions must have been in darkness. But the rule is a familiar one at law. Bac. Abr., Damages, D; *James* v. *Morgan*, 1 Lev., 111; *Thornborough* v. *Whitacre*, 6 Mod., 305; *Cutler* v. *How*, 8 Mass., 257; *Same* v. *Johnson*, *Id.*, 266; *Baxter* v. *Wales*, 12 *Id.*, 365.

As to the cases cited against the doctrine of inadequacy; *Parker* v. *Palmer*, 1 Ch. Cas., 41, is not much relied upon by the gentleman himself. It is, indeed, as he says, very obscure, and does not decide the point. *London* v. *Richmond*, 2 Vern., 421-3, was a fall of property in value subsequent to the bargain; and the anonymous case cited by Ld. Thurlow, in *Mortimer* v. *Capper*, 1 Bro. Ch. Cas., 158, was denied to be law, by Sir Samuel Romilly, in *Mortlock* *v. *Buller*, 10 Ves., 298, and [***480** correctly. Ld. Thurlow says: "I remember a case of a contract for a piece of ground, which was to be inclosed for £20, and upon a bill for specific performance, the defense was, that it was worth £200. And although the contract was to be performed *in futuro*, yet, neither party knowing the value, the Master of the Rolls decreed a performance." It was a case of gross inadequacy, and can never be supported. As to the principal case, the agreement was perfectly fair; and the Lord *Chancellor* says, in *Mortimer* v. *Capper*, p. 157, "to decree for you, I must lay it down as a rule, that where a bargain depends upon a contingent event, which chance both the parties know, if the event turns out against one of the parties, he must be discharged from his contract." This is clear where the party runs the risk of the contingency; and the final opinion is far from sustaining the gentleman's doctrine. The case was referred to a master to ascertain the value of the annuity, which was the subject of purchase; and the *Lord Chancellor* puts it on the fairness of the price. All this will be seen at the close of the case. It virtually overrules the anonymous case cited.

The case of *Adams* v. *Weare*, 1 Bro. Ch. Cas., 567, is the one principally relied on against us; but it will be found that this case is contradictory and obscure. The vendee purchased with a view to building a mill. The vendor knew nothing of this according to the case; but from Ld. Thurlow's opinion, it was plainly in the contemplation of both parties. At page 568 he says he was not very anxious to discuss the point what bargains the court should execute; that every agreement should be performed unless waived; that the rule should be fixed, and not rest on loose expressions, such as "hard" and "unconscionable," which expressions, unless properly applied, mean little or nothing. That is true. No words mean anything unless properly applied. He then goes into the particulars of the bargain; it was objected that, when the bargain was made, the price was three fourths more than the value; "but," says he, "for aught I know to the contrary, it may be the value." To warrant the erection of the building, consent from the Corporation *of Bristol [***481** was necessary, and the consent of a Mrs. Day; and both parties supposed this might be obtained without difficulty. The vendee agreed to procure it. The value must have been connected with the probability of obtaining it. All the vendee did was to ask Mrs. Day's consent; and the court rely upon this fact; and notice particularly, at page 569, where it looks like the main ground; and the *Chancellor* said if that consent should be obtained, the plan might yet be carried into effect. It did not appear but that the mill might have been built, had a competent premium been tendered to Mrs. Day; and thus the case turned on Ld. Thurlow's inability to decide whether the fair value was given or not. If an authority for the other side, it is opposed to his former opinion in *Mortimer* v. *Capper*, 1 Bro. Ch., 156.

It is said *Collier* v. *Brown*, 1 Cox, 428, decides the abstract point, that inadequacy is no objection. The court say (pp. 431-2): "The parties bargained with their eyes open and that no imposition or surprise was proved in the case; that Mary Turner was very well satisfied with her bargain until she found she could get more for the premises; that, under these circumstances, mere inadequacy of price (where it cannot be used as evidence of fraud) is not, of itself, sufficient to prevent the court from administering its usual equity; for if it were, it might be difficult to draw the line, or to say that whenever a better offer is made, it shall not be reason why a former agreement should not be executed." Thus the court expressly declare that they take the peculiar circumstances of the case as a guide, and they state the circumstances under which they say inadequacy is not enough. In *Emery* v. *Wase*, 8 Ves., 517, Ld. Eldon said he did not deny that mere inadequacy, though considerable, was not enough; but, he adds, "very considerable difference in value, is not inconsiderable evidence that the contract was not made with great care and attention;" and specific performance was denied on another ground. The *dictum* in relation to simple inadequacy was not called for. In *Coles* v. *Trecothick*, 9 Ves., 246, Ld. Eldon said: "Inadequacy is quite out of the question. The cases of reversions and **482***] *interests of that sort go upon very different principles. In some, the whole duty of making good the bargain, upon the principles of this court, is upon the vendee; as in the instance of heirs expectant. Inadequacy of price does not depend upon a person giving *pretium affectionis*, from any peculiar motive, beyond what any other man would give, the reasonable price." The property was sold for £20,000, and the offer was £25,000; in refer- to which, he speaks of the *pretium affectionis*, and says that, "unless the inadequacy of price is such as shocks the conscience, and amounts, in itself, to conclusive and decisive evidence of fraud in the transaction, it is not, itself, a sufficient ground for refusing a specific performance." Inadequacy, as he admits, was really out of the question; and the *dictum* in relation to it was *obiter*. Is it true, as he says, that inadequacy, in order to prevail, must be such as to shock the conscience? He not only travels beyond the case, but beyond the law, as it had been long settled by his predecessors; unless it be understood in reference to the particular case, which was an auction sale. So it must be considered; otherwise it goes beyond his own opinion in *White* v. *Damon*, 7 Ves., 31. There (p. 35) he says, "the plaintiff is not affected with anything beyond suspicion; the sale taking place at an auction, without any fraud, surprise or mistake; the estate being offered upon any price he would bid, and without more he became the purchaser. I am inclined to say, that a sale by auction, no fraud, surprise, &c., cannot be set aside for mère inadequacy of price. It will be very difficult to sustain sales by auction, if this court will not specifically perform the agreement." He ought to be understood as using language with the same view in both cases. *Livingston* v. *Byrne*, 11 Johns., 566, lays down the same doctrine.

In *Burrowes* v. *Lock*, 10 Ves., 470, a specific execution was directed, it is true, without regard to inadequacy; but the property in question was already vested in trust. The bargain was executed so far, and the case came within the principle applicable to setting aside contracts. Being executed in trust, refusing to carry it into complete execution would have *been equivalent to setting it aside. [***483** *Floyer* v. *Sherard*, Amb., 18, gives the true solution of that case. "The next objection," says the court (p. 19), "was, as to our giving relief; for in many cases, the court will not set an agreement aside, and yet not extend any relief. But in the present case, there is no difference between setting it aside, and not giving relief." Again; "in a case of this kind, the court is as much bound to give its relief as if it was a legal title, and an action brought at law." So in *Burrowes* v. *Lock*, there was no chance of reaching the case at law; and in such case the refusing to carry into execution, or setting aside, stand upon the same ground. It does not appear, by the case, that there was any covenant upon which the party could have had a remedy at law, or if a warranty of title was implied, there was no question made but the vendor had a complete title: so that this case comes to a question of inadequacy upon an effort to set aside the contract. In *Western* v. *Russell*, 3 Ves. & B., 187, the Master of the Rolls said: "It is then alleged that the estate was sold greatly below its fair value, and upon that ground there can be no specific performance. Here, again, it is unnecessary to determine, as a general question, whether inadequacy of price might or might not be a ground for refusing performance; the case before the court being that of the proprietor of an estate not alleged to have been under any incapacity or deficiency of judgment, or to have been led by accident or design into a misapprehension of the value." This part of his opinion contains all that is material to the case then under consideration. He does not profess to decide upon the ground of inadequacy, but places the decree on entirely a different foundation. Nor does he presuppose that inadequacy was an insufficient ground; but this is connected with surprise. The question of inadequacy, alone, was carefully shunned. Nor was the question decided in *Cadman* v. *Horner*, 18 Ves., 10. The Master of the Rolls said the allegation of inadequacy was shaken by the defendant's own testimony; and he accordingly took this ground. He would not stop to inquire where the weight of authority lay, but examined the question whether *there [***484** was inadequacy in fact. *Kien* v. *Stukeley*, 2 Bro. P. C., 396, 398, decides that inadequacy alone is a sufficient objection.

But the case of the respondents does not stand upon inadequacy alone. There are other important circumstances interwoven with it, which, in the language of the *Chancellor*, are sufficient to overcome the scruples of the most cautious mind. The agreement was obtained from an habitual drunkard, and it is in vain to talk of such a man's acuteness in making a bargain. This is a point sufficiently put in issue. The appellant does not pretend that he was surprised with the defense upon this ground; nor was he, in fact, so surprised. The examination of witnesses was full to this question, by himself, after which he should not be heard to make the objection. [Here the counsel examined the testimony to this point.] That reasonable doubts exist as to the fairness of the transaction, is enough to resist a bill for specific performance. In the language of one of the cases read, "it must be above all objection." It is not necessary, as upon a bill to set the contract aside, that positive unfairness should be shown. The distinction is taken in *Cook* v. *Clayworth*, 18 Ves., 12; *Id.*, 14, *note*, that the court will not set aside a contract on the ground of intoxication, unless it was procured by the party who seeks to take advantage of it; though it is not necessary to establish this fact in order to avoid its execution. In *Dunnage* v. *White*, 1 Swanston, 138, even in a contract made with the view to a family arrangement, Sir T. Plumer says (pp. 149, 50) "of the incompetency of J. E. L. there is no satisfactory evidence; the solicitor who attests the deed proves that he was sober and under no mental disability, and without regard to undue influence, the evidence is certainly not sufficient to impeach the deed; but as to his general description, there is strong testimony, and all on one side, that he was dissolute, illiterate, addicted to intoxication; that he had recently passed from a low station into the possession of property to which he was not apparently destined; that his course of life rendered him extremely subject to imposition. Such habits, though not constituting absolute **485***] incapacity, lay a ground for a strict *examination, &c." So here, if there was not a total alienation, Ellison's faculties must have been impaired, and an inability produced.

But the appellant did not and could not perform the agreement, at the time stipulated by him, nor during Ellison's lifetime. The Newburgh lots being then incumbered to their full value, and there being no waiver of time, or indulgence granted, by Ellison in his lifetime, nor by the respondents since his decease.

One bound to sell in fee simple must covenant against incumbrances. 1 Madd. Ch., 339. A mortgage is such an incumbrance as to excuse a bargainee from completing his purchase. *Butler* v. *O'Hear*, 1 Des. Eq., 382; *Judson* v. *Wass*, 11 Johns., 525. We are met by the argument that the mortgage is now paid, and it is enough that the vendor can make a good title at the coming in of the master's report, or even at the final decree. This position was considered and refuted in *Alley* v. *Deschamps*, 13 Ves., 225, where the *Chancellor* entered into the subject very fully, and pronounced it an extravagant doctrine.

The right should be the same, both at law and in equity. A Court of Chancery is resorted to merely because the remedy is different; but it must be founded on the same right as the remedy at law. If the party is unable to perform at the day, it is true he may be relieved; and there are two cases in which this may be done. 1. Even where the delay is occasioned by circumstances over which the party seeking an execution has no control, he may be relieved, unless the delay be so great as to amount to an abandonment, if the time of execution is not made material by the contract, or no change of circumstances accrue. In one case of this kind an Act of Parliament was waited for, to enable the party to convey, this being necessary to warrant the grant of a reversion from the Crown. But 2. Where the party is in fault, the whole depending on him, a different rule prevails. This point was considered in *Kien* v. *Stukely*, Gilb., 155. In *Fordyce* v. *Ford*, 4 Bro. Ch. Cas., 494, the performance was placed on the ground of acquiescence, and there was no *considerable delay; [***486** but the Master of the Rolls denied that a vendor was to take his own time.

It is said the appellant is without remedy at law, in this case, from the lapse of time. If so, it was his own fault. I refer to *Lloyd* v. *Collett*, 4 Bro. Ch. Cas., 469; 4 Ves., 689, 690, *note b*, S. C. In the latter book, Ld. Loughborough is reported to have said: "There is nothing of more importance than that the ordinary contracts between man and man, which are so necessary in their intercourse with each other, should be certain and fixed, and that it should be certainly known when a man is bound and when not. There is a difficulty to comprehend how the essentials of a contract should be different in equity and at law. It is one thing to say the time is not so essential that in no case in which the day has by any means been suffered to elapse, the court would relieve against it and decree performance—the conduct of the parties, inevitable accident, &c., might induce the court to relieve. But it is a different thing to say the appointment of a day is to have no effect at all, and that it is not in the power of the parties to contract that if the agreement is not executed at a particular time, the parties shall be at liberty to rescind it. In most of the cases, there have been steps taken. Is there any case in which, without any previous communication at all between the parties, the time has been suffered to elapse? I want a case to prove that where nothing has been done by the parties, this court will hold, in a contract of buying and selling, a rule that certainly is not the rule at law, that the time is not an essential part of the contract. Here no step has been taken, from the day of the sale, for six months after the expiration of the time at which the contract was to be completed. If a given default will not do, what length of time will do? It is true, the plaintiff must have considered himself bound after the day. So he was. He could not take advantage of his own neglect. He says, "by my own default this contract is void in law —I cannot succeed at law—on the contrary, the other party is entitled to recover back the money he has paid in expectation of the execution of his contract—therefore an equity arises to me." An equity out of his own neglect! *It is a singular head [***487** of equity." So, in this case, the party is not able to perform, because he does not make himself so. In *Benedict* v. *Lynch*, 1 Johns. Ch., 370, 375, the *Chancellor* acknowledged the rule as laid down by Ld. Loughborough, and repeats and adopts it in terms; and (p. 375) he declares the general rule to be, that a party coming after the day for performance cannot be heard, unless he justify the delay by a substantial excuse; and where he has omitted to perform by the day, without such excuse, and there has been no acquiescence on the other side, he will not be relieved; in support of which he cites Newl. on Cont., 342, and Sugd. L. of V, 3d Lond. ed., 268; *Milward* v. *Earl Thanet*, 5 Ves, 720, in *note*, S. P.

The only questions are, what was to be performed by the appellant, and whether his omission was excused. He has done nothing; and before he could call for an execution of the contract, he should have put himself in a situation to perform it on his part, by cancelling the mortgage. True this was done before bill filed, but the appellant should have been ready, in this case, at the day. I cite to this point *Colson* v. *Thompson*, 2 Wh., 336. *Hepburn* v. *Auld*, 5 Cr., 262, was cited by *Mr. Henry*, to show that time was immaterial; and it is true the general doctrine is laid down there, and in *Hepburn* v. *Dunlop*, 1 Wh., 179. These cases may be supported on the ground of waiver, though they seem more properly to come within the distinction we have advanced, that where the party cannot be able to perform by any act exclusively his own, he shall be excused; but not where the fault arises entirely from his own neglect. Suppose we admit, then, that the appellant's remedy is gone at law—the whole loss is owing to himself. To permit one to claim equity for want of a remedy at law, which he himself has thrown away, would be most extraordinary. The appellant calls on the court to relieve him, because he has not done his duty. The rule, that equity will relieve, upon the ground of there being a want of all remedy at law, does not apply. The cases where equity has disregarded time are those where the party has lost his remedy, without his own mere neglect. **488***] It is, indeed, *a strange equity, as Ld. Loughborough said, which is to grow out of the negligence of the party who seeks it.

But suppose, for the sake of argument, that equity would originally have relieved, under such circumstances; it will not do so where the specific performance becomes a hardship, from a change of circumstances. The plans for improvement, which would alone prevent almost a total loss of the property, are defeated by Ellison's death. His wife and children cannot enter into his commercial views. Take what is said in *Seton* v. *Slade*, 7 Ves., 274, for a guide—"The title to an estate requires so much clearing and inquiry that unless substantial objections appear, not merely as to the time, but an alteration of circumstances affecting the value of the thing, or objections arising out of circumstances, not merely as to time, but the conduct of the parties during the time, unless the objection can be so sustained, many of the cases go the length of establishing that the objection cannot be maintained." Take what is here said as a criterion, the court cannot help seeing that here is a change of circumstances. The expectation, if any, of a rise in value, from the establishment of a Navy Yard at Newburgh, is defeated.

The counsel have great difficulty in seeing how, if inadequacy alone be an insufficient objection, it should be different, when taken in connection with lapse of time, or the other circumstances in the case, any one of which would not, alone, be a sufficient defense. But the *Chancellor* is not singular in taking this ground. Both Powell and Sugden take the same view of it, holding that, in all cases where the price is inadequate, the court will seize upon delay, connect it with inadequacy, and refuse to interfere upon the two grounds together. 2 Pow. on Cont., 229; Sugd. L. of V., 2d Am., from 5th Lond. ed., 190. These authors both think inadequacy alone not sufficient; but otherwise, when connected with lapse of time. Possession being taken does not vary the case. This was holden in *Savage* v. *Taylor*, Cas. *t.* Talb., 234, cited by the *Chancellor*. The true principle of this case is contained in the opinion of the *Chancellor*, and his words, relative to the taking possession, need not be accounted for, by supposing *that he had some edition of the work [***489** not seen by the gentleman. That it was taken is evident both from the opinion and the decree. In *Whorwood* v. *Simpson*, 2 Vern., 186; *Alley* v. *Deschamps*, 13 Ves., 225, and *Rochfort* v. *Creswick*, 2 Bro. P. C., 296, possessions had also been taken, and in the last two cases held a long time, yet a specific performance was refused.

Mr. S. Jones, same side, entered into a very full examination of the cases cited by the Atty-Gen., vindicated his views, and enforced and illustrated his arguments. He said the doctrine, as stated by the *Lord Chancellor*, in *Radcliffe* v. *Warrington*, 12 Ves., 331, 332, that enforcing specific performance is not a matter of course; that the jurisdiction is not compulsory upon the court, but the subject of discretion; that the question is not what the court might do; but what it may do under the circumstances, runs through all the cases to the period of our Revolution. It is true, that where the matter is peculiarly the subject of equity jurisdiction, as a legacy, the *Chancellor* has no more discretion than exists at law; because, to exercise it might take away all relief; otherwise, if a remedy may be had in either court. The exercise of discretion is safe, because the party to whom relief is denied may still go to law. If at the Revolution this was the law of England, we adopted it by our Constitution; and if it has been shown that subsequent to this period the English *Chancellors* followed new rules, this court were not bound to follow them. He said this not to disparage the decisions of the English courts. Reason on the other side of the Atlantic is the same as here; but if the English rule has undergone no alteration with us, it is the safest to abide by it. He agreed that *obiter dicta* of Ld. Eldon had thrown doubts upon the question, but nothing more. There is no case, even in England, deciding directly that inadequacy is an insufficient objection to a specific performance.

In *Mortimer* v. *Capper*, 1 Bro. Ch., 158, a case is cited, and in P. Wms. are several cases in which a great change in the value of the property, even after the bargain, was held *enough to deny a specific execution. [***490** And *Ex parte Minor*, 11 Ves., 559, will be found a case in which the same ground was taken, even as to an auction sale.

The principle, that a sot is never in a fit situation to do business, is not only sustained by the authorities, but recognized by the Statute (sess. 44, ch. 109) giving over the management of his affairs to the town officers.

Cases had been cited to show that there can be no exercise of discretion, where the remedy was gone at law; but these were cases in which the remedy is exclusively equitable, like *Atty-Gen.* v. *Day*, 1 Ves., 218, 221, which related to the execution of an order made upon a master's report; and the party never could have gone to law. On this ground relief was granted. Talking of discretion does not always presuppose an existing present remedy at law. There are cases where it will be exercised, though there be no such remedy. In *Hick* v. *Phillips*, Prec. in Ch., 575, there was none, and yet the court exercised their discretion in denying a specific performance.

Mr. J. V. Henry, in reply. I presume it would not have been contended that the appellant lost all remedy by default, in not tendering a deed on the 1st of June, and by not then being in a capacity to convey, if there were no inadequacy in the case. As to the impediment arising from the mortgage, I cite Pow. on Cont., 266–7, where the author says: "It will make no difference, in respect to performance in specie, although it be evident, from the person's own showing who institutes the suit, that he had not, at the time of entering into the agreement respecting which the suit is preferred, a good title to the hereditaments which are the subject of it." He relies on *Longford* v. *Pitt*, 2 P. Wms., 629, where the Master of Rolls said: "It is enough that the party have title at the time of the decree; which is always the single subject of inquiry on reference." He illustrates his doctrine by the case where an Act of Parliament was required to make the title perfect.

It is said that there is a distinction between a defect removable by the act of the party, and
491*] some other power; that, in *the latter case, he is more favored. Why so? Is not one more blamable, when he contracts to sell an estate in the power of another, than where it is under their own control exclusively? In *Wynn* v. *Morgan*, 7 Ves., 202, the general principle is advanced, that time is not material, in the eye of a court of equity, and that it is enough that the party seeking performance have a title at the hearing. I admit it is different, where time is of the essence of the contract, as in the case of the South Sea stock agreements. A want of title is certainly more material than a mere lapse of time for a few days; and yet it has been uniformly held that the former should be relieved against. This was so in *Wynn* v. *Morgan*, 7 Ves., 202; *Mortlock* v. *Buller*, 10 Ves., 315; *Jenkins* v. *Hiles*, 6 Ves., 646, and *Davis* v. *Hone*, 2 Sch. & L., 352. In *Day* v. *Newman*, 2 Cox, 77, which has been triumphantly cited against us, the Master of the Rolls explicitly declares (p. 83) that lapse of time is no objection. *Clute* v. *Robison*, 2 Johns., 595, recognizes the same rule. The decree was reversed in that case, upon the express ground that though the party had no title when he first came to perform, yet the objection was obviated at the time of the decree. *Hepburn* v. *Auld*, 5 Cr., 262, establishes the same point.

That the appellant is without remedy at law, is a powerful reason in favor of a specific performance. At law, the appellant must have averred performance, or a tender of performance, on the 1st of June. This was a condition precedent. We could not perform at that day, and therefore our legal remedy is gone. Newl. on Cont., 89, says that courts of equity afford assistance, as to land or real estate, principally in those cases where courts of law are incapable of giving to the party the remedy which he seeks; though, he says, that contracts relating to stocks and personal chattels are an exception. In *Flint* v. *Brandon*, 8 Ves., 163, the Master of the Rolls says: "It is only where the legal remedy is inadequate or defective, that it becomes necessary for courts of equity to interfere." In *Errington* v. *Aynesley*, 2 Bro. Ch., 341, it is said (p. 343): A specific performance is only decreed where the party wants *the thing in specie, and cannot [*492
have it in any other way." *Davis* v. *Hone*, 2 Sch. & L., 347, S. P. Mitford, in his Treatise on Pleadings, pp. 95–6, advances the same doctrine.

I have given several cases in which it was held, that because the party was remediless at law, he should, therefore, be relieved in equity. Other reasons are, that several of the respondents are infants. They are trustees, and both at common law and by the Statute of Anne (1 R. L., 148, sec. 7), the remedy is confined to a court of equity alone. This contract is one of exchange. The specific thing is in question; and the case is distinguishable, in this respect, from most of those where money was the consideration on one side.

I know not what use gentlemen intended to make of 1 Madd., 339, as to what covenants are necessary in a deed. We have never refused to give a deed, including all the covenants contemplated by our contract. These are broader than Ellison agreed to enter into on his part. In *Butler* v. *O'Hear*, 1 Des., 382, the party could make out a title at the hearing; and *Judson* v. *Wass*, 11 Johns., 525, and *Hasbrouck* v. *Tappen*, 15 Johns., 200, merely show the strictness which prevails at law. In *Alley* v. *Deschamps*, 13 Ves., 225, there was not only a change of circumstances, but the party had lain by for three years, without any excuse of his default. This was held an abandonment, upon the peculiar facts of the case. *Kien* v. *Stukeley*, Gilb., 155, confirms our doctrine that, to make lapse of time material, it must be of the essence of the contract. An intention to pay in South Sea stock was frustrated by delay. That this is the sense of the rule appears also from *Lewis* v. *Ld. Lechmere*, 2 Eq. Cas. Abr., 20, pl. 17. Time was there deemed material, because the stock fell Where is the analogy between that and this case? Here is land of ascertained value. There was stock continually fluctuating in its price. *Lloyd* v. *Collet*, 4 Bro. Ch. Cas., 469, is remarked upon in Newl. on Cont., 242. That author says, if considerable time has elapsed, without sufficient reason to excuse the delay, courts of equity now decline decreeing a specific performance *and [*493
states *Lloyd* v. *Collet* as illustrative of the position. There were repeated applications in that case, to perform, and the contract was held to be abandoned. In *Milward* v. *Earl Thanet*, 5 Ves. 720, *note b*, the parties differed as to the construction of the agreement; and there was a delay of seven years. That the party must be ready, desirous, prompt and eager, as said by that case, is a figurative expression, which means merely that he must

not be negligent. Possession was delivered in the present case. There was a part execution. *Colson* v. *Thompson*, 2 Wh., 336, was a case of gross neglect, in not effecting a survey. *Hepburn* v. *Dunlop*, 1 *Id.*, 179, says nothing about the lapse of time, but contains the principle, that if the title be good at the decree it is enough. Sugden, 190, is, I admit, against us, if the text were to stand by itself; but the cases on which it is bottomed are of contracts where either time was of the essence of the contract, or there was fraud or abuse of confidence. To have been borne out by the cases as to time, he should have qualified his rule, by providing that it should be of the essence of the agreement. 2 Pow. on Cont., 229, 230, presents a class of cases where the contract should not have been executed, even if there had been no delay. *Rochfort* v. *Creswick*, 2 Bro. P. C., 296, was tried by the rule as to fairness and honesty; and in *Harrington* v. *Wheeler*, 4 Ves., 686, cited also in Newl. on Cont., 243, 244, there was a lapse of six years; no act done towards execution, and, in the meantime, the vendor had agreed to convey to a third person. *Benedict* v. *Lynch*, 1 Johns. Ch., 370, is also cited. It will merely be necessary to read the caption of that case to see that it cannot apply. The agreement was declared to be void, in terms, by the parties; and the *Chancellor* relies upon this express provision. He thinks that the parties may make the time material by express agreement, though it had been formerly held otherwise; and he also relies upon the fact that there was no excuse for the delay. The want of this excuse is included in his general rule laid down at pages 375, 376. That rule is correct. It excepts a case of acquiescence. We are suffered to remain in possession without objection; and fall directly **494***] within the qualification. *He afterwards repeats the same idea; and the case has no application, until it be shown that Seymour has released his claims. So far from this, here was a cotemporaneous delivery of possession by both parties. We say that where the time slips by, being of the essence of the contract, it is never an objection to a specific execution, unless the party, who alone can be injured, promptly refuses to complete the purchase on this ground. *Hick* v. *Phillips*, Prec. in Ch., 575, was an effort to impose copyhold upon the party instead of freehold. *Hanger* v. *Eyles*, 21 Vin., 540, A, pl. 1; 2 Pow. on Cont., 230, S. C., was an utter incapacity to convey at the day; and *Pincke* v. *Curteis*, 4 Bro. Ch., 328; Newl. on Cont., 231. S. C., was not only an omission at the day, but this was followed by communication between the parties, and there was no effort to procure a performance, and no acquiescence in the delay by the party injured, yet a performance was decreed. Newland (p. 246) states the case of *Guest* v. *Homfray*, 5 Ves., 818, too strongly. The cases stated by him are mostly of auction sales, where time is material; and the case from 5 Ves., 818, admitted delay as an objection, because no title could be made out; and the vendee, for that reason, declined going on.

On the whole, the cases are not opposed to the doctrine for which we contend. In no case, where time was not of the essence of the contract, has a short delay been holden any objection, especially if imputable to an incumbrance, or want of title, which may be removed. A bill cannot be filed till after the day passes. If delay be a sufficient objection, why all this doctrine in relation to lapse of time? The party may always file his bill at a short day, as was done in this instance; and if the incumbrance is removed before the decree, it is enough. Ellison is as such in fault as Seymour. The former took no steps towards the performance of the contract, though he did no act to disaffirm it.

Shall the incumbrance and delay, then, though nothing in themselves, become effectual when added to inadequacy, which is also nothing, and, when taken together, make a whole, which is to constitute a defense? It would be like adding and giving effect to a series of cyphers.

*Occasional intoxication is no de- [***495** feuse, unless it has resulted in a total prostration of the mind. 1 Pow. on Cont., 29, 30.

Mr. Jones. We do not rely upon occasional intoxication as constituting an objection. Our position is, that habitual intoxication, producing mental debility, disqualifies the party to contract, the same as any other disease of the mind.

Mr. Henry. *Cook* v. *Clayworth*, 18 Ves., 12, contains the whole doctrine upon this subject, and I shall content myself with referring to that case. The note at page 14 of that book is relied on against us; but when this speaks of intoxication as a disability, it means a state of actual intoxication at the time of the contract. Habitual intoxication, or mental disability from any other cause, is not proved.

These parties, then, stood on a footing of perfect equality, so far as capacity and means of judging were concerned; and is it to be tolerated that mere inadequacy, not sufficient to evince fraud, shall defeat a bill for specific performance? The consequences would be monstrous. A large landholder sells to a farmer at $1 per acre payable by installments. The day of paying one of these installments passes; and the land was in fact worth $2. Shall the vendor have it in his power to decline a conveyance upon such ground? One wishing to exchange a commercial for an agricultural life, selects his residence, and purchases of the farmer, at $40 per acre, what was worth but $20. On becoming sick of his bargain, may he be off? This is a plain case of the *pretium affectionis;* and yet the *Chancellor's* doctrine allows a place for repentance. This is inadequacy, *per se.* The same rule must be extended to large speculations in cities where the price of the subject falls. The only safe rule is the one for which we contend, that the inadequacy must be such, *per se*, or connected with other circumstances, as shall be proof of fraud; otherwise, what shall be the standard in a country where real estate fluctuates in value as it does here? Allowing the objection of inadequacy *per se*, makes the *Chancellor* the arbiter of every bargain.

I propose briefly to examine the cases on this subject, as they arise in chronological order. *Parker* v. *Palmer*, 1 Ch. *Cas., 42, is [***496** not, as supposed by gentlemen, given up. It is not, as supposed, barren of fact. It is a strong case. The execution of a mere bet upon contingency was decreed, though inadequacy was conceded. *Phillips* v. *Bucks*, 1 Vern., 227, 229, lays down a general position which runs through a number of cases; but there had not been fair and open dealing. *Berney* v. *Pitt*, 2 Vern., 14, was an unconscionable bargain with an heir for his expectancy; and in *The Marquis of Normanby* v. *Berkly*, 5 Vin., 539, not a single fact is stated; and the general position taken is, what we admit, that the contract must be fair. It is supposed that a jury might mitigate the damages. So far it is not law; and the whole case is rendered of doubtful authority by such a position. A jury cannot mitigate, unless the contract betrays absolute folly. Even there, the rule prevails in no case except where there is fraud or imbecility. *Green* v. *Green*, 5 Vin., 538, pl. 19, was a dealing in relation to a mere expectancy, and yet the court refused to set it aside. *Young* v. *Clerk*, Prec. in Ch., 538, illustrates the danger of depending for a guide upon the general rules laid down in cases, without going to the circumstances. We are told, on the authority of this case, that the contract must be free from all exception, by reason of undervalue. The *Lord Chancellor* said that the contract was unreasonable, or founded in fraud, and dismissed the bill, and left the party to law. The facts show fraud—viz.: a concealment of the leases—a palpable *suppressio veri*, one branch of the very definition of fraud. It it not a case of mere inadequacy, though it was relied on as such, and is, undoubtedly, a leading case upon which the doctrine contended for on the other side is founded. In 5 Vin., 533, pl. 32, will be found a string of cases, from Ld. Harcourt's manuscript tables, containing the principle that equity will not carry unreasonable agreements into execution. At page 538, pl. 21, a specific execution was denied, because the plaintiff had shuffled, and a distinction was drawn, which runs through all the cases, between stock and land contracts, and the reason is given. The same page, 548, pl. 9, says: "Contract for S. S. stock, at an unreasonable price, set aside," **497***] referring to *the case of *Thompson* v. *Harcourt*, 2 Bro. P. C., 415. The result given is inaccurate; and it shows how little reliance can be placed upon these manuscripts. *Rochfort* v. *Creswick*, 2 Bro. P. C., 296, respects the fairness of the agreement; one of the qualifications of the rule which we laid down in the opening. *Kien* v. *Stukely*, Gilb., 155, was a contract for lands, at 40 years' purchase, which were not worth more than 15. The intention was, to pay in South Sea stock, and a specific execution was denied, on the ground that the time had elapsed, and the stock fallen. That was a case where time was of the essence of the agreement.

Gentlemen persist that *Thompson* v. *Harcourt*, 2 Bro. P. C., 415, is correctly considered by the *Chancellor* a mere case of inadequacy. What we say is, that he should not have placed it on the ground of inadequacy alone. The contract, in that case, could not have been executed at the opening of the books, and the vendor could never, therefore, have succeeded at law; yet the court say to the purchaser upon a bill for execution, 'You shall pay at the rate of 920 *per cent.* on the £290;' and leave the case there. The contract was not only executed, but this was done by the halves. Powell, a man of deep learning, in his Treatise on Contracts (2d Vol., p. 232), says, of this case, that the execution of the contract was decreed by chancery, on the ground that a subsequent change in value or circumstances could not impair its validity, and that this decree was affirmed in the House of Lords. He does not, therefore, understand it as the *Chancellor* does. This case was decided in 1722. Now I refer to *Squire* v. *Baker*, 5 Vin., 549, pl. 12, decided in 1726, only four years after, where it is said: "A written agreement being unreasonable, the court would not carry it into execution, but decreed that it be delivered to the party for whose benefit it was designed, that he may have an opportunity to make the most of it at law." Now, I ask, how does this last consist with *Thompson* v. *Harcourt*? Yet the *Chancellor* cites both cases as supporting the same position. *Savage* v. *Taylor*, Cas. *t.* Talb., 234, went upon the unfairness of the party, and the facts will be seen *clearly to warrant [***498** that ground. Inadequacy is not even mentioned. *Barnardiston* v. *Lingwood*, 2 Atk., 133, contains the general proposition only, that the bargain being hard is an objection to a specific performance. But the agreement was made while the vendor was in distress, and there was, in fact, misapprehension. The court say, if the agreement had been fair they would have decreed a conveyance. Accordingly, in *Goring* v. *Nash*, 3 *Id.*, 187, 188, it is said, the discretion which the court exercised is not arbitrary, but referrible to general rules, *Buxton* v. *Lister*, 3 *Id.*, 386, is relied on against us; but it merely reiterates the general rule, that the agreement should be certain, fair and just. This was a case of personal property. In *Joynes* v. *Statham*, *Id.*, 388, there was circumvention. The same spirit pervades the whole of Ld. Hardwicke's decisions. See, also, *London* v. *Nash*, *Id.*, 512; S. C., 1 Ves., 12, where a specific execution was holden oppressive, and an issue directed to ascertain the damages. In *Underwood* v. *Hitchcox*, 1 Ves., 279, he says, "the rule, that decreeing specific performance is discretionary, is well known; that to warrant this, it should be in writing, fair in all its parts, and for adequate consideration." The case depends particularly upon the policy of the English courts, who give all possible effect to family settlements. At p. 280 it is treated upon this ground, and said the estate was intended by the uncle as a benefit to the defendant and his family.

Faine v. *Brown*, cited by counsel in 2 Ves., 304, was a case where, if a stranger had been a purchaser, the vendor would have lost half his estate. To decree a specific preformance would have been equivalent to decreeing a penalty. Besides, the vendor was intoxicated at the time. In 1 Fonbl., Newland and Powell, this case is not mentioned at all, with reference to the question of inadequacy. If the purchaser had been the brother himself, Ld. Hardwicke would still have told him he was a volunteer, and not entitled to relief. *Pope* v. *Roots*, 7 Bro. P. C., 184; 1 *Id.*, 370, Toml. ed., is not law. It will be seen, by 2 Pow. on Cont., 76, 62, and Newl. on Cont., 82-5, that it has been overruled in its broad sense, and has resulted in this, that no after inequality can

499*] prevent a *specific performance, if the contract was for adequate consideration when made. *Mortimer* v. *Capper*, 1 Bro. Ch. Cas., 156, before cited, proves this rule conclusively. The bargain was fair, and though the inadequacy was great, it was executed. *Heathcote* v. *Paignon*, 2 Bro. Ch. Cas., 175, repeats the doctrine, reviews the last case, and speaks of resting the question of specific performance on the market price, as an absurdity. It takes the difference between the effect of mere inadequacy, and the evidence arising from gross inadequacy. It is said, "here is no evidence of distress—nothing but inadequacy of value—and if that could be made the rule, the least circumstance which varied the next case which occurred might make the difference;" thus giving the rule for which we contend, in the most luminous manner. The parties stood on equal ground—the contract should have been executed, and it was executed accordingly.

Day v. *Newman*, 2 Cox., 77, is correctly relied upon, as giving force to the objection of simple inadequacy. Ld. Alvanley and Ld. Rosslyn are noted as being the only *Chancellors* who had recognized this doctrine, or attempted to break in upon the opposite rule. Newland on Cont., 66. To my mind there was evidence of overreaching in the vendor, and imbecility in the vendee. It was, in fact, a case of constructive fraud, arising from inadequacy and overreaching, though Ld. Alvanley chooses to deny this, and places the case upon the foundation of simple inadequacy. Yet, in the same year (1788), a correct view of the subject had been taken by the Court of Exchequer, in *Collier* v. *Brown*, 1 Cox, 428. In that case it was insisted (*Id.*, p. 431) that inadequacy alone was an objection, but denied by the court, in so many words, and the rule stated as we contend for it. *Collet* v. *Wollaston*, 3 Bro. Ch. Cas., 228, decided in 1791, was an agreement to assign stock; and by leaving the party to law he would get the value. *Perkins* v. *Wright*, 3 Harr. & M'H., 324, quoted by gentlemen, is plainly not law. It even goes the length of impeaching the contract, from a subsequent accidental change of value; against which the rule is now clearly settled, by cases respecting annuities, destruction by fire, or by earth-**500***] quakes. **Poole* v. *Shergold*, 2 Bro. Ch. Cas., 118, *Jackson* v. *Lever*, 3 *Id.*, 605.

White v. *Damon*, 7 Ves., 30, was an auction case. Ld. Rosslyn had decreed against a specific performance, on the ground of inadequacy; and Ld. Eldon denies his doctrine, going on the ground that it is an auction sale; but the broad proposition which he lays down after this, denies the objection and general inadequacy. *Flint* v. *Brandon*, 8 Ves., 163, has no application; but in *Emery* v. *Wase*, *Id.*, 505, 517, Ld., Eldon confirms his former doctrine, saying that mere difference of value, though considerable, is no objection. The refusal to decree an execution in that case, was on the ground that the court will never compel the husband to exercise his authority over his wife for that purpose. Again; in *Coles* v. *Trecothick*, 9 Ves., 246, Ld. Eldon says, inadequacy does not depend on one's giving *pretium affectionis*, and to make it available it must be such as shocks the conscience. The *pretium affectionis* does not mean attachment merely, but any peculiar motive which leads to a purchase, even for the sake of selling again. The odious appellation of fraud can never be applied to such speculations. Try the rule by this case. Admitting that Ellison purchased with a view to the Navy Yard, and was disappointed, and allowing that he gave too much, should a specific execution be, therefore, denied? Sir Samuel Romilly, in citing *Tilly* v. *Peers*, 10 Ves., 301, from his own notes, adds to what is mentioned by the *Chancellor*, of that case, that on a cross-bill it appeared to be a case of clear fraud; and it is on the latter ground that we must take performance to have been denied. *Mortlock* v. *Buller*, the principal case, beside being one of an auction sale, went on the ground that the agent had no power to sell, and had imposed upon the trustees. There would have been a breach of trust, also, had the trustees conveyed. It is the rather to be inferred, that the case cited by Sir Samuel Romilly went on the ground of fraud disclosed in the cross-bill, because in *Western* v. *Russell*, 3 Ves. & B., 187, 190, A. D. 1814, he denied that inadequacy is a defense, and says he pressed it in vain in *Mortlock* v. *Buller*, and it never had been holden sufficient.

*I forgot to notice, in the order I [***501** had prescribed to myself, the case of *Adams* v. *Weare*, 1 Bro. Ch. Cas., 568, decided in 1784, which was a case of 60 years' purchase, upon the faith that the vendee could make the subject worth what he gave, by obtaining certain mill privileges. The inadequacy was plain, but as there was no evidence of fraud or mistake, a specific execution was decreed, and the *Chancellor* lays down our rule strongly.

Mason v. *Armitage*, 13 Ves., 25, merely qualifies the rule for which we contend, by admitting a mistake to be a defense. In *Willan* v. *Willan*, 16 Ves., 83, surprise is mentioned as another qualification; and the *Chancellor* enters fully into the distinction for which we contend between the force of circumstances which will operate to set aside an agreement, on the one hand, or deny its execution on the other. *Cadman* v. *Horner*, 18 Ves., 10, gives misrepresentation as another qualification of our rule; and does not touch the question whether inadequacy is a defense, *per se*. In *Buckle* v. *Mitchell*, *Id.*, 111, Sir W. Grant, Master of the Rolls, says, "a contract for a purchase is an equitable title; and the person having such title is, in equity, to most purposes, considered as the complete owner of the estate. It is true that equity does not in every case lend its aid to carry a contract for a purchase into execution; but it does not arbitrarily execute one contract and refuse to execute another. Some grounds must be laid to prevent the party from obtaining, in this case, the assistance which the court usually gives in cases of the same general description."

Western v. *Russell*, 3 Ves. & B., 187, is a case parallel with the present in all its features. The marginal note is this: "Inadequacy of consideration no ground for resisting the execution of a contract to sell; the vendor not being under any incapacity, deficiency of judgment, or led by accident or design into a misapprehension of the value." Sir Samuel Romilly denies, *arguendo*, that inadequacy is a defense; and Sir W. Grant, Master of the

Rolls, says, virtually, that inadequacy of price cannot be urged where everything is perfectly fair; but that it can be used only as auxiliary to other proof of fraud, incapacity, or the like. **502***] These *being out of the question, he refused to consider inadequacy. The inadequacy there was very great. We come within the precise terms of that case, except that the inadequacy here is not near so striking. The case of *Howell* v. *George*, 1 Madd. Ch., 1, proceeded on the ground that the interest of the wife and son were to be affected; and the *Chancellor* would not compel the defendant to control them. Another ground was the intrinsic difficulty upon the words of the power. The rule is laid down there, generally, that the court will not decree a specific performance where the case is hard, &c. But it really goes on the mistake of the party in supposing that he has an estate in fee when it was only for life, and sanctions one qualification of the rule which we advanced in the outset—that of mistake. In 2 Pow. on Cont., ed. of 1790, p. 228, it is said: "But exorbitancy, uncoupled with circumstances of fraud, has not been determined to be a ground for the Court of Chancery to refuse its interposition on behalf of the vendor of an estate." Not one case can be found except *Day* v. *Newman*, 2 Cox, 77, opposed to this position. Newl. on Cont., 65 and 66, treats the point as somewhat unsettled, and considers several of the authorities, which have been cited in the course of the argument.

The case of *Howorth* v. *Deem*, 1 Eden, 351, cited on the other side, did not involve the question of inadequacy. It related to a family settlement; and *Johnson* v. *Hill*, 1 Vern., 271, was the case of an heir selling his expectancy, which rests on grounds peculiar to itself. *Hick* v. *Phillips*, Prec. in Ch., 545, was cited as a case of overvalue; but, plainly, it did not go on that ground, though it is true that *Young* v. *Clerk* was there cited; but this was to show that the court have a discretion to refuse a decree of performance generally. 1 Madd. Ch., 9, *n.*, cites *Faine* v. *Brown* for the same purpose. *Vaughan* v. *Thomas*, 1 Bro. Ch. Cas., 556, was a case of personal property, and *Collet* v. *Wollaston*, 3 *Id.*, 228, a case of stock. The 1st edition of Madd. Ch. does not, as supposed on the other side, vary substantially from his last, in relation to this subject. The phrase is essentially the same in both edi- **503***] tions, because *there was no material change in the principle of the cases upon which that writer relied. *Simmons* v. *Hill*, 4 Harr. & M'H., 252, goes merely to discretion in refusing to decree a specific performance, without placing it on the ground of inadequacy. *Carberry* v. *Tannehill*, 1 Harr. & J., 224, was a case of youth and great ignorance in the vendor. The *Chancellor* adverts to these grounds particularly; and the same remark applies to *Clitherall* v. *Ogilvie*, 1 Des., 250. In addition to ignorance and youth, there was great precipitancy; and the inadequacy was gross, so as to evince fraud. The note to that case (p. 258) will show that it does not rest upon the objection of mere inadequacy. *Campbell* v. *Spencer*, 2 Binn., 129, is also cited, but it militates against the gentlemen. The right to a specific execution was, in that case, tried by a jury. There was no great inadequacy; nor did Yeates, *J.*, who tried the cause, hold the contract to be void. He left it to the jury, who found against the contract. There was evidence from which they might have inferred fraud, and for this reason the court denied a new trial. But they agreed with Yeates, *J.*, upon the point of inadequacy. *Franklin* v. *Osgood*, 2 Johns. Ch., 1, was an attempt to set aside a sale. The case did not call upon the *Chancellor* for a discussion as to the effect of inadequacy upon a bill to enforce performance. What he said as to this was, therefore, entirely gratuitous. Both *Pope* v. *Roots*, 7 Bro. P. C., 184, and *White* v. *Nutt*, 1 P. Wms., 60, are considered by Newland in his Treatise on Contracts, 85, 86, as showing that subsequent circumstances of change are no objection, and he gives a variety of instances, farther illustrative of this position; as the death of one on whose life an annuity depended—destruction by fire, &c., in all which specific execution was decreed. What the *Lord Chancellor* says in *Rose* v. *Cunynghame*, 11 Ves., 554, confirms this idea. The estate is considered as executed in the vendee; and the decree operates as a mere confirmation.

Now why go to the jury? Can they mitigate damages in consequence of a change of value? Bac. Abr., Damages, D, to which we are referred for this, cites cases of mere cheat, or extreme folly and weakness. But could the jury divide *the loss even if the New- [***504** burgh lots had been sunk? They have no discretion. They are not arbitrary judges in matters of contract. Could they, in this case, give an amount in damages to the appellant short of the value of the farms, admitting that his remedy at law was good? The measure of the damages is the worth of the thing, on the day when the conveyance was to be made.

SAVAGE, *Ch. J.* On the 14th day of Jan., 1820, William Seymour and Thomas Ellison entered into an agreement under seal, by which Ellison agreed to convey to Seymour two farms in the Towns of Montgomery and Walkill, in the County of Orange, containing by estimation 799 acres of land; and Seymour agreed to convey to Ellison an equal undivided third part of certain lots in the village of Newburgh; the conveyances to be executed on or before the 1st of June then next. It was further agreed that the parties might respectively take possession of the premises so to be conveyed to them. The parties did take possession accordingly; and on the 3d of Aug., 1820, Ellison died without the conveyances being executed. The bill was filed against the respondent, as the heirs of Thomas Ellison, to compel the performance of the above contract. It was resisted in the Court of Chancery on three grounds:

1. Inadequacy of price.
2. Debility of Ellison's mind produced by habitual intoxication.
3. The inability of the appellant to fulfill on his part.

The *Chancellor* dismissed the bill on all these grounds, and expressed an opinion that inadequacy of price may, of itself, and without fraud or other ingredient, be sufficient to authorize the court to refuse its aid in enforcing the performance of a contract for the sale of land; though it might not be sufficient to set aside the contract.

These are the principal points in the case, on which the defense rests. The testimony is very voluminous, and I shall not now enter into a detailed statement of it. The weight of evidence, in my judgment, establishes the difference in value, between the farms and the **505***] lots, at $5,000 and *upwards; and that Ellison was, in the month of Jan., 1820, and before and after, of intemperate habits. Some of the witnesses represented him as incapable of doing business; and others thought him capable, except when intoxicated. It also appears, that, both in Jan. and June, 1820, the village lots were incumbered by a mortgage to the amount of $5,000, and so continued till shortly before filing the bill.

It is asserted by elementary writers that the power of enforcing agreements specifically will not be exercised but to subserve the cause of justice; and that whenever the bargain is a hard one, bordering on oppression; where there has not been perfect fairness; where any facts have not been concealed which should been disclosed; or where any unfair advantage has been taken; in those cases equity will not decree a specific performance, but leave the party to his remedy at law. Reeve's Dom. Rel., 386; Newl. on Cont., 223-4.

The cases in which a court of equity decrees specific performance of contracts, are those where damages recovered at law would not answer the intention of the parties in making the contract. 2 Sch. & L., 347.

In my judgment, His Honor, the *Chancellor*, is correct in saying that it is not a matter of course, in all cases, to decree specific performance of contracts. Cas. *t.* Talb., 236; 12 Ves., 331; 1 Ves., Jr., 566. It requires the exercise of a sound discretion upon a view of all the circumstances. That discretion must, indeed, not be arbitrary and capricious. It must be regulated upon grounds that will make it judicial. 7 Ves., 35. If the contract has been entered into by a competent party, and is, in its nature and circumstances, unobjectionable, it is as much a matter of course to decree specific performance, as it is to give damages at law. 9 Ves., 608.

The appellant's counsel maintain that inadequacy of price, alone, is no ground for refusing to enforce a specific performance, unless it amounts to evidence of fraud. The ease of *Thompson* v. *Harcourt*, 2 Bro. P. C., 415, A. D. 1722, is claimed as an authority by both **506***] parties. As I understand *it, it supports the proposition advanced by the appellant's counsel. The case was substantially this, so far as it is applicable here: during the infatuation which prevailed on the subject of the South Sea scheme, and on the 18th of June, 1720, Thompson agreed with Harcourt, that he would, on the next opening of the books of the Company, transfer to him £1,000 South Sea stock, and Harcourt agreed to pay Thompson £9,200 for it, which is 920 *per cent.* The books were opened on the 5th Oct. Thompson represented to Harcourt that he had the £1,000 ready to transfer (though, in fact, he had but £290). And Harcourt not being prepared to pay the £9,200, another agreement was entered into, by which the time was extended to the next transfer day after Christmas, upon certain terms. That day was the 1st May, 1721, and Thompson not having the stock, procured it of another, to be returned on certain conditions. On that day the stock was tendered to Harcourt, but refused by him, and then retransferred to the person from whom it had been procured for the purpose of the tender. Thompson then prosecuted at law upon the contract; and Harcourt filed his bill to be relieved against it. In the meantime the bubble had burst; and it was enacted by Parliament that all contracts for the sale and purchase of the stock, unperformed on the 29th Sept., 1721, where the seller had not the stock on the day of the contract, or within six days after, should be void as to so much as the seller was not possessed of. Thompson then filed a cross-bill, praying a specific performance. Both causes were heard at the same time, and the court decreed that Harcourt should pay Thompson 920 *per cent.* for the £290 stock which he actually held of his own. This decree was on the bill for relief; and the cross-bill, which was for specific performance, was dismissed without costs. Thompson appealed because he was not allowed the 920 *per cent.* on the whole £1,000; but the appeal was dismissed, and the decree affirmed. The only reason why the 920 *per cent.* was not allowed, on the whole, must have been because he was the owner of stock to £290 only. The decree proceeded upon the Act of Parliament. So far as the court acted on the contract, they must *be understood as decreeing a specific [***507** performance. In that case there was no pretense of fraud or circumvention. It seemed to rest on inadequacy only; and that arising from subsequent circumstances; the stock being worth 920 *per cent.* at the time of the contract. There were other facts and points in the case to which I have not referred, as they have no bearing on the present question.

In *Barnardiston* v. *Lingwood*, 2 Atk., 133, A. D. 1740. Barnardiston, being distressed for money, conveyed to Lingwood, his (B's) interest, being a remainder in tail after the death of his uncle, worth £300 *per annum*, for the sum of £300. A bill for relief was filed, and a cross-bill for a specific performance. Ld. Hardwicke dismissed the cross-bill; and says that in the case of a hard bargain, when it is not absolutely executed, but executory only, the constant rule of the court is not to carry it into execution.

In *Buxton* v. *Lister*, 3 Atk., 383, A. D. 1746, the bill was to enforce a contract for timber sold at £3,050, when it was worth no more than £2,500. Ld. Hardwicke objected, at first, on the ground that the thing in controversy was a chattel; but finally decided on the merits; and dismissed the bill upon the ground of hardship without costs, on Buxton giving up the agreement, saying that if he was to dismiss it upon the misrepresentation (which was fully shown) he would dismiss it with costs. In the course of his remarks, he uses the language quoted by His Honor, the *Chancellor*, "that nothing is better established, than that the court will not decree a performance of an agreement, unless it is fair and just in all its parts; and that it is in the discretion of the court whether they will decree a performance."

In the same year (1746) the cause of *Joynes* v. *Statham* came before him, on a bill for specific performance of an agreement for a lease of a house, which was signed by the defendant only, and contained a stipulation to pay £9 rent, yearly. The defendant insisted, and offered to prove, that the agreement should have been, to pay the rent clear of taxes; but the plaintiff, who wrote it, omitted that clause. Lord Hardwicke admitted the evidence, observing, "that the constant doctrine of this court is, that it is in their discre- **508***] tion *whether, in such a bill, they will decree a specific performance, or leave the plaintiff to his remedy at law."

In *London* v. *Nash*, 1 Ves., 12, more fully reported 3 Atk., 512, A. D. 1747, Ld. Hardwicke refused to decree specific performance, on the ground that the court is not obliged to do this, where it will be attended with great loss and hardship to one of the parties. The bill, in that case, claimed a performance of an agreement to new build certain houses, which the defendant had agreed to do, but, instead of building, had thoroughly repaired them. It is also observed that, even if the defendant intended to evade his contract, still a specific performance would be hard, and all that the city wanted was to be compensated in damages. The *Chancellor*, therefore, directed an issue.

In *Underwood* v. *Hitchcox*, 2 Ves., 279, A. D. 1749, Ld. Hardwicke says, the rule of equity, in carrying agreements into a specific performance, is well known; and the court is not obliged to decree every agreement entered into, though for valuable consideration in strictness of law, it depending on the circumstances. And undoubtedly, every agreement, of which there should be a specific performance, ought to be in writing, certain and fair in all its parts, and for adequate consideration. And he refused, in that case, to decree performance, because it was too hard to decree the defendant to make a surrender of the copyhold estate (which was the thing in controversy) for so inadequate a consideration. He referred to the rule laid down in *Atty-Gen.* v. *Day*, 1 Ves., 220, where he says that decreeing performance is discretionary, when the party has his election of two remedies, in equity, or at law; and, even if there is no other remedy, it should not be done, if there are strong and material objections against it. Ld. Hardwicke's rule was recognized by Ld. Erskine, in *Mason* v. *Armitage*, 13 Ves., 37, A. D. 1806.

The case of *Faine* v. *Brown*, cited by counsel in *Ramsden* v. *Hylton*, Ves., 307, A. D. 1750, was admitted to be an authority supporting the *Chancellor's* decree, if it was correctly stated. Ld. Hardwicke, in that case, said that, independent of the circumstance of intoxica- **509***] tion when the contract was *entered into, the hardship, alone, of losing half the purchase money, if carried into execution, was sufficient to determine the discretion of the court, not to interfere, but leave the parties to law.

In *Day* v. *Newman*, at the Rolls (2 Cox, 77), performance was refused, on the ground of inadequacy alone; but in *Collier* v. *Brown*, 1 Cox, 428, decided the same year (1788), in the Court of Exchequer, though there was some inadequacy of price, a performance was decreed. An estate worth £400 or more was sold for £275. The price first asked was £300; but the owner was not much acquainted with the estate, and supposed she was selling to the tenant, till after the contract was executed. She was also very old, yet the court was of opinion that the parties bargained with their eyes open, and as there was no imposition or surprise in the case, mere inadequacy of price (when it could not be used as evidence of fraud) was not, of itself, sufficient to prevent the court from administering its usual equity.

Three years afterwards the same court, in *Tilly* v. *Peers*, cited by Sir Samuel Romilly, from his own note, in *Mortlock* v. *Buller*, 10 Ves., 301, declared that, laying out of consideration all circumstances of fraud, the court would not enforce a hard bargain. We have not the facts upon which the decision was founded; but it seems, from the remarks of Baron Thompson, that it was a clear case of fraud.

White v. *Damon*, 7 Ves., 30, A. D. 1801-2, was the case of property sold at auction for £1,120, worth £2,200. A bill was filed for a specific performance; and though Ld. Rosslyn first dismissed the bill on the ground of inadequacy, it was not finally decided on that ground. It was before Ld. Rosslyn, and afterwards, on a petition for a rehearing, before Ld. Eldon. They both, however, agreed in the general proposition that it is not a matter of course to carry an agreement into execution, but rests in discretion.

In *Coles* v. *Trecothick*, 9 Ves., 246, A. D. 1804, Ld. Eldon declared that unless the inadequacy of price is such as shocks the conscience, and amounts in itself to conclusive evidence of fraud in the transaction, it is not a sufficient ground for *refusing a specific per- [***510** formance. He had just been recapitulating the facts. It was a case of sale of real estate by an auctioneer, and Trecothick had surveyed the premises, and valued them at £23,000—had told the auctioneer not to sell for less than £19,500—and had agreed they should go for £20,000; but he refused compliance with the contract, because another offer of £25,000 had been subsequently made; and if the declaration of his Lordship was made in allusion to those facts, it certainly cannot be questioned.

The case of *Mortlock* v. *Buller*, 10 Ves., 292, A. D. 1804, was also the case of a sale by an auctioneer of an estate for £26,500, worth £34,900. The question of inadequacy was noticed by the counsel, and much discussed. Ld. Eldon did not decide upon it, but refused the specific performance upon other grounds. He, however, seems to adopt the doctrine of Ld. Alvanley, that the court is not bound to execute every contract; that if there was any sort of surprise that made it not fair nor honest to call for an execution, he would not give the extraordinary relief of a specific performance; neither would he order the contract to be delivered up, but would let the purchaser go to law.

So in *Willan* v. *Willan*, 16 Ves., 83, A. D. 1809, the point of inadequacy was not raised. Ld. Eldon remarked that there are many cases where equity will not disturb an agreement which has been executed, though it would have refused to carry it into execution.

In *Western* v. *Russell*, 3 Ves. & B., 193, A. D. 1814, there was great inadequacy. The purchase was stated by counsel to be at one tenth of the value. The Master of the Rolls does not, indeed, decide on that point; but he argues strongly against its sufficiency, as a ground to refuse specific performance. There was, in that case, no pretense of incapacity. The vendor set his own price, and obtained it; and though he lived a year and a half afterwards, expressed no dissatisfaction. Yet it was proved that in 1809, when the purchase was made, the estate was worth double the price. The Master of the Rolls, after noticing these facts, remarks that the court would treat men's con- **511***] tracts with *great levity, if, on such a state of circumstances, it should refuse to carry them into execution.

In *Griffith* v. *Spratley*, 2 Bro. Ch. Cas., 179, *n.*, it was decided that inadequacy alone was not sufficient to set aside a transaction.

Having thus noticed most of the cases cited by His Honor, the *Chancellor*, I shall proceed to state some of those cited by the counsel.

In *London* v. *Richmond*, 2 Vern., 423, A. D. 1701, the bill was filed to compel the performance of a lease. One objection was that the rent reserved was £7,000 *per annum*, and the real value not £300; and that it was against the rules of equity to decree in specie such a hard and unreasonable bargain. But the Lord Keeper Wright said, as a beneficial bargain will be decreed in equity, so if it happens to be a losing bargain, for the same reason, it ought to be decreed.

Adams v. *Weare*, 1 Bro. Ch. Cas., 567, A. D. 1783, on appeal from the Rolls, was a bill for the specific performance of an agreement to purchase a mill seat. The purchaser had agreed to give a large price, in the view of building a mill, which depended on the consent of the Corporation of Bristol. The contract was absolute in its terms, and the vendor had refused to annex any condition. The vendee could not obtain the consent of the Corporation, and refused compliance with his contract. The Master of the Rolls had decreed performance, and *Lord Chancellor* Thurlow said he thought he had done right; for no case could be cited where parties have made a bargain with their eyes perfectly open and no surprise whatever, as in that case, in which the court had refused to decree a specific performance. He added, "here is no mistake of the object; and as to the greatness of the price, Adams (the vendor) had a right to ask a large sum, and the other had agreed to give it, with a view to the intended purpose of erecting and working his mill."

In *Mortimer* v. *Capper*, 1 Bro. Ch. Cas., 156, A. D. 1782, the question was whether equity would enforce the performance of an agreement for a piece of land against the heirs of the vendor, where part of the consideration was an annuity of £50, for the vendor's life, and he **512***] had died two days after making *the agreement. The whole consideration was £200, and the annuity £50. The ground was worth £1,300; and it was contended that the agreement was too hard, and ought not to be carried into execution. The *Lord Chancellor* said: "I remember a case of a contract for a piece of ground, which was to be inclosed, for £20, and upon a bill for specific performance, the defense was that it was worth £200; and although the contract was to be performed *in futuro*, yet neither party knowing the value, the Master of the Rolls decreed performance." In relation to the case before him, however, he said: "I think, if the price be fair, the contract ought not to be cut down merely because the annuity, which is a contingent payment, never became payable;" and he ordered a reference to a master, to inquire into the real value of the estate and of the annuity.

In *Emery* v. *Wase*, 8 Ves., 518, A. D. 1803, the question was whether a husband should be compelled to procure his wife to execute his contract; and Ld. Eldon, *arguendo*, says: "I do not deny that mere difference in value, though considerable, is not, of itself, a sufficient ground for refusing a specific performance of a contract; but very considerable difference in value is not inconsiderable evidence that it was not made with great care and attention."

In *Burrowes* v. *Lock*, 10 Ves., 470, A. D. 1805, Edward Cartwright was entitled to £288, and assigned it to the plaintiff, to whom he was indebted £132, and by whom he was pressed for satisfaction of the debt. The costs of the transaction were £10 paid by the plaintiff; and Cartwright had previously conveyed away one tenth, so that £142 were given for what was worth £260. The Master of the Rolls decreed performance, saying: "If fraud is out of the case, I do not know that I can set aside this contract, or refuse to act upon it, merely on the ground of inadequacy of price."

In *Cadman* v. *Horner*, 18 Ves., 10, A. D. 1810, the plaintiff prayed a specific performance of a contract, which was resisted on the ground of inadequacy and misrepresentation; and on those two grounds it was denied. But the Master of the Rolls expressed no opinion upon the question of inadequacy alone.

*The case of *Poole* v. *Shergold*, 2 Bro. [***513** Ch. Cas., 118, decides that the difference arising from the calamities of the times ought not to rescind a contract; and *Jackson* v. *Lever*, 3 Bro. Ch. Cas., 605, that a contract for the sale of land, for an annuity for the life of the vendor, shall be performed by the vendor's heirs, though he died without receiving any part o it.

The object of the last two cases, I presume, was to show that, although the Navy Yard was not established at Newburgh, and although Ellison died before the application to enforce the contract, yet neither of these circumstances can constitute a defense to the present action.

Many cases have also been cited by the counsel for the respondents, some of which I shall examine. I will first, however, consider a little further some of the above cases.

The case of *Thompson* v. *Harcourt* I have considered an authority for the appellant. As I before remarked, it was claimed by the counsel on both sides. It was considered by the *Chancellor* as a case in favor of the respondents. Perhaps, therefore, I am mistaken in my reading of it, but I think not. It was in the House of Lords. The reporter has not given the opinion of the judges, and we must infer the ground of decision, from the case, the decree, and the points argued by counsel. The case was decided 13th Feb., 1722. On the 9th Nov., in the same year, the case of *Kien* v. *Stukeley* was decided (which I shall hereafter refer to on another point), in which a specific performance was refused. Both these cases grew out of the South Sea speculation, or were connected with it. In the first, where 920 *per cent.* was decreed to be paid, it appeared that when the contract was made, it was fair and equal: that stock, at one time, was 1,000 *per cent.* above par. The inadequacy arose, therefore, from subsequent circumstances, and did not exist at the time of the contract. In the latter case, lands were sold for 40 years' purchase, which, at the time, were worth only 15 years' purchase: and the vendee expected to pay in South Sea stock. The inadequacy here existed at the time of the contract; and must **514***] have been one ground, at *least, of the decree. Both cases were decided by the same court, and within nine months of each other; and, in my opinion, are perfectly reconcilable upon the relative difference of time at which the inadequacy arose. So in *London* v. *Richmond*, the rent was agreed upon, on a calculation of the quantity of water which certain pipes would discharge. This was greatly overrated, yet the court compelled performance. The lessee should have calculated better; though, I confess, I am not satisfied with that case.

In *Adams* v. *Weare* the seller was explicit, and when the purchaser said he would give the price, if the consent of the City of Bristol could be obtained, the seller told him, "Sir, I will have no if in the case. You must purchase absolutely or not at all." In that case, it was admitted that the inadequacy existed at the time of the contract, and was known to both parties; and the court would not permit the purchaser, afterwards, to be off from his contract, because he did not succeed in his speculation.

Not so in this case. The appellant avers that the lots were worth the consideration given, or very near it, long before anything was ever said about a Navy Yard at Newburgh; and on the other hand, the inadequacy is shown to have existed at the time of the contract, and not to have arisen from subsequent circumstances. It does not appear that the expectation of a Navy Yard was the sole inducement to the purchase. It is stated, by one witness, that Ellison intended to build stores and sloops, and go extensively into commerce.

Johnson, Ex'r of Hill, v. *Nott*, 1 Vern., 271-2, A. D. 1684. In this case Hill bought of the defendant a contingent estate, at an under value. Nott had previously brought his bill, to be relieved, and was relieved by Ld. Nottingham; but, upon a rehearing, before Lord Keeper Guilford, that decree was reversed. Johnson then brought his bill for a specific performance; and the Lord Keeper said that a contract which carries an equity to have it decreed in specie, ought to be without all objection.

In *Vaughan* v. *Thomas*, 1 Bro. Ch. Cas., 556, A. D. 1783, the plaintiff agreed with the defendant for an annuity worth nine years purchase, for the consideration of five years' purchase, and brought *his bill to [***515** compel a specific performance; but the court said that if they assisted the plaintiff, they should give sanction to a very unconscientious bargain, and that, under this view of the case, he was by no means entitled to their aid.

In *Collett* v. *Wollaston*, 3 Bro. Ch. Cas., 228, A. D. 1791, the plaintiff had purchased, at auction, the reversionary interest of £2,000 South Sea stock, subject to the life of a man 45 years of age, and £1,200 South Sea annuities, for £215; and filed his bill for an assignment and transfer. The Master of the Rolls said, the reversionary interests seeming to be sold for a very low price, he would direct an inquiry into their value, before he decreed a specific performance of the purchase. *Vide*, also, several cases 5 Vin., 539 to 549, adhering to the rule in *Normanby* v. *Beckley*, that the contract must be fair and reasonable in every particular.

In *Clitherall* v. *Ogilvie*, 1 Des., 257-63, A. D. 1792, the defendant entered into a written contract to sell the plaintiff certain lands, for £3,500, which were worth three times that amount. On further inquiry as to the value of the property, he declined executing the conveyances; and the bill was brought for a specific performance. The court, after a full discussion and examination of the cases on the subject, took notice of the distinction between setting aside an unreasonable contract, after it is executed, and compelling a specific performance; and, recognizing Ld. Hardwicke's rule in *Underwood* v. *Hitchcox*, declared, that on full consideration of the case, and all the circumstances (although there was no proof of fraud or imposition), the sum for which the land was agreed to be sold was grossly inadequate to its real value; and that, being an unreasonable contract, and a very hard bargain, it would be unreasonable and unjustifiable to decree a specific performance; and left the plaintiff to his remedy at law.

In *Ward* v. *Webber*, 1 Wash., 229, A. D. 1794, President Pendleton, delivering the opinion of the court, says: "It is true that the court will never decree iniquity; and there are instances where they have refused to decree hard bargains, though fair; but these are rare, and are generally cases of glaring hardships. For, in general, the court will not undertake *to estimate the speculations of parties [***516** in a contract, but will deem them the best judges of their own views, and will compel a performance, though they may be eventually disappointed in their expectations."

In the case of *Campbell* v. *Spencer*, 2 Binn., 133, A. D. 1800, there was no fraud or imposition; nor does it appear that there was inadequacy to any great degree; but it was a foolish bargain, whereby a farmer agreed to sell his farm for the remnant of a store of goods; and *Ch. J.* Tilghman and *Judge* Breckenridge both say, they would not enforce the contract, nor declare it void, but leave the plaintiff to his action upon it. *Judge* Breckenridge placed reliance upon its being a hard bargain, attended with suspicious circumstances.

In the case of *Osgood* v. *Franklin*, 2 Johns. Ch., 23, A. D, 1816, the *Chancellor* remarks, "there is a very important distinction, which runs through the cases, between ordering a contract to be rescinded, and decreeing a specific performance. Though inadequacy of price is not a ground for decreeing an agreement to be delivered up, or a sale rescinded (unless its grossness amount to fraud), yet it may be sufficient for the court to refuse to enforce performance. It is not uncommon for the court to refuse to enforce for inadequacy, and at the same time to refuse to rescind."

Chancellor Dessaussure, who was not on the bench when the cause of *Clitherall* v. *Ogilvie* was decided, has added a valuable and learned note to the report of that case, which he concludes by observing: "It is agreed, on all hands, that the court is not bound to decree a specific performance in every case where it will not set aside the contract, nor bound to set aside every contract of which it will not decree the specific performance. The court will not decree specific performance, where there is any surprise, making it not fair and honest to proceed and call for specific performance."

Having thus taken a cursory view of some of the principal cases on the point under consideration, and having also noticed the *dicta* of some learned jurists, I shall be justified in the remark, that the question is one upon which very great men have differed, and have admin-
517*] istered the equity of the *court upon diametrically opposite principles. The one class maintain that the court will not lend its aid to enforce the performance of contracts, unless they are fair, just and reasonable, and founded on adequate consideration. The other class maintain that unless the inadequacy of price is such as shocks the conscience, and amounts in itself to decisive and conclusive evidence of fraud in the transaction, it is not of itself a sufficient ground for refusing a specific performance.

The most distinguished of those who support the latter doctrine is Ld. Eldon. To him may be added Sir William Grant, Lord Keeper Wright, and probably some others. The former doctrine was declared or acted upon by the Lds. Somers, Macclesfield, Northington, Guilford, Talbot, Harcourt, Hardwicke, Alvanley, Erskine, Rosslyn and *Chief Baron* Eyre, in England; and in this country it has been adopted by the Court of Chancery of S. C., the Court of Appeals of Va., and the Court of Chancery of this State; and I believe there is no American decision to the contrary. Among American jurists, of distinguished celebrity, who have maintained this doctrine, are *Chancellor* Dessaussure, of S. C., *President* Pendleton of Va., the late *Ch. J.* Reeve, of Conn., and last, though not least, the late *Chancellor* Kent, *justum et tenacem propositi virum*—a man whose stern integrity, superior talents and extensive erudition, have rendered him an ornament to the courts over which he has presided in his native State; and who may, without arrogance, but with the most perfect complacency, look back upon his twenty-six years of judicial labors, and say—

Exegi monumentum ære perennius;
Regalique situ pyramidum altius:
Non omnis moriar; multaque pars mei
Vitabit libitinam.

If we determine this question by the prevailing practice of courts of equity (it has not, indeed, been uniform), we must decide in favor of the rule as laid down by Ld. Hardwicke. If we determine it by the reason and propriety of the two propositions, there is certainly great weight in the consideration that, in enforcing contracts, the court, if it acts at *all, must act *ex rigore*, and cannot [***518** weigh the equities of the parties; whereas a jury, in a court of law, can mitigate the damages according to equity and good conscience. It seems, indeed, paradoxical, to send parties from a court of equity to a court of law, to obtain equity; but it arises from the peculiar construction and practice of the courts.

Again; if we call to our aid the opinions of men among the most celebrated for their learning and talents, of the times in which they respectively lived, we find a great preponderance in favor of sending hard and inequitable bargains to a court of law.

Upon authority therefore, as well as upon principle, I am clearly of opinion, that a court of equity ought not to lend its aid in enforcing an executory contract unless it is fair, just, reasonable and equal in all its parts, and founded upon adequate consideration.

It is undoubtedly well settled that inadequacy of price, alone, is not a sufficient reason for setting aside a contract executed, unless its grossness amount to fraud; but there is a wide difference between enforcing an executory contract, and setting aside a contract deliberately executed; and the two subjects admit of very different views and considerations.

The next ground of defense is, that Ellison's mind was debilitated by habitual intoxication. The witnesses agree as to the fact of his habitual intemperance, for some years before his death; but they differ in their opinions as to the effect produced by it upon his capacity to transact business. The fact is before the court; and our acquaintance with mankind supersedes the necessity of evidence to prove that habitual inebriety, in most cases, debilitates the mind. As like causes produce like effects, it would require strong proof to show that Ellison was an exception to the general rule. It also appears that this contract was unknown to his family and friends. It was made by Drake Seymour, on behalf of his brother. And though the character of Drake Seymour rebuts the idea of fraud or imposition upon a man under intoxication; yet it is well known that interest has a controlling influence *over the minds of many, per- [***519** haps of most men, even of correct principles; and may, and often does, induce them to make bargains which conscience cannot approve.

The third ground of defense is, that the appellant was unable on the day appointed to give a title to the lots, on account of incumbrances.

The appellant's counsel contend, that it is sufficient, if he was able to give a title at the time of the decree; and so it was decided by the Master of the Rolls, in *Langford* v. *Pitt*, 2 P. Wms., 630, A. D. 1731. He said that the direction of the court, in all cases, was, to inquire whether the seller can, not whether he could make a title at the time of executing the agreement. In *Wynn* v. *Morgan*, 7 Ves., 202, A. D., 1802, it was decided that where the time, at which the contract was to be executed, is not material, and there is no unreasonable delay, the vendor, though not having a good title at the time the contract was to be executed nor when the bill was filed, but being able to make a title at the hearing, is entitled to a specific performance.

In *Brashier* v. *Gratz*, 6 Wh., 528, A. D. 1821, *Ch. J.* Marshall says, the rule that time is not of the essence of a contract, has been recognized in courts of equity; that a failure to perform on the day does not deprive a purchaser of his right to demand a specific performance at a subsequent day, when he shall be able to comply with his part of the engagement. But the rule is not universal. Circumstances may have changed; and the other party may be placed in a worse condition; and then the court would leave the parties to their remedy at law. The party who is ready, may file his bill requiring the other to perform or rescind; and the court will compel him to do one or the other. If, then, a bill for a specific performance be brought by a party who is himself in fault, the court will consider all the circumstances of the case, and decree according to those circumstances.

In *Hepburn* v. *Auld*, 5 Cr., 262, A. D. 1809, the same point had been so ruled; though *Mr. Justice* Livingston expressed his dissent on the point of dispensing with time. 1 Wh., 195-196, S. C.

520*] *In *Butler* v. *O'Hear*, 1 Des., 398, the court say, lapse of time, unattended with other circumstances, is not, of itself, a sufficient ground for it to refuse its aid to compel a specific performance of an agreement; that it was sufficient if the plaintiff could then make title.

In *Judson* v. *Wass*, 11 Johns., 525, A. D. 1814, which was a case of the sale of land, at auction, one of the conditions being that the money should be paid in seventy-five hours, the conveyance to be dated on the day of sale; the premises were incumbered with a mortgage; and the court said that in every sale of that kind, there is a condition, that the purchaser shall not be bound to part with his money, unless the seller is able to give him a title according to the terms of the sale. That, however, was an action at law, and is not applicable here.

In *Waters* v. *Travis*, 9 Johns., 466, A. D. 1812, the late *Ch. J.* Spencer, who gave the opinion of this court, says, the lapse of time, when no material inconvenience has been suffered, can be urged only on the ground that it is evidence of abandonment of the agreement.

In the case now under consideration, I am inclined to the opinion that the appellant, not being in a condition to give a good title on the 1st of June, 1820, is, of itself, no objection to a specific performance. The conveyances were to be simultaneous acts; or rather, by the terms of the contract, Ellison was first to convey. The language of Seymour's covenant is: "In consideration of which premises (the conveyance by Ellison) the said William Seymour doth by these presents covenant and agree, &c."

But it seems that when there is great inadequacy of consideration, the vendor is held to great strictness, as to time, in the performance on his part. In the case of *Kien* v. *Stukely*, 2 Bro. P. C., 396-398, A. D. 1722, Stukely, on the 20th July, 1720, sold lands by contract to Kien for forty years purchase, when they were worth only fifteen years purchase, and £120 were paid; Kien intending to pay the residue in South Sea stock, which was then worth 1,000 *per cent.;* and the title was to be made out on the 29th Dec., then next. The title was not made out by the day and Kien declined the purchase. On a bill filed by Stukely, performance was decreed; but on *appeal to the House of Lords, this [***521** decree was reversed. By the report in Brown, the decree seems to rest on the ground of inadequacy; and the point relating to time is not stated; but from a report of the same case by *Baron* Gilbert (Gilb., 155-156), it seems to have been decided on the ground of the vendor not having made out his title to the premises sold by the day stipulated in the contract. The decision is understood by Sugden in his Treatise on Vendors, p. 281, as having been made upon both grounds, and he has deduced from it this principle; that when the price is unreasonable or inadequate, or the contract is in other respects, inequitable, equity will not assist either party, if he has permitted the day appointed for completing the contract to elapse without performing his part of the agreement.

On the whole case, therefore, I am of opinion:

1. That on the question of decreeing specific performance of executory contracts, the Court of Chancery must exercise its discretion—not an arbitrary, but a sound judicial discretion. If the contract be free from objection, it is the duty of the court to decree performance. But if there are circumstances of unfairness, though not amounting to fraud or oppression, or if the inadequacy of consideration be so great as to render the bargain hard and unconscionable; on either ground the court may refuse its aid to enforce the contract, and leave the parties to contest their rights in a court of law.

If it is asked what degree of inadequacy is necessary to constitute the bargain a hard one; it might be asked, in answer, what degree of inadequacy is necessary to constituted fraud—to shock the conscience, and produce an exclamation?

The truth is, that neither the one nor the other admits of a definite answer. It must be determined by the judgment of the court; and as there is certainly a difficulty in ascertaining the precise point, there is much less danger in stopping short of it, than in going beyond it. To me it seems a solecism in language, to say that a party, who has obtained *an in- [***522** equitable bargain, shall be received, in a court of equity, to demand its performance.

2. In the next place, though the incompetency of Ellison arising from habitual intemperance is not clearly established, yet enough appears to raise a doubt on the subject, and to cast a suspicion upon the fairness of the transaction. The authorities cited, on the question of setting aside contracts obtained from persons while under the influence of intoxication, are not applicable. None of them state that a

contract so obtained ought to be enforced in equity, by decreeing a specific execution.

3. And, although lapse of time, when not of the essence of a contract, or an incapacity to make title on the day stipulated, are not insuperable obstacles in the way of obtaining the specific execution of a contract, provided title can be made before the decree; yet, when connected with inadequacy of price, they will justify the court in withholding the exercise of its extraordinary powers in compelling a specific performance.

I concur, therefore, with His Honor, the *Chancellor*, and am of opinion that his decree should be affirmed.

WOODWORTH, *J.*, not having heard the argument, gave no opinion.

Clark, Earll, Gardiner, Green, Mallory M'Call, Morgan, Ward and *Wright, Senators*, concurred in the opinion of the *Chief Justice*.

SUDAM, *Senator*. In this case, it cannot be necessary for me to enter into a detailed statement of the facts. I shall merely take a general view of the claims of the appellant, and of the defense set up by the respondents, and then proceed to the consideration of the questions submitted to the court by the counsel who have so ably and ingeniously argued this cause.

William Seymour, the appellant, and Thomas Ellison, the father of the respondents, on Jan. 14, 1820, entered into an agreement for the exchange of one third of certain lots owned by Seymour, in the Village of Newburgh, **523***] *for certain farms, owned by Ellison, in Montgomery and Walkill. The property is particularly described in the article between them. By this agreement, Ellison covenanted with Seymour, that he would on or before the first day of June next ensuing its date, by sufficient conveyances, grant, bargain and sell, &c., the farms to the appellant, in fee simple; in consideration of which Seymour covenanted and agreed that he would, on or before the 1st day of June ensuing the date, sufficiently grant, bargain and sell to Ellison, the equal undivided third parts of the Newburgh lots, with the wharves, buildings, &c. The articles of agreement contain the following clause: "And it is hereby further agreed by and between the said parties, that it shall be lawful for them respectively to enter into and upon the said premises to them respectively intended to be granted and conveyed, and to have and receive the profits thereof to their own use respectively."

The bill states, that in pursuance of this agreement Seymour entered into possession of, and received the rents and profits of the property to be conveyed to him by Ellison, and Ellison entered into the possession of the property to be conveyed to him by Seymour; and that Ellison's heirs at law have, since his death, continued in possession; that Seymour, during the lifetime of Ellison, was always ready to convey to him, according to his contract, but that Ellison, for several months previous to his death, was incapable of transacting business; and that he died about the 3d Aug., 1820, intestate, leaving Harriet Ellison, his widow, and the respondents, his heirs at law; that all his children, except Mary Jane Delancy, are infants, under the age of 21 years; and that, by reason of their infancy, they cannot convey, according to the terms of the contract; that Mrs. Ellison, the widow of Thomas Ellison, died before the time of filing the bill.

The prayer of the appellant is, that the respondents may be decreed to execute a deed, according to the true intent and meaning of the covenant entered into between the appellants and Thomas Ellison, in his lifetime.

The respondents admit: 1. That their father, Thomas Ellison, entered into covenant with Seymour, the appellant; *but [***524** they leave him to prove whether he had a sufficient title to the property to be conveyed by him. 2. They insist that he had previously conveyed a portion of it to his sister, Esther Seymour, or to some other person, for her use or benefit. 3. That his title was very questionable. 4. That the bargain for the exchange was unconscionable, inasmuch as the lands to be conveyed by Ellison to Seymour exceeded the value of the lands to be conveyed by Seymour to Ellison by several thousand dollars. 5. That the appellant could not make a good title to the premises, because they were incumbered by a mortgage remaining uncanceled at the death of Ellison. 6. That the appellant did not, on or before, or subsequent to the day specified, tender a deed, in pursuance of the article. 7. That Ellison, from the 14th Jan., 1820, until the 1st June, 1820, "was, in all respects, as capable and competent to transact business, as he was for several weeks and months previous to the 14th Jan., 1820." Then the respondents, after stating their age, and denying that the appellant was ready and willing to execute and deliver a deed to Ellison in his lifetime, and leaving him to his proof, submit themselves to the decree of the court.

In the decree entered in this cause by His Honor, the *Chancellor*, he refuses to direct a specific performance of the contract by the heirs at law of Ellison, "from the great inadequacy in value of the lots in the Village of Newburgh, which Seymour contracted to convey to Ellison, for the two farms in Orange Co., which Ellison contracted to convey to Seymour, as mentioned in the pleadings and proofs; and also, from the habits of intoxication in which Ellison had indulged in the last years of his life, and the mental debility produced thereby; and also, from the want of readiness and ability in Seymour to convey a good and unincumbered title to the said lots in the Village of Newburgh, at the time fixed for the performance of said contract, or at any time thereafter, during the lifetime of Ellison."

The respondents, in support of this decree, make the following points:

*1. That the bargain was hard, dis- [***525** proportionate and unequal in its terms.

2. That during the time of the negotiation, and at the time Ellison entered into the contract, he was not in a fit state of mind to form such an agreement, or to understand his rights or appreciate his interests; and that the bargain was secretly and unfairly obtained by the appellant.

3. That the appellant did not and could not perform the agreement on his part, as stipulated by him, in the lifetime of Ellison, because the appellant's lands were incumbered

to their value; and there was no waiver of time, or indulgence given, by Ellison in his lifetime, nor by the respondents since his decease.

The first point made by the respondents, that this contract for exchange of lands was hard, disproportionate and unequal in its terms, is the main point in the cause, and has been so treated by the *Chancellor* in his opinion. He assumes it as a fact, that "at the date of the agreement, the village lots were not worth half the value of the country farms," and says: "We may make an ample advance of the one, and an ample diminution of the other, in value, if we were to fix the one third of the Newburgh lots at $6,000, and the farms at $12,000.

The decision, upon the evidence given as to the difference in value between the property to be conveyed by the appellant to the father of the respondents, may decide the cause, without entering into the consideration of the other points; but I think our decision must depend mainly on other evidence; for it cannot be sustained, in my opinion, that mere inequality in value, which is not so gross as to strike the moral feeling of an indifferent man, would be sufficient to warrant the *Chancellor* in withholding a decree for specific performance. I admit that the exercise of the power, in a Court of Chancery, to enforce the specific performance of contracts for the sale or the exchange of land, rests in the sound discretion of the court; but this is a sound legal discretion; and not the exercise of an arbitrary power, interfering with the contracts of individuals, and sporting with their vested rights. I also admit that the party claiming the spe-
526*] cific performance must present a case fair, just and reasonable; that the contract must be founded on adequate consideration; and that it must be free from fraud, misrepresentation, deceit or surprise.

To determine whether, in fact, the agreement for exchange was hard, unequal, and disproportionate, and whether it was free from fraud, surprise, &c., it will be necessary to examine, with as much brevity as possible, the history of this transaction.

On the 3d of Jan., 1818, Drake Seymour, the brother of the appellant, sold to Ellison, the father of the respondents, the one equal undivided third part of the lot first described in the articles of agreement, lying on the east side of Water St., for the sum of $12,500, cash. This bargain was made verbally, in the year 1817, and completed, by the delivery of the deed, in Jan., 1818; and the negotiation concerning it was kept up from Apr., 1817, to Jan., 1818, when it was consummated. In Mar., 1818, Ellison agreed to purchase of Samuel Sands Seymour his undivided third part in the same lots, lying east and west of Water St., for $13,825, he taking, in part payment, a mortgage which Ellison held against one Tallman, and Ellison agreeing to guaranty, that, on foreclosure, the mortgaged premises should produce the principal and interest due. This contract was signed and sealed by the parties.

In Mar., 1818, Ellison informed Drake Seymour "that he had only to purchase the part of the lot belonging to the appellant, to own the whole," and made propositions to the witness (Drake Seymour), to be submitted to his brother. Both in the years 1818 and 1819, Drake Seymour frequently saw Ellison in relation to the purchase of the appellant's one third of the lots; and from the time Ellison first proposed to purchase from the appellant, to the time when a verbal contract was concluded for the exchange, more than 18 months had elapsed; and about 1 year and 10 months had elapsed before it was reduced to writing and signed by Ellison and the appellant. On the conclusion of the verbal agreement, Ellison authorized the appellant to take possession of the farms, and possession was taken accordingly. In *Jan., 1820, the appellant [*527
sent by Drake Seymour, to Ellison, at N. Y., the articles of agreement in question, already executed on his part. They were handed to Ellison, to be executed by him. He requested that they might be left with him for examination, to see if they were in conformity with the verbal agreement. He examined them, found them correct, and executed them the day after.

By the evidence of Samuel M'Coun, who was employed by Ellison to estimate the value of the farms, it distinctly appears that he understood from Ellison, that he and the appellant were negotiating for the exchange. In various conversations, he told M'Coun "that he was negotiating an exchange with the appellant, and that he wished M'Coun to make up his mind upon the value of the two farms, to be exchanged for the Newburgh lots. That he (Ellison) did not wish M'Coun to appraise the appellant's lots in the village of Newburgh; but that he would do that himself." It is also in evidence that Ellison, during the summer, resided in New Windsor, in the County of Orange, adjoining the Village of Newburgh, and that he was well acquainted with the property of the appellant, proposed to be exchanged for his two farms. It also appears that Ellison had a favorable opinion of Newburgh as a business place; and he may have been influenced by the consideration that property there would rise in value, in consequence of the expected establishment of a Navy Yard.

That the contract was deliberately made, there can be no doubt. M'Coun says, expressly, that Ellison told him "he would not conclude the bargain between him and the appellant, until he had seen him" (M'Coun), and ascertained his opinion of the value of the farms.

We here find a purchase by Ellison, in Jan., 1818, of one third of the Newburgh lots east of Water St., for the sum of $12,500, on a negotiation commenced in April preceding, and at a time when, according to the pleadings and proofs, there is no pretense of incompetency. About Mar., 1818, Ellison purchased from S. S. Seymour, his undivided third in the Newburgh lots, lying east and west of Water St., for the sum of $13,825. About the same time he *informed Drake Seymour that he [*528
had purchased one third of S. S. Seymour, and talked of exchanging the farms for the like share of the appellant. In addition, he informed Benjamin Case and John Anderson that he had purchased the shares of Drake and S. S. Seymour; and that he also intended to purchase the share of the appellant; and he told Anderson how he intended to render the property valuable to himself.

The whole presents a very strong case, and one in which the contract should be carried into effect, unless some controlling rule of decision in our equity courts shall require the contrary.

There can be no doubt, from a review of the evidence, that Ellison made his bargain, well knowing all the facts, in relation to the Newburgh lots, as well as his farms proposed to be exchanged for them. His own agent (M'Coun) ascertained the value of the farms. He said he would himself appraise the value of the lots in Newburgh. It could not be pretended, that after a purchase of two thirds of the whole property, he had never examined the premises, or that he had not ascertained the situation and comparative value of the Newburgh lots; for it is admitted by all parties, that at the time of his purchase from Drake Seymour, and his agreeing to purchase of S. S. Seymour, he was not incompetent to transact business of any kind. Immediately after this, the negotiation for the one third of the appellant's lots commenced, and that negotiation continued for 18 months before it was verbally concluded, and for one year and ten months before it was reduced to writing. There is, therefore, no pretense, in my opinion, that Ellison was not fully acquainted with the premises, proposed to be exchanged with him by the appellant. Besides having before become the purchaser of two thirds of the lot on the east side of Water St., and the one third of the lot of S. S. Seymour, on the west side of the same street, and having paid, in each instance, a sum exceeding the price he had agreed to pay the appellant, we have the positive testimony of Drake Seymour that throughout the whole of the negotiation he was perfectly competent to transact business. **529***] He was in a situation *deliberately to form his opinion, and unquestionably he did do so, as to the value of the Newburgh lots; and from his previous purchases, he must have ascertained their value, to his own satisfaction. Under the advice of his agent, he knew the value of the property to be conveyed by him to the appellant. We must take it, then, that Ellison, deliberately and with his eyes open, entered into the contract which the appellant now seeks to enforce by a decree of a court of equity.

I am, therefore, of opinion, from a review of the whole evidence, that this contract was, at the time the negotiation was first entered into, and at the time the articles were first executed by Seymour and Ellison, certain, fair and just, in all its parts.

The next question which presents itself to the consideration of the court is, whether the contract between the appellant and Ellison is so hard, unreasonable, or unequal, that this court will not aid to enforce it.

In reviewing this part of the case, it will be the duty of the court to investigate the evidence as to the value of the Newburgh lots, and the farms to be exchanged for them. Should they arrive at the conclusion that mere inadequacy in value, where there is no fraud, misrepresentation, imposition or concealment of facts, is of itself sufficient to avoid the contract, it will save a great deal of the labor and investigation which might otherwise be required. I admit, however, that where the inadequacy of price in a contract is so flagrant and palpable as to convince a man at the first blush that one of the contracting parties had been imposed on by some false pretense, such a contract ought not to be enforced by this, or any other court of equity. It is not to be denied, that it is the settled doctrine of the Court of Chancery, that it will not carry into effect, specifically, a contract where the inadequacy of price amounts to conclusive evidence of fraud. In this view of the case, therefore, as well as in reference to the objection of mere inadequacy, I shall briefly examine the evidence of value.

*It may be proper to premise, that [***530** there is a distinction between a Court of Chancery, refusing to decree the specific performance of a contract, and setting it aside. *Mortlock* v. *Buller*, 10 Ves., 292. It is also well settled, that a court of equity will not disturb an agreement that has been executed, although they would not have decreed a specific performance. *Willan* v. *Willan*, 16 Ves., 83. In the first case, the court would leave the party to his remedy at law. In the second, they would refuse to interfere by directing the agreement to be canceled, the party having consummated his own act. But if there should be fraud, circumvention, deceit or misrepresentation, a Court of Chancery would order the contract to be delivered up to be canceled. This case, then, being free from fraud, concealment and misrepresentation, and from the charge of a hasty and unadvised contract, one important question appears to be, can a court of equity interfere, under such circumstances, to avoid the contract? For, in my opinion, not to carry this contract into effect is to avoid it wholly. It would be well to consider whether this is a case coming within the rule. For if it be true that the respondents must rest the decree of the *Chancellor*, principally, on the inadequacy in value of the property to be exchanged; and if it be true that, in order to avoid such a contract, the inadequacy of price must amount to conclusive evidence of fraud (*Western* v. *Russell*, 3 Ves. & B., 187; *Willan* v. *Willan*, 16 Ves., 83; *Coles* v. *Trecothick*, 9 Ves., 246, per Ld. Eldon), I do not see in what manner the opinion of His Honor, the *Chancellor*, can be supported.

There is no question so well calculated to generate a variety of opinion, as that which regards the value of a village lot, or a farm in the country; and unless the disproportion should be gross and palpable, it would be very difficult to estimate how much more had been given by A for a lot than the price at which B would value it.

This, by the proofs, is the precise case before us. The average value of the appellant's interest in the lots at Newburgh, as sworn by six witnesses, is $10,856; and this is corroborated by the fact that the father of the appellant estimated *the lot east of Water [***531** St., several years since, at $30,000. The average of the farms, as sworn to by witnesses, is $12,686, and the difference about $2,186, according to the highest estimate made by the witnesses of the respondents. The lowest estimate of the Newburgh lots, by the respondents' witnesses, is between $5,000 and $6,000.

That a difference of opinion should exist among the witnesses, both as to the value of the lots in Newburgh and the farms of Ellison, is very natural. Every person, at all acquainted with the price set upon real property, and that which is paid when sales do take place in the country, and in country villages, must be aware to what extent an honest difference of opinion does and always will exist. One will venture his fortune in the purchase of property which, in his judgment, will lay the foundation for a comfortable settlement of his family, while his immediate neighbor, with the same knowlege of all the circumstances, pronounces the purchase rash and injudicious. There is scarcely an instance in which a great difference of opinion does not exist, upon the point, whether the purchaser has a good bargain or not. In the country, and in country villages, there is no settled criterion by which property can be estimated. It is not an uncommon circumstance for men to hold on upon real estate, in the hope of getting their price, until the law interferes, and the sheriff is compelled to solve all scruples on the subject. In the present case, Ellison, a man of fortune, and competent to carry into effect his plans for the improvement of the two Newburgh lots, impressed with the idea of the growing importance of that village, and influenced, in all probability, by the expectation of the establishment of a Navy Yard in its vicinity, and being the owner of two thirds of the premises in question, exchanges certain farms in the country for the lots in Newburgh. He does this deliberately, freely, and with a full knowledge of the situation of his own property and that which he agreed to take in exchange. There is no ground for saying that there was, in this case, either fraud, surprise, misrepresentation, or deceit. The bargain was conducted by him throughout with great deliberation, and he consummated it with his eyes open. Under such circumstances, we are **532***] *called on to say, that mere inadequacy of price, and where there is much contradictory evidence, is of itself sufficient to prevent the Court of Chancery from decreeing the specific performance of the contract.

In the case of *Coles* v. *Trecothick*, 9 Ves., 246, Ld. Eldon observed, that inadequacy of price, unless it amounted to conclusive evidence of fraud, was not itself a sufficient ground for refusing a specific performance; and although this was the case of an auction sale the opinion was pronounced on the general question. In *Mortlock* v. *Buller*, 10 Ves., 292, the *Lord Chancellor* declined giving an opinion on the doctrine of inadequacy. In *Western* v. *Russell*, 3 Ves. & B., 187, the defense was gross inadequacy of consideration. The Master of the Rolls said that it was not necessary to determine the general question whether inadequacy of price might not be a ground for refusing performance, and he decided the case upon its special circumstances, and held that, as the vendor was not alleged to be under any incapacity or deficiency of judgment, and set his own price and obtained it, and never expressed any dissatisfaction, but accused the purchaser of delay, the agreement should be carried into execution. *Chancellor* Kent admits that Ld. Eldon and the Master of the Rolls had thrown doubt and distrust on this doctrine that inadequacy of price is of itself sufficient to prevent a specific execution.

In *Collier* v. *Brown*, 1 Cox, 428, it was expressly held on a bill for specific performance, that if the parties bargained with their eyes open and without imposition or surprise, mere inadequacy of price was not of itself sufficient to prevent the court from administering its usual equity. This is the doctrine of common sense and common honesty; for it may be asked with great propriety, what right have we to sport with the contracts of parties fairly and deliberately entered into, and prevent them from being carried into effect?

I cannot assent to the doctrine, that inadequacy of price may of itself, and without fraud or other ingredient, be sufficient to stay the application of the power of a Court of Chancery, *to enforce a specific perform- [***533** ance of a private contract to sell land.

To establish this doctrine in the State of N. Y. would, to my mind, be sanctioning a principle which would lead to very injurious results. Every member of this court must be well aware how much property is held by contract; that purchases are constantly made upon speculation; that the value of real estate is fluctuating; and that there, most generally, exists an honest difference of opinion in regard to any bargain as to its being a beneficial one or not. To say, when all is fair, and the parties deal on equal terms, that a court of equity will not interfere, does not appear to me to be supported by authority (*Day* v. *Newman*, 2 Cox, 77; *Willan* v. *Willan*, 16 Ves., 83; *Western* v. *Russel*, 3 Ves. & B., 187; *Mortlock* v. *Buller*, 10 Ves., 292), and unless I am bound down by some rigid rule of law, I, for one, cannot consent to its introduction into our equity code.

I have not had time to analyze all the cases which have been cited, so as to bring them in review before the court. The earlier cases are very loosely reported; and we cannot, either from the decisions made, or from the opinions of the court, form a satisfactory judgment on the particular facts; and from the doubts and disapprobation of Sir William Grant, the Master of the Rolls, and of Ld. Elden, I feel myself warranted in saying that the point is unsettled in England. Nor can I perceive why a contract for the sale of land, which is fair in all its parts, should not be carried into effect as much as any other contract. In principle there is not and there ought not to be a difference.

There may be such inadequacy of price as, of itself, to be an evidence of fraud. But wherever this does not exist, and resort is had to the testimony of witnesses, and they differ in their valuation, as in the present case, the contract should be executed. In the case before the court, the average value of the farms by six of the respondents' witnesses is $12,686. Six witnesses on the part of the appellant (and men, too, of great respectability), value the Newbugh lots at $10,856. The difference is $1,830. How is it possible for any Chancellor to decide upon the relative weight of such *evidence? What can clearly be ex- [***534** tracted from such a state of the case is, that it is much better to carry the contract into effect than that the rule of equity should depend on the judgment of a single individual. It is impossible for any court to appreciate all the considerations which influence men who enter into speculations of this kind. I admit that the case might present a different aspect if all the witnesses agreed in opinion. But here is a difference of opinion among some of the most respectable people of Newburgh, as to the value of the lots; and the witnesses for the appellant are supported by the former purchases made by Ellison when he was as sane as he ever was.

There is another circumstance which has considerable weight with me, and it is that this contract is for the exchange of real property. It cannot be denied that, in such cases, each party is anxious to put a high nominal value on his own land. It is a transaction wholly different, in this respect, from that of a cash sale. Although the Newburgh lots did not produce an income proportionate to the value put upon them by the appellant, yet the same objection existed as to the farms; for it appears by the evidence of Colden that they were very much out of repair.

Upon the whole, I am of opinion that there is not in the present case such an inadequacy of price as, of itself, amounts to conclusive evidence of fraud; that the contract between the appellant and Ellison, in his lifetime, was entered into with a full knowledge of all the circumstances by Ellison, and after much deliberation; and that it is fair in all its parts; and that the respondents ought to be compelled, specifically, to carry it into effect. *Coles* v. *Trecothick*, 9 Ves., 246.

I have not entered at large into the consideration of the question raised on the argument, as to the incompetency of Ellison; because it appeared to me that the weight of testimony, on that point, was clearly with the appellant; and all the facts in the case show that he concluded the bargain with great care and deliberation. If Drake Seymour is to be believed (and I think he is entitled to the most implicit credit), Ellison was perfectly competent to transact busi-
535*] ness *throughout the whole negotiation, and when he was not so, the subject was never mentioned to him. Indeed, his own agent, M'Coun, says that when intoxicated he never knew him attempt to do business. Where a general incapacity is proved, it is the duty of the adverse party to show competency when the contract was executed; but in the present case all the evidence goes to show Ellison's competency to transact business when the negotiation commenced; and Drake Seymour expressly swears to it when the contract was executed.

As to the third point, that the appellant was not in a situation to give a good title to the village lots, either when he contracted or when the deeds were to be exchanged, I am somewhat at a loss to reconcile the decree of His Honor, the late *Chancellor* with itself. He says on this point, "that the appellant was in default on the 1st of June, 1820. He ought to have shown himself able and ready to convey on that day;" and that he was in default because the property was incumbered by a mortgage of $5,000.

In conclusion, however, he says that he heard no evidence as to the complainant's title; that in the case of a specific performance, it is the usual course of the court to refer the inquiry as to title to a master. In my judgment, this inquiry extends not only to the actual title but to incumbrances upon the property. In fact, the master is to inquire whether the party can make a deed according to his contract. If he can, it is sufficient, although he was not in a situation to do so when he entered into the contract or at the time for performance; though it might be otherwise, where one party had been quickened by the other, or where time is of the essence of the contract, as where it relates to stocks or other personal chattels. 2 Pow. on Cont., 266, 267; 3 Eq. Abr., 690; 2 P. Wms., 630, 631; 7 Ves., 202; 10 Ves., 315; 6 Ves., 646; 2 Cox, 77; 2 Johns., 595, 614.

The appellant's remedy is lost at law, because the property was covered by a mortgage. But that is no objection in a court of equity. Newl. on Cont., 89. It is the peculiar privilege of courts of equity to interfere where the remedy *is defective at law, if it be not against [***536**
conscience; and if a contract be fair, it should be enforced. 8 Ves., 163; 2 Sch. & L., 347, 352; 9 Ves., 608.

I do not see anything in this cause which looks like an abandonment of the contract. It is clearly distinguishable from the cases in 1 Des., 382, and 13 Ves., 238. Here was no necessity for punctuality, as the parties had taken possession according to the contract. Indeed, the state of Ellison's health was a sufficient excuse for not offering to convey at the day. I am satisfied that the general rule is as laid down by the appellant's counsel; and that this case does not come within the exceptions to it.

The cause must, therefore, be remitted to the Court of Chancery, that the *Chancellor* may direct a master to inquire whether the appellant can give to the respondents a clear and unincumbered title of the Newburgh lots; and if he can, a decree for a specific performance, according to the contract, must be entered against the respondents.

Bowman, Bronson, Burrows, Burt, Cramer, Dudley, Haight, Lynde, M'Intire, Redfield, Thorn, Wheeler, and *Wooster, Senators*, concurred.

A majority of the court being for a reversal, it was thereupon ordered, adjudged and decreed, that one of the masters of the Court of Chancery be directed to inquire whether the said appellant has and can give a good title to certain lands in the town of Newburgh, in the County of Orange, which, by certain articles of agreement set forth in the appellant's bill of complaint, and proved in the said cause, the said appellant had agreed to convey to the said Thomas Ellison, deceased, in his lifetime; and if His Honor, the *Chancellor*, upon the coming in of the report of the said master, shall be of opinion that such title can be given, that a proper decree be made for the specific performance, by the appellant and the respondents, of the said articles of agreement, and for the execution, by the proper parties, of all necessary conveyances, with suitable covenants for assuring the title, and requiring the appellant and respondents to procure all proper persons to join in such conveyance; and that *the respondents, in that case, pay to [***537**
the appellant his costs in the Court of Chan-

cery, to be taxed; and it was further ordered that the record be remitted, &c.

For affirming, 10; for reversing, 14.

N. B. Sutherland, J., was absent, through indisposition; and took no part in deciding this, or any of the causes during this session.

Reversing—6 Johns. Ch., 222.
Cited in—5 Wend., 654; 9 Wend., 346, 548; 3 Johns., Ch., 608; 1 Paige, 246; 11 Paige, 380; Hoffm., 40; Clarke, 406; 2 Sand. Ch., 299; 9 N. Y., 544; 25 N. Y., 202; 36 N. Y., 331; 41 N. Y., 396; 57 N. Y., 158; 76 N. Y., 369; 2 Trans. App., 367; How. Cas., 752; 17 Barb., 166; 21 Barb., 389; 25 Barb., 537; 57 Barb., 564; 26 How. Pr., 219; 31 How. Pr., 41; 33 How. Pr., 369; 15 Abb. Pr., 359, *n.*; 1 Abb. N. S., 303; 4 Abb. N. S., 61; 21 Kan., 299; 104 Mass., 416; 33 Am. Rep., 184 (23 Kan., 474); 37 Am. Dec., 415 (11 Ohio, 109); 39 Am. Dec., 412 (4 Scam., 287).

JOHN WHELAN, *Appellant*,
v.
WILLIAM WHELAN AND JOSEPH WHELAN, *Respondents*.

When Equity will Set Aside Conveyance on Ground of Undue Influence—What must be Alleged in the Bill—Conveyance, by Father to Children—Inadequate Consideration—False Representations, by Children—Conveyance Closely Scrutinized in Equity—Fraudulent Conveyance, Void—Set Aside in Equity, as to Innocent Persons, who have Acquired Interests Under it—Marriage, as Consideration—Parties in Equity—Trust—Statute of Frauds.

W., a man 74 years of age, owning a considerable real estate, the father of seven children, and whose wife was sickly and irritable, was troubled for several years with dissensions among his children about the management of his property, his wife taking part with all his children on one side, except Wm. and J., two of his sons, who took part with him; and the dissensions ran so high that the mother and the children who took part with her, departed, leaving W. and his two sons, Wm. and J., in possession of the property, the management of which was confided by their father to them, as it had been for some time before the family was broken up. W. was credulous and easily led by Wm., and shortly after his wife left him, he was sued in a justice's court for her board; and on asking Wm.'s advice, Wm. told him that if he intended giving him anything he wished he would do it; that, as he and his mother were conducting, he would soon have nothing to give. W.'s fears being alarmed by a belief that his wife would dissipate his property, in order to place it beyond the reach of debts which she might contract, he was induced to convey most of his real and personal estate to these two sons, in fee, amounting to more than $9,000, and a farm, &c., to Wm., in trust for another son; but which trust was declared by parol only. Though he had before declared an intention to give all his estate to Wm. and J., by way of advancement; and though they executed to him a bond and mortgage to secure his and his wife's maintenance, and $50 a year, &c., during their lives; yet, held, that the conveyance, executed under such circumstances, was void, as being caused by fraud, undue influence, and unfounded alarm, excited or countenanced by Wm.; and being also for an inadequate consideration; and though J. might have had no part in bringing it about; yet, held, that it was also void as to him.

To warrant relief, for any cause, in a court of equity (*e. g.*, undue influence in procuring a conveyance), it must be stated in the bill; but the charge need not be direct; it is sufficient if, on a hearing upon the *pleadings and proofs, the [*538 ground of relief can be gathered from an examination of the whole bill.

A conveyance obtained by children from a father will not be sanctioned by a court of equity, if it appear to have been caused by an abuse of confidence reposed by him in his children, who, for the purpose of p curi g it took advantage of his age, imbecility and partiality for them, the conveyance being also for an inadequate consideration.

A conveyance by a father 74 years of age, his wife being nearly 70 years of age, and in delicate health, to his two sons, of real and personal estate worth more than $9,000, taking from his sons a bond and mortgage to secure his and his wife's maintenance, and an annuity of $50, during their lives; held to be for a consideration grossly inadequate; it not appearing to be intended as an advancement.

If a representation be made by one to another who is going to deal in a matter of interest upon the faith of that representation, the former shall make it good.

He who bargains, in a matter of advantage, with a person, placing confidence in him, is bound to show that a reasonable use has been made of that confidence.

One falsely supposing his estate in danger, conveys it to his sons, who know that it is not in danger, but neglect to set the grantor right—this concealment is a sufficient ground for avoiding the conveyance.

Where a grant is made by an aged father to his children with whom he lives, who have the management of his property, and in whom he reposes particular confidence, if a court of equity sees that any arts or stratagems, or any undue means, or the least speck of imposition, or the least scintilla of fraud entered into the bargain, it will avoid the grant.

A deed procured by fraud or undue influence is void and will be set aside in equity, not only as against the one who practiced the fraud or exerted the influence, but as to third persons who have acquired interests under it, though they may be perfectly innocent; thus undoing the whole transaction.

Marriage is a valuable consideration; and a voluntary deed ceases to be so, if a marriage be induced by its provisions; but it should appear in evidence that is was the cause of the marriage. The mere fact that one holding a voluntary conveyance of property marries, will not make the conveyance good.

Whether a marriage induced by a conveyance or settlement obtained by fraud or undue influence will make it good, *quære*.

All persons concerned in the demand, or who may be affected by the relief prayed, ought to be parties to a bill in equity, if within the jurisdiction of the court; but to a bill filed against one to set aside a deed of bargain and sale of land absolute on its face, although the parties agreed by parol that it should be in trust for another, the latter need not be made a party; for the trust not being declared by writing, is void.

A trust must be manifested and proved in writing, or it is void within the Statute of Frauds.

Citations—6 Ves., 182, 278; 1 Sch. & L., 209; 14 Ves., 273, 280, 289; 1 Mer., 644; 1 Dick., 84; 2 Dick., 504, 761; 2 Ves., 627; Wilm., 64; 12 Johns., 536; 5 Johns. Ch., 12; 3 Ves., 696.

*APPEAL from the Court of Chancery. [*539 The appellant filed his bill in the court of Chancery Apr. 29, 1822, praying that a conveyance executed by him to the respondents, Jan. 19, 1821, for his farm, situated at Johnstown, in Montgomery Co., and a bill of sale of personal property thereon, and a conveyance of another farm in St. Lawrence Co., and the personal property thereon, might be set aside. The bill alleged that the appellant was a native of Ireland, of the age of seventy-five years; that he had resided in Johnstown

---

NOTE.—*Undue influence—When conveyance set aside, because of.* Compare Sweet v. Bean, 67 Barb., 91; Neihcisel v. Toerge, 4 Redf., 328; Seguine v. Seguine, 4 Abb. Ct. App. Dec., 191; 3 Keys, 663; 35 How. Pr., 336; Brand v. Brand, 39 How. Pr., 193, 275; Brice v. Brice, 5 Barb., 533; Brown v. Torrey, 24 Barb., 583; Brady's Appeal, 66 Pa. St., 277.

Inadequate consideration. See Seymour v. Delancey, *ante*, 445 *note*.

Marriage, as consideration. See Verplanck v. Sterry, 12 Johns., 536, *note*.

Parties in equity. See Hickock v. Scribner, 3 Johns. Cas., 311, *note*.

thirty-five years ; that he had seven children—Charles, of the County of St. Lawrence ; John, Martha and Elizabeth, the last being the wife of W. Carr, who reside in the State of Indiana; Mary, who resides in Ireland, and Joseph and William, the respondents, resident at Johnstown. That his farm at Johnstown contained 350 acres, was of the value of $8,000, upon which the appellant and his wife resided till the autumn of 1820. That some time previous to 1820, in consequence of advanced age and imbecility of body, he resigned the management of the principal part of his real and personal estate to his sons, John, Joseph and William, who resided upon and occupied his farm ; that his son-in-law, W. Carr, leased the farm in 1819 and left it in the autumn of 1820. That for some time before the appellant was involved in a family quarrel or contention, which arose from unnatural jealousies and dissensions between his children, respecting the use and occupation of his estate ; that his wife, Martha, aged about sixty-eight years, in delicate health, and peevish in her disposition, took an active part in favor of some of the children, in opposition to the views and wishes of the appellant, which ultimately produced a dispersion of his family in the fall of 1820, by the removal of his daughter Martha, W. Carr and Elizabeth, his wife, to the State of Indiana, his son John having previously removed there, his wife leaving home and taking lodgings with Mrs. Shurtliff, in the village of Johnstown—the appellant and the respondents thus being left in the sole possession of his farm. That the appellant owned a farm in St. Lawrence Co., N. Y., on which his son Charles then resided. That he was called upon to pay **540***] the board of his wife *at Mrs. Shurtliff's, some months thereafter, which, by the advice of the respondents, he declined ; and shortly after Mrs. Shurtliff commenced an action against him in a justice's court. That he left the defense of the suit to his son William, whom he directed to ascertain the amount of the demand against him, who informed him, on his return from attending on the suit, that Mrs. Shurtliff's demand was $75, and that the appellant's wife had contracted a debt of about $100, at Campbell's, a merchant in the village of Johnstown. That William feigned to be very much cast down, upbraided him with not having advertised his mother pursuant to his previous advice, and said that if she was permitted to go on in that way she would soon dissipate his whole estate, and unless the appellant should immediately do something to prevent it, the respondents would be forced to leave him. That the appellant was in great distress of mind, and sorely grieved at these representations of William, confirmed by Joseph, and asked what was to be done to prevent his wife Martha from dissipating his whole estate. William proposed that he should convey to him and Joseph his whole real and personal estate, which would put it out of the reach of his wife and the persons dealing with her, and that she would return home if people would no longer trust her ; that to secure his maintenance they would give him a mortgage of $5,000 upon the farm, and a bond to pay him $50 a year, keep a good horse, and furnish him with all things necessary for his comfort and convenience, and indemnify him against the maintenance of his wife ; that he, confiding in the representations of the respondents, and desirous of saving his estate, agreed to the proposition. That he proposed to the respondents to go to Johnstown to draw the writings, to which they objected, alleging that the lawyers there were all combined against them in favor of their mother, and proposed to go to the office of Mr. Reynolds, at Amsterdam, in the same county, who was an entire stranger to them, all of which was falsely and fraudulently represented to him, as an excuse to decoy him out of the reach of his old friends and acquaintances, who probably would have advised him from an act so improper and inconsiderate. That Jan. 19, *1821, the appellant, William, the re- [***541** spondent, and one John Clary, the particular friend of William, went to Amsterdam, about twelve miles from his residence, and called upon Mr. Reynolds to draw a deed of his farm to the respondents ; that before the deed was executed William called him aside and reminded him of his title to about 100 acres of land in St. Lawrence Co., on which his son Charles had resided for twelve years, and insisted that this farm should also be conveyed to him, in trust for Charles—that as he trusted the respondents with all the rest, they could safely be trusted with that also. That he, confiding in their honesty and good intentions, consented to put in the deed the farm in St. Lawrence Co., and also all his personal property in Johnstown, and in the use and possession of his son Charles, in consequence of the like persuasions and representations ; that the deed thus drawn was then and there executed and delivered ; that a mortgage was then drawn on the farm in Johnstown, and a bond, in the penalty of $5,000, from the respondents to the appellant, conditioned for the maintenance of the appellant and his wife during their lives, and to pay the appellant an annuity of $50. That the appellant did not execute the conveyances for the purpose of defrauding his creditors, or of hindering or defeating the collection of any existing demand, but, on the contrary, it was understood and expressly agreed that the respondent should pay all debts due from him, which were few in number and small in amount ; that they had, however, paid little or no attention to his debts. That William took all the writings then executed, including the bond and mortgage, and that they were all put into a trunk in the house where the parties lived, and to which he (Wm.) had access at all times ; that the appellant had been deprived of the possession of the bond which accompanied the mortgage, and that he believed William had possessed himself of it, with all title deeds and other papers belonging to the appellant, and had either concealed or destroyed them, so they were out of his possession or power to regain them ; that when the respondents were informed that the bond and other p p s had been taken out of his possession, *they denied having any knowl- [***542** edge of them, and mocked him by offering to give new ones ; that they fraudulently detained the originals, and concealed them from him. That the personal property conveyed, and since in possession of the respondents, was worth $400. That at the time of the conveyances the respondents lived with the appellant, have since married, and still continued to live on the Johnstown farm, without permitting the appellant to exercise any acts of ownership. That after the conveyances his wife returned home, remained there a short time, then went and lived with one Wells, afterwards with John Clary, and finally, in Mar., 1822, the respondents lodged her with one John Taylor, a poor man, occupying a log hut on the farm; and that she was in a helpless condition, as well as the appellant, the respondents insisting on their living with them, or at such places as they designated. That he remained in the family of the respondents until about three weeks before he filed his bill, when he thought it most prudent and safe to depart; and he took up his abode with Henry Cuyler, where he was at the filing of the bill, without the means of making him a compensation.

The bill then charged: 1. That the appellant was induced, by the persuasions and false representations of the respondents that their mother was spending the whole estate, to execute the deed for the purpose of preventing it, and upon no other motive. 2. That at the time he executed the deed, he did not intend to make any settlement or disposition of his estate whatever, more than to remove it out of the reach of his wife Martha, so that she might not by her extravagance spend or incumber it. 3. That there was no other moving cause to execute the deed but the persuasion and representation of the respondents of the absolute necessity of so doing, to prevent the whole estate being dissipated by their mother, and that the bond and mortgage were proposed to be given by the respondents merely to give color to the transaction; and that the terms of these were altogether dictated by them, and acceded to by him, he not believing that the plan was to make him wholly dependent on the respondents for a living. 4. That **543***] the respondents have *not complied with the condition of the bond. 5. That three or four years since the respondents purchased a farm adjoining the appellant's for the sum of $2,000; that the complainant, to assist them in paying for it, loaned them, at different times, $800 and upwards; and that, about a year ago (in the spring of 1821), he borrowed of their brother-in-law, T. Goff, $170, for which he gave his note, which note the respondents pretend to have purchased, and to hold as a debt against the appellant, and that they refuse to pay him his annuity. 6. That on or about June 8, 1820, and while his wife Martha was from home, the respondents moved and persuaded him to give one or both of them a conveyance of the Johnstown farm, for the purpose of preventing his wife from running him in debt, and incumbering his estate; that in Aug. or Sept. following, William being dangerously ill, and his life despaired of, the respondent's reconveyed this to him, but yet pretend that they will avail themselves of the conveyance to them, and withhold the deed from the appellant.

The bill prayed for a reconveyance to the appellant, &c., and for an injunction, and was sworn to by the appellant.

The respondents, Nov. 7, 1822, answered separately. Joseph admitted all the preliminary facts stated by the appellant; but denied that he ever made any false representations to his father, to induce him to execute the deed to himself and William, in Jan., 1821, or that he knew the intention of his father, to execute such a deed, until it had been completed at the office of Mr. Reynolds.

William denied telling the appellant that his wife had contracted a debt of $100, or any other sum, with Campbell, or that he ever called on Mrs. Shurtliff respecting her demand for board, until after the deed of Jan., 1821, was executed, or that he had informed the appellant that he had done so, or that her demand was $75, or that he had told the appellant that if his wife was permitted to go on in this way, she would, in a short time, involve him in debt, and dissipate his whole estate, or anything to that effect, otherwise than as hereinafter mentioned by him. He admitted that on the evening of his and his father's return from Albany, about Jan. 18, 1821, they found a copy of a *sum- [***544** mons against the appellant in favor of Mrs. Shurtliff; that the appellant then asked him what was to be done; that he then told his father, as he had often told him before, that if he had anything to give him, he wished to know it; otherwise, he would abandon the farm; that, as the appellant and his wife were acting, they would soon have little enough for themselves. That the complainant answered, he had always intended the farm and the personal property for the respondents; and it was then agreed that a deed should be executed to them for the real, and a bill of sale for the personal estate, which was accordingly done, and the bond and mortgage executed as mentioned in the bill. He detailed what passed at the office of Mr. Reynolds in his presence and that of John Clary; that, as near as he could recollect, the appellant stated to Mr. Reynolds that he owned a farm in Johnstown; that his wife refused to live with him; that he was apprehensive she would run him in debt; that the merchants would trust her, and he should have to pay her debts: that he had understood he should be charged $5 a week for her support, and, at that rate, he could not support her, and he was determined to provide for her maintenance on the farm, and get rid of all his estate, so that he could be kept in jail but for a limited period; that he intended his farm, and the personal estate upon it, for the respondents, and he might as well give it to them to-day as to-morrow; and then stated what his sons were to give, and secure to him for the farm, and the personal property. That he, at the same time, conveyed the farm in St. Lawrence Co., on which the appellant's son Charles lived, to William, who promised that he would do with it, and convey it to Charles, as the appellant should direct; and that he has always been, and still is ready to do so.

Both of the respondents admitted that Jan. 20, 1821, they received from the appellant, a bill of sale of the personal property on both the farms; the personal property on the farm in Johnstown to belong to the respondents; and that in St. Lawrence to be held for Charles, or to be disposed of for the benefit of him as 545*] the appellant might direct; *that the personal property of which they possessed themselves does not exceed $245 in value; and that they have never possessed themselves of that in St. Lawrence Co.

William admitted that they were to pay all his father's debts, except the debt due Goff, which he and Joseph were bound to pay; and that they have complied with this part of the agreement. He denied that he took away the bond and mortgage, executed to the appellant, or that they were, to his knowledge, placed in an unlocked trunk in the house, as charged in the bill.

Joseph further answered, that when he executed the bond and mortgage, he believed the conveyance to William and himself to be an absolute deed, subject only to the claims secured by the bond and mortgage. And he denied that the bond and mortgage were intended as a mere cover to the transaction, or that they were proposed by William; but that, on the contrary, the transaction was fair, &c.

Both answered that immediately after the deed was executed, they took absolute possession of the farm; and that the appellant, for about ten months afterwards, was satisfied with the transaction. That they respectively married in May, 1821, and February, 1822, and lived together on the farm. That in 1821 their mother came to reside with them, and continued with them about four months; that she then lodged with Wells, of Amsterdam, till the winter of 1821-2. She then removed to John Clary's, where she continued till Apr. or May, 1822, and then removed to O. Taylor's, where she continued till the bill was filed, when she came to reside with the respondents. That they never refused to pay Wells for her board. They admitted the conveyance in June, 1820, by the appellant to them, of the farm at Johnstown; that a mortgage thereon was executed for $3,000, by William, to the appellant; and that, on the request of the latter, they reconveyed to him in Sept. following, William being then dangerously ill. That they know of no consideration or cause for this conveyance to them, unless it was in consequence of an expected prosecution from one Lobdell, and to defeat his recovery.

546*] *William further answered that in Feb. or Mar., 1822, he was charged with being in possession of the bond and other papers. He denied that he ever had them after their execution, or that he knew where they were, until a few days before the filing of the bill. He supposed the bond had been sent with the mortgage to be recorded, or that Alexander M'Call had it: but he had since been informed that the bond was with his papers, at Hugh M'Call's; and that it was, with other papers, delivered to him in June, 1821, although he had no recollection of it.

Both admitted that on the purchase of the farm adjoining their father's, for $2,000, he gave them $500 towards the purchase money; that this was in 1817; that he at the same time borrowed $170 of Golf, which they are bound to pay.

Both insisted: 1. That they purchased the farm for a good and valuable consideration, being the bond and mortgage executed by them; that the conveyance was not procured by representations that their mother was spending the whole estate, or any other false representations or persuasions; but that the appellant, of his own free will and accord, conveyed to the respondents, by way of settlement and advancement. 2. That it was in pursuance of a previous contract, well understood and agreed upon, that the conveyance was made; and that the persuasions and representations of the respondents, of the necessity of the conveyance to prevent their mother from dissapating the estate, were not the only moving cause for making the conveyance and bill of sale.

Joseph admitted that he had held himself out as a *bona fide* purchaser for a good and valuable consideration secured to the appellant; and that the principle consideration for making the conveyance and bill of sale, was the natural love and affection which he had for the respondents. That, previous to the conveyance, he had made no contract or agreement with the appellant, respecting the purchase of the farm; and that the appellant executed the deed on a contract well understood between him and William.

Both admitted that the manner of using and occupying the appellant's real and personal estate had been a source of contention in his family for a number of years; and it was *difficult for any of his children to [*547 have his good opinion for any great length of time. That he frequently changed his opinion and wishes respecting them, and as often wished to give one or the other a greater share in the management and use of his estate. That their mother had sometimes appeared to favor those children the most whom the appellant, at the time, was most inclined to oppose; so that it was difficult for any one of the children to enjoy the good opinion of the appellant and his wife at the same time. And that the dissensions in the family had induced some of the children to remove, at the times mentioned in the appellant's bill.

The cause having been put at issue in the Court of Chancery, by a general replication to both answers, witnesses were examined on both sides.

Testimony for the appellant (*taken in 1823*).

Daniel Wells had been acquainted with the appellant for 15 years, and believed him to be credulous and easily persuaded, by those whom he believed to be his friends. Witness had heard and believed that the appellant's wife had been badly treated, and suffered to wander abroad. She lived at witness' house about nine weeks, and Joseph Whelan refused to pay for her board.

Marcus T. Reynolds had known the appellant and William Whelan for about two years. Jan. 19, 1821, they came together, with John Clary, to witness' office, and either the appellant or William requested him to draw the deeds, but which he did not remember. He did not recollect distinctly all the conversation that passed. The appellant stated he had been prosecuted for the maintenance of his wife, and that a recovery had been had against him, and that he was fearful he would be harassed with law suits from time to time, for his wife's board and maintenance, But the witness did not know that the law suit was the cause of the conveyances, though he believed the reasons assigned by the appellant were among the inducements to the conveyances. That he drew the deed of the farm in question, and subscribed his name as a witness; and after its execution, some conversation took place between the appellant and William, relative to 548*] the St. Lawrence farm. Conveying *it to Charles Whelan, who lived upon it, was talked of, or to his children; but it was finally conveyed to William, in trust for Charles and the children, to be conveyed to such of them as the appellant should direct. That the appellant appeared not to be prepared or anxious to exact a stipulation from them for the support of himself and wife, until (after the conveyance executed) the propriety of this had been suggested to him; and then the parties agreed upon the terms of the bond and mortgage mentioned in the pleadings, which the witness drew.

Rebecca Cuyler had been acquainted with the parties for 14 years, during which time they had been in easy circumstances. The appellant and his wife lived at variance for several years, in consequence of strife and jealousy between the appellant and his children, about the use and management of his real and personal estate. The appellant's wife left her family, and went to reside with Mrs. Shurtliff, in the fall of 1820.

Jacob A. Cuyler had been acquainted with the parties for 15 years, and they were in easy circumstances. He knew the manner in which the family had lived. The appellant and his wife had lived at variance, arising from strifes and jealousies between the appellant and his children, about the use and management of the real and personal estate. He had found the appellant easily led by William. In the family strife the appellant and the respondents were usually on one side, and the appellant's wife and the other children opposed to them. In his opinion, the appellant's real estate in Johnstown was worth $9,000, and would have rented for $250.

Margaret Taylor had been acquainted with the parties for 13 years; and did not believe the appellant could have been easily persuaded by any person but his son William. For the last two years, the appellant's wife had been treated with coldness and neglect, and suffered to wander abroad and seek her living among strangers. Heard William say he would not pay anything for her maintenance while abroad; and heard her request William to furnish her with diet more suitable to her state of health, who said he would do so when he should go to Albany.

549*] *Henry Cuyler had been acquainted with the appellant and his family for 30 years. He concurred with the other witnesses as to contention in the family and its cause, and as to their circumstances in life. He had found the appellant easily led by William, who with Joseph were the appellant's friends and advisers in 1819–20, when there was great strife and litigation in the family. He concurred as to appellant's wife wandering abroad, and the respondents refusing to pay for her board, because they had means provided for her to live at home. He considered the real estate worth $8,000, and the personal about $170. He heard the appellant say he had conveyed the farm to the respondents to prevent unlawful claims against him by means of his wife.

D. P. M'Naughton had known the family for 25 years; and concurred as to their strifes, &c., and their circumstances as to property; that the appellant was easily led by his son William: and as to the respondents' siding with the appellant in family disputes. He was present when the bill of sale and the bond and mortgage were executed. The appellant said it was a hard case for him to make an assignment of his property; for it was done for the express purpose of preventing Martha, his wife, from spending his estate. The appellant directed William to take the papers to the clerk's office, have them recorded, and return them He heard William request his mother, who lived at Henry Cuyler's, to go home; otherwise, he told her, he would not provide for her; but said if she would go home she should have a room and be treated as a mother. She declined going home. This witness agreed with J. A. Cuyler as to the value of the real estate.

Alexander M'Call, aged 21 years, had known the parties from his infancy, and they had been good livers. He concurred with the other witnesses as to the strife in the family and its cause. The appellant was a credulous man, and easily persuaded by those whom he believed to be his friends. Witness' father, Hugh M'Call, had in his possession the deed, bond and bill of sale. He testified that the real estate was worth $8,000, the personal about $200; and the yearly rent of the real would have been about $250.

*Hugh M'Call had known the parties [*550 and the family 24 years, and concurred as to the value of their property, their strife and its cause. He stated that the appellant's wife boarded at Mrs. Shurtliff's; and William said that the price of her board was $5 per week. That William left with the witness the deeds and bill of sale with the bond; and which were afterwards taken away by William, as the witness was informed by one of his children and believed. He heard the appellant demand the bond of William, who told him to ask Alexander M'Call for it. Witness then asked William whether he had not the bond, whereupon he left the witness and the appellant, without giving any answer.

Nancy M'Intire had been acquainted with the appellant and his family for 30 years, lived near them, and they had always been good livers. The appellant's wife had been ill treated by the family for a number of years.

Charles Whelan, a son of the appellant, of Louisville, in St. Lawrence Co., concurred as to the strifes of the family and the cause. The appellant was a man credulous and easily persuaded to anything by those he supposed his friends; and he might be persuaded to do an act dictated to him when any fear of difficulty might threaten him or his property. He heard William say that the appellant had, by his advice, put his property out of his hands to prevent the creditors of Martha his wife from getting anything from him for her board and maintenance abroad. That Feb. 24, 1823, the witness advised William to settle this controversy, and remove on to his own farm, giving up possession to the appellant. But William said that he would not; that he had now got the old man into the situation he wanted him; that he had worked to get him into that situation for ten years; and that he would not give up an acre, unless the appellant would come to his terms.

Testimony for the respondents (taken in 1823).

John Clary, aged 38 years, has been acquainted with the family from his nativity. He heard the appellant say at Mr. Reynolds' office, Jan. 19, 1821, and afterwards at the appellant's house, and a number of time subse-
551*] quent, *that he intended to convey his property in Johnstown to his sons Joseph and William. He had also said the same thing at the house of the witness. He was present at the appellant's house when the bond and mortgage were executed, and, with Duncan P. M'Naughton, subscribed his name as a witness to them; at which time he heard the appellant say he had conveyed his farm in Johnstown to the respondents. He went in company with the appellant and William to the office of Mr. Reynolds, at the request of both parties, Jan. 19, 1821. There he heard the appellant, William being present, say to Mr. Reynolds, that he came to convey his farm in Johnstown to Joseph and William; that he did so for the purpose of saving it from the creditors of his wife; that he had been sued for her board the day previous by Mrs. Shurtliff; that the reason he came to Reynolds was because he could not trust the people of Johnstown; and that he had been informed that if he was not a freeholder they could not confine him more than 30 days on the limits for debt. The deed in question was then drawn, and executed, and was witnessed by the deponent and Mr. Reynolds. After the execution of this deed, the appellant stated that the people in Johnstown would still know that he was a freeholder in the County of St. Lawrence; and therefore it would be necessary for him to convey his farm there to some person, as it would not be safe to convey it to his son Charles, he being in debt. That he would convey it to William in trust for Charles and his children, and by William to be conveyed as Charles should direct. He did not hear William say anything to induce the appellant to make the deed to him; nor did the witness say anything to induce him to make the conveyance. He had heard the appellant say, "I protest to God, a child belonging to me shall not have one cent's worth of my estate, but my sons Joseph and William; for the others robbed me of all I had; they have not left me a chair to sit on." He concurred with the other witnesses as to the strife in the family and its cause. The contentions in the family had taken place within the last four years. The appellant's wife resided with the witness, in Mar. and Apr., 1821, about five weeks, there being no contract as to the price of her board. Joseph and William were to pay
552*] the witness, and had *paid a part. He had heard the respondents say they could as well support her at home, and find her all that would be necessary for her comfort; and William stated that he could not maintain her abroad. She had been weakly and out of health for several years; and peevish and irritable in her feelings. Previous to going to Mr. Reynolds, the family had always had their business done at Johnstown Village. The appellant was a perfect stranger to Mr. Reynolds; but William appeared to be acquainted with him. The distance from the appellant's to Mr. Reynolds' was about ten miles; and to Jobustown Village about four miles. Witness was present when the bill of sale was executed; the reasons assigned for which were the same as those for conveying the real estate. The strife in the family had the effect to drive some of them abroad.

Mary Kane heard the appellant, in 1820, and at several times after, say that he meant to convey his farm and property to Joseph and William; and in April or May, 1821, he said he had given them a great bargain, for he had let them have the farm for a mere trifle, in comparison with what he ought to have had for it, or was offered for it before. That he now only got the support of himself and wife and $50 a year; and Joseph might now see (contrary to what his mother had wished to make him believe) that the appellant had not sent for him to make a negro of him; for he had done well by him. That in Oct., 1821, the appellant said he was satisfied with what he had done in regard to conveying his property to the respondents.

Thomas Goff saw the appellant at Albany in the fall of 1820, and he said he intended to convey all his property in Johnstown to Joseph and William. That his son John and his son-in-law William had taken away almost all his property, and left him considerably in debt; and he would give the remainder to the respondents, who remained with him to take care of him; that this was in consideration of their good conduct, and he would reserve enough to live on. He applied to the witness for a loan of $1,000, and offered to give him good security, which he supposed was his farm. He is a brother-in-law of the respondents, who married his sisters.

*Catharine Goff heard the appellant [***553**
say, in the winter of 1821, that he conveyed, or would convey his property to the respondents; and he found fault with his son John, and son-in-law, William Carr; stated that they had robbed him, and left him nothing but the house and land; and should not have a cent's worth more of him.

Mary Hannesey, sister to the respondents' wives, lived in the respondents' families in the summer of 1821, and till the month of Aug., 1822; heard the appellant say that Joseph Whelan's wife used the old lady better than her own daughter ever did; that the old woman wanted a considerable attention to make her comfortable; that he had conveyed his estate to the respondents, and was perfectly satisfied; that he expected no more than $50 a year; that in Mar., 1822, he demanded his rent of the respondents, who replied they would pay him his rent, if he would deliver up to them a certain bond. He said he would close the bond upon them. They replied, the bond was good for nothing. On the same day he said to the witness, it was astonishing the boys would not give him his rent; but he was glad he had not received it; for then he could not get back his land. The appellant's wife, from bodily infirmities, made herself very unhappy in the family; often complained of ill treatment and bad usage without a cause; had heard the respondents try to coax their mother to live at home.

The consideration stated in the deed of the Johnstown farm was $5,000.

Upon the above pleadings and proofs, the *Chancellor* dismissed the appellant's bill; for which he assigned the following reasons:

THE CHANCELLOR. The complainant seeks to annul his own conveyances to two of his sons. These conveyances are valid, unless they were obtained by fraud; the answers of the defendants deny all fraud; and after a careful consideration of all the proofs taken in the cause, I am of opinion that no fraud is proved.

The testimony most favorable to the complainant, is that of Charles Whelan, who
554*] states, that *Feb. 24, 1823, the defendant, William Whelan, declared in substance, that he had worked ten years to get his father into his present situation, and that he would not give up the farm.

This testimony does not show that fraud was practiced in obtaining these conveyances. But this witness, who is another son of the complainant, can not be impartial, since, if his father should prevail in this suit, he may well expect to receive some portion of the property —and he himself says that he has no reason to expect anything more, in that event, than a son may expect from a father, or a child's portion.

Upon the whole case, it does not appear that these conveyances were obtained by fraud; and the suit must, therefore, be dismissed.

The complainant in making these conveyances of all his property, has been very improvident, but he had power to dispose of his property, and he is not at liberty to revoke his own conveyances from mere repentance. I have no power to vary or dispense with the principle, that such a conveyance is valid against the grantor, when it is free from fraud. But the question of costs is in the discretion of the court. And as the complainant is now poor, and unable to pay costs, and has became so by his imprudent generosity to his two sons, the defendants, it will, I think, be a reasonable exercise of discretion to dismiss the suit without costs against the complainant.

After entering the appeal in this cause, and before the argument on the merits,

Mr. H. Cunningham, the solicitor and counsel for the appellant in the court below, and who argued the cause there, moved this court for a rule allowing the appellant to prosecute here in *forma pauperis*, which was opposed by,

Mr. D. Cady, but granted.

Owing to *Mr. Cunningham's* engagements as a member of the House of Assembly, then in session, he did not argue upon the merits.

555*] **Mr. H. Bleecker*, for the appellant. These conveyances were executed under such circumstances that a Court of Chancery ought to set them aside. The weakness and incapacity of the appellant, and the influence of the respondents over him, will be found abundantly established by the evidence. They were always on his side in the quarrels which disturbed this old man of 75—they were his sons, his agents in the management of the property, in whom he implicitly confided. He was easily led, and exhibits great mental weakness in the silly notions which he formed as to the amount which might be recovered of him for his wife's board, and the probability that it might ruin a man of his estate. He was prejudiced against all his family except the respondents, who, it is plainly inferrible, seized on a favorable moment, and induced him to disinherit all his other children. The evidence of any intention to convey to these sons, before the fatal summons was served on him at the suit of Mrs. Shurtliff, is extremely slight, and wholly disproved by the entire evidence. It was that trifling circumstance which worked him into a state of alarm, and enabled the respondents to profit by his fears; and it is plain that these formed the whole or the principal ground of the conveyance.

Whether there is fraud actually proved or not, the consideration was so grossly inadequate, as to warrant an inference of fraud (*Guynne* v. *Heaton*, 1 Bro. Ch., 8, 9), independent of delusion or mistake. Here is much besides inadequacy. All was conducted by the advice of William, even to the conveyance of the farm in St. Lawrence; and the conduct of the sons, afterwards, places their original motives in a very questionable point of light. Even the bond securing their father's maintenance and small annuity is withheld.

For the effect of fraud upon a conveyance, I refer to *Underhill* v. *Harwood*, 10 Ves., 209; *Boyd* v. *Dunlap*, 1 Johns. Ch., 482, and *Wendell* v. *Van Rensselaer*, *Id.*, 350. In the latter case the *Chancellor* refused to set aside the deeds, but from his reasoning, and the cases cited, it is evident he would have interfered and set them aside, had a case strong as the present been made out. *Huguenin* v. *Basely*, 14 Ves., *273, was a voluntary settlement by [***556**
a widow, upon a clergyman and his family, compassed by his undue influence over her, having first got the management of her affairs. This was set aside, on the same grounds of policy as are applicable to the relation of guardian and ward. One who is the actual guardian of another, or one who is placed in a relation holding the same degree or influence, should come within the same salutary rule. The court decided the case last cited upon the principles and authorities advanced by Sir Samuel Romilly, and the other counsel concerned for the complainant, to which I refer as a lucid exposition of the doctrine on this head. *Hatch* v. *Hatch*, 9 Ves., 292, and *Chesterfield* v. *Jansen*, 2 Ves., Sr., 155, both contain principles applicable here; and in *Griffin* v. *De Veulle*, 3 Wood. Lect. App., 16, a deed was set aside, under circumstances less strong than those presented by the present case.

In determining whether there be fraud, the court will look to all the circumstances of the case, the weakness of the appellant, and the relation of the parties. 1 Madd. Ch., 224. Proof of actual fraud is not necessary, but may be inferred from such relation, or other circumstances. *Evans* v. *Llewellin*, 1 Cox, 333, 339; *Wright* v. *Proud*, 13 Ves., 136, 137. Misrepresentation, age, inexperience, parental influenee, confidence, a confiding temper, improvidence, distress and negligence, in the vendor are grounds for setting aside a sale. *Wyatt* v. *Grove*, 2 Sch. & L., 492; *Murray* v. *Palmer*, *Id.*, 474; *Carpenter* v. *Herriot*, 1 Eden, 338; *Bowes* v. *Heaps*, 3 Ves. &. B., 119; *Wharton* v. *May*, 5 Ves., 27, 67; *Griffiths* v. *Robbins*, 3 Madd. Ch., 191; *Gibson* v. *Jeyes*, 6 Ves., 267, 278.

Mr. A. Spencer, same side, would give the gentlemen who were to answer notice that he should, in reply, rely on the following authorities: to show that if void as to Williams, the deeds were so as to Joseph, though the latter might not be implicated in the fraud, *Huguenin* v. *Basely*, 14 Ves., 273, 288; to show the effect of the *suppressio veri*, undue advantage and inadequacy of price, 1 Madd. Ch., 308; *Jervois* v. *Duke*, 1 Vern., 19; *Broderick* v. *Brod-*
557*] *erick*, 1 P. Wms., 239; *James* *v. *Graves*, 2 *Id.*, 270; *Bowles* v. *Stewart*, 1 Sch. & L., 209; 1 Madd., Ch., 211; 1 Fonbl., 113; Newl. on Cont., 365-6; that the conveyances should be set aside, notwithstanding the grantor's object was to screen his estate from the payment of his debts, *Young* v. *Peachy*, 2 Atk., 258; that the vendor's acquiescence is no objection, *Murray* v. *Palmer*, 2 Sch. & L., 486; *Crowe* v. *Ballard*, 1 Ves., Jr., 215; *Roche* v. *O'Brien*, 1 Ball & B., 330; that the respondents cannot avail themselves of the Statute of Frauds, as to the use in favor of Charles in the St. Lawrence farm, though this was not declared in writing, 1 Madd. Ch., 305; and that the marriage of the respondents will not vary the case, if the conveyances were originally invalid for fraud, *Sterry* v. *Arden*, 1 Johns. Ch., 271.

Messrs. D. Cady and *B. F. Butler*, for the respondents. We shall insist that the decree of the *Chancellor* should be affirmed, for the following, among other reasons:

1. Because there is nothing in the pleadings or proofs which shows that the respondents, or either of them, possessed or exerted any such influence over the appellant, as should avoid his deed to them.

2. Because, if any such influence existed, the appellant has not, by his bill, made that the ground upon which he asks relief; but he rests his claim for relief upon the ground that the respondents had practiced a fraud upon him, by making false representations respecting debts contracted by his wife, and thus obtained a conveyance from him of his estate in Johnstown. That charge being positively denied by the respondents, and not supported by the proof, the complainant can be entitled to no relief.

3. Because, if it appears from the pleadings and proofs, that the respondents were unmarried at the time the appellant conveyed the estate in Johnstown to them, and that they both, soon after they took possession of the estate, were married to women, to whom, or to whose friends and connections, the appellant had declared the respondents were the owners of the estate, it would be "against public policy, and contrary to equity and good conscience," to permit him now to avoid that conveyance.

558*] *4. Because the deed for the farm in the County of St. Lawrence was given to the respondent, William Whelan; and it appears from the proofs that it was given in trust for Charles Whelan and his children, and to be conveyed to such person as Charles Whelan should direct. Charles Whelan, therefore, is a necessary party to any question respecting the validity of that deed; and without his being a party no decree for a reconveyance can legally be made.

There is much irrelevant matter in the bill. Many of the charges relate to a time long after the deed was executed; and their admission by the answers, or establishment in proof could have no possible influence. *Morris* v. *Burroughs*, 1 Atk., 404. What has the ill usage of the mother, for instance, to do with the case? But these charges are denied by the answers, and there is a failure to establish them in proof. There is very little testimony to any of them, and that is slight, general, imperfect and can weigh nothing against the positive denial in the answers.

Many cases have been cited as to undue influence, and this transaction has been placed in a variety of shapes. Sometimes it has been likened to a deed from a ward to his guardian; sometimes like one from a *cestui que trust* to a trustee, or a client to his attorney; and sometimes the case has been precisely inverted, by making it like a deed from a child to a parent—not from a parent to his children. But there is obviously no sort of analogy in any of the cases relied upon. They are those where influence or overreaching may be presumed, and upon principles of policy, is presumed by the law. *Morse* v. *Royal*, 12 Ves., 371. If a case could be found of undue influence exercised by a child, over a father, or presumed without proof, it would, we admit, go to make out the appellant's case; but we believe both the cases and the rational presumption are rather the other way, and in favor of the father's influence over the child, and this, we presume, is the first time that the contrary was ever pretended. (*Vide Middleton* v. *Kenyon*, 2 Ves., Jr., 391, 413.)

In simple truth, the deed was an advancement to these children, long in contemplation, and deliberately executed; *a species [*559
of conveyance highly favored in the law, and good even without any other consideration. A deed to a stranger, without pecuniary consideration, inures to the use of the grantor, but it is otherwise where the consideration of blood intervenes. There the use passes to the grantee, without any other consideration.

Huguenin v. *Basely*, 14 Ves., 273, is so much relied upon for the appellant, that we are referred not only to the case but the argument. What is the case? One of mere imposition, influence and fraud, exerted over a female, who was a stranger to the value of the estate which she granted, and who resided thousands of miles from it. The letter, incorporated in the report, was considered as decisive evidence of undue influence. Reliance was placed by counsel, upon the defendant's being the spiritual guide of the plaintiff, on the authority of Pothier; and this author, with the concurrent authority of Ld. Hardwicke, is cited against the exercise of bounty to an *administrateur*, or one managing the affairs of another. To apply the argument and principles of that case, the facts should have some analogy to the present; but none can be shown. Here the appellant had resided on his farm for 35 years, was perfectly acquainted with its value,

and had tried the temper and capacity of the respondents, his children, to whom he makes the advance. *Griffiths* v. *Robins*, 3 Madd., 191, was the case of a female donor, 84 years of age, nearly blind, dependent upon and placing a confidence in the donee, granting her estate, and reserving a very inadequate annuity. That is not this case. The appellant was capable of managing his own affairs. He secures to himself and wife a comfortable living, beside $50 annuity, and the payment of all his debts, out of a farm which would rent for only $250, a sum, in itself, utterly inadequate to the purposes of their maintenance. *Lewis* v. *Pead*, 1 Ves., Jr., 19, is much more analogous. Mrs. Lewis, when 75 years of age, leased for 99 years to Jones, a stranger, for £70, a very inadequate rent, the premises being worth £130; and Jones boasted that he had made a bargain worth £800. On a bill filed by her son to set aside the lease, per Buller, *J.*: "There must
560*] be some substantial *ground for supposing fraud stated and proved. Her being old is no proof that she was imposed upon. She did not choose to acquaint even her own attorney with her reasons for granting this lease. There is no sort of fraud in the original concoction of the business. We have seen the greatest abilities displayed at a greater age than 75; therefore, that alone can be no ground to presume imposition. She had a right to make this contract; and though the reasons of her favor to this man do not appear, that does not signify; and it appears she lived on bad terms with her son the plaintiff.

We do not deny that there may be such influence of the son over the father as to avoid a deed; but what is the proof of influence in this case, if it is to be deemed in issue, which we deny? None of the witnesses state any particular facts or instances, from which influence is to be inferred. All is mere general opinion. Even in a case of confirmed lunacy, a host of opinions will not prove it, but the facts and grounds of inference must be stated. Coop. Med. Jur., 289. It is enough that these children sided with their father in the family controversies? He was morally and legally the head of the family, and it was the duty of all the children to side with him. These did so under all circumstances; and is this to be imputed to them as a crime? If they were scoundrels for siding with him, he was the greater one, and has no right to allege this against his children. Every presumption is in favor of a deed from a father to his son, till positive fraud be shown. 1 Bos. & P., 120. An attorney, while carrying on a law suit, is not allowed to take a deed from his client; but it is otherwise if the client be the father of the attorney.

It is enough that undue influence is out of the question, as not being charged in the bill. The complainant cannot go beyond the allegations there. *Gouverneur* v. *Elmendorf*, 5 Johns. Ch., 82, *James* v. *M'Kernon*, 6 Johns., 559. All fraud is denied, and there is not the semblance of proof to establish it. To do away the answer, there should be two witnesses contradicting it, or, what is equivalent, one witness and potent circumstances. *Woodcock* v. *Bennet*, 1 Cow.,
561*] *711. The pretended misrepresentations relate to Mrs. Shurtliff, and the affair of board and the law suit; but William never saw her till after the deed, and could have made no representations on the subject. The farm must be lost, it seems, because certain facts were suppressed; but it must be shown first that they were known. The appellant talked to Mr. Reynolds about $5 per week for his wife's board, but his knowledge was not and could not have been derived from William. All which was said as to this and the $100 debt, and the consequent danger of dissipating the estate, was mere matter of opinion, and not the subject of the *suppressio veri*. Nor is there evidence that the facts were untrue. This should be shown, and that William knew them to be untrue.

Charles Whelan is obviously interested, and his testimony must be laid out of view. The appellant deliberately approved of what he had done, long after the conveyance; and the case is stripped of everything like surprise, the grounds which courts of equity usually lay hold of, in these cases, to set aside conveyances, as in *Evens* v. *Llewellen*, 1 Cox, 333. For five years the appellant had been saying to the respondents, "This farm belongs to you;" and avowing his intention to convey it to them, among his neighbors. He did convey the same land in 1820. On William's falling sick, this was annulled. Everything shows deliberation. We are told that he was alarmed by the summons and the law suit. Were these calculated to alarm a man worth $8,000? He must have known that at the worst the recovery could not exceed $50; and the most that can be said is, that had it not been for the summons he would not have conveyed on that very day, but reserved the same act till some short time after.

Inadequacy of price is also insisted on. We ask a case where a deed from a father to a son was ever impeached for that cause. It might be a good objection in the mouth of a creditor; but as between the parties, even had the deed been to a stranger, it could not be alleged, unless so gross as to shock the judgment. This is the ordinary case of an aged agriculturalist *withdrawing himself from active life. [*562
and placing his concerns in the hands of his children. It is calculated to excite no surprise —it is what thousands have done before. The whole income of the estate would not maintain the parents, if we add the expense of clothing and sickness.

It is said, that if the deed be void as to William it is so as to Joseph. This is grounded on the rule, that if it be void in part it is void in the whole. And we do not quarrel with the principle; because, taken in its full extent, it is a two edged sword, and is accompanied with the qualification, that if it be impossible to set aside a deed without doing as much injustice as justice, the court will not interfere. But the principle does not apply, except the whole be acquired by fraud: as in *Huguenin* v. *Basely* 14 Ves., 288, the case relied upon. There were third persons claiming through the fraudulent grantee. Nor does the rule apply when the good can be severed from the bad. One gives a bond, in the penalty of $3,000, conditioned to pay three persons $500 each—because one of the $500 happens to be for usury, shall it destroy the honest claims of the others, which rest on distinct grounds, and can be clearly ascertained and separated? It is the same of the present case, which is a deed to tenants in common—their interests are distinct—each may eject, give leases for their respective moieties, or distrain. Suppose a deed executed to a fair purchaser and his fraudulent attorney, conveying equal portions—would the court set aside the whole, in order to punish the attorney? William never requested a deed for Joseph, as to whom there is not a pretense of influence, or even a request on his part.

In support of the third point, we refer to *Verplank* v. *Sterry*, 12 Johns., 559, and *Sterry* v. *Arden*, 1 Johns. Ch., 271. The latter case was cited on the other side, as stopping with the position that a voluntary conveyance may be made good by marriage; but it does not deny the same effect as to deeds voidable on other grounds. We refer particularly to *Brown* v. *Carter*, 5 Ves., 862, 878. There the son, tenant in tail, just as he came of age joined his father in charging the estate with £3,000 for the use of the latter, and in resettling it, taking **563***] back to himself only an estate *for life, remainder to his first and other sons, &c., and he married and acquiesced till the death of his father; and though there was no probability of issue, it was held that all equity in favor of setting the conveyance aside was gone by the marriage, &c., and the conveyance was holden good even as against creditors. The court say they would have interfered had the marriage been out of the question. The principle of that case is, that the court will protect marital rights with the greatest jealousy; and is the same which governed a case of dower, in *Oliver* v. *Richardson*, 9 Ves., 222. A settlement procured by a fraud in which the wife was not concerned, will be protected. *Barrow* v. *Barrow*, 2 Dick., 504. The principle of the latter case also applies not only to the wife of Joseph, but to himself. Both were strangers to the pretended fraud, and indeed were ignorant of the whole transaction.

Here was a long acquiescence on the part of the appellant, with which the marriages are undoubtedly connected. The wives saw the sons in possession, claiming title, and the father acquiescing. *Murray* v. *Palmer*, 2 Sch. & L., 479, is relied on to show that this cannot be urged; but that was a case where the acquiescence was in ignorance of the party's rights, and induced by fraud.

A conveyance entirely without consideration, if there be no fraud, cannot be set aside, except by creditors, unless for duress. 1 Madd. Ch., 216, 324.

Mr. A. Spencer, in reply. Three years ago the appellant was comparatively a wealthy farmer; and the bill seeks to set aside an act by which he is stripped of everything, and thrown upon the charity of his neighbors. Against this, several formal objections have been made. Our bill is sometimes too large, and sometimes too small; but the court will not listen to such objections, unless forced upon them. They often refuse to hear a point not made in the court below. But in the progress of the cause they will find no difficulty in reaching the merits. We rely that the bill charges positive fraud; and this is established in three ways—1. By the answer; 2. By positive proof; and 3. By the intrinsic *nature of the transaction. We also [***564** rely, that the conveyances were executed under delusion and misapprehension, and that these were induced by misrepresentation or suppression of the truth.

As to the objection that our bill contains too much, we agree with the case of *Morris* v. *Burroughs*, cited from 1 Atk., 404, that the deeds cannot be avoided by subsequent circumstances, considered merely as such; yet they may be resorted to in order to show *quo animo* the act was done, as you would look to an escape in a prosecution for felony. We use them here to show an original design to deprive the appellant of subsistence. Indeed, the course has been acquiesced in by the respondents, who have not moved to strike out the matter for impertinence, and have even gone into proof upon that head. The fact, for instance, that William withheld the bond for the appellant's maintenance, is admitted in the answer, and M'Call gives in evidence in relation to it. When required to pay the $50, an order on Charles for the use of the farm which William held in trust is offered; or payment is refused till the old bond and mortgage are given up, though known to be good for nothing. They maltreat the mother, and drive her from the house, refusing to make provision for her, falsely pretending inability to support her away from home. And the answer, denying that they refused to pay Wells for her board, is directly contradicted.

Suppose the court should think there is no charge of undue influence in the bill, the utmost they will do is to order it dismissed without costs. *Beekman* v. *Frost*, 18 Johns., 544. *Cui bono*, then, is the objection made? For the benefit of lawyers. I do not deny that the relief must be *secundum allegata et probata*; but nothing technical is necessary. Though a bill properly consists of nine heads, and a matter may more properly be charged in the stating part, yet this requisition is merely formal, and it may be set forth in any other part, or collected from the whole bill. Originally the bill was a mere petition, containing the substance of the case, which is yet sufficient, though a more formal way is found convenient and safe for the pleader. If enough appear on the whole bill to warrant the relief, it will be granted. The *party is not under the necessity [***565** of using the epithet to characterize the influence made use of. It is enough that he state facts, without christening them "undue influence." If the bone and marrow be found in the bill, it is enough. Undue influence is a conclusion of law which need not be stated, especially in equity, where the rules of pleading are most enlarged and liberal.

I proceed, then, as to both heads of fraud and undue influence; for they are blended in the bill. The appellant's age, his emigration from Ireland, his property, the domestic broils in which he was involved, resulting in a partial dismemberment of his family; the quarrels among his children in relation to the use and management of his estate, the desertion of his wife in the fall of 1820, her going to Mrs. Shurtliff's, the suit for her board, the summons, the agency of William in that affair, his return, representing the charge of $5 per

week for board, and the debt to Campbell, William's advice which is yielded to, going to Reynolds', having no intention to settle the estate, but induced by alarm and persuasion. These facts, charged in the bill and made out in proof, show the appellant much in the power of the respondents. Great influence is inferable, and which was exerted for a most pernicious purpose. The respondents were his sole reliance, and had the management of his property; and had an overruling influence upon his mind. We admit and charge, that William was the only actor in the scene; but it is singular that he should have kept the whole an entire secret from Joseph, as he says in his answer. Both say they had the principal management of the appellant's affairs at the time; both impute the strife in the family to disagreement between the appellant and his wife, the respondents being dutiful and attentive on their part. Both knew of the suit and service of the summons, and what took place on that occasion; admitting that William went to Shurtliff's, denying that he had misled his father—companions throughout all these proceedings and acquainted with all, except the fact charged that William exerted his influence to procure an immediate conveyance—a very singular exception, at the least. William, in one breath, denies having charged his father and mother with dissipating the es-
566*] tate; *and in the next he admits it. The father then throws himself upon his son's advice. And suppose he had said nothing to influence him—nothing charged in the bill—but stood by and heard his father make the strange resolutions which he formed upon the imaginary terrors by which he was surrounded. Indeed, all this is admitted by the answer; and it is admitted what is equivalent to the matter charged. It cannot be evaded by the pretense that it is not the same. I charge fraud by false dice. This is denied in the answer, and attributed to false cards. Shall this form a defense, or shall it be taken for the same, in substance? Seeing his father deluded and fearful, he seizes the favorable moment; he does not, indeed, he says, use the words charged; but, "to save the farm, you must, if you have anything to give, give it now." This in the absence of all the family. "I tell you, that as you and mother are acting, you will soon have nothing to give." Surely he admits substantially the whole that is charged. The whole of his answer, so far as particulars are charged, is conceived in falsehood, and not to be believed, except where it makes for us. It admits that his father stated to Reynolds his difficulty and danger, adding (falsely according to Reynolds' evidence) that he at the same time declared his previous intention to give his estate to his sons; and he might as well convey it at that time as any other. Both admit that the debts to be paid were trifling, which is indeed inferable from their not showing what they amount to. They insist on the conveyance as an advancement; and then, by way of negative pregnant, deny that the only moving cause was fear of the estate being dissipated, wrought through William's representations. Does not this admit that it was part of the moving cause? Accusing the appellant and his wife with waste and impending ruin, and urging him to give then, or that he would abandon the appellant, is admitted by William's answer. This, in itself, was the creation of an alarm which he knew to be false and ill-founded. There was no conduct calculated to produce ruin, or to excite the barbarous threat of desertion on the part of William. Sometimes the answer insists on the deed as having been executed for a valuable consideration; *at others, upon a spirit of love, [*567
affection and advancement so excessive as to give everything away to such dutiful children. The parties hurry off to a stranger, the appellant laboring under the delusion that everybody at Johnstown was combined to ruin him—a stranger who could know and suspect nothing of the fraud; and call upon him to draw the papers. William stands by and hears the lunatic and unfounded representations of his father to Reynolds, giving them countenance and sanction by his silence, and joining in the request. Everything was sudden; and it is fairly inferable that all was moved by William, who the day before had returned from Albany, and who must have told his father what he related to Reynolds. How could his father acquire this knowledge through any other channel? William was the confidential agent who managed the entire business. The father looked for information nowhere else. But be this as it may, the man who stands by, and takes advantage of an erroneous impression, knowing it to be such and omitting its correction, is as guilty as the one who excites it. Add, then, the evidence of M'Naughton, and Charles Whelan, and a strong case of undue influence and fraud is established.

Charles is not so far interested as to disqualify him. His expectations are no more than that of any child. He expects a child's portion. Clary mentions no other motive as being assigned by the appellant to Reynolds, than that of keeping his property away from his creditors and devesting himself of freehold. William answers as if the agreement to maintain his father was matter of previous arrangement; but Reynolds says that the old man did not appear to expect anything of that kind, till suggested by William, doubtless with a view to color the transaction. So perfectly confiding was the appellant, that he had not thought of indemnity; and the answer of William is false in saying there was any agreement to that effect. Being false in so many particulars, this answer must be rejected *in toto*. It comes emphatically within the rule, *falsus in uno, falsus in omnibus*.

The facts bring these parties within the principle which required the whole of this business to have been done with *great [*568
deliberation, publicly, and under the advice of mutual friends. It is said we do not show actual imbecility. This is not necessary. Here is a man 75 years of age. We have the authority of the Constitution that at 60 a man begins to go down hill; and on this ground he is excluded from the superior benches of justice. The respondents should have rescued the appellant from the operation of this general rule, by showing that he was an exception. Besides, credulity is a confirmation of the mind as fatal as general imbecility. All the witnesses agree that the appellant was very cred-

ulous and easy of persuasion to any purpose, especially by William. Cooper is relied on, that general opinion as to his state of mind is not enough; but it is so *prima facie*. Inquiry into particulars belonged to the other side, who should have pointed their interrogatories in such a manner as to show the conclusions of the witnesses destitute of premises. Not having done this, the intendment is that they are well founded.

Fraud consists of anything which deceives another; cunning, device, trick, suppression of truth in any manner so as to cloud the mind. Several cases have been cited, of a class which arises from the relation of the parties, and consequent influence. Seeing this situation, the law throws its shield around the party. It is objected that these cases do not apply to the appellant, going merely against the abuse of parental authority. What, if so? What do we read cases for? For the sake of the rule which they establish, to be applied to other cases coming within the principle of those cited. In *Gibson* v *Jeyes*, 6 Ves., 266, an attorney had sold an annuity to his client, to the disadvantage of the latter; and on a bill filed to set it aside, on the ground of the relation which existed between the parties, Ld. Eldon (p. 278), after enumerating the very great precautions under which alone such a sale could stand, and declaring that if the party would mix the character of vendor with that of attorney, he shall be holden to manifest that he has given all that reasonable advice against himself that he would have given against a third person, proceeds: "Is it asked where this rule is to be found? I answer in that great rule of the **569***] court, that he *who bargains in a matter of advantage, with a person placing confidence in him, is bound to show that a reasonable use has been made of that confidence; a rule applying to trustees, attorneys, or anyone else." Was the appellant dealing with one in whom he confided? He then comes within the principle of the case cited. It is not even necessary that we should show the abuse. It is enough to show the confidence. In the language of Ld. Eldon (*Id.* 278), that circumstance throws upon the one in whom confidence is placed the whole *onus* of the case. He must show affirmatively that everything was fair. In *Chesterfield* v. *Janssen*, 2 Ves., Sr., 155-6, Ld. Hardwicke enumerates four species of fraud. The 2d, he says, "may be apparent from the intrinsic nature and subject of the bargain itself; such as no man in his senses and not under delusion would make, on the one hand, and as no honest or fair man would accept, on the other; which are inequitable and unconscientious bargains; and of such even the common law has taken notice, for which, if it would not look a little ludicrous, might be cited *James* v. *Morgan*, 1 Lev., 3." A fourth species of fraud, which he mentions and comments upon at large, is one arising from an attempt to impose on third persons, and from the relation of the parties; and in the latter case he says fraud is matter of presumption to be rebutted by the other side. *Young* v. *Peachy*, 2 Atk., 258, goes fully to the same point. *Griffiths* v. *Robins*, 3 Madd., 191, will be found most strikingly analogous to the present, both in fact and principle. I invite the particular attention of the court to that case, and especially to the language of the *Vice-Chancellor*. The whole is directly applicable; and, if to be respected as authority, disposes of this cause. The case of *Gee* v. *Spencer*, 1 Vern., 32, is also directly applicable. There was a suit in chancery touching a rectory owned by three sisters. The husband of one of whom, fearing to be in law, and made to believe that he should be forced to pay costs, released £1,000, the arrears upon his share of the rectory, to the other two sisters who were to bear the charge of the suit. This release was set aside on the ground that a misapprehension *in the party shall avoid his [***570** release. This case is cited with approbation in 2 Pow. on Cont., 202.

Lewis v. *Pead*, 1 Ves., 19, cited on the other side, was decided by Buller, *J.*, sitting for the *Lord Chancellor;* and though a good common lawyer, he was not familiar with the principles of equity. Taking his decision, however, as authority, it is no more than that the age of 75 does not, *per se*, evince inability.

I thank gentlemen for the case of *Middleton* v. *Kenyon*, 2 Ves., Jr., 391. It contains all our premises, and all our conclusions, though the transaction was affirmed. What is that case? The elder Middleton, having incumbered his estate by his extravagance, in order to relieve himself by raising a very large sum, parted with certain interests in an estate to his son, in consideration of the latter contributing his own interest in the same estate, to relieve his father. The conveyance was to three trustees, of whom Ld. Kenyon was one, and a defendant in chancery. The ablest counsel were consulted, and the whole affair was conducted with ample time, and the greatest deliberation; but after the best possible arrangement, the father took it into his head that there had been misapprehension; and that, too, after long acquiescence, and large interests acquired, *bona fide*, by third persons, in the course of executing the trust. At page 408, the *Lord Chancellor* lays down the precise ground upon which we go, that any bargain may be declared null and set aside, upon grounds of undue practice or influence exerted, or on the ground of mistake.

The force of the different pretenses set up by the respondents—sometimes that the deed was for natural love and affection, and sometimes for valuable consideration—is shown and illustrated by *Clarkson* v. *Hanway*, 2 P. Wms., 203. The consideration appearing on the face of the deed, is a pecuniary one of $5,000, the value probably which the respondents choose to fix on the bond and mortgage for maintenance, &c., and the case last cited shows that they cannot now press into their aid the consideration of natural love and affection, because it falsifies the deed. At least, it strengthens *the proof of fraud, by showing that [***571** the deed carries a disguise.

As to the marriages, it is plain from the case of *Sterry* v. *Arden*, 1 Johns. Ch., 271, and *Huguenin* v. *Basely*, 14 Ves., 273, that they cannot be taken into the account, provided there be fraud in the case, though a marriage may supply the mere want of a valuable consideration. But here there is no proof that the father ever heard of the intended marriages of the respondents, or that the wives ever heard of the conveyance; and no injurious consequences or disappointment to them can arise from setting aside the conveyance. The respondents already had farms, to the purchase of which the father contributed.

The facts do not warrant the inference that Charles is a necessary party. The proof of the trust is by parol; and it resulted to the grantor, who had the sole direction of it between Charles and his children. It was not limited to him specifically, but to him or his children, as the father might direct. No interest passed out of the father, and it was not such a trust as Charles could enforce in a court of equity. *Steere* v. *Steere*, 5 Johns. Ch., 1.

The declarations of the appellant, made to witnesses before the conveyance, that he intended his property for the respondents, were general, and might as well relate to a will as to a deed.

WOODWORTH, *J.* The bill seeks to be relieved against two conveyances executed by the appellant—the one for a farm in Johnstown, the other for 100 acres of land in the County of St. Lawrence.

Relief is claimed, on the ground of undue influence and fraud. The respondents object that the former is not alleged in the bill, and consequently not in issue.

The bill charges the respondents with fraudulent artifices, management, and undue influence, in obtaining the deeds. It is, however, sufficient, if from an examination of the whole bill, the facts stated show that the respondents necessarily had undue influence or control over the appellant, so that the parties did not treat on equal terms. The rule that re-
572*] quires *everything essential to the appellant's right to be alleged, is then satisfied. His equity will then appear, and the court may administer the relief to which he is entitled. Whether undue influence has been used, is an inference from the facts alleged and proved, and does not require the averment of the pleader to put them in issue. It is enough if they authorize the court to draw the conclusion.

I will briefly state some of the leading features of this case. The appellant is far advanced in years. He is probably not exempt from the infirmities incident to mind and body in the last stage of human life. In this second childhood, a surrender of business into other hands becomes indispensable. Something like a guardianship of the person and property is in most cases necessary. The appellant had reared a numerous family. For several years there appears to have been much family contention, arising from dissensions between his children with respect to the use and management of his estate. The appellant's wife took part with some of the children. She and her husband lived unhappily, and separated. The bill alleges that the appellant had committed the management of his estate chiefly to his sons, John, Joseph and William; that after his wife left her home, the farm was in the exclusive possession of the appellant and the respondents. It is in proof that the appellant was very credulous, and easily persuaded by those whom he believed his friends; that he was easily led by William: that in the family strifes the appellant and the respondents were on one side—the wife and the other children in opposition; that the appellant could be persuaded to do any act dictated to him, when apprehensive that his property was in danger. It cannot be doubted that he was placed in a situation highly favorable to the views of the respondents. They had full opportunity for operating on his hopes and fears. A contract obtained from one party, so much in the power of the other, cannot be sanctioned, if confidence has been abused, if there is inadequacy of price, or the inference is plain, that advantage has been taken of age and imbecility, and the partiality of a parent has been artfully made use of to strip him of his property, and reduce him to a state of dependence and want.

*It does not appear that Joseph [***573**
was an active agent in procuring the deeds. The transaction was between the appellant and William. The first question is, whether fraud or undue influence was practiced by the latter.

The farm is valued at $9,000. The appellant's debts were trifling. His wife boarded with Mrs. Shurtliff. The bill alleges that she charged, as William stated, $5 per week for his mother's board; that the appellant was sued by her in a justices' court; that William observed, if his mother was permitted to go on in that way she would involve the appellant in debt, and dissipate his whole estate; and that unless the appellant would immediately do something to prevent it, the respondents would leave him. That he asked the respondents what could be done. William advised the appellant to convey to him and his brother the whole estate, real and personal. That to prevent such consequences he consented to the proposition.

The respondent, William, in his answer, admits, that in Jan. 1821, he returned from Albany with the appellant, and found that Mrs. Shurtliff had commenced an action by summons. That the appellant asked him what should be done? That he then told the appellant, as he had often done before, that if the appellant had anything to give him, he wished to know it, otherwise he would abandon the farm; that as the appellant and his wife were acting, they would soon have little enough for themselves. That thereupon it was agreed that the appellant should execute a deed of the farm. The question here arises, what induced the appellant, at this time, tó devest himself of all his property? The answer is obvious—his fears that his estate would be swept away for debts contracted by his wife.

It is scarcely necessary to say that the supposition was groundless. His wife had been at board 13 weeks. The demand was afterwards settled for $25. A summons had issued to collect this small debt. This statement is enough to satisfy every mind that the appellant was bereft of ordinary understanding. If his ignorance and imbecility of mind were so great as to entertain such apprehensions, for such a cause, it is evident he would become an easy prey to any designing *knave who [***574**
happened to possess his confidence. How does William treat these suggestions? Every motive of duty towards a parent required him not to give a false coloring. He was bound not only to speak, but to speak truly. But

such a course would not answer the purpose in view. He had too much discernment not to perceive that this was the favorable moment to profit by the appellant's fears. Instead of quieting the idle apprehensions of his father, he renews his request. "If you have anything to give, I wish to know it; otherwise I will abandon the farm"—and adds, that as the appellant and his wife were acting, they would soon have little enough for themselves. The impression such remarks were calculated to make cannot be mistaken. It was, in substance, saying, "Your estate will be dissipated by the expense of supporting your wife, and the only way to avoid it is to give me your property." The allegation was untrue in point of fact. There was no ground for alarm. The conduct of William on this occasion was not only undutiful, but fraudulent. The appellant was thereby deceived, and became the dupe of the artifice practiced on him. The proceedings at Mr. Reynolds' office are in exact accordance with the view I have taken. William admits that the appellant stated to Reynolds he was apprehensive his wife would run him in debt; and the merchants would trust her; that he understood he should be charged $5 per week for her board; that he was determined to get rid of all his estate, so that he could not be kept in jail but a short time.

The question here occurs, from whom did the appellant derive his information? Reynolds testified that the appellant stated he had been prosecuted for the maintenance of his wife; that a recovery had been had against him, and he was fearful he should be harassed with law suits, from time to time, for his wife's board and maintenance. He believed the above were among the inducements to convey his estate. Clary testified that the appellant declared he made the conveyance for the purpose of saving it from his wife's creditors. William stands by and does not attempt to remove these erroneous impressions. Had the business been fairly explained, I doubt not that Mr. Reynolds would **575***] have informed the appellant *there was no cause for alarm. The next day, when the bond and mortgage and bill of sale were executed, M'Naughton testifies that the appellant declared it was a hard case for him to make an assignment of his property—it was done for the express purpose of preventing Martha, his wife, from spending his estate. Here also William is silent. He suffers his father to remain under the delusion. He perceives his unwillingness to reduce himself from affluence to dependence; and yet quietly takes possession of the papers, and permits the fraud to be carried into effect. A strong confirmation of the fraudulent intentions of William, is derived from his declarations to Charles Whelan, in 1823. "He had got the old man into the situation he wanted—that he had worked to get the appellant into that situation for these ten years."

There is another fact that marks the influence of William over the appellant, as well as his incapacity to protect himself. Mr. Reynolds says, after the appellant had conveyed his property to the respondents, he appeared not to be prepared or anxious to exact a stipulation from them for the support of himself and wife, until the propriety of this had been suggested to him. At length a bond and mortgage were prepared, with condition to give the appellant and wife a comfortable support, in sickness and in health, and the sum of $50 annually, during life; but that the respondents should not be required to provide such support except in their own dwelling-houses, which they or one of them should occupy. As the appellant seemed not to have thought of any consideration to be paid, nor anxious to require any, he was of course willing to accept any thing William would give. The specter of law suits, his wife's debts, and imprisonment, had so haunted his imagination, that his own future support seems to have been lost sight of; or, if not, he reposed on the filial affection of his favorite sons. The consideration, then, was grossly inadequate, and not suited to the exigency of the case. It may well be considered as one item that gives the character of fraud to this transaction. There is no ground for upholding this deed on the principle that this was an advancement, or that it was founded on natural love *and affection. All the [***576** declarations of the appellant of his intentions respecting the respondents, must be considered as relating to his future bounty. They can have no effect in supporting the present deed.

The principles which govern a court of equity, abundantly prove that the appellant is entitled to relief. In *Evans* v. *Bicknell*, 6 Ves., 182, the *Chancellor* observed, it is a very old head of equity that if a representation is made to another person, going to deal in a matter of interest, upon the faith of that representation, the former shall make that representation good if he knows it to be false. So also in *Gibson* v. *Jeyes*, 6 Ves., 278, it is laid down as a general rule in equity, that he who bargains in matter of advantage, with a person placing confidence in him, is bound to show that a reasonable use has been made of that confidence—a rule applying to trustees, attorneys or anyone else. We cannot shut our eyes to the fact that William well knew that the appellant's large real estate was not in danger of being wasted, by the inconsiderable expense of paying his mother's board in the country, and supplying her wants for a few years—she then being nearly seventy years of age, and in delicate health. The supposition would be puerile, and inconsistent with the intelligence and management discovered by William, in effecting his object. The appellant, in great distress, makes inquiry what is to be done. He seems to be entirely ignorant that his estate and person were not in danger. William had the power to make known to him his true situation, but he withholds the information. It would, therefore, be unconscionable to hold the appellant to the bargain; this concealment is alone a sufficient ground for avoiding it. When transactions of this kind are between parties standing in such relations to each other, they ought to be conducted with all imaginable fairness. In *Bowles* v. *Stewart*, 1 Sch. & L., 209, it was held that concealment of a material fact was sufficient to avoid a release obtained by the person whose duty it was to make the disclosure. I fully subscribe to the reasoning of Sir Samuel Romilly in *Huguenin* v. *Basely*, as applicable to this part of the case; that "if the court sees that any arts or stratagems, or any *un- [***577** due means have been used; if it sees the least speck of imposition at the bottom; if there be the least scintilla of fraud, this court will, and ought to interpose; and by the exertion of such a jurisdiction, they are so far from infringing the right of alienation, which is the inseparable incident of property, that they act upon the principle of securing the full, ample and uninfluenced enjoyment of it."

From this examination, it seems to me, there is little difficulty in deciding that the respondent William procured the deed from the appellant to the respondents by fraud and imposition; and that so far as he is concerned, it ought to be held utterly null and void.

The next question is, whether the fault of William, in procuring the deed, renders it void as to Joseph, the other respondent. It is a general rule, that in ordinary cases of fraud, equity undoes the whole transaction, and replaces the parties in their former situation. *Daubney* v. *Cockburn*, 1 Mer., 644.

The case of *Bennet* v. *Wade*, 1 Dick., 84, is very much in point. The facts were briefly these: Sir John Leigh was seised of a large real estate; his mind was so weak that he was easy to be imposed upon; the defendant was a surgeon and apothecary, who attended him, took advantage of this weakness, and prevailed on him, then aged sixty, to marry Wade's daughter, aged sixteen, and to execute a settlement in favor of his daughter. The daughter dying soon after, Wade obtained a will from Sir John in his favor, and also indentures of lease and release as he alleged in consideration of the will. After the testator's death, Wade set up the deeds, under which the defendant's claimed beneficially, and they entered on the estates. A part of the estate was conveyed to Wade in fee; a bill was filed to set aside the deeds, and a cross-bill to establish them. It was argued on the part of the plaintiffs, that whatever fraud or imposition had been practiced on Sir John Leigh, by the defendant Wade, they were not privy to or concerned in it; that it would be hard to involve the innocent with the guilty, and punish them, by setting aside the deeds *in toto*. But Ld. Hardwicke **578***] was of *opinion that the deeds were founded in fraud, and being so, it vitiated the whole; that they were obtained from Sir John Leigh, by fraud, imposition and circumvention, by means of the undue influence of the defendant Wade over his weakness; and that the same ought to be set aside. This case fully establishes the principle, that the respondent Joseph cannot be protected. So, also, in *Davidson* v. *Russell*, 2 Dick., 761, the question was, whether a deed could be set aside in part for fraud, and the rest established. Lord Thurlow was decidedly of opinion it could not. He directed the contract to be set aside, and observed, there could be no hesitation; though it appeared that innocent persons were interested under it. This cause was afterwards reheard and affirmed by Ld. Loughborough, in 1794.

In *Huguenin* v. *Basely*, 14 Ves., Jr., 289, the same doctrine is recognized. Ld. Eldon observes: "I should regret that any doubt could be entertained, whether it is not competent to a court of equity to take away from third persons the benefits which they have derived from the fraud, imposition or undue influence of others." The case of *Bridgeman* v. *Green*, 2 Ves., 627, was considered by his Lordship as an express authority that it is within the reach of the principle of this court, to declare that interests so gained by third persons cannot possibly be held by them. This last cause afterwards came before the Lords Commissioners, and *Lord Ch. J.* Wilmot expresses himself thus: "There is no pretense that Green's brother or his wife was party to any imposition, or had any due or undue influence over the plaintiff; but does it follow from thence that they must keep the money? No., Whoever receives it must take it tainted and infected with the undue influence and imposition of the person procuring the gift. His partitioning and cantoning it out amongst his relations and friends, will not purify the gift, and protect it against the equity of the person imposed upon. Let the hand receiving it be ever so chaste, yet if it comes through a polluted channel, the obligation of restitution will follow it." Wilm., 64; 14 Ves., 289.

It is unnecessary to pursue this doctrine through all the cases, to be found in the books. It is believed that the rule is *firmly [***579** established. If it were otherwise; that a person could evade the principle, by giving interests to third persons, instead of reserving them to himself, it would be almost impossible ever to reach a case of fraud. The deed, then, is bad *in toto*, and must be set aside as to both the respondents.

But it is contended, that inasmuch as the respondents were unmarried at the time the estate was conveyed, and afterwards married, and the appellant declared to the friends and connexions of their wives that the respondents were the owners of the estate, it would be against public policy and contrary to equity and good conscience, to permit him now to avoid that conveyance.

The evidence of Thomas Goff is, that in 1820 the appellant stated that he intended to convey all his property in Johnstown to the respondents. Catharine Goff testified that the appellant said he had conveyed or intended to convey his farm. But there is no testimony that any declarations were ever made to the respondents' wives, before their marriage; nor does it appear that the conveyance made by the appellant was among the inducements to the marriage. Indeed, it does not appear that they had any previous information or knowledge respecting the transaction between the appellant and the respondents.

The facts, then, do not present the question raised by the counsel, or form any objection to the interference of the court. Marriage is a valuable consideration; and if the grantee of a voluntary deed gains credit by the conveyance, and a person is induced to marry on account of the provisions made in the deed, the conveyance, on the marriage, ceases to be voluntary. This principle was decided in *Sterry* v. *Arden*, 12 Johns., 536.

In the case of *Barrow* v. *Barrow*, 2 Dick., 504, cited by the respondents' counsel, it was held that a settlement in consideration of marriage, procured by fraud and imposition in which the wife was not concerned, should not be set aside. In that case, the daughter of the person who practiced the fraud revolted at first, but was prevailed on to marry the person who made the settlement, although his intel- **580*]** lect *was quite impaired, and he in a state of childhood. The court refused to interfere, on the ground that there was a valuable consideration proceeding from the party not privy to the fraud.

The remaining inquiry is, whether Charles Whelan is a necessary party, in consequence of the deed given by the appellant to William in trust for Charles. All persons concerned in the demand, or who may be affected by the relief prayed, ought to be parties, if within the jurisdiction of the court. The question here is, whether Charles Whelan could enforce the execution of the trust. If he could not, he is not a necessary party. The farm in St. Lawrence Co., on the face of the agreement, was conveyed unconditionally to William. He admits in his answer, that he agreed to convey it to Charles, as the appellant should direct. There was no declaration or evidence of trust in writing, and the deed is absolute. This case cannot be taken out of the Statute of Frauds. A trust need not be created by writing, but it must be manifested and proved by writing. The nature of the trust, and the terms and conditions of it, must sufficiently appear; so that the court may not be called on to execute the trust, in a manner different from that intended. *Steere* v. *Steere*, 5 Johns. Ch., 1; *Foster* v. *Hale*, 3 Ves., Jr., 696. It follows then that Charles Whelan could not compel the execution of the trust. The deed for the St. Lawrence farm rests on the same foundation as the conveyance to the respondents jointly. I am of opinion that the decree of His Honor, the *Chancellor*, be reversed; and that a decree be entered, declaring that the deed from the appellant to the respondents for the farm in Johnstown, and the deed to William Whelan for the St. Lawrence farm, be annulled and held for nought, and that the appellant recover against the respondents his costs in the court below, to be taxed.

Savage, Ch. J. Bowman, Bowne, Burrows, Burt, Clark, Cramer, Earll, Gardiner, Green, Haight, Keyes, Mallory, M'Call, M'Intyre, Morgan, Nelson, Stranahan, Thorn and *Wheeler, Senators*, concurred.

581*] *SUDAM, *Senator*, went into a very full examination of the pleadings. He said the points for the consideration of the court are:

1. Whether the conveyance of Jan. 19, 1821, was fraudulent and void by reason of William's false representations; or by his suppression of the truth when he was bound to speak.

2. If not, was the appellant so much under the influence of the respondents, or either of them, that the conveyance was not the execution of a free, unbiased purpose of bounty?

3. Whether the court can compel a reconveyance of the St. Lawrence farm; Charles Whelan not being a party to the bill.

Upon the first point he went at large into the facts connected with and immediately preceding the conveyance, as those upon which the opinion of the court must rest. The subsequent transactions, he said, may be regarded as circumstances, but not of primary importance, in the decision of the cause. They may aid in the conclusion, but cannot be the basis of our judgment. The Johnstown farm was worth at least $8,000, and the personal property there amounted to about $400; but there is no evidence as to the value of the St. Lawrence farm, or the personal property upon it. The respondent was 74 years of age, and his wife about 67, at the time of the conveyance. According to the admissions of the answers, he had, some time previous to the spring of 1819, resigned the charge of his real estate at Johnstown to his sons, John, Joseph and William; the reason of which, as stated by William, was to make them men of business; though Joseph says he did not know the reason. How long they had occupied the farm does not appear. In 1819 Carr, the appellant's son-in-law, came into possession, and occupied it till the fall of 1820; when all the children then at home, except the respondents, removed to Indiana, leaving the respondents in full possession, with the appellant. About the same time, Martha, the appellant's wife, left the house, and took lodgings with Mrs. Shurtliff. The respondents admit there had been dissension in the family, but *deny, in the first part of their **[*582** answer, that it arose from disagreement as to the management of the farm. In June, 1820, the appellant had, of his own motion, executed a deed of the farm in question to Joseph and William, taking a bond and mortgage from William alone, for $3,000. These papers were drawn at Johnstown, and the transaction was known to Joseph. In Sept. following, William being dangerously ill, this was rescinded, on the mere request of the father, the respondents releasing to him all their right, the appellant thus becoming reseised of the farm about the time his wife and children left him. Cut off from all communication with the rest of his family, the appellant continued to reside with Joseph and William till Jan., 1821; when, on the latter returning from Albany, they found the copy of the summons from Mrs. Shurtliff. In relation to this, William admits that his father asked him what was to be done; to which he replied, and had often told him before, that if he had anything to give him he wished to know it, otherwise he would abandon the place—that as the appellant and his wife were acting, they would soon have little enough for themselves. That it was then agreed, as the father had long intended, to execute the conveyance and bill of sale. On the 19th, William and his father, with John Clary, who appears to have been a mutual friend, went to the office of Mr. Reynolds, an attorney and counselor at law, an entire stranger, ten miles distant, for the purpose of having the proper conveyances drawn. William's answer, as to what passed there, concurs, in the main, with the evidence of Mr. Reynolds as to the cause of the conveyance. That it was owing to fear of the wife's extravagance, and the consequent law suits. But Reynolds omits the declaration of the father, set up in the answer, that he had intended the farm for his sons, and might as well give it to them to-day as to-morrow; and his mentioning the consideration he was to receive. So far from this, he appeared not to be prepared or anxious to exact any stipulation from the respondents, for his and his wife's maintenance, till the propriety of this had been suggested to him; and then he and William agreed on the bond and mortgage.

583*] *This is the evidence of a person wholly disconnected with the parties, swearing in direct contradiction to William, as to any moving cause beyond the fears of the father. If the conveyance was the mere consummation of a prior intent, why did the appellant devest himself of all his real estate, including that in St. Lawrence? And where is the force of the other motive assigned by William, that the appellant wished to devest himself of all freehold, to evade imprisonment for debt, when the respondents both admit that they were to pay all subsisting debts, and were to prevent future ones by maintaining both the appellant and his wife? It is clear that the appellant acted under erroneous impressions in regard to his legal liability; that his object was not to advance any of his children, or settle his estate. But he conveyed because he believed, from information, that it was necessary to prevent his estate being squandered by his wife, and to insure only a temporary imprisonment for debts contracted by her. John Clary's testimony goes distinctly to these two causes. True, according to his testimony, the appellant protested to God, that a child belonging to him should not have one cent, except the respondents; for the others had robbed him of all he had, and had not left him a chair to sit on. This declaration is made at the very moment when he is conveying a valuable estate in Johnstown, and a farm in St. Lawrence, with the personal property there, for the use of his son Charles. If this evidence proves anything, it is, that the appellant was influenced by considerations different from those set up by the respondents; and indeed, that he knew not what he said, or what he did. His declarations were directly at variance with the truth and with his acts. He declared that he could not trust the people of Johnstown; which was the reason of his applying to Mr. Reynolds. Clary was also present when the bill of sale was executed, and he states that the reasons for this were the same as for conveying the real estate. This comes from a witness produced by the respondents. M'Naughton was also present with all the parties, and witnessed the bill of sale and bond and mortgage; and the appellant complained that his case was a hard one; that
584*] *the whole was done for the express purpose of preventing his wife from spending the estate.

Was here, then, misrepresentation by William, or a studied silence on the part of the respondents when they ought to have spoken, which led to and confirmed the opinion of their father in the fancied danger to his estate? Had William before said anything to strengthen that opinion? Upon a careful and laborious analysis of the evidence, I am of opinion that the appellant's case has been made out, on this point. The sole management of the appellant's affairs was in the hands of his sons. Aged, weak, credulous and solitary, he looked to them for advice. Deserted by the rest of his family, whom he abhorred for fancied injuries, and to whom he believed he could never be reconciled, he was left dependent upon these two sons. To the feuds and distractions of his family, was added the pursuit of his property by legal process. He goes for advice and consolation to William, the most favored of his two remaining children, and the one in whom he particularly confided. And who but William, under such circumstances, would have added poignancy to a father's wretchedness by a threat of desertion mingled with harsh reproof, and by advice which was immediately followed by a conveyance of his estate? The facts which the appellant stated as the cause of the alarm which led to the conveyance, must have been derived from one or both of the respondents. At any rate, his fears were countenanced by them both. Both were present when the bill of sale and mortgage were executed, and both then heard the true cause assigned by the appellant. As his children and confidential agents, they were bound in duty to set him right, and to see that he did not act upon such motives. In my opinion, here was palpable delusion and fraud; and the deed should be set aside for that reason.

I have arrived at this conclusion, independent of Charles Whelan's evidence. Though I think him competent, the prospect he has of a portion of his father's property, and his stating a conversation between him and William alone, undoubtedly go to his credit; yet he is so entirely supported by the other facts, I think him entitled to much credit. And if he *is to be believed, the case presents [*585
positive proof of a preconcerted fraud, compassed by the labor of years.

2. But there is another point in the cause well worthy of consideration. It is that the respondents had an undue influence over the appellant, to such an extent as to preclude our saying that he conveyed the farm and personal property at Johnstown as a free, unbiased act of bounty.

The counsel for the respondents meet this point, firstly by saying that it is not made a substantive allegation in the bill; and if this be so, it cannot be available here. The bill charges that the appellant was led to convey by the false representations and persuasions of the respondents that his wife was spending the whole estate; that he conveyed, not for the purpose of making a settlement or disposition of his estate, but for the purpose of removing it out of her reach; and that there was no other moving cause for the conveyance than the persuasion and representation of the respondents that such a step was absolutely necessary to prevent the estate being dissipated by the mother. The bill also states the dissensions in the family, with their cause, and the manner in which the appellant lived with the respondents. The parties have gone on to examine witnesses to the point of undue influence, and I think properly; for, in my opinion, it is substantially involved and sufficiently stated in the bill, though not named undue influence, in terms.

I have already adverted generally to the situation of the property and the family, their dissensions and ultimate dispersion, and the age of the appellant and his wife, the latter of whom was in delicate health for several years, of an irritable and peevish disposition, and had taken part with several of the children, against their father, in the dissensions of the family, which arose relative to the use and enjoyment of the real estate at Johnstown. The answers admits, that previous to the lease of 1819, under which Carr possessed the farm, John, William and Joseph had the management of it, and that during this lease, the appellant and respondents resided in a log house, on the same farm, while the wife resided with Carr at the homestead. The answers admit the **586***] previous *agency and management of the estate, the separation of the family during the lease, and its dispersion after the lease had expired—virtually saying that the appellant was under the keeping of the respondents, and residing with them for some years previous to the transaction in question. It is abundantly in proof, that the appellant was a credulous man and easily led, especially by William, who, with Joseph, uniformly took sides with his father, in the dissensions of the family, against its other members. Taking into account the age of the appellant, the double relations of parent and child and principal and agent, the general credulity of the appellant, and the case with which he might be led by William, connected with the circumstances attending the conveyance, and the case is brought most emphatically within the principle of those cases cited by the counsel for the appellant which forbid a contract between persons holding certain relations to each other, which imply, from their nature, an influence and confidence, too great to be trusted in the hands of one who may wield them to his own advantage. It was, indeed, truly said at the bar, that no case had been shown in which a conveyance from a parent to one of his children had been set aside for these or the like causes; but that relief had been refused in such cases. These refusals were in cases of English family settlements, where provisions were made for children, which the court adjudged to be reasonable in reference to the estate of the party making the settlement. No case can be cited, in which an aged man, under the custody and influence of one of his relations, disposed of his whole estate to such relation in exclusion of others having equal natural claims upon his bounty, where a court of equity would not look into the transaction with an eagle eye. Besides, the English decisions are doubtless influenced by their law recognizing the rights of primogeniture and entailment. In this country these rights are unknown. But it is not sought here to avoid the deed, because the whole property is given to the respondents. That the appellant clearly had a right to do, if he chose. But the objection is, that when he made this conveyance he was, and had been for some time, so much under the influence of the respondents, that he would take their sug- **587***] gestions* as his rule of conduct; so that the conveyance was not his act but theirs—it was not the result of his own free will, but an act done under the pressure of circumstances, aided by the suggestions or advice of the respondents. At any rate they made no attempt to correct the erroneous impressions under which the appellant labored, though they were acting as his agents in relation to his real and personal estate, and indeed were bound to this by other powerful considerations of duty. They have, in a word, betrayed the trust and confidence reposed in them, and made a profit of their treachery. The view of the case is, I think, fully supported by the answers and evidence. It is also a remarkable circumstance, that this conveyance was only about four months after the reconveyance to him of this very property, by William, of whom he had before taken a bond and mortgage of $3,000. The first conveyance, it seems, was for fear of a judgment, and the property was, on the appellant's request, surrendered by the respondents. According to their account, they received the first deed without inquiry, William alone gave the mortgage, and the whole property was readily surrendered. Would these things have taken place, if, as pretended, it had been the long and settled purpose of the appellant to convey by way of advancement? The truth seems to be, that he had surrendered himself as well as his estate, to the charge of the respondents. His age, his education, his infirmities, and his passions, all combined to make him a fit subject to be operated upon by trifling causes. He had no benefit from the advice of counsel, or of any one except Clary, who was also the friend of the respondents. From these considerations, followed by the hurried, secret and suspicious manner in which the business was transacted, I feel constrained to say, that if there ever was a case in which a court of equity ought to avoid a deed for undue influence, this is one.

3. William having submitted, in his answer, to reconvey the St. Lawrence farm, and there being no written declaration of trust, I can see no reason why we should not adjudge a reconveyance. On a bill filed by Charles, or his children, William might set up the Statute of Frauds, and defeat *a conveyance; [***588** and he admits that this farm was given to him in trust for such purposes as the appellant should direct.

Though Joseph appears only to have assented to the act of William, yet I think the deed is void as to both.

I am, therefore, of opinion that the decree of His Honor, the *Chancellor*, should be reversed; and that a reconveyance of the two farms should be decreed.

Bronson, Dudley, Lynde, Redfield, Ward, Wooster and *Wright, Senators*, dissented.

A majority of the court being for a reversal, the following order was thereupon entered:

"It is ordered, adjudged and decreed, that the decree of the Court of Chancery, appealed from, be and the same is hereby reversed. And it is further ordered, adjudged and decreed that the deed and conveyance executed by the appellant to the respondents, on the 19th day of January, 1821, and in the pleadings in this cause mentioned, whereby the appellant conveyed to the respondents in fee, a certain farm of land in the town of Johnstown, in the County of Montgomery; and also another deed and conveyance executed by the appellant to the respondent William Whelan, on the day and year last aforesaid, and also in the said pleadings mentioned, and whereby the appellant conveyed to the said William Whelan, one of the respondents, in fee, a farm of land in the County of St. Lawrence; and also a bill of sale of certain personal property, executed by the appellant to the respondents, and also in the said pleadings mentioned; are, and the same are hereby declared to be, respectively, fraudulent, null and void. And it is further ordered, adjudged and decreed that the respondents forthwith deliver up to the appellant the said several and respective deeds to be canceled; and that the respondents, also, by a competent deed of conveyance for that purpose, release and convey to the appellant, in fee, all their right, title and interest, of, in, and to the said farm of land in the said town of Johnstown, in the said pleadings mentioned, with proper and **589***] *apt covenants against their own acts and transactions since the said 19th day of January, 1821, whereby the title to the said farm may be impaired, or in anywise incumbered. And it is further ordered, adjudged and decreed, that the respondent William Whelan, in like manner, release and convey to the appellant, in fee, all his right, title and interest of, in and to the said farm in the County of St. Lawrence, in the said pleadings mentioned, with like covenants; the said deeds to be settled by a master of the Court of Chancery, if the parties disagree respecting the same. And it is further ordered, adjudged and decreed that if it be referred to a master to take and state an account of the value of the annual rent of of the said farm in Johnstown, from the said 19th day of January, 1821; in which account the respondents shall be debited the value of the said rents from the said time until the taking of such account, if the respondents shall then be in possession of the said farm; but if they shall have yielded up the possession thereof to the appellant, then to the time of so yielding up the same; and the respondents shall be credited for the board, maintenance, support and clothing of the appellant and his wife during the time they or either of them were maintained and supported by the respondents, since the said 19th day of January, 1821; and the respondents shall also be credited for any moneys paid to or advanced for the said appellant since the day and year last aforesaid; and also, that the respondents be credited the balance of any permanent and beneficial improvements made on the said farm in Johnstown since the said 19th day of January, 1821. And the said master shall also take and state an account of the value of the goods and personal property conveyed by the said bill of sale by the appellant to the respondents, and which have been sold, disposed of, or appropriated to the use of the respondents, and which shall not be delivered up by the respondents to the appellant before the taking of such account. And it is further ordered, adjudged and decreed that the appellant shall deliver up to the respondents, to be canceled, the bond and mortgage given by them to the appellant to secure the maintenance of the appellant and his wife, and mentioned in the pleadings in **590***] *this cause. And it is further ordered, adjudged and decreed that the appellant recover of the respondents his costs, to be taxed in the prosecution of this suit in the Court of Chancery, and that this cause be remitted to the Court of Chancery, to the end that this decree may be carried into execution."

For reversal, 23; for affirmance, 7.

Undue Influence. Distinguished—61 Ill., 518.

Cited in—4 Cow., 706; 1 Paige, 177; 3 Edw., 39; 3 Sand. Ch., 426; 2 N. Y., 251; 10 N. Y., 459; 26 N.Y., 12; 35 N. Y., 595; 75 N. Y., 102; 17 Hun, 304; 1 Barb., 539; 5 Barb., 540; 6 Barb., 549; 9 Barb., 602; 40 Barb., 529; 65 Barb., 356; 2 T. & C., 29 *n.*; 39 How. P., 265; 1 Redf., 246; 7 Leg. Obs., 159; 8 How. (U. S.), 410; 1 Wood & M., 101, 353; 33 Cal., 440; 44 Mo., 537; 67 Mo., 197; 65 Mo., 415; 19 Am. Dec., 407; 50 Am. Dec., 509 (2 G. Greene, 55); 31 Am. Rep., 436 29 Am. Rep., 615 (1 McArth., 558).

Also cited in—4 Cow., 706; 2 N. Y., 251; 10 N. Y., 459; 6 Barb., 549; 9 Barb., 602; 50 Am. Dec., 509 (2 G. Greene, 55).

RICHARD UDALL, Impleaded with EDWARD M. L. KENNEY, *Appellant*, *v.* ELIZA S. KENNEY, *Respondent.*

Settlement by Father, in Favor of Infant Daughter—Marriage of Daughter, During Infancy—Assignment of Property, by Daughter and Husband—Assignee, Having Knowledge of Trust—Equity of Wife, How and When Protected in Court of Chancery—Marital Rights of Husband.

The wife's equity, as it is called, cannot be disposed of by the husband, without first making suitable provision for her support.

Though the wife should join her husband in the assignment of it, this will not render the disposition valid, she being an infant.

The only way in which she can herself dispose of it, is by consent in court, or out of court, on an adequate provision being made for her:

Otherwise as to a wife's choses in possession or in action. Of the former the husband is absolute owner by the marriage; and so of the latter, when reduced into his possession.

It seems, that when the property of the wife is the subject of an action at law, equity will not interfere, by injunction or otherwise, so as to prevent the husband getting possession till he make proper provision for his wife.

But if the aid of a court of equity be necessary to enable the husband to get possession of his wife's property, the court will see, when he comes there for that purpose, that he first make a suitable provision for her; or it will interfere, at her suit, to prevent his getting possession, in any way, till such provision is made.

So of the general assignee of the husband, by his own act, with or without valuable consideration or by operation of law.

So of a specific assignment for valuable consideration, with or without notice of the wife's equitable claim.

Cases on the last three heads considered in chronological order, by Savage, *Ch. J.*

In all these cases, the extent of the provision for the wife is properly the subject of reference to a master and must depend on circumstances; and the husband, or his assignee, is entitled to what remains after provision made.

The general rule is, that the interest or income of his wife's equitable property may be received by the husband, while he lives with and maintains her.

*But if he neglects to do this, or if he ran [*591 away with and married her while she was a ward of the court; or has shown incapacity to manage his concerns or a disposition to squander his wife's property, the court will direct the interest to be paid to her, or to a trustee for her benefit.

While, however, he has a right to receive the interest or income of his wife's property, he may transfer that right to another for valuable consideration, who shall not be holden to account to the wife, especially if such right of the husband or assignee be sanctioned by an order of court.

It seems that inadequacy of price, alone, is not a sufficient ground for setting a contract aside.

Bank stock was settled by a father by deed declaring a trust in favor of his infant daughter, and by an order of the Court of Chancery was placed in the hands of the Assistant Register of that court, as trustee to execute the trust in her favor. She married, and an order of the court was made to pay the dividends of the stock to the husband. Within a year after the marriage, and while she she was an infant, she and her husband transferred the stock for a valuable consideration, the assignee knowing at the same time of the deed of settlement and the infancy of the wife; whereupon an order was made that the dividends should thereafter be paid to the assignee till the wife came of age, or the further order of the court. On a bill filed, by the wife, against the husband and assignee, the Court of Chancery declared the assignment null and void, so far as it respected the wife's equity; and decreed that the assignee should account for the dividends received by him under the order. And the husband having misbehaved himself, the dividends were directed to be paid to the wife, until she came of age, with liberty for her then to apply for such suitable provision, out of the property, as might be determined on the usual reference to a master. On appeal to the Court of Errors, the decree was affirmed, except so much as directed the assignee to account for dividends received anterior to the decree; and the wife in the meantime having come of age, the record was remitted with directions to the court below to make the proper reference, and determine what would be a suitable provision—the overplus, if any, to be paid to the assignee. And the *Chief Justice* intimated, in delivering the opinion of the court, that if the wife had no fortune beside the stock, which was $8,000, the whole would not exceed a reasonable provision.

Citations—1 Vern., 7, 18; 3 Vern., 270; 1 P. Wms., 382, 458, 459, *n.*; 2 P. Wms., 608; 9 Mod., 102; 2 Atk., 96, 207, 417; 1 Atk., 280; 1 Bro. Ch., 51, 52, 50 *n.*; 2 Dick., 647, 491; 4 Bro. Ch., 326; 2 Ves., Jr., 607; 3 Ves., 506; 4 Ves., 19, 515, 799; 1 Jack. & Walk., 456; 11 Ves., 12; 1 Des., 263; 2 Johns. Ch., 206; 2 Ves., 562; 3 Atk., 20.

APPEAL from the Court of Chancery. The pleadings and proofs with the decree, and the late *Chancellor's* reasons in its support, are stated in the report of the same case, as it stood in the court below, under title of *E. S. Kenney* v. *Udall & Kenney*, 5 Johns. Ch., 464. All the facts material to the view taken of the case here, will be found in the opinion of Savage, *Ch. J.*, who delivered the opinion of this court.

592*] **Mr. J. V. Henry*, for the appellant, premised, that under the impression of duty which the *Chancellor* felt to protect this young married woman, he had gone very great lengths; and had cut down everything, even his own order for the payment of the dividends. He contended that the case of *Earl of Salisbury* v. *Newton*, 1 Eden, 370, cited by the *Chancellor*, was distinguishable from the present. Notwithstanding *Like* v. *Beresford*, 3 Ves., 506, which he considers as settling the question of the wife's right to her equity against a particular assignee, for valuable consideration, he admits that it was a litigated point in *Wright* v. *Morley*, 11 Ves., 12. In *Jewson* v. *Moulson*, 2 Atk., 417, the wife had never been in the receipt of the fund. The cases cited by the *Chancellor* of a claim to the wife's equity by the assignees of a bankrupt husband, will of course not be relied on, as they go upon the ground that the assignment is general, and by operation of law. *Beresford* v. *Hobson*, 1 Madd. Ch., 262, goes farther for the wife than any other case; but even there she did not get the whole: whereas all is here declared void by the *Chancellor*, in the face both of the assignment and his own order.

That this assignment cannot be rescinded for inadequacy of price, or as a fraudulent, or unconscionable bargain, he cited Newl. on Cont., 357–8 and 360–5; *Franklin* v. *Osgood*, 14 Johns., 559, per Platt, *J.*; 1 Fonbl., B. 1, ch. 2, sec. 9; 1 Madd. Ch., 98.

He then stated the following points, and cited and commented upon the authorities which follow them respectively:

1. That the stock in question was a vested interest in the wife, subject to the limitation over on the contingency of her dying without issue before 21. And the husband having, at law, an absolute right to all the wife's personal estate in possession, and a qualified right to her choses in action, had therefore power to dispose of the stock. 1 Roper on Legacies, 182, 183, 184, 203; *Lumb* v. *Milnes*, 5 Ves., 517, 519; Com. Dig., Baron and *Feme*, E, 3; *Sir Edward Turner's* case, 1 Vern., 7; *Pitt* v. *Hunt*, *Id.*, 18; *Tudor* v. *Samyne*, 2 Vern., 270; *Duke of Chandos* v. *Talbot*, *2 P. Wms., 608; *Lord* [*593 *Carteret* v. *Paschal*, 3 P. Wms., 199; *Bates* v. *Dandy*, 2 Atk., 207; *Jewson* v. *Moulson*, *Id.*, 417; *Hawkins* v. *Obin*, *Id.*, 549; *Grey* v. *Kentish*, 1 Atk., 280; *Countess of Strathmore* v. *Bowes*, 1 Ves., Jr., 28.

2. Such disposition being made by the husband, the wife cannot be admitted to impeach it, on the ground that it was unfairly or improperly obtained. That right belongs to the husband only, or those claiming under him; and as he does not seek to do this, nor even unite with his wife as complainant in the cause, the court ought not to interfere to set it aside.

3. The court does not interfere with the legal rights of the husband, but will suffer him, if he can without its aid, to obtain at law the possession of her estate. The stock in question was legal property.

An action would have lain against the husband for its value, had he refused to complete the transfer. *Morris* v. *Mechanics' Bank*, 10 Johns., 484; *King* v. *Bank of England*, Doug., 523.

4. The objection that the wife is a ward of the court, is unfounded, the wardship having ceased on her marriage; and the court below having even acted on that principle, by directing the dividends to be paid to Kenney in his character of husband. *Mendes* v. *Mendes*, 1 Ves., Sr., 89, 91, per Ld. Hardwicke, C.

5. That even if the stock was equitable property, yet a specific assignment of it, by contract, for a valuable consideration is valid, and not subject to an equity of the wife, for a provision. *Sir Edward Turner's* case, 1 Vern., 7; S. C., 1 Eq. Abr., 58, pl. 2; *Pitt* v. *Hunt*, 1 Vern., 18; S. C., 1 Eq. Abr., 58, pl. 3; *Povey* v. *Amhurst*, Gilb., Eq., 80; S. C., 2 Eq. Abr., 132; *Duke of Chandos* v. *Talbot*, 2 P. Wms., 608; *Bates* v. *Dandy*, 2 Atk., 207; *Hawkins* v. *Obin*, *Id.*, 549; *Grey* v. *Kentish*, 1 Atk., 280; *Saddington* v. *Kinsman*, 1 Bro. Ch., 51; *Wirsal* v. *Marlar*, 2 Dick., 647; *Earl of Thomond* v. *Earl of Suffolk*, 1 P. Wms., 469; *Clinton* v. *Hooper*, 1 Ves., 173; *Wright* *v. *Morley*, [*594 11 Ves., 12; *Hyde* v. *Price*, 3 Ves., 473; Newl. on Cont., 131–2.

6. But if otherwise, the equity is only to part and not to the whole; and the full amount of the principal advanced by the appellant, with the interest thereon, ought, at least, to be reimbursed him. *Packer* v. *Wyndham*, Prec. in Ch., 412; *Squib* v. *Wyn*, 1 P. Wms., 378; *Lord Carteret* v. *Paschal*, 3 *Id.*, 197, 199; *Jewson* v. *Moulson*, 2 Atk., 417; *Earl of Salisbury* v. *Newton*, 1 Eden, 370; *Franco* v. *Franco*, 4 Ves., 515, 529; *Pryor* v. *Hill*, 4 Bro. Ch., 138; *Burdon* v. *Dean*, 2 Ves., Jr., 607; *Oswell* v. *Probert*, *Id.*, 680; *Brown* v. *Clark*, 3 *Id.*, 166, 168; *Prindle* v. *Hodgson*, *Id.*, 617; *Macauley* v. *Phil-*

lips, 4 *Id.*, 15; *Lumb* v. *Milnes*, 5 *Id.*, 517; *Lady Elibank* v. *Montolieu*, *Id.*, 737; *Wright* v. *Morley*, 11 Ves., 12. The counsel said that these cases show, not only the rights of the husband in the wife's property generally, but also as to the wife's equity, from them it would appear never to have been doubted, either in the case of general or particular assignees of the husband, that they shall hold subject only to a reasonable provision for the wife.

7. That the appellant is, at any rate, entitled to the dividends on the stock which were directed to be paid to the husband, free of all her claims until she attained 21.

Mr. Talcot, Atty-Gen., and *Mr. B. F. Butler*, for the respondent, insisted upon the following points in support of the decree, and cited and commented upon the authorities following them respectively.

I. The deed of settlement executed by Hewitt, the father of the respondent, directing the dividends as they accrued to be paid to her during her minority and the stock to be transferred to her at the age of 21, clearly contemplated a personal enjoyment by her of the stock; and therefore the assignment was in direct violation of the trusts declared by the deed of settlement, and consequently void. *Hyde* v. *Price*, 3 Ves., 437, recognized as never having been questioned in *M. E. Church* v. *Jaques*, 3 Johns. Ch., 103; *Stone* v. *Lidderdale*, 2 Anst., 533, where the assignment of an officer's half **595***] pay was held void both in equity *and at law. Sugd. on Pow., 111, 112; Clancey's Rights of Women, 52, 53, 382–384; Roper on Revocations, &c., with Tracts upon the Law of Baron and *Feme*, 230, 301. The case of *Jaques* v. *M. E. Church*, 17 Johns., 548, the counsel said, merely sets up the general power of the wife to dispose of her separate property, without denying that a trust may be limited to her in such terms as to take away that right.

II. The assignment was also void, as against the equitable right of the respondent to have the stock secured for her separate use. This right, usually called the wife's equity, is perfectly reasonable and just; is well understood in courts of equity; and has been uniformly admitted and admistered by them for more than a century.

The counsel said there were four classes of cases in support of this point:

1. Of the wife's equity as against her husband: *Wiltham* v. *Waterhouse*, Toth., 91; *Ash* v. *Forrest*, *Id.*, 116; *Gibbons* v. *Moulton*, *t.* Finch, 346; *Id.*, 361; *Id.*, 367; *Mico* v. *Powell*, 1 Vern., 39; *Oxenden* v. *Oxenden*, 2 Vern., 493; *Harrison* v. *Buckle*, 1 Str., 239; *Gardener* v. *Walker*, *Id.*, 503; *Winch* v. *Page*, Buuh., 86; *Milner* v. *Colmer*, 2 P. Wms., 638; *Adams* v. *Pierce*, 3 *Id.*, 11; *Brown* v. *Elton*, *Id.*, 202; 1 Eq. Abr., 64, G, and the cases there cited; *Bond* v. *Simmons*, 3 Atk., 20; *Tomkyns* v. *Ladbroke*, 2 Ves., Sr., 591, 593; *Jewson* v. *Moulson*, 2 Atk., 417; *Ex parte Coysegame*, 1 Atk., 192; *Grey* v. *Kentish*, *Id.*, 280; *Meals* v. *Meals*, 1 Dick., 373; *Ellis* v. *Ellis*, 1 Suppl. to Vin. Abr., 475, F, pl. 4; *Roberts* v. *Roberts*, *Id.*, 576, F, p. 5; S. C., 2 Cox, 422; *Clinton* v. *Hooper*, 1 Ves., Jr., 173, 181, 185; *Lady Elibank* v. *Montolieu*, 5 Ves., 737; *Murray* v. *Lord Elibank*, 10 Ves., 84; S. C., 13 Ves., 1; *Carr* v. *Taylor*, 10 Ves., 574; *Howard* v. *Moffat*, 2 Johns. Ch., 206; *Glen* v. *Fisher*, 6 *Id.*, 33; *Davison* v. *Atkinson*, 5 T. R., 434.

2. Of the wife's equity as against the general assignees of the husband: *Vandenanker* v. *Desbrough*, 2 Vern., 96; *Parker* v. *Dykes*, 1 Eq. Abr., 54, B; *Jacobson* v. *Peer Williams*, *Id.*; S. C., 1 P. Wms., 382; *Grey* v. *Kentish*, 1 *Atk., 280; *Ex parte Coysegame*, *Id.*, [***596** 192; *Worsal* v. *Marlar*, 2 Dick., 647; S. C., 1 Cox, 153, under title of *Warrall* v. *Marlar*, and *Bushnan* v. *Pell*; *Pryor* v. *Hill*, 4 Bro. Ch., 138; *Bosvil* v. *Brander*, 1 P. Wms., 458; *Id.*, 459, *note* 1; *Burdon* v. *Dean*, 2 Ves., Jr., 601; *Oswell* v. *Probert*, *Id.*, 680; *Brown* v. *Clark*, 3 *Id.*, 166; *Freeman* v. *Parseley*, *Id.*, 421; *Lumb* v. *Milnes*, 5 *Id.*, 517; *Carr* v. *Taylor*, 10 *Id.*, 574; *Milford* v. *Milford*, 9 *Id.*, 87.

3. Of the wife's equity as against a voluntary particular assignment: Clancey's Rights of Women, 267; *Jewson* v. *Moulson*, 2 Atk., 420, per Lord Hardwicke.

4. As against the specific assignee for a valuable consideration: *Saddington* v. *Kinsman*, 1 Bro. Ch., 44; *Povey* v. *Brown*, Prec. in Ch., 325; *Jewson* v. *Moulson*, 2 Atk., 417; *Pope* v. *Cranshaw*, 4 Bro. Ch., 326; *Like* v. *Beresford*, 3 Ves., 506, 512; *Macaulay* v. *Philips*, 4 Ves., 19; *Wright* v. *Morley*, 11 Ves., 17; *E. S. Kenny* v. *Udall*, the decision appealed from, 5 Johns. Ch., 464; *Haviland* v. *Myers*, 6 *Id.*, 25; *Haviland* v. *Bloom*, *Id.*, 178; *Earl of Salisbury* v. *Newton*, 1 Eden, 370.

III. The equity of the respondent is materially fortified by the circumstance, that her marriage was clandestine, at a time when she was of a very tender age, a ward of the Court of Chancery, and her husband a bankrupt. *Butler* v. *Freeman*, Ambl., 301; *Eyre* v. *Countess of Shaftsbury*, 2 P. Wms., 118; *Stackpole* v. *Beaumont*, 3 Ves., 98, per *Ld. Chancellor*; *Like* v. *Beresford*, *Id.*, 506; Laws N. Y., sess. 38, ch. 106, sec. 1; *Call* v. *Coults*, 1 Ves. & Bea., 303; *Stevens* v. *Savage*, 1 Ves., Jr., 154; *Winch* v. *James*, 4 Ves., 386; *Chassaing* v. *Parsonage*, 5 Ves., 15; *Wells* v. *Price*, 5 Ves., 398; *Millet* v. *Rowse*, 11 Ves., 419.

IV. The case is fortified still farther by the facts that the consideration actually paid by the appellant for the assignment was neither meritorious nor fair; but grossly inadequate; and that in procuring it, a most oppressive advantage was taken of the husband's pecuniary distresses and necessities.

*V. On the whole, the decree is war- [***597** ranted by the pleadings and proofs in the cause, and is in conformity to the settled law of a court of equity, on the subject.

Mr. Henry, in reply, reviewed the cases cited for the respondents, and remarked that the whole class of cases which went to deny the husband a right to dispose of the wife's equity, proceeded upon the ground that it could not be reached at law, but only by the aid of this court. They were English cases, and therefore went upon the law as it stood there. It is otherwise in this country as to legacies which, in whatever shape they may be devised, are recoverable by an action at law. The Statute (1 R. L., 315–16, sec. 19) which gives this right has been in existence ever since 1743 (1 S. & L., 315; V. S., 229; 2 J. & V., 386; 1 K. & R., 540), and cuts up, at once, all the English doctrine as to the wife's equity in a legacy. It is no longer a mere equitable right. The husband may proceed at law; and a court of equity, therefore, will not and cannot restrain him, according to the doctrine of all the cases.

SAVAGE, *Ch. J.* June 21, 1814, Thomas Hewitt, of the City of N. Y., being possessed of 310 shares in the capital stock of the Bank of America, executed a deed of settlement, by which, among other things, he transferred all his shares in the B. of A., to the president, directors and company of that Bank, in trust for the uses and purposes in the deed expressed; one of which is follows: "In further trust to pay my daughter Eliza the interest or dividends accruing on eight thousand dollars of the said stock or shares, as the same accrues, for her education; and to transfer the principal thereof to her, at the age of 21 years." "If my said daughter Eliza dies under 21, and without issue, then the principal to go to my said son Thomas." It was also further provided that if the Bank should be about to be dissolved, then they should transfer the shares to Jonathan Burrall, Henry Remson and Richard Riker, to hold upon the same trusts. Thomas Hewitt died Oct. 12, 1814, leaving the deed of settlement in full force. Sidney Hewitt, the **598***] mother of Eliza, was appointed, *by the Court of Chancery, guardian of her person, and Isaac L. Kip, Assistant Register, her trustee to receive the dividends and pay them over to Sidney Hewitt, the guardian. Mrs. Kenny supposes she was, therefore, a ward of the Court of Chancery. Jan. 19, 1818, Eliza intermarried with her present husband, Edward M. L. Kenney. She was then a little over 16 years of age, and was at a boarding-school, where she had been placed by her mother. Sidney Hewitt, the mother and guardian, had been applied to for her consent to the marriage, but she refused it except on condition that it should be postponed for two years. Upon the marriage taking place the guardian was displeased, but became reconciled in about a week.

Feb. 9 following, Kenney was authorized by a rule of court, founded on and reciting the marriage, to receive the dividends until the further order of the court; and by virtue of this order, he did receive one or more dividends. He became much embarrassed, and proposed to pledge or sell the stock. One Ezra L. Ingraham offered his services in effecting some negotiation, with a view to raise money. The appellant, Udall, became the purchaser, for the nominal price of $5,000, under circumstances which I shall hereafter advert to, and took an assignment, dated Dec. 12, 1818, executed by Kenney and his wife, who was still an infant; and paid, as he alleges, $4,500. Mrs. Kenney avers that only $150 were applied to her use.

June 17, 1819, an order was granted, founded upon the sale to Udall, directing the dividends after Jan. 1, 1819, to be paid to him until Mrs. Kenney should arrive to the age of 21, or the further order of the court.

Nov. 11, 1820, she filed her bill, praying: 1. That the assignment to Udall might be declared null and void, as respects her individual rights to the stock, and that Udall might assign it to some proper person, as trustee for her. 2. That he might account for the dividends received by him. 3. That an order might be made, revoking the order of June 17, 1819. 4. For such disposition of *the stock as [***599** would secure it for her own support and maintenance, and place it beyond the control of her husband.

Aug. 10, 1821, the *Chancellor* declared the assignment to be void, as respected Mrs. Kenney's rights; rescinded the former orders for paying dividends to Kenney and Udall respectively; directed payment to Mrs. Kenney's solicitor, to the amount of the costs, and then Mrs. Kenney herself; directed the Bank not to permit a transfer of the shares; and leaving Mrs. Kenney, when 21 years of age, to apply for the stock, or so much as justice shall require, to be settled for her separate use and support. To reverse this decree is the object of the present appeal.

The determination of this cause, independent of the fairness or unfairness of the transaction, must depend upon the extent of the marital rights. The signature of the wife to the assignment gave it no additional validity. She was, on account of her infancy, incapable of doing any act disposing of her property or dispensing with her rights; and, on account of her coverture, she is presumed to have acted under the coercion of her husband. The assignment, therefore, must be considered as the act of the husband alone.

The interest of the husband was acquired by virtue of the marriage.

It is not disputed that a husband, in virtue of his marriage, becomes absolute owner of the goods and chattels of his wife, and may, consequently, dispose of them, including not only her choses in possession, but in action, when the latter are reduced into possession. And the authorities go so far as to say that if the husband can obtain possession of the wife's choses in action without the aid of a court of chancery, he will be permitted to do so, and then to dispose of them at his discretion. But where the property of the wife is under the care of the court, and the husband cannot enjoy it without the authority of the court, care will be taken that before it is placed at the husband's disposal, a suitable provision shall be made out of it for the wife's support.

That the general assignees of the husband stand in no better situation than the husband himself admits of no dispute. But the cases are not perfectly agreed as to the situation of *an assignee of a specific chose in ac- [***600** tion, or an assignee for valuable consideration. A concise review of the decisions will, therefore, be of service in arriving at a correct conclusion.

It was determined by the Lords, in *Sir Edward Turner's* case, 1 Vern., 7, A. D. 1681, on appeal from chancery, that a term, assigned in trust for a *feme sole*, might be disposed of by the husband after marriage; but if it had been assigned for the use of the wife, by consent of the husband, then he could not meddle.

In *Pitt* v. *Hunt*, 1 Vern., 18, *Chancellor* Nottingham decreed according to this case, though contrary to all previous adjudications, and so admitted by the counsel.

In *Tudor* v. *Samyne*, 2 Vern., 270, A. D. 1692, the same doctrine was held, upon the authority of *Turner's* case.

In *Jacobson* v. *Williams*, 1 P. Wms., 372, A. D. 1717, before *Lord Chancellor* Cowper, an infant, entitled to a legacy of £1,000, intermarried with J. S. at 18 years of age, without the knowledge or consent of her father. J. S. becoming a bankrupt, the plaintiffs claimed the legacy as assignees. This claim was denied as to the principal sum, upon the ground that they stood in no better situation than the bankrupt himself, to whom the court would not have allowed it without a provision for the wife and children. For the same reason it was said the assignees had a right to the interest during the husband's life. But, at a subsequent day, the *Chancellor* dismissed the bill, upon the ground that the legacy depended on a contingency which had not ceased when the assignment was executed on the commissioners; therefore nothing passed, not even the interest.

In *Bosvil* v. *Brander*, 1 P. Wms., 458, A. D. 1718, a *feme sole*, mortgagee, married a tradesman who became a bankrupt, and the commissioners assigned all his estate, real and personal. Then the husband died, and his widow filed her bill to have the benefit of the mortgage. But the Master of the Rolls decreed against her, on the ground that as there was a covenant to pay the money, the legal estate was vested in the assignees. It was said, however, that if the husband or the assignees had asked the aid of equity to enforce the mort-
601*] gage, *the court would have refused this, unless some provision had been made for the wife.

In *Duke of Chandos* v. *Talbot*, 1 P. Wms., 608, A. D. 1731, before King, *Chancellor*, the question was whether a legacy of £1,000, given to Dorothy Doliman, payable at her age of 25 years, and assigned by her and her husband for £750, before she became of age, was a good assignment; and it was decided that, being a personal thing, the husband alone might assign it, and as to its being a contingency, that was no objection, for a possibility of a term might be assigned by the husband alone; and *Theobalds* v. *Duffoy*, 9 Mod., 102, was cited.

In *Bates* v. *Dandy*, 2 Atk., 207, A. D. 1741, the husband had borrowed money, and pledged two mortgages, to which his wife had an equitable title, and promised in writing to assign them as security. But dying without baving made the assignment, Ld. Hardwicke held that the husband's promise to assign amounted, in equity, to an assignment *pro tanto*, the residue belonging to the wife. And it is then declared that the husband may assign the wife's chose in action, or a possibility that the wife is entitled to, as well as her term, if the assignment be for valuable consideration.

In little more than a year afterwards came the case of *Jewson* v. *Moulson*, 2 Atk., 417, A. D. 1742, which has been fully stated by His Honor, the *Chancellor*, in his opinion. The husband assigned to the defendant, for an honest debt, the share of his wife in her father's estate, which depended on the contingency of her arriving at 21 years of age. He afterwards assigned the same to trustees for the benefit of all his creditors. Ld. Hardwicke said that the equity was extremely plain against the husband and his general assignees; that the court will not suffer the husband to take the wife's portion till he makes a reasonable provision for her; and he dates this doctrine as far back as the 14th of Charles I. He further remarked that if the husband could obtain possession of his wife's chattels without the aid of the court, he knew of no instance in which it had interfered; but he expressed a doubt whether an injunction would not be granted, *at the wife's request, to stay [*602 execution till provision be made for her. He then refers to several previous cases, and mentions *Tudor* v. *Samyne*, *Bosvill* v. *Brander* and *Bates* v. *Dandy*, in which, he observes, the assignee for valuable consideration had got the better of the wife's equity. The circumstances of the case were much relied on, the wife's infancy; that the assignment was not of a particular thing, but her whole fortune; the clause of survivorship; the requisite aid of the court to obtain possession of her fortune; and the presumed knowledge of Moulson, the creditor of all these facts, as well as of the rule in equity as to making provision for the wife out of her own fortune. He lays great weight upon several facts which were parallel with those in this case—that the wife's whole fortune was assigned; that the husband was in debt before he married—ran away with his wife clandestinely. And he says, if an assignee for valuable consideration is to be protected, all the care and guardianship which the court extends to infants would be entirely defeated. He, therefore, determined not to allow the whole to the creditor, without making provision for the wife. The parties settle by dividing the fund, and Ld. Hardwicke confirmed the agreement.

In these cases the doctrine is, that when the husband or his assignees come into equity to obtain possession of the wife's choses in action, the court will compel them to do equity. It seems, however, that if the wife's fortune is the subject of equitable cognizance, it is immaterial, in this view, who asks the aid of the court. The same consequences follow, in whatever shape the matter is brought forward. Accordingly, in *Grey* v. *Kentish*, 1 Atk., 280; S. C., 1 P. Wms., 459, *n.*, A. D. 1749, corrected, the wife's property was, by a decree of chancery, vested in South Sea annuities. The husband assigned it as security for £150, and became bankrupt. The wife petitioned that the annuities might be transferred to her. Ld. Hardwicke said that a husband cannot assign a possibility in law, but equity will support such an assignment for valuable consideration. This was not an assignment, but a pledge, and as the particular and general assignees *took with notice of the equity [*603 of the wife, it was decreed to her.

In *Saddington* v. *Kinsman*, 1 Bro. Ch., 51-2, A. D. 1779, Ld. Thurlow said that in the case of an assignment for valuable consideration, no provision is made for the wife; but the cause was never decided. He referred to *Gayer* v. *Wilkinson*, 1 Bro. Ch., 50, *note*, which denied that a wife's equity passed by a bankrupt assignment, and asked the counsel whether they knew of any case in point which contradicted it.

In *Worrall* v. *Marlar*, and *Bushnan* v. *Pell*, 1 P. Wms., 459, *note*, A. D. 1784, Sarah Worrall, the wife of an insolvent debtor, was entitled, by bond from her father, to a share of his estate. The father, by will, after the insolvency of her husband, gave her £8,000, in lieu of her claim by virtue of the bond. She filed her bill, praying that the £8,000 might be settled upon her, to her separate use, and the use of her children. Bushnan, her husband's assignee, filed his bill, praying for an account under the bond, and to elect as the husband might if he had not become insolvent. Ld. Thurlow was clearly of opinion that the interest of the wife was assignable, but that the claim of the creditors extended only to the interest taken under the bond; and as to that under the will, the assignee should make proposals for a settlement on the wife and children. His Lordship added that he had considered the several cases on the subject, and did not find it any where decided, that if the husband make an actual assignment, by contract, for a valuable consideration, the assignee should be bound to make any provision for the wife out of the property assigned; but that a court of equity has much greater consideration for an assignment actually made by contract, than for an assignment by mere operation of law. In the latter case, the creditor stood in the place of the husband, as respects the wife's equity. After proposals had been made, one half the amount due on the bond was decreed to the creditors, and the residue of the £8,000 to the wife.

It will be seen, that the decision of this case did not require the observations of Ld. Thur-
604*] low, relative to assignees *for valuable consideration. What he said on that subject was, therefore, altogether *obiter*. At all events, he was mistaken in supposing that there were no cases establishing the wife's equity, as against assignees for valuable consideration. There is a short note of this case in 2 Dick., 647, under title of *Worsal* v. *Marlar*.

The doctrine of the wife's equity will be found distinctly declared, as against the husband, in a great number of cases, cited by the counsel for the respondent, but it cannot be necessary even to name them here. The cases already commented on, leave no doubt as to the doctrine and practice of the court to sustain the wife's equity against her husband, his assignees by operation of law, and his voluntary assignees. And the only question in the case is as to an assignee for valuable consideration.

In *Gayner* v. *Wilkinson*, 2 Dick., 491, A. D. 1783, the plaintiffs, as assignees of the husband, claimed a contingent legacy given to the wife but not reduced into possession in the life of the husband. Ld. Bathurst remarked that there is a difference between an assignee for a consideration, and the assignees of a bankrupt, because a general assignee must sue in his own name, but a particular assignee must sue in the name of the husband. He adds that if the husband dies before the subject of the assignment is recovered, the assignee will lose all legal remedy, and must come into chancery for its assistance; that particular assignment have been sometimes supported, but not generally; that the court will not strip a widow and children; that the interest of the wife was not such a legal interest as the husband could assign; and he dismissed the bill. He cited *Wenman* v. *Mason*, where the wife had joined her husband in the assignment, and yet she was allowed a settlement of £300.

In *Pope* v. *Crashaw*, 4 Br. Ch., 329, the Master of the Rolls said he hoped it would be understood that a husband cannot by assigning his wife's property bar her of any equity she may have in it. That he should never subscribe to the contrary doctrine.

In *Burdon* v. *Dean*, 2 Ves., Jr., 607, A. D. 1795, the right of the wife to her equity was distinctly admitted and allowed.

*The case of *Like* v. *Beresford*, 3 Ves., [***605**
506, A. D. 1797, was much stronger than the present in favor of the assignee for valuable consideration. The wife was entitled to a legacy, in bank stock, on the day of her marriage. She eloped with Beresford, in Oct. 1780, and about the same time a bill was filed in her name, against the trustee, and the stock was transferred to the name of the Accountant-General. The real object of the bill was to make the wife a ward of the Court of Chancery. Beresford filed his bill to obtain the stock; and during the pendency of the suit borrowed money of one Roberts, and conveyed the stock to him in trust to sell and pay himself, and to pay over the residue to Beresford. Beresford also became indebted to Like, the plaintiff, for money and necessaries furnished to him and his wife; in consideration of which, and of moneys to be advanced by Like, Beresford, by deed of assignment of Mar., 1783, conveyed the stock to Like, subject to Roberts' claim. The whole, being upwards of £5,000, was decreed to trustees, for Mrs. Beresford; and the object of Like's bill was, to obtain payment of his demand out of the dividends accrued subsequent to the marriage. It was insisted, for the plaintiff, that whatever is the rule as to the husband's right to assign his wife's fortune for valuable consideration, at least he should be allowed the dividends accrued, and that he might, for valuable consideration, assign an equitable estate in the wife's property. But the Master of the Rolls decreed against the plaintiff, relying on the declaration of Ld. Hardwicke, in *Jewson* v. *Moulson*, that the right of the husband to assign would put an end to the equity of the wife. Much weight was placed on the fact that the wife was a ward of the court.

In *Macaulay* v. *Philips*, 4 Ves., 19, A. D. 1798, speaking of the decision in *Like* v. *Beresford*, the Master of the Rolls says, the guard of a court of equity upon the wife's interest would be very singular, if the husband, not being entitled at law, might assign it for valuable consideration to another person, who would be entitled in equity; and it never was decided that the husband could by such assignment or any other means deprive her of her equity.

*I will notice but one other case on [***606**
this point. In *Johnson* v. *Johnson*, 1 Jac. & W., 456, the doctrine of the two last cases is adhered to. The Master of the Rolls admits that an assignment for a valuable consideration is sufficient to bar the right of the wife, surviving; but that it does not however, take away her equity. All this, he adds, is too clear to admit of any doubt.

It appears, therefore, to be established beyond all dispute, that the personal property of a *feme covert* which is under the protection and control of the Court of Chancery, cannot be taken from her without her consent in open court, or by a suitable provision being made for her out of the property. And it matters not whether the application for the property be made by the husband, or his assignee in law, or his assignee for a valuable consideration. Whether the court will extend its aid to property which the husband or his assignee can reduce to possession at law, is not absolutely decided; nor does that question arise here.

To the case already mentioned may be added, *Wright* v. *Morley*, 11 Ves., 12, and *Franco* v. *Franco*, 4 Ves., 515, in England; and in this country, *Ex parte Beresford*, 1 Des., 263, and *Howard* v. *Moffatt*, 2 Johns. Ch., 206. And, on the whole, I fully concur with His Honor, the late *Chancellor*, when he says: "I consider the wife's equity, as against any assignment whatsoever and to whomsoever, to be now too well settled to be shaken."

As to the amount of the wife's estate which shall be secured to her, that is a proper subject of reference to a master, and must necessarily be determined by the circumstances of each particular case. The rule is, that an adequate provision be made for the wife, and the children if there are any. What shall be considered adequate must depend entirely on circumstances. In some cases the whole has been allowed the wife—in one case an annuity of £40 *per annum*—in another the interest of £8,000. In other cases, the half has been assigned, by agreement, and sanctioned by the court; and again, £100, out of an annuity of £260, was decreed to the assignee of the husband. This
607*] part of the subject is *herein nowise important, except so far as relates to that part of the decree of His Honor, the *Chancellor* which rescinds the previous orders of the court, allowing the dividends of the stock in question to be paid first to Kenney and afterwards to Udall, and directs those accruing subsequent to filling the bill to be paid to Mrs. Kenney herself, after payment of the costs, till the further order of the court.

The general rule undoubtedly is, that the interest of the wife's property may be received by the husband, where he lives with and maintains her, but not when he leaves her unprovided. *Watkyns* v. *Watkyns*, 2 Atk., 96; *Sleech* v. *Thorington*, 2 Ves., Sr., 562; *Wright* v. *Morley*, 11 Ves., 12.

In *Bond* v. *Simmons*, 3 Atk., 20, Ld. Hardwicke said that when a husband has received a great part of his wife's portion, and only a small part remains, and the husband is so perverse that he will not make a competent settlement on the wife, the court will not only stop the payment of the residue, but will even prevent his receiving the interest of that residue, that it may accumulate for the benefit of the wife, unless he is starving for want of maintenance. And in *Bullock* v. *Menzies*, 4 Ves., 799, the court refused to give the wife any part of the interest of her own property, because she refused to live with her husband, when he was willing to receive and provide for her.

In some cases a reference has been directed, to ascertain the fact of the husband's providing for his wife. If that fact be material in this case it is pretty clear, from the pleadings and proofs, that the husband has totally neglected his duty in this respect. So far from providing for his wife, it appears to have been his object to squander the whole of her patrimony as fast as possible. He, therefore, does not come recommended to the favor of the court, and in justice to the wife, it ought to direct the payment of the dividends either to her or to some trustee for her benefit.

But the question here is not between the husband and wife. The appellant claims to be a *bona fide* purchaser, by contract, for valuable consideration. Admit, for the present, that he is so. What did he purchase? Clearly, nothing but the right to be substituted for the husband, as to his interest *in the [***608**
wife's property. In *Wright* v. *Morley*, Sir William Grant, reasoning on the subject, asks: "If the husband has but the right of reducing the wife's interest into possession, how can he, for valuable consideration or otherwise, convey more than he has? If he parts with it for valuable consideration, and the assignee acquires a right different from that which the husband had, he parts with something different from what he has;" and he might have said more than he has. And in this instance, if the claim of the appellant be allowed on account of his character of *bona fide* purchaser for valuable consideration from the husband, by that very purchase he has, in connection with the husband, stripped this infant wife, probably of her whole fortune, and reduced her to beggary—from competence, if not affluence, to absolute penury. But he has chosen to put himself in the situation of the husband. The court will leave him there.

That the appellant is a *bona fide* purchaser for valuable consideration is at least questionable. It is not necessary to impute to him absolute fraud; but the facts of the case show that an unconscientious advantage was taken of Kenney's situation. The stock was offered to him at a bargain; and had he contracted with persons on an equal footing with himself, notwithstanding the enormous speculation, the inadequacy alone would not induce the interference of the court. *Vide Seymour* v. *Delancy*, *ante*, 445. Nor is it necessary now to interfere solely on that ground. But it is certainly true, from his own showing, that he took at least $2,000 from these poor, distressed and improvident people; making due allowance for every risk he run, with the exception of the claim of the wife's equity. By advancing money before the terms were absolutely settled between him and Kenney, he placed him in a situation which compelled him afterwards to submit to such conditions as might be imposed. The appellant entered into the purchase after an examination of the deed of settlement. He acted against the advice of counsel, and, as must be presumed, whatever may be the fact, with a full knowledge of the wife's rights. His subsequent purchase of his own *bond, for [***609**
half the amount secured by it, as the *Chancellor* justly observes, marks the character of the whole transaction.

The appellant has, however, actually parted with his money, to a certain amount, and justice requires that it should be refunded to him by the husband; and this may be done out of the wife's property, provided there is sufficient after making an adequate settlement upon the wife. To discuss this subject further might be premature. I have no hesitancy, however, in saying that if the stock in question is her whole fortune, it is not too much for her support; and it should be settled upon her, for the support of herself and children, if any.

The result of my researches and reflection on this case is—

1. That the wife has an undoubted right to an adequate provision for her, and her children, if any, out of her equitable property, as against her husband or any assignee of the husband. And when it is necessary to come into a court of equity, for its aid in obtaining possession of such property, the court will see that proper provision shall be made.

2. That though, in general, a husband who lives with and maintains his wife is entitled to receive the dividends or interest of her estate, yet when the husband deserts his wife, or neglects or refuses to provide for and maintain her, or when he has misbehaved himself, and ran away with a ward of the court, and, I would add, when he has shown a total incapacity to manage his concerns, or a disposition wantonly to waste his wife's property, in such cases the court ought to direct the interest to be paid, either to the wife or to a trustee for her benefit.

I am, therefore, of opinion that the decree of His Honor, the late *Chancellor*, be affirmed, except so far as it rescinds the former orders of the Court of Chancery, directing the dividends to be paid first to Kenney, and afterwards to Udall, and that part directing the dividends which accrued before the decree to be paid to Mrs. Kenney. By the order of Feb. 9, 1818, the dividends were directed to be paid to Kenney till the further order of the court; **610***] and by the *order of June 7, 1819, the dividends which accrued after Jan. 1, 1819, until Mrs. Kenney should arrive at the age of twenty-one years, or till the further order of the court in the premises, were to be paid over to Udall. It seems to me just, therefore, that the appellant should have received the dividends until Aug. 10, 1821, when the decree was made.

The amount which will be an adequate settlement for the wife must, of course, be asoertained by a master of the Court of Chancery. The amount actually paid by the appellant ought also to be ascertained by a master. And on the coming in of his report, should there be anything left after making a competent provision for the wife, it is perfectly equitable and proper that the surplus be applied to the reimbursement of the amount actually advanced by the appellant.

Woodworth, J., and *Bowne, Bronson, Burrows, Burt, Clark, Cramer, Dudley, Earll, Gardiner, Green, Haight, Lynde, Mallory, M'Intyre, Morgan, Nelson, Redfield, Sudam, Thorn, Ward, Wheeler* and *Wright, Senators*, concurred.

Bowman, M'Call and *Wooster, Senators*, dissented.

A majority of the court concurring in the opinion of Savage, *Ch. J.*, it was thereupon ordered, adjudged and decreed that the assignment of the bank stock and dividends in the pleadings mentioned, made by Edward M. L. Kenney, the husband of the respondent, Eliza S. Kenney, to the appellant, Richard Udall, on the 12th day of December, 1818, was and is subject to the equity of the respondent, Eliza S. Kenney, to an adequate settlement and provision therefrom; and that the right and equity of the said respondent to such settlement and provision, out of the said bank stock, remain wholly unimpaired; and that the decree of the Court of Chancery made in this cause on the 10th day of August, 1821, so far as the same declares such equity of the said respondent, be, and the same is hereby affirmed. But inasmuch as it appears to this court that the appellant, Richard Udall, was entitled, under the orders of the Court of Chancery *referred to in the pleadings, [***611** and directing the dividends of the said stock to be paid to the said Edward M. L. Kenney, and afterwards to the said appellant himself, to receive the said dividends until the date of the said decree so made in this cause by the said Court of Chancery—it is ordered, adjudged and decreed that so much and such part of said decree as rescinds the said orders, and directs the dividends on the said stock which were received since the said 11th day of November, 1820, and prior to the making of the said decree, to be paid to the solicitor for the said respondent, be, and the same is hereby reversed; and that the same be paid to the appellant. And it is further ordered, adjudged and decreed that the record in this cause be remitted to the Court of Chancery; and that it be referred to one of the masters of that court, to ascertain and report as to the fortune and estate of the respondent, Eliza S. Kenney, derived from her father, Thomas Hewitt, or otherwise, and the disposition thereof; and, generally, as to the property, estate, condition and circumstances of the said Eliza S. Kenney and her husband, Edward M. L. Kenney, at the time of their marriage, and also at the time of making such report; to the end that such competent and adequate settlement and provision may be made, for the separate use and maintenance of the said respondent, and her children, if any she has, or may have, out of the aforesaid bank stock, and the dividends which accrued thereon after the said decree, as may be just, regard being had to all the circumstances of the case, as the same shall appear on the coming in of such report; and that the surplus, if any, be decreed to the appellant, &c.

For affirming, 24; for reversal, 3.

Cited in—2 Paige, 304; 4 Paige, 74; 6 Paige, 369; Hoffm., 467; 13 Hun, 438; 18 Barb., 162; 60 Barb., 302; 9 How. Pr., 280; 37 How. Pr., 245; 38 Cal., 278; 15 Mich., 66; 31 Am. Dee., 259; 32 Am. Dec., 376; 9 N. H., 309.

---

*WALTER F. OSGOOD ET AL., [*612
Plaintiffs in Error,
v.
THE PRESIDENT AND DIRECTORS OF THE MANHATTAN COMPANY, *Defendants in Error.*

Acts or Admissions of Executors—Not Evidence Against Heirs or Devisees—Improper Admission of Evidence as Ground of Reversal.

A petition to the surrogate by executors, for a sale of real estate of their testatrix, accompanied with a sworn account of the personal estate, is not evidence to show the insolvency of the ancestor at the time she conveyed the real estate in question to certain persons, in an action by a creditor against her heirs and devisees, seeking to show that such conveyances were voluntary and fraudulent, whereby the subject of them became assets in the defendants' hands.

Even a judgment against executors is not evidence against the heir.

To make the confessions of one man evidence against another, they must have a joint interest in possession.

The confession of a grantor, or his executors, after the grant, are not admissible, in evidence, to prejudice the rights of the grantee.

Whether the confession of one of a corporation aggregate be evidence against the company, *quære*.

If improper evidence be given in the court below, though it be merely cumulative, the judgment will be reversed.

Citations—16 Johns., 89; 1 Munf., 437, 455, 456; 5 Johns., 412; 6 Johns. Ch., 360; 1 Hayw., 397, *n.*; 1 Esp. *N. P.*, 135; 3 Johns., 536; 10 Johns., 66; 11 East, 578; 3 Day, 493; 6 Johns., 267-269.

ERROR from the Supreme Court. The action in that court was *assumpsit*, by the President and Directors of the Manhattan Co. against Walter Franklin Osgood, Edmund Charles Genet and Martha B., his wife; Samuel Osgood and Juliana, his wife; Susan K. Osgood, De Witt Clinton and Maria, his wife; John L. Norton and Sarah, his wife, and Hannah Clinton, which Walter, Martha, Juliana and Susan, were alleged, in the declaration, to be heirs and devisees, and Maria, Sarah and Hannah; heirs of Maria Osgood, deceased. The action was upon two promissory notes, the one dated July 25, 1814, for $6,000, payable at 90 days, the other Aug. 10, 1814, for $500, payable in 60 days, both indorsed by Maria Osgood. The memorandum was of Oct. Term, 1815. The defendants, De Witt Clinton and Maria, his wife; John L. Norton and Sarah, his wife, and Hannah Clinton, pleaded *riens*
613*] *per descent*. *and the plaintiffs took judgment of assets *quando acciderent*. The other defendants, Walter F. Osgood, Edmund C. Genet and Martha B., his wife; Samuel Osgood and Juliana, his wife, and Susan K. Osgood, pleaded the general issue, and also, as to the said Walter, Martha, Juliana and Susan, *riens per descent* or devise, to which the plaintiffs replied assets at the time of the commencement of the suit by descent and devise. The cause was tried before the late *Mr. Justice* Van Ness, at the N. Y. sittings, in Dec., 1816.

Samuel Osgood, the elder, was seised of several houses and lots of land in the City of N. Y., and made his will, dated Feb. 8, 1792, by which he devised to his wife, Maria Osgood, all the estate, both real and personal, of which he was then possessed, or might be possessed at the time of his decease, and appointed her sole executrix. He afterwards purchased some lots of land at Greenwich, and died Aug. 23, 1813. Maria Osgood was, before and at the time of his death, seised, in her own right, of three several houses and lots of land, situate in Cherry St., in the City of N. Y., which she conveyed by three several deeds, bearing date May 31, 1814, in consideration of love and natural affection, to her three daughters, the defendants, Martha B., Susan K. and Juliana, respectively.

Maria Osgood made her will July 27, 1814, by which, after several specific bequests of money and chattels, and particularly several bequests to Walter F. Osgood, she devised the residue of her real and personal estate to her children, the defendants, Martha B., Juliana, Walter F. and Susan K. Osgood, and appointed the defendants, Walter F. Osgood, Samuel Osgood and Edmund C. Genet her executors. The testatrix died Oct. 8, 1814, and the notes in question, which afterwards fell due, remained unpaid. The real estate devised was heavily incumbered by mortgages.

A variety of evidence was produced at the trial, to show that at the time of the conveyance to her daughters Mrs. Osgood was insolvent; and for that purpose, the plaintiffs also produced the petition of her executors to the Surrogate *of the City and County of [*614
N. Y., dated Jan. 10, 1816, stating that the personal estate of the testatrix was insufficient to pay her debts, and requesting the aid of the surrogate in the premises, pursuant to the statute in such case made and provided; to which was attached an account between the executors and the estate, with an account of the personal property and debts of the testatrix, omitting to say when they arose, or whether due when Mrs. Osgood conveyed. These accounts were sworn to by the executors; but before any order was made by the surrogate upon the petition, they declined proceeding further, alleging that they had acted under a misapprehension. The admission of this testimony was objected to on the part of the defendants, but it was received by the judge, and the defendants excepted. A considerable part of the debts of the testatrix consisted of indorsements for the accommodation of Walter F. Osgood.

The judge charged the jury strongly in favor of the plaintiffs upon the point whether the deeds from Mrs. Osgood to her daughters were voluntary, fraudulent and void as to creditors; and the estate embraced by them was, consequently, as to the plaintiffs, assets by descent or devise, under the issued joined on the plea of *riens per descent* or devise, in the hands of the defendants, who were parties to that issue.

The jury found a verdict for the plaintiffs, on which the court below gave judgment, in Jan. Term, 1818; and the cause came here upon a bill of exeeptions, containing the above point upon the admission of evidence, with others which it is not necessary to notice.

The reasons in support of the judgment below were rendered, as in 15 Johns., 167–168, S. C.; 1 Cow., 65, S. C., upon a question of amendment.

Mr. S. Jones, for the plaintiffs in error. The judge decided erroneously, in admitting the petition and schedule presented to the surrogate by the executors of Maria Osgood, as competent evidence to show that she was indebted May 31, 1814, and also (subsequently to that day) at the time of her death; and especially in admitting the petition *and sebed- [*615
ule as evidence against those who had never signed, or in any way admitted or recognized them as true.

In chancery, the answer of one defendant will not be listened to as evidence, even against his co-defendant. This is upon a principle which applies with much greater force here, where admissions out of court, by third persons, not parties, are insisted upon as taking away the rights of these grantees. *Phœnix* v.

Dey, 5 Johns., 412; *Grant* v. *U. S. Bank*, 1 Cai. Cas., 121; *Leeds* v. *Mar. Ins. Co.*, 2 Wh., 380. The answer of a minor by his guardian is never received as evidence against the former; nor will the confession of one partner implicate another, unless made during the continuance of the joint business, and in relation to the partnership estate. The petition and schedule, though sworn to, were no more than a mere *ex parte* deposition; and it is a most dangerous relaxation of the rules of evidence, to say that this shall be evidence against a stranger. What connection is there between executors and heirs which makes the acts of the former evidence against the latter? Their rights and liabilities are entirely distinct. *Jackson* v. *Hoag*, 6 Johns., 59. In *Mason's Devisees* v. *Peters' Admrs.*, 1 Munf., 437, it was decided that even a judicial recovery against an executor is no evidence against a devisee or heir. Is a mere admission of higher authority than a judgment at law, upon the very question in dispute? True, as against the executors themselves, the evidence would be admissible; but it cannot be so against a mere stranger; nor would the admission of one coheir be evidence against another who should be party in the very suit where it was offered, unless both should be so connected in the pleadings as to be incapable of severance. Beside, what renders the decision in this case more strikingly erroneous is, that Walter F. Osgood, one of the executors who petitioned, was interested to charge the real estate conveyed.

Again; this petition and schedule were not the highest evidence which the nature of the case admitted. The original evidences of debt should have been produced; and why not file a bill of discovery, and ask the heirs them-
616*] selves *for the amount of the debts, instead of relying on the acts of strangers? *Johnson* v. *Beardslee*, 15 Johns., 3, was relied upon by the court below; but the promise of executors, who were also heirs, was there received merely to take the case out of the Statute of Limitations. It is well settled that evidence will be received to take a case out of the statute, which is too slight to establish a debt. Phil. Ev., 192; 15 East, 34, 35, and 4 Johns., 461, are also relied upon; but these authorities do not apply. It may be that where there is a joint interest, a declaration by one is evidence against all who are parties to the suit in which it is offered; that is to say, where they all constitute one person. Where there is a privity, or a joint demise, or the plea of the defendants admits a joint demand, perhaps the same rule applies. The authorities cited by the court will support a class of cases where a witness makes a declaration against his interest, and dies. You may then give it in evidence; but even this is limited to a case where he could testify to the fact, if alive. No excuse but death will then answer. Absence, sickness, &c., will be unavailable. The principle of these authorities has no application to the present question.

Mr. J. V. Henry, for the defendants in error. The petition and schedule objected to were the act of Maria Osgood's executors. She is the person under whom the defendants claim; and her executors, appointed by her, were acting within the sphere of their official duty, recognized and required of them by the Statute (1 R. L., 450, 451, sec. 22). They had power, by this Statute, to obtain a surrogate's order, and sell this very real estate which the defendants complain was affected by their act. As the personal representatives of the testatrix, they rendered an account of her debts with a view to a payment of her creditors. They confined themselves to the personalty, and in this view their acts are the most satisfactory evidence of what she owed. No person could perform this duty except the executors, and for this purpose they stood in her place. Suppose we had offered to show an oral admission of the executors, that when Mrs. Osgood *executed [***617** this conveyance she was indebted to the Manhattan Co. $10,000. Would not this evidence be admissible? Recollect it was not offered to charge the defendants below directly with a debt, but to establish the collateral fact of insolvency? One of the executors, Walter F. Osgood, and Mrs. Genet, the wife of another; and Juliana, the wife of Samuel Osgood, were also devisees, having a common interest with the other defendants, in the land; and their acts were received merely as evidence, *prima facie*, that Mrs. Osgood was indebted—nothing more. We are asked, why not file a bill of discovery? For what end? Had we done this, we should have been referred to the surrogate's office. *Mason's Devisees* v. *Peter's Adm'rs*, 1 Munf., 437, does not apply; because, in that case, the judgment was offered as direct and conclusive evidence to charge the realty. Here it was merely one item in the proof to show the intent of the conveyance. It was not to charge the defendants with a debt, though this might be the consequence of establishing the fraudulent intent. Several analogous cases are cited in 1 Phil. Ev., 191-193. Among these are the entries and declarations of deceased persons. The signing a bill of lading by a master of a vessel, is admissible to charge the insurer, at the suit of the consignee. *Haddow* v. *Parry*, 3 Taunt., 303. So declarations by a person having a joint interest with the party (1 Phil. Ev., 72, 2 Am. ed.), or by a rated parishioner upon a question of settlement, are admissible. *The King* v. *The Inh. of Hardwick*, 11 East. 578; Gilb. Ev., 59, Lond. ed., 1791, *note v*, states a case of covenant against two defendants, and the affidavit of one was received as evidence against both. Suppose a partner of the ancestor should acknowledge a debt due from the firm—would not this be clearly admissible in evidence against his heirs or personal representatives? The objection, however, if it prevails, will merely be the foundation of a new trial.

Mr. Talcott, Att'y Gen., in reply. It is not disputed, that in order to charge these defendants, it was necessary to show that the ancestor was insolvent when she conveyed; *or, [***618** at any rate, so much in debt as to authorize an inference of fraud. This was clearly necessary, to warrant the court in setting aside a conveyance to the children. To support this allegation, a statement signed by the executors, one only of whom is a devisee and heir, is produced. The petition is dated in May, 1816, and, at the close, a list of debts is given, without a single date by which to determine whether they arose before or after the alienation. Yet it was received to prove an indebtedness, not at the time when the inventory was made (for this was utterly immaterial), but that the grantor was insolvent two years before. Upon what principle, if admissible at all, can this schedule be received to make her indebted in 1814, when she conveyed?

But it was not admissible for any purpose against the defendants below; and if so, no matter what other evidence was given—there must be a new trial. *Marquand* v. *Webb*, 16 Johns., 89.

In the first place, it was not the best evidence. The creditors themselves should have been called, and the proper documents produced and proved by witnesses, to establish the debts where there were such. The executors did not know what the debts were. They had probably been told that they were so much; but, on oath, the creditors might not have sworn to it.

Again; it is enough that the suit was against heirs and devisees, but the acknowledgment by executors; and the question is, not whether one may charge property, by his confession, in which he is interested, but property in which he has no manner of interest. It is said that the evidence was not to charge the defendants with a debt; but this is a mistake. It was to make them liable in every sense of the word. Even their persons were to be made liable to a *ca. sa.* It is also said these executors were acting in reference to personal property, and hence their acts did not affect the realty. We complain that their acts were made to have the latter effect. The decision of the court below puts it in their power to charge the realty, and they have done so. The case of *Mason's Devisees* v. *Peter's Adm'rs*, 1 Munf., 437, is conclusive. So far as the cases cited 619*] *from Phillips apply, they are not disputed; but how is it to be shown that Samuel Osgood or Genet were, in the least, interested? True, they intermarried with heirs or devisees; but they could not confess away their wives' rights. Walter F. Osgood is, in fact, interested, to have the conveyances set aside at the suit of creditors, as it would relieve him from the heavy incumbrances, by mortgage, upon the lands devised to him as one of the residuary devisees. Indeed, he gets nothing by the will unless the conveyances are avoided.

But it is not true that the confession of one will bind another, because the one happens to be interested. How is this with regard to joint trespassers, who have an equal interest? Clearly, one cannot confess away the other's rights. So of a promissory note, signed by two jointly; the admission of one will not charge the other. So the admission of an indorser, though against his interest, is not evidence to charge the maker. *Hemings* v. *Robinson*, Barn., 436, 3d ed. But it is said that the confession of one, having a joint interest, is evidence against another having the same interest. If so, you must first show that such a joint interest exist. This depends here upon the conveyances being void, to establish which the evidence was offered; and the proposition to admit it is a perfect *petitio principii*. *Mooers* v. *White*, 6 Johns. Ch., 360, is all fours with this case. The Statute of Limitations was set up by the defendants, who were executors and devisees; but the evidence was, that one of the executors, as such, had acknowledged the debt within six years. This was overruled by the *Chancellor*, as the suit was to affect the real estate. He said, even as to the Statute of Limitations, that the executor, as such, could do no act to waive it as between the creditor and the heir. 6 Johns Ch., 373. In this case, the evidence was admitted, not merely to take the estate from heirs and devisees, but from grantees. No matter whether the grantee be a child of the grantor, or a stranger. The principle is the same. It is still a question whether an executor can make an acknowledgment having a retroactive effect to take the estate away from a grantee.

*Again; suppose Mrs. Osgood alive. [*620 Could she herself confess away the estate granted? No. This is clear, not only upon principle but authority. *Phœnix* v. *Dey*, 5 Johns., 412. Why so? A contrary rule would place the grantee in the power of the grantor at any distance of time, and under any change of circumstances. This is a conclusive answer in itself. In *Arnold* v. *Bell*, 1 Hayw., 397, in *note*, there was an attempt of this kind. The confessions of the grantor, made after the grant were offered in evidence; but overruled on the ground that, though evidence against himself, they were not so against anybody else. If he cannot make the confession himself, it is very clear that he cannot delegate the power of doing it to his executors.

Even an acknowledgment of record by one joint promisor is not evidence against another. *Grey* v. *Palmers*, 1 Esp. *N. P.*, 135. One copartner cannot bind another by his confession that they were partners (*Whitney* v. *Ferris*, 10 Johns., 66); nor by striking a balance after a dissolution. *Hackley* v. *Patrick*, 3 *Id.*, 536; *Smith* v. *Ludlow*, 6 *Id.*, 267. The *King* v. *Hardwick*, 11 East, 578, went on peculiar grounds. A rated parishioner made the confession which was admitted against the parish, and Ld. Ellenborough said he was substantially a party to the suit, and it was like receiving the admission of one of an aggregate company or corporation. Even this doctrine has been denied by very respectable authority. *President, &c.*, v. *Hart*, 3 Day, 493. But whether the case cited on the other side be law or not, it has no resemblance to the present one.

The admission of this evidence, then, being erroneous, as observed by the gentleman, a *venire de novo* must issue.

SUDAM, *Senator*. One of the questions presented for the consideration of the court, is, whether the petition to the surrogate by the executors of Mrs. Osgood, stating that the personal estate of the deceased was insufficient to pay her debts, and requesting the aid of the surrogate in the premises, pursuant to the statute, &c., to which was annexed a statement *of her personal effects, sworn to by [*621 the executors was properly admitted by the judge at the circuit, as evidence of her insolvency at the time she executed to her daughters the deeds of the lots in Cherry St. This testimony was admitted by the judge who presided at the circuit; and his decision was confirmed by the Supreme Court. It now comes to this court on a bill of exceptions to his opinion on this and other points.

Having myself arrived at the conclusion that this evidence should not have been received, it will be unnecessary for me to consider the other points in this cause.

In order to make out their case, the plaintiffs below were bound to show affirmatively, that the defendants were the heirs and devisees of Mrs. Osgood. To do this, they were compellable to make out, in proof, that the voluntary conveyances to her daughters were void under the Statute to Prevent Fraudulent Conveyances, as to creditors, by reason of her insolvency when she executed the deeds; and the petition and schedule were offered as *prima facie* evidence of this.

It will be recollected that this petition was never acted on; and that the executors declined proceeding upon it, on the ground that they had made it out under a misapprehension. The statement of the debts offered to the surrogate did not specify the time when they were contracted; so that we cannot, from this, decide whether they arose before or after the conveyances were executed; and it was made by persons having only an interest in right of their wives, in the premises in question, except Walter F. Osgood, who was, in fact, interested to avoid his mother's conveyance.

It is well settled that if improper evidence be given, although it may be cumulative only, the judgment must be reversed; for we cannot say what effect such evidence may have had on the minds of a jury. *Marquand* v. *Webb*, 16 Johns., 89. This evidence should not, in my opinion, have been admitted, at all, against either the heirs or devisees, admitting that the insolvency of Mrs. Osgood, at the time of executing the deeds, rendered them void as to creditors. Upon this point, I do not mean to

622*] give an opinion; but the acts *of executors ought not to bind heirs or devisees, unless in the case of an actual decree of sale by the surrogate. In the present case, too, the executors themselves, after presenting the petition declined acting upon it. Under such circumstances, especially, the petition and schedule should not be received against the heirs and devisees; and particularly in this case, where it goes to charge them personally with the debt of the ancestor. The form of entering judgment for the plaintiffs below, whether against the lands of the ancestor, or against his land and the person of the defendants, cannot alter our decision.

Even a judgment against an executor is no evidence against the heir. *Mason's Devisee* v. *Peters' Admr.*, 1 Munf., 437, 455, 456. If this is inadmissible against the heir, merely to fix the amount of the demand, upon what principle can it be said that an *ex parte* statement by executors (though under oath) shall be evidence for a much more important purpose; to avoid a conveyance of real estate, and charge the persons and estates of heirs and devisees as upon a false plea.

It was the duty of the plaintiffs below substantially to make out their case, before the defendants could be called upon for their defense; and to effect this, it was necessary for them to prove that the conveyances by Mrs. Osgood to her daughters were void. Could this be done by admissions of executors, or any other persons who were not grantees? I think not. Mrs. Osgood's own confessions, after she had executed the deed to her daughters could not have been admitted. *Phœnix* v. *Dey*, 5 Johns., 412. And it will be contended that executors, named in her will, can make an admission of more effect than her own? It appears to me this point is settled by the opinion of the late *Chancellor* in *Mooers* v. *White*, 6 Johns. Ch., 360, and *Arnold* v. *Bell*, 1 Hayw., 397, *note*.

It will be recollected that the conveyances to the daughters were in severalty. There could, therefore, be no joint interest in them till they were avoided. To accomplish this, any acts done by the executors, without the concurrence of the devisees, could not be used as evidence upon any principle. *To [*623 warrant receiving the admissions of one in prejudice of another, they must have a joint interest in possession, not a mere community of interest. *Grey* v. *Palmers*, 1 Esp. *N. P.*, 135; *Hackley* v. *Patrick*, 3 Johns., 536; *Smith* v. *Ludlow*, 6 *Id.*, 267; *Whitney* v. *Ferris*, 10 *Id.*, 66.

The case cited at the bar, of *The King* v. *Hardwick*, 11 East, 578, does not affect the question. There the admission of a parishioner, liable to be assessed for taxes, was received, on the ground that the parish was an aggregate company of which he was a member. Beside, I think the ground upon which that case was put very questionable, at least; and I find, that in Conn., it has been directly overruled as to a corporation aggregate. *Hartford Bank* v. *Hart*, 3 Day, 493.

On the whole, I am of opinion that the evidence was improperly admitted; that the judgment must, therefore, be reversed; and the record be remitted, and a *venire de novo* issue from the court below.

The Court being unanimously of this opinion, it was thereupon ordered, adjudged and decreed that the judgment of the Supreme Court be reversed, with costs in error, to be taxed, for the plaintiff in error; and that the transcript be remitted to the said Supreme Court, and that the said court award a *venire facias de novo*.

SANFORD, *Chancellor*, being a stockholder in the Company, gave no opinion.

Criticised—12 Wend., 41.

Cited in—6 Cow., 455; 8 Cow., 708, 751; 5 Wend., 46; 8 Wend., 16; 18 Wend., 503; 1 Paige, 36; 8 Paige, 144; 10 Paige, 368; 1 N. Y., 522; 26 N. Y., 278; 29 N. Y., 503; 35 N. Y., 59; 45 N. Y., 3, 804; 47 N. Y., 188; 2 Lans., 172; 10 Hun, 473; 15 Hun, 547; 4 Barb., 535; 5 Barb., 407; 7 Barb., 587; 8 Barb., 534; 16 Barb., 544; 26 Barb., 362; 32 Barb., 34; 48 Barb., 329; 3 Abb. Pr., 158; 2 Abb. N. S. 388; 2 Hall, 50; 1 Duer, 431; 6 Duer, 146; 3 Bos., 516; 2 Daly, 163; 1 Bradf., 15; 3 Bradf., 243; 1 Redf., 327; 3 Co. R., 245; 2 Wood & M., 153; see 38 Cal., 283, 284; 99 Mass., 129; 87 Pa., 455; 22 Am. Dec., 610, 611; 49 Am. Dec., 351.

PETER THALLHIMER, *Plaintiff in Error*, *v.* GEORGE BRINCKERHOFF, *Defendant in Error.*

Champerty and Maintenance—What Interest will Render Maintenance Lawful—Relationship between Suitor and Maintainor—History and object of Laws against Champerty, &c.—Form of Action—Parties.

NOTE.—*Champerty and maintenance—Offense of.* Compare Van Dyck v. Van Beuren, 1 Johns., 345, *note*; 2 Parson's on Contracts, 765.

Parties in equity. See Hickock v. Scribner, 1 Johns. Cas., 311, *note*.

H. T., who claimed land as heir at law of his father, and who was about to commence suits to recover the possession of it, entered into an agreement with the plaintiff, who had married his sister, by which he covenanted in consideration of the premises, &c., to convey to the plaintiff the one fourth part of the property which should be recovered; and the plaintiff, in consideration of such covenant, &c., promised H. T. to pay, bear and sustain the one half of
624*] all the expenses which might occur *in the prosecution of the intended suits, &c. The defendant who drew the agreement, and subscribed it as a witness, as attorney of H. T., and the plaintiff brought actions of ejectment against the persons in possession of the land; and afterwards, by virtue of a power of attorney from H. T., for that purpose, but without the knowledge of the plaintiff, compromised with the tenants, and received from them a large sum of money.

In an action of *assumpsit* for money had and received to the use of the plaintiff, brought by him to recover one fourth part of the money so received by the defendant: held, that the agreement between the plaintiff and H. T., was valid, and not illegal and void within the provisions of the Act to Prevent and Punish Champerty and Maintenance (sess. 24, ch. 87; 1 R. L., 172), and that the plaintiff could, therefore, recover against the defendant.

Held, also, that general *indebitatus assumpsit* for money had and received was the proper form of action.

Held, also, that the non-joinder of H. T. was no objection.

History of the law in relation to champerty, maintenance and barratry.

It was a principle of the common law that a chose in action could not be transferred; but this is now reversed; though at this day a part of a chose in action cannot be transferred.

The common law rule never prevailed in courts of equity.

To maintain the suit of another, is unlawful, unless the person maintaining has some interest, in the subject of the suit, distinct from what he may acquire by the agreement to maintain, or is connected with the suitor in some social relation; but where one has such an interest, whether it be great or small, vested or contingent, certain or uncertain, he may maintain. So, where there is consanguinity or affinity between the suitor and him who gives aid to the suit, the latter may maintain.

The relation of landlord and tenant, master and servant, acts of charity to the poor, and the exercise of the legal profession, are also cases in which it is not unlawful to maintain.

The law against champerty, &c., were intended to prevent the interference of strangers having no pretense of right in the subject of the suit, and standing in no relation of duty to the suitor.

The above rules and exceptions extend both to champerty and maintenance—the latter being the generic term, including champerty, which is maintenance in a particular form, viz.: upon a contract to divide the subject of the suit.

A husband whose wife may, by possibility, be heir of one who claims land, may maintain the suit of the claimant, brought to recover the land, upon an agreement to have part of the land.

Citations—4 Inst. tit. 16; 2 Code, tit. 59; 5 Dig. tit. 1, 79; 4 Inst. tit. 1-33; Huber. Praelect., 457, 1478; Wood's Civ. Law, 341; 4 Bl. Com., 135; 1 Leon., 167; Co. Litt., 114 *a*; 4 D. & E., 340, 341; Stat. 32 H. VIII.

ERROR from the Supreme Court, upon a bill of exceptions. Judgment was rendered for the defendant below, who was also the defendant in this court, upon facts which are, to every material purpose, detailed in the
625*] report of the *same cause, as it came before the Supreme Court (20 Johns., 386) in Jan. Term, 1823.

Mr. S. G. Huntington, for the plaintiff in error:

1. The agreement between Teller and the plaintiff was legal and binding upon the parties. The objection is, that the plaintiff was guilty of maintenance or champerty, by the act of entering into it, and that it is, therefore, void. Maintenance is defined to be an officious intermeddling in a suit that no way belongs to one, by maintaining or assisting either party with money or otherwise, to the disturbance of the community, by stirring up suits. 4 Bl. Com., 134, 135; 3 Burn., *J.* 116; 2 Chit. C. L., 233, *note a*; 5 Com. Dig., 16, Maintenance, A. Champerty is a specie of maintenance, being a bargain with a plaintiff or defendant to divide the land or other matter sued for, between them, if they prevail at law. 3 Burn., *J.*, 116; 4 Bl. Com., 134, 135; 2 Chit. C. L., 223, *note a*; 5 Com. Dig., 16, Maintenance, A, 1, 2. If a man have any interest in the subject of the agreement about which the suit is to be brought or is depending, this is not maintenance, be the interest never so remote. Hawk. P. C., B. 1, ch. 83, secs. 1, 13, 17, 18, 21, 22; *Wickham* v. *Conklin*, 8 Johns., 220; 3 Burn., *J.*, 117; Bac. Abr., Maintenance, B.

Here is, we contend, such an interest in the plaintiff as legally entitled him to make this arrangement. Teller admitted, by his agreement, under seal, that the plaintiff intermarried with his sister, and had an equitable, though not a legal interest in the subject of the agreement; that this interest in the plaintiff was a consequence of the marriage. No such interest could have been communicated, unless there had been, at least, an equitable one in the wife. Our case, then, is made out by the agreement itself, which must be taken as conclusive between the parties, and upon all claiming under them. 1 Phil. Ev., 355, 2d Am. ed.

The plaintiff, then, having an interest, all the authorities agree that he may maintain the action. The extent of the interest is nowhere made the criterion: 2 Roll. Abr., 115; Bro. Abr., Maintenance, pl. 7, 14, 17. Nor is it necessary *that the interest should be vested [*626 or certain—a contingent interest is enough. 2 Roll. Abr., 117; 1 Hawk. P. C., B. 1, ch. 83, secs. 13, 14.

The case states that Thallhimer married the sister, not a sister of Teller, thus implying, in terms, that she was his only sister; nor is there evidence that he had any other. He having no children (and it is not shown that he had any) she was the next heir. Being the next heir, or one of the next heirs, her husband had a clear right to contract. Indeed, a mere possibility of future interest is enough. 15 Vin., 162, Maintenance, H; 1 Hawk., B. 1, ch. 83, secs. 13, 14; *Id.*, ch. 84, sec. 19; Bro., Maintenance, 15, 18; 1 Bac. Abr., 576, tit. Champerty; 2 Inst., 563, 564.

2. But if the agreement were illegal, the defendant cannot take advantage of it. Teller, having acted under the agreement, has no right to object; and if so with him, it is the same with the defendant, who acts under him, and is bound by the relation of attorney. He can do nothing except what Teller authorizes him to do. Suppose that, at the circuit, the defendant's counsel had set up the Statute of Limitations, but the defendant himself had risen and told them to waive this, and declined all advantage from it; would not the counsel have been bound by his acts? Certainly. To defend upon such ground, they must maintain an authority to do it, derived from their client. So with the defendant here. He should have shown that his client authorized him to withhold from us our just due upon the agreement—that Teller objects to our recovery, and

authorizes him to do so. He, for aught that appears, is willing that we should have the full benefit of the arrangement. There is no evidence that Brinckerhoff ever settled with him. The inference, in the absence of proof to the contrary, is, that he is perfectly willing to do us justice.

3. The money received by the defendant was, as to one fourth part, received by him to the use of the plaintiff.

Messrs. H. Blecker and *A. Van Vechten*, for the defendant in error, made the following points: 1. That Henry R. Teller should have been joined with the plaintiff in the action.
627*] *Ziele* v. **Exrs. of Campbell*, 2 Johns. Cas., 382. 2. An action of *assumpsit* cannot be sustained for the money claimed by the plaintiff, because, by the agreement between Teller and him, the plaintiff was to have one fourth of the land, not the money received for it. The *casus fœderis*, between the parties never occurred. 3. The agreement was void, within the Statute to Prevent Champerty and Maintenance, and the plaintiff can derive no right of action from it against the defendant. 4. The plaintiff ought to have proved notice to the defendant, to pay the proportion of the money claimed.

It is true, the first, second and third points were not expressly made at the circuit; but we have a right to present them here, especially those which it is plain could not have been obviated by any additional proof. *Beekman* v. *Frost*, 18 Johns., 544. This is clearly so with the objection of the non-joinder, and the form of the action, being for money instead of the breach of the special agreement. Both of these objections arise from the nature of the transaction.

The third point is the principal one. As to this the defendant was not put upon his defense. It is said, he should have proved this and that; but the obvious answer is, that he had no chance to prove anything. The cause was arrested upon the insufficiency of the plaintiff's proof; and it would be unreasonable to infer anything against the defendant, for lack of evidence, which the circuit judge pronounced to be idle and unnecessary.

The agreement was void. The Statute (1 R. L., 172, sec. 1) provides that no officer or other person shall take upon him any business that is or may be in suit, to have any part of the thing in plea or demand; and no person, upon any such agreement, shall give up his right to another; and every such conveyance or agreement shall be void; and every person who shall maintain any plea or suit in any court, for lands, &c., to have part or profit of them, shall be punished by fine and imprisonment; but this Act shall not prohibit any person to have counsel of persons duly licensed, or of his parents and next friends. We rely upon these provisions. The other sections of the Statute provide against buying titles, and simple maintenance. The latter is merely aiding
628*] *another in a suit. Champerty is where a man agrees to maintain the suit upon condition to have part of the thing in dispute This was the view taken of the subject in *Jackson* v. *Ketcham*, 8 Johns., 479. The court say the established doctrine is, that a purchase, or even gift of the land, while a suit is pending concerning it, if it be made with the knowledge of the suit, and be not the consummation of a previous bargain, nor founded on the ties of blood, is within the purview of the Statute. An agreement, in contemplation of a suit, is equally void as if it had been the consummation of a contract founded in maintenance. This is obvious from the words of the Statute, as cited and commented upon in the last case. If the agreement relate to what is or may be in suit, it is void. The court adopt the ancient doctrine, in its full extent, and say that our Statute is even more explicit, in avoiding the agreement, than the old ones, of which it is a transcript. West., 1, ch. 25, 28, 49, and 28 Edw. I., ch. 11.

It was said, in the court below, that here was no adverse possession; but this is immaterial. Even if Teller had been in possession himself, a defendant in ejectment, or expecting to be a defendant, it is plain, from *Jackson* v. *Ketchum*, the agreement would have been void, as an act of champerty. The Statute forbids one taking upon himself anything in plea or demand; and the present is the very case within its contemplation and its terms. You could not illustrate the offense in plainer and stronger language than is presented by the bill of exceptions. The agreement looks to an adverse possession, if this were necessary. Suits were to be brought for the purpose of getting into possession. These would have been unnecessary had there been no adverse possessors of the land. Had the possession been in acknowledged subserviency to Teller's title, there would have been no sharing of expense in order to vindicate the right. But, we repeat, it is enough that the business was, or might be, in suit, and that the plaintiff was to have a part of the thing in demand. No explanation, however, was offered, to take the case out of the Statute. If adverse possession be an ingredient of the offense, why was it not negatived by proof at *the trial? If suits [***629**
for the recovery were not necessary, why was this not shown?

All that has been set up in vindication of the agreement is, that the plaintiff intermarried with the sister of Teller, and thus acquired an equitable interest. It is true, that a certain interest would take the case out of the 9th section of the Statute, which relates not to champerty, but maintenance. But even if this be holden maintenance, here is no such interest as will form an exception. *Wickham, q. t.* v. *Conklin*, 8 Johns., 220, cited on the other side, was a case of mere maintenance; and an exception was allowed. This was on the ground that the defendant, Conklin, was a *cestui que trust* of the land in dispute, and prosecuted for his own benefit. He had a plain, definable, equitable, subsisting interest, which might be enforced. Not so here, Thallhimer had no right but what he was to acquire by force of the agreement itself. It is said this admits the wife's interest. Not so. It admits the facts stated in it—and these show no interest whatever. Does an admission that A is the sister of B show her to be his heir? The amount of the admission in the agreement is, that she had a just right, not equitable. Had it stated an equitable right as the consequence of the relation, the conclusion would have been false.

How could Mrs. Thallhimer ever have enforced a right growing out of these circumstances? Teller is admitted to be the heir at law. It appears his father died before the Statute of Descents, and he was the sole heir, being the eldest son. A court of equity could not assist her. The interest is altogether ideal and intangible. The right to real estate is settled by the law, and there can be no right not founded on this basis. The law can draw no conclusion of right from such premises as are stated here, and the inference sought for has nothing to support it. Suppose a man attempts to devise land by an instrument attested by two witnesses only; could it be pretended that the devisee had any equitable or legal right? His friends might think so, but the law would treat him as perfect stranger. 2 Bl. Com., 13. It would never allow an exception which could be satisfied by the mere fancy of the **630***] claimant, but refers to such *an interest, only, as itself would recognize and enforce; otherwise its provisions might be evaded at pleasure. If Mrs. Thallhimer had such a right as the law acknowledges, on the ground taken, that she might possibly inherit; uncles, cousins, &c., come within the same rule. All the relations may possibly inherit. Would this remote chance entitle them to bring suits for the land? A defendant may thus lie at the mercy of a whole community of relations, bringing suits upon an agreement to divide the spoil. Indeed, the moment you go beyond the heir, you launch beyond all rule, and virtually repeal the Statute. Then if the interest does not take the case out of the Statute of Maintenance (the 9th section), *a fortiori* it will not out of the Statute of Champerty (the 1st section).

Does the case come within the exception in favor of licensed counsel, or parents, or next friends? 1 R. L., 172, sec. 1. Does taking counsel excuse the buying and selling, or contracting to have part of the thing in dispute? The enacting clause prohibits this to all, including counsel and friends. Among all the authorities cited, there is but one which mentions an exception in the case of champerty, where the thing may be conveyed. That is 1 Hawk., B. 1, ch. 84, sec. 19. This was cited and relied on by His Honor, *Judge* Woodworth, who dissented from the court below. 20 Johns., 401. And if this be law, it is against the plain terms of the Act. Hawkins is writing under the general head of maintenance, of which he treats champerty as a subdivision; and this section 19 is the only one in which he has mentioned such an exception under this head. He cites Lord Coke, and all that he says is taken from the Year Books. The two offenses of champerty and maintenance may have been confounded in this single instance; for certainly other authorities are plainly to the contrary. It has been repeatedly decided under the English Statute, that even attorneys or counsel cannot agree to have part of the thing about which they are litigating as a compensation for their services; and why not so as to a next friend. Indeed his advice must always be entirely gratuitous. He cannot take fees. Why not the same in one case as in the other, **631***] as to sharing *the spoil? Both are placed on the same footing by the Statute of Maintenance, and both are, in terms, shut out by the Statute of Champerty. The exception cannot be extended by construction. But, most likely, when Hawkins makes this exception of the son, he must mean the heir. Thus the 2 inst., 564, upon which he relies, says: "In like manner, and by the like reason, if the father be demandant in a *præcipe*, he may promise and contract with the son to secure him the land after the recovery, and is not any champerty within this Act, and so of any other ancestor and his heir apparent." It is plain that Coke means "heir," or why should he add, "so of any other ancestor, or heir apparent?" In ch. 88, secs. 13, 14, Hawkins speaks first of remainder-men and reversioners having a vested interest, or an interest which it is in no man's power to deprive them of; and he concludes, "therefore, an heir apparent, or the husband of such heir may maintain the ancestor." Is it not fair to conclude that here, also, when he speaks of an heir he means one who has a vested interest as heir? The *Chief Justice* who delivered the opinion of the court below understands Ld. Coke to mean, merely, that the pendency of a suit shall not prevent a father making provision for his son out of the thing in demand.

If the exception be not limited to the heir apparent or presumptive, we ask again, where are you to stop? The whole range of kindred may maintain suits with impunity. To whom did it belong to show that Mrs. Thallhimer was heir apparent or presumptive? It does not follow from her being the sister of Teller. The agreement does not make out even this plausible case. For aught that appears, other persons were heirs of Teller. One fourth is to be conveyed; but how does it appear that Thallhimer had an interest in this or any other portion? We mention this to show that the estimate of interest was merely arbitrary—that the sister had no real interest. When the heir is allowed to maintain, this relates to the subject of his immediate expectancy or descent. If Mrs. Thallhimer had any interest, instead of being promoted, it was cut off by the agreement. The land would have gone to her; but this agreement turns it over *absolutely to [***632** her husband, leaving her a mere contingent interest in one third of this fourth, as dowager. It is evident that all this language, relating to her interest, was inserted in the agreement colorably to avoid the Statute. All the authorities cited against us, perhaps with the single exception we have mentioned, relate to maintenance. The 1 Hawk, ch. 83, sec. 20, says, "one cannot justify laying out his own money in the cause, unless he be either father, or son, or heir apparent to the party, or the husband of such an heiress;" though the same section agrees that a remote relation may stand by and counsel at the bar. This is to the same effect as the 14th section of that chapter. It is said that a contingent interest is enough. What this contingent interest must be, will appear from sections 13 and 14 of the same chapter. The contingency must be such as is settled and fixed when the event happens, and the heir alone is an exception to this rule. True, it is said, in 15 Vin., 162, H, pl., 9, that a brother may maintain, but the reason is given, viz.: because he is heir presumptive. Accordingly, the same book says, a brother of the half blood cannot, because there is no immediate possibility of his inheriting. (*Id.*) The distinction between an heir apparent and presumptive, will be found in 2 Bl. Com., 208. The authorities in 15 Vin. Abr., 168, O, pl., 9, and Bro., Maintenance, pl. 18, p. 74, and elsewhere, must be understood in reference to one of these heirs, when they say that the husband of a cousin who may be heir has a right to maintain. This relates to a cousin who is heir presumptive. Could a father maintain the suit of his son-in-law? Besides, these cases mean maintenance properly so called, and as contradistinguished from champerty. The section quoted by *Mr. Justice* Woodworth, in the court below (1 Hawk., B. 1, ch. 83, sec. 20), will be seen not to embrace the present case.

The maintenance was not in consideration of the relationship of these parties, but of the land. It was matter of profit on both sides. We deny that even heirs may contract in this manner.

Then, if Thallhimer had a right to maintain within the authorities, they will not justify him 633*] in this act of champerty; *and though the court might not punish him criminally, for thus leaguing to vindicate even a fancied right of his own or his wife's, they will declare the agreement void.

We are told, in the language of Buller, *J.*, in *Master* v. *Miller*, 4 T. R., 340, that our doctrine is harsh; but this is a subject for the Legislature. The language there does not apply. It related to an assignment of a chose in action, and the question was of maintenance, not champerty.

It is said the right to object does not lie with the defendant; but we answer, the agreement is void within the express terms of a statute; and being so, it is as no agreement. Even a party may make the objection. Teller himself might do so; and, *a fortiori*, his agent. The ground and policy of the objection is, that the agreement is unlawful and criminal, and even if Teller has consented that the defendant should hold the money to the plaintiff's use, this will not legitimate the transaction, and render that good which was corrupt and void in the beginning. This would enable the parties to repeal a statute. That the defendant may object, we cite *Whitaker* v. *Cone*, 2 Johns. Cas., 58; *Belding* v. *Pitkin*, 2 Cai., 147, and *Hunt* v. *Knickerbacker*, 5 Johns., 327. It is clear that the plaintiff could never have recovered the land. Then how can he recover the money? In addition to the authorities already cited to this point, and which were referred to by the *Chief Justice* in the court below, we rely on *Briggs* v. *Lawrence*, 3 T. R., 454; *Clugas* v. *Penaluna*, 4 *Id.*, 466; *Morck* v. *Abel*, 3 Bos. & P., 35. No act or contract in contravention of law can be made the foundation of an action.

Mr. S. Jones, in reply. I stand here to vindicate a contract made in perfect good faith, with a professional gentleman, the legal agent of the plaintiff; and which has been acted under for a number of years. He was the common attorney of Teller and Thallhimer; as such he has received their money respectively. He claims to withhold it, and unless there is some unbending law to which morality itself must yield, I trust we shall recover. The land 634*] to be recovered *belonged to the common ancestor of Teller and his sister; and both had a fair and equitable right to it. It is true that Teller might have maintained the action alone; but in the prosecution of the contemplated suits, the names of all the ancestor's children might also have been used. Instead of taking either course, money was received for the land expected to be obtained. We affirm the transaction, put ourselves upon the court and jury, and show a plain right, unless the agreement is impeachable upon the ground of legal invalidity. How does Brinckerhoff defend himself? By showing that he has accounted for the money? There is no pretense of this. After having acted under the agreement, his counsel object that it is illegal; and a majority of the court below have sustained the objection. Convinced that the dissenting judge was right, we bring our writ of error.

We are met at the threshold by several preliminary objections. One is, that the action should have been in the joint names of Teller and Thallhimer. But even if they had been partners, and the party as here, omitted to take advantage of the non-joinder, either in pleading or at the trial, we might have recovered in severalty. This is clearly the rule as to joint defendants, who must plead the non-joinder in abatement; and it is the same in regard to the plaintiff, where there is a total omission to object. The defendant was properly met by this answer in the court below. Even if the action should have been joint on the face of the bill, yet if the objection had been made at the circuit, it might have been obviated. We might have shown that the defendant had settled with Teller, reserving the money for which we sue, in his hands 'for our use. This would have been a severance. But the parties have separated their rights by the terms of the agreement. Thallhimer was to have one fourth —Teller three fourths; and the suit could have been brought in no other form. The action for money had and received is an equitable action, favored by the courts; and not to be defeated by the technical rules applicable to many other actions.

We are also told that the money was not received in pursuance of the agreement; that this embraced land only. *and the [*635 *casus fœderis* has not occurred. This goes to the merits of the case. If Teller could, by a separate power, defeat our agreement, then, it is true, we cannot recover at all. But how is this? Suppose Teller had recovered the land, and afterwards sold it in defiance of our right; if the agreement be valid, should we have no remedy for the money? Will gentlemen deny a position, so well known to the law, that in such a case the money would be substituted for the land—that we might affirm the sale and recover the money received upon it? The present is that case. By this act of sale, Teller is made our debtor. So of Brinckerhoff, the actual receiver of the money. True we might have disavowed the act, and proceeded against Teller upon the special agreement; but we had, also, a right to affirm it, which we do by prosecuting our action in this form. Brinckerhoff is discharged from the claims of Teller by our recovery. If he had liens upon the money, this should have been shown. His fair credits would have been allowed.

It is said we were bound to give him notice.

Of what? Not to pay the money over to Teller? This would have been so provided he had paid it over—which is not pretended. There was no use in giving notice. Had he paid over without this, I admit we should have been driven to our action against Teller, the principal.

But all these formal objections were clearly answerable at the trial by other evidence. The case cited from the 18 Johns., therefore, does not bear gentlemen out. It is of an objection which goes to the whole ground of action; and which, on its face, is final, conclusive and unavoidable by any possible explanation.

The only objection taken, was, that the agreement was void. This is fairly before the court, and I shall proceed to consider it. This agreement recites that Teller was heir to the lands described, his intention to sue for their recovery, that the plaintiff intermarried with his sister, who was justly entitled to a part of them, though not legally. Now, were all these recitals true, or does it lie with our own agent, who has acted under them to declare them **636***] *false? If true, Thallhimer had, by the intermarriage, a just right to a part of the land. It is said if Teller was sole seised, then Mrs. Thallhimer could not be entitled in any way; but is this so? Suppose the land held adversely at the death of the ancestor, who made his will devising one fourth to his sister, but which could not take effect on account of the adverse possession—would she not be entitled, in the language of every man? And would not the heir to whom the right should descend, be a scoundrel for withholding it? Might not such a claim be called just? And would not its justice be recognized by the law? Would an agreement to perfect such a right, by a fair course of litigation, deserves the epithet of injustice or corruption? Would it be void in law? If so, law is not morality. We have, I think, presented one case of just right, though without strict legal title. Suppose others: that the ancestor had died in possession having made a will which is lost; that Teller the heir knew this fact, but as the document was gone, nothing remained to show the right; or suppose the heir at the death bed of his father, who declared, in the hearing of all his children, that he intended his land for them equally; or suppose the ancestor died the day before an Act passed altering the course of descent from the eldest son to the children in equal moieties, by which the whole descends according to the ancient rights of primogeniture: the next day, the Legislature declare the old rule partial and unjust; shall it be penal for parties to use the same language, in either of the cases supposed, and make arrangements to be at a joint expense in the prosecution of such a right, technically belonging to one, but justly to all? Here is the last case precisely—an honest attempt by Teller to carry the provisions of our Statute of Descents into effect. He made a law for himself, in order to do an act of justice to his sister. Having the whole right, and entitled to the several possession, he treats with his brothers and sisters. The recovery required expense; was it right that he should pay the whole? No. Accordingly, the sister assumes the proper share of expense, and he puts the whole on the same footing as if it had descended in common. For aught we know, the same agreement *was made with other [***637** brothers and sisters of the family. Is this agreement, then, subject to the criticisms which have been made upon it? When you look at an agreement with a view to its construction, you must take it as it is. The strongest consideration must have been that of consanguinity. Why give one fourth of $50,-000 for one half of ten or a dozen lawsuits? The distinction attempted to be drawn between the husband and wife is without foundation. In law they are one. We are to intend that the compromise was for less than the value. Would Teller have made such an arrangement with a stranger? He would have found men enough who, if the agreement had been lawful, would have assumed the same responsibility for one tenth of the land. The rights of primogeniture have been declared unnatural and unjust, by a statute, almost the first which passed after the Declaration of Independence. The contract was to equalize the land. Does it contravene the law as it stood at the time?

The 1st and 3d sections of the Statute of Champerty, &c. (1 R. L., 172-3), are relied upon as embracing and avoiding the agreement. If you take the words of the 1st section, in their broadest sense, and take a case where the bargain turns upon the consideration of having a part of the thing in demand, without any other motive, it might be void. But is this so, if any other motive be mixed with it? To bring the case within a statute so highly penal, must not the agreement be an act founded upon the naked consideration of a part of the thing in demand? Must not maintaining be the sole ground of the part received? If not so, the motive takes away the guilt. What was the evil intended to be remedied? I cannot express this better than was done by *Mr. Justice* Woodworth, who dissented from the judgment below, and I, therefore, refer the court to what he says (20 Johns., 400). The Act was levelled against strangers, not relatives, either by interest or blood. It was aimed against intruders, or, to adopt the language of the old Act itself, against impertinent intruders. It never was intended to restrain the son from protecting the father, or the brother from advocating the cause of the brother. I appeal to the *language [***638** of *Mr. Justice* Buller, in *Master* v. *Miller*, 4 T. R., 340. "It is curious (says he), and not altogether useless, to see how the doctrine of maintenance has, from time to time, been received in Westminster Hall. At one time, not only he who laid out money to assist another in his cause, but he that, by his friendship or or interest, saved him an expense which he would otherwise be put to, was held guilty of maintenance. Bro., tit. Maintenance, 7, 14, 17, &c. Nay, if he officiously gave evidence, it was maintenance; so that he must have had a subpœna, or suppress the truth. That such doctrine, repugnant to every honest feeling of the human heart, should soon be laid aside, must be expected. Accordingly, a variety of exceptions were soon made; and, amongst others, it was held, that if a person has any interest in the thing in dispute, though on contingency only, he may lawfully maintain an action on it." 2 Roll. Abr., 115. There may have been some reason, in early times, why these statutes should have been so construed; for in the reigns when they passed, it was not unusual for lords to buy up contested claims against each other, or against commons, when at variance with them, with a view to persecute and oppress the farmers of the country and others. Very soon, however, exceptions were introduced. The first was interest. If you take the strict words, they embrace every one, whether interested or not. Yet this exception was well established soon after the passage of the Act. On this head, the series of cases is unbroken; and when we passed the Statute we adopted the exception. The very definition of the offense, which implies an officious intermeddling, and which was the evil intended to be remedied, precludes the operation of the statute. In some of the books the definition is stated to be an officious act of maintenance, not warranted by the interest of the party interfering. In *Wickham* v. *Conklin*, 8 Johns., 220, this distinction is recognized. The case decides that one having an interest cannot be guilty of maintenance. Where is the origin of this exception? There is none in the words of the Act, yet it is universally acknowledged to exist. Upon what authority do gentlemen deny us the right to go beyond the words of **639***] *the Act? With what consistency do they deny this, and at the same time admit their exception? Is it not confined to maintenance. It extends to champerty. It embraces both offenses. You are never guilty of either, when the inducement is to protect your own interest, and the contract is not a naked one to defray expenses, and have a part of the thing in demand. An opposite construction is at war with the strongest principles of human nature. This induced the courts to make the exception.

The exception founded upon considerations of blood depends on the mixed principle of interest and affection. A relation may, by possibility, inherit; and we have cited various authorities, where this is enough. In 15 Vin. Abr., Maintenance, H, it is said: "Some books say, generally, that a man may maintain his blood" (9 Hen., VI., 64); that is to say, all who are of kin to him. Again; "So it is of him to whom the land may descend" (19 Edw., IV., 3 *b*). And several corresponding instances are put under the same head (I). Reference is made to the Year Books, whence the doctrine has been handed down to us unimpaired. The distinction in the Y. B. is not in favor of the heir apparent only. It is general that a parent may maintain for his son; but a brother, of the half blood, cannot maintain his brother. Why? Because he is considered a mere stranger. The exception does not exist as to him, because he cannot by any possibility inherit.

It is said our authorities mostly relate to maintenance. Be it so. What is champerty? A species of maintenance, which latter is the generic term. Hawkins, B. 1, ch. 83, secs. 2, 3, defines maintenance to be of two kinds, *ruralis* or *curialis;* and he includes champerty, in terms, as being one of the subdivisions of the second head. Every case, therefore, applying to one species, applies also to the other. There is no substance in the distinction; and though it is said the 1st section concerning champerty, embraces everybody, it is the same of the 9th section, which relates to other kinds of maintenance. An offense under one section, would be subject to the same rules as one under the other. *Indeed, the 9th section is more [***640** general and comprehensive than the first.

The two cases cited by His Honor, *Judge* Woodworth, from Viner, obviate the objection that the contract was with Thallhimer, instead of his wife. Her right to maintain is transferred to him, and continues in him, so long as his interest is continued by the marriage, or a tenancy by the curtesy. Indeed, it has become an axiom, that any one having an interest may maintain; the ground of which is, that it would be absurd for a statute to deny one the right of protecting his own property.

It is said this must be a certain and definite interest, such as the law will enforce. But what kind of interest is that of the heir apparent or presumptive, which gentlemen admit forms an exception? The law will no more protect his interest, than it will that of the most remote expectant. His interest may be defeated by the ancestor at any time. A vested right, then, of which gentlemen speak, is not the only exception; nor is the certainty of the right the principle upon which it depends. Why is not our rule that kindred shall be excepted, equally certain? We all know what the word "kindred" means. It is a good consideration, as contradistinguished from a valuable one, and every lawyer knows that a deed, which would be void to a stranger, would be good between kindred. Courts act upon this distinction every day. Counsel advise upon it. You have only to inquire whether the parties are related. Acting upon such a rule would not, as gentlemen apprehend, repeal the Act, unless you find a man related to all the world. Why should not a brother, or uncle aid his brother or nephew? Must one stand by and see his relative stripped of his estate? He has a chance of inheritance which may become absolute the next day. The court, in *Wickham* v. *Conklin*, 8 Johns., 220, sanction this distinction.

But how does it appear that Mrs. Thallhimer is not, at least, heir presumptive, admitting the necessity of showing her to be so. Who is she? The sister of Teller, the owner. If he have no children, she is heir presumptive, though he may have other brothers or sisters. In the absence of *other proof, is it [***641** not fair to presume that she is heir presumptive? It lay with the other party to impeach the agreement, by showing that she was not so.

But it was enough that she was the sister, and consequently of the blood of Teller.

It was asked, suppose the father had attempted to devise to her by a will imperfectly witnessed, would it be lawful for her to maintain the suit of the heir, upon a contract to have part? I answer, unhesitatingly, yes. A court, I trust, will never be found to restrain an heir from perfecting such an imperfect will, by carrying into effect the lawful intent of the testator. It was asked, may a father maintain for his son-in-law, in consideration of part to be recovered. I answer this question also in the affirmative. The books agree that he may maintain for his son; and it follows that he may for the son's wife, in whose estate the son is interested. So of the daughter's husband.

Again; the saving in the 1st section of the Statute, in favor of counsel, parents and friends, extends to this case. To determine this construction we must refer to the authorities, and we ask no better for this purpose, than the one cited on the other side. 2 Inst., 563, 564. Ld. Coke there speaks of *prochein amies*. The Statute means not merely counsel, but aid and assistance. It would be idle for it to except mere advice, whether of counsel or friends. Hence the cases make a distinction between legal counsel and the aid of friends. Gentlemen put the case, that counsel cannot take part of the thing in controversy; but they wrongly infer that it is the same of friends. The opposite is the fair inference, and this accords with the opinion of the court below. They cite the 2 Inst., 564, which declares, that though the father be impleaded, he may infeoff his son, for his assistance, maintenance and comfort; for this is nature's profession. What is the meaning of this exposition, but that though counsel may not take part, yet the son may. He may enfeoff, &c.: that is, he may convey part in consideration of the son's aid. The language of the exception in the Act is, next friends; and the father is included in the words of the exception by way of example merely. The law **642***] of nature, as *Coke says, makes it the duty of relatives to support each other. Why did the Act make the exception if it meant merely counsel. It is made in the very Statute which speaks of taking a part of the thing in demand. This Act was framed from a variety of old statutes, by searching which, it will be observed that this exception is attached immediately to a clause prohibiting champerty. The original Act was express, that one might take counsel of a pleader for his fee, or of his next friends. Art. *super chart.* 28, Edw. I., ch. 11. The offense is, taking a part of the thing in demand. The exception of the advice of friends would be an idle exception. Our construction is, that you are not only at liberty to advise with your friend, but to give him a part of the thing in controversy. The terms giving liberty to take counsel allow this. It is the officious intermeddling that the Statute intended to guard against.

I ask a case in the whole round of 300 years where a relative was ever prosecuted for maintenance. I challenge the production of any case of champerty in a near relative; and I do hope the decision of this court will restore the rule as we contend for it—a rule which the case in the court below has, for the first time, broken in upon. The father may maintain the son, and yet, by the English law, the estate would escheat before he could inherit it.

But let the agreement be what it will as to other persons, Brinckerhoff cannot object to it. I seek not to enforce a contract null and void; but the defendant, a professional man, understanding his rights perfectly, has admitted everything necessary to make out a complete case against him. He knew, professionally, that the Act was not one of champerty. He went on, and instituted suits under the agreement, as attorney of Teller and Thallhimer. The agreement did not consider the suits certain. For aught the parties supposed, the lands might have been surrendered on sight of the title. The recital that Thallhimer's wife being Teller's sister, she was, therefore, in justice entitled, is conclusive upon the defendant, in whose mouth it does not lie to say there was no interest except what arose out of the contract. He recites, it is true, that she had no legal interest, *that is, not the [***643** legal title. It is enough that she had a just one. Who can say, that by some act of Teller's own, even prior to the marriage, he had not made her interested? I am speaking of the defendant's acts—his declarations in the agreement, of which he cannot deny one word. He admits a previous interest acquired by marriage. If so, it must have subsisted before the agreement; and the court will intend as against him, that some act was done by which an interest was lawfully conferred. Then it comes to this—two parties having an interest in certain property, the legal title to which is vested in one, agree, that when the property is recovered it shall go to both, according to their respective rights. It is the duty of the court to seize on every intendment in favor of sustaining an agreement, such as this, made between near relations.

THE CHANCELLOR. Champerty, maintenance and barratry were defined as offenses, in very early stages of the English law. These practices seem to have been then common in England, and they were denounced not only as sins very heinous in themselves, and highly injurious to the peace of society, but also as offenses which actually interrupted the course of public justice. The excitement of suits is an evil, when suits are unjust; but when right is withheld, and the object of a suit is just, to promote the suit is to promote justice. That a resort to the public tribunals for justice, should produce injustice, can be true, only where the administration of justice is weak or corrupt, or where the laws are very imperfect. Where the administration of justice is firm, pure, and equal to all, and where the laws give adequate redress for groundless suits, it is not easy to conceive, that mischief can arise from opening the courts of justice to all suitors, or from contracts by which the fruits of a suit may be divided between him who has the right of action, and him who has contributed advice, expense or exertion, to institute the suit, or prosecute it to effect. The right of litigating may be abused, and proper remedies for groundless and vexatious litigation must exist; but the remedies for the abuse of this right should be such as not to impair the *free use of the right itself. As the [***644** justice or injustice of the claim cannot be known before the termination of the cause, the checks upon unjust litigation must, in general, consist, not in excluding the suit or the suitor from the courts, but in redress following the decision of justice upon the merits of the cause.

The Roman law, by its provisions for preventing groundless and vexatious suits, required that the plaintiff should take an oath that the suit was not commenced from malice, and that he believed his cause to be legal and just. The defendant was required to swear, that in his belief the plaintiff had no just claim. The advocates on both sides were required to take similar oaths. If the plaintiff failed in his suit, he was fined in a sum, which was sometimes a tenth part of the demand; and in cases of great malice and vexation, the plaintiff was farther punished by a decree of ignominy. Inst., bk. 4, tit. 16; Code, bk. 2, tit. 59; Dig., bk. 5, tit. 1-79; Inst., bk. 4, tit. 1-33; Huber. Prælect., 457, 1478; Wood's Civil Law, 341.

The English doctrine of maintenance arose from causes peculiar to the state of the society in which it was established. The great reason for the suppression of champerty and maintenance was an apprehension that justice itself was endangered by these practices. Blackstone, 4 Com., 135, speaks of this offense as preverting the process of law into an engine of oppression. In the case of *Slywright* v. *Page*, 1 Leon., 167, it was, said by the whole Court of C. P., that the meaning of the Stat. of the 32 Hen. VIII. concerning maintenance, was "to repress the practices of many who when they thought they had title or right to any land, for the furtherance of their pretended right, conveyed their interest in some part thereof to great persons, and with their countenance, did oppress the possessors." The power of great men, to whom rights of action were transferred, in order to obtain support and favor in suits brought to assert those rights; the confederacies which were thus formed; and the oppression which followed from the influence of great men, in such cases, are themes of complaint, in the early books of the English **645***] law. While the *power of nobles and great men was felt in the administration of justice, these practices seem to have produced real and great evils. In that state of things, instead of invigorating and purifying the administration of justice, as the direct remedy for such evils, the laws concerning champerty and maintenance were established, as penal regulations intended to operate upon the parties to these transactions.

In modern times, and since England has enjoyed a pure and firm administration of justice, these evils are little felt; and champerty and maintenance are now seldom mentioned, as occurring in fact, or as producing mischief in that country. The Statute for the Limitation of Actions, the Statute of Frauds, the extension of the action for malicious prosecutions, and the costs given against unsuccessful parties, have all taken place since the law of maintenance was established, and all these alterations have contributed to prevent or punish groundless and vexatious litigation.

It was a principle of the common law, that a right of action could not be transferred by him who had the right to another. When we seek the reason of this rule, we find it in the motive already mentioned, an apprehension that justice would fail, and oppression would follow, if rights of action might be assigned. "Nothing," says Coke (Co. Litt., 114 *a*); "nothing in action, entry or re-entry can be granted over; for so, under color thereof, pretended titles might be granted to great men, whereby right might be trodden down, and the weak oppressed." Feeble, partial and corrupt must have been the administration of justice where such a reason could have force. In early times this rule concerning rights of action was vigorously enforced. As the entire right of action could not be assigned, so no part of it could be transferred, and no man could purchase another's right to a suit, either in whole or in part. Hence the doctrine of maintenance, which prohibits contracts for a part of the thing in demand, was adopted as an auxiliary regulation, to enforce the general principle which prohibited the transfer of all rights of action. But the rule of the common law, that rights of action cannot be assigned, has in modern times been reversed; the apprehension that justice *would be trodden [***646** down if property in action should be transferred, is no longer entertained; and the ancient rule now serves only to give form to some legal proceedings. In the courts of equity this rule was never followed, and those courts have always considered and treated the rule as unjust, and have supported assignments of rights of action. Experience has fully shown, not only that no evil results from the assignment of rights of action, but that the public good is greatly promoted by the free commerce and circulation of property in action, as well as of property in possession.

The general law, both in England and here, now is, that rights of action may be transferred; and as the laws concerning maintenance are still in force, the present state of the law is, that while an entire right of action may be transferred to a purchaser, with complete effect, a contract to transfer a part of a right of action is void. The primary rule forbidding the assignment of a right of action has ceased, but the auxiliary sanction concerning the assignment of a part of such a right remains in force. The English judges, feeling that the original reasons for the law of champerty and maintenance had ceased, have gradually mitigated that law by interpretations and exceptions; and the present state of English opinion on this subject may be seen in 4 T. R., 340, 341; where Buller, *J.*, expresses himself in terms which do not disguise his contempt for the whole doctrine of maintenance.

In many of the States of this Union these laws are not in force, and the want of them, is said to be no inconvenience.

These observations are made to show that in examining the English law, and English authorities concerning champerty and maintenance, we must, in order to ascertain the sense and extent of their doctrines, bear in mind the state of society which produced them, the evils for which they were intended to afford a remedy, and the different state of things to which they are now applicable. It is only by this recurrence to history that we can trace the true reasons of the English law; the causes of the horror with which the maintenance *of suits was viewed in [***647** early times; the decline and fall of the rule of the common law, that things in action were not vendible; and the different views, which at different times have had influence upon the judicial expositions of the law of maintenance in England.

Our Statute concerning Champerty and Maintenance is a compilation of the several English statutes relating to the same subjects, and it declares certain contracts void. This Statute, throughout, makes or supposes a distinction, which before prevailed in the rules of the common law, between maintenance which is innocent and that which is unlawful. To maintain the suit of another is unlawful, unless the person maintaining has some interest on the subject of the suit, or unless he is connected with the suitor in some social relation. These are the exceptions to a general rule, and they are exceptions which rest upon the strongest ground of reason as well as the support of authority.

Where the person promoting the suit of another, has any interest whatever in the thing demanded, distinct from that which he may acquire by an agreement with the suitor, he is, in effect, also a suitor, according to the nature and extent of his interest. To deny to such a person the benefit which he might receive from a suit conducted mainly or partly for the benefit of another, would be to close the temple of justice against all persons not parties to the suit, and yet having interests in the subject of litigation, which may be affected by the determination of the cause. It is, accordingly, a principle, that any interest whatever in the subject of the suit, is sufficient to exempt him who gives aid to the suitor from the charge of illegal maintenance. Whether this interest is great or small, vested or contingent, certain or uncertain, it affords a just reason to him who has such an interest to participate in the suit of another, who also has or claims some right to the same subject. Bac. Abr., tit. Maintenance, B, and the several authorities there cited.

Where there is consanguinity or affinity between the suitor and him who gives aid to the suit, the voice of nature, and the language of the law equally declare that such assistance is **648***] *not unlawful maintenance. The relation of landlord and tenant, that of master and servant, acts of charity to the poor, and the exercise of the legal profession, are all cases in which it is not unlawful to give aid in the conduct of suits before the courts of justice.

Upon all such cases these laws were never intended to operate. They were intended to prevent the interference of strangers having no pretense of right in the subject of the suit, and standing in no relation of duty to the suitor. They were intended to prevent traffic in doubtful claims, and to operate upon buyers of pretended rights, who had no relation to the suitor or the subject otherwise than as purchasers of the profits of litigation.

It has been urged that champerty and maintenance are distinct offenses, and that champerty is illegal, in many cases, in which maintenance in other modes would be lawful. If principles are considered, it seems to be of little moment, whether he who maintains the suit of another receives his reward from the subject of the suit, or from any other property of the suitor Champerty is one species of maintenance; but the authorities do not declare contracts for a part of the thing in demand, universally unlawful. The distinction made by the books between interference which is illegal and that which is lawful, consists in the rule and the exceptions already stated; and where maintenance is lawful, as in the case of interest in the subject, or relation to the suitor, a contract to divide the subject of the suit, which is maintenance in a particular form, is also legal.

In this case the wife of Thallhimer was the sister of Teller, and this relation, recited in the contract, evidently led Thallhimer and Teller to the contract itself. Thallhimer did not obtrude himself into the concerns of a stranger, but he agreed to give aid to his relative, as he might justifiably do. He was not the promoter of litigation in which he had no concern. His wife might inherit Teller's lands; and this reason, alone, exempts the contract before us from the imputation of champerty or illegal maintenance. It is immaterial to this question, whether the contingencies which must occur before Teller's sister could inherit, were such *as to render that event [**649** probable or not. She might become the owner of these lands, as the heir of Teller; and this potential interest was a sufficient reason that her husband should join in measures to recover the lands.

The charge of champerty or maintenance, being the only objection made to this agreement, and that objection not being applicable to this case, the agreement is valid. The action now brought against Brinckerhoff is *assumpsit* for money received by him for the use of Thallhimer. The contract not transferring any right in the lands themselves to Thallhimer, the legal title remained in Teller, who had power to bring suits, to compromise the claim, and to release the legal title. Teller did compromise the claim and did release the legal title to the possessors of the land for a sum of money; this was done by Brinckerhoff acting under a power from Teller, and the money was received by Brinckerhoff. After these facts had occurred, there never could be a conveyance of any right in the lands from Teller to Thallhimer; and the agreement could have effect, only by considering the money received, as substituted for the land, in respect to the rights of Thallhimer under the contract. The construction gives effect to the contract, and must be adopted as the sense of the contract itself, and as a necessary consequence from the events succeeding the contract, which rendered any conveyance of a right in the lands impossible The compromise was valid, both in respect to Teller and the possessors of the land; and if this agreement now has any effect, it must operate upon the money received, as it might have operated upon the land, had the land itself been specifically recovered. If this contract could be defeated by acts of Teller and Brinckerhoff, in which Thallhimer had no part, and over which he had no control, the most flagrant injustice would be done to Thallhimer. The sense of the contract evidently is, that in the event of success, Thallhimer shall have one fourth part of the property, whether the fruits of the claim should be realized in one species of property or another.

*The rights of Thallhimer in this [***650** suit arises from his agreement with Teller, from the act of Teller in authorizing the compromise, and from the acts of Brinckerhoff in commencing the actions of ejectment, in making the compromise and receiving the money. In commencing the actions of ejectment, Brinckerhoff acted as the attorney of both Thallhimer and Teller. In making the compromise, he acted as the agent of Teller, in respect to the possessors of the land; for Teller having the legal title, he alone could give a power to compromise. But as Brinckerhoff had full knowledge of the rights of Thallhimer under the agreement, he may be justly regarded, in making the compromise, as the agent of both Thallhimer and Teller, in respect to their rights and according to their respective interests. In these circumstances, the action for money received for the plaintiff is entirely proper; the use of that form being to allow the introduction of the express contract and all the acts of the parties; and also to give effect to any tacit promise which law and justice may infer from all the facts of the case. The agreement determines that Thallhimer's share of the money is one fourth part; and Brinckerhoff had not paid, as he ought not to have paid, this fourth part to Teller. This share is money belonging to Thallhimer, and remaining in the hands of Brinckerhoff. Thus, the objections made to the form of this suit appear to be destitute of weight.

My opinion is, that the judgment of the Supreme Court should be reversed, and that the cause should be again sent to trial.

The Court being unanimously of this opinion, it was thereupon ordered, adjudged and decreed that the judgment of the Supreme Court in this cause be reversed, with costs in error to be taxed for the plaintiff in error; and that the transcript be remitted to the said Supreme Court; and that the said court award a *venire facias de novo.*

Doubted—31 Am. Rep., 57 (60 Ala., 582).
Cited in—6 Cow., 94; 4 Wend., 310; 8 Wend., 635; 9 Wend., 536; 20 Wend., 221; 5 Den., 312; 5 N. Y., 347; 14 N. Y., 296; 14 Barb., 450; 19 Barb., 439; 22 Cal., 95.
See 6 Cow., 90.

651*] *WILLIAM SHARPSTEEN, *Plaintiff in Error,*

v.

WILLIAM M. TILLOU, *Defendant in Error.*

Construction of Will—Power, to Executors to Sell Realty—Object of Power being Frustrated, Power Fails—Whether Power Survives Death of one Executor.

H. made his will, by which he devised his house, &c., to his wife, and a comfortable maintenance so her, out of the income of his real estate, so long at she remained his widow; to his two sons, E and I., the use and improvement of all his real estate, except their mother's maintenance during her natural life; and directed that after her decease, all his real estate should be sold; and gave to his two sons, E. and I., £150 a piece, and to his five sons all the rest of his estate of all kinds, to be equally divided between them, and appointed L. D. and his son I. executors for the purposes in his will mentioned. L. and D., strangers to the family, alone, proved the will, and took upon themselves its execution. The testator died, leaving a widow and his five sons, and the children of a deceased daughter. The widow having died, I. having also died without issue, and E. and another son having died leaving issue, the two executors, L. and D. sold the real estate. Held, that the objects of the testator, having been, in a great measure, defeated, and his intentions in giving the power frustrated, the power itself failed; and the sale was consequently void, so far as it depended upon the power; but the two surviving sons having also conveyed all their interest to the grantee of the executors; held that their conveyance passed two fifths of the real estate; that the power being inoperative, the real estate descended to the heirs at law.

The purpose of a testator, in giving a power by his will to sell real estate, must be ascertained from all the provisions of the will; and the objects of the power must be considered in connection with the power itself.

A power to sell real estate in a will fails when its objects are unattainable.

Where one directs his executors to sell land, it seems this is a naked authority, not coupled with an interest. There is no estate vested in the executors as such: and on the death of one executor, the power would not survive at common law. Opinion of the Supreme Court, not considered on error.

It seems that the 11th section of the Act Concerning Wills (1 R. L., 366) merely provides for the case of an executor who refuses to act; but where executors are directed to sell the land, thus having a naked authority, if one die, though he never qualified as executor, the power is gone. (*Id.*)

It seems that where land is devised to executors to be sold, the survivor or survivors might sell at common law. (*Id.*)

Citation—6 Johns., 73.

ERROR from the Supreme Court upon a special verdict. The action in the court below was brought by Tillou against Sharpsteen, upon covenants of seisin contained in two deeds *in fee, from Sharpsteen [*652 and his wife to Tillou, for two several parcels of land in the Town of Washington, Dutchess Co., dated Mar. 16, 1819. The cause was tried at the Dutchess Circuit, where the jury found a special verdict; that after the deeds were executed, the plaintiff below, on or about Apr. 1, 1819, entered upon and occupied the premises for a short time; that Moses Hallock, deceased, was, at the time of his death, seised in fee of the premises in question; that he died in 1803, leaving a widow and several children his heirs at law, having made his last will; that Phebe Hallock, who was the only witness sworn on the trial to establish the will, swore that herself, Edward Hallock and John Allen were subscribing witnesses to the will; that Edward was the son of Moses Hallock, the testator, and Edward is now deceased; that Phebe, the witness, was his wife, and now his widow; that John Allen is infirm and unable to attend court, and is unfit to give testimony from loss of mind; that the will was duly executed by Moses, the testator, and witnessed by the above named witnesses, in presence of each other and the testator; that, by this will, the testator directed his executors to pay his debts, &c., gave to his wife, if she outlived him, the best room in his house, two cows, her choice of one of his horses, all his household furniture, she to have a good comfortable maintenance out of the income of his real estate as long as she remained his widow; then, after several legacies, he gave to his two sons, Edward and Isaac M., the use and improvement of all his real estate, except their mother's maintenance, during her natural life; and directed that, after her decease, all his real estate should be sold; and gave to his two sons, Edward and Isaac M., £150 a piece; and

NOTE.—*Power to executors to sell—Failure of intent of testator—Power fails, when.* Compare above case with Jackson v. Jansen, 6 Johns., 73; Slocum v. Slocum, 4 Edw., 613.

then, his will was that his five sons, Isaiah, Peter, Obadiah, Edward and Isaac M. have all the rest of his estate, of all kinds, not before disposed of, to be equally divided between them. He then appointed Phineas Lounsberry, Samuel Doughty and his son Isaac M. his executors for the purposes in his will mentioned; that Doughty and Lounsberry, two only of the executors, ever proved or took on them the execution of the will; they did this Sept. 3, 1803; that the testator, at his death, left a **653***]*widow, Bridget Hallock, and five sons, before named, and six grandchildren, the children of his deceased daughter Miriam; that Obadiah died in the year 1810, leaving four children who are yet alive; that Isaiah and Peter are now living; that Edward died in 1810, leaving Phebe his widow and three children, two of whom are living, and one dead; that Isaac M. died in June, 1817, without issue, was never married, nor did he leave any last will or testament; that Bridget, the widow of Moses Hallock, died in the spring of 1818; that the children of Miriam are living; that Lounsberry and Doughty, as acting executors of the will of Moses Hallock, executed a deed for the premises in question to the defendant below, William Sharpsteen, dated Aug. 29, 1818; that Isaiah Hallock and Peter Hallock also executed their deed to the defendant below, William Sharpsteen, for the premises in question, dated May 21, 1818; but whether, &c., and if, &c., the jury assessed the damages at $3,578.56, being three fifths of the consideration money in the deeds to the plaintiff below, with interest.

On this verdict the Supreme Court gave judgment for the plaintiff below, with $225.54 costs, making with the damages $3,803.80, in Jan. Term, 1823, for which they gave their reasons as follows:

Reasons for the judgment in the court below.

The intention of the testator, in directing a sale, seems to have been, among other things, to provide for Edward and Isaac, by securing to them £150 each, out of the avails of the farm, in the first instance, and then an equal share with the other sons. This cannot be carried into effect, because Edward and his wife being witnesses, the devise to him is void. 1 R. L., 367; 4 Johns., 311; 1 Johns. Cas., 163. Thus one object in view, when the power to sell was created, cannot be attained. Isaac also died before his mother. As to him the £150 are lapsed, for it was a personal devise to him solely. If the sale by the executors is held valid, they cannot make distribution according to the will.

The subsequent events are such, that had they been foreseen by the testator a sale would not have been directed. In construction of these powers, the intent is much regarded. **654***] *If the object in creating the power ceases, the lands descend to the heirs at law. 6 Johns., 73. On this ground we think the sale by the executors cannot be supported.

On another ground, the sale is void. This is a naked authority to sell, not coupled with an interest. There is no previous estate created and vested in the executors as such. On the death of one executor, the power at common law would not survive. *Bergen* v. *Bennet*, 1 Cai. Cas., 16.

The 11th section of the Statute Concerning Wills (1 R. L., 366) provides for the case when part of the executors refuse to act, and makes valid all sales made by executors who take charge of the administration of the will. It leaves untouched the case of one of the executors dying before the sale. The Statute recognizes the distinction between lands devised to executors, to be sold, and a devise directing them to sell the lands. In the former case, no statute provision was necessary to sanction a sale by surviving executors. In the latter, the Legislature left the power, in the event of the death of one of the executors, to the operation of the common law. But whether the power was with or without an interest, all the executors must join, if living. The Statute was passed to provide a remedy in case of refusal to act.

The defendant, however, having a sufficient conveyance from the two of the sons of Moses Hallock, the plaintiff is entitled to recover three fifths of the consideration money, only, and interest.

Mr. J. Tallmadge, for the plaintiff in error, contended that the judgment in the court below should be reversed, for the following reasons:

1. Because the power to sell contained in the will was sufficient, and well executed by the two surviving executors; and their deed was effectual to pass the entire estate.

2. Because, if the power to sell was insufficient, or not well executed, yet the will was not void, but contained a good devise in fee, and the deed from Peter and Isaiah Hallock, the two surviving sons, conveyed a greater interest in the premises than two fifths, as declared in the judgment of the court.

*He said, the judgment was errone- [***655** ous, both in fact and law. If, as the Supreme Court assume, the power was void, then the judgment was for too much, provided the will is to operate for any purpose. The court say the devise to Isaac M. lapsed in consequence of his dying before the mother. If so, it descended to the other children of the testator, the grantors, Isaiah and Peter taking each one fifth of that share, which also passed by the deed, and should have been deducted from the verdict. The court disregarded the several lapses, which happened by the death of the several heirs, three or whom died in the lifetime of their mother. Edward and his wife witnessing the will, the devise to them being therefore void, this descended, in equal shares, to all. The interest of Isaiah and Peter, being two fifths also, in this share, passed by their deed. But taking the principles assumed by the court below, and allowing the will to be void, still they have given judgment for too much, by one fifth of Isaac M.'s share, who died without issue.

But the principles assumed in relation to this will, by the court below were not correct. The testator professes to disposes of all his estate, real and personal. After bequeathing several legacies, and making several devises, he disposes of all the residue of his personal estate to his five sons, and provides for the sale of his real estate, and the distribution of the avails. Two of his sons were to have £150 each, and the five to take the residue. Now suppose the power to sell was void, or incapable of execution, the whole passed to the five sons under the residuary clause. Though a power to sell be inoperative, there is nothing to prevent a residuary clause, embracing the fee, taking full effect. The court had no right to pronounce the will void *in toto*, because a part of it failed. Then Isaiah and Peter took two fifths under this clause; and, by the death of Isaac without issue, they took two fifths of his share which passed by the deed. This makes the judgment erroneous for so much.

But the court erred in saying that the power became void. They go on the ground that where a power is given by the will to sell, and the object fails, the power goes with it; and they maintain and illustrate the position, by **656***] the case of *a power to sell for the maintenance of a widow, who dies before the sale. *Jackson* v. *Jansen*, 6 Johns., 73. This is a very different case. Where a beneficial interest in the sale is given to several, because one dies, it does not follow that the power ceases as to all. If the object totally fails, the power fails also. Not so as to a partial failure; and the power shall be executed for the residue. Here the object still remains as to two of the devisees, who are living.

The court say, that in the construction of these powers the intent is to be regarded. This is admitted in its fullest extent, and is, undoubtedly, applicable to the whole will. Here was a clear intent not to die intestate. The court will almost disregard and break down the words of a power and a will, providing for a sale of lands, in order to effectuate this intent. *Jackson* v. *Given*, 16 Johns., 167. No intendment should be received, to defeat the intent not to die intestate, so plainly manifest upon this will. Yet the court below have totally disregarded it. Miriam's children are let in, to share in the descent, though the ancestor expressly excluded them.

As to the number of executors necessary to execute the power—if this power be annexed to the office of executor, all the authorities agree that it may be executed by those only who take the trust. This will does annex the power to the office. The testator directs the payment of his debts, and without saying by whom, the sale of his real estate. He then appoints his executors, in terms, for the purposes mentioned in the will. All the authorities agree that where no one is designated to sell, the executors, as such, are to do it. It belongs to them *virtute officii*. It is only where persons are specifically designated as a kind of attorneys for the purposes of the sale, that the strict doctrine advanced by the court below prevails. I contend, therefore, that the power was well executed by the survivors. *Osgood* v. *Franklin*, 2 Johns. Ch., 1, 20, 21; 14 Johns., 527; S. C., on appeal, *Id.*, 553; *Jackson* v. *Ferriss*, 15, *Id.*, 346; *Jackson* v. *Jansen*, 6 *Id.*, 73. All the authorities are referred to in these cases. *Davoue* v. *Fanning*, 2 Johns. Ch., 254; *Blatch* v. *Wilder*, 1 Atk., 420; and Sugd. on **657***] *Pow., 167, &c., are direct authorities to show that executors are the proper persons to sell lands not expressly directed to be sold by others, especially where the avails are intended to pay legacies. Here the avails were to be distributed among the children—a disposition in the nature of a legacy. In *Lessee of Zebach* v. *Smith*, 3 Binn., 69, the will ordered thus: "The executors, namely: A, B and C, shall be empowered to sell my land, &c., and to give a good right." Two of the executors refused to act, and one only sold. The court held this well, and said that one might sell alone in all cases where the power is annexed to the office of executor. *Id.*, 73.

The court say that the 1 R. L., 366, sec. 11, provides for the case when part of the executors refuse to act, leaving untouched this case, where one of the executors dies before the sale. In *Davoue* v. *Fanning*, 2 Johns. Ch., 254, the *Chancellor* said: "If all the executors named had the power by the will, then the sole acting executor has the power by the Statute (1 R. L., 366), on the neglect or refusal of the rest of the executors to act." The Statute declares, expressly, that if part refuse to act, all the power to sell shall devolve on those who qualify and take the trust; and the court say that the power is gone notwithstanding, if he who stands out die before it is fully consummated. This we deny. The full power passes instantly to those who take the trust; and no subsequent events can defeat this effect. The executor refusing is considered as having never existed; and this reasoning will be found strengthened, by comparing the Statute as it first passed (1 Jones & Var., 153) with the subsequent revisions. The survivor is expressly declared, by the old Act, to possess the power; and without this, the evil of the old law is not fully remedied.

Mr. G. Bloom, for the defendant in error, contended: 1. That the two surviving executors had not power to sell at the time of the conveyance to Sharpsteen. 2. That the judgment of the Supreme Court was correct, as to the rule of damages adopted by them.

*He said the power did not survive [***658** to the two executors. It became a naked power by the death of one, the survivors being strangers to the family, and having no interest in the subject. It does not appear that there were any debts to pay, or other charges against the estate. There were no practicable objects to be attained by the sale, after the widow's death. This will directs the executors to sell. There is no unqualified command to do this. All the authorities agree that a power conferred by such language is a naked one. "If a man, by his will, direct his executors to sell his land, this is but a bare authority to sell, without interest; for the land, in the meantime, descends to the heir at law, who, until the sale, would, at common law, be entitled to the profits—and being but a naked authority, if one of the executors die, the power, at the common law, would not survive." *Bergen* v. *Bennet*, 1 Cai. Cas., 16; Pow. on Dev., 291 to 310; 3 Salk., 277; Co. Litt., 113 *a*; *Id.*, 181 *c*; *Id.*, 236. It is a general rule that a power not coupled with an interest is a naked power. A power simply collateral, and without interest, or a naked power, is when, to a mere stranger, authority is given to dispose of an interest in which he has no estate whatever. Pow. on Pow., 8, 10, 12; Butler's *note*, 298 to Co. Litt., 342 *b*; *Edwards* v. *Sleater*, Hardr., 415, 416. In all the cases cited against the position for which I contend, there was a power coupled with an interest, or a trust committed, capable of execution at the time.

It is agreed that the intention is much regarded in the construction of these powers. What was the testator's intention in the instance before us? First, to provide for the widow, by leaving her in charge of Edward and Isaac his sons; second, to provide for them, by giving each, on a sale of the estate, $375. The latter object could never be accomplished by the sale. Edward and his wife being witnesses, the devise to them was void (1 R. L., 367, sec. 12; *Jackson* v. *Denniston*, 4 Johns., 311; *Same* v. *Woods*, 1 Johns. Cas., 163), and Isaac died before his mother, without heirs, and without a will. Of course, his share lapsed, and diffused itself among all the brothers and sisters. Toll. L. E., 171, 2, 3, 305, 304. Indeed, whether it lapsed or vested, **659***] *can make no difference, because it would descend in the same manner, at his death, to his brother's and sister's children. The provision for both, then, failed. The intention of the testator was defeated. Beside, the gift to Edward and Isaac was personal—not to them and their heirs. The farm was sold for $3,000, fifteen years after the testator's death. Taking out $750, would leave only $450 to each of the five sons. Edward never took any interest in this, and Isaac died before the sale. How the executors could substitute takers of the sale money, so as to fulfill the testator's intention, it is impossible to conceive. Every member of the family would get more or less than the testator intended.

Again; when every material object contemplated by a testator, in framing his will, fails, the will itself must, of consequence, fail, and the property be regulated by the statute of descent and distribution. Could the testator here have been foreseen the changes which have occurred in his family, will any one suppose that he would have left such a will?

The court below were correct in saying that our Act (1 R. L., 366) does not apply to a survivorship of executors, but leaves the case as it stood at the common law.

If the court, however, should think that the power did not survive to Lounsberry and Doughty, and yet consider the will good, then they will affirm the judgment of the Supreme Court in part and reverse it in part, exercising a discretion as to the costs. *Waters* v. *Travis*, 8 Johns., 566; *Anonymous*, 12, *Id.*, 340. The judgment was founded on the supposition that the will is void, and that Peter and Isaiah conveyed only two fifths of the farm; whereas, if the will be good, they were entitled to two fifths of the whole, and also two fifths of Edward's and two fifths of Isaac's lapsed shares. This would lessen the amount of the judgment some, but not to any considerable amount.

THE CHANCELLOR. The objects which the testator seems to have contemplated, in directing that his real estate should be sold after the decease of his widow, have been, to a great extent, defeated by himself, by rules of law, and by events which occurred after his death. **660***] His son Edward, being a *witness to the will, could take nothing under it, and all the beneficial intentions of the testator towards this son are ineffectual. If the bequest of £150 to his son Isaac M. is considered as payable from the product of the real estate when sold, and such is the sense of the will, this contingent legacy fails—Isaac M. having died before the power to sell was or could be exerted. The intended dispositions of the money which should arise from the sale of the real estate are, to a great extent, impossible; and in these circumstances, the intentions of the testator in giving the power, are frustrated This power to sell cannot be disjoined from the other provisions of the will; the purposes of the testator in giving the power, as in other respects, must be ascertained from all the provisions of the instrument, and the objects of the power must be considered in connection with the power itself. In the case of *Jackson* v. *Jansen*, 6 Johns., 73, the Supreme Court held that where the object of a testator in giving a power to sell had ceased, the power itself also ceased. In this case I am of opinion that by the total nullity of the will in respect to the portions of the estate intended for Edward, and by the failure of the legacy of £250 to Isaac M., the objects of the power had so far failed that there was not a valid power to sell, in 1818, when a sale was made by two of the executors. The power fails, because its objects are unattainable.

It is urged by the counsel of Sharpsteen, that if the power to sell failed, the five sons of the testator took the land, as devisees. But this seems not to be the sense of that clause of the will, by which the testator gives all the rest of his estate not before disposed of to his five sons. The testator had before made dispositions of all his real estate, and his intention concerning the residue must be understood to exclude his land. He had, indeed, previously disposed of all his movable estate; but whether the terms "movable estate" were used by him to comprehend all his personal estate, or in some sense more restricted, is uncertain. The testator, in making the final bequest of the residue of all his estate, seems to *have [***661** supposed that his land would be sold, and might produce a sum greater than would be sufficient to discharge the legacies; and upon that supposition, he probably meant to dispose of such an excess. But his intentions declared by this will are to a great extent null, and the last disposing clause of the will seems not to be a devise in fee of his land.

The land of Moses Hallock, not being devised in fee, and being subject only to the temporary charges made in the will, descended by his death to his heirs at law. His heirs were five sons and six children of a deceased daughter. Each of his five sons, therefore, took a sixth part, and the children of his deceased daughter took another sixth part of his land.

Isaac M. Hallock died in 1817, intestate, and without issue. His heirs were his brothers Isaiah and Peter, the children of his deceased sister, those of his deceased brother Edward, and those of his deceased brother Obadiah. The share of Isaac M. in the land of his father thus descended in five portions, Isaiah and Peter each taking a fifth part of that share.

Isaiah and Peter, as heirs of their father, each took a sixth part, and as heirs of their brother Isaac M., each of them took a fifth part of his sixth part of the land. These fractions added, and more simply expressed, are two fifths of the whole; and the result of all these descents gave to Isaiah and Peter the same proportion of the whole, which they would have taken had the land descended by the death of Moses Hallock in five shares, instead of six. Isaiah and Peter were thus, severally, owners of one fifth part of the land, May 21, 1818, when they conveyed all their title to Sharpsteen, and he then acquired a title to two fifths of the land in question.

The conveyance from the executors being void, for want of a sufficient power; the conveyance from Isaiah and Peter being valid, to the extent of their rights; and their rights embracing two fifths of the subject, the title conveyed by Sharpsteen to Tillou has failed, **662***] in respect to the three fifth *parts of the land. I am, accordingly, of opinion that there is no error in the decision of the Supreme Court.

The Court being unanimously of this opinion, it was therefore ordered, adjudged and decreed that the plaintiff take nothing by his writ; and that the defendant go thereof without day. And it was further ordered adjudged and decreed that the defendant recover against the plaintiff his costs to be taxed, in defending the writ of error in this cause; and that the record be remitted, &c.

Cited in—21 Wend., 441; 4 Edw., 617; 1 N. Y., 358; 50 N. Y., 435; 66 N. Y., 174; 69 N. Y., 13; 7 Lans., 238; 6 Hun, 221; 1 Barb., 101; 49 Barb., 133; 33 How. Pr., 234; 2 Bradf., 113.

THE PRESIDENT, DIRECTORS AND COMPANY OF THE BANK OF UTICA, *Plaintiffs in Error,*

v.

A. K. & G. M. SMEDES AND A. CAMFIELD, *Defendants in Error.*

Negotiable Paper—Duty of Banks in Collecting—Consideration, for Undertaking to Give Notice to Indorsers—Pleading and Practice—Powers of Corporations—When Demand Notes should be Presented.

The indorsement and delivery of a promissory note to a bank, on its request, is a sufficient consideration for an undertaking, on the part of the Bank, to charge the indorser by a regular notice of non-payment; and if they neglect to do this, the holder or owner of the note, to whom the promise is made, may maintain an action against them, and recover damages for neglect.

A count for such neglect would be good as a count for a misfeasance, the receipt of the note, and neglect to perform the undertaking, being properly a mismanagement of the business undertaken. The acceptance of the note by the Bank may well be considered the first step in the execution of the contract, and no other consideration is necessary.

Objections, not taken in the Supreme Court, cannot be taken in the Court of Errors.

A corporation may make any contract, to do an act at any place, if such contract be within the scope of its general power.

It seems that a statute incorporating a bank is, in its nature, a public statute.

The declaration stated that the Bank of Utica had, pursuant to the Act of the Legislature, passed Apr. 10, 1815, established an office of discount and deposit in Canandaigua. Held, a sufficient recital of the Act in pleading, though it should be considered a private Act; especially after verdict.

The declaration alleged that the defendants had undertaken to charge the first indorser of notes payable on demand; and set forth this first indorsement of the notes to the plaintiffs as having been made on a day certain—the indorsement and delivery of the notes, by the plaintiffs, to the *de- [*663 fendants, about six months thereafter—and their undertaking at the latter time. Held sufficient, especially after verdict, though the declaration did not aver that the demand of payment was made within a reasonable time.

What is a reasonable time, within which a note payable on demand should be presented for payment, in order to charge an indorser, depends on all the facts of the case, to be proved at the trial.

The power of a verdict, to cure formal defects in pleading, should be liberally applied.

Citation—Act, April 10, 1815.

ERROR, from the Supreme Court. The cause was tried in the court below at the Ontario Circuit, in June, 1821, before the late *Mr. Justice Yates*, the venue, which was originally laid in the County of N. Y., having been changed by an order of the court.

The declaration, the only part of the proceedings questioned upon the writ of error, consisted, besides the money counts, of three special counts, the first of which was as follows:

City and County of New York, *ss.* The President, &c., of the Bank of Utica was summoned to answer A. K. Smedes, &c., of a plea of trespass on the case, &c.; and thereupon the said A. K. Smedes, &c., by Evert A. Bancker, their attorney, complain for this, to wit: that whereas, on the 14th day of February, 1818, and before and since that time, at the 1st ward in the City of New York, and in the County of New York, A. K. Smedes, G. M. Smedes and Abiel Camfield, plaintiffs, were merchants and copartners in trade, under that name, style and firm of A. & G. Smedes & Camfield; and whereas, also, the before named defendants, the President, &c., of the Bank of Utica, on the day and year aforesaid, and before and since that time, pursuant to the Act of the Legislature of the State of New York, passed the 10th day of April, A. D. 1815, had established an office of discount and deposit in Canandaigua, to wit: at the 1st ward in the City of New York, and in the County of New York, and were then and there transacting and doing business as bankers, by virtue of the Act aforesaid, under the name, style and description of the Utica Branch Bank in Canandaigua; and whereas, also, on the 12th day of August, A. D. 1817, at, &c., *to wit: at, &c., Punder- [*664 son B. Underhill and Harris Seymour were merchants and copartners in trade, under the name, style and firm of Underhill & Seymour; and whereas, also, on the said 12th day of August, A. D. 1817, the before named P. B. Underhill and H. Seymour, at, &c., to wit: at, &c., or one of them, for and in the name of the said firm of Underhill & Seymour, made a certain note in writing, commonly called a promissory note,

NOTE.—*Duty of banks as collection agents—Consideration for their undertaking to charge indorsers of negotiable paper deposited with them for collection.* See Allen v. Suydam, 20 Wend., 321; Allen v. Bank, 22 Wend., 215.

Corporation—Powers of. See People v. Utica Ins. Co., 15 Johns., 358, *note.*

Note payable on demand—When should be presented for payment. See Furman v. Haskin, 2 Cai., 369; Conroy v. Warren, 3 Johns. Cas., 259, *notes.*

Public and private statutes. See Jenkins v. Union Turnpike Road, 1 Cai. Cas., 86.

bearing date the same day and year last aforesaid, and then and there delivered the said note to a certain John C. Spencer; by which said note, the said P. B. Underhill and H. Seymour, under the name and signature of Underhill & Seymour, promised to pay to the order of the said John C. Spencer, by the name and description of John C. Spencer, Esquire, at the Utica Branch Bank, $1,237, with interest from date, for value received; and the said J. C. Spencer, to whom, or to whose order, the payment of the said sum of money mentioned in the said note, was to be made as aforesaid, afterwards, and before the payment of the said sum of money mentioned in the said note, or any part thereof, and also before the time limited, and appointed by the said note for the payment thereof, to wit: on the same day and year last aforesaid, at &c., to wit: at &c., indorsed the said note in writing, with his proper name and signature of J. C. Spencer, and by that indorsement, ordered and appointed the contents of the said note to be paid to the before named A. K. Smedes, &c., the before named plaintiffs; and then and there delivered the said note, so indorsed, to the said A. K. Smedes, &c.; and the said A. K. Smedes, &c., to whom, or to whose order, the payment of the said sum of money, mentioned in the said note, was to be made as aforesaid, afterwards, and before the payment of the said sum of money, mentioned in the said note, or any part thereof, and also before the time limited and appointed by the said note, for the payment thereof, to wit: on the day last aforesaid, at, &c., to wit: at, &c., indorsed the said note in writing, with the name and signature of the said firm of A. & G. Smedes and A. Camfield, and, by that indorsement, ordered and appointed the contents of the said note to be paid to the before named defendants, The President,
665*] *&c., at the Utica Branch Bank in Canandaigua; and the said plaintiffs, for the more effectual recovery and collection of the moneys in the said note specified, according to the tenor and effect of the said note, and of the said indorsements so made thereon as aforesaid, afterwards, to wit: on the 14th day of February, A. D. 1818, at, &c., to wit: at, &c., caused the said note to be deposited at the office of discount and deposit established by the defendants, pursuant to the statute in such case made and provided, under the name and style of the Utica Branch Bank at Canandaigua, aforesaid, to be collected by the said defendants, in behalf of them, the before named plaintiffs. And the said President, Directors and Company of the Bank of Utica, in the village of Utica, the before named defendants, thereupon, to wit: on the said 14th day of February, A. D. 1818, at, &c., to wit: at, &c., in consideration that the said plaintiffs had so indorsed and deposited the said note for collection, in manner and form aforesaid, thereupon assumed upon themselves, and then and there faithfully undertook to present the said note, and demand payment of the sum of money specified in the same, from the said P. B. Underhill and H. Seymour, according to the tenor and effect of the said note, and of the several indorsements so made thereon as aforesaid; and in case default should be made in the payment of the said sum of money in the said note mentioned, or of any part thereof, by the said P. B. Underhill and H. Seymour, as aforesaid, then the before named defendants, The President, &c., in the village of Utica, further assumed upon themselves, and then and there, in consideration of certain reasonable fees and rewards, to be, therefore, paid by the said plaintiffs to the said defendants, they the said defendants undertook, according to the usage and custom of merchants, well and truly to notify, or cause notice to be given, to J. C. Spencer, the before named indorser, of the non-payment and protest of the said promissory note, and by such notice, by force of the statute in such case made and provided, render the said J. C. Spencer liable as indorser for the payment of the said sum of money, in the said *note specified, according to the [*666 tenor and effect of the said note, and of the said indorsement, so by the said J. C. Spencer thereon made, as aforesaid. And the said plaintiffs, in fact, say, that the said P. B. Underhill and H. Seymour, afterwards, to wit: on the 14th day of February, A. D. 1818, at, &c., to wit: at, &c., did neglect to pay the said sum of money in the said note specified, according to the tenor and effect of the said note, and of the said indorsements, so thereon made as aforesaid, and did then and there wholly refuse and make default therein; and although it became and was the duty of the said President, &c., under and by virtue of the said undertaking, to cause due notice to be given of the non-payment and protest of the said promissory note, to the said J. C. Spencer, indorser as aforesaid; yet the said President, &c., not regarding their duty in that behalf, nor their undertaking aforesaid, in form aforesaid made, but contriving and fraudulently intending to injure and defraud the before named plaintiffs, A. K. Smedes, &c., in this behalf, did not nor would well and truly notify, or cause due notice to be given to the said J. C. Spencer, indorser as aforesaid, of the non-payment of the said promissory note, by the said P. Underhill and H. Seymour, but wrongfully and injuriously, afterwards, to wit: on the 14th day of February, A. D. 1818, at, &c., to wit: at, &c., wholly neglected and refused so to do; and by reason of the default and neglect of the defendants aforesaid, the said A. K. Smedes, &c., for want of evidence of such due notice to the said J. C. Spencer, indorser as aforesaid, have not only failed and been defeated in their suit subsequently instituted in the Supreme Court of Judicature of the People of the State of New York, for the recovery of the moneys in the said promissory note specified, from the said J. C. Spencer, indorser as aforesaid; but in pursuance of the judgment had and obtained against them, the before named plaintiffs in the suit aforesaid, and entered up in favor of the said J. C. Spencer, in the said Supreme Court, &c., on the 4th day of October, A. D. 1819, at, &c., to wit: at, &c., have been compelled to pay and did pay, on, &c., $29.12 to the said J. C. Spencer, as well for his costs and charges in and about his *defense in the said [*667 action, as for the sheriff's fees and poundage in serving a writ of *fi. fa.* issued in pursuance of, and by virtue of the judgment aforesaid; and the said plaintiffs, by reason of the said judgment so had and obtained against them, were

further rendered liable and are still liable, to pay a large sum of money, to wit: the sum of $75, for their costs and charges accrued in and about the prosecution of the said action, to wit: at, &c., and have lost and been deprived of the means of recovering the same from the said J. C. Spencer, indorser as aforesaid, to the damage, &c., $2,000, of all which the said defendants, on, &c., at, &c., had notice.

The 2d count was substantially the same with the 1st, except that the consideration of the promises by the defendants below was alleged to be that the plaintiffs had, at the defendant's request, employed them to present and demand the note of the makers, and had, at the defendant's like request, employed them, for certain reasonable fees and rewards, &c., to protest and give notice, &c.

The 3d count was as follows: "And whereas, also, heretofore, to wit: on the said 14th day of February, 1818, at, &c., in consideration that the said plaintiffs, at the special instance and request of the said defendants, would indorse and deliver to them, the said defendants, a certain other promissory note in the words and figures following, to wit: 'Canandaigua, August 12th, 1817. Six months after date, we promise to pay to the order of John C. Spencer, Esq., at the Utica Branch Bank, twelve hundred and thirty seven dollars, for value received, with interest from date. Underhill & Seymour, Dolls. 1,237.00;' which said note had been, theretofore, to wit: on the said 12th day of August, A. D. 1817, at, &c., to wit: at, &c., according to the statute in such case made and provided, and agreeable to the usage and custom of merchants, duly indorsed by the said J. C. Spencer (to whom or to whose order the said note was made payable), to the before named plaintiffs, and had also, according to the usage and custom of merchants, been duly indorsed by the before named plaintiffs, to the said defendants, or order, with intent that the said de-668*]fendants might, as the holders *thereof, according to the usage and custom of merchants, and by the force of the statute in such case made and provided, receive and collect the moneys in the said note specified, for the account, use and benefit of the said plaintiffs; and in case the said note should not be paid by the said P. B. Underhill and H. Seymour, at the time and place specified in the said note, according to the tenor and effect thereof, and of the indorsements so thereon made as aforesaid, with the further intent that they, the said defendants, should then and there, according to the usage and custom of merchants, and by force of the statute in such case made and provided, protest or cause to be protested the said promissory note, and notify or cause to be notified the said J. C. Spencer, indorser as aforesaid, of the non-payment of the said sum of money in the said note mentioned, according to the tenor and effect of the said note and of the indorsements so thereon made as aforesaid, they, the said defendants, undertook and then and there faithfully promised, that they, the said defendants, would duly present the said note to the said P. B. Underhill and H. Seymour, the drawers thereof, at the Utica Branch Bank in Canandaigua, on the said 14th day of February, A. D. 1818; and in case the said P. B. Underhill and H. Seymour should make default, or neglect to pay the said note, the said defendants undertook and then and there faithfully promised to protest, or cause the said note to be protested for the non-payment thereof, and duly to notify, or cause due notice to be given, to the said J. C. Spencer, indorser as aforesaid, of the neglect and default of the said P. B. Underhill and H. Seymour, in not paying the said sum of money in the said note specified, according to the tenor and effect thereof, and of the indorsements so thereon made as aforesaid. And the said plaintiffs, in fact, say that they, the said plaintiffs, confiding in the promise and undertaking aforesaid, by the said defendants, in form aforesaid made, did afterwards, to wit: on the 14th day of February, A. D. 1818, deliver to the said defendants, at their office of discount and deposit, styled the Utica Branch Bank in Canandaigua, the said note indorsed as aforesaid, for the purpose aforesaid. Yet the said defendants, not* [*669 regarding the said promise and undertaking, but contriving and intending to injure the said plaintiffs, in that behalf, did not, nor would notify, or cause due notice to be given to the said J. C. Spencer, indorser, as aforesaid, of the neglect and default then and there made of the said P. B. Underhill and H. Seymour, in failing to pay the said sum of money in the said note mentioned, according to the tenor and effect thereof, and of the said indorsements so thereon made, as aforesaid; but did then and there wholly fail and make default therein; by means whereof the plaintiffs have wholly lost and been deprived of the said sum of money in the said note mentioned, to the great damage of them, the said plaintiffs, to wit: of, &c., of which premises the said defendants, afterwards, to wit: on, &c., at, &c., had notice."

Plea, the general issue.

There was a general verdict for the plaintiffs below, upon all the counts in the declaration, for $1,610.03, upon which the court below gave judgment in Jan. Term, 1823, for the reasons given, 20 Johns., 377 to 385, S. C., where the evidence necessary to sustain these counts was very fully considered by Woodworth, *J.*, who delivered the opinion of the court upon a case made. There being no special verdict or bill of exceptions, the evidence was not before this court; but the cause went entirely upon the sufficiency of the declaration. Much of *Judge* Woodworth's opinion will, however, be found applicable to the questions raised here.

Mr. P. S. Parker, for the plaintiffs in error, remarked, generally, that where there is a substantial defect in a declaration the defendant may avail himself of it by demurrer, motion in arrest or writ of error. The verdict in this case is general, upon all the counts, three of which are special; and if either be defective in substance, our writ of error is sustained. It is true, courts have gone as far as possible in the amendment of the proceedings below, by entering the verdict upon the good counts, if warranted by the minutes of the circuit judge. Nothing of that kind, was, however, done in this case.

*1. There does not appear, in any [*670 part of the declaration, an authority in the defendants below to transact banking business at Canandaigua. There is no statute recited or set forth giving them such authority, and there is no public Act to that effect. It will hardly be contended that a bank has an incidental right to establish offices of discount and deposit, nor is there anything in the original charter of the Bank of Utica giving them such a right. Then, if there was any authority to do this, it should have been specially shown. The plaintiffs below did not seek to recover of any officer of the branch, but of the mother bank—not for the act or omission of the Bank, but for the fault of an individual. If the Bank of Utica had no right to erect this office, they are not liable; and in all cases, where a party seeks to establish a right in virtue of a private Act, as this must be, he must plead the Act as he would any other record. True, the declaration refers generally to an Act authorizing the establishment of an office at Canandaigua, but the Act itself should be set forth specially, to show the connection between the mother bank and the agent. 1 Chit. Pl., 218; 1 Bl. Com., 86; Bac. Abr., Statute, L. Here even the title of the statute is not mentioned.

2. The 1st and 2d counts of the declaration set forth a note payable on demand; and no cause of action could arise against the defendants below, for negligence in not presenting such a note for payment, and in omitting to notify the indorser 6 months after it was due. No time of payment being specified in the notes, they were due and demandable immediately. *Thompson* v. *Ketchum*, 8 Johns., 192; *Herrick* v. *Bennett*, *Id.*, 374; *Sheehy* v. *Mandeville*, 7 Cr., 217. The notes are stated, in both these counts, to have been made and dated Aug. 12, 1817; to have been indorsed by Spencer at that time; and to have been deposited in the Bank, Feb. 14, 1818; at which time the defendants below promised to make demand and give notice. What duty was imposed upon the defendants? Of what avail were a demand and notice at that late day? Two months and a half have been holden an unreasonable delay. This must depend on 671*] circumstances; *such as the distance between the residence of the holder and the other parties. In this case, there would be a material difference as to time between a residence of the drawers in S. C., and the village of Canandaigua; and nothing appears that they did not reside at the latter place. But suppose they resided at the City of N. Y., at the date of the note—a demand might have been made, and the usual time of communication, which is but a few days, between these places, would have carried notice of non-payment to Canandaigua. There is an allegation that the plaintiffs below brought a suit against the indorser, and were defeated, with costs, for want of due notice. This appears, on the face of the declaration, to have been their own fault. Chit. on Bills, 350.

3. There is no sufficient consideration set forth in the 3d count. The promise relied on was a *nudum pactum*. There is a wide distinction in this respect, between a nonfeasance and misfeasance. In the latter case, an action lies for negligence, though the undertaking be without consideration; otherwise for a nonfeasance. In such case, a full and plain consideration must be clearly stated, to warrant an action. *Thorne* v. *Deas*, 4 Johns., 84. In the case cited all the authorities are stated and considered.

That error will lie upon one count substantially bad, though the others be good, if the verdict be general, the court are referred to *Hopkins* v. *Beedle*, 1 Cai., 347; *Grant* v. *Astle*, Doug., 730; *Cheetham* v. *Tillotson*,, 5 Johns., 430, and *Trevor* v. *Wall*, 1 T. R., 151.

The distinction upon which we rely, between a nonfeasance and misfeasance, is admitted by His Honor, *Judge* Woodworth, who delivered the opinion of the court below upon the case made. He admits, that ordinarily, in the former case, there must be a complete consideration appearing upon the face of the declaration; but he considers that banks form an exception. Where is the distinction? Suppose this had been the case of an individual banker or broker; would not the case be precisely the same in principle? Is it true, of them, that the mere delivery of the paper, and the expected benefit to be derived from deposit, funds, facilities, &c., would form a legal consideration? If not, why *otherwise [*672 as to incorporated banks? The learned judge adverts to the case of *Elsee* v. *Gatward*, 5 T. R., 143. Now, in that case, the judges agree, that if Gatward had performed he might have had an action for his compensation against Elsee; but this expectation of benefit was not allowed to form a consideration. Having done nothing towards the work, though it was in the line of his business as a carpenter, yet this circumstance did not make out a consideration. How is it possible to distinguish the two cases? The very point decided in *Thorne* v. *Deas*, 4 Johns., 96, was, that an action will not lie in such a case. In this case, we admit, that if the Bank had got the money in their vaults, they would have been liable; but they were as much at liberty to attempt obtaining it or not, as Gatward was to undertake or omit the building. The only consideration alleged by this count is, that the plaintiffs would deliver the notes to be collected for the plaintiffs' benefit. This is no consideration at all. The delivery of the notes was no benefit to the defendants. It does not appear by the declaration that they could possibly derive any benefit.

4. The 3d count does not aver the non-payment of the note by the makers. This was an essential averment, and payment not being negatived, we have a right to infer that it was made at the day.

5. Neither of the counts aver that the makers were insolvent. Without this, the plaintiffs below could have sustained no damage.

Mr. S. M. Hopkins, for the defendants in error. The note in question, in fact, fell due Feb. 14, 1818, as averred in the 3d count. The opinion of the court below was given upon the merits of the case, as they appeared at the circuit, and has very little bearing upon the form of the declaration, which, alone, is questioned here. The informalities in the record were never brought to the view of the court below in any shape; and this furnishes us with one answer to the writ of error. It is, that the defendants below should have taken their objections in the Supreme Court, by demurrer or motion in arrest. We are not to be met, for 673*] *the first time, with them here. This was determined in the late case of *Colden* v. *Knickerbacker*, 2 Cow., 31, which holds that, to warrant reviewing a point here, it must have been expressly passed upon by the court below.

It is admitted that the 1st and 2d counts aver a sufficient consideration; but there is a clerical mistake, in not setting forth the note as payable at 6 months. In the 3d count, however, the note is truly set forth; but this is said to be defective, in omitting to aver a sufficient consideration. The law does not require a full consideration. The merest trifle is sufficient. An attorney who engages to defend a suit for $5 received, is bound to a faithful discharge of his duty, and is fully amenable for all the damages arising from his neglect. Equally so, if he engages to defend upon the express or implied promise of his client to pay him the reasonable or legal fees. If he simply engage to defend a cause, without anything farther, it is a mere naked promise; but if anything be done by the client, or any liability incurred, the attorney will be bound. The slightest loss or inconvenience on the part of the promisee makes a sufficient consideration. 1 Com. on Cont., 16, 17. This is fully exemplified in the books. An executor is not bound without assets; yet if he promise the creditor, "prove your debt and I will pay it," he is bound, on the condition being performed. A delivery of goods, in which one has only a special property (*Bind* v. *Plain*, Cro. Eliz., 218), or mutual acceptance of bills to the same amount, is also a good consideration. So intermarriage with a third person. *Brown* v. *Garborough*, Cro. Eliz., 63. So performance of what the promisee was previously bound to do by an award. *Foster* v. *Scarlet*, Cro. Eliz., 70. So a promise to show a deed. *Sturlyn* v. *Albany*, Cro. Eliz., 67; S. C., *Id.*, 150. Doing an act for the benefit of a third person, at the defendant's request. *Hunt* v. *Bate*, Dy., 272 *b*. In the margin of this page the plaintiff's sealing a lease is mentioned as a consideration, though it was of no consequence to the defendant. Now, in the 3d count it is thus set forth: "In consideration that the said plaintiffs, at the special instance and request of the said defendants, would indorse and deliver to 674*] them, the *said defendants, a certain other promissory note, in the words and figures following," &c. (setting forth the note in question, and that it was indorsed and delivered). Here is a consideration, within the cases, fully stated. The indorsement and delivery put it upon the defendants to make the demand and give the notice; otherwise, the plaintiffs' remedy against the indorser would be gone forever. The plaintiffs ceased to hold the note. They had put it out of their power, therefore, to make the demand, at the request of the defendants; and the mere fact that they had incurred this inconvenience was enough. The consideration is not merely formal, as supposed. The distinction between nonfeasance and misfeasance is founded on the case of *Coggs* v. *Bernard*, 2 Ld. Raym., 909, and I had supposed this case would be cited. It has not been; and I presume, for the reason that it would make decidedly against the plaintiffs in error. The receipt of the property, and beginning the act about it, was holden enough, in that case, to bind the bailee to its prudent management, according to the terms of the bailment. Having the note in their possession, controlling it exclusively, and not acting at the proper time, became a deceit upon us, which worked a lasting injury. If the act is commenced it must be finished—it must be well, truly, faithfully and correctly done, according to the nature of the act to be performed—otherwise an action lies. In this case, an attorney undertakes to charge an indorser. *Coggs* v. *Bernard* is, that if you begin the trust, you must go through with it. I retain an attorney to defend, put my papers in his hands, and he omits to appear, by which I am damnified, in the loss of my cause, or otherwise—was it ever doubted that he would be liable? Here the papers are delivered, and no notice given; yet, say the bailees, "we might act our pleasure, and ruin you with impunity—we have a right to go on, and do the business at the halves, and yet you have no remedy for our carelessness." Is this to be tolerated? In *Coggs* v. *Bernard* there were two objections—one, a want of consideration; the other, that the defendant was not shown to be a common carrier. The objection, and all the reasoning in that cause, presupposed and admitted that the being a common *car- [*675 rier, whose business it is to convey goods, would have been sufficient to sustain the action. Here is a common collector; and His Honor, *Mr. Justice* Woodworth rightly held that the Bank was liable, on the ground that this was in the ordinary course of their business, of which they made a profit. This abundantly appeared upon a consideration of the merits.

But if all the defects imputed to this declaration exist, they are cured by the verdict. The objection is to a title defectively set forth —not a defective title. *Rex* v. *Landaff*, 2 Str., 1011. In *Small* v. *Cole*, 2 Burr., 1159, 1161, the demise was laid as having been made 30 years after the memorandum; yet the court held that this defect was cured by the verdict. Denison, *J.*, gave as a reason, that no doubt a proper title was proved upon the trial. Com. Dig. Pleader, C., 87, refers to various cases of the like character. One defect complained of is, that our declaration does not allege a neglect to pay the note. But we say the defendants caused no notice to be given that payment was not made—an averment of non-payment which, to be sure, is somewhat circuitous and argumentative, but no ground of objection upon error. It is a mere formal defect, scarcely objectionable by special demurrer. No position is better settled, than that a verdict shall cure all that which may be supposed, from the record, to have been proved at the trial. Neglect was essential to maintain the action before the jury, and must have been proved. The omission, therefore, is cured. *Hornsey* v. *Dimocke*, 1 Vent., 119; *De La Barre* v. *Jones*, Hardr., 222; Bull. *N. P.*, 321; *Hall* v. *Douglass*, Barn., 452; *Huffam* v. *Ellis*, 3 Taunt., 415. Indeed, it is a negative averment, which it lay with the defendants to disprove. If this be not done, it is received as proved from the nature of the issue.

We must not, however, be considered as admitting that this declaration is substantially defective; for we do not think this can be maintained. On the subject of what consideration is necessary, we also refer to Com. Dig., Action upon the case upon *assumpsit*, B. 1, 2, 3. In *Anonymous*, 2 Vent., 45, the considera-**676***] tion alleged and held good was, *that the plaintiff paid to the defendant so much money, who assumed to pay a like sum into court and appear—a case much like the present. The Bank received a note, equivalent in itself to money, which, in the ordinary course of things, would produce to them its face in cash, from which they might have derived a benefit as a deposit. They are, at any rate, benefited as much as the attorney was in Ventris, though they forthwith pay out the money. Again; if, in consideration that you will pay A such a sum of money, I promise to pay B the same sum, this binds me to the payment, though I derive no benefit from the consideration. Com. Dig., Action upon the case upon *assumpsit*, B, 11. Again; if the plaintiff will permit the defendant to receive money of A, which he owes the plaintiff, the defendant promises to give the plaintiff a bill of exchange for so much; this shall bind, though A become insolvent and never pay; for the plaintiff, perhaps, would not have delayed, had it not been for the defendant's promise. *Ib.*

We admit that the doctrine of nonfeasance and misfeasance is left in a little confusion by the books, some expressions giving color to the positions advanced against us. It is said, for instance, that if one take charge of brandy, and spill a portion of it, which implies feasance, he is liable; but if the bailee, who receives it, totally omit doing anything whatever by which it is lost or spilled, he is not liable. The latter position is not warranted by the cases. *Coggs* v. *Bernard* is, that the bailee is not liable if he do nothing; that is, if he never even receive the property. Suppose a revenue law required brandy to be deposited in a public store; or that, otherwise, it should be forfeited—I deliver the brandy, with the documents and key, to one, for the purpose of having it stored, and he staves the pipes and wastes the brandy—it is admitted he would be liable. Suppose, again, that he receives them, and then refuses to stir, by which the brandy is forfeited to the government, by reason of not being deposited; the loss is equally serious—the consideration equally adequate—and yet shall it be said the bailor must abide the loss? In *Elsee* v. *Gatward*, 5 T. R., 143, 148, Ld. Kenyon recognized what Powell, *J.*, said in **677***] *Coggs* v. *Bernard*, *that "an action will not lie for not doing a thing, for want of a sufficient consideration; but if the bailee will take the goods into his custody, he shall be answerable for them; for the taking of the goods into his custody is his own act." So here, the defendants take the note, which is the same as delivery of goods, and they are liable, no matter what name you give to the omission, whether nonfeasance or misfeasance.

As to the clerical error in the 1st and 2d counts, which omit to set forth the time the notes had to run, it is true they are mentioned as bearing date Aug. 12, and as being indorsed Feb. 14; but the time is laid under a *scilicet*, and is immaterial. There can be no intendment that the notes were indorsed an hour before they were delivered, or that they lay an unreasonable time with the plaintiffs below. The proof must have been regular, and might have proceeded in total disregard of the time, which was mere form. Beside, it does not lie with the Bank to say that a presentment and notice would do us no service, after having expressly promised, upon good consideration, to perform these acts for us. Being notes payable on demand, no particular time is fixed by the law within which these acts should be done. The time, it is admitted, must depend on circumstances, which may, in certain cases, warrant a greater delay than six months. All this was proper matter of proof upon the trial. *Losee* v. *Dunkin*, 7 Johns., 70; *Furman* v. *Haskin*, 2 Cai., 369; *Loomis* v. *Pulver*, 9 Johns., 244; *Hendricks* v. *Judah*, 1 *Id.*, 319. Various circumstances would excuse a delay of strict notice. It might have been waived by the indorser. These are matters which are never spread upon the record, and cannot come fairly in question here.

The statute under which the parties proceeded is sufficiently set forth; but if not so, the imperfection is cured by the verdict. Beside, we do not admit that Acts in relation to banks are private. They are treated as public in all our judicial proceedings, where it has never been thought necessary to recite them at large. Our courts have decided that their bills are a legal tender, unless specially objected to, and *their charters concern the currency of [***678** the country. *Holland's* case, 4 Rep. 76; —— v. ———, 2 Show., 318; *Cade* v. *Hillary*, Lutw., 1407, 1410; *The King* v. *Buggs*, Shin., 428, 429. In *People* v. *Utica Ins. Co.*, 15 Johns., 363, in answer to an information in nature of a *quo warranto*, the defendants pleaded the Act incorporating them as an insurance company, not as a private but a public Act; and no exception was taken for this reason.

Mr. S. A. Foot, in reply. This is certainly a case of the first impression. There has been none, either in England or this country, where a bank has been charged under circumstances like the present. This court are called upon to make a precedent, and I need not remark that it should be well considered. The single ground of complaint is, that the Bank gave no notice to the indorser, by which the plaintiffs below sustained damage. The Bank made an honest attempt to save the note, by employing an agent to give notice. Neither party are in moral default; and the case, therefore, presents a close contest, upon a legal question, which shall sustain the loss.

It is said we are estopped to call upon this court for its interference, because we did not interpose our objections in the court below. We present them with the record and the opinion of the court. How does it appear that we did not move in arrest of judgment? This is not to be determined by the assertion of counsel. Can it be ascertained by the printed opinion of the court? Suppose there should be no formal opinion, or the court below should forbear to notice what we did object there, must we be concluded? Is it meant that this court cannot notice objections which that court were pleased to think unimportant, and therefore did not mention? I see no other way but to look at the record, see what objections might have been made, and consider them, at least, *prima facie*, as made. We are referred to *Colden* v. *Knickerbacker*, 2 Cow., 31. What was that case? The defendant had allowed judgment to pass by default; the question came up 679*] on a record of *the default: and it was seen that he had not even placed himself in a condition to take the objections raised. The record must be the only test. The question cannot be tried by affidavit. But if this be not so, and the court should seek for the best lights they have, the opinion below, it does appear from this, that the objections upon the case related not only to the evidence, but the pleadings. *Mr. Justice* Woodworth, who gave the opinion, felt himself constrained to lay the 1st and 2d counts out of view as not reaching the case; and to make the whole depend upon the third count. What does this mean, unless the pleadings were drawn in question? Substantially, they were as much in question as here. The whole declaration was before the court, who restricted the case to the 3d count. With leave of this court, however, I shall consider all the questions which might have been raised in the court below, relying upon the rule which I first advanced as the correct one.

It will not be denied that where one count is substantially defective, and the verdict is general, the judgment should be reversed. I would barely observe in relation to the 1st and 2d counts, that it is true, as contended by the other side, that the note should have been presented in a reasonable time, and that this was matter of proof at the trial; but the declaration should have averred expressly, that afterwards, to wit: on such a day, being within a reasonable time after the making or indorsement, they were presented for payment, and notice of non-payment given. The counts neither contain this averment, not set forth the circumstances, to show whether these steps were taken in a reasonable time or not. Omitting this, no loss is shown, as a consequence of the default.

As to the 3d count, upon which the principle question arises, I shall not stop to review the cases, and draw the distinction between nonfeasance and misfeasance, because I am sure it will be found that *Mr. Justice* Woodworth assumed the sensible ground in the court below. In a word, nonfeasance is not doing; misfeasance is entering upon the undertaking, doing, but doing negligently. In the first case, a consideration is necessary; in the latter, not. 680*] In the *first, the contract is merely honorary; as to the second, if you will be kind and generous, and enter upon the act of kindness and generosity, you shall be holden to perform faithfully. If you merely say you will be so, it is a different thing. Woodworth, *J.*, says of this declaration, "the 3d count is the only one on which the plaintiffs can rely; and that is for a nonfeasance, which cannot be supported, unless founded on a valid consideration." 20 Johns., 379. To the same effect is the language of Kent, *Ch. J.*, in *Thorne* v. *Deas*, 4 Johns., 99. "But none of these cases," says he, "nor, as far as I can discover, do any of the *dicta* of the judges in them, go so far as to say, that an *assumpsit* would lie for the nonperformance of a promise, without stating a consideration for the promise." Woodworth, *J.*, also defines, and well defines, what shall constitute a consideration. It is either an injury to one party, or a benefit to the other (20 Johns., 380); that is, if the promisee be injured or the promisor benefited. Here the single consideration is, that the plaintiffs below would indorse and deliver over the note to the defendants below for collection. Was this such a prejudice to the holders, or benefit to the Bank as would make a binding consideration, and render them liable for omitting performance? Neither the counsel nor the court below pretended that this alone was sufficient, but they put it on the ground of expectation. It was the probable or expected benefit to the Bank, arising from the course of their business, the hope that it would result in the receipt of the money due, and its temporary use; and the judge enters into a disquisition upon the manner of doing business in banks, to show that the expectation was a reasonable one. But it is essential to the validity of the declaration, that not only the promise but the consideration should be distinctly and fully set forth there. Now, the consideration mentioned, and relied on by the court, does not appear in the 3d count at all. It is the act of indorsement and delivery, not the expectation, which is averred. To conform to the opinion of the court below, the addition should have been made, "and also in consideration of the use of the money to be received till withdrawn." The real consideration, upon which the *court below pro- [*681 ceeded, is a perfect nonentity here. The court below forgot this. They forgot that they could not rely upon a consideration not made the foundation of the judgment by pleading. It may be thought that the benefit to have been derived from the use of the money was not a distinct and independent fact necessary to be averred, but that it resulted from the allegation of indorsement and delivery. A moment's reflection will show the contrary. It may be the course of the Bank to keep such moneys separate from the general fund; but whether they do so or not, is a question of fact. This may or may not be their practice. It depends on their mode of doing business; and the temporary use of the money may or may not result from its receipt. Again; it may be no benefit to the Bank, even if it be intended that they would use it; or the benefit may not equal the risk of receiving, paying out, exchange, &c. If not, it can constitute no legal consideration. Thus, the temporary use itself, and the benefit of that use, are both of them independent facts, which it is necessary to aver; and it would introduce a single laxity in pleading, to say that mere matters of proof shall be the subject of judicial intendment.

But suppose we are mistaken in saying that the consideration is not sufficiently set forth; will an expectation of benefit, from performing the promise, constitute a consideration? It appears to me that the ease of *Elsee* v. *Gatward*, 5 T. R., 143, furnishes a complete answer. It cannot be said that, in that case, a benefit was not equally matter of expectation from a performance by the promisor; yet all the judges agreed that the promise was a *nudum pactum*. This case is stronger against the action than that. There the carpenter must certainly have been paid, if he had performed the services. Here, it is not pretended that the receipt of the money would have conferred anything more than a contingent benefit. It might or might not have resulted in an advantage to the promisors. The benefit intended by the cases, which is to form a consideration, must be a benefit either actually received, or resting in a present, legal, vested right to it. Take the **682***] case, stated on the other side, *of an attorney or counsel employed to manage a cause. The client tells his counsel, "I cannot pay you; but the cause stands high on the calendar; and if you argue it ably, you will probably be retained in several causes which stand lower upon the same calendar." Suppose the counsel to promise upon such a consideration; would he be bound to perform? The case of the attorney directly retained is different. Certain fees are allowed him by the law; on his accepting a retainer, his client incurs the legal liability to pay those fees, and he must, therefore, appear and defend or prosecute according to his engagement, or pay damages for the neglect. So of common carriers. They are allowed, by law, certain fees; and it is enough, in complaining of nonfeasance, to allege that the defendant was a common carrier, or a common porter, and that the article was delivered by the promisee and accepted by the promisor. No other consideration is necessary, because, by the law, he may exact and enforce a reward. This is not so of the Bank. It is not one of their legal duties to notify indorsers. This is the proper business for a notary public. The Bank can recover no reward, while the notary is entitled to his fees. The Bank is like the carpenter, not the attorney, carrier or porter. Ld. Kenyon draws this very distinction in *Elsee* v. *Gatward*.

The indorsement and delivery, so far from being an injury to the plaintiffs below, was a benefit; and so intended by the parties. The note was payable at the Bank. Suppose they had refused to receive it in any shape. The Smedes must have been at the expense of employing some other agent to attend at the Bank during the whole third day of grace. The Bank relieved them from this expense by engaging a notary.

Again; the Bank of Utica, not being connected by any statute which is set forth with the Bank at Canandaigua, the former cannot be liable, unless it has assented to the latter doing business in this way for the former. All this should have been averred. The connection between the two banks should have been exhibited upon the pleadings, either from a statute or a contract of agency. The rule is **683***] inflexible, that a *private statute must be set forth at large in pleading. Bac. Abr, Statute, F; *Boyce* v. *Whitaker*, Doug., 87; *Dive* v. *Manningham*, Plowd., 65; *Read* v. *Potter*, Cro. Jac., 139; *Jenkins* v. *Union Turnp. Co.*, 1 Chi. Cas., 93; *Wright* v. *Paton*, 10 Johns., 300; *Holland's* case, 4 Rep., 76.

It is said, however, that all our objections to this declaration are cured by the verdict. The rule upon this head is, that if a matter essential in pleading be alleged in terms too general to stand the test of a demurrer, and a certain specific fact is necessary to support it, that fact will, after verdict, be intended to have been proved at the trial; but the rule goes no farther. The law will only imply means to substantiate a general allegation. This is what it means by a title defectively set forth. Here is a defective title. Nothing either general or special is alleged. The want of averring non-payment specifically may be cured by the rule, as to the effect of the verdict, but nothing more. The law knows nothing about individual rights, gifts or franchises. If all the effects claimed from this verdict are to be recognized, it is certainly a most sovereign remedy. It will not only supply defects in a general allegation, but make a case out of whole cloth.

It is said this Act is public, because it concerns the currency of the State. But this is very indirectly and distantly. The charter is still a franchise. Suppose a statute gives a private banker certain privileges, would the Act be public, because it affects the currency? There is a clause at the end of almost every bank charter, declaring it a public Act. Would this be necessary, if these acts are, in their own nature, public?

THE CHANCELLOR. The principal question raised in this cause, is one which was discussed before the Supreme Court, and was there determined. It is, whether any sufficient consideration for the promise stated in the 3d count appears from the declaration, or not. Upon this question, I concur with the Supreme Court in their opinion, that this count is good, considered as a count for nonfeasance. The reasons of the Supreme Court, in support of this opinion, are *just and conclusive. But the [***684** 3d count may also, I think, be as properly considered a count for misfeasance. The truth of the transaction, even as it is stated in this count, was as much a mismanagement of the business undertaken as it was a total neglect to perform it. The reception of the note by the Bank for collection, may well be considered as the first step in the execution of the contract, on their part, and in this view no other consideration was necessary.

Upon the other objections made by the plaintiffs in error, it might be sufficient to say that they do not appear to have been presented to the Supreme Court; and that by the decisions and practice of this court, such objections cannot be entertained here. I will, however, state my opinion upon some of the most important of those objections.

It is urged that there is no public law establishing an office of the Bank of Utica at Canandaigua; and that the Act of Apr. 10, 1815, authorizing this Bank to establish an office at Canandaigua is a private Act, which is not set forth in the declaration. The Act incorporating the Bank of Utica is declared to be a public Act; and the action is against this Bank. This Corporation may make any contract within the scope of its general powers, and may bind itself to do an act at Canandaigua or any other place; and wherever the engagement may be broken, the Bank will be equally liable. But I am not prepared to admit that a law incorporating a bank, without declaring the law to be a public Statute, is a private Act, which must be recited in every suit against the Corporation. These institutions are public in their nature and character, and their operations affect the whole community. But without pursuing this inquiry, I am of opinion that the Act of Apr. 10, 1815, authorizing the Bank of Utica to establish an office at Canandaigna, is sufficiently set forth in the declaration in this cause. The declaration states that the Bank of Utica had, pursuant to the Act of the Legislature passed Apr. 10, 1815, established an office of discount and deposit, in Canandaigua. This allegation, though not a full recital of the Act, must be sufficient, at least, after a verdict.

685*] *Another objection is, that the note stated in the first two counts of the declaration appears as a note payable on demand, and that it is not alleged that any demand of payment from the makers, was made within a reasonable time. What was a reasonable time, would depend upon all the facts of the case, as they must have appeared at the trial. The decisive answer to this objection, and to some others which have been urged, is, that they are made for the first time, after the trial of the cause and a verdict by a jury. All these objections may have been made, and all these defects, if they are such, may have been supplied by sufficient proofs at the trial. The established rules of our law authorize, and justice and public convenience require, that the power of a verdict to cure formal defects in pleading should be liberally applied.

I am, accordingly, of opinion that the judgment of the Supreme Court should be affirmed.

The Court being unanimously of this opinion, it was thereupon ordered, adjudged and decreed that the judgment of the Supreme Court be affirmed; and that the defendants in error, according to the statute in such case made and provided, recover their double costs for their defense of the writ of error, to be taxed; and also their damages for the delay and vexation, to be assessed—which said damages shall be calculated at and after the rate of seven *per cent.* upon the amount of the judgment in the Supreme Court, so as aforesaid rendered, from the return of the *postea* in the Supreme Court, to the day of such assessment; and that the amount of such damages and costs be inserted in the *remittitur*; and that the record be remitted, &c.

Affirming—20 Johns., 372.

Bills, notes and checks—Duty of banks as collecting agent. Cited in—9 Wend., 48; 11 Wend., 475; 15 Wend., 487; 22 Wend., 228; 7 N. Y., 461; 15 N. Y., 168; 69 N. Y., 387; 8 Barb., 399; 41 Barb., 346; 66 Barb., 162; 27 How. Pr., 60; 17 Abb. Pr., 367; 9 Bos., 463; 6 Rob., 350; 4 How., U. S., 325; 4 McLean, 130; 38 Mo., 64; 34 Am. Dec., 294; 25 Am. Rep., 210.

Public act, what is. Cited in—2 Keyes, 406; 35 How. Pr., 51, 132; 3 Abb. N. S., 481; 4 Abb. N. S., 4; 6 Rob., 328; 7 Rob., 398; 43 Am. Dec., 116 (Morris, 482).

Also cited in—11 Wend., 405; 23 Wend., 556; 10 Barb., 372.

686*] *JACOB BARKER, *Plaintiff in Error*,

v.

THE PEOPLE OF THE STATE OF NEW YORK, *Defendants in Error.*

Constitutionality of Law to Suppress Dueling—Exclusion from Office, &c.—Nature of Legislative Power, as to Punishment of Crime.

The Act to Suppress Dueling, passed Nov. 5, 1816, (sess. 40, ch. 1), which declares that any person convicted of challenging another to fight a duel, &c., "shall be incapable of holding or being elected to any post of profit, trust or emolument, civil or military, under this State, is constitutional; and a conviction and judgment of disqualification under it, are, therefore, legal and valid.

The provision in the Constitution of the U. S., that cruel and unusual punishment shall not be inflicted, is a restriction upon the government of the U. S. only; and not upon the government of any State.

The Constitution of the U. S. does not regulate the punishment of crimes against a State.

The State Legislature cannot establish arbitrary exclusions from office, or any g[illegible] regulation requiring qualifications which the State Constitution has not required.

The power of the State Legislature, in the punishment of crimes, is not a special grant or limited authority, but a part of the legislative, or sovereign power of the State, to maintain social order, and to take life, liberty and all the rights of both when the sacrifice is necessary.

The provision in the State Constitution, that the judgment upon impeachment shall not extend farther than a removal from office, and disqualification to hold office, is a restriction, not an authority.

The power of the State Legislature, over crimes, is a power to produce the end by adequate means;

But there are numerous regulations in the Constitution which operate as restrictions upon this power.

Examples.

Eligibility to office is not so secured.

Infliction of disqualification to hold office, as a punishment, is not incompatible with that part of the Constitution, which provides that each house shall be the judge of the qualifications of its own members.

Citation—Act, Nov. 5, 1816, sec. 1.

ERROR to the Supreme Court. In Feb., 1822, Jacob Barker, the plaintiff in error, was indicted in the Court of General Sessions of the Peace, of the City and County of N. Y., for sending a challenge to David Rogers, to fight a duel. The indictment contained five counts; the four first of which alleged the offense to have been committed by Barker, in the City of N. Y., on various days, in the months of Jan. *and Feb., 1822, "against the form of **[*687** the statute in such case made and provided," being founded on the "Act to Suppress Dueling," passed Nov. 5, 1816. The 5th count was for a similar offense at common law. The plaintiff in error was tried on the indictment, at the Court of General Sessions held in the City of N. Y., in May, 1822. The jury rendered a general verdict of guilty, and the Dist. Atty. having entered a *nolle prosequi* in the 5th count (for the offense at common law), the court thereupon gave judgment that the plaintiff in error, "for the offense aforesaid, as charged in the first, second, third, and fourth counts of the said indictment, whereof he is convicted, be incapable of holding, or being elected to any post of profit, trust or emolument, civil or military, under the State of N. Y."

A writ of error was brought, on this judgment to the Supreme Court, which, in Jan. Term., 1823, affirmed the judgment of the General Sessions. *Vide* S. C., 20 Johns., 457, which contains the reasons assigned to this court in support of the judgment.

Mr. B. F. Butler, for the plaintiff in error, argued,

1. That the Act of Nov. 5, 1816, "to Suppress Dueling," on which the judgment is founded, is contrary and repugnant to the provisions and spirit of the Constitution of this State, in force at the time of its enactment.

2. It is also repugnant to the Constitution of the U. S.

3. It is repugnant to those parts of the amended Constitution of this State, which relate to the right of suffrage, and which became in force and took effect from the last day of Feb., 1822; and being so repugnant, was abrogated by the amended Constitution.

He said that before an an examination of the points, it might be useful briefly to to consider the history of the Act in question. The subject of dueling had, before the passage of the Act, been presented in such a variety of lights to the Legislature, that they felt themselves called upon for some vigorous provisions against it. The old Statute of 1813 (2 R. L., **688***] 192) *being found ineffectual, the Act of Nov. 5, 1816 (sess. 40, ch. 1), passed the two houses at the previous winter session, and was sent to the Council of Revision. This Act, besides imposing the penalty of disfranchisement for sending a challenge, &c., provided than an oath should be taken by all officers afterwards appointed, and solicitors, attorneys, counsel, &c., afterwards admitted that they had not and would not, violate the Act. This was by the 2d section; and doubts being entertained as to its constitutionality, it was laid over among the files of the Council till the Nov. session, at which time it was approved by a majority of the Council and became a law from that date. Notwithstanding this decision of the Council, doubts were still entertained as to its constitutionality; and in the case of *Dox*, a member of the Assembly from Genesee, the question was discussed in the Legislature, and he was denied a seat, because he would not take the oath. A few days after this a bill passed the Assembly repealing the 2d section, but it was rejected by the Senate. During the pendency of the bill, the constitutional power of the Legislature to make such a law was fully discussed; but the objection was confined to the 2d section. At the session of the late Convention, however, the subject was taken up; the 6th article of the new Constitution abolishes the oath; and whatever might have been thought on this subject before, it is now, we believe, pretty generally conceded that the 2d section, at least, was unconstitutional. This history is useful, as it establishes that, in the fervor of the times, the Constitution was violated in the 2d section; and admonishes us, that from the same cause, it might possibly have been violated in the 1st.

In discussing the points proposed it is proper to inquire, generally, what power the Legislature possess under the Constitution of this State. The late *Ch. J.*, in delivering the opinion of the court below, says, that they possess all power, not expressly forbidden by the Constitution of this State, or of the U. S., which relates to the prevention of crime, or the well ordering of society. From this we, with very great deference, dissent. We contend that they possess the power only, which is expressly con- **689***] ferred by the *Constitution, or that which results from its provisions by necessary implication. This construction has universally been applied to the Constitution of the U. S. It is said by the *Ch. J.*, not to apply here, because our State Constitution contains no enumeration of powers. There are but few prohibitions in the State Constitution. Our rule admits that when the Legislature are not expressly prohibited, they possess all power not repugnant to any express provision or the fundamental principles of a free government, or, in other words, the spirit of the Constitution. Thus the true will be found to lie between the two extremes of a power limited by enumeration, or left entirely at large. Indeed, this rule is admitted, in effect, by the *Ch. J.*; for, notwithstanding the broad terms of the axiom with which he sets out, he goes on to argue that there is no repugnancy between the provisions of the Act and those of the Constitution—at any rate, beyond that provision which makes the Assembly judges of their own members. He admits that such a repugnancy would destroy the Act *pro tanto*. The 3d article of the original Constitution erecting a Council of Revision, with powers to guard against the passage of laws contrary to the spirit of the Constitution, implies also that such a distinction exists. There are certain Acts which the Legislature cannot pass, though not expressly prohibited, and though not inconsistent with any express provision of the Constitution. *Calder* v. *Bull*, 3 Dall., 386; *Fletcher* v. *Peck*, 6 Cr., 87, 135; *Green* v. *Biddle*, 8 Wh., 1, 88. There is nothing which prohibits devesting one man of his freehold and giving it to another; no provision against retrospective laws; yet no law can be passed devesting a freehold, because it is inconsistent with those principles of liberty on which all free governments are founded.

We contend that the Act of Nov. 5, 1816, was contrary to several express provisions of the original Constitution, particularly the 9th, 10th and 12th articles. The first clause of the 9th article makes the Assembly judges of its own members. No particular qualification was required *in a candidate for that house; [***690** though it was, perhaps, implied that they should have the same qualifications as the elector. But the 10th section required a Senator to be a freeholder, which could not be varied by any Act of legislation. Could they, for instance, have defined the qualification more particularly by saying that the freehold intended should amount to $250? This would violate the rule that an express provision excludes implication. If the Legislature had power to require other qualifications, they might subvert the freedom of election. In effect, the Dueling Act did require a qualification unknown to the Constitution. Jan. 1, 1822, the plaintiff in error was eligible to a seat in the Assembly or Senate. In the latter he once held a seat. He is now, according to the judgment of a Court of Sessions, ineligible to either branch of the Legislature. How has he become so? The Constitution does not recognize the disqualification imposed. It is the same thing as an Act requiring 20 years residence of the candidate in a particular county or a freehold of the value of $1,000, or the membership of a cotton factory, as a qualification. Suppose he should present himself to the House of Assembly as a member of that body, could they say, "you have all the constitutional qualifications, all which the people required, but not such as the Legislature have seen proper to demand;" and for that reason exclude him? Do the House of Assembly longer retain the power of judging in cases coming within this Act? No. If the Act be valid, their power is discontinued; and the judiciary are to determine the qualifications of members. The late *Ch. J.* seems to admit that this consequence could not follow, and that the Act is so far void. The 17th and 20th articles prescribing the qualifications of the Governor and Lieutenant-Governor, are equally violated.

So of the 29th article, providing that town officers, &c., shall be continued eligible as heretofore; though there may be some doubt whether this be not confined merely to the manner of their election. The utmost extent of legislative power is to render a man ineligible to such offices alone as are created by the Legislature or left by the Constitution for them to create or control.

691*] *Can this judgment be good in part and void in part? The late *Ch. J.* seems to think it may; and this is true even in criminal cases, where the judgment consists of several distinct and independent branches; as where it imposes a fine of $15 and imprisonment for 30 days. *In the Matter of Sweatman*, 1 Cow., 144. So in civil cases where it is divided into costs and damages; but when the judgment is entire, and the good cannot be distinguished from the bad, it must be reversed *in toto*.

This Act is also repugnant to the 13th article, which forbids the disfranchisement of any member of this State, unless by the law of the land or the judgment of his peers. On this head, the late *Ch. J.* remarks, that "if the Dueling Act is not otherwise unconstitutional, then the injunctions of this article have been complied with; for the Act is the law of the land, and the verdict is the judgment of the plaintiff's peers." This is a case of the *petitio principii;* for though the judgment was under a statute, it does not follow that the proceeding was according to the law of the land, unless the Act was unconstitutional. If it violated the Constitution, it was void, and the trial was not such an one by the plaintiff's peers as is known to the law. It is begging the whole question in controversy. Suppose the Legislature to pass a law devesting you of the title to one of your farms, and conferring it upon your neighbor; this is equally the law of the land, because it has the form of an Act of the Legislature. Suppose they should pass an agrarian law, providing that no man shall hold more than 100 acres of land; but if he buys more, it shall be forfeited to his nearest neighbor who has no land; and a jury should find this fact, and a court give judgment of forfeiture: this would be equally an ouster of private right by the law of the land, and the judgment of his peers. The Act must be not only formally, but constitutionally good, or any act which your peers may do under it is a nullity, and as if they had never acted at all.

The late *Ch. J.* said he did not perceive the application of the 33d article. It was expressly stated by the plaintiff, in his argument before the court below, that this article confined the disfranchisement or sentence of ineligi-

692*] bility *to the impeaching power. *Vide* 20 Johns., 457. It gives this power to the Senate; and the plaintiff wishes to be understood as contending, that when a constitution or statute creates a power, and places it in the hands of a particular tribunal, to be exercised in a particular manner, all other tribunals, and all other courses of proceeding, other than those which are enumerated, are virtually excluded.

The late *Ch. J.* himself thinks that the enumeration of offenses in the new Constitution, for which one may be deprived of his vote, excludes, by necessary implicatien, all others. Now, by the 39th article of the old Constitution, ministers of the gospel were ineligible. Take the late *Ch. J.'s* own rule, that this enumeration excludes all other causes of ineligibility; and this article, alone, would be sufficient ground from which to infer the invalidity of the judgment below. Suppose the Legislature should exclude other classes—lawyers or physicians, for instance—would the provision be valid? Here they have excluded duelists, who, at times, form a very considerable class of the community.

The Act is repugnant to the spirit of the Constitution. We have already explained what we mean by this. It is a repugnancy to those principles which lie at the bottom of every free government. We do not believe that the people ever intended to confer this arbitrary power of disfranchisement. We do not believe it, because the power is too mighty to be intrusted with any republican Legislature. If they do possess it, they are omnipotent, like the British Parliament, and able to subvert the liberties of the people. If they may disfranchise in this, they may in any other case. A simple assault and battery is an offense of the same legal grade as sending a challenge, not to mention a great number of other ordinary misdemeanors of the same rank, some of which are committed very frequently, and almost with impunity. The Legislature may go on in this way, without end, disfranchising one and another, till the State would be reduced to very narrow limits in its selection of officers. Working, sporting, or traveling on Sunday, or profane cursing and swearing, may be followed by the same consequences. They may create new offenses, and impose ineligibility, by *their Acts to protect game [***693** and fisheries. We are not to repose on the remoteness of the probability that these things will come to pass. It is the power which is in question—not what they will do, but what they may do. Did the people who delegated the right to frame our original Constitution, suffering as they were at the moment under the lawless encroachments of British myrmidons, intend to leave this matter at such loose ends, intrusting their Legislature with a power to disfranchise the whole community?

Another fundamental principle of all free governments is, that punishments shall be proportioned to the nature of the offense. This is so treated not only by all enlightend writers on the subject, but it is incorporated as a maxim in various Constitutions of the U. S. Cruel or unusual punishments are not to be inflicted. 8 Am. to Const. U. S.; 18 art. Bill of Rights in Const. N. H.; 14 sec. of 8th art. Const. Ohio. And though not, in terms, a part of our State Constitution, it is one of its fundamental principles, as much as the rule that the freehold of one man shall not be arbitrarily devested and conferred upon another. We do not speak of the power to prescribe punishments, cruel or unusual in themselves, but the act of imposing penalties, of the same undistinguished severity, upon all offenses, without distinction as to their nature. The Statute in question imposes the same penalty on all who commit the offense of sending a challenge, whatever may be its extenuating circumstances, in whatever class of society it may be committed, whether among the bar, the Army, the Navy, &c. All are alike disqualified from becoming members of the Legislature. The man against whom the sentence is pronounced becomes a slave in a nation of freemen, for an offense, which under some circumstances, should be excused. Its moral guilt depends upon those circumstances. This law, like the tyranny of Procrustes, seizes the victim, and adapts him to the bed of justice. A whole life of atonement, for a juvenile freak, can not rescue him from lasting disfranchisement and disgrace. No matter how warm the blood, or great the provocation—whether the challenge be given or accepted—and though the challenge or acceptance be immediately **694***] withdrawn, the *same consequences follow. Such a law violates the eternal principles of morality and of natural justice itself.

It is said, by the late *Ch. J.*, that disfranchisement is not an unusual punishment. He does not allude to ineligibility, and we think he is mistaken in saying so of disfranchisement, inflicted by the Legislature. We presume he must have alluded to attainders, which are now prohibited by the Constitution of the U. S. He says it was the consequence of treason, and of infamous crimes; but at any rate, such a consequence is very different from ineligibility. Till the adoption of the late Constitution, there was nothing of this to prevent a citizen's voting or being elected. Again; it may be answered, that he speaks of the matter as it stood at the common law, which, though adopted by the Constitution, is, in this respect, altered by the Bill of Rights. Probably the Statute (1 W. & M., ch. 2) which passed in England, containing the same clause, referred to certain cruel punishments which were inflicted about the last of the second James. 4 Bl. Com., 378. But these had long been discontinued, and were not known in this free country, when it was reiterated by the Constitution of the U. S., and the declaration of rights in our own State. 1 R. L., 48, sec. 8. The punishment in question was unknown to the common law, as it respects this offense. So far, at least, it was unusual; and we have already shown, that applying it to a crime of this grade is cruel.

All the arguments drawn from the old, apply with still greater force under the new Constitution. The trial in the Court of Sessions took place in May, 1822; and by the 9th article of the amended Constitution, all its parts which relate to the right of suffrage and the time of election were then in force. By the 2d section of the 2d article, laws may be passed excluding from the right of suffrage persons who had been or might be convicted of infamous crimes. The late *Ch. J.* admits that this enumeration, by necessary implication, denies the power in any other case; and that the offense of which the plaintiff has been convicted is not an infamous one; but he limits its operation to the direct right of suffrage, and distinguishes this from eligibility. We *do not contend that the [***695** right of voting and being voted for are convertible; but we do contend that they are common, and that the citizen who has one must necessarily enjoy the other. We shall not stop to comment on the right of suffrage, or examine the full import of the term. It may certainly be extended, however, to the right of voting in the Legislature upon the passage of a law; but we are willing to concede, for the purpose of the present argument, that it means voting at an election. Now, though you may deprive the plaintiff of his own personal vote, you cannot deny his fellow citizens the right to vote for him—nor the right to vote for himself; which, under certain circumstances, might become a duty. If the Legislature can disqualify for one offense, they may for another; and thus the argument returns, that this may be extended from one to an hundred, and so on to every member of the community.

In determining a constitutional question of this character, which concerns the liberty of the citizen, every construction should be in favor of that liberty; and if a doubt exist in the mind of the court, this great principle should be applied, and judgment be rendered for the plaintiff in error.

Talcott, Atty-Gen., for the defendants in error. The question for the court to decide is not whether the Act under consideration, or any part of it, be inexpedient, but whether the Legislature had a constitutional power to pass the particular section in question. I do not controvert the right of this or any other court, to entertain the inquiry. I admit it is their duty—but I do say, that the court will come to a conclusion against the validity of the Statute, upon such grounds, with great reluctance, and not till all doubt be removed from their minds. *Dartmouth College* v. *Woodward*, 4 Wh., 625; *Calder* v. *Bull*, per Iredell, *J.*, 3 Dall., 399. I do not controvert the gentleman's limitation of legislative power to that which is consistent both with the letter and spirit of the Constitution. It is not necessary for me to contend that the Legislature have any power inconsistent either with its words or its spirit, or which is repugnant to the principles of civil liberty. This *Act is perfectly consistent with [***696** all three; and in showing it to be so, I shall not follow the gentleman, with any minuteness, into his doctrine of remote consequences, or examine the force of the language in all the various constitutional provisions which he has considered; but I shall rely mainly on the evidence to be derived from practical construction, by men who have framed and acted upon Constitutions containing the same principles with our own. In N. J., an attempt to bribe a judge or justice is punished with fine and imprisonment, and disqualification to hold any office of honor, trust or profit, under that State, Laws N. J., 1821, pp. 249, 250. In Pa., sending or carrying a challenge for, or becoming a second in a duel, is punished with forfeiture of all the rights of citizenship for 7 years. 4 Laws Pa., 389, Act of 1794. The Act of 1806, 7 Laws Pa., 665–6, re-enacts this law, as to persons sending or accepting a challenge; and as to persons carrying, it does not deprive them of all rights of citizenship, but only disqualifies them to hold any office of trust or profit under the Commonwealth. In Delaware, a person elected member of Assembly upon a promise to serve for nothing, or less than the law allows for services, is declared by statute incapable of serving for that year. 1 Laws Del., 148. In Va., by a law of 1695 (*vide* 1 Stat. at L., 131), collectors and their officers receiving, and persons giving bribes, were declared forever incapable of any office or employment within the Colony; and the same disqualification followed, for bribery in relation to any other duties concerning the customs. *Id.*, 191. In 1705, a law passed that collectors, &c., receiving a bribe to defraud the customs, should forever afterwards be disabled from holding the office, and also be disabled from holding any office or employment relating to the customs. 3 *Id.*, 232. In 1785 a law was passed, that if any person elected to serve in the General Assembly, should bribe an elector, he should be expelled, and disabled to be re-elected during the term of 3 years. 1 Rev. Code, 22. By a law of 1790, the penalty declared for selling a public office, or for taking anything for a vote in the appointing to any such office, was, **697***] in one case, the *loss of the office held, and in the other, incapacity of voting for any candidate for the office sold; and if the offender was a member of Assembly, expulsion and perpetual disqualification from being elected; and the person agreeing to buy was declared incapable of serving in the office purchased. 1 Rev. Code, 52. Another law declared that if candidates for the Legislature gave money, meat, drink or other reward, to promote their election, they should be expelled, and disabled to be elected for three years. 1 Rev. Code, 389. By a law of 1810, an oath similar to the one prescribed by the Act in question here, was made necessary for all officers; and a challenger, or acceptor of a challenge, was made incapable of holding or being elected to any post of profit, trust or emolument, civil or military. The Statute of Conn. is to the same effect. Rev. Law. Conn., 1821, p. 161, secs. 52, 53. So in Vt. (A. D. 1801, 1 Laws of Vt., 367), whose statute also denies the offender the privilege of a freeman generally. *Ib.* The Statute of Mass. is the same, except in limiting the disqualification to 20 years. Vol. I., Laws Mass., 367, A. D. 1801. The oath prescribed by the Statute of Ill., on this subject, is like ours; and the offender is made incapable of holding, or being elected to any post of profit, trust or emolument, civil or military. A. D. 1819, Laws of Ill., 32. By a Statute of the U. S., if any person give any bribe or reward, to obtain a judgment or decree of a U. S. judge, on any matter in controversy, both the giver and receiver are subject to fine and imprisonment, at the discretion of the court, and are perpetually disqualified, by conviction, to hold any office of trust or profit under the U. S. 2 L. U. S., Colvin's ed., 97, sec. 21, A. D. 1790.

If the Statute in question be a violation of the fundamental principles of free government, it is singular that almost every statute book in the U. S. should exhibit examples of the same extravagance, among jurists profound in their learning, and patriots ardent in their attachment to liberty.

*Too much stress is laid by the other [***698** side upon an enumeration of particular qualifications. The Governor, says the original Constitution, must be a freeholder. This certainly disqualifies those who are not freeholders; but does it also imply that no other disqualification can exist beyond the one mentioned? The 13th article declares that no citizen of this State shall be disfranchised, unless by the law of the land, or the judgment of his peers. There is a similar provision in the Constitution of the U. S. The argument of the late *Ch. J.*, on this head, it seems, is to be a *petitio principii.* There will be little difficulty, I imagine, in determining between the gentleman and the *Ch. J.*, whether he who assumes the Act to be constitutional, and therefore good, or the one who assumes it to be unconstitutional, and therefore void, may be fairly charged with begging the question. The 33d article, which relates to impeachments, is no more than what the Constitution of the U. S. contains—the 8th amendment of which also provides that cruel and unusual punishments shall not be inflicted. If ineligibility be a cruel and unusual punishment, as supposed upon the other side, the 8th amendment would repeal that branch of the same Constitution which sanctions disqualification as one consequence of a conviction upon impeachment. The several States have gone on, in the face of these provisions in the Constitution of the U. S., imposing disfranchisement and ineligibility in the same manner as is done by the Statute in question.

It is said that punishments should be proportioned to the nature of the offense. This is obviously a mere question of expediency. Indeed, the argument demands what can never be exactly reached by any human code. How is the punishment of any crime to be proportioned to all the circumstances of each particular case? A man may be guilty of burglary in various degrees, yet the punishment is the same in each. One starving in the streets breaks a house for bread—is he equally guilty with the one who does the same without motive? Executive clemency, alone, can grant relief, and to that it is reserved.

*We are told that this Act is repug- [***699** nant to that part of the Constitution which determines the right of suffrage. It appears to me that this objection is answered most conclusively by the late *Ch. J.* The complaint is, that we contract the right of the voter. All that this proves is, that the person disqualified is placed in the same situation as every other person—who, if he votes for one that is ineligible, loses his vote. The alarm, it seems, is that this sentence of ineligibility may be extended to every member of the community. But what is the nature of our government? It lays out general lines—it cannot reach every case, or look to every extreme. The late *Ch. J.* places this matter upon its proper ground. The Legislature have power to pass all laws for the well ordering of society which are not forbidden by the Constitution. The gentleman supposes extreme cases, to which the Legislature never can go. They must enjoy an extensive discretion in every government; and it is true that any system may be abused, but by reasoning against the possible abuse of power, we deny all power except that of Deity. Even the Christian religion has been perverted to the worst of purposes. When we come to the point supposed by the gentleman, there is a redeeming spirit in the people, which will restrain and correct those who feel power and forget right.

Mr. Butler, in reply. The amount of the gentleman's argument, as derived from other States, is, that because they have violated the Constitution, or the fundamental principles of government, we may, therefore, do the same. It is not necessary to look beyond our own Constitution and that of the U. S. But when we do, we find but two classes of cases in which disfranchisement and ineligibility have been sanctioned by statutes. These are cases of dueling and bribery, from which we must except all the statutes which passed under the Colonial Governments, they being instances which certainly carry no force, as examples, to legislators who act under the new constitutions. Beside, the statutes passed upon these subject, since must stand or fall by the provisions of the particular state constitution under which they 700*] *passed. Some of the constitutions in the neighboring States are broader than ours on this head. Their laws, too, in relation to dueling, have doubtless grown out of the effervescence of the moment, like ours; and they have never been enforced. In Md. the Legislature has lately repealed such a law, as unconstitutional. All the state laws, in relation to dueling, probably stand on the same ground both of principle and policy. This is the first time the question upon their validity has been raised anywhere; and, as to bribery, though the Constitution gives no express authority to punish it by disfranchisement or ineligibility, there are sufficient indications, in almost all the constitutions, of an intent to confer such a power. Indeed, it is consistent with the very terms of some of them. The question, however, as to the validity of any of these statutes, has not been judicially passed upon, and I deny the force of such proof.

When I urged the danger that the rights of suffrage might be impaired or destroyed by multiplying cases of ineligibility, I expected to be met with the objection of extreme cases. The Atty-Gen. does not and will not deny that if the Legislature have power, in the case under consideration, to inflict the punishment of ineligibility, they have it equally in all others, in assault and battery or any other common law offenses. Can the consequence suggested, then, be properly called an extreme case? It seems that our security must lie in the patriotism and intelligence of the Legislature, or the control of their constituents. We say the people have not chosen to rest it there. The security of their liberties reposes upon the provisions of their Constitution, express or implied, a surer and better foundation.

I thank the Atty-Gen. for his allusion to the abuses of the Christian religion, in one of his illustrations, and will pursue it. I put the case of the Legislature annexing this punishment of ineligibility to the violation of the Christian Sabbath, or to profane swearing. Is it supposing an extreme case, to say that they may, within forty years, impose this disability as a punishment for those very common offenses? Had the same thing been supposed, when the original Constitution was adopted, in relation to this offense of *sending [*701 a challenge, might it not have been treated as an extreme case with just as much propriety? Yet the force of circumstances has produced this Act, and may, with just as much probability, result in the same thing, with regard to a breach of the Sabbath. No doubt there are many who think a violation of the Christian Sabbath an offense great as sending a challenge, at least, under some circumstances. Suppose a similar statute in relation to the former offense (it was, too, an offense at common law), could it be maintained as constitutional? If so, the very abuses of religion to which the Atty-Gen. alludes may return upon us.

THE CHANCELLOR. The 1st section of the Act of Nov. 5, 1816, to Suppress Dueling, prescribes that "the person convicted shall be incapable of holding or being elected to any post of profit, trust or emolument, civil or military, under this State;" and the objection now made is, that this punishment is inconsistent with the Constitution.

The Constitution of the U. S. provides that cruel and unusual punishments shall not be inflicted. This provision is one of the amendments to that Constitution, which were adopted soon after the Constitution itself had been ratified. Like other amendments adopted at the same time, it is a restriction upon the Government of the U. S., intended to deprive that Government of a power, which it had or might claim, under the original Constitution. In the language which accompanied these amendments, when they were proposed and adopted; "these further declaratory and restrictive clauses were added to the Constitution, in order to prevent misconstruction, or abuse of its powers." The solicitude of the people and of the States then was, not to limit the power of the States, but to limit the power of the Union, and by new provisions to give security to rights, which were supposed to be in danger from the new and untried system of national government. The danger apprehended was by the parts from the new government of the whole; and not by any State from its own government. Each State was then at liberty, as it now is, to provide by its *own [*702 Constitution, that cruel and unusual punishments shall not be inflicted by its own government. Accordingly, several of the States, in their Constitutions established since the adoption of this Amendment to the Constitution of the Union, have provided that cruel and unusual punishments shall not be inflicted. This provision is found in the Constitutions of Ohio, Tenn., Ind. and Me. The Constitutions of Del., Ky., Miss. and Ala., also established since the adoption of the amendment in question, provide that cruel punishments shall not be inflicted. Other state constitutions are silent upon the subject of punishments, either cruel or unusual. It is most evident that the States which have imposed these restraints upon their own governments, conceived that they were at liberty to do so or not; and that, in their conception, the Constitution of the Union contained no such restraints upon state governments, in the punishment of crimes against States. To consider this amendment as operating upon the several States would be to render nugatory and null the like provision in the Constitutions of very many of the States; and at the same time, to force upon all the States which have not adopted such a provision a rule which they may think inexpedient, and which they, at least, have thought unnecessary in their own internal economy. This provision concerning punishments is, therefore, as a part of the Constitution of the Union, a restriction upon the Government of the Union; and as a part of any state constitution, it is a restriction upon the government of the State which has established it. The Constitution of this State imposes no such restriction upon punishments. Without inquiring whether disqualification to hold office is a punishment either cruel or unusual, I consider this provision of the National Constitution inapplicable to offenses against a State.

The Constitution of the U. S. provides that no State shall pass any bill of attainder, or *ex post facto* law; but that Constitution does not regulate the punishment of crimes against a State.

In considering the question before us, it seems to me to be of little importance whether **703***] we examine it in reference *to the late Constitution of this State, or by that which now exists. The principles and provisions of both instruments, so far as they concern this question, are nearly the same; but as parts of the existing Constitution were in force when this conviction took place, and as it has been urged at the bar that this judgment is more clearly repugnant to the existing Constitution than it may have been to the preceding instrument, I shall inquire whether this judgment is or is not repugnant to the Constitution now in force.

Eligibility to public trusts is claimed as a constitutional right, which cannot be abridged or impaired. The Constitution establishes and defines the right of suffrage; and gives to the electors, and to various authorities, the power to confer public trusts. It declares that ministers of religion shall be ineligible to any office; it prescribes, in respect to certain offices, particular circumstances, without which a person is not eligible to those stations; and it provides that persons holding certain offices shall hold no other public trust. Excepting particular exclusions thus established, the electors and the appointing authorities are, by the Constitution, wholly free to confer public stations upon any person, according to their pleasure. The Constitution giving the right of election and the right of appointment—these rights consisting, essentially, in the freedom of choice; and the Constitution also declaring that certain persons are not eligible to office; it follows from these powers and provisions that all other persons are eligible. Eligibility to office is not declared as a right or principle by any express terms of the Constitution, but it results as a just deduction, from the express powers and provisions of the system. The basis of the principle is the absolute liberty of the electors and the appointing authorities to choose and to appoint any person who is not made ineligible by the Constitution. Eligibility to office, therefore, belongs, not exclusively or especially to electors enjoying the right of suffrage. It belongs equally to all persons whomsoever, not excluded by the Constitution. I therefore conceive it to be entirely clear that the Legislature cannot establish arbitrary exclusions from office, or any general regulation requiring *qualifications which the Constitution [***704** has not required. If, for example, it should be enacted by law that all physicians, or all persons of a particular religious sect, should be ineligible to public trusts; or that all persons not possessing a certain amount of property should be excluded; or that a member of the Assembly must be a freeholder; any such regulation would be an infringement of the Constitution; and it would be so, because, should it prevail, it would be, in effect, an alteration of the Constitution itself. But the question before us is not at all of this character. The Legislature have made no such general regulation. They have prescribed that incapacity to hold public trusts shall be the punishment of a particular crime, and the question here is, whether they have power to prescribe such an incapacity as a punishment or not.

The power of the Legislature in the punishment of crimes is not a special grant, or a limited authority to do any particular thing, or to act in any particular manner. It is a part of "the legislative power of this State," mentioned in the first sentence of the Constitution. It is the sovereign power of a State, to maintain social order, by laws for the due punishment of crimes. It is a power to take life and liberty, and all the rights of both, when the sacrifice is necessary to the peace, order and safety of the community. This general authority is vested in the Legislature, and as it is one of the most ample of their powers, its due exercise is among the highest of their duties. When an offender is imprisoned, he is deprived of the exercise of most of the rights of a citizen; and when he suffers death, all his rights are extinguished. The Legislature have power to prescribe imprisonment or death, as the punishment of any offense. The rights of a citizen are thus subject to the power of the State, in the punishment of crimes; and the restrictions of the Constitution upon this, as upon all the general powers of the government, are, that no citizen shall be deprived of his rights, unless by the law of the land or the judgment of his peers, and that no person shall be deprived of life, liberty or property without due process of law.

*The Constitution has, in one case, [***705** limited punishment. When an officer of the State is convicted upon impeachment, the judgment cannot extend farther than removal from office and disqualification to hold office. This provision stands here, a restriction, not an authority. As the punishment is not to extend farther than removal and disqualification, the sense of the terms and the known course of proceedings in the country from which we derive the history and practice of impeachments, both show that this provision is a mere limitation of a greater power, a power to inflict other punishments, as well as removal and disqualification. Impeachments of public officers, a peculiar species of accusation, made and tried in a peculiar manner, are to extend no farther in their effect than to discharge an officer from his trust, and to render him incapable of holding office; but if the cause for which the officer is thus punished is a public offense, he may be, also, indicted, tried and punished, according to law—the Constitution leaving the definition of the offense, and its particular punishment, in this case, as in all others, to the general power of the Legislature. This part of the Constitution concerning judgment on impeachments, is therefore a limitation of the power of the Court for the Trial of Impeachments, and not a restriction upon the general power of the Legislature over crimes.

The power of the State over crimes is thus committed to the Legislature, without a definition of any crime, without a description of any punishment to be adopted, or to be rejected, and without any direction to the Legislature concerning punishments. It is, then, a power to produce the end by adequate means —a power to establish a criminal code, with competent sanctions—a power to define crimes and prescribe punishments by laws, in the discretion of the Legislature.

But though no crime is defined in the Constitution, and no species of punishment is specially forbidden to the Legislature, yet there are numerous regulations of the Constitution which must operate as restrictions upon this general power. The whole Constitution must be supported; and all its powers and rules must be reconciled into concord. A law **706***] *which should declare it a crime to exercise any fundamental right of the Constitution, as the right of suffrage, or the free exercise of religious worship, would infringe an express rule of the system; and would, therefore, not be within the general power over crimes. Particular punishments would also encroach upon rules and rights established by the Constitution. Though the Legislature have an undoubted right to prescribe capital punishment, and other punishments which produce a disability to enjoy constitutional rights, yet a mere deprivation of rights would, even as a punishment, be, in many cases, repugnant to rules and rights expressly established. Many rights are plainly expressed, and intended to be fundamental and inviolable, in all circumstances. A law enacting that a criminal should, as a punishment for his offense, forfeit the right of trial by jury, would contravene the Constitution, and a deprivation of this right could not be allowed in the form of a punishment. Any other right thus secured, as universal and inviolable, must equally prevail against the general power of the Legislature to select and prescribe punishments. These rights are secured to all; to criminals, as well as to others; and a punishment consisting solely in the deprivation of such a right, would be an evident infringement of the Constitution. Any punishment operating as an infringement of some rule thus expressly established, or some right thus expressly secured, would be unconstitutional, and all punishments which do not subvert such rules and rights of the Constitution are within the scope and choice of the legislative power.

But while many rights are consecrated, as universal and inviolable, the right of eligibility to office, is not so secured. It is not one of the express rules of the Constitution, and is not declared as a right, or mentioned in terms as a principle, in any part of the instrument. Important as this right is, it stands, as the right to life itself stands, subject to the general power of the Legislature, over crimes and punishments. As a right flowing from the Constitution, it cannot be taken away by any law declaring that classes of men, or even a single person not convicted of a public offense, shall be ineligible to public stations; but as a right not expressly secured by the Constitution, *it may be taken from [***707** convicted criminals when the Legislature, in their plenary power over crimes, deem such a deprivation a necessary punishment. To say this is to say, in substance, that the right in question may be forfeited by crimes when the Legislature so direct. If this right is taken from none but malefactors, in punishment for offenses declared by law, and ascertained in the due course of justice, the sense of the whole Constitution is maintained; and the public, it may be presumed, will not find their choice of agents much abridged by the exclusions from office, which their own legislators, courts and juries may thus add to those specified in the Constitution.

Each house of the Legislature is the judge of the qualifications of its own members, and it is said that this provision of the Constitution is infringed by the disqualification in question. The sense of this provision is, that each house shall decide upon the qualifications of its own members without interference or control from any other authority; but this part of the Constitution does not define any qualification which shall be allowed or required by either house. The only qualification made requisite by the Constitution for a Senator, is that he shall be a freeholder; and in respect to members of the Assembly, no qualification whatever is required by the Constitution. Whether the Legislature can exclude from public trusts any person not excluded by the express rules of the Constitution, is the question which I have already examined: and according to my views of that question, there may be an exclusion by law, in punishment for crimes; but in no other manner, and for no other cause. If, then, a disqualification for crime is constitutional, each house of the Legislature, bound to support the Constitution, would give effect to the disqualification. But as the authority of each house is exclusive and supreme in all questions concerning the qualifications of its own members, if either house should consider such a disqualification unconstitutional, or for any reason whatever should disregard it, the opinion of the house would prevail, in respect to the seat and rights of any member declared ineligible by the courts. The disqualification pronounced by the courts would then *fail to produce an exclu- [***708** sion from the Legislature; but it would, nevertheless, be effectual to exclude from all other public stations. Its effect in respect to all other public employments, must be decided by the tribunals of justice. Thus, the same question, must for different objects, receive decisions from different jurisdictions; and under one Constitution and one system of laws, the same decision may be expected from all the public authorities. But if the Senate or the Assembly on one side, and the courts of justice on the other, should make opposite decisions respecting such a disqualification, both decisions would prevail in different respects. The power of each house of the Legislature to judge of the qualifications of its own members, does not determine or illustrate what is or is not a qualification; the Statute to Suppress Dueling does not propose to deprive, nor can any law deprive, the several houses of the Legislature of their exclusive jurisdiction; and this part of the Constitution, is therefore not infringed by the judgment of disqualification now in question.

It has been strongly urged that the power to prescribe this species of punishment may be abused. That such a power may be abused cannot be denied, since all power intrusted to men is subject to abuse. The power to declare crimes and prescribe punishments is high, indefinite and discretionary and, therefore, affords ample room for abuse. Yet the Legislature, by their Acts, instead of any tendency to severity, show a strong disposition to mildness in the use of their power over crimes and punishments. That disqualification to hold public trusts will become a frequent punishment seems not probable, the Legislature having hitherto adopted this punishment only in the two cases of bribery and duels. But whatever may be the danger of abuse, the punishment itself is not unconstitutional. The remedy for abuse of the legislative power, in enacting laws which may be unwise, while they are not unconstitutional, is not in the courts of justice. It is found in other parts of the system, in frequent elections and in the due course of the legislative power itself, which alike enacts and repeals laws, in pursuance of public opinion. That this punishment is little *consonant to the genius of our insti- [*709 tutions; that there is an ample choice of punishment for crimes, without adopting this; that the electors and the appointing powers should enjoy their free choice for public stations, without legal exclusions even for crimes, are reasons of great force; but they are reasons upon which the Legislature must decide.

My opinion upon the whole case is, that the punishment of incapacity to hold office, prescribed by the Act to Suppress Dueling, is not inconsistent with the Constitution; and that this cause has been rightly determined by the courts through which it has passed.

Bowman, Burt, Clark, Dudley, Earll, Gardiner, Haight, Lynde, Mallory, M'Call, M'Intyre, Redfield, Sudam, Thorn, Ward, Wooster and *Wright, Senators,* concurred.

OGDEN, *Senator*, dissented.

For affirmance, 18; for reversal, 1.

Cited in—10 Wend., 457; 2 Hill., 247; 13 N. Y., 418; 50 N. Y., 458; 39 How. Pr., 358; 2 Park., 539; 48 Ind., 347.

[END OF APRIL SESSION, 1824.]

CASES ARGUED AND DETERMINED

IN THE

Court for the Trial of Impeachments

AND THE

CORRECTION OF ERRORS

OF THE

STATE OF NEW YORK,

IN FEBRUARY, 1825.

713*] *THE NORTH RIVER STEAMBOAT COMPANY, *Appellants,*

v.

JOHN R. LIVINGSTON, *Respondent.*

Constitutional Law—State Grant, of Exclusive Right of Navigation—Power of Congress, to Regulate Commerce—"Coasting Trade" Included—"Internal Commerce of the State"—Nature and Powers of General Government—Ferries— Taxation — Injunction — When Judge Excused from Sitting.

The Acts of the Legislature of this State, granting to Robert R. Livingston and Robert Fulton the exclusive navigation of all the waters within its jurisdiction, with boats moved by fire or steam, for a term of years, are repugnant to that clause of the Constitution of the U. S., which authorizes Congress to regulate commerce, so far as those Acts prohibit vessels licensed according to the laws of the U. S., for carrying on the coasting trade, from navigating those waters by means of fire or steam.

The terms "coasting trade" mean commercial intercourse, carried on between different districts in different States, different districts in the same State, or different places in the same district, on the sea coast, or on a navigable river.

The power to regulate commerce among the States, conferred by the Federal Constitution, extends to the coasting trade.

What is meant by the terms "internal commerce of the State."

The Constitution of the U. S. should be so construed as best to promote the great objects for which it was made—avoiding the two extremes of a liberal, or strict construction.

Commercial defects in the Articles of Confederation considered, with the objects of the Federal Constitution on that head.

The powers given to the General Government are to be first satisfied. Some of these are exclusive—some concurrent; and when concurrent, the provisions of the General Government are paramount.

For certain purposes, the General Government is a single consolidated one. In this character, Congress executes its powers.

Congress have no right, under their power of regulating commerce, to interfere with the ferries of the State, except so far as they are used for carrying on the coasting trade;

Nor can they interfere with the navigation upon our canals, or inland lakes or rivers;

But, under their taxing power, they may tax canal boats, or any other property.

An injunction should not be granted, in order to secure a claim to statute privileges, if the right be doubtful.

An order of the Court of Chancery was, as to part of the right, against the appellants, from which they appealed, and, as to another part in their favor, from which neither party appealed; held, that though the respondent could not question that part of the order which was for the appellants, yet he might argue against the reasons and ground upon which it was made, it appearing that if they failed, there could be no foundation for the appeal.

*A judge allowed to withdraw from his seat, [*714 he being interested.

So where he had relations who were interested.

But this privilege was denied to a judge, who requested to withdraw, upon the ground that he had formed and expressed an opinion.

Citations—9 Johns., 507; 4 Johns. Ch., 150; 17 Johns., 488; 4 Wh., 122; 16 Johns., 248; 9 Wh., 203, 204; 1 Johns., 435; Act, Sept. 1, 1789; Act, Feb. 18, 1793.

APPEAL from the Court of Chancery. After the decision in the *Steamboat Co.* v. *Livingston,* 1 Hopk. Ch., 151, June 14, 1824, refusing an injunction against an indirect intercourse between the Cities of N. Y. and Albany, to be carried on by the defendant's steamboat, The Olive Branch, by way of N. J., the plaintiffs by leave of the court below, upon petition presented, and an order made, June 28, 1824, amended their bill, so as to charge the defendant, that, though on the first passage of his boat from N. Y. to Albany, he caused her to stop opposite and adjoining the City of Jersey, in the State of N. J., yet such stopping was collusive and fraudulent, and intended to evade the operation and effect of the laws of this State, granting an exclusive right of navigation by steamboats, and not for any *bona fide* purpose of commercial intercourse; and that since her first trip, although she had performed upwards of 50 passages between the Cities of N. Y. and Albany, yet she had never, in the course of any of them, stopped at, opposite, or adjoining any port or place in the State of N. J., but had prosecuted such passages direct

---

NOTE.—*Constitutional law—Regulation of Commerce—Powers of Congress—When concurrent and when exclusive.* See Gibbons v. Ogden, 17 Johns, 488; S. C., 9 Wh., 1, and *notes* Law. ed.

from a wharf in the City of N. Y., to a wharf in the City of Albany, &c., stopping always at intermediate places upon the Hudson, where it was probable that passengers might be procured. The amended bill then prayed an injunction against such direct intercourse; and all such indirect intercourse, by way of N. J., unless in the prosecution of a *bona fide* voyage, or for the purpose of a *bona fide* commercial intercourse, to or with some place in N. J., and not for the purpose of evading the laws of this State relative to steamboats.

Order to show cause, &c.

This amended bill, being duly verified by various affidavits, copies of the petition, order for amendment, &c., and affidavits were, pur- **715*]** suant to the order, served upon the *defendant July 1, 1824; on the 6th, the motion for an injunction was argued before the *Chancellor;* who, July 9, 1824, made an order, that, so far as the complainants asked an injunction, to prohibit the navigation of the steamboat Olive Branch to or from another State, the motion should be denied; and it was further ordered that an injunction should issue, restraining the defendant from navigating the steamboat Olive Branch, in the waters between the Cities of N. Y. and Troy, when there was no voyage made by the boat to or from another State.

July 19, 1824, the plaintiffs appealed to this court, from so much of the order as denied an injunction, to prohibit the navigation to or from another State.

For a statement of the case in the court below, previous to presenting a petition to amend, with the opinion of His Honor, the *Chancellor* upon it, see 1 Hopk. Ch., 150, 198 to 212.

The reasons in support of that branch of the last order, to which the appeal immediately related, were thus assigned by,

THE CHANCELLOR. Since the decision of the former application for an injunction, the complainants have amended their bill; and several affidavits are also now laid before the court. From the amended bill and these affidavits, it appears, that since the voyage upon which the former application was founded, The Olive Branch has been constantly engaged, and is now employed in navigation between the Cities of Albany and N. Y., without proceeding to any other State.

Upon the facts now before the court, the complainants ask an injunction, to restrain the defendant from navigating the Hudson, in any direct voyage between ports in this State; and also, from navigating circuitously, by stopping in N. J., unless such stopping shall be in the prosecution of a voyage or commerce intended in good faith, and not for the purpose of evading the state grant.

One object of this application, is, to prevent a circuitous navigation through another State, **716*]** where the sole purpose of *the passage to or from another State, may be to continue the voyage to other ports in this State, and where the circuitous voyage would not take place, if a direct voyage between ports in this State were free.

For the complainants, it is urged that a circuitons navigation through another State is a fraud upon their right; that fraud vitiates everything; and that when it is evident, that a circuitous voyage through another State would not take place, if a voyage confined to a State were open, such a circuitous voyage should be regarded and treated as a fraud, and should not be permitted.

That the rights of one should be so used, as not to encroach upon the rights of another; that things which the laws do not permit to be done directly, cannot be done by artifice or circuity; and that fraud cannot prevail; are general principles, which are clear and undisputed. But have these principles any application to this case? The solution of this question must depend upon the true nature and extent of the different rights, which are here in question.

The right of the defendant is derived from a law of the U. S.; and that of the complainants from a law of a State; and to a great extent, these laws are in conflict with each other. Between such laws and such rights, so far as conflict exists, there can be no action like that of opposing powers; no equal rights entitled to equal support; and no reconciliation of adverse rights to the same thing. The law of the U. S. is supreme; and the law of the State is wholly without efficacy, so far as the supreme law extends. The state law is annihilated, so far as the ground is occupied by the law of the Union; and the supreme law prevails, as if the state law had never been made. The supremacy of constitutional laws of the Union, and the nullity of state laws inconsistent with such laws of the Union, are principles of the Constitution of the U. S. Thus, this case is entirely different from any of those, in which various rights derived from one lawgiving source, may exist together, and all may claim scope for their exercise.

What then is the right which has been adjudged to belong to steam vessels licensed for the coasting trade? It is, as I understand the *Supreme Court of the U. S., a right of **[*717** free intercourse by navigation, from State to State; a right to navigate freely, from one State to another, in all cases. It is the same right which a licensed vessel using sails has to proceed from State to State. It is not merely a right to transport merchandise or passengers, or to carry on commerce in any particular manner; but it is a right to engage in everything which constitutes the coasting trade, and for that purpose, to navigate from State to State, whatever may be the intention of any particular voyage. This seems to me to be the meaning of the Supreme Court; and such being the right conferred by a law of the Union, this right must have its full effect, notwithstanding any law of a State.

The complaint now made is, that a right given by a law of the State, may be impaired or impeded in its effect, by the exercise of a right given by a law of the Union. The answer to this complaint is, that so far as the law of the Union acts upon the case, the state law is extinguished; and that such opposing rights to the same thing, cannot co-exist under the Constitution of our country.

If a vessel may in this manner, do that circuitously, which the same vessel may not do directly, this effect is produced by the division of legislative powers between different governments, and by express laws which distinct governments have enacted. It is one of the results of that complex system of government, which has no parallel, in its peculiar structure and the distribution of its powers. If a vessel may navigate between this State and another, it is because a law of the Union, has made such a voyage lawful; and if the same vessel may not navigate between two ports of this State, it is because a law of the State, has made such a voyage unlawful. The law of the State is, that all its waters are subject to an exclusive right of navigation; and the law of the Union, as it is expounded by the Supreme Court, is, that a licensed vessel may navigate the same waters in any voyage to or from another State. These laws are to a great extent, inconsistent; but in a certain other extent, they are not incompatible. Those waters of this State, which are not navigable to or from another State, remain subject in effect, **718***] *to the exclusive grant of this State, because from their situation, the right to navigate from State to State, cannot be there exercised. In those waters of this State, which are navigable to or from another State, the law of this State no longer excludes licensed vessels navigating to or from another State. Where from the contiguity of waters of this State to other States, a voyage to or from an adjoining State may be easily made a circuitous voyage through an adjoining State; may, as a fact, be little more than a direct voyage within this State. But the two cases are still different, and are governed by different laws, made in virtue of distinct powers of legislation. If the laws now in question operate in this manner, it is because navigation between this State and others is subject to the legislation of the Union; while navigation wholly within the State is subject to the legislation of the State, so far as the laws of the State may operate in subordination to those of the Union. The effect of these different laws, thus understood, is to open those waters of the State, which are the theater of navigation between this State and other States, whenever such a navigation takes place, and in no other case; and to leave the navigation of those waters in other cases, and the navigation of waters which are wholly internal, in all cases, subject to the state grant.

If the several rights which are here claimed, had emanated from one government possessing all the powers which are divided between the Union and the States, the argument concerning fraud and circuity would be applicable to rights so arrayed against each other; and the courts of justice might then so enforce and protect such rights as to reconcile them equitably with each other. But when one right is derived from a law of the Union, and an opposing right from a law of a State, all the judges of this country are bound to ascertain the extent of the right given by the law of the Union, and to give effect to that right as fully as if the state law had not been made. The interference of a state law with a constitutional law of the Union, is ascertained, not for the purpose of reconciling repugnant provisions and opposing rights, but in order to declare the state law null.

719*] *For these reasons, I am of opinion that the doctrines concerning fraud can have no application to this case, or to any analogous case, arising under a constitutional law of the Union and a law of a State. The Constitution of the U. S. gives the principle, which must govern all such cases. The law of the Union first has its full operation; and so much only of the state law, as is not abrogated by the effect of the supreme law, remains. This principle destroys all incongruities, and is the only legitimate test of which such cases are susceptible. The right given by a law of the Union, to navigate from State to State, cannot be abridged or restricted by a state law; and whenever a case of navigation between this State and another takes place, the state grant is extinct, as an impediment or objection to such a voyage.

In my examinations of this subject, I have endeavored to ascertain what has been adjudged by the Supreme Court of the U. S., and to discuss those questions of the controversy which that court has not determined. The Supreme Court has fully determined the question of navigation from State to State; and in everything concerning that question, I follow the Supreme Court. In respect to navigation within the State, in cases not comprehended by the decision of the Supreme Court, I have given my reasons for thinking that a license for the coasting trade does not confer any right inconsistent with the state grant. The general result from the decision of the Supreme Court, the former decisions of the courts of this State, and all the views which have been taken, is, that the state grant remains in force, in those cases in which the right to navigate from State to State, does not intervene; and that where this paramount right intervenes, the law of this State is wholly void. The portion of the state grant which remains, is that fragment of the right granted which may have effect, after the law of the Union shall first have had its full operation; and nothing more of the state grant can remain in force. The state grant is in force, only when and where the right to navigate from State to State is not exercised.

So far as the complainants ask an injunction to prohibit the navigation of The Olive Branch to or from another State *the applica- [***720** tion is refused; and an injunction to restrain the defendant from navigating that vessel, in the waters between the Cities of N. Y. and Troy, when there is no voyage to or from another State, is granted.

Mr. T. J. Oakley, for the appellants, said the decretal order, in part appealed from, consisted of two distinct branches: so far as the motion below related to an injunction against a fraudulent intercourse between N.Y. and Troy, by way of N. J., it was denied; but so far as it related to a direct intercourse between those cities, it was granted. The latter was upon the principle, that the state laws are operative, and confer upon the appellants an exclusive right to the direct navigation. In this branch of the decree, both parties have acquiesced; neither has appealed; and he supposed that, for all the purposes of the present discussion, it must be laid entirely out of view, with the principles upon which it was bottomed; and that the attention of the court would be directed, exclusively, to the ground upon which the voyage by the way of N. J. was allowed. By not appealing, he supposed the respondent had conceded the validity of the state laws in respect to internal navigation; and would not be allowed to question them here. He mentioned this, because it might be important to understand how counsel would consider it; and he did not know how to obtain the direction of the court upon the subject. To his mind it was clear, that not having appealed from that part of the order which was against the respondent, gentlemen could not now oppose the reasons upon which it was founded.

Mr. J. V. Henry, for the respondent, did not wish the gentleman to remain in the dark, as to the course which the counsel for the respondent intended to pursue. With leave of the court, they should contest the whole grounds upon which the order, in both its branches, proceeded. No concession made by counsel, or omission to appeal, could alter the constitutional ground. If the counsel for the respondent could prove that the Supreme Court of the U. S., in *Gibbons* v. *Ogden*, 9 Wh., 1, had **721***] made a decision *embracing and definitively settling the controversy in their favor as to both branches of the order, they have a right to do so. He had contended for this in the court below, and intended to pursue the same train of argument here. He was not precluded by the decree. The whole subject came up by the appeal made in behalf of the Company; and upon this ground, counsel had a right to consider all the arguments with which it was connected.

Mr. A. Van Vechten, same side, would add one word to what had fallen from his associate. Gentlemen come here to get rid of an order allowing them an exclusive right to a direct intercourse, with their boat, between N. Y. and Troy; but giving the respondent a common right with them to ply between those cities by way of N. J. From the latter branch of the order they appeal. Now, if we show that they have already got more than they are entitled to, this court will not enlarge the order in their favor. If it turns out that they have no right to either branch of the decree, upon any ground, or in other words, if all fails them, they cannot retain a part. They are certainly bound to establish an exclusive right within this State, before they can set up one in N. J. If they fail in the former, the latter goes of course. True, we cannot appeal, till the final hearing. The order is technically binding till then; but the principle of the whole order remains open. The two questions which it involves cannot be separated.

Mr. Henry briefly examined the several reported cases in relation to the steamboat controversy, concluding with that of *Gibbons* v. *Ogden*, in 9 Wh., 1, with a view to show that the subject was completely opened by that decision, which, in his opinion, disposed of both grounds; and in order to show that the discussion was not to be limited by the maxim *stare decisis*, upon the supposition that any decision heretofore made by this court was not completely done away by the decree of the U. S. Court.

Mr. Oakley had barely alluded to the difficulty which the case presented, for the purpose of learning of gentlemen what course *they intended to pursue, or, if it was [***722** proper, taking the direction of the court. He did not intend now, and perhaps it would be unnecessary at any stage of the discussion, to follow the gentleman in a review of the authorities to which he had referred. This might be material, if the court should consider the questions open upon both branches of the decree. He would like to understand if the court thought gentlemen had a right to contend that an order against them, from which they had not appealed, was erroneous. True, they may appeal from the final decree. So may the appellants; but the time has gone by for questioning this interlocutory order on their part. This being a court whose jurisdiction is strictly appellate, they cannot notice anything which does not come up in the form of an appeal. The exclusive right of the appellant within the State is conceded. It is out of the question as to this cause, and the respondent must be silent upon it. He is estopped by his own neglect; and the only inquiry which this court will make is as to the ulterior right of indirect navigation.

Mr. T. A. Emmet, for the appellants, said the difference between counsel related to a simple matter of practice; not how the question concerning the last branch of the order should be discussed (for that would be settled when they reached it in the course of argument), but whether it should be examined at all. This court directs its attention to the matter appealed from. The order appealed from has a double aspect, only one of which is looked to by the appeal. This injunction is merely interlocutory process, which may be dissolved at the final hearing in the court below. The respondent may then apply for its dissolution, and if refused, he may appeal. But the 15 days, to which the appeal from an interlocutory order is limited, have gone by; and whether gentlemen can now get it up by a side wind is the question. He had always thought that whenever a party was dissatisfied with an order or decree, if he intended to be relieved from it, he must appeal or be concluded. If both parties are dissatisfied, both must appeal.

*TALLMADGE, *President*, did not [***723** understand the counsel for the respondent as claiming to disturb the order for an injunction. On the contrary, they acquiesce in this; but they claim to maintain the proposition that no injunction whatever should be granted by way of answer to the appeal which claims an injuction as to a particular branch of navigation. In discussing the narrower proposition, they claim to go into the broader one as material in its support.

WOODWORTH, J., should, for himself at any rate, considering the nature and importance of this controversy, which related to a great constitutional question, be inclined to hear the counsel at large, reserving the point of practice. But he did not feel any difficulty in saying that the ground of the whole order was fairly open to discussion in the form which the matter now assumed. To be sure, the respondent's counsel had precluded themselves from a direct appeal by their acquiescence beyond the period of limitation; but suppose they satisfy the court, not only that the respondent has a right to the indirect navigation by way of N. J., but establish the broader proposition, that they have a right in all respects equal to that of the appellants. This, to be sure, would go to the order for an injunction, which is unappealed from; but it would also be the most powerful reason in answer to the appeal.

SUTHERLAND, *J.*, said the respondent was content with the whole order, and willing to submit to its operation, provided it could be entirely retained. The appellants are, however, dissatisfied with a part, and come here to reverse it; and all the respondent now claims is the right to answer, "Here was an order, one branch of which was for you and one branch for me; you come to reverse the latter, and claim the whole. I now put you to your whole title. I insist you have no title whatever. The whole fails, and, of course, you have no right to a part."

SAVAGE, *Ch. J.*, was clear that counsel should be at liberty to go into the whole question. If they could maintain the respondent's title to a general and unqualified navigation **724***] *between N. Y. and Troy, this certainly included the lesser proposition that he might navigate on the same route by way of N. J., and would be conclusive against the appeal.

The other members of *the Court* being unanimously of this opinion, the cause was then argued at large by

Mr. Oakley, for the appellants;

Messrs. Van Vechten and *Henry*, for the respondent; and,

Mr. Emmet, in reply.

The arguments did not differ materially from those used by the same counsel and by *Mr. Haines* in the court below, which will be found well reported by Mr. Hopkins in his first volume of Chancery Reports, 151 to 198, to which the reader is referred. And I omit them here, the rather because they are mostly noticed in the learned and eloquent opinions of *Mr. Justice* Woodworth and *Ch. J.* Savage, who, it will be seen, with other members of the court, differed as to the order which should be made here.

Previous to the argument,

COLDEN and SPENCER, *Senators*, were allowed, on their request, to withdraw from their seats in court—the former, on the ground that he was interested, and the latter on the ground that he was related to persons having an interest, in the event of the cause.

OGDEN, *Senator*, in the course of the argument, said he had long since formed an opinion upon the questions under discussion, which he had freely expressed to others, and endeavored to enforce with what little power of argument he was master of. And he asked leave, for this reason, to withdraw from his seat, and take no part in the decision.

SUTHERLAND, *J.*, did not think Mr. Ogden could be excused on this ground. The question is one of law, not of fact; and a judge having **725***] formed and expressed an opinion, *did not come within the principle which would make this a cause of challenge to a juror.

WOODWORTH, *J.*, understood Mr. Ogden not only to have formed an opinion, but to be so wedded to that opinion that he could not yield it. As a juror, upon a question of fact, he clearly would not be received; and though being a judge, he could not be challenged for this cause; yet, he inclined to think the court might, in their discretion, excuse him. But,

A majority of *the Court* overruled the request of Mr. Ogden, and he continued in his seat.

WOODWORTH, *J.* The appellants are entitled to all the interest and property, which Robert R. Livingston and Robert Fulton had, to the exclusive right and privilege of navigating steamboats on that part of the waters of the Hudson River, between N. Y. and Troy. This right has frequently been questioned in the courts of this State. Every objection that the ingenuity of counsel could suggest, has heretofore been presented for consideration, and overruled by our highest court of justice.

It would be a waste of time minutely to review those decisions. They must be considered as of binding authority, until a higher tribunal shall have pronounced them erroneous. On this point there is probably no difference of opinion. Wretched, indeed, would be the state of the community if it were otherwise. Individual rights would depend on the fluctuating opinions of different men, sitting in the same courts—what is declared to be law to-day, might not be law to-morrow. The evils growing out of such a system are too apparent to require comment. It must, however, be understood, that this doctrine is not to be carried so far as to sanction error. It will sometimes happen that the principle upon which a cause ought to be decided, has been overlooked, or mistaken—sometimes the rule, as settled by former adjudications, has been misapplied. In these and similar cases, it is undoubtedly proper to review and correct; but it is always expected that manifest error be pointed out. If precisely the same questions have been before decided, *and the same arguments con- [***726** sidered, they have the highest claim to conclusiveness in the courts where they were pronounced.

That the decisions on the exclusive right of Livingston and Fulton are of this character, is abundantly manifest. In the cause of *Livingston* v. *Van Ingen*, 9 Johns., 507, the several Acts of the Legislature granting this monopoly, are decided to be constitutional and valid. It is true, that the effect of a license under the U. S., for carrying on the coasting trade, was not then drawn in question—the respondents had not obtained any such license; but it was objected, that the state laws interfered with the power given to Congress, "to regulate commerce with foreign nations and among the several States, and with the Indian tribes." It was held that all the internal commerce of the State, by land and water, remained entirely and exclusively within the scope of the original sovereignty. In the case of *Ogden* v. *Gibbons*, 4 Johns. Ch., 150, it was decided that these Acts were constitutional, and that the license gave the vessel an American character, while the right of the individual procuring the license, to use the vessel, as against another individual, setting up a distinct and exclusive right, remained precisely as it did before. The decree was affirmed by this court. 17 Johns., 488. The Supreme Court of the U. S. reversed that decree, and it is contended that the reversal was upon the grounds litigated in the cause now before us. If this be so, it becomes our duty to give that decision its full effect, as proceeding from a court of paramount and controlling jurisdiction.

Before I proceed to discuss this point, it is proper to observe that the extent of the decision in the case of *Gibbons* v. *Ogden* is to be limited, as it was in *Sturges* v. *Crowninshield*, 4 Wh., 122. The court there say, that their opinion is confined to the case actually under consideration. In the case of *Mather* v. *Bush*, 16 Johns., 248, the Supreme Court of this State proceeded on that ground, and held that between that case and *Sturges* v. *Crowninshield* there was a material and manifest distinction; that a full and fair effect to the decision in *Sturges* v. *Crowninshield*, ought to be given, so **727***] far, and so far *only, as that court had actually decided; that it would be unfit and irregular to analyze the reasoning and illustrations in the opinion delivered, any farther than to show that the point then presented was not intended to be decided; and that we were not called upon to take a step in advance of the Supreme Court of the U. S. To the opinion delivered in *Mather* v. *Bush* I fully assented, both as to the result and the reasons assigned. On further reflection, I see no cause to recede from the ground then taken. I proceed to inquire—

First. What was the precise point in issue, in the case of *Gibbons* v. *Ogden*, and what was decided?

Second. Does the case before us present the same question?

Third. If the respondent has the right to navigate his steamboat from N. J. to N. Y., under a license to carry on the coasting trade, is he in the fair exercise of that right, by proceeding from N. Y. to N. J., and from thence to Albany, unless the voyage shall be for the purpose of carrying on such trade *bona fide*, and not for the purpose of evading the state grant?

The bill of Ogden alleged, that by virtue of his exclusive right, he run a steamboat, called The Atalanta, between the City of N. Y. and Elizabethtown Point; that the defendant, Gibbons, was the owner of two boats impelled by steam, and in contravention of the exclusive right of the plaintiff, had set in motion the said boats, and employed them in the transportation of passengers, between the City of N. Y. and Elizabethtown; and that they then actually navigated between those places. An injunction was granted, restraining the defendant from navigating his boats on the waters of this State, between Elizabethtown and N. Y. The answer admitted that the boats were intended to navigate between N. Y. and Halsted's Point, in N. J.; and that they did run, and continue so to do, until restrained by the injunction. The defendant averred that his boats were duly enrolled, and licensed under the laws of the U. S., to be employed in carrying on the coasting trade; and insisted, that under the license, they might lawfully be **728***] employed in *the coasting trade, between parts of the same State, or of different States, and could not be excluded or restrained therein, by any law or grant of a particular State, on any pretense to an exclusive right to navigate the waters of any particular State by steamboats. The residue of the answer presents a distinct ground of defense, not connected with the present inquiry.

The preceding is a concise statement of the pleadings, on which the Supreme Court of the U. S. adjudicated. What, then, was in issue between these parties? Certainly not whether the license conferred a right to navigate between two points in this State, when the voyage is not a continuation of a passage to or from another State. The reasons in support of this proposition appear to me conclusive. Ogden claimed no right to a navigation of that description. He merely claimed the right to run his boat from Elizabethtown to N. Y. His purchase extended no farther. The bill complained of the invasion of this right solely. If the answer sets up a right more extensive than that asserted in the bill, it puts in issue only so much as applies to the case made by the bill. What goes beyond, may or may not be well founded. Let it be either, it seems necessarily to follow, that the plaintiff is not called on to admit or deny it. As to him, it may be considered as irrelevant matter, unless the whole case made by the answer depends on one and the same principle. The answer alleges a right, under the license, to navigate steamboats from N. Y. to Elizabethtown. This meets the case made by the bill. If it also claims a right under the license, to navigate from N. Y. to Albany, without reference to the commencement or termination of the voyage in N. J., in this respect it goes beyond the bill, and is not matter in issue between the parties, unless the decision of the first necessarily decides the second. If the two questions are not precisely the same; if there are well founded doubts whether the establishment of the right to navigate between N. Y. and N. J. proves the right to navigate the whole extent of the Hudson; and more especially, if there are substantial grounds of argument to resist the right claimed, in the latter case, which do *not [***729** apply to the other, it cannot safely be said that a decision on one controls the other. It requires a clear and explicit adjudication of the higher tribunal, on the point, before the respondent is entitled to rest on the ground of authority.

I have supposed that Gibbons claimed, in his answer, the right set up by the respondent. I think it manifest, however, that he did not. A right to employ his boat in the coasting trade, between different States, is all that seems to be claimed. If this protected the defendant, in running his boats from Jersey to the City of N. Y., against the exclusive privilege of the plaintiff, it was all the defendant desired, and all that necessarily came in question. The boats were employed in that navigation only, and for that purpose the answer alleges they were intended. To that extent the decision of the Supreme Court of the U. S. is definite and certain. The defendant run no boat under the circumstances presented in the case before us. It was, therefore, a mere speculative question, whether the exclusive privilege must yield to the license, in such a case. I admit it was incidental to, and in some degree, but not inseparably, connected with the right to run boats from Elizabethtown to N. Y. Unless, therefore, the Supreme Court of the U. S., in language not to be mistaken, have considered the two cases to be the same, or that the license would equally extend to authorize a navigation between two places within the State, I am not disposed to anticipate, or go in advance of their opinion. Resort, then, must be had, in the first place, to the decree itself, and then to the reasoning upon which it is founded.

The language of the decree is, that the license to carry on the coasting trade gave full authority to navigate the waters of the U. S., by steam or otherwise, for the purpose of carrying on the coasting trade, any law of the State of N. Y. to the contrary notwithstanding. This was the point decided, and nothing more. It was all the appellant required, to obtain a reversal. *Ch. J.* Marshall observes, "the coasting trade is a term well understood; the law has defined it, and all know its meaning **730***] perfectly; the *Act describes, with great minuteness, the various operations of a vessel engaged in it; and it cannot be doubted, that a voyage from N. J. to N. Y. is one of those operations." This, then, is the basis upon which the decree rests. It is a particular specification of the point decided by the court. The remaining parts of the decree, where general terms are employed, must be understood as conforming to that specification. It is analogous to the principle which governs in the construction of other instruments. Where there is a particular recital, or enumeration of particulars, to which the instrument is to apply, subsequent general words shall be qualified by the particular recital. When, therefore, the court afterwards declare, "that so much of the several laws of the State of N. Y., as prohibits vessels licensed according to the laws of the U. S., from navigating the waters of the State of N. Y., by means of fire or steam, is repugnant to the Constitution, and void," does it authorize a navigation for carrying on a trade wholly internal, within the waters of a State? Evidently not, unless the coasting trade is declared to extend, not only to commerce between the States, but also to internal commerce within the State. When, therefore, the decree speaks of navigating the waters of the State by fire or steam, the words, "for the purpose of carrying on the coasting trade" are necessarily understood. So, also, in the last clause, where the court say, that the "decree of this court, which perpetually enjoins Gibbons from navigating the waters of this State, by steam or fire, is erroneous," must receive the same construction; so that the whole decree may hold an uniform language, and correctly state the precise point involved in the decision.

But it is contended that the opinion delivered embraces the present case, and sanctions the right claimed by the respondent. I have already suggested my views, as to the reasoning and illustrations which courts may assign in support of their judgments, and that, generally speaking, we tread on unsafe ground, if we depart from the point actually decided.

In discussing the general nature of the power to regulate commerce among the States, and **731***] the effect of a license to *carry on the coasting trade, the right of the State over its internal commerce was considered. But it is nowhere asserted, in the opinion delivered, that the license to carry on the coasting trade extends to the commerce of a State purely internal. If, from the reasoning, we may conjecture, or even think it probable, that the superior tribunal may, on a future occasion, carry the doctrine to that extent, we are not justified in reversing what has been solemnly and repeatedly adjudged in our own courts on such grounds. It must either be on the ground of an express decision by paramount authority, or that, on a consideration of the new points of view, in which the question is presented, we are satisfied the former decisions are erroneous.

The *Ch. J.* considers the power of regulating commerce, as extending to the regulation of navigation, and that commerce "among the several States," comprehends every species of commercial intercourse; that it cannot stop at the external boundary line of each State, but may be introduced into the interior. But it was "not intended to say that these words comprehend commerce, which is completely internal, which is carried on between man and man in a State, or between different parts of the same State, and which does not extend to, or affect other States." And, again, he observes, "the enumeration of the particular classes of commerce to which the power was to be extended, would not have been made, had the intention been to extend the power to every description. The enumeration presupposes something not enumerated; and that something, if we regard the language or the subject of the sentence, must be the exclusively internal commerce of a State. The genius and character of the whole government seems to be, that its action is to be applied to all the external concerns of the nation, and to those internal concerns which affect the State generally, but not to those which are completely within a particular State, which do not affect other States, and with which it is not necessary to interfere for the purpose of executing some of the general powers of the government. The completely internal commerce of a State, then, may be considered as reserved for the State itself."

*Commerce, then, among the States, [***732** as explained by the Supreme Court of the U. S., does not include internal commerce. It is that which proceeds from one State to another. A voyage in the prosecution of such a commerce may be continued from port to port, and place to place, on the internal waters of the State. Thus, a voyage direct from Elizabethtown to Albany, is commerce among the States, and the vessel may touch at any intermediate port. In the opinion delivered, the question is put, "can a trading expedition, between two adjoining States, commence and terminate outside of each? And if the trading intercourse be between two States, remote from each other, must it not commence in one, and terminate in the other, and probably pass through a third? Commerce among the States must, of necessity, be commerce with the States." This language seems to me incapable of being mistaken. In discussing the constitutional powers of Congress, under the clause to regulate "commerce among the States," the *Ch. J.* kept steadily in view, a commerce directly from one State to another, and that, so far as that was concerned, all state regulations in collision must yield. The general expressions in the opinion, "that the power of Congress must be exercised whenever the subject exists, and if it exists within the States, then the power of Congress may be exercised within a State," are all to be understood as qualified and limited, so as to protect the commerce from one State to another.

The whole scope of the reasoning is, to show the extent of the power of Congress on this subject; that it is, in its nature, exclusive, and consequently does not admit of participation by the States. It is conceded, in the opinion delivered, that the direct power of Congress to regulate commerce among the States, does not operate on the internal commerce of a State, but that such internal commerce may be considered as reserved for the State itself.

I have attempted to show what species of commercial intercourse is intended by the words "commerce among the States." If I am correct in the construction put upon the reasoning of the *Ch. J.*, it follows, that a navigation from port to port, where the *termini* of
733*] the voyage are both *within a State, is not within the direct power given to Congress, but is under State control, except in certain cases, which I will directly point out. In pursuing this subject, it must be kept in mind, that I am not examining this as an original question, but to ascertain what ground is covered by the decision of the Supreme Court; to that extent it will receive our sanction.

The opinion clearly maintains, that although the States have the power of legislating on the subject of their internal commerce, and no direct power is given to Congress on this subject; yet that a collision may sometimes take place, and consequently that the law of Congress, if within their delegated powers, being the supreme law of the land, must prevail. This collision did exist in the case of *Ogden* v. *Gibbons;* for although it be admitted that the State has a right to regulate its internal commerce, the power is subject to this qualification, that whenever that regulation interferes with the power of Congress, so far as it interferes, it is inoperative and void. The Supreme Court considered the steamboat monopoly as the exercise of a right strictly commercial, and that, therefore, it must yield to a paramount law of Congress, made in pursuance of the Constitution. By the license under that law, Gibbons was authorized to navigate from N. J. to any port or place in this State. To that extent the state law is in collision, and to that only has the decree reference in the following sentence: "that so much of the several laws of the State of N. Y. as prohibits vessels licensed, according to the laws of the U. S., from navigating the waters of the State of N. Y. by means of fire or steam, is repugnant to the Constitution and void." It was argued that a construction put on the words, "commerce among the States," like that which obtained the sanction of the Supreme Court, would subvert state inspection laws, health laws, turnpike roads and ferries. But it was answered, as to these, that although having a considerable influence on commerce, the right to pass them was not derived from the power to regulate it, but formed a portion of that mass of legislation within a State, not surrendered to the General Government. Certain it is, that according to the explanation given *by the court, of the terms "commerce [***734** among the States," they cannot be defended as commercial regulations. It is because they are not so considered, that they are not affected by a law of Congress. On this ground Gibbons could not set up a ferry between the City of Jersey and N. Y.; it would not be a commerce within the meaning of the Constitution, and consequently the state grant of the ferry would be valid. These points I consider as decided, and do not feel myself at liberty to question them.

The opinion delivered, supposes that the subjects of internal state regulations may be also affected in another way by the General Government. The proposition is thus laid down: "If the legislative power of the Union can reach them, it must be for national purposes; it must be where the power is expressly given for a special purpose, or is clearly incidental to some power expressly given." 9 Wh. 203, 204. It is here proper to remark, that the Act of Congress for licensing vessels to be employed in the coasting trade must be considered as an Act passed in the exercise of their express powers; it is to give effect to those powers exclusively. It does not profess to call in aid of the express power, any incidental power, nor can it be collected from the Act, whether Congress claim the right of interfering with the purely internal commerce of the State, in consequence of any incidental power. Admitting that Congress may, on this principle, support the right to pass laws, in collision with the internal regulations of a State, the only consequence is, that so far, and to that extent, the general and state governments have concurrent powers; and no question can arise upon them, until they come in conflict. There is nothing, then, in the principle which bears upon the present question; for Congress have not yet attempted to exercise any incidental power, at variance with the State right to regulate its internal commerce.

The example given by the *Ch. J.*, as to the manner in which the incidental power may be exercised, as I understand it, has an important bearing upon the principal question, what is commerce among the States? He says (page 204): "If Congress license vessels to sail from one port *to another in the same [***735** State, the Act is supposed to be necessarily incidental to the power expressly granted to Congress, and implies no claim of a direct power to regulate the purely internal commerce of a State, or to act directly on its system of police." The case put, seems to be the very case under consideration, "a vessel sailing from one port to another in the same State." This is an implied admission that it does not fall within the express power of Congress to regulate commerce among the States, and could only be reached, if reached at all, by the exercise of what is called a power incidental to the power expressly given.

According to the view I have taken, the question to be decided is narrowed down to a single proposition: does the direct power of Congress to regulate commerce among the States, include the right of regulating commerce between two points in the same State, when there is no voyage to or from another State? I have endeavored to show that it does not; and that if there is an incidental power, which, when called into action, might bear on internal state legislation, the answer is, it is not exclusive, and no such power has yet been exercised: when it is, it will be time enough to consider its validity.

It does not seem to me that the law of Congress, or the license granted under that law, can make any difference, according to the view taken by the Supreme Court; for it necessarily results, that if Congress have the exclusive power to regulate commerce among the States (and so it is held), the States have no power at all to legislate on the subject. Their Acts must be void, whether Congress had passed any law regulating the coasting trade or not. The right, it is true, to carry on the coasting trade, is held to be derived from the license; but if it were not so, the same consequences would result as respects the appellants. Their claim for an injunction would then rest on a law, inoperative and void, so far as it comes in collision with the constitutional power of Congress. It could not be supported, whether the license gave a right to the respondent, or was only evidence of the character of the ves-
736*] sel. The whole question depends *on this: what is meant by the expression, "commerce among the States?"

But the Act of Congress, and the license under it, may, I apprehend, be advantageously considered, for the purpose of fortifying the construction given to the powers of Congress on this subject.

I consider the Act Regulating the Coasting Trade as a plenary exercise of the powers of Congress under the Constitution, so far as navigation, or a commerce by water, is concerned. The Act has given no definition as to the extent of this right. The sense of Congress seems to be, that the "coasting trade" is co-extensive with the direct power "to regulate commerce among the States." It does not assert any other or greater right. Does, then, the coasting trade, within its legitmate meaning, apply to a commerce carried on by a citizen of a State, exclusively on the internal waters of the same State?

When words are employed, which had previously received a known interpretation, they are to be construed in that manner, unless a different intent is plainly indicated. When the Constitution of the U. S. was adopted, it found the States in the possession and exercise of a coasting trade; each State had a right of prescribing its own regulations; the citizens of one State, when navigating the waters of another State, were obliged to conform to its regulations. Subject to these, they might navigate from one State to another, and to any port or place within a State. This was the coasting trade as generally understood. A voyage proceeding from another State to this State would be the coasting trade, whether the vessel terminated her voyage at the City of N. Y., or proceeded on her voyage to Albany. It would, within the meaning of the terms, be a coasting trade, although the internal waters of the State form no part of the coast. The trade had reference to an intercourse between States, which might be carried into the interior of a State, if there were navigable waters: but with respect to a trade purely internal, between different parts of the same State, I am not aware that it was ever considered within the meaning *of those terms. It would [*737 have been novel, I apprehend, if not unintelligible language, to speak of the coasting trade on the Hudson River. It seems, therefore, to my mind, a fair inference that Congress never contemplated that the license gave a right to navigate the internal waters of a State, unless in the prosecution of a coasting trade from State to State; but intended to limit it to a commerce of the latter description.

The grievance in this case is, that the respondent navigates a steamboat from N. Y. to Albany, notwithstanding the exclusive right of the appellants. The injunction does not, according to the view I have taken, interfere or come in collision with the license.

But it is contended that this is a coasting trade from State to State, inasmuch as the boat of the respondent on her voyage from N. Y., stops in N. J., and from thence proceeds to Albany. The appellants allege that it is collusive and fraudulent, intended to evade the operation of the laws of this State, and not for any *bona fide* purpose of commercial intercourse. In confirmation of this, they charge that the respondent's steamboat stopped adjoining the City of Jersey, but did not land or take on board any goods, wares, merchandise or passengers whatever. On this state of facts, the question recurs, what is authorized by the license? It is a coasting trade from one State to any other port or place in another State. The law of the State excluding the entry of such vessels is in collision, but the collision exists only when the trade is carried on. The meaning of the license is, that you may enter the waters of N. Y. for the purpose of trade; a state law cannot prevent your entry. If for other purposes, the license cannot be called to your aid. I think this evident from the following considerations:

It is commerce only among the States that Congress is authorized by the Constitution to regulate. The license cannot have a more extensive operation than the power from which it is derived; consequently it can only act upon commerce. The commerce specified is the coasting trade, and to that it is confined. To say that a vessel proceeding from N. Y. to the wharf in the City of Jersey, without any *communication with the shore, [*738 without landing or taking on board goods or passengers, is a trade within the meaning of the license, is to my mind a gratuitous assertion; but when to this is added, that the touching at N. J. seems to have been for the purpose of fraudulently evading the laws of the State, and not for any *bona fide* purpose of commercial intercourse; when it is evident that the inducement was to bring the respondent within the decision in the case of *Ogden* v. *Gibbons*, some of the landmarks of the law must be removed before the doctrine can be sanctioned. No principle is better settled than this—what cannot lawfully be done directly cannot be done indirectly. This circuitous voyage was in evasion of the laws of this State; the touching at N. J. was colorable only. The affidavit of the respondent has not denied that it was an evasion. Indeed, the whole scope of the respondent's argument has been directed to show that the *Chancellor's* opinion is incorrect, in considering a voyage commencing and terminating in this State, as not protected by the license; while that part which relates to touching at a port in another State, in the course of the voyage, has scarcely been urged. It may be laid down as a general principle, that whenever an act is done *in fraudem legis*, it cannot be the basis of a suit, in the courts of the country, whose laws are attempted to be infringed. *Jackson* v. *Jackson*, 1 Johns., 425. The fraudulent act is considered as no act; it is the same as if nothing had been done; and although I do not think it necessary to lay any stress on the intention with which the act was done, because the facts do not constitute a coasting trade, yet I think the principle applicable, both as it respects the Act of Congress and the laws of this State. The attempt is to convert into a *bona fide* coasting trade, what is so in point of form, and colorable only; and to make it the basis on which to resist successfully the laws of this State. Neither can succeed. The respondent must abide the decision of the court on the other grounds.

My opinion is, that the decree of His Honor, the *Chancellor*, be reversed, and that an injunction issue restraining the respondent from navigating the steamboat Olive Branch in the waters between the City of N. Y. and Troy, **739***] when *there is no voyage made to or from another State in good faith, for the purpose of carrying on the coasting trade, and when no such *bona fide* trade or commerce shall be actually carried on.

Sutherland, J., and *Crary, Haight, Lake, McMichael, Nelson, Thorn* and *Wilkeson, Senators*, concurred.

SAVAGE, *Ch. J.* The appellants filed their bill in the Court of Chancery, charging the respondent with a violation of their exclusive right to navigate the internal waters of this State, by navigating on those waters, from N. Y. to Albany, with his steamboat, The Olive Branch, for the purpose of carrying passengers. They prayed an injunction to restrain and prevent such navigation.

The opposition to the motion for an injunction rested upon a copy of the enrolment of the steamboat Olive Branch, and a license for the coasting trade, and also the affidavit of the defendant, relying upon an intercourse with the State of N. J. The plaintiffs allege that the intercourse with the State of N. J. was collusive and fraudulent, and not a *bona fide* voyage to or from another State.

The *Chancellor* granted the injunction to restrain the defendant from navigating directly from N. Y. to Troy, when there is no voyage made by the steamboat to or from another State; but denied the injunction to prohibit the navigation to or from another State. The latter part of the decree, only, is appealed from.

The respondent denies any title in the appellants, to an exclusive right of navigation with steamboats, in the waters of this State; and contends that unless their right be first established, the question of fraud or no fraud is altogether immaterial. Under this view of the rights of the respondent, the whole question has been argued by counsel before this court. I proceed, therefore, to inquire, whether the appellants have any right to the exclusive navigation of the waters of this State, with vessels propelled by steam; and, particularly, whether they have such right in the waters of the Hudson River.

*The appellants have all the right [***740** which was granted to Livingston and Fulton. The validity of that grant is denied. It has been asserted by the courts of this State, and denied by the Supreme Court of the U. S. The point of inquiry, then, will be, whether any part of the grant is still valid; and if any, whether it exists as to the waters of the Hudson River.

Upon the argument of this cause, the counsel agreed in urging upon the court the propriety of adhering to former decisions, not overruled, upon the ground that a court of *dernier resort* can not review its own decisions, and that its adjudications must remain the law, until altered by legislative authority. It will be useful, therefore, before entering into any discussion as to the constitutionality of the laws in question, to ascertain precisely what has been judicially determined, both by this court and the Supreme Court of the U. S.; that while we adhere with firmness to the decisions of this court, deliberately made, we may recede, with respectful submission, from so much as has been overruled by the superior tribunal.

The constitutionality of the laws relative to steamboats, was first drawn in question in the case of *Livingston* v. *Van Ingen*, 9 Johns., 507. In that case, the title of the plaintiffs was substantially like that of the appellants here. The defendants were charged with violating the plaintiffs' exclusive right, by navigating with steamboats between N. Y. and Albany. The defense in that case differs from this, inasmuch as no coasting license was shown. The defense rested on the ground that, by the adoption of the Constitution of the U. S., the State had parted with all right to legislate on the subject, and that, therefore, the Acts were unconstitutional and void. This defense was unanimously overruled by the court, on the broad ground of the constitutionality of the laws; but as no decision can be considered absolute authority, except upon a state of facts similar to those adjudicated upon, the case of *Livingston* v. *Van Ingen* is an authority so far as the facts are similar; but when they differ, no farther authority than the reasoning of *the [***741** judges is applicable, and then only as the opinions of learned men on the question.

In the case of *Gibbons* v. *Ogden*, 17 Johns., 488, Ogden, the complainant, in the Court of Chancery, charged the defendant, Gibbons, with an infringement of the exclusive grant to Livingston and Fulton, which he, Ogden, held under an assignment, by his (Gibbons') navigating with his steamboats, The Stoudinger and The Bellona, between N. Y. and Elizabethtown Point. The defendant justified, on the ground that his boats were above 20 tons burthen, and had been duly enrolled and licensed under an Act of Congress; and he insisted, that under such licenses his boats might be lawfully employed and navigated in the coasting trade, between ports of the same State, or of different States, and could not be excluded or restricted by any law or grant of any particular State. This defense was overruled by the late *Chancellor*, who did not consider the license as conferring any right whatever. He held that the license only gave the vessel an American character, but left the owner of the vessel precisely where he was before the license, in respect to the exclusive grant claimed by Livingston and Fulton, and their assigns. When the cause was brought into this court, by appeal from the decretal order of the *Chancellor*, *Mr. Justice* Platt, who delivered the unanimous opinion of the court, agrees with the *Chancellor* in the opinion, that the only effect of the license is to determine the national character of the vessel, and the rate of duties which she is to pay; and he adds, that "such a vessel, coasting from one State to another, would have exactly the same right to trade, and the same right of transit, whether she had the coasting license or not;" and the order of the *Chancellor* was affirmed, on the ground that the question had been settled in the case of *Livingston* v. *Van Ingen*. The decree of the *Chancellor*, which was affirmed in this court, declares the several Acts of the Legislature of the State of N. Y., granting the exclusive right, to be valid, notwithstanding the objections taken by the defendant; "and that the complainant is well entitled to the right exclusively to navigate the waters for the purpose mentioned in the said bill of **742***] complaint, with boats moved by *steam or fire; and that the defendant cannot lawfully navigate the same, with the steamboats of him the said defendant, &c., under the respective enrolments and licenses, &c."

When this decree, and the whole proceedings, were carried into the Supreme Court of the U. S., that court was of opinion that the several licenses to the steamboats, The Stoudinger and The Bellona, to carry on the coasting trade, &c., "give full authority to those vessels to navigate the waters of the U. S., by steam or otherwise, for the purpose of carrying on the coasting trade, any law of the State of N. Y. to the contrary notwithstanding; and that so much of the several laws of the State of N. Y., as prohibits vessels licensed according to the laws of the U. S., from navigating the waters of the State of N. Y., by means of fire or steam, is repugnant to the said Constitution, and void." The decree, was, therefore, reversed.

The facts in the two cases cited were not similar to each other, nor to this case. In the first, that of *Livingston* v. *Van Ingen*, the controversy was as to the validity of the State grant, within the bounds of the State; but the effect of a license, under the Act Regulating the Coasting Trade, could not be considered, because it was not a fact in the case. In the second case, that of *Ogden* v. *Gibbons*, the effect of a coasting license was considered, both by the Court of Chancery and by this court, and the license was adjudged to give no right whatever. In this opinion both courts erred, as is proved by the decision of the Supreme Court of the U. S.; by which it is settled that a steamboat navigating with a coasting license, performing a voyage from a port of another State to a port in this State, is authorized to navigate the waters of this State, the laws of this State to the contrary notwithstanding.

But though, whether a steamboat may, under the authority of a license, navigate the waters of the Hudson within this State, in opposition to the grant to Livingston and Fulton, is a question which has not been decided, in terms, by this court, or the Supreme Court of the U. S.; yet it seems to me to have been virtually decided by both *courts. In this court, [***743** the only effect of the license was declared to be that of giving an American character, and that it conferred no right in a case of intercourse between this State and the State of N. J. Of course it could have no effect where the intercourse was entirely within the State. In the Supreme Court of the U. S., the language of the decree is, that "the several licenses to carry on the coasting trade, give full authority to those vessels to navigate the waters of the U. S., by steam or otherwise, for the purpose of carrying on the coasting trade." I agree that the decision of the court is to be considered in reference to the facts of the case, and that the facts in that case were different from this, inasmuch as there the voyage was from a port in another State. Certain points, however, were decided, which were, in a degree, necessary to the main decision given in the cause.

Some of the points decided by the Supreme Court are,

1. That the power to regulate commerce among the States is exclusive.

2. That commerce means not only traffic, or the exchange of commodities, but also intercourse; that it includes navigation.

3. Congress has power, of course, to regulate navigation. This regulation of commerce and navigation must take place within the States; the waters of the U. S. are necessarily the waters of some particular State—Congress must act on the subject where it exists.

4. That though the right of intercourse does not depend on the Constitution and laws of Congress, yet Congress has power to regulate that right, and has done so, by "An Act for Enrolling and Licensing Ships or Vessels to be Employed in the Coasting Trade and Fisheries, and for Regulating the Same," passed Feb. 18, 1793.

5. That this Act implies, unequivocally, an authority to licensed vessels to carry on the coasting trade; the license is the language of the Legislature, and transfers to the grantee all the right which the grantor can transfer.

6. That what is meant by the coasting trade is defined in the Act of 1793.

*7. That steamboats are to be enrolled [***744** and licensed in the same manner as vessels propelled by wind, and are entitled to the same privileges.

It is also intimated, and an opinion expressed, though not judicially decided, that the transportation of passengers is equally a branch of the coasting trade as the transportation of goods; that Congress has power to license vessels to sail from one port to another in the same State; and that this power implies no claim of a direct power to regulate the purely internal commerce of a State, or act directly on its system of police.

From these premises it seems to me to follow, as a corollary, that vessels with a coasting license, are authorized to navigate, for the purpose of carrying on the coasting trade in all the navigable waters of the State in which the coasting trade can exist.

If I am correct in these inferences, they lead necessarily to the decision of this cause, and then the objection, that we ought not to go in advance of the Supreme Court, is altogether inapplicable. Before proceeding to apply these principles, it is proper to settle the meaning of certain words and phrases used in this controversy. What, then, do we understand by commerce among the States? In what does the coasting trade consist? And what is internal commerce? Do they interfere with each other, or where is the boundary that marks the limit of each?

It has been contended that commerce among the States, means a voyage from State to State, commencing in a particular State and terminating, as respects the authority of the license, at the boundary line of the State entered; and that the subsequent progress of the vessel is under state regulations. If this were correct, then the vessel making a voyage from a port in one State to a port in another, must navigate subject to the regulations of the State in which she commences her voyage, until she touches the boundary line of such State; and at the same moment when she leaves the jurisdiction of the one State, she enters the jurisdiction of the other, and then navigates subject to the regulations of the State she has thus entered, until **745***] she completes her *voyage. Hence she is under the control of state regulations during her whole voyage, except perhaps at the moment of passing the boundary line. By this construction, Congress is ousted of its jurisdiction altogether; and that clause of the Constitution which gives them power to regulate commerce among the States, becomes a dead letter. The Supreme Court says, "commerce among the States cannot stop at the boundary line of each State, but may be introduced into the interior.' Again,' "commerce among the States must, of necessity, be commerce within the States." In the same opinion, we find as full a definition of the term as the facts of the case required, and beyond that it was not necessary to go. Accordingly, it is said, "comprehensive as the word 'among' is, it may very properly be restricted to that commerce which concerns more States than one." Again; "the genius and character of the whole government seem to be that its action is to be applied to all the external concerns of the nation, and to those internal concerns which affect the States generally; but not to those which are completely within a particular State, which do not affect other States, and with which it is not necessary to interfere for the purpose of executing some of the general powers of the government. The completely internal commerce of a state, then, may be considered as reserved for the State itself."

It is evident, from these expressions, that the Supreme Court was of opinion, that over a part of the internal commerce of the States Congress has power. Precisely how far that power extends, it did not become necessary to decide; but from the expressions, completely internal, exclusively internal, and purely internal, it is clearly inferrible, that all that part of the internal commerce of a State which is not exclusively internal, is subject to the regulation of Congress. How far, then, within the State, does that commerce extend, which is not completely internal? If all commerce, which enters the exterior lines of a State, is internal, and exclusively so, then all commerce would be included, as well foreign as among the States, which is directly contrary to the decision, and to the Constitution. The counsel for the appellants *contended, if a steam vessel [***746** from another State, with a coasting license, has a right to enter a port in this State, that, at the exterior port, the voyage is terminated as between the States, and that she cannot proceed to any other place within the State, except in subjection to the exclusive grant. His Honor, the *Chancellor*, decides that such a vessel may proceed to any port in this State, and depart from any port in this State and proceed to another, and touch at intermediate places; and that the navigation which is subject to the state grant is that which takes place between any two points in this State, when the voyage is not a continuation of a passage to or from another State. The Supreme Court says, "if Congress license vessels to sail from one port to another, in the same State, the Act is supposed to be necessarily incidental to the power expressly granted to Congress, and implies no claim of a direct power to regulate the purely internal commerce of a State, or to act directly on its system of police."

The power of Congress to license vessels to sail from one port to another in the same State, is here distinctly asserted, as incidental to the power directly granted. It seems, also, to be, impliedly at least, admitted, that this is a regulation of commerce within a State, and subject to state legislation. It is elsewhere asserted that the power to regulate commerce with foreign nations, and among the States, is necessarily an exclusive power. From what is here said, it seems that the incidental power to regulate commerce within the State, is a concurrent power; and if so, it is admitted, that in case of collision, the law of Congress must prevail. But the opinion here seems to consider the purely internal commerce as not affected by the act of licensing vessels to sail from port to port within the State. If this be so, then the internal commerce over which the State has exclusive control, is something existing where coasting vessels cannot come, or have no right to navigate, as in the case of a ferry within the State. And hence it follows, that the commerce among the States, which Congress has power to regulate, either directly or incidentally, is that commerce which may be carried on *by vessels regularly [***747** licensed by the laws of Congress; or, in other words, the coasting trade.

This brings me to the inquiry, what is the coasting trade? The answer to this inquiry, is to be found in the laws of Congress, the first of which is entitled, "An Act for Registering and Clearing Vessels, Regulating the Coasting Trade, and for other purposes," passed Sept. 1, 1789; but more particularly in "An Act for

Enrolling and Licensing Ships or Vessels to be Employed in the Coasting Trade and Fisheries, and for Regulating the Same," passed Feb. 18, 1793. It cannot be necessary to enter into a minute analysis of the sections of this last mentioned Act; a general reference to some of its provisions being sufficient for my present purpose.

This Act contains, in the 1st section, a prohibition to all vessels, except those authorized as is therein provided, from carrying on the coasting trade. The license then gives the authority, or the Act regulates a right previously existing (and it is, in my judgment, immaterial which, for the purpose of deciding this controversy), and particularly specifies the mode of carrying on trade in certain vessels, on the coast or a navigable river, between districts in different States, and districts in the same State, and different places in the same district. This, then, is the definition given by Congress to the term "the coasting trade." *Ch. J.* Marshall so understands it, when he says: "The coasting trade is a term well understood. The law has defined it, and all know its meaning perfectly. The Act describes, with great minuteness, the various operations of a vessel engaged in it."

According to the definition of the coasting trade, as extracted from the Act of Congress, of Feb. 18, 1793, it means commercial intercourse carried on between different districts in different States, between different districts in the same State, and between different places in the same district, on the sea coast or on a navigable river. Agreeably to this definition, a voyage in vessel of suitable tonnage, from N. Y. to Albany, is as much a coasting voyage as from Boston to Plymouth or New Bedford. In both the *termini* are in the same State, and within the navigable **748***] waters of the *U. S., though in one the navigation is upon a river; in the other on the ocean. The Government of the U. S. have no jurisdiction (the District of Columbia and the Territories excepted), where a State has not also jurisdiction for State purposes; and I can see nothing in the nature of our governments which excludes the authority of Congress from our navigable rivers. They are arms of the sea. As well might La. shut the mouth of the Mississippi, or Va. the Chesapeake, as N. Y. the Hudson. In corroboration of this construction, is the fact that all vessels employed in navigating the river take a coasting license. I am aware it is said that the license is given, not under the power to regulate commerce, but the power to lay and collect taxes. When Congress have power to do the same act by virtue of distinct powers, they may exercise which they please; and when they profess to act under the power to regulate commerce, as they do in this Act, there is no necessity to resort to any other. I need not, therefore, inquire whether the license does not more properly emanate from the taxing power. Under whatever power it is issued, it proves that the vessel has complied with the regulations of Congress respecting the coasting trade, and is entitled to all the privileges of coasting vessels. A discussion of this question is superseded by an express adjudication. The language of the Supreme Court is: "To the court it seems very clear, that the whole Act on the subject of the coasting trade, according to those principles which govern the construction of statutes, implies, unequivocally, an authority to licensed vessels to carry on the coasting trade." Again: "The license must be understood to be what it purports to be, a legislative authority to carry on the coasting trade."

What, then, is internal commerce?

An answer to this inquiry will necessarily lead to some repetition. It is contended by the appellants, and is decided by the *Chancellor*, that it comprehends all that navigation where the *termini* of the voyage are both within the same State. *Ch. J.* Marshall has said, that the word "among" may properly be restricted to that commerce *which concerns more [***749** States than one. Again: "the enumeration presupposes something not enumerated; and that something, if we regard the language or the subject of the sentence, must be the exclusively internal commerce of a State. The genius and character of the whole government seem to be, that its action is to be applied to all the external concerns of the nation, and to those internal concerns which affect the States generally; but not to those which are completely within a particular State, which do not affect other States, and with which it is not necessary to interfere for the purpose of executing some of the general powers of the government. The completely internal commerce of a State, then, may be considered as reserved for the State itself." What is here said, it must be admitted, conveys no definite idea of what is the completely or exclusively internal commerce alluded to. In a subsequent part of the opinion, an explanation is to be found. When speaking of inspection laws, he observes, "They form a portion of that immense mass of legislation which embraces everything within the territory of a State not surrendered to the General Government; all which can be most advantageously exercised by the States themselves. Inspection laws, quarantine laws health laws of every description, as well as laws for regulating the internal commerce of a State, and those which respect turnpike roads, ferries, &c., are component parts of this mass. No direct general power, over these objects, is granted to Congress: and, consequently, they remain subject to state legislation. If the legislative power of the Union can reach them, it must be for national purposes; it must be when the power is expressly given for a special purpose, or is clearly incidental to some power which is expressly given. It is obvious, that the government of the Union, in the exercise of its express powers—that, for example, of regulating commerce with foreign nations and among the States—may use means that may also be employed by a State, in the exercise of its acknowledged powers; that, for example, of regulating commerce within the State. If Congress license vessels to sail from one port to another in the same State, the Act is supposed to be necessarily incidental to the *power expressly granted to Congress, [***750** and implies no claim of a direct power to regulate the purely internal commerce of a State, or to act directly on its system of police."

A definition of what is meant by internal commerce, appears, in part, by the above extract from the opinion of the Supreme Court. To extend it to all its various subjects, would here be entirely useless. The object of the present inquiry is completely answered, by showing what is not that purely internal commerce spoken of as exclusively subject to state legislation: and I trust I have already shown that the navigation of the Hudson, a public navigable river, is not included in such internal commerce; but that it composes a part of the coasting trade, and is, therefore, subject to the regulation and control of Congress.

In my judgment, then, the case of *Gibbons* v. *Ogden* decides that the commerce subject to the control of Congress is the coasting trade, which includes the transportation of passengers. That the coasting trade may lawfully be carried on by licensed vessels, in all the navigable waters of the U. S., including all rivers approachable from the coasts. If this be so, then The Olive Branch was engaged in a lawful trade, and had a perfect right to the navgation of the Hudson. I will, therefore, detain the court but a moment, while I add a few general remarks.

Much difference of opinion exists, on the question of construction to be given to the Constitution of the U. S.; some contending that it should receive a liberal construction, and others that it should be construed strictly. In my judgment, it should be so construed as best to promote the great objects for which it was made. This end will be best answered by avoiding either extreme of the rules of construction, and keeping steadily in view the purposes for which the government was instituted, "to form a more perfect union, establish justice, insure domestic tranquility, provide for the common defense, promote the general welfare, and secure the blessings of liberty." Under the Articles of Confederation, the States were sovereign and independent—too much so for the mutual safety and prosperity of the whole. The States, therefore, in adopting the Federal Constitution, parted with **751***] *a portion of their individual sovereignty, in order to give the head of the confederacy stronger powers, by which to draw closer together the different parts of this widely extended government. Before that time, the several States imposed what duties they pleased not inconsistent with public treaties, and were perfectly sovereign and independent, as to regulating all other commerce within their respective limits, subject to one restriction only, to wit: that the people of other States should enjoy therein all the privileges of trade and commerce, subject to the same duties, &c., as the inhabitants of such State, provided such restrictions did not prevent the removal of property to another State, of which the owner should be an inhabitant, and that no duties should be laid on property of the U. S., or either of them.

This power of regulating commerce led to many difficulties and embarrassments, as we learn from the history of the times; and to prevent a recurrence of those commercial difficulties, was one great and leading inducement to the adoption of the present Constitution. Any power, therefore, given to Congress, short of the power to regulate that commerce to which the people of the U. S. had access, would not have secured the object so desirable to be attained: and it never could have been intended that, within the territory of a particular State, Congress should define the rights and privileges of citizens of other States, while the State Legislature should define the rights and privileges of its own citizens, in relation to the same subject. The framers of the Constitution never supposed that they were splitting the jurisdiction over the subject, and leaving it liable to most of the difficulties which previously existed. If the several States may still regulate commerce, within the limits of their States, to the exclusion of Congress, there is nothing left for Congress to act upon. If the power of Congress is limited to voyages commencing in one State and terminating in another, then its jurisdiction is much abridged, and much of the Act Regulating the Coasting Trade should be repealed.

*To show the understanding of those [***752** who framed and adopted the Constitution, we have only to look at the Acts of Congress immediately consequent upon its adoption. And we find that at the first session of the first Congress, one of the first Acts passed, is "An Act for Registering and Clearing Vessels, Regulating the Coasting Trade, and for other purposes," passed Sept. 1, 1789, containing substantially the provisions of the Act of 1793. By this Act, licensed vessels are authorized to trade from district to district. By what authority did Congress undertake to regulate the coasting trade? The coasting trade is a term not found in the Constitution. It need not be contended to be the execution of the power to collect taxes, &c.; for it has been decided to have been an execution of the power to regulate commerce. What commerce? Surely not foreign commerce, nor among the Indian tribes? It must mean, then, "commerce among the several States." Congress, then, passed the Act Regulating the Coasting Trade, under the power to regulate commerce among the several States. This was a contemporaneous exposition of the Constitution with which all were satisfied; and it was not then thought that state boundaries had any effect or influence upon this kind of navigation. It was not then thought that the coasting trade, or commerce among the States, must consist of voyages from State to State only; that was the discovery of later times. It was then thought that commerce among the States meant among the people of the States; that this commerce was internal as related to the Government of the U. S. and its citizens, and as contradistinguished from foreign commerce. It was at that time supposed that the Constitution intended to guaranty to the citizens of the whole U. S. an equality of commercial rights and privileges. Hence the restriction on Congress, that "no preference shall be given by any regulation of commerce or revenue to the ports of one State over those of another;" and hence, also, the subsequent provision, that "the citizens of each State shall be entitled to all the privileges and immunities of citizens in the several States." The framers of the Constitution though it unnecessary to declare the converse of the *last provision, to wit: [***753** that the citizens of each State shall be entitled within their own State, to all the privileges and immunities which citizens of other States enjoy within such State.

How is this fact under the principle contended for by the appellants? Citizens of other States, coming from a port in their own State, have a right to navigate freely with their steamboats, in our waters and from port to port, while our own citizens are excluded from such navigation from port to port, unless the voyage extends out of the State. I mention this as an inconsistency growing out of the construction contended for. One leading object of the Constitution was to secure an equality of commercial rights to the citizens of the General Government, in whatever State they might reside. We ought not to forget that we are the citizens of two distinct, yet connected governments. Each has its proper sphere of action. The powers given to the General Government are to be first satisfied. Some of these powers are exclusive, and some concurrent; but when concurrent, the provisions of the General Government are paramount. Whether powers are exclusive or concurrent, is to be determined more by the nature of the power itself, than by the phraseology of the Constitution. Under the old Confederation, the States retained the character of independent and sovereign States; under the present Constitution, for certain specified purposes, the distinction of States is partially lost, and we become a single, consolidated government. It is in this character that Congress executes its powers; and having, in this character, power to regulate commerce among the States, that power must necessarily reach the subject where it exists; and so far as navigation is concerned, it exists where the coasting trade exists, and is, therefore, subject to the regulations of Congress.

We are told that there is great danger of encroachment by the General Government, and that the state governments will be swallowed up by it; and therefore that the state laws should be supported. My answer is, if such danger exists, the States should not provoke a termination of their existence, by encroach- **754***] ments *on their part; nor should they submit to usurpation. There is no difficulty in harmonizing, if each government will be content with the powers possessed by it. But why should we more apprehend an abuse of power, or an act of usurpation, by the general than by the state governments? Both are constituted by the representatives of the people. Every member of the National Legislature is a citizen of some State, and of course feels his state partialities and perhaps jealousies; and should be presumed, in the absence of proof to the contrary, equally jealous of the rights of his constituents, as the members of our State Legislatures. I am fully sensible of the propriety of preserving the state governments, with all their rights and powers; but this is by no means inconsistent with conceding to the General Government its appropriate powers.

We were cautioned upon the argument, to beware how we admit the authority of Congress to regulate navigation within the waters of the Hudson, as we should thereby abandon the right to license ferries and receive tolls on our canals. The Supreme Court expressly disavows any authority in Congress to interfere with the purely internal commerce or police of a State. Ferries may be subject to the Acts of Congress, so far as they are used for carrying on the coasting trade; but those ferries which are the subjects of state grant, if they can be called commercial regulations at all, belong clearly to the internal commerce of the States. We are told that the grant to the plaintiffs is only a ferry from Albany to N.Y. If the exclusive grant be really a right of ferry, the plaintiffs may occupy with their boats every ferry in the State, and thus destroy the rights of all others. But there is no pretense for denominating their grant a ferry. To speak of a ferry from N. Y. to Albany, is as great an abuse of terms, as to talk of a ferry from New Orleans to St. Louis or Pittsburgh, or even from N. Y. to Liverpool. Those ferries over which the State exercises its appropriate authority, are not connected with the coasting trade; they are not, in the constitutional sense, commercial regulations. But if they were, they belong to that exclusively internal commerce over which Congress has no control. Our right to *regulate naviga- [***755** tion upon our canals rests upon a still firmer basis. They are no part of the navigable waters of the U. S., within the Act Regulating the Coasting Trade, or the Constitution. Congress may, indeed, under the taxing power, impose taxes upon canal boats, as they may upon every species of property within the States; but that gives them no direct power to regulate the navigation upon our canals, or upon our inland lakes and rivers. The authority of Congress to regulate navigation is confined to our coasts, bays and navigable rivers.

If I am correct in the views which I have taken of this subject, an injunction cannot be granted, whether the respondent carried on what has been denominated a fraudulent intercourse with N. J. or not. I forbear, therefore, an examination of that part of the decree of His Honor, the *Chancellor*, which relates to such intercourse.

But even if the conclusions which I have drawn from established premises, be not admitted as absolutely correct and conclusive, is there no doubt on the subject? After the highest judicial tribunal in our country has said that "so much of the several laws of the State of N. Y. as prohibits vessels licensed according to the laws of the U. S., from navigating the waters of the State of N. Y. by means of fire or steam, is repugnant to the said Constitution and void," can it be pretended that the claim of the appellants is no longer doubtful? The plea in the case of *Gibbons* v. *Ogden* distinctly asserted the right to navigate between different places in the same State. This was part of the issue; yet the court broadly assert the right of licensed vessels "to navigate the waters of the U. S. by steam or otherwise, for the purpose of carrying on the coasting trade, any law of the State of N. Y. to the contrary notwithstanding." In *Livingston* v. *Van Ingen*, the late *Chancellor* Kent says, "injunctions are always granted to secure the enjoyment of statute privileges, of which the party is in the actual possession, unless the right be doubtful." This is undoubtedly the correct rule, and the true result of an examination of the adjudged cases.

756*] *If anything were wanting, in addition to the express and unequivocal language of the Supreme Court of the U. S., to show that the appellants have not a clear right, free from doubt, it is found in the peculiar situation in which an injunction will place the citizens of this State. They are forbidden rights, which are open to, and may be enjoyed freely by all the world beside. If the injunction is granted it cannot secure to the appellants their monopoly. The citizens of other States, with their steamboats, have full right to navigate our waters and carry on a profitable business, commencing or terminating their voyage in their own State; while our own citizens must stand with their arms folded and look on, unless they, too, terminate their voyages without the State. If this deplorable state of things necessarily results from the Constitution and laws of our country, it must be submitted to, with what grace we can; but is it not a powerful argument to prove that the reasoning, which leads to such a result, is unsound?

For these reasons, I am of opinion that an injunction ought not to be granted; and that that part of the decree of His Honor, the *Chancellor*, refusing an injunction, be affirmed.

Bowman, Brayton, Burrows, Burt, Clark, Cramer, Dudley, Earll, Ellsworth, Gardiner, Keyes, Lefferts, Lynde, Mallory, McCall, McIntyre, Morgan, Redfield, Ward, Wooster, Wright, Senators, concurred.

OGDEN, *Senator*, gave no opinion.

A majority of *the Court* concurring with the *Chief Justice*, it was thereupon ordered, adjudged and decreed that that part of the decree of His Honor, the *Chancellor*, appealed from, be affirmed, with costs, &c.

For affirmance, 22; for reversal, 9.

Affirming—Hopk., 144.
Cited in—1 Wend., 560; 12 Wend., 317; 15 Wend., 131; 4 Den., 479; 27 N. Y., 445; 2 Sandf., 398; 69 Ill., 102; 30 Am. Dec., 40.

[END OF FEBRUARY SESSION, 1825.]

REPORTS OF CASES

ARGUED AND DETERMINED

IN THE

UPREME COURT,

AND IN THE

COURT FOR THE TRIAL OF IMPEACHMENTS

AND

THE CORRECTION OF ERRORS,

IN THE

STATE OF NEW YORK.

BY ESEK COWEN,

COUNSELOR AT LAW.

VOL. IV.

1836.

CASES

ARGUED AND DETERMINED

IN THE

SUPREME COURT

OF THE

STATE OF NEW YORK,

IN

FEBRUARY TERM, 1825, IN THE FORTY-NINTH YEAR OF OUR INDEPENDENCE.

COMPTON v. JONES.

Assignment of Specialty—Promise to Pay Assignee—Assumpsit *by Assignee, on Promise.*

A promise to pay the assignee of a chose in action, entitles him to sue in his own name, in *assumpsit*, though the contract assigned be a specialty.

ON demurrer. The declaration was in *assumpsit*. The 1st count stated, that Feb. 4, 1823, the defendant made, &c., his certain deed, &c., dated, &c., and delivered the same to one S. T. Wood, by which he, for value received promised to pay Wood, or bearer, $500, in four equal annual installments from the date; that Wood afterwards, &c., for a valuable consideration to him (Wood) paid, assigned and transferred the deed, &c., to the plaintiff, thereby constituted him the bearer thereof, and authorized and directed him to demand and receive of the defendant the contents of the deed, &c., for his own benefit; that afterwards, and before the payment, &c., the plaintiff gave notice to the defendant of the assignment, &c.; that, in consideration of the premises, afterwards, &c., in consideration that the plaintiff would accept and agree to the defendant's promise in the declaration after mentioned, the defendant promised the plaintiff to pay him the money mentioned in the deed, averring that $250 had become due before the commencement of the suit.

14*] *General demurrer and joinder.

Mr. C. M. Lee, in support of the demurrer, relied on what this court said in *Andrews* v. *Montgomery*, 19 Johns., 162, 165 viz.: that *assumpsit* cannot be supported where there has been an express contract, under seal; but the party must proceed in debt or covenant.

Mr. Z. A. Leland, contra, cited *Fenner* v. *Meares*, 2 Bl., 1269, and Cowen's Treatise, 35.

SAVAGE, *Ch. J.*, remarked that what was said by the court in the authority cited by the defendant's counsel, was intended of a case where the action was brought by the party to the specialty. And the whole *Court* were clear that the action was sustainable, being on a promise to the assignee.

Judgment for the plaintiff.

Cited in—5 Wend., 203, 349; 9 Wend., 318; 3 Hill, 89; 67 N. Y., 175; 2 Barb., 351; 23 Am. Rep., 109 (67 N. Y., 162).

SHATTUCK v. CHAMBERLIN.

Practice—Offer of Costs Should be to Attorney.

An offer of costs, on stipulating to try a cause, should be made to the defendant's attorney, not to his counsel.

THIS cause being at issue, the plaintiff noticed it for trial; but neglecting to bring it on at the circuit, his attorney tendered a stipulation to try at the next circuit, to the counsel for the defendant, and offered to pay the costs; notwithstanding which,

Mr. Z. A. Leland now moved for judgment as in cases of nonsuit, on the ground that the offer to pay costs should have been made to the attorney.

Mr. W. M. Oliver, contra.

Curia. The offer to pay costs was insufficient, as being made to the defendant's counsel. It should have been to the attorney. He, alone, is in general able to know the amount of the costs, and authorized to receive them. The motion must be granted, unless the plaintiff stipulate.

Rule accordingly.

*HALL v. COE. [*15

Action for Malicious Prosecution—Venue.

In an action for a malicious prosecution in a neighboring State, the plaintiff may lay his venue in any county of this State, and retain it there, on stipulating to give material evidence arising in the county where it is laid, though the defendant have a greater number of witnesses residing in the county, to which he moves to change the venue.

And this, too, though the cause of action in another count, in trover, in the same declaration, arose in the county to which he moves to change the venue.

MR. P. S. PARKER moved to change the venue from the County of Chenango to the County of Steuben. He read an affidavit of the defendant, stating that the declaration consisted of two counts—the first in trover—the second for a malicious prosecution. That the cause of action in the first count arose in the County of Steuben, &c., and that in the second count in the State of Pa., &c. That the defendant had 12 witnesses residing in Steuben, &c.

Mr. J. Platt, contra, would not enter the lists as to the number of witnesses; but though the cause of action in the first count arose in Steuben, that in the second arose in Pa. Being for a malicious prosecution, and sounding in tort, it did not come within the rule that the number of witnesses is to control; but had the cause of action arisen in Chenango, the plaintiff might have retained the venue by stipulating to give material evidence arising in that county.

He submitted, whether it was not the same thing here. The cause of action arose, it is true in Pa.; but this entitles the plaintiff to lay his venue in any county in the State, and to retain it, upon the fiction that the cause of action arose there, provided he will stipulate. This stipulation will be satisfied by proof that the cause of action arose in a foreign country. *Gerard* v. *DeRobeck*, 1 H. Bl., 280.

Curia. Retain your venue, on stipulating to give material evidence arising in the County of Chenango,

Mr. Platt expressing his willingness to do this,

Rule accordingly.

16*] *JACKSON, ex dem. PRINDLE,
v.
LYTLE.

Ejectment—Leave to Enter into Consent Rule—Costs.

To obtain leave to enter into the contest rule specially, the defendant in ejectment must apply to the court, and is, therefore, entitled to have the costs of such application taxed in his final bill of costs, if he be successful.

So if the plaintiff discontinue.

MR. S. STEVENS moved for a retaxation of costs. The plaintiff having discontinued this suit, on payment of costs, the defendant's attorneys included in the bill the costs of making a motion for leave to enter into the consent rule specially, at the last February Term of this court, amounting to $9.32. These costs were objected to by the plaintiff's attorneys, on the taxation, but were taxed by the commissioners.

The attorneys for the parties now submitted whether the defendant is entitled to these costs. They stipulated that the facts reported in S. C., 2 Cow., 442, be taken as a part of this case (without affidavit); by which it appears that the application to enter into the consent rule was granted without costs.

Mr. J. Willard, contra, said the court having decided, in the case cited, that the entering into a consent rule was not a matter of course, and the plaintiff having refused to do it, without an application to the court, the costs of the motion should abide the event.

In the case of a necessary application to the court, in the progress of a cause, when the course and practice of the court is not to enforce payment of the costs by attachment, they abide the event.

Thus, the costs of a motion for a reference, for a commission, for a rule to change the venue, of motions in real actions, motions for attachment against the sheriff, &c., where costs are not awarded by the rule, make a part of the general costs of the action, and abide the event of the suit.

The defendant did not come to ask a favor, nor to be relieved from a rule obtained against him. The application was in the ordinary course of the cause.

**Mr. S. Stevens*, in reply. The costs [*17 objected to are those of the motion—not of the consent rule. Had the affidavit presented to the plaintiff's attorneys been sufficient, it is evident, from the case reported in 2 Cow., that costs would have been given. The court say the consent rule cannot be made special as a matter of course, but should be on application to the court; especially where the affidavit is so general and loose as the one which was served on the plaintiff's attorneys. It was, then, the fault of the defendant's attorneys that they did not obtain costs, which must be considered as finally denied by that motion. In the case of motions to change the venue, for a reference, for a commission, &c., no costs are given, one way or the other: and they stand on the same footing with any other ordinary step in the cause.

Curia. We think the case not distinguishable, in principle, from the ordinary one of allowing, in the final taxation, the costs of motions to change the venue, to refer the cause, or for a commission. If the party incurring these costs succeed, he recovers them as a part of the general costs in the cause, upon the ground that it is necessary to move the court. It is so in this case. The defendant must apply to the court for leave to enter into a special consent rule. Had he been successful upon a trial, these costs would, therefore, be allowed; and a discontinuance of the suit is the same in principle as to this question.

Rule accordingly.

ROSE *v.* SMITH AND DAVIS.

Misconduct of Jury in Justice Court—Assignable as Error in Fact—Practice.

Misconduct of a jury in a justice's court, properly assignable as error in fact, and if found, the course is to move court specially for judgment of reversal, on producing the *postea*, &c.

That spirituous liquors was circulated among the jury, while sitting as such, even though by consent, is cause for reversing the judgment.

ON *certiorari* to a justice's court, the affidavit upon which the *certiorari* was founded, charged misconduct in the jury, *in [*18 drinking spirituous liquor. To this part of the affidavit the justice returned that he knew nothing of the fact. Whereupon, the plaintiff assigned for error, specially, that while the jury were sitting together at the trial, they drank of spirituous liquor, conveyed to them by the defendants, without the knowledge of the plaintiff; that one of them became intoxicated. And upon issue, the jury at the circuit found that spiritous liquor was circulated among the jury in the justice's court, while sitting as such; that one of the jurors, in the justice's court, was disguised with liquor, given to him during the trial; and that, during the trial, the plaintiff in error objected to the circulation of a liquor among the jurors, while sitting.

A motion was now made for judgment of reversal, upon producing the *N. P.* record, with the *postea* and copy of the minutes of the circuit, &c. And *Kellogg* v. *Wilder*, 15 Johns., 455, was cited, to show that there was sufficient cause, upon the finding of the jury, for reversing the judgment. *Harvey* v. *Rickett*, *Id.*, 87, was also cited, to show that the misconduct should be taken advantage of by assignment of error in fact; and *Brown* v. *Lerow*, 2 Cow., 525, to show that judgment, in this case, is not of course, but should be on special motion.

For the defendants in error it was insisted that the verdict was substantially for the defendant, to whom the *postea* should be delivered. The assignment of errors alleged that the liquor was furnished by the defendants. This is not verified by the verdict. Without it the judgment should not be reversed. It is a material allegation that the defendants found the liquor. Bac. Abr., Verdict, O, pl. 23, 31; 2 Rol. Abr., 707, pl. 49; *Smith* v. *Thompson*, 1 Cow., 221, and the note to that case, where all the cases are collected, as to the misbehavior of jurors.

Should the court render judgment for the plaintiff, it would present a novel case; one not found in all the books; a case where either party may set aside a judgment, on error, for the same cause. In this case, if the plaintiff can reverse the judgment, the defendants may do the same; for neither party is in fault.

19*] *The assignment is, that one of the jurors was intoxicated; the finding, that he was disguised, which is not according to the issue. It is indefinite, and unworthy of legal notice.

Mr. H. Lathrop, for the plaintiff in error.

Mr. J. Brackett, for the defendants in error.

Curia. This matter comes properly before us by an assignment of error in fact, issue and verdict; upon which the application for judgment should be special. The circulation of spirituous liquor among the jury was, of itself, fatal, on error; and we have decided, that even consent of parties will not cure it. The matter really to be tried, then, was not whether the circulation of the liquor was procured or consented to by the defendants, but whether such a thing took place for any cause, no matter what. In an inferior court, it is impossible to correct this practice by moving for a new trial, as may be done in a court of record. To avoid the evil of intoxication, effectually, it has, therefore, been thought necessary to interfere, and set aside the judgment, wherever on error, it appears that spirituous liquor has circulated among the jury. The present is a flagrant case. Not only was liquor freely circulated, but one of the jury was, in the language of the verdict, disguised with liquor.

Judgment reversed.

Cited in—1 Hill, 209; 2 Hill, 393; 15 Barb., 49; 62 Barb., 617; 7 How. Pr., 69.
See—7 Am. Rep., 306 (27 Iowa, 494); 30 Am. Rep., 406 (48 Iowa, 536).

RIPLEY v. BENEDICT.

Action of Covenant in C. P.—Judgment for Defendant—Subsequent Action in Supreme Court on Same Instrument for Same and Additional Breaches—Proceedings Stayed, till Costs of First Action Paid.

The plaintiff sued in the C. P. in an action of covenant; and judgment being against him, on demurrer to the declaration, upon certain breaches, he sued in the Supreme Court, upon the same covenant, for the same breaches, and others; though the latter accrued after the action in the C. P. commenced; yet, held, the same cause of action as the first, and proceedings stayed till costs of first action paid.

THE plaintiff had sued the defendant, in covenant, in the C. P. of Saratoga Co., upon articles of agreement, *assigning [***20** certain breaches. Upon demurrer to the declaration, the C. P. gave judgment against the plaintiff, with leave to amend on payment of costs; which he did not do, but sued for the same breaches here; assigning also a further breach, which the plaintiff's attorney swore had happened after the commencement of the suit in the C. P., and of which he could not, therefore, avail himself in the first suit. The costs of the first suit not having been paid, it was now moved to stay proceedings here till the plaintiffs should pay the costs of the suit in the C. P.

Mr. W. L. F. Warren, for the motion.

Mr. P. H. M'Omber, contra.

Curia. The first action was on the same instrument as the present, which also includes the same cause of action as the first. The addition of another cause of action does not so materially change the ground as to destroy the identity of the two causes. They are still the same; and it is no answer to the application to say that the plaintiff goes here for the same cause and more. The proceedings must stay till the costs of the first action are paid.

Motion granted with costs.

BRAINARD v. PHILLIPS.

[S. C., 2 Cow., 440, by the title of Phillips v. Brainard.]

Justice's return to *certiorari* taxed, on affirmance of judgment, in the defendant's bill of costs.

Where a motion to set aside a *certiorari* is denied without costs, these are not taxable as a part of the defendant's general costs, upon affirmance.

ON *certiorari* to a justice's court, the judgment was affirmed; and the defendant had procured to be taxed in his bill of costs, the drawing and copying the return of the justice; and a motion for retaxation was moved for upon this ground, among others.

Curia. The general practice has been to tax this item in the defendant's bill. As to this,

Motion denied.

*A motion had been made by the defend-[***21** ant to set aside the *certiorari* for irregularity but denied without costs, which were also taxed as the defendant's general costs in the cause; and it was insisted that these were properly taxable, like the costs of a motion to change the venue for a commission, reference, &c. But,

Per Curiam. They do not stand upon the same ground. The cases mentioned are necessary steps in the ordinary course of the cause. Here was a motion improperly made. It was, to be sure, denied without costs; probably under some peculiar circumstances in the case, by which our discretion as to costs was guided. These, however, were finally disposed of upon the motion. As to this,

Retaxation ordered.

Mr. M. Brainard, for the motion.
Mr. J. A. Spencer, contra.

Cited in—14 How. Pr., 266.

THE PEOPLE, ex rel. GREEN, v. THE JUDGES OF ONONDAGA COMMON PLEAS.

Notice of Set-off need not Claim Balance, to Entitle Defendant to Judgment.

A notice of set-off need not expressly claim a balance in the defendant's favor, in order to warrant his recovering one.
It is enough to warrant this, that it set forth his demand in the usual form.

ON a reference in the court below, between Green, plaintiff, and Hall, defendant, the referees had certified a balance in favor of the defendant of about $80, which the C. P. had, on motion, refused to set aside, and they rendered judgment thereon.

This court had, at a previous term, on various grounds granted an alternative *mandamus*, commanding the court below to set aside the report, &c.

Now, upon the return, different questions were made; and, among other things, it was objected in behalf of Green, that the defendant's notice of set-off in the court below, did not, in terms, claim that a balance was due to him over and above the plaintiff's demand.

22*] **Mr. J. A. Spencer*, for the plaintiffs.
Mr. G. C. Bronson, for the defendants.

Curia. This was not necessary. The right to a balance in the defendant's favor followed, upon the common notice, as a legal consequence. They need not claim a balance in terms.

Peremptory mandamus *denied.*

Cited in—6 Wend., 525.

MORAN v. DAWES.

Bill of Exceptions—Does not Prevent Rule nisi *for Judgment—Notice, for Taxation of Costs.*

Though a bill of exceptions be a stay of proceedings, yet, like a certificate of probable cause, it does not prevent a rule *nisi*, for judgment.

A notice of taxing costs is not such a proceeding as the court will set aside.

THIS cause was tried at the last circuit in the City of N. Y., and a verdict found for the plaintiff. Certain exceptions were taken by the defendant, at the trial; and the circuit judge signed and sealed a bill of exceptions, at the defendant's request; notwithstanding which, the plaintiff had proceeded, on the 2d day of the present term, to enter a rule for judgment *nisi*, &c., and had given notice of taxing costs.

Mr. A. Spencer (*Mr. J. V. Henry*, same side), now moved to set aside the rule, and all subsequent proceedings, for irregularity. He said the bill of exceptions, *per se*, stayed all proceedings. This had been holden, upon the construction of the statute.

Mr. W. Sampson, contra, said the statute did not operate as an absolute stay of proceedings. The court would regulate its effect by rule and they had done so, in one respect, by their general rule of last October Term, touching frivolous bills of exception, which he read from 3 Cow., 439.

Mr. Henry said *Hasbrouck* v. *Tappen*, 15 Johns., 182, is in point for the motion.

Mr. Sampson. The party had a right to his rule *nisi*, as upon a certificate to stay proceedings on a case made. *Hackley* v. *Hastie*, *3 [*23 Johns., 252. The taxation of costs is a step out of court for the mere purpose of liquidating the amount. It may be a mere speculation on the part of the plaintiff. For aught that appears, he may never proceed for the costs at all; but content himself with the damages. There was no need of the defendant's coming here.

Mr. Spencer. The taxation of costs and signing the roll are usually simultaneous acts; and we had a right to suppose they would be so in this instance.

WOODWORTH, *J.* I think there is no doubt that the plaintiff might take his rule *nisi*, as upon a certificate of probable cause. True, the court decided in *Hasbrouck* v. *Tappen*, that a bill of exceptions, *per se*, stayed the proceedings; but they did not consider its effect as to the rule for judgment.

Mr. Henry. Suppose we are successful in our motion for a new trial, the court must then reverse their rule.

WOODWORTH, *J.* This rule is merely contingent in its terms, and is not at all inconsistent with the defendant's rights upon the bill.

SAVAGE, *Ch. J.* The same objection of reversing the rule would hold upon a case made, and certificate of probable cause; yet it has never been allowed.

SUTHERLAND, *J.* A motion is pending in this cause, and has been argued, to treat this bill of exceptions as a frivolous one within the rule referred to. Suppose that motion succeeds; it appears to me important that the party should have a right to his rule *nisi*, so that he can immediately take the effect of the decision. So in all cases. If this be not so, he must wait four days after we have passed upon his case. The notice to tax the costs is not a proceeding which we can set aside.

Motion denied, with costs.

24*] *MARTIN AND WEBBERS, *Executors*, v. SARLES, Administrator of REYNOLDS.

Judgment against Administrator on Plea of Payment—Will not be Let in to Plead Plene Administravit.

An administrator, who goes to trial upon a plea of payment, though in good faith, and not knowing the effect of a finding against him upon that plea on verdict against him, will not be relieved, by being let in to plead *plene administravit*, although he swear that he has a good defense upon this plea.

THE defendant having filed an inventory, as administrator, was sued upon a bond of his intestate; and being advised by the family of the intestate that the bond was paid, retained an attorney, pleaded payment, and defended on this ground at the circuit, in Apr., 1824, by his counsel, when a verdict passed against him.

Mr. S. A. Foot, on an affidavit of Sarles, that he did not understand the legal effect of this plea of payment, as subjecting him to a personal liability for the debt, on its being found against him; that it was pleaded in good faith; and that he had fully administered when the suit was brought—moved to set aside all proceedings, on terms, and that the defendant be let in to plead *plene administravit*. It appeared that judgment had been entered on the verdict, in May Term, 1824, a *fi. fa.* returned *nulla bona*, and a *capias ad respondendum* served on the defendant, issued and returnable in Oct. Term last, with a view to charge him personally. He swore that he did not understand, till the *capias* was served that these proceedings would have the effect to charge him.

WOODWORTH, *J.* Can it be proper, after a party has thus had the chance of a trial, to allow him to come in at any distance of time for relief?

Mr. Foot. Laches are out of the question, for the consequences were not known to the defendant.

WOODWORTH, *J.* He had counsel.

Mr. Foot. He could derive no benefit from his counsel, for he did not dream of this consequence. He was misled by the family into a belief that he could not make out payment, and accordingly instructed his counsel to rely upon this. The court frequently relieve against mistakes of practice, and it appears to me their interference here would be warranted on the same principle.

25*] *SUTHERLAND, *J.* Suppose a party suffers judgment by default, and then comes, after a lapse of several terms, for relief, on the ground that he did not know the affect of the judgment.

Mr. Foot. That would be a palpable case of negligence. Here is a case in which a mistake might very well happen; and *Phillips* v. *Hawley*, 6 Johns., 129, shows that the court will relieve an administrator, even where there has been laches, on the ground that his attorney was ignorant that through the want of a plea he would be charged personally.

WOODWORTH, *J.* You do not make out that case.

SUTHERLAND, *J.* We must presume, at any rate, that the defendant's attorney and counsel understood the effect of a finding against this plea, till the contrary is shown.

Mr. Foot. Being ignorant of the want of assets, he did not advise with his counsel; and the court will relieve him from the consequences of this mistake, upon principles which would govern a court of equity in a similar case. 3 Bac. Abr., 37, Executors and Administrators, M., pl. 1 n. *d*, and the cases there cited. One of the cases cited in Bacon holds, that finding a plea against the executor is not always conclusive; and if the plea was *bona fide*, a court of equity will relieve. It now seems to be settled, though formerly doubted, that court will notice and relieve against mistakes of law, as well as of fact. *Hunt* v. *Rousmanier*, 8 Wh., 174.

WOODWORTH, J. The defendant here says no more than any one may say, in truth, with respect to the effect of a plea of *plene administravit*, and many other pleas. If we allow this excuse, there will be no end to litigation. He went to trial with his counsel, having every opportunity for instruction as to the law of his case. And,

Per totam Curiam, without hearing *Mr. E. Williams*, who was to have argued on the other side,

Motion denied.

---

*THE PEOPLE v. DOUGLASS. [*26

Conduct of Jury in Trial for Murder—Separation—When Cause for Setting Aside Verdict.

A jury, impaneled to try a prisoner, upon an indictment for murder, were allowed to leave the court-house during the trial, under the charge of two sworn constables; and having left the court-house, two of them separated from their fellows, went to their lodgings, a distance of 30 rods, ate cakes, took some with them on their return, and drank spirituous liquor, though not enough to effect them in the least, and one of them conversed on the subject of the trial; they returned, heard tne trial through, and joined in a verdict of guilty. Held, that the verdict should be set aside, and a new trial granted.

The mere separation of a jury, though impaneled to try a capital offense, and though they separate contrary to the directions of a court, will not, of itself, be a sufficient cause for setting aside the verdict;

But if there be the least suspicion of abuse, the verdict should be set aside.

Citations—2 Roll., 85; Va. Cas., 271; 1 Chit., 401, 426; 2 Hayw., 238.

AT the last Court of Oyer and Terminer in Steuben Co., Douglass was convicted of murder. The trial commenced Jan. 11, 1825. About 2 P. M. the jury had liberty to retire from the box, under the charge of two sworn constables, and the direction of the court to keep together, and return speedily. This was before the trial had concluded. The jury retired to consider on their verdict about 11 P. M., and returned a verdict of guilty about 4 the next morning. After the conviction, a motion was made in the Court of Oyer and Terminer for a new trial, on the ground that two of the jurors, while out under the care of the constables, separated from their fellows, ate, drank whisky, put cakes in their pockets, and conversed with bystanders on the subject of the trial. The prisoner was thereupon re-

why should there be a difference in favor of felony, or even a capital felony? We answer, because in the latter case, the life of the accused is at stake. Society is about inflicting a punishment which can neither be recalled nor mitigated; about sending a human being into eternity. This very circumstance admonishes to greater caution. This distinction is kept up in various other respects. Peremptory challenges are allowed to the accused. The form of administering the juror's oath is more solemn; a plea in abatement, though overruled, results merely in judgment of *respondeas ouster;* while in a case of misdemeanor it is final. The rules of evidence, we agree with the Atty-Gen., must be the same in all cases; but this does not reach the question before the court, which is one as to the form—the guards which the law has imposed with a view to protect the life of the accused.

WOODWORTH, *J.*, in delivering the opinion of the court, spoke nearly as follows:

33*] The question whether a new trial *is to be granted to the prisoner, will depend on the facts disclosed by the affidavits, as to the misconduct of the two jurors, Lamb and Swartwout. It is alleged that they separated from their fellows, while the jury were out under the charge of the constables, and ate, drank spirituous liquor, and conversed on the subject of the trial. Anciently the utmost rigor and strictness were observed in the manner of keeping the jury: and when once charged with a cause, they never could be discharged till they had agreed on their verdict; but the practice has been much relaxed in modern times, in both these particulars. In *Parke's* case, 2 Rol., 85, at *nisi prius*, a juror was challenged and withdrawn, and afterwards went out, mingled with the jury, and stayed with them above half an hour; but the court held, that this should not set aside the verdict, unless it was shown that the jury had new evidence given after they went out of court; but that it was a misdemeanor in him who was challenged, and punishable.

On looking into the books, we do not find that mere separation of the jury has ever been held a sufficient cause for setting aside a verdict, either in a civil or criminal cause, if we except, perhaps, the case of *The Commonwealth* v. *M'Caul*, Va. Cas., 271. The question has been learnedly examined in several cases, and especially in that of *King* v. *Wolf*, 1 Chit., 401. That appears to be a case which excited very great interest, and led to the utmost research of the counsel, and the Court of K. B. It was ably argued, and all the judges delivered their opinions *seriatim.* It was the case of a trial for a conspiracy, which commenced on the morning of Apr. 20, 1819, at Guildhall, before Abbot, *Ch. J.*, and continued till 11 at night, when the evidence being closed on the part of the prosecution, but the case being unfinished, the court informed the jury they might retire to their families; but especially warned them not to have any communication with any person, concerning the matter in issue. They retired accordingly, and the next morning assembled, heard the case through, and at a late hour in the afternoon found the defendants guilty. No abuse being pretended, the naked question *was presented, whether a separation, *per se*, was a sufficient ground for avoiding the verdict; and it was held, after great deliberation, that it was not. The court admitted the ancient strictness which prevailed in this respect, but said it had been much relaxed; that it frequently became necessary, from the very great length of modern trials, that the jury should separate; that from the mere fatigue and exhaustion which jurors frequently undergo, it is a course not only essential to the rights of the public, but of mercy to defendants, whose causes must be unsafe in the hands of a jury entirely shut out from comfortable refreshment and relaxation, perhaps for several days. Best, *J.*, in particular, speaks of the same rule being applicable to trials, for the highest criminal offenses. "Suppose (says he) in the case of a trial for capital felony, some of the jury, by accident, get out of the box, and the prisoner, in the result of the trial, is acquitted; the consequence of the argument; the prisoners would be a mistrial, and the man must be put on his trial again." 1 Chit., 426. What the K. B. would have said of a capital case, it is true, does not directly appear, because the case under consideration was one of a misdemeanor. But the reasoning of the judges is equally applicable to both cases; and we think that the mere fact of separation, unaccompanied with abuse, should not avoid the verdict, even in a capital case. A decision was cited to this effect from Conn. but we do not rely upon that, because the latitude allowed to jurors, in all respects, is there very great, and their courts do not profess to be guided in this practice by the rules of the common law. The decisions in this country are not uniform. Several cases were cited on the argument from the N. J. Reports, in which the separation of the jury was held irregular, but not sufficient to vitiate the verdict. These cases were not capital: but they go strongly to support the general principle. *State* v. *Carstaphen*, 2 Hayw., 238, was a criminal case, and the same doctrine was holden. The case of *The Commonwealth* v. *M'Caul*, Va. Cas., 271, does, however, go the length of saying, that the court should guard against the possibility of abuse, by setting aside the verdict *if any of the jury depart from the control of the officer; but the court did not profess to go upon any adjudged case in England; and we think the English cases are founded on the better reason. These are uniform, that though the jury separate, if there be no farther abuse, this shall not vitiate the verdict though it would be a contempt of the court, if contrary to their instructions, and would be punishable as such.

[*34

[*35

In the case at bar, the jury retired before the trial had closed, under the care of two sworn constables; and it is alleged, on the part of the prisoner, that two of them not only separated from their fellows, but also drank whisky, and conversed freely on the subject of the trial.

Three of the witnesses, through whom it is sought to fix on Lamb and Swartwout the charge of having drank whisky and conversed on the matter in issue, having deliberately contradicted what they had sworn as to conversations, I think they should not receive credit even for what they say in relation to the drinking of these jurors. Their testimony properly comes within the maxim, *falsus in uno, falsus in omnibus*. Besides, one of them is shown to have been a notorious drunkard himself. He was in a state of intoxication during most of the session, and at the very time when he pretends to have heard and seen things implicating the two jurors. But the case is very different with Wheeler, who thinks he saw both Swartwout and Lamb drink some kind of spirituous liquor while out. This witness stands unimpeached; and the exculpatory affidavit of Swartwout, one of the jurors, is not explicit. He confines himself to a literal denial that he drank whisky, but Wheeler's affidavit, that he drank some kind of spirits, may still be correct.

Admitting, however, that the weight of evidence is against drinking—admitting that Wheeler's and Swartwout affidavits cannot be reconciled—I think that in a case of life and death, the question upon the misbehaviour of the jury should be beyond all doubt. Clearly we should disregard the fact of eating, as forming any ground for setting aside the verdict; for though this might be a contempt of court, being without their leave, yet an opportunity to take reasonable refreshments would always 36*] be granted, at a proper season; *and the circumstance of their being obtained somewhat irregularly, could not prejudice the prisoner. But here the doubt is, whether there was not farther abuse in drinking spirituous liquors. This should not be tolerated in any shape, in the jury, during the progress of the trial; and we have uniformly held that it vitiated the verdict in a civil cause, even where the liquor was given to the jury by consent. It will not do to weigh and examine the quantity which may have been taken by the jury, nor the effect produced. In this case, it is not at all probable that either of these jurors was, in the least, under the influence of strong drink; but being doubtful whether they may not have drank something, we ought not, especially in a case of life and death, to sustain the verdict.

We cannot lay down any general rule for all cases like this which may arise. They will be attended with different circumstances. We do mean to be understood, however, as saying, that the mere separation of the jury, without any farther abuse, is not sufficient ground for setting aside a verdict; though it may deserve severe reprehension from the court. In this case, we think there is not a total failure of proof that the two jurors drank, though perhaps the balance of evidence may be against it.

SUTHERLAND, *J.* I concur in the result of the opinion delivered. I do not think the evidence before us is to be weighed and balanced with the same nicety as would be proper in a civil cause. All we have to do, in a case like the present, is to inquire whether in the conduct of the jury, that prudence and circumspection has been observed which becomes them on so solemn an occasion as that which commits to their hands the life of a fellow being. There is no difference among us, that the mere fact of drinking spirituous liquor is enough to set aside the verdict. It will never do to hold a rule short of this; that where any one of the jury, in the course of the trial, drinks spirituous liquor, we will set aside the verdict, on this ground alone. In this case, I think there is little doubt that two of the jurors did drink, though probably not in such quantities as in the least to disqualify them for a *dis- [*37 charge of their duty. Here are four witnesses who concur in the fact that the two jurors drank; and none of them have ever contradicted themselves, as to this fact, in any subsequent conversation, though three of them have given statements at war with their affidavits, in other respects. Swartwout contents himself with denying that he drank whisky; but does not, and indeed could not in truth, deny this of his co-juror, Lamb; though he might, if true, have done so with the same propriety that he denies Lamb's holding conversation with any one on the subject of the trial. As to the latter, he could not speak with absolute certainty. At one time he was six rods from Lamb, when he might have conversed unheard by Swartwout; though if during the time of their separation he had his eye upon Lamb, he might have negated the fact of his drinking. He has not even gone so far as to say that he did not see Lamb drink. Though three of these witnesses have, subsequent to their making affidavits in behalf of the prisoner, contradicted themselves in relation to some of the material facts to which they swore, I do not think that, on this summary application addressed to the court, we are warranted in utterly rejecting their testimony, upon the maxim *falsus in uno, falsus in omnibus*. It is enough that we are brought to entertain a reasonable doubt upon the facts in question. It is not like the case of a civil trial, or indeed of any trial, where witnesses may be compelled to attend and undergo a cross-examination. But, on the whole, I think the evidence conclusive that the jurors whose conduct is in question, or one of them, did drink spirituous liquor of some kind.

As remarked by *Mr. Justice* Woodworth, it is impossible to lay down any general rule, which shall guide in all the various circumstances with which cases like this may be attended; yet I have no hesitation in saying that where the separation of a jury is contrary to their duty towards the court, and there is the slightest suspicion of abuse, their verdict should be set aside. The separation here was unusual and unwarrantable. It was perfectly proper for this jury to go out under the care of the constable, and a jury cannot, in *such [*38 a case, be always immediately under the eyes of the officers. The purpose is plain for which they were suffered to leave the box. It was not for the purpose of going to their meals; and they received from the court the usual strict charge as to their demeanor. Yet they departed entirely from the care of the officer, and the instructions they had received, and went a distance of thirty rods, to their lodgings. This was not necessary. It was improper; and I think a separation under these circumstances, in itself, enters with great weight into the cause for granting a new trial, in which we are unanimous.

SAVAGE, *Ch. J.* I concur in the opinion that a new trial should be granted; and without recapitulating the evidence, would merely observe that in a civil suit, at this day, it is perfectly clear that a separation of the jury, without and even contrary to the direction of the court, would not, of itself, warrant us in setting aside their verdict. The ancient strictness, in this respect, has been much relaxed, as will be seen by the uniform current of modern decisions. Yet upon so grave a question as that of the life or death of a fellow citizen, I am not prepared to say that the separation of the jury, contrary to the instructions of the court, and mingling with the throng about the court-house, should not affect their verdict. But I do not deem it necessary for me to express an opinion upon this point, because I think it abundantly proved that these two jurors not only separated from their fellows, and ate and took cakes with them on their return, but that they also drank whisky. That Lamb also conversed on the subject of the matter in issue, is not fully negatived by Swartwout. He admits that he heard Lamb in conversation on the steps of the jail, he does not know on what subject; but another witness tells us that it related to the trial. This was while Swartwout was at the distance of five or six rods from Lamb, on the way to the court house. It is true that the witness who speaks to that conversation, and renders details, has given a different history; but his affidavit is somewhat confirmed by the circumstances stated in Swartwout's affidavit. I think **39***] I am warranted, from the *proof, in adding to the other misconduct of these jurors, that conversation was held by some bystander, at least with Lamb, upon the subject which he was engaged in trying. It has been properly observed that there is very great difficulty is laying down a general rule which shall govern in these cases. But I am willing to say, that in no case, where it appears that any of the jury separate from their fellows contrary to the direction of the court, make use of strong drink, and converse upon the matter which they are impaneled to try, would it be safe to sanction their verdict. The prisoner must be remanded to the County of Steuben, and a new trial had at the next Court of Oyer and Terminer in that county.

Rule accordingly.

Disapproved—48 Iowa, 539 (30 Am. Rep., 406).
Denied—44 Am. Rep., 551 (61 Cal., 164).
Cited in—7 Cow., 563; 2 Wend., 355; 7 Wend., 423; 1 Hill, 208, 211; 19 N. Y., 560; 20 N. Y., 552; 40 N. Y., 5; 5 Barb., 303; 13 Abb., N. S., 231; 9 How., Pr., 11; 1 Park., 260; 3 Park., 43; 4 Park., 503; 4 Bos., 510; 24 Ind., 155; 35 Ind., 500; 58 Ind., 299; 30 Ill., 273; 12 Kas., 546; 20 Am. Dec., 619; 21 Am. Dec., 714 (9 Conn., 47); 1 Am. Rep., 303, 306 (27 Iowa, 494); 9 Am. Rep., 761 (35 Ind., 496); 28 Am. Rep., 413 (1 Tex. Ct. App., 248); 30 Am. Rep., 406 (48 Iowa, 530).

WHITNEY
v.
SPENCER AND GRANT, Impleaded with HERRICK.

Bond Conditioned to Pay Judgment, or Surrender Defendant in Execution—Issue of Execution by Plaintiff—Condition Precedent.

In declaring on a bond, conditioned to pay a judgment in three months, or surrender the body of the defendant in execution, at the suit of the plaintiff, in 30 days thereafter, the taking out execution by the plaintiff within the 30 days, is a condition precedent, and must be shown in the declaration.

If performance of the condition of a bond be prevented by the omission of the obligee, the obligor is discharged.

Citation—10 Johns., 27.

ON error from the C. P., of Delaware. In that court the plaintiff declared against the defendants in debt, for $100, upon a bond dated July 27, 1818, with condition, after reciting that a judgment had, on the day of the date, been rendered in favor of the plaintiff, against one Stockton, for $50, with costs, that if Stockton should well and truly pay the judgment at the expiration of 3 months from the date of the bond, or surrender Stockton's body in execution within 30 days thereafter, then the bond to be void, &c. The declaration then averred that Stockton did not pay the judgment at the expiration of the 3 months, nor at any time afterwards, nor did he, within 30 days thereafter, surrender his body in execution, agreeably to the condition of the bond. The defendants pleaded, 1. That no execution issued on the judgment, at any time before the commencement of the plaintiff's suit. 2. That Stockton was ready, *within the County [***40** of Delaware, to be surrendered by the defendants whenever execution should be issued against him.

General demurrer to both pleas and joinders, upon which the court below gave judgment for the defendants.

Mr. L. Monson, for the plaintiff in error, said it could not be pretended that the second plea was good. A readiness to surrender when execution should issue, cannot be considered a performance.

As to the question upon this declaration, and whether it was necessary to aver that execution issue in proper time to enable the defendants to perform, though the cases in this court, perhaps, are not uniform, yet the weight of authority, both here and in England, is decisive that where one stipulates for the act of a third person it must be literally performed, unless prevented by the act of God, or of the obligee himself. This was held in *Mounsey* v. *Drake*, 10 Johns., 27, in relation to a bond almost word for word like the present. The condition of of the bond there was, that the defendant should pay the debt or surrender his body to the sheriff; and though he offered to surrender himself to the sheriff in due time, according to the condition of the bond, an actual surrender was held necessary. At page 29 of that volume several cases are cited and considered by the court, and they say there are various other cases to the same point. The court will find the authorities uniform on this subject. 1 Saund., 215, 216, *n.* 2; Bull. *N. P.*, 164–5; Co. Litt., 209, *a*; Reeve's Dom. Rel., 113; 2 Mod., 304; *Ackerly* v. *Vernon*, Willes, 160; Selw. *N. P.*, 525, 526, and the cases there cited; 6 T. R., 719, 720, 722, per Ld. Kenyon, *Ch. J.*, and Lawrence and Grose, *JJ.*

According to these authorities, it is not enough that Stockton did all in his power. Nothing is an excuse for the non-performance, save the act of the law, the act of God, or the act of the obligee himself. Here was no condition precedent to be performed by the obligee.

WOODWORTH, *J.* But do not the terms of the bond imply that the obligee should sue out

41*] his execution, so as to *enable the defendants to surrender? If this be so, your declaration is bad within the authorities cited. The obligors were prevented in their performance, by the omission of the obligee.

Mr. Monson read the case of *Mounsey* v. *Drake*, and insisted that the same objection existed in that case. The obligors might have paid the debt; and they can no more excuse themselves here, for the want of an execution, than in that case.

Mr. S. Sherwood, contra, said this case could not be distinguished from that of *Tuttle* v. *Kip*, 19 Johns., 194, upon which latter case he relied as being conclusive for the defendants in error.

Mr. Monson said that case went upon the construction to be given to the 8th section of the Act Extending the Jurisdiction of Justices of the Peace. Sec. 41, ch. 94. Nothing appears upon this record that the bond was given under that section. It might as well relate to any other court, and the case cannot be distinguished from *Mounsey* v. *Drake*.

Curia. We think differently. In *Mounsey* v. *Drake*, the condition was general to surrender to the sheriff. Here it is to surrender in execution. No one could sue out this execution except the plaintiff. It was, therefore, his own fault that the surrender did not take place.

Judgment affirmed.

Cited in—1 Den., 571; 15 Barb., 348.

RAYMOND v. HINMAN.

Capias ad respondendum tested by mistake at Utica, when it should have been Albany, is amendable.

The *capias ad respondendum* was, by a clerical mistake, tested in Oct. Term, 1824, at Utica, whereas it should have been Albany, where the court was held.

Mr. J. A. Spencer moved to set it aside as irregular.

Mr. P. Ruggles moved to amend.

42*] **Mr. Spencer* objected, that being *mesne* process, it was not amendable.

Curia. The objection has never been extended to the place of teste in *mesne* process. The plaintiff may amend.

Rule accordingly.

Cited in—4 Daly, 523; 49 Am. Dec., 743 (3 Texas, 261).

HAYES v. BAYLEY.

Judgment, on Report of Referees—Rate of Taxation of Costs.

In *assumpsit*, and judgment for the plaintiff, on the report of referees for less than $250, the costs of opposing the motion to set aside the reference upon the merits, like other costs in the cause, must be taxed at the C. P. rate only.

They are the costs of an ordinary proceeding in the cause, and properly included in the final bill.

IN *assumpsit*, the cause was referred, and the referees reported in favor of the plaintiff $52.52. The attorney for the defendant being dissatisfied with the report, moved to set it aside upon the merits, and the cause was placed upon the calendar, noticed for argument at several terms, brought to a hearing, the motion denied, and judgment rendered for the plaintiff upon the report. The plaintiff's attorney noticed the costs for taxation, charging C. P. costs for all services, &c., except those which related to opposing the motion to set aside the report, for which he charged at the rate of Supreme Court costs, and the commissioner taxed them accordingly.

A motion was now made, in behalf of the defendant, for a retaxation, upon this ground.

Mr. B. Whiting, for the motion.

Messrs. D. Beecher and *J. A. Spencer*, contra.

Curia. The whole of these proceedings, upon the motion, were in the ordinary course of the cause, and properly included in the final bill, among the general costs, like the expenses of the reference and the other usual expenses in the course of the suit. They all, therefore, stand on the same footing as to the rate at which they should be taxed. The whole must be reduced to C. P. costs.

Motion granted.

---

*JACKSON, ex dem. FIELD, v. SINCLAIR. [*43

Verdict, Subject to Opinion of Court—Stipulation that Either Party may Turn it into Special Verdict or Bill of Exceptions—Time for Election—Practice.

On a verdict for the plaintiff, subject to the opinion of the court on a case, and a stipulation that either party may turn it into a special verdict or bill of exceptions, the party against whom judgment is rendered is entitled to a reasonable time to elect, under the stipulation and make up and settle the verdict or bill. The party in whose favor the judgment is rendered should, at least, give notice thereof to the opposite party, and wait a reasonable time for him to make his election, or should apply to the court for leave to proceed, &c.

THIS case was tried June 12, 1822, and a verdict taken for the plaintiff by consent, subject to the opinion of the court on a case, to be turned into a special verdict or bill of exceptions by either party. The case, as made and settled, contained a stipulation to this effect. It was argued at February Term, 1824, and decided Nov. 13, in the same year, when the court gave judgment for the plaintiff, whose attorney perfected judgment, and filed his record on the 20th, and on the 21st of the same month issued a writ of possession, which was executed immediately, by dispossessing the tenant of the defendant, and putting Field, the lessor in this suit, in possession. The defendant's tenant thereupon agreed to become the tenant of Field, at the same rent upon which he had before held of the defendant. The affidavit of the defendant's attorney stated that he intended to bring error; but owing to unavoidable delay in obtaining from the plaintiff's attorney the documentary evidence exhibited by the plaintiff upon trial, the defendant's attorney had not had sufficient time to finish the bill of exceptions. On these facts,

Mr. J. Platt, for the defendant, moved that the writ of possession, and all subsequent proceedings, be set aside for irregularity, and that a writ of restitution issue.

Mr. A. Spencer, contra, admitted that the plaintiff's attorney had been somewhat precipitate, but insisted that he was regular, notwithstanding the stipulation. He said this was in the alternative that the case might be changed into a bill of exceptions or special verdict; and no election was made by the plaintiff's attorney between the two. The court may relieve, but it should be on terms. The defendant should be required to give bail in error, and perhaps to pay the costs.

44*] *WOODWORTH, *J.* It cannot be that the plaintiff's attorney was warrantable in this hasty proceeding. Here was a decision pronounced at the last moment of the term; and the plaintiff should have taken no step till the defendant had a fair opportunity to make his election between a verdict and a bill of exceptions, and procure the verdict or bill to be settled. An application to the court frequently becomes necessary to this end. There is, I believe, no settled course, in practice, which this matter should take, as to time or manner; but it is clear that the party ought not to be precluded all benefit from his stipulation, by the unreasonable haste of his adversary. He must, in some fair and equitable way, have the benefit of it.

SUTHERLAND, *J.* Here has been great haste, but still I do not think we ought to relieve the party, unless he now elect whether he will have a verdict or bill of exceptions, and show a *bona fide* intention to prosecute a writ of error.

Mr. Platt. The attorney swears to that intention. As I understand the practice, this stipulation is itself a stay of all proceedings, at least, for a reasonable time after the decision. We elect to proceed by bill of exceptions.

WOODWORTH, *J.* I have no doubt the issuing a writ of possession was irregular. I remember a case in which I was counsel, wherein it was held that the plaintiff was bound by this stipulation to wait a reasonable time, at least, or to apply to the court for leave to proceed notwithstanding the stipulation.

SAVAGE, *Ch. J.* There can be no doubt that we ought to set aside this writ of possession; but we will think further upon the question as to the terms, if any, upon which this should be done, and the ulterior relief to be given.

At another day,

WOODWORTH, *J.*, said that the court, on conferring upon this motion, held the proceed-
45*] ings after judgment to be altogether *irregular. There is no settled course of practice on this subject; but the party against whom the judgment is rendered should, at least, have fair notice, and a reasonable chance to make an election, or the court should be moved in relation to the matter, before the execution is proceeded upon. The execution must be set aside, and a writ of restitution issue, with costs, on the defendant's stipulating to bring no action for the trespass. The defendant's attorney may take twenty days within which to make and serve a bill of exceptions; and, moreover, the lessor of the plaintiff must pay to the defendant the rent which the former may have received of the tenant.

Rule accordingly.

Cited in—61 N. Y., 618.

ATKINSON *v.* HOLCOMB.

Action of Replevin—Venue.

Replevin is a local action; and, in general, the venue will not be changed from the county where the cause of action arose.

Whether there be any exception to this rule, as where the action is in nature of an ordinary action of trespass, *de bonis asportatis*, *quære*.

If this be an exception, yet the plaintiff may retain his venue upon the usual stipulation.

IN replevin. *Mr. J. Platt* moved to change the venue from the County of Monroe to the County of Rensselaer on the ground that the defendant had twenty-five witnesses living in the latter county.

Mr. S. M. Hopkins, contra, read an affidavit that the cause of action arose in Monroe, and insisted that replevin was a local action. The place is material and traversable. 2 Chit. Pl., 364, *notes c* and *e*; Gilb. Repl., 125. Even on a plea of *non cepit*, the place is considered material (1 Saund., 347, *n.* 1); and if the plaintiff is driven to lay his venue in Rensselaer, the cause of action having in fact arisen in Monroe, he must be nonsuited at the trial.

At any rate, the action being for a tort, the plaintiff may retain his venue by stipulating to give material evidence, arising in the County of Monroe. *Serially* v. *Wells*, 1 Cow., 196; *Ross* v. *Lown*, 8 Johns., 354; *Duryee* v. *Orcutt*, 9 *Id.*, 248.

Mr. Platt, in reply. Where replevin is [*46 to reclaim chattels distrained for rent, or cattle distrained *damage feasant*, it is, to be sure, a local action, because it relates immediately to lands, like trespass *quare clausum fregit*. The authorities cited on the other side prove this, and nothing more. The plaintiff does not show this action to be for any cause relating to land. It is an appropriate remedy to recover chattels tortiously taken by one private person from another, and may be substituted for trespass *de bonis asportatis*, where the owner chooses to have the specific chattel, instead of damages. For aught that appears, it is no more local than any action of trespass *de bonis asportatis*.

Per Curiam. The only difference which the determination of this motion can make in the rights of the plaintiff lies between considering the action in nature of a trespass *de bonis asportatis*, and properly an action of replevin. In the former case, he may retain his venue upon the usual stipulation—in the latter, it cannot be changed, in any view upon the facts disclosed, because it is in its nature local. It is true that replevin lies for a trespass *de bonis asportatis*, or for a wrongful distress either for rent or *damage feasant*. In general, however, it is a local action, the place being material and traversable; and we have looked into all the authorities upon the question, to see if there be any exception. We find none; and without saying whether it might not stand on the same footing as an action of trespass *de bonis asportatis*, where it appeared upon the motion to have been brought for that cause, we deem it our duty to treat it as, *prima facie*, local. Where nothing appears, therefore, of the particular nature and object of the action, as in this case, but merely that it is an action of replevin, we hold it within the general rule; and the motion must, therefore, be denied.

Motion denied.

Cited in—5 Wend., 292; 3 Daly, 456.

47*] *TUCKER ET AL. v. LADD AND LADD.

When Plea Not Set Aside as False—Affidavit Taken before Notary in Another State.

The court will not set aside a plea, on the ground of its being false, unless it also appear to be intended artfully to draw the plaintiff into a course of special pleading which may compromit his rights, and not then, if the defendant swear that he expects to be able to prove it.

Affidavit taken before a notary public of N. H. allowed to be read.

MR. B. F. BUTLER, for the plaintiffs, moved to strike out the second plea of the defendant. It was a plea of set-off; and he read affidavits showing that it was false and unfounded in point of fact; and he also insisted that a set-off can not be pleaded under the Statute of this State. *Alsop* v. *Caines*, 10 Johns., 396; *Caines* v. *Brisban*, 13 *Id.*, 9. The defendants had also given notice of setting off the same matters stated in the plea. He cited *Steward* v. *Hotchkiss*, 2 Cow., 634; *Richmond* v. *Tallmadge*, 16 Johns., 312, per Kent, *Chancellor*, and 1 Archb. Pr., 121.

Mr. H. Bleecker, contra, proposed to read an affidavit of one of the defendants, taken before a notary public, at Portsmouth, in the State of N. H., attested by his hand and seal of office, the deponent residing in that State.

Mr. Butler, objected to this; but,

Per Curiam. We have been in the habit of receiving affidavits thus taken, under such circumstances.

Mr. Bleecker then read the affidavit, which stated that the defendant expected to be able to prove all the material allegations in the special plea.

Curia. We do not interfere to set aside a plea merely on the ground of its falsity, unless it be also apparent that it is intended to entrap the plaintiff; being of a doubtful character, and calling for a course of special pleading, which may compromit his rights. We said no more in *Steward* v. *Hotchkiss*. In this case, if, as insisted, the plea is plainly defective, the plaintiffs might have demurred. But it is 48*] enough that *the defendant swears he expects to be able to prove his plea. The motion must be denied with costs.

Rule accordingly.(b)

Overruled—6 Cow., 35.
Cited in—4 How. Pr., 157.

(b) Since the decision in Richley v. Proone, 1 B. & C., 286, both the C. P. and K. B. of England have brought their practice of setting aside false pleas on motion, within the qualification which this court have acted upon in the only two reported cases going to the question, viz.: Steward v. Hotchkiss, 2 Cow., 637, and the present case. Young v. Gadderer, M. T., 1823; 1 Bing., 380.

*CHANDLER v. BRECKNELL. [*49

When Action for False Imprisonment Ordered Discontinued—Mesne *Process against Body Tested out of Term, not Amendable.*

A *capias ad respondendum*, tested out of term by mistake, set aside on the defendant's stipulating, on payment of costs, to discontinue an action of false imprisonment which he had brought against the plaintiff.

Mesne process against the body tested out of term is not amendable.

MR. GRIFFEN moved to set aside the *capias ad respondendum*, tested Oct. 30, 1825, returnable the 3d Monday of Feb. next, on the ground that it was tested out of term, no term of Oct., 1825, having passed.

Mr. P. Gridley, contra, moved to amend; and he read an affidavit showing that the wrong test arose from a clerical mistake.

Curia. We have never gone so far as to allow an amendment of *mesne* process against the body, where it is tested out of term. Let the *capias* be set aside, on the defendant's stipulating not to bring an action of false imprisonment.

Mr. Griffen. An action is already brought.

Curia. Then you must discontinue it, on payment of the costs of your action.

Rule accordingly.

Cited in—10 Wend., 214; 15 Wend., 301; 18 Wend., 677; 5 Hill, 247 (*n.*); 2 Den., 185; 16 N. Y., 446; 18 Barb., 271; 4 Daly, 522.

EX PARTE CHAMBERLAIN.

Trial for Misdemeanor—Witnesses for Defendant, Need Not Attend unless Fees Paid.

Witnesses for the defendant, in a prosecution for a misdemeanor, are not bound to attend the trial unless their fees are paid as in civil cases; otherwise as to prosecutions for felony.

This court will not grant a *mandamus* to compel an inferior court to punish a man for a contempt, unless the civil rights of an individual are implicated in the proceeding.

When this is not the case, every court must be the judge whether a contempt has been committed against it.

MOTION for a *mandamus* to the justices of the General Sessions of the Peace of the County of Oneida, commanding them to attach and punish John Garter, for non-attendance in that court as a witness. Chamberlain had been indicted *for an assault and battery, [*50 which was tried at the February Term of that court, 1825. He subpœnaed Garter to attend as a witness in his behalf; he neglected to appear, and was attached; but was discharged by the court, upon his answering, to the interrogatories, that no fees had been tendered to him.

Against the motion, the 2 R. L., 29, which prescribes the fees of witnesses, and the 1 R. L., 524, sec. 20, which makes it obligatory on witnesses to attend, upon being subpœnaed, and paid for travel to and from court, and one day's attendance, were cited; also 1 Ch. C. L., Phil. ed., 613. But it was replied that these apply to civil causes only; that the Statute (1 R. L., 497, sec. 12) provides, that all persons charged with crimes shall be entitled to have counsel, and compulsory process to compel the attendance of witnesses; that this wholesome provision of the law would be virtually denied the person charged with a crime, and confined in jail, without friends or money, should the doctrine acted upon by the court below prevail.

Messrs. E. Allen and *J. A. Spencer*, for the motion.

Mr. H. Denio, contra.

Cur. adv. vult.

At a subsequent day,

The Court said they had looked into this subject, and thought the distinction lay between misdemeanor and felony; that in the former case the defendant must tender his witnesses their fees, as in civil cases; but that in prosecutions for felonies they were compellable to attend without fees. They should have denied this motion at once, on the ground that it sought for a *mandamus* to compel an inferior court to punish for a contempt, had the matter rested there; for every court must be the sole judge whether a contempt has been committed against it or not; but as the private rights of an individual were also implicated, they had for that reason looked into the merits.

Motion denied.

Cited in—5 Abb. Pr., 89.

51*]*PARDEE v. REID AND ARNOLD.

Filing Special Bail—Notice.

The plaintiff's attorney is not bound to regard the filing a special bail piece, unless he have notice of it; and though special bail be actually in, without notice, the filing common bail, and entry of a default, after the ordinary time, is proper, even within the four days after special bail is filed.

THE *capias ad respondendum* was returned the 1st day of last October Term; the declaration was filed *de bene esse*, and rule to plead entered, and notice thereof affixed in the clerk's office, Nov. 10, 1824; and Dec. 10 thereafter, common bail was filed, and a default entered. But Dec. 6, a special bailpiece had been filed by the defendant, notice whereof was afterwards given, but not till Dec. 20, and after the default had been entered.

Mr. M. T. Reynolds, for the defendant, moved to set aside the default as irregular, it having been entered before the four full days had expired after filing special bail. He cited 1 R. L., 324, sec. 5, and *Leispenard* v. *Baker*, 6 Johns., 323.

Mr. S. A. Foot, contra.

Curia. The plaintiff's attorney was not bound at his peril to know whether special bail was in. To require this, would drive him to a search in all our clerk's offices. Special bail is not regularly in, until notice is given to the plaintiff's attorney. This case is as if no special bailpiece had been filed; and double the time for putting in special bail having elapsed, the filing common bail and entry of the default were regular. The motion must be denied.

Motion denied.

JACKSON, ex dem. DAVIS ET AL., v. BROWNSON.

Notice of Motion.

A notice for the next term, generally, is sufficient, and if it add a particular day for the motion, which is several times forward, this may be rejected as surplusage.

MR. M. T. REYNOLDS moved for judgment as in case of nonsuit, upon a notice of motion which was thus: "Take notice *that I shall move this Honorable Court, [*52 at the next term thereof, to be holden at the Capitol in the City of Albany, on the 3d Monday in October next," &c. The notice was dated Jan. 28, 1825, and served in season for this term.

Mr. A. Conkling, contra, objected that from the terms of the notice the time for making the motion would not arrive till October Term, next.

Curia. It is impossible that the plaintiff's attorney could have been misled by this notice. It is first general for the next term after its date and service. The words "on the third Monday of October next" must be rejected as surplusage.

Mr. Conkling thereupon stipulated.

Cited in—13 How. Pr., 536.

SHAW v. AYRS, Impleaded with AYRS.

Opposition to Motion for Reference.

Manner of showing how questions of law will arise so as to oppose motion for a reference.

MR. C. M. LEE moved for a reference on the usual affidavit.

Mr. W. M. Oliver, contra, produced a sworn copy of the declaration, which consisted of two special counts only, upon an agreement. The declaration recited that the plaintiff being possessed of certain goods and notes belonging to one Stoddard, who owed the plaintiff, he, at the request of the defendants, promised to deliver the goods to them, in consideration of which premises the defendants promised to receive the goods and notes, and pay the plaintiff the demands which he then had or should thereafter have against Stoddard, provided that the plaintiff should purchase no demands against Stoddard after Dec. 29, 1823. The declaration averred that the plaintiff had always been ready to deliver the goods and notes.

It appeared from the second count of the declaration, as well as by an affidavit produced by *Mr. Oliver*, that this *agree- [*53 ment was in writing, setting forth the consideration as it was stated in the declaration, and signed by the defendants only. The affidavit of one of the defendants also stated that a question of law would arise, viz.: whether the plaintiff could recover without an actual delivery of the goods—this being, as would be contended, a condition precedent upon the agreement which would be proved (though not perhaps distinctly appearing to be such upon the face of the declaration); and this, especially, as the agreement was executed by the defendants only.

Curia. Here is no averment of delivery or of an offer to deliver the goods and notes; and a question of law may very well arise upon the proof, whether the contract in question was such as to bind the defendants, without any further act or consideration than a mere promise to deliver the goods. It is sworn that this question will arise, and the manner in which it may arise sufficiently appears from the declaration and affidavit.

Motion denied.

Cited in—10 How. Pr., 352; 13 How. Pr., 439; 39 Super., 416; 5 Daly, 71.

BISSELL *v.* HOPKINS.

Judgment—Action of Trover—Writ of Error—Affirmance—Interest and Double Costs.

On verdict and judgment for the plaintiff in trover, error and judgment of affirmance, the defendant in error has both interest from the time of the judgment below, and also double costs, the execution being actually delayed by the writ of error.

In trover the plaintiff may recover interest on the value of the goods from the time of the conversion.

Citations—2 Cow., 579; 3 Cow., 379; 13 Johns., 590

ON ERROR from the Livingston C. P. The action below was trover by Hopkins against Bissell. Verdict and judgment for the plaintiff, upon which Bissell brought error to this court, where the judgment was affirmed. (S. C., 3 Cow., 166.) Bail in error having been put in, and the execution stayed, the question was now submitted to the court, whether the defendant in error should have not only his double costs, but also interest from the time of the rendition of the judgment below till its affirmance here.

Mr. O. Hastings, for the plaintiff in error.

54*] **Mr. F. Tracy*, contra.

Curia. The defendant in error is entitled to both interest and double costs. 2 Cow., 579; *Stone* v. *Burt*, 3 Cow., 379. The only objection which is made to allowing interest is, that as the action below was for a tort, no interest could be recovered there; and such is the general rule. *Gelston* v. *Hoyt*, 13 Johns., 561. But this was an action of trover, in which interest is recoverable upon the value of the goods from the time of the conversion.

Rule accordingly.

Cited in—43 How. Pr., 285; 1 E. D. S., 487.

HUMPHREY & HUMPHREY *v.* COTTLEY.

Practice—Bill of Particulars—What it Should State.

Practice upon requiring a farther bill of particulars.

The party, under an order for a bill of particulars, must state the time when the items of his demand arose with as much particularity as possible. If he cannot give the day, he should give the month, year, &c.

THIS was an action of trover. June 2, 1824, an order was made by the Hon. J. T. Irving, first judge, &c., requiring the plaintiffs to show cause before him at his office, at the City Hall, N. Y., on the 10th, why they should not deliver to the defendant, or his attorney, an account in writing of the particulars of the plaintiff's demand. This order was served on the agent of the plaintiff's attorney, but did not reach him till the 12th. On the 10th the order was made absolute that the plaintiffs deliver a bill of particulars to the defendant or his attorney; and that in the meantime all proceedings on the part of the plaintiffs be stayed. This order being duly served, the plaintiff's attorney delivered a bill, which, after the title of the cause, ran thus: "And the said plaintiffs, in pursuance of an order of the Hon. John T. Irving, deliver the following account and particulars for which this suit is brought, that is to say: for 2 sticks of timber 24 inches square, 70 or 80 feet long, 100 sticks of round hemlock and pine timber called dock sticks," &c., proceeding in this form, without giving dates or mentioning any time within which the plaintiffs' claims for the several items arose. On the 26th July the judge made an order for a further bill of particulars, requiring the plaintiffs to state the *precise date and times when the several [*55 articles specified in the declaration came to the defendant's possession, or were converted by him. After this, the defendant's attorney made an affidavit that he had conferred with his clients, and from the facts he had gathered from them, and by a conversation with the witnesses, he could not comply with the last order, so far as to give the precise dates and times when the articles specified in the declaration came to the defendant's hands or were converted to his use. Upon this affidavit and the above facts,

A motion was now made to set aside the second order of the judge. On the part of the defendant an affidavit was read to show that a statement of the time was necessary to enable him to prepare for his defense.

Mr. H. Carter, for the motion.

Messrs. King and *Randall*, contra.

Curia. In a bill of particulars, the date of the items should always be given with as much particularity as possible. If the precise day cannot be stated, the month or year probably can. This is a matter in relation to which the judge who grants the order must exercise a sound discretion on hearing both parties, under all the circumstances of the case. The motion must be denied.

Motion denied.

Cited in—2 Wend., 579; 59 N. Y., 184; 8 How. Pr., 332; 48 How. Pr., 176; 49 How. Pr., 40; 37 Super., 317; 41 Super., 357; 17 Am. Rep., 343, 346 (59 N. Y., 176).

PACKARD ET AL. *v.* HILL.

Setting Aside Default—Costs.

Where, after a regular default, the defendant makes an affidavit of merits, which he shows to the plaintiff's attorney, with an affidavit showing a clear right to set it aside on terms; and offers to plead and to pay all costs, &c., if the plaintiff's attorney refuse to comply with such offer, it seems, this court will not allow him costs, on his coming here to oppose the motion to set aside the default, beyond what were offered: otherwise, where there are special circumstances, leaving it doubtful whether the court would set aside the default upon the papers shown to the attorney.

A REGULAR default for want of a plea having been taken, the defendant's attorney procured an affidavit of merits to be made by the special bail, the defendant being absent from the State, and he himself made an affidavit accounting for the default, which papers he exhibited to the plaintiff's attorney, offering to
56*] *pay the costs of the default, and take short notice of the trial, so that no time should be lost. On these facts,

A motion was now made to set aside the default, which was opposed; and it was contended in behalf of the defendant, that he should take his motion without paying the costs of opposing, or of any step on the part of the plaintiffs since the offer made.

Mr. A. S. Garr, for the motion.

Mr. H. D. Sedgwick, contra.

Curia. In an ordinary case of an affidavit of merits, and an application and offers like these to the plaintiff's attorney, we should doubtless grant a motion to set aside a default without costs, subsequent to the offer: but this is not that case. The affidavit of merits is not made by the defendant, and there are some other circumstances which perhaps required the plaintiff's attorney, out of a just regard to the rights of his clients, to meet this motion here. Under the circumstances, the usual terms must be imposed, which are payment of all costs including those of opposing this motion. The defendant must also plead issuably, *instanter*, and take four days notice of trial, for the circuit now sitting in the City of N. Y.

Rule accordingly.

Cited in—2 Hun, 292½; 4 T. & C., 522; 48 How. Pr., 140.

MAY *v.* RICHARDSON ET AL.

Order of Bill of Particulars—Application for Judgment of Non Pros.

On an order for a bill of particulars becoming absolute against the plaintiff, the defendant may move for a rule that the plaintiff furnish a bill in so many days and pay the costs of the motion, or that judgment of *non pros.* be entered.

SEPT. 30, last, an order for a bill of particulars was made absolute against the plaintiff upon a regular order to show cause, and served on the agent of the plaintiff's attorney, Oct. 9.

A motion was now made for judgment of *non pros.*, and that the plaintiff pay the costs of this motion.

Mr. J. S. Tallmadge, for the motion.

Mr. A. C. Paige, contra.

57*] **Curia.* Upon an order for a bill of particulars absolute against the plaintiff, the defendant moves this court, who make a rule for judgment of *non pros. nisi.* As the party disobeying the order is in fault, it is reasonable that he should pay the costs of the motion. In this case, let the plaintiff deliver a bill in 20 days, and pay the costs of this motion or judgment of *non pros.* may be entered.

Rule accordingly.

Cited in—4 How. Pr., 307; 2 Co. R., 129.

HEPBURN *v.* HOAG & HEPBURN.

Action on Bond—Claim of Set-Off—Practice.

Whether a set-off be admissible in an action on a bond for performance of covenants, *quære.*

Where in debt on a bond for performance of covenants, the jury were directed by the judge to find for the plaintiff, and to certify at the same time the sum due from him to the defendants; held, that the certificate was a nullity; and that the plaintiff might take judgment.

The Statute (1 R. L., 315) authorizes a certificate of a balance in favor of the defendant only where the verdict is for him; and if by mistake of the judge the verdict be for the plaintiff, and the jury certify a balance for the defendant, the proper mode of correcting this is on a case.

The practice being mistaken, however, time may be given to make a case.

Citations—1 R. L., 315.

DEBT on bond in the penalty of $2,000, conditioned to pay money, and also to support the plaintiff, his mother and sister, alleging a breach in the latter particular. Plea, *non est factum*, with notice of set-off. On the trial, at the Columbia Circuit, the plaintiff relied solely on the breach in not maintaining the plaintiff, which, up to the time of the suit brought, was proved to be $10. The defendants then, under a notice of set-off, proposed to prove demands against the plaintiff; but the judge refused to permit this, thinking the nature of the plaintiff's demand precluded it; but he afterwards allowed the defendants to establish their demand with a view to have the question settled by this court, and directed the jury to find for the plaintiff $10, and also to certify what they found due to the defendants, which they did at $500. The cause was tried Sept. 30, 1824. At the next term, the plaintiff perfected his judgment, as upon a verdict for himself.

Mr. E. Williams now moved to set off the plaintiff's damages and costs against the $500, certified for the defendants.

Mr. C. Bushnell, contra, objected that the verdict being for the plaintiff, the certificate of the jury was a nullity. It is *allowed [***58**
by the Statue only when the verdict is for the defendant. If the defendants had intended to avail themselves of their set-off, they should have made a case, upon the mistake of the judge and obtained a new trial. But the set-off is not admissible against damages upon a bond for performance of covenants; it is confined to a bond for the payment of money.

Mr. E. Williams, in reply, insisted that if a case were necessary, it lay with the plaintiff to make it. This was substantially a verdict for the defendants.

Curia. We cannot determine, in this form, whether the set-off was proper or not. It should have been brought before us as an enumerated motion, upon a case. The Statute (1 R. L., 315) is plain that the jury cannot certify a balance in favor of the defendant unless the verdict be for him. Here was a general verdict for the plaintiff, and a distinct certificate of a larger balance due to the defendants. This certificate is a mere nullity; and the plaintiff was regular in taking a judgment upon his verdict. But as there seems to have been a mistake of the practice, by the defendants' attorney, and there may be some question whether the set-off be not admissible, we stay the proceedings of the plaintiffs, and give the defendants 30 days, within which to make a case, and bring up the question, if they choose.

Rule accordingly.

Cited in—6 Cow., 616.

SHUFELT v. ROWLEY.

Action, for Assault and Debauching Plaintiff's Daughter—Costs, Rate of.

In trespass for assaulting and getting the plaintiff's daughter with child, the gist of the action is the loss of service. It is not technically an action of assault and battery; and if the plaintiff recover less than $250 he is entitled to a C. P. costs only, within the Statute. (1 R. L., 344, sec. 4.)

To warrant a taxation of costs for the travel of witnesses, the amount of travel should appear by affidavit; otherwise not a single day's travel can be allowed.

IN trespass, one count was for making an assault upon the plaintiff's daughter, and maltreating, debauching and getting her with child, with a *per quod*, &c. and another count was in trespass *quare domum fregit, et alia enor-* **59*]** *mia*, &c. *generally. General verdict for the plaintiff for $100 damages; and the commissioner taxed Supreme Court costs. He also allowed for witnesses, one day going and one day returning, when nothing appeared upon the affidavit of their attendance, as to where they resided, or how far they actually traveled.

Mr. E. Williams, moved for a retaxation on both grounds.

Mr. C. Bushnell, contra, insisted on Supreme Court costs, as the action was for an assault and battery. He insisted that it came within the proviso in 1 R. L., 344, sec. 4. He said, in relation to witnesses' fees, the practice is to tax for one days' going and one returning, of course.

Mr. Williams, said that by the 4th section 1 R. L., 344, all personal actions, not there excepted, carry C. P. costs only, unless the damages exceed $250. This not one of the excepted cases.

Curia. This is not technically an action of assault and battery. The gist of the action, is the loss of service; and the title to land not coming in question, the plaintiff is entitled to C. P. costs only. The practice, insisted on, of allowing for the travel of witnesses, without actual travel being shown by affidavit, is erroneous. For aught that appears, the witnesses in this case, may have all resided within a few rods of the place of trial. The affidavit should show the probable amount of travel. There must be a retaxation, on both grounds.

Rule accordingly.

Cited in—2 Paige, 466; 5 Lans., 458; 45 Barb., 43; 59 How. Pr., 394; 8 Abb., N. C., 155; 46 Sup. Ct., 43.

*BANDER v. COVILL. [*60

Notice of Trial — Defect — Court will Inquire Whether Attorney was Misled by.

In determining the sufficiency of a notice of trial, e. g., a notice for the day before the circuit is appointed to commence, the court will not only look to the face of the notice, but other circumstances, to see whether the opposite party was, in fact, misled by the mistake.

THE plaintiff's attorneys noticed this cause for trial and inquest by a notice, dated Nov. 3, 1824, that it would be tried at the next Circuit Court to be held in and for the Country of Rensselaer, at &c., on 3d Monday of Nov. instant, whereas the circuit was appointed for, and commenced on the next day, the 3d Tuesday of that month; but it appeared by various conversations between the counsel of the parties, which took place in the course of the circuit, that the defendant's counsel, or attorney, was not misled by the mistake. The plaintiff's counsel took an inquest by default, which,

Mr. J. Payne, for the defendant, moved to set aside, for the defect in the notice.

Mr. A. Conkling, contra, cited *Quick* v. *Merrill*, 3 Cai.; 133, and *Wolfe* v. *Horton*, *Id.*, 86.

Curia. In determining the sufficiency of this and the like notices, it is a general rule that we will inquire whether the attorney or party was misled by the defect. Now though these circuits are not appointed by law, yet notice is required to be published, and the attorneys, especially where, as here, they live directly in the neighborhood of the circuit, must look to it. But we will also examine the question whether the party, his attorney, or counsel, have, in fact, been misled; and it appears clearly, in this case, that they have not. The motion must be denied.

Motion denied.

Cited in—50 N. Y., 179; 13 How. Pr., 536; 9 Abb. Pr., 162; 2 Hilt., 470.

*PHELPS AND HOWARD, Overseers of the Poor of PREBLE, [*61

v.

BRONSON ET AL.

Judgment by Default—Common Bail, Filed nunc pro tunc.

Where a plaintiff takes a judgment by default, but inadvertently omits to file common bail, the court, on motion, will always give liberty to do this *nunc pro tunc*.

SEVERAL questions were made, upon cross motions, as to the regularity of the proceedings to judgment; one of which was, whether the plaintiff's attorney should be suffered to file common bail for the defendants, *nunc pro tunc*, they having been arrested, and the ordinary return of *cepi corpora* having been made, and the default, though regular in other respects, being, by inadvertence, without a common bailpiece being first filed; and as to this,

Per Curiam. There is no doubt that when a plaintiff takes his default, but inadvertently omits to file common bail, in a case proper for it, he should always be permitted to make his proceedings good by doing this *nunc pro tunc*. Upon such a case being presented by affidavit and notice of motion, it is a matter of course to grant a rule that it may be done.

Rule accordingly.(a)

Cited in—3 Barb., 608.

(a) *Vide* 2 Cow., 43, per Sudam, *Senator*.

EX PARTE HARRISON.

Appeal Bond—Form of, in Various Cases.

Form of bond on appeal by plaintiff from a judgment against him for costs only, before a justice, under the Statute (sess. 47, ch. 238, sec. 36). It need not be conditioned to pay the judgment below, or surrender, &c.
So if plaintiff appeal on account of the judgment in his favor being too small.
So if defendant appeal for the smallness of the judgment in his favor.
Otherwise, if a party appeal from a judgment against him for both damages and costs.
How the bond should be in such case.
Bond is, in all cases, to be in the penalty of double the judgment, whether for costs only, or damages and costs.

Citation—19 Johns., 171.

HARRISON sued Adams before a justice of Onondaga Co., who gave judgment for the defendant. Upon which the plaintiff appealed to the next Court of C. P. for that county; gave due notice of appeal to the justice, July 24, 1824; paid the costs recovered by the defendant; and executed and delivered to the justice a bond in these words: "Know all men by these presents, that we, William Harrison, Samuel Forman and Morehouse Hickok, 62*] are held and firmly *bound unto John Adams, in the sum of seven dollars ninety-six cents, to the payment whereof we bind ourselves, jointly and severally, firmly by these presents. Sealed with our seals. Dated July 24, 1824. The condition of this obligation is such, that whereas the above named William Harrison, by Samuel Forman, as his next friend, heretofore brought a suit before Thaddeus Patchen, Esq., a justice of the peace in and for the County of Onondaga, against the above named John Adams, which suit came on to be tried before the said justice and a jury, on the 17th day of July instant, at which time a judgment was rendered therein, on the verdict of the said jury, in favor of the said Adams, against the said Harrison, for the costs of suit amounting to three dollars and ninety-eight cents; and whereas the said William Harrison has appealed from the said judgment, to the Court of Common Pleas in and for the County of Onondaga; now, therefore, the condition of this obligation is such, that if the said William Harrison shall prosecute the said appeal with all due diligence, to a decision in the Court of Common Pleas, and in case judgment shall be rendered against such appellant, shall pay such judgment, including costs of the appeal, then this obligation to be void; otherwise to be and remain in full force and virtue." Signed and sealed by the obligors. On this bond was indorsed, "I approve of the within bond and securities. July 24th, 1824. T. Patchen, J. Peace."

Aug. 2 the justice made his return which was filed with the bond in the clerk's office of Onondaga, Aug. 14; and on motion of the appellee, at the next September Term of the Onondaga C. P. they quashed the appeal, for a defect in the bond, and on the ground that it did not conform to the Statute (sess. 47, ch. 238, sec. 36.)

Mr. B. D. Noxon, now moved for a *mandamus*, commanding the C. P. to vacate the rule, and proceed in the appeal.

Mr. J. R. Lawrence, contra, insisted that the bond was defective within the Statute (sess. 47, ch. 238, sec. 26), in not providing for the payment of the judgment recovered before the justice *and the interest. This, he said, is [*63 made necessary, by that section, in all cases. Again; *In the Matter of David Marsh*, 19 Johns., 171, this court decided that the word "judgment," as used in the Act of 1818, did not comprehend the costs. If the costs cannot be considered a part of the judgment, in a case like this, where there are no damages, the bond can have no penalty; and so it is no security to the appellee for the costs of the appeal, as the appellee cannot recover beyond the amount of the penalty. The provisions of the Acts of 1818 and 1824 are alike in this respect; and the decision of this court cited, when applied to this case, proves that it is not a case contemplated by the Statute. The party should not be allowed to harass his adversary by an appeal, without any security for costs.

Mr. Noxon, in reply, said it would be idle to give a bond for the payment of the judgment and interest which had been already paid, at the time of appealing; and as to the decision cited, it merely went to regulate the cases, under the old Act, in which an appeal would lie. The late Act gives one in all cases; and a little discrepancy between this general provision and the form of the bond, will not do away the express words of the Act.

Curia, per WOODWORTH, *J.* The Statute requires that the bond be in double the amount of the judgment; if costs only are adjudged against a party, it follows that it must be in double the amount of the costs; if damages and costs, then double the amount of both. In the *Matter of David Marsh*, 19 Johns., 171, it is true this court held that the costs were not to be considered a part of the judgment. But that was for the purpose of the right to appeal, the Statute of 1818 giving an appeal only when the damages recovered were over $25; consequently, if it required the addition of the costs to make out a sum exceeding $25, an appeal would not lie. But under the Act of 1824, an appeal is given in every case; and when the amount of the judgment is spoken of, it has reference to the costs as well as the damages.

*The first part of the section regulating [*64 appeals declares that the party appealing shall give a bond with a condition, to prosecute the appeal, with due diligence, to a decision in the Court of C. P.; and in case judgment shall be rendered against the appellant, to pay such judgment, including costs of the appeal. This applies to cases: 1. Where the plaintiff may recover before the justice, but being dissatisfied with the amount recovered, appeals; 2. Where a defendant has judgment in his favor for costs only, and appeals because a balance is not found in his favor, or where a balance is found in his favor, and he claims a greater; and 3. Where the plaintiff appeals, when the judgment is in favor of the defendant for costs merely. In all these cases, the condition of the bond has nothing to do with the costs, damages, or debt, recovered in the court below; because, as to the costs, they are paid before the party can appeal, and as to the damages in favor of the appellant, he seeks to get rid of them by the appeal. But when the party against whom damages are found appeals, then the condition is to pay the debt or damages, with interest and costs of appeal, if the appeal shall not be prosecuted with diligence, or that the appellant shall surrender his body in execution on the judgment. The sentence is obscure; but the meaning is, if the suit is not prosecuted with due diligence, the appellant shall pay, or surrender his body; and in case judgment shall be rendered against the appellant, he shall pay or surrender in like manner. This construction is necessary in order to make the latter clause consistent with the former, to effectuate the intent of the Legislature, and to avoid an absurdity which would arise from adhering to a literal construction; which would be, that if the appellant prosecuted with diligence, he would not be obliged, by the bond, to pay or surrender, although he might fail in the appeal. The words, "or in case judgment shall be rendered against the appellant," in the condition of the bond, applicable to the first class of cases, are necessarily to be understood in the second, after the words, "if such appeal shall not be prosecuted with all due diligence."

65*] *In the present case, judgment was in favor of the defendant for costs; and consequently, as the bond is the form prescribed by the first part of the section, it complies with the Act; and the court below erred in quashing the appeal.

Motion granted.

Cited in—5 Cow., 291; 9 Cow., 229; 3 Barb., 608.

HAMLIN AND BENEDICT v. BOUGHTON ET AL.

Sale on Execution—Receipt by Deputy-Sheriff Discharges Defendant—Practice.

A sale of goods by a deputy-sheriff and a receipt of the proceeds operate as a payment to the sheriff, and discharge the defendant.

The court, however, will not order satisfaction to be entered of record, until the money is paid to the plaintiff; but will stay all proceedings against the defendant, leaving the plaintiff to his remedy against the sheriff.

IN this case, it appeared that the judgment for the plaintiffs had been satisfied, by various payments, and some sales of property on credit, by the consent of both parties. These sales had been made by a deputy of the sheriff of Ontario, to whom the execution was directed. It was delivered to the deputy, who sold upon it; and the proceeds of the sales had been received by him.

A motion was now made, in behalf of the defendants, to enter satisfaction upon the judgment, or to stay execution, whichsoever the court might direct. No notice of the motion had been served on the sheriff.

Mr. W. Hubbell, for the motion.

Mr. B. Whiting, contra.

Curia. The plaintiffs are bound to give credit, in some shape, for the money received by the deputy. An entry of satisfaction upon the record, however, might deprive them of all remedy against the sheriff. For the present, therefore, we direct a stay of all further proceedings against the defendants, which will not interfere with the plaintiffs' remedy against the sheriff.

Rule accordingly.

*EX PARTE THAYER. [*66

Discharge, Under Act Abolishing Imprisonment for Debt—Extends, to What.

A discharge under the Act to Abolish Imprisonment for Debt in Certain Cases, sess. 42, ch. 101, extends to judgments in actions for wrongs.

THAYER made an affidavit that he was and is an insolvent debtor, and that he presented a petition (made out as required by the Act of Apr. 7, 1819, with the other papers required by that Act) to the first judge of Yates Co. where the deponent resided, but the judge refused to receive the papers, on the ground that it appeared by the deponent's inventory that he owed but one debt, which was due upon a judgment in the C. P. of Ontario Co,, recovered against the deponent for an assault and battery. Upon this affidavit,

Mr. H. A. Wisner now moved for a *mandamus* commanding the judge to receive and act upon the application.

Mr. W. M. Oliver, contra, said he supposed the Statute contemplated a discharge from debts due upon contract only. The words of the Act, sess. 42, ch. 101, sec. 3, giving the terms of the discharge, confine it to a debt or debts, due, &c., or contracted for before that time, though payable afterwards. By the 2d section the insolvent is to state the consideration of the debts which he owes, in the account of his creditors, before the judge has jurisdiction. Both sections taken together, would seem to imply that the discharge was not intended for that class of debts due upon judgments for wrongs, but such as arose upon contract. These alone can properly be said to have a consideration. It appeared to him that the insolvent should be put to his application under the 4th section of the "Act for Relief of Debtors with Respect to the Imprisonment of their persons," 1 R. L. 349, which he can make, if the plaintiff should think proper to charge him in execution.

Mr. E. Cowen, in reply, said that the words of the discharge are general, debt or debts, which clearly include all demands upon judgment for whatever cause. Besides, one object of the Statute was equality in the distribution of the debtor's *property among all his creditors. [*67 All his property passes, by the assignment in trust for the creditors. If judgment creditors for a tort are not included, those claiming upon contract would take the whole, and exclude the former from their dividend. This would be unjust; but it followed from the ground taken against the motion. If a judgment for a tort could not be made the foundation of a petition, it could not be be considered in a division of the insolvent's estate. There can be no difficulty in stating the consideration. It is the injury for which the judgment was obtained.

The Court were clear that the words "debt" or "debts," used in the Act, extended to demands due on judgment, whether upon tort or contract; and they said it had so been holden before.(a)

Motion granted.

Cited in—24 Wend., 367; 31 How. Pr., 127; 2 Daly, 115; 1 Leg. Obs., 328.

(a) See People v. Marine Court of N. Y., 3 Cow., 366, where the same construction was given to the Act for the Relief of Debtors with Respect to the Imprisonment of their Persons, 1 R. L., 348.

THE PEOPLE

v.

HALLETT, Sheriff of HERKIMER.

Nominal Damages, not Allowed in Judgment by Default in Debt—Costs.

Nominal damages are not given in a judgment by default in debt:

And so where judgment was for the plaintiff by *nil dicit* for $250, the penalty of a bond; held, that the plaintiff could not add nominal damages to raise it above $250, in order to carry Supreme Court cos s.

IN the original suit, the plaintiff recovered in debt on bond, in the penalty of $250, conditioned to pay $150. The judgment was by default for want of a plea. This suit was an attachment against the defendant for not returning the *fi. fa.*, and it being agreed that the costs upon the attachment must follow at the same rate with those in the original cause, it was submitted upon this ground. (*Vide People* v. *Chapman*, 1 Cow., 214.)

Mr. M. Hoffman, for the defendant, relied on the words of the Act Concerning Costs, 1 R. L., 344, sec. 4, and insisted that 6 cents nominal damages, for the detention of the debt cannot be regarded.

Mr. P. Gansevoort, contra, cited *Clapp* v. *Reynolds*, 2 Johns. Cas., 409, where the damages were held to make part of the amount for **68***] *the purpose of costs, in an action upon a penal bill. He insisted that the nominal damages might be taken into the account, upon the question of costs. To show that nominal damages were allowable, he cited Caines' Practical Forms, 215, sec. 10.

Curia. No nominal damages are given in a judgment by default in debt.(a) The judgment consists of the debt and costs—nothing more. The costs must be taxed at the C. P. rate.

Rule accordingly.

Cited in—9 Cow., 653 (*n*).

(a) And so are the entries in Lill. Ent., 473, 483, 503; Tidd. Pr. Forms, 169–70, on *mutuatus*. So of debt on bond. (*Id.*) So in 5 Wentw., 165–6, 414; 10 *Id.*, 427–8, 453; 7 *Id.*, 402. Nominal or other damages are given by verdict in debt. Lill. Ent., 257, 379; Tidd. Pr. Forms, 186–7. And hence, Clapp v. Reynolds, 2 Johns. Cas., 409, was probably the case of a verdict; and what is said by Buller, J., in Lord Lonsdale v. Church, 2 T. R., 398, and by Lord Kenyon, *Ch. J.*, in Wilde v. Clarkson, 6 T. R., 304, or nominal damages, must also be understood in reference to a recovery by verdict.

THE PEOPLE

v.

HALLETT, Sheriff of HERKIMER.

Attachment for not Returning Execution—Costs.

The costs of an attachment for not returning an execution where the judgment in *assumpsit* is less than $250 must be taxed at the rate of C. P. costs.

Citation—1 Cow., 214.

IN the original suit (*Spencer* v. *Sprague*) the plaintiffs recovered judgment in *assumpsit*, and had execution for damages to $191.24, and costs to $28.96, upon which the defendant in this suit was attached for not returning the execution; and the only question was, whether there should be a retaxation, the costs against the defendant having been taxed as Supreme Court costs.

Mr. M. Hoffman, for the defendant, moved for a retaxation, and cited *People* v. *Chapman*, *Sheriff*, 1 Cow., 214.

Mr. W. Esleeck, contra.

Curia.* This case comes within the [*69** pinciple of *People* v. *Chapman*, cited for the motion. Though in form a suit by the people, it is really in favor of the party; and C. P. costs only are allowable. The rule is the same, whether the attachment be for neglect to return *mesne* or final process.

Motion granted.

SNOWDEN

v.

ROBERTS, Impleaded with HAYES, ALLISON and SMITH.

Motion, to Supersede Habeas Corpus Cum Causa. *—Practice—When Cause Removable from C. P. by* Habeas Corpus*—Practice, when Cause Removed by One of Several Defendants.*

A motion to supersede a *habeas corpus, cum causa*, will be heard, though the writ be not returned.

Though a *habeas corpus cum causa* be not properly directed, it lies with the court below to object to this; not with the party; who cannot move to supersede it on this ground, after the court below have acted upon it.

Though the sum in question do not exceed $500, in a cause in the C. P. of N. Y. (*vide* sess. 46, ch. 207), yet if it appear by affidavit that the title to land will come in question, the cause is removable by *habeas corpus*.

One of several defendants returned, taken in the court below, may sue out a *habeas corpus*; but, to avoid a *procedendo*, he must put in bail for all the defendants, according to the 10th general rule of October Term, 1796.

Citations—4 T. R., 499; Stat., sess. 46, ch. 207; 1 Str., 527; 11 Johns., 199; 1 Dunl. Pr., 225.

AN action of trespass *quare clausum fregit* had been commenced against the defendants in the C. P. in the City of N. Y., by

Snowden; and the *capias ad respondendum* returned their *cepi corpora*. The damages were laid at $500 only, both in the *capias* and declaration, both of which were against all the defendants jointly. Issue being joined and the cause noticed for trial, Roberts alone sued out a *habeas corpus* in the cause, directed by mistake, "to the Judges of the Court of Common Pleas," without saying of what court, and the writ then ran thus: "We command you that you have the body of Elijah J. Roberts, who is impleaded with Jacob Hays, Robert Allison, and Daniel Fell Smith, detained in your prison, &c., together, &c., at the suit of Thomas Snowden," &c. The writ of *habeas corpus* was returnable at the present term; but not yet returned. Roberts appeared separately from the other defendants in the court below, by his attorney, and the other defendants appeared by their attorney. The *habeas corpus* was allowed by the commissioner, upon an affidavit that the title to land would come in question in the cause; and it was sued out at the instance of Roberts alone; and the court 70*] below received *it as a *supersedeas*, and refused to go on with the trial, at their last January Term, when it was filed.

Messrs. Blunt and *Johnson* now moved to supersede the writ of *habeas corpus*: 1. Because the amount demanded was only $500. To warrant a *habeas corpus* to the C. P. of the City of N. Y., the amount demanded should exceed that sum. (Laws, sess. 46, ch. 207.) 2. Because the *habeas corpus* had no direction. It should be directed to the judges of the court in which the record is. (Tidd. Pr., 336.) And though the court may not quash the writ, it not being returned, yet, for a misdirection, they will supersede it. *Woodcraft* v. *Kinaston*, 2 Atk., 318. In *Daniel* v. *Phillips*, 4 T. R., 499, the court did not deny that a misdirection would be fatal, if objected to before the return; though they held that a return would cure the defect. 3. Only one defendant is ordered to be brought up by the writ. *Fry* v. *Carey*, 1 Str., 527; *Youle* v. *Graham*, 11 Johns., 199.

Mr. S. M. Hopkins, contra, objected that the *habeas corpus* not being returned, there is no cause in court. The proper course would have been for the party to move for a *mandamus*, commending the court below to proceed in the cause, but the court will not set the writ aside. *Clark* v. *Lawrence*, 1 Cow., 48-8. The cause involving a question of title, the amount of damages does not govern. (Laws, sess. 46, ch. 207.)

The defect in the direction is supplied by filing the writ with the court of N. Y. At any rate, the objection as to this is formal, and the writ may be amended. *Gordon* v. *Valentine*, 16 Johns., 145. That one of several defendants may remove a cause by *habeas corpus*, he cited *Fry* v. *Carey*, Str., 527, and 1 Dunl. Pr., 224-5.

Curia. The motion to supersede the writ is proper, though it be not returned. We, therefore, disallow the preliminary objection. But the motion must be denied upon the merits. The court below have received and acted upon the writ, and it does not lie with the party to 71*] object after this. **Daniel* v. *Phillips*, 4 T. R., 499. At most the objection is of mere form, and might be obviated by amendment. The court below are the proper party to object.

The exception that the suit was for $500 only, is removed by the affidavit, that the title to land would come in question. The Statute, sess. 46, ch. 207, which denies a *habeas corpus* to the N. Y. C. P., when the sum does not exceed $500, excepts the case where the title to lands or tenements will come in question.

One of several defendants may remove a cause by *habeas corpus*. On the return of the writ, if the defendant do not, upon being ruled, proceed according to the 10th general rule of October Term, 1796, the plaintiff may issue a *procedendo*. The only difference in the proceedings between a sole defendant and where there are several, is, that in the latter case the one who sues out the *habeas corpus* must see that bail is in for himself and his co-defendants. *Fry* v. *Carey*, 1 Str., 527; *Youle* v. *Graham*, 11 Johns., 199; 1 Dunl. Pr., 225.

Motion denied.

VAIL *v.* SMITH.

Record of Inferior Court, as Evidence in Supreme Court—Variance—Amendment of.

It seems that an exemplification of a record of an inferior court of this State is evidence in the Supreme Court, and that it is not necessary to remove the record there by *certiorari*, to make it evidence, even on a plea of *nul tiel record*.

The declaration set forth a judgment as of October Term, 1813, *prout patet per recordum*. On *nul tiel record*, the judgment produced was of October Term, 1814; held, a fatal variance.

But it appearing that the judgment was entered as of October Term, by mistake, the plaintiff was, on the trial, allowed to withdraw his record, in order that he might move to amend it.

The text of the record is the evidence which must control as to the time when the judgment is entered; and it cannot be corrected, on the trial, by the judge's date of signing the judgment in the margin.

DEBT, on a judgment of the Albany C. P. The declaration set forth a judgment of the Court of C. P. in favor of the plaintiff, against the defendant, as of the 3d Tuesday of Oct., 1813, *prout patet per recordum*, &c. Plea, *nul tiel record*.

**Mr. J. Payn* moved to bring on the [*72 trial by record; and he produced an exemplification of the record of a judgment in the C. P. of the County of Albany, in favor of the plaintiff, against the defendant, the *placita* whereof was of the 3d Tuesday of Oct., 1813, and the cause was continued upon the record to the 3d Tuesday of Oct. next (1814), but the record was signed Oct. 22, 1813.

Mr. I. Hamilton, for the defendant, objected that the evidence was inadmissible. He said, this being the record of another and an inferior court, it should be brought here by a *certiorari*. That upon a plea of *nul tiel record*, the record itself is necessary, or the tenor of it; and it can come here by *certiorari* only, for the purpose of being evidence. An exemplification merely is not sufficient. *Woodcraft* v. *Kinaston*, 2 Atk., 317, 318.

WOODWORTH, *J*. I believe we have always considered an exemplification sufficient.

Mr. Hamilton. There is a variance. The declaration sets forth a judgment of October

Term, 1813. This record is continued to October Term, 1814.

Mr. Payn, in reply. The variance evidently arises from a mere mistake of the attorney in making up the record. He has inadvertently drawn the *placita* as of the term at which judgment was rendered, instead of the term at which the writ was returnable; and the continuance being to Oct. next, produces the variance. The declaration is of the term at which judgment was actually rendered, as appears by the signing in the margin. The day is altogether immaterial, as in other cases. *Brooks* v. *Bemiss*. 8 Johns., 455. But if otherwise, the court will allow us to withdraw the record, move the C. P. to amend, and bring on the cause at another day.

73*] **Curia*. The text of the record must be taken as evidence of the time when judgment was rendered; and cannot be corrected by the note in the margin of the day when it was signed. In this view, there is a fatal variance between the declaration and the evidence; but the plaintiff may withdraw his record, and move the C. P. to amend.

Rule accordingly.

THE PEOPLE, ex rel. KNAPP,

v.

THE JUDGES OF THE COURT OF COMMON PLEAS OF THE COUNTY OF WESTCHESTER.

Alternative Mandamus *Commanding C. P. to Seal Bill of Exceptions—Form of—What Sufficient—Service of—Motion to Quash Before Return.*

Form of an alternative *mandamus*, to a Court of C. P. commanding them to seal a bill of exceptions. It did not set forth the bill; yet held sufficient.

It was served in vacation, by showing each judge separately, the original *mandamus*, and delivering him a copy; held, a good service.

A motion to quash an alternative *mandamus* may be made before the writ is returned.

Citation—1 Johns., 64.

A *MANDAMUS* was issued out of this court in these words: "The people, &c., to the judges, &c., of Westchester, greeting: Whereas, it has lately been represented to us, in our Supreme Court of Judicature, before our justices thereof, on the part and behalf of Jonas Knapp, that at a Court of Common Pleas held in and for the County of Westchester, at, &c., on, &c., a certain suit, then and there pending, in the said Court of Common Pleas, before you, the said judges, wherein Jonas Knapp was appellee, and Sylvanus Knapp appellant, was argued before you, the said judges, and a judgment of nonsuit rendered therein by you 74*] the said judges; *and that the said Jonas Knapp, by his counsel, learned in the law, did then and there except to the opinion of you, the said judges in the said suit, and to the judgment therein by you so rendered as aforesaid, and did then and there write his exceptions, and tender the same to you, and request you to affix your seals to the same, to which said exceptions, you, the said judges, refused to affix your seals: Whereupon, we, being willing that justice should be done in the premises, do command you, that you, the said judges, do affix your seals to the said bill of exceptions, according to the statute in such case made and provided; or, in default thereof, that you make known to us, in our Supreme Court of Judicature, before our said justices thereof, at the Capitol, in the City of Albany, on the 3d Monday of February next, why you have not done the same. Witness, John Savage, Esq., &c., at, &c., the 30th day of October, A. D. 1824."

It appeared by an affidavit of the first judge of Westchester, that this writ was served by showing the judges, each of them, in vacation, the original which the attorney retained, and at the same time delivering to each a copy.

Mr. E. Williams, for the defendants, moved to quash or supersede the *mandamus*; 1. On the ground that it is defective in form, in omitting to set forth or recite the bill of exceptions. In *Sikes* v. *Ransom*, 6 Johns., 279, this court say, that our Statute is the same as the English, in relation to bills of exceptions; that the Supreme Court can issue the writ, as well as the chancery in England. The court then refer to the English forms, and say that they can be the same in the Supreme Court; that the writ, after reciting the complaint, commands the judges, *si ita est, tunc sigilla, vestra*, &c., and if it be returned *quod non ita est*, the answer would be sufficient. In Bull. *N. P.*, 316, it is said, if the judges refuse to sign the bill, the party grieved by the denial may have a writ upon the Statute, commanding the same to be done *juxta forman statuti*; it recites the form of an exception taken and overruled, and it follows, *vobis præcipimus quod si ita est tunc sigilla vestra apponatis*; and *if it be re- [*75 turned, *quod non ita est*, an action will lie for a false return, and thereupon the surmise will be tried, &c.

From these authorities, it is evident that the *mandamus* must recite the bill of exceptions tendered, that the judges below may see whether the bill they are required to seal comprises the same matters as that tendered; and that they may be able to return specifically, *quod non ita est*, or otherwise, according to the fact.

Nothing appears upon the *mandamus* but what the C. P. did right in directing a nonsuit; or, if otherwise, there is not that point of law stated which would be the subject of a bill. The contrary, rather, appears, and that there is no point of law to which a bill of exceptions can be taken. (2 Cai., 168.)

The counsel also objected to the manner of service, as irregular.

Mr. J. Edwards referred to Bac. Abr., *mandamus*, B, to show that a motion to quash the writ would not lie before a return made and filed. The manner of service was right as settled by this court in *People* v. *Supervisors, etc.*, 1 Johns., 64. The bill of exceptions need not appear in the writ. It is always tendered to the judges at the trial, and, in practice, it is served on them with the *mandamus*. If not done, or the service is, in any manner, irregular, it may be cause for refusing a peremptory *mandamus*, but is no cause for quashing or superseding the writ. The form of a *mandamus* to set aside a rule, as drawn by counsel, in *Blunt* v. *Greenwood*, which is given at length in 1 Cow., 22, was not more explicit than this. The judges should make a return upon which issue may be taken, and should not be allowed to quash the writ upon their affidavit.

He concluded, by moving that a peremptory *mandamus* issue.

Curia. It is objected that a motion to quash the writ will not lie till it is returned. Such is the general rule; but a case is cited, *The* 76*] *People* v. *Judges and Supervisors*,*1 Johns., 64, by which it appears that the service of an alternative *mandamus* may be by delivering a copy, at the same time showing the original. The party thus having a right to retain the writ, the judges must make a return without it. The writ itself cannot be returned by them; and we think the case an exception to the rule. The motion is, for that reason, in time. We think, however, it was not necessary to recite the bill of exceptions in the writ; the motion to quash or supersede it is, therefore, denied; but as the defendants may not have had time to prepare a return, we give them to the next term for this purpose, when, if the return be not made, a peremptory *mandamus* must go.

Rule accordingly.

Cited in—7 Wend., 537; 10 Wend., 31; 58 N. Y. 160; 3 How. Pr., 165; 5 How. Pr., 380; 28 Hun, 546.

EX PARTE STAATS.

Collection, by Attorney—Failure to Pay, Proceeds to Client—Attachment.

Where a bond was left with an attorney of this court, to the end that he should write to the obligor and obtain the money; but without any express direction to bring a suit in default of payment, the attorney having received the money without suit, and neglected to pay it over, on demand, to his client: held, that he received the bond to collect in his character of attorney; and that an attachment should issue against him, unless he paid over the money.

THE relator, Staats, had left a bond with J. W. Edmonds, Esq., an attorney of this court, to the end that he should write to the obligor to pay to him (Edmonds). for the use of Staats, who was the obligee, the money due upon the bond; but he did not direct Mr. Edmonds to commence a suit upon it, in case the obligor should make default in paying according to such written request. The obligor paid the money to Mr. Edmonds, who had neglected to pay it over to the obligee, though repeatedly requested by the obligee to do this. Mr. Edmonds made affidavit that he was poor and unable to raise the money to pay the obligee, but was willing that the obligee should take all his property; that he had offered to assign good demands to the obligee which he believed were collectable, in payment of the money, which had been refused, &c. Upon these facts,

Mr. J. L'Amoureaux moved for a rule that Mr. Edmonds show cause why an attachment should not issue against him. He cited *People* v. *Smith*, 3 Cai., 221, and *People* v. *Wilson*, 5 Johns., 368.

Mr. J. W. Edmonds, in person, contra.

**Curia.* The motion must be granted. It [*77 is plain that this bond was left with Mr. Edmonds in his character of attorney, though no specific directions were given to bring a suit. It turned out that there was no need of a suit. The money was paid in; and the relator is entitled to our aid in obtaining it, in the same manner as if collected by suit.

Rule to show cause.(a)

Cited in—4 Hill, 45; 51 Barb., 243; 4 How. Pr., 242; 14 Abb. R. S., 251; 2 Co. R., 116.

(a) In the Matter of Knight, 1 Bing., 91, C. B., Mich., T., 1822; De Wolf v. ——, 2 Chit. 63.

NOTE.—*Attorney and client—Failure of attorney to pay over money collected—Remedy of client—When summary relief granted.* See People v. Smith, 3 Cai., 221, *note.*

*JACKSON, ex dem. PIONIER ET AL., [*78
v.
SCHAUBER.

THE SAME, ex dem. THE SAME,
v.
DIFFERENT DEFENDANTS IN TEN OTHER CAUSES.

Stay of Proceedings, in Several Actions, by Same Plaintiff Against Different Defendants, Involving Same Questions—Verdict in one Case—Motion for New Trial—Practice.

Where several causes, in favor of the same plaintiff, though against different defendants, concerning the title to property, depend on the same questions and the same evidence, either p y may move that only one of the causes be tried and that the others abide the event; and if the fact that the questions and evidence are the same in all, be not disputed by affidavit, the motion will be granted; otherwise, if that fact be denied, or appear to be doubtful.

And where several causes, concerning the title to land, in favor of the same plaintiff, against different defendants, were noticed for trial, and one was tried, in which the plaintiff was nonsuited, upon which his counsel gave notice to the defendants' counsel, that, as all the causes depended on the same questions, the others would not be tried, and a case was made, and an order obtained to stay proceedings in the cause tried, with a view to a motion for a new trial; and on motion for judgment as in case of nonsuit, the plaintiff's attorney swore that the title and evidence of the plaintiff were the same in all the causes; held, that unless the defendants would file affidavits, in 20 days, that the questions and evidence were not the same in all the causes, the motion should be denied; and that the causes untried should abide the event of the one last tried; and that if such affidavits should be filed, that then the plaintiff should pay costs of the circuit, &c.

EJECTMENT, for land in the County of Saratoga. The first cause, and two of the others, were noticed for trial, at the December Circuit, in Saratoga, 1823, when the first was tried, and a verdict taken therein for the plaintiffs subject to the opinion of this court on a case. The two other causes were not brought to trial at that circuit. All the causes, except the first, were noticed for trial at the Saratoga Circuit in June last, one of them brought on to trial, and the plaintiff nonsuited; when his counsel declined preceding to trial with the others, and they were not tried. The nine remaining causes were again noticed for trial, at the last December Circuit in Saratoga, and one of them tried, and the plaintiff being nonsuited, he declined proceeding to trial in the other causes, of which he gave the defendants' counsel, in each, notice on the morning of the day following the trial. Before the trial, the defendants' counsel stated to the circuit judge, in open court, in the presence of the plaintiff's counsel, that cases had been made in the two causes first tried, which were then pending and undetermined by this court (which was the fact), and requested the judge to postpone the trial of all the causes till decisions could be had upon the cases so made; the judge asked the defendants' counsel if he would consent to let the causes then noticed for trial abide the decision of the court on the cases made, to which he replied in the negative, though the plaintiff's counsel consented. The affidavit of the plaintiff's attorney stated that the title and **79***] evidence of the plaintiff in *support of it was the same in each of these causes. A case was also made in the cause last tried, with a view to set aside the nonsuit, &c., and the circuit judges had stayed the proceedings by a certificate of probable cause.

Mr. A. Van Vechten now moved for judgment as in case of nonsuit, in all these causes except such as had been tried.

Mr. L. H. Palmer, contra.

Curia. Where a number of causes are brought and all depend upon the same title, as here, and the questions to be litigated, and the evidence, are the same in all, it is competent for either party to make an application to this court, before the circuit arrives, that only one of the causes be carried down to trial; and that the plaintiff be not prejudiced by his omission to try others; and, in a clear case, that they abide the event of the cause to be tried. In passing upon such a motion, the court would be guided by the admissions of the party against whom the motion should be made. If the affidavits of the parties should agree that the points of inquiry and the evidence would be the same in all the causes, the motion would be granted. If they should disagree, though they should only leave the matter in doubt, the motion would be denied. Here neither party has applied for our direction—all the causes were noticed; an offer was made but not acceded to, at the circuit, that eight of them should abide the event of the ninth, which the plaintiff contemplated trying. It was tried; the plaintiff was nonsuited, a case is made and proceedings stayed till a decision here. The plaintiff's counsel gave notice the morning after the trial that he should not try the remaining causes; and on the defendants moving for judgment as in case of nonsuit, they are met by the affidavit of the plaintiff's attorney that the questions to be tried were the same in all the causes. The only dispute here is about the costs, which must depend on the fact that the questions and evidence were or were not the same in all the causes. If the former be the fact, it cannot be just that the plaintiff should be required to go through with the formality of a trial in each; and repeated decisions of this court have pronounced him not in default, **80***] for taking *the course which he has pursued. The only difficulty arises from the form in which these motions for judgment, as in case of nonsuit, are brought forward. Owing to this, the defendants have not yet been heard upon the question, whether according to their views of the matter, the questions and evidence will be the same in all. Under the circumstances, therefore, we direct a rule to be entered, that the causes untried abide the event of the cause of *Jackson* v. *Lyon* (the cause last tried), unless the defendants shall, within 20 days, file an affidavit that the last causes not tried do not depend on the same questions and on the same evidence as the cause last tried; and if they file such affidavit, then that the lessors of the plaintiff pay to the defendants their costs of the last circuit, &c.

Mr. Van Vechten said the causes did not depend on the same questions and the same evidence; and an affidavit to that effect would be filed.

Cited in—2 Wend., 211.

EX PARTE CHRYSLIN.

Appeal from Justice Court—Compliance with Forms, Necessary—Appeal Bond—Amendment in C. P.

An appeal to to the court of C. P. from a justices' court, cannot be received unless the forms of proceeding for that purpose, required by the 36th section of the Fifty Dollar Act, sess. 47, ch. 238, be strictly complied with.

Thus, if the clause in the appeal bond, required by the Act relative to paying the judgment in the justice's court, with interest, &c., be omitted, the appeal cannot be received nor have the C. P. power to amend the bond.

After they are duly possessed of the cause, they may, however, amend as in ordinary cases.

Citations—Act, sess. 47, ch. 238, sec. 36; 3 Cow., 251.

HICKOK and Hamilton sued Chryslin before a justice of the peace of the County of Onondaga, and recovered judgment against him for $34.99 damages and costs, from which the defendant appealed to the next Court of C. P. of that county, gave the proper notice, paid the costs, and gave a bond with a surety approved by the justice, payable to the plaintiffs, with a penalty of $70 conditioned, after reciting the j d m and that the defendant had appealedu tgusent" that if the above bounden Jacob Chryslin shall prosecute the said appeal with all due diligence to a decision in the Court of C. P., and shall, moreover, pay to the said Morehouse Hickok and Robert Hamilton the judgment to be rendered on such appeal with interest thereon, and their, *the said More- [***81** house & Robert's costs of such appeal, provided costs be awarded against him the said Jacob; or that said Jacob will surrender his body in execution of said judgment to be rendered on said appeal, provided judgment shall be rendered against said Jacob, then, &c., otherwise, &c." Sep. 15 last, being within the time required by law, the justice made due return to the appeal which, with the bond, was filed in the Clerk's office of Onondaga County. At the last September Term of the C. P. of that county, the cause was called upon the appeal, and Chryslin, the appellant, appeared by his attorney; and the appellees appeared by their attorney, and moved the court to quash the appeal, on the ground that the condition of the bond was defective: which motion was opposed. The court decided that the condition of the bond did not conform to the statute, &c. The counsel for the appellant then moved to amend the bond; but the court overruled the motion and quashed the appeal, though it was agreed by the counsel of both parties, that if the bond was defective this arose from a mere clerical mistake, and that the appeal was prosecuted in good faith.

Mr. H. Baldwin, for the relator, now moved for an alternative *mandamus*, commanding the judges to vacate the rule quashing the appeal, and proceed to a hearing. He said the only objections raised related to the condition of the bond. The first is, that it omits the clause "to pay the debt or damages recovered before the justice, together with the interest thereon, and costs of such appeal, if such appeal shall not be prosecuted with all due diligence," &c. (Sess. 47, ch. 238, sec. 36.) The second is, that the condition should not be in the alternative, to pay the debt or damages and costs, or surrender the body in execution, &c.

The object of requiring the first clause was merely to compel the appellant to appear. He did appear, and the Statute was, in this, substantially complied with. As to the second objection, the Statute is obscurely worded; but it is supposed the bond is a substantial compliance with it.

But as to both objections, we say it lay exclusively with the justice to pass upon the **82*]** validity of the bond. Not only *the sureties but the bond is also to be approved of by the justice. Such is the fair import of the section in question. The justice having approved the bond, the matter becomes *res judicata*, and the C. P. have no power to call its validity in question.

If, however, the bond was defective, we had a right to amend, not only upon general principles, but on the authority of *Tompkins* v. *Curtis*, 3 Cow., 251.

The motion was not opposed; but,

Per Curiam. The bond was defective. The clause relative to paying the judgment below, with interest and costs of the appeal, &c., was omitted, which is a material part of the condition required by the Statute. This being so, the Act is peremptory that the appeal shall not be received. It had no force or effect whatever. (Sess. 47, ch. 238, sec. 36.) The court had no discretion. It seems to be the intention of the Legislature that the party shall not be heard on appeal, unless he comply strictly with the terms of the Act. The court below acquired no jurisdiction of the appeal. There is no cause concerning which he can interfere. In this view they have no power to amend the bond. After being possessed of the cause, they may exercise the ordinary power of amending, as we held in the case cited, of *Tompkins* v. *Curtis*; but they cannot do this till the cause is before them. The motion must be denied.

Rule accordingly.

Cited in—4 Cow., 541; 17 Wend., 69; 6 Leg. Obs., 318; 1 Co. R., 53; 13 Mich., 222.

VAN ANTWERP, Sheriff of ALBANY,
v.
NEWMAN.

Writ of Error—Practice—Form of Recognizance of Bail—Delay in Return of Writ of Error—Insufficient to Allow Execution to Go.

A writ of error is a writ of right and need not be allowed by a judge.

Filing it with the clerk and entering its receipt, is a sufficient allowance; and will stay execution, if bail be in.

No particular form of a recognizance of bail in error is necessary; and where it was drawn up in the form of a bond, with a proper penalty and condition, and acknowledged before a judge, who certified the acknowledgment in this form: "Signed, sealed and delivered, in the presence of J. W.," the judge held, that this was sufficient.

Mere delay to have a writ of error returned, for nearly a year, is not a sufficient ground for allowing the defendant in error to proceed with his exetion.

MR. J. L'AMOUREUX, for the the plaintiff, moved for leave to take out execution in this cause, notwithstanding the writ of error *brought by the defendant upon the judg- [***83** ment of this court for the plaintiff. (*Vide* S. C., 2 Cow., 543.)

The security given to stay execution was in this form: "Know all men by these presents that we, Lewis Newman, John Nelliger and John Hinckley, are held and firmly bound unto Cornelius Van Antwerp, Esquire, Sheriff of the City and County of Albany, in the sum of one thousand and twenty three dollars and fifty-two cents, of the money of account of the United States of America, to be paid unto the said Cornelius, his attorney, executors, administrators or assigns; for which payment we bind ourselves, our heirs, executors and administrators, firmly by these presents. Sealed with our seals, and dated the thirtieth day of March, in the year of our Lord one thousand eight hundred and twenty-four."

The condition of the above recognizance is such, that if the said Lewis Newman doth and shall prosecute to effect the writ of error, brought in the Court for the Trial of Impeachments and the Correction of Errors, against the said Cornelius Van Antwerp, Sheriff as aforesaid, upon a judgment in our Mayor's Court of the City of Albany, and which was reversed by our said Supreme Court; and also pay and satisfy, if such judgment of the Supreme Court shall be affirmed, the costs to be adjudged upon such judgment, and all costs and damages to be awarded for delay of execution, then the above recognizance to be void, otherwise to remain in full force and virtue.

LEWIS NEWMAN, (L. S.)
JOHN NELLIGER, (L. S.)
JOHN HINCKLEY. (L. S.)

Signed, sealed and delivered
in the presence of,
JOHN WOODWORTH."

To this was subjoined the following:

* "I approve of the above persons as [***84** sufficient sureties for the prosecution of the writ of error in the within mentioned cause. March 30th, 1824. JOHN WOODWORTH."

The writ of error was in the usual form, issued out of the Court of Chancery, tested Mar. 30, 1824, returnable without delay, and was filed in the clerk's office of this court, April 10, 1824. On the same day, notice of this was given to the plaintiff's attorney. The defendant's attorney had not yet caused the writ of error to be returned. This writ had been issued and filed, without being allowed by a judge.

Mr. L'Amoureux said, though the court could not quash the writ, they might prevent its delaying execution. Here had been a delay of nearly a year since the writ was filed. It had not even been returned. This alone would be a ground for suffering execution to go. (2 Dunl. Pr., 1139, 1141, and the cases there cited.)

2. The writ should have been allowed by a judge.

3. The recognizance is altogether defective. It does not refer to a writ of error from this court, but from the Mayor's Court. It is in the form of a common bond, and has never been acknowledged.

Mr. L. H. Palmer, contra.

Curia. The mere delay, in this case, is not a sufficient ground for our allowing execution to go.

It is not necessary that a writ of error should be allowed by a judge. It is a writ of right; and the proper officer is bound to issue it of course, on the application of the party. The English books speak much of allowing a writ of error, but this does not mean a judicial act. There the writ is delivered to the clerk of the errors, who enters its receipt, whereupon the party takes of him a note or certificate that he has allowed the writ. This is what the books **85***] *mean when they speak of allowance. With us, the English idea of allowance of the writ is seldom complied with, beyond the receipt of it by the clerk of the court to which it is directed.(*d*) The filing it with him, and his entering the receipt of it, is an allowance, and stays execution, if bail be in.

As to the recognizance, the party here drew a bond, with an adequate penalty, and a proper condition. With this he goes to a judge, in whose presence it is executed. The judge witnesses it, and certifies, substantially, that it was acknowledged in his presence. The proceeding was somewhat informal. The instrument is not technically worded; but it was a virtual compliance with the Act. The words "signed, sealed and delivered, in the presence of" the judge, is equivalent to saying that it was acknowledged before him. It was, in fact, so acknowledged. It was the act of the party and his bail. It is a sufficient warrant for drawing up a regular recognizance roll; and we think it fully available to the plaintiff, should he find it necessary to resort to it by action.

Motion denied.

Cited in—9 Cow., 229; 3 Barb., 608.

(*d*) In note to Gravall v. Stimpson, 1 Bos. & P., 479 *n. a.*, the allowance of a writ of error is defined to be, its delivery to the clerk of the errors; and Meriton v. Stevens, Barn., 205, and Sykes v. Dawson, *Id.*, 209, support that definition. *Vide*, also, Payne v. Whaley, 2 Bos. & P., 137.

SHERMAN, by his Guardian, E. SMITH,

v.

JAMES McNITT.

Action of Slander—Rule, Allowing Plaintiff to Try only One of Several Actions, Does not Apply to.

The rule which allows a plaintiff to try only one of several causes, where the questions and the evidence are the same in all, without being subjected to costs for not trying the others, does not apply to actions of slander, &c., where the question is one of damages, to be determined by a jury, but is confined to questions of property.

AFTER the decision (February Term, 1824), in 2 Cow., 452, the plaintiff carried this cause down to trial, and *obtained a ver- [*86 dict; and in settling the general bill of costs between the parties, the same question now arose again, upon a motion for retaxation, which was determined then; and the additional fact was now shown to the court, that both the causes of *Sherman* v. *McNitt* and *Sherman* v. *Wilson*, mentioned in that report, were actions of slander; and now, in speaking of that case,

WOODWORTH, *J.*, who delivered the opinion of the court, said: "It does not appear, by the report, that the two causes were actions of slander. Whether this fact appeared upon the affidavits, we do not remember; but, at any rate, our attention was not called to the circumstance, nor did we advert to it. The plaintiff now claims the costs of the circuit, upon the ground that as both causes depended on the same question, and that against Wilson had been tried, and was to be further considered upon a case made, it was regular to let the other go off till the decision of this court should be obtained. This is the rule where all the causes involve the same questions, and the same evidence, in relation to a right of property, like that in Mr. Palmer's causes, decided at the present term. *Jackson* v. *Schauber*, *ante*, 78. But it is obvious that the rule cannot apply to actions of slander. The question is one of damages upon which there is no certain rule, and which belongs almost exclusively to the jury. The plaintiff having tried one cause, in which he obtains a verdict for a certain amount, may still go before another jury, in another cause, and litigate the same question, and demand a heavier sum, and perhaps have it allowed, on precisely the same state of facts as appeared on the first trial. This is not that kind of question over which courts ordinarily exercise any control upon a motion for a new trial; nor would it be proper, in any such cases, for the court to order that one cause should abide the event of the other. It now appears that these are actions of slander; and it follows that the plaintiff was in default for not trying both his causes, pursuant to notice."

Rule accordingly.

S. C.—2 Cow., 452.

---

*KETCHUM, Executor, &c., [*87

v.

KETCHUM.

Actions by Executor—Liability for Costs.

An executor declared upon a promissory note, and for money lent, &c., in the lifetime of his testator, laying a promise to himself as executor, after his testator's death. Being nonsuited upon the trial, held, that he should not pay costs.

So of an *insimul computassent*, with him, touching accounts of the testator.

The general rule is, that if the executor sue as such, when he might have sued in his own name, if he fail, he shall pay costs; otherwise, if he necessarily sue as executor.

And this depends on the inquiry, whether the cause of action accrued wholly after the testator's death, or wholly or partially before. If wholly after, the executor pays costs on his failure, as in trover upon his own possession, or *assumpsit* for money had and received to his use, or debt for an escape upon his own judgment and execution as executor. Otherwise, if the demand accrued wholly or partially before, as in *assumpsit* upon a promise to testator. So, if this be followed by a promise to the executor to pay the same debt. In both cases the action should be by the executor in his representative character. And so of debt for an escape from his testator's judgment and execution, though the escape was after his death.

Citations—5 T. R., 234, 235; 6 Mod., 91, 181; 1 Salk., 207.

THE declaration was in *assumpsit* upon a promissory note, made by the defendant to the testator; also for money lent by him to and paid for the defendant, and for money had and received by the defendant to the use of the testator, in his lifetime; with an averment that, in consideration of the indebtedness to the testator, the defendant, after the testator's death, promised to pay the several sums, so due the testator, to the plaintiff, as his executor. On the trial, evidence was offered by the plaintiff, and received by the judge, touching promises made by the defendant to the plaintiff after his testator's death, in order to support the plaintiff's action, as appeared to this court by the certificate of the circuit judge. At the circuit, the judge directed the plaintiff to be nonsuited, and a nonsuit was accordingly entered.

Mr. D. Buel, Jr., now moved that judgment be entered against the plaintiff for costs. He said it is well settled, that in action of trover, brought by administrators, where the declaration charges a conversion after the death of the intestate as well as before, and the jury find a verdict for the defendant, and the judge certifies that evidence was given applicable to the count for a conversion after the intestate's death, the defendant is entitled to costs; be- **88***] cause there was *no necessity of suing in a representative character. *Admrs. of Tilton* v. *Williams*, 11 Johns., 403; *Hollis* v. *Smith*, 10 East, 293.

The same rule, in actions of *assumpsit*, was long since adopted, even in England, where the courts have leaned against making the personal representatives liable for costs; *Marsh* v. *Yellowly*, 2 Str. 1106; whereas this court has given a construction to the Statute of Costs more severe against them. *Brown* v. *Lambert*, 16 Johns., 148; *Hogeboom* v. *Clark*, 17 *Id.*, 268. That an executor must pay costs, where he is nonsuited, in an action upon an *assumpsit* to himself, was decided in *Thornton* v. *Jett*, 1 Wash., 138.

It is only when executors or administrators must necessarily prosecute in their representative character, that they are exempted from costs on nonsuit, &c. (2 Dunl. Pr., 721, and the cases there cited.)

Mr. E. W. Walbridge, contra. Costs are never allowed against executors, upon a nonsuit, where they are obliged to sue in their representative character. *Cook* v. *Lucas*, 2 East, 395; *Bittersall* v. *Groote*, 2 Bos. & P., 253; *Hawkes* v. *Saunders*, 3 Burr., 1586; *Hollis* v. *Smith*, 10 East, 293; *Hayworth* v. *David*, Cro. Jac., 229; *Wilton* v. *Hamilton*, 1 Bos. & P., 445; *Admrs. of Tilton* v. *Williams*, 11 Johns., 403. In this case, it was necessary that the plaintiff should sue as executor; and the case cannot be distinguished, in any respect, from that of *Wilton* v. *Hamilton*, 1 Bos. & P., 445, where costs were denied.

Indeed, executors and administrators should always be exempt from costs, when prosecuting the right of their testator or intestate, though they be nonsuited. Some authorities hold this to be the rule in all cases where the action will lie in the name of the person whom they represent; though the injury be done, or the promise made to them personally, after the death of the testator or intestate. *Cookerill* v. *Kynaston*, 4 T. R., 277, 280–1, per Buller, *J.*

Curia*. The rule is, that where an [*89** executor or administrator unnecessarily sues in his representative character · that is, where he might have brought the action in his own name; if he is nonsuited, or there shall be a verdict against him (5 T. R. 234–5), he shall pay costs. The mere change of the form of action shall not protect him. In this rule the counsel agree; and it is abundantly supported by the cases cited on both sides. Then the only question is, whether Ketchum, the plaintiff in this suit, necessarily described himself as executor. On looking into the cases, we think he did. The case of *Goldthwayte* v. *Petrie*, 5 T. R., 234–5, we think, draws the correct distinction. It lays down the rule as established, that where an action is brought by an executor, as such, for transactions arising in the lifetime of his testator, he is not liable to pay costs, though he fail in the action. That was an action brought to recover money alleged to be received after the death of the testator, to the use of Goldthwayte's wife, as executrix; the whole transaction, as declared upon, took place after the testator's death; the money was averred to have been received, and the implied promise to have arisen afterwards; there was no cause of action whatever set forth against the defendant, as having accrued before; and the verdict being for him, the executrix was holden to pay the costs. There she might have sued in her own name, without mentioning her representative character at all; but it is different where there is a full and complete cause of action during the testator's or intestate's lifetime. There a promise, after his death, to pay the debt, will not inure to the executor or administrator, in his individual character. It is merely a confirmation of the demand due in a representative character. *Jenkins* v. *Plombe*, 6 Mod., 91; *Id.*, 181; S. C., 1 Salk., 207, by the title of *Jenkins* v. *Plume*, cited by the court, and recognized as law in *Goldthwayte* v. *Petrie*, contained a similar doctrine. The distinction which we now take was there much considered, and very fully illustrated. In its outline, that case was the same as *Goldthwayte* v. *Petrie*, being an action by executors, for money had and received to their use as such, after the testator's death. Holt, *Ch. J.*, said *the receipt [***90** was in the plaintiff's own right; and, in any view the debt ought to be looked upon as a new debt, contracted since the death of the testator. He illustrated his remarks by the familiar case of trover upon the executor's own possession, in which it is now fully settled, that if he fail he must pay costs. He then mentions a case much like the present; a case where a balance is struck on an accounting between an executor and the debtor, upon matters of account which arose in the testator's life; and there, he says, though a new action accrues, yet the executor shall not pay costs, if he be defeated. It is still in the right of the testator. No new contract is made. The whole is a mere ascertaining of what was due before. Yet the law always implies a promise upon a balance struck; but the promise is to the executor as such, and the action should still be in his name. So in another case put by Holt, "if judgment and execution be in testator's life, and escape in executor's time, upon a nonsuit in action by the executors for this escape, he shall not pay costs; but if he had judgment and execution in his own time, and an escape had happened, for which he brings an action and is nonsuited, he shall pay costs." The whole court agreed upon the case of the *insimul computassent*, as appears by the report both in 6 Mod. and in Salkeld. The distinction, therefore, seems to lie between an entire and a partial cause of action arising after the testator's death. And there is reason in such a distinction. In the former case, the executor knows, or ought to know, the merits of the cause, and should be holden to sue, upon the peril of costs. In the latter case, he cannot understand the whole subject; and therefore the law holds him to no more than his own expenses. Then what is this case? A promissory note, and money had and received, lent and paid, &c., all in the testator's lifetime; and in consideration of this, a promise to the executor, as such, that the money should be paid. This is not so strong a case against the executor as an *insimul computassent*. Here cannot be said to be a new action; and we think the plaintiff was under a necessity to sue in his representative character. The cause of action was complete during the life of his tes-**91***] tator. It is not *like the case of trover upon his own possession, an escape upon his own judgment and execution, or money received immediately to his use, &c.; and, on the whole, we are clear against allowing costs.

Motion denied.

Cited in—4 Cow., 552; 5 Cow., 268; 5 Wend., 92; 9 Wend., 303, 490; 18 Wend., 637; 1 Den., 627; H. & D., 387; 1 Lans., 305; 11 Barb., 248; 14 How. Pr., 485; 5 Abb., N. S., 199; 3 Sand., 661; 2 Daly, 423; Co. R. N. S., 89; 20 Wis., 386.

ROWAN *v.* LYTLE.

Practice—Certiorari—*When Special Assignment of Diminution, Necessary—Service of Assignment—Negligence of Attorney.*

It seems, that in order to warrant the issuing a *certiorari*, on error, to bring up any proceedings *dehors* the record, the plaintiff in error must first assign the diminution specially and serve it upon the defendant or his attorney as in ordinary cases of an assignment of errors.

The court may award a *certiorari* to support the judgment, at any time.

Form of rule for this purpose.

Whether a *certiorari* on alleging diminution should be allowed by a judge, *quære.*

Where an attorney has been negligent in not informing himself of an irregularity for several terms, he cannot move to set aside the proceedings.

ON a writ of error to the C. P. of Washington Co., returnable in May Term, 1828, but not actually returned and filed in the clerk's office of this court till October Term, 1823, the plaintiff's attorneys, at the same term of Oct., filed an allegation of diminution, and entered a rule awarding a writ of *certiorari* which was immediately issued, and filed with the clerk of the court below, returnable at the February Term of this court, 1824. Jan. 28, 1824, the plaintiff's attorneys served the defendant's attorneys with an assignment of errors, but without notice of any rule to join in error, nor had any such rule been entered; and the defendant's attorneys, the next day, served a joinder in error, of *in nullo est erratum*, upon the plaintiff's attorneys. The cause had been noticed for argument at May, August and October Terms last; but no error book served on the defendant's attorneys, till just as one of them was starting from his residence in Salem, Washington Co., to attend the last August Term; and the issue being young, he did not examine the error book till since the last October Term; but supposed that it contained a mere copy of the record in the court below. On examining it, however, he found that the minutes of the clerk containing the verdict of the jury, and also two rules for judgment, had been certified. The action below was replevin, for various articles of personal property, brought by Rowan against Lytle; and the jury found part of the property in Rowan and part in Lytle; thus giving a double verdict, upon which the parties had respectively entered rules for judgment. These were certified.

Mr. S. A. Foot, for the defendant, [***92** now moved to set aside the suggestion on diminution, and all subsequent proceedings, for irregularity; and he took several grounds: 1st. That diminution was not regularly alleged. He said an assignment of errors is either general or special. When the plaintiff in error relies upon any defect, which does not appear upon the face of the record, he must assign such defect for error, specially, and pray a *certiorari* to verify it. (1 Archb. Pr., 228, 229; Tidd. Pr., 1109, 2 Ld. Raym., 1441; *Id.*, 1156; *Id.*, 1398; 2 Saund., 101, *q.* in *note*, where all the cases are reviewed.) A copy of this special assignment should then be served on the defendant's attorney, who may come in and confess the error by pleading *in nullo est erratum*, which will supersede the necessity of a *certiorari* (Tidd. Pr., 1111); and if the defendant does not plead *in nullo est erratum*, then is the time for the plaintiff to sue out his *certiorari* to verify his assignment: and if the return to this does not bring up all the proceedings, the defendant in error may, before joining in error, enter a suggestion of the fact, pray a *certiorari*, have a return of the proceedings omitted, and then pleaded *in nullo est erratum*. (*Id.*, 1114.) If there be no *certiorari* prayed, to verify the error assigned, the court will disregard it. (2 Archb. Pr., 229.) The form of an assignment of errors alleging diminution is given in Tidd's Appendix, 307, and in *Burr* v. *Waterman*, 2 Cow. 36, 38, *note*. Farther as to the practice subsequent to alleging diminution, he cited 1 Archb. Pr., 229; Tidd. Pr., 1110; 2 Ld. Raym., 1047; Tidd. Pr., 1112; 2 Saund., 101 *r*, *note*; and contended that the whole practice was at war with a secret *ex parte* assignment, writ and return; that, at any rate, whether the allegation should precede or follow the assignment of errors, the defendant in error should have notice of it; a copy of the suggestion should have been served at least as early as when the copy of the assignment of errors was delivered.

2. The second ground he took was that the *certiorari* should have been allowed by a judge; that it stands on the same footing as a writ of **93***] error, or *habeas corpus*, neither of *which can be issued without an allowance (1 R. L. 140, sec. 1).

3. He also objected that the *certiorari* was returnable out of term, viz.: the 1st Monday of Feb.; whereas it should have been the 3d Monday; and the court will not allow an amendment. (2 Str., 765, 819; 2 Saund., 101 *r*.)

4. Should the court be against the defendant upon all these grounds, he then asked a *certiorari*, on the part of the defendant, on entering a suggestion that a judgment had been entered on the verdict rendered in favor of the plaintiff, this not appearing upon the present return. The court may issue a *certiorari*, even after diminution alleged by the plaintiff, and one *certiorari* returned and *in nullo est erratum* pleaded. *Berkley* v. *Howard*, 2 Str., 907.

Mr. S. Stevens, contra, said the delay in making the motion was not excused. Where the objection sounds in irregularity, delay should be fully and clearly excused. The inattention of the attorney is not such an excuse as the court will receive.

It is not necessary to have a writ of this kind allowed. It is a writ of right not of grace. A writ of error from this Court to the C. P. is never allowed; and this is as much a writ of right, as a writ of error. (1 R. L., 143, sec. 1; 2 R. L., 148, sec. 12.) The *certiorari* issues upon a rule of this court, the entry of which is equivalent to an allowance. It is like the case of a *habeas corpus* or *certiorari* issued upon a special application to, and a rule of this court ordering it.

The defendant has appeared and pleaded, the cause has been noticed for argument for three successive terms; and he comes too late with a motion to set aside the previous proceedings for irregularity.

As to the practice; the allegation of diminution, and the assignment of errors are separate pleadings. In the allegation of diminution, nothing is said of any error in the record, or that any error whatever exists; but merely that there were certain proceedings in the cause not **94***] returned with the *writ of error; and it then prays that they may be certified. On the *certiorari* being returned, the plaintiff assigns errors both in the record and in the matters certified; and the defendant joins in error. By our practice, the defendant has a right to join in error immediately, on being served with a copy of the assignment; and after *in nullo est erratum* pleaded, no *certiorari* can go. Thus the practice contended for would altogether deprive the plaintiff of his *certiorari*. (2 Dunl. Pr., 1156.) There is no necessity for notice that the *certiorari* has issued. The defendant might as well contend for notice of issuing the writ of error. The first notice of either may be the assignment of errors upon the matters brought up, unless, in case of the writ of error, the party wishes to make it a *supersedeas* to execution or a stay of proceedings. The rule for a *certiorari* is a rule of course; and the attorney need no more give notice of his intention to enter it, than in the case of any common rule.

The Court, in delivering their opinion, did not enter much into the practice which should be pursued by the party in issuing a *certiorari*. They inclined to think however, that the English practice as contended for by *Mr. Foot* should be pursued. They said that this practice was to assign errors in the record, removed by the writ of error, and by the same instrument to allege diminution and pray a *certiorari*. This seemed to be the more reasonable, because on serving the defendant's attorney with a copy of this assignment and allegation, he may come in and confess the diminution assigned; and thus supersede the necessity of a *certiorari*. But they were clear that the defendant in error should have looked to all these objections for irregularity, earlier. They were merely technical; and were waived by the delay.

They said no substantial injury could arise to the defendant from retaining the proceedings as far as they had gone. He now applied on his part to enter a suggestion upon the roll and take out a *certiorari*; and they saw no objection to this. It was true that, after *in nullo est erratum* pleaded, neither party could as of course have a *certiorari*, yet the court might award this writ to affirm the judgment at any *time. (1 Archb. Pr., 229.) They al- [***95** lowed the defendant, therefore, to take a rule for this purpose.

RULE: That the motion to set aside the suggestion of diminution made, and the *certiorari* issued by the plaintiff be denied; and it is further ordered, that the defendant have leave within 20 days to enter a suggestion that judgment has been entered on the verdict rendered in favor of the plaintiff in the court below; and that thereupon a *certiorari* issue; and that no costs be allowed on this motion.

Cited in—7 Wend., 480; 6 Lans., 153; 24 How. Pr., 282; 1 Daly, 300; Blatchf. Prize, 254; 2 Blatchf., 94.

THE PEOPLE *v.* CLARK.

Practice—Quo Warranto.

The general rules of the court, in relation to pleading, amending, &c., are applicable to proceedings upon an information in nature of a *quo warranto*.

IN February Term, 1824, the Atty-Gen. obtained leave to file an information against the defendant in nature of a *quo warranto*, to which the defendant appeared and pleaded. The Atty-Gen. demurred specially to the plea, entered the usual common rule, to join in demurrer, and served a copy of the demurrer upon the defendant's attorney, with notice of the common rule so entered. The defendant's attorney thereupon entered the usual common rule to amend his plea, filed an amended plea, and served a copy on the Atty-Gen., with notice of the rule. This the Atty-Gen. declined receiving, unless the defendant would consent that he should amend by adding a new count to the information. This being declined, the Atty-Gen. treated the amended plea as a nullity; and on the ground that it was irregular to take a rule to amend, of course, entered the defendant's default for want of a joinder in demurrer; and the cause now came before the court on cross motions.

Mr. Talcott, Atty-Gen., moved for judgment of *ouster*, against the defendant.

Mr. S. Stevens, for the defendant, moved to set aside the default for irregularity, on the **96***] ground that the defendant had *regularly amended his plea; and the Atty-Gen. should have answered it.

The Atty-Gen. denied that the amendment was regular; and insisted that the general rule of the court, as to amending of course, did not apply.

Mr. A. Hascall said that if the defendant's attorney had mistaken the practice, he had been led into the mistake by the Atty-Gen., who had entered a rule, of course, to join in demurrer. He thought the general rule for amending equally applicable with the one for pleading. At any rate, the Atty-Gen. should not have treated the rule to amend, as a nullity. He should have moved to set it aside. The defendant may, at least, come in on terms.

The Atty-Gen. said there was no affidavit of merits.' But he did not wish the defendant to be precluded from making a defense, if he had any. All he desired was, that the people should have leave to amend, as he had proposed they should do by consent; and that the defendant should then be heard. Accordingly, if the court should think the defendant ought to be let in, he wished to be understood as moving for leave to add another count to the information.

Curia. We see no reason why the parties should not proceed according to the general rules and practice of the court as to pleading, amending, &c. We are referred to no case which is against this. The Atty-Gen. entered a common rule to join in demurrer, and we think rightly; and that the defendant was right in entering his common rule to amend. The Atty-Gen. may take the rule which he asks, and proceed against the defendant upon an amended information. The defendant may plead to this *de novo*.

Rule accordingly.

NOTE. The Atty-Gen. mentioned to the court the case of *King* v. *Glemmon*, in 2 Rolle, 41, where it was held that the defendant could not change his plea without the consent of the **97***] King's attorney, if a term had *arrived since the plea was put in; though the King had altered the pleadings on his part; but,

The Court said they never should hold a defendant to all the strictness of that case.

Cited in—18 Wend., 602; 44 Mo., 226.

PEOPLE
v.
RICHARDSON, Clerk of WAYNE COUNTY.

Practice—Quo Warranto.

The process upon an information in nature of a *quo warranto*, is either a *venire facias* and *distringas*, or a subpœna and attachment.

It is irregular to proceed against the defendant by a rule to appear.

Citation—1 R. L., 108, sec. 4.

THE Atty-Gen. having proceeded to enter an appearance for, and to take a default against, the defendant, pursuant to a rule obtained on an *ex parte* application for the purpose, at the last term, as mentioned in S. C., 3 Cow., 357.

Mr. J. C. Spencer, for the defendant now moved to set it aside, as irregular.

He read an affidavit, showing that no process had been served; and he did not know till this term, when he saw the note of the case in 3 Cow., that the subject had even been mentioned to the court; but supposed the Atty-Gen. had entered a rule of course for the defendant to appear and plead as he would have done upon a *scire facias*. He contended that no citizen could be pursued to judgment, without due process of law (1 R. L. 47, secs. 2, 3); and that a rule upon the party is not process applicable to a proceeding upon an information in nature of a *quo warranto*. The Statute Authorizing an Information requires the relator to proceed in the manner usual upon such information. (1 R. L. 108, sec. 4.) These informations and the manner of proceeding upon them were well known to the common law before the Statute passed, and must be adhered to. The information uniformly prayed process against the defendant. (Trem. P. C., 446, 429; 6 Wentw. Plead., 28, 29, &c.) This process is either a subpœna and attachment, or *venire facias* and *distringas*. Bac. Abr., Informations, D, Com. Dig., *quo warranto*, C, 2; 2 Morg. Att'ys Vade Mec. 106; *Rex* v. *Mayor*, &c., of Hertford, 1 Salk., 374; S. C., 2 Salk., 669; *King* v. *Trinity House*, 1 *Sid., 86; [***98** *King* v. *Ginever*, 6 T. R., 594; 2 Kyd on Corp., 404, 438; *Commonwealth* v. *Sprenger*, 5 Binn., 353.

The defendant may not only be ousted of his office, but is subject to a fine, as in other criminal prosecutions for a misdemeanor. *Rex* v. *Mayor and Alderman*, 1 Ld. Raym., 426. And the original process may be pursued to outlawry. (Com. Dig., Utlagary, 486, B; 2 Kyd on Corp., 438–9.) This seems to constitute the only distinction between the original process. If the people do not mean to proceed to outlawry, they may go on by subpœna and attachment; otherwise by *venire facias*, *distringas*, &c. (4 Bl. Com., 318; 1 Chit. C. L., 350, 351.) Our Statute is like the English; and, of course, the cases of construction upon that apply here. The only cases in which a defendant shall be holden to answer without process, are actions against officers of the court which are founded upon the theory of their being always in court; and of ejectment which is a mere creature of practice.

Mr. Talcott, Atty-Gen., admitted that the practice in England is to bring the defendant in by process. He said he would agree, that if that was to govern, and this court had not, and could not establish a practice of their own, differing from the English, the proceedings in this case are irregular. The general rule of this court, upon a proceeding by *scire facias*, sanctions a course much like the present. On the writ being served, and indeed on two writs returned *nihil*, the plaintiff may at once take

NOTE.—Quo warranto. See, generally, People v. Van Slyck, *post*, 297, *note*; People v. Tibbits, *post*, 358, *note*; People v. Utica Ins. Co., 15 Johns., 358, *note*.

a rule, of course, that the defendant appear and plead at a short day, or that his default be entered. This is mere matter of practice. The defendant by the rule, has had full notice, which is not always allowed upon a *scire facias.*

To be sure, said the Atty-Gen., the practice pursued in this instance has never been judicially passed upon by this court, but it has long been followed; and he mentioned the case of *People* v. *Kipp,* in which this court (August Term, 1822) granted leave to file an information, in nature of a *quo warranto,* against **99*]** *the defendants; and on motion, made a rule at the same term, of which this is almost a literal copy. [Here the Atty-Gen. read the rule in that case.] To this rule, the late *Ch. J.* Spencer, who had held the office of Atty-Gen., had been a long time upon the bench, and, I need not say, was well acquainted with the practice of the court in all its branches, assented. And the learned counsel for the defendants did not think of questioning the regularity of the proceeding.——

SUTHERLAND, *J.* I think we had that very case before us, when we granted your rule at the last term.

The 4th section of the Statute, the title of which is, "An Act for Rendering the Proceedings upon Informations in Nature of a *quo warranto* more Speedy and Effectual," provides that the defendant shall appear and plead as of the same term in which the information shall be filed, unless the court shall give further time. One object of the Statute was to avoid delay; and its beneficial ends would be entirely defeated in many cases arising under our Constitution and laws, the provisions of which make many offices of very short duration if the prosecutor shall be put back to the dilatory process of the common law.

Mr. Spencer, in reply. The Atty-Gen. agrees with me that the settled practice of the K. B., which is also the law of this court, requires that process should issue. The statute gave a new remedy, unknown to the common law; and if this remedy is to be more speedy, it is an additional reason why the party should have due notice upon process, at the hands of the proper officer of the court. It is said the defendant must answer as of the same term at which the information is filed. The provisions of the Act may be inconsistent with themselves, but this will not warrant judicial legislation. The Act, however, by a "more speedy" remedy, may mean merely that the 15 days between the test and return of process, required by some of the cases which I cited, be dispensed with.

100*] *The case of a *scire facias,* mentioned by the Atty-Gen., is not an original proceeding. It is always founded upon a record, showing that the party had before been in court, and confessed the debt, or that it had been adjudged against him in a course of litigation; or it is intended, like a rule, to hasten proceedings in a cause wherein he has previously appeared.

Nor does it follow, because Mr. Kip and his associates, or other defendants, may have appeared gratuitously upon a rule, or slept upon their rights, that the whole practice is to be overturned.

Cur. adv Vult.

Curia. We have looked into the Statute Relative to Informations in Nature of a *quo warranto,* with the authorities which relate to it. The 4th section (1 R. L., 108) declares that the Atty-Gen. may proceed, after filing the information, in such manner as is usual in cases of informations, in the nature of a *quo warranto.* We think this clause refers to the process by which the defendant is to be brought into court; and, at any rate, we see nothing in the statute which dispenses with the ancient practice in this respect. In England the course is perfectly well settled. The Atty-Gen. must proceed either by *venire facias* and *distringas,* or subpœna and attachment. This subject, it is true, has been several times before the court; but it was upon motions entirely *ex parte,* the matter passed without discussion, and the court did not go into the law of the question which is now presented. Nothing was decided which has the force of binding authority. The subject is fairly open, and we see no necessity for departing from the English practice. The judgment by default must be set aside.

Rule accordingly. (*a*)

Cited in—4 Cow., 390; 18 Wend., 603; 21 Wend., 250; 57 N. Y., 320; 17 Barb., 25; 26 Barb., 352; 4 Duer, 419; 38 N. J. L., 284; 18 O. St., 286; 23 O. St., 127; 5 Kan., 222; 70 Ill., 27; 80 Ill., 511; 14 Mich., 247; 15 Mich., 330; 22 O. St., 361.

(*a*) **This proceeding by information in nature of a *quo warranto*** is becoming a common one, upon which many of the profession may be called to advise. Yet it is a subject of which our books of practice and of a reference have taken but little notice; and it is, most likely, owing to this, that the *most eminent practitioners must be **[*101** times at a loss what course to pursue, without many great trouble in examining many books, through which the cases and entries are scattered. These considerations led me to suppose that not only would the report of new cases of practice on this head be acceptable to the profession, but that a summary classification and note of the older authorities might not be deemed useless.

Cases in which this information lies. These will be seen, generally, by the Statute (1 R. L., 108, sec. 4) made to regulate the proceedings; though the power of the court to grant the information was not derived from this Act. It was intended merely to regulate the proceedings, in the cases mentioned by it. Bull. *N. P.*, 211. For the common law power, as well as that conferred by the English Statute, see Bull, *N. P.*, 210, 211, 212; Com. Dig. *Quo Warranto,* A, B; 2 Morg. Att'ys Vad. Mec., 103-4-5, and the cases there cited. Also, 3 T. R., 596, 599, *n. a*; 2 East, 308; 6 T. R., 560; 6 East, 359; 5 T. R., 85; 4 East, 337; 3 T. R., 596; 4 *Id.*, 240, *n.*; 3 East, 119; 4 East, 327; 6 East, 356. In King v. Highmore, 5 B. & A., 771, an information was granted to try the right to the office of bailiff; though not a corporate office. The words of our statute are broader than the English, as to the kind of office or franchise, for the usurpation of, or intrusion into which, the remedy is given. The English Statute is recited in Bac. Abr., Informations, D; 2 Hawk, P. C., ch. 26, sec. 14, 15, 16. The Statutes of this State to Regulate the Proceedings, and to extend the Statute of Amendments and Jeofails to these proceedings, are in 1 R. L., 108-9, sec. 4, 5, 6, and 121, sec. 10.

In Mass., this information lies to inquire into the election of an officer or member of a corporation, on the relation of any one interested in, or injured by the election or admission. Commonwealth v. U. F. Ins. Co., 5 Mass., 230. So against officers appointed by the Executive, as well as those holding corporate offices or franchises. The Same v. Fowler, 10 *Id.*, 290; S. C., 11 *Id.*, 339. The jurisdiction belongs to the Supreme Judicial Court. *Ib.* Where one is appointed by the governor, to an office which does not exist, this information lies. *Ib.* The writ of assize of novel disseissin does not lie to recover the office of *Chief Justice* of a district. Whittington v. Polk, 1 Harr. & J., 236.

In this State it has been decided that where a person is in office by color of right, the remedy is not by *mandamus* to admit another having lawful claim; but by information in the nature of a *quo warranto*. People v. Corporation of N. Y., 6 Johns. Cas., 79; People v. Turnpike Co., 2 Johns., 190, also cited *post*. An information lies against an incorporated company for carrying on banking operations, without authority from the Legislature. People v. Utica Ins. Co., 15 Johns., 358. For privileges and immunities of a public nature which cannot be legally exercised without a legislative grant are franchises, although they never existed in the people, or could be exercised by them in their political capacity. *Ib.* **102***] An information was *filed to try the election of a county clerk in N. J., and the right of a deliberative assembly to reconsider their proceedings discussed and passed upon by the court. State v. Foster, 2 Halst. 101. This information will lie against a corporation or an individual. Cas. K. B., 225; Bull. *N. P.*, 212.

In what Courts. In England this information is filed in the K. B. 2 Sull. Lect., 168-9. In Mass., in the Supreme Judicial Court. Commonwealth v. Fowler, 10 Mass., 290. In this State, in the Supreme Court.

Nature of the proceeding. Though a criminal proceeding in form, yet in substance it is but a civil one. Rex v. Francis, 2 T. R., 484; 2 Kyd on Corp., 439; Commonwealth v. Browne, 1 Serg. & R., 385, per Tilghman, *Ch. J.*

When leave to file this information will be granted. It is not granted of course, but depends on the sound discretion of the court upon the circumstances of the case. Bac. Abr., Informations, D; King v. Trevenen, 2 B. & A., 339; People v. Sweeting, 2 Johns., 184. The Statute (1 R. L. 108, sec. 4) mentions leave of the court—so of the English Statute—as to leave under those Statutes, the following cases have been decided: It will usually be granted, where the right, or the fact on which the right depends, is disputed and doubtful. Rex v. Latham, 3 Burr., 1485; 1 Bl., 468. Or where the right turns upon a point of new or doubtful law. Rex v. Carter, Cowp., 58; Rex v. Godwin, Doug., 397. Or where there is no other remedy. Cas. K. B., 225; Bull. *N.* P., 212. It does not seem to be a reason for refusing an information, that the objection to the defendant's title arises from a defect in the title of some other person, through whom he claims, provided the application be made within proper time (8 Mod., 216); for it is admitted that where judgment of ouster has been given against a person through whom a title is claimed, that may be a reason for granting an information to impeach the derivative title (2 Str., 1109; Andr., 389; 5 Burr., 2601; Cowp., 500, *arguendo*); and that the title of the defendant may be impeached by an issue introduced on the record, respecting the title of the person under whom he claims, though the latter has not been ousted on an information filed against him. *Ib.* It may, or may not be possible to impeach the original right on which the derivative title depends, by an information filed against the person who claimed to exercise that right. Whatever may be the case, where that may be done, but in fact has not been done, it has been decided, that where it cannot be done, the original right may be impeached in an information against the person whose derivative title depends upon it. Rex v. Mein, 3 T. R., 596; 2 Kyd on Corp., 435-6. It is no objection to an information against an alderman, that the relators, who opposed his election, afterwards made no opposition to his election to the principal office of magistracy, which required that the defendant shou d be an alderman as a qualification for the higher office; or that they attended at, and concurred in corporate meetings, whereat he presided or attended in his official character. King v. Clarke, 1 East, 38. Nor is it an objection, that the relators in an information **103***] which would *operate, in its effect, to dissolve the Corporation, attended corporate meetings at which the Mayor was elected, whose election they impeach on the ground that the Corporation was dissolved by the loss of an integral part; and that they voted for another candidate, and afterwards attended other corporate meetings, at which such Mayor presided. King v. Morris, King v. Stewart, 3 East, 213. So a previous knowledge of the fact, in the person on whose affidavit the motion is made, will not be a ground for refusing the information, if he was under no obligation of remonstrating against the proceedings, if he be in fact merely a witness, not relator; as in the case of an application on the affidavit of the town clerk. Rex v. Binsted, Cowp., 75. Nor will the relator's concurrence in the election of the defendant, be any ground for refusal, if the objection was matter of substance, not of form in the election. Rex v. Smith, 3 T. R., 573. And where the application is made on the affidavit of several persons, all of whom, but one, concurred in the election of the defendant, if that one will avow himself the relator, and render himself responsible for the costs, his being joined with others who concurred in the election, will be no reason for refusing the information. Rex v. Simmons, 4 T. R., 223. Where the application is made for the purpose of enforcing a general Act of Parliament, which interests all the corporations in the kingdom, it is no objection that the party applying is not a member of the Corporation. Rex v. Brown, 3 T. R., 574, *n.* The abandonment of a former information, for the same cause, is, of itself, no reason for refusing an information, as that may have been by collusion. Rex v. Bond, 2 T. R., 771. The court will make the rule for an information in nature of a *quo warranto* absolute, though the party has, since the rule obtained, resigned his office, and his resignation has been accepted. Rex v. Warlow, 2 Maule. & S., 75. Rules to show cause or informations were granted, in various cases, in 8 Mod., which it may be useful to consult, by way of illustration, at pages 132, 135, 165-6, 35, 36, 215-16, 234.

When it will not be granted. If the defendant can show that his right has already been determined by *mandamus* (2 Hawk. P. C. Ch., 26, sec. 9); or that it depends on the right of those who voted for him, which has not yet been tried (*Ib.*); or that the person upon whose right the defendant's title depends has enjoyed his franchise so long, that the court would not permit it to be impeached in this mode of proceeding, the information will be denied. Rex v. Stevens, 1 Burr., 433; Rex v. Peacock, 4 T. R., 684. So if the defendant's right have been acquiesced in for a length of time (Bac. Abr., Informations, D). The time within which a corporate office might be impeached by a *quo warranto*, was, by the common law, indefinite; it varied with the circumstances of each particular case. Rex v. Powell, 8 Mod., 165; Rex v. Pike, *Id.*, 286, cited 1 T. R., 4, *n.*, and 3 T. R., 311; Rex v. Williams, 1 Str., 677; and *vide* 1 T. R. 1; *Id.*, 3, and *note* there, 3 *Id.*, 310, 311; 2 T. R., 767. And it was for some time, thought better that it should be unsettled. Rex v. Latham, 3 Burr., 1485-6, per Ld. Mansfield. At length, however, the court set a limit to their discretionary power, and confined it, in analogy, to other cases of limitations, within 20 years. Winchelsea causes, 4 Burr., *1962, 2022, [***104** 2121; Rex v. Rogers, *Id.*, 2523; and, at length, to six years. Rex v. Dicken, 4 T. R., 282; Rex v. Peacock, 4 T. R., 684; R. G., Hil. T., 1791; 4 T. R., 284. And the last period was confirmed by Parliament. Stat. 32, Geo. III, 58 and *vide* Rex v. Autridge, 8 T. R., 467. If the person from whom the title was derived be dead, it seems the information should not be granted, Rex v. Sperring, 1 T. R., 4, *n.*; or the parties have acquiesced. King v. Stacey, 1 T. R., 4, per Buller, J. So where so great a number of derivative titles would be affected by a judgment against the defendant, that it would tend to dissolve the Corporation. Rex v Carter, Cowp., 59, per Ld. Mansfield. So where the franchise no way concerns the public (as all those which relate to the government of a corporation, or the election of members of Parliament (case of the Borough of Horsham, Hil., 30 Geo. III., 3 T. R., 599, *n.*; Rex v. Mein, *Id.*, 598-9; King v. Bingham, 2 East, 308; and fairs and markets, &c., are said to do—2 Hawk, Ch. 26, sec. 9); but is wholly of a private nature, as a cony-warren. Rex v. Sir William Lowther, 2 Ld. Raym., 1409; S. C., 1 Str., 637; Ibboston's case, Cas. t. Hardw., 248; Rex v. Caan, Andr., 15; 1 Bott., pl. 326; Rex v. Shepherd, 4 T. R., 381. So where two sets of churchwardens are sworn in. Rex v. Dawbeny, 2 Str., 1196. And *quære* as to fairs and markets. Rex v. Marsden, 3 Burr., 1812; 1 Bl., 579; Ibbotson's case, Cas. t. Hardw., 248; Hardr., 162 *arguendo.* So, if the election by which the defendant claims is agreeable to the charter, or he has never acted under the election, or there has been but a mere claim, and no use of the franchise. Rex v. Ponsonby, Say., 245; Rex v. Whitwell, 5 T. R., 85. But swearing in is a user, though it be defective. King v. Tate, 4 East, 337. So, if it appear that the time, for which the officer was elected, will expire before the inquiry can have any effect. People v. Sweeting, 2 Johns., 184, Commonwealth v. Athearn, 3 Mass., 285. So where the persons on whose affidavits the motion is grounded, have lain by without recently prosecuting, though with full knowledge of the fact (Rex v. Wardroper, 4 Burr., 2024, per Aston, *J.*); or have concurred with the rest of the Corporation in a resolution not to take advantage of a flaw in the defendant's title (Rex v. Mortlock, 3 T. R., 300); or where the prosecutor stands in the same circumstances with the defendant (per Ld. Kenyon, *Ch. J.*, in Rex v. Bond, 2 T. R., 771; Rex v. Cudlipp, 6 T. R., 503); or where the persons in whose name the application is made, are wholly unconnected with the Corporation. Rex v. Stacy, 1 T. R., 3, and *note* there. So where the application is manifestly frivolous and vexatious; and the court will, in such case, discharge the rule with costs. 2 Str., 1039; 2 Burr., 780; 3 T. R., 301. The court will not grant an information to try the validity of an election to the office of church-warden, because it is no unsurpation on the Crown. Rex v. Shepherd, 4 T. R., 381. So where the relator had agreed not to enforce a by-law upon which he now grounded his attempt to impeach the defendant's title. Rex v. Mortlock, 3 T. R., 300. It is a valid objection, that the relator was present, and concurred, at the time of the objectionable election, though he was then ignorant of the objection. King v. Trevenen, 2 B. & A., 339. So where the relator is indigent, and there are strong 105*] reasons to suspect that *he is applying not on his own account, or at his own expense, but in collusion with a stranger. *Ib.* So where the circumstances throw suspicion on the motives of the relator, and the consequence will be to dissolve a corporation. *Ib.* The court will not grant this information to enforce a claim for damages against a turnpike company, done to the relator's property in laying out a road, though the Act require the Company to pay the damages. People v. Turnpike Co., 2 Johns., 190. A secondary and incidental ground for the information, resorted to by way of forlorn hope, after the original and main ground has failed, will be listened to with distrust; and the court, in their discretion, may disregard it, though it might be a good ground if brought before the court in the first instance. Rex v. Osbourne, 4 East, 327, 336. *Quo warranto* will not lie against a County Treasurer, to show by what authority he holds the office, if he has been, *de facto*, elected by the justices in Quarter Sessions. Rex v. Treasurer of Herefordshire, 1 Chit., 700. Rule, to show cause why information in nature of a *quo warranto* should not be filed against an ordinary, discharged. Hays v. Harley, 1 Rep. Const. Court, S. C., 267. It will not be granted against a person exercising a corporate franchise, to which he has been legally elected, though he has committed an offense which might amount to a forfeiture, until he has been removed by the Corporation. Rex v. Heaven, 2 T. R., 772. It was denied on the oath of a town clerk, who swore that he had not sworn the defendants; because he had entered that he had sworn them on the record. Rex v. Williams, 1 Str., 677.

The affidavits on which the motion is founded. These should not be entitled in any cause. King v. Pierson, Andr., 313, per Page and Probyn. *JJ.*; King v. Cole, 6 T. R., 642, per Lord Kenyon, *Ch. J.*; Haight v. Turner, 2 Johns., 371-2. On affidavit that the relator did not believe that the defendant had been duly sworn in, though the affidavit to show cause did not expressly allege that he had been sworn, but stated that he appeared, by the Corporation books, to have been sworn in, the court denied an information. King v. Newling, 3 T. R., 310. If sufficient appear to draw the merits of an election to a corporate office in question, the court will grant the information, though the deponents swear only to their information and belief that the defendant was admitted a freeman, &c., this not being denied by the defendant, on showing cause. King v. Harwood, 2 East, 177. The form of the affidavits for the rule to show cause are given at length in Commonwealth v. Douglass, 1 Binn., 77. If the affidavit in support of the rule omit a material fact, which is stated in the affidavit filed on the other side, the latter may be read by the prosecutor in support of his rule. Rex v. Mein, 3 T. R. 596. On application upon the ground that the defendants were elected contrary to the provisions of a particular charter, the affidavit must state that the charter was accepted, or that the usage has been in conformity to it; and the affidavit being ill for omitting this, the court refused leave to amend it, but put the party to a new application. King v. Barzey, 4 Maule & S., 253.

106*] **The rule thereupon.* It is usual to proceed by u e to show cause, on *ex parte* affidavits; but the court have a discretion as to this; and where the whole case had been disclosed by the defendant's answers in chancery, and the answers of others favorable to them, touching the subject of the application, the Supreme Court looked into the answers, and granted a rule for an information in the first instance. People v. Kip, 1 U. S. Law Journal, 286.

Rule to inspect books. Upon a rule to show cause, the court will grant a rule for the inspection of books belonging to the Corporation. Bull. *N.* P., 210.

Affidavits on showing cause. These may be entitled. King v. Pierson, Andr., 313, per Page & Probyn, *JJ.*; King v. Cole, 6 T. R., 640, 642, per Lord Kenyon, *Ch. J.* Or they may not be entitled, at the defendant's choice. King v. Cole, 6 T. R., 642, per Lord Kenyon, *Ch. J.* If these affidavits, and the cause shown do not put the matter beyond dispute, the rule will be made absolute. Bull. *N. P.*, 210. The court will judge, from all the circumstances of the case, who is the real relator. Per Lord Kenyon, *Ch. J.*, in Rex v. Cudlipp, 6 T. R., 509.

Showing cause. Unless the cause shown be such as puts the matter beyond dispute, the court will make the rule absolute for the information, in order that the question concerning the right may be properly determined. Bull. *N. P.*, 210. But, it seems, the court will not grant the rule for an information on the last day of the term. Rex v. Davies, Say., 241.

The information.. A sufficient variety of English precedents will be found in 6 Wentworth's Pl., 28 to 234. These are, for usurping or intruding into the offices or stations of Alderman, p. 28; of Mayor, 40, 50, 107, 161, 119, 214; of Bailiff of a Borough, 60; Master of the Company of Coopers, 63; Burgess, 71, 146, 154, 184, 188, 194, 200, 209, 225, 234; Commonalty Steward, 81; Freeman of a Borough, 84, 137; of a City, 132; Commoner, 175; Freemen of Coventry, 180; 2 Kyd on Corp., 403.

*This is the form, whether the information [*107 be brought for an usurpation without any original title, or for a subsequent forfeiture, where the original title is not disputed. *Id. & vide* Co. Ent., 527, 564, *per tot. quo war.* v. Mayor, &c., of London.

*15 Johns., 362, gives the form of the in- [*108 formation, &c., at length, in People v. Utica Ins. Co. See, also, the substance of an information in Conn. State v. Tudor, 5 Day Cas., 329. It need not show a title in the people to have the particular franchise exercised; but calls on the intruder to show by what authority he claims it; and if the title set up be incomplete, the people are entitled to judgment. 15 Johns., 388, per Spencer, *J.*, who cites 2 Kyd on Corp., 399, and 4 Burr., 2146-7. The Act to Incorporate the Utica Ins. Co., passed Mar. 29, 1816, sess. 39, ch. 52, does not authorize the Company to institute a bank, issue bills, discount notes and receive deposits, such powers not being expressly granted by the Legislature, and not being within their intention, as collected from the Act of Incorporation; and the Company having assumed and exercised those powers, they were held to have usurped a franchise; and on an information in nature of a *quo warranto* being filed by the Atty-Gen., judgment of *ouster* was rendered against them. *Id.*, 358. In Mass., the Solicitor-General, in an information against one for usurping a public offiee, recited an order of the House of Representatives, requesting him to file such information, and stated that he filed it by virtue of, and in compliance with this authority; and, on the ground that the Legislature had no right to give this construction, it was moved to quash the information; but the court held, that the act of filing the information should be deemed to emanate from the official authority of the Solicitor-General, who might, *ex officio*, file the information. Commonwealth v. Fowler, 10 Mass., 290. The form of the information is given in that case, with the plea in bar. *Id.*, p. 295. Every citizen who pays taxes, has such an interest as will authorize an information in the nature of a *quo warranto*, to be filed at his suggestion, to inquire by what authority the collector holds his office. Commonwealth v. Browne, 1 Serg. & R., 382. It may be filed to inquire into the election or admission of an officer or member of a corporation, when moved for by any person interested in, or injured by such election or admission, if it were unduly made. Commonwealth v. F. & M. Ins. Co., 5 Mass., 230. It may also be moved for by the Atty-Gen., *ex officio*, or on the authority of the Legislature, but it is confined to one of these three ways. *Ib.* One appointed by the Executive to an office *which does not exist [*109 may be removed by information in nature of a *quo warranto*. Commonwealth v. Fowler, 10 Mass. 290.

The general proceeding is by information for the King, by his Attorney-General, against any usurper of franchises, &c., to show *quo warranto* he uses them. Co. Ent., 527 *b.* So against him who exercises a power unlawfully; as, if a Mayor, &c., admits to freedom persons who have no right; for there is no other remedy. 1 Salk., 374. If the information be for using a franchise by a corporation, it should be against the Corporation. King v. Cusacke, 2 Roll., 113, 115. If for usurping to be a Corporation, it should be against the particular persons. *Ibid.* But it will not lie at all, merely for encouraging such an usurpation. Rex v. Marsden, 2 Burr., 1812. It will not lie on the relation of an individual against a corporation as a body. This should always be by, and in the name of the Atty-Gen. Rex v. Corp. of Carmarthen, 2 Burr., 869. If, on the relation of a private person, it should be against the several individuals, to show by what authority they claim their respective franchises. *Ib.* If the information be at common law, there is no relator, nor ought there to be judgment for costs, but only a *capiatur pro fine.* Bull. *N. P.*, 211. It is not necessary to state in the information that leave of the court was granted to file it. Cowp., 501. By the statute, one information may be filed to try the rights of different persons. 1 R. L., 108, sec. 4. A *quo warranto* was brought for vexation, upon forty-eight points, and the court being moved in it, ordered that the prosecutor should waive that *quo warranto*, and should bring a new one, and therein insist on only three points, but that he might proceed to trial upon his new *quo warranto*, in such time as he might have done upon the old. (Hill, 22 Car. B. R.), to the end that he might not be delayed in his proceedings by being put to bring the new *quo warranto.* 2 Lill. Pr. Reg., 509, B. On moving to file an information, the court will judge from all the circumstances of the case who is the real relator. Per Lord Kenyon, *Ch. J.*, in Rex v. Cudlipp, 6 T. R., 509. It seems that though an information may be granted on the application of a stranger, yet he ought to make out a strong case. Rex v. Kemp, 1 East, 46, *n.* An information does not lie against a mere servant of a corporation, whose office does not affect any franchise, or other authority holden under the Crown. Rex v. Bedford Corp., 6 East, 356.

Consolidation. After rules have been made absolute for several informations, the court will give leave to consolidate them at the instance of the defendants. Rex v. Foster, 1 Burr., 573. But, without the defendant's consent, the court will not consolidate several distinct informations for several distinct offices; for there must be an information against each to enable each to disclaim. Rex v. Warlow, 2 Maule & S., 75.

Of quashing the information. This cannot be done on motion, even with the consent of parties. Rex v. Edgar, and the same v. Bricknell, 4 Burr., 2297.

The process. The principal case decides that this should be a *venire facias* and *distringas*, or subpœna and attachment; and some books speak indifferently of these two kinds of process. *Vide* 2 Kyd on Corp., 438.

110*] *In the Commonwealth of Pa. v. Sprenger, 5 Binn., 353, the court awarded a *venire.* In that State the 9 Anne, ch. 20, had not been enacted as late as 1817. 3 Serg. & R., 52. In a note by Siderfin (Le Roy v. Trinity House, 1 Sid., 86), which is much referred to by the books, he says, it appears, on comparing the precedents in Coke's Entries, 527, 528, &c., that there is this difference between a *quo warranto* and an information in nature of a *quo warranto*, in respect to the process. Upon an information, it seems, the process shall be *venire facias* and *distringas;* but upon a writ of *quo warranto*, it is summons; and for default of appearance, that the liberties shall be seized. 2 Kyd on Corp., 438, says the process usually issued to bring the defendant into court, is a writ of subpœna, and if that be disobeyed, an attachment; but if the defendant cannot be served with a subpœna, it is said, the process is *venire facias* and *distringas;* which looks as if a *venire* and *distringas* were to follow a subpœna; and for this he quotes Sid., 86, which he altogether misapprehends in this p c : and at a previous page, 404, he refers to Coke's Entries, the same authority on which Siderfin relies in his note, and says that, according to these entries, the process usually awarded against individuals is a *venire facias* which is followed by a *distringas;* and in this he is right and according to the entry itself, which at 527, is an award of a *venire* against certain individuals named, who claim to be a body politic; though from the hasty search which I have made, I do not find any entry of a *distringas.* These entries touching *quo warranto* are voluminous, and follow from p. 527 to 564, in very large double folio pages. At p. 536, I find the entry of a *distringas* as the first process against the Corporation, viz.: Mayor, Commonalty and Citizens of London. This is also mentioned in 2 Kyd, 404. the entry of the *venire* is thus immediately at the close of the information: "Whereupon the sheriff is commanded, that he cause to come," or, "that he omit not, &c., but that he cause to come, &c., to answer, &c." The entry of the *distringas* is thus: "whereupon it is agreed (*concordat' est*) that the aforesaid Mayor and Commonalty and Citizens of ——, be distrained by all their lands, &c., so that, &c., to answer to our Lord the King in the premises, and the sheriff is commanded, that he distrain them in form aforesaid, so that, &c.," at such a day, &c. (and see 2 Kyd on Corp., 404). In Rex v. Mayor and Aldermen of Hertford, 1 Salk., 374, it is said the process is subpœna and *distringas.* This case was up several times. It is reported in Carthew, 503, as The King v. The Town of Hertford, where it is stated that the first process out of the Crown office was a *venire facias* in the nature of a summons (though Salkeld says it should be a subpœna. This *venire* was followed by a *distringas*, and an *alias* and *pluries distringas;* which was conceded on all sides to be the right course, for though a motion was made to set the writs of *distringas* aside, this did not relate to the nature of the process. The writs of *distringas* and the motion to set them aside are also mentioned in Holt, 320, S. C., entitled as in Salkeld. Com. Dig., *Quo Warranto*, C, 2, says the process is *venire* and *distringas*, and cites Co. Entr., 1 Sid. and 1 Salk., *supra;* and so says 2 Morg. Att'ys Vad. Mec., 106, 107 on the same authorities as Comyn. But Morgan says (*Id.*, 107) that the first process against a corporation shall be a summons and afterwards a *distringas in infinitum.* He says this on [*111 the authority of Carthew, *supra*, where the first process is stated to be a *venire* in nature of a summons. Thus the *venire* and distress infinite appears to be the predominant process in all cases; though in the report of King v. Mayor, &c., of Hertford, 1 Ld. Raym., 426, subpœna and *distringas* are mentioned as the proper process. In Commonwealth v. Fowler, 10 Mass., 290, 291, the process was summons.

How the defendant should be named. If an usurpation be by a corporation, the process shall be against them by their corporate name. 2 Morg. Att'ys Vad. Mec., 107, citing the case of the *quo warranto* against the City of London, 16, Treby's Argument. If it be for usurping to be a corporation, it shall be against the natural persons who usurp, or by a name which comprehends them. *Ib.*, citing *Id.*, 69, and Pollexfen's Argument. And see 2 Rolle, 115.

Teste and return of process. In King v. Town of Hertford, Carth., 503, the *venire* was returnable in Easter Term, 11 Will. III., upon which a *distringas* issued, returnable *crast.* Trinity; and upon that return a second *distringas* was made returnable in fifteen days, in the same Trinity Term; and upon this being returned, a third *distringas* was made, tested in that term, and returnable in Mich. Term, Anno 11 Will. III.; and it was moved that the two last might be set aside for irregularity; for that the process in these cases should be made returnable *de termino in terminum*, and not quicker; but that in Trinity Term there issued two writs of *distringas*, which should not be; and above forty precedents to this effect, in the crown office, were insisted on. But Holt, *Ch. J.*, answered, that crown office work was, like church work, very slow in its progress, it being usual for clerks to make all such process out together, and of the same test and return from term to term; but no law required that it should be so; and the motion was denied. S. C., 2 Salk., 699, S. P.; S. C., 1 Ld. Raym., 426, S. P.

Of the issues upon the distringas. It was moved in last case that the court would make a special rule to estreat the issues upon the several writs of *distringas*, but no such rule was made; but the issues were left to be estreated in due time, according to the course of the court. And in the report of the same case, in Holt, 320, this estreating in due time is said to be to send them up into the Exchequer the last days of the two issuable terms; though the court agreed that in an extraordinary case they might make a rule for this purpose.

Of the seizure nomine districtionis *for non-appearance.* As the process in the proceeding by *quo warranto* was dilatory, while this was conducted before the old justices in Eyre, if the party did not appear at a certain stage, the franchise or subject of the writ might be seized, on process to the sheriff, as a distress, and the defendant was put to come in and replevy it, as he would any other distress. When the justices in Eyre ceased, and the jurisdiction of this writ passed to the K. B., the same practice prevailed there, and some of the ancient cases look as if the franchise, &c., should be forfeited forever, unless it was replevied at a short day: though by a modern case, which underwent much discussion, and was

112*] finally *determined by the Lords, on writ of error, it was held that this had never been the law. But it was agreed by the same case, that the subject of the suit might be seized. The argument for the conclusive effect of the seizure, was founded principally on the Y. B., 15 ed., 4, which is there reported at length; but the summary given by Jenkins, in his Centuries, 141, and *vide* 2 Kyd on Corp., 502, S. C., is thus: "A *quo warranto* is brought in the King's Bench; the defendant being summoned makes default; and another default at the return of the *venire facias;* judgment shall be that the franchise shall be seized into the King's hands; and not that it shall be forfeited; for it does not yet appear whether there be cause of forfeiture. No man shall finally lose his land, or his franchise, on any default, if he has never appeared." And with this summary the Parliament agreed. In that case a judgment was given, that the market aforesaid be taken and seized into the King's hands, *quousque,* &c. 2 Kyd on Corp., 497. And the sheriff was commanded to seize the market, according to the form of the judgment aforesaid, &c., and to show, at the next term, how he executed the writ; when he returned that he had seized the market into the King's hands, according to the form of the writ. *Id.*, 498. This same practice was introduced upon the information in nature of a *quo warranto*; and a similar judgment was given and executed, upon such an information, against the City of Chester, in Hil. Term, 35 & 36 Charles II., the form of which see in 2 T. R., 518. 2 Kyd on Corp., 494, S. C. The judgment there was of seizure, *quousque*, &c., *i. e.*, until the said court shall further order. The great and labored cause of The King v. Emery, 2 T. R., 515, 569, turned mainly upon the effect of this judgment. The K. B. held it final; but afterwards, in Parliament, the judgment was reversed, a note of which reversal is in 4 T. R., 122, but no part of the case there given. The report of the case in the House of Lords, on error, occupied 2 vols. quarto; but a sufficient abstract, as to this point, is in 2 Kyd on Corp., 496 to 511. At p. 510, the *Ch. B.* Eyre, who delivered the opinion of the House of Lords, said he conceived the effect of the judgment and seizure by the sheriff, laid the King's hands on the franchise of being a corporation, and upon other franchises in the information, so that the Corporation could not use its liberties; the action of its vital powers was suspended; and in this situation he had no doubt that a *custos* might be appointed; that the Corporation in that case might have been restored, on paying a fine to the King, and were restored by pardon, &c. See an examination of this question, at large, with all the cases, in The King v. Emery, above cited from 2 T. R., 515, and 2 Kyd on Corp., 496, &c.

Whether the defendant can be pursued to outlawry. Vide 2 Kyd on Corp., 438, 439, who concludes that he may.

Who may defend. If the defendant suffer the rule to show cause to be made absolute, or suffer judgment by default, others whose title may be affected by the judgment may be let in to defend his title, on undertaking to do this at their own expense, and indemnifying him against all costs, &c. Bac. Abr., Informations D; 3 T. R., 310.

Time to plead. The court may allow to each, as well prosecutor as defendant, such convenient time 113*] to plead, reply, rejoin or demur, as they *shall think reasonable. 9 Anne, ch. 20; 2 Lill. Prac. Reg., 510, B, and see the next head. To this effect is the Stat. 1 R. L., 109, sec. 6.

Imparlance. There is an entry of this, 15 Johns., 363; People v. Utica Ins. Co. In Herring v. Brown, Comb., 11, 12, Williams moved for a second imparlance in a *quo warranto*, and said it was granted in the case of the City of London; but the court denied it; for Astry said by the course of the court, they were to have but the common imparlance; and per *Cur.*, being *ex. gratia*, we may grant or deny it as we see cause. See the next previous head of time to plead.

Of the plea. The defendant may plead in abatement; but he must verify it by affidavit as in other cases of dilatory pleas (1 R. L., 524, sec. 23; 2 Kyd on Corp., 439; Rex v. Jones, 2 Str., 1161); and this must be entitled. 2 Str., 1161. Whether he may plead a misnomer in his addition, *quære. Vide* 2 Kyd on Corp., 438, 439, and Rex v. Mayor of Hedon, 1 Wils., 244, as to the right of outlawry, upon which such a plea seems to depend. There is such a plea in 6 Wentw. Plead., 51.

The Statute (4 Anne, ch. 16, sec. 4; 1 R. L., 519, sec. 9) allowing the defendant to plead more than one plea, with leave of the court, does not extend to information in nature of a *quo warranto*. There is no instance in which the court have given such leave (Rex v. Newland, Say., 96); and see what is said by Sir Fletcher Norton and Ld. Mansfield, in Rex v. Leigh, 4 Burr., 2146, and a *note* to that case which mentions Rex v. Brisco, as going to the same point with Sayre. But under the Statute 32 Geo. III., ch. 58, sec. 2, the defendant may plead several pleas. Rex v. Autridge, 8 T. R., 467. This Statute is there recited in a *note*. There is no such Statute in this State. As to the construction of that Statute, see Rex v. Stokes, 2 Maule & S., 71.

The plea in bar should set out the defendant's title at length, and conclude with a general traverse, "without this, that he usurped, &c." Rex v. Blagden, Gilb., 145. And where the title set forth is bad but the user confessed, this amounts to a confession of the usurpation. Rex v. Philips, 1 Str., 394, 397, cited 1 Burr., 302, 305. The defendant may either disclaim as to all the franchises mentioned in the information, or plead as to all; or plead as to part and disclaim as to part. 2 Kyd on Corp., 405.

*A variety of English forms for these pleas [*114 are in 6 Wentw. Plead., 28 to 242, among which are a plea in abatement for a wrong addition, p. 51; of disclaimer, 83; that the defendant was elected by a casting vote according to custom, 29, 36; a custom on vacancy to elect a commonalty steward, and that the defendant was duly elected, 82; plea setting out a charter and the defendant's regular election, 150; the like, setting out a by-law, 157, with other pleas reciting customs, usages, by-laws, &c., from 28 to 242. For form of plea in N. J., see State v. Foster, 2 Halst., 101. The substance of a plea in Conn., see State v. Tudor, 5 Day Cas. Err., 330. For the form of a plea in this State, see People v. Utica Ins. Co., 15 Johns., 363 to 365, setting forth the title to a franchise under an Act. The plea was adjudged insufficient in substance. The form was not questioned.

It is not sufficient for the defendant, in a *quo warranto*, to plead that such a subject hath a lawful interest to hold a leet, without making any title to himself; for the writ is *quo warranto* he claims, &c. 2 Leon., case 31. *Nor is it enough [*118 to plead *non usurpavit libertates prædictas*, but the plea should also say *nec earum aliquam.* 3 Leon., case 135. The defendant must either justify or disclaim; and not guilty and *non usurpavit* are not good pleas; for they do not answer to the nature of the charge which is to show by what warrant or authority. Bull, *N. P.*, 211; Cas. K. B., 225. The defendant should show a full title to himself. Com. Dig., *Quo Warranto*, ch. 4, cites 9 Co., 24 *b*; 2 Leon., 28; Hardr., 456. As if the King grant *bona felonum*, or other franchises, which lie in charter, to an Abbot, &c., whose possessions come back to the Crown, and the King regrants *bona felonum*, &c., *adeo plene prout abbas habuit;* in a *quo warranto* against the grantee, he should plead the first grant to the Abbot, the reunion in the Crown, and afterwards the regrant, &c. (*Ib.*, cites R., 9 Co., 26 *a*, per Popham, 2 *J.*, Cont. Mo., 297.) In pleading the King's charter, he ought not to say he granted and confirmed, for this is double. *Ib.* cites Sid., 86. In pleading the grant of an office, he should show it an ancient office (*Ib.*, cites 1 Sid., 86, and qualifies it with *semble*); and allegee the thing done to be appurtenant to his office (*Ib.*, cites 1 Sid., 86); and in pleading a grant to an Abbot he should show for what estate. *Ib.*, cites R. Mo., 297. In pleading a privilege to himself as copyholder, he should plead it in him who has the freehold, at least. *Ib.*, cites R. Yelv., 191. But it is sufficient that the plea be as general as the information; as if a *quo warranto* be for using a market, toll, &c., it is sufficient to make title to the market, toll, &c., without saying how much the toll was. *Ib.*, cites Palm., 81. If he claim a franchise as appendant to a manor which came to the King by the attainder of B., and afterwards was granted to him, it is sufficient to say that B., *fuit debito modo attinctus. Ib.*, cites 3 Leon., 72, *semb.* So if he claims franchises by prescription, and others by charter, he may conclude *eo warranto utitur* generally: for it shall be taken distributively. *Ib.*, cites R. Mo., 398. That a man may prescribe *tenere placito*, but not to have cognizance of pleas, &c., and as to the distinction between what may be prescribed for, and what must be pleaded by way of grant, see 1 Salk., 183-4, Bull. *N. P.*, 212; 5 Co., 109; 9 Co., 24. Several general rules relative to pleading are laid down in Sir Edmund Bacon's case, Latch, 45, which was *quo warranto;* but as they are equally applicable to other cases, they are found in the books upon pleadings in general. And see also the various cases collected in Keilw., from 137 to 158; Cro. Car., 311, pl. 2; Rex v. Knight, 4 T. R., 419, 425; Rex v. Birch, 4 T. R., 608; Rex v. Clarke, 2 East, 75; Rex

v. Mein. 4 T. R., 480, for cases of and pleadings in *quo warranto*, relative to various corporate titles.

Replication and Demurrer. After plea, the Atty-Gen. demurs or replies, and the subsequent proceedings are in the same manner as in civil actions. 2 Kyd on Corp., 406. Where several things are necessary to constitute a complete title in the defendant, the Crown may take issue on each, and if any one of the issues, on a fact material to the title, be found against the defendant, there shall be judgment of ouster, and the defendant shall pay the costs on all the issues. Bac. Abr., Informations, D, cites Rex v. Hearle, 1 Str., 627; 2 Ld. Raym., 1447; Rex v. Downes, 1 T. R., 453. The replication should not take issue on the general traverse, without this, **119***] *"that he usurped, &c.," but should be to the special matter, that the defendant may know how to apply his defense. *Ib.*, cites Rex v. Blagden, Gilb., 145. The court will not interfere summarily to set aside a replication because it goes to a point not insisted on in the information. Rex v. Brown, 4 T. R., 276.

For English forms of replications denying customs, usages, &c., see 6 Went. Plead., 28 to 242, at different intervals. For demurrers, *Id.*, 113, 106, 62, 52, 152, &c. Also, People v. Utica Ins. Co., 15 Johns., 365. Whether the prosecutor can demur to part of the plea and reply to the rest, *quære*. Rex v. Ginever, 6 T. R., 733, *note*. *Semb.*, he may demur to the whole and plead to particular parts. *Ib.* Form of replication in N. J., State v. Foster, 2 Halst., 101.

Rejoinder and joinder in demurrer. For forms of rejoinder see 6 Went. Plead., 58, &c.; of joinder in demurrer. People v. Utica Ins. Co., 15 Johns., 365; 6 Went. Plead., 114, 62, 52, 152, &c. Rejoinder in N. J., State v. Foster, 2 Halst., 103.

Surrejoinder. For the form of this see 6 Went. Plead., 58.

Rules to plead, reply, &c. These are of course, and the same as in ordinary proceedings. People v. Clark, *ante*, 95. In England they have rules to plead peculiar to this and like informations, grounded on the practice of the crown office. But they are rules of course. The practice there is fully exhibited in Rex v. Ginever, 6 T. R., 594, and the *notes* there.

Suggestion that sheriff is interested and prayer that distringas may be directed to a coroner. 6 Went. Pl., 106–7.

Of amending the pleadings, and other proceedings. These are the same as in ordinary actions; rules of course may be entered for this purpose, in the same manner. People v. Clark, *ante*, 95. And amendments on special motion appear to have always stood on the same footing as in other actions. Com. Dig., *Quo Warranto*, C, 4; Sid., 54; Rex v. Blatchford, 4 Burr., 2147. Indeed, there is a greater reason for allowing the defendant to amend his plea, or withdraw and substitute another, as he cannot plead double; and this matter was so considered in Rex v. Blatchford, 4 Burr., 2147, where the defendant was allowed to withdraw his plea and plead *de novo* just before the trial, upon payment of costs, pleading within a week, and taking short notice of trial, with liberty for the prosecutor to reply *de novo*, and this was done without affidavit of any particular circumstances, or any particular reasons given for the amendment. See opinion of Ld. Mansfield on that motion, *Id.*, 2148. The Atty-Gen. was allowed to amend the information by adding a new count, on motion. People v. Clark, *ante*, 95. The Statute of Amendments and Jeofails are extended to all the proceedings on informations in nature of a *quo warranto*. 1 R. L., 117, 121, sec. 10.

Trial and evidence. The practice and rules relative to these are generally the same as in ordinary cases. What is peculiar as to evidence arises mostly out of the law touching the old British corporations, and has little application here. Buller in his Treatise of *Nisi Prius*, 211, 12, 13, has collected a few cases of this kind, only three of which, from **120***] 4 Co., 78; Comb., 316, and *1 Salk., 168, properly come under the head of evidence. The others more properly belong to a treatise on corporations. Other cases of evidence, peculiar to this proceeding, are Rex v. Hebden, 2 Str., 1109; and see Andr., 389; Rex v. Grimes, 5 Burr., 2598, 2601; Rex v. Spearing, 1 T. R., 4 *n.*; Cowp., 503, 507; Rex v. Mein, 3 T. R., 596; 4 T. R., 480; Rex v. Robins, 2 Str., 1069; Cowp., 502; Doug., 374.

There is now no doubt that a new trial may be granted, be the verdict for the people or defendant. 2 Kyd on Corp., 445; and *vide* Rex v. Bennet, 1 Str., 101; Rex v. Corporation of Brecknock, 8 Mod., 201; Rex v. Francis, 2 T. R., 484; 3 Wood. Lect., 355. But a new trial will not be granted for misdirection, where it appears that the term of office, in the defendant, respecting which, the information was filed, has expired, and a new annual election of officers made. State v. Tudor, 5 Day Cas. in Er., 329. Where the issue in on the legality of the election, evidence may be given of conversations and transactions previous to the election, if they were connected with, and might have an influence on it, though no previous notice thereof has been given. Commonwealth v. Welper, 3 Serg. & R., 29. The place where the process should be returned and trial held, see Commonwealth v. Smead, 11 Mass., 74. Motion for a new trial for variance between pleading and proof, &c., Rex v. Rowland, 3 B. & A., 130. The court will order a change of venue on the ground of local prejudice. Rex v. Emery, 1 T. R., 363, &c.; 3 Wood. Lect., 341. And the court may, in its discretion, order a trial at bar. The King v. Emery, 1 T. R., 363.

Bill of exceptions. For this a form is given in 6 Went. Plead., 130, 133.

Postea. For a form of this, see 6 Went. Plead., 240.

Repleader. Where the defendant pleads a bad title, which results in an immaterial issue, and a verdict for him, the rule, as to awarding a repleader, is the same as in ordinary actions. 1 Str., 394, 397, cited 1 Burr., 302, 305.

The judgment. This seems to be the same, and subject to the same varieties, at common law, as on the writ of *quo warranto*. 2 Kyd on Corp., 406.

If the defendant's plea be confessed, the judgment is to allow the franchises. Com. Dig., *Quo Warranto*, C, 5, cites Co. Ent., 535 *b*, 537 *a*, 549, 564. But a confession by the Atty-Gen. does not bind the King where the matter is not private, but concerns the public. *Ib.*, cites 1 Roll., *112. So a [***121** confession by the Atty-Gen., if it be not after the plea upon record, does not bind the King. *Ib.* cites Sav., 19, *Semb.* So a confession by the Atty-Gen. does not conclude the King or the court, in a point of law, but only as to the fact (*Ib.*, cites 2 Bulstr., 296); as to which a judgment is conclusive against the King (Hardr., 129), and generally on a judgment against the King in this proceeding, he is forever bound. 1 Roll., 112.

On disclaimer, by the defendant, the Atty-Gen. prays "that whereas the said ———, by his plea, has disavowed and disclaimed all and singular the liberties, &c., above specified, judgment may be given for the King, and that the said ———, with the said liberties and franchises, or any of them, may no way intermeddle, but may hereafter be altogether excluded from the same," and judgment is accordingly given in that form. 2 Kyd on Corp., 407; Co. Ent., 27 *b*.

With respect to the form of the judgment for the King, at common law, there are several nice distinctions, and considerable dispute in the books; as whether it should be of seizure, ouster, or mixed of both; and whether it should be of *capias pro fine*, or *quod sit in misericordia*, &c., but, to all practical purposes, these distinctions are, I conceive, abolished by the Statute of this State (1 R. L., 108, sec. 5), which declares the form of the judgment for the people. As the curious reader may, however, desire to look into the common law cases on this head, he will find them fully collected and briefly stated in 2 Kyd on Corp., 407 to 409. There cannot be judgment against a corporation, but in their politic capacity. 4 Mod., 58.

Judgment is for costs against the relator or defendant, according to the event of the suit. 1 R. L., 108–9, sec. 5.

Where several things are necessary to constitute a complete title in the defendant, the Atty-Gen. may take issue on each; and if any one of the issues on a fact material to the title be found against the defendant, judgment of ouster shall be given against him. As where being elected and sworn are both necessary to the title, and the jury find against the being sworn, and for the election. Rex v. Hearle, 1 Str., 582, 625, 627; 2 Ld. Raym., 1447. This is affirmed on error, and is recognized in Rex v. Reeks, 2 Ld. Raym., 1447; and see, also, Rex v. Latham, 3 Burr., 1485, 1487, per Ld. Mansfield, at the last page. It is said in the 2 Lill. Prac. Reg., 509, C, that if several privileges are granted in a charter, and there is a forfeiture of the charter, for an abuser of one of the privileges, and a *quo warranto* is brought, and judgment upon it, this is a forfeiture of the whole charter.

Upon information in nature of a *quo warranto* against one for claiming the office of alderman, if he disclaim, and judgment of ouster be given against him, he is concluded from showing to a second information for exercising the same office, that he was duly elected before such first information and judgment of ouster, and that he was afterwards sworn in by virtue of a peremptory *mandamus*. But, *semble*, if the election to the office were good, and only the first swearing in irregular, the first judgment should not have been an absolute judgment of ouster; but either a judgment of *capiatur pro fine* only, for the temporary usurpation, or a 122*] judgment **quousque*, &c. King v. Clarke, 2 East, 75, and see 2 Str., 952. If judgment be against the principal franchise, all incidental and subordinate franchises are also gone. Palm., 82. The judgment in a *quo warranto* is final; for it is in nature of a writ of right. 1 Sid., 86. A judgment *quod capiantur* amounts to the same thing as a judgment *quod capiuntur* in the indicative mood, like the judgment in debt *quod recuperet*, which is the same with *quod recuperat* (said *arguendo*, in Sir James Smith's case, Carth., 218, as appears by the following entries and cases: Rast. Ent., 54; Co. Ent., 538, 559; 9 Rep., 98; 15 ed., 4, 7; Ryley, 277; Maynard's ed., 2, 16, 24). What judgment may be given in Mass., see Commonwealth v. U. F. M. I. Co. of Newburyport, 5 Mass., 230, and Commonwealth v. Fowler, 11 *Id.*, 339.

For forms of judgment, see 6 Went. Plead., 13, 89, 161, and 242. The form of the judgment in Mass. is given at length in Commonwealth v. Fowler, 11 Mass., 339, as drawn up under the direction of the court.

Judgment rolls complete. 6 Went. Plead., 234 to 242, contains the roll from the *placita* to the judgment. So *Id.*, 153 to 161.

Costs. In England costs are not given against the defendant, except where the information relates to a corporate office; but this is upon the particular wording of the Statute 9 Anne, ch. 20, which is clearly not so broad as the N. Y. Statute. Rex v. Wallis, 5 T. R., 375. The court will not stay proceedings until the prosecutor give security for costs, on the ground that the relator is in insolvent circumstances, where it appears that he is a corporator, and no fraud is suggested. Rex v. Wynne, 2 Maule & S., 346. The Statute 9 Anne, ch. 20, had not (in 1817) been re-enacted in Pa., and it was therefore held, in Commonwealth v. Woelper, 3 Serg. & R., 52, that neither party could recover costs, the information being at common law.

Execution. If judgment be for the people, the regular course is, to issue a writ of seizure to the sheriff, which, after reciting the proceedings, commands him to seize the liberties into the people's hands (*vide* 2 Kyd on Corp., 410, cites Co. Ent., 539 *b*); and thereon the sheriff shall return a seizure, Co. Ent., 540 *b*. But this writ, in point of fact, has not always issued. 2 Kyd on Corp., 410. The usual process by *fi. fa.* or *ca. sa.* goes for the costs, either against the relator or defendant, according to the event. 1 R. L., 108, 109, sec. 6.

Writ of error. For the form of this writ, see 6 Went. Plead., 153. This is a writ of Error from the the K. B. to Parliament.

Return thereto. Same book, 153.

By an Act passed Apr. 21, 1825 (since writing the above), one of the justices of the Supreme Court may, in vacation, grant leave to file an information in nature of a *quo warranto* against any corporation, on notice or otherwise in his discretion; on filing which, the Atty-Gen. may issue process. On this process being returned duly served, the clerk may enter the defendant's appearance; whereupon, the proceedings against them shall be the same as in the case of private persons. When an issue of fact is joined, the cause shall be entitled to a prefer- 123*] ence at the circuit; *and on its coming before the Supreme Court, on demurrer, special verdict, bill of exceptions, demurrer to evidence, or case, it shall be preferred, so that it may be argued and determined at the term for which it shall be noticed.

The Supreme Court, on the application of any person or persons, natural or corporate, who may be aggrieved by, or complain of any election, or any proceedings, act or matter, in or touching the same, on notice, shall proceed in a summary way to hear the affidavits, proofs and allegations of the parties, or otherwise inquire into the matter or cause of complaint; and thereupon establish the election so complained of, or order a new election, or make such order and give such relief, in the premises, as right and justice may appear to require; and may order an issue or issues to try the rights of the parties to the office, offices or franchise in question, or may give leave to the Atty-Gen. to exhibit an information or informations in nature of a *quo warranto*, pursuant to the act for rendering the proceedings upon writs of *mandamus*, and informations in the nature of a *quo warranto*, more speedy and effectual, passed Feb. 6, 1788.

In case any such issue shall be ordered, or any such information be permitted to be filed, it shall be lawful for the court to make such further order, for prescribing and limiting the times for the respective parties to plead and proceed therein, and for giving preference to any issue, to be made up or joined therein, and for expediting the ulterior proceedings, if any, so as to cause the same to be proceeded upon, and a final determination thereon to be had, with the best and most convenient speed that may be; and the court shall cause the same to be expedited by all such ways and means, as a due regard to the ends of justice will admit, and the case may require.

On information by the Atty-Gen. against a corporation, or any person or persons claiming to be a corporation, or to be officers of a corporation, if judgment shall finally pass against the defendants, full Supreme Court costs shall be awarded, to be collected by execution or attachment.

As this Act relates merely to the mode of proceeding against corporations or corporate offices, the ancient practice, it will be perceived, must still be resorted to in all other cases.

---

*REES *v.* OVERBAUGH. [*124

Action on Bond from which Seals had been Torn —Practice.

The plaintiff's attorney in declaring on a bond from which the seals had been torn by mistake, inadverently made profert and gave oyer, and went to trial, on *non est factum*, where the objection was taken, for the variance; but the circuit judge reserved the point, and the verdict being for the plaintiff, this with other points was put into a case with a view to move for a new trial; and, on motion, before the case was argued, it not appearing that the defendant had been misled by the form of declaring, the plaintiff was allowed to amend, by adapting his declaration to the fact.

Citation—18 Johns., 510, 512.

DEBT on bond, from which the seals had been torn off by mistake. The plaintiff's bond in the declaration; and served a copy of attorney inadvertently made profert of the the bond on the defendant's attorney, thus treating it as a perfect bond; and he went to trial on the plea of *non est factum*. At the trial, before *Judge* Walworth, at the last Montgomery Circuit, the defendant's counsel objected that the bond being without the original seals was not evidence under the declaration; that the plaintiff, instead of making profert, should have excused himself from doing this, upon the circumstances, and have shown the excuse by the declaration. The judge refused to nonsuit the plaintiff on the ground that the profert was mere matter of form, and might be amended on application to the Supreme Court; and he permitted the plaintiff to show in evidence how the seal was torn off. This being done, a verdict was found for the plaintiff. The defendant made a case containing this and other points, upon which he purposed to move for a new trial.

Mr. M. T. Reynolds, for the plaintiff, now moved to amend, by adapting the declaration to the case made in evidence; and he relied mainly on *Sargent* v. *Dennison*, 2 Cow., 515.

Mr. A. Conkling, contra, said this was the common case of a mistake in the form of declaring. The attorney supposed this to be the correct mode. The objection was taken upon the trial, and overruled by the judge upon a speculation of what the Supreme Court would do upon a motion to amend. A case is made, and it is a very clear one upon this point, and presents a verdict, in other respects, not only against law, but against evidence. Take the case of fraud, and no *scienter* alleged in declaring; yet the judge admits evidence to show the *scienter* upon the ground which he took here; would the court allow the plaintiff's attorney **125***] to amend? We *have no objection to the amendment, if it be on the terms of giving us a new trial.

SUTHERLAND, *J.* Suppose this the only point in your case, upon which we should grant you a new trial, clearly the plaintiff might then move to amend, before going down to a second trial.

Mr. Conkling cited *Paine* v. *Bustin*, 1 Stark., 74, which he said was in point against the motion.

Mr. Reynolds, in reply, said it was not proper here to speak of the merits. As to form, he certainly did not ask the court to go so far as they had done in *Sargent* v. *Dennison*. If he had averred the loss, he need not even have given a copy of the bond; so that the mistake was a benefit to the defendant. Giving over entitled him to a copy, and he had it. The whole is a mere quibble about form. There is no pretense of the defendant being misled. To entitle him to a new trial, he should show an injury; not a possibility of one.

SUTHERLAND, *J.* May we not allow you the amendment on the argument of the case? Will it not be the same thing to you if allowed then? The proceedings must probably be stayed till that time.

Mr. Reynolds. It will not be the same thing; because the parties there cannot be put to show, on affidavit, whether the defendant was misled by the omission. We may there hear it urged that he was injured; and perhaps this will be intended in the absence of explanation. We here call on him to show the injury; and he has a chance to speak. Besides, if we amend, it is on payment of costs; and they will go on increasing, to the argument of the case.

WOODWORTH, *J.* Here could not possibly have been any surprise upon the defendant; and I think you are entitled to amend.

126*] *SAVAGE, *Ch. J.*, was also inclined to grant the amendment without further examination; but,

Mr. Conkling expressing himself with considerable confidence that the court would find, on looking into the subject, that they had not yet gone so far, they took the papers and delayed deciding the motion for the present; but at another day,

The Court said that they had examined the cases. The old authorities were very strict, but had been entirely disregarded of late. They thought that not only the case cited by the plaintiff's counsel would bear out this amendment; but the rule laid down in *Lyon* v. *Burtis*, 18 Johns., 510, 512, would fully justify it.

Motion granted.(a)

Cited in—6 Cow., 631; 20 Wend., 670; 10 Paige, 112.

(a) *Vide* 2 Archb. Pr., 235-6.

THE PRESIDENT, &c., OF THE BANK OF CHENANGO, v. ROOT AND KEELER.

Attorney Sued with Another—Practice—Joint Indorsers—Whether Notice to Both Necessary to Charge Either.

An attorney, sued with a common person, is not entitled to be served with the papers in the cause, if he give no notice of defending.

Whether two joint indorsers not partners, must both have notice in order to charge either, *quære*.

The court intimated strongly that they must, but the point was not finally decided.

THE defendant, Root, an attorney, being sued with another by *capias* the plaintiff had proceeded to judgment against him, as a common person, by filing the declaration, and affixing notices, &c., in the clerk's office, &c. He had given no notice of appearance to the plaintiff's attorney, either in his own name, or that of any other attorney, nor that he should defend the cause. On this state of facts, the defendant had given notice of a non-enumerated motion to set aside the default of irregularity. The affidavits in opposition to the motion gave the same history, and went on to detail other particulars, viz.: that the action was against Root and Keeler as indorsers of a promissory note made payable to them jointly, and indorsed with their hands and names respectively. Root had received a regular notice as indorser; but Keeler had not; in consequence of which a verdict had been found for him. A rule for judgment by default, &c., had been entered against Root.

*Mr. Talcott, Atty-Gen., moved to [***127** set aside the proceedings for irregularity.

The first ground he took was, that the papers should have been served on Root in the same manner as upon an attorney retained in the cause, and he cited *Brown* v. *Childs*, 17 Johns., 1.

Mr. J. A. Collier, contra, said the rule did not apply to an attorney sued with others. It never prevailed even in England, where an attorney's privilege is much greater than here.

SUTHERLAND, *J.* We have decided to the same effect, over and over again.

WOODWORTH, *J.* The being joined with common person, as defendant in the same process, takes away the attorney's privilege. This we have often decided. *Gay* v. *Rogers*, 3 Cow., 368.

Mr. Talcott. This is true as to the service of the writ; but I am not aware that the rule has been extended to the service of subsequent papers. This does not depend on the common law, but on the practice of the court.

He next took the ground that here could be no judgment for the plaintiff, upon the whole record. The contract of the defendants was joint; and a verdict for one is equivalent to a verdict for both. The note was payable to them jointly, and their indorsement was, in its very nature, joint. The plaintiff must succeed against all or none, the contract being entire. (Tidd Pract., 803-4, and the cases there cited.)

Mr. Collier said this point could not be raised on a non-enumerated motion. If the defendant relies upon the proceedings at the circuit, he should bring up the matter by a motion in arrest, or at any rate wait till the coming in of the *postea*. But,

The Court said that they would hear the motion on its merits, and consider of the preliminary point.

128*] *WOODWORTH, *J.*, said it came to the simple question, whether you can maintain an action against one of two joint indorsers, if notice be not given to the other.

Mr. Collier. Root cannot complain of a judgment against him. He received notice, and was duly charged as indorser. The condition of his indorsement was, "give *me* notice."

WOODWORTH, *J.* "Give *us* notice."

Mr. Collier. I put the case of a second indorser. He cannot complain that no notice was given to the first.

SUTHERLAND, *J.* Your case is of several indorsements. Would the property of this note have passed by the separate indorsement of either Root or Keeler?

Mr. Collier. It would not.

SUTHERLAND, *J.* Does not this show a joint notice necessary?

Mr. Collier. I think not.

WOODWORTH, *J.* Each of the defendants stands upon the joint rights of both.

SUTHERLAND, *J.* Like joint obligors in a bond. If one be discharged, you cannot go against the other.

WOODWORTH, *J.* If you are right, then you should have had a verdict and judgment against Keeler. The notice to Root would have been sufficient for both.

The Atty-Gen. said that *Carrick* v. *Vickery*, 2 Doug., 653, *note*, had been overruled.

At another day,

The Court said they were clear that the defendant Root, having given no notice that he would appear and defend the cause, and being joined with others, might be treated as a common person. As to the other branch of the

129*] motion, they *thought it true, as a general proposition, that a notice to one of two joint indorsers, they not being partners, would not affect the other; but they would not now decide the point. The facts on which that objection was grounded, principally came out in the plaintiff's affidavits, who was probably not anticipating the ground now taken; and there might be circumstances to take the case out of the general rule. If there were any such he should have a fair opportunity to show them. Besides, all the facts appear of record, and the defendant might, and perhaps properly should, have brought up the matter by way of motion in arrest of judgment. They denied the motion, but without costs.

Motion denied.

Cited in—1 Wend., 33.

RAYMOND *v.* MERCHANT.

Writ of Error—Bail—Judgment for Costs Only.

The Act Concerning Writs of Error (1 R. L., 143, sec. 2), which requires the plaintiff in error to give bail for the debt or damages and costs, extends to a judgment for the defendant, for costs only.

Citations—1 B. & P., 249; 1 Cow., 15, 18, 21.

JUDGMENT being for the defendant on demurrer, *vide*, S. C., 3 Cow., 147, he had taken out of the Register's office in chancery, a writ of error, and filed it with the clerk of this court, but had not put in bail in error. The defendant had, therefore, disregarded the writ of error, sued out a *fi. fa.* which had been returned *nulla bona*, and now,

Mr. I. Hamilton moved for leave to prosecute the bond which the plaintiff had given with sureties to pay the defendant's costs, the plaintiff being a non-resident of the State. He said that, as no bail had been put in, the writ of error did not interrupt his proceedings, to collect the judgment, in any way.

Mr. S. A. Foot, contra, moved to set aside the *fi. fa.* for irregularity. He said that at common law, the writ of error was, in itself, a stay of proceedings; and operated as a *supersedeas* to the execution at any time before it was executed. *But being frequently [*130 brought for the mere purpose of delay, the Statute (1 R. L., 143, sec. 2) was passed, providing that no execution, in any personal action, should be a stay unless the plaintiff in error gave bail. Although this section is general, that execution shall not be stayed in any personal action, yet when the same section comes to speak of the terms in which the bail is to be given, it is evident that it can apply to cases only in which judgment is for the plaintiff in the court below. The condition of the recognizance is, to prosecute the writ of error to effect; "and also to pay and satisfy, if such judgment shall be affirmed, the debt or damages and costs, to be adjudged upon such judgment, and all costs and damages to be awarded for the delay of execution." The Statute then goes on, in a distinct section (sec. 3), to provide for error in dower and ejectment. As to these cases, the introductory part of the section is equally general, and would seem to require bail in all cases, be the judgment for or against the plaintiff; but when it comes to speak of the recognizance of bail, we find it conditioned to pay costs and damages; and in order to ascertain these damages, the court are to award a writ of inquiry. So it is evident that both these sections can apply only to writs of error, brought to reverse judgments for the plaintiff. They are unqualified that a recognizance must be given in language which would be inapplicable to a judgment for the defendant. In personal actions, the object was to prevent delay in collecting the debt or damages—in dower and ejectment, to avoid delay in obtaining possession of the thing in dispute. The Legislature never counted the delay anything as to a mere bill of costs; and the same view seems to be taken of the subject by the books of practice. They have not given directions for a recognizance of bail, where mere costs are concerned. Though the sections in question set out with general words, these are clearly restrained, not only by the terms in which the recognizance is required to be given, but by the nature of the subject and the evil to be avoided. I find no trace of any proceeding to give bail in a case like this, either in the English or American books.

Mr. Hamilton, in reply. All the [*131 reasoning upon the other side is confined to a mere criticism upon the terms of the recognizance. The words of the Statute are admitted to be general and peremptory, clearly embracing this case. The whole should be taken together, and all the court have to do is to construe the words "debt or damages and costs" disjunctively, as to the costs, when the judgment is for these only; and the Statute has its full effect. The first part of the section should control. The mere costs of a defense may be larger in amount than the debt or damages which a plaintiff may recover. The evil of delay is, therefore, the same in both cases, and no distinction I believe, has ever been made, in practice, by the profession. But the word "damages" includes "costs," and so the court have frequently holden. Our Statute of Dockets (1 R. L., 501, sec. 3), requires the clerk to docket all judgments for debt or damages, under which the practice has always been to docket judgments for costs only. The 8th section of the same Statute (1 R. L., 502) contemplates a judgment for costs being so perfected as to be a lien on lands. The two sections are considered together, with the intent and object of the Statute. So it should be here. That the court frequently consider costs as damages, is a familiar proposition, in support of which no case need be adduced. The recognizance is not only for the damages, &c., below, but for the costs on error. Is a party to be deprived of all security for these also?

Cur. adv. vult.

Curia. We find no decision applicable to this question; and it must, therefore, depend upon the meaning of the Statute to be gathered from its language and object. Its language is general, and embraces writs of error which are prosecuted upon a judgment in any personal action. It is supposed that the condition which the Statute requires to be inserted in the recognizance, that the plaintiff in error shall pay the debt or damages and costs, restricts its meaning to those cases only where the judgment upon which the writ of error is brought shall be for the plaintiff below; or at any rate for something besides costs, as the wording would be partially inapplicable to a **132***] *judgment for costs merely. In fixing the form, the Legislature probably had an immediate eye to the common case of a debt or damages and costs; but their intention, as indicated at the beginning of the section, cannot have full effect, without a construction which reaches the present case. There certainly can be no good reason why bail should be required where nominal damages with costs are given; and yet should be denied for costs alone. The latter case is equally within the mischief intended to be remedied; and the Act should be construed liberally with a view to suppress the mischief. *Ablett* v. *Ellis*, 1 Bos. & P., 249, per Eyre, *Ch. J.*, and Buller, *J.*, acc.

The question, however, is novel, and the recognizance was omitted upon the belief that it was not necessary. The motion of the plaintiff is to set aside the *fi. fa.*; that of the defendant, to prosecute the security heretofore given. Strictly, the defendant's motion should be granted and the plaintiff's denied; but, under the circumstances of the case, the plaintiff may take a rule that both motions be denied on the plaintiff's filing, within 20 days, a proper recognizance to prosecute the writ of error; and on payment of all the costs of both motions. If the costs be not paid, the defendant may enter his rule to prosecute.

We do not mean by this indulgence to be understood as innovating at all upon the ordinary rule, limiting the time of putting in bail on error. *Vide Blunt* v. *Greenwood*, 1 Cow., 15, 18, 21. We depart from it in this instance, only upon the peculiar circumstances presented by the case.

Rule accordingly.

---

*EX PARTE STEVENS. [*133

Several Judgment Liens on Same Land—Sale of Land on Execution on one Judgment for Less than Amount of Judgment, Extinguishes Lien of that Judgment—Subsequent Sale on Execution on Senior Judgment—Junior Judgment Creditors, no Right to Redeem More than Fifteen Months After First Sale—Who Entitled to Conveyance from Sheriff.

A sale of land upon a judgment and execution, though for only a part of what is due upon the judgment, with the lapse of fifteen months from the time of sale, and a conveyance by the sheriff, destroys the lien of the judgment, even for the balance remaining due; and the judgment creditor for the balance cannot, therefore, redeem the land from a purchaser under a senior judgment, within the Stat., sess. 43, ch. 184, sec. 3.

Such a sale and conveyance, also, destroys the lien of all junior judgment creditors; so that they cannot redeem from a purchaser under any judgment older than the one upon which the conveyance is made.

Thus, where M. had judgment, then C., and then S., all against F., which bound his land: C. sold the land for part of his judgment; then M. sold; C. waited 15 months from his (C.'s) sale, and took a conveyance, and then, within 15 months from the time of M.'s sale, paid M his bid, &c., and claimed to redeem as creditor for his (C.'s) balance; and S., also in proper time, paid M.'s bid, &c., and claimed to redeem: held, that both C.'s lien for his balance, and S.'s lien by judgment, were devested by the sale and conveyance on C.'s judgment; and that neither could redeem.

Citation—8 Johns., 333.

MR. J. R. LAWRENCE (*Mr. I. Hamilton* same side) moved for a *mandamus*, commanding Jonas Earll, Jr., Esq., late Sheriff of the County of Onondaga, to convey certain premises to Robert Stevens.

The facts agreed upon by the counsel for the parties interested were as follows: Mar. 23, 1822, all the right and title of Henry Field to lot No. 46, in Camillus, Onondaga Co., was sold by Hezekiah L. Granger, Esq., then sheriff of that county, under a *fi. fa.* issued on a judgment in the Supreme Court, in favor of George Leitch, deceased, against Field and one Brackett, for $1,843.54, docketed Oct. 20, 1819, and bid off by Nathan Gorham at $1,000, of which a certificate was made and filed pursuant to the statute. Gorham gave his note for the bid to Cumpston, the administrator of Leitch, payable in 6 years, with interest. Before the payment of the note, Cumpston discovered that Nathan Munro was the owner of two judgments against Field, older than Leitch's, which were a lien on the premises sold; and Cumpston deducted the amount of these judgments from the note (the balance of which was paid by H. & J. Dodge's bond and mortgage). These two senior judgments were in the C. P. of Onondaga Co.; one in favor of the trustees of the town of Camillus against Field and one Clark, for $106.37, docketed Nov. 25, 1817; and the other in favor of Anthouy Johnson and others against Field, for $137.24, docketed Dec. 10, 1817. July 3, 1823, Jonas Earll, Jr., late Sheriff of the County of Onondaga, under two writs of *fi. fa.* issued **134***] upon these judgments, *sold the same premises to Nathan Munro for $84.70, being the balance due on both judgments, of which he was the assignee and owner, and of which sale a certificate was given according to the statute. Sept. 6, 1823 (no redemption having been made upon the first sale), Gorham took a deed from Granger as sheriff; and Dec. 19, 1823, conveyed the premises by deed of quit-claim, to H. and J. Dodge, for the consideration of the sum due on the note to Cumpston, deducting Munro's bid; and the Dodges paid the balance due on the note, by their bond and mortgage upon these and other premises. July 24, 1824, Cumpston, the administrator of Leitch, with money furnished by the Dodges, and for their sole benefit, paid to Munro the amount of his bid, $84.70, with 10 *per cent.* interest from the day of sale, claiming to redeem as a judgment creditor, in order to perfect the title of the Dodges; and Oct. 2, 1824, Robert Stevens, as assignee of another judgment in the Onondaga C. P., in favor of Jacob Campbell against Field, docketed Aug. 28, 1820, paid to Jonas Earll, Jr., the sheriff who sold to Munro, the amount of Munro's bid, with 10 *per cent.* interest from the day of sale, which money still remains in the hands of the sheriff, and claimed to redeem the premises from Munro as a judgment creditor of Field. Earll, however, refused to convey to any person unless upon the order of the Supreme Court.

It was agreed by the counsel that a *mandamus* should issue, commanding the sheriff to convey to such of the claimants as, upon the above state of facts, they should think entitled.

Messrs. Lawrence and *Hamilton*, for Stevens, made the following question: Can a plaintiff redeem as a judgment creditor, after having sold the land which he seeks to redeem, upon the judgment in virtue of which he seeks to redeem? *i. e.*, is the balance of the judgment, over the amount bid, a lien on the lands sold, so as to enable the plaintiff to redeem? They contended that it was not; and if so, Cumpston was not entitled to the deed. The sale extinguished all further lien of the judgment upon the premises sold under it. To this, the **135***] *case of *Hewson* v. *Daygert*, 8 Johns., 333, is express. The court say that the sale of land on the first installment of a judgment, extinguished the lien of the judgment, as to that land. (*Id.*, 334.) Having no lien, there is an end of the question; for without this, he could not redeem. *Erwin* v. *Schriver*, 19 Johns., 379; *Marsh* v. *Wendover*, 3 Cow., 69; *Hurd* v. *Magee*, *Id.*, 35; *Dickenson* v. *Gilliland*, 1 Cow., 481. It is reasonable that this should be as we contend; for if the balance still remain a lien, no one would be safe in purchasing at a sheriff's sale. The owner could sell the land a second time; and if a second, then as many times as be pleased, on repeated balances, till his judgment was satisfied, though the property might be of trifling amount. The sale to Gorham was subject to Munro's judgments, which were deducted when he came to pay his bid. The sale to him is, therefore, entitled to no peculiar favor. It is his neglect that he did not pay up these judgments; or he might have redeemed as grantee, within the year.

No attempt being made by Gorham or the Dodges to redeem as grantees within the year, their right also fails. *Van Rensselaer* v. *Sheriff of Onondaga*, 1 Cow., 443.

Then the right of Cumpston, Leith's administrator, being out of the way, as also that of the grantees, Stevens' right was complete; and the sheriff should be commanded to convey to him.

Messrs. H. F. Mather and *D. Kellogg*, contra, contended that Cumpston's lien remained, notwithstanding the sale upon his judgment. At any rate, after the sale to him, and the conveyance in pursuance of it, all the lien which Stevens had upon his judgment was taken away. The argument, therefore, that without a lien no one can redeem, will, at least, affect Cumpston and Stevens equally. And if Cumpston's judgment is gone for the purpose of lien, Munro is entitled to the deed. Stevens does not come within any of the provisions of the statute. Cumpston's judgment was older than his; and the sale and conveyance upon it clearly ousted Stevens of all lien. Thus, the rights of Cumpston and Stevens both fail.

*WOODWORTH, *J.*, who delivered [***136** the opinion of the court, spoke to this effect:

The two judgments which belong to Munro were docketed in 1817; another, belonging to Cumpston, was docketed in 1819, and another, belonging to Stevens, in 1820; all being against Field, who owned the premises in question at the time of docketing. On Cumpston's judgment, the sheriff sold these premises to Gorham Mar. 23, 1822; and after the expiration of the 15 months executed a conveyance (Sept. 6, 1823). The bid of Gorham not amounting to the sum due on Cumpston's judgment, he still remained a judgment creditor of Field. July 22, 1823, before the deed of conveyance was due to Gorham, Munro purchased the premises, upon his judgments, and took a certificate of sale. July 24, 1824, Cumpston claimed, as judgment creditor for his balance, to redeem of Munro, and paid to him the requisite sum; and Oct. 2, 1824, Stevens, claiming to redeem upon his judgment, paid the proper sum to the sheriff, for Munro's use. This offer of Stevens to redeem was after the 15 months from Gorham's purchase had elapsed, but within 15 months from the sale to Munro, so that Stevens came in season to redeem of Munro, provided his judgment was a lien; and Cumpston was also clearly in time, if his balance was a lien. Their respective rights depend entirely upon this question of lien. If they show no right of lien, we have repeatedly decided that they cannot redeem, however meritorious their pretentions may be in other respects.

First, then, as to Cumpston. His lien is clearly gone. His judgment was once a lien, and continued so for 15 months after the sale to Gorham; but after the lapse of that time, it ceased to be so. A deed was executed to the purchaser, who took all the right which a sale and conveyance upon the judgment could give. This right was complete as to that judgment; and took from it all lien. In principle, it is the case of *Hewson* v. *Daygert*, cited by the counsel for Stevens. The court decided, in terms, that after a sale upon the first installment of the judgment, the lien of the other installments was gone. Unless this were so, the most man- **137***] ifest *injustice to the purchaser might intervene. Both upon principle and authority, we are bound to hold that Cumpston's balance was not a lien, when he made the effort to redeem.

Then had Stevens a right to redeem? He comes as a junior judgment creditor; his judgment was a lien when the sale was made to Gorham; but he neglected to redeem. The 15 months elapsed after Gorham's purchase upon a judgment senior to Stevens'. A perfect title passed to Gorham, by which all junior liens were subverted. Stevens should have redeemed of Gorham. Not having done so, he is concluded. His lien is gone, and was so when he came to redeem of Munro.

But Cumpston paid the money directly to Munro. Whether his acceptance of the amount gives Cumpston an equitable right, it is not necessary to decide. The remedy upon this ground, if any, belongs to another forum.

Neither Cumpston nor Stevens are entitled to a conveyance. We think the sheriff should convey to Munro.

Rule accordingly.

Cited in—5 Hill, 229; 1 Den., 635 (*n.*); 4 Den., 139; 1 Barb., 388, 578; 3 Barb., 72; 4 Barb., 126; 29 Mich., 139.

Ex PARTE THE OVERSEERS OF THE POOR OF THE TOWN OF GATES, in the County of MONROE.

Pauper—When County Chargeable with Maintenance of.

The county cannot be charged with the maintenance of a pauper, under the 25th section of the Act for the Relief and Settlement of the Poor (1 R. L., 279), without a previous adjudication by two justices, pursuant to the 7th section of the same Act, that the pauper has no settlement in this State.

Citations—1 R. L., 280, 284, 287, secs. 7, 16, 25; Stat., sess. 40, ch. 177, sec. 3; 7 Johns., 89; 1 Cow., 205; 8 Johns., 323.

AT a previous term a rule had been obtained to show cause why a *mandamus* should not issue to the Supervisors of the County of Monroe, commanding them to audit and allow to the Overseers of the Town of Gates, in that county, the expenses which they had paid towards the maintenance of certain transient paupers having no residence in this State.

On showing cause it appeared that the account being presented to the Board of Super- **138***] visors, they referred the matter *to a committee, who called on the two justices who made the several orders of maintenance upon which the disbursements claimed by the Overseers had been incurred, and ascertained that there had been no attempt towards an adjudication concerning the last legal settlement of any of the paupers by two justices, pursuant to the 7th section of the "Act for the Relief and Settlement of the Poor," passed Apr. 8, 1813. That no more had been done, in any case, than for the single magistrate to whom the application was made, and before whom the pauper had been brought, to examine him on oath concerning his last place of residence or settlement, and his circumstances; that in several cases no examination whatever was made, on oath, as to the settlement or circumstances of the pauper; and that in one case the justice adjudged the pauper to have no legal settlement in this State from the brogue or accent of his tongue, without any further examination.

The Board rejected the accounts on two grounds: 1. That an adjudication by two justices was necessary. 2. That if not, there should, at least, be an examination on oath, by the single magistrate, which there had not been in several of these cases.

Mr. I. Hills. The counsel for the Supervisors, on showing cause, requested the court to review what they had said on granting an alternative *mandamus*, in *Ex parte Dow*, 1 Cow., 205, and insisted that, although in *Adams* v. *Supervisors of Col.*, on which the court in *Dow's* case relied as authority, no adjudication was made by two justices, yet the point was not distinctly raised by counsel, nor was this circumstance expressly adverted to by the court. He insisted that there was the same reason for requiring an adjudication of two magistrates, in order to charge the county, under the 25th section of the "Act for the Relief and Settlement of the Poor" (1 R. L., 287), as to charge a town within this State under the 16th section. In neither case did the statute expressly require an adjudication of two justices; but to warrant a proceeding upon the 16th section it has been holden necessary. *Voorhis* v. *Whipple*, *7 Johns., [***139** 89. The counsel contended that the principle of that case was applicable to a proceeding against the county, upon the 25th section, to which the same practice should, therefore, be extended.

Cur. adv. vult.

WOODWORTH, *J.*, delivered the opinion of the court to the following effect:

In determining the question raised, he said, it is necessary to look at the provisions of three several sections of the "Act for the Relief and Settlement of the Poor," viz.: the 7th, 16th and 25th (1 R. L., 280, 284, 287). The 7th section provides that if any overseer of the poor shall have reason to believe that any stranger is likely to become chargeable to his town, he shall apply to two justices, who shall examine the stranger and others, on oath, relating not only to the abilities, but the last place of his legal settlement, with a view to his removal. That section also contemplates an inquiry, by the justices, whether the pauper be settled in this State or not; for if he have no settlement, and came in by way of the City of N. Y., he may be sent to that city. A subsequent Statute (sess. 40, ch. 177, sec. 3) also provides that paupers coming into this State after the passage of that Act, having gained no settlement here, may, on a similar examination, be transported out of the State. These removals must, in all cases, be preceded by an adjudication as to the place of settle-

ment, either in this State or out of it. The 16th section provides that if the pauper come from one town in this State to reside in another town in this State, where he is taken so sick, &c., that he cannot conveniently be removed, the overseers of the town where he is taken sick shall give notice of this fact to the overseers of the town where he is settled, &c., and request them to maintain him, &c.; and if they do not do it, the expense of maintenance may be summarily collected of them by a warrant of distress, to be issued by two magistrates. This section, in itself, contains no provision that an adjudication of settlement shall be made before the warrant for a distress goes. But in *Voorhis* v. *Whipple*, 7 Johns., 89, this court held that it presupposed the
140*] pauper's *last place of legal settlement to have been ascertained according to the provisions of the 7th section; and to give the 16th section any other construction would lead to great abuse and oppression. Then comes the 25th section. This provides that when any pauper belonging to any city or town in this State shall apply for relief, an overseer of the poor and a justice shall inquire into his state and circumstances, and if it appears that he requires relief, the justice shall give to the overseer a written order for a weekly or other allowance. And further, the overseer and justice are to proceed in the same manner in relation to a pauper not having any settlement in the State, with this addition—that if they find the pauper so sick, &c., as not to be removable, or when it shall be impossible to make any order of removal, the money expended upon the order for relief shall be a charge upon the county, to be allowed by the Board of Supervisors. Upon an examination and order for relief, under this section, not accompanied by any adjudication of settlement by two justices, the Supervisors of Monroe were moved to allow the accounts in question. To this they demurred; appointed a committee of examination, who found that what had been done by way of inquiry as to settlement had been conducted in a very informal and careless manner. In several cases no oath was administered, and in one the brogue or accent of the pauper's tongue was made the sole test of his residence.

On the whole, upon a careful examination of the several sections mentioned, we are satisfied that the case of *Voorhis* v. *Whipple* extends, in principle, to the present case. That was an attempt to charge a neighboring town in this State with the maintenance of a pauper settled there, but who could not be removed. For this purpose the warrant of distress, mentioned in the 16th section, was issued without a previous adjudication of two magistrates; and on the question coming up on *certiorari*, the court say: "The inducement to the enacting of the 16th section of the Act for the Settlement and Relief of the Poor was to relieve the town where a pauper happened to be taken sick or lame, so as not to be able to be
141*] removed back to the place of his *last legal settlement; but in providing for this summary relief to the town actually burdened with the pauper, it presupposes that the place of his last legal settlement has been ascertained, according to the provisions of the 7th section, to wit: by an order of two justices, making an adjudication upon the fact, after having themselves examined the pauper on oath. To give the 16th section any other construction would lead to great abuse and oppression. Towns might be charged, if the manner of proceeding in this case be sanctioned, with the payment of large sums of money unjustly, and without the examination of the pauper himself, which is essentially requisite to find out his last legal settlement." Much of this reasoning applies to the principal case, which depends upon construction. It is admitted that there is no express statutory provision on the subject, but the several sections in question should be so construed as not to work injustice. At best, the examination must be *ex parte* in the first instance. The trial, in one case, is upon a question of right between two towns; in the other, between a town and the county. The same solemnities should be adhered to in both cases. The powers of the single magistrate and overseer relate merely to the circumstances of the pauper, and the impropriety or impossibility of removing him. In *Dow's* case, 1 Cow., 205, we were moved for a *mandamus* upon the ground taken here. There had been a literal compliance with the terms of the 25th section, in the same manner as there appeared to have been in the previous case of *Adams* v. *Supervisors of Col.*, 8 Johns., 323, and without entering into the subject at large, we granted an alternative *mandamus*. On more mature reflection we are satisfied that the impression we then entertained on the subject was wrong; and that a county cannot be charged under the 25th section, except by an adjudication of two justices that the pauper has no settlement in this State, made pursuant to the 7th section. The rule to show cause must, therefore, be discharged.

Rule discharged.

Cited in—5 Cow., 653; 7 Cow., 221; 1 Wend., 501; 2 Wend., 292.

---

*DAVIS *v.* ADAMS. [*142

Pleading and Practice.

A plea will not be set aside as frivolous merely because the court have held one precisely like it, bad on demurrer, or on motion for judgment *non obstante veredicto*.

Nor can the plaintiff treat it as a nullity, and enter a rule, of course, for judgment, as by default, or confession by *nil dicit*.

The defendant has a right to retain it on the record, and have it passed upon, with a view to bring a writ of error.

But under the special circumstances of the case, the court allowed the plaintiff, on the subject coming up on a non-enumerated motion, to enter judgment as upon a demurrer and joinder.

Citation—2 Cow., 626.

ASSUMPSIT on two promissory notes, made at Alexandria, in the District of Columbia. The defendant had pleaded the same plea as he had done in the cause of *Whittemore* v. *Adams*, 2 Cow., 626. At first, the plaintiff demurred and the defendant joined in demurrer; but on seeing the report of the first case, the plaintiff at the last term, by S. M. Hopkins, his counsel, moved to set aside the plea as frivolous, which I opposed for the defendant, and the motion was denied by the court; but they allowed Hopkins to withdraw his demurrer, which he did; and thereupon the plaintiff treated the plea as a nullity, and immediately entered a rule of course for judgment of *nil dicit.* This I moved to set aside as irregular, upon an affidavit that the plea was put in in good faith; and that the attorney desired to retain it upon the record with a view that he might bring a writ of error, which motion was opposed by Mr. Hopkins, but granted with costs; whereupon the plaintiff treated the plea as a confession of the action by *nil dicit* and entered a rule for judgment generally; and that the clerk assess damages. At the present term I moved to set aside this last rule for irregularity, which was opposed by Mr. Hopkins.

Curia. The plaintiff should either have retained his demurrer, and gone to argument upon the calendar, or confessed the defendant's plea, taking a judgment, to be levied of his goods and chattels; or have taken issue, suffered a verdict for the defendant, and then moved for judgment *non obstante veredicto,* as was done in *Whittemore* v. *Adams.* The defendant is entitled to retain his plea upon the record, and have it passed upon by the court, with a view to his writ of error. The rule for judgment must be set aside, with costs; but under the special circumstances of this case, the plaintiff may enter up judgment as upon the demurrer and joinder heretofore interposed in the cause.

Rule accordingly

Cited in—5 How. Pr., 249; 3 Co. R., 242.

143*] *HAYES *v.* BAYLEY.

Practice—Costs.

Where the plaintiff recovers, in the Supreme Court, a sum which carries C. P. costs only, he is not allowed counsel fees, at the Supreme Court rate.

Semb., he cannot be allowed counsel fees, as such, for any service of counsel there being no rate fixed for the service of counsel in the C. P.

Citation—1 Cow., 170.

AFTER the retaxation ordered, *ante*, p. 42, in this cause, the plaintiff's attorney retaxed his costs; and the commissioner allowed the plaintiff a counsel fee of $3.75, being at the Supreme Court rate, on opposing the motion to set aside the report of referees; though the costs properly allowable in the cause were C. P. costs only. This the plaintiff claimed on the authority of *Alcott* v. *Phelps*, 1 Cow., 170; contending that though there was no counsel fee allowed in the C P., yet it should be allowed here; and that it must be at the Supreme Court rate, as none was established in the C. P.

A motion was now again made for a retaxation.

Mr. B. Whiting, for the motion.

Messrs. D. Beecher and *J. A. Spencer*, contra.

Curia. We said in *Alcott* v. P*helps* that the plaintiff might charge for all necessary services, on a recovery of less than $250, at the C. P. rate, and we allowed a *nisi prius* record; but there is no rate established in that court for a counsel fee. It by no means follows from this, that the plaintiff is entitled to its allowance, and that too, at the Supreme Court rate. It is a service entirely unknown to the C. P., and to which there is no rate in that court applicable. The counsel fee must be stricken out.

Rule accordingly.

THE PEOPLE
v.
ROSSITER, Gentleman, one, &c.

Discharge, under Insolvent Act—People not Bound by.

A discharge under the Act to Abolish Imprisonment for Debt, &c. (sess. 42, ch. 101), does not extend to a debt due the people of this State.

Nor, *semb.*, does any insolvent or bankrupt law, unless the people are named in it.

JUDGMENT was obtained against the defendant, an attorney of this court, for clerk's fees due to the plaintiffs, under a *ca.* *sa.*, upon which judgment he was im- [*144 prisoned, after he had obtained his discharge under the Act to Abolish Imprisonment for Debt in Certain Cases. (Sess. 42, ch. 101.) The assignment was executed after the debt arose; and now, on an affidavit showing these facts,

Mr. J. R. Lawrence moved that he be discharged. He relied on the broad and unqualified words of the 3d section—that the debtor shall be exempt from imprisonment, for or by reason of any debt or debts, due at the time of making the assignment, &c. Here is no exception, he said, of debts due to the people; and none should be implied.

Mr. Talcott, Atty-Gen., contra, said that general words would not bind the people. They are not named; and the rule as to them, under this Act, is the same which prevails as to the King, under the English Bankrupt Laws. He is not bound, because not named.

Curia. The motion must be denied. The people are not bound by an Act of this kind, unless they are named in it. The rule is the same as in England. The King is not bound by a Bankrupt Law unless named (*a*); and the people are the King for the purposes of this rule.

Motion denied.

Cited in—19 Wall., 239; Crabbie, 316, 30 N. J. E., 684.

(*a*) Anonymous, 1 Atk., 262; Rex v. Pixley, Bunb. 202. This question is fully examined in reference to the Statute of Limitations by *Mr. Justice* Story in U. S. v. Hoar, 2 Mas., 311-12, &c., and *vide* U. S. v. Wilson, 8 Wh., 253, that a state insolvent law shall not bind the U. S.

NOTE.—*Bankrupt and Insolvent Laws—Discharge under—Government not bound by unless specially named in Act.* See People v. Herkimer, 4 Cow., 345; Commonwealth v. Hutchinson, 10 Pa. St., 466; United States v. Herron, 20 Wall., 251 (full discussion per Clifford J.).

A fine imposed for violation of an injunction is not released by discharge under the bankruptcy law. Spalding v. State of N. Y., 4 How., 21; Spalding v. People, 7 Hill, 301.

Statutes of Limitation—Whether binding on government. See People v. Gilbert, 18 Johns., 227, *note.*

FULLER v. ROOSEVELT.

Amendment of Bill of Particulars.

After a cause is at issue, and noticed for trial three times, a judge at chambers has no power to allow an amendment to the plaintiff's bill of particulars. This power belongs to the court, exclusively.

AFTER this cause had been noticed for trial a third time, and pending the circuit for which it was last noticed, the plaintiff discovered that it was necessary for him to amend his bill of particulars by adding new items; and on an affidavit of the circumstances, **145***] he applied to the Recorder of N. *Y. who granted him leave to do this, on paying to the defendant his costs of the (then) circuit. Upon papers showing all the proceedings before the Recorder,

Mr. J. I. Roosevelt, Jr., moved to vacate this order as irregular. He said the Recorder had not power to grant it. This could only be done by the court. A new bill of particulars, substantially varying the ground of action, should be subject to the same rules as to amending, which apply to the introduction of a new count in the declaration. This will not be allowed after two terms from the commencement of the action. *Aubeer* v. *Barker*, 1 Wils., 149. Here have been seven terms. This rule is approved in *Sackett* v *Thompson*, 2 Johns., 206, 207. The amendment was granted in *Heneshoff* v. *Miller*, on the ground that a new cause of action was not introduced. In *Jackson* v. *Murray*, 1 Cow., 156, the court refused to allow the addition of a new demise, on the ground that it introduced a new cause of action, as to which the Statute of Limitations had attached. At any rate, as the amendment introduced new items, not embraced in the first bill, it should not have been granted, without payment of all the costs incurred in the defense after the first bill was delivered.

Mr. S. S. Gardner, contra. This court has made no decision declaring the extent of the power which a judge at chambers has over bills of particulars. In *The King* v. *Wilkes*, 4 Burr., 2527, Ld. Mansfield, the very day before the trial, amended the information. Bills of particulars, though considered a part of the pleadings are not construed with the same strictness; and no evil can result from giving a judge at chambers power over them. If the bill be not sufficiently specific, he may make a second order for a further bill. (1 Cow., 574, *note.*) Why not then grant the plaintiff an order to amend where he has made a mistake? At any rate, the court will now permit the plaintiff to amend, as the facts are fully before them.

Curia. We think the Recorder did not possess the power to allow this amendment. It **146***] was not a chamber power *at this stage of the cause; but belonged to the court. The order must be vacated; but the whole case being now before us, we allow the amendment, on payment of the costs of this motion.

Rule Accordingly.

THE PEOPLE, ex rel. HOLLEY, v. THE SUPERVISORS OF THE COUNTY OF COLUMBIA.

Constable—When Entitled to Fees for Attending Court.

A constable summoned and actually attending court, under the Statute (sess. 42, ch. 27), is entitled to his fees, though he do not actually serve as constable. It is enough that he is attending and ready to serve; and it is no objection to allowing him his fees that he was a deputy-sheriff, and attended court as such.

AN alternative *mandamus* had been issued, and served upon the defendants, commanding them to audit and allow the account of Holley, for his services as a constable in attending the Court of Oyer and Terminer, and the Court of C. P. and General Sessions of the County of Columbia; he having been duly summoned to attend, by the sheriff, and having attended accordingly, pursuant to the Act of the 5th Mar. 1819, sess. 42, ch. 27.

The return stated that Holley was an acting deputy of the sheriff, during all the time for which he claimed pay as constable; that he attended as a deputy not as constable; did not carry a staff, or perform any of the duties, pertaining to the office of a constable. Upon this ground they denied him fees as constable.

Mr. C. Bushell moved for a peremptory *mandamus.*

Mr. T. Bay, contra.

Curia. It is enough that he was summoned, and attending ready to perform his duty as constable, if called on. The Statute is peremptory that he shall have $1.25 a day for travel and attendance.

Rule for peremptory mandamus.

NOTE. A similar rule was made, on similar grounds, in the cause of *The People, ex rel. Waterman*, against the same defendants.

Distinguished—66 N. Y., 595.
Cited in—6 Hun, 93; 64 Barb., 504.

---

*WARNER v. SHAFER. [*147

Practice—Costs.

The attorney for the party who demurs is not entitled to make out, and charge a copy of the demurrer book for himself.

ON *certiorari* to a justice's court. There was a demurrer to the assignment of errors, and judgment for the defendant; and in taxing the costs the commissioner allowed not only a draft of the demurrer book, but a copy for the defendant's attorney. On this ground among others,

Mr. H. Hamilton, for the plaintiff, moved for a retaxation.

Mr. T. Lawyer, contra.

Curia. Here are both a draft of the demurrer book, and a copy for the defendant's attorney charged and allowed; or in other words two copies for himself. This was unnecessary. The draft would have answered him every useful purpose. The charge for the copy is wrong and should be deducted.

Rule accordingly.

Cited in—24 Am. Dec., 638 (4 Vt., 549).

JACKSON *v.* PEER.

Action for Mesne *Profits—Security for Costs.*

Where the section for *mesne* profits is brought in the name of the nominal plaintiff in ejectment, the court will stay proceedings on his part, till security for costs be filed.

Citation—Runnington, 439.

TRESPASS for the *mesne* profits of land recovered in an action of ejectment, brought by Jackson, as nominal plaintiff, on the demise of M. S. and J. A. Freeman, against the defendant. The present action was also in the name of Jackson, the nominal plaintiff in the ejectment.

Mr. J. Houghton, for the defendant, moved that all proceedings on the part of the plaintiff be stayed until security should be given for answering the defendant's costs, and cited Runn. on Ej., 439, and *Frary* v. *Dakin*, 8 Johns., 353.

Mr. A. Dixon, contra.

Curia. It seems, by Runnington, 439, to be the practice of the English courts to require **148***] security for costs, where *the suit for *mesne* profits is brought in the name of the nominal plaintiff. We grant the rule as moved for.

Motion granted.

MANN

v.

GERARDUS Q. CARLEY, sued by the name of GRAUTIS Q. CARLEY, Impleaded with WALTON and DE GROFF.

CHAPIN

v.

GERARDUS Q. CARLEY, who is sued by the name of QUARTUS Q. CARLEY, Impleaded with DE GROFF, WALTON and MEACH.

*Practice—Defendant, Sued by Wrong Name—Appearance—*Capias, *etc., Set Aside for Irregularity—Plea in Abatement.*

Grantis and Gerardus are different names.
So are Quaratus and Gerardus.
A defendant, sued by a wrong name, may plead the misnomer in abatement, after he has appeared and given notice thereof specially.
And in a case where he moved before appearance the court set aside the *capias* and subsequent proceedings for irregularity.
But they refused to do this in a case where the defendant had appeared, though specially.
And they will not hereafter do it in any case—having adopted a general rule, that, hereafter, the misnomer of the defendant shall in all cases be pleaded in abatement.
There are only three ways for the defendant to appear in a cause, viz.: by putting in special bail, filing common bail, or causing his appearance to be entered. Giving notice of retainer is not an appearance.

THE *capias ad respondendum* in the first cause, returnable at the last October Term, was issued against Carley, by the name of Grautius Q. Carley, whereas his real name was Gerardus Q. Carley. The *capias* contained no *ac etiam*, and was served on Carley and Walton. Carley's attorney gave notice of retainer, entitled, "*Gerardus Q. Carley*, who is sued by the name of *Grantis Q. Carley*, impleaded, &c., ads. *John M. Mann.*" A declaration, indorsed *de bene esse*, was delivered to the agent of the defendant's attorney Dec. 13, last. The declaration was against the defendant by his right name, stating that he was sued by the name of Grautis Q. Carley. The notice of this motion was served on Dec. 20, last, with an order to stay proceedings, &c.

At an early day in the present term,

Mr. A. C. Paige for Carley moved to set aside the *capias* and all subsequent proceedings, on the part of the plaintiff in the first cause, for irregularity.

He said it is now well established that proceedings in a cause will be set aside for a misnomer of the defendant, where the application is made before the time for pleading in abatement has expired. *Smith* v. *Innes*, 4 Maule & S., 360; *Wilkes* v. *Lorck*, 2 Taunt., 399; *Greenslade* v. *Rotheroe*, 2 New *Rep., [*149 or 5 Bos. & P., 132; *Doo* v. *Butcher*, 3 T. R., 611; *Corbett* v. *Bates*, *Id.*, 660; *Delanoy* v. *Cannon*, 10 East, 328; *Dring* v. *Dickenson*, 11 East, 225; 1 Dunl. Pr., 236. The case of *Smith* v. *Innes*, 4 Maule & S., 360, was distinguished, by the court, from *Binfield* v. *Maxwell*, 15 East, 159, upon the ground that the motion was not made in the last case, till after the time for pleading in abatement had expired. *Smith* v. *Patten*, 6 Taunt., 115, and *Oakley* v. *Giles*, 3 East, 167, are distinguishable for the same reason. In *Delanoy* v. *Mannon*, 10 East, 328, the same distinction was made. *Murray* v. *Hubbart*, 1 Bos. & P., 645, is not against the motion, as there the defendant appeared, by putting in bail in his right name, without stating that he was sued by the name mentioned in the writ.

That a misnomer may be pleaded in abatement, is well settled. *Oakley* v. *Giles*, 3 East, 167; 1 Chit. Pl., 250; Bac. Abr., Misnomer, F; *Eichorn* v. *Le'maitre*, 2 Wils., 367; *Shadgett* v. *Clipson*, 8 East, 328; *Cole* v. *Hindson*, 6 T. R., 234; *Holdipp* v. *Otway*, cited by Lawrence, *J.*, in *Blackwell* v. *Fleming*, 7 T. R., 443, *note a*; *Smith* v. Patten, 6 Taunt., 115; *Binfield* v. *Maxwell*, 15 East, 159; *Smith* v. *Innes*, 4 Maule & S., 360; *Delanoy* v. *Cannon*, 10 East, 328; *Jones* v. *Macquilan*, 5 T. R., 195; 1 Dunl. Pr., 436; 2 Chit. Pl., 458, 462, 4, 6. And whenever a misnomer can be pleaded in abatement, a motion may now be made to set aside the proceedings for irregularity. *Smith* v. *Innes*, 4 Maule & S., 360–1.

There is clearly a misnomer in this case. Gerardus and Grautis are different names. Shakepear and Shakspeare, *King* v. *Shakspeare*, 10 East, 83; Agnes and Anne, 2 Roll. Abr., 135; Richard James, and James Richard, *Jones* v. *Macquilan*, 5 T. R., 195; Ralph and Randall, Randulphus and Randalphus,

Bac. Abr., Misnomer, A, have been holden different names. See also 1 Chit. Pl., 440. The law notices only one Christian name. A middle letter is no part of the name. *Franklin* v. *Talmadge*, 5 Johns., 84.

150*] *The notice of retainer, served on the plaintiff's attorney, by the attorney for Carley, did not cure the defect in the process. The notice was drawn in such a manner as to reserve the right of taking advantage of the misnomer. (Tidd's Pr., 582, *note i;* 1 Dunl. Pr., 175; *Id.*, 237–8.)

The writ being unbailable, is no reason why Carley should not be allowed to take advantage of the misnomer. He is not considered in court. It is the same as if he had not been sued at all; *Greenslade* v. *Rotheroe*, 5 Bos. & P., 132, per Mansfield, *Ch. J.;* and the plaintiff has no right to have an appearance entered, or common bail filed in the right name, and then to declare in that name. *Doo* v. *Butcher*, 3 T. R, 611; *Delanoy* v. *Cannon*, 10 East, 328; *Dring* v. *Dickenson*, 11 East, 225; *Corbett* v. *Bates*, 3 T. R, 660. The case of *Symmers* v. *Wason*, 1 Bos. & P., 105, was overruled in *Delanoy* v. *Cannon*, 10 East, 328; and the positions laid down in Chitty's Pleadings, 250–1 and 440, as to the manner of evading the effect of a misnomer, will be found not fully sustained by the decisions which he cites. In *Smith* v. *Innes*, 4 Maule & S, 360, the misnomer was James instead of John; and Innes had signed the bail-bond with the initials of his Christian name, thus J. Innes; yet this was held no objection to the motion.

A notice of retainer is not an appearance. An appearance is only by putting in special bail, filing common bail, or having an appearance entered. 1 Dunl. Pr., 300, 301; 6 Rule of April Term, 1796; 1 Dunl. Pr., 163, 4, 5; *De Wandelaer* v. *Coomer*, 6 Johns., 328; *Redmond* v. *Russell*, 12 *Id.*, 154.

Mr. J. Platt, contra, said that in truth here was no misnomer. The only distinction of sound arose from the difference between the Yankee and Dutch pronunciation. The former gives the name Grautius, the latter Gerardus, which would enable us to reply to a plea in abatement, that the defendant is known as well by the name we have called him, as the one which he claims. That would be a conclusive answer to a plea, and should be equally so to a motion. *Petrie* v. *Woodworth*, 3 Cai., 219. This is one of the corruptions which **151***] *have arisen from the migration and settlement of our eastern brethren, among the descendants of Holland, whose fathers founded the State, and whose pride it would have been to have secured the original pronunciation, to their remotest posterity. But the gentleman has mistaken the remedy. If we are not permitted to avail ourselves of this corruption of sound; if the ancient pronunciation is to be protected by our courts of justice, and our citizens punished for departing from it, this will only be done where the abuse has been accompanied with greater violence than was practiced in this instance. Here has been no arrest with a view to imprison, or hold to bail. The process was unbailable, and the defendant indorsed his appearance. The cases of the gentleman will not any of them be found to apply to such a case. If the defendant be held to bail, then, say the cases, he may, before the time for pleading in abatement has expired, move to be discharged on common bail (1 Dunl. Pr., 236); or a judge at his chambers will discharge him on the same terms. This is the meaning and spirit of the cases cited. Here, nothing more than common bail was ever exacted; the mere entry of an appearance. In such a case, the court should put this Gerardus or Grautis, to his plea in abatement. 2 Chit Pl., 464; *Oakley* v. *Giles*, 3 East, 168.

Cur. adv. vult.

The facts in the second cause were the same as in the first; except that the *capias* was bailable, and Carley had put in special bail, the bailpiece beginning thus: ———*ss.* "Gerardus Q. Carley, sued by the name of Quartus Q. Carley, impleaded, &c." A special notice of bail was given. After the argument, but before the decision of the motion, in the first cause,

Mr. A. C. Paige, for Carley, also moved to set aside the *capias* and all subsequent proceedings in the second cause. He urged the same arguments as before, and cited the same authorities.

Messrs. J. Edwards and *W. Hubbell*, contra.

Mr. Edwards* read an affidavit of [*152** the plaintiff's attorney, that the misnomer was by mistake; and that he had made out, and filed an original bill, and a *præcipe* for a *latitat*, in both of which the parties were described by their right names.

The counsel then argued that a misnomer should not be treated as an irregularity. They did not find that a similar case had ever been before this court. It is said in 1 Dunl. Pr., 236, that proceedings will be set aside, where the defendant is sued by a wrong name, if application be made before the time for pleading in abatement has expired. The book does not say that this will be so, whether bail has been put in or not; but by referring to the cases cited, they will be found to be those in which bail had not been entered by the defendant. We admit there are several cases of the kind, where the Court of K. B. have set aside proceedings, the plaintiff having declared against the defendant by his right name, as sued by a wrong name, first filing common bail for the defendant by his right name; but we do not find any case where the defendant had entered special bail by his right name, although stating that he was sued by another name, in which proceedings have been set aside. In *Binfield* v. *Maxwell*, 15 East, 158, where the defendant applied after the time for pleading in abatement had expired, the motion was denied; and one reason assigned by the court was, that there was no doubt that the defendant was the person really intended to be sued. That reason applies to this case.

But the Court of C. P. in England have adopted a rule different from the K. B., in relation to misnomer. In *Symners* v. *Wason*, 1 Bos. & P., 105, a case precisely similar to this in every feature, that court refused either to set aside the proceedings, or to discharge the bail. If this court have not already settled a practice for themselves, that of the C. P. will best promote justice, and be found nearer in conformity with the principles of our own

practice. The defendant, through mistake, is arrested by a wrong name; he appears and puts in bail by his right name, stating that he had been arrested by a wrong name, there being no doubt that he was the person really in-
153*] tended; *the plaintiff declares against him by his right name, stating that he had been arrested by the wrong one; the defendant is regularly in court; the declaration is against him. What is the substantial injury complained of? We can see none. By putting in bail, he has, at any rate removed all difficulty. In *Murray* v. *Hubbart*, 1 Bos. & P., 645, the defendant was arrested by the name of Francis, and appeared and put in bail by the name of Samuel; the plaintiff declared thus: "Samuel Hubbart, arrested by the name of Francis Hubbart, was attached to answer George Murray, &c.;" the defendant pleaded the misnomer in abatement; but the plaintiff treated the plea as a nullity, and signed judgment. The court refused to set aside the judgment, and said: "The case, therefore, comes to this—that so long as it is the practice of the court to issue the *mesne* process first, and to allow an original to be sued out afterwards, if necessary to substantiate the proceedings, no advantage can be taken, after appearance, of a misnomer in the *mesne* process."

If, then, the proceedings cannot be sustained as regular, they may be amended. That this would be so in the C. P. appears by the case last cited. Amendments are allowed, not only in civil, but even in criminal cases, where there is anything to amend by. In this case an original bill has been filed against the defendant, by his right name. The *capias* presupposes this to have been done; and after judgment, and a writ of error brought, the party may file an original bill, *nunc pro tunc*, as of course. (1 Dunl. Pr., 112, 113, and the cases there cited.) The plaintiff may now amend his *capias* and declaration, if necessary, by the original on file. In *Mestær* v. *Hertz*, 3 Maule & S., 450, it was decided that the appearance of the defendant, in the same manner as here, was of itself, sufficient for the plaintiff to amend his *capias* and declaration by. In the case at bar, there is no necessity of amending the declaration. It is against the defendant by his right name, by the name in which the suit was commenced, and the name in which he has put in bail. Indeed, we may ask what occasion then to amend the *capias*, which was
154*] only the means of bringing *him into court? If, however, an amendment of either *capias* or declaration, or both, is deemed necessary, we have enough to amend by. The principle originally advanced by Ld. Hardwicke, and which runs through all the subsequent cases, is "that "an amendment shall or shall not be made, as shall best tend to the furtherance of justice."

If the original bill in this court is to be considered the same as the original writ in England, as to the subsequent proceedings, then the case cited of *Murray* v. *Hubbart* shows that we have been regular and that no amendment is necessary.

Mr. Paige, in reply, said the defendant's appearance had not cured the mistake in the writ; for he has appeared in the manner required in order to reserve the right of taking advantage of the misnomer. (Tidd's Pr., 582, *note* 1; 2 Amer. ed.) Simply putting in bail, either in the right or the wrong name, would estop the defendant from pleading the misnomer in abatement. To preserve this right, he must appear specially, as was done in this instance. (*Id.*, 1 Dunl. Pr., 175, 237, 238, and the cases there cited.) That this appearance does not cure the mistake is farther proved by the fact that no plea in abatement was ever interposed without such an appearance, or, what is equivalent, the filing common bail or entering an appearance in the same special form. 1 Chit. Pl., 412; 1 Dunl. Pr., 376; *Venn* v. *Calvert*, 4 T. R., 578; *Allaire* v. *Ouland*, 2 Johns. Cas., 53, 56. The defendant must always appear before he can plead, either in abatement or in bar. A plea before appearance is a nullity. (*Id.*, *Ibid.*) What further confirms this position is, that a plea in abatement for a misnomer may be put in by attorney. (1 Chit. Plead., 412; 2 *Id.*, 416; Tidd Pr., 582-3.) If, then, the appearance does not estop the defendant, to plead in abatement, it does not prevent him from having the proceedings set aside on motion; for the latter proceeding can be adopted whenever a plea in abatement would be proper. In *Smish* v. *Innes*, 4 Maule & S., 360, it is evident that the defendant must have appeared, or the notice of declaration would not have been served on him. *And [***155** see what Blosset says, *arguendo*, in *Rex* v. *Sheriff of Suffolk*, 4 Taunt., 819. The plaintiff has no right to declare as he has done here, except where the defendant appears generally, by his right name. *Doo* v. *Butcher*, 3 T. R., 611; *Murray* v. *Hubbard*, 5 Bos. & P., 645. Whenever he appears specially, as Carley has done, it is notice to the plaintiff that he intends to take advantage of the misnomer.

Both causes were continued under advisement, till the other non-enumerated business of the term was mostly disposed of; when,

WOODWORTH, *J.*, delivered the opinion of the court:

After stating both cases, and wherein they differed, he said the motions under consideration were novel—he believed without precedent in this court, and not of very ancient date in the English courts. There had, however, within a few years been several cases of the kind both in the K. B. and the C. P., to which the court had been referred, at the bar. He should not now advert to them particularly. The court had examined them with a good deal of care; and for himself he confessed that he had bestowed more labor, and had found more perplexity in coming to a result, satisfactory to his own mind upon these motions, than he had experienced in all the other non-enumerated business of the term, extensive, important and complicated as it had been.

The cases in which motions to set aside proceedings for a misnomer of the defendant will be entertained, are different in the different courts of K. B. and C. P; and they have not always been exactly uniform even in the same court. But, in general, they agree that where the defendant moves to set aside the proceedings, before appearance, he is entitled to relief in that form; and we dispose of these motions

according to that test. The usual course is to plead the misnomer in abatement. Without saying whether this would be a more beneficial course to the defendant, it is, at any rate, the fairer one; and we are not disposed to countenance the present form of proceeding, by doing more than we feel ourselves bound to do
156*] by the authorities. *These are uniform in declaring that where the defendant moves, before he has appeared in any manner, the practice is to set aside the *capias*, and the subsequent proceedings of the plaintiff, for irregularity. That the defendant is misnamed has not been denied. If the fact had been contradicted or, perhaps, if it had been shown that defendant was generally known as well by the name of Grautis as Gerardus, of course we should not interfere. In truth, these names are different. They cannot be considered the same with any of the authorities. We do not think the cases warrant the distinction, contended for by the counsel for the plaintiff in the first cause, between process bailable and process unbailable.

Then, has the defendant appeared at the suit of Mann in any way? We think not; a mere notice of retainer is not an appearance. This can only be by putting in special bail, filing common bail, or by causing an appearance to be entered. No other mode of appearance is known in our practice. In the cause at the suit of Munn, therefore, we grant the motion.

The cause at the suit of Chapin stands on a different ground. The defendant was sued by the name of Quartus—a clear misnomer; but he appeared. True his appearance was special. The *capias* issued with an *ac etiam* against Quartus; the defendant appeared by a bailpiece in this form. "Gerardus Q. Carley, sued by the name of Quartus Q. Carley, is delivered on bail, &c.," and a corresponding special notice of bail was given by the defendant's attorney. This was a good appearance in the action. It was available to the plaintiff and entitled him to declare. Had the defendant appeared without reciting the bailpiece and notice the misnomer, he would even been estopped to plead it in abatement. But this special form is given in the books, and has the effect of saving to the defendant, not his motion to set aside the proceedings, but his plea in abatement—to which he may resort. In these cases of special appearance the plaintiff declares by the right name, of which he has notice from the defendant, and thus drives him to his plea in abatement. After the defendant has appeared, in any form, we will not entertain a motion. The
157*] motion is, *accordingly, denied in the last case; but the defendant may plead the misnomer in abatement, if he choose.

It is not improbable that we may, on further reflection, adopt some general rule of practice, denying these summary applications in cases of misnomer which may hereafter arise; but whatever reluctance we may feel at granting the motion in either of these cases, it would be improper to adopt any such rule and apply it to them. The motion is granted in the first, but denied in the second cause.

Rules accordingly.

NOTE. The following general rule was afterwards adopted by *the Court:*

February Term, 1825.

ORDERED that, in future, *the Court* will not entertain a motion to set aside the process or proceedings in a cause, on the ground of a misnomer of the party arrested; but will leave him to his remedy, of a plea in abatement.

Cited in—1 Wend., 71; 7 How. Pr., 26; 11 How. Pr., 139; 22 How. Pr., 520; 7 Bos., 694; 46 Ind., 478.

ANONYMOUS.

Practice—Enumerated Motion, Noticed but not Made—No Costs Allowed.

No costs are allowed for preparation and attendance to oppose a motion to bring on a demurrer as frivolous, noticed but not made.

So of all enumerated motions.

MARCH 16, 1825. *Mr. J. L. Viele* (the bar having finished their non-enumerated business of the term, which was to be moved pursuant to notice) moved for the costs of preparation and attendance to oppose a motion to bring on an argument as upon a frivolous demurrer, which had been noticed, but not made.

Curia We cannot allow you costs. The motion noticed is an enumerated one, a case in which we never give costs of attending to oppose. We do this in non-enumerated motions alone, where only one side has a right to notice them.

Motion denied.

*ROSS [*158
v.
LUTHER, Sheriff of CLINTON.

Commencement of Suit—Delivery of Writ to Messenger, to be Delivered to Coroner on Ceriatn Contingency—Suit not Commenced until Writ Actually Delivered to Coroner—Amendment of Teste of Writ.

The issuing the writ is the commencement of the suit.

Where the plaintiff's attorney delivered a *capias ad respondendum* to an agent or messenger, with directions to deliver it to the coroner, on his ascertaining that a prisoner was off the jail liberties: held, that the writ was not issued, and the suit therefore not commenced, on the agent or messenger determining to deliver it accordingly, and going in search of the coroner, but only by the actual delivery of the writ to the coroner. A writ wrongly tested, as to the name of the *Ch. Justice*, is amendable; and where this mistake is in a *ca. sa.* the sheriff cannot object it in an action for an escape.

Citations—17 Johns., 63; 18 Johns., 14, 496.

DEBT for the escape of Wait, a prisoner on *ca. sa.*, from the jail limits of Clinton Co., tried at the Clinton Circuit July 4, 1823, before Walworth, *Ch. J.* The main question arising upon the case, related to the time at which this suit should be deemed to have been commenced. The *ca. sa.*, was also wrongly tested in the name of Kent, *Ch. J.* The time of commencing the suit depended on the testimony of St. John. B. L. Skinner, who testified

NOTE.—*Commencement of suit—What constitutes.* See Lowry v. Lawrence, 1 Cal., 69, *note.*

that Feb. 7, 1820, at half past 9 P. M., according to the coroner's watch, he delivered the *capias ad respondendum* to him (the coroner) and immediately proceeded rapidly in a cutter the distance of 2½ miles from the limits, to a tavern, where he found Wait.

The defendant's counsel then insisted that the making out the *capias ad respondendum* was the commencement of the suit, and offered to show that it had been made out some time before its delivery to the coroner; but the judge decided that neither the making out of the writ, nor its actual delivery to the coroner, was the commencement of the suit; but that the suit was commenced when the writ was actually put in motion for the coroner, with a certain and determined intention of delivering it to him to be served.

Skinner then further testified that he was a clerk in the office of the plaintiff's attorney; and that the writ had been filled up sometime before; and left with him to be issued, when it could be ascertained that Wait was off the limits; that some time in the fore part of the evening, when the process was delivered, he took it, and went out of the office with an intention of delivering it to the coroner, if he could be satisfied that Wait was out, but not otherwise; that about 9 o'clock P. M. he ascertained, to his satisfaction, that Wait had escaped from the limits, made up his mind to deliver the process, and went in pursuit of the **159***] coroner for the purpose. *Witnesses were then called by both parties, to the time when Wait was off the limits.

The judge charged the jury that the suit must be considered as commenced when Skinner started to deliver the writ to the coroner, after he had determined absolutely to deliver it, and not when he first took it from the office, his intention not then being fixed; and he left it to the jury to say, from all the evidence, whether Wait was off the limits when such absolute determination was formed and Skinner started to deliver the writ—directing them that if they found this in the affirmative, they should render a verdict for the plaintiff; otherwise, for the defendant. The jury returned a verdict for the defendant.

Mr. J. Edwards, for the plaintiff, now moved for a new trial, and contended that the suit was not commenced, in judgment of law, till the process was actually delivered to the coroner. Skinner, he said, was the plaintiff's agent, under whose control the process continued, till it passed from his hands. An intention of his could not amount to the commencement of a suit, any more than that of the plaintiff, if the process had been in his own hands. In this respect the case is distinguishable from *Bronson* v. *Earl*, 17 Johns., 63; *Burdick* v. *Green*, 18 Johns., 14, and *Visscher* v. *Gansevoort*, 18 Johns., 496. In the latter case the court say: "We cannot admit that the messenger, or bearer of the writ, shall have it in his power to decide whether the suit shall be commenced by any event subsequent to the delivery of the writ to him, short of its being actually put into his hands, or left at the office of the coroner." That is this case. Besides, the rule would be inconvenient and dangerous, which shall erect the plaintiff's agent into a judge to determine by his secret resolve, without any open definite act, when the suit shall be commenced.

Mr. J. A. Collier, for the defendant, said the delivery of the writ to the coroner was certainly not the only criterion which determines the commencement of the suit. This is apparent from the cases cited, in one of which (*Burdick* v. *Green*) putting the process into the post-office, directed to *the officer, was said [***160** to be a commencement (18 Johns., 20, per Platt, *J.*); and in another (*Bronson* v. *Earl*), a delivery to the officer's wife was holden sufficient. The judge here decided according to *Burdick* v. *Green*, in which the court say that intention may be inquired into. According to the English rule, the suit is commenced whenever the writ is sealed; and perhaps since the case of *Filkins* v. *Brockway*, 19 Johns., 170, and *People* v. *Singer*, 1 Cow., 41, S. P., the filling up of process should now be deemed the commencement of the suit in this State. These cases decide that a seal can be used but once; that process begins to perform its office as soon as it is made out; and they seem to contradict the former cases. If this be so, the suit was clearly commenced prematurely. No escape had taken place.

Mr. S. A. Foot, in reply, said it is perhaps to be regretted that anything short of an actual delivery of the writ to the officer should have been allowed to acquire a right to the plaintiff, though it might be otherwise for the purpose of saving a debt from the Statute of Limitations. The court would have found it much more safe never to have departed from the case of *Bronson* v. *Earl*. If the commencement of the suit rests on mental resolution, it tempts to perjury. It is true that intent is considered in *Burdick* v. *Green*; but there ought, at least, to be an overt act, by which it shall be clearly manifested. In *Visscher* v. *Gansevoort*, the court do not, indeed, question *Burdick* v. *Green*; but they require a distinct act, the parting with the process, so as to put it beyond the party's control. The act must be absolute; it must be more than intention, or the mere act of the mind. If the party, or his agent, be the carrier, he should be required actually to deliver the writ to the officer before the suit shall be considered as commenced.

WOODWORTH, *J.* The judged charged the jury that the suit must be considered as commenced when Skinner started to deliver the writ to the coroner, after he had determined absolutely to issue it; and not from the time when he first took it from the office, without any certain intention of delivering it.

*If the law was correctly laid down, [***161** there is no ground for disturbing the verdict on the question of fact. From the evidence, it is somewhat doubtful whether Wait was out of the limits when the agent determined to deliver the writ, and went in pursuit of the officer.

The delivery of a writ to the wife of a coroner is a sufficient commencement of an action against the sheriff. *Bronson* v. *Earl*, 17 Johns., 63. In that case, however, it appeared that the writ was put into the hands of a person to be delivered to the coroner to be served, at such time as the prisoner should be found to have left the jail limits. There was no evidence of an absolute intention to deliver the writ before the time of its actual delivery, so that the question in this cause did not come under consideration. In *Burdick* v. *Green*, 18 Johns., 14, it was held that the issuing of the writ is the commencement of the suit, in all cases where the time is material so as to save the Statute of Limitations. By this general proposition, is not intended that the mere filling up of the process is such commencement. The same case explains the rule; that it is not necessary to show the writ was actually delivered to the sheriff; but it is sufficient if it appear that the writ was made out, and sent to sheriff or his deputy by mail or otherwise, with a *bona fide*, absolute and unequivocal intention of having it served. The same doctrine is recognized in *Visscher* v. *Gansevoort*, 18 Johns., 496. These cases decide the law applicable to the case under consideration.

Skinner testified that he was a clerk in the office of the plaintiff's attorney; that the writ had been filled up some time previous, and left with him to be issued when he could ascertain that Wait was off the limits. There was not, then, an absolute intention that the writ should be delivered to the coroner in the first instance. It was committed to Skinner to exercise his discretion; he became satisfied about 9 o'clock that Wait was off the limits; and then made up his mind to deliver it to the coroner, which was done a half hour afterwards. Skinner was merely an agent or messenger, with power from the plaintiff to decide on the **162***] time when *to deliver the writ. It does not appear that he had any other authority. It was not competent, therefore, for him to decide from what time the suit should be considered as commenced. In *Visscher* v. *Gansevoort* it was decided that the messenger or bearer of the writ has not the power to decide whether the suit shall be commenced by any event subsequent to the delivery of the writ to him, short of its being actually put into the hands, or left at the office of the coroner. It follows, then, conclusively, that the determination of Skinner to deliver the writ, absolutely, is of no avail; and the suit was not commenced until the actual delivery to the coroner.

The judge, therefore, erred in supposing that the decision of Skinner to deliver the writ was the test. He ought to have charged the jury that, on the facts, the suit was not commenced in judgment of law until the coroner received the writ. The consequence is, that the plaintiff is entitled to a new trial, with costs to abide the event.

SUTHERLAND *J.* The suit cannot be considered as having been commenced, until the actual delivery of the writ to the coroner. When the witness, Skinner, who was the clerk of the plaintiff's attorney, left the office with the writ, he had no absolute intention of delivering it to the coroner. He states that the took it with an intention of delivering it to the coroner, if he could be satisfied Wait was off the limits, but not otherwise. That afterwards, he made up his mind to deliver it to the coroner, as he learned sufficient to satisfy him he ought to issue the writ; and he went immediately in pursuit of the coroner, for the purpose of delivering it to him, but was about half an hour before he found him.

The clerk is to be considered as the agent or messenger of the attorney, and as acting in obedience to his orders when he took the writ and left the office with it. That his instructions had been given him at some previous time, and not at the precise moment when he left the office, cannot vary the case. He left the office, then, with instructions to deliver the writ, if Wait was beyond the limits. This case is, then, precisely within that of *Visscher* v. *Gansevoort*, in which the court say, "when the attorney issued the writ, *the inten- [***163** tion to commence the suit was not absolute, positive and unequivocal; and we cannot admit that the messenger or bearer of the writ shall have it in his power to decide, whether the suit shall be commenced by any event subsequent to the delivery of the writ to him, short of its being actually put into the hands, or left at the office of the coroner.

The judge, therefore, erred in charging the jury that the suit must be considered as commenced, "when the clerk started to deliver the writ to the coroner, after he had determined absolutely to issue it."

The execution having been tested in the name of *Ch. J.* Kent, instead of *Ch. J.* Thompson, did not render it void. It was amendable, and the sheriff could not avail himself of the irregularity.

SAVAGE, *Ch. J.*, concurred.

New trial granted, with costs to abide the event.

BALLOU *v.* SPENCER AND SPENCER.

Special Partnership — What Constitutes — Contract, for Sale of Land to Two — Part Payment to be Made, in Notes Indorsed by Purchasers — One Purchaser Cannot Bind Others by Indorsement.

A and B enter into a contract with C for a conveyance from him to them of a farm, and that they will pay a part in good negotiable promissory notes to be indorsed by them; held, that this does not constitute them special partners, so that one can bind both by an indorsement in the name of both, without the knowledge and assent of the other.

Citations— 4 Johns., 251; 1 Esp., 30; 3 T. R., 757.

ASSUMPSIT, tried before Rochester Circuit Judge, at the Madison Circuit, July 7, 1823.

The action was brought to recover the amount of the following promissory note: "Lenox, May 1st, 1821. For value received, I promise to pay Ichabod S. Spencer, or bearer, one hundred and fifty dollars, with interest, in one year from date. Witness my hand,

WILLIAM BARRIE."

The note was indorsed thus: "I. S. & J. A. Spencer."

The declaration in the cause consisted of three counts. The first stated the defendants to be partners in law, and to have indorsed the note as such partners. The second stated them

NOTE.—*Partnership—What constitutes—Power of Partners.* See Post v. Kimberly, 9 Johns., 470, *note;* Wetmore v. Baker, 9 Johns., 307, *note;* Dai v. Halsey, 16 Johns., 34, *note;* Bruen v. Mraquand, 17 Johns., 58, *note;* Foot v. Sabin, 19 Johns., 155, *note;* Reynolds v. Cleveland, *post*, 282, *note.*

to be the bearers of the note, and as such bearers to have indorsed it, without saying they were partners. The third count consisted of the usual money counts.

It was admitted by the counsel for the defendants that the indorsement on the back of the note was in the handwriting of one of the defendants, namely: I. S. Spencer; but de-
164*] nied *that the other defendant, J. A. Spencer, was bound by the indorsement.

The plaintiff then offered in evidence a sealed contract executed by the defendants and one Charles Stroud, in the words following:

"Articles of agreement, made this 17th Apr., 1821, between Charles Stroud of one part, and Ichabod S. Spencer and Joshua A. Spencer of the other part, as follows: the said Charles agrees to sell and quitclaim his right and title to lot number eighty-two, in the Canastota tract, to the said Ichabod S. & Joshua A., their heirs and assigns forever, for one thousand dollars, to be paid as hereafter mentioned; and when the payments are made, to give them a quitclaim deed. And said Ichabod S. & Joshua A. agree to pay said Charles, as and for the purchase price of said premises, one thousand dollars, in manner following to wit: three hundred and forty four dollars and sixty seven cents is paid down, and the residue shall be paid, say in three weeks or sooner, in good negotiable promissory notes due or to be due within one year; and in cases where said Charles is not acquainted with the drawers, so as to be satisfied of their responsibility, the said Ichabod S. & Joshua A. shall indorse said notes. The said Ichabod S. & Joshua A. to have the possession or use and profits of the premises, from henceforth, and the said Charles to take the same on equal shares, for one year; the above contracted land only includes one hundred and thirty six acres, of which the said Charles is now possessed, so that he excepts Eleazer Lewis' twenty acres and Job Lockwood's thirty-six acres, sixty one hundreths, to convey himself. In witness, &c."

The plaintiff then proved by Charles Stroud, a party to this contract, that the note in question was delivered to him by Ichabod S. Spencer, one of the defendants, in part pay of the purchase money, for the land mentioned in the contract, and in compliance with that part of the contract, which states that good negotiable promissory notes should be turned out in payment for the land; that he received this on the contract; that it was indorsed at his request, by Ichabod S. Spencer, one of the de-
165*] fendants, in the name of both; that *J A. Spencer was not present when he received the note from I. S. Spencer, and he did not know that he knew of the indorsement.

The judge determined that the evidence was not sufficient to entitle the plaintiff to recover of J. A. Spencer, and ordered the plaintiff to be nonsuited for this cause, with leave to make a case for the opinion of the Supreme Court. The plaintiff, accordingly, under the direction of the court, was nonsuited, with leave to move to set the nonsuit aside.

Mr. C. P. Kirkland, for the plaintiff, insisted that by the agreement with Stroud, the defendants became partners, *pro hac vice*. One was, therefore, authorized to indorse in the name of both. Each trusted the other to do any act in performance of the contract, which contemplated a joint indorsement. One might, doubtless, have paid in the joint property of both; and a release of the covenant by one would have bound the other.

But if the defendants were not constituted special partners by the agreement, it is presumable, from the facts proved, that J. A. authorized I. S. Spencer to indorse in the name of both; and the judge should, at least, have left the cause to the jury upon the question of this fact. *Ely* v. *Adams*, 19 Johns., 313.

Mr. J. A. Spencer, contra. There is no evidence that the defendants were ever partners, as averred in the first count, or that they were bearers as averred in the second. I. S. Spencer had no right, under the agreement, to use the other defendant's name by indorsing it upon a note. As well might it be said that he could bind his joint contractor in the agreement by any other new and distinct contract. The indorsement spoken of by the agreement is, in its nature, the actual indorsement of both. The note was payable to I. S. Spencer alone. He was the owner. Taking the agreement in reference to such a note, it could mean only a second indorsement by the other defendant, I. S. Spencer being liable in the first instance. It does not appear that the other defendant ever saw or heard of the note in question.

*Besides, there was no demand of [***166**
payment or notice to the indorser proved. The nonsuit is not confined by the case to the question of partnership, but goes upon the whole case.

Mr. Kirkland, in reply, said the want of demand and notice not being made a point at the trial, could not now be insisted on.

SAVAGE, *Ch. J.* I think the nonsuit was right. There is no evidence whatever in the case to show that the defendants were partners. The agreement did not make them so; nor their joint interest in the land purchased of Stroud. The note in question was payable to I. S. Spencer, alone. J. A. Spencer is not shown to have had any interest in it. There is no ground whatever to charge him; nor, indeed, either of the defendants; for no demand upon the maker or notice to the indorser was proved, or any excuse shown for the omission.

SUTHERLAND, *J.*, concurred.

WOODWORTH, *J.*, dissenting. The defendants agreed to purchase a lot of land of Charles Stroud for $1,000—a part of the consideration to be paid down, and the residue in negotiable promissory notes. In cases where Stroud was not acquainted with the drawers, and not satisfied of their responsibility, the defendants stipulated to indorse. This contract constituted a joint concern in the purchase, and in the securities to be given for the payment. A partnership may exist in a particular concern or business, which, although it does not make out a general partnership, the partners are liable, where the business is connected with such particular concern. A general rule applicable to both general and special partnerships is, that in transactions relating to the joint concern, one of several partners may bind the rest. He may issue notes and indorse bills for the common benefit, without applying to the rest in every particular case. In special partnerships, the power of the individuals composing them, can only be exercised within the compass of that particular business to which 167*] the partnership relates. It is *analogous to the power of an agent appointed for a special purpose, who, if he exceed his authority, cannot bind his principal. This doctrine is well settled by a variety of cases. *Livingston* v. *Roosevelt*, 4 Johns., 251 ; 1 Esp., 30 ; 3 T. R., 757. If, then, one individual, in a limited partnership or concern, may indorse notes for the common benefit in relation to that concern, I apprehend there can be no doubt of the right of either of the defendants to make the indorsement in question. It was authorized not only by the fact that they were joint purchasers, and were jointly to make payment, but by an express covenant that the defendants should indorse, if the responsibility of the drawers was not satisfactory to the person of whom they purchased. Within the principles laid down, and the authority derived from the special agreement between the parties, either of the defendants was authorized to indorse for both. Whether J. A. Spencer was present, or subscribed his name, is immaterial. In judgment of law, the indorsement was obligatory on both.

The note was received in part payment, and indorsed at the request of Stroud. The contract was thereby executed on the part of the defendants, and placed them on the footing of indorsers.

It does not appear by the case that any question was raised at the trial, whether the note could be given in evidence under the counts in the declaration, or whether there had been a demand and notice. As to the first, the evidence supported the second count, which avers that the defendants, being bearers of the note, indorsed it, without saying they were partners. It was sufficient to show that the indorsement was legally binding on both defendants. No objection appears to have been made at the trial, on this ground. From the case, it may be inferred that proof of a demand and notice were not offered, in consequence of the decision of the judge that J. A. Spencer was not liable. The indorsement was considered as not binding on him. Had this been correct, it was useless to produce evidence of a demand and notice.

Under the circumstances, it cannot now be determined, whether the plaintiff could prove 168*] a demand and notice, or *not. The presumption is, that this question was not raised, as the judge evidently disposed of the cause on another ground. I think the nonsuit should be set set aside and a new trial granted, with costs to abide the event.

Motion denied.

Cited in—15 Wend., 193.

JACKSON *v.* LOOMIS.

Action of Trespass—Value of Improvements, in Mitigation of Damages.

In an action of trespass for *mesne* profits against a *bona fide* purchaser, he shall be allowed against the plaintiff, in mitigation of damages, the value of permanent improvements made in good faith, to the extent of the rents and profits claimed by the plaintiff.

Citations—1 Johns. Cas., 281; 2 Johns. Cas., 441; 1 Johns. Ch., 387-8; 8 Wh., 81, 82; 5 Co., 30.

TRESPASS for *mesne* profits, tried at the Washington Circuit, July 15, 1823, before Walworth, Circuit Judge. On the trial, the plaintiff produced in evidence an exemplification of a record of recovery, in an action of ejectment, duly signed and filed Mar. 5, 1822, by which it appeared that the demise in the declaration was laid Feb. 2, 1818 ; and it was admitted by the defendant, that a writ of possession had been issued on the judgment, and the lessor of the plaintiff put into possession of the premises, July 15, 1822. Robert Wilcox was then sworn as a witness on the part of the plaintiff, and testified that he knew the premises recovered in the action of ejectment ; that about 32½ acres were cultivated lands ; that the annual worth or value of the 32½ acres, over and above taxes and ordinary repairs, was $2 per acre, amounting in the whole to $65 *per annum.*

The defendant then offered to prove that May 1, 1812, he entered into possession of the premises as a *bona fide* purchaser, for a valuable consideration, by virtue of a deed from one James Wells, who had been reported the owner of the premises, and had been in the possession for many years previous to the sale to the defendant ; that the defendant continued to possess and enjoy the premises peaceably, without interruption, until Feb. 2, 1818, when the lessor of the plaintiff in the action of ejectment claimed the premises by virtue of a sale under a mortgage, executed by Wells anterior to the date of the deed under which the defendant held the premises, and commenced the action of ejectment as mortgagee ; that the defendant *resisted the claim until it [*169 was finally decided against him in the Court for the Correction of Errors. That from Feb. 2, 1818, to the time of the decision, the defendant had expended, in labor and advances in making permanent, useful and beneficial improvements upon the premises, a sum more than equal to the value of the annual income from Feb. 2, 1818, until possession of the premises was delivered ; that the improvements made by the defendant consisted in digging and gathering stones from the soil on the premises, and building stone walls or fences around the premises, and forming them into convenient lots. Which evidence the counsel for the dedendant insisted should be admitted and allowed as decisive to entitle the defendant to a verdict, and to bar the plaintiff from a recovery, and at all events, that it should be admitted and allowed in mitigation of damages. But the counsel for the plaintiff insisted that the evidence was not sufficient, and could not be admitted or allowed either to entitle the defendant to a verdict, or in mitigation of damages. The judge refused to receive the testimony, either for the purpose of entitling the defendant to a verdict, or in mitigation of damages, and the jury gave a verdict for the plaintiff for $287 damages. To this opinion the defendant excepted, and the question now came before the court on a bill of exceptions, by way of motion for a new trial.

Mr. J. L. Wendell, for the defendant. Trespass for *mesne* profits is an equitable action, intended to do justice to the plaintiff by putting him in as good a situation as he would have held, provided he had not been dispossessed. If waste has been committed, the damages may be increased accordingly, beyond the measure of the rent, to an extent which will make him whole. And, on the other hand, if improvements are made of a permanent and beneficial nature, and the defendant entered in good faith, a jury are bound, as honest men, to deduct their value from the damages. We do not claim, by way of set-off, an allowance for all the improvements. We are aware that this is inadmissible; and that we cannot go beyond answering the claim for damages. Nor **170***] *do we pretend that where a defendant enters with knowledge he has no title, he should be even allowed to mitigate damages by improvement; nor do we ask an allowance for improvements, which are merely showy and unsubstantial, or unappropriate to the premises. These, we agree, should be disallowed, because not beneficial. Suppose a defendant entering in good faith, and by labor and expense, changing that which was worthless before into a valuable farm; turning, for instance, a barren marsh into a fruitful field; would it not be revolting to every feeling of justice, that a plaintiff should take damages upon the basis that he had himself made the improvements—that the defendant should not only lose his labor, but pay the income which that labor had created?

In *Moore* v. *Cable*, 1 Johns. Ch., 387, 388, the party, standing in the place of a mortgagee, entered without right, and with full knowledge that this was so. To give a mortgagee an indefinite latitude in improving the estate, might entirely defeat the title of the mortgagor. Besides, the case is distinguishable in another point of view. The mortgagee knows that he may not be deprived of his lands. He improves for his own benefit. Yet the *Chancellor* allowed the mortgagee, in that case, what was denied to us in this. At any rate, the plaintiff ought not to recover for the annual value of the land as enhanced by the defendant himself.

Mr. R. Weston, contra: The question presented by the case is, whether, after denying the plaintiff's title, and putting him to an expensive litigation in its support, the defendant can finally turn round upon him in an action for *mesne* profits, and demand a deduction of improvements. This question has, I believe, never been directly decided; but it has been repeatedly held, that the damages in an action for *mesne* profits necessarily follow a recovery in ejectment. They are an inseparable incident. Even a recovery of the same premises in a cross-ejectment, will not protect the defendant. The annual value of the land is the measure of the damages, whatever may have been the views of the defendant in taking possession. The land, no matter what may be its **171***] *increase of value, and whether it arise from the labor of the defendant or any other cause, belongs to the plaintiff, with all its permanent improvements: and he is entitled to the rent. It is well settled that the defendant can have no action for the price of his labor; a promise to pay him for it would be *nudum pactum;* and to allow a deduction would be making substance yield to form. Had the land been voluntarily surrendered six years ago, the defendant could have recovered nothing for his improvements; but by obstinately holding out, and maintaining possession to the last, he gains the use of the land.

Mr. Wendell, in reply, said he had omitted to cite *Murray* v. *Gouverneur*, 2 Johns. Cas., 441, which was an action for the *mesne* profits, and where Kent, *J.*, said, "as to the sums expended by the appellant for repairs, it may be left for liquidation in an action for the *mesne* profits if the respondents should think proper to sue for the rents and profits. The action for *mesne* profits is a liberal and equitable action, and will allow of every kind of equitable defense."

Mr. Weston would merely say, that the remark of Kent, *J.*, was *obiter*. The question here in controversy did not arise in that case.

Curia, per SAVAGE, *Ch. J.* Though I find no cases in point upon the question presented, either in England or this State, there are several which bear upon it. In the case of *Van Allen* v. *Rogers*, 1 Johns. Cas., 281, the defendant held the premises under a contract with the devisor of the plaintiff. In an action for *mesne* profits, the defendant offered to prove that, by permission of the general owner, he built a house, barn and store then occupied by the plaintiff. The court say the improvements were made antecedent to the plaintiff's title; if the defendant is entitled to compensation, he must seek it from the personal representatives of the devisor—not from the plaintiff. They do not say what they would have held, if the original owner had brought the suit. In *Murray* v. *Gouverneur*, 2 Johns. Cas., 441–2, Kent, *J.*, who *gave the opinion of the court, [***172** says, "as to the sum expended for repairs, it may be left for liquidation in an action for the *mesne* profits, if the respondents should think proper to sue for the rents and profits. The action for *mesne* profits is a liberal and equitable one, and will allow of every kind of equitable defense." In *Moore* v. *Cable*, 1 Johns. Ch., 387–8, the question was, whether a mortgagee in possession was entitled to his improvements against the mortgagor applying to redeem. The *Chancellor* decided he was not, but that the mortgagee should not be holden to allow for rents and profits, which had exclusively arisen from his own expenditures in improvements; and that he should be allowed for necessary repairs, though not for clearing land.

There is certainly no reason, in general, why the owner of land should be compelled to pay for improvements which he neither directed nor desired, as a condition on which he is to gain possession of his property. But when an occupant has taken possession under a *bona fide* purchase, and made permanent improvements, it is very hard for him to lose both land and improvements. If the plaintiff is not content with acquiring possession of his property in an improved condition, after he has neglected to assert his title for a number of years, it is certainly equitable that the defendant should be allowed the value of his improvements, made in good faith to the extent of the rents and profits claimed. This view of the subject is fully supported by *Green* v. *Biddle*, 8 Wh., 81, 82, and the authorities there cited, especially *Coulter's* case, 5 Co., 30. Most clearly the defendant should not be compelled to pay an enhanced rent in consequence of his own improvements. The defendant is entitled to a new trial.

New trial granted. (a)

Cited in—5 Cow., 264; 59 N. Y., 52; 61 N. Y., 397; 4 Sand., 487; 1 Sawy., 26.

(a) The value of improvements made by the defendant may be set off against a claim of *mesne* profits; but profits before the demise laid should be first deducted from the value of the improvements. Hylton v. Brown, C. C., Apr., 1808, Pa.; Whart. Dig., Eject., I, pl. 74, p. 188, M. S. Rep.

173*] *THOMAS v. WOODS.

Assignment of Bond and Mortgage, Payable in Installments, with Annual Interest—Covenant by Assignor, to be Accountable if Assignee Could not Collect of Obligor by Due Process of Law—Delay of Assignee to Sue Obligor, after Installment Fell Due—Interest in Arrear—Balance, Left Due After Foreclosure and Sale—Responsibility of Assignor—Pleading.

W. assigned a bond and mortgage, payable by installments, with interest annually to T. and covenanted that if T. should not be able to procure and enforce payment at the times, and in the manner therein specified, by due process of law, W. would be accountable to him for what should remain due. The first installment became due Mar., 1, 1814; but T. did not sue the mortgagor until after the next May Term, when certain interest had been in arrear for several years. The suit was pursued to judgment, and a *fi. fa.* and an *alias fi. fa.* returned *nulla bona*, &c., and in the meantime, T. foreclosed the mortgage, which still left a balance unpaid, including the interest in arrear; and from the evidence, it appeared probable that the mortgagor had been unable to pay this balance before and ever since the installment became due; in an action by T. against W., held that T. should not recover the interest in arrear for several years, this being forfeited by delay; but that he might recover the residue; suffering a term to elapse after it fell due, not being an unreasonable delay as to this, under all the circumstances of the case.

One covenants to pay a debt, if it cannot be collected of another by due process of law; it is a compliance with the condition, if the covenantee exert reasonable diligence to collect, under all the circumstances of the case; and if he suffer a term to elapse after the debt falls due without suit, it being apparent that the covenantor has sustained no injury by the delay, he is liable. Nor is it necessary to issue a *ca. sa.* against the principal debtor, if it be apparent that it would be of no avail.

It is enough that the covenantor have notice of the failure to collect after due process of law. There is no need of demand or request.

Otherwise, it seems, if the covenant be to pay on request, expressly.

In an action on such a covenant, averring notice, the defendant must deny this by plea, or it will be taken as admitted upon the record.

A plea of *non est factum* puts in issue the execution of a deed only. All other material averments in the declaration are admitted.

Citations—1 Cal., 427; 19 Johns., 69, 71, 72; 1 Cow., 98; 10 Johns., 47; 1 Saund., 33.

COVENANT, tried at the Washington Circuit, July 15, 1823, before Walworth, Circuit Judge. The declaration stated that Feb. 8, 1809, one Joshua Streeter and Adah, his wife, for $2,400, mortgaged to the defendant certain premises to secure the payment of $1,200, and interest, according to the condition of a certain bond executed therewith by Streeter; that afterwards, Aug. 27, 1810, the defendant assigned the mortgage to the plaintiff, in which assignment it was agreed by the defendant that in case the plaintiff should not be able to procure or enforce the payment of the money secured by the mortgage and bond, by due process of law, the defendant should stand accountable to the plaintiff for such sum or sums of money as should remain due, in manner and at the several times specified in the bond.

The declaration then averred: 1. That the bond was dated the same day and year with the mortgage, and conditioned to pay $1,200, with interest, to commence from Apr. 1, thereafter, as follows: $500 in five years from Mar. 1, then next; $400 in nine years from *Mar. 1, then next; and the remaining [*174 sum of $300, in thirteen years from Mar. 1, then next, and the interest on the whole sum, or any such sum as should from time to time remain due of the $1,200, annually, Mar. 1, in each year; the first interest to be paid Mar. 1, 1810. 2. That Mar. 1, 1814, the sum of $913 became due and was unpaid; and the plaintiff being unable to procure payment without suit, caused a suit to be commenced in the Supreme Court, on the bond against Streeter, in the name of the defendant, and in October Term, 1814, obtained judgment for $2,400 of debt and $24.67 costs, issued a *testatum fieri facias* to the sheriff of the County of Washington, to which he returned that Streeter had not any goods or chattels, lands or tenements in his bailiwick, whereof he could cause to be made the debt and damages, or any part thereof. 3. That the plaintiff being unable to procure payment of the mortgage, foreclosed it; and Dec. 30, 1814, sold the premises to John P. Reynolds for $905, being the highest sum bid; that the costs and charges of sale were $50.84, and deducting this, together with the costs of obtaining the judgment from $905, there remained $829.49 to be applied on the mortgage. 4. That Mar. 1, 1818, there became due on the bond and mortgage $430.20, over and above the $829.49, which being unpaid, an *alias testatum fieri facias* was issued on the judgment, to the sheriff of the County of Washington, who returned that Streeter had not any goods or chattels, lands or tenements in his bailiwick, whereof he could cause to be made the debt and damages, or any part thereof. 5. That Streeter is insolvent, and has been so since Mar. 1, 1814. 6. That the defendant had notice of the proceedings against Streeter and of his insolvency.

To this declaration the defendant pleaded: 1. That the assignment was not his deed. 2. That Mar. 1, 1814, Streeter was not insolvent, but from thence hitherto was solvent, and able to pay all sums of money as they fell due, according to the condition of the bond. 3. The same. 4. That the plaintiff might have procured and enforced *payment of [*175 the sums of money on the bond and mortgage by due process of law.

On the trial, the plaintiff proved the mortgage and bond, upon which there were the following indorsements of payments:

June 16, 1810,	$60 00
Sep. 22, 1810,	16 64
Apr. 23, 1811,	91 00
Apr. 1, 1813,	84 00
	$251 64

The assignment, foreclosure, judgment, the several writs of *fi. fa.* and returns set forth in declaring, being also proved (the memorandum of the judgment record being of August Term, 1814), the plaintiff rested; and the defendant moved for a nonsuit, objecting that the plaintiff should have proved notice of Streeter's default, and a demand of payment, to which the plaintiff's counsel answered that it was averred in the declaration and not denied by the plea. The defendant also insisted that a suit should have been brought for the default in payment of a part of the interest in 1811, thirty-six cents, the whole in 1812, and that a suit for the installment due in Mar. 1814, should have been commenced before May Term. The court reserved the questions, and refused the nonsuit.

Ebenezer Russell, a witness on the part of the defendant, testified that Joshua Streeter had been deputy-sheriff and jailer of the County of Washington, in the Town of Salem, for several years past; that the witness, as Treasurer of the County of Washington, paid him on

Feb. 2, 1815,	$ 12 34
Feb. 10, 1816,	644 67
Feb. 18, 1817,	801 73
Sep. 23, 1818,	1,151 64
Jan. 18, 1819,	611 75
Mar. 23, 1820,	706 16
Feb. 1, 1821,	525 71
	$4,628 82

176*] *That the above sums were audited to Streeter, by the supervisors of the County of Washington, for keeping the prisoners during those years, and some little repairs to the jail; that a very small part of it was for services rendered the county as constable; that Streeter frequently drew upon the witness as treasurer before he was entitled to receive the amount audited, and the witness paid such drafts on the credit of the fund; and he did not hesitate to advance $200 or $300 before the amount was audited, and when Streeter became entitled to receive the amount audited, such drafts were accepted by him, and his receipts taken for the whole amount audited for the year; that in 1816 or 1817, he advanced to John Beaty about $600 for Streeter, which was due for provisions furnished him for the prisoners, and some money.

John Doty, a witness for the plaintiff, testified that he had been acquainted with Joshua Streeter for some time; that as early as 1814 he was unable to pay his debts; that he was his (witness') deputy-sheriff for many years; did not know of his owning any real property since 1811; that since 1814 he has had but a trifling personal property, and that generally covered by execution; that he had no means of supporting the prisoners except by the money paid him from the county; that in 1811, if he had been prosecuted for $70 or $80, it might have been collected; that in 1814, if he had been prosecuted for $400 or $500, it could not have been collected; had known of judgments against him since 1812 or 1813, the executions against him previous to 1820 were generally *arranged, except one in favor of Barney of about $100, which was obtained as early as 1814 or 1815, which had not been paid; but he did not know that any execution was issued on it. At the time Streeter was in the receipt of the money from the Treasurer of the County of Washington, which was necessary for the support of the prisoners in jail, he was the deputy and jailer of the witness, and was in the receipt of considerable sums of money for fees.

Hiram Lawrence, a witness for the defendant, testified that in the years 1813, 1814 and 1815, he should think a judgment of about $100 might have been collected of Streeter; *that he could not recollect when he [***177** returned from Philadelphia, after driving the last horses; but since that time he had been reputed insolvent; that before 1814 the witness held a note against him of about $150, which witness sold to one Todd, and guarantied the payment; that Todd sued Streeter on the note and obtained judgment; and an execution was issued after the sale on the mortgage, and he understood Todd got the money. This was all the knowledge witness had of the payment, except that he had never been called on by Todd upon his guaranty.

Zacheus Atwood, a witness for the plaintiff, testified that he had known Streeter for 19 years; that he went to Philadelphia with a drove of horses previous to the last war, and that from that time he has been reputed to be insolvent; that he has had but little personal property since then; that in 1814 he had two horses, and afterwards he had two in his possession for some years; he kept the jail and received much money in the course of his business.

Jesse L. Billings, a witness for the plaintiff, testified that Streeter went to Philadelphia with the last drove of horses, previous to 1815, and he thinks it was in 1811; and on his return it was reported that he lost his pocket-book and the money, and from that time he was reputed insolvent. If judgment on the bond had been obtained in August Term, instead of October Term, 1814, and a *ca. sa.* had been issued after a *fi. fa.*, he thinks the debt could not have been collected.

A verdict was taken for the plaintiff, by consent, for $586.86, subject to the opinion of the Supreme Court on all the questions arising upon the case.

Mr. J. Crary, for the plaintiff, opened the cause. After stating the facts, he cited *Ten Eyck* v. *Tibbits*, 1 Cai., 443. He said the plaintiff has a right to recover the whole sum yet due on the bond and mortgage. There has been no neglect which amounts to a forfeiture of the whole or any part. Due process of law means no more than commencing a suit, and following it to judgment. To shield himself from *paying, pursuant to his guaranty, [***178** the defendant should show a loss by our neglect. This could not be, for Streeter was insolvent throughout; and there could be no loss by an omission to sue. But there has been no omission. We proceeded at the very first moment that we could do it with effect. Woods guarantied the payment of the interest, and the several installments from time to time as they fell due. Will it be said a term intervened between the money falling due and a suit brought? The answer is that Streeter was never worth one dollar.

Messrs. S. Stevens and *D. Russell*, contra. Whether Streeter was solvent or insolvent is wholly immaterial. The plaintiff was bound to proceed diligently under the covenant, as a condition to any claim upon the defendant. It is not for the plaintiff to say, under this covenant, whether it was incumbent upon him to proceed. He had no right to judge of the defendant's ability; no discretion in the business. An installment fell due in Mar., 1814, but no suit was brought till after May Term. Here, then, was the loss of a term; and according to both the English cases, and those recently decided by this court, the whole claim was forfeited. The condition goes to the whole sum; even a failure as to the interest is enough. *Rees* v. *Berrington*, 2 Ves., Jr., 540; *Nisbet* v. *Smith*, 2 Bro. Ch., 578-9; *Ex parte Smith*, 3 *Id.*, 3, 4; *Moakley* v. *Riggs*, 19 Johns., 69, 72; *Kies* v. *Tifft*, 1 Cow., 98; *Straton* v. *Rastall*, 2 T. R., 366, 370; *Darbyshire* v. *Parker*, 6 East, 3, 10. Some of these cases, it is true, relate to sureties, and the defendant is no more than a surety.

Again; notice and demand of payment were necessary. The defendant was liable to pay only on the default of the mortgagor, of which notice should be given. *Morris* v. *Kirke*, Cro. Eliz., 73-4; *Devenly* v. *Welbore*, *Id.*, 85; *Obaston* v. *Garton*, *Id.*, 91; *Applethwart* v. *Northley*, *Id.*, 229; the case of *An Hostler*, Yelv., 66; 1 Saund., 33, *n.* 2; *Selman* v. *King*, Cro. Jac., 183; *Bradley* v. *Toder*, *Id.*, 228-9; *Hill* v. *Wade*, *Id.*, 523; *Rumball* v. *Ball*, 10 Mod., 38. The defendant was not the original debtor. 179*] This is always a *reason why he should have notice. His undertaking is collateral. 1 Dunl. Pr., 262; *Ernst* v. *Bartle*, 1 Johns. Cas., 319, 327; *Bowdell* v. *Parsons*, 10 East, 359. It may be said, as it was at the trial, that notice is averred, and not denied; but notice alone is not competent. There should have been a demand.

Again; the verdict is for too much. In casting interest, small payments, less than the interest due at the time, have been deducted when paid, and the interest cast on the balance. *Connecticut* v. *Jackson*, 1 Johns. Ch., 13; *Stoughton* v. *Lynch*, 2 *Id.*, 209.

Another objection is, that though the plaintiff was, by the legal effect of the covenant, bound to proceed at his own costs, we are charged with these.

The plaintiff should not only have proceeded by *fi. fa.*, but this should have been followed up by a *ca. sa.* The process should have been complete. There was no way of testing the defendant's ability, but by a rigid course of execution.

Mr. Crary, in reply. We aver notice of all our proceedings to Woods; the precise balance or deficiency is set forth; and notice of this is included in the averment. This is not denied by plea, and therefore stands omitted upon the record. An actual demand was not necessary. It was the defendant's duty to pay on learning the extent of the failure. *Non est factum*, and Streeter's insolvency only, are the issues. Every material averment, not denied, is admitted. *Gardner* v. *Gardner*, 10 Johns., 47; Tidd. Pr., 593; Peake Ev., 266.

As to the objection of laches, it certainly can have no weight. At all events, it cannot extend beyond the particular sum or installment which was the subject of the neglect. This is settled by the case cited of *Ten Eyck* v. *Tibbits*, 1 Cai., 443. In that case, one entire installment was not prosecuted for at all; and the court presumed it paid. But I repeat, we are confined to no particular time in commencing our suit. Due process of law means a suit commenced and carried on to judgment, generally. The words *or sense denote [*180 no particular time at which this is to be done. If the business is managed prudently, the trust on our part has been properly executed, and the defendant has no right to complain. It was in the plaintiff's discretion whether he would go to a *ca. sa.* Woods gave no directions to have this extreme remedy tried; and without some farther act or agreement on the part of Woods, such a step would have endangered our rights. Had we committed the debtor in execution, this would have extinguished the demand; and Woods might have pleaded it in discharge of an action against him. As to the objection that costs are included, it is true only as to those of foreclosure. We have defrayed the costs of the action ourselves.

WOODWORTH, *J.* The defendant assigned to the plaintiff a bond and mortgage against Joshua Streeter; and covenanted, that in case the plaintiff should not be able to procure or enforce payment, at the times and in the manner therein specified, by due process of law, the defendant would be accountable to him for such sum or sums of money as should remain due.

The bond bears date Feb. 8, 1809, and is conditioned for the payment of $1,200, with interest, to commence Apr. 1 thereafter; $500, payable Mar. 1, 1814; $400, Mar. 1, 1818; and $300, Mar. 1, 1822; the interest payable annually Mar. 1 in each year.

This action is commenced to recover the balance of principle and interest due Mar. 1, 1818. The declaration avers, that Mar. 1, 1814, $913 became due; that a suit was commenced against Streeter in the Supreme Court, and judgment obtained in October Term, 1814; that a *testatum fieri facias* issued to the sheriff of Washington, where Streeter resided, who returned that the defendant had no goods or chattels, lands or tenements. It also avers that the plaintiff foreclosed the mortgage and sold the mortgaged premises, Dec. 30, 1814, for $905; and after deducting $50.84 for costs, there remained $829.49 to be applied to the mortgage. The next averment states, that Mar. 1, 1818, $420.30 became due, over and *above [*181 the sum before received, and that the plaintiff issued an *alias fieri facias* to the same county, which was returned in like manner as the first. The declaration then alleges that Streeter was insolvent, and had been so since Mar. 1, 1814, and that the defendant had notice of the proceedings against him, and of his insolvency.

The defendant pleaded *non est factum*, and that the plaintiff might have enforced payment by due process of law, and took issue as to the insolvency of Streeter.

The verdict was taken, by consent, for $586.-86, subject to the opinion of the court, the amount to be reduced, if necessary, to such sum as the plaintiff is entitled to recover.

At the trial, the bond was given in evidence;

and by the indorsements on the back, it appears that the interest for 1810, 1811 and 1813, except 36 cents, was received; but there is no evidence that the interest for 1812 had been paid by Streeter, or that any prosecution was commenced previous to 1814. For this omission, the defendant contends that the plaintiff has not complied with the contract, and consequently, that he is exonerated. There is no doubt that the defendant is not liable for the interest of 1812, by reason of the neglect to prosecute for upwards of two years thereafter. When this interest fell due, the plaintiff, to whom it was payable, had a right to receive it from Streeter, or remit it to him, or, if he chose, to forbear a prosecution, and thereby incur the risk of loss, by exonerating the defendant to that extent. He was authorized so to do, within the fair construction of the assignment. It is immaterial to the defendant, provided no claim for its payment can be enforced against him. It would be a forced and unnatural construction, to suppose the parties intended that nothing short of actual payment should suspend a suit against Streeter, although the same object was attained, so far as the defended is concerned, if the plaintiff by any other act relinquished his hold upon him. I apprehend this objection cannot be supported upon any principle of law or justice.

In *Ten Eyck* v. *Tibbets*, 1 Cai., 427, the bond assigned was payable by installments; the **182***] plaintiffs covenanted to use *all due diligence, and to take all legal measures by prosecution at law. The first installment was payable May 1, 1798, but no action was commenced until May 1, 1799, when the second became due. In the action to recover against the assignors, no notice was taken of the first installment; the plaintiffs did not claim to recover it of the defendants; but, among other things, it was urged by them that it was the duty of the plaintiffs to have proceeded, and that if the installment had not been paid or sued for, the plaintiffs lost all right to look to the defendants for any future sums. The objection was not regarded. Thompson, *J.*, says, "it is a sufficient answer to say that no demand is made of the defendants for that installment; any delay or laches of the plaintiffs in this respect, can only be alleged when a demand is made upon the defeudants." On this point Radcliff, *J.*, concurred, and Lewis, *Ch. J.*, seems not to have noticed the objection.

The action against Streeter was not commenced until May vacation, 1814. It is contended that it ought to have been commenced previous to that term. By the terms "due process of law," I understand all ordinary legal measures, prosecuted with good faith. In considering the question of due diligence, I think it relevant to look at the testimony relative to Streeter's responsibility in Apr., 1814. He had been jailor and deputy-sheriff a number of years. Sheriff Doty testified that as early as 1814 he was unable to pay his debts; he did not know that he owned any real estate; since that time he has had but trifling personal property, and that generally covered by execution; and that he had no other means of supporting the prisoners, than with the money paid him by the county. One witness thought that in 1814 and 1815 a judgment of $100 might have been collected; but several other witnesses stated that he had been reputed to be insolvent from the time he went to Philadelphia with a drove of horses, which appeared to be previous to the last war. Another witness thought if the judgment had been obtained in August Term, instead of October, and a *ca. sa*, issued after a *fi. fa.*, the debt could not have been collected.

*These facts render it highly proba- [***183** ble, that had the suit been commenced Apr. 1, 1814, the result would have been the same. Do they not show reasonable diligence in point of time? Every question of due diligence must be decided by a view of all the facts and circumstances. What would be a lache in one case, might be reasonable diligence in another. It will not be contended that due diligence requires a prosecution to be commenced, in every case on the day the money is payable. If a party intends that, he will guard his contract as in the case before cited, where the plaintiffs covenanted to prosecute "immediately after the several sums of money become due." There is no such stipulation in this case. I entirely concur with the reasoning of *Mr. Justice* Thompson on this point, in the case cited. He observes, "If there were any circumstances, whereby any loss might probably be sustained for want of due diligence in procuring payment of the first installment, it might have been proper evidence for the defendants to have availed themselves of, on the issue with respect to due diligence." I think the evidence satisfactory, that no loss has thereby been sustained. A reasonable discretion, as to time, was intended to be vested in the plaintiff by the language of the assignment; the strict construction contended for by the defendant would, I apprehend, be a departure from the obvious import. I conclude, then, that the plaintiff is not chargeable with neglect by omitting to commence the action until May vacation, 1814.

The case of *Moakley* v. *Riggs*, 19 Johns., 69, is not applicable. There the defendant undertook that the note was good and collectable after due course of law. The plaintiff sued the indorsers, but not the maker, and averred that the maker was discharged, under the Insolvent Act, 17 months after the note become due. The defendant demurred, and the court held that this neglect discharged the defendant. Whether the maker was possessed of property during the 17 months did not appear. They could not presume that he was not, nor could they say the money might not have been collected if a suit had been instituted when the note fell due. They were not called on to express an opinion, whether the *plaintiff [***184** could pass a term with safety; for, however that might be, there was no doubt that 17 months would discharge from the guaranty. The expression, that a term should not have been lost, may be regarded in that case as an *obiter dictum*. Admitting, however, that it is to be considered as authority, it must be understood as applicable to the case then under consideration, where there was no evidence to show that the money could not have been collected by due course of law. It would not, I apprehend, have been laid down as a rule, had the facts corresponded with this case. In the case of *Kies* v. *T. & S. Tifft*, 1 Cow., 98, the facts were these ; the defendants gave a note to the plaintiff, payable Feb. 1, 1820, and the plaintiff assigned to the defendants a mortgage against Lewis and Tifft, the last installment of which was payable on the same day. By a condition to the note underwritten, the defendants agreed that if the mortgage should be collected by the time set forth, then the note to be payable at the time therein specified; if not, the note was not payable until the money was collected on the mortgage by due course of law. It did not appear that the defendants had ever prosecuted Lewis, the mortgagor. Aug. 8, 1820, Kies commenced his action on the ground that the defendant had not used due diligence. It was not pretended that Lewis was not of sufficient ability to pay. The court held that the defendants were liable, that they ought not to have suffered a term to pass without a prosecution, particularly as they were so directed by the plaintiff. This case is also clearly distinguishable from the present. There was no insolvency of the mortgagor proved, or that he was destitute of property, nor that the premises mortgaged, were not abundantly sufficent to satisfy the debt. No cause is assigned for not prosecuting. The inference is, that the defendants did not elect so to do, and consequently could have no well founded complaint for being held liable to pay the note.

The next objection is, that the plaintiff has not proved notice of the proceedings to the defendant, and a demand of payment. The declaration avers notice of the proceedings against Streeter and his insolvency ; the truth of this **185***] averment *is admitted by the pleadings. By the plea of *non est factum*, the execution of the instrument only is put in issue ; all the other material facts are thereby admitted. (10 Johns., 47).

The other pleas put in issue the solvency of Streeter, and that the plaintiff might have enforced payment by due process of law. The averment of notice is not traversed. It was, therefore, unnecessary to offer further evidence on that point, at the trial. The liability of the defendant rested on this, that the plaintiff had done all that the covenant required of him.

If the facts, of which the defendant was notified, are, in judgment of law, sufficient to charge him, then his duty required him to pay without a demand. By the express terms of the covenant, he is to pay, if the plaintiff cannot obtain payment by due process of law. After knowledge of this, to insist on a demand, is to make a requisition not required by the contract. There is a difference between a mere duty and a collateral sum. Where the first is promised to be paid on request, no actual request is necessary ; but it is on a promise to pay a collateral sum upon request ; and had the contract in this case contained that stipulation, the plaintiff could not recover without proving it ; but it is not provided for, and was, therefore, unnecessary to be proved. (1 Saund., 33).

It is also objected that the facts proved on the trial do not show that the money could not have been collected of Streeter in 1814. I have, in some measure, anticipated this objection. It may safely be conceded that they do not conclusively establish that fact; but do they not remove all reasonable doubt on this subject, and satisfy the mind, that in the exercise of a sound discretion, the plaintiff might well consider it immaterial whether a suit was commenced a term sooner or later ? If there is sufficient ground for deeming the difference of time immaterial, which I think there is, then there was no want of due diligence in permitting the May Term to pass without a suit.

It is also urged that a *ca. sa.* ought to have issued after the return of a *fi. fa.* The contract does not, in my view, *require it, when [*186 it is evident that no benefit could be derived by issuing that process, nor any injury to the defendant sustained by the omission. The certain consequence would have been, the accumulation of costs to be paid by the plaintiff, without any prospect of remuneration. It is enough that all reasonable measures be pursued, such as a prudent man would take in conducting his affairs with skill and judgment. To take every possible step, and exhaust every legal process, to no valuable purpose, does not seem to be demanded by the contract of the parties. I am of opinion that the plaintiff is entitled to judgment.

SUTHERLAND, *J.*, after stating the facts. It is contended on the part of the defendant that the plaintiff is not entitled to recover. 1. Because he has not used due diligence in prosecuting Streeter, the obligor. 2. Because he has not used all legal means to collect the money from him, no *ca. sa.* having been issued on the judgment. 3. Because he has neither averred or proved a demand of payment from the defendant of the sum in arrear, before suit brought.

The first installment and all the interest which became due upon it having been paid, and constituting no part of the plaintiff's demand in this action, whether he was guilty of laches or not in the collection of that installment, cannot effect his present claim. The evidence establishes, beyond all question, the insolvency of Streeter Mar. 1, 1814 ; and that he had no real property to be affected by a judgment. The principal question in this case arose in the case of *Ten Eyck* v. *Tibbits*, 1 Cai., 427. That was also an action of covenant upon an assignment of a bond payable by installments. The covenant was substantially like the one in question. The plaintiff's action was founded on the non-payment of the second installment ; and in his declaration he neither averred payment of the first installment, nor took any notice of it. It was objected that if the first installment was not paid at the day it was the duty of the plaintiff to have commenced a suit and obtained a judgment for the penalty, which would have operated as a security for the subsequent installment; and that he ought *affirmatively to have shown, [*187 either that it was paid at the day or that a suit was commenced. In answer to this, Thompson, *J.*, in his opinion says : "It is sufficient that no demand is made of the defendant for that installment; and the presumption is that that it has been paid. Any delay or laches of the plaintiffs in this respect, however, it appears to me, can only be alleged when a demand is made upon them for that installment. If there were any circumstances (shown) whereby any loss might probably be sustained for want or due diligence in procuring payment of the first installment, it might have been proper evidence for the defendant on the issue with respect to due diligence, &c. The other judges were of the same opinion.

But in the case before us, admitting the question of laches as to the first installment to be open, I think it may well be doubted whether the plaintiff was in default. It does not appear when the proceedings for foreclosing the mortgage were commenced. The sale was in Dec., nine months after the first installment became due. There is nothing in this fact from which the presumption necessarily arises that there was any delay in instituting the proceedings. Every presumption is in favor of the diligence of the plaintiff, and it is for the defendant affirmatively to make out a neglect of duty. The sale may have been postponed for want of bidders; or it may have been delayed for other justifiable reasons. It can hardly be contended that it was the duty of the plaintiff simultaneously to prosecute the bond and foreclose the mortgage. He must do both if necessary, before he can resort to the defendant. But he may first try the effect of the one and if that is unavailing, then resort to the other. Here the foreclosure produced more than sufficient to pay all that became due previons to Mar. 1, 1818; and if no suit had been commenced by the plaintiff on the bond, I am not prepared to say that his right would have been affected by the omission, unless it appeared that it had been injurious to the defendant. But here a suit was commenced in *M*ay vacation after the installment became due; that is, within two months. This is *prima facie* sufficient. Where the plaintiff resided at the time does not appear. He may have lived in **188***] *a remote part of the State from which process could not, without extraordinary care and diligence, have been issued and served before the *M*ay Term. Reasonable diligence is all that is required.

The *dicta* in *Moakley* v. *Riggs*, 19 Johns., 72, and *Kies* v. *Tifft*, 1 Cow., 98, "that a term must not be permitted to elapse before suit is brought," must be taken in connection with the fact in those cases. There was great and unnecessary delay in both.

In relation to the second installment, the only laches imputed to the plaintiff is in not issuing a *ca. sa.* A *testatum fi. fa.* was issued immediately after it became due, which was returned *nulla bona*, and the declaration avers that the defendant had notice of the fact. This court has held that where a party undertakes to pay the debt of a third person, if it cannot be collected from him, it is necessary to issue not only a *fi. fa.* but a *ca. sa.*, against the original debtor, before recourse can be had to the surety. I do not well see how this case is to be distinguished from that. The fact that here the proceedings are in the name of the guarantor, and that if the body of Streeter, the obligor, had been taken in execution, it would have been a satisfaction of the debt as between him and Woods, does not appear to me to vary the case. That is a risk which Woods assumed if, by the terms of the covenant, it was the plaintiff's duty to issue a *ca. sa.* before he could resort to him. The taking of Streeter in execution would not have affected the plaintiff's right of action against Woods.

It is no answer to say that Streeter was insolvent, and that there is no reason to suppose that a *ca. sa.* would have produced the money. Upon that point the witnesses entertained different opinions; and it is the right of the defendant to insist that the effect of it shall be determined, not by the opinion of witnesses, but by actual experiment. By the terms of the defendant's covenant the issuing of a *ca. sa.* against Streeter was a condition precedent to his liability; and it was incumbent on the plaintiff to show a performance of that condition, or that its performance was dispensed with by the defendant before he can resort to him. *Moakley* v. *Riggs*, 19 Johns., 71-2, per Spencer, *J.*

*It was not necessary for the plaintiff to aver or prove a demand of payment from the defendant before suit brought. The declaration contains all that was necessary to be averred on that point; notice to the defendant of the issuing a *fi. fa.* against Streeter, and a return of *nulla bona*, and that Streeter was insolvent. If those facts established the position that the money could not be collected from Streeter by due process of law (as the plaintiff supposed), this was enough. The defendant's liability then immediately accrued. It was no part of the contract that payment should be demanded before suit brought. Notice of the facts from which the defendant's liability necessarily resulted was all that was necessary to be averred. The bringing of the action was a sufficient demand. [***189**

But upon the second point I have come to the conclusion, though with reluctance, that the defendant is entitled to judgment.

SAVAGE, *Ch. J.*, concurred with *Mr. Justice* Woodworth: and proceeded to estimate the amount which the plaintiff ought to recover, according to the principles laid down by him. And a majority of *the Court* finally concurred in a judgment for the plaintiff for $476.60.

Judgment for the plaintiff.

Cited in—9 Cow., 312; 1 Wend.,461; 5 Wend., 308; 11 Wend., 105, 634; 13 Wend., 545; 14 Wend., 233; 21 Wend., 58; 5 Barb., 504; 6 Barb., 552; 14 Barb., 78, 582; 24 Barb., 511; 31 Barb., 94; 38 Barb., 106; 56 Barb., 82; 18 How. Pr., 283; 2 Hall, 489; 4 E. D. S., 476; 39 Mich., 713; 33 Am. Rep., 448 (39 Mich., 710).

---

*CLARK *v.* PHELPS ET AL. [*190

Laying out Highway—Powers of Commissioners—Cannot Lay out Highway Through Buildings, etc.—Right of Owner of Cultivated Land to Appeal from Decision of Commissioners—Right, Personal—Effect of Delay, on Part of Judges in Hearing Appeal—Practice.

By the Act to Regulate Highways (2 R. L., 270, sec. 1, 16), the Commissioners of Highways are authorized to lay out public highways, through land lying in a state of nature, or through improved or cultivated land, commonly so called; but this provision does not authorize them to lay out a highway through buildings, mills or manufactories, or fixtures, yards, &c., appurtenant to them, without consent of the owner.

Accordingly, where Commissioners laid out, and opened a road through a corn crib, mill yard, and the tenter bars of a fulling mill, held that they were liable to the owner in trespass.

The right of the owner of improved or cultivated land, through which the Commissioners have laid a highway, to appeal to three judges of the Court of C. P., under the 36th section of the Act (2 R. L., 282), is personal to such owner, whose private rights cannot be affected by an appeal in behalf of any other person, through whose land the same road may also have been laid. If there be several owners, each may appeal for himself.

It is the duty of the judges to whom such appeal is made, to convene and decide it as soon as may be, on a day, &c., which they shall agree upon, of which they should give notice to the parties, who then, and not till then, are bound to attend, or be concluded.

An appeal suspends the powers of the Commissioners; and till their acts are affirmed by a decision, they cannot open the road. If they do so, they are trespassers.

When one C., through whose land a road was laid, appealed to three judges; then M., through whose land the same road passed, appealed to three judges, two of whom were the same judges appealed to by C.; and C. appeared before the last Board, and objected to their proceeding, on the ground that his appeal was first; but his objection was overruled; and he then stated his reasons against the proceedings of the Commissioners, in passing over the ground through which the road ran; and the judges affirmed the acts of the Commissioners; held, notwithstanding, that their decision was void, and of no effect as to C.; and that he was entitled to select the three judges who were to pass upon his rights.

After C.'s appeal, one of the judges to whom he appealed went abroad, and did not return till after M.'s appeal was decided; and no further proceedings were had by C.; and the Commissioners laid out and opened the road; yet held, that C.'s appeal continued in force, and was not to be deemed discontinued or abandoned by the neglect of the judges to convene and hear it; and that the Commissioners were trespassers.

If the Commissioners deem the judges dilatory, they should apply to them to fix a day for the hearing.

After the appeal, the judges become actors, and if they do not proceed, it cannot be imputed as a lache to the party.

Where a road is laid out through improved land, on the petition of twelve men, upon the proceeding coming in question before a court, it will be intended that they were 12 reputable freeholders, within the words of the Act (2 R. L., 275, sec. 16), until the contrary be shown. Per Woodworth, *J.*, interrupting *Mr.* Platt, *arguendo*.

Citation—2 R. L., 270.

TRESPASS *quare clausum fregit*, tried July 16, 1823, at the Tompkins Circuit, before Nelson, Circuit Judge.

The plaintiff proved that the defendants, in Nov., 1821, opened a road through his land, and in doing so pulled down a corn crib which the plaintiff had used as such for several years; and ploughed and scraped 12 or 15 rods through the plaintiff's mill yards; and erected a bridge across Salmon Creek; so as to injure the plaintiff's water privileges for mills; ploughed and scraped close to the rear of the plaintiff's dwelling-house, and cut up his door yard with wagons and teams in carrying stone and timber for the bridge. The plaintiff had, on his premises, a saw mill, fulling mill and **191***] *carding machine. In June, 1821, the plaintiff had agreed with a carpenter to build him a dwelling-house, pointing out the spot where it now stands as the site. Some of the timber was procured in Aug. and the dwelling-house finally erected before the actual opening of the road, but after it was laid out. The road cut off about two rods of the plaintiff's tenter bars, erected for carrying on the business of his fulling mill; but it was in fact worked and traveled so as not to interfere with the tenter bars of the dwelling-house.

The defendants justified as Commissioners of Highways, and proved that they had, Aug. 14, 1821, laid out the road according to the provisions of the Act to Regulate Highways, on the petition of 12 freeholders; and that they had proceeded according to the directions of the 16th section of that Act (2 R. L., 275.)

The plaintiff then proved that he appealed from this act of the Commissioners to R. Smith, S. Crittenden and J. Sutton, three of the judges of the C. P. of Tompkin's Co., giving them notice of his appeal, Aug. 21, 1821. *Judge* Smith declined attending to hear the appeal till after his return from the late State Convention, of which he was a member, when he promised to give the plaintiff notice, &c. This was never done.

The defendants proved that in the meantime, Andrew Myers, through whose improved land the same road ran, appealed to Crittenden, Sutton and Gere, three of the judges of Tompkins Co., Crittenden and Sutton being two of the judges to whom the plaintiff had appealed, who, Sept. 22, 1821, met and heard and decided the appeal affirming the proceedings of the Commissioners; that the plaintiff appeared before them with counsel, and apprised them of his appeal, and objected to their proceeding; but afterwards went with the judges on the line of the road, through his premises, and pointed out his objections; and was present when the decision was made; that proper notice had been given to the plaintiff, to remove his fences previous to the opening of the road.

The plaintiff offered to prove that the road ran through *his mill yards, so as to [***192**
deprive him of the beneficial use of his mills; but this evidence was overruled: and under the direction of the judge, the jury found for the defendants. The only question of fact submitted to them was, whether the road did not run through the plaintiff's garden, occupied as such for four years before the road had been laid out.

Mr. J. Platt, moved to set aside the verdict, and for a new trial. He insisted:

1. That the Commissioners had no power, under the Act to Regulate Highways (2 R. L., 270), to destroy the plaintiff's mill site, or lay out a road through a building of any kind. This Act creates their office, and defines their power. The language of the 1st section is general. By this, their authority as to the nature of the ground is unlimited in terms, but it refers to the limitation in the 16th section, which confines their power to improved or cultivated land; or, as they are called, in another part of this section, inclosed or improved lands. What is the meaning of these terms? They are not technical, and must, therefore, be understood according to their ordinary acceptation, which is merely land brought from its wild uncultivated state, and made capable of present use, for the purpose of crops. The various provisions of the 16th section relate to land of this description. The whole of this section is a mere proviso to the 1st. It was assumed by the Legislature, that to run a road through wild lands rather conferred a benefit than worked an injury to the owner; but in reference to improved, inclosed or cultivated lands, it was otherwise. The court will, however, in construction, limit the description according to the nature of the case, the subject-matter, and the power of the Legislature. From these

we think there is an implied restriction to wild lands, or improved or cultivated lands, properly so-called. The Legislature had no power to burden other lands. There is a proviso in this 16th section, that a road shall not be laid through a garden, or orchard of a certain age or growth. No adequate mode of assessing damages is provided for the injury to building, mill seats and the like; and it would be **193***] injurious to them, to suppose *they intended to confer a power to lay roads through a building, without any adequate provision for compensation. The power extends merely to improved or cultivated land, in the sense for which we contend. Look at the great caution which they have exercised relative to the demolition of buildings, in laying out streets in the City of N. Y. Express words were deemed necessary to confer this power, and the most cautious provisions were adopted against its abuse. It would be absurd to call a corn crib improved or cultivated land. So of the mill seat, in its natural state. The tenter bars were necessary for the enjoyment of the fulling mill. The Legislature thought that a garden or orchard might have come within the power given, and therefore inserted an express exception of these. Why was this done? They were considered as peculiarly dear to the owner, being generally appurtenant to his dwelling-house. Shall we be told that the Legislature have guarded the appurtenance, but have left the building unprotected? That they have carefully saved the incident, without intending to protect the principal? That a paltry cabbage or potato patch shall be held sacred, while the dwelling-house may be destroyed? It is a well settled rule of construction, that, though a statute may be couched in such general terms, as by a full and extended construction to take away private property, it shall be restricted in it operation to other objects. The court will intend that the Legislature did not mean to do injustice to the individual, and adopt such a construction as is consistent with the rights of the subject. *Gardner* v. *Trustees of N.*, 2 Johns. Ch., 162; *The People* v. *Platt*, 17 Johns., 195, 315; *Bradshaw* v. *Rogers*, 20 Johns., 103, 106; *Varick* v. *Corp. of N. Y.*, 4 Johns. Ch., 53; Bac. Abr., Statute, I, pl. 10, p. 391; *Wales* v. *Stetson*, 2 Mass., 143, 146. The 39th section of the Act to Regulate Highways also affords a strong inference against the power set up in this case. It provides for the removal of fences in all cases where a road is laid out through inclosed lands. This shows plainly that the Legislature had in view ordinary inclosed fields merely; and it is inconsistent with any other construction than the one for which we contend.

194*] *These fences are to be removed on a notice of 60 days only. If the removal of a building was contemplated, the operation may, in many cases, be very dilatory and expensive. The mere materials of some houses would sell for $5,000. Yet there is no power to extend the time, and no provision for the extraordinary expense.

2. It nowhere appears, in the proceedings, that the freeholders who petitioned to have the road laid out were reputable freeholders, in the language of the 16th section of the Act.

WOODWORTH, *J.* This is clearly to be intended, till the contrary is shown; and we so held in a case lately before us.

3. We had appealed from these proceedings, by which the power of the Commissioners was suspended. They had no jurisdiction till our appeal was determined. The second appeal could have no effect upon our rights. *Prior in tempore, potior est in jure*, applies. The 36th section, which gives the right of appeal, has prescribed no limit of time for deciding upon it. This right is given in severalty to each and every one aggrieved by the act of the Commissioners, and the decision of the judges is made conclusive in the premises. Though there may be an appeal on account of the public inconvenience, in which case a single one may settle the question for that purpose, it was also intended for the more important end, if vindicating private right. Meyers had a right to appeal in his own name; but the determination in his case should not be allowed to affect ours. Our rights are to be decided upon our own appeal, and that only. We had a right to the services of *Judge* Smith as a constituent member of the Board. This Board were limited to the subject-matter of the particular appeal. On that alone could the decision be final and conclusive within the meaning of the Statute. Our rights are not to be litigated through Meyers, the decision of whose appeal ought not to affect us upon any principle. It was a matter over which we had no control; we had no chance to counteract any abuse of our rights, because we were not a party. Meyers *might [***195** have stated that the road was beneficial to him; that he appealed because his neighbor Clark was injured, and such an admission, which we had no right to contradict, should have produced an instantaneous decision against the appeal. The inquiry would be "what business have you with Clark's interests?" The Board would be right in saying, "you agree with the public that the road should be laid; and, as between you and them, there is no issue. There is nothing for us to decide."

SUTHERLAND, *J.* Does not the Statute require the judges, on appeal, to examine and dceide upon the entire road laid out by the Commissioners?

Their power can only be co-extensive with the subject-matter of the appeal. The time has been, and that, too, since the passage of the Act of which this is a revision, when a single town was so large that a road might be laid through it by the Commissioners, affecting hundreds of farms. The appeal is from the Commissioners of the town; and the rights of several different individuals are usually involved in the inquiry. The law requires notice to none beside the Commissioners. By all others, the discovery that there is an appeal may be merely accidental. The appellant may select three judges, some of whom may be inimical to the rights of his neighbors, though indifferent as to his own. We are deprived of this right of election, as well as of notice. There are two modes of assessing damages provided, after the decision upon appeal, if it should be against the appellant. One of these must be elected by the party interested, within 30 days after the determination of the appeal. (2 R. L., 282, 3, sec. 38.) Of this privilege we may also be deprived for want of notice, if the appeal of a third person is to affect us. It cannot be that the Legislature intended to act with such a total disregard to private right. Each proprietor should have a chance to act and speak for himself. Without this, the right of appeal would be a mockery.

Mr. J. A. Collier, for the defendant. This is the ordinary case of a road laid out through **196***] improved lands on petition, *without the consent of the owner; an appeal and confirmation by the judges. Upon this, the defendants, the Commissioners, gave the plaintiff notice to remove his fences, and after waiting the 60 days, without obedience being yielded to their notice, they go on, as they lawfully might, and open the road themselves. Clark, the plaintiff, appeared before the judges to whom Meyers appealed, was heard there upon his objections to the road; the judges passed upon the merits of these objections; and then the plaintiff, finding that they were overruled, instead of resorting to his *certiorari*, commences an action of trespass against the Commissioners, who, throughout this business, did no more than their duty.

The bold ground is taken, that the improvements in question are of a nature not coming within the jurisdiction of the Commissioners. It is admitted, however, that the words of the Statute are general: that they reach the case; and it is sought in vain to find any express exception of it. An implied qualification is, however, sought for in the 16th section. It is said to result from the nature of the provisions found there, giving a different mode of proceeding in the two cases of waste and improved lands; but it is admitted that nothing is expressly taken out of the power of the Commissioners, except gardens and orchards of a certain age; and it would seem to follow that, in relation to all other improvements, their power is unlimited. The court cannot legislate other exceptions into existence. The provisions for assessing damages are even more liberal than in the instance put of demolishing buildings in the metropolis. The party may elect between a jury of the vicinage, and commissioners to be appointed by a judge of the C. P. The law secures an impartial constable (2 R. L., 284, sec. 45), and an impartial jury. None of the jurors who certify in favor of the road are allowed to sit in assessing the damages (sess. 40, ch. 43, sec. 1), and the right of appeal is given from the assessment of the Commissioners to three judges of the C. P. (*Id.*, sec. 2.) These instances indicate a most scrupulous care in the Legislature to guard the rights of the individual. The Commissioners had a right to act, unless it be true that **197***] *private property cannot be taken for public use, even with the most ample provision for compensation.

The measure upon which the court are called to animadvert, by giving a very narrow construction to the Act, is said to be the unwarrantable destruction of a fixture. This fixture is, in plain English, a mere corn crib, slightly built. We contend that Commissioners may interfere with any improvements, except gardens and orchards. It would be lamentable that a flourishing village must be deprived of a very necessary road, because a corn crib or mill site happen to intervene. All this comes in very properly upon a calculation of damages. The exceptions of gardens and orchards may have been merely arbitrary. There does not seem to be any reason in the exception; but surely it cannot follow that houses and fixtures are, therefore, to be excepted. They are demolished every day in the City of N. Y. for public purposes. In *Goodell* v. *Jackson*, 20 Johns., 725, 6, 7, the language of the Court of Errors will be found to constitute an able argument against the narrow construction contended for.

The decision upon the appeal was final and conclusive, till reversed on *certiorari*. The plaintiff did not prosecute his own appeal with due diligence. He should have applied to some other judge on being informed that Smith could not attend to the appeal. The business, in its nature, required immediate attention, and could not be postponed to suit the individual convenience of the judge. When jurisdiction was given to the judges by Meyers' appeal, the plaintiff should have applied to another judge, if he could not trust those selected by Myers, and associated him with the others as one of the Board of Appeal. Suppose *Judge* Smith had gone to Europe—were proceedings to be suspended till his return? Does the mere fact of giving notice to three judges that an appeal is made to them, confer exclusive jurisdiction? The notice to Smith was necessarily conditional. Myers had the same rights as the plaintiff; and unless he had appealed before Smith's return, would have lost his remedy by lapse of time. Suppose Smith had died; must the proceedings *be hung up forever? [***198**
At any rate the plaintiff might waive the right of nomination; and he has done this.

Any one aggrieved has a right of appeal. *People* v. *Champion*, 16 Johns., 61. And the 36th section 2 R. L., 282, makes the decision on appeal conclusive. The road is finally established by the Board of Appeal till altered by an equal power. (2 R. L., 282, sec. 37.) The reason of this provision is, that the Board are supposed to have all the facts relating to the entire road laid out, before them on a single appeal. Anyone wishing to impeach the road may be heard before them. Is it possible the Legislature intended that the Commissioners should be harassed by a series of appeals, separate and numerous as the individuals interested may be? At this rate few roads could be laid out short of several months litigation. The first decision must conclude as to the whole road; and a decision to the contrary would virtually defeat the Act by rendering its execution impracticable. The individual may not stop at the judges of the C. P., but may sue out a *certiorari* to this court; and upon the basis contended for, 50 or 100 writs of *certiorari* might be brought upon the same road. Some might be affirmed and some reversed. The two extremes of the road may be established and the middle gone. These great inconveniences cannot be avoided, unless the act of the Commissioners is considered entire—all its parts standing or falling together upon one review, co-extensive with the subject matter.

The maxim, *prior in tempore potior in jure*, relied on for the plaintiff, applies with the greater force against him. The decision establishing our right was first in time, the judges having jurisdiction of the subject-matter. Myers exercised proper diligence. The idea that notice to the plaintiff was unnecessary and legally inefficient, is a mistaken one. In *Com. of Kinderhook* v. *Claw*, 15 Johns., 537, it was held that notice must be given to all parties interested. But if this be otherwise, the remedy is with the Legislature only. By the 42d sess., ch. 127, sec. 1, a road once established by three judges may be revoked by other judges. This can only be where the Commissioners have decided in favor of the **199***] *road. If they withhold their assent, and the judges reverse their decision, and adjudge the road to be laid out, it is the business of the Commissioners to go on and open it. *People* v. *Champion*, 16 Johns., 61; *The Same* v. *Commissioners of Salem*, 1 Cow., 23. If several appeals may be had, one set of judges may lay out the road, and another may refuse it. The 39th section expressly protects the Commissioners in all their acts consequent upon an appeal and confirmation. All these provisions show, most clearly, that the Legislature never contemplated more than one appeal.

If the judges acted improperly in going into the merits upon Myer's appeal, after the plaintiff had raised the question of jurisdiction on the ground of his prior appeal, he should have come to this court on *certiorari*. *Beach* v. *Furman*, 9 Johns., 229; *Butler* v. *Potter*, 17 *Id.*, 245; *Freeman* v. *Cornwall*, 10 *Id.*, 470. He has been deprived of no right. He had every chance to elect the mode in which his damages should be assessed; and though he suffered the 30 days to pass without an election, the Commissioners were equally bound to see that he had his pay upon the assessment of a jury. *In the matter of Johnston*, 19 Johns., 272.

Mr. Platt, in reply. To say that the Commissioners are expressly protected by the mandate of the judges, begs the question of jurisdiction. If the Commissioners had no power to lay the road, the act of the judges cannot help them to it; and the whole proceeding is void.

The plaintiff did not submit his rights to the second Board of Judges. He objected expressly to their taking cognizance of the matter, on the ground that he had made an appeal in his own name; and his going to the merits, after being overruled, was not a waiver.

It is conceded that if no compensation is provided for the injury to buildings and fixtures, even an express power to the Commissioners would be void. This must depend on the 16th section, which I think I have shown, narrows down the injury to what is cultivated lands? These words I have defined. They mean a close cultivated for agricultural pur- **200***] poses. *I deny that a graveyard, for instance, would be included in the term "improved, inclosed or cultivated lands," as used by the 16th section. Would a church be included? If a witness should swear that a lot was uncultivated, what would be understood by this? Merely that crops were not raised upon it. Inclosed and improved lands are used in various parts of the Statute in the same sense. Does a corn crib, tenter bars and mill seat come within these terms? The Commissioners act under limited powers, which should be construed, if possible, consistently with private right. These powers are perfectly susceptible of such a construction. This is the first time we hear of their exertion upon buildings and fixtures, &c. The total absence of such attempts is a practical construction of the Statute, sanctioned by an acquiescence of the whole community.

There was no unnecessary delay by the plaintiff in urging on the appeal. It was no more than reasonable, under the circumstances, that he should be indulged till *Judge* Smith's return. He had a right to select three judges, out of the five appointed by government. This narrow right of selection should not be fettered by a rigid construction. Because a judge is necessarily absent a short time on business, to wait for his return should not operate as a waiver. Presenting the petition, or giving notice of the appeal, must, in practice, be received as conclusive evidence of a *bona fide* intention to prosecute it with effect, as rapidly as circumstances will admit. It is not necessary to speculate upon the consequence of *Judge* Smith's death. Probably the court will say that such an event, being the act of God, should work no injury, and require the substitution of another judge. At any rate, when there is an appeal, there must be a decision before the road can be opened.

SUTHERLAND, *J.* Suppose one appeals, and declines going forward with it, what remedy have the public, or other individuals, who may be interested in hastening a decision?

This would, perhaps, depend, in some measure, on the question, whether the appeal be on account of the private *or the public [***201** injury. If, for the private, there may be 100 appeals or more; whereas, if an individual appeals in behalf of the public, one single decision would settle their rights. But, in either case, on application to this court, by any relator who should be interested, Your Honors would see that the judges should not unreasonably delay proceeding upon the appeal.

The distinction between a case ended by one appeal and a case depending on several, hangs upon the difference between an appeal in right of the public and in right of an individual. In the former case, the appellant is in the nature of a relator upon a *mandamus* or information; the whole subject-matter is covered by the proceeding; whereas the appeals against private injuries must be as distinct from each other as actions of trespass. The decision, as to Myers, is an affirmance *pro tanto* merely. It reaches so much of the road, only, as runs upon his farm. The Commissioners must wait till all appeals are out of the way. To be sure, there may be delay; and there should be. The subject-matter is a private right. The object is to devest it; and if more obstacles were in the way, I should rejoice at it. If a road be laid without petition, through wild or uncultivated lands, several appeals would also lie; and in either case, if a part of the road be affirmed, and part reversed, the public must take the consequences. If embarrassed by such a result, there is then a summary power to discontinue the part which is held good, if it should be deemed not worth the preserving. Each appeal, however, would usually be considered in reference to the propriety of retaining the whole, or only part of the road; and cases might very well arise, in which it should be reversed in part and affirmed in part, like a judgment. If a road be wholly refused, it is not final. It does not preclude the Commissioners afterwards going on, and laying out a road upon a change of circumstances requiring this to be done.

Had the judges affirmed Myers' appeal, leaving ours pending, the supervisors of the county might have refused to assess the damages of the former, till the event of the second appeal was known. If these decisions operate **202***] *pro* **tanto* only, which I think must be holden clear, the same inconveniences arise, whether there be one, two or more appeals. The 37th section 2 R. L., 282, does not apply to a case like the present. That relates to a refusal of the Commissioners to lay out the road, and their being overruled on appeal, and the road laid out. They are then finally bound. But if they lay out in the first instance, and their proceedings are reversed, all is at large, and the Commissioners may, in their discretion, proceed *de novo*.

It is said we should proceed by *certiorari*. Unfortunately, we are not parties to the appeal. Not being bound by it, we cannot question it. The court would tell us, "the decision is void as to you;" and quash the writ as unnecessary and officious. The mere fact that the law does not require notice to third persons, is of itself conclusive evidence that the party stands upon the merits of his own appeal alone.

Curia, per WOODWORTH, *J.* The Commissioners are authorized by the 1st section of the Act to Regulate Highways (2 R. L., 270), to lay out new roads under the restrictions therein mentioned. The 16th section specifies the exceptions, which are, that a road shall not be laid out through improved or cultivated land, without the consent of the owner, unless upon the application of twelve freeholders on oath; nor through any orchard or garden without the like consent, if the orchard be of the growth of four years, or the garden shall have been cultivated for the like period.

It follows, from these provisions, that the Commissioners may lay out new roads over land laying in a state of nature, and over such as are improved or cultivated within the meaning of those terms, as used in the Act. In all other cases, authority is not given. The exception implies the right, in the first case, because, by restricting the powers of the Commissioners where lands are improved or cultivated, it implies that no limitation was intended where there was no cultivation or improvement. It will be conceded that the words of the Act, taken most extensively, may include every species of improvement. The erection of **203***] dwelling-houses, *barns and out houses, mills and manufactories, are improvements of great value. There is no exception in terms, denying the right of the Commissioners to prostrate such buildings for the purpose of laying out roads; yet it has never been urged that such a right existed; nor am I aware that it has ever been exercised, without the consent of the owner. The reason is obvious; it is because such improvements, although highly beneficial, were not within the view of the Legislature; they did not so understand the terms, "improved or cultivated land." These terms are to be taken in the popular sense, according to the general understanding of the community, when distinguishing what is called wild land, or land in a state of nature, from that which has been cultivated and improved. The terms, to "improve or cultivate," may be considered synonymous. To cultivate is defined, "to improve the product of the earth by manual industry." When speaking of improved land, it is generally understood to be such as has been reclaimed, is used for the purpose of husbandry, and is cultivated as such, whether the appropriation is for tillage, meadow or pasture. The more valuable improvements on land comprising buildings and their immediate appurtenances, could not have been in contemplation, as appears evident by the exception itself. When, therefore, the exception protects a garden or orchard of four years, and is silent as to other improvements, the removal of which would be attended with greater inconvenience and loss to the owner, it goes far to give a construction to the meaning of the words. A fair inference may be drawn from this provision that the Legislature intended to confine the power of laying out roads within the limits I have stated. It became necessary to guard the right of the owner with respect to a garden and orchard; for they fall within the terms "improved and cultivated." A garden is formed by cultivation of the land strictly; the land on which an orchard is planted, is g[illegible]y used in like manner. If the Act had been silent as to these, there would be nothing opposed to their appropriation by the Commissioners, if they deemed it proper. Could the Legislature intend that a garden should be protected, and yet allow every other *appendage to the dwelling-house to [***204** be removed? That barns and out houses be taken down to give place to a road? Can a construction be tolerated, that the Commissioners, under this section, have power to prostrate court-yards, fences, trees and shrubbery, contiguous to a dwelling-house? Was it intended that the ground immediately adjoining mills and manufactories, indispenably necessary for the enjoyment and use of those establishments, might be converted into a road, and leave the owner to his damages, to be assessed under the Act? Can the Commissioners take from a manufactory the adjoining ground, which is actually used and occupied by the various machinery and their appendants, essential to such use, and in the absence of which the business cannot be carried on without loss or great inconvenience? I apprehend not. Grounds used in this manner may be said to be improved for those particular purposes; but they are not improved or cultivated land within the meaning of the Act. If this exposition of the Statute be correct, then the defendants had not authority to lay out the road in the manner they have done. The corn crib was a necessary appendant to the dwelling; the string of tenter bars appurtenant to the fulling mill, fixed two feet in the ground, for the purpose of hanging cloth, was necessary to be placed in the manner stated in the case. The road cuts off a portion of these bars and the corn crib. It seems, however, that it was worked and traveled so as not to interfere with the former. The plaintiff also offered to prove that the road includes so much of the yards of the saw mill and fulling mill as to deprive the plaintiff of their beneficial use. This was overruled. In the preceding particulars, it appears to me that the ground was appropriated in such a manner as not to fall within the description intended by the Act; and consequently, the Commissioners ought not to have included such parts in the road laid out.

But if this construction is not well founded, then the question is, whether the plaintiff's appeal has been disposed of. If it has not, the defendants were trespassers in opening the road. The plaintiff appealed in season to three judges, and, by the 36th section, it became
205*] their duty to *convene as soon as might be, and decide upon the appeal. When notice of the appeal was served on *Judge* Smith, he was about leaving home for the Convention, and agreed with the plaintiff to attend to it on his return. He was to fix on the time and give the plaintiff notice. Another of the judges states that the plaintiff informed him the business was to remain until Smith returned. It does not appear that any further proceedings have been had on this appeal; but shortly after it was made, Myers, through whose land the road also passed, appealed to three judges; two of whom were the same persons named by the plaintiff. They confirmed the laying out of the Commissioners, and it is now contended that this is conclusive on the plaintiff. When the judges met to decide the appeal of Myers, the plaintiff was present, and objected to their proceedings, as his appeal remained undetermined. The judges determined to proceed. The plaintiff went on to the ground with the judges, and pointed out his objections; but there is no evidence that at any time he waived his appeal. The plaintiff probably supposed that the appeal of Myers would affect his interest, and that it would be conclusive on him; but he was mistaken. His appeal was then in full force, and could not be abandoned without his consent. No such consent can be inferred from his accompanying the judges and stating his objections. As he was not bound to regard the proceedings of Myers, is was not a waiver, express or implied. The plaintiff never appealed to the judges selected by Myers; they could not gain jurisdiction of the appeal by implication. The Statute contemplates that the appeal be made expressly, and that the party appealing name the judges. Under such circumstances, it would be a perversion of the Act to consider the plaintiff's appeal before them.

The true construction of the Act is, that every person conceiving himself aggrieved may appeal. Such are the words, and such evidently the intent. A road may extend through a town—it may pass through twenty farms. The owner of land at one extremity may have good cause to appeal, so far as he is concerned; but he has no interest or con-
206*] cern *with the owner of land at the other extreme point, six miles distant. The questions are altogether disconnected. One may show sufficient cause to reverse as to him; and, in the other case, it may appear that the road ought to be confirmed. It would, therefore, be absurd and unjust that the merits of both appeals should be tried at the same time and by the same persons, unless by consent. Each individual has the right of selecting three judges, who are to convene and decide; but if the doctrine contended for be correct, then the party regularly bringing forward the first appeal has the exclusive right of selection, and the other persons are obliged to acquiesce.

But it is said that no further proceedings have been had under the plaintiff's appeal, and therefore it is at an end. It will be seen the judges are to convene; it is implied that they are to notify the parties, who then, and not till then, are bound to give their attendance. The judges have not done this. If the Commissioners deemed the proceedings dilatory, and had they applied to the judges to convene and appoint a day, it would have been done; but it was omitted. As to the plaintiff, it was agreed between him and *Judge* Smith to wait until his return from the Convention, and then he was to give the plaintiff a week's notice. There is no proof that this has been done. After the appeal, the judges become actors and are required to proceed; if they do not, it cannot be imputed as a lache to the party appealing. The appeal, then, is still pending; and no authority existed for entering on the plaintiff's land. By the 39th section, 60 days are given to remove fences after the decision on the appeal. For these reasons, I am of opinion that the verdict be set aside, and a new trial granted with costs to abide the event.

New trial granted.

Cited in—2 Wend., 384; 8 Wend., 80; 3 Hill, 460, 608; 4 Paige, 523; 6 Paige, 86; 5 N. Y., 572; 24 N. Y., 564; 6 Barb., 612; 27 Barb., 97; 13 How. Pr., 127.

---

*JACKSON, ex dem. CADWELL [***207**
ET AL.,
v.
KING AND KING.

Voluntary deed—Valid as against Grantor's Heir—Attempt to Avoid Deed, on Ground of Grantor's Mental Disability—Burden of Proof—What Degree of Imbecility Renders Person Incapable of Contracting—Mental Weakness, as Evidence of Fraud—Distinction as to Proof of Fraud in Equity and Law.

A voluntary deed is good as against the grantor's heir.

Where an act is sought to be avoided on the ground of mental disability, the proof lies with him who alleges it.

Till the contrary appears, sanity is to be presumed. But after a general derangement is shown, it then is incumbent on the one who insists that the act is valid, to show sanity at the very time when it was performed.

What shall constitute that derangement, or imbecility of mind which renders a party incapable of contracting.

Idiots and lunatics, or persons *non compos*, are of this description; and the disability is confined to these.

One *non compos* is one who has wholly lost his understanding; and of such persons only, till since the Revolution, did even the Court of Chancery entertain jurisdiction.

It does not follow that because, according to the modern doctrine of the Court of Chancery, one would be the proper subject of a commission in nature of a writ *de lunatico inquirendo*, that his acts are void or voidable in a court of law.
The question as to the validity of a deed executed prior to such a commission, would not be at all affected by it.
For, to affect a deed at the common law, an entire loss of the understanding must be shown. The common law has drawn no line to show what degree of intellect is necessary to uphold it.
Such a distinction shown to be impracticable.
But mere weakness of understanding is an item in the proof of fraud.
Against this, a court of equity will relieve, when it can be collected from the circumstances.
So will a court of law, where fraud is clearly established.
But courts of equity and law have not always concurrent jurisdiction in cases of fraud.
The distinction goes upon the kind and degrees of evidence.
E. g., at law, fraud must be proved, not presumed. Whereas, in equity, it may be presumed, from the relative situations of the parties, inadequacy of price, want of correct information, &c.

Citations—16 Johns., 189; 5 Johns., 159; 4 Co., 123; Co. Litt., 247 *a*; 2 Madd., 569, 573; 2 Johns. Ch., 232; 12 Ves., 445; 3 P. Wms., 129; Pow. Cont., 30; 1 Fonbl., 60, 61; 1 Burr., 396; 3 Co. Inst., 84; 18 Ves., 483; 1 Ves. & B., 98; 2 Ves., 155; 1 Br. Ch., 1; 2 Br. Ch., 150.

EJECTMENT, for lands in Washington Co., tried before Walworth, Circuit Judge, at the July Circuit in that county, 1823.

At the trial, it was admitted by the defendants' counsel, that Moses Cadwell, deceased, was seised in fee of the premises in question in his lifetime, and that the defendants were in possession of them at the time of suit brought.

The plaintiff then proved by Lucretia Cadwell, that 45 years before the trial she was married to Cadwell, and had issue by him several sons and daughters, the lessors of the plaintiff; that Cadwell left her twenty-three years before the trial, and went off with one Elizabeth Healy, the wife of one Daniel Healy, with whom he lived till the time of his death, in Nov., 1821; that Elizabeth Healy had two daughters, Betsy and Lydia, who lived with Cadwell till they married—Betsy to James W. Smith, and Lydia to Henry K. Higgins.

The defendants then produced in evidence a deed of bargain and sale of the premises in **208***] question, executed by Cadwell, *being then a little more than 50 years of age, to James W. Smith, dated July 1, 1816, expressed to be for the consideration of $2,500, but a small part of which was actually paid; also, a deed of bargain and sale of the premises in question, with full covenants, from Smith to the defendants, dated May 29, 1819.

The only question upon the trial was, whether Cadwell, when he executed the deed to Smith, was of sufficient capacity to convey, the lessors of the plaintiff alleging that he was incompetent by reason of mental incapacity; and the defendants denying the allegation. To this question a great variety of evidence was heard, which I shall not recite; because, for the purpose of presenting the legal questions in the cause, it is sufficiently detailed in the opinion of the court.

Upon the question of incapacity, the judge charged the jury that to render the deed invalid, they must be satisfied that Cadwell was not in a situation to transact that particular business rationally; not, on the one hand, that he should be capable of doing all kinds of business with judgment and discretion; nor, on the other, that he should be wholly deprived of reason, so as to be incapable of doing the most familiar and trifling work; that if they were satisfied that his mind and memory were in such a situation, at the time of executing the the deed, as to render him wholly incompetent to judge of his rights and interests in relation to that transaction, the deed was void; and it was their duty to find a verdict for the plaintiff; otherwise, to find for the defendant.

Under this charge, the jury found for the plaintiff.

Mr. J. L. Wendell moved for a new trial. He contended that the judge ought not to have submitted the general question of capacity or incapacity to the jury, at the time when the deed was executed; but whether the bargainor came within a class of disqualifying cases known and defined by the law. Being of full age, the grantor was of capacity to convey, unless he was *non compos*, that is to say, an idiot or lunatic. One *non compos* is described by the law as one who never had reason, or who from some cause has totally lost it. *2 [***209** Madd. Ch., 568, Am. ed., 1817, and the cases there cited; *The Matter of Barker*, 2 Johns. Ch., 232, 236. The jury should have been told so; the nature of the incapacity required should have been pointed out to them; and their attention drawn to the simple inquiry whether Cadwell, in point of fact, came within the legal description. Saying that he was not capable of conveying, because he was mentally incapable at the time, is laying down a new rule, which certainly is not sanctioned by authority. Till *Barker's* case such a doctrine was unknown in this country, even in chancery, upon the execution of a commission in the nature of a writ *de lunatico inquirendo*, which admits a greater latitude of inquiry into mental capacity than was ever indulged by the more certain and rigid rules of common law. These rules never pronounce a disqualification to be made out, until a complete deprivation of reason is clearly shown. 2 Madd. Ch., 572, Am. ed., 1817, and the cases there cited; 1 Harr. Ch., 738; *The Matter of Barker*, 2 Johns. Ch., 236. The case being put on this simple ground, a discreet jury cannot well err. But if the power to convey is to depend upon any degree of incapacity short of this, the title to real estate is left alarmingly insecure. In this case, the jury have set aside the deed upon a very slight balance of testimony, at the most, in favor of imprudence, partial loss of memory, childishness or folly. A large number of witnesses deny his incapacity. Nothing like a general derangement of mind was made out by the plaintiff. It was, therefore, not necessary for the defendants to call a single witness; for the law always presumes sanity until general derangement is shown. *Van Alst* v. *Hunter*, 5 Johns. Ch., 158.

But admitting the charge of the judge to have been correct, the verdict is against the weight of evidence. [Here the counsel went into the testimony at large.]

Mr. A. Spencer, same side, would here apprise the opposite counsel of certain authorities which he should use in reply. As to the rules by which the court would be governed in granting a new trial, *Bright* v. *Eynon*, 1

Burr., 390, he said was a leading case. Ld. **210***] Mansfield there said, erroneous *general verdicts, for which a new trial should be granted. mostly included legal consequences as well as propositions of fact. In drawing these consequences, the jury might mistake, and infer directly contrary to law; and he adds, that "the reasons for granting a new trial must be collected from the whole evidence; and from the nature of the case considered under all its circumstances." He also cited on the same subject, *Halsey* v. *Watson*, 1 Cai., 24; *Jackson* v. *Sternbergh*, *Id.*, 162; *Jackson* v. *Laird*, 8 Johns., 489; *M'Connel* v. *Hampton*, 12 Johns., 234; *Wilkie* v. *Roosevelt*, 3 Johns. Cas., 206. It the last case, he said, two new trials were successively granted, because the verdicts were contrary evidence upon a question of usury.

To show that the deed was good as to the heirs, though voluntary, and that it was not within the Statute against Fraudulent Conveyances, he cited *Jackson* v. *Garnsey*, 16 Johns., 189.

Allowing the deed to be voluntary, or intended as a will, a greater degree of capacity is not necessary than would be required for the making a will. As to what this degree should be, writers have not drawn the line definitely; but a less degree of capacity than can be pretended from the evidence in this cause is sufficient. A good principle on this head is laid down in *Ex parte Holland*, 11 Ves., 11. It is there said by the *Lord Chancellor*, that the strongest mind may be reduced by the delirium of a fever, or any other cause, to a very inferior degree of capacity, which would yet admit of making a will.

In *Van Alst* v. *Hunter*, 5 Johns. Ch., 160, a case where, as usual, the evidence differed upon the point of incapacity, the *Chancellor* said, "the control which the law gives to a man over the disposal of his own property, is one of the most efficient means which he has, in protracted life, to command the attentions due to his infirmities." And he goes on to examine the facts in reference to this proposition.

It is said in Swinburne on Wills, pt. 2, sec. 4: "But if a man be of a mean understanding, neither of the wise sort nor of the foolish, but indifferent, as it were betwixt a man and a fool, yea, though he rather incline to the fool- **211***] ish sort, so that, *for his dull capacity, he might worthily be called *grossum caput*, a dull pate or a dunce; such an one is not prohibited to make a testament." At pt. 2, sec. 5, it is said that old age is of itself no incapacity, unless it produce mere childishness or idiocy, as where the testator forgets his own name. In *Hathorn* v. *King*, 8 Mass., 372, the court instructed the jury, "that if they should think that the testatrix, at the time of dictating the will, had sufficient discretion for that purpose; and that at the time of executing the will she was able to recollect the particulars she had so dictated, they might find her of sound and disposing mind and memory at the time of executing." In *Ex parte Cranmer*, 12 Ves., 445, an inquisition was returned, that the person alleged to be lunatic was "so far debilitated in his mind as to be incapable of the general management of his affairs, &c." And in commenting upon this return, the *Lord Chancellor* adverted to the delicacy of the question which might arise with reference to the liberty of the subject; and held it dangerous and improper to act upon such a return; and he asks, "how can I tell what is so far debilitated in his mind as not to be equal to the general management of his affairs?"

Mr. D. Russell, contra. This is a question between the heirs at law of Cadwell, and persons holding under a grant of land from him, without anything like an adequate consideration, to one having no affinity with him. It was Cadwell's property; and unless disposed of understandingly, it passed to his heirs, the lessors. The motion is to set aside the verdict as contrary to evidence; and it is important to inquire, in the first place, what is necessary to deprive him of a disposing power? Technical idiocy or lunacy is not required. It is enough that he was in such a state of imbecility as not to be capable of acting under a proper apprehension of his rights and duties. To determine upon this position, we must look at the facts whence it is to be inferred. Whenever a case appears, upon which a court of equity would interfere, in order to prevent an act of delusion or folly, this court will interpose and avoid the act, if it is completed. No matter in what cause the incapacity may originate, whether it *be old age, intemperance [***212** or disease. There are various infirmities which may debilitate the human mind, upon which a court of equity will grant a commission of lunacy, with a view to prevent the alienation of property, much short of a positive and absolute privation of reason. We contend that the true inquiry is, would a court of equity, under the circumstances of this case, have thrown its protecting influence into the scale, had it been seasonably and properly applied to, against the grant in question. Would it not have placed Cadwell under the care of a committee. The evidence certainly shows great imbecility; and that a court of equity would so have done, we refer to *The Matter of Barker*, 2 Johns. Ch., 332, and the cases there cited. The *Chancellor* says: "A court of chancery is the constitutional and appropriate tribunal, to take care of those who are incompetent to take care of themselves. There would be a deplorable failure of justice, without such a power. The object is protection to the helpless; and the imbecility of extreme old age, when the powers of memory and judgment have become extinct, seems as much as the helplessness of infancy, to be within the reason and necessity of the trust." The case was then put to the jury in a proper shape. Whether the rule cited be ancient or modern, is immaterial; so long as it is a part of the law, it clearly exists. In Highmore on Lunacy, 101, Am. ed., 1822, it is said: "The faith of every contract, rests upon the capacity of the contracting parties." Was the grantor of sufficient ability to grant? Again: "It is of the essence of every contract, not so much that it is valid, as that the parties are in a sufficient capability to bind themselves; for every alienation of a man's right, all contracts between man and man, &c., ought to be done with sound judgment." (*Ib.*) *Webster* v. *Woodford*, 3 Day, 90, establishes the position once

controverted, that "a man may show that he was *non compos mentis* in avoidance of his deed." A great variety of cases are there collected and discussed, applicable to the case under consideration. Lunacy once being established, Highmore gives the nature and extent of the returning reason, necessary to give effect
213*] to the act done. "Where the *existence of derangement is shown in general, the partiality of its operations, in the particular instance, should be manifestly and incontestibly proved, in order to prevent the application of its general effect." (*Id.*, 102.) Again: "General lunacy being established, the proof is thrown upon the party, alleging the lucid interval; and must establish a restoration of mind, sufficient to enable the party soundly to judge of his act." (*Id.*, 123, 4.) There is hardly a case so bad, but that some witnesses may be obtained in favor of sanity.

Wilkie v. *Roosevelt* is relied on as warranting a new trial. The difference is, that there was a case of palpable usury, but where the evidence is doubtful, courts uniformly refuse to award a new trial. In *Walker* v. *Smith*, 4 Dall., 389, 391, this was refused, though the court were far from being satisfied with the conclusion to which the jury had come from the evidence. In *Wait* v. *M'Neil*, 7 Mass., 261, the court refused to do this, though the verdict was against the positive testimony of a witness, unimpeached, except from some slight circumstances, having a tendency to lessen his credibility, or showing that the witness might be mistaken. In *Hurtin* v. *Hopkins*, 9 Johns., 36, the court say they will not grant a new trial, when there is no other ground for the motion than that the jury have misunderstood or disregarded the evidence, where the verdict is for the defendant in a penal action, or an action penal in its nature. They require evidence of partiality or corruption. (Opinions in the Mayor's Court, 12 and 13 S. P.)

Mr. A. Van Vechten, same side. Every application for a new trial is addressed to the discretion of the court. It is not enough that more light may possibly be elicited by a new trial, but the granting or refusing it must, in a great measure, depend on the particular circumstances of each case. This is Ld. Mansfield's doctrine, and the doctrine of this court. Admitting there may be doubt upon the facts, *cui bono*, a new trial? There is always a possibility, that a party may make out a better case, with a second chance. There is no material distinction, in this respect, between ac-
214*] tions *of ejectment and other actions sounding in tort. The reason upon which some of the cases have excepted ejectment, as calling more emphatically for a new trial, is not very powerful; for, though the possession is changed, a new action may be brought, by the losing party, and the title tried *de novo;* whereas, in other actions, the judgment is final and conclusive. One would, therefore, suppose that the facilities for a new trial should be greater in the latter. I admit that this is not a case of technical lunacy; but it certainly presents the want of a sound disposing mind in Cadwell, which, according to Ld. Coke and other writers, and cases both ancient and modern, should avoid the conveyance.

[Both *Mr. Russell* and *Mr. Van Vechten* examined the evidence to this point, at large, in the course of their respective arguments.]

Mr. A. Spencer, in reply. I am sensible that where the verdict is merely against the weight of evidence and the charge of the judge is right, the leaning of the court will be in favor of supporting the verdict; but in a mere question of property, if they perceive that the verdict is clearly against the weight of evidence; they will set it right. If they are satisfied that the jury have been excited by passion, led away by an appeal to the feelings, or misguided by prejudice, it is the duty of the court to interfere and grant a new trial upon this ground. I was aware that in citing cases, and laying down rules from the books, I was saying nothing new; but the nature of the case requires that familiar principles should be adverted to; for, while I admit, in the language of the counsel on the other side, that the granting a new trial is a matter of discretion, depending in some measure on the circumstances of each case as it arises, I must be understood to mean a sound legal discretion, guided and controlled as far as possible by the books of authority. No heirs or anybody else, can call this act, of giving the deed, in question, if the grantor was capable of executing it; and this involves an inquiry into the nature and extent of the capacity of which a grantor or devisor should be possessed. It is an inquiry which has its *bearing on all classes [***215**
of society; and the court will not forget that wills are generally made and valuable estates settled by persons *in extremis;* on their sick beds, or laboring under the weakness and imbecility of old age. These considerations are neither of them enough to invalidate the act. To say so, would be to impugn most wills or deeds in the nature of wills.

I referred to *Ex parte Holyland*, 11 Ves., 11, and I beg leave to remind the court again of what was said there by Ld. Eldon. A failure of memory is not a sufficient objection. If the testator is capable of doing an act of thought and judgment, it is enough. In *Van Alst* v. *Hunter*, 5 Johns. Ch., 148, 158, the court will find all the authorities to this point collected from the common and civil law. In that case the devisor's memory was extremely depreciated; and *Chancellor* Kent's remarks will be found directly applicable to the present case. He says, "the failure of memory is not sufficient to create the incapacity, unless it be quite total or extend to his immediate family and property. The Roman law (Code 6, 24, 14, and *note* 55) seemed to apply the incapacity only to an extreme failure of memory; as for a man to forget his own name—*fatuus præsumitur qui in proprio nomine errat.* The want of recollection of names is one of the earliest symptoms of a decay of memory; but this failure may exist to a very great degree, and yet 'the solid power of understanding' remain." I have greatly deceived myself, in the strictest examination I have been able to give this evidence, if, with respect to Cadwell, at the time he gave the deed in question, there was not as perfect an understanding, judgment and deliberation as in any common case. The burden of showing a want of capacity lies upon the plaintiff; and if we can rebut his evidence by showing a general capacity, or a lucid interval accompanying the act, or sufficient mind in the bargainor to comprehend what he was doing, the case on the part of the defendant is made out. If we have succeeded in neutralizing the evidence, the conclusion of law is that he was sane. He was only about 50 years of age, according to the testimony of Simpson; and if the plaintiff wished mental 216*] decrepitude to *be inferred from old age, he should have shown the bargainor to have been a much older man. None of the witnesses ascribe his failure of capacity to this cause; while, on both sides, they agree that he was an eccentric old man, fond of humor and calling men by strange names; (and he adverted to the outlines of the testimony).

With regard to the general law, there is no difference between the counsel for the plaintiff and myself. At common law, always, a man must have mental capacity to convey. The only dispute between us is, as to the degree of capacity. I admit that this was the true question before the jury; that no technical disability need be shown. It is enough if soundness of mind and memory were wanting.

Curia, per WOODWORTH, *J.* If the deed from Cadwell to Smith is valid the plaintiffs cannot recover. The execution appears to be sufficiently proved, by the subscribing witnesses; and there was an acknowledgment before a master in chancery. If voluntary, it is good between the parties; for the heir cannot set up the want of consideration in the deed from his ancestors. (16 Johns., 189.) But it is contended that Cadwell was *non compos*, or not of sound mind. The rule applicable to such cases is, that where the act of a party is sought to be avoided, on the ground of mental disability, proof of the fact lies upon him who alleges it, and until the contrary appears, sanity is to be presumed. One of the qualifications of this rule is, that after a general derangement has been shown, it is then incumbent on the other side to show that the party who did the act was sane at the very time when it was performed. *Jackson* v. *Van Dusen*, 5 Johns., 159.

The first question is, have the plaintiffs established the fact of general derangement, so as to impose on the other party the necessity of showing competency, or a lucid interval at the time the deed was executed. It becomes material to inquire what constitutes that derangement, or imbecility of mind, that renders a party incapable of contracting. Idiots and lunatics, or persons *non compos*, fall within this description. I apprehend the disability 217*] applies exclusively *to such. Ld. Coke defines *non compos mentis*, "to be a person who was of good and sound memory, and by the visitation of God had lost it," or, "he that by sickness, grief, or other accident, wholly loseth his understanding." *Beverley's* case, 4 Co., 123; Co. Litt., 247 *a*. The deeds of all such persons are void; for the terms "*non compos*," of unsound mind, are legal terms, and import a total deprivation of sense. (2 Madd., 569.) Prior to our Revolution, the Court of Chancery in England entertained jurisdiction in such cases only; mere imbecility of mind, not amounting to idiocy or lunacy, not being considered as sufficient to interfere with the liberty of the subject over his person and property. Latterly, a different doctrine has prevailed. The Court of Chancery has entertained jurisdiction in such cases. In the matter of *Barker*, 2 Johns. Ch., 232, the cases on this subject are reviewed. It was considered as founded in good sense and the necessity of the case, for the protection of a numerous class of persons, whose minds have sunk under the power of disease, or the weight of age, and were liable to become the victims of folly or fraud. This enlarged jurisdiction seems to have sprung up since the time of Ld. Hardwicke, and, as Mr. Maddock observes (2 Madd. Ch., 573), "was rather arbitrarily introduced, so much so, that it has more than once been hinted that legislative provision on the subject would be proper." Without, however, questioning the propriety of assuming jurisdiction in such cases, it may be observed, that the doctrine, if well founded, does not prove that a deed fairly obtained from a person, who might be a fit subject for a commission in the nature of a writ *de lunatico inquirendo*, could be awarded in a court of law. Indeed, the contrary is strongly implied; for the ground of interference is, as Ld. Erskine observes (12 Ves., 445), to protect a party in his second state of infancy. By such a proceeding, the right of a party to contract, who is incapable of managing his affairs, by reason of a partial derangement of mind, is taken for granted.

The question of the validity of a deed executed prior to a commission of this nature, would not in the least be affected by such commission. It must be shown that the grantor *was *non compos*, within the [*218 legal acceptation of the term; that it was not a partial, but an entire loss of the understanding; for the common law seems not to have drawn any discriminating line by which to determine how great must be the imbecility of mind to render a contract void, or how much intellect must remain to uphold it. The difficulty of making such discrimination is apparent. If a man has sufficient capacity to work his farm, or tend his mill skillfully, will the law deny him the right of selling either? I apprehend not. How is a purchaser to protect himself, if the *quantum* of intellect is the criterion by which to determine whether the contract is valid? He may act with the utmost integrity, and yet be in danger; for although it be established that the party with whom be dealt had understanding deemed sufficient for the provident management of his affairs, by this rule the contract would be void. But weakness of understanding is not, of itself, any objection in law to the validity of a contract. If a man be legally *compos mentis*, he is the disposer of his own property, and his will stands for a reason for his actions. *Osmond* v. *Fitzroy*, 3 P. Wms., 129; Pow. on Cont., 30; 1 Fonbl., 60.

According to this doctrine, the plaintiff has failed to invalidate the deed on the ground that Cadwell was *non compos*. The testimony adduced at the trial clearly shows that he is not included in the legal definition of that term. It is abundantly proved, by a number of witnesses, that he was perfectly rational, and possessed his ordinary intelligence at various times, when they saw, conversed and transacted business with him, up to the time of executing the deed; and from their intimate acquaintance, they pronounced him, in their opinion, of sound mind.

It is true, a number of the plaintiff's witnesses consider him of unsound mind, and incapahle of managing his concerns; but, on examining this testimony, it will be found that the opinion rests on specific facts, which do not warrant an opinion to that extent. Much seems to have been inferred from the fact that he did not recollect persons coming to his mill; that he took no part in the settlement of his accounts, although present; that he indulged **219***] in idle stories; *that he talked of turning the water back, so as to obtain the benefit of it a second time; that he was incoherent and unconnected in his statements; and greatly affected by very trivial circumstances. I admit these are proofs of a weak or impaired understanding; but they do not satisfactorily prove anything more. From the same witness it may be collected, that in some respects, at least, he was rational. It seems to be conceded that, during all this time, he was a miller, and did the work well: for there is no complaint. No witness states that he was deficient in conducting this business. This alone proves that he had memory and judgment. The taking of toll correctly, grinding the different kinds of grain, so as to satisfy customers, and bestowing the care necessary to prevent confusion, is of itself satisfactory proof that he had competent understanding in this respect. Besides, he bought, sold and took notes. He, at different times, after the deed was given, mentioned his inducement for making the conveyance. The cause for so doing is always stated in the same way. It cannot be correctly said that in his situation it was unnatural or absurd. The fact that he had deserted his wife and children twenty years before, shows very clearly that they would not be the objects of his bounty.

On the whole, it appears to me that Cadwell had memory and judgment to a moderate extent; and was not disabled, by law, from selling his farm and giving the deed. The plaintiffs have failed in showing a general incapacity; at most, they have shown only a want of understanding on some occasions. There is not sufficient within the rule, to impose on the defendants the necessity of proving that he was sane when he did the act.

The next question is whether the evidence makes out a case of fraud or imposition. In discussing this point it is conceded that, although mere weakness of understanding is insufficient, it furnishes strong ground of suspicion that when persons in such a state execute conveyances, they are acted upon by improper influence and, therefore, wherever fraud can be collected from the circumstances **220***] of the transaction, *equity will interpose and relieve against it. Courts of law have also a concurrent jurisdiction with courts of equity, where the fraud can be clearly established; and will relieve by making void the instrument. *Bright* v. *Eynon*, 1 Burr., 396; 1 Fonbl., 61.

But courts of law have not, in all cases of fraud, a concurrent jurisdiction. Ld. Coke, in 3 Inst., 84, in speaking of the jurisdiction of courts of equity as to frauds, covin and deceit, seems to admit that all frauds are not relievable at law. The distinction between legal and equitable jurisdiction upon fraud is this: that at law it must be proved, not presumed; so that equitable jurisdiction may be exercised upon an instrument unduly obtained, when a court of law could not enter into the question. (18 Ves., 483.) In *Butcher* v. *Butcher*, 1 Ves. & Bea., 98, Ld. Eldon observes that some judges have said that a deed cannot be fraudulent unless it be fraudulent both in law and in equity; but to that doctrine he could not agree, though a strong inclination had been evident to say whatever is equity ought to be law—an opinion acted upon by *Mr. Justice* Buller, who had persuaded Ld. Mansfield to act upon it, until it was reformed by Ld. Kenyon, with the assistance of the same judge; yet the clear doctrine of Ld. Hardwicke and all his predecessors was that there are many instances of fraud that would affect instruments in equity of which the law could not take notice. The broad ground assumed by Ld. Mansfield, 1 Burr., 396, is that courts of equity and courts of law have a concurrent jurisdiction to suppress and relieve against fraud. This doctrine has, however, been subsequently qualified, according to the distinction taken by Ld. Eldon, and is founded in good sense. I am not aware of any express adjudication in our courts. But in 4 Des. Ch., 684, it is sanctioned. It was there held that fraud may be presumed in equity, but must be proved at law. In accordance with these principles, a variety of cases have been decided, and relief afforded in equity, where, from the nature of the transaction and the situation of the parties, fraud and imposition might be presumed. 3 P. Wms., 129; Powell on Cont., 31. So, also, in *Chesterfield* v. **Jansen*, 2 Ves., 155, Ld. Hardwicke [***221** describes one species of fraud that may be presumed from the circumstances and condition of the parties contracting. And this, he says, goes further than the rule of law, which is that fraud must be proved, not presumed. Inadequacy of consideration is also a badge of fraud, or a fact connected with other circumstances from which fraud may be inferred. (1 Bro. Ch. Cas., 1.) So, also, a conveyance obtained from persons uninformed of their rights will be set aside, though no actual fraud be proved. (2 *Id.*, 150.) In these and many other cases that might be cited, equity considers the instruments as obtained fraudulently from the circumstances and relation of the parties, although no actual fraud is proved. Yet in none of these cases has it been decided that a court of law would declare the instrument void.

If the preceding doctrine be correct, it follows that the facts disclosed in this case are not of a character to entitle a court of law to declare the deed void. I have not discovered any evidence of actual fraud by the grantee of Cadwell, or that any deception was practiced, or inducements held out to gain the title. If the plaintiffs are entitled to relief, it must be in equity, on the ground of age, imbecility, the consideration and nature of the contract from which fraud is to be inferred. I apprehend, however, that enough is not shown to set aside the deed in that court. Cadwell appears to have been the actor, and to have understood the transaction. He takes care to provide for himself, his wife, and the woman with whom he had cohabited, and in consequence of age and infirmity, is willing to surrender the property into other hands—not to a stranger, but one who had married a person reared in his family, and to whom he probably considered himself *in loco parentis*. There is nothing so surprising or unusual in such a course as to excite suspicion; and as imbecility of mind, singly, is not sufficient, I incline to think that relief would be denied. Be that as it may, a court of law is not the proper forum.

On the whole, I am of opinion that the verdict be set aside, and a new trial granted.

New trial granted.

Cited in—5 Cow., 510; 3 Wend., 631; 21 Wend., 143; 24 Wend., 86; 26 Wend., 298; 9 N. Y., 392; 25 N. Y., 70; 49 N. Y., 121; 51 N. Y., 31; 19 Hun, 488; 7 Barb., 322; 14 Barb., 494; 24 Barb., 586; 43 Barb., 456; 53 Barb., 182; 63 Barb., 464; 9 Abb. Pr., 286; 12 Abb. N. S., 299; 7 Daly, 223; 11 Wall., 233; 34 Ind., 435; 34 Wis., 136; 2 Am. Rep., 203 (48 N. H., 133); 10 Am. Rep., 341 (49 N. Y., 111); 10 Am. Rep., 555 (51 N. Y., 27).

222*] *DICKEY

v.

THE NEW YORK INSURANCE COMPANY.

Marine Insurance—Abandonment—Injury, Exceeding One Half—Repairs—State of Facts, at Time of Abandonment, Determines Right—True Cause for Abandonment must be Assigned—Effect of Lien for Repairs.

If the injury to a ship, by the perils insured against, exceed one half her value, the insured may abandon to the underwriters as for a total loss, which cannot afterwards be turned into a partial one. Accordingly, the abandonment may be enforced, though the ship afterwards be repaired by the master, and proceed on her journey.

But the abandonment must be before the vessel is fully repaired and able to proceed on her voyage. If she be, in fact, repaired, the abandonment is void, though this be not known to the assured.

It is the actual state of things, therefore, at the time of the abandonment, and not the state of the party's information, that decides the validity of an abandonment.

Where a ship bound to Antwerp was insured, and repaired, on account of sea damage, at Port Louis, in the Isle of France; and the expense of a part of the repairs was defrayed by a sale of the cargo, and the residue charged upon the remainder of the cargo by a *respondentia* bond; held, that no lien was thereby created upon the ship which could be taken into the account in estimating the insured's right to abandon as for a total loss.

In making an abandonment the assured is bound to assign the true cause; *e. g.*, if he abandon on account of sea damage only, he cannot avail himself of the fact that the ship was afterwards incumbered by the expense of repairs. As to the latter, he should make a new abandonment.

Where a ship has sustained damage by the perils insured against to more than one half her value, her restoration, in order to devest the right of abandonment, must be complete and perfect; and if, though in fact restored, she still remain subject to a lien for the expense of her repairs to more than half her value, this is not such a full and beneficial restoration as to take away the right to abandon.

Items included in, and manner of estimating the amount of repairs, deducting one third new for old, after first deducting the value of the old materials. Per Savage, *Ch. J.*

Citations—10 East, 341; 1 Cai., 21; 4 Cr., 29; 4 Binn., 287; 1 Johns., 181; Phil. Ins., 407, 401; Doug., 231; 3 Johns. Cas., 182; 1 T. R., 608, 613, 615, 616; 2 Burr., 697, 1213.

ASSUMPSIT upon a policy of insurance, on one half the body, tackle, apparel and other furniture of the ship Frances Henrietta, Allyn, master, valued at $20,000, on a voyage from Antwerp to one or more ports in the India or China Seas; and at and from the port or ports of lading to N. Y., or a port in Europe, not north of Holland; tried before Woodworth, *J.*, at the N. Y. sittings, in June, 1822.

The declaration was varied in its counts, to meet a total or partial loss. The evidence was that the ship proceeded on her voyage July 1, 1818, for Batavia, in the Island of Java, where she arrived in good condition Dec. 2 in the same year; that she sailed thence with a full cargo, a considerable portion of which belonged to the plaintiff, bound to Antwerp, in Holland, Jan. 24, 1819; but while sailing on her voyage, from Feb. 20 to Mar. 4, she encountered a succession of winds and tempestuous weather, became leaky, and was so much broken and damaged that it was necessary for her preservation to proceed for Port Louis, in the Isle of France, where *she arrived [*223 in distress Mar. 7, 1819. Here the ship was regularly surveyed; and the surveyers reported that she should be unloaded immediately, as well for her safety and the safety of her cargo as for enabling them to ascertain the damages she might have sustained. The cargo was thereupon partially unladen and put into the custom house of St. Louis, and a second survey held Mar. 16, when it was thought necessary farther to unlade. The unlading was accordingly resumed, and continued to the 20th, when, on a third survey, it was recommended that the ship should be entirely unloaded, which was accordingly done, by the 27th, with the exception of some few articles, and the ship placed in the usual and proper situation for undergoing a final survey and repairs. Here she was further unladed, but not entirely so, when, on the 28th and 29th, the wind was very severe, and finally increased to a severe hurricane. On the 30th the ship was driven on shore, and suffered very great additional injury. Apr. 14, 1819, a fourth survey was held, and the surveyors reported that all the ship's injury had arisen from the above causes, and recommended the proper repairs. These repairs were commenced May 7, 1819, and prosecuted with due diligence, under the direction of the master.

A portion of the cargo, consisting of rice, principally belonging to the plaintiff, together with certain ship materials, were, on the 5th and 22d Apr. and June 3, 1819, sold under the direction of the Court of Admiralty of the Isle of France, to defray the expenses of repairs, amounting in net proceeds to $10,972.50. This being the only part of the cargo which could be sold without great sacrifice, and not

NOTE.—*Marine insurance—Right of abandonment—When it accrues.* See Dupuy v. United Ins. Co., 3 Johns., Cas., 182; Abbott v. Broome, 1 Cai., 292, *notes.*

Actual facts at time of abandonment determine right. Mumford v. Church, 1 Johns. Cas., 147, *note.*

near paying the expenses of the repairs, the master was obliged to borrow of one Reush $8,925, upon *respondentia* of the cargo, and he executed a *respondentia* bond accordingly, which also bound him to the payment personally. The *respondentia* bond was made payable ten days after the arrival of the ship at a port in the Netherlands. The repairs being completed, and the residue of the cargo reshipped, and certain goods taken on board upon freight, by permission of the Court of
224*] Admiralty, *June 28, 1819, the ship being tight, stanch and strong, set sail from Port Louis for a port in Holland, and arrived at Antwerp Oct. 1, 1819, where the cargo was delivered in good order to the consignees, and where the averages upon the vessel, freight and cargo, in the premises, were regulated and settled under an appointment and order of the tribunal of commerce of Antwerp, according to the usage and law of Holland; and by that tribunal ordered to be carried into execution. The cargo was afterwards sold at Antwerp by the consignee, who charged the sum due on bottomry in account with the plaintiff.

In the meantime, July 6, 1819, while the ship being in good repair, was prosecuting her voyage from Port Louis to Antwerp, the plaintiff caused to be delivered to the defendants the following letter of abandonment:

"NEW YORK, 6th July, 1819.

To the President and Directors of the New York Ins'ce Co.

Gentlemen:

I have advice from the Isle of France, dated 12th April last, that my ship Francis Henrietta had put into that port in distress on the 7th of March; and that on the 28th and 29th of March, she was under the influence of a hurricane that parted her cables and drove her on shore, beating over a bed of hard sand and coal, by which she has suffered great damage, as well in the hull, as to her rigging, spars, &c., leaving the lower masts only standing. In consequence of this disaster, and the great injury sustained to the voyage this ship was pursuing, I am obliged to abandon my interest therein to my underwriters, and you are hereby required to take notice, that I abandon to your office so much of the ship and cargo as you have insured; and that I shall claim from you thereon a total loss.

Respectfully,
yr. ob. st.,
ROB. DICKEY."

This letter was, in due season, followed by a delivery of the usual preliminary proofs.
225*] *The ship sailed from Antwerp for N. Y., Dec. 5, 1819, having in freight 20 hogsheads of madder, and 40 or 50 boxes of muskets. Being a foreign bottom, she had not been able to procure a cargo at Antwerp. She arrived in the port of N. Y. Jan. 4, 1820, after having sustained some additional damage from a succession of violent and tempestuous weather in the course of her passage.

The whole disbursements of the ship at Port Louis amounted to $20,191.74, including repairs estimated at $14,281.72.

The plaintiff's counsel read in evidence a copy of the *respondentia* bond from the master to Reush, dated at Port Louis, June 6, 1819, in the penal sum of £3,914 9*s*. 6*d*., the condition whereof recited that the master had, for the use and payment of the repairs and expenses incurred in that harbor upon the ship, taken up, and received of Rensh, $8,925, current money of Mauritius, fixed between the parties at £1,957 4*s*. 9*d*. sterling, to run at *respondentia* on the cargo of the lading of the ship, to proceed to a port in the Netherlands, &c.; and for the further security of Rensh, the master thereby consented and agreed, for himself, his heirs, &c., to engage and assign over to Rensh the several wares and merchandise, laden, or to be laden, on the ship, and which wares and merchandise were, by the bond, declared to be thus mortgaged and assigned over, and not to be delivered to any other use or purpose whatever till payment of the bond.

The condition of the bond then, was that if the master should pay the money borrowed, at the expiration of ten days after the arrival of the ship at a port in the Netherlands, or in case of loss, the customary due on salvage, then the bond to be void, &c.; otherwise, &c.

The plaintiff also proved that Holland was, in 1818, 1819 and 1820, governed by the *Code de Commerce*, part of the Civil Code of France; and read in evidence articles 190 and 191, of the *Code de Commerce*.

A verdict was taken for the plaintiff, for $20,000, subject to a case, and with liberty to either party to turn it into a *special [***226**
verdict, or bill of exceptions; the amount of the verdict to be increased or diminished, and subject to adjustment, as the court should direct; and if a balance should appear in favor of the defendants, then a verdict and judgment to be entered accordingly, &c.

This cause was argued at the last May Term; and the only question made at the bar was, whether the plaintiff was entitled to recover as for a total or partial loss.

Mr. D. B. Ogden, for the plaintiff, contended that he was entitled to recover for a total loss. He said he did not rely on an actual, but should contend that a technical total loss was shown. It will not be denied that the *bona fide* expenses and repairs, incurred in consequence of the perils insured against, exceed one half the value of the vessel; and so far, there can be no difference upon the propriety of our claim; But it will be said that the abandonment was too late; that it should have been before she left the Isle of France, in full repair, to proceed on her destined voyage.

To be good, the abandonment must be founded on such a state of facts as will justify the party in considering the loss total. At what time is it necessary that these facts should exist? When the information reaches the assured, or when the abandonment is made? The supposed or actual state of the subject, at the time of abandonment? We say the belief of the assured is to govern, if the ground of his belief was once true; though such grounds may, at the time he abandons, have ceased to exist. To decide otherwise, would overturn the first principles in the law of insurance. In all cases of a technical total loss, it is optional with the assured, whether he will abandon or not. If the whole subject be destroyed, no abandonment is necessary. If these positions be true, does it not follow that the assured must await the proper information? Without this he cannot act; and it is idle and tantalizing to give him the right to elect, and yet deny him the means of exercising it beneficially or properly. The only means he can have is information received. Shall the whole effect be destroyed, because the vessel was repaired before the abandonment took place? If so, all **227***] *the talk about notice and election in the books is a dead letter, in those instances where a vessel is injured at so great a distance that the assured cannot keep his eye upon her.

We are aware that some cases lay down a contrary rule; but none of them go the length contended for here. *Bainbridge* v. *Neilson*, 10 East, 329, was a case of capture, and almost immediate recapture; and, even under such circumstances, the doctrine that the assured could not abandon on information received, after the vessel was reclaimed, was considered somewhat novel, as will be seen by a report of the same case, in Campbell. (1 Campb., 237, S. C.) This case has been followed as to capture, but no other ground of abandonment. *Dorr* v. *N. E. M. Ins. Co.*, 4 Mass., 221, 229; *Fitzsimmons* v. *N. P. Ins. Co.*, 4 Cr., 185, 201; *Alexander* v. *Balt. Ins. Co.*, *Id.* 370, 372, and *Mumford* v. *Church*, 1 Johns. Cas., 147; 1 Cai. Cas., 21, S. C., are all cases of technical total loss by capture. *Smith* v. *Robertson*, 2 Dow., 474, 482, questions the doctrine even as to capture; and in *M'Ivers* v. *Henderson*, 4 Maule & S., 576., the distinction is taken, that in those cases where, on capture, a recovery of the property defeats the abandonment, there must be a restitution of the ship in an undamaged state; and the same distinction is holden in the C. P. *Hudson* v. *Harrison*, 3 Brod. & Bing., 97, 105. "If the insured, while he has a right to consider the loss as total, elect to abandon, this will fix the nature of the loss; and no subsequent event can render it partial." (2 Mar., on Ins., 589.) Dickey was bound, after he received information of the loss, to abandon the very first opportunity. *Mitchell* v. *Edie*, 1 T. R., 608; 2 Mar. on Ins., 591. The abandonment relates to and takes effect from the loss. The master, from that time, is the agent of the underwriters. In going on to repair, he acts for the benefit of all concerned; but he is never considered the agent, or rather arbiter, who is to decide whether there shall or shall not be an abandonment. (1 T. R., 613, 614.) This is vested, by law, in the discretion of the assured solely. We admit that, if the assured goes on and repairs, it might be a waiver; but this must be done by himself, through his express orders, or legal agent; otherwise, you deliver him over to the control of a stranger.

The only case directly against us, is *Humphrey* v. *Un. Ins. Co.* in the C. C. U. S. Mass., a note of which is given by Mr. Phillips. (Phil. on Ins., 401.) If that case be correctly **228***] reported, we *have only to say that *Judge* Story (a thing we admit not very usual with him) was most clearly in an error. He is made to speak of the assured's electing to repair, and thereby losing his right to abandon. Now, it is extremely difficult, to see how the assured could elect to repair, when he knew nothing of the repairs which were going on, and neither he, nor the law for him, ever created an agent, who was authorized to do this.

But suppose that case to be law; its principle must be, that the loss turns out in fact to be partial, the ship being restored, and proceeding on her voyage. Such is the rule, we have seen, even in case of capture. If we can show that she never was restored, the case does not apply. To make out payment for the repairs, all the cargo which could be sold to the least advantage at Port Louis was disposed of; and the master was obliged to hypothecate the residue. This was perfectly within the master's general power the case being one of necessity. *U. Ins. Co.* v. *Scott*, 1 Johns., 106; Abb. on Ship., 2 Am. ed., 157, pt. 2, ch. 3, sec. 29. The only difference between the opposite counsel and us must relate to the consequences of the *respondentia* upon the cargo. This must be decided not by the law of the U. S., but Holland, to which the contract had reference; and where the vessel was when the claim was enforced. (*Vide* Abbott on Ship., 2d Am. ed., 133, 4, pt. 2, ch. 3, sec. 9.) The owners of the hypothecated cargo had a lien over on the ship. (*Id.*, Hall's Maritime Loans, 92, 93, 95.) The loan was not repaid. It was not made on the credit of Dickey. Can it be said, then, that the ship was, to all intents, restored to him? No. He was still liable to lose his ship by an enforcement of the lien. In point of fact, she was never under his control, nor restored to his possession.

Mr. Emmet, same side, read that part of the *Code de Commerce* referred to by the case, to show the law of lien at Antwerp; and cited *Consequa* v. *Willings*, 1 Pet. C. C., 301.

Mr. J. Duer, for the defendants. The case sought to be made out by the plaintiff is certainly one of the first impression; and we had supposed that at this time of day, the law was so well settled, that the right to abandon depends on the state of facts at the time of the abandonment, as to preclude all argument. At most, it is barely necessary to refer to and *briefly review the cases on which we [***229** rely. They are all collected by Mr. Phillip's, in his treatise on Insurance (Phil. on Ins., 436, &c.), and it cannot be necessary for us to refer to the books which contain them. Gentlemen are mistaken in supposing that the rule began with *Bainbridge* v. *Neilson*, 10 East, 329. The same rule, in substance, was laid down and acted upon by Lord Mansfield in *Goss* v. *Withers*, 2 Burr., 689, though in more general terms. It is the same thing in this country, whether the loss has, at the time of the abandonment, ceased to be a technically total one or not. If the ship be repaired and proceeding on her voyage, in either event the right of abandonment is gone. The assured takes this risk. True it is otherwise in England. To prevent an abandonment, the property must not only be restored, but in such a condition as that the loss ceases to be total; and *Smith* v. *Robertson*, 2 Dow., 474, 482, was a case of the latter kind. None of the cases cited give countenance to the argument that the rule for which we contend is confined to cases of capture. The reason upon which we go is equally applicable to every other case. The true principle is stated by Kent, *Ch. J.*, in *Schieffelin* v. *N. Y. Ins. Co.*, 9 Johns., 21, 26. It may be that the property restored is in such circumstances as not to take away the right to abandon; but they must be peculiar; and the exceptions very few under our adjudged cases.

Abandonment is, in all cases, founded on an inability to proceed in the voyage. There is no reason, in any case, for turning a partial loss into a constructive total one, except the probability that the vessel will, in the end, be actually lost. If she is restored and in the act of earning freight, the only object as it respects the vessel, why should the owner be allowed more than a compensation to the extent of his actual loss? This principle runs through and connects all the cases on the subject of abandonment.

The distinction between an absolute and constructive loss is well settled, and familiar to every lawyer. Strictly speaking, there cannot be a total loss without an actual destruction of the subject, or a devesting the property by condemnation. This strictness, would, however, be hard; because, though not actually **230***] lost, it may be in such a condition *as will probably result in a loss; and it would be unreasonable and hard to drive the party to an actual experiment. He is, therefore, allowed to abandon while the probability exists. So capture will probably lead to condemnation; and upon the same principle, the assured may abandon before waiting to hear the sentence. It was to provide for these and the like cases that the insured is allowed to disentangle himself from a losing speculation, by throwing the risk on the underwriter. These cases are usually either capture, shipweck or any combination of facts showing that the voyage is not worth pursuing; and the two questions always present themselves—is the vessel in the possession of the owner? And is she capable of pursuing her voyage? On capture, restoration is contingent; and stranding and shipwreck do not always give the right to abandon. The vessel is for the time disabled; but if she be restored immediately, she should be repaired; and the shipwreck or stranding should be such that a total loss may be calculated on, or a loss of the voyage expected from the delay. The class of cases which have created the greatest doubt and difficulty is the last. Most of the cases I have already cited are to this; and though some of them deal in generalities, and may admit of equivocation, yet, in their progress, they have disentangled themselves from every subtilty and settled down upon the plain simple practical rule for which we contend.

The master's being agent for the assurer depends on the inquiry whether the abandonment was properly made, and to say he was agent in this case begs the question. Till abandonment, he is the agent of the assured only. Phil. on Ins., 407, 468; *Jumel* v. *Mar. Ins. Co.*, 7 Johns., 423, 4. After abandonment, he becomes the agent of the assurers (*Id.*); but this is always on the ground, that the abandonment is effectual, as being warranted by the facts existing at the time it is made.

It is said on the authority of Ashurst, *J.* (1 T. R., 608, 613, 614), the master's act cannot prejudice the right to abandon; but it cannot be possible that he ever intended to be understood in the sense contended for. It would go to the extent, that if the loss were once total, it must always remain so, though the master by his seasonable exertions, and in the exercise of a most imperious *duty, had changed [***231** its character into a loss slightly partial. Take the case of a capture, and an immediate ransom or compromise by the master—was it ever asserted or supposed that this does not take away the right to abandon? In that case he restores by money—in another by repairs. And are not both cases the same in principle? They are also the same upon authority. *Parsons* v. *Scott*, 2 Taunt., 370. If, in any case, the master is agent for the assurer before abandonment, it is in the case of a plain total loss, by which the voyage is palpably gone. In that case he acts for those concerned; but while he is engaged in the prosecution of the voyage, or with a view to its prosecution, he is always the exclusive agent of the assured.

If the right to abandon depended wholly upon the amount paid for the expense of repairs, &c., true it would be perfect, without regard to the time or the state of the vessel, even though fully repaired by the owner himself, and engaged in the prosecution of the voyage. No reason could exist against making his election by the ultimate amount of repairs determined on actual estimate; yet the cases are uniform that he cannot do this; that he has an election either to abandon or repair; and cannot do both. *Martin* v. *Crockatt*, 14 East, 465; *Thompson* v. *The R. E. Ins Co.*, 1 Maule & S., 30, per Ld. Ellenborough; *Wood* v. *L. & K. Ins. Co.*, 6 Mass., 482, per Parsons, *J.* This class of cases is alone conclusive.

Again; the assurer has a right to repair and put the ship on her voyage. This also takes away the right to abandon; *Hamilton* v. *Mendes*, 2 Burr., 1209, per Ld. Mansfield; *Dacosta* v. *Newnham*, 2 T. R., 407; *Seton* v. *Del. Ins. Co.*, Cond. Marsh., 562, *note* 92; 5 Serg. & R., 509; and to this there are a series of authorities, which cannot be shaken. If this right does not arise from the nature of the contract, the insurer may always make it a part of the policy by express provision, and issue general instructions to repair.

An abandonment should, at any rate, always be made while the loss exists, in order to enable the assurers to determine whether they will repair what becomes their own property in virtue of the abandonment. *Martin* v. *Crockatt*, 14 East, 465. It is the assurers, not the master, who are to determine this question. There is good reason why this should be so; the assurer has nothing to do with the cargo; and he will always guide himself by his own interest as owner, if the property devolves on him. If the cargo be lost, he may not repair. So, where in *any case the freight will not be [***232** enough to indemnify him. Whereas, if the owner of the vessel be also owner of the cargo, he may lose sight of the interest of the underwriters upon the ship, in his attention to the cargo. Though the freight may be inadequate, yet he may repair and charge the underwriter with the loss.

If the right rests with the amount of money paid, why has it never been applied to any other case? Why not to capture and ransom? Is any trace of the doctrine to be found in such cases? There must have been frequent opportunity to apply it; yet it never was insisted on. The expense of repairs to one half is, in truth, in all cases mere *prima facie* evidence of incapacity to proceed on the voyage.

It is said the vessel was not restored beneficially. Suppose this, for the sake of the argument, to be so. If the ground of abandonmemt, for which we have contended, be the true one, it is immaterial whether the bond upon the cargo would affect the vessel or whether it would not. If properly borrowed, the underwriters are accountable for it, with marine interest; but no case shows that a mere lien is good cause of abandonment, or can be insisted on as an actual total loss. There was such a lien in *Da Costa* v. *Newnham*, 2 T. R., 407; but it was not noticed as a ground of abandonment, either by the counsel or the court.

But was there a lien? If the master borrows money, on his own credit, a lien accrues to him; if he sells a part of the cargo, the proprietors of the goods sold have a lien; or the lender may have a lien, if he loan on the credit of the ship; but this is where he has taken no other security. Here no lien accrued; none was left to be implied; for the debt was secured by an express contract. There are various modes by which a lien may be extinguished. (*Code de Com.*, Art., 193.) Novation is one (Code Civil, B. 3, ch. 5, sec. 2); the substitution of a new debt or a new debtor. (*Id.*) Here the master and owner might have been bound; but taking a *respondentia* bond extinguished all implied liability. (Poth. on Obl., ch. 2; 1 Evans Poth., 380.) The implied lien of the civil law, is like one at the common law. A security by bond or express contract destroys it.

233*] *If, however, it existed at all, it was in favor of the owner of the cargo, of whom the plaintiff was the principal one, and he also owned the ship; and to give him a lien over, would be to say that one may have a lien on his own goods. If the abandonment had been effectual, and the ship transferred by it to the underwriters, a lien might then have existed in the hands of Dickey. The claim, as it now stands, assumes that an abandonment was well made; that this created the lien—and then, that the lien thus created goes back and forms a cause for the abandonment—thus reasoning in a complete circle.

Mr. G. Griffin, same side, also argued against the distinction insisted on by the counsel for the plaintiff between abandonment in case of capture, and other cases; and he cited *Church* v. *Bedient*, 1 Cai. Cas., 21; *Hallet* v. *Peyton*, *Id.*, 28; *Penny* v. *N. Y. Ins. Co.*, 3 Cai., 155, and *Schieffelin* v. *N. Y. Ins. Co.*, 9 Johns., 437; *Adams* v. *Del. Ins. Co.*, 3 Binn., 287; *Marshall* v. *Del. Ins. Co.*, 4 Cr., 202; *Alexander* v. *Bal. Ins. Co.*, *Id.*, 370; and *Smith* v. *Universal Ins. Co.*, 6 Wh., 185, as setting the rule that the right of the parties depend upon the state of facts; not the information at the time of the abandonment. He said, in the late digest of the Reports of Pennsylvania (Whart. Dig., 333, Ins., H, *c*), several manuscript cases are collected as supporting the rule, which is thus laid down: "It is the actual state of things, at the time of the abandonment; and not the state of the party's information, that decides the validity of the abandonment." No distinction is made between the capture and any other cause. Phillips concedes that the weight of authority in support of the rule is irresistible. (Phil. on Ins., 436–7.) What reason is there for confining the rule to capture? If a restoration in that case oust the right to abandon, why not in others? An embargo or blockade are good cause to abandon while they continue; but on raising them the cause ceases. So of a sunken vessel, as in *Shaw* v. *Felton*, 2 East, 109. While she is in this condition, no doubt the owner might abandon; but suppose, before the abandonment takes place, she is raised and the hole in her bottom repaired, is not the right gone? It is one of the excellencies in the law of insurance, that it is not bound down by technicalities. The principle there, at least, is *universal, that when the [***234** cause ceases, the effect ceases. In *M'Masters* v. *Schoolbred*, 1 Esp., 237, damage and repair to £60, *per cent.* were mixed up with capture, yet the restoration was held to take away all to abandon. *Humphrey* v. *Union Ins. Co.*, Phil. on Ins., 401, is in point against the distinction. The talking about an election to repair is censured as absurd in that case; but it was perfectly proper. The owner is considered as repairing by the hand of the master, his agent; and the judge goes upon the maxim *qui facit per alium, facit per se.* Even the bottomry bond on which the vessel was sold was not allowed to vary the principle of abandonment. This is always, either because the loss, *prima facie*, breaks up the voyage, or because there are not sufficient funds to repair. The presumption and the want of funds are met and repelled, in this case, by the fact of repairing. We offer to pay all that has been expended, and, in honesty, the assured can ask no more.

It is said the captain was the agent of the underwriters; or that, if not so, he had no power to change a total into a partial loss. Both the position and corollary are negatived by *Doederer* v. *Del. Ins. Co.*, C. C., Apr., 1807, M. S. Whart. Dig., 337, Insurance, H., *f*, pl. 182; Condy's Marsh., 534 *b*, S. C. That case adjudges that the captain continues the agent of the assured, after capture, until the abandonment is made, and may, as such, prejudice him by his acts; that he is the agent of the insurer, only when he acts for the benefit of all concerned. Then when does the transition of character occur? Plainly when the relation is changed by a valid abandonment, which presupposes a state of facts justifying it at the time. A deduction cannot be made to fortify the premises. The plaintiff has attempted this; and literally seizes on the conclusion to fortify his major proposition. Remaining the agent of the assured, is the captain to be taught by him not to touch the vessel by repairing the injury done by storms, ransoming from capture, or raising a sunken ship, for fear of changing a total into a partial loss? Is not this a monstrous doctrine? His duty, as settled by law, is directly the contrary; and he has faithfully pursued it in this instance, on consultation with, and under the direction of surveyors who recommended the repairs.

*It is said, here is a lien, and the [***235** French Code is relied on (*Code de Commerce*, Livre 2, tit. 1, art. 190, 191); but the law is universal, that when one is entitled to an implied lien, it is waived by entering into a special contract to secure it. His remedy must be confined to his special contract; and his lien is gone forever. Bull. *N. P.*, 45; *Cowell* v. *Simpson*, 16 Ves., 275. This doctrine is derived from the civil law, on which the continental systems are based. (And *vide Code de Commerce*, art. 320.) Instead of relying on the general law of lien, a *respondentia* bond is given, and is confined in its effect to the particular articles mentioned in it. (*Id.*)

But this lien was never enforced. The vessel proceeded to her home port with her cargo, where the bills were all finally discharged, or might have been so, out of Dickey's own funds, by his consignee. The vessel was not stopped one moment. The lien is a mere phantom conjured up to convert the loss from a partial to a total one. A lien or peril on paper, or in mere name, is no ground of abandonment. A substantial injury should arise. In *Humphrey* v. *Union Ins. Co.*, Phil. on Ins., 401, there was a bottomry bond, not merely on the cargo, but the vessel itself; and yet it was denied as a ground of abandonment.

But it is enough for us that this lien was not set up as the foundation of an abandonment in the letter of Dickey. The law is well settled that you cannot abandon generally, but must put your finger on the clause, and point it out specifically. *Suydam* v. *Mar. Ins. Co.*, 1 Johns., 190–2; S. C., *Id.*, 138. The letter cannot be eked out, and made to meet this cause by construction. The plaintiff should have told us of the lien in terms and by name. He did not do it, because he did not dream of its being an injury; and we hear nothing of it in the voluminous evidence of the master.

[The counsel for the defendants also examined the items of expense, and contended that the repairs in question did cost one half the ship's value.]

Mr. T. A. Emmet, in reply. Our case is far from being one of the first impression. I think we shall show it already decided, or, at least, dependent on old principles. We rely on *Goss* v. *Withers*, 2 Burr., 683; *Hamilton* v. *Mendes*, *Id.*, 1198, and *Mills* v. *Fletcher*, Doug., 231. The rule laid down in these cases has been 236*] *highly approved by the ablest writers on commercial law (Evans' Essays, 53, tit. Abandonment; Park on Ins., 194, tit. Abandonment); and the decisions of our own courts founded on them, leave no room to entertain the later cases opposed to them.

We admit the general position, that insurance is a contract of indemnity; but to attain this, the law has adopted a general rule applicable, without farther examination, to all cases attended with certain circumstances. The familiar case of deducting one third new for old, in case of sea damage, is one example under that rule, which in *Dunham* v. *Com. Ins. Co.*, 11 Johns., 315, was adhered to, for the sake of preserving it unimpaired, even at the expense of manifest injustice. Another rule of the same character is, that under certain circumstances, the assured may abandon and claim for a total loss, which comes within the conventional rule of indemnity; and goes upon the idea that no measure can be established to reach every case. In these cases the assurer is not allowed to controvert the rule, by saying that an adjustment, as for a partial loss, will give an indemnity. (Mar. on Ins., 599, 560.) This is an old rule, ingrafted in the commercial code of every country; and recommended as well by the highest equity, as the most universal adoption.

But the application of the rule to this case is denied; and gentlemen would confine its operation to certain cases of reason and justice which they suggest. One of the gentlemen says it is founded on the presumed innavigability of the ship, and on this his whole argument is founded. A little reflection would have taught him otherwise; for the rule applies as well to goods as ships, of the former of which innavigability cannot be predicated. *Parsons* v. *Scott*, 2 Taunt., 363, 373, per Lawrence, *J.* The rule began with goods; and if afterwards extended to ships, as being in *pari ratione*, the reason must be sought in something not applicable to ships. Different rules apply to each. Several cases will warrant the abandonment of a ship, which will not apply to goods; and they sometimes complicate to such a degree, as makes it difficult to say, when they do apply to the one or the other. The three cases from Burrow and Douglass, decided in Ld. Mansfield, establishing the rule, that "if the voyage be lost, or not worth pursuing" (*Hamilton* v. *Mendes*, 2 Burr., 1198), which is wrongly put in the conjunctive, "lost and not worth pursuing, *in *Falkner* v. [*237 *Ritchie*, 2 Maule & S., 293, does not apply to both cases, but must be taken distributively, and in reference to two different situations of the ship. "The loss of the voyage" alludes to the innavigability of the ship; the "not being worth pursuing," the damage it has received, though it may still continue navigable. In these two senses it is considered by Buller, *J.*, in *Mitchell* v. *Edie*, 1 T. R., 615, and by Ld. Ellenborough, in *Thompson* v. *The R. Exch. Ins. Co.*, 1 Maule & S., 30; and the distinction is highly reasonable and derives countenance from several other books. *Rhinelander* v. *Ins. Co. of Pa.*, 4 Cr., 45; Weskett on Ins., tit. Abandonment, sec. 23; *Hamilton* v. *Mendes*, 2 Burr., 1201, per Aston, *arguendo*, adopted *in hæc verba* by Park on Ins., 194.

According to these authorities, where the ship is damaged to one half its value, the voyage ceases to be worth pursuing. To make a distinction between individual instances, would be inconvenient, as opening a door to management and fraud. To avoid this, the law generalizes, declaring that the loss of one half, accompanied by an abandonment, shall, in themselves, constitute a technical total loss. It sets up a positive rule, and will not allow the reason and fitness of the thing to be examined, with a view to each individual case. If the objection in this case, that a plaintiff, in honesty, can ask nothing more than an estimate of and allowance for his apparent loss, have any weight, it is an argument against the rule itself, and not a case coming within the rule. The same remark was made in *Hamilton* v. *Mendes*, but it was misdirected, if meant to be pointed at the rule. The case was one of capture and immediate recapture, with little or no damage; and for what little damage there had been sustained, the underwriters had offered to pay. The arguments used in that case by Ld. Mansfield are introduced into almost every discussion arising upon a claim for a technical *total loss; but they never apply, for in that case it had not happened.

[He examined the facts in the case under consideration, and insisted that the real loss was much more than one half the value of the ship; and that a recovery as for a partial loss would not amount to a complete indemnity; that there are several items always contemplated in a valid policy, and among others the great delay, **238***] which could not be covered *by estimates upon the principles of a partial loss; and with a view to which the plaintiff should, in honesty and fairness, recover as for a total loss to the extent of the valuation in the policy.]

True, it was intimated in *Brown* v. *Smith*, 1 Dow., 349, and *Smith* v. *Robertson*, 2 *Id.*, 474, that delay of the voyage does not form a ground of abandonment of the ship; but it clearly comes in aid of the rule that the assured may abandon when the voyage is not worth pursuing.

We are told that the abandonment was too late; that it should relate to the state of facts at the time of the abandonment; and that repairing and proceeding upon the voyage, turned a technical total loss into a partial one. I do not intend to examine the question whether the right to abandon depends on the state of facts, or information, at the time it is attempted; because, according to the view which I have taken, the facts were never so much altered as to deprive the plaintiff of that right. Nor do I feel authorized, after the decisions of our courts upon the subject, to contend that the state of information is to govern. Different opinions upon the question have, however, existed among great men; and I do feel warranted in saying, that where facts are urged to do away the state of the information, they should be clear beyond all doubt, and the alleged alteration of circumstances should be closely scrutinized. This is required by the state of this commercial country, trading extensively to the most distant parts of the world, our merchants being, for months together, in the greatest uncertainty as to the fate of their adventures. It was natural to say, that where the facts are plainly and entirely changed by a sudden recapture, or the speedy raising an embargo, the party should be holden to the state of facts. Such an event often leaves but little trace of damages behind; and Story, *J.*, means no more than this in *Smith* v. *Universal Ins. Co.*, 6 Wh., 186. Even in case of capture, if the salvage exceed one half the value of the ship, a restoration will not devest the right to abandon. This may be clearly gathered from the cases cited, decided by Ld. Mansfield. And there is a marked difference which should lead to a more **239***] careful preservation *of the right in the case of sea damage. Where there is a capture, the insurer pays the whole amount of damage sustained; while in that of sea damage, he comes off by paying two thirds of it, under the rule which deducts one third new for old. In the case of *M'Masters* v. *Schoolbred*, 1 Esp., 237, relied on as one illustration by gentlemen, there was no abandonment; and, of course, no question was or could be raised, whether there was a technical total loss. Had there been an abandonment, it is plain, from the opinion of Ld. Kenyon, that it would have been sustained, and an attempt was made to show an offer to abandon. Besides, if *Bainbridge* v. *Neilson*, 10 East, 329, relied upon by gentlemen, be law, *M'Masters* v. *Schoolbred*, as understood by them, is overruled. If it is still to be regarded as authority, it supports the rule for which we contend. There was no abandonment in *Da Costa* v. *Newnham*, 2 T. R., 407, and there does not appear to be a loss of 50 *per cent.*

The utmost that can be said of the power of the captain over the rights of the parties, is, that he is the agent of all concerned. *Mitchell* v. *Edie*, 1 T. R., 608, 613, 614; *Jumel* v. *Mar. Ins. Co.*, 7 Johns., 412, 423, per Kent, *Ch. J.* He has no power to control the assured's right of abandonment. If he succeed in diminishing to less than 50 *per cent.* or entirely removing the damage, the underwriter may well have the benefit of this; but if he merely change the character of it, his act has no effect between the parties. He cannot take away the election of the assured. The rule giving a right to this election is a positive one, *Smith* v. *Bell*, 2 Cai. Cas., 153, 157, per Lansing, *Chancellor*; and the reason applies with just as much force after the captain has completed the repairs as before. Applying the funds of the owner towards the repairs does not diminish the injury. Nay, they make a loss which renders the voyage not worth pursuing, and come to the same thing as if they had never been done. The underwriters cannot say, that for a loss of 50 *per cent.* the assured shall not abandon and convert it into a total loss. We have seen the rule, that he may do so, is precise, technical and positive. The repairs merely change one prospective damage into another. They merely substitute new debts due to people other than the assured. The debt due from the underwriters was, in truth, just as much when the vessel left Port Louis, and was proceeding on her voyage *as when she was wrecked [***240** there; and in *Ralston* v. *The Union Ins. Co*, 4 Binn., 386, the very point decided was, that where the loss is more than 50 *per cent.* the assured may abandon, even after the vessel has been not only repaired, but has reached her port of destination. In *Peters* v. *Phenix Ins. Co.*, 3 Serg. & R., 25, the same point was decided; and in *Coolidge* v. *Gloucester Mar. Ins. Co.*. 15 Mass., 314, it will be seen by a comparison of the dates, that the assured was allowed to abandon after the ship was fully repaired. In the case of *The Argonaut*, Pamphlet, lately decided by *Judge* Story, the same doctrine is held by him; and he denies that *Thornely* v. *Hebson*, 2 B. & A., 513, is law. This last case, decided by *Judge* Story, is in contradiction to *Humphrey* v. *Un. Ins. Co.*, said to be decided by him in Phillips on Insurance, p. 401.

As to the lien; the *Code de Commerce*, 190, 191, speaks the marine law of the world, if we except England, where her courts of admiralty have been restrained in the exercise of it. (Abbott on Ship., 135, 6.) Nor is it necessary to inquire whether our district courts would allow a recovery upon the lien. In every other country, the ship is bound to make good the loss of the cargo, arising from its being appropriated to repairs; and the lien may be enforced by a proceeding *in rem*, without regard to the question who owns the ship or who owns the cargo. Admit what is contended, that by the 320th article of the *Code de Commerce*, the borrower cannot, after taking the *respondentia* bond, have recourse to the ship, but is confined to his remedy against the cargo; as soon as he goes to the cargo, the owners of this may go to the ship. It comes indirectly to the same thing. The loss is removed but one step; and it is not material whether the captain or consignee has the right of lien. If the ship is bound by it, some one has it; and its existence is the only point. The same argument answers the objection of a novation or substitution. The effect of the *respondentia* is a direct lien upon the ship, as if she had herself, in the first instance, been bottomed for the expenses. *Humphrey* v. *Union Ins. Co.*, Phil. on Ins., 401, is relied on; but this goes upon the idea of an election to waive the abandonment by the owner's direction to repair. Here was no such direction. So long as the lien exists, **241***] the ship cannot be considered *as restored. This idea is maintained by *Da Costa* v. *Newnham*, 2 T. R., 407, and *Smith* v. *Williams*, 2 Cai. Cas., 110, decides that bottomry upon a ship takes away the insurable interest *pro tanto*.

It is said the plaintiff had funds at Antwerp, by which the ship was or might have been relieved; but the right to use those funds in the payment of debts depends on assuming that there was no right to abandon. It is the opposite side, then, that reasons in the entirely vicious circle. The ship, not the plaintiff, was the debtor. Had not the plaintiff appropriated his funds to pay debts, the ship must have been sold for this purpose at Antwerp. But the debts to be paid at Antwerp were, in truth, the debts of the underwriters. It was for the very purpose of enabling the plaintiff to avoid the payment of those debts, that the law gave him a right to abandon. This right continued. The rule could not cease to exist when everything remained in debt, and heavily incumbered. Suppose the plaintiff had sold the whole adventure, how would the parties have bargained? The amount of the various liens must have been deducted from the value of the ship, and the balance would have formed the price. Can it be possible that this ship was beneficially restored, when it could not have been sold short of first raising liens to very nearly its value? In this view, the case is directly within *Goss* v. *Withers*, 2 Burr., 683, and *M'Iver* v. *Henderson*, 4 Maule. & S., 576, which leaves the law where *Goss* v. *Withers* had placed it; and obviates every part of the objection taken. The case of *Patterson* v. *Ritchie*, *Id.*, 393, 396, per Ld. Ellenborough, is also with the plaintiff upon this point of lien. Indeed, substitute sea damage for capture, and it is precisely this case.

WOODWORTH, *J.* This is an action on a valued policy for $10,000, on one half of the ship Frances Henrietta. Mar. 7, 1819, the vessel put into Port Louis, in the Isle of France, in distress, where the cargo was taken out; and she was afterwards repaired, at an expense exceeding half the value. June 28 the vessel having been repaired, sailed for a port in Holland, and arrived at Antwerp Oct. 1, following. July 6, 1819, the plaintiff abandoned his interest to the defendants, and claims to recover for a total loss.

*The first question is, whether the [***242** state of facts as they existed at the time of abandonment, or the supposed state of things at the time, must govern in deciding whether there has been a total or a partial loss. On this point, it seems to me, that as well the nature of the contract, as the authority of adjudged cases, require us to adopt the former. For the purpose of establishing a uniform rule, the assurer is liable for a technical total loss, if the repairs exceed one half the value of the ship, and this can never be turned into a partial loss, if the insured abandons before the repairs are made. His right is *stricti juris*, and may be enforced although it may turn out that the ship was subsequently repaired, and proceeded on her voyage. The construction of the contract binds the assurer in such a case. He must then do the best he can with the property thrown on his hands. The measure of indemnity, thus far, is well defined and certain; but a very different case is presented, when that which at one time gave a right to abandon has ceased to exist; when the injury on which the right is founded has been repaired; and the vessel in every respect as capable of performing the voyage as before any damage was sustained. It would be repugnant to consider the loss total, when the final event has decided that it is partial. If the peril be over, and the subject insured in safety, the assured cannot elect to abandon, because he has no right to abandon when the thing is safe. (Park, 209). On this principle of the law of insurance, the real state of facts must be the criterion to determine to what extent the assured has a right te recover. If the information received is to govern, this principle is subverted, and the responsibility of the underwriters greatly enlarged. In the words of Ld. *Ellenborough*, 10 East, 341, "it would be to make them answerable, not for the actual loss sustained by the insured, whom they have undertaken to indemnify, against the risk stated in the policy, but for a supposed total loss, which had in fact ceased to exist." The question is well settled on authority. In *Church* v. *Bedient*, 1 Cai. Cas., 21, it was held that on a capture, restoration and abandonment, the fact of restoration, though unknown at the time of abandoning, takes away the right of abandonment and *claim for a total loss. It was there [***243** considered, that, from the mere act of abandonment, no positive right could be derived to the insured, unless it be combined with total loss. If, in the final event, it should prove an average loss, the act of abandoment would be nugatory.

This reasonable principle was sanctioned by the Supreme Court of the U. S., in the case of *Rhinelander* v. *Ins. Co. of Pa.*, 4 Cr. 29. The question was also decided in 4 Binn., 287. The court there held that there is nothing in the nature of the contract, from which it may be inferred that the rights of the parties are to depend upon supposed losses.

We must then look to the state of things at the time of abandonment. The voyage was not broken up; the vessel had been repaired, and was on her way to the port of destination; the technical loss did not continue to July 6, 1819. The plaintiffs had been placed in the same situation, in respect to the vessel, as they were before the injury happened. She arrived safely at Antwerp. The plaintiff's case is one that may frequently happen when the damage is sustained at a great distance from the assured. Months pass before information can be received. In every case where there is information of technical total loss, it it advisable to elect to abandon, if the assured wishes to cast the property upon the underwriter. It may or may not become effectual, but it places the assured in a situation to make the loss total upon the contingency that the state of facts correspond with the information received. Why should it be otherwise? Indemnity is the object, and that is obtained if the insurer pays the damages for repairs.

Where the technical total loss continues, it is true that more than an indemnity may, in many cases, be recovered. For the sake of a uniform rule, this consequence is sometimes unavoidable. In that particular instance, the general nature of the contract is made to yield to the greater benefit derived from an inflexible rule; but when the case does not come strictly within it, when the vessel is in the same, or perhaps in a better state than before the injury, it would change the contract of insurance from its original object, in-
244*] demnity, *to allow the insured to abandon, and in this manner protect himself for depreciation in the value of the vessel, or the consequences of an unfavorable market. But it is contended that the vessel was not beneficially restored, and therefore the loss continued. That will depend on the question, was there a lien on the vessel? Undoubtedly the assured has a right to claim that his possession shall be absolute and perfect. He is not bound to relinquish his claim for a total loss, if in reality there is a lien or incumbrance attached to the vessel. But the abandonment was not put on this ground; it is stated to be in consequence of the disaster, and the great injury to the voyage. In making the abandonment the assured must assign the true causes. If he assign an insufficient cause, he is bound by it, and cannot avail himself of a subsequent event without a new abandonment. This was so held in *Suydam* v. *Mar. Ins. Co.*, 1 Johns., 181.

The master paid for repairs at the Isle of France. In doing this, besides selling a part of the cargo, he was obliged to borrow money on *respondentia*, on the cargo. The vessel was not pledged for the payment. She must, therefore, be considered as beneficially restored; no impediment was placed in the way of prosecuting the voyage to a successful termination.

The plaintiff, then, is entitled to recover for a partial loss only. In adjusting this loss, the defendants must pay the amount expended for repairing the ship, with interest, deducting one third new for old; and also the difference between the amount of sales of a part of the cargo at St. Louis, for the purpose of repairing the ship, and what it would have produced at the port of delivery in Europe, together with marine interest on that part which was pledged; the residue of the expenses at the Isle of France to be settled as general average, to which the vessel, freight and cargo are to contibute—the defendants paying the ship's proportion of general average.

SUTHERLAND, *J.*, concurred.

*SAVAGE, *Ch. J.* The important [***245** question is: had the plaintiff a a right to abandon when the offer was made?

To decide this question correctly, it is necessary to inquire,

First. Whether the repairs at the Isle of France exceeded a moiety of the value of the ship, so as to constitute a technical total loss.

Second. Whether that loss continued total at the time when the offer to abandon was made.

Third. Whether the plaintiff lost his right to abandon by repairing.

1. It is perfectly well settled that if the ship be injured by any of the perils insured against, and the repairs will cost more than half the value of the vessel, the injury amounts to a technical total loss, and the insured may abandon. (Phil. on Ins., 401, and the cases there cited.)

It becomes necessary to ascertain the amount of the repairs, as it is denied that they did amount to half the value of the vessel; and I shall state what items of expense at the Isle of France I consider as belonging to repairs. By the case of *Dupuy* v. *United Ins. Co.*, 3 Johns. Cas., 182, it seems that the agent's commissions might be properly included in the estimate of repairs. But in this case the expenditure for repairs, rejecting commissions, exceed half the value. Take the following items:

Copper nails,	$861 42
" "	425 25
Rope, hemp, &c.,	139 17
Oil,	8 00
Ship-chandlery and cable,	1,085 23
Ship carpenter's bill,	14,444 72
White lead,	42 00
Old junk,	10 00
Cables,	345 00
	$17,360 79
Deduct old copper,	1,464 09
	$15,896 70
Deduct ⅓,	5,298 90
Amount of repairs,	$10,597 80

rejecting several items properly chargeable to the ship.

*The repairs, therefore, have exceed- [***246** ed half the value of the vessel, as valued in the policy; and it is not pretended that the value was greater at the port of necessity.

2. But it is contended, that as the vessel was actually repaired, and on her voyage when the offer to abandon was made, it is like the restitution of a captured vessel, which being restored before abandonment, the right to abandon is lost.

It is well settled that the right to abandon depends on the state of facts existing at the time the offer is made and not on the information of the assured; and it is equally well settled, in cases of capture, that if, before abandonment the vessel is restored, the underwriter is not liable for a total loss, unless the voyage be lost or not worth pursuing, or the salvage exceed half the value. So far as an analogy exists in this case, to cases of capture, is there anything equivalent to restoration? The vessel indeed, was afloat, and in the prosecution of her voyage when the assured offered to abandon, but under an incumbrance exceeding half her value; and therefore was not restored. There can be no doubt that the master had the right to sell a part of the cargo in case of necessity, and to borrow money upon bottomry or *respondentia*; and in this case I understand the law to be, that the vessel was bound to indemnify the cargo against the *respondentia* bond. This *respondentia*, and the expenses paid by the sale of the cargo, constituted such an incumbrance upon the vessel that the owner cannot be said to have his ship restored to him. Would a captured ship be considered as restored by being returned to the possession of the assured, subject to the payment of salvage exceeding 50 *per cent.* of her value? On the other hand, it is said that it never can be proper to convert a partial into a total loss; that all the assured can ask is indemnity; and all the insurers ought to pay is the amount of the plaintiff's loss. If, therefore, the defendants pay the plaintiff his expenses in procuring the restoration of his vessel, what more can he ask? Had the defendants, by an agent at Port Louis, made the necessary advances for the repairs, and the vessel had thus been restored to the **247***] plaintiff without any sacrifice on *his part, would he then have had a right of abandonment? And if not, would the offer of the defendants to pay all those expenses and losses as soon as informed of them, rebut any claim or right of the plaintiff to abandon. These questions are answered by *Mr. Justice* Story, who says the offer to repair has never been relied on to defeat an indisputable vested right to abandon; but an offer to bear all expenses is a proper ingredient in considering whether the owner has a right to abandon. *Peel* v. *Merch. Ins. Co.*, Phil. on Ins., 407.

In my judgment the plaintiff had a right to abandon, unless, by repairing the vessel, he signified his election not to do so.

3. This point has been decided by *Mr. Justice* Story, in *Humphrey* v. *Union Ins. Co.*, Phil. on Ins., 401, U. S. C. C. Mass., May, 1823. In that case, a ship from Messina to Boston, sustained a sea damage which made it necessary to put into Lisbon, where she was repaired by the master, at an expense exceeding half her value; and the vessel was bottomed for the expense. The owner abandoned, on hearing of the accident, which was only a few days before the arrival of the vessel at Boston. Proceedings were instituted on the bottomry bond, and the vessel sold; but the sale did not produce enough to satisfy the bond. It was held that this was a partial loss; and that the assured by electing to repair, had lost his right to abandon.

This is a case exactly in point; and if it is received as authority, decides the one now under consideration. I find no case, exactly in point, decided the other way, though there are both cases and principles which seem to lead to a different conclusion. A state of things must often occur in which it becomes necessary for the master to act without consulting the owner. The accident may happen, as here, at a distance, which renders such a communication impossible. It then becomes the duty of the master to act; and in *Milles* v. *Fletcher*, Doug., 231, Ld. Mansfield expressed an opinion, that if the master had acted as would have been right, in case the vessel and cargo were his own, the underwriter must answer for the consequences. Hence, it would seem *to follow that it depends [***248** on the propriety of the course adopted, whether the master acted as the agent of the plaintiff or defendant; and that if it was for the benefit of the ship and cargo to repair, then the plaintiff should not be prejudiced by the acts of the master. "Till the assured have been informed of what has happened, and have had an opportunity of exercising their own judgment, no act done by the master shall prejudice their right of abandonment." *Mitchell* v. *Edie*, per Ashurst, *J.*, 1 T. R., 613. The master is, therefore, not to judge of the propriety of an abandonment, nor is he the agent of the assured for that purpose.

The language of writers on insurance, and of courts, in discussing the question whether the assured is entitled to abandon, seems to suppose that an abandonment may be made after the ship is repaired. In the cases of wrecks or stranding, how can it be known that the expense of setting the vessel afloat will exceed half the value, until that expense has been incurred? In the case of repairs, generally, the estimates of surveyors may be relied on; but even should the master know that the repairs will exceed half the value of the vessel, may it not still be proper for him, as the agent of all concerned, to make the repairs? He is not bound to know whether the owner will chose to abandon. The assured is, in no case, obliged to abandon. He may do so in certain cases; and he must make his election in a reasonable time after information of the event which gives him the right; but the master is not to calculate or speculate on what his election may be. It is the master's duty, therefore, to make the repairs, where it would be his interest to do so were he the owner of both ship and cargo. In the case of *Dupuy* v. *United Ins. Co.*, 3 Johns. Cas., 182, the voyage was from N. Y. to St. Sebastians and back. The vessel was obliged by a storm to put into Kinsale, where she was repaired at an expense exceeding half her value. It does not appear expressly that she was repaired before she was abandoned, but it may be inferred. On the other hand, it is contended, and with great force, that the abandonment should be made before repairs; that the insurers may elect whether to repair or not; that they may prefer to *sell the stranded vessel for what [***249** she will bring, rather than repair, when, perhaps, as in this case, the repairs may cost more than the vessel, when repaired, will be worth; and that as the master is not the agent of the assured to determine whether to abandon or not, so neither should he be the agent of the insurers to determine whether to repair or not, in a case where the amount of repairs may be cause of abandonment.

On this point, the opinion of *Mr. Justice* Story is entitled to great consideration; and I am content to take the rule as laid down by him, that the assured can in no case abandon after making repairs; that by electing to repair, he loses his right to abandon.

This rule is supposed to be most consonant to the contract of insurance and the principles of justice. It has been doubted by very learned jurists, whether an abandonment ought ever to have been permitted in any case. (*Vide Mitchell* v. *Edie*, per Buller, *J.*, 1 T. R., 608, 615, 616.) It is now too late to discuss that question; but in a case where the right is not supported by an express adjudication, and is denied by such respectable authority; and when we have the authority of Ld. Mansfield for saying, that "in late times the privileges of abandonment has been restrained for fear of letting in frauds. (2 Burr., 697, *Id.*, 1213), we shall be justified in adopting the rule as laid down in *Humphrey* v. *Un. Ins. Co.*

In my opinion, therefore, the plaintiff is entitled to recover for a partial loss only.

Judgment accordingly.

Affirmed—3 Wend., 658.

Cited in—5 Cow., 66; 6 Cow., 330; 3 Paige, 332; Hoffm., 103; 26 N. Y., 479; 5 Duer, 370; 2 Sand., 487; 131 Mass., 249; 15 Am. Dec., 432; 36 Am. Dec., 451 (3 Ala., 18).

250*] *OAKLEY *v.* CRENSHAW.

Factor—Payment of Balance by, to Principal—When Factor thereby Assumes Outstanding Debts and Releases Principal from Obligation to Refund Advances.

The payment of a balance of account, by a factor or commission merchant to his principal, after the sales made, and for the purpose of closing the accounts between the parties, is an assumption of the outstanding debts; and consequently the principal is no longer accountable, or bound to refund advances though the debtors finally fail to pay for goods sold on commission, the proceeds of which were looked to for reimbursement.

Citation—3 Johns. Ch., 600.

ASSUMPSIT for money advanced, tried at the N. Y. sittings, in June, 1822, before Woodworth, *J.*, when a verdict was taken for the plaintiff, subject to the opinion of this court upon a case, as follows: May 22, 1815, the defendant, a merchant at Richmond in Va., shipped by the shooner Octavo, to the plaintiff, a commission merchant in N. Y., 27 kegs of tobacco, consigned to the plaintiff to be sold on account of the defendant, which the plaintiff received. June 9, 1815, the plaintiff received of the defendant 27 other kegs of tobacco by the schooner Traverse the Ocean, for sale on account of the defendant. The last parcel was first sold; and the plaintiff, by letter of June 17, 1815, inclosed to the defendant the account of sales, stating net proceeds $880.03, due per average Sep. 27 (then) next, and wrote: "If you want the money, I will remit you on your allowing me 1½ per cent. as a guarantee for amount outstanding, you to have the benefit of exchange to the extent that is in favor of your bill, should it be drawn by you on me." The defendant drew accordingly, and his bill was paid, July 15, 1815.

But 4 kegs of the first parcel were sold till Oct. 20, 1816, when the remaining 23 kegs were sold by the plaintiff to E. Whitaker, for $854.27, on the usual term of credit, on the sale of tobacco, at that period at N. Y. Sept. 26, 1815, the defendant wrote to the plaintiff thus: "In a letter written the 12th inst. I advised you of my intention to draw for $600, at 60 days, on account of the tobacco in your possession. Not having heard from you since, I have given Mr. Robinson a draft for that sum, which you will please accept. The season being near at hand, I hope you will be enabled to make an advantageous sale of my tobacco, &c." This bill was accepted and paid by the plaintiff, Nov. 28, 1815. Oct. 26, preceding, the plaintiff had inclosed to the defendant an *account of sales of the [*251 parcel first received, and wrote thus: "I have now to hand you an account of sales of your tobacco; net proceeds, $918.98, due per average 11th February next; errors and outstanding debts excepted; also statement of accounts showing $344.50 balance. I would remark, that I consider the sale of your tobacco rather chance than otherwise, at the price obtained, &c." For this balance, the defendant drew a bill on the plaintiff, which he refused to accept; and by his letter of Feb. 1, 1816, assigned as a reason, disappointment in not receiving moneys from the country, and among others from Whitaker; saying that when paid, he would advise the defeudant, in which event, he advises him to draw for $2.86 less. Apr. 16, 1816, the plaintiff wrote: "Last evening, I received in part pay of note of Whitaker, which included yours, among other sums. Although it would be but right that you should have only your proportion; yet I am desirous not to have the account stand open. Therefore, you may draw for $341.32, being net sum, after deducting sundry postages." This sum was shortly afterwards paid, on the defendant's draft, as proposed by the letter. In Apr., 1816, the plaintiff accepted Whitaker's draft for $4,000 in favor of one Neeland, and took a bond and warrant of Whitaker as a counter security. It appeared in proof that, at the time of the sale to Whitaker, he was a man in good credit, who had been long a customer of the plaintiff, and in the habit of purchasing tobacco from him; and that he made use of every effort to collect the money of Whitaker without success. Whitaker afterwards failed and took the benefit of the Insolvent Act. In Apr., 1817, the plaintiff caused to be presented to the defendant an account current, charging him with the amount of the several drafts paid on his account; with the charges on the tobacco; with 1½ *per cent.* on the guaranty on tobacco by The Traverse the Ocean, and crediting the several sums received from sales of the tobacco, and showing a balance due to the plaintiff of $652.59. This account the defendant refused to pay, stating as the ground of his refusal, that the plaintiff had guarantied the sale to Whitaker. This was the only objection he made when the account was presented; but he *added, [*252 generally, that he should resist the payment on every ground he could.

Mr. D. B. Ogden, for the plaintiff, insisted that there was no guaranty of the sales as to that part of the tobacco received by The Octavo; and the money being paid on the faith of Whitaker's debt, which had failed, the plaintiff was entitled to recover. The defendant was the principal debtor. Whitaker was looked to as a mere surety.

Mr. W. Slosson, for the defendant, insisted that the authority given by the plaintiff, by his letter of Apr. 16, 1816, to draw for the $341.32 balance, especially after having, by his letter of Feb. 1, declined payment and the acceptance and payment of the draft drawn pursuant to that authority, was a full settlement of the account between the parties.

The payment of a balance of account by a factor to his principal, is, in law, an assumption of the outstanding debts; and closes the transactions between them, especially when done, as in this instance, after the sales made, with full knowledge of all circumstances and for that express purpose. *Consequa* v. *Fanning*, 3 Johns. Ch., 600, 5 Res.; *Simpson* v. *Swan*, 3 Campb., 291.

Curia, per SAVAGE, *Ch. J.* There was no agreement to guaranty the sale of the tobacco by The Octavo; but merely to advance $600, before the sale of any part of this consignment, except the 4 kegs. The plaintiff would clearly be entitled to recover, was it not for his payment of the balance, the $341.32. Feb. 1, 1816, the plaintiff wrote to the defendant, "as soon as the funds of yours are received, you shall have prompt advice thereof;" and Apr. 16, writing again, and alluding to his letter of Feb. 1, he says: "Last evening, I received in part pay of note of Whitaker, which included yours among other sums. Although it would be but right that you should have only your proportion, yet I am desirous not to have the account stand open. Therefore you may draw for $341.32, &c." This seems **253***] to me a final *settlement and assumption of the debt due from Whitaker. About this time, the plaintiff accepted a draft of Whitaker for $4,000, and took counter security. If he did not intend to assume this debt of the defendant, he surely ought to have informed him. *Consequa* v. *Fanning*, 3 Johns. Ch., 600.

Judgment for the defendant.

Cited in—5 Cow., 475.

DONELY v. ROCKFELLER AND FELLER.

Bond, by Putative Father for Support of Bastard — When Overseers can Maintain Action on— Order of Filiation as Evidence.

An action on a bond given by a putative father and his sureties, to the Overseers of the Poor, to indemnify a town against the maintenance of a bastard child, will not lie, unless the Overseers show that they have been damnified by an actual payment of money or other disbursement in support of the child.

A mere liability to maintain the child is not sufficient.

An order of filiation against the putative father, charging him with a weekly payment of money, or payment of money for past expenses, &c., is not admissible evidence in such an action.

Citations—10 Johns., 345; 7 Johns., 168, 169, 358; 4 Mass., 627; 6 Johns., 158, 189; 5 Johns., 357, 133; 9 Johns., 367, 368; 3 Cow., 313; 1 H. Bl., 253; 1 R. L., 306, sec. 2, 1; 16 Johns., 155.

ERROR from the C. P. of Columbia. The action in the court below was debt on a penal bond, dated Nov. 2, 1817, executed by A. Doucly and two others, to Rockfeller and Feller, as Overseers of the Poor of the town of Clermont, and conditioned to indemnify as well such Overseers, as all and every the other inhabitants, &c., against all costs, charges, rates, assessments, damages and expenses whatsoever, for or by reason of the birth, education and maintenance of a bastard child, begotten by one John Donely, one of the co-obligors on the body of Hannah Lasher, an inhabitant of Clermont, &c. The declaration averred that the child was born Apr. 1, 1818, and was living when the action was commenced, Aug., 1821; but that neither the defendant, nor his co-obligors, or either of them, had indemnified as well the plaintiffs, as Overseers, &c., but had refused and neglected, &c., and that the plaintiffs Jan. 1, 1818, and on divers other days and times, &c., were obliged to lay out and expend large sums of money, viz.: $100, in and about the lying-in expenses of Hannah Lasher, and in and about the birth, education and maintenance of her child; and that the successor of Feller, one of the plaintiffs, also was obliged to expend other $100 for the same purpose.

The only evidence given at the trial, in support of the plaintiff's action, besides the bond, was an order of filiation, dated Apr. 25, 1818, made by two justices upon John Donely, charging him with the payment of $16, lying-in and *other past expenses, and 56 [***254** cents weekly thereafter. But no actual disbursements by the Overseers, or either of them, on account of the child, was shown; on the contrary, it appeared that the child had been supported by the mother, aided by several sums which had been paid in for her use, under the order of filiation, and which were indorsed upon the order. The sums due by the order had, however, run in arrear till, at the time of the trial, about $50 was due.

The reading of this order in evidence was objected to; but the objection was overruled. The defendant's counsel moved for a nonsuit, which was denied; and the court charged in favor of the plaintiffs below, and the jury found a verdict accordingly, and assessed the damages at $50.61. The defendant excepted to the decisions and charge of the court, and the cause came here on a bill of exceptions.

Mr. D. B. Tallmadge, for the plaintiff in error. Both breaches aver that the plaintiffs below have not been indemnified, and specify the consequences, which are two payments of $100 each, at several times, towards the maintenance, &c., of the child. Not one cent has been expended. The averments are entirely unsupported. The bond in question is, in every sense, one of indemnity merely; and I need not cite authorities to show that actual, certain, specific damage must be shown by the plaintiffs to entitle them to a recovery. They must have been put to expense, and obliged to pay by reason of the matter against which the security was taken, or, at least, the damages should have been liquidated by a judgment against them, rendering their liability fixed and inevitable. This doctrine receives the plainest illustration by the decisions touching the liability of bankrupts and insolvents. Suppose the defendant had been discharged under the Insolvent Act, and the next day the plaintiffs had been obliged to expend money for the maintenance of the child—it is clear that the discharge would be no bar to the action. The reason is, that the discharge would be obtained before the right of action accrued. It depends on the fact of payment. *Chilton* v. *Whiffin*, 3 Wils., 13; *Griffith* v. *Harrison*, 1 Salk., 196, 197.

255*] *Here is no evidence that the Overseers were ever even liable to pay. The mother maintained the child; but the law implies no promise on the part of the Overseers to pay her for this. *Stevens* v. *Howard*, 12 Johns., 195; *Brooks* v. *Read*, 13 *Id.*, 380; *Olney* v. *Wickes*, 18 *Id.* 122; *Rouse* v. *Moore*, *Id.*, 407. But mere liability to pay, if it existed, could not be enough. Such a position would, in its consequences, make the putative father and his sureties liable to a suit the day after a bond is given, for some speculative amount which such officers may fancy they will be bound to pay; but which, in the event, may never devolve upon them.

The order of filiation was improperly received in evidence. It was, as respects the surety, *res inter alios*. No such order was necessary; and it could form no test of the amount due. It fixes the sum to be paid by the putative father for past expenses, which were paid; and then requires a prospective payment of 56 cents weekly. This was conclusive upon nobody concerned in the bond, not even upon the Overseers. Suppose they had been obliged to pay $2 weekly, this could be recovered notwithstanding the order; and if they had paid but 25 cents, they could demand no more. That the order has nothing to do with the damages, was settled in *Falls* v. *Belknap*, 1 Johns., 486.

Mr. C. Bushnell, for the defendant in error. The child was an inhabitant of Clermont, and the order of filiation and payment under it were conclusive evidence of the putative father's liability. *Falls* v. *Belknap*, 1 Johns., 486, 491; *Hays* v. *Bryant*, 1 H. Bl., 253; *Sweet* v. *O. of Clinton*, 3 Johns., 26; *Wallsworth* v. *Mead*, 9 *Id.*, 367; *People* v. *Relyea*, 16 *Id.*, 155. It was admissible in evidence as well against the surety as the putative father himself. *Wallsworth* v. *Mead*, 9 Johns., 368; *People* v. *Relyea*, 16 *Id.*, 155; *Kip* v. *Brigham*, 7 *Id.*, 169; S. C., 6 *Id.*, 158; 1 Evans' Poth., pt. 4, ch. 3, sec. 3, art. 5, pl., 61, p. 562; *Maybee* v. *Avery*, 18 Johns., 352, 354.

256*] *There can be no doubt that the liability of the town to support, and actually providing for the child, would be equivalent to the payment of money, and sustain the action, if the bond were to be regarded as a mere private bond of indemnity. *Hays* v. *Bryant*, 1 H. Bl., 253. Here the child has been provided for; the putative father has from time to time made payments; and the fair intendment from the evidence is, that the provisions was at the expense of the town.

But where a bond is given to indemnify public officers against official and involuntary liability, that liability, fixed after delinquency of the principal, is sufficient to sustain an action on the bond, without payment; and a contrary rule would often work a ruin to the officer. *M'Intyre* v. *Woods*, 5 Johns., 357; *Kip* v. *Brigham*, 6 *Id.*, 158; 7 *Id.*, 168, S. C.; Com. Dig., Escape, E; *Sheriffs of Worwich* v. *Bradshaw*, Cro. Eliz., 53; *Tillman* v. *Lansing*, 4 Johns., 45.

WOODWORTH, *J.* The declaration is on a bond, with condition to indemnify and save harmless the plaintiffs in the court below from all costs, charges, damages and expenses, by reason of the birth, education and maintenance of a bastard child. The breaches assigned are, that the defendant has not indemnified the plaintiffs and their successors in the premises, and by means thereof they were obliged and did pay divers sums of money; that is, $100, for the lying-in expenses, and for the maintenance of the child; and further, that the successor in office of Feller, one of the plaintiffs, and Rockfeller, the other plaintiff, were obliged and necessarily did expend divers sums, to wit: $100, in and about the birth, education and maintenance.

The defendant pleads: 1. That the plaintiffs were not obliged to expend the money alleged in the breach. 2. Payment. 3. That the defendant did indemnify and save harmless the plaintiffs; and concludes to the country.

The plaintiff in error contends that no evidence was offered in the court below of the expenditure of money, by the plaintiffs, and consequently that the assignment is not supported.

*In looking at the pleadings, it seems **[*257** to me that the first issue substantially is, whether the plaintiffs were liable to pay the money alleged; for, although they, in the assignment, say they were obliged to pay and did pay and expend the money, the defendant in his plea negatives merely the first part of the allegation, to wit: that they were not forced and obliged to pay. The plea is silent as to the allegation that they actually did pay and expend the money. That the plaintiffs in the assignment understood the expressions, "forced and obliged to pay," as importing no more than that they were liable to be called on to make advances, is very evident, by the next sentence, which is, that they did pay and expend. This would have been repetition and useless, if "obliged to pay" means that they actually made payment, as the counsel for the plaintiff construe the breach, in order to raise the principal question relied on. I think, therefore, that on this issue the plaintiffs below were required to show that the child was a charge; that, in the relation they stood, it became their duty to see that provision was made for its maintenance, and what was the necessary sum accrued for its support to the time of bringing the suit. I apprehend such proof would have been sufficient, whether the plaintiffs had actually made the advances or not. If this doctrine be well founded, it seems to follow, conclusively, that the allegation of actual payment need not have been made, being impertinent and irrelevant, and had the defendant expressly alleged non-payment, or even admitting that the plea, in its present form, is so to be understood, the issue would be immaterial in that respect; and if found for the defendant, would, of itself, oppose no obstacle in the plaintiff's way. It will be remembered that this is a bond to indemnify public officers. The plaintiffs, as Overseers of the Poor, were bound to provide for the child, who was born in and chargeable to the town of Clermont. The child continued a charge upon the town; and the presumption of law is, that the plaintiffs, as their duty required, made suitable provision. *Hartwell* v. Root, 19 Johns., 345.

The bond was given to indemnify and save harmless the agents of the town, or, in other **258***] words, to pay whatever might *be reasonably required of the plaintiffs for support and maintenance. The construction to be given to a bond of indemnity to a public officer is not that he shall first advance his own money or that of the town, and then seek remuneration, but that the party covenanting shall, in the first instance, make advances so as to relieve the officer from the burden. The policy of the law has, therefore, wisely distinguished such a case from that of a bond of indemnity from one individual to another, where the party indemnified must first pay the money before he can sustain an action for any more than nominal damages. (7 Johns., 358; 4 Mass., 627.) It is on this principle that a sheriff, who has taken a bond for the liberties of the prison, which is, in effect, a bond of indemnity (6 Johns., 189), is entitled, after judgment against him for the escape, to recover the whole amount in damages without first making payment. *Kip* v. *Brigham*, 7 Johns., 168; 5 Johns., 357, 133; 6 Johns., 158.

The plaintiffs offered in evidence the order of filiation, made subsequent to the bond, which was objected to, but properly admitted, because it was an adjudication, on the subject-matter, against which the bond was to indemnify and conclusive, until reversed, upon the surety well as the putative father. It fixed the extent of the defendant's liability, and was equivalent to a judgment for the $16 and the 56 cents weekly. It rested with the defendant to show himself exonerated from the payment. *Wallsworth* v. *Mead*, 9 Johns., 368; 7 Johns., 169; 6 Johns., 168.

From the view I have taken of this case, the plaintiffs were entitled to recover a sum sufficient to satisfy for the expense of maintenance, without showing they had paid the amount of such expenses. The order reduced to certainty the sum to be paid, and in so doing is to be considered as a decision made by competent authority, that so much was requisite for the child's support. In consequence of this, it was the duty of the plaintiffs to cause relief to be administered to that extent at least.

On the whole, I am of opinion that the judgment in the court below should be affirmed.

259*] *SUTHERLAND, *J.* The plaintiff in error contends that the plaintiffs were not entitled to recover without proof of the expenditures alleged, and the exception appears to me to be well taken. This is strictly a bond of indemnity; no more—and there is nothing in the case to show that the plaintiffs below have been damnified in any respect. It is distinguishable from the cases of bonds for the jail liberties, relied upon by the counsel for the defendants in error. They are conditioned that the debtor shall remain a true and faithful prisoner, within the liberties of the jail; and the condition is broken, in terms, the moment he goes beyond the limits. *Non damnificatus*, therefore, to such an action on such a bond would not be a good plea; *M'Clure* v. *Erwin*, 3 Cow., 313; but it would undoubtedly be good in this case. In *Hays* v. *Bryant*, 1 H. Bl., 253, which was an action on a bond with a condition similar to this, the plea was *non damnificatus;* the plaintiff had actually expended money in support of the child; and the defense was, that it was paid voluntarily; no justice's order for the payment or allowance having been made. The court held that such an order was not necessary; that the parish officers were legally bound to maintain the child; and having actually expended money in its support, were entitled to recover on the bond. No action has, I believe, ever been sustained upon such a bond without this actual expenditure; and I think that nothing short of it will support the action.

The order of filiation, if properly received in evidence, does not vary the case. I incline to think, however, that it was not admissible at all. Where a bond is given, no order is necessary to warrant the expenditure. At most, it merely establishes the liability of the putative father, which is also admitted by the act of giving the bond. Had money been actually paid, the order might have been evidence to show that the sum paid was reasonable and proper; but for that purpose only.

SAVAGE, *Ch. J.* The Statute (1 R. L., 306, sec. 2,) points out two different courses which the putative father may pursue. One is by directly giving a bond to indemnify the town, *with sureties; the other by entering [***260** into a recognizance to appear at the next General Sessions of the county, and to perform such order as shall be made pursuant to the Statute. There is a third remedy which the town may adopt, by an order of filiation alone, without any other security. (*Id.*, sec. 1.) This order of filiation has no connection with a boud of indemnity. Here the bond was taken in the first instance, and the order made afterwards. In an action upon this bond, the plaintiffs below were bound to show a damnification by payment of the money for which they sued. A mere liability to pay is not sufficient. The order was the subject of a distinct action. *Wallsworth* v. *Mead*, 9 Johns, 367. And had there been a recognizance to abide the order, an action of debt would have lain against the sureties in that. *People* v. *Reylea*, 16 Johns., 155. But when the plaintiffs elected to sue the bond, they were bound to follow up its terms by establishing actual damage. Suppose the defendants had pleaded *non damnificatus*, must not the plaintiff have replied damage and shown how they had been damnified? The order of filiation had nothing to do with this suit, and was improperly admitted. The judgment must be reversed, and a *venire de novo* issue from the Columbia C. P.

Judgment reversed.

Reversed, 8 Cow., 623.
Cited in—7 Cow., 238; 44 Barb., 213.

THE PEOPLE v. P. C. VAN WYCK.

District Attorney—Liability, for Clerk's Fees—Rights to Compensation.

A district attorney is not liable for clerk's fees accruing in the course of suits, for fines and forfeitures upon recognizances, pursuant to the Act of

Apr. 21, 1818 (sess. 41, ch. 283, sec. 7. Laws N. Y. Vol. IV. p. 307 *c*), unless such fees are in fact collected by him.

The Board of Supervisors are not bound to allow him a compensation for services, under that section, but only for those which arise in the course of criminal proceedings, viz.: such as are provided for district attorneys in the Statute of 1813, 2 R. L., 21, or by the Act (sess. 41 ch. 283, sec. 9), which do not extend to suits upon recognizances, &c.

Citations—12 Johns., 444; 18 Johns., 122; Act, April 21, 1818 (4 Laws N. Y., 307 *c*); Act April 9, 1813; Act, April 6, 1810.

ASSUMPSIT, against the defendant, an attorney of this court, for fees of the clerks of this court, upon the Statute 1 R. L., 243.

261*] *The defendant pleaded that these fees, if any, accrued for services done, and materials and other necessary things found and provided, in certain suits at law, prosecuted for and in the name of the plaintiffs, to recover certain fines and forfeitures due and owing to them, in which suits the defendant officiated as public prosecutor, in the capacity of district attorney for the County of N. Y., he being at the time district attorney.

Another plea was to the same effect, adding that no costs or moneys whatever had been recovered and collected of the defendants.

Demurrer to both pleas, and joinder.

Mr. Talcott, Atty-Gen., in support of the demurrer. Before the Statute, 1 R. L., 243, sec. 4, giving a salary to the clerks, no doubt the defendant would have been liable for fees at their suit individually. That Statute provides that the clerks of this court shall render an account of all fees without exception to the Comptroller, who has it in charge by the same act to see that they are collected. The people come in as the successors or assignees of the clerks. By the Act of Apr. 21, 1818, 4 Laws N. Y., 306, sess. 41, ch. 283, sec. 6, district attorneys are thereafter to be paid all fees and disbursements by the counties. The Supervisors are bound to allow for the fees in question; and if this defense prevail, the defendant succeeds in throwing upon the people, what they have charged upon the several counties.

At any rate, the defendant does not go far enough. He should not only say that the fees arose in the course of public prosecutions, but show, in particular, what suits they were and the kind of services which he called on the clerks to perform. For aught that appears, a great variety of unnecessary labor may have been demanded of the clerks under pretense of these suits, for which the defendant would be liable, allowing his defense for those which were necessarily performed. If he succeed, it must be on the ground that circuity of claim is to be avoided; that if he is liable, yet he may demand reimbursement of the plaintiffs, **262***] which *would be an idle ceremony. To make out a bar on this ground, he should show fully and clearly the specific services, that the court may see judicially, whether they were proper. It does not follow, that because they were performed in the course of the causes, the plaintiffs are to allow them.

Mr. Van Wyck, in person, contra, said he had defended this suit upon the broad ground that a public prosecutor is not liable to the officers of the State for services which he demands of them. He is certainly not bound to advance money for them out of his own pocket. If he is liable to the clerks of the Supreme Court, he is equally so to clerks of counties, sheriffs and constables, a thing which was never heard or thought of. All these officers are bound to work for the people without pay, unless there be an express provision for them. (2 Bac. Abr., Fees, A, p. 463.) Witnesses for the State were allowed no fees at the common law, as is evident from the Statute (sess. 42, ch. 248, sec. 7), providing that the treasurer shall pay them. If we are correct, in saying these disbursements cannot be charged, the county are not liable to pay; and although the proceeds of the recognizances are given to the counties, this works no change as to the district attorney's liability to pay clerk's fees in the first instance. The suits prosecuted are still in the name of the people, and for the people; and they are the true plaintiffs in the suits. A public agent is not personally liable. *Walker* v. *Swartwout*, 12 Johns., 444; *Olney* v. *Wickes*, 18 *Id.*, 122. If unnecessary services have been done, the Attorney-General should have replied this fact. Till this is shown, it will be intended that the public prosecutor has done his duty.

The Atty-Gen., in reply, said the bill of costs are usually made up in these prosecutions for fines and forfeitures, the same as in a civil suit. A retaining fee, other items of service by the attorney, and clerk's fees, are charged to the defendant, and paid by him over to the district attorney, who has no right, when called on by the clerk, to claim them as a godsend to himself. The services *are no [***263** longer done for the people, but only a part of the people. The fines go to the counties (sess. 41, ch. 283, sec. 7), who are relators, merely using the name of the people, like the relator upon a sheriff's or administrator's bond, who is allowed to sue in the people's name, but is bound to pay costs as an individual. Here it is claimed that the people have given up all these debts to the counties, and yet are required to pay for collecting them. This should be at the proper costs and charges of the assignee; at least, the district attorney should have shown due diligence to collect of the defendants, and that he had failed.

WOODWORTH, *J.* By the Act of Apr. 9, 1813, 2 R. L., 16, the fees of the clerks of the Supreme Court, in civil causes, are regulated. When the services specified are performed, they are entitled to compensation. But it by no means follows that when a public officer is required by law to institute and conduct prosecutions, in behalf of the people, and is necessarily obliged to resort to the clerk to seal the process, and perform other services incident to such prosecutions, that the claim for compensation is against the officer. If this were the case, it would seem to subvert the known and established rule, that where a public agent or officer acts ostensibly within the line of his official duty, his contracts are public, not personal.[1] *Walker* v. *Swartwout*, 12 Johns., 444; *Olney* v. *Wickes*, 18 *Id.*, 122.

The fees of the clerk generally accrue from services rendered for attorneys in the causes

1.—See note to Gill v. Brown, 12 Johns., 385, Law. ed.

of individual suitors. In such cases the attorneys are liable. But in the case before us, the defendant was district attorney. By the 7th section of the Act of Apr. 21, 1818, 4 Laws, N. Y. 307 *c*, it is declared that fines and recognizances, which may be imposed and forfeited in any of the counties within this State, shall be collected by the district attorneys thereof, and paid to the county treasurer, for the use of the county. This Act imposed a duty. So far as the personal service of the district attorney extended, he was bound to perform it; but it never could have been intended, nor does the Act require a construction, that he was also bound to make advances of
264*] his *own money to the different officers of court and witnesses, so as to enable him to bring such causes to a termination. If such had been the intent, it is reasonable to suppose that some provision would have been made for the ultimate remuneration of the officer; at least, in cases where there was a failure to recover. But, in this respect, the law is silent. The 6th section declares that the compensation which is allowed by law to district attorneys shall be paid by the respective counties, and that their accounts be taxed by any officer authorized to tax costs in the Supreme Court. Here is the only provision for payment; and that has reference to the fees allowed by the Act of 1813, for conducting public prosecutions, and does not include fees for services in civil suits. When, therefore, the Act speak of compensation allowed by law, it necessarily means such fees as the Act of 1813 specifies; for there is no other Act on the subject. The 9th section of the Statute of Apr. 1, 1818, does not reach the case. If the defendant had made application for compensation to the Supervisors of the county, they might correctly answer, the county is entitled to the fines when collected; but with the costs accrued we have no concern; for the Act has not required us to make any allowance. Whether the clerk would have been justifiable in refusing, till paid, to file the papers and affix the seal to process, in the causes commenced by the district attorney, it is not necessary to decide. It is enough that, in our opinion, if he rendered his services, the officer is not bound for payment.

The Act has not provided in what manner the fees shall be paid. The claim for compensation must, as in other cases not specifically provided for, be addressed to the justice of the Legislature.

If the preceding view be correct, with respect to the clerk, prior to the passing of the Act of Apr. 6, 1810, I think that subsequent to that period, the argument against the defendant's liability becomes more conclusive; for, by that Act, a salary is allowed to the clerks, and the amount of fees are directed to be paid to the Treasurer of the State.

If the plaintiffs are entitled to recover, an officer who is directed to perform services for
265*] the State, and in the exercise *of that duty, is obliged to resort to the office of the State for the purpose of filing his papers and sealing process, is placed on the same footing as an attorney for private suitors; and that, too, although it turns out that nothing can be recovered against the persons prosecuted. Such a principle would indeed place the State on advantageous ground, and distinguish the case from the law applicable to principal and agent; but it cannot be supposed. When an agent acts within the scope of his authority, and renders services for his principal, he is entitled to be paid by both for his disbursements and services. Suppose the principal happened to be the owner of the horse rode by the agent, in traveling to perform his agency, or the owner and occupant of the ferry over which he crossed, would it be contended that he should pay his principal for these aids? For what purpose could the law sanction such a claim, when it is evident that if the agent paid the principal for such charges, he would be entitled to recover them back, as expenses necessarily incurred? This would be the case between individuals. The present case is distinguished in this, and the State cannot be prosecuted; yet the principle is the same. If the defendant had succeeded and recovered the costs, then he would have become liable for these fees on the ground of money had and received; but not otherwise. One of the pleas avers that no costs or moneys have been recovered or collected, which the demurrer admits. The objection that due diligence ought to have been averred cannot be sustained; for, until the contrary appears, we are to presume that a public officer has done his duty.

I am of opinion that the defendant is entitled to judgment.

SUTHERLAND, *J.*, concurred.

SAVAGE, *Ch. J.*, having been Comptroller, in whose office the fees in question stood charged to the defendant, and having also directed this suit to be brought, gave no opinion.

Judgment for the defendant.

Cited in—1 Wend., 17; 1 Hill, 366; 32 N. Y., 476; 14 Barb., 56; 28 How. Pr., 24; 18 Abb. Pr., 11.

---

*JACKSON, ex dem. WALSH, [*266
v.
COLDEN.

Foreclosure—Advertisement and Sale, to Mortgagee or Assignee—Foreclosure, Complete without deed—Mortgagor or Assignor cannot Object that Acknowledgment was Taken without the State—Usury—Assignment of Mortgage at Discount of more than Lawful Interest—When Usurious—Whether Mortgagor Entitled to Notice to Quit.

A foreclosure under the Act Concerning Mortgages (1 R. L., 312), by an advertisement and sale, is complete without a deed of conveyance where the mortgaged premises are purchased by the mortgagee or his assignee.

It does not lie with the mortgagor or assignor of the mortgage, to object that the power of sale was not regularly acknowledged and recorded.

A mortgage created for the purpose of being assigned upon a loan of money, and assigned accordingly upon a loan at discount of more than 7 *per cent.* is not usurious unless the assignee know, at the time of the assignment, of the purpose for which the mortgage was made.

The mortgagor, in order to warrant ejectment against him, is not entitled to notice to quit after foreclosure. At any rate, the advertisement of sale operates as a sufficient notice to quit.

A commissioner to take the acknowledgment of deeds, has no power to take the acknowledgment out of the State; though,

Semble, he may take the acknowledgment in any county within the State, though out of the county for which he is appointed.

Citations—1 R. L., 375, secs. 7, 8, 9, 10; 2 Cai., 61; 2 Johns. Ch., 611; 4 Johns., 215, 216; 1 Cai. Cas. Err., 17, 18; 3 Johns., 422; 2 Johns., 75; 6 Johns., 272; 17 Johns., 176, 300; 15 Johns., 44, 355.

EJECTMENT for lot No. 126, in Pittstown patent, in the town of Hoosick and County of Rensselaer, tried at the Rensselaer Circuit, Dec. 13, 1822, before His Honor, the late *Ch. J.* Spencer.

On the trial, the plaintiff introduced the following evidence: 1. A mortgage of the premises in question, executed by John Vander Speigle and Laura, his wife, to Colden, the defendant, dated Jan. 22, 1819, acknowledged before Asher Armstrong, a commissioner to take the acknowledgment of deeds, on the same Jan. 22; and by Laura, his wife, on the 29th of the same month: and recorded in the clerk's office of the County of Rensselaer, the same Jan. 29, to secure the payment of $4,500, one half Mar. 1, 1820, and the other half Mar. 1, 1821, with interest payable annually Mar. 1. The commissioner, who was sworn as a witness, stated that this acknowledgment was taken at Bennington, Vt. 2. An assignment of this mortgage by Colden to Walsh, dated Feb. 2, 1819, expressed to be in consideration of $4,500, acknowledged Nov. 9, 1821, and recorded in the clerk's office of Rensselaer Co. Nov. 26, 1821. By this assignment, Colden covenanted to make good to Walsh any deficiency of $4,500, which might remain on a sale of the premises by virtue of the power in the mortgage. 3. The affidavit of Gardiner Tracy, stating that he had advertised the mortgaged premises in question for six months in the newspaper called the Lansingburgh Gazette; and the affidavit of Will- 267*] iam Walsh, stating that he *affixed a copy of the advertisement on the outer door of the court-house in the City of Troy Feb. 6, 1821; and also the affidavit of Jacob C. Lansing, stating that he acted as auctioneer, and sold the premises by virtue of the mortgage (and that the sale was a fair, open and public sale) at the place mentioned in the advertisement, Aug. 9, 1821; and that the premises were bid off by Walsh, the lessor of the plaintiff, and assignee of the mortgage, for $3,000. These affidavits were duly taken and recorded in the clerk's office of the County of Rensselaer, Aug. 22, 1821.

The plaintiff then having proved the defendant in possession, rested.

The defendant's counsel moved for a nonsuit, on the ground that the foreclosure was imperfect, as the lessor was the purchaser, and could not convey the premises under the foreclosing sale; and that no notice to quit had been shown. The judge ruled that though he thought the foreclosure inoperative, there being no deed or foreclosure; yet the plaintiff might recover under the assignment without showing a notice to quit, to which opinion the defendant's counsel excepted.

The defendant then introduced in evidence, 1. A deed of defeasance executed by Vander Speigel to Colden, dated Jan. 22, 1819, for the premises in question, acknowledged before Asher Armstrong, a commissioner, the same day it bore date, reciting that Colden, by his indenture of that date, conveyed to Vander Speigel, in fee, the same premises; that Vander Speigel on the same day, by bond and mortgage of the same date, conveyed to the defendant for the purpose of securing the purchase money of the premises; and that it was the defendant's intention to assign the mortgage; and declaring that if the defendant should pay the holder or assignee of the bond and mortgage the money secured by them according to their condition, or furnish money to Vander Speigel to do the same; then the conveyance from the defendant to Vander Speigel to be void, and the premises revest in the defendant, &c. 2. A deed in fee of the premises in question *from the defendant to Vander [*268 Speigel, dated Jan. 22, 1819, with full covenants, duly acknowledged before Asher Armstrong. 3. A bond of indemnity executed by the defendant to Vander Speigel, dated Jan. 22, 1819, reciting the deed of defeasance, bond and mortgage; and binding the defendant, in case a sale of the premises should prove insufficient to pay the amount of the bond and mortgage, to save Vander Speigel harmless against the deficiency.

The defendant then proved that the mortgage was sold by Colden to Walsh at a discount of 5 *per cent.*, and that interest was to be calculated between them so as to allow Walsh 12 *per cent.* from that time to the time when the mortgage should become due; that the assignment, bond and mortgage were to be deposited with a third person, and in case the defendant paid back the money advanced upon the assignment, with interest, and $50 premium, within three months after the advance; the mortgage, &c., and assignment were to be delivered back and the assignment canceled. In speaking of this transaction afterwards, Walsh declared that this was what Colden called "raising the wind."

Considerable testimony was then offered by both parties, the defendant seeking to show that the lessor of the plaintiff knew of the above transaction between the defendant and Vander Speigel: and that they were for the purpose of enabling the defendant to raise money by loan upon the assignment of the mortgage, and the plaintiff seeking to avoid any evidence of this fact. It is not necessary to state this testimony. Suffice it to say, the court, as will be seen by their opinion, did not think it established the fact of the lessor's knowledge.

A verdict was taken for the plaintiff, subject to the opinion of the court on a case.

Mr. D. Buel, for the plaintiff:

1. The sale of the premises by virtue of the power in the mortgage was perfect. No deed of foreclosure was necessary. The Statute 1 R. L., 375, sess. 36, ch. 32, sec. 10, sanctions a sale to the mortgagee or assignee, who cannot convey to himself. The sale was not a judicial act; but the mere execution of a trust. The *evidence that the trust is executed, [*269 consists of the various affidavits touching the advertisement and sale, which are to be recorded. (1 R. L., 374, secs. 7, 8.) For what other purpose is this required by the Statute? The reason why a sheriff's sale of land is in-

valid without a written conveyance is, that the omission is within the mischief of the Statute of Frauds. *Simonds* v. *Catlin*, 2 Cai., 61; *Jackson* v. *Catlin*, 2 Johns., 248; *Catlin* v. *Jackson*, 8 *Id.*, 520. He is not bound even to return the execution; but here we have the same anthenticity as in case of a sale under the Act for the Partition of Lands by authority of the Supreme Court, Court of C. P., or Court of Chancery; in which latter case no release is necessary (1 R. L., 510, sec. 5; *Young* v. *Cooper*, 3 Johns. Ch., 295), or any other judicial sale. It is equivalent to a strict foreclosure in equity. *Bergen* v. *Bennet*, 1 Cai. Cas., 1, 20; *Jackson* v. *Henry*, 10 Johns., 185, 195. I do not mean a foreclosure by sale, which is a modern practice in the Court of Chancery; but the English foreclosure, whereby the title vests in the mortgagee or assignee by act and operation of law. In this case a deed is never executed. The object and effect is merely to shut out all parties in interest from the right of coming to redeem. All the proceedings are, by statute, made matter of record; and become evidence of a nature as high and conclusive as the recorded decree of a court of equity. The 10th section of the Statute of Mortgages, 1 R. L., 375, was passed long after the general Statute Relative to Sales under the special power (*vide* 1 K. & R., 482, sec. 5, 6; sess. 31, ch. 156, sec. 5), but not a word is said of a written conveyance. True the 6th section supposes a conveyance, but it is evident, on comparing this with the 10th, that none is deemed necessary when the purchase is by the mortgagee or assignee. One reason for requiring a deed upon a sheriff's sale, doubtless, was that without it the Registry Acts might be evaded in recording counties. This evil cannot exist where all the proceedings are recorded in the proper office. Besides, here is the writing made necessary by the Statute of Frauds. The assignee took all the interest of the mortgagee. This was made a matter of record, as well as the mortgage; and, by pursuing the record, the purchaser finds that all outstanding equity is extinguished.

2. The commissioner to take acknowledgments and proof, &c., has all the power given by a former Statute (1 R. L., 369) to a judge **270***] *of the Supreme Court or Court of C. P. (sess. 41, ch. 55.) In neither Statute is the officer limited in the execution of his functions to any particular place. His jurisdiction is not territorial, so far as the mere acknowledgment is concerned. *Jackson* v. *Humphrey*, 1 Johns., 498, which will, doubtless, be relied on against us, related to the proof of the deed, and involved the question whether an oath could be administered out of the State—an act local in its nature, according to the doctrines of the criminal law, which considers a venue within the State essential, and to be made out in proof, should an indictment for perjury become necessary. In that case, Emmott, counsel, who argued against the act of the judge, conceded that had his act been the mere taking an acknowledgment, it would have been valid, though without the State. Suppose the commissioner to have stood on the N. Y. side, and the cognizors on the Vt. side of the State line during the acknowledgment, would not the objection be deemed rediculous?

3. But the acknowledgment is not a necessary part of the mortgage, except so far as the *feme covert* was concerned. It is only necessary to warrant the recording; and the plaintiff is, therefore, entitled to recover under the assignment. *Jackson* v. *Chase*, 2 Johns., 84, 87; *Weaver* v. *Belcher*, 3 East, 449; *Berry* v. *Mut. Ins. Co.*, 2 Johns. Ch., 611; *Jackson* v. *Dubois*, 4 Johns., 216. The legal estate passed to the assignee, and he may maintain ejectment. *Smartle* v. *Williams*, 1 Salk., 245.

4. Notice to quit was unnecessary. The relation of the parties was that of assignor and assignee, not mortgagor and mortgagee, to which last alone the doctrine of notice to quit applies, where a mortgage is in question. *Jackson* v. *Laughhead*, 2 Johns., 75; *Jackson* v. *Chase*, *Id.*, 84; *Jackson* v. *Fuller*, 4 *Id.*, 215; *Jackson* v. *Wheeler*, 6 *Id.*, 272. There must be either a tenancy, or *quasi* such, to require notice; and even then a disclaimer forfeits the right. *Jackson* v. *Deyo*, 3 *Id.*, 422. Colden holds adversely. In this character, no one can demand notice; no presumption can arise that he is in by consent of the lessor of the plaintiff, which is the notion upon which notice is required to a mortgagor.

5. Here was no communication for the loan, when the mortgage was created; and selling it at a discount was not usurious, unless accompanied with an usurious intent. There must be a design to evade the Statute of Usury. *Wycoff* v. *Longhead*, 2 Dall., 92; *Munn* v. *The Com. Co.*, 15 Johns., 44; *Bush* v. *Livingston*, 2 Cai. Cas., 66. The case does not come within *Munn* v. *The Commission Co.*, *15 [***271** Johns., 44, and *Powell* v. *Waters*, 17 *Id.*, 176. Those cases go on the ground that the lender knew the purpose for which the paper was created. This will be obvious by recurring to the authorities (*Jones* v. *Hake*, 2 Johns. Cas., 90; *Wilkie* v. *Roosevelt*, 3 *Id.*, 66; *Id.*, 206, S. C.) upon which the latter cases are founded, in all of which knowledge appears. Suppose the broker of negotiable paper made to procure a loan, tell the lender upon discount that the paper is valid; would he be allowed to gainsay this? Knowledge is always of the essence of usury. *Barclay* v. *Walmsley*, 4 East, 55; *Floyer* v. *Edwards*, Cowp., 112 to 116; *Nevison* v. *Whitley*, Cro. Car., 501; *Buckley* v. *Guildbank*, Cro. Jac., 678; *Bush* v. *Buckingham*, 2 Vent., 83; *Livingston* v. *Bird*, 1 Root, 303; Ord. on Usury, 59 to 62.

At any rate, the court have never gone so far as to say that a mortgage and bond created to raise money, and sold at a discount, even with knowledge, shall, for that reason, be holden usurious and void.

But, if void for usury, the transaction was only so as between the original parties, and the defendant cannot lie still, suffer a foreclosure and then avail himself of the usury in this manner. *Jackson* v. *Henry*, 10 Johns., 185.

Mr. J. V. Henry, same side, as to the point of usury, cited *Fuller's* case, 4 Leon., 208; *Murray* v. *Harding*, 3 Wils., 394; *Le Grange* v. *Hamilton*, 4 T. R., 613 and 615, and Ord. on Usury, 74, 75, 76, and the cases there cited.

Messrs. L. Mitchell and *A. Van Vechten*, for the defendant:

1. The foreclosure was inoperative and void. Only one practice has obtained in relation to

this summary mode of foreclosing upon the power contained in the mortgage. A deed of conveyance is, and always must be, executed through a third person, where the mortgagee or assignee becomes the purchaser. The 6th section contemplates a conveyance, and the 10th was merely to remove a doubt whether the mortgagee, &c., being a trustee, could purchase for his own benefit. It was not intended to alter the forms of doing the business. One acting under a power must give the same title, and convey in the same form as his principal. A mortgagee does not convey in his own right. The title is not in him, but the mortgagor, from whom the power is derived. One cannot give a deed to himself; but the same form should be pursued as in *Jackson* v. *Henry*, 10 Johns., 185–187.

272*] *2. The power was never properly acknowledged. Of course, it was never properly recorded; a ceremony made essential by the Statute, 1 R. L., 374, sec. 6, to the validity of the sale. The power of the officer is confined to his own State. Commissioners are mere county officers. The case of *Jackson* v. *Humphrey*, 1 Johns., 498, is conclusive, and cannot be distinguished. The commissioner wants the power; and it is the same thing whether the object be proof or acknowledgment. The purposes of the Act are the same in each case—to give effect to the deed. The extreme case put on the other side of the commissioner and cognizor on different sides of the state line, will not help the matter. When a state officer is out of his territorial limits, he ceases *quoad* any act done there to be a state officer.

3. Notice to quit should have been given. No matter what the form of doing this business, the court cannot but see that Colden was the real mortgagor. The ceremonies which passed between him and Vander Speigel were mere form. Colden was the owner of the land throughout. The title never passed from him. Allow him as to Vander Speigel, to be a mortgagee in possession, the assignment to Walsh was, at most, a mortgage, and established the relation of mortgagor and mortgagee between Colden and him. It was a sub-mortgage; and a notice to quit was equally necessary, as if it had been a principal one. The agreement that the money should be repaid within a certain time, and the assignment canceled was plainly made out in proof. Clearly, Colden's interest might have been sold on execution. Indeed, no interest whatever passed to Vander Speigel. Being at first a mortgage, it always continued so. 1 Pow. on Mort., 146, 152, 157; *Mellor* v. *Lees*, 2 Atk., 495; *Howard* v. *Harris*, 1 Vern., 33; S. C., *Id.*, 190.

4. The assignment was void for usury. Here was a loan of money, upon an assignment by way of mortgage, to become void on repayment of an extravagant per centage, and $50 premium. The transaction with Vander Speigel was a cover for usury. The assignment was to lie three months as a mere escrow, to await the repayment. Walsh was secured at all events for his money by Colden's personal covenant for the deficiency. The court will look at the real substance and nature of the **273***] transaction. Walsh and *Colden stood in the relation of lender and borrower. No doubt here was a loan at an illegal *per cent.* the very definition of usury. The court will not suffer it to be disguised by the shape in which the business was done. Knowledge in Walsh was not necessary to make the assignment void. This was not deemed necessary in the cases cited on the other side. It is enough that the instrument is to derive its existence from the usurious act; and the case is the same in principle, whether it be a mortgage, a note, or bill of exchange. Knowledge or a corrupt agreement is necessary to be shown, only where the offender is prosecuted as a criminal. *Dunham* v. *Dey*, 13 Johns., 44.

The recorded affidavits of sale are said to be sufficient evidence even to satisfy the Statute of Frauds. But they are no more than *prima facie* evidence of sale; none at all of the conveyance. For aught that appears from these, the consideration money may never have been paid. The premises may be set up and sold again for want of payment. It is a deed of conveyance only which can safely be received as the final execution of the power. All the facts proved by the affidavits are revocable in their very nature. The rule is universal that a freehold cannot pass short of a writing under seal. The analogy to a case of strict foreclosure does not hold. There the right of redemption is cut off by a decree. If this be so as to the mortgagee upon a statute sale, why not the same as to any other purchaser, to whom a deed has always been holden necessary.

Mr. J. V. Henry, in reply. The court will not extend the case of *Jackson* v *Humphrey*, 1 Johns., 498. Were the office of commissioner judicial, it would be proper to confine him to the territory for which he is appointed. But it is merely ministerial, at least in taking acknowledgments. Suppose a commissioner of one county should take an acknowledgment in another; is there a doubt that it would be valid? The Statute recognizes the taking acknowledgments and proofs, in foreign countries, by a judge of another State or the U. S; evidently regarding this power as personal, not territorial. The Legislature never contemplated confining the proof or acknowledgment to state boundaries, *with the view to [***274** prosecution, for a crime which might be committed in acknowledging or proving a deed.

But the mortgage was good on its face. So was the acknowledgment. Is it to be tolerated that Colden, the party who imposed them upon Walsh, shall now be permitted to gainsay them? Beside, the registry of the power is not necessary to the validity of the sale as between the parties. *Bergen* v. *Bennet*, 1 Cai. Cas., 17.

Must the mortgagee, then, stand by, and see the premises sacrificed upon the bid of another. Such is the effect of the doctrine contended for. Cases may exist, in which the bidding cannot be properly confined to another. To avoid this evil, the Legislature have empowered him to purchase, to avoid the effect of Hamilton and Tompkins' reasoning in *Bergen* v. *Bennet*, *Id.*, 10, 11. Had it not been for this statute provision, the complete loss of the property to the mortgagee might be the consequence; and the argument that he cannot deed to himself, is conclusive that no conveyance is necessary. The Statute would not sanction a nugatory thing. It intended that the purchase should, in itself, without deed, operate as an extinguishment of the equity of redemption, except as to creditors by judgment or decree, whose rights are expressly saved. The sale and conveyance are treated by the statute as distinct things. Suppose, after the sale, Vander Speigel had filed his bill to redeem, and these proceedings had been pleaded in bar; would they not be considered a complete bar in equity? The mortgagee already has the legal estate after forfeiture. The Statute gives the form of cutting off the equitable one by an extrajudicial sale. Foreclosure, both in equity and at law, is considered in this light. In neither case is a deed necessary.

If the foreclosure was complete, what becomes of the defense of usury? It must have been pleaded to a bill for foreclosure; and at law, it must be shown by bill before the sale is made, provided the purchase be *bona fide*.

Notice to quit is out of the question, for the assignment was absolute on its face. No interest whatever was left in Colden. It was, at most, an equitable mortgage, in virtue of the parol agreement to cancel on repayment. To this, the doctrine to quit has no application. **275***] In truth, it *is neither a mortgage at law or in equity, but a mere contract of purchase and repurchase. If, however, a notice was necessary, the advertisement in the newspaper was a sufficient notice within the rule. *Jackson* v. *Lamson*, 17, Johns., 300.

There is no similarity between the case of a promissory note, created for the purpose of discount, and this mortgage. In the former case, the note had no legal existence, and cannot be enforced at law or in equity, till it takes effect by the discount itself. Its legal existence depends on the discount being a fair one. Here the mortgage was complete and available at law, independent of the discount. But if, as contended, the whole between Colden and Vander Speigel was mere ceremony and goes for nothing, and the sale be considered absolute, the objection is put down by another view. It was the same as selling the land itself at an undervalue. This is not usury. If the mortgage was valid in its inception, all the cases agree, that subsequent usury will not vitiate it.

SUTHERLAND, *J.* The plaintiff claims title to the premises in question, under a mortgage given by John Vander Speigel to the defendant, bearing date Jan. 22, 1819, which was assigned by the defendant to the lessor of the plaintiff, Feb. 2d, in the same year.

The mortgage was foreclosed under the statute, and the premises sold Aug. 9, 1821, to the lessor of the plaintiff, he being the highest bidder; and this action is brought to recover the possession of the mortgage premises thus sold.

The plaintiff's title is resisted on several grounds: 1. It is contended that the foreclosure was void; first, because it was not, and could not be consummated by a deed; the owner of the mortgage, in whose name the deed must be given, having himself become the purchaser. Secondly, because the acknowledgment of the mortgage was taken out of the State, by a commissioner of the State, and the power to sell, therefore, was not properly recorded. 2. It is contended that the contract under which the assignment to the lessor took place was usurious; that he cannot, therefore, recover *under the assignment, if the [***276** foreclosure should be held void and inoperative; and 3. That the defendant was entitled to notice to quit.

I am inclined to the opinion that the lessor of the plaintiff acquired a valid and legal title under the foreclosure, although no deed was executed upon the sale. The Statute 1 R. L., 375, sec. 10, provides that no title to mortgaged premises, derived from any sale, made in virtue of a special power for that purpose contained in the mortgage, shall be questioned, impeached or defeated, either at law or in equity, by reason that the mortgaged premises were purchased in by the mortgagee or his or her assignee, or by his, her or their legal representatives, or for his, her or their benefit or account; provided that the sale was, in every other respect, regular, fair and with good faith. Here is an implied statute authority to the mortgagee, or his assignee, to become a purchaser, not only by his agent, but in his own person. The Legislature must have been aware that the owner of the mortgage is the person who makes the sale: and in whose name the conveyance to the purchaser must be given; and when they authorized the mortgagee, or his assignee, to become a purchaser, they must have contemplated a sale without a deed, as none in such cases can be given.

The other provisions of the Act are adapted to meet a contingency like this, and to guard against the objection on general principles, as well as those which grow out of the Statute of Frauds, to a foreclosure without deed.

The 7th, 8th and 9th sections of the Act provide for perpetuating the evidence of the regularity of the sale. The affidavit of the printer who published the advertisement, and of the person who put it on the door of the courthouse, and also of the person who acted as auctioneer at the sale, stating the circumstances of the sale, after having been duly acknowledged and certified, may be recorded at full length in the book of mortgages, in the clerk's office of the county where the lands lie; and the record of either of the affidavits is made, *prima facie*, evidence of the facts set forth in it.

The affidavit of the auctioneer generally, and I believe universally, has a copy of the advertisement of sale attached *to it; and [***277** states that the sale was fair and public; and made at the time and place mentioned in the advertisement; to whom the premises were struck off, and for what sum.

Although the Statute is not imperative that these affidavits shall be recorded, yet the obvious importance to the purchaser, of putting the evidence which they contain beyond the reach of casualty, has rendered the practice of recording them universal. In this case, they were actually recorded within a fortnight after the sale; and the affidavit of the auctioneer, by reference to the advertisement attached to it, contains a particular description of the premises sold, the time and place at which the sale took place; and states that the premises were struck off to William Walsh, the lessor of the plaintiff, who was the highest bidder, for $3,000.

This is clearly a sufficient note, or memorandum in writing, to take the case out of the Statute of Frauds; and obviously distinguishes it from that of *Simonds* v. *Catlin*, 2 Cai., 61. The point there decided was, that sheriffs' sales upon executions were within the Statute of Frauds; and would not pass an estate without a deed or note in writing, signed by the sheriff; and that the return of the sheriff, in that case, upon the execution, was not a sufficient deed or note in writing within the Act; because it did not contain the requisite certainty. Kent, *Ch. J.*, who delivered the opinion of the court, says: "It does not appear what estate was sold, whether an estate for years, for life, or in fee, nor is there any certainty as to the thing sold. It was stated to be all that farm or tract of land in Pompey, in the tenure and occupation of the defendant; but there was no estimation of the quantity of land sold, nor in what part of the town it lays, or how marked or bounded;" and he says, "in all cases of sheriffs' sales, the thing sold must be specified with so much precision, as that, from the description, it can be reduced to a certainty." The affidavit of the auctioneer does contain all the particulars in which the return of the sheriff was here held to be defective; and clearly, in my judgment, removes the objection growing out of the Statute of Frauds.

278*] *If the Statute, then, by authorizing the mortgagee, or his assignee, to become the purchaser at the mortgage sale, has impliedly dispensed with the necessity of a deed to pass the estate in such a case, since none can be given; and if there is a sufficient note in writing to take the case out of the Statute of Frauds, then the equity of redemption of the mortgagor was regularly foreclosed; and the whole estate vested in the lessor of the plaintiff by the mortgage sale.

Whether the acknowledgment was void or not, on account of its having been taken in Vt., by a commissioner of this State, it is not material to decide; though I incline to the opinion that it would have been void, between different parties. But it does not lie in the mouth either of Colden or Vander Speigel, after having procured the acknowledgment to be thus taken, and the mortgage, with the power of sale to be recorded, to question the authority of the commissioner. They have affirmed his authority; and shall not be permitted now to question it as against a *bona fide* purchaser under the power. But the acknowledgment and registry of the mortgage are not necessary to its validity, as between the original parties; nor would an entire omission to record the power, affect the sale as between them. *Berry* v. *Mut. Ins. Co.*, 2 Johns. Ch., 611; *Jackson* v. *Dubois*, 4 Johns., 216. *Mr. Justice* Kent, in *Bergen* v. *Bennet*, 1 Cai. Cas., 17, 18, says, the only use in recording the power is for the benefit of the purchaser; and it does not lie with the mortgagor to object to the validity of the sale, by reason of that omission.

The mortgage having been, therefore, regularly foreclosed, and the lessor of the plaintiff become the purchaser, neither the question of usury nor the necessity of notice can arise. The lessor's title is derived from the mortgage, in which there is no pretense of there having been usury; and not under the assignment, in which the usury is alleged to have taken place.

The mortgagor in possession has never, I believe, been held to be entitled to a notice to quit from the purchaser under the foreclosure of the mortgage. There is no privity, nor anything like the relation of landlord and tenant, subsisting *between them (3 Johns., [***279** 422; 2 Johns., 75, 84; 4 Johns., 215; 6 Johns., 272); but if there was, the case of *Jackson, ex dem. Bennet*, v. *Lamsen*, 17 Johns., 300, has settled that the notice of sale under the power is equivalent to six months notice to quit.

It was urged on the argument that this was not an operative mortgage, as between Vander Speigel and Colden; that it was made for the purpose of enabling Colden to raise money, and falls within the principle established by this court in *Munn* v. *Commission Co.*, 15 Johns., 44; *Bennett* v. *Smith*, 15 Johns., 355, and *Powell* v. *Waters*, 17 Johns., 176, that if a bill or note be made for the purpose of raising money upon it; and it is discounted at a higher premium than the legal rate of interest; and when none of the parties whose names are on it, can, as between themselves, maintain a suit on the instrument when it becomes mature, provided it had not been discounted, that then such discounting would be usurious, and the instrument void. Admitting that this principle may be applicable to specialties, as well as to negotiable paper, it must be with the qualification that the person purchasing knew that the specialty was not operative, being made for the purpose of raising money. The evidence in this case does not establish the fact that Walsh knew of the circumstances attending the creation of the bond and mortgage when he became the purchaser of it.

His application to Vander Speigel to know if he had any objection to his purchasing the bond and mortgage; and Vander Speigel's reply that he would as soon pay him as Colden, or any other person, afford satisfactory evidence that he at that time believed the bond and mortgage to be fair and valid; and there is nothing in the case to show that he learned the real nature of the transaction, before he completed the purchase, or until the winter of 1821.

This view of the case renders it unnecessary to consider whether the assignment of the mortgage to Walsh was usurious or not.

WOODWORTH, *J.*, concurred.

*SAVAGE, *Ch. J.*, doubted upon the [***280** question of usury; but as to the other points he remarked as follows:

1. By the Act Concerning Deeds (1 R. L., 369), and the Act Authorizing Commissioners to be Appointed to take the Proof and Acknowledgment of Deeds, passed Mar. 24, 1818, sess. 41, ch. 55, it seems to have been the policy of the Legislature to provide officers authorized to take the proof or acknowledgment of deeds in all places where they could possibly be necessary. But it does not necessarily follow that they are confined to their territorial limits. The judges of the Supreme Court of the U. S. have, of course, jurisdiction throughout the U. S.; and the judges of the superior courts of the several States, within their States. There is nothing prohibiting those officers from acting within the limits of this State or of any other State. The trust, as to them, seems to be a personal one, arising

from that weight of character supposed to be connected with the offices they respectively hold. The Commissioners, by the Act of 1818, have the same powers which a master in chancery or a judge of the C. P. previously had. Their jurisdiction, no doubt, extended throughout the State; and but for the ease of *Jackson* v. *Humphrey*, 1 Johns., 498, I should have contended that their authority was not limited by territory. It was there decided that a judge could not take proof in Canada, because he could not administer an oath out of the State, nor could the witness be convicted of perjury. These objections would lie equally well to an act by any other officer out of the State. We certainly could not convict a witness in this State who had sworn falsely in Vt., before the *Ch. J.* of that State; and if he should be indicted in that State for perjury thus committed, might it not be well urged that he had not offended against the laws of that State? And that the *Ch. J.*, in administering an oath to him acted extrajudicially, and without authority under the laws of that State? There is, however, one argument to be drawn from the Act of 1818, in favor of confining the officers named in the Act to their several appropriate jurisdictions. The commissioners first received their authority from the Act of Mar. 24, 1818, the 5th section of **281***] *which provides that when a deed is proved or acknowledged before a C. P. judge or commissioner, and such deed is to be recorded in a different county from that in which the judge or commissioner resides, no record shall be made of it, unless accompanied by a certificate from the clerk of the county in which such judge or commissioner resides, stating that such person is judge or commissioner, and that the signature is genuine; and the 6th section provides that nothing in this Act shall extend to deeds proved or acknowledged out of the State. Now, whether the 6th section is construed to extend to the whole Act or to the 5th section, it seems to show the intention of the Legislature on this question. If it relates to the whole Act, then it expressly denies the power of the commissioners out of the State. If it has relation only to the certificate of the county clerk mentioned in the 5th section, then, if the commissioners possess the power contended for, this would follow, that when acting, in their own counties, their signatures, and official existence must be proved by the county clerk; but when acting out of the State, no such proof is required; that is, when they act out of the State, greater credit is to be given to their official acts than when acting within it; an absurdity not to be imputed to the Legislature.

I apprehend the Legislature never intended the commissioners should execute their offices out of the State. But that point is not very material in this case. The acknowledgment is necessary in order to warrant the record; but the recording a mortgage or power of sale is not necessary to their validity as between the parties.

2. The proceedings and sale under the Statute are a species of foreclosure of the equity of redemption; and I confess I can see no necessity for a deed, unless when a third person purchases. The mortgagee has the legal estate. It is true, for some purposes, the mortgagor is deemed to be the owner and to be seised until after foreclosure; but he cannot set up title in himself against the mortgagee after condition broken. In *Bergen* v. *Bennett*, 1 Cai. Cas., 1, and *Jackson* v. *Henry*, 10 Johns., 185, the assignee conveyed to his own agent, and the court consider it equivalent to a purchase *by the assignee. [***282** The first case happened before, and the last after the passage of the Act authorizing the mortgagee, &c., to purchase. In both cases the conveyance was deemed valid. If so, would not a deed from the assignee to himself be valid? Such a deed would certainly be an useless ceremony, if it be true that the mortgagee or assignee already has the legal estate.

3. A notice to quit, after a six months' notice of the foreclosure and sale, was clearly not necessary. There was nothing like the relation of landlord and tenant existing between these parties. The assignee, holding the legal estate, was entitled to recover against any person holding under, or by title derived from the mortgagor, which was the case of this defendant.

The objection that the mortgage was not a valid instrument, upon any other ground than that of usury, ought not to be listened to when coming from the very man who had transferred it as a valid mortgage to the lessor of the plaintiff. To allow it, would be permitting the defendant to take advantage of his own fraudulent conduct.

Judgment for the plaintiff.

Cited in—8 Wend., 22; 17 Wend., 343; 24 Wend., 92; 4 Den., 44; 1 Paige, 52; 68 N. Y., 162; 12 Barb., 20; 20 Barb., 562; 14 Abb. Pr., 421; 118 Mass., 560.

REYNOLDS AND REYNOLDS
v.
P. & S. CLEVELAND, Impleaded with S. I ANDRUS.

Partnership—Proof of Limited Partnership—Liability of Partner, for Articles Furnished Firm when Vendor Ignorant of Partnership—Pleading.

What is sufficient proof of a limited partnership.

Partners are all liable for articles furnished for the benefit of the firm, though the vendor does not know of the existence of the firm, and though he suppose himself dealing with, and give credit to an individual partner by charging him alone in his books.

NOTE.—*Partnership—Liability for purchases by one partner for benefit of the firm.*

The partnership is liable for purchases for the benefit of the firm, though the vendor did not know of the existence of the firm. In addition to the above case of Reynolds v. Cleveland, see Griffith v. Buffum, 22 Vt., 181; Given v. Albert, 5 Watts. & S., 333; Tucker v. Peaslee, 36 N. H., 167; Poole v. Lewis, 75 N. C., 417; Roth v. Moore, 19 La. Ann., 86; Baxter v. Clark, 4 Ired. L., 127; Bisel v. Hobbs, 6 Blackf., 479; H. R. & E. R. R. Co. v. Walsh, 85 Ill., 58; Ruppell v. Roberts, 4 Nev. & M., 31; Bottomley v. Mettall, 5 C. B. N. S., 222; Robinson v. Wilkinson, 3 Price, 538. See, also, Beekham v. Drake, 9 M. & W., 79; 11 M. & W., 315; Everett v. Chapman, 6 Conn., 347. But see Watt v. Kirby, 15 Ill., 200; Sinklear v. Lambert, 5 Phila., 36.

See, generally, Ballou v. Spencer, *ante*, 163 and cases and *notes* there cited; Le Roy v. Johnson, 2 Pet., 186, *note* in Law. ed.

And so it seems, though the agreement be reduced to writing between the vendor and the individual partner, and signed by the latter with his own name only.

On a sale, with warranty of the article sold, upon a credit for cash, after the credit has expired, the goods being delivered, and the contract thereby executed, the vendor may, in a suit for the price, declare in general *indebitatus assumpsit*, for goods sold.

Citations—1 Esp., 29; 4 T. R., 728; 7 Johns., 36, 311; 1 Cow., 290, 359, 378, 390; 10 Johns., 132; 4 Bos. & P., 351; 5 Mass., 391; 4 Binn., 4; 1 Chit., 338; 1 Bos. & P., 397; 4 T. R., 720, 726, 728; Doug., 371; Watson, L. P., 46, 168, 169.

ASSUMPSIT for two run of buhr millstones. The declaration contained the common counts for the millstones, at a price stated, and a *quantum meruit*. The defendants severally pleaded *non assumpsit*, with other pleas.

283*] *The cause was tried before Savage, *Ch. J.*, at the Albany Circuit, Apr., 1823.

The plaintiffs proved by Joseph Spencer, that in Jan. 1820, and before and after, the defendants were reputed partners in a mill at Rochester; and that S. Cleveland had the direction and management of it. They also gave in evidence a letter from S. Cleveland to Jno. Townsend, Albany, dated at Rochester, June 14, 1819, requesting him to sell, on credit, castings for a flour mill, to be built at Rochester; and stating that Mr. Patterson had recommended to get the castings of him; another letter from S. Cleveland dated at Rochester, July 20, 1819, to Townsend, acknowledging that he had been apprised of his prices and credit; acceding to them, and inclosing a bill and directions relative to the castings, and stating that the gentlemen concerned with him were S. I Andrus and P. Cleveland.

The plaintiffs then called Erastus Corning, who testified that he was acquainted with the defendant, P. Cleveland; that all the defendants were reputed to be partners and joint owners in a mill at Rochester in 1820; that in Jan. of that year, P. Cleveland bought of the house in Albany, to which the witness belonged, on credit, bolting cloths for the mill at Rochester, which were charged to the firm; that a suit was brought against all the defendants for the amount of the bolting cloths, and a judgment recovered against them, which was collected; and that when he bought the bolting cloths, he told the witness, that he wanted to purchase two run of buhr millstones for the same mill. The witness told him that the plaintiffs were in the habit of furnishing millstones, on the recommendation of the witness; and if he wished, the witness would send for the plaintiffs. The witness was in the habit of acting as the agent of the plaintiffs in the sale of their millstones. P. Cleveland stated that the millstones were for the Company at Rochester, and gave the witness the names of the three defendants as constituting the Company; and referred the witness to Mr. York, for their standing and responsibility; that one of the plaintiffs, on being sent for, called at the witness' store, where P. Cleveland stated, in the

284*] presence of the witness, the *size and quality of the stones he wished to purchase, and inquired the price; and the plaintiff agreed to make them for $660. P. Cleveland also stated to the plaintiff that the stones were for the mill at Rochester; that the plaintiffs, in this instance, relied altogether upon the witness in giving the credit, which would not have been given to P. Cleveland individually. P. Cleveland requested the plaintiff to go with him to his lodgings, and reduce the agreement to writing, to which the plaintiff agreed. The memorandum of the agreement was afterwards delivered to the witness by Mr. York, through whom it was sent by P. Cleveland, to enable the witness to obtain the stones and forward them which he did, to the Company in Rochester, in July, 1820. P. Cleveland told the witness that the stones were received there, and that the Company would soon pay for them. The agreement was left by Mr. York with the witness; but he does not know what has become of it. It had been called for by P. Cleveland, or some person for him, but could not be found. It was an agreement with P. Cleveland, and contained a warranty of the quality of the stones. There was no signature to it beside that of P. Cleveland. It was not signed by the plaintiffs or either of them.

The defendant's counsel moved for a nonsuit, on the ground that the plaintiffs ought to have declared on the special agreement; and also that as the agreement was made with P. Cleveland individually, the action could not be sustained against all the defendants. The motion was overruled.

The defendants then called H. G. Wheaton, who testified that he went to the plaintiffs with the defendant S. Cleveland; and that one of the plaintiffs stated that there was an agreement in writing concerning the millstones; that by the agreement, the plaintiffs undertook to provide the stones and to warrant them; and P. Cleveland undertook to pay for them; that one of the plaintiffs showed his book in which there was a charge of the millstones to Mr. Cleveland of Ogdensburgh. This book was produced, on notice for that purpose, and contained a charge of the millstones thus: *1820, January [***285**
21, sold to Mr. Cleveland, of Ogdensburgh, two run of 5 feet stones, at 330 per pair———660."

Corning was then again called, and testified that P. Cleveland lived at Ogdensburgh, and S. Cleveland at Rochester; that one of the plaintiffs agreed to warrant the stones. The witness supposed that this plaintiff depended on the witness for the responsibility of the purchasers of the stones; but the witness did not make the bargain. That was made by one of the plaintiffs and P. Cleveland. The witness would not have recommended the plaintiffs to trust P. Cleveland alone; who, at the time he purchased the bolting cloths, said that the stones were for the mill at Rochester; that the witness did not know that the plaintiffs had knowledge of any person concerned besides P. Cleveland. Nothing was mentioned when the plaintiff was present, and when he conversed with the plaintiff in the store of the witness, about any other persons concerned in the mill.

The plaintiff then called D. Sibley, who testified that he was acquainted with S. Cleveland and the defendant, Andrus; and had heard S. Cleveland say that the defendants were jointly responsible for all of the machinery in the mill; that P. Cleveland had lately removed to Rochester.

The judge charged the jury that Corning had acted as a sort of agent for both parties;

that they should inquire whether the stones were delivered in consequence of the written agreement; that if they were delivered to the firm the plaintiffs were entitled to recover.

The jury found a verdict for the plaintiffs for the price of the stones, and the interest.

Mr. H. Bleecker, for the defendants, now moved for a new trial. He said the contract was with P. Cleveland individually, and the suit should, therefore, have been against him alone. *Manahan* v. *Gibbons*, 19 Johns., 109; 112; *Livingston's Exrs.* v. *Tremper*, 11 *Id.*, 101, 1 Chit. Pl., 31, 32; *Yates* v. *Lansing*, 8 Johns., 289. It was a special agreement in writing with warranty; and the suit should have been brought upon the agreement which was not reached by the common counts. Had this been a covenant, clearly the partners could not be sued; and is not the remedy equally controlled by a special agreement? Are not the plaintiffs **286***] holden to proceed against *the actual contracting party, whether they knew of the firm or not? The agreement being special, differs the case from one of dormant partners. There the recovery is upon the implied contract? 1 Mont. on Partnership, Am. ed., 160, and the cases there cited. Here is no room for implication. All the stipulations between the parties are express. *Evans* v. *Drummond*, 4 Esp., 91, 92; *Reed* v. *White*, 5 *Id.*, 122; *Newmarch* v. *Clay*, 14 East, 239; *Mead* v. *Tomlinson*, 1 Day, 148; *Ripley* v. *Kingsbury*, *Id.*, 150, *note a; James* v. *Hackley*, 16 Johns., 273. The remedy on the warranty, for instance, would be confined to P. Cleveland alone, for he alone was the vendee, and responsible for the price. The plaintiff should have declared on the special agreement, averring that the warranty had been fulfilled on their part, as a condition precedent. No recovery could be had, unless the stones were as warranted. It makes no difference whether the plaintiffs knew of the partnership or not. P. Cleveland could not plead a recovery in this suit in bar to a future action against him alone. The partners never supposing themselves liable as such, the fair presumption is, that, as between them and P. Cleveland, they have closed the concern, accounting to him for this purchase as an individual one; and they ought not to suffer through the false appearance held out by the plaintiffs. The plaintiffs could not resort to the general counts. *Robertson* v. *Lynch*, 18 Johns., 451, 456. That these were inapplicable, he cited *Raymond* v. *Bernard*, 12 Johns., 274; *Fenton* v. *Halloway*, 1 Stark., 126; *Linningdale* v. *Livingston*, 10 Johns., 36; *Jennings* v. *Camp*, 13 *Id.*, 94, 97, and *Clark* v. *Smith*, 14 *Id.*, 326.

The judge erred in charging that Corning was the agent of both parties. *Guy* v. *Oakley*, 13 Johns., 332, 334; *Foot* v. *Sabin*, 19 *Id.*, 154.

The verdict is against the weight of evidence; and the judge should have directed the jury to find a verdict for the defendants.

Mr. W. Esleck, contra. The partnership of the defendants was fully established by the letters and confessions. Then the acts of P. Cleveland are binding on all. It was not his intention that credit should be given to him alone. If it was, why did he disclose the names of his copartners? The contract being signed by him alone, can make no difference. If it was a contract for the benefit of the firm, all are bound; and those not named may be sued as dormant partners. Admit that the plaintiffs knew of the firm. They also knew that the stones were for the benefit of the mill; and that all the partners would be liable. *Saville* v. *Robertson*, 4 T. R., 720, 728. The delivery being to all *the defendants, gives [***287** character to the transaction (*Id.*, 1 Com. on Cont., 277; Watson's L. of P., 129); and even the promissory note of P. Cleveland would not have discharged the firm (*Schermerhorn* v. *Loines*, 7 Johns., 311; Watson's L. of P., 130; 1 Esp. Dig., pt. 1, 228, Gould's ed.), unless the plaintiffs had declared expressly that they had intended to look to him alone. If this had been so, we admit, they having at the same time a knowledge of the firm, this written agreement might have operated against him only. The form of entry in the book is by no means conclusive as to whom the credit was given. It is certainly not so strong as the case of taking an individual promissory note.

The contract being executed by a delivery, the general counts are proper. 1 Ch., pl. 338, and the cases there cited; Bull *N. P.*, 139; *Payn* v. *Bacomb*, Doug., 651; *Kelley* v. *Foster*, 2 Binn., 4; *Alcorn* v. *Westbrook*, 1 Wils., per Dennison, *J.*, 117; 1 Dunl. Pr., 270; *Tuttle* v. *Mayo*, 7 Johns., 132; *Linningdale* v. *Livingston*, 10 *Id.*, 36; *Porter* v. *Talcott*, 1 Cow., 359. The cases cited against us upon this point, are where the contract was still open and executory when the action was brought.

As to the questions raised upon the evidence, it is a sufficient answer that the jury have passed upon it. They have decided that the defendants were partners, and that credit was given to them as such.

Mr. Bleecker, in reply, said, that although Andrus was not arrested, yet the existence of the firm must be as clearly established as if he had been regularly brought into court. The claim is treated by the plaintiffs as joint, against all three; and unless it is made out in that shape, the verdict should be for the defendants. Now the letters or declarations of the Clevelands cannot be received to implicate Andrus, from whom we hear nothing about his being a partner.

WOODWORTH, *J.*, after briefly stating the facts. It is contended by the defendants, that the contract was made with P. Cleveland individually, and that the suit ought to have been against him alone. He was the ostensible person who made the contract. It is also evident that Reynolds did not know there were other persons connected with him, as partners in the mill. I presume Reynolds was satisfied as to his responsibility, without making any particular inquiry. Corning says, in this instance, they relied altogether on him in giving the credit; that the credit would not have been given to P. Cleveland individually, but no communication was made to the plaintiffs respecting the partners. That the defendants *were jointly concerned at the time, [***288** and that the stones were received is not questioned. From this statement, it appears to me that all the defendants are liable. A partnership is a joint undertaking to share in the profit and loss. The defendants stood in that relation to each other, not as general partners, but as jointly concerned in erecting a mill and procuring machinery; they were partners to this extent (1 Esp., 29), and became jointly responsible for articles purchased by one of the partners and applied to the benefit of the concern. This law is well settled, that if one partner order goods himself, without disclosing the names of the other partners, and the goods be afterwards delivered to them all, they are all liable; because the delivery and the sale are considered as forming one entire contract. In such case, the one partner, who buys the goods, does not contract for himself, but on account of the partnership. This doctrine is fully recognized in the books. *Saville* v. *Robertson*, 4 T. R., 728; *Schermerhorn* v. *Loines*, 7 Johns., 311; *Muldon* v. *Whitlock*, 1 Cow., 290. It cannot be pretended that the plaintiffs have done any act to discharge the partners. Admitting that a special contract had been signed by the plaintiffs and P. Cleveland, it would not have that effect, unless it appeared that the plaintiffs had taken him exclusively for their debtor, knowing that there were other partners.

It is also urged that the action ought to have been commenced on the special agreement in writing.

I have not discovered any evidence that there was a written contract signed by the plaintiffs. The writing delivered to Corning had not their signature; it is from that fact to be inferred that Cleveland merely noted down by way of memorandum, that Reynolds was to deliver the stones and warrant them. When Reynolds afterwards admitted that there was an agreement in writing, the presumption is, he had reference to the paper delivered to Corning, for there is no legal evidence of the contents of any other. If Reynolds had in his possession a written contract, he was not called on to produce it. Without that, the defendants cannot give parol evidence of the contents.

289*] *But if it be admitted that there was a written contract corresponding with the statement of Reynolds, it is not a valid objection to the recovery. Where the evidence is sufficient to support the general count, supposing the plaintiff had not declared on the special agreement, he is entitled to recover without any attempt to support the agreement. (7 Johns., 36; 10 Johns., 132; 4 Bos. & P., 351; 5 Mass., 391.) There is no special agreement laid. Does the evidence support the general count? The plaintiffs agreed to deliver the stones for a certain price; after delivery the defendants become liable in *indebitatus assumpsit*.

The plaintiffs might declare by a general count, in the same manner as if there had been a delivery in the first instance, and not an agreement to deliver. That part of the agreement relating to a warranty, is a distinct subject. It may or may not entitle the defendants to an action to recover damages. It is not, however, so connected with the sale of the mill stones, that the plaintiffs' right to recover for the goods sold, is in the least obstructed by the fact of a warranty. The evidence, therefore, is clearly sufficient to support the general count; for the contract was executed on the part of the plaintiffs. There was nothing more for them to perform. When the contract is executed on the part of the plaintiff, he may declare generally. The law raises a duty for which *assumpsit* will lie. (4 Binn., 4; 1 Cow., 378; 1 Chit., 338; 1 Bos. & P., 397.)

I am of opinion, that the motion for a new trial be denied.

SUTHERLAND, *J.* The partnership of the defendants, at the time when the contract for the mill stones was made by P. Cleveland; and also when they were delivered, is sufficiently established by the evidence; so that they were, in fact, purchased for the use of the firm, though the existence of the firm does not appear to have been known to the plaintiffs; and they were, therefore, charged to P. Cleveland only. Independent of the written, special agreement, and striking that out of the case, I think it is clear that the defendants are liable. The contract was for the benefit of the firm; and within the scope of the partnership. The *partnership was in a mill, and the [*290 contract for the millstones, an article of indispensable necessity in the prosecution of the business. It was a contract, therefore, which each partner had authority to make for the whole. It is then, in principle, a case of dormant partners, in which a contract within the scope of the partnership, made by the ostensible partner in his own name, is sought to be enforced against the firm. There can be no doubt of the liability of the firm in such a case. Though the goods be furnished on the credit of the ostensible partner only, the law implies a promise to pay for them, on the part of all those who are entitled to a share in the profits. *Saville* v. *Robertson*, 4 T. R., 720, 726, 728, per Ashurst and Buller, *JJ.*; *Hoare* v. *Dawes*, Doug., 371; Watson L. P., 46, 168, 169. In *Schermerhorn* v. *Loines*, 7 Johns., 311, it was held that where a person supplied stores to a ship, of which there were several owners, on the order of one of them, who acted as ship's husband, and took his note in payment, and gave a receipt in full, it was no discharge of the other owners, especially as it did not appear that the plaintiffs knew, at the time, that there were other owners; and the note not having been paid, a recovery was had against all the partners upon the original cause of action. The same principal was established in *Muldon* v. *Whitlock*, 1 Cow., 290.

But it is said the action should have been upon the written memorandum of the agreement, made at the time of the sale. What that memorandum was, is very imperfectly disclosed by the evidence. Corning, however, who is the only witness that ever saw it, swears expressly that it was not signed by Reynolds; and that it was left in the possession of P. Cleveland; and contained a warranty of the quality of the stones on the part of Reynolds; that it was sent to the witness by P. Cleveland, to enable him to obtain the stones, and forward them to the defendants. This evidence leaves it extremely questionable whether the memorandum contained any agreement whatever on the part of P. Cleveland to pay for the stones. It was left in his possession, not to be signed by Reynolds, although it is said to contain a warranty on his part. It does not appear to have specified either the price *or the terms of payment. It [*291 was probably no more than a memorandum on the part of Cleveland, himself, of the quality and description of the stones; and that the plaintiff had agreed to warrant them. The parties agreed upon the description and price of the stones in the presence of Corning, when Cleveland proposed that they should go and reduce it to writing; upon which they left the store of Corning; and the only exidence that they did reduce it to writing, is, that P. Cleveland, some time afterwards, sent the memorandum in question to the witness. It does not appear to be in the handwriting of Reynolds; and it is expressly shown that it was not signed by him. There is not a particle of evidence that he ever saw, heard of or assented to it. I do not think, that upon this evidence, a jury would be warranted in saying that there was any written contract between the parties. This view of the subject disposes of the objection.

But admitting a special agreement to have been shown—everything which, so far as appears it imposed upon the plaintiffs to do, has been done by them. The stones were delivered to the plaintiffs, and nothing remains to be done except the payment of the consideration money, on the part of the defendants. In such cases the general count of *indebitatus assumpsit* is sufficient without noticing the special agreement. This subject was maturely considered by the court, and all the cases looked at in *Porter* v. *Talcott*, 1 Cow., 359.

But it is said that the special contract contained a warranty on the part of the plaintiffs; and if they had declared specially they must have averred and shown performance on their part. If it had been averred, I apprehend the delivery of the stones to the defendant, and their acceptance of them, without complaint, would be *prima facie* evidence of a compliance with the contract in that respect. That is shown in this case. If they were not made according to contract, the defendants were at liberty to show it.

SAVAGE, *Ch. J.*, concurred in the result of these opinions.

New trial denied.

Cited in—3 Lans., 491; 13 Barb., 233; 2 Rob., 136.

292*] *SHUMWAY ET AL. v. STILLMAN.

Action on Judgment of Another State—Defense, Want of Jurisdiction in that State—Pleading—Record, Prima Facie *Evidence of Jurisdiction.*

In an action upon the judgment of a neighboring State, the defendant may show by plea, that the court had no jurisdiction of his person, or the subject-matter of the suit.

But where the defendant to a declaration on such a judgment pleaded that at the time of the commencement of the suit and when the judgment was rendered, and during all the intermediate time, he was and ever since has been, an inhabitant of and resident in the City of Schenectady, and County of Schenectady, State of N. Y.; held bad on general demurrer—this plea not being inconsistent with the fact of his having actually appeared in person, or otherwise, and defended the suit.

The record of a judgment in a neighboring State is, *prima facie*, evidence that the court by which it was rendered had jurisdiction; and, to do away the effect of the record, the contrary should be clearly and fully shown.

The only plea of the general issue, applicable to a declaration upon the judgment of a neighboring State is *nul tiel record*.

Citations—7 Cr., 481; 15 Johns., 141; 19 Johns., 162; 9 Mass., 467, 470; 1 Mass., 399.

DEBT on judgment in favor of the plaintiffs against the defendant recovered in the Circuit Court of C. P., at Worcester, in the Commonwealth of Mass., June 19, 1820. The defendant pleaded, that at the time of the commencement of the suit in which the recovery of the judgment was obtained, and at the time when the judgment was rendered, and during all the time between the time of the commencement of the suit and recovery of the judgment, and ever since he was, has been and still is an inhabitant of and resident in the City of Schenectady, County of Schenectady, and State of N. Y.

General demurrer and joinder.

Mr. B. F. Butler, in support of the demurrer, said that *nul tiel record* was the only appropriate plea. *Mills* v. *Duryee*, 7 Cr., 481; *Hampton* v. *M'Connell*, 3 Wh., 234; *Borden* v. *Fitch*, 15 Johns., 121, 140. But admitting the principle of the plea to be good, it is insufficient in not answering all that it assumes to answer. It does not show that the defendant was not actually arrested. It should have denied actual arrest, personal notice and voluntary appearance. Either of these might well be, though the defendant as alleged in the plea, was all along an inhabitant of, and resident in the City of Schenectady. The record is, *prima facie*, evidence of jurisdiction in the court of Mass., and all the facts, questioning this, should be fully stated.

Mr. A. C. Paige, contra, conceded that upon the authorities cited, the merits of a judgment of a sister State were not inquirable into; that in this sense, *nul tiel record* is the only proper plea; but he said it is also well settled that the jurisdiction of its courts may be questioned, either as to the *persons or subject-mat- [*293 ter. *Borden* v. *Fitch*, 15, Johns., 141, 142, 143; *Pawling* v. *Bird's Executors*, 13 *Id.*, 207; *Bissell* v. *Briggs*, 9 Mass., 462, 469; *Kilburn* v. *Woodworth*, 5 Johns., 37, 41; *Robinson* v. *Ward's Ex'rs.*, 8 *Id.*, 86; *Fenton* v. *Garlick*, *Id.*, 197; *Bartlett* v. *Knight*, 1 Mass., 408. In order to make a such a judgment the foundation of an action, the defendant must, at the commencement of the suit, have been within the jurisdiction of the court; and while there, must have been personally served with process. His continued residence in Schenectady, as averred by the plea, is inconsistent with his having been within the jurisdiction of the Mass. court at any time, for the purpose of the judgment. *Bartlet* v. *Knight*, 1 Mass., 401, 409; is in point for this plea. It is drawn in the very words of the one in that case.

WOODWORTH and SUTHERLAND, *JJ.*, inquired whether the averment in the plea did not still leave it open to be implied that the defendant might have been in Mass., and duly served with process there.

NOTE.—*Judgment of sister state—How far conclusive under Federal Constitution—How far examinable—Question of jurisdiction—Recitals in record, effect of.* See Hitchcock v. Aicken 1 Cai., 460; Pawling v. Wilson, 13 Johns., 192, *notes.*

Effect of foreign judgment. Vandenheuvel v. United Ins. Co., 2 Johns. Cas., 451; Pawling v. Wilson, 13 Johns., 192, *notes.*

The legal inference is, that he was not in Mass. when the suit was commenced. If not there, the proceeding must have been *in rem;* and in such case, even a subsequent voluntary appearance will not confer jurisdiction. *Bissell* v. *Briggs*, 9 Mass., 462, 468; *Pawling* v. *Bird's Ex'rs.*, 13 Johns., 192, 207. If the defendant was arrested, or appeared by attorney, or any other way by his own act, this should have been replied by the plaintiff. In *Kilburn* v. *Woodworth*, 5 Johns., 37, 41, the proof was no more than we have averred; yet this court held it sufficient to negative the jurisdiction of the foreign court.

But the declaration is defective in substance. It should have averred that the defendant was within the jurisdiction of the court at the commencement of the suit; and that, while there, he was served with process. *Kibbe* v. *Kibbe*, Kirby, 119.

At any rate, if the plea is defective, the court will allow us to amend; and this without payment of costs.

He also cited *Buttrick* v. *Allen*, 8 Mass., 273.

Mr. Butler, in reply, said that an averment of actual residence in Schenectady would not have been enough; for, notwithstanding this, the defendant might have appeared by appointing an attorney. This plea, however, is still weaker. Actual residence is not pretended. He might have been a resident in this State, and yet have been personally in Mass. defending the suit through all its stages. The word **294***] *"resident," does not imply actual "inhabitancy." It may be a mere right of settlement. Instances of this occur under our poor laws, 1 R. L., 279. The word "resident" is synonymous with "inhabitant." *Rosevelt* v. *Kellogg*, 20 Johns., 210.

Curia, per SUTHERLAND, *J.* The questions which arise upon the demurrer are: 1. Whether any plea than that of *nul tiel record* can be pleaded in a case like this. 2. Admitting that is competent to show that the court which rendered the judgment, had no jurisdiction over the person of the defendant, is that fact shown with sufficient certainty by the plea in question?

The Supreme Court of the U. S., in *Mills* v. *Duryee*, 7 Cr., 481, decided that *nil debet* was not a proper plea to an action of debt, upon a state judgment, prosecuted in another State; and that in that particular case, as it it was presented to the court, *nul tiel record* was the proper plea. But I do not understand the court, in the opinion delivered by *Mr. Justice* Story, as deciding or intimating that *nul tiel record* is the only proper plea to such an action. The only general proposition upon the subject of pleading, which I conceive to have been established by that case is, that *nul tiel record* is the only proper general issue in an action of debt upon a state judgment; and this necessarily resulted from the conclusion to which the court came, that by the provisions of the Constitution and the law of Congress upon that subject, judgments of the state courts are to be considered and treated as records. *Judge* Story says, "the pleadings in an action are governed by the dignity of the instrument on which it is founded. If it be a record, conclusive between the parties, it cannot be denied but by the plea of *nul tiel record.*" And in order to show that the record in that case was of this description, that is, conclusive between the parties, he says, "in the present case, the defendant had full notice of the suit, for he was arrested and gave bail; and it is beyond all doubt that the judgment of the Supreme Court of N. Y. was conclusive upon the parties in that State:" putting the conclusiveness of the judgment between the parties upon the ground that the defendant had notice of the *suit and appeared to it; implied- [***295** ly admitting that the judgment would not be conclusive, where the court had not acquired jurisdiction over the person of the defendant; and that in such a case, *nul tiel record* was not the only proper plea.

This point not having been decided by the Supreme Court of the U. S., I cannot entertain a doubt upon principle, that, in an action upon a state judgment, it is competent for the defendant to show, by a special plea, that the court in which the judgment was rendered had no jurisdiction either of the subject-matter, or of the person. In *Borden* v. *Fitch*, 15 Johns., 141, the court say, "to give any binding effect to a judgment, it is essential that the court should have jurisdiction of the person and of the subject-matter; and the want of jurisdiction is a matter that may always be set up against a judgment, when sought to be enforced, or where any benefit is claimed under it. The want of jurisdiction makes it utterly void, and unavailable for any purpose. In *Andrews* v. *Montgomery*, 19 Johns., 162, *Ch. J.* Spencer, in delivering the opinion of the court, says that this court, in *Borden* v. *Fitch*, did not believe that the decision in *Mills* v. *Duryee* was intended to be carried so far as to preclude the party, against whom it was rendered, from showing that such judgment was fraudulently obtained, or that the court had not jurisdiction of the person of the defendant. With these qualifications (he says), we are bound by the authority of that case to consider a judgment, fairly and regularly obtained in another State, a full and conclusive evidence of the matter adjudicated. The same principle was held by *Ch. J.* Parsons, in *Bissell* v. *Briggs*, 9 Mass., 467. He says, "the public acts, records and judicial proceedings contemplated (by the Constitution and laws of the U. S.), and to which full faith and credit are to be given, are such as were within the jurisdiction of the State, whence they shall be taken. Whenever, therefore, a record of a judgment of any court of any State is produced as conclusive evidence, the jurisdiction of the court rendering it is open to inquiry. If it should appear that the court had no jurisdiction of the cause, no faith or credit whatever will be given to the judgment." And again: "if a court of any State should render *judgment against [***296** a man, not within the State, nor bound by its laws, nor amenable to the jurisdiction of its courts, if that judgment should be produced in any other State against the defendant, the jurisdiction of the court might be inquired into, and if a want of jurisdiction appeared, no credit would be given to the judgment.

Against the principle of the plea, therefore, in my opinion, there is no objection. But,

2. Does the plea state enough, to show that

the court, which rendered the judgment, had not jurisdiction of the person of the defendant?

Every presumption is in favor of the jurisdiction of the court. The record is, *prima facie*, evidence of it, and will be held conclusive, until clearly and explicitly disproved. Now the plea, in this case, may be literally true, and yet the defendant may have been personally served with process, in the State of Mass.; may have entered special bail in the action; may have appeared and litigated the cause either in person or by attorney upon the trial; and may have been present in court when the judgment was rendered. It merely states that the defendant's domicil, from the commencement of the suit, until the rendering of the judgment, was in Schenectady, in the State of N. Y. Now, as is said by *Ch. J.* Parsons, in *Bissell* v. *Briggs*, 9 Mass., 470, an inhabitant of one State may, without changing his domicil, go into another; he may there contract a debt, or commit a tort; and while there he owes a temporary allegiance to that State, is bound by its laws, and is amenable to its courts. This plea, therefore, entirely fails in showing the want of jurisdiction in the court which rendered the judgment.

This plea was probably taken from that in *Bartlet* v. *Knight*, 1 Mass., 399. But in that case the plea contained the further allegation, that the defendant, at the time of making the promise, and at the time of the recovery of the judgment was an infant; and that case was determined on the ground that the judgment was nothing more than a foreign judgment, and liable to be impeached, not on the ground of the want of jurisdiction only, but on any **297***] other ground which *showed the plaintiff ought not to have recovered. No objection was taken to the plea on the ground that the want of jurisdiction was not sufficiently stated. The court seem to have given more weight in their judgment to the fact of infancy, than the want of jurisdiction.

I am of opinion that the plaintiff is entitled to judgment, but the defendant may amend his plea.

Rule accordingly.

Cited in—3 Wend., 269; 5 Wend., 156; 6 Wend., 449; 10 Wend., 673; 13 Wend., 416; 16 Wend., 39; 17 Wend., 485; 8 N. Y., 262; 18 N. Y., 96; 28 N. Y., 653; 41 N. Y., 275; 53 N. Y., 600; 76 N. Y., 83; 6 Barb., 615; 10 Barb., 111; 4 Abb. Pr., 166; 1 Hall., 162; 4 Bradf., 208; 7 Allen., 460; 59 How. Pr., 514; 2 Kan., 81; 15 Kan., 286; 37 Mich., 350; 17 Am. Dec., 365 (6 Pick., 232); 21 Am. Dec., 175, 176; 22 Am. Dec., 619; 25 Am. Dec., 319 (5 G. & J., 500); 39 Am. Dec., 433, 434 (4 Scam., 536); 44 Am. Dec., 691 (3 Gilm., 397); 21 Am. Rep., 72 (79 Penn., 354); 29 Am. Rep., 368 (6 Neb., 419); 32 Am. Rep., 277 (76 N. Y., 78).

THE PEOPLE, ex rel. VAN VOAST,
v.
VAN SLYCK.

Quo Warranto—*When it Lies—Duties of County Boards of Canvassers—Practice—Attendance of Inspectors at Elections—Duties of Inspectors—Preference of* Quo Warranto *Proceedings on Calendar—Pleading.*

An information in nature of a *quo warranto* lies against one intruding into the office of Sheriff, in consequence of an unlawful decision of the County Board of Canvassers, in his favor, convened pursuant to the 10th section of the Act for Regulating Elections, passed Apr. 17, 1822, sess. 45, ch. 250.

The duties of the Board are ministerial, not judicial. A *certiorari*, therefore, is not the proper remedy.

The Act does not require that one of the Town Inspectors be appointed to preside at the election.

All the Inspectors attending, equally preside, and have equal powers.

Some one of these must be appointed by a majority of those who preside, to deliver the statement of the town vote to the County Clerk, and attend the County Board of Canvassers as a member.

This appointment may be written or parol. A written appointment is preferable.

If the statement of the town votes be delivered to the County Clerk by a Town Inspector, and the fact of his being so is not questioned by the Canvassers, he ought not to be excluded; for the delivery of the statement, and his attendance to perform the duties of a Canvasser are, *prima facie*, evidece that he was regularly appointed.

The certificate of appointment, if in writing, is good evidence, though not signed by a majority of the Town Inspectors till after the town poll closed.

The Inspector appointed may be one of the appointers himself, and sign the certificate.

If the votes of a town are improperly excluded, by which a majority of votes are canvassed and allowed to a candidate for the office of Sheriff, who receives a certificate, takes the oath of office, &c., and acts as Sheriff, judgment of ouster will be given against him, on an information in nature of a *quo warranto* being filed *ex relatione* the one who had the actual majority of votes.

A special verdict in an information in nature of a *quo warranto* allowed a preference in argument on the calendar.

Pleadings in an information in nature of a *quo warranto*, against one who unlawfully intruded into the office of Sheriff, viz.: The information, plea, setting forth the defendant's title under the Act Regulating Elections, sess. 45, ch. 250. Replication and issues at length.

Citations—3 Johns. Cas., 79; 2 Johns., 184.

[NOTE.—The court allowed this cause a preference on the calendar, on the ground of its being upon information, in nature of a *quo warranto*.]

SCHENECTADY COUNTY, to wit: Samuel A. Talcott, Atty-Gen. of the people of the State of N. Y., who sues for the said people in this behalf, comes here into the Supreme *Court of Judicature of the State of [***298** New York, before the justices of the people of the State of New York, of the Supreme Court of Judicature of the same People at the Capitol in the City of Albany, on Saturday, Jan. 18, A. D. 1823, in January Term, and for the said people of the State of N. Y., at the relation of Gershom Van Yoast, of the City of Schenectady, according to the form of the Statute in such cases made and provided, gives the court here to understand and be informed, that the office of Sheriff of the County of Schenectady hath been for a long time heretofore, to wit: for the space of ten years last past, and upwards, and still is a public office, and an office of great trust and pre-eminence within the

NOTE.—Quo warranto *against usurper of a public office.*

An information in the nature of a quo warranto *lies to correct the unlawful usurpation of a public office.* People v. Mayor, &c., of N. Y., 3 Johns. Cas., 79; People v. Sweeting, 2 Johns., 184; People v. Bartlett, 6 Wend., 422; Lewis v. Oliver, 4 Abb. Pr., 121; Mayor, &c., of N. Y. v. Conover, 5 Abb. Pr., 171; People v. Thacher, 55 N. Y., 525; 14 Am. Rep., 312; People v. Scannell, 7 Cal., 432; People v. Forquer, 1 Ill., 104; People v. Head, 25 Ill., 325; Clark v. Commonwealth, 29 Pa. St., 129; State v. Utter, 14 N. J. L., 84; Strong, Petitioner &c., 37 Mass. (20 Pick), 484; Commonwealth v. Dearborn, 15 Mass., 125; Commonwealth v. Fowler, 10 Mass., 295; Commonwealth v. Allen, 128 Mass., 308; Parker, v. Smith, 3 Minn., 240;

State of N. Y., to wit: at the City and in the County of Schenectady aforesaid; and that Harmanus A. Van Siyek, of the County of Schenectady aforesaid, without any legal warrant, grant or right whatsoever, hath, for the space of fourteen days now last past, and more, held, used and executed the said office of Sheriff of the County of Schenectady, without any legal warrant, grant or right, and still doth hold, use and execute the said office, to wit: at the city and in the county aforesaid; and that the said Harmanus A. Van Slyck, for and during all the time last above mentioned, without any legal warrant, grant or right whatsoever, at the City and in the County of Schenectady, has claimed and still does claim, to be Sheriff of the County of Schenectady aforesaid, and to have, use and enjoy all the liberties, privileges and franchises to the office of Sheriff of the County of Schenectady aforesaid, belonging and appertaining, which said office, liberties, privileges and franchises, he, the said Harmanus A. Van Slyck, for and during the whole time last above mentioned, upon the said people hath usurped, intruded into and unlawfully held, and still doth usurp, intrude into and unlawfully hold; that is to say, at the City and in the County of Schenectady aforesaid, in contempt of the people of the State of N. Y., and to their great damage and prejudice, and also against their dignity.

And the said Harmanus A. Van Siyek, by Alonzo C. Paige, his attorney, comes, and having heard information, complains that he is, by color thereof, grievously used and dis- **299***] quieted, *and this unjustly; because, protesting that the said information, and the matters therein contained, are not sufficient in law; to which said information the said Harmanus is not bound by the law of the land to answer; yet for plea, in this behalf, the said Harmanus saith, that true it is, that the office of Sheriff of the County of Schenectady hath been, for the space of ten years last past, and upwards, and still is a public office, and an office of great trust and pre-eminence within the State of New York, to wit: at the City and in the County of Schenectady aforesaid, as in the said information is suggested; but the said Harmanus further saith, that an election was held in the several towns and ward of the said County of Schenectady, for the election, among other officers of the State of New York, and of the said County of Schenectady, of Sheriff of said County of Schenectady, on the first Monday of Nov., A. D. 1822, and continued from day to day, for three successive days, including said first Monday of Nov., pursuant to an Act of the Legislature of the people of the State of New York, entitled an Act for regulating elections, passed Apr. 17th, 1822. And the said Harmanus further saith, that after the said election, to wit: on the Tuesday next following the said election, such of the Inspectors of Elections as did attend, and had been appointed by a major part of the Inspectors, who had presided at the said election in the several towns and wards in the said county, according to the direction of the said Act, to attend at the clerk's office in said county, and in person to deliver to the clerk of said county, at the office, or to his deputy, or to the keeper of said office, a true copy of the statement of the votes given at said election, in the respective towns and wards in said county, in which they were respectively Inspectors as aforesaid, for (among other officers) the officer of Sheriff aforesaid, did attend at the office of the clerk of said county, and in person, did deliver to the clerk of said county, a true copy of the statement of votes or certificate of the Inspectors of the respective towns and wards of said county, of the votes given as aforesaid, for the officers aforesaid; and they, the said Inspectors, so attending as aforesaid, having been appointed as aforesaid, and baving respectively *attended in person as aforesaid, at [***300** the time and place aforesaid, and having delivered their respective statements or certificates of the votes given as aforesaid, to the clerk of said county as aforesaid, did then and there, to wit: on the said Tuesday next following said election, at the office of the said clerk, according to the directions of, and in the manner required, by the aforesaid Act of the said Legislature, together with the clerk of said county, form themselves into a Board of Canvassers, and appoint one of their number, to wit: Simon A. Groot, chairman, and the clerk of said county, to wit: Jelles A. Fonda, was present at and acted as secretary of said Board, and as one of the members thereof; and the said Harmanus further saith that the said Board of Canvassers, being so formed, and organized as aforesaid, did then and there proceed in the manner, and at the time required by the aforesaid Act, to calculate and ascertain the aggregate amount or whole number of votes given as aforesaid, and delivered to the said clerk as required by the said Act, for the respective candidates voted for as Members of Assembly, Sheriff, Clerk and Coroners of said county, respectively, at said election; and did thereupon determine, conformably to the aforesaid statements or certificates of votes given as aforesaid, and delivered as aforesaid, to the clerk aforesaid, by the Inspectors of Election of the several towns and wards in said county, as aforesaid, appointed as aforesaid, upon the persons respectively duly elected, by the greatest number of votes in said county, as Member of Assembly, Sheriff, Clerk and Coroners of said county; and the said Board of Canvassers did then and there further, in pursuance of the direction of said Act, make and cause to be subscribed by their aforesaid chairman and secretary, with

Commonwealth v. Messer, 44 Pa. St., 341; Commonwealth v. Small, 26 Pa. St., 31.

In proceedings upon information to try title to a public office, the court will not go behind the returns of the canvassers, their action being ministerial, not judicial. See above case of People v. Van Slyck. "It is the *election*, and not the certificate of the canvassers that gives the *right* to an office." People v. Cook, 8 N. Y., 83. See, also, People v. Seaman, 5 Den., 409; People v. Vail, 20 Wend., 12; People v. Ferguson, 8 Cow., 102; People v. Pease, 30 Barb., 588; Atty-Gen. v. Barstow, 4 Wis., 567; State v. Steers, 44 Mo., 223. But see Commonwealth v. Baxter, 35 Pa. St., 263.

Quo warranto *lies against a corporation for usurping a public franchise*. See People v. Utica Ins. Co., 15 Johns., 358, *note*; People v. Tibbits, *post*, 358, *note*.

For a full discussion of the remedy against usurpers of public offices, see High Extr. Leg. Rem., secs. 623–646, and authorities there cited. For the present New York practice, see Code Civ. Pro., secs. 1797 &c., and 1948 &c.

their proper names and handwriting, a certificate of such determination, and caused the same to be recorded in a book kept in the office of the clerk of said county for that purpose, and a true copy thereof, subscribed as aforesaid, to be delivered to each of the persons so elected to the respective offices of Member of Assembly, Sheriff, Clerk and Coroner of said county; and the said Harmanus further saith, that the said Board of Canvassers of the said **301***] County of *Schenectady, so formed and organized as aforesaid, for the purpose aforesaid, upon calculating and ascertaining the aggregate amount or whole number of votes given and delivered as aforesaid, for the respective candidates for the offices of Sheriff, Clerk and Coroner of said county, at said election as aforesaid, among other things required of them by law, did thereupon determine conformably to the statements or certificates delivered as aforesaid, to the clerk as aforesaid, that he, the said Harmanus A. Van Slyck, was duly elected by the greatest number of votes in said county, as Sheriff of said county ; and that said Board of Canvassers, upon such determination as aforesaid, did then and there, among other things required of them by law, make, and cause to be subscribed by their chairman and secretary aforesaid, with their proper names and handwriting, and to be recorded in the clerk's office of said county, as aforesaid, a certificate of such determination, that the said Harmanus had been duly elected as aforesaid as Sheriff of said county as aforesaid ; and that a true copy of said certificate of said Board of Canvassers, so made and subscribed as aforesaid, was by the said Board of Canvassers, caused to be delivered to him, the said Harmanus, so elected as aforesaid, to the said office of Sheriff of said county as aforesaid, to wit: at the City and in the County of Schenectady aforesaid ; which said certificate the said Harmanus brings here into court. And the said Harmanus further saith, that having been duly elected Sheriff of said county as aforesaid, and having received a true copy of the certificate of the determination of the Board of Canvassers, in the premises as aforesaid ; he, the said Harmanus; thereafter, to wit : Jan. 1, A. D. 1823, at the City of Schenectady, in said county, in due form of law, entered into a boud to the people of the State of New York, in the penal sum of five thousand dollars, with two sureties, to wit : John Haverly and Christian Haverly, of the Town of Glenville, in the county aforesaid, being freeholders in said county, jointly and severally, in said sum of five thousand dollars, to answer to the people of this State, and the **302***] parties, *if any should complain, according to the Act in such case made and provided ; which said bond was then and there duly filed in the office of the clerk of said County of Schenectady, he, the said clerk of the said county, then and there judging of, and determining the competency of said sureties. And the said Harmanus further saith, that, upon filing said bond in the office of the clerk as aforesaid, to wit: Jan. 1, A. D. 1823, at the city and in the county aforesaid, he, the said Harmanus did, in due manner and form, take and subscribe the oath for the due execution and faithful discharge of the duties of the office of Sheriff of said county, as by law in such case is required, before Jelles A. Fonda, Esquire, clerk of the said County of Schenectady, who then and there had a lawful and competent authority to administer the same in that behalf. And the said Harmanus further saith, that at the time of the said election, and on the said Jan. 1, A. D. 1823, he, the said Harmanus, then was, and still is, a substantial freeholder, to wit : at the town of Rotterdam, in said County of Schenectady. And thereupon, he, the said Harmanus, to wit : on the said Jan. 1, A. D. 1823, was then and there duly elected, appointed, qualified and admitted, according to the several statutes in such cases made and provided, into the said office of Sheriff of said County of Schenectady, by reason of which said premises, he, the said Harmanus, then and there became and was and still is Sheriff of said county, to wit : at the County of Schenectady aforesaid, by virtue whereof, the said Harmanus, for all the time in said information in that behalf mentioned, hath used and exercised, and still doth use and exercise, the said office of Sheriff of the said County of Schenectady ; and hath there claimed and still doth claim, to be Sheriff of said County of Schenectady, and to have, use and enjoy all the liberties, privileges and franchises, to the said office of Sheriff of the County of Schenectady aforesaid, belonging and appertaining, as it was lawful for him to do. Without this, that the said Harmanus hath usurped the said office, liberties and franchises upon the said people of the State of New York, in manner and form, as, by the said information, is above supposed ; all which said several matters *and things, he the said Harmanus is [***303** ready to verify, as the court shall consider ; whereupon he prays judgment, and that the aforesaid office, liberties, privileges and franchises, in form aforesaid claimed, by him, the said Harmanus, may, for the future, be allowed to him, and that he may be dismissed and discharged by the court hereof, and from the premises aforesaid. And the said Samuel A. Talcott, Esquire, Atty-Gen. of the people of the State of New York, who for the said people, at the relation of the said Gershom Van Voast, prosecuted in this behalf, being present here in court, and having heard the said plea of the said Harmanus A. Van Slyck, by him above pleaded in bar read, for the said people, saith, that for anything by him, the said Harmanus A. Van Slyck, therein alleged, the said people ought not to be barred from having and maintaining their aforesaid information against him ; because, protesting, that the said plea of the said Harmanus A. Van Slyck, and the matters therein contained, are insufficient in law to bar the said people from having and maintaining their aforesaid information against the said Harmanus A. Van Slyck, for replication nevertheles, in this behalf the said Atty Gen. saith, that, true it is, that an election was held in the several towns and wards of the said County of Schenectady, for the election (among other officers of the State of New York, and of the said County of Schenectady) of Sheriff of said County of Schenectady, on the first Monday of Nov., A. D. 1822, and continued from day to day, for three successive days, including said first Monday of Nov., pursuant to an Act of the Legislature of the people of the State of New York, entitled "An Act for Regulating Elections," passed Apr. 17, 1822; and after the said election, to wit: on the Tuesday next following the said election, such of the Inspectors of Election as did attend, and had been appoined by a major part of the Inspectors, who had presided at the said election, in the several towns and wards in the said county, according to the directions of the said Act, to attend at the clerk's office in said county, and in person to deliver to the clerk of said county, at the office, or to his deputy, or to the keeper of said **304***] office, a true *copy of the statement of the votes given at said election, in the respective towns and wards in said county, in which they were respectively Inspectors as aforesaid, for (among other officers) the office of Sheriff aforesaid, did attend at the office of the clerk of said county, and in person did deliver to the clerk of said county a true copy of the statement of votes, or certificate of the Inspectors of the respective towns and wards in said county, of the votes given as aforesaid for the officers aforesaid. But the said Atty-Gen., for the said people further saith, that the Inspectors attending as aforesaid, having been appointed as aforesaid, and having respectively attended in person as aforesaid, at the time and place aforesaid, and having delivered their respective statements or certificates of the votes given as aforesaid, to the clerk of said county as aforesaid, did not then and there, to wit: on the said Tuesday next following said election, at the office of the said clerk, according to the directions of, and in the manner required by, the aforesaid Act of the said Legislature, together with the clerk of said county, form themselves into a Board of Canvassers, and appoint such chairman, and have such secretary, as in the said plea of the said Harmanus is mentioned; and this the said Atty-Gen. prays may be inquired of by the country, and the said Harmanus doth the like, &c. And the said Atty-Gen. further saith, that the said supposed Board of Canvassers did not, at the time, place and in the manner in the said plea alleged, proceed to calculate and ascertain the aggregate amount or whole number of votes given as aforesaid, and delivered to the said clerk as required by the said Act, for the respective candidates voted for as Members of Assembly, Sheriff, Clerk and Coroners of said county respectively at said election; and this, &c. And the said Atty-Gen. further saith, that the said supposed Board of Canvassers did not determine, conformable to the aforesaid statements or certificates of votes given as aforesaid, and delivered, as aforesaid, to the clerk aforesaid, by the Inspectors of Election of the several towns and wards in said county appointed as aforesaid, upon the persons respectively duly elected by the greatest number of votes in said county, as Member of Assem- **305***] bly, *Sheriff, Clerk and Coroners of said county; and this, &c. And the said Atty-Gen. further saith, that the said supposed Board of Canvassers did not, at the time and place, and in the manner in the said plea, for the purpose mentioned, cause to be subscribed, by the supposed chairman and secretary, such certificate of such determination, as in the said plea is alleged; and this, &c. And the said Atty-Gen. further saith, that the said supposed Board of Canvassers did not cause such supposed certificate of such supposed determination, as in the said plea is alleged, to be recorded in a book kept in the office of the clerk of said county for that purpose; and this, &c. And the said Atty-Gen. further saith, that the said supposed Board of Canvassers did not cause a true copy of such supposed certificate, subscribed as in the said plea is alleged, to be delivered to each of the persons so elected, to the respective offices of Member of Assembly, Sheriff, Clerk and Coroner of said county; and this, &c. And the said Atty-Gen. further saith, that the said supposed Board of Canvassers of the said County of Schenectady did not determine, conformably to the statements or certificates delivered as aforesaid, to the clerk aforesaid, that he, the said Harmanus, was duly elected by the greatest number of votes in said county, as sheriff of said county, as in the said plea is alleged; and this, &c. And the said Atty-Gen. further saith, that the said supposed Board of Canvassers did not make and cause to be subscribed by their supposed chairman and secretary, and to be recorded in the clerk's office of said county, a certificate of a determination that the said Harmanus had been duly elected sheriff of said county, as in the said plea is alleged; and this, &c. And the said Atty-Gen. further saith, that a true copy of said last mentioned supposed certificate of said supposed Board of Canvassers, made and subscribed as in the said plea is alleged, was not, by the said supposed Board of Canvassers, caused to be delivered to the said Harmanus as in the said plea is supposed; and this, &c. And the said Atty-Gen. further saith, that the said Harmanus was not elected Sheriff of the said County of Schenctady, as in the said plea is supposed; *and this, [***306** &c. And the said Atty-Gen further saith, that true it is that the said Harmanus, at the time and place for that purpose in the said plea mentioned, did enter into such bond in such penal sum, with such sureties and condition, and that such bond was filed in such office as in the said plea alleged; and also that the said Harmanus did, on the day and year, and at the place in the said plea alleged, take and subscribe such oath before the said Jelles A. Fonda, as is also in the said plea alleged; and further, that the said Harmanus, on the said Jan. 1st, A. D. 1823, was, and still is a substantial freeholder, to wit: at the place in the said plea for that purpose mentioned; but the said Atty-Gen. further saith, that the said Harmanus was not, on the said Jan. 1st, or at any time since, nor is he now, Sheriff of the said County of Schenectady, as in the said plea is alleged; and this, &c.

Upon the above pleadings, the cause was tried before Duer, Circuit Judge, at the Schenectady Circuit, in Sept., 1824, when the jury found a special verdict as follows: that at the election mentioned in the pleadings, the defendant received 758 votes, and that the relator received 768 votes, from the electors, for the office of Sheriff of the County of Schenectady, which votes were duly canvassed and estimated by the Inspectors, of Election, at the re-

spective polls held in the several wards and towns of the county; and the names of the several candidates voted for at such election were set down in writing with the number of votes, in words at full length, given for the candidates for the said office of Sheriff, and certified and subscribed by the Inspectors with their own proper names thereto; and that the Inspectors did, within two days thereafter, cause to be delivered to the respective town clerks, and clerk of the City of Schenectady, in the County of Schenectady, in the several towns and wards in which such votes were taken, one copy of the statement to be by them respectively entered of record in their office; that the poll books and ballots made and taken at the election were immediately, upon the making and subscribing the statement or certificates, destroyed by the Inspectors; that before the commencement of the election, the Secre-
307*] tary of *State did cause the Act of the Legislature, entitled "An Act for Regulating Elections," passed Apr. 17, 1822, to be printed and distributed to the clerks of the respective counties of this State, and did prepare certain forms for carrying this Act into effect, in pursuance of the directions of the 30th section; and further that among the forms prepared by the Secretary of State, was one in the words and figures following; that is to say, "No. 25 —form of appointment by the Inspectors of Election of one of their own body [section IX]. We, the inspectors of election in the town of [or in ward of the City of] in the County of do appoint , one of the said Inspectors, to preside at the election to be held this day, and the two succeeding days in the said town [or ward] for [specify the officers to be elected] and to do and perform such other duties as appertain to him, as presiding inspector, by virtue of the Act for Regulating Elections. Dated, &c.

} Inspectors of Election."

"NOTE.—This appointment must be made before the poll is opened." Which form was printed with, and annexed to the Act, and distributed by the Secretary therewith, to the several county clerks of this State. That in all the towns and wards of the County of Schenectady, except in the town of Niskayuna, a majority of the Inspectors who presided at the election did, before the poll of election was opened, appoint one of their number to preside at the election, and did subscribe, and give to the person so appointed to preside, a certificate in the form above prepared and distributed by the Secretary of State, with the blanks left by the Secretary, properly filled up, as to names, date and place. That Jacob C. Van Vranken, Peter D. Van Vranken and Cornelius E. Tymesen were Inspectors of and presided at and held the poll of the election in the Town of Niskayuna, one of the towns of the county; and that Jacob C. Van Vranken and Peter D. Van Vranken, after the close of the poll in the last mentioned town, did appoint Tymesen to attend at the clerk's office of the County of Schenectady, and in person to deliver to the
308*] clerk at the office, or to the deputy *or keeper of the office, a true copy of the statement of votes so given at the election in the Town of Niskayuna, certified by him and the other Inspectors, and to perform the duties prescribed for the persons so appointed in and by the 10th section of the Act. But that the Inspectors of Election in the Town of Niskayuna did not, at the time of making the appointment of Tymesen, make or subscribe any certificate in writing, that he was appointed for any of the last mentioned purposes. That the Inspectors of Election in the Town of Niskayuna did at the time of his appointment, deliver to Tymesen a true copy of the statement of votes given, at the said election in the Town of Niskayuna, certified by all the Inspectors who attended the election in the town, with which, last mentioned certificate, he did, after his appointment, to wit: on the Tuesday next following the election, at one o'clock in the afternoon of that day, attend at the clerk's office of the County of Schenectady; and did, in person, deliver the last mentioned certificate to the clerk, with whom the same has ever since remained; of which delivery, all the Canvassers herein next mentioned at the time of their meeting had notice. That on Tuesday next following the election, at the hour of one o'clock in the afternoon, the following persons, having been duly appointed and received certificates in writing of that fact, to attend at the clerk's office of the County of Schenectady, for the purpose expressed in the 10th section of the Act, did also attend at the clerk's office, and did deliver to the clerk true copies of the statements of votes taken at the election in their respective towns and wards, duly certified; that is to say, John F. D. Vedder, from the town of Duanesburgh (and thus naming the Inspectors who attended from their respective towns). That these Inspectors, together with Tymesen, from the Town of Niskayuna, and Jelles A. Fonda, the County Clerk, being on the day and hour last mentioned, and before four o'clock in the afternoon of the same day, so assembled and attending at the County Clerk's office for the purpose, did form themselves into a Board of Canvassers, and did appoint Simon A. Groot chairman of the Board, and Jelles A. Fonda being present, was secretary thereof. *That imme- [*309 diately after the appointment of the chairman, the several persons so attending the Board were required to produce written certificates of their appointment as members, from the majority of the Inspectors of their respective towns and wards: and that all the Canvassers so attending did produce such certificates, except Tymesen, who told the Canvassers that he had received no such written certificate of appointment from the Inspectors who held the poll of the election in the Town of Niskayuna; but that he was so appointed without writing; whereupon the Canvassers did determine by a vote, that Tymesen had no right to a seat as a member of the Board of Canvassers, and did exclude him from the board. That after this determination of the Canvassers, and before the hour of four o'clock in the afternoon, Tymesen did procure a paper writing in the following words: "We, the Inspectors of the Election in the Town of Niskayuna, in the County of Schenectady, do appoint Tymesen, one of the Inspectors of said election, to preside at the election to be held in the said town,

for the officers to be elected in the said county, on the fourth day of November, and the two succeeding days, in the year one thousand eight hundred and twenty-two, to do and perform all such duties as appertain to the said election, by virtue of the Act Regulating Elections. Dated this fourth day of November, 1822." Which was signed by Jacob C. Van Vranken and Cornelius E. Tymesen, as Inspectors of Election of the Town of Niskayuna, on the Tuesday next following the election. That Tymesen did offer this writing to the Canvassers, and did again claim a seat with them, as a member of the Board of Canvassers, before the hour of four o'clock in the afternoon of the Tuesday next following the election, and did inform the Canvassers, so assembled as a Board of Canvassers, that himself and Jacob C. Van Vranken were a majority of the Inspectors who had presided at the poll of the election in the Town of Niskayuna; but the said Canvassers did a second time, by vote, determine, that Tymesen had no right to a seat with the Board, and did exclude him therefrom, alleging, among other reasons, for exeluding him, that the writing was not subscribed by a majority of the Inspectors, who
310*] had presided at the poll *of the election in Niskayuna, exclusive of Tymesen. That after this determination, and after the hour of four o'clock of the afternoon of the Tuesday next following the election, they, with the exception of Tymesen, proceeded to calculate and ascertain the whole number of votes, which were given at the election for the several persons voted for as Governor, Lieutenant-Governor, Senator, a Representative in the Congress of the U. S., Member of Assembly, Sheriff, Clerk of the County and Coroners, at the election in the first and second wards in the City of Schenectady; and then adjourned the further canvass of the votes of the county and their meeting until nine o'clock in the forenoon of the following day. That after this adjournment, and before the hour to which the Canvassers had adjourned their meeting, Tymsen procured another paper writing or certificate in the words following: "We, the majority of the Inspectors actually presiding at the election in the Town of Niskayuna, in the County of Schenectady, on the fourth day of November instant, and the two succeeding days, in the said town, for Governor, Lieutenant-Governor, four Senators, an Assemblyman, Sheriff, County Clerk, four Coroners and one Representative to Congress, do certify that we did, on the sixth day of November instant, appoint Cornelius E. Tymesen, also actually presiding at said election, to do and perform such duties as appertain to him by virtue of such appointment, and as are prescribed in the 10th section of the Act for Regulating Elections, passed April 17th, 1822. Dated 12th November, 1822;" which last mentioned certificate was signed by Peter D. Van Vranken and Jacob C. Van Vranken as Inspectors. That Nov. 13, A. D. 1822, at the hour of nine o'clock in the forenoon, being the day and hour to which the canvass of the remainder of the votes of the county, and the meeting of the Canvassers were adjourned, and immediately after the Canvassers had met, and were about to continue the canvass of the remainder of the votes, Tymesen, accompanied by Jacob C. Van Vranken and Peter D. Van Vranken, did appear before the Board, and Tymesen did present the last mentioned certificate to the Canvassers, and Jacob C. Van Vranken and Peter D. Van Vranken offered to the *Board to make oath, that Tymesen [*311
had been appointed by the Inspectors who presided at the poll in the Town of Niskayuna, at the election, to attend with a certificate of the votes of the Town of Niskayuna, at the clerk's office of the county, as a member of the Board of Canvassers, and Tymeson did claim a seat at, and to be a member of the Board, and to act as one of the Canvassers of the votes of the county, so given at the election; but a majority of the Canvassers refused to receive any evidence of the appointment of Tymesen as one of the Board, alleging, among other reasons therefor, that such proof ought to have been offered previous to the hour of four o'clock in the afternoon of the Tuesday next following the election; and did, thereupon, a third time, by vote, determine that Tymesen had no right to a seat at the Board as a member thereof; and did again exclude him therefrom. That the remaining Canvassers did proeeed to calculate, estimate and ascertain the remainder of the votes given at the election; and having completed such estimate and calculation, and ascertained the amount of votes given at the election, a motion was made by one of the Canvassers, and seconded by another, that they should calculate, estimate and ascertain the number of votes given in the Town of Niskayuna, which motion the chairman refused to put to vote. Whereupon, one of the Canvassers made a motion, that the chairman and secretary of the Canvassers should sign a certificate of the result of the canvass of the votes of the county, as it had been obtained by excluding the votes of the Town of Niskayuna, and from canvassing the votes given in the other towns and wards of the said county, which was carried by the votes of a majority of the Canvassers; and that thereupon, the chairman and secretary did sign a certificate, which commenced with the following words: "At a meeting of the Board of Canvassers, duly organized and held in and for the County of Schenectady, at the clerk's office in the City of Schenectady, in said county, on the 12th and 13th days of November, in the year 1822, pursuant to the Act entitled 'An Act for Regulating Elections,' passed April the 17th, 1822, Simon A. Groot was chosen chairman, and Jelles A. Fonda, clerk of the said *county, was, *ex officio*, secretary of the [*312
said Board, the following persons appeared and constituted the said Board, they being Inspectors of Elections in the several wards and towns in the said county, and having been respectively appointed by the major part of the Inspectors of their respective wards and towns to preside at an election held therein, on the fourth day of November, 1822, and the two succeeding days inclusive, for the purpose of choosing one Member of Assembly, one Sheriff, four Coroners and one Clerk; that is to say, John N. Marselis, of the first ward, Simon A. Groot, of the second ward, none admitted of the Town of Niskayuna. The certificates and statements of the votes of the Town of Nis-

kayuna were denied acceptance. The Inspectors had neglected the necessary appointment for a presiding Inspector, pursuant to the 10th section of the Act Regulating Elections, passed April 17th, 1822. Harmanus A. Van Slyck, of the town of Rotterdam (and so of each town). The Board then proceeded to calculate and ascertain the whole number of votes, given at such election, in the said county for the several persons voted for the offices above specified; any thereupon the said Board do, according to the Act aforesaid, set down in writing the names of the several candidates so voted for at such election, for any and every of the offices aforesaid, and the numbers of votes in words written at full length, which were given at such election, for the said candidates respectively." That the said certificate then contained a statement of the votes given in each town and ward of the county, except in the Town of Niskayuna, for (among other officers) the candidates for the office of Sheriff, by which statement it appears that the defendant received at the election, in the towns and wards of the county, exclusive of the votes of the Town of Niskayuna, 732 votes for the office of Sheriff, and that Gershom Van Voast, the relator, received in the towns and wards of the county, exclusive of the votes of the Town of Niskayuna, 719 votes for the office of Sheriff; and that the defendant and Gershom Van Voast, each received more votes than any other candidates for the office of Sheriff at the election. **313***] That the last mentioned *certificate, after detailing the votes of the respective candidates for the offices of Assemblyman, Clerk, Sheriff and Coroners, in each town and ward of the county, except the Town of Niskayuna, concludes, so far as relates to the office of Sheriff, in the following words: "And do certify, determine and declare, conformably to the statements or certificates, made and delivered by the Inspectors of Elections of the several wards and towns in the said county, that Harmanus A. Van Slyck, by the greatest number of votes in the said county, was duly elected Sheriff of the said county. In testimony whereof we, the chairman and secretary of the said Board of Canvassers, have hereunto set our hands, this thirteenth day of November, in the year one thousand eight hundred and twenty-two." That the last mentioned certificate is entered by the County Clerk at full length, in a book by him provided for that purpose, and kept in his office; and further, that a true copy thereof, subscribed by the chairman and secretary, was delivered to Van Slyck, and another copy thereof published in the newspaper, printed in the county. That in the Town of Niskayuna, the defendant and Van Voast each obtained more votes than any other person for the office of Sheriff; and that the defendant obtained for the office 26 votes only, and Van Voast 49 votes, which was duly certified in the certificate so signed by the Inspectors of the Election, and delivered to Tymesen, and by him delivered to the County Clerk as before mentioned. That the Canvassers did reject and refuse to canvass and estimate the votes given in the Town of Niskayuna, at the election, and certified and delivered to the County Clerk, and that the votes given in the Town of Niskayuna for Van Voast, added to the votes given for him in the several towns and wards of the county, for the office of Sheriff, give him a majority of ten votes for the office of Sheriff, over any other person voted for at the election. That the defendant upon receiving the copy of the certificate signed by the chairman and secretary, Jan. 1, A. D., 1823, took the oath and gave the security prescribed by law, and entered upon the office of Sheriff of the County of Schenectady; and held this office ever since; and that the defendant, at the *time of the election, and Jan. 1, 1823, [***314** was a freeholder. But whether, &c.

Mr. S. W. Jones, for the plaintiffs. Unless the defendant shows a clear right, he cannot hold. The 8th section of the 4th article of the new Constitution provides, "that sheriffs, &c., shall be chosen by the electors of the respective counties, once in every three years.

To make a choice of the defendant within this provision, there should be a majority of legal votes; whereas the verdict finds a majority the other way; and falsifies the certificate of the Board of Canvassers, which is indeed untrue upon its face.

The Board proceeded under the notion that an appointment of a president was necessary for the Town Board, and that this should be certified to the County Board. This was not necessary. The Secretary of State was mistaken in his construction of the 10th section of the Act for Regulating Elections, sess. 46, ch. 250, sec. 10. The words are, "that one of the said Inspectors, who shall actually preside at such election in each of the towns and wards of this State, to be appointed for that purpose by the major part of the Inspectors who so preside, shall, on, &c., attend at the clerk's office, &c." In the 9th section or any previous sections there is no allusion to a presiding Inspector; and it is plain from the several provisions in relation to the proceedings of the Town Board, that all and each of them are to be considered and treated as presidents within the meaning of the 10th section. Either of them may be appointed after the poll has closed; and no particular form of appointment is necessary. The secretary directs, in his note, that the appointment should be made before the opening of the poll. Suppose the one then appointed should be sick, die, or otherwise incapable of attending, must the votes be lost?

WOODWORTH, *J.* I think there is nothing in the Act that requires this proceeding.

There are several cases in which certificates are made necessary by the Town Board, but a president, as such, is not *once mentioned. [***315** The Inspectors are treated as having the same equal authority throughout, and in every respect.

The Court told *Mr. Jones* that he need not pursue this point any further for the present; but they would hear the other side upon it.

Mr. Jones then cited the following authorities to show than an information, in nature of a *quo warranto*, was the proper remedy in this case: *King* v. *Godwin*, Doug., 398; *Rex* v. *Vice-Chancellor of Cambridge*, 3 Burr., 1647; *People* v. *Sweeting*, 2 Johns., 184; *People* v. *Mayor &c., of N. Y.*, 3 Johns. Cas., 79; 1 R. L. 107. The granting of a *mandamus* and an information in nature of a *quo warranto*, be said, depend much upon the same principles; the one being to admit an officer improperly excluded; the other to oust one who has usurped an office illegally, in order to make way for the rightful candidate. (2 Esp. Dig., 343, Gould's ed.; 2 Hawk. P. C., ch. 26, sec. 9.)

Messrs. A. C. Paige and *M. T. Reynolds*, for the defendant. If the canvass were an original proceeding in this court, there might be no difficulty in saying that the defendant should not hold his place as Sheriff; but there is an insuperable impediment to their interference at this stage, and in this manner. The certificate of determination of the Board of Canvassers is conclusive evidence of the legal election of the defendant. It can neither be impeached nor contradicted. The only guard against misconduct is provided by the 19th section of the Act. If the canvassers willfully violate their oath, they are subject to the penalty of $500. This court might, for the reason relied on in this case, review every canvass of an election, not excepting that of Governor, Lieut.-Govcruor, &c., by the State Canvassers. Upon the same ground, an information would lie against a member of either house of the Legislature; for if this court have jurisdiction, it can be taken away only by express provision. When organized pursuant to the 10th section, a majority of the County Board are, by the same section, to determine &c., upon the person or persons duly elected, &c., as Sheriff, &c. The **316***] authority here is judicial; and it *is plain, from the whole Act on this subject, the Legislature intended that the determination should be as far binding and conclusive as a judgment in a court of justice.

Very great inconveniences will result from a contrary construction. Suppose the defendant to be ousted; a new Sheriff cannot be immediately chosen; the Board cannot be convened; they are *functus officio;* their powers are limited. As a body, they must be made up of the town boards, which are continually changing; and, if otherwise, they can do no Act after the Tuesday, or some adjourned day next succeeding the election. They cannot again convene. No subsequent board can perform their duties. No process can be issued to restore Van Voast, and the county must for a time remain without a Sheriff. The coroners cannot take the county. Their powers are inadequate, being principally judicial; seldom ministerial. (5 Com. Dig., Officer, G., 5 to 13; 1 Bl. Com., 348–9; 1 R. L., 420, 1, sec. 5.) In his ministerial capacity he acts strictly as a substitute for the Sheriff in the case of his death, partiality, &c. What, in the meantime. is to become of the jail and the prisoners? Is the door to be thrown open to them? If the court sees that such a consequence must follow, they will not interfere. It is a maxim that if the right of an individual conflict with the public safety, the former must yield.

By the 14th section of the Act Regulating Elections, the judges of this court are, upon certain events, to act as State Canvassers; and the powers of State and County Canvassers are conferred in nearly the same terms. Would you interfere and grant an information upon a canvass of two of your own body? You must do it upon the principle relied on here. The Legislature, obviously, never intended that this court should exercise the power of review. The case is one of the first impression. Not one case of an information in nature of a *quo warranto* to try a right to the office of Sheriff can be produced. There is but instance in the books of such a proceeding against an elective public officer, and that was a supervisor (*People* v. *Sweeting*, 2 Johns., 184), where it was refused on the ground that the term of office had nearly expired. Admitting, however, that it will lie in that case, it does not *fol- [***317** low that it will lie against a Sheriff. There is no Board, as in this case, vested with judicial powers. The justices of the town are to preside, with authority to say who shall vote, but not who is elected. The canvass is a ministerial act. (2 R. L., 127, sec. 2, 3.) The case of *Rex* v. *Vice-Chancellor of Cambridge*, cited from Burrow, 1647, was a proceeding by *mandamus*. But admitting the principle to be the same, it will be found, on examining that case, that the power of the Canvassers was not judicial. The Statute R. L., 418, 19, sec. 1, requires that the county should be assigned to the new Sheriff. This is done. Suppose the defendant to be ousted of his office, to whom shall he assign? The Statute requires that he should assign to his successor. Here he has none. It requires that the assignment should be by the Sheriff. Being ousted of his office, no one is left to perform that duty. The court will look to the interests of the public. The K. B. have denied a *certiorari* to remove an assessment of the land tax. *Rex* v. *King*, 2 T. R., 234. So of a poor rate, on the ground of general inconvenience. (2 Str., 932, 975.) And they will act upon the same principle in this case. The defendant has prisoners in custody, whom he cannot hold—perhaps both himself and bail will be left without accountability to creditors. At any rate, he is regularly in; and the hazard and loss of an ouster should not be visited upon his head, who is found to be in regular possession of the office, by the act of a Board of Canvassers.

Suppose an Inspector had not attended from the Town of Niskayuna, would the court interfere, because the Constitution requires a majority? Where is the court to stop? Will they descend to the towns and look to their proceedings? Because an improper vote may have been received, will they examine and deduct it? Is this practicable? Beside, the ceremony of a canvass is indeed an idle one, if liable to be thus overturned. It has no binding force, and might as well have been omitted altogether by the Act.

If this court have jurisdiction to review the determination of the Board of Canvassers, their reviewing power can only *be ex- [***318** ercised through the medium of a *certiorari*; and until reversed in this form, it remains valid and conclusive, and cannot be questioned by an information in nature of a *quo warranto*. A *certiorari* is necessary to reverse an improper appointment of a constable by two justices. *Wood* v. *Peake*, 8 Johns., 69. The reason is, because the 2 R. L., 127, sec. 5, conferring this power of appointment, creates a judicial authority, from the exercise of which a *certiorari* lies. *Wildy* v. *Washburn*, 16 Johns., 49. And the power conveyed by the Statute in question is as plainly so as that given by the earlier Statute in relation to the appointment of a constable. For the cases in which a *certiorari* will, in general, lie, and is necessary, the court are referred to *Smith* v. *Lewis*, 3 Johns., 168-9, per Kent, *Ch. J.*; *Lawton* v. *The Comrs. of H W. of Cambridge*, 2 Cai., 179; *Learned* v. *Duval*, 3 Johns. Cas., 141; *People* v. *Runkel*, 6 Johns., 334; *Rex* v. *Inhabitants of* —— *in Glanorganshire*, 1 Ld. Raym., 580; *Cross* v. *Smith*, 1 Salk., 146; 1 Bac. Abr., *Certiorari*, B; *Rex* v. *The Inhabitants of Great Marlow*, 2 East, 244. The certificate of determination was a record, the history of a judicial decision, unimpeachable for defect or illegality; and no averment is admissible against it. 1 Chit. Pl., 353-4, 480-1; 1 Phil. Ev., 218, 219, ed. 1820, and the cases there cited; *M'Lean* v. *Hugarin*, 13 Johns., 184. The writ of *certiorari* is the only known and acknowledged process to reverse the judicial decision of an inferior tribunal. A *quo warranto* is inapplicable, except when the power to be reviewed is ministerial.

But the Board of Canvassers decided correctly in refusing the Inspector from Niskayuna his seat; and in refusing to canvass the votes from that town. The attending Inspector should have been appointed on the first day of the election; and that appointment should have been made in writing and signed by a majority of the Inspectors. The forms of instruments and proceeding, promulgated by the Secretary of State, were sanctioned by the Statute, sess. 45, ch. 25, sec. 30, by which it was made his duty to furnish them. There should be a written appointment in the hands **319***] of the *attending Inspector, to inform the Board of his authority. The act of appointment should be written; and, at any rate, made out during, or immediately after the election, not at any distance of time. These successive certificates were a mere recital of what was previously done.

An information in the nature of a *quo warranto* against a Sheriff cannot be brought on the relation of an individual. Van Voast has no interest in the question, because this court have no power to restore him; and where an individual has no interest, he cannot be received as relator. *Rex* v. *Williams*, 1 Burr., 402, 407; 3 Bl. Com., 262, 263, 264, *note* 1; *Rex* v. *Wallis*, 5 T. R., 375; *Rex* v. *Marsden*, 3 Burr., 1812, 1816, 1817; *Rex* v. *Hall*, 1 Barn. & C., 237; *Commonwealth* v. *U. F. & Mar. Ins. Co., etc.*, 5 Mass., 230. The proceeding should be in the name of the people, without a relator.

The defendant was bound to take the office or be indicted and punished. *Rex* v. *Wallis*, 5 T. R., 375, 381, per Buller, *J.*; 5 Jac. L. Dict., 377, 8, ed. 1811, tit. *Quo Warranto*; 1 Bl. Com., 341; 2 Chit. C. L., 267, *note x*; *Atty-Gen.* v. *Read*, 2 Mod., 300, arg. for the plaintiff; 6 Com. Dig., Viscount, A, 2. And there is a difference made in several of the cases just cited between one compelled to take a burdensome office and one claiming and coming in as a volunteer. The defendant was made Sheriff by the act of others.

If judgment be rendered against the defendant, the fine should be merely nominal. The information in nature of a *quo warranto* is for the purpose of trying a civil right; and the treatment of it as a criminal proceeding is formal merely. *People* v. *Utica Ins. Co.*, per Spencer, *J.*, 15 Johns., 387; 3 Bac. Abr., Informations, A, p. 636, ed. 1813; *Rex* v. *Shepherd*, 4 T. R., 385; 3 Bl. Com., 262, 264, *note* 1. This is the first proceeding of the kind against a Sheriff. The town certificate of appointment was signed by two only of the inspectors, one of whom was the carrier of the votes; and the supplemental certificates were entirely unavailing. The secretary's directions were taken as the guide; and all proceeded in good faith. The reasons fully *appear [***320** for every step that was taken. The fine goes to the people, and is no benefit to the relator. Under these circumstances, there is nothing to take the case out of the general rule that the fine should be nominal only.

Mr. A. Van Vechten, in reply. The question is, whether the defendant was elected or canvassed into office. If the latter, he is not Sheriff. It is admitted that the election was regular. The work was well done, so far as that was concerned. We deny that the act of the County Board was judicial. It was merely ministerial. They are required to cast up the votes as returned; and anyone who understands arithmetic can do this. They have power to do nothing more. The addition gives the result. They are not to say who are or who are not competent voters, or whether the votes are to be received and counted, but merely to fix the majority from the return made, and declare the result upon the certificate of the Town Inspectors, who are required to certify the votes at full length. Is this a judicial act? Then every schoolmaster in the State becomes a judge if he happens to be chosen an Inspector. Some degree of judgment must be exercised, to be sure, but not that sort of judicial discretion, we trust, which is to control the Constitution. *Rex* v. *Vice Chancellor of Cambridge*, 3 Burr., 1647, is decisive that the election, not the decision of the Canvassers, confers the right.

The votes are to be certified by the Town Inspectors, two copies made, one to be deposited in the town clerk's office before the canvass commences, and another to be delivered by the County Clerk to the Inspector appointed to attend the County Board; this also before the canvass commences. The mere possession of this copy by the Inspector is, at least, *prima facie* evidence of his appointment. No new officer is to be elected. The Inspectors of the town are all and each of them presidents; and the right to deliver the votes and act as a member of the County Board is incident to the office of Inspector. Tymeson had a statement of votes duly canvassed. This informed the Board of all it was requisite they should know. If there was fraud or anything surreptitious on the part of the Inspector, it then lay with the Board to show it.

*The secretary could impose no [***321** form not required by the election law. The member of the County Board is to be appointed by his fellow Inspectors. This is all which the Act requires. No writing is necessary. No particular time is required; and are we gravely to be told that the power given to the secretary, to prescribe the forms of proceeding, enables him to do away or neutralize the Act? The secretary thought it a good thing to have a president; and it might be well enough; but the Inspectors have indulged in a bolder fancy, and have made the omission avoid all the proceedings.

I have said a certificate is to be filed in the town clerk's office. Is not this a judicial act as well as that of the County Canvassers? If so, here would be record against record, an estoppel by which the County Board should have been governed. This alone would answer the notion of conclusiveness. Because the court examine the county canvass, it is a *non sequitur* that they may go back to the town poll. Everything there has been regularly done. The maxim of law is that there is no law without a remedy. The right to interfere with wrongful elections by *mandamus* or *quo warranto* existed at common law, and is recognized and regulated by Statute, 1 R. L., 107. The former is to compel admission when the office is vacant; the latter to oust when it is improperly filled. The Statute extends to any office or franchise in the State, being much broader than the English. An information has repeatedly been allowed in relation to public elective offices. *People* v. *Mayor, &c., of N. Y.*, 3 Johns. Cas., 79; *People* v. *Sweeting*, 2 Johns., 184. The last case was that of a Supervisor; and it was not questioned that the information would have lain, had not the term of office nearly elapsed before it was applied for. Yet no substantial distinction exists between the powers of the Inspectors at town meeting, in reference to the Supervisor, and those of the County Board as to the Sheriff. It is merely counting and estimating the votes in either case.

It is not necessary to reconvene the County Board in order to restore Van Voast. The verdict of the jury and the judgment of this court will answer every requisite purpose.

322*] *This court have nothing to do with the consequences. If the defendant be an usurper, he must be ousted. The court have no dispensing power; and if the facts found warrant it, they are in duty bound to pronounce judgment of ouster. It is asked, how do you get Van Voast in? It might as well be asked how you get the defendant out. If the court have the means of executing their judgment by the proper officer, then there is no difficulty in either. All Van Voast has to do on ouster of the defendant is to give security and take the oath of office. The custody of the county devolves, in the meantime, to the jailer *de facto*, who must give over the jail to the Sheriff *de jure*. Gentlemen need be under no concern as to the *modus operandi*. We will see to it, and endeavor to be sufficiently advised of the manner in which our rights are to be enforced and maintained.

Van Voast was the proper relator. In the view we have taken, he has the highest interest, and is receivable upon gentlemen's own principles. He has the right, and is the only one who would come in and assume the responsibility for costs.

A *certiorari* is inapplicable. It would be no remedy. We are necessarily here by information in order to show the falsity of the decision. A *certiorari* would presuppose the truth of the record. We aver its falsity. To whom can a *certiorari* issue? Gentlemen say the Board is dissolved, and it cannot go to them. On *quo warranto* the facts are tried by a jury, the court give judgment of ouster; the rightful claimant comes in, and the court will either give judgment to this effect or grant a *mandamus* to the proper authority, compelling them to receive him.

It is, perhaps, difficult to determine whether an information lies to try the title of the Govcruor and State officers. The Governor is the representative of the State; and an appeal from the State Canvassers may not exist. It is a case, perhaps, to which neither the common or statute law extends. But it by no means follows that the court have not power in this instance. Because a case may be put a little puzzling, it does not deprive the court of jurisdiction. The Constitution gives the right to Congress, Senate and Assembly to determine *all questions upon the election **[*323** of their members, and impliedly excludes the jurisdiction of the court in those cases.

Curia, per Woodworth, *J.* This is an information in nature of a *quo warranto*, filed against the defendant, who, as is alleged, intruded into, and unlawfully holds the office of Sheriff of the County of Schenectady.

The remedy by information is adapted to this case. The Statute is comprehensive in its terms. It extends to all persons who shall usurp, intrude into or unlawfully hold and execute any office or franchise within this State. The jurisdiction of the court cannot well be doubted, when the question relates to a public office. The decision of officers acting ministerially is sought to be reviewed. In *People* v. *Mayor of N. Y.*, 3 Johns. Cas., 79, and *People* v. *Sweeting*, 2 Johns., 184, the court entertained jurisdiction; in one case where the relator claimed to have been elected to the office of Alderman; in the other, to that of Supervisor; and considered an information as the proper remedy to try the rights of the parties.

It was contended on the argument that the decision of the Board of Canvassers was conclusive, until reversed; and could only be reviewed by *certiorari*. This objection cannot prevail. The duties of the Canvassers are ministerial. They are required by the Act to attend at the clerk's office, and calculate and ascertain the whole number of votes given at any election; and certify the same to be a true canvass. This is not a judicial act, but merely ministerial. They have no power to controvert the votes of the electors. If they deviate from the directions of the Statute, and certify in favor of a Sheriff not duly elected, he is liable to be ousted by information. The trial is had upon the right of the party holding the office. The certificate is not conclusive. The court will decide upon an examination of all the facts.

The question then is, have the Canvassers complied with the duties enjoined on them by law? I am clearly of opinion they have not.

A certificate of the election in Niskayuna was signed by *all the Inspectors, and **[*324** one of their number appointed to deliver it to the clerk of the county. This was done within the time limited by law. When the Board met to calculate the votes, the Inspector from Niskayuna was excluded, on the ground that he did not produce written evidence of his appointment. The Statute declares that one of the Inspectors of Election, who shall actually preside at such election, to be appointed by a major part of the Inspectors who shall so preside, shall, in person, deliver to the clerk a copy of the statement of votes. It is then made the duty of the Inspectors, who attend at the clerk's office, to ascertain the whole number of votes given for the respective candidates at the election.

The 10th section of the Act does not require that one of the Inspectors be appointed to preside at the election. All the Inspectors attending equally preside, and have equal powers. The meaning of the Act is, that some one of the Inspectors, who attended the election, shall be appointed to deliver the certificate, and attend at the clerk's office of the county. It is not necessary to make this appointment until the votes of the town are canvassed.

Although an appointment by writing is to be preferred, it is not indispensable. The Statute is silent as to a written appointment. If an objection is taken when an Inspector presents himself at the Board of Canvassers, the evidence of his appointment may be either by writing or parol. If the statement of the votes of the town are delivered to the clerk by an Inspector, and the fact of his being an Inspector is not questioned by the Canvassers, he ought not to be excluded; for the delivery of the statement, and attendance to perform the duty of a Canvasser is, *prima facie*, evidence of an appointment for that purpose. The Canvassers, therefore, erred in excluding the Inspector from Niskayuna on his first application.

But if this were not sufficient, the certificate produced, before the hour of 4 o'clock Nov. 12, was evidence that the person producing it had been regularly appointed. The Act gives the power of appointment to the major part of the Inspectors who shall preside. The person **325***] *appointed is not excluded from participation; and consequently he may constitute one of the majority who confer on him the appointment. A second certificate signed by all the Inspectors was produced the next day, before the canvass was finished. The Inspectors from Niskayuna attended personally; and offered to make oath. The Board then decided not to receive any evidence, because not offered previous to four o'clock P. M. of the day preceding. The votes of Niskayuna were not calculated. Excluding that town, the defendant had a majority of votes, and was declared duly elected. If the votes of Niskayuna had been canvassed, the relator would have been found to be elected.

The several decisions of the Board of Canvassers are manifestly erroneous; and call for the interposition of this court. The defendant was not duly elected Sheriff, but unlawfully holds that office. It is the opinion of the court that judgment of ouster be entered; and that the relator recover his costs of prosecution.

Judgment of ouster.

Distinguished—70 N. Y., 527.

Cited in—20 Wend., 14; 3 Hill, 47; 5 Hill, 621; 5 Den., 411; 8 N. Y., 82; 27 N. Y., 55, 84; 55 N. Y., 197; 5 Hun, 44; 14 Barb., 296; 30 Barb., 598; 25 How. Pr., 502; 26 Cal., 214; 30 Cal., 337; 61 Ind., 409; 44 Mo., 227; 16 Mich., 321.

JACKSON, ex dem. MURPHY ET UX.,
v.
VAN HOESEN.

Estate for Life—Effect of Words "Bargained and Sold"—Tenant for Life—Power of Alienation—Conveyance by—Tenant for Years.

The words "has bargained and sold," in a conveyance sealed, are operative to pass an estate for life.

Tenant for life, unless restrained by condition, may aliene his whole estate or any less estate.

If lands are conveyed to a natural person, without words of limitation, an estate for the life of the grantee passes, unless the grantor be tenant for his own life only. Then only an estate for the life of the grantor passes. Reason of this distinction.

If tenant for years convey without limitation, his whole estate passes.

Citations—10 Johns., 337, 338; 1 Cruise Dig., Estate for Life, sec. 95; 4 Cruise Dig., Deed, ch. 24, sec. 42; Dyer, 307 *b.*; 2 Bac. Abr., A. 559; Co. Litt., 42 *a*, *b*, 183 *a*.

EJECTMENT for a farm in the Town of Taghkanic, in the County of Columbia, tried at the Columbia Circuit, June 30, 1823, before Betts, Circuit Judge; when a verdict was taken for the plaintiff, subject to the opinion of the court on a case.

May 27, 1798, Henry W. Livingston executed a lease of the premises in question, to John Murphy and Eve Connor, his wife, for their lives. John Murphy died about the year 1814, leaving the lessors of the plaintiff his heirs at law; and they are also his administrator and administratrix under letters dated Feb. 26, 1814.

The defendant claimed under and gave in evidence an *instrument in writing, [***326** commencing in the usual form of articles of agreement, dated Apr. 28, 1800, interchangeably signed and sealed by John Murphy, in his lifetime, and Jacob Van Hoesen, the father of the defendant—which, after naming the parties and date, ran thus: "witnesseth, that the said John Murphy of the first part has bargained and sold unto the said Jacob, the farm, &c." (the premises in question); and these words, "has bargained and sold," were the only operative words. Murphy also declared by this instrument that Van Hoesen "is to have possession of the above premises on the 1st day of May next." The instrument then provided for paying the consideration money by installments.

Jacob Van Hoesen took possession accordingly, and continued in possession till about 1815, when he died, leaving the defendant his heir at law, who continued in possession to the time of the trial.

The instrument in writing, executed by John Murphy and Jacob Van Hoesen, was left with one F. Hanson till about two years before the trial, who also testified that he filled up a printed blank lease for the premises from John Murphy to Jacob Van Hoesen, dated Jan. 20, 1814, for the parties named in it.

When the instrument of Apr. 28, 1800, was executed, Murphy's name was stricken out of the rent book as tenant, by the agent of Livingston the landlord, and Van Hoesen's inserted as tenant of that farm; and the rents have always since been paid by Van Hoesen and his heirs.

Mr. E. Williams, for the plaintiff. The instrument in writing of Apr. 28, 1800, was executory and not a present lease or conveyance; and was to have been followed up by a lease, which was never executed. It, therefore, passed no interest. 4 Cruise Dig., Deed, ch. 33, sec. 34, pp. 428, 429; *Blandford* v. *Marlborough*, per *Lord Chancellor*, 2 Atk., 545; *Jackson* v. *Kisselbrack*, 10 Johns., 336, 337; *Roe* v. *Ashburner*, 5 T. R., 163, 167; *Doe* v. *Smith*, per Lord Ellenborough, 6 East, 535; *Goodtitle* v. *Way*, 1 T. R., 735.

327*] *At any rate, if it could be construed into a sub-lease or conveyance *in præsenti*, it passed only an estate for the life of the bargainee, there being no words of limitation or of inheritance. Then the death of the bargainee terminates the estate. (Co. Litt., 42 *a*, *Id.*, sec. 283; *Id.*, 183 *a*, *b*.)

Mr. J. Sudam, for the defendant. The instrument of Apr. 28, 1800, contains apt words of conveyance, "has bargained and sold," and operates as an assignment or conveyance of the premises. *Jackson* v. *Kisselbrack*, 10 Johns., 336, and the cases there cited. Where the estate intended to be passed by a conveyance is not mentioned, it is deemed to pass an estate for the life of the grantee, if the grantor had power to sell such an estate. (1 Cruise Dig., Estate for Life, sec. 4, 5, pp. 60, 61; Co. Litt., 42 *a*, sec. 56.) Murphy, having only a life estate in the premises could not convey for the life of his grantee; and the law will so construe the conveyance as to have it pass the estate which he had in the premises. (Co. Litt., 42 *a*, *Id.*, sec. 283; Wood's Inst., 128–9, 269.) The court will also be guided by the acts of the parties, the long possession, the payment of rent, and the change of the tenant's name in the rent roll. There is no doubt, from the context, that Murphy intended to devest himself of all his interest. The authorities relied on against this, are where a question might arise between the tenant and the reversioner upon the effect of a common law conveyance. No such question can arise upon conveyances which take effect upon the Statute of Uses.

Curia, per SAVAGE, *Ch. J.* The questions arising in this case are:

1. Was the article an agreement for a lease, or was it a lease in itself?

2. If it was an instrument conveying a present interest, what estate passed by it?

As to the first question, it is unnecessary to examine the numerous cases to be found on the subject. They are many of them cited in *Jackson* v. *Kisselbrack*, 10 Johns., 337, which I consider decisive of this question. In that **328***] case a *memorandum of an agreement was made, by which the grantor "set and to farm let" to the defendant certain premises; and the agreement contained a covenant that they should be surveyed, and then the defendant was to take a lease. The late *Ch. J.*, in giving the opinion of the court, says that the last circumstance has generally given a character to the instrument of an agreement for a lease as contradistinguished from a present demise. He adds, that none of the cases contradict the position, that where there are apt words of present demise, and to them are superadded a covenant for a further lease, the instrument is to be considered a lease, and the covenant as operating in the nature of a covenant for further assurance. This case is much stronger. Here are apt words of conveyance. The contract seems to be complete, and no provision is made for any further conveyance. If the assertion be true, "that there is no case of a present demise by apt words followed by a possession, in which the instrument has not been held to pass an immediate interest" (per Spencer, *J.*, *Id.*, 338), then certainly an immediate interest passed by the instrument under consideration.

John Murphy had an estate for the lives of himself and wife, and though the case is silent on the subject, I presume the wife is still living. The plaintiff, then, is entitled to recover, unless John Murphy conveyed away his whole estate. What estate did he convey? Every tenant for life has the power of alienating his whole estate, or of creating any estate less than his own, unless restrained by condition. If he seeks to create a greater estate, the effort must necessarily be void for the excess, as no one can give what he has not. (1 Cruise Dig., Estate for Life, sec. 95.)

If lands are conveyed to a natural person without any words of limitation whatever, he will take an estate for his own life, unless the grantor be only tenant for his own life; in which case the grantee will take an estate for the life of the grantor only. (4 Cruise Dig., Deed, ch. 24, sec. 42.) But if a tenant for years conveys without limitation, his whole estate passes. *Fenton* v. *Forster*, Dyer, 307 *b*; and *vide* 2 Bac. Abr., Estate for Life and Occupancy, A, p. 559. *Ld. Coke (Co. [***329** Litt., 42 *a*, and 183 *a*) gives as a reason, the maxim in law, that every man's grant shall be taken by construction of law most forcibly against himself; and is so to be understood that no wrong be thereby done; for it is another maxim in law, *quod legis constructio non facit injuriam*. And therefore, if tenant for life make a lease generally, this shall be taken an estate for his own life that made the lease; for if it should be a lease for the life of the lessee, it would be a wrong to him in reversion. The law will intend the lease to be such an one as he may lawfully make rather than that an injury may accrue to any one. (Co. Litt., 42 *b*.)

Whether, therefore, the estate conveyed be for the life of the lessor or lessee, as both are dead, it is at an end; and as the lease to John Murphy has not expired, the plaintiff is entitled to recover. I have taken no notice of the fact of Murphy's name being stricken from the landlord's rent book, as that only shows the opinion of his agent; nor of the unexecuted lease, as that was not prepared by the direction of the defendant.

Judgment for the plaintiff.

Cited in—3 Barb. Ch., 245.

DEWEY v. OSBORN.

Ejectment—Lessor may Bring Trespass against Defendant, after Judgment before Hab. Fac. Poss. *Executed—Rights of Disseisee after Re-entry—Record of Recovery in Ejectment—Evidence, of what—Several Demises—In whose name, Trespass Brought.*

A lessor in an action of ejectment may bring trespass *quare*, &c., against the defendant or his servants for an injury done to the freehold, intermediate the verdict and *hab. fac. poss.* executed.

After the re-entry of the disseisee, the law supposes the freehold all along to have continued in him; and he may maintain trespass against the disseisor and his servants.

The record of recovery in ejectment is conclusive evidence of title in the lessor of the plaintiff, from the time of the demise laid, against the defendant and his servants; who cannot, therefore, in bar of an action of trespass, show title in another after that time.

Where there are several separate demises in a declaration in ejectment, an action of trespass against the defendant or his servants may be maintained in the name of that lessor upon whose title the recovery was had; and where it appeared that the sheriff delivered possession to one of the several lessors under the *hab. fac. poss.* this was held *prima facie* evidence that the recovery was upon his title.

Citations—11 Co., 51; Hob., 98; 20 Vin. Abr., T, pl. 5, p. 465; 3 Bl. Com., 210; 1 Chit. PL, 177; Cro .Eliz., 540; 3 Cai., 261, 263; 12 Johns., 184; 6 Bac. Abr., Trespass, C, pl. 3, p. 566; Peake Ev., 38; 1 Phil. Ev., 222-3; Runn. Ejec., 439, 441; 2 Burr., 667, 668.

TRESPASS *quare clausum fregit*, tried July 18, 1823, at the Washington Circuit, before Walworth, Circuit Judge. The plaintiff gave in evidence an exemplification of a record of judgment in favor of James Jackson *ex dem.* Thaddeus Dewey and John Goodwin against James Barker, Jr., docketed in this 330*] court, Aug. *10, 1821; and also a writ of possession tested Aug. 10, 1821, returnable on the first day of the then next term of this court; upon which was indorsed the return of the sheriff of the County of Washington, that, by virtue of the writ of possession, he had, Aug. 10, 1821, caused the possession of the premises in the writ of possession mentioned to be delivered to Dewey.

The plaintiff then proved by Henry Thorn, Esq., that he made the service of the declaration in ejectment about four or five years ago upon Barker; that Barker was then in possession of the premises, and had been in possession for several years then next preceding; and that he continued so in possession until the execution of the writ of possession; that the witness was present at the time when the sheriff turned Barker out of possession, and put Dewey in possession.

Jonathan Rice, a witness for the plaintiff, testified that James Barker, Jr., was in possession of about 120 acres of lot No. 24, in the Artillery patent, in the Town of Fort Ann, in June, 1821, and had been for a number of years previous to that time; that there was a small framed house, a small barn and a corn house on that part of the lot so possessed by Barker; that in May or June, 1821, the buildings were moved off the lot on to an adjoining lot owned by James Barker. That the defendant's oxen were there, and helped draw the buildings; did not see the defendant do anything to aid in moving the buildings; thought they were removed on Saturday, and it was before July 1, 1821.

Benjamin Eastman, a witness for the plaintiff, testified that he knew the premises; was present when the buildings were removed; had since heard the defendant say he had assisted in removing them, and expected he should have trouble about it. He did not recollect the words the defendant made use of, but drew this conclusion, that he expected trouble, from the fact that Chester Dewey had forbidden them removing the buildings. James Barker, Jr., was then in possession of the land from which the buildings were removed; and had been, for many years, using it as his own. The house was worth $150 or $200 as it stood, but after prepared for removing, from $50 to $100. *The buildings were drawn into the [*331 adjoining lot owned by old Mr. James Barker, who occupied the land from which the buildings were drawn for twenty or thirty years before James Barker, Jr., went into possession. He succeeded to the possession of his father. The defendant and other neighbors were invited to assist in removing the buildings, and the witness, with the others, attended in consequence of such invitation. He heard some one say that Dewey had recovered the land, but did not hear the defendant say anything about it, and did not know that he knew it. The defendant told him that he came there to assist James Barker, Jr., to remove his buildings, and said he had assisted; that he had a yoke of oxen there, and expected to get into trouble about it, in consequence of the recovery of the plaintiff against James Barker, Jr. That James Barker, Jr., had been in possession for eight years previous to the removal of the buildings, and that the witness saw him remove grain from off the premises after the buildings were removed. That previous to the removal of the buildings, the recovery of the plaintiff against James Barker, Jr., was the subject of conversation among the persons assembled there to assist in the removal. That after the barn and corn house were removed, and before the house was removed, while the company was assembled for the removal of it, Chester Dewey, the son of the plaintiff, came there and said his father had recovered the premises, that they belonged to him, and he had sent him (Chester Dewey) to forbid the removal of the buildings. That the defendant was in a situation to have heard what Chester Dewey said, and it was spoken publicly.

Chester Dewey was also produced as a witness on the part, of the plaintiff, and swore that the action of ejectment against James Barker, Jr., at the suit of the plaintiff, his father, was tried at the Washington Circuit, June 4, 1821, and the buildings were removed from off the premises on Saturday of the next week; and that he, by the direction of his father, the plaintiff, came to the premises at the time they were removing the buildings, and before the house was removed off the premises, and forbid the company from removing *them, [*332 and informed them that his father had recovered the premises, and that they belonged to him.

It appeared in evidence that the premises from which the buildings were removed were the same which had been recovered in the ejectment suit by Dewey the plaintiff, and from which James Barker, Jr., had been turned out of possession by virtue of the writ of possession.

The plaintiff then rested his cause, and the defendant applied for a nonsuit, which was overruled.

The defendant then offered to prove that James Barker, Jr., put the buildings on the premises for his own use, while he was in possession, claiming to hold the land independent of any right derived from the plaintiff; but this testimony was objected to and overruled. The defendant then gave in evidence a deed of the premises in question from Adam Patterson to James Barker, dated Feb. 4, 1796. The defendant then called Abraham Boyce, who testified that James Barker, the elder, went into possession of the premises about the time of the date of the deed, and continued in possession until his son, James Barker, Jr., took possession under him, about eight years since; that the witness never heard Barker say anything about the title of the land until within about fifteen years; since which time he had claimed to be the owner, and witness has heard him say that he had a better title than anybody in this country. The defendant, in bar of the action, then offered to prove that James Barker, Jr., held under James Barker, Sr.; and that the defendant, in what he did, in relation to the removal of the buildings, acted under the direction and at the instance of James Barker, the grantee; but this testimony was objected to by the plaintiff, and the court decided that the defendant had not shown sufficient to found an adverse possession in Barker, and the testimony was overruled. The defendant then introduced several witnesses to show the value of the buildings, and the jury, under the direction of the court, found a verdict for the plaintiff for $55 damages.

333*] **Mr. D. Russell* now moved for a new trial. He said:

1. The record produced should not have been admitted as evidence. This was the only evidence of title; but ejectment is a possessory action, and can give no right against a third person till consummated by possession. The ejectment neither establishes title nor possession. Osborn was not a party nor privy to the suit, and against any other the record cannot be received. (Peake's Ev., 38.) Suppose the verdict had been the other way, could Osborn, the defendant, have set up the record against Dewey, in an action of trespass brought by him? The rights of the parties must be reciprocal. This is the test of admissibility of a record. It must be such as may be used by either party. *Andrews* v. *Herring*, 5 Mass., 210; *Fowler* v. *Collins*, 2 Root, 231; *Turpin, Admr.* v. *Thomas' Representatives*, 2 Hen. & Munf., 139. The record would show neither a right of entry nor of property, even against Barker, who might have brought his cross-action the next moment.

2. Dewey was at most a tenant in common with others, according to his own showing; and could not recover, if at all, beyond a moiety of the damages equal to his interest, which could not have been more than one half.

3. Again; the remedy is misconceived. Trespass *quare clausum fregit* can only be maintained by the person who has the possession in fact at the time the injury complained of was committed. The mere right of possession is not enough; and for an injury to the freehold, Dewey is the last who ought to sue, because the ejectment establishes no more than a possessory right. Even for an injury to the freehold, the tenant alone can have trespass. *Campbell* v. *Arnold*, 1 Johns., 511, 512; 2 Phil. Ev., 133; *Stuyvesant* v. *Tompkins*, 9 Johns., 61; 11 Johns., 569, S. C., in error; *Wickham* v. *Freeman*, 12 Johns., 183; *Douglass* v. *Valentine*, 7 Johns., 273.

4. The decision of the judge was incorrect. The deed from Patterson and the evidence of Boyce established both claim to, and color of title in Barker sufficient to destroy all presumption that the grantee, Barker, Sr., held under Dewey. The possession was clearly adverse. There was *a claim of right; **[*334** and is there a doubt that 20 years having run, the possession would have barred an ejectment? Twenty years possession is a title. *Taylor* v. *Horde, per* Ld. Mansfield, 1 Burr., 119. Here the possession commenced in 1796. Barker then took possession under color of title, and possessed till 1821, which forms a complete presumption of title in him. *Smith* v. *Lorillard*, 10 Johns., 338, 356. Why, then, were we not allowed to show that we did the act complained of by direction of Barker, the elder, who had the right?

5. At any rate, whether the possession was adverse or not, was a question which should have been submitted to the jury.

Mr. A. Van Vechten, contra. We do not controvert any of the legal positions on the part of the defendant. But they do not apply. Here was a recovery in ejectment consummated by a delivery of possession to Dewey; and the question is whether a man who has recovered in ejectment may, between verdict and judgment, be stripped of all the permanent improvements upon the land, through the tenant and the assistance of his neighbors whom he calls in.

It is said the record is not evidence of right. This position takes for granted the main point involved in it, viz.; that the defendant was a stranger; whereas, he was one of the defendant's assistance in the mischief. The agents must abide the recovery against the principal. If the recovery was conclusive against Barker, it is equally so against all who come to aid and assist him.

The recovery in ejectment, consummated by the execution of a writ of *hab. fac. possess.* before this suit was commenced, gave the plaintiff a right of action for intermediate trespasses committed on the premises. This is plainly so as to the defendant in ejectment (1 Ch. Pl., 177; *Richard Lifford's* case, 11 Co. Rep., 51; *Holcomb* v. *Rawlins*, Cro. Eliz., 540; 3 Bl. Com., 210); and whatever is evidence against him is so against the present defendant. He identifies himself with the original defendant. He was a joint trespasser with Barker, and liable either jointly or severally. He came, not to *exercise his own rights, but those of **[*335** Barker. Trespass is usually brought in the name of the lessor for the *mesne* profits, and the plaintiff may go for all the consequences of the original tortious entry; all the wrongful acts which followed. *Goodtitle* v. *North*, Doug., 584. The record, in such a case, is conclusive evidence; and can it be pretended that the assistance of half a dozen servants shall shut out the record as against them? It is always conclusive evidence of title, from the day of the demise laid in the declaration. *Van Alen* v. *Rogers*, 1 Johns., Cas., 281; *Benson* v. *Matsdorf*, 2 Johns., 369.

[WOODWORTH, *J.* I think there can be no doubt that the right to recover against the defendant in ejectment, for all the wrong he has committed, follows the judgment in ejectment; and so of all those concerned as his servants, who come to his assistance after ejectment brought.]

The record is, to be sure, evidence of nothing more than that the right has been litigated and finally decided on; but it is conclusive on the defendant, and all claiming under him. *Blasdale* v. *Babcock*, 1 Johns., 517; *Kip* v. *Brigham*, 7 *Id.*, 168; *Waldo* v. *Long*, *Id.*, 173; *Jackson* v. *Randall*, 11 *Id.*, 405; *Outram* v. *Morewood*, 3 East, 346; *Barney* v. *Dewey*, 13 Johns., 224; *Jackson* v. *Stone*, *Id.*, 447; *Case* v. *Reeve*, 14 *Id.*, 79; Runn. on Eject., 438, 439, 441, 442; *Aslin* v. *Parkin*, 2 Burr., 667. The last of these cases declares that possession is a part of the title; and therefore the recovery cannot be controverted. After the recovery, the lessor is deemed to have all along been in possession. *Goodtitle* v. *Tombs*, 3 Wils., 118. Admitting that judgment gives a mere possessory right, this is sufficient, according to the defendant's argument, who insists that the one having possession should bring the action. And according to Ld. Mansfield, in *Aslin* v. *Parkin*, the record establishes the right to the possession and the possession itself. The rule that the record is evidence only against parties or privies is well established. But when one comes in under the defendant, he is so far privy as to be concluded. Strangers alone are excepted—those who stand entirely independent of the **336***] *party. The record would, doubtless, be reciprocally evidence for or against the plaintiff according to the verdict. Had it been for the defendant, it might have been used in this action to evince a want of right in the plaintiff. He had brought the action, examined and cross examined witnesses and submitted his rights to the jury. The judgment was followed by a writ of possession, executed in favor of Dewey, who still remains in possession. Certainly this record is evidence, and stands conclusive until contradicted by a cross ejectment or recovery.

True, if the demise had been joint from Dewey and Goodwin, this action should have been joint, and only a moiety of the damages could have been recovered. But this was not so; it was several, and the recovery on the demise of Dewey alone.

Possession was delivered to Dewey alone. He is the one in possession and entitled to the possessory action of trespass. The effect of the recovery is to make the defendant a trespasser *ab initio*.

The adverse possession was in Barker, Sr., if in anybody. This cannot be used to aid Barker, Jr.

Mr. Russell, in reply. It is not necessary to deny the main positions of the other side. All the authorities cited as to the effect of the recovery relate to the remedy against the tenant himself, for the *mesne* profits. *Benson* v. *Matsdorf*, 2 Johns., 369, is a fair sample.

We had a right to defend under Barker, Sr., in whom the title, *prima facie*, resided, and who stood entirely independent of the ejectment. The evidence was admissible under the general issue. *Dodd* v. *Kyffin*, 7 T. R., 350; *Argent* v. *Durrant*, 8 *Id.*, 403; 2 Phil. Ev., 138-9. That the younger Barker suffered judgment against the consent of Barker, Sr., does not effect the right of the latter, who was in from 1796; that Barker the younger did not set up Barker, Sr.'s, title does not preclude our doing it here. If he had cut down all the timber upon the lot, could Dewey for that reason maintain trespass against him? No privity is shown between the two Barkers. To bind the defendant, *a privity of estate [***337** should be shown between him and the defendant in ejectment. The suit cannot operate against a mere stranger. *Blasdale* v. *Babcock*, 1 Johns., 517, cited on the other side, went upon privity of interest and notice neither of which is shown here.

Although nominally in favor of James Jackson, the action is, in truth and substance, in behalf of the lessors named; and shall one of these be permitted to recover for the whole? Suppose the present action in favor of Jackson, the nominal plaintiff, as it might be; clearly he could not bring successive actions for each lessor. The remedy cannot be divided in this manner. Could he recover the entire damages in successive actions? This would be still more unjust and absurd. And can this injustice be worked in another form, by bringing the action in the name of the several lessors? The right of Goodwin, upon the record, appears to be equal with Dewey's. The most favorable light in which he can be viewed is as a tenant in common; and the rule is inflexible in that case, that he can recover only according to his moiety. *Austin* v. *Hall*, 13 Johns., 286.

Case v. *De Goes*, 3 Cai., 261, decides that strangers shall not be made liable in trespass by the relation and overreaching of a suit. It is said the defendant was the mere servant of Barker; but there is no foundation for this position in point of fact. We expressly offered to justify under Barker, the elder. That the defendant came to assist young Barker did not preclude his setting up a right in another, which had been consummated by time.

The form of the action is misconceived also. If there be a remedy, it is by an action on the case.

Curia, per SUTHERLAND, *J.* The defendant acted as the servant and under the direction of Barker, in removing the buildings, which constitutes the trespass complained of. It was committed after verdict and before judgment in the ejectment suit, and the action was not brought till after the writ of possession was executed.

The first question which arises is, whether a lessor in ejectment, after he has recovered and been put into possession, *can main- [***338** tain an action of trespass against the defendant, or his servants, for an injury done to the freehold, at this stage of the ejectment suit, and while the defendant continues in possession.

The general proposition, that trespass *quare clausum fregit* can be sustained only by the person who had the actual possession when the injury was committed, cannot be questioned. But it is also true, that in case of disseisin, the disseisee, after he has regained possession by re-entry may maintain trespass against the disseisor and his servants, for acts intermediate the disseisin and re-entry; for, as to them the law, after the re-entry, supposes the freehold to have continued in the disseisee. The proposition is thus laid down and illustrated in *Lifford's* case, 11 Rep., 51: "If one disseises me, and during the disseisin, he cuts down the trees or grass, or the corn growing upon the land, and afterwards I re-enter, I shall have an action of trespass against him *vi et armis*, for the trees, grass, corn, &c.; for, after my regress, the law, as to the disseisor and his servants, supposes the freehold always continued in me." And see *Moore* v. *Hussey*, Hob., 98; 20 Vin. Abr., Trespass, pl. 5, p. 465; 3 Bl. Com., 210; 1 Chit. Pl., 177; *Holcomb* v. *Rawlins*, Cro. Eliz., 540. In the last case it was held, that after re-entry the disseisee could maintain trespass not only against the disseisor, but against his grantee. The only difficulty upon the point, is whether the remedy shall extend to a stranger who comes in by title under the disseisor, or be confined to the disseisor and his servants. That the remedy lies against the latter is unquestionably now the settled law, though otherwise, it seems, as to strangers. *Case* v. *De Goes*, 3 Cai., 261, 263; *Wickham* v. *Freeman*, 12 Johns., 184. The contrary position in 6 Bac. Abr., Trespass *c*, pl. 3, p. 566, that the disseisee of land cannot maintain an action of trespass *quare clausum fregit*, for an injury done thereto betwixt the time of the disseisin and his re-entry," if it be intended of the disseisor as well as strangers, clearly is not law. The action for the *mesne* profits is an action of trespass, and is founded on the principle of possession by relation of the re entry. The damages in that action are **339*]** *not limited to the rent. Extra damages may be given. (Runn. on Eject., 439, and the cases there cited.) Whether the plaintiff's remedy for the *mesne* profits is affected by the bringing of this action, is not now a subject of inquiry. I think this action may be maintained.

The record of the recovery in ejectment was competent evidence against the defendant in this suit. He was the servant of the defendant in the ejectment, and acted by his orders. A judgment is evidence, not only against the party, but also against those claiming or acting under him. (Peake Ev., 38; 1 Phil. Ev., 222-3.)

The evidence of the elder Barker's title was properly rejected. The defendant being the servant of Barker, the defendant in the ejectment, whatever concludes him is conclusive against the present defendant. Now the recovery in ejectment, as between the lessor and the defendant in that suit, was undoubtedly conclusive evidence of the lessor's title, from the time of the demise laid in the declaration. Runn. on Eject., 441; *Aslin* v. *Parkin*, 2 Burr., 667, 668.

I am inclined to think that the evidence of adverse possession in James Barker, Sr., should also have been excluded; but as nothing like an adverse possession was made out, whether it was or was not properly admitted is immateria.

There is nothing in the case to show that the plaintiff was a mere tenant in common, and recovered in the ejectment suit in that character. There was a demise from Goodwin as well as the plaintiff; but this does not appear to have been joint; and the case states that the possession was delivered to Dewey. I think we are to intend that the recovery was on his demise; and he was, therefore, entitled to recover the whole damages.

Motion denied.

Cited in—5 Cow., 264 *note*, 410; 8 Cow., 222; 8 Wend., 592; 6 Hill, 331; 34 N. Y., 365; 36 N. Y., 170; 61 N. Y., 394; 1 Trans. App., 310; 8 Hun, 570; 18 Barb., 497; 1 T. & C., 94; 4 Sand., 487; 44 Ind., 295; 15 Am. Rep., 237 (44 Ind., 290).

---

*THE TRUSTEES OF THE VILLAGE OF NEWBURGH [*340

v.

GALATIAN AND GRISWOLD.

Bond of Indemnity Against Costs and Expenses of Certain Act—Obligor Liable for Costs of Defending Groundless Suit—Also for Costs Incurred by Another and Recovered of Obligee—Notice to Obligor to Defend—Evidence—Covenant for Quiet Enjoyment—Bond of Indemnity, not Given Against Illegal Act, is Void.

A bond to save harmless and indemnify against the costs and expenses of a certain act extends to the costs of defending a groundless suit for the act, in which the obligee succeeded.

The obligors having notice of the suit in which the expenses are incurred, are bound to defend it; and if they do not, the recovery is conclusive against them.

So if the costs are incurred by another, who sues the obligee for them, who gives notice to the obligor to defend; the recovery against the obligee is conclusive against the obligor as to the amount of damages.

The rule that a covenant for quiet enjoyment is not broken until a lawful suit and eviction, is technical, applying to that particular covenant; and does not extend to a bond of indemnity.

A bond of indemnity against an act palpably illegal, is void; otherwise of an act *prima facie* legal and *bona fide*.

Citations—3 Johns., 471; 5 Johns., 120; 8 Johns., 198; 1 Johns., 517; 6 Johns., 158; 7 Johns., 168; 19 Johns., 284.

DEBT on bond in the penalty of $1,000, conditioned that the defendants should pay the plaintiffs all such sums of money as should or might be paid, laid out and expended by the plaintiffs, in repairing and improving a certain street in Newburgh, called First St.; that is to say, that part or section of First St. between Colden St. and Hudson's River, so as to construct and make a safe and convenient passage and way for wagons, carts and carriages, in and along First St. to the road and highway leading to George Gardner's dock, near First St.; and should, moreover, save, defend, keep harmless and indemnified, from time to time and at all times after the date, the Trustees of the Village of Newburgh, for the time being,

NOTE.—*Contract of indemnity against illegal act—When void.* Compare Coventry v. Barton, 17 Johns., 149, *note.*

their agents, workmen and servants, and each and every of them, and also the overseers of streets, roads and highways of the village, and each and every of them, of, from and against all actions, suits, costs, damages and demands whatsoever, for or by reason, or on account thereof. Plea by Galatian: 1. *Non est factum*; 2. Performance; 3. *Non damnificatus.*

To the 2d plea the plaintiffs replied, setting forth the commencement of a suit by one Gardner against the former Trustees, for repairing and improving First St., as mentioned in the bond, in which they expended $770.83 about their defense, which the defendants in this suit, though requested, refused to pay; and that these Trustees having gone out of office, sued their successors for the costs expended, and in October Term, 1821, recovered $859.33, besides costs; that the present plaintiffs expended $83.09 in defending the suit in favor of their predecessors, of which the present defendants had notice, and they were requested to defend it; but though requested to pay, had not paid, &c.

To the 3d plea the replication was substantially the same.

341*] *Rejoinders denying the suits and payments.

The issues were substantially the same as to Griswold.

The cause was tried at the Orange Circuit, July 1, 1823, before Duer, Circuit Judge.

At the trial, the execution of the bond being admitted, the plaintiffs proved the suits and disbursements mentioned in the replication. In the suit brought against the plaintiffs' predecessors, the verdict was for the defendants; and the principal question was, whether the condition of the bond embraced the expense of suits improperly brought for the cause mentioned in the condition, and in which the Trustees succeeded; or whether it was not confined to well founded suits.

Other testimony was given and other questions raised, which will sufficiently appear from the opinion of the court. The documentary and other proof was very voluminous; but it is not material, for the purpose of the questions decided, to state it. Griswold produced and proved his discharge as an insolvent debtor, under the Body Act. The case was argued by,

Mr. T. J. Oakley, for the plaintiffs, and,

Messrs. C. H. and P. Ruggles, for the defendants.

For the plaintiffs, it was argued that the defendants had notice of the suit against them. This was admitted by the course of pleading and the recovery was conclusive. *Blasdale* v. *Babcock*, 1 Johns., 517.

The defense of the first suit was for the benefit of the obligors, who stood in the relation of sureties, and were bound to pay the costs of the defense. Their liability was like that of an indorser on an accommodation note. *Powell* v. *Trustees of Newburgh*, 19 Johns., 284, 287.

For the defendants, it was argued that the bond could not be considered as an indemnity to the Trustees against the wrongful or illegal acts of strangers, or against groundless suits; but must have reference to some claim of right, which might be set up in opposition to the Trustees, against the contemplated repairs; and as they had succeeded, and recovered their *costs, they could not be considered as [*342 having been legally damnified, within the import of the bond. It was likened to a covenant for quiet enjoyment. *Van Slyck* v. *Kimball*, 8 Johns., 198. The words are general. To make them operate as an agreement to indemnify against wrongful suits, they should be expressly and specifically pointed to such a case. *Perry* v. *Edwards*, 1 Str., 400; Vin. Abr., Condition, Z, *a*, pl. 6, and *note* there; *Foster* v. *Mapes*, Cro. Eliz., 212; *Broking* v. *Cham*, Cro. Jac., 425; *Leigh* v. *Gotyer*, *Id.*, 444; *Lloyd* v. *Tompkins*, 1 T. R., 671; *Dudley* v. *Folliot*, 3 T. R., 584.

In *Simpson* v. *Griffin*, 9 Johns., 131, a payee indorser who had been sued and paid the debt with costs, was denied the recovery of those costs against the maker.

In reply, it was said that the case of *Van Slyck* v. *Kimball*, 8 Johns., 198, and *Korts* v. *Carpenter*, 5 Johns., 120, and *Waldron* v. *M'Carty*, 3 *Id.*, 471, the cases on which *Van Slyck* v. *Kimball*, 8 *Id.*, 198, is founded, go upon a technical rule, applicable only to covenants for quiet enjoyment. *Perry* v. *Edwards*, 1 Str., 400, was a covenant for the quiet enjoyment of personal property, and went upon the same technical doctrine with a similar covenant relative to real estate.

That the bond was not void as being to indemnify against an illegal act, *Blackett* v. *Crissop*, 1 Ld. Raym., 278, was cited.

Curia, per WOODWORTH, *J.* The defendants' covenanted to pay all sums of money expended in the improving First St., and to indemnify the plaintiffs from all actions, suits, costs and damages on account thereof. It evidently was the intention of the parties that the plaintiffs should be completely indemnified for all lawful acts in the discharge of their duty. It could not be foreseen that groundless suits would not be commenced against them. They knew that if drawn into litigation in such cases, expenses would necessarily accrue; and therefore, to guard against such a contingency, resorted to this covenant. If the bond is not to be construed in this manner, the indemnity is imperfect. To the plaintiffs *the [*343 injury is the same, whether they are subjected to costs and expenses, by a party having a well founded claim, or by one who has not. In either case they must defend, and in so doing are obliged to incur costs. The only difference would be that, in the first case, they would be subjected to costs and damages, in the latter to costs only. The plaintiffs, as Trustees, may have proceeded with all requisite caution, and discharged their duty in good faith; and yet it might happen that some individual received an injury, in consequence of the improvements made, for which he would be entitled to maintain his action. If the plaintiffs had been guilty of gross negligence, or willfully or maliciously injured the property of others, there would be no remedy on the bond. A stipulation to indemnify for such acts would be against law, and void. The plaintiffs were prosecuted by Gardner, who had no cause of action against them. The suit was instituted with a view to recover damages by reason of the acts of the plaintiffs in making the improvements on First St. That the condition extended to such a case is, to my mind, manifest. It is true that a covenant to indemnify against all demands, dues and damages, is tantamount to a covenant for quiet enjoyment, which goes to the possession and not to the title; and that the latter is broken only by an entry and expulsion from, or some actual disturbance in, the possession, without which no action can be maintained. (3 Johns., 471; 5 Johns., 120; 8 Johns., 198.) These cases were cited on the argument as analagous to the one before us, but they do not apply. Covenants for quiet enjoyment of land, or to indemnify against incumbrances, have been settled by a series of decisions and acted upon. They manifestly imply that the possession of the person indemnified shall be actually disturbed. An eviction must be shown. But in the present case, as well the intention of the parties, derived from the bond, as the expressions used, require a different construction. The indemnity is more extensive. The plaintiffs are to be protected against all costs to which they might be subjected on account of making the improvement. It is neither expressly or by implication put on the ground that a recovery must be had against the 344*] Trustees. If this view *be correct, the inquiry is, whether the plaintiffs have shown enough to enable them to recover.

The issue joined, is substantially, whether the former Trustees were sued by Gardner for making repairs and improvements on First St.; and whether they had paid the cost and expenses by reason of such prosecution. I think the plaintiffs have sufficiently established the affirmative. The suit of Gardner was professedly commenced to recover damages for the acts of the plaintiffs, as Trustees of Newburgh. The first count in his declaration alleges an obstruction of the old road between Water St. and First St.; the second count alleges that the plaintiffs filled up a sluice, and turned the water, by which Gardner was injured. It is true that Gardner abandoned the second count on the trial, but that is no answer to any part of the plaintiffs' demand, for they were bound to come prepared to defend against all the counts—they all had reference to the improvements made; the plaintiffs could not mistake the nature of the claim. Walter Case testified that the sluice was in the center of First St.; when, therefore, Gardner stated in his second count that the *gravamen* was, the stopping up the sluice, they were apprised that it pointed to the repairs made, equally with the first count. Whether Gardner gave any evidence under the second count becomes immaterial. The costs in question are for resisting the claim until it was abandoned. Shutting up the old road was connected with, and formed a part of the improvements. Selah Reeve, a witness, testified that the work was done under his superintendence; that First St. was raised from 2 feet 6 inches, to 3 feet, where it crossed Gardner's old road; and that after the improvement the old road became useless.

It may be observed that the reasonableness of the costs, or whether the suit of Gardner might have been defended at less expense, does not seem to be drawn in question; nor does it appear what were the items constituting the bill of costs. If the defendants on the pleadings and case are liable, the amount is ascertained; it is the sum recovered of the plaintiffs and their costs in making a defense.

*The breach assigned by the plaintiffs is, that the former Trustees incurred costs, in the defense of Gardner's suit, to $770.83; that they prosecuted the plaintiffs to recover the same, and did recover $859.33; that the plaintiffs expended $83.09 in the defense, of which the defendants had notice. The rejoinder is, that Gardner did not prosecute as stated in the replication, that the plaintiffs have not been obliged, nor have they paid such costs. That Gardner commenced such action and failed, is fully shown. The plaintiffs proved that they paid the amount; that they were obliged to do so, is evident by the record of recovery against them. The defendants were requested to defend that suit, and refused or omitted. It is, therefore, conclusive upon them. (1 Johns., 517; 6 Johns., 158; 7 Johns., 168.) They cannot now litigate the question whether the costs claimed by the former Trustees, and recovered against the plaintiffs, were extravagant or not. They might have shown in the former suit what deductions, if any, ought to be made; not having done so, we are not to intend that more was recovered than necessary costs and expenses. [*345

I have considered the facts stated in the case of the former Trustees against the plaintiffs, *Powell* v. *Trustees of Newburgh*, 19 Johns., 284, as evidence in this cause. The stipulation is, that it might be read in evidence as competent proof that the judgment before mentioned was obtained upon the facts therein stated. This is a sufficient admission of those facts, without farther proof.

I am of opinion that the plaintiffs are entitled to judgment; but no execution to be issued against the body of Griswold.

Judgment for the plaintiffs.

Cited in—12 Wend., 311; 24 N. Y., 109; 3 Lans., 275; 6 Barb., 470; 15 Barb., 349; 40 Barb., 241; 26 Ind., 88.

THE PEOPLE
v.
HERKIMER, Gentlemen, one, &c.

Statute—People not Bound by General Words of—Judicial Notice.

The people have succeeded to the rights of the King, the former sovereign of this State. They are not, therefore, bound by general words in a statute restrictive of prerogative, without being expressly named. *E. g.*, the Insolvent Law.

The courts will take judicial notice of public statutes.

Citations—11 Co., 74; Bac. Abr., Prerogative, E, pl. 5; 18 Johns., 229.

ASSUMPSIT. The declaration was, that June 1, 1822, the defendant was indebted to the plaintiffs in $200, *as well as for work, [*346 labor and services, before that time, done and

NOTE.—*People not bound by insolvent law or statute of limitations unless expressly named.* See People v. Rossiter, *ante*, 143, *note*.

performed by the clerks of this court, for the defendant, at his special instance and request, as for divers materials and other necessary things used in and about that work, before that time found and provided by the plaintiffs at the like special instance and request; and being so indebted, &c., promised, &c.

Plea, that after the premises, &c., to wit: Dec. 11, 1818, in the Town of Danube, in the County of Herkimer, the defendant became insolvent, &c., and in conjunction with so many of his creditors, whose just debts amounted in value to at least two thirds of all the moneys owing by him, presented their petition to Nathan Smith, Esq., first judge, &c., praying that the defendant might be discharged, &c., agreeably to the provisions of the Act for Giving Relief in Cases of Insolvency, &c. (going on and setting forth a regular assignment and discharge Mar. 20, 1819, pursuant to that Act); that the promises, &c., were made before that time, &c.

General demurrer and joinder.

Mr. Talcott, Atty-Gen., in support of the demurrer.

The questions are:

1. Is a debt due to the people affected by a discharge under the Insolvent Act?

2. If it is, then is this discharge properly pleaded in bar of the action, without averring that the debt accrued after the passing of the Act?

On the first question: The people are not expressly included in the general provision of the Act, and nothing shall be taken against them by implication. Where the people are not named they are not bound. *People* v. *Gilbert*, 18 Johns., 229. The general rule of the common law is, that Acts made for the advancement of the public good, of religion and justice, bind the King, though not named in them. Of other Acts he may take advantage, if he pleases; but he cannot be devested of any right, power or interest, unless the Statute is made by express words to extend to him. (11 Co., 68; 5 Co., 14; 7 Co., 32.)

This doctrine has been applied to the Bankrupt Law, which contains the words as general as our Insolvent Law; and it is holden **347***] *that the King is not bound by it, and his debt not discharged by it; though an assignment by the commissioners of the bankrupt's property saves it from a subsequent execution on behalf of the King, because it transfers the title from the debtor to another person. *Audley* v. *Halsev*, Sir Wm. Jones, 202; *Rex* v. *Pixley*, Bunh., 202; *Anon.*, 1 Atk., 262; Cooke's Bankrupt Laws, ch. 8, sec. 13.

But even if the discharge does affect the debt of the people, the defendant could not plead it in bar of the action without averring that the promises were made after the passage of the Act.

This court, as well as the Supreme Court of the U. S., have held a discharge no bar to a suit on contracts made before the Act. The time, therefore, is material to support the defendant's plea, and he should have alleged that the promises were made before the enactment of the Statute; instead of which he only avers in the beginning of his plea, that they were made before Dec. 11, 1818; and in the concluding part, that they were made before Mar. 20, 1819. The defendant cannot help himself by referring to the day laid in the declaration; for, in declaring on implied contracts, the time is wholly immaterial; the plaintiff may lay what day he pleases, and the day stated in the declaration can never be insisted on as binding on him. If the defendant wishes to make the time material, it must be done by his plea.

Without averring that the promises were made after the passing of the Act, the discharge can only be pleaded in bar of execution against the person, as in England, under the Insolvent Acts of that country. (*Vide* Precedents, 2 Chit., 430, 431; 2 Ld. Raym., 1262–3; 3 Went., 196–200, 202; Lill. Entries, 108.)

Mr. O. G. Otis, contra. An assignment of all the defendant's property was made in trust for the benefit of all his creditors, of whom the people were a part. It is to be intended that the people took the benefit of the dividend, like every other creditor. The discharge may, therefore, be presumed beneficial to them; and if beneficial, then they are bound, although not named in the Statute. (1 Bl. Com., 264; 11 Rep., 71, 74.)

The court must see, from the date of the Statute giving clerk's fees to the people, compared with the date of the Insolvent Act in *question, that the latter preceded the [***348** promises set forth in the declaration.

Curia, per SAVAGE, *Ch. J.* It is a maxim of the common law, that when an Act of Parliament is made for the public good, the advancement of religion and justice, and to prevent injury and wrong, the King shall be bound by such Act, though not named; but when a Statute is general, and any prerogative right, title or interest would be devested or taken from the King, in such he shall not be bound, unless the Statute is made by express words to extend to him. (11 Co., 74, Bac. Abr. Prerogative, E, pl. 5.) The Acts of Limitation and of Bankruptcy have been held, in England, not to bind the King. And the same doctrine was adopted by this court in *People* v. *Gilbert*, 18 Johns., 229, so far as relates to the Statute of Limitation. The reason of that case applies to the Insolvent Acts, and the same rule must prevail. That the people of the State, being the sovereign, have succeeded to the rights of the King, the former sovereign is also held in the case last cited. This disposes of the demurrer in favor of the plaintiffs. Were it necessary to decide the other question, I should incline to consider the plea sufficient, on the ground that the court are to take notice of all public Acts. They, therefore, know that the law, giving the clerk's fees to the people, was passed at the same session with the Insolvent Act; and the services must, necessarily, have been rendered afterwards.

Judgment for the plaintiffs.

Cited in—3 Hun, 167; 14 Hun, 586; 8 Barb., 194; 5 T. & C., 268; 7 How. Pr., 250; 20 Wall., 263; 9 Bank. Reg., 545.

349*] *BRADLEY v. COVEL.

Tenancy at Will—From Year to Year—Notice to Quit—Holding Over—Implied Agreement as to Rent.

A tenancy at will is held to be a tenancy from year to year, merely for the purpose of a notice to quit.

A shorter notice (*e. g.*, 3 months) will terminate the tenancy; but in such case, where the holding is at a stated rent, the notice turns the tenancy at will into a tenancy from year to year, running from the expiration of the first notice; and imposes the necessity of giving a notice to quit of six months, terminating on a day in the year corresponding with the termination of the first notice, in order to warrant an ejectment; and the holding over upon the tenancy from year to year is at the former rent.

Where a tenant holds over after such notice without any new stipulation, the law implies an agreement that it should be at the former rent.

This case distinguished from Abeel v. Radcliff, 15 Johns., 507.

Citations—7 Johns., 4, 5; 5 T. R., 471, 472; 15 Johns., 505, 507.

ASSUMPSIT, for the use and occupation of a house and lot in Troy, tried before Spencer, late *Ch. J.*, at the Rensselaer Circuit, Dec., 1822.

The facts were these: the defendant's wife went into the house in Sept., 1819, with the plaintiff's consent, to hold it free of rent, without limitation of time, she engaging to pay the ground rent, which was due to one Vanderheyden. To this the defendant assented, and paid the ground rent, which was $6.25 *per annum*, up to May 1, 1822. This he did June 22, 1822. But Oct. 26, 1820, the plaintiff gave notice to the defendant and his wife to quit the premises, within three months from that time; and now, on proof that the premises were in fact worth from $100 to $140 *per annum*, claimed a rent accordingly, for the time subsequent to the expiration of the notice; and to this effect the judge charged the jury, holding the notice to quit to be sufficient. Verdict for the plaintiff, $137. The defendant's counsel excepted to the decision of the judge.

Mr. J. P. Cushman, for the defendant, moved for a new trial. He said the defendant was a tenant from year to year, and entitled to 6 months notice to quit. The defendant's wife possessed more than a year, before the notice to quit was given. Then the rule is plain. A tenant from year to year is entitled to six months' notice, ending at the commencement of the current year. (Woodf. L. & T., 182; Esp. 39.) The moment the second year begins, the tenant has a right to hold to its end. (1 T. R., 163.) Holding for an indefinite period, should be construed a tenancy from year to year (1 Johns., 325–6), which cannot be vacated without a half year's notice. (3 Burr., 1609; **350***] 1 T. R., 159; 3 Wils., 25.) If *a tenant possess as a mere occupant, with the plaintiff's license, he is entitled to notice. (1 Johns., 325.)

At any rate, if the notice terminated the tenancy, the holding over was on the former rent. (5 T. R., 472; 13 Johns., 299; 15 *Id.*, 507.)

If there was no permission, the plaintiff should have brought trespass for the holding over. (2 Bl. Com., 147, 149.) If there was permission, it was according to the former rent; and, in either view, the plaintiff cannot recover.

Mr. E. Wilson, Jr., contra. The defendant was a tenant at will (2 Bl. Com., 146, and authorities there cited; 1 R. L., 78); and the notice to quit was a legal determination of the estate (2 Bl. Com, 146, and authorities there cited; *Phillips* v. *Covert*, 7 Johns., 1, 5); after which the tenant holding over was bound to pay the real annual value of the premises. *Abeel* v. *Radcliff*, 15 Johns, 505. Courts incline to turn tenancies at will into tenancies from year to year, merely for the purpose of a notice to quit, to enable the party to bring an ejectment. For every other purpose, they retain their true character of tenancies at will. *Phillips* v. *Covert*, 7 Johns., 4, per Kent, *Ch. J.*

Curia, per WOODWORTH, *J.* The notice to quit terminated the tenancy at will, and converted it into a tenancy from year to year. A tenancy at will is held to be a tenancy from year to year, merely for the sake of a notice to quit; and the landlord cannot recover possession without giving six months' notice; but this notice is not necessary for any other purpose. *Phillips* v. *Covert*, 7 Johns., 4, 5. The question then is, on what terms shall the defendant be considered as holding, after the tenancy at will ceased. Though he could not be ousted on such a notice, yet he must be considered as holding over; for his interest was at an end. The rule seems to be, in such cases, that where there is no new stipulation, an implication arises of a tacit consent on both sides, that the tenant shall hold from year to year at the former rent. *Doe* v. *Bell*, 5 T. R., 472, per Ld. Kenyon, *Ch. J.*; *Abeel* v. *Radcliff*, 15 Johns., 505. This manner of terminating a tenancy at will is of but little *use; for [***351** it leaves the landlord, as to the rent, in the same situation as before, and imposes the necessity of a six months notice to quit on the day of the year corresponding to that on which the first notice expires. Without this, the landlord would still be unable to sustain an ejectment. *Doe* v. *Bell*, 5 T. R., 471. With this consequence, however, we have nothing to do.

What then, was the former rent? Although the plaintiff was not, in fact, to receive anything, yet the defendant was to pay the ground rent to the landlord paramount, namely: $6.25, this being all that was exacted for lot and building. This was virtually so much rent to be paid to the plaintiff, who owed it to Vanderheyden. I do not perceive on what principle the plaintiff can claim more. The case is not like that of *Abeel* v. *Radcliff*, 15 Johns., 507. There the first rent was for the lot merely. Afterwards buildings were erected; and the court held that the annual value of both land and buildings was the proper measure of damages. Here the rent of $6.25 was for the whole. There must be a new trial, with costs to abide the event.

New trial granted.

Cited in—7 Cow., 751; 8 Cow., 15; 2 Wend., 513; 4 Wend., 328; 13 Wend., 483; 15 Wend., 406; 51 N. Y., 313; 70 N. Y., 186; 7 Hun, 201; 3 Barb., 579; 14 Barb., 257; 32 Barb., 567; 35 Barb., 168; 5 How. Pr., 88; 19 How. Pr., 31; 5 Rob., 261; 40 Ind., 527; 42 Ind., 220; 10 Am. Rep., 326 (49 N. Y., 24); 10 Am. Rep., 612 (51 N. Y., 309); 26 Am. Rep., 571 (70 N. Y., 180).

NOTE.—*Landlord and Tenant—Tenancy from year to year—What constitutes notice to quit.* See Jackson v. Wilsey, 9 Johns., 267, *note.*

HINCKLEY v. EMERSON.

Action, for Killing Dog—What, a Justification.

If one's dog chases or worries cattle, an action lies against him, if he have notice that his dog is in the habit of doing this.
But no one has a right, for this reason, to kill the dog, except he worry sheep, and thus be brought within the Statute, 1 R. L., 169.
To justify killing him, except in the case of sheep, it is necessary to show that he could not otherwise be separated.
When a dog attacks a person, he may be killed as a common nuisance.
And so if he attack, and actually kill domestic animals on the owner's land.

Citations—1 R. L., 169; Cro. Jac., 45; 3 Lev., 28; 1 Saund., 84; 13 Johns., 312; 1 Esp., 203, 487; Cro. Car., 254.

ON *certiorari* to a justice's court. In the court below Emerson declared against Hinckley, in trespass, for killing his (Emerson's) dog; to which Hinckley pleaded the general issue; and justified the killing as necessary to preserve his property.

The plaintiff proved that the defendant shot the dog near the defendant's gate. The wit- 352*] ness swore that he set the *dog on the defendant's hogs; but he did not hurt them. Afterwards the dog attacked the hogs of his own accord. The witness called him off, and took him by the ear to lead him to the plaintiff's shed; when the defendant came with his rifle, the witness let go his hold, and the defendant shot the dog. The witness had several times set him on cattle, when they came under the plaintiff's shed; but was directed by the plaintiff to be careful that he did not injure them. He swore that the dog was worth $10 or $15.

The defendant offered to show, in bar of the action, that the dog had habitually chased and worried the cattle, hogs and geese of the defendant, on his premises, within the plaintiff's knowledge; but the justice decided that the action could not be defeated by such evidence, though the damages might be mitigated. Judgment for the plaintiff.

Mr. W. L. F. Warren, for the plaintiff in error.

Mr. W. Metcalf, contra.

Curia, per WOODWORTH, *J.* If the plaintiff's dog had worried or injured the defendant's cattle on his land, an action would lie, if the plaintiff had previous notice that his dog was in the habit of being thus vicious. But except in the case of worrying or killing sheep, a case provided for by Statute, 1 R. L., 169, I do not know that any one beside the master has a right to kill the dog. It seems to be law that where a dog chases and kills one's domestic animals on his land, he may kill the dog. *Wadhurst* v. *Damme*, Cro. Jac., 45; *Barrington* v. *Turner*, 3 Lev., 28. But if the dog merely chases or bites an animal, in order to justify killing the dog, it is necessary to show that he could not otherwise be separated. *Wright* v. *Ramscott*, 1 Saund., 84. But where a dog is ferocious and attacks persons, he may be killed, being considered a nuisance. *Putnam* v. *Payne*, 13 Johns., 312. The Statute, allowing dogs that attack sheep to be killed, recognizes the common law doctrine as above laid down. And *vide Breck* v. *Copeland*, 1 Esp., *203; *Boulton* v. *Banks*, Cro. Car., 254; [*353 *Kinnion* v. *Davies*, *Id.*, 487. The judgment must be affirmed.

Judgment affirmed.(a)

Cited in—17 Wend., 500; 1 Den., 498; 1 N. Y., 516; 17 Barb., 586; 4 Park., 392; 60 Ill., 214; 11 Kan., 484 (15 Am. Rep., 355); 38 Wis., 389 (20 Am. Rep., 10); 49 Am. Dec., 347.

(a) This cause was decided in October Term, 1824.

GENERAL RULE.

February Term, 1825.

ORDERED, That after the present term of this court, no cause be entered on the calendar of enumerative motions, unless the note of the time when the question arose (a) be filed in the clerk's office of this court, at the place where the court is to be held, before the Tuesday next preceding the term.

(a) *Vide* the 1, 2 and 3 Rules, January Term, 1799.

[END OF FEBRUARY TERM, 1825.]

CASES

ARGUED AND DETERMINED

IN THE

SUPREME COURT

OF THE

STATE OF NEW YORK,

IN

MAY TERM, 1825, IN THE FORTY-NINTH YEAR OF OUR INDEPENDENCE.

M'KEE *v.* NELSON.

Action for Breach of Promise—Evidence.

In an action for a breach of a marriage promise, a witness may be asked his opinion, whether, living with the plaintiff, and from an observance of her deportment, &c., he is of opinion that the plaintiff was sincerely attached to the defendant.

The father of the defendant may be asked, if he did not remonstrate with the defendant against the marriage; but shall not be allowed to specify immoral conduct, as the ground of such remonstrance, unless he personally knows the ground to be true.

Unchastity or immorality in the plaintiff may be given in evidence by the defendant.

After a question has been repeatedly asked and answered without objection, in the course of a trial, it is too late to object to its repetition, on the ground that the answer is in itself inadmissible.

ACTION for breach of promise of marriage. On the trial at the City of N. Y., before Edwards, Circuit Judge, Feb. 9, 1825, the plaintiff proved the progress of the intimacy between the parties, and finally a promise of marriage, and the defendant's refusal to execute it. And in the course of the examination of witnesses, W. J. M'Kee and Margaret M'Kee, witnesses for the plaintiff, expressed their opinions that the plaintiff was, from what they saw, much attached to the defendant. This passed without objection. Thomas M'Kee, also a witness for the plaintiff, expressed the same opinion, without objection.

Afterwards, in the course of the trial, the plaintiff's counsel interrogated Thomas M'Kee, Margaret M'Kee and Robert M'Kee, whether, living in the same house, and constantly associ-
356*] ating *with the plaintiff as a member of the family, and from an attentive observance of the whole deportment during the courtship, and at the time of the defendant's deserting her, it was their opinion or not, that the plaintiff was sincerely attached to the defendant. To this question, the counsel for the defendant objected; but the judge overruled the objection, observing, that whether the plaintiff's affection was sincere or not could only be gathered from an attentive observation of her conduct, and was not susceptible of any other proof than what had been already given, and was then offered by the plaintiff.

To this decision the counsel for the defendant excepted.

The counsel for the defendant proposed to interrogate the father of the defendant, whether he and the defendant's mother did not, after the promise had been made, and before its breach, remonstrate with the defendant against his marrying the plaintiff; and whether they assigned to the defendant any and what reasons why he ought not to marry the plaintiff. To this question the plaintiff's counsel objected. The judge decided that the question might be put, whether the father and mother did not strenuously remonstrate with the defendant against the marriage; but not as to the reasons of the remonstrance; *i. e.*, as to any particular facts stated on which the remonstrance was grounded, which might affect the moral character of the plaintiff, unless the witness had a personal knowledge of the truth of those facts. To this decision the plaintiff's counsel also excepted; and a bill of exceptions, including both points, have been sealed, and a verdict found for the plaintiff,

Mr. D. Graham, for the plaintiff, now moved to bring it to a hearing as frivolous.

Mr. G. Griffin, contra.

Curia. We think the judge's decision founded in good sense, and in the nature of things. We do not see how the various facts upon which an opinion of the plaintiff's attachment must be grounded are capable of specification, so as to leave it, like ordinary facts, as a matter of inference, to the jury. It is true, as a general rule, that witnesses are not allowed *to give their opinions to [*357
a jury; but there are exceptions, and we think this one of them. There are a thousand nameless things, indicating the existence and degree of the tender passion, which language cannot specify. The opinion of witnesses on this subject must be derived from a series of incidents, passing under their observation, which yet they never could detail to a jury. Were there nothing more in the case, therefore, we think there is no ground for the bill.

But we are not left to this ground. The objection came too late. It was certainly waived. The same opinion had been repeatedly expressed, in the same manner, in the course of the trial, by different witnesses, without any sort of objection. Just as the trial is drawing to a close, on these questions being put, the objection is made for the first time. The answer would have been a mere iteration of what had passed without objection, at intervals, during the whole previous course of the trial. At least, under the circumstances, it was altogether immaterial. It could not change the complexion of the case.

The answer of the father as to particular facts was also clearly inadmissible. Want of chastity or immoral conduct may be shown, but it is matter of proof. The effect of allowing the father to answer as to particulars might have been, by a side wind, to get that in which was untrue, resting merely in conjecture; and thus to work a prejudice in the mind of the jury. This cannot be tolerated. A new trial must be denied.

Rule accordingly.

Cited in—1 Wend., 197; 4 Wend., 326; 10 Wend., 340; 17 Wend., 163; 5 Den., 85; 9 N. Y., 187, 388; 17 N. Y., 344; 24 N. Y., 256; 7 Barb., 326; 3 T. & C., 426; 10 How. Pr., 293; 3 Abb. N. C., 234, *note*; 3 Park., 57; 5 Daly, 81; 5 Leg. Obs., 214; 12 Leg. Obs., 49; 35 Ind., 58; 117 Mass., 134; 40 Am. Dec., 487 (12 Ohio, 483); 50 Am. Dec., 333 (6 Ga., 324); 6 Am. Rep., 565 (49 N. H., 399); 22 Am. Rep., 458 (56 N. H., 227).

ANONYMOUS.

Costs — When Non-payment Constitutes Contempt—Costs on Motion.

To bring a party into contempt for non-payment of costs, the rule should be entered expressly directing him to pay costs.

The rule that where a motion is denied, costs follow of course, unless the contrary be expressed, is merely directory to the clerk; and to subject a party to their payment, the clerk should enter the rule for costs.

MR. J. HOOKER, moved for an attachment for the non-payment of costs. He produced a rule by which a motion made by the party against whom he moved was denied, but
358*] the *rule did not say with costs. He relied on *Jackson* v. *Gayer*, 2 Cow., 484, that where a motion is denied, costs follow of course, unless the contrary be expressed.

Curia. That rule is merely directory to the clerk, that unless we express the contrary, he should enter the rule with costs. If this was the fact, you should have seen to it that the rule was entered correctly. It should contain an express order to pay the costs, to bring the party into contempt.

Motion denied.

THE PEOPLE, ex rel. ISRAEL, *v.* TIBBETS ET AL.

Quo Warranto—*Lies Against Person Usurping Office of Corporation—Office Being Annual, no Objection—Powers of a Corporation, to Regulate Qualifications of Voters.*

The remedy by information, in nature of a *quo warranto*, lies against persons who have usurped or intruded in the office of Directors of an Insurance Company, or any other Corporation.

So against persons who intrude into any office or offices created for the government of a Corporation.

So it lies against persons who usurp the right to be a Corporation. To be a Corporation is a franchise.

The court will not deny leave to file an information in nature of a *quo warranto* against persons who unlawfully intrude into offices, on the ground that the offices are merely annual; and that, therefore, it is doubtful whether, according the course of the court, a trial can be had before the office expires; provided the application for leave to file the information be made at the earliest opportunity, after the offense complained of is committed.

The Act incorporating The Franklin Fire Ins. Co., gave a vote for each share of stock; but provided that no share should entitle the holder to vote, unless the stock should have been held by him at least 60 days next and immediately preceding an election; and that the major part of Directors should constitute a Board, and have power to make such by-laws, rules and regulations as to them should appear needful and proper respecting the election, &c., and they passed a by-law requiring a transfer of stock to be registered in order to be effectual. And about a month preceding the annual election, they passed another by-law, reciting that it might happen that stock might be sold within 60 days next immediately preceding an election, but not transferred on the books of the Company at the time of the election; and that the seller, in whose name it might stand, might offer to vote upon it, though he might have no beneficial interest in it; and enacting that such voting would be a violation of the Act of Incorporation; and that it should be the duty of the inspectors of the election, whenever they should or might suspect, that the stock proposed to be voted upon, had been sold or bargained for, or contracted to be sold within the 60 days, but not transferred on the books, to require the person proposing to vote to adduce satisfactory proof to the inspectors, either by his own oath or affirmation taken before some competent officer, or other proof that the stock had not been sold, or the beneficial interest, or any part of it, parted with by any bargain, or contract of sale, within the 60 days; and in default of such proof to reject the vote. Held, that this by-law was void; that the vendor might vote, notwithstanding the transfer within 60 days, the same being unregistered; and it appearing that certain candidates for the office of Director were elected in consequence of this by-law being enforced, the court allowed an information in nature of a *quo warranto* to be filed against them.

A Corporation have no power, by a by-law, to demand an oath of a stockholder in its funds, in order to test his qualifications as a voter.

Citations—1 R. L., 108; 2 Bl. Com., 37; 15 Johns., 386-9; 1 Str., 303; 9 Ann. C., 20; U. S. Law. Journal, 286; 2 Burr., 869; 1 Bl., 187; 2 Johns., 184.

MR. TALCOTT, Atty-Gen., at the last term, moved for leave to file an information in nature of a *quo warranto* *against [*359 Tibbets *et al.*, President and Directors of the Franklin Fire Ins. Co., on affidavits, that Jan. 10, 1825, at Wall St., in the City of N. Y., between 12 at noon and 2 P. M., an election was held for Directers; that there were two sets of candidates; one list being headed by the name of Tibbets, the other by that of Israel; that by the 4th section of the Company's charter, it is provided that the Directors should, at all times, during their continuance in office, be stockholders of the Company in their own right; and that no share should entitle the holders to vote, unless the stock should have been held by him, at least 60 days next immediately preceding an election; and by the 8 section, that the major part of the Directors shall constitute a Board, and have power to make and prescribe such by-laws, rules and

NOTE.—Quo warranto *against corporation—Against officers of.*

An information in the nature of a quo warranto *lies against a corporation for usurping a public franchise.* People v. Utica Ins. Co., 15 Johns., 358, *note*; People v. Manhattan Co., 9 Wend., 351; People v. Mayor of N. Y., 32 Barb., 35; 10 Abb. Pr., 144; 19 How. Pr., 155; Cochran v. McLeary, 22 Iowa, 75; State v. Southern, &c., R. R. Co., 24 Tex., 80; State v. Ramos, 10 La. Ann., 420; State v. Turnpike Co.,

regulations, as to them shall appear needful and proper respecting the election and meeting of Directors, the transfer of shares, the management and conducting of the business of the Corporation, and all matters appertaining thereto; provided that such by-laws, &c., should not be repugnant to the Constitution and laws of this State or of the U. S.; that they had passed a by-law requiring the transfer of stock to be registered, in order to its being effectual; that immediately after 12 at noon, Jan. 10, 1825, the inspectors of the election began to receive proxies for the Tibbets list, which were objected to by Mr. Dey, a counselor at law, in behalf of various stockholders, on the ground that some of them were sealed and some of them not sealed, some with witnesses and some without, and some in the name of executors and administrators, without proof that they were the parties represented, whereas they should have been accompanied with the surrogate's certificate; and he demanded an inspection of them, which was denied, on the ground that the inspectors would judge, and that there was not time for Mr. Dey to inspect them; and he particularly objected that no one had authority to vote on the stock of Enos Collins, of Halifax; but the ballot for this and various other stock, represented by proxy, were put into the box without allowing Mr. Dey a chance to examine the authority upon which they were received, and
360*] *upon the ground that the inspectors were satisfied. Various other objections in the course of the election were made by Mr. Dey to votes by proxy; but in no instance was he allowed to examine the authority upon which they were given, nor were any of his objections allowed.

That previous to the election, a small book had been made out and furnished to the inspectors, containing the amount of stock and names of those who held it, entitled to vote, and also other stock and the names of those who held in not entitled to vote, which they made their guide in the receipt of ballots; that on one Wells offering to vote for the Israel list on three proxies, representing 480 shares, they refused his ballots on the authority of this book, saying that a part, at least, of the stock he represented had been sold by the persons in whose names he appeared. He denied this, and Mr. Dey demanded the stock ledger to test the fact, declining to receive the small book as evidence; that the inspectors, however, declared themselves bound by this book, saying they had not the control of the stock ledger, and that Mr. Dey was not a stockholder; and in answer to several demands made of the ledger for the same purpose by stockholders, the inspectors said they should not have it; and no books of the Company were produced to show how the stock offered to be voted upon stood.

That on Mr. Wells reiterating his demand to vote, the copy of a by-law of the Company was produced and exhibited to Mr. Dey, passed Dec. 13, 1824, in these words: "Whereas, in and by the Act to incorporate this Company, it is provided that the Directors shall be elected by the votes of the stockholders or their proxies, but that no share shall entitle the holder to vote at an election of Directors, unless the same shall have been held by him at least 60 days next immediately preceding such election; and whereas it may happen that stock may be sold within 60 days next immediately preceding an election, but not transferred on the books of this Company, at the time of such election, and that the seller, in whose name it may have stood, may offer to vote on such stock, either by himself or by his proxy, although he may have no beneficial interest therein at the time either *of such election or of executing [*361
such proxy; it is, therefore, hereby declared, that to allow stock so circumstanced to be voted on, either by the person in whose name it has so stood, or by his proxy, is a violation of the spirit and contrary to the true intent and meaning of the said Act of Incorporation; and that it appearing needful and proper to pass a by-law prohibiting all such voting, in order to provide an adequate remedy in the premises, be it, therefore, enacted, and it shall be and hereby is made the duty of the inspectors, at any election of Directors, whenever they shall or may suspect that any of the stock, on which any of the vote or votes may be offered, has been sold or bargained for, or contracted to be sold within the 60 days next immediately preceding such election, but which shall not have been transferred on the books of this Company, to require the person offering such vote or votes, to adduce satisfactory proof to the said inspectors, either by his own oath or affirmation taken before some competent officer, or other proof, that such stock has not been sold, or the beneficial interests therein, or any part of such interest parted with by any bargain, or contract of sale, within the 60 days next preceding such election. And that, unless such proof be adduced, no such vote or votes shall be received or allowed by the said inspectors."

That Mr. Dey objected that this by-law had no force, because it was passed within 30 days previous to the election; that no notice of it had been published; that it was fraudulent and void, and the stockholders not bound by it; that the inspectors admitted no notice had been given of the law; that on the ground of this by-law, and the small book, they refused the votes of Wells; that the same ground was taken against several other proxies; that upon being questioned, repeatedly, at different times during the election, whether the inspectors insisted the party objected against should swear, the inspectors replied they asked no man to swear: he might swear or not just as he pleased; they were bound by the by-law, and if he (the voter) would furnish the proof, they would look at it; that it was not till about half past

---

21 N. J. L., 9; Commonwealth v. Delaware, &c., Co., 43 Pa. St., 295.

An information lies against a corporation for a mis-user or non-user of corporate franchises. People v. Manhattan Co., 9 Wend., 351; People v. Geneva College, 5 Wend., 211; People v. Kingston and Middletown Turnp. Road Co., 23 Wend., 193; People v. Bristol and Rensselaerville Turup. Road, 23 Wend., 222; Commonwealth v. Commercial Bank, 28 Pa. St., 383; State v. Paterson, &c., Turup. Co., 21 N. J. L., 9; State v. Real Estate Bank, 5 Ark., 595; Commonwealth v. James River Co., Va. Cas., 190; High Ext. Legal Rem., secs. 647-677.

For the use of this remedy against the usurper of a public office, see People v. Van Slyck, *ante*, p. 297, *note*.

one P. M. that Mr. Dey was enabled to obtain **362***] *a copy of the by-law; after which several votes made affidavits on which their votes were received; and some were refused, because the affidavit did not exactly conform to the by-law. A proxy on 50 shares given by the executors of J. T. Glover, deceased, being objected to, S. Glover, one of the executors, made affidavit that the executors, "are at present the *bona fide* owners of 50 shares of the capital stock, &c., and that they have been such owners as aforesaid for a period of more than 60 days prior to this date;" that the inspectors determined not to receive the vote, because the affidavit did not conform to the by-law: soon after declared that it was 2 o'clock, and the vote was finally rejected. That upwards of 800 other shares were denied votes on the same ground; that a considerable number of shares were allowed votes by the inspectors, without any proof under the by-law, though stockholders friendly to the Israel list objected that such stock had been sold.

That the Tibbets list finally prevailed and was elected by a majority of only 186 votes over the Israel list; and that this success was owing to the rigid adherence to the by-law on the part of the inspectors; that most of the Directors thus elected had also been Directors during the preceding year.

Several affidavits were read against the motion, showing that, shortly previous to the passage of the by-law, it was known that sundry persons were making collusive purchases of stock at a very high price, within 60 days previous to the election, for the avowed purpose of effecting a change in direction of the Company; stipulating in their contracts that the stock should not be transferred till after the election, because the transfer would disqualify the stock to be voted on; that to prevent such a consequence, the by-law was passed, under the advice of eminent counsel, including the late *Chancellor* Kent; that the list of stock entitled to vote, or disqualified under the by-law, was made out by the Secretary of the Company by which the inspectors were guided; that the inspectors believed the list to be correct in every particular; that several shares, suspected by the Directors to have been the subject of a collusive contract of sale, had, since the election, been actually transferred on **363***] the books; *that it was the invariable custom in conducting the election of chartered companies, in the City of N. Y., to furnish the inspectors with a list of the stock qualified and not qualified to vote; that this very much facilitates the business of the election; that in this instance it was not furnished, for the purpose of controlling the decision of the inspectors; but as containing information confidently belived to be correct, and to put them on inquiry as to the qualifications of the various persons who might offer to vote, either in person or by their proxies; that such lists were generally considered *prima facie* but not conelusive evidence; and the list, in this instance, was so treated; that no undue partiality was exhibited by the inspectors in favor of the Tibbets list, but that the election was fairly conducted, according to the by-law; that the proxies objected to by Mr. Dey were correct, &c.; that in several instances, the contracts of sale aimed at by the by-law were accompanied with the agreement that the purchaser should vote on the stock sold by proxy.

The cause was argued at the last term.

The affidavits for and against the motion having been read,

Mr. S. Jones opened the argument for the motion. He said that *prima facie*, every share in the Company was entitled to one vote, and unless this right was repelled by clear evidence; unless there was a defect either in ownership or the appointment of proxies, or some misconduct amounting to a disqualification, the votes for the Israel ticket should have been received. The defeat of this ticket was mainly effected by by the magic operation of the by-law. The inspectors properly established for their government the rule to be found in the charter of the Company, that the stock of the individual offering to vote must have been held by him during 60 days, next and immediately preceding the election; but they then came to the question, what is to be deemed a holding. They answered that the voter must have the stock, not only in his name, but the entire right must be vested in him during that time; not even contracted to be sold; that one may have both the legal and nominal interest, and yet *be without the right to vote. This [***364** we deny. The book of stockholders or of transfer was the proper evidence. Who is the literal holder? Is it not the man in whose name the stock stands? The language of the charter is, that each share held by the voter 60 days, &c., may be voted upon by him. It is admitted that the stock had stood in the names of the persons rejected. They stood on the books; they had been stockholders beyond all doubt, and there was no evidence that they had transferred their stock, except the *ex parte*, unofficial list, constantly resorted to by the inspectors. Did the Legislature mean to disqualify one, because he had made some contract about his stock within the 60 days? The Act may be satisfied short of this. Its object was to prevent any change of voters within that time. It meant that though one sold his stock within the 60 days, yet he might still vote upon it. The Act did not mean that it should be wholly unrepresented. Till transferred upon the books, the legal title continued in the former holder. The Act does not require that the voter should hold the stock in his own right. There is a clause in the same section requiring, for the purpose of being a Director, a holding in one's own right, showing that the Legislature understood the distinction between trustees and *cestuis que trust*, and spoke accordingly. Holder, here, stands simply and alone. Shall we be told that though a stockholder could not transfer his right to a third person, yet he lost it himself? Why should it have this effect any more than the mere pledge of stock for a loan? On what is the right to vote founded? Upon stock. If my vendee allows me to retain the stock in my name, I am his trustee, and vote under his direction. Shall my *cestui que trust* be deprived of his votes? I may remain such trustee for years, or months, or a shorter time. The Act contemplates this case, and attaches no other disability than ineligibility to the office of director. The inspectors admitted the votes of executors and administrators, who are mere trustees, yet they never thought of inquiring whether the holder died within the 60 days.

Every stockholder may vote by proxy. One, by leaving his shares standing in the name of **365***] the vendor, constitutes *him, *ipso facto*, his proxy. Suppose a treaty, or understanding, by which A is to become a purchaser 6 months after the next election, upon the faith of which the vendor gives a proxy to the contemplated vendee so as to comply with the form of the Act; would not this be good? It is the same thing if, on a sale *in presenti*, the parties agree that the stock shall remain in the name of the vendor with the view that he shall vote at the election. The voting is a part of the consideration. The vendor asks less for the stock, perhaps, by reason that he retains the right to vote. Suppose it is a transfer of one third of the vendor's interest in the stock, must he lose his entire vote? No. If every one of these shares, the right to vote upon which was questioned and overruled, had been absolutely sold but suffered to stand in the name of the respective vendors, they would still have had a right to vote, unless plain fraud against the vendee was made out.

No one would have a right to object against the vote, except the vendee, by reason of duress or fraud. The President or Directors cannot do it, for the sake of holding their offices. The objection must come from some one who can compel the change of the vote. A court of equity would enforce the reservation by the vendor of a right to vote. The plain intent of the Legislature was that the Directors should be chosen by the stock. This is the cardinal object to be followed; nor should a single share be excluded upon mere presumption. This should not be admitted unless upon a plain rule laid down by the Act, from which there is no escape. To make this Act operate as a prohibition, there must be a plain, full and actual transfer apparent upon the books.

If the Statute has not sanctioned the disqualification contended for, it cannot be created by a by-law. Such a by-law is in restraint of right, and the Corporation must show that it accords with the express powers given to the Company. The power to make by-laws is conferred by the 8th section, which, to be sure, mentions the transfer of stock as one subject; but it is left to other parts of the law to deter- **366***] mine *who is a holder. The Company cannot determine this, therefore, the law settles it.

Mr. Wells' case is a complete illustration of the doctrine contended for against us. On his offering to vote, the inspectors turned to a book and told him he had sold out. This being denied and the stock standing in the proper names the inspectors had no right to reject the votes. At all events, they were bound to produce proof of the transfer. They showed no document establishing the pretended transfer. Not a particle of proof was offered, and nothing is now shown to make it out. It was necessary to show affirmatively that the stock had been sold. Instead of this, they called on Wells under the by-law, to prove negatively that it had not been sold. They never told Wells what evidence they had. The stock book was out of the way; and all they pretended to produce was the list furnished by the secretary. If an abstract is evidence, the original book should be accessible, that its truth may be seen by all. If he had sold he might have repurchased. The denial of Wells was as good as the assertion of the inspectors. The vendee might have become insolvent before the transfer was complete, in which case it might have been revoked. Till the consideration is paid, there is no change of the property.

The authority to pass by-laws regulating elections extends merely to the due ordering of the election in point of form; not the qualifications of the voters. The Corporation can neither superadd to nor detract, from their rights. Besides, if the right to vote could be affected by the by-law, it passed too late, only about 30 days before the election. One half of the stock of the Company might have been sold during the preceding 30 days, the right to vote upon which must be referred to the charter; yet the by-law is made to operate without regard to time, to affect previously vested rights. Accordingly, it assumes a declaratory language. It does not enact simply, but declares, that certain transfers are not contrary to the letter, but the spirit of the charter. The mere suspicion of the inspectors was made a sufficient objection; *and they, accord- [***367** ingly, may suspect every one who comes to vote against them.

They put down in a list all whom the Directors told them to suspect. The appearance of the name upon the list of suspected persons is deemed sufficient, until the suspicion is removed by an affidavit made before some person having competent authority to administer an oath. This was intended to meet every case of a partial or total, conditional or absolute transfer. The oath required is voluntary and extrajudicial. The by-law could not be complied with, for no one has authority to administer a voluntary oath.

Besides being retroactive, the by-law was kept secret. It was exhibited for the first time during the hours of the election. It was fraudulent. Had it been known to the voters, they might have rescinded the disqualifying contracts; and they doubtless would have done so indignantly, even at a sacrifice of half their interest.

The Corporation had no right to require an oath by a by-law or in any other form. (2 Kyd on Corp., 112.) They have no greater power than an individual.

The negative could not be reached by legal proof, whereas the affirmative was susceptible of proof, and the burden of showing the transfer lay with the inspectors from the nature of the issue. In the case of *People* v. *Kip* 1 U. S. Law Jour., 236, which will be found in point for the present application, this court decided that a by-law less arbitrary than the present, but directed to the same object, was void.

Mr. J. V. Henry said the validity of the election certainly depended upon the by-law. If that is void, the election cannot be sustained. We agree that this depends upon the question, who are to be considered stockholders for the purpose of voting, within the true intent and meaning of the charter; and we deny that where there is a full and perfect transfer, the vender can vote though the assignment be not entered upon the books.

An entry in the books is not necessary for the purposes of a transfer. The voter should have not merely a nominal but a beneficial in-
368*] terest. This is *the meaning of the charter. The holder for 60 days before the election must be the beneficial holder during that time; and neither the assignee nor assignor, within that period, have the right to vote. The vendees knew, or which is the same thing, were bound to know all this when they purchased. The Act did not intend to tolerate a course of stock jobbing just before the election, and the case under consideration is a complete illustration of the evil. This court in *Bank of Utica* v. *Smalley*, 2 Cow. 770, decided that an assignment of bank stock was complete as between the parties to it, though the charter expressly provided that the transfer should first be entered in the bank books. They declare that this was necessary only in reference to the rights of the bank; that the property vested in the assignee absolutely, as it respected the vendor, without any entry.

If we are correct in saying that the charter of this Company intended to exclude all persons from voting unless they are beneficial holders what then, we ask, is there which is improper about this by-law? It is good within the authority conferred by the 8th section. Where a transfer is absolute, the vendee may insist on a conveyance presently. The control of the vendor is virtually gone. It is conceded that the vendee who buys within the 60 days cannot vote, and upon what principle shall this be allowed to the vendor who has parted with his interest and has no further concern in the affairs of the Company?

The Company had power to pass the by-law in question. Bac. Abr., By-Laws, A *Rex* v. *Spencer*, 3 Burr., 1838, per Wilmot, *J.* True, a corporation cannot pass a by-law requiring an oath as to the due observance of statutes. (Bac. Abr., By-laws, E, Am. ed. of 1813.) The passage cited from 2 Kyd, 112, relates merely to the admission of a member. Not a word is quoted denying the power to impose an oath touching the rights of property. The by-law in question relates merely to the beneficial ownership. The case of *People* v. *Kip*, cited from the Law Journal, does not apply. The language of the charter under which the Company there acted, differs from the one now
369*] under *consideration in respect to the qualifications of voters. It declared expressly that the one in whose name the stock stood for a certain time before the election, should be entitled to the vote. The charter disregarded the beneficial ownership. In this case the word is held; and we have shown it not enough that the voter is the mere nominal holder. Here the beneficial, there the mere nominal holding, was looked to. The test is different. The by-law rightfully contemplates either a partial or total alienation of the stock, and on suspicion of this, it puts the voter to his oath. Upon what ground can such a law be censured as inquisitorial? It admonishes the voter, if he is owner, to say so on oath before some one competent to administer it. If he is not owner, to remain silent. It establishes the only test by which the truth can be known, in a way sufficiently summary for the purposes of an election. This by-law subjects the party to no forfeiture or penalty. It deprives him of no right. It is no more than what a court of equity would require upon a bill filed by one of the parties. Yet no one ever dreamed of the proceeding being inquisitorial when exercised by that court, where the most important rights are every day determined by an appeal to the party's own oath. The transfer is a matter of confidence and secrecy between the vendor and véndee. No evidence is within the power of the inspectors. The by-law does not stop with the oath of the party. He may introduce other proof. This is spoken of as being impossible; not so. Suppose the sale conditional on its face; let him prove this, and it negates an absolute sa e.

If this provision be void, it does not vitiate other independent provisions of the by-law. It may be rejected as surplusage, and the good parts of the by-law be allowed to stand without it. The transfer of a part of the stock operates as a disqualification *pro tanto*, but if the by-law be void so far as it relates to a partial transfer, it may be good as to a total one and the rest be rejected as surplusage.

If the by-law be in conformity to the spirit of the charter, it would still have been idle, if without the provision for proof by the oath of the party. This must, from the nature of *the proceeding, be called for, and [***370**
suspicion must be made a ground for the call. It is pointed at secret transfers. If there be full, open, perfect knowledge of the transfer, absolute proof is easily accessible, or no proof at all might be necessary. If the Legislature intended to permit these speculations in stock, within 60 days preceding the election, then the by-law is void, otherwise it is good. If good, there was a discretion incident to the power of passing it, as to all the legal means by which it should be carried into effect, and no choice was left with the Directors, whether they would enforce it or not. The legislative power resided in other hands. The law was not clandestinely passed. All the stockholders might have had access to the books of the Company, and have seen and examined it.

In *People* v. *Kipp* the by-law contemplated an oath to be administered by the inspectors themselves. Here competent authority is required. We ask, if a voluntary oath before competent authority is criminal, or inadmissible, what becomes of notarial oaths, and the thousands of oaths which are administered to test, or to settle private rights, in a course of dealing among a commercial community?

The granting leave to file an information is matter of sound discretion. Bac. Abr., Informations, D; *Rex* v. *Grosvenor*, 2 Str., 1196; *Rex* v. *Marsden*, 3 Burr., 1812, 1816, per Ld. Mansfield, *Ch. J.*

Where a corporation is private in its end, no information will be filed to determine the right of its officers. *Ib.* The subject-matter should be such as concerns the public. This is evident from the nature of the proceeding. There is not only judgment of ouster, but a fine for the misdemeanor.

The charter, or franchise itself, is a different thing from the officers under it. It concerns the public that no franchise should be usurped;

but where a franchise confessedly exists, the objects of which are merely private, the courts should treat the question of office arising in the company as equally private. It is like the mere question of appointing an agent by any individual. It is only when an office concerning the public is usurped, that the court should interfere. Our Statute, on which this applica-
371*] tion is grounded *(1 R. L., 108, sec. 4), is nearly a transcript from that of 9 Anne, which has uniformly been confined in construction to a usurpation upon the public. In a matter of mere private right, the party should be left to his action on the case, if he is wrongfully deprived of his corporate office. When our Statutes are transcripts of the English Statutes, the construction of both is the same. *Taylor* v. *Delancy*, per *Curiam*, 2 Cai. Cas., 151; case of *Yates*, per Kent, *Ch. J.*, 4 Johns., 359. And this, though there may be a slight difference of phraseology between the two. Here is nothing relating to police or magistracy; nor does it come within the principle of *People* v. *Utica Ins. Co.*, 15 Johns., 386 to 389. There was an usurpation of banking powers, a franchise affecting the public. It did not relate to the mere officers of the Corporation. But there is a difference even between the officers of a bank, which relates to the currency of the country, and a mere private corporation, like an insurance company.

Mr. A. Van Vechten, same side. The Statute requires that a motion for leave should precede the filing of the information. The reason is, that the court may see whether a proper case for an information is made out. Every prosecution of this kind is brought forward with a double aspect. It looks both to an ouster from the franchise or office, and a fine for the misdemeanor; but are these objects applicable to the violation of a mere private office—a matter resting between individuals? The variance of our Statute from the English, consists merely in the introduction of the words "office" and "franchise," generally into our Statute, which, as used there, relates to the exercise of a public right, and not a corporation concerning a private object. In the latter case, the law always puts the party aggrieved to his action on the case. Hence the distinction. It runs through the law. Public rights are vindicated by an information, or other criminal proceeding, at the suit of the people; private right, by action, at the suit of the person injured. It is a *non sequitur* that a franchise for a mere private purpose wants this extraordinary protection by information, because it is a
372*] franchise. *Take the case of religious corporations, summarily created under the general Statute—does an information lie? This never was pretended. Indeed it was denied in *Rex* v. *Dawbeny*, 2 Str., 1196, on the ground that the incorporation is private, and the right should be settled by action; and the same thing was held in *Rex* v. *Marsden*, 3 Burr., 1812, 1818. In *People* v. *Utica Ins. Co.*, 15 Johns., 386, and in *Same* v. *Kip*, 1 U. S. Law Jour., 286, it is true that an information was held to lie; but the first related to a franchise, and the last to offices which affected the pecuniary concerns of the community.

Again; where the remedy must be ineffectual, the court will not interfere, even in relation to a public officer. This was held in *People* v. *Sweeting*, 2 Johns., 184, of one who had intruded into the office of town supervisor.

[WOODWORTH, *J.* In that case, there were but about three months of the year for which the officer was elected, remaining at the time of the motion.]

The offices in question here are annual; and nearly two months of the year have gone. All experience denies the possibility of trying this right within the time for which the Directors are chosen. The court will not grant the information where the proceedings must be so palpably nugatory. 3 Bac. Abr., Informations, D; *Rex* v. *Williams*, 1 Burr., 402, 407.

It is said the power given in the charter for the Company to regulate elections, regards merely the form of proceeding. Gentlemen mean, I suppose, the manner of voting, whether by ballot or otherwise, and the creation of inspectors, &c. But it will not be denied that the Directors are so to regulate the election as to effectuate the intention of the Legislature. It is a general rule, in relation to these matters, that the electors and elected should possess the same qualifications. The Directors are required to hold in their own right; and the general rule must be left to its operation, unless it be plain that the Legislature have created a *distinction by ex- [***373**
pressly conferring a right to vote upon the nominal holder. The court will not infer such an absurd intention. The nominal holder is under no tie of interest to the Company. He may wantonly and capriciously vote against the interest of his *cestui que trust*. One object of the Statute, in requiring the holding for 60 days previous to the election, was to prevent the election bring wrested from the old stockholders, who were presumed better acquainted with the concerns of the Company, by surprise. Are voters obtained here, by contract, on the spur of the occasion, as that kind of men who should control corporate elections? Though the transfer be private, if a dividend is claimed by the transferee, it cannot be withheld. The entry upon the books does not affect the rights of the vendor and vendee, as between each other. The power to make by-laws must, from its nature be as extensive as the objects to be effected by the Corporation. It is incidental to every corporation and need not be expressed in the grant. By requiring the voters to hold for sixty days previous to the election, the charter intended to disqualify all others, and the by-law in question accords with the spirit of the charter, in as much as it is calculated to prevent the imposition of fraudulent voters. The second volume of Kyd on Corporations (112) is cited against the power to administer an oath; but the oath there treated of was one imposed upon admission into the Company; an oath not sanctioned by the charter in express terms, nor necessary to its end. All oaths are not forbidden. The case of *Rex* v. *Decan' et Capitul' Dublin*, 1 Str., 539, per Eyre, *J.*, and *City of London* v. *Vanacker*, 1 Ld. Raym., 496 to 500; S. C., 1 Salk., 142, sanction the power to impose a voluntary oath, through a by-law of the Company, where it is proper for the purposes of the institution. The distinction is, that the Corporation have no right to create the officer by whom the oath

is to be administered. It must, from its nature, be voluntary. There is no power to compel its administration. But it must be taken before some person competent by law to administer oaths. The cases upon which we rely, and the **374***] case of *People* v. **Kip*, 1 U. S. Law Jour., 286, are reconcilable upon his distinction. The by-law in the latter case required the voters to submit to the inspectors as to the sufficiency of the oath.

It is said here was no absolute sale—not bargains for stock, but bargains for votes. Be it so. This we say was a fraud, and properly met through the by-law. Nor can it make any difference that the oath was negative. It is good, according to the case cited from Ld. Raymond, 496, though it contain a negative, provided it conform to the spirit of the charter. And if there be anything in the by-law, which does not so conform, *quoad hoc*, the court will disregard and reject it. The stock books are an uncertain and delusive test; for it is conceded that the person in whose name the stock stands may have no kind of interest; and there certainly can be no greater fraud than his voting for Directors under such circumstances. The certificates of stock are better. Upon these, some indorsement must appear showing a transfer, if any such in fact exist. But the oath of the elector is still more satisfactory, and is the test usually resorted to at all our elections.

It is said that denying a trustee all right to vote would effect the rights of executors and administrators. To this we answer, there is no danger of fraud in such cases. The holder comes in by act and operation of law. The Act was intended to defeat voluntary sales, and absolutely prevent their being used for the purposes of fraud. The distinction between the two cases is strong and palpable.

This question is not, as supposed, one between the vendor and vendee of the stock. The sales, though they may be valid as to them, may yet be void as to the Company, who have an interest in the votes to be given.

The Atty-Gen., in reply, said he was surprised to hear the objection that this court have no right to interfere. It is said this proceeding is only applicable to the usurpation of a franchise belonging to the people, or intrusion into some public office; that it comes with a double object; that it is mixed of a civil and criminal character, seeking not only an ouster **375***] *of the offices but a fine for the intrusion. But this is not necessarily so. There is a variety of different franchises which form the subject of an information in nature of a *quo warranto*, as to some of which judgment of seizure may be given and some not. The latter class is where the people cannot exercise the franchise in question. The present is not a case of seizure. We need not contest the proposition, in terms, that an information will not lie where it goes to a mere private right. It may be true, with the qualifications allowed by the gentlemen. In some of the authorities cited, church-wardens are mentioned as not subject to this proceeding; but they are, in truth, canonical officers; their election is in virtue of a canon of the English church. The instance of incorporations, in this country, to promote religious objects was unfortunate; for it has been expressly adjudged that an information lies against the officers of such an incorporation, who may be ousted, and a fine imposed. *Commonwealth* v. *Woelper*, 3 Serg. & R., 29. The imposition of a fine in such a case implies that these are to be considered public officers. *Rex* v. *Marsden*, 3 Burr., 1812, was a case of conflicting markets; but the application was not denied upon the point of private right. The question is barely mentioned, but the court forbear to intimate any opinion. It is sufficient, however, to say that these cases of gentlemen upon private right do not apply, because the question here is not of that character. The usurpation and injury are to be public, as in *Latham's* case, 3 Burr., 1485. No remedy could be had by any individual of this Company, as such. Against whom could an action be brought? Not against the inspectors, unless they acted maliciously. Against the Directors for passing a void law? They, too, deny all malice, which takes away our remedy as to them. But suppose an action lies for the mistake, what would it avail the plaintiff? Could damages be given? And what is to be their measure? Who can estimate the amount? Nothing short of the general superintending power of the court will reach the evil.

But whatever may be the rule upon the British Act, there can be no dispute upon our own. When the English cases *say [***376** that the information must relate to a public matter, they evidently go on the narrow words of the Statute of Anne. Our Act is more comprehensive. It extended this remedy to an intrusion into, or a usurpation of any office or franchise.

Is not the conduct of corporations, however, a matter of public concern? Is it correct, in terms, to say the officers of a corporation are mere private agents? But if private, the information may be granted if there be circumstances of a public nature connected with their duties. What is a corporation? It is the creature of a Statute; it is derivable from the people only. One incident is the power to make by-laws. In this case the Directors are invested with that power. It is a part of the corporate franchise to be governed by laws made in a particular manner. The body of the corporation have a right to insist that these laws shall be properly made. This right of making laws is a branch of the highest prerogative which the people themselves possess. I had supposed this question at rest by the case of *People* v. *Kip*, cited from the Law Journal.

[WOODWORTH, *J.* The question was not made by the counsel; but the court entertained no doubt of their right to interfere in that case.]

The right was not questioned at any stage of that controversy; but a plea was put in, and an issue taken. That case is spoken of as involving a higher degree of importance; because it related to a bank, which is connected with the pecuniary concerns of the community. But can that consideration constitute a distinction to affect this case? Will the court adopt, as a practical ground of action, the extent of the influence which a corporation may have upon the community. In *Commonwealth* v. *Union F. & M. Ins. Co.*, 5 Mass., 230, the information was for the purpose of dissolving the charter. It was brought forward by a relator, to whose capacity an objection was made; in answer to which, the court said: "Informations of this nature are properly grantable for the purpose of inquiring into the 377*] election or admission of an officer *or member of a Corporation, when moved for by any person interested in, or injured by, such election or admission, if the same was unduly made. And upon such information, if the election or admission was illegal, judgment of a motion might be entered, and a fine might also be imposed on the party who had usurped upon the Commonwealth;" thus laying down a doctrine repeatedly recognized and well understood by the books.

If the question in *People* v. *Sweeting*, 2 Johns., 184, were new, I should certainly submit whether, late as that application was made, the information might not have properly been allowed, for the purposes of a fine. *Rex* v. *Williams*, 1 Burr., 407–8, sanctions an information for one single act of usurpation; and it will be seen by 2 Hawk., P. C., ch. 26, sec. 14, that the Statute of Anne was passed with reference to annual offices. This is the reason, says the book, why that Statute hastened the issue, by requiring the defendant to plead as of the same term when the information is filed. But the extent of the delay is, in this case, a mere matter of speculation; and it is enough that the relator is willing to take the risk of it upon himself.

Then, as to the main question. We say the object of this provision for a 60 day holding related merely to the form or shape in which the stock should be represented. It was to prevent delay and confusion at the election, by transfers made just before it commenced, and give the Directors 60 days to make out the list of voters from the books—so as to have a certain and easy guide, on the day of election, corresponding with the stock book, as it stood 60 days before. We agree there is no distinction, in general, between electors and elected: but it is enough that the Statute has expressed an exception. The argument on the other side is, that by a transfer within the 60 days, the vendor loses his right, but the vendee acquires no right to vote—thus making a portion of the stock wholly unrepresented. What do gentlemen mean by a transfer? Do they mean an absolute executed sale? If so, the argument does not reach this case. If they mean a sale not yet consummated, we say the ownership remains in the vendor. Suppose an executory 378*] contract to be *consummated after the election; who is the voter? Is there a transfer? The transfer may be merely by parol, perhaps. If the vendor be not the stockholder, there is none who can hold; and if all the stock should be sold in this way, there would be no stockholders left; and not a soul to carry on the concerns of the corporation. Suppose a contract of sale which the parties agree should be executed 25 years hence, is the right of voting suspended during all that time? In truth, it is much like the question between the mortgagor and mortgagee in a popular election. The one who has possession of the land must vote there; the one who possesses the stock here. In *Stockdale* v. *South Sea Co.*, 2 Atk., 141, it is said: "The Company have no more right to inquire who is the true proprietor, when the trust does not appear, than a lord of a manor into a right to a copyhold estate when no trust appears; for the person whose name is entered in their books is, to all intents and purposes, with regard to the Company, the proprietor." Suppose one agrees to sell land *in futuro*, does not the vendor continue the freeholder till the deed is executed? Again; suppose the contract to transfer stock within the 60 days—though the transfer day passes, the property is not changed till an actual transfer; nor can the contract for a sale of stock be specifically enforced in a court of equity. Newl. on Cont., 90, 91; 1 Madd., 402, last ed.; *Nutbrowne* v. *Thornton*, 10 Ves., 161; *Mason* v. *Armitage*, 13 *Id.*, 37. In the case cited from the U. S. Law Journal, the court say the inspectors should not go beyond the books. Indeed they use the same language, in substance, as does Ld. Hardwicke in *Stockdale* v. *South Sea Co.*, 2 Atk., 141. So much—supposing the sales in this case executed. But it is plain, from the papers on both sides, that they were merely executory.

Now, suppose either an executory or executed contract a disqualification; was not the by-law inquisitorial? The general power to pass by-laws does not, as supposed, depend on the question whether its object be beneficial or injurious to the corporation. It may be highly beneficial and yet void. The power depends upon the charter; and I deny that, under this charter, any by-law can be made to test the qualifications *of electors. The [*379 Directors can provide no means for this object unless they fairly result from the provisions of the charter. We are supported in this position by the cases cited on the other side, from Str., 539, and Ld. Raym., 496. To the same point is Carth., 482, S. C., as in Ld. Raymond. There the counsel say the oath in question was not imposed, but merely voluntarily. They did not pretend to maintain the doctrine that the corporation might impose an oath. The objection was raised in Ld. Raym., 498. It arose upon a by-law of the city requiring as an excuse for any one elected sheriff, that he should swear and produce compurgators that he was not worth £10,000. It is said, at page 498, to be unreasonable, because it imposes an oath, &c. At page 500 this is answered that it was a favor to the defendant, &c., and Holt, *Ch. J.*, goes on to show how.

The sheriff was compellable to serve without the by-law; and it was passed for his ease and excuse. By simply making an affidavit, he was excused from a burden. It was not demanded of him as a preliminary to his exercise of a corporate right, and the court put the question on that ground. That very distinction settles this question in our favor; and it is also plainly settled by *People* v. *Kip*, cited from the U. S. Law Jour. The ground that the oath was illegal is there distinctly decided. It is a mistaken supposition that the manner of taking the oath was different from that prescribed in the present case. The words were precisely the same, as will be seen by the original papers. The affidavit was to be taken before any one competent to administer an oath. This is a stronger case against the Directors. Mere suspicion is made the ground of rejection; and the by-law makes no provision for absentees, as, it will be seen, was the case in *People* v. *Kip*. One who holds a proxy from another residing in England never could get in a vote under this law, if his constituent should unfortunately be suspected by the inspectors.

The law is also void, as being retroactive, involving cases of transfer made before its passage. 2 Kyd on Corp., 112, 113; *Jackson* v. *How*, 19 Johns., 80.

380*] *The provision in the by-law, for other proof of ownership, is subject to the same objection as the voluntary affidavit. Such proof must be by voluntary oath, if had at all: besides the intrinsic absurdity of requiring an impossibility, the proof of a negative, which no sensible system of jurisprudence ever did require, or ever will, in a question of property. The production of a stock certificate will not better the proof beyond the books. It may be in the hands of one having no manner of right. Besides, it would be inadmissible. Proof, in law, means legal proof, or proof on the oath of a disinterested person. *Van Steenburgh* v. *Kortz*, 10 Johns., 167; *Brown* v. *Hinchman*, 9 *Id.*, 75. The word "proof" is used in the by-law, and taking it in its legal signification, it never could reach a negative. The voter is required to negative, not merely that the sale is conditional or executory, but that there was ever any sale at all.

The cause having remained under advisement to the present term,

SAVAGE, *Ch. J.*, now stated the facts—upon which facts, he said, three questions had been made at the bar. The first respected the power and duty of the court to grant the information in this particular case: the second, what should be deemed a holding within the words of the charter, so as to constitute a voter; and the third, the validity of the by-law, requiring an oath of the voter, or other proof as the test of his qualification.

The Statute, 1 R. L., 108, gives the remedy by *quo warranto* against any person who shall usurp, intrude into, or unlawfully hold or execute any office or franchise within this State. To be a corporation is a franchise (2 Bl. Com., 37), for the usurpation of which an information always lies. (15 Johns., 386 to 389; 1 Str., 303.) And the question is, whether an intrusion into offices, created for the government or exercise of the franchise, is equally within the Act as an usurpation of the franchise itself. The 9 Anne, ch. 20, seems to treat a corporate office as, in itself, a franchise. The words of our Statute are even broader than those of the English; and if, as was agreed upon the argument, they embrace cor-

381*] porate *offices which have an extensive influence upon society, it is difficult to perceive any reason for limiting their operation to these only, in exclusion of the less important offices of the same description. There is certainly nothing requiring this in the Act itself. The words of the 9 Anne are, "that in case any person or persons shall usurp, intrude into, or unlawfully hold and execute, the office or franchise of mayor, bailiff, portreeve, or other office within a city, town corporate, borough or place, in England or Wales," it shall be lawful, with leave, &c., to file the information. To these words the K. B. did, at one time, consider some few mere private offices or franchises an exception; but later cases leave it doubtful whether any such exception now exists. No such distinction upon our Statute has ever been judicially recognized; nor do we feel warranted in governing ourselves, upon these applications, by the greater or less degree of public consequence attached to the office in question. Such a rule would be fluctuating, uncertain, and, indeed, could never be reduced to practice. The question was not even raised in *People* v. *Kip*, dedecided by this court in August Term, 1822, and reported in the U. S. Law Jour., 286. Nor do we think it can well admit of any doubt. Indeed, the case would seem to be within the English Statute, which it is said extends to offices relating to the government of a Corporation. *Rex* v. *Corporation of Curmarthen*, 2 Burr., 869; S. C., 1 Bl., 187.

In *People* v. *Sweeting*, 2 Johns., 184, there had been great delay in making the motion. The office of town supervisor, to which it related, would expire in the short term of three months; it was impossible that an issue could have been sooner tried; and the court, in their discretion, under the circumstances of that case, denied the information. Here the motion was brought before us at the term next after the election. We cannot refuse it upon the mere chance that a trial may fail. To do this would be equivalent to a refusal in all cases, where the office is annual; a length to which we presume the court did not intend to go, and to *which it was not necessary they [***382** should go, in *People* v. *Sweeting*. On the whole we are clear, upon the nature of the case, as to our right of allowing the information to be filed; and that the lapse of time is not such as to require us, in the exercise of a sound discretion, to deny it.

The second and third questions we shall not discuss at large, because we think they are both disposed of by *People* v. *Kip*. That case was said, at the bar, not to apply; the qualification of the voter being that he should have held, in his own name, the stock on which he sought to vote, for a certain number of days before the election: whereas, it is here that he should have held simply, without providing that it should be in his own name. If there be any distinction, it is in favor of the present application. The provision in that case was more sedulously restrictive upon the voter, requiring not only a holding, but a holding in a particular manner, or to be evinced by a particular species of evidence. The case cannot, therefore, be distinguished, at most, in favor of these officers, by any difference of wording in the Statute upon which it proceeded from the one now under consideration. On reflection, we are satisfied with the decision in that case.

Rule granted.(a)

Cited in—63 Barb., 571; 25 How. Pr., 416; 44 How. Pr., 454; 14 Abb. Pr., 79; 16 Abb. Pr., 392; 28 Cal., 506; 70 Ill., 27; 27 Am. Dec., 37, 46 (2 Green Law. 222.)

(a) IN SUPREME COURT—AUGUST TERM, 1882.

THE PEOPLE OF THE STATE OF NEW YORK, at the relation of JACOB BARKER, THOMAS HAZARD, JR., and THOMAS M. HUNTINGTON,

v.

LEONARD KIP, DAVID ROGERS, JOHN C. MORRISON, DUNCAN PHYFE, THOMAS DARLING, THOMAS BROOKS, CHARLES TOWN, ALEXANDER MCMUIR, PETER A. JAY and ABRAHAM B. MEAD.

Mr. Samuel A. Talcott, Atty-Gen. of the People of the State of N. Y., moved, on Tuesday the 8th instant, for leave to file an information in the nature of a *quo warranto* against the defendants above named, who claim to be the Directors of the North River Bank of the City of N. Y. This motion was founded on a bill in chancery recently filed against the defendants and others, by James D. P. Ogden, Jacob Barker and others, and on the answers to that bill, and also on an affidavit showing that the relators above named are stockholders in the North River Bank.

On Friday, *Ch. J.* Spencer delivered the opinion of the court, to the following effect:

383*] "*These applications being generally founded on the *ex parte* affidavit of the relators, it has of late years been usual in the English Court of K. B., and in this court, to afford the defendant an opportunity of being heard against granting leave to file the information. A rule to show cause is, therefore, generally entered; and leave is afterwards granted or refused, as circumstances shall appear upon cause shown. In the present case, the application is for leave to file the information in the first instance. There is no doubt that the court are bound to exercise a reasonable discretion on the subject; and this cause comes before us in a manner so peculiar, that we think it proper to except it from the general rule. The application does not rest upon a mere *ex parte* affidavit. The evidence placed in our hands comes from the defendants themselves, or from a source most favorable to them. We have the sworn answers of the defendants to a bill in chancery, filed in relation to the very election complained of. We have, also, the answers of the inspectors of that election. Upon a rule to show cause, nothing could be alleged by the defendants against granting leave to file the information, which is not already urged on their part, in the papers presented to the court. We have looked into the answers, and we find the defendants and the inspectors admitting a state of facts, which not only render it proper to grant leave as applied for, but which seems to us imperiously to require it at our hands. To give time under such circumstances, would be an abuse of the discretion vested in this court. We will briefly advert to a part of the case as admitted by the defendants and inspectors. A controversy existed among the stockholders of the Bank, a portion of whom were desirous to effect a change in the direction. A few days before the election, a by-law was passed by the Board of Directors, of which Board most of the defendants were members and then present, authorizing any stockholder to challenge the votes offered at the election; and if supported by affidavits or other probable cause, to the satisfaction of the inspectors, that they might then require the person whose vote should be challenged, to make oath in answer to the cause of challenge, the sufficiency of which should be determined by the inspectors; and if such oath was refused, that the vote should be rejected. Under this by-law, votes given upon the proxies of several persons, who appeared, from the books of the Bank and the certificates of the cashier, as stockholders to a large amount, were challenged, on the ground that the persons, in whose names the stock stood, and who held the certificates of the Bank, were not the exclusive owners, but that some third person or persons had an equitable interest therein. This was considered by the inspectors as good cause of challenge; and the persons whose proxies were thus objected to, were required, notwithstanding the most urgent remonstrances to the contrary, to make affidavits in writing in answer to these allegations, and to answer, under an oath prescribed by men who did not themselves act under the solemn obligations of an oath, to various verbal interrogatories, and to submit to a sort of inquisatorial examination at variance with the fundamental principles of our civil and political institutions, at the pleasure of the inspectors. In this manner votes upon a great number of shares were entirely disregarded by the inspectors. It is evident, from the answers, that if *all the votes [*384 received into the hands of the inspectors from persons duly authorized to give such votes, had been estimated by the inspectors, that the result would have been different from that declared by the inspectors; as, in such case, the persons whose seats are now contested, could not have been certified to have been elected.

Without entering any further at this time into the facts disclosed, we are unanimously of opinion that the by-law, and the proceedings under it at the election, were most illegal and reprehensible. The Act of Incorporation provides, 'that each stockholder shall be entitled to one vote in each share of the stock in the bank, which he shall have held in its own name at least fourteen days previous to the time of voting. (Sess. 44, ch. 146, sec. 8.) Further than this, the inspectors had no right to inquire, as it was not competent for the Directors to pass any by-law at variance with the positive provisions of the Act incorporating the Bank. We, therefore, feel ourselves called upon to grant the motion; more especially as the Statute contemplates in cases of this sort, the most speedy and effectual proceedings, which a due regard to the rights of parties and the proper administration of justice will permit."

Leave granted to file the information *instanter*.

Counsel for the plaintiffs, *Mr. S. A. Talcott*, Atty-Gen., and *Mr. Benjamin F. Butler*.

Counsel for the defendants, *Mr. Samuel Jones*.

Cited in—27 Am. Dec., 37, 46 (2 Green Law, 222).

THE PEOPLE, ex rel. ISRAEL,
v.
TIBBETS ET AL.

Statute — Construed Strictly, When it Affects Vested Rights—Rule does not Apply if it Affects the Remedy Merely — Pleading—Quo Warranto.

The 10th section of the Act to Prevent Fraudulent Bankruptcies by Incorporated Companies, and to Facilitate Proceedings Against Them, &c., passed Apr. 21, 1825 (sess. 48, ch. 324), applies to an information in nature of a *quo warranto*, which the Atty-Gen. had moved to file before the passage of the Act, but which the court did not give leave file till after its passage.

A statute altering the mode of proceeding in point of form, in a suit pending when the Act passed, so as to prevent a delay and hasten the time of trial, is not unconstitutional.

Such an Act will be construed liberally, and general words, not expressly prospective, will be applied to a pending proceeding.

The rule that a statute should not be so construed as to effect vested rights, does not apply to a statute which alters the form of the remedy merely.

Under the 10th section of the Act to Prevent Fraudulent Bankruptcies by Incorporated Companies, and to Facilitate Proceedings Against Them, &c. (sess. 48, ch. 324), the court will make a rule for the defendant to appear as well as to plead, &c., within a certain time without process, on giving leave to file an information in nature of a *quo warranto*, under the 9th section of that Act.

Form of the rule to appear, plead, &c., under the 10th section.

Whether a suit by information in nature of a *quo warranto*, shall be considered as commenced on moving to file the information, and before it is actually filed, *quære*.

The court will construe a statute strictly to prevent its interfering with vested rights.

NOTE.—1. *Construction of statutes affecting the remedy*. 2. Quo warranto.

1. *Though statutes affecting vested interests are strictly construed*, where such statutes affect the remedy merely they are not generally within the rule. See above case of People v. Tibbets; Matter of Smith, 10 Wend., 449; Gildersleeve v. People, 10 Barb., 35. Statutes affecting remedy on foreign contracts valid. See Nash v. Tupper, 1 Cai., 402, *note*.

2. *Quo warranto*. See, generally, People v. Utica Ins. Co., 15 Johns., 358, *note*; People v. Tibbets, *ante*, p. 358, *note*; People v. Van Slyck, *ante*, p. 297.

Citations—Act, Feb. 6, 1788; 1 R. L., 485, sec. 5; Act, April 21, 1825.

AFTER the preceding opinion in this case was delivered,

Mr. Talcott, Atty-Gen., upon the same papers, moved to file the information under **385***] the 9th section of the "Act *to Prevent Fraudulent Bankruptcies by Incorporated Companies, to Facilitate Proceedings Against Them, and for other purposes," passed Apr. 21, 1825 (sess. 48, ch. 325), since the above motion in this cause was argued; and for a rule to expedite the proceedings, according to the provisions of that Act.

He said the old Statute had evidently contemplated a more rapid proceeding than could be had at common law. It expressly authorized the court to require a plea from the defendant, as of the same term at which the information was filed. But the Legislature saw that, in consequence of the decision at the last term in *Richardson's* case, *ante*, 97, putting the cause back to the common law process, the proceedings upon the old Statute would not be sufficiently rapid to answer the purposes of justice; and, for that reason, immediately interfered. Perhaps, however, independent of the last Statute, this court might make the same rule against the defendants which they made in *Richardson's* case, 3 Cow., 357, on the *ex parte* application. There the defendant had not appeared when the rule was made which was afterwards set aside. Here the defendants have come into court and argued against the motion, which is a sufficient appearance for the purpose of enabling the court regularly to make such a rule upon them, admitting we are holding to the proceeding upon the old Statute.

The Act of Apr. 21, 1825 (secs. 8 and 9), provides for two cases—one where the information is filed by direction of a single judge in vacation, with or without notice of the application. In such case, on the process being returned served, the clerk is to enter the defendant's appearance. Another case is, where, upon reasonable notice, a motion is made, and leave granted by the court, in term, to file an information under the old Act of Feb. 6, 1788. And by the 10th section, in both these cases, the court are authorized to make rules for expediting the pleading; and the expression, among others, is, "to make such further order for prescribing and limiting the times for the respective parties to plead and proceed therein," &c. This provision extends to both cases. **386***] In the 9th section, which *contemplates leave of the court, there is no provision at all for process; but within this general power of making rules as to pleading and proceeding, an authority to fix the time within which the defendant shall appear, and the manner of his appearing, is included. It can hardly be sdpposed that a summary mode of compelling an appearance should be provided, as to an information filed upon the order of a single judge, and yet that the Legislature meant to deny this where the proceeding to obtain leave was more deliberate, by notice and motion in court.

Mr. G. Griffin, contra. The question is, simply, whether the Act applies to this proceeding, which was commenced before the Statute passed. To give it such a construction would be contrary to the spirit of the Constitution. It may well be doubted how far it is competent for the Legislature to pass an Act like the present, so as to affect present or future proceedings against corporations. It looks too much like outlawing one class of the community by a statute. Upon this point we shall not enlarge at this stage of the proceeding; but would barely ask the court to look into *Holden* v. *James*, 11 Mass., 396.

At any rate this Act cannot have a retroactive operation upon proceedings instituted several weeks, and indeed months before it passed. The general rule is certainly against this. "*Nova constitutio futuris formam imponere debèt, non præteritis.*" (2 Inst., 292; Bract., lib. 4, fol. 228.) The rule is clear, where the words of the Statute are general, that it shall not have a retrospection to take away rights. *Gilmore* v. *Exr. of Shooter*, 2 Mod., 310; *Couch* v. *Jeffries*, 4 Burr., 24, 60; *Duffield* v. *Smith*, 3 Serg. & R., 590; *Bedford* v. *Shilling*, 4 *Id.*, 401; *Dash* v. *Van Kleeck*, 7 Johns., 477. That the Legislature may, in certain cases, by express words, modify or control pending proceedings, need not be denied for the present, but they have not professed to do so. Where the words are equivocal, the construction should always be against this. But by looking at different parts of the Act, it will be seen that they intended to make it prospective. The attention *of the court has been [***387** drawn by the Atty-Gen. to three sections only, the 8th, 9th and 10th. But a previous section, the 4th, which relates to the civil remedy against corporations, and which abridges the proceedings in the same way as the sections relied on, is made, in terms, to embrace only suits which should thereafter be prosecuted. It was not deemed necessary to repeat this, in the subsequent sections relied on, but it is plainly implied. The prospective words are to be taken as connecting themselves with the subsequent sections. The 8th section itself is, in the future tense, "that when the Atty-Gen. shall proceed," &c. In the 9th section, "that it shall be the duty of the Supreme Court, &c." So in the 10th section, "that it shall be lawful for the Supreme Court, &c." Thus the general rule is fortified by the prospective words in every section relied upon. The 14th section authorizes the court to award Supreme Court costs against the defendants, if judgment shall go against them. This is a provision penal in its nature; and to give it effect would be violating the Constitution, which forbids the passage of *ex post facto* laws.

The defendants, here, have a vested right to a certain mode of proceeding, and to certain rights or privileges which cannot be taken away in this manner. The penalty which they were formerly subject to cannot be enhanced. One having a right to a penalty cannot be deprived of that right by an Act of Parliament, pending an action to recover it. Such was the case of *Couch* v. *Jeffries*, 4 Burr., 24, 60.

Mr. T. A. Emmet, same side. The Atty-Gen. admits there is a difference between a case where an information is filed under the order of a single judge, and the case of one filed under a rule of the court; and we contend that the subsequent proceedings have respect to, and connect themselves with, this difference. Will it be denied that a suit was commenced at the last term? Can it be doubted that the cause was so far pending as to give application to the rule that the Statute shall not act prospectively? Who can say, that had we known of this Statute we should have appeared to the motion? That we should not 388*] rather have put the Atty-Gen. *to the process required by *Richardson's* case? It is obvious from the 9th section that the late Statute did not mean to repeal the Law of 1788. That law is referred to by this section, as still existing in all its branches, and among other things, for the purpose of the proceedings. The object of the late Statute was merely to provide for a new case. In February Term, the proceeding was completely within the Statute of 1788. At the present term, the court delivered their opinion. In the meantime, an Act passed making it, perhaps, a matter of regret that we appeared at all. Should not the order made at the present term relate to the last, and be considered as made then? To deny the application of the late Act to this proceeding would, at least, be a judicious exercise of the discretion which the court are called upon to exert, and which they always have power to exert upon the proceedings on the information, as well as whether it shall be filed.

It was necessary that the Atty-Gen. should have power to file the information in vacation. This is the case provided for; and the Legislature intended to leave informations granted in term time, which proceed under the Act of 1788, to be entirely regulated by that Act. Wherever the word "information" occurs in the late Act, it means an information filed under its own special provisions. The power to give preference and expedite other proceedings refer to an information thus filed. The Act should be construed strictly.

The 9th section introduces a proceeding in which the right to a trial by jury is forgotten to be a part of our Constitution. True, it gives an issue, which we trust will never be denied. The court may decide summarily, direct an issue, or grant leave to file an information under the Act of 1788. Then comes the 10th section regulating the proceedings. This is, "that it shall be lawful for the Supreme Court, in case any such issue shall be ordered, or any such information directed, &c.", to make order for expediting the proceeding. This evidently refers to one of the two previous modes, viz.: a summary proceeding, or an issue directed.

Mr. S. Jones, in reply. The two Statutes being in *pari materia*, are connected by their 389*] very nature. We have a right *to go on under the old Act and apply the new one to it. The court will hardly pass upon the constitutionality of a law in this summary way, but refer the question to a subsequent stage of the proceedings, when it can be more deliberately and formally considered in a shape which shall give the party, thinking himself aggrieved, a remedy on error.

Suppose the suit to have been commenced at the last term, we deny the want of power in the Legislature to interfere; and we deny the rule that general and comprehensive words, embracing the case, shall be construed to steer clear of the proceeding. The rule is, simply, that a statute shall not be so construed as to vary antecedent vested rights; but was it ever before heard that an Act could not be passed applying to the mere form of a pending suit or proceeding? This is done every day. The Legislature may give a new rule which shall entirely alter the course of proceeding. Nay, the court itself, without legislative authority, may do the same thing. It is mere matter of practice invading no right, interfering with no privilege; and *Couch* v. *Jeffries*, cited from 4 Burr., 2461, goes upon this distinction. The word "hereafter," relied on, is in the 4th section, entirely independent of those we rely upon, and relates to a distinct proceeding—the civil remedy for a debt. There is not the least ground for saying that it should be read in connection with the 8th, 9th and 10th sections. When the Legislature come to a different class of cases, they use different words, having a present import.

The Statute had two different objects in view. The 8th section relates to corporations, the 9th to the officers of corporations. It should be so construed as to suppress the mischief and advance the remedy; and every statute to prevent delays in the administration of justice is to be liberally and beneficially applied. Then the 10th section confers the fullest and most ample powers to hasten the proceedings whenever any information is filed.

In *Duffield* v. *Smith*, 3 Serg. & R., 590, 598, an Act passed after an action of trespass brought, was sought to be *so construed as to [*390 devest the right. This was denied because the right was vested. It was a matter of right, not of mere form. The case of *Bedford* v. *Shilling*, 4 Serg. & R., 401, went upon the same distinction.

The court may not only make a short rule to appear and plead, but may make a rule as to all the subsequent pleadings and proceedings, bringing them within a shorter time than usual, so as to effectuate the intent of the Legislature in making the remedy as speedy as possible.

The last day of term, SUTHERLAND, *J.*, being absent,

WOODWORTH, *J.*, said all the members of the court had examined the Statute and the questions submitted upon it, and were unanimous that the motion must be granted. The remaining judges were authorized to say that Sutherland, *J.* (who had this morning departed for his residence), unhesitatingly concurred in this opinion. The court had adopted no written opinion, but he would briefly state the views they entertained upon the subject.

The court had thought it a proper case for an information, according to an opinion which they had expressed at the present term, upon papers submitted at the last; and the relator now applies, upon the Statute since passed, for a rule that the defendants appear; and he also moves that the court should make a short rule for pleading, in order that an issue may be speedily joined. The Act of 1788 declared upon what terms an information should be filed, but left the proceedings upon it to their usual and ancient course. The only provision in that Act expressly hastening the proceedings is in the 1st section, which enables the court to require a plea as of the same term at which the information should be filed. This indicated an intention that a case of this kind should be proceeded in with more than ordinary diligence; but the provision was inadequate to the object, inasmuch as it left the preliminary steps, the process to compel the defendant's appearance, to be pursued according to the rules of the common law—a proceeding so dilatory as to render the suit in many cases altogether inefficient. This was held to be the course, at the last term, in *Richardson's* case, *ante*, 97, after a full examination **391***] of the subject. *The authorities spoke so plain a language as left the court no room for doubt. The Act now in question was obviously passed to remedy this defect. There cannot be a question that it applies to all informations filed against corporations or their officers; and the only question which can arise is, whether the Act is to be deemed so entirely prospective as to steer clear of the present case. The defendants insist that it is so, and ground themselves mainly upon the argument that a contrary construction would take away vested rights.

It is also said that this construction is deducible from the language of the 4th section, which is prospective in terms. This is true of that particular section; but it was well answered at the bar, that it relates entirely to a distinct subject, and that the sections relied upon are altogether disconnected with and independent of it; that the former relates to the civil, the latter to the criminal remedy against corporations, and the plain difference of expression by the Legislature, in relation to these different subjects, is a strong argument against the construction for which the defendants contend. The Legislature thought it rather too severe and rigorous a proceeding, to change the course of the civil remedy for debt, in suits already brought; and hence they made it expressly prospective. Not so as to a proceeding for intrusion or usurpation.

It is not necessary to inquire whether a suit might properly be said to be commenced when this motion was made. The information was not yet filed, and it may well be doubted whether it is perfectly correct, in technical meaning, to say that before process issued, or even an information filed, which is in the nature of a bill or plaint, that an action is commenced. Admitting, however, that it was commenced, for all the purposes of this question, there is no invasion of private right in the case within the rule which struggles against giving statutes a retroactive effect. The words of the 9th section are, that it shall be the duty of the Supreme Court, upon the application of any person, or persons, or body corporate, &c., to proceed forthwith, and in a summary way, &c., to inquire as to the election **392***] complained of, &c., *order an issue, &c., or direct the Atty-Gen. to file an information under the Act of 1788. Then the next section is, that it shall be lawful for the Supreme Court, in case any such issue shall be ordered, or any such information directed or permitted to be filed, to make order for prescribing and limiting the times for the parties to plead and proceed therein, for giving preference to the issues, and for expediting the ulterior proceedings, so as to cause the same to be proceeded upon, and the final determination thereof to be had with the best and most convenient speed that may be, and to cause the same to be expedited by all such ways and means as a due regard to the ends of justice will admit, and the case may require. This applies to all cases whether any incipient proceedings may have taken place before the passage of the Act or not. Whenever the relator comes forward with his application, at whatever stage of the proceedings, he may have the benefit of the Act, by the expedition of his case as its exigency, and the ends of justice may demand. The Act looks to the end of the term for which the offices endure. In respect to corporations, this term is usually a single year, and without a speedy hearing the suit will be entirely nugatory.

If it were true that the Statute interfered with vested rights, the court would feel bound to give it the very strictest construction; but there is no such thing. What right is taken away? Are the defendants devested of their defense upon the merits? Their saying that the proceeding is hastened in point of form makes nothing for them. They have no right to complain of this. It is complaining that he is put upon his defense to-day, whereas he had a right to delay till to-morrow; a singular head of vested right—a right to delay justice. Are not the Legislature competent to take away or abridge such an evil? It is most important that they should possess this power. The pretense of the defendants does not merit the name of right. It relates to the remedy. The Act merely says that, under its regulations, the questions between the parties may, peradventure, be brought to trial *six [***393** months earlier than they otherwise would have been. This is a very usual subject of legislative interference Indeed, as was said at the bar, the court might do the same thing independent of the Legislature. Suppose they were to make an order that all rules to plead should be 10 days instead of 20, would it lie with the parties interested to gainsay this? The Legislature are in the habit of changing the form of proceeding, to try rights, in various ways. Take a single instance. Ejectment may now be brought for the people instead of the former more dilatory form of a writ of escheat or intrusion. The former is much the more summary remedy, and was itself instituted by the courts, and applied to various cases where a more dilatory form prevailed according to the ancient practice. This remedy was given to the people by an Act of the Legislature (1 R. L., 485, sec. 5), which Act, too, sanctioned ejectments pending at the time of its passage. Would it be competent for defendants in possession, or against whom ejectments were brought, when that Act passed, to object that the remedy against them was thus made too speedy, and demand to be proceeded against by the old writ? To complain that the alteration hurrying them on to trial was a violation of the Constitution or of vested rights? At this rate, every statute by which the collection of debts or the trial of rights is rendered more speedy, or effectual, would be inapplicable and void in reference to subsisting rights. We are clear that short rules for pleading should be granted.

It is true that nothing is said in the Act as to compelling an appearance where the proceeding is against officers. The right to make a rule for the defendants to appear, depends upon the construction which should be given to the words of the 10th section. The power of the court is, not only to make rules for pleading, but rules to proceed; and the whole is to be done so as to cause the matter to be proceeded upon, and the final determination thereof to be had, with the best and most convenient speed that may be. The court are to cause the same to be expedited by all such ways and means as a due regard to the ends of justice will admit, and the case may require. If the Act meant to confer no summary 394*] *power of compelling an appearance, it would use a most inconsistent language. This department of the proceedings in which the greatest delay must intervene, would be wholly unprovided for. The intention of the Act must have been, that the cause should be put in such a situation, as would enable the relator to proceed immediately.

The court order the following,

RULE: That the Atty-Gen. have leave to file an information or informations, in the nature of a *quo warranto*, under the Act entitled "An Act to Prevent Fraudulent Bankruptcies by Incorporated Companies, to Facilitate Proceedings Against Them, and for other purposes," passed Apr. 21, 1825, against Elisha Tibbets, &c., to try by what warrant, or authority, the said last named persons, or any of them, claim to hold and exercise the office of Directors of the Franklin Fire Ins. Co. And it is further ordered, that within 20 days after filing such information and notice thereof to the defendants, the appearance of the defendants be entered in the book of common rules; and that the defendants plead to the said information or informations within the same time; and further, that all subsequent pleadings, if any, on the part of the defendants, shall be served within ten days after service upon them of the pleading to be answered; and if the defendants shall neglect to plead, or answer, within the times above limited, their default or defaults may be entered; and thereupon, judgment of ouster shall be given against them, or such of them as make default upon motion to be made to this court, unless such defaults are set aside.

Reviewed—71 Me., 383.
Cited in—46 Am. Dec., 459 (4 Gilm., 221).

SNYDER *v.* SDYDER.

Practice—Failure of Plaintiff to Reply to Plea of Statute of Limitations.

Where the plaintiff neglected to reply to a plea of the Statute of Limitations; and went to trial a *nisi prius* record omitting it; but the defendant had the full benefit of the defense upon the Statute, at the trial; the court refused to set aside a verdict for the plaintiff for irregularity; but suffered him to amend.

MR. G. A. SHUFELDT, for the defendant, moved to set aside the verdict, &c., in this cause, for irregularity; upon affidavits showing these facts; that the declaration contained three *counts—the first upon a prom- [*395 issory note, the second for goods sold, &c., and the third for money lent, &c; that to the 1st count the defendant pleaded the general issue, and to the 2d and 3d the Statute of Limitations; and that without replying to this last plea, the plaintiff noticed the cause for trial, and tried it upon the *N.* P. record, containing no plea except the general issue; but the defendant appeared by his counsel at the trial, and with the plaintiff's consent, insisted upon and had the full benefit of the Statute of Limitations in his defense, as if an issue had been joined upon the plea. Verdict for the plaintiff.

Mr. K. Miller, contra, insisted that it was too late for the defendant to make this objection, after having appeared at the trial, and taken the full benefit of the defense upon the Statute. He had sustained no injury. At any rate, the court would allow the plaintiff to amend, by filing a replication *nunc pro tunc*, and amending the *N.* P. record accordingly. And,

The Court were clear that the amendment, as prayed by *Mr. Miller*, should be granted.

Rule accordingly.(*a*)

(*a*) The same point was virtually decided by the English C. P. in the late case of Cook v. Burke, 5 Taunt., 164. And see 2 Saund., 319, *note* 6, by Sergt. Williams; and Grundy v. Mell, 4 Bos. & P., 28, often cited as 1 New Rep. The principal case seems to be within the Statute of Amendments and Jeofails. 1 R. L., 118, sec. 6.

---

*HAMLIN *v.* HART. [*396

Practice—Costs.

The plaintiff can in no case have costs in a suit originally brought in the Supreme Court, in an action of *assumpsit*, unless he recover more than $50.

He cannot have costs, though the accounts of both parties exceed $400.

To entitle him in such case to costs, he should sue in the C. P.

ASSUMPSIT. On a reference, the report was in favor of the plaintiff for $22, the accounts of both parties exceeding $400. And upon this, the question was, whether the plaintiff should have costs or whether he should pay costs to the defendant.

Mr. A. Sampson, for the plaintiff.
Mr. F. M. Haight, for the defendant.

Curia. The plaintiff must pay costs to the defendant. It is true the suit could not be brought in a justice's court, the whole accounts on both sides exceeding $400. But the plaintiff, in order to recover costs, must have sued in the C. P. In *assumpsit*, the plaintiff can in no case have costs in the Supreme Court in a suit originally brought there, unless he recovers more than $50 damages.

Rule accordingly.(*a*)

Cited in—6 Cow., 612.

(*a*) See 1 R. L., 344, secs. 4, 5, and sess. 47, ch. 238, secs., 1 33.

VISCHER, Widow, *Demandant*, *v.* CONANT, *Tenant*.

Dower—When View Granted—Bill of Particulars.

In dower *unde nihil habet*, view is not of course.

In general a view will not be granted, unless boundaries are in question.

If, in real actions, the tenant wish a more definite knowledge of the extent of the demandant's claims, than he can obtain from the count, he should obtain a bill of particulars, as in the action of ejectment.

Citations—20 Johns., 276; Booth on R. A., 38; Park. Dow., 286; 1 R. L., 86, 87, sec., 21; Col. Cas., 46; 2 Archb. Pr., 48, 49, 189.

DOWER *unde nihil habet*, of land in Massena, in the County of St. Lawrence. The count was in the usual general form, without showing any land in certain; and now, after a special imparlance, and before plea,

Mr. S. M. Hopkins moved for a view, on an affidavit of the tenant, that he was seised in his *demesne* as of fee, of several lots of land in Massena, purchased by him of different persons; and none of the conveyances or titles, **397***] for which, *were received by him of the demandant's husband, in whose rights he claimed, or from any person claiming under him, as the deponent believed; that he was also possessed of several lots or tracts of land, in the same town, as tenant at will; that he did not know of what lands dower was sought in this suit; that he had procured the records of St. Lawrence Co., and of the State, in the office of the Secretary of the State, to be searched, and could not find that the demandant's husband had ever been seised in fee of any lands in the Town of Massena.

Mr. J. M'Kown, contra, said it was not a matter of course, in the action of dower, to grant a view. *Ostrander* v. *Kneeland*, 20 Johns., 276. Indeed, view could not formerly be had in dower *unde nihil habet* at all. (Booth, 38.)

Mr. Hopkins said this was the only way in which the tenant could obtain notice of the extent to which the demandant claimed.

Curia, per SAVAGE, *Ch. J.* It was decided in *Ostrander* v. *Kneeland*, 20 Johns., 276, that in dower *unde nihil habet* view cannot be demanded of course; and it has been doubted whether it lies at all (Booth on R. A., 38, and *note*, Anthon's ed.; Park on Dower, 286); though the better opinion seems to be that it does. (Park on Dower, 286, and the authorities there cited in *note*.) And this is plainly implied by the Statute, 1 R. L., 86–7, sec. 21, which denies it "when the dower in demand is of land that the husband aliened to the tenant, or his or her ancestors, where the tenant ought not to be ignorant what land the husband did alien to him or her." In this case, the tenant denies that, to his knowledge or belief, the dower demanded is of lands, claimed by him, directly or indirectly, under the husband; and it is, thus far, we think, a case proper for a view. But is a view necessary? In such case only is it to be granted. (1 R. L., 86.) And upon this question we must be governed by the circumstances of the case. This is the course in ejectment, where the form of the declaration is equally general as in this action. For the *purposes of view, the [***398** two cases are precisely similar; and we think the same practice should be followed in each upon the question of granting it. This court have decided that they would not grant a view in the latter action, unless it appear that boundaries will come in question. *Wickham* v. *Waters*, Col. Cas. 49. And it is difficult to perceive how a view can be necessary in any other case. To ascertain the precise premises for which the plaintiff is proceeding, the constant course, in an action of ejectment, is to obtain a bill of particulars, which may be done at any time before trial, on application to a judge or commissioner. (2 Archb. Pr., 48, 49, and the cases there cited.) This will answer all the purposes of a view in the present case. The object of the tenant is to be advertised in which of the several tracts in Massena whereof he is possessed, the dower in demand lies. This proceeding, to obtain a bill of particulars, seems applicable to all actions in which the plaintiff declares generally, without specifying particularly his cause of action. (2 Archb. Pr., 198.) The only difficulty, in this stage of the proceeding, will be in saving to him his plea of non-tenure, if the claim should happen to relate to those lands of which he is not seised. For this purpose he should have obtained the order for particulars during his imparlance. Under the circumstances of this case, however, we will, if he wish it, grant him a special imparlance to the next term, to the end that he may obtain the particulars of the demandant's claim, as in other cases.

Mr. Hopkins said, as he did not wish the specification with a view to a plea, but merely to the trial, he would plead the present term, and take the course mentioned by the court to obtain a bill of particulars to inform the defendant as to the trial.

Motion denied.(a)

Cited in—6 Cow. 579; 59 N. Y., 184; 49 How. Pr., 41; 17 Am. Rep., 343, 346.

(*a*) There have been three decisions, previous to the one in the principal case, upon the question when a view shall be granted in real actions, viz.: Inh. of Gravesend v. Voorhis, 1 Johns. Cas., 237; Haynes v. Budd. *Id.*, 335, and Ostrander v. Kneeland, 20 Johns., 276. *It is plain that the Stat- [*399 ute, 1 R. L., 86, applies to real actions generally, writs of right as well as dower; and this being so, the reasoning of the court in Ostrander v. Kneeland, and the principal case, seems to do away the two former cases.

WALLIS *v.* MURRAY.

When Plaintiff Entitled to Copy of Paper in Defendant's Possession.

The court will order the defendant to allow the plaintiff to take a copy of a paper in his possession, on which the suit is founded, though the plaintiff once had a counterpart, which is lost.

It is not necessary to show that it was delivered to the defendant, to hold as trustee of the plaintiff.

The Supreme Court will grant this rule, as to such a paper, in all cases where chancery would entertain a bill of discovery.

Citations—11 Johns., 245, *n.*; 3 Cow., 17, 18, *n. a*; 19 Johns., 268; 2 Archb. Pr., 186.

MR. ROOSEVELT, for the plaintiff, moved for a rule that the defendant furnish the plaintiff's attorney, at the plaintiff's expense,

with a true copy of the written contract on which this action is founded. He read affidavits showing that the action is *assumpsit* brought to recover the price of a large quantity of merchandise sold to the defendant by the plaintiff's agent, under a written contract special in its provisions; that one part was re-
400*] tained by the plaintiff's agent; *and the counterpart of the defendant; that the part retained by the agent had been lost; that a paper produced and annexed to the affidavits was believed to be a copy; but the plaintiff's agent and attorney, not being certain of this, feared that the action might fail on account of a variance between the declaration to be filed and the contract to be proved in evidence at the trial; and that the counterpart, or a copy of it, was necessary to enable the plaintiff to declare with accuracy; that though one Canning was named in the contract as one of the parties, he, in fact, entered into it as the agent of the plaintiff.

Mr. P. W. Radcliff, contra, read an affidavit of the defendant, neither admitting nor denying that the paper annexed to the plaintiff's affidavits was a true copy of the agreement; but stating that when he entered into the contract, he then, and for some time afterwards, supposed it was with Canning in his own right, and not as agent for the plaintiff; that the counterpart was delivered to the defendant as his own property, and for his own use, and not as trustee for Canning or any other person; that he had, as he believed, fully complied with the agreement on his part; that Canning had, before the commencement of this suit, made a statement in writing concerning the matters in controversy, which he had delivered to the defendant, who had returned it to Canning—all of which was before any dispute had arisen touching the subject of this suit; that the statement may be material to the defendant in his defense, as he is advised by counsel and believes; that he has applied to the plaintiff's attorney for a copy of that statement, which had been denied.

Mr. Roosevelt cited *Denslow* v. *Fowler*, 2 Cow., 592, and the cases cited in the note to that case, *note a*; *Jackson* v. *Jones*, 3 Cow., 17, and *People* v. *Vail*, 2 Cow. 623.

Mr. Radcliff relied on the same authorities, and especially *Street* v. *Brown*, 6 Taunt., 602. In *Morrow* v. *Saunders*, 1 Brod. & Bing., 318, it was expressly sworn that there was but one copy and never had been any other, that it was
401*] only *upon an affidavit going thus far that the court would grant the motion. Mr. Cowen, in his note to *Denslow* v. *Fowler*, omitted to notice that circumstance. In Dunlap's Practice, 1 Dunl. Pr., 616–7, the rule is laid down in the same manner.

Curia, per SAVAGE, *Ch. J.* The power of the courts in England, to compel a party to produce or furnish copies of papers to his adversary, is said, by the latter cases, to rest on the idea that the paper in question was left with the party required to furnish it as a trustee for the other; and the motion has been denied where a counterpart was kept by the party applying. Why this trust should give jurisdiction more than an accidental loss of a counterpart once existing, it is difficult to perceive. If the courts go upon the analogy to equitable relief, accident is as plain a ground as trust. This court have certainly, in practice, been confined to neither ground. In *Lawrence* v. *Ocean Ins. Co.*, 11 Johns., 245, *note*, a rule was granted to produce numerous items of written evidence in an insurance cause, complicated in its details, and important on account of the amount involved. In *Jackson* v. *Jones*, 3 Cow., 17, deeds of the party were ordered to be deposited for inspection, on an allegation that thereby the adverse party hoped to be enabled to prove them forgeries. The same thing has been done of a promissory note. *Brush* v. *Gibbon*, *Id.*, 18, *note a.* In *Willis* v. *Bailey*, 19 Johns., 268, this court declare the principle upon which they proceeded in *Lawrence* v. *Ocean Ins. Co.*, viz.: that the necessity of the rule to enable the defendants to defend themselves was fully shown on affidavit; and they adopted the principle that from the facts shown the defendant would be entitled, on a bill of discovery, to the information sought. It is said the K. B. acted on the same principle in the time of Ld. Mansfield. (2 Archb. Pr., 186.) When the court, in *Willis* v. *Bailey*, say they do not mean to adopt the English practice, they allude to the proceeding before a judge at chambers. The only restriction intimated by that case relative to the subject-matter is, that the paper ordered to be produced must constitute, in itself, a cause of action. They say that the English practice has not gone beyond this.

*There is no doubt that, on a bill of [***402** discovery, the plaintiff would be entitled to all that he asks, and even more—a discovery of the contents of this paper and the oath of the defendant as to its execution. Nor is there any doubt that the paper will be necessary, to enable the plaintiff to proceed in his cause with safety. The paper itself constitutes a cause of action; and on the whole we grant the motion, on condition that the plaintiff deliver a copy of the statement asked for by the defendant.

Rule accordingly.

Cited in—9 Wend., 459; 2 Hall, 578; 12 Leg. Obs., 139.

THE PEOPLE, ex rel. GREEN,
v.
THE JUDGES OF THE C. P. OF ONEIDA COUNTY.

Mandamus—*Costs.*

Mandamus to a Court of C. P., commanding them to vacate a rule is a new suit; and on the defendants' succeeding, they shall have a retaining fee taxed against the relator.

AN alternative *mandamus* issued to the defendants, commanding them to set aside a rule made by the Oneida C. P. On their return, a peremptory *mandamus* was denied; and on taxing costs, the commissioner allowed a retaining fee against the relator.

A motion was now made to retax the bill, on the ground that this and other items in the bill were improper.

Mr. R. N. Morrison, for the motion.

Mr. T. E. Clark, contra.

Curia. The retaining fee was properly taxed. This is in no sense a mere continuation of the cause below, but a new suit.

Motion denied.

403*] *THE PEOPLE, ex rel. KNAPP,

v.

THE JUDGES OF THE COURT OF C. P. OF THE COUNTY OF WESTCHESTER.

Alternative Mandamus — *Service of — Return.*

Alernative *mandamus* to the judges of the C. P. is in nature of a rule to show cause, may be served in vacation by showing the original and delivering a copy, the judges should return without waiting to receive the writ, and the relator should cause this to be filed.

THE defendants not having yet made return to the alternative *mandamus* issued in this cause, for which purpose time was given them at the last term. (*Vide ante,* 73, S. C.)

Mr. Jas. Smith now moved for peremptory *mandamus.*

Mr. E. Williams, contra, said the judges could make no return till they were possessed of the writ itself, and he read affidavits that this had not been furnished. They deemed this essential.

Curia. The judges did not understand the purpose for which we made the rule giving time at the last term. We considered the alternative *mandamus* in the nature of a rule to show cause; that it might be served by showing the original, and delivering a copy in vacation. It follows, that the judges might have made a return without the writ. We give them to the next term, at which time they are to make a return. The relator must then file the original writ.

Rule accordingly.

Cited in—7 Wend., 537; 13 Wend., 655, *n.*; 45 Am. Dec., 356 (10 Mo., 117).

ROOT *v.* KING ET AL.

Action for Libel—Change of Venue.

The change of venue in an action for a libel dispersed in several counties, depends on the same principles as in an action on contract; and a change of venue will accordingly be denied, unless there is a decided preponderance of witnesses, or some other strong circumstances in favor of the change.

Citations—2 Cai., 245; 2 Johns., 453; 3 Johns., 139; 8 Johns., 354; 9 Johns., 248; 1 Tidd, 547, 548; 2 Archb. Pr., 176.

MR. J. I. ROOSEVELT, for the defendants, moved to change the venue from Delaware to N. Y. or Albany. He read an affidavit of the defendants, that the action was for a libel published of the plaintiff in his character of Lieut.-Governor; that the justification would rest on proof as to the appearance and conduct of the plaintiff, at a particular time, whilst he was presiding over the Senate at Albany; that **404*]** the *defendants have ten witnesses at N. Y. and Long Island, material, &c., and a greater number at Albany.

Mr. Talcott, Atty-Gen., contra, read an affidavit of the plaintiff that he had many witnesses residing in the County of Delaware, where he resides, necessary and material, &c.; the number of the witnesses he did not know, nor could he at present ascertain, but believed it would exceed ten; that he had no witnesses, as he was aware, in N. Y.; that if the defendants should justify, he would need the testimony of many Senators, present at the time and place mentioned in the libel, who could attend with less travel at Del. than N. Y.; and that the libel was circulated in Del.

He said the venue was optional with the plaintiff, the action being for a libel dispersed in several counties. (1 Duul. Pr., 410.) It does not appear that the cause of action arose any more in N. Y. than Del., which is necessary in order to change the venue, the action arising *ex delicto. Serially* v. *Wells,* 1 Cow., 196. Indeed it did arise in Del. At any rate, the plaintiff may retain his venue on stipulating to give material evidence arising in Del.

If the convenience of the parties is to be consulted, it is to be remarked that the change would be directly against the convenience of the plaintiff. He has no witnesses in N. Y. This does not appear to be so with the defendants in relation to Del.

As to witnesses living in other counties, it appears by the plaintiff's affidavit, that they can attend with more convenience in Del. than N. Y. In such a case the venue will not be changed, but on special ground; as where witnesses of both parties reside in the county to which the defendant wishes to take the venue. (1 Dunl. Pr., 411.) The contrary appears in this case.

If the plaintiff's witnesses live in the county where the venue is laid, the venue will be retained, unless there is a great and striking preponderance against him. (1 Dunl. Pr., 411.) The contrary appears in this case.

Curia,* per SAVAGE, *Ch. J.* In *Clinton* v. *Croswell,* 2 Cai., 245, the libel was published in a newspaper printed in Green Co.; but it had also been published in N. Y., where the plaintiff resided. On a motion to change the venue from N. Y., where it was laid by the plaintiff, to the County of Green, it was contended to be of more importance to an individual to protect his character in the place of his residence than at a distance. The court said there was no ground for the application, and denied it. In *Manning* v. *Downing,* 2 Johns., 453, this court laid down the general principles on which venues are changed in transitory actions; that the change depended on the convenience of suitors and the saving of expense to the parties; and they would not allow the plaintiff to retain his venue by stipulation, when it was shown that the defendant had witnesses in a distant county. In *Nicholson* v. *Lathrop,* 3 *Id.,* 139, which was an action for a libel, the venue was laid in Albany. The defendant moved to change it on the ground that the libel was published by the defendant in a paper printed in Utica, where he resided, the plaintiff being a resident in Herkimer; and also on the ground that the defendant had a number of witnesses in Oneida and Herkimer. It did not appear that the [*405**

plaintiff had any witnesses in Albany. The court allowed the plaintiff 20 days within which to elect whether he would lay his venue in Oneida or Herkimer. In *Ross* v. *Lown*, 8 *Id.*, 354, the court again recognized the general principles of convenience and saving of expense, and said they would not, in an action sounding in contract, permit the plaintiff to retain his venue by a stipulation; but in that case, which was trespass *de bonis asportatis*, they allowed him to retain it on stipulating to give material evidence arising in the county where he laid his venue, though his witnesses were only half as numerous as the defendant's, and the cause of action arose in the county where the defendant wished the cause tried. In *Duryee* v. *Orcutt*, 9 *Id.*, 248, the court recognized the same principle, and add: "There are transitory actions in which the venue is altogether optional with the plaintiff. In this **406***] class *we have placed, generally, all actions on contract. It includes, also, all actions arising beyond sea or out of the State; for libels dispersed in several counties; for escapes, or false returns against a carrier on a specialty, note or bill of exchange; and whenever the cause of action is not wholly or necessarily confined to a single county. In these cases the venue will not be changed but upon special grounds, as where the witnesses of both parties reside in the county to which the defendant wishes to bring the venue. If the plaintiff's witnesses reside in the county in which he has laid the venue, unless there is a great and striking preponderance against him, the venue will not be changed."

This case places the action for a libel dispersed in several counties upon the same footing as transitory actions arising on contract, and it is viewed in the same light by the English practice. (1 Tidd, 547-8; 2 Archb. Pr., 176.) We do not see special grounds sufficiently strong, in this case, to require a change of the venue, either in the balance of number or convenience of the witnesses or parties. The preponderance is rather in favor of the plaintiff.

Motion denied.

Cited in—6 Cow., 591.

MILLS *v.* McCOY ET UX.

Action for Malicious Prosecution—Variance between Declaration and Proof—When Objection may be Made—Acquittal Works a Discharge in Law and Fact.

A judge at the circuit is bound to notice an objection for a substantial and material variance between the declaration and evidence, though not made till after the defendant's counsel has closed his summing up to the jury.

In a declaration for a malicious prosecution, setting forth a search-warrant, detention, indictment and acquittal, the search-warrant, detention, &c., are mere matter of inducement, and need not be proved.

Declaring that the search-warrant commanded to bring the person, whereas it commanded to bring both the person and goods, is no material variance, the declaration not professing to set forth the search warrant in *hæc verba*.

Declaring that the defendant caused the plaintiff to be carried before O. and detained till she gave bail, whereas she was in fact first committed for want of sureties by H., and afterwards brought before O. and bailed, is no variance.

Declaring that the plaintiff was acquitted on an indictment, and that the prosecution was ended and determined, and setting forth a judgment of the court to this effect, whereas the record stopped with a verdict of not guilty, and did not contain any judgment of acquittal, is no variance.

On a verdict of acquittal, if the defendant be in prison, he is immediately discharged, and if out on bail, his recognizance is, *ipso facto*, discharged without any further entry.

CASE for slander and malicious prosecution.

On the trial at the circuit various testimony was adduced on both *sides; [***407** and after the defendants' counsel had closed summing up the testimony to the jury, and the plaintiff's counsel had risen to reply, the counsel for the defendants objected that there was a variance between the allegations in the counts for malicious prosecution and the documentary proof produced to support it fatal to the plaintiff's right to sustain the action, and moved the court so to rule. The court declined considering the objection, on the ground that it was too late, and the defendants' counsel excepted.

Mr. G. Griffin (*Mr. W. M. Price*, same side) now moved to bring on the argument upon the bill of exceptions as frivolous.

Mr. D. Graham, contra.

Curia. We think it was the duty of the judge to listen to the objection if there was anything in it. If the variance was substantial, and such as could not be amended, the objection did not come too late. On the other hand, if it was merely formal, we should consider the objection, at any stage, as going for nothing.

At another day,

Mr. Graham pointed out the following variances:

1. The declaration set forth a warrant thus: that upon a certain charge of petit larceny (specifying it) made before one James Hopson, a police justice, &c., "she, the said Catherine McCoy (one of the defendants), falsely and maliciously, and without any reasonable or probable cause whatever, caused and procured the said James Hopson, so being, &c., to make and grant his certain warrant under his hand and seal, in the name of the people of the State of N. Y., for the apprehending and taking of the body of the said plaintiff, with a certain cotton sheet, value of one dollar and fifty cents, several pillow cases, a feather pillow, several towels, &c., and for bringing her, the plaintiff, before him, the said James Hopson, or some other justice of the peace for the City and County of N. Y., at the police office in the City Hall of the said city, to answer the said charge, and to be dealt with as the law directs."

*That the plaintiff was arrested and [***408** detained in custody, until afterwards, &c., the defendant, Catherine McCoy, falsely, &c., caused and procured the plaintiff to go and appear, &c., before Smith Orcutt, a certain other special justice, &c., and the plaintiff then and there to be detained until she, with Homan and Cornell, her bail, had signed and acknowledged a certain recognizance, &c. (setting it out), to appear at the next General Sessions, &c.

That then, falsely, &c., and without any reasonable or probable cause whatever, the defendant, Catherine McCoy, caused the plaintiff to be indicted of the larceny charged.

That afterwards, at the General Sessions, held at, &c., before, &c., the plaintiff was in due manner acquitted of the premises in the indictment charged by a jury of the City and County of N. Y., whereupon it was afterwards adjudged by the court that the plaintiff should depart thence without day; and the plaintiff was and is duly discharged and acquitted of and from the premises in the said indictment specified; and the prosecution is wholly ended and determined, to wit: at, &c.

The search-warrant in evidence was thus: "State of New York, and City and County of New York, *ss.* To any constable or marshal of said city: Whereas information, on oath, hath been given me, James Hopson, one, &c., by Catherine McCoy, of No. 275, Greenwich St., in the 3d ward of the said city, that the following articles, to wit: a cotton sheet, value of one dollar and fifty cents, several pillow cases, a feather pillow, several towels, &c., have lately been feloniously taken, stolen and carried away by Margaret Mills, as is supposed, in the city and ward aforesaid; and that the said Catherine McCoy has a probable cause to suspect, and does suspect that the said articles, or part thereof, are now concealed in the house of George Mills, on the Green Hill, in the 7th ward. These are, therefore, in the name, &c., to command and authorize you, with proper assistance, in the day time, to enter into the house of the said George Mills, situate as aforesaid, and there diligently to search for the said articles; and if the same, or any part thereof, shall be found you are likewise commanded to bring the same, so found, together **409***] *with the said Catherine, or the person in whose custody the same shall be so found, before me, or some other justice of the peace for the said city, to be dealt with as the law directs. Given, &c., the 11th May, 1824," &c.

The warrant of commitment was thus: "City and County of New York, *ss.* By James Hopson, Esquire, one, &c., to the constables and marshals, &c. These are, in the name, &c., to command you, &c., to convey to the said prison the body of Margaret Mills, and deliver her to the keeper thereof; and you, the said keeper, are hereby commanded to receive into your custody, in the said prison, the body of the said Margaret, who stands charged before me, on the oath of Catherine McCoy, with having within 4 weeks last past, at the City of New York, feloniously taken, stolen and carried away, one cotton sheet, value one dollar and fifty cents, several pillow cases, one feather pillow, several towels and other articles; and that you safely keep the said Margaret in your custody, in the said prison, until she shall be thence delivered by due course of law. Given, &c., May 11th, 1824."

The recognizance before Orcutt was then given in evidence.

A record of the indictment and trial was then produced in evidence, ending, however, with the verdict of acquittal, not followed by any judgment of the court.

Mr. Graham cited the following authorities:

1. As to the variance between the search-warrant as set forth in the declaration, and that submitted in proof—2 Campb., 270; 8 East, 328; 7 Taunt., 399.

2. Between the commitment, and that proved —Archb. Plead., 125.

3. Between the description of the court, and the finding of the bill as averred and proved—2 Camph., 193; Archb. Plead., 125; 4 T.R., 590.

4. Between the averment of the plaintiff's acquittal, and determination of the suit, and the record of acquittal.

Curia, per WOODWORTH, *J.* All that part of this declaration, which relates to the search-warrant and commitment *is mere in- [***410** ducement, and even less than inducement. It might have been stricken entirely out of the record, and the cause of action would have been complete upon the indictment, trial and acquittal. There was then no need of proving either the search-warrant or *mittimus*. But if otherwise, the variance complained of is merely formal and unsubstantial.

The variance now pointed out as to the search-warrant is, that the declaration speaks of it as commanding to bring the person merely; whereas the warrant, in fact, calls not only for the person, but the goods found, and commands that both should be forthcoming before the magistrate. The declaration does not profess to set forth the warrant in *hæc verba;* and the bringing of the goods was, obviously, a matter entirely unimportant to the prosecution, unless, by the form of the declaration, it had been made matter of description.

The alleged variance as to the *mittimus* is, that the declaration says the defendant caused the plaintiff to be brought before Orcutt, detained and recognized; whereas, upon a *mittimus*, Hopson committed her, and she was afterwards let out by Orcutt on bail. This is substantially the same thing. The legal effect of the *mittimus* was to detain her till bailed by a magistrate.

There is no variance between the style of the court in the declaration, and that contained in the record which was given in evidence.

The only doubt is, whether the record should not have contained a formal judgment of acquittal, in order to have satisfied that part of the declaration which sets forth the judgment, and says the plaintiff was duly discharged and acquitted, and that the prosecution was wholly ended and determined.

We think this was not necessary. The record ends with the finding of the jury—not guilty. This works a discharge in law, and in fact; for the moment this verdict is pronounced, the defendant, if in prison, is set at large, and if out on bail the recognizance is considered as *ipso facto* void, and no discharge is ever, in practice, entered. No entry is usual, upon the main record, beyond the verdict of not guilty; and * it is *prima facie*, evi- [***411** dence of an acquital and determination of the prosecution, within the words of the declaration.

Judgment for the plaintiff.

WELLS ET AL. *v.* MARSHALL.

MORRISON ET AL. *v.* THE SAME.

Fi. Fa.—*Preference over Attachment.*

A *fi. fa.* delivered to the sheriff takes preference

of an attachment levied before the *fi. fa.* but after the delivery of the *fi. fa.* to the sheriff.

Citation—18 Johns., 311.

IN the first cause, a *fi. fa.* against the goods of the defendant was delivered to the Sheriff of Ulster, Apr. 18, 1825. On Tuesday evening, Apr. 19, the plaintiffs in the second cause obtained an attachment against the goods of the defendant, from a justice of Ulster, under which early on Wednesday morning, the 20th, a constable levied on, and took into his custody, the defendant's goods, the *fi. fa.* not yet being levied; but, on the same day, the sheriff went to the defendant's dwelling-house and levied on all the goods to be found.

And the question was, which process should take preference.

By agreement of the parties, the sheriff had sold all the defendant's goods; and they now requested this court to direct the disposition of the money in his hands. Judgment had been duly obtained on the attachment for $30. The constable had notice of the *fi. fa.* and was forbidden, by one of the plaintiff's named in it, to remove the goods.

Mr. C. G. Dewitt, for Wells &c., insisted that the *fi. fa.* took preference, by the delivery, though the attachment was first levied, and cited *Lambert* v. *Paulding*, 18 Johns., 311, which he said was decisive.

Mr. J. Sudam, contra, cited 2 Eq. Cas. Abr., 381; 12 Johns., 162, 403, 407; 4 East, 1, 523; and 3 Maule. & S., 371.

Curia. The case of *Lambert* v. *Paulding* is decisive that the *fi. fa.* must take preference.

Rule accordingly.

Cited in—10 Abb. Pr., 94; 5 Bos., 536; 41 Am. Dec., 207, 208 (1 Gilm., 636).

412*] *MORAN *v.* DAWES.

Debauching Female Servant—Form of Action for—Proof of Relation of Master and Servant.

In general, the plaintiff has his election to bring case or trespass, for debauching his female servant.

Case is, in all cases, a proper remedy.

To establish the relation of master and servant in this action, the slighest acts of service are sufficient.

Citations—2 T. R., 168; 2 Phil. Ev., 157; 5 Bos. & P., 476; 2 Maule & S., 436; Reeve's Dom. Rel., 293; 5 East, 47, *n. a*; 1 Chit. PL, 137, 138; 2 Chit. Pl., 267, *n. u*; 1 BL Com., 429; 3 Bl. Com., 142; 3 Serg. & R., 315; Selw. *N. P.*, 1083, *n.* 17; 2 T. R., 167-8; Ld. Raym., 1032; 1 H. Bl., 555; 10 Johns., 115; 8 Co., 146; 6 Bac., 560, 561.

CASE for seducing and debauching Jane Moran, the daughter and servant of the plaintiff, *per quod servitium amisit;* tried before Edwards, Circuit Judge, at the N. Y. Circuit, Jan. 12, 1825.

On the trial, Jane Moran, a witness for the plaintiff, testified that she was the daughter of the plaintiff, and at the time of the connexion between her and the defendant, she was over the age of 21 years. That she then lived with her mother in Rector St., in the City of N. Y., in a house owned by her brother; that her brother, mother and sister, also resided there; that her mother was the mistress of the house; that they had a common table; that each, out of their earnings, supported the establishment; she, and her brother and sister furnished money out of their earnings, which made a common fund in the hands of her mother, who out of this fund, purchased the necessary articles for the family, the mother rendering her services only; that the witness sometimes made up garments for her mother gratuitously, as a daughter would; and that she assisted her mother in her household affairs.

That while living with her mother in this way, the defendant, in the absence of the mother, and the other occupants of the house, entered her room in the day time, about midday, while she was lying on her bed asleep, and had carnal knowledge with her, first by force and against her will, but she yielded before the conclusion.

The plaintiff having rested here, the defendant's counsel moved for a nonsuit, on the ground that the action should have been trespass, and that the relation of mistress and servant was not established. The judge overruled the motion, and the defendant excepted.

Mr. A. Spencer moved for a new trial; and to show that the action should have been trespass, he cited *Ditcham* v. *Bond*, *2 [*413 Maule & S., 436; *Woodward* v. *Walton*, 5 Bos. & P., 476, and *Crosby* v. *Leng*, 12 East, 409.

To show that the relation of mistress and servant was not established, he cited *Postlethwaite* v. *Parkes*, 3 Burr., 1878, and *Bennett* v. *Alcott*, 2 T. R., 166.

Mr. C. D. Colden, contra, to show that case was proper, cited 2 Chit. Pl., 266, 268; Archb. Civ. PL, sec. 5, p. 25; 1 Chit. Pl., 137; 1 Bl. Com., 429, and *note* by Christian; and *Martin* v. *Payne*, 9 Johns., 387. He admitted there was some confusion in the English authorities, but thought they were all reducible to the proposition that the plaintiff may, at his election, bring case or trespass.

To show that the relation of mistress and servant was established, he cited 3 Bl. Com., 142, *note* by Christian; Selw. *N. P.*, 967; and 2 Phil. Ev., 156, 157.

Curia. The relation of mistress and servant; between the plaintiff and her daughter, was sufficiently made out at the trial. The slightest acts of service are sufficient, as merely milking cows. *Bennett* v. *Alcott*, 2 T. R., 168. So it is said making tea for, or attention to the plaintiff, during sickness. (2 Phil. Ev., 157.) Mr. Phillips very judiciously remarks, that otherwise the action might be confined to families in the lower ranks of life, where the daughter is literally a servant; and could never be extended to the higher order, where it is generally more wanted; and where the injury is often of a more aggravated kind. (*Id.*)

As to the form of the action; in England, trespass *vi et armis* seems to have predominated. *Woodward* v. *Walton*, 5 Bos. & P., 476; *Ditcham* v. *Bond*, 2 Maule & S., 436; Reeve's Dom. Rel. 293. Yet the right to bring case, laying the injury with a *per quod servitium amisit*, has there, not only been judiciously recognized, but very able writers upon English law treat this as the most proper form. *Satherwaite* v. *Duerst*. 5 East, 47, *note a;* 1 Chit. Pl., 137, 138; 2 *Id.*, 267, *note u*, and cases there cited; Christian's *notes* to 1 Bl. Com., 429, and 3 *Id.*,

142. Mr. Chitty has given the precedent of a declaration in this form of action. (2 Chit. Pl., 267.) Case is uniformly brought in Conn. **414***] (Reeve's *Dom. Rel., 293.) And though trespass was holden to lie in Pennsylvania, yet case was pronounced the most appropriate remedy. *Ream* v. *Rank*, 3 Serg. & R., 315. Perhaps, with certain qualifications, the remark made at the bar, that the plaintiff may elect between trespass and case, is correct. Where the seduction is accompanied with actual violence upon the person of the daughter, or an illegal entry, upon the plaintiff's close, or into his house, probably, in the first case, trespass would lie for the assault within the case of *Ditcham* v. *Bond;* and in the last there is no doubt, trespass *quare clausum, vel domum fregit,* would lie. And in each case, damages for the seduction and loss of service may be laid as matter of aggravation. But it is clear, we think, both upon principle and authority, that case is, without exception, a proper remedy. (Selw. *N. P.*, 1033, *note* 17, cites 2 T. R., 167, 8, per Buller, *J.*, and per Holt, *Ch. J.*, Ld. Raym., 1032.) Neither the injury to the person of the child, nor the property of the plaintiff, are, in truth, ever taken into the account. They are little more than a mere fiction, adopted in order to sustain the remedy by trespass. The direct injury may be waived in all cases; and the declaration framed to meet the consequential injury, disregarding entirely every consideration, except the loss of service, and the more important one of seduction and disgrace. A very usual case may be supposed, in which, if we are to be governed by the technical rules relating to an action of trespass, the father would be remediless, for the most aggravated form of the injury, unless he has an election. The seducer is received at the dwelling of the father on the footing of a suitor; he thus having a license to enter the house, of which he avails himself to accomplish the seduction, with the consent of the daughter. It could hardly be said that trespass and assault would lie for such an act. The father is then put to his remedy by trespass *quare domum fregit,* laying the seduction, &c., by way of aggravation. The defendant does not become a trespasser *ab initio;* for license was given by the party. A person who is guilty of abusing an authority in fact, does not thereby become a trespasser *ab initio;* but it is otherwise where a license is given by law. (6 Bac., 560, 561, **415***] *and the cases there cited; 8 Rep., 146.) The defendant may, therefore, justify the entry. It is a rule that the trespass itself being justified, this also reaches the matter laid in aggravation; *Taylor* v. *Cole*, 1 H. Bl., 555; and thus the defeudant would be acquitted of the entire charge against him. It cannot be that the law ever intended to trammel this remedy by imposing upon the party such an absurd result. It marks the limit of the prosecution, by confining it to one holding the relation of master, *Nickleson* v. *Stryker*, 10 Johns., 115, from which it looks directly to the consequential injury as the vital spark of the action; thus reducing the case to the plain and familiar principle which marks the distinction between trespass and case. On the whole, we are all perfectly clear that case was well brought; and the motion for a new trial must be denied.

New trial refused.

Cited in—1 Wend., 450; 10 Wend., 340; 32 N. Y., 235; 5 Lans., 456; 2 Barb., 187; 9 Barb., 525; 24 Barb., 629; 44 Barb., 594; 7 How. Pr., 281; 4 Bos., 627.

WRIGHT AND ELY v. HOOKER.

Error in Advertisement of Land for Sale on Fi. Fa.—*Action against Sheriff—Sale Vacated on Motion.*

Sale of real estate under a *fi. fa.* vacated, &c., on motion in behalf of the deputy-sheriff who sold; an action having been brought against the sheriff for the penalty given by the Statute, 1 R. L., 505, sec. 13, he having misdescribed the land in the advertisement by mistake; on paying the costs of the motion, and of the suit against the sheriff, the deputy having acted in good faith.

A DEPUTY of the Sheriff of Oswego had, by mistake, advertised the defendant's farm for sale at the house of the defendant, upon a *fi. fa.* under a wrong description; but he sold the farm and gave a certificate of sale by a full and correct description including the No. of the lot. The sale took place, not at the defendant's actual dwelling-house, but at his late dwelling-house on the farm sold, from which he had removed a few months before; but to which the deputy made affidavit he expected he would shortly return, as he informed him that such was his intention, and he owned the house at the time of the sale. The deputy also swore that he sold without discovering the error in description; that he could not ascertain the number of the lot which was, therefore, omitted in the advertisement; and the misdescription was in the length of one of the boundary lines, being, as he believed, by mistake of the printer, advertised as 78 chains and 50 links long, whereas it should have been 28 *chains and 50 links; that he be- [***416** lieved, from repeated conversations with the defendant, that he fully understood where the sale was to be; that the proceedings were in good faith. Hooker had sued the Sheriff of Oswego, Otis Hart, for the penalty given by the Statute, 1 R. L. 505, sec. 13, for selling real estate without duly advertising it.

Several affidavits were read on the part of Hooker to rebut the allegation of good faith.

It appeared that the plaintiff, Wright, bid off the farm by his agent; no money was paid, but the amount bid was indorsed as received by the sheriff on the *fi. fa.*, and a return made accordingly.

On personal notice of the motion served on the defendant and on the plaintiff's attorney,

Mr. J. Platt, in behalf of the deputy, moved to vacate the sale, certificate, receipt and return upon the *fi. fa.*

Mr. G. C. Bronson, contra.

The Court being satisfied that the proceedings were in good faith, granted the motion, on payment of all the costs of opposing this motion, and the costs in the action brought against the sheriff.

Rule accordingly.

Cited in—8 How. Pr., 81.

BRADT v. KOON.

LAWRENCE v. BRADT.

Judgment for Costs—Attorney's Lien.

An attorney obtains judgment for costs in favor of A against B, the latter has no right to set off a judgment purchased by him against A after the judgment obtained in A's favor, so as to defeat the attorney's lien.

The court will protect the attorney's lien to the same extent as the rights of an assignee.

IN the first cause, Bradt had recovered in this court $70. In the second cause, Lawrence had recovered $53.81 in the Mayor's Court of the City of Albany, which was assigned to Koon; and now,

Mr. J. Koon moved to set off $53.81, the last judgment against so much of the first, and cited **417***] *Schermerhorn* v. *Schermerhorn*, *3 Cai., 190; *Hall* v. *Odie*, 2 Bos. & P., 28; *Cooper* v. *Bigelow*, 1 Cow., 206, and *Chamberlin* v. *Day*, 3 Cow., 353.

Affidavits were read in opposition to the motion, showing that the judgment against Koon was obtained upon a stipulation to pay certain costs in a cause brought by Bradt against Koon, wherein *Mr. J. T. B. Van Vechten* was attorney for Bradt; and these costs were due and unpaid to Mr. Van Vechten; that this was known to Koon when he took an assignment of Lawrence's judgment. Upon these facts,

Mr. J. T. B. Van Vechten submitted that the beneficial interest in the whole judgment was in him, and that Bradt was a mere trustee for his benefit; that his equity was like that of an assignee, whose rights Koon perfectly understood. That an attorney has a lien upon the costs nominally due to his client, but really to the attorney, which lien the court will protect to the same extent as if the right was acquired by assignment, he cited *Martin* v. *Hawks*, 15 Johns., 405. And on the authority of that case,

The Court said the motion must be denied.

Motion denied.

Cited in—13 Wend., 653; 28 N. Y., 240; 11 Hun, 25; 4 Barb., 50; 5 How. Pr., 349; 2 Wall., Jr., 479; 46 Ill., 481; 28 Am. Dec., 498.

EX PARTE LAWRENCE.

Judgment—Lien on Realty—Right of Creditor to Redeem—Effect of Levy on Personalty.

A levy on personal property sufficient to satisfy a *fi. fa.* is an extinguishment of the judgment on which it issued.

The judgment, therefore, ceases to be a lien on real estate, and the judgment creditor has no right, as such, to redeem under the Act, sess. 43, ch. 184, sec. 3.

Citations—2 Ld. Raym., 1072; 1 Salk., 322; 4 Mass., 403; 12 Johns., 207; 7 Johns., 428-9; 3 Cow., 35, 69.

TOLL obtained judgment against Chandler, and bid off Chandler's land in Camillus, Onondaga Co., on a *fi. fa.*, at $30, May 8, 1823. Drake having a junior judgment for $82.55 against Chandler and one Hopping, assigned it to Lawrence, who sued out a *fi. fa.*, on which the sheriff made $43 by a sale of Chandler's personal property; and then levied on Hopping's personal property to an amount sufficient to satisfy the *fi. fa.*, and took a receipt for it. The sale of Hopping's property was delayed from time to time, by Lawrence's directions, till, in Aug., 1824, Lawrence claimed of the sheriff to redeem, as a judgment creditor of Chandler, the land sold, upon the senior judgment, to Toll; but the sheriff denied his right to redeem, and would not receive the money, or give a conveyance; and in Sept. last, *he sold Hopping's personal property, [***418** and collected the residue of Lawrence's *fi. fa.* pursuant to his directions.

A *mandamus* was now moved for, to the Sheriff of Onondaga, commanding him to convey to Lawrence.

Mr. G. Lawrence, for the motion.

Mr. B. D. Noxon, contra.

Curia. Clearly this motion must be denied. The levy on the personal property of Hopping, to an amount sufficient to satisfy Lawrence's execution operated *per se*, as an extinguishment of his judgment. This has been often held. *Clerk* v. *Withers*, 2 Ld. Raym., 1072; S. C., 1 Salk., 322; *Ladd* v. *Blunt*, 4 Mass., 403; *Hoyt* v. *Hudson*, 12 Johns., 207; *Reed* v. *Pruyn*, 7 *Id.*, 428-9. Lawrence's judgment ceased to be a lien from the time of the levy, and of course he could not redeem. *Matter of Hurd*, 3 Cow., 35; *Matter of Marsh*, *Id.*, 69.

Motion denied.

Cited in—7 Cow., 21; 2 Wend., 298; 6 Wend., 563; 7 Wend., 221; 14 Wend., 262; 16 Wend., 351, 445; 23 Wend., 499; 2 Den., 355; Hoffm., 149; 7 Barb., 73; 22 Barb., 524; 3 How. Pr., 263; 8 Abb. Pr., 237; 1 Leg. Obs., 60; 3 Wall., 699; 42 Ind., 310; 40 Am. Dec., 73 (7 How., Miss., 386); 49 Am. Dec., 59 (11 S. & M., 249).

JACKSON v. PEER.

Practice—Plea Puis Darrein Continuance—*Amendment.*

A plea *puis darrein continuance* may, in general, be pleaded without being verified by affidavit.

And the defendant may enter a rule of course to amend such a plea, as in other cases.

So he may enter a rule of course to reply or that the plaintiff be *non prossed.*

Under a rule of course to amend his plea, the defendant may alter it so as to modify, or vary entirely, the ground of defense taken by the original plea.

Citation—9 Johns., 250.

TRESPASS for *mesne* profits, in the name of the nominal plaintiff, on a recovery in ejectment in this court, *ex dem. Freeman.* The cause being at issue, upon a plea of the general issue, and noticed for trial at the Chautauqua Circuit in Aug., 1824, the defendant there interposed a plea *puis darrein continuance*, duly verified by oath, that the writ of possession in the ejectment suit had been vacated by a rule of this court, and the possession of the premises in question yielded up and restored to the defendant. To this plea the plaintiff demurred *instanter*, and served a copy of the demurrer on the defendant's attorney: and moved the court for a *trial of the issue in fact, which [***419** had been joined in the cause; but the judge declined trying it. No rule to join in demurrer was ever entered. Afterwards the defendant's attorney entered a rule of course to amend the plea *puis darrein continuance;* and Oct. 30, 1824, served a copy of the amended plea on the plaintiff's attorney. This plea, in addition to the *vacatur* and restitution pleaded in the first, averred that Sept. 16, 1824, Freeman, the lessor, had caused the judgment in the ejectment to be vacated, set aside and altogether held for nothing. Nov. 19, 1824, the attorney for the plaintiff returned this copy to the defendant's attorney, objecting that it was irregular, and that the plaintiff's attorney was not bound to receive it. This was soon afterwards returned to the plaintiff's attorney by mail. The defendant's attorney having entered a rule to reply to the amended plea, gave notice of this to the plaintiff's attorney, and proceeded to judgment of *nol pros.*, for want of a replication, in the same manner as in the ordinary course of a cause, upon the usual plea. He then caused the defendant's costs to be regularly demanded of Freeman, the lessor, Apr. 14, 1825, delivering him at the same time a copy of a *ca. sa.* for the costs, with a copy of the taxed bill, and showing him the original *ca. sa.* and taxed bill. And now,

Messrs. P. *De Witt* and *J. Houghton*, for the defendant, moved for an attachment against the lessor of the plaintiff for non-payment of costs.

Messrs. R. Sedgwick and *A. Dixon*, contra, moved to set aside the *nol pros.*, for irregularity, insisting that a plea *puis darrein continuance* cannot be amended of course in any respect; and that at any rate, it cannot be amended so as to make it an entire new plea, setting forth additional matter, which would, in itself, constitute a defense. They cited 18 Johns., 310; Bull. *N. P.*, 309; 2 Dunl. Pr., 628-9; 1 Chit. Pl., 638; 2 Tidd, 778; Yelv., 181; Freem., 252; Gilb. C. P., 105; 1 Str., 493; 1 Ld. Raym., 266, and Col. Cas., 87.

They also insisted that the plea, not being verified by affidavit, was a nullity. (Tidd, 777.)

420*] **Messrs. Dewitt* and *J. Houghton*, to show that the plea need not be verified by affidavit; cited *Bancker* v. *Ash*, and *Lawrence* v. *Ash*, 9 Johns., 250, and they insisted that this plea, as well as any other in the ordinary course of the cause, might be followed by a rule of course to reply.

Curia. Both these motions depend upon the regularity of the plea, and the proceedings under it. The amended plea *puis darrein continuance* was not void for want of being verified by affidavit. (9 Johns., 250.)

The 4th rule of April Term, 1796, is general, that the rule to plead or answer shall, in all cases, be a rule of 20 days after notice of its entry, except in certain specified cases not including pleas *puis darrein continuance;* and we see no objection in policy or convenience, against its being extended to these pleas. The 8th rule of that term is also general that the defendant may amend a special plea which is demurred to; and we think that, in spirit as well as terms, it embraces a plea *puis darrein continuance*. This is not the case of adding a new plea, but a mere alteration of an old one. Under a rule of course to amend, the defendant has a right to alter his plea in substance, so as to modify, or vary entirely the original ground of defense.

The plaintiff's motion must be denied, and the defendant's granted, but without costs on either side.

Rule accordingly.

Cited in—7 Wend., 262; 3 How. Pr., 300; 1 Co. B, 65.

EX PARTE BOARD.

Practice—Sale of Lands on Fi. Fa.—*Redemption.*

One who comes to redeem from a judgment creditor under Act, sess. 43, ch. 184, sec. 3, may pay the money either to the sheriff or the creditor.

The sheriff may receive current bank bills even against the express directions of the creditor.

So he may allow an assignee to redeem, *de bene esse*, without demanding present evidence of the assignment.

M. DENTON recovered against A. Stickney $360, in the Orange C. P.; and the judgment was docketed, Apr. 23, 1822, and Dec. 1, 1823, assigned *to D. Denton, H. [***421** Seely & D. Roe. P. Board then recovered against the same Stickney $316.68 in the same court; and the judgment was docketed Sept., 1823; and in Feb. following assigned to C. Board. J. Steward then recovered against Stickney $50.74, before a justice of Orange Co.; and the transcript was filed in the clerk's office of Orange Oct. 17, 1823; and Jan. 15, 1824, he assigned to D. Roe.

Jan. 7, 1824, certain lands of Stickney were sold by the Sheriff of Orange, on three writs of *fi. fa.* issued on judgments docketed before either of the above, and bid off by D. Roe at $350, who received a certificate of sale, upon which he was entitled to a deed, unless the lands should be redeemed, Apr. 7, 1825. At 11 o'clock P. M. of this day, J. B. Booth presented himself to the sheriff to redeem in behalf of C. Board, assignee of P. Board's judgment; and produced the requisite evidence of his (C. Board's) right to redeem, and tendered the requisite amount in specie, which the sheriff received. D. Roe then immediately came to the sheriff and demanded of Mr. Booth an account of the sum due upon C. Board's judgment. Mr. Booth answered $180, whereupon Roe handed the sheriff $200, stating to Mr. Booth that he redeemed upon the judgment in favor of M. Denton, and that in favor of Steward, for the benefit of himself, H. Seeley and D. Denton, the assignees.

Mr. Booth insisted that the sheriff should require from Roe the exhibition of an assignment of the judgments upon which he redeemed, objected to his receiving bank notes, and insisted that he should take nothing but specie. The sheriff refused to comply; but informed Mr. Booth that if he wished to redeem over against Roe, he would accept current money; and Roe told Booth that if he wished to redeem further, he would immediately give him the amount due upon his (Roe's) judgments. But Booth did not require the amount, nor express a wish to redeem further; and declined receiving from the sheriff the money which he had paid with the money paid by Roe; and C. Board, also, afterwards, declined receiving this money, though offered to him by the sheriff. On these facts,

422*] *Mr. *H.* G. *Wisner* moved for a *mandamus*, commanding the Sheriff of Orange to convey to C. Board.

He insisted:

1. That according to the true construction of the Statute, the money should have been paid to the judgment creditor, not the sheriff.

2. That if otherwise, the sheriff was the mere agent of the creditor, and had no right to receive bank bills contrary to the instructions of his principal.

3. The evidence of the assignment was wanting.

Mr. O. Hoffman, contra.

Curia. It is clear from the Statute (nor has it ever been doubted in the great number of cases which have been before us involving the question) that the sheriff may receive the money. The Statute leaves it optional with the one who comes to redeem, to pay the money to either the sheriff or the judgment creditor.

The sheriff is not merely a naked agent, subject to the absolute control of the creditor as to his conduct. He had a discretion, as he would have on a sale upon execution, though in both cases he is *quasi* agent; and he was right in receiving the current bank bills of the country.(*a*)

He was also right in trusting (though this was also in his discretion) as to the fact that the one who came to redeem was a regular assignee, and as such entitled to redeem. He may receive the money, *de bene esse*, and satisfy himself afterwards of the truth. It now appears that there is a subsisting judgment which has been regularly assigned. This is enough. The motion must be denied.

Motion denied.

Cited in—7 Cow., 582; 20 Wend., 559; 26 Cal., 663; 82 Ind., 302.

(*a*) *Vide* M'Donald v. Neilson, 2 Cow., 139.

423*] *SPRINGSTED

v.

JAYNE, Impleaded with JAYNE.

Death of Plaintiff, after Verdict, before Judgment—Practice.

The court will not order proceedings to stay till administration granted, where the plaintiff dies intermediate the verdict and judgment, though the defendant have made a case for a new trial.

In such case, the cause proceeds the same as if the plaintiff had lived. His death works no change in its course.

If judgment is rendered for him, it relates to the term next after the trial.

THIS cause was tried at the Orange Circuit in the summer of 1823, and a verdict given for the plaintiff. The defendant made a case for the purpose of moving for a new trial, which was noticed for argument at this term, by the attorney for the plaintiff. In the last autumn the plaintiff died intestate, and no administration of his estate having yet been granted,

Mr. H. G. Wisner, for the defendant, moved for a rule that all futher proceedings on the part of the plaintiff be stayed till an administrator should be appointed.

Mr. T. J. Oakley, contra, said that this would be of no use to the defendant, nor did the death of the plaintiff vary the situation of the parties. Should judgment be for the plaintiff, it would relate to and be entered up as of the term next after the verdict was rendered. In the eye of the law the plaintiff's death worked no change whatever in the cause. Every thing, even the attorney, remained the same; and all should be treated as if Springsted was still alive, until the question as to the new trial should be granted.

And of this opinion was *the Court;* and they denied the motion.

Motion denied.

Cited in—4 Barb., 524; 9 How. Pr., 244; 20 How. Pr., 375; 2 Abb. Pr., 296; 3 Sand., 662; Co. R. N. S., 90.

---

*SHOOK [*424

v.

FULTON ET AL., Executors of PHILIPS.

Pleading—Practice.

Where the defendant pleads two distinct pleas, neither of which is, in itself, a defense, though both together would be; and the plaintiff replies separately, and goes to trial, and the pleas are found for the defendant, judgment shall be for him; for the cause is with him on the whole record; and the court will consider the two pleas substantially one; though, in form, two; and to avail himself of the defect, the plaintiff should demur.

ASSUMPSIT. The defendants pleaded a judgment recovered and outstanding in favor of Dubois and others, for $274.24, without concluding *et hoc paratus est verificare per recordum;* and then proceeded thus: "And for further plea in this behalf, by leave of the court first had and obtained, according to the term of the statute in such case made and provided, the said defendants further say" (going on and pleading a debt to, and retainer therefor, by Fulton, one of the executors to $122; and then proceeded thus): "And the said defendants, executors as aforesaid, further say they have duly and fully administered all and singular the goods and chattels which were of the said Philips, deceased, at the time of his death, which ever came to their hands to be administered, except goods and chattels to the value of $332, &c., which were not sufficient to satisfy the several debts aforesaid due, and owing on the said judgment, and also due to the said Fulton, &c.; and this, they, the said defendants, are ready to verify, &c.; praying judgment.

The plaintiff put in two distinct, full replications, viz.: 1. *Nul tiel record*, as to the judgment; and 2. Assets beyond what were admitted, sufficient to satisfy the plaintiff's claim.

A motion was made at the last term to bring on the trial by record upon the first replication; but some difficulty being started as to the effect of the defendants' pleading, the court refused to give judgment until the issue of fact should be disposed of; and they directed that the matter should be then moved again.

It was now admitted by both parties that the debt due to the plaintiff was $145.01, and that the assets in the defendant's hands were no more than $163 over and above what would pay the debt due to Fulton, the executor, the sum which he claimed by his plea to retain.

425*] **Mr. G. A. Shufeldt* (*Mr.* P. *Ruggles* same side) insisted that, upon the form of the pleadings, the plaintiff was entitled to judgment.

Messrs. J. W. Wheeler and *E. Williams*, contra.

Curia. No doubt, taking the judgment and the retainer to be pleaded separately, they would be bad. Neither would be a full answer to the plaintiff's declaration. The plaintiff has treated them as distinct by putting in two separate and distinct replications; but this does not make them so. The verdict of the jury, on the state of facts before us, would be, that the testator promised as averred in the declaration; but that the defendant, Fulton's plea of retainer is true. Then comes the record verifying the plea of a judgment recovered, so that all the issues are in favor of the defendants. On the whole record, the cause is with them. In form, the pleas are separate; but we cannot avoid seeing that, in substance, they are one. We will not suffer the plaintiff to entrap the defendants by taking issue in this way, going down to trial, and then coming in, on the ground of this form, to work a substantial injury to the defendants. If he considered the pleas bad in form, he should have demurred, when the defendants might have amended. Upon this state of the case, we should give judgment for the defendants. But as the plaintiff may have mistaken his course, he may withdraw his replications, and enter judgment for assets *in futuro*, on paying all the costs accerned subsequent to the filing of the replications, and the costs of this motion. If he do not elect to do this within 30 days, the defendants may then take judgment.

Rule accordingly.

Cited in—15 Wend., 467,

426*] *PELL AND WIFE v. GRIGG.

Variance Between Declarations and ac etiam—*Discharge of Bail.*

If the declaration be for a cause of action different from the *ac etiam*, the special bail may move for an *exoneretur*, which will be ordered with costs.

THE *ac etiam* in the *alias capias ad respondendum*, on which the defendant was arrested, was thus: "For speaking, uttering and publishing certain slanderous, scandalous and actionable words against the said Joseph and Sarah, to their damage, &c." The defendant having been holden to bail below upon a judge's order, put in bail above. The declaration was for maliciously suing out an attachment under the Absconding Debtor Act, against Mrs. Pell, upon false representations, and affidavits wrongfully procured; and upon the false affidavit of the defendant, &c.

Mr. H. A. Fay moved that an *exoneretur* be entered on the original bailpiece, for the variance between the *ac etiam* and the declaration; and cited Tidd Pr., 242; 2 H. Bl., 278; 2 Bos. & P., 358.

Mr. H. A. Western, contra, believed that the bail were discharged by the variance; but insisted that the motion was unnecessary, and should, therefore, be denied. The variance exonerated the bail by its own operation, and would be a defense in an action on the recognizance. At any rate costs should not be allowed against the plaintiff

Mr. Fay, in reply, said the bail were entitled to a discharge of record. Without this formality they would be liable to a suit. The delay to apply for this would, by-and-by, be insisted on as a waiver of the objection.

The Court, without assigning their reasons, granted the motion, with costs.

Rule accordingly.

Cited in—9 Wend., 479; 35 Barb., 210; 13 Abb. Pr., 106.

---

*JACKSON, ex dem. HOWELL ET AL., [*427
v.
JOHN AND MARY DELANCEY.

Competency of Witness—Widow of Grantor with Warranty—When Competent to Support Title of Grantee—Conveyance by Bargain and Sale—Consideration for—Bargain and Sale to Vest in futuro, *void—Covenant to Stand Seised.*

The widow of a grantor of land with warranty, he having died insolvent, is an admissible witness in support of the title of the grantee, on being released by him, and without her releasing her interest in her husband's personal estate.

The grantor in a quitclaim deed is a competent witness in support of the grantee's title.

A pecuniary consideration is essential to give effect to a conveyance of lands, as a bargain and sale. A conveyance expressed to be in consideration of the future performance of certain conditions, though one of them be to pay money, is not valid as a bargain and sale.

A bargain and sale of a freehold to vest *in futuro*, is void; though otherwise, it seems, of a covenant to stand seised.

When a deed states a consideration, and does not say, for other considerations, none other than the one expressed can be shown.

A deed cannot operate as a covenant to stand seised, unless the consideration of blood or marriage be expressed on its face.

Citations—1 Cow., 622; 7 Johns., 342; 16 Johns., 47; 7 Mass., 384.

EJECTMENT for a lot of ground in the Bowery, City of N. Y., tried before Edwards, Circuit Judge, at the N. Y. Circuit, July 1, 1823.

John Deitz, being seised in fee of the premises in question, died, leaving the lessors of the plaintiff his heirs at law. During his lifetime, Deitz executed and delivered to Abraham Buice, his son-in-law, a deed of the premises in question, which, so far as is material here,

---

NOTE.—*Real property — Deeds — Consideration — Bargain and sale.*

A deed, to operate as a bargain and sale, must have a pecuniary consideration. Jackson v. Florence, 16 Johns., 47; Jackson v. Sebring, 16 Johns., 515; Jackson v. Cadwell, 1 Cow., 622; Jackson v. Pike, 9 Cow., 69; Corwin v. Corwin, 6 N. Y., 342; Schott v. Burton, 13 Barb., 173; Cheney v. Watkins, 1 Harr & J., 527; Okison v. Patterson, 1 W. & S., 395.

The consideration must be more than nominal. Du-was thus: "To all to whom these presents shall come, or may concern. Know ye, that I, John Deitz, of, &c., in consideration of the performances hereinafter mentioned, have given, granted, alienated, enfeoffed and confirmed; and by these presents, do give, grant, aliene, enfeoff and confirm unto my son-in-law, Abraham Buice, all my estate, real and personal; and the reversion, &c., to have, &c., to the said Buice, his heirs, &c.; provided always, and upon this special trust and confidence, nevertheless, and upon this express condition, that he, the said Abraham Buice, his heirs, executors, administrators and assigns, shall and do permit and suffer me to be and remain in possession, and to use and enjoy all and every my said estate, both real and personal, during my natural life, without paying or yielding anything therefor, or in respect thereof, and not otherwise; and further, that from and after my decease, the said Abraham Buice, his heirs, &c., shall well and truly pay unto Frederick Howell, £100, and also deliver unto the said Frederick Howell two feather beds and all my wearing apparel; and further, that during my natural life, the said Abraham Buice, his heirs, &c., shall and will find and provide me with good meat and drink, washing and lodging; and the said Abraham Buice is to occupy and, be in possession of my house, situate at the corner of Eagle St., for which he is to allow me £60 a year during my nat- **428***] ural *life; and further, I am to assist the said Abraham Buice in repairing the buildings; and further, I do hereby promise that I will pay and discharge all debts and incumbrances on my said estate, except £345, which is to be paid out of my estate, for which I am to allow the said Abraham Buice interest after my debts are paid; and that from and after my decease, he, the said Abraham Buice, his heirs, &c., shall or lawfully may have, hold and enjoy the premises hereby given and granted, and every part, &c., and dispose thereof, and convert the same to his and their own proper use and behoof, &c."

Abraham Buice and his wife, by deed of indenture, dated July 11, 1803, conveyed the premises in question to Peter Crawbuck, with covenants of seisin and quiet enjoyment, a covenant against incumbrances, and for further assurance, Crawbuck conveyed to one of the defendants.

In the course of the trial, Margaret Buice, the widow of Abraham Buice, who had died since the execution of the deed to Crawbuck, was offered as a witness by the defendant, but objected to on the ground of interest. The defendant thereupon executed to her a general release, and especially a release of all claims by reason of her being a grantor in the deed from her husband. The objection was persisted in, on the ground that her interest consisted in a claim to a residuary share in her husband's personal estate. The defendant then proved that her husband died insolvent, and she was sworn.

Peter Crawbuck was also offered as a witness on the part of the defendant. He was objected to, as being the immediate grantor of Mary Delancey, one of the defendants: but it did not appear that the deed, by which he conveyed, contained any covenants, and he was sworn.

The defendant examined Margaret Buice, Peter Crawbuck, and other witnesses, to show that Buice had fulfilled the conditions in the deed from Deitz; that Buice intermarried with the grantor's daughter, and that the conveyance was judicious, under the circumstances of the case, &c.

Verdict for the plaintiff, subject to the opinion of the court on a case, with leave to turn it into a special verdict.

*On the argument at the bar, [***429** *Messrs. A. Burr* and *L. Mitchell*, for the plaintiff, argued five different points which they made upon the case, among which were these two:

1. That the evidence of Mrs. Buice and Crawbuck should have been rejected.

2. That the deed from Deitz to Buice was void, both as a common law conveyance, and under the Statute of Uses; because, first, there is no consideration, either of blood or money; second, because it pretends to convey an estate of freehold to commence in future; third, because the subject of the conveyance was not sufficiently located or described.

To show that the deed from Deitz could not be valid as a covenant to stand seised, there being no consideration of blood expressed, or existing in fact, they cited *Jackson* v. *Florence*, 16 Johns., 47, and the cases there cited; *Jackson* v. *Cadwell*, 1 Cow., 622; Vin. Abr., Uses, Z, *a*, pl. 8; Cruise Dig., Deed, ch. 12, sec. 20; *Jackson* v. *Sebring*, 16 Johns., 515; *Wallis* v. *Wallis*, 4 Mass., 135.

That no other consideration could be shown than what is expressed, *Maigley* v. *Hauer*, 7 Johns., 341; *Schermerhorn* v. *Vanderheyden*, 1 Johns., 139; *Howes* v. *Barker*, 3 *Id.*, 506.

That an estate of freehold cannot be conveyed to commence *in futuro*, *Barwick's* case, 5 Rep., 95, 3 res.; *Roe* v. *Tranmer*, 2 Wils., 75; *Pray* v. *Pierce*, 7 Mass., 384.

That the deed cannot take effect as a bargain and sale, for want of a pecuniary consideration, *Jackson* v. *Sebring*, 16 Johns., 515; *Jackson* v. *Alexander*, 3 Johns., 488; *Jackson* v. *Cadwell*, 6 Cow., 622; there being no livery of seisin. (Shep. Touch., 209, 220; Litt., sec. 59.)

As to the effect of the condition in the deed,

---

voll v. Wilson, 9 Barb., 487; Hayes v. Kershow, 1 Sandf. Ch., 258.

"But the better doctrine seems to be, that any valuable consideration, a *quid pro quo*, acknowledged or proved, will be sufficient to sustain a bargain and sale." 3 Washb. Real Prop., 370, citing Jackson v. Leek, 19 Wend., 339; Jackson v. Pike, 9 Cow., 69; Jackson v. Alexander, 3 Johns., 484, 492; Jackson v. Schoonmaker, 2 Johns., 230; Shep. Touch., 223; Deen v. Hanks, 5 Ired., 30.

· *Though a pecuniary consideration is necessary* to support a deed of bargain and sale, it need not be money alone. Jackson v. Pike, 9 Cow., 69.

On the question of the creation of estates *in futuro*, see, Jackson v. Sebring, 16 Johns., 528, Jackson v. McKenney, 3 Wend., 233; Rogers v. Eagle Fire Ins. Co., 9 Wend., 611; Jackson v. Staats, 11 Johns., 337, 351; Mardan v. Chase, 32 Me., 329; Hawes v. Stebbins, 49 Cal., 369; Brewer v. Hardy, 22 Pick., 376; Barrett v. French, 1 Conn., 354; Welsh v. Foster, 12 Mass., 93; Green v. Thomas, 11 Me., 321; Corwin v. Corwin, 9 Barb., 219; Jackson v. Cadwell, 1 Cow., 622; 3 Washb. Real Prop., 372.

On the consideration clause of deeds, see generally, Bower v. Bell, 20 Johns., 338, *note*.

they cited *Butler* v. *Lady Bray*, Dy., 189, 190; Shep. Touch., 219, 220.

Messrs. R. Bogardus and *J. O. Hoffman*, contra, insisted that the testimony of Mrs. Buice and Crawbuck was admissible (*M'Don-*
430*] *ald* *v. *Neilson*, 2 Cow., 139); and that the deed in question was valid and effectual under the circumstances and facts in the case; and a bar to the lessors of the plaintiff, who claim as heirs at law of the grantor. They insisted that this was a conditional estate in fee, vesting presently, and defeasible by condition subsequent. (2 Bl. Com., 154; Co. Litt., 201.) They never had contended that this was a covenant to stand seised; because it wanted the consideration of blood upon the face of the deed; but it was a bargain and sale, supported by a pecuniary consideration. It is not necessary for the deed to say that money is paid. That it is to be paid is enough. (Dy., 336 *b*, 337 *a*.) Suppose the grant to be of a freehold to commence *in futuro;* the conveyance is good under the Statute of Uses, and this has been so held, ever since the decision in *Jackson* v. *Dunsbagh*, 1 Johns. Cas., 91. At page 96 this very case is put by Lewis, *Ch. J.*, who delivered the opinion of the court. He says, "here is a conveyance to the bargainee, to take effect at the decease of the bargainor, which creates a resulting use to the latter, during life, with a vested use in remainder to the bargainee in fee, both uses being served in succession out of the seisin of the bargainor. An authority to this effect will be found in Saunders on Uses and Trusts, 133, where it is said that if a man bargains and sells his lands after seven years, the grant is good, and until it takes place the use results." (Bac. on Uses, 63.)

The description is sufficiently certain. On the whole, it refers to the lot as being in the possession of Buice.

Curia, per SAVAGE, *Ch. J.* In my opinion, the judge properly admitted the testimony of Mrs. Buice. Her interest, if any, was extremely remote and contingent. Crawbuck was properly admitted, if his conveyance was merely a quitclaim; though otherwise, if he had warranted the title. How the fact was, the case does not inform us; and it lay with the plaintiff to show the warranty, if it existed.

But the important question is upon the validity of the deed from Deitz to Buice. It cannot operate as a bargain and sale for want of pecuniary consideration (1 Cow., 622); and if
431*] *it cannot operate as a covenant to stand seised, it is void, because it purports to convey a freehold *in futuro*. (7 Mass., 384.) It certainly cannot operate as a covenant to stand seised, for want of the considerations of blood or marriage. It is settled, that where there is a consideration stated in a deed, and it is not said "for other considerations," you cannot enter into proof of any other; for that would be contrary to the deed. (7 Johns., 342.) The consideration stated in this deed is as follows: "in consideration of the performances hereinafter mentioned." Those performances were expressed by way of condition to this effect: 1. That the grantor should occupy and enjoy for life. 2. That after his death, Buice should pay Frederick Howell £100, &c. 3. That Buice should find and provide for the grantor, meat, drink, &c. 4. That Buice should occupy one house and pay £60. In consideration of performing these things, after the death of the grantor, Buice was to have an estate of inheritance.

The case then comes within the principle of *Jackson* v. *Florence*, 16 Johns., 47, unless the stipulation, or rather condition, that £100 be paid to Howell, distinguishes it. In that case, the lessor was a blind and infirm old man, and the consideration was his support for life. Here Deitz was an old man, extremely intemperate, and the only pecuniary consideration is a condition to be performed after the grantor's death, until which event the estate is not to vest. There was no covenant whatever, on the part of Buice, to perform the conditions; and his going into possession of one house and lot cannot raise an implied agreement to perform them. He was to pay rent for the use of the house. It was, then, perfectly optional with him to perform the conditions or not.

It was contended on the argument that the conveyance was of a present estate absolutely, to be defeated by the non-performance of conditions subsequent. It is certain, however, that no estate passed till the death of the grantor. The support of the grantor must have been his inducement for making the deed. The grantee was under no obligation to afford such support, nor was he obligated to make the payment. *The deed, then, when ex- [***432**
ecuted, was inoperative and void.

The premises in question are not designated by the deed, except under the general description of all my estate. Such a description has been adjudged insufficient in a sheriff's deed, but the same considerations do not apply as between individuals. On the whole, however, I am of opinion that, all other objections aside, the deed in question is inoperative as a bargain and sale, for two reasons: 1. Because there is no pecuniary consideration; and 2. Because it purports to convey an estate in fee simple; to commence *in futuro*, without any other less estate to support it.

Judgment for the plaintiff.

Cited in—9 Cow. 72; 9 Wend., 614; 12 Wend., 63; 22 Wend., 143; 6 Paige, 531; 36 N. Y., 436; 2 Trans., App., 310; 7 Barb., 177; 9 Barb., 221; 47 Ind., 104; 102 Mass., 536; 17 Ohio St., 660; 3 Am. Rep., 497 (102 Mass., 533).

FARLEY *v.* CLEVELAND.

Statute of Frauds—Promise to Pay Debt of Another—New Consideration.

Where a promise to pay the debt of a third person, arises out of some new consideration of benefit to the promisor, or harm to the promisee, moving to

---

NOTE.—*Statute of Frauds—Promise to pay the debt of another on a new and original consideration.*

At common law, prior to the enactment of the Statute of Frauds, a promise to pay the debt of another, whether oral or written, was binding only when supported by a legal consideration. The statute did not assume to alter the character of the promise, by dispensing with the consideration. Its purpose was simply to require the evidence of such promise to be in writing. On principle, every promise to pay the debt of another, whether prior, collateral or subsequent, must be supported by a legal consideration, and is within the

the promisor, either from the promisee or the original debtor, such promise is not within the Statute of Frauds, 1 R. L., 78, sec. 11, though the original debt still subsist, and remains entirely unaffected by the new agreement.

Thus where M. owed F. and C. in consideration that M. delivered to him hay to the value of the debt, promised by parol to pay F; held, that this was not within the Statute.

The English and American cases establishing, illustrating and explaining this rule, collated and examined, per Savage, *Ch. J.*

Citations—8 Johns., 29, 376; Rob. Frauds, 232; 2 Ld. Raym., 1085; Cowp., 227; 2 T. R., 80; 1 H. Bl., 120; 2 Wils., 94; 12 Johns., 291; 4 Johns., 222; 1 Wils., 305; 3 Burr., 1886; 2 Str., 873; 7 Johns., 463; 3 Johns., 210; 10 Johns., 412; 15 Johns., 425; 18 Johns., 12.

ON ERROR from the Washington C. P. Farley sued Cleveland in the court below, declaring specially, that one Moon, Nov. 22, 1815, gave the plaintiff a promissory note for $100, with interest, payable June 1 thereafter; that Jan. 1, 1817, Cleveland, in consideration of 15 tons of hay (value $250) sold and delivered by Moon to him, at the instance, promised to pay the note of Moon to Farley.

On his trial, the plaintiff offered to prove the note, and that in the spring of 1817 Moon absconded, just before which the defendant promised to pay Moon's note to the plaintiff, in consideration of 15 tons of hay, worth $10 per ton, to be delivered by Moon to him; that the hay was thereupon delivered to the defendant, and in consideration thereof, he promised the plaintiff, by parol, to pay the note; that the next day Moon absconded.

The C. P. nonsuited the plaintiff, on the ground that the promise being to pay the debt 433*] of another, and not in writing, *was void within the Statute of Frauds; and that was the only question made on the argument here.

Mr. D. Russell, for the plaintiff in error, said the delivery of the property constituted a new and distinct consideration, and thus took the case out of the Statute; and he relied on *Schermerhorn* v. *Vanderheyden*, 1 Johns., 139, and the cases there cited, that a promise to one for the benefit of another, will maintain a suit in the name of the one for whose benefit it is made. He said in *Leonard* v. *Vredenburgh*, 8 Johns., 29, the cases were considered and classified by Kent, *Ch. J.*, and his third class of cases, which he says is not within the Statute, embraces the present one. It is, "when a promise to pay the debt of another, arises out of some new and original consideration of benefit or harm moving between the newly contracting parties." (*Id.*, 39.) The arrangement operated as an extinguishment of Moon's debt; and the note was retained merely as evidence of the consideration of the defendant's promise; and to show the extent of the plaintiff's claim. He also cited *Skelton* v. *Brewster*, *Id.*, 376; *Myers* v. *Morse*, 15 Johns., 425; *Chaplin* v. *Rogers*, 1 East, 192; *Hinde* v. *Whitehouse*, 7 *Id.*, 558; *Elmore* v. *Stone*, 1 Taunt., 457; Rob. on Frauds, 232, and *Stadt* v. *Lill*, 9 East, 348.

Mr. J. Willard, contra, said the rule is, that wherever the liability of the original debtor is not destroyed by the promise of the third person, the promise is collateral and within the Statute; *Simpson* v. *Patten*, 4 Johns., 422; *Jackson* v. *Rayner*, 12 *Id.*, 291; *Leonard* v. *Vredenburgh*, 8 *Id.*, 29; *Fish* v. *Hutchinson*, 2 Wils., 94; and he also cited 1 H. Bl., 120; 2 Ld. Raym., 1085; 2 T. R., 80.

He said Farley's remedy against Moon continues unimpaired. In all the cases cited on the other side, the liability of the original debtor was discharged; and that discharge constituted the whole or a part of the consideration of the promise. In such case the promise is original. There is nothing left to which it can be collateral. (3 Burr., 1886; 7 Johns., 463; 8 *Id.*, 376.)

*There is, if the promise be in truth [*434 an original one, a variance from the declaration, which sets it forth as collateral.

Mr. Russell, in reply, said there was no substantial variance; but if otherwise, the objection could not be listened to here, because omitted in the court below.

---

statute. The time of making the promise is not a proper test to determine whether it is within the statute. Whether the promise is to pay the debt of another, is the only test within its language and intent. Unfortunately this plain construction has not always been followed. The questions of time and consideration, added as tests, have introduced confusion and conflict of authority. Mallory v. Gillett, 21 N. Y., 412; Wait Act. & Def., Vol. 7, pp. 13-21.

"*In all these cases, founded upon a new and original consideration of benefit to the defendant, or harm to the plaintiff, moving to the party making the promise, either from the plaintiff or the original debtor, the subsisting liability of the original debtor, is no objection to the recovery.*" Above case of Farley v. Cleveland. See, also, Leonard v. Vredenberg, 8 Johns., 29, *note*; Skelton v. Brewster, 8 Johns., 376; Goold v. Phillips, 10 Johns., 412; Olmstead v. Greenley, 18 Johns., 12; Gardiner v. Hopkins, 5 Wend., 23; Elwood v. Monk, 5 Wend., 235; Meech v. Smith, 7 Wend., 315; Lawrence v. Fox, 20 N. Y., 268; Johnson v. Gilbert, 4 Hill, 178; Mallery v. Gillett, 21 N. Y., 412; Cardell v. McNeil, 21 N. Y., 336; Baker v. Bradley, 42 N. Y., 316; Mason v. Hall, 30 Ala., 599; Todd v. Tobey, 29 Me., 219; Dyer v. Gibson, 16 Wis., 557; Cross v. Richardson, 30 Vt., 641.

An agreement upon a new consideration moving from the creditor, or any other than the debtor, is within the statute. Simpson v. Patten, 4 Johns., 422; Jackson v. Rayner, 12 Johns., 291; Smith v. Ives, 15 Wend., 182; Packer v. Wilson, 15 Wend., 343; Watson v. Randall, 20 Wend., 201; Stern v. Drinker, 2 E. D. Smith, 401; State Bank v. Mettler, 2 Bosw., 392; Nelson v. Boynton, 44 Mass. (3 Met.) 396.

Forbearance was the new consideration in several of the above cases.

"The new or original consideration may move to the promisor as well from the debtor as the creditor, the fundamental requisite being that such consideration must not be one wholly existing or moving between the debtor and the creditor." Mallory v. Gillett, 21 N. Y., 427.

Where a third person assumes the indebtedness of another on a new consideration (*e. g.*, the discharge of the original debtor), the agreement is not within the statute. Jennings v. Webster, 7 Cow., 256; Baker v. Bradley, 42 N. Y., 316; Wood v. Corcoran, 83 Mass., (1 Allen) 406; Stone v. Symmes, 35 Mass. (18 Pick.), 467; Britton v. Angier, 48 N. H., 420; Yale v. Edgerton, 14 Minn., 194; Kutzmeyer v. Ennis, 27 N. J. L., 371; Warren v. Smith, 24 Tex., 484; Brown v. Brown, 47 Mo., 130; 4 Am. Rep., 320; Goodman v. Chase, 1 B. & Ald., 297; Butcher v. Stewart, 11 Mees. & W., 857.

Where the promisor agrees to pay the debt of another, his motive being that such payment will also pay his own debt, the agreement is not within the statute. Goetz v. Foos, 14 Minn., 265; Cotterell v. Stevens, 10 Wis., 422; Bessbears v. Rowe, 46 Mo., 501; Tibbetts v. Flanders, 18 N. H., 284.

On the sale of a note, a guaranty of payment, made by the owner, is not within the statute. Cardell v. McNeil, 21 N. Y., 336; Dauber v. Blackney, 38 Barb., 432; Mobile &c. Ry. Co. v. James, 57 Ga., 198; Wyman v. Goodrich, 26 Wis., 21.

Curia, per SAVAGE, *Ch. J.* That part of the Statute which relates to this case, is as follows: "No action shall be brought whereby to charge the defendant upon any special promise to answer for the debt, default or miscarriages of another person, unless the agreement upon which such actions shall be brought, or some memorandum or note thereof, shall be in writing," &c. Our Statute is a transcript of the 29 Charles II. The English decisions, therefore, upon that Statute, are entitled to consideration. We have been referred to several, before noticing which, the three classes of cases mentioned by Kent, *Ch. J.*, in *Leonard* v. *Vredenburgh*, 8 Johns., 29, should be attended to. These are: 1. Where the promise of the defendant is collateral to the principal promise, but made at the same time. 2. Where the collateral promise was subsequent to the original indebtedness, and was made upon no other consideration but the liability of the original debtor. 3. Where the promise arises out of some new consideration of benefit or harm, moving between the newly contracting parties, or, as expressed by Mr. Roberts (Rob. on Frauds, 232): "If it spring out of any new transaction, or move to the party promising upon some fresh and substantive ground of a personal concern to himself." The first class needs no other consideration than the original debt to which it is collateral; the second does; and the third is not within the Statute at all. In the first two cases the consideration must be in writing, as well as the promise; in the third, all may rest in parol, as in ordinary cases.

Buckmyr v. *Darnall*, 2 Ld. Raym., 1085, belongs to the first class. The defendant had promised the plaintiff to return his horse, if he would let him to one English, to ride to Reading. This was held to be collateral, because English was liable on the original bailment; **435***] and hence it must be *in writing. So, also, in *Jones* v. *Cooper*, Cowp., 227, the promise was to pay the plaintiff, if the debtor did not, which was clearly within the Statute. In *Matson* v. *Wharam*, 2 T. R., 80, the defendant applied to the plaintiff to sell goods to one Coulthard, and said, "I will see you paid." This was held to be void, being merely by parol. In *Anderson* v. *Hayman*, 1 H. Bl., 120, the defendant said, "use my son well, charge him as low as possible, and I will be bound for the payment of the money, as far as £800 or £1,000." The goods were charged to the son. The promise was held to be collateral and void, being by parol.

In this court, the case of *Leonard* v. *Vredenburgh*, as decided, belongs to the third class. The defendant promised in writing to guaranty a note of one M. Johnson for $500, on which the guaranty was written.

The case of *Fish* v. *Hutchinson*, 2 Wils., 94, belongs to the second class. The plaintiff had sued one Vickars, and the defendant in consideration that the plaintiff would stay his action, promised to pay him the money owing to him by Vickars. The court decided this promise to be within the Statute, as the original debt was still subsisting. So, also, in the case of *Jackson* v. *Rayner*, 12 Johns., 291, in this court, the defendant in the court below, promised the plaintiff below (who had sued the defendant's son), that he, the defendant, would pay the debt, as he had taken his son's property, and meant to pay his honest debts. The court decided that a promise in writing was necessary; and emphasized the fact, that the original debt of the son was still subsisting. This case was decided on the authority of *Simpson* v. *Patten*, 4 Johns., 222, which will be hereafter noticed.

The third class mentioned by Kent, *Ch. J.*, as not within the Statute, has been illustrated by the following cases: In *Read* v. *Nash*, 1 Wils., 305, one Tuack, the plaintiff's testator, had sued one Johnson for an assault and battery, and the cause being at issue, the defendant promised that if Tuack would withdraw the record, he would pay him £50 and the costs. This was held an original promise, and that there was no debt, default or miscarriage. In *Williams* v. *Leper*, 3 Burr., 1886, the plaintiff was proceeding to distrain *the goods [***436** of one Taylor, his tenant, for three quarter's rent, being £45, when the defendant, who was agent for Taylor's creditors, to sell the goods under an assignment of them, promised the plaintiff to pay the rent in arrear if he would desist from distraining. It was contended that this promise should have been in writing, and that Taylor still remained liable till actual satisfaction. Ld. Mansfield said the landlord had a legal pledge—he had a lien upon the goods, and that the statute did not apply. The case of *Simpson* v. *Patten*, 4 Johns., 222, came here on *certiorari*. Patten had sued Simpson in the court below on a promise that if he, Patten, would forbear to sue, one J. S. Simpson would pay the amount of J. S.'s note, as soon as he could sell an acre of land of J. S., which he, Simpson, was authorized to sell. Simpson had sold the land, and a recovery was had on the parol promise. This court reversed the judgment, saying that a promise to pay the debt of a third person must be in writing, notwithstanding it is made on sufficient consideration. They said nothing about this promise being an original undertaking. In support of their opinion, they cite some of the above cases, and *King* v. *Wilson*, 2 Str., 873, where Raymond, *Ch. J.*, held that a parol promise to pay the debt of another, in consideration of forbearance, was void by the the Statute of Frauds and Perjuries. In the cases of *Simpson* v. *Patten* and *Jackson* v. *Rayner*, there was a good consideration, that of indefinite forbearance, and in both cases funds of the original debtor were placed in the hands of the defendants by which they had the means of performing their promises; but the original debt was still subsisting. The case of *Slingerland* v. *Morse*, 7 Johns., 463, was very much like the case of *Williams* v. *Leper*. The plaintiff had distrained the goods of his tenant, and the defendants promised in writing to deliver them six days after demand or pay $450. It was contended that the writing should have contained a consideration, according to *Sears* v. *Brink*, 3 Johns., 210, considering the case as within *Ch. J.* Kent's second class; but the undertaking was held to be original. The plaintiff had a lien which he relinquished; and as this took the case out of the statute no writing was necessary. **Skelton* v. *Brewster*, 8 Johns., [***437** 376, came here on *certiorari*. Brewster had levied on the property of one W. S. by virtue

of an execution. W. S. delivered all his goods to Skelton, who, in consideration of this, and that the plaintiff would discharge W. S. from the execution, promised to pay $25. In this case the court said, "the promise of the defendant below to pay the judgment against a third person was founded on a new and distinct consideration, which was the delivery of the goods of such person, and the plaintiff's discharge of the judgment;" and they held it an original promise. This case differs from *Simpson* v. *Patten*, and *Jackson* v. *Rayner*, in no essential particular, except that, in those cases, the original debtor remained liable. In this case he was discharged. In those cases the promises were held to be within the Statute—in this, not. It would seem, therefore, that the liability of the original debtor was a controlling fact. But in *Gold* v. *Philips*, 10 Johns., 412, the liability of the original debtor was overlooked or not deemed important. In that case the plaintiffs had a demand against one Aaron Wood. Wood sold his farm to the defendants, and they agreed to pay Wood a certain sum. The rest of the consideration was composed of Wood's debts, which the defendants agreed to pay, and among them was the demand of the plaintiffs. The defendant wrote to the plaintiffs as follows: "Gentlemen, an arrangement has been made between us and Aaron Wood by which we are to be accountable to you for the balance due from him to you, on account." The court say, "the promise of the defendants was not within the Statute of Frauds. It had no immediate connection with the original contract, but was founded on a new and distinct consideration. The distinction noticed in *Leonard* v. *Vredenburgh* applies to this case, and takes it out of the statute. The defendants made the promise in consideration of a sale of lands made to them by Wood; and they assumed to pay the debt of the plaintiffs, as being by arrangement with Wood, part payment of the purchase money. Here was a valid assumption of the debt of Aaron Wood." In this case the original debtor was not dis-
438*] charged, and the property *purchased of Wood had passed to another person who had made a similar promise. In the case of *Myers* v. *Morse*, 15 Johns., 425, the plaintiffs were liable as indorsers of one H. M. They also held a note drawn by H. M. and indorsed by the defendant on which he was liable. It was agreed by the plaintiffs that they would not hold the defendant liable on the note held by them; in consideration whereof, he promised to indemnify the plaintiffs against one third of any loss which they might sustain as indorsers of H. M. This was held to be an original promise, founded upon the new consideration moving between the newly contracting parties. The case of *Olmsted* v. *Greenly*, 18 Johns., 12, was this: the plaintiff was liable as indorser for B. & H. for $1,000. B. owed the plaintiff $150, and it was agreed between the plaintiff, defendant and B., that B. should place in the defendant's hands, in cash, $600, and in goods, $1,500; and that the defendant should pay the note indorsed by the plaintiff, and indemnify him against all damages and costs by reason of that indorsement: and should also pay the plaintiff the debt due him from B. The plaintiff averred that B. had the money and goods, and that the plaintiff caused them to be put in the defendant's hands for the purposes mentioned. The court said, this is not a case within the Statute of Frauds. It is not a mere collateral undertaking, on the part of the defendant, to pay the debt of Bristol; but was an original contract on an independent consideration, received by the defendant by the procurement of the plaintiff. The plaintiff has the same ground of action as if he had delivered his own goods to the defendant as the consideration of the promise.

These cases do not entirely agree unless they are distinguishable by the circumstance that in some of them forbearance to sue the original debtor is the whole or a principal part of the consideration for the promise; and in the others, the whole consideration is something new, moving to the party making the promise. Thus, in *Simpson* v. *Patten*, and *Jackson* v. *Raynor*, the promise was founded as well upon the forbearance of the plaintiffs to sue the original debtor, as upon property of the debtor being placed in the hands of *the de- [**439**
fendants, out of which the debts might be paid; but in the cases of *Gold* v. *Philips*, *Myers* v. *Morse* and *Olmstead* v. *Greenly*, no allusion is had to the effect to be produced upon the original debtor. The promise in those cases was predicated upon value received by the defendants, either from the plaintiffs or the original debtor.

The case under consideration is, in principle, very much like the case of *Gold* v. *Philips*. The defendant had, in that case, purchased land of the original debtor, which was the consideration moving to the defendant. In this the defendant purchased hay, which was the consideration moving to him. So, too, in *Olmstead* v. *Greenly*, the original debtor placed money and goods in the defendant's hands, with which he promised to make certain payments and to pay the plaintiff's debt. It was averred that this was done by the procurement of the plaintiff, which is the only difference between that case and this, if the hay was not absolutely sold by Moon to the defendant. In all these cases, founded upon a new and original consideration of benefit to the defendant, or harm to the plaintiff, moving to the party making the promise, either from the plaintiff or the original debtor, the subsisting liability of the original debtor is no objection to the recovery.

I am, therefore, of opinion that the court below erred; that the judgment be reversed and a *veniré de novo* awarded.

Judgment reversed.

Affirmed—9 Cow., 639.

Cited in—5 Wend., 237; 7 Wend., 318; 12 Wend., 521; 13 Wend., 122; 20 Wend., 204; 2 Den., 55; 4 Den., 98; 2 N. Y., 234; 12 N. Y., 300; 20 N. Y., 270; 21 N. Y., 419, 422; 46 N. Y., 461; 69 N. Y., 286; 77 N. Y., 95; 3 Barb., 212; 4 Barb., 133; 7 Barb., 177; 15 Barb., 253; 16 Barb., 565, 649; 23 Barb., 616; 27 Barb., 85; 35 Barb., 155; 16 How. Pr., 566; 17 How. Pr., 295; 23 How. Pr., 532; 45 How, Pr., 38; 5 Abb., N. S., 50; 2 Bos., 398; 2 Rob., 49; 2 E. D. S., 404; 3 E. D. S., 70; 1 Leg. Obs., 398; 22 How. (U. S.), 43; 22 Cal., 190; 12 Mich., 12; 36 Mich., 325; 13 Minn., 381; 24 Minn., 516; 46 Mo., 503; 36 N. J. L., 146; 45 Pa. St., 188; 37 Am. Dec., 150 (3 Metc. 332); 43 Am. Dec., 734, 737; 44 Am. Dec., 507 (10 Ala., 755); 46 Am. Dec., 360 (Fla., 301); 47 Am. Dec., 546 (1 Strob., 5); 49 Am. Dec., 639 (3 Strob., 177); 7 Am. Rep., 372 (46 N. Y., 456); 21 Am. Rep., 383 (59 Mo., 204); 24 Am. Rep., 597 (36 Mich., 320); 25 Am. Rep., 199; 44 Am. Rep., 230 (86 Ind., 352).

440*] *THE ONEIDA MANUFACTURING SOCIETY
v.
LAWRENCE ET AL.

Sale of Chattels—Warranty—What Constitutes—Latent Defects—When Vendor Responsible for, without Warranty—Sale by Sample—Pleading—Evidence.

No particular phraseology is necessary to constitute a warranty of goods; but an assertion or affirmation concerning the thing sold, to be evidence of a warranty, should be positive and unequivocal, one which the vendee relies on, which is understood by the parties as an absolute assertion, and not the expression of an opinion.

In ordinary sales, where the vendee has an opportunity of examining the commodity, the vendor is not answerable for any latent defect, without fraud or an express warranty, or such a direct affirmation or representation as is tantamount to a warranty, and not the expression of an opinion.

But in the case of sales by sample, the vendor is held responsible, that the quality of the bulk of the commodity shall be equal to the sample shown.

Declaration upon a warranty of cotton, that it was good merchantable cotton, free from dirt and all filthy matter; proof that the defendant produced a sample of good merchantable cotton, free, &c. (as in the declaration), and stated that it was good upland cotton, and that the sample was true, or that it was prime upland Georgia cotton: held, no variance.

To entitle the exemplifications of a commission and depositions to be read in evidence, there must be an accompanying certificate of a judge, or other officer, authorized by the Statute, 1 R. L., 520, sec. 11, to receive and open commissions.

Every sale of packed cotton must be considered in the nature of a sale by sample, which amounts to a warranty that the whole bulk shall compare with the specimen exhibited. Per Savage, *Ch. J.*, on the authority of Nott & M'Cord, 540-1.

Citations—3 T. R., 57-8; 19 Johns., 290; 2 Cai., 48; 20 Johns., 196, 202-3, 357; 1 Johns., 96, 129; 4 Johns., 421; 2 Nott & McC., 538, 540-1; 5 Johns., 355, 395; 4 Camph., 145.

ASSUMPSIT, upon an express warranty of cotton. The declaration was, that the defendants promised that the cotton was good merchantable cotton, free from dirt and all filthy matter.

The cause was tried July 17, 1823, at the Oneida Circuit, before Williams, Circuit Judge.

At the trial, it was proved that the defendants sold the cotton to the plaintiffs by bill, as twenty-five bales of Georgia upland cotton; the plaintiffs' witness swore that one of the defendants (Dec., 1820, or Jan., 1821) sold the cotton to the agent of the plaintiffs, presenting him with samples of the cotton, declaring they were drawn from the bales in the warehouse of the defendants, and that it was good upland cotton, and that those were true samples. The defendants' witness, who spoke of the sale, said the defendant represented it as prime upland Georgia cotton. The plaintiffs' agent had no opportunity to inspect it.

The cotton turned out to be far inferior to the sample and representation, being foul and damaged. It had been packed with a mixture of water, which had stained the cotton and rotted a part of it.

An exemplification of a commission to examine witnesses executed in Ga., with the return, was offered in evidence by the defendants; but objected to, and excluded by the judge, on the ground that there was no certificate or indorsement among the papers offered and exemplified, of any *judge or [*441 other officer, authorized by statute to receive and open commissions, that he had received and opened this, or by whose hands it was received.

Verdict for the plaintiffs. Damages, $736.99.

Mr. J. Platt moved for a new trial:

1. He contended that there was a variance between the contract declared on and the one proved; and he cited the following cases as illustrative of the great strictness with which courts bind down the plaintiff in his proof to the exact words of his count, viz.: *Snell* v. *Moses*, 1 Johns., 96; *Perry* v. *Aaron, Id.*, 129; *Bristow* v. *Wright*, Doug., 665; *King* v. *Pippet*, 1 T. R., 235; *Parkinson* v. *Lee*, 2 East, 314; *Symonds* v. *Carr*, 1 Camph., 361; *Clarke* v. *Gray*, 6 East, 564; *Hands* v. *Burton*, 9 *Id.*, 349; *Goulding* v. *Skinner*, 1 Pick., 162.

2. To show that the declaration of the defendants did not amount to a warranty, he cited *Chandelor* v. *Lopus*, Cro. Jac., 4; *Seixas* v. *Woods*, 2 Cai., 48; Sugd. L. V., 3; *Heermance* v. *Vernoy*, 6 Johns., 5; *De Freeze* v. *Trumper*, 1 *Id.*, 274; *Holden* v. *Dakin*, 4 *Id.*, 421; *Davis* v. *Meeker*, 5 *Id.*, 354; *Jendwine* v. *Slade*, 2 Esp., 572; *Willings* v. *Consequa*, 1 Pet. C. C., 317; *Sands* v. *Taylor*, 5 Johns., 395; *Swett* v. *Colgate*, 20 Johns., 196; 2 Com. on Cont., 265; Coop. Just., 609; *Parkinson* v. *Lee*, 2 East, 314.

3. He said the Statute, 1 R. L., 520, sec. 11, is merely directory as to the duty of the judge on receiving and opening the commission; his certifying is not essential to its being evidence, and his omission should not prejudice the party. All the Statute requires is, that it should be executed in a certain manner—that this should appear on its face; but being filed with the clerk and exemplified, the intendment is, that it was properly received and opened, until the contrary is shown.

Mr. Talcott, Atty-Gen., contra, insisted that there was enough proved to authorize the inference of a warranty by the jury; and for this he relied mainly on *Chapman* v. *Murch*, *19 Johns., 290, and cited *Bradford* v. [*442 *Manly*, 13 Mass., 139, in which the court decided that a sale by sample is tantamount to a warranty; that the article sold is of the same kind with the sample; also, *Gardiner* v. *Gray*, 4 Camph., 144, where it was held that when goods are sold, by written contract, as goods of a certain denomination, there is an implied warranty that they are of a merchantable quality of the denomination mentioned in the contract; and *Rose* v. *Beatie*, 2 Nott & M'C., 538, 540, 541.

He said the contract was set forth in the declaration, according to its substance and effect, which is enough. It need not be literally pursued. *Bristow* v. *Wright*, Doug., 665, 666, per Ld. Mansfield; *West* v. *Andrews*, 1 Barn. & Cress., 77.

That the commission and depositions were inadmissible, he cited *Jackson* v. *Hobby*, 20 Johns., 357.

Curia, per SAVAGE, *Ch. J.* The questions are:

NOTE.—*Sale of chattel—Warranty—What sufficient to constitute.* See Chapman v. Murch, 19 Johns., 29.

Latent defect—Warranty not implied. See Seixas v. Woods, 2 Cai., 48, *note*.

Sale by sample. See Sands v. Taylor, 5 Johns., 395.

1. Did the defendants warrant the cotton, and if so, what was the warranty?

2. Is the contract proved as laid?

3. Was the commission properly rejected?

There is no particular phraseology necessary to constitute a warranty. The assertion, or affirmation, of the vendor, concerning the article sold must be positive and unequivocal. It must be a representation which the vendee relies on, and which is understood by the parties as an absolute assertion, and not the expression of an opinion. (3 T. R., 57, 58; 19 Johns., 290.) *Seixas* v. *Woods*, 2 Cai., 48, is a leading case on this subject. The law is there fully recognized, that a sound price does not imply a warranty, and that, as to any latent defects in the article, the rule *caveat emptor* applies, unless there is a warranty. Nothing is there said, however, as to what expressions shall constitute a warranty. It appeared that the defendant was agent for a house in New Providence, from which he received the wood in question. It was invoiced as braziletto; he advertised it as such, sold it as such, described it as such in the bill of parcels, and the plaintiff's agent selected it from other wood, sup- **443***] *posing it to be braziletto, and both parties supposing that the wood was, in fact, braziletto. These facts did not, in the opinion of the court, constitute a warranty. The late case of *Swett* v. *Colgate*, 20 Johns., 196, 202, 203, was decided on the same principle. The next case after *Seixas* v. *Wood* was that of *Snell* v. *Moses*, 1 Johns., 96, in which the plaintiffs endeavored to recover for fraud. They purchased blue guineas, for which the cartman inquired, and received three bales of blue goods, described as blue guineas in the bill of parcels. No intimation is given in this case on the question of what would constitute a warranty. In *Perry* v. *Aaron*, 1 Johns., 129, there was an express warranty, and the court, in granting a new trial, do not state whether it was on the ground of a variance between the count and the proof, or on the ground of merits. In *Holden* v. *Dakin*, 4 Johns., 421, the defendant's clerk sold the plaintiff paints of an inferior quality for good paints; but the kegs had not been opened since the defendant purchased them. The court say here was no express warranty. All that was proved upon the trial was that the clerk of the vendor sold the paints for good paints, and at a fair price; but this was not sufficient to raise a warranty. If a warranty was to be inferred from these circumstances, it would be universal, upon every *bona fide* sale at the usual price, unless there was a stipulation to the contrary. Such was the civil law; and such is now the law of S. C., 2 Nott & M'C., 538. In *Davis* v. *Meeker*, 5 Johns., 355, the court say, "the assertion of the defendant that the wagon was worth more than its real value, furnishes no ground of action." In the case of *Sands* v. *Taylor*, 5 Johns., 395, Spencer, *Ch. J.*, says: "It has been frequently decided here, that on the sale of a commodity, no action can be sustained for any difference in quality between the thing contracted for and the thing delivered, unless there be fraud, or a warranty. I am disposed to confine this rule to the case of a sale where the thing sold is exhibited, and am ready to admit that on sales by sample

444

there is an implied warranty that the sample taken in the usual way is a fair specimen of the thing sold."

*So, also, in *Gardiner* v. *Gray*, 4 [***444** Campb., 145, Ld. Ellenborough says: "Where there is no opportunity to inspect the commodity, the maxim of *caveat emptor* does not apply. He (the purchaser) cannot, without a warranty, insist that it shall be of any particular quality or fineness; but the intention of both parties must be taken to be, that it shall be salable in the market under the denomination mentioned in the contract between them."

In the case under consideration, the sale was by sample, for, though the plaintiffs' agent saw the bags in which the cotton was packed, yet he had no opportunity of inspecting the bulk of the commodity. He could only see the samples. In this respect, the present case differs from those of the blue guineas, the barilla and the braziletto. Every sale of packed cotton must be considered in the nature of a sale by sample, which amounts to a warranty that the whole bulk shall compare with the specimen exhibited. (2 Nott & McCord, 540, 541.)

From an examination of the cases, some of which I have stated, I am safe in laying down the rule, that in ordinary sales, when the vendee has an opportunity of examining the commodity, the vendor is not answerable for any latent defect, without fraud or an express warranty, or such a direct affirmation or representation, as is tantamount to a warranty, and not the expression of an opinion; but in cases of sales by sample, the vendor is held responsible that the quality of the bulk of the commodity shall be equal to the sample shown.

In the case of *Gardiner* v. *Gray*, where a sample of waste silk was shown, to enable the purchaser to form a judgment of the commodity, but not as a warranty, Ld. Ellenborough held, that under such circumstances, the purchaser has a right to expect a salable article, according to the description in the contract. He adds, "without any particular warranty, there is an implied term in every such contract. Where there is no opportunity to inspect the commodity, the maxim *caveat emptor* does not apply." It seems to me, therefore, that whether the production of the samples in this case be construed a warranty that the bulk is of the same *quality, or whether they were [***445** shown to the plaintiff's agent to enable him to form a judgment of the quality of the article, the defendants are bound, either that the article shall be equal to the samples, or that it shall be a salable one, of the description contracted for.

This is the main point in the cause. I am of opinion there was no substantial variance between the contract as laid and proved; and the desposition was properly rejected within *Jackson* v. *Hobby*, 20 Johns., 257.

I am, accordingly, of opinion that the plaintiffs are entitled to judgment.

Judgment accordingly.

Criticised—5 N. Y., 85, 98, 104.

Cited in—6 Cow., 357; 8 Cow., 27; 9 Wend., 26; 12 Wend., 419, 575; 17 Wend., 271; 18 Wend., 441; 5 N. Y., 98, 104; 51 N. Y., 201; 6 Barb., 562; 7 Barb., 20; 22 Barb., 135; 24 Barb., 554; 44 How. Pr., 115; 4 E. D. S., 205; 1 Hilt., 267; 36 Ill., 87; 23 Am. Dec., 89-98 (3 Rawle, 23); 27 Am. Dec., 134, 135, 163; 34 Am. Dec., 109 (4 How., Miss., 59); 10 Am. Rep., 598.

THE PEOPLE, ex rel. FOGALSONGER, v. THE JUDGES OF THE COURT OF C. P. OF THE COUNTY OF ERIE.

Judgment, against Executors or Administrators, by Confession—Proof of Assets—Practice—Forms of Judgments and Executions against Executors and Administrators.

A judgment against executors or administrators, by confession, is conclusive proof that they have assets sufficient to satisfy it.

The plaintiff may, after issuing a *fi. fa. de bonis testatoris, vel intestoris*, and a return of a *devastavit* by the sheriff, issue a *fi. fa. de bonis propriis*, of course, and without the formality of a *scire fieri* inquiry, or an action of debt suggesting a *devastavit*.

The different forms of judgment against executors and administrators, considered, according to the different pleas which they interpose, and the forms of execution upon these.

The rule on this head in Lansing v. Lansing, 18 Johns., 503, explained and qualified.

If, on a *fi. fa. de bonis intestatoris*, issued upon a judgment by confession, against an administrator, he do not produce assets, this justifies the sheriff in returning a *devastavit*.

Citations—18 Johns., 503; Cro. Car., 518, 527; 6 Mass., 393; 1 Saund., 219 *a*, 336, *n.* 10; Cro. Jac., 647, 671; Tidd., 933, 1019; Dy., 210, *n.*; 5 Rep., 32; 1 Johns. Cas., 276, 278; 3 T. R., 685, 687, 689; 2 Str., 732.

A *MANDAMUS*, tested May 9, 1821, was directed to the defendants, reciting that an execution had issued out of the C. P. of Niagara (now Erie) on a judgment against Pierce, Raymond and Smith, administrators, &c., of C. Smith, deceased, at the suit of the relator, tested Nov. 10, 1819, and returnable the 20th of that month, with an indorsement directing the sheriff to levy of the proper goods and chattels of the defendants $100, and interest from Aug. 25, 1816; that the defendants, at their February Term, 1820, by rule, ordered this execution to be set aside for irregularity; and commanding them to vacate the rule, or show cause, &c., at, &c., on the first Monday of Aug., 1821.

To this the defendants returned a judgment before them in 1816, in favor of the relator **446***] against the defendants below. *Pierce, &c., as administrators of C. Smith, rendered on a *cognovit actionem* in 1816; a *fi. fa.* for a balance due on that judgment of $100, tested Aug. 28, 1819, returnable the 3d Tuesday of Nov., then next, *de bonis intestatoris*.

To this, the sheriff returned thus: "The within named G. Pierce, C. W. Raymond and A. Smith have no goods or chattels in my bailiwick, which were of the within named Cushman Smith, at the time of his death to the value of the damages within mentioned, or any part thereof, but divers goods and chattels which were of the said Cushman, at the time of his death, to the value of the damages within mentioned, after the death of the said Cushman, came to the hands of the said defendants to be administered, which said goods and chattels the said defendants have, before the coming of this writ to be directed, eloigned, wasted and converted to their own use."

The return then set forth the *fi. fa.* tested and returnable as stated in the *mandamus*, reciting the first *fi. fa.* and return and commanding the sheriff to levy the damages, *de bonis propriis*; and that the judges set this execution aside as irregular. General demurrer and joinder.

Mr. J. Platt, in support of the demurrer, contended, that after judgment by confession against administrators, and return of *nulla bona* and *devastavit* on a *fi. fa. de bonis intestatoris*, it was regular to issue a *fi. fa. de bonis propriis* without a *scire fieri* inquiry; and he cited the following authorities: 1 Saund., edited by Sergt. Wms., 219, *note* 8; Rast. Ent., 323, 326; Tidd., 929; 2 Archb. Pr., 133; *Rock* v. *Leighton*, 1 Salk., 310; *Ramsden* v. *Jackson*, 1 Atk., 292; *Ewing* v. *Peters*, 3 T. R., 685, and *Platt* v. *Robins*, 1 Johns. Cas., 276.

Mr. J. A. Collier, contra, said nearly all the authorities would be found in 1 Saund., 219, *note* 8, cited on the other side. He would, however, refer the court to the following in particular, which would show the difference between the ancient and modern practice: *Stubbs* v. *Rightwife*, Cro. Eliz., 102; 1 Saund., 305, 306; Lill. Ent., 667; *Morfoot* v. *Chivers*, 2 Ld. Raym., 1395; Com. Dig., Administration, 1, 3; **Mounson* v. *Bourn*, Cro. [**447** Car., 518; S. C. *Id.*, 527; *Proctor* v. *Chamberlaine, Id.*, 564; *Herne* v. ———, 1 Lev., 7.

Curia per SAVAGE, *Ch. J.* In considering this question, it is proper to look into the form of the judgment against an executor. This should be according to his liability. So far as this arises from pleading, I take the rule to be as follows. If he plead *ne unques executor*, or a release to himself, and the issue be found against him, the judgment is, that execution issue in the first instance, *de bonis testatoris si, et si non, de bonis propriis*, for both debt and costs; and the reason is that he pleaded a plea which he knew to be false, and thus unnecessarily delayed the plaintiff. The rule laid down in *Lansing* v. *Lansing*, 18 Johns., 503, is right as to that case; but it is too broad, and should be accompanied with this qualification, that if the executor suffer judgment by default, or give a *cognovit actionem*, or plead any other plea but the two above named, and the issue be found against him, the judgment is *de bonis testatoris si*, for the whole debt or damages and costs, *et si non*, then *de bonis propriis* for the costs. *Mounson* v. *Bourn*, Cro. Car., 518; 6 Mass., 393, contra. If the executor plead *plene administravit*, either general or special and *nulla bona*, or *nulla bona ultra*, and the plaintiff be satisfied of the truth of the plea, or, on issue joined, it be found for the defendant, then the judgment is for assets *quando acciderint*. 1 Saund., 336, *n.* 10; *Bull* v. *Wheeler*, Cro. Jac., 647; *Bridgman* v. *Lightfoot, Id.*, 671.

As the regularity of the second execution issued in the court below, the ancient practice of the K. B. and C. P. differed. In the former, upon *nulla bona* and a *devastavit*, returned by the sheriff, an execution issued immediately *de bonis propriis*. (Tidd, 933, 1019; Dy., 210, *n.*) The better practice was to issue a *scire facias*, and obtain an award of execution *de bonis propriis*. The most usual pratiee was, not to have a *devastavit* returned, but *nulla bona* only, and then to see a special *fi. fa. quod de bonis testatoris, &c., et si constare poterit quod de vastavit, tunc de bonis propriis*. In the C. P., the *practice was to suggest a *devastavit* in [***448** the *fi. fa. de bonis testatoris*; and direct the sheriff to inquire by a jury, whether a *devastavit* had been committed: and if it was found by the inquistition, then a *scire facias* issued; and unless a good defense was made, an execution *de bonis propriis* was awarded. In *Pettifer's* case, 5 Rep., 32, the judgment of the C. P. was reversed by the K. B., upon the ground that the sheriff was not responsible for a return of a *devastavit* upon an inquisition, whereas he would be, upon a return on his own responsibility. Afterwards, in *Mounson* v. *Bourn*, Cro. Car., 527, the practice of the C. P. was confirmed, and finally it became the practice of both courts, on a return of *nulla bona*, without a *devastavit*, to issue a *scire fieri* inquiry, upon which, if an inquisition was found against the executor, then he was warned to appear; upon the return, he might traverse the inquisition, and if found against him, an execution *de bonis propriis* issued. An action of debt suggesting a *devastavit* is much more common in both courts. In either mode of proceeding, the executor is entitled to the same defense; but in neither can he avoid the consequences of pleading a false plea, confessing judgment, or suffering it to go by default. Either is an admission of assets, with this exception, that when *plene administravit* is pleaded, and found against the executor, he is liable to the extent only of assets found to be in his hands nuadministered. (1 Saund., 219 *a*; 1 Johns. Cas., 276; 3 T. R., 685.)

It is an established principle, that if a party omit on the first opportunity, to plead matter in bar, he shall not be permitted to do so in a subsequent proceeding founded on the original action. (2 Str., 732; 3 T. R., 689; 1 Johns. Cas., 278.) Ld. Kenyon, in *Eweing* v. *Peters*, 3 T. R., 687, 688, thought the law hard, which made a previous judgment conclusive upon an executor, and pointed out a discrepancy between the law and the judgment, which is *de bonis testatoris*, while by this very judgment the executor is absolutely concluded; and by another proceeding, either in *scire facias* or debt, he shall be charged personally. It was observed by Buller, *J.*, that though the executor 449*] confess assets, yet *the judgment should be *de bonis testatoris*; for though the judgment be evidence of assets, yet there is no reason to levy on the executor's goods unless he hath wasted; "and that being matter of fact, it must appear upon record, and judgment must be given thereupon, before his own goods can be affected." Although, therefore, the sheriff may return a *devastavit*, yet the return ought not to supply the place of an adjudication of the court, and hence the necessity of a *scire facias* or a *scire fieri* inquiry, or an action of debt.

I confess, to my mind, this distinction appears more like a matter of technical formality than of substance. In the present case, the defendant, by confessing a judgment, admitted assets. By not producing those assets to the sheriff upon the *fi. fa. de bonis intestatoris*, he has committed a *devastavit*, and justified the sheriff in his return. What defense can he make either to an inquisition or an action? Certainly none. It is unreasonable that the plaintiff should be driven to his *scire fieri* inquiry, upon which he gets no costs, unless the defendants appear. It is unreasonable that he should be put to an action to obtain what cannot possibly be denied him. This has always been treated by the courts as a matter of practice, under their control, in relation to which, they may establish their own rules; and it is undoubtedly so. That an execution *de bonis propriis* should go of course, at least upon this return of the sheriff, results from principles the most plainly established. Such a course unites convenience, expedition and the most perfect safety to the rights of parties, with the least expense. I feel myself impelled to yield to these considerations, and am, accordingly, of opinion that the second execution was regular and that, consequently, judgment should be for the plaintiffs upon this demurrer.

Judgment for the plaintiffs.

Cited in—12 How. Pr., 391; 2 Abb. Pr., 436; 3 How. 44 (U. S.), 61.

---

*JACKSON, ex dem. JOHNSON ET AL., [*450
v.
TALLMADGE.

Survey—Actual Location and Possession under, Prevails over Map—Discretion of Court, to Hear Evidence after Summing up Commenced.

Where a tract of land was surveyed, by direction of the Surveyor-General, and a map made, the lines of which did not agree with the survey, and the land was then patented to W., who gave deeds with the map annexed; but extensive locations were made and possession taken in the patent according to the survey; held, that such possessions should not be disturbed; but that the survey, and practical location under it, should prevail over the map.

After the regular examination of witnesses upon a trial is through, and the counsel for the defendant has commenced summing up, it is in the discretion of the judge whether he will hear further evidence.

Citations—17 Johns., 31; 7 Johns., 241.

EJECTMENT for land claimed to lie in the northeast section of township No. 10, in Watkins' & Flint's purchase, in the County of Tioga, tried at the circuit for that county, July 22, 1823, before Nelson, Circuit Judge.

It was admitted, at the trial, that the lessors of the plaintiff owned the northeast section, and the defendant the southest section, and the only question was as to the true line between them. It was admitted that both parties claimed title by deed of conveyance from John W. Watkins, the patentee, to which was annexed an original or printed map of the purchase. In 1791, Lawrence Vrooman was employed by the Surveyor-General to run out the tract into townships and quarter townships. He employed three assistants, giving them directions how to run. They did not, however, comply with these directions, but the map was made out upon the supposition that they had run correctly. This produced a difference between the map and survey, but extensive prac-

---

NOTE.—1. *Location of boundaries.* 2. *Reopening the case to admit further evidence.*

1. *Long acquiescence in erroneous location of boundaries is evidence of an agreement.* Rockwell v. Adams, 7 Cow. 761; Jackson v. Murray, 7 Johns., 5; Jackson v. Dieffendorf, 3 Johns., 269; Jackson v. Veddar, 3 Johns., 8; Jackson v. Ogden, 7 Johns., 238; Jackson v. Bowen, 1 Cai., 358; Jackson v. Freer, 17 Johns., 29; Baldwin v. Brown, 16 N. Y., 359; Corning v. Troy Iron and Nail Factory, 44 N. Y., 577; Pierson v. Mosher, 30 Barb., 81; Smith v. McAllister, 14 Barb., 434; Davis v. Judge, 46 Vt., 655; Taught v.

tical locations in the patent were made in disregard of the map, and according to the survey. The patent to Watkins, was dated June 25, 1794. The question was which should prevail, the map or survey; if the former, the plaintiff was entitled to recover; if the latter, the defendant. The premises in question were actually occupied from 15 to 17 years under the survey. A number of witnesses were examined upon the question, whether the lessors of the plaintiff had acquiesced in the survey.

After the regular examination of witnesses was through, and while the defendant's counsel was summing up to the jury, the plaintiff's counsel offered further evidence upon the question of acquiescence, which the judge refused to receive, on the ground that it was too late.

The judge charged in favor of the survey and against the map line; and the jury found a verdict for the defendant.

451*] **Mr. J. Blunt* moved for a new trial. As to the effect of the actual location, he referred to, and considered the cases of *Davis' Lessee* v. *Keeper*, 4 Binn., 161, 166; and *Jackson* v. *Cole*, 16 Johns., 257.

That the further evidence should have been received, he cited *Alexander* v. *Byron*, 2 Johns. Cas., 318, and *Mercer* v. *Sayre*, 7 Johns., 306.

Mr. J. Talmadge, in person, contra, cited John. Dig., Patent, II, pl. 14, 15, 16, 22, and *Jackson* v. *Freer*, 17 Johns., 29.

Mr. J. A. Collier, in reply.

The Court thought the verdict should not be disturbed; and,

SAVAGE, *Ch. J.*, who delivered their opinion, after stating the facts, adverted to and relied on *Jackson* v. *Freer*, 17 Johns., 31. He said the question there, as stated by Spencer, *Ch. J.*, was, "which shall prevail, the actual location of the lots on the ground, by marking and numbering trees at the corners, and by marking the lines of the lots, or the courses and distances which the map represents the lots as entitled to?" The court decided in favor of the actual location. The survey was considered as the act of the parties, though made by the agent of the Surveyor-General, as in this case. In *Jackson* v. *Ogden*, 7 Johns., 241, it was said, that when the map and survey do not agree, a practical location, acquiesced in, is entitled to great weight.

In this case, the evidence of acquiescence in the location by the lessors of the plaintiff, was not very conclusive; and further testimony on that subject might have been satisfactory. Such was offered after the counsel had commenced summing up, but rejected. It was, doubtless, discretionary with the judge to receive or reject it; and I cannot say that his discretion was not properly exercised. From the case as it stands, I think a new trial should be refused.

New trial denied.

Cited in—9 Cow., 68; 6 Wend., 281; 18 Wend., 163; 6 Barb., 132; 4 Bos., 509; 2 Wood & M., 148; 20 Am. Dec., 582 (5 N. H., 280).

---

*BARNS v. GRAHAM. [*452

Note Payable in Ponderous Articles—Tender, Where and How Made.

Upon a note payable in ponderous articles, at a day certain, without specifying any place of payment, to make a tender, the promisor ought to seek the promisee before the day, and know of him where he will have the articles delivered; and then if he appoint a reasonable place or such an one as might have been in the contemplation of the parties when they contracted, offer the articles there.

If the note be payable, either generally or at a certain place, the articles should not be tendered in bulk, mixed and undistinguishable from others of the kind; but should be separated and distinguished; so that the promisee may know what to take.

Citations—8 Johns., 477; Co. Litt., 210 *b*.

ERROR from the Yates C. P. The action below was *assumpsit*, by Graham against Barnes, on the following note: "For value received of Orison Graham, I promise to pay him, or bearer, the sum of $127, in good merchantable lumber, an equal proportion clear stuff, in one year from the 15th day of May next, with lawful interest; as witness, &c., at Italy, this 26th day of October, 1822. *N. B.* Said lumber is to be of good white-pine timber." (Signed) Timothy Barns.

The defendant below offered to prove that when the note became due, he had at his saw-mill in Italy, where both parties lived, a sufficient quantity of lumber, of the quality described, to pay the note; but the plaintiff below did not call to demand it; and that the lumber was in bulk, and not sorted or separated from other lumber at the mill.

This evidence was objected to, by the plaintiff below, and overruled by the court, as not amounting to proof of a tender.

Messrs. P. *S. Parker* and *A.* P. *Vosburgh*, for the plaintiff in error, made the following points:

1. The parties to the instrument, being both residents of the town of Italy, it was incumbent on the plaintiff below to have demanded at the mill of Barns, the lumber stipulated to be paid, no place having been appointed in the contract for the payment.

2. As no place was appointed for the payment, or delivery of the lumber, it should have

---

Holway, 50 Me., 24; Columbet v. Pachees, 48 Cal., 395; Ball v. Cox, 7 Ind., 453; Coyle v. Cleary, 116 Mass., 208; Hathaway v. Evans, 108 Mass., 267; Savage v. Foy, 7 La. Ann., 573; Chew v. Morton, 10 Watts., 321; Prim v. Raboteau, 56 Mo., 407; McArthur v. Henry, 35 Tex., 801.

Acquiescence for many years is conclusive evidence of an agreement. From fifteen years upwards have been held conclusive. For instances, see authorities above cited.

The time required by the Statute of Limitations is necessary unless the jury infer an agreement. Jackson v. McConnell, 19 Wend., 175.

In cases of uncertainty parties are bound by their actual location—especially after long acquiescence. Jackson v. Murray, 7 Johns., 5; Rockwell v. Adams, 7 Cow., 761; Jackson v. Ogden, 7 Johns., 238; Jackson v. Smith, 9 Johns., 100; Jackson v. Freer, 17 Johns., 29.

See, generally, on practical location of boundaries, Jackson v. Dysling, 2 Cai., 198, *note*.

2. *Reopening the case to admit further evidence.*

After the parties have rested, or after they have commenced summing up, the admission of further testimony is in the discretion of the court. See, Mathews v. Whitney, 12 Wend., 396, *note*.

NOTE.—*Tender of chattels—When necessary—What sufficient.* See Slingerland v. Morse, 8 Johns., 474, *note*.

been left to the jury, whether, under all the circumstances of the case, it was not the understanding of the parties, at the time of making the contract, that Graham should receive the lumber at Barns' mill; and they cited Chip. Cont., 24, 25; *Coit* v. *Houston*, 3 Johns. Cas., 243; *Slingerland* v. *Morse*, 8 Johns., 474, and 2 Poth. Obl., Newbern ed., 1802, pt. 3, p. 28, art. 3.

453*] **Messrs. W. M. Oliver* and *H. A. Wisner*, contra, contended:

1. That, as no place of payment was specified in the note, the tender should have been made at the house of the payee, or at the place of making the note; or, at least, that the maker should have called upon, and requested the payee to name a convenient place of delivery. (Chip. Cont., 26, 28; 9 Johns., 477; Cow. Treat., 483, and cases there cited.)

2. But, should it be thought that the maker's mill was the proper place of payment, then the lumber should have been measured, separated, and specifically designed. (8 Johns., 477.) The effect of a tender, when properly made, is, to pass the property in the specific articles tendered, from the debtor to the creditor, and the debtor afterwards holds them as a bailee. (*Id.*, 15 Johns., 351.) If any act remains to be done to prepare the goods for delivery, the property does not pass. (*Id.*, Cow. Treat., 479, and cases there cited.) These authorities say that, if "any act remains to be done, such as weighing, measuring, &c., the goods do not pass; for the tenderee will not be able to identify the goods, or maintain an action of trover for them." (And *vide* 3 Johns. Cas., 243; 7 Johns., 124; 5 Johns., 119.)

Curia, per SAVAGE, *Ch. J.* The court below decided correctly. When a note is payable in ponderous articles, and no place is designated, the law does not seem to have perfectly settled the place. In *Slingerland* v. *Morse*, 8 Johns., 477, this court appear to adopt the doctrine of Ld. Coke (Co. Litt., 210 *b*) that in such case, the obligor must seek the obligee before the day, and know where he will appoint to receive them, and there they must be delivered; yet they hold that the obligor is not bound to deliver the articles at an unreasonable place.

In this case, the defendant below made no effort of that kind, nor did he separate the property he intended to tender in payment of the note. Suppose, the night after the note fell due, a fire had consumed all the lumber at the mill; must the payee have lost it to the **454*]** extent of his demand? *How could he know which part to preserve had he been present at the fire?

The defendant below should, before the day of payment, have called on the plaintiff to know where the lumber should be delivered, and then have actually delivered it there, if the delivery at that place would have been reasonable, and within the probable contemplation of the parties when the note was given; as at the plaintiff's house, in the same town, where he might wish to use the lumber; though the defendant ought not to be obliged to carry it to market for the plaintiff. But the defendant did not do enough, even if the lumber had been payable at his mill. He should have counted it out, having regard to the quality of the lumber specified in the contract.

Judgment affirmed.

Cited in—4 Wend., 317, 528; 5 Wend., 190; 11 N. Y., 90; 9 Barb., 159; 5 How. Pr., 232; 21 Minn., 458; 49 Pa., 45; 21 Am. Dec., 164, 211; 26 Am. Dec., 544 (11 Me., 398).

FRYE *v.* LOCKWOOD.

Involuntary Payment, to an Agent—Payment over to Principal—When not Bar to Action against Agent.

In general where money is paid to an agent to be paid over to his principal which is accordingly paid over without notice not to do so, no suit will lie against the agent to recover it back; but the money must be paid with the intent to pass it to the credit of the principal.

And the rule does not extend to an agent who obtains money illegally by compulsion or extortion; and especially where a suit brought to recover it of the agent is defended at the risk and expense of the principal.

Thus, where a deputy-marshal of the U. S., upon a warrant, demanded money, as due for a fine imposed by a pretended court-martial of the U. S., whose proceedings were *coram non judice* and void, which money was paid on demand, paid over to the marshal, without notice not to do it, and a suit was brought against the deputy to recover it back, and the suit was defended by the marshal or Secretary of War; held, that the action lay against the deputy.

Such a payment is not voluntary, within the meaning of the rule, that a voluntary payment of money will not constitute a ground of action.

Citations—4 Burr., 1984; Cowp., 567; 3 M. & S., 344; 4 T. R., 553; 9 Johns., 201; 1 Taunt., 359; 1 Campb., 397.

ASSUMPSIT, for money had and received. The action was to recover back $100, money paid by the plaintiff to the defendant, upon the ground that it was wrongfully collected by him from the plaintiff, under pretense of its being a court-martial fine, imposed under the circumstances detailed in *Mills* v. *Martin*, 19 Johns., 7, which see.

The cause was tried at the Orange Circuit, July 2, 1823, before Duer, Circuit Judge.

It was agreed that the money, since the decision in *Mills* v. *Martin*, could not have been legally collected by the defendant; but his counsel insisted that the action would not lie against him, on the ground that the president of the court-martial certified the fine to the marshal of the district where *the **[*455** plaintiff resided; and that the defendant in aid, and as the assistant of Seymour, a deputy-marshal, demanded the fine of the plaintiff, which he voluntarily paid to the defendant, with the fees of collection, which fine was immediately remitted by the defendant and Seymour, and paid over to the marshal; that both the defendant and Seymour were deputies of the marshal, for the purpose of serving and executing court-martial certificates; and that the suit was defended by the marshal or Secretary at War.

NOTE.—*Money paid to agent by mistake or by compulsion—When may be recovered from agent, although paid by him to principal.* See Hearsey v. Pruyn, 7 Johns., 179, *note*.

What is involuntary payment? See Hall v. Shultz, 4 Johns., 240, *note*.

These facts being proved, and it not appearing that the defendant had notice not to pay over the fine, a verdict was taken for the plaintiff, subject to the opinion of the court on a case, with liberty to either party to turn it into a special verdict.

Mr. E. Williams, for the plaintiff :

1. The money was extorted from the plaintiff, under color of process, upon a proceeding purporting to be judicial, but which was void. This cannot be called a voluntary payment.

2. Notice to the defendant not to pay over the money to his principal, was not necessary.

Mr. T. J. Oakley, for the defendant, said the plaintiff having paid the money voluntarily, cannot recover it back in an action of *assumpsit;* and at any rate, the defendant being a deputy-marshal, and having paid the money over to his principal before action brought, and without notice not to do this, an action cannot be maintained against him, but should be brought against the marshal ; and he cited 1 Selw. *N. P.*, Wheat. ed., 71, 72, *note;* 1 Chit. Pl., 25, and the cases there cited; *Greenway* v. *Hurd*, 4 T. R., 553; *Sadler* v. *Evans*, 4 Burr., 1984; *Pelo* v. *Blades*, 5 Taunt., 657; *Edwards* v. *Hodding*, *Id.*, 815, and *Ripley* v. *Gelston*, 9 Johns., 201.

Mr. Williams, in reply, said here was no agent of any government. Both principal and agent are trespassers, and the law will not recognize the relation of principal and agent, for any purpose of protection. The payment was not with intention that the money should **456***] go to the government, or the *marshal. *Ripley* v. *Gelston*, 9 Johns., 201, and *Cox* v. *Prentice*, 3 Maule & S., 344, are in point for the plaintiff as to the effect of paying over. The defendant was bound to know the law ; and knowing this, he knew there was no right to pay over the money.

Curia, per SUTHERLAND, *J.* Where money is paid to an agent, for the purpose of being paid over to his principal, and is actually paid over, no suit will lie against the agent to recover it back. In *Sadler* v. *Evans*, 4 Burr., 1984, the defendant was the receiver of the rent of Lady Windsor, and in that character demanded from the plaintiff, and received a certain rent, for which he gave a receipt, stating that he received it for the use of Lady Windsor. The rent, in truth, was not due to Lady Windsor, but having been paid for the purpose of being paid over to her, it was held that it could not be recovered back from the agent. In *Buller* v. *Harrison*, Cowp., 567, and *Cox* v. *Prentice*, 3 Maule & S., 344, the agent had not paid over the moneys to his principal. The case of *Greenway* v. *Hurd*, 4 T. R., 553, which was principally relied on by the defendant's counsel, seems to be placed by Ld. Kenyon, more on the ground of the want of the notice, required by statute to be given, before an action could be sustained, than upon the principle that the defendant was exempt from liability as being an agent; and Buller, *J.*, seems to put his opinion on the ground that the payment by the plaintiff was voluntary on his part.

In *Ripley* v. *Gelston*, 9 Johns., 201, the Collector of the Customs was held liable in an action for money had and received, for duties which had been illegally exacted by him, although the duties had been paid over by him to the U. S. The court there adopted the true distinction. They say the cases which exempt the agent from the suit, if he has paid over the money to his principal, without notice, do not apply. The money was paid by compulsion ; it was extorted as a condition of granting the clearance, and not paid with the intent or purpose that the collector should pass it to the credit of the U. S. And they rely upon *Snowden* v. *Davis*, 1 Taunt., 359.

*In *Townson* v. *Wilson*, 1 Campb., [***457** 397, Ld. Ellenborough says, if any one gets money into his hands illegally, he cannot discharge himself by paying it over to another. But it is not necessary to rely on that principle in this case ; for it was proved on the trial that the defendant admitted he had no interest in the defense ; that it was conducted either by the Secretary of War or the marshal. In such a case, even if the liability of the defendant were more questionable, I should hesitate before I would drive the plaintiff to a new action, against the very persons who now in truth defend this.

Judgment for the plaintiff.

Cited in—29 Barb., 92; 52 Barb., 579; 56 How. Pr., 482; 8 Bos., 155; 2 E. D. S., 234; 41 Wis., 131.
See 4 Cow., 470, *post.*

GRISWOLD
v.
STEWART ET AL., Heirs and Terre-tenants of WALTON.

*Death of Party—Entry of Judgment by Default at Term Commencing thereafter—Judgment Void—Relation—*Sci. Fa *on such Judgment against Terre-tenants—*Practice.

A judgment by default, entered at a term which commences after the defendant's death, is void.

It is not made good by any statute; and is not good by relation; for,

A judgment does not relate back to a period beyond the first day of the term at which it is entered.

On a *scire facias* upon such a judgment against the terre-tenants, they may show by plea that the judgment was so entered; for,

The rule, that one cannot contradict a record, applies only to such as are parties or privies to the record, and may bring error; and,

The rule that one cannot to a *scire facias*, plead any matter which he might have pleaded to the original action, is also limited to parties or privies.

Citations—1 Chit. Pl., 354; 16 Johns., 55; Bac. Abr. Error, B; Cro. Eliz., 199; 1 Ld. Raym., 669; 2 Salk. 600, 2 Mod., 308; 8 Johns., 77; Cowp., 727; 2 Str., 1043; 17 Car. 2, c. 8; Tidd., 847, 849; 1 R. L., 144, sec. 5; 312; Act April 15, 1814 (sess. 37, ch. 200, sec. 40); 8 and 9 Wm., 3 ch. 11.

ON *scire facias* against Stewart and others, setting forth a judgment of this court in favor of the plaintiff, against Walton, for $5,-866.02 debt and costs, Oct. 29, 1813; that execution thereof still remained to be made; that Walton was dead; and commanding the Sheriff of Columbia Co. to warn the heirs and tenants of all the lands in his bailiwick, whereof Walton, or any other person or persons, in trust for him, were seised Oct. 29, 1813, or at any time after, to show cause, &c.

why the debt and costs should not be made of those lands and tenements;

Stewart, being warned as one of the tenants on the day of the rendition of the judgment, appeared and pleaded two pleas, one of which, and the only one which it is important to notice, was thus: that the suit in which the judgment was obtained against Walton, was commenced by bill, he being an attorney and counselor of this court; and that he died before the rendition of the judgment, to wit: **458***] *Oct. 5, 1813; and that the judgment was obtained by default, and without issuing any writ of *scire facias*.

General demurrer and joinder.

Mr. J. Lynch, in support of the demurrer, said the plea is bad: 1. Because it impeaches the validity of record. 1 Chit. Plead., 354; *Hayward* v. *Ribbans*, 4 East, 310; *Horsy* v. *Daniel*, 1 Lev., 161; *Moses* v. *Macferlan*, 2 Burr., 1007, *arguendo; Drake* v. *Mitchell*, 3 East, 251, 258. According to the record, Walton appeared and must have been alive. 2. Because it sets up matter of defense which existed prior to the judgment. *M'Farland* v. *Irwin*, 8 Johns., 77, 79; *Cook* v. *Jones*, Cowp., 727, 728; *Bush* v. *Gower*, 2 Str., 1043.

Mr. D. Cady, contra. The judgment was absolutely void as to every one except parties or privies, and all who could not bring error. *Warter* v. *Perry*, Cro. Eliz., 199; *Proctor* v. *Johnson*, 2 Salk., 600; S. C., 1 Ld. Raym., 669.

Error could not have been brought by Stewart the terre-tennat. (Bac. Abr., Error, B.)

At any rate the judgment does not relate to a day when Walton was living, and is no lien on land which had ceased to be his, when the judgment was entered. *Heapy* v. *Parris*, 6 T. R., 368. The lands had descended; and it is only of lands, whereof he was seised at the rendition of the judgment, that execution could be had. (1 R. L., 500, 501, sec. 2.)

Curia, per SUTHERLAND, *J.* The rule, that records cannot be impeached in pleading, is founded on the consideration that the regular and orderly way of trying their validity is by writ of error; and that it might lead to great abuse, to permit the solemn judgments of a court of record to be incidentally called in question in pleading, when a more direct and satisfactory mode of testing their validity exists. 1 Chit. Pl., 354, and the cases there cited; *Green* v. *Ovington*, 16 Johns., 55.

The reason of the rule shows its limitation. It is confined to parties or privies, who alone can bring error. (Bac. Abr., Error, B, and the cases there cited.) It does not apply to strangers. Thus, in *Warter* v. *Perry*, Cro. Eliz., **459***] *199, which was *scire facias* against bail, they pleaded that the principal was dead the day of the judgment given; and the objection was taken that the plea went to avoid the judgment as being erroneous; but the plea was held good, because the bail could not have a writ of error to reverse the judgment. So in *Proctor* v. *Johnson*, 1 Ld. Raym., 669, the question was, whether a *scire facias* lay at common law, against the terre-tenants on a judgment in ejectment. It was held that it did; and Holt, *Ch. J.*, said, "upon the *scire facias* the terre-tenants will have notice; and they, being strangers to the judgment, may falsify." (S.C., 2 Salk., 600.) The case of *Randall and his Wife*, 2 Mod., 308, establishes the same doctrine. That was an action of debt upon an administration bond; and the defendants pleaded a judgment recovered against the intestate, and *nil assets ultra*. The plaintiff replied that there was an action against the intestate, but that he died before judgment, and that after his death judgment was obtained, and kept on foot *per fraudem*. The defendants traversed the fraud, but did not answer the death of the intestate, and the plaintiff demurred. The replication was held good; because, the judgment being manifestly bad, and the plaintiff a stranger to it, he had no other way to avoid it but by plea.

But it is said the plea is bad, because the matter of defense which it sets up existed prior to the judgment, within the cases of *M'Farland* v. *Irwin*, 8 Johns., 77; *Cook* v. *Jones*, Cowp., 727, and *Bush* v. *Gower*, 2 Str., 1043. The rule, that nothing which was a defense to the original action can be pleaded in *scire facias*, applies only to the original parties or to privies, not strangers. This is evident from the reason and nature of things.

If, then, the defendant has a right to set up this matter of defense, is it not conclusive, to show the judgment which is sought to be enforced, absolutely void as against the defendant? It was a judgment by default, not by confession or verdict, and therefore not within the Statute of 17 Car. 2, ch. 8; Tidd, 847; 1 R. L., 144, sec. 5, which provides that the death of either party, between verdict and judgment, shall not be alleged for error, so as the judgment be entered within *two terms after the [***460** verdict; nor within the Act of Apr. 15, 1814, sess. 37, ch. 200, sec. 40, which has a provision similar to the last in relation to judgments entered by confession, after the death of the defendant; so that they be entered in two terms after the signing a plea of confession in actions pending during the defendant's lifetime; nor is it within the 10th section of the Act concerning Executors and Administrators, 1 R. L., 312, which provides that judgment shall not abate by the death of either party, after interlocutory judgment (8 & 9 Wm. III, ch. 11; Tidd, 847); for the representatives of the deceased were not brought in and made parties by *scire facias*, which was necessary by that statute.

Nor can the judgment be supported on the ground of relation. It cannot relate back to a period anterior to the term as of which it was entered. (Tidd, 849, and the cases there cited.) It was entered on the 29th Oct., 1813; *i. e.*, during the October Term, which commenced on the third Monday of that month. Walton died on the 5th, about a fortnight before the term commenced. The judgment is, therefore, void, and the demurrer, consequently, well taken. If void, it was no lien on the lands of the defendant—a conclusive objection against an execution upon land in the hands of the terre-tenants.

Judgment for the defendant.

Reviewed—7 Fed. Rep., 557.
Cited in—13 Wend., 594; 5 N. Y., 440; 10 N. Y., 169; 26 N. Y., 354; 2 Barb., 154; 13 How., 122.

461*] *MARSH v. LAWRENCE.

Confession of Judgment before Justice—What Sufficient Specification—Bill of Sale for Security to Vendee—Possession of Vendor, not Evidence of Fraud—Equity of Redemption, not Liable to Execution—Priority of Executions—Sale on Junior Execution, Valid—Supreme Court will not Interfere, Summarily, as to Application of Money Levied on Execution, by another than its Own Officers—Whether Levy Presumed.

What shall be deemed a valid confession of judgment before a justice under the Statute, sess. 41, ch. 94, sec. 7.

Form of a confession, specification and affidavit under that Statute recognized as valid.

A specification, stating generally that the debt is due from the defendant to the plaintiff, for money paid by the latter, as security for the former, is sufficient.

A bill of sale, or assignment of goods, declaring that the object is to secure the vendee as surety for the vendor, and that in case the vendee shall become liable, that he may turn the goods out on execution, or that they should be at his disposal at private sale, accounting to the vendor for the proceeds, is in nature of a mortgage, the possession of the vendor consistent with the face of the deed, and therefore not evidence of fraud as to creditors.

An equity of redemption in goods cannot be taken and sold on execution.

A justice's execution was levied on goods, which were sold; but previous to the levy, a *fi. fa.* against the same goods had been delivered to the sheriff; held, that the levy and sale upon the justice's execution changed the property of the goods, and the sheriff could not afterwards take them.

If a sheriff having two executions, sell on a junior one, the sale is valid.

The Supreme Court will not interfere summarily, and direct how money levied on execution by a constable, or other person, not their own officer, shall be applied.

Otherwise, as to their own officers.

Whether a levy will ever be presumed as between conflicting executions (doubted by Sutherland, J., interrupting Noxon, *arguendo*).

It seems that a levy will be presumed in no case, unless where a want of it would be gross negligence in the officer. Per Sutherland, J., interrupting Noxon, *arguendo*.

Citations—Sess. 41, ch. 94, sec. 7; 1 R. L., 502; 12 Johns., 163, 403; 4 East, 523, 538; 1 Ld. Raym., 252; 18 Johns., 311.

ERROR from the C. P. of Onondaga, where the cause came by appeal from a justice's court, by which judgment was rendered against Marsh for $30.

The action below was trover by Edmund Lawrence against Marsh for a horse. The cause was tried in the C. P. in Aug., 1822, when the jury found a special verdict, that in the term of Nov., 1818, in the C. P. of Onondaga, one Hutchinson recovered a judgment of $1,010, the penalty of a judgment bond and costs, against M. Curtis and Joab Lawrence, which was docketed Dec. 11, 1818; that a *fi. fa.* issued thereon, and was delivered to Bronson, a deputy-sheriff, Sept. 28, 1819, at 8 A. M., who levied upon the personal property of Curtis and Lawrence, and sold Lawrence's property Sept. 15, 1821, to $450.30, which was paid to Hutchinson; and Jan. 15, 1822, Hutchinson received $240.90, in full of his judgment. That the judgment was given for a debt of Curtis, Lawrence being the surety; that under date of May 10, 1820, Curtis executed a bill of sale of the horse in question, with divers other personal property particularly mentioned in it, reciting that Lawrence had thus become security, and providing *that the articles [*462 should be at the disposal of Lawrence, in case he should be made liable on the judgment; that he might turn them out to be sold on the execution, or take them into his own possession, and dispose of them at private sale, accounting to the vendor for the proceeds. That this instrument was made out in 1821, and was sent by Curtis to Lawrence Sept. 15, 1821, without any request of Lawrence for that purpose at that time, though Lawrence had frequently requested Curtis to secure him; that the bill of sale was intended to include all the personal property of Lawrence holden by the execution, and was antedated by mistake; that Lawrence never took possession of the property, or any part of it. That Nov. 30, 1821, a judgment was rendered before N. H. Earll, Esq., a justice of Onondaga, in favor of Lawrence, against Curtis, for $100.32, on a written confession, in these words: "*Joab Lawrence* v. *Medad Curtis*. Medad Curtis, the defendant, in this cause, hereby certifies, that he is indebted to the plaintiff in this cause, in the sum of $100 over and above all demands in favor of the defendant against the plaintiff; and that the same is due for money paid by him to James Hutchinson, as security for him, the defendant. Witness, &c., November 30th, 1821. (Signed) Medad Curtis." That the judgment confessed was for part of the money raised by a sale of Lawrence's property; and Curtis made affidavit before the justice thus: "Onondaga County, *ss.* Medad Curtis, the above named defendant, being duly sworn, saith, that the above statement is true, and that the judgment confessed in the above cause is not for the purpose of defrauding creditors, and that he honestly and truly owes that sum to Medad Curtis." That Dec. 1, 1821, execution was issued on the judgment by consent of Curtis, and delivered to J. Bronson, a constable, who, Dec. 3, 1821, levied on Curtis' property, including the horse, having then the bill of sale, which was delivered by Joab Lawrence to his son Edmund Lawrence (the defendant in error), the appellee in the court below, and by him delivered to Bronson, to have the property specified in it, levied upon by him, on the justice's execution. That Dec. 15, 1821, Bronson sold the *horse [*463 on this execution to Edmund Lawrence (the defendant in error) who took him into his possession. That other articles besides those mentioned in the bill of sale were also levied on and sold. That when the horse was sold, he was in Curtis' barn, but had been taken out and shown, and several bids made on him, &c. That in August Term, 1820, of the Onondaga C. P., Jonas Earll, Jr., recovered judgment against Curtis, for $102.47, docketed Aug. 29, 1820; upon which a writ of *fi. fa.* was issued and returned *nulla bona*; and Nov. 30, 1821, an *alias fi. fa.* tested Nov. 29, 1821, and returnable the 4th Monday of Feb. thereafter, was delivered to Elisha Marsh (the plaintiff in error), the appellant below, a deputy-sheriff of Onondaga; that Dec. 18, 1821, Marsh took the horse in question from Edmund Lawrence, and advertised and sold him previous to this suit being commenced before the justice. That Curtis had possession of, and used the horse, from Nov. 30 to Dec. 15, 1821, Marsh and Curtis residing within 100 rods of each other in the same village. That Marsh knew nothing of the constable's sale, till the day he took the horse. That the execution in favor of Earll was returned satisfied by Marsh; but whether, &c.

The Court of C. P. gave judgment for the plaintiff (the appellee) below.

Mr. B. F. Butler, for the plaintiff in error.

1. The property of Curtis was bound from the time when the *alias fi. fa.* was delivered to Marsh, the deputy. The defendant in error relies on the general principle advanced in *Payne* v. *Drew*, 4 East, 523, that till actual levy, the property, notwithstanding the delivery of the execution to the sheriff, remains in the defendant, subject to be levied upon by any other process. We understand this court have followed *Payne* v. *Drew*, in *Hotchkiss* v. *M'Vicker*, 12 Johns., 403. There is a distinction, however, between the sheriff's right to maintain trover, and his right to seize the property. But admitting the constable's lien could not be devested by any act of the sheriff, while that lien existed; that the sheriff could not take the property out of the constable's hands, **464***] *because it was in custody of the law, the reason had ceased in this instance, for it was sold and had passed into the hands of the defendant in error. The lien had, therefore, ceased. It is extremely well settled that the defendant in the execution cannot, by any voluntary sale or assignment of his own, defeat the lien which is created by the mere delivery of the execution; but the sheriff may take the property wherever he can find it in his county, before the return day of the execution. *Haggerty* v. *Wilber*, 16 Johns., 287; *Lambert* v. *Paulding*, 18 *Id.*, 311; *Beals* v. *Allen*, *Id.*, 363. Now, if the defendant, Curtis, could not prevent the sheriff's following the property by a direct sale, shall he be permitted to work that consequence indirectly by voluntarily creating a judgment, and procuring a judicial sale. In a word, shall he be permitted to do that indirectly, which the law will not allow him to do directly—to do that by operation of law, which he cannot do by his own acts? There is no more reason for protecting the purchaser in one case than in the other. The goods are subject to the previous lien, like lands to the judgment first docketed. The delivery of a *fi. fa.* to the sheriff has the same effect upon the defendant's goods as the docket of a judgment upon his hands. Unless this be so, the plaintiff in the execution is without remedy. The purchaser of the goods is not a sufferer. He is bound to inquire, and know of all executions in the sheriff's hands; and the omission to do so is his own fault. There is the more reason that he should be holden to this in the case before the court; for you have no control over the money in the hands of the constable, he not being your officer, but an officer of the inferior court. Besides, a previous levy by the sheriff should be presumed.

2. The defendant in error can claim no rights under the bill of sale, for several reasons. One is, because it was never executed. Joab Lawrence did not know of it, nor assent to it; another, he waived it by selling under the execution; another, it was fraudulent and void as being a general sale, and the possession never changed; *Sturtevant* v. *Ballard*, 9 Johns., 337, and the cases there cited; another, that the sole was to Joab Lawrence. How can it be made to *inure to the benefit of Ed- [***465** mund Lawrence, the defendant in error, who was a stranger to the transaction, so as to enable him to maintain trover?

3. The judgment in favor of Joab Lawrence was void. The confession was defective within the Statute, sess. 41, ch. 94, sec. 6, 7. The written confession and specification are not sufficiently definite to satisfy the 7th section of the Act. The oath was not in due form. The specification should, at least, be as particular as was required by the Act passed at the same session, in relation to confessions in courts of record. Ch. 259, sec. 8; *Lawless* v. *Hacket*, 16 Johns., 149. By the Act now in question, the defendant is required to set forth the particular items of the demand. The specification is too general. It is no guide to creditors, who were actually concerned in this case, and therefore the doctrine in *Griffin* v. *Mitchell*, 2 Cow., 548, 550, cannot be replied to us. The Statute (7th sec.) declares the judgment void if it want the proper specification; and *Woodcock* v. *Bennet*, 1 Cow., 711, reviewed all the cases, and declared that where the judgment is void, even purchasers *bona fide*, will not be protected.

Mr. B. D. Noxon, contra. The assignment of the property was by way of mortgage, and it has been often decided that a continuing possession of the vendor being consistent with the contract, is, in such case, no evidence of fraud. That the transaction was morally right, appears by the special verdict. Edmund Lawrence, though not nominally a party, was really so. The bill of sale was delivered to him. At any rate he was the agent—as such, had possession of the property and might maintain trover. He was a bailee. It appears from the verdict that the claim upon the mortgage was never abandoned; at least, the verdict does not find that it was, and, therefore, the equity of redemption was sold.

The confession, specification and oath, though not formal, are a substantial compliance with the Statute. The cause and item of indebtedness are given. It is for money paid as security, and could not be more specific.

*Here is no room to presume a pre- [***466** vious levy by the sheriff. The doctrine of presumption comes in only where the execution has been a long time in the sheriff's hands. The verdict finds there was no levy, and none was indorsed on the execution.

[SUTHERLAND, *J.* It is, at least, questionable whether a levy should ever be presumed as between conflicting executions; and I do not think it could be presumed here, upon any ground. It is done, I believe, only in cases where a want of it would be gross negligence in the officer.]

If there be any presumption here, it is against the levy.

I had almost supposed the gentleman had given up his claim upon the point of the previous delivery of the execution; as he put himself on *Payne* v. *Drew*, 4 East, 523, which, if law, is certainly against him. But he seemed to suppose that case merely went against trover by the sheriff. Our Statute is the same as the English; and our common law is the same

touching the effect of the delivery of an execution. *Payne* v. *Drew* decides that where there are two equal authorities, the one first actually levied or executed takes preference. It is agreed that the sheriff had not such a lien as would sustain trover. This is the settled law. *Hotchkiss* v. *M'Vicker*, 12 Johns., 403. The cases cited from 18 Johnson, are, that the defendant cannot defeat the execution by voluntary assignment; and where he removes the property, and it is sold on an execution subsequently delivered, not that the sale shall be defeated, but merely that the money, the avails of the sale, shall be applied under the direction of the court, according to the date of the delivery of the executions. This leaves the sale to stand good. Such was the case of *Lambert* v. *Paulding*, 18 Johns., 311. That case is stronger for us then *Payne* v. *Drew*. The objection, that the defendant was doing indirectly, through a judgment confessed, what he could not do directly, will not avail. It cannot be pretended that there was any fraud in the proceeding. Where two executions are in the same sheriff's hands, and he sells on the younger, even there the sale would be valid.
467*] *Smallcomb* v. *Cross*, *Carth., 419, 420; 1 Salk., 320; 1 Ld. Raym., 251; *Sandford* v. *Roosa*, 12 Johns., 162, 163, 164.

Curia, per WOODWORTH, *J.*, after stating the case. The specification filed with the justice was substantially a compliance with the Statute, sess. 41, ch. 94, sec. 7.

The bill of sale must be considered in the nature of a mortgage, and the possession of Curtis consistent with it. It provides that the articles conveyed should be at the disposal of Joab Lawrence, that he should have the right to turn them out to be sold on the execution of Hutchinson, or dispose of them at private sale. Lawrence, then, had the right of taking possession at any time when he should think proper. Curtis had no right to detain them for any definite period. He was subject to the pleasure of Lawrence. He had, indeed, an equitable interest, in the nature of an equity of redemption, in the goods, and a right to any surplus, if they were sold. If this be so, I do not perceive that they could be considered, in judgment of law, the goods and chattels of Curtis, so as to be subject to the execution of Earll. That could not attach on an equity, which was all that remained in Curtis. If, therefore, it be conceded that the defendant in error acquired no title under his purchase, still he had the lawful possession of the horse, and might well maintain an action against the plaintiff in error, who derived no authority from the execution to make the levy and sale. I incline to think that the decision of this cause might be placed on that ground.

If, however, I am mistaken on this point, then the question arises, whether the C. P. execution of Earll, having been delivered to the sheriff before the justice's execution was levied, is entitled to a preference. If the property was bound from the time of the delivery, and the defendant in the execution could not make a valid sale of it afterwards, the law will not permit him to do the same thing indirectly, by confessing a judgment and authorizing a judicial sale.

But a more difficult question is presented here, and that is, whether the purchaser, under the justice's execution, is *not pro- [***468** tected. I am not aware that this point has been decided by our courts.

The statute declares that no writ of execution shall bind the property of the goods, but from the time the writ shall be delivered to the sheriff. (1 R. L., 502.) The meaning of these words is, that after the writ is so delivered, the defendant cannot make an assignment, or do any act to devest the right of the sheriff to take the goods. The delivery does not alter the property; but, both before and since the Statute of Frauds, it continues in the defendant until execution executed. (12 Johns., 403.) The delivery of the execution does not, however, in every case, authorize the sheriff subsequently to take the goods and sell them. In *Payne* v. *Drew*, 4 East, 538, Ld. Ellenborough very fully and accurately examined the cases on this subject and observed, that "the sense in which, and the extent to which goods are said to be bound, is, that it (the *fi. fa.*) binds the property as against the party himself, and all claiming by assignment from, through, or under him; but it does not so vest the property in the goods, absolutely, as to defeat the effect of a sale thereof, made by the sheriff under an execution." A sheriff cannot maintain trover for goods taken out of the possession of the party against whom the execution issued, until he has made a levy. He has only a right to seize the goods, if he can find them. (12 Johns., 403.)

It is well settled, that if two writs of *fieri facias* are delivered to the sheriff, and he sells under the junior execution, such sale cannot be avoided, and the party has no remedy but against the sheriff. The property of the goods is bound by the sale, and cannot be taken by the execution first delivered. The reason given is, "that sales made by the sheriff ought not to be defeated; for if they were, no man would buy goods levied upon by a writ of execution." (1 Ld. Raym., 252; 4 East, 523; 12 Johns., 163, 403.)

The present case is distinguished by this; that here are different officers. But, if the principle be sound, it follows that any junior execution, first levied, and a sale under it, confers a good title on the purchaser. If the executions are in the hands of the same officer, the plaintiff in the first execution *has [***469** a perfect remedy against him; for it is his duty to sell on the first, and if he does not, he is answerable. If the executions are in the hands of different officers, then the liability of the sheriff to whom the first execution was delivered, would depend on the question, whether he had been guilty of negligence in not having made a levy before the sale under the second execution. If there be no negligence, I apprehend the party would be without redress, unless the money produced by the sale under the second execution happened to remain in the hands of the sheriff, when an application was made to the court for a rule directing to whom it should be paid over. This was done in *Lambert* v. *Paulding*, 18 Johns., 311. If, however, it should appear that the money actually raised on the second execution, had been paid over to the plaintiff in that execution, this remedy would fail, and consequently, the lien arising by the first delivery would become ineffectual. Whatever might be the result of an application against an officer of the court, directing him to pay over money, the execution of this summary jurisdiction would not be used to enforce such an application against an officer of another court, over whom this court has no control. But if otherwise, it does not affect the present question, which is between the sheriff and the purchaser under the second execution. The general principle, it appears to me, goes the whole length of upholding the title of the purchaser under the second execution, provided the levy and sale were perfected, before a levy on the first. The fact that one execution issued from this court, or the C. P., and the other from a justice's court, cannot change the principle which governs.

In the ease of *Lambert* v. *Paulding*, it appeared that the vessel was bound by an execution delivered to the Sheriff of N. Y. It was removed to Westchester, and there levied on and sold. The title of the purchaser was not even questioned. It was conceded on the argument that the property in the vessel acquired by the purchaser remained undisturbed. The claim was, that the proceeds in the hands of the sheriff were subject to the lien, and the court directed the sheriff to pay them over. **470***] This case is very much in point. *The only difference is, that the purchaser derived his title from a constable's sale, and not from a sheriff's. But the constable, in this case, had the same right to levy and sell the horse, that the Sheriff of Westchester had to sell the vessel. If so, the purchaser's title is valid. It was not, then, competent for the sheriff to take the horse, by virtue of his execution, from the premises of the defendant in error; and the judgment must be affirmed.

Judgment affirmed.

Cited in—3 Wend., 500; 8 Wend., 347; 9 Wend., 34; 1 N. Y., 28, 296; 11 N. Y., 510; 28 N. Y., 577; 40 N. Y., 103; 5 Barb., 392; 16 Barb., 49; 25 Barb., 634; 19 How. Pr., 482; 25 How. Pr., 65; 12 Abb. Pr., 102; 2 Duer, 105; 11 Leg. Obs., 339; 41 N. J. L., 287; 41 Am. Dec., 207, 208 (1 Gilm., 636); 32 Am. Rep., 206 (12 Vroom., 281).

CLARKSON *v.* EDES.

Maritime Law—General Owner of Vessel—Right to Maintain Action for Freight—Lien—Where Owner Does not Part with Possession and Control of Vessel, His Lien for Freight Remains—Question Determined by Charter-party.

When the general owner of a vessel parts with his ownership and possession in the vessel to a charterer, the latter is considered owner, and the former has no lien for freight;

Otherwise, where he does not part with the possession and control of the vessel.

In the latter case, he may maintain an action for the freight, in the name of the master, on the bills of lading.

Or he may enforce his claim by detaining the goods till payment, the law giving him a lien for the freight.

Where the general owners agreed to freight and let a schooner to D. Edes, master, to proceed from N. Y. to Havana, thence to Curaçoa, thence to Jacmel, and thence to N. Y.; the owners covenanting that she should be tight, strong, well manned, victualed and appareled during the voyage; that D. might load, and discharge from on board, such cargo or cargoes, or parts thereof, in either of the ports or places, as by them should be ordered; the schooner to proceed as soon as dispatched by D. at either or any of the ports or places mentioned, direct and without delay to the next port or place, D. agreeing to deliver and receive the cargoes, or parts thereof, at all the places along side, and within reach of the vessels; to pay the owners at the rate of $325 per month, at the end of every month, if in port, or on her arrival (if required), with all port charges except at N. Y.; also to advance what might be necessary for expenses, if wanted; sufficient room in the hold to be allowed for the provisions, wood and water, and for storage of the cables; and on the vessel arriving at Havana, or any other port mentioned, if D. should request it of the master or commander, the vessel to return direct to N. Y., in which case the voyage to be deemed ended, as if she had visited all the ports; held, that the general owners did not, by this contract, part with the ownership and possession of the vessel to D. so as to preclude their lien for freight; and that they might sue the consignee for the freight on the bill of lading, in the name of the master; and that a payment to the charterer, with notice of the owner's claim, would not protect the consignee.

Whether the general owner has parted with the ownership and possession to the charterer, must be determined from the charter-party.

Citations—8 Cr., 49, 50; 2 B. & A., 511, 512; 1 Cr., 214, 237; 18 Johns., 157, 162; Cowp., 143; 7 Taunt., 14; 1 Johns., 238; 8 Johns., 276; 8 Wh., 605.

ERROR from the C. P. of the City of N. Y.

The action in the court below was *indebitatus assumpsit*, by Edes against Clarkson, for freight, primage and average, in respect to goods, &c., carried, &c., in a schooner called Thetis, the plaintiff master, from Havana to N. Y., and for care and attendance, &c., about loading and unloading the goods, &c. The cause was tried in May Term, 1824, in the court below, before Irving, first judge.

On the trial, the plaintiff gave in evidence, two bills of lading, one of goods shipped by The Thetis, by Drake and Mitchell, of Havana, for N. Y., deliverable in good order, &c., at *N. Y. (dangers and and accidents of [***471** the seas excepted), to Clarkson, or his assigns, he or they paying freight, &c., dated Jan. 27, 1824; the other, of goods shipped by Clark & Co., on board The Thetis, for the same voyage, deliverable in like good order, &c. (with like exception), to Clarkson, or his assigns, he or they paying freight, &c., dated Jan. 21, 1824. The defendant below admitted the receipt of the goods, and that he gave a receipt, reciting that a controversy existed between the owners and one Charles Douglass, as to which was entitled to the freight, and promising to hold it for the party who should prove to be legally authorized to receive it.

NOTE.—*Lien of a chartered ship for freight.*

Under a contract by bill of lading or charter-party, the ship is bound to the cargo and the cargo to the ship for the performance of the contract. The lien on the cargo for freight belongs to the ship, and can only be enforced by the party having the possession and control of the ship. Where the owner surrenders the possession and control of the ship to the charterer, the latter is considered owner for the voyage, and the former has no lien for freight.

Contra, where the owner retains possession and control. Lander v. Clark, 1 Hall, 355; Holmes v. Pavenstedt, 5 Sandf., 97; Mactaggert v. Henry, 3 E. D. Smith, 390; Pickman v. Woods, 23 Mass. (6 Pick.), 248; Palmer v. Gracie, 4 Wash., 110; Drinkwater v. Brig Spartan, Ware, 149; Ruggles v. Buckner, 1 Paine C. C., 358; Marcardier v. Chesapeake Ins. Co., 8 Cr., 39; Raymond v. Tyson, 58 U. S. (17 How.), 53; Belcher v. Copper, 4 Man. & G., 502.

The plaintiff then rested, and the defendant, for the purpose of his defense, read a charter-party, which was admitted to be correct, and to be executed by the owners of the schooner, and by Douglass, and that the freight for which this suit is brought was earned by the schooner, on the voyage made under the charter-party, which was as follows:

"This charter-party, made and concluded this 10th day of November, A. D. 1823, between William Lockwood & Co. and John Bulkley & Son, of the City of N. Y., of the first part and Charles Douglass of the aforesaid city, of the second part, witnesseth, that the said parties of the first part have hereby agreed to freight, and to let to the said party of the second part, the whole of the schooner called The Thetis of N. Y., of the burthen of 99 $\frac{1}{9}\frac{1}{5}$ tons, whereof Thomas Edes is master, for the following voyage, viz.: to proceed from hence to the port of Havana; at and from thence to Curaçoa, with the privilege of touching, if necessary, at a port or place on the south side of St. Domingo, on her way to the aforesaid port of Curaçoa; at and from thence to Jacmel, St. Domingo, and from thence back to N. Y. The parties of the first part engage, that the said schooner shall be tight, strong and well manned, victualed and appareled, and shall be so kept during the continuance of said voyage; that the party of the second part may load and discharge from on board said schooner, such cargo or cargoes, or parts thereof, in either or any of the above ports or places, as by them shall be ordered. The said **472***] schooner to *proceed as soon as dispatched by the said second party, at either or any of the aforesaid ports or places, direct and without delay, to the next port or place, the usual dangers of the seas excepted. The party of the second part doth hereby agree to deliver and receive the cargoes or parts thereof, as may be at all and exery place alongside and within reach of the vessel's tackles, she being first anchored or moored at the usual place at each port. In consideration of which, the party of the second part agrees to pay to the parties of the first part, or to their agents or assigns, at and after the rate of $325 for every calendar month, payable at the expiration of every month, if in port, or immediately on her arrival thereafter (if required by the parties of the first part), in the currency of the place wherever she may be, together with all and every port charge, excepting at the port of N. Y.; and also to advance from time to time, on account of the charter, whatever moneys may be required for the necessary expenses or disbursements of the vessel, if any should be wanted. For the true and faithful performance of said voyage, the parties hereunto bind themselves each to the other; that is to say, the parties of the first part, the said schooner, her tackle and apparel, and the said party of the second part, the cargo or cargoes to be ladened on board, in the penal sum of $1,000 lawful money of the U. S. In witness whereof, they have hereunto interchangeably set their hands and seals on the day and the year first above written.

It is understood that sufficient room in the hold of said vessel is to be allowed for the necessary provisions, wood and water during the voyage above mentioned, and also for storage of the cables.

It is also further agreed and understood, by the parties to the foregoing instrument of writing or charter-party, that, upon the arrival of the said schooner Thetis, at the port of Havana, or at any other of the foreign ports or places mentioned in the foregoing instrument, if the party of the second part shall request of the master or commander, the immediate and direct return of said schooner from Havana, or from any of the other of said ports, directly to the port of *N. Y., said master or [***473** commander shall be obliged so to do; and upon the arrival and discharge of said schooner, in the port of N. Y., said voyage, alluded to in the foregoing instrument of writing shall be deemed to have been concluded and completed, as effectually as if said schooner had visited or touched at all the ports mentioned in the foregoing charter-party. In witness, whereof, the parties have interchangeably set their hands and seals hereto."

The defendants then gave in evidence the receipt in full by Douglass for the freight received of Clarkson, the defendant below, dated Apr. 10, 1824. This payment was made on Douglass' indemnifying Clarkson against the plaintiff's claim.

Upon this proof, the plaintiffs counsel submitted, that the owner under the charter-party had the sole right to freight, of the consignees; that the payment by Clarkson to Douglass was not *bona fide*, and that this was the only question for the jury.

On the part of the defendant, it was contended, that Douglass had the sole right to collect the freight under the charter-party; but that, if the owners had a lien on the goods of the consignees, they had lost it on the possession of the goods coming to the defendant; and, that they could not maintain a suit on the bills of lading for the freight, but must look to the charterer under the charter-party, or to the defendant on the special agreement entered into by him with the plaintiff; thirdly, that, even if the owners had a right to collect the freight, there was an equal right in Douglass; and, as Douglass had first received it, the payment was good; fourthly, that, before the owners could have a right to collect the freight, they were bound to show by the terms of the charter-party, that they had demanded payment of the monthly freight of Douglass, who refused to pay it; fifthly, inasmuch as the bills of lading did not make the freight payable to the master, he had no claim for it under the facts.

The judge gave his opinion, that it was evident from the defendant's receipt of Feb. 18, 1824, that the cargo for which this freight was claimed was received by the defendant with a knowledge that a controversy existed between the owners of the vessel and the charterer, Douglass, as to which *was entitled to [***474** receive it, and that the defendant was to be accountable to the one who should be adjudged lawfully entitled; his payment was with a view to this accountability; the more so, as he took an indemnity. That this accountability was evidently to depend on the decision of some court; and the only question, therefore, would be, who was the owner and possessor of this vessel for the voyage. That if the general owners were to be in possession of the vessel, and have the control of her during the voyage, they were entitled to the freight. That this would depend on the construction of the charter-party, the various provisions of which he examined; and held, that they had not parted with the ownership and possession. That being both owners and in possession, they were entitled to receive the freight and to enforce the claim, either by detaining the goods until the freight was paid, or by bringing an action on the bills of lading.

To this opinion the defendant's counsel excepted, a verdict was found for the plaintiff for $109.74, on which judgment was rendered in the court below, and the cause came here upon a bill of exceptions.

Mr. T. A. Emmet, for the plaintiff in error, contended:

1. That the owners had no right to look to any other than Douglass for the moneys due under the charter-party. *Hutton* v. *Braggs*, 7 Taunt., 14; *Christie* v. *Lewis*, 2 Brod. & Bing., 410. And he distinguished this from *Hooe* v. *Groverman*, 1 Cr., 214; and he also cited as bearing upon this point, *Gracie* v. *Palmer*, 8 Wh., 632, per Johnson, *J.; Chandler* v. *Belden*, 18 Johns., 157, per Spencer, *J.;* 1 Com. on Cont., 359–60; Doug., 104; Abbott, 228; *Faith* v. *E. I. Co.*, 4 B. & A., 630, and *Tate* v. *Meek*, 8 Taunt., 280, 293.

2. The owners had, at any rate, no other right than a mere lien on the property, and having parted with this, had no right to sue.

3. If the owners might sue, the charterer had the same right; and he, having first carried his right into effect, deprived the owners of their's as against Clarkson.

Mr. J. Anthon, contra, contended:

1. That the bills of lading being in the common form, the freight money was, from the 475*] *nature of the instrument, payable to the owners; Abbott, pt. 3, ch. 2; and the master may collect it in his own name. *Ib.*

That Messrs. Lockwood & Co. and Bulkley & Son were to be considered the owners, he cited *Marcadier* v. *The Chesapeake Ins. Co.*, 8 Cr., 49, per Marshall, *Ch. J.; Christie* v. *Lewis*, 2 Brod. & Bing., 435: *Gracie* v. *Palmer*, 8 Wh., 605; *Saville* v. *Champion*, 2 B. & A., 511, per Abbott, *Ch. J.; Hooe* v. *Groverman*, 1 Cr., 237; Abbott, pt. 3, ch. 1; *Faith* v. *East Ind. Co.*, 4 B. & A., 637, per Parke, *arg.;* 2 B. & A., 510, Campbell, *arg.*

2. Though the owner's lien be gone, the right of action on the bill of lading remains.

Mr. Emmet, in reply, cited *Yates* v. *Railston*, 8 Taunt., 293.

[And both the counsel examined at large, the different clauses of the charter-party, and the cases cited, in reference to the question who should be deemed owner.]

WOODWORTH, *J.* The plaintiff below was master of the schooner Thetis, and declared for the freight of certain goods. On the arrival of the vessel at N. Y., the goods were delivered to the plaintiff in error, who gave a receipt, promising to pay freight to the party legally authorized to receive it. This arrangement was made in consequence of a controversy between the owners of the vessel, and one Douglass, to whom to whom they had executed a charter-party for the voyage, both claiming a right to the freight. The defendant in the court below gave in evidence the charter-party, and proved that Apr. 10, 1824, he paid the amount of freight to Douglass, on receiving a bond of indemnity. The judge held the only question to be, who was the owner and possessor of the vessel for the voyage; and that if the owners of the vessel were to be considered in possession, they were entitled to receive the freight, and that would depend upon the construction of the charter-party; that, in his opinion, the owners had not parted with the ownership and possession; and were entitled to receive the freight, and to enforce their claim, either by detaining the goods until payment, or by bringing an action on the bills of lading.

*To this opinion the defendant ex- [*476 cepted.

The right to collect the freight is exclusive in one or the other of the parties. This right may be enforced by insisting on the lien until payment, or by resorting to an action, which may be sustained in the name of the master, on the bills of lading, for the benefit of the owners and possessors of the vessel. Whether payment to the charterer exonerated the defendant, necessarily depends on the question, whether, by the terms of the charter-party, he had the control, navigation, and possession of the vessel for the voyage. From an attentive consideration of the various clauses and provisions of the charter-party, I am of opinion that the general owners had not parted with the ownership and possession of the vessel, and consequently they were entitled to receive the freight.

The law is correctly laid down in *Marcadier* v. *Chesapeake Ins. Co.*, 8 Cr. 49. It is, that "a person may be owner for the voyage, who, by a contract with the general owner hires the ship for the voyage, and has the exclusive possession, command and navigation of the ship. But where the general owner retains the possession, command and navigation of the ship, and contracts to carry a cargo on freight for the voyage, the charter-party is considered a mere affreightment, sounding in covenant; and the freighter is not clothed with the character or legal responsibility of ownership. In the first case, the general freighter is responsible for the conduct of the master and mariners during the voyage. In the latter case the responsibility rests on the general owner."

The construction must be on the whole instrument, in order to determine whether the owner intended to part with the possession.

The first clause declares that the parties of the first part had agreed to freight, and to let to the party of the second part, the whole of the schooner Thetis. This expression, taken singly, would undoubtedly import that Douglass had the possession and control of the vessel. In *Marcadier* v. *Chesapeake Ins. Co.*, the language is substantially the same. The charter-party contained these *words: [*477 "Hath granted, and to freight let the brig, excepting and reserving her cabin for the accomodation of the captain." Yet the court held that the ownership and possession were retained by the general owner, in consequence of subsequent clauses, which compare with those in the charter-party in question.

The second and third clauses are, that the party of the second part may load and discharge from on board the schooner such cargo, in either of the ports or places, as, by them, shall be ordered; and that the party of the second part agrees to deliver and receive the cargo or parts thereof, as may be, at all and every place, along side and within reach of the vessel's tackles, she having first anchored.

It seems to me that these clauses are inconsistent with the idea of actual ownership and possession in the freighter. If that had existed, there was no necessity for such stipulations; but, on the ground that the general owners (although stipulating that the vessel should be employed for the voyage, in carrying freight for the charterer) still retained possession and control of the vessel, the clauses are intelligible and proper in requiring the charterer to conform to them. In *Saville* v. *Campion*, 2 B. & A., 511, such a clause was considered as conelusive that the possession was retained by the general owner.

The fourth clause, which provides that sufficient room in the hold is to be allowed for the necessary provisions and water during the voyage, goes far to determine the meaning of the contract. From this, it is plainly to be inferred that the general owners considered themselves as having possession of the vessel, and that they were to navigate her, and therefore made this reservation to enable them to perform.

The vessel was to be navigated at the expense of the general owners, which shows very clearly that their ownership and possession continued. If it had been otherwise, such a provision in the contract would not have been inserted.

It is also provided that the vessel shall be tight, strong and well manned, victualed and appareled during the voyage. If the doctrine contended for by the plaintiff in error be correct, what concern had the general owner with **478***] manning *and victualing the vessel? The cases of *Hooe* v. *Groverman*, 1 Cr., 237, and *Marcardier* v. *Chesapeake Ins. Co.*, 8 Cr., 50, are very decisive to the effect of such a clause.

There are other parts of the charter-party which serve to strengthen this construction, but I consider it unnecessary to notice them.

There is no doubt that the owner may waive his right to receive the freight, and if the charter-party clearly show that he intended to resort to the charterer solely, the right cannot be enforced. In the case of *Chandler* v. *Belden*, 18 Johns., 157, the stipulation was to receive $500, in advance, and the residue in three equal payments at 30, 60 and 90 days from the end of the voyage. This was held to be a waiver of the lien: but in the present case no such intent is indicated. Whatever remained unpaid at the return of the vessel, was then due and payable.

The judgment should be affirmed.

SUTHERLAND, *J.*, concurred.

SAVAGE, *Ch. J.* The important inquiry is, who was the owner of The Thetis, for the voyage in question? Doubtless, when the charterer becomes owner for the voyage there is no lien of the general owner for freight. It exists only when the carrier for freight is also owner for the voyage. The question of ownership must be determined by the charter-party, the contract between those claiming the ownership. It is substantially this:

1. The owners, Lockwood & Co. and Bulkley & Son, agreed to freight and to let to Charles Douglass, the vessel, Thomas Edes, master, to proceed from N. Y. to Havana, thence to Curaçoa, thence to Jacmel, and thence to N. Y.

2. The owners covenant, that the vessel shall be tight, strong, and well manned, victualed and appareled, and so kept during the voyage, and that Douglass may load and discharge from on board the schooner, such cargo or cargoes, or parts thereof, in either or any of the above ports or places, as by them shall be ordered; the schooner to proceed *as [***479** soon as dispatched by the party of the second part, at either or any of the ports or places mentioned, direct and without delay to the next port or place. The party of the second part agrees to deliver and receive the cargoes, or parts thereof, at all the places along side, and within reach of the vessel's tackles.

3. In consideration whereof, Douglass agrees to pay the parties of the first part, at and after the rate of $325 per month, at the end of every month, if in port—or on her arrival (if required), with all port charges, except at N. Y.; also to advance what may be necessary for expenses, if wanted. The parties bind themselves; *i. e.*, the owners, the vessel, tackle and apparel, and Douglass, the cargo, &c., in the penalty of $1,000.

4. Sufficient room in the hold was to be allowed for the provisions, wood and water and for storage of the cables.

5. On the vessel's arriving at Havana, or any other port mentioned, if the party of the second part shall request of the master or commander, the direct return from such port to N. Y., he shall be obliged so to do; and upon her return to N. Y., the voyage to be ended, as if she had gone to all the ports.

In *Vallejo* v. *Wheeler*, Cowp., 143, the charterer was considered the owner. The facts of the case are not fully stated; but it appears that the charterer had appointed the master, and that the owner of the hulk had nothing to do with the voyage. In *Hutton* v. *Bragg*, 7 Taunt., 14, the owner let his ship to the charterer from London to the Cape of Good Hope and back—the master having liberty to reserve the cabin for his sole use, and the usual accommodation for the crew and ship stores. The charterer covenanted to pay a certain sum in freight, for the voyage out and home. The C. P. held the charterer the owner for the voyage. In this case, the charter-party was in terms of letting to him, as remarked by Abbott, *Ch. J.*, in *Saville* v. *Campion*, 2 B. & A., 512. In this last case, *Hutton* v. *Bragg* was doubted, and it was held that the owner had not parted with the possession of his ship. The contract was that the commander should take on board a full cargo for *the freighter, reserving room for the [***480** provisions and cables; proceeding to Madeira, there to receive from the freighter's agent such goods as he might think fit to load; thence to

Madras or Calcutta, and thence to London—all the cabins, except one, to the freighter, who should send a supercargo; the freighter to pay, after the voyage was complete, £14 per ton upon the ship's registered tonnage, and the time of payment specified; the supercargo to direct the stowage of the goods laden, but in no other manner to interfere with the captain's authority.

The question seems to have been the most fully examined by the American courts.

In *Hooe* v. *Groverman*, 1 Cr., 214, the owner had "granted, and to freight letten," the whole tonnage of the vessel. Marshall, *Ch.J.*, places some weight on this phraseology, and also on the covenants by the owner, to deliver the cargo; that the vessel was to be kept and manned by him, and that the charterer was to pay the freight. He says the owner, Groverman, is to be considered the owner for the voyage. Again; in *Marcadier* v. *Chesapeake Ins. Co.*, 8 Cr., 49, it is said by *Mr. Justice* Story, who delivered the opinion of the court: "A person may be owner for the voyage, who, by a contract with the general owner, hires the ship for the voyage, and has the exclusive possession, command and navigation of the ship. Such is understood to have been the case of *Vallejo* v. *Wheeler*. But when the general owner retains the possession, command and navigation of the ship, and contracts to carry a cargo on freight for the voyage, the charter party is considered as a mere affreightment, sounding in covenant, and the freighter is not clothed with the character, or legal responsibility of ownership." In the case of *Gracie* v. *Palmer*, 8 Wh., 605, the owners let, and the charterers hired the vessel to freight for the voyage. Then followed several covenants, by the owners, to navigate the ship, to load and unload the cargo, &c. *Mr. Justice* Johnson, who delivered the opinion of the court, says: "The ship owner, who lets his ship to hire to another, whether manned and equipped or not, enters into a contract totally **481***] different from him who engages *to employ her himself in the transportation of the goods of another. In the former case he parts with the possession to another, and that other becomes the carrier. In the latter, he retains the possession of the ship, although the hold may be the property of the charterer; and being subject to the liabilities, he retains the rights incident to the character of a common carrier." In *M'Intyre* v. *Bowne*, 1 Johns., 238, *Mr. Justice* Thompson says: "It appears the assured equipped the brig, hired the master and crew, paid them, furnished the provisions and other necessaries for the voyage, excepted half the cabin, the privilege of 20 barrels on account of the master, &c. Under such circumstances, I should not consider A. & B. (the charterers) as owners for the voyage." In *Hallet* v. *Col. Ins. Co.*, 8 Johns., 276, the court say, the master of the vessel was to be considered as owner *pro hac vice*, or for the voyage insured. There was a complete letting of the entire vessel for the voyage. The master was to victual and man her at his own cost. He had the whole management and control, &c. In *Chandler* v. *Belden*, 18 Johns., 162, the only point decided is, as to the owner's lien, which was held to be waved by an express agreement regulating the time and manner of paying freight, by stipulations in a charter-party, and especially as the cargo was deliverable before the period of payment arrived.

These cases do not decide the present question; but they do decide that the general owner has a claim and lien for the freight, and that must continue, unless the owner has parted with it, either by constituting the charterer owner for the voyage, or by postponing payment beyond the time when the goods are to be delivered.

The question who was owner, must be determined by the charter-party. Was it, then, the intention of these parties that the owner should relinquish his ownership for the voyage? He first lets the whole of the vessel, and if the charter-party had stopped here, there could be very little doubt on the question. Second. The owners covenant that the vessel shall be strong, well manned and provided during the voyage, and that Douglass may load, &c. Why this permission, *if [***482** Douglass was the owner? Had that been the understanding of the parties, surely the charterer would have the right to load and unload what cargo he pleased, when and where he pleased, without a covenant from those who had parted with all interest in their vessel. The owners further covenant that the vessel shall proceed so soon as dispatched, &c. From this, it seems, the owners directed the movements of the vessel. They then had the control and navigation of her. The charterer agrees to deliver and receive the cargoes along side, &c. To whom was he to deliver? To his own agent? To himself? Such a covenant would be preposterous. But if the captain is considered the agent of the owners, then indeed there is great propriety in the covenant.

It was urged, in argument, that the clause providing for sufficient room in the hold to be allowed for provisions, &c., shows that the charterer was in possession of the vessel. I do not draw that inference. I think it proves that the charterer had the right to occupy the whole vessel with his goods, excepting that part reserved or allowed for provisions, water, cables, &c.

But the last provision in the charter-party seems to me to settle the question, if there be any doubt upon its previous parts. On the vessel arriving at Havana, she was to return, if the charterer requested it. Now why request his own servant to obey him? If the charterer was in possession, and had the control and navigation of the ship, surely this covenant is nonsense. Not so, on the supposition that the owners retained the possession.

I am of opinion, that the judgment of the court below be affirmed.

Judgment affirmed.

Cited in—11 Wend., 665; 78 N. Y., 51 7 Hun, 137; 12 Hun, 528; 11 Barb., 506; 26 How. Pr., 197; 30 How. Pr., 389; 17 Abb. Pr., 75; 1 Abb. N. S., 177, 438; 1 Hall., 375; 5 Sand., 100; 4 Rob., 67; 3 E. D. S., 398; 17 How. U. S., 62; 11 Wall., 601; 14 Wall., 612; 1 Cliff., 139; 1 Sum., 569; 2 Sum., 597; 2 McLean, 423; 2 Wood & M., 166; 26 Mich., 88; 22 Wis., 276.

483*] *THADDEUS DAN ET AL.
v.
BENAJAH BROWN.

Proof of Execution of Will—Revocation of Will —Parol Declarations of Testator—Admissible when Part of Res Gestæ—*Revocation by Cancellation—Parol Evidence of Contents of Will —Proof to Admit—Admissions of Party.*

One of the subscribing witnesses to a will of lands, may prove its execution, on a trial at law.

And this, though the will be lost, or not produced in court.

And where a witness to a lost will proved its due attestation by three witnesses, but had forgotten the name of one of them, having no doubt, however, that he was a competent witness, this was holden sufficient.

The parol declarations of a devisor will not amount to a revocation of a will of lands; nor can they be received upon a question of revocation, unless they relate to the *res gestæ*. They are then evidence to show the intent with which the act was done.

To revoke a will by cancellation, this must be done *animo revocandi*. The slightest degree of cancellation, &c., with intent to revoke, will operate as a revocation.

To warrant giving parol evidence of a will not shown to be destroyed, it must be first proved that diligent search for it has been made, by or at the request of the party interested, at the place where it is most likely it would be found—as among the papers of the devisor at his residence, if the will do not appear to have been deposited in any public office.

This search may be proved by a party in the cause, who made the search, though he be interested, as it is merely addressed to the court, in order to let in secondary proof.

The admission of a plaintiff or defendant will, in general, affect none but himself, and not his co-plaintiff or defendant, unless they are his partners.

Thus, in partition, by several tenants in common against others, on a plea of *non tenent insimul*, the admission of one of the plaintiffs, that a will was lost, shall not be received to affect his co-plaintiffs.

The confession of one tenant in common of lands is not evidence against his co-tenant.

Citations—Com. Rep., 531; 12 Johns., 33, 185, 192; 4 Burr., 2514; 2 Bl., 1044.]

ON petition of partition, under the Act for the Partition of Land, 1 R. L., 507. The plaintiffs presented their petition, to the Supreme Court, for the partition of certain lands lying in the County of Rensselaer. The defendants pleaded *non tenent insimul*, and annexed to the plea a notice that Benajah Brown, Sr., previous to his death, made and executed his will, in due form of law, for the passing of real property, and at the time of his death left the same will unrevoked and uncanceled, by which he devised to the defendants the whole of the real property mentioned in the petition. The cause was tried at the Rensselaer Circuit in July, 1823, before Duer, *C. J.*

On the trial the seisin of Benajah Brown, deceased, as stated in the petition, being admitted by the defendants, and the plaintiffs having proved his death while so seised, and 484*] *that the plaintiffs, parties to this suit, except those claiming in right of their wives, were his heirs at law, being his children, except Sellick, who was his grandchild.

James Mallory was called by the defendants, and testified that he had been well acquainted with Benajah Brown, deceased; that he made his will Nov. 9, A. D. 1816, at the office then occupied by the witness and William L. Marcy, in Troy; that the will was drawn by Mr. Marcy; that after it was executed, Brown delivered it to the witness for safe keeping; that the witness gave a receipt for the will, on the day it was executed, which he then had, and that he ascertained the date of the will from the receipt; that in the summer or fall of the year 1821, Brown called upon the witness to get the will, and stated that he wished to add a codicil to it. The witness delivered the will to him. He further testified, that since the death of Brown, in a conversation with Jared Betts, one of the plaintiffs, he told the witness that the will could not be found; that James Brown had been up at Brunswick, from Westchester, and looked for the will in the desk where he supposed it was left, and it could not be found there.

Thomas Clowes, Surrogate of Rensselaer, called by the defendants, testified that Harvey Betts, Thaddeus Dan and James Brown applied to him on the subject of the administration of the estate of Benajah Brown, deceased; that Betts and Dan said they presumed there had been a will, that search was made, but it could not be found; and the witness stated a long conversation between these persons, as to the existence, search for and probable loss or concealment of the will; that they finally petitioned for letters of administration and made affidavit that Benajah Brown died intestate, upon which letters were granted; that James Brown stated that his father told him, a few days before his death, that his will was in his desk at Brunswick, locked up with other papers, which he specified, and stated where he had left the key of the desk; that he found it there, and unlocked the desk with it, but did not find the will. Benajah Brown resided at Brunswick, Rensselaer Co., but died in Westchester, on a visit to his children, in 1822. The defendants *then offered to prove the [*485 contents of the will, on the ground that they had proved its existence and loss, or satisfactorily accounted for the non-production of it. The plaintiff's counsel objected, but the court overruled the objection.

William L. Marcy was then called as a witness, who testified that in the autumn of 1816 Benajah Brown, now deceased, called, in company with James Brown, one of the defendants, on James Mallory (who at the time occupied an office with the witness) to draw a will for him. Mr. Mallory requested the witness to draw the will, which he did, and after he had drawn and engrossed it, Brown, deceased, executed it in the presence of three witnesses, and those three witnesses signed their names to the will in the presence of the deceased, and of each other. The witness was one of these witnesses, and James Mallory was another, and who the third witness was he could not recollect; but from the circumstances of the deceased depending upon him to see that the will was properly executed, he has no doubt that the third witness was a credible witness. At least he is satisfied he must have though so, at the time of the execution of the will; and he thinks the third witness must have been a person of his acquaintance, and

NOTE.—*Wills—Evidence.*

Before secondary evidence of the contents of a will can be introduced, proof of search for it in the places where it would be likely to be found, must be given. Jackson v. Hasbrouck, 12 Johns., 192, *note.*

have been called upon by him to witness the execution of the will.

The counsel for the defendants were proceeding to prove by this witness the contents of the will, to which the counsel for the plaintiffs objected, upon the ground that the defendants had not shown who were the three witnesses in whose presence the will was executed, and had not proved the due execution of the will; but the judge decided that the defendants had sufficiently proved the execution of the will, and were entitled to prove its contents by parol. Upon this, Mr. Marcy testified that, by the provisions of the will, the deceased devised one sixth part of all his real and personal estate to each of his sons, James, Weed, Seth, Jotham and Silas, and one sixth part to James Brown, his son, in trust. The avails of this, during the life of Benajah, one of the defendants, were to be paid to him and to his children, and after his death the remainder
486*] of the sixth part was to be *paid to his children, and that the devise of the real and personal property was charged with the payment of $200 to each of the daughters of the deceased, and the like sum to Sanford Sellick, his grandson.

Upon this testimony, the jury found a verdict for the defendants.

Mr. J. Paine, for the plaintiffs, moved for a new trial; and contended:

1. That the execution of the will was not sufficiently proved. The witness must be able to testify to all which the Statute of Wills requires. One of the requisites is, that the witnesses should be credible. This should appear. The heir does not know them. Their names should be given, that the heir may know what witnesses he is to meet, and the jury pass upon their credibiltiy. 1 Phil. Ev., 377, Am. ed. of 1820, and *note b; Jackson* v. *Le Grange*, 19 Johns., 386, 388; Bull. *N. P.*, 264.

2. That the declarations of Benajah Brown, made during his last illness, were inadmissible to prove the execution of his will, or to repel the presumption that it had been destroyed by him. *Jackson* v. *Kniffen*, 2 Johns., 31; Rob. Frauds, 307; *Doe* v. *Perkes*, 3 B. & A., 489, 491; 2 Phil. Ev., 196, 197.

3. If the will was destroyed by any person before the death of Benajah Brown, it ceased to be a will. Rob. Wills, 21; *Lawrence* v. *Kete*, Alleyn, 54; *Havard* v. *Davis*, 2 Binn., 406; 1 Eq. Cas. Abr., 402.

4. That the verdict was against law and evidence.

Mr. A. Spencer, same side, said he should rely on *Gray* v. *Pentland*, 2 Serg. & R., 23, 25, 26; *Jackson* v. *Root*, 18 Johns., 60; 1 Phil. Ev., Am. ed., 1820, p. 346, and *Williams* v. *Younghusband*, 1 Stark., 139, to show what degree of strictness was necessary in the proof of loss; *Wilson* v. *Boerem*, 15 Johns., 286, and *Rex* v. *Inh. of Morton*, 4 Maule & S., 48, that declarations *in extremis* are inadmissible, except in cases of homicide. *Goodright* v. *Glacier*, 4 Burr., 2512, as to what acts are necessary to destroy a will; to the same purpose, *Pemberton* v. *Pemberton*, 13 Ves., 290. He also
487*] *cited *Burthenshaw* v. *Gilbert*, Cowp., 49; Gilb. on Dev., 115, and 1 Phil. Ev., Am. ed., 1820, p. 173.

Messrs. J. P. Cushman and *A. Van Vechten*, contra. The will was sufficiently proved. It was with Mallory four years, when the devisor took it, with the view to a codicil. He afterwards declared that it still existed, and several of the plaintiffs stated that it could not be found. This evidence was not objected to, and the whole case must rest on the sufficiency of the proof of loss. As to this, the court are referred to *Livingston* v. *Rogers*, 1 Cai. Cas., xxvii; *Jackson* v. *Lucett*, 2 Cai., 365; *Jackson* v. *Hasbrouck*, 12 Jobus., 192; *Jackson* v. *Frier*, 16 *Id.*, 193, 196, and *Caufman* v. *Presbyt. Con. of Cedar Spring*, 6 Binn., 59. Having proved the loss, we went to the proof of execution. This was made out with all the requisite formalities. The circumstance of loss does not vary the mode of proof. One witness is enough, *Jackson* v. *Le Grange*, 19 Johns., 388, whether the will be produced or not; and it is for the heir to impeach him by calling the other witnesses. The word "credible," in the Statute, 1 R. L., 364, when it speaks of the witnesses, means, at any rate, no more than competent; and competency is always to be presumed till the heir show the contrary. The witnesses may be entire strangers to each other, or subscribe at different times, and it would be hardly possible to reach the strictness demanded of us. Who of the legal profession, when they write and attest wills, charge themselves with names? If not, and the will happen to be lost, it must be unavailable, unless the proof in the present instance be enough. The hardship upon the heirs is no answer. The presumption is always in favor of supporting the will. *Bond* v. *Seawell*, 3 Burr., 1773. Suppose the names obliterated, or eaten out by rats, how are we to know them? Yet it cannot be denied that the will may, notwithstanding, be established. Where all the witnesses are dead, yet the will may be proved, You intend that the execution was regular from proof of the handwriting. 8 Vin., 125, Will, N. 7; *Hands* v. *James*, Com., 531.

*Has the will been revoked? This [*488 cannot be pretended, as to any mode of revocation pointed out by the statute, which is express that the will shall not be revoked in any other way. Implied revocations are all confined to alterations in the devisor's circumstances.

As to the act of revocation, the declarations of the devisor are admissible, whether before, at or after the act. This is no infringement of the statute. To what is it addressed? To the *quo animo*. Suppose a case of tearing. The question immediately arises *quo animo* is this done? And most of the cases cited in 2 Phil. Ev., 197, relied on against us agree that this may be shown by the devisor's declarations. The case of *Bibb* v. *Thomas*, 2 Bl., 1044, and *Brady* v. *Cubit*, 2 East, 534, and *note, a*, go distinctly to this.

We deny that the will must be in existence at the devisor's death. Suppose it had been accidentally burnt, or the heir had destroyed it, is its effect gone? In the case cited against this, of *Lawrence* v. *Kete*, Alleyn, 54, the question was put to the jury; and the case is the less satisfactory, because it arose before the Statute relative to the Attestation of Wills. Shep. Touch,, 411, is a direct authority that the loss in the devisor's lifetime, only has the effect to throw the burden of proving the contents upon the heir; and what was said in *Goodright* v. *Harwood*, 3 Wils., 512, 513, admits the doctrine fully. *Havard* v. *Davis*, 2 Binn., 406, S. P., cited on the other side.

The declarations of James Brown cannot now be objected to as incompetent; because they were admitted at the trial without objection. All that can now be done is to deny their sufficiency. They certainly fortify the legal presumption, in itself very strong, that the will existed.

It will not be pretended that the admissions of Betts and others were incompetent. They were parties to the issue of *non tenent insimul*, and were of course competent. True we might have examined James Brown as a witness to the loss of the will. So might the opposite party; and because he is a competent witness, it does not follow that the plaintiff's admissions against themselves are not competent. If Brown's declarations are not evidence *per se*, **489***] they are so as *being made in the presence of Betts and Dan, who joined in the same declarations. What the declarations were worth was for the jury to say.

Mr. Spencer, in reply, would not inquire whether it was necessary to show the name of the third witness; nor whether the destruction of the will in the devisor's lifetime, without his consent, would have destroyed it; but he considered the evidence at large (the whole of which I have not thought it necessary to detail), in order to show that the will was in truth canceled or destroyed during the devisor's lifetime, and with his consent. He denied, upon the authority of the cases of *Pemberton* v. *Pemberton*, 13 Ves., 292, and *Doe* v. *Perkes*, 3 B. & A., 489, before cited, that the declarations of the testator could have any effect in setting up a canceled will. He said they are mere hearsay evidence, inadmissible, unless a part of the *res gestæ*. The act of cancellation implies the *quo animo*. The law intends that it was done with intent to destroy the will. If gentlemen are correct, it must be done in the presence of witnesses. The presumption of an intention to revoke had often been held to follow the act of cancellation or destruction. To rebut this, and defeat the title of the heir, the proof should be clear and convincing. (Gilb. on Dev., 115.)

Curia, per WOODWORTH, *J.* The will of Benajah Brown was proved by one of the subscribing witnesses. He stated that it was executed in presence of himself, James Mallory, and another person, whose name he did not recollect; but had no doubt of his being a credible witness. This was all the evidence that could be expected, under the circumstances of the case. It was, *prima facie*, sufficient. In the case of *Hands* v. *James*, Com., 531, where all the witnesses were dead, it was submitted to the jury to determine whether the witnesses to the will set their names in the presence of the testator, merely upon circumstances, without any positive proof, upon the ground that there could not, probably, be any express proof, as few are usually present beside the devisor and witnesses, and from the nature of the case, the proof must be circum- **490***] stantial. It was observed that *three witnesses had set their names, and it must be intended that they did it regularly; that one witness was an attorney of good character, and may be presumed to understand what ought to be done, rather than the contrary. Here the attorney drew the will, subscribed it as a witness, and testifies to everything but the name of the third witness. It seems to me that from this, the presumption of due execution is irresistible.

The execution of the will being established, the next question is, whether there was any evidence that it was canceled. On this point I lay no stress upon the declarations of the testator. They were made long after the execution of the will, and shortly before his death. They are not evidence, unless they relate to the *res gestæ*, or to an act done; as where, by mistake, the will is torn or thrown into the fire. The declarations of the testator are, in such cases, evidence, where they show the *quo animo*. (12 Johns., 33.) The act of canceling is, in itself, equivocal, and will be governed by the intent. The rule is, that if the testator lets the will stand until he dies, it is his will; if he does not suffer it to do so, it is not his will. It is ambulatory until his death. (4 Burr., 2514.) There must be a canceling *animo revocandi*. Revocation is an act of the mind, which must be demonstrated by some outward and visible sign of revocation. The statute has prescribed four. If any of them are performed in the slightest manner, joined with a declared intent to revoke, it will be an effectual revocation. (2 Bl., 1044.) The evidence here does not warrant any such intent. The testator, several months before his death, called for the will and wished to add a codicil. There is no other act that indicates an intent to make the least alteration. No act was done, or dissatisfaction expressed upon which to raise a presumption. The most that can be urged is, that the testator expressed a desire to make some alteration by way of codicil, from which it is rather to be inferred that the general features of the will were approved, and that an additional, or greater provision, was contemplated, for some of the objects of his bounty. The conclusive answer is, that all this was inchoate. It rests merely in an intent expressed *at one [***491** time, and to a single individual. We are left entirely to conjecture, whether the testator ever afterwards did a single act to warrant the presumption of canceling the will in whole or in part. I, therefore, consider the will as remaining in force at the testator's death.

The more important question is, whether it sufficiently appears that there has been diligent search for the will where it was most likely to be found, so as to warrant the introduction of secondary evidence. The general rule is, that to entitle a party to give parol evidence of the contents of a will, when there is not conclusive evidence of its destruction, it must be shown that diligent search has been made in those places where it would most probably be found. (12 Johns., 192.)

In examining this question, I will first consider the place where the will was most likely to be found. The will not having been recorded, no resort need be had to a public office. It is last traced to the hands of the testator, who resided in Brunswick. His desk and other papers were there. He died from home on a visit to his children in Westchester. I think the defendants are bound to show due search among the papers of the deceased, at his usual place of residence; and if, on such search, the will cannot be found, parol evidence is admissible. James Brown might have been examined as a witness to the court, on this collateral point, but he was not. The question then rests on the evidence introduced by the plaintiff. Any declarations of Brown, independent of that, are not evidence.

James Mallory testified that Jared Betts, one of the plaintiffs, informed him that the will could not be found; that James Brown had been up to Brunswick, and looked for the will in the desk, where he supposed it was left, and it could not be found. This is certainly a very explicit admission by one of the plaintiffs. Harvey Betts and Thaddeus Dan stated to the surrogate that they presumed there had been a will, but it could not be found; and that search had been made. The plaintiff's counsel introduced the petition and affidavit of Brown, Betts and Dan, to obtain administration. These, **492***] *however, are silent as to the question whether due search had been made.

The defendants, who claim under the will, were called on to prove that they had made diligent search. Search by other persons, and not at their request, will not suffice. The admission by Jared Betts and Thaddeus Dan to the surrogate, was, not that Brown, or either of the defendants, had made search, but generally, that the will could not be found. In what manner and by whom search was made, they do not state. It was an admission that did not exonerate the defendants from giving affirmative proof of search made by them or some of them.

The only evidence remaining is the statement made by Jared Betts on another occasion. Although this admission might have been sufficient to conclude him, if he had been the only plaintiff, it ought not to affect the interest of the other plaintiffs who claim as tenants in common with him. If an ejectment is brought by tenants in common, the plaintiff may give in evidence the separate titles of the several lessors to separate parts of the premises, and recover accordingly. (12 Johns., 185.) But it would seem an unjust rule which would suffer one tenant in common to admit away the rights of others. As far as I have been able to discover, an admission by a party to the record is evidence against him who makes it; and where there are partners, against them also, but not against others who happen to be joined as parties to the suit. The cases which speak of the admission as proper evidence, will be found to have reference to a sole plaintiff or defendant. The confession, then, of Jared Betts, that Brown had made search, was no evidence to dispense with the production of the will, and furnished no ground to admit secondary evidence, so far as the other plaintiffs were concerned. On this point, the verdict should be set aside and a new trial granted.

New trial granted.

Proof of contents of lost or destroyed will. Cited in—6 Cow., 382; 11 Wend., 602; 13 Wend., 493; 1 Sand. Ch., 237; 26 N. Y., 437; 45 Barb., 451; 30 How. Pr., 235.

Declarations of one tenant in common, inadmissible against his co-tenant. Cited in—4 Barb., 536; 39 Barb., 325; 63 Pa. St., 63.

Will—Proof of what necessary to. Cited in—9 Cow., 220; 1 Wend., 413; 12 Hun, 347; 1 Barb., 538; 19 Am. Dec., 525.

Probate—Competency of witnesses, on. Cited in—5 N. Y., 134; 3 Bradf., 242; 29 Am. Dec., 246 (3 Porter, 51).

Revocation of wills. Cited in—9 Cow., 220; 6 Wend., 189; 11 N. Y., 161; 3 Bradf., 97.

Will—Attestation clause, proof of facts attested. Cited in—51 Barb., 262; 2 Bradf., 74, 284.

---

*HAMMON [*493

v.

C. HUNTLEY, B. HUNTLEY AND W. PARK, Executors of P. HUNTLEY.

Effect of Confession by Executor, of Debt Due from Testator.

The confession by an executor, of a debt due from his testator, is not admissible as evidence in a suit for the debt, against his co-executor, to establish the original demand.

Otherwise, to take it out of the Statute of Limitations.

Citations—3 Johns., 536; 6 Johns., 269; 15 Johns., 4; 3 Bac. Abr., 31; Toller, 367.

ASSUMPSIT for land sold and conveyed by the plaintiff to the testator. The declaration also contained the general money counts. The cause was tried before Nelson, Circuit Judge, at the Otsego Circuit, Sept. 16, 1823.

The declaration did not lay any promise from the executors to the plaintiff, since the testator's death; but merely averred a promise by the testator. This suit was against the three executors; and in the course of the trial, after a variety of conflicting evidence, upon the question, whether the testator and the executors, since his death, had not paid the plaintiff in full for the land sold, the plaintiff's counsel offered in evidence a letter purporting to be written after the commencement of this suit, by C. & B. Huntley, two of the defendants, to the plaintiff, acknowledging a balance of $240 to be due from the testator's estate to him; and promising to pay it. This evidence was objected to by the defendant's counsel, on the ground that the declaration averred no promise from the executors: but the testimony was admitted. Several witnesses on the part of the plaintiff swore that the signature to the letter was in the hand and name of C. Huntley. There was but little evidence on the part of the defendants to oppose this, and the cause passed to the jury on the question of fact, whether the letter was genuine or not. This was the main evidence on which the plaintiff's cause depended; and the judge charged the jury, that if they believed it to be genuine, they would find for the plaintiff, which they did, for the amount acknowledged by the letter to be due.

A motion was now made in behalf of the defendants, for a new trial, upon the above facts, as well as upon the ground of evidence showing the forgery of the letter, discovered since the trial, the particulars as to which are sufficiently stated in the opinion of the court.

*For the defendants, the following [*494 points, among others, were taken:

1. That the proof of the letter was inadmissible, on the ground that there was no promise laid from the executors, since the testator's death. To this was cited, 7 T. R., 182, 183; 3 East, 409; Willes, 29; 5 Binn., 573, and 1 Dunl. Pr., 56.

2. That the handwriting of only one of the defendants was proved.

Mr. D. Andrews, for the motion.

Messrs. I. Seelye and *W. G. Angel*, contra.

Curia, per WOODWORTH, *J.* This cause comes before the court on a case, and an application for a new trial on the ground of newly discovered evidence. The question is, whether an admission by one of the executors, that a certain sum was due from the testator to the plaintiff, is sufficient evidence to authorize a verdict against all the executors. It would undoubtedly be sufficient to take the case out of the Statute of Limitations. Does it establish the original demand against the testator, so as to make all the executors responsible for the acknowledgment of one?

The acknowledgment of one partner, after the dissolution of the partnership, of a previous debt, will bind the other partner, so far as to prevent him from availing himself of the Statute of Limitations; but it will not be evidence of an original debt. (3 Johns., 536; 6 Johns., 269; 15 Johns., 4.)

Where several persons are appointed executors, they are esteemed in law but as one person, and the acts done by one of them, which relate to the delivery, gift, sale, payment, possession or release of the testator's goods, are deemed the acts of all; for they have a joint authority over the whole. (3 Bac. Abr., 31.) But it is equally clear that one executor shall not be charged with the *devastavit* of his companion; and shall be no further liable, than for the assets which come to his hands.

If the admission of one executor is enough to establish the original demand, it seems to contravene the spirit of the rule which exoncrates him from a charge for the *devastavit* of his co-executor. The consequences of such a **495***] doctrine are, that *all the executors may be made liable, when in fact no debt against the testator existed.

In the present case, suppose the executors, when the suit was commenced, were satisfied the plaintiff had no demand; could prove none, and that, therefore, they omitted the plea of *plene administravit*; if this evidence is competent against all, then all the executors became liable ultimately for the recovery, although there may be a deficiency of assets. At this rate there would be no safety in any case, unless the plea of *plene administravit* were interposed. An executor could not repose securely on the strongest and best founded conviction that the demand was unfounded, when his companion could, at any moment, make an admission which would conclude his fellow. If this be the law as between executors, it is of dangerous tendency, and may well be considered an anomaly. Each executor may control and dispose of the chattels of the deceased; but cannot, I apprehend, affect his companion, so as to make him personally liable. It is held that if one executor confess a judgment, it shall not conclude and bind the rest. (Toll., 367.) It follows that he cannot do indirectly what he is prohibited from doing directly. If such evidence is competent against both, it is, in effect, clothing one with power to do an act which shall give a right of recovery. Whether this is done by confessing judgment, or by making admissions that may be used as evidence to produce the same result, is in my view, the same thing.

The verdict is clearly founded on the letter containing the acknowledgment. As the handwriting of only one of the executors was proved, I think it not sufficient to sustain the verdict.

On another ground, a new trial should be granted. There is certainly doubt and mystery hanging over this case. The plaintiff proved that he had in his possession a letter purporting to have been signed by two of these executors. He testified that he forwarded it to his attorney by delivering it to the mail-carrier. It has not since been heard of. The defendants have sworn that it is a forgery; and that on examining at the postoffices in Virgil and Burlington, for which the *letter was [***496** designed, it appears that all the letters from the former to the latter place had been received. In the exercise of a sound discretion, I think enough is shown to require the granting a new trial, on the ground of surprise. A verdict, under the circumstances of this case, should not be conclusive. There is a strong negative evidence, making it improbable that such a letter was written. The transaction requires the scrutiny of another trial.

New trial granted.

Cited in—5 Wend., 561; 14 Wend., 97; 19 Wend., 493; 5 Hill, 239; 11 N. Y., 181; 79 N. Y., 418; 3 Hun, 322; 3 Barb., 548; 4 Barb., 535; 5 Barb., 407; 10 Barb., 566; 15 Barb., 174; 22 Barb., 69; 3 Redf., 406; 36 N. J. L., 45; 21 Am. Dec., 243; 49 Am. Dec., 44 (11 S. & M., 9); 13 Am. Rep., 418 (36 N. J., 44).

VAN BEUREN AND VAN GAASBECK, Executors of GROEN, *v.* VAN GAASBECK.

Interest on Account—Allowable when—Running Account as Set-off to a Bond.

Interest is not allowable on an unliquidated account for goods sold and work done, unless there be an agreement express or implied to allow interest.

And where the defendant owed the plaintiff's testator, on a security drawing interest, which lay unpaid for more than 30 years, and during all this time the defendant had an account accumulating against the plaintiffs' testator for work done and goods sold, at short periods, which had never been liquidated or settled, amounting in the end, to more than the principal sum due by the bond; held, that interest should be allowed on the bond, but not on the account; and that the latter should not, in adjusting the balance, be allowed from time to time, as payment on the bond.

Rule of set-off the same at law as in equity.

Citations—4 Johns. Ch., 437; 3 Cow., 393; 1 Dick., 428; 3 Johns. Ch., 601, 358.

DEBT on bond, given by the defendant to the testator, tried at the Ulster Circuit, Nov. 1823, before Betts, Circuit Judge.

NOTE.—*Interest—When allowable on account.* See Newell v. Griswold, 6 Johns., 45 *note*.

The bond was dated Feb. 6, 1786, and conditioned to pay $712.50, Feb. 6, 1787, with interest at and after the rate of 6 *per cent. per annum*, on which was indorsed £9, Nov. 19, 1794, and £29 in 1813, and £29 in the same year.

The defendant claimed to set off an account in his favor, against the testator, running from July 1781, to May 1820, containing charges in almost every month of the intermediate years, for some small articles of service, or goods sold, such as usually pass in trade and interchange of labor, between farmers, amounting to $1,187.50.

Both the bond, the indorsements and the account, after deducting a small amount of the plaintiffs, were admitted; and it was agreed that the balance should be set off against the bond; and the only question was whether interest should be allowed on the bond, and for how long, and whether, without making the account apply from time to time as payment upon it; or whether interest should not be allowed upon the account, which had never been footed up or settled.

497*] *A verdict was taken for the plaintiff for $1,000, subject to the opinion of this court upon the above points. The balance to be struck by a referee named by the parties, according to the rules to be laid down by the court.

The judge at the circuit, decided that the bond drew interest from its date, at 6 *per cent.* and no more, and that interest should be denied on the account.

Messrs. Ruggles and *Hasbrouck*, for the plaintiffs.

Mr. J. Sudam, for the defendant.

Curia, per WOODWORTH, *J.* The bond is conditioned for the payment of interest, at the rate of 6 *per cent. per annum.* The contract for the parties is not confined to the time limited for the payment of the principal, but is general, and continues until the contract ceases to operate. (4 Johns. Ch., 437.)

At the trial, the defendant exhibited an account against the plaintiff's testator, commencing in 1781 and ending in 1820, which was admitted. An account of the plaintiffs against the defendant was also admitted, and it was agreed that the balance should be considered applicable, as a set-off against the plaintiff's demand.

The only question is, whether the defendant is entitled to interest. The bond is dated in 1786, payable in 1787, and the charges in the defendant's account are subsequent to that period, with the exception of a small part.

From the nature of the transaction, it is probable that, had the question been disposed of by the testator in his lifetime, the apparent equity of allowing interest, on the defendant's account, or considering the advances made as payment at the time, would not have been disregarded. The court, however, are called on to apply a general rule, which cannot notice the supposed hardship of a particular case.

Considerable stress is put by the defendant's counsel, on the fact that the account was not disputed. This cannot be a material fact. I cannot perceive any just cause for allowing a party a benefit, when the account is not disputed, that would not equally be allowable in a case where it was disputed, *but [***498** clearly and satisfactorily proved. The true question is, has the account been liquidated, or was there an agreement, express or implied to pay interest? Admitting on the trial, that the balance claimed was correct, is no evidence of a previous liquidation upon which to allow interest. It does not appear that any communication ever took place between the parties respecting the accounts, from their commencement to their termination. They must, therefore, be considered as unsettled and unliquidated. (3 Cow., 393.) If the defendant had not been indebted to the testator on a security carrying interest, his equity would be the same. If he had prosecuted as plaintiff, no interest would be allowed. The fact that he was holden to pay interest to the testator, cannot affect the principle which is to govern. It shows, indeed, the consequences arising from his negligence and inattention to his rights, which might have been avoided, but nothing more. It presents no fact upon which the court can infer an implied agreement to pay interest, that would not equally apply to every just account of long standing.

But it is contended that the court are authorized to order rests to be made, in stating the account by referees, under the Statute of Set-off, in the same manner as is done by the Court of Chancery. At common law, if the plaintiff was indebted to the defendant in as much, or even more than the defendant owed to him, yet he had no method of striking a balance. The only way of obtaining relief was by going into a court of equity. I am not, however, aware, that when resort was had to that court, the question of interest, on unsettled and unliquidated accounts, was governed by a different rule from that which was sanctioned at law. I have always supposed that, in this respect, the same rule prevailed. In the case of *Borret* v. *Goodere*, 1 Dick., 428, Ld. Camden observed, there is no instance where interest is given on an open mutual account, without some particular circumstances. So also, in *Consequa* v. *Fanning*, 3 Johns. Ch., 601, it was held that unsettled accounts do not bear interest of course, until liquidation. Indeed, it may be laid down as an established proposition that a court of equity follows the same general rules as a court of law, in relation to set-off. **Duncan* v. *Lyon*, 3 Johns. Ch., [***499** 358. The Statute concerning Set-off and reference are remedial; but confer no power on the court to relax the general rules of law. The question of interest is the same, whether a cause is tried by referees or a jury, or whether an account is pleaded by way of set-off, or constitutes the plaintiff's cause of action.

The doctrine, then, of rests, ought not to be applied; because the law does not allow interest on unliquidated accounts; and equity follows the same rule.

Accounts have frequently been directed, by the Court of Chancery, to be taken with annual rests. Where an executor, administrator or trustee profits from the use of the trust funds, or negligently suffers the trust money to lie idle, he will be charged with interest; and the court will exercise its discretion as to making annual rests. But this is altogether distinct from the claim of interest on unliquidated accounts not containing charges for money. To allow rests in this case, for the purpose of calculating interest, would, in my view, be arbitrary, not warranted by any rule of law, or sanctioned by the practice of a court of equity in analogous cases. I am of opinion that the defendant's account, without interest (after deducting the amount of the testator's account), be allowed as a set-off against the balance due on the bond; and that the referee agreed on making the calculation accordingly.

Rule accordingly.

Cited in—6 Cow., 195; 43 N. Y., 246; 53 N. Y., 590; 3 Hun, 218; 10 Hun, 181, 526; 5 T. & C., 677; 3 Bos., 575; 19 Hun, 87; 129 Mass., 91, 434; 18 Wis., 368; 10 S. C., 133; 37 Am. Rep., 311, 375 (129 Mass., 425).

GENERAL RULE.

IN SUPREME COURT, MAY 21, 1825.

ORDERED, that when there shall be a stipulation in a case, giving either party leave to turn the same into a special verdict, or bill of exceptions, the party to whom that right shall be reserved, shall have thirty days after the adjournment of the court, at the term when judgment shall be given, to prepare and serve such special verdict, or bill of exceptions. *And if the same shall not be [*500 agreed to by the party upon whom the same shall be served, he shall have twenty days to prepare and serve amendments; and in case such amendments shall not be agreed to, the same shall be settled by one of the justices of this court, on a notice to be given within ten days after service of such amendments. And in case such special verdict, or bill of exceptions, shall not be served within the said thirty days, the prevailing party shall be at liberty to perfect his judgment and proceed thereon. And in case no amendments shall be proposed and served within the said twenty days allowed for that purpose (or within such further time as shall, upon special application, be allowed by one of the justices of this court), the special verdict or bill of exceptions shall be deemed assented to, as prepared and served.(a)

(a) *Vide* Jackson v. Sinclair, *ante*, 43, and Van Dyck v. Van Buren, 1 Cai., 13.

[END OF MAY TERM, 1825.]

CASES

ARGUED AND DETERMINED

IN THE

SUPREME COURT

OF THE

STATE OF NEW YORK,

IN

AUGUST TERM, 1825, IN THE FIFTIETH YEAR OF OUR INDEPENDENCE.

HARWOOD v. FRENCH.

Action in Justice Court—Failure of Defendant to Plead—Certiorari.

Where, in a suit under the Act for the More Speedy Recovery of Debts to the Value of Fifty Dollars (sess. 47, ch. 238), the defendant omits to plead, and judgment is rendered, a *certiorari* lies.
In such case, no appeal to the C. P. lies.

ON *certiorari* to a justice's court. The justice returned that French declared against Harwood, who was brought before him on a warrant issued Mar. 10, 1825. Harwood, objected to any proceedings, on the ground of his privilege, he having attended a court of special sessions as a party, and not having had time to return home before his being arrested upon the warrant; and made other objections, all of which were overruled. He refused to plead; and the justice examined the plaintiff's witnesses, and gave judgment against him for $5 and costs. And now,

Mr. Edward Allen moved to set aside the *certiorari* as having issued contrary to the provisions of the Act for the More Speedy Recovery of Debts to the Value of Fifty Dollars, sess. 47, ch. 238, sec. 36, p. 294. He read a clause of the Statute, which is, "that no writ of false judgment, or writ of *certiorari*, shall be allowed, or be of any force or effect, except in cases where remedy by appeal is not provided for by this Act, to remove any judgment, order or proceeding whatsoever, to be rendered, had or made by virtue of this Act, **502***] into the *Supreme Court of Judicature of this State." He contended that this suit had been tried within the meaning of the subsequent clause of the same section, giving an appeal in all suits which shall be tried before a justice; and that the defendant might, otherwise, evade the Act by omitting to plead, and yet put the plaintiff to do precisely what he would be obliged to do on an issue; for he is always bound to prove his demand, though no plea be interposed. *Cudner* v. *Dixon*, 10 Johns., 106.

Mr. J. A. Spencer, contra, said the proceedings of the plaintiff were entirely *ex parte*. There was nothing which could be called a trial—no litigation—no more than a mere inquest before the sheriff on a writ of inquiry.

SUTHERLAND, *J.* The 38th section of this Act contemplates an issue, in order to which there must be pleadings on both sides. When the cause goes to the Court of C. P., on appeal, there are no new pleadings. It proceeds upon those in the court below. The issue joined below is to be heard and tried in the C. P.

Mr. J. Platt, same side with *Mr. Spencer*, said the Statute certainly did not mean to abolish the remedy by *certiorari* entirely. It provides that no *certiorari* shall be brought, except in cases where an appeal is not provided for.

This expression implies that an appeal does not apply to every cause which may be decided by the justice; and the present case is one exception in the contemplation of the Legislature.

Curia. The only question is, whether the defendant before the justice could appeal. If he could not, it is clear that a *certiorari* lies. On looking into the Act, we think this a case to which the remedy by appeal is inapplicable. It lies in those cases only where there is a trial, either by the justice or a jury. Technically speaking, here has certainly been no trial. Nor has there, we think, been one within the meaning of the Act. It speaks of an issue joined by pleading, upon which alone the cause is to be heard in the Court *of [***503** C. P. Here was no issue—no pleadings on which the Court of C. P. could proceed to a trial, properly so called. In point of form, only one party could be heard, except as to the mere question of the amount of damages. The proceeding must be in nature of an inquest. No *venire* could issue, or jury be convened and sworn, to pass upon any issue between the parties. The motion must be denied.

Motion denied.

Cited in—1 Wend., 316; 4 Cow., 536.

SPAWN v. VEEDER.

Amendment of Bill of Particulars after Trial—Practice—Costs.

The plaintiff allowed to amend his bill of particulars, after his cause tried, a new trial granted, and two notices of trial after this, the cause being noticed for trial at the time of the amendment.
This allowed on terms of paying all costs, if the defendant changed his defense;
If not, then costs of the motion.

MR. S. A. FOOT, for the plaintiff, moved for leave to furnish an amended bill of particulars to the defendant.

It appeared from the affidavits read on both sides, that the declaration was served Aug. 1, 1822, with a bill of particulars, on the defendant's attorney; that issue was joined Aug. 20, 1822; and the cause tried Apr., 1823. The bill proved very defective on the trial. A verdict was rendered for the plaintiff; but a new trial was granted upon the merits, in February Term, 1824. The cause had since been twice noticed for trial, and now stood noticed for the Albany Circuit. The first bill was defective in consequence of the plaintiff's attorney not being fully instructed by his client, who lived 400 miles from him. But lately he had procured full and correct instructions, which enabled him to furnish the requisite particulars.

Mr. J. M'Kown, contra.

Curia. These amendments are much a matter of discretion. The plaintiff's attorney has not been very diligent in procuring proper information from his client; but it will further the ends of justice to grant the amendment. We save the defendant from all costs resulting to him from the mistake. If he chooses to change his plea so as to vary his defense, he may do so; and then the plaintiff must first **504***] *pay him all costs from the plea down to this time inclusive. If not, the amendment is granted on the plaintiff's paying the costs of this motion.

Rule accordingly.(a)

Cited in—6 How. Pr., 394; 4 Duer, 230; 6 Daly, 220.

(a) *Vide* Fuller v. Roosevelt, *ante*, 144. In Rex v. John Wilkes, Esq., a criminal information for a libel was amended in a material part by Ld. Mansfield, at his chambers, the day before trial, without the defendant's consent. His Lordship consulted and produced many precedents in favor of the amendment.

MILLER AND M'EWEN v. GREGORY.

Practice.

Capias ad respondendum not bailable, returnable out of term, is void, and not amendable.

THE *capias ad respondendum* was, by mistake, made returnable on Sunday, May 15, 1825; and for this reason, Sunday being out of term, or rather after the last return day,

Mr. J. Platt moved to set it aside, and cited *Bunn* v. *Thomas*, 2 Johns., 190; *Cramer* v. *Van Alstyne*, 9 *Id.*, 386; and 6 Mod., 251, 252, per Holt, *Ch. J.*, in *Davy* v. *Salter*.

Mr. T. J. Oakley, contra, read an affidavit that the *capias* was not bailable, and contended that this took the case out of the rule which made *mesne* process void, because more than a term intervenes between the test and return, viz.: the danger of a protracted imprisonment; and he moved to amend; but,

Per Curiam. This makes no difference. We cannot look to see whether a long return may or may not work a long imprisonment. The form of the *capias* is the only thing in question. It is fully settled that *mesne* process against the body, returnable out of term, is void, and cannot be amended. The motion must be granted on the defendant's stipulating not to bring false imprisonment.

Rule accordingly.

Cited in—10 Wend., 214; 15 Wend., 301; 18 Wend., 677; 2 Den., 285; 18 Barb., 271; 23 Barb., 601.

---

*PHILIPS v. CASWELL. [*505

Return to Certiorari *Written by Plaintiff's Attorney.*

The return to a *certiorari* will not be set aside because the attorney for the plaintiff in error wrote it, if he acted as the mere amanuensis of the justice.

Citation—3 Cow., 20.

ON *certiorari* to a justice's court, it appeared that the attorney for the plaintiff in error wrote the return; but he swore that the justice voluntarily and without request came to his office and desired him to write it, which he did, the justice dictating the whole of the facts.

A motion was now made to set aside the return as irregular. *Fox* v. *Johnson*, 3 Cow., 20, was relied on.

Mr. W. Baker, for the motion.

Messrs. G. H. Feeter and *N. S. Benton*, contra.

Curia. We think the attorney, in this case, comes within the character of a mere amanuensis for the justice. Such an exception to the rule established by *Fox* v. *Johnson* was mentioned by the court; and we think it does not come within the reason of the rule. The motion is denied.

Motion denied.

Cited in—4 Cow., 537 (*n*).

EX PARTE VAN HOESEN.

Bond on Appeal from Justice Court—Practice.

On appeal from a justice's court, the bond required by the statute may be executed by attorney.
And to a motion to quash the appeal for want of a proper bond the exhibition and proof of the power before the Court of C. P., and filing it, is a sufficient answer. The court may then order the power to be filed with the clerk.

MR. J. PLATT moved for a *mandamus* to the judges of Columbia C. P., commanding them to vacate a rule quashing an appeal from the Justice's Court of the City of Hudson, brought by Van Hoesen against M'Kinstry.

The case was this: Van Hoesen appealed from a judgment against him for damages and costs in favor of M'Kinstry; and the appeal bond was executed in the name of Van Hoesen, by A. L. Jordan, as his attorney. M'Kinstry moved the C. P. to quash the appeal, and the affidavits there were contradictory upon the question whether Jordan presented his **506***] *authority to execute the bond to the justices of the court below; but it appeared to the C. P. that he had a written authority for that purpose when the bond was executed, which was there exhibited on the motion, and proved. The C. P. quashed the appeal, and thereupon Van Hoesen's counsel offered to file, and did file the bond with the clerk; but the court held this insufficient.

Mr. Platt cited Laws, sess. 47, ch. 238, secs. 36, 37.

He contended that the bond was well executed; it was enough that the authorization was proved when the fact of execution was contested. It need not even be in writing. This is according to the principles of the common law. The Statute is silent. A power of attorney to execute a mortgage need not be recorded. *Wilson* v. *Troup*, 2 Cow., 195. This is upon the principle that the power to execute is no part of the deed.

Messrs. D. B. Tallmadge and *E. Williams*, contra. If the appeal was not prosecuted according to law, it was the right and the duty of the C. P. to quash it. The approbation which the justices are authorized to indorse on the bond, relates merely to the sufficiency of the surety. A proper bond must be executed, according to the Statute cited, within ten days after the judgment rendered; and unless this be done, the appeal cannot be received. It must be a perfect bond within the ten days Is a bond given by an attorney, but not accompanied by the power to execute it, sufficient? All bonds cannot be given by attorney. Where there is a judgment, and the execution is to be prevented, the law may very properly demand a signing in person. The sheriff should see this done in the case of a limit bond, and a bond to prosecute a writ of error must be given in person. The Act expressly authorizes the notice of the appeal to be signed by the party or his attorney; but when speaking of the bond there is no such alternative. This language implies the distinction for which we contend. May it, as the gentleman contends, be one half in writing and the other by parol? Is a man to be driven round the country to search both for the attorney who executes, and the witnesses, **507***] to *prove his parol authority? It should, at any rate, have been in writing, and actually filed, before the court could entertain the appeal. It was an integral part of the bond—nay, the vital principle of its existence. The party could never enforce it without the use of the power, which should be furnished in the first instance, without driving the party to his motion in order to obtain it. In other cases, the attorney is bound to show his power in the most full and distinct manner. The *onus* lies with him; and if he fails to do this, he is personally liable. *White* v. *Skinner*, 13 Johns., 307. But,

The Court were clear that the motion must be granted; and,

WOODWORTH, *J.*, said the statute speaks of a bond; but whether this be executed in person or by attorney, it is the same thing. Indeed, there are many cases where the party cannot execute in person, as in case of sickness or necessary absence; and the statute would never impose the strictness contended for without excepting such cases. Yet there is no exception. Requiring the party to execute the bond in person would, in various cases, work an absolute deprivation of right. It is enough that the bond was, in point of fact, valid in its creation. To be sure, it was reasonable in the court below to require that the authority should be filed. On its production, and being proved, they might have compelled the party to file it, as one of the papers relating to the motion before them. They should have done so, and retained the cause. It was afterwards filed, and still remains on file. The statute is clearly satisfied, and the motion should be granted.

Motion granted.

---

*ANDREWS AND JEROME [*508

v.

HERRIOT.

Lex Loci—*Seal*—*Form of Action, Determined by* Lex Fori.

Covenant will not lie in this State, on a contract to be performed in Pa., with a scrawl and the word "seal" in the *locus sigilli*, though, by the law of that State, this constitutes a seal.

The form of the action relates to the remedy, and is governable by the *lex fori*.

Citation—2 Cai., 362.

ACTION of covenant tried before Throop, Circuit Judge, at the Onondaga Circuit, 1823. The declaration was in covenant on a contract between the parties to be performed in the State of Pa. Plea, *non est factum*.

On the trial, the contract offered in evidence was signed with the name of Herriot; but in-

---

NOTE.—1. *Seal—What sufficient.* See Warren v. Lynch, 5 Johns., 239, *note*.

2. *Conflict of laws—Foreign contracts*—LEX LOCI *and* LEX FORI.

The *lex loci contractus* governs the nature, validity, construction and effect of foreign contracts; the *lex fori* the remedy. See Nash v. Tupper, 1 Cai., 402, *note*; Lodge v. Phelps, 1 Johns. Cas., 139, *note*; 2 Kent. Com., pp. 453-463, notes and authorities there cited; Story Conf. L., sects. 556-583, notes and numerous authorities there cited; Parsons' Cont., vol. 2, pp. 582-592, notes and authorities there cited; 1 Wait Act. and Def., 129, and authorities there cited; Dickinson v. Edwards, 77 N. Y., 573, and authorities there cited and distinguished; see also the full note at the end of the above case of Andrews v. Herriott, *post*, p. 510.

In addition to the grounds upon which this doctrine is generally rested, it may be said, that courts are created for the administration of the remedies of their own jurisdiction. If they should attempt to administer the remedies of other jurisdictions, their acts would be extrajudicial and of non effect. But the proper construction of every contract depends upon the law with reference to which it was made. Such law forms an important part of the facts and conditions surrounding the parties, which must be considered in determining their intent. Hence the courts look to the *lex loci contractus*, not to enforce law foreign to their jurisdiction, but to discover the *intent* of the parties, that they may apply to such intent the remedies of the *lex fori*. The *lex loci contractus* is not enforced because it is law, but because it forms a part of the contract.

stead of wafer or wax, there was a scrawl with the word "seal" in the *locus sigilli;* and the concluding words of the contract purported a seal in the usual form. A counselor at law of the State of Pa. was sworn as a witness for the plaintiff, and testified that, by the common law of that State, such a mark was a seal.

The defendant's counsel objected to the contract being read in evidence; but the objection was overruled, and the contract read to the jury.

A verdict was finally taken for the plaintiff, subject to the opinion of the court, upon this and other points which arose in the course of the trial.

Mr. V. Birdseye, for the plaintiff, insisted, that as the contract was to be performed in Pa., the court would notice the law of that State in giving it a construction. The effect of the instrument, not merely the remedy upon it, is the question; and the *lex loci* applies. *Meredith* v. *Hinsdale,* 2 Cai., 362, is in point. That was an action of debt upon a Pa. bond; and it was sustained upon the very ground assumed here. The contract should be carried into effect according to the intention of the parties. They intended that it should operate as a specialty everywhere. That the law of the State where the contract is to be performed shall govern, without regard to the place of its execution, is abundantly proved by the authorities. *Thompson* v. *Ketcham,* 4 Johns., 285, and the cases there cited. This law settles the nature and effect of the contract. It is important that it should be so, for a variety of reasons; and one is, for preserving due pref-

509*] erence in the distribution of *the estates of deceased persons. The remedy is another thing. On determining the degree of the contract, that is left to our own law, so that the *lex fori* is not affected. On determining that the scrawl is a seal, the *lex fori* comes in, and says that the action should be covenant, a remedy already known to the law of the State. The agreement therefore gives no new remedy.

The case of *Warren* v. *Lynch,* 5 Johns., 239, although it denies that, according to our own law, anything short of wax and wafer will constitute a seal, leaves *Meredith* v. *Hinsdale,* unimpaired as to the only point decided by it.

He also cited *Jones* v. *Logwood,* 1 Wash., 42: *Baird & Briggs* v. *Blaigrove, Id.,* 170; *Austin's Admx.* v. *Whitlock's Exrs.,* 1 Munf., 487; *Newbold* v. *Lamb,* 2 South., 449: *Adam* v. *Kers,* 1 Bos. & P., 360; *United States* v. *Coffin,* Bee's S. C., 140, and Jac. L. Dict., Seal.

Mr. Birdseye was proceeding to the other points in the cause, but the court told him they were impressed so strongly against him upon the one which he had already argued, that he need not proceed farther for the present. But as the point was an important one, they would look into it farther, and examine the cases cited; and if they should then entertain any doubt, they would call upon him to resume his argument.

Mr. N. P. Randall, for the defendant, referred the court to *Jackson* v. *Wood,* 12 Johns., 242; *Scoville* v. *Canfield,* 14 Johns., 338; 1 Phil. Ev., 415, 16, *note, a,* and the cases there cited; and *Whittemore* v. *Adams,* 2 Cow., 626.

On the same day, at the commencement of the afternoon session,

THE CHIEF JUSTICE informed *Mr. Birdseye* that the court had examined the question during their recess; that *Mr. B.* was fully supported by *Meredith* v. *Hinsdale,* if that were now to be received as law; but the current of authority, *since the decision of that [***510** case, had been uniform and unbroken, that the *lex loci contractus* governs only as to the construction of the contract, and has nothing to do with the remedy, which is controlled entirely by the *lex fori.* We are satisfied that *Meredith* v. *Hinsdale* was decided without proper attention to this distinction. The dispute is merely upon the remedy; that is to say, whether the action shall be covenant or *assumpsit* upon a given contract, between two persons within the jurisdiction of the court. The substance and effect of the recovery is the same in either form. We are satisfied that we cannot sanction *Meredith* v. *Hinsdale,* without overturning the entire class of cases which distinguish between the different effects of the *lex loci* and the *lex fori.* We are so firmly fixed in the conclusion to which we have come, that it will be useless to argue the other points. Being against the plaintiff upon the first, this decides the cause.

Judgment for the defendant.(a)

Cited in—6 Cow., 47; 5 Wend., 482; 6 Wend., 485; 12 Wend., 443; 14 Wend., 250; 23 Wend., 98; 3 N. Y., 270; 15 N. Y., 90, 227; 20 N. Y., 113; 27 N. Y., 74; 35 N. Y., 658; 43 N. Y., 429, 433; 49 N. Y., 576; 5 Barb., 441; 12 Barb., 634, 645; 22 Barb., 128; 30 Barb., 435; 33 Barb., 75, 118; 34 Barb., 335; 36 Barb., 613; 41 Barb., 553; 18 How. Pr., 337; 10 Abb. Pr., 77; 12 Abb. Pr., 14; 5 Abb. N. C., 135; 40 Super., 360; 8 How. (U. S.), 464; 8 Pet., 373; 13 Pet., 327; 1 Wood & M., 176; 2 Wood & M., 465; 6 Blatchf., 546; 16 Mich., 73; 9 Minn., 66; 106 U. S., 133; 45 Pa., 494; 23 Am. Dec., 571 (4 Gill & J., 332); 27 Am. Dec., 139; 39 Am. Dec., 299, 300 (1 P. & B., 65); 42 Am. Dec., 199 (13 Ohio, 209); 30 Am., Rep., 512 (55 Miss., 153).

(a) *The* LEX LOCI *and* LEX FORI, to which the above case looks, have probably come more frequently under review in this country than in any other. That the attention of our courts should often be drawn to them, results from the political confederacy of the States, which, while it supports among them close and extensive connections in business and policy, yet holds them, sufficiently distinct and independent to call into continual exercise that rule which expounds and gives effect to contracts, and other transactions, according to the state law under which they are made, or take place; but stops there, and carefully distinguishes between construction and right, on the one hand, and remedy on the other. The general rule is acknowledged by the law of nations, and by all the local writers and adjudications relating to it; but the difficulty of its application has been very considerable. Hence the great variety of cases and comments to which it has given rise, the embarrassments of the most able and ingenious counsel, and the importance of looking with attention to the rules and adjudged cases upon the subject, not only in England and other foreign countries, but of sister States, and especially of the U. S., whose courts are, on this head, emphatically the arbiters of state differences.

This subject in itself deserves a treatise, but I can do nothing more here than to arrange and refer to the authorities, giving the substance of some of them. Huberus, in his title *De Conflictu Legum* has broken the ground the most effectually, I believe, of all the European writers; but even yet, it must be considered as but little more than broken for the use of the American student. Mr. Wheaton, *arg.,* 3 Johns. Ch., 202, speaks of Huber as having originated the distinction between the *lex fori* and the *lex loci* **contractus,* and his remarks on the [***511** *lex loci* generally are well known to form the text upon which our lawyers proceed. Ld. Mansfield used to cite him with approbation, and Mr. Hargrave declared that his writings on the civil law were much esteemed. Note 44 to Co. Litt., 79 *b.* He was quoted, approved and relied upon in Desesbats

v. Berquier, 1 Binn., 336, and the late *Chancellor* Kent, in Holmes v. Remsen, 4 Johns. Ch., 469, says that Huber's Essay "*De Conflictu Legum* is everywhere received as containing a doctrine of universal law." In truth, he is referred to as authority in almost every case where the *lex loci* has been seriously in question. A sufficient extract, for the purpose of the present subject, was translated, and read in the argument of Emory v. Greenough, 3 Dall., 369, 370; and furnished by Mr. Dallas, the reporter, in a note to that case (*Id.*, p. 370 to 377). Thus being very generally in the hands of the profession, it need not be repeated here. Suffice it to say, that this extract takes ground broad enough to embrace the whole superstructure of European and American authority relative to the *lex loci* and *lex fori*. It is true that some few of his examples have been overruled by our cases, owing to his erroneous application of principles; but this is no more than will be found true of several cases adjudged upon the same principles, in England, Scotland and this country.

The cases divide themselves into several classes:

1. *The* lex loci contractus. The general proposition upon this head will be found in almost all the cases from which I shall extract the point decided; but it is more generally laid down, and supported, as follows: that the law of a place where a contract is made, or to be performed, is to govern as to the nature, validity, construction and effect of such contract: that being valid in such place, it is to be considered equally valid, and to be enforced everywhere, with the exception of cases in which the contract is immoral or unjust, or in which the enforcing it in a State would be injurious to the rights, the interest or convenience of such State or its citizens; and, on the contrary, if a contract be void, or be discharged by the law of the place where it is made or to be performed, it is to be considered as void or discharged everywhere, and to be enforced nowhere. Hub. *ubi. supra*, 3 Dall., 371, *n.*; Pearsall v. Dwight, 2 Mass., 84; Greenwood v. Curtis, 6 *Id.*, 358; Blanchard v. Russell, 13 *Id.*, 1; Prentiss v. Savage, 13 *Id.*, 20; Inh. of Medway v. Inh. of Needham, 16 *Id.*, 157; Inh. of West Cambridge v. Inh. of Lexington, 1 Pick., 506; Lodge v. Phelps. 1 Johns. Cas., 139; Smith v. Smith, 2 Johns., 235; Ruggles v. Keeler, 3 *Id.*, 263; Thompson v. Ketcham, 4 *Id.*, 285; 8 *Id.*, 189; Warder v. Arell, 2 Wash., 282; Van Reimsdyck v. Kane, 1 Gall., 375; Sherrill v. Hopkins, 1 Cow., 103, and several cases there cited by Sutherland, *J.*, pp. 105–10; Powers v. Lynch, 3 Mass., 77; Baker v. Wheaton, 5 *Id.*, 509; Grimshaw v. Bender, 6 *Id.*, 157; Winthrop v. Carlton, 12 *Id.*, 4; Hull v. Blake, 13 *Id.*, 153; Barrell v. Benjamin, 15 *Id.*, 354; Watson v. Bourne, 10 *Id.*, 337; Vanschaick v. Edwards, 2 Johns. Cas., 355; Courtois v. Carpentier, C. C., Apr., 1806, MS.; Whart. Dig., Foreign Laws, &c., pl. 5; Smith v. Mead, 3 Conn., N. S., 253; Medbury v. Hopkins, *Id.*, 472; Male v. Roberts, 3 Esp., 163; Harper v. Hampton, 1 Harris and Johns., 453; S. C., *Id.*, 662.

512*] *But as the laws of contracts, &c., in foreign States or countries are not admitted *ex proprio vigore*, but only *ex comitate*, the judicial power will exercise a discretion with respect to the laws they may be called upon to sanction; for if they be manifestly unjust, or calculated to injure their own citizens, they ought to be rejected. Blanchard v. Russell, 13 Mass., 6, per Parker, *Ch. J.* Accordingly an exception is, where it would be dangerous, or inconvenient, or of immoral tendency to enforce the foreign contract here. 3 Dall., 371, *note;* Pearsall v. Dwight, 2 Mass., 89; Prentiss v. Savage, 13 *Id.*, 25.

In pursuance of the above rules, a contract of marriage, though it would be invalid by our law, will yet be held valid here, if so by the law of the country where celebrated, unless indeed it be incestuous by the law of nature. 3 Dall., 373, 374, *note;* Ilderton v. Ilderton, 2 H. Bl., 145; Compton v. Bearcroft, Bull, *N. P.*, 114; Inh. of West Cambridge v. Inh. of Lexington, 1 Pick., 506; Greenwood v. Curtis, 6 Mass., 378, per Parsons, *Ch. J.;* Inh. of Medway v. Inh. of Needham, 16 *Id.*, 157; Decouche v. Savetier, 3 Johns. Ch., 190; Gordon *alias* Dalrymple v. Dalrymple, before the Consistorial Court of London, Dodson's Rep., 6, per Sir W. Scott.

And the rights and incidents of the marriage, in the country where celebrated, shall follow and be allowed everywhere; as communion of goods, common risk of profit and loss, *donation mutuelle*, dower, jointure, inheritance, &c. *Id.*, and *vide* Royal Bank of Scotland v. Cuthbert, 1 Rose's Cas. Bank. App., 481, per Ld. Meadowbank.

A sale of goods (*e. g.*, negroes) by one in a foreign country, lawful there, though interdicted in Mass., will be enforced, or upheld by the courts of Mass. 3 Dall., 372, *note;* Greenwood v. Curtis, 6 Mass., 358, 378. So if one lawfully, in a foreign country, sell goods in a manner, or on grounds which would not be lawful here, our courts will uphold the sale. Grant v. M'Lachlin, 4 Johns., 34.

Personal rights obtained or communicated by the law of a place accompany the person. Thus, if one of the age of 21 may convey his real estate in the county where he comes to that age, he may do the same where 25 years are required. 3 Dall., 375, 376, *note*. But whether the right to couvey real estate do not come within the *lex loci rei sitæ*, *post;* and whether this rule extend beyond personal estate, *quære*.

The rate of interest or damages is governed by the *lex loci*. 1 Dall., 191, per Shippen, *President;* Slacum v. Pomery, 6 Cr., 221; Winthrop v. Pepoon, 1 Bay, 468; Lanusse v. Barker, 3 Wh., 101, 146; Kissam v. Burrall, Kirby, 326; Fanning v. Consequa, 17 Johns., 511; James v. Allen, 1 Dall., 191; Winthrop v. Carleton, 12 Mass., 4; Gaillard ads. Ball, 1 Nott & M'C., 67.

So one's liability as maker, indorser, acceptor, or other party to a promissory note or bill of exchange. Powers v. Lynch, 3 Mass., 77; and *vide* Hicks v. Brown, 12 Johns., 142, 143; Slacum v. Pomeroy, 6 Cr., 221; Hull v. Blake, 13 Mass., 153.

So the construction of foreign marriage settlements. Cowp., 174; Feaubert v. Trust, Prec. in Ch., 207.

*So the terms of payment, between a captain and his crew, Johnson v. Machielsne, 3 Campb., 44, the time when a suit shall be brought for seamen's wages (*Ib.*), and time of payment of a bill of exchange. Chit. on bills, Phil. ed. of 1821, p. 120, 1, and the authorities there cited. [*513

A note given in Mass., as a premium on a policy of insurance, on a vessel engaged in the African slave trade, being void by the law of that State, is void in S. C. Touro v. Cassin, 1 Nott & M'C., 173. A note void for usury in Mass., is so here. Van Schaick v. Edwards, 2 Johns. Cas., 355. If void for gaming in France, it is so in England. Robinson v. Bland, 2 Burr., 1077. The acceptance of a bill of exchange at Leghorn, void there, held so in England. Burrows v. Jemino, 2 Str., 732.

So a sale or agreement to sell goods in a foreign country, prohibited by its laws (3 Dall., 372, *note*), is void everywhere.

But foreign revenue laws will not be noticed here; and accordingly, a foreign contract, void for want of a stamp where made, will not, for that reason, be held void here. Ludlow v. Van Rensselaer, 1 Johns., 94; but *vide* Alves v. Hodgson, 7 T. R., 237, and Clegg v. Levy, 3 Campb., 166, contra. Yet if the contract, thus made void by the Revenue Law of a foreign country, is to be executed there, or one is carrying on business with that country, and violates its revenue laws, the courts of that country will not aid him to enforce such contract. Scriba v. Ins. Co. of N. A., C. C., Oct., 1807; Whart. Dig. Foreign Laws, &c., p. 287, pl. 3.

Nor shall the penal laws or laws of forfeiture in one's country operate upon his rights or liabilities in another. Folliott v. Ogden, 1 H. Bl., 123, 135; Scoville v. Canfield, 14 Johns., 338; Warder v. Arell, 2 Wash., 295, per Roane, *J.;* Commonwealth v. Green, 17 Mass., 515; Inh. of West Cambridge v. Inh. of Lexington, 1 Pick., 506. Yet it was held in Camp v. Lockwood, 1 Dall., 393, that any one whose property had been confiscated in Conn., could not, in Pa., recover a debt embraced by the Act of Confiscation; and *vide* Negro David v. Porter, 4 Harr. & M'H., 418.

Personal disabilities follow the person. Thus, when young men, prodigals, married women, &c., of a country are considered subject to curators by the law, or unable to contract, they are to be so considered elsewhere, both in their rights and disabilities; 3 Dall., 375, 376; Thompson v. Ketchum, 8 Johns., 189; Male v. Roberts, 3 Esp., 163; and if they be unable to commit crimes in Friezeland, it is the same thing in Holland. 3 Dall., 375, 376, *note*.

Authorities, showing that a contract shall be explained, &c., by the law of the place where it is to be performed; and the rules by which we are to determine the place of performance. Lanusse v. Barker, 3 Wh., 101, 146; Robinson v. Bland, 1 Bl., 247, 258; S. C., 2 Burr., 1077; Melan v. Duke of Fitz James, 1 Bos. & P., 138; Searight v. Calbraith, 4 Dall., 324, 327; Van Reimsdyk v. Kane, 1 Gall., 371, 375; Ludlow v. Van Rensselaer, 1 Johns., 94; Smith v. Smith, 2 Johns., 235; Thompson v. Ketchum, 8 *Ibid.*, 189; Harrison v. Sterry, 5 Cr., 289; Slacum v. Pomeroy, 6 *Ibid.*, 221; Fanning v. Consequa, 17 Johns., 511 *Sherrill v. Hopkins, 1 Cow., 103, [*514

108; 3 Dall., 374, *note;* Powers v. Lynch, 3 Mass., 77; Scriba v. Ins. Co. of N. A., C. C., Oct., 1807, Whart. Dig. Foreign Laws, &c., p. 287, pl. 3; Coolidge v. Poor, 15 Mass., 427; Champant v. Ranelagh, Prec. in Ch., 128; Eq. Cas. Abr., Interest Money. E, and the cases there cited; Ranelagh v. Champante, 2 Vern., 395; Smith v. Mead, 3 Conn., N. S., 353; Potter v. Brown, 5 East, 124; Harper v. Hampton, 1 Harr. & J., 453; S. C., *Id.*, 622; Touro v. Cassin, 1 Nott & M'Cord, 173; Lewis v. Fullerton, 1 Randolph, 15, 23.

The discharge of, or defense against a contract, in the place where it is made or to be performed, is the same everywhere. Thus, if infancy be a defense against a contract made in Jamaica, it is so here (Thompson v. Ketchum, 8 Johns., 189); or if against a contract made in Scotland, it is so in England. Male v. Roberts, 3 Esp., 163. If a tender and refusal in the county where the contract is made, produce a forfeiture of the debt, it is so everywhere. Warder v. Arell, 2 Wash., 282, 295, &c. A S. C. contract paid in paper money there, which depreciated, was held a payment in England (Anon., 1 Bro. Ch. Cas., 376); and a tender in assignats, upon a contract made in France, being lawful there, was held lawful in Pa. Searight v. Calbraith, 4 Dall., 325, 327. So a tender of bills on the Vt. State Bank in Conn., upon a note payable to the Bank, pursuant to a statute of Vt. Vt. State Bank v. Porter, 5 Day, 316. The promissory note of a third person taken for goods sold in N. Y., the maker becoming insolvent before the day of payment, being a discharge in N. Y., where the contract was made, was held to be so in Conn. Bartsch v. Atwater, 1 Conn., N. S., 409.

A voluntary payment of a debt by a citizen of this State to an executor or administrator, regularly appointed by a foreign government, though he could not sue here, it seems, shall be held valid, and protect the debtor against a second suit for the same money. Williams v. Storrs, 6 Johns. Ch., 353; Doolittle v. Lewis, 7 *Id.*, 45.

Discharges of contracts by operation of law, are also governed by the *lex loci contractus.* In Quin v. Keefe, 2 H. Bl., 55, the question arose whether an Irish bankrupt certificate of discharge from a contract made in Ireland, was a discharge in England. The point was treated as a novel one in the C. B., and went off upon a formal defect in the plea. Since that time the effect of foreign bankrupt certificates and insolvent discharges has been the subject of much discussion, both in foreign notions and in the U. S.; and the attention of courts has been mainly drawn to two different branches of the proceeding, viz.: the assignment or *cessio bonorum,* contested between the assignees and particular creditors who were seeking satisfaction by foreign attachment or other proceeding against the bankrupt or his goods; or the discharge, contested between particular creditors and the bankrupt.

The assignment of the bankrupt or insolvent, is at length considered as a general sale of goods by his own act *bona fide,* and available like any other honest sale against all who claim by lien or sale 515*] subsequent. This depends *upon the *lex domicilii,* and will be considered under that head in its due order.

The certificate or discharge, we have said, depends on the *lex loci contractus, i. e.,* the law of the place where the contract is made, or to be performed. Thus, the drawer of a bill of exchange at Baltimore on London (though payable to a British subject resident in England), having been declared a bankrupt, and discharged from his debts as such, this was holden to bar an action in the English K. B. And the case was expressly put on the ground that the cause of action having arisen in the U. S., and the contract not to be performed elsewhere, and having been followed by a discharge here, it should be deemed discharged everywhere. Potter v. Brown, 5 East, 124. The earlier cases of Ballantine v. Golding, Cooke's Bank. Law, 515, and Smith v. Buchanan, 1 East, 6, proceeded upon the same principle. In the latter case an insolvent discharge of Md. was denied any effect upon a debt contracted in England; the other common law cases have almost uniformly gone upon the same distinction. Van Raugh v. Van Arsdain, 3 Cai., 154; Ewart v. Coulthard, cited *Id.*, 154, 155; 1 Johns., 119, per Spencer, *J.*; Watson v. Bourne, 10 Mass., 337; M'Millan v. M'Neill, 4 Wh., 209; Smith v. Smith, 2 Johns., 235; Hicks v. Hotchkiss, 7 Johns. Ch., 297; Mather v. Bush, 16 Johns., 238; Blanchard v. Russell, 13 Mass., 1; Bradford v. Farrand, *Id.*, 18; Walsh v. Farrand, *Id.*, 19; Proctor v. Moore, 1 Mass., 198; Clarke's Ex'rs v. Van Riemsdyk, 9 Cr., 153; Millar v. Hall, 1 Dall., 229; Hicks v. Brown, 12 Johns., 142; Babcock v. Weston, 1 Gall., 168; Van Riemsdyk v. Kane, 1 *Id.*, 371, 377, 380; Baker v. Wheaton, 5 Mass., 509; Harris v. Mandeville, 2 Dall., 256; M'Menomy v. Murray, 3 Johns. Ch., 435; Buel v. Shethar, cited in 3 Day, 82; Smith v. Brown, 3 Binn., 201; Walsh v. Nourse, 5 *Id.*, 381; Vanuxem v. Hazlehursts, 1 South., 199-202, per Kirkpatrick, *Ch. J.*; Rowland v. Stevenson, 1 Halsted, 149.

Stein's case, in the Court of Session, Scotland, went further, and gave an English bankrupt certificate the effect to discharge all debts arising either in England or Scotland. 1 Rose's Cas. Bank., App., 462. The effect of the certificate is mentioned at p. 486; and *vide* M'Kim v. Marshall, 1 Harr. & J., 101, and Harrison v. Young, *Id.*, 102, *note.*

It was formerly holden that a discharge under an Insolvent Law of this State was, upon the express words of the Statute, a discharge from all contracts, wherever made; Penniman v. Meigs, 9 Johns., 325; but that case has since been overruled as unconstitutional by M'Millan v. M'Neill, 4 Wh., 209; and the operation of the *lex loci contractus* restored in all its force. Hicks v. Hotchkiss, 7 Johns. Ch., 297, 312; Mather v. Bush, 16 Johns., 233; Sherill v. Hopkins, 1 Cow., 103.

But a statute of the U. S. may still give an universal effect to a discharge, without regard to the place where the contract was made. Murray v. De Rottenham, 6 Johns. Ch., 52; Harrison v. Sterry, 5 Cr., 289, and *vide* 4 Johns. Ch., 488.

*An insolvent discharge, even at the place [*516 of the contract, shall not always operate to discharge it, where the creditor is without the jurisdiction of the law by which it is granted. Thus, a temporary Insolvent Law of Jamaica, by which debtors were released from all demands against them on surrendering their effects for the benefit of their creditors, the effects to be distributed only among such creditors as should apply within thirty days after public notice of the surrender, was holden inoperative as to a creditor residing in Mass., though the contract was made in Jamaica, and to be performed there. The court put it on the ground that such a law could not be intended by the Legislature to operate beyond the bounds of Jamaica—the Act being manifestly partial or unjust to foreign creditors, the notice being short, and no provision being made that it should reach them in such season as would enable them to participate in its advantages. Prentiss v. Savage, 13 Mass., 20. The comity of nations does not require that such a discharge should have effect in a foreign country. The fair principles of the contract would be violated by it. *Id.*, 24. The same principles were recognized in Tappan v. Poor, 15 Mass., 419. In order to take effect, the foreign discharge must, though granted where the cause of action arose, have been complete and executed before action commenced. If granted after, it is not pleadable like a domestic discharge. *Id.*

2. *Of the* LEX DOMICILII. The first question which occurs under this head is, what shall constitute the domicil of the person, so as to give effect to its law? In most cases this is of easy solution; but it is not always so. The general rules will be found accurately and fully laid down by Rush, *President,* in Berquier v. O'Daniel, 1 Binn., 349, 351, *note,* or more broadly by Ld. Thurlow, in Bruce v. Bruce, in the House of Lords, 2 Bos. & P., 230, *note.* They are that a man's being at a place is *prima facie* evidence that he is domiciled there; and those who contest this may show that he was there as a traveler, or on particular business, or on a visit, or for the sake of his health, &c. *Id.* His mode of living is not material, whether on rent, at lodgings, or in the house of a friend. The apparent or avowed intention of constant residence, not the manner of it, constitutes the domicil. Minute circumstances, in inquiries of this sort, are taken into consideration; as a man's immediate employment; his general pursuits and habits of life, his friends and connections. There is no fixed period of time necessary to create a domicil. It may be acquired after the shortest residence under certain circumstances; and under others, the longest residence may be insufficient for the purpose. Though declarations are good evidence that one has changed his domicil, yet no fixed views of change can be equivalent to the actual abandonment of one domicil, and the acquisition of another. The domicil of origin arises from birth and connections. A minor, during pupilage, cannot acquire a domicil of his own. It follows that of his father, and remains until he acquires another, which he cannot do until he becomes a person *sui juris.* 2 Binn., 251, 252, *note*; Somerville v. Somerville, 5 Ves., 750. The domicil of origin remains until clearly abandoned, and another taken. Somerville

v. Somerville, 5 Ves., 750. Ld. Somerville had two domicils, the family seat in Scotland and a leasehold house in London; and, upon circumstances, the former, which was also the domicil of origin, **517***] prevailed. **Id.* Where the father is dead, the domicil of the children follows that of the surviving mother. Potinger v. Wightman, 3 Meriv., 67.

The four cases above cited from 2 Bos. & P., 230; 1 Binn., 349, *note*; 5 Ves., 750, and 3 Mer., 67, contain together a complete treatise on what is to constitute a domicil, both in the view of our own and foreign jurists, with full references and illustrations. Instead of repeating these, I refer to the cases themselves.

The domicil being ascertained, "it is," says Ld. Loughborough, "a clear proposition, not only of the law of England, but of every country in the world, where law has the semblance of science, that personal property has no locality. The meaning of that is, not that personal property has no visible locality, but that it is subject to that law which governs the person of the owner. With respect to the disposition of it, with respect to the transmission of it, either by succession or the act of the party, it follows the law of the person. The owner in any country may dispose of his personal property. If he dies, it is not the law of the country in which the property is, but the law of the country of which he was a subject, that will regulate the succession. For instance, if a foreigner having property in the funds here dies, that property is claimed according to the right of representation given by the law of his own country."

Sill v. Worswick, 1 H. Bl., 690; Bruce v. Bruce, 2 Bos. & P., 229, *note*; Guier v. O'Daniel, 2 Binn., 349, *note*; Somerville v. Somerville, 5 Ves., 750; Potinger v. Wightman, 3 Mer., 67, before cited, and Stevens v. Gaylord, 11 Mass., 256; Pipon v. Pipon, Amb., 25; Thorne v. Watkins, 2 Ves., Sr., 35; Milne v. Morton, 6 Binn., 361, per Tilghman, *Ch. J.*; Balfour v. Scott, 6 Br. P. C., 550, Toml. ed.; Harvey v. Richards, 1 Mas., 381, also recognize these principles, and apply them to questions of distribution of intestates' estates arising between different countries.

The same principles are recognized in Dixon's Ex'rs v. Ramsay's Ex'rs, 3 Cr., 319, and Decouche v. Savetier, 3 Johns. Ch., 190; Jac. Law Dict., Domicil, and Vattel, B. 2, ch. 8, secs. 108-111. So in Desebats v. Berquier, 1 Binn., 336, which held that a will of personal property must be executed according to the *lex domicilii*; and that if void by that law, it will not pass personal estate in another country, though executed with all the formality of its laws. 3 Dall., 371, 372, *note*, S. P.

These principles are also fully examined in Holmes v. Remsen, 4 Johns. Ch., 460, and at p. 474, mentioned as applicable to the estates of lunatics, on the authority of Ld. Hardwicke.

Various other cases give the general doctrine, and apply it in different ways. Burn v. Cole, Amb., 415; Bempde v. Johnstone, 3 Ves., Jr., 198; Hog v. Lashley, 6 Br. P. C., 577; Drummond v. Drummond, *Id.*, 601; Richards v. Dutch, 8 Mass., 506; Dawes v. Boylston, 9 *Id.*, 337; case of a British legacy to the wife of a foreign husband, mentioned by the *Lord Chancellor* in Campbell v. French, 3 Ves., 323; Latimer v. Elgin, 4 Dess., 26, 31, 32, upon a title to slaves.

518*] *In Harvey v. Richards, 1 Mas., 408, Story, *J.*, refers to several books of the Civil Law and foreign jurists, upon this subject, as well as to several of the common law cases.

The question is (*Id.*, 409, &c.) taken up and discussed, as to how far it is the right and duty of a foreign forum to decree distribution according to the law of another country, and whether it is bound to dismiss a suit for that purpose and turn the parties round to the courts of the intestate's domicil. In 1 Mas., 409 to 430, the cases upon this point in England, Pa., and Mass., which are apparently conflicting, are considered and reconciled; and the conclusion is, that the courts of one country may decree distribution according to the laws of another: but that, under certain circumstances, they should not do this; as where full justice cannot be done for want of parties, &c., in which case, they may direct assets to be remitted, to be distributed by the tribunal of the domicil, &c.

But the greater share of litigation upon this head has grown out of the conflicting regulations of different commercial countries relative to bankrupts; and is usually grounded on the effect due to the claims of assignees under Bankrupt Laws and Statutes of Insolvency. The rights of the assignees have generally been considered in reference to some particular creditor of the bankrupt, who after an act of bankruptcy, or assignment at the domicil of the bankrupt, commences a suit in a foreign country, either against the person of the bankrupt in the ordinary way, upon his going into that country, or (more generally) by foreign attachment, or other process against the bankrupt's property there in possession or in action. In Sill v. Worswick, 1 H. Bl., 665, for instance, both the bankrupt and creditor being residents of England, the latter, after an act of bankruptcy, but before the assignment, sent to his agent in the Island of St. Christopher, and attached and obtained payment of his own debt, which was contracted in England, from a debt due to the bankrupt in St. Christopher. The assignees in England sued the creditor there for the money, as money had and received to their use; and they recovered upon the principles before cited at large from that case, as laid down by Ld. Loughborough. He applied the *lex domicilii* to the case of the bankrupt, considering the assignment in the same light as a voluntary one made by him; Holmes v. Remsen, 4 Johns. Ch., 487, same proposition vindicated; and therefore, as passing all his property everywhere, and among it, the very debt of the bankrupt, which the creditor had collected by the process of foreign attachment. The avails of it were, consequently, money had and received to the use of the assignees. The same doctrine was held upon a foreign attachment taken out after assignment in England, in Hunter v. Potts, 4 T. R., 182. Here, at page 192, Ld. Kenyon acknowledges and vindicates the *lex domicilii* as the foundation of his opinion. In Solomons v. Ross, and Jollet v. Duponthieu, 1 H. Bl., 131, 132, *note*, the same principles were applied by the English Court of Chancery. These cases preferred a bankrupt assignment in Holland, to a foreign attachment in England. Neal v. Cottingham, 2 H. Bl., 132, *note*, preferred an English bankrupt assignment to a foreign attachment in Ireland. These cases given in the note to H. Bl. do not profess to inquire whether the creditor was domiciled in the same country with the bankrupt or not; nor of the place where the debt arose.

*Ld. Loughborough's reasoning in Sill v. [***519** Worswick, 1 H. Bl., 693, shows how far the rule is to be qualified by the law of the foreign country. He says: "It by no means follows that a commission of bankrupt has an operation in another country, against the law of that country. I do not wish to have it understood that it follows, as a consequence, from the opinion I am now giving (I rather think that the contrary would be the consequence of the reasoning I am now using), that a creditor in that country, not subject to the Bankrupt Laws, nor affected by them, obtaining payment of his debt and afterwards coming over to this country, would be liable to refund that debt. If he had recovered it in an adverse suit with the assignees, he would clearly not be liable. But if the law of that country preferred him to the assignee, though I must suppose that determination wrong, yet I do not think that my holding a contrary opinion would revoke the determination of that country, however I might disapprove of the principle upon which the law so decided. But another case may possibly occur, of a suit brought against the bankrupt personally; and a case of this sort was stated in the argument, Waring v. Knight. I have not been able to get a particular account of that case. It is shortly stated in Cooke's Bank. Law, 372, that a person having committed an act of bankruptcy, had gone over to Gibraltar, that a commission of bankrupt was taken out against him, and that the defendant brought an action against him in Gibraltar, and obtained judgment, and under the judgment, payment of his debt. Whether the person was resident in Gibraltar prior to the bankruptcy; whether the debt was contracted at Gibraltar; whether he appeared to the commission in England, none of these circumstances are stated. But the decision would undoubtedly be very materially varied by these circumstances. Ld. Mansfield held, that the defendant having recovered the debt against the bankrupt, who was personally present at Gibraltar, was not answerable to the assignees for the money."

According to these views of Ld. Loughborough, the rights of the assignees and the creditor who sues in a foreign country, after the act of bankruptcy or assignment, depend upon the principle of the *lex domicilii* as applied to the bankrupt on the one hand and the creditor on the other. He puts the case upon the question, whether the foreign court in which the attachment is sued, the creditor residing within its jurisdiction, would, on notice of the assignment, and its being set up as a defense, prefer the title of the assignees, and hold the attaching creditor barred. 1 H. Bl., 692, 693. Ld. Kenyon places the ques-

tion in the same view, in Hunter v. Potts, 4 T. R., 192, and both agree that the claim of the assignees must depend on the question, whether the assignment would be recognized as operative by the law of the foreign country; and the latter holds, that, uncontradicted by proof of a contrary law in the foreign country, the *lex domicilii* of the bankrupt shall prevail. Harrison v. Sterry, 5 Cr., 289, as explained in Holmes v. Remsen, 4 Johns. Ch., 488, S. P.; 2 H. Bl., 409, S. P.; M'Intosh v. Ogilvie, 4 T. R., 193, *note*, may be supported by these principles; and most of the other cases upon the same question, which has been as before observed, often up between assignees and attaching creditors, will, I believe, be found to accord with the rules above cited. Phil-
520*] lips v. Hunter, *2 H. Bl., 402; Holmes v. Remsen, 4 Johns. Ch., 460; Smith v. Buchanan, 1 East, 11, per Ld. Kenyon, *Ch. J.*; *Ex parte* Blakes, 1 Cox's Ch., 398; Le Chevalier v. Lynch, Doug., 170; Royal Bank of Scotland v. Cuthbert, in the Court of Session, Scotland, 1 Rose's Cas.' Bank., App., 462, and especially the reasoning of Ld. Robertson, pp. 477, 479, on the merits; Selkrig v. Davies, 2 Dow, 230; S. C., 2 Rose's Cas. Bank., 291, by the title of Selkrig v. Davis; Parish v. Seron, in the City Court of Dunkirk, France, reported in Coop. Bank. Law, *addenda*, XXVII; Bird v. Caritat, 2 Johns., 342.

Chancellor Kent, in Holmes v. Remsen, 4 Johns. Ch., 460, laid down a further qualification of the above rules. It was this, that the doctrine of relation in regard to bankrupts is a mere positive rule of municipal policy, and the rule of comity among nations does not require its adoption. This places bankrupt assignments and ordinary insolvent assignments upon the same footing. These, not any relation to the act of bankruptcy, are to be regarded as devesting the bankrupt's title.

In Pa., the application of the *lex domicilii* to an English bankrupt assignment was denied; Milne v. Morton, 6 Binn., 353, and preference given to an attachment, though subsequent to the bankrupt assignment. *Ibid.* So in Conn. Taylor v. Geary, Kirby, 313. So in Md. Burk v. M'Clain, 1 Harr. & M'H., 236; Wallace v. Patterson, 2 *Id.*, 463; Ward v. Morris, 4 *Id.*, 330. So in N. C. McNeil v. Colquhoon, 2 Hayw., 245. So in S. C. Topham's Assignees v. Chapman, 1 Con. Court, S. C., 283. And the general proposition, that the Bankrupt Law of a foreign country cannot operate a legal transfer of property in this, was broadly and distinctly laid down by the Supreme Court of the U. S., in Harrison v. Sterry, 5 Cr., 289, 302. This proposition is also very ably supported by *Mr. Justice* Platt, in Holmes v. Remsen, 20 Johns., 254 to 267, where he takes issue with the late *Chancellor's* reasoning upon the same case when before him. 4 Johns., Ch., 460. *Judge* Platt thinks that, at any rate, the rules of comity adopted and vindicated by the *Chancellor*, cannot, with propriety, be extended by us beyond our sister States, or by England beyond Scotland and Ireland; and he treats it as a mere rule of comity—not of international law.

In all questions arising between the subjects of different States, each is to be considered as a party to the authoritative acts of his own government. Consequa v. Fanning, 3 Johns. Ch., 587; S. C., 17 Johns., 511, on appeal.

3. *Of proceedings in foreign courts of justice.* It is a general rule, that judgments or decrees by the courts of foreign nations, having jurisdiction, are conclusive on the same question, passed upon by them, arising incidentally here. 3 Dall., 372-3, *note*, 3 Johns., 168-9, per Kent, *Ch. J.*; Cas. t. Hardw., 83, per Ld. Hardwicke, *Ch. J.* Thus, the defendant being indicted in England for murder at the Cape of Good Hope, was allowed to plead an acquittal by a court having jurisdiction there. Roche's case, Leach Cr. Cas., 138; Hutchinson's case, cited 1 Show.,
521*] 6, and 2 Str., *733, S. P. So a foreign decree establishing a marriage is conclusive on the marriage coming incidentally in question here. 1 Ves., Sr., 159, per Ld. Hardwicke. So a decree vacating the acceptance of a bill of exchange. Burrows v. Jemino, 2 Str., 733; S. C., Vin. Abr. Evidence, A. *b*, 13, pl. 9, under Title of Burrows v. Temineaw. So a decree for the sale of goods. Grant v. M'Lachlin, 4 Johns., 34.

Collection of money by foreign attachment is a bar. Thus, where I owe a debt to or have funds of a foreigner, and a creditor of the foreigner sues me as garnishee by foreign attachment, by which I am compelled to pay the debt, the authorities are uniform that, having once paid the debt upon due process of law, this shall bar all claim of my creditor, whether he sue me for it in the country where the attachment issued or any foreign country. This proposition is deducible from several cases cited under the previous head of the *lex domicilii* in which the same thing was held as to actions between the assignees of bankrupts and garnishees. There are also other cases to the same effect, at the suit of assignees or creditors in their own names. Cleve v. Mill, 1 Cooke B. L., 303; Embree v. Hanna, 5 Johns., 101; Savage's case, 1 Salk., 291; Holmes v. Remsen, 4 Johns. Ch., 467; M'Daniel v. Hughes, 3 East, 367; Holmes v. Remsen, 20 Johns., 229.

A judgment upon foreign attachment is a bar to a suit here by assignees under the Absconding Debtor Act, though the attachment under that Act issued before the money came to the hands of the garnishee, and before the foreign attachment issued against him. Holmes v. Remsen, 20 Johns., 229.

And where the maker of a note was sued as garnishee in Ga., and compelled to pay the money as debtor to the maker of the note; though it was indorsed *bona fide* to a citizen of Mass., before the suit in Ga. was commenced; yet, held, by the court in Mass., on a suit by the indorsee, that the proceedings in Ga. were a bar, the note having been made in Ga. And the court relied much on the ground of the *lex loci contractus.* Hull v. Blake, 13 Mass., 153.

A proceeding by foreign attachment will abate or bar a suit here, accordingly as it is pending, or carried to judgment, in the same manner as a suit commenced here for the same cause, Brook v. Smith, 1 Salk., 230; Chevalier v. Lynch, Dougl., 170; Cleve v. Mills., 1 Cooke B. L., 303; Embree v. Hanna, 5 Johns., 102; Savage's case, 1 Salk., 291; La Chevalier v. Dormer, Doug., 170; Fisher v. Lane, 3 Wils., 297, questioned in Embree v. Hanna, 5 Johns., 102, 103. Nathan v. Giles, 5 Taunt., 558.

In *assumpsit*, it may be given in evidence under the general issue, when a bar; 1 Chit. Pl., 480, and the authorities there cited; Burrows v. Temineaw, Vin. Abr., Evidence, A, *b*, 13, pl. 9; M'Daniel v. Hughes, 3 East, 367; Nathan v. Giles, 5 Taunt., 558; otherwise in an action on a specialty. 1 Chit. Pl., 480, and the authorities there cited.

A suit pending in a foreign country between the same parties, commenced by process against the person, will not abate a suit here for the same cause, like a proceeding by foreign attachment; Brown v. Joy, 9 Johns., *221, and the cases there cited; [*522 but if it be carried to judgment, it is a bar. *Id.*, Griswold v. Pitcairn, 2 Conn. N. S., 85.

The cases in England, and most of those decided by the courts in the U. S., hold that a decree of condemnation by a foreign Court of Admiralty is, like other foreign decrees, on coming incidentally in question here, conclusive. Park on Ins., 462, &c., and the cases there cited; Cond. Marsh., 392, 393, and the cases there cited. Hughes v. Cornelius, 2 Show., 232, is the leading English case. This has been followed by numerous others. Bernardi v. Motteux, Doug., 575; Mayne v. Walter, Park, 363; Barzilla v. Lewes, *Id.*, 359; Salloucci v. Woodmas, *Id.*, 362; Same v. Johnson, *Id.*, 364; De Souza v. Ewer, *Id.*, 361; Calvert v. Boville, 7 T. R., 523; Geyer v. Aquilar, *Id.*, 681; Rich v. Parker, *Id.*, 705; Christe v. Secretan, 8 *Id.*, 192; Garrels v. Kingston, *Id.*, 230; Pollard v. Bell, *Id.*, 430; Helstrom v. Rhodes, *Id.*, 444; Bird v. Appleton, *Id.*, 562; Price v. Bell, 1 East, 663; Kindersley v. Chase, Park, 5th ed., 363; Oddy v. Boville, 2 East, 473; Baring v. Cleggett, 3 Bos. & P., 201; Lothian v. Henderson, *Id.*, 499; Baring v. The Royal Ex. Ass. Co., 5 East, 99; Bolton v. Gladstone, *Ibid.*, 155; Fisher v. Ogle, 1 Campb., 418; Donaldson v. Thompson, *Ibid.*, 429.

There are also many American cases to the same effect. Groning v. Union Ins. Co., 1 Nott. & M'C., 537; Bailey v. South Car. Ins. Co., *Id.*, 541, 542, &c., *note*; Starke v. Woodward, *Id.*, 329, 330, *note*; Goix v. Low, 1 Johns. Cas., 341; Croudson v. Leonard, 4 Cr., 434; Gray v. Swan, 1 Harr. & J., 142; Dempsey v. Ins. Co. of Pa., 1 Binn., 299, *note f.*; S. C. 4 Yeates, 119, by title of Browne v. President, &c., of the Ins. Co. of Pa.; Baxter v. N. E. Mar. Ins. Co., 6 Mass., 277; S. C., 7 *Id.*, 275; Robinson v. Jones, 8 *Id.*, 536; Cheriot v. Foussat, 3 Binn., 220; Armroyd v. Williams, C. C., Apr. 1811, MS.; Whart. Dig., Evidence, E, pl. 64; Stewart v. Warner, 1 Day, 142; Brown v. Un. Ins. Co. at New London, 4 Day, 179; Laing v. United Ins. Co., 2 Johns. Cas., 174.

An exception was, when it related to a warranty of American property in a policy which contained an express provision that the warranty should be proved, if required, in a particular place. Calbraith v. Gracie, C. C., Apr. 1805, MS., 1 Binn., 296, *note*; Calhoun v. The Ins. Co. of Pa., 1 Binn., 293. Or when, on its face, it appeared to be for insufficient cause. Fitz Simmons v. Newport Ins. Co., 4 Cr., 185.

In this State, such a decree has long been treated, under any circumstances, as an exception to the general rule; being considered mere *prima facie* evidence, though incidentally in question. Vandenheuvel v. U. Ins. Co., 2 Cai. Cas., 217; S. C., 2 Johns. Cas., 451; Johnston v. Ludlow, 2 Johns. Cas., 481; Laing v. U. Ins. Co., *Id.*, 587; Radcliff v. U. Ins., 9 Johns., 277; N. Y. F. Ins. Co. v. De Wolf, 2 Cow., 66.

And if enough appear on the face of the decree to impeach it, it is not even *prima facie* evidence. Johnston v. Ludlow, 1 Cai. Cas., 21.

And in Mass., if it do not distinctly state the cause of condemnation, it is mere *prima facie* evidence. 523*] Robinson v. Jones, 8 Mass., *536, and *vide* Maley v. Shattuck, 3 Cr., 488, and Bailey v. S. Car. Ins. Co. 1 Nott. & M'C., 541 to 546, S. P.

So in Pa., Vasse v. Ball, 2 Dall., 270: S. C., 2 Yeates, 178, and *vide* Crousillat v. Ball, 3 Yeates, 375; S. C., 4 Dall., 294, where they have adopted, by statute, the rule of this State. 5 Sm. Laws, 49.

If the action here be directly on a foreign judgment or decree, all the authorities agree, that it is no more than *prima facie* evidence. Duplein v. De Roven, 2 Vern., 540; Walker v. Witter, Doug., 1; Crawford v. Whittal, *Id.*, 4, *note*; Galbraith v. Neville, *Id.*, 6, *note*; Sinclair v. Fraser, stated in Doug., 5, *note*, and also cited in The Duchess of Kingston's trial, 11 Harg. St. Tr., 122; 5 East, 475, *note b*, and what is said there of Galbraith v. Neville, per Ld. Mansfield, in Herbert v. Cook, Willes, 37, *n. a*; Philips v. Hunter, 2 H. Bl., 410, per Eyre, *Ch. J.*; Bartlet v. Knight, 1 Mass., 401; Buttrick v. Allen, 8 Mass., 273; Bissell v. Briggs, 9 *Id.*, 462; Stevens v. Gaylord, 11 *Id.*, 265; 3 Johns., 168, 169, per Kent, *Ch. J.*; Taylor v. Bryden, 8 Johns., 173; Hubbell v. Cowdrey, 5 *Id.*, 132; Smith v. William, 2 Cai. Cas., 110, 119; James v. Allen, 1 Dall., 191; Hitchcock v. Aicken, 1 Cai., 460; Betts v. Death, Addis., 265; Stoddard v. Allen, N. Chipman, 44; King v. Van Gilder, 1 D. Chipman, 59.

Judgments and decrees of neighboring States are, however, made an exception to this rule by the Constitution (art. 4, sec. 1), and laws (1 U. S. Laws, old ed., 115; 2 *Id.*, new ed., 102) of the U. S. After various decisions of the state courts, placing them as to their effect, on the same footing as foreign judgments (*vide* the cases last above cited from the State Reports) and some decisions giving them full effect. *Vide* Armstrong v. Carson's Executors, 1 Dall., 302; Green v. Sarmiento, U. S. C. C., 1 Pet., 74; Jacobs v. Hull, 12 Mass., 25; and Betts v. Death, Addis., 265. The question was put at rest by Mills v. Duryee, 7 Cr., 481, in the Supreme Court of the U. S. This case made them of the same dignity and conclusive effect in each State, as in that where rendered. Since that case, several others havs followed to the same effect. Clark's Executors v. Carrington, 7 Cr., 308; Hampton v. M'Connel, 3 Wh., 234; Buford v. Buford, 4 Munf., 241; Borden v. Fitch, 15 Johns., 121; Andrews v. Montgomery, 19 Johns., 162; 1 Pet., 155; Commonwealth v. Green, 17 Mass., 515; Gibbons v. Livingston, 1 Halst., 236, 275, 283, 284.

But the Constitution, statute, &c., is confined to civil judgments, &c., and a judgment in a criminal prosecution, in one State, can have no validity or effect in another; nor can its consequences, direct or incidental, extend into another State. Commonwealth v. Green, 17 Mass., 515. Thus, a foreign conviction of one for an infamous crime, does not render him an incompetent witness. *Ib.* So of a conviction in a neighboring State. *Ib.*

A judgment of a neighboring State on foreign attachment is not conclusive evidence of the debt, even in a suit between the same parties. Phelps v. Holker, 1 Dall., 261; Betts v. Death, Addis., 265.

All the cases agree, both as to foreign and state judgments or decrees, that in order to make them effectual to any purpose, the court in which they 524*] *are rendered must have jurisdiction. As to the source from which this jurisdiction must emanate, it is enough that the court be one *de facto*, deriving its authority from those in whom the power of the country is vested. Bank of N. A. v. M'Call, 4 Binn., 371. Upon this principle, the proceedings of a court in the late unacknowledged Government of St. Domingo were recognized as valid. *Ib.* And *vide* Ingraham's Heirs v. Cock. 1 Overton's Tenn., 22, 28, &c., as to the Franklin Government.

For the manner of proving the lines of a State, *vide* State v. Evans, *Id.*, 220.

Being properly organized, the forum proceeds according to its own laws; and if these sanction a foreign attachment against a garnishee, even for the debt of a deceased foreigner, other governments will not, therefore, hold the proceeding void. Bank of N. A. v. M'Call, 4 Binn., 371.

But if the suit be commenced and carried to judgment without personal notice to the defendant, the whole is void; and will not be received even as *prima facie* evidence in support of an action. Buchanan v. Rucker, 9 East, 192; S. C., 1 Campb., 63; Kibbe v. Kibbe, Kirby's 119; Butrick v. Allen, 8 Mass., 273; Pawling v. Wilson, 13 Johns., 192; Borden v. Fitch, 15 *Id.*, 121; Kilburn v. Woodworth, 5 *Id.*, 37; Phelps v. Holker, 1 Dall., 261; Robinson v. Executors of Ward, 8 Johns., 86; Cavan v. Stewart, 1 Stark., 525.

And it is the same thing, though notice be given to the defendant, if he be out of the State at the time. Fenton v. Galick, 8 Johns., 194.

The jurisdiction of the court even of a neighboring State, and especially of a foreign country, may always be questioned. Rose v. Himely, 4 Cr., 241; Borden v. Fitch, 15 Johns., 121; Pawling v. Wilson, 13 *Id.*, 191; Andrews v. Montgomery, 19 *Id.*, 162, per Spencer C. *J.*; Snell v. Foussat, 3 Binn., 241, *note*; Cheriot v. Same, *Id.*, 220; Bartlet v. Knight, 1 Mass., 401; Bissell v. Briggs, 9 Mass., 467, per Parsons, *Ch. J.*; Shumway v. Stillman, 4 Cow., 292; Cavan v Stewart, 1 Stark., 525.

The jurisdiction may be questioned on the general issue, pleaded to debt or *assumpsit* on the judgment. Bissel v. Briggs, 9 Mass., 462; Stevens v. Gaylord, 11 *Id.*, 266.

If the source of the court's authority be unusual, it lies on the one who would support the sentence to prove its legitimacy; but if its origin does not appear, it will be presumed legitimate. Snell v. Foussat, C. C., Apr., 1825; 3 Binn., 239, *note*; Cheriot v. Poussat, *Id.*, 220. And *vide*, also, Hudson v. Guester, 4 Cr., 225, as to proving loss of jurisdiction.

For the manner of pleading non-residence of the party, in order to show want of jurisdiction of the person in a foreign court, *vide* Smith v. Rhoades, 1 Day, 168; Shumway v. Stillman, *ante.*, 292. In Walker v. Maxwell, 1 Mass., 104, it was held that in pleading, the proceedings of a court in R. I., upon a statute, it should be particularly set forth. It is not enough to say generally, that they were pursuant to the statute, &c.

If the foreign court have jurisdiction, its proceedings cannot be impeached for error, on coming incidentally in question here. Tarlton v. Tarlton, *4 Maule. & S., 20. And in an action directly [*525 upon the judgment, the court will intend jurisdiction, and that the proceedings were regular until the contrary be clearly shown. Molony v. Gibbons, 2 Camph., 502; Shumway v. Stillman, *ante*, 292. But its justice may be impeached upon the general issue, Stevens v. Gaylord, 11 Mass., 266.

The decree must be complete, definite, certain and final in the sum to be paid; Saddler v. Robins, 1 Campb., 253; but being so, an action will lie even on the decree of a foreign Court of Chancery, the same as on a judgment at law. *Ib.*

The judgment or decree may be avoided for fraud, or where it is obtained in evasion of the laws of the country in which it is sought to be enforced. Jackson v. Jacksou, 1 Johns., 424; Buford v. Buford, 4 Munf., 241; Borden v. Fitch, 15 Johns., 121.

4. *Of foreign statutes.* These have not *proprio vigore*, the force of law, beyond the limits of the State enacting them. Pearsall v. Dwight, 11 Mass., 88.

5. *Of foreign criminal laws.* These cannot, *ex vigore suo*, have any force or effect beyond the State which enacts them. Commonwealth v. Green, 17 Mass., 515; Inh. of West Cambridge v. Inh. of Lexington, 1 Pick., 506.

6. *The manner of proving foreign laws, including the common law of the different States.* Where an act is *malum in se*, and an offense at common law, courts will presume it forbidden by the laws of the country where it was performed, until the contrary is shown; and upon this principle the Supreme Judicial Court in Mass. held a contract made in N. Y., to be void as founded in champerty, without requiring proof that it was forbidden here. Thurston v. Percival, 1 Pick., 415. But it is otherwise of a mere positive law; and accordingly, where infancy was set up as a defense to an action upon contract made in a foreign country, it was held necessary to show by evidence that it was a defense by the law of that country. Male v. Roberts, 3 Esp., 163; Thompson v. Ketchum, 8 Johns., 189. Yet in Legg v. Legg, 8 Mass., 99, the court, on a question whether a marriage in Vt., passed the wife's choses in action to the husband, said, "We must presume the laws of Vermont to be similar to ours on this subject, unless the contrary is regularly shown;"

and the same was held in Md., even as to real property. Harper v. Hampton, 1 Harris & Johns., 687.

The general rule is, that the law of a foreign country must be proved; and will not be judicially noticed by our courts. Freemoult v. Dedire 1 P. Wms., 429, 431; Feaubert v. Turst, Prec. Ch., 207; S. C., 1 Br. P. C., 38; S. C., Vin. Abr. Foreign, C., pl. 1; Mostyn v. Fabrigas, Cowp., 174; Ganer v. Lady Lanesborough, Peake, 17; Melan v. Duke of Fitz James, 1 Bos. & P., 138; Collet v. Ld. Keith, 2 East, 273; Male v. Roberts, 3 Esp., 163; Talbot v. Seeman, 1 Cr., 38; Church v. Hubbart, 2 *Id.*, 187.

526*] *Various other cases go to the same doctrine. They hold that the common or unwritten law is to be proved by parol, but that statutes or written laws must in general, be proved by copies authenticated under the government seal, which was noticed judicially in Anon., 9 Mod., 68. This rule, with its exceptions and illustrations, may be gathered from the following cases: Kenney v. Clarkson, 1 Johns., 385, 394; Walpole v. Ewer, 2 Cond., Marsh., 762; Boehtlinck v. Schneider, 3 Esp., 58; Hulle v. Heightman, 4 *Id.*, 75; Frith v. Sprague, 14 Mass., 455; Livingston v. Maryland Ins. Co., 6 Cr., 274; Robinson v. Clifford, 2 Cond. Marsh., 706, a *note*; S. C., Whart. Dig., Evidence, F, pl., 82; Seton v. Del. Ins. Co., *Id.*; *Id.*, Clegg v. Levy, 3 Campb., 166; Miller v. Heinrick, 4 Campb., 155; Consequa v. Willings, 1 Pet., 225, 229; Smith v. Elder, 3 Johns., 105; Richardson v. Anderson, 1 Campb., 65, *note a*; Brush v. Wilkins, 4 Johns. Ch., 520; Lessee of Albertson v. Robeson, 1 Dall., 9; Young v. Bank of Alexandria, 4 Cr., 384 Livingston v. Maryland Ins. Co., 6 Cr., 274; Woodbridge v. Austin, 2 Taylor, 367.

In Latimer v. Elgin, 4 Dess., 26, 32. Mr. Haywood's Reports were received as evidence of the common law of N. C.

7. *Manner of proving state statutes.* This is matter of positive regulation by statute, &c., upon which several decisions have been made. Const. U. S., Art. 4, sec. 1; 1 U. S. Laws, old ed., 115, 2 *Id.*, new ed., 102; Craig v. Brown, 1 Pet., 352; Thompson v. Musser, 1 Dall., 458. Poindexter's Exrs. v. Barker, 2 Hayw., 173; U. S. v. Johns., 4 Dall., 413, 416; Thompson v. Musser, 1 Dall., 462; Biddis v. James, 6 Binn., 321; Commonwealth v. Frazer, cited 6 Binn., 323; Commonwealth v. Longchamps, Whart. Dig., Evidence, F, pl., 80; State v. Stade, 1 D. Chipman, 303; Elmore v. Mills, 1 Hayw., 359, 360.

8. *Manner of proving foreign judgments, decrees, &c.* This should, in general, be by proving the handwriting of the foreign judge who signs them, and the authenticity of the seal affixed. Henry v. Adey, 4 Esp., 229, 3 East, 221; Buchanan v. Rucker, 1 Campb., 63; Flindt v. Atkins, 3 *Id.*, 215; Alves v. Bunbury, 4 *Id.*, 28.

The foreign court must certify with a seal, if it have one, though it be old and disused. Cavan v. Stewart, 1 Stark., 525; and if there be no seal, the record or proceedings must, at least, be authenticated in the usual manner, or in some mode known to the foreign government. Alves v. Bunbury, 4 Campb., 28; Black v. Braybrook, and Appleton v. Braybrook, 2 Stark., 6, 7.

Since the Union, an Irish judgment is properly pleadable as a record, but it can be proved only by an examined copy on oath. Collins v. Ld. Viscount Matthew, 5 East, 473; S. C. 2 Smith, 25.

Our own decisions give directions for almost all the different modes of proof upon this head, which it may be necessary to resort to. Smith v. Blagge, 1 Johns. Cas., 238; Delafield v. Hand, 3 Johns., 310; Vandervoort v. Smith, 2 Cai., 155; Yeaton v. Fry, 5
527*] Cr., 335; *Gardner v. Col. Ins. Co., 7 Johns., 514; Butrick v. Allen, 8 Mass., 273; Hadfield v. Jameson, 2 Munf., 53; Church v. Hubbart, 2 Cr., 238, &c.; Marshall v. Union Ins. Co., C. C., Apr., 1810, MS.; Whart. Dig., Evidence, E. pl. 72; Assuria v. Ins. Co. of Pa., C. C., Oct., 1812, MS., *Id.*, pl. 73; Houquebies v. Girard, C. C., Oct. 1808, MS., *Id.*, pl. 74; Russel v. Union Ins. Co., C. C., Apr., 1806, MS., *Id.*, pl. 75; Dederer v. Del. Ins. Co., C. C., Apr., 1807, MS., *Id.*, pl. 76; Gardere v. Col. Ins. Co., 7 Johns., 514; Pepoon v. Jenkins, 2 Johns. Cas., 119; Young v. Gregory, 3 Call., 446. Hadfield v. Jameson, 2 Munf., 53; Griswold v. Pitcairn, 2 Conn. N. S., 85; Messonier v. Union Ins. Co. of Charleston, 1 Nott & M'C., 168; Hincle v. Carruth, 1 Conn. S. C., 471.

9. *Manner of proving state judgments, decrees, &c.* This is also matter of positive regulation, as to which the authorities follow: Const. U. S., Art. 4, sec. 1; 1 U. S. Laws, old ed., 115; 2 *Id.*, New ed., 102; Smith v. Blagge, 1 Johns. Cas., 238; Note to Alston v. Taylor, 1 Hayw., 394, 395; Ellemore v. Mills, 1 Hayw., 359; Murray v. Marsh, 2 Hayw., 290; Pepoon v. Jenkins, 2 Johns. Cas., 119; Ferguson v. Harwood, 7 Cr., 408; Drummond v. Magruder, 9 Cr., 122; Craig v. Brown, 1 Pet., 352; Turner v. Waddington, C. C., Oct., 1811, MS.; Whart. Dig., Evidence, C, pl. 18; Frey v. Wells, 4 Yeates, 396; Thurston v. Murray, 3 Binn., 326; Haight v. Morris, 2 Halsted, 289; Thompson v. Bullock, 1 Bay, 364, 366.

To make the record, &c., conclusive, it should be authenticated according to the Act of Congress. If this be not so, however, but it be authenticated in the same manner as foreign records may be, it is still testimony, but sinks to the degree of *prima facie* evidence. Baker v. Field, 2 Yeates, 532, and Ralston v. Cummins there cited. *Semb.* that, in this light, a sworn copy is admissible. Collins v. Ld. Matthew, 5 East, 473; S. C., 2 Smith, 25.

A justice's judgment in a neighboring State, is not within the Act of Congress, but must be proved, and has the same effect as a foreign judgment. King v. Gilder, 1 D. Chipman, 59. A copy certified by the justice was received in evidence. *Ib.*

Of the LEX LOCI REI SITÆ. This governs real property, the title to which can be acquired and lost only in the manner prescribed by the law of the country where it is situate. U. S. v. Crosby, 7 Cr., 115; Cutter v. Davenport, per *Cur.*, 1 Pick., 86; Robinson v. Campbell, 3 Wh., 212; 4 T. R., 192, per Lord Kenyon, *Ch. J.*; *Id.*, 184, where Law. *arg.*, cites the authorities from the law of nations and the civil law; Brodie v. Barry, 2 Ves. & B., 131; Selkrig v. Davis, 2 Rose Cas. Bank., 291; S. C., 2 Dow, 230; Clark v. Graham, 6 Wh., 577; Kerr v. Devisees of Moon, 9 Wh., 565; M'Cormick v. Sullivant, 10 *Id.*, 192, 202; Darby v. Mayer, *Id.*, 469; Harper v. Hampton, 1 Harr. & J., 687; Latimer v. Elgin, 4 Dress., 26, 31, 32.

Thus, where one Nelson, of Grenada, according to the law of that place, conveyed land in Mass., by writing before a notary public without *seal, [528
the seal being a requisite formality in Mass., held that the conveyance was void, U. S. v. Crosby, 7 Cr., 115; and in Selkrig v. Davis, 2 Rose Cas. Bank., 291; 2 Dow., 230; it was held that a commission of bankrupt and assignment in England, though they passed the bankrupt's personal estate in Scotland, would not affect his real estate there.

In deciding on state statutes concerning land, the Supreme Court of the U. S. adopt the construction given by the state court, if that can be ascertained. Polk's lessee v. Wendell, 9 Cr., 87, 98.

Clark v. Graham, 6 Wh., 577, applied the *lex loci rei sitæ*, to a deed and Kerr v. Devisees of Moon, 9 *Id.*, 565, to wills of land in a neighboring State. So M'Cormick v. Sullivant, 10 *Id.*, 192, 202.

A mere change of sovereignty does not vary the private rights of real property, existing before the change, whether they were acquired by individual or state grant. Mutual Assistant Society v. Watts' Exr., 1 Wh., 279, 282.

The courts of every Government or State have the exclusive authority of construing its local statutes; and their construction will be respected in other Governments or States. Elmendorf v. Taylor, 10 Wh., 153, 159.

If the laws of another State are in question, in a court in Md., even concerning real property in the neighboring State, and there is no proof what the law of the latter is, the court of Md. will presume it to be the same with theirs. Harper v. Hampton, 1 Harr. & J., 687.

How far the *lex loci rei sitæ*, in reference to the evidence of the execution of wills of real estate, proved and recorded according to the laws of the different States, is modified by the provisions of the Constitution and laws of the U. S., in respect to the faith and credit, &c., to be given to the public Acts, records and judicial proceedings of each State, in every other State, *quære*. Darby v. Mayer, 10 Wh., 469.

10. *Of the* LEX FORI. The great difficulty upon this head, has been to run a plain practical line between cases of the *lex loci contractus*, *lex domicilii*, &c., on the one hand, and the *lex fori* on the other; for, though it is universally conceded that the latter must govern the remedy; Fenwick v. Sears, 1 Cr., 259; Dixon's Exrs. v. Ramsay's Exrs., 3 *Id.*, 319, 323; Nash v. Tupper, 1 Cai., 402; Ruggles v. Keeler, 3 Johns., 286; Pearsall v. Dwight, 2 Mass., 84; Smith v. Spinola, 2 Johns., 198; Van Reimsdyk v. Kayne, 1 Gall., 371; Bird v. Caritat, 2 Johns., 342; Sicard v. Whale, 11 Johns., 194; Courtois v. Carpentier, C. C., 1806, MS., Whart. Dig., Foreign Laws, &c., pl. 5; 1 Bos. & P., 142, per Heath, *J.*; Doran v. O'Reilly, 3 Price, 250; Anon., 7 Taunt., 244; yet the courts of different countries have not unfrequently confounded the remedy with the right; and rendered it very difficult for counsel to advise, not merely of

new subjects not yet adjudged to belong to the one or the other, but sometimes of those to which the distinction has been judicially applied. An instance of the latter was Meredith v. Hinsdale, 2 Cai., 362, overruled by the principal case; and it would, perhaps, be questionable, after the more enlightened 529*] view of the distiction taken by *modern cases, whether an agreement between two foreigners, that their contract should be enforced only by the tribunals of their own country, would oust our courts of jurisdiction, as was held in Gienar v. Mayer, 2 H. Bl., 603; or that a party not liable to arrest in a suit upon his contract brought in the country where it was made, should, for that reason, be discharged on common bail in a suit upon the same contract in another country, as was held in Melan v. Fitz James, 1 Bos. & P., 138, from which Ld. Kenyon afterwards dissented. 2 East, 455; Talleyrand v. Boulanger, 3 Ves., 447. S. P., as in Melan v. Fitz James; Conframp v. Bunel, 4 Dall, 419, S. P.

The principles adopted in Whittemore v. Adams, 2 Cow., 626, &c., and several of the cases there cited, would seem utterly to exclude the influence of foreign laws upon the jurisdiction or practice of our courts.

The form of the action (as in the principle case), must clearly be determined by the *lex fori*. An action is, "the form of a suit given by the law to recover a thing." *Termes de la ley*, Action. It is a species of the remedy, which is called in its definition, "the action or means given by the law for the recovery of a right. Cunningham's Law Dict., Remedy; Jac. Law Dict., Remedy.

We administer justice according to our laws and the laws prescribed by our Legislature. 14 Johns., 340; Bird v. Caritat, 2 Johns., 345. And accordingly, where a statute of Conn. declared that in a suit brought there by an assignee of a chose in action, the plaintiff should, on proof of certain facts, be nonsuited, the law was holden inapplicable to a suit by such assignee in this State.

The question of proper parties must be settled by the law of the forum. A foreign Corporation may sue here. Henriques v. Dutch West India Co., 2 Ld. Raym., 1532; 1 Str., 612; Silver Lake Bank v. North, 4 Johns. Ch., 370-2; The Society for the Propagation of the Gospel, &c., v. Wheeler, 2 Call., 105; Bank of Marietta v. Pindal, 2 Randolph, 465; Portsmouth Livery Co. v. Weston, 10 Mass., 91. So a foreign sovereign or nation. Nabob of Arcot v. East India Co., 4 Bro. Ch., 180.

But persons coming *en autre droit*, under the appointment of foreign laws, cannot be parties. To entitle them to be received, as such, they must have their appointments repeated under our laws. This has been held of foreign guardians; Morrel v. Dickey, 1 Johns. Ch., 153; of foreign executors and administrators. *Id.*, 156; Tourton v. Flower, 3 P. Wms., 369; Lee v. Bank of England, 8 Ves., 44; Goodwin v. Jones, 3 Mass., 514; Riley v. Riley, 3 Day., 74; Fenwick v. Admrs. of Sears, 1 Cr., 259; Dixon's Exrs. v. Ramsay's Exrs., 3 Cr., 319; Doolittle v. Lewis, 7 Johns. Ch., 45; Williams v. Storrs, 6 *Id.*, 353; Lewis v. M'Farland, 9 Cr., 159; Doe v. Same, 9 *Id.*, 151, 152; Langdon v. Potter, 11 Mass., 313; Borden v. Borden, 5 *Id.*, 67; Stevens v. Gaylord, 11 *Id.*, 256; Cutler v. Davenport, 1 Pick., 81; Kerr v. Devisees of Moon, 9 Wh., 565; Darby's Lessee v. Mayer, 10 *Id.*, 465; Admrs. of Dodge v. Wetmore, Brayton, 92; Lee v. Havens, *Id.*, 93.

But the objection does not apply to an executor to whom land is devised. Doe v. M'Farland, 9 Cr., 151, 152. Nor to the executor of a mortgagee. Doolittle 530*] *v. Lewis, 7 Johns. Ch., 45. They may enforce their claims here to lands in this State devised or mortgaged, without a domestic probate, because they do not come merely as executors. Yet it was holden that a foreign executor could not assign a mortgage of land in Mass. Cutler v. Davenport, 1 Pick., 81.

It was said by the late *Chancellor*, that foreign bankrupt assignees may sue here in their own names; Holmes v. Remsen, 4 Johns. Ch., 460, 485; but the contrary was held as to a court of law, in Bird v. Caritat, 2 Johns., 342; and *vide* Milne v. Moreton, 6 Binn., 353. In Dawes v. Boylston, 9 Mass., 337, 346, the Supreme Court of Mass. explicitly deny the right of English bankrupt assignees to sue there; and *vide* Bird v. Pierpont, 1 Johns., 118. In Raymond v. Johnson, 11 Johns., 488, this right was denied to an insolvent assignee of N. J.

That the above cases, as to parties, go upon the *lex fori*, *vide* Dixon's Exrs. v. Ramsay's Exrs., 3 Cr., 391; Bird v. Caritat, 2 Johns., 345, and Milne v. Moreton, 6 Binn., 353.

A promissory note payable to order, though made in a country where it is not negotiable, may yet be negotiated here, and the indorsee may sue in his own name, Lodge v. Phelps, 1 Johns. Cas., 139; S. C., 2 Cai. Cas., 321; Milne v. Graham, 1 Barn. & Cresw., 192, S. P., on the ground that the note was within the spirit of the Statute of 3 & 4 Anne ch. 9, 1 R. L., 151.

Though distribution of the deceased's personal estate is to be according to the *lex domicilii*; yet the payment of his debts is to be according to the order, and in the manner prescribed by the law of the country where the assets are administered. This being matter of remedy, is subject to the *lex fori*. Harison v. Sterry, 5 Cr., 299, per Marshall, *Ch. J.*, Milne v. Moreton, 6 Binn., 361, per Tilghman, *Ch. J.*

And the same rule prevails as to heirs in one State, though the assets arise by a sale of lands of their ancestor lying in another. The avails were decreed, therefore, to the specialty creditors, in such a case. Hamilton v. Heirs & Exrs. of Haynes, Cann. & Norw., 413.

Foreign Statutes of Limitation are in no case available here, but our own Statutes of this kind are applicable to all actions. They belong to the *lex fori*. Decouche v. Savetier, 3 Johns. Ch., 97; Nash v. Tupper, 1 Cai., 102; Ruggles v. Keeler, 3 Johns., 263; 1 Gall., 376, per Story, J.; Pearsall v. Dwight, 2 Mass., 84; Byrne v. Crowninshield, 17 *Id.*, 55; Medbury v. Hopkins, 3 Con., N. S., 472; S. C., Harper v. Hampton, 1 Harr. & Johns., 453, *Id.*, 622.

It is now fully settled, that an insolvent discharge of the person relates merely to the remedy; and if granted in another State, or a foreign country, it will not, under any circumstances, or at any stage of the cause, be noticed by our courts or allowed to operate here for any purpose. White v. Canfield, 7 Johns., 117; Tappan v. Poor, 15 Mass., 419; Watson v. Bourne, 10 *Id.*, 337; James v. Allen, 1 Dall., 88; Sicard v. Whale, 11 Johns., 194; Peck v. Hozier, 14 Johns., 346; Whittemore v. Adams, 2 Cow., 626; Woodbridge v. Wright, 3 Con. N. S., 523; Vanuxhern v. Hazlehursts, 1 South., 202, per Kirkpatrick, *Ch. J.*

*The same line which divides the *lex loci* [*531 and *lex fori* of foreign countries, exists between the U. S. and the several States; and accordingly, it has been lately held that the 34th section of the Judiciary Act of 1789, ch. 20, 2 U. S. Law, new ed., 70, providing that the laws of the several States, except, &c., shall be regarded as rules of decision in trials at common law, in the courts of the U. S., in cases where they apply, does not extend to the process and practice of those courts. It is a mere legislative recognition of the principles of universal jurisprudence as to the operation of the *lex loci*. This distinction was established and illustrated at large in Wyman v. Southard, 10 Wh., 1.

11. *Law of crimes.* The Legislature of one State cannot define and punish crimes committed in another. State v. Knight, Tayl., 65. A statute doing this was declared unconstitutional and void. *Ib.*

12. *Of the power of one State over the fugitives from the justice of another.* See the opinion of Kent, *Chancellor*, in Washburn's case, 4 Johns. Ch., 106; S. C., 3 Wheeler's Crim. Cas., 473, and the opinion of Tilghman, *Ch. J.*, in Commonwealth v. Deacon, 2 Wheeler's Crim. Cas., 1.

ROGERS *v.* M'GREGOR.

Trespass Quare Clausum Fregit—*Title to Land Involved—Costs.*

In trespass *quare clausum fregit*, where the title to land comes in question, the plaintiff is entitled to single costs, though he recover less than $50 damages.

IN trespass *quare clausum fregit* in this court, the plaintiff at the circuit recovered only $32.50; but the circuit judge certified that the title to land came in question; and,

Mr. E. Cowen, for the plaintiff, moved for single costs.

Mr. J. B. Lathrop, contra, said the action might have been brought in a justice's court; and submitted whether it was not within the Statute, sess. 47; ch. 238, sec. 33, providing that if the plaintiff in any suit which may be brought in any court of record shall fail to recover a sum exceeding $50, he shall not recover any costs of the defendant, provided the suit so brought might have been commenced in a justice's court. He said a justice had jurisdiction, and had the suit been prosecuted in a justice's court, the defendant could only oust him of jurisdiction by pleading title specially. This he might not have done.

532*] **Curia.* We must take the case as it stood at the circuit without inquiring what might possibly have been the defendant's course before a justice, had the suit been brought in a justice's court. On this particular cause, which in fact did involve the title to lands, a justice had no jurisdiction. The case, as made out at the trial, must be the criterion.

Motion granted.

Cited in—10 How. Pr., 409.

CANFIELD & LOSEY *v.* LINDLEY.

Change of Venue—Witnesses Residing in Adjacent State.

That witnesses reside in a neighboring State, near the place where the venue is laid, is not a reason for retaining it.

IN covenant, *Mr. J. Dickson* moved to change the venue from the City of N. Y. to the County of Monroe, on an affidavit stating the residence of three material witnesses in the latter county.

Mr. G. C. Bronson, contra, opposed this on the plaintiff's affidavit that he had one witness in the City of N. Y., and three in the State of N. J. near the City of N. Y., whose attendance he expected to procure at the circuit; but,

Per Curiam. We do not remember its ever having been held, that the fact of witnesses' residing in a neighboring State is to weigh with us in fixing the venue. A commission may yet be necessary to examine them.

Motion granted.

Cited in—2 Wend., 282; 6 Wend., 542; 4 Hill, 68, (*n*).

JACKSON, ex dem. TEN EYCK ET UX., *v.* CLARK.

Practice—Costs.

Separate papers, for motions for judgment as in case of nonsuit in different causes, in favor of the same nominal plaintiff, on the same demise, though against different defendants, the attorneys for the parties being the same in each, and the motions depending on the same cause, arising simultaneously, will not, in future be taxed.

THERE were eleven causes on the same demise against different defendants, and the same attorneys in each; and the defendant's attorney had prepared eleven different sets of papers, for eleven different motions for judg-
533*] ment as in *case of nonsuit, on the same ground, and for the same cause arising at the same time; and the question was, whether the defendants should, respectively, on the plaintiff's stipulating, be entitled to have the expense of all these papers taxed against him.

Mr. B. Perkins, for the defendants.

Mr. J. M'Kown, contra.

Curia. We are not aware that we have denied costs for any part of the papers when actually made out under these circumstances, though we have held, that in like cases, where they were in fact consolidated, they should not be taxed as separate sets. *Jackson* v. *Garnsey*, 3 Cow., 385 (*infra*); *Jackson* v. *Keller*, 18 Johns., 310; *Boyce* v. *Thomson*, 20, *Id.*, 274. It is competent, though not necessary, to come here upon distinct papers, and we allow them to be taxed in this instance; but we wish the bar to understand that this will not be done hereafter in the like cases. Here are the same plaintiff, the same lessors, and though different defendants, the same attorneys in all the causes; and the same motion is made in each, on the same grounds, and the causes of the motions arose at the same time. One set of papers would, in truth, have answered every purpose, and in future no more will be taxed.

Rule accordingly.

Cited in—11 Wend., 173; 19 Wend., 83; 1 Den., 683; 1 Blatchf., 158.

BRISBIN, Administrator, *v.* M'LAUGHLIN.

Assignment of Errors—Allegation of Diminution—Practice.

The plaintiff in error may assign common errors, and allege diminution at the same time, and take out a *certiorari*, and enter his rule to join in error.

If the defendant does not join in error according to the rule, the plaintiff may enter a default, though the *certiorari* be not returned.

ON ERROR from the C. P. of N. Y. The plaintiff assigned errors specially in the record, alleging diminution, and sued out a *certiorari* in order to verify the diminution; but without waiting to have it returned, entered a default for *not joining in [***534**
error. The assignment of errors, and notice of the rule to join in error, were served May 18, 1825; the *certiorari* filed with the clerk of the C. P. June 9, 1825; and the defendant's default was entered the same day.

Mr. J. W. Patterson now moved to set aside the default for irregularity.

Mr. W. Mulick, contra, said the plaintiff had a right to proceed against the defendant in error in the same manner as if there had been no *certiorari* in the case. When diminution is alleged in the Court of Errors, according to the second rule of that court, the defendant may join in error, and then, unless it turn out that the plaintiff has caused it to be returned within a certain time, he loses all benefit of the diminution upon the argument. The rule is, in effect, the same in this court, though the course to be pursued, in applying it, is different. Under a general assignment of error in the record, and *in nullo est erratum* pleaded, the plaintiff cannot insist on the want of any of the out works of the record; as the original writ, bill, &c., but is confined to argue from the record itself. *Graddell* v. *Tyson*, 2 Ld. Raym., 1441. To avail himself of any defect *dehors* this, he must allege diminution (*Ib.*), which is to be served on the defendant with the other asssignment of error, and sue out a *certiorari* to verify the truth of the allegation. (*Vide Rowan* v. *Lytle*, *ante*, 91.) It is true that in such a case the plea of *in nullo*, &c., would be a confession of the error ; but in order to avoid this circumstance, the defendant should immediately take a rule against the plaintiff in error to return his *certiorari*, and in case he docs not, he loses the benefit of the special assignment. *Smith* v. *Stonehard*, 1 Salk., 267. If not returned within the rule, which is one of four days, the defendant may then give a joinder of *in nullo*, &c., and enter a *non misit breve* on the record, without taking any notice of the diminution. This renders the assignment of errors, as to that part, of no effect. (2 Sell. Pr., 378 ; 1 Archb. Pr., 231 ; 2 Ld. Raym., 1156 ; Tidd., 1112 ; 2 Dunl., 1150.)

535*] **Curia.* It does not appear from the papers before us, whether the plaintiff in error gave the common assignment of errors at the same time with the allegation of diminution ; but this was probably so, and we will intend it, until the omission is shown affirmatively. He was right in giving the common assignment before the *certiorari* was issued, and alleging diminution at the same time, as the foundation of the *certiorari*. Although he issued a *certiorari* to verify the allegation, he might afterwards waive it, and proceed upon the common assignment. He has done so by taking the default. The force of the *certiorari* is probably spent, and the reversal, therefore, stands upon the face of the record, as nothing *dehors* this is brought up. But be this as it may, the plaintiff had a right to the effect of his rule to join in error, the defendant having omitted to take any step on his part.

Motion denied.

NOTE. *The Court* did not say how the defendant should have proceeded—whether by taking issue on the common assignment alone, or pleading *in nullo est erratum* to the whole, and trusting to the want of a return, upon the argument, as the Court of Errors may do in the like cases, according to their second rule (see 1 Archb. Pr., 231 ; Tidd, 1112, for a similar rule in the House of Lords); or immediately taking a four day rule against the plaintiff to return the writ according to the practice of the K.'s B., as laid down in 2 Sell. Pr., 378, and *vide* 2 Salk., 267 ; 2 Ld. Raym., 1156 ; Tidd, 1112.

Cited in—7 Wend., 480.

536*] *BALDWIN *v.* GOODYEAR.

Practice in Justice Court—Refusal of Adjournment—Certiorari *Quashed—Appeal.*

Where the defendant, in a justice's court, pleaded in abatement, upon which issue was taken, but the justice denied an adjournment to the defendant, for the purpose of obtaining evidence to prove his plea ; whereupon he pleaded the general issue, and went to trial on the merits, upon which judgment was against him, and then brought a *certiorari* to correct the error of refusing to adjourn, and an appeal to the C. P. upon the merits; held, that the appeal only would lie; and the *certiorari* was quashed.

ON *certiorari* to a justice's court. Goodyear sued Baldwin in the court below, by summons, Apr. 6, 1825. Baldwin pleaded his privilege as an attorney and counselor of the Court of Errors, then sitting. On which, Goodyear took issue, and Baldwin requested an adjournment, to enable him to procure evidence to show the truth of the plea. This was denied. Baldwin then pleaded the general issue ; the cause was tried and judgment rendered against him. From this judgment he appealed to the C. P., and also brought his writ of *certiorari* to this court, which it was now moved to set aside ; and the Statute, sess. 47, ch. 238, secs. 36–38, pp. 294, 295, was relied on as denying a *certiorari* in this case.

Mr. J. L. Woods, for the motion.

Messrs. S. S. Baldwin and *H. Stephens*, contra.

Curia. The statute cited puts the party either to his appeal or *certiorari*. Clearly he is not entitled to both. The plaintiff in error supposes that he may bring a *certiorari* upon a formal error of refusing to adjourn, and have his appeal upon the merits. But whenever an issue is joined, he is confined to his appeal alone. Here where two successive issues—first on the matter in abatement and on this being passed upon and overruled, issue was taken and a trial had upon the merits. Both were the proper subject of appeal, and may be reviewed by the Court of C. P. It is only where there is no issue that a *certiorari* will lie.(a)

Motion granted.

Cited in—1 Wend., 316.

(a) *Vide* Harwood v. French, *ante*, 501.

---

*HUNTER *v.* GRAVES. [*537

Return to Certiorari—*Drawn by Attorney for Defendant in Error.*

A return to a *certiorari* will not be set aside merely on the ground that it was drawn by the attorney for the defendant in error ; *aliter*, if drawn by the plaintiff's attorney.

MOTION to set aside the return to a writ of *certiorari* to a justice's court, on the ground that the return was drawn by the attorney for the defendant in error ; and *Fox* v. *Johnson*, 3 Cow., 20, was relied upon.

Mr. J. B. Lathrop, for the motion.

Mr. C. P. Kirkland, contra.

Curia. The farthest we have gone is in *Fox* v. *Johnson*. We do not allow the attorney of the plaintiff in error to interfere in drawing the return, except as a mere amanuensis; (a) because he is seeking to reverse the judgment. The defendant's attorney is seeking for its affirmance, which is more favored by the law. The mere fact, therefore, that the defendant's attorney drew the return, without any abuse being shown, is not sufficient ground for setting it aside.

Motion denied.

Cited in—30 How. Pr., 376.

(a) *Vide* Philips v. Caswell, *ante*, 505.

JACKSON, ex dem. LOOP ET AL.,
v.
HARRINGTON.

Settlement of Case—Service of Case, Before Notice of Argument.

A case which becomes settled by lapse of time, after the amendments are served, or by arrangement between the parties must be drawn out, copied and served at or before giving notice of argument, in the same manner as where it is settled by a judge.

Otherwise it will, on motion, be stricken from the calendar of the term.

MR. D. KELLOGG, for the defendant, moved to strike this cause from the calendar for the term, on the ground that the plaintiff's attorney had not served the amended case when he gave notice of argument, nor afterwards. The plaintiff's attorney had made and served a case on the defendant's attorney, who had served the plaintiff's attorney with amendments, to which the plaintiff's attorney did not object, nor did he give any notice of referring 538*] the case to be settled by the *circuit judge who tried the cause. He relied on *Peck* v. *Peck*, 14 Johns., 219, and *Delamater* v. *Smith*, 16 Johns., 2.

Mr. A. Gibbs, contra, said it was not necessary to serve a case, where the party making it adopted the amendments served, as in this instance. The rule of the court extends merely to cases settled by a judge. He cited rule 6, January Term, 1799, and rule of January Term, 1816. Here the party is in full possession of the case, without service of a copy. The case is within the reason of *Van Buskirk* v. *Burr*, 20 Johns., 275, where the court held that demurrer books need not be served till the argument comes on. He also cited *Jackson* v. *Case*, 12 Johns., 431, and relied on *Peck* v. *Peck*, 14 *Id.*, 219, as showing that the rule upon which the defendant's counsel applied, was confined to cases settled by the judge.

Curia. There was, perhaps, some reason to suppose so from the authorities; but we think the practice should be the same, without regard to the manner of settling the case. This will preclude all disputes upon the argument as to the frame of it. The transcriber may mistake the precise import or place of the proposed amendment; but if the case be copied, and served, at least as early as the notice of argument, it gives a fair chance for correction, before the cause is called upon the calendar. We deny this motion, without costs; but in future, the course must be the same in regard to cases amended or settled by agreement, or by the lapse of time, as those settled by the judge. In all these cases, they must be drawn out, copied and served at or before giving notice of argument.

Motion denied.

Cited in—5 Cow., 22; 2 Wend., 211.

539*] *LYON v. BURTIS.

Certificate of Probable Cause—Practice.

An appeal lies from a circuit judge either granting or refusing a certificate of probable cause.

But the court will not hear an argument upon it.

Mr. A. Burr, for the plaintiff, having given notice of a motion for that purpose, moved to vacate the order or certificate of probable cause of Betts, Circuit Judge, who tried the cause, staying the proceeding, for the purpose of enabling the defendant to move for a new trial.

Mr. S. Jones read an affidavit showing that the case had been settled by the judge, and once noticed for argument; and contended that it could not be heard till it was reached in course of the calendar; but,

The Court said they would hear the motion; and this was the practice, whether the appeal was from a circuit judge refusing or granting an order.

Mr. Jones then proposed to argue the cause; but,

Per Curiam. We will listen to such points as you choose to suggest, either at the bar or in writing; but we do not hear the cause argued at this stage of it. We look into it merely to see whether there be probable cause to stay the proceedings.

The case was, accordingly, submitted.

Cited in—5 Cow., 439; 4 Hill, 556; 5 How. Pr., 309; 6 How. Pr., 466; Co. R. N.S., 26.

VAN RENSSELAER v. HAMILTON ET AL.

Practice—Costs.

Nisi Prius record taxed as costs of the circuit, though the cause was noticed and carried down at a previous circuit.

Plaintiff allowed per folio for engrossing notice of special matter on the *N. P.* record.

But not allowed for notice of inquest after affidavits of merits filed.

THIS cause had been put off at the circuit on motion of the defendants, on the usual terms of paying the costs of the circuit; and, the costs having been taxed, on motion for retaxation, the following items were held to be properly allowed as a part of those costs:

*Dr. *Nisi Prius* record, fol. 4, and engrossing, - - - - $1 26 [*540
Enrolling pleadings thereon, fol. 225, at 1s., - - - - - 28 12½

These were allowed, although the cause had once been carried down at a previous circuit, when a *N. P.* record was prepared.

The plaintiff was also allowed per folio for engrossing the defendant's notice of special matter in their defense, upon the *N. P.* record.

But *the Court* refused to allow a charge for the notice of inquest, because there had once before been a notice of inquest and an affidavit of merits was then filed; and they held that this extended to the cause throughout, so that afterwards, a notice of inquest was not proper; but only a notice of trial.

Mr. J. A. Dunlap, for the motion.
Mr. E. Williams, contra.

Cited in—6 How. Pr. 466; 5 Hill, 554.

EX PARTE SHETHAR.

Appeal from Justice Court to C. P.—When C. P. May Refuse to Proceed.

If the court of C. P., at any stage of a proceeding upon appeal from a justice's court, become satisfied that the Statute (sess. 47, ch. 236, sec. 36) was not complied with in bringing the appeal, they may refuse to proceed; as where, on the trial, they are satisfied that the appeal bond was executed without authority.

In this and the like cases, they are without jurisdiction.

Citations—Stat. sess. 47, ch. 238, sec. 36; 4 Cow., 80.

MOTION for a *mandamus* to the Judges of Alleghany C. P., commanding them to vacate a rule dismissing an appeal to them from a justice's court, brought by Shethar against Crook. The cause proceeded to trial, and after the appellant, Shethar, who was plaintiff before the justice, had gone through with his evidence to the jury, the appellee objected that the appeal bond purported to have been executed by Shethar, by his attorney. The justice had indorsed his approval of the security. The appellee insisted that the court should not proceed without proof of the attorney's authority to execute it; to which it was answered that the justice having approved the security, the court became possessed of the cause and should hear no evidence except what was pertinent to the issue; but the court directed that unless the appellant proved the **541***] authority of the attorney they *should dismiss the appeal; and no proof being produced, they discharged the jury.

Mr. F. Tracy, for the motion.

Curia. We think the court below were right in refusing to proceed. They may inquire into their authority or jurisdiction at any stage of the proceedings. The Statute (sess. 47, ch. 238, sec. 36) under which this appeal was brought, is peremptory that the appeal shall not be received or be of any force or effect unless a bond is given, and the other accompanying requisites complied with. A bond, good in form merely, without any power to execute it, is void, and as nothing; the court would be without jurisdiction, and a trial would be a nugatory thing, *coram non judice*. The case is within the principle of *Ex parte Chryslin*, decided last February Term, 4 Cow., 80; and the motion must be denied.

Motion denied.

Cited in—6 Cow., 46; 9 Cow., 229; 17 Wend., 69; 3 Barb., 608; 45 Mo., 120.

KEEP *v.* TYLER.

Change of Venue—Practice.

On obtaining a rule to change the venue, the defendant must follow this up with serving a certified copy on the plaintiff's attorney.

Till this be done, the plaintiff has a right to consider the original venue as the place of trial.

A mere notice of the rule is not sufficient.

MOTION for judgment as in case of nonsuit. The venue was laid in the County of Cortland; but, at the last February Term was changed, by rule of this court, to the County of Delaware, and notice of the rule, but not a certified copy, served on the agent of the plaintiff's attorney. The default, on which the present motion was founded, was the not trying in Delaware.

The motion was opposed on the ground that a certified copy of the rule had not been served; and *Thompson* v. *Douglass*, 2 Johns. Cas., 226, and *Smith* v. *Sharp*, 13 Johns., 466, were relied on for this.

Messrs. Sherwood and *Parker*, for the motion.

Messrs. Ross and *Gray*, contra.

**Curia.* The mere granting the mo- [*542 tion did not work a change of the venue. The practice is to follow this with the service of a certified copy of the rule. An ordinary notice seems not to be sufficient. . Till the proper notice, the plaintiff may disregard the rule, and consider the venue as remaining in Cortland.

Motion denied.

Cited in—4 Hill, 70 (*n*).

IN THE MATTER OF THE APPLICATION OF THE MAYOR, ALDERMAN AND COMMONALTY OF THE CITY OF NEW YORK, for extending Mercer Street, in the late 8th, now 9th Ward of the City.

Conveyance of Land—What Not an Implied Grant of Way.

A grant of land as abutting in the rear upon a certain street, which was merely laid down as such upon a map, but not actually opened, the land being accessible by a street in front, is not an implied grant of way in the supposed street in the rear; nor is it an implied covenant to open the street in the rear.

Citations—19 Johns., 181; 4 Mass., 590.

MR. ULSHOEFFER moved to confirm the report of the Commissioners of Estimate and Assessment.

Mr. S. Jones, contra, opposed the application, on the ground that the Commissioners had mistaken the law in estimating the value of lands taken for the improvement. They supposed that certain land belonging to the heirs of Elizabeth Depeyster, deceased, over which the contemplated improvement extended, were subject to a right of way in virtue of a conveyance in fee from the owners. The deeds of conveyance to several purchasers of lands were, in terms, bounded in front by Broadway, and in the rear on Mercer St., this latter being a space voluntarily left by the owners, which they called Mercer St., laid down as such on a map of the city, though not laid out by the corporation; and in reference to which the owners conveyed. This space is the same taken by the Corporation for Mercer St.; and the Commissioners thinking the deed contained a constructive covenant for a perpetual right of way to the alienees, refused to allow the alienors anything beyond a nominal compensation for the land. The alienees knew that Mercer St. had not been officially or otherwise opened, at the time of their purchases, but was merely laid down on the map as before mentioned.

*He said that a covenant could not [*543 be implied from the mere description, the office of which is only to define the limits and contents of the premises. Nor do the grantees acquire a right of way from necessity over the grantor's land. This can be only where the premises granted are inaccessible in any other way. Its being the private way of the grantor, gives the grantee no right. The former may shut it up when he pleases. The term "Mercer St." was mere description, and had reference to a street expected to be laid out when the proper time should arrive. It was a precaution against continuing the lots conveyed over the future street ground. With this view the map was framed.

It never could be opened as a public street but by the Corporation; and they had a right to say that no public street should be laid there.

He commented upon *Holmes* v. *Teller*, 3 Lev., 305; *Fowle* v. *Bigelow*, 10 Mass., 379; *Roberts* v. *Karr*, 1 Taunt., 495, which he said would be relied on by the counsel for the Corporation; and insisted that they were not at variance with the principles for which he contended.

He argued that, at any rate, the right of soil remained in the claimants, and they should have been paid more than a mere nominal consideration. And to this point he cited and relied upon *Cortelyou* v. *Van Brunt*, 2 Johns., 357, 363; *Jackson* v. *Hathaway*, 15 Johns., 447, and *Underwood* v. *Stuyvesant*, 19 Johns., 181.

In *Clap* v. *M'Neil*, 4 Mass., 580, he said the very point in question was decided in favor of the claimants.

Mr. Ulschoeffer, in reply, said the Corporation, by 2 R. L., 414, would take the absolute fee of Mercer St., on its being laid out; but the Commissioners thought its value nominal only, on account of the perpetual easement or right of way created by the deed. The street appeared upon the map, and the grantees doubtless purchased in reference to it, and paid a higher consideration, upon this account. The fair import of this description is a covenant to open the street without compensation. The grantor was as much holden that the lots should bound on a street in the rear, as upon Broadway in front.

544*] *He cited *Holmes* v. *Teller*, 3 Lev., 305; *Roberts* v. *Karr*, 1 Taunt., 495; *Fowle* v. *Bigelow*, 10 Mass., 375, and *Jackson* v. *Hathaway*, 15 Johns., 452, 491, 545.

At another day,

The Court said they had examined the questions presented by this case, and the authorities cited; and were satisfied that the Commissioners had proceeded upon a wrong principle; that the mere abuttal upon Mercer St. did not amount to an implied grant of way. *Underwood* v. *Stuyveysant*, 19 Johns., 181. And they adopted what was said upon a similar point, by Parsons, *Ch. J.*, in *Clap* v. *M'Neil*, 4 Mass., 590. *The Court* holding that the claimants were entitled to compensation without regard to the supposed easement, the matter was again referred to the Commissioners for review upon this principle, and the present motion denied.

Rule accordingly.

Overruled—2 Wend., 474; 23 N. Y., 66.
Cited in—1 Wend., 271; 8 Wend., 106; 11 Wend., 499; 18 Wend., 411; 6 Paige, 193, 624; 1 Edw., 470; 5 Rob., 204; 1 Sand., 342; 5 Duer, 148; 4 Allen, 210; 31 Am. Dec., 383.

EX PARTE SANDERS.

Discontinuance of Highway—Practice.

A public highway having been laid out by three judges of the C. P. on a petition to discontinue it, they discontinued only a part, and *certiorari* was brought from their decision; held, that the *certiorari* did not suspend proceedings as to that part of the road which they had not directed to be discontinued, but that the Commissioners were bound to go forward and open this part.

And a *mandamus* to compel them to do this was granted, notwithstanding the *certiorari*.

MR. H. MARKELL moved for a *mandamus* to the Commissioners of Highways of the Town of Minden, in Montgomery Co., commanding them to open and improve a road laid out by three of the judges of the Court of C. P. of that county. A *certiorari* had been brought upon the determination of the judges, which was affirmed in this court. On the petition of sundry inhabitants of Minden, to discontinue the whole road, the three judges of the C. P. had discontinued a part of it; and from their determination a *certiorari* was brought, and is now pending in this court. The object of the motion was to compel the Commissioners to open and improve the part not discontinued.

Messrs. J. W. Cady and *S. M. Hopkins*, contra, insisted that though the judges had decided upon only a part of the road, yet the **certiorari* went to the whole, and sus- [***545** pended all proceedings of the Commissioners till it should be passed upon. The 37th section of the Act to Regulate Highways, 2 R. L., 282, gives the judges a right to proceed upon petition only; and they must grant an entire discontinuance of the road when the petition prays this. Nothing was said in the petition about an alteration of the road; and when the Statute speaks of discontinuance, it means a total one. It is to correct the error of partially discontinuing, and extend the effect of the petition to the whole road, that the *certiorari* is brought. Being before the court in this form, they will not interfere by *mandamus*.

Mr Platt, in reply, denied that the judges were confined to the petition, or bound to discontinue *in toto*. The section referred to, expressly gives them a right to alter the road, which is equivalent to saying that they may partially discontinue it. But suppose they did exceed their jurisdiction, then the old road, as first laid, remains in force *quoad hoc*. It is the part only which remains untouched that we seek to open.

Curia. Clearly the *certiorari* can have no effect upon the part not embraced in the decision of the judges. As to this, the Commissioners are bound to proceed. Should the determination of the judges be reversed, *non constat* that any part of the road would then be discontinued. The necessary effect of the reversal would by no means be to discontinue the whole road; on the contrary, it might result in a confirmation of the whole.

Motion denied.

Cited in—19 Wend., 65.

---

*WOOSTER v. PERRY. [*546

Practice—Costs for Copying Certain Matter into Nisi Prius Record.

Prima facie, the plaintiff's attorney is right in copying the defendant's notice of special matter into the *N. P.* record and judgment roll, and may have this service taxed.

If it be, in truth, unnecessary, on showing this to the taxing officer, he should strike it out.

ON a verdict for the plaintiff, he had procured the costs of entering the defendant's notice of special matter, on the judgment roll and *N. P.* record, to be taxed by a commissioner, which,

Messrs. A. Loomis and *O. G. Otis*, for the defendant, moved to have stricken out of the bill. They said the notice constituted no part of the record, *Vaughan* v. *Havens*, 8 Johns. 109; and where papers are unnecessarily copied into a record, they will not be allowed in taxation. *Jackson* v. *Mather*, 2 Cow., 584. The notice was not necessary in the record, even at *Nisi Prius*. If denied, it must be proved by affidavit or orally.

Mr. M. Hoffman, contra, said the notice was, in fact, engrossed upon the *N. P.* record and judgment roll, with the suggestion that it had been given with the general issue. Though not technically a plea, and therefore not of record without a proper suggestion, yet it often is, and always may be, material as a part of the record in determining the admissibility of evidence, and on bill of exceptions, &c. Besides, the counsel who try the cause rarely serve the papers, and cannot prove the notice. If in the *N. P.* record, it should also be in the judgment roll.

Curia. *Prima facie*, it is proper to make the notice of special matter a part of the record. It is true, that under certain circumstances, this might be altogether useless—in which case, it should be stricken out on taxation. But nothing of this was shown to the taxing officer or to us; and the motion must be denied.

Motion denied.

Cited in—3 Wend., 312.

547*] *VAN ALSTYNE *v.* WIMPLE.

Submission to Arbitration—Award of Costs—Taxation.

A cause was submitted by the parties to arbitrators, who awarded costs of suit, to be taxed. These were taxed *ex parte* by a commissioner. On motion for retaxation, held, that the cause being out of court, they had no further control over the costs upon summary application.

Held, also, that the taxation would not be conclusive in an action on the bond or award.

THIS cause had been commenced in this court, but was, pursuant to agreement of the parties, submitted to arbitrators by a general submission of all matters in difference; and the arbitrators had (*inter alia*) awarded that Wimple should pay to Van Alstyne the costs of this suit, to be taxed. Van Alstyne had procured them to be taxed by a commissioner *ex parte*, and without notice to Wimple.

Mr. G. C. Bronson moved for a retaxation.

Mr. J. A. Spencer, contra, opposed this, on the ground that the cause was out of court by the submission and award.

Mr. Bronson, in reply, admitted this to be so, but it did not follow that the court would deny a retaxation. They will not do this, as between attorney and client, though long after a cause is ended; because the taxation would be conclusive between them. So here the taxation will be final and not inquirable into in an action on the award. The items of the bill are never inquirable into at the circuit. The award is good as to the costs. Though the arbitrators cannot, in general, refer the amount of a demand to a third person for liquidation, yet a bill of costs is an exception.

Curia. By the submission of these parties without a rule, the cause is out of court, and there is no provision that it should be made a rule. Without saying whether the taxation can have any effect, it is clearly not such an official one as will shut out all inquiry at the circuit, in an action upon the bond or award. The submission deprives us of summary jurisdiction over the costs. The right of taxation, as between attorney and client, stands upon a different ground, viz.: the power of the court over their own officers. The motion must be denied.

Motion denied.

---

*EX PARTE ROOT. [*548

Motion for Mandamus *Denied—Costs—*Cap. ad Resp. *Set Aside—Lapse of more than One Term between Test and Return, Ground for.*

Where on motion for a *mandamus*, upon notice, the case is clear against the relator, the court will deny it with costs.

Where more than a term intervened between the test and return of a *capias ad respondendum*, held, that it was void.

THE Court of C. P. of Erie Co. had, on motion, set aside a *capias ad respondendum*, at the suit of Root against M. K. St. John, administratrix, &c., on the ground that more than one term intervened between the test and return; and now, on an affidavit of this fact, and notice of the motion served on the attorneys of Mrs. St. John in the court below,

A motion was made for a *mandamus* to compel the judges of that court to vacate the rule, which this court were clear should be denied; and then the question was raised whether the denial should be followed with costs.

Mr. J. Root, for the motion.

Messrs. White and *Bennet*, contra.

Curia. The general practice, on denying motions of this kind, has been not to give costs, especially where the motion is merely *ex parte*. But where notice of the motion is given to the adverse party, which he opposes rightfully, as in this instance, and the law is plain against the relator, we see no reason why costs should not follow the denial. Such is the present case. The C. P. decided according to a known and well settled rule of practice.

Motion denied, with costs.

Cited in—8 Abb. Pr., 291.

REEDER, Assignee of H. SEELY, an Insolvent Debtor, *v.* B. SEELY.

Suit en Autre Droit—*Discontinuance—Costs.*

One who sues *en autre droit*, in good faith, though without proper grounds, may discontinue without costs.

E. g., the assignee of an insolvent debtor.

MR. ASGILL GIBBS moved for judgment as in case of nonsuit.

Mr. W. M. Oliver, contra, read affidavits showing that at the time of H. Seely's discharge, the defendant was and still is insolv-
549*] ent, *and utterly unable to pay the demand sought to be recovered by this action, though not actually discharged under the Insolvent Act, which was unknown to the plaintiff when this suit was commenced; and moved for leave to discontinue without costs.

Mr. Gibbs, in reply, said that the plaintiff should not be allowed to do this, after the defendant had appeared.

Curia. The plaintiff sues *en autre droit;* and for the purposes of this motion stands on the same footing as an executor, who may discontinue without costs.(a) The motion must be granted.

Motion granted.

Cited in—9 How. Pr., 344; 5 Abb. Pr., 230; 1 Sheld., 428.

(a) *Vide* Phœnix, Admr. v. Hill, 3 Johns., 249.

HENDERSON

v.

DAVID BALLANTINE AND ALEXANDER JOHNSON.

Variance between Court and Writ, as to Christian Name of Defendant—Default, Set Aside.

Default against the defendant, for want of a plea set aside, for variance between the writ and count in the Christian name of one of the defendants, the writ being Alexander and the count Andrew.

IN replevin, the writ was against the defendants by their true names of David and Alexander; their attorney gave notice of retainer to the plaintiff's attorney, but had not otherwise taken any steps in the cause, and no appearance was entered. The count filed, and the copy served on the defendants' attorneys, were in the name of Andrew instead of Alexander Johnson, as one of the defendants; upon which the plaintiff's attorney took judgment by default.

A motion was now made to set the default aside as irregular, for this variance.

Mr. S. R. Hobbie, for the motion, cited Dunl. Pr., 236, 291, 400, 436; 1 Chit. Pl., 241, 249, 439; 12 Johns., 430; 1 Bos. & P., 105; 1 Dunl. Pr., 134, 163, 331; 2 *Id.*, 876, 882; 1 R. L., 92, 324; 1 Cow., 210; 6 Johns., 328; 3 Cai., 96.

Mr. S. Sherwood, contra.

Curia. The motion must be granted for the variance between the writ and count.

Motion granted.

Cited in—7 How. Pr., 26.

550*] *JACKSON, ex dem. CULVER,

v.

BROWN.

Amendment of Venire.

A *venire* for the circuit amended, by adding a seal, and making out and filing a sheriff's return thereto, *nunc pro tunc*.

AT the last Tompkins Circuit, the plaintiff was nonsuited, the defendant neither appearing at the trial, nor confessing lease, entry and ouster. After the circuit, the defendant discovered that the plaintiff's attorney had, by mistake, gone to trial upon a *venire* without any seal; and that the sheriff had omitted to make a return upon it; and for these causes,

Mr. C. P. Kirkland moved to set aside the nonsuit, and all subsequent proceedings, for irregularity. He relied mainly on *People* v. *M'Kay*, 18 Johns., 212.

Mr. W. M. Oliver, contra, moved to amend, by affixing a seal to the *venire*, and causing the sheriff to make out a return *nunc pro tunc*.

Curia. Take your motion to amend in both particulars, on payment of costs.

Rule accordingly.

Cited in—1 Wend., 17; 3 Barb., 18; 6 Barb., 313; 2 Abb. Pr., 225; 4 E. D. S., 374; 4 Daly, 522; 35 Mo., 196; 56 Ind., 224; 49 Am. Dec., 744 (3 Texas, 261).

CHAMBERLIN, Admr.,

v.

SPENCER AND SPENCER.

Action by Administrator—Costs.

Where an administrator goes for money had and received to his use after the letters of administration granted, he may sue in his own name; and if he recover less than $50, must pay costs to the defendant, which may be set off against the damages.

Citations—5 T. R., 234-5; 6 Mod., 91, 181; 1 Salk., 207, 314; 4 Cow., 87.

ASSUMPSIT for money had and received by the defendants to the use of the plaintiff, after the death of his intestate, and after the plaintiff had taken out letters of administration. The plaintiff sued as administrator for a trover and conversion of the goods of his intestate, recovered judgment, and retained the defendants as attorneys, to bring debt on that judgment. They did so, obtained a second judgment, and collected the money, for the balance of which this action was brought in the name of the plaintiff as administrator, who recovered a verdict at the circuit for $26.63.

Mr. J. A. Spencer, for the defendant, moved to set off these damages against the defendants' costs; and read an affidavit, *that the [*551 defendants had procured the costs to be regularly taxed, and had offered the plaintiff's attorney to set them off, which he declined. He cited 1 R. L., 343, sec. 2; 12 Johns., 289; 2 *Id.*, 377; 4 *Id.*, 190; Bac. Abr., Costs, E, 3; 3 Burr., 1584; 16 Johns., 148; 6 Mod., 181-191; 17 Johns., 268; 2 *Id.*, 377; Hullock's L. C., 199, and the cases there cited; 6 Mod., 92; S. C., 11 *Id.*, 174; *Id.*, 135; Tidd Pr., 893; 8 Johns., 379; 2 Johns. Cas., 209; Laws N. Y., sess. 47; ch. 228, secs. 1, 33; 4 T. R., 280; 5 *Id.*, 234; 7 *Id.*, 354.

Mr. Edward Allen, contra, cited Tidd Pr., 893, 894; *Id.*, 897; 1 Salk., 207; 11 Johns., 403.

Curia. The plaintiff might have sued for the money in his own name, and is, therefore, liable for costs. *Goldthwayte* v. *Petrie*, 5 T. R., 234-5, and *Jenkins* v. *Plombe*, 6 Mod., 91, *Id.*,

181; S. C., 1 Salk., 207, are in point. These cases were fully considered and adopted in *Ketchum* v. *Ketchum*, 4 Cow., 87. The only case against them is *Eaves* v. *Mocato*, 1 Salk., 314; but this has never been acted upon; and there is reason to believe, from the mention of it in *Jenkins* v. *Plume*, *Id.*, 207, that it was wrongly reported; being an action on an *insimul computassent;* and not, as mentioned in the report, for money had and received. The motion must be granted.

Motion granted.

Cited in—1 Lans., 306.

MORSE, Administrator, v. M'COY.

Executor—When not Liable for Costs for not Going to Trial.

An executor is not liable to pay costs for not going to trial, if he show due diligence to be prepared for trial, but fail without his fault: as where he has sought to subpœna a material witness, but failed by reason of his keeping out of the way.

Other cases in which an executor shall pay, or be excused from costs.

Citations—4 Johns., 190; 4 Burr., 1584, 1929; 16 Johns., 148; 3 Burr., 1584; 3 Johns., 249; Barnes, 133; 1 Salk., 314, 207, 208; 4 Cow., 87; Tidd., 893; 2 Arch., 131; Toller, 440; 2 Dunl., 723; 2 Johns., 480.

MR. J. L. VIELE moved for judgment as in case of nonsuit, for not proceeding to trial at the last Saratoga Circuit, pursuant to notice.

Mr. G. W. Kirkland, contra, read an affidavit showing, as an excuse, that the plaintiff had **552***] endeavored to subpœna and *procure the attendance of a material witness on his part, but that the witnes industriously kept out of the way of the subpœna—had not attended the circuit; and that, in consequence of this, the plaintiff could not be ready to try.

Curia. An executor or administrator, plaintiff, is liable for costs on *non pros.* *Rudd* v. *Long*, 4 Johns., 190; *Hawes, Executrix*, v. *Saunders*, 4 Burr., 1584; so on judgment as in case of nonsuit. *Brown, Executor*, v. *Lambert*, 16 Johns., 148. These were cases of judgment unaccompanied with any excuse. The first is put on the ground of neglect, expressly, which, indeed, a mere *non pros.* implies. In the last a judgment was perfected, when, it seems, the plaintiff came with an excuse, which it was held too late to receive. It is also well settled, as a general rule, that an executor or administrator must pay costs for not going to trial pursuant to notice. *Hawes, Executrix* v. *Saunders*, 3 Burr., 1584. In all these cases, he is, *prima facie*, liable for costs. Neglect will be presumed, until he show the contrary. But the total absence of neglect certainly forms an exception to this rule. Where the executor or administrator shows this to the court, they will allow him to discontinue without costs; *Phœnix Admr.*, v. *Hill*, 3 Johns., 249; which, for most purposes, is the same as a *non pros.*, or judgment in case of nonsuit. And the court will not presume, on a motion to discontinue, that he knowingly brought a wrong action. (*Ib.*) It was also held in *Ogle* v. *Moffat*, Barnes, 133, that he shall be exempt from paying costs for not going to trial according to notice, where his inability to proceed arises without his own wilful default. He is not liable for costs on a nonsuit at the trial. *Eaves* v. *Mocato*, 1 Salk., 314; S. C. *Id.*, 207, cited *Jenkins* v. *Plume*, *Id.*, 208, per Holt, *Ch. J.; Ketchum* v. *Ketchum*, 4 Cow., 87. The proposition laid down in *Ogle* v. *Moffat*, was afterwards adopted by Yates, *J.*, and Ld. Mansfield, in *Bennet* v. *Coker*, 4 Burr., 1929, and carried into the English books of practice (Tidd, 893, 2 Archb., 131, Toller, 440), and our own (2 Dunl., 723).

*The authorities all go on the ques- [***553** tion of laches. If the executor or administrator proceed in good faith, he may get rid of his action without costs, by moving to discontinue, which is the form in which his fairness is to be tested; or he may go on to trial, where though he be nonsuit, or a verdict pass against him, he is not subject to costs. The motion for judgment as in case of nonsuit, is the only opportunity afforded him for showing to the court that the omission to try was not his fault. The plaintiff has fully excused himself in this case, and is neither bound to stipulate, *Marseles* v. *Clapper*, 2 Johns., 480, nor pay costs. But, *prima facie*, he was bound to do both. The defendant was, therefore, right in coming here, and the motion must be denied, without costs on either side.

Rule accordingly.

Cited in—5 Cow., 14; 1 Wend., 34; 1 Paige, 83; 22 Hun, 463; 2 Barb., 376; 2 Leg. Obs., 261.

MUMFORD v. ARMSTRONG.

Arrest on Ca. Sa.—*Voluntary Escape—Second Arrest—Sheriff can Receive only Money or its Equivalent, on* Ca. Sa.

One who escapes from a *ca. sa.* though with the consent of the sheriff, may be again arrested on a second *ca. sa.*

The sheriff can receive nothing in satisfaction of a *ca. sa.* but money or its equivalent.

If he discharge the party arrested, on receiving his draft upon a third person, this is a voluntary escape.

Citation—1 Cow., 46.

JUDGMENT of nonsuit having been obtained against the plaintiff, the defendant's attorney issued a *ca. sa.* for the costs, to the Sheriff of Oneida, who arrested the plaintiff, received his draft on E. B. for the money, which he was directed by an indorsement on the *ca. sa.* to receive, and discharged the plaintiff; whereupon the defendant's attorney issued another *ca. sa.* upon which the plaintiff was again arrested.

A motion being made to set this last execution aside, the following authorities were cited: *Bank of Orange* v. *Wakeman*, 1 Cow., 46, 47, and *note a*, at the end of that case; Vin. Abr., Execution, X, *a*, pl. 10; 1 Sel. Pr., 536; 2 Dunl. Pr., 832, 833.

Mr. J. Bradish, for the motion.

Mr. L. F. Stevens, contra.

Curia. In the *Bank of Orange* v. *Wakeman*, 1 Cow., 46, we held that the sheriff's taking a promissory note for the money upon a *fi. fa.* in his hands would not operate as payment, even though he returned the execution satis-

554*] fied. *The draft, in this instance, not being a payment, the act of permitting the defendant to go at large was a voluntary escape, and the plaintiff clearly had a right to issue another *ca. sa.* and proceed to the second arrest.(*a*) The sheriff could receive nothing in payment but money, or its equivalent.

Motion denied.

Cited in—6 Cow., 468; 1 Wend., 368; 19 Wend., 191; 20 Wend., 605; 18 Hun, 265; 9 Barb., 22; 2 How. Pr., 258; 2 Abb. Pr., 186; 4 E. D. S., 230.

(*a*) See 1 R. L., 426, sec. 24; 8 Johns., 361.

CHAPIN *v.* DE GROFF ET AL.

Change of Venue.

The venue will not be changed, if the motion be made after issue joined, provided it appear that the plaintiff may lose a trial by the delay.

Citation—8 Johns., 447.

MR. A. C. PAIGE moved to change the venue in this cause from the County of Ontario to the County of Schenectady, on the usual affidavit.

Mr. J. C. Spencer, contra, read an affidavit showing that issue was joined before the last May Term, viz.: Apr. 27 preceding; that May 25, the defendant's attorney procured an order to stay all proceedings on the part of the plaintiff till the last day of the present term, which was founded on the affidavit to change the venue. This order was served on the plaintiff's attorney on the 2d day of June last; previous to which he had forwarded to the defendants' attorney a notice of trial for the Ontario Circuit, to be held on the 3d Monday of June. He contended that the application was too late; and cited *Delevan* v. *Baldwin*, 3 Cai., 194, and *Kent* v. *Dodge*, 3 Johns., 447.

Curia. This motion might have been made at May Term; instead of which the defendant lies by, without excuse, till May 25. He then obtains an order to stay proceedings, which carries the plaintiff over the Ontario Circuit, and produces the loss of a trial. If the defendant will wait till after issue joined, before he moves to change the venue, it behooves him to see that the plaintiff cannot lose a circuit by the delay. *Kent* v. *Dodge*, 8 Johns., 447.

Motion denied.

Cited in—11 Wend, 186; 22 Wend., 617; 4 Hill, 63 (*n.*); 12 Hun, 85; 4 How. Pr., 89.

555*] *TURNER *v.* DEXTER.

Amendment to Plea.

On a motion to amend, the court inquire no farther into the merits of the amendment, than to see that it is not frivolous.

And they allowed a defendant to amend by adding a notice of special matter, though it was doubtful whether it was a defense at law, or belonged exclusively to equity.

MOTION for leave to add to the plea of *non est factum*, a notice of special matter, to be given in evidence as a defense, which was set forth at large in the defendant's affidavit. The action was covenant. The defendant's attorney omitted to plead, or give notice of the special matter, supposing this unnecessary, till a few days before the circuit at which the cause was noticed for trial, when counsel advised to give the notice, but the plaintiff's attorney refused to receive it.

Mr. O. G. Otis, for the motion.

Mr. I. S. Talmage, contra.

The argument against the application went mainly on the ground that the matter set forth in the notice was not a defense. But,

Per Curiam. The matter set forth in the notice proposed to be given is not frivolous; though there is doubt, perhaps, whether the defendant can avail himself of it at law, and must not go to his bail in equity. But on applications to amend, we will not inquire into the merits of the amendment, further than to see that it is not plainly frivolous.

Motion granted on terms.

Cited in—5 Rob., 628.

---

*THE COLUMBIAN MANUFACTURING COMPANY [*556

v.

VANDERPOEL.

Property of Manufacturing Corporations Subject to Taxation.

The real and personal estate of manufacturing companies are by the Act for the Assessment and Collection of Taxes, passed Apr. 23, 1823, sess. 46, ch. 262, sec. 14, rendered subject to taxation; and that Act virtually repeals the Act for the Encouragement of Manufactures Within this State, passed Feb. 28, 1817, sess. 40, ch. 64.

Citations—Act, Feb. 28, 1817; Act, April 23, 1823.

TRESPASS against the defendant, for taking certain bales of cotton sheeting, manufactured and owned by the plaintiffs, from their possession in the town of Stuyvesant, County of Columbia. The defendant was collector of that town, and had a tax list of the town for A. D. 1823, and a warrant in the usual form to collect the taxes. This list, among others, included a tax of $149 against the plaintiffs, assessed upon their property in the Town of Stuyvesant, on an estimation as follows:

	Non-residents.	No. of Acres.	Quality of land.	Real estate.	Personal.	Total of.	Tax.
Columbiaville Manufacturing Company:		20	2d	30,000	20,000	50,000	$149

The plaintiffs refused to pay the tax, on the ground that their property was exempted from taxation. To collect the tax by virtue of his warrant, the defendant levied on and sold the above bales of cotton.

Messrs. C. Bushnell and *A. Spencer*, for the plaintiffs, cited Laws N. Y., sess. 40, ch. 64; *Id.*, sess. 46, ch. 262, sec. 4; Journals of the Assembly, sess. 47, A. D. 1824, p. 187, Rep. Atty-Gen.; *Brown* v. *Compton*, 8 T. R., 430, 431, 433; *Jackson* v. *Smith*, 5 Johns., 115; *Van Slyck* v. *Taylor*, 9 *Id*, 146; *Suydam* v. *Keys*,

13 *Id.*, 444; *Cable* v. *Cooper*, 15 *Id.*, 152, 156, 157, and *Bigelow* v. *Stearns*, 19 *Id.*, 39.

Messrs. J. and *A. Vanderpool*, for the defendant, cited Laws N. Y., sess. 46, ch. 262, secs. 3, 4, 14–16, 69; and *People* v. *Utica Ins. Co.*, 15 Johns., 380.

Curia, per SUTHERLAND, *J.* The question in this case is, whether the Act of Feb. 28, 1817, exempting the buildings, machinery and the manufactured articles in the hands of the manufacturer of every cotton, woolen or linen **557***] manufactory *within this State, is repealed by the Act for the Assessment and Collection of Taxes, passed Apr. 23, 1823.

The latter Act was intended as a revision of all the laws upon the subject of taxation; and it was obviously the intention of the Legislature to embrace in it, either in terms, or by reference, all the subsisting legal provisions upon that subject.

The 3d section of the Act contains an enumeration of certain species of property, belonging to certain classes and individuals, which it declares shall be exempt from taxation. Neither the real, nor personal property of manufacturing societies is mentioned in that section.

The 14th section provides that all incorporated companies receiving a regular income, &c., shall be considered persons within the meaning of the Act, and assessments shall be made and taxes imposed and levied upon them, and collected in the same manner as upon individuals; and that the cashiers of banks, secretaries of insurances companies, and secretaries or treasurers of all manufacturing companies shall make and deliver to the assessors, &c., a list containing the real estate occupied by such company, if any; and the amount of capital actually paid in (except, &c.), and the assessors shall insert in their assessment roll, opposite to the name of such company, the amount of such real and personal property.

The next section makes it the duty of the cashier, treasurer or secretary, as the case may be, to pay the amount of the tax imposed upon such company.

The language of the 14th section is as broad and comprehensive as it is capable of being made; and in terms renders the real and personal estate of all manufacturing companies subject to taxation. Does it not then, in relation to the Act of Feb. 28, 1817, fall within the general principle that *leges posteriores, priores contrarias abrogant?* The one declares that all the buildings, machinery, &c., of every cotton, woolen and linen manufactory, shall be exempted from taxation; the other that the assessments shall be made and taxes imposed, levied and collected upon all incorporated companies, &c., as upon individuals; that the sec- **558***] retaries *or treasurers of all manufacturing companies shall deliver a list of the real estate occupied by such company, and the amount of capital actually paid in, to the assessors, who shall insert it in their assessment, roll, &c.; and that the secretary or treasurer shall pay the tax imposed upon such company. Two statutes more directly repugnant to each other, could not well be penned; and though the latter Statute is not couched in negative terms, yet, it appears to me, necessarily to imply a negative, and virtually to repeal the former.

But it is supposed by the counsel for the plaintiffs, that the 4th section of the Act of 1823, expressly recognizes the existence of the Act of 1817, and saves and perpetuates it.

This section provides that all real and personal estate of whatsoever description, household furniture, except as above exempted, goods, chattels, &c., bank stock, and all other kinds of stock, and all such property, real and personal, as is not exempted by some law of the U. S., or of this State, or by the Constitution of this State, shall be subject to taxation under the meaning of this Act.

The argument is, that this exemption has nothing to operate upon, unless it refers to the Act of 1817; that it cannot relate to laws subsequently to be passed, because the Legislature must have known that any subsequent law exempting property from taxation, would be valid and effectual without it. In that aspect, therefore, it was entirely useless. It certainly was so; but not more useless or unavailing than the accompanying provision in relation to property exempt by the laws of the U. S., or the Constitution of this State. The Legislature must equally have known, that however general and absolute the terms of their law might be, it could not affect property which either a law of the U. S., passed under the authority conferred upon Congress by the Constitution, or the Constitution of this State had exempted, or should exempt from taxation. The Constitution of this State, and the laws passed by Congress, under the authority conferred by the Constitution of the U. S., are paramount, and need no saving clause to secure their operation and effect. These considerations show that the provisions in the 4th section, relied on by the plaintiffs, were probably *inserted as matter of form, or from [***559** abundant caution, and not from a mature consideration of their necessity and effect.

At all events, if the subsequent provisions of the Act are so clearly contrary to the Act of 1817, that the repugnancy could not have escaped the attention of the Legislature—so contrary as to show that they must have known the latter virtually repealed the former, it would be doing violence to the principles of sound construction applicable to statutes, to sustain a law, which the Legislature had thus clearly manifested their intention to repeal, upon the strength of so questionable a clause as that relied upon.

I am, therefore, of opinion that the property of the plaintiffs was liable to taxation, and that they have no cause of action against the defendant.

Judgment for the defendant.

Cited in—4 Hun, 649; 67 Barb., 264; 1 Abb. Pr., 22; 5 Rob., 629; 4 E. D. S., 696; 2 Daly, 408; 2 Paine, 219.

BURT *v.* STERNBURGH.

Judgment of Court of Concurrent Jurisdiction—Conclusive Evidence of What, in Subsequent Suit, as to Same Matter between Same Parties in another Court.

The judgment of a court of current jurisdiction directly upon the point is as a plea, a bar: or as evidence conclusive between the same parties upon the same matter, directly in question in another court.

Thus, where B. brought trespass *quare clausum fregit* in May, 1816, laying the trespass with a *continuendo* between Nov. 1, 1814, and Nov. 24, 1815, and recovered; and then brought trespass against the same defendant for a subsequent injury to the premises in question in the former suit; held, that the record in the former suit, followed by parol evidence that the premises in question were the same in both, was conclusive evidence of the plaintiff's title in the second action; that it operated against the defendant by way of estoppel, whether it was pleaded, or given in evidence in the second suit.

But held, also, that the defendant might, in the second suit, have shown title in himself by alienation, or adverse possession, acquired since the time in question in the former suit.

Cit i s—3 Cow., 120; 11 State Trials, 261; 3 Burr., 1353; 2 Barn. & Ald., 662; 3 East, 353.

TRESPASS *quare clausum fregit*, tried at the Schoharie Circuit, Sept. 17, 1823, before Duer, Circuit Judge.

The action was commenced Dec. 2, 1816. At the trial, the plaintiff proved that the defendant had cut timber on land, which the plaintiff insisted was lot 8, in the subdivision of lot 133, in the old Schoharie patent; that the cutting was west of the east line of lot 8, as thus claimed; that the defendant resided on and possessed a farm adjoining this line; that the heavy timber cut by him was principally pine, and was cut in the summer or fall of 1816; and certain underbrush, before that time. That the defendant claimed the *locus in quo* as his **560***] own, and had, about five *years before the trial, cleared it off and fenced it, claiming it as part of his farm.

The plaintiff then offered in evidence an exemplification of a record of a judgment in the Supreme Court, in an action of trespass *quare clausum fregit* between the same parties, Burt being plaintiff and Sternburgh defendant, in which a verdict was rendered for the plaintiff for $23 damages and $91.92 costs, the trespass being laid with a *continuendo*, between Nov. 1, 1814, and Nov. 24, 1815, and the pleadings the same as in this cause, in all things, except as to the time of committing the trespass. It appeared from that record that the suit was commenced as of May Term, 1816, and tried at the Schoharie Circuit, in Nov., 1818, before His Honor, *Mr. Justice* Platt. The plaintiff also offered to prove that the injury for which the recovery was had in that case was a trespass upon the *locus in quo* in this suit, and that on a former trial, the defendant attempted to defend himself under a title derived from George W. Featherstonhaugh. The plaintiff insisted that this record and proof were conclusive evidence of the plaintiff's title in the cause then on trial. The defendant's counsel objected that they were not conclusive, but the judge decided that they were. The exemplification was then read in evidence, and John Adams, Esq., was sworn as a witness for the plaintiff, and testified that the injury for which the former recovery was had, was a trespass committed upon the same land now in controversy; that on the former trial, the defendant attempted to defend himself under a title derived from George W. Featherstonhaugh, and claimed the premises as lying in Weyfield and Clifford's patent; and that the plaintiff claimed them as lying in the old Schoharie patent; and that it was conceded on that trial, in which the witness officiated as counsel, that in case the premises were in the old Schoharie patent, then the plaintiff was entitled to recover; but in case they were in Weyfield and Clifford's patent, then the defendant was entitled to a verdict.

Peter Mann was then called, and testified that the trespass in the former suit was upon the same spot of ground as the one proved in this cause.

*The defendant then objected that [***561** the plaintiff had not shown that he had the possession of the *locus in quo* when the trespass was committed. This objection was also overruled by the judge.

The defendant then offered to prove that the *locus in quo* was not within the old Schoharie patent, but was within a patent granted to Weyfield and Clifford, and that the defendant had the title to the *locus in quo*, at the time when the trespass complained of in this suit was alleged to have been committed. This evidence was also objected to by the plaintiff's counsel, and overruled by the judge; and the jury, under his charge, gave a verdict for the plaintiff for $56 damages and 6 cents costs.

Mr. D. Cady, for the defendant, now moved for a new trial. He relied mainly on what was said by Ld. Ellenborough, in *Outram* v. *Morewood*, 3 East, 357, and contended that the record of the former cause, and the evidence under it, could not be deemed conclusive of both the plaintiff's title and possession, after the period embraced by the *continuendo*. The point decided, related to the title for that period of time only. Besides, on the first trial, the defendant claimed title under Featherstonhaugh. In the present, he sets up a different one. The record is conclusive only as to the very point tried; and *Gardner* v. *Buckbee*, 3 Cow., 120, which will be relied upon, decides no more than this.

Messrs. H. Hamilton and *A. Spencer*, for the plaintiff, subscribed to the doctrine of Ld. Ellenborough, in *Outram* v. *Morewood*, and relied upon it as an authority for the plaintiff. His Lordship undoubtedly did, in that case, set up a distinction between the effect of a former recovery when pleaded, and when offered in evidence, making it, in the former case, conclusive as an estoppel; in the latter not so. But *Ld. Ch. J.* De Grey, in the *Duchess of Kingston's* case, 11 St. Tr., 262, held it conclusive either way; and this court recognized his doctrine in *Gardner* v. *Buckbee*, cited for the defendant. All the defendant could show, as to title, was, that he had acquired a new one since the former trial.

*The counsel also cited *Gelston* v. [***562** *Hoyt*, 3 Wh., 246; Peak. Ev., 34; 1 Phil. Ev., 129, 134, and 1 Chit. Pl., 492, 494.

Curia. Per SUTHERLAND, *J.* In *Gardner* v. *Buckbee*, 3 Cow., 120, we adopted the language of *Ch. J.* De Grey, in the case of *The Duchess of Kingston*, 11 St. Tr., 261, that the judgment of a court of concurrent jurisdiction, directly upon the point, is as a plea, a bar, or as evidence conclusive between the same parties, upon the same matter, directly in question in another court. In that case, the former judgment was not pleaded, but was given in evidence under the general issue;

and the counsel for the defendant there contended that the later cases had overruled the opinions of Ld. Mansfield, in *Bird* v. *Randall*, 3 Burr., 1353, and of *Ch. J.* De Grey, in the case of *The Duchess of Kingston*, that a former judgment is as conclusive in its operation when given in evidence as though it were pleaded. The case of *Vooght* v. *Winch*, 2 Barnw. & Ald., 662, was relied upon. But we considered those opinions too well supported, both by principle and authority to admit of discussion.

It is well remarked by Ld. Ellenborough, in *Outram* v. *Morewood*, 3 East, 353, that the operation and effect of a former recovery, if it operate at all, as a conclusive bar, must be by way of estoppel; that it is not the recovery, but the matter alleged by the party, and upon which the recovery proceeds, which creates the estoppel. The recovery of itself, he continues, in an action of trespass, is only a bar to the future recovery of damages for the same injury. But the estoppel precludes parties and privies from contending to the contrary of that point or matter of fact, which, having once been distinctly put in issue by them, or by those to whom they are privy in estate or law, has been on such issue joined, solemnly found against them. In that case, the question which the defendant wished to contest was, whether certain coal mines, in relation to which the action was brought, were, at the time of making a certain conveyance by Sir John Zouch, part and parcel of the coal mines included in that conveyance. The plaintiff showed, by his replication, that the precise **563***] point *had been raised between the same parties in a former action, and decided in his favor; and the court held that the defendant was estopped from again raising that question; that the point was conclusively settled between the parties by the verdict.

In this case, it was shown that the former trial was between the same parties for a trespass committed by the defendant, upon the same premises for a trespass upon which this action was brought; that the defendant then attempted to defend himself, under a title from George W. Featherstonhaugh, and contended and endeavored to prove that the *locus in quo* was in a patent granted to Weyfield and Clifford, and not in the Schoharie patent, as was contended by the plaintiff; and it was admitted on the former trial that if the premises were in the Schoharie patent, the plaintiff was entitled to recover; if in the Weyfield and Clifford patent, that the defendant was entitled to a verdict. The former verdict must then have turned on that point; and it was in favor of the plaintiff. Yet that was the precise question which the defendant sought again to agitate in this case. He offered to prove that the *locus in quo* was in the Weyfield and Clifford patent, and that he had title to it when the trespass was alleged to have been committed. The decision of the judge, that the former recovery, and the evidence offered by the plaintiff, were conclusive evidence of the plaintiff's title, must be understood as having been made after the defendant had disclosed the defense and title on which he relied; and as determining nothing more than that, in relation to that title, founded on the allegation that the premises were in the Weyfield and Clifford patent, the recovery and evidence were conclusive. The offer on the part of the defendant, was nothing more than to show that the premises were not in the Schoharie, but in the Weyfield and Clifford patent. If this is the fair construction of the case, of which I have no doubt, I think the decision of the judge was correct. The defendant was estopped from again opening that question.

But he certainly was not concluded by the former verdict from showing title in himself, acquired subsequently to that trial, or indeed any other title than one depending on the *point settled in the former cause. He [***564** might have shown that the plaintiff's title had been extinguished, either by alienation or a subsequent adverse possession. But I repeat, I understand his offer was simply to show that the premises were not in the Schoharie patent, but in the patent of Weyfield and Clifford, and that, therefore, the plaintiff had no title. That was impugning the verity of the former verdict which he had no right to do. This case can not be distinguished in principle, from *Gardner* v. *Buckbee* and *Outram* v. *Morewood*.

Motion for a new trial denied.

Cited in—6 Cow., 692; 8 Wend., 45; 18 Wend., 122; 2 Hill, 480; 6 Hill, 125; 3 Den., 361; 3 N. Y., 523; 4 N. Y., 75; 6 N. Y., 143; 68 N. Y., 449; 79 N. Y., 398; 2 Keyes, 631; 1 Abb. App. Dec., 181; 3 Barb., 173; 13 Barb., 161; 36 Barb., 94; 42 Barb., 663; 11 Abb. Pr., 16; 5 Sand., 142; 6 Bos., 547; 3 Daly, 46; 18 How. U. S., 302; 24 How. U. S., 579; 2 Wall., 42; 7 Wall., 96; 1 Wood. & M., 182; 50 Ind., 420; 22 Am. Dec., 619.

JEWELL ET AL. *v.* SCHROEPPEL.

*Contract under Seal for Performance of Certain Work—Work Done in Different Manner from that Provided in Contract—*Assumpsit *Lies for Work and Labor—Evidence, of Promise to Pay for Labor—Former Action of Covenant by Employer and Recovery of Damages, no Defense.*

If there be a special agreement under seal, to do work and it be done, but not pursuant to the agreement either in point of time, or in any other respect, the party who did the work may recover upon the common count in *assumpsit* for work and labor.

If, when the time of performance arrives in such case, the party goes on, with the knowledge and assent of his employers, to complete the work subsequently, this is evidence of a promise to pay for the work. So if he do not object.

And it is no objection to his bringing *assumpsit*, that his employer had previously sued him in covenant for not performing in time, and recovered damages.

The workman cannot maintain covenant, unless he perform the work strictly within the time.

Where the terms of a special agreement are performed, a duty is raised for which a general *indebitatus assumpsit* will lie; but as long as the special contract remains unrescinded or unperformed the party cannot recover under the common counts.

Citations—3 T. R., 590, 592, *n. b*; 8 Johns., 392; 15 Johns., 204; 9 Johns., 115; Bull. *N. P.*, 139; 2 Phil. Ev., 83, *n.*; 8 Mass., 287; 3 Johns. Ch., 23.

ASSUMPSIT, tried at the Oneida Circuit, July, 1823, before Williams, Circuit Judge.

The declaration set forth a special agreement, and added the common count for work, labor and materials found.

At the trial, a sealed contract was given in evidence, dated Sept. 6, 1818, between the plaintiffs and defendant, by which the former covenanted with the latter to complete a certain mill within 10 months, and a canal and mill-dam within 13 months from that date; and the latter covenanted with the former that, on the work being completed within these times, he would pay them a certain sum, &c.

It was further in evidence, that though the plaintiffs commenced the respective parts of the work before the respective times for their completion mentioned in the specialty, the canal and dam were not completed within the 13 months; but the plaintiffs, with the defendant's knowledge and approbation, prosecuted and completed them afterwards.

565*] *It also appeared that the defendant had prosecuted the plaintiffs in a former suit, for not fulfilling their covenants contained in the specialty, and recovered a judgment for damages.

The jury having found for the plaintiffs $349.54.

Mr. J. Platt, for the defendant, now moved for a new trial; and he took several objections, among which were: 1. That the proof at the trial did not support the special agreement stated in the declaration. 2. That if proved, there was no consideration to support it. 3. That, at most, the evidence only made out an agreement to enlarge the time of performing the sealed contract, and the remedy should have been covenant. 4. That the former recovery was a bar. He cited 1 Chit. Pl., 94; *Clark* v. *Smith*, 14 Johns., 326; *Champlin* v. *Butler*, 18 *Id.*, 169; *Robertson* v. *Lynch*, *Id.*, 451, and *Andrews* v. *Montgomery*, 19 *Id.*, 162.

Mr. G. C. Bronson, contra, cited *Fleming* v. *Gilbert*, 3 Johns., 528; *Lawrence* v. *Dale*, 3 Johns. Ch., 23, 42; *Philips* v. *Butler*, 8 Johns., 392; *Littler* v. *Holland*, 3 T. R., 590; *Brown* v. *Goodman*, *Id.*, 592, *note*, *b*; *Freeman* v. *Adams*, 9 Johns., 115; *Hasbrouck* v. *Tappen*, 15 *Id.*, 204; *Keating* v. *Price*, 1 Johns. Cas., 22; *Felton* v. *Dickenson*, 10 Mass., 287; *Alcorn* v. *Westbrook*, 1 Wils., 117, per Dennison, *J.*; *Robson* v. *Godfrey*, 1 Stark., 277; S. C., 1 Holt *N. P.*, 236; 2 Phil. Ev., 83, in *note*; *Bank of Col.* v. *Patterson*, 7 Cr., 299; Bull. *N. P.*, 139; *Cook* v. *Munstone*, 4 Bos. & P., 355, per Mansfield, *Ch. J.*; *Linningdale* v. *Livingston*, 10 Johns., 36; *Raymond* v. *Bernard*, 12 *Id.*, 274; *Jennings* v. *Camp*, 13 *Id.*, 94; *Gillet* v. *Maynard*, 5 *Id.*, 85, and *Towers* v. *Barret*, 1 T. R., 133.

Curia, per SUTHERLAND, *J.* The charge of the judge is not stated in the case, and must, therefore, be presumed to have been correct; and the verdict must be considered as given under proper directions from the court.

The special contract stated in the declaration, is nothing more than a parol enlargement of the time of performance of the original agreement, and a promise to pay the price originally **566***] *stipulated, upon the work being completed at a subsequent day, within a reasonable time after the new agreement.

It is abundantly settled that the plaintiffs, inasmuch as they had not performed within the time stipulated by the original contract, could not recover upon the covenants contained in it. They could not, in such an action, give evidence of an extension of the time. *Littler* v. *Holland*, 3 T. R., 590, and *Brown* v. *Goodman*, *Id.*, 592, *note*, *b*; *Philips* v. *Butler*, 8 Johns., 392; *Hasbrouck* v. *Tappen*, 15 *Id.*, 204; *Freeman* v. *Adams* 9 *Id.*, 115.

If they can recover at all, it must be in the form of action which they have adopted.

I do not think it material to inquire whether the evidence supports the special count or not, as I see no legal objection to their recovery upon the common counts. It is a case of an executed, not an executory contract, performed according to its terms, except in point of time. The jury must have so considered it: and although the evidence upon that point is somewhat contradictory, I think the balance of testimony is in favor of the plaintiffs.

I consider it well settled, that if there be a special agreement to do a piece of work, and the work be done, but not pursuant to such agreement, either in point of time or any other respect, the party can recover upon the common counts. Where the terms of a special agreement are performed, a duty is raised for which a general *indebitatus assumpsit* will lie; but as long as the special contract remains unrescinded or unperformed, the party cannot recover under the common counts. Bull. *N. P.*, 139; 2 Phil. Ev., 82, *note*, where most of the cases are well collected and stated; 10 Mass., 287.

It appears in the case from the testimony of W. Blanchard, that he was employed by the plaintiffs to finish the canal and dam in July, 1820; that his instructions were to work until the defendant was satisfied; that the defendant was present when he commenced working; and that before he quit, H. W. Schroeppel, the son and agent of the defendant, accepted the work as completed, and did not object that any part of it was defective. I am inclined to think that *this testimony, connected with [***567** other circumstances in the case, would authorize a jury to believe that a special agreement of the nature stated in the declaration, was in fact made; but, at all events, it strengthens and confirms the plaintiffs' right to recover under the common counts. If the defendant intended to rescind the contract, it was his duty then to have spoken. *Lawrence* v. *Dale*, 3 Johns. Ch., 23. By permitting the plaintiffs, after knowing that the work was not completed in time, to proceed and finish it, he waived all right to object on that ground, and the law imputes a promise, on his part, to pay what the labor was reasonably worth.

The recovery of Schroeppel against the plaintiffs does not affect their right in this suit. One of the breaches assigned in the former case was, that the work was not completed within the time limited by the contract. If the plaintiffs sustained any injury from that circumstance, it was a fair subject of damages. But the judgment in that case is evidence of nothing that can affect the plaintiffs' right in his action.

Motion for new trial denied.

Cited in—2 Wend., 405, 590; 6 Wend., 432; 7 Wend., 111; 11 Wend., 484, 665; 12 Wend., 388, 412; 14 Wend., 99; 16 Wend., 635, 642; 21 Wend., 633; 24 Wend., 63; 9 N. Y., 98, 528; 12 N. Y., 370; 17 N. Y., 230; 3 Lans.,

524; 4 Barb., 621; 9 Barb., 376; 12 Barb., 376; 14 Barb., 177; 20 Barb., 487; 60 Barb., 148; 6 T. & C., 255; 41 How. Pr., 404; 4 Duer., 305; 33 Super., 367; 1 E. D. S., 397; 20 Am. Dec., 629, 653; 23 Am. Dec., 705 (6 N. H., 15); 26 Am. Dec., 716 (6 N. H., 486); 27 Am. Dec., 324 (2 Watts, 451).

THE PRESIDENT, DIRECTORS AND COMPANY OF THE BANK OF CHENANGO

v.

HYDE, JOHNSON AND W. WHITNEY.

Loan of Money by Attorney—Promissory Note by Borrower and Another, Deposited with Bank as Security—Recovery against Borrower, for Money Lent—Failure to Collect—Action by Bank against Makers of Note, Sustained—Act Forbidding Attorneys to Purchase Choses in Action, Does not Apply—Judgment against Borrower, no Bar.

H., J. & W. drew a promissory note to be discounted at the Chenango Bank, and payable to the Bank. On the Bank declining to discount it, B., an attorney at law, at the request of H., advanced him the money, and it was agreed between them that the note should be left at the Bank, as the agent or trustee of B., for his security. B. afterwards sued and recovered against H. for money lent, but could not collect his judgment. He then brought an action in the name of the Bank against all three of the makers; held, that he should recover: that this was not the purchase of a chose in action by an attorney at law, and therefore void within the Act, sess. 41, ch. 259, sec. 1, &c., that the note was not void and without consideration, and was properly left as security; this not changing the liability of the parties from what it would have been, had the note been regularly discounted by the Bank; that the Bank did not exceed its powers in taking the note as agent or trustee for B., nor was the judgment against H. a bar to the suit upon the note.

Citations—Act, April 1, 1818; 17 Johns., 176; 15 Johns., 55; 20 Johns., 288; 10 Johns., 198; 1 Kyd. Corp., 70; 2 Cow., 699; 18 Johns., 459; 3 East, 251; 13 Johns., 241; 2 Binn., 146; 14 Johns., 404.

ASSUMPSIT, tried at the Chenango Circuit, Aug., 1823, before Nelson, Circuit Judge. **568*]** *The suit was commenced in January Term, 1821, and was brought to recover the amount of a joint and several promissory note made by the defendants, dated Jan. 1, 1819, for $300, payable to the Bank of Chenango, or order, at 63 days. Plea, the general issue.

The execution of the note being admitted on the trial, J. L. Fenton, Cashier of the Bank, a witness for the defendant, testified that Hyde, one of the defendants, called at the Bank, about the date of the note, and presented it for discount. That it was not discount day, and the note was, besides, objected to as not being in the form required by the rules of the Bank. Hyde went in pursuit of James Birdsall, who came to the Bank, and it was agreed between Birdsall and Hyde, that Birdsall should advance the amount of the note to Hyde; that the note should be delivered to the Bank to be retained by them as the agent of, and as a security to, Birdsall for the money advanced. Hyde said he would endeavor to procure another note, satisfactory to the Bank, in two weeks, and present it for discount. The witness gave encouragement that this might be done; and Hyde agreed, if it was, that the money should be paid to Birdsall, for the money advanced by him. The witness did not know that Hyde was principal in the note, except from his name appearing first on the note, which was usually the case with principals upon notes presented to the Bank.

The defendant's counsel then produced a note, which he received of Birdsall to use on the trial, signed by Hyde, one of the defendants, dated Mar. 8, 1819, payable to the defendant, Johnson, or order, at the Bank of Chenango, 63 days after date, for $300, and indorsed by Johnson and Thomas Whitney. The witness stated that about 90 days after the first transaction, Birdsall called at the Bank and offered this last note to be discounted, which was declined. That the Bank never had any interest in the notes, except as the holder of the first note by agreement, as trustees or agents of Birdsall, as he had before stated. That the first note was delivered over to Birdsall for prosecution, after the Bank had refused to discount the second note, and that the suit was commenced in the name of the Bank by their consent, and *for the **[*569** benefit of Birdsall, under the agreement which he had stated.

It was admitted that before this action was commenced, a suit was instituted by Birdsall against Hyde, for the money advanced by him at the Bank, in which Birdsall declared for money lent only, and obtained judgment in August Term, 1819; that an execution had been issued to the Sheriff of Broome, who had levied $62, besides his fees, and returned, as to the residue, *nulla bona.*

The defendants' counsel then read in evidence a letter from Birdsall to Hyde, dated Mar. 2, 1819, thus: "Your note has not been sent to the Bank as was agreed, and of course, I am compelled to lie out of my money that I advanced. It is now due, and immediate payment is expected;" also another letter from the same to the same, dated Apr. 7, 1819, thus: "The bearer informs me, that the course of business in our Bank was not accurately understood by you and your friends; and that probably, in consequence of that, you had not met the expectations of the Bank We discount at 63 days, notes drawn by an individual or firm, and indorsed by two respectable indorsers; and it is expected, in every case, that the note will be paid up when due; and if the Bank is in a situation to discount, notes so paid will have a preference. If not paid when due, the note is protested, thus adding to the expense, and evidencing the want of punctuality in the maker. The paper of those who suffer their notes to run over the time cannot be considered so good as new paper. The Bank, in three or four instances, have discounted joint notes, to save the drawers, who resided at a distance, from a second journey; and in a few instances in which they have done so, they have found it disadvantageous to the Bank; and of course, no notes in that form can be discounted hereafter. When notes have run over the time of payment, no new notes for the same persons can be discounted, till the old are paid up. These are the regulations in almost all the banks; and in one like ours, with a small capital, they are indispensably

NOTE.—*Accommodation paper—Diversion of.* See Denniston v. Bacon, 10 Johns., 198, *note.*

necessary; as without punctuality in the customer, the Bank cannot do business advantageously. The loan of $300 that I made to
570*] *you was a very unfortunate one for me. For two weeks, the Board would have discounted a note in proper form; but as none came, I have been compelled to lie out of the money, when I could very illy spare it. I cannot procure the discount of the one you sent me. The $5 was received and will be applied on your note. I have been obliged to borrow the money from individuals, that I lent you, and am now extremely in want of it. If you can pay it next Tuesday, it will save me the trouble of borrowing it over again, as I shall then have to pay it where I have borrowed it; and longer than that time it is impossible for me to wait. It is an object to obtain foreign money, particularly current; and if your notes in the Bank could be paid up next week, I presume the Board would renew them for a part or the whole."

Thomas Whitney, a witness for the defendants, testified that in the winter and spring of 1819, and for 6 or 9 months afterwards, Hyde was in good circumstances, and able to pay the money; but in the latter part of that year, and about the time when Birdsall's execution issued, became embarrassed, and was understood to be insolvent; though it was understood that he had property concealed, but did not pay debts; and since that period, he had been the principal part of the time in possession of personal property, which he used and claimed as his own, sufficient to satisfy the judgment.

The defendants' counsel offered to prove by this witness, that the second note was made and indorsed for the benefit of Hyde alone, as a circumstance from which to infer that the first was for his benefit, and the other defendants mere sureties. This testimony was objected to by the plaintiffs' counsel and overruled.

It appeared that the former suit was commenced Apr. 23, 1819; the execution issued Sept. 28, 1819; and that Hyde's personal property was sold in Jan., 1820; that an *alias fi. fa.* was issued July 26, 1822, upon which $41.54 was collected, and the execution returned *nulla bona* as to the residue.

It was admitted that Birdsall, at the time he loaned or advanced the money, was an attorney and counselor of this court.

571*] *Upon this evidence, the defendant's counsel insisted that the plaintiffs were not entitled to recover; that Birdsall, being an attorney, had no right to advance the money; that it was not necessary that this should be pleaded. But the judge decided that the plaintiffs were entitled to recover; and the jury, under his direction, found for the plaintiffs $339.43.

It was agreed that if this court should be of that opinion, the verdict should stand; otherwise, a new trial should be granted.

Mr. J. A. Collier, for the defendants, insisted:

1. That the advance of the money by Birdsall, who was an attorney, whether it be considered as a purchase of the note, or that this was a pledge, was contrary to the Statute, and the whole contract was consequently void; and cited 1 R. L., 417, and Laws N. Y., sess. 41, ch. 259, sec. 1.

2. This defense was admissible under the plea of *non assumpsit;* and no special notice necessary. (1 Chit. Pl., 469, 70; Lawes' Pl., *Assumpsit*, 520.)

3. The note having been drawn for discount at the Bank, and rejected, was invalid, and without consideration; and no suit can be maintained by the payees; nor could one of the makers, without the knowledge or consent of the others, change the contract by virtually substituting other payees; or convert the note to any different object than was contemplated at the time of making it. *Marvin* v. *M'Cullum*, 20 Johns., 288; *Denniston* v. *Bacon*, 10 *Id.*, 198.

4. The Bank being incorporated for a definite and distinct object, could not legally be trustees for Birdsall, in business disconnected with their banking concerns; and going, as they do in this business, beyond the scope of their corporate powers, no suit can be maintained in their names. 1 Plowd., 103; 1 Kyd. on Corp., 72; *Beatty* v. *Mar. Ins. Co.*, 2 Johns., 109; *People* v. *Utica Ins. Co.*, 15 *Id.*, 358; *N. Y. F. Ins. Co.* v. *Sturgess*, 2 Cow., 664.

5. Birdsall, by prosecuting Hyde to judgment and execution, for money lent, treated the transaction, as in truth it was, a contract between himself and Hyde; and is estopped to *consider it an advance upon the note, [*572
or as a contract by which Johnson and Whitney were bound.

6. The judgment in the separate suit against Hyde was an extinguishment of any demand against him upon the note, and afforded him a valid defense to this suit. The defendants were, therefore, entitled to judgment, as the plaintiffs failed to show a joint liability in all. *Manahan* v. *Gibbons*, 19 Johns., 109; *Robertson* v. *Smith*, 18 *Id.*, 459.

Mr. B. F. Butler, contra, cited, as to the first point, *Williams* v. *Matthews*, 3 Cow., 252, and *Van Rensselaer* v. *Sheriff of Albany*, 2 *Id.*, 501.

As to the third point, *Brown* v. *Mott*, 7 Johns., 461; *Powell* v. *Waters*, 17 *Id.*, 176; *Chenango Bank* v. *Curtiss*, 19 *Id.*, 326.

As to the sixth point, *Drake* v. *Mitchell*, 3 East, 251; *Chipman* v. *Martin*, 13 Johns., 240; and *Day* v. *Leal*, 14 *Id.*, 404.

Curia, per SUTHERLAND, *J.* There is no force in the objection, that the advance of the money by Birdsall to Hyde, under the circumstances of this case, was a violation of the Act of Apr. 1st, 1818, prohibiting attorneys and counselors from purchasing choses in action, or lending or advancing money upon them, for the purpose of having them placed in their hands, or the hands of another person for prosecution. It was a mere loan of money, upon a security which had no legal existence or validity, before it was placed in the hands of Birdsall. In the hands of Hyde, it was not an available instrument. He was one of the makers; and it became a promissory note, or chose in action, only on its delivery to Birdsall or the Bank, for his use. If this was a purchase within the Statute, then an attorney can in no case lend money, and take a note as security. That the instrument was drawn and signed by the makers, before the Bank or Birdsall were

applied to for the money, does not alter the transaction. It took its inception when it passed to them; and if there had been usury exacted upon the transfer, it would have destroyed the note in the hands of any subsequent *bona fide* holder. *Powell* v. *Waters*, 17
573*] Johns., *176; *Munn* v. *Com. Co.*, 15 *Id.*, 55; *Marvin* v. *M'Collum*, 20 *Id.*, 288. The facts in the case conclusively repel the supposition that the consideration or inducement on the part of Birdsall, for advancing the money, was the placing the note in the hands of the Bank for collection. I apprehend the Statute, in prohibiting the purchase of choses in action, means pre-existing securities, or demands. The term buying and purchasing can, in strictness, be applicable to such only. On this ground, therefore, without deciding whether the Statute prohibits the purchase of choses in action by attorneys or counselors, when they are not purchased for the purpose of collection, it is clear that it has no application to this case.

Nor is the validity of the note affected by the circumstance that it was drawn for the purpose of being discounted at the Bank of Chenango. It was made to raise money on. It did not change the responsibility of any of the parties to it, that the money was advanced by Birdsall, instead of the Bank. The case of *Powell* v. *Waters*, 17 Johns., 176, is decisive upon this point. In *Denniston* v. *Bacon*, 10 Johns., 198, which was cited by the defendant's counsel, the contract was essentially changed, and on that ground the note was held invalid. The Bacons made their note to Gere and Elliot, the latter informing them by letter that he had made an agreement at the Bank that they should discount it; and that 20 *per cent.* should be paid in 56 days, 20 *per cent.* in 112 days, and the residue in 168 days. When the note was offered, the bank refused to discount it, and Elliot then indorsed it to Denniston, who brought the suit for Elliot's benefit, as it was expressly admitted. The court held that between those parties, the letter of Elliot, and the note, formed but one contract; and that the defendants were not responsible, because the note was not discounted on the terms stated in the letter, but the whole amount was exacted at the expiration of 60 days. Had it been discounted on the terms originally proposed, by another bank, or an individual, the transaction would not have been questioned. The case of *Marvin* v. *M'Cullum*, 20 Johns., 288, which was also cited for the defendants, has no application to this point.

574*] *But it is said the suit could not be maintained in the name of the Bank; that they could not legally be trustees for Birdsall, this not being within the scope of the powers conferred by their Act of Incorporation. The general proposition that a Corporation can have no other capacities than such as are necessary to carry into effect the purposes for which it was established, is undoubtedly true. 1 Kyd on Corp., 70; *N. Y. F. Ins. Co.* v. *Ely*, 2 Cow., 699. But I apprehend the Bank, in this case, has not transcended its powers. Upon the face of the transaction there is nothing exceptionable. It appears to be a loan by a bank upon a promissory note; but the proof shows that it was, in truth, a loan by Birdsall; and the reason of the note being in the name of the Bank, and left in their possession, is satisfactorily accounted for. It was intended to be discounted by the Bank; but they refusing to discount it, Birdsall advanced the money, and now brings the suit in the name of the nominal payees. The question is, not whether the Bank has a general authority to act in the capacity of a trustee; but whether the *bona fide* holder of a promissory note, in which the bank is nominally the payee, has a right to sue in the name of the Bank. I apprehend, if the Bank had refused the use of its name, a court of equity would have compelled it to allow such use on proper terms.

Nor was the judgment in the separate suit of *Birdsall* v. *Hyde*, for money lent, an extinguishment of his liability upon the note. If that suit had been upon the note, instead of the original advance, the doctrine contended for by the defendant's counsel would have applied. The judgment, in that case, would have been a bar to any subsequent suit against Hyde upon the note; and of course against his co-defendants, who would be charged only jointly with him. The case of *Robertson* v. *Smith*, 18 Johns., 459, would then have applied with decisive force in favor of the defendants.

But in *Drake* v. *Mitchell*, 3 East, 251, it was held that where one of three joint covenantors gives a bill of exchange for part of the debt secured by the covenant, on which bill judgment is recovered, such judgment is no bar to an action of covenant against the three. Grose, *J.*, says, "the *note or bill, not having [***575** been accepted as satisfaction for the debt, could only operate as a collateral security; and though judgment has been recovered on the bill, yet not having produced satisfaction in fact, the plaintiff may still resort to his original remedy on the covenant."

In *Chipman* v. *Martin*, 13 Johns., 241, this court decided that a judgment on a covenant for the payment of rent is not, without actual satisfaction, an extinguishment of the rent; and the lessor may, notwithstanding the judgment, distrain for the same rent for which the judgment was obtained. It was held to be a case of concurrent remedies, where the party may pursue all until satisfaction is produced. It was likened to the case of a bond and mortgage, in which a recovery upon the bond will not preclude the mortgagee from bringing his action of ejectment, and recovering possession of the land. The same principle is recognized and illustrated in *Bantleon* v. *Smith*, 2 Binn., 146. In *Day* v. *Leal*, 14 Johns., 404, it was held that a collateral security of a higher nature (as a bond and warrant of attorney), executed by one of the makers of a note, on which judgment has been entered, did not, as long as the judgment was unsatisfied, extinguish the original contract.

If Hyde was individually liable to Birdsall for money lent, then the note in question was a collateral security, and the judgment upon the original cause of action, without satisfaction, is no bar to an action on the note.

Nor is the fact of Birdsall's prosecuting and obtaining judgment against Hyde, individually, for money lent, evidence that he advanced the money upon his credit, and not upon the note. Hyde was the individual with whom the transaction took place. It was natural for Birdsall to call upon him for payment in the first instance, if he supposed he had a right to resort to him individually.

Upon the whole case, therefore, I am of opinion the plaintiffs are entitled to judgment.

Judgment for the plaintiffs.

Cited in—5 Wend., 69; 9 Wend., 172; 1 Den., 410; 2 Paige, 511; 32 N. Y., 557; 65 Barb., 576; 5 Duer, 94; 1 Bos., 337; 1 Sweeny, 122; 28 Hun, 30; 31 Am. Dec., 587 (10 Yerg., 417); 37 Am. Dec., 228 (12 N. H., 549); 36 Am. Rep., 312 (71 Me., 270).

576*] *RUSSELL

v.

DOTY, Sheriff of WASHINGTON.

Action for Removing Goods, from Demised Premises, on Execution, Leaving Rent Unpaid—Statute Extends to all Goods on Premises—Landlord's Lien Co-extensive with Right of Distress—Rent Payable in Advance, may be Distrained for—Actual Possession, Unnecessary to Enable Owner to Give Lease—Defendant Remaining in Possession after Sale on Execution, Presumed to be Tenant of Purchaser.

The Statute, sess. 36, ch. 63, sec. 12; 1 R. L., 437, providing that goods shall not be removed by execution from the demised premises till one year's rent paid, extends to all goods upon the premises, whether they belong to the tenant or any other person. The specific lien of the landlord on goods upon the premises for a year's rent is, under this Statute, co-extensive with his right of distress; *i. e.*, goods which he might distrain cannot be removed by execution till the year's rent be paid.

Rent may be payable in advance by contract, and may be distrained for, or will entitle the landlord to, a specific lien against an execution, under the Statute.

One need not be actually possessed of land in order to be enabled to give a lease of it. The undisputed right of possession is enough: as where one purchases land at sheriff's sale, and the defendant in the execution has not actually surrendered the possession, yet the purchaser may give a valid lease to a third person before acquiring possession by ejectment.

After a purchase of land on execution, if the defendant remains in possession, the presumption of law, as between the purchaser and all third persons, is that he remains in possession as tenant of the purchaser, and in subordination to his title.

Citations—13 Johns., 344; Woodfall, 238, 564, 563; 1 R. L., 437; 1 M. & S., 245; 18 Johns., 1; Gilb. on Rents, 25; 2 Bac. Abr., tit. Distress (C); 2 T. R., 600; 6 Mod., 214; 8 Ann. C., 14; 2 Wils., 141; 5 Binn., 505.

CASE upon the Statute, sess. 36, ch. 63, sec. 12; 1 R. L., 437, for removing goods in execution, leaving the rent unpaid; tried at the Washington Circuit, June, 1822, before the late *Mr. Justice* Yates.

At the trial it appeared that the plaintiff purchased the demised premises, which are situate in Salem, Washington Co., at a sheriff's sale upon a judgment and execution against James Nichols, and received a conveyance dated Apr. 17, 1819. The plaintiff then produced a lease of the premises from himself to Charles Nichols, dated Apr. 24, 1819, for one year, at a rent of $150, payable May 1 after the date of the lease. A deputy of the defendant swore that he received an execution against James Nichols in the fall of 1819, by virtue whereof he took and removed the goods in question (value more than $150) from a store on the demised premises, after having notice from the plaintiff that his rent was due; and without first paying the rent. Charles and James Nichols were both in the store when the goods were taken. The latter built the store, and the former resided in Vt., but he continued the business of the store from the spring of 1819, having that spring purchased James' goods at a sheriff's sale upon an execution against James. James, since that time, had occupied a room in the back of the store, and was frequently in the store.

The plaintiff having here rested his cause, the defendant's counsel moved for a nonsuit, on the ground, 1. That the plaintiff could not make a lease till he was in possession. 2. *That the execution was not against [*577 the tenant, but James Nichols. 3. That the rent was not due in respect of occupancy, but merely in respect to the parties' agreement. The court overruled the motion, and the defendant's counsel excepted.

A variety of testimony was then gone into to show that the sale of James' property to Charles in the spring of 1819 was fraudulent and void as to creditors; after which the judge intimated to the defendant's counsel that the plaintiff was entitled to recover, if the questions of law had been correctly decided. The defendant's counsel declined going to the jury, who found for the plaintiff $184.23 damages.

Mr. J. Crary now moved for a new trial. He said that by the purchase at the sheriff's sale the plaintiff acquired a mere right of possession, and had no right to give a lease, without showing that he obtained actual possession. *People* v. *Brinkerhoff*, 13 Johns., 340.

Beside, this is not a case within the statute. The defendant and tenant must be the same. This is evident from the provision that the sheriff may levy not only the amount of the execution, but the rent also, and pay the whole to the plaintiff. The Statute, 1 R. L., 437, sec. 12, never intended that the goods of a third person should be sold by the sheriff to pay the tenant's rent. The right of the sheriff to make the rent out of property on the demised premises was not intended to be as broad as the landlord's right of distress. It is the tenant's goods alone which the Statute means. These were not his, but James'; and the lease was evidently a mere cover for the property. The statute does not extend beyond the landlord and his immediate lessee; and it was expressly held in *Bennet's* case, 2 Str., 787, that it does not protect the ground landlord against an execution upon the goods of a sublessee. (S. C., Woodf. L. & T., 566.)

The rent was not due within the meaning of the statute; and the landlord cannot claim unless it be due. *Trappan* v. *Morie*, 18 Johns., 1; *Buckley* v. *Taylor*, 2 T. R., 600, went upon the custom of the country, that rent might be *demanded in advance. As against [*578 creditors, the rent should always be due upon occupancy. A contrary rule would facilitate fraud.

Mr. D. Russell, contra. The question of fraud cannot be raised here. It belonged exclusively to the jury, before whom the gentleman shrunk from its investigation.

A voluntary entry, on a purchase at a sheriff's sale, is equivalent to a recovery in ejectment, and execution executed. The Statute of Uses carries the constructive, which, in this instance, was consummated by actual possession taken peaceably. After a purchase at sheriff's sale, the tenant is in under the purchaser.

The Statute, 1 R. L., 437, sec. 12, is general in its terms, and embraces all the property upon the premises demised. Had the Legislature intended an execution against the lessee alone, they would have said so.

Rent may be made payable in advance. The gentleman shows no authority, proving that the time of payment is not under the control of the parties, as in other cases; and *Williams* v. *Howard*, 3 Munf., 277, is in point, that rent may be made payable in advance, by contract.

[On this point he was stopped by the court.]

The statute should be liberally and beneficially construed for the landlord. It was intended to give him a specific lien on the property against all executions to the extent of a year's rent, in every case where he may distrain. *Henchett* v. *Kimpson*, 2 Wils., 140; *Binns* v. *Hudson*, 5 Binn., 505, 506.

Curia, per SUTHERLAND, *J.* It is not ueeessary that the owner of land should be in the actual possession of it, to enable him to give a valid lease. The undisputed right of possession, I apprehend, is sufficient. Here James Nichols has never questioned the plaintiff's right to give the lease. On the contrary, the evidence warrants the inference that Charles Nichols went into possession of the store with the assent of James immediately after the purchase. James appears to have surrendered the possession of the store, and to have been per-
579*] mitted *by the plaintiff to occupy a single room in the back part of it.

It is true that the plaintiff could not have obtained the possession of the premises against the will of James Nichols, without an action of ejectment. (13 Johns., 344.) But the tenant had a right voluntarily to surrender the possession. And I apprehend that, as between a purchaser of land at sheriff's sale and all third persons, if the defendant remains in possession after the sale, the presumption of law is, that he remains as the tenant of the purchaser, and in subordination to his title. It is not for strangers to say that he holds in hostility to the true owner.

Nor is it material whether the property taken belonged to James Nichols, the defendant in the execution, or to Charles, the tenant of the plaintiff. The statute is express, that no goods or chattels whatsoever, in or upon the demised premises, shall be liable to be taken by virtue of any execution, &c., unless the party at whose suit the execution is sued out shall pay to the landlord of the premises, or his bailiff, all and every sum or sums of money due for rent, at the time of taking the goods or chattels by virtue of the execution; not exceeding, however, one year's rent. Whether the statute would extend to property casually upon the premises, belonging to strangers, which the tenant did not claim to own, so as to protect it from execution, may perhaps be questionable. It certainly would not, if it appeared to have been placed there with the fraudulent intent of protecting it from execution, and the landlord was a party to the fraud. But where the property is claimed by the tenant, and is upon the premises in his actual possession, it is clearly, both by the letter and spirit of the Act, protected from execution, until the rent is paid. The landlord had a right to look to and rely upon it as security for his rent; and the legal presumption is, that he did rely upon it. He was not bound to inquire into the claims of third persons to the property. He had a right to distrain it; and it would seem to have been the intention of the Legislature to give the landlord a specific lien, co-extensive with his right of distress, to the amount of one year's rent. (Woodf., 563.) No terms could have *been used more [***580** comprehensive than those of the 12th section of our Act, 1 R. L., 437. "No goods or chattels whatsoever, in or upon the demised premises, shall be liable to be taken by virtue of any execution;" not an execution against the tenant only, but against any other person. The 13th and 14th sections of the Act, which authorize the landlord to seize any goods which may have been removed from the premises, and impose a penalty on tenants, and others removing goods, to defraud the landlord of his rent, are expressly confined to the goods of the tenant, and do not extend to any other goods which may be upon the premises.

In this case, therefore, I repeat, it is immaterial whether the goods removed belonged to James or Charles Nichols. They ostensibly belonged to Charles. They were purchased by him at sheriff's sale, and had ever since the purchase been in his exclusive possession. There is no evidence that the sale was fraudulent and colorable. If the defendant intended to take that ground, he should have gone to the jury upon it. It was a question for them to decide. He voluntarily declined submitting the cause to the jury, thereby admitting that there were no facts in dispute, and that the whole merits of the case were embraced in the questions of law decided by the judge, and to which he excepted. To those exceptions, therefore, he must now be confined. The property removed is, by the course of the trial, admitted to have belonged to the tenant.

But it is objected that the rent in this case was not due within the meaning of the statute.

It is well settled that the landlord can claim from the party suing out the execution, or the sheriff, only the amount of the rent due at the time of the levy. The English courts, as well as our own, have thus expounded the statute. (1 Maule & S., 245; 18 Johns., 1.) The defendant contends that the rent must be due in virtue of actual occupancy, and not in advance, in consequence of an agreement, in order to give the landlord a specific lien under the statute. Rent may be reserved in advance, so as to give the landlord either a right of action, or right to distrain for it, immediately upon *the tenant entering into possession. [***581** (Gilb. on Rents, 25; Woodf., 238; 2 Bac. Abr., tit. Distress, C; 2 T. R., 600; 6 Mod., 214.) The case of *Buckley* v *Taylor*, 2 T. R., 600, involved the very question whether rent payable in advance, either by contract or the custom of the country, was due within the 8 Anne, ch. 14, which is like the 12th section of our Act; and Erskine contended there, as it has been contended here, that the provisions of that statute only extended to rent which had become due in respect of the actual occupation of the tenant. But the court held otherwise. Buller, *J.*, says: "In general, the landlord cannot distrain till the rent becomes due (that is, until the end of the year); but if the agreement be otherwise, I see no objection to it in point of law. If the tenant take a lease, and agree that the rent shall be payable on a particular day, the law gives the landlord a power of distraining on that day." That rent, surely, must be due for which the landlord has a right to distrain; and there is nothing in the terms of the statute, or in the reason or nature of the case, from which it is to be inferred that the Legislature intended to confine the specific lien given to landlords by the 12th section of the Act to rent which had become due by actual occupancy. It has always been held that this statute was to have a liberal construction. (Woodf., 564; 2 Wils., 141; 5 Binn., 505.) I am, therefore, of opinion that the motion for a new trial must be denied.

New trial refused.

Overruled—6 Wend., 392; 2 Hill, 450.
Cited in—6 Cow., 107; 4 N. Y., 272; 71 Ill., 332; 37 N. J. L., 94.

PENDLETON v. DYETT.

Action for Rent—What will Sustain Plea of Eviction.

To sustain a plea of eviction, in bar of an action for rent, the tenant must show an actual expulsion, before, and that it continued till after the rent due.

That the landlord is guilty of a nuisance, as bringing lewd women near the premises which are so situate that the tenant and his family are broken of their rest, and otherwise so much annoyed that he is obliged to leave the demised premises, and keep away on that account, is not sufficient to bar the landlord's claim for rent.

Eviction of the whole, or any part of the demised premises, is a good plea in bar, to an action either of debt or covenant, for rent.

Citations—Cruise Dig. tit. 28, Rents, ch. 3; 3 Woodfall, 412-13; 1 Saund., 203, 204, n (2); Styles, 446, 432; Hob., 326; 1 Ld. Raym., 369; 1 Cowp., 242.

COVENANT for rent upon a lease dated dated Oct. 15, 1818, given by the plaintiff to the defendant, for the term of two, three, **582***] *five or eight years, but not for a less term than two years, of two rooms, or the whole of the second floor, and two rooms chosen by the defendant on the third floor of a certain house or store in Beaver St., corner of William St., in the City of N. Y., at a rent of $425 *per annum*, which the defendant covenanted to pay, and entered into possession of the demised premises.

The defendant pleaded:

1st. *Non est factum.*

2. That before any of the rent became due, to wit: on, &c., the plaintiff entered upon the demised premises, and ejected, expelled, put out and amoved the defendant, and kept and continued him so ejected, expelled and amoved from thence hitherto.

Replication, denying the expulsion and issue.

The cause was tried at the N. Y. Circuit, June 19, 1823, before Edwards, Circuit Judge.

On the trial, the counsel for the defendant produced receipts for rent Feb. 1, 1820, and offered to prove that about that time the plaintiff introduced into the house demised lewd women or prostitutes, and continued this practice from time to time and at sundry times, keeping and detaining them in there all night for the purpose of prostitution; that such women would frequently enter the house in the day time, and after staying all night, would leave it by daylight in the morning; that the plaintiff sometimes introduced other men into the house, who, together with him, kept company with the lewd women or prostitutes during the night; that on such occasions the plaintiff and the women, being in company in certain parts of the house not included in the lease, but adjacent and in the plaintiff's occupation, were accustomed to make a great deal of indecent noise and disturbance, the women often screaming extravagantly so as to be heard throughout the house, and by the near neighbors; and frequently using obscene and vulgar language, so loud as to be understood at a considerable distance; that such noise and riotous proceedings, being frequently continued all night, greatly disturbed the rest of persons sleeping in other parts of the house, and particularly in the parts demised; that these practices were matter of conversation and reproach *in the neighbor- [***583** hood; and were of a nature to draw, and did draw, odium and infamy upon the house as being a place of ill fame, so that it was no longer reputable for moral or decent persons to dwell or enter there; that all these practices were by the procurement or permission and concurrence of the plaintiff. That the defendant, being a person of good and respectable character, was compelled by the repetition of these practices to leave the house, and did leave it for that cause, about the beginning of Mar., 1820; and did not return. That a respectable man of the name of Fox, to whom part of the house had been underlet, left it for the same cause.

This evidence was objected to, and overruled by the judge, as inadmissible upon the issue; and the defendant's counsel excepted. Verdict for the plaintiff, damages $362.52.

Mr. H. W. Warner, for the defendant, moved for a new trial, and cited *Hunt* v. *Cope*, Cowp., 242. That an eviction is a good defense, he said, there is no doubt. The evidence offered should have gone to the jury, who would have been authorized to presume an eviction. If the conduct of the lessor be such as to make it improper, inconvenient or useless for the tenant to remain in possession, this is equivalent to an eviction.

Mr. J. A. Dunlap, contra, said the evidence offered was no defense to the action; and if otherwise, it was inadmissible under the plea.

In support of the first point, he cited 3 Cruise Dig., 348, tit. Rents, ch. 3; Co. Litt., 148 *b*; Ld. Raym., 369; Cro. Eliz., 341; Cro. Jac., 425; 3 Johns., 48; T. Jones, 148; 1 T. R., 671; 7 Johns., 376; 13 *Id.*, 105; Esp. Ev., 142.

To the second point, 1 Phil. Ev., 153; Esp. Ev., 131; 2 Lev., 143; Hob., 326.

Curia, per SUTHERLAND, *J.* Eviction of the

whole or any part of the demised premises, is a good plea in bar to an action either of debt or covenant for the rent. In this all the authorities agree. (Cruise Dig., 28, tit. Rents, ch. 3; Woodf., 412, 413; 1 Saund., 204, *n*, **584***] and cases there *cited.) The plea in this case is unexceptionable in point of form. It is according to the established precedents. *Salmon* v. *Smith*, 1 Saund., 203, 204, *n*. 2. It states that the plaintiff (who was the defendant's lessor), entered into and upon the demised premises, and ejected, expelled, put out and amoved the said defendant from the possession thereof, and kept and continued him so ejected, expelled, &c., from thence hitherto. The only question in the case is, whether the evidence offered by the defendant, and which was rejected by the judge who tried the cause, supported the plea, or was of a character which ought to have been submitted to the jury, for them to decide whether it made out the fact of eviction or not. No actual ouster or turning out of possession is pretended. The proof offered does not show an entry by the lessor upon the premises. It does not make out even a trespass. The acts complained of as amounting to an eviction were committed in a different part of the same house, with which the demised premises had no connection, except that the approach to each was by a common entrance. They operated not upon the physical safety of the tenant, or the physical condition of the demised premises; but upon the moral sense and feeling of the defendant. The acts were most exceptionable in themselves, and if they could not be abated, the defendant had not only a moral right, but it was his moral duty, to abandon the scene of riot and prostitution. But they could have been abated. The law afforded a prompt and sufficient remedy. The police of the city, upon the complaint of the defendant, would have instantly taken the plaintiff and his associates into custody, and punished them by fine and imprisonment as often as the offense was repeated. There was no moral necessity, therefore, for abandoning the premises. Suppose the plaintiff had been in the habit of exhibiting himself either in the common passage, or in the street opposite the premises in question, in indecent attitudes, or in a state of offensive nakedness, so that the defendant and his family could not leave his house without witnessing the disgusting exhibition; would this cause have supported a plea of eviction? They would both stand upon the footing of nuisances, **585***] which the *plaintiff or any other citizen might cause to be abated. But if, instead of taking that course, he should abandon his house, it must be considered a voluntary and not a compulsory act.

But I apprehend there can be no eviction without an actual entry. Such is the form of the plea, and the proof must sustain it. The very definition of the term eviction, is an expulsion of the lessee out of all or some part of the demised premises; and Sergeant Williams says, that to occasion a suspension of the rent, the plea must state an eviction or expulsion of the lessee by the lessor, and a keeping him out of possession, until after the rent became due; otherwise it will be bad. (1 Saund., 204, *n*. 2.) If a constructive expulsion, without entry, may constitute an eviction, which will operate as a suspension of the rent, why is the averment of an entry contained in all the precedents, and why do all the cases agree, that without such averment the plea would be bad? Thus, in *Timbrell* v. *Bullock*, Styles, 446, it is said that, to make a suspension of rent reserved upon a lease for years, the lessor must oust the lessee of part of the thing let, at least, and hold him out until after the day on which the rent is made payable by the lease; and if the lessee re-enters the rent is revived. A re-entry presupposes an actual ouster or expulsion. So, in *Page* v. *Parr*, Styles, 432, which was an action of covenant for rent, the defendant pleaded in bar, that the plaintiff entered into a part of the land demised, before the rent became due, and so had suspended his rent. The plaintiff replied that the defendant re-entered and so was possessed as in his former estate. To which replication there was a demurrer. And Rolle, *Ch. J.*, held the demurrer well taken, on the ground that the replication did not state that the defendant, after re-entry, continued in possession until the rents were due; and judgment was given for the defendant. According to the case of *Salmon* v. *Smith*, 1 Saund., 204, and *note* 2, the plea would be now held bad for omitting to state that the defendant was kept out of possession until the rent became due. But this case also clearly contemplates an actual entry or ouster by the lessor, as necessary in order *to suspend the rent. So, in *Reynolds* [***586** v. *Buckle*, Hob., 326, which was an action of debt for rent, the defendant pleaded that before rent due the plaintiff entered upon him; but did not say that he did expel him, or hold him out; and the plea, on that ground, was declared to be, of itself, an insufficient bar. But in that case it was cured by the verdict. *Bushell* v. *Lechmore*, 1 Ld. Raym., 369, also decides that a mere entry or trespass without an eviction will not suspend the rent. Upon this point all the cases concur. *Hunt* v. *Cope*, 1 Cowp., 242, is a strong case. There the defendant pleaded that the lessor, with force and arms, entered upon the demised premises and demolished a summer-house, being a part of the premises, by means whereof the tenant had been deprived of the use of the summer-house, &c. This plea was held to be bad, because it did not aver an actual eviction or expulsion of the lessee. The defendant's counsel urged that the facts in the plea amounted to an eviction, on the ground that an actual entry was stated, and a destruction of a portion of the premises; and if an eviction could be constructively pleaded, this would seem to be good. But all the courts held it bad, and Aston, *J.*, says all the cases in the books suppose the lessee to be put out of possession. Therefore, merely saying that he was deprived of the enjoyment of the premises, is not sufficient. If it is necessary to state, in terms, that the lessee was turned out of possession, in order to make a good plea of eviction, it would seem to follow that the proof in support of the plea must be substantially of the same character. Ld. Mansfield, in *Hunt* v. *Cope*, says that the facts there stated might have been sufficient for the jury to have found for the defendant under a good plea of eviction. But there, it will be recollected, an actual entry, and a physical destruction of a portion of the premises, are averred; and if an actual ouster can be inferred from circumstances, it surely might in that case; yet Ld. Mansfield considers it as matter of doubt.

In the case before us, there was not only no actual entry, but no assertion, either express or implied, of a right of entry on the part of the lessor, or of any other right or control over the demised premises. The disturbance suf- **587*]** fered *by the lessee was the cousequence of conduct on the part of the lessor which partook of the nature of a nuisance, and which he had the power of abating at pleasure. He was not, therefore, constrained by any necessity, either moral or physical, to abandon the premises; and, in judgment of law, so far as this action is concerned, his abandonment must be considered voluntary. The evidence offered was properly rejected by the judge. The motion for a new trial must be denied.

New trial refused.

Reversed—8 Cow., 727.
Cited in—2 Wend., 566, *n.*; 7 Wend., 215; 24 Wend., 293; 3 Den., 457; 4 N. Y., 219; 5 Lans., 200; 10 Hun, 155; 22 Barb., 165; 12 How. Pr., 62; 14 How., 117; 5 Abb. Pr., 3; 1 Hilt., 325.
See 43 N. J. L., 482; 46 Am. Dec., 729 (13 Met., 177); 8 Am. Rep., 325 (106 Mass., 201).

JACKSON, ex dem. SWARTWOUT ET UX.,
v.
COLE.

*Ejectment—Parol Declarations, of Party in Possession, as Evidence—Evidence of Forfeiture by Attainder—*Prima Facie *Evidence that Title was once in Party Attainted—Adoption of Location and Enumeration by Act of Forfeiture as Evidence of Title—Exemplified Copy of Copy as Evidence—Conditions to Proper Performance of Official Act—When Deemed to have been Performed—When Conveyance from Trustee to* Cestui que Trust *Presumed—Acts of State Officers as Evidence against State—Proof of Documents from Comptroller's Office.*

The parol declarations of one in possession of lands, as to the nature and extent of his interest, no legal title being shown in him, are admissible against him as evidence, and against those who claim under him, unless it appear that there is higher testimony as to the matter sought to be shown by parol.

Where, in ejectment, the defendant gave evidence to show that certain lands of D. C., under whom the lessors of the plaintiff claimed title, were forfeited by an Act of Attainder, held, that this was *prima facie* evidence that the title to the premises in question was once in D. C.; and that the plaintiff might, without further proof of title in D. C., proceed to deduce a title from him.

Where an Act for vesting certain lands of D. C. in C. C. referred to a location and enumeration of the lands of D. C. made, &c., and delivered to the Commissioners of Forfeitures, and directed them to be appraised by such persons as the Commissioners of Forfeitures should appoint, and the appraised value to be paid either to the Commissioners, or Treasurer, &c.; as against the State, the location and enumeration, thus adopted by the Act, are conclusive that the lands mentioned in them belonged to D. C.

An exemplification of a copy of the certificate of the appraisers, filed in the Treasurer's office, having an indorsement by the Treasurer upon it, that the original had been delivered to C. C., deceased, and it being shown that it could not be found among the papers of C. C., was held admissible in evidence, though it was the exemplified copy of a copy.

This copy having been furnished to the Treasurer by the Commissioners of Forfeitures for his information, and as his guide under the Act for vesting the land in C. C., may be regarded as an original for some purposes, and especially as against the State, the Treasurer having indorsed upon it all he did under it.

Where a State officer, *e. g.*, the Treasurer, does an act which would be a violation of his duty unless certain terms or conditions had first been performed by an individual; as between the State and the individual, such performance shall be deemed, *prima facie*, to have taken place.

Under what circumstances a conveyance from a trustee to a *cestui que trust* is to be presumed.

To what extent the acts of state officers, as the Treasurer, Surveyor-General, &c., shall be evidence against the State.

Manner of proving documents from the Comptroller's office.

Citations—7 Johns., 186; 10 Johns., 336, 358; 16 Johns., 302; 6 Johns., 19; 4 Johns., 230; 12 Johns., 96; 18 Johns., 330; Act, Oct. 22, 1779; Act, April 21, 1787; Act, Jan. 27, 1789; 4 T. R., 682; Cowp., 46; 3 Burr., 1901; Doug., 721; 11 Johns., 456.

EJECTMENT for one fourth of the south part of lot No. 10, in Glen's purchase, in Herkimer Co., tried at the circuit in that county, before Williams, Circuit Judge, July 8, 1823.

*On the trial, the plaintiff read in evi- **[*588** dence a deed from J. O. Hoffman, Eliza Ann Colden and T. Cooper, to Cole, the defendant, dated Jan. 21, 1798, for 400 acres of land, in lot No. 10, Glen's purchase, including the premises in question.

James Cochran, a witness for the plaintiff, testified that he knew T. Cooper; that he died four or five years ago; that he also knew Catharine, the wife of T. Cooper; and that she died in 1796 or 1797, leaving issue a son, Colden Cooper, who died without issue several years ago, and a daughter, Alice Ann, who is married to Swartwout, the lessor. That Cole, the defendant, a few days before the trial, called on him to subpœna him as a witness, and said he wanted to prove the death of Mrs. Cooper; that he was sued by Swartwout and wife for part of his land; that when he bought the land, Cooper only had signed the deed; but that the land belonged to his wife. He also said that if Mrs. Cooper had signed the deed, he should have been perfectly safe.

It was further proved that Mrs. Cooper was the daughter of David Colden; that she was born about the year 1775; that she married T. Cooper in 1792, and died in 1796 or 1797. That David Colden had four children, Mary, wife of J. O. Hoffman, C. D. Colden, Eliza Ann Colden and Mrs. Cooper.

The defendant's counsel then read the Act of Attainder of Oct. 22, 1779, by which David Colden was attainted by name.

The plaintiff's counsel then read in evidence an Act, entitled "An Act for Vesting the Estate of D. Colden, deceased, not already sold, in Cadwallader Colden," passed Apr. 21, 1787;

NOTE.—*Evidence.* 1. *Declarations of one in possession of lands, as to the nature and extent of his interest—When excluded.*

In connection with above case of Jackson v. Cole, see Jackson v. Belknap, 12 Johns., 96; Jackson v. Denison, 4 Wend., 558; Sheldon v. Van Slyke, 16 Barb., 26; Burlingame v. Robbins, 21 Barb., 327.

2. *Conveyance by trustee, after many years, presumed.* See Jackson v. Moore, 13 Johns., 513, *note.*

the 1st section of which vested all the lands of D. Colden in C. Colden, in trust for the children of D. Colden, and gave the trustee power to maintain suits in his own name. The 2d section provided that C. Colden should pay to the Commissioners of Forfeitures, or to the Treasurer, the appraised value of the lands in public securities, and should also deliver to the Surveyor-General certain papers belonging to the office of the Surveyor-General of the Colony, and make and file an affidavit of the **589***] delivery of such papers. *The Act also gave C. Colden, the trustee, power to mortgage or sell enough of the lands for the repayment of such moneys as he should advance.

The defendant's counsel objected that it was not proved that the conditions of this Act had been complied with.

The plaintiff's counsel contended that no one but the people could take advantage of the non-fulfillment of the conditions of the Act of 1787; and so the circuit judge decided.

But to show the conditions complied with, the plaintiff read a certified paper from the Comptroller's office, sealed by the Comptroller's seal.

This paper contained the copy of an appraisement of the lands of D. Colden, made pursuant to the Act of 1787, in which the premises in question were included, and at the bottom of it was a copy of a certificate by the Commissioners of Forfeitures, dated Aug. 23, 1788, that it was a copy of the appraisement. Then followed a certificate from G. Barker, the (then) Treasurer, by which it appeared that C. Colden had paid the appraised value of the lands, and that the Treasurer had given him a receipt for the money.

It was proved that the lands mentioned in the appraisal were generally held under the children of D. Colden, or some of them.

Morse, a witness, swore that he had compared the paper from the Comptroller's office with the one on file, and that it was a true copy; that the State had never made any claims to these lands; that he had searched among the papers of C. Colden, deceased, the trustee, and that the original of the paper from the Comptroller's office could not be found.

The plaintiff's counsel then read in evidence an exemplified copy of the will of Lieut.-Gov. C. Colden, from the office of the Surrogate of N. Y.; and also a certificate from the Surrogate that the original was not in his office, and a like certificate from the Secretary of State, that the original will was not among the probate papers deposited in his office.

This will directed Gov. Colden's executors to divide his lands equally among his children. **590***] The plaintiff's counsel *then read in evidence an exemplification of the partition deed made by the surviving executor of this will, dated Oct., 1787, by which it appeared that the premises in question fell to the share of the testator's son, David Colden. It was proved that all the lands of Lieut.-Gov. Colden were held pursuant to this partition deed.

The whole of the above evidence was received subject to all legal exceptions.

The defendant was admitted to be in possession, and the jury, under the direction of the judge, found a verdict for the plaintiff for an undivided fourth part of the premises. The additional facts, necessary to present the points decided, will be found in the opinion of the court.

A motion was now made to set aside the verdict, and for a new trial.

Mr. M. Hoffman, for the defendant:

1. No title in the lessors was made out. The testimony was not sufficient to establish the seisin of D. Colden. The testimony of Cochran cannot be received as to title. (6 Johns., 20.) The very act of subpœnaing witnesses to defend the suit, instead of admitting the rights of the lessors, denied them.

If the title was once in D. Colden, it vested in the people by the Act of Attainder; and if the Act of 1787 devested the people of their estate, it vested the legal estate in C. Colden, not in the children of D. Colden. The former had power to sell or mortgage. The legal estate, therefore, would not be executed by the Statute of Uses, but would remain in his heirs. Cruise Dig., Trust, ch. 1, sec. 26; 1 Ves., 142; 2 Saund., 11, *n.* 17; 3 Bos. & P., 174; 2 T. R., 648.

2. C. Colden never complied with the conditions of the Act of 1787; and therefore the title never vested in him. The conditions are all precedent, and until performed the title remained in the State.

3. The paper from the Comptroller's office was improperly received. It was a certified copy of a copy relative to an appraisal of and payment for lands. Such a copy is not evidence. (1 Dall., 64.) Inquiry and search for the original should have been made among C. Colden's heirs.

4. The will of Lieut.-Gov. Colden was not properly authenticated. The exemplification was from the Surrogate of *N. Y.; but [***591** by the Act concerning Wills, 1 R. L., 368, this should have been from the Court of Probates.

The testimony of Cochran will doubtless be much relied on; but it could not be understood to mean anything more than that the defendant had a title to his farm from Cooper, and that a claim was now set up to it as his wife's land.

There is nothing from which a conveyance from C. Colden to the children of D. Colden can be presumed.

Mr. J. O. Morse, contra:

1. The evidence of Cochran, alone, made out a perfect right of recovery in the lessors. The defendant held by virtue of a deed from one of the daughters of D. Colden, and the husbands of two other of his daughters. He took the deed in 1798. Mrs. Cooper having died the year before, T. Cooper, one of the grantors, had no interest except his estate by the curtesy, which expired with him.

Again; both the partition deed and the paper from the Comptroller's office, show that the premises belonged to D. Colden before his attainder; and the Act of 1787 vests all his lands in C. Colden, in trust for the children of D. Colden.

2. It was not necessary for us to show the conditions of the Act of 1787 complied with. None but the people can take advantage of a non-compliance. (Com. Dig., Condition, O; 3 Atk., 134; Co. Litt., 214 *a.*) Had they been a party to this suit, they could not object the non-compliance, without showing office found.

People v. *Brown*, 1 Cai., 416. The State has made no claim to any of these lands since 1787; but suffered them to be held by the children of D. Colden. Such a lapse of time will warrant a presumption that the conditions have been complied with.

3. It was not necessary, in order to make out our case, to resort to the will of Lieut.-Gov. Colden. The partition and possession under it proved, *prima facie*, at least that the title was in D. Colden, independent of the will.

The defendant is estopped to object that the estate did not pass and become executed by the Statute of Uses. By his act of taking a title from Cooper, he acknowledged his estate; and we claim under him. Besides, "an estate in a trustee shall not be set up against the *cestui que trust*; anything shall rather be presumed." (Cowp., 36, per Ld. Mansfield.) The statute, however, did execute the use. The authorities **592***] *cited on the other side are where the trustees had power to sell the whole estate. In this case the power was to sell only a part, and the power to mortgage a part operated, at most, as a mere charge on the land, and the fee was left to be executed in the *cestuis que use*, subject to a lien which is regarded by the law as merely personal. If, however, the trustee ever had the legal estate, it was only for a sufficient time to reimburse himself; and this object having been answered, it is now in the *cestuis que use*. (1 Cruise Dig., tit. 12, Trust, sec. 5; 3 East, 162.)

Mr. D. Cady, same side. It would be difficult to state an admission more full or unequivocal than the one made by the defendant to Cochran. The declarations of a party in possession as to his title, are evidence against him, and all claiming under him. (4 Johns., 230, 234.) This proposition is illustrated by a variety of cases in our reports, less strong than the present one. (12 Johns., 96; 18 *Id.*, 332.) The case cited against us from 6 Johns., 20, was an attempt to prove a transfer of title by parol. To allow this, would overrule the Statute of Frauds; but no such consequence follows from receiving the acknowledgment of a defendant who shows no title, as *prima facie* evidence of title in the lessors.

Again; offering the Act of Attainder in evidence was an affirmation that D. Colden once owned the land. To repel this, we read the Act of 1787. The defendant now says D. Colden never owned the premises. Why then did he show the Act of Attainder?

But we show a title in D. Colden. The Commissioners of Forfeitures furnished the Treasurer of the State with a copy of the location and appraisal, made pursuant to the Act of 1787. This included the premises in question. The Treasurer received from C. Colden, the trustee, the value of these lands.

The writing from the Comptroller's office was not a copy of a copy within the meaning of the rule relied upon. The memorandum made on the copy by the Treasurer, constituted it, in one sense, and for the purpose of the present investigation, an original document. It was, at least, *prima facie* evidence.

593*] **Curia*, per SUTHERLAND, *J.* I think the plaintiff is entitled to recover. The deed from Cooper to the defendant, and his admissions to Cochran that the estate belonged to Mrs. Cooper, and that if she had signed the deed with her husband, his title would have been good, were sufficient, *prima facie*, to establish the fact that Cooper was only tenant by the curtesy, and that the estate belonged to his wife, of whom Mrs. Swartwout, one of the lessors of the plaintiff, is the sole heir. The admissions of the defendant do not fall within the class of cases in which it has been held that parol acknowledgments, as to the title of real estate, are inadmissible. I think it will be found, in all those cases, either that a title had been previously made out, which it was sought to devest by the parol admissions, contrary to the provisions of the Statute of Frauds, or it appeared from the acknowledgments themselves that there had been written conveyances, and that the admissions, therefore, were not the best evidence that existed in the case. Thus, in *Jackson* v. *Vosburgh*, 7 Johns., 186, after the plaintiff had established his title, the defendant offered to prove a parol disclaimer, by the lessors of the plaintiff, of any right to the premises. So in *Jackson* v. *Kisselbrack*, 10 Johns., 336, the defendant claimed title under an agreement between him and the lessor of the plaintiff, which was held to amount to a lease or present demise. He also proved the payment of rent. The plaintiff then offered to show that the defendant had disclaimed holding under him, and had expressly denied his title. The court say, if an interest passed to the defendant by the agreement, no subsequent disclaimer by parol can abrogate it; for a freehold interest can not be devested by words *in pais*. In *Brant* v. *Livermore*, 10 Johns., 358, after the lessors of the plaintiff had established their title to the premises in question, the defendant offered to show that two of the lessors, since the commencement of the suit, had disclaimed all interest or ownership in the land. The court say parol evidence of a disclaimer to a title to real property, otherwise valid is inadmissible. So in *Jackson* v. *Cary*, 16 Johns., 302, the defendant had established a clear title; and it was attempted on the part of the plaintiff to *show that she had repeat- [***594** edly admitted that she had only a life estate, and that the grantor of the plaintiff had a right to convey the fee subject to her life estate. *Ch. J.* Spencer says the parol declarations made by the defendant avail nothing; for, though parol declarations of tenancy have been received, with certain qualifications, parol proof has never yet been admitted to destroy or take away a title.

In *Jackson* v. *Shearman*, 6 Johns., 19, it appeared from parol admissions that there had been a written conveyance; and the court excluded the parol proof, saying that the extent of the title transferred, &c., rested upon higher evidence than upon parol proof of acknowledgment by the party. It rested upon the written assignment of the lease.

But where the party in possession has not established a legal title, his declarations, and the declarations of those under whom he claims, as to the nature and extent of their interest, or as to the right of the plaintiffs, have repeatedly been received in evidence. Thus, in *Jackson* v. *Bard*, 4 Johns., 230, declarations of a party under whom the defendant claimed, showing a distrust of his own right, and an admission of the title of the plaintiff, were held admissible. So also in *Jackson* v. *Belknap*, 12 Johns., 96, and in *Jackson* v. *M'Vey*, 18 Johns., 330, the defendant was allowed to give evidence of the declarations of one of the lessors, to show under what title he held.

But independently of the admissions of the defendant, the evidence of title in the lessors of the plaintiff was, *prima facie*, sufficient. That the premises in question were once the property of David Colden, appears to me to be admitted by the course of the defense upon the trial. Before the plaintiffs had attempted to connect themselves with David Colden, or to show that he was the owner of the property, and the source of their title, the defendant introduced the Act of Oct. 22d, 1779, by which the land and real estate of David Colden were declared to be forfeited to, and vested in the people of this State. This evidence had neither force nor pertinency, unless the premises in question were a part of the lands so forfeited. It proceeded upon the admission that the plaintiff had made out a title, *prima facie*, and **595*]** was *intended to show a title out of the plaintiff, and in the people of the State. To repel this evidence, the plaintiff read the Act of Apr. 21, 1787, for vesting the estate of David Colden, not already sold, in Cadwallader Colden, in trust for the children of David Colden, of whom Mrs. Cooper was one. The Act refers to a certain location or enumeration of the lands of David Colden, made by Cadwallader Colden, Aug. 1, 1786, and delivered to the Commissioners of Forfeitures of the western district; and directs them to be appraised by such appraisers as the Commissioners should appoint, and the appraised value to be paid, either to the Commissioners or to the Treasurer of the State for the time being; and certain maps and papers which were in the possession of David Colden at the time of his death, and which belonged to the office of the Surveyor-General, were to be procured, and delivered by Cadwallader Colden to the Surveyor-General, &c., before the Act could take effect. As against the State, the location thus referred to and adopted by the Act, would be conclusive evidence that the lands mentioned were the lands which belonged to David Colden. It was those lands that were to be appraised and paid for. The location is spoken of in the Act as having been delivered to the Commissioners of Forfeitures.

The exemplification of the copy of the certificate of the appraisers was competent evidence; and it established the fact that the premises in question were included in the location delivered to the Commissioners by Cadwallader Colden, of the lands of David: that they had been appraised pursuant to the Statute, and the appraised value paid into the Treasury of the State. It was objected to this document, that it was but the copy of a copy. It however appears from the certificate of G. Barker, the Treasurer, indorsed on the document that the original certificate had been delivered to Cadwallader Colden, and it was shown by Mr. Morse that they were not to be found among the papers of Mr. Colden. This was sufficient to authorize the introduction of secondary evidence.

But although this certificate is styled a copy, it may well be considered an original for certain purposes. It was the *evidence **[*596** furnished by the Commissioners of Forfeitures to the Treasurer, as to what lands of David Colden were included in the location mentioned in the Act, and of their having been appraised pursuant to the Act, in order that he might know what amount to receive from the trustees. The Treasurer considered it as affording competent evidence upon those points, as his voucher or authority for receiving payment pursuant to the Statute. He accordingly indorsed upon it all that he did under it; the amount received; that he gave a receipt for it to Mr. Colden; but that he gave no deed or conveyance, Mr. Colden resting his title upon the certificate of the appraisers, and upon his receipt for the money; and put it on file in the office. As against the State, it is certainly to be considered an original document, and as verifying all that is contained in it. So far as the Treasurer's certificate is concerned, it is original; and proves the payment of the appraised value of the land in the State, from which a previous compliance on the part of the trustee, with all the other requirements of the Act, is necessarily to be inferred.

In *Jackson* v. *Belknap*, 12 Johns., 96, the lessor claimed title under a deed from the Surveyor-General, which was given under and pursuant to the provisions of an Act of the Legislature, authorizing the Surveyor-General to sell such lands of one Weatherhead as one Cockburn should discover to have become forfeited by the attainder of Weatherhead; and which had been previously discovered. This Act, and the deed from the Surveyor-General, were held to afford *prima facie* evidence that the lands mentioned in the deed were lands discovered by Cockburn, and which had been forfeited by the attainder of Weatherhead. The court say the Surveyor-General was a public officer, executing a special trust reposed in him by the Act. He was only authorized to sell such land as Cockburn should discover to him to have become forfeited by the attainder of Weatherhead. It is to be presumed, therefore, that due inquiry was made by him; and the title given, in pursuance thereof, is to be received, in the first instance, as given conformably to the requisites of the Act. So in this case, the fact that the officers of government, *whose duty it was to see the provis- **[*597** ions of the Act of 1787 carried into effect, and complied with on the part of the trustee, have proceeded as they could not, consistently with their duty, have done, unless the trustee had performed whatever was incumbent on him to do, is *prima facie* evidence of performance on his part. The Act of Jan. 27, 1789, passed for the relief of Cadwallader Colden, assumes, and takes it for granted, that he had complied substantially with the Act of 1787. I am, therefore, of opinion that it was sufficiently shown that the premises in question were included in the location delivered by Cadwallader Colden to the Commissioners, as mentioned in the Act; that the title of David Colden to the lands was recognized by the Act; and that it was, therefore, unnecessary for the plaintiff to give further evidence on that point; and that a compliance on the part of the trustee with the conditions of the Act was *prima facie*, established.

But it is said, if the provisions of the Act of 1787 were complied with, then the legal estate in the lands of David Colden, mentioned in the Act vested in Cadwallader Colden, and is not shown to have been transferred to the heirs of David. Whether the trust created by the Act of 1787 was executed in the children of David Colden by the Statute of Uses, or not, I do not deem it material to decide; for admitting that it was not, I am clearly of opinion that a conveyance from the trustee to the *cestui que trust*, is, under the circumstances of this case, to be presumed, if such conveyance was necessary to vest the legal estate in them.

The children of David Colden were, by the very terms of the Act, the individuals intended to be benefited by it. The lands of David were declared to be vested in Cadwallader in trust for them. The power given to the trustee to sell or mortgage a portion, if necessary, in order to pay the appraised value of the State, was a power given for their benefit. If the trustee advanced it, he was authorized to sell or mortgage for his indemnity. There is no evidence that the money paid by the trustee to the Treasurer was his own money, and not money raised and advanced by the heirs. But **598***] *if such be the presumption of law, then it is fairly to be intended, after this lapse of time, either that it was subsequently repaid by the heirs, or that the trustee exercised the power given to him by the Act, and sold enough of the estate to reimburse all his advances. If so, then the purpose for which the legal estate was vested in him was accomplished; and it became his duty to convey it to the heirs; and the law will presume that he did his duty. (4 T. R., 682; Cowp., 46; 3 Burr., 1901; Doug., 721; 11 Johns., 456.) This presumption derives confirmation from the fact, as testified to by Morse, that many portions of the land of David Colden, mentioned in the location and appraisement, had been held for upwards of thirty years under his heirs; and also from the circumstance that the defendant himself, as early as 1798, took a conveyance for the premises in question from one of the daughters of David Colden, and the husbands of two others.

Indeed, it may be questionable whether this is not such a recognition of the legal title of h heirs as to preclude the defendant from denying that it passed from the trustee to the *cestui que trust*.

Holding, as I do, that the Act of 1787 recognizes the lands, mentioned in the location of Cadwallader Colden, as the lands of David Colden, to be appraised and paid for; and that the proceedings under that Act sufficiently identify them, and show the premises in question to be a portion of them, it becomes nuneoessary to trace the title of David Colden farther back. All the testimony, therefore, in relation to the will of Lieut.-Gov. Colden, and the partition and holding in conformity to it, becomes immaterial.

I am, therefore, of opinion that the plaintiff is entitled to judgment for one undivided fourth part of the premises in question.

New trial denied.

Cited in—4 Wend., 560; 14 Wend., 626; 10 N. Y., 544; 16 Barb., 32; 21 Barb., 330; 22 Barb., 165; 46 Barb., 160; 11 Mich., 243; 38 Mich., 330; 28 Am. Dec., 554; 15 Am. Dec., 435, 456.

---

*JACKSON, ex dem. STEWART, [*599
v.
TOWN.

Purchaser at Sheriff's Sale under Judgment against Party not in Possession—What he must Show to Recover in Ejectment—Where Party against whom Judgment was Recovered is in Possession, this Sufficient—Conveyance by Defendant before Judgment—Consideration—Construction of Registry Acts.

To recover in ejectment under a purchase at sheriff's sale, on a judgment against a party not in possession, the plaintiff must prove against the one found in possession, that the party against whom the judgment was rendered had some right, title or interest in the premises sold. And it was held not enough to show that such party held adversely for less than 20 years, but abandoned the premises before judgment, to which she never returned; though a few months after abandoning, she conveyed to the defendant in ejectment, who afterwards entered under the conveyance.

An equitable or legal seisin must be shown, on which a judgment can attach, and be a lien, in order to warrant a sale of real estate under it.

When the party against whom the judgment is recovered is the actual possessor, this is sufficient of itself; for actual possession is *prima facie* evidence of title; and he cannot show title in another.

If one convey, before judgment against him, the land conveyed cannot be sold under the judgment; and the law will intend such conveyance to be *bona fide*, and for valuable consideration, till the contrary is shown.

Even if the deed be founded on natural love and affection, it will not be void within the 13 Eliz., as against creditors, if it be not shown that the grantor was indebted to such a degree that the settlement will deprive the creditors of an ample fund for payment of their demands.

And a deed upon such a consideration is good within the 27 Eliz., as against subsequent purchasers,

But not in either case, if a fraudulent use be made of it.

The Registry Acts are not confined in their operation to subsequent immediate purchasers from the same grantor; but one purchasing mediately from him; *e. g.*, under a judgment, is protected.

The Registry Acts are remedial, and should be liberally and beneficially construed.

But the purchaser is not protected by these Acts, unless the grantor, mediate or immediate, had some interest which could pass by the prior recorded deed under which the purchaser claims the protection of the Acts.

Citations—1 R. L., 370, 500: 1 Cai. Cas., 66; 2 Bl. Com., 196; 3 Cai., 188; 12 Johns., 536; Cowp., 713; 4 Johns., 216; 13 Johns., 471.

EJECTMENT for 60 acres of land in Cherry Valley, Otsego Co., tried at the December Circuit for that county, 1824.

On the trial, the plaintiff proved that Eleanor Town, the mother of the defendant, had been in possession of the premises in question, claiming them as her own, and exercising acts of ownership over them, till Nov. 1, 1820, when she removed off them. The defendant moved on in Apr. or May, 1824. It did not appear who had possession in the intermediate time.

The plaintiff then proved that one Darly recovered judgment in slander, against Eleanor Town, for words spoken in May, 1822, at the February Term of the Otsego C. P., 1823, then docketed, for $90 damages and costs; and that under an execution issued upon this judgment, the premises in question were sold to the lessor of the plaintiff, the attorney of Darly, and the sale accompanied with the usual certificate, May 7, 1823; that Aug. 9, 1824, the sheriff executed a conveyance to the lessor, which was duly acknowledged and recorded. The defend- **600***] ant then gave in *evidence a deed in fee of the premises in question, from Eleanor Town to the defendant, who is her daughter, dated Mar. 30, 1821, for a money consideration, a part of which, it was proved, had been paid. The defendant was then 19 years of age It did not appear that the lessor, when he purchased under the execution, had any notice of the deed; and it had never been recorded.

Mr. A. Stewart, for the plaintiff, contended that Otsego being a recording county, 1 R. L., 370, sec. 4, and the defendant's deed not being recorded, it was void against a *bona fide* purchaser at sheriff's sale. *Jackson* v. *Terry*, 13 Johns., 471; *Jackson* v. *Dubois*, 4 *Id.*, 222. As to such purchaser, nothing passed from Eleanor Town to the defendant.

Mr. I. Seelye, for the defendant. The plaintiff did not prove enough to entitle him to recover. Eleanor Town abandoned the premises in 1820, and never returned to them. She had possession before, and claimed title; but this was not an interest upon which a judgment in 1823 would attach.

A purchaser at sheriff's sale cannot, at any rate, by having his deed of land, on which the judgment never attached, first recorded, acquire a title against one who purchased before the judgment. The judgment debtor must be seised at the time of docketing the judgment, or at some time afterwards. A purchaser at sheriff's sale, under a judgment which is not a lien, is not a *bona fide* purchaser within the Recording Act. A grantee in fee is not obliged to record his deed to guard against the effect of a subsequent judgment docketed; or as against any person other than the original grantor. (2 Binn., 502; 15 Johns., 262.) One is bound to record only as against subsequent mortgages, or *bona fide* purchases from the grantor. This has virtually, I think, though not directly, been decided by the court. (4 Johns., 216.)

The plaintiff was the attorney of Darly in the slander suit, and cannot be considered a *bona fide* purchaser. (3 Johns. Ch., 147, 344; 15 Johns., 262.)

A judgment creditor is not a purchaser, within the meaning of the Registry Acts. (4 Cruise Dig., 343, ch. 21, sec. 2; 2 P. Wms., 491; 1 Sch. & L., 160; 2 Binn., 497; *Id.*, 502.)

601*] **Curia*, per WOODWORTH, *J.* Eleanor Town, the mother of the defendant, was in possession of a farm, claimed it as her own, and exercised acts of ownership until Nov. 1, 1820, when she removed from the premises. Who succeeded her does not appear. These facts constitute a good adverse possession, during the time she occupied; but the moment she removed, the continuity of the adverse possession was broken, and, in judgment of law, the possession was in him who had title. There is no evidence of title in Eleanor Town, nor how long her adverse possession continued. To derive any benefit from the latter, it must appear to have been for at least 20 years. That not being pretended, the fact is not established that she ever had any right or title to the premises.

In February Term, 1823, Darley recovered against her a judgment for words spoken in May, 1822; the premises were sold on an execution issued on this judgment, and the lessor, who was attorney for Darley, became the purchaser. The certificate of sale is dated May 7, 1823. Aug. 9, 1824, the land not being redeemed, the sheriff executed a deed, which was recorded the day after.

The first question arising in this case is, does the evidence introduced by the plaintiff entitle him to recover? In my opinion it clearly does not. Whenever real estate is sold under an execution, against a party not in possession, and the purchaser brings an action of ejectment against the person found in possession, it cannot be questioned that the plaintiff is bound to prove on the trial that the defendant in the execution had some right, title or interest in the premises sold.

The 1st section of the Act, 1 R. L., 500, declares that lands, tenements and real estate may be sold, and the judgment shall be a lien on the same. The form of the execution would seem to imply a legal seisin, but cannot control the declared intent of the Legislature, which makes every species of real estate liable to sale. When a statute speaks of a seisin, an equitable may be as well intended as a legal one; the term is applicable to both. (1 Cai. Cas., 66.) It is evident, then, that a seisin must be shown *upon which the judg- [***602** ment attached in order to recover the possession. Where the defendant in the execution is the possessor, it is of itself sufficient; for actual possession is, *prima facie*, evidence of a legal title. (2 Bl. Com., 196.) He cannot show title in another, for the plaintiff comes into exactly such estate as the debtor had; and if it was a tenancy, the plaintiff will be a tenant also, and estopped in a suit by the landlord from disputing his right, in the same manner as the original tenant. This was so held in *Jackson* v. *Graham*, 3 Cai., 188.

There is, then, a failure on the part of the plaintiff to make out any right in Eleanor Town to the premises; and consequently, from his own showing, nothing passed by the sale.

If, however, the defendant has produced proof which sufficiently establishes the right of Eleanor Town, the plaintiff may avail himself of the evidence; for the judgment of the court must be founded on the whole case.

The defendant gave in evidence a deed from Eleanor Town to Lydia Town, her daughter, the defendant, then 19 years of age, executed Mar. 30, 1821, for a money consideration, and proved that a part of the consideration had been paid. Does this additional fact remedy the defect in the plaintiff's proof? After an attentive consideration of its efficacy, I think it does not. Separating this act from everything relating to the former possession of Eleanor Town, with which it does not appear to have any connection, it does not furnish evidence of any right in her at the time the conveyance was made. The case is silent as to the fact, in whom was the title vested; and and as to possession, that had been abandoned several months previously. It does not appear that Eleanor Town had even a right of possession to transfer to the defendant. How, then, can it be said that she took anything under the deed? It purports to convey all the right, and, as against the grantor, would estop her from asserting a right to dispossess the defendant; but nothing more. Here, then, as it seems to me, is an insuperable difficulty in the plaintiff's way. His deed is necessarily inoperative, unless the judgment was a lien; and **603***] that cannot *be, unless there is a legal or equitable seisin. Eleanor Town not having either, nothing could pass by the sale to the plaintiff. It would be a perversion of the Statute, authorizing the sale of lands, tenements or real estate, to adjudge that a case of this kind was within its provisions.

But there is another answer equally conclusive; if it be admitted that at the date of the deed Eleanor Town had seisin of the premises, then she parted with all her right and title,and the deed is valid, if not fraudulent and void against creditors and subsequent purchasers. There are no circumstances disclosed to establish fraud. It does not not appear that the grantor was indebted at the time, and the deed was executed more than a year before the speaking of the words for which the damages were given. The deed was given for a money consideration, a part of which was paid. We cannot intend that the consideration was inadequate, or that the payment was not well secured. If it was intended to attack the transaction as fraudulent, on either of these grounds, proof of the facts ought and probably would have been brought before the court. In the absence of proof, it may be presumed the plaintiff rested on other grounds. We are to intend, on the facts before us, that the deed was *bona fide*, and for valuable consideration, and consequently valid against the claims of creditors and subsequent purchasers. In this view of the case, it becomes unnecessary to consider how far the law would protect the defendant, provided it had been a conceded point that the mother made the deed to her daughter on the consideration of natural love and affection. In that case, it would unquestionably have been good against creditors, according to the construction given to the 13 Elizabeth, because it is free from the imputation of fraud. This question was very ably examined by *Ch. J.* Spencer, in *Verplank* v. *Sterry*, 12 Johns., 536. It was there held that to impeach a voluntary settlement, made on a meritorious consideration, it is necessary that the seller should not only be indebted,but should be insolvent, or in doubtful circumstances at the time; that if the grantor be not indebted to such a degree, as that the settlement will deprive the creditors of an ample **604***] fund for the payment of *their debts, the consideration of natural love and affection will support the deed, although a voluntary one, against his creditors. The Statutes 13 and 27 Eliz. contain the general proviso annexed to our Statute, excepting from their operation those deeds only which are *bona fide*, and upon good consideration. The same learned judge observed in the case referred to, that the deed from Arden to Mrs. Sterry had these two circumstances; it was *bona fide*, and it had a good consideration, that of love and natural affection; and was saved by the express proviso of the statute. I entirely subscribe to the doctrine, that neither a creditor under the 13th, nor a subsequent purchaser under the 27 Eliz., can impeach a conveyance *bona fide*, founded on natural love and affection, free from the imputation of fraud, and where the grantor had, independent of the property granted, an ample fund to satisfy his creditors; with this qualification, however, that if a fraudulent use is made of a settlement, it may be carried back to the time when the fraud commenced, as was held in *Doe* v. *Rutledge*, Cowp., 713. If the grantor continues in possession, and receives the rents and profits, or if there are other circumstances subsequently, calculated to deceive the subsequent purchaser, without doubt they would contaminate the deed; but without them it would be valid. If this view be correct, it follows that had the deed in question been founded on love and affection merely, the plaintiff could not, on the facts before us, as a creditor or subsequent purchaser, have defeated its operation. A *fortiori*, he cannot, when it is shown not to rest on a meritorious, but valuable consideration, and is not contaminated with fraud.

If, then, the deed has not been successfully assailed on this ground, by its legal operation all the right and title of Mrs. Town was transferred to the defendant long before the judgment attached. After Mar. 30, 1821, there was no interest remaining in her that was the subject of sale. She had no lands, tenements or real estate within the meaning of the Statute; and consequently, the was nothing to give life or effect to a sheriff's deed, which solely derives its efficacy *from the [***605** fact that the defendant in the execution had an interest liable to be sold.

But it is contended that a *bona fide* purchaser at a sheriff's sale, without notice of a prior deed not recorded, is protected by putting his deed on record. It is true that the deed to the defendant has not been recorded. I will briefly inquire whether that fact is material. It has been urged, on the argument, that the statute is confined in its application to a purchaser from the same grantor. The words used in the Act are, "any subsequent *bona fide* purchaser or mortgagee for valuable consideration." (1 R. L., 370.) The statute is remedial, and ought to be liberally construed. To say that the second deed must, in all cases, be given by the same grantor, is too limited a construction to remedy the evil the Legislature had in view. The intent being to guard the fair subsequent purchaser against secret outstanding conveyances, why should not the statute apply, where the second deed was obtained mediately from the same grantor as well as to cases where it was immediately given by him? If a defendant confesses a judgment, he thereby indirectly authorizes a sale and the execution of a deed. If judgment is obtained against him, without a plea of confession, although it cannot be said that the defendant assented to the judgment and sale, yet they are founded on his delinquency. The non-payment of the debt due from the debtor, is the foundation of the judgment and sale. Whether willingly or unwillingly, the whole proceeds from the fault of the debtor, who is to be considered as the source from whence the purchaser derives his claim. It would, therefore, seem not to be a forced construction of the statute, to apply it to such cases. In either case, the reason for protecting the purchaser is the same. I therefore concur in the opinion expressed in *Jackson* v. *Dubois*, 4 Johns. 216, and *Jackson* v. *Terry*, 13 Johns., 471. In the first case, *Mr. Justice* Spencer observed that a mortgage not registered had a preference over a subsequent judgment docketed. But if the land should be sold by the sheriff, under the judgment, prior to the registry of the mort- **606*]** gage, a *bona fide* purchaser *at the sheriff's sale would be protected against the mortgage. It was not necessary to the decision of that case to lay down the doctrine; nevertheless, I think it correct for the reasons already given. The case in 13 Johns. expressly decides, that if after land has been sold on execution, and a conveyance made by the sheriff, and before such conveyance is recorded, the former proprietor conveys it to a *bona fide* purchaser, for a valuable consideration, who has his deed first recorded, such subsequent purchaser will gain a priority. The doctrine in this case supports the proposition laid down in 4 Johns. It turned on priority of recording. Terry, the defendant, derived title under a judgment prior to the date of the deed from James Turner to the lessor of the plaintiff, and yet failed because his deed had not been first recorded. If a sheriff's deed is within the Recording Act, it seems to me clear that the principle of this case, which entitled Merrit to recover on a junior title first recorded, would entitle a purchaser at sheriff's sale, whose deed was recorded, to a preference over a prior unregistered mortgage. I consider the law correctly laid down in both cases; but they do not decide the present question. In each of those cases, the defendant in the execution had an interest liable to be sold. In the first, Sammons was mortgagor, and had an interest upon which the judgment was a lien; in the second, the deed from Archibald Turner to James Turner was fraudulent and void as against creditors; consequently, the judgment against Archibald became a lien, having been entered before James Turner made a *bona fide* sale to Merrit. These facts were essential, in order to maintain the proposition that a sheriff's deed is within the Recording Act. In the present case, Eleanor Town had no title, and the judgment was no lien. I cannot perceive that the plaintiff acquired anything more than if the sheriff had sold and conveyed the same premises on an execution against John Doe or Richard Roe, who were utter strangers. A subsequent *bona fide* purchaser within the meaning of the Act, must be one with whom the grantor in the first deed actually conveyed, or who did or suffered some act which, by the operation of law, authorized a sale and con- **607*]** veyance; and if *the deed was in consequence of a sale under a judgment, then that the property sold was a legitimate subject of such sale.

These principles decide the plaintiff's claim. Eleanor Town has not conveyed to the plaintiff, nor done any act authorizing a valid conveyance. There was no lien on the premises, and no authority was given by law to sell and convey. How liberal and extensive soever may be the construction of the statute, and giving full effect to the cases referred to, I think it demonstrable that the present case is not within the letter or spirit of the 4th section of the Act concerning Deeds and, consequently, that the defendant is entitled to judgment.

Judgment for the defendant.

Cited in—8 Cow., 436; 9 Cow., 84, 124, 192; 1 Wend. 504; 6 Wend., 225; 8 Wend., 626; 11 Wend., 433; 15 Wend., 595; 10 N. Y., 542; 24 N. Y., 633; 59 N. Y., 346; 6 Barb., 69, 126; 19 How. Pr., 483; 1 E. D. S., 333; 7 Leg. Obs., 148; 94 Ill., 60; 21 Am. Dec., 313; 39 Am. Dec., 255 (1 Rob., 123); 50 Am. Dec., 324 (6 Ga., 103).

M'NEILLY v. RICHARDSON.

Advance of Money by Pliff. to Deft. to be Used for Particular Purpose—Money Used for Different Purpose—Deft. not Chargeable until Day of Payment—Discharge in Insolvency Does not Affect Debts Accruing after Petition Presented—When Affects Debtors Residing out of U. S.

The plaintiff, resident in Ireland, drew a bill of exchange in favor of the defendant, resident in N. Y., for money, to be employed in building a vessel, and prosecuting a particular adventure, pursuant to a previous agreement.

The defendant received the bill, May 27, 1818; and the money was paid to him upon it, July 29, 1818. The defendant built the vessel, but employed her in a different adventure from the one agreed on. June 22, 1818, he petitioned for his discharge under the Act for Giving Relief in Cases of Insolvency, 1 R. L., 460; which was granted, his property being assigned, &c., Aug. 12, 1818; held, that the money was recoverable as money had and received to the plaintiff's use; and that the debt, not accruing till after the defendant petitioned, was not affected by the discharge.

Where one advances money to another, to be employed in a particular manner, and he appropriates it to a different object, it may be recovered back as money had and received to the use of him who advances it.

A discharge under the Act for Giving Relief in Cases of Insolvency, does not affect debts which are contracted after the time of presenting the petition.

Nor will the discharge affect creditors residing out of the U. S., unless the 8th section of the Act be pursued.

Citation—1 R. L., 460.

ASSUMPSIT, for money had and received to the plaintiff's use, tried before Woodworth, J., at the N. Y. sittings, Apr. 23, 1822, when a verdict was taken for the plaintiff, for $2,794.84, subject to the opinion of the court on the following case:

The plaintiff, resident in Ireland, sent to the defendant, a resident in the City of N. Y., a bill of exchange drawn by Cressy & Dawson, of Lawrence Town in Ireland, on Abraham Bell, of the City of N. Y., merchant, in favor of the defendant, dated Mar. 19, 1818, for $2,210, payable at 60 days' sight. The bill was accepted *May 27, 1818, and paid to the **[*608** defendant July 29, 1818. The amount of the bill was received by the defendant on account of the plaintiff.

The counsel for the defendant then produced the discharge of the defendant under the Insolvent Act of this State, entitled "An Act for Giving Relief in Cases of Insolvency;" and relied upon that discharge in bar of the plaintiff's action. The discharge was dated Aug. 12, 1818.

The counsel for the plaintiff then produced the petition of the defendant, with the accompanying document, under the Act, from which it appeared that the petition was presented to the Recorder of the City of N. Y. June 22, 1818; that the creditors were required to show cause Aug. 12, 1818; and on that day the defendant executed an assignment of his estate and obtained the discharge. It further appeared, that in the account of the creditors of the defendant, the plaintiff was not represented as a creditor, nor was the bill of exchange included in the inventory of the defendant's estate.

The judge being of opinion that the discharge was not a bar to the plaintiff's right to recover, the counsel for the defendant called Hugh Hill, who testified that he was well acquainted with the parties; that he saw the plaintiff in Belfast in 1817 and 1818; that he had a conversation with him relative to the business in which the witness and the defendant, and the plaintiff and the plaintiff's brother were concerned; that the plaintiff admitted the agreement between them to be that the defendant was to build a vessel, load it with tobacco and send it to Ireland on their joint account; that the bill was remitted on account of that concern; that the witness also advanced $2,000 on the account of the concern; that he did not consider that either himself or the plaintiff was to be concerned in the vessel, if it was not loaded with tobacco and sent to Ireland; that the defendant had admitted to the witness that instead of sending the vessel to Ireland with a cargo of tobacco, he loaded her with a different cargo and sent **609***] *her to Havana; that the defendant has never rendered any account to the witness as part owner of the vessel or cargo; that the witness had seen the plaintiff in Ireland after the vessel was finished, and understood from him that it was called the Retrieve.

John White testified that the defendant built the schooner Retrieve, which cost, as near as the witness could tell, about $10,000; that the witness was employed as superintendent; that she was sent on a voyage to Havana, which the witness had understood was a losing one.

The counsel for the defendant then offered to go into an examination of the accounts of the voyage; from which, as he stated, it would appear that the voyage had been a disastrous one, and that the defendant had lost a large sum of money.

The judge rejected this evidence.

Mr. G. Brinckerhoff, for the plaintiff. The insolvent discharge was no bar. When the defendant petitioned, he held the bill as agent or factor of the plaintiff; and the money which he received under it was holden in the same way. This the law will intend, as it was his duty so to consider and hold it. That property holden as agent, factor or trustee, will not pass under a bankrupt assignment, is abundantly settled by the authorities. (10 Johns., 63, 289; 2 Vern., 638; Paley on Ag., 79; 3 Maule & S., 576, per Ld. Ellenborough, *Ch. J.*)

The money being advanced to the defendant on account of a special adventure, and no part appropriated to that or any other object, he is accountable for money had and received. (5 T. R., 226, per Ld. Kenyon, *Ch. J.*; 1 East, 554; 9 *Id.*, 12; Willes, 404.)

Mr. S. Jones, for the defendant. The bill was paid to the defendant July 29. The avails then became a part of his own funds. The bill was no longer a chose in action. The assignment and discharge which took place in Aug., *operated on all debts due from [***610** the defendant before the assignment, and this among the rest. The plaintiff might have come in for his dividend. If the money received on the bill was kept distinct from the defendant's, as trust money, it lay with the plaintiff to show it.

But the money was appropriated by the defendant. So far as the building of the schooner was concerned, the contract was literally pursued. Nor does it appear but that changing the destination of the vessel was proper under the circumstances. War, or other cause for this, might have intervened. The change will be intended to have been proper, till the contrary be shown.

Curia, per WOODWORTH, *J.* The money was advanced by the plaintiff to be applied in a particular adventure. He never consented to a different appropriation. The defendant has, on his own risk and on his own responsibility, undertaken a different voyage, and chosen a different cargo. With the profit or loss of this concern the plaintiff had no connection. This is a sufficient reason for excluding evidence to prove the defendant's loss. The money not being applied according to the contract, the plaintiff was entitled to a return of it, as money had and received to his use. The defendant must be considered as holding the bill in trust for the plaintiff to the day of payment. Until that time he was not the plaintiff's debtor in any amount. A bill was resorted to by the plaintiff as the medium by which to make the remittance. The defendant, it seems, was to receive the money for a particular object, and would not be chargeable till the day of payment, unless he had made himself liable on the ground of negligence.

The question then, is, whether the discharge was a bar. The petition was presented June 22, 1818. The plaintiff was not named as a creditor, nor the bill of exchange inserted in the inventory.

I think it very clear that the discharge is no bar to the plaintiff's action. The whole scope of the Act, 1 R. L., 460, has reference to creditors and debts due, or to become due, *when the petition is presented. The [***611** 1st section of the Act gives the right of petitioning for a discharge, to the insolvent and his creditors who shall have the debts owing to them. All subsequent proceedings are predicated on this fact. The existing state of things at the time of presenting the petition is the criterion. Persons who subsequently become creditors, are necessarily excluded from a participation of the insolvent's property, and are not affected by the discharge. It seems to me that a different construction would defeat the plain intent of the Act. Suppose an insolvent at the time of presenting his petition, was indebted $1,000, for two thirds of which sum the creditors became petitioners; subsequent to this, and before the assignment, the insolvent contracts debts to the amount of $1,000 more; the doctrine contended for would, in that case, discharge the insolvent when, in fact, less than one third of the creditors in amount petitioned for the discharge. The intention of the Act is to exonerate the debtor from debts then due; and, consequently, subsequent creditors are not affected. Again; the insolvent is required to deliver an account of his creditors, and the moneys owing to them. This necessarily excludes subsequent creditors.

The 6th section declares that upon producing a certificate from the assignee, the officer shall discharge the insolvent from all such debts due at the time of the assignment or contracted for before that time, though payable afterwards. The words "such debts," refer to those upon which the proceedings under the Act are had. They alone are discharged.

The 19th section provides for a distribution of the insolvent's estate; and directs that a just and equal distribution be made to creditors, whose debts are discharged by the Act; which seems to imply that there may be others who cannot participate in the distribution.

In the present case, the plaintiff did not reside in the U. S. By the 8th section, it is expressly enacted that debts due to creditors residing without the U. S. are not to be discharged, unless the foreign creditor petition, or *receive a dividend, or two thirds of [*612 all the insolvent's debts including foreign debts shall have been signed off. There has not been a compliance with these requisitions. I am of opinion that the plaintiff is entitled to judgment.

Judgment for the plaintiff.

Cited in—7 Wend., 71; 8 Wend., 349; Edm., 188; 2 Hall, 537; 2 Daly, 116.

[END OF AUGUST TERM, 1825.]

CASES ARGUED AND DETERMINED

IN THE

Court for the Trial of Impeachments

AND THE

CORRECTION OF ERRORS

OF THE

STATE OF NEW YORK,

IN JUNE AND JULY, 1825.

JOHN MURRAY AND JAMES B. MURRAY, *Appellants*,

v.

JOHN G. COSTER, ET AL., *Respondents*.

Bill for Account and Discovery—Plea of Statute of Limitations, Overruled—Defendant Cannot Repeat Overruled Matter in Second Answer.

• After a plea of the Statute of Limitations to a bill for an account and discovery, with an accompanying answer, is overruled, and the defendant ordered to put in a full and perfect answer, he will not be allowed to repeat in his second answer the same matter contained in the plea which had been overruled, though he add matter in his second answer sufficient to sustain the defense upon the Statute; but he must put in a full and perfect answer.

Points and matters not decided or passed upon by the whole court:

1. To what extent a defendant may, by answer, refuse to answer, noticed per Colden, *Senator*, and particularly examined by Savage, *Ch. J.*, who argues that he should be allowed thus to refuse in all cases.

2. When the Statute of Limitations is sufficiently pleaded by answer, examined. Per Savage, *Ch.* J.

3. In what cases, after matter has been pleaded and passed upon by the court, it may again be set up by the defendant in a plea or answer. Per Sutherland, *J.*, and Colden, *Senator*.

4. Subsequent confessions, not admissible in evidence to explain former ones. Per Colden, *Senator*.

5. How far a defendant shall be allowed to explain away facts, admitted in one answer in chancery, by a subsequent one. Per Colden, *Senator*.

6. How far an offer of compromise, or admissions connected with it, is evidence. Per Colden, *Senator*.

7. General object and course of pleading in chancery. Per Savage, *Ch.* J.

Citations—3 P. Wms., 91, 94; 2 Vern., 701; 2 Ves., 491, 492; 1 Ves., 246, 247; 1 Atk., 450, 493; Mitf. Pl., 11, 15, 244, 248; 2 Madd., 299; 2 Anstr., 410; 2 Ves., 247; 4 Johns. Ch., 209, 214, 215; 11 Ves., 306; 1 R. L., 186; 2 Atk., 612; 2 Cox., 224; 1 Johns. Ch., 73; 2 Ves. Jr., 454; 3 Br. Ch., 205; 16 Ves., 387; 2 Br. Ch., 252; 3 Atk., 105; Eq. Drafts, 389; 15 Johns., 571.

APPEAL from the Court of Chancery. The history and statement of this case may **618***] *be gathered from S. C., 5 Johns. Ch., 525; S. C., 7 *Id.*, 157; and 20 S. C., Johns., 567, 610; on appeal from the decision in 5 Johns. Ch., 522. It now came up on appeal from the order mentioned in 7 Johns. Ch., 173, overruling certain exceptions to the master's report.

The following brief review of the case is, however, deemed proper in this place:

John G. Coster and others, the respondents, as assignees of the Columbian Ins. Co., in June, 1821, filed their bill against John & James B. Murray, the appellants, calling upon them to account for one third of the proceeds of certain linens purchased at Copenhagen in 1813, by one George Dickinson as the agent of the Company, and James B. Murray as agent of the appellants. The bill charged that these linens were purchased on the joint account of the Insurance Company and the Murrays, the Company advancing one third and the Murrays two thirds of the purchase money; and that the net proceeds of the linens were to be divided in the same proportion. That the linens were shipped from Copenhagen by James Murray to the U. S., and came to the hands of the appellants, who sold them and received the proceeds. That in June, 1814, the respondents demanded from the appellants the one third of the linens or their proceeds. That the appellants admitted that they had received and sold the linens, and a few weeks thereafter rendered to the respondents an account of sales, in which they charged for insurance and commissions more than $2,000, to which the respondents objected. That they repeatedly urged the appellants to pay them the one third of the proceeds of the linens, which they neglected or refused to do until May, 1821, when being threatened with a prosecution, the appellants proposed that an interview should be had between the counsel of the parties, which accordingly took place. That the counsel for the appellants proposed that they should pay to the respondents the principal amount of the one third part of the proceeds of the linens, without interest. That this proposition was declined by the respondents.

*To this bill the appellants put in a [***619** plea of the Statute of Limitations, and an answer in support of that plea denying any promise to pay within six years. The cause was heard upon the pleadings, and the *Chancellor* (Dec. 11, 1821) overruled the plea and answer, on the ground that it was a case of trust, and therefore not affected by the Statute of Limitations; and ordered the appellants to put in a full and perfect answer. (5 Johns., Ch., 532.)

Upon appeal to this court, the decree was, in Nov. 1822, affirmed; not, however, on the ground taken by the *Chancellor;* but because the answer contained such an admission of the respondents' debt as to defeat the operation of the Statute of Limitations, which, therefore, was no bar. (20 Johns., 603 to 610.) The original plea and answer being thus overruled, and the appellants being ordered to put in a full and perfect answer, they filed their second answer within the time limited by the order of the Court of Chancery; but instead of fully answering the charges in the bill, stating an account and making the discovery sought for, they set up the Statute of Limitations, as a bar to the discovery, account and relief sought, and confined their answer to an explanation of those charges in the bill which, if unanswered, would have defeated the plea of the Statute. (7 Johns., Ch., 167.) To this answer the respondents filed seven exceptions, and the appellants not submitting to put in a further answer, the exceptions were referred to a master, who reported that they were well taken. (*Id.*, 168.) The appellants excepted to the report of the master (*Ib.*), but the *Chancellor* overruled the exceptions and confirmed the report, directing the appellants to answer the first six exceptions allowed by the master; and upon the 7th exception, that a certain part of the first answer should be stricken out. (*Id.*, 173.) The cause came here on appeal from this order.

The only point now decided was the same as that in S. C., 7 Johns. Ch., 167.

The facts necessary to the understanding of some other points, adverted to or discussed by several of the judges, are sufficiently stated in their opinions.

The reasons of the late *Chancellor* in support of the order were rendered as in S. C., 7 John. Ch., 170, 173.

620*] *The cause was very fully argued at the last session, in January, 1825, by,

Mr. J. V. Henry, for the appellants, and

Mr. Talcott, Atty-Gen., for the respondents.

But the authorities, and the different views of counsel, are so fully presented in the former reports of the cause above referred to, and were now so thoroughly considered by the judges in giving their opinions, that it is not deemed necessary to repeat them.

SUTHERLAND, *J.*, after stating the ease. The first and principal question which arises, is, whether the appellants, after their plea of the Statute of Limitations had been overruled, were at liberty to insist on the same matter by way of answer. If it should be held that they were not, then the exceptions to the answer are, clearly, well taken—as the appellants, being deprived of their bar to the relief sought, were bound to answer fully to all the matters contained in the bill.

But if they were entitled to set up the same defense by way of answer, which had been passed upon and overruled, when offered by way of plea, it still remains to be considered, whether, having undertaken to answer, they were not bound to make discovery, and answer fully as to everything that would not take away or destroy the defense of the Statute of Limitations.

The general position, that if a plea is overruled, the defendant may insist on the same matter by way of answer, is certainly to be found in treatises on the practice and proceedings in chancery, of high and established character. But, like most other general propositions, it is subject to limitations and exceptions; and the extent to which it is true, can only be accurately understood by an examination of the cases from which it professedly derives its authority, and from a consideration of its bearing and effect upon other general principles of fundamental truth and importance in the administration of every system of justice. The cases which were cited and relied on by the defendant's counsel to *sustain their position, are *Harris* v. [***621** *Ingledew*, 3 P. Wms., 91; *Stephens* v. *Gaule*, 2 Vern., 701; *Finch* v. *Finch*, 2 Ves., Sr., 491; *East India Co.* v. *Campbell*, 1 Ves., Sr., 246, and *The Earl of Suffolk* v. *Green*, 1 Atk., 450.

Harris v. *Ingledew*, 3 P. Wms., 91, was a case of a bill filed by the simple contract creditors of William Ingledew, after his death, to compel a sale of his real estate for payment of his debts; he having devised his real estate subject to the payment of his debts. The bill was filed against the devisees and others who had purchased portions of the real estate from them. One of the defendants who had thus purchased, pleaded that he was a purchaser for a full and valuable consideration, but omitted in his plea to deny notice of the will of William Ingledew. The plaintiff replied, and took issue on the plea; and the question was, whether the plaintiff, by replying to the plea, instead of setting it down to be argued, and excepting to it, had not admitted it to be a good defense in law, provided it was true in fact. And the counsel of the defendant, among other reasons which he urged in support of his position, contended that if the legal efficacy of the plea was not admitted by the replication, "the defendant might be tricked by the plaintiff, who having found that the defendant had made a slip in his plea, might decline setting it down for argument, and reply to it, in which case the defendant would be without remedy; for he could do no more than prove his plea; whereas, if such plea had been set down to be argued, on its being overruled, the defendant might still have helped himself by putting all his defense in his answer. The Master of the Rolls in deciding this point, simply says, the constant course is, in case a plea be replied to, that the defendant need only prove his plea, &c.; and takes no notice of the consideration which had been urged by counsel. He neither adopts nor repels it. This case, therefore, furnishes no authority in support of the position for which it was cited. But if the language of the counsel in that case had, in truth, been the language of the court, as the *Chancellor*, in his opinion, seems to suppose it was, it would not affect this case; first, for the reason assigned by the *Chancellor*, "that it does not appear that the court would not *have required the answer to meet [***622** fully all the charges in the bill." But, secondly, and I think principally, because a purchase for a valuable consideration, without notice of a previous charge, is both in form and substance a very different defense from a purchase for a valuable consideration, merely. In overruling the latter, therefore, when offered by way of plea, the court would not have passed upon and decided the former. No reason, therefore, could exist, why it should not be put forth as a defense, by way of answer, if it was originally proper matter for an answer.

In *Finch* v. *Finch*, 2 Ves. Sr., 491, all the court decided was, that a defendant, whose answer had been reported to be insufficient, and who, without excepting to the report, had submitted to answer again, was not precluded from insisting on the same matter in his second answer. Ld. Hardwicke said that it was not a proper manner of bringing the matter before the court; but that the defendant was not absolutely precluded by the forms of the court from doing it; that where there are several exceptions, the court has always said, that as this matter has not undergone the judgment of the court, they shall be suffered to go into it. If it was a single exception, perhaps it would be another matter. That it was not like a second demurrer, or a second plea, which cannot be put in a second time, if overruled. Yet, he remarked, "the court frequently allows the defendant, after it has overruled a plea, to insist on the same matter by answer; and that comes on the merits at hearing the cause." Taking the well established distinction, that the court will not, after a demurrer or a plea is overruled, grant leave to put in a second demurrer or a second plea, containing the same matter; but that it will sometimes, after a plea is overruled, permit the defendant to insist on the same matter by answer. And if he answer fully, his right again to insist on the same matter may be reserved for discussion on the hearing upon the merits, instead of being determined upon exceptions. But if he set up the same matter in order to protect him from discovery, his right to avail himself of it ought to be determined upon exceptions, and not upon the hearing on the merits. In the first case, it may, perhaps, be put in without leave having **623***] been first obtained; *in the latter, it clearly ought not. The case of *Finch* v. *Finch*, therefore, decides nothing that has any application to this case; and the illustration used by Ld. Hardwicke seems to me very clearly to show that, in a case like this, he would not have listened to a defense by way of answer, which had undergone the judgment of the court, and been overruled by way of plea.

E. I. Co. v. *Campbell*, 1 Ves., Sr., 246, was an information brought in the name of the Atty-Gen., to compel the defendant to discover how he came by the possession of certain goods in the East Indies; whether it was not by fraud or violence; and whether they were not the property of the Indians. The defendant pleaded that he could not discover how the goods came to his possession, because it would subject him to a fine or corporal punishment, or to the penalties in the Act of Parliament, for carrying on trade within the jurisdiction of the E. I. Co. The plea having been overruled, he put in a demurrer, which was, in substance, the same as his plea. The court sustained the demurrer, but evidently upon the particular circumstances of the case. They say it was an out of the way bill, and of a dangerous nature, by persons having no right, and founded on supposition. And after contending that a demurrer after a plea was not within the notion of two dilatories, they conclude by saying, "but supposing it to be dilatory, a court of equity must not, merely for form's sake, be a court of inquisition to do great injustice." And by way of illustration, they remark that a plea may be overruled, as a plea of purchase, without notice for want of form, covering too much and yet it may be insisted on in the answer. This is the only observation that has any relation to a case like this, and the distinction between the case put and this will at once be perceived. If a plea be overruled for want of form, its merits have not been considered, or passed upon by the court, and if it was originally proper for an answer, there may be no objection to its being presented in that shape after it has been overruled as a plea, on some collateral point of form.

Earl of Suffolk* v. *Green*, 1 Atk., [*624** 450, was the case of a bill filed to perpetuate the testimony of witnesses to a bond, given by the plaintiff's ancestor. The bill charged that the defendant, Green, who was the obligee in the bond, was very aged and infirm, and that the bond was usurious. The defendant demurred to so much of the bill as sought discovery, and also to perpetuate the testimony. The demurrer was held to be bad so far as it related to perpetuating the testimony, though good as to the discovery. But a demurrer that is bad in part, is void *in toto*. It was, therefore, overruled, but liberty was expressly reserved to the defendant to insist by way of answer, against making any discovery touching the usurious contract, charged by the bill. So far, therefore, as any inference is to be drawn from this case, it is against the right to insist by way of answer, upon any defense which has been overruled on demurrer, even on the ground of informality, unless liberty to insist on it is expressly reserved.

In *Stephens* v. *Gaule*, 2 Vern., 701, the plaintiff filed his bill to redeem a mortgage, and charged that the defendant pretended to be a jointress, and in nature of a purchaser from her husband; whereas, her husband was only an assignee of a mortgage and had no other title. The defendant pleaded her title, and denied notice of the mortgage; but did not answer whether her husband had any other title than as assignee of a mortgage; and the plea was overruled by Ld. Harcourt. Exceptions being taken to this answer, on the ground that it omitted to state whether the husband of the defendant had any other title than as assignee of the mortgage, *Ld. Chancellor* Cowper allowed the answer to be sufficient.

The first observation to be made upon this case is, that the plea was overruled by Ld. Harcourt, and the answer was decided to be sufficient by *Ld. Chancellor* Cowper. He probably thought the plea had been improperly overruled. But the decisive objection to the case as an authority upon the point now under discussion, is, that the objection does not appear to have been taken, that the defense set up in the answer had already been overruled

625*] in the plea. *For aught that appears, liberty to insist upon the same defense may have been reserved when the plea was overruled, or subsequently granted; or it may have been permitted simply, because it was not objected to.

These are all the cases cited by Ld. Redesdale (Mitf. Plead., 244) to support the position that if a plea is overruled, the defendant may insist on the same matter by way of answer. They certainly show that, under certain circumstances, it is admissible. But there is not one of them that countenances the idea that a defense which is proper for a plea, after it has been presented in that shape, and discussed and maturely considered by the court, and finally overruled upon the merits, may again be presented by way of answer. The remark of the *Chancellor* is, therefore, just, "that there is no foundation in authority for such an answer in any of the cases which have a bearing on the question."

The object of plea is to prevent further proceedings, at large, by resting on some point founded on matter stated in the plea; Mitf. Plead., 15; and the defense proper for a plea must be such as reduces the cause to a particular point, which will bar the plaintiff's demand, and then it is of use; because, by having the judgment of the court upon that point, the parties are saved the expense of an examination of witnesses (2 Madd., 299); or as *Ch. B.* Macdonald expresses it, in *Freeland* v. *Johnson*, 2 Anst., 410: "The meaning of a demurrer or plea is to intercept, in an early stage, a cause which must ultimately end in nothing; a demurrer, by something in the bill; a plea, by matter *dehors*. If a plea could be repeated," he observes, "it would not do its office; it would not have the effect of saving litigation, but would encourage defendants to try it as a daily experiment to save time." It is, therefore, an established principle in chancery, that the same matter cannot be a second time pleaded, although the first plea was overruled on a ground of form. You may move for a rehearing, or for leave to amend; but you cannot again plead the same plea. The reason or principle on which this rule is established is, that a plea is, in truth, only an excuse for not answering, on
626*] *the ground of some conclusive bar. If it is decided to be insufficient, the effect and the presumed object of putting it in, is delay. It shall not, therefore, be repeated. But if it be overruled on a point of form, the court may grant leave to amend, or the defendant may avail himself of the same matter in his answer, if his answer is full and perfect in other respects. He will then have the benefit of it on the hearing; and if it should be decided against him, the complainant will not be again delayed. And it may be that it would not be ground of exception to an answer that it contained the same matter which had been overruled in a previous plea, even on the merits. If the answer was full, the question might be reserved to the hearing. But the court, I apprehend, would not again take the matter into consideration, if it had already been solemnly decided upon the plea. However this may be, it is most manifest that there is no distinction in principle, between a second plea, which contains the same defense that had been overruled in a former plea, and an answer containing merely the same matter. The effect is the same, if it be decided that the matter in the answer is not sufficient to bar relief, or protect the defendant from discovery, and he be directed to make a full and perfect answer, and the complainant is a second time delayed upon the same ground, which is the precise objection to a second plea. I should, therefore, apprehend, with the *Chancellor*, that if a second plea be not admissible, it must be equally inadmissible, when it comes in a varied shape in point of form, but in the same shape, and with the same pretensions in point of substance.

These general considerations have a peculiar force when applied to this particular case. The decree or order of Dec., 1821, overruled the plea of the Statute of Limitations and the answer accompanying it, and directed the defendant to put in a full and perfect answer to the bill. It certainly was the intention of the *Chancellor* by that decree, finally to dispose of the Statute as a bar to the discovery and relief sought by the bill. If it had not been, he would, according to the established course of the court, instead of overruling the plea, have directed it to stand for an answer, with *liberty to the respondents to except. [*627
The appellants supposed that if that decree was sustained, the defense of the Statute of Limitations was gone. If not, why did they appeal from the decree? If, according to its terms and spirit, its only operation was to strike from the records of the cause the paper on which the plea was written, and not to dispose of the defense itself, and to leave them at liberty again to present it in the shape of an answer, why did they not put in their answer at once? Why appeal from the decree, when it was a matter of perfect indifference to them whether it was affirmed or reversed, as it only affected the form and not the substance of their defense? If they have now a right to set up the Statute of Limitations by way of answer, they had a right to do it the moment the decree of Dec., 1821, was pronounced. That decree was simply affirmed without being altered or modified by this court. The proceedings of this court also showed that they supposed that, by affirming the decree of the *Chancellor*, the question of the Statute of Limitations was put at rest, and that such was their intention.

After the decree of affirmance was pronounced, on the ground that the answer of the appellants contained such an admission of the respondents' debt as to defeat the operation of the Statute of Limitations, their counsel moved the court so to modify the decree, as that the cause might be sent back to the Court of Chancery, without prejudice on the point on which the court had grounded their decision; and so that the defendants might amend their answer upon that point. The motion was denied, and Spencer, *Ch. J.*, whose opinion upon this motion prevailed, said, "Independent of all that relates to the negotiation between the counsel of the parties, the answer contains a sufficient admission of the debt to take it out of the operation of the Statute. An amendment, therefore, of the answer would avail nothing. If the court had the power, he should not be for exercising it, in order to let in the Statute of Limitations in this case, where the party has made such a clear admission of the debt as is contained in the answer." *Ch. J.* Spencer, therefore, supposed that the object and effect of the application, if granted, **628***] *would be to enable the appellants again to set up the defense of the Statute of Limitations; and he was for denying the motion on the very ground that they ought not again to be permitted to set up the Statute. And such undoubtedly was the opinion of a majority of the court who concurred with him. Under such circumstances, I fully assent to the corectness of the observation of the *Chancellor*, "that after a plea of the Statute has been once technically pleaded, and formally discussed, considered and overruled, and again solemnly discussed and overruled upon appeal, and a full and perfect answer required by the order of both courts, and an effort to have the decretal order so modified as to allow the plea to stand for an answer, denied, it surely cannot, upon any reasonable principle, be permitted to the party to escape from the order in this way, and bring the very same matter into discussion. I am, therefore, of opinion upon this ground, without considering the other point in the cause, that the decree of His Honor the *Chancellor* should be affirmed.

WOODWORTH, *J.*, concurred.

COLDEN, *Senator*. The most material question to be decided, appears to me to be embraced by the second point submitted by the counsel for the appellants, to wit: "that the answer (that is the last answer) is a bar to the relief sought. If it be so, then unquestionably, the appellants are right in their conclusion, that it protects them from an account, and from a discovery as to all such parts of the bill as are referred to in the first six exceptions to the answer. If they are so protected, the master was wrong in allowing these exceptions; and the order or decree of the *Chancellor*, requiring a further answer from the appellants, cannot be sustained.

If the last answer be a bar to an account and discovery, as the appellants contend, it must be so because they have a right, in this second answer, again to set up the Statute of Limitations; and to insist on new or explanatory matter, to show that in their former answer they had made no admission which would prevent the statute from being a bar. The **629***] **Chancellor* decided that they having first pleaded the statute, and that plea having been overruled, they were thereby precluded from insisting on the statute a second time by way of answer, or at least that they could not do this without leave.

I cannot doubt the correctness of the *Chancellor's* decision. If, in this case, the statute may, as a matter of course, be insisted on by way of answer, after it has been overruled as a plea, it will follow that in every case a party may first plead any matter in bar, and when that is overruled, or (as in case before us) even after an appeal to this court, and a decree against it, he may, at the end of all this litigation, send his adversary nearly back to the commencement of the suit.

There is, in my opinion, no necessity for allowing a course which must lead to so much delay, vexation and expense. If, after a plea has been overruled, it should happen that the plea or the answer by which the party intended to support it was insufficient, through some omission or mistake, he might apply in the court below for leave to amend. So, in this case, if the matter set up in the second answer would afford just grounds to support the plea of the statute, the appellants ought to have applied to the Court of Chancery for liberty to bring them under its consideration.

I do not think the suggestions of the appellants well founded, that this course could not have been pursued, because the plea and answer were overruled, and therefore could not have been amended. The whole matter was under the control of the *Chancellor*, and there was nothing to prevent his modifying the decree as he might think right.

The appellants asked for a modification of the former decree of this court after it had been pronounced, and this court would have had no hesitation in making the modification, if it had appeared to them that justice required that they should do so.

But I put my opinion in this case on other grounds. Let it be admitted, and I take the fact to be so, that the appellants, in their first answer, made admissions, in order to support their plea, which clearly deprived them of the benefit of the statute. Can they be permitted in their second answer *again to set [***630** up the statute and to allege new matter, which is entirely to do away the force of their first admissions?

If a person in conversation, or in writing, make declarations which are an admission of the validity of a claim against him, he will not be permitted to give evidence of subsequent declarations or writings which may contradict or explain away his first admissions. And most assuredly a party cannot be permitted to do this, after, in a course of litigation, he has been made to feel the force of his original declarations.

It seems to me extraordinary, that the appellants should insist that they have a right, as a matter of course, by a second answer, to cancel the admissions which they put on record under oath in their first answer. There can be no rule of law which will authorize so great a violation of justice and common sense. To allow a party, when he may find that he has made an incautious admission, to contradict himself by a new answer, would be to hold out too great a limitation to the consciences of men. To adopt the words of Ld. Nottingham, in answer to an application to enlarge publication, "it would be of dangerous consequence, if people, after seeing where a cause pinched, should then be at liberty, to bolster up the faulty part."

The appellants cannot expect to be allowed, by their second answer, to vary or control their admissions in the first answer, unless they can succeed in establishing the position, so strenuously urged by their counsel, that the overruling the plea and the first answer, annihilated that answer, so far that it must be entirely overlooked, although it forms a part of the record before the court. I do not believe there is any technical rule which obliges justice to be so blind to matters which are spread before her, by those whose controversy she is to decide.

But again, the order of the Court of Chancery, and the decree of this court, requires that the appellants should put in a full and perfect answer. Why were this order and this decree made? Because the appellants had never answered the bill. They had pleaded **631***] the statute, and set forth certain *facts in support of their plea. This, though it be technically called a plea and answer, is, in fact, no answer to the bill. The whole amounts only to a plea; and so far from being an answer, it is but a claim, on the part of the appellants, to be exempt from any obligation to answer.

After it has been decided that they are not entitled to this exemption, how do they comply with the order to make a full and perfect answer? They do it in no other way than by again setting up their right to be exempt from answering, and attempting to support that right by allegations in explanation or contradiction of their former averments. In the one case, they set up the statute by plea, and in the other by answer. But, in truth, they are, in the latter, but repeating their former defense. The first and second answers are in fact the same. They both insist that the appellants ought not be compelled to answer. It is not possible, in my opinion, that this variance in form can so essentially change the effect of two things between which there is no substantial difference.

Suppose the appellants had, under the order to put in a full and perfect answer, again pleaded the statute, and that in other respects their second answer had been as it now is, I presume it would not be contended for a moment that they had complied with the order. In the first and second answer, so far as respects the statute, they put it forward as a bar, substantially in the same words; but in the former instance they claim the benefit of it as a plea, and in the latter "they pray that they may have the benefit of the said statute in the same manner, and to the same extent, as if they had pleaded the said statute in bar to the relief, discovery and account sought for, and prayed in the said bill."

I think, therefore, the *Chancellor* was well warranted in saying, as he has done in his opinion, "that the second answer was nothing more, in substance and effect, than a repetition of the plea of the Statute of Limitations, after that plea had been overruled, and the decretal order overruling it, requiring the defendants to put in a full and perfect answer to the bill, affirmed in the Court of Errors."

This reasoning brings me to a conclusion **632***] which enables *me to render my judgment in this case. But I should not treat the distinguished counsel who were engaged in this case with due respect if I did not more particularly notice their learned and elaborate arguments, and the authorities they cited. I have looked into all the cases to which we were referred that were within my reach, and I can find no authority that appears to me inconsistent with the opinion I entertain.

I admit, as has been said in our own courts, as well as in the English courts, that the Statute of Limitations may be a very conscientious plea, and I admit that it may be so in this case. But if it be, its conscientiousness must arise from matters not disclosed by the pleadings. I agree with a Senator who, in giving an opinion in this case on a former occasion, said that the claim on the part of the respondents as presented to the consideration of the court, addresses itself to the moral sense in a character of strong and prevailing equity; but I admit, as he did, that the appellants are entitled to the benefit of this defense, however technical it may be, if founded upon principles which are established for the government of a court of chancery.

The position taken by the appellant's counsel, and in support of which many authorities were cited, that after a plea is overruled, a defendant may insist on the same matter by way of answer, cannot be true as a general rule, and in the full meaning of the terms in which it is expressed. For example, it cannot be contended that one who has in due form pleaded the Statute of Limitations, and whose plea has been overruled, can answer that he has not promised within six years.

I take the rule and the meaning of the authorities to be this: that where a matter which might be a sufficient bar has been informally pleaded, and the plea has been overruled on that account, the defendant may, with leave of the court, insist on the same matter by way of answer. Where a plea is overruled for some informality or insufficiency in the plea itself, or in the answer to support the plea, then the matter pleaded, in the language of the books, has never undergone the judgment of the court, *Finch* v. *Finch*, 2 Ves., Sr., 491; that is, the court *has never decided [***633** that the matter on which the party intended to rely, might not be a bar. The judgment of the court, in such a case, applies only to the form. But where a plea is overruled on the ground that the party had placed himself or that he stood in such a situation that the matter pleaded could not be a bar, in my opinion, a defendant will never be allowed again to bring the same matter before the court, by way of answer. And even where the plea is overruled for want of form, I apprehend that a defendant cannot insist upon the same matter in his answer without leave. The reason of imposing upon him the necessity of asking this leave is, that the court may grant it or not, as it may understand that the plea was overruled for defect of form, or because the matter insisted upon could not, however it might be put before the court, be a bar.

So, in the case above cited, of *Finch* v. *Finch*, the language of the *Ld. Chancellor* is, "the defendant would not be precluded from insisting on the same matter in his answer, for the matter (that is, whether what the party intended to rely upon would be a sufficient bar or not) had not undergone the judgment of the court."

In the cases of *E. I. Co.* v. *Campbell*, 2 Ves., Sen., 247, Lord Hardwicke says, "a plea may be overruled as a plea of purchase, for want of form, as covering too much, and yet it may be insisted on in the answer."

The case of *Stephens* v. *Gaule*, 2 Vern., 701, which was much relied upon by the learned counsel for the appellants, seems to me to be entirely reconcilable with the above mentioned cases, which were also cited by him.

The report is very short, and it must be acknowledged, not very explicit.

The defendant had not stated in her plea that her husband, under whom she claimed as a purchaser without notice, had or pretended to have title, or that he was in possession, which is necessary to support a plea of this nature. The plea, therefore, was insufficient and informal, and was overruled on that account. She afterwards answered, and again insisted that she was in as a purchaser without notice, but stated that her husband was in possession, and claimed to be so by descent from his mother. *Ld. Chancellor* King allowed the **634***] *answer. This case, then, is one where the plea and not the matter of the plea had undergone the judgment of the court. It will be observed, that in this case there was nothing in the second answer inconsistent with what the widow had set up in her plea and answer. Had she in her first answer admitted notice or want of consideration, or any other fact that would have shown that she is not entitled to protection as a purchaser, would she have been permitted to set up a defense to which she had shown she was not entitled?

How does it stand as to the case which we are deciding? The plea of the appellants was in due form; but in their answer they stated facts which, in the opinion of this court, showed they were not entitled to the benefit of the statute. They asked this court for permission to amend their answer, but were refused; because, as the *Chief Justice* said, they had made admissions which no amendment could cure. This court has, then, decided on the matter of their plea. It was overruled, not for informality, but because, after what they had said in their first answer, the statute, according to the judgment of this court, could never be a bar. This, then, was *res adjudicata*, which the appellants cannot, in my opinion, be permitted again to bring into question.

It will be perceived, that if my view of this case be correct, there is no necessity for examining several questions, the discussion of which occupied much of the time of the court on the hearing.

It was contended by the counsel for the respondents that a defendant cannot refuse to answer, by answer; and that if he submits to answer at all, he must answer fully. It must be admitted that these are general rules; but it must also be conceded that there are many exceptions to them. In the case of *Philips* v. *Prevost*, 4 Johns. Ch., 215, *Chancellor* Kent allowed the defendant to insist, by answer, on lapse of time as a bar to the account, discovery and relief prayed for by the bill, on the ground that in that case the Statute of Limitations could not have been pleaded; and that this defense could not have been made otherwise than by answer. He says, "there cannot be any inflexible rule upon this subject. The reason and convenience of the case must determine **635***] when and how far *the application of the general rule is to be controlled." The counsel for the respondents has, with great learning and ability, undertaken to point out all the exceptions which are admitted to the above mentioned rules. I will not venture to say that the case in question falls under any of these exceptions. I am happy to think myself relieved from the necessity of giving any opinion on points upon which Ld. Eldon and *Chancellor* Kent have declared it impossible to reconcile the numerous authorities. If this were an original answer, then it would be incumbent on us to consider what Ld. Eldon, in *Shaw* v. *Ching*, 11 Ves., 306, calls "this distracted point;" but if we confirm the former opinion of this court, that the appellants, by their first plea and answer, were precluded from setting up the Statute of Limitations as a bar to the account, discovery and relief sought by the bill, we have only to decide that the second answer does not comply with the order of the *Chancellor*, confirmed by this court, that the appellants should put in a full and perfect answer.

For the same reasons, I do not find myself called upon to notice, although I have examined the many cases which were cited, as to the admissions of the defendant which were relied upon to take the case out of the Statute. That no advantage shall be taken of offers made by way of compromise; that a party may, with impunity, attempt to buy his peace, are well established rules of law (2 Campb., 106, *note;* 13 Johns., 288), to which our reason and our feelings at once assent. But I am not prepared to admit that what a party may state as a fact, though the statement may be made in the course of a negotiation for a compromise, or may be connected with an offer to purchase peace, will not be as binding as if the fact had been disclosed in any other way. If a man says to me, I do not admit that I owe you any thing, but rather than be sued I will give you a hundred dollars, it would be most unjust to suffer me to avail myself of this offer to recover against him. But if one tells me, it is true, I justly owe you a hundred dollars, and will give you fifty if you will give up your debt, I apprehend there is no rule of law so absurd and unjust as to prevent my availing myself of my debtor's confession, because he connected with it an offer of compromise.

*So, if the appellants have admitted [***636** by their answers, that they had the linens, and that they have never accounted or paid for them, in my opinion, they are bound by this admission, though it may have been made in the course of a negotiation for a compromise, and though they may have understood that the negotiation related to the breaking up of the voyage of The Egeria, or to a claim of the respondents for the proceeds of the linens.

But this is not, in my opinion, now open for discussion, because this court, of the last resort, has decided that the appellants, in their first answer, did make such an admission as the respondents were at liberty to avail themselves of, and such as precluded the appellants from sheltering themselves under the Statute of Limitations.

The master's report as to the seventh exception, allowed by the master, and also by the *Chancellor*, seems to have been acquiesced in by the appellants. For, although one of their points be, that there was no foundation for the allowance, by the master, of the seventh exception, yet I do not recollect that a word was said on the hearing to this point by either of the counsel. I presume that this exception was passed over, because there was no room to question that the parts of the answer to which it refers were, as the master reports, irrelevant. I am of this opinion. I think the *Chancellor* was right in disallowing all the exceptions to the master's report; and I am, therefore, in favor of affirming his decree.

Bowman, Brayton, Burrows, Burt, Clark, Cramer, Dudley, Earll, Elsworth, Gardiner, Haight, Keyes, Lake, Lefferts, McCall, McIntyre, McMichael, Morgan, Thorn, Wilkeson, Wooster, Senators, concurred.

SAVAGE, *Ch. J.*, after stating the case. There are three questions necessary to be discussed, to arrive at a satisfactory conclusion in this cause.

First. The plea having been overruled, were the appellants at liberty to insist on the same matter by way of answer?

637*] *Second. If they answer at all, were they not bound to answer fully? and,

Third. Does the answer contain matter which bars the relief sought?

I will here premise, that when the plea was overruled by the *Chancellor*, he discussed and decided two points. 1. That the case did not come within the exception to the 5th section of the Statute of Limitations, as an action concerning the trade of merchandise, between merchant and merchant, their factors or servants (1 R. L., 186); and 2. That it was a clear case of trust, and therefore the Statute was no bar. On this last point the plea was overruled. When the cause first came here, Spencer, *Ch. J.*, delivered the opinion of the court, in which the point first decided by the *Chancellor* is concurred in, on the ground that the exception in the statute is not applicable to a case where all the items of an account are on one side, and that the reason and principle of the exception embraced open and current accounts where there were mutual dealing and mutual credits. On the second point, the decision of the *Chancellor* was overruled; and the doctrine of Ld. Hardwicke (2 Atk., 612) was recognized and approved, that a trust is, where there is such a confidence between parties that no action at law will lie. It was added, that in this case there was a clear remedy at law, and had the objection been made, the bill would have been dismissed. It was a case, therefore, in which the party had a right to plead the statute. The decree of the *Chancellor* was, however, affirmed, on the ground that the answer accompanying the plea admitted the claim to be subsisting and unsatisfied, and thereby defeated the operation of the Statute.

When the answer now under consideration came before the *Chancellor*, he allowed the exceptions to it upon the ground that the same matter had undergone the judgment of the court, in the shape of a plea.

1. This brings me to the examination of the first question I propose to discuss, to wit: whether the appellants were at liberty to insist on the same matter by way of answer, which had been overruled by way of plea.

638*] *The object of pleading, in any court, is to present the complaint of the plaintiff, and also the grounds on which that claim is resisted by the defendant, that the court may decide upon the precise point in issue.

If the bill is supposed to contain no cause of action, the defendant may demur. If he does not choose to rely upon the weakness of the plaintiff's title, but wishes to set up some cause for which the suit should be dismissed, delayed or barred, he may plead or answer. If a demurrer is overruled, he must make a new defense, not by demurrer, to the same extent as the former, but he may defend himself by plea or answer. After a plea has been overruled, defense may be made by demurrer, by new plea, or by answer; but the new plea should not contain the same matter as the plea overruled. Such a course would be calling upon the court for a rehearing, contrary to its settled practice. (Mitf. Plead., 11-14.)

But it is contended by the counsel for the appellants, that though the plea be overruled, the same matter may be insisted on by way of answer; and this proposition is laid down in a work of high authority (Mitf. Plead., 3d ed., 248), which cites, in its support, 2 Ves., 492, and 1 Atk., 450. The latter is the case of *Suffolk* v. *Green*, decided in 1739, which has no connection with this question, any further than what arises from analogy existing between a demurrer and plea. Ld. Hardwicke overruled a demurrer on the ground of its insufficiency, but without prejudice to the defendant's insisting upon the matter relied on by way of answer. In *Finch* v. *Finch*, 2 Ves., Sr., 491, decided in 1752, the first answer was reported insufficient; the defendant submitted to make a further answer, which was also reported insufficient; and the question was whether, by submitting to answer further, without excepting, the defendant had precluded himself from insisting on the same matter by his second answer. Ld. Hardwicke held he was not, and assigned as a reason, that the matter had not undergone the judgment of the court. He adds, it is not like a second demurrer, or dilatory, or a second plea, which cannot be put in a second time if overruled; yet, notwithstanding, the court frequently allows *the defendant, after a plea has been [***639** overruled, to insist on the same matter by answer which was overruled as a plea; and that comes on the merits at hearing the cause.

To support this doctrine of Ld. Hardwicke, the reporter refers to *Harris* v. *Ingledew*, 3 P. Wms., 94. In that case a bill was filed by certain creditors of William Ingledew to compel a sale of his real estate devised subject to the payment of his debts. One of the defendants pleaded that he was purchaser for valuable consideration, but omitted in his plea to deny notice of the will of William Ingledew. And it was argued that the plaintiff having joined issue on the plea, he had admitted it to be good; that had the plaintiff set it down to be argued without taking issue, the want of a denial of notice would have been a good exception; and it was argued that, if it were otherwise, the defendant might be tricked by the plaintiff's replying to it, and he could do no more than prove it; whereas if such a plea had been set down to be argued and overruled, the defendant might still have helped himself by putting all his defense in his answer. The only answer made by Sir Joseph Jekyl, Master of the Rolls, to this argument, is, that, in case a plea be replied to, the defendant need only prove his plea; and here it is the plaintiff's own fault, for he had it in his election, to have it set down to be argued; wherefore, if the defendant proves what he has pleaded, the bill is to be dismissed against him with costs. The Master of the Rolls seems to adopt the reasoning of the counsel, and supports the general proposition that matter overruled as a plea may still be urged in the answer; and the plea in the case of *Harris* v. *Ingledew* is a strong instance to show the reasonableness of the rule. The plea was admitted to be defective, because the defendant had not denied notice of the will of Ingleden, which subjected his estate to the payment of his debts. Had that plea been overruled for that cause, it would certainly have been highly unjust that he should not have an opportunity to supply that fact in his answer. This same doctrine is asserted by the Court of Exchequer, in *E. I. Co.* v. *Campbell*, 1 Ves., Sr., 247. And in *Hoare* v. *Parker*, 2 Cox, 224, where a plea overruled was insisted on by way of answer, **640***] the *Ld.* **Chancellor* asked if there were any instances, after a plea overruled, of the same thing being allowed to be insisted upon by answer; and to show that it might be done, Scott cited *Harris* v. *Ingledew*, and *Finch* v. *Finch*; but His Lordship said those were cases of bills of relief, but he knew no instance of the same being done in bills of discovery only; thus admitting, that in bills of relief such was the proper and common practice. In the case under consideration, relief is asked for. It is not a case of discovery. None was necessary. The respondents had all the evidence they wanted. *Vide*, also, *Stephens* v. *Gaule*, 2 Vern., 701.

2. It is contended, however, that when a defendant submits to answer, he must answer fully. In the English courts, this question has been decided both ways, and by very learned and highly respectable Chancellors and judges. The late *Chancellor* Kent has reviewed most of the cases in *M. E. Church* v. *Jaques*, 1 Johns. Ch., 73, and *Phillips* v. *Prevost*, 4 *Id.*, 209. He came to the conclusion that if the defendant submits to answer, he must answer fully; but that the rule was subject to exceptions. The only two which he mentions in *M. E. Ch.* v. *Jaques*, are, that of an innocent purchaser, as in *Jerrard* v. *Saunders*, 2 Ves., Jr., 454; and the denial of a copartnership, as in *Jacobs* v. *Goodman*, 3 Bro. Ch., 205. To these exceptions he added another in *Phillips* v. *Prevost*, to wit: where the plaintiff has no title.

In the equity side of the Court of Exchequer, I understand the rule is, and always has been, that a defendant may answer in part, and object to a further answer. It is in the Court of Chancery alone where the conflict has existed between what has been called the old and the new rule. The whole dispute is about the form of pleading, and if once settled, it is a matter of very little moment which way it is settled. The objection stated by Ld. Eldon to the new rule in *Somerville* v. *Mackay*, 16 Ves., 387, arises out of the practical inconvenience, that, in chancery, the defense is not judged of, in the first instance, by the court itself, but goes to a master upon exceptions to the answer, and then to the court upon exceptions to the report; **641***] in my *judgment, a very useless ceremony, and a practice which calls for correction. The late *Chancellor*, upon the able review which he has given of this question in *Phillips* v. *Prevost*, has adopted, as a general rule, that established by Ld. Thurlow, in *Cookson* v. *Ellison*, 2 Bro. Ch., 252, where the plaintiff had made one a party defendant who had no interest, and was a mere witness. He did not demur, but answered part, and was therefore compelled to answer fully. Yet, in *Green* v. *Winter*, cited 4 Johns. Ch., 214, the *Chancellor* virtually overruled this very case. The defendant had disclaimed all interest, and the only difference was, that Ellison had answered part; but neither had demurred or pleaded. In the latter case, the *Chancellor* very properly decided that the defendant was not bound to answer further. He adds: "I could not perceive the propriety, or feel the necessity of requiring a further answer merely to serve the curiosity or convenience of the plaintiff. Nor can I perceive the good sense of requiring long accounts and schedules from a defendant, when a defense is set up in the answer which meets the title. If the matter of defense should fail, the defendant might then be required to answer further." In the same case he remarks that "the defendant may insist upon the benefit of the Statute of Limitations in his answer as well as by plea." That this has been repeatedly done, he cites *Lacon* v. *Briggs*, 3 Atk., 105; *Prince* v. *Heylin*, 1 Atk., 493, and Eq. Drafts, 389.

If, therefore, the general rule first laid down in *Cookson* v. *Ellison* be established, with its exceptions already admitted, another exception should be added, to wit: where a defense is set up which meets and controverts the title. Take for an example this very case. I proceed on the supposition that the Statute of Limitations is well pleaded. Where can be the necessity or propriety of going at length into accounts or dealings of long standing, when a recovery is barred by lapse of time? For whose benefit is such an investigation to be instituted? It is not pretended that any discovery is wanted to aid a suit at law; and if it were, I understand the rule to be now settled, that matter which bars the relief, bars also the discovery.

*It was urged upon the argument, [***642** by the respondent's counsel, that if the general rule were, that a defendant might avail himself by answer of the same matter overruled as a plea, yet it ought not to be permitted in this case, because a motion was made here, and denied, the effect of which would have been an amendment similar to the one now sought for. In my judgment the result of that motion should have no influence in deciding this question of pleading. The court merely expressed an opinion on the plea then before it, but did not prejudge the further pleadings nor the rights of the parties. If the result of that motion should have any effect, it should be in favor of receiving the answer—as otherwise the appellants may, through the inadvertence of counsel, lose the benefit of a defense to which they are entitled by the laws of the land.

3. I shall, therefore, proceed to inquire whether the answer now put in contains any defense to the claim of the respondents. His Honor, the late *Chancellor*, considered it nothing more than a repetition of the former plea of

the Statute of Limitations, which had been overruled. If he is correct in this position, his decree should be affirmed. A comparison of the two answers will enable us to form an accurate opinion on that point.

That part of the first answer, which this court considered an omission of the debt, is the offer made by the appellant's counsel to pay one third of the proceeds of the linens, explicitly stating at the same time, that they were discharged from all liability by virtue of the Statute, and that they reserved the right to avail themselves of the Statute in their defense if the offer was refused. This was thought not to come within the rule laid down by Spencer, *J.*, in *Sands* v. *Gelston*, 15 Johns., 571, who says, "though indeed the defendant may admit that what the plaintiff claims as a debt has never been paid, if he protests against his liability, it would be an outrage on common sense, to infer a promise to pay, in the face of his denial of his liability to pay."

In the present answer the appellants have presented the same matter, accompanied by these other explanations: 1 A denial of their admission of any claim of the respondents. 2. **643***] *That in the conversation which led to the attempt to compromise, the subject of the linens was not mentioned; and that the interview between the counsel of the parties had relation to a supposed claim for the breaking up the voyage of the ship Egeria. 3. That the appellants instructed their counsel to do no act which might be construed into any admission of a claim by the respondents. 4. That the offer was intended for the purpose of putting an end of any claim against the defendants, or either of them; and for purchasing their peace, and of compromise, and for no other purpose. 5. They expressly deny an intention to admit any liability to pay any claim on account of the linens.

It is, however, contended that the claim is still admitted, and the second answer does not, in effect, vary from the first. The objection taken by Spencer, *Ch. J.*, in giving the opinion of this court upon that answer, was, that there was an offer to pay the whole demand; and no denial of the justice of the claim. Here the appellants enter their protest against the validity of the demand, and say, under oath, that the offer was not to pay the whole demand; but to compromise a pretended claim for breaking up a voyage for the purpose of purchasing their peace. I know of no case which has gone so far as to decide that an offer made under such circumstances, and with such explanations and reservations, and when so much pains were taken to negate the idea of liability, should be construed into a promise to pay. And it would be strange, indeed, if defendants, understanding their rights, and having the benefit of counsel, should promise to pay a demand, when in the same breath they deny their liability. Upon the best consideration I am able to give the subject, I can see no ground for the allegation that this answer contains an admission of the demand.

If courts can, by one refinement after another, entirely fritter away the statutes of the State, further legislation will be useless.

I am of opinion that the decree of the *Chancellor* be reversed; because, 1. The appellants had a right to put into their answer, among other things, the same matter which, standing alone, was overruled as insufficient in a plea. 2. *That their answer containing a bar [***644** to the relief sought, is a bar to the discovery; and they may, therefore, object to answer fully to the charges in the bill. 3. The answer under consideration contains a complete defense to the complaint of the respondents.

CRARY, *Senator*, concurred with the *Chief Justice* in the result of his opinion. He was not prepared to go into the subject; but felt it his duty to protest against what appeared to him a positive violation of an existing statute. Such he felt still bound to consider the Statute of Limitations; though it had been greatly broken in upon by our courts. He had read and listened with attention to the opinions of judges in all the various stages of this cause; and he acknowledged their learning. He had seen the appellants begin with a clear defense under the Statute of Limitations. They retained counsel from the very first moment to manage that defense, and instructed them not to waive it, though they were willing they should buy peace. With a view to this object, they negotiated in the spirit of their instructions. They have struggled at every stage to preserve the defense of the appellants unimpaired, but our court have found themselves so crippled and impotent as to be unable to give the appellants the benefit of it. Enough has been got out of them from term to term, in answers on oath drawn under the advice of counsel, urging the defense, too, at every step to defeat that defense. This is the ground assumed by the respondents; but it was a ground which he could not yield. He felt that it was equivalent to a complete repeal of the statute.

Greenly, *Lynde* and *Redfield*, *Senators*, concurred.

A majority being for affirmance, it was thereupon ordered, adjudged and decreed that the decree of His Honor, the *Chancellor*, in this cause be affirmed, with costs to the respondents to be taxed, upon the appeal to this court, and that the appeal, record and proceedings be remitted, &c.

Affirmed—7 Johns. Ch., 167.
Cited in—2 Paige, 414; 20 Barb., 475; 38 Ind., 541.

---

*EDWARD PERKINS, *Appellant*, [***445**

v.

THE WASHINGTON INSURANCE COMPANY OF THE CITY OF NEW YORK, *Respondents*.

Insurance—Appointment of Agent, with Power to Make Contracts Under Certain Conditions—Destruction of Premises, after Contract by Agent, Before Ratification by Company—Liability of Company—How Corporation may Appoint Agent—General Doctrine of Agency—Effect of Receipt for Premium of Insurance—Neglect of Agent to Remit Premium.

Where an Insurance Company in the City of N. Y. appointed R., a surveyor in Savannah, Ga., and by their president empowered him to make contracts of insurance, to take effect from the time when the premium should be paid, and should be received at N. Y., provided the office should recognize the rate of premium and be otherwise satisfied with the risk; and R. advertised, at Savannah, the terms on which the Company would insure, and subscribed himself as agent of the Company at Savannah, mentioning that they would insure through him, &c., and P. paid the usual premium of insurance on certain goods Jan. 5, 1820, to R., who gave P. a receipt for the money, describing himself as agent of the Company, and specifying the consideration and object of the receipt; but before the premium was received at N. Y., the goods were consumed by fire; and P. afterwards tendered the premium to the Company, and demanded that they should indemnify him or execute the contract of insurance; held, that they were bound to comply, though the premium had not been received by them before the loss; and that the premium being according to their established rates, it did not lie with the Company arbitrarily to say they would not recognize the rate of premium, or would not be satisfied with the risk; and they were accordingly deemed to indemnify the assured.

One may become the agent of a corporation in the same manner as he may of an individual, without any deed or writing.

A mere warrant of survey given by an insurance Company does not authorize the surveyor to do any act binding upon them.

Where a principal objects to the act of his agent, as unauthorized, the question is not what power he intended to give his agent, but what power the third person who dealt with the agent, and who insists on his acts as valid, had a right to infer that he possessed from his own acts and those of his principal. Per Colden, *Senator*.

A receipt for a premium of insurance signed by the president or secretary of an insurance company is as binding as a policy; and it is the common custom in the City of N. Y. to insure by receipts of this nature, signed by some officer of the company. The only difference between the effect of these and of a policy is, that the former must be enforced in chancery and the latter at law. Per Colden, *Senator*.

It is a well settled rule in chancery, that what one is legally bound to do, shall be considered as done, by all those having a right to claim its performance. Per Colden, *Senator*.

This rule applied to the case of an obligation to insure, depending on the receipt of a premium by the insurer, from his agent, whose duty it is to remit the premium presently. Per Colden, *Senator*.

646*] *When the obligation of the insurer depends on his actually receiving the premium from his agent, but the agent neglects to remit it, by reason whereof the obligation does not attach, an action lies by the insured against the agent; and the measure of damages will be the amount which was to have been insured. Per Colden, *Senator*.

APPEAL from the Court of Chancery. Oct. 9, 1821, the appellant filed his bill in that court against the respondents, stating that Jan. 5, 1820, and since, the appellant being the owner of a certain stock of dry goods, groceries, &c., in a storehouse in the City of Savannah, applied to Henry P. Russell, of Savannah, the agent of the respondents, an incorporated *Insurance Company in the City of N. Y., for insurance upon this stock; that Russell, on the same Jan. 5, agreed that the respondents should become insurers on the stock, for one year from that day for $5,000, at a premium of 2½ *per cent.*, the premium to be paid on that day; and that the Company should execute a policy in the usual form; that the premium was accordingly paid to Russell, with $3.50 for the expense of a survey and policy; that Russell gave a receipt for these sums, declaring the object, consideration and purpose as above set forth, and signed the receipt, "John P. Russell, agent of said Company;" that on the morning of Jan. 11, an extensive and destructive fire broke out in Savannah, and consumed the greater portion of the goods; that the appellant gave notice to Russell of the loss, offered the usual preliminary proof and demanded a policy of insurance; but Russell stated that he had not forwarded the premium to the Company, and had not received a policy from them, and he intimated that the Company would not consider themselves bound by what had been done; that proper notice with the usual proofs were, in May, 1820, given to the respondents in the City of N. Y.; but they had refused to execute a policy or indemnify the appellant to the amount lost, although the appellant had, Apr. 28, 1821, tendered to their President the amount of the premium.

*The bill prayed that the respondents [*647 might be decreed to pay the amount agreed to be insured, or to execute the policy, &c.

To this bill the respondents answered, admitting all the material facts charged, except Russell's agency. They denied that he was agent, or had power or authority to act for them otherwise than as a surveyor. They admitted that they had appointed him surveyor for them in Savannah, &c., of buildings insured, or in which goods offered for insurance were kept: and empowered him to state to applicants at Savannah the probable rates, according to the nature of the risk at which insurance might be expected to be effected by them; always, however, reserving to themselves the power and control to abide by, or to vary the rates so stated by him, or entirely to decline such insurance, when the proposal for such insurance and his report or survey should be presented to them for their deliberation. That they permitted him to receive the probable premiums and transmit them to the respondents, in order to prevent unnecessary delay in effecting insurance; but absolutely denied that they ever appointed him their agent for insuring or effecting any insurance against loss or damage by fire.

To this answer the appellant filed a general replication; and testimony was taken on both sides, mainly to the question whether Russell was agent, as alleged in the bill, for the purpose of contracting to insure in the name of the Company. The proofs need not be recited here, because they are briefly stated by the *Chancellor* in his reasons for the decree, and are gone very fully into by the judges who delivered the opinion of this court.

The cause was brought to a hearing in the Court of Chancery, on the pleadings and proofs, Nov. 27, 1822; and Dec. 28 thereafter, the *Chancellor* decreed that the appellant's bill should be dismissed; for which he assigned his reasons as follows:

KENT, *Chancellor*. The essential point in this case is, whether Henry P. Russell was authorized to bind, and did bind, the defendants to insure the goods of the plaintiff, at the rate *and upon the terms specified in the [*648 receipt which Russell gave to the plaintiff, Jan. 5, 1820. The counsel for the plaintiff contends that Russell was the general agent for the defendants at Savannah, for the purpose of receiving premiums, and agreeing to make insurances, and that they were bound by his acts. The other side insist that Russell was not their agent for that purpose; that he was only their surveyor, to survey and return a description of the property offered for insurance, to state to applicants the probable rates of insurance, and to receive from persons willing to pay, the premiums he might think fit to name, and to transmit the same to the defendants; and that they reserved to themselves a right to deliberate and act upon the application, and to accept or reject the proposal and premium in their discretion; that in receiving the money, Russell acted as the agent of the applicant, and that there was no contract of insurance in any case until the proposal had been received and accepted by the defendants, accompanied with a receipt of the premium at their office.

Russell's appointment was strictly that of "surveyor, for the defendants, of buildings and goods offered to be insured in Savannah." This appointment bore date Dec. 11, 1818. Under the appointment as surveyor, Russell, Feb. 18, 1819, published in the papers at Savannah, that "insurances by the defendants might be effected by application to him, who had a table and classes of hazards, and rates of annual premiums, to be exhibited, and that he was authorized to say insurance would be effected as favorable to the assured as those of any company in the U. S.; and that he would attend to the surveying the property, and would obtain the policies from the defendants with the least possible delay." The proposals he signed as "agent for Savannah;" and he says that this advertisement he published at his own suggestion, and he does not know that it ever came to the knowledge of the defendants.

I apprehend that the defendants are not bound by any assumed power contained in these proposals, made and published without their authority. But the proposals do not, in fact, assume any authority to make contracts **649***] of insurance *binding on the Company. He was to receive applications, and through him as the medium of communication, insurances might be effected. He was authorized to say insurances would be effected on the most favorable terms; that he possessed the rates of premium, and he would attend to surveying the property and obtaining the policies. There is nothing in all this, that, upon any necessary and sound construction, carries the idea that he himself could make valid and binding contracts of insurance, in the first instance, without the subsequent sanction of the defendants. He was, evidently, from his own account, to act only as a surveyor, with authority to receive and communicate applications, and to receive and communicate the answers.

He had blank printed proposals of a circular nature, and without signature issued by the Company, and one of these he affixed upon his store. It was a general outline of the classes of hazards and rates of annual premiums, and conditions of insurance. One of the conditions was, that "all applications for insurance must be made at the office of the Company;" and another, "no insurance will be considered as made or binding until the premium is paid, and that every policy of insurance made by the Company shall be sealed with its seal, and signed by the President and Secretary."

Hitherto we have discovered nothing that will justify the conclusion that Russell had authority to make a contract of insurance binding on the Company. And if we recur to the correspondence between them, we shall equally fail in discovering the power contended for in this case.

In a letter from Russell to the defendants, dated Apr. 9, 1819, he observed, that "there is a difficulty, owing to the distance from N. Y., in getting along with insurances here, and I have written to Mr. Swords on the subject. Unless I am furnished with blank policies ready signed, or unless my receipt for the premiums as agent is made binding on the Company until the policies can be obtained from the office, I suspect but little can be done in the way of insuring, for I find that applicants want the risk to commence as soon as the premium is paid." The answer from the defendants, by Mr. Swords, their President, was dated Apr. 27, 1819, and states, that "the Company had never furnished *agents [***650** or surveyors with blank policies. The Board will never saction it. The most and best that can be done is, that all insurances that you may agree to make, and for which the premium you shall charge, shall be actually paid, and shall be received here, the office will consider as insuring at the time of the payment to you, so that in case of accident between such time of payment and the receipt of the money here, the Company will indemnify such loss; provided, however, that the office shall recognize the said rate of premium which you shall charge, and shall be otherwise satisfied with the risk. The Company will, in no case, guarantee the transmission of money for a premium. Insurances are effected here, only, on the actual payment of the premium to one of its officers."

By another letter from the defendants, by their secretary of the date of Apr. 28, 1819, they say, "no insurance shall be binding until the premium is received at this office. The reason of this rule is, that the Company will not be responsible for the risk of sending the premium either by land or water. I am authorized, however, to assure you, that in all cases where the risk is accepted, on the receipt of the premium here, they will execute the policy to take effect from the time the premium was received by you, if the same shall be requested in the letter accompanying the survey."

By these letters, the Company expressly declared that the receipt of the premium by the Company, at their office in N. Y., was indispensable, and that the insurance was to be effected there only. The Company were to recognize the rate of premium, and to be satisfied with the risk, and then, and on the receipt of the premium, the contract was to be made by them, and then it might relate back to the date of the receipt of the premium by Russell, if that was the pleasure of the other party. It was impossible for the Company in more expressive language to have retained in their own hands their right to bind themselves, or more pointedly denied that right to their surveyor.

It appears, by the testimony of Russell, that in several instances the rate of insurance agreed on (and conditionally of course) by him was satisfactory to the Company, and confirmed *by them, and the policies made [***651** to bear date with the receipt of the money at Savannah. But Russell himself, evidently considered his agreement, with the applicants, as not binding on the defendants. In his letter to the Company of Dec. 18, 1819, he says, "I herewith forward to you two more applications for insurance which I presume will be accepted by the Company at the rates of premium which I have named, as I wish to do nothing which they will not confirm. I have fixed the premium agreeably to that established by them for buildings of this description. I forward three or four surveys. If they are received I will thank you to inform me as soon as may be, whether the others are accepted by the Company, as in that case we wish the insurances effected as soon as practicable. It will be desirable, in every instance, that policies be forwarded with as little delay as possible after the receipt of the premium."

This letter was written only a few days before the plaintiff made application to Russell, and paid the rate of premium agreed on; and I cannot perceive either in the written documents or in the usages or practice of the Company, any authority in Russell to bind the defendants in a contract of insurance, before they had seen the terms, or exercised their judgment upon them, and accepted of them, and actually received the premium.

It is extremely probable that if the terms and premium had been received in this case, before notice of the fire, they would have been accepted, and the policy would have been issued. And so we may say that, in ten thousand other cases, property lost by fire might have been insured upon the usual terms, if application had been made and received in due time. The question here is, was a valid contract made by the defendants so as to fix the risk upon them from the receipt of the premium by Russell? If his agency in agreeing to the rate of insurance and receiving the premium, did not of itself, and forthwith, irrevocably bind the defendants, it is certain that they are not bound; for they did nothing afterwards in ratification of that agreement. I consider that Russell was strictly the agent of the plaintiff in receiving and undertaking to transmit the 652*] premium; for the defendants *had repeatedly declared that they would not consider the premium as paid until received at their office. It would be unjust, as respects the defendants, to bind them without their assent, and contrary to their declared will explicitly communicated to Russell; nor can they be fairly accused of any deception towards the public, or charged with holding out to the world that Russell was invested with absolute powers to bind them. There was nothing in all the documents or letters he possessed to warrant such a conclusion, and if the plaintiff dealt with him in confidence that the agreement with him was binding, he did it without due examination, and at his own peril.

The only circumstance that seems to give any color to the claim, is, that the defendants in several instances allowed the policies to relate back and cover the property from the time the premium was received by Russell, so as to assume the intermediate risk. But this was in pursuance of their letters of the 27th and 28th of April, in which they promised to do it if the same should be requested, and always with the proviso, that the premium had been actually received by them, and the rates of premium approved of, and the risk adjudged to be satisfactory. The important right of the Company by their Board of Directors to deliberate upon the terms stated, and to judge of the expediency of the risk, was always reserved; and it is a right so essential to the safety and credit of every insurance company that we ought not to consider it as having been renounced, unless we are warranted by the clearest proof. If the Company were bound definitively by the act of Russell, in this case, they were equally so in every other case, in which the premium was paid to him; and the office of insurance, upon that construction, was transferred to Savannah, and Russell substituted for the Board of Directors, provided for by their charter. A deduction so alarming, and so repugnant to the duty of the directors of the institution, ought to rest on positive proof, and not on presumptions raised in opposition to the declared purpose of the Company.

Upon the whole, I see nothing in this case that can justify me in saying that the agreement between the plaintiff and *Rus- [*653 sell, Jan. 5, 1820, was an agreement to which the defendants were a party, or by which they were concluded.

If no loss had intervened, and the defendants, upon information of the survey and rates of premium and payment of the premium, had in their discretion determined that the risk was not acceptable, I apprehend they would have been deemed in the lawful exercise of a right of deliberation, and that the risk would not and could not have been enforced against them, contrary to their will. The circumstance of a loss occurring before they had time to deliberate could not, in reason and justice, impair their rights, and make that act binding which otherwise would not have been deemed so. The interpretation of contracts, and the administration of justice, ought to rest on general and fixed principles, and not on views of temporary hardship or expediency. I am, accordingly, of opinion that the bill ought to be dismissed.

The cause was argued, at the last session of this court, in January, by

Mr. D. B. Ogden, for the appellant, and

Mr. T. A. Emmet, for the respondents,

Upon the single point whether Russell should be considered the legal agent of the respondents for the purpose of binding, and whether he did bind the respondents to insure. But their views are so fully incorporated in the opinions of the late *Chancellor*, already given, and of the judges who delivered the opinion of this court, that they need not be given here. In the course of the argument, *Randall* v. *Van Vechten*, 19 Johns., 60; *Bank of Col.* v. *Adms. of Patterson*, 7 Cr., 297, 299, and *Munn* v. *Com. Co.*, 15 Johns., 44, were cited, for the appellant, to show that the respondents might, though a corporation, contract by an agent not appointed by their corporate seal; and *Whitehead* v. *Tuckett*, 15 East, 400, as to the nature and effect of a general agency, was also cited for the appellant.

And for the respondents, 1 Madd. Ch., 325, 2 Lond. ed., and the authorities there cited, to show that if the transfer of the *direc- [*654 tion of the Company to an agent in Savannah was illegal, the court would not compel a specific execution of a contract made in pursuance of such an authority; and Paley on Agency, 144, ed. by Neil Gow, to show the nature and effect of a general agency.

WOODWORTH, J. Jan. 5, 1830, the appellant paid to Henry P. Russell $106.25, for the purpose of insuring $5,000 on his stock of dry goods and groceries, in the city of Savannah, against loss or damage by fire. Russell subscribed a receipt describing himself as agent of the respondents; and acknowledged that he had received fifty cents for the expense of the policy, and $3 for taking the survey and transacting the business. Jan. 11, 1820, the goods were consumed by fire. The respondents deny that, on the facts appearing in this cause, there is any liability on their part, to compensate for the loss.

The material question is, whether Henry P. Russell was the agent of the respondents, and in that capacity had the authority to bind them to insure the appellant's goods; and a concise view of some of the leading facts becomes necessary, in order to arrive at a correct conclusion.

Dec. 11, 1818, the respondents appointed Russell surveyor. The power was limited to this object solely. Feb. 10, 1819, Russell caused to be published in a newspaper printed at Savannah, the proposals of the Company; and added that insurance might be effected by application to him; and that he would obtain policies from the office with the least possible delay. To this notice Russell subscribed his name as agent for the City of Savannah. It appears by the depositions that subsequently, and previous to Jan. 5, 1820, he agreed to insure for a number of individuals, and received the premiums, which were transmitted to the respondents; and that in every instance, save one, the Company confirmed the insurance, and transmitted policies bearing date at the time the receipt was given to the applicant for insurance. It also appears, that Russell applied to the respondents for an enlargement of his powers as agent. In his letter dated Apr. 655*] *9, 1819, to Mr. Hawes, the Secretary, he observes: "There is a difficulty, owing to the distance from New York, in getting along with insurances here. Unless I am furnished with blank policies, ready signed, or unless my receipt for the premiums, as agent, is binding upon the Company until the policies can be obtained from the office, I suspect but little can be done in the way of insuring; for I find that applicants want the risk to commence as soou as the premium is paid." Apr. 28, 1819, Mr. Hawes writes in reply, that "the Directors are aware of the difficulty of making insurance at a distance, and will obviate it, as far as consistent with the principle they had adopted, which was that no insurance shall be binding until the premium is received at their office in New York." He assigned as the reason of the rule, that the Company would not be responsible "for the risk of sending the premium either by land or water;" and that in all cases when the risk is accepted, the policy is to take effect from the time when the premium was received by the agent.

Apr. 27, 1819, Mr. Swords, President of the Company, wrote to Russell as follows: "All insurances that you may agree to make, and for which such premiums as you may deem proper to charge, shall be actually paid, and shall be received here, the office will consider as insuring at the time of the payment to you; so that in case of accident between such time of payment, and the receipt of the money here, the Company will indemnify such loss; provided, however, the office shall recognize the rate of premium which you shall charge, and shall be otherwise satisfied with the risk."

After this review, we may safely dismiss the inquiry, what were the original powers conferred on the agent. It may be conceded that they were no greater than those of surveyor, strictly; and that he could not, in that capacity, bind his principal by an agreement to insure. The limited nature of such an appointment, it was soon perceived, could answer no beneficial purpose. It is to be presumed that very few, if any, would be disposed to advance the premium, and wait an indefinite period before the policy should attach. Russell communi- *cates the difficulty to the President, [*656 who is to be considered the organ of the Company communicating their assent to the enlarged powers of the agent; and particularly, as it is not pretended that his letter to Russell was unauthorized.

According to the instructions thus given to the agent, when and in what cases were his agreements to insure, binding on the respondents? Upon payment of the premium to the agent, the applicant for insurance was subject to the following contingencies; first, that the premium should be received at the office in N. Y.; secondly, that the rate of premium should be recognized at the office; and lastly, that the Company should be otherwise satisfied with the risk.

As to the first, no doubt can arise; for it depends on the fact whether the money has been received or tendered at the office in N. Y. As to the second, it was undoubtedly intended that if the rate of premium taken by the agent, conformed to the rules and regulations of the Company, and was not less than the uniform rate before taken in other and similar cases which had invariably received the sanction of the respondents, the applicant would be entitled to a policy of insurance commencing on the day the premium was paid; for, although it is provided that the office shall recognize the rate of premium, it must be understood as having referred to the rules and regulations sanctioned by the Board of Directors, and the power vested in the agent. The right of the Company to exercise their judgment whether the agreement of the agent to insure, corresponded with the instructions given, cannot be questioned. But, from the nature of the case, it seems necessarily confined within such limits. It cannot be urged that the Company reserved or intended to reserve the right of arbitrarily refusing to subscribe a policy, when every prerequisite which they had themselves prescribed had been fairly and honestly complied with. It must, then, be confined within the bounds I have already traced; and if so, when the agent presents a case, having received the premium, the fair implication of the proviso is, that the Company shall act upon it; and if they decline to act, or point out any objection, the presumption is, that none exists, 657*] *within the true intent of the proviso inserted in the instructions. It is very evident to my mind that the respondents did not repose themselves on any objectionable features in the conduct of the agent, but on an absolute right of refusal, which they conceived was vested in them, without assigning any cause. This is inferable from that part of their answer wherein they state, "that not considering themselves bound by any such alleged agreement for insurance, they did not examine into, and therefore neither they nor their officers or agents did at any time object to the sufficiency of the proofs; nor did they, in any way, intimate or pretend that there had been any unfairness or fraud on the part of the appellant in obtaining the insurance. It is also remarkable that no suggestion is made, that the rate of insurance was not conformable to the general usage of the Company. Can it be doubted that, had the loss not have happened, previous to the time when the premium was offered to be paid in the City of N. Y., that this policy would have been signed as readily as others which had been transmitted by the agent?

These remarks are equally applicable to the third and last proviso, "the Company shall be otherwise satisfied with the risk." The question upon this should be considered in the same manner, as if application had been made for the policy before any loss sustained. What reasons could have been assigned for dissatisfaction with the risk? If any existed, it was the duty of the respondents to point them out. Not having done so, it is not uncharitable to suppose that they declined acting as in ordinary cases, in consequence of the loss, erroneously supposing that a literal adherence to the words of the instructions would shield them against the appellant's claim to compensation. It is not unnatural, in controversies between individuals, for them, however upright, to seize on every plank that may possibly lead to safety. Hence it comes, no man is a proper judge in his own cause; and that courts are established to measure out equal and exact justice to contending parties.

The only remaining inquiry is, whether the agreement to insure between the appellant and Russell, the agent, was within the instructions given by the respondents, and agreeable to 658*] *their rules and regulations. The insurance was at 2½ *per cent.* premium, on dry goods and groceries. It does not appear whether the store-house which contained the goods, was included in the first, second or third class of hazards. Supposing it to have been the last, the rate of insurance on such buildings, not having goods hazardous therein, is stated at from 175 to 200 cents on the $100. Goods hazardous, which includes groceries, are charged with 12½ cents in addition to this premium. The rate, then, paid by the appellant was equal to the highest sum claimed by the respondents in their proposals for insurance. I apprehend, therefore, that there is no well founded objection to the rate of insurance. This is evident from the acts of the respondents in uniformly accepting former risks, upon contracts of insurance made on the same, or not more favorable terms. The only risk rejected was not on the ground that the premium was too small, but that the application was for six months insurance and the premium paid for that time only; whereas an insurance for six months is always chargeable with three quarters of a year. If, then, we look at the instructions given, the proposals issued containing the rates of insurance, and the acts of the respondents in reference to similar cases, the conclusion seems to be irresistible that the risk and rate of premium were entirely satisfactory. The premium was also tendered in N. Y. and refused, which is a compliance with the first part of the proviso. This, in my view, removes every obstacle in the appellant's way.

I am of opinion that the decree of His Honor, the *Chancellor*, be reversed; and that the respondents be decreed to pay to the appellant the amount agreed to be insured.

SAVAGE, *Ch. J.*, and SUTHERLAND, *J.*, concurred.

COLDEN, *Senator*. The question in this case is, whether Russell was so far the agent of the respondents as to bind them to an insurance for which he was paid a premium by the appellant, Jan. 5, 1820. For this premium he then signed, as agent for the respondents, a receipt *purporting that they should [*659 insure the appellant; and that the insurance should take effect from the date of the receipt.

I believe it is now perfectly well settled that a person may become the agent of a corporation, as he may of an individual, without any deed or writing. Were it not so, there could be no safety in dealing with a corporation, unless it were with a full Board of Directors. They would have all the advantages of employing agents, and be under no responsibility for their acts. The cases cited by the appellant's counsel seem to me to be conclusive on this point, and to render any further discussion or illustration of it unnecessary.

Long before the premium in question was paid to Russell he had received from the respondents what their President, in his letter inclosing it, called "a warrant," under the corporate seal, whereby Russell was appointed "surveyor of The Washington Ins. Co. of such buildings as should be offered for insurance in the said Company."

If this were the extent of the authority given by the respondents to Russell, then, unquestionably, no act of his would be binding on the Company; for I do not see that a survey made by him could be, in anywise, obligatory.

But most certainly he exercised other powers, not only with the consent and approbation of the respondents, but by the direction of their President. These powers were such as well warranted him in assuming the title of agent, and such as leave us no reason to be surprised that the respondents should have known that he was in the habit of calling and signing himself their agent, without their objecting to his doing so until the present controversy arose. Two of the letters of Russell to the respondents, which are exhibits in the cause, are signed by him as agent. These letters relate to premiums received and transmitted by Russell. And the receipt of the letters and of the premiums are acknowledged in subsequent letters of the respondents.

So little were the acts of Russell directed by

the power given to him by the warrant, that it is hardly necessary to refer to that instrument in the further examination of the cause.

660*] *Russell was acknowledgedly not only the agent of the respondents to make surveys, but to agree to make insurances, to charge such premiums as he should think proper, to receive the premiums, and to remit them to the respondents at N. Y. That he was the agent of the respondents, for these purposes, appears from the letter of the President of Apr. 27, 1819, which is an answer to the one from Russell of the 9th of the same month applying for signed blank policies, which were refused. It is true that, by the same letter, it appears that the Company intended to reserve a right to judge of the rate of premium and of the risk. I shall, in the sequel, advert to this part of the letter. I only refer to it at this time to show that the respondents never intended to confine the powers of Russell to those of a surveyor, or supposed that they were limited to those conferred by the warrant.

That Russell was the agent of the respondents, to receive premiums and to transmit them to the Company, not only appears from the letters already mentioned, but is acknowledged in the answer. The words of the answer to which I now refer are as follows: "They permitted him, as in their said answer afterwards particularly mentioned, to receive from such persons as were willing to pay the same to him the sums which he might think fit to name as the probable premiums, and to transmit the same to the respondents in the City of N. Y., in order to prevent any unnecessary delay in effecting the insurance."

If they permitted Russell to receive and remit premiums, they authorized him to do so.

This acknowledgment of the respondent is not qualified by any subsequent part of the answer, farther than by a denial that they authorized or intended Russell to be their agent to make insurances. But, on the contrary, they aver that they refused to give him such powers when he applied for them.

This would be conclusive against the appellant if the points were what powers the respondents intended to give to Russell. But that is not the case. The question is, what powers were the citizens of Savannah, and the
661*] appellant as *one of them, justified, from the acts of Russell and of the respondents, in presuming he possessed. It might have been very far from the intention of the respondents to authorize their agent to bind them to an insurance at his pleasure. It might have been very imprudent in the Company to have renounced the important right of deliberating on the expediency of a risk. To keep these matters under the control of the Directors may be very essential to the credit and safety of every insurance company. In all this I entirely agree with His Honor, the late *Chancellor*. But if the Directors have incautiously given to their agent, or suffered him to exercise, too large a power, they must bear the consequences of their own imprudence. I am not disposed to sacrifice the just claims of one who confided in the respondents, to their safety or to the support of their credit.

I will presume that it is established that Russell was the agent of the respondents to receive premiums and to remit them to the Company at N. Y. Then we are to inquire whether the respondents were bound by the receipt, as if the payment had been made to themselves.

It will not be questioned that if the premium had been paid at the office of the Company in N. Y., and the President or Secretary had signed the receipt which was given by Russell, the insurance would have been as binding as if a policy had been executed. Receipts of this nature are in common use. Much of the insurance made in this city is done, in the first instance, by similar receipts signed by some officer of the corporation. They are intended to give immediate effect to the insurance, and supply the place of a formal policy until one can be prepared. It has been decided that these receipts are as binding as a policy could be. In truth, the receipt answers all the use of a policy, except that the latter authorizes the assured, in case of loss, to sue in a court of law, instead of being obliged to resort, as in this case, to a court of chancery.

The letter from the President of the Company to Russell which inclosed his appointment as surveyor also covered the printed proposals of the Company. From these Russell, as he says in his answer to the second direct interrogatory, *framed an adver- [*662
tisement, which is one of the appellant's exhibits, inviting the citizens of Savannah to make insurance through him with the respondents. To this advertisement he put the names of the President and Secretary.

The respondents aver in their answer, and we must therefore believe, that this advertisement was unauthorized by them, and that they never had knowledge of it till after this controversy arose. But although they disclaim the advertisement, yet they admit in their answer that they sent the printed proposals, which are an exhibit, to Russell. And he testifies that these proposals, together with the letter, which was written on the back of them, he pasted on a piece of pasteboard, and hung it in his store for the information of those who might choose to read it.

These proposals, after a preface which gives assurances of the solidity of the Company, and of the fairness, candor and liberality which the Directors meant to practice, proceeds to state a number of articles, for the information and government of those who meant to do business with the Company. The fifth of these articles is in the following words: "No insurance is to be considered as made or binding until the premium is paid." It is to be observed that here is no intimation, as to where, or to whom the premium is to be paid. There is nothing from which those who read the proposals as they were stuck up in the office of Russell, could understand that the payment of a premium to an agent of the Company authorized to receive the same, would not be as binding as if it had been paid at the office of the respondents, in N. Y.

I presume it will be admitted, that all persons dealing with the respondents, and who had knowledge of this article of the proposals, would be authorized to infer from it, a converse proposition, to wit: that every insurance would be considered as made and binding when the premium was paid.

How then does the case stand? The appellant found Russell the agent of the respondents, to accept propositions to insure his property, and to receive payment of the premium. He also found a declaration of the respondents, which was, in effect, that when the premium was paid, the insurance was to be considered as binding.

663*] *I think the appellant was authorized to conclude, when he had paid the premium to the agent of the respondents in Savannah, that the respondents were bound to make good to him any loss he might subsequently sustain.

I cannot think that anything was communicated to him from which he was to understand that his property was to remain uninsured, until Russell should have collected so large an amount of premiums as he might think worth while to remit to his constituents. Russell says it was not his practice to send on these premiums immediately; that with respect to the premium in question, he pursued his usual course of waiting until he had got a considerable sum of money for the purpose of purchasing a bill of exchange to make the remittance.

In my view of the subject, it is entirely immaterial how far the respondents intended to limit the agency of Russell. If they meant that those who dealt with him should understand that he had a limited agency, it was their business to have made known the bounds which they had prescribed to him. But, on the contrary, their authority to him to receive premiums, and their notice that the payment of a premium should be binding, I think, left them without the power to disavow Russell's acts.

It appears to me, however, that the case may be put on another footing, no less unfavorable to the defense of the respondents. I apprehend it is a well settled rule of the Court of Chancery, that whatever a party was under a legal obligation to perform, shall, as to all persons who had a right to claim the performance, be considered as having been performed. In other words, no person shall be allowed any advantage from his own or his agent's laches.

As the respondent's admit Russell was authorized to receive premiums, and to remit them, it was his duty to remit the premium he received from the appellant without delay. If he had done so, the respondents must have received it before they had news of the fire, which did not happen till Jan. 11. Had the premium been duly remitted, there is no doubt but that policy would have been made; because there is no intimation on the part of the respondents 664*] *that there was any objection to the risk, or to the premium. I think, therefore, the Court of Chancery would have been well warranted in considering the case as if the premium had been transmitted to the respondents in due time, and had, as it must have been, received by them before they had news of the fire.

Suppose an action had been brought against Russell for not sending the premium in due time, can there be a doubt but that the appellant would have recovered in a court of law; and that the measure of damages would have been the amount which was to have been insured, and for which the premium was paid. The plaintiff, in such an action, would only have had to show that if the premium had been duly forwarded, the risk would have been taken, and he would have had the benefit of an insurance. And so in this case, when Russell, who was the agent of the respondents to receive and remit the premium, has withheld it, I think the respondents are to be held responsible, as they would have been, if he had performed his duty.

It will be seen that I take but little notice of the correspondence between Russell and the respondents, by which it may appear that they intended to limit his agency. I disregard it, because it does not appear that the appellant ever had any knowledge of this correspondence.

But if we regard this correspondence, I confess I find myself entirely at loss to reconcile the defense, which the respondents have made in the court below, with principles of justice and equity.

In Russell's letter of Apr. 9, 1819, he applies for ready signed blank policies, or to have his receipt for premiums made binding on the Company, until policies could be obtained from the office. The answer to this letter is from the President of the Company, and is dated the 28th of the same month. In this answer, the President, after objecting to furnish blank policies, says, "the most and best that can be done, I think, is this, that all insurances that you may agree to make, and for which such premiums as you may think proper to charge, shall be actually paid and received here, the office will consider as inuring at the time of *the [*665 payment to you, so that in case of accident between such time of payment, and the receipt of the money here, the Company will indemnify such loss, provided, however, the office shall recognize the rate of premium which you shall charge, and shall be otherwise satisfied with the risk."

Now what is the actual state of things? Russell has agreed to make an insurance for the appellant, for which he has thought proper to charge a certain premium, which has been actually paid, and which has been received at the office of the respondents. I say received there, because it has been tendered to them. But an accident between the date of the receipt and the tender of the money here has happened.

What then can the defendant say, consistently with the President's letter, why they should not make a policy which shall inure at the time of the payment to Russell?

All that this letter of the President will permit them to say is, that the office did not recognize the rate of premium, and were not otherwise satisfied with the risk. But can they honestly and conscientiously say this? Was this the truth? Was it not the truth that the loss had intervened, and therefore they would not make the policy? If they may make the excuse they offer in the case, then they might have made it in every case where a loss happened between the payment of the premium to their agent, and the receipt of the money here. In other words, whenever they received an account of a loss before the premium came into their hands, however long their agent might have chosen to retain it, they would not make a policy; and so, it will be seen, that the President's undertaking that a policy should inure from the time of the payment to the agent, if we give to his letter the construction the respondents contend for, is a perfect fallacy. But the respondents should, in my opinion, be obliged to recognize the rate of premium which was charged and to be satisfied with the risk, unless they can show some objections to the one or the other. This they do not pretend to do. There is not the least pretense that if the loss had not happened, they would not have taken the premium, and made the policy.

666*] *I cannot consent to suffer the respondents thus to evade the spirit of the agreement, made with their express authority by their agent.

I am sure the equity of the case is against them; and I do believe that this is an instance where law and equity coincide.

I confess, it is with much diffidence that I dissent from the great legal authority by which the decree in this case was pronounced. Were I in a situation to ask advice, instead of being obliged to render a judgment, I might be governed by an opinion deserving such high consideration. But as it is, I am not at liberty to yield to feelings of respect; and must decide according to my own convictions.

My opinion is that the decree of the *Chancellor* should be reversed.

The Court concurring unanimously in the result of these opinions, it was thereupon ordered, adjudged and decreed, that the decree of the Court of Chancery be reversed and vacated. And it was further ordered, adjudged and decreed that it be referred to one of the masters of that court, to ascertain and report the balance justly due to the appellant in this cause, for the amount insured on the stock of dry goods and groceries, &c., belonging to the appellant, mentioned in the pleadings in this cause, and interest on the same to be calculated from Apr. 15, 1820. And it was further ordered, adjuged and decreed that upon the coming in and confirmation of the report, the respondents be decreed to pay to the solicitor of the appellant, the appellant's costs in the Court of Chancery, to be taxed, and also the balance reported to be due to him on account of said insurance and interest, together with the interest on the same from the date of the report; and that the record be remitted, &c.

Reversing—6 Johns. Ch., 485.
Distinguished—6 Abb., N. C., 463.
Cited in—21 Wend., 300; 23 Wend., 22; H. & D., 406; 9 Paige, 501; Hoffm., 353; 4 Sand. Ch., 409; 8 N. Y., 357; 10 N. Y., 454; 16 N. Y., 267; 17 N. Y., 454; 27 N. Y., 559; 30 N. Y., 86; 50 N. Y., 249; 4 Lans., 438; 5 Lans., 75; 4 Barb., 373; 6 Barb., 580; 20 Barb., 476; 22 Barb., 535; 29 Barb., 314; 43 Barb., 384; 27 How. Pr., 272; 4 Abb. Pr., 181; 2 Duer, 347; 2 Rob., 393; 9 How. (U. S.), 405; 6 Wall., 132; 20 Wall, 401; 4 McLean, 50; 31 Mich., 420; 43 Mo., 115; 36 Wis., 603; 47 Wis., 371; 31 Am. Dec., 719 (7 Porter, 454); 3 Am. Rep., 304 (7 Bush, 81).

667*] *ELIJAH HOPKINS, Impleaded with COMFORT CARPENTER, *Appellant*,

v.

MARGARET M'LAREN, *Respondent*.

Bill in Equity against Assignee of Mortgage, to have it Canceled on Ground of Payment—Hearing—Mortgage Found to have been Redelivered to Mortgagee for Breach of Condition—Mortgagee Made Party by Supplemental Bill, Not Affected by Proofs Between Original Parties—Former Recovery in Ejectment by Complainant on Question of Payment, not conclusive—Nature of Supplemental Bill—Lis Pendens—*Purchaser* Pendente Lite.

Where the owner of an equity of redemption filed her bill against an assignee of the mortgagee, to have it delivered up and canceled, on the ground that it was paid, and that she had recovered in an ejectment against the assignee upon the point of payment; and the assignee answered the bill, and proofs were taken, and the cause brought to a hearing; when it was discovered that the mortgagee had assigned the mortgage conditionally; and that since the bill filed, the mortgage had been redelivered to him for a violation of the condition; and he was thereupon brought in and made a party upon supplemental bill; upon which he answered both the original and supplemental bill at large, denying payment of the mortgage; to which the plaintiff put in a general replication, and brought the cause to a hearing, without taking any proofs, as between her and the mortgagee; held, that the facts set up in the answer of the mortgagee must be taken, on the hearing, as true; and that he was not affected by the proofs taken between the original parties; but should have been allowed to prove the truth of his answer.

Held, also, that the recovery in ejectment was not conclusive against him.

The bill filed against him was a supplemental bill, in nature of an original one, and entitled him to a new defense; otherwise, it seems where a supplemental bill is in nature of a bill of revivor, and seeks merely to bring in parties who claim, under the original parties, the same interest by the same title. Per Colden, *Senator*.

The doctrine of *lis pendens* applies only where a third person attempts to intrude into a controversy, by acquiring an interest in the matter in litigation pending the suit. The reason and illustration of this rule. Per Colden, *Senator*.

A verdict and judgment in ejectment is never conclusive, even between the immediate parties, except in an action for mesne profits. Per Colden, *Senator*.

A purchaser, *pendente lite*, coming in as a party, after publication passed, would be bound by the previous proofs. Per Savage, *Ch. J.*

Citations—3 Johns. Ch., 423; 4 Johns. Ch., 363, 364; 1 Johns. Ch., 483; 2 Atk., 175; 2 Madd. Ch., 405; 2 Johns. Ch., 158, 155, 444, 445; 2 P. Wms., 483; Mitf. Pl., 68.

APPEAL from the Court of Chancery. The respondent, Apr. 1, 1818, filed her bill, in that court, against Comfort Carpenter, stating that Feb. 13, 1816, she recovered a judgment against one Enos Cook, for $122.06, sued out a *fi. fa.*, purchased certain premises mortgaged by Cook, at auction, upon the *fi. fa.* for $126.-38, and took a sheriff's deed dated July 8, 1816. That these premises were mortgaged by Cook to Elijah Hopkins, the *appellant, by [*668 indenture of mortgage dated Jan. 4, 1816. That this mortgage had been paid to the appellant. That Jan. 2, 1817, and after it was paid, the mortgage was assigned by the appellant to Comfort Carpenter, who had notice that it was paid. That the respondent prosecuted an action of ejectment for the premises, which was defended by Carpenter, the assignee; but it appearing in evidence that the mortgage had been paid, the respondent recovered. The bill then sought a discovery by special interrogatory, whether the mortgage had been paid; prayed a subpœna against Carpenter, alone; and alleged that he had advertised the premises for sale under the power in the mortgage; and prayed an injunction against the sale, and for general relief.

July 18, 1817, Carpenter answered, denying that the mortgage had been paid; but that a balance was still due. That Hopkins, the appellant, Mar. 8, 1817, $533.36 being then due on the mortgage, assigned it to Carpenter, for the consideration of that sum, secured to be paid. He admitted the trial, defense and recovery in ejectment; and that he had since advertised the premises for sale.

The cause having been put at issue by a general replication, witnesses were examined on both sides.

Hopkins, the appellant, having been examined as a witness, in behalf of Carpenter, and it appearing that he was interested, his testimony was suppressed by the *Chancellor*, Nov. 30, 1820.

The cause having afterwards come to a hearing (March Term, 1822), and an objection being taken by Carpenter, for want of proper parties, the *Chancellor* directed the cause to stand over, without prejudice, to the end that Hopkins, the respondent, might be made a party defendant. The order of suppression recited that Carpenter was insolvent, and had absconded; that Hopkins, the appellant, still claimed an interest in the mortgage, and that the suit in chancery was defended at his expense, and for his benefit.

Aug. 1, 1822, the respondent filed her supplemental bill against Hopkins, the appellant, **669***] stating substantially *the same facts as were stated in her original bill: and further, that the assignment from Hopkins to Carpenter was conditional; that the premises were advertised for sale for his benefit, and that the condition not having been performed, the assignment had become void; and that a part, or the whole of the mortgage was due to Hopkins.

Hopkins, Sept. 24, 1822, answered, that Mar. 8, 1817, he assigned the mortgage to Carpenter, for the consideration of $533.36, he (Carpenter) paying that sum to Hopkins, by certain installments; and that it was provided in the assignment, that if Carpenter failed to pay the installments, or any part thereof, at the day, the assignment should be void, and the mortgage should be redelivered to Hopkins. That Carpenter had failed to pay any part of the consideration except $124.20, and that Mar. 1, 1820, the assignment and mortgage were accordingly redelivered by Carpenter to Hopkins. He admitted the trial, verdict and judgment in ejectment; but averred that the defendant's evidence to repel the proof of payment was rejected by the judge at the circuit. He denied that the mortgage had been paid; admitted the facts charged in the supplemental bill, and answered the original bill at large.

A general replication to this answer was filed, and without taking any testimony as between the respondent and appellant, the cause was brought to a hearing, March Term, 1823, against both defendants; and the *Chancellor*, May 5, 1823, decreed that, by the verdict in the ejectment, and the proofs in the cause, payment of the mortgage was sufficiently made out; and that the mortgage, &c., should be delivered up to be canceled, &c.

The additional facts, necessary to be understood, will be found detailed in the opinions of the judges.

From this decree Hopkins appealed.

The cause having been decided by the late *Chancellor*, whose term of office had since expired, no reasons were rendered by him to this court, in support of the decree.

Mr. J. Platt*, for the appellant, con- [*670** tended:

1. That the verdict and judgment in ejectment were not conclusive, as *res judicata*.

2. That the evidence arising from the pleadings and proofs, as between Carpenter and the respondent, did not prove that the mortgage was paid.

3. That the *lis pendens* between the respondent and Carpenter did not invalidate the redelivery of the mortgage by Carpenter to Hopkins; because the original assignment of the bond and mortgage by Hopkins to Carpenter was conditional; and the condition being broken by the default of Carpenter, the whole interest in that security reverted to Hopkins as original mortgagee.

4. That Hopkins having been made defendant subsequent to the proofs taken in the cause between the respondent and Carpenter, whose proofs were not evidence against Hopkins, who is the real party in interest as mortgagee; and his answer, denying all the facts on which the equity of the respondent's bill depended, remains in full force as evidence for the appellant. *Hammersly* v. *Lambert*, 2 Johns. Ch., 432; Wyatt's P. R., 193; 1 Harr. Pr., 503; 2 Madd. Ch., 421, 422, Lond. ed.; Mitf., 59; *Hewatson* v. *Tookey*, 2 Dick., 799; 2 Madd. Ch., 1st ed., 141; Jac. Ch. Pr., 139.

Mr. J. Hamilton (*Mr. J. R. Lawrence*, same side), contra, said that Hopkins and Carpenter were, in truth, but one. Hopkins remained in the dark, putting forward Carpenter to defend the suit; and on its arriving nearly to a close, comes forward to overturn the proceedings, and compel the respondent to travel over the whole ground again. This is not to be tolerated. If the forms of the Court of Chancery required that he should be heard, in an ordinary case, this is a fraud upon those forms, and Hopkins is not entitled to the benefit of them. But we deny that he was entitled to an examination of witnesses, upon any ground. He was concluded by what had been done before he was made a party. Coming in upon a supplemental bill, and claiming under the original defendant, he could not gainsay the proofs in the cause, even had he all along been ignorant of its pendency. Coop. Pl., 73-83; Cooke B. L., 559; *Boeve* v. *Skipwith*, 2 Ch., 75; S. C., *Vin. Abr., Chancery R., *a*, pl. 3; [***671** *Lewellen* v. *Mackworth*, 2 Atk., 40; *Thorn* v. *Germand*, 4 Johns. Ch., 364, 365; *Ensworth* v. *Lambert*, *Id.*, 605; *Shephard* v. *Merril*, 3 *Id.*, 423; Mitf., 60-63; *Jones* v. *Jones*, 3 Atk., 111; 2 Suppl. to Vin. Abr., Chancery, R, *a*, pl. 3, p. 50.

At any rate, no proof could be taken, except upon the new matter charged in the supplemental bill; and this was not necessary, because it was admitted by the appellant's answer. Hind Ch., 43, 44; 1 Har. Ch., 149, 150; *Boyd* v. *Dunlap*, 1 Johns. Ch., 483.

The *lis pendens* operated as notice, and the redelivery of the mortgage from Carpenter to Hopkins was, therefore, void. *Walker* v. *Smallwood*, Amb., 676; *Mead* v. *Ld. Orrery*, 3 Atk., 243, per Ld. Hardwicke; *Le Neve* v. *Le Neve*, *Id.*, 648; *Daniels* v. *Davison*, 16 Ves., 249; *Heatly* v. *Finster*, 2 Johns. Ch., 158, 161;

Chesterman v. *Gardner*, 5 *Id.*, 29; *Cook* v. *Mancius*, *Id.*, 89, 96; *Sorrell* v. *Carpenter*, 2 P. Wms., 482, 483; *Bishop of Winchester* v. *Paine*, 11 Ves., 194; *Murray* v. *Ballou*, 1 Johns. Ch., 566; *Murray* v. *Lilburn*, 2 *Id.*, 441.

As to the effect of the verdict and judgment, they referred to 1 Phil. Ev., 223 and 226, 227; and insisted that Hopkins should be estopped, for he might have come in as landlord, and was privy to the ejectment. *Mabee* v. *Avery*, 18 Johns., 352; *Calhoun's Lessee* v. *Dunning*, 4 Dall., 120; *Duncan* v. *Lyon*, 3 Johns. Ch., 356. They insisted that the decision on the ejectment was at least equivalent to a verdict on a feigned issue, by which the *Chancellor* may hold the parties concluded. *Kemp* v. *Mackrell*, 2 Ves., 579; *Waters* v. *Travis*, 9 Johns., 468.

In addition to these arguments and authorities, the respondent's counsel submitted the following printed points to the court:

1st. That the mortgage was paid or satisfied to Hopkins; that this fact is abundantly established as well from the pleadings and proofs in the cause, as also by the verdict and judgment in the ejectment suit. That Carpenter took an assignment from Hopkins with notice **672***] that the mortgage was *satisfied; that the mortgage was afterwards kept on foot by preconcert and combination between Carpenter and Hopkins, in order to defraud the respondent. Carpenter was put by Hopkins, as his assignee, in his place and stead. That Carpenter was ostensibly the absolute owner of the mortgage; that he, as such, was the only person the respondent would be required or expected to make a defendant. That Carpenter thus standing in the shoes of Hopkins, litigating the fact of the payment of the mortgage, when Hopkins was afterwards brought in on supplemental bill, and the cause brought on to a hearing, the acts of Carpenter as his representative, contesting the same matter in dispute, were binding upon Hopkins. There was such a privity of contract and estate or interest in the mortgage between these two men, as to render the verdict in ejectment, under the circumstances of the case, binding and conclusive against Hopkins as well as against Carpenter.

2d. The re-assignment or redelivery of the mortgage by Carpenter to Hopkins pending the suit, was void, and could not operate to the prejudice of the respondent's right to a decree, founded upon the testimony already given in the cause. Such re-assignment or redelivery was not only a fraud upon the respondent, but done in *fraudem legis*, and by a fraudulent conspiracy between Hopkins and Carpenter to deprive the respondent of her remedy, and elude the justice of the court in respect of any decree it should make for the relief of the respondent. Equity can never uphold a re-assignment under such circumstances.

3d. That Carpenter having been put in possession of the mortgage by Hopkins himself, with power to advertise, to foreclose and to collect or receive the money upon it, the circumstance of Hopkins' having been made a defendant with Carpenter, subsequent to the proofs taken in the cause, does not prevent those proofs from having the same operation and effect against Hopkins as against Carpenter, inasmuch as no change of interest which could affect the questions litigated between Carpenter and the respondent had occurred to entitle Hopkins to any examination of the same or of different witnesses; and more especially ought the appellant *to be pre- [***673** cluded from setting up such right in this court, or objecting here that those proofs are not evidence against Hopkins, without showing that he has taken the proper measures in the Court of Chancery to procure such examination of the same or other witnesses as to avoid the force and effect of their testimony by applying to the *Chancellor* for an order for that purpose, or otherwise proceeding in that court to obtain such examination, or to preclude the complainant from the benefit of any examination of witnesses therein, or without showing some order or decision of the Court of Chancery against him upon the point, at war with some settled rule of equity.

4th. The answer of Hopkins admits the material facts charged in the supplemental bill, and therefore it became unnecessary for the complainant to examine witnesses as to those facts. His answer, as to all the facts recited from the original bill, was irregular, impertinent, and unworthy of regard; and for the respondent to have proceeded upon the supplemental bill and answer, to the examination of witnesses, as to facts put in issue on the original bill and answer, would likewise have been irregular, and such testimony would, on motion, have been suppressed.

SAVAGE, *Ch. J.*, after stating the facts. Two questions arise upon this case:

1. Whether the proofs taken in the cause could be regularly used as against the appellant, they having been taken before he was a party; and,

2. Whether those proofs, if admissible, prove the fact of payment.

It is contended on the part of the appellant, that those proofs cannot be used, because he had no opportunity to examine witnesses. To this, it is answered that having succeeded to the rights and liabilities of Carpenter, he is entitled to no other privileges than Carpenter. In 1 Madd. Ch., 141, it is said that if a defendant be added after publication passed, the cause, as to such defendant, must be heard on the bill and answer only; and Jacob's Ch. Pr., 139, is cited to support that *dictum*; and it was *urged at the bar, that at any [***674** rate, a defendant brought in on a supplemental bill, is to answer only the matters charged in that bill; and as to these, if they are denied in the answer, proofs may be taken, and the cause brought to a hearing, as on original bills. In *Shephard* v. *Merril*, 3 Johns. Ch., 423, the *Chancellor* refused an amendment to the bill after publication passed; but gave leave to add new charges by supplemental bill. And it is hardly supposable that such leave would have been granted, if the plaintiff could not support his charges by proof, should they be denied by the answer. The same practice was afterwards recognized in *Thorn* v. *Germand*, 4 Johns. Ch., 363, 364. In Mitford Pl., 58, 59, it is said that "a supplemental bill must state the original bill, and the proceedings upon it; and if the supplemental bill is occasioned by an event subsequent to the original bill, it must state that event, and the consequent alteration with respect to the parties; and, in general, the supplemental bill must pray that all the defendants may appear and answer to the charges it contains; or if the supplemental bill is not for discovery merely, the cause must be heard upon the supplemental bill at the same time it is heard upon the original bill, if it has not been heard; and if it has been heard upon the original, it must be further heard upon the supplemental bill." Nothing is here said as to the cause being heard upon the pleadings merely, without proof. In *Boyd* v. *Dunlap*, 1 Johns. Ch., 483, the *Chancellor* says: "Liberty to re-examine witnesses, rests in discretion, and is to be governed by circumstances."

But whatever the rule may be, as to a plaintiff's right to examine witnesses upon the answer to a supplemental bill, in this case none were examined. The respondent filed a general replication, and went to a hearing without examining a single witness. Admitting that the appellant was, in strict practice, bound to answer only the charges in the supplemental bill, and not those in the original; yet he has answered the latter charges. He has denied them; and the question arises, is not that answer to be taken as true, the respondent having neither examined witnesses to disprove it,
675*] *nor excepted to the answer as containing irrelevant or improper matter.

Had Hopkins simply answered the charges in the supplemental bill, he would have been bound by the previous proofs taken in the cause, especially, if he is to be considered as a purchaser *pendente lite*. *Garth* v. *Ward*, 2 Atk., 175. Lord Hardwicke asks: "So in the case of a mortgagor who comes here for redemption, if during such suit he should assign the equity of redemption, and, in the final hearing of the cause, there should be a decree against the mortgagor, will not the assignee of the equity of redemption be bound by this decree?" In 2 Madd. Ch., 405, this rule is laid down: "Where a supplemental bill is brought after publication, it is irregular to examine witnesses to a matter that was in issue, and not proved in the original cause; nor can such proofs be read; and if there be no proof as to the new matter in the supplemental bill, it will be dismissed." This must be understood, probably, of a case where the facts in the original bill are not answered in the supplemental.

From the best examination I have been able to give the subject, admitting, in a case like the present, the answer is to be confined to the supplemental bill, and that the proofs taken on the original bill are to stand; yet the respondent having gone on to a hearing, leaving the answer to the supplemental bill not disproved, nor stricken out for impertinence, I am satisfied that she has been irregular. The *Chancellor*, and of course this court, on appeal, is bound to consider the facts in the answer to the supplemental bill admitted by the complainant.

On the second point I will barely remark, without going into detail, that the evidence is far from being satisfactory on the question of payment. The appellant shows a valid instrument under seal, on which there appears to be due to him $125 and interest, and a liability to indemnify to at least $400 more; and the only evidence to counteract this claim rests on loose circumstances and declarations rather equivocal.

*To show payment, by which a par- [***676**
ty is to lose his lien for such a demand, the proof, if not positive, should at least be satisfactory.

Under the circumstances of this case, the verdict in ejectment should have little weight; as the appellant avers, and this is not contradicted by the proofs, that the evidence offered to disprove the payment was rejected by the court before which the ejectment was tried.

I am, therefore, of opinion that the decree of His Honor, the *Chancellor*, should be reversed.

WOODWORTH and SUTHERLAND, *JJ.*, concurred.

COLDEN, *Senator*. In this case the *Chancellor* has decided that the mortgage given by Enos Cook to the appellant was satisfied. He draws this conclusion from proofs taken before the appellant was a party in the cause; and from a verdict in an ejectment suit between the respondent and Carpenter.

He has also decided that the appellant having become repossessed of the mortgage pending the suit below, between the respondent and Carpenter, the suit might proceed as if the mortgage had remained in the hands of Carpenter, and as if the appellant had no interest in the controversy.

The answer of the appellant, to which there was a general replication, denies that the mortgage was satisfied, and avers that he holds the same as security for a considerable amount yet due upon it. If the appellant ought not to be concluded by the testimony taken before he became a party, and if, after he was made a defendant, he had a right to produce witnesses to support his answer, then it is unnecessary to examine how far the testimony, as between the respondent and Carpenter, is sufficient to establish the payment of the mortgage.

The only questions, therefore, which I think it necessary to decide, are:

1. Whether the appellant should not, after he was made a defendant, have had an opportunity of examining witnesses, as if he had been an original party to the suit.

*2. Whether his repossession of the [***677**
mortgage, pending the suit below, was such an acquisition of it as subjected his title to the mortgage to the rules which govern, where property in controversy is taken while the right to it is in litigation.

3. And lastly, whether the appellant was concluded by the verdict and judgment in the ejectment suit.

It is important to notice that the appellant is not a volunteer in the cause. He was examined as a witness, by the defendant, Carpenter, and testified that the mortgage was an outstanding unsatisfied security in his hands. His testimony was suppressed, by an order of the *Chancellor*, on a petition of the respondent, stating that the appellant appeared to be deeply interested in the event of the cause; and that he claimed to be the owner of the mortgage by reason of failure in performing the conditions of the assignment of the mortgage by the appellant to the defendant, Carpenter; and that the appellant, either jointly with the defendant, Carpenter, or solely, was interested in the subject-matter of the suit.

After this, when all the testimony, on which the cause was finally decided, was before the court, and when the cause was on hearing, upon the suggestion of the defendant, Carpenter, the *Chancellor* ordered that the cause should stand over, without prejudice, to the end that the respondent might bring in Hopkins as a party defendant.

If Hopkins' denial of payment, when he was brought in, gave him no right to controvert the fact and to prove his allegations, there does not seem to be any satisfactory reason why he should have been made a party. His denial could not help the respondent; and the cause seems to have stood before the *Chancellor* on precisely the same ground, when he directed Hopkins to be made a party, that it did subsequently. But when it appeared to the *Chancellor*, by the showing of the respondent, that Hopkins claimed to be owner of the mortgage, and that he was jointly or solely interested in the suit, I think the *Chancellor* could not have done otherwise than compel the respondent to make him a party. When he answered, it appeared that the allegations of the 678*] *respondent, as to his claim of interest, were true. It would seem that a party, so circumstanced, should be entitled to produce his testimony; and should not be concluded by examinations which had been taken in a proceeding of which he was not, by legal intendment, conusant.

But it is said the decree against the appellant, without giving him an opportunity to examine witnesses or to question those which had been examined, was correct, because the rights of the respondent, as against the mortgage in the hands of the defendant Carpenter, were not affected by a re-assignment or redelivery of the mortgage by the defendant Carpenter to Hopkins, pending the suit.

Certainly, if there had been an unconditional assignment of the mortgage to Carpenter, and Hopkins had taken a voluntary assignment of it, while it was in litigation in the court below, he must have been content to have been represented by Carpenter, and must have abided by the proceeding and any decree that might have been made against him. But this was not the case. The mortgage was assigned to Carpenter, long before the commencement of the suit, upon the express condition, that in case of failure in any of the payments, which Carpenter had agreed upon as the consideration for the assignment, then the assignment was to be absolutely null and void, and the mortgage was to be redelivered to the assignor. The appellant then, never ceased to have an interest in the mortgage. If Carpenter did not pay, as the appellant avers in his answer, and as he possibly might have proved if he had been allowed the opportunity to examine witnesses, the appellant would have been entitled to a reassignment and redelivery of the mortgage. Can it be, because a suit to which the appellant was a stranger was depending between the respondent and Carpenter, that the appellant was not at liberty to avail himself of the terms and conditions of his assignment?

The doctrine of *lis pendens* applies only where a third person attempts to intrude into a controversy, by acquiring an interest in the matter in litigation pending the suit.

The rule as given by *Chancellor* Kent, in the case of *Murray* v. *Lilburn*, 2 Johns. Ch., 445, is, that "any interest *acquired in the [*679 subject-matter of a suit, pending the suit, is so far considered as a nullity, that it cannot avail against the plaintiff's title."

The reason of the rule is, that if a transfer of interest, pending a suit were to be allowed to affect the proceedings, there would be no end to litigation; for as soon as a new party was brought in, he might transfer to another, and render it necessary to bring that other before the court, so that a suit might be interminable. But this reason has no application to a third person, whose interest subsisted before the suit was commenced, and who might have been made an original party.

So that neither the rule, nor the reason of the rule applies to the case under consideration. The interest of the appellant in the mortgage was not a voluntary acquisition by him pending the suit. His interest subsisted long before the suit was commenced, and ought not, in my opinion, to have been considered as a nullity.

In the cases of *Walker* v. *Smalwood*, Amb., 676, and *Sorrel* v. *Carpenter*, 2 P Wms., 483, cited by the respondent's counsel, the conveyances were made after the commencement of the suit. In *Heatley* v. *Finster*, 2 Johns. Ch., 158; *Murray* v. *Finster*, *Id.*, 155, and *Murray* v. *Lilburn*, *Id.*, 444, the defendants claimed under a trustee, in virtue of certain transactions between them and the trustee, after bills were filed charging the trustee with fraud in relation to these transactions—the defendants having notice that a charge of fraud was the ground of the suits. The court decided that these transactions, *pendente lite*, were invalid.

The bill in this case, as against the appellant, is an original bill in the nature of a supplemental bill. To such a bill it is said in Mit. Pl., 68, 2 Eng. ed., a new defense may be made. The pleadings and depositions cannot be used in the same manner as if filed or taken in the same cause.

Where a supplemental bill is in the nature of a bill of revivor, and seeks merely to bring parties who claim under the original party to the suit, and claim the same interest by the same title, that the original party did, then there may *be equity in binding and con- [*680 cluding the new party by testimony taken previously to his having been made a defendant.

But where, as in the case under consideration, there is no privity or connection between the new party and the original defendant, where he may not know, and has no interest to support the title of the new party, it seems to me that it would be a very unjust rule which would oblige the new party to abide by the testimony taken while he was a stranger to the suit, and would prevent his producing witnesses to support the title he sets up.

I forbear to examine this point further: because, putting the redelivery of the mortgage to the appellant out of question, and supposing that the mortgage had always remained in possession of Carpenter, I think it appeared in the Court of Chancery, as well by the showing of the respondent as by the answer of the appellant, that he was so far interested that he ought to have been made an original party;

and that when he was subsequently brought in, he had the same right to produce witnesses, and to prove his case, that he would have had if he had been made a defendant at the commencement of the suit.

The third reason assigned for concluding the appellant by the testimony taken before he was a party, is that the fact that the mortgage was paid and satisfied in Feb. 1816, by Enos Cook, was put in issue and established by the verdict of a jury upon a trial in an ejectment, founded upon the mortgage.

We understand from the respondent's bill, that she having recovered a judgment against Cook, sold the mortgaged premises, under an execution issued on that judgment, and became the purchaser, at the sheriff's sale, for $126.38. That she thereupon brought her ejectment, to which a defense was made by Carpenter as the assignee of the mortgage. That it appeared to the court that the mortgage was satisfied, and the respondent recovered judgment.

I do not find that the appellant had any notice of this suit. But if the appellant ought not to be concluded by the proceedings in the Court of Chancery, to which he was not a party, as I think he should not be, he ought not to be bound by the event of the suit at common law.

681*] *I do not understand that a verdict in ejectment is conclusive as to any point, even between the same parties, unless it be in the action for *mesne* profits. And so far as I have been able to examine the cases cited by the respondent's counsel from Phillips and and other authors, they are to this effect.

Suppose, after the verdict in the ejectment suit, Hopkins, or even Carpenter himself, had discovered testimony that would, beyond all doubt, have shown that the mortgage was unsatisfied; might not either of them have brought a new ejectment, or have resorted to a court of equity? I cannot think they would have been precluded from doing so because the fact of payment was put in issue in the suit between the respondent and Carpenter; the more particularly, when the common law court excluded evidence of a settlement between the mortgagor and mortgagee which showed how much was due on the mortgage. This evidence could only have been excluded on the ground that, as Hopkins was not a party to the record, the memorandum between him and Cook, of Jan. 2, 1817, was *res inter alios acta*.

Now it would be very unjust, as it appears to me, that this testimony should be excluded in the court of common law, on the ground of the appellant's not being a party to the record, and yet that he should be concluded, in the Court of Chancery, by the event of that suit, on the ground that though he was not in the record he was a party in interest.

My opinion is, that the decree be reversed, and that the record be remitted to the Court of Chancery, under such an order as shall admit the appellant to prove his answer, as if he had been an original party to the suit.

I have come to this conclusion, without any other want of confidence in its correctness, than its being in opposition to the high authority to which it is opposed. But we are placed in a situation where we must take care that our habitual respect for that authority has not an undue influence, and where we are bound to decide according to our own understandings and intelligence, however we may estimate the talents, learning and experience by which the judgments, brought to our review, are declared.

The Court* (except Morgan, *Senator*) [*682** being for a reversal, it was thereupon ordered, adjudged and decreed that the decree of His Honor, the *Chancellor*, be reversed, and the record remitted, &c.

Cited in—11 Wend., 459; 1 Paige, 18; 48 N. Y., 603; 3 Keyes, 491; 1 Abb. App. Dec., 459; 3 Lans., 132; 8 Hun, 381; 6 T. & C., 604; 3 Abb. N. S., 238.

WILLIAM FELLOWS, Impleaded with JOHN FELLOWS, THOMAS FELLOWS and ROSWELL DAY, *Appellant*,

v.

ABIGAIL FELLOWS, Administratrix, AND JEREMIAH RUNDLE, Administrator, of EZRA FELLOWS, Deceased.

Bill in Equity—Charge of Conspiracy to Defraud Creditor—Pleading—Joinder of Parties—Demurrer—Purchase of Land by Administrators upon Decree in Favor of Intestate—Power of Equity to Reach Debtors' Property—To Prevent Multiplicity of Suits.

The bill charged that several defendants combined and confederated among themselves, and with the debtor of the complainants, against whom they had obtained a decree for their debt, to defraud the complainants, by taking a conveyance and transfer to each, in separate parcels, of all the debtor's real and personal property, without consideration, and with intent to avoid execution upon the decree; and that they accordingly received such conveyances and transfer of all the debtor's property which they held for him or for their own use. To this bill one of the defendants answered, denying the combination between himself and the other several alienees and transferrees of the debtor's property, and demurred to the residue of the bill, because it was for several distinct matters and causes, in many of which the defendant, thus answering and demurring, was not interested or concerned: held, that the defendants were properly joined, and that the demurrer should be overruled.

This was held, as well because there was one connected interest, centering in the point in issue in the cause, or one common point of litigation, as that the joinder tended to prevent multiplicity of suits.

The general rule is, that where a bill is filed concerning things of distinct natures, against several persons, it is demurrable; but unconnected parties may join in a suit where there is one connected interest among them all, centering in the point in issue in the cause.

An administrator who purchases land upon judgment or decree in favor of his intestate, holds it as a trustee, and may be compelled to account for the land itself to his *cestuis que trust*.

He may, in his representative character, call in the aid of a court of equity to perfect his title. Per Woodworth, J.

Of the power of a court of chancery to reach a debtor's property in the hands of third persons. Per Woodworth, J.

It is a favorite object of equity, to prevent multiplicity of suits. Hence all persons interested are to be made parties. Creditors may join in compelling *executors, &c., to account, or one [***683** creditor, or more, may sue for the benefit of the whole. Per Sutherland, J.

But equity will not permit several plaintiffs by one bill, to demand several matters perfectly distinct and unconnected, against one defendant; nor one plaintiff to demand several matters of different natures against several defendants; otherwise, if the defendants have a common interest, centering in the point in issue in the cause, or where one general right is claimed by the bill. Illustration of these propositions. Per Sutherland, J.

It is not sufficient that the parties have an interest in some one or more items in an account charged. Per Sutherland, J.

The rule that multifarious matters shall not be joined in the same suit, is a rule of convenience. Per Colden, *Senator*.

The rule in Brinkerhoff v. Brown, 6 Johns. Ch., 139, "that a bill may be filed against several persons, relative to matters of the same nature, forming a connected series of acts, all intended to defraud and injure the plaintiffs, and in which all the defendants were, more or less, concerned, though not jointly in each act," considered, recognized and applied. Per Savage, *Ch. J.*, Sutherland, *J.*, and Colden, *Senator*.

Citations—2 Madd., 234, 294; 2 Anstr., 469-477; 2 Sch. & L., 370; 5 Johns., Ch., 388; 1 Madd. Ch., 91; 5 Ves., 682; 20 Johns., 554; Coop. Eq. Pl., 182; Mitf., 146; 2 Harr. Ch. Pr., 289; 1 East, 227; 1 Atk., 282; 2 Ves., Jr., 486; 2 Dick., 677; 18 Ves., 71; 6 Johns. Ch., 139, 157; 3 Cow., 537.

APPEAL from the Court of Chancery. Feb. 4, 1823, the respondents filed their bill in that court, against William Fellows, the appellant, John Fellows, Thomas Fellows and Roswell Day, charging that Nov. 24, 1815, Ezra Fellows, the intestate, was seised of 214 acres of land in Stillwater, Saratoga County, 150 acres of which were incumbered with a life lease from the intestate to his father, John Fellows, and a part by a mortgage of $700, and another part by a mortgage of $55; and the whole by a judgment of $200. That before Nov. 24, 1815, the intestate with John Fellows, his father, and Roswell Day, two of the defendants below, agreed that the intestate should convey to Day all his (the intestate's) right in the 214 acres; that Day should pay the incumbrances and work the 150 acres on shares for the father; and should pay the intestate $3,500.

That shortly before Nov. 24, 1815, one Martin Adsit proposed to purchase the 214 acres for $8,239, payable thus: $2,000 in 10 days, $3,000 May 15, then next, and the residue (to be secured by bond and mortgage on the premises) in annual payments of $500 each, with interest. That Nov. 24, 1815, it was 684*] agreed *between the intestate and his father, with Day's assent, that the 214 acres should be sold and conveyed by the intestate to his father by quitclaim deed; who should convey to Adsit, and that the intestate should receive for his proportion of the purchase money, $1,000 of the first payment, $1,000 of the second, and the first, third and fifth installments of $500 each, with interest, to be secured by the bond and mortgage of Adsit. That the intestate, Nov. 24, 1815, quitclaimed accordingly. That he received the two first payments of $1,000 each. That Nov. 24, the father gave the intestate a written memorandum of the agreement, as to the three last installments, which he was to receive, promising to pay the $1,500 out of Adsit's bond and mortgage, as the installments should be received by him in their turn, or that the intestate might take Adsit's bond and mortgage for his share, in his own name.

That the father conveyed to Adsit, taking the bond and mortgage in his own name, for the whole purchase money, except what had been paid, without the intestate's knowledge or consent, with intent to defraud him of the $1,500, his due.

That in further pursuance of his fraudulent intent, the father, Mar. 17, 1817, canceled and delivered up to Adsit, his bond and mortgage, and received as a substitute the promissory note of Raymond and Jesse Adsit, sons of Martin Adsit, the mortgagor, payable to John Fellows (the father) or bearer, with interest, at the several times when the installments would fall due,—which notes the drawers secured by bond and mortgage, to the intestate's father, on 107 acres of the farm sold by him to M. Adsit; all without the intestate's consent, and in violation of the original trust and agreement, &c.

That Feb. 15, 1819, the intestate filed his bill in the Court of Chancery against the father, who was, Feb. 16, served with an injunction forbidding him to transfer the notes; that Nov. 10, 1820, Ezra Fellows, the intestate, dying, the respondents obtained letters of administration. That Dec. 30, 1820, they filed their bill of revivor; and May 17, 1821, the *suit was revived by an order of the [*685 Court of Chancery. That Apr. 27, 1822, the Court of Chancery rendered a final decree, declaring that the intestate was entitled to the $1,500, in question, with interest; that the father had violated his trust in giving up the bond and mortgage to be canceled, and that he had fraudulently converted the $1,500 to his own use; and that he should pay the respondents $2,012.24, with costs.

That William Fellows and Thomas Fellows, sons, and Roswell Day, son-in-law of John Fellows, the father, were well acquainted with and had full knowledge of the agreement for the sale of the farm between the intestate and his father, and of the proportion which the intestate was to receive, and the time and manner in which, and the source from which, he was to receive it; that they knew of the bill filed, of the injunction, progress of the suit and decree.

That John Fellows, the father, apprehending that a decree would be made against him, came to a fraudulent determination, and entered into a secret and fraudulent combination with William, Thomas and Roswell, his sons, and son-in-law, so to manage and conceal his (John Fellows') property as to delay and defraud the respondents, and to retain for his own use, in the hands of William, Thomas and Roswell, his sons, and son-in-law, or for their use respectively, the money due the respondents, and all his (John Fellows') own property; and that for that purpose, after the injunction served upon him, and before the hearing, he voluntarily, fraudulently and without any fair or valuable consideration, transferred and delivered to his son William two of the notes drawn by Raymond and Jesse Adsit; and to his son Thomas two others, one of which he had given up to the drawers, and received another of the same tenor and date drawn by them payable to himself—which notes William and Thomas continued to hold at the time of filing the bill against them, or they had received and held the amount fraudulently.

That after the exhibition of the bill against

him by the intestate, John Fellows, the father; also, in pursuance of the same fraudulent combination, voluntarily, fraudulently and with-
686*] out *any fair and valuable consideration, or under color of some pretended debt, conveyed to Day one of his farms of about 40 acres, lying in Malta, Saratoga Co., worth about $1,500, which was held by Day for the use of the father; that this was done to prevent its being taken and sold on execution upon the decree; that with the same intent, and for the same purpose, he conveyed his other farm of four acres, in Malta, worth about $500, to his son Thomas, without any consideration.

That July 27, 1822, the respondents sued out a *fieri facias* upon their decree, directed to the Sheriff of the County of Saratoga, upon which he levied only $20 out of the father's personal property; and that the land conveyed to Day had been sold upon the *fi. fa.* to the respondents, for $300, and that conveyed to Thomas Fellows for $50, upon which the sheriff returned to the *fi. fa.* that he had levied $353; and *nulla bona et terræ*, as to the residue. That Thomas Fellows had paid the respondents the $50 which they bid for his lot, in order to redeem it.

That the respondents had applied to the defendants below in a friendly manner, &c., but that they, combining and confederating, &c., all which, &c.

The bill concluded by praying that the conveyances to Thomas Fellows and Roswell Day might be declared void and delivered up to be canceled; that an account might be taken of the money paid and received on the notes, and this decree to be paid to the respondents, to the amount of the decree in their favor, with interest thereon, and for general relief.

To this bill the defendants demurred severally; and the appellant assigned for causes of demurrer that the bill was exhibited against the appellant, John Fellows, Thomas Fellows and Roswell Day, for several distinct matters and causes, in many whereof, as appeared by the bill, the appellant was not, in any manner, interested or concerned; by reason of which distinct matters the bill was drawn out to a considerable length, and the appellant compelled to take a copy of the whole; that by joining the appellant with the other defendants below, and distinct matters together, which did
687*] not *depend on each other in the bill, the pleadings, order and proceedings would in the progress of the suit, be intricate and prolix, and the appellant put to unreasonable and unnecessary charges in taking copies, although several parts of the bill no way related to or concerned him, &c.

The appellant also answered, and denied that he ever did, at any time, combine with the other defendants below, all or either of them, so to manage and conceal all, or any part of the property of John Fellows, as to delay and defraud the respondents and to retain in the hands of Thomas Fellows, Roswell Day and the appellant, all or either of them, for the use of John Fellows, or for the use of Thomas Fellows, Roswell Day and the appellant, all or either of them, all or any part of the money belonging to the respondents, arising from the sale of the farm mentioned in the bill, or all or any part of the property of John Fellows, as stated in the bill.

And he also denied all, and all manner of unlawful combination, &c. (in the usual form).

The demurrers were brought to a hearing in August Term 1823, when His Honor, the *Chancellor*, overruled them, and ordered the defendants below to put in a good and sufficient answer in six weeks.

From this decree, William Fellows appealed; and now the *Chancellor* assigned the reasons for the decree as follows:

SANFORD, *Chancellor*. The object of this suit is to obtain satisfaction of a decree against John Fellows, from his property. The bill alleges that all his property has been transferred by him, without consideration and fraudulently, in parcels, to three persons; that is to say, one part to his son William, another part to his son Thomas, and another part to his son-in-law, Roswell Day. John Fellows and these three persons are made defendants; and they all demur to the bill, alleging that they are impleaded together, for distinct matters.

A complainant is not permitted to demand by one bill, several matters of distinct natures, against several defendants. (Mitf., 146, 147; 1 Harr., 289.)

The matter demanded by the bill, is the property of John Fellows; but this property, having been divided into three *parts, [*688
is now held in portions, by the other defendants. Each of these defendants, by his demurrer, confesses that his share of the property was conveyed to him without consideration, by fraud, and for the purpose of screening it from the complainants' demand. When these defendants thus admit that this property is now in their hands, without any right whatever, against the complainants, they may justly be considered as also admitting that the same property is now one subject of demand, as it clearly was before the transfers were made.

If, however, instead of one matter in demand, here are three, they are all of the same nature, in respect to the questions which they now present. Each one of three defendants holds a portion of the property of John Fellows, by fraud, and by a fraud of the same kind. The right of the complainants is against the whole property, and their right against all portions of it, is of one nature. The claims of the three defendants, who now hold the property in portions, are of one character, each of them holding under a fraudulent transfer, made by John Fellows, in like manner in each instance.

This, therefore, is not a case of several matters of distinct natures, in the sense of the rule, upon that subject.

Each of these defendants has subjoined to his demurrer an answer, denying combination with the other defendants. Such an answer is a sufficient denial of the general charge of combination, made in the bill; but all the fraud specially alleged in the bill stands confessed. The defendants deny that they combined to defraud the complainants, but they admit that they did defraud the complainants, by the transfers of the property, and by holding it in separate portions.

The bill expressly alleges that John Fellows

had determined to transfer all his property, in order to defraud the complainants. From the allegations of the bill, from the relation of these defendants to each other, and from the course and nature of these transactions, it sufficiently appears, and may be taken as a fact, that each of these defendants had knowledge of the conveyances to the other defendants, and of the fraudulent object of all the convey-
689*] ances. *In this respect, all the defendants were privy to a scheme of fraud, of which the consummation consisted in separate conveyances of separate parts of the property. If the manner of accomplishing this fraud cannot deprive the complainants of their rights, it should not deprive them of their remedy; and these defendants cannot justly claim the benefit of the rule concerning distinct matters of different kinds, when their own fraud has produced the separation in question. The conveyances by the father to three others of his family are the very fraud which forms the basis of the suit, and such a fraud cannot prevail against either the right or the remedy of the complainants. The separation of the property into portions, is a part of the fraud; and to allow that such a separation shall render separate suits necessary, would be to allow success to the fraud itself, so far as multiplicity of suits may impede the recovery of a just demand. When the matters in question are thus rendered several by fraud, the fraudulent parties have no claim to the benefit of the rule which forbids that distinct subjects shall be blended in one suit. The circumstances of this case form a sufficient connection between the defendants, in respect to the property in demand, to enable the complainants to join them in one suit.

Mr. S. G. Huntington, for the appellant:

1. The respondents' claims are founded on several matters of distinct natures, which they have introduced into their bill against several defendants. No matter in what form the bill may bring forward these matters, if the claims are in their nature distinct, and should have been the subject of a separate suit against each defendant, the respondents cannot make them joint by treating them so in their bill. The appellant denies all fraud by his answer, all combination or connection with the other defendants, in the fraud charged, and all joint design to withhold the claim of the respondents. This leaves him alone, and standing upon his individual rights. If any design against the respondents' rights was formed, it began and ended in the mind of John Fellows, the father, and never was communicated to the appellant. The denial is, that the defendants ever combined with John Fellows, or that
690*] *he combined with them. This does away all joint equity against the defendants.

Indeed, William Fellows, Roswell Day and John Fellows are not charged with jointly combining. For aught that appears in the bill, John Fellows conveyed to William Fellows at one time, and to Roswell Day at another—neither William nor Roswell knowing what the other was about. To warrant joining them as defendants, in relation to the land, the bill should certainly show that they were jointly privy to the fraud. They are not, as to this, charged with following up any fraudulent design. All combination and joint design among the defandants, are confined, on the face of the bill, to the transfer of the notes to William and Thomas Fellows and Roswell Day. Taking the averments in the bill, and answer together, it is impossible for the court to deduce any connection between the defendants. No joint decree is prayed for; and it must, from the nature of the case, be against the defendants severally, according to the property in their respective possessions.

If things of a distinct nature are joined in a bill against different defendants, it is good cause of demurrer. (2 Madd. Ch., 234, 1st ed.; 1 Harr. Pr., 392, 8th ed.; Mitf. Pl., 147, 3d ed.; Eq. Drafts, 422, 423.) No doubt has ever been entertained that a demurrer will lie for this cause, if accompanied with an answer denying all combination. (Coop. Eq. Pl., 182, 183; Mitf. Pl. 147, 3d ed.) The proposition for which we contend is illustrated in the two books last cited; and the question was fully considered in *Whaley* v. *Dawson*, 2 Sch. & L., 367, 370; *Dilly* v. *Doig*, 2 Ves., Jr., 486, and *Brinkerhoff* v. *Brown*, 6 Johns. Ch., 139, 149.

2. The respondents have also joined pretended claims, in their own right, with other pretended claims in the right of the intestate. It is not averred that the respondents bid for the land in a representative character. As to this, they must, therefore, come in their own right. Where an administrator bids upon an execution of his intestate, it must, from the nature of the transaction, be in his own right. (Toll. L. E., 239, 2d Lond. ed.) He cannot throw the purchase upon his *cestuis que trust*. Nothing is said that the heirs or *distributees [***691** of the intestate even knew of the purchase. To warrant blending this with matters *en autre droit*, their assent should be shown affirmatively. They were not bound to submit, and have the land thrown upon them for better or for worse. Sudg. L. V., 35, Am. ed., 1820; *Beardsley* v. *Root*, 11 Johns., 464; 1 Madd. Ch., 269, 1st ed.; 2 *Id.*, 384; *Ex parte Bennet*, 10 Ves., Jr., 381, 400; *Earl of Winchelsea* v. *Norcliffe*, 1 Vern., 435, 437; *Nelthorp* v. *Pennyman*, 14 Ves., 517; *Prowse* v. *Abingdon*, 1 Atk., 484; Toll. L. E., 182; Bac. Abr., Guardian, G.

3. The complainants have not made a case which entitles them to discovery or relief. A discovery could be of no avail for the purposes of the bill. The notes in question were all *res judicatæ*, before the commencement of this suit. The intestate filed his bill, which was followed up by his personal representatives; and a degree obtained, not for the notes themselves, but their value. This decree declares that the notes were appropriated to the use of the defendant, in that suit, and directs him to account for the value. A *fieri facias* was issued upon the decree. This operated to transfer the property in the notes like an action of trover. If the *Chancellor* could not originally reach these notes in the hands of John Fellows, can they now be pursued beyond him, in the hands of the defendants? An injunction was obtained against the transfer of the notes; and the intestate, having neglected to take a degree for them specifically in the first instance, cannot now follow them. Having the cause before them, the court will look into and decide the whole merits of the case. *Le Guen* v.

Gouverneur, 1 Johns. Cas., 436; *Bush* v. *Livingston*, 2 Cai. Cas., 66; *Beebe* v. *Bank of N. Y.*, 1 Johns., 529. And they will hear an objection in this court, which was not taken below, if they see that, upon its being taken there, it could not have been obviated. *Beekman* v. *Frost*, 18 Johns., 544.

Mr. J. L. Velie, for the respondents. The appellant contents himself with the simple denial of combination, and by his demurrer admits all the rest of the case—all the specific **692***] allegations *of fraud; that the intestate was drawn into a court of chancery to enforce the trust against his father, and that after the decree, and with a view to defeat the claim of his heirs, they fraudulently received a transfer of the very subject of that suit, and all the real property of the defendant, with knowledge, and with consideration. They then gravely come into a court of equity, and ask if there be relief. If there be none, if there be any technical bar, it is a very great slander upon our system of jurisprudence.

We admit the rule, that where the matter in litigation depends upon distinct rights, in different individuals, they cannot be joined, but it has no application to this case. We present a transaction to the court founded upon and progressing in fraud, and whether one defendant may have obtained $500 and another $1,000 of the subject to which we are entitled, can make no difference—it does not alter the nature of our claim or their defense. We ask that the property of John Fellows may pay his debts. The defendants admit themselves to be *quasi* agents of John Fellows. As between them and a creditor, they have no claim as owners.

The rule relied upon against the joinder will be found in the authorities cited on the other side. We rely on *Whaley* v. *Dawson*, 2 Sch. & L., 367; *Brinkerhoff* v. *Brown*, 6 Johns. Ch., 139, and the authorities cited in the latter, as decisive for the respondents. The result of that case is, that a bill may be filed against several persons, relative to matters of the same nature, forming a connected series of acts, all intended to defraud and injure the plaintiffs, and in which all the defendants were, more or less, concerned, though not jointly, in each act.

The want of alleging that the respondents purchased upon the execution as administrators, does not vary the case. Indeed, they could purchase in no other character. When administrators purchase under the circumstances disclosed, equity will always compel them to account. Suppose they buy at half the value of the property, and the judgment remains unsatisfied, are they to profit by the speculation? **693***] *But without regard to the other circumstances, we have a claim upon the decree and execution in the first suit. This was a lien on all John Fellows' property. It was so as to all which he retained in his hands; and all which he transferred without consideration. The transfers were merely void; and, in the eye of the law, the whole continued in him, as to the respondents. The demurrer, which admits the fraudulent transfer, virtually admits all these legal consequences.

These few simple principles, it appears to us, decide this cause. If the argument for the appellant is to prevail, the situation of creditors will be very difficult. By dividing the subject of dispute into ten parts or more, the debtor may drive the creditor to as many suits; and the whole object must be three times expended in the pursuit.

Mr. A. Van Vechten, same side. This being a speaking demurrer, should be overruled for that, if for no other reason. *Edsell* v. *Buchanan*, 2 Ves., Jr., 83.

Every rule laid down by His Honor, the *Chancellor*, is agreeable to equity and the principles of law. The defendants admit a series of facts establishing a fraudulent result, in which they were agents. By taking property under the circumstances disclosed, they have united themselves in the fraud, and they cannot escape by the general denial of combination, when they admit specific facts which clearly show it. It was necessary to join them. The same proof applies to all. Indeed, it is enough that the transfer was without consideration, and void as against creditors. The whole property is John Fellows' right, in the hands of the other defendants. The rule relied upon does not demand identity of person; the identity of subject-matter is enough.

The objection assigned by the demurrer, that prolixity and intricacy and expense are promoted by a single suit, is not true in fact. Only three names are added by this, and three several bills would be much more voluminous and require more copies.

*The respondents are correctly styled [***694** administrators. They obtained the decree as such, sued out execution and bid off the property as such, and they could not devest themselves of that character. 1 Madd. Ch., 91, 1st ed.; *Campbell* v. *Walker*, and *Whelpale* v. *Cookson*, 5 Ves., 682; *Lister* v. *Lister*, 6 *Id.*, 631; *Ex parte Bennett*, 10 *Id.*, 381, 392; *Sanderson* v. *Walker*, 13 *Id.*, 601; *Holdridge* v. *Gillespie*, 2 Johns. Ch., 30; *Hart* v. *Ten Eyck*, *Id.*, 104; *Davoue* v. *Fanning*, *Id.*, 252; *Hendricks* v. *Robinson*, *Id.*, 311; *Howell* v. *Howell*, 4 *Id.*, 118; *Van Horne* v. *Fonda*, 5 *Id.*, 388.

The objection that the notes were *res judicata*, under the decree, can avail nothing. Suppose a bill filed for a specific chattel, which, before the decree, is sold and converted into money by the defendant, and the decree is for the money; does it follow that you cannot follow the subject into which it is changed, or the chattel itself into the hands of the person who bought it? The *Chancellor* would find means to make any party who has disposed of it account for its value.

Mr. S. A. Foot, in reply. It is true, that by demurring we admit the fraud; but we deny combination; and the whole is thus reduced to a mere point of law. It is unbecoming in gentlemen to introduce an informal proceeding, and then charge the fault upon the law. We are litigating a rule of pleading; and one reason why the law objects to the unnecessary joinder of parties defendants, is, that in this way a plaintiff may deprive one of the testimony of the other. Unless there be a joint liability, or joint right in parties, they are witnesses for each other; and the reason of the rule in equity is, so far, the same as that which prevails in trespass at law. There a defendant, clearly innocent, or disconnected with the others, is preliminarily acquitted by the jury.

Here we must resort to a demurrer; for answering and suffering publication to pass would work a complete deprivation of the testimony, which we might want at the hands of our co-defendants.

What then is the test by which to determine whether there should be a joinder? If, to warrant this, there should be a joint liability in whole or in part, we must prevail. If re-
695*] mote *connection, without joint liability, be enough, perhaps we must give up the cause. It seems to us, that in the cases decided by the Court of Chancery, this idea of joint liability has been left too much out of view. In *Brinkerhoff* v. *Brown*, 6 Johns. Ch., 139, the fraudulent combination was not denied; and we are satisfied that the *Chancellor* could not have made some remarks which he had done in that case, had he fully examined Ld. Kenyon's remarks in *Berkley* v. *Presgrave*, 1 East, 220, 226, 227, whom he admits to be a great master of equity practice. He says the rule is the same both at law and in equity; and we assert, without fear of contradiction, that no case can be found sustaining a joint bill upon distinct and separate rights or liabilities, where each person claims or is liable for his own acts alone. There must be a common point of controversy, the decision of which effects the whole, and will settle the rights of all. It is not enough that there is a common source of title. One has a patent and contracts to sell ten different farms to ten different men; he cannot file a bill against all, jointly, to compel a specific performance. Yet here is a common source of title. A merchant sells goods to one in Plattsburgh, and to another in N. Y.; he cannot sue them jointly for the price. All that gentlemen can allege, in this case, is a common source of title. One of the defendants purchases at one time a distinct subject, and another at a subsequent time, from the same man. There being but one decree, and a sale of the whole subject-matter to the respondents, does not connect the liability of the defendants. Here not only the persons, but the subject-matter is entirely distinct. One is proceeded against for land, and the other for notes. Does a joint suit follow, as contended, because individuals, living perhaps in different parts of the country, happen to do different acts which may produce a fraudulent result? Where a man fraudulently sells one of his farms to A at Buffalo, and another to B in the City of N. Y., can C., a creditor, join them in a suit? To warrant this, it is necessary to show that A is accountable for the act of B, of whom he never heard.

696*] *In what character does the law intend that these respondents purchased under the execution? Clearly in their own right, not as administrators. This is evident from the very cases cited on the other side; and the bill is multifarious in this respect.

His Honor, the *Chancellor*, assumes that each of the defendants had knowledge of the conveyance to the other. He infers this from the course of the transactions. With deference, we conceive that no such inference is warranted by the case stated in the bill. No such knowledge is charged in any part of it. Indeed, we conceive, that a suit might as well be brought against two persons jointly, one of whom had bought fraudulently, and the other fairly. The separation of interests could not be more distinct in the case supposed, than the one under consideration.

WOODWORTH, *J.* It is material to ascertain what facts in the bill are admitted by the demurrer. Whatever is not covered by the answer, is necessarily admitted. The denial is, that the appellant did not combine with the other defendants, to defraud or delay the respondents. Excluding this charge, as not admitted, the following facts alleged in the bill are conceded: that all the defendants in the court below were acquainted with and had full knowledge of the agreement made for the sale of the farm between Ezra Fellows and John Fellows, and the proportion of the purchase money that Ezra Fellows was to receive; that they had knowledge of the filing of the bill against John Fellows, and the service of the injunction restraining him from selling or disposing of the notes in question. The bill also charges that John Fellows, under the apprehension that a recovery would be had against him, came to a fraudulent determination, and entered into a fraudulent and secret combination with the defendants, so to manage and conceal the property as to delay and defraud the respondents; and that, in fulfillment of this fraudulent design, without any valuable consideration, he transferred two of the notes to his son William, and two others to his son Thomas; and also conveyed 40 acres of land in Malta to his son-in-law Roswell Day, and 4 acres to his son Thomas.

Now, on looking at the answer, it will be seen that the *denial extends to this [***697**
merely; that the appellant did not combine with the other defendants below to defraud; that is, according to the legal and grammatical meaning of the term, they did not join together or agree to act in concert, for the purpose of consummating this fraud. Admitting that there was no formal agreement that they should all unite in the act, yet it stands confessed that all had intimate knowledge of the whole transaction. They knew the justice of the respondents' claim against John Fellows, and knowing this, William Fellows, Thomas Fellows and Roswell Day consented to become actors, and severally took transfers of separate parcels of John Fellows' property, which transfers are admitted to have been made fraudulently, and without consideration.

Granting that there was no express agreement between the parties to defraud, the demerit, in a moral point of view, was not the less that they acted individually, and not in concert. Whether, in a legal point of view, the objection that several distinct matters are alleged, in which the appellant is not interested, can prevail, I will briefly examine.

The general rule will not be questioned, that where a bill is filed concerning things of distinct natures, against several persons, it is demurrable; but unconnected parties may join in a suit, when there is one connected interest among them all, centering in the point in issue in the cause. (2 Madd., 234; 2 Anst., 469, 477.)

In the present case, the object is to reach the property of John Fellows, in the hands of the appellant and the other defendants. This property was fraudulently parceled out, and con

veyed to three individuals. But for the fraudulent acts of the appellant, and the other defendants, the respondents might have obtained the fruits of their decree against John Fellows. The claim against all is of the same nature. The fraud alleged against each one of the defendants is the same. The question to be decided is, in every respect, the same. The transfer being fraudulent, the property was not changed by being put into the hands of the defendants. The respondents seek the property of John Fellows, which the defendants hold without title. They are, therefore, all neces-
698*] sarily *concerned in the thing to be recovered, although they set up distinct interests to separate parcels.

I am clearly of opinion that this is not a case within the rule relied on by the appellant; but must be considered as falling within that class of cases where there is a common interest among all, centering in the point in issue in the cause. Ld. Redesdale, in *Whaley* v. *Dawson*, 2 Sch. & L., 370, observes, that in the English cases, where demurrers, because the plaintiff demanded in his bill matters of distinct natures against several defendants not connected in interest, have been overruled, there has been a general right in the plaintiff covering the whole case, although the rights of the defendants may have been distinct. In such cases the court proceeds on the ground of preventing multiplicity of suits, where one general right is claimed by the plaintiff against all the defendants. A demurrer lies where the subjects of the suit are, in themselves, distinct. Here the subject is the property of John Fellows, in the hands of the defendants. The case does not afford ground for a demurrer within the authorities cited.

It is also objected that the respondents have connected in the bill, claims in their own right, and in their right as administrators.

I do not so understand the bill. The whole of the proceedings were in their right as administrators. The purchase by the respondents at the sheriff's sale, was in the character of administrators. They were agents and trustees, and could not devest themselves of the trust. The *cestuis que trust* were entitled to take the land at their election; and the respondents, having purchased in this manner, may, in their representative capacity, call in the aid of the court to perfect their title. (5 Johns. Ch., 388; 1 Madd. Ch., 91; 5 Ves., 682.)

The power of the Court of Chancery to assist a judgment and execution creditor to discover and reach the property of his debtor, in whosesoever hands it has been placed, I have considered as well settled, since the case of *Hadden* v. *Spader*, 20 Johns., 554. There can be no well founded objection on this ground.
699*] I consider this case much *stronger; for here the appellant does not stand as a mere bailee, but as having no colorable ground of claim to the notes or the avails of them.

On every ground upon which this cause can be viewed, I am of opinion that the decree of His Honor, the *Chancellor*, be affirmed.

SUTHERLAND, *J.* The object of the bill is to enable the respondents to reach the property of John Fellows (against whom they have a decree), fraudulently transferred by him to the other defendants, and thus put beyond the reach of the execution of the respondents. The object is a legitimate one, and to the accomplishment of which a court of equity will readily lend its aid. The power and authority of the Court of Chancery, to grant the aid and relief asked for, is fully established by the case of *Hadden* v. *Spader*, 20 Johns., 554, decided by this court. If the allegations in the bill be true, here is a most iniquitous attempt, on the part of a debtor, to put his creditor at defiance, and defraud him of his just debt, by a voluntary and fraudulent distribution of his property among his children. That the respondents are entitled to relief, is clear; and the only question is, whether they must seek it by separate suits against each of the individuals implicated in the transaction, or whether they are at liberty to bring them all into court in one suit.

It is a favorite object with a court of equity to prevent multiplicity of suits. For this purpose it is a general rule, in chancery, that all persons materially interested must be made parties. Creditors are permitted to unite in calling on the representatives of a deceased debtor, for an account of the assets of the estate—or one or more of them may prosecute the suit, in behalf and for the benefit of the whole. The forms of proceeding in chancery, and the power of the court to mold its decrees, so as to suit the various equities of the case, as established by the proof, enable it advantageously to settle, and adjust in a single suit, rights and interests which, according to the rules of pleading in the courts of common law, would necessarily result in various issues, incapable of being tried in a single cause, and disposed of by a single judgment.

*But notwithstanding this disposi- [*700
tion of a court of equity to prevent the multiplication of suits, it will not permit several plaintiffs to demand, by one bill, several matters perfectly distinct and unconnected against one defendant; nor one plaintiff to demand several matters of different natures against several defendants. And the reason of this rule is said to be, that such a proceeding would tend to load each defendant with an unnecessary burden of costs, by swelling the pleadings with the statement of the several claims against the other defendants with which he has no connection; Coop. Eq. Pl., 182; Mitf., 146; 2 Madd. Ch., 294; 2 Harr. Ch. Pr., 289; 1 East, 227; and also to prevent confusion and to preserve some analogy to the comparative simplicity of declaration at common law. But where several persons, although unconnected with each other, are made defendants, a demurrer will not lie if they have a common interest centering in the point in issue in the cause. (2 Anst., 477; 2 Madd. Ch., 294.) Nor will it lie, where one general right is claimed by the bill, though the defendants have separate and distinct rights. Thus, in the *Mayor of York* v. *Pilkington*, 1 Atk., 282, it was held that a bill to quiet the plaintiff in a right of fishery might be brought against several defendants, although there was no privity between them and the plaintiff, and they claimed distinct rights. The plaintiff claimed a general right to the fishery extending to all the defendants; and it was held that they might avail themselves of their several exemptions

and distinct rights upon an issue to try the general right. The bill was sustained for the sake of peace and to prevent a multiplicity of suits. A bill against several unconnected defendants to establish the custom of a mill, and a right to tithes, has been sustained upon the same general principle; and that it was for the establishment of a right liable to invasion by all the world. *Whaley* v. *Dawson*, 2 Sch. & L., 370. But the proprietor of a copyright cannot proceed in one bill against several booksellers, between whom there is no privity or connection for a violation of his right. This was so held in *Dilly* v. *Doig*, 2 Ves., Jr., 486; and the *Ld. Chancellor* remarks that he does not remember any case upon patent rights where a number of persons acting all separately, upon **701***] *distinct grounds, have been permitted to be brought before the court in one bill; and he takes the distinction between a bill to establish a right of fishery, or the custom of a mill, and the case then before him. So, also, if an estate is sold in parcels to different purchasers, the vendor cannot unite them all in one bill for a specific performance, nor can they unite in one suit against the vendor for the same purpose; for each contract is separate and independent, and each case must depend on its own peculir circumstances. *Rayner* v. *Julian*, 2 Dick., 677; Coop. Eq. Pl., 182. In the case of *Ward* v. *Duke of Northumberland*, 2 Anst., 469, the bill was held bad, not only because a considerable part of it related merely to the private concerns of the Duke, with which Ld. Beverly had no concern; but it was bad as against the Duke alone, because, although he was interested in every part of it, it was in different characters; individually and solely as to some and in the character of executor, and jointly with Ld. Beverly as to others. But *Ch. B.* M'Donald there recognizes the principle, "that unconnected parties may be joined in a suit where there is one common interest among them all, centering in the point in issue in the cause.

It is not sufficient, as was held in *Saxton* v. *Davis*, 18 Ves., 71, that the parties have a common interest in some one or more items in an account charged. The contrary position was taken in that case by the counsel for the complainants; but it was conclusively answered by Sir Samuel Romilly, that if that were sufficient, the objection to a bill as multifarious could never be sustained. They must have a common interest, not in a particular item, or insulated charge in the bill, but in the point in issue in the cause. And this seems to be the general test laid down in all the elementary writers, and acknowledged by all the cases in England. The only difficulty is in its application.

This question was fully considered and discussed by the late *Chancellor* in *Brinkerhoff* v. *Brown*, 6 Johns. Ch., 139, which was a case very analogous, in many respects, to the one now before the court. The complainants, in **702***] *that case, were several distinct and unconnected judgment creditors of the Genesee Manufacturing Co.; and the object of their bill was to obtain satisfaction of their debt out of the property of the Company, which they alleged had been withdrawn from the reach of their executions by the fraudulent acts of the defendants, some of whom were the trustees of the Company: and one object of the bill was to charge the trustees individually, for neglect of duty, and fraud. With that charge, it was said, the defendants who were not trustees had no concern. Another object was, to charge others of the defendants as stockholders and another, to redeem certain personal property purchased by two of the defendants, with which the other defendants were not shown to have any concern. The bill charged that five of the defendants fraudulently confessed a certain judgment in which the other two were not alleged to have had any interest, and the bill was demurred to as multifarious, on these among other grounds. The *Chancellor*, after stating the facts in the case, remarks, "it thus appears, from the bill, that all the defendants were not jointly concerned in every injurious act charged. There was a series of acts on the part of the persons concerned in this company, all produced by the same fraudulent intent, and terminating in the deception and injury of the plaintiffs. The defendants performed different parts in the same drama, but it was still one piece, one entire performance, marked by different scenes; and the question now occurs whether the several matters charged are so distinct and unconnected, as to render the joining of them in one bill a ground of demurrer." After considering all the English cases he observes, that "the principle to be deduced from them is, that a bill against several persons must relate to matters of the same nature, and having a connection with each other, and in which all the defendants are more or less concerned, though their rights in respect to the general subject of the case may be distinct." And in relation to that particular case he goes on to remark that, "when we consider that the plaintiffs are judgment creditors, having claims against the Genesee Co. perfectly established, and not the subject of litigation in this suit; and that the general right claimed *by the bill is a [***703** due application of the capital of that Company to the payment of their judgments; that the subject of the bill, and of the relief, and the only matter in litigation is the fraud charged in the creation, management and disposition of that capital, and in which charge all the defendants are implicated, though in different degrees and proportions, I think we may safely conclude that this case falls within the reach of that principle, and that the demurrer cannot be sustained." He accordingly overruled it. These observations are as just and pertinent in their application to this case as to that in which they were used. Here the respondents are judgment creditors of John Fellows, having their claims perfectly established by a decree in chancery, and not the subject of litigation in this suit. Here, also, the general right claimed by the bill is a due application of the property of John Fellows to the payment of their judgment. Here, also, the subject of the bill and of the relief, and the only matter in litigation is the fraud charged in the management and disposition of that property; and in which charge all the defendants are implicated, though in different degrees and proportions. Here the defendants, therefore, have one common interest among them all, centering in the point in issue in the cause, and distinct matters, of different natures, are not demanded by the bill. It is one matter—the property of John Fellows; and the point in issue upon which the rights of all the parties must depend is, whether the transfer of that property to his sons and son in-law, who are his co-defendants, was fraudulent or not. Why may not that question be tried as well in one as in three suits? The transfer to each is alleged to have been made with the same fraudulent intent, at the same time; to have been received by each without consideration, with a full knowledge of the fraudulent motive with which it was made and an entire acquiescence and participation in it. It was in truth but one transaction, in which the defendants all participated. The evidence in relation to each must be substantially the same. Neither the pleadings nor the proofs are essentially varied or enlarged from what they would necessarily have been been, had the bill been filed against one of the defendants only. If all the parties 704*] *to a fraudulent transaction like this, cannot be called to an account in one suit, it is in the power of dishonest debtors, by a distribution of their property in minute portions among their relations and friends, to defraud their creditors and set them at defiance with impunity. The expense and delay of separate suits would render their prosecution worse than useless, for all purposes of indemnity or relief. The establishment of such a doctrine would be most mischievous; and I am persuaded that it has as little foundation in authority, as it certainly has in the large and comprehensive principles of substantial justice and equity.

The other point, made on the part of the appellant, that the respondents have joined and connected claims in their own right, and claims in their right as the representatives of Ezra Fellows, is unfounded in fact. It grows out of that part of the bill in which the respondents state the proceeding upon the execution and the sale of the real and personal estate; and that they became the purchasers, at such sale, of the lot which had been conveyed to Roswell Day and Thomas Fellows. The first objection is, that they do not state in the bill that they purchased as administrators. That allegation is in the same form with every other charge in the bill. It commences by stating the respondents to be the representatives of Ezra Fellows, and in all the subsequent parts, they designate themselves simply as your oratrix and orator, without adding their description of administrators. But that is to be understood throughout, and was unnecessary to be stated. If, then, they purchased as administrators, it is not for the defendants to question their authority. It is to be presumed in this stage of the cause, that they purchased at the request and for the benefit of the heirs, and a court of equity would compel them to account to the estate.

I am, therefore, of opinion that the decree of His Honor, the *Chancellor*, should be affirmed.

SAVAGE, *Ch. J.* In *Brinkerhoff* v. *Brown*, 6 Johns. Ch., 157, the late *Chancellor*, after a full examination of the cases cited on the argument of this cause, deduces from them this principle: "That a bill against several persons *must relate to matters of the [*705 same nature, and having a connection with each other, and in which all the defendants are more or less concerned, though their rights in respect to the general subject of the case, may be distinct. The cases cited, in my judgment, warrant this rule. In *Dilly* v. *Doig*, 2 Ves., Jr., 486, it was held that two booksellers, who had been guilty of an invasion of the plaintiff's copyright, could not be joined as defendants in the same bill, on the ground that there was no privity. The *Lord Chancellor* says, however: "If the defendant against whom you had got the injunction had transferred his books to another, I would have followed it." Now, it is fair to infer, that if the bookseller enjoined had sold his books to several persons who were privy to the injunction, and all of whom took the books with the express purpose of defrauding the plaintiff, though each might have no interest in the books sold to the other, yet they would have been so far connected as to be properly joined in one suit.

In the case put by Ld. Kenyon, of an estate sold in parcels to several individuals, who could not be permitted to unite in a bill for a specific performance, there is a distinct contract with each individual which may admit of very different considerations. Not so in the case now before the court. There was, in the hands of John Fellows, certain property in the custody of the law, sequestered, if I may use the expression, and set apart to answer the demand of Ezra Fellows. This fact was perfectly known to all the defendants; and each of them, separately, as we are to intend (for they have denied the combination and confederacy), conspired with John Fellows to defraud the respondents, by collusively taking separate parts of the property, and holding it for the benefit of John Fellows. There was no privity between William Fellows, Thomas Fellows and Roswell Day; but there was privity between each of them and John Fellows. If, then, we take the rule as laid down by the counsel for the appellant, "that there must be a common point of litigation, the decision of which affects the whole, and will settle the rights of all," still this case comes within it. The common point of litigation is the fraudulent transfer of the property *by John Fellows to the other de- [*706 fendants. If the source of their title be corrupt, the property is taken with the taint of corruption, and though the person receiving it may have been innocent of all fraud, yet he must suffer a loss in consequence of the impure channel through which it came. This point was so decided, at the last term of this court, in *Whelan* v. *Whelan*, 3 Cow., 537. And if so, with respect to an innocent person, *a fortiori*, a partaker in the corruption shall not retain what he has thus received. In my opinion, therefore, the appellant here comes within the rule relied on by the respondents. The matters are not distinct. They are component parts of one corrupted body.

On this point (and this I consider the only point in the case) I am of opinion that the decree of His Honor, the *Chancellor*, be affirmed.

There is no ground for the allegation, that

the respondents come in two capacities. They acted throughout as the representatives of Ezra Fellows—as trustees for those interested in the estate—and to whom they are accountable for the land, purchased with the estate in the respondents' hands.

COLDEN, *Senator*. It is not denied that, under the case made by the bill, the respondents may be entitled to relief; but it is contended that the Court of Chancery could make no decree in their favor in this case, because the appellant was impleaded in the court below with other defendants.

It is admitted to be a rule of equity pleading, that matters which are distinct and of different natures cannot be joined in the same bill.

It often happens that it is not easy to ascertain whether the matters, which are the subject of a suit, are or are not distinct and of different natures; and therefore it is frequently difficult to determine when the rule I have mentioned is to be applied. It is this difficulty which has given rise to the numerous cases that have been cited in the argument.

I shall not attempt to reconcile these authorities, or to do more than to ascertain whether the general rule be applicable to the case now under consideration, so as to preclude the respondents from maintaining their suit.

707*] *The counsel for the appellant could not avoid admitting that if there were a joint liability on the part of the defendants below, the demurrer could not be sustained. And they also very properly, as it appears to me, admitted that if the defendants below were parties to the fraud, which is the *gravamen* of the bill, and acted in concert to accomplish it; there was such a connection between them as would render them jointly responsible. Then the question which we are to decide is, in my opinion, reduced to this: whether the facts stated in the bill warranted the *Chancellor* in concluding that all the defendants below were parties and confederates in the fraud, which it is alleged was practiced by the father, in transferring his real and personal property to his son-in-law and to the brothers of Ezra.

It is expressly stated in the bill that each of the defendants below were acquainted with all the transactions of the father, in relation to the property in question, from the time of the sale to Adsit till it came into their hands. They had full knowledge of the proceedings in the revived suit against the father, and of the injunction which was granted in that suit. They advised and aided the father in the management and defense of that suit. They took from the father, without giving him any consideration, a voluntary conveyance, in different parts, of all his property, each of them knowing that such transfer was made with a view to defraud, and that it would defraud Ezra. To William, the appellant, the father transferred two of the Adsit notes; to Thomas two other of the same notes, which notes, or their proceeds, it is averred, these sons fraudulently retain. To the son-in-law, the father conveyed a farm in Malta, as the bill charges; fraudulently, voluntarily and without consideration, and with a view to avoid the effects of a decree against him in the pending suit; and in the same way, and with the same views, he conveyed another piece of land in Malta to his son Thomas.

It is expressly charged in the bill, not only that this property was transferred to, but that it is held by the grantees, with a view to defeat the claim of their brother Ezra.

*Now, if we take the allegations of **[*708** the bill to be true, it seems to me that we cannot hesitate to say that the defendants below were jointly concerned in practicing the fraud, which was intended to defeat, and which has hitherto defeated, the just claim of the respondents.

I say the just claim, because, although we have heard from the counsel that the farm at Stillwater originally belonged to the father, and that his object was to make a distribution of it among his children, yet no such facts appear on the record. We know of no owner of the farm prior to Ezra.

We may apply to this case, in my opinion, with great propriety, the words of the *Chancellor* in *Brinkerhoff* v. *Brown*, 6 Johns. Ch., 139; "there was a series of acts on the part of the persons concerned, all produced by the same fraudulent intent, and terminating in the deception and injury of the respondents. The appellants played different parts of the same drama, but it was still one piece, one entire performance, marked by different scenes." Other expressions of the *Chancellor*, in the same case, are not less adapted to the present occasion. "The subject of the bill," says he, "is the fraud charged, in which charge all the defendants are implicated, though in different degrees and proportions." The connection between the defendants in that case, and their co-operation in the transactions which were the foundation of the suit, were certainly less obvious than is the participation of the defendants below in the acts against which relief is sought in the present instance.

It is hardly necessary to stop to point out the great difference between the case presented by the bill and the cases cited by the counsel for the appellant, in which it is decided that independent, unconnected holders of different parts of property which a complainant may claim, either on the ground of its having been fraudulently transferred to them, or on any other ground, cannot be made the subject of a single suit.

But it is said, that though the demurrer would, if it stood alone, admit the allegations of the bill, and would, therefore, acknowledge the fraud, and the co-operation of the defendants below in its perpetration; yet there is in this case an *answer; and that the answer **[*709** denies the fraud, and the charges in the bill from which it is deduced. If this were so, I think there would be no hesitation in deciding that the suit against the defendants jointly could not be maintained. But so far from this being the case, the answer does no more than deny the general and formal charge of combination. It appears to be drawn with great care not to deny any one of the facts which are stated in the bill as evidence of the fraud, and from which the conclusion that the appellant, William, acted in concert with his father and brothers and brother-in-law, with a design to defraud Ezra, results. Had the appellant said in his answer that he knew nothing of the agreement between Ezra and his father, that he was not privy to the relinquishment of the bond and mortgage to Adsit, and the substitution of the Adsit notes, and the new mortgage; that he was ignorant of the proceedings in the original, and in the revived suit; that he and the other defendants below were not their father's agents or advisers in the management of that suit; that the transfer in the notes and the conveyances of the lands were made for a good or valuable consideration, and without any design to defeat the claim of the respondents, then the interest of the defendants would have been distinct and separate; there would have been no joint liability; and though a demurrer might not have been proper, if the answer had met these charges, as it would then have covered the whole bill, yet such an answer, if it would not have defeated the claim of the respondents, would at least have been fatal to this joint suit.

But the answer we have now before us is, as I have said, no more than a denial of the combination; and indeed, amounts only to the general denial of fraud and confederacy, which is the usual conclusion of all answers, and which is always insufficient where, as in this case, fraudulent acts are particularly charged.

There is another ground on which, in my opinion, this demurrer must fail. It is charged in the bill that the notes were transferred, and the conveyances made to secure them as the effects of John Fellows, and with respect to **710***] the lands, *it is averred that they are held for his use and benefit. These charges are not denied by the answer, and are, therefore, admitted by the demurrer. The defendants below, then, took and yet hold the property or the proceeds, as trustees for the grantor. I apprehend a court of equity would never allow trustees, under these circumstances, to set up their title or trust, against the claim of a creditor of the *cestui que trust*.

Again; if the property be the property of John Fellows, in the hands of the defendants below as his trustees, though they hold different parcels of it, the suit is not for separate and distinct matters, any more than it would be if it were against John Fellows himself solely, and claimed from him money, notes and lands.

It has been objected that the defendants below are not proper parties, inasmuch as they claim in their representative characters, and the transaction shows that if they have any title, it is in their own right. But it appears to me that the complainants had no connection with these affairs but as administrators. This and another point made here, viz.: that the notes were *res judicata*, do not appear, from the *Chancellor's* opinion, to have been raised when the cause was before him. They do not seem now to have been much relied upon by the counsel for the appellant, and I am not prepared to say that the demurrer can be sustained on either of these grounds.

The rule that multifarious matters shall not be joined in the same suit, seems to me to be all that requires consideration for the decision of this case.

This is a rule of convenience; and however necessary its general observance may be, yet, though in this case it were to be admitted that the matters are distinct, and of different natures (which in my opinion they are not), still it is obvious that justice may be administered between the parties in this suit, without subjecting the appellant or his co-defendants to any of the embarrassments, the fear of which is the foundation of the rule. Nevertheless, if it appeared clearly to be applicable to the case, we could not refuse the appellant the advantage of it. But when it is so apparent that justice may be done, although there should be error in *not allowing the demurrrer, [***711** there is less reluctance in deciding that it must be overruled.

My opinion is, that the decree of His Honor, the *Chancellor*, should be affirmed.

This being the unanimous opinion of *the Court*, it was thereupon, ordered, adjudged and decreed that the decree of His Honor, the *Chancellor*, in this cause, be affirmed, with costs to the respondents, to be taxed upon the appeal to this court; and that the record and proceedings, &c., be remitted, &c.

Cited in—5 Paige, 67; 4 Edw., 214, 219; 4 Sand. Ch., 36, 275; 17 N. Y., 607; 35 N. Y., 324; 53 N. Y., 305; 1 Barb., 122; 16 Barb., 331; 20 Barb., 383; 33 Barb., 35; 50 Barb., 59; 66 Barb., 14, 299; 20 How. Pr., 426; 31 How. P., 506; 56 How. Pr., 456; 1 Abb. Pr., 427; 6 Abb. Pr., 111; 7 Abb. Pr., 68; 10 Abb. Pr., 37; 11 Abb. Pr., 433; 12 Abb. Pr., 48; 6 Abb. N. C., 217; 4 Bos., 546; 40 Super., 267; 10 Bank. Reg., 190; 2 McLean, 314; 3 Lean, 420; 26 Cal., 360; 44 Cal., 319; 9 Minn., 186, 187; 10 Minn., 205; 31 N. J. Eq., 757; 18 Wis., 570; 23 Wis., 494; 38 Wis., 189; 37 Am. Dec., 557 (2 Humph., 327); 40 Am. Dec., 103 (1 S. & M., 423); 44 Am. Dec., 719 (3 Gilm., 518); 13 Am. Rep., 527.

NEWMAN, *Plaintiff in Error*,
v.
VAN ANTWERP, *Defendant in Error*.

Power of Court as to Costs.

This court, on granting a rule that the writ of error and transcript from the Supreme Court be not received, pursuant to the first rule of this court, has no power to award the costs of the motion.

Till the writ of error be returned, the Court of Errors are not in possession of the cause, so as to render any judgment.

The power of this court to give costs, upon a writ of error, depends upon Statute, 1 R. L., 346, which does not provide for costs on a mere *ne recipiatur*.

Citation—1 R. L., 343, 346.

ON moving for, and taking a rule that the writ of error and transcript in this cause be not received, under the first general rule of this court. (16 Johns., 603.)

Mr. W. Sampson, for the defendant, moved also for the costs of the motion; and to support this branch of the application, he relied on *Webb* v. *Brown*, 19 Johns., 453.

COLDEN, *Senator*. The power of this court to give costs on a writ of error depends upon the Statute concerning Costs. (1 R. L., 343.) Sections 13, 14 and 15 of this statute (*Id.*, 346), provide for costs upon affirmance, reversal, nonsuit, discontinuance and quashing the writ of error; but I am aware of no statute which gives costs upon a mere rule not to receive the writ. It is true that costs were given in the case cited; but the point was not made by counsel; and probably not thought of by the

712*] court. We are not yet possessed *of the cause; and have no materials before us on which to frame a record of judgment.

Cramer, Gardiner, Haight, Keyes, Lake, Lynde, McCall, McIntyre, Wilkinson and *Wright, Senators*, concurred.

SANFORD, *Chancellor*. I should regret such a want of power in this court. If there be no means of punishing a party in costs, who brings his writ of error and delays his adversary, without cause, there is a defect in the law. This may not be technically a discontinuance; but I incline to consider it one, within the 13th section of the Statute, 1 R. L., 346, and am disposed to follow the case cited. I agree that the court should not give costs, unless they are authorized to do so by the statute. When a writ is issued, there is a cause commenced and pending, which is susceptible of a discontinuance.

Bowman, Burt, Dudley, Earll, Ellsworth, Greenly, Lefferts, McMichael, Redfield and *Wooster, Senators*, concurred.

The Court being equally divided, the casting voice was given by,

TALLMADGE, *President*. I think costs are not warranted by the statute. To my mind, this is neither a nonsuit nor discontinuance. The penalty imposed by the first rule of the court, upon which the defendant in error comes here, is, that in default of returning the writ of error and transcript, the plaintiff in error shall lose the benefit of the writ. Nothing is there said of costs, or that any judgment shall be rendered. The course under the rule is to proceed summarily, by a motion, for a mere *ne recipiatur*. I think we are not possessed of the cause, for the purpose of rendering any judgment whatever, properly so called, until the writ be returned. This may be a *casus omissus* in the statute; but the question is not very important. The costs on a motion of this kind cannot much exceed a retaining fee. I think they cannot be allowed.

Rule accordingly.

Cited in—10 Wend., 575.

713*] *GENERAL RULE.

JULY 6, 1825.

ORDERED, that whenever an appeal or writ of error shall be brought on for argument, and the reasons of the court below shall not be annexed to the case, the cause shall not be heard, unless it shall be made to appear by affidavit that application was made for such reasons, and that the same could not be obtained.

RECEPTION OF GENERAL LA FAYETTE.

ON the evening of July 3, the business of the court not being yet completed, and the President being informed that

GENERAL LA FAYETTE

Would be pleased to visit the court, they adjourned to 10 o'clock, A. M. of the next day, at their chamber in the City Hall. The court having assembled accordingly, the General soon after appeared, and having been seated, was addressed by the President as follows:

GENERAL LA FAYETTE: The Senate of this State, now assembled as a court of ultimate appeal, have directed me, on their behalf, and in behalf of the people of this State, whom we represent, to congratulate you on your safe return to this city, and to tender to you renewed assurances of high respect.

Gratitude for your public services has been evinced from all classes of society; it is steady and unceasing; and will, as it has heretofore, attend you in every vicissitude of life. But your presence with us on the day of this anniversary, recalls scenes which have passed, and awakens all our sensibilities.

In the helpless infancy of our country, and before it had obtained a place amongst the nations of the earth; and when we were oppressed and borne down by the strong arm of tyranny, you came to our succor. You generously put *your life and fortune [*714 upon the cause of our country. You aided our fathers to establish that independence, the jubilee of which we have this day assembled to commemorate.

In the pride of your youth, and in the vigor of manhood, you came clad in arms, to support our just cause, and partake in the perils of our fathers; it is their childrens' joy, in this day of their strength and prosperity, and when the veil of time is closing on the fullness of your years, to acknowledge you as their benefactor. Our mothers taught us in our infancy to lisp your name; our fathers have instructed us to emulate your example.

Your recent tour throughout this country has enabled you to witness the progress of improvement, and to contrast in your recollection our present with our past condition. The relative condition of a people enslaved, and a people in the full enjoyment of freedom, is here strongly exemplified. The wilderness has vanished before the arm of independent industry. The ignorance of subjects has given away to the intelligence of freemen. Plenty has taken the place of want. Prosperity and strength have been substituted for poverty and weakness. The two millions and a half of subjects whom you came to enfranchise, and to aid in the day of their adversity, now count about eleven millions of hardy freemen, all uniting with one accord in this celebration. In alluding to the progress of improvement, it will not be forgotten that the Marble Hall, in which we are now assembled—an edifice, splendid, even as a monument of the arts, and which the growth of this city has already left short of its center—occupies the place which was a common waste without the city, when you toiled in our cause, and was then used as an open field, upon which mercenary troops were marshaled, and sent forth in battle against our fathers.

Such is the character of the blessings which flow from freedom; such are some of the results proceeding from that independence, and those republican institutions which we enjoy, and which you assisted to establish; and to which you first sealed your devotion, with a portion of your blood at the Brandywine. It was the participation in such a cause, and the performance of such deeds, by which you merited the gratitude and gained the devoted 715*] friendship of this nation. *That friendship has attended you in every subsequent event of your life, and it has ever found you, in the hour of temptation and of trial, faithful to liberty, good order, and a government of laws. The enthusiasm of youth might have attached you to our cause; the firmness of manhood and the spirit to withstand oppression might have sustained you when suffering in the prison of Olmutz, but a virtuous love of rational liberty could alone have enabled you to resist the temptations of power and the workings of ambition, when a mighty Revolution had placed you at the head of the National Guards of France, and invited you to wield the power of that wonderful people.

It was then that the danger awaited you. It was then that the love of principle prevailed over the love of power, and virtue triumphed over ambition.

It is at such moments, in the possession of power and apparent prosperity, when human weakness is most exposed. It was in such moments, when a Cæsar, a Napoleon and an Iturbide fell! It was in such moments when a Washington, a La Fayette and a Bolivar triumphed.

Gen. LA FAYETTE immediately replied in the following terms:

It is to me, sir, an inexpressible but deeply felt gratification, on this solemn anniversary day, to be able to celebrate the joyful jubilee of this great and good City of New York; where, for the first time after an absence of forty years, I have enjoyed the happiness to find myself again on American ground; and where was begun, near eleven months since, that series of welcomes from the American people, and their representatives, which will fill every one of the remaining days and the last instant of my life with a most lively sense of gratitude and delight.

Now, sir, that gratification is completed, when I am admitted to appear before this respected body, to offer to the gentlemen of the Senate my profound acknowledgments for the favors bestowed upon me by the two branches of the Legislature, and to receive from them those highly valued marks of their approbation and friendship, expressed by you, sir, in so kind and flattering terms, for which I beg you, Mr. President, *and all of you, [*716 gentlemen, to acccept my warm and respectful thanks.

The Fourth of July has been the era of a new social order, hitherto unexampled, and founded on the sovereignity of the people; on the plain rights of man; on the practice of unalloyed self-government. Its results have exceeded the most sanguine expectations; its problem has been happily and practically solved; and another problem remains to be solved; how long other nations will prefer paying, at an immense price, the aristocracy and despotism of a few privileged oppressors, to blessings of freedom and equal rights, under the economical and truly representative institutions.

At every step of my visit through the twenty-four United States, on which you are pleased to congratulate me, I have had to admire wonders of creation and improvement. Nowhere can they be more conspicuous than in the State of New York, and in the prodigious progress of this city. Those western parts which I had left a wilderness, I have found covered with flourishing towns, highly cultivated farms, active factories, and intersected by the admirable canal, already becoming the communication of an immense trade; all in consequence of independence, freedom, and a republican spirit.

No higher honor could be bestowed on me, than to have associated my name to the two great names you have mentioned. To the first of them, sir, whose place is above all men in my filial heart, my principal boast is, to have been an adopted son, a faithful disciple. Of the other, no man can be a more exalted admirer than I am; and permit me to observe, that what my friends and myself have only attempted in the other hemisphere, has been, in South America, and under the liberating auspices of his talents and virtues, happily effectuated. But in every testimony from the people of this State, and their representatives, I am to acknowledge a benevolent kindness, which, if it exceeds my merits, is equaled by the sentiments of my everlasting devotion, respect and gratitude.

[END OF THE SUMMER SESSION, 1825.]

APPENDIX.

The volume being closed a little short of the usual number of pages, thus enabling me to present the profession with the following case without enhancing the price, is my excuse for this appendix; if laying before them such an able and luminous discussion of their professional rights and duties in matters relative to which they are frequently called to advise, require any excuse. It is true the decisions of our circuit courts cannot be considered as of binding authority; but it is certainly not presuming too much on their utility as precedents, to say that now and then one of them, which is made upon full argument and deliberation, is, at least, as high evidence of the law as thousands of *Nisi Prius* decisions in England, much more hastily made; and which are published and daily quoted as authority on both sides of the Atlantic.

IN THE COURT OF EQUITY FOR THE FOURTH CIRCUIT OF THE STATE OF NEW YORK.

SETH AND ALPHEUS HAWLEY AND URIAH MARVIN

v.

JOHN CRAMER, HOUSE & MYERS, KNICKERBACKER & STEWART AND WILLIAM DE WOLF.

Entry of Judgment, on Bond and Warrant of Attorney, for Benefit of Several Creditors—Levy, on Real Estate—Agreement, by three Creditors, to Authorize Agent to Attend Sale and Purchase for their Benefit—Sale, by Agent, to Bona Fide *Purchaser—Purchaser Acquires Title—The three Creditors Accountable to Remaining Creditors for Share of Profits—When Attorney may Purchase—Application, to Set Aside Purchase by Agent or Trustee—Must be in Reasonable Time—When Right of Action Barred in Equity—Parties—Notice—Jurisdiction of Equity—Having Gained for One Purpose, Retains for All.*

A debtor, being in failing circumstances, and owing to five of his creditors $7,540, in separate and distinct debts, gave them a judgment bond, in which all their debts were included; and C, as their attorney, entered upon the judgment, and issued an execution, upon which the real property of the debtor was advertised for sale by the sheriff. Three of the creditors attended the sale, in the absence of the other two, and agreed not to bid against each other, but to employ an agent to bid in the property and to divide the profits of the purchase between them, in proportion to their respective debts; and for this purpose they employed C., the attorney, who bid in the property for $625, which was less than one fifth of its cash value; and a few days thereafter the attorney sold the premises for $3,600, and divided the profits, arising from the resale, among the three creditors, to the exclusion of the other two; held, that the purchase, by the attorney, as agent for three of his clients only, was fraudulent, as against the other two, who were absent at the sheriff's sale. But as the resale was made to a *bona fide* purchaser, who had no notice of the fraud; also, held, that both sales must stand; and that the three creditors, who made the fraudulent purchase, must account 718*] to the other two, for their *shares of the proceeds of the last sale; in proportion to the amount of their several interests, in the judgment, at the time of the sheriff's sale.

An agreement between persons having separate and distinct interests, not to bid against each other, at the sheriff's sale, but to divide the profits of the purchase, is against public policy; and is a fraud upon other persons interested in the sale.

It seems that an attorney, who issues an execution, cannot become a purchaser at the sheriff's sale, either on his own account, or as the agent of a third person, without the consent, and against the interest of his client; and leaving the client's debt unsatisfied.

Where the client, himself, is not prohibited from purchasing, the attorney may purchase, with his assent; and neither the defendant in the execution or a third person can object to the validity of such a purchase.

A purchase, made by a person standing in the situation of agent or trustee for the sale, however fair and honest it may have been, must be set aside, on the application of the *cestui que trust*, or principal, if such application is made within a reasonable time.

If the application is not made within a reasonable time, it will be considered as a waiver or adandonment of the right.

What shall be deemed a reasonable time has not been settled by any fixed rule; and seems to depend upon the exercise of the sound discretion of the court, under all the circumstances of each particular case.

A person who is incapacitated from purchasing on his own account, cannot purchase as the agent of a third person; neither can he become a purchaser through the intervention of another.

The shortest period which a court of equity is bound to consider an absolute bar to a suit respecting real estate, in analogy to the limitation of actions at law, is twenty years.

In cases of implied trusts in relation to personal property, or to the rents and profits of real estate, where persons claiming in their own right are turned into trustees by implication, the right of action in equity will be considered as barred in six years, in analogy to the limitations of similar actions at law.

A dormant partner, who has never been known in the transactions to which the suit relates, need not be made a party.

The purchaser of a chose in action takes it subject to all equities, although a *bona fide* purchaser without notice.

Whatever is sufficient to put a purchaser on inquiry is, in equity, considered as conveying notice.

A bond given by a debtor to his creditor is *prima facie* evidence of his indebtedness, even as against third persons.

An objection to the jurisdiction, on the ground that a perfect remedy existed at law, should be raised by demurrer to the bill, or insisted on by the defendant in his answer. It is too late to make the objection at the hearing, unless the court be wholly incompetent to afford the relief sought by the bill.

Where courts of equity once had jurisdiction of a case, they still retain it, though the original ground of jurisdiction, the inability of the plaintiff to recover at law, no longer exists.

*Courts of equity have concurrent jurisdic- [*719 tion with courts of law in all matters of account.

Where a court of equity has gained jurisdiction of a cause for one purpose, it may retain it generally.

Citations—2 Vern., 692, 764; 2 Johns. Ch., 271, 369, 252, 512; 3 Conn., 146; 1 Johns. Ch., 267, 344; 2 Ves., Jr., 200, 440; 2 Sch. & L., 474, 599; 8 Johns., 520; 2 Cai., 56, 54, 40, 37; 9 Johns., 505; 17 Johns., 388; 10 Johns., 596; 16 Ves., 324; 6 Johns., 194; 3 Johns. Cas., 32; 4 Johns. Ch., 254, 121; 8 Ves., Jr., 352; 8 Wh., 441; 10 Ves., 381, 423; 11 Johns., 464; Code Civ. Dis. Francais Liv. 3, tit. 6, ch. 2, art. 1596, 7; 1 Cox. Cas., 140; 14 Ves., 91, 214, 517; 5 Ves., 682, 707; 6 Ves., 266, 625, 631; 5 Johns., 47, 48; 2 Cow., 191; Sug. Vend., 431; 18 Ves., 120, 311; 12 Ves., 373; 4 Br. Ch., 350; 4 Desaus. Ch., 503, 702, 716; Cooper Ch. Cas., 201; 1 Cai. Cas., 1; 3 Binn., 64; 2 Hen. & Munf., 245; 2 Br. Ch., 400; 4 Ves., 417; 4 Binn., 44; 9 Ves., 292; 12 Johns., 141; 2 P. Wms., 307.

THE bill in this cause was filed in Nov., 1823. The defendants appeared and put in their several answers, to which, replications were filed; and witnesses were examined. The material facts in the case, are fully stated in the opinion of the court. The cause was brought to hearing, on the pleadings and proofs, at the stated term of the court, in Mar., 1825; and was argued with much ability, by

Mr. W. Hay, for the complainants, and

Mr. S. G. Huntington, for the defendants.

A final decree in the cause was made at the July Term, 1825; and the following opinion was filed by the circuit judge, as containing the reasons on which that decree was founded:

WALWORTH, *Ch. J.* "The facts in this case, as they appear from the pleadings and proofs, are substantially these: John M. Berry of Moreau, in the County of Saratoga, was indebted to the complainants, S. & A. Hawley, in the sum of $1,300, and to Marvin in the sum of $500. He was also indebted to the defendants, House & Myers, $1,820; Stewart & Knickerbacker $520, and to DeWolf $950. One Isaac B. Payne was also supposed to be holden as indorser and surety for Berry in the sum of $2,450, including a small debt actually due to him from Berry.

August 6, 1816, Berry being in failing circumstances, to secure the payment of these several sums, he gave to all those creditors a joint bond, in the penalty of $15,000, conditioned to pay $7,540, with interest; and also gave a warrant of attorney to confess judgment on the bond. The defendant, Cramer, witnessed the bond; on the back of which was a memorandum of the amount due to the obligees respectively. A judgment was entered in the Supreme Court, on the bond and war- **720***] rant, the 9th day of the same *month, by Cramer and his partner, Given, as attorneys for the obligees. At the execution of the bond and warrant, it was known to all the parties that the $2,450, included therein, was not all due to Payne; but that it principally consisted of debts for which he was holden as Berry's surety. One of these debts was a note from Berry to William Given, indorsed by Payne. On this note the drawer and indorser were both sued, and separate judgments obtained against them thereon; and a *fieri facias* was issued on the one against Berry, to the Sheriff of Saratoga, in Oct. 1816, for the amount of that judgment and interest. In Feb. 1817, the Hawleys paid Given the amount due on the note, together with the costs of both suits, and protest, and took an assignment of both of his judgments; and in Mar. thereafter, the execution was satisfied, by a sale of Berry's personal property; which was bid off by one of the Hawleys.

The debt to Knickerbacker & Stewart was reduced to $301 by payments from Berry. The amount actually due to Payne, including all the Berry debts for which he was made responsible as his surety, was ascertained to be only $890; and for that sum he afterwards assigned to De Wolf, all his interest in the $15,000 judgment. In Mar. 1817, Cramer and Given, as attorneys for the plaintiffs, and at the request of House, Knickerbacker and De Wolf, issued an execution on the judgment, with a direction to levy $7,557.75 and interest, &c. By virtue of this execution the sheriff levied on all the real property of Berry, a farm in Moreau worth $5,000; and Aug. 8, it was advertised to be sold at Waterford, Sept. 23, 1817.

Shortly before, or at the sale, the Waterford creditors, who with Cramer are the defendants in this suit, without the knowledge of the complainants, mutually agreed that Cramer, the attorney should attend the sale as their agent, and bid upon the farm, at his discretion, for their separate benefit. He did, accordingly, attend the sale as the agent of the Waterford creditors, in the absence and without the knowledge of the other persons interested in the judgment, and bid off the farm for $625. Dec. 26, *1817, by direction of the [***721** Waterford creditors, Cramer sold the farm to Hugh Peebles for $3,600, in cash; which was the full value of the farm, exclusive of a mortgage of $1,400 which Peebles held thereon. Cramer gave a quitclaim deed of the farm and received the $3,600, for the defendants, out of which they permitted him to retain $38.12 for the costs of suit and sheriff's fees, and also $20 claimed by him to be due on an older judgment, belonging to him, against the premises. They also left in Cramer's hands what they considered the complainants' shares of the $625, after deducting the $58.12 therefrom, and divided the residue of the $3,600 among themselves; but in what proportions or by what ratio does not appear, except that De Wolf admits he received from $1,818 to $1,840, as his proportion. Before the filing of the bill, Cramer paid to the Hawleys $94.19, as their proportion of the proceeds of the sale, and which was received without prejudice to their further claims; and he admits he has still in his hands $41.22, for Marvin, which he is and ever has been ready to pay over to him, as and for his share.

A preliminary question has been raised by the counsel for the defendants, of which I will first dispose. It is alleged in the answer of House and Myers, that one Reynolds was jointly interested with them in their debt as a partner. And it is now insisted that he should have been made a party to the suit.

It might, perhaps, be considered a sufficient answer to this objection, that Reynolds was not a party to the judgment against Berry, and has never been known in the transactions connected therewith; and therefore, as to the parties in this suit, he must be considered a dormant partner. But what is conclusive against the defendants, on this point, is the fact, that the statement of the interest of Reynolds, in the answer, is not responsive to anything contained in the bill and, therefore, is not evidence for the defendants. And they have produced no proof whatever to show that he was, in fact, a partner, or a party in interest.

On the part of the Hawleys, it is insisted that the Given debt, with the two bills of cost thereon, being covered by *the amount [***722** inserted in the judgment bond for Payne, they as assignees of the debt, are entitled to a priority; or at least to stand in the place of Payne, *pro tanto*.

So far as it respects the principal debt, and the costs of the suit against the drawer of the note, the Hawleys can have no pretense of claim on the fund raised by the sale of the real estate of Berry. The evidence is conclusive that the whole amount of the judgment against the drawer of the note was raised by the sale of his personal property, which was bid off by Alpheus Hawley; who also gave a receipt in full of the execution. As to the cost of the suit against the indorser (about $35), under all the circumstances connected with that transaction, I think it may be fairly presumed to have been an advance of that amount, by the Hawleys, for the benefit of Berry, without any intention on their part of holding Payne responsible therefor; and without any expectation of being reimbursed out of the property secured by the $15,000 judgment. They have, therefore, no claim to be substituted in the place of Payne for the amount of that cost.

Neither can the claim of the defendant De Wolf, for the whole $2,450, under the assignment from Payne, be sustained in a court of equity In his answer De Wolf denies all knowledge of the actual amount due from Berry to Payne at the time of the assignment. But this is not sufficient to entitle him to the whole amount, as a *bona fide* purchaser without notice. He was the purchaser of a mere chose in action; and took the right of Payne subject to all the equities which existed against that right, in the hands of Payne. *Coles* v. *Jones*, 2 Vern., 692; *Turton* v. *Benson*, 2 *Id.*, 764; *Tourville* v. *Naish*, 3 P. Wms., 307; *Livingston* v. *Hubbs*, 2 Johns., Ch., 512. But on the principles which are applicable to purchasers of the legal estate, De Wolf cannot be considered a *bona fide* purchaser for this whole amount. Being a party to the bond and warrant, he is constructively chargeable with notice of the real situation of Payne's debt. Besides, he had actual information of that which was sufficient to put him on inquiry; and whatever is sufficient to put a party on **723***] inquiry is, in equity, considered *as conveying notice. (3 Conn., 146.) On this ground, in *Sterry* v. *Arden*, 1 Johns. Ch., 267; *Chancellor* Kent held a purchaser chargeable with constructive notice, who had only heard that the vendor had made some provision for his daughter, out of the property. And this principle is fully supported by the English authorities.

In *Taylor* v. *Stibert*, 2 Ves., Jr., 440, Ld. Rosslyn says: "It has been determined that a purchaser being told particular parts of an estate were in possession of a tenant, without any information as to his interest, and taking it for granted it was a lease from year to year, was bound by a lease the tenant had, which was a surprise upon him. That was rightly determined; for it was sufficient to put the purchaser upon inquiry that he was informed the estate was not in the actual possession of the person with whom he contracted." And these remarks of Ld. Rosslyn are quoted with approbation by Ld. Redesdale, as containing a doctrine which had never been doubted. *Crofton* v. *Ormsby*, 2 Sch. & L., 599.

De Wolf, in his answer, admits that at or about the time of executing the bond and warrant, which was many months previous to his purchase of Payne's right, he was informed that the $2,450 was not all due to Payne, but was intended to cover indorsements and responsibilities for Berry, and which he might thereafter be compelled to pay. And with this knowledge, if De Wolf did, in fact, as he alleges in his answer, purchase of Payne without ascertaining how much was actually due, it was *crassa negligentia*. Payne sold to him his right in the judgment for $890, the exact sum due; and if De Wolf was not informed that was the real amount due, he must have remained intentionally and willfully ignorant of that fact, for the purpose of obtaining more than his fair proportion of the proceeds of the judgment. And it appears by his answer that he has, in truth, obtained more than his fair proportion; even as between him and his co-defendants in this cause. Under such circumstances he has no reason to complain of any hardship in the application of the maxim *caveat emptor*, to his purchase of Payne's interest in *the judgment. The assignment must [***724** be permitted to stand only for the $890 actually due; and the residue of the $2,450, together with the amount paid by Berry to Knickerbacker and Stewart, must be considered as stricken out of the judgment. It appears from the testimony of Payne, that the assignment was made after the sale of the personal property, which was in March, 1817: and if the $890 included in the interest on Payne's claim up to that time, which is not at all improbable, De Wolf will still get a dividend on a few dollars more than his equitable right in the judgment.

It follows, from the reduction of De Wolf's claim under the assignment, to the real amount which was due to Payne, that the amount left in the hands of Cramer for the complainant's shares of the purchase money bid at the sheriff's sale, is less than they were actually entitled to, even if they are to be concluded by that sale. And if they are limited to their proportions of the $625 bid at that sale, there can be no propriety in permitting Cramer to retain out of that amount the $20 alleged to be due him on an older judgment. If the purchase by him as the agent of the Waterford creditors was a *bona fide* and legal purchase, it was a purchase subject to all prior incumbrances; and if any such existed, the Waterford creditors should have paid them without deducting the amount from the purchase money in which other persons had an interest. As well might they claim to deduct from that purchase money the whole amount of the mortgage to Peebles, which was also an older incumbrance on the premises sold. The costs and sheriff's fees, only, being deducted from the amount bid, would leave $586.88 to be distributed; and the whole amount due on the judgment, exclusive of interest, was $5,761. Considering these as the basis of distribution, the proportionate share of the Hawleys would exceed $130, and that of Marvin would be something more than $50. But the amount left in Cramer's hands for the Hawleys was only $107.16, and for Marvin $41.22, of which the latter has received nothing; and the former for some cause which is unexplained, have been paid only $94.19. Admitting, therefore, that the complainants have no claim beyond this amount they have an *unquestionable right to a decree for [***725** an account of the net proceeds of the sheriff's sale, and for the payment of their respective proportions thereof.

But the defendants insist that this part of the claim is barred by the Act of Limitations. The

sheriff's sale was in Sept., 1817; the bill of the complainants was filed in Nov., 1823, and the appearance of all the defendants was entered Dec. 8, thereafter, and within six years after the sale to Peebles. The sheriff's deed is not among the exhibits in the cause, and has not been read in evidence. It does not, therefore, certainly appear at what time the sale was consummated by the execution of a deed. But I think it may be fairly inferred, from the facts in the case, that the deed was not actually executed until about the time of the sale of the farm to Peebles. In ordinary cases, the execution of the sheriff's deed will have relation to the back time when the sale actually took place; and it is the usual practice to date them at that time, though executed afterwards. But this relation, which is a fiction of law, is never to be adopted when third persons, who are not parties or privies, will be prejudiced thereby. *Heath* v. *Ross*, 12 Johns., 141. The Statute of Limitations could not begin to run until the purchasers became legally liable for the purchase money, which was not until the actual execution of the deed by the sheriff. It has been frequently decided by the Supreme Court that a sheriff's sale is within the Statute of Frauds; and that the execution of the deed is necessary to devest the title of the defendent in the execution. These decisions have been sanctioned by the highest judicial tribunal in the State. *Catlin* v. *Jackson*, in Error, 8 Johns., 520. The execution on which the farm was sold, is in evidence, but there is no return thereon, neither is there any receipt or memorandum to show that any money was ever received by the sheriff or by any other person on the execution. The necessary inference from these facts, taken in connection with the answers of the defendants, is, that no money was paid or received on account of the farm until the sale to Peebles. And the attempt by the defendants, at that time, to apportion to the com-
726*] plainants *their shares of the proceeds of the sheriff's sale, is a sufficient admission of their liability to account, to take the case out of the Statute of Limitations.

Another objection which has been urged by the defendant's counsel is, that there is no evidence to support the averment in the complainant's bill, that Berry was indebted to them in the sums therein stated—the defendants in their answers having denied all knowledge of such indebtedness.

The defendants all admit, by their answers, that in the bond and warrant given by Berry, there was included the sum of $1,300, as and for a debt of that amount due from him to the Hawleys, and $500 as and for a debt of of that amount due to Marvin. The bond executed by Berry has been proved and is an exhibit in the cause; and that, taken in connection with this admission in the answers of the defendants, is *prima facie* evidence of the debts due to the complainants, as stated in their bill. The defendants, by their answers, do not even pretend that they have any reason to believe these sums were fraudulently inserted in the bond and warrant, when no such debts were really due. If the defendants had any reason to suspect that the sums, thus included in the bond and warrant, were not real and *bona fide* debts due from Berry to the complainants, or that any part of the same had been paid to them by Berry, they might have set up that defense in their answer. In which case the defendants would have been permitted to establish the fact by proof at the hearing or by a cross-bill, they might have called on the complainants to disclose the consideration and grounds of such indebtedness, and the payments, if any, which had been made thereon. The bond, as against Berry, is conclusive evidence of the debts, unless some fraud or mistake in the transaction could be shown. And it must, at least, be *prima facie* evidence of the indebtedness as against third persons; especially where such third persons are parties to the same instrument.

Another objection has been made by the defendants' counsel which goes to the jurisdiction of the court. It is urged that if the complainants have any subsisting claim against any of the defendants, they have a complete and ample remedy at law.

*Although the counsel, on the argu- [***727** ment, appeared to have but little confidence in this objection, yet, as it has been made one of the formal points in the cause, it may be proper that I should give it some consideration. This objection to the jurisdiction is made, for the first time, at the hearing. It was neither raised by demurrer to the bill, nor insisted on as a ground of defense, in the answer of the defendants. They have thus submitted the cause to the cognizance of the court, and they now come too late with this objection to its jurisdiction, unless the court be wholly incompetent to grant the relief which the complainants have sought by their bill. *Ludlow* v. *Simond*, 2 Cai. Cas., 56, per Kent, *Ch. J.*; *Id.*, 40, per Thompson, *J.*, and *Underhill* v. *Van Cortlandt*, 2 Johns. Ch., 369.

If the defendants were not too late with this objection, it would still be somewhat doubtful whether the complainants had a remedy at law, against their co-plaintiffs in the judgment, to recover their equitable proportions of the amount raised by the sale, though I am inclined to the opinion that they might have recovered against them, respectively, in actions for money had and received, within the principles which by modern decisions have been applied to that action. But the remedy at law was doubtful, and would have required a multiplicity of actions; either of which grounds would be sufficient to authorize the interference of a court of equity. Neither does it follow, of course, that this court is ousted of jurisdiction in all cases where the party has a perfect remedy at law. The proposition is undoubtedly correct as a general principle; but the rule is subject to many exceptions. There is a great variety of cases where courts of equity have concurrent jurisdiction with courts of law; and such is the case in all matters of account. Per Thompson, *J.*, in *Ludlow* v. *Simond*, 2 Cai. Cas., 37, and per Kent, *Ch. J.*, in *Post* v. *Kimberly*, 9 Johns., 505. The extension of the equitable principles upon which actions for money had and received may be sustained in courts of law has not devested the courts of equity of their ancient jurisdiction in all matters of account. It is an established principle, that where a court of equity once had jurisdiction, *it will still insist on [***728** retaining it, though the original ground of jurisdiction, the inability of the party to recover at law no longer exists. Per Spencer, *Ch. J.*, in *King* v. *Baldwin*, 17 Johns., 388. And the late *Chancellor* Kent, while delivering his opinion in the Court of Errors, in *Ludlow* v. *Simond*, observes: "I should regret exceedingly that any opinion which might be given by this court should tend to embarrass the benign and well settled jurisdiction of chancery, in the unlimited cognizance of accounts." (2 Cai. Cas., 54.)

Again; the complainants had a right to come into this court for a discovery of the amount paid to the defendants by Berry; to ascertain the proceeds of the judgment, which had been received by them respectively; to ascertain the amount which was actually due to De Wolf, under the assignment from Payne; and to settle the rights and proportions of the respective parties in the distribution of the fund.

And it is a settled rule in equity, that when the court has gained jurisdiction of the cause for one purpose, it may retain it generally. Per Spencer, *J.*, in *Rathbone* v. *Warren*, 10 Johns., 596.

Another objection contained in the written points of the defendants, but which was not mentioned on the argument, is, that the complainants are improperly joined.

This objection could not have been intended to be seriously urged; for there is no rule in equity which is better settled than the one that all persons having an interest in the distribution of the fund or in the subject-matter of the suit must be made parties, either as complainants or defendants, if within the jurisdiction of the court. And although there are exceptions to this rule, those exceptions are only by way of excuse for not bringing all the parties in interest before the court. In *Cockburn* v. *Thompson*, 16 Ves., 324, Ld. Eldon mentions a variety of cases of this description. The objection that there is a misjoinder of complainants can only be sustained where several persons file a joint bill, for separate and distinct causes of action, having no connection with each other; neither as it respects the rights of the complainants, or the rights of the defend-
729*] ants. *In this case, the subject-matter of the suit, in respect to all the parties, is the same; though their rights and liabilities may be separate and distinct, as it respects the distribution of the fund; and it would have been a valid objection that either of the parties to the judgment, and who had a subsisting interest in the subject-matter of the suit, was not a party.

Having disposed of these preliminary questions, I proceed to the examination of the one of more importance, the principal one in the cause, and which has probably produced this suit.

Have the complainants any claim beyond their proportionate shares of the amount of the bid at the sheriff's sale?

I have examined this question with much care and attention, not so much on account of the effect which my decision may have upon the interests of the parties to the suit, which should always be a subject of secondary consideration with the court, as on account of the important principles which are involved in that decision. After a full investigation of the subject, I have arrived at the conclusion that the validity of the purchase at the sheriff's sale cannot be sustained; and, consequently, that the complainants are entitled to their proportionate shares of the amount which was received by the defendants, on the subsequent sale of the farm to Peebles.

But though, under all the circumstances of this case, I am compelled to pronounce the purchase at the sheriff's sale fraudulent and void as against the complainants, upon the principles of equity, there is nothing in this decision which necessarily implicates the characters of the defendants. The transaction was a contest by creditors to obtain a preference in the collection of their just demands which were due from a debtor who was insolvent. And though these defendants, for the purpose of securing such preference, acting under a mistaken impression as to their legal rights, have made a purchase which is deemed constructively fraudulent, as being contrary to public policy and inconsistent with the equitable rights of the complainants, it is still perfectly *reconcilable with the moral hon- [***730**
esty of the persons concerned in making such purchase.

The complainants allege that the purchase at the sheriff's sale was fraudulent and void as against them:

1. Because the execution was issued without their knowledge or consent.

2. Because they were not informed of the time and place of sale; and,

3. Because John Cramer, one of the attorneys for the plaintiffs, and whose name appeared upon the execution as such attorney, became the purchaser, by collusion with the other defendants, at a sum far below the real value of the property; and this in the absence and without the knowledge or consent of the complainants. And in connection with this is the point arising out of the facts stated in the answer, as to the agreement made by the defendants with each other, previous to and at the sale.

Before I proceed to the examination of these points, I will barely remark that as it satisfactorily appears that no money was paid to the sheriff by the defendants, or by Cramer, the agent of the Waterford creditors, on the sale upon the execution; and the purchase being made with the moneys due on the judgment, a part of which purchase money belonged to the complainants, it might be questionable whether a trust in their favor, *pro tanto*, was not created by such purchase. But as this has neither been made a point in the cause, nor discussed at the hearing, I shall not go into the examination of that question.

1. It is admitted in the answers of some of the defendants, that the execution was issued at the request of House, Knickerbacker and De Wolf, in the absence of the complainants; and probably, at the time, it was without their knowledge. But the defendants all deny any fraudulent intent in taking out the execution, and the complainants have produced no evidence whatever to contradict this point of the answers. And all suspicion of fraud, or of any improper object in issuing the execution, is rebutted by the fact that it remained nearly five months in the sheriff's hands before the

farm was advertised for sale thereon. Besides, 731*] there can be no doubt *of the right of either of the parties interested in the judgment to call for an execution, without consulting their co-plaintiffs, unless there was some express agreement or understanding to the contrary; and none is pretended in this case.

2. It appears that the farm was advertised for sale in the manner prescribed by law, in a public newspaper of the county. And whether that paper was published at Waterford, as both parties have supposed in their pleadings in this cause, or at Ballston Spa, as the proofs would seem to indicate, is wholly immaterial. In the absence of all evidence to the contrary, I am also bound to presume that the officer complied with the other requisites of the Statute, by affixing up notices, of the time and place of sale, at three of the most public places in the town where the land was to be sold. This was legal notice to all persons interested in the sale. But in addition to this legal notice, the answer of De Wolf is positive, that, before the sale, he gave actual notice to Marvin of the time and place when it was to be made, and requested him to attend, or to make some arrangement in relation to the property. This part of the answer is responsive to the bill, and being uncontradicted, is conclusive evidence of the fact. The testimony of Given is nearly as positive, as to the information which he communicated to Alpheus Hawley. And though it is probable Hawley may have mistaken the day, or even possible that Given unintentionally misinformed him as to the time, yet neither of those circumstances could form any sufficient ground for impeaching the validity of the sale.

3. The defendants have expressly denied the existence of any fraud or fraudulent intentions, in the employment of Cramer to purchase in the property for them on the execution. But this general denial is not sufficient in this case, though it may be sufficient to rebut the presumption of any corrupt intention on the part of the defendants. If a party, in his answer, admit the existence of facts which render the transaction, in which he has been engaged, legally or constructively fraudulent as against the complainants, his general denial of all fraud will not counteract or alter the 732*] legal *effect of such admission. It may rebut the presumption of a corrupt intention to defraud, but it cannot affect the legal conclusion which the court is bound to draw from the facts admitted.

In this case, from the admission of the defendants, there can be no doubt of the fact that the Waterford creditors agreed not to bid against each other at the sheriff's sale; and that they also agreed to employ Cramer, one of the attorneys for all the parties on the record, as their separate agent to bid in the property for their joint benefit in the proportion to their respective interests in the judgment; and to exclude the complainants from any participation in the benefits arising from the purchase, beyond their proportions of the amount actually bid at the sale.

If the plaintiffs in the judgment are to be considered as having distinct and separate interests therein, and as respecting different rights, their agreement not to bid against each other, but to unite in the purchase, was, of itself, against public policy and was constructively fraudulent, not only as against their co-plaintiffs, but also as against Berry, the defendant in the execution.

In *Doolin* v. *Ward*, 6 Johns., 194, the Supreme Court of this State decided that an agreement by two persons that they would not bid against each other at an auction, that one should buy in the articles, and they would afterwards divide the same equally between them, was against public policy, and was void, as tending injuriously to affect the character and the value of sales at auction. In *Jones* v. *Caswell*, 3 Johns. Cas., 32, Radcliff, *J.*, observes: "The law has regulated sales on execution with a jealous care, and enjoined such proceedings as are likely to promote a fair competition. A combination to prevent such competition is contrary to morality and sound policy. It operates as a fraud upon the debtor and remaining creditors, by depriving the former of the opportunity which he ought to possess of obtaining a full equivalent for the property which is devoted to the payment of his debts, and opens the door for oppressive speculations." And these principles are expressly recognized and fully sanctioned by the late *Chancellor*, in *Troup* v. *Wood*, 4 Johns. Ch., 254. *In the present case, can there be [*733 any doubt that the sacrifice of the Berry farm, for about one sixth of its actual value in cash, was the immediate and inevitable result of this agreement, entered into by the five Waterford creditors, representing three distinct and separate interests in the judgment; and this, too, in the absence and without the knowledge of the other persons who were interested in the sale? Had this illegal agreement not been entered into, there is no probability that either of them would have suffered the property to be sold at such an enormous sacrifice, and leave their debts unpaid.

But this is not the only objection which the complainants urge against the validity of the purchase. They also complain that the Waterford creditors employed the attorney on record to make the purchase; that they seduced him from the allegiance which he owed to all the plaintiffs in the execution as their common agent for the collection of the amount due on the judgment; and that they engaged him to become the separate agent of a part of his clients, in a speculation not only inconsistent with but directly opposed to the interests of the rest, and contrary to the duty which he owed to the whole collectively. And here the important question arises, which I will now consider.

Can the attorney on record, who issues an execution, become a purchaser at the sheriff's sale on such execution, either for his own benefit, or as the agent of others, against the interest and without the consent of those for whose benefit the execution issued?

I consider the fact that the purchase was made by the attorney, without the consent and against the interest of some of his clients, or those for whose benefit he is supposed to act as attorney, as important in this case. For notwithstanding, the court, in *Howell* v. *Baker*, 4 Johns. Ch., 121, said that the rule disqualifying solicitors and attorneys from purchasing at sales brought about by their agency, had strong pretensions to be applied to the case of an application by the defendant in an execution to set aside a purchase made by the plaintiff's attorney, the late *Chancellor*, inten- 734*] tionally *avoided deciding that point, though it was directly before him in that suit. I think the doctrine has never been carried to that extent, even in the decisions of the English courts, which have gone the farthest on this subject. The reasons why the attorney or agent is not permitted to purchase, is because it is supposed to be inconsistent with the duty which he owes to those for whom he is employed to act; and from the relation which exists between the agent and his principal; or between the attorney and his client. But these reasons cannot apply to the defendant in the execution. The plaintiff's attorney owes no allegiance to the defendant, and is under no obligation of duty to take care of his interest; neither is there any confidential connection existing between them. There can be no doubt of the right of a plaintiff to purchase on his own execution. And I think there can be as little doubt of the right of the attorney to purchase for his client, with his assent; or to purchase for himself, or as the agent of a third person, with the like permission. There are cases in which the client, himself, is not permitted to purchase, and in all such it may be proper to extend the like prohibition to his attorney or agent. The case of a solicitor to a commission of bankruptcy, in England, is one of this description. The assignees are not permitted to become purchasers of the bankrupt's effects; and the same rule is applied to the solicitor to the commission, who is their agent in the management of the estate. He cannot purchase, even by permission of the assignees, without the consent of all the parties interested in the fund arising from the sale. *Ex parte James*, 8 Ves., Jr., 352.

All the cases, on the subject of purchases by persons standing in the situation of actual trustees for the sale, were ably and elaborately reviewed by *Chancellor* Kent, in *Davoue* v. *Fanning*, 2 Johns. Ch., 252. It would, therefore, be considered presumption in me to go over that ground, and I shall not attempt it; but content myself with observing that the principles there settled, by him, have been sanctioned by the highest court in the Union. *Wormley* v. *Wormley*, 8 Wh., 441. In all such cases, the rule appears now to be fully settled, 735*] that the purchase, however *fair and honest it may have been, must be set aside on the application of any of the parties in interest; provided such application be made within a reasonable time after the sale; which is to be judged of by the court, under all the circumstances of the case. And the fact that the purchase was made by the trustee through the intervention of a third person, or that the trustee purchased as agent for another, makes no difference in the legal effect of the transaction, or in the application of the general rule. A person who is incapacitated from purchasing on his own account, cannot in any case, or under any circumstances, buy as the agent of a third person. *Ex parte Bennet*, 10 Ves., Jr., 381.

So far as I have been able to discover, the question, whether an attorney can become a purchaser without the consent of his client, for whose benefit the sale is made; or whether he stands in the same situation as regards his client, as the trustee or other agent does in relation to his *cestui que trust* or principal, has not been judicially settled in any of the courts of this country. In the English courts the rule is frequently referred to by counsel, as being perfectly settled, and well understood. But even there I have been able to find but few reported cases, except in bankruptcy, where a purchase by the attorney has been set aside, notwithstanding it was perfectly fair in all its circumstances. The fact that lands are not there sold under judgments in the common law courts, and that sales made by order of the courts of equity are examined and passed upon by the court, on the coming in of the master's report of the sale, will, probably, account for the small number of cases that appear in the English reports. The case of *Owen* v. *Foulkes*, mentioned in a note to *Lacy's* case, 6 Ves., Jr., 631, was a purchase by the solicitor in the cause; a bill filed by creditors; the purchase perfectly fair; the solicitor bidding openly in the presence of very respectable persons concerned for mortgages and creditors, and declaring that he was bidding for himself; the sale, at that time, being also necessary. The reporter says, "but the general rule prevailed." And the sale was set aside, as has been done in a number of cases there mentioned, where the purchase has been made by the solicitor to the commission in bankruptcy.

*By the Roman law, guardians were [*736 prohibited from purchasing the property of their wards; agents and attorneys, the property intrusted to their care and management; and generally, all persons, having a trust or charge, were disabled from purchasing the property which was the object of such trust. And the disability was extended to their children and other persons under their control. And the new Civil Code of France has carried the principle to its fullest extent. The 1596th article, under the title "*Que peut acheter au vendre*," having prohibited on sales at auction or to the highest bidder, guardians from becoming purchasers of the goods which they have in guardianship; agents from purchasing goods of which they have the charge of the sale; administrators, those things the settlement whereof is committed to their care and administration; and public officers, the goods of the nation of which they have the ordering of the sale, &c.; the next article prohibits the judges of the courts, and their petitioners, or suitors, the attorneys, registers, bailiffs, notaries and other officers, &c., (*Les juges, leurs suppleants, les commissaires du gouvernement, les substitutes, les greffies, huissiers, avoues, defenseurs officieux, et notaries*), from becoming the purchasers of anything connected with the suits litigated in the tribunals, within the jurisdiction of which, they exercise their functions; under the penalty of having the sale made void, and of paying the costs with damages and interest. (Code Civil, *Des Francais*, Liv. 3, tit. 6, ch. 2, art. 1596, 1597.)

The principles of the French Code, so far as it relates to attorneys, are sustained by Ld.

Thurlow, in *Hall* v. *Hallet*, 1 Cox. Cas., 140. In speaking of an assignment of certain debts, made by an administrator to an attorney who had been employed generally in the management of the legal business of the estate, he declared that if the decision rested upon the simple fact of the assignment only, the assignee should not be entitled to any advantage from the purchase of the debts ; for no attorney could be permitted to buy things in a course of litigation, of which litigation he has the management. And in the case of the petition of Frances James, in bankruptcy, 8 Ves., 352,
737*] Ld. Eldon set *aside a purchase made by a solicitor, who had been employed by the assignees in the business of the estate ; although the sale was perfectly fair, and the purchase sanctioned by most of the persons interested in the estate—the amount bid, being, at the time of sale, considered the full value of the premises. He observes, "this doctrine, as to purchases by trustees, assignees, and persons having a confidential character, stands much more upon general principle than upon the circumstances of any individual case. It rests upon this, that the purchase is not permitted in any case, however honest the circumstances—the general interest of justice requiring it to be destroyed in every instance—as no court is equal to the examination and ascertainment of the truth, in much the greatest number of cases."

But it is supposed, by the counsel for the defendants, that the case of *Beardsley* v. *Root*, in the Supreme Court of this State, 11 Johns., 464, and *Nelthrop* v. *Pennyman*, in the English Court of Chancery, 14 Ves., Jr., 517, have established the doctrine that attorneys may become purchasers without the consent and against the interests of their clients. In the first case, the Supreme Court decided that the attorney for the plaintiff, as such, without other authority, had no right to make a purchase for the client, especially under the circumstances of that case, where the client would have to pay the amount due upon an older judgment. And the attorney, having made such purchase when it was absolutely necessary for the protection of his client's interests, and having taken a deed in his own name, the court held him liable to his client for the amount bid on his execution. In the other case, Ld. Eldon refused to discharge the solicitor in the cause from a purchase of the property, which had been made by him to prevent the sale at an undervalue. And he declared that the solicitor purchasing under such circumstances must keep the property, if the court thought he ought to keep it. This last case was not a contest between the attorney and client, but it was an application to be relieved from the purchase, that there might be a resale ; and other parties in the cause, besides his own client, had an interest in the question and
738*] *might hold him to his purchase. Neither of these cases establish the right of the attorney to purchase for himself, as against his client. They are both founded upon a principle which is well settled, both in equity and at law, that a person cannot be relieved from the consequences of his own illegal act. Any person, who is a party in interest, and who supposes himself injured by the illegal act, may apply for redress, if he thinks proper to do so. If a resale of the property is ordered, it is to be put up again at the price bid by the former purchaser ; and if nothing further is bid he may be compelled to take the property and to account for the proceeds of the first sale. *Whelpdale* v. *Cookson*, 5 Ves., Jr., 682 ; *Ex parte Reynolds*, 5 Ves., Jr., 707 ; *Ex parte Lacy*, 6 Ves., Jr., 625 ; *Jackson* v. *Van Dalfsen*, 5 Johns., 48. If an attorney is not authorized to purchase for his client in any case, or under any circumstances, without an express authority for that purpose, it does not necessarily follow that he has the right to purchase for himself, or as the agent for a third person. He still has a duty to perform, in the execution of the trust reposed in him as attorney. I incline to the opinion that there may be cases in which it would be the duty of the attorney to purchase for his client if it became absolutely necessary to do so, in order to prevent a very great sacrifice of property, and a certain and irreparable loss to his client. And this seems to be the opinion of the court in *Beardsley* v. *Root*, though I admit it must be an extreme case, to justify such an interference by the attorney, without consulting his client.

But in this case, although Cramer had no authority to purchase for the complainants, he had, in virtue of his character of attorney in the execution, the power to direct and control the proceedings thereon. When he found that the interests of a part of his clients were about to be sacrificed, in their absence, in consequence of the combination among the other plaintiffs in the execution, he could have apprised the officer thereof, and requested him to postpone the sale. And if the sheriff had refused to adjourn the sale, under such circumstances, and had proceeded to sacrifice the property, the court would have set aside the proceedings as fraudulent *and oppress- [***739**
ive on the part of the officer. *M'Donald* v. *Neilson*, 2 Cow., 191, per Savage, *Ch. J.* It was urged by the defendant's counsel that Marvin had no right to complain because he was requested by De Wolf to attend the sale and bid upon the property, and he declined attending. What his reasons were, for not attending, does not appear. His debt was small, when compared with most of the others, and he probably supposed the property would sell for something like its fair value. He had a right to presume the sale would be conducted in good faith, under the immediate observation of his attorneys, both of whom resided at the place where the sale was to be made. He could not anticipate that there would be a combination among the other creditors, to prevent a fair competition, or which would have the effect to destroy all competition among themselves, and thus reduce the amount of the bids. Much less could he anticipate that one of those attorneys, with the knowledge that such an arrangement had been entered into, would not only suffer the property to be thus sacrificed, but that he would also become the agent of the purchasers to bid in the property for them. And certainly that attorney mistook the duty which was imposed upon him by the relation in which he stood to the complainants, when he consented, under such circumstances, to

make the purchase as the agent of the Waterford creditors, without first letting the complainants know that he would no longer attend to their rights, in the collection of the judgment. It is true Cramer, in his answer, says he was only employed to enter judgment and issue execution. But I do not understand him to mean that there was any special agreement or understanding that he should do that and nothing more; but only as intending to say, there was nothing said about any further services. This would leave him the full control of the execution, on a retainer to enter the judgment and to issue execution, as in ordinary cases.

There are strong reasons, on the ground of public policy, against permitting the attorney to become the purchaser, either for himself or as agent of another, in any case, where it
740*] *can possibly interfere in any manner with the rights of his client. And I strongly incline to the opinion that the only safe rule is, to set aside all such purchases, as of course, on the application of the client, where the purchase has been made without his knowledge and consent, if any part of his debt remains unsatisfied. But it is not necessary that I should go that length for the decision of this case. It is not necessary for me to carry the doctrine to the extent to which it is carried by the Napoleon Code, which is only an extension of the principles of the Macedonian Decree of the civil law; or even to the extent to which it has been carried in the English courts; where the sale would be set aside without showing any unfairness or want of consideration in the purchase. It will be sufficient if I apply to this case the general principles which regulate and are applicable to the dealings between attorney and client. The rule, as I understand it, is this: an attorney, retaining that character, may contract with his principal, where the principal is acting in his own right, and not as agent or trustee for another; or he may purchase at public auction, or private sale, in cases where his client is interested in the proceeds of such sale, provided the purchase is made with the knowledge and consent of his client. But in all cases where the relation of attorney and client exists, and which is in any manner referable to the subject of the purchase, whether such purchase be made by the attorney on his own account, or as the agent or for the benefit of others, the purchaser must be subject to the *onus* of making it fully manifest that no advantage has been taken of the client. Testing the present case by this rule, the purchase at the sheriff's sale could not be supported, even if the attorney had bid with the knowledge and permission of the complainants. The property was purchased at a very great undervalue, leaving their debts unsatisfied. Under such circumstances it would still be incumbent on the purchaser to satisfy the court, beyond all doubt, that the attorney was ignorant of the value of the property, or that he fully apprised the complainants of its real value before the sale. If the attorney knew that Peebles wished to become a purchaser of the property, and that
741*] *he was willing to pay its real value, or something near that value, it would be necessary for him to show that his clients were informed of that fact, before he could be permitted to sustain a purchase to himself, at an undervalue. But though sufficient was stated in the bill to create a suspicion that he was aware of the fact, which is all that was necessary to throw upon the defendants the burden of removing such suspicion, the attorney does not deny his knowledge of the fact; but contents himself with only denying that he has any recollection that Peebles apprised him of his intention to attend the sale and that he promised to give him notice of the time and place. If he had only heard the fact from some other source, he would be bound to communicate that information to his clients, before he could be permitted to purchase at so great an undervalue, even with their consent. And if he had no such knowledge or information, it should have been fully and explicitly denied in his answer. And before he could become the purchaser, as the agent of the Waterford creditors, it would also be indispensably requisite that he should give information to the complainants that he was employed to bid for those creditors; and also of the agreement which they had made not to bid against each other, and to divide the profits of the purchase in proportion to their debts. (Sudg. L.V., 431.) Again; the property was bid in, by the attorney, for about one sixth part of its known cash value; and this total inadequacy of price when taken in connection with the other circumstances of this case, is sufficient to vacate the sale. As between parties perfectly independent of each other, where no confidential relation exists between them, and where no undue influence has been exercised, mere inadequacy of price, unless it be so great as to be evidence of fraud, is not sufficient to avoid a purchase; especially where the sale was at public auction. But the rule is otherwise where the relation of attorney and client exists, between the purchaser and the person interested in selling. In contracts between attorney and client, if there is a great inadequacy in the price paid on a purchase by the attorney, the contract will not be sustained in a court of equity. *Gibson* v. *Jeyes*, 6 Ves. Jr., *266; *Wood* v. *Downes*, 18 Ves. Jr., [***742**
120; *Morse* v. *Royal*, 12 Ves., Jr., 373; *Montesquieu* v. *Sandys*, 18 Ves., Jr., 311; *Newman* v. *Payne*, 2 Ves., Jr., 200; S. C., 4 Bro. C. C., 350; *Butler* v. *Haskell*, 4 Desaus. Ch. 702.

It is true that in *Wendell* v. *Van Rensselaer*, 1 Johns. Ch., 344, *Chancellor* Kent refused to set aside a deed given to an attorney, although there was a great inadequacy of consideration. But it will be seen by a reference to that case that the attorney had not been employed as such in relation to the property in question. In the language of an English *Chancellor* he was not attorney in *hac re;* neither was he the general agent of Wendell, in relation to his property. Under the circumstances of that case, Van Rensselaer, not being the attorney of Wendell in relation to this matter, might become the purchaser, as he was under no obligations of duty to advise in relation to that transaction. But, even in that case, the *Chancellor* declares that if he had been able to discover the least scintilla of fraud or imposition, on the part of Van Rensselaer, in procuring the deeds, he should annul the transaction.

But it has been urged, in this case, that the

complainants have lost their remedy by lapse of time. In cases of implied trusts, in relation to personal property, or the rents and profits of real estate, where persons claiming in their own right are turned into trustees by implication, or by operation of law, it is a general rule that the right of action, in equity, will be considered as barred in six years, in analogy to the limitation at law. And probably if the commencement of this suit had been delayed a few days longer, the complainants would have lost all remedy by the operation of the Statute of Limitations. In cases of this description, independent of the Statutes of Limitation, if the person entitled to relief against an improper purchase acquiesce for a long time, without making any objection, or bringing a suit, equity will not grant relief. But in this case there has not been any acquiescence of either of the complainants: neither is the length of time sufficient to bar their claim. The Statute of Limitations cannot apply to this case, because the suit was commenced, and the appearance **743***] of the defendants *actually entered therein, within six years after the land was converted into money, by the sale to Peebles. The shortest limitation of actions at law, in this State, respecting real property, is twenty years; and by analogy that would be the shortest period which a court of equity would be bound to consider as an absolute bar to the equitable rights of the complainants upon the land, while it remained in the hands of the defendants.

But in cases of this kind courts of equity have frequently refused relief where the suit was commenced within the twenty years; not, however, on the ground of any analogy to the limitation of actions, of the like nature, at law, but on the principle that acquiescence, for a great length of time, after the party was in a situation to enforce his right, and with a full knowledge of the facts, was evidence of a waiver, or abandonment of the right. In all cases like the present, the application to set aside the sale, or for other relief, must be made within a reasonable time; but what is a reasonable time cannot well be defined so as to establish any general rule and must, in a great measure, depend upon the exercise of the sound discretion of the court, under all the circumstances of each particular case. In *Gregory* v. *Gregory*, Coop. Ch. Cas., 201, the Master of the Rolls refused to set aside a purchase, by a trustee, after a lapse of eighteen years. In *Bergen* v. *Bennet*, 1 Cai. Cas., 1, the Court of Errors refused the application, after sixteen years acquiescence. In *Butler* v. *Haskell*, the Court of Chancery of S. C. did not consider eleven years an unreasonable delay, and in many cases relief has been granted after a much longer period. *Purcell* v. *M'Namara*, 14 Ves., 91; *Pickett* v. *Loggon*, 14 Ves., 214; *Hatch* v. *Hatch*, 9 Ves., 292; *Murray* v. *Palmer*, 2 Sch. & L., 474.

Having arrived at the conclusion that the validity of Cramer's purchase, for the Waterford creditors, cannot be sustained, and that the remedy has not been lost by lapse of time, I now come to the last question in the cause: to what relief are the complainants in this case entitled. It is urged by the defendant's counsel that, if the purchase by the attorney was illegal, it was a fraud upon the whole world, *and that the only remedy is by a resale,[***744** on the execution.

The premises having been purchased, by Peebles, *bona fide*, without notice of any fraud or illegality in the sheriff's sale, the purchase made by him must be sustained; and of course there can be no resale upon the execution. (Per Brakenridge, *J.*, 3 Binn., 64.) The remedy in cases like the present goes to the persons who had an interest in the property before the sale, and no other person can apply to set the sale aside. 2 Hen. & Munf., 245; 5 Johns., 47. In this case the whole value of the property, being insufficient to satisfy the judgment on which it was sold, no person, except the complainants, could have any interest in the remedy, unless it might be Berry, the defendant in the execution. He has no interest in the distribution of the fund raised by the sale to Peebles and, therefore, is not a necessary party to this suit. And it may not be too late for him to compel the plaintiffs, in the judgment, to allow the whole amount of the purchase money, paid by Peebles, towards satisfying the judgment, if the purchase at the sheriff's sale should be considered illegal, as against him.

In cases of purchases by trustees, or others who are not authorized to purchase without the consent of their principal or *cestui que trust*, the rule of equity is, that if the purchaser has not devested himself of the property, it is to be put up again, at the amount of the former bid, together with he value of beneficial and lasting improvements, made thereon after the sale, and if it brings nothing more, he is to be holden to his purchase. But if he has parted with the estate, he may be compelled to account for all the property which has been made by him on the resale. 4 Des. Ch., 503, per James, *Ch.*; *Davoue* v. *Fanning*, 2 Johns. Ch., 271; *Randall* v. *Erington*, 10 Ves., 423; *Lester* v. *Lester*, 6 Ves., 631; 4 Binn., per Tilghman, *Ch. J.*, 44; *Ex parte Reynolds*, 5 Ves., 707; *Fox* v. *Macreath*, 2 Bro. Ch. Cas., 400; *Ex parte Lacy*, 6 Ves., 625; *Butler* v. *Haskell*, 4 Des. Ch., 716; *Ld. Hardwicke* v. *Vernon*, 4 Ves., 417. And according to the decision in *Fox* v. *Macreath*, he must pay interest upon the profits which he has made upon the sale.

*I shall, therefore, decree that the [***745** complainants, respectively, are entitled to their ratable proportions of the amount which was raised by the sale to Peebles, of the Berry farm; deducting therefrom the costs and sheriff's fees, and the balance due on Cramer's judgment, amounting in all to $58.12. And that they are entitled to interest, on the amount of such ratable proportions, from the time of the last mentioned sale, excepting on such part thereof as was left in the hands of Cramer for their use. The apportionment to be made agreeably to the principles, and on the amounts or sums, above settled as due to the respectives parties. That the defendant Cramer pay to the complainants the amount received for them, respectively, which has not already been paid over by him. And that the other defendants pay to them the residue of their proportionate shares, respectively, and the interest thereon as aforesaid, together with the costs of the complainints in this suit to be taxed. And inasmuch as they have not disclosed the amount of the purchase money, received by them respectively, in such a manner as to enable me to decree contribution among them, I shall direct that the complainants have execution against them, jointly, for the amount due, with the costs. And if any of them shall be compelled to pay more than what he or they shall consider their just and equitable proportion thereof, he or they may go before the clerk of this court, or a master in chancery, on the foot of the decree, and obtain a report of the amount, which has been received and paid by the said Waterford creditors respectively, and a statement of the acount between them, on the principles of the decree in this cause; to the end that, on the coming in of the said report, such further decree may be made, for an equitable contribution between them, as shall be just; and that the usual liberty be given to the master to examine the parties and others on oath, and to compel the production of books and papers, on the taking of such account.

The following decree was entered in the cause:

"This cause having been heard on the pleadings and proofs, at the stated term of this court, **746***] in Mar. last, and *the same being duly considered by the court, it is this day ordered, adjudged, declared and decreed, and this court, by virtue of the authority therein vested, doth order, adjudge, declare and decree that the complainants, S. H. & A. H., have no right or claim to any part of the proceeds of the judgment against B. in favor of the said complainants and others, for $15,000 of debt, besides damages and costs, entered in the Supreme Court of Judicature, on the 9th day of August, 1816, in the said pleadings and proof particularly mentioned, over and above their original debt, included therein; for an account of the assignment of the judgments in favor of W. G. against P. and against the said B. in the said pleadings also mentioned. And it is further declared and decreed, that the assignment made by P. to W. D. W., one of the defendants, of the interest of the said P. in the said judgment, in favor of the complainants and others, against B. was not valid for any greater sum than $890, which was the whole amount that was actually due on the said judgment, to the said P. for debts due from, and responsibilities incurred for the said B. And it is, therefore, decreed that the said assignment from P. of his interest in the said judgment, be permitted to stand for the said sum of $890, with the interest thereon as hereafter mentioned, only; and that the residue of the sum of $24.50, included in the said judgment for P's. supposed debts and responsibilities, together with the sum of $219, paid by the said B. to K. & S., before the sheriff's sale under the said judgment, be considered as stricken out of the said judgment. And it is further adjudged, declared and decreed that the relative proportions, rights and interests of the parties respectively, in the said judgment, against B. at the time of the sale of the Berry farm, under the said judgment, were as follows, to wit: there was due to S. & A. H. $1,300, to U. M. $500, to H. & M. $1,820, to K. & S. $301, and to W. D. W., for his original debt and for the amount due to him under the assignment from P. $1,840, with interest on the said sums, respectively, from the 6th day of August, 1816. And it appearing to this court, by the said pleadings and proofs, that the defendant, J. C., at the sheriff's *sale, on the execution [***747** issued upon the last said mentioned judgment, became the purchaser of the Berry farm, as the agent of the other defendants, under an illegal agreement, between such defendants, not to bid against each other, at the said sheriff's sale, but to employ the said J. C. to bid for them jointly, and to divide the profits which might be made on such purchase, between them, in proportion to their respective debts; and it further appearing to this court that at the time of the said purchase, the said J. C. was the attorney, as well of the complainants as of the said defendants on the execution upon which the said sheriff's sale was made; and that he made the said purchase, as agent of the other defendants in this cause, in consequence of such illegal agreement between them, and in the absence of the complainants, and without their knowledge or consent; and that the amount bid at the said sheriff's sale, and for which the said premises were struck off to the said attorney, was less than one fifth of the known cash value of the said farm: whereby nearly the whole of the complainants' debts, secured by the said judgment, remain unsatisfied; it is, therefore, further adjudged, declared and decreed that the said purchase of the Berry farm, by the said J. C., as the agent of the other defendants, was illegal, fraudulent and void, as against the complainants in this cause. But it further appearing to this court that after the said illegal and fraudulent purchase of the said Berry farm, to wit; on the 26th day of December, 1817, and within six years before the time of filing the bill of the complainants, and of the entering the appearance of the defendants, in this cause, the said J. C., as agent of the said other defendants, sold the said Berry farm to H. P. for the sum of $3,600; and that the said H. P. purchased *bona fide*, and actually paid the purchase money, without notice of such illegality or fraud, in the purchase at the sheriff's sale; it is further decreed and declared that the said sheriff's sale, and the said sale to the said H. P., be permitted to stand and remain valid, for the protection of the legal and equitable rights of the said *bona fide* purchaser; and that the said complainants are, in equity, entitled to their ratable proportions of the purchase *money, received on the sale to [***748** the said H. P. And it is further declared and decreed that the costs of entering the judgment and issuing the said execution, and the sheriff's fees on the same, and the balance of an older judgment against the said B., in favor of the said J. C., which was a lien on the said farm, and which costs, sheriff's fees and balance, amount to $58.12, were properly retained by the said J. C., and paid out of the moneys received on the said sale to H. P. And that out of the residue of the moneys received on the said sale to H. P., amounting to the sum of $3,541.88, the said S. & A. H. were entitled to receive the sum of $799.24, and the said U.M. was entitled to receive $307.40, as their respective ratable proportions of the said purchase money, in proportion to the amounts due them on the said judgment against B. And it further appearing to the court that, of the sums which

the complainants were so entitled to receive, the defendant J. C. received and has in his hands, for the use of the said U. M. $41.22; and that he also received for the use of the said S. & A. H., the sum of $107.16, of which sum he has paid over to them $94.19, and that the residue, $12.97, remains in his hands for their use; it is further ordered, adjudged and decreed that the said J. C. pay over to the said complainants, respectively, the said sums of money so remaining in his hands for their use. And the said other defendants, H. & M., K. & S. and W. D. W. having divided the residue of the money which belonged to the said complainants, among themselves; and not having disclosed the amount thereof, which they have severally and respectively received, in such manner as to enable the court to decree contribution, among them, in the payment of the same, to the complainants; it is further ordered, adjudged and decreed that the said five last mentioned defendants are jointly and severally liable for the payment thereof to the said complainants, together with the interest thereon from the time they so received and divided the same between them, at the time of the sale to H. P. And it is, therefore, further ordered, adjudged and decreed that the said five last mentioned de-
749*] fendants pay to the said *S. & A. H. $692.08 for their proportion of the residue aforesaid; and that they also pay to them interest thereon, at the rate of seven *per cent. per annum*, for the said 26th day of December, 1817, until they so pay the same; and that the said last mentioned defendants also pay to the said U. M., for his proportion of the said residue, the sum of $266.18, together with the interest thereon, at the rate and from the time last aforesaid, until they shall so pay the same; and that the said five last mentioned defendants also pay to the complainants their costs of this suit to be taxed; and that the said complainants have execution for the said sums, so adjudged to them, with the interest, as aforesaid, and costs, agreeable to the course and practice of the court.

And it is further ordered and decreed that if any of the said five last mentioned defendants shall, under this decree, be compelled to pay more than his or their equitable proportion of the said sums, so adjudged to the said complainants, or of the costs of this suit, such defendant or defendants may apply to a master in chancery, or to the clerk of this court, on the foot of this decree, and obtain a report of what has been received and paid out by the said last named defendant, respectively, and a statement of the account thereof between them, on the principles of this decree, to the end that on the coming in of the said report, such further order and decree may be made for an equitable contribution among the said defendants, as shall be just. And the usual liberty is given to the said master or clerk to examine the parties, and all other parties on oath, as witnesses, and to compel the production of books and papers, upon taking such account, as he shall deem proper and necessary."

Agreement, to prevent bidding at auction sale, void. Cited in—5 Lans., 357; 1 McLean, 300; 17 Am. Rep., 27 (57 Ill., 416).

Trustee—Personal transactions in relation to trust—Cannot be allowed to profit by. Cited in—1 Paige, 397; 9 Paige, 241, 663; 11 Paige, 115; Clarke, 466; 3 Sandf. Ch., 62; 14 N. Y., 91; 22 N. Y., 349; 44 N. Y., 241; 52 N. Y., 235; 3 Keyes, 305; 1 Abb. App. Dec., 385; 1 Trans. App., 149; 27 Hun, 302; 18 Barb., 47; 33 Barb., 593; 59 Barb., 13; 66 Barb., 222; 21 How. Pr., 201; 26 How. Pr., 220; 36 How. Pr., 160; 4 Abb. Pr., 113; 5 Abb. N. S., 315; 6 Bos., 451, 462; 39 Super., 533; 41 Super., 269; 22 Wall., 340; 3 Wood & M., 487, 490, 491; 28 Mich., 106; 24 Minn., 499; 69 Mo., 261; 36 Wis., 550.

Knowledge of facts, sufficient to put one on inquiry, will keep him from being bona fide *purchaser.* Cited in—1 Barb. Ch., 232; 39 N. Y., 74; 50 N. Y., 351; 76 N. Y., 390; 6 Trans. App., 350; 4 Abb. N. C., 116; 2 Black, 390; 5 Bank Reg., 264; 10 Bank Reg., 177; 36 Cal., 437; 110 Mass., 395.

Jurisdiction of equity—Cannot be objected to, after plea. Cited in—2 Paige, 510; 1 Barb. Ch., 130; 3 Barb. Ch., 574; Hoffm., 15, 417; Clarke, 331; 35 N. Y., 103; 31 Barb., 74; 45 How. Pr., 240; 55 How. Pr., 212; 2 2 Leg. Obs., 384; 17 Wall., 288; 5 Bank Reg., 15; 88 Ill., 147.

Minor or cestui que trust *must disaffirm within reasonable time.* Cited in—24 Minn., 499; 44 Wis., 483.

Also cited in—27 N. Y., 567; 54 Barb., 377; 41 Am. Dec., 220 (7 Blackf., 218).

REPORTS OF CASES

ARGUED AND DETERMINED

IN THE

SUPREME COURT,

AND IN THE

COURT FOR THE TRIAL OF IMPEACHMENTS

AND

THE CORRECTION OF ERRORS,

IN THE

STATE OF NEW YORK.

BY ESEK COWEN.

COUNSELOR AT LAW.

VOL. V.

1837.

CASES

ARGUED AND DETERMINED

IN THE

SUPREME COURT

OF THE

STATE OF NEW YORK,

IN

OCTOBER TERM, 1825, IN THE FIFTIETH YEAR OF OUR INDEPENDENCE.

ANONYMOUS.

Practice—Papers to be Filed.

Papers upon which a motion is made or opposed should be filed by the attorney. It is his duty to file them, of course, without any motion for that purpose; and the court will compel him to do this upon suggestion.

It does not lie with the party who made an affidavit to support or oppose a motion, to object that it is sought to be filed with a view to prosecute him for perjury.

THIS cause had been submitted to referees (under the Statute) who reported for the plaintiff; whereupon the defendant's attorney moved to set the report aside, upon several affidavits made by the defendant before commissioners in the City of Albany; and the motion was heard upon the calendar, and granted several terms ago; but the defendant's attorney omitted to file the affidavits upon which the motion was founded. The plaintiff wishing to prosecute the defendant for perjury in his affidavits, applied for and obtained an order of Savage, *Ch. J.*, directing the defendant's attorney to file them with the clerk at Albany; but he, under the defendant's direction, refused to do this.

Mr. E. Livingston, Dist. Atty., of Albany, now, upon an affidavit of this, and that the order had been served, moved to make it a rule of this court.

Mr. J. Lansing, contra, objected that no notice of the motion had been given by the plaintiff's attorney; and though he admitted that, in the case of a non-enumerated motion, it is the duty of the attorney to file the affidavits; yet he said the practice among the bar had been **14***] different in relation to enumerated *motions. Beside, the defendant ought not to be compelled in this manner to criminate himself. This was not only so at common law; but under the express provisions of the Constitution, art. 6, sec. 7.

Curia. A formal notice of motion is not necessary. We would order you to file the affidavits, upon an informal suggestion that you had omitted to file them. All motions stand upon the same footing in this respect, whether enumerated or non-enumerated. It is the duty of the attorney to file the original papers with the clerk at the time of making or opposing the motion. Though copies are furnished, it is upon the originals that the judgment or decision is founded. It does not lie with the defendant, in answer to this application, to say that filing the affidavits will criminate him. The question is between the court and the attorney. The motion must be granted.

Motion granted.(a)

(a) Mr. Livingston informed me that he relied for his practice on what Yates, *J.*, said in Rex v. Wilkes, 4 Burr., 2571.

PURDY, Executor of PURDY, *v.* PURDY.

Practice—Discontinuance by Executor—Costs.

Executor allowed to discontinue without costs, on motion, after having stipulated to try, and noticed his cause for trial, but omitting to try it because he discovered at the circuit that he could not succeed, it also appearing that the action was commenced in good faith.

A cross motion for judgment as in case of nonsuit denied without costs.

Citation—4 Cow., 551.

MR. J. PIERSON moved for judgment as in case of nonsuit, for not proceeding to trial, pursuant to notice, at the last Reusselaer Circuit. The plaintiff had stipulated to try at that circuit.

Mr. H. P. Hunt, contra, read an affidavit showing that the cause had been commenced and prosecution in good faith, till the last Rensselaer Circuit, when the plaintiff discovered for the first, on the examination of a witness sworn in a cross cause by the defendant against the plaintiff, that the action in this cause could not be sustained; and moved for leave to discontinue without costs.

Curia. The motion to discontinue without costs must be granted. The case comes within the principle of *Morse* v. **M'Coy*, 4 Cow., [***15** 551. The motion for judgment as in case of nonsuit is denied, without costs.

Rule accordingly.

Cited in—1 Paige, 83; 2 Barb., 376; 9 How. Pr., 344; 5 Abb., 230.

WRIGHT *v.* JEFFREY.

Practice—Special Bail.

Putting in special bail without process, warrants the plaintiff's proceeding against the defendant, as if process had been served.

And where the *capias ad respondendum* was returnable on Sunday; yet held, that putting in special bail, though without knowledge of the defect, was a waiver of it.

And so, it seems, even if it had been served on Sunday.

Citation—1 Cow., 209.

THE *capias ad respondendum* was returnable on Sunday; and without knowing this fact, the defendant had put in special bail.

Mr. H. Stephens, for the defendant, moved to set aside the *capias*, and all subsequent proceedings.

Mr. J. C. Wright, contra.

Curia. The motion must be denied. It was not material whether the defendant had knowledge of the defect or not when he put in special bail. Putting in bail would have warranted the plaintiff in proceeding without any process. The case is not within the Statute, or the rule of public policy which forbids any ministerial act in the course of a cause to be performed on Sunday. It is probably a mere clerical mistake of the return day. It was taken for granted, however, by *Vanderpoel* v. *Wright*, 1 Cow., 209, that even in that case, which was the service of a *capias* on Sunday, an appearance would have cured the defect.

Motion denied.

Cited in—1 Wend., 37; 56 Barb., 113; 67 Barb., 388; 1 E. D. S., 390; 2 E. D. S., 39; 3 Daly, 108; 3 Co. R.; 171; 27 Mich., 38.

OGDEN *v.* PAYNE AND HOLMES.

Practice—Affidavit to put off a Cause—Discretion of Court.

The ordinary affidavit is sufficient to put off a cause at the circuit, unless circumstances of suspicion appear from counter affidavits, or otherwise.

It is not a circumstance of suspicion requiring more than the ordinary affidavit, that the witness, on account of whose absence the defendant applies to put off the cause, is the attorney of the plaintiff.

THIS cause, which was *assumpsit*, being noticed for trial at the last Saratoga Circuit, **16***] the defendant's counsel, on an *affidavit of Payne, that H. F. L., the attorney for the plaintiff, was a material witness for him in the cause, as he was advised by counsel and verily believed to be true; that he could not safely proceed to trial without his testimony; that he had endeavored to subpœna him, but he had gone a journey, as he was informed, to Philadelphia, and that he could not serve him with a subpœna, moved to put off the trial on the usual terms; but it appearing that Mr. L. was the attorney for the plaintiff, the judge required the defendants to state, by affidavit, what they expected to prove by him, in order that it might be seen whether the facts he would be called on to prove were not communicated to him professionally in the course of the cause. This the defendants' counsel declined to do; and the judge ordered the trial to proceed. Whereupon the defendants' counsel declined to appear, and an inquest was taken by default.

Mr. L. H. Palmer, for the defendants, now moved to set aside the inquest, for irregularity.

Mr. E. Cowen, contra, cited 3 Burr., 1514.

Curia. No doubt according to the case cited from Burrow, the judge has a discretion in certain cases, whether he will put off the trial upon the common affidavit. This is a very rational rule; and it is important that it should sometimes be exercised to prevent delay; but the rule does not attach, unless, by counter affidavits or otherwise, circumstances of suspicion are made to appear. Nothing of the kind appeared in this instance. It is the common case of a motion to put off the trial, for the absence of a material witness, whose attendance ordinary diligence could not procure. The action was *assumpsit*. We do not see that suspicion could attach from the mere fact that the witness was the attorney for the plaintiff. There is nothing unusual in such a circumstance, and the defendants should not be holden to disclose particulars. It might give the opposite party an undue advantage, and should not be required in the usual case.

RULE: That the inquest be set aside and a new trial granted, on payment of the costs of the circuit to the time of applying *to [***17** the d to put off the trial; and that the residue of the costs abide the event of the suit.

Cited in—7 Cow., 384; 1 Wend., 37; 8 Wend., 71; 6 Hun, 75; 3 How. Pr., 50; 51 How. Pr., 353; 3 Abb. N. S., 296, 305; 4 Bos., 668; 6 Rob., 511; 7 Rob., 27; 37 Super., 427; 1 E. D. S., 390; 3 Co. R., 171.

EX PARTE CARMICHAEL.

Redemption on Judgment, by Attachment, before a Justice.

A creditor, upon a judgment obtained by attachment before a justice, may redeem lands sold on *fi. fa.* upon a previous judgment.

A judgment upon attachment before a justice has the same force with any other except as to the defendants' right of set-off.

CERTAIN real estate of one Draper having been sold on a judgment and *fi. fa.* in favor of Pumpelly, in this court, Carmichael afterwards, and within 15 months after the sale, obtained judgment for more than $25 against the same Draper, filed a transcript, &c., and offered to redeem as a judgment creditor. But the sheriff refused to receive the money, on the ground that Pumpelly might contest the right to redeem upon the judgment, it being upon attachment.

A motion was now made for a *mandamus* commanding the sheriff to convey to Carmichael.

Mr. S. Mack, for the relator.

Mr. W. Platt, contra.

Curia. There is no force in the objection that the judgment was by attachment. It was of equal force with one rendered upon personal notice, except as to the defendant's right of set-off. The motion must be granted.

Motion granted.

Cited in—8 Wend., 346.

SCHOOLCRAFT AND CHAPMAN
v.
LATHROP.

Practice—Effect of Taking the Benefit of Insolvent Act Pending Suit—Costs.

The plaintiff taking the benefit of the Insolvent Act pending the suit is no cause for staying the proceedings till security for costs filed, if his assignees are within the jurisdiction of the court.
It is well settled, that where judgment is against the plaintiff in a suit carried on for the benefit of an assignee, the latter is liable for the costs.

Citations—7 T. R., 292; 4 Johns., 484; 6 Taunt., 123; 2 Cow., 460.

AFTER verdict for the plaintiffs, they respectively obtained their discharge under Statute of Insolvency, after assigning all their property for the benefit of their creditors. The cause being noticed for argument on the part of the plaintiffs upon a bill of exceptions taken by the defendant at the trial,
18*] *It was now moved that all proceedings on the part of the plaintiffs should be staved till security for costs filed.

Mr. I. Hamilton, for the motion.

Mr. S. S. Lush, contra.

Curia. The cases are not uniform upon this question. *Vide Webb* v. *Ward*, 7 T. R., 292; *Ketcham* v. *Clark*, 4 Johns., 484; *Snow* v. *Townsend*, 6 Taunt., 123. But it is now the well settled practice that where one is beneficially interested in the demand of the plaintiff, as assignee, and the suit is carried on for his benefit upon judgment against the plaintiff, such assignee is liable for the costs (see *Waring* v. *Baret*, 2 Cow., 460), and their collection may be enforced by attachment. This suit going on for the benefit of the assignees, who are within the jurisdiction of the court, the security of the defendant is complete under that rule; and we deny the motion without costs.

Rule accordingly.

Cited in—18 Wend., 674; 20 Wend., 632; 1 Hill, 632; 15 Abb. Pr., 196; 43 N. J. L., 150.

BRACKET v. ALVORD.

Action for Rent—When Transitory.

Where the action for rent is founded on privity of contract, as between the lessor and lessee, it is transitory; otherwise, if on privity of estate, as where an assignee is a party.

MR. J. PLATT, for the defendant, moved to change the venue from the County of Onondaga to the County of Oswego. The affidavit upon which he moved was defective, in not stating that the defendant's witnesses residing in the latter county were material as advised by counsel, but he relied on the action being local. The affidavit stated that it was an action for rent upon a lease given by the plaintiff to the defendant of lands in Oswego.

Mr. J. Edwards, contra, cited 1 Dunl., 244.

Curia. The distinction is that where the action for rent is founded on privity of contract, as between lessor and lessee, there the action is transitory; but if on privity of estate, as between the lessor and the assignee of the lessee, or the assignee *of the lessor [*19 and the lessee, &c., it is local.(a) The motion must be denied.

Motion denied.

(a) Corp. of N. Y. v. Dawson, 2 Johns. Cas., 335, and the cases there cited.

EX PARTE HAYWOOD.

*Practice—Statute—When Appeal Lies under—*Mandamus.

Under the Act, sess. 47, ch. 238, secs. 36, 38, an appeal lies in all cases, whether the judgment of the justice be upon an issue of law or fact.

Citations—Act, sess. 41, ch. 94, secs. 17, 18, p. 82; Act, sess. 47, ch. 238, secs. 36, 7, 8, pp. 294-296.

HAYWOOD sued Miller before a justice of Columbia; Miller pleaded the general issue and a special plea. To the latter there was a demurrer, upon which the justice gave judgment against Haywood, who appealed to the Columbia C. P.; but that court quashed the appeal upon the authority of *Peters* v. *Parsons*, 18 Johns., 140, and *Breese* v. *Williams*, 20 *Id.*, 280. And now,

Mr. D. B. Tallmadge moved (*ex parte*) for an alternative *mandamus* commanding that court to set aside the rule by which they ordered the appeal to be quashed, and to proceed upon the appeal. He said the cases relied upon were under the Act of 1818, sess. 41, ch. 94, secs. 17, 18, p. 82, which differed from the late Act, sess. 47, ch. 238, secs. 36-38, pp. 294-296. And,

The Court were clearly of this opinion. They said the cases cited went upon the construction of the 17th, 18th and 19th sections of the Act of 1818, but the provisions of the Act of 1824 are materially different. The 38th section provides expressly that all issues in law upon appeal shall be tried by the court, and all issues of fact by a jury. The pleadings are in all cases to be the same as those before the justice. There can be no mistake, therefore, as to the intention of the Legislature that an appeal is the remedy in all cases, whether the judgment be upon an issue of law or of fact. Let an alternative *mandamus* go.

Motion granted.

---

*EX PARTE WARD. [*20

Practice—New Trial.

A judge of the C. P., counselor, &c., may consent to a new trial without having been present at the trial.

IN trover, by Ward against Esty, in the Ontario C. P. Howell, first judge, a counselor at law of this court, was not present at the trial or any part of it; but the verdict being for the plaintiff, he consented, on a motion afterwards made, that a new trial should be granted on the merits.

Mr. J. C. Spencer now moved for a *mandamus* commanding that court to set aside their rule for a new trial, and proceed to judgment. He contended that the true construction of the proviso in the 3d section of the Act concerning the Courts of C. P., 2 R. L., 141,

142, is that the judge who is counselor, and assenting to the new trial, shall be present at the trial. How can he judge whether the verdict be against evidence if he has not heard it? By the section cited, these courts are to hear, try and determine. If the counselor did not hear, how can he judge as to a new trial? Will it be said that he can obtain a competent knowledge from the notes or reports of the other judges, or from affidavits? Such never could have been the intention of the statute. Suppose a judge newly appointed after a trial; ought he to be permitted to award a new trial?

Mr. M. H. Sibley, contra.

Curia. The proviso relied upon is "that no new trial shall be granted otherwise than for irregularity, unless one of the judges present and concurring shall be of the degree of counselor at law in the Supreme Court of this State." This presence and concurrence are referable to the time of granting the motion; not the time of trial. It must depend on the judge's own discretion upon the means of information and circumstances of the case, whether he will interfere. We deny the motion, but without costs.

Motion denied.

21*] *STRONG

v.

PLATNER ET AL., Executors of PLATNER.

Practice—New Trial—Affidavits in Support of.

On a motion for a new trial on account of newly discovered evidence, or to set aside the report of referees upon the merits and other enumerated motions, founded upon affidavit, counter affidavits may be read without being previously served on the party moving.

MR. E. WILLIAMS moved for a new trial, on the ground of newly discovered evidence, and for the misconduct of a juror.

Mr. B. F. Butler, contra, offered counter affidavits.

Mr. Williams said this being a calendar motion, counter affidavits should not be read, unless served upon the party moving. That the affidavits offered had not been served.

SUTHERLAND, J. We held, at the last term, that on moving to set aside the report of referees, upon the merits, which is a calendar motion, counter affidavits might be read without being served; and,

Per Curiam. There is no difference, in this respect, between enumerated and non-enumerated motions.

The affidavits were read, accordingly.

STOKES

v.

CAMPBELL, an Infant, by J. CAMPBELL, his Guardian, Impleaded with T. CAMPBELL.

Practice—Motion to Amend, Plea Allowed after Reversal of Judgment on Demurrer—Costs.

On reversing a judgment of the C. P., given for the defendant on a demurrer to one of his pleas, he was allowed to amend his plea upon payment of costs.

THIS action was originally commenced in the C. P. of the City and County of N. Y. The defendant pleaded two pleas, one of which was demurred to by the plaintiff, upon which judgment was given for the defendant in the court below. On error to this court, the judgment was reversed.

A motion was now made to amend the plea, so as to put the cause at issue upon both pleas, and have a trial at the circuit. And it was insisted that the defendant below ought not to be prejudiced by the decision there for him. The C. P. would have allowed an amendment if they had deemed the demurrer well taken. Dunl. Pr., 533, 534, and the cases there cited.

**Mr. A. S. Garr*, for the motion. [*22

Mr. E. Baldwin, contra.

The Court granted the motion, on payment of costs.

Motion granted.

HONAY & CHAPMAN *v.* CHESTERMAN.

Practice—Notice of Argument.

If the party making a case do not serve a copy of it upon the opposite party, at least four days before the term at which it is noticed for argument by the opposite party, on an affidavit of this fact and of service of notice of argument, the relief sought by the case will be denied.

Citations—14 Johns., 219; 4 Cow., 537.

MR. J. L. WENDELL, for the defendant, moved to bring on the motion for a new trial, on a case made, in its order on the calendar.

S. A. Foot, contra, read an affidavit made by the plaintiff's attorney, of the service of a notice of argument by the plaintiff's attorney on the defendant's attorney; also an affidavit that the defendant's attorney, who made the case, had not served a copy of it on the plaintiff's attorney on or before Oct. 15, the term commencing on the 17th; and moved that the motion for a new trial be denied upon this ground.

Curia. Take your motion. It is the settled practice, that the party who makes the case must serve a copy on the other party. *Peck* v. *Peck*, 14 Johns., 219; *Jackson* v. *Harrington*, 4 Cow., 537. If this be not done at least four days before the term, the consequence is, that on the opposite party showing this fact by affidavit, the motion upon the case must be denied, provided the party moving for the denial have noticed the argument on his part.

Motion, for a new trial, denied.

Overruled—6 Cow., 609.

---

*BEEKMAN *v.* REED. [*23

Practice—Notice of Motion.

A motion, though on the calendar must be noticed for the particular term at which it is intended to be made.

A notice of a motion for a particular term, and that if not then made it will be continued on the calendar, from term to term, until it shall be made, is insufficient.

MR. S. A. FOOT moved to bring on the argument of this cause upon affidavits made for the purpose of a motion to set aside the report of referees upon the merits. The cause was on the calendar; and he read the proof of the service of a notice that a motion would be made to set aside the report, upon the affidavits, at the last August Term, at the Academy in Utica; and if it should not then be made, that the cause would be continued on the calendar from term to term, until it should be brought on.

Mr. J. M'Kown objected that the notice of the motion was insufficient for the present term.

Curia. The notice is insufficient, and we cannot hear the motion. The regular practice is to notice for the particular term at which the motion is to be made, and we must not allow this course to be departed from, where no reason is shown for it. Causes cannot be continued in this manner by a single notice running from term to term.

Motion denied.

STAFFORD ET AL. v. RICE.

Witnesses—One Whose Name Appears on Negotiable Paper Competent to Prove it Void in its Inception.

One whose name appears upon negotiable paper may, notwithstanding, be a witness to prove that it was void in its inception, for usury, or other cause. Winton v. Saidler, 3 Johns. Cas., 185, contra, is not law.

Citations—3 Johns. Cas., 185; 17 Johns., 176.

ASSUMPSIT, tried at the Washington Circuit, June 16, 1825, before Duer, Circuit Judge.

The plaintiffs, on the trial, produced in evidence a promissory note, made by the defendant, to Samuel Topliff, or bearer, dated Feb. 16, 1820, for $44.99, payable six months after date, the execution of which was admitted.

The defendant then called Samuel Topliff as a witness, who was objected to by the plaintiffs counsel, and rejected by the judge.

The defendant then offered to prove by 24*] Topliff, that at *the time the note was given, he, the witness, had no interest in it; but took it for the benefit, and on the behalf of the plaintiffs; and immediately afterwards transferred and delivered it to the plaintiffs, and advised them of all the facts relative to the making of the note, and upon what consideration it was made. This evidence was also objected to by the plaintiffs' counsel, and rejected by the judge. The jury found a verdict for the plaintiffs for $60.64.

Mr. S. Stevens, for the defendant, now moved for a new trial. He contended, that though the payee might not be a competent witness for the indorsee, or the one to whom he had transferred the note by delivery, yet he was clearly a competent witness for the maker. His interest, if he has any, is against the party calling him. In the case before the court, he could have been received to testify for either party, being in fact a mere conduit or agent through whom the note passed to the plaintiffs. He was equally indifferent with any third person. The only ground of objection must rest upon the rule, *quod nemo allegans suam turpitudinem est audiendus.* (17 Johns., 176.) But the facts offered in evidence were such as to disprove any turpitude on the part of the witness; and, if any existed, to fix it on the plaintiffs. In *Tuthill* v. *Davis*, 20 Johns., 285, the court seem even to question, whether *Winton* v. *Saidler*, 3 Johns. Cas., 185, upon the authority of which the maxim cited was applied to indorsers and others, whose names appear upon negotiable paper, is to be considered as law. But it is enough that nothing immoral or illegal was offered in proof. The witness was certainly competent to prove anything else.

Mr. Jacob Lansing, contra. The offer of proof by the payee was general and indefinite; and had he been received to testify, would have reached the fact of usury, or any other illegal consideration. The cases have not gone so far as to allow one, whose name appears upon negotiable paper, to impeach it by proof of any fact which may render it void *ab origine.* He must be confined in his testimony to such matter as arose subsequently to the giving of the note by *which it is discharged; [*25 as payment, release, &c. The plaintiffs rely on the case of *Winton* v. *Saidler*; and it was upon the authority of that case that the judge excluded Topliff.

WOODWORTH, *J.* *Winton* v. *Saidler* is not law. It is now several years since that case has been acted upon; and in *Powell* v. *Powers* it was directly overruled.

SUTHERLAND, *J.* Under the later decisions, a witness, whose name appears upon negotiable paper, may be received to prove usury in its inception.

SAVAGE, *Ch. J.* *Winton* v. *Saidler* has been repeatedly overruled, and can no longer be considered as law.

Mr. Lansing agreed that if that case was not law there must be a new trial; and,

Per totam Curiam,
New trial granted.

Cited in—3 Wend., 416; Hoffm., 549.

THOMAS v. BULKLEY, Manucaptor of COFFIELD.

Practice—Surrender of Principal by Bail—Sickness of Principal.

Bail may surrender their principal, and obtain an *exoneretur*, on motion, after the 8 days allowed, *ex gratia*, for surrender, if the surrender within that time was prevented by the sickness of the principal; and this, though no order to stay proceedings, or rule for enlarging the time to surrender, was obtained within the 8 days, the sickness of the principal not being known to the bail within that time.

Citation—1 Johns. Cas., 413.

THE bail in this case having become fixed by a return of the *ca. sa.* in the original cause, of *Thomas* v. *Coffield*, a *capias ad respondendum* was issued to the Sheriff of the City and County of N. Y., against the bail, and served,

NOTE.—*Competency of witnesses—Parties to bills and notes, as witnesses, against validity.* See Baker v. Arnold, 1 Cai., 258, *note*; Woodhull v. Holmes, 10 Johns., 231, *note*.

returnable the 4th day of August last. Aug. 15, the bail received a letter from his principal, dated and bearing its post mark at Edenton, N. C., Aug. 8 (in reply to letters written by the bail, on the 10th and 25th of July preceding, requesting him to surrender himself), stating that he had been so ill with a fever, that he could not before peruse or answer the letters from the bail, Aug. 16, the bail procured an order staying all proceedings in the suit against him, for the purpose of moving this court for further time to surrender. After this, the principal started for the City of N. 26*] Y.; but on his way *suffered a relapse; and did not reach the city till Oct. 13, when (as soon as his health would permit, Oct. 19, 1825) he surrendered himself to the Sheriff of N. Y., in exoneration of his bail.

Mr. E. Cowen, for the motion, cited *Boardman* v. *Fowler*, 1 Johns. Cas., 413; *Livingston* v. *Bartles*, 4 Johns., 478, and *Rathbone* v. *Warren, Id.*, 310.

Mr. A. Van Vechten, contra, said that sickness could not be received as an excuse for not surrendering the principal; and will not be listened to, even where the application is made before the expiration of the 8 days. *Wynn* v. *Petty*, 4 East, 102; *Grant* v. *Fagan, Id.*, 189; *Olcott* v. *Lilly*, 4 Johns., 407.

Curia. We should, clearly, have enlarged the time to surrender this sick man, had his sickness been known to the bail, and disclosed to us within the eight days allowed, *ex gratia*, for surrender, after the return day of the *capias* against the bail; and the case would then have finally come to an *exoneretur*. The facts not being known to the bail within that time, he could neither obtain an order to stay proceedings, nor apply to the court to give the further time. He has, therefore, been guilty of no laches; and by ordering an *exoneretur*, we are only doing directly what would, had not unavoidable circumstances intervened, ultimately have been obtained in another way. We think the bail should not be prejudiced by the sickness of his principal, especially as the plaintiff will not suffer by his discharge, which must granted on payment of costs. There is no case in this court precisely in point; but we think the principle of *Boardman* v. *Fowler*, 1 Johns. Cas., 413, applies. Let an *exoneretur* be entered, on payment of the costs of the action against the bail, and of opposing this motion.

Rule accordingly.

Cited in—20 How. Pr., 20; 10 Abb. Pr., 280; 12 Abb. Pr., 84; 79 Pa., 332; 21 Am. Rep., 64.

27*] *Ex parte EASTABROOKS.

Practice—Appeal Bond.

The appellee in the C. P. cannot object that the appeal bond is in the penalty of more than double the judgment before the justice.

THE Court of C. P. of Warren Co. quashed an appeal from a justice's court, brought by Eastabrooks against Rockwell, because the penalty of the appeal bond was more than double the amount of the judgment rendered by the court below.

A motion was now made for a *mandamus*, commanding the Court of C. P. to vacate the rule quashing the appeal, and to proceed in the cause.

Mr. W. Hay, Jr., for the motion.

The motion was not opposed; but,

The Court said they were very clearly of opinion that the penalty being more than double the amount of the judgment, was no objection; though its being less, was so, because it might abridge the rights of the appellee. It may be for his benefit, but cannot possibly injure him, that the bond is for more. And they awarded an alternative *mandamus*.

Rule accordingly.

Cited in—17 Wend., 70; 62 N. Y., 116; 1 Hun, 525; 3 T. & C., 629; 2 Co. R., 52.

DAVENBAGH *v.* M'KINNIE.

Practice—Production of Paper, by Third Party.

The court will not, on motion, compel a third person, no way interested in the suit, to produce a private paper of his own, for the inspection of a party.

IN WASTE. One Ellis was the grantee in, and had possession of, a deed constituting a link in the plaintiff's deduction of title; and on an affidavit that he withheld the inspection of this deed from the plaintiff, by means whereof he was embarrassed in setting out his title in the declaration, and could not safely try his cause,

Mr. A. C. Paige moved for a rule upon Ellis, requiring him to allow the plaintiff's attorney to take a copy of this deed, and cited *Wallis* v. *Murray*, 4 Cow., 399; 19 Johns., 268; 2 Camph., 94, *note;* 12 Johns., 225; 1 Campb., *562, per Sir J. Mansfield; 11 Johns., [*28 245; 2 Archb. Pr., 196, and 4 Taunt., 157, 161.

Mr. J. J. Danforth said, whatever the court might do, if this deed were in the hands of the party, they would never call upon a third person in this form to produce a paper. He is liable to be called on by a subpœna *duces tecum*. But this being an action for a tort, the court will not even compel a party to produce papers for the inspection of his antagonist; and so this court held in *Denslow* v. *Fowler*, 2 Cow., 592.

Curia. If the action were upon contract, and the motion unobjectionable on this ground, we would not grant this application. It is aimed against a third person not interested in the cause; and seeks to pry into his private papers. If the plaintiff deem it material, he must compel its production by subpœna *duces tecum*, or in some other way than by motion.

Motion denied.

WILLARD AND PLATT *v.* THE MAYOR, &c., OF HUDSON.

Practice—Costs.

A brief, attorney, and counsel fee, not allowable on a motion of course in partition, and other real actions.

IN PARTITION. It was submitted to the court, whether the attorney for the plaintiffs should be allowed in taxation of costs upon a judgment against the defendants, a brief, and an attorney and counsel fee on each ordinary motion in the course of the cause; and,

Mr. C. Bushnell, for the plaintiffs, contended that he should; that in a real action there is no common rule, or rule of course; but all motions must be made in open court, and must stand on the footing of any special motion as to the costs.

Mr. E. Williams, contra, said that these were motions of course, though made in open court. Special motions, properly so called, are founded on affidavit or other proof, of which the opposite party must be apprised, and have notice
29*] *of the motion. The ordinary motions in real actions, do not imply opposition; and there is, therefore, no need of a brief and fees for argument as upon special motions.

Curia. These charges cannot be allowed. They are inadmissible, except upon such motions as require notice to the adverse party, being founded upon special cause. The ordinary rules, taken in the progress of a real action, are as much rules of course as those which are entered in the common rule book. The only difference is in the form of moving them, and the time of entry, which is in open court, and within the term.(*a*)

Rule accordingly.

(*a*)—See 1 Reg. Gen., April Term, 1796.

EX PARTE VASQUES.

Practice—Submission to Arbitration—Time of.

A submission to arbitration, may, within 1 R. L., 125, be made a rule of court, as well after, as before the award.

VASQUES and M'Reever had submitted certain matters in difference to arbitrators, and agreed that the submission should be made a rule of the Court of C. P. of the City and County of N. Y. The arbitrators having awarded the payment of a sum of money to Vasques, he applied to the C. P. for a rule enforcing the award; which the court declined to grant, on the ground that the submission not being made a rule of court before the award the parties should be left to their usual remedy by suit.

A motion was now made for a *mandamus*, commanding the Court of C. P. to make the submission a rule of court; and 1 R. L., 125; *Knight* v. *Carey*, 1 Cow., 39, and the *notes* to that case, were cited.

Mr. J. M'Kown, for the motion.

Curia. We see no reason for the distinction taken by the Court of C. P. The practice ap-
30*] pears to be *well settled that the submission may be made a rule of court as well after as before the award. Let an alternative *mandamus* go.

Rule accordingly.

CHANDLER *v.* BICKNELL.

Practice—Motion for Judgment as in Case of Nonsuit—Opposition to.

It is not a good ground of opposition to a motion for judgment as in case of nonsuit, that the judge allowed the plaintiff to withdraw a juror, because of an unexpected defect in his proof.

THE plaintiff unexpectedly failing at the trial to establish by proof the absence from the State of a subscribing witness to the bond on which this suit was brought, so as to let in secondary evidence; on his motion, the circuit judge allowed him to withdraw a juror; and the cause went off for the circuit. And now,

Mr. J. Platt, for the defendant, moved for judgment as in case of nonsuit.

Mr. C. P. Kirkland, contra, insisted that where the circuit judge allows the plaintiff to withdraw a juror, this excuses him both from payment of the costs, and a judgment of nonsuit; and he cited Tidd, 785; 1 Archb. Pr., 174.

Curia. We do not see why this case should not stand on the same footing, as if the cause had gone off at the circuit, for want of sufficient testimony on the part of the plaintiff, without a jury being sworn. We might refuse to nonsuit the plaintiff, or excuse from stipulating; but not from costs. There must be the usual rule *nisi*.

Motion granted.

*EX PARTE C. & A. THOMPSON. [*31

Practice—Control of Execution, Issued by County Clerk, on Judgment by Justice, by the C. P.

The C. P. may set aside, or otherwise control an execution issued by the county clerk, on a judgment rendered by a justice of the peace, transcribed, and docketed by the clerk of the county.

THE Court of C. P. of Saratoga were moved to set aside the docket, or record of a justice's judgment against C. & A. Thompson, in favor of Newcomb, and the execution thereon issued by the county clerk; upon affidavits, that before the transcript was filed, the judgment had been paid and satisfied by the Thompsons. This motion was denied by the C. P. upon the ground that they had no jurisdiction of the matter.

A motion was now made for a *mandamus*, commanding that court to take cognizance of the motion.

Mr. J. Bloore, for the motion.

The motion was not opposed; but,

The Court said they had no doubt that the Court of C. P. had jurisdiction of the case—that the execution was their process. That the merits of the motion were not before this court; but on the single point of jurisdiction, they granted a

Rule to show cause.(*a*)

Cited in—21 Am. Dec., 310 (6 Wend., 213).

(*a*) See Sholts v. Judges of Yates, 2 Cow., 506, 508.

EX PARTE BROWN.

Practice — Non-enumerated Motion — Time of Hearing.

A non-enumerated motion will not, in general, be heard after the hearing of non-enumerated motions has been closed for the term, though the cause of the motion arose so late, that it could not be noticed four days before such close.

A notice of such a motion may be for a day which happens after the close of non-enumerated business: but it is at the peril of the party; and if this business be closed before the day arrive, he cannot make the motion, but must pay costs.

Where the cause of the motion arises thus late, it seems the safer course is to obtain a judge's order to stay proceedings.

But in a case where such an order cannot have any effect, the court will hear the motion, after the non-enumerated business is closed.

The Supreme Court will not interfere by *mandamus*, to control the mere chamber business of a judge of the C. P.

NOV. 8. After the court had finished the regular hearing of non-enumerated motions for the term,

32*] **Mr. A. Spencer* moved for a *mandamus* to the first judge of the Court of C. P. of the City and County of N. Y., commanding him to vacate certain orders which he had made on the 1st inst., discharging one Smith upon common bail, in certain actions brought against him in that court by Brown. Notice of the motion had been given for to-day.

Mr. J. L. Wendell, contra, objected that it was too late in term for the motion, the non-enumerated motions being closed.

Mr. Spencer said, the cause of the motion had arisen so late that 4 days' notice of the motion could not be given for a day in term preceding the close of the non-enumerated motions; and that as no operative order could be given at chambers by a judge of this court. to stay the proceedings in the court below, or control it in any way upon the subject of the motion, it was an exception to the general rule.

Curia. We have generally refused to hear non-enumerated motions after that class of business is closed for the term; and this though the cause of the motion may have arisen too late to admit of a notice at an earlier day. The notice may be given for any day in term, if there be an excuse for not giving it for the first; but it is at the peril of the party. If the business close before the day of the notice arrive, he must take his order from a judge or commissioner to stay proceedings, and renew his notice for the next term. We have this very term, given costs for attending to oppose a motion under these circumstances, though counsel were in court prepared to make it pursuant to the notice. But we consider the present motion an exception to our general rule. An order to stay proceedings would be inoperative. We will, therefore, hear the motion.

The motion was accordingly heard; but,

The Court on the merits of the application being further disclosed; said they must deny it, being clear against interfering by *mandamus*, touching the mere chamber business, of a judge of the C. P.

Motion denied.

Cited in—1 Wend., 79; 18 Wend., 515; 3 Abb. Pr., 66.

33*] *EX PARTE DAVIS AND SOWLE.

Practice—Jurisdiction of the C. P. on Appeal under Defective Bond—May Award Costs.

Though a C. P. cannot entertain jurisdiction of a cause on appeal, if the bond be defective; yet, on quashing the appeal for that cause, the parties being before them, they have jurisdiction of the person; and may award the costs of the motion.

ON dismissing an appeal as irregularly brought, by Davis and Sowle against Waugh, from a justice's court to the C. P. of Monroe, the parties being in court, and the motion being opposed, that court awarded costs of the motion against the appellants; and now,

Mr. J. Platt moved for a *mandamus*, commanding that court to vacate the rule, on the ground that they had no jurisdiction for any purpose; and he cited *Ex parte Shether*, 4 Cow., 540, and *Ex parte Chryslin, Ib.*, 80; also Laws, sess. 47, ch. 238, sec. 36, p. 295.

The motion was not opposed; but,

Per Curiam. These parties were before the court, who we think, had jurisdiction over their persons for the purpose of costs.(*a*)

Motion denied.

Cited in—8 Abb. Pr., 291; 1 Wall. Jr., 188; 2 Wood & M., 420.

(*a*) In like manner, this court sometimes give costs against one who moves for a *mandamus*, if the motion be opposed, though it be denied; and therefore no cause be commenced. *Ex parte* Root, 4 Cow., 548.

JACKSON, ex dem. HOWELL,
v.
DELANCY.

Practice—Writ of Error, in Ejectment, Does not Stay Action for Mesne *Profits.*

A writ of error, by the defendant in ejectment, will not protect him against an immediate action for the *mesne* profits.

IN ejectment, the judgment being for the plaintiff, and a writ of possession executed, at the last term, the defendant moved for and took a rule for leave to turn the case made in this cause into a special verdict, for the purpose of bringing a writ of error; and the rule was, also, that until the writ of error should be determined, no action for the *mesne* profits should be brought; and now, on producing a certified copy of the rule; and on notice of a motion for that purpose,

Mr. A. Burr moved to modify the rule of the last term, so as to permit the plaintiff to proceed for the *mesne* profits; and *he [*34 cited *Roe* v. *Jones*, 1 H. Bl., 84; Adams on Eject., 329.

Mr. R. Bogardus, contra.

Curia. It appears, by the authorities cited, to be well settled that a writ of error will not stay an action for *mesne* profits. No particular circumstances exist to take this case out of the general rule. We think the modification applied for should be allowed.(*a*)

Motion granted.

(*a*) Donford v. Ellis, 12 Mob., 138, S. P.

THE PEOPLE, ex rel. S. & O. TITUS,
v.
THE JUDGES OF THE COURT OF C. P. OF THE COUNTY OF DUTCHESS.

Practice—On Appeal to the C. P. Parties need not Execute the Appeal bond—Two Parties—Two Partners.

On appeal to the C. P. from the judgment of a justice, the party need not execute the appeal bond.

It is sufficient, if executed by competent sureties.
One of two parties cannot bind the other, by executing an appeal bond for both.
So of two partners.

ON appeal from a justice's court by S. and O. Titus, against Schermerhorn, the C. P. of Dutchess dismissed the appeal, on the ground that the appeal bond was executed by only one of the appellants, being signed and sealed by him thus: "Stephen & Obediah Titus. (L. S.)"

On the judges showing this for cause, a motion was now made for a peremptory *mandamus*, commanding them to set aside their rule dismissing the appeal; and to proceed upon it.

Mr. H. Swift, for the motion.

Mr. T. J. Oakley, contra, said the Statute, sess. 47, ch. 238, sec. 37, required the bond to be signed by the party appealing. The word "party" is often used in the same section; and in a sense which, it cannot be doubted, extends to all the parties. Thus, either party conceiving himself aggrieved may appeal. The party appealing is to serve a notice signed by the party appealing &c. So the word "appellant," although grammatically singular, was doubtless intended, as used in this section, of all the parties who appeal. Thus, in case judgment is rendered against the appellant, the 35*] bond is that *he shall pay, &c. If the judgment may have been rendered against the appellant before the justice, the further condition shall be added, &c., and so in various other instances (which he put), where party or appellant, in the singular, has a plural meaning. Is the case before the court an exception? It would seem to be necessary that the party should himself execute the bond, in order to signify his assent to the appeal, and give the C. P. the jurisdiction. The Statute concerning Writs of Error, 1 R. L., 143, sec. 2, expressly provides for an absent party, and requires three sureties; when otherwise, two would be enough.

Curia. Clearly one of two men, though partners, cannot bind the other by specialty upon the footing of his general authority. But we think there is no necessity for the party to give the bond, provided the security is fully competent without him. (The main object of the bond is, not to give the court jurisdiction, though it is made incidentally necessary, for this purpose, by the statute; but to make the appellee secure in recovering his demand. This purpose is just as well answered without the party, as with him, provided competent sureties execute the bond.) The court below erred, and the motion must be granted.

Rule for a peremptory mandamus.

Overruled—7 Cow., 428.

EX PARTE HOLBROOK, FESSENDEN, ADAMS AND LEE.

Practice—Appeal Bond—Execution by Attorney.

A general power to defend a cause will not authorize the attorney to execute an appeal bond in the name of his client.

ON appeal to the C. P. of Jefferson Co., by Holbrook, Fessenden, Adams and Lee, against W. & I. Symonds, the court quashed the appeal, because the appeal bond was executed by C. Rice, as attorney for Holbrook and Fessenden. It appeared in that court, that the bond was duly executed by the other two appellants; and that Rice had a power from *Holbrook and Fessenden, who resided [*36 in Vt., to do everything necessary and proper to be done in defending any suit or suits brought or which might be brought against them. The bond was duly executed by the proper surety, approved by the justice who tried the cause.

Mr. S. M. Hopkins moved for a *mandamus*, commanding the Court of C. P. to set aside the rule quashing the appeal, and proceed upon it. He noticed the argument in the last cause, which had been drawn from the provision of the Statute concerning Writs of Error, in favor of absent persons. But he said this provision was not necessary. The English Statute relative to Writs of Error upon judgments in dower or ejectment, from which ours was taken, contained no such provision; and yet an absent party had been excused from entering into the recognizance. Good security by third persons was holden enough. (2 Crompt. Pr., 349-351.) But in this case the attorney had authority to execute the bond.

Mr. Talcott, Atty-Gen., contra, said a general authority to defend would not extend to the execution of a bond.

One of several parties cannot appeal. It would be dangerous to allow such a practice, by which his co-party may be condemned in an increased judgment, without his knowledge or consent. The case from Crompton was one of a recognizance not executed by a party at all. Will this court go so far in the case of an appeal? We trust they will not legislate, because the English courts have done so.

This cause was argued after the next preceding one of *People* v. *The Judges*, but before that was decided. In this case, also,

The Court held the bond to be sufficient; and,

SUTHERLAND, *J.*, remarked, in giving the opinion of the court, that it involved the same point with that; for it was clear that a general power to defend all causes, &c., would not authorize the attorney to execute an appeal bond in the name of his client.

Rule for a mandamus.

Cited in—7 Cow., 428; 11 Abb. Pr., 72.

*BENEDICT *v.* RIPLEY. [*37

Practice—Amendment to Plea.

A defendant cannot amend his plea of course under the 8 Reg. Gen. of April Term, 1796, unless it be demurred to.
And then, he cannot add a new plea.

IN covenant, the plaintiff declared, assigning several breaches, to which the defendant pleaded two pleas, tendering an issue to the country, which were not demurred to. Nearly two years after, he entered a rule to amend, and pleaded, under the rule, four additional pleas.

Mr. W. L. F. Warren, for the plaintiff, moved to set aside the rule, and the pleas under it, as irregular. He cited 8 Reg. Gen.

April Term, 1796; under which, he said, the defendant could not amend his plea of course, at any time, unless it be demurred to. That a plea could not be added, he cited 18 Johns., 310; Duul. Pr., 695, 292.

Mr. P. H. M'Omber, contra.

Curia. Clearly the defendant could not amend his plea at any time. The 8 Reg. Gen. of April Term, 1796, is the only authority for amending of course. Under this rule you cannot amend a plea unless it be demurred to; and then you cannot add a new plea. The motion must be granted.

Motion granted.

Cited in—9 How. Pr., 141; 22 How. Pr., 231; 13 Abb. Pr., 270.

BLAKE, by his Guardian, *v.* HALL.

Practice—Certiorari, *Removes the Record Itself.*

A *certiorari* removes, in contemplation of law, the record itself, and where the plaintiff appeared in the C. P. by guardian, and the defendant appeared there and the plaintiff had filed a declaration; held, that he might proceed against the defendant in the Supreme Court, on the removal of the cause by *certiorari*, by immediately taking a rule against him to plead, and for want of a plea, take a default.

Citation—3 Cai., 86.

THIS cause was removed by *certiorari* to this court from the C. P. of the City and County of N. Y., after the plaintiff had declared in the court below. After the return of the *certiorari*, Aug. 23 last, the plaintiff entered with the clerk of this court a rule to plead to the declaration in the court below, of which he gave the defendant notice; and for want of a plea within the usual time, entered a default. Neither special nor common bail had been **38***] *filed in this court; nor had the defendant appeared here in any other form; nor had the plaintiff, who was an infant, and sued below by his guardian, had any guardian or next friend appointed in this court.

Mr. J. M'Kown moved to set aside the proceedings for irregularity. He contended that the plaintiff should have commenced his proceedings *de novo*, by having a guardian appointed, awaiting the defendant's appearance, and declaring in this court. He admitted that *Wolfe* v. *Horton*, 3 Cai., 86, was against this; but *Rex* v. *North*, 2 Salk., 565, on which alone the case in Caines went, does not decide where the proceedings are to begin in the court above; and the English authorities are against the practice pursued in this case. (Tidd, 349, Riley's ed., *Ib.*, 6th ed., 411; Bac. Abr., *Certiorari*, K; 4 Vin. Abr., 359, pl. 4; Lee's Dictionary of Pr., 286.)

Mr. B. F. Butler, contra cited 1 Dunl. Pr., 223.

Curia. A *certiorari* is in nature of a writ of error, and removes, in contemplation of law, the record itself. This was held in *Wolfe* v. *Horton* 3 Cai., 86. It follows that the cause is here, on the return of the *certiorari*, in the same situation as to the appearance of the parties, and other incidents, as it stood in the court below. And it proceeds here directly from the point at which it stopped below. The English practice appears to be different; but the practice of this court has been settled ever since the case of *Wolfe* v. *Horton*.

Motion denied.

LANSING ET AL., Executors, &c.,
v.
QUACKENBUSH.

Sale of Land on a fi. fa. *Remedy.*

Where the defendant has no title to land sold on a *fi. fa.* for which the sheriff has given a certificate of sale to the purchaser, and indorsed the sum bid on the *fi. fa.* relief will not be granted on motion; but the purchaser should go to a court of equity.

THE plaintiffs having sued out a *fi. fa.* against the defendant, upon a judgment of this court, to the Sheriff of Essex, *he sold [***39** certain lots of land supposed to belong to the defendant, situate in that county, at certain prices bid for each lot by Jacob Lansing, one of the plaintiff's and gave him a certificate of sale, specifying each lot and the sum for which it sold. The amount, in the aggregate, was $4,096, which he indorsed as paid upon the *fi. fa.* Before the sale, the defendant represented to the purchaser that he had title to certain of these lots, which sold for the greater portion of the sum indorsed; but which it turned out, on inquiry, belonged absolutely to another.

Mr. J. Lansing (*Mr. S. M. Hopkins* same side), therefore, now moved to amend, by reducing the amount of the indorsement to the amount bid for those lots to which the defendant had title, and striking from the certificate the lots to which he had no title.

Mr. S. Stevens, contra.

Curia. Clearly there must be a remedy in this case; but we do not grant it upon this motion, because we think the more proper forum, is a court of equity.

Motion denied.

Cited in—12 Wend., 253; 9 Paige, 40; 3 Barb. Ch., 587; 39 Super, 539; 4 McLean, 616; 59 Ind., 204; 66 Ind., 338; 49 Am. Dec., 214 (3 Barb. Ch., 528).

EX PARTE TAYLOE.

1. Habeas Corpus—*Court not Concluded by Finding of Coroner's Inquest.* 2. *Bail—Not Allowed, in Cases of Manslaughter, where there is no Reasonable doubt of Prisoner's Guilt.* 3. *Power of Supreme Court, in Relation to Bail.* 4. *Practice.*

The Supreme Court have the same powers in relation to bail as the English K. B.; and may let persons charged with criminal offenses to bail, in all cases whatsoever.

Upon the return of a *habeas corpus ad subjiciendum*, with the body of a prisoner, against whom a coroner's inquest have found an inquisition of murder or manslaughter, the court are not concluded by the finding; but will look into the depositions to see whether a crime has been committed, its nature, and the strength of proof by which the accusation was supported.

Though the crime appear to be but manslaughter, it is not of course to allow bail.

But if the guilt or innocence of the prisoner appear to be indifferent, he may be bailed.

Though the warrant of commitment be defective, the court will not discharge the prisoner finally for that reason: but if a crime be made out upon the depositions, the course is to discharge *pro forma*, but remand upon a special rule. Form thereof.

If there be no reasonable doubt of the guilt of a prisoner charged with committing a felony, he ought not to be bailed, even by Supreme Court.

Citations—Hawk., bk. 2, ch. 15, sec. 40 and 80; 2 Str., 911, 1242, 851; 1 Salk., 104; 2 T. R., 77, 267; 3 East,

157, 163, 165; 15 Mass., 277; 1 Wheel. Crim. Cas., 443, 446-7; 1 Chit. C. L., 98, 99, 113; 1 Roll., 268; Ld. Raym., 381; 3 Bulstr., 113; Com. Dig. Bail, F, 3; 4 Bl. Com., 181, 191, 299; Co. Entries, 354, 356; Kelyng, 89; 1 Str., 499; 6 St. Tr., 195; Foster C. L., 255, 277; 1 Hale P. C., 479; 1 East, C. L., 224; Dyer, 179, pl. 42 (2 Eliz.).

CHARLES TAYLOE was committed to the common jail of the County of Columbia, during the present term, for having slain one **40***] *Crandall; but the warrant of commitment did not recite enough to show a proper cause of commitment; and the court, at an early day in the present term, granted a *habeas corpus ad subjiciendum*, returnable before them, with a view to inquire whether the prisoner should be bailed. Upon the return of this writ, it appeared that a coroner's inquest, having inquired into the case, had returned an inquisition of manslaughter; and the depositions upon which Tayloe was committed, and on which the inquisition was founded, presented substantially this case; that Oct. 19, 1825, Crandall, the deceased, was standing near the Academy in Kinderhook, Columbia Co.; and was ordered by one of the students, a little boy, to leave the place where he stood, the little boy supposing that he (Crandall) wished to look into the dressing room of the scholars, it being the day of the public school exhibition. Crandall refused to go away at first, and the little boy threatened to bring other boys, who should compel him to depart. But this was not done, and he soon went away. Shortly after he was met in the street by the little boy and a large boy, at some distance from the Academy. An angry conversation was held between them, followed by a scuffle. Other students were sent for and arrived; and among these was the prisoner. All the school boys present then attacked the deceased, and the prisoner threw a stick at him. The deceased defended himself as well as he could. He alternately retreated and pursued some of the boys, who came out against him. At length he obtained a piece of board, with which he defended himself, and assailed his adversaries. Among others, he struck the prisoner with this piece of board; whereupon the prisoner stabbed him with a jack knife in the abdomen, giving him a wound, of which he died. After stabbing Crandall, and while standing a short distance from him, the prisoner admitted that he had done so, and said he would do it again on like provocation.

Mr. B. F. Butler moved that the prisoner be let to bail. He said that, at the utmost, the evidence made out a mere case of manslaughter. In applying the English practice, upon the sub- **41***] ject *of bail, to this court, it would be necessary to distinguish when the books speak of the K. B., whose high powers this court possesses, and classes of inferior magistrates, who are numerous, and possess the power of letting to bail in certain specified cases only. No doubt many cases, or rather *dicta*, which may be cited against this application, refer to the inferior magistrate; not to the Court of K. B. or a judge of that court, who undoubtedly possess the power, in their discretion, to bail in all cases whatsoever. (1 Chit. C. L., 98; Com. Dig., Bail, F, 4; 2 Hall., P. C., 129; 2 Hawk. ch. 15, secs. 40, 80.) The page of Chitty, just cited, gives the general rule in relation to manslaughter; and in *People* v. *Goodwin*, 1 Wheeler Crim. Cas., 443, before Spencer, late *Ch. J.*, after laying down the same rule, he says (*Id.*, 448) it "is adapted to all who can comply with its terms; and it is the misfortune of those who cannot give the necessary security." Several cases are there cited by the *Ch. J.*, in which bail has been allowed upon a charge of homicide. There are three cases in Coke's Entries, 354 to 356, which were copied from the rolls of the court, by which it will be seen that the power was exercised, in the reign of Elizabeth, to bail in cases of murder. And it appears by two of these entries, that the offenders, after being bailed, were convicted of manslaughter. The book, at the pages cited, purports to be copied from rolls of the K. B. then in actual existence; the number of the roll is given, as well as the dates and places of the several offenses, and the initials of the offenders; and it shows the power of the court to be very ancient, as well as that it will be exercised on actual indictment even for murder—not confined to cases of doubt, but where the prisoners were finally convicted. The entries are, *de gratia Curiæ speciala*, the offender is delivered on bail, &c., after the award of a *capias*, and an arrest. The only exception in case of manslaughter seems to be where a party is guilty by his own confession, or notoriously guilty, as the books say, which, in manslaughter, can only be upon his own confession. (2 Hawk. ch. 15, sec. 80.)

*The counsel also cited *Lisle's* case, [*42 Kelyng Cr. Cas., 89; 1 Bulst., 85; *King* v. *Poynes*, 3 Bulst., 113; *Herbert & Vaughan's* case, Latch, 12; also Selfridge's Trial, p. 8, 2d ed., who, he said, was bailed after an indictment for manslaughter; a stronger case than this, where no indictment is found.

It would not be denied, he said, that the court might look into the depositions, to see whether a manslaughter had been committed, notwithstanding the inquisition. He denied that the deposition made out manslaughter. But, at any rate, it could not but be seen, that if there was manslaughter in the case, it was of the very lowest grade. He was aware that there was no such things as legal degrees of manslaughter; but like every other offense, it was attended with different degrees of moral turpitude, and was more various in this respect than any other crime. It presented innumerable shades, from murder, the highest offense against the life of a fellow being, down to excusable homicide. It was upon this principle that the Legislature had allowed a great latitude of discretion to the court, who are to fix the punishment; and this court are warrantable in looking to these considerations, when called on to allow bail.

Mr. J. Wilcoxon, Dist. Atty., contra, relied upon *King* v. *Marks*, 3 East, 157, as a case in point, against bailing the prisoner. He said the K. B. held, in that case, that they might remand, though the warrant of commitment was defective, the depositions making out a felony. In that case, the prisoners were committed on a charge of felony upon the Statute against Administering, being present at or assisting in the Administration of Unlawful Oaths. The court looked into the deposition: and although they admitted the law to be doubtful, yet they inclined against the prisoners and thinking that they might be guilty within the Statute, they were, therefore, remanded by special rule, because the warrant was defective. The court looked to see whether a felony had probably been committed, without reference to the degree of moral guilt; and inclining that the offense made out was within the Statute, **43***] they deemed it their duty to *remand; leaving the question of law to be afterwards discussed upon a more full state of facts.

Now here is a plain felony of some kind—at least a manslaughter; and we do not hesitate to say, a technical murder. There can be no doubt that this assemblage of boys, followed by the affray, was a riot; and brings the case within the rule laid down in 1 Hawk., ch. 29, sec. 10; that "if a man happen to kill another in the willful commission of any unlawful act, which necessarily tends to raise tumults and quarrels, and consequently cannot but be attended with the danger of personal hurt to some one or other, as by committing a riot, robbing a park, &c., he shall be adjudged guilty of murder." Being thus engaged in an unlawful act, though Crandall had given the first blow, yet the stabbing was murder. *King* v. *Oneby*, 2 Ld. Raym., 1485; S. C., Toml. Dig., 79. The offense shall not be reduced to manslaughter unless the blow or offense be such as to deprive the party of his reasoning faculties at the time. (Toml. Dig., 79, tit. Homicide, II.) Indeed, there have been various convictions of murder, upon a slaying after very great provocation. 1 Hall. P. C., 455; 4 Bl. Com., 199; Kelyng, 5; *Regina* v. *Mawgridge, Id.*, 119. And in *Brown's* case, Leach Cr. Cas., 151, the offense was turned into manslaughter, only upon the ground that the prisoner had reason to fear his own destruction, had he not taken the life of his adversary.

If, on looking into the depositions, the court should conclude here has been a murder, clearly they will not allow bail. And so we contend if the prisoner be guilty of manslaughter. That there was a manslaughter committed, seems to be very slightly contested by the prisoner's counsel. The court are to exercise a sound legal discretion; and they will not bail, even for manslaughter, unless there be very great doubt of guilt. *King* v. *Marks*, 3 East, 157; *People* v. *Goodwin*, 1 Wheeler Crim. Cas., 443.

Mr. Talcott, Atty-Gen., same side. We admit the power of this court, in its discretion, to bail in all cases whatsoever; but this discre- **44***] tion is judicial, and will be guided *by previously adjudged cases. The rule as laid down in 1 Chit. C. L., 98, 99, is the true one—that "it is not usual for this court to bail, in case of a felony, unless when in consequence of the defect of the commitment, and of the examination and depositions, it appears doubtful whether any offense has been committed." A defect in the *mittimus* alone has been shown not to be a ground of bail. This has not and will not be denied.

Is this application, then, warranted by any of the adjudged cases? We agree that in looking to these a distinction should be kept in view between this high tribunal and the inferior magistrates, whose powers, in regard to bail, are limited; but is there a single case presenting the strong circumstances of the present against the prisoner, a plain manslaughter, at least, and, beyond much doubt, a technical murder, in which bail was allowed? The rolls copied into Coke's Entries, which are relied upon, could not, in their nature, present the facts upon which the court proceeded to bail. The depositions or evidence were no part of the record. Beside the fact that guilt or innocence hangs indifferent between the prisoner and the Crown, there are various other circumstances by which the court might have been guided, in letting to bail. One is, a session past. *Fitzpatrick's* case, 1 Salk., 103. So even after conviction, where the prisoner is entitled to his clergy, he may be bailed; *Lisle's* case, *Id.*, though this was denied in one instance. *King v. Keat, Id.* So, if the prisoner's life be in danger from imprisonment. *Lord Aylesbury's* case, *Id.* But these and the like circumstances aside, it is enough that the evidence affects the prisoner, in the case of murder. *Anon.*, 1 Salk., 104. The practice being thus settled, that it is not a matter of course to bail, leaves no doubt that in the cases cited from Co. Entries, there must have been special grounds for the entry upon the roll, which could not appear there. In one of those very cases, the prisoner finally pleaded a pardon. This is plainly one case in which the court will bail. *Armstrong* v. *Lisle*, 12 Mod., 108. Indeed, they will do so in the case of an approver, who merely has a right to a pardon. *Rex* v. *Rudd*, Cowp., 331, 334. All these, and the *like cases, are plainly exceptions to [***45** the general rule, that the court will not bail where the guilt is plain. The 2 Hawk., ch. 15, sec. 80, cited for the prisoner, also supports the rule. He says if the prisoner be notoriously guilty of manslaughter, not by confession merely, as the counsel for the prisoner have it, but by confession or otherwise, he cannot be bailed. Bulstr., 85, is not at all inconsistent with this rule; and *King* v. *Poynes*, 3 Bulstr., 113, supports it strongly. *Herbert & Vaughan's* case, Latch., 12, presents a set of special circumstances; and Selfridge's application for bail passed without objection. *Goodwin's* case was singularly special in its circumstances; and on examining it, the court will find its general doctrine against bail in a case like the present. That case was once up before the Sessions of N. Y., and Mr. Colden, the then Mayor, considered it very fully, and limited the exercise of the power to bail to the instances, in which we admit it may be exercised. After an indictment for manslaughter, he held that the prisoner could not be bailed till something was shown from which he might be presumed innocent. (1 Wheeler Crim. Cas., 435, 437.) Afterwards the case came on for trial upon the indictment; the jury disagreed; and the late *Ch. J.*, in the same case and same book (p. 443), considers the guilt and innocence of the prisoner as standing so far indifferent as to warrant his being bailed. It is said, in Com. Dig. Bail, F. 3, that the K. B. will not bail in manslaughter, unless there be a reasonable cause. Bail was denied to two English noblemen indicted for manslaughter. (Styles, 371.)

We have been referred, through *Goodwin's* case, to two cases in Strange, *Rex* v. *Dalton*, 2 Str., 911, and *Rex* v. *Magrath*, *Id.*, 1242. In

Rex v. *Dalton* we have only the *dictum* of a single judge, at his dwelling-house; no particular circumstances are stated; and the instance put there of *Clifton's* case sustains the right of the court to deny bail on the ground of the offense being murder, though the coroner's inquest calls it manslaughter, if the depositions will carry it beyond mere manslaughter. *Rex* v. *Magrath* comes to us also equally naked of all circumstances; and the only point
46*] *in question was, evidently, whether the court would look beyond the inquisition, in order to see the real facts. That case refers to one, for its support, in which the application was denied (*Anon.*, 1 Salk., 104), upon the very principles for which we contend; and leaves a very fair inference that there must have been circumstances not mentioned by the reporter. Indeed, Strange's cases generally too much deserve the criticism of *Mr. Justice* Foster, that he is overstudious of brevity, omitting many of the material circumstances upon which cases turned. When *Goodwin's* case was before the N. Y. Sessions, the Mayor declared there was not a single English case cited which questioned the rule upon which he proceeded. But suppose the cases in Strange to question it; are they to sweep away the long settled doctrine upon this question, and arrest the whole current of decisions both before and since? That these cases are not now considered authority in England, in their naked state, I refer to *King* v. *Jones*, 1 Barn. & Ald., 209, where counsel deemed it necessary to show on a mere commitment, before indictment, for a manslaughter, that the deceased fell in a fight provoked by himself. Upon this proof, the court allowed bail. That case does no more than follow up *King* v. *Marks*, 3 East, 157, already stated by my associate counsel. Ld. Ellenborough, in that case, puts the question upon doubt as to the truth of the charge; and the judges all concur with him in putting the case upon its doubtful character, either in law or fact, or both.

In this view of the matter, it is not material whether the case be murder or manslaughter. The rule is the same in England, as to both, for they are both, capital.

If there be any distinction in this country, we then say the prisoner should not be bailed, because he is guilty of murder. The authority cited by *Mr. Wilcoxon* shows it a murder, if it followed a riot. That here was a riot, I refer to 1 Russell on Crimes, 354, 355; 1 East P. C., 257, sec. 33. Where homicide is committed, it will be intended to be murder, and it lies with the offender to reduce it to an inferior crime, by proof on his part. It is not enough
47*] for this purpose, to say *that the affair was sudden. The act must arise from a provocation legally sufficient. It must arise from a cause which overrules and controls human reason. The cause must be adequate to the effect. Wherever it appears that the crime was, at the moment, though in consequence of a sudden quarrel, deliberately and intentionally executed, the killing is murder in the first degree. *Commonwealth* v. *Dougherty*, 1 Browne Pa., Appendix, XVIII.

In this case the attack did not proceed originally from the deceased. It came from the prisoner. The deceased was almost continually on the retreat. Was it ever heard of, that the blow which is necessary for one's defense should mitigate the crime of the adversary who kills him, from murder to manslaughter? The blows which the deceased gave were mere efforts of self defense. To mitigate the crime, they must clearly appear to have proceeded from a provocation not sought by the party. Nor is it every attack, however trifling and disproportionate, which will have this effect. The law, indeed, makes great allowance for human frailty. It will not inquire whether the precise pound of flesh has been taken. But if a man will take punishment into his own hand, it will see to it that he shall exercise it in mercy.

It has been intimated, and how far it may hereafter be insisted on I know not, that the killing in this case was no more than mere excusable homicide. I will not detain the court by citing cases on a point so plain. Because jurors may have relaxed the rules of law in *Selfridge's* and *Goodwin's* and other cases, these furnish no reasons for the court to do so. To reduce the crime to manslaughter, there must be a sudden affray conducted on equal terms. 1 Russel's Cr. L., 613, 646, 647, 660, 661, 1 East C. L., 215, 234-236; 2 Ld. Raym., 1496: Foster C. L., 295; *Brown's* case, Leach, 151; *King* v. *Snow*, *Id.*, 155. *Commonwealth* v. *Dougherty*, 1 Brown Pa., Appendix, XXII, XXIII.

At a subsequent day, the Atty-Gen. mentioned to the court, 1 Chit. C. L., 113, as relating to the course the court usually take when a motion is made for the allowance of bail upon a charge of homicide.

**Mr. E. Williams*, in reply. When [*48 my associate counsel admitted that we cannot call upon the court to bail the prisoner as a matter of right, but of discretion, he conceded all that can be claimed. In this country, I may say, that a prisoner is, *prima facie*, entitled to bail; and it lies with the people to show circumstances, which take the case out of the rule. I know there were English cases which might be urged against this rule; but they are more properly attributable to the extreme severity of the British penal code. It is conceded to us that this court may bail in all cases; but it is denied that they ever will do it in cases of felonious homicide, unless induced by extenuating circumstances; or rather where, from the proof, guilt or innocence, appears to be indifferent. The rule, as laid down by the late *Ch. J.*, in *Goodwin's* case, is undoubtedly the true one: "That the judges will in general exercise the power of bailing in favor of a prisoner in every case not capital." (1 Wheeler Crim. Cas., 445.) Then in all cases not capital, the power of bailing is to be exercised. If the prisoner is forthcoming to take his trial, the end of the law is answered. And the doctrine applies with peculiar force to the crime of manslaughter; which is not only never capital, under our system of criminal law, but ranges through an infinite variety of light and shade, from mere excusable homicide to malignant murder. If you disallow bail, the offender may be punished for the crime before he is tried, with a severity as great, and for a term nearly as long, as after the sentence of the law is pronounced. Sup-

pose an homicide felonious in a mere technical sense—all but justifiable—a case in which the offender would, of course, be pardoned ; ought the prisoner to be bailed either before, or after the trial ? Actual pardon is seldom granted till after trial ; and shall he in the meantime be confined with the same rigor as the most atrocious criminal though it be seen that on conviction he will be pardoned of course ? All this for the mere sake of form and show ! The English criminal code is founded in terror; ours in reformation. It may be important in England to secure the criminal as a pageant. With us the object is to make punishment certain, in order to reform. It lies with the pub-
49*] lic prosecutor *to show that the case is an exception to these principles.

It is said that, to warrant bail, the guilt and innocence of the prisoner must hang in equal scales. Who holds the scales ? If the law, they are always equal. If the judge, different opinions may prevail at different times upon the same circumstances. If the rule be one of law, there must be some evidence to which the law can apply itself. After conviction, the matter is adjudged against the prisoner ; and not till then does the law esteem him guilty, unless it be upon confession deliberately made in the face of the court. But it is here said the crime may be substantiated in any other way. This is not so. After conviction, if there be mitigating circumstances, entitling the party to a pardon or to a new trial, he may yet be bailed ; and it is here, only, that the doctrine contended for against us can apply, under our mitigated system of criminal punishment. The reason having ceased with us, the severity of the English law has ceased also, as it would under their own government in a like case. Shall we demand the extravagant security of personal inprisonment, upon the mere fiction that a crime is capital, when the semblance of such a character has been legally abolished ?

Are affidavits, showing the probability of guilt, enough to call for the exercise of the English rule ? *Goodwin's* case, 1 Wheeler Crim. Cas., 434, was decided by an inferior court, which proceeded mainly upon the ground that a coroner's inquisition of murder had been found upon the case. This they considered as *prima facie* evidence that there was murder, though the regular grand inquest had found manslaughter merely. Another reason given against bail was somewhat more popular than legal ; that to allow bail would be placing the poor and rich upon an unequal footing. The preference of the rich man to the poor one, pervades not only our criminal but our civil jurisprudence. The one can give bail or pay his debts ; the other cannot, and must be imprisoned ; yet, I imagine, this was never before urged as a reason why the rich man should be denied bail altogether. When the case of *Goodwin* afterwards came before the
50*] *late *Ch. J.*, a man who was never yet accused of wanting firmness in the administration of justice, he viewed the matter in this light ; and in his own clear and forcible manner laid down and vindicated the rule which we have cited, and by which we are willing to abide in the decision of this cause. It is evident from the report of Selfridge's trial; that both the court and the Atty-Gen. of our neighboring State, Mass., considered the law as perfectly well settled in favor of bail, as a matter of course upon an indictment for manslaughter. If this be a mere technical manslaughter, it is not only the right, but the duty of the court to bail. Selfridge's trial also places the law of self defense on a very high and elevated ground, and contains all I could wish to say on the subject of the nature and mitigated character of the offense charged against the prisoner. If the act be merely rash and indiscreet, it is manslaughter ; if the mere effect of passion, it is manslaughter ; if deliberate, and evincing a depraved heart, it is murder. It is not necessary that human reason should be dethroned, to reduce the act of killing below murder. The mere tilting the bench on which the prisoner sat, was, in one case, held enough; and the father, who pursued and killed the man that had abused his child, was, out of respect to human frailty, held guilty of manslaughter merely.

The counsel also considered the depositions at large, and insisted that the offense in proof did not amount even to manslaughter.

SAVAGE, *Ch. J.* The power of this court to bail, in all cases of crimes punishable by our laws, is not questioned. And whether the prisoner is to be bailed or remanded, rests in the discretion of the court. That discretion is to be guided by the circumstances of the case, and a consideration of the authorities applicable to those circumstances.

The writ was allowed in this case, for a defect apparent upon the face of the warrant of commitment. No affidavit, therefore, was necessary on the part of the prisoner, stating the circumstances which he might consider as entitling him to relief. But in all cases on *habeas corpus*, previous to indictment, the court *will look into the deposition before [*51
the magistrate, or before the coroner's inquest; and though the commitment be full and in due form, yet if the testimony proves no crime, the court will discharge or bail ; and though the commitment be defective, yet, if the depositions contain evidence of an offense not bailable, the prisoner will be remanded.

The coroner's inquest has charged the prisoner with having committed that species of felonious homicide which is in law denominated manslaughter. This offense differs from murder, in the absence of malice.

Murder is well defined to be, the voluntarily killing any person, of malice aforethought, either express, or implied by law. Manslaughter differs in this : that though the act which occasions the death be unlawful, or likely to be attended with bodily mischief, yet the malice, either express or implied, which is the very essence of murder, is presumed to be wanting ; and the act being imputed to the infirmity of human nature, the punishment is proportionably lenient.

The counsel for the prisoner contend that the facts, as proved by the depositions, do not amount to manslaughter ; but even if they do, yet, unless the prisoner's guilt be established by his own confession, he is entitled to bail, and we are referred to several authorities on the subject, some of which I shall notice.

(Hawk., bk. 2, ch. 15, secs. 40, 80.) The rule,

as here laid down, I take to be the correct one on the question of bail. It is this—that persons convicted of felony, or who have confessed their guilt, or are notoriously guilty of treason or manslaughter, by their own confession or otherwise, are not to be admitted to bail, without some special motive to induce the court to grant it. For, says the learned writer, bail is only proper where it stands indifferent whether the party be guilty or innocent of the accusation against him, as it often does before his trial; but where that indifferency is removed, it would, generally speaking, be absurd to bail him.

Two cases are cited from Strange, to show that bail is a matter of course in manslaughter.
52*] In *Rex* v. *Dalton*, 2 Str., *911, before Ld. Raymond at chambers, he is made to say that if the depositions amounted only to manslaughter, he would bail, though the coroner's inquest had found it murder; that *Ld. Mohun's* case, in Salk., 104, was in point; and that the Lords bailed him after an indictment for murder.

In *Rex* v. *Magrath*, 2 Str., 1242, the whole report is this: "He was committed for manslaughter; and it appearing to be no more, upon the depositions before the coroner, the court admitted him to bail, according to Salk., 104." Both these cases are supposed to be supported by *Ld. Mohun's* case, in 1 Salk., 104, which was as follows: "If a man be found guily of murder by the coroner's inquest, we sometimes bail him, because the coroner proceeds upon depositions taken in writing, which we may look into. Otherwise, if a man be found guilty of murder by a grand jury; because the court cannot take notice of their evidence, which they, by their oath, are bound to conceal." This case, as reported, certainly proves nothing. No circumstances are given; and for aught that appears, the court, on examining the depositions, might have been satisfied of the prisoner's innocence, or that the offense was below the degree of felonious homicide. And in *Keath's* case, 1 Salk., 103, the same court said that, in manslaughter, after conviction, no bail is allowed till clergy had. Even *Ld. Mohun's* case has in one instance at least, been disregarded, if not overruled. In *Rex* v. *Action*, 2 Str., 851, the court refused to look into the despositions, and remanded the prisoner.

These cases from Salkeld and Strange are, when fully considered, of little or no weight. Nor have they been followed in more modern times. In *King* v. *Wyer*, 2 T. R., 77, the prisoner's counsel moved that he might be bailed, on the ground that the offense charged was not felony, but the court being of opinion that the offense was felony, the prisoner was remanded. In *King* v. *Marks*, 3 East, 163, Ld. Ellenborough says: "As it appears, then, from the depositions, that there is a *corpus delicti*, within the meaning of the Act of Parliament, which constitutes it felony, it is our duty to remand the prisoner." The other judges all concurred;
53*] *and Le Blanc said, "if upon the depositions returned, the court see that a felony has been committed, and that there is a reasonable ground of charge against the prisoners, they will not bail, but remand them."

The cases in this country, which may be considered as authority, are but few. In *Selfridge's* case the prisoner was bailed without opposition, but on what circumstances we are not informed. It is surely not the practice of the Supreme Court of Mass. to bail of course in such cases, as appears by *Trask's* case, 15 Mass., 277. He was refused bail, as it was uncertain whether Sampson, whom he had wounded, would not die. The case of *People* v. *Goodwin*, before the late *Ch. J.* Spencer, at chambers (1 Wheeler Crim. Cas., 443), was much relied on by the prisoner's counsel. The practice of bailing, as laid down by *Ch. J.* Spencer, is undoubtedly correct. He cites the cases from Strange and Salkeld, but does not follow them. He lays down the law from Hawkins, substantially, as before quoted; and upon that law he evidently acted in admitting the prisoner to bail. He says: "It appears to me, that from the facts before me, this conclusion is inevitable, that it is quite doubtful whether the prisoner is guilty. And I think it stands indifferent whether he is so or not." He alludes to the circumstances of the trial, and to the fact that the jury could not agree, from which he draws an inference in favor of the prisoner's innocence. He then adds: "In such a case, as I understand the law, he is entitled to be bailed," thus distinctly placing the exercise of his discretionary power to bail, upon the probability of the prisoner's innocence. *Ch. J.* Spencer does not say that persons charged with the offense of manslaughter are entitled to bail of course; but it is quite indifferent whether he is guilty. If the facts in this case now before the court afford the same presumption of innocence, and it appear to the court from the depositions, that is quite indifferent whether he is guilty, then, in my opinion, he ought to be bailed; otherwise, not.

This necessarily leads to an examination of the testimony. I shall, however, not enter into it in detail, but merely *state the sub- [*54
stance. Oct. 19, last, Crandall, the deceased, a lad of 17, was at the Academy in Kinderhook. He was ordered by one of the students, a small boy, to leave the place where he was. He refused, but soon went away—the boy threatening to bring other boys to compel him. Shortly after, the deceased was met in the street, at some distance from the Academy, by the same student and a larger boy. An angry conversation ensued, and a scuffle. Other students were sent for, and came; and among them was the prisoner. The school boys all attacked the deceased, and the prisoner threw a stick at him. The deceased defended himself as well as he could. He retreated at times, and at times pursued some of the boys. At length he obtained a piece of board, with which he defended himself, and assailed his adversaries Among others, he struck the prisoner with this piece of board, and thereupon the prisoner stabbed him with a jack knife, in the abdomen, of which wound he died.

The depositions containing these facts show an offense which, in by judgment, is manslaughter at the least.

The contest in the books is, not whether death under such circumstances is manslaughter, but whether it is not murder.

As we think the warrant is defective, the prisoner must be remanded upon a special rule.

SUTHERLAND, *J.* I have very little to say in addition to the remarks made by the *Chief Justice.* The power of this court to bail in all cases whatsoever is indisputable, and was conceded by the counsel for the people. Hence, in whatever manner the court may exercise this power, it can never be alleged that the act is void for excess. But it is important that we should be governed, as far as may be, by rules. The necessity of confiding such a power to any court is a subject of regret; but it is necessary in this as well as some other cases. It is clear, however, that the general rules which govern and confine the common magistrate in letting to bail, should never be departed from, except in extraordinary cases. Is the present case within those rules? The object of arrest and imprisonment is not to
55*] *punish the delinquent; but to secure his forthcoming, to abide the punishment which may be inflicted by the sentence of the law, upon conviction, as was justly remarked by the late *Ch. J.*, Spencer, in *Goodwin's* case. (Wheeler's Crim. Cas., 446, 447.) The principal consideration is, whether the nature of the crime be such as that a recognizance would operate to secure the prisoner's appearance. If so, it is proper to receive bail as a substitute for imprisonment. Where the punishment is directly, or in effect pecuniary merely, as by fine or temporary imprisonment for a misdemeanor, it is accordingly a matter of course to receive competent bail, proportioned to the probable amount of the ultimate penalty. There is little or no difficulty in saying what the amount should be; and it may, at any rate, be made perfectly adequate to the object. But when the punishment is either capital, or imprisonment may follow for a considerable length of time, in the State Prison, at hard labor, or other degrading circumstances, for a crime involving moral turpitude, these are far different considerations; and the law proceeds upon this difference in allowing or denying bail. If capital, bail should not in general be allowed, because no pecuniary consideration can weigh against life; and where guilt is clear, and a rigorous and disgraceful imprisonment may follow for a great length of time, the presumption is strong that the accused will not appear and surrender himself to the demands of justice, to avoid a mere forfeiture of property. The safest course, therefore, in cases of felony, where the guilt of the criminal is clear, is to deny bail. Hawkins, B. 2, ch. 15, sec. 40, expresses himself more clearly and correctly to this point than any other author upon criminal law. He lays down the rule in terms, that in cases of felony, bail should be allowed only where the guilt or innocence of the prisoner is indifferent. His words are, "for bail is only proper where it stands indifferent, whether the party be guilty or innocent of the accusation against him." And he follows this with the distinct proposition, that where the guilt is not indifferent, in general, it would be absurd to bail him. Several of the authorities have been considered by
56*] the *Ch. J.*; and others will *be commented upon by *Mr. Justice* Woodworth. I shall not, therefore, go over them. I would merely observe, that I have found no case at war with the position of Hawkins. Of the two cases from Strange, *Rex* v. *Dalton*, 2 Str., 911, and *Rex* v. *Magrath, Id.*, 1242, relied upon by the counsel for the prisoner, it is enough to say that there is, in the report, a total destitution of circumstances. Sufficient might, and probably did appear of the proof, to make them fit cases for bail. It is perfectly evident to me, on looking into those cases, and the cases upon which they were bottomed, that they were not reported with a view to settle the weight of proof which would warrant letting the prisoner to bail; but rather to show what kind of proof is admissible upon the return of the *habeas corpus*. *Rex* v. *Magrath* gives the authorities upon which both that and *Rex* v. *Dalton* proceeded. These were *Clifton's* case and *Ld. Mohun's* case, 1 Salk., 104. In the first, bail was refused, because the crime was thought to be murder, although the inquisition was manslaughter. The only point decided in *Ld. Mohun's* case was, that the court would look into the depositions, upon the return of the *habeas corpus*, to see whether they warranted the finding of the inquest; and in the two cases cited from Strange, the attention of the reporter seems confined to this single point. He, therefore, very naturally omits to notice the degree of the proof. His object was to show that the finding of the inquest should not be conclusive; though this would be otherwise, if an indictment had been regularly found by a grand jury; that the depositions before the coroner, being in writing, and taken publicly, may be looked into with propriety; whereas, if the finding had been by a grand jury, who had pronounced the crime to be murder, this should not be questioned, upon a motion for bail; because the evidence before the grand jury is taken orally, and in secret, and should not be disclosed. An indictment, found by them, is, therefore, very properly distinguished from the finding before the coroner. The indictment must be taken as conclusive upon the degree of the crime. The opinion of the *Ch. J.*, in *Rex* v. *Dalton*, wherein he says generally, that if the crime amounted to *manslaughter merely, bail might be [***57**
received, goes beyond the point intended to be presented by the reporter; and must be taken in reference to some facts, not mentioned by him, because he did not think them material. But if otherwise; if the *Ch. J.* intended to be understood as laying down the rule broadly, and in the abstract, that bail should be allowed of course in a case of manslaughter, his opinion is opposed to repeated authorities of more modern date. From these, I feel fully warranted in saying that we ought not to bail a prisoner, accused of manslaughter, unless there be a reasonable doubt of his guilt. *Selfridge's* case is not inconsistent with this rule. In the history of his trial, some of the circumstances which preceded it are mentioned. Among these, his actual confinment for four months previous to the indictment, appears. If the practice in the State of Mass. was to bail of course in manslaughter, he would never have been committed at all, or would have been immediately let out on bail. True he was finally bailed after indictment, but the particular circumstances which warranted this are not detailed in the report. I see it was proved, in the course of the trial, that the prisoner's

health was very feeble. Indeed there may have been many circumstances combined with this consideration, to satisfy the Atty-Gen., and the court, that no objection could be made; and what is material in weighing this authority, none was made to his being bailed.

In this case, upon the *ex parte* depositions, which we have examined, I do not think there is any rational doubt that the prisoner is guilty of manslaughter. It is true, they are *ex parte*, and for that reason, neither the depositions nor the opinion which we give, can or ought to influence the final determination upon his guilt or innocence; but they are the only medium through which we can look at the case; and afford the only lights to guide our discretion in granting or refusing bail. We speak of them in this view. Upon the evidence before us, on which alone we can act, I think the prisoner ought not to be let to bail.

WOODWORTH, *J.* Had this been an ordinary case, I should have contented myself with the **58***] simple expression of *an opinion. It is, however, important not only to the individual, whose liberty is involved in the decision we are to make, but as presenting several grave questions, in which the community at large have a deep interest.

These questions are: 1. On the supposition that the crime of manslaughter has been committed, can the prisoner be bailed? 2. Does the evidence before the court make out a case of manslaughter?

Upon the first question, the power of this court, in their discretion, to admit persons to bail in all cases whatsoever, was admitted upon the argument, and is abundantly proved by authority. (1 Chit. C. L., 98; 3 East, 163.) It was also conceded, and the same authorities prove, that the prisoner cannot claim bail as a matter of right. The inquiry follows, in what manner is the discretion of the court to be exercised? To say that bail must be allowed of course, where it may be collected from the evidence, that a felony has been committed, would leave no room for discretion, and utterly subvert the principle upon which the right to bail rests. Accordingly, the rule laid down by the later and more approved authorities is, that unless it be doubtful whether a felony has been committed; and if, from the depositions, the court can collect that a felony has been committed, they will not bail the prisoner. (1 Chit. C. L., 99; 3 East, 157; 2 T. R., 257.) The court look at the depositions, to see if enough is charged to justify a detainer of the prisoner, and put him upon his trial. (1 Chit. C. L., 113.) Hawk., B. 2, ch. 15, sec. 80, says: "It is difficult to find an instance where persons notoriously guilty of treason or manslaughter, by their own confession, or otherwise, have been admitted to bail, without some special motive to induce the court to grant it." And he cites 1 Roll., 268; Raym., 381; 3 Bulstr., 113. In Com. Dig., Bail, F, 3, it is said, "the court will not bail in treason, murder, manslaughter, &c., unless there be a reasonable cause;" and many cases are cited in support of the position. The law is laid down to the same effect in 4 Bl. Com., 299; and in *King* v. *Marks*, 3 East, 165, the rule is advanced in these cautious and qualified terms: The court "will bail whenever there is any doubt on the law, or the fact of the case."

*Indeed, the whole current of author- [***59** ities in the English books sanction this doctrine; and it cannot be overthrown by a few ancient cases, where, by the report, it seems bail was allowed in manslaughter, without special cause shown. As to the cases in Co. Ent., 354 to 356, there may, as was observed at the bar, have been important circumstances which are not disclosed; and which could not properly be disclosed by the record. The compiler does not profess to give anything more than the mere form of the entry. We have a right to presume from the later authorities that a proper case for bail was made out. *Lisle's* case, cited for the prisoner from Kelyng, 89, is stated generally to be a case of manslaughter; but the degree of proof is not given; and it would perhaps be sufficient to say, as of the entry in Coke, a proper case should be presumed to have been made out. But that case is contrary to Dyer, 179, pl. 42 (2 Eliz.) The words of the case in Dyer are: "A man found guilty of felonious homicide, before judgment, it was moved whether he was bailable; and held he was not, for the intendment of the law of bail is, that it stands indifferently whether he be guilty or not, until trial." As to the cases of *Rex* v. *Dalton*, 2 Str., 911, and *Rex* v *Magrath*, *Id.*, 1242, we are fortified in the belief that there was probably an omission to state the circumstances, by what *Mr. Justice* Foster says in his Crown Law, 294, of another case as reported by Strange. He complains that Strange was over studious of brevity; and instances *Rex* v. *Tranter*, 1 Str., 499, which, from the facts reported, seems to be a case of murder, and yet was held manslaughter; but by a report of the same case in 6 St. Tr., 195, it appears that important circumstances were omitted by Strange. At most, these cases in Strange are solitary ones, and cannot stand against the uniform unbroken current of modern authority. The rule was well settled before it came under consideration in *Goodwin's* case, decided by the late *Ch. J.* Spencer (1 Wheeler Crim. Cas., 446), a jurist eminently deserving the encomium bestowed upon him by the prisoner's counsel. He found himself obliged to do no more than apply a rule which was well settled. He adverted to the cases in Strange, but was not *gov- [***60** erned by them; he uses nearly the same qualified language, which I have cited from the *King* v. *Marks*, 3 East, 165. If it be doubtful whether the prisoner be guilty, or if he may be innocent, in such case, as he understood the law, he was entitled to bail. Undoubtedly, the true rule of law is here laid down by the *Ch. J.;* and it is expressed with his usual precision and perspicuity.

The case of *Selfridge* was cited by the counsel for the prisoner. If that case had been discussed and decided by the court upon the question of bail, it cannot weigh against the English authorities and our own. But the application to admit him to bail passed without opposition. The attorney and Solicitor Gen. are to be considered as consenting that he should be let to bail. They were in possession of all the testimony; and making no opposition to his going at large upon bail, the court might, from this circumstance alone, have inferred probable innocence. If, in the principal case, the Atty-Gen. had arisen in his place, and stated to us that he had examined the testimony, and was convinced that it presented a question of so much doubt that bail would be proper, we should hardly have deemed it our duty to inquire farther. In *Selfridge's* case the event proved the propriety of the course which was taken. Upon the trial, the following question was submitted by *Judge* Parker, in his charge to the jury: "whether the accused could probably have saved himself from death, or enormous bodily harm, by retreating to the wall, or throwing himself into the arms of friends who would protect him. This is the real stress of the case." The prisoner was acquitted.

The nature of the punishment must also be regarded, in deciding this question: if guilty, the prisoner must suffer corporal imprisonment. When, therefore, the circumstances afford strong presumption of guilt, the accused, if bailed, would probably be induced to flight, in order to evade the punishment.

Again; it was argued for the prisoner, that though his case be one of clear manslaughter, yet it is at most technically so, and is, in truth, of such a mitigated character as to admit of bail. But there is no authority which war-
61*] rants us, upon *the question of bail, in being guided by the apparent degree of moral guilt. If it be clear that the offense has been committed, the prisoner must be remanded. The degree of criminality, or moral delinquency, to be gathered from the mitigating circumstances of the case, can be considered and weighed by that tribunal alone which is to fix the extent of the punishment.

According to the view which I have taken of the case, it becomes unnecessary to say whether the depositions make out the crime of murder; because I am perfectly well satisfied that if they show manslaughter, beyond all reasonable doubt, we ought not to bail.

2. Manslaughter is the unlawful killing without malice express or implied. (4 Bl. Com., 191.) To excuse a homicide, the person killing must have no other probable means of escaping from his assailant. (4 Bl. Com., 181.) "He who would excuse himself upon the foot of self defense, must show that, before a mortal stroke given, he had declined any further combat, and retreated as far as he could; and that he killed his adversary through mere necessity." (Foster Cr. L., 277.) And in such case, "it mattereth not who gave the first blow." (*Id.*, 1 Hale P. C., 479.) "The fact of killing being proved, the necessity of so doing must be proved by the prisoner, unless it appears by the evidence produced against him." (1 East C. L., 224; Foster C. L., 255.) "If one seeing two fight, takes part with one of them, and kills the other, it is manslaughter."

The case must be tested by these principles. The tender years of the prisoner are not now in question. He is admitted to be above the age of discretion, after which he is legally capable of crime; his youth can weigh nothing except in estimating the measure of his punishment. We are under the necessity of looking into the testimony, and of making such remarks as are due to the case, upon the facts as they are now presented. If the conclusions which we express prove finally prejudicial to the prisoner, such a consequence is to be deprecated, but it arises from his own act in making the present application.

What, then, is the case before us? I will merely glance at *it, so far as may be [*62 necessary to justify the opinion we have formed. There is no reason to conclude that the deceased commenced the combat. He acted on the defensive, after Gleason approached him with the boys from the Academy. A conflict then ensued between the deceased and these boys, which was, for a while, conducted by the former without the use of any weapon. His stick was laid aside—sometime after which, he obtained a piece of board, with which he defended himself. While thus employed, the prisoner voluntarily and unnecessarily engaged in the affray, joining the combatants in hostility to the deceased; and indeed, must be considered as making the first assault. If not, how came he engaged? It is true that the deceased struck him with the piece of board; but there is no evidence that his life was in danger, or that great bodily harm was likely to ensue, either from the blow or the instrument made use of. It does not appear that the prisoner retreated, and was pursued by the deceased, or that the deceased struck the prisoner more than once. It does not appear that the weapon would probably produce death, nor, by the effect produced, that great bodily harm was experienced by the prisoner.

On the law and the facts before us, therefore, I concur in the opinion that the application to let the prisoner to bail must be denied; and this on the ground that the depositions present a case of manslaughter, at least, clearly made out.

RULE.

SUPREME COURT.
IN THE MATTER OF CHARLES TAYLOE.

Charles Tayloe being brought into court, in custody of the keeper of the jail of the County of Columbia, by virtue of a writ of *habeas corpus*, it is ordered that the said writ and the return made thereto be filed; and upon reading the several depositions taken before Lucas Hoes and Barent Hoes, justices of the peace in and for the said County of Columbia, and their warrant of commitment thereupon; and also the depositions taken before Samuel Clary, a coroner in and for said county, upon an inquest taken upon *the body of one Eber [*63 L. Crandall; and the inquisition found by the jury, and upon hearing counsel as well for the people as the prisoner, it is ordered, that the said Charles Tayloe be discharged from his imprisonment by virtue of the warrants in said return mentioned; and that he, the said Charles Tayloe, be recommitted to the said keeper of the jail of the County of Columbia aforesaid, for unlawfully, wickedly and feloniously stabbing and killing the said Eber L. Crandall, on or about the nineteenth day of October last past, at Kinderhook, in the said County of Columbia, to be, by the said keeper, kept in safe custody, without bail or mainprize, until he shall be thence discharged by due course of law.

Cited in—8 Barb., 162; 10 How. Pr., 571; 3 Abb. Pr., 306; 8 Abb. N. S., 28; 1 Park., 236; 2 Park., 573; 4 Park., 652; 1 McLean, 437; 5 Blatchf., 308; 37 Am. Dec., 334; 25 Am. Rep., 648 (53 Ala. 495).

DEPAU
v.
THE OCEAN INSURANCE COMPANY.

Marine Insurance. 1. After Vessel is Repaired, Insured Cannot Abandon as for a Total Loss. 2. Sale of Part of the Cargo, to Defray Expense of Repairs—No Lien on the Vessel. 3. Settlement of General Average, in Foreign Port—When Conclusive. 4. Defects, Prior to Insurance, not Amounting to Unseaworthiness, not Considered.

After a vessel is repaired, and successfully pursuing her voyage, the assured cannot abandon as for a technical total loss.

Where part of a cargo is sold at a port of necessity, to defray the expense of repairs upon a ship, this creates no lien upon the ship, for such expenses.

When a general average is fairly settled in a foreign port, though not the port of necessity, but the port of destination, which the assured is obliged to pay, this is conclusive as between him and the underwriters.

If the defects in a vessel, existing previous to effecting a policy of insurance, be not such as to render her unseaworthy, they cannot be take into consideration, in determining whether the expense of her repairs exceed half her value.

Citations—2 Cai., 85; 4 Cow., 244; 2 T. R., 407; 11 Johns., 323.

ASSUMPSIT on a policy of insurance, tried at the N. Y. Circuit, Nov., 1823, before Edwards, Circuit Judge.

The action was brought to recover as for a total loss, on a policy dated July 28, 1820, underwritten by the defendants, in favor of the plaintiff, upon one half of the ship Manchester Packet, on a voyage at and from Havana to Rotterdam, at a premium of 2½ *per cent.*, the sum subscribed to the policy being $2,000; and one half the vessel valued by the policy at the sum insured.

The ship proceeded on the voyage insured, in good condition, according to several of the plaintiff's witnesses; and after encountering a variety of severe weather, a number of the crew having died, and the ship being in a leaky condition, she was compelled to put into Halifax, where she arrived Sep. 6, 1820; underwent several surveys, and was finally repaired and ready for sea, Nov. 17, at an expense of more than half her value. Nov. 18, she sailed for Rotterdam, where she arrived in the latter part of Feb., 1821.

64*] *Certain sugars, a part of her cargo, were sold at Halifax for the purpose of raising funds, to pay the expenses of the repairs; and at Rotterdam the averages, both general and particular, of these expenses were stated and certified.

Here, a bottomry bond to secure the balance of these expenses, and the port charges at Rotterdam was executed; upon which the ship was afterwards, on her arrival at N. Y., arrested, libeled and sold, the net proceeds proving insufficent to discharge the amount due on the bond by about $100.

Dec. 8, 1820, the plaintiff abandoned as for a total loss.

The plaintiff having rested, the defendants' counsel offered to prove that the greater part of the repairs at Halifax, were on account of injuries existing before the policy attached; and to designate in proof, what injuries happened before, and what after that time; what injuries were old, and what accrued during the voyage; and that the expenses of repairs incurred for injuries during the period covered by the policy did not amount to a moiety, so as to constitute a technical total loss.

This testimony was objected to, and overruled by the judge; but he said he would allow proof that any items of the repairs, or expenses at Halifax, were not necessary to render the vessel seaworthy.

To this opinion the defendants' counsel excepted.

The defendants' counsel then, among other things, objected that certain cables procured at Halifax were not chargeable; and that the assured had no right to abandon, after the vessel had been repaired, and was in the due prosecution of her voyage; and that the abandonment could not be aided by the subsequent events of the voyage.

A verdict was taken, by consent, for the plaintiff for $3,000 damages, subject to the opinion of the the court upon a case, and subject to adjustment upon the basis to be fixed by the court, with liberty to either party to turn it into a bill of exceptions.

Mr. W. Slosson*, for the plaintiff, ad- **[*65 mitted that, to test the right of abandonment, we must look to the actual state of the ship at the time of the abandonment; not to the information of the assured; according to the case of *Dickey* v. *N. Y. Ins. Co.*, 4 Cow., 222. But here, no abandonment was necessary; for there was an actual total loss. The cases of *Gordon* v. *Bowen*, 2 Johns., 150, and *Mullett* v. *Shedden*, 13 East, 304, show that this may be, though the property physically remain; and the last case shows that a loss by adjudication, as in the principal case, is total in fact. *Da Costa* v. *Newnham*, 2 T. R., 407, is an illustration of this proposition.

The evidence as to the antecedent injuries, which did not produce unseaworthiness, was inadmissible. *Depeyster* v. *Col. Ins. Co.*, 2 Cai., 85.

Messrs. G. Griffin and *J. O. Hoffman*, contra, relied on *Dickey* v. *N. Y. Ins. Co.* as conclusive, that after the ship was repaired, and on her voyage, the assured could not abandon.

As to the average, the foreign adjustment is not conclusive, though it might be otherwise had it been made at the port of necessity. It should not conclude, when made at the port of destination, unless compulsory.

Mr. T. A. Emmet, in reply, said the rules of adjustment were different in different countries, and the only way to do justice is to adopt the foreign adjustment, when fairly made. If this adjustment could have been enforced at Rotterdam, it is valid here. The distinction between a port of necessity and of destination,

---

NOTE.—*Marine Insurance.*

1. *Abandonment—Time for.* See Earl v. Shaw, 1 Johns., Cas., 313, *note*; Mumford v Church, 1 Johns., Cas., 167, *note*; Roget v. Thurston, 2 Johns., Cas., 248, *note*; Smith v. Steinbach, 2 Cai. Cas., 158, *note*.

2. *Foreign adjustment—How far Conclusive.* See Lenox v. United Ins. Co., 3 Johns., Cas., 178, *note*.

is in favor of the latter. He cited Phil. on Ins., 375, 379, and *Strong* v. *N. Y. F. Ins. Co.*, 11 Johns., 323.

Curia, per Savage, *Ch. J.* There can be no controversy as to the fact, that the expense of the repairs exceeded one half the value of the vessel; and the cables most be considered and paid for as a part of her repairs.

That the insurer is not at liberty to show that the vessel had received part of the injury 66*] anterior to the voyage, has *not been disputed since the decision of *Depeyster* v. *Col. Ins. Co.*, 2 Cai., 85, unless she was, in fact, unseaworthy.

Assuming these points in favor of the plaintiff, had he, under the circumstances of the case, a right to abandon for a technical total loss?

In *Dickey* v. *N. Y. Ins. Co.*, 4 Cow., 244, it was decided that the assured could not abandon after the vessel was repaired and successfully pursuing her voyage. In that case, however, the vessel was considered as restored, the *respondentia* being no lien on the ship. In this case, the bottomry was executed at Rotterdam after the voyage had terminated, on account of the sugars sold at Halifax, and port charges at Rotterdam. In the case cited, the master sold part of the cargo at the Isle of France, and was obliged to borrow money upon *respondentia* on the cargo; and the court say: "The vessel was not pledged for the payment; she must, therefore, be considered as beneficially restored; no impediment was placed in the way of prosecuting the voyage to a successful termination. The plaintiff, then, is entitled to recover for a partial loss only." This case is not to be distinguished in principle. Here the master paid for the repairs at Halifax. To enable him to do this, he sold part of the cargo. No bottomry or *respondentia* was executed; no money was borrowed; and according to the case cited, there was no lien on the ship. She was, then, beneficially restored. She did, in fact, prosecute her voyage; and was in the prosecution of her voyage, Dec. 8, 1820, when the offer to abandon was made. In *Da Costa* v. *Newnham*, 2 T. R., 407, the vessel was never beneficially restored. A bottomry bond was executed to raise money, with which to make the repairs—under process upon which, she was subsequently sold. In that particular the case differs from the principal one.

According to the principles settled by this court, the plaintiff can recover for a partial loss only.

He is entitled to the amount expended for repairs, deducting one third new for old; and 67*] also the difference between *the price for which the sugars sold at Halifax and what they would have sold for at Rotterdam; the residue of the expenses at Halifax to be borne upon the principles of general average; the defendants to pay the ship's proportion of that average.

Strong v. *F. Ins. Co.*, 11 Johns., 323, decides, that when a general average is fairly settled in a foreign port, and the insured is obliged to pay his proportion of it, he may recover the amount from the insurer, though the average may have been settled differently abroad, from what it would have been at the home port. The averages settled at Rotterdam, upon which money was paid, or the bottomry bond given must, accordingly, govern.

Rule accordingly.

Cited in—6 Cow., 330; 15 Wend., 461; 3 Paige, 332; 1 Hall, 448; 2 Sand., 80; 5 Duer, 368; 1 Story, 471; 3 Sum., 393; 131 Mass., 250.

JACKSON, ex dem. VAN WYCK, v. SEWARD.

Fraud—Settlement by Way of Advancement to Children, by Person Indebted, Fraudulent, as against Creditors, if such, Prior to Settlement —Rule Applies to Debt Due as Guarantor, though Contingent at Time of Settlement— When Presumption of Fraud, Repelled by Circumstances.

A voluntary settlement or conveyance by way of advancement to children, after marriage, by a person indebted at the time, is fraudulent and void as against all his creditors, who were such prior to the settlement or advancement; and that without regard to the amount of their debts, or the extent of the property settled, or the circumstances of the person who makes the settlement or advancement.

This rule applies to a debt due from a person as guarantor: though it be contingent, till after the settlement or advancement; and though it be such a debt at the time as could not be proved under an English commission of bankrupt, or under our Insolvent Acts.

But with regard to debts contracted subsequent to the settlement, or advancement, it seems that the presumption of fraud, arising in law, may be repelled by circumstances.

A father, having guarantied the payment of a certain judgment against S., who had lands bound by the judgment, which, at a fair value, might well be supposed sufficient to pay the judgment, then disposed of all his real estate, by giving to his son a full covenant deed, and taking a bond to himself for an annuity for his life; and the son, also, in consideration of the deed, gave separate bonds to two of his sisters for their portions; after which the property of S. was exhausted by execution, and proved insufficient to pay the judgment; and the father was sued upon his guaranty, and had judgment against him, on execution upon which, the real estate, thus conveyed for the benefit of his children, was sold. On ejectment by the purchaser, though the jury found against all actual fraud; yet held, that the advancement was fraudulent in law, and void as against the debt due by the guaranty.

Reade v. Livingston, 3 Johns. Ch., 481, in equity, considered, and its doctrine applied to a court of law.

Citations—18 Johns., 425; Keb., 499; 3 Co., 82; Rob. Fraud. Conv., 459; 3 Johns. Ch., 481, 500; 1 Day Conn., 525.

EJECTMENT, commenced in May, 1822, for a farm in Fishkill, Dutchess Co., tried before Betts, Circuit Judge, at the Dutchess Circuit, July 7, 1823.

The suit was brought against Philander Seward and William Seward, jointly; the latter of whom died in July, 1822, and the suit was continued against the former, the present defendant.

*On the trial these facts appeared: [*68 Apr. 16, 1818, William Seward, being aged and infirm, was seised in fee of the premises in question, being a valuable farm of more than 200 acres; and being so seised, by deed of bargain and sale, dated on that day, conveyed them to the defendant, his son, for the consideration expressed, of $10,000, with full covenants.

NOTE.—*Fraud in fact and in Law.* See report of this case in the Court of Errors, 8 Cow., 406, *note*.

The true consideration, however, was as follows: certain bonds from the defendant—one to his sister, Rebecca Swartwout, for $2,277.50; another to his sister, Electa Dodge, for $2,175—both bearing even date with the deed, and payable 6 months after the death of his father William; another in the penalty of $10,000, bearing the same date, to his father, conditioned to pay him an annuity of $500, in half yearly payments, on which were indorsed, in the father's handwriting, the payment of these annuities, in Apr., of the years 1819, 1820, 1821 and 1822.

The lessor of the plaintiff had, after the execution of this deed, recovered a judgment in this court, against William Seward, the father, in an action tried at the Dutchess April Circuit, 1820, for $2,980.04 damages and costs, which was docketed Sept. 13, 1820. That action was commenced in Aug., 1819: and was bottomed on a covenant of guaranty executed by William, the father, to the lessor of the plaintiff. This covenant was dated before the deed, viz.: Nov. 6, 1817; and guarantied that a certain judgment in this court of about $2,700, against William Seward, Jr., in favor of the father, and by him assigned to the lessor of the plaintiff, was collectable. Executions were kept running upon this judgment against William Seward, Jr.'s property, in different counties, till after the deed to the defendant in this cause was executed; and in Feb., 1819, and not before, the property of William Seward was exhausted. Evidence was also given that he had a large real estate situate in different counties, which might fairly be supposed sufficient to satisfy the judgment against him, until it was sold upon execution, on which property the judgment was a lien at the time of the assignment.

69*] *A *fi. fa.* having issued on the judgment against the father, by virtue thereof, the premises in question were sold at auction, and conveyed to the lessor of the plaintiff Feb. 19, 1820, by the Sheriff of Dutchess.

Much evidence was given as to the good faith and honesty of the deed to the son, which was so strong in favor of the deed that the counsel for the plaintiff declined going to the jury upon it.

A verdict was, therefore, taken for the plaintiff, subject to the opinion of this court, upon the single question, whether the deed was fraudulent in law, as against the lessor of the plaintiff.

Mr. P. Ruggles, for the plaintiff, now insisted, among other things,

1. That the lessor of the plaintiff was a creditor within the Statute against Fraudulent Conveyances. (1 R. L., 75, sec. 2.) To which point he cited *Jackson* v. *Myers*, 18 Johns., 425, and the cases there referred to.

2. That the deed was voluntary, fraudulent and void within that Statute. *Reade* v. *Livingston*, 3 Johns. Ch., 481, and the cases there cited.

Mr. J. Tallmadge, contra, said that all actual fraud was negatived by the verdict. The deed to the defendant was not voluntary, and therefore was not fraudulent in law, within the meaning of the cases. The obligation contracted by the grantee was indeed an adequate consideration. But there being perfect *bona fides* in fact, it is only necessary for the court to see that there was such a pecuniary consideration as would carry the use. One dollar would have been sufficient for this purpose. The inadequacy of consideration is merely evidence of fraud, not fraud *per se*.

But even if voluntary, the deed is not, for that reason, necessarily void. It may still be valid, even as to prior creditors. And the late *Chancellor* is not borne out, by his cases, in the strong *dictum* that the legal presumption of fraud in such a conveyance cannot be repelled. (3 Johns. Ch., 500.) To show that the intent is always to be considered, the counsel cited Rob. Fraud. Conv., 190; 8 T. R., 530; Shep. *Touch., 67; 6 East, 257; 2 Bl. Com., [*70 297; 5 Ves., 384; 2 Atk., 600; 2 Bro. Ch., 90; Newl. on Cont., 384, 385; 5 Ves., 384; and Cowp., 432, 708.

But the debt against William Seward, Sr., did not arise till after he conveyed to the defendant. The guaranty was conditional. Nothing was due upon it till the property of W. Seward, Jr., was exhausted by execution, in Feb., 1819. The debt not being due from the father till this time, it is the same as if it had been contracted after the execution of the deed to his son; and the charge of fraud is repelled by the proof, that till after the deed all parties had every reason to suppose the estate of William Seward, Jr., sufficient. (3 Johns. Ch., 501.) In this view, actual fraud alone was the question. To this point, and that the debt of the father was contingent, and could not even have been proved under a commission of bankruptcy, till after the deed, the counsel cited Bac. Abr., Bankrupt, E; Johns., Dig., Insolvent, II, and the cases there cited; 1 Johns. Cas., 73; 9 Johns., 127; Doug., 92; 3 T. R., 539; 3 Atk., 410; Prec. Ch., 377; Gilb. Eq., 37, and 15 Johns., 261.

Mr. T. J. Oakley, in reply, denied that here was anything paid by the grantee as a consideration for the land. The annuity was no more than a fair rent, and the grantee would, therefore, lose nothing. Being a voluntary conveyance, it is fraudulent in law, notwithstanding the finding of the jury; though we admit it would not be so as to debts contracted after the deed was executed. As to these, the question would turn upon the fraudulent intent, and the finding would perhaps be conclusive. He referred to 1 Madd. Ch., 217, 1st Am. ed., and the cases there cited.

Curia, per SUTHERLAND, *J.* It is admitted that there was no actual fraudulent intent on the part of William Seward, in making conveyance to his son, the defendant, Apr. 16, 1818. But it is contended that the conveyance was voluntary and, therefore, fraudulent, in judgment of law as against the lessor of the plaintiff, who was a prior creditor.

1. Was Van Wyck a creditor within the Statute?

*2. If a creditor, was the conveyance [*71 fraudulent as against him?

The case of *Jackson* v. *Myers*, 18 Johns., 425, and the authorities there cited, appear to me to establish the position that Van Wyck stood in a relation to William Seward, which entitled him to the protection of the Statute. Whether he was strictly a creditor or not, within the meaning and provisions of the English Bankrupt Act, I do not think it material to inquire; for our Statute for the Prevention of Frauds is not confined to creditors only, but it avoids all conveyances, &c., devised and contrived with the purpose and intent to delay, hinder or defraud creditors and others of their just actions, &c., &c.

Now, most of the cases cited by the defendant's counsel upon this point, were decisions under the English Bankrupt Acts; and, admitting them to establish that the lessor of the plaintiff would not be considered a creditor under those Acts, it would not follow that he is not entitled to the protection of our Act for the Prevention of Frauds. In *Jackson* v. *Myers*, 18 Johns., 425, it was held, that although the plaintiff had no debt or demand against the grantor in the fraudulent conveyance at the time it was executed, but merely an action *in maleficio* pending, the deeds were fraudulent within the true construction of the Statute. And in *Mountford* v. *Ranie*, Keb., 499, the conveyance was held fraudulent, although the plaintiff had become a creditor only by the escape of a prisoner, and although the bond on which the judgment was obtained, had been given many years subsequent to the conveyance.

The question of creditor or not, cannot turn on the ground of contingent liability when considering this Act. If it should, all indorsers and sureties would be deprived of its protection. It was said in *Twyne's* case, 3 Rep., 82, and reiterated by this court in *Jackson* v. *Myers*, that the Statute extends not only to creditors but to all others who had cause of action or suit, or any penalty or forfeiture. And it has always been held that the Statute was entitled to a liberal construction for the suppression of fraud.

72*] *The demand in this case, fundamentally, as it is expressed by Roberts, in his Treatise on Fraud. Conv., 459, arose before the conveyance. It arose upon a covenant prior in date to the conveyance, for the performance of a collateral, and if you please, contingent act. But it cannot be said that the covenantor was ignorant of his liability, so as to exempt him from the imputation of fraud under the statute, if he has made a voluntary conveyance.

2. Was the conveyance in this case voluntary? The consideration expressed in the deed is $10,000. The consideration proved is an annuity to the grantor of $500 during his life; and the bonds of the defendant to his sisters, the daughters of the grantor, for about $4,500, payable in six months after his death. The annuity is proved to have been paid for four years. The bonds have not been paid. The grantor died in July, 1822. The essence of the transaction is the same as though the grantor had conveyed all his estate to his children, either in equal or unequal proportions, reserving an annuity from each, proportioned to the respective portions of the estate. Instead of giving any portion of his farm to his daughters, he gives the whole to his son, and charges it with the sums intended for the advancement of his daughters. The annuity paid to the grantor cannot inure by way of pecuniary consideration to the support of the deed. The payments were subsequent to the conveyance. The annuity was in the nature of rent for the use of the farm, and cannot be considered the consideration for the conveyance. It is a deed of gift to his children; so intended by the grantor in perfect truth and honesty, and so understood by all the witnesses whom he consulted, or to whom he explained his views and wishes.

Is such a conveyance valid against a prior creditor? *Chancellor* Kent, in *Reade* v. *Livingston*, 3 Johns. Ch., 481, has discussed this question with his usual learning and ability; and after analyzing all the cases, he comes (*Id.*, 500) to this general conclusion: "that if the party be indebted at the time of a voluntary settlement, it is presumed to be fraudulent, in respect to such debts; and no circumstances will permit those debts to be affected by the settlement, or repel the legal presumption of fraud." The presumption *of law in [*73 this case does not depend upon the amount of the debts or the extent of the property in settlement, or the circumstances of the party. "There is," he observes, "no such line of distinction set up or traced in any of the cases. The attempt would be embarrassing, if not dangerous, to the rights of creditors, and prove an inlet to fraud. The law has, therefore, wisely disabled the debtor from making any voluntary settlement of his estate, to stand in the way of his exististing debts. This is the clear and uniform doctrine of the cases."

With respect to the claims of subsequent creditors, he held that the presumption of fraud arising from the circumstance that the party was indebted at the time, may be repelled; that it is repelled by the fact of those debts being secured by mortgage, or by a provision in the settlement; that if no such circumstances exist, the subsequent creditor may show prior indebtedness; that as to subsequent debts, there is no necessary legal presumption of fraud, from a voluntary conveyance; and that there must be proof of fraud, in fact; and that the indebtedness at the time of the conveyance, in order to be available to a subsequent creditor, must be such, in its circumstances and amount, as to justify the conclusion of fraud.

The *Chancellor* considers the case of *Salmon* v. *Bennett*, 1 Day Conn., N. S., 525, as against the current and weight of English decisions; and as not intended to conform to those decisions upon the statutes against fraudulent conveyances. It would be worse than useless, for me to follow the *Chancellor* in his analysis of the English cases. I have looked into most of them, and am satisfied that, so far as is necessary for the decision of this case, the conclusions which he has drawn are fully warranted, not only on the ground of authority, but by considerations of the soundest policy and wisdom.

Judgment for the plaintiff.

Reversed—8 Cow., 406.
Limited—18 Wend., 375.
Cited in—5 Wend., 696; 4 Hill, 279; 2 Paige, 58; 1 Edw., 326; 24 N. Y., 627; 5 Barb., 410; 3 Rob., 348; 9 Leg. Obs., 119; 35 N. J. L., 135; 29 N. J. E., 559; 54 Wis., 308.

74*] *JACKSON, ex dem. SWARTWOUT ET UX.,
v.
JOHNSON.

THE SAME v. BRAINARD.(a)

Ejectment—1. Lands Vested in Trustee in Trust for Female Infant and Others, by Act of Legislature. 2. Adverse Possession—What amounts to—Must be Hostile in Inception, and Possessor Must Claim Entire Title. 3. Statute of Limitation—Does not Run Against One Under Disability—Where Several Disabilities Exist it does not Run till All are Removed. 4. Tenancy by the Curtesy—What Constitutes. 5. Seisin—May be by Tenant in Possession. 6. Witnesses—Lessor of Plaintiff Allowed to Prove Loss of Deed. 7. Champerty and Maintenance.

A, in 1787, was vested by Act of the Legislature, with certain lands in fee in trust for B., a female infant and others, he having power to sell, &c. May 12, 1790, he contracted by his attorney to sell a farm to R., on his (R.'s) paying, &c.; and R. took possession under the contract and began to improve the land; but soon assigned his contract to J., who, in 1790, succeeded him in the possession. B., the female *cestui que trust*, being still an infant, intermarried with C. Apr. 7, 1792; and Nov. 5, of the same year A. conveyed all the trust property (including the land contracted for by R.) to the *cestui que trust*. Afterwards, Dec. 13, 1793, A., the trustee, by his attorney, conveyed the fee to J. During the same year, but at what time in the year it did not appear, B. had issue, a son, born alive, by her husband C., and afterwards, Sept. 30, 1795, a daughter. B. died in July, 1797, having attained the age of 21, C., her husband, surviving. The son died intestate and unmarried, in 1816; and his father, the husband of B., died in 1817, the daughter surviving. On ejectment, *ex dem.* the daughter against J., who had held claiming title, from the date of his deed of Dec. 13, 1793; held first, that his possession was not adverse, so as to avoid the deed to the *cestuis que trust* for champerty or maintenance; secondly, that his possession was adverse from the date of his deed; but thirdly, as B., the owner, was then under disability, both of infancy and coverture, the Statute of Limitations should not run against her till both these disabilities were removed; that she, or her heirs, should have, in any event ten years after the removal of her disabilities, and at least 20 years after the adverse possession commenced within which to enter or bring ejectment; and fourthly, that C. was tenant by the curtesy whether the adverse possession or disseisin took place before, or after, issue of the marriage; and fifthly, that this suspending the right of entry or action of her heirs, they had yet ten years within which to bring ejectment, after the estate by the curtesy terminated by the death of her father, in 1817.

It seems that a conveyance in fee, to one in trust for others, coupled with power to sell or mortgage, for the purpose of reimbursing to the trustee, certain moneys to be expended about the trust property, does not carry the possession or legal estate to the *cestui que trust* by virtue of the Statute of Uses.

It seems that where A. contracts to convey land to B. on certain conditions being performed, and afterwards conveys accordingly, this is evidence that the previous conditions were performed by B.

A possession and claim of land under an executory contract of purchase, is not such as an adverse possession as will render a deed from the true owner void of champerty or maintenance; nor is it such an adverse possession as if continued for 20 years, will bar an entry within the Statute of Limitations; and especially, it is no sense adverse, as to the one with whom the contract is made.

To constitute an adverse possession, it must not only be hostile in its inception but the possesor must claim the entire title; for if it be subservient to, and admit the existence of a higher title, it is not adverse to that title.

Yet, it seems, that where one enters under a contract for a deed with A., and afterwards takes a deed from B., his possession from this time is adverse to A., and if continued for 20 years, will bar A.'s entry.

The disability which entitles a party to the benefit of the proviso in the Statute of Limitations, must exist when the right of entry or action first accrues; and if several disabilities exist together, the Statute does not begin to run until the whole are removed.

If several disabilities exist together, in the owner of an estate, as infancy and coverture, when the advese possession commences against her, she, or if she die, her heirs have at least ten years within which to enter or bring an action, after both disabilities are removed; and they are entitled to full 20 years for this purpose, from the time when the adverse possession commenced. Thus, if the disabilities should be removed within three years after the adverse possession commenced, they would not be barred under 17 years. So if the disabilities should not be removed till 20 years after the adverse possession began, they would still have 10 years to enter or bring ejectment. And thus, 30 years adverse possession or more, may be necessary to bar an entry or ejectment.

And though these disabilities be removed, if the right of entry or ejectment be suspended by the intervention of a particular estate, existing at the time of their removal, as a tenancy by the curtesy, initiate, during their existence, and consummate *eo instanti* that they determine, the owners still have 10 years to enter or bring ejectment after the particular estate determined.

Cumulative or successive disabilities, such as are mentioned by the proviso in the Statute of Limitations, are not allowed to stand in the way of the Statute; but the intervention of a partieular estate is not within the rule. Thus, if the disseisin happen during infancy and coverture, and afterward, before or at the determination of these disabilities, an estate by the curtesy intervene, it is not within the rule; but the rightful owner shall have yet 10 years to enter or bring ejectment, after the estate by the curtesy is determined.

The Statute of Limitations does not run against remainder-men or reversioners, during the continuance of the particular estate. It was aimed at those who may be guilty of laches in omitting to enter or bring actions; which cannot be said of remainder-men and reversioners, who have no right in law to do either. And this, whether the particular estate exist at the time of the disseisin, or arise subsequently, provided that in the latter case it be immediately preceded by a disability or disabilities within the proviso of the Satute.

Four things are necessary to constitute a tenancy by the curtesy: marriage, seisin of the wife, issue and death of the wife. But it is not necessary that seisin and issue should concur together at one time; and therefore if the wife become seised of lands during the coverture, and then be disseised, and then have issue, the husband shall be tenant by the curtesy of these lands; and on his wife's death may enter as such; and during her life he is called tenant by the curtesy initiate. So if the wife become seised after issue, though the issue die before her seisin.

As to what shall amount to a seisin, it is enough that the wife have a tenant in possession who holds at will, or who entered under a contract to purchase her estate.

And it seems that the rule which requires actual seisin applies only to cases where it is not complete till entry; as where the estate comes to the wife by descent or devise; not where it comes by purchase, and is transferred into possession by the Statute of Uses.

The lessor of the plaintiff sworn as a witness, at the circuit without objection, in order to prove the loss of a deed.

(a) These causes were decided in August Term, 1825.

NOTE.—1. *Adverse possession. What constitutes.* See Jackson v. Smith, 13 Johns., 406, *note, and notes there cited*; Jackson v. Sharp, 9 Johns., 163, *note*; Brandt v. Ogden, 1 Johns., 156, *note*.

2. *Statute of Limitations. Does not run against reversioner or remainder-man* till after determination of the particular estate. Jackson v. Schoonmaker, 4 Johns., 390; Jackson v. Sellick, 8 Johns., 262; Fogal v. Pirro, 10 Bosw., 100; 17 Abb. Pr., 117; Gibson v. Jayne, 37 Miss., 164; Foster v. Marshall, 22 N. H., 491; Bell v. McCawley, 29 Ga., 355; Bailey v. Woodbury, 50 Vt., 166; Woodson v. Smith, 1 Head, 276; Higgins v. Crosby, 40 Ill., 260.

Citations—4 Cow., 587; Act, Apr. 21, 1787; 4 Johns., 230, 390, 402; 1 Cow., 605, 610; 9 Johns., 180, 181; 3 Johns. Ch., 137, 129, 138; 18 Johns., 44, 45, 448; 4 Taunt., 826; 6 East, 50, 80; 4 Day, 298; 2 Cow., 27; 4 Mass., 182; 4 T. R., 300; Plowd., 353, 375; 1 Co. Inst., 29, 30 *a*, 39 *a*; 8 Co., 36; 13 Co., 23; 1 Cruise Dig. tit. 5, ch. 1, secs. 10, 11, 25, p. 107, 112, 113; 8 Johns., 262, 269; 3 Atk., 469; Cruise, 110, 11, 12, sec. 24; 107, ch. 1, sec. 11; 112, sec. 25; 2 Bl. Com., 238, 312, 338; 1 Johns., 156.

EJECTMENTS, to recover an undivided fourth part of lots 5 and 10 in Colden's tract, in Croghan's patent, in the town of Burlington, in Otsego Co., tried at the circuit in that County, Sept., 1823, before Nelson, Circuit Judge.

It was admitted that Cadwallader Colden and David Colden were, Mar. 15, 1770, seised of 1483 acres of land, of which the premises in question were a part.

75*] *The plaintiff gave in evidence a deed from Cadwallader Colden to David Colden, dated Dec. 12, 1775, and by which lots 5 and 10, with others, were released to David Colden.

It was admitted that David Colden's name was in the Act of Attainder of 1779.

The plaintiff's counsel then read in evidence an Act of the Legislature passed Apr. 21, 1787, the 1st section of which vested the estate of David Colden, not already sold, in Cadwallader Colden, his heirs, executors and administrators, in trust for the children of David Col-
76*] den, and authorized *Cadwallader Colden to bring actions for the recovery of the property in his own name.

The 2d section was in the form of a proviso, that Cadwallader Colden should pay into the Treasury, in three months, such sums as the land should be appraised at, and deliver to the Surveyor-General certain papers belonging to his office and make a certain affidavit.

The 3d section directed the Commissioners of Forfeitures to have the lands mentioned in a certain location of the lands of David Colden made by Cadwallader Colden, appraised; and authorized Cadwallader Colden, when the terms of the Act should be complied with, to sell or mortgage enough of the land to repay himself any money he might have advanced.

The plaintiff's counsel then read in evidence an Act of the Legislature passed Jan. 17, 1789, by which the time of payment to the estate was extended.

He then read in evidence a copy of a paper from the Comptroller's office, a certificate from the Surveyor-General, and an affidavit made by Cadwallader Colden before the *Ch. J.*, by which it appeared that the conditions of the Act of 1787 had all been complied with.

He further read a deposition of Cadwallader D. Colden, taken by consent, by which it appeared that David Colden died in the year 1784, leaving five children, viz.: Cadwallader D., still living; Alice Criste, Mary, Elizabeth Anne, and Catharine. Alice Criste was born in 1768, and died intestate in 1788, without having been married. Mary was born in 1770, married J. O. Hoffman, and died in 1797, leaving children. Elizabeth Anne was born 1774, was married to E. W. Laight in 1799, and died intestate in 1800, without having had a child.

That Catharine, the fourth daughter, was born Nov. 20, 1775, married Thomas Cooper, Apr. 7, 1792, and died intestate in July, 1797, leaving her husband, Thomas Cooper, and a son Colden, and a daughter, Alice Anne, by him living.

That Alice Anne was born Sept. 30, 1795, and Married Dec. 22, 1814, to Samuel Swartwout who, with Alice Anne, his wife, are the lessors of the plaintiff.

*That Colden Cooper was born in 1793, **[*77** and died intestate without having been married, Nov. 21, 1816. Thomas Cooper died in Nov. or Dec., 1817.

It also appeared from this deposition, that Cadwallader Colden, the trustee under the Act of 1787, Nov. 5, 1792, gave the deponent (the son of David Colden) a deed for his undivided fourth of the trust lands (which deed was produced), and also that Cadwallader Colden, on the same day executed to Catharine Cooper, the fourth daughter of D. Colden, a deed for her undivided fourth part. Also, that Catharine Cooper's deed was, in all respects, similar to the deed produced. That these deeds were intended as a full execution of the trust.

The witness recollected the place where the deeds were signed. It was at Mr. Hoffman's. The parties assembled there for the purpose. A copy of this deed was annexed to the case.

The deposition also stated that long previous to the execution of these deeds, and as early as 1790, Cadwallader Colden, the trustee, had been paid for all his advances, out of moneys of the children of David Colden, received from England; that none of the trust lands were sold to raise this money, or for the repayment of any money raised for this purpose; that Cadwallader Colden never pretended to have any claims on those lands after this money from England was received and paid.

The money from England was received in the months of Feb. and June, 1790. In the deed from Cadwallader Colden, the trustee, to Cadwallader D. Colden, there was an exception as to the Otsego lands, in the covenant, that he had done nothing to incumber or impair the title. This (as appeared from the deposition), as the deponent understood, was because some of these lands had been sold by William Cooper, of Cooperstown.

S. Swartwout, the lessor, was sworn as a witness, and proved the loss of the deed from Cadwallader Colden, the trustee, to Catharine Cooper.

*It was admitted that the defendant, **[*78** in the first cause, was in possession of part of No. 10, and the defendant in the second cause, of part of No. 5. and lease, entry and ouster in both causes were confessed. The plaintiff then rested.

The defendants then gave in evidence a power of attorney from Cadwallader Colden, the trustee, to William Cooper, of Cooperstown, dated, Jan. 30, 1790, authorizing William Cooper to sell his (Cadwallader Colden's) lands and also any lands Cadwallader Colden was intrusted with.

The defendant in the first cause then read in evidence an article or contract from William Cooper, as attorney for Cadwallader Colden, to one Matthew Rogers, dated 12 May, 1790, by which it was agreed, that if Rogers paid a certain sum of money by the year 1800, with interest annually, he should receive a deed for the whole of No. 10. This article is more particularly recited in the opinion of Sutherland, *J.*

The defendant in the first cause proved that he, as assignee of the contract to Rogers, went on to No. 10, in 1790; that he had built a log house that summer, and cleared a part of it; and had ever since been in possession, claiming it as his own. He also gave in evidence a deed in fee from William Cooper, as attorney for Cadwallader Colden, to him, dated Dec. 13, 1793, for the premises in question, given in pursuance of the article.

The defendant in the second cause gave in evidence a similar article to one T. Morse, and proved that one Giles, as assignee of Morse, entered in 1790, and cleared a part, and built a log house; that he continued there till 1794, and then sold to the defendant, who had continued in possession ever since, claiming the land as his own. He also gave in evidence a deed in fee from William Cooper, as attorney for Cadwallader Colden, to himself, for the premises in question, dated Jan. 6, 1795, executed pursuant to the article to Morse.

Verdicts were taken for the plaintiff for a fourth of the premises in question, subject to the opinion of the court upon the above case.

Mr. J. O. Morse, for the plaintiff, made the following points:

1. The plaintiff has shown a perfect title in the lessors.

79*] *2. The defendants' possession did not become adverse, till after the death of Thomas Cooper, who was tenant by the curtesy.

1. Title is shown in the lessors; for it is proved, First. That in 1770 D. Colden and C. Colden were seised in fee. Second. That in 1775, C. Colden released to D. Colden half the tract of which the premises in question are part. Third. Although the lands of David were forfeited by the Act of 1779, the Act of 1787 vests them in Cadwallader Colden, in trust for the children of David. Fourth. In 1792, C. Colden, the trustee, conveyed to Catharine Cooper, one of the children of David, her share, of which the premises in question are part. Fifth. Catharine Cooper died in 1797, leaving her husband, Thomas Cooper, survivor, who was tenant by the curtesy. Sixth. Thomas Cooper died in 1817, and the estate of Mrs. Swartwout then vested, her brother Colden having previously died.

2. The possession of the defendants, under the contracts to Rogers and Morse, was not adverse. *Jackson* v. *Camp*, 1 Cow., 605.

It cannot be said that the deed from C. Colden to Mrs. C. Cooper, in 1792, was void for champerty. The case of *Jackson* v. *Bard*, 4 Johns., 230, is decisive on this point. The cases are exactly parallel. In the case of *Cooper* v. *Stower*, 9 Johns., 331, it was decided that a contract to sell and convey, does not even give a license to enter; but it was agreed that till the contract was executed by all the purchasers, and a certain bond given, no timber should be cut; and the court say, that with this addition, the most that could be implied was a permission to enter and occupy as tenants at will, till the consideration money was paid.

The defendants in these causes, then, while occupying under the contracts of Morse and Rogers, the consideration money not having been paid, are to be considered, at most, no better than tenants at will, or *quasi* tenants at will, to C. Colden, or to his *cestui que trust*, Mrs. Cooper.

Their possession, then, did not destroy the operation of the deed to Mrs. Cooper, in 1792; and if this was an operative and valid deed, it is not necessary to inquire whether *the [*80 trust created by the Act of 1787 was executed by our Statute of Uses.

But it may be said, perhaps, that the defendants' possession became adverse when they took their deeds, the first in 1793, and the second in 1795.

For the sake of the argument, we are willing to admit that their possessions did, in their nature, become adverse; but it is denied that they began to operate against Mrs. Cooper.

We admit that there cannot be a succession of disabilities. We say, in the language of Kent, *Chancellor*, in *Demarest* v. *Wynkoop*, 3 Johns. Ch., 136: "If several disabilities exist together at the time the right of action accrues (or at the time the adverse possession commences), the Statute does not begin to run until the party has survived them all."

In our cases, Mrs. Cooper was, at the date of the defendants' deed, laboring under two disabilities, infancy and coverture.

In 1796 she became of age, and her disability as an infant, perhaps, then ceased; but her disability, as a *feme covert* continued as long as she lived. This disability she did not survive. The Statute, therefore, did not begin to run against her.

This is undoubtedly the true doctrine on this subject; and there is nothing that militates against it, except it be a mere *dictum* of *Ch. J.* Swift, of Conn. (2 Conn., N. S., 33).

The rule laid down by *Chancellor* Kent is supported by Chambre, *J.*, in *Cotterell* v. *Dutton*, 4 Taunt., 830.

If, then, the Statute did not begin to run against Mrs. Cooper in her lifetime, the intervention of her husband's life estate, as tenant by the curtesy, would further prevent it, so that in fact it never began to run against Mrs. Swartwout, till after the death of her father.

A contrary rule would be the height of injustice. It would compel the reversioner to bring his suit during the continuance of the particular estate, which is impossible. *Jackson* v. *Schoonmaker*, 4 Johns., 402; 7 East, 311.

*If the Statute does begin to run, the [*81 proviso is a nullity. "If there be no right to enter during a particular estate, in such a case, the Statute never attaches." (Ballan., on Lim., 49.)

Possibly, however, it may be contended that Mrs. Cooper was never seised of these lands, in such a manner as to constitute her husband a tenant by the curtesy.

The rule which now exists on this subject is, that there must be a constructive possession in fact. *Jackson* v. *Sellick*, 8 Johns., 271.

In 1792 C. Colden conveyed these lands to Mrs. Cooper. The persons then on the lands, as has been shown on the authority of *Cooper* v. *Stower*, 9 Johns., 331, were her tenants at will, or *quasi* such. She could have maintained trespass against them on the authority of that case. She had, therefore, a constructive seisin in fact.

In *De Grey* v. *Richardson*, 3 Atk., 469, curtesy was allowed in a case precisely like these.

In *Sterling* v. *Pennington*, 7 Vin., 149, pl. 11, the wife was denied possession during the coverture, and yet curtesy was allowed.

Again; it will not be pretended but that from the year 1787 Mrs. Cooper had a trust estate in these lands. The lands were then wild. An actual entry was not necessary. *Jackson* v. *Sellick*, 8 Johns., 271.

A husband shall be tenant by the curtesy of a trust estate of freehold in the wife. *Watts* v. *Ball*, 1 P. Wms., 108; Cruise Dig., tit. XII., Trust, ch. 11, secs. 8, 9; *Chaplin* v. *Chaplin*, 3 P. Wms., 229; Com. Dig., Estate, D, 1.

Messrs. I. Seelye and *R. Campbell*, contra.

1. If the Act of 1787 vested in the children of D. Colden, by the Statute of Uses, an estate in fee, or if it is vested by the payment of money to the trustee in 1790, the Statute of Limitations began to run against Mrs. Cooper before her marriage.

Giving the deeds to the defendants, is full evidence that every part of the contracts was performed. *Jackson* v. *Camp*, 1 Cow., 605.

82*] *Where a possession is taken under a contract, and the contract consummated by a deed, the possession is adverse from the first. The possession being adverse in 1790, operated on the rights of Mrs. Cooper, then an infant.

The proviso in the Statute of Limitations saved her rights until that disability was removed; but cumulative disabilities are not within the proviso. (18 Johns., 40; 3 Johns. Ch., 129, 138; 4 Taunt., 826; 6 East, 80; 4 Day, 298; Plow., 353; 4 Mass., 182; 4 T. R., 300; 2 Conn., 27.)

If title first accrue to an infant 16 years old, he is not within the proviso, nor obliged to bring his action in 10 years after he comes of age; for in all cases a person has 20 years.

If Mrs. Cooper was seised in 1790, the Statute began to run against her. She was of age in 1796. She and her heirs had 15 years to bring an action. The Statute having begun to run, no subsequent disability can stop it. (2 Conn., 27, 33, per Swift, *Ch. J.*

2. But if Mrs. Cooper was not seised till the date of the deed to her from C. Colden, in 1792, this deed gave her no right; for it was void for champerty. At the date of this deed, the defendants had been three years in possession under the contracts. C. Colden could sell nothing but a right of action.

If Mrs. Cooper would have been compelled to bring an action to get possession, the deed must be void; for such an action cannot be sold. It is directly in face of the Statute, and void at common law. (1. R. L., 172; 3 Johns. Cas., 101; 2 Johns. Cas., 41, 58; 5 Johns., 489; Co. Litt., 214; 11 Johns., 91; 9 *Id.*, 55.) The lessors, therefore, showed no right.

3. The adverse possession certainly began to operate on the execution of the deeds to the defendants. Mrs. Cooper was then an infant and *covert*. She was of age in 1796, and died in 1797. She had 20 years from the date of the defendant's deeds, and her heirs ten years from her death.

It does not appear from the case that Mrs. Cooper had a child at the date of Johnson's deed, Dec, 1793. Of course, Thomas Cooper was not then tenant by the curtesy.

83*] *The case states that Colden Cooper was born in 1793; but the time in that year is not stated. The tenancy by the curtesy must have existed when the adverse possession commenced. It cannot arise during the existence of an adverse possession.

4. When the adverse possession commenced in *Johnson's* case, T. Cooper had not acquired even an incohate right by the birth of a child. His life estate did not commence till the death of his wife in 1797, if at all. (1 Binn., 10.)

The *dictum* that the Statute does not begin to run in such a case as this, is not correct. It can only be true that the Statute never runs out, and forms a bar during that disability, nor until ten years afterward. (Op. of *Ch. J.* Swift, 2 Conn., 27, 33.)

The Statute did, therefore, begin to run, and the life estate of tenancy by the curtesy, not being in existence when the adverse possession commenced, will not stop the Statute.

This, therefore, distinguishes the case from those of *Jackson* v. *Schoonmaker*, 4 Johns., 390, and *Jackson* v. *Sellick*, 8 Johns., 262.

5. The decisive answer to the plaintiff's claim is, that Thomas Cooper never was tenant by the curtesy. Here was no seisin in deed, and in fact. This is necessary. (1 Inst., 29 *a*; 1 Cruise, 107, sec. 10; Perkins, 464, 470.)

There has been no relaxation of this rule, except where lands are wild, as in *Jackson* v. *Sellick*, 8 Johns., 265. If, however, T. Cooper and wife should be deemed seised in law, that seisin was in trust for the defendants; and the husband of a female trustee cannot be tenant by the curtesy. (1 Madd. Ch., 268; 1 Cruise, Dig., 471, title, XII., Trust, ch. 1, sec. 30.)

Where articles are entered into for the purchase of an estate, a trust immediately results to the purchaser. (3 Johns. Ch., 316; 1 Madd. Ch., 389–391.)

Mr. D. Cady, in reply. It cannot be necessary to discuss the questions, whether the Act of Apr. 7, 1787, created such a trust in C. Colden as was executed in the children of D. Colden, by the Statute of Uses; nor whether they *became seised of the legal estate [***84** in 1790, when all the money which their trustee had advanced on account of the trust estate was repaid. It is enough to show that it was vested in them by their trustee Nov. 5, 1792.

The husband of Mrs. Cooper, the *cestui que trust*, could not, even by his dissent, make void a deed executed by the trustee in pursuance of the trust. But there is no pretense that he dissented.

In 1 Inst., sec. 1, 3 *a*, it is said, "a *feme covert* is of capacity to purchase of others, without the consent of her husband; but the husband may disagree thereto and devest the whole estate; but if he neither agree nor disagree the purchase is good." The law, then, requires that the husband should do an act clearly manifesting his dissent to the purchase.

What are the facts which are supposed to prove the adverse possession upon which the defendants rely for a defense? Were it conceded that Dec. 13, 1793, the possession of the defendants became adverse to all the world, and so continued from that time to the present, it would not furnish them with a shadow of a defense. Unless their possession was commenced in hostility to the title of C. Colden, and continued adverse down to Nov. 5, 1792, when he executed a deed to Mrs. Cooper, his *cestui que trust*, no one of the objections taken by the defendant's counsel, and founded upon adverse possession, can be supported.

The court say, in the case of *Smith* v. *Burtis*, 9 Johns., 180, "a possession, for ever so long a time, stripped of the circumstance that it is accompanied with the claim of the entire title, will not amount to an adverse possession, barring those who have the real and legitimate title." The fact of possession and the *quo animo* it was commenced or continued, are the only tests; it must necessarily be exclusive of any other right." In the case of *Brandt* v. *Ogden*, 1 Johns., 158, the court say, "in order to bar the recovery of a plaintiff who has a title by a possession in the defendant, strict proof has always been required, not only that the first possession was taken under a claim **85***] hostile to the *real owner; but that such hostility has continued on the part of the succeeding tenants.

In these cases, the court were speaking of such an adverse possession, as would, if continued 20 years, bar the person having title; but the possession which will make void a deed executed by a person having the title, must be of the same character. Suppose Johnson had remained in possession 20 years, as assignee of the contract to M. Rogers; would that possession have protected him against an ejectment brought by C. Colden? Could he have alleged that he entered claiming the fee in hostility to the title of C. Colden? So far from this, C. Colden, on the trial of such ejectment, need not have given any other evidence of his title than the contract to Rogers, and proof that the defendant entered and claimed as assignee of that contract. *Jackson* v. *Dobbin*, 3 Johns., 223; *Jackson* v. *Reynolds*, 1 Cai., 444.

. The counsel for the defendant have introduced what is deemed a new test, in order to determine whether a possession be or be not adverse. They assume that if the defendant had committed such an ouster or disseisin as would compel C. Colden, or the children of D. Colden, to bring an action to get possession, then the deed must be void! Indeed! is this the rule? A tenant at will or at sufferance, if he be obstinate, cannot be turned out of possession but by action; and is it to be taken for granted that he will be obstinate, and that his possession renders it unlawful for his landlord to sell the estate? The law requires strict proof in order to show that a possession is adverse. Without such proof, the possession is always presumed to be in subordination to the title, and to be held for the rightful owner. (9 Johns., 166, 167; 3 Johns. Cas., 124.)

The case of *Jackson* v. *Bard*, 4 Johns., 231, bears directly upon the point under discussion; and in the case of *Jackson* v. *Camp*, 1 Cow., 610, the court say, "that the agreement (to purchase) had not placed Dyer in a situation to commence holding adversely, until he had performed the condition." When Johnson, **86***] as the assignee of the agreement *with Rogers, entered, it was altogether uncertain whether he ever would perform the conditions upon which the agreement would take effect, and there is no evidence in the case that he ever did pay a cent before the deed of Nov. 5, 1792, to Mrs. Cooper. He did not enter claiming title in himself, but claiming the title to be in C. Colden, from whom he intended to acquire it.

A deed given in Dec., 1793, by C. Colden, can furnish no evidence that the article of sale was performed, against his grantee, in a deed given in Nov., 1792. Beside, the agreement was for the conveyance of 525 acres of land, and the deed is for but 100 acres. It is idle, therefore, to say that the deed was given in pursuance of the contract, or that it furnishes evidence that the contract was performed. It is rather evidence that the agreement with Rogers was abandoned, and a new agreement substituted in its stead. It cannot, however, be important whether the defendant did or did not perform the agreement under which he entered. Suppose he had regularly paid the interest up to the time when C. Colden conveyed to Mrs. Cooper, would such payment have rendered his possession adverse, so that C. Colden could not give a valid deed to his *cestui que trust?* If C. Colden had been seised of the land in his own right, and covenanted to convey it to the defendant in the year 1800; and the defendant had paid the interest to Nov., 1792, C. Colden might have been considered a trustee for the defendant; and had C. Colden then given a deed to another, the deed would have passed a valid title at law, but the purchaser might have been charged with the trust, and compelled in a court of equity to convey the land to the defendant. But in this case, C. Colden was trustee for the children of D. Colden, before he made any agreement with the defendant's assignor, Rogers. There is good reason for saying that the defendant purchased with notice of that trust. The papers which the defendant would have to produce, to show his own title, would prove the trust. *Hamilton* v. *Royce*, 2 Sch. & L., 315. But whether he is chargeable with notice of the trust or not, Mrs. Cooper had the first equity, and the first title at law.

*But suppose the agreement made by [***87** Wm. Cooper with Rogers was a valid agreement, as against the children of D. Colden; neither C. Colden nor his attorney could, after he had conveyed the estate to his *cestuis que trust*, give a valid deed to Johnson. The defendant should have looked to them for a title.

The Statute against Champerty and Maintenance has no application to a deed given by a trustee to his *cestui que trust* in pursuance of the trust. Their titles constitute but one, and it must be immaterial, as to other persons, whether their titles be united in one person or not. There can be no danger, that a *cestui que trust* will purchase in his own title at an undervalue for the purpose of litigation or oppression. The intent of the Statute was "to restrain all persons from transferring any disputed right to strangers." (3 Bac. Abr., 326. Maintenance.) "Whoever has a reversion or remainder vested in him may lawfully take any conveyance which will strengthen his estate." May not a *cestui que trust* do the same.

Why did the execution of that deed to Mrs. Cooper give the character of hostility to the defendant's possession? If the defendant, when that deed was executed, was in possession, admitting the title of C. Colden, and intending to purchase that title, he did not commence to hold in hostility to it, the moment it was transferred to Mrs. Cooper. No; he continued to hold under the same title, as her tenant at will.

To support their branch of the argument upon the Statute of Limitations, the defendant's counsel are driven to the necessity of insisting that T. Cooper was not tenant by the curtesy. So confident are we that T. Cooper was tenant by the curtesy, and that, during his life, the descent to the children of Mrs. Cooper was suspended, that I do not deem it necessary to examine whether the construction put upon the Statute of Limitations by the defendant's counsel be or be not correct.

The law is not, that to make the husband tenant by the curtesy, the seisin of the wife must be after the birth of issue. (1 Cruise Dig., 107, chap. 1, sec. 11; *Id.*, 113, sec. 25.) **88***] *The time when the seisin of the wife commences, whether before or after issue had, is immaterial. Thus, Ld. Coke says (1 Inst., 30 *a*): "If a man takes a woman seised of lands in fee and is disseised, and then has issue, and the wife dies, he shall enter and hold by the curtesy. So if he has issue before the descent of lands upon his wife." These authorities are enough to show that it is wholly immaterial whether Colden Cooper was born before or after the deed given to the defendant. Nay; if he had never been born, it would not have varied the right of the lessors.

The question is, was Mrs. Cooper, at any time during the coverture, so seised as to entitle her husband to be tenant by the curtesy? This question must be answed in the affirmative, unless Cadwallader Colden was so disseised that he could not convey a legal title to his *cestui que trust*, Mrs. Cooper, Nov. 5, 1792. That he was not so disseised, has, it is believed, been sufficiently shown.

It requires the same seisin in the wife, to enable her heir to take by descent, as it does to entitle her husband to be tenant by the curtesy. (1 Cruise Dig., 112, ch. 1, sec. 24.) A seisin in law is said not to be sufficient for either purpose. A seisin in law, as distinguished from a seisin in deed, applies only to cases in which the title of the person claiming is not complete till entry. Thus, a person who claims as heir or devisee has only a seisin in law, before entry; and if before entry, a stranger enters, it is an abatement, not a disseisin. (3 Bl. Com., 167.) "In descents of land which are cast upon the heir by the act of the law itself, the heir has not *plenum dominium*, or full and complete ownership, till he has made an actual corporal entry into the lands; and if he die before entry made, his heir shall not be entitled to take possession; but the heir of the person who was last actually seised." (2 Bl. Com., 312.) But when a person claims under a deed or conveyance, to which effect is given by the Statute of Uses, "he is put at once into corporal possession of the land, without ever having seen it, by a kind of parliamentary magic." (2 Bl. Com., 338.) In this case Mrs. Cooper did not claim as heir, devisee or feoffee, and there was no necessity that she should **89***] enter in order to *enable her heirs to take, or her husband to be tenant by the curtesy. She claimed either under a legislative grant, or under a deed from her trustee, in either of which cases was entry necessary to give *plenum dominium*. The case put by Ld. Coke, 1 Inst., 29 *a*, to show that the husband shall not be tenant by the curtesy, where the wife has only a seisin in law, is where lands descend to the wife, she has issue, and dies before entry. But the literal construction of this rule has been departed from, both in England and in this country. (1 Cruise Dig., 110, sec. 16.)

In the case of *Jackson* v. *Sellick*, 8 Johns., 262, the court held that, as to lands, the possession followed the title, and that to entitle the husband to be tenant by the curtesy, it was not necessary that he should enter during the coverture. In the case of *Jackson* v. *Howe*, 14 Johns., 405, 406, the court held that, as to wild lands, the heir need not enter in order to become the stock from which a descent might be claimed.

Here the possession of the defendant was the possession of Cadwallader Colden, which was transferred to Mrs. Cooper, and she had a right to consider the defendant as holding for her. At all events, she had a right so to consider him till he took a deed in 1793. And were it conceded that she and her husband were then disseised, and so continued till her death, it would present the very case in which Ld. Coke says that the husband "shall enter and hold by the curtesy."

SUTHERLAND, *J*. The lessors of the plaintiff made out a clear paper title to the premises in question, and are entitled to recover, unless the deed from Cadwallader Colden to Mrs. Cooper, of Nov. 5, 1792, was void under the Statute of Champerty and Maintenance, or their rights barred by adverse possession.

The questions which arose in the suit of the same lessors against Cole, 4 Cow., 587, whether the trust in favor of the heirs of David Colden, created by the Act of 1787, was executed by the Statute of Uses; or if not, whether a conveyance from the trustee to the *cestuis que trust* was to be presumed are excluded from this case; because an actual conveyance from their *trustee is proved; and the first ques- [***90** tion which arises is, whether that conveyance was valid. It bears date Nov. 5, 1792; and it is contended by the defendant that it was void; because, at the time of its execution, the premises in question which, among others, it purported to convey, were in the actual possession of the defendant, under a contract of sale made between Cadwallader Colden, by his attorney William Cooper, and one Matthew Rogers, May 12, 1790. It appears that the defendant, as the assignee of that contract, entered upon a part of the premises which it contains, in the summer of 1790, made a small clearing and erected a log house; that Dec. 13, 1793, he took a deed from William Cooper, as the attorney of Colden, and has remained in the possession down to the time of the trial.

This, it is said, was an adverse possession from the time of the defendant's entry in 1790; but if not so, then that it became adverse upon the receiving of his deed in 1793.

So far as the question of maintenance is concerned, it is not material whether the defendant's possession became adverse or not, upon receiving his deed in 1793. If the lands conveyed to Mrs. Cooper by the deed of Nov. 5, 1792, were not then held adversely to the grantor, the deed was not void on the ground of champerty and maintenance. The adverse possession must exist at the time of the conveyance, in order to avoid it. If the defendant's possession was not then adverse to Cadwallader Colden, under whom he entered, it was, in judgment of law, the possession of Colden; and his conveyance would not be affected, either by the terms or the principles of the Act against Champerty and Maintenance. In the view of that Act, it would be valid, whatever might be its legal effect and operation.

Was the defendant, then, Nov. 5, 1792, in possession of the premises in question, holding them adversely to Cadwallader Colden? By the contract with Rogers, he was to have a deed for his land from Colden, upon his paying him £262 10*s*, with interest, annually, on or before May 12, 1800. The contract does not, in terms, authorize Rogers to enter upon the land. It **91***] contains no *words of present demise. It recites that Rogers, by his obligation, bearing even date with the agreement, was indebted to Colden in the sum of £262 10*s*, and covenants that in consideration thereof, the said Colden will convey to the said Rogers, the premises mentioned therein, if the said Rogers shall pay the said sum of £262 10*s*, with interest, annually, on or before May 12, 1800. Rogers, therefore, or his assignee, was not entitled to a deed until the land was paid for. He did not enter, claiming the whole title. The contract itself admits the title to reside in Colden, and that it was to remain in him until Rogers' part of the agreement was performed. Now, admitting the deed to the defendant, given in 1793, to be evidence of performance on his part, it is evidence of performance only at the time it was given, and not at any antecedent period. In 1792, therefore, when the deed to Mrs. Cooper was given, the defendant had not performed, and was not entitled to a conveyance. Such a possession has never been considered adverse. In *Jackson* v. *Bard*, 4 Johns., 230, one Barton, in May, 1798, entered into articles of agreement with Dickenson and Harris for the sale of certain premises. Soon after one Smith purchased a portion of the premises from Dickenson, by contract, and paid him $25 and entered into possession. Mar. 8, 1799, Barton gave a deed to Dickenson and took back a mortgage. Barton foreclosed the mortgage, and the lessor of the plaintiff became the purchaser, and took a deed from Burton on the mortgage sale. The tenant in possession under Smith forbid the sale, and it was contended that the possession of Smith was adverse at the time of the giving of the mortgage, so as to render it void and prevent its operation. But the court held it not to be adverse to Barton's title. They say Dickenson could not have set up against Barton an adverse holding; and Smith, who claimed under him, must be considered as standing in the same situation.

In *Jackson* v. *Camp*, 1 Cow., 605, the same principle is distinctly recognized. One Dyer made a contract for land with the agent of the proprietors in 1792, and entered under it. In 1794 he received his deed. In 1796 *he [***92** sold a part of it to the defendant. It appeared that he took possession under his contract, of land which the deed did not cover, and the defendant sought to retain it, on the ground of adverse possession. The possession taken under Dyer's contract was held not to be adverse on several grounds. But, among others, the court say, the agreement (made by Dyer with the agent) "did not put him in a situation to commence holding adversely, until he performed the condition. The land still belonged to the proprietor of the township. Whether he ever would perform was contingent. He entered on the lot, it is true, but it was necessarily subject to the right of turning him off, if he neglected to make full payment. The possession, therefore, when taken, had not the characteristics to constitute it adverse. It was not hostile in its inception. On the non-performance, Dyer would become liable to be turned out as a trespasser, and responsible in that character for the *mesne* profits." These observations are entirely applicable to this case, and are decisive of the question of adverse possession, at the time of the giving of the deed from Cadwallader Colden to Mrs. Cooper in 1792. That deed, therefore, was not void on the ground of champerty or maintenance.

A possession, in order to be adverse, must be accompanied with a claim of the entire title. If it appear that the title claimed is subservient to, and admits the existence of, a higher title, the possession is not adverse to that title. *Smith* v. *Burtis*, 9 Johns., 180. Now, in this case, the agreement between Colden and Rogers is an admission on the part of Rogers that the legal title remained in Colden; for it provided for the conveyance of that title to Rogers at a future period, upon certain contingencies. If Rogers had not performed the agreement, it would have afforded all the evidence of title which would have been necessary to enable Colden to recover the possession from him, in an action of ejectment. Colden might, perhaps, be considered as the trustee of Rogers, holding the legal estate in trust for him, upon performance on his part; and if Colden's estate in the land had been absolute and in his own right, and not in trust for the heirs of David Colden, his grantee would probably have *taken [***93** it subject to the trust for Rogers, and might, perhaps, have been compelled in equity to convey. It may well be doubted whether, in a case like this, where the legal estate has been united to the older equitable interest, chancery would interfere in favor of a younger equity. But that inquiry is irrelevant here, for in this action the legal title must prevail.

But if the defendant had not such an adverse possession Nov. 1, 1792, as to render the conveyance to Mrs. Cooper, of that date, void, it is contended that his possession, at all events, became adverse to the lessors of the plaintiff Dec. 13, 1793, when he received his deed from Cadwallader Colden; and that the claim of the lessors of the plaintiff is barred by the Statute of Limitations. It is answered that Mrs. Cooper was, at that time, both an infant and *feme covert*; that her coverture continued until her death in 1797; that the descent to her children was suspended during the life of Thomas Cooper, her husband, who was tenant by the curtesy, and who survived until 1817. In reply, it is denied that Mrs. Cooper ever was so seised as to constitute her husband tenant by the curtesy. In order to create such a tenancy, it is said that there must be a seisin in fact, either in the wife or the husband in her right. But admitting there was a sufficient seisin, then it is contended that in Dec., 1793, when the defendant's adverse possession commenced, Cooper was not tenant by the curtesy, as it is not shown that Colden Cooper, his son, was then born; that his life estate did not commence until the death of his wife, in 1797; and that the Statute having commenced running in 1793, could not be impeded by any subsequent disability.

It is well settled that cumulative disabilities are not allowed or protected by the statute; that a party can only avail himself of the disabilities existing when the right of action first accrued. *Demarest* v. *Wynkoop*, 3 Johns. Ch., 138, and the cases there cited and examined by *Chancellor* Kent, and *Jackson* v. *Wheat*, 18 Johns. 45, where the doctrine is fully recognized.

It is also clear, both from the words and pol-
94*] icy of the *Statute, and the repeated expositions which have been given to it, that if 20 years have elapsed since the right of action accrued, and 10 of those years have been free from disability, the right of entry is barred; that is, the party is not entitled to 20 years after the disability ceases to bring his action, but to 10 years only, provided, at the expiration of those 10 years, twenty years have elapsed since the right of entry or action accrued.

Thus, in this case, Mrs. Cooper, in 1793, when the defendant's adverse possession commenced, was an infant and *feme covert*. She was, at all events, entitled to 20 years to bring her action; and if her coverture continued also for 20 years, she was entitled to 10 years after it ceased. The Statute would have protected her for 30 years. But if her infancy and coverture had ceased at any time within ten years after the defendant's entry, then she was barred at the expiration of 20 years, because she had more than ten years free from disability. Her infancy, in fact, terminated in 1796, and her coverture in 1797, when she died. If her husband had not a life estate as tenant by the curtesy, so that her lands then descended to her heirs, their right of entry terminated in 1813, being 20 years from the commencement of the defendant's adverse possession, and more than 10 years after the determination of the disabilities, and death of their ancestor. Kent, *Ch. J.*, in *Smith* v. *Burtis*, 9 Johns., 181, considers this the true exposition of the Statute; and although he says that the question did not necessarily arise in that case, and therefore he did not wish the opinion on that point then expressed by him, to be considered definitive, subsequent reflection and examination confirmed him in that opinion; for he reiterates it in the case of *Demarest* v. *Wynkoop*, already referred to. *Vide*, also, 4 Taunt., 826; 6 East, 50; 4 Day, 298; 2 Conn., 27; 4 Mass., 182; 4 T. R., 300; Plowd., 353.

Unless, therefore, Thomas Cooper was tenant by the curtesy of his wife's lands, so as to suspend their descent to her heirs, the claim of the lessors of the plaintiff is barred by the Statute of Limitations.

*It seems to be supposed by the coun- [*95
sel for the defendant, that unless the life estate of Cooper had vested, by the birth of a child, previous to the commencement of the adverse possession in 1793, although he might subsequently have become tenant by the curtesy, the heirs of Mrs. Cooper could not avail themselves of this new disability, to avoid the bar of the Statute of Limitations; that it would fall within the principle of cumulative or successive disabilities, which are not allowed by the policy of the Act.

It is clear that the birth of a child at any time during coverture, whether before or after the commencement of the defendant's possession, would constitute Cooper tenant by the curtesy of all the lands of his wife, of which, during coverture, she was so seised as to support such an estate. Ld. Coke, 1 Inst., 30 *a*, says, "four things belong to an estate of tenancy by the curtesy, viz.: marriage, seisin of the wife, issue, and death of the wife. But it is not necessary that these should concur together all at one time; and therefore if a man taketh a woman, seised of lands in fee, and is disseised, and then have issue, and the wife die, he shall enter and hold by the curtesy. So if he hath issue which dieth before the descent." *Vide*, also, 8 Rep., 36, *Paine's* case, (*a*) 13 Rep., 23; *Menvil's* case; 1 Cruise Dig. tit. 5, Curtesy, ch. 1, sec. 11, 25, pp. 107, 112, 113.

Cooper then had a life estate in the premises in question, which was initiate, as it is expressed (Co. Litt., 30 *a*), upon the birth of a child in 1793; and became consummate upon the death of his wife in 1797, and continued until his death in 1817.

During the existence of this particular estate, the lands of Mrs. Cooper did not descend to her heirs, so as to give them a right of entry. The question then recurs, whether this particular estate, which arose, or was created subsequent to the commencement of the adverse possession in 1793, was a cumulative disability, of which the lessors of the plaintiff cannot avail themselves under the Statute, by way of excuse for not having brought their action within thirteen years after the death of their ancestor; the period *within which [*96
they must have brought it, if this estate by the curtesy had not existed.

The Statute declares that no person shall make any entry into lands, but within 20 years next after his right or title descended or accrued; provided, that if any person, entitled to make such entry, be, at the time such right or title first descended or accrued, within the age of 21 years, *feme covert*, &c., such person and his heirs shall or may after the said 20 years be expired, make such entry, as he or they might have done before the expiration of the said 20 years, so as such person, within ten years after such disability removed, or the heir or heirs of such person, within ten years after his death, make such entry. Now, it is most obvious that the heirs here contemplated are such heirs as have a right of entry. The object of the Statute was to punish parties guilty of laches in the assertion of their right, by a forfeiture of them. The proviso was in-

(*a*) Cited sometimes, 8 Rep., 35 *b*, and of some editions, p. 67.

tended to save those who, in judgment of law, had a reasonable excuse for their delay; and give to them and their heirs 10 years after the disability should be removed, to bring such action, or make such entry as they might have brought, or made within the 20 years. But the parties in reversion in this case could not have made entry, or brought any action to recover the possession during the 20 years. The Statute would work great injustice if it were held to affect the rights of reversioners or remainder-men, during the continuance of the particular estate. Such was the view of the Statute taken by this court, in *Jackson* v. *Schoonmaker*, 4 Johns., 390, and *Jackson* v. *Sellick*, 8 Johns., 262. In the first case, it is said that neither a descent cast nor the Statute of Limitations will affect a right, if a particular estate existed at the time of the disseisin, or when the adverse possession began; because a right of entry in the remainder-man cannot exist during the existence of the particular estate. And the laches of a tenant for life will not affect the party entitled. The reason given shows that the circumstance that the particular estate existed at the time of the disseisin, or when the adverse possession began, can vary the case. It applies with equal force to a case where it accrued subsequently.

97*] *In *Jackson* v. *Sellick* the adverse possession commenced in 1772, when Vincent Matthews was tenant by the curtesy; the estate in reversion being in his daughter, then an infant. She married Beekman in 1783; and Matthews, the tenant by the curtesy, died in 1784. Beekman, the husband, died in 1807; and his widow, the daughter of Matthews, was the lessor of the plaintiff. When the adverse possession commenced, the only disability that existed, independent of the estate by the curtesy, was the infancy of the lessor. Her coverture did not commence until 1783, the particular estate having terminated in 1784. It was contended that the lessor being then of full age, and having a right of entry, was bound to exert it; and that she could not avail herself of her coverture; and it was urged that her coverture was a second or cumulative disability, which was never allowed. But the court held, that during the particular estate no right of entry had descended to the lessor; that the Statute, therefore, did not begin to run until the death of the tenant by the curtesy; that coverture was the first disability; and they reiterate the language used by them in *Jackson* v. *Schoonmaker*, that the Statute of Limitations does not affect the right of a remainder-man during the continuance of the particular estate. If the right of remainder-men or reversioners are not affected by the Statute, then, during the life of the tenant by the curtesy, it could not have run against the lessors, for they had no right of entry until his death. If Mrs. Cooper, then, was so seised as to constitute her husband tenant by the curtesy, the right of the lessors are not barred by the Statute of Limitations, and they are entitled to recover.

It is said to be indispensable that there should be an actual seisin of the land, either by the wife or by the husband in her right, in order to constitute him a tenant by the curtesy; that a seisin in law is not sufficient to support such an estate; it must be in fact and in deed.

This is, undoubtedly, the general language of the English authorities. (Co. Litt., 29 *a*; Cruise, Dig., 108, tit. 5, ch. 1, sec. 10.) But this rule, in its literal strictness, has not been adhered to either in England or in this country.

*In *De Grey* v. *Richardson*, 3 Atk., [*98 469, Ld. Hardwicke ruled that the husband was entitled to hold, as tenant by the curtesy, an estate tail descended to his wife from her brother, which was leased for years; and on which leases there were large arrearages but no rent paid during the life of the wife. So that the possession of a lessee for years is so far the possession of the person entitled to the inheritance, even before the receipt of rent, as to entitle the husband to curtesy. And several other cases in which the relaxation of the rule is exemplified, are collected in 1 Cruise Dig., 110–112.

In this court, *Jackson* v. *Sellick*, 8 Johns., 270, it was held not to apply to wild and uncultivated lands; that in relation to them, actual occupation was not necessary to sustain an estate by the curtesy; that the possession follows the title so as to enable the owner to maintain trespass, and with equal reason, to sustain an estate by the curtesy.

But it is suggested by the counsel for the plaintiff, and I think with great force, that the rule requiring an actual seisin applies only to cases in which the title of the person claiming is not complete till entry. Thus, a person claiming by descent or devise, has only a seisin in law before entry, and if he die before entry, the inheritance will go, not to his heir, but the heir of the person last actually seised. Upon such a seisin of the wife, there could be no estate by the curtesy. Her issue would not be capable of inheriting from her; and the rule seems to be, that, to enable the husband to be tenant by the curtesy, the wife must have such seisin, as will enable her issue to inherit from her. (1 Cruise Dig., 112, sec. 24.)

Now, in all the cases in which an actual seisin of the wife has been held necessary, it will be found that she claimed either as heir or devisee and not by virtue of a deed or conveyance to which effect is given by the Statute of Uses.

Where the Statute executes the estate, as is said by Blackstone, 2 Com., 238, the party intended to be benefitted, is put at once into corporal possession of the land without ever having seen it, by a kind of parliamentary magic. Here the wife did not claim as heir or devisee, but under a deed from *Cadwallader [*99 Colden; and I apprehend, with the counsel for the plaintiff, that no actual entry was necessary in order to enable her heirs to take, or her husband to be tenant by the curtesy.

I am, accordingly, of opinion that the plaintiff is entitled to recover in both causes.

SAVAGE, *Ch. J.* I propose to consider the rights of the parties, at the several different stages of their title.

In 1787 the title to the premises in question, and other lands, is admitted to have been vested in the people of this State. The Act of that year was a conditional grant of these lands to C. Colden, in trust for the heirs of D. Colden.

The title, however, did not vest until the conditions were performed, which was in Feb., 1790. C. Colden was authorized to sell the lands to reimburse advances which it was contemplated he would make, and in fact did make. He took the legal estate, and the heirs only an equitable one. In May, 1790, he contracted to sell the premises in question to Rogers. This contract he had a right to make, and was, in fact, the only person who could convey the title. The defendant, Johnson, went into possession as assignee under the contract, and acquired an equitable interest in the land; but his possession was surely not adverse to the true title. He was considered, in law, a tenant at will to the owner of the estate, C. Colden.

Such was the relation of the parties, till Nov. 5, 1792, when C. Colden, who had, in 1790, been reimbursed his advances, put an end to his trust by conveying the legal estate to the children of D. Colden. Between the trustee and *cestuis que trust* there was no difficulty. Their title was the same. Before the conveyance of 1792, they severally held different component parts (if I may so express it) of the same title. The legal estate was in C. Colden, while the equitable estate rested in the heirs of D. Colden. His (C. C's) acts were valid and binding upon those heirs, and when he conveyed to them the legal estate, they took it subject to such equitable interests as the defendant and others had acquired in the lands, by virtue of **100***] the acts of *the trustee. So far from an adverse possession, which would invalidate the conveyances from C. Colden to the heirs, there existed a tenancy. (4 Johns., 230.) That relation was transferred from the trustee to the heirs. They might have enforced the performance of the contract, and were bound on their part to give the title on the terms and conditions contained in it.

While such were the relations between these parties, the defendant, Johnson, Dec. 13, 1793, received a deed from Cooper as attorney for C. Colden. At this time C. Colden had no interest in the lands; and as the defendants are presumed to have been conusant of the conveyance in 1792, receiving this deed was an act of disloyalty to the true landlords; and may, therefore, be considered, with propriety, the commencement of a holding adverse to the title of the lessors.

It is contended that the execution of the deed is evidence of the performance of the contract by the defendants; and so it would be, undoubtedly, if it had been given by the owner of the title in pursuance of the contract. But under the circumstances of this case, the deed of C. Colden can have no more legal operation upon the title of the defendant than if it had been executed by John Stiles. It evinces, however, an intention to hold under a title hostile to that of the lessors, and is, therefore, adverse. That a possession taken at first under the true title may subsequently become adverse, seems to be conceded by several decisions of this court. (1 Cow., 610; 18 Johns., 488.) And this, I apprehend, is an exception to the rule as we find it laid down in *Brandt* v. *Ogden*, 1 Johns., 156, that the possession must be adverse in its inception. After Dec. 13, 1793, the defendant claimed the entire title, exclusive of any right in another, and this claim was in hostility to the title of the lessors. Whether Mrs. Cooper had a right of action against the defendant on the execution of the deed to her, in 1792, would depend on the payment of the interest by the defendant. Supposing that to have been done, which we are warranted in assuming, as the case is silent on the point, it follows that Mrs. Cooper had no right of action against the *de- [***101** fendant, until Dec. 13, 1793, when he disclaimed her title by taking a deed from another, and as respects the rights of the parties, a stranger.

I assume, then, what to me seems undeniable, that Dec. 13, 1793, the defendant's possession became adverse, and that the Statute of Limitations would then have commenced running but for the disabilities of Mrs. Cooper. At this time she was an infant and a *feme covert;* and it is perfectly well settled that if several disabilities exist, when the right of action accrues, the Statute does not begin to run till the party has survived them all. (3 Johns. Ch., 138, 1 Plowd., 375.) It is equally well settled that cumulative disabilities cannot be allowed. Two disabilities were existing when the right of action accrued—infancy and coverture; and the provisio in the Statute gives ten years in which an action may be brought, after such disabilities removed. The last of these disabilities was removed by the death of Mrs. Cooper in July, 1797. Her infancy had ceased in Nov. 1796.

According to the construction given to the Statute (3 Johns. Ch., 137), the party has, in every event, twenty years to make his entry; and if under disability when the right accrues, he has ten years, and no more, after the disability ceases. If twenty years were not to be allowed, and the heirs of Mrs. Cooper were confined to ten years after the death of their mother, their right would have been barred in 1813, though the twenty years would not expire till 1817. But as the Statute did not intend to place those persons named in the proviso in a worse condition than those who were under no disability whatever, it is a reasonable construction of the Statute, that twenty years shall be allowed them at all events. It may happen that this proviso will give to some thirty years, while others, under similar disabilities, may have but the twenty years. Such would be the situation of the lessors of the plaintiff, were there no intervening life estate, to suspend further the operation of the statute.

It becomes important, then, to inquire whether Thomas Cooper was tenant by the curtesy; and if so, what effect *the [***102** existence of his life estate has upon the rights of the parties.

To constitute this estate, four things are necessary—marriage, seisin, issue born alive, and the death of the wife. The marriage in this case took place Apr. 7, 1792. According to the view which I have taken, the wife became seised of the legal estate Nov. 5, 1792. She had one child in 1793, and another in 1795; and died in 1797, when the husband's estate became perfect.

It is objected, however, that the wife could not have that seisin, in fact, which is necessary to make the husband tenant by the curtesy. It has been settled by this court in the case of *Jackson* v. *Sellick*, 8 Johns., 269, that a wife who had the legal title to wild and uncultivated lands, had such a seisin as was sufficient to constitute her husband tenant by the curtesy. Here, however, there was an actual entry by the tenant of the wife; for it has also been adjudged by this court, that a purchaser by contract holds as tenant at will. It is immaterial at what period, during coverture, the wife become seised; whether before issue or after. Nor is it material, whether the issue be living at the time of the seisin. So, if the wife be seised, and disseised before issue, yet if she have issue after the disseisin, the husband shall hold as tenant by the curtesy. (Co. Litt., 29, 30.) The husband's title does not become perfect till the death of the wife, though, for some purposes, it is supposed to commence at the birth of a child. He is then called tenant by the curtesy initiate, but not consummate till the death of the wife.

Assuming, then, that there was such seisin in Mrs. Cooper as entitled her husband to hold as tenant by the curtesy, it becomes necessary to inquire, whether the existence of that estate prevents the operation of the Statute of Limitations. In *Jackson* v. *Schoonmaker*, 4 Johns., 402, it was decided that "neither a descent cast nor the Statute of Limitations will affect a right, if a particular estate existed, at the time of the disseisin, or when the adverse possession began; because a right of entry in the remainder-man cannot exist dur-
103*] ing *the existence of the particular estate; and the laches of a tenant for life will not affect the party entitled. An entry, to avoid the Statute, must be an entry for the purpose of taking possession; and such an entry cannot be made during the existence of the life estate." In that case, the disseisin happened after the tenancy by the curtesy was consummate; and hence, possibly, the peculiar phraseology of the court, when they say, "if a partienlar estate existed at the time of the disseisin, or when the adverse possession began." I apprehend the doctrine is equally true, that the right of a reversioner or remainder-man is not affected by the Statute, if the particular estate existed when the right accrued. And the same reason may be given for the one as the other; because the right of entry never existed in him, in reversion or remainder, during the continuance of the particular estate. When did the Statute become operative? Not till the death of Mrs. Cooper, as that event terminated the coverture. But the same event which subjected her heirs to the operation of the Statute, consummated the particular estate which precluded them from any right of entry; *et impotentia excusat legem.*

Before the Statute can, by any reasonable construction, be made to operate, there must be some laches on the part of those asserting a right of entry; and the policy of the Statute gives to every claimant at least ten y s, within which laches shall not be imputed.ear

At what period of time, I would ask, was it in the power of the heirs of Mrs. Cooper to have asserted their rights, before 1817, when Thomas Cooper died? Their infancy, I admit, is no excuse for them, as successive disabilities are not allowed. The Statute was not operative till the death of Mrs. Cooper. It is true, indeed, that more than twenty years have elapsed since the adverse possession commenced; and more than ten years since the last disability was removed, which existed when the dissesin took place; but I would ask, when were the claimants guilty of laches? They were not bound to make an entry or claim till the death of Mrs. Cooper. And from that period, till the death of the tenant for life, the law would not permit them to enter. *Shall laches, then, be imputed [***104**
to them? Certainly not. Whether Colden Cooper was born before or after the disseisin, seems to me not to change the rights of the parties. The lessors of the plaintiff have brought their action within ten years after the operation of the Statute upon their claim, and are not barred by it. Having, in my opinion, shown a right to one fourth of the premises, they are entitled to judgment for so much.

WOODWORTH, *J.*, dissenting in the first cause. I am of opinion that a legal title to one undivided fourth part of the premises in question was conveyed to Catharine Cooper by the deed from Cadwallader Colden, of Nov. 5, 1792. At this time the possession held under a contract to sell, given by William Cooper, as attorney for Cadwallader Colden, was not adverse; because the purchase rested in contract, and the conditions were not yet performed. An adverse possession cannot commence under a contract to purchase, as has been frequently decided upon reasons fully assigned. The adverse possession of Johnson commenced Dec. 13, 1793, when Cooper conveyed to him. At that time Catharine Cooper was an infant and *feme covert.* She died in July, 1797, leaving a son born in 1793, since dead without issue; and Alice, one of the lessors of the plaintiff, born Sept. 30, 1795.

The question is, whether the plaintiff is bound by the Statute of Limitations. It is contended that Mrs. Swartwout had but ten years from the death of her mother to bring a suit, because Thomas Cooper was never tenant by the curtesy; and consequently there was no suspension of the Statute. The argument is founded on this, that it does not appear that Colden Cooper was born before the deed executed to the defendants, and if he was not, it is contended that there was not such a seisin in the wife as would make the husband tenant by the curtesy; or, in other words, that it must be an actual seisin after the birth of issue; and that a previous seisin during the coverture and before issue, is insufficient. The law on this subject is otherwise. According to Ld. Coke, if a man takes a woman seised of lands, and is disseised, and then *has issue, and the wife dies, he [***105**
shall enter and hold by the curtesy. (1 Cruise Dig., 107, ch. 1, sec. 11; *Id.*, 112, sec. 25.) So that whether the birth of Colden Cooper was before the deed of 1793 or not, is immaterial as to the question whether Thomas Cooper was not tenant by the curtesy at some period during the coverture. Mrs. Cooper did not take as heir or devisee, in which cases it might be necessary for her to make an actual entry, in order to enable her heir to take by descent, or her husband to be tenant by the curtesy. The title was not cast on her by act of law; but she took under a deed to which effect is given by the Statute of Uses by which she was

put in corporal possession, there being no adverse holding at the time. (2 Bl. Com., 312, 338; 1 Inst., 29.)

But admitting this proposition to be correct, the material point is this: when did the right of entry first accrue, and what were the existing disabilities at that time? The answer is, the adverse possession commenced Dec. 13, 1793. The only disabilities then existing were infancy and coverture. No tenancy by the curtesy existed at that period; for it is not shown that Colden Cooper was then born. The birth of a child is necessary to constitute this estate. The husband at that moment had no estate that could be continued beyond the côverture; for, on the death of his wife without issue, the estate would have immediately descended to her heirs. Whether he would ever have a greater right was altogether contingent and uncertain. He had not even an inchoate right as tenant by the curtesy; consequently, the proviso in the Statute applied to coverture and infancy only, and gave ten years after those disabilities were removed. But the party has in any event 20 years to make his entry, and as Mrs. Cooper died in 1797, four years after her disseisin, the effect of the proviso would be to give her heirs sixteen years after her death. The sixteen years ended in 1813. The law is well settled that the right of entry is not barred until all the disabilities, existing when the right of action accrued, are removed; that there cannot be cumulative disabilities; for when the Statute first begins to run, all subsequent disabilities are disregarded. It is, then, evident, that although Thomas Cooper afterwards became a tenant by the curtesy, it does not interpose

106*] any additional barrier to *prevent the operation of the Statute. The following authorities establish the doctrine laid down: 3 Johns. Ch., 129; 18 Johns., 44; 8 *Id.*, 262; 2 Conn., 27; 6 East, 80; 4 Mass., 182; Plowd., 353. As the deed to the defendant, Johnson, bears date Dec. 13, 1793, and by the testimony of Cadwallader D. Colden, it appears that Colden Cooper was born in 1793, it is highly probable that his birth was previous to the disseisin. Had this been shown, then Thomas Cooper would have had a contingent estate as tenant by the curtesy; and in the event of his surviving his wife it would have become absolute. But on the facts before us I am of opinion that the defendant, Johnson, is entitled to judgment.

Judgment for the plaintiff in both causes.

Adverse possession—Persons under legal disability. Cited in—6 Cow., 727; 4 Denio, 209; 43 N. Y., 548; 71 N. Y., 193; 2 Abb. Pr., 312; 17 Abb. Pr., 128; 10 Bos., 113; 67 Mo., 603; 59 Pa. St., 303; 39 Am. Dec., 299; 1 Pim. & B., 65; 39 Am. Dec., 333 (5 Ala., 407).

Cannot commence from holding under contract to purchase unless it is fully performed. Cited in—15 Wend., 181; 73 N. Y., 566; 6 Barb., 128; 12 Barb., 356; 14 Barb., 454; 7 W. Dig., 99.

Adverse possession—What amounts to. Cited in—12 Wend., 675; 14 Wend., 229; 70 N. Y., 152; 17 Barb., 666; 11 Abb. N. S., 111; 6 Abb. N. S., 97; 3 Abb. N. C., 346; 3 Duer, 40; 1 Rob., 471; 5 Rob., 311, 717; 1 Sheld., 166.

Also cited in—5 Cow., 484; 6 Cow., 755; 2 Wend., 368; 17 Wend., 46; 3 Hill, 186; 4 Denio, 209; 43 N. Y., 548; 59 N. Y., 139; 71 N. Y., 193; 79 N. Y., 321; 19 Hun, 251; 10 Barb., 400; 28 Barb., 367; 37 Barb., 250; 17 Abb. Pr., 128; 36 Ohio St., 589.

SARGENT *v.* ——.

1. Action by the Mother, for Seduction of Daughter, Sustained, though at time of Seduction Daughter was in the employ of Another, She Having Returned to her Home, Prior to Birth of Child. 2. New Trial—Grounds for. 3. Excessive Damages—Damages for Bringing up Child, not Allowed. 4. Jurors—When Affidavits of, Admissible. 5. Proof of an Alibi.

Where the defect, or objection, appears upon the face of the declaration, the remedy is by motion in arrest—not for a new trial, even though, upon motion for a nonsuit at the circuit, the judge reserve the point.

Where a widow bound her daughter an apprentice, who was seduced, upon which the indenture was canceled by consent, and the daughter returned to the mother's house, and lay in, there: held that an action on the case lay for the seduction at the suit of the mother.

Courts will not set aside verdicts in this, and the like action, for excessive damages, unless they are so very excessive as to warrant an inference of prejudice, partiality, passion or corruption in the jury.

Affidavits of jurors, may be received to show that they adopt a principle in estimating damages not allowed by law; otherwise, as to the personal misconduct of any of the jury.

As where, in case, by the mother for seducing her daughter, they allow her a sum for bringing up the daughter's child, the fruit of the illicit connection. Damages should not be allowed on this ground.

Where, in such an action, the daughter swore that she was gotten with child on the evening of Friday, June 13, a time when the defendant was in fact 30 or 40 miles distance from her, it appearing by the defendant's affidavit, &c., that he could not know, and had no reason to suppose she would fix on that time; so that he could be able to meet the evidence by proof of an *alibi*, and accordingly he did not attempt to prove the *alibi* upon the trial: held, that he should have a new trial, in order to produce evidence to this point, the case not coming within the objection that the evidence was merely to impeach the testimony of a witness: for it would go to disprove the main fact in question upon the trial: nor was it within the objection, or being cumulative.

Where the testimony is contradictory, and the credibility of witnesses are in question, it is the peculiar province of the jury to weigh and determine upon it. The court will not, therefore, interfere with their verdict, on the sole ground, that it is against the weight of evidence.

Citations—3 Johns., 182, 282, 271, 113; 4 Johns., 406, 425, 488; 1 Johns., 509; 9 Johns., 51, 387; 5 East, 49; 3 Burr., 1878; 10 Johns., 117, 446; 3 Bl. Com., 142, *n.* 13; 2 Ld. Raym., 1032; 2 T. R., 168, 281; 1 Salk., 206; Stat. 22 and 23 Car. II.; Cro. Car., 141, 163, 307; 8 Johns., 370; 15 Johns., 496; 4 T. R., 651; 12 Johns., 235, 6, 237; 5 Taunt., 277; 11 East, 22; 2 Archb. Pr., 222; 5 Johns., 207, 249; 3 Cai. 57; 4 Bos. and P., 329; Tidd. Pr., 817; 1 T. R., 11; 5 Burr., 2657; 2 Bl., 803; 1 Burr., 383; 1 R. L., 139.

CASE for seduction tried at the Otsego Circuit, Feb. 12, 1824, before Nelson, Circuit Judge.

*The declaration was entitled of [*107 May Term, 1882; and stated that Eliza Bowen,

NOTE.—*Seduction—Who may maintain action for.* The doctrine of the above case of Sargent v.——, is disapproved in Bartley v. Richtmyer, 4 N. Y., 38. See also, George v. Van Horn, 9 Barb., 523; Heinricks v. Kerchner, 35 Mo., 378; Vossel v. Cole, 10 Mo., 634.

The action is based on loss of service. The parent cannot maintain it unless the daughter was in his employ, or subject to his command at the time of her seduction. Bartley v. Richtmyer, 4 N. Y., 38, and authorities there cited; Nickleson v. Stryker, 10 Johns., 115; Mulvehall v. Milward, 11 N. Y., 343; Ball v. Bruce, 21 Ill., 161; Greenwood v. Greenwood, 28 Md., 369.

A mere temporary absence from home at the time of the seduction does not bar the action. Lipe v.

the daughter of the plaintiff, a widow, was, Sep. 27, 1816 (then aged 11 years, 3 months and 3 days), bound by indenture, as servant to P. F. of the town of Butternuts, in Otsego Co., till 18 years of age; that she was debauched by the defendant, May 31, 1821, while at service with P. F. under the indentures, and becoming pregnant, the indentures were canceled by the parties, Aug. 18, 1821, and the daughter returned to the service of the plaintiff, and that Feb. 24, 1822, while yet an infant under 21, and in the service of the plaintiff, she was delivered of a male child, *per quod*, &c.

The daughter was, as usual, the principal witness for the plaintiff, upon the trial; and swore that she first saw the defendant, who dined at her master's house, she waiting upon the table, on Friday, June 8, 1821. He, at that time, said nothing to her. The next time she saw him was on the afternoon of the Sunday following, June 10. He came to her master's that day, while the family were gone to church, leaving her and Julia Edson, another servant in the family, at home. He came into the kitchen door where they stood, asked for a drink of water, went with them into the kitchen, and staid some time; they all three went together up stairs into the school room, where there was a bed; and after Julia had left them and gone down, the defendant there had connection with her. He kissed both her and Julia in the kitchen, when the witness ran up stairs, and Julia followed her, and the defendant came up after them. They all sat down on the bed a few minutes, when Julia got up, went out, and left the defendant alone with the witness, who did not ask Julia to stay, but only asked her, as she went out at the door, not to leave the witness alone. They remained in the room 10 or 15 minutes. The defendant held her fast, and asked her to stay, but she did not suspect what he wanted of her. She did not know that the door was locked after Julia went out. The defendant had connection with her twice in the school room after Julia went out. He promised her (and **108***] she believed him) that if *anything happened, he would take care of her for life. The next time the defendant saw her was Wednesday evening, June 13. He came to her at her master's wood-house, where she was picking up chips. No previous appointment had been made; but on his request, she went with him to the alders, on the bank of a neighboring creek, where she had connection with him once. They were there about half an hour or three quarters. She believed that at that time she became with child by him.

This witness having proved the other facts recited in the declaration, the plaintiff rested. Her mother resided in Boston, Mass., where the child was born.

The defendant's counsel then moved for a nonsuit, on the ground that the action was not sustainable by the mother, as the injury was alleged and proved to have been committed while the daughter was an indented servant of P. F.

The judge denied the motion, but reserved the point.

The defendant's counsel then read a deposition of P. F. the master, taken by consent; and introduced several witnesses, viz: Julia Edson, a servant with the daughter; Richard Hughes and Crowell Gifford, hired men at her master's in 1820 and 1821; Caty Edwards, intimately acquainted with her, in the spring of 1821, and Doct. Wing, a physician in the town of Butternuts.

P. F., Julia Edson, and Caty Edwards proved several instances of loose, familiar and improper conduct in the daughter, especially with the men servants of P. F., in consequence of which he had made up his mind to discharge her in Apr. 1821, but was deterred by her humble and supplicating entreaties and promises of amendment; and Hughes and Gifford proved positively that she had had carnal connection with men, a little time before that sworn to by her with the defendant.

Witnesses were also sworn on the part of the plaintiff, who proved that Julia Edson, Caty Edwards, Hughes and Gifford had repeatedly admitted, in general terms, either that the daughter's conduct had been proper, or that they knew nothing against her.

*The counsel for the plaintiff, in [***109** summing up, admitted that the plaintiff did not claim there was any seduction; but they contended that the facts showed the defendant to be the father of the child.

Verdict for the plaintiff for $920 damages.

A motion was now made in behalf of the defendant for a new trial, not only upon the above case; but also because, as was now shown by affidavit, the plaintiff's counsel upon the trial, in summing up to the jury, beside claiming for expense and loss of service, told the jury that they should find a sum for the plaintiff sufficient to support and bring up the child till it was of an age to support itself; which, not being corrected by the judge in his charge, two of the jury swore was allowed by the jury; and one of them swore that this made $900, out of the $920 which they found —$20 being all they would have allowed for

Eisenlerd, 32 N. Y., 229; Keller v. Donnelly, 5 Md., 211; Wallace v. Clark, 2 Overt., 93.

It is only necessary to show that the parent has the legal right at the time to command the services of the daughter, and slight evidence of loss of service is a sufficient basis for the action. Mulvehall v. Milward, 11 N. Y., 343; Clark v. Fitch, 2 Wend., 459; Martin v. Payne, 9 Johns., 387; Kennedy v. Shea, 110 Mass., 147; 14 Am. Rep., 584; White v. Murtland, 71 Ill., 252; 22 Am. Rep., 100; Updegraff v. Bennett, 8 Clarke (Ia.) 72; Boyd v. Bird, 8 Blackf., 113. See, also, Griffiths v. Teetgen, 28 Eng. L. & Eq., 371; Bennet v Alcott, 2 T. R., 166; Rist v. Faux, 4 B. & S., 409.

After the death of the father, the mother may maintain the action. Badgley v. Decker, 44 Barb., 577; Furman v. Van Sise, 56 N. Y., 435; 15 Am. Rep., 441, *note*; Gray v. Durland, 51 N. Y., 424; Keller v. Donnelly, 5 Md., 211; Coon v. Moffett, 2 Pen. (N. J.), 583. But see Heinricks v. Kerchner, 35 Mo., 378; South v. Denniston, 2 Watts, 474.

The action may be maintained by any person standing *in loco parentis* to the person seduced. Bracey v. Kibbe, 31 Barb., 273; Certwell v. Hoyt, 6 Hun, 575; Ingersoll v. Jones, 5 Barb., 661; Davidson v. Goddall, 18 N. H., 423; Ball v. Bruce, 21 Ill., 161; Kelley v. Donnelly, 5 Md., 211; Fernsler v. Moyer, 3 Watts & Serg., 416; Blanchard v. Ilsley, 120 Mass., 487; 21 Am. Rep., 535; Manvell v. Thomson, 2 Car. & P., 303; Edmondson v. Machell, 2 T. R., 4.

Where the daughter is in the employ of another, and her father cannot command her services, he cannot maintain the action. Dain v. Wycoff, 7 N. Y., 191; White v. Murtland, 71 Ill., 252; 22 Am. Rep., 100; Speight v. Oliviera, 2 Stark., 495. But see Dain v. Wycoff, 18 N. Y., 45.

expense and loss of service; and that they allowed nothing for violating the daughter's chastity, or corrupting her morals.

Another ground of the motion was surprise upon the trial, that the daughter should have sworn to the connection by which she became pregnant on the evening of Wednesday, June 13, 1821; whereas the defendant could prove by several witnesses (and he produced their affidavits to this effect) that he was traveling in a wagon, a considerable distance from her master's, on his way to Albany, at the very time of this alleged connection; and had been so traveling during the whole of June 13, 1821.

Other particulars, both as to the case and affidavits, will be found stated in the opinion of the court.

T. J. Oakley, for the defendant:

1. The action was not sustainable by the mother. The relation of mistress and servant did not exist at the time of the injury. The master alone could sue. The mother had no right to recall the child to her service. Had she left her mother, without an intention to return, though not indented, this action would not lie at the suit of the mother. *Martin* v. *Payne*, 9 Johns., 387; 3 Bl. Com., 142, and 110*] *Christian's *note* 13, citing 4 Burr., 1878; Selw. *N. P.*, 1083, 1084. The seduction is the *gravamen;* and this must be followed by, and combined with loss of service. Neither is sufficient of itself to sustain the action. Neither the whole, nor any part of the cause of action, could be transferred from the master to the mother, by canceling the indentures.

2. It was impossible for the defendant to anticipate the bearing and importance of the newly discovered evidence; and in that sense it was out of his power to produce it. This part of the case is plainly within *Jackson* v. *Laird*, 8 Johns., 489.

3. I am aware of the general rule, which forbids the affidavits of jurors, in impeachment of their verdict; but I apprehend the rule relates to an impeachment, by showing some personal misconduct, not to a plain misconception of the principle or law of the case. In *Smith* v. *Cheetham*, 3 Cai., 57, the court received affidavits of the confession of the jury as to their misconduct. The reasoning of Livingston, *J.*, is certainly very forcible in favor of going this length, and indeed receiving their affidavits, And Kent, *Ch. J.*, who was opposed to him, received the affidavits of the constable as to the manner in which the verdict was formed. The court may certainly then hear of this from affidavits; and our view of the case is sanctioned by the introduction to the opinion which Woodworth, *J.*, delivered in *Williams* v. *Baldwin*, 18 Johns., 489. It is evident, from his language, that the court must have inquired into the principles upon which the jury proceeded; and probably through affidavits of the jurors themselves.

To say that affidavits must in all cases be excluded, under the notion of some technical rule, is certainly losing sight of good sense. I think it will be found, that all the cases excluding jurors' affidavits, go upon the impeachment of their conduct.

4. The damages are excessive, and the verdict against evidence.

**Mr. S. A. Foot*, contra. The error [*111 upon which the defendant's counsel sought to nonsuit us upon the trial, appears upon the face of the declaration. It is not, therefore, the subject of such an objection; but be it ever so great a defect, the remedy is only by moving in arrest of judgment *Meyer* v. *M'Lean*, 1 Johns., 509; *Smith* v. *Elder*, 3 *Id.*, 105, 113; *Van Vechten* v. *Graves*, 4 *Id.*, 403.

But the cause of action is well stated. The daughter was to serve till 18, not 21, and the indentures were canceled before 18. Fictions and construction have been resorted to in support of this action. There need not be an actual, but the constructive relation of master and servant, is enough. Absence from the father's house is no objection, if the child be under age; *Nickleson* v. *Stryker*, 10 Johns., 115; and though I need not, yet I might, in this case, ask the court to go on the mere relation of parent and child. The disgrace and moral desolation of families, evil example, the violation of the good order of society, &c., always enter into this action.

In *Martin* v. *Payne*, Spencer, *J.*, puts the case of a daughter absent at a boarding school; and *Judge* Reeve, in his treatise on Domestic Relations, 292, puts the very case under consideration, as forming the proper subject of an action upon general principles. Here, too, the master has abandoned the child, and turned her over to the parent. Should the action in such a case, or indeed; in any case, depend upon the mere volition of the master? There was an intention to return, within the cases. There was an actual return, and consequential damages, the object of an action on the case, as contradistinguished from trespass. Three justices might have dissolved the contract of binding (1 R. L., 139), and the parties have done no more than would have been done under the Statute.

Suppose a daughter seduced by the master himself, and discharged by the justices, or by consent of parties, is it to be endured that the injured parent shall have no remedy? Yet she has none, if all depends upon the will of the master.

The court will not interfere in actions of this kind, either upon the ground of excessive damages, or that the verdict *is against the [*112 weight of evidence. *Coleman* v. *Southwick*, 9 Johns., 45; *Southwick* v. *Stevens*, 10 *Id.*, 443; *Ward* v. *Center*, 3 *Id.*, 271; *Jarvis* v. *Hatheway*, *Id.*, 180, 183; *Feeter* v. *Whipple*, 8 *Id.*, 369; *Woodward* v. *Paine*, 15 *Id.*, 493.

It is well settled, that where the party comes upon newly discovered evidence, he must show due diligence to obtain it in the first instance. The least laches are an objection. *Hollingsworth* v. *Napier*, 3 Cai., 186. It is never allowed where the newly discovered evidence goes to impeach a witness. *Bunn* v. *Hoyt*, 3 Johns., 255; *Duryee* v. *Dennison*, 5 *Id.*, 248; *Shumway* v. *Fowler*, 4 *Id.*, 425; *Halsey* v. *Watson*, 1 Cai., 24, 25. *Shumway* v. *Fowler* was this very case.

Another decisive objection to the newly discovered evidence is that it is cumulative.

The affidavits of the jurors are clearly not receivable. *Dana* v. *Tucker*, 4 Johns., 487. In no case can a verdict stand, if the party be allowed to go round to the jury, and fish out of a few of them some strange reason for their finding.

But it was proper to allow damages for bringing up the child. It being born out of the State, the overseers and justices of Butternuts, or any other town in this State, could give no relief.

Mr. Oakley, in reply. The general rule may be, as stated by the plaintiff's counsel, that where the defect appears of record, the remedy is by motion in arrest; and not for a new trial. But it cannot apply where the point is reserved by the judge, and spread upon a case. Beside, will not the court give a new trial, when they see, in any form, that neither by the declaration, nor the proof in its support, can the plaintiff ever be entitled to recover?

All the cases, and especially *Nickleson* v. *Stryker*, cited on the other side, are explicit, that, to entitle the plaintiff to this action, there must be a present right of service in him; that the relation of master and servant must exist either actually or constructively, at the time of **113***] the seduction. Where *the child is apprenticed, no right of this kind exists in any but the master named as such in the indentures. *Martin* v. *Payne* goes upon the present right of service. It admits that the want of this right would deprive the parent of the action. The illustration put there, of a daughter at a boarding school, most powerfully enforces this very distinction. The daughter here was the servant, both *de jure* and *de facto*, of P. F. Whether of full age is not the criterion. Age is looked to only to decide the constructive relation. Although the daughter be under age, the relation of servant to her parent ceases when the truth is known that she is the indented servant of another. If the master himself commit the injury, the law would dissolve the indentures, and then the right of action would arise. That case makes nothing in favor of a claim against a third person.

I had always supposed that where a plaintiff brings an action on the case, he must make out his whole case. It is the act of the defendant which makes him liable—the seduction. Expenditure, loss of service, disgrace, &c., are mere items of damage, mere consequences resulting to the mother, while the case remains with P. F. There are various instances of this, and the like actions, by one standing in *loco parentis*. *Edmonson* v. *Machell*, 2 T. R., 4, was one where the question came up on the rule of damages to be adopted in reference to that relation. But whenever the question has arisen upon the right of action, it has always been put upon the relation of master and servant existing at the time.

Mr. Foot here mentioned the case of words not slanderous of themselves, but resulting in loss to the party of whom they are spoken. He said the Statute of Limitations ran in such a case only from the time when the damage arose; not from the time of speaking the words. This had been holden of a loss of marriage by speaking words.

Mr. Oakley. In the case put, there is no act which, *per se*, would make the party liable at all. The special damage alone is the cause. But follow the illustration from the doctrine of slander. Suppose one to hold a particular **114***] character *or relation, which alone enables the slander to affect him, but which he abandons before action; could he yet sue for the words? I should suppose not.

The new evidence upon which we move goes to disprove the main fact in the cause by proving another directly inconsistent with it. The defendant, conscious of no connection whatever with this female, who pretends she was seduced by him, could not fix upon any time when he was out of the County of Otsego as the one which she would take for the time of the offense. Nor is the evidence cumulative. The fact of an *alibi* was not set up, or attempted to be proved on the trial.

Courts will always interfere where the jury have mistaken the law. True, they generally examine into this on the case made; but where it appears equally plain in any other way the same result should follow. The argument upon this point is a mere dispute about form.

SUTHERLAND, *J.* This is an application for a new trial on the following grounds:

1. That the action cannot be sustained by the mother (the present plaintiff) at all, because the daughter, at the time when the alleged injury was committed, was an indented apprentice and in the actual service of her master; and the subsequent canceling of the indentures could not transfer the right of action, which previously belonged to the master, to the mother.

2. That the verdict is against the weight of evidence; and,

3. That the damages are excessive.

A new trial is also moved for on the ground of newly discovered evidence, which will be subsequently considered.

Whether the declaration discloses a good cause of action in favor of the present plaintiff or not, is a question which cannot arise upon this motion. If it does not disclose a good cause of action, it is apparent upon the record, and must be taken advantage of by motion in arrest of judgment. This ground of objection is founded upon the alleged error of the judge who tried the cause, in refusing to nonsuit the plaintiff. But the judge at the trial was only authorized to try *the [***115** issues of fact between the parties, and was not to decide upon the pleadings, or whether the facts set forth in the declaration, if true, would or would not entitle the plaintiff to judgment on the coming in of the *postea*. *Ward* v. *Center*, 3 Johns., 271; *Smith* v. *Elder*, 3 Johns., 113; *Van Vechten* v. *Graves*, 4 Johns., 406; *Meyer* v. *M'Lean*, 1 Johns., 509.

But it may be desirable to the parties to have the opinion of the court expressed upon the point whether the present plaintiff can sustain this action, as that question will undoubtedly arise, and be regularly brought before the court, in the event of a new trial being granted upon any of the grounds on which it is now asked.

In *Martin* v. *Payne*, 9 Johns., 387, the daughter, at the time of her seduction, resided in the family of her uncle, with the consent of her father, and worked for her uncle when she pleased, for which he agreed to pay her; but there was no agreement for her continuance with him for any definite time. Previous to her seduction she had no expectation of returning to her father's house to reside; yet, being under age, and having returned immediately after her seduction, and he having supported her and borne all the expenses incident to her confinement, it was held that he was entitled to an action on the case against her seducer for debauching her *per quod servitium amisit*. Spencer, *J.*, in delivering the opinion of the court, says, "in the present case the father had made no contract for hiring out his daughter, and the relation of master and servant did exist from the legal control he had over her services; and although she had no intention of returning, that did not terminate the relation, because her volition could not affect his right." And he remarks that the case of *Dean* v. *Peel*, 5 East, 49, is the only one in which the right of the father to maintain an action for debauching his daughter whilst under age has ever been denied; and that he considered it a departure from all former decisions upon the subject. Where the daughter is over twenty-one years of age, and in the service of another, the action is not maintainable. (3 Burr., 1878.) She must, **116***] when of age, be in her father's *service, so as to constitute in law and in fact the relation of master and servant, in order to entitle the father to maintain an action for debauching her. *Nickleson* v. *Stryker*, 10 Johns., 117.

It must be conceded that if the indentures of apprenticeship had not been canceled or voluntarily rescinded by the parties, the mother could not have maintained this suit. It is not founded upon the relation of parent and child, but of master and servant; and where the latter relation does not exist, either in fact or in judgment of law, no loss of service can be alleged or proved, without which an action on the case for seduction cannot be sustained. The apprentice, by suffering herself to be debanched and thereby rendered incapable of performing her part of the indentures, virtually abrogated them by putting it in the power of the master to have them dissolved and discharged at his pleasure. It is expressly provided by the 11th section of the Act concerning Apprentices and Servants, 1 R. L., 139, that it shall be lawful for three justices, &c., upon application or complaint made upon oath by any master or mistress against any apprentice or servant, touching or concerning any misdemeanor, miscarriage or ill behavior, &c., to hear, examine and determine the same, and to punish the offender by commitment, &c., or otherwise, by discharging such apprentice or servant by warrant or certificate under their hands and seals, &c. That the offense in this case is one for which the apprentice or servant would have been discharged there can be no doubt. And it is equally clear that the parties had a right voluntarily to abandon a contract which would have been canceled upon application to the competent authorities. I consider the indentures, therefore, as legally canceled from Aug. 18, 1821, when, by the mutual consent of the parties, they were given up. She then returned to the house of her mother, and from that period, at least, the relation of mistress and servant was restored between them.

In an action of trespass on the case, for an injury like this, the real cause of action is the expenditure of money and [the loss of service consequent upon the seduction. Hence the *action cannot be sustained for seduc- [***117** tion unless it is followed by pregnancy or the loss of health and, consequently, of service. (3 Bl. Com., 142, *note* 13.) The *per quod* is the gist of the action. But trespass may be maintained where the defendant illegally enters the father's house, and debauching his daughter may be stated and proved as an aggravation of the trespass, although it may not have been followed by the consequences of pregnancy.

Where the action is trespass, whether it be followed by pregnancy or not, the illegal entry is considered the gist of the action, and the loss of service, &c., merely as consequential. If the trespass, therefore, be not proved, the plaintiff cannot in such case recover. 2 Ld. Raym., 1032; *Bennett* v. *Alcott*, 2 T. R., 168, per Buller, *J.*; 3 Bl. Com., 143, *note* 13.

It would seem, according to these principles, not to be material who was entitled to the services of the female at the time of the seduction, when the action is case. But the real inquiry is, upon whom has the cousequential injury fallen—the expense attending her confinement and the loss of her services?

Suppose a daughter hired out by her parent for a month, or six months, and debauched during her service, but the fact not known nor the consequences of it apparent until after the expiration of her term of service and her return to her father's house, is there no remedy in such a case? If there is, it must belong to the parent. For if the circumstances of the case would support trespass in the name of the master, the recovery would be nominal merely, as he could not aver or prove the consequential injury by way of aggravation. Or suppose the case put by counsel upon the argument, that an indented or hired servant is debauched by her master, has the parent no redress? The supposition is not to be endured. It cannot, therefore, be necessary, according to the theory or just principles by which this action is regulated, that the parent, in order to sustain it, should be entitled to the services of the daughter at the very instant when the act is committed which subsequently results in a *loss of service or neces- [***118** sary pecuniary disbursements. The latter circumstances constitute the real *gravemen*; and if that fall upon the parent, it entitles him to the legal redress. In *Brown* v. *Gibbons*, 1 Salk., 206, it is said if a man bring trespass for beating his servant, *per quod servitium amisit*, it is not an action of assault and battery, within the Statute of 22 and 23 Car. 2, but is an action founded on the special damage. So in slander, where the words are not actionable in themselves, and special damage is alleged, that is considered the cause of action for some purposes. (Cro. Car., 141, 163, 307.)

The very act of prostitution may be considered an abrogation of the contract or indentures of service, at the election of the master; and when he makes his election, as taking effect by relation, from the time when the act was committed.

I am, therefore, very clearly of opinion that the parent, in this case, can sustain the action.

There is no ground for interfering with the verdict as being against the weight of evidence, upon the fact of seduction. It was positively and circumstantially sworn to by the daughter; and although, as to some of the particulars, she was contradicted by Miss Edson, and her veracity may be considered as impeached by other witnesses, still the jury believed her; and it was their peculiar province to decide upon the credibility of conflicting witnesses. Under such circumstances, particularly in actions of this nature, the court never disturb the finding of a jury. (3 Johns., 182, 282; 8 Johns., 370; 15 Johns., 496.)

Nor do I think we are authorized to interfere on the ground of the excessiveness of the damages, although they appear to us much larger than they should have been. There were no aggravating circumstances in the case; no arts of seduction were used, for none were necessary. The character of the daughter had long been considered loose and abandoned. There were no wounded feelings, or blasted reputation to aggravate the moral impropriety of the defendant's conduct, and to call for exemplary damages. We should have been better satisfied with a verdict, barely sufficient to re-
119*] munerate *the plaintiff for her actual loss. But the damages are not so flagrantly outrageous and extravagant as necessarily to evince intemperance, passion, partiality or corruption on the part of the jury; and where that is not the case, the court will not undertake to set their judgment on a question of damages, in an action of this nature, in opposition to the judgment of the jury. It is the judgment of the jury, and not of the court which is to determine the damages in actions for personal injuries. *Coleman* v. *Southwick*, 9 Johns., 51; *M'Connell* v. *Hampton*, 12 Johns., 235, 236; 10 Johns., 446. In *Duberley* v. *Gunning*, 4 T. R., 651, which was an action for criminal conversation, the evidence showed that the husband had been guilty of gross negligence and inattention to the conduct of his wife, with respect to the defendant. That he had suffered many indecent familiarities between them in his presence, while he was engaged in similar conduct with another woman; and Ld. Kenyon charged the jury that those circumstances, if they did not entirely take away the ground of action, went very far in mitigation of damages. The jury, notwithstanding the charge, found a verdict for the plaintiff for £5,000. Upon a motion for a new trial, on the ground of the excessiveness of the damages, Ld. Kenyon admitted that the damages were much larger than they ought to have been, and that he should have been satisfied with nominal damages; but he observed he had known instances of much greater damages given in that kind of cases, which were never got rid of by granting new trials; that he had never known an instance in which a new trial had been granted, in such a case, upon the ground of excessive damages; and although he felt great difficulties on the one side as well as the other, he had not courage enough to make the first precedent of granting a new trial under such circumstances. *Mr. Justice* Buller was of opinion, in that case, that the defendant was entitled to a verdict; that the conduct of the husband was such as to authorize the conclusion of his consent to the prostitution of the wife. He was for granting a new trial; yet the other judges agreed with Ld. Kenyon, that even in *such a case, [*120
they were not authorized to set aside the verdict.

The present action is of the same nature and character, as an action for criminal conversation, which Spencer, *J.*, in *M'Connell* v. *Hampton*, 12 Johns., 237, considered as exempted by peculiar considerations from the interference of the court on the ground of excessive damages. I have found no case in which a verdict, in such an action, has been set aside on such grounds. I am very far from saying that the court would, in no case, interfere in such an action, on account of the enormity of the damages; but the case must be of a very peculiar and extraordinary character to justify their interference. *Hewlet* v. *Cruchley*, 5 Taunt., 277; *Irwin* v. *Dearman*, 11 East, 22; 2 Archb. Pr., 222, and cases there cited; *Hutcheson* v. *Peck*, 5 Johns., 207, per Van Ness, *J.* The verdict in this case is by no means as excessive and enormous, as in the case of *Duberly* v. *Gunning*.

Upon the case, therefore, I think the motion for a new trial must be denied.

But upon the ground of mistake in the jury, as to the principles upon which their verdict was made up, and also of newly discovered evidence, I am inclined to think a new trial should be granted.

Two of the jurors swear that the jury, their fellows, as well as themselves, came immediately to the conclusion that the plaintiff was entitled to nothing but her actual expenses and the loss of her daughter's services during her confinement; that it was clearly proved that she had been very profligate and corrupt before the defendant knew her; that they estimated the actual expenses at $20, and gave the $900 to pay the expense of maintaining, supporting and bringing up the child, till it was of sufficient age to maintain itself; and in that way, the jury gave a verdict for the plaintiff for $920; that the jurors supposed it was proper to give enough to bring up and educate the child, as the plaintiff's counsel, in addressing the jury, expressly claimed a right to recover on that principle, which was not denied by the judge in his charge; nor did he notice or comment on it at all.

*The plaintiff has produced no affi- [*121
davit from any of the other jurors, denying this statement. It then stands admitted not that one or two jurors estimated the damages on that principle; but that it was an error common to all the jury, resulting from what they considered the implied assent of the judge, to the correctness of the rule of damages as claimed by the counsel for the plaintiff. This is, in effect, equivalent to a misdirection of the judge. It is clearly the duty of the court to interfere in such a case, if the facts come properly before them. The plaintiff is under no legal obligation to support and educate the child; nor can she be compelled to appropriate the proceeds of this verdict to that purpose; nor will it afford the defendant any exemption from his liability to provide for the child, when called upon in the regular and due course of law.

I must confess that, upon the argument, I was strongly inclined to think the affidavits of the jurors were inadmissible; but, upon looking into the cases, I have come to a different conclusion.

In *Dana* v. *Tucker*, 4 Johns., 488, the court say, the better opinion is, that the affidavits of jurors are not to be received to impeach a verdict; but that they may be admitted in exculpation of the jurors, and in support of their verdict. The affidavit disclosed that the jurors settled the amount of the verdict by each marking down such sum as he thought ought to be allowed, and dividing the aggregate amount by twelve. This case overrules that of *Smith* v. *Cheetham*, 3 Cai., 57, in which similar affidavits were held admissible by Spencer and Livingston, *JJ.*, *Ch. J.* Kent dissenting. The decision in *Dana* v. *Tucker* is undoubtedly in accordance with the latest authorities in England. *Owen* v. *Warburton*, 4 Bos. & P., 329; Tidd. Pr., 817, and the cases there cited; 1 T. R., 11. The English courts have also refused to receive the affidavits of jurors to explain the grounds of their verdict; and show that they intended something different from what they found. (5 Burr., 2667; 2 Bl., 803; 2 T. R., 281; 1 Burr., 383; Tidd Pr., 817, contra.)

I think the affidavits may be received here, without impeaching the principle of either class of those cases.

122*] *They are not introduced to show any impropriety in the conduct of the jurors, or that the verdict is not such as they intended; but to show a misconception of the rule of damages, as derived from the charge of the judge, taken in connection with the argument of counsel. It was natural for the jury to infer from the silence of the judge upon this point (which was the most important, and indeed the only point of any difficulty in the case), his assent to the correctness of the rule of damages, as laid down by the counsel. They acted upon that supposition. Their error was one into which they were led by the court. It was in the nature of a misdirection. The fact that they were so misled, can be derived from no other source than the jurors themselves. If the judge had expressed the opinion which the jurors understood him to entertain, the verdict would have been set aside for a misdirection. I repeat, that the affidavits impute no impropriety of conduct to the jurors, nor do they contradict the verdict as recorded. In such a case I find no authority against receiving them; and I am inclined to the opinion, though not without some hesitation, that, under the circumstances of this case, they may be safely admitted; and that the defendant, on that ground, is entitled to a new trial, as also on the ground of the newly discovered evidence.

The defendant was guilty of no laches in not being prepared to prove on the trial, that he was not in the town of Butternuts on the day when the witnesses swore she became pregnant by him. Upon the supposition that he never had connection with the witness, and that her whole story is a fabrication; still, knowing that he was in the neighborhood about the time when, according to the birth of the child, it must have been begotten, he could not have anticipated that she would allege the connection to have taken place at a period subsequent to his leaving the neighborhood; and consequently was not, in the exercise of ordinary diligence and discretion, bound to be prepared to show when he did leave it.

Nor is the effect of the testimony merely to impeach the witness. It establishes a fact which (if the witness is to be understood as swearing that her pregnancy took place on Wednesday, June 13, shows conclusively that the *defendant could not have been the [***123**
father of the child. It does not contradict her in an incidental circumstance, the only effect of which is to diminish the credit to which she is entitled when she speaks to the main fact in the cause, without having any direct bearing on that fact, as in *Shumway* v. *Fowler*, 4 Johns., 425, and *Duryee* v. *Dennison*, 5 Johns., 249, and the cases there cited; but it disproves, or has a direct tendency to disprove, the existence of the main fact itself. It is, in truth, proof of an *alibi*, which I apprehend has never been considered as merely impeaching a witness.

I am, therefore, on these grounds, for granting a new trial.

New trial granted.

Seduction, action for, by whom it will lie. Disapproved—4 N. Y., 45.
Approved—15 Am. Rep., 443 (56 N. Y., 435).
Cited in—1 Wend., 450; 2 Wend., 464; 51 N. Y., 429; 2 Barb., 188; 5 Barb., 665; 9 Barb., 525; 24 Barb., 624; 29 Barb., 127; 50 Barb., 104, 214; 10 Kan., 523; 20 Am. Dec., 643.

Damages in case of. Cited in—10 Wend., 340; 9 Hun, 513.

Affidavit of jurors cannot be received to show mistake in verdict. Distinguished—21 Wis., 369; 20 Am. Rep., 547 (63 N. Y., 364).
Cited in—6 Cow., 54; 1 Wend., 30; 9 Wend., 253; 1 Den., 369; 25 Cal., 400; 40 Am. Dec., 166 (13 N. H., 462).

New trial granted to enable party to prove alibi. Cited in—10 Wend., 296; 43 Barb., 209; 4 How. Pr., 268; 2 Abb. N. S., 111.

When court will interfere because damages excessive. Cited in—8 Cow., 215; 12 Barb., 496; 18 Barb., 221; 47 Barb., 53; 3 Abb. Pr., 105; 1 Hilt., 148; 8 Minn., 171.

JACKSON, ex dem. VAN SCHAICK ET AL.,
v.
DAVIS.(*a*)

1. *Witnesses—Person interested, or a Party, Competent to Prove Death of Subscribing Witness.* 2. *Evidence—Ancient Deed.* 3. *Landlord and Tenant—Relation Attaches to Successors of Tenant—They are Bound by Acts and Acknowledgments of Predecessors—Non-Demand and Non-Payment of Rent for 20 Years—Effect of—Presumption of Conveyance—When not presumed—Tenant cannot Question Landlord's Title, but may Show its Termination—Attornment.* 4. *Award of Commissioners under Statute.*

An interested person, and even a party, are competent to prove the death of a subscribing witness to a lease, in order to let in secondary proof of its execution.

If an objection which can be obviated by further proof be not taken or not persisted in at the trial, it will not be received as the ground of a motion for a new trial.

It seems that, in order to entitle a deed to be read in evidence, as an ancient deed, without further evidence of its execution, proof that part of the premises contained in it have been possessed under it for thirty years, is sufficient even as against one in possession of another part.

(*a*) This cause was decided at August Term, 1825.

When the relation of landlord and tenant is once established, it attaches to all who may succeed the tenant, immediately or remotely.

And the succeeding tenant is as much affected by the acts and acknowledgments of his predecessor, as though they were his own.

Though one purchase and take of a lessee, and, in fact, enter upon the premises under an absolute conveyance in fee, yet, in judgment of law, he enters as tenant to the lessor.

The mere non-payment and non-demand of rent for 20 years will not raise a presumption that the landlord's title is extinguished by a conveyance to the tenant or otherwise.

Mere length of time will not raise a presumption in the nature of evidence. It must arise from some facts or circumstances within that time.

Where the possession of one is not inconsistent with the title of another, a conveyance from that other is never to be presumed for the purpose of quieting the possession; *e. g.*, the possession of a tenant consistently with a lease.

The decision in Jackson, *ex dem.* Waldron, v. Welden, 3 Johns., 283, giving effect to an attornment or purchase by a tenant with the consent of his landlord, in consequence of the land being awarded to another, under the Act of Mar. 11, 1793 (3 Green. L. N. Y., 81 to 84), is confined to an actual attornment of purchase, with such consent; but where, after the award of the commissioners, certain proprietors of Van Schaick's patent, not parties to the act or award, declared, of land which they had leased (before the Act passed), that, by the award of the commissioners, they had lost their title to it, and did not claim rent for it; but the tenant instead of attorning to or buying under another patent, to which the land was awarded, set the proprietors of both patents at defiance, claiming the land as a gore between them; in ejectment by his landlords against him, held, that he was, notwithstanding, concluded, and could not dispute their title.

In ejectment by a landlord against his tenant, the latter cannot show, in his defense, that the landlord has acknowledged, by parol that the title was in another.

But if he has actually purchased of or attorned to another, with his landlord's consent or encouragement, this throws the burden of proving title upon the landlord, the same as if the action had been against a stranger holding adversely.

A conveyance in fee, by a tenant for years, is a disseisin of the landlord or not, at his election. For the sake of the remedy, he may consider the grantee a disseisor; but the tenant cannot constitute himself so in spite of his landlord.

Though a tenant cannot dely his landlord's title, yet he may show that it has terminated, either by his own limitation or by conveyance, or by operation of law.

The award of commissioners under the Act of Mar. 11, 1793, to settle the limits, &c., between the Kayaderosseras patent, the Halfmoon patent, and the Shannondhoi or Clifton Park patent (3 Gr., 81, sess. 16, ch. 57), was operative upon such persons only as petitioned for the Act; whether proprietors of, purchasers from, or lessees under the patents. And see, on the same subject, Statutes, sess. 18, ch. 57, 3 Gr., 222; and sess. 16, ch. 15, 3 Gr., 21.

Citations—1 Bl., 532; 2 Dall., 116; 16 Johns., 193, 305, 20 Johns., 144; Phil. Ev., 349, 119, *n. a*; 3 Johns., 283; 223, 499, 386, 292; 2 T. R., 53; 1 T. R., 700, *n.*; Woodfall, 484, 487; 1 Cai., 444; 2 Johns. Cas., 223; Bull. *N. P.*, 110; 7 Johns., 283, 186; 12 Johns., 242; Runn., 276; 3 Burr., 1071; 1 Cowp., 214; 10 Johns., 336, 358; 6 Johns., 21; Cruise Dig., 367; 1 Burr., 112; Stat. 4 H. VII., ch. 24; Act, March 11, 1793; 4 T. R., 682; Act, April 7, 1795; Act, Jan. 9, 1793.

EJECTMENT, for land in the Town of Halfmoon, Saratoga County, tried at the Saratoga Circuit, July 30, 1823, before Wal-
124*] worth, *Circuit Judge; when a verdict was taken for the plaintiff, subject to the opinion of this court, on a case to be made, with liberty to either party to turn it into a bill of exceptions, or special verdict.

A case was accordingly made and argued in October Term, 1824, by,

Messrs. S. G. Huntington and *A. Van Vechten*, for the plaintiff, and,

Messrs. J. L. Viele and *S. A. Foot*, for the defendant.

But the facts in the cause, the arguments of counsel, and the cases cited, are so fully stated and considered by the court in the course of their opinion, as to render an account of them in the usual place, little more than repetition. They are, therefore, omitted.

The following are the written points delivered to the court, and discussed by the counsel:

On the part of the plaintiff:

1. Derick Lane was a competent witness to prove the death of the subscribing witness.

2. The execution of the lease by John C. Cornell, for lot No. 3, was sufficiently proved.

3. The judge was correct in refusing to nonsuit the plaintiff, on the ground that he had not proved the payment of rent within twenty years.

*4. The Act of Mar. 11, 1793, and the [*125 award of the commissioners, were no bar to this suit.

5. The plaintiff is entitled to a verdict for the whole premises.

6. The testimony of Joshua Palmerton was properly rejected.

7. The defendant ought not to have been permitted to go into evidence of his purchase and holding, without producing conveyances.

On the part of the defendant:

1. The plaintiff failed to show title to lot No. 3, as he could not prove his lease.

2. The plaintiff ought to have proved payment of rent, or some direct acknowledgment of tenancy, within twenty years; and a nonsuit ought to have been granted, for want of such proof.

3. The relation of landlord and tenant has never existed between the lessors of the plaintiff and defendant.

4. The Act of the Legislature of 1793, and the award under it, are valid and conclusive upon the lessors.

5. The testimony of Palmerton should have been admitted.

6. The defendant made out a perfect adverse possession, commencing in 1798; and, as to the interest of Christina Van Schaick, at least no disability was shown.

Curia, per SUTHERLAND, *J.* This action is brought to recover lot No. 4, and the one half of lot No. 3, in the Halfmoon, or Van Schaick patent.

The lessors of the plaintiff produced a lease of lot No. 4, from Christina Van Schaick, and John G. Van Schaick and Anna, his wife, to Alexander Brevoot, dated Jan. 1. 1784, for 70 years, reserving an annual rent of £4. This lease was duly acknowledged and recorded.

They also offered in evidence a lease of lot No. 3, from the same lessors, to John C. Connell, of the same date, for the same term, and reserving the same rent. This lease was not recorded; and one principal question in the case is, whether it was sufficiently proved to entitle it to be admitted *in evidence. [*126 The death of one of the subscribing witnesses was proved by Guert Van Schoonhoven; and Aaron Lane was offered as a witness to prove the death of the other. He was objected to, on the ground of interest; and it was admitted that his wife was interested in the Van Schaick patent; and that he had agreed to pay his proportion of the expense of this and other suits, which might be commenced to try the Van Schaick title. He was, however, admitted by the judge, and proved the death of the other subscribing witness to the lease. The plaintiff then proved the signature of Connell, the lessee, to the lease. The defendant still objected to the reading of the lease, without further proof of its execution; and the plaintiff undertook to prove twenty years' possession under the lease. After the evidence on this point was concluded, he rested his cause; and the defendant moved for a nonsuit, on the ground that the plaintiff had not proved the payment of any rent within twenty years. The court denied the motion, and decided that the evidence was, *prima facie*, sufficient to entitle the plaintiff to recover one third of the premises, on the demise of John G. Van Schaick.

The defendant then went into proof of the proceedings under the Act of Mar. 11, 1793, to ascertain and settle the limits and boundaries between the patent of Kayaderosseras, the patent of Halfmoon, or Van Schaick patent, and the patent of Clifton Park. It was admitted that, according to the decision of the commissioners under that Act, the premises in question were in the patent of Clifton Park; but the constitutionality and validity of that Act, so far as it affected the rights of the plaintiff, were denied.

A verdict was taken for the plaintiff, subject to the opinion of the Supreme Court.

1. Lane was a competent witness. Evidence of the loss of a paper, or the death of a witness, is addressed to the court, for the purpose of laying a foundation, for the admission of secondary evidence; and it is well settled that it is no objection to a witness, when offered with this view, that he is interested in the cause, or even that he is a party to the record. (1 Bl., 532; 2 Dall., 116; 16 Johns., 193; 20 Johns., 144.)

127*] *2. The objection to the proof of the execution of the lease by Connell, for lot No. 3, as the case stands, appears finally to have been abandoned by the defendant. After the death of the subscribing witnesses, and the signature of Connell to the lease, were proved, the defendant objected to the sufficiency of the proof. The case states that the plaintiff thereupon undertook to prove twenty years' possession, and upwards, under the lease; and after stating the evidence given, says: "The plaintiffs here rested their cause, and the defendant thereupon moved for a nonsuit, on the ground that the plaintiffs had not proved the payment of any rent within twenty years." The very ground of the application for a nonsuit presupposes the lease to have been proved, and seems to admit that the plaintiff had succeeded in making out the twenty years' possession in correspondence with the lease; but that the fact of tenancy, which might be inferred from the proof, was rebutted by the circumstance that no rent was proved to have been paid within twenty years; that a surrender of the lease was, therefore, to be presumed. There is nothing in the case to show that the sufficiency of the proof of the lease was finally objected to by the defendant. If the objection was not taken or persisted in upon the trial, it cannot be taken here; for it is of a nature which might have been removed by further evidence.

But I am inclined to think there was sufficient evidence of a possession accompanying the lease to entitle it to be read as an ancient deed, it being more than thirty years old. (Phil. Ev., 349; 3 Johns., 292.) John C. Connell, the lessee, died in 1801, and Isaac Connell, his son, testified that, at the time of his death, he was in possession of that part of lot No. 3, which Nehemiah Davis owned and occupied at the time of the trial. Joshua Mandeville testified that the defendant admitted to him that he had sold the south half of No. 3 to his son Nehemiah. Mandeville also testified that in the spring of 1823 Nehemiah was in possession of the south half of No. 3, and claimed compensation for damages done to the south half, in laying out a road through it. This evidence conclusively establishes that John C. Connell, the *lessee, died in [***128** possession of the south half of No. 3 in 1801. Samuel Stewart testified that, as administrator of the estate of John C. Connell, he, in the same year, 1801, sold a leasehold estate in the half of lot No. 3 to the defendant; that he either gave him a quitclaim deed or assigned the lease. He presumed that he assigned the lease, though he was not confident. It was a lease from the Van Schaicks to Connell for a term of years. The sale from the defendant to his son Nehemiah, of the south half of lot No. 3, and his possession down to the time of the trial, complete the evidence of a possession of the south half, under and consistent with the provisions of the lease; and would seem to bring it within the rule, which entitles an ancient deed to be read without proof of its execution.

But it is objected that the possession proved does not extend to the north half of No. 3, the premises in question. Let it be recollected that the question now is, whether the Van Schaicks ever gave a lease to Connell for lot No. 3; not whether the defendant holds under that lease. That will be subsequently considered. Now, I apprehended, that it cannot be necessary, in order to entitle an instrument to be read as an ancient deed, to prove a corresponding possession of every portion of the premises which it purports to convey. A possession of part under the deed affords evidence of its authenticity of as high a character as though that possession extended to the whole. I am, therefore, inclined to think that this lease was entitled to be read as an ancient deed.

But again; the defendant admitted to Mandeville that both lots, Nos. 3 and 4, were leased by the Van Schaicks; and that one of them was leased to Connell; and that he purchased that lot from Connell. And the testimony of Stewart shows that the defendant purchased from the estate of Connell a leasehold interest only in lot No. 3, under the Van Schaicks; and he believes that interest was conveyed to him by an assignment of the lease given by the Van Schaicks to Connell. Is not the defendant, then, concluded from denying that lot No. 3 was originally held by Connell under a lease from the Van Schaicks? And the only object of introducing the lease was to prove that fact. It is true *the defendant, at [***129** the same time, denied that the Van Schaicks had any title to the lot, or that he owed them any rent. The bearing and effect of that denial will be considered hereafter.

Andrew Brevoort appears to have immediately entered into possession of lot No. 4, under his lease, and also to have been in possession of the north half of lot No. 3, previous to 1792, when he died. Richard Davis testified that in 1792 he purchased, from the representatives of Brevoort, lot No. 4 and the north half of lot No. 3; that he purchased it as land leased by the Van Schaicks; that he soon after sold it as such to Stephen Van Denburgh, and assigned the lease to him; and various sales and transfers are proved, until it came into the possession of the defendant, about twenty five years before the trial. This evidence shows, conclusively, that the defendant derived the possession of lot No. 4 and the north half of lot No. 3 from persons who acknowledged that these lots were leased by the Van Schaicks, and that they held as their tenants. The testimony of Isaac Connell and of Richard Davis, and the defendant's admissions to Mandeville, show a clear and explicit acknowledgment of the Van Schaick title. The defendant is as much affected by the acts and acknowledgments of his predecessors, in the possession of the premises, as though they were his own. *Davies* v. *Pierce*, 2 T. R., 53; 1 T. R., 760, *note;* Woodf., 484; 1 Cai., 444; 2 Johns. Cas., 223; 3 Johns., 499, 223.

When the relation of landlord and tenant is once established, it attaches to all who may succeed to the possession, through or under the tenant, either immediately or remotely.

But it is said that, although a person succeeding a tenant is to be presumed to have taken as tenant also, yet he may repel that presumption by showing that he did not take in that character; and that the testimony of James Davis, in this case, shows that the defendant purchased the premises in question, not as leasehold property, but in fee absolute. Davis' testimony upon this point is by no means explicit. He states that he made the contract for the farm, on behalf of the defendant; that **130***] Teachout, the vendor, possessed *and claimed it as his own; that he said he had a good title, and would give a good deed; but whether he gave a deed with covenants of warranty, or only a quitclaim, does not appear. Admitting, however, that he purchased and entered upon the premises under an absolute conveyance in fee, he still, in judgment of law, entered as the tenant of the Van Schaicks. This precise point arose in the case of *Jackson* v. *Scissam*, 3 Johns., 499. The fact of tenancy, in that case, was made out by proof of the confessions of one Smith (from whom the defendant derived the possession), that he entered under one of the lessors of the plaintiff. The defendant, to repel the presumption that he entered in the same character, produced and proved a deed from Smith to him, for the consideration of £300, with full covenants; and there was no evidence that the defendant knew, or had any reason to suppose, that Smith derived his possession from the lessors; and yet the court held that Smith's acknowledgments, if they were evidence of a tenancy in him, were conclusive against the defendant. Indeed, that point was not disputed, and is too clear upon principle, as well as authority, to admit of discussion. *Vide Jackson* v. *Cole*, 4 Cow., 587.

But it is said, that admitting the defendant, and those from whom he derived his possession to have entered under the Van Schaicks, an abandonment of the title, on the part of the Van Schaicks, is to be presumed, inasmuch as there is no proof of the payment of rent, or any acknowledgment of tenancy within twenty years. Satisfaction of the rent might possibly be presumed, as payment of a bond will be, after a forbearance of twenty years, unexplained on the part of the obligee. So, where a mortgagee has never entered into possession of the mortgaged premises, and no demand of payment has been made of either principal or interest, for twenty years, it has always been held sufficient to warrant the presumption that the mortgage has been satisfied. (Bull. *N. P.*, 110; 3 Johns., 386; 7 Johns., 283; 12 Johns., 242; 1 Phil. Ev., 119, *note a.*) But the analogy between this case and those of bonds and mortgages, appears to me to be confined to the rent, and not to extend to the title of the landlord. There is a material distinction between the presumption *of the payment [***131** of money, and the execution of a release or the extinguishment of a right to rent, which can only be by deed. Payment is presumed, after a great lapse of time, in analogy to, and upon the principle of the Statute of Limitations, because the evidence of the fact may reasonably be presumed to be lost. But where the relation of landlord and tenant is once established, under a sealed lease, the mere circumstance that the landlord has not demanded the rent, cannot justify the presumption that he has extinguished his right to it, by a conveyance of the interest in remainder or reversion to his tenant. The presumption sought to be indulged in this case, is not a presumption of law, which cannot be contradicted; but is a presumption in the nature of evidence; and mere length of time will never raise such presumption. It must arise from some facts or circumstances which took place within that time. (Woodf., 487; Runn., 276; 2 Burr., 1071.) Now, here there are no such facts or circumstances; but, on the contrary, all the circumstances in the case tend to repel such presumption. It cannot arise from the defendant's possession, for that is consistent with the title of the lessors of the plaintiff as landlords; nor from the decision of the commissioners, that the premises in question were in the Clifton Park patent, for if their award was legally binding and operative upon the lessors, so as to transfer their title, whatever it might be, to the proprietors of Clifton Park patent, then there is neither necessity nor room for the indulgence of presumptions of any kind. If the award was not binding upon the lessors, then the fact of its having been made cannot justify, or raise a presumption that they have abandoned any right or interest which may previously have belonged to them. Every presumption of this kind is repelled by the acts of the defendant himself. It is in proof that he repeatedly denied the title, both of the Van Schaicks and the proprietors of Clifton Park, and claimed the premises in question, on the ground of possession merely, as being part of a gore between those patents, and covered by neither. He never pretended to claim under the award of the commissioners, or on the ground of a release or conveyance from the lessors of the plaintiff, in accordance with it.

132*] *This does not fall within the class of cases where a release or conveyance is to be presumed, for the purpose of quieting the possession. The defendant's possession, as tenant, is not inconsistent with the plaintiff's title; and it still comes back to the inquiry whether, admitting him to have come into possession as tenant, an extinguishment of the landlord's right is to be presumed, from the mere circumstance that no rent has been demanded within twenty years. The case of *Eldridge* v. *Knott*, 1 Cowp., 214, is very much in point. It was there held, that a release or extinguishment of a quit-rent, is not to be presumed from mere length of time, short of fifty years, the period fixed by statute as a bar to the demand. And the reasoning of Ld. Mansfield and of *Mr. Justice* Aston, shows conclusively, that under the circumstances of this case, no such presumption can be indulged. In *Jackson* v. *Welden*, 3 Johns., 283, which was a case very similar to this, and involved a question of title between the Van Schaick and Kayaderosseras patents, under the Act of 1793, the plaintiff attempted to recover on the ground of the tenancy of the defendant. But it appeared that the defendant, after the commissioners had decided that his lot belonged to the Kayaderosseras and not to the Van Schaick patent under which he originally entered, had purchased from the Kayaderosseras proprietors. It also appeared that the lessor of the plaintiff had declared that he had given up all claim to the land, and that he did not blame the defendant for having purchased under the Kayaderosseras patent; that he had exacted no rent after the determination of the commissioners; and that, with a full knowledge that another of the tenants had agreed to purchase under the Kayaderosseras patent, he told him that a title under that patent would be valid. The court held that under the circumstances of that case, the lessor of the plaintiff must be deemed to have been privy to, and to have assented to the defendant's attornment to the proprietors of the Kayaderosseras patent; and that such an attornment being valid under the Statute, terminated the tenancy; and that the plaintiff, therefore, could not recover on the ground of the prior tenancy of the defendant; but must produce his title.

133*] *Joshua Palmerton was offered in the principal case, to prove that after the decision of the commissioners, and before the defendant went into possession, one of the lessors of the plaintiff told the witness that they had lost their title by that decision; and that they did not now claim or receive rent for any of the lands lying northwest of the line settled by the commissioners, and that they declined, for that reason, to sell the witness a lot which they formerly claimed, lying in the gore. This evidence, I think, was properly rejected by the judge. The defendant did not pretend to claim under the Clifton Park patent, in pursuance of the award of the commissioners. He had taken no title under the proprietors of that patent, the lessors' assent to which might be presumed from the evidence offered, connected with other circumstances in the case, and thus create a valid attornment, but he claimed in hostility to both patents. In *Jackson* v. *Welden*, the abandonment which it was held might be presumed, was in favor of the Kayaderosseras patent, in conformity to the award of the commissioners; for the defendant had purchased under that patent, and the plaintiff was driven to proof of his title, in order that the defendant, if evicted, could have his remedy on his covenant against the Kayaderosseras proprietors. In this case, the declarations offered to be proved were not made to a tenant, but to a stranger. They are not shown to have been communicated to the defendant, or to have influenced his conduct. It would be dangerous to permit the title to real estate to be affected by such casual declarations, made to persons, and under circumstances, which did not impose upon the party any peculiar obligation to speak with caution and accuracy.

In *Jackson* v. *Vosburgh*, 7 Johns., 186, the defendant, who was shown to have entered as tenant, offered to prove that the lessors had disclaimed any right to the premises; and that he had been in the actual possession of the premises, in his own right, for more than thirty years before the bringing of the suit. The court say such a disclaimer as was there set up could be of no validity; and such evidence, if admissible, would lead to fraud and perjury, and be destructive of *title to [***134** property; and it was held inadmissible, even for the purpose of disproving the fact of tenancy, although the thirty years' possession under claim of title, was held admissible for that purpose. *Jackson* v. *Kisselbrack*, 10 Johns., 336, and *Brant* v. *Livermore*, 10 Johns., 358, reiterate the doctrine that evidence of a parol disclaimer of title to real property is inadmissible. In *Jackson* v. *Cary*, 16 Johns., 305, *Ch. J.* Spencer says, that although parol declarations of tenancy have been received with certain qualifications, parol proof has never yet been admitted to destroy or take away a title; and that to allow parol evidence to have that effect would be introducing a new and most dangerous species of evidence, in direct hostility to the principle of the Statute of Frauds. 6 Johns., 21; 4 Cruise Dig., 367; *Vide Jackson* v. *Cole*, 4 Cow., 587.

The point of adverse possession was substantially abandoned upon the argument. If the defendant entered as tenant of the Van Schaicks, and there has been no abandonment of their title (as I have endeavored to show), nor any act of disloyalty on the part of the defendant (and none is shown until he refused to pay rent when demanded by Mandeville in 1822), then there could be no adverse possession.

The conveyance in fee of the tenant, was a disseisin of the landlord or not, at his election. For the sake of his remedy, he had a right to consider the grantee a disseisor. But he cannot constitute himself a disseisor in spite of his landlord. Ld. Mansfield says, in *Taylor* v. *Horde*, 1 Burr., 112: "If the lessee, for life or years, makes a feoffment, the lessor may still distrain for the rent, or charge the person to whom it is paid as a receiver, or, bringing an ejectment, choose whether he will be considered as disseissed." And he remarks that, except the special case of fines with proclamations, and the construction of the Statute of 4 Hen. VII., ch. 24, for the sake of the bar, he cannot think of a case where the true owner, whose entry is not taken away, may not elect (by pursuing a possessory remedy) to be deemed as not having been disseised.

This brings us to the consideration of the effect and operation of the award of the com- **135*]** missioners, under the Act of *Mar. 11, 1793, upon the title of the plaintiff. For although a tenant cannot deny the title of his landlord under which he entered, it is competent for him to show that it has terminated, either by its original limitation, or by conveyance, or by the judgment and operation of law. *England* v. *Slade*, 4 T. R., 682.

The Act in question professes, on its face, to have been passed upon the petition and application of the proprietors, and the agents for the proprietors, of the respective patents of Kayaderosseras, Halfmoon and Clifton Park. It recites, as the inducement to the passing of the Act, that the proprietors and agents had made such joint application, by their petition to the Legislature, with which it appeared reasonable to comply. It is apparent that the Legislature supposed all the parties interested in those patents were petitioners for the Act; and the subsequent Act of Apr. 7, 1795, exempting the lessees and purchasers in those patents from the operation of the Act of 1793, upon the express ground that they were not parties to the petition, and had had no opportunity to be heard, or show cause why it should not have been granted, is a strong expression of the opinion of the Legislature that the first Act was intended to operate, and did, in fact, operate only on those who had petitioned for it. The Van Schaicks were not parties to that petition; and it is evident, therefore, that the Act was passed under a misapprehension of the material facts which are assigned as the reasons for its passage.

The Act of Jan. 19, 1793, to ascertain and settle the limits and boundaries between the patent of Kayaderosseras and the Halfmoon patent (and for which the Van Schaicks, as well as other proprietors, petitioned) expired by its own limitation in one year. *Id.*, sec. 7. It was never acted under by the commissioners; and I do not perceive how it can be brought in aid of the subsequent Act of Mar. 11, of the same year. In the absence of all proof of a ratification on the part of the Van Schaicks of the proceedings of the commissioners, I should entertain very serious doubts of their being concluded by the award. And the fact of Mr. Van Vechten's having appeared before the commissioners as counsel for the claimants under the Van Schaick patent, is **136*]** *not of itself sufficient to warrant the presumption of their assent and submission to the award.

But admitting the award to be binding, as between the proprietors of the Halfmoon and Clifton Park patents, I apprehend the defendant in this case is excepted from its operation, in consequence of the relation in which he stands to the lessors of the plaintiff, by the express provisions of the Act of Apr. 7, 1795. That Act was passed for the relief of such persons as may have held land, either by lease or purchase, in either of the patents, when the Act of Mar. 11, 1793, was passed, and who did not unite in the application to the Legislature for its passage. After reciting the agreements and petitions for the Act of 1793; and that the proprietors of the Halfmoon and Clifton Park patents had, previous to such agreements and petitions, leased part of the lands supposed to be within these patents, for terms of years, for life and lives, and in fee; and had also sold part of the lands supposed to be in one or both of the patents; and had executed leases and deeds for the lands so leased and sold, to sundry persons, not being parties to the agreements or petitions, and who had no notice of the intended application to the Legislature, it enacts, "that the title of no person whomsoever, claiming lands in either of said patents, by lease or by purchase in fee simple, and who did not unite in an application to the Legislature for an Act entitled, &c., passed Mar. 11, 1793, and who did not subscribe such agreements and petitions as aforesaid, shall be bound or anyways affected by the determination of the commissioners, &c., made in pursuance of the provisions in the said Act contained; anything in the said Act to the contrary, notwithstanding." It will be recollected that the premises in question were leased to Connell in 1784 for seventy years. There is no pretense that he, or any one claiming under him, united in the application for the Act of 1793. He held the premises under the lease in 1795; and not being a party to the Act of 1793, or award of the commissioners, his is the very case for which the Act of 1795 intended to provide. If the title of the tenant was not bound, or affected by the determination of the commissioners, the rights of the landlord were, of *course, unimpaired; and neither **[*137** the original lessee, nor those who have succeeded to his rights, can set up the proceedings under the Act of 1793, in bar of the title of their lessor.

I am, therefore, of opinion that the plaintiff is entitled to judgment.

Judgment for the plaintiff.

Cited in—5 Cow., 349; 7 Cow., 325; 9 Cow., 192; 4 Wend., 638; 7 Wend., 376; 14 Wend., 626; 25 Wend., 458; 9 N. Y., 24; 35 N. Y., 471; 48 N. Y., 274; 53 N. Y., 293; 65 N. Y., 30; 71 N. Y., 193; 26 Barb., 408; 46 Barb., 461; 47 Barb., 526; 51 Barb., 16; 63 Barb., 95, 101; 67 Barb., 413; 2 Bos., 578; 1 Hilt., 405; 3 Wood. & M., 96; 62 How. Pr., 283; 99 Mass., 16; 21 Wis., 61; 17 Am. Dec., 518; 28 Am. Dec., 554; 35 Am. Dec., 106 (9 Scam., 245); 40 Am. Dec., 172 (14 N. H., 19).

WITHY *v.* MUMFORD.

Covenants of Warranty Run with the Land—Action on, may be Sustained by Assignee of Covenantee or His Heirs.

A covenant of warranty runs with the land. It is intended for the benefit of, and accordingly an action may be sustained upon it by the assignee of the covenantee or his heirs.

A grants to B, who grants to C, both grants being with warranty; then C is evicted by a title paramount to A's title; held that C may bring covenant directly against A; or he may sue B; who, on payment, &c., may sue A; and so of any successive number of warrantors.

Citations—Co. Litt., 384 *b*; 5 Co., 17; Cro. Car., 503; 2 Johns., 1; 4 Cruise Dig., 452-457; 14 Johns., 89; 2 Mass., 460; 1 Conn., 244.

ON demurrer to the declaration. This was of a plea of breach of covenant; and stated that Feb. 21, 1814, the defendant, by indenture between him and one Harnden, did grant, &c., to Harnden in fee, certain lands (describing them); and that he did covenant, &c., with Harnden, his heirs and assigns, &c., to warrant and defend the premises, &c., against all persons claiming, &c.; that on the day of the execution of this indenture, Harnden entered into possession of the premises, &c.; and afterwards, Mar. 12, 1817, by indenture between him and the plaintiff, conveyed the same premises to the plaintiff, in fee, who entered, &c.; but was afterwards evicted by certain persons having lawful title, before the defendant conveyed to Harnden. And so, &c.

The defendant craved oyer of the indenture between Harnden and the plaintiff, which was granted; and the indenture set forth contained a covenant of warranty from Harnden to the plaintiff, his heirs and assigns. For this cause,

Demurrer and joinder.

Mr. J. A. Collier, in support of the demurrer, cited *Kane* v. *Sanger*, 14 Johns., 89, as a case in point for the demurrer. He said the very question is there examined and decided by Spencer, the late *Ch. J.*, who delivers the opinion of the court. The action should have been brought by Harnden. He also cited *Greenby* v. *Wilcocks*, 2 Johns., 1.

138*] **Mr. S. Sherwood*, contra, denied that the point was necessarily involved in *Kane* v. *Sanger*. It is true, he said, the late *Ch. J.* laid down the proposition taken by the demurrer; but this was evidently done on very little reflection. The point was not discussed. He takes it for granted that where a warrantor conveys the land with warranty, his grantee cannot sue the original warrantor; but must look to his immediate covenant of indemnity. For this, he cites 2 Mass., 460, containing a *dictum* of *Ch. J.* Parsons, who cites no authority. The *dictum* itself is put as a mere illustration; and when critically examined, cannot be understood as supporting the position which it is relied upon to prove. Clearly, the case of *Kane* v. *Sanger* is not law, if it decides what the counsel supposes. *Greenby* v. *Wilcocks*, 2 Johns. 1; *Middlemore* v. *Goodale*, Cro. Car., 503, 505; Co. Litt., 385 *a;* Shep. Touch., 198, tit. Warranty, sec. 12; Vin. Abr., Covenant, H, pl. 2; *Id.*, K, pl. 6.

Curia, per SAVAGE, *Ch. J.* The point on which the defendant relies, is that the deed from Harnden to the plaintiff containing a covenant of warranty, he cannot sue as assignee.

In the days of Ld. Coke the law was understood differently. He says, "if a man enfeoffeth A, to have and to hold to him, his heirs and assigns: A enfeoffeth B and his heirs; B dieth, the heir of B shall vouch as assignee to A; so as heirs of assignees, and assignees of assigns, and assignees of heirs, are within this word (assigns); which seemed to be a question in Bracton's time. And the assignee shall not only vouch, but also have a *warrantia cartæ.*" (Co. Litt., 384, *b*, and the authorities there cited.)

The same doctrine is found in *Spencer's* case, 5 Rep., 17, and in all the books. That the covenant to warrant and defend, is a covenant which runs with the land, and that the assignee is entitled to the benefit of all such covenants, is a proposition which needs not the citation of an authority for its support. The doctrine will be found, however, in 4 Cruise, Dig., 452–457.

*The case of *Middlemore* v. *Goodale*, [***139** Cro. Car., 503, was an action by the assignee on the covenant for further assurance. The defendant pleaded a release from J. S., with whom he made the covenant, which release was executed after the commencement of the suit. All the court agreed that the covenant ran with the land, and that the assignee should have the benefit of it.

From these authorities, it is clear that the covenant of warranty runs with the land, and is intended for the benefit of the grantee, his heirs or his assigns, according to the language of the covenant itself.

But it is contended by the defendant, that though the assignee of the grantee may generally resort to the original grantor, for a breach of the covenant happening after the assignment, yet he has not such remedy when he has a warranty from his immediate grantor. There is surely nothing in the covenant of warranty itself to justify such a doctrine; nor is there any reason growing out of the acts of the parties, why the assignee, by taking a warranty from his immediate grantor, should lose his claim upon the first grantor. It cannot operate by way of release. If this were the consequence, a quitclaim deed would often be a better conveyance than one with full covenants.

It is contended, however, that this doctrine is supported by authority, and the cases of *Greenby* v. *Wilcocks*, 2 Johns., 1, and *Kane* v. *Sanger*, 14 Johns., 89, are cited.

The case of *Greenby* v. *Wilcocks* decides that an action upon the covenant of seisin cannot be brought by the assignee, because the grantor, having no title when the covenant is made, it is broken immediately, before the assignment, and when broken, becomes a mere chose in action and, as such, is incapable of assignment. This being the only reason given, it would seem to follow that whoever was owner of the land, which was the *substratum* of the covenant, would be entitled to prosecute for the breach of a covenant running with that land, if broken while the land was in his hands. This case, therefore, proves nothing against the plaintiff's right of recovery in the principal case, but rather supports it. The plaintiff, an assignee, has been evicted. The covenant *remained unbroken till af- [***140** ter the assignment to him. He has been damnified; not the original grantee, Harnden; and if the defendant's doctrine be correct, Harnden may recover damages which he never sustained, and may pocket the money; while the plaintiff, upon whom the whole loss has fallen, can recover nothing, if Harnden be unable to respond. Such a doctrine I should hold utterly untenable, were it not for what was said by the late *Ch. J.* Spencer, in the case of *Kane* v. *Sanger*.

That was an action of covenant, brought to recover damages for an eviction of the plaintiff's grantees. The counsel for the plaintiff seems not to have argued the main point, but placed his right to recover upon a variance between the defendant's notice and proof. Spencer, *J.*, in delivering the opinion of the court, says, "it is a general rule, that where covenants run with the land, if the land is assigned or conveyed, before the covenants are broken, and afterwards they are broken, the assignee or grantee can alone bring the action of covenant to recover damages; but if the grantor or assignor is bound to indemnify the assignee or grantee, against such breach of covenant, then the assignor or grantor must bring the action;" and he cites 2 Mass., 460.

In a subsequent part of the opinion, he admits, that to avoid circuity of action, a release from the plaintiff's grantees to the defendant would have been a bar to the suit, but for the circumstance that they had given the plaintiff mortgages; and the mortgages reinvested the title in the plaintiff; so that, in effect, there were no assignees. The plaintiff having conveyed away the property, and received it back, stood as if no conveyance had ever been executed by him. These mortgages had been assigned to Morris; and it was a fact in the case that the suit was brought by the direction and for the benefit of Morris; so that the recovery, after all, was virtually in favor of the assignee.

The remark, therefore, that the assignee, with warranty, could not maintain an action, as assignee, for a breach after the assignment, was not called for. It professes to be supported by no authority but the case of *Bickford* v. *Page*, 2 Mass., 460, per Parsons, *Ch. J.* **141***] With the greatest deference, *I do not understand such doctrine to be there asserted. The case itself was an action by the covenantee, against the covenantor, and breaches were assigned upon the covenants of warranty, of seisin, and against incumbrances. The defendant pleaded that the plaintiff, before suit brought, had conveyed to one Roberts, without any covenants making him liable for any defect of title. The plaintiff, in his replication, set out his deed to Roberts, being a release with warranty against himself, his heirs and assigns. To this replication the defendant demurred. No incumbrances were shown nor any eviction. The court, therefore, decided that the plaintiff ought to recover on the covenant of seisin, on the ground that this covenant having been broken before the plaintiff's release to Roberts, it was a chose in action, unassignable in its nature and, therefore, did not pass to Roberts by the release. Parsons, *Ch. J.*, in the course of delivering the opinion of the court, advances the doctrine relied on by the late *Ch. J.* of this court, in these words: "It is a general rule, that when a feoffment or demise is made of land with covenants that run with the land, if the feoffee or lessee assign the land, before the covenants are broken, and afterwards they are broken, the assignee only, can bring an action of covenant, to recover damages, unless the nature of the assignment be such, that the assignor is holden to indemnify the assignee against a breach of the covenants by the feoffor or lessor. This rule is founded on the principle that no man can maintain an action to recover damages who can have suffered no damages."

Here, it is distinctly asserted that the grantee, who is also the assignor, can maintain no action for damages if he is himself not liable to his assignee. Why? Because he can have suffered no damages. The assignee, who has suffered damages, and he only, can bring the action in such a case. But if the assignor has covenanted to warrant the assignee, and has actually sustained damage, in consequence of his covenant, by a recovery against him, then he has his remedy over against his grantor. Having been damnified, he is thereby reinvested with his original rights. Then he will have suffered the damages which he seeks to recover on the *covenant to himself; [***142** and in such a case the assignee is not the only person who, under any circumstances, may prosecute the original grantor. That this is what *Ch. J.* Parsons meant, is evident, from what he lays down as the foundation of the rule. The reason he gives is, that no man can recover damages, who has sustained none. Mere liability is not enough. Actual damage must have been suffered by the assignor, to authorize the action by him. To place any other construction upon the language of *Ch. J.* Parsons, is to render him inconsistent with himself, besides making him stem the whole current of authority.

This subject has been very fully discussed in *Booth* v. *Starr*, 1 Conn. N. S., 244. The facts were, that J. Booth conveyed with warranty to S. Booth a lot of land in Hudson. Booth conveyed to a third person, he to a fourth, and he to the fifth grantee—all with covenants of warranty and seisin. The last grantee was evicted, but the plaintiff, S. Booth, was not damnified. Swift, *J.*, states the question to be, whether, in the case of a covenant of warranty, annexed to lands, an intermediate covenantee can maintain an action against a prior covenantor, without having been sued by, or satisfied the damages to the last covenantee who has been evicted.

The question was discussed with great learning and ability and at considerable length, and the court expressly decided that the last covenantee, who has been evicted, may prosecute any or all of the preceding covenantors till he obtain satisfaction; but that no intermediate covenantee can sue his covenantor till he himself has been compelled to pay damages upon his own covenant.

In this case, the plaintiff might have sued Harnden, his own immediate grantor. He did not choose to do so. Harnden may have been dead, or insolvent, or the plaintiff may have had other reasons for preferring a direct resort to the defendant. It is sufficient for his purpose that he had a legal right to do this.

*In the case of *Garlock* v. *Closs*,(a) [***143** decided by this court, in May Term, 1824, a similar action was sustained by an intermediate covenantee, who had been damnified,

(a) GARLOCK v. CLOSS—May Term, 1824.

COVENANT. The declaration stated that the defendant Closs conveyed land (describing it) to J. G. Garlock, who conveyed to Dieffendorf, who conveyed to Conkling, who conveyed to H. Garlock, the plaintiff, who conveyed to Walradt, all with warranty; that Walradt was evicted under a deed from the Comptroller, upon a sale for taxes charged on the land, before the defendant conveyed: and that the plaintiff had paid Walradt the value of the land, with the costs of a suit brought for its recov-

though the property had passed through four different grantors, with warranty, down to himself. The plaintiff is entitled to judgment.

Judgment for the plaintiff.

Cited in—10 Wend., 184; 19 Wend., 337; 21 Wend., 124; 3 Den., 295; 1 Paige, 414; 4 Paige, 582; 40 N. Y., 286; 22 Hun, 463; 1 Barb., 405; 13 Barb., 281; 6 How. Pr., 25; 1 Duer, 197; Co. R. N. S., 188; 22 Am. Dec., 780 (5 Ohio, 154); 27 Am. Dec., 232 (1 Dev. & B., 94).

144*] *SPENCER *v.* TILDEN ET AL.

1. *Usury—Contract to Sell Cows for Double the Number to be Returned in Four Years, Not Usurious. 2. Inquiry into Alternative Consideration Allowed to Determine Whether a Penalty or Liquidated Damages. 3. Parol Evidence, not Admitted to Vary Express Terms of Written Contract.*

Selling cows, &c., on a contract to return double the same number and description, at the end of four years, is not usurious.

So of sheep, to double in three years. *Vide note*, at end of the principal case.

In an action on a written promise, not sealed, to pay and deliver $360, or 12 cows, &c., expressed to be for value received; held, that the value of the consideration, and of the cows, to be delivered, might be inquired into with a view to see whether the sum expressed was intended by the parties as a penalty, or as liquidated damages; and it appearing that the sum expressed was much beyond the value of either; held, that it was in nature of a penalty, and that the plaintiff must be confined to the value of the cows to be delivered, with interest, as the measure of his damages.

A promise in writing, was to deliver 12 cows, with 12 calves, which come of said cows, on, &c.; held, that in an action against the promisor, he could not show that at the time of signing the contract the promisee declared (calling witnesses to his declaration) that he would, notwithstanding, receive 12 cows with calf, or with calves by their sides; and that the defendant, on the day stipulated, tendered 11 cows, with calves by their sides; and one cow with calf, which calved the evening after the tender; as this would be to vary the express terms of the written contract.

ASSUMPSIT, tried at the Oneida Circuit, July, 1823, before Williams, Circuit Judge.

The action was upon a written contract in these words:

"April 15th, 1819. For value received, we promise to pay and deliver to John Spencer, or bearer, three hundred and sixty dollars, or twelve good middling cows, and twelve good calves which come of said cows above mentioned, to be paid and delivered at the dwelling-house of said Spencer's now is in, four years from the date, in Verona. Said cows not to exceed eight years old; nor under four years old. As witness our hands.

JOHN TILDEN.
ITHIEL TILDEN."

The execution of this contract was proved by the plaintiff, at the trial; and also that interest upon the $360, from Apr. 15, 1823, to the *quarto die post* of August Term following, would be $7.87; and the plaintiff claimed to recover $367. 87.

The defense was, 1. Usury; 2. Performance.

The evidence to sustain the defense of usury was, that the plaintiff, a few days before the date of the agreement, agreed with the defendants to let them have six cows for four years; and that the defendants, at the end of the term, should return him twelve cows with calf, or with calves by their sides, or pay him $30 each for the six cows. The plaintiff admitted it was more than the cows were worth; but said he would put them at that sum, so as to be sure and have the cows again. He said, at the same time, that his bargain was as good as 25 *per cent.* interest. That accordingly, the *plaintiff afterwards delivered six [*145 cows to the defendants, one or two of the cows having calves by their sides, and the residue being with calf; and the defendants executed the contract in question. This was on the day of its date. The plaintiff then reiterated that his bargain was as good to him as 25 *per cent.*, and the defendants answered that it was more. The plaintiff replied it was worth 25 *per cent.*, but he did not wish them to take the cows. The defendants also proved that the cows which they then received were not so good as middling cows, and were not then worth more than $19 each—in the whole, $114. The defendants also proved (though this was objected to by the plaintiff as immaterial) that twelve good middling cows, with calves by their sides, would, on Apr. 15, 1823, have been worth $204.

To sustain the defense of performance, the defendants offered to prove that the plaintiff, on the parties coming together on the day of executing the contract in question, produced it ready written; that the defendants objected to its terms, and that it should have been for twelve cows, either with calf, or with calves by their side; that the plaintiff said this should make no difference; and if the defendants would sign the contract as it was, he would take twelve cows either with calf or with

ery, with the costs of an action by Walradt against him upon his covenant.

Demurrer and joinder.

Mr. J. Lynch, in support of the demurrer, made this point, among others:

It appears that H. Garlock, at the time of the eviction, was the grantee of Conkling, with warranty. The suit should, therefore, have been brought by the plaintiff against Conkling, and not against the defendant.

In support of this point, he relied on Kane v. Sanger, 14 Johns., 89, cited in the principal case.

Mr. A. Conkling, contra, took the same ground against that case as was taken in the principal case by *Mr. Sherwood;* and cited Shep. Touch., 176, 198; Com. Dig., Covenant, C. 3; Baylye v. Hughes, Cro. Car., 137; Bac. Abr., Covenant, E, pl. 2, 5; Middlemore v. Goodale, Cro. Car., 503; Co. Litt., 384 *b*, and Booth v. Starr, 2 Conn. N. S., 244.

Mr. Lynch, in reply, said he was not prepared, nor did he think it necessary, to defend the decision of this court in Kane v. Sanger. No case or *dictum* had been produced negativing the distinction there taken.

Judgment for the plaintiff.

See also, Campbell v. Lewis, 3 B. & A., 392; Kingdon v. Nottle, 1 Maule & S., 355; *Id.*, 4 Maule & S., 53, and King v. Jones, 5 Taunt., 418.

NOTE.—*Usury, loan or sale of chattels.*

There must be a loan or forbearance of money to constitute usury. Perrine v. Hotchkiss, 2 Lans., 416.

In a bona fide *loan of chattels*, any compensation may be reserved. Bull v. Rice, 5 N. Y., 315; Cummings v. Williams, 4 Wend., 679; Hall v. Haggart, 17 Wend., 280.

Contracts for the sale of notes, or other personal property on time, when not used as artifices for evading the usury laws, are not usurious, though the profit exceeds the rate allowed by law. Dry Dock Bank v. American, &c. Co., 3 N. Y., 344; Thomas v. Murray, 32 N. Y., 605; Goldsmith v. Brown, 35 Barb., 484; Morrison v. McKinnon, 12 Fla., 552; Gilmore v. Ferguson, 28 Iowa, 220; First Nat. Bank v. Owen, 23 Iowa, 185.

calves by their side, and called witnesses to what he said. Whereupon the defendants signed the contract; and on the day for its performance, drove to the place of performance twelve good middling cows, eleven having calves by their sides, and one being with calf and which actually calved on the evening of the same day. That these cows, in all respects, answered the terms of the agreement, with the single difference that one of them had not a calf by her side. These offers were made, upon the ground that that the plaintiff had committed a fraud upon the defendants in the above transactions; but the evidence was rejected by the judge, on the ground that it went to vary a written contract by parol; and that the tender was not a compliance with the written contract.

The plaintiff then proved that, at the date of the contract, cows were about one fifth **146***] higher than in 1823; and that the *usual practice of letting cows was to double in four years—the party letting, usually taking part of all risk of accidents. The defendants objected to the proof of usage, but the objection was overruled.

The judge then said, that if it was agreed, or intended by the parties, that the plaintiff should receive above 7 *per cent.* interest, the note would be void for usury; and he should consider that as a question of fact for the jury to decide. If the plaintiff was entitled to recover at all, the $360 were to be considered in the nature of a penalty; and the plaintiff could not recover above the twelve cows and calves when they became due, with interest to the *quarto die post* being $208; and hereupon a verdict for that sum was taken for the plaintiff, subject to the opinion of this court on the above case, and under an agreement that they should give judgment, or set aside, or modify the verdict, accordingly as they should hold the law to be.

Mr. S. Beardsley, for the plaintiff:

1. Here was no usury. The sale was of property *bona fide*, upon a special agreement. The seller took all the risk of the market as to the value of the cows at the time of the payment. To constitute usury, there must be a loan upon excessive interest, to be repaid at all events. Ord, Usury, 29, 69–72; Vin. Abr., Usury, C, 10; *Fountain* v. *Grymes*, Cro. Jac., 252; *Roberts* v. *Trenayne*, *Id.*, 507, 508; *Earl of Chesterfield* v. *Jansen*, 1 Wils., 292, per Burnett, *J.; Richards* v. *Brown*, Cowp., 776, 777. Here, the cows had actually depreciated in value, at least, one fifth.

As to the high price of $360, it is enough that the contract was in the alterative, to pay that sum or deliver the cows.

By the latter, the defendants might have saved themselves, which takes away the inference of usury arising from this feature of the contract. *Tate* v. *Wellings*, 3 T. R., 531; *Maddock* v. *Rumball*, 8 East, 304; *Bank of Chenango* v. *Curtiss*, 19 Johns., 326. Inadequacy of price can only be insisted on as a badge of usury, where there is a loan. (Ord, Usury, 74, 75.) Where there is a loan of money, and a sale of goods at a very low price, the value **147***] of which is fluctuating *in the market, this is not evidence of usury. *Stuart* v. *F. & M. Bank*, 19 Johns., 496.

2. The $360 were not in the nature of a penalty; but the sum agreed to be paid. That sum is no more a penalty than the sum in any large promissory note, given for a small consideration. The question whether a sum of money agreed to be paid, is in the nature of a penalty, must depend on the facts to be collected from the face of the contract. The intent of the parties must be gathered from the agreement itself. Newl., Cont., 307; Com., Cont., 541; *Dennis* v. *Cummins*, 3 Johns. Cas., 297, 298; Holt, *N. P.*, 45, *note*. The nature and effect of the contract could not be varied by parol. This can only be done where its words are equivocal, or there is a latent ambiguity. Where a contract is in the alternative, to pay a sum of money, or do any other act, the money is always in the nature of liquidated damages. *Slosson* v. *Beadle*, 7 Johns., 72. A new trial should be granted, so that the damages may be assessed correctly, at $360, and the interest.

3. Here was no valid performance, or tender of performance.

Mr. C. C. Bronson, contra. This being a case subject to the opinion of the court, they come in the place of the jury; and we are entitled here to every fair inference, from the facts stated in the case. The usage set up on the trial cannot sanction usury. Here was a loan. It was no more a sale than the loan of money itself. True the defendants might sell or dispose of the cows as they pleased. So might they of money, if they had borrowed that instead of cows; and one may fluctuate in the market as well as the other. Where the specific thing is to be returned, the lender may always charge what he pleases; not so where the return is in kind. (Ord, Usury, 26–29.) The loan may be in money, or what is equivalent to it; and there may be usury, where there is apparently a mere sale. (Ord, Usury, 29.) Nothing is more usual, than an attempt to disguise usury, in this and other forms: but they will not avail. 7 Bac. Abr., Am. *ed., 195. Usury, C; [***148** *Pollard* v. *Scholy*, Cro. Eliz., 20; *Glisson* v. *Newton's Exrs.*, 1 Hayw., 336; *Atkinson* v. *Scott's Exrs.*, 1 Bay, 307; *Cutler* v. *Johnson*, 8 Mass., 266. The letting of cattle, with large increase, in Mass., is excepted from the Statute of Usury. 8 Mass., 259, Dana, *arguendo*, which shows the sense of the Legislature there, that otherwise such contracts would be void. Inadequacy of price, on sale, is evidence of usury. (Ord, Usury, 77; 2 Ves., Sr., 155.) So, if there be a mere colorable contingency in the contract. *Clayton's* case, 5 Rep., 70.

If here be no usury, yet the plaintiff should recover no more than the value of the property he parted with and lawful interest, estimated at $149.12, and this on the ground that the agreement was a hard and unconscionable one, affording a gain to the plaintiff, and producing a loss to the defendants of 40 *per cent.* At any rate, he should recover no more than the value of the twelve cows, and the calves by their sides, and interest, the sum for which the verdict was taken. *Dennis* v. *Cummins*, 3 Johns. Cas., 297, was decided against the sum being considered as liquidated damages, on the ground that it was extravagant, and out of all proportion with the sum really and honestly due. As much appears upon the face of this contract for the government of the court, as on the contract in that case.

Mr. Beardsley, in reply, said, though it be true that money may fluctuate in the market, this is to a trifling amount; and ordinarily a loan, with a view to this, would be colorable. Not so of goods. You might as well say, that every sale by a merchant at a high price would be usurious.

Curia, per SAVAGE, *Ch. J.* The contract was not usurious, though the plaintiff was a very hard and unconscionable creditor. The interest and principal were both put at hazard to a considerable extent. It was uncertain in 1819 what would be the value of the cows in 1823. If the hazard be slight, and merely colorable, it will not take the case out of the Statute; but I do not consider it so in this case. Here was no negotiation for a loan of money. It was *a bargain by which the plaintiff was pretty certain of making a handsome profit; but by which he might lose.(a) [*149

*I think the $360 in the contract must be considered as a penalty. The verdict is, therefore, right, and the plaintiff entitled to judgment for the $208.(b) [*150

Judgment for the plaintiff.

Cited in—7 Cow., 309; 4 Wend., 681; 13 Wend., 590; 17 Wend., 281, 454; 5 Den., 141; 4 Sand. Ch., 309; 4 N. Y., 372; 5 N. Y., 317; 60 N. Y., 412; 2 Barb., 667; 12 Barb., 381; 14 Barb., 145; 65 Barb., 282; 51 How. Pr., 38; 16 Abb. N. S., 405; 1 E. D. S., 489, 581; 30 Am. Rep., 29 (9 S. C., 344).

(a) *May Term*, 1825.

HOLMES *v.* WETMORE.

ON *certiorari* to a justice's court. Wetmore sued Holmes in the court below, on the following agreement:

"WHITESTOWN, August 26th, 1819. Ebenezer Holmes received of Ezra Wetmore ten ewe sheep, for which I promise to deliver twenty sheep, of as good a quality; three years from the date.

EBENEZER HOLMES."

Plea, the general issue.

On the trial, sheep, in Aug., 1822, were proved to be worth one dollar. The justice gave judgment for the plaintiff for $20 damages and the costs.

Judgment affirmed.

HAMLIN *v.* FITCH. Kirb, Conn., 260.

ACTION on a note dated Feb. 28, 1785, by which the defendant promised to pay the plaintiff $16,839, in final settlement certificates, within 6 months from the date. On issue, the jury found that the note was given for the loan of this $16,839 in final settlement certificates; and that it was corruptly agreed between the parties that the defendant should give the plaintiff $1,000 in lawful money, for the loan, beyond the legal interest, for the 6 months; and that the note was given in pursuance of this agreement; and therefore void. This finding was in the language of the issue.

On motion for judgment for the plaintiff; *non obstante*, &c.

The Court, *Judges* Dyer and Pitkin dissenting, gave judgment for the plaintiff according to the motion, saying: "To bring a contract within the Statute, and the mischief it was made to prevent, it must be clearly for the repayment of a greater value than the amount of the loan, with an advance thereon, at the rate of 6 *per cent. per annum*. That it be of a greater quantity, though of the same kind of article, is not sufficient. If the article be of a fluctuating value, and from such change or diminution of its value as from its nature or the course of trade, it is subject to, it may not at the time of repayment, be worth more, or so much. A loan of 100 bushels of salt, for example, in the year 1783, when it was at twelve shillings, to repay double the quantity, at the end of one year, when it might have been worth but four shillings, would not come within the statute, be the price what it might at the year's end. Nor would it make a difference, if it was to repay 106 bushels of salt, and a sum of money, besides, provided both of them might not amount to more than the value of the loan, and 6 *per cent.* interest thereon.

With regard to the final settlement certificates, said to be loaned in this case; it is matter of public notoriety that they were, at the time of the contract, in a state of rapid depreciation; and that, having no funds to rest upon, for principal or interest, it was wholly uncertain how low they would fall, and whether, at the end of six months, they would, if considered as merchandise (as they must be, to bring them at all within the description of the statute), be worth half so much as they were when loaded; in which case, the plaintiff, instead of gaining three hundred pounds, would lose that sum, and the defendant gain it. The loss by the depreciation was at the plaintiff's risk. As he received in the £300 a premium for the risk, the rule of damages upon this note, would be the market value of the certificates, at the time they were to be repaid. So was the case of Lathrop v. West determined in this county, where the loan was of depreciating continental bills; and a sum in hard money was taken as a premium for risking the depreciation upon them. There the depreciation happening to exceed the premium, the plaintiff lost the whole interest, and part of the principal, as might have been the case here. The contract in this case, though in the form of a loan, was really in nature of a specnlation and bargain of hazard. It depended upon a contingency, to wit: that of depreciation, whether all, or how much of the principal, or value loaned, should be repaid, and which of the parties the speculation should ultimately favor; which takes the contract entirely out of the Statute; 2 Burr., 891; Show., 8; Comb., 125; Holt, 738; though it may leave a question, how far the premium taken for the risk in this case, was unconscionable; and could be relieved against in equity."

The two dissenting judges recited the Connecticut Statute of Usury, which, as to the point decided, is the same as the Statute of this State.

The case of Morrisset v. King, 2 Burr., 821, seems to go upon much the same principle; and see Shipwith v. Gibson, 4 Hen. & Munf., 490.

(b) This doctrine, which converts damages apparently stipulated, or fixed by the parties, into a penalty, came from the civil law through the Court of Chancery; and has at length obtained a firm hold in the courts of common law. It is obvious that, in order to enforce it, courts must disregard the particular expressions of the parties; for the moment we agree that a party may, by calling a real penalty liquidated damages, or throwing it into the form of an alternative in a contract, or substituting its payment for some specified default, secure the whole to himself, without regard to the real damage, we bring back the oppressive rule of the common law. The griping creditor will always use the particular form, or phraseology of contract, which will secure him his pound of flesh; unless the courts interfere, in all cases, and tell him that, from the very nature and essence of *his bond, whatever he claims, and in whatever shape, or upon whatever footing, if it be, in truth, plainly beyond the legal amount of damages, so far it shall be no more than nominal. Hence, it seems, that the rule laid down by Mr. Holt, in his note to Barton v. Glover, Holt *N. P.*, 43, 45, is, notwithstanding the doubt of Gibbs, *Ch. J.*, in that case, the true one, viz.: "Where a sum of money, whether in the name of a penalty or otherwise, is introduced in a covenant or agreement, merely to secure the enjoyment of a collateral object, the enjoyment of the object is considered as the principal intent of the deed or contract, and the penalty only as accessory, and therefore only to secure the damage really incurred." Within the spirit of this rule is Dennis v. Cummins, 3 Johns. Cas., 297, and Slosson v. Beadle, 7 Johns., 72, does not depart from it. Some of the cases in England, put by Holt, in his note, look like an exception to this rule; but the courts of that country will find themselves obliged to come back to it, or give it up. A plain, positive, settled exception, depending on the form of the contract, would destroy it. The rule is no more than what is laid down in the civil law, as deduced from a decision of Dumoulin by Pothier (*vide* 1 Ev. Poth., 210), that the penalty "being stipulated in lieu of damages, it is contrary to its nature to be carried beyond the limits which the law, respecting damages, prescribes." Nor can the courts enforce this rule without looking freely to the contract; not only, as it appears upon its face, but the comparative value of [*151 the consideration and thing to be performed, as they did here in the principal case; for if they confine themselves to the language of the parties, it is so easy to disguise the real case by fair words, that the rule becomes nothing. The right to redeem from under the penalty (to be made fully effectual) must be held inherent in the contract, like the equity of redemption in a mortgage; and not controlled even by the express intention of the parties. Mr. Evans, in his notes to Pothier, acknowledges the difficulty of deducing any general rule from the cases, which he considers at large (*vide* 2 Ev. Poth. 93-98); but, at page 98, he gives the form of a contract, in so many words, which, he suggests, may secure the creditor's object, and evade the scrutiny of courts. If he be right, all the creditor has to do, is to make his debtor sign a contract copied from Mr. Evans; and he may thus cripple or overreach all the courts of law and equity. But I imagine their rules were not framed so loosely and inconsiderately, as to be overthrown by a mere transposition of words or sentences.

152*] *GLEASON *v.* PINNEY.

Assumpsit *on Note for Certain Sum Payable in Specific Articles—Sum Expressed, the True Measure of Damages.*

In an action on a note for a certain sum of money, payable in specific articles, at a certain price, the sum expressed, not the value of the articles, is the true measure of damages.

Citations—3 Conn., 58; 2 Johns., 235, 242.

IN ERROR to the Onondaga C. P. The action in the court below was *assumpsit*, by Pinney against Gleason, upon several notes, due at different times, in this form:

"For value received, I promise to pay John Pinney, seventy-nine dollars, fifty cents, on the first day of August, 1822, in salt, at fourteen shillings per barrel, in good boating order. Liverpool, June, 30th, 1820.

ARA GLEASON."

On these several notes, if the sum due upon them was calculated in the dollars and cents expressed with interest, the balance due to the plaintiff below, at the time of the trial (May, 1824), over and above the defendant's payments and set-off proved upon the trial, would have been $87.60; but if the sum due upon the notes was calculated at the cash value of the salt, when they respectively became due, with interest to the time of the trial, then no balance would have been due to the plaintiff below; but the verdict should have been for the defendant.

These facts being found specially by the jury, the court below rendered judgment for the plaintiff for the $87.60 with costs.

The only question now, on error, was, whether the money, or the value of the salt, was the proper measure of damages.

Mr. B. D. Noxon, for the plaintiff in error.

Mr. S. Beardsly, contra, cited *Brooks* v. *Hubbard*, 3 Conn. N. S., 58.

Curia, per SAVAGE, *Ch. J.* The Court of C. P. adopted the true measure of damages. The defendant below acknowledged by his several notes, the amount of the debt due in dollars and cents. The delivery of the salt was the mere mode of payment. He might have
153*] avoided the payment *of the whole sum by this delivery; but not having done so, he should not be discharged by paying less than the debt which he has agreed to be due. This precise question was very fully considered in *Brooks* v. *Hubbard*, cited by the counsel for the defendant in error; and the rule acted upon in this case, holden to be the correct one. The same rule was recognized by this court in *Smith* v. *Smith*, 2 Johns., 235, 243. The judgment must be affirmed.

* *Judgment affirmed.*

Reversed—5 Wend., 393.
Cited in—4 Hill, 165; 3 Bos., 188.
See, 5 Cow., 411.

*The reporter afterwards found that this should have been "*Judgment reversed.*"

NOTE.—*Note for certain sum payable in specific articles. Measure of Damages.* See Pinney v. Gleason (reversing the above), 5 Wend., 393, *note.*

THE PRESIDENT, DIRECTORS AND COMPANY OF THE BANK OF UTICA *v.* HILLARD.

Witness—Rule as to Competency of—Mere Clerk of Bank not Compelled to Produce Bank Books on a Duces Tecum—*Party to Note Competent to show Invalidity in its Inception*

The clerk in a bank is not bound to produce its books, on a subpœna *duces tecum.*

Where it appeared that a bank had kept books or memoranda, in which they entered the time, manner and terms of discounting notes; held, on a suit by the bank against an indorser, upon discount that it was not competent for him to show the custom of of the bank, under the direction of the cashier, to take an usurious discount in all cases, from the creation of the Bank till after the particular note had been discounted, without first showing that notice had been given to the Bank to produce the books and memoranda on the trial, which had not been complied with.

The general rule, as to the competency of witnesses, is, that every person not interested in the event of the suit, nor incapacitated by his religious tenets, nor by the conviction of an infamous crime, is a competent witness. All other circumstances affect his credit only.

The maker, or other person, whose name appears upon a promissory note, is within this rule, a competent witness to show that it was void in its creation for usury, or other cause.

Citations—1 T. R., 296; 7 T. R., 597, 601; 3 Johns. Cas., 185.

ASSUMPSIT on a promissory note, by the Bank as indorsee against the defendant as indorser. The note was made by one Samuel Jones, dated Aug. 24, 1821, for $2,000, payable to the defendant, or order, at the Utica Bank, 90 days after date, and discounted by the plaintiffs.

The cause was tried at the Oneida Circuit, Oct. 4, 1824, before Betts, *Circuit Judge.*

The signatures of the maker and indorser being admitted, the plaintiffs called Thomas Colling as witness, who proved the usual demand and notice.

The defendant's counsel then stated their defense to be that the note was usurious; and proceeded to the cross-examination of Colling, who testified that he had been clerk of the Utica Bank for 10 or 12 years; and that he had been *served with a subpœna *duces te-* [*154
cum to produce the books of the Bank, in which were entered the time and manner of the discount of the note in question; and all the

NOTE.—*Competency of witnesses. Parties to bills and notes.* See Baker v. Arnold, 1 Cai., 258, *note*; Woodhull v. Holmes, 10 Johns., 231, *note.*

memoranda made by him or the plaintiffs respecting the discount or manner of discounting that note, or any notes of which it was a renewal. He was then called upon by the defendant's counsel to produce the book, or books, memoranda, &c., pursuant to the subpœna; to which he answered, that he had not brought them. The defendant's counsel then requested a delay, till the books and papers could be produced from the Bank; whereupon the counsel for the plaintiff objected that the witness was not bound to produce them, upon the ground that he was not the proper officer to be called upon for that purpose; and they objected to the delay. The judge sustained the objection, holding that the president or cashier should have been subpœnaed; and refused the delay requested; to which the defendant's counsel excepted.

Colling then testified, that from marks made upon the note by himself, he knew that it was discounted in renewal of a former note, for the like amount then in the Bank; and that, as a clerk of the Bank, it was made his duty to compute the amount of interest received on notes discounted at the Bank; but that he had not examined the books of the Bank, to see what sum was received by the plaintiffs for discount upon this note in particular; nor did he know the amount; nor did he know or recollect whether he did make the calculation of the amount of discount in that particular instance; as he was frequently absent from the Bank, and in such cases, it was done by one of the other clerks.

The defendant's counsel then offered to prove by the witness, that, in pursuance of general directions from the cashier of the Bank, the interest received by it, upon all notes discounted at the Bank, from its creation down to several months after discounting the note in question, had been computed by the standard of 30 days to a month, and 360 days to the year, without a single exception; and that by this standard, the interest received at the time of discounting the note would amount to $36.18. To this evidence the plaintiff's counsel objected; and it was rejected by the judge 155*] *on the ground that a general rule, practiced in other cases, was not evidence of the amount of discount in this particular case; and the defendant's counsel excepted.

They then offered Jones, the maker, as a witness, who was objected to by the plaintiff's counsel, as interested. He swore on his *voir dire*, that he and the defendant had been joint indorsers of a promissory note, made by one Moryan, for $2,000, which the plaintiffs had discounted for Moryan's benefit; that it had been from time to time renewed; that it was an accommodation note; and on failure of Moryan, it was agreed between the witness and the defendant, that the witness should become maker, and the defendant indorser, of the note in question, in renewal of Moryan's note; and that each should pay one half of the former, which was made and indorsed accordingly; and that he had since paid the plaintiffs $1,000, which were indorsed on the note in question. Whether this was in full of his half, he did not know; and this suit was brought by the plaintiffs, at his request, he having agreed to pay them the costs, if they should fail to recover them of the defendant. Upon this evidence, the judge rejected the witness as incompetent, and the defendant's counsel excepted.

Verdict for the plaintiff for $1,331.84 damages.

Mr. J. A. Spencer, moved for a new trial, and insisted:

1. That Colling was bound to produce the books, &c., under the subpœna *duces tecum*. The president pays no attention to the *minutiæ* of business carried on in a bank; nor is the cashier exclusively concerned in these. It is not necessary to inquire whether the clerk had a right to carry these papers abroad, on a private request. He was certainly bound to produce them on the demand of the law. They are, for the purpose of evidence, the papers of the court, and the cashier could not control them when required by the court. The bookkeeper of a merchant may be called on by subpœna, to produce the books of his principal. He has the possession and care of them, as bailee and agent. So of this clerk. The books, being in his possession and power, were subject to the subpœna.

*2. The general direction of the [*156 cashier, and the practice of the Bank, were, at least, competent evidence for the jury. Whether they would have been conclusive or satisfactory, is not the question. The evidence went to show that an usurious discount had been taken in all cases, this being directed by the proper officer of the Bank, whose directions, it is to be presumed, were obeyed. The whole includes all its parts. If taken in every instance, the proposition includes the particular one under consideration.

3. Jones' interest was in favor of the plaintiffs. He was, therefore, the best possible witness for the defendant, by whom he was offered. At any rate, his interest, as to costs, was of his own creation, without our consent. He could not, in this way, deprive us of his testimony. It is like the familiar case of a wager, by a witness, upon the event of a suit, which never is allowed to disqualify him, unless made with the consent of the party who offers him. The witness was accountable to the Bank, as maker, at all events, if we look merely to the face of the note; and on the Bank recovering against the defendant, the witness was accountable, as maker, to the defendant. This produces a balance of interest. The record in the present cause, if the defendant succeeds, will not be evidence to protect the witness against the Bank. That is the criterion of interest. But when we look to the agreement between these parties, which was to share half and half, in the payment of the $2,000; and when we see that the witness had paid his share it produces a strong interest, preponderating against us. That the witness had an actual feeling in favor of the plaintiffs' success, is evident from his having agreed to pay the costs, upon their failure to collect of the defendant.

Mr. J. Platt, contra:

1. The Bank being a party, their officers were not compellable to produce the books in any way. A party may always withhold a paper, and put his adversary to prove it the best way he can.

2. Colling did know the amount of discount. He was often absent, and did not know who made the calculation upon this particular note. **157***] Then, he is asked, as to the *custom which prevailed at the Bank to take usury. More than the bare statement of such a proposition is not necessary to show its fallacy.

3. Jones was interested in two points of view. His relation to the parties, as maker, was enough; and he is interested at least to the amount of the costs, which the defendant could recover over against him; in the event of the plaintiffs succeeding in this suit. The suit is on a mere accommodation indorsement. This will always be intended, as to an indorser, till the contrary is shown. But the agreement by the witness with the defendant, to pay one half the $2,000 note, creates another interest which would exclude him. The recovery in this suit would be evidence in favor of the defendant, in a suit against the witness for contribution. It would be essential testimony, and in itself, conclusive, to a certain extent, in such a suit. (Phil. Ev., 43, 44, 48; 3 T. R., 32, 36; 4 East, 582; 1 Str., 632; Cowp., 621.) If we are guided by the face of the paper, the interest is not balanced. The witness is interested to prevent a recovery against the defendant, to whom, in that event, he must pay not only principal, but the costs which we recover. *Pierce* v. *Butler*, 14 Mass., 303, 312; *Jones* v. *Brooke*, 4 Taunt., 464.

Mr. Spencer, in reply. Colling connected himself with the note by his marks upon it. He did the business; and it was certainly competent for him to say that he acted in reference to the custom of the Bank, and the direction of the cashier. Could this chain of circumstances leave any doubt of the usury?

The note was not made for the accommodation of the witness. We suppose this would not be intended; but must be shown affirmatively; and that there are, therefore, no costs in question, between the defendant and the witness. The maker is never liable to the indorser for the costs of a suit, on a note given in the ordinary course of business. (9 Johns., 131.) But it is enough that this matter was disposed of by arrangement between them; each being liable for one half. Costs could not be **158***] recovered in the face of *this agreement. But if otherwise, the witness was liable to the plaintiffs for their costs by express agreement. Go as this cause will, it seems he must pay costs, according to the ground taken on the other side. The doctrine of contribution goes on a joint undertaking; and does not apply between maker and indorser. In this view, the recovery here against the defendant would not be necessary, or even admissible, against the witness, in an action over. The note, having taken it up, would be enough in themselves. The recovery would be no proof that a farthing had been contributed. But it is clear that not one shilling ever can be recovered of the witness by the defendant in any event. The witness has done all that he agreed to do; that was, to pay one half the note.

Curia, per SAVAGE, *Ch. J.* The obligation of Colling to produce the books, upon the *duces tecum*, depends on the question, whether they were in his possession and under his control. He was the mere clerk of the plaintiffs, and in that character had no such property in or possession of the books, as imposed the obligation to bring them. They were under control of the cashier, who might forbid their removal, or place them beyond the reach of the witness.

It does not appear that the general direction from the cashier, and the custom of the Bank, were the best evidence in the power of the defendant. The books and memoranda themselves might have been produced on notice for that purpose to the plaintiffs. Had this notice been given, and not complied with, I incline to think the inferior evidence would have been, *prima facie*, sufficient. It would then be fair to presume that the witness could not state the contents of the books in relation to this note, because he had been careful not to know them, or refresh his memory on the subject. As the matter stood, I think the judge decided correctly.

Was Jones, the maker, a competent witness? It is contended that he was interested in the costs. Originally, both the witness and defendant were indorsers and sureties on paper *of Morgan, upon whose failure they [***159** substituted the note in question, agreeing to share the loss equally between them. The witness, it seems, had fulfilled his part of the arrangement, or nearly so; and this suit was brought at his instance, and on his undertaking to indemnify the plaintiffs against the costs, to collect the payment of the residue from the defendant. Admitting Jones' liability to the defendant for a part of these costs, he is, on the other hand, liable to the Bank for the whole, in case of their failure to collect of the defendant. His interest is, therefore, neutralized.

Jones was, then, a competent witness, unless he is to be excluded on the ground of policy. Before *Walton* v. *Shelly*, 1 T. R., 296, the rule and its exceptions were, that every person was a competent witness who was not interested in the event of the cause, rendered infamous by crime, or excluded for infidelity. By that case, a new exception was introduced, "that no party, who has signed a paper or deed, shall ever be permitted to give testimony to invalidate that instrument, which he hath so signed." This exception, continued a prevailing one, in England, though not universally so, till it was overruled in *Jordaine* v. *Lashbrooke*, 7 T. R., 597, 601, where the reasoning in *Walton* v. *Shelly*, was considered, and the ancient rule re-established—Ashurst, *J.*, still adhering to the opinion he had given in *Walton* v. *Shelly*. He was the only judge on the bench, in 1798, who had also been there in 1786. The doctrine advanced by Ld. Kenyon, in the latter case, is, "that when a witness is infamous, and the record of his conviction is produced, or when he is interested in the event of the cause, he cannot be received; but to carry the rule beyond that, would be extending it further that policy, morality, or the interests of the public require." This has ever since been the law in England. But this court, in *Winton* v. *Saidler*, 3 Johns. Cas., 185, adopted *Walton* v. *Shelly*, which has also been adopted in most of the U. S. In *Winton* v. *Saidler*, the question is ably discussed by the judges, who delivered their opinions; and the decision made by a bare majority of the court.

160*] *Without intending to enter at large into the arguments on this subject, I would barely remark, that those who have maintained the doctrines lying on each side of the question, have been influenced by the arguments of Ld. Mansfield, on the one hand, and Ld. Kenyon on the other. The former seems to found his argument on a maxim of the civil law: "*nemo allegans suam turpitudinem est audiendus*," applying it in this way; every person who has signed an instrument, has thereby declared that he knows of no objection to it; and should not afterwards be permitted to contradict this declaration. The allegation of the frauds, which might thus be practiced, is met by Ld. Kenyon, with supposing that greater ones may be practiced on parties and strangers, by getting the names of all who may be witnesses of fraudulent paper; and then the guilty will stand entrenched in the forms of law. Supposing the danger which we are to apprehend on the score of fraud to be equally great on the one hand as the other, I can see no good reason for refusing to parties who may be innocent, the benefit of disclosing the whole truth. I cannot believe that justice will be promoted or the morals of community improved, by permitting these, guilty of frauds, to protect themselves from the testimony of the only witnesses who are supposed to have a knowledge of the facts.

This court has been gradually receding from the decision in *Walton* v. *Shelly*; and I am free to declare that I entirely deny the propriety of the exception adopted in that case; and consider the old rule, with its ancient exceptions, the only correct one. See *Stafford* v. *Rice*, *ante*, 23. That rule is, that every person not interested in the event of the suit, nor incapacitated by his religious tenets, nor by the conviction of an infamous crime, is a competent witness. All other circumstances affect his credit only.

In my opinion, the judge erred in excluding the witness; and a new trial should be granted on that ground, with costs to abide the event of the suit.

New trial granted.

Distinguished—1 Blatchf., 241.
Cited in—7 Cow., 385; 1 Wend., 557; 3 Wend., 416; Hoffm., 549, 550; 14 How. Pr., 30; 1 Hall, 510; 1 Blatchf., 240; 71 Ill., 198; 37 Am. Rep., 426 (70 Mo., 62).

NOTE.—In consequence of a defect in the papers which I had obtained in *Gleason* v. *Pinney*, *ante*, 152, I was led to report the judgment, as one of affirmance; whereas it was, in fact, a reversal of the judgment below; Savage, *Ch. J.*, dissenting upon the grounds there reported as the opinion of the court.—REPORTER.

161*] *WENDELL

v.

THE PRESIDENT, DIRECTORS AND COMPANY OF THE WASHINGTON AND WARREN BANK.

Statute—Construction of.

Under the 10th section of the Act incorporating the Washington and Warren Bank, sess. 40, ch. 185, the person whose bills, &c., are refused payment in specie, may recover, not only the principal sum due, with the usual interest, at 7 *per cent.*; but also 10 *per cent. per annum*, on the same principal from the time payment is demanded, till it is made.

Citations—4 Johns., 119; 12 Johns., 17.

IN *assumpsit*, the facts were thus: the plaintiff was the owner, and held bills of the defendants, to $1,200, which June 1, 1820, he presented to the defendant's cashier within banking hours, and demanded payment in specie, which the cashier refused. This suit was for the principal, damages and interest. The defendants paid into court, the principal and ten *per cent. per annum* damages, since the demand; and the only question was, whether, under the Statute incorporating the defendants (sess. 40, ch. 185, sec. 10,) the plaintiff should also recover legal interest on the same principal, at 7 *per cent.*

Mr. J. L. Wendell, for the plaintiff, insisted that he should, and cited *Hendricks* v. *Franklin*, 4 Johns., 119.

Mr. B. F. Butler, contra.

Curia, per SAVAGE, *Ch. J.* The section in question provides that the defendants shall be liable to pay for all notes, bills, &c., the payment of which shall have been demanded, as the bills in this case were, and which shall not have been paid in specie, damages at the rate of 10 *per cent. per annum*, until they shall be paid or otherwise satisfied. I think the Legislature intended this 10 *per cent.* as an addition to the sum of principal and interest which was already recoverable at law. They intended this, by way of punishment to the defendants, and compensation to the plaintiff, for his loss and disappointment. There is certainly some analogy between this case and that of protested foreign bills of exchange, upon which the drawer is bound to pay, not only interest and 20 *per cent.* damages (4 Johns., 119), but the difference of exchange. (12 *Id.*, 17.) The plaintiff must have judgment for $336, over and above what has been paid into court.

Judgment accordingly.

Cited in—6 Cow., 215.

---

*VAN ALSTINE *v.* WIMPLE. [*162

Statute of Frauds—Naked Fee, not an Interest of any value and not a Consideration for a Promise—If Part of an Entire Promise is Void by the Statute, the Promise is Void.

After a sale of V.'s land on *fi. fa.* to O. for $42, and before the sheriff conveyed, W. agreed verbally with V. and O. to take the land of O. and give V. $600, of which he paid $200: and the sheriff conveyed to O., who conveyed to W., who afterwards sold part of the land for $600, and acknowledged the agreement with V: in *assumpsit* by V. against W. for the $400 remaining unpaid, held, that the agreement was within the Statute of Frauds, and void, because not in writing and also for want of consideration.

Intermediate a sheriff's sale of land on *fi. fa.* and giving a deed, though the naked fee remain in the debtor, yet this is not an interest of any value; and so no consideration for a promise.

If part of an entire promise be void by the Statute of Frauds, the whole is void.

Citations—2 Vent., 223; 7 T. R., 197; 8 Johns., 253; 4 Johns., 240; 14 Johns., 358; 1 Johns. Ch., 339; 2 Johns. Ch., 405; 5 Johns. Ch., 1; 2 Cai., 63; 2 Johns., 248.

INDEBITATUS *assumpsit*, for land bargained and sold by the plaintiff to the defendant. The declaration also contained the usual counts for goods, work, money, and on an *insimul computassent*. The cause was tried at the Madison Circuit, Mar. 10, 1824, before Williams, *Circuit Judge*.

On the trial, the plaintiff proved that about 30 acres of land belonging to him, was, Sept. 25, 1815, sold at sheriff's sale, on a *fi. fa.* against him, upon a judgment in favor of one Hopkins, to one Olcott, on a bid of $42. That after the sale, but before Olcott had taken a deed from the sheriff, it was verbally agreed between the plaintiff and defendant, with Olcott's assent, that he should relinquish his purchase to the defendant; that he should, however, take his deed from the sheriff, and then convey to the defendant; who agreed to pay the plaintiff $600, of which he paid $200 down. The plaintiff was to have two years within which to redeem the land, by repaying the $200, with interest: but if this was not done, then the defendant agreed to pay the plaintiff the remaining $400. Shortly after, the sheriff conveyed to Olcott; who conveyed to the defendant pursuant to this arrangement; and the defendant afterwards in Apr., 1817, sold and conveyed 16 acres of the land to one Vanduzer, for $600. The plaintiff never redeemed, or offered to redeem the land; but brought this action for the $400, and interest. After the suit was commenced, the defendant acknowledged the debt.

Verdict for the plaintiff, subject to the opinion of the court, upon the questions, among others, whether the agreement was void, as not being in writing, within the Statute of Frauds; and if valid in this respect, yet whether it was not void for want of consideration.

163*] **Mr. J. A. Spencer*, for the plaintiff, said there could be no doubt that general *indebitatus assumpsit* would lie for lands sold and conveyed.

Mr. G. C. Bronson, for the defendant. This is admitted.

Mr. Spencer. When this bargain was made, the fee was still in the plaintiff. The estate did not pass till the sheriff's deed was executed. *Simonds* v. *Catlin*, 2 Cai., 61, 63. *Jackson* v. *Catlin*, 2 Johns., 248. *Van Rensselaer* v. *Sheriff of Onondaga*, 1 Cow., 443. An interest in the land passed to, and became executed in the defendant. So far the contract is valid and unavoidable. The defendant has sold a part of these lands, and converted them into money, after which he acknowledged the debt; and we are not only entitled to recover upon the special agreement, or for lands sold, but upon the counts for money had and received, and the *insimul computassent*. (1 Chit. Pl., 341; 2 T. R., 370: 2 Burr., 1008.) The purchase money was a lien on the land, which lien the defendant has impaired, converting a portion of the land into money, by sale to a *bona fide* purchaser; for which money he should account in this action. *Garson* v. *Green*, 1 Johns. Ch., 308.

Mr. G. C. Bronson, contra. The plaintiff retained no interest whatever, legal or equitable, after the sheriff's sale; and of course could convey none to the defendant. There was, therefore, no consideration for this promise. But the contract is void within the Statute of Frauds. 1 R. L., 78, secs. 11, 12; *Hall* v. *Shultz*, 4 Johns., 240; *Sherrill* v. *Crosby*, 14 *Id.*, 358; *Botsford* v. *Burr*, 2 Johns. Ch., 405; *Movan* v. *Hays*, 1 *Id.*, 339; *Steere* v. *Steere*, 5 *Id.*, 1; *Crawford* v. *Morrell*, 8 Johns., 253; *Harris* v. *Stapleton*, 7 T. R., 201; Rob., Frauds, 100; Sugd. L. V., 70.

Curia, per SUTHERLAND, *J.* So far as the agreement professed to bind the defendant to reconvey the land, upon being repaid the $200 advanced by him, it was clearly within the Statute of Frauds, and void at law. It was a contract for the sale of lands, and comes within the very words of the *Act. It has been [***164** repeatedly held, that if part of one entire contract be void under the Statute of Frauds, the whole is void; that the party shall not be permitted to separate the parts of an entire agreement, and recover on one part, the other being void—and this, although the part which was void, and could not have been enforced, has been actually performed. Thus, in *Ld. Lexington* v. *Clarke*, 2 Vent., 223, the declaration stated that Brady, the former husband of Mrs. Clarke, was tenant at will to the plaintiff, at an annual rent of £320; that at the time of his death, one half year's rent was due; that Mrs. Clarke, while sole, before her second marriage, in consideration that the plaintiff would permit her to enjoy the premises until the next Lady day, and permit her to remove certain posts, rails, &c., fixed on the premises by her husband, promised to pay the £160 in arrear, and also £260 more. The £160 were paid before suit brought; and it was held that this part of the agreement being void, as it was to pay the debt of another, and not in writing, the residue was void also, although, had it stood by itself, it might have been enforced. The same doctrine was held by Ld. Kenyon, in *Chater* v. *Beckett*, 7 T. R., 197; and by this court, in *Crawford* v. *Morrell*, 8 Johns., 253. The cases of *Hall* v. *Shultz*, 4 Johns., 240; *Sherrill* v. *Crosby*, 14 *Id.*, 358; *Movan* v. *Hays*, 1 Johns. Ch., 339; *Botsford* v. *Burr*, 2 *Id.*, 405, and *Steere* v. *Steere*, 5 *Id.*, 1, have also some bearing upon this point.

But I am also inclined to think that there was no consideration to support the promise of the defendant to pay the plaintiff the $600 for the land, and that on this ground he is not entitled to recover. If the legal effect and character of the transaction be the same as though the defendant had been the purchaser at the sheriff's sale, instead of Olcott, to whose rights he succeeded, which appears to me to be the case, then it seems to me very clear, that the defendant's agreement was without consideration. If the sheriff's deed had been executed and delivered, it will at once be conceded that there would have been no consideration for the promise. And the fact that the naked fee remained in the plaintiff until the deed was executed, does not, in my judgment, *alter [***165** the case. (2 Cai., 63; 2 Johns., 248.) All his beneficial interest in the land was gone. No act or assent on his part was necessary to the consummation of the title of the purchaser. It was not in his power to prevent it. The purchaser could compel the sheriff, at any moment, to execute the deed.

Suppose the plaintiff, after the sale, and before the execution of the deed (both being on the same day), had conveyed the land in question to a third person; would his deed have passed either the legal estate, or any equitable interest to his grantee? If not, how can any consideration to support the promise of the defendant, be implied from the fact that, at the moment of making the promise, the naked fee remained in the plaintiff?

I am, therefore, of opinion that on either of these grounds the defendant is entitled to judgment. If the plaintiff has any remedy, it must be in equity.

Judgment for the defendant.

Cited in—9 Cow., 270; 10 Wend., 440; 5 Den., 247; 10 N. Y., 235; 30 N. Y., 298 (*a*); 36 N. Y., 539; 43 N.Y., 552; 44 N. Y., 90; 45 N. Y., 420; 2 Trans. App., 373; 1 Barb., 518; 10 Barb., 371; 25 Barb., 448; 47 Barb., 175; 53 Barb., 68; 64 Barb., 257; 4 Bos., 154; 39 Super., 151; 2 E. D. S., 407; 4 E. D. S., 161; 25 Ind., 542; 37 Ohio St., 408; 11 Am. Rep., 504 (36 Md., 336).

CRITTENDEN *v.* WILSON.

Cumulative Remedies—Building of Dam under Authority of Statute—Action, for Overflowing Plaintiff's Land.

An Act authorizing one to build a dam on his own land, upon a creek or river which is a public highway, merely protects him from an indictment for a nuisance. If, in doing this, he flow his neighbor's land, he is liable to an action, even though the Act provide a summary mode of appraising and paying the damages arising from such a consequence.

If a statute give a remedy in the affirmative, without a negative expressed or implied, for a matter which was actionable at the common law, the party may still sue at the common law, as well as upon the Statute: for this does not take away the common law remedy.

Citations—Act, April 12, 1813 (2 R. L., 286); 17 Johns., 195; 2 Inst., 200; Com. Dig., Action upon Stat., C.

ON demurrer to the defendant's pleas. The action was case, for overflowing the plaintiff's land, in consequence of the defendant's erecting a mill-dam across the Otselic Creek or River, at Willet, in the County of Cortland. To this declaration the defendant interposed two pleas, each being, in substance, that he was authorized to build the dam, by an Act of the Legislature, passed Mar. 22, 1822, adjoining his land, and that he complied, on his part, with all the requirements and provisions of the Act, which he set forth at large in his pleas. By these, it appeared that the 2d section of the Act provided that it should be the duty of the Court of C. P., of Cortland Co., once in every three years, if required by any person **166***] who had sustained any damage *by his land being flowed by the dam, to appoint three respectable freeholders of Cortland Co., who should, once in every year, appraise the damages sustained in consequence of the dam; and that the damages so appraised, should be paid by the defendant, &c., within 60 days after the appraisement, who should also pay the expenses of the appraisement.

Demurrer and joinder.

Mr. J. A. Collier, in support of the demurrer, contended that the Act was unconstitutional and void; and he cited the new Constitution, art. 7, sec. 2.

Mr. J. A. Spencer cited the general canal law of the State, and several Acts concerning Local Canals, Dams, and Roads; also the Act concerning Highways in general—all of which, so far as they relate to the remedy for damages, he said, the principle contained in the demurrer would avoid; also, *People* v. *Platt*, 17 Johns., 195; *Rodgers* v. *Bradshaw*, 20 Johns., 735; *Id.*, S. C., 103, and 2 R. L., 286, declaring the creek in question a public highway. But,

Mr. Collier, in reply, said the Acts and authorities cited related to public objects. This Act was to further a mere private purpose, and was plainly unconstitutional. At any rate, the remedy given by the Statute is merely cumulative.

Curia, per SUTHERLAND, *J.* It is contended that the Legislature had no authority to authorize the erection of a dam, in such a manner as to overflow the land of third persons; or, if they had, that they had no right to take from such persons the privilege of having their damages assessed by a jury, and direct them to be assessed by appraisers.

The Otselic River was declared a public highway by the Act of Apr. 12, 1813, 2 R. L., 286. No individual, therefore, had a right to obstruct it by dams, or other erections, without a grant from the Legislature. The right of the Legislature to make such grant is too clear to be disputed. The grantee, of course, takes it subject to the restriction, *sic utere tuo ut alienum non lædas.* The Legislature, in this instance, have not assumed the right of authorizing the defendant *to erect a dam, [***167** which shall cause the lands of his neighbor to be overflowed. The Act anticipates that such may be the consequence, and makes it an express condition of the grant, that the defendant shall pay all damages which may result from it; and prescribes the mode in which they shall be ascertained. If there had been no express provision in the Act for the payment of damages, the defendant would still have been liable to pay them; and the only effect of this provision is to enforce the duty of making compensation by additional sanctions, as the grant or license may be avoided, if the defendant should fail to pay the damages in the manner prescribed by the Act. The effect of the

---

NOTE.—*Cumulative Remedies,*

A statute granting a new remedy does not take away a pre-existing remedy without express words or necessary implication. The new remedy is cumulative. Jackson v. Bradt, 2 Cai., 169; Scidmore v. Smith, 13 Johns., 322; Colden v. Eldred, 15 Johns., 220; Farmers' Turnpike Co. v. Coventry, 10 Johns., 389; Wheaton v. Hibbard, 20 Johns., 290; Wetmore v. Tracy, 14 Wend., 250; Susquehannah, &c., Turnpike Co., v. People, 15 Wend., 267; Clark v. Brown, 18 Wend., 213; Platt v Sherry, 7 Wend., 236; Stafford v. Ingersol, 3 Hill, 38; Waterford, &c., Turnpike Co., v. People, 9 Barb., 161; Livingston v. Van Ingen, 9 Johns., 571; Renwick v. Morris, 7 Barb., 575; Tremain v. Richardson, 68 N. Y., 617; Behan v. People, 17 N. Y., 516; 7 Abb. Pr., 82; 16 How. Pr., 153; People v. Stevens, 13 Wend., 341; Lane v. Salter, 51 N. Y., 1; Collison v. Newcastle & Darlington Ry. Co., 1 Car. & K. 546; Litchfield v. Simpson, 8 Q. B. 65.

Where a right is created by the statute, and a remedy is expressly given, such remedy is exclusive. Almy v. Harris, 5 Johns., 175; McKeon v. Caberty, 3 Wend., 494; People v. Hazard, 4 Hill, 207; Pennington v. Townsend, 7 Wend., 276; Dudley v. Mayhew, 3 N. Y., 9; Smith v. Lockwood, 13 Barb., 209; First Ntl. Bank v. Lamb, 57 Barb., 434; St. Pancras v. Battenburgh, 2 C. B. (N. S.), 477. See, also, Small v. Herkimer Mfg. Co., 2 N. Y., 330; Mil s v. Stewart, 41 N. Y., 384. See generally, People v. City of Brooklyn, 69 N. Y., 605; People v. Hall, 80 N. Y., 117; Almy v. Harris, 5 Johns., 175, *note.*

grant is merely to authorize the defendant to erect a dam, as he might have done, if the stream had been his own, without grant. In such a case, he would have been responsible in damages for all the injury occasioned by it to others. The dam could not be indicted as a public nuisance, and abated. The only remedy for those injured would have been by action. *People* v. *Platt*, 17 Johns., 195.

Was it then the intention of the Legislature, by making it a condition of the grant, that the defendant should pay the damages which might result to third persons from his dam, to be ascertained in the manner pointed out by the 2d section of the Act, to deprive those who might sustain injury, of their remedy by action? I think it is clear that such was not the intention of the Legislature. Their object was to provide a summary remedy for those who might be injured by the dam, by which they might be remunerated more expeditiously, and with less expense, than by the ordinary course of law. They made it a condition of the grant that the grantee should, within sixty days, pay the damages which the appraisers should assess. They had a right to impose that condition; it was assented to by the defendant. He, therefore voluntarily waived his right to a trial by jury. It was the condition upon which the privilege of erecting or continuing his dam was conferred upon him. But there is nothing in the Act which, either in terms or by necessary implication, makes it compulsory upon those who may be injured to have their damages as-
168*] sessed under the Act, or deprives *them of their pre-existing common law remedy by action. The Act is not couched in negative terms. The remedy which it provides is cumulative merely, and not exclusive. "If a statute gives a remedy in the affirmative (without a negative expressed or implied), for a matter which was actionable by the common law, the party may sue at the common law as well as upon the Statute; for this does not take away the common law remedy." (2 Inst., 200; Com. Dig., Action upon Statute, C.)

It is unnecessary to consider whether the Legislature had a constitutional right to deprive persons who might be injured by the defendant's dam, of their remedy by action, as I am very clearly of the opinion that they have not undertaken to exercise such authority in this case.

The plaintiff is entitled to judgment upon the demurrer, with leave to the defendant to amend.

Judgment for the plaintiff.

Cited in—4 Wend., 670; 15 Wend., 208; 5 Barb., 86; 6 Barb., 76, 318; 9 Barb., 173; 13 Barb., 34; 24 Barb., 365; 27 Barb., 522; 4 How. Pr., 7; 18 How. (U. S.), 432; 1 Wall. Jr., 292; 36 N. J. L., 342; 28 Am. Dec., 526; 34 Am. Dec., 186, 192 (2 Harr., 129); 2 Am. Rep., 62; 38 Am. Rep., 411 (83 N. Y., 178).

JACKSON, ex dem. CLARKE, v. RANDALL.

Ejectment for Dower—Proceedings to Admeasure Dower, no Evidence of Title and Seisin of Husband.

In ejectment for dower, admeasured on application to the surrogate, under the Act, 1 R. L., 60-62, the proceedings are no evidence of title, nor of anything more than that the part assigned belongs to the widow, after a title is shown to the whole. The plaintiff must prove his title, the same as in any other actions of ejectment; and the defendant may impeach it.

Citations—9 Johns., 246; 17 Johns., 125; 10 Johns., 368.

EJECTMENT, for lands assigned to the lessor of the plaintiff as dower, pursuant to the Statute, 1 R. L., 60-62, on her petition to the Surrogate of Otsego Co., tried at the Otsego Circuit, Sept., 1823, before Nelson, *Circuit Judge.*

At the trial, the intermarriage of the lessor of the plaintiff with Samuel Tyler, and his death, about three years before the trial, being proved by the plaintiff, his counsel then gave in evidence the proceedings before the surrogate; by which it appeared that certain lands, particularly described in the proceedings, situate in Pittsfield, Otsego Co., had been admeasured and assigned to the lessor of the plaintiff, as dower, upon the seisin of her husband, during coverture, by admeasurers, appointed according to the statute, &c., and that the report of the admeasurers was filed before the commencement of this suit; that the defendant had due notice of the petition, and consequent proceedings, for admeasuring and assigning the dower.

*The defendant's counsel then of- [***169**
fered to prove that he was, when the proceedings before the surrogate were commenced against him, not seised of any freehold in the premises, but was merely a tenant from year to year; which was objected to by the plaintiff's counsel, and excluded by the judge.

The counsel for the defendant also insisted that notice to the defendant of the proceedings before the surrogate was insufficient, and should have been given to the tenant of the freehold; which objection was overruled by the judge.

The defendant's counsel then offered to show an outstanding title in a third person, and that the lessor of the plaintiff had no right to dower. This offer being objected to by the plaintiff's counsel, was overruled by the judge, and the jury found for the plaintiff.

Mr. J. M'Kown, for the defendant, moved for a new trial; and cited *Matter of Martha Watkins*, 9 Johns., 245; *Matter of Esther Gardinier*, 10 *Id.*, 368, and *Jackson* v. *Hixon*, 17 *Id.*, 123, 126.

Mr. G. C. Bronson, contra, cited *Coates* v. *Cheever*, 1 Cow., 460.

Curia, per SUTHERLAND, *J.* The judge erred in holding these proceedings conclusive evidence of the title and seisin of the husband. In *The Matter of Martha Watkins*, 9 Johns., 246, the court say, the proceeding of the surrogate, under the Act, are founded on the assumption that the widow is entitled to her dower out of the estate in question, and that it is only to be designated and set off. There is no provision for trying, before the surrogate, the title to dower; and the admeasurement to be made, in pursuance of his order, cannot affect, or prejudice the right to dower, or the legal or equitable bar to it. Those rights, if litigated, remain open for investigation in the ordinary course of justice. The admeasurers are not to do execution as the sheriff does, on a writ of *habere facias possessionem.* If the right to dower be denied, the party may protect his possession notwithstanding the admeasurement, and drive her to her action at law.

170*] *Until the admeasurement is reversed on appeal, it is conclusive in an action of ejectment, as to the part belonging the widow, if she is entitled to dower at all. But it was admitted by the plaintiff's counsel, in *Jackson* v. *Hixon*, 17 Johns., 125, that the proceedings before the surrogate were no evidence of title. The seisin of the husband was proved in that case; and the proof was admitted to be necessary. This is like any other ejectment suit. The plaintiff must make out his title; and the defendant is at liberty to impeach it. (10 Jonus., 368.) A new trial must be granted, with costs to abide the event of the suit.

New trial granted.

Cited in—5 Cow., 302; 6 Cow., 317; 4 Wend., 632; 9 Wend., 310; 14 Wend., 255.

BULL *v.* FOLLETT.

1. *Indenture of Apprenticeship Between the Ward and His Guardian, and the Master, Binds the Guardian to See that the Apprentice Fulfills his Duties.* 2. *Covenant—No Precise or Formal Terms Necessary.*

An indenture of apprenticeship between a ward and his guardian and the master, declaring the duties of the apprentice in the usual form, and concluding thus: "for the true performance of all and singular the said covenants and agreements the said master, apprentice and guardian have hereunto interchangeably set their hands and seals," &c., binds the guardian to see that the apprentice fulfills all his duties to his master.

No precise or formal terms are necessary to constitute a covenant. The inquiry always is, what was the intention of the parties.

Citations—10 Johns., 99; 14 Johns., 374; 2 Mass., 228; Doug., 518; 8 Mod., 191.

COVENANT on indentures of apprenticeship, tried June 16, 1822, at the Ontario Circuit, before Throop, *Circuit Judge*.

The indenture proved at the trial was thus: "This indenture, made the 7th day of April, A. D. 1816, witnesseth, that F. M. Follett, a minor, aged 15 years, the 1st February, 1816, of his own free, will, &c., with the consent of N. Follett (the defendant), his guardian, doth by the presents, bind himself to J. Bull (the plaintiff), to learn the trade, &c., of a hatter, &c., to serve, &c., from the date hereof, until the 1st February, A. D. 1822; during which time the said apprentice, his said master shall faithfully serve, &c.," and concluded thus: "for the true performance of all and singular the said covenants and agreements, the said master, apprentice and guardian, have hereunto interchangeably set their hands and seals, the day and year first above written.

Sealed, &c. J. BULL. (L. S.)
F. M. FOLLETT. (L. S.)
N. FOLLETT. (L. S.)"

171*] *The plaintiff declared against the defendant, the guardian, alleging, as a breach, the departure of the apprentice from the service of the plaintiff; and that so the defendant had not kept his covenant.

After the indenture was proved at the trial, the judge, on the motion of the defendant's counsel, refused to hear further proof, and nonsuited the plaintiff, on the ground that the defendant was not bound by any of the coveuants in the indenture.

A motion was now made to set aside the nonsuit, and for a new trial.

Mr. S. M. Hopkins, for the defendant, cited *Whitley* v. *Loftus*, 8 Mod., 190; *Branch* v. *Ewington*, Doug., 518, and *Mead* v. *Billings*, 10 Johns., 99.

Mr. J. C. Spencer, contra, cited *Ackley* v. *Hoskins*, 14 Johns., 374, and *Blunt* v. *Melcher*, 2 Mass., 228.

Curia, per SUTHERLAND, *J.* In *Mead* v. *Billings*, 10 Jobus., 99, the terms of the indenture were, "that for the true performance of all and singular the covenants and agreements aforesaid, the said parties bind themselves, each unto the other. In witness, &c., interchangeably set their hands and seals, &c." And it was executed by the master, the father and the apprentice. The father was there held to be bound for the son, and to be responsible in an action of covenant for the son's act, in leaving his master before the expiration of the term. Here, the terms used are, "for the true performance of all and singular the said covenants and agreements, the said master, apprentice and guardian have hereunto interchangeably set their hands and seals, &c." The words "bind themselves each unto the other," as used in *Mead* v. *Billings*, are here omitted; but that omission does not appear to me to alter the construction or legal effect of the instrument. The intention of all the parties, the guardian as well as the master and apprentice, to be bound by the covenants, is clearly to be inferred from the terms used; and that is all that is necessary. No precise or formal terms *are necessary to con- **[*172** stitute a covenant more than any other agreement. The inquiry always is, what was the intention of the parties. Here they declare that they have interchangeably set their hands and seals not in witness generally, of what they have done, as in *Ackley* v. *Hoskins*, 14 Johns., 374, but specifically, for the true performance of all and singular the aforesaid covenants and agreements—that is, to bind them to the performance of those covenants. The phraseology used leaves no reasonable doubt of the intention of the parties, mutually and interchangeably to be bound by the covenants.

In *Ackley* v. *Hoskins* the court held that the terms of the instrument, "In witness whereof, the parties have interchangeably set their hands and seals, &c.," were satisfied so far as the guardian was concerned, by considering them as referring to his consent to the covenants and agreements of his ward. But here the guardian has expressly declared that he signed and sealed the instrument, not merely to manifest his assent to the acts of his ward, but for the true performance of all the preceding covenants and agreements. In *Blunt* v. *Melcher*, 2 Mass., 228, the terms used were, "In testimony whereof the said parties have to these indentures interchangeably set their hands and seals." This was held not to amount to a covenant on the part of the guardian, for the same reasons that were assigned by this court in *Ackley* v. *Hoskins*.

Branch v. *Ewington*, Doug., 518, and *Whitley* v. *Loftus*, 8 Mod., 191, are, that although it is not necessary for the parent or guardian to bind himself for the good conduct, &c., of the apprentice; yet, if the language of the indenture evinces his intention to do so, he shall be held responsible.

I am, therefore, of opinion that the nonsuit ought to be set aside and a new trial granted, the costs to abide the event.

Motion granted.

Cited in—7 Wend., 45; 2 Hill, 597.

173*] *JACKSON, ex dem. Dox,

v.

JACKSON.

1. *Evidence—Objection to Admissibility, too Late on Motion for New Trial—Evidence, to Vary a Written Contract, Inadmissible—2. Adverse Possession—Possession, of Heir or Tenant of Mortgagor, not Adverse to Mortgagee or his Assignees.*

The admissibility of evidence, if not objected to at the trial, cannot be questioned on a motion for a new trial.

One in possession, claiming either as heir or tenant of a mortgagor, has not such an adverse possession as will avoid a deed to the mortgagee, or his assignee, upon a foreclosure.

In ejectment by the mortgagee, or his assignee, or a purchaser under a mortgage expressly conditioned for the payment of money, evidence that the mortgage was given to indemnify the mortgagee as special bail for the mortgagor, and that no damage had followed his being bail, is inadmissible.

So are the admissions of the mortgagee that the mortgage was not a lien, unless it appear that a subsequent mortgagee was misled by the admission.

Citations—Cowp., 47; 18 Johns., 45; Cro. Eliz., 697; 3 Wils., 275; 8 Johns., 189; 6 Johns., 20; Johns. Dig., 213.

EJECTMENT, for lots Nos. 4 and 5 on the west side of Water St., in the Village of Geneva, tried June 22, 1824, before Throop, *C. J.*

At the trial, it appeared that the defendant claimed the lots as the heir of his father Elias Jackson; and had resided on them for about sixteen years. The most of this time he resided with his mother, who died in possession a few years before the trial. She resided on a part of the premises, which she claimed as tenant in dower. She was reputed to be the widow of Elias Jackson, who, Apr. 16, 1796, mortgaged the premises in question to one Annine. The mortgage was expressed to secure £620, payable May 20 following, on which day it was registered. It was assigned to one Stoddard Nov. 2, 1803, and the assignment was acknowledged and registered in the clerk's office of Ontario Co.; and Stoddard assigned to the lessor of the plaintiff, July 21, 1823. This assignment was also acknowledged and recorded in the same clerk's office July 22, 1823. The equity of redemption of the mortgage was duly foreclosed under a special power of sale, and the title conveyed by the lessor of the plaintiff to his agent, and by the latter to the lessor of the plaintiff, Feb. 7, 1824. Whether the mortgagor was still alive was left doubtful by the testimony. He had left the country long since, and the reports as to his death were contradictory.

The defendant offered to show that the mortgage from Elias Jackson was, in truth, given to Anuine, to indemnify him as special bail in a suit against Elias Jackson; and that Annine had never sustained any damage in consequence of being bail; that Annine, shortly after the mortgage was given, being inquired of by a subsequent mortgagee of Jackson, declared that his mortgage was not then a lien on the premises.

*On objection by the plaintiff, to this [*174 evidence, it was rejected by the judge.

Verdict for the plaintiff.

A motion was now made for a new trial, on several grounds, which were all overruled by the court. The only questions which it is deemed material to notice are, whether the defense offered was admissible, and whether there was an adverse possession in the defendant, so as to defeat the deed to Dox, the lessor of the plaintiff.

Mr. E. Williams, for the defendant, as to the first question, cited *Clarke* v. *Henry*, 2 Cow., 324. He said there was an adverse possession in the defendant, and a descent cast; and the deed to Dox was, therefore, void.

Mr. J. C. Spencer, contra, cited *Mease* v. *Mease*, Cowp., 47; *Wells* v. *Baldwin*, 18 Johns., 45; *Meads* v. *Lansingh*, Hopk. Ch., 124; *Jackson* v. *Shearman*, 6 Johns., 19, and *Jackson* v. *Collins*, 3 Cow., 89.

Curia, per SUTHERLAND, *J.* It was made a point, in behalf of the defendant, upon the argument, that the evidence to show that the widow of Jackson claimed to hold the premises while she continued in possession, in right of her dower, and also the evidence in relation to the death of Jackson, were improperly admitted. The evidence was not objected to upon the trial, and the propriety of its admission cannot now be questioned.

But it is perfectly immaterial whether Jackson, the mortgagor, was dead or alive. The defendant professed to derive all his title from him. He supposed him dead and, therefore, claimed as his heir. But if he was alive, then the defendant was merely his tenant. In neither case could his possession be adverse to that of Jackson, or his mortgagee.

The only question in the case is as to the admissibility of the evidence offered by the defendant.

The case of *Mease* v. *Mease*, Cowp., 47, is conclusive against its admissibility. That was an action of debt upon bond, conditioned for payment at a day certain. The defendant pleaded that it was given as an indemnity to the *plaintiff's testator against another [*175 bond, and that he had not been damnified—to which plea the plaintiff demurred; and the plea was held by Ld. Mansfield to be clearly bad. He held that the agreement stated in the plea, being against the express condition of the bond, it therefore could not be given in evi-

NOTE.—*Parol evidence—When admissible.*

For a full discussion, see Jackson v. Bowen, 1 Cal., 358, *note*. See, also, McKinstry v. Pearsall, 3 Johns., 319, *note*; Sears v. Brink, 3 Johns., 210, *note*; Jackson v. Root, 18 Johns., 60, *note*; and *notes* there cited: Bowen v. Bell, 20 Johns., 338, *note*; Thomas v. M'Daniel, 14 Johns., 185, *note*; Jackson v. Hasbrouck, 12 Johns., 192, *note*; Jackson v. Todd, 3 Johns., 300, *note*.

dence. It is to be remarked that, for aught that appears, the agreement was in writing. The plea merely stated the fact. How it was to be made out was not disclosed.

The case of *Wells* v. *Baldwin*, 18 Johns., 45, is also very analogous to this. That was an action of debt upon a bond conditioned for the payment of money on a fixed day. The defendant pleaded that the bond was given as collateral security for the performance, by the defendant, of a certain contract or agreement between the parties; and stated a satisfactory reason for not performing. The plea was held bad upon demurrer; and *Ch. J.* Spencer, who delivered the opinion of the court, after having considered several of the cases, concludes by saying that it would be against the strong current of authority to admit such a defense. And it is fairly to be inferred that, in his opinion, it was immaterial whether the agreement was in writing or by parol. He says, had the defendant entered into a bond without condition and taken from the plaintiff a defeasance in a separate instrument, referring to the bond, &c., then the defeasance might have been pleaded. But here the bond is with a condition that the defendant shall pay certain sums of money at fixed times; and it would be contradicting and impugning the bond to admit proof that instead of paying the money stipulated in the condition, the plaintiff was not to be paid, unless he cleared certain lands in a particular manner. *Hayford* v. *Andrews*, Cro. Eliz., 697; *Meres* v. *Ansel*, 3 Wils., 275, and *Thompson* v. *Ketchum*, 8 Johns., 189, are also in point against the admissibility of this defense.

Proof of the confessions of Annine, that his mortgage was not a lien on the land, were properly rejected. (6 Johns., 20; Johns. Dig., 213, and the cases there referred to.) As between Annine and the subsequent mortgagee, to whom the declarations are alleged to have
176*] been made, the proof *might have been admissible on the ground of fraud, if shown to have misled or injured him; but not between Annine and third persons.

The motion for a new trial must be denied.

New trial refused.

Cited in—14 Wend., 617; 2 Den., 315; 1 Sandf. Ch., 37; 4 N. Y., 491 (a); 10 Barb., 104; 2 Wood. & M., 148; 31 N. J. E., 551.

WATTLES ET AL.,
v.
MARSH, Sheriff of ONONDAGA.

Writ of Habeas Corpus ad Testificandum *to Bring up a Prisoner in Execution on a* Ca. sa. *—Form of—When and by Whom Allowed—Writ, Valid on its Face, Protects Officer who Executes it.*

The first judge of a county, of the decree of counselor at law in the Supreme Court, may allow a *habeas corpus ad testificandum*, to bring up a prisoner in execution upon a *ca. sa.*

This writ may be allowed to bring up a prisoner under a *ca. sa.*, to testify in relation to his own application to a first judge, for a discharge pursuant to an act of insolvency.

And if valid on its face, though irregularly or erroneously allowed, the sheriff will be protected in his obedience to it.

Form of the writ.

Though it do not say to testify, yet if it have words equivalent, this is sufficient.

So, though it do not specify a place of return within the county, as at the office of the first judge, for this is to be intended.

The alteration of the writ, after it is executed, without the knowledge or privity of the sheriff, will not deprive him of the right to give it in evidence for his justification, though such alteration be made by the deputy who executed it.

If a *habeas corpus ad testificandum* be issued by an officer of competent authority, and be not void on its face, the sheriff is bound to obey it.

Citation—18 Johns., 48; 5 Johns., 357; 3 Esp., 283; 3 Burr., 1340; 4 East, 587; 13 Johns., 444; 19 Johns., 397; 1 Cow., 309.

DEBT against the defendant for the escape of one Frederick Lasher, from the jail limits of Onondaga Co., where he was confined on a *ca. sa.* at the suit of the plaintiffs; tried July 11, 1823, at the Onondaga Circuit, before Rochester, *Circuit Judge.*

The alleged escape was the defendant's deputy, taking Lasher from the limits, and having him before the first judge of Onondaga, Dec. 17, 1822, to testify concerning his own application for a discharge under the Act to Abolish Imprisonment for Debt in Certain Cases.

To justify this, the defendant's counsel offered in evidence a writ of *habeas corpus ad testificandum*, in these words:

"The People of the State of New York, by the Grace of God free and independent, to the Sheriff of the County of Onondaga, greeting: We command you that you have the body of Frederick Lasher, detained in our prison, in your custody, as it is said, under safe and secure conduct, before Joshua Forman, Esquire, first judge of the Court of Common Pleas in and for the County of Onondaga, on the seventeenth day of December next, at ten o'clock in the forenoon, there to testify and answer unto those things that may be there required of him, pursuant to the Act, entitled 'An Act to Abolish *Imprisonment for Debt in Certain [***177** Cases;' and immediately after the said Frederick Lasher shall have answered what may be inquired touching his application for the benefit of the said Act, that then you return him to our said prison, under safe and secure conduct, and have then there this writ. Witness Ambrose Spencer, Esquire, *Chief Justice* of the Supreme Court, at the Academy, in the Town of Utica, the third Monday of October, in the year eighteen hundred and twenty-two.

AR. BREESE, Cl'k.

JOHN WILKINSON, Atty."

It was indorsed thus:

"Allowed December 16th, 1822.

J. FORMAN, first judge of Onon. Com. Pleas, a counselor, &c."

The plaintiff's counsel objected to reading the *habeas corpus* in evidence, unless the defendant showed some proceedings had been pending before *Judge* Forman in some lawsuit or otherwise, wherein Lasher might have been improved as a witness. The judge overruled the objection, and permitted the writ to be read in evidence; after the defendant had proved by *Judge* Forman, that he allowed it, and that he was first judge of the Court of C. P. of the County of Onondaga, and of the

NOTE.—*Ministerial officers—How far protected by process.* See Warner v. Shed, 10 Johns., 138, *note.*

On the general subject, see Henderson v. Brown, 1 Cai., 92, *note*; Seaman v. Patten, 2 Cai., 312, *note*; Wallsworth v. M'Cullough, 10 Johns., 93, *note.*

degree of counselor at law of the Supreme Court, at the time of allowing it; and also had proved by Nicholas P. Randall, that the writ was in the hands of Elisha Marsh, a deputy of the Sheriff of the County of Onondaga, on the morning of Dec. 17, 1822, and before Lasher left the jail liberties to go to Syracuse. Randall also swore that he went to Syracuse, and that after he had been there a short time, Lasher and the deputy-sheriff came to Syracuse together, and remained together during the time they were at Syracuse; and that after the hearing of the insolvent application of Lasher, the witness and they returned by the nearest and most direct route to the jail liberties, and arrived there about 4 o'clock in the afternoon of the 17th.

The plaintiff's counsel further proved by *Judge* Forman, that the writ was allowed by him on the application of John Wilkinson, Esq., who, at the time, acted as counsel for **178***] Lasher; *and *Judge* Forman did not recollect whether there was any affidavit or not, but rather thought there was not. John Wilkinson, a witness for the plaintiffs, testified that he got the writ allowed by *Judge* Forman, without any affidavit, and sent it to Lasher, or to Marsh, the deputy-sheriff, and he did not recollect which; and that he did not know that the deputy-sheriff had any knowledge that he acted as counsel for Lasher. Elisha Marsh, the deputy-sheriff, a witness for the plaintiffs, testified that he received the writ of Lasher, on the morning of Dec. 17, 1822, inclosed in a letter; that Lasher at the time of delivering the letter to him, in which the writ was inclosed, told him he had a letter for him, from Mr. Randall. The witness, at that time, knew that Randall was the attorney who had made the application of insolvency; that, on opening the letter, he found, instead of a letter from Randall, that the writ of *habeas corpus*, in Wilkinson's handwriting, was inclosed. He further testified that he did not know upon whose application the writ issued; that he knew that the writ was in the handwriting of Wilkinson, but did not know that he was attorney or counsel for Lasher on the application.

John Wilkinson further testified that the words "testify and" were not in the writ at the time it was allowed; but that some time after Dec. 17, 1822, Marsh the deputy-sheriff, called upon him, the witness, and told him that the sheriff was sued for the escape of Lasher, and that *Judge* Earll said he thought the writ, as it was, would be a good justification for the sheriff, but that the words "testify and" ought to have been in the writ; that thereupon the witness, at the request of the deputy-sheriff, made the alteration by interlining the words "testify and."

The counsel for the plaintiffs then contended that the writ ought not to be received as evidence, on the ground of the alteration, and that it was no justification for the sheriff; which objection was overruled by the judge.

The judge charged the jury, that if they believed that the defendant, or the deputy, knew the writ had been obtained on the application of Lasher or his counsel, they should find for **179***] *the plaintiffs; otherwise, for the defendant; and they found for the defendant.

A motion was now made for a new trial, on the grounds:

1. That the application being made for the writ, by the insolvent himself, without affidavit, it was irregular; and afforded no justification to the sheriff.

2. In the form in which it was allowed, it was not an *hab. corp. ad testificandum;* nor was any place mentioned where the sheriff was to have the body.

3. The alteration of the writ by the deputy, after it was allowed, rendered it absolutely void, and inadmissible in evidence.

4. A judge, at his chambers, has no authority to allow an *hab. corp. ad testificandum.* It can be allowed only on motion in open court. *Judge* Forman, therefore, having no jurisdiction, the sheriff was not protected.

Mr. B. D. Noxon, for the plaintiffs, cited to the first point, *Thelluson* v. *Coppinger*, 3 Esp., 283; *Suydam* v. *Keys*, 13 Johns., 444; *Rex* v. *Roddam*, Cowp., 672, and Tidd Pr., 739; also 1 R. L., 463, sec. 7, and sess. 42, ch. 101, secs. 4, 7, p. 117.

To the third point, Cruise, Dig., Deed, ch. 22, secs. 3, 4; Bac. Abr., Forgery, A; 3 Chit. Cr. L., 1023; *Jackson* v. *Malin*, 15 Johns., 293; *Masters* v. *Miller*, 4 T. R., 320; S. C., 2 H. Bl., 141; *Woolley* v. *Constant*, 4 Johns., 54.

To the fourth point, *Ex parte Wilson*, 6 Cr., 52; *Ex parte Bolman*, 4 *Id.*, 75, 93; *Ex parte Burford*, 3 Cr., 448; *Chapman* v. *Welles*, Kirby Conn., 137; *Matter of Edward Price*, 4 East, 587; *Rex* v. *Burbage*, 3 Burr., 1440; *People* v. *Goodhue*, 2 Johns. Ch., 198; Comb., 17, per *Ch. J.*, in *Palmer* v. *Allicott; Rex* v. *Levir*, Comb., 47, per *Cur.*, and *Adams* v. ———, 3 Keb., 51.

Mr. S. Beardsley, contra, as to the first point, cited *Jones* v. *Cook*, 1 Cow., 309; Laws, sess. 41, ch. 195, p. 173, in connection with 1 R. L., 322; 1 Dunl. Pr., 477; *Hassam* v. *Griffin*, 18 Johns., 48; *Currie* v. *Henry*, 2 Johns., 433; *Hines* v. *Ballard*, 11 *Id.*, 491.

*As to the second point, Bac. Abr., [***180** Sheriff, M, pl. 2; *Noble* v. *Smith*, 5 Johns., 357; *Hassam* v. *Griffin*, 18 *Id.*, 48; 1 R. L., 354; *Perkin* v. *Proctor*, 2 Wils., 382; *Parsons* v. *Lloyd*, 3 *Id.*, 341; *Jones* v. *Cook*, 1 Cow., 309; *Bissell* v. *Kip*, 5 Johns., 89, 100; Laws, sess. 42, p. 116.

As to the third point, 1 R. L., 463, sec. 7.

Curia, per SUTHERLAND, *J.* There was nothing upon the face of the writ showing it to be void, or to have been issued without competent authority. The omission in the writ, of the words "to testify," was not material. It still appeared to be a *habeas corpus ad testificandum.* It directed the sheriff to bring the prisoner before the officer, to answer unto those things that might be there required of him, pursuant to the Act, entitled An Act to Abolish Imprisonment for Debt in Certain Cases. Under that Act he would be required to answer only as a witness. It was substantially good, and was in the words of the statute. The omission of a place in the writ where the prisoner was to be brought, did not render it void. He was directed to be brought, before Joshua Forman, Esq., first judge of the Court of C. P., in and for the County of Onondaga. If the words, at his office, in said county, had been added, it would have been, in terms, sufficiently explicit; and I think they are fairly to be understood.

The writ was allowed by an officer of competent authority to allow writs of *habeas corpus*. He had the same powers as a judge of the Supreme Court at chambers; and the case of *Hassam* v. *Griffin*, 18 Johns., 48, shows that a *habeas corpus ad testificandum* may be allowed by a judge at chambers, to bring up a prisoner charged in execution. (And *vide* 5 *Id.*, 357.)

If a writ was issued by an officer of competent authority, and was not void on its face, the defendant was bound to obey it. (5 Johns., 357; 3 Esp., 283; 3 Burr., 1340; 4 East, 587.) Whether the writ was regularly issued or not; whether upon the application of the creditor, or the insolvent, the sheriff had no means of **181***] knowing, and was not *bound to inquire. Admitting it to have issued erroneously, there being no defect of jurisdiction in the officer, it is a justification to the sheriff. (13 Johns., 444; 19 Johns., 39; *Id.*, 7; 1 Cow., 309.)

The alteration of the writ, subsequent to its execution, could not deprive the sheriff of his justification under it, if it was originally sufficient to justify him. The alteration was made without his authority; and he was not responsible for the act of his deputy in that respect. But the principle relied on by the defendant's counsel, does not apply to a case like this.

The motion for a new trial must be denied.

New trial refused.

Cited in—1 Keyes, 524; 4 Abb. App. Dec., 599.

BROWN *v.* BENNETT.

Pleading—Assault and Battery—Various Pleas —Effects of—Evidence Under.

Where the plaintiff declared in assault and battery; and the defendant, after pleading not guilty, pleaded, *son assault demesne*, to which the plaintiff replied *de injuria*, &c., and the defendant also pleaded that the plaintiff was beating one C, and that the defendant, *moliter manus*, &c., to prevent injury to C, to which the plaintiff replied that he was constable, and had a warrant against C., and had arrested him; and that the defendant was aiding him to escape; that C. got into the defendant's carriage, who was driving him off, and therefore the plaintiff seized C. and drew him out of the carriage, which was the same assault upon C. mentioned in the defendant's plea; upon the trial, the defendant abandoned this last plea, and relied upon *son assault demesne* and the plaintiff would have shown the facts stated in his replication to the last plea, under the general replication *de injuria*, &c., to the first plea, and that when the defendant was about driving C. off in his carriage, the plaintiff seized the lines of the horses, and prevented him, and seized C., &c. But,

Held, that these facts were inadmissible in evidence, upon *de injuria*, &c.; and that they should have been specially replied.

De injuria, &c., takes issue merely upon the excuse (in this instance, *son assault*, &c.) set up by the defendant's plea.

If the plaintiff have new facts, or circumstances justifying his own assault, in answer to the plea of *son assault*, &c., he should reply, setting them out specially; and cannot give them in evidence under the general replication, *de injuria*, &c.

Citations—1 Chit. pl., 563-4; 2 W. Bl., 1165; Carth., 280; 2 Chit. pl., 643, *n.* (*t*), (*u*); 5 Com. Dig. Pl., F, 18; 7 Johns., 111; 20 Vin., 440; Comb., 227.

TRESPASS, assault and battery, tried before Williams, *Circuit Judge*, at the Oneida Circuit, July 24, 1823.

The declaration contained two counts. The first charged that the defendant May 24, 1822, with force and arms, &c., made an assault upon the plaintiff to wit: at Vernon, &c., and then and there with his hands, fists and feet, *and with clubs, stones, whips and [***182** sticks, and with the wheels of carriages, gave and struck the plaintiff a great many violent blows and strokes, on and about his head, face, breast, back, shoulders, arms, legs and divers other parts of his body; and also, then and there, with great force and violence, shook, pulled and dragged about the plaintiff. By means, &c., the plaintiff was, &c., and became, &c., and was hindered, &c., and was forced to pay, &c.

The second count was in the usual form, for a common assault and battery.

The defendant pleaded, 1st, not guilty to the whole declaration; 2d, *son assault demesne* in the common form, to the first count in the declaration. The 3d plea was to the first count in the declaration, and stated, in substance, that the plaintiff made an assault upon one Ambrose Cadwell, and was beating him, &c.; and the defendant, to preserve the peace, and to part the plaintiff from Cadwell, and prevent him from further beating him, gently laid his hands upon the plaintiff, as he lawfully might do, &c. And because the plaintiff continued to beat Cadwell, and attempted with great force, &c., to throw him out of a carriage in which he was riding, to and upon the ground, to the great and immediate danger of the life and limbs of Cadwell; the defendant thereupon, to preserve the peace and to save and deliver Cadwell, &c., did, necessarily and unavoidably, beat the plaintiff, as mentioned in the first count, which are the same trespasses, &c. 4th. *Son assault demesne*, in the common form, to the 2d count in the declaration. 5th. The same plea to the 2d count as the third plea was to the first count.

To the 2d plea (*son assault demesne*) the plaintiff replied *de injuria*, &c., generally, and in the common form.

To the 3d plea he replied, in substance, the due issuing of a warrant by Simeon Bingham, Esq., a justice of Oneida Co., in favor of one Rowland Wilson against Cadwell, under, and in pursuance of the Act for the Recovery of Debts to the Value of Twenty-five Dollars, which warrant was delivered to the plaintiff, who was a constable of Vernon, in Oneida Co., to be executed, &c.; that he took Cadwell on *the warrant, and carried him be- [***183** fore the justice, and that before he was duly discharged, he attempted to escape from the plaintiff's custody, against his will and consent, and that the defendant aided and abetted Cadwell in such attempt to escape. That Cadwell got into the defendant's carriage, who was furiously driving him off, &c., wherefore the plaintiff gently laid his hands upon Cadwell, to prevent his escaping; and because Cadwell resisted with strong hand, &c., the plaintiff, as such constable, &c., pulled Cadwell out of the carriage, as he lawfully might, &c., doing no unnecessary damage, and exerting no unnecessay force, &c., which is the same, &c., mentioned in the third plea.

To the 4th plea (*son assault demesne*,) the plaintiff replied *de injuria*, in the common form.

To the 5th plea, the plaintiff replied in the same manner as to the third plea.

Upon the trial of the cause, the counsel for the plaintiff offered to prove that the plaintiff, May 23, 1822, was constable of the town of Vernon, and, as such officer, had a warrant, which had been duly issued by Simeon Bingham, Esq., a justice of the peace of that town, at the suit of Rowland Wilson, against Ambrose Cadwell, by virtue of which warrant, he had arrested Cadwell, and had him in custody; and that while the plaintiff so had Cadwell in his custody, the defendant attempted to rescue Cadwell from such custody, and for that purpose persuaded Cadwell to get into the carriage of the defendant, for the purpose of driving him off, out of the custody of the plaintiff; that the plaintiff remonstrated against such conduct, and endeavored to dissuade Cadwell and the defendant from pursuing their intention. That the defendant well knew that Cadwell was in the plaintiff's custody, and that he told Cadwell to get in his carriage, and that he would bear Cadwell out in it, and would stand between him and all harm. That Cadwell accordingly did get into the defendant's carriage, and that the plaintiff, for the purpose of preventing the escape of Cadwell, stepped his foot upon the nave of the defendant's carriage wheel, and took hold of the lines of the defendant, and also took hold of Cadwell to take him from the carriage. That the defend-
184*] ant *then immediately placed himself between the plaintiff and Cadwell, for the purposed of preventing the plaintiff from taking Cadwell out of the carriage, and started his horse, and threw the breast of the plaintiff with great violence across the wheel of the carriage, and dragged him along the highway between the wheel and the body of the carriage; that the plaintiff, for the purpose of stopping the movement of the carriage, took hold of the defendant's rains; and that the defendant struck the plaintiff across his face with the butt of his whip.

To this evidence of the warrant and arrest, the counsel for the defendant objected, and said that he relied upon his plea of not guilty, and his 2d and 4th pleas of *son assault demesne;* that the offer of the plaintiff showed that he made the first assault upon the defendant, in wrongfully seizing his lines; and that the plaintiff could not, under his replication of *de injuria*, &c., justify the assault upon the defendant, by proving the warrant and arrest; but that the plaintiff, if he wished to give such evidence, should have replied specially, and stated it in his replications.

The defendant offered no evidence, and did not claim or pretend to justify under his 3d or 5th pleas.

The judge overruled the evidence offered by the plaintiff of the warrant and arrest, upon the ground that the plaintiff could not give this evidence under the general replications of *de injuria*, &c., but should have replied? them specially. The plaintiff then offered to give the same evidence under his replications to the 3d and 5th pleas of the defendant. To this the defendant objected, and it was overruled, upon the ground that he had not claimed or attempted to justify under the 3d and 5th pleas, and the plaintiff thereupon submitted to a nonsuit.

Mr. J. C. Spencer, for the plaintiff, now moved to set aside the nonsuit, and for a new trial. He said that *son assault demesne* was mere matter of excuse, to which *de injuria sua*, &c., might always be replied. (8 Co. Rep., 67 *a;* Yelv., 157; Cro. Jac., 224; Salk., 637, 638; Willes, 54, 99, 204; 1 Chit. Pl., 563, 579, 584; 2 Saund., 294, *note* 1; 6 Bac. *Abr., [***185** Trespass, 1, pl. 4, Replication; 4 Johns., 159; 5 *Id.*, 112; T. Raym., 50; 12 Johns., 291.) If the general replication was all that the plea called for, it followed that the evidence offered was proper.

Mr. G. C. Bronson, contra, admitted the legal position taken, that *de injuria* was a proper replication; but said it is quite another question, as to what might be evidence under it. The plaintiff's counsel has argued the question as if we had demurred to the replication. Evidence of a right to make the assault varies from the replication, which is merely a traverse that the plaintiff made the first assault. It is but an issue upon that fact. We say he should have replied the warrant with the arrest, and carried us to an issue upon that. The other pleas did not help him. We had a right to consider them mere form, and not rely upon them at all, and we did so. He cited, 7 Johns., 111; Carth., 280; 1 Chit. Pl., 582, 584; 2 *Id.*, 642, *note, t, u;* 2 Bl., 1165.

Mr. Spencer, in reply, admitted that, had the action been against Cadwell, it might have been necessary to reply specially. Not so as to the third person. The warrant and arrest, as to them, were mere matter of excuse; not of right. There is not a case at war with this distinction.

Curia, per SUTHERLAND, *J.* The evidence was properly rejected. The general replication, *de injuria*, &c., denies that the plaintiff made the first assault, &c., as alleged in the plea of *son assault*. Where the plea, therefore, is true in fact, and the plaintiff relies upon special circumstances or facts to justify the assault, which he admits he first made, he must set them out specially in his replication, and not reply generally *de injuria*. (1 Chit. Pl., 563, 564.) When in fact, therefore, the plaintiff made the first assault or whenever, in answer to the defendant's plea of *son assault*, he relies upon new matter, he should not reply generally *de injuria*, but should state such new matter specially. *Sayre* v. *Earl of Rochford*, 2 W. Bl., 1165; Carth., 280; 2 Chit. Pl., 643, *note, t, u;* 5 Com. Dig., Pl., F, 18. He cannot give it in evidence under the general replication of *de injuria*. In *Collier* v. *Moulton*, 7 Johns., 111, *Ch.* **J.* Thompson says, if the defend- [***186** ant had pleaded *son assault* instead of giving notice of it under the general issue, and the plaintiff intended to avail himself of the *moliter manus*, &c., he must have replied specially; for he could not give it in evidence under the general replication, *de injuria sua propria*. 20 Vin., 440; *King* v. *Peppard*, Comb., 227.

The evidence being properly rejected under the general replication, and the defendant having given no evidence under his third plea, to which the special matter offered in evidence was replied specially, it could not be admitted under that replication. The nonsuit, therefore, was properly ordered; and the motion to set it aside, and for a new trial must be denied.

Motion denied.

Cited in—38 N. J. L., 100.

LEIBER AND COLVIN v. GOODRICH.

Promise to Pay in Paper Currency, not a Promissory Note—Statute.

A note payable in Pa. or N. Y. paper currency to be current in the State of Pa., or the State of N. Y., is not a promissory note for the payment of money within the Statute, 1 R. L., 151.

Citations—Chit. Bills, 58; 4 Mass., 245; 19 Johns. 120; 19 Johns., 144.

ON demurrer to the declaration. The plaintiff declared, for that the defendant, June 1, A. D. 1817, at Painted Post, to wit: at Utica, in the County of Oneida, made his certain promissory note in writing, &c., dated the day and year, aforesaid, &c., by which he promised to pay one Samuel Lamphear, or bearer, the sum of $200, in Pa. paper currency, or N. Y., to be current in the State of Pa. or the State of N. Y. (meaning thereby, current money of the State of N. Y. or Pa.), with interest in two years from the date, to be paid at the maker's dwelling house in Painted Post; that Lamphear, after &c., assigned and delivered this note to the plaintiffs &c.

General demurrer and joinder.

And the question was, whether this was a promissory negotiable note, for the payment of money, within the Statute, 1 R. L., 151.

Mr. C. P. Kirkland, in support of the demurrer, cited Chit. Bills, 58; 9 Johns., 120; 19 *Id.*, 144; 4 Mass., 245.

187*] **Mr. J. Platt*, contra, cited 9 Johns. 120; 1 Johns. Ch., 231; 12 Johns., 395, 220; 1 Cr., 133.

Curia, per SUTHERLAND, *J.* Payment in any bank bills generally current in the State of Pennsylvania, although not current in this State, would satisfy the terms of the note. Its legal effect, therefore, is the same as though it had been payable merely in bank bills, current in the State of Pa. Are such bills known, approved of and used in this State as cash? I believe that, in truth, most of the Pa. bills pass only at a discount in this State. But if the fact be otherwise, it certainly is not so notorious that we can officially take notice of it. The note, therefore, is not payable in cash, but in something differing in value from cash. Of course it is not negotiable under the Statute. (Chit. Bills, 58.) In *Jones* v. *Fales*, 4 Mass., 245, the note was payable in foreign bills, and the court held that they would officially understand those terms to mean the paper of country banks, and that they would judicially take notice that such paper, from various causes, might differ in value from cash. York State bills, and bank notes current in the City of N. Y., have been held to be equivalent to lawful current money of the State. *Keith* v. *Jones*, 9 Johns., 120; *Judah* v. *Harris*, 19 Johns., 144, and the cases there cited. We may officially take notice that our own bank paper is, in conformity with common usage and common understanding, regarded as cash. But we cannot be supposed judicially to know the value of the paper currency of other States.

Nor can we intend, from the geographical situation of Painted Post, where the note was payable, that bank bills current in Pa. were of as much value there as the bills of our own State. And if such were admitted to be the fact, I am not prepared to say that it would alter the case, unless, from the fact of their being current in that place, their general currency is necessarily to be inferred; which cannot be pretended.

*I am, therefore, of opinion that the [***188** note was not negotiable, and the defendant is entitled to judgment on the demurrer.

Judgment for the defendant.

Cited in—23 Wend., 74; 2 Hill, 427; 2 N. Y., 543; 39 N. Y., 101; 43 N. Y., 212; 60 N. Y., 270; 2 McLean, 12; 1 Kan., 36; 47 Wis., 560; 35 Am. Dec., 547; 4 Am. Rep., 245 (29 Iowa, 501); 19 Am. Rep. 179 (60 N. Y., 265; 15 Am. Rep., 164 (27 Mich., 191); 32 Am. Rep., 779 (47 Wis., 551).

MALCOM, *Demandant*, v. ROGERS, *Tenant.*

1. Co-heirs Tenants in Common Under Statute —May join or Bring Separate Actions for Shares. 2. Construction of Statute—"Shall or May"—When Imperative and when Permissive.

Co-heirs under the Statute of Descents, 1 R. L., 52, sec. 3, are tenants in common; and though they may join in a real action, pursuant to the Statute, 1 R. L., 80 sec. 2, they are not compellable to join; but may bring several actions for their respective shares or interests.

The words "shall or may," when used in a statute, are imperative, only when the public interest and rights are concerned; but when a statute declares that an individual or individuals 'shall or may" do certain acts, or have a certain remedy, which is intended for his or their own benefit, he or they have a discretion to do the act, or pursue the remedy or not.

Record in a writ of right, from the end of the count, to demurrer and joinder inclusive, upon a plea in abatement of nonjoinder of demandants.

Citations—Co. Litt., 197 *b*; Litt., sec. 311; 2 Bl. Com., 187, 194; Com. Dig. tit. Abatement, E, 10 F, 6; Adams on Ej., 186; Runn. on Ej., 222; 2 Cal. 169; Stat. 52 Hen. III., ch., 29; 1 R. L., 79, sec. 2; 5 Johns. Ch., 112; 2 Salk., 609; 14 Car., 2 Ch., 12; Stat. 23 Hen. VI.; 3 Atk., 211; 1 Vern., 152.

IN a writ of right; the count began thus: "Richard M. Malcom, &c., demands against George P. Rogers, the one equal undivided tenth part; and also the one equal undivided ninth part, of another equal undivided tenth part, or two messuages, &c., and set forth that the demandant's father, William Malcom, was seised of the whole of these messuages, &c., in his *demesne* as of fee; and died, leaving three sons and seven daughters (naming them), among whom were the demandant, and William A. and Abigail; that William A. died without issue, whereby his share descended to the demandent and his surviving brothers and sisters, and to William M., the sole son and heir of Abigail, who died before William A. The demandant, therefore, claimed the one undivided tenth, as the heir of his father; and the one undivided ninth of the other undivided tenth, as the heir of his brother, William A., deceased, who was the heir of William Malcom. (See this count, at length, in 1 Cow., 11, *note*, *m.*)

After a special imparlance(*a*) the defendant pleaded in abatement to the writ, that neither

---

NOTE.—*Negotiable paper—Medium of payment of. An instrument payable in specific articles not negotiable—Negotiable paper must be payable in money only—"Bank bills"—"Currency," &c.* See Saxton v. Johnson, 10 Johns., 418, *note.*

(*a*) *Vide* 1 Cow., 12, *note n.*

the brothers and sisters surviving, nor William M., were named in the writ, nor sued together with the demandant.

General demurrer and joinder.(b)

189*] *Mr. S. M. Hopkins, in support of the demurrer. By the express provision of the Statute of Descents, the demandant, his brothers, sisters and nephew, are tenants in common; 1 R. L., 52, sec. 3; and it is against the policy of the common law that they should join. The court might otherwise have ten different titles to try in one action. This was 190*] the clear, *well settled and universal rule of the common law, as to real actions, for land. Litt., sec. 311.; 1 Inst., 197 b; 2 Bl. Com., 194; Com. Dig., Abatement, E, 10; *Jackson* v. *Bradt*, 2 Cai., 169.

But the Statute concerning the process and proceedings in Assizes, and other actions, 1 R. L., 79, 80, sec. 2, does provide, that if a person die leaving several heirs, either in the same or different degrees, they shall or may recover in one writ or action. The plea must stand or fall by these words, "shall or may," which, it will be said, mean "must." We deny that, in good English, shall or may mean must, and we deny that they mean so here, in good law, or common sense. Here are ten heirs. One may be himself a deforciant; one may have released, and one will not join; and the cotenant is thus deprived of his remedy. The distinction between the cases in which "shall" and "may" are to be deemed imperative, or potential, in law, is so fully considered, with the authorities, by the late *Chancellor*, in *Pres-*
191*] *ident &c.* *v. *Miller*, 5 Johns. Ch., 101–113, that we shall do no more upon this branch of the subject, that refer to that case.

Mr. J. Platt, contra. This is a mere question of practice, and both convenience and policy would seem to require that the plea should be sustained. The right of all these heirs may as well be tried in one, as in ten actions; and the court will, if they do not feel themselves bound by law to do otherwise, establish such a rule as shall prevent, not promote, a multiplicity of suits.

These heirs are not tenants in common, within the sense of the rule contended for. The reason of that rule is founded on the idea that tenants in common may claim by distinct titles. In England they never acquire by descent. Those who did acquire in this manner, parceners for instance, generally stood in no need of severance, and were required to join. (Com. Dig., Abatement, E, 8, and the authorities there cited); or proceed by summons and severance. (Booth on R. A., 26.) Tenants in gavelkind were compellable to join. (Com. Dig., Abatement, E, 8, and the authorities there cited.) Our statute is, that the land shall descend to sons as tenants in common, in the same manner as if they were all daughters. These words are significant, and place them on the same ground as parceners.

Our Statute, 1 R. L., 80, sec. 2, is a transcript of the Statute 52 Hen. III., ch. 29, which has never been considered as authorizing English heirs to sever. The rule, notwithstanding the Act, has continued uniform there. I do not so much mean to insist that "shall or may" mean "must," as that our Statute of De-

(b) The record, after the close of the count, as in 1 Cow., 11, 12, is thus: "And now at this day, that is to say, on the first Monday of Aug., &c. (1823), until which day, the said George P. Rogers saving to himself all advantages and exceptions, as well as to the jurisdiction of the court, as to the writ and count, aforesaid, had leave to imparle thereto, before the justices of the people of the State of N. Y., of the Supreme Court of Judicature of the same people, at the Academy, in the Town of Utica, in the County of Oneida, comes the said George P. Rogers, by Gabriel Winter and and Thomas Bolton, his attorneys, and defends the right, &c., and prays judgment of the writ aforesaid; because he says, that it appears by the count aforesaid of the said Richard M. Malcom, that the said William Malcom, deceased, the late father of the said Richard M. Malcom, died seised of the whole of the messuages and land aforesaid, with the appurtenances in his *demesne* as of fee and right, without devising the same, leaving lawful issue three sons and seven daughters, to wit: Samuel B., Frances Elizabeth C., Ann S., Catharine B., Margaret B., Agnes, Abigail and the said Richard M. and William A., and no other lawful issue, and that thereupon, the right to the said one equal undivided tenth part, above demanded, of the said messuages and land, with the appurtenances, descended and came from the said William Malcom, to the said Richard M. Malcom, who now demands the same as son and heir, in respect to the said one equal undivided tenth part, of the said William Malcom, deceased; and that, thereupon, also one other equal undivided tenth part of the said messuages and land, with the appurtenances, descended and came from the said William Malcom, to the said William A., also as son and heir in respect to the same of the said William Malcom, deceased; and that because the said William A. died without issue, after the death of his said father, leaving the said Richard M., Samuel B., Frances, Elizabeth C., Ann S., Catharine B., Margaret B. and Agnes, his said brothers and sisters and William M., the only lawful child and heir of his said sister Abigail, who was then deceased, the right to the one equal undivided ninth part of the said last mentioned one equal undivided tenth part, which, so as aforesaid, descended and came to the said William A., descended and came to the said Richard M. Malcom, as brother and heir, in respect to the same, of the said William A., deceased, and that the said Richard M. also demands the same, as brother and heir, in respect to the same, of the said William A. deceased; and because the said Samuel B., Frances, Elizabeth C., Ann S., Catharine B., Maragaret B., Agnes, and William M. are not named in the said writ, nor do prosecute together with the said Richard M. Malcom, in this behalf, the said George P. Rogers prays judgment of the said writ, and that the said writ may be quashed, &c.

And the said Richard M. Malcom saith, that the said plea of the said George P. Rogers, and the matters therein contained, in manner and form as the same are above pleaded and set forth, are not sufficient in law to quash the said writ, and that he, the said Richard M. Malcom, is not bound by the law of the land to answer the same: and this he is ready to verify. Wherefore, for want of a sufficient plea in this behalf, the said Richard M. Malcom prays judgment that the said writ may be adjuded good, and that the said George P. Rogers may answer further, &c.

On or about this day, to wit: on the third Monday of October (1823), until which day the said George P. Rogers, saving to himself all advantage and exception to the writ and count aforesaid, had leave to rejoin to the plea, by the said Richard M. Malcom, above pleaded, by way of reply to the said plea, by the said George P. Rogers, above pleaded, before the justices of the people of the State of N. Y., of the Supreme Court of Judicature of the same people, at the Capital in the City of Albany, come, as well the said Richard M. Malcom, as the said George P. Rogers, by their respective attorneys aforesaid; and the said George P. Rogers says, that his said plea, by him above pleaded, and the matters therein contained, in manner and form as the same are above pleaded and set forth, are sufficient in law to quash the aforesaid writ of the said Richard M. Malcom; which said plea, and the matters therein contained, he, the said George P. Rogers, is ready to verify and prove, as the said court here shall direct and award; wherefore, inasmuch as the said Richard M. Malcom hath not answered the said plea, nor hitherto in any manner denied the same, the said George P. Rogers, as before, prays judgment of the said writ, and that the same may be quashed, &c.

But because, &c. (*curia advisare vult*, &c.).

scents does not vary the remedy of heirs here, either from that of English parceners, or heirs in gavelkind. *Stedman* v. *Bates*, 1 Ld. Raym., 64, holds that parceners must join in avowry, thus contradicting *Osmer* v. *Sheafe*, 2 Lutw., 1210. They are, though several persons, all one heir. (Co. Litt., 164 *a;* 2 Bl. Com., 187, 188.) The statute intending to create a kind of descent like that which prevailed in gavelkind and coparcenary, it makes no difference that the heirs are in different degrees. (Litt., **192***] sec. 241 ; Co. *Litt., 163 *a*, 164 *a;* Com. Dig., Parceners, B.) Runn. on Eject., 223, gives the reason why parceners cannot sever. It is because they come in as one heir, and the possession must be joint. And the same doctrine is found in *Jackson* v. *Sample*, 3 Johns. Cas., 235, and in Adams on Eject., 186, 187; though there is a distinction between pos sessory and droitural actions. (3 Johns. Cas., 235 ; 12 East, 39.)

Mr. Hopkins, in reply, said the remedy could not depend upon the question, whether all the tenants in common came to their right or possession by the same act or means. All may claim by one conveyance ; yet it never was disputed that such may, nay must, sever in a real action. This alone destroys the doctrine set up on the other side. When our Statute of Descents says that lands shall descend in the same manner as if the heirs were all daughters, it merely means in such shares as daughters would take. It goes to the quantity, not the nature of the estate.

Curia, per SUTHERLAND, *J*. The general rule is, that tenants in common cannot join, or be joined, in real or mixed actions, unless in the case where some entire or indivisible thing is to be recovered. (Co. Litt., 197 *b*.) Their freeholds are several, and they claim by several and distinct titles. (Litt., sec. 311 ; 2 Bl. Com., 194 ; Com. Dig., tit. Abatement, E, 10, F, 6.) Their is neither a privity of title, nor an union and entirety of interest, as between joint tenants, which render it necessary for the latter to unite, generally, in all real and mixed actions. It was formerly held that tenants in common could not join in making a lease; and that a recovery in ejectment could not be had upon their joint demise ; but that a separate demise by each must be laid ; else, as their estates and titles are different and independent of each other, it would be permitting the plaintiff to try several and distinct titles in one issue, at the same time. (Adams on Eject., 186; Runn. on Eject., 222.) This rule was relaxed as to ejectment in *Jackson* v. *Bradt*, 2 Cai., 169.
193*] *By the 52 Hen. III., ch. 29, and the Statute of this State for giving Further Remedy and Regulating the Process and Proceedings in Assizes and other actions, 1 R. L., 79, sec. 2, it is provided, "that if any person hath died, or shall die, leaving several persons, his or her heirs, either in the same degree, or in different degrees, all such heirs shall or may recover in one writ or action, as heirs of the deceased person." This Statute undoubtedly authorizes the bringing of a joint action by heirs, who are tenants in common. But the question here is, whether it is imperative upon them to unite, and takes away all discretion upon the subject.

The Statute was intended for the benefit and relief of heirs. Such is the scope and general character of its provisions ; and the language used in this particular section, I am inclined to think, according to established principles of construction, leaves it discretionary with heirs to bring joint or several actions, according to their own views of their own interests.

In *N. T. Co.* v. *Miller*, 5 Johns. Ch., 112, one point presented was, whether the plaintiffs were bound by an Act of the Legislature, passed in 1815, to remove their gate from the Walkill Bridge. The words of the Act were, "that it shall and may be lawful for the president, directors and company, to remove the toll-gate, &c." The *Chancellor* held that the statute was not imperative ; but that it left it to the discretion of the company to remove their gate or not ; and he considered the true rule of construction applicable to statutes in such cases to be, that the word "may" means "must or shall," only in cases where the public interest and rights are concerned, and where the public or third persons have a claim *de jure* that the power should be exercised.

So in *Rex* v. *Barlow*, 2 Salk., 609, it was said that where a statute directs the doing of a thing for the sake of justice or the public good, the word "may" is the same as the word "shall." That was a case under the 14 Car. II., ch. 12, which gave power and authority to the churchwardens, &c., to make an assessment to reimburse the constables. The statute was held to be imperative. Both the public and the constables *had an interest in having the [***194** authority exercised. The Statute of 23 Hen. VI., which says the sheriff may take bail, is construed the same as though it had said he shall, upon the principle already stated. The case of *Stamper* v. *Millar*, 3 Atk., 211, and *Backwell's* case, 1 Vern., 152, illustrate the same principle. In the latter case, the Lord Keeper declared that though the words in the Act of Parliament, under which the application for a commission of bankruptcy was made, were, that the *Chancellor* may grant it, yet that "may" was in effect "must," and it had been so resolved by all the judges.

In the case now under consideration, the public has no direct or immediate interest in the question ; nor have third persons a vested right. or, as *Chancellor* Kent expresses it, a claim *de jure* to call upon the plaintiff to exercise the authority given by the statute to sue jointly with his co-tenants. It is a power given for the benefit of the heirs, which they may exercise, or not, at their discretion. It is permissive merely, and not compulsory.

It was said upon the argument that the English Statute was the same as ours, and that under their statute, co-parceners and tenants in gavelkind (who are co-parceners by particular custom, instead of common law), may be compelled to join. Co-parceners and tenants in gavelkind might sue and be sued jointly at common law ; and they are not at all affected by the statute. The properties of their estates are like those of joint tenants, not of tenants in common. They have an unity of interest, title and possession. All the parceners make but one heir ; and have but one estate among them. (2 Bl. Com., 187.) And although their estate is created in England in the same manner as a tenancy in common may be created under our laws, the properties, qualities and incidents of the two estates are in no respect similar.

I am, therefore, of opinion that the demandant is entitled to judgment.

Judgment of respondeas ouster.

Cited in—1 Hill, 547; 3 Hill, 615; 6 Hill, 638; 41 N. Y., 424; 46 N. Y., 203; 52 N. Y., 27; 62 N. Y., 479; 2 Keyes, 411; 8 Hun, 535; 7 Barb., 64; 17 Barb., 156; 32 Barb., 386; 5 How. Pr., 50; 6 How. Pr., 224; 10 How. Pr., 239; 8 Bos., 630; 1 Leg. Obs., 247; 4 Leg. Obs., 146; 9 How. (U. S.), 259; 4 Wall., 446; 48 Mo., 178; 11 Min., 101; 8 Am. Rep., 90 (48 Mo., 167).

195*] *MILLER v. WATSON.

Warranty of Title—Breach of—Eviction Necessary—Promise to Pay a Debt Secured by Promise of Higher Nature, is Void.

Where W. gave M. a deed with warranty, and afterwards admitted that the title had failed, and promised M. to refund the consideration money which he had received, and stated a balance due, yet held that *assumpsit* would not lie to recover it, but that M. should be put to his action on the covenant.

And no eviction of M. being proved, held that there was no consideration to sustain the promise.

Where a debt is secured by an instrument of a higher nature, as by deed or record, a promise to pay it is void.

Citations—3 Cai., 114; 4 Johns., 117; 2 T. R., 100; 4 Bos. & P., 104; 2 Str., 1027; Cro. Jac., 506, 598; Com. Dig., 207, Action upon the Case upon *Assumpsit* (F, 1); 1 Chit. Pl., 94, *n.* (*b*).

GENERAL *indebitatus assumpsit* for work, &c., money, &c., and on an account stated, tried at the Seneca Circuit, Sept. 22, 1823, before Throop, *Circuit Judge.*

On the trial the plaintiff proved that his agent called on the defendant concerning certain land sold and conveyed by the defendant to the plaintiff, and for which the consideration money had been paid by the plaintiff. An action of ejectment had been brought against the plaintiff for this land. The defendant admitted that the title had failed, and struck a balance of what would be due to the plaintiff, which he promised to pay. This was subscribed by the defendant thus: "Errors excepted, 15th July, 1816, E. Watson;" and delivered to the agent. The principal and interest of the balance, at the time of the trial, amounted to $1,549.85.

The defendant gave in evidence a deed with a covenant of warranty, from him to the plaintiff, of the land in question, for the consideration of $655, dated Dec. 15, 1810.

The defendant's counsel then objected that the plaintiff could not recover, there being no proof of eviction from the land, and, therefore, no consideration to support the promise; and that the plaintiff should be confined to his remedy upon the covenant in the deed. The judge overruled the objection, on the ground that the defendant had acknowledged that his title had failed, which was a sufficient consideration; that the defendant's promise was, therefore, valid; and the jury found for the plaintiff $1,549.85 damages.

Mr. J. C. Spencer, for the defendant, now moved for a new trial, and he cited 2 Cai., 188, 192; 1 Rep., 1; Cro. Jac., 196; 1 Salk., 211; Doug., 654; 7 Johns., 26; 15 *Id.*, 234; 1 Chit. Pl., 302; 7 Johns., 36; 1 Chit. Pl., 94, 95, *note b;* 2 Johns. Ch., 519; Cowp., 128, 129; 2 T. R., 100; Moore, 340; 1 Roll. Abr., 570; 7 Johns., 21; 8 *Id.*, 384; 3 Cai., 111; 4 Johns., 1; 3 Johns., 509; 1 Dall., 428.

**Mr. A. Gibbs*, contra, cited 1 Cai., [*196 47; 3 Johns., 506; 2 T. R., 100; 2 Saund., 134; 19 Johns., 147.

Curia, per SUTHERLAND, *J.* This action cannot be sustained. The parol promise of the defendant, on which it is founded, was simply to repay the consideration money, which he had received from the plaintiff, with interest. That he was bound to do by his covenant of warranty, if the defendant had been evicted. The deed from the defendant to the plaintiff bore date Dec. 15, 1810. The promise proved was made July 15, 1816, less than six years after the giving of the deed, when no interest had accrued, which the plaintiff was not entitled to recover in an action upon the covenant of warranty. (3 Cai., 114; 4 Johns., 117.) The promise, therefore, was simply, in judgment of law, to perform the covenant; and it is well settled that when a party has a security of a higher nature, he must found his action upon it; and that, in general, where there has been an express contract under seal, *assumpsit* will not lie upon a promise to perform it. The action must be either debt or covenant upon the contract itself. There is an anonymous case in Cowp., 128, in which it was held by Ld. Mansfield and *Mr. Justice* Ashurst that a promise by a defendant to pay a judgment obtained against them, in consideration that the plaintiff would stay execution, will not support an *assumpsit.* Ld. Mansfield observed that it was a new species of action, and an attempt to turn a judgment debt into a debt upon simple contracts. (*Vide*, also, 2 T. R., 100; 4 Bos. & P., 104; 2 Str., 1027; Cro. Jac., 506, 598; Com. Dig., 207, Action upon the Case upon *Assumpsit*, F, 1; 1 Chit. Pl., 94, 95, *note b.*)

Now it is clear that there was a good consideration to support the promise. The defendant's deed does not appear to have contained any other covenant than the covenant of warranty. And upon that covenant there can be no recovery without eviction. There is no evidence of an eviction in this case, except what is to be derived from the admission of the defendant that the title had failed, and that he would be compelled to refund the consideration money received; *and the [*197 further fact that an ejectment had been commenced against the defendant. This certainly was very equivocal evidence in relation to a fact which, if it existed, the plaintiff must have had the means of establishing by clear and explicit testimony. The defendant may

---

NOTE.—*Covenants*—1. *Warranty—Only broken by an eviction.* See Vanderkarr v. Vanderkarr, 11 Johns., 122, *note.*

2. Assumpsit—*When it does not lie.*

The action of assumpsit *does not lie on a specialty.* Dubois v. Doubleday, 9 Wend., 317; Hinkley v. Fowler, 15 Me., 285; Porter v. R. R. Co., 37 Me., 349; Holmes v. Smith, 49 Me., 242; Gazzum v. Ohio Ins. Co., Wright (Ohio), 214; Tullis v. Sewell, 3 Ohio, 510; McCargo v. Crutcher, 23 Ala., 575; Marine Ins. Co. v. Young, 1 Cr., 332.

3. *Merger*—See, generally, Day v. Leal, 14 Johns., 404, *note.*

have been mistaken in the opinion that his title had failed. The ejectment suits may have been discontinued, and the plaintiff may have retained the quiet and undisturbed possession of the premises to the present hour. I do not think a jury would be authorized in finding the fact of eviction upon this testimony. If there was no eviction, the promise of the defendant was without consideration. Admitting that there was a cloud upon the title, or that it had entirely failed, the hostile claim may have been quieted, and purchased in by the plaintiff for a very small portion of the consideration money; or the defendant may himself have quieted the title.

The form of action adopted by the plaintiff dispenses with the averment and proof, on his part, of any of the circumstances which show that the defendant's covenant has been broken, and that he has been damnified. I am, therefore, inclined to think that there was no legal consideration to support the promise of the defendant; and if the plaintiff has been damnified, he must seek redress upon the covenant of the defendant.

There must be a new trial, with costs to abide the event.

New trial granted.

Cited in—7 Cow., 40; 4 Wend., 269; 1 Hill, 149; 1 Sandf. Ch., 313; 3 Barb., 228, 433; 5 Barb., 321; 6 Barb., 166; 30 Barb., 341; 3 Rob., 213.

J. WRIGHT *v.* T. WRIGHT.

Award, not Containing all Matters Submittted, Void, where Bond of Submission Contains an Ita Quod *Clause—Pleading.*

Upon a general bond of submission to arbitrators, with an *ita quod* clause, if they do not award on all the matters in controversy between the parties, of which they have notice, the award is void *in toto*; adjudged upon plea that they had omitted to pass upon a certain matter; replication setting forth an award which, on its face, excluded this matter, demurrer and joinder.

Citations—Cro. Jac., 200, 354, 399; Kyd Aw., 174-176; 8 Co., 98 *b*; Hob., 49; Cro. Eliz., 838, 858; Dy., 216, 217; Benl., 107; Willes, 268; 14 Johns., 106.

ON demurrer to the replication. The pleadings were thus: declaration on a bond made at the Town of Constable, in the County of Franklin. The defendant prayed oyer of
198*] *the bond and condition, and set them out in *hæc verba*, by which it appeared that the bond was from the defendant to the plaintiff, in the penalty of $5,000, dated June 15, 1824, and conditioned to abide the award of certain arbitrators upon the usual general submission: "So as the award, &c., be made, &c., on or before the 1st day of July next, then, &c." After pleading *non est factum*, the defendant pleaded, secondly, "that the said arbitrators did not within, &c., make any legal, sufficient and final award, &c., of and concerning all the matters and controversies in the said condition mentioned; but, on the contrary thereof, the said arbitrators made a partial and insufficient award of and concerning the premises in the said condition mentioned, by leaving therein a controversy between the said T. and J. relative to a house and shed in the said Town of Constable wholly undecided and undetermined, although the said arbitrators had notice of the said controversy previously to the making of the said award, and were requested to decide the same." Replication: "That the arbitrators, &c., after, &c., and within the time limited, &c.; that is to say, on the said 1st day of July, at, &c., did, &c., make their award, &c., of and concerning the premises in the said condition mentioned, &c., and ready, &c., and did, &c., award and order in the words, &c., following, to wit: indorsed upon the said writing obligatory, &c. We, &c., do, in the first place, say that we do not take into consideration the house and shed, nor pass no order upon it. As to the remainder of the counts, after hearing the observation of parties, testimony of witnesses, and pleading of counsel, do order, adjust and declare that, on final conclusion, we say that we find for J. Wright $61.75, against said T., and costs, of which, &c."

General demurrer and joinder.

Mr. A. Wheeler, in support of the demurrer.

Mr. J. Parkhurst, contra, cited *M'Kinstry* v. *Solomons*, 2 Johns., 57; *Martin* v. *Williams*, 13 *Id.*, 264; *Jackson* v. *Ambler*, 14 *Id.*, 96; and *Cox* v. *Jagger*, 2 Cow., 638.

**Curia*, per SUTHERLAND, *J.* It is a [*199
general rule, that where the bond of submission contains an *ita quod* clause, the award will be void, unless it comprehend all the matters submitted. This rule is invariable, where the particular matters submitted are specified in the bond. But where the submission is general, and an award concerning one or more things is made, it will be presumed, until the contrary be shown, that nothing else was referred to the arbitrators, or brought before them by the parties. *Middleton* v. *Weeks*, Cro. Jac., 200; *Ormelade* v. *Coke*, *Id.*, 354; Kyd on Aw., 174-176, and the cases there cited; 8 Rep., 98 *b*; Hob., 49; *Risden* v. *Inglet*, Cro. Eliz., 838. But if arbitrators award in relation to one or more things, and say that they will not meddle with the rest, the whole is void; because they have not pursued their authority; *Barnes* v. *Greenwel*, Cro. Eliz., 858; Dy., 216, 217; Benl., 107; Kyd on Aw., 174; and in such a case, it is immaterial whether the submission was general or special; for, if general, it appears on the face of the award that the arbitrators had notice of the matters which they refuse to decide.

The case of *Bradford* v. *Bryan*, Willes, 268, is precisely in point. That was a general submission with an *ita quod* clause. The suits and controversies of the parties appear to have been in relation to tithes. The award was, that the defendant should pay to the plaintiff a certain sum of money in full of all demands; and that the plaintiff should pay to the defendant a certain other sum of money for all tithes and Easter duties whatsoever (except tithes of calves, &c.), and that the parties, on receipt of the sums, should execute general releases to each other of all demands whatsoever ("except the said tithes of calves, for which the defendant was at liberty to prosecute if he thought fit"). Upon general demurrer, the award was holden to be void *in toto*, for not determining all the matters in dispute between the parties.

The present case cannot be distinguished from that. The award shows that the arbitrators had notice of the house and shed, as a matter in controversy. Such notice is ex-
200*] pressly *averred in the plea; and also that the arbitrators were requested to decide upon this branch of the subject. It must, therefore, have been brought before them by the parties, for the purpose of being adjudicated upon.

It is not like the case of *Berry* v. *Penring*, Cro. Jac., 399, where the award was, that all suits and actions shall cease, and all matters be determined, except in relation to a partienlar bond; which was awarded to stand in force. It was contended that this was not an award in relation to the bond. But the court held, and most clearly they held correctly, that this was not a disclaimer to meddle with the bond, but an express award that it should stand in force and be satisfied. *Jackson* v. *Ambler*, 14 Johns., 106, per Spencer, *J.*

The plea is somewhat informal, and possibly, upon special demurrer, might have been held bad; but it is good in substance. I am, therefore, of opinion that the defendant is entitled to judgment.

Judgment for the defendant.

Ctied in—5 N. Y., 486; 27 N. Y., 230; 71 N. Y., 213; 74 N. Y., 113; 3 Barb., 61; 7 W. Dig., 215; 69 Ill., 181.

JACKSON, ex dem. MURRAY ET AL., *v.* DENN.

Ejectment—Prior Possession, Short of Twenty Years, Under Claim of Right.

In ejectment, a prior possession, short of 20 years, under a claim of right, will prevail over a subsequent possession, short of 20 years, if the first be not relinquished.

Citations—10 Johns., 338; 16 Johns., 325; 2 Johns., 22; 3 Johns., 383; 4 Johns., 208.

EJECTMENT for part of lot No. 93, in the Township of Junius, tried at the Seneca Circuit, Mar. 6, 1824, before Throop, *C. J.*

On the trial, the plaintiff proved by H. W. Dobbin, that he, the witness, was in possession of the premises in question from 1805 to 1808, claiming possession of the whole of lot 93. He then gave in evidence a conveyance in fee, by deed poll, of lot 93, from Dobbin to the lessors of the plaintiff, for the consideration of $50. That Dobbin continued his possession about 4 years after, when he was succeeded by another tenant under the lessors of the plaintiff; and this last was succeeded by a series of tenants down to one Quivy, who was in possession under a lease in the summer of 1821, or 1822. After this the premises were left vacant, there being no house upon
201*] them; and the defendant entered *into possession in Dec., 1822, and built a log house, where he resided in Apr., 1823.

A witness testified that Quivy took under a lease in writing from the lessors of the plaintiff, which the witness had in court, and the defendant objected that this lease should be produced; but the objection was overruled. Other facts are mentioned in the opinion of the court.

The defendant moved for a nonsuit, on the ground that neither the lessors, nor any one under them, were in the actual occupancy of the premises when the defendant took possession, nor indeed from the summer of 1822; and the judge directed a nonsuit accordingly.

A motion was now made to set aside the nonsuit, and for a new trial.

Mr. J. A. Collier, for the plaintiff, cited 2 Johns., 22; 4 *Id.*, 202; 10 *Id.*, 338; 16 *Id.*, 325.

Mr. H. V. R. Shermerhorn, contra, cited 1 Greenl. ed. L. N. Y., 55; 2 *Id.*, 281, 332, by which, he said, it would appear that the premises in question belonged to the people of the State, they lying in the military tract.

Curia, per SUTHERLAND, *J.* The nonsuit must be set aside. The lessors of the plaintiff showed a continued possession in themselves and the one from whom they derived it, under a claim or assertion of right, from 1805 to 1821 or 1822. In Dec., 1822, the defendant entered, without pretending any right or title, the premises being then vacant. This action was brought in Apr., 1823. The reason of the premises being vacant is given by Thomas Mumford, a witness for the plaintiff, who testified that he was the agent of the lessors, with authority to lease or sell the lot; that he had leased it for several years to different tenants; that he last leased it to one Quivy, who, after the expiration of his lease, held over, with the consent of the witness, who never knew that he had left the premises, until informed that the defendant had entered. This shows that the possession had never been abandoned by the lessors, without the *animus revertendi*.

*In *Smith* v. *Lorillard*, 10 Johns., [*202
338, the rule is thus stated: "A prior possession, short of 20 years, under a claim, or assertion of right, will prevail over a subsequent possession, short of 20 years, where no other evidence appears on either side." It is, however, to be understood, that the prior possession of the plaintiff had not been voluntarily relinquished, without the *animus revertendi*; and that the subsequent possession of the defendant was acquired by mere entry, without any lawful right. (16 Johns., 325; 2 *Id.*, 22; 3 *Id.*, 383; 4 *Id.*, 208.)

Motion granted.

Cited in—15 Wend., 176; 5 Lans., 211, 214.

JACKSON, ex dem. BARCLAY and BAYARD, *v.* BLODGET.

Mortgage not an Independent Debt—Assignment of the Bond or Debt Passes the Mortgage—Payment to Mortgagee after Assignment of Debt.

The assignment of a bond, or debt, secured by mortgage, passes the interest in the mortgage.

The debt is the principal, and the mortgage but an accessory, which cannot exist as an independent debt.

If, therefore, after the assignment of a bond secured by mortgage, though the mortgage be not delivered, and notice of such assignment to the ob-

NOTE.—*Mortgage—Accessory to debt—Transfer of debt passes interest in mortgage, whether latter is assigned or not.* See Green v. Hart, 1 Johns., 580, *note*. See, also, Jackson v. Willard, 4 Johns., 41; Jackson v. Merscreau, 11 Johns., 534; Langdon v. Buel, 9 Wend., 80; Kortright v. Cady, 21 N. Y., 343; Parmelee v. Dan, 23 Barb., 461; Bolen v. Crosby, 49 N. Y.,

ligor, he pay the debt to the mortgagee, and take a discharge, this is in his own wrong, and void as to the assignee.

Citations—2 Burr., 978; Barnard Ch., 90, 93; 1 Johns., 590; 4 Johns., 43; Pow. Mortg., 1115, 6.

EJECTMENT, for part of lot No. 79, in the Township of Virgil, and County of Cortland, tried at the circuit in that county, Sept. 22, 1823, before Rochester, *Circuit Judge.*

On the trial, the plaintiff gave in evidence a mortgage from one Hopkins to Barclay, one of the lessors of the plaintiff, of the premises in question, dated July 20, 1815; which was proved and registered on the same day. This mortgage was conditioned for the payment of 450 bushels of rye and four barrels of pork, according to the condition of a bond bearing the same date. He then gave in evidence an assignment, indorsed upon the bond, from Barclay to one Rice, dated Aug. 28; 1815, reciting that Rice had become bail to the sheriff for Barclay, at the suit of one Johnson, and stating that in consideration of Rice's undertaking as bail, he did thereby assign, &c., all his right, &c., in the bond to Rice, upon the condition, that if he should pay Johnson's demand with costs, so as to indemnify Rice, then the assignment to be void; otherwise, to be of force, so far as to indemnify Rice.

It was admitted that Rice gave Hopkins notice of this assignment within three days after it was executed.

The plaintiff then offered in evidence an assignment indorsed on the bond from Rice to **203***] Bayard, one of the lessors *of the plaintiff, dated Feb. 12, 1817, and declaring that in considertion of Bayard's indemnity to Rice, against his obligation as bail, he did thereby assign, &c., his right, &c., in the bond to Bayard. The introduction of this assignment as evidence was objected to, but it was admitted, and the plaintiff then proved an assignment of both mortgage and bond from Barclay to Bayard, dated May 23, 1817, duly proved, and registered by the clerk of Cortland Co., June 28, 1817.

The defendant then gave in evidence a written power of attorney, dated Nov. 8, 1815, by which Barclay appointed one Cole his attorney, to ask, demand, sue for and recover all that was due or owing to him from Hopkins, and Parnham, Shevalier, Coburn and Abby; and to receive all sum or sums of money due to him from Shevalier, Coburn and Abby, and to release and discharge the same, and to do all things, touching the premises, as himself could do, were he personally present at the doing of the same.

The defendant then offered in evidence a receipt given by Cole to Hopkins, dated Oct. 28, 1816, of 450 bushels of rye and 4 barrels of pork, and expressed to be the sum in full to satisfy the mortgage.

The plaintiff objected to this receipt as evidence, on the ground that the assignment to Rice, and notice to Hopkins, operate as a revocation of Cole's authority, and that the payment was not in good faith; and the court sustained the objection.

The defendant then gave in evidence a regular discharge of the mortgage, dated Apr. 10, 1817, signed and sealed by Cole in Barclay's names, attested by two witnesses, acknowledged and registered in the Cortland clerk's office, sufficient in form to discharge the mortgage according to the statute, &c.

It was admitted that the defendant was in possession as the tenant of one Messenger, and a deed in fee, of the premises in question, from Hopkins to Messenger, dated Dec. 10, 1818, duly proved and recorded, was given in evidence.

*It was also admitted that, at the [***204** time of the several assignments, the mortgage was in possession of Cole, and was by him delivered to Hopkins, when the discharge was executed, and by the latter delivered to Messenger when he received his deed.

Verdict for the plaintiff, subject to the opinion of the Supreme Court.

Mr. L. F. Stephens, for the plaintiff. The discharge was void. Cole's authority did not reach such a case. Besides, a statute discharge cannot be given by attorney. The clerk who records it has nothing before him showing the authority. *Jackson* v. *Hopkins*, 18 Johns., 487, decides that this very power could not be recorded. If so, it was void. It could operate as notice to no one, within the Statute, 1 R. L., 373.

The payment to Cole was in fraud of the rights of the parties. The bond was previously assigned, and carried the mortgage as its incident. (1 Johns., 580.)

Cole's power to receive the debt was revoked by the assignments and notice to Hopkins, these acts being inconsistent with the power.

Mr. H. Stephens, for the defendant. The plaintiff seeks to recover against a *bona fide* purchaser, upon a latent equity, though the latter took from a grantor having all the evidences of payment about him.

Jackson v. *Hopkins* goes on the ground that the power was not duly proved. On the trial of this cause the due execution of the power was not disputed. But the right to register is not material. The payment of the mortgage was in itself a discharge. It was not delivered with the assignments. Barclay had a right to separate the bond and mortgage, by assigning one and retaining the other. The bond was the principal; the mortgage a mere collateral security. At any rate, the assignees are guilty of gross neglect in not getting possession of the mortgage, and leaving it behind to impose upon the purchaser from Hopkins; and if there be any loss, they should bear it. The

---

183; Perot v. Levasseur, 21 La. Ann., 529; Smith v. Moore, 11 N. H., 55; Northy v. Northy, 45 N. H., 144; Donley v. Hays, 17 Serg. & R., 400; Harris v. Mills, 28 Ills., 46; Willis v. Farley, 24 Cal., 497; Perkins v. Stone, 23 Tex., 563; Ladue v. R. R. Co., 13 Mich., 396. But see, Young v. Miller, 6 Gray, 152. In Ill. forclosure proceedings by assignee must be brought in the name of the mortgagee. Burland v. Kipp, 55 Ill., 376.

The assignment of the interest of the mortgagee in the mortgaged premises, without an assignment of the debt, is a mere nullity. Jackson v. Bronson, 19 Johns., 325.

The assignment of part of a mortgage debt passes a proportionable interest in the mortgage. Pattison v. Hull, 9 Cow., 747. See, generally, Hurt v. Wilson, 38 Cal., 263; Cathcart's Appeal, 13 Pa. St., 416; Lindsey v. Bates, 42 Miss., 397; Waller v. Tate, 4 B. Mon., 529; Perry v. Roberts, 30 Ind., 244.

subsequent assignment of the mortgage by Barclay, without its being delivered and the 205*] *registry of that assignment, could not alter the case. This was an unofficial registry, and was notice to nobody. *James* v. *Morey*, 2 Cow., 246. The mortgage was paid before the assignment, and Bayard took subject to all previous equities.

Curia, per SUTHERLAND, *J.* The bond from Hopkins to Barclay was assigned by Barclay to Rice Aug. 28, 1815, and notice of the assignment was given by Rice to Hopkins within three days thereafter.

The power of attorney from Barclay to Cole, to ask for and receive, &c., all that was due from Hopkins and others to Barclay, was given Nov. 8, 1815, more than two months after the assignment from Barclay to Rice. So far, therefore, as this demand against Hopkins was concerned, the power of attorney was a nullity. There was nothing due from Hopkins to Barclay upon it. The debt had become the property of Rice, and Hopkins had notice of it. Any payment, therefore, from Hopkins to Cole, upon this bond, was a payment in his own wrong, and in fraud of the rights of the assignee. If Hopkins had no right to make the payment, Cole certainly had no right to receive it; and any discharge, either of the debt or the mortgage, as between Hopkins and Rice, was a mere nullity. The power of attorney to Cole contained no express authority to discharge the mortgage. If he possessed that power, it was because it was implied in the authority given to receive what was due from Hopkins, and to give a receipt or discharge for it. But nothing being due from Hopkins to Barclay upon this bond, it having been previously transferred, there could be no implied authority to discharge the mortgage; which did not constitute a distinct and independent debt, but was merely collateral to the bond.

It is very clear that if Cole had no authority to receive payment of the bond, he had none to discharge the mortgage. Whether the assignment of the bond, therefore, to Rice carried with it the mortgage as its incident or not, the acknowledgment of satisfaction by Cole was an unauthorized and void act.

206*] *It is not pretended that Barclay expressly reserved the mortgage when he assigned the bond to Rice for the purpose of discharging it. What, then, was the legal operation of that assignment upon the mortgage? Was it, *ipso facto*, a discharge? If it was not, then the mortgage must have accompanied the bond, although not expressly named in the assignment; for it could not exist as an independent security in the hands of one person, while the bond belonged to another. The debt (the evidence of which was the bond) is the principal; the mortgage the accessory; and *omne principale trahit ad se accessorium* It is said by Ld. Mansfield, in *Martin* v. *Mowlin*, 2 Burr., 978, that a mortgage is a charge upon the land, and whatever will give the money, will carry the estate in the land along with it, to every purpose; that the assignment of the debt, or forgiving it, will draw the land after it as a consequence, though it were only by parol. *Richards* v. *Syms*, Barnard. Ch., 90, 93. This opinion of Ld. Mansfield was expressly recognized by the Court of Errors, in *Greene* v. *Hart*, 1 Johns., 590. There the mortgage was delivered to the assignee with the note, which was assigned. But Spencer, *J.*, who delivered the unanimous opinion of the court, says: "Had the mortgage not been delivered, nor anything said about it, I should have considered the respondent (the assignee), on the failure of the mortgagor to pay the note, entitled to the aid of the mortgage." He observes that it was competent to the parties to agree that the mortgage should not be resorted to by the holder of the note; but the proof of such agreement lies on the appellant, and it should be explicit.

So in *Jackson* v. *Willard*, 4 Johns., 43, which was a case involving the question whether lands mortgaged can be sold on an execution against the mortgagee, before foreclosure, it is observed by Kent, *Ch. J.*, that "the mortgage, before foreclosure, is but an incident attached to the debt, which cannot be detached from its principal; that the mortgage interest, as distinguished from the debt, has no determinate value, and is not a fit subject of assignment. If it should be assigned, the assignee must hold the interest at the will and disposal of the creditor who holds the bond. The control over *the mortgaged premises must essential- [*207 ly reside in him who holds the debt. It would be absurd in principle, and oppressive in practice, for the debt and the mortgage to be separated, and placed in different and independent hands. (Pow. on Mort., 1115, 1116.) The mortgage is the accessory, and *accessorium non ducit, sed sequitur principale*."

The mortgage in this case, therefore, although not expressly named, accompanied the bond, in judgment of law, when it was assigned to Rice, and vested in him all the rights of the mortgagee. There is no necessity, therefore, of resorting to the subsequent assignment of the mortgage itself by Barclay, except as affording evidence that he had not complied with the condition mentioned in the original assignment of the bond, upon which that assignment was to become void; and that the assignment, therefore, though originally conditional, as between Barclay and Rice, had become absolute.

The defeudant, or those for whom he holds, claim as grantees of Hopkins, under a deed of Dec. 10, 1818; and seem to put forth as a ground of equity, at least that the mortgagee, or his assignees, by leaving the mortgage in the hands of Cole, had been guilty of laches, and enabled him and Hopkins to perpetrate a fraud upon an innocent purchaser. There is nothing in this case to show that the grantee of Hopkins was an innocent purchaser—that he had not full notice of all the facts in the case. But admitting that he had not, it would not vary the legal rights of the parties.

I am of opinion that the plaintiff is entitled to judgment.

Judgment for the plaintiff.

Cited in—9 Cow., 751; 9 Wend., 84; 6 Hill, 239; 1 Paige, 71; 4 N. Y., 410; 36 N. Y., 45; 42 N. Y., 346; 44 N. Y., 57, 233; 49 N. Y., 187; 61 N. Y., 118; 64 N. Y., 44; 2 Keyes, 265; 1 Abb. App. Dec., 521; 1 Trans. App., 64; 4 Hun, 125; 6 Barb., 138; 12 Barb., 119; 13 Barb., 232; 31 Barb., 516; 6 T. & C., 388; 6 How. Pr., 164; 31 How. Pr., 3; 34 How. Pr., 130; 17 Abb. Pr., 344; 3 Daly, 238; Co. R. N. S., 313; 16 Wall., 274; 18 Wall., 154; 4 Ben., 442; 91 Ill., 86; 13 Mich., 396; 1 Am. Rep., 539 (42 N. Y., 334); 21 Am. Rep., 585 (64 N. Y., 41).

JACKSON, ex dem. GORMAN ET AL., v. HOOKER AND HOOKER.

New Trial Granted on Newly Discovered Evidence, though Cumulative Merely—Exception to General Rule.

New trial granted in ejectment for land in the military tract, on the ground of newly discovered evidence; though this was cumulative merely, and tended to impeach a witness sworn at the first trial. Ejectments for military lots are, in this respect, an exception to the general rule.

Citations—8 Johns., 489; 12 Johns., 354; 14 Johns., 186.

EJECTMENT, for part of lot No. 94, in the Town of Truxton (late Fabius), in the County of Cortland, tried at the Cortland **208***] *Circuit, the 29th and 30th of June, 1824, before Walworth, *Circuit Judge.*

A verdict was found for the defendant; and a motion was now made for a new trial, on grounds which are sufficiently stated in the opinion of the court.

Messrs. D. Woods and *J. A. Spencer*, for the plaintiff, cited 14 Johns., 186; 12 *Id.*, 354; 8 *Id.*, 489; 3 Burr., 1771.

Mr. S. Forman, contra, cited 2 Cai., 155; 3 *Id.*, 182, 307; 1 *Id.*, 24; 6 Johns., 425; 5 *Id.*, 248; 2 Cai., 129.

Curia, per SUTHERLAND, *J.* This is an application, on the part of the plaintiff, for a new trial, on the ground of surprise, and also of newly discovered evidence. The action was brought to recover possession of a part of lot No. 94, in the Town of Truxton (formerly Fabius), in the County of Cortland. The lot was patented to Richard Gorman, a soldier, in the N. Y. line, during the Revolutionary War. The lessors of the plaintiff were the children of James Gorman, who, they contend, was the brother, and heir at law, of Richard. Whether he was, or was not so, was the turning point in the cause.

The evidence on the part of the defendant tended to show that the grandparents of the lessors never had but two children—a daughter, named Molly, and James, the father of the lessors. The evidence was very contradictory, and left it extremely doubtful what the fact was.

The testimony of Sarah Gorman, taken under a commission in New Hampshire, was introduced on the part of the plaintiff. She testified that she was the mother of the lessors and the widow of James Gorman; that she had always understood from Hannah Gorman, the mother of her husband, that Richard Gorman was her son, and the brother of James. That she, the witness, knew Richard, her husband's brother. That he spent one day at he husband's house, after he was 21 years of age, and the witness was 76 years of age.

To repel this evidence, the defendants produced Increase M. Hooker, who testified that in Aug. 1813, Sarah Gorman *(the wit- [***209** ness, whose testimony has just been stated) told him that there never had been such a man as Richard Gorman; that sometime during the Revolutionary War, a man came to her house who called himself Peter Gorman, and claimed to be the brother of James Gorman, her husband; but that he was not his brother, and that he afterwards changed his name to Richard Gorman. Hooker further testified that he went, at the same time, to the house of Joseph S. Gorman, a son of Sarah Gorman, who confirmed, in every respect, the story told by his mother.

This is the testimony by which the lessors of the plaintiff allege they were surprised. They allege that it is an entire fabrication, and produce the affidavit of Sarah Gorman, positively denying that she ever held such conversation with Hooker. They also show that Joseph S. Gorman, who, Hooker alleged, told him the same story, was at that time, and during the whole of the years 1813 and 1814, a soldier in the Army of the U. S., in the late War, and was not in N. H. where Hooker alleges the conversation took place. They account for not producing the affidavit of Joseph, by showing that he is somewhere in the western country, but where they do not know.

The newly discovered evidence is cumulative merely, upon the point of James being the brother of Richard, but it is important.

The lessors of the plaintiff are not chargeable with any negligence in not being prepared to repel the evidence of Hooker. They were not bound to anticipate that a story so entirely irreconcilable with the deposition of Sarah Gorman, their witness, would be imputed to her. She was beyond the jurisdiction of the court, and was probably too old to be produced on the trial, even if she was within its jurisdiction. The testimony of Hooker may have decided the cause with the jury. It was calculated to make a deep impression on them.

I am inclined to think the ends of justice will be best answered by giving the plaintiff an opportunity of repelling or explaining this testimony. It will not be going further than this court has repeatedly gone, in granting new trials relative *to military lots. That [***210** class of cases is considered peculiar, and as exempt from the ordinary rules in relation to granting new trials. But the motion must be granted, on payment of costs. *Jackson* v. *Laird*, 8 Johns., 489; *Jackson* v. *Crosby*, 12 Johns., 354; *Jackson* v. *Kinney*, 14 Johns., 186.

New trial granted, on payment of costs.

Cited in—5 Wend., 122; 34 Barb., 295.

NOTE.—*New trial—Newly discovered evidence—Conflict of evidence.*

Newly discovered evidence, which is merely cumulative, not a ground for a new trial unless clear that it would change the result. See Halsey v. Watson, 1 Cai., 24 *note*; Wilkie v. Roosevelt, 3 Johns. Cas., 206, *note*.

In ejectment for military bounty lands where the identity of the soldier is the principal question, a new trial may be granted on newly discovered evidence, which is merely cumulative, or to admit evidence to impeach a principal witness. These cases are deemed exceptional and the general rule does not apply. Jackson v. Crosby, 12 Johns., 354; Jackson v. Kinney, 14 Johns., 186.

STRONG v. STEBBINS.

Distress—Construction of a Statute Concerning—Penal Statutes, Strictly Construed—Ownership Presumed in One Having Possession of Goods.

An action will not lie for the penalty given by the 14th section of the Statute Concerning Distresses, Rents and the Renewal of Leases, 1 R. L., 437, 438, for the removal or concealment of goods not the property of the tenant, though they be liable to distress.

The Act contemplates physical aid or assistance, directly or indirectly in the removal, or concealment of the goods. Merely advising their removal will not subject to its penalty.

Nor will the removal, or concealment, of a part of the goods, subject to the penalty of removing or concealing the whole.

A penal statute is not to be enlarged by construction.

A tenant being in possession of goods, the intendment of law is, that he is the owner; and the *onus* of proving the contrary lies upon him who has removed them, to avoid a distress.

DEBT, to recover the penalty given by the 14th section of the Act Concerning Distresses, Rents and the Renewal of Leases, 1 R. L., 437, 438, for willfully and knowingly aiding or assisting the tenant, in the fraudulent conveying and carrying away goods and chattels, and in keeping and detaining them off and from certain premises demised by the plaintiff to one Ambrose.

The cause was tried at the Monroe Circuit, Sept. 27, 1824, before Rochester, *Circuit Judge*.

The main question upon the trial was, whether the acts of the defendant were such as brought him within that section of the Statute upon which the action was founded.

As to this, the tenant, who was called as a witness by the plaintiff, testified that the amount of property removed was about $120; that it consisted of household furniture; that it was removed, to avoid a distress, and for the joint benefit of himself and the defendant, who had a judgment against him. That the goods were removed in the night; and the defendant advised that they should be placed in such a situation that his brother Eber, who had receipted the property to the sheriff upon the defendant's execution on his judgment, might get it; and that it might be applied on the defendant's judgment. That about $2 worth of the property was taken to the defendant's; and it was agreed by the defendant that his clerk **211***] or brother might be called *up in the night to receive property brought there. A part of the property was removed to the house of one Lamb, who afterwards purchased it for $20, and gave his note to the defendant for that amount. The defendant had notice that the rent was due.

The defendant's counsel moved for a nonsuit, on the ground that the defendant merely advised, without aiding or assisting in the removal; but the judge overruled the motion, on the ground that the advising of a removal, and an actual removal pursuant to such advice, with a view to have the goods applied on the defendant's judgment, was aiding and assisting within the meaning of the Statute; and he charged the jury accordingly, who found for the plaintiff, $240.

In the course of the trial, the defendant's counsel objected, that it did not appear that the goods removed were the property of the tenant; but the judge decided that this made no difference; that it was enough if they were distrainable.

A motion was now made for a new trial.

Mr. J. H. Gregory, for the defendant.

Mr. R. Beach, contra.

Curia, per SUTHERLAND, *J.* The evidence clearly establishes that the defendant instigated and advised the removal, knowing that rent was due; and with a view to put the goods beyond the reach of the landlord. But there is no proof that he aided or assisted in the removal, in any other way than by receiving $2 worth of the property; and agreeing that his clerk, or brother, might be called up at night to receive any of the property that might be brought to his house. There is no evidence, however, that any was brought there, and received pursuant this arrangement, or in any other way, except the trifling amount already mentioned.

The judge was clearly wrong in the opinion that the tenant need not own the goods. The Statute, upon which the *action was [***212** brought, is express upon this point. But the error is not material. The tenant being in possession, the presumption of law is, that he was the owner; and there was nothing to show that they did not belong to him. If the action had been against the tenant, the *onus* would have lain on him, to show that they were not his goods; and so of the present defendant.

I am also inclined to think that the judge erred in the opinion expressed by him upon the other point, relative to the defendant's agency in the affair.

This is a penal action. The Statute giving it is not to be enlarged by construction. It appears to me to contemplate physical aid or assistance in some way, either directly or indirectly, in removing or concealing the goods. If the defendant's servants, by his direction, or with his knowledge and assent, had assisted, that would have rendered the defendant liable; or if the goods had been removed to his house, and received and concealed by him, he knowing the object and circumstances of the removal, that would have brought him within the Act. It provides that every person, so offending, shall forfeit and pay to the landlord, &c., from whose estate such goods, &c., were so carried off, &c., double the value of the goods by him carried off, or concealed as aforesaid. If the evidence is to be considered as establishing the fact that the defendant received and concealed $2 worth of the goods, that would not make him liable for the whole.

I do not think the mere advising the removal of the goods is sufficient to subject a party to the penalty given by the Statute. The judge, therefore, in my opinion, erred in his charge to the jury; and a new trial must be granted, with costs to abide the event.

New trial granted.

Cited in—11 Wend., 147; 2 Hill, 450; 50 N. Y., 317; 4 Lans., 23; 1 Leg. Obs., 107.

---

*SMYTH *v.* BRADSTREET. [***213**

Action, for Fees, by Commissioner to make Partition—Does not Lie till Fees are taxed by Court—Joinder of Commissioners in the Action.

A commissioner, to make partition under the Act for Partition of Lands, 1 R. L., 507, cannot maintain a suit for his fees, or compensation, till taxed by the court.

In an action by a commissioner, under the Act, for his fees and disbursements, his co-commissioner is not a competent witness for the plaintiff.

Whether the commissioners must join or sever in their action for fees, or disbursements, *quære*. And see the authorities as to the claim being joint, the necessity of joinder, and the consequences of non-joinder, fully collected by *Mr. A. Burr, arguendo*, for the defendant.

In partition, under the Act for the Partition of Lands, 1 R. L., 507, the amount of compensation to the commissioners must be determined by the court, as per 1 R. L., 512, sec. 9.

Citations—1 R. L., 512, sec. 9; 16 Johns., 92; 4 Johns., 293; 11 Johns., 57; 4 Mass., 653.

ASSUMPSIT, tried at the Delaware Circuit, Sept. 2, 1823, before Nelson, *Circuit Judge.*

The declaration contained the usual money counts, and counts for work, labor, care, diligence and materials found, &c.

At the trial, the plaintiff proved certain services performed by himself and Bartlet, Peak and Bostwick, commissioners in several causes at the suit of the defendant, for the partition of lands, prosecuted in this court, who granted rules appointing them for that purpose, certified copies of which were served on them by the defendant; that $3 per day would be a reasonable compensation; and $1 per day for expenses, and various disbursements to flagmen, &c. Bostwick & Peak were offered as witnesses for the plaintiff. They were objected to, but the objection was overruled and they were sworn.

The defendant's counsel moved for a nonsuit, on these, among other grounds: 1. That the commissioners could not maintain separate suits. 2. That they could not recover upon a *quantum meruit*, but their fees should be fixed by the court. The judge overruled the motion, and the jury found for the plaintiff.

Mr. A. Burr, for the defendant, now moved for a new trial on these points, among others: 1. That the commissioners could not maintain separate suits. 2. One commissioner was not a competent witness for the other relative to their fees or expenses. 3. The compensation of the commissioners could not be recovered in an action upon a *quantum meruit*, but must be adjudicated and fixed by the court.

To the first point, he cited *Decker* v. *Livingston*, 15 Johns., 482; 1 Tidd Pr., 8; 1 Chit. Pl., 3-7, 9; *Dob* v. *Halsey*, 16 Johns., 40; 2 Str., **214***] 820; 1 Saund., *163; 1 Dunl. Pr., 34; *Eccleston* v. *Clipsham*, 1 Saund., 153, and *note* 1; *Anderson* v. *Martindale*, 1 East, 497, 501; *Hill* v. *Tucker*, 1 Taunt., 7; *Townsend* v. *Neal*, 2 Campb., 190; 1 Roll. Abr., 31, pl. 9; *Vaux* v. *Steward*, Styles, 156, 157; *Vaux* v. *Draper*, *Id.*, 203; 2 Saund., 116 *b*, 1; *Thimblethorp* v. *Hardesty*, 7 Mod., 116; *Rolle* v. *Yates*, Yelv., 177; *Savile* v. *Roberts*, 1 Ld. Raym., 380; *Graham* v. *Robertson*, 2 T. R., 282; 1 Chit. Pl. 6, *note y; Southcoat* v. *Hoare*, 3 Taunt., 87; *Phillips* v. *Bonsall*, 2 Binn., 138, 143; *Dunham* v. *Gillis*, 8 Mass., 462; *Ziele* v. *Campbell's Exrs.*, 2 Johns. Cas., 384; Co. Litt., 180 *b;* Bac. Abr., Joint Tenancy, K; *Scott* v. *Godwin*, 1 Bos. & P., 73; 1 Chit. Pl., 10; 15 Johns., 433, per *Cur.*

As to the second point, 16 Johns., 92, 95, per *Cur.; Swift* v. *Dean*, 6 Johns., 523; *Gage* v. *Stewart*, 4 Johns., 293; *Butler* v. *Warren*, 11 *Id.*, 57; *Maynard* v. *Webb*, 16 *Id.*, 92; *Emerton* v. *Andrews*, 4 Mass., 653.

As to the third point, *Andrews* v. *Montgomery*, 19 Johns., 162; 1 Chit. Pl., 94; *Scott* v. *Elmendorf*, 12 Johns., 318; *Virany, Exr.*, v. *Warne*, 4 Esp., 47; 1 R. L., 510, sec. 6; *Id.*, 512, sec. 9.

Messrs. S. Sherwood and *A. Parker*, contra, cited 5 Johns., 252; 9 *Id.*, 114; 15 *Id.*, 260.

Curia, per WOODWORTH, *J.* The plaintiff declared in *assumpsit*, for work, labor and services, as a commissioner in the partition of lands; and for money and materials provided. At the trial, an account was exhibited, containing a charge for services, at $3 per day; and $1 per day for expenses; and such other advances as had been made for the hire of flagmen, &c. The plaintiff proved by one of the commissioners, the services performed, and moneys paid, and that $3 per day was reasonable. The defendant objected to the evidence; but the objection was overruled, as was also a motion for a nonsuit; and there was a verdict found for the plaintiff.

The services have been so far per- [***215** formed as to entitle the plaintiff to payment; but the question is, whether he has not prematurely resorted to this action.

The 9th section of the Act, 1 R. L., 512, sec. 9, declares that the commissioners shall be allowed such sum for their services as the court shall direct, which shall be paid by the petitioners, and shall be allowed as part of the costs, to be taxed. The manner of obtaining payment, then, is prescribed by the Statute. That refers the *quantum* of compensation to the court in which the proceedings are had. If so, the amount is not a proper subject of liquidation by a jury. If the plaintiff in the partition should tax his costs, to enable him to obtain contribution from the several owners, for the expenses incurred, he would not be authorized by the Act to insert in the bill the damages found by the verdict; but would be confined to the allowance made by the court. The proper course is, for the commissioners to apply to the court, who, under the Act, would certify the sum to be allowed. After this, the defendant would be liable to an action; and the amount allowed by the court would be the measure of damages. Whether, in that case, the commissioners must join, or might sever in their actions, is not a point now necessary to be decided.

There is, also, an objection to the competency of the witnesses produced. One commissioner was called to prove not only the services of his fellow commissioner, but the money paid for flagmen, &c. The money thus paid by the plaintiff, in this cause, was a charge for which the other commissioners were holden to contribute a proportion; for the money paid to the men employed must be considered as paid for the benefit and assistance of all the commissioners; and, from the nature of the trust, the employment must be presumed to have been by the assent of all. It follows that Bartlet and Bostwick were interested in this part of the demand; for if the plaintiff succeeded, by their testimony, in recovering the disbursements, they thereby became exonerated. The commissioners proved a fact which they had a direct interest to establish. The law on this point is well settled. *Marquand* v. *Webb*, 16 Johns., 92; *Gage* v. *Stewart*, 4 *Id.*, 293; **Butler* v. *Warren*, 11 *Id.*, 57; [***216** *Emerton* v. *Andrews*, 4 Mass., 653.

I am of opinion that the verdict should be set aside, and a new trial granted, with costs to abide the event.

New trial granted.

Cited in—18 Wend., 497; 26 Barb., 351.

JACKSON, ex dem. TEED ET AL.,
v.
HALSTEAD.

Ejectment by Assignee of Lease—Estoppel—Adverse Possession—Grant of a River, does not Include the Soil or Islands.

One assigned a lease; and then took a reassignment, with certain exceptions, both the assignment and reassignment being indorsed on the lease, and afterwards assigned the whole; under which last assignment, the assignee claimed the whole, in ejectment, against one claiming, and in possession under the exception. On the plaintiff's producing the lease in evidence with the assignment and reassignment thus indorsed, the genuineness of the latter being established; held, that the assignment, when thus taken in connection with the reassignment, might be read without being proved by a subscribing witness; and that the one taking under the reassignment, which was in nature of a sub-lease, and all claiming under him, were estopped to question the genuineness of the assignment.

To constitute an adverse possession of land, not included in a grant of it, so as to avoid a conveyance by the real owner, there must be a *pedis possessio*, or substantial inclosure; but the inclosure need not be by an artificial fence, or other erection. A river, a mountain or continued ledge of rocks, &c., or other natural obstruction, sufficient to prevent the intrusion of cattle, is enough.

A grant of a river, *eo nomine*, will not pass the soil of the river, or an island within it.

If one grant *aquam suam*, the soil will not pass; but only the piscary within the water, according to Co. Litt., 4 *b*, and Com. Dig., Grant, E, 5.

Citations—3 Johns., 234; 10 Johns., 477; 1 Johns., 156; 1 Cow., 285; Co. Litt., 352; 4 Co., 53; Co. Litt., 4 *b*; Com. Dig., Grant, E, 5.

EJECTMENT, for part of farm No. 14, and a part of Delaware River, adjoining it, in lot No. 41, in the Hardenburgh patent, tried at the Delaware Circuit, June 7, 1824, before Walworth, *Circuit Judge.*

On the trial, the plaintiff deduced a title by a lease in fee dated Jan. 1, 1793, from one Desbroses to Ingersol, who assigned the lease to Levi Palmer, Nov. 4, 1801. This lease was of certain premises, described as beginning at the southerly side of the Delaware River, at a birch tree; and running several courses round certain land on the southerly side of the river, to the river, at a tree standing on the low lands, west from the place of beginning, "and thence easterly, up said river, as it winds and turns (including the same), to the place of beginning, containing 130 acres of land." Under these words, the plaintiff claimed a small island in the Delaware, opposite the shore, which was confessedly included; and proposed to show that the defendant was in possession of this Island; but the judge overruled the evidence.

Palmer was the common source under which both parties claimed title; and the plaintiff **217***] proved an assignment of *the lease from him (Palmer) to Jennings, dated Oct. 17, 1811, who devised one half of all his real estate to his wife in fee, and the other half to her for life, remainder over in fee. She intermarried with Teed, and they were both named as lessors of the plaintiff.

The defendant, in order to deduce a title from Palmer to himself, relied on an assignment indorsed upon the lease, dated Mar. 14, 1806, from Palmer to Ebenezer Bennett, being before the assignment to Jennings and a reassignment, also indorsed on the lease from Bennett to Palmer dated Feb. 12, 1807. This reassignment contained an exception of 8 acres and 17 rods, as sold by Bennett to Halstead, the defendant. The assignment to Bennett was not proved by the subscribing witness; and the plaintiff's counsel objected, on this ground, to its being read; but the judge held that, taken in connection with the reassignment, it was to be considered as in proof; and it was accordingly read.

The defendant then gave in evidence a sub-lease in fee from Bennett to himself, dated Apr. 7, 1806, for two small lots of land, parcel of the premises contained in the original lease, describing them particularly; but the description did not include a small strip of land lying immediately on the bank of the river, though it was intended to include this; and the defendant claimed to have possessed it adversely at the time of, and so as to avoid the assignment from Palmer to Jennings.

The circumstances constituting this adverse possession are stated at large in the opinion of the court, with such other particulars as, in connection with the above, will sufficiently elucidate the nature of the controversy, and render a further history here unnecessary.

The judge said he should charge that, as to the strip of land, a good adverse possession was made out; that the assignment to Jennings was, therefore, void *pro tanto;* that he had established a good title to the land described in the sub-lease; and that the Island did not pass to Ingersol by the words of the original lease; upon which, the plaintiff submitted to a nonsuit, with leave to move to set it aside.

Mr. S. Sherwood* now moved to set [*218** aside the nonsuit, upon the several grounds taken at the trial. As to the adverse possession relied on by the defendant, he cited *Jackson* v. *Camp*, 1 Cow., 609, 610.

Mr. Talcott, Atty-Gen., contra. To show that the descriptive words of the original lease, including the same, did not reach the land of the river and the island, he cited Co. Litt., 4 *b*, and Com. Dig., Grant, E, 5; and that the assignment from Palmer to Bennett was admissible in evidence without being proved by the subscribing witness, *Rex* v. *Inh. of Middlezoy*, 2 T. R., 43; *Pearce* v. *Hooper*, 3 Taunt., 62; *Betts* v. *Badger*, 12 Johns., 233, and *Jackson* v. *Kingsley*, 17 *Id.*, 158.

Mr. Sherwood, in reply, denied that the cases cited would warrant reading the assignment; though he should not insist so much upon this objection, as that the judge erred in excluding the Island from the original lease, and in holding that an adverse possession was established.

Curia, per WOODWORTH, *J.* The plaintiff made out a title to farm number 14, as described in the leases given by Desbroses to Ingersol, and claimed to recover of the defendant three certain parcels alleged to be in his possession; and described on the map annexed to the case as follows: one lot of 6 acres, adjoining the Delaware River; one lot of 2 acres, 17 rods, a strip of land lying between the north bounds of the last lot and the river; and also a small island, claimed as included within the bounds of the original lease.

The defendant claimed title from the same source. On the back of the lease produced by the plaintiff, was written an assignment from

Levi Palmer to Ebenezer Bennett, dated Mar. 14, 1806. The plaintiff objected to its introduction, unless proved by the subscribing witness. The judge admitted it without such proof; because there was a reassignment from Bennett to Palmer, of Feb. 12, 1807, also indorsed, which was not questioned. It is proper here to state that the reassignment from Ben- **219***] nett contained an *exception and reservation of 8 acres, 17 rods, being the two parcels first described. As between Bennet and Palmer, the acceptance of a conveyance by the the latter from the former, containing a reservation of part, was an admission of the right of Bennet to the portion excepted; and Palmer, being a sub-lessee, was estopped from alleging the contrary. Co. Litt., 352; *Rawlyns'* case, 4 Rep., 53. Besides, the acceptance of a reassignment, indorsed on the same paper that contained the assignment, seems to be an explicit acknowledgment of the authencity and genuineness of the latter. It is not, therefore, admissible that Palmer, or those claiming under him, be permitted to deny the execution. The judge was correct in receiving the evidence.

Oct. 17, 1811, Palmer conveyed to Jennings, the premises described in the original lease, without making any exception. The lessors of the plaintiff are the representatives of Jennings. They acquired no title to the 8 acres and 17 rods.

With respect to the island, the plaintiff's right depends on the expression in the original lease. The farm demised lies on the south side of and adjoining the river. The last course but one extends to the river; "thence up the said river as it winds and turns (including the same) to the place of beginning." The question is, what do these words grant? It is laid down in Co. Litt., 4 *b*, that "if a man grant *aquam suam*, the soil shall not pass; but the piscary within the water passeth therewith." The same rule is recognized in Com. Dig., Grant, E, 5. No right, then, to the Island was acquired; and all testimony, as to the defendant's possession of that part of the premises in question, was properly excluded.

The plaintiff is entitled to recover the small parcel of land lying between the 2 acres and 17 rods and the river; unless the deed from Palmer to Jennings is inoperative, in this respect, by reason of an adverse possession, at the time it was executed. The boundaries in the defendant's conveyance do not include this parcel. He cannot, therefore, rest on the ground of a good constructive possession; but must make out a *pedis possessio*, or actual oc- **220***] cupancy, with *claim of title. The adverse possession must be marked by a substantial inclosure, and continued down, to render it available. (2 Johns., 234; 10 *Id.*, 477; 1 *Id.*, 156; 1 Cow., 285.)

It appears, by the defendant's testimony, that a saw-mill and dam, formerly erected on the premises, have gone to decay. The commencement of the fence, near the flat stone designated on the map, is about one rod from the river, and leaves some ground not inclosed. But it is in proof that the fence, at this place, is as near to the river as the wash of the floods and the make of the ground will permit. To apply the rule so strictly as to require the fence to be placed on the very margin of the river, where it would be liable to be swept away by the rise of water, would be unnecessarily rigid, and not within the reason of the rule defining what shall constitute an adverse possession. It must be perfectly obvious that such a location is evidence of a claim to the water's edge. With respect to the residue of the fence, it appears to have been built as near to the river as the land would permit. There is no valid objection on this ground. The fence was not continued the whole extent to the upper corner. McGilvery says it was discontinued in some places, where the bank and the growth on it, of themselves, formed a sufficient obstruction to cattle; that the northerly line is a high bank, unfit for cultivation, and covered chiefly with hemlock. Kinney, the surveyor, says the upper corner of the lot was not inclosed.

From the whole of the evidence, I understand that the small parcel was inclosed by a fence on all sides, excepting on the northerly line, where it extended a part of the way only; and at that portion of the line where it did not continue, the high bank served as a substitute. For the purpose of notoriety, as well as good husbandry, this was a substantial inclosure. Why require a fence, where nature had formed a sufficient barrier, to prevent the intrusion of cattle? The defendant sufficiently marked the extent of his possession. Suppose a lot of land is bounded on the one side by a navigable river, or a continued ledge of rocks, or a mountain of difficult ascent or descent, and that the other sides are *well inclosed; [***221** would not this, with a claim of title, constitute an adverse possession? It certainly would, because, in such a case, everything had been done that could reasonably be required to proteet the crop, or denote exclusive occupancy. The case before us is analogous. The defendant's possession was adverse when Palmer assigned to Jennings, and so continued to the time of commencing the action.

The assignment, then, being in relation to this parcel void, the title never passed from Palmer; and, as he is not a lessor, the plaintiff cannot recover. Had there been a demise from him, the defendant's adverse possession would have been unavailing, as it falls short of 20 years.

I am of opinion that the motion to set aside the nonsuit be denied.

Motion denied.

Cited in—2 Wend., 524; 3 Barb., 367; 21 Barb., 482; 29 Barb., 324; 34 Barb., 532; 22 How. Pr., 215; 45 How. Pr., 367; 20 Wis., 432; 38 Am. Rep., 508 (84 N. Y., 215).

JACKSON, ex dem. HUNT ET AL.,
v.
LUQUERE.

Wills—Mere Efflux of Time Insufficient to Admit a Will Without Proof—But 30 Years Possession Under a Will Entitles it to be Read as an Ancient Will, Without Further Proof—Other Circumstances May Entitle it to be Thus Read—Construction of Words, "Equally Divided."

To prove the execution of a will, it is not enough to account for the absence of the three subscribing witnesses, and prove the handwriting of one only; but, under such circumstances, proof of the handwriting of all three of the witnesses, and that of the testator, would be proper to be left to the jury, from which to infer that the formalities required by the statute had been observed.

Mere efflux of time, as 30 years or more, from the date of a will, does not entitle it to be read without further proof.

But possession of 30 years, under a will, entitles it to be read as an ancient will, without further proof, the same as a deed; and it seems that it is not necessary to show that all the devisees were thus in possession under the will, but the possession of a part under it is sufficient.

A possession of part under the will, for less than thirty years, accompanied with proof satisfactorily accounting for the absence of all the subscribing witnesses, as where they are dead; and proof of the handwriting of one, and the acts of the devisees of the land in question—as possessing it, claiming under the will, and executing deeds of partition reciting the will, and the like; are also sufficient to entitle it to be read in evidence, without further proof.

Under a devise of land to two daughters, "to be equally divided between them, share and share alike, and to be to them for and during their natural life; and after their death, then to be to their, and each of their children; and to be divided between them, share and share alike;" held, that this conveyed a mere tenancy in common for life to the two daughters, without the power to make partition binding upon, or in the least affecting their respective children.

Held, also, that, on the death of one, the other surviving, the remainder, in an equal undivided moiety of the whole land devised, vested in possession in the children of the former *per stirpes*, and not *per capita*; and that immediately, without waiting for the death of the survivor.

The words "equally to be divided," in wills or deeds, go to the quality, not the limitation of the estate.

Citations—Phil. Ev., 383; Com., 531; 4 T. R., 709; 9 Ves., 5; 2 East, 183; 3 Johns. Cas., 283; 3 T. R., 85; 1 P. Wms., 14; 1 Atk., 493, 494; 2 Atk., 122; 3 Atk., 525, 731; 1 Ves., 115; 2 Ves., 252, 257; Willes, 341; 1 Salk., 391, 392; 2 Bl. Com., 122, 169, 193; Co. Litt., 198 *b*, sec. 318; Cro. Eliz., 718; 5 Bac., 699, 862; 1 Co., 62; Poph., 6; 31 Hen. VIII., ch. 1; 32 Hen. VIII., ch. 32; Act, Feb. 6, 1788; 2 Greenl. Laws N. Y., 13.

EJECTMENT for land in Brooklyn, Kings Co., tried at the circuit in that Co., May 30, 1822, before Woodworth, *J.*

222*] *The lessors of the plaintiff, Elizabeth, wife of T. Hunt, and Sarah Colwell, are the granddaughters of Aert Middagh, by Margaretta, one of his daughters, and claimed under the will of their grandfather Middagh, dated Jan. 7, 1777, by which he devised certain land, including the premises in question, to his "two daughters, Margaretta and Magdalena, to be equally divided between them, share and share alike; and to be to them, for and during their natural life; and after their death, then to be to their, and each of their children; and to be divided between them, share and share alike." This will contained various other devises to different persons; among which was one of a small piece of land to the devisor's son John. The will was dated Jan. 7, 1777. The devisor was seised in fee of the land devised, and died during the Revolutionary War, leaving his daughters, Margaretta and Magdalena—the former having died lately, and Magdalena still surviving.

The plaintiff having proved the above facts on the trial, except the execution of the will, in order to show this, he proved the death and handwriting of Wyckoff, one of the subscribing witnesses; and that Patience Titus, the second witness, was dead, and that J Crawley, the third, went to England about 30 years ago, was reputed to have died there, and had not been heard of since. He followed this evidence with an exemplification of the probate of the will under the official seal, and a certificate of the surrogate of the City and County of N. Y., dated May 28, 1822.

The defendant's counsel admitted that the paper purporting to be Aert Middagh's will, was procured from the surrogate, but objected to either the will or exemplification being read in evidence. The judge rejected the paper purporting to be the original will, but allowed the exemplification to be read.

The plaintiff also proved that the devisor's son John entered into the part devised to him after the devisor's death.

The defendant then offered in evidence a deed of partition reciting the will, dated Oct. 18, 1793, between Margaretta and Magdalena, by which the premises in question were conveyed by the former to the latter in severalty.

*The plaintiff's counsel objected to [***223** this deed as evidence, on the ground that the plaintiff did not claim title under Margaretta: but the judge allowed it to be read, subject to the objection of the counsel, and charged the jury that it was a good defense to the action. The jury found for the defendant.

The additional facts, necessary to understand the points decided, will be found stated in the opinion of the court.

Mr. T. A. Emmet, for the defendant, moved for a new trial, principally on the grounds, 1. That the paper produced on the trial, and purporting to be the original will, should have been read; and 2. That the deed of partition was improperly admitted in evidence, the rights of the lessors of the plaintiff not being affected by it.

That the original will was sufficiently proved, he cited 4 T. R., 709, *note; Jackson* v. *Laroway*, 3 Johns. Cas., 283; *M'Kenire* v. *Frazer*, 9 Ves., 5; *Milward* v. *Temple*, 1 Campb., 375; 1 Phil. Ev., 403, 404, 420; *Jackson* v. *Burton*, 11 Johns., 64, and 1 R. L., 368, sec. 21.

That the lessors of the plaintiff took as purchasers, on the death of Margaretta and, therefore, that the deed of partition was improperly admitted in evidence, it not being binding on them, &c., he cited *Salisbury's* case, 2 Vent., 365; *Hamell* v. *Hunt*, Prec. in Ch., 163, 164; *Ward* v. *Everard*, 1 Salk., 391; *Fisher* v. *Wigg*, 1 P. Wms., 14; S. C., 5 Cruise Dig., 455, 458; *Rancliffe* v. *Parkins*, 6 Dow, 149.

Messrs. D. B. Ogden and *S. Jones*, contra, cited *Hay* v. *Earl of Coventry*, 3 T. R., 83, 85, &c., per Ld. Kenyon, *Ch. J.*, and 9 Ves., 5, *notes* 1 and 2 to the Am. ed., and the cases there referred to.

Curia, per WOODWORTH, *J.* At the trial, the plaintiff proved the handwriting of Cornelius Wyckoff, one of the subscribing witnesses, and his death; that another witness had been dead many years; and that the third went to England about thirty years ago, and had not been heard of since. There was no evidence offered to prove the handwriting of the testator, or that of Patience Titus, or John Crawley. This *evidence, *per se*, is [***225** not sufficient to prove the execution of the will. It is necessary, in every case, to establish the fact that the testator executed in the presence of three witnesses; or, in cases where such proof does not exist, to give other evidence from which it may be presumed. This may be done by calling one or more of the witnesses, to prove the execution agreeably to the statute; or, if the witnesses are dead, proof of their handwriting, and that of the testator, is proper to be left to the jury, upon the question whether, under such circumstances, it may not be presumed that the formalities of the statute were observed. (Phil. Ev., 383.) It is decided in *Hands* v. *James*, Com., 531, that when three witnesses have set their names, it must be intended they did it regularly. If, however (the witnesses being all dead), the handwriting of one or two of them is established, it raises no other presumption but that so far as related to their attestation, the will was well executed. They may have subscribed their name in the presence of the testator and the other witnesses; but the testator may have acknowledged his signing to the witnesses separately. It seems, therefore, to follow, that nothing short of proving the handwriting of all will be sufficient. Proof of the handwriting of one witness raises no presumption that either of the others subscribed his name. Cases arising on other instruments do not decide the case of a will. There it is enough if the party executed, but here he must execute in a particular manner or his will is utterly void.

The mere efflux of time has never, I apprehend, been adjudged sufficient to admit a will to be read without proof. The note to *Doe* v. *Brabant*, 4 T. R., 709, is very short and unsatisfactory. It is said that the Master of the Rolls had decided that a will above 30 years years old should be read without proof. I do not find that this doctrine is supported by the cases, and therefore think it can only be correct when the antiquity of the instrument is connected with possession or other circumstances. A doctrine repugnant to this, and resting merely on the existence of the instrument for more than 30 years, has never been **225***] judicially recognized in this *State; and, if introduced, would be an experiment of very dangerous tendency.

The case of *M'Kenire* v. *Fraser*, 9 Ves., 5, was relied on. Upon examination, it is far from being satisfactory. The handwriting of two of the witnesses was proved, and no account could be given of the third. The will being above 30 years old, and the testator having been dead for twenty years, an objection was made to the proof of the will. The Master of the Rolls said he could not see any distinction in this respect, between a will and a deed, except that the former, not having effect till the death, wants a kind of authentication which the other has; that is, from the nature of the subject; "but, in this case," he added, "I think the proof sufficient; for, in a late case, in the Court of K. B., *Cunliff* v. *Sefton*, 2 East, 183, inquiry of the same kind was held sufficient." The case referred to in 2 East was an action on a bond, attested by two subscribing witnesses; and, after diligent inquiry, no account could be obtained of one of them. Proof was then received of the handwriting of the other witness, one of the plaintiffs. If the rule applied, in the present case, there was this defect: here the witnesses were known; they are now dead; no attempt was made to prove the handwriting of two of the witnesses. There was then a want of diligence. Where a witness cannot be found, nor any account of him obtained, nothing more can be done but when he is ascertained, and the reason of his non-production is satisfactory, then not only due diligence, but the rule that the best evidence that the case admits of shall be adduced, demands the proof of his handwriting if practicable.

The case of *Jackson* v. *Laroway*, 3 Johns., Cas., 283, decides that a will concerning real property may, under certain circumstances, be given in evidence, as an ancient deed; and it is laid down as a general rule, that a deed appearing to be of the age of thirty years, may be given in evidence without proof of its execution, if possession be shown to have accompanied it; and where no possession has accompanied it, if such account be given of the deed as may be reasonably expected, under all the circumstances, of the case, *and will [***226** afford the presumption that it is genuine. The rule is founded on the necessity of admitting other proof, as a substitute for the production of witnesses, who cannot be supposed any longer to exist. Where no possession appears, other circumstances are admitted to account for it, and raise a legal presumption in its favor. In that case, the admission of the will of Leonard Lewis was on the latter ground; for there had been no actual possession under it by the plaintiff. It is true that the peculiar situation of the property afforded an explanation of the want of possession. Yet, had possession under the will been deemed the only test, it is manifest that the court would not have allowed the will to be read. The decision, then, is put, not on the ground of possession, but other facts proven, which raised the presumption that it was genuine. These appear to have been the indorsements on it, and proof of the handwriting of the clerks and one of the judges who certified. They were not received as proof of the due execution of the will, but with a view to show the antiquity of the instrument, and that it existed at the periods when these certificates bear date. The law of this case has never been overruled and, so far as applicable, must govern the present.

The paper offered as the will of Aert Middagh bears date January 7, 1777. By it, he devised his property to his five children, in different proportions.

I will first examine how stands the question of possession under the will. The testator devised to his son John one acre and a half of land, joining to the south side of his land and the remainder, which joined the acre and a half, he devised to his daughters, Margaretta and Magdalena.

By the evidence stated in the case, it appears that John Middagh owned a house and lot in his father's lifetime, and never claimed more; and that the acre and a half devised, adjoined his house and lot on the south; that Aert Middagh died possessed of all the property described in the map made by Jeremiah Lot, and annexed to the case, except the lot where John Middagh's house stood. John Read testified that he never heard or knew that John Middagh exercised any control over any part of the land south of his lot, until *after his father's [***227** death, when he built four houses, next to each other, on the ground south of the place, where his own house stood. I think the possession thus taken by John Middagh, after his father's death, must be considered as taken under the will; for he disclaimed any right previously. It is not stated when his possession commenced, or when the houses were built, but it may be inferred that it was soon after his father's death. There is no evidence to show how long this possession continued. If it had been for 30 years, that fact would have been sufficient to admit the will to be read.

I consider, then, the evidence thus far as establishing the proposition that a possession under the will, in one of the devisees, is made out.

It cannot, I think, be shown, that under the rule of 30 years possession, is meant that where there are ten devisees of separate parcels of a testator's estate, to ten individuals, a possession in each devisee of more than 30 years, must be made out, before the will can be read as an ancient will.(a) When Margaretta and Magdalena entered on the premises under the will, does not appear; but the deed from the former to the latter, dated Oct. 10, 1793, is satisfactory evidence that it was as early as that day. This was nearly 30 years previous to the trial. I admit it is short of the period entitling a party to rest on length of possession; yet it is a circumstance connected with the other proofs, going to support the presumption of the antiquity and genuineness of the will. I cannot forbear remarking, it is matter of surprise that evidence more full and conclusive, as to the holding and length of possession under the will, by the different devisees, had not been laid before the court. I incline, however, to think that enough is shown to warrant the reading of it in evidence. My opinion is not founded on a possession of 30 years under the will; for to that extent it is not made out; but on the other alternative, that there are circumstances which raise the presumption that it is genuine. They are the following: The handwriting of one of the subscribing witnesses, long since dead, is sat-
228*] isfactorily *proved. The evidence of the possession of John Middagh, and the acts of Margaretta and Magdalena, tend to show the antiquity of the instrument, and its probable authenticity, as fully as they were shown in *Jackson* v. *Laroway*. I am, therefore, of opinion that, according to the doctrine laid down in that case, the will ought to be received in evidence on the footing of an ancient deed.

The next question is, whether the rights of the plaintiff are affected by the partition between Margaretta and Magdalena. This will depend on the construction of the words in the will: "I give unto my other two daughters, Margaretta and Magdalena, the remainder of my land which joins the acre and a half, to be equally divided between them, share and share alike; and to be to them for and during their natural life; and after their death, then to be to their and each of their children; and to be divided between them share and share alike." In the construction of wills, I adhere to the rule laid down by Ld. Kenyon, in *Hay* v. *Earl of Coventry*, 3 T. R., 85. "The general rule which is laid down in the books, and on which courts alone can, with any safety, proceed in the decision of questions of this kind, is to collect the testator's intention from the words which he has used in his will; and not from conjecture. It is not necessary that any technical or artificial form of words should be used in a will; but we must collect the meaning of the testator from the words which he has used; and cannot add words which he has not used." Whenever words have received a judicial determination, the security of titles requires that such construction be adhered to. The words "equally to be divided," in wills, go to the quality of the estate, and not to the limitation of it. They create a tenancy in common. So, also, in deeds, which receive their operation from the Statute of Uses; but not in common law conveyances. (1 P. Wms., 14; 1 Atk., 493, 494; 2 Atk., 122; 3 Atk., 525, 731; 1 Ves., 115; 2 Ves., 252, 257; Willes, 341; 1 Salk., 391, 392.)

If the construction put on these words be correct, then, it follows, that Margaretta and Magdalena, being tenants in common for life, had no other power or control over the property devised than is given by law to persons holding *such estates. They cannot claim [***229** that the words "equally to be divided" are directory as to a partition. The testator meant nothing more than the signification which the law attaches to those words. If, however, they are considered as directory, that partition be made between the tenants in common, I perceive no cause for believing that the testator intended that those in remainder should be affected by the acts of the tenants for life. I cannot suppose that, in that event, he had anything more in view than that Margaretta and Magdalena should divide the premises for and during their lives, so that each might have a separate possession. It is highly improbable that the testator intended to sanction the division to be made between the daughters as binding on their children. A division by consent might have been very unequal, at the time when it would be made. Circumstances may have greatly changed the relative value, at the decease of either of the tenants for life, when the children of the deceased tenant would, in my opinion, become entitled to their share. Why should the property devised to them be accepted, thus fettered and impaired in value, by the act of the tenant for life? I cannot assign a motive, to induce the testator so to subject the property devised to his grandchildren. They were equally objects of his bounty. The power now claimed, as derived from the will, was not necessary for the beneficial enjoyment by the daughters. It was enough for them to divide for themselves, so long as their estates continued. I cannot, therefore, construe these words as implying an intent that a division made by the testator's daughters should be binding and conclusive on their children.

But it is contended that if no power was given to divide, so as to effect those in remainder, then the children of the daughters would take *per capita*, so that if Margaretta had one child, and Magdalena ten, they would take equally. I think this is a mistaken view of the devise. The latter clause is, "and after their death, then to be to their, and each of their children, and to be divided between them share and share alike." The argument supposes that, by

(a) *Vide* Jackson v. Davis, *ante*, 123, S. P. as to a deed.

denying the power of the tenant for life to 230*] bind those in remainder, the *devise is to receive such construction; and further, that as long as either of the daughters are alive, the grandchildren can take nothing. I consider the will as giving a tenancy in common, for life, to each of the daughters, with no other powers than such as are incident to that estate; and the words, "after their death," are to be understood, that upon the death of either, the quantity or portion of the estate of which the daughter, so dying was seised as a tenant in common for life, became vested in her children, as tenants in common in fee.

What, then, were the powers of the daughters, as to a partition? As a general proposition, it may be laid down that partition, so as to affect the inheritance, is not one of the incidents to a tenancy for life. (2 Bl. Com., 122.) The estate devised to the grandchildren is a vested remainder, though to be enjoyed *in futuro*, which nothing can defeat or set aside. (2 Bl. Com., 169.) It would, therefore, seem to be inconsistent with the nature of the estate, to turn that, which was a tenancy in common in all the land devised to Margaretta and Magdalena, to a tenancy in common in the divided share of the tenant for life.

Tenants in common are compellable, by statute, to make partition; which they were not, at common law. (2 Bl. Com., 193; Co. Litt., 198 *b*, sec. 318.) The partition between Margaretta and Magdalena, was voluntary, and undoubtedly valid as between themselves; but its operation was necessarily limited by the power incident to an estate for life, by the common law. The law is correctly laid down in *Pledgard* v. *Lake*, Cro. Eliz., 718; 5 Bac., 862. The case was this: A, tenant for life, remainder to B, in tail; he, in remainder, lets for years, to begin after the death of tenant for life; the tenant for life afterwards suffers a recovery, with voucher of him in remainder in tail, and dies. It was held that the lease shall take place; for the lessee may falsify the recovery, either by the common law or statutes; for the tenant for life hath no power to bar him in remainder, without his assent or concurrence, as the tenant in tail in possession hath. (1 Co., 62; Poph., 6.) The principle of this case applies to the one before us. The tenant for life had no power 231*] *to change or alter the tenancy in common, which those in remainder held in the premises devised to Margaretta and Magdalena. A partition does not change the claim, by confining it to a divided parcel. The partition was not made in pursuance of any statute; nor was it sanctioned by consent of those in remainder. In England, by the Statute 31 Hen. VIII., ch. 1, joint tenants, and tenants in common, of estates of inheritance, were compellable to make partition. The 32 Hen. VIII., ch. 32, gave the like remedy to joint tenants and tenants in common, for life or years. (5 Bac., 699.)

The Act of Feb. 6, 1788, to compel joint tenants and tenants in common to make partition (2 Greenl., ed. L. N.Y., 13), contains substantially the same provisions. The 2d section of this Act declares that tenants in common for life, and where one has an estate with others that have estates of inheritance or freehold, may be compelled to make partition; but that no such partition shall be prejudicial to persons, other than such as be parties to the same. The tenants for life could not, by their individual act, prejudiee the rights of the lessors of the plaintiff.

I am, on the whole, of opinion that a new trial be granted, with costs to abide the event.

New trial granted.

Criticised—17 Wend., 126.

Cited in—5 Cow., 374; 1 Wend., 413; 7 Wend., 374; 11 Wend., 602; 4 Den., 214; 4 N. Y., 63; 5 N. Y., 134; 62 N. Y., 552; 1 Keyes, 268; 2 Abb. App. Dec., 36; 1 Barb., 108; 2 Barb., 131; 6 Barb., 115; 11 Barb., 539; 45 Barb., 451; 33 How. Pr., 488; 30 How. Pr., 235; 17 Abb. Pr., 133; 10 Bos., 119; 1 Bradf., 293; Tuck., 419, 442; 63 How. Pr., 313.

WHEELER *v.* RAYMOND.

1. *Set-Off — Action on a Judgment, in Name of Judgment Creditor, for Benefit of Assignee— Defendant cannot Set-Off Debt Due from Assignee.* 2. *Pleading.*

In an action on a judgment, in the name of a judgment creditor, for the benefit of an assignee of the judgment, the defendant cannot set off a debt due to him from the assignee.

It seems that a plea of set-off is inadmissible under our Statute, 1 R. L., 515; but the defendant can avail himself of it by notice only, with the general issue.

Whether a notice of set-off is available with the plea of *nul tiel record*, to a declaration in debt on judgment, *quære.*

In an action by one in his own name, for a debt due to him in trust for another, the defendant cannot set off a demand against the *cestui que trust.*

Where W. assigned a judgment to L. and K., who gave notice to the debtor, and then assigned to R., who assigned to another, notice of the last two assignments not being given to the debtor; in debt on this judgment by the last assignee, in the name of W.; held, that the debtor could not set off a demand due to him from R, while the latter owned the judgment.

Citations—8 Johns., 152; 1 R. L., 515; Stats. 2 and 8, Geo. II.; 3 Johns., 263; 1 T. R., 623, 621, 2; 10 John., 396; 13 Johns., 22.

ON demurrer to the rejoinder. The declaration was in debt on a judgment of this court in January Term, 1820, for $1,039.30.

*Plea, that Sept. 18, 1820, the plaint- [*232 iff, by an instrument in writing, sealed, and set forth by the plea, *in hæc verba*, acknowledged to have been fully satisfied for all claims or demands he had against the defendant, by virtue of the judgment, and consented on his, (the plaintiff's) part, that the sheriff should discharge the defendant from imprisonment.

Replication, as to parcel of the judgment, viz.: as to $189.84, and $353.50—$543.34; that after the judgment was recovered, and before this suit was commenced, viz.: Feb. 1, 1820, the plaintiff assigned the $189.84 to Samuel Lush, whereof the defendant, on the same day, had notice; and that Lush, Feb. 6, 1820, before this suit was commenced, assigned that portion of the judgment to Jonathan Roberts; and further, that Feb. 1, 1820, and before this suit was commenced, the plaintiff as signed to Elias Kane, $353,50, other parcel of the judgment, whereof the defendant, on the same day, had notice; and that Kane, before this suit was commenced, viz.: Feb. 7, 1822, assigned the $353.50 to Jonathan Roberts; and the whole $543.34, part of the judgment, being thus vested in Roberts, that he (Roberts), before this suit was commenced, to wit: Aug. 25, 1822, assigned the $543.34 to Jonathan E. Robinson; and that this suit was commenced, and is prosecuted for his benefit. No notice to the defendant of the assignment to Roberts or Robinson was averred; and as to the residue, not assigned, the plaintiff entered a *nolle prosequi.*

Rejoinder, that Jonathan Roberts, before the exhibiting of the bill of the plaintiff in this behalf, to wit: Feb. 7, 1822, was indebted to the defendant in $3,000, for the work, &c., for goods, &c., and for money, &c. (to the usual effect of a general notice of set-off), and that the defendant was willing to set off so much of the debt due to him, as should amount to the sum claimed by the plaintiff, in behalf of the assignee.

General demurrer and joinder.

233*] **Mr. W. H. Maynard*, in support of the demurrer.

Mr. E. Cowen, contra.

Curia, per WOODWORTH, *J.* The questions presented by the demurrer are:

1. Whether, in a court of law, a set-off can be allowed against a *cestui que trust*, in an action commenced by the trustee; and,

2. If it can, whether the form of pleading is not confined to the general issue, with notice.

The general doctrine, that the rights of an assignee of a chose in action will be protected, and that the court will look to the parties in interest, is well established. This, however, must be understood as applicable to cases where the principle may be enforced, without departing from the forms of proceeding in a court of law. In *Tuttle* v. *Beebe*, 8 Johns., 152, the defendant was permitted to set off two bonds executed by the plaintiff to third persons, and by him assigned to the defendant. In this case, the Statute for the Amendment of the Law, 1 R. L., 515, interposed no impediment; for the plaintiff on the record was the debtor, and the person liable to pay the money on the bonds assigned. A different case is presented, when the set-off relied on is not against the plaintiff, but the *cestui que trust.*

The question, then, is, has the Statute provided for such a case. If it has not, it will not be pretended that the defense is valid at law. The Act has reference to persons dealing together, or being indebted, and having demands against each other. In such cases, when one sues the other, a set-off is allowed. But can it be said that a set-off against a *cestui que trust* will satisfy these words? The plaintiff on the record is a stranger to the set-off. It is not a demand against him; and seems not to be within the provisions of the Act. I admit that the statute should be construed liberally; but that will not justify the court in extending it to cases not foreseen when it passed and, perhaps, on that account, not provided for. Ours is substantially the same as the English Statute, 2 and 8 Geo. II.; ex- **234***] cept that, by the *latter, the set-off may be pleaded in bar, or given in evidence under the general issue; and no provision is made for the recovery of the defendant's demand, when it exceeds the plaintiff's. By our statute the defendant is allowed to plead the general issue only, with notice; and if it appears that the plaintiff is over paid, then the jury shall find a verdict for the defendant, and certify to the court how much they find the plaintiff indebted to him, more than the sum demanded; and the defendant shall have judgment and execution for the balance.

This part of the statute plainly shows that the set-off must be against the plaintiff on the record; for, in all the cases where a set-off is permitted, the right is expressly given; and the jury are required to certify the balance due to the defendant. The court have no authority to restrict the plain words of the Act; and decide that, in certain cases, a defendant may have judgment and execution for the sum certified; but in others, like the present, so much only shall be set off, as will satisfy the plaintiff's demand. The court have no such dispensing power; and, as it is a conceded point that no balance can be certified, judgment entered, or execution issued against Wheeler, the plaintiff, for money that Roberts may be in arrear to the defendant, I have no hesitation in saying the case is not provided for by the Act.

In *Ruggles* v. *Keeler*, 3 Johns., 263, the defendant in the court below proved that the note had been sold to Walker Lewis; and offered to prove as a set off, that Lewis was indebted to the defendant. This was objected to, on the ground that it was more than six years since a right of action accrued to the defendant. The evidence was excluded. On a writ of error, the judgment was reversed. This court held, that the defendants may set off demands against the plaintiff, arising when both parties resided in Conn., and which, if sued for there, would be barred by the Statute of Limitations in that State, provided six years had not elapsed since the plaintiff came into this State. The question, whether a set-off against Lewis was admissible, allowing the demand not to be barred, was never raised by the counsel, *nor [***235** considered by the court. It is not, therefore, an authority on the point before us.

The English Statute may be satisfied by allowing a set off against a *cestui que trust*, of so much of a debt due from him to a defendant, as will satisfy the plaintiff's demand. On this ground, I apprehend, the court enforced the right of an assignee of a chose in action, against the *cestui que trust*, in the case of *Bottomley* v. *Brooke*, referred to by Ashurst, *J.*, in *Winch* v. *Keeley*, 1 T. R., 623. The defendant pleaded that the bond was given for securing money lent to him by Mrs. Chancellor, and was given by her direction to the plaintiff, in trust for her; and that Mrs. Chancellor, before the action brought, was indebted to the defendant in more money than the amount of the bond. To this plea there was a demurrer, which was withdrawn by the advice of the court. *Vide* 1 T. R., 621, 2, Lawrence *arguendo*. They did not look to the plaintiff, on the record; but to the person beneficially interested. It is evident the court considered the statute as placing no impediment in the way of the defense. But our statute gives right to a defendant, who interposes a set-off, which cannot be exercised against the *cestui que trust;* and, consequently, it cannot be extended to such a case.

The case of *Alsop* v. *Caines*, 10 Johns., 396, is in point. The defendant pleaded a set-off against Riley; in action by Alsop and others, and averred that Riley was the person beneficially interested; that he, by the plaintiff, sold the goods to the defendant; and that Brannan, one of the plaintiffs, by the direction of Riley, assigned the demand to Fairchild. It was held that a court of law could not recognize and settle such interfering and complicated trusts; and that the statute allowing set-offs did not apply to the case; inasmuch as the defendant could not have judgment and execution against the plaintiff for any balance due from him. It was also held that the defendant, instead of pleading the set-off in bar, ought to have pleaded the general issue, and given notice of the set-off, according to the directions of the Act. The judgment in that cause was afterwards affirmed in the Court of Errors. (13 Johns., 22.) Cantine, *Senator*, was **236***] *of opinion that the defendant might avail himself of the right of set-off, though not by special plea; but admitting the plea to be good, he considered the replication good also. Sanford, *Senator*, was of opinion that whether the plea was good or bad, the replication was sufficient. No other opinions were delivered. It is manifest that the doctrine laid down in the court below was not overruled—at least, there is no evidence of the fact to be collected from the report; for both the Senators, who delivered opinions, concurring that the replication was good, it may be presumed the judgment was affirmed on that ground. Had no other opinion been delivered than that of Mr. Cantine, it could not be ascertained that a single member of the court considered the defense available in any shape. The decision of that point did not become necessary, according to the view taken. The plea of set-off in bar was considered bad by the court below, as not being authorized by the statute. The decision on error may have turned on this; but whether it did or not, it cannot be collected that the doctrine of the Supreme Court was overruled.

I am, on the whole, of opinion that the defense is not available at law.

It becomes unnecessary to consider whether a defendant may interpose a plea of set-off, when the action is commenced on a judgment, on the ground that the general issue, in such case, being *nul tiel record*, there cannot be a trial by jury. The defense not being available by any form of pleading, the plaintiff is entitled to judgment on the demurrer.

Judgment for the plaintiff.

Affirmed—9 Cow., 295.
Cited in—6 Cow., 694; 7 Cow., 452; 9 Cow., 299; 3 Wend., 18, 402; 5 Wend., 350; 7 Wend., 226; 1 Hill, 554; 1 Page, 112; 39 Am. Dec., 300 (1 Pinn., 226; 1 Burr., 65).

237*] *JACKSON, ex dem. BOGERT ET AL.,
v.
KING.

*Evidence—Registers of Births, &c., Competent to Prove Pedigree—Hearsay, Showing General Reputation, Admissible for Same Purpose—Proof of Identity—*Prima Facie *Evidence that Patentee of Land and Ancestor Were Same Person.*

The general rule is, that registers of births, marriages and burials are competent evidence, on a trial, to prove a pedigree; and when the original is of a public nature (*e. g.*, the records of the Reformed Dutch Church in the City of N. Y), a sworn copy is admissible.

Hearsay in the family, and among relations, tradition, and any thing which shows a general reputation, is also admissible to establish a pedigree.

Producing letters patent to one, and then tracing a descent from one of the same name, are, *prima facie*, evidence that the patentee and ancestor are the same person; and it lies with the defendant to rebut this, by showing another of corresponding name, age, &c., or in some other way.

The nature and force of evidence derived from a register of births, marriages, &c., in establishing a pedigree; and what is sufficient, connected with proof of search in the register, its dates, and other evidence as to the family, to require the question of pedigree to be submitted to a jury, and *prima facie*, sufficient to establish it.

Proof of identity, either of the plaintiff or defendant, with one named in the contract, &c., proved, is never necessary in the first instance. Producing the contract, bearing the same name with the party in the suit, is, *prima facie*, sufficient; and throws it upon the other party to produce evidence against the identity.

Citations—Peak., 9; Cowp., 591; 3 T. R., 723; 8 Johns., 128; 15 Johns., 226; 13 Johns., 518; 1 Campb., 196; 4 Campb., 34.

EJECTMENT for land in Halfmoon, in the County of Saratoga, tried at the circuit in that county June 9, 1824, before Nelson, *Circuit Judge.*

On the trial, it appeared that the defendant, and those under whom he claimed had possessed the land for 30 or 40 years, but no adverse possession was made out; and the main question was, whether certain testimony, which will be found stated at large in the opinion of the court, was admissible to establish the pedigree of the lessors of the plaintiff. Certain parts of the evidence were objected to as inadmissible, by the defendants' counsel. They were, however, received by the judge; but on hearing the whole of the testimony which the plaintiff produced, he directed a nonsuit, on the ground that William Appel, from whom the plaintiff claimed to derive title, was not sufficiently indentified with the one of the same name in the patent under which they claimed. The case at bar, therefore, involved the two questions, whether the testimony was competent to show pedigree; and, also, whether there there was sufficient to go to the jury upon the identity of the patentee.

The whole is so fully stated by the court, that it need not be farther noticed here.

Mr. J. L. Wendell, for the defendant, moved to set aside the nonsuit, and for a new trial; and he cited *Jackson* v. *Goes*, 13 Johns., 518, 523; *Daniel* v. *North*, 11 East, 372; *Jackson* v. *Boneham*, 15 Johns., 226, 228; *Berkeley Peerage* *case, 4 Campb., 401, 409; 1 Phil. [***238** Ev., 186; *Rich* v. *Johnson*, 2 Str., 1142.

NOTE.—*Evidence of pedigree.*

Family records, church registers, registers of births, marriages and deaths, &c., are competent to prove pedigree. Jackson v. Cooley, 8 Johns., 128; Jackson v. Browner, 18 Johns., 37; Russell v. Jackson, 22 Wend., 277; People v. Fulton Fire Ins. Co., 25 Wend., 205; Canjolle v. Ferrie, 26 Barb., 177; 23 N. Y., 90; Arms v. Middleton, 23 Barb., 571; Hunt v. Johnson, 19 N. Y., 279; Greenwood v. City of New Orleans, 12 La. Ann., 426; Barry v. Waring, 2 Har. & G., 103; Kennedy v. Doyle, 92 Mass. (10 Allen), 161; Ryerson v. Grover, 1 N. J. L., 458; Clark v. Trinity Church, 5 Watts. & S. 266; Collins v. Grantham, 12 Ind., 440; Wiseman v. Cornish, 8 Jones (N. C.) L., 218; Clara v. Ewell, 2 Cr. C. C., 208, Lewis v. Marshall, 5 Pet., 469; Blackburn v. Crawford, 3 Wall., 175.

Contra, when recent, and the party who made them is in court or can be produced. Leggett v. Boyd, 3 Wend., 376; Kobbe v. Price, 14 Hun, 55; Curtis v. Patton, 6 Serg. & R., 135; Campbell v. Wilson, 23 Tex., 252. See, generally, Greenl. Ev., Vol.I., secs. 103-105, notes and authorities there cited.

Messrs. G. W. Kirtland and *S. G. Huntington*, contra, cited 1 Phil. Ev., 321, 325, 326; Adams on Eject., 55, 56, 252, 253; 2 Bl. Com., 209; Peak. Ev.; 309, 310, 355; Pow. on Dev., 184; Rob. on Wills, 297; 11 Mod., 128; 8 East, 566; 2 Phil. Ev., 188; 15 East, 294, *note a*; 5 Burr., 2604; 1 Cai., 84; Cowp., 217; 1 Campb., 196; 4 Campb., 34; Woodf. L. & T., 489; 2 W. Bl., 1099; 3 Johns. Cas., 109, 118; 10 Johns., 377; Cowp., 102; 2 Johns., 573.

Curia, per WOODWORTH, *J.* Sept. 10, 1708, a patent was granted to William Appel, including the premises in question. The lessors of the plaintiff claim to be his heirs at law.

At the trial, a sworn copy of certain entries of baptisms and marriages, in the records of the Reformed Protestant Dutch Church in the City of N. Y., was given in evidence, to prove the pedigree of the lessors of the plaintiff; by which it appeared, that May 26, 1695, one William Appel and his wife had a son baptized by the name of Simon; that in 1719, Magdalena, and Sept. 24, 1721, Gertruig, daughters of Simon Appel, were also baptized; and that Aug. 25, 1743, Magdalena Appel was married to Abraham Pelts.

In almost all the books, which treat on the subject of evidence, it is laid down that the register of births, marriages and burials is competent evidence; and wherever an original is of a public nature, and admissible in evidence, an examined copy will equally be admitted. (Phil., 320, 306; Peake, 86; Bull. *N. P.*, 247.) This rule is necessary, as well for the security of the instrument as for the convenience of the public. In addition to this, the hearsay evidence of pedigree was competent, and, of itself, sufficient.

Baron Gilbert, in his treatise on Evidence, 112, lays down the rule, that hearsay is good evidence to prove who is the grandfather, when he married, what children he had; of which **239***] *it is not reasonable to suppose the party has better evidence.

Bogert testified that, from conversation in his family and among his relations, from his infancy, he always understood and had been informed that Magdalena Pelts was the daughter of one Simon Appel, and that Simon was the oldest son of one William Appel. Testimony as to pedigree is not to be tested by the ordinary rules of evidence. It forms an exception to the general rule. Hence it is, that anything which shows a general reputation is admissible to establish it. (Peake, 9.) In Cowp., 591, *Goodright* v. *Moss*, Ld. *Mansfield* held that tradition is sufficient in point of pedigree. Ld. *Kenyon* observed, in the case of *King* v. *Inh. of Eriswell*, 3 T. R., 723: "I admit that declarations of the members of a family, and perhaps of others living in habits of intimacy with them, are received in evidence as to pedigrees; but evidence of what a mere stranger has said, has ever been rejected in such cases." This doctrine was also sanctioned by this court, in *Jackson* v. *Cooley*, 8 Johns., 128. In *Jackson* v. *Boneham*, 15 Johns., 226, a sworn copy of the records of the Town of Stonington, which contained the date of the marriage of the parents of the lessors, and the time of the birth of their children, was admitted. In the opinion delivered, Thompson, *Ch. J.*, says, "we do not perceive any objection to the admission of a sworn copy of the records, as evidence of the family."

If, then, the evidence was properly received, the question to be decided is, whether William Appel, mentioned in the records of the church, is to be considered the person to whom the patent issued. In order to test this point, let us suppose that an ejectment had been commenced by William Appel, in his lifetime, to recover the possession, and that he was the only lessor; would not the production of the patent be all that was necessary, in the first instance, to make out a title? I apprehend this question has been decided by our courts. In *Jackson* v. *Goes*, 13 Johns., 518, letters patent to Peter Shultz, one of the lessors, were produced. The defendant proved that there was another person of the same name, who was too young, during the Revolutionary War, to be *a soldier; and that the lessor himself [***240** had not been a soldier. Upon that evidence it was held that the defendant was entitled to judgment. By this statement, it will be seen that no question was raised whether the plaintiff was bound in the first place to prove his identity, as well as produce his patent. On the contrary, the right of the defendant to go into this evidence was alone contested. The counsel for the defendant admitted, on the argument, that the lessor, on producing the patent was, *prima facie*, entitled to recover. Spencer, *J.*, observes: "In this action, whenever the plaintiff introduces a deed conveying the premises to a person, of the name of his lessor, it is, *prima facie*, evidence that the lessor is the real grantee: the burden of disproving this, and repelling the presumption, is thrown on the defendant; and he may prove that the deed was granted to a different person of the same name." Thompson, *Ch. J.*, observed that it was always open to a defendant in ejectment, to show that the lessor was not the person intended by the patent, though he may bear the same name. The cases cited by the defendant's counsel from 1 Campb., 196, and 4 Campb., 34, seem to contravene this rule. In the first case, the action was to recover copyhold premises. It appeared that certain persons of the same name with the lessors had been admitted as tenants in fee. It was contended that evidence of the identity of the persons admitted ought to be given. Ld. Ellenborough was of that opinion, holding that there was not sufficient evidence of the admission of the lessors. In the latter case, the issue was *non est factum*; the witness produced was unacquainted with the defendant, and testified merely that a person executed the bond, in the name of the defendant. This case does not apply; for the proof was manifestly defective; the witness not knowing that the person who signed the bond, was of the same name with the defendant. Dampier, *J.*, observed, "that some evidence of identity was indispensably necessary; and that even presuming that the person who executed, was of the same name, he asked, how did it appear that it was the defendant sued in the action? These were *Nisi Prius* cases; and however respectable, cannot be regarded as a rule of *decision here, in opposition to the [***241** practice recognized and acted upon in our own courts. The rule we have adopted is, that proof of identity may always be admitted, when the fact is questioned—leaving to the defendant the right of showing that the plaintiff is not the person intended. As far as I am acquainted, the course of practice in this State has corresponded with this rule. I have never known a case, where a plaintiff, having the name of a patentee or grantee, was received to go further than the production of his deed or patent, unless the presumption of identity was first repelled by the defendant; nor where the production of a bond or note on trial, was not holden, *prima facie*, sufficient, against a defendant of the same name with the obligor or maker.

If, then, William Appel, described in the records, had been the lessor, his identity would be presumed until disproved by the defendant, because there is no proof that there ever was another person of that name. The presumption cannot be affected, whether he stands before the court as a lessor or the ancestor, under whom the lessors of the plaintiff claim. The presumption is not founded on the circumstance that an action happened to have been commenced, but on this: the patent is to William Appel; there was a person of that name, and no other or different person is proved to have existed. On the principles laid down, the conclusion is, that William Appel, described in the records, was the patentee.

The next question is, whether the evidence of pedigree, derived from the records of baptisms, was sufficient. They prove that William Appel had a son named Simon; that one Simon Appel had a daughter Magdalena baptized in 1719; and another daughter, Gertruig, baptized in 1721. That Simon Appel, mentioned in the extract of baptism in 1719, was the son of William. is, I think, to be presumed. The presumption is considerably fortified by the fact that William appears to have been one of the sponsors. But it may be asked what is the use of allowing the registers of births, marriages and baptisms? If A claims that B is his ancestor, as grandfather; that such an-
242*] cestor has been dead a *century, and his son C half a century; it cannot be expected that living witnesses can be produced, to prove the relationship of past generations. He may, then, resort to the register. What fact does that establish? It may appear that B was married; that he had a son C afterwards baptized; that C afterwards had a son A baptized; on the face of the register, it does not appear that A was the son of C, or that C was the son of B; but it is the best evidence the nature of the case admits; and because greater evils are apprehended from the rejection of such evidence than its admission, the law has relaxed the general rules and allowed the exception. But after all, the evidence would be unavailing, unless the law presumed that the persons named in the register were the ancestors of the claimant, they all bearing the same names—and no evidence being adduced that there had ever been other persons of that name. From the search made by Bogert, the witness, in the book of records, for a great number of years, and nothing appearing to show that there was ever any other William or Simon Appel; from the fact that Simon had a daughter, Magdalena, and that a person, of her name, was married in 1743 to Abram Pelts; from the dates of the several baptisms and marriages being at such distance of time from each other as to be consistent with the claim, I think it may be presumed that these persons are descended of William Appel in a direct line. The testimony of Mrs. Van Deusen proves that Magdalena Pelts, the grandmother of one of the lessors, was the widow of Abram Pelts. She died in 1795. Her age is not stated. It is evident, however, she was far advanced in years, as her granddaughter was born in 1771. It is a reasonable presumption, that she is the person whose marriage is certified to have taken place in 1743.

From the preceding view, it follows that the judge erred in directing the nonsuit. The evidence produced by the plaintiff was, *prima facie*, sufficient to entitle him to recover.

Whether the presumption that William Appel, named in the certificate as the patentee, has been repelled by the evidence, on the part of the defendant, is a question of fact, proper for the consideration of the jury, under the direction *of the court. The declara- [***243**
tions of Mrs. Pelts, and the long acquiescence, were circumstances bearing on this question. It would be premature, in this court, to express an opinion now as to the weight of testimony on this point, until a jury have passed on it.

With respect to the possession, it was not adverse at its commencement, nor at any subsequent period. Schauber, the first possessor, declared he had no title. He sold to William King, from whom the defendant received the possession. There is evidence that valuable improvements have been made, but none that the possessors claimed title.

I am of opinion that the nonsuit be set aside, and a new title granted, with costs to abide the event.

Motion granted.

Cited in—9 Cow., 150; 19 Wend., 442; 18 N. Y., 92; 8 Barb., 582; 52 How. Pr., 284.

DUNLOP AND MEIGS *v.* PATTERSON.

1. *Witnesses—Objection to Competency of, too Late after Appeal to C. P. 2. Charge of Court, should Include such Views as to Credibility of Witnesses as the Law Requires the Jury to Consider.*

Under the former Statute, sess. 41, ch. 94, sec. 17-19, allowing and regulating proceedings upon appeal to the C. P. from a justice's court; whether a witness sworn in the court below, without objection to his competency on the ground of interest, could be excluded in the C. P. on that ground, *quære*.

A witness not sworn in the court below was inadmissible to prove such interest in the C. P.

It seems that error will not lie for the mere omission of a court to charge the jury upon a part of the evidence or matter of law, to which the attention of the court was not drawn by the party.

But if they comment upon a piece of testimony given to the jury; and leave it generally open for the jury to pass upon, without adding such views, as to its credibility, as the law requires the jury to consider, the judgment will be reversed.

Thus, where the material fact in a cause depended, for its proof, upon the testimony of F., a single unsupported witness, who swore to that fact; but upon whose cross-examination it was plain that he had perjured himself, either in the cause pending or in a former cause relative to the same matter; and the court charged the jury that he was competent: that they might give his testimony such weight as they thought it deserved; that it was in some measure supported by R. (a witness who had agreed with the testimony of F. in a collateral, immaterial fact); and, therefore, entitled to that additional weight; held, that the jury should have been instructed to disregard F.'s testimony; that the court erred in not so instructing them; and the judgment was, for that cause, reversed on error, upon a bill of exceptions presenting this point.

Citation—4 Laws, sess. 41, ch. 94, sec. 19, p. 83.

ON ERROR from the Albany C. P. The action was trover, originally brought by the defendant against the plaintiffs in error, for the sloop or boat William, in a justice's **244***] *court of the County of Albany. A verdict being for the plaintiff in that court, the defendants there brought and prosecuted an appeal to the Albany C. P., pursuant to the former Act, sess. 41, ch. 94, secs. 17-19, and the cause coming on to be tried there, Orin Fuller was offered as a witness on the part of Patterson, the appellee. The appellants objected to his introduction, on the ground that he was interested in the event of the suit; and proposed to establish his interest by the testimony of John O. Cole, who was not sworn before the justice's court. His introduction as a witness being objected to, on this ground, he was excluded by the C. P., who gave as an additional reason, that it did not appear by the justice's return that Fuller was objected to as being interested, in the justice's court. The counsel for the appellants excepted to this decision.

Fuller being sworn, stated that he had purchased the boat as agent for the appellee, and swore to various facts tending to show that it belonged to him—as that he bought it with the appellee's property, being in trade on commission for the appellee, with a sign importing a commission store. Among other things, however, he acknowledged, in a course of cross-examination, that he was a witness in a cause between other parties, in which the property of the same boat was in question, on which occasion he swore that the boat was his own property, and afterwards told the same story to Meigs; when, in truth, at each time, he knew (as he said) it belonged to the appellee. This witness was supported, as to a few collateral facts, by the testimony of Valentine W. Rathbone; but not upon the main question, as, to whom the boat belonged.

The additional facts necessary to an understanding of the points decided, both here and in the court below, will be found stated in the opinion of the court.

The C. P. denied a motion to nonsuit the appellee; and charged the jury that Fuller was a competent witness whose testimony should go to the jury, who might give that weight to it which they thought it deserved; "that his testimony was in some measure supported by that of Valentine W. Rathbone and, therefore, entitled to that additional weight; and that if the jury believed the testimony of Orin Fuller, **245***] that *is, that he was actually trading upon commission under the said plaintiff, and was trading with the funds of the said plaintiff, and that the boat in question was purchased by the said Orin Fuller, for the said plaintiff, and with the money or goods of the said plaintiff, then they ought to find a verdict for the said plaintiff, for the value of the said boat, but if they believed, from the testimony before them, that the said Orin Fuller was not trading upon commission under the said plaintiff, nor with his funds, but was trading with his own funds, and had bought the said boat with his own money or goods; and had put up his sign, and held out to the world that he was trading as a commission merchant, merely to defraud his creditors, they ought to find a verdict for the defendant."

To this charge the appellants' counsel excepted; and the jury found for the appellee $50 damages; and the appellants brought error to this court.

Mr. J. T. B. Van Vechten, for the plaintiffs in error.

Messrs. Vanderheyden and *Van Antwerp*, contra.

Curia, per WOODWORTH, *J.* I incline to the opinion that the Court of C. P. decided correctly, in disallowing the testimony of Cole, to prove Fuller an interested witness. He was sworn before the justice, and no objection taken to his competency. When a cause was brought before the court by appeal, the Act in question declared that the parties should proceed to the hearing on an examination of the same witnesses named in the return, that were sworn and testified before the justice, unless they should have been objected to, and illegally admitted. (4 Laws, sess. 41, ch. 94, sec. 19, p. 83.) The intention of the Act was, that the merits of the cause should be tried on appeal, by the same witnesses and testimony given in the court below. If objections to the competency of a witness could have been raised, for the first time, on the appeal, the consequence might have been that the evidence upon which the recovery was had would have been excluded; and if so, there could not have been a trial of the merits upon the same testimony. *Such a construction of the [***246** Act would have given an undue advantage to the party omitting to take the objection to the competency of a witness *in limine*, and reserving it, to exclude him in case of an appeal. It is obvious that such a course might operate as a surprise upon the adverse party, when, perhaps, the objection might have been obviated, if taken in the court below. Besides, how could it have been known that the appellant was not apprised of the interest of the witness on the first trial? If it was known, the omission to object might well have been considered a waiver.(a)

The next question is, was the charge of the Court of C. P. correct. In deciding this point, we cannot take into view any omission of the judge to charge the jury on matter of law which may be deemed essential—especially when the attention of the court was not called by the counsel to the points alleged as material to be given in charge. *Vide Douglass* v. *M'Allister*, 3 Cr., 298; *Smith* v. *Carrington*, 4 *Id.*,

(a) The frequent questions made under the Act here, in questions as to the admission of evidence upon appeal, in reference to what evidence was received by the justice, cannot now arise. The late Act, sess. 47, ch. 238, does not prohibit the introduction of testimony on appeal, as upon an original trial, without regard to the evidence in the justice's court.

62; *Wasse* v. *Smith*, 6 *Id.*, 226; 17 Johns., 218; Reg. Gen. Dist. Court Phila., Wharton's Pa. Dig. Error, A. The exception, then, applies to the opinion delivered. If that is correct, as far as it proceeds, the exception is not well taken.

The court stated to the jury that Fuller's testimony was competent; that they might give it such weight as they thought it deserved; that it was, in some measure, supported by Rathbone and, therefore, entitled to that additional weight.

After an attentive consideration of the evidence given by Fuller, it seems to me that this part of the charge was manifestly erroneous. The jury, it is true, are judges of fact and the credibility of witnesses; but in the exercise of this power, they must be governed by the judgment of law on the facts. If the law has adjudged that certain facts render a witness unworthy of credit, the jury cannot rightfully give credit to his testimony or found a verdict upon it. They have no arbitrary discretion. It is their duty to follow the advice of the court as to the law. In this case, the charge gave **247*]** *them the most extensive range. Their attention was not called to the fact that Fuller, by his own admission, had sworn falsely. According to himself, on a former trial, he testified that the boat in question was his own property; and subsequently declared the same thing to Meigs; and that, at the time he so testified, it was, in truth, the property of Patterson. On the trial in this cause he testified that it was not his property, but belonged to Patterson. No reason whatever is assigned for this prevarication and disregard to truth. He was not, therefore, a credible witness, unless supported as to the material fact which he attempted to establish. The law will not permit either life or property to be put in jeopardy by such testimony. If it would, there must be but little security for either. A stronger case could scarcely be made out, than that of a witness who, by his own statement, appears to be guilty of false swearing. This imputation is warranted by the circumstances disclosed in the case; for it cannot be pretended that he, who was the purchaser of the boat, did not know whether the purchase was for himself or another person. If he knew his testimony was false, either on the first or second trial, how could the jury safely rest on such testimony? But it was said that he was, in some measure, supported by Rathbone. This I apprehend to be a mistake. Rathbone's testimony was immaterial and irrelevant. He proved the sale of goods to Fuller on account of Patterson, for which the latter agreed to pay, but says nothing in relation to the right of property in the boat. Fuller may have testified truly in this respect, but it neither impeaches nor supports the testimony in question. When the court instructed the jury to give the evidence the weight they thought it deserved, this implied that they had an uncontrolled discretion, to do as their judgments might direct, without any legal restraint as to the manner of exercising it. Under such a charge different jurors would probably form different opinions, founded on considerations not recognized by the law. The court ought to have charged the jury that the testimony of Fuller was so strongly impeached as to justify them in disregarding it altogether; that the unsupported testimony of a single *witness, who swore at one time in di- **[*248** rect contradiction to the testimony given by him at another, in relation to the same transaction, was not entitled to credit, and ought not to be regarded. If the charge had been of such a character, it is probable the result of the trial would have been different.

My opinion is that this exception is well taken; that the judgment be reversed, and a *venire de novo* issue in the court below.

Judgment reversed.

Limited—29 N. Y., 528; 40 N. Y., 6; 74 N. Y., 504; 62 Barb., 679.

Cited in—29 N. Y., 492; 74 N. Y., 504; 2 Keyes, 549; 3 Keyes, 230; 3 Abb. App. Dec., 49; 15 Barb., 594; 25 Barb., 198; 47 How. Pr., 199; 2 Abb. N. S., 191; 16 Abb. N.S., 345; 1 Rob., 413; 8 Daly, 215; 7 W. Dig., 524.

JACKSON, ex dem. LANSING,
v.
LAW & NELSON.

Tender—When and How to be Made—Effect of—of Money Due on a Judgment Does not Discharge it or Creditor's Lien—Statute.

A tender of the money due upon a judgment does not discharge it, or take away the lien of the judgment creditor; but he may still redeem upon it, as a judgment creditor, within the Statute, sess. 43, ch. 184, sec. 3.

A tender must be made before suit brought.

After judgment, the only way to make a tender effectual, is to bring the money into court, and move for, and obtain a rule to enter satisfaction upon the record; and in the meantime, an order may be obtained restraining the sale of property on execution upon the judgment, if the sheriff refuse the money upon its being tendered, it being his duty to receive it.

It is always the duty of the sheriff to receive money tendered upon a *fi. fa.* and forbear to sell.

The effect of a tender, when made in season, is merely to discharge the debtor from subsequent interest.

The principal is never discharged by a tender, unless under peculiar circumstances; as where there is not, after tender and refusal, any remedy to enforce the payment of the debt or performance of the duty.

Even a tender of money, upon a judgment, if followed up with the proper means to render it available, will bar a claim of interest.

Whether it will have this effect, if not so followed up, *quære.*

Citations—Act, sess. 43, ch. 184, sec. 3; 6 Bac., 156, 452, 458; Bro., Tender, pl. 9; 1 Inst., 207.

EJECTMENT for land in Hebron, Washington Co., tried at the circuit in that Co., July 14, 1823, before Walworth, *Circuit Judge.*

The premises in question had formerly belonged to one Quackenbush; and Apr. 14, 1821, they were sold on a *fi. fa.* against Quackenbush, upon a judgment docketed in 1806 to Law, the defendant. The lessor of the plaintiff redeemed upon junior judgments against Quackenbush; and took a sheriff's deed of conveyance, July 13, 1822. One question at the trial was, whether these judgments were valid, and operative as a lien, at the time of redemption. They were in favor of one Whiteside; and the defendant proved that previous to the sale already mentioned, *May **[*249** 6, 1818, the sheriff was proceeding to sell the premises in question, on writs of *fi. fa.* upon the Whiteside judgments, and others; when Law, the defendant, a junior judgment creditor, tendered to the sheriff, Lansing, the lessor, being present, a quantity of untold bank notes, upon the Whiteside executions, in order to compel the sheriff to sell on executions upon judgments younger than Law's. The tender was not objected to, on account of its being in bank notes, nor because the money was not counted. The sheriff swore, at the trial, that he had no doubt they were sufficient in amount; and accordingly proceeded to sell upon executions, on the junior judgments, Lansing becoming the purchaser.

It was upon the two Whiteside judgments, which were afterwards assigned to Lansing, the lessor, that he redeemed and obtained his conveyance.

Verdict for the plaintiff, subject to the opinion of this court.

The above, with the further particulars, stated in the opinion of the court, will fully present the question decided.

Mr. J. Lansing, for the plaintiff. The tender was with a view to compel a sale on a junior judgment. This is not sufficient. A tender should be absolute with the simple intent to pay the debt; otherwise, it is bad. *Eastland* v. *Longshorn*, 1 Not. & M'C., 194; *Cole* v. *Blake*, Peake *N. P.*, 179; 1 Esp. Dig., pt. 1, p. 300, Gould's ed., and the cases there cited. We admit that Law was privy to the judgment, and had a right to make payment; but it was too late to make a valid tender. A tender cannot be made upon a judgment. It must precede the commencement of a suit. Even the party, Quackenbush, could not have made a tender after the suit commenced; and the rights of the privy are certainly no greater than those of the party under whom he comes in. *Bothy's* case, 6 Rep., 31; 1 Inst., 206–208. Again; the levy was made, and the property of Quackenbush in the custody of the law; after which a tender cannot be made. *Pilkington's* case, 5 **250***] Rep., *76; *Pilkington* v. *Hastings*, Cro. Eliz., 813; *Firth* v. *Purvis*, 5 T. R., 433. To make the tender complete and effectual, the defendant should have shown the sheriff's refusal to receive the money: and proved, in the language of the plea, that he was *touts temps prist, et uncore prist;* and bring the money into court. Unless all this is done, the whole proceeding is nullity. *Rose* v. *Russell*, Kirby, 293; Cow. Treat., 486, &c., where all the authorities to this point are collected. Had the sheriff still persisted in selling, the defendant, to save himself, must have bid the whole amount of the Whiteside judgments. Besides, a mere tender, in any view, would have been insufficient. This must have been followed up by a motion, and satisfaction of the judgments upon the record. A mere tender of money never discharges the debt. Bac. Abr., Tender, E; *Wolcott* v. *Van Santvoord*, 17 Johns., 248, 253.

The only case which can be relied on against us, is that of *Jackson* v. *Crafts*, 18 Johns., 110, which was the case of a tender to the assignee of a mortgage, to prevent a statute sale. But, in that case, the tender was made to the creditor, and kept good. The land was not, as here, in the custody of the law; and no suit, in legal contemplation, was commenced. The whole was *in pais*. The lien was created, and might be discharged by the parties. Such is the rule in relation to a conditional grant of lands. (1 Inst., 207 *a*.)

Messrs. J. Crary and *D. Russell*, contra. The person redeeming upon the statute must have a lien upon the land at the time. The judgment upon which Law purchased, having been obtained before the Statute Authorizing a Redemption was passed, it does not apply, though the sale was after its passage. *Dash* v. *Van Kleeck*, 7 Johns., 477. In this view, the title passed to Law absolutely. Besides, the sale on junior judgments, though after the advertisement upon the Whiteside executions, passed the title; and the plaintiff must look to the sheriff. *Sandford* v. *Roosa*, 12 Johns., 162.

The effect of the tender was to take away the lien, though we admit the debt or duty remained. It became personal *upon [***251** Law, who should have had notice that Lansing was assignee, when he came to redeem. But it is enough that the tender discharged the lien. This is settled by *Jackson* v. *Crafts*, 18 Johns., 110, 115. The payment of the money to the sheriff by Lansing inured to the benefit of Law. Lansing cannot pretend that he was a *bona fide* purchaser of the Whiteside judgment. The tender was with his knowledge. It was not conditional, and was properly made to the sheriff. He held the executions, and was the proper person to enforce and receive payment. The tender being made, the object of the execution was answered; this not being to enforce a sale of the land, but the payment of the debt.

In *Jackson* v. *Crafts* the tender was to the agent. No matter where the money afterwards remains. It is the tender, not the subsequent disposition of the money, to which the law looks.

Mr. Lansing, in reply, as to the necessity of keeping the money tendered ready at all times, down to the period of pleading, or giving it in evidence, cited *Horn* v. *Luines*, per Holt, *Ch. J.*; 12 Mod., 354; *Brownlow* v. *Hewley*, Ld. Raym., 82; *Giles* v. *Hartis*, *Id.*, 254; *Horne* v. *Lewen*, *Id.*, 643; 2 Roll. Abr., 524, *Touts temps prist*, D.

Curia, per WOODWORTH, *J.* The premises in question were sold Apr. 14, 1821, under a judgment recovered by John Williams, against Gerrit Quackenbush, Feb. 15, 1806. John Law, one of the defendants, became the purchaser. May 29, 1815, two judgments in favor of John Whiteside against Quackenbush, were docketed; and July 13, 1822, assigned to the lessor of the plaintiff, who, on the day last mentioned, redeemed the lands sold under the judgment of Williams, in the manner prescribed by the Act, and received a deed from the sheriff.

The material question arising in this case is, whether the judgments in favor of Whiteside were, at the time of the redemption, a lien on the land. On the part of the defendants, it appeared that in 1817 executions were issued on the judgments of Whiteside, and also on judgments in favor of other *plaintiff's, to [***252** the Sheriff of Washington Co.; that in May, 1818, the sheriff proceeded to sell the right of Quackenbush; and thereupon, John Law, being a judgment creditor, tendered to the sheriff bank notes, on the Whiteside executions, for the purpose of compelling him to sell upon executions issued on junior judgments. The sheriff, who was examined as a witness, states that the money was not counted, but he had no doubt that the quantity was sufficient; that in consequence of this tender he did not sell on the executions of Whiteside, but sold the premises on two junior executions to Jacob Lansing, the lessor. The case does not state that the sheriff refused to accept the money tendered, but I understand that the fact is so. He suspended the sale under the executions of Whiteside, but did not receive payment. Afterwards, Lansing, having become the assignee of the judgments, redeemed under them the land sold by virtue of the judgment of Williams. There are a number of other facts in the case not deemed material to the decision of the cause.

By the 3d section of the Act concerning Judgments and Executions, sess. 43, ch. 184, any creditor, who shall have a decree in chancery, or a judgment at law, against a defendant, has a right to redeem. It seems to me that, at law, the lien did not cease by reason of the tender. It is undoubtedly the duty of a sheriff to receive the money on a *fieri facias*, when offered; and if refused, on application to the court, a summary remedy would be applied, restraining the sheriff from making a sale, or by directing satisfaction to be entered of record, on payment to the plaintiff. No attempt, however, was made by Law to obtain a discharge of the judgment, after the tender made to the sheriff. He cannot, therefore, claim that the judgment was satisfied; and if it was not, Lansing had a right to redeem under it. The doctrine of tender is not applicable; for that cannot be made after an action is commenced; 6 Bac., 452; Bro., Tender, pl. 9; and in cases where a tender is made in season, and the creditor refuses, the effect is merely to discharge the dêbtor from subsequent interest. (6 Bac., 458.) The principal is never discharged, unless under peculiar circumstances; as where there was not, after the tender and **253***] refusal, any remedy *to enforce the payment of the debtor, the performance of the duty. (6 Bac., 156; 1 Inst., 207.) The effect of the tender, in this case, is to bar the damages or interest. To that extent it would have been available, if Law had applied for redress. The debt still remains due, and the judgment in force. Law never brought the money into court, but still retains it. His omission to claim the interference of the court has left the plaintiff in possesssion of a valid judgment, which the Statute authorized him to use in the manner he has done. On the question before us, admitting that the tender discharged all subsequent interest, it does not affect the title; for the judgment was a lien until wholly paid. If any part remained due, it continued a lien. If the defendant is subjected to loss by the redemption, it is imputable to his want of vigilance in not following up the tender by an application to this court, where ample redress might have been obtained. I am of opinion that the plaintiff is entitled to judgment.

SAVAGE, *Ch. J.*, dissented.

Judgment for the plaintiff.

Affirmed—9 Cow., 641.
Distinguished—65 N. Y., 320.
Cited in—7 Cow., 558; 4 Den., 486; 1 Edw., 636; 19 N. Y., 384; 1 Barb., 384; 22 Am. Rep., 612-617 (65 N. Y., 314).

EVE TROVINGER *v.* M'BURNEY.

Future Illicit Intercourse, not a Valid Consideration for a Promise—Purpose to Continue Illicit Relation Must be Clearly Proved.

A promise by the putative father, to pay for the board of a woman and her bastard child; the purpose of both parties, express or tacit, being to facilitate a continued state of cohabitation between the promisor and the woman, is void.

But the purpose must be clearly proved; and is not to be inferred from a previous cohabitation between them, with the knowledge of the promisee. This fact is not sufficient ground for the jury to infer consent to a subsequent cohabitation, in a case where the woman is the daughter of the promisee. It makes nothing towards such an inference and should not be submitted to the jury.

Citations—1 Esp., 13; 5 Ves., 291; 1 Campb., 348.

ASSUMPSIT, for meat, drink, &c., found and provided, and work and labor, in and about the nursing &c., of Catharine Trovinger, the plaintiff's daughter, and James M'Burney, and Susan M'Burney, infant children of Catharine, at the defendant's request, and on his promise to pay, &c., tried at the Steuben Circuit, Oct. 1, 1823, before Nelson, *Circuit Judge*; when a verdict was found for the plaintiff.

The facts are sufficiently stated in the opinion of the court.

*The main defense on the trial was, [***254** that the services, board, &c., of the plaintiff, were performed and bestowed with the view of encouraging and facilitating the continuance of the defendant, in a state of prostitution with the plaintiff's daughter, Catharine; and therefore, formed no legal consideration for the defendant's promise; but the judge, who tried the cause, did not deem the testimony upon this point even strong enough to be submitted to the jury.

Another question was, whether the parties had fully accounted together concerning the subject-matter of this suit and a promissory note been executed by the plaintiff for the balance; or, whether her giving the note was not presumptive evidence that her demand was paid.

Mr. J. C. Spencer, for the defendant, now moved for a new trial; and cited *Girardy* v. *Richardson*, 1 Esp., 13; 1 Selw. *N. P.*, 79; *Gray* v. *Matthias*, 5 Ves., 286; *Holman* v. *Johnson*, per Ld. Mansfield, Cowp., 343; 1 Phil. Ev., 113; *Decker* v. *Livingston*, 15 Johns., 479; *Van Vlieden* v. *Welles*, 6 *Id.*, 85.

Messrs. J. Platt and *E. Allen*, contra, cited *Turner* v. *Vaughan*, 2 Wils., 339; *Bowry* v. *Bennet*, 1 Campb., 348; *Lloyd* v. *Johnson*, 1 Bos. & P., 340; Exodus, ch. 22, v. 16.

NOTE.—*Contracts—Consideration—Illegal—Immoral.*

The general rule is, that where the consideration, or any part thereof, is illegal, the contract is void. Trustees v. Gallatin, 4 Cow., 340; Sherman v. Barnard, 19 Barb., 291; Moore v. Remington, 34 Barb., 427; Saratoga Bank v. King, 44 N. Y., 87; Carlton v. Bailey, 27 N. H., 230; Deering v. Chapman, 22 Me., 488; Perkins v. Cummings, 68 Mass. (2 Gray), 258; Buck v. Albee, 26 Vt., 184; Filson v. Himes, 5 Pa. St., 452; Coulter v. Robertson, 14 Smedes & M., 18; Chandler v. Johnson, 39 Ga., 85; Kottwitz v. Alexander, 34 Tex., 689; Brua's Appeal, 55 Pa. St., 294; Dumont v. Dufore, 27 Ind., 263; Armstrong v. Toler, 11 Wh., 258, *note in Law. ed.*; 2 Kent, Com., 468, notes and authorities there cited.

All contracts, whether under seal or not, made in consideration of future illicit sexual intercourse, are utterly void. Wait v. Day, 4 Den., 439; Fellows v.

Curia, per WOODWORTH, *J*. The first question to be decided is, whether the consideration for the defendant's promise was illegal and void.

The plaintiff's daughter became the mother of an illegitimate child. The defendant was the reputed father, and promised to pay the plaintiff for their board. About two years after another child was born, of which the defendant was, also, the father. Shortly afterwards he made a similar promise. The plaintiff knew that the defendant, before the birth of the first, and until after the birth of the second child, frequently visited her daughter at the plaintiff's house and, during all that time, frequently cohabited with her.

From this statement, it is obvious that the daughter was placed in a situation requiring
255*] support; and it was the duty *of the defeudant to provide for her. If, however, the party contracting to board, either expressly or tacitly assented, that, during that period, the illicit intercourse might be continued; or, if it appears that the contract was made for the purpose of facilitating a continued prostitution, it would thereby become tainted, and deprive the plaintiff of her action.

In order to decide this question correctly, it is necessary briefly to consider the circumstances under which each promise was made.

After the birth of the first child, the defendant stipulated to pay for boarding. This, *per se*, was a lawful and commendable act, and formed a valid contract. But it is objected that the plaintiff knew, during the time, that the defendant visited the daughter and, previous to the birth, cohabited with her. This objection, it is true, greatly implicates the character of the plaintiff, and justly subjects her to the imputation of an immoral woman, regardless of the reputation of her child; for it is not alleged that she took measures to prevent the cohabitation, or even expressed her disapprobation. But it must be remembered that all this had passed. The daughter had become a charge upon some one, and needed assistance. The defendant having assumed to afford that assistance, he ought not to be exonerated, unless the previous censurable conduct of the plaintiff will warrant a presumption that she agreed to board her daughter and daughter's child, for the purpose of subsequent prostitution. I do not consider myself at liberty to draw such a conclusion from the facts disclosed. The simple circumstance, that the plaintiff had knowledge of the previous cohabitation, and did not discountenance it, seems to me calculated to awaken remorse for the past—when, perhaps the omission, on her part, to discharge an incumbent duty of her daughter, had been the cause of her incontinence and subsequent disgrace. However that may be, past transgressions do not furnish legal grounds for presuming an intent to sanction their repitition. Something more is necessary.

If, then, the contract is not impeached for this cause, it is very clear that it cannot be affeted by subsequent improprieties *on [***256**
the part of the plaintiff, not shown to have been in contemplation when the contract was made.

With respect to the second assumption to pay, the remarks already made are equally applicable. There is this difference, however, in the two cases; in the latter, it does not appear that the defendant ever cohabited with the daughter after the contract was made. The witness says, that soon after the birth of the second child, the defendant made the promise; and the plaintiff knew of the cohabitation before the birth of James, and until after the birth of Susan. The question is, how long after? Was it subsequent to the promise, which is stated to have been made "soon after" the birth? This cannot be affirmed. The evidence leaves the fact undecided. It would, therefore, be a perversion of law and justice, to impute an immoral act on such ground.

Whenever anything is done directly in furtherance of immorality, the maxim, *ex turpi causa, non oritur actio*, applies; as in *Girardy* v. *Richardson*, 1 Esp., 13, where the rooms were let for the exrpess purpose of prostitution. In the case of *Gray* v. *Matthias*, 5 Ves., 291, a voluntary bond, given during cohabitation, to a woman, previously of a very loose life, was held to be unimpeached, although the parties cohabited together until the death of the obligor; but a second bond, expressly securing a continuance of the connection, by an annuity in case of separation, was held to be void at law. This shows, very clearly, that the party's previous course of life, however abandoned, and connection after the contract, do not invalidate it. The test is, does it appear by the contract itself, or was there any understanding of the parties, though not expressed, that the connection was to continue?

Emperor, 13 Barb., 92; Lady Cox's case, 3 P. Wms., 339; Walker v. Perkins, Burr., 1568; Coolidge v. Blake, 15 Mass., 427; Walker v. Gregory, 36 Ala., 180; Walraven v. Jones, 1 Haust. (Del.), 355; Baldy v. Stratton, 11 Pa. St., 316; Singleton v. Bremar, Harp., 201; Winebrinner v. Weisiger, 3 T. B. Mon., 35; Sherman v. Barrett, 1 McMull., 147.

Contracts for the performance of immoral acts, or for the promotion of immorality, are void. Forsythe v. State, 6 Ohio, 21; Spalding v. Preston, 21 Vt., 9; Brua's Appeal, 55 Pa. St., 294; Merrick v. Trustees, 8 Gill., 59; Armstrong v. Toler, 11 Wh., 258, *note in Law. ed.*

Past seduction and cohabitation will not support a parol promise. Fisher v. Bridges, 3 Bl. & B., 642; Jennings v. Brown, 9 Mees. & W., 496; Beaumont v. Reeve, 8 Q. B., 483.

A sealed instrument, given in consideration of past illicit sexual intercourse, can be enforced. Bunn v. Winthrop, 1 Johns. Ch., 329; Self v. Clark, 2 Jones, Eq., 309; Howell v. Fountain, 3 Ga., 176; Winebrinner v. Weisiger, 3 T. B. Mon., 35; Wyant v. Lisher, 23 Pa. St., 338; Turner v. Vaughan, 2 Wils., 339; Annandale v. Harris, 2 P. Wms., 432; Mathew v. Hanbury, 2 Vern., 187; Lady Cox's case, 3 P. Wms., 339; Nye v. Mosely, 6 Barn. & C., 183.

A promise by putative father, to support bastard *child*, is not illegal *per se*, and may be enforced. Hook v. Pratt, 78 N. Y., 371; S. C., 34 Am. Rep., 539, *notes*; S. C., 13 Hun, 396; Haven v. Hobbs, 1 Vt., 238; Holcomb v. Stimpson, 8 Vt., 141; Flanegan v. Garrison, 28 Ga., 136; Robinson v. Crenshaw, 2 Stew. & P., 276; Jennings v. Brown, 9 Mees. & W., 496; Smith v. Roche, 6 C. B. (N. S.), 223.

"It seems to have been held in England, formerly, that while a promise in consideration of future illicit cohabitation was certainly void, a promise in consideration of past cohabitation, especially if grounded upon seduction by the promisor, was sufficient. It appears to be now held, that the consideration is equally insufficient in either case." Citing, Beaumont v. Reeve, 8 Adol. & Ell. N. S., 483; Binnington v. Wallis, 4 Barn. & Ald., 650; Jennings v. Brown, 9 Mees. & W., 496; Annandale v. Harris, 2 P. Wms., 432; Walker v. Perkins, 1 W. Bl., 517; Eastwood v. Kenyon, 11 Adol. & Ell., 438.

See, generally, Armstrong v. Toler, 24 U. S. (11 Wh.), 258, *note in Law. ed.*

The case of *Dillon* v. *Jones*, cited in 5 Ves., 291, and commented on by Macdonald, *Ch. B.*, who delivered the opinion of the court, was this: the parties had cohabited together for some time, when a bond for £3,000 was given. They lived together afterwards until they quarreled. The defendant was asked whether the security was given as the price of prostitution? She said no—no consideration of that kind was coupled with it; adding, "but perhaps he might mean to attach me." Ld. Bat-**257***] hurst would *not interfere, but upon the terms of paying the money into court. This case shows that the fact of there being any understanding must be proved. It is much stronger than the present. The appearance of the transaction might well excite suspicion, that he who was cohabiting with a woman at the time he bound himself to pay her a large sum of money, intended a continuance of that connection, and that this entered into the views of the parties when the contract was made. Yet the law will not allow the inference of an illicit purpose from such facts. In the case of *Bowry* v. *Bennett*, 1 Campb., 348, the defense was, that the articles sold were for the purpose of enabling the defendants to carry on her business of prostitution. Ld. Ellenborough held, it must not only be shown that the plaintiff had notice of the defendant's way of life, but that he sold the clothes, to enable her to carry it on. It is evident, therefore, to my mind, that enough has not been shown to render this contract void, and that the question ought not to have been submitted to the jury.

The next question is, whether the giving of the note amounted to a discharge of the plaintiff's claim. No presumption of this kind can arise, for the plaintiff's demand was not allowed when the note was given. This appears clearly from the evidence.

Whether the plaintiff consented to give the note as the balance due to the defendant, and look exclusively to her daughter, on the promise she made, was, in substance, submitted by the judge to the jury, and found against the defendant. I think they judged correctly. My impression is that the plaintiff never intended to discharge the defendant until paid. Her daughter stated that by her settlement with the defendant, she was to pay those charges; and that this appeared to satisfy the plaintiff. This amounts to but little at most. The plaintiff said nothing; and, if concluded, it must be because the opinion of a witness is to be substituted for facts.

The motion for a new trial must be denied.
New trial refused.

Cited in—17 Wend., 176; 5 Lans., 155; 4 E. D. S., 580.

258*] *THE PEOPLE *v.* SMITH.

Malicious Killing of Cow—Indictment Lies for.

An indictment lies for maliciously, wickedly and willfully killing a cow, the property of another.

Acts injurious to private persons which tend to excite violent resentment, and thus produce a disturbance of the peace, are indictable.

Citations—1 Dall., 355; 5 Binn., 277; 1 Mass., 59.

THE defendant was indicted for maliciously, wickedly and willfully killing a cow, the goods and chattels of John Dibble; and found guilty at the General Sessions in Delaware Co. The cause was brought to this court by *certiorari*, with a view to obtain their opinion, whether the offense charged be indictable.

Mr. S. Sherwood, for the defendant, cited 4 Bl. Com., 5, 6; 3 *Id.*, 120; 2 Hawk. P. C., 301, ch. 25, sec. 4; *Rex* v. *Buck*, 1 Str., 679; S. C., Sess. Cas., 370: *Rex* v. *Channel*, 2 Str., 793; S. C., Sess. Cas., 366; *King* v. *Leginham*, 1 Mod., 71; *Rex* v. *Wheatley*, 2 Burr., 1125; 4 Com. Dig., Indictment, E; *Rex* v. *Combrune*, 1 Wils., 301; *Anonymous*, 6 Mod., 88; *Rex* v. *Atkins*, 3 Burr., 1706; *Rex* v. *Bake*, *Id.*, 1731, and *Queen* v. *Crisp*, 6 Mod., 175.

He said the cases which went to sustain indictments for killing animals, and other private injuries, proceeded on the ground of secrecy, or of great cruelty, operating as an evil example, or tendency to a breach of the peace. *Respublica* v. *Teischer*, 1 Dall., 335, 337; *Commonwealth* v. *Taylor*, 5 Binn., 277, 280; *People* v. *Stakes*, 1 Wheeler Crim. Cas., 111. *Isaac Ross'* case, 3 City Hall Recorder, 191. The case of poisoning a dog, cited in *Respublica* v. *Teischer*, 1 Dall., 338, by M'Kean, *Ch. J.*, as being in 12 Mod., 337, he had not been able to find, and presumed that no such case existed. A statute was deemed necessary in Mass. for the punishment of incendiaries, *Commonwealth* v. *Macomber*, 3 Mass., 254, and in this State, for the criminal punishment of trespasses on lands. (1 R. L., 525, 526.)

He cited also Stat. 9 Geo. I., ch. 22; Cr. Cir. Comp., 84, 85; 2 Chit. C. L., 1087.

Mr. J. A. Collier, contra, cited *Anonymous*, 3 Salk., 187; 4 Bl. Com. 5, and Christian's *note*, 3; *State* v. *Council*, 1 *Overton, Tenn., [***259** 305; *Commonwealth* v. *Leach*, 1 Mass., 59; Russell on Crimes, Am. ed., 1682, *note; Commonwealth* v. *Taylor*, 5 Binn., 277, 280, and *Respublica* v. *Teischer*, 1 Dall., 335.

Curia, per WOODWORTH, *J.* There is no precise line by which indictments for malicious mischief are separated from actions of trespass. Blackstone, in the 4th vol. of his Commentaries, speaks of the former as done, not *animo furandi*, or with an intent of gaining by another's loss; but either out of a spirit of wanton cruelty, or black and diabolical revenge. It cannot be expected that the mere liability to damages will operate on a mind so depraved. The injury may be committed when none but the person injured is a witness. The perpetrator may be insolvent; and thus gratify his malice with impunity, if there is no redress otherwise than by civil action. This would be contrary to the policy of every well regulated government, which is to protect the citizen in his right, by restraining and punishing the wrong-doer. The offense is distinguishable from an ordinary trespass in this: that it is not only a violation of private right, without color or pretense, but without the hope or expectation of gain. Such an act discovers a degree of moral turpitude dangerous to society, and, for their security, ought to be punished criminally. It is an evil example of the most pernicious tendency, inasmuch as the act is an outrage upon the principles and feelings of humanity. The direct tendency is a breach of the peace. What more likely to produce it, than wantonly killing, out of mere malice, a useful domestic animal ?

Acts injurious to private persons, which tend to excite violent resentment, and thus produce a disturbance of the peace, have always been held indictable. Thus sending a challenge to fight a duel, or publishing a libel, are indictable offences.

It appears to me that the offense stated in this indictment is a proper subject of criminal prosecution. It was so held in *Respublica* v. *Teischer*, 1 Dall., 355, a case precisely like the present. M'Kean, *Ch. J.*, observed that the
260*] *poisoning of chickens, cheating with false dice, fraudulently tearing a promissory note, and many other offenses of a similar description, had been indicted in Pa. This case is approved in *Commonwealth* v. *Taylor*, 5 Binn., 277. In *Commonwealth* v. *Leach*, 1 Mass., 59, the defendants were indicted for poisoning a cow. The only question raised was, whether the sessions had jurisdiction. There was not even a suggestion, by the court or counsel, that the offense was not indictable.

I entertain no doubt that the conviction in this case was warranted by the principles of the common law; and judgment should be given against the defendant.

Judgment accordingly.

Cited in—19 Wend., 419; 5 Den., 280; 24 How. Pr., 351; 5 Park., 192, 575; 21 Am. Rep., 456 (72 N. C., 201).

[END OF OCTOBER TERM, 1825.]

CASES

ARGUED AND DETERMINED

IN THE

SUPREME COURT

OF THE

STATE OF NEW YORK,

IN

FEBRUARY TERM, 1826, IN THE FIFTIETH YEAR OF OUR INDEPENDENCE.

GRAVES ET AL. v. JOICE.

Action for Mesne Profits—Record in Ejectment Suit Conclusive Evidence of Plaintiff's Title—Matters of Defense in Original cannot be shown in Mitigation of Damages.

In an action for *mesne* profits, the record in the ejectment suit is conclusive evidence of title in the plaintiff; and where the declaration, consent rule, writ of possession and return, in the ejectment suit were all in the usual general form; the plaintiff being nonsuited on account of the defendant's not confessing lease, entry and ouster; in an action for the *mesne* profits, held, that the defendant could not show, in mitigation of damages, that the plaintiff brought the ejectment to recover only a small undivided part of the premises in question; but that this was matter of defense in the original action only.

Citation—4 Cow., 168.

TRESPASS for *mesne* profits; tried at the Schoharie Circuit, Oct. 26, 1824, before Duer, *Circuit Judge.*

On the trial, the plaintiffs produced the exemplification of a record of a judgment of nonsuit, for not confessing lease, entry and ouster, in an action of ejectment, for land in Blenheim, Schoharie Co., in which they were named as lessors, against the defendant. The declaration stated the day of ouster to have been May 3, 1821, and described the premises in the usual general form; and the judgment, which was general, for the plaintiff's term yet to come in the whole premises, was docketed Feb. 18, 1824. The plaintiffs, also, produced the exemplification of a writ of possession, containing the same general form of description as the declaration; and the return of the sheriff indorsed, that he had caused the plaintiff to have the possession of his several terms yet to come, of, in and to the several tenements, &c., within mentioned, &c.

The plaintiffs then proved that by virtue of this writ, a deputy-sheriff went with Graves, **262***] one of the plaintiffs, to a *farm, called the M'Kinney farm, situate in Blenheim, which was posessed by the defendant when the ejectment was commenced. That the deputy understood from Graves that he claimed only a part of this farm. The deputy delivered possession, by putting the tenant, his family and goods out of the house, and placing the goods in the street; that the annual value of the farm was about $75.

The defendant's counsel then offered to prove that the plaintiffs had often and uniformly admitted that the ejectment was brought, not for the whole farm, but only one-third of a fourth part of it. To this the plaintiff's counsel objected; but the evidence was received by the judge, on the ground that it was important for both parties to show for what the ejectment was, in fact, brought for the purpose of ascertaining the amount of the damages.

The proof offered was accordingly received; and the plaintiff's counsel admitted the facts to be as sworn to by the defendant's witnesses; and that, if admissible, the damages should be reduced accordingly; and the counsel for both parties agreed on the proper sum for which the verdict should be, upon the different views which they entertained, as to the admissibility of the evidence; and a verdict was taken for the plaintiffs, subject to the opinion of this court.

Mr. J. Powers, for the plaintiffs, was stopped by the court.

Mr. L. Munson, contra, said it was perfectly plain, from the case, that the plaintiffs were, in fact, entitled to but very small damages; that the proceedings in ejectment, which are so very general in point of description, should not be conclusive on the defendant as to the quantity of land recovered. In this, as in many other particulars, the form should yield to the substance and truth of the case. These are the objects of an action of ejectment; but here it is sought to be used for the purpose of working a wrong. We agree that nothing can be set up in the action for *mesne* profits which would be a bar to the original action; but the proof in question merely goes to the amount of damages.

*[WOODWORTH, *J.* But these must [***263** always be according to the title established at the trial in the ejectment. This record shows title to the whole land, not to a part only. Whether you are to recover the whole, or only a part of the interest in the land in controversy,

is a question which relates to the title—as to which the record in ejectment is conclusive. The circumstances might have been such as to warrant an application to this court, to limit the extent of the recovery in the original action; but it appears to me that it would be overturning all rule to allow that question to be tried in an action for *mesne* profits.]

The record in ejectment is, generally, no evidence as to the extent of the plaintiff's interest. No doubt this court will interfere summarily, and restore the lands which the plaintiff has wrongfully taken upon a writ of possession.

If he has taken a several possession, when he is only entitled to one in common, they will do this in the same manner as they will control the extent of an entire possession. And cannot both be as safely and properly done by the judge and jury at the circuit, in the action for *mesne* profits? This action is declared to be a liberal one, allowing every equitable defense. Per Kent, *J.*, in *Murray* v. *Gouverneur*, 2 Johns., Cas., 441. The cases establish the mere general proposition that the title cannot be controverted; not that its extent is unquestionable. The latter enters into the amount of damages, the great object of the action. It is impossible for the defendant ever to recover the money back, which will be wrongfully taken from him by this action; and the court will, if possible, therefore receive the defense. He also cited Adams on Eject., 192, and the cases in *note h.*

But *the court* (absent SUTHERLAND, *J.*), without hearing *Mr. Powers*, in reply, were clear that the plaintiff should recover the whole *mesne* profits at the highest estimate; and,

Per WOODWORTH, *J.* The defendant being in possession of the M'Kinney farm, entered into the consent rule generally; and there being nothing to narrow this in the course of the
264*] *ejectment, the plaintiff recovered the whole. If there is nothing to the contrary in the proceedings in the original action, the consent rule being general, the plaintiff recovers all the land of which the defendant is possessed; and he can recover nothing beyond the possession. It would certainly be violating all precedent to allow of this defense. It was a defense which peculiarly belonged to the action of ejectment. This matter should have been put right at the trial in that action. Nothing is more usual than for the judge to interfere there, and limit the terms of the verdict to the right as proved in evidence.

SAVAGE, *Ch. J.* Neither the judge nor jury in this action had anything to do with the manner of taking possession, or the extent to which it is taken under the writ of possession. To admit either would be to attack the record in a collateral way. If you may question the effect of the record as to one half, you may do the same as to three fourths; and the same principle would extend to the whole; and destroy the rule, that in an action for *mesne* profits the record is conclusive. It has been well observed by *Judge* Woodworth, that all this is confined to the trial of the ejectment. The general proposition that the action for *mesne* profits is an equitable action, relied on by the counsel for the defendant, relates to the measure of damages upon the title, as it appears by the record and proceedings in the original cause. It cannot be extended so as to intrench upon or overthrow that title. That the rule is viewed in this light, will be seen by a case lately before us; *Jackson* v. *Loomis*, 4 Cow., 168.

Judgment accordingly.(a)

(a) *Vide* Aslin v. Parkin, 2 Burr., 668; Van Alen v. Rogers, 1 Johns. Cas., 283; 1 Phil. Ev., 236, ed. of 1820; Baily v. Fair Play, 6 Binn., 450; Goodtitle v. Tombs, 3 Wils., 118; Benson v. Matsdorf, 2 Johns., 369, 371; Jackson v. Randall, 11 Johns., 405; Same v. Stone, 13 *Id.*, 447; Dewey v. Osborn, 4 Cow., 339.

---

*JACKSON, ex dem. SINCLAIR ET AL., [*265
v.
BAILEY.

Amendment of Declaration, After Nonsuit.

Amendment, as to the place laid in a declaration in ejectment, granted after the plaintiff had been nonsuited at the trial for variance.

EJECTMENT for land in the Town of Moriah, Essex Co., brought to trial at the last circuit in that county; when the plaintiff was nonsuited, on the ground that the declaration described the land as lying in the Town of Crown Point in that county.

Now, on an affidavit, that this was a mistake of the attorney, which was not discovered till after the jury were sworn.

Mr. S. Stevens, for the plaintiff, moved to set aside the nonsuit, and to amend the declaration.

Mr. D. Russell, contra, said it was too late to amend, after the plaintiff had been nonsuited for the variance; but,

The Court granted the motion, on payment of costs.

Rule accordingly.

COUCH *v.* ASH.

Imprisonment for Debt—Statute.

Under the Act to Abolish Imprisonment for Debt in Certain Cases, sess. 42, ch. 101, a new promise to pay the debt, made after the discharge, will not restore the right to imprison the defendant.

ASSUMPSIT. The defendant pleaded his discharge under the Act to Abolish Imprisonment for Debt in Certain Cases, sess. 42, ch. 101. Replication, that after the discharge, the defendant undertook and promised the plaintiff to pay the sum mentioned in the declaration. Rejoinder and issue upon that fact.

The cause was tried upon this issue at the last Ulster Circuit, before Betts, *Cir. Judge*; and a verdict found for the plaintiff.

Mr. J. Sudam, for the defendant, moved that notwithstanding the verdict, judgment should be against the defendant *de bonis* only; and cited *Wilson* v. *Kemp*, 3 Maule, & S., 595.

**Mr. C. H. Ruggles*, contra, cited 3 [*266
Chit. Pl., 474, 475, and the Statute 54 Geo. III., ch. 28.

Curia. Let the judgment be for the plaintiff, with a special entry on the record, exempting his person from imprisonment.

Rule accordingly.

Cited in—27 Am. Dec., 284 (4 Rawle, 452).

IN THE MATTER OF DE PEYSTER, an Absent Debtor.

Absconding Debtor Act—When Proof of Debt Received from Creditors—What Creditors Entitled to Dividends.

After the second dividend under the Absconding Debtor Act, 1 R. L., 157, no creditor can be received to prove his debt.

To entitle a creditor to a dividend, he must have been such at the time of the first publication of the proceedings under the Act, pursuant to the 2d section.

Citations—1 R. L., 162, secs. 17, 19; 1 Johns., 174.

ON petition by the Trustees of De Peyster, an absent or absconding debtor, under the Act "for Relief against Absconding and Absent Debtors," 1 R. L., 157, for instruction; and on the application of certain creditors of De Peyster residing in London; the following case was presented to the court:

The trustees had made two dividends, and recently advertised a third and final dividend. The London creditors did not hear of the proceedings in this matter till after the second dividend; but they afterwards came in and claimed their full dividend before the final distribution should be made. The trustees also anticipated that claims to the final dividend would be interposed by persons who had become creditors since the issuing of the attachment.

Mr. G. Brinckerhoff, for the London creditors, cited 1 R. L., 164, sec. 27; 1 Johns., 165, 173, 174, and the cases there cited.

Mr. H. S. Jones, for the Trustees, cited 1 R. L., 162, sec. 19.

Curia. The 19th section declares, that if any creditor neglects to give notice of or deliver an account of his demand to the trustees until after distribution, pursuant to the 17th section, he shall not be entitled to any dividend; but if he shall comply before the second distribution, he shall have the sum he would have been entitled to on the first distribution, before any second dividend be made.

The trustees are required, by the 17th section, to give notice to all the creditors to come **267***] in and prove their debts, *within a certain time, when the first dividend is to be made. Now, we have seen that, by a subsequent section, if they neglect doing this before the first, they shall be received before the second dividend; but no provision of this kind is made in reference to the third. Taking these various enactments into view, we are satisfied that creditors who neglect to prove their demands till after a second dividend are precluded from all share of the debtor's estate in the hands of the trustees. An opinion to this effect was expressed in *Peck* v. *Randall*, 1 Johns., 174; though the question does not appear to have been presented by the case.

This ground would, in the particular case before us, preclude the claim of all who became creditors after the attachment issued. But we have no hesitation, on this head, in answering the question put to us by the trustees, on broader ground. We are of opinion that no person can be entitled to a dividend who was not a creditor at the time of the first publication of notice of the attachment, pursuant to the 2d section of the Act.

Motion of the London creditors denied.

Cited in—3 Abb. App. Dec., 237; 12 How. Pr., 349.

A. BARKER AND E. MANN, Executor and Executrix of J. MANN,
v.
BAKER.

Practice—Trover by Executors—Costs.

In trover by executors, on a conversion after the testator's death, if they be nonsuited, &c., at the trial, they must pay costs.

For they may declare in their own right.

Where executors may declare in their own right they shall pay costs on nonsuit, &c.

Citations—2 Saund., 47 *k*; 7 T. R., 354; 10 East, 293; 11 Johns., 403; 4 Cow., 87.

IN trover for a pair of horses. The declaration contained three counts. The first alleged the trover and conversion in the testator's lifetime; the second alleged the trover in the plaintiff's lifetime, and the conversion after his death; and the third, both trover and conversion after his death.

On the trial, at the last Monroe Circuit, the plaintiffs proved that after the testator's death, the horses were found in the defendant's possession, and were demanded by the plaintiffs, but the defendant refused to deliver them. A strong case being made out by the defendant, the plaintiffs submitted to a nonsuit.

Mr. J. C. Spencer*, for the defendant, [*268** now moved for costs. He cited *Ketchum* v. *Ketchum*, 4 Cow., 87; *Jenkins* v. *Plombe*, 6 Mod., 91; *Id.*, 181; 1 Salk., 287; *Hollis* v. *Smith*, 10 East, 293; *Bollard* v. *Spencer*, 7 T. R., 354; *Admrs. of Tilton* v. *Williams*, 11 Johns., 403.

Mr. A. Samson, contra, cited *Cockerill* v. *Kynaston*, 4 T. R., 277.

Curia. In trover by executors, where the conversion, which is the gist of the action, is after the death of the testator, they must pay costs, if they fail. (2 Saund., 47 *k*.) It is true that in *Cockerill* v. *Kynaston*, relied on by the plaintiff's counsel, costs were denied to the defendant, and the case is not distinguishable from the present. But in a subsequent case, *Bollard* v. *Spencer*, 7 T. R., 354, Ld. Kenyon said there was some mistake in *Cockerill* v. *Kynaston*; and the plaintiffs having declared on a possession after the testator's death, were holden, on being nonsuited, to pay costs. In *Hollis* v. *Smith*, 10 East, 293, the pleadings were like the second and third counts of this declaration. Ld. Ellenborough said the question was, whether the plaintiffs need declare as administrators; that it certainly was not necessary to declare in that form; that on the death of the intestate, the plaintiffs were, in point of law, the owners of the goods; and whether possessed of them or not, they might declare as other persons; and judgment was given against them for costs.

The rule that executors, when prosecuting in right of the testator, shall not pay costs, applies to cases where it is necessary to sue in their representative character. *Admrs. of Tilton* v. *Williams*, 11 Johns., 403. The general doctrine on this head was very fully considered in *Ketchum* v. *Ketchum*, 4 Cow., 87.

In the principal case, the whole evidence of the trover and conversion was of a time subsequent to the testator's death. The defendant must take his judgment for costs.

Motion granted.

Cited in—9 Wend., 490; 1 Den. 627; 1 Lans., 305; 14 How. Pr., 485; 5 Abb. Pr., 231; 5 Sand., 395; 20 Wis., 386.

269*] *FISH *v.* WRIGHT.

Practice—Stay of Proceedings—Costs.

Where the cause is noticed for trial, and the defendant then obtains an order to stay proceedings, with a view to move for a reference, the motion will not be granted, except on the terms of paying the costs of preparing for trial to the time when the order was served.

ON motion for a reference, in behalf of the defendant, it appeared that the cause, being at issue, had been noticed for trial by the plaintiff's attorney, for Nov. 29, last; but on the 26th the defendant's attorney served him with an order to stay proceedings, made with a view to this motion.

The Court agreed that the motion must be granted; but one question was, if it should not be on payment of the costs of the plaintiff, in preparing for trial.

Mr. C. F. Ingalls, for the defendant.

N. B.—Mr. Doe, contra, cited *Budd* v. *Malburn*, 1 Cow., 47.

Curia. We think this question comes within the decisions of this court, in the case cited, and other cases, where orders to stay, with a view to the change of venue, are obtained, after the cause is noticed for trial. The defendant may take the effect of his motion; but this must be on payment of the costs of the notice, and preparation for trial, to the time when the order was served.

Rule accordingly.

JACKSON, ex dem. HOOKER, *v.* YOUNG.

Omission of Sheriff to File Certificate of Sale, does not Prejudice Purchaser—Statute.

The sheriff's omission to file the certificate of sale according to the Statute, sess. 43, ch. 184, sec. 1, will not prejudice the purchaser.

This Act is not a condition precedent; but the Statute is merely directory.

EJECTMENT, tried before Throop, *Circuit Judge*, Dec. 13, 1824, at the Oswego Circuit.

The lessor of the plaintiff claimed title to the premises in question, as the assignee of the purchaser, at a sheriff's sale of those premises; and gave in evidence, the sheriff's deed, reciting the sale in Dec., 1822, at public vendue, to J. H.; and a sealed assignment of his right to receive a deed, to the lessor of the plaintiff. The original assignment from J. H. to the lessor of the plaintiff was also given in evidence.

270*] *The defendant's counsel moved for a nonsuit, on the ground that it did not appear that a certificate of the sale had been filed in the clerk's office, pursuant to the Statute, sess. 43, ch. 184, sec. 1. This motion being denied, the defendant then offered to prove that no such certificate had been filed in the clerk's office. This testimony was excluded by the judge; and a verdict was then taken for the plaintiffs, subject to the opinion of the court.

Mr. Talcott, Atty-Gen., for the plaintiff, cited *Young* v. *Taylor*, 2 Binn., 227; *Jackson* v. *Rosevelt*, 13 Johns., 97; *Jackson* v. *Vanderheyden*, 17 *Id.*, 167.

Mr. B. F. Butler, contra, said the object of the statute in requiring the certificate to be filed was, to give the debtor and his creditors such information as might be necessary, to guide them in redeeming the land sold. This important object would be defeated, unless the sheriff is holden to great strictness in filing the certificate. But,

The Court, without hearing *Mr. Talcott*, in reply, were clear that the statute was merely directory; that the filing of a certificate was not a condition precedent to the giving of the the deed, and passing the title; and that the sheriff's omission should not prejudice the purchaser.

Judgment for the plaintiff.

Cited in—4 Wend. 590; 6 Wend., 487; 2 N.Y., 68 (*a*); 8 N. Y., 89; 24 N. Y, 587; 34 N. Y., 273; 1 Keyes, 517; 1 Hun, 54; 10 Barb, 480; 14 Barb., 291; 1 T. & C., 375; 3 T. & C., 136; 74 Ind., 491; 40 Mich., 236; 45 Mo., 441; 45 Am. Dec., 858 (10 Mo., 117).

CANFIELD AND CRANE, Ex'rs of WARING, *v.* WESTCOTT.

Contract for Sale of Land—Proviso for Benefit of Vendor—Election.

In articles for sale of land, by which the vendee covenants to pay, and the vendor covenants to convey on payment, and the vendee agrees that if he fails in his covenant, the contract shall be void; on action by the vendor for the money no part having been paid; held, that the action lay; the contract being void only at the election of the vendor.

So if the contract contain a general proviso, that if the vendee do not perform, it shall be void; it is voidable only, at the election of the vendor.

ON demurrer to the declaration. This was in covenant on articles of agreement under seal, dated Mar. 21, 1820, between the defendant and the testator; whereby the defendant covenanted to pay the testator $416, with interest, &c., in four equal annual payments, the first installment to be paid on or before the first day of Jan., 1825, &c., as the consideration of a lot of land. The testator covenanted that as soon as the defendant had fulfilled all the covenants on his part, he, the testator, would convey the lot to the defendant. The declaration averred that the *first two [*271 installments were in arrear, and unpaid; and claimed to recover the whole with interest.

The defendant craved and had oyer of the articles, whereby it appeared, that after the mutual covenants above mentioned, the defendant bound himself, by the same articles, to settle on the lot in the season of 1820, and make various improvements; to commit no waste, &c. The articles then proceeded thus: "the said Daniel (the defendant) hereby agrees, that should he fail in performing any part of the above covenants, that this contract shall become void, and of no effect; and that the said party of the second part (the testator) shall and may re-enter, and take possession of the said premises, without hindrance and molestation."

General demurrer and joinder.

Mr. J. Steele, in support of the demurrer, insisted that by the plaintiff's own showing the agreement was void; that it was to become so by its own provision, if any of the defendant's covenants should not be kept; and the plaintiffs had shown the happening of this contingency. But,

The Court, without hearing *Mr. J. Platt*, who was to have argued against the demurrer, were clear that judgment must be for the plaintiff. They said the provision that this agreement should be void, was for the benefit of the vendor. On the vendee's default, the vendor might, therefore, consider the agreement void at his own election; or affirm it, and brings his action on the covenants; and they said this had been often so held in much stronger cases; as where the provision in the articles was general and positive, in the words of both parties, that if the vendee failed to perform, the contract should be void.

The *Chief Justice* told *Mr. Steele* he might withdraw the demurrer and plead, if he had any other defense.

But *Mr. Steele* said he had not; and,

The plaintiff had judgment.(a)

Cited in—7 Wend., 214; 24 Wend., 326; 10 N. Y., 442; 51 N. Y., 58; 74 N. Y., 214; 7 Lans., 351; 11 Hun, 478; 10 Barb., 376; 37 Barb., 34; 64 Barb., 557; 14 Abb. N. S., 107; 1 Leg. Obs., 103; 38 Cal., 251; 20 Ind., 436; 36 N. J. L., 155.

(a) May Term, 1823.—MANCIUS *v.* SERGEANT.

ON ERROR to the C. P. of Columbia. The declaration in the court below was in covenant by Mancius against Sergeant, on articles of agreement, by which Mancius covenanted, on Sergeant's fulfill-
272*] ing his covenants after *mentioned, to convey to him. He then covenanted to pay, &c., by installments; and the articles then provided, that if Sergeant should fail to perform his covenants, Manelus should be released and discharged from his covenants; and that Sergeant should forfeit his payments, if any. The declaration averred a total non-performance on the part of Sergeant.

General demurrer and joinder.

The C. P. gave judgment for the defendant below.

Mr. E. Williams, for the plaintiff in error.

Mr. C. Bushnell, contra.

Curia, per SAVAGE, *Ch. J.* That the intent of the parties is to be the governing consideration in the construction of every contract, cannot be denied; nor that such intent (when doubtful) is to be collected from the whole instrument, and the nature of the contract; every part of it having meaning and effect if possible.

What, then, was the meaning of the parties when they entered into this contract? Did they intend it should be a *felo de se*, or that the defendant below might make it so, or valid and operative at his election? What inducement could the plaintiff below have for making such a contract?

The covenants by the defendant below were absolute; and on his performance, the plaintiff below would have been bound; but the clause providing for a forfeiture of previous payment was totally inoperative until, at least, one payment made. The whole clause providing for the vendor's discharge from his covenants, and the for feitureof the vendee's payments, is clearly a condition in favor of the former; not the latter. The vendee was bound to pay at all events. If he had failed, even after having made payments, the vendor might consider the contract at an end, and sell the land to another. If, however, he chooses not to do so, but hold the vendee to his contract, he has an undoubted right to enforce it by compelling payment. A contrary doctrine would be allowing the vendee to take advantage of his own negligence, without any advantage to the vendor, but rather an injury; as he is, in the meantime, prohibited from selling the land to any other purchaser.

Judgment reversed.

Cited in—5 Cow., 273, *n.*; 51 N. Y., 58; 11 Hun, 478; 37 Barb., 34.

CHURCH *v.* AYRES.

AFTER the decision in Mancius v. Sargeant, a question of the void clause was submitted to the Supreme Court, between Church, plaintiff, and Ayers, defendant. The case was this: Ayers paid Church $5 for land; and by articles between the parties acknowledging this payment, covenanted to pay upwards of $400 more within nine years, by equal annual installments, with interest, annually, &c. The articles then had this clause; "and in case default shall be made in any of the payments of the above principal or interest, at any of the annual periods above stipulated for the payment thereof, this agreement shall be absolutely null and void." The articles *then proceed to provide that if Church [*273
should not enforce the payments, or annul the contract, Ayers would pay interest upon interest, &c.

The money not being paid pursuant to the contract, Church brought covenant, alleging the breach; and Ayers demurred.

Mr. H. Welles, in support of the demurrer.

Mr. S. S. Haight, contra.

SAVAGE, *Ch. J.*, in delivering the opinion of the court, after recognizing the same general principles as in Mancius v. Sergeant, that the intent is to govern, &c., and every part of the contract is to have effect, proceeded as follows: "It seems to me very clear, in this case, that it was the intention of the parties, that on the failure of the defendant to pay, according to his stipulation, it should be optional with the plaintiff, to avoid the contract, or not. A further provision is made in his favor, in case he shall not avail himself of the clause in question. It is a settled principle, that a party in whose favor a provision is made by the contract, may waive it if he pleases.

The very point now raised was decided by this court, on the same state of pleadings, in Van Rensselaer v. Fitch. The case is not reported, but I have been favored by the late *Ch. J.*, with the demurrer book, and the decision of the court. Van Rensselaer sued Fitch on an article of agreement, as follows: "First; the said party of the second part (Fitch) agrees to purchase of the said party of the first part (Van Rensselaer) the lands hereinafter mentioned; and to pay him for the same, the sum of $32.96, in one year from the date hereof, with interest on the same till paid; otherwise, these presents to be void both at law and in equity." Van Rensselaer then covenanted that the money being paid, he would convey. To a declaration on this contract, the defendant demurred; and judgment was rendered for the plaintiff.

The present is even a stronger case for the plaintiff. The authority cited is in point, and a similar judgment must be given."

Judgment for the plaintiff.

Cited in—51 N. Y., 58; 11 Hun, 478; 37 Barb., 34.

EX PARTE SMITH.

Habeas Corpus—*State Magistrate May Commit for Further Examination Touching Crime Against the United States—Form of Commitment.*

Form of commitment to jail, for further examination, by a justice.

A state magistrate may commit for further examination touching a crime against the U. S.

On *habeas corpus*, a prisoner who had been committed by a state magistrate for further examination, touching a robbery of the U. S. mail, was remanded, without any cause being shown by the Attorney-General; the prisoner having been in custody but a short time.

SMITH was committed on this warrant: "Police office, City of Albany. The jailer will receive, and safely keep *for fur- [*274
ther examination, George W. Smith, who is charged with having been engaged in, or ac-

cessory to a robbery of the United States mail. March 14, 1826.

J. O. COLE, Justice of the Peace."

The warrant was not sealed.

Mar. 16. The prisoner being brought up by *habeas corpus*.

Mr. J. V. N. Yates moved that he be discharged. The affidavit of the prisoner, on which the writ was allowed, stated that he understood the charge against him to be that of robbing the mail between Baltimore and Philadelphia; and that, on making due inquiries, he found that he was not confined on any process, nor on the demand, as far as he could learn, of the Executive of any State; nor upon any process from any of the U. S. courts.

Mr. Yates said, that from the view he had taken of the case, it was unnecessary to criticise the order of commitment made by the police magistrate. The offense being against a law of the U. S. (U. S. Const., Art. 3, Ingersol Dig., 688), a state magistrate has no jurisdiction. (1 Wh., 330.) This general position would, probably, not be disputed by the Atty-Gen. He would, most likely, contend that the state magistrate might commit for trial before the U. S. tribunals; but the decision cited from Wheaton involved this question also. He admitted that Congress had, in terms, conferred this power upon state magistrates; *vide* 4 Laws U. S., 302, sec. 35; but the case in Wheaton, and *U. S.* v. *Lathrop*, 17 Johns., 4, both concur in denying that they could constitutionally do this. The courts of the U. S. have exclusive jurisdiction. If the magistrate acts judicially, of which he supposed there could be no doubt, he comes within the cases cited. This court had, he was aware, in a similar case, remanded prisoners, in order to secure their forthcoming, on the demand of the U. S.; *People* v. *Lynch*, 11 Johns., 554, *note;* but this was contrary to the views taken of the subject in the more recent cases. The prisoner cannot be remanded, if there is a want of jurisdiction.

275*] *The offense was committed out of this State; and there is also a want of jurisdiction on this ground.

Mr. Talcott Atty-Gen., declined reading affidavits to justify the detention of the prisoner, on the ground that this might lead to disclosures unfavorable to the prosecution. He admitted that the state tribunals had not the power finally to try for the crime charged; but we could detain the prisoner till his trial should be provided for by the proper authority; and that should be for such reasonable time as would enable the General Government to apply for and take the prisoner into their custody. This had been held of a foreign government, to whom we were bound only by the law of nations. *In the Matter of Washburn*, 4 Johns. Ch., 106. And is our obligation less, in reference to our own federative government? Heath, *J.*, in *Muir* v. *Kaye*, 4 Taunt., 43, said that such has always been the law, even as to nations properly foreign. That we may detain and deliver up offenders for crimes against other States, has never been questioned; and this court have holden it to be their duty to do so.

This commitment is merely for further examination. No formality is necessary in such a commitment. It may be by a verbal warrant; no crime need be specified. The order in question is in the usual form, and is sanctioned by the authorities. The prisoner may be committed to the county jail, or otherwise secured for this purpose, and detained a reasonable time, according to the exigencies of each particular case. Twenty days, or more, may not be an unreasonable time. (1 Chit. C. L., 73, 74.)

Mr. Yates, in reply, did not deny that a magistrate might commit for further examination, but insisted that this depends on his having jurisdiction. If that be wanting, he certainly cannot commit for examination, or for any other purpose. The doctrine of *Chancellor* Kent, taken in the extent contended for by the Atty-Gen., is fraught with much mischief. It would warrant a magistrate in detaining for examination, till proof could be obtained from the Cape of Good Hope, or any other distant quarter of the world. The comity *of nations will certainly not demand [***276** this in relation to any crime short of murder; and it was held not to reach a case of that aggravated nature, by *Ch. J.* Tilghman who, with the case of *Washburn* before him, refused to act upon it. The remedy given by the Constitution of the U. S. is fully adequate. The fugitive must be demanded by the Executive, to warrant his being delivered up.

SUTHERLAND, *J.* But the Governor of another State may know nothing of the arrest. A reasonable time must be allowed for giving him notice.

WOODWORTH, *J.* Detaining a prisoner by state authority, in order that he may be delivered over for prosecution to the U. S., is, by no means, an unusual exercise of power. This court has repeatedly sanctioned such a proceeding, and in one case very lately.

Mr. Yates. At any rate, this is a matter of discretion with the court; and they should require proof of the Atty-Gen., that there is, at least, probable cause for the detention.

SAVAGE, *C. J.* If here had been unreasonable delay, that would be a ground of discharge, unless probable cause could be shown. But a very short time has elapsed since the commitment; and we are clear, that, for the present, the prisoner must be remanded for further examination.

Rule accordingly.

Cited in—16 Barb., 307; 42 Barb., 223; Edm., 452.

EX PARTE G. SMITH.

Act to Abolish Imprisonment for Debt—Extent of.

A discharge under the Act to Abolish Imprisonment for Debt, &c., sess. 42, ch. 101, extends to one committed to jail for not fulfilling an order of filiation and maintenance, within 1 R. L., 306, sec. 1.

Citations—9 Johns., 368; 9 Johns., 127.

SMITH having been committed to jail in Columbia, for not performing an order of filiation and maintenance, for a *weekly [***277** sum of money, made pursuant to 1 R. L., 306, sec. 1; and being afterwards discharged under the Act to Abolish Imprisonment for Debt, &c., sess. 42, ch. 101; and the sheriff refusing to set him at liberty, on the production of the discharge,

Mr. D. B. Tallmadge moved for a *habeas corpus* to bring him up, in order that he might be discharged by this court. He said the question in these cases is, whether the debt be due to the people or to individuals. In the latter case, the discharge under the Insolvent Act is operative. *Rex* v. *Wakefield*, 13 East, 190. Judgment for a tort creates a debt within the meaning of the Act. *Ex parte Thayer*, 4 Cow., 66. An action lies on this order. *Wallsworth* v. *Mead*, 9 Johns., 368.

Mr. C. Bushnell, contra, agreed that the court should finally dispose of this question without the formality of a *habeas corpus*. He said that all the sheriff and overseers wished was to be instructed in their duty. This case is *sui generis*. Actual payment of any sum in gross would not discharge the prisoner. And if the insolvent discharge operates for the amount due, it cannot reach the arrears which may hereafter accrue. A discharge affects no debt which cannot be proved, and be the subject of a dividend.

Curia. We think this is a case within the meaning of the Act. The order imposes a mere civil obligation, for which an action would lie. It is in the nature of a judgment for so much, payable by weekly installments. *Wallsworth* v. *Mead*, 9 Johns., 368. Another effect of the order is, to impose on the putative father the obligation of giving surety to perform it, if he has neglected the actual performance. For default of both, he is imprisoned. He is in execution for not performing one of two things, both of which are, in their nature, civil obligations; and both of which were due at the time of the assignment. His imprisonment was for or by reason of a debt, due at the time of the assignment, in the words of the Insolvent Act. It is for such a case that the Act was **278***] intended. The debt itself *is not discharged; but only one remedy for the debt. Whether the putative father may not yet be sued and imprisoned for arrears upon the order accruing after the assignment, in analogy to the case of rent, and within the reason of *Lansing* v. *Prendergast*, 9 Johns., 127, it is not necessary now to decide.

Motion granted.

GRAY *v.* THORNBER.

Practice—Supersedeas—*Statute.*

Delivering a *ca. sa.* to the sheriff is good cause against a *supersedeas* under the Statute, 1 R. L., 353, sec. 12; but if it appear to have been returned *non est inventus*, a *supersedeas* will be granted, unless it be followed up by an *alias*.

The court may, under special circumstances, give time to issue an *alias*.

Citations—8 Johns., 379, 382; 3 Johns., 446.

THE defendant having been surrendered, in discharge of his bail, to the Sheriff of N. Y., Oct. 29; Mar. 7, the Recorder of N. Y. made an order upon the plaintiff, to show cause, on the 11th, why a *supersedeas* should not issue upon the Statute, 1. R. L., 353, sec. 12.

On showing cause, it appeared that a *ca. sa.* had been delivered to the sheriff, Mar. 4, returnable that day; but the defendant was not actually arrested upon it; and the sheriff returned it *non est inventus;* though the defendant had continued in his custody on the limits, after the surrender, and was so in his custody when he returned the *ca. sa.*

The recorder refused to make an order which should be absolute for a *supersedeas* until Mar. 21, to the end that the opinion of the Supreme Court might be taken in the case.

Mr. S. M. Hopkins moved to set aside the order of the recorder. He said it was a sufficient answer to the application for a *supersedeas*, that the defendant had been charged in execution at the time of showing cause. (Col. Cas., 42; 1 Cai., 67). It is enough that an execution is delivered to the sheriff. *Minturn* v. *Phelps*, 3 Johns., 446. It is not the fault of the plaintiff, if a sheriff will not arrest a man in his custody. In *Minturn* v. *Phelps*, putting a *ca. sa.* in the postoffice, directed to the sheriff, was held sufficient.

Mr. J. E. Lovett*, contra, relied on [*279** the case of *Tracy* v. *Whipple*, 8 Johns., 379, 382, as in point against the motion.

Curia. *Tracy* v. *Whipple* is decisive that the mere delivery of a *ca. sa.* to the sheriff, against a person on the limits, is not, *per se et eo instanti*, an arrest, so as to charge the sheriff for an escape; but is that material to the present question? The plaintiff has made an ineffectual attempt to charge the defendant. The execution was returned *non est*, and he might have issued an *alias ca. sa.* on the 11th. That would have been good cause, under the authorities cited for the motion. He did not do so, but seems to rely on the sheriff's liability. In *Minturn* v. *Phelps*, 3 Johns., 446, had it been shown to the court that the *ca. sa.* had miscarried, or had not been executed, or not received by the sheriff, till after the return day, is there a doubt that a *supersedeas* would have followed?

We think the recorder decided correctly.

Mr. Hopkins said there had been a misapprehension of the practice on the part of the plaintiff's attorney, and moved for a stay of proceedings until he should be able to communicate with him, so that he might yet charge the defendant in execution. He said that in a case so circumstanced, this might be done, as he was confident he could show upon authority, if time should be allowed.

As to this,

Cur. adv. vult.

Time was, afterwards, allowed accordingly.

SYMONDS *v.* CRAW.

Practice—Non Pros—*Bill of Particulars.*

A plaintiff may be *non prossed* as to his common counts only, leaving him to proceed upon his special count, for not furnishing a bill of particulars.

Furnishing a bill of particulars after a regular notice of a motion for judgment of *non pros.*, for not delivering one pursuant to a judge's order, is an answer to the application, provided the costs be paid up to that time; but not otherwise.

MR. E. GRIFFIN, for the defendant, moved for judgment of *non pros.*, for not delivering a bill of particulars pursuant to *an [***280** order. The declaration contained one special count with the general counts; and the order was founded upon and related to the latter.

After this motion was noticed, the plaintiff furnished a bill, but did not pay the costs.

Mr. J. Steele opposed the application, insisting that the plaintiff could not be *non prossed* as to a part of the counts. Besides, he said, a bill had been furnished; and, in either view, the motion must fail.

Curia. We think differently. The motion must be granted as to the common counts, unless the plaintiff pay the costs of this application within thirty days. Furnishing a bill of particulars after notice given, would have been an answer to the present application, had the costs of the motion been paid up to the time of the bill furnished.

Rule accordingly.

Cited in—4 How. Pr., 307; 2 Co. R., 129.

ADAMS v. SMITH AND PARMETER.

Practice—Sale, by Sheriff, of Property not Belonging to Defendants.

Where the sheriff sold property on a *fi. fa.* against the defendants and indorsed the amount of sales upon the execution; but the property turned out to belong to a third person, who recovered its value in an action against the sheriff and the plaintiff jointly; the court ordered the indorsement stricken out, and that an *alias fi. fa.* should issue for the whole.

THE sheriff had sold certain personal property on a *fi. fa.* in this cause, and indorsed the amount of sales upon it as received. Afterwards it turned out that the property did not belong to the defendants, or either of them; and the value of the property was recovered by the owner, in an action against the sheriff and the plaintiff jointly.

A motion was now made to strike out the indorsement; and for leave to issue a *fi. fa.* for the whole amount of the judgment.

Mr. P. L. Tracy, for the motion.

Mr. R. Beach, contra.

Curia. The motion must be granted.

Motion granted.

Cited in—4 Den., 165; 3 Barb. Ch., 588; 14 N. Y., 278; 40 N. Y., 401; 4 McLean, 616; 23 Cal., 362; 59 Ind., 204; 16 Minn., 16; 22 Minn., 231; 49 Am. Dec., 214 (3 Barb. Ch., 528).

281*] *WILLIAM v. BROWN.

Practice—Notice.

If a notice of presenting a petition in partition, and of moving to appoint commissioners, mention a wrong place, this will be rejected as surplusage. No place need be mentioned in such notice.

IN partition, the notice of presenting the petition and moving for the appointment of commissioners, was October Term last, at the City Hall of the City of N. Y., instead of the Capital in the City of Albany. A rule having been taken upon that notice,

Mr. L. F. Stevens now moved to set it aside.

Mr. T. Mumford, contra.

Curia. If the place of moving had been entirely omitted the notice would, notwithstanding, have been good. The place of our terms is fixed by a public law, of which every one must take notice at his peril. The addition of a wrong place, by mistake, is mere surplusage, and may be rejected. The motion must be denied, with costs.

Motion denied.

YOUNGS v. VAN SCHAICK.

Practice—Costs.

In assumpsit removed by *habeas corpus* from the Mayor's Court of Albany, to the Supreme Court, the plaintiff is entitled to Supreme Court costs, where he recovers more than $50, though less than $250.

ASSUMPSIT, commenced in the Mayor's Court of the City of Albany, where the plaintiff declared for $800; and the defendant removed the cause into this court by *habeas corpus*. The cause being here referred, and the referees having reported $144.21 for the plaintiff, he claimed the taxation of Supreme Court costs before the commissioner, *Judge* L'Amoureaux, who asked the advice of this court, whether they should be taxed at the Supreme Court or C. P. rate, upon the Stat. 1 R. L., 344, sec. 4.

Mr. W. Esleeck, for the plaintiff.

Mr. I. T. B. Van Vechten, for the defendant.

Curia. The plaintiff is entitled to Supreme Court costs.

---

*JACKSON, ex dem. SWARTWOUT [*282 ET UX., v. STILES. CHAMBERLAIN, *Tenant*.

THE SAME, ex dem. THE SAME, v. THE SAME, in five other actions of ejectment, against different tenants.

Practice—Rule, that Several Ejectment Causes Should Abide Result of One to be Noticed for Trial.

Several ejectment causes, depending on the same questions, and substantially the same evidence, directed to abide the event of such cause among them, as the plaintiff should notice for trial.

MR. I. SEELYE moved to consolidate these causes, on an affidavit of the partner of the attorney for the tenants, that he was well acquainted with the titles of both parties, &c., that he was informed and believed, and had good reason to believe, that the lessors had caused these actions to be brought on the same grounds, and the same title which they set up in *Jackson* v. *Johnson*, *ante*, 74, that the plaintiff's claim of title in all these causes is the same, and derived from the same source; and that the plaintiff's evidence on the trial would be substantially the same in each. That, as he was informed and believed, the tenants all claimed title from the same source; and that the same evidence would be adduced by all the tenants, on the trial, varying only in the manner of conveying down the title to them. That the venues were all laid in the County of Otsego, and the demises all laid on the same day. That he verily believed that a trial in one would settle the plaintiff's rights in all the other causes.

The motion was founded on the authority of *Jackson* v. *Shauber*, 4 Cow., 78 ; and,

Messrs. J. O. Morse and *D. Cady*, contra, agreed that, within the cases cited, one of these causes should determine the whole ; and the question was, whether the court would designate the cause to be tried, or the attorney for the plaintiff should elect, on noticing for trial.

Mr. Seelye insisted that the court should name the cause in the rule.

Mr. Cady said this would be unsafe, for the defendant in the cause named might die before the notice of trial served, and the cause thus be abated.

283*] *RULE. "That all the causes abide the event and final determination of the one which the plaintiff may elect to notice for trial; and that whatever judgment may finally be rendered in the cause thus noticed for trial, shall be entered in all the other causes ; and the party prevailing shall be at liberty to make up and file records therein accordingly."

OLIVER
v.
THE TRUSTEES OF THE FIRST PRESBYTERIAN CHURCH in SPRINGFIELD.

Misconduct of Jury — Improper Separation — Verdict Set Aside.

Where a jury procured their separation, by pretending to the constable that they had agreed upon a sealed verdict when in truth they had not: and conversations out of doors were afterwards carried on in the the presence of some of them relative to the suit, by persons not on the jury ; and on assembling they were sent out again though this was objected to by the plaintiff ; and then they returned with a verdict for the defendant ; held, that the verdict should be set aside.

Where the jury improperly separate, and this is followed by the the slightest suspicion of abuse the verdict will be set aside.

THIS cause having been submitted to the jury at the last Otsego Circuit, they retired under the sworn charge of the constable. It being late in the evening when they retired, they had liberty from the court (by consent of parties) to seal their verdict and disperse, rendering it next morning. They accordingly told the constable they had agreed, and dispersed ; the next morning delivered a paper purporting to contain their verdict, which was, on opening it, found to contain these words : "The jurors, after due deliberation, do not agree." Signed by all the jurors.

Before the jury reassembled to deliver the above paper, some of them were seen in a bar-room, where the cause was much talked of.

On the paper being delivered, the judge, after explaining certain testimony, as to which the jury disagreed, directed them to retire and reconsider the case ; which they did, though this course was objected to by the plaintiff's counsel ; and afterwards they returned a verdict for the defendant.

Mr. I. Seelye now moved to set this verdict aside.

Mr. A. Stewart, contra, cited *Smith* v. *Thompson*, 1 Cow., 221, and the cases there cited in the note ; *People* v. *Douglass*, 4 Cow., 26 ; *Ex parte Hill*, 3 Cow., 355.

Curia. In the cases cited of verdicts sustained, notwithstanding the separation of the jury, there was no suspicion *of abuse ; [***284** and indeed, it appeared affirmatively, that there was nothing that followed the separation which could be injurions to the party seeeking to get rid of the verdict. The present case is far different. After practicing a fraud on the constable, several of the jurors are found in a public bar-room, where the subject of the suit was much talked of in their presence ; and it is not pretended that they did not listen to the conversation, and might not have been influenced by it. This is not to be tolerated. Here is not only suspicion of abuse, and we have uniformly held that the slightest suspicion of this sort, will vitiate the verdict, but we think the circumstances of this case, in themselves, amount to a positive abuse. They evince that want of respect in the jury to the obligations imposed upon them by their situation, which cannot be sanctioned consistently with the rights of parties. They procured their separation by a very unbecoming artifice, thus placing themselves in a situation to be practiced upon and influenced by conversation out of doors. Such conversation was carried on in the presence of some of them. Indeed, it is difficult to see how the suspicions which attach to this case could be explained away. The motion must be granted, with costs to abide the event.

Rule accordingly.

Cited in—2 Wend., 355 ; 7 Wend., 422 ; 4 How. Pr., 255 ; 9 How. Pr., 13 ; 44 How. Pr., 363 ; 4 Bos., 510.

EX PARTE HUNT.

Paupers — Grandparents to be Supported by Grandchildren—Mandamus.

The Statute, 1 R. L., 286, sec. 21, requiring a grandchild to support his indigent grandparents, extends to the case of his indigent maternal grandparents.

AT their last August Term, the General Sessions of Washington Co. made an order on Hunt, among others, pursuant to the Statute, 1 R. L., 286, sec. 21, to maintain W. S. and E. his wife, paupers, on the ground that Hunt's father married the daughter of the paupers ; and that Hunt was the son of that marriage.

Mr. D. Russell moved for a *mandamus*, commanding the sessions to vacate their order. He said the statute does not compel a man to maintain the indigent parents of his wife. (1 Bl.,

NOTE.—*Misconduct of jury—When verdict set aside for.*

The verdict will be set aside for any misconduct of the jury where it appears that injury has resulted to the party complaining, but not otherwise. Smith v. Thompson, 1 Cow., 221 ; Horton v. Horton, 2 Cow., 589 ; Wilson v. Abrabams, 1 Hill, 207 ; People v. Hartung, 8 Abb. Pr., 132 ; Hackley v. Hastie, 3 Johns., 252 ; Blackley v. Sheldon, 7 Johns., 32 ; Anthony v. Smith, 4 Bosw., 503 ; Hager v. Hager, 38 Barb., 92 ; Henlow v. Leonard, 7 Johns., 200 ; Thayer v. VanVleet, 5 Johns., 111 ; Roberts v. State, 14 Ga., 8 ; Langworthy v. Myers, 4 Iowa, 18 ; Wright v. Rogers, 3 N. J. L., 547 ; Crane v. Sayre, 6 N. J. L., 110 ; Drake v. Newton, 23 N. J. L., 111 ; Oram v. Bishop, 30 N. J. L., 153. But see Brant v. Fowler, 7 Cow. 562 ; Demund v. Gowen, 5 N. J. L., 687 ; Lester v. Stanley, 3 Day (Conn.), 287. See, generally, Harvey v. Rickett, 15 Johns., 87, *note* ; Smith v. Cheetham, 3 Cai., 57, *note*.

Com., 448, Christian's *note;* Reeve Dom. Rel., **285***] *284 ; 2 Ld. Raym., 1454 ; 1 Str., 190 ; 4 T. R.,118 ; Kirby, 156.) Now, if the father of Hunt was not bound to maintain the paupers, clearly Hunt himself ought not to be bound. He would be bound to maintain the indigent parents of his father. If of his mother, also, a most unreasonable burden is thus imposed.

The motion was not opposed, but,

Per Curiam. The statute is, that the children and grandchildren shall maintain their indigent parents and grandparents. The paupers are the maternal grandparents of Hunt. He is thus within the terms of the statute; and we see no reason, in principle or authority, why he should be exempted. The authorities cited, exempt the son-in-law, on the ground that the statute means natural relations only, which is not this case. We have nothing to do with the question of expediency.

It is questionable whether a *mandamus* lies, the matter being *res judicata* in the court below. But whether it does or not, we are clear against the relator on the merits.

Motion denied.

THE PEOPLE, ex rel. HAYWOOD,
v.
THE JUDGES OF COLUMBIA.

Practice—Mandamus.

Under the Act, sess. 47, ch. 238, sec. 36, 38, an appeal lies in all cases, whether the judgment of the justice be upon an issue of law or fact.

ON returning the *mandamus* granted in *Ex parte Haywood, ante,* 19, the facts were the same in substance as in that case; and *The Court* ordered a peremptory *mandamus.*

Mr. D. B. Tallmadge, for the plaintiffs.

Mr. C. Bushnell, for the defendants.

286*] *EX PARTE WEED.

Practice—Appeal Bond, must Recite Precise Amount of Judgment.

An appeal bond must recite the precise amount of the judgment before the justice.

ON appeal from a justice's judgment to the C. P. of St. Lawrence, the justice's return stated a judgment before him, in the cause of *Weed* v. *White,* of $4.25 for the defendant; but the appeal bond recited a judgment in a cause between the same parties, of $5.00 for the defendant.

The trial coming on, the C. P. refused, for the above reason (and another which it is not material to notice) to proceed in the trial, and quashed the appeal.

A motion was now made for a *mandamus* to compel them to proceed with the trial.

Mr. H. Allen, for the motion.

Mr. S. Wright, Jr., contra.

Curia. The C. P. were right in quashing the appeal for the variance. There might well be two judgments between the parties—one for $5, and the other for $4.25. In an action by the appellee upon the bond, the judgment recited by it could not, without matter *aliunde,* appear to be the same as the one revised upon the appeal. We do not say whether such matter could be received; but, at any rate, he ought not to be put to such a doubtful remedy, as this bond would afford him. We have uniformly required great strictness in prosecuting these appeals, and we felt ourselves justified in this course, from the language of the statute.

Motion denied.

---

*EX PARTE METZLER, Assignee of [*287
P. H. WENDOVER, Sheriff, &c.

Practice—Motion, to Set Aside Proceedings on Bail-bond—Affidavits—Irregularity.

On a motion to set aside the proceedings on a bail-bond, affidavits made in support of the motion, and entitled in the original cause, attached to an order to stay proceedings entitled in the bail-bond suit, with a notice of motion, showing the real object of the application, may be read.

Where the bail below became bail above, and the plaintiff excepted, and then took an assignment of the bond, and commenced an action upon it: held, that the proceeding was irregular, and should be set aside, with costs.

THE case will appear from the following opinion of Irving, first judge of the C. P. of the City and County of N. Y.:

COMMON PLEAS.

LEWIS VOSS and HIRAM PIERCE, ads. JOHN W. METZLER, Assignee of P. H. Wendover, Sheriff, &c.

THE SAME ads. THE SAME.

These are actions commenced on the bail-bonds, and the present application is to set aside all proceedings in these suits. The application is founded on several depositions taken in the original suits. These depositions were submitted to me in vacation, and I thought them sufficient to order a stay of proceedings in the bail-bond suits. Copies were accordingly served on the adverse party, with copies of the orders to stay, entitled in the bail-bond suits fully set out, and accompanied with a notice in the bail-bond suits of the present application. In the title to this notice, the defendant has omitted to state the character in which the plaintiff sues; but the parties to the suit are correctly named, and the body of the notice shows both its applicability and its object. All the questions, therefore, submitted to me relate to suits actually in existence, and which have an immediate connection with each other. The case, therefore, in 2 Cow., 509, where the affidavits were entitled in suits that had no existence, is not analogous. Indictments for perjury would lie upon the depositions before me, if they were false.

By these affidavits, it appears that Hiram Pierce was bail below. That Dec. 1, 1825, he became bail above and, therefore, complied with the condition of the bond he had entered into with the sheriff. The bond was not forfeited. If the plaintiff was dissatisfied with the bail, he should have ruled the sheriff after excepting to its sufficiency. But it certainly was not competent for him first to except to the bail, thereby declaring it insufficient; then,

288*] *immediately thereafter, to take an assignment of the bail-bond, thereby admitting it to be sufficient; and then to commence a suit upon such bond as forfeited. It cannot be correct that a man should be sued for not doing that which he actually did a day or two before, and against the sufficiency of which the party now prosecuting him objected. It appears to me, that if the plaintiff excepts to the bail who was bail below, and afterwards becoming satisfied of his sufficiency, takes an assignment of the bail-bond, he ought to apply to the court for leave to withdraw his exception; but he certainly ought not to put the bond in suit. The having already complied with its conditions, must surely be available to the party sued. (1 Salk., 97; 7 Mod., 62, 117; 1 Tidd, 222, 245, and cases cited there; Rich. Prac. C. P., 118.)

In the original suits between Voss and Metzler, the exceptions taken to the bail were not abandoned after assignments of the bail-bonds had been taken. Suits were prosecuted on these bonds; the bail entered were required to justify; the suits on the bail-bonds have never yet been discontinued; and the bail thus prosecuted has been compelled to apply to this court for relief. It is obviously just that he should have it with costs, for being obliged to make this application.

It is, therefore, ordered, that all the proceedings by the plaintiff in the above bail-bond suits, respectively, be set aside; that the plaintiff pay to the defendants their costs in these suits respectively, and also of the present application for relief; and for the preparation of the depositions on which the same is founded.

A motion was now made for a *mandamus*, commanding the judges of the C. P. of N. Y. to vacate the above rule.

Mr. D. Graham, for the motion.

Mr. C. C. King, contra.

The Court said the reasoning of *Judge* Irving was perfectly satisfactory; and they denied the motion.

Rule accordingly.

289*] *SEYMOUR

v.

DEYO, Sheriff of ULSTER.

Practice—Motion, to Set Aside Nonsuit—Costs.

The court will not hear a motion to set aside a nonsuit at the trial, the plaintiff having since died and the only effect obviously being merely to unsettle the question of costs.

IN debt for an escape, the plaintiff was nonsuited at the circuit, Mar., 1824, and a case was made with a view to set the nonsuit aside, which was now on the calendar. After May Term last the plaintiff died; and,

Mr. C. H. Ruggles now moved for a rule that the cause should be stricken off, and that the defendant have judgment for costs.

Mr. J. Sudam, contra.

Curia. We cannot hear the question upon the nonsuit argued, merely to unsettle the question as to costs. This would be its only effect. Granting a new trial rests in the sound discretion of the court; and we have refused to do this, where it was plain that the only effect would be a recovery of nominal damages. The present case is analogous in principle; and the motion must be granted.

Rule accordingly.

Cited in—7 Wend., 422; 18 Wend., 544; 9 How. Pr., 245; 3 Sand., 661; Co. R. N. S., 89.

CUNNINGHAM

v.

BROWN & M'KENZIE, Manucaptors of SHEPHERD.

Practice—Discharge of Principal under Body Act—Exoneretur.

A judge at chambers, or a commissioner, &c., may order an *exoneretur*, on the discharge of the principal under the Body Act, in the same manner as on an actual surrender.

The discharge is conclusive, and cannot be questioned, as against the bail, for irregularity of fraud.

DEBT on recognizance of bail. The *capias* was returnable Oct. 20, last. Being served on the defendants, Mr. Bucklin, a commissioner to do the chamber duties of a judge of the Supreme Court, made an order on the 24th, for the plaintiff to show cause before him on the 27th why an *exoneretur* should not be entered on the bailpiece.

*This order was founded on the discharge of Shepherd, the principal, under the Act to Abolish Imprisonment for Debt, in Certain Cases, granted July 2, preceding; Shepherd had gone to Michigan; and had been there most of the time since his discharge. [*290

The order for the *exoneretur* was opposed, on the ground that the insolvent discharge was surreptitiously obtained, that the proceedings before the commissioner were irregular; and that the insolvent had fraudulently concealed his property, and made a false inventory, &c., so that the discharge was void by the statute. But Mr. Bucklin ordered the *exoneretur* on payment of costs.

Mr. J. Piatt now moved to set it aside. He said a judge or commissioner has no power to order an *exoneretur*, especially during term time, as this was, without an actual surrender. And if the commissioner had the power to discharge, the papers before him showed that the discharge was fraudulent and void.

Messrs. D. Tillinghast and *A. Spencer*, contra. No doubt, a judge at chambers may order an *exoneretur* on actual surrender. A discharge under the Insolvent Act is equivalent to a surrender. (1 Cai., 9–11.) It is the same thing, in effect, and gives the judge jurisdiction. An actual surrender would have been a very idle ceremony; for, on producing the discharge to the jailer, he could not have detained the principal one moment.

This discharge was conclusive, at least, as respects the bail, who, it is not pretended, were parties to the irregularity or fraud, or even knew anything about it. But the discharge cannot be questioned in this collateral way. It is so as to a discharge under the two-thirds Act. (1 Cow., 50); and the rule in relation to the Body Act is the same, except on the mere question of holding to bail. (1 Cow., 228.) They also cited 1 Tidd, 240-242.

For these reasons,

The Court were clear against the motion, and denied it, with costs.

Rule accordingly.

291*] *THE PEOPLE, ex rel. HOLLY,
v.
THE SUPERVISORS OF COLUMBIA.

THE SAME, ex rel. WATERMAN,
v.
THE SAME.

Practice—Mandamus—*Costs.*

Costs are not usually given, on granting an alternative or peremptory *mandamus* on motion.

If the party will secure costs, he should go to his demurrer, or issue of fact.

ON taking the rule both for the alternative and peremptory *mandamus* in this cause, it was entered by the attorney with costs, which the defendants refused to pay; and now moved to strike out the rule. (See the report of these cases, 4 Cow., 146.)

Mr. T. Bay, for the motion.

Mr. C. Bushnell, contra.

Curia. Costs were not ordered in these causes; and generally we do not give them, on granting either an alternative or peremptory *mandamus* on motion. If the relator wishes to secure costs, he must go to his demurrer or issue of fact.

Motion granted.

Cited in—13 Wend., 132.

EX PARTE CORWIN.

Practice—Appeal Bond Void, Unless Double the Damages and Costs.

An appeal bond must be in the penalty of double the damages and costs recovered before the justice, or it is void.

Citations—4 Cow., 61; 19 Johns., 171.

THE Court of C. P. of Onondaga made a rule quashing an appeal; because the penalty of the appeal bond was only double the amount of the damages recovered before the justice; but not in double the damages and costs.

Mr. J. R. Lawrence moved for a *mandamus* commanding them to vacate the rule; and proceed in the appeal.

Mr. B. D. Noxon, contra.

Curia. We have been pressed to reconsider the view which we incidentally took of this question in *Ex parte Harrison*, 4 Cow., 61, and apply *The Matter of Marsh*, 19 Johns., 171, to the bond under the late Act. And it was said, at the bar, that the Legislature could not have 292*] meant *that the costs should be considered in the penalty; because they have, in all cases, required them to be paid preliminarily to the appeal. But the penalty has no influence upon the sum to be recovered under the bond. The statute is, that the penalty of the bond must, in all cases, be in double the amount of the judgment. Now suppose a judgment for costs only, without damages; unless the costs, although paid, are in such a case, to be reckoned in forming the penalty, the bond must be without one; and thus the intention of the Legislature would be entirely defeated, as to a very numerous class of cases adverted to in *Ex parte Harrison*. We see no reason whatever for reconsidering the rule laid down in that case, and the motion must be denied.

Motion denied.

THE PEOPLE, ex rel. PARISH,
v.
THE SUPERVISORS OF ST. LAWRENCE.

Statute—Assessment of Damages by Commissioners, Conclusive on Board of Supervisors.

The assessment of damages by commissioners appointed under the 16th section of the Act to Regulate Highways, 2 R. L., 275, is conclusive upon the Board of Supervisors, who are bound to proceed and levy such damages; and cannot inquire whether they be too high or not.

A ROAD being laid out through the improved land of the relator, his damages were appraised by commissioners, according to the 16th section of the Act to Regulate Highways, 2 R. L., 275, at $750. The oath and award of the commissioners being presented to the defendants, they proceeded to inquire into the merits of the relator's claim, as whether it was not extravagant; and though requested by him to cause the sum awarded to be levied, they postponed the consideration of the subject to their next annual meeting.

A motion was now for a *mandamus* commanding the defendants to raise, levy and collect the money.

Mr. J. M'Kown, for the motion.

Curia. Clearly the Supervisors have nothing to do with the merits of the appraisal. The statute declares that the whole of the damages, &c., shall be presented to the Board of Supervisors, &c., who shall cause the same to be raised, levied and collected, in the same manner as the other town *charges are by [*293 law directed to be raised, levied and collected. The award of the commissioners, they having jurisdiction, is conclusive upon the Board as to the amount. The motion must be granted.

Motion granted.

Cited in—1 Wend., 324; 10 Wend., 587; 3 Barb., 336; 4 Barb., 76; 13 Barb., 443; 20 Barb., 297; 20 How. Pr., 497; 43 Ind., 348; 19 Am. Dec., 507.

EX PARTE CALDWELL, an Absconding Debtor.

Practice—Attachment.

A foreign creditor is entitled to an attachment under the Absconding Debtor Act. 1 R. L., 157.

CALDWELL fled from his creditors in Paisley, Scotland, to the City of N. Y. Being pursued hither by Crawford, one of his Scotch creditors, he concealed himself; and an attachment was taken out against him under the Act for Relief against Absconding and Absent Debtors, 1 R. L., 157.

Mr. S. A. Foote now moved to supersede the attachment, on the ground, among others, that foreign creditors are not within the statute. He cited *Matter of Fitzgerald*, 2 Cai., 318.

Mr. J. Platt, contra, cited 6 Johns. Ch., 186, and the 20th section of the Act in question, as conclusive.

Curia. The court must have overlooked that section when they decided *Fitzgerald's* case cited from Cai. That section sanctions this proceeding in express terms. And the motion must be denied.

Motion denied.

Cited in—6 Cow., 605; 23 N. Y., 179, 180; 2 Barb., 437; 3 How. Pr., 209.

294*] *ROE *v.* SWART.

TEN EYCK *v.* THE SAME.

Practice—Issuing Execution on Judgment, Before Expiration of 10 Years, does not Extend the Lien.

The issuing of an execution, before the 10 years after docketing a judgment have expired, and a sale under it after the ten years, will not extend the lien of the judgment as against subsequent judgment creditors, &c.

JUDGMENT in the first cause was docketed against the defendant Aug. 28, 1813; and a *fi. fa.* delivered to the sheriff July 20, 1823. Judgment in the second cause was perfected against the defendant in 1818; and a *fi. fa.* issued to the same sheriff July 1, 1825, who sold lands of the defendant on both executions, Sept. 23, 1825, being more than ten years from the perfecting of the first judgment. Now,

Mr. C. H. Ruggles moved for a rule applying the avails of the sale to the execution on the last judgment; and he cited 1 R. L., 500; Act of Apr. 3d, 1821; 5 Laws, 245 *c.*

He said if an execution is allowed to prolong the lien, the statute might be defeated by the party, who could extend the lien indefinitely by merely issuing an execution.

Mr. W. Mulock, contra.

Curia. The statute is that all judgments thereafter to be rendered, should cease to be a lien or incumbrance on any real estate, as against *bona fide* purchasers, or subsequent incumbrancers, by mortgage, judgment, or otherwise, from and after ten years from the time of docketing. The words leave no room for doubt or construction; and the motion must be granted. Clearly the plaintiff cannot enlarge the lien by the mere act of issuing execution.

Motion granted.

Cited in—18 Wend., 624; 1 Hill, 643; 44 How. Pr., 258; 14 Abb. N. S., 62; 35 Super., 66; 37 Cal., 133-136.

ANONYMOUS.

Practice—Court Requests Abstracts of Facts by Counsel.

The advantage of furnishing the court with an abstract of the facts on a non-enumerated motion, where the papers are prolix, and the facts numerous and complicated.

MAR. 24. *Curia*. Papers were delivered to us in this cause some days ago, upon a motion for a *mandamus* against a sheriff, commanding him to execute a conveyance of land. *They amount to about half a quire of [*295 paper, and go into a minute, complicated and tedious detail of judgments, redemptions and a series of incidental transactions, which it becomes necessary for us to examine and arrange before we can decide the points presented. No abstract was furnished to us; and we have not time, at the present term, to make one for ourselves. Of course, the matter must remain undecided till the next term.

We take this occasion to suggest to the bar, that, in case of this character, it would facilitate and expedite the right understanding and decision of the motion, and save us much labor, if, in addition to the points and authorities, counsel would furnish us with an abstract of the facts of the case, according to their understanding of them. We mean by this, such a sketch or outline as every gentleman would naturally form for his own use, in the progress of his examination as counsel. It gives the court a bird's eye view, which they can very readily and accurately fill up and correct from the body of the papers; while it will not, in general, add much to the labors of counsel.

BROMAGHAM ET AL. *v.* CLAPP.

Practice—Object of Suits in Partition—Rights Ascertained—Possession not Awarded—Adverse Possession—Parties to Such Suit need not be Actually Seised.

The object of a suit in partition under the Statute, 1 R. L., 507, is, to ascertain the several rights of the parties; but possession is not awarded.

Though the plaintiff's right of entry be destroyed by adverse possession when the suit in partition is commenced, yet, when the court see that such possession was short of 25 years and, therefore, no bar to a writ of right, they are bound to proceed under the statute, and ascertain the rights of the parties.

To warrant proceedings in partition, it is not necessary that all the parties should be actually seised when the suit is commenced.

Citation—1 R. L., 509.

IN partition, under the Act for the Partition of Lands, passed Apr. 12, 1813, 1 R. L., 507. The proceeding was for partition of a farm in Schodack, Rensselaer Co., of which the plaintiffs claimed to be seised in fee as tenants in common, each of one ninth part. The petition was presented to this court Aug. 9, 1823; and was served on the defendant about 3 months before. Plea, that the defendant, at the time of preferring the petition, and at the time of *pleading, was *sole* seised and possessed [*296 in his demesne as of fee, &c., and traversing the tenancy in common. To this plea was annexed a notice that he had been so seised for 25 years previous to the exhibiting of the petition, adversely to the claims of the petitioners, and all other persons. Replication, that the plaintiffs were seised in fee, &c., as tenants in common *modo et forma*, &c., and issue.

The cause was tried at the Rensselaer Circuit June, 1824, before Betts, *Ch. J.*, when it appeared that William Bromagham, the father of the plaintiffs, being seised in fee of the premises in question, died intestate about Jan. 15, 1799; leaving the plaintiffs, three of his children, and six others, his children and heirs at law; nine in the whole. Previously, in May, 1795, he had been declared a lunatic; and in August, then next following, Peter, his son, was appointed his committee by the Court of Chancery; and took possession of his real and personal estate. In Oct., 1802, Peter, having purchased the right of his brother Isaac, contracted to sell the whole of the premises in question to the defendant in fee; and May 3, 1803, conveyed the whole in fee to the defendant. Sometime in Mar. next before, the defendant had entered; and has continued in possession, claiming title ever since. Jemima Martin, one of the plaintiffs, was covert-baron in 1803; but her husband died thirteen years before this suit was commenced.

A very long case was made and argued at the bar, involving several questions of fact, and various points beside those presented above; but it is not deemed material to notice them. A verdict was taken at the circuit, for the plaintiffs, subject to the opinion of the court.

Mr. J. V. N. Yates, for the plaintiffs:

1. The defendant has not established such an adverse possession as to bar our right of recovery. He has not shown an adverse possession for 25 years, as set up in his plea, nor even for 20 years; but if for either, it was not, under the circumstances, such an adverse possession as to bar a tenant in common. It was not adverse in its inception.

297*] *2. In this case, the mere right, or seisin in fee, is in question. This arises out of the pleadings. The defendant sets up a sole seisin in himself; but he fails to establish it. *Nase* v. *Peck*, 3 Johns. Cas., 128. Besides, partition, in its very nature, draws in question the *jus proprietatis*, Vin., Partition, R, pl. 3, U, pl. 2, 6; *Lucet* v. *Beekman*, 2 Cai., 385; *Cook* v. *Allen*, 2 Mass., 462, not merely the right of possession. In this view, a clear adverse possession, of at least 25 years, must be shown, to constitute a bar; which will hardly be pretended.

3. In any view, Jemima's right is not barred; she having been covert when her title accrued; and she continued so to 1813.

Messrs. J. Edwards and *S. A. Foot*, contra, contended that a clear adverse possession, of at least 20 years before suit brought, was established. The plaintiff's right of entry being gone partition will not lie. It is a possessory action. *Lloyd* v. *Gordon*, 2 Har. & McH., 254, 260. Twenty years is, therefore, a bar. There is an adverse possession of 25 years; which is sufficient to bar this suit, if it is to be considered in the nature of a real action, involving the mere right of property.

But the plaintiffs have mistaken their remedy. Proceedings in partition cannot be had under the statute, unless the parties are all seised at the time of commencing them. Here all the plaintiffs were disseised. They should have brought ejectment; obtained possession or seisin, in common; and then have brought partition.

Curia, per SAVAGE, *Ch. J.* The plaintiffs are each entitled to one ninth of the premises in question, unless they have parted with their interest; or are barred by the Statute of Limitations.

Peter, by virtue of his appointment as committee of the lunatic, was entitled to the real estate; but after his father's death, he had no interest, except as one of the heirs at law, and as the assignee of Isaac, whose right he had purchased; he could, therefore, convey no greater title to the defendant.

*It is contended, however, that the [*298 possesssion has been so long adverse that the plaintiffs are barred. If the possession was adverse from the death of the lunatic, then twenty four years had elapsed when this suit was commenced, which was in May, 1823. But I apprehend the possession of one tenant in common inures to the benefit of all his co-tenants, unless there has been an actual ouster, or something tantamount thereto. (3 Cruise, Dig., 485.) The defendant's possession was adverse from May 3, 1803, when he was in possession, claiming title under a conveyance of the whole. This was a trifle more than twenty years before the present suit was commenced. The possessory right, therefore, is gone as to all the plaintiffs; for though Jemima Martin was covert in 1803, yet her husband died thirteen years before this suit was commenced. She was barred in ten years after the disability was thus removed.

But though the possession and the right of possession are thus gone from the plaintiffs, they have a remedy by writ of right. In this action of partition, the several rights of the parties are ascertained, and their portions designated; but possession is not awarded. If the plaintiffs had lost all remedy, it would be useless for the court to inquire into the right. But their remedy is not gone till twenty five years' adverse posesssion shall have elapsed. It is, therefore, the duty of the court, in the language of the statute, to "ascertain and determine the respective rights of the parties, &c., and g judgment that partition be made according thereto," &c.

The plaintiffs are each entitled to one ninth of the premises in question. The j , must, accordingly, be for the plaintiffs [illegible] ninths; and that commissioners be appointed to make partition, &c. (1 R. L., 509.)

WOODWORTH, *J.*, having formerly been concerned as counsel, in relation to the rights in question in the cause, gave no opinion.

Judgment accordingly.

Cited in—22 Wend., 588; 22 Mich., 74; 25 Minn., 542.

---

*JACKSON, ex dem. SITZER, [*299
v.
WALTERMIRE.

Action for Dower—Same Evidence of Seisin in Husband Necessary, as is Required in an Action in Ejectment by the Heir—Prima Facie *Evidence of Seisin—Effect of Proceedings in C. P.*

The proceedings to set off or assign dower by the Court of C. P., under the Act, 1 R. L., 60, are merely evidence of the location of the land to be recovered. All the other facts, as seisin of the husband, &c., must be proved in the ordinary way, as in an action of dower.

The same evidence of seisin which would entitle the heir to recover in ejectment, will sustain an action for dower.

Actual possession of the husband, or his receipt of rent, is *prima facie*, evidence of seisin, in an action for dower.

Where it appeared, by parol, that the husband bought a farm, paying something towards it, taking possession, and selling to another, who succeeded him in the possession; and so through several tenants down to the defendant, who was in possession; held, that this was, *prima facie*, evidence of the husband's seisin, and sufficient to entitle his widow to recover dower, though no deeds were shown.

Citations—2 Phil. Ev., 187; 1 Cai., 190; 2 Johns., 123; 9 Johns., 245; 17 Johns., 123; 5 Cow., 168.

EJECTMENT for dower, admeasured and set off to the lessor of the plaintiff, pursuant to the Statute, &c., 1 R. L., 60, by the Court of C. Pl. of the County of Columbia; tried at the circuit in that county in 1824, before Duer, *Circuit Judge*.

The plaintiff, after giving in evidence the proceedings of the Court of C. P., admeasurers, &c., by which dower was set off to her, as the widow of Frederick Sitzer, of a farm situated in Ghent, Columbia Co., in the occupation of the defendant; and after proving her intermarriage with, and the death of her husband, gave in evidence a notice served on the defendant's attorney to produce, on the trial, a deed from Peter Lawrence to Frederick Sitzer, given thirty years ago, or thereabouts; a deed from Sitzer to Abner Wilcox, given a few years thereafter; a deed from Wilcox to Isaac Wright, given a short time after the last mentioned deed; a deed from Wright to Jacob Residorph, given a few years after the last mentioned deed; a deed from Residorph to Benjamin Traver, given a few years after the last mentioned deed; and a deed from Traver to the defendant, given a few years after the date of the last mentioned deed; all given for, and including the farm in possession of the defendant.

The defendant declining to produce the deeds, or any of them, upon this notice, the plaintiff proved by parol, that Sitzer, the husband, purchased of one Lawrence, who had resided on the farm four or five years, and paid him some money; that Sitzer sold the farm to Abner Wilcox, who succeeded Sitzer in possession; that John Youngs and Isaac Wright lived upon the farm a short time under Wilcox, and as his 300*] *tenants; that Wilcox sold the farm to Jacob Residorph, who succeeded to the possession of Wilcox, Youngs and Wright; that Residorph sold to Benjamin Traver, who succeeded to the possession of Residorph; that Wilcox had often declared, while in possession, that he had bought the farm of Sitzer; that Youngs and Wright, while in possession, declared that they held under Wilcox; that Residorph, while in possession, declared that he bought of Wilcox, and Traver that he bought of Residorph; that the defendant bought of and succeeded to the possession of Traver.

The defendant moved for a nonsuit, on the ground that the evidence of seisin of the husband was insufficient; and the judge granted the motion.

Mr. A. Vanderpoel, for the plaintiff, now moved to set aside the nonsuit, and for a new trial. He said the seisin proved was sufficient to entitle the plaintiff to recover. We proved the possession of the husband in his own right, and payment by him of the consideration money. This is, *prima facie*, evidence of seisin. It is not necessary for the widow to introduce the title deeds of the husband. The law presumes it not in her power to produce them. *Bancroft* v. *White* 1 Cai., 190. The defendant holds under a title derived from the husband. This, of itself, is, *prima facie*, evidence of the husband's seisin. *Embree* v. *Ellis*, 2 Johns., 119; *Andrews' Lessee* v. *Fleming*, 2 Dall., 93; *Bassler* v. *Niesly*, 2 Serg. & R., 352.

But we produce the ordinary proof of seisin. This is by establishing an actual possession. (Jac. Law Dict., Seisin; Co. Litt., 152.) Dower follows such a seisin. (2 Bl., Com., 134.) If a seisin in fee is alleged, it shall be intended a lawful seisin till the contrary appear. *Meriton* v. *Benn*, Lutw., 1337, 1343.

The widow is dowable of all lands which may descend to the heir. (2 Bl. Com., 134.) Is there a doubt that the heir of the husband might have recovered upon this proof, if the land had not been conveyed? In such a case, clearly, a mere possession is presumptive evidence of seisin. (2 Phil. Ev., 187.) In ejectment, a possession, though short of twenty years, is enough to entitle the plaintiff to recover. *Jack-*son* v. *Hazen*, 2 Johns., 22; *Smith* v. [*301 *Lorillard*, 10 *Id.*, 338. Though ejectment be a possessory action, yet the proof is the same in real actions involving the mere right. *Nase* v. *Peck*, 3 Johns. Cas., 128.

Messrs. D. B. Tallmadge and *E. Williams*, contra, contended that the proof of seisin was insufficient. The cases cited are of ejectment —a mere possessory action, so far as they relate to the proof of possession. Those relating to the claim of the tenant under the husband are where the claim was by deed. Nothing of this kind is shown here. We have a mere transfer of possession from one to another, accompanied with parol declarations. These are admissible no farther than they relate to the tenancy or possession; not for the purpose of showing title, which is essential to constitute a seisin as contradistinguished from a mere possession.

Curia, per SAVAGE, *Ch. J.* It is urged, and I think correctly, that the same evidence of seisin should entitle the widow to recover her dower as would be sufficient to authorize a recovery by the heir. In such case, "the seisin of the deceased is proved by showing his actual possession of the premises, or by proving his receipt of rent from the person in possession. This is presumptive evidence of a seisin in fee, and sufficient until the contrary appears." (2 Phil. Ev., 187.) The rule laid down by Kent, *J.*, in *Bancroft* v. *White*, 1 Cai., 190, is this: "The former husband of the demandant, for some years previous to Nov. 1, 1786, was possessed of the premises, and used them as his own, and not in the right of another. He then, for a valuable consideration, conveyed the same in fee with a covenant of warranty; and the lands have passed by subsequent conveyances in fee to the present tenant. This is sufficient evidence, in the first instance, of seisin in the husband. The wife is not bound to produce her husband's deeds; because it is not presumed to be in her power; and in the present case the tenant claims in fee under title derived from the husband. The marriage and death of the husband being proved, there is no question in the case." In *Embree* v. *Ellis*, 2 Johns., 123, Thompson, *J.*, says, *"The principal question in this [*302 case is, whether a sufficient seisin in the demandant's husband has been shown, to entitle her to dower. Lewis Morris, the son, had been possessed of the premises in question, by receiving the rents and profits thereof, for ten years. He then conveyed them in fee to the demandant's husband, who continued in possession for ten or twelve years, until they were sold under an execution against him; and purchased by Lewis Morris, the son. These facts were clearly sufficient, *prima facie*, to entitle the demandant to a recovery."

The same evidence of title is required in this case, as if there had been no proceedings before the C. P. They merely locate the premises, but determine nothing as to the right. *Matter of Watkins*, 9 Johns., 245; *Jackson* v. *Hixon*, 17 *Id.*, 123; *Jackson* v. *Randall*, *ante*, 168.

In this case, it appears that between thirty and forty years ago, the husband bought the farm, and paid something towards it. He sold to Wilcox, and from him it passed through the hands of Residorph and Traver to the defendant, who purchased from Traver, and is now in possession under that title. The possession accompanied every conveyance. No deeds are shown, though notice was given to produce them. And no objection was made to the parol testimony of the above facts.

In my opinion, this was, *prima facie*, enough. The nonsuit must be set aside, and a new trial granted.

Rule accordingly.

Cited in—4 Wend., 632; 17 Wend., 165; 2 Hill, 342; 1 N. Y., 245; 2 Abb. App. Dec., 53; 4 Barb., 185; 3 Redf., 38; 39 Wis., 188.

303*] *MEAD AND ROGERS v. ENGS.

Negotiable Paper — Notice of Non-payment — Time to Give—Reasonable Diligence Sufficient —To Whom Notice should be Given.

Notice of non-payment of a bill of exchange, &c., must generally be given by an indorser to the indorser next before him, by the next post after he himself has received notice of the dishonor; and so on to the drawer. But this rule is not inflexible. It means the next convenient and practicable post; and one dealing in bills or notes is not bound to watch the postoffice constantly, for the purpose of receiving and transmitting notices. Reasonable diligence and attention is all that the law exacts.

Accordingly, where R., residing at Bristol, R. I., Oct. 21, sent notice of non-payment of an inland bill, to S., his immediate indorser at Providence, by the post which reached there on the same day, at 5 P. M.; and S. received the notice on the morning of the 22d, and put a notice in the postoffice, in the afternoon of the same day, for his indorser at N. Y., although a mail had previously left Providence at 1 P. M. of the same day for N. Y.; and this letter was post marked the 23d, and was taken by the post of that day in the morning, and reached the indorser at N. Y., in the due course of the mail; there being no laches imputed after this: held, that the drawer was not discharged.

One to whom a bill or note is indorsed merely as agent to collect (*e. g.*, a bank), is a holder for the purpose of giving and receiving notice of non-payment; and he is not bound to give notice of non-payment directly to all prior parties; but may notice his next immediate indorser, who is bound to notice his indorser, &c., in the same manner as if the bill or note had been negotiated for a valuable consideration.

If an indorser receive notice from any one who is a party, he is liable to any subsequent indorser, though he may have received no notice from him, Per Sutherland, J.

Citations—18 Johns., 239, 240; 3 Bos. & P., 599 602; 9 East, 347; 1 Campb., 246, 349; 6 East, 9, 10; Chit. Bills, 405, 401, 291, 295, 408; 20 Johns., 382; 2 Taunt., 38; 15 East, 291; 2 Campb., 373, 208; 5 Mass., 167; 3 Johns. Cas., 90; 2 Johns., 204.

ASSUMPSIT, on an inland bill of exchange, by the plaintiffs, as indorsees, against the defendant, as drawer, tried at the N. Y. Circuit, Jan. 18, 1825, before Edwards, *C. J.* The bill was dated at N. Y., June 17, 1823, and drawn on one Bourne, Bristol, R. I., for $400, at four months, by the defendant, payable to his own order; and by him indorsed to the plaintiffs. It was duly accepted and left at the Freemen's Bank, Bristol, for collection. The bill was due Oct. 20, 1823; payment demanded on that day by a notary, who protested it for non-payment; and returned it to Richmond, the Cashier of the Bank. Richmond sent the bill and protest by the next mail, Oct. 21, at 2 P. M., to Smith, Cashier of the Roger Williams Bank, Providence, from whom he had received it for collection; and where the mail arrived at 5 P. M. of the same day. Smith received the bill and protest, Oct. 22, Wednesday, and forwarded them by the first mail after so receiving them, to Flewelling, at N. Y., the immediate indorser of the R. W. Bank. Flewelling received them Oct. 25, in the morning, inclosed in Smith's letter, which was postmarked at Providence, Oct. 23. In 1823, a mail left *Providence for N. [*304 Y., by the way of Hartford, on Tuesday, Thursday and Saturday mornings, about 8 o'clock; and arrived at N. Y., in about 48 hours. Another mail left Providence for N. Y., by way of Saybrook, on Monday, Wednesday and Friday, at 1 P. M.; and arrived at N. Y., in about 36 hours; and of course, Smith did not deliver his letter at the postoffice in Providence early enough on Wednesday for the mail which left there at 1 P. M.

These facts appearing at the trial, the defendant offered evidence that it was the custom of N. Y. banks, which received bills or notes for collection, to give notice of payment directly to all prior parties; but the evidence was excluded.

The defendant's counsel objected, among other things, that Smith was guilty of laches, 1st, in not obtaining the letter of Richmond on Tuesday, the 21st; and 2d, in not forwarding the bill and protest to Flewelling by the Wednesday's mail (22); and 3d, that the notary at Bristol should have given direct notice to all the parties entitled to receive it.

The judge left it to the jury, whether Smith had sent the bill and protest to N. Y. by the next mail after he received them; and charged that it was not necessary for Smith to give direct notice to all parties, as contended by the defendant's counsel. Under this charge, the jury found for the plaintiff for $457.34 damages.

Mr. H. Ketchum now moved for a new trial: 1. Because the judge improperly overruled the evidence offered of the custom of banks in the City of N. Y., to give notice of non-payment to all the prior parties interested, on bills or notes left with them for collection. *Renner* v. *Bank of Col.*, 9 Wh. 581.

NOTE.—*Negotiable paper—Notice, by holder, of dishonor—Time to give.* See Bryden v. Bryden, 11 Johns., 187, *note, and other notes there cited*; Stafford v. Yates, 18 Johns., 327, *note*.

2. The charge of the judge was against law. *Morgan* v. *Woodworth*, 3 Johns. Cas., 89; *Morgan* v. *Van Ingen*, 2 Johns., 204.

3. On the ground of laches; and that the judge should have charged the jury that it was Smith's duty, in the exercise of ordinary **305*]** *diligence, to have received the bill and protest on the evening of the 21st, or the opening of the postoffice on the morning of Oct. 22.

4. That the verdict was against evidence.

As to the 2d point, he said diligence was a question of law; *Smedes* v. *Bank of Utica*, 20 Johns., 382; *Bank of Utica* v. *Smith*, 18 *Id.*, 230; and should not, therefore, have been left to the jury.

We admit that English bankers receiving notes or bills for collection, may give notice in the same manner as if they were indorsed to them for a valuable consideration; but the rule has never been adopted with us; and, indeed, is virtually overruled by *Smedes* v. *Bank of Utica* and *Bank of Utica* v. *Smith*.

Mr. B. F. Butler, contra, said the only serious question in the case is, whether the notary was bound to give direct notice to all concerned; or whether it might be given circuitously through the indorsers to each in his turn. This case is not an exception to a bill transferred in the ordinary course of business; as to which, it is admitted, an indirect notice would be good; and that the notice here given would be sufficient, the authorities are abundant. Chit. Bills, Phil. ed., 291, 295, 401, 407; *Haynes* v. *Birks*, 3 Bos. & P., 399; *Langdale* v. *Trimmer*, 15 East, 291; *Jameson* v. *Swinton*, 2 Campb., 373; *Rickford* v. *Ridge, Id.*, 537, 539, per Ld. Ellenbrough, *Robson* v. *Bennett*, 2 Taunt., 387; *Colt* v. *Noble*, 5 Mass., 167; *Tunno* v. *Lague*, 2 Johns. Cas., 1; *Morgan* v. *Van Ingen*, 2 Johns., 204; *Darbyshire* v. *Parker*, 6 East, 3.

The judge was right in referring the question of diligence to the jury. *Chapman* v. *Lipscombe*, 1 Johns., 294.

Curia, per SUTHERLAND, *J.* No laches are imputed after the bail and protest reached Flewelling. The law does not require the holder of a bill or note to give the earliest possible notice of its dishonor. It requires of him only an ordinary and reasonable diligence. *Bank of Utica* v. *Smith*, 18 Johns., 240, per Spencer, J.; 3 Bos. & P., 602. Nor is he bound the **306*]** *moment he receives notice of the dishonor of a bill to lay aside all other business, and dispatch notice to the prior parties to the bill. If reasonable diligence is used it is sufficient. *Scott* v. *Lifford*, 9 East, 347; S. C., 1 Campb., 246. Ld. Ellenbrough, in *Darbyshire* v. *Parker*, 6 East, 9, observes, there must be some reasonable time allowed, for giving notice, and that, too, accommodating itself to other business and affairs of life. Otherwise, it is saying that a man who has bill transactions passing through his hands, must be nailed to the postoffice, and can attend to no other business, however urgent, till this is dispatched.

I do not think the cashier at Providence is chargeable with laches in not having received the bill and protest from Bristol, until the morning of the 22d. It did not arrive until after 5 o'clock on the preceding day, when, with commercial men generally, and especially with banks, the business of the day is considered as closed. In our large commercial towns there is scarcely an hour in the day in which mails are not received; and if it is the duty of all those who have any interest in bills or notes, to omit no act by which they may receive the earliest possible intelligence in relation to them, then, as Ld. Ellenborough observes, they must be in constant attendance at the postoffice. So rigid a rule is not required by considerations of commercial policy, and there is no authority in favor of it. Reasonable diligence and attention are all that the law exacts.

Nor do I think the cashier at Providence was bound to forward the bill and protest by the mail which left there at one o'clock of the day on which he received the letter. At what hour they were received by him does not appear; and he states very positively in his deposition, that they were forwarded by the first mail after they were received; that he is well acquainted with the course of the mails between Providence and N. Y; and that the bill was sent with as much expedition as the course of the mails would permit. But from his letter bearing the Providence postmark of the 23d, it is fairly to be persumed that it was not put in the postoffice in season for the mail which left there at 1 o'clock P. M. on the 22d. Either the witness, who swears that there was such a mail, *must be mistaken, in that fact, or the **[*307** cashier must have fallen into an error; or he did not receive the letter from Bristol until after 1 o'clock. The latter supposition is very improbable. I think the cause must be decided upon the assumption that he received the bill on the morning of the 22d, and forwarded it to N. Y. by putting it into the postoffice in the afternoon of the same day, a mail having, in the meantime, left there at 1 o'clock.

It is well established in England, that where the parties to a bail or note reside in London, or in an adjacent village within the limits of the two-penny post, each party has an entire day after that on which he was informed of the dishonor, to give notice to the immediate indorsers; and Mr. Chitty seems to consider it in all cases sufficient, whether the parties reside in London or elsewhere, if each forward notice on the day after that on which he received information of the dishonor. (Chitty Bills, 408, Phil. ed.) But I think he is not supported by the authorities on which he relies, in this general position.

The general rule, I apprehend, is more correctly stated by *Mr. Justice* Lawrence, in *Darbyshire* v. *Parker*, 6 East, 10. This is, that where the parties live in different places, notice shall be sent by the next post. But if, in any particular place, the post should go out so early after the receipt of the intelligence, as that it would be inconvenient to require a strict adherence to the general rule, then, in such case, it would not be reasonable to require the notice to be sent till the second post. Ld. Ellenborough, however, in the same case (page 9), seems to consider the question unsettled, whether a party is in any case bound to communicate by the next post the intelligence he had received by the post on the same day, although there was a reasonable time between the coming in and going out of the post on the same day. Grose, *J.*, observes, "when it is said in the books that notice must be sent by the next post to a party living at another place, that cannot be taken literally in all cases, but must mean the next convenient, the next practicable post. It cannot be meant to apply to a case where the post goes out the next minute after advice received."

308*] *I conceive the general rule to be, therefore, that notice must be sent by the next post after intelligence of the dishonor of a bill is received. But this rule is, undoubtedly, subject to the qualifications stated by *Justices* Lawrence and Grose. (And *vide* 20 Johns., 382.)

The facts in this case bring it within the exception to the rule. The cashier was not bound, in the exercise of due diligence, to have prepared and forwarded notice by the 1 o'clock mail. It is not reasonable to demand from him the neglect of his other official duties, to prepare his letters and notices during the usual banking hours.

Although the Providence and Bristol banks had no interest in the bill, and were mere agents to collect it; yet, for the purpose of receiving and transmitting notices, &c., they are to be considered the real holders. This is perfectly settled in England, and, I believe, is according to the established usage in this country. *Haynes* v. *Birks*, 3 Bos. & P., 599; *Robson* v. *Bennett*, 2 Taunt., 38; *Langdale* v. *Trimmer*, 15 East, 291; Chit. on Bills, 405, Phil. ed.; *Scott* v. *Lifford*, 9 East, 347; S. C., 1 Campb., 349.

This precise question was settled in Mass., in the case of *Colt* v. *Noble*, 5 Mass., 167. The plaintiff, in that case, purchased from the defendant, a master of an American ship then at Madras, and bound to Portsmouth, in N. H., which was the place of his residence, a bill drawn by W. Cox, in favor of the defendant, on Cox and Greenwood, in London. The defendant indorsed the bill to the plaintiffs. They sent it to their agents in London to obtain payment from the drawers. The bill was protested for non-payment, and the agents returned it to the plaintiffs at Madras, but gave no notice of its dishonor to the defendant in America. The plaintiffs, however, in a reasonable time after they received the bill from their agent, sent notice of its dishonor to the defendant. And the defense was that the defendant should have had notice of the dishonor of the bill direct from London, and not by the way of Madras. *Ch. J.* Parsons delivered the opinion of the court, by which the notice was held good.

309*] *If the drawer or indorser of a bill of exchange receive due notice of its dishonor from any person who is a party to it, he is directly liable upon it to any subsequent indorser, although he may have received no notice of its dishonor from him. (2 Camph., 208, 373; Chitty, Bills, 401, and *seq.*, *Id.*, 291, 295, &c.; 18 Johns., 239; 3 Johns. Cas., 90; 2 Johns., 204.)

The evidence of custom, which was rejected by the judge, was in no respect material. It is prudent and probably customary for the holders of bills of exchange to give notice of their dishonor to all the parties to the bill. They may not wish to run the hazard of some of the parties being discharged by the omission of such notice. But if the holder is satisfied with the responsibility of his immediate indorser, there is no necessity for his giving notice to any previous party; and if such notice is given by the other parties to the bill, the holder may recover against any of them.

Motion for a new trial denied.

Cited in—3 Wend., 277; 1 Hill, 265; 2 Hill, 457; 20 N. Y., 410; 34 N. Y., 130; 23 Hun, 631; 41 Barb., 345; 27 How. Pr., 59; 55 How. Pr., 161; 17 Abb. Pr., 366; 2 Hall, 119; 4 Duer, 208; 7 Bos., 475; 6 Daly, 564; 4 How. (U. S.), 346; 17 Wis., 154; 36 Am. Rep., 507 (13 Vroom., 28); 41 Am. Rep., 402 (87 N. Y., 590).

GRANT AND HURD, late Overseers of the Poor of PAWLINGS, DUTCHESS Co.,

v.

FANCHER AND DEAN, Overseers of the Poor of PATTERSON, PUTNAM Co.

Overseers are a Quasi *Corporation—Their Successors may Collect Debts Due Them in Their Official Capacity—Successors may also be Sued on Their Contracts or for Their Neglect of Duty.*

Overseers of the Poor are a *quasi* corporation; and their successors may sue for a debt or duty due to their predecessors in their official capacity.

And where they contract a debt, or neglect a duty which devolves upon them as Overseers, by which they become liable to another, and then go out of office, they cannot be sued as late Overseers; but the action should be against their successors.

Whether, where a pauper, having no residence in this State, on the application of Overseers of the Poor, is removed by an order of justices to another town, and the order being reversed, they, on request, refuse to take back the pauper or provide for him, by which the town to which he is removed is put to expense in his maintenance, are liable to an action at the suit of the Overseers of the Poor of the injured town, *quære*.

Whether, on the reversal of such order, the injured town should not procure an order to remove the pauper back to the town whence he was sent, and thus relieve itself, *quære*.

Citations—18 Johns., 125, 418; 1 Cow., 670, 260; 15 Johns., 281, 440; 2 Salk., 488.

ON ERROR from the Dutchess C. P. The action in the court below was case by Fancher & Dean, Overseers of Patterson, against Grant & Hurd, late Overseers of Pawlings. The declaration was that Jan. 2, 1817, Helen Fleming, a pauper having no legal settlement in this *State, was removed [*310 by an order of justices, on the application of the defendants below, from Pawlings to Patterson; that the order adjudged her to be settled in Patterson, where she was received upon it by the Overseers of that town, the predecessors of the plaintiffs below, who provided for her until, &c.; but they, the plaintiffs' predecessors, afterwards appealed to the next General Sessions of Dutchess, who reversed the order at their October Term, 1817, of which the defendants below had notice. That the defendants were Overseers at the date of the order, and continued so to the 1st Tuesday of Apr., 1819; that they had not, however, removed the pauper back to Patterson in a reasonable time after the order was quashed, or taken care of her, though requested to do one or the other; by reason whereof the plaintiffs, as Overseers, were injured, &c., and they and their predecessors had expended moneys, &c., in her support, &c.

On general demurrer to this declaration the court below gave judgment for the plaintiffs there, and the damages were assessed on writ of inquiry.

Mr. N. P. Tallmadge, for the plaintiffs in error, insisted that Overseers of the Poor are not a corporation, and cannot sue or be sued. *Smith* v. *Voorheese*, 1 Penn. N. J., 272; *Gould* v. *Bailley*, *Id.*, 6. But the plaintiffs below, if able to sue, cannot sue for injuries to their predecessors. At any rate, if Overseers are to be considered a corporation, the defendants cannot be sued as late Overseers. Those who were such at the commencement of the suit were alone liable.

Mr. H. Swift, contra. Overseers of the Poor are, from necessity, a *quasi* corporation; and possess a capacity to sue commensurate with their public trusts and duties. (18 Johns., 407.) The plaintiffs below are the only persons entitled to receive the damages done to the town.

But there is no such necessity that Overseers should be considered a corporation for the purpose of being sued. They are arrested, holden to bail, and judgment and execution goes against them in their private capacity. Their indemnity is from the town on whose account they pay the money. Indeed, for aught that appears, the defendants below
311*] *might have been Overseers when the action was brought.

At any rate, if a corporation as to the contracts of their predecessors, they ought not to be considered so as to torts. The suit in question was for a wrong, a nonfeasance. Those only who do an injury ought to defend it. A prebendary may have a remedy against his predecessor for neglect in repairing. (1 Kyd on Corp., 222.)

Curia, per SAVAGE, *Ch. J.* It is objected by the plaintiffs in error:

1. That the plaintiffs below were not a corporation, and could not sue or be sued.

It is now too late to discuss that question. In *Pittstown* v. *Plattsburgh*, 18 Johns., 418, it is said "they (Overseers of the Poor) are the public agents and trustees of the towns in respect to their poor; and must necessarily, without express authority from the Legislature, possess a capacity to sue commensurate with their public trusts and duties." And the general proposition is laid down that "where a public office is instituted by the Legislature, an implied authority is conferred on the officer to bring all suits as incident to his office which the proper and faithful discharge of the duties of his office require."

2. It is objected that if the plaintiffs below possessed a capacity to sue, they could not sue for acts done in the time of their predecessors.

This point has been also settled by an express adjudication. In the case of *Jansen* v. *Ostrander*, 1 Cow., 670, the supervisor of a town was allowed to prosecute in his own name on a bond given to his predecessor in office. In this case, as well as in *Pittstown* v. *Plattsburgh*, the town officers are considered as *quasi* corporations, so far as is necessary for each to perform their several trusts imposed upon them by their several offices.

3. It is said, if the defendants are to be sued as a corporation, they should not be sued as late Overseers.

How far the successors in office are liable for the acts of their predecessors in office, it is not necessary now to decide. In the case of *Todd* v. *Birdsall*, 1 Cow., 260, the latter sued Todd & M'Cord, Overseers of Cortland, before a justice, *for goods delivered to a per- [***312**
son who kept a pauper of the town, for the use of the pauper, upon the written request of one of the Overseers of the Poor of the preceding year, and recovered; and this court affirmed the judgment. The court say: "In the present case the question is, whether the action can be sustained against the defendants, who now represent the interests of the town in relation to the poor; and for whose benefit the advance was made. It seems highly expedient that legal liabilities incurred by their predecessors in office for the support of the poor ought, upon a sound construction of their duties and powers, to devolve upon them. It is incident to their office, which, in this respect, may be viewed in the nature of a corporation."

In these cases, strictly speaking, it is not the officers of the town, but the town itself, which is the corporation. The officers represent the various interests of the town; and the only difficulty that exists is, that the officer becomes personally liable, and has no certain remedy against the town for indemnity. It is much to be regretted that the Legislature have not made some proper provision on the subject.

In *King* v. *Butler*, 15 Johns., 281, the Overseer made himself personally responsible by an absolute promise, and a recovery was had against him. But in *Olney* v. *Wickes*, 18 Johns., 125, the Overseer was not held responsible in his private character, because he contracted expressly in his official capacity. Unless, therefore, the successors were liable, there would be no remedy.

These cases do not decide the case now before the court; but they seem to settle this principle; that when an Overseer acts officially, the liability incurred devolves upon his successor, in matters of contract, when his acts are clearly within the scope of his authority; but when he exceeds his authority, he is personally responsible.

The defendants in the court below, if liable at all, were so not on any express contract, but for an omission of duty. It is contended that it was incumbent on them, as the representatives of their town, to have taken back the pauper, which they had improperly and illegally imposed upon Patterson. If this liability be admitted, it seems to me to raise *an [***313**
implied *assumpsit* only on the part of the town offending. There seems to me nothing like a tort, in this omission of duty, admitting it to have been so, any more than there is in the non-performance of any duty imposed by law, or the non-payment of any contract implied by law. There surely is nothing like a personal assumption of a liability which is, in its nature, merely official.

In the case of express contracts, when they appear to be made by officers acting in an official capacity, there is no personal liability, as in *Olney* v. *Wickes*; but it devolves upon the incumbents of the office, as in *Todd* v. *Birdsall*.

The case is not stronger against the defendants below, than if they had expressly agreed, in their official character, to pay to Patterson the expenses of the pauper; and in such case, the two authorities last referred to show that the action should have been brought, not against the late, but the present Overseers.

If I am correct in this position, the judgment must be reversed, and the discussion of the other questions becomes unnecessary. I may be permitted to remark, however, that perhaps the question, whether an action lies at all in the case presented by the declaration, is not perfectly settled, though that is not here made a point. When the case of *Pittstown* v. *Plattsburgh*, 15 Johns., 440, first came before the court, it presented just such a case on the part of the plaintiffs; and the court expressed a strong opinion that the action was maintainable, as the pauper had been thrown upon Pittstown by the procurement of Plattsburgh; and as the pauper, having no settlement in the State, Pittstown was not bound to procure an original order to send him back; and their power to do so was questionable. When that case came again before the court (18 Johns., 418), it was after a trial, when the fact was shown that the pauper had a settlement within the State. The court then decided that Pittstown was bound to send the pauper to the place of his settlement; and therefore, could not sustain the action. They again say, that if the averment had been proved that the pauper had no settlement within the State, the action would have been maintainable. It is, however, subsequently in-
314*] timated, *upon the strength of Chalbury and Chipping Farringdon (2 Salk., 488), that Pittstown might have sent the pauper back to Plattsburgh, after the reversal of the order; and that is assigned as one of the grounds upon which judgment was given for the defendants. If Patterson could have sent back the pauper in question to Pawlings, there is no ground for this action, in any shape.

I am of opinion that the defendants below were not liable; and the judgment must be reversed.

Judgment reversed.

Cited in—4 Wend., 408; 12 Wend., 118; 32 N. Y., 477; How. Cas., 675; 66 Barb., 71; 7 Abb. N. S., 355; 1 Sweeny, 227.

See 13 Johns., 496.

JACKSON, ex dem. THE PEOPLE, v. ETZ ET AL.

*Ejectment, by the People, for Escheated Lands—There must be no Reasonable Doubt of Failure of Heirs—Evidence—Hearsay—When Admissible—*Prima Facie, *of Failure of Heirs—Of National Character—Alien Soldiers' Heirs, Though Born of a Slave Mother, may Inherit Grant for Military Services in Revolutionary War.*

In ejectment, by the people, for escheated lands *propter defectum sanguinis*, the jury should be satisfied beyond all reasonable doubt, that the tenant whose lands are claimed as being escheated, died without heirs.

Hearsay evidence of finding the body and burial of one supposed to be dead, is inadmissible; though otherwise as to the fact of his death.

That one was missing at a particular time, with a report and general belief of his death, is, it seems, *prima facie*, evidence of his death.

Evidence is inadmissible to support the testimony of a witness by showing the consistency between his former declarations and his evidence on the trial, unless he is first impeached.

The rule is, that a witness cannot be supported by evidence in chief; but if he is impeached, it may be heard in reply.

In ejectment for escheated land, proof that a man's intimate acquaintances for several years never heard him speak of his family, father, mother, wife or children, is, *prima facie*, evidence that he has no heirs, if the place of his birth be unknown to them, and there appear no clue to better evidence; but this may be overthrown by very slight proof of heirs.

That one is reputed to be an Irishman, and has the accent or brogue of an Irishman, and is reported to be an Irish deserter, is, *prima facie*, evidence that he is an Irishman.

A grant of land to an alien soldier for military services during the Revolutionary War, and who died during that war, enables his heirs, though aliens, to inherit.

So of a slave. His heirs, though born of a wife who was a slave, may inherit under such a grant. Per Sutherland, J., upon the authority of Jackson v. Lervey, not reported.

Citations—15 East, 293, 294, *n*; 8 East, 542; 4 Mass., 702; Bull. *N. P.*, 294, 1 Phil. Ev., 180, 212, 213; 15 Johns., 226; 18 Johns., 39; 4 Campb., 415; 20 Johns., 703.

EJECTMENT for 450 acres of lot No. 77, Tully, now Preble, Cortland Co., tried at the Cortland Circuit, Sept., 1824, before Rochester, *Circuit Judge.*

At the trial, the Atty-Gen. produced a patent to one John Tool for 500 acres in lot 77, in Tully, dated 13 Sept., 1790, which passed the Secretary's office, Aug. 29, 1791. He then produced the office copy of the balloting book, which, among the returns of dead of the different regiments, was thus: "John Tool, of the 4th Regiment, Fowler's Company, died 26th March, 1779."

*The Atty-Gen. then proceeded, by [***315** various witnesses, to identify this John Tool, the patentee thus described in the balloting book; contending that he was an Irishman, a foreigner by birth, and that he died without heirs, whereby the premises in question escheated to the State.

The defendant sought to show, by various witnesses, that Tool's being returned dead was a mistake; that in truth he had deserted from the American service, and lived several years after the American War, having a wife and children; but it was agreed by both parties that he was an Irishman, who deserted from the British service, during the Revolutionary War, and enlisted into the American Army, and that the patent in question was granted in consideration of his enlistment and military services, according to the law of this State.

In the course of the trial, several questions arose and were decided by the judge, which, with the facts, are sufficiently noticed in the opinion of the court.

Verdict for the plaintiff.

Mr. E. Williams, for the defendant, moved for a new trial.

Mr. Talcott, Atty-Gen., contra.

Curia, per SUTHERLAND, *J.* The right of the State to recover the premises in question, depends upon the fact, whether John Tool, the soldier to whom they were patented, died without heirs capable of inheriting his estate.

If he left no heirs, it is immaterial whether he was a forcigner or an American citizen. His land would escheat *propter defectum sanguinis.*

If he was an alien himself, and left only alien heirs the question arises, whether this case, from the nature and circumstances of the grant, forms an exception to the general rule, that aliens are incapable of taking by descent.

Although the patentee was a foreigner, if he left natural born descendants, they would be entitled to take by inheritance, and the escheat would be defeated.

The judge correctly charged the jury, that, unless they were satisfied beyond a reasonable **316***] doubt, that John Tool died *without heirs, they must find for the defendant. They, notwithstanding, found for the plaintiff; and their verdict appears to me to be clearly against the weight of evidence.

There is no evidence of the existence of more than one John Tool. The John Tool spoken of by the defendants' witnesses, corresponds in age, in personal appearance, in his dialect, habits and manners, with the soldier of that name described by the witnesses for the plaintiff. They were both between twenty-five and thirty years of age, of about the same height, of light florid complexion, sandy hair and whiskers. Both spoke with a strong Irish accent, and appeared to be Irishmen by birth. They were both remarkably jovial and noisy; sociable and fond of liquor, but not drunkards. Both were great talkers, and both were said to be Irish deserters. The John Tool, spoken of by the defendants' witnesses, enlisted at Nobletown, in the winter of 1776; and the plaintiff's witnesses first saw there John Tool in the barracks at Fishkill, in the winter or spring of that year. All the plaintiff's witnesses agree that they never knew but one John Tool; and he belonged to Fowler's Company, and was stationed, in the winter of 1779, at Fort Plain, on the Mohawk River, where they all saw and knew him. Col. McKinstry knew the John Tool of whom the defendants' witnesses speak, at Nobletown, before he enlisted; and the individual whom he there knew, and who was there enlisted, he afterwards saw at Fort Plain, in the uniform of a soldier. He told him he belonged to the army, and wished Col. McKinstry to aid him in obtaining a furlough.

The identity of these individuals I consider, therefore, established, with all the certainty which human testimony, both direct and circumstantial, is capable of affording. Did this John Tool die at Fort Plain in the spring of 1779? The story of the plaintiff's witnesses, that Tool was lost or missing in returning from Diffendorf's tavern to the camp, on the night of St. Patrick's; and that it was afterwards generally reported and believed that he was dead, is perfectly consistent with the evidence on the part of the defendants. Both parties admit that he left his companions on the night of St. Patrick's, 1779, and was not afterwards **317***] seen alive in *camp. The plaintiff alleges that he died on that night; and the defendant that he deserted and returned to his family at Nobletown.

Three witnesses on the part of the defendant, Pixley, White and Col. M'Kinstry, swear that they were well acquainted with Tool before he enlisted. That in the spring of 1779 he returned to Nobletown, where his family, as well as the witnesses, resided. That he admitted his desertion on the night of St. Patrick's; and related particularly the manner and circumstances, together with his motives for leaving the army. His story, as related by them, corresponds in every particular with the account given by the plaintiff's witnesses, up to the time of his separation from his companions in returning to camp. He feigned himself drunk, and let his comrades go ahead; and then made the best of his way home. Nathan Rowley, another witness, has often heard him tell the story of his desertion. There is nothing improbable or unnatural in this relation; and the considerations, which the witnesses state prevented the neighbors of Tool from taking him up as a deserter, are such as were calculated to have that effect.

These witnesses cannot be mistaken in the material facts to which they have sworn. The story told by Tool puts the fact of his identity beyond the possibility of question. We must believe that he returned to Nobletown, and gave the account of himself to which they have testified; or that four witnesses have willfully and deliberately perjured themselves. I do not see that human charity can find any escape from this conclusion.

I have already remarked, that so far as the general reputation and belief of Tool's death at Fort Plain is concerned, it is not inconsistent with the narration given by the defendants' witnesses. Having been a faithful soldier, as Capt. Fowler says, they did not suspect him of desertion; but supposed he had either perished in a severe snow storm, or been destroyed by the savages. He was, of course, returned dead, and he always said that they would think he was dead.

*What, then, are the facts and cir- [***318** cumstances proved on the part of the plaintiff, independent of general reputation, which tend to establish the fact of his having died at Fort Plain?

Several witnesses testify that eight or ten days after Tool was stated to have perished, it was said, or reported, that his body was found. But Johnson, Sandford and Sparks are the only witnesses who pretend to have seen and recognized his body. They, however, swear that eight or ten days after Tool was missing news came to the Fort that a soldier was found dead. That they went to see the body and found it was Tool. That a grave was dug, and he was buried on the spot where he was found. These witnessses undoubtedly believe what they have sworn to. The testimony of Johnson, however, is subject to the remark, that by his own admission his memory is nearly gone; that he recollects no other fact or circumstance which occurred at that period. He could name no other soldier who died during the war; and he recollected the name of only one who belonged to his regiment. He was 74 years of age; and from the general character of his testimony, appears to have been a superannuated and imbeeile old man; and if he were unsupported by other witnesses, I should think his testimony, from the considerations which I have stated, entitled to very little weight. But he is corroborated by Sandford and Sparks; and to the character of their testimony there appears to be no just exception. Capt. Fowler, however, swears that he never heard that Tool was seen dead or alive after he was first missing; and Ensign Morell never heard that he was found.

Now, under the circumstances of this case, which of these witnesses are most likely to be mistaken? Those who swear to having seen the dead body of Tool, or those who testify that they saw him in life and health, long after the period when he was said to have died, and heard from his own lips the account of his escape—corresponding in every particular with the facts proved in the case up to Mar. 17, 1779, when he was supposed to have perished?

The plaintiff's witnesses must be mistaken. The body which they saw must have been that **319***] of some other soldier. *The change which death produces in the human countenance is such as to render mistake natural and probable. Those who supposed it to be the body of Tool, believed that it had been exposed for ten days. The general belief that Tool was frozen to death on the night of St. Patrick's, followed by the finding of a dead body within a few days after, would naturally give rise to the report that Tool's body was found, and all who came to see it would come with the previous impression that it was Tool. And unless there had appeared some striking dissimilarity in the size or prominent features, such impression would not be likely to be removed. The more minute characteristics of Tool would not be expected to be found, after an exposure for such a length of time.

The verdict, therefore, is, in my judgment, decidedly against the weight of evidence. For if Tool, the patentee, did not die at Fort Plain, but escaped and returned to Nobletown, then it was most clearly proved that he was married, and had several children born in this State, some of whom were living at the time of the trial. The plaintiff, therefore, could not recover on the ground of an escheat.

The hearsay evidence of the finding of the body, and the burial of Tool, was improperly admitted. Proof of the general report, and belief of his death, on the night of St. Patrick's, was not objected to, and seems, from analogy to cases of pedigree, &c., to be admissible. The fact that a soldier, or any other individual was missing at a particular time, accompanied with a report and general belief of his death, must be, in many cases, not only the best, but the only evidence, which can be supposed to exist, of his death. It is, perhaps, reasonable that it should be held, *prima facie*, sufficient. *Doe* v. *Griffin*, 15 East, 293. But a report that the body of a particuliar individual was found, and buried at a particular time and place, carries on the face of it an admission, that, if it is well founded, it is not the best evidence which exists in the case; for the body must have been found and buried by human agents, who are presumed to be competent and capable of testifying to the facts, especially if they did not occur at a very remote period. Particular and insulated facts cannot be proved **320***] by hearsay or general reputation. *The evidence of them is not to be supposed to exist only in general reputation, and hearsay; as it is in cases of pedigree, prescription and custom. Although a pedigree, may be proved by hearsay, the place of birth cannot. *Rex* v. *Erith*, 8 East, 542; 15 East, 293, 294, *note*; *Bartlet* v. *Delprat*, 4 Mass. 702; Bull. *N. P.*, 294; 1 Phil. Ev., 180; *Jackson* v. *Boneham*, 15 Johns., 226; 18 Johns., 39; *Berkley Peerage* case, 4 Camph., 415, per Mansfield, *Ch. J.*

In this case the hearsay testimony of Reeve is of the loosest character. He says, when he was sick, "news came that Tool was missing; and after 8 or 10 days, it was said Tool was found. That several soldiers went to the funeral, and when they returned, it was reported that Tool was found and buried. It does not amount to a general report; nor does it appear who said or reported that he was found and buried; nor, of course, whether those by whom it was said or reported had the means of knowing the fact. What effect this testimony had with the jury, it is impossible to say. It was calculated to corroborate the direct testimony of the finding and burial of Tool, and in that way undoubtedly had its weight.

The evidence offered to support the testimony of Col. M'Kinstry, by showing what he had before said, to be consistent with his testimony, was properly rejected. There was no attempt to impeach his general character, or to show that he had been inconsistent with himself in giving different accounts of the transactions to which he testified. I know of no exception to the rule that a witness cannot be supported by evidence in chief. If impeached, it is admissible in reply. (1 Phil. Ev., 212, 213, N. Y. ed., 1816; Bull. *N. P.*, 294.)

I am inclined to think that the proof was, *prima facie*, sufficient to show that Tool died without heirs, if the evidence on the part of the defendant is to be excluded from the case, on the ground that it relates to a different person, or is unworthy of credit. He was never heard to speak of his family, father, mother, wife or children. What better evidence, then, does the nature of the case admit? Of whom are inquiries to be made? The place of his birth is not known. *Most of the witnesses think he was an [***321** Irishman; but he never spoke of the place of his nativity; nor does there appear to be any clue by evidence of a higher or more satisfactory character.

Very slight proof, I admit, on the part of the defendant, that the patentee had relatives or connections, would counterbalance this negative evidence. But in the absence of any such proof, I think the evidence on the part of the plaintiff may be considered, *prima facie*, sufficient. The witnesses were not transient acquaintances of Tool. Some of them were his fellow soldiers and companions for more than two years.

I am also of opinion that there was sufficient evidence, *prima facie*, that Tool was a foreigner. Every witness in the cause testifies that he was reputed and believed to be an Irishman —had the appearance and dialect of an Irishman; some say he was reputed to be an Irish deserter.

But admitting that he left alien heirs, could they inherit the premises in question? It is contended that the patent and laws of this State vested the title in the heirs of John Tool; and conferred upon them, whether natives or aliens, the capacity to hold. I consider this to be the doctrine of the Court of Errors in *Goodell* v. *Jackson*, 20 Johns., 703. That was the case of a patent granted to an Indian soldier, who served during the Revolutionary War. And the principal question was, whether the son of the patentee, being an Oneida Indian, was competent to take and hold as heir, the lands thus granted to his father.

The Supreme Court held that the Oneida Indians were to be considered as citizens of this State, and not a distinct and independent people. That the son of the soldier was, therefore, entitled to take and hold by descent as a citizen, and was not subject to the disabilities of alienism. The Court of Errors, however, in the opinion delivered by *Chancellor* Kent, maintained that the Oneida Indians did not form an integral part of the people of this State, but that they were a distinct community, possessing, and recognized both by this State and the U. S., as possessing many, if not all the attributes of a distinct and independent, though a depressed and degraded people. The *Chancellor* **322***] says, "if, *therefore, the case turned upon the question, whether William, the Indian heir, was a citizen or an alien in 1783, I should not be in favor of the conclusion drawn by the Supreme Court. But I do not place the cause upon that ground, for the reasons which have already been mentioned. I take it (he continues) as a given point, that the patent issued according to the direction, and under the authority of the statute mentioned in it; and then, I say, that the grant to John Sagoharase and his heirs, rendered the Indian heir competent to take, though an alien; and his title was not liable to be impeached on account of his civil or political condition."

In the case of *Jackson* v. *Lervey*, lately decided by this court, the patent issued to Peter Slingerland, a slave, who was a soldier in the Revolutionary Army, and died during the war, leaving a child born of a woman also a slave. From this child, the defendant was a *bona fide* purchaser; and it was held that the patent, taken in connection with the laws under which it issued, was to be considered as a legislative grant, conferring upon the soldier, though an alien or a slave, the capacity to take and transmit the land to his heirs. The court say, "can it be supposed that the party thus granting, in express terms, to the soldier and his heirs, intended to raise the question of disability, arising from alienism or slavery? The soldier being dead, when the patent issued, it was, in effect, a grant to his heirs. What heirs were intended? Evidently, the persons who stood in such relation to him, as would entitle them to inherit, provided the soldier had been a freeman and a citizen." Upon the authority of these cases, therefore, without repeating the arguments and considerations upon which the decisions were founded, I consider it a matter of indifference, if the patentee left heirs, whether they were aliens, or native American citizens.

New trial granted.

Cited in—7 Wend., 370; 7 N. Y., 310; 28 N. Y., 40; 4 Lans., 441; 7 Lans., 239; 4 Hun, 544; 12 Barb., 358; 28 Barb., 331; 26 How., 244; 11 How. (U. S.), 490; 1 Cliff., 105; 1 Allen, 484; 17 Mich., 435.

*REYNOLDS v. SHULER. [*323

What Amounts to a Conversion—Restoration, not a Protection from an Action, though it will go in Mitigation of Damages—Mortgagee in Possession may Maintain Trover—Landlord and Tenant—Distress.

If one undertake to exercise dominion over personal property, in exclusion or defiance of the owner's right, it is a conversion.

Thus, where S., a bailiff, distrained goods in R.'s coal house, as the goods of G., and sold them, but did not remove them; held, that this was a conversion.

But the restoration to or repossession of goods by the plaintiff before suit brought, will go in mitigation of damages.

A mortgagee in possession of chattels, may maintain trover for their conversion.

As between landlord and tenant, the latter may, during the term, remove copper stills, kettles, steam tubs, &c., erected by him for the purpose of carrying on the business of the distillery, though fixed to the building.

And he may sell or mortgage such articles. But if mortgaged, and the mortgagee take possession, and remove them, the rent being unpaid, the landlord may follow and distrain them within thirty days thereafter.

And if separated by the tenant, or his agent, they are liable to distress. A mortgage of goods is not a sale of them *bona fide* (so as to prevent their being followed as a distress), within the proviso of the 13th section of the Statute, 1 R. L., 437.

To warrant distraining goods removed off the demised premises it is not necessary that the rent should have fallen due within thirty days next before their removal; but they may be distrained at any time within thirty days after their removal, if the rent be then due, or become due within thirty days after the removal; or within thirty days after the rent shall have become due, if the rent did not fall due till after thirty days from their removal.

Citations—6 Bac. Abr., 677, 678, 680; 6 T. R., 298; 6 East, 540; 6 Mod., 212; 7 Johns., 254; 10 Johns., 175, 176; 4 T. R., 260, 567; 12 Mod., 212; Bull., *N. P.*, 34, 46; 5 Johns., 258; Powell on Mortg., 55, 56; 1 Atk., 477; 6 Johns., 5; 1 Salk., 368; 3 Atk., 12, *n.*, p. 16; Ambl., 113; 17 Johns., 116; 2 East 90; 3 East, 50; 4 Esp., 33; Co. Litt., 47 *b*; Woodf., 389, 384; 3 Bl. Com., 6, 10, 9; 4 Barn and Ald., 206; 3 Com. Dig., 557, Distress. C; 4 T. R., 565; 1 R. L. 437; 3 Cow., 270; Act, April 13, 1820; 1 R. L., 437.

TROVER, for certain copper stills, or kettles, steam tubs, coolers and a worm, tried at the Montgomery Circuit, July 23, 1823, before Walworth, *Circuit Judge.*

On the trial, these facts were proved: one Gilman, a distiller, had mortgaged the articles in question, to the plaintiff, to secure a sum of money; and default having been made in the payment, the plaintiff caused them to be removed into his possession. The articles were placed by Gilman and Taylor in a stone distillery, which they held under a lease for years, and then in possession of Gilman, for the purpose of carrying on the distilling business. When the plaintiff's agent took the articles, they were found affixed to the building; the kettles or boilers being masoned up in brick arches and the steam tubs and coolers, with the worm, were all connected with the boilers by logs and braces affixed to the building. He broke up the arches and took out the kettles and other articles, and removed them to the plaintiff's coal house.

May 15, 1822, within thirty days after the removal by the plaintiff, Shuler distrained the articles so removed, as bailiff of Duncan the Stewart and Charles Tullock, landlords of Gilman and Taylor, for $68.74, a balance of rent

324*] *which fell due Nov. 1, preceding. The lease under which this distress took place, was dated Aug. 24, 1820, and was for the term of four years ; and included the still.

The plaintiff admitted that he removed the articles, knowing the rent to be due.

The defendant sold them at auction, the rent not being paid at the plaintiff's coal house, but they had not been actually removed by the purchaser when this suit was commenced. The plaintiff forbid the sale, claiming that they were fixtures and not liable to distress.

A motion was made for a nonsuit, on the ground that no conversion was proved ; but it was overruled; and the jury, by consent, found a verdict for the plaintiff for $193.50, subject to the opinion of this court on a case ; and with liberty to either party to turn it into a special verdict or bill of exceptions.

Mr. M. T. Reynolds, for the plaintiff:

1. The property could not have been distrained before removal. Things annexed to the freehold cannot be distrained, as furnaces, cauldrons, &c. (Bradby on Distr., 214.) So of things which cannot be restored in the same plight as when taken. (*Id.*, 212; Co. Litt., 47.) The anvil in a smith's shop is privileged, because it is affixed to the freehold. (4 T. R., 566, per Ld. Kenyon.) And so of things generally, which are thus affixed. (*Id.*, per Buller, *J.*) Trespass lies for taking fixtures as a distress for rent. (4 B. & A., 206.)

2. The severance by the plaintiff, and immediate removal, could not give the landlord any greater right to distrain than he had before.

3. Besides, here was a *bona fide* sale and removal before distress. The statute authorizing a distress after removal, expressly excepts such a case. (1 R. L., 437, sec. 13.) It does not apply to the goods of any one beside the tenant. (Bradby on Distr., 137, 138.)

The plaintiff, for the purpose of this suit, is to be considered the absolute owner. (Pow., Mortg., 51 ; 1 Atk., 167, 477 ; 1 Ves., Jr., 348, 378 ; 5 Johns., 260 ; 2 Cai. Cas., 200.)

325*] *4. The conversion was sufficiently proved. (7 Johns., 254 ; 6 Bac. Abr., 677 ; 1 Johns., 65; 10 *Id.*, 172; 1 Chit. Pl., 155; 6 East, 540 ; 6 Mod., 212 ; 6 T. R., 298.)

5. The landlord could not distrain after thirty days from the time when the rent became due. Laws, sess. 41, ch. 228, sec. 7 ; *Burr* v. *Van Buskirk*, 3 Cow., 263.

Mr. D. Cady, contra. There was no sufficient evidence of a conversion. (12 Mod., 344 ; 6 East., 538 ; 4 T. R., 263, 264.) The plaintiff has never been disturbed in his possession. At any rate, the damages should not have been more than nominal. The goods should have been considered as returned, and the damages reduced accordingly, though there might have been a technical conversion. (5 Mass., 105, 106 ; 14 Johns., 278 ; 6 Mod., 212.

Whatever the tenant may remove from the premises may be taken for rent. (Woodf., ch. 13, sec. 1, p. 389.) And no doubt these articles might have been so removed. (*Id.*, p. 281 ; 1 Atk., 477 ; 1 Salk., 368.) But if they were not such as the tenant could remove, then the plaintiff has no title, and cannot recover. (9 Johns., 362.)

Burr v. *Van Buskirk* did not call for the decision whether a landlord may distrain after thirty days from the time of the rent falling due. It turned on other points. The statutes there considered are not inconsistent, but may well stand together.

Curia, per SUTHERLAND, *J.* The first question which arises is, whether there was sufficient evidence of a conversion of the goods in question by the defendant.

It is not necessary to a conversion that there should be a manual taking of the thing in question by the defendant. It is not necessary to show that he has applied it to his own use. If he undertakes to exercise a dominion over it, in exclusion or in defiance of the plaintiff's right, that is, in law, a conversion, whether it be for his own or another person's use. Hence, a redelivery of the thing will not protect him from the action. (6 Bac. Abr., 677.)

*In *Shipwick* v. *Blanchard*, 6 T.R., 298, [*326 the defendant entered upon the premises of the plaintiff, and gave him written notice that he seized and distrained his goods for rent. The plaintiff paid the rent, and then brought an action of trover, for taking the goods, the defendant having no right to distrain. It was contended by Chambre & Holroyd, for the defendant, that trover would not lie, because there was no taking in fact, but only a notice to the plaintiff, that the things were taken without any removal of them, or actual laying hands on any part of them. But it was answered by Law, that if a party claim and assert a dominion over goods, especially turning the possession of them to his own profit, that is a clear possession in law, to subject the wrongdoer to an action of trover ; and the action was sustained.

In *M'Combie* v. *Davies*, 6 East, 540, Ld. Ellenborough reiterates, with approbation, the opinion of Ld. Holt, in *Baldwin* v. *Cole*, 6 Mod., 212, that the very assuming to one's self the property and right of disposing of another man's goods, is a conversion.

In *Bristol* v. *Burt*, 7 Johns., 254, in which most of the cases are considered, the same doctrine is recognized and established. Also in *Murray* v. *Burling*, 10 Johns., 175.

The undertaking to sell, under color of legal process, another man's goods, is an assumption of a right to dispose of them, of the highest and most unequivocal character. It must, almost of necessity, bring a charge upon the party, to a greater or less extent ; and that, in the opinion of Buller, *J.*, in *Syeds* v. *Hay*, 4 T. R., 260, is sufficient.

If the property in question, therefore, was the plaintiff's and was not liable to be distrained, no matter what became of it subsequent to the sale, Trover may be maintained, to recover his damages. In estimating those damages, it may be proper to inquire, what became of the property after the sale? If the plaintiff repossessed himself of it before suit brought, it would not deprive him of his action, though it would diminish his damages. For it is well settled that trover lies for damages for the conversion of a chattel, notwithstanding it is restored before suit brought. The action *is not to recover the thing, [*327 but damages for the conversion. The restoration or recovery of the property goes only in mitigation of damages. 6 Bac. Abr., 678-680; 12 Mod., 212; Bull., *N. P.*, 46; *Ogden* v. *N. Y. F. Ins. Co.*, 10 Johns., 176, per Thompson, *J.* The plaintiff is to be presumed to have acquired the possession of the property in question, with the knowledge and assent of Gilman, who had mortgaged it to him. Indeed, this is fairly to be inferred from the evidence. He was then a mortgagee in possession; and as such, had a sufficient property in the goods, to enable him to maintain trover for their conversion. (5 Johns., 258; Pow. Mortg., 55, 56.)

The next question is, whether the property was liable to be distrained for rent, before its removal by the plaintiff. The old rule, that whatever was attached to the freehold became part of it and could not be taken away, has been very much relaxed by modern determinations, as between landlord and tenant. Thus, it was held by Ld. Hardwicke, in *Ex parte Quincy*, 1 Atk., 477, that a tenant, during the term, may take away chimney pieces, and even wainscot, if put up by himself. And if a man lets a house where there is a copper, or a brewhouse, where there are utensils, unless there was some consideration given for them, and a valuation set upon them, they would not pass. And he adds, several sorts of things are often fixed to the freehold, and yet may be taken away—as beds fastened to the ceiling with ropes, or nailed; yet no doubt they may be removed. *Heermance* v. *Vernoy*, 6 Johns., 5. In *Poole's* case, 1 Salk., 368, it was held by Ld. Holt that a soap-boiler, during the term, might remove the fats, coppers, &c., which he had set up for the convenience of his trade; and that he might do it at common law, in favor of trade, and to encourage industry. In *Lawton* v. *Lawton*, 3 Atk., 12, it was held that a fire engine set up for the benefit of a colliery, by a tenant for life, was to be considered a part of his personal estate, and to go to the executor. And Ld. Hardwicke observes, that what would have been held to be waste in Henry VII.'s time, as removing wainscot fixed only with screws, and marble chimney pieces, is now allowed to be done; and he adds, cop-
328*] pers *and all sorts of brewing vessels cannot possibly be used without being as much fixed as fire engines. And in brewhouses especially, pipes must be laid through the walls, and supported by walls; and yet, as they are laid for the convenience of trade, landlords will not be allowed to retain them. *Vide note* 1, to that case, page 16; *Dudley* v. *Warde*, Amb., 113; Bull. *N. P.*, 34; 2 East, 90; *Elwes* v. *Maw*, 3 East, 50, per Ld. Ellenborough, in which this subject is very ably discussed, and all the cases considered. (4 Esp., 33; Woodf., 280, 281; 17 Johns., 116.) These cases very conclusively establish that the tenant in the case now under consideration, had a right at any time during his term to remove the articles in question from the demised premises.

The question then arises, whether the proposition (which as a general rule is undoubtedly true), that things fixed to the freehold cannot be distrained (Co. Litt., 47 *b;* Woodf., 389), applies to a case like this.

The reason of the rule is, that they savor of the realty; and the right of distress is confined to personal chattels. (3 Bl. Com., 6, 10; Woodf., 384.) The anvil of the smith, and millstones are privileged, because they are attached to the realty. (4 T. R., 567, per Ld. Kenyon.) And the privilege continues, although they may be temporarily removed from their places for the purpose of repairs; because such removal is a matter of necessity; and they still continue, in judgment of law, the one a part of the forge, and the other of the mill. (Woodf., 389.)

So, it is said, caldrons and furnaces, or the doors and windows of a house, cannot, for the same reason, be distrained.

But suppose the anvil, the millstone, the caldron or furnace, or the doors and windows of a house, broken up and separated from the freehold, not temporarily, for the purpose of repair, but permanently for the purpose of being sold, and still remaining on the demised premises, would they not be liable to be distrained? They would have ceased to be a part of the freehold, or to savor of the realty. They *would be simply per- [***329**
sonal chattels; and, as such, unquestionably liable to distress.

If the reason of their original exemption be supposed to be, that they could not be severed from the freehold without detriment and, therefore, could not be restored to the owner in the same condition in which they were taken (a distress at common law being merely in the nature of a pledge or security, and not of execution or satisfaction; 3 Bl. Com., 9; Co. Litt., 47 *b;* Woodf., 389); still, that reason ceases when they are actually severed, not by the landlord, but by the tenant or his agent. So at common law, sheaves or shocks of corn on the ground, &c., could not be distrained; but if loaded on a cart, they might, for they then cease to savor of the realty, and may be safely restored. (3 Bl. Com., 9; Co. Litt., 47 *b;* 4 B. & Ald., 207, per Abbot, *Ch. J.*; 3 Com. Dig., 557, Distress, C; 4 T. R., 565.)

There was a period, then, after the articles in question were separated from the realty, when they were upon the demised premises, and subject to be distrained for rent as the property of the tenant. They were removed by the plaintiff and followed by the landlord, within the time prescribed by the statute.

The mortgage was not a sale of the chattels, within the proviso of the 13th section of the Act concerning Distresses, 1 R. L., 437.

But the rent distrained for in this case, fell due more than thirty days before the distress was made. The warrant is dated the 15th of May, 1820; and directs the bailiff to distrain for $68.74, for rent due Nov. 1 (then) last.

It is contended, on the authority of *Burr* v. *Van Buskirk*, 3 Cow., 270, that the landlord's right to pursue and distrain property removed from the premises, is limited to 30 days after the rent falls due.

Such, undoubtedly, was the opinion expressed by *Mr. Justice* Woodworth in that case. He considered the 7th section of the Act of Apr. 13, 1820, as altering the law in that respect. The determination of that point was not necessary to the decision of the cause. It was a point raised and *discussed; but the [***330**
judgment of the court would have been the same, whatever might have been its opinion upon that particular question. I then doubted.

the correctness of the construction given by *Mr. Justice* Woodworth, to the 7th section of the Act 1820, sess. 43, ch. 194; and I believe it was then distinctly understood, that the question was to be considered open for future consideration.

By the 13th section of the Act of 1813, 1 R. L., 437, the landlord had a right (if the tenant removed his goods and chattels from the demised premises leaving the rent unpaid) to take and seize them, wherever they could be found, at any time within 30 days after their removal, as a distress for the arrears of rent; provided such seizure was made after such rent had become due and payable. If the tenant, therefore, removed his goods more than 30 days before the rent fell due they could not be followed for the purpose of distress. The 7th section of the Act of 1820, sess. 43, ch.194, p. 178, authorizes the landlord, at any time within 30 days next after his rent shall have become due, to pursue and seize all such goods and chattels of the tenant as may have been conveyed away, &c., without any restriction as to the time of their removal; and repeals so much of the 13th section of the Act of 1813 as is repugnant to the 7th section of the Act of 1820. These sections are to be construed together, and effect is to be given to both, so far as they are capable of standing together. The latter was not intended as a substitute for the former, but as an amendment of it. It provides for a case omitted in the former Act. It does not take from the landlord the right to pursue the property of the tenant, in any case where he before possessed it; but it gives him authority to follow and seize it, in a case in which, by the old Act, he could not.

Taken together, their construction appears to me to be this: the landlord shall, in no case, pursue and seize the goods, &c., until his rent is due. If rent was due at the time of their removal, or becomes due within 30 days thereafter, he must pursue and seize them within 30 days after their removal. But if no rent is due when the goods are removed, nor becomes due within 30 days thereafter, then he may **331***] *pursue and seize them at any time within 30 days after his rent does become due.

SAVAGE, *Ch. J.*, said he concurred in the opinion of Sutherland, *J.* The declaration in the 6th section of the Act of 1820, "that nothing in this Act contained, shall be construed to impair the rights of any landlord or lessor, under existing laws," seems expressly to countenance the construction given by him to the 7th section, and though the 7th section, and the 13th section of the Act of 1813, may admit either of the construction given in *Burr* v. *Van Buskirk*, or the one now given, that which allows both to stand should be preferred, especially when the Legislature declare that they do not mean to lessen or impair the landlord's remedy. The construction given in *Burr* v. *Van Buskirk* certainly does impair the landlord's remedy very essentially.

Judgment for the defendant.

Cited in—7 Cow., 738; 1 Wend., 309; 8 Wend., 613; 10 Wend., 322, 14 Wend., 204; 20 Wend., 642; 21 Wend., 395; 23 Wend., 467, 495; 25 Wend., 398; 44 N. Y., 112; 45 N. Y., 794 (6 Am. Rep., 174); 49 N. Y., 314; 57 N. Y., 33; 4 Hun, 628; 22 Hun, 48; 54 Barb., 422; 49 How. Pr., 268; 2 Sand., 66; 1 Duer, 366; 1 Daly, 326; 71 Ill., 282; 47 Pa., 121; 24 Am. Dec., 110.

THE PEOPLE *v.* THE COUNTY OF NEW YORK.

Interest—Runs on Arrears of Taxes Due from a County to the State—Payment of Amount of Principal Made Generally, does not bar an action for Amount of Interest.

Interest runs on arrears of taxes owing by a county to the State, to be calculated after thirty days from the time when the account current is made up, and rendered by the Comptroller, pursuant to the Statute, sess. 38, ch. 29, sec. 4.

Payment of the amount of principal money due from a debtor will not prevent an action to his creditor, for the amount of the interest; unless the payment be made, and received specially in extinguishment of the principal. If made generally, it applies first to extinguish the interest; and the balance may be sued for, as principal.

Citations—3 Cow., 393; Act. Oct., 24, 1814 (sess. 38, ch. 29, sec. 4); Act. sess. 45, ch. 127, sec. 5.

CASE agreed and submitted. During the years 1815, 1816 and 1817, the County of N. Y. became indebted to the people of the State in the amount of $165,466.75 for balance of state taxes, which were laid upon the County, during those years. These balances the County Treasurer neglected to pay. May 22, 1817, an account was stated by the Comptroller exhibiting the above sum as then due to the State; and then, and frequently since he requested payment; and the accounts current furnished annually since 1817, have contained a charge of interest. The Treasurer, in reply, stated that the taxes had not been fully collected; and for that reason he was unable to pay. But no formal demand, in pursuant of the Act of Oct. 24, 1814, sess. 38, ch. 29, was ever made by the Comptroller *upon the Treasurer, re- [***332** quiring him to pay the balance in his hands, within thirty days from the first day of May, in each of the years in which the balances acerned; and a copy of the account stated by the Comptroller was never delivered to the Atty-Gen. to be prosecuted against the Treasurer. No notice was ever given to the supervisors of the county by the Comptroller, that there was any balance due the State for taxes from the Treasurer, prior to the month of May, 1820, except the notices to the Treasurer. The Treasurer died in Feb., 1819. Jan. 25, 1821, $22,362.95 were paid; and Aug. 9, the further sum of $188.45, which, together with $6,841.55, claimed on account of interest, would be in full of the claim of the State on account of taxes and interest, prior to May 31, 1821.

Upon this case, the question submitted was, whether the County of N. Y. was liable to pay interest on the balances, and if so from what time.

Mr. M. Ulshoeffer, for the defendants, denied that interest would be collectable, were this a question between individuals arising upon a contract. *Calton* v. *Bragg*, 16 East, 224; *Haviland* v. *Bowerbank*, 1 Camph., 50, 129; *Pease* v. *Barber*, 3 Cai., 266; *People* v. *Gasherie*, 9 Johns., 71.

The delay in the collection of taxes may be very great. Various officers are concerned, who may be negligent; and it may be a long time before the Treasurer can compel the payment of the money by process of law. Not one word is said in the statutes about making a defaulting collector pay interest upon whose promptitude the Treasurer must depend. (*Vide* 2 R.

L., 401. sec. 156; *Id.*, 513, secs. 12, 13; *Id.*, 400, sec. 255; *Id.*, 350, sec. 51.) The State Comptroller may charge interest on taxes on real estate, but no such authority is possessed by the County Treasurer, or the collectors; nor are they bound to pay interest.

Suppose the late County Treasurer to have been negligent about proceeding against the collectors, he would only be liable for the balance in his hands. (Laws, sess. 38, ch. 29, sec. 4, proviso.)

333*] *But if the Treasurer had been liable for interest, it does not follow that the county is so. The county was not a party to his fraud or negligence. It is liable only, by statute, sess. 38, ch. 29, sec. 5. Section 4 of the same statute prescribes the terms, on which the county are to be liable. The Comptroller is required to take certain steps against the County Treasurer, which were not pursued in this case. Notice was not given to the supervisors. The county stood in the relation of surety to their Treasurer; and were entitled to have him faithfully pursued by the creditor; otherwise, they are discharged. *People* v. *Jansen*, 7 Johns., 332, 339.

But the principal of the taxes has all been paid. Interest alone remains, for which an action will not lie. *Tillotson* v. *Preston*, 3 Johns., 229.

This question as to interest has been settled by legislative exposition. It was deemed necessary, by a late Act (Mar. 29, A. D. 1822, sess. 45, ch. 127, sec. 5), to enable the counties to raise interest on arrears of taxes due to the State. This Act was passed on the recommendation of the Comptroller. (Ass. Journ., sess. 45, p. 245.) The proviso in the Act shows that before its passage, no charge of interest existed or could be made against the county.

Mr. Talcott, Atty-Gen., contra. *Tillotson* v. *Preston*, 3 Johns., 229, was a case of payment in satisfaction of the principal, and does not apply. The payments here were properly applied to extinguish the interest in the first instance. Indeed, if interest was due to the plaintiffs, the Comptroller had no power so to apply the money as to deprive them of a remedy for it.

The late Act of Mar. 29, 1822, sess. 45, ch. 127, sec. 5, was not intended to confer the right to interest. The State had this right before; and the report of the Comptroller, on which that Act was founded, presupposes the right. (Ass. Journ., 1822, pp. 243, 245.) The intention of the makers of a statute should always be regarded in its construction. (Plowd., 205, 232, 366.)

334*] *Upon the general doctrine of interest, the charge is clearly allowable. It is sufficiently supported by the cases cited on the other side. And see the cases collected in 5 Day ed. Esp. *N. P.*, 114; 5 Ves., 801; 1 Hen. & Munf., 211; 3 Johns. Cas., 310; 3 Cai., 234; 15 Johns., 409; *Thomas* v. *Weed*, 14 Johns., 255; *Kane* v. *Smith*, 12 Johns., 156.

The Statute, sess. 38. ch. 29, sec. 3, p. 32, fixes the time when the money should be paid by the county. This is on or before Mar. 1; by which time it presumes the taxes to have been paid to the county. From that time interest should be paid.

The *People* v. *Jansen* has no application. Besides being distinguishable in its circumstances, even supposing this to be a case of surety, a decisive answer is, that the county is the original debtor, acting by their agent the Treasurer; and chargeable with his default, though they may have no actual notice.

Curia, per SAVAGE, *Ch. J.* The subject of interest upon contracts having lately been very fully considered by this court in *Reid* v. *Rensselaer Glass Factory*, 3 Cow., 393, I abstain from an examination of the cases cited on this head. They will be found collected and commented on in that case. I will, however, remark that the English rule, as laid down by the late cases, is not admitted to be correct, but expressly denied. It is certainly reasonable that when money is due, and withheld against the consent of the creditor, the debtor should pay interest as a compensation to the creditor, who has lost the use of his money. Whether the debtor has, in the meantime, used the money, or received interest for it from others, in whose hands it may have been, or kept it on deposit, is surely a matter with which the creditor has no concern. His loss is neither augmented nor diminished by the loss or gain of the debtor. The creditor has lost the use of his money, which is equal to the lawful interest; and without recovering that, he is not indemnified.

It will surely not be considered inequitable that whenever the debtor knows precisely what he is to pay, and when he is to pay, he shall be charged with interest, if he neglects to pay.

*Such was the situation of these par- [*335 ties. The defendants knew perfectly well the amount of the tax due from the county to the State; and they also knew that they were bound to make payment by a certain day in each year. They were then clearly bound to pay interest, unless they are protected by some exception from the general rule.

Generally, in the accounts between the State and the several counties, where taxes on non-resident lands properly designated, are received in payment, the county cannot know the precise amount due, until the taxes have been examined by the Comptroller, and either admitted or rejected by him. Hence, the propriety of an account current, showing the balance. Until this is shown, there is, in fact, an unliquidated account between the parties. Of course, no interest is chargeable, until the balance is ascertained; and, in this case, none should be charged until the county had notice of the balance, and an opportunity to pay it.

What shall be a reasonable time from the stating of the account, we may infer from the Act of Oct. 24, 1814, sess, 38, ch. 29, sec. 4, which gives the Treasurer thirty days.

It has been contended, however, that this Act shows that no interest is collectable at all; because interest is not mentioned by it in prescribing proceedings against the County Treasurer, where he has improperly detained moneys in his hands. If it were admitted that interest is not collectable in that case, it would not determine the question between these parties. The Legislature might think it proper to excuse that officer from the payment of interest; though it would be perfectly equitable and legal to compel its payment. But it is a sufficient answer to that argument that the Act contemplates an entirely different proceeding from the present—a proceeding against an individual who receives the money as the agent of the county, whose sureties whould most probably be compelled to pay for his defalcation. This is a proceeding against the original debtors, who have neglected to pay the amount of their debt; who are supposed to have retained the money in their own hands; and therefore, come within the general principle; and are not entitled to that commiseration which is some- **336***] times *extended to sureties by indulgent and compassionate creditors.

It is contended, however, that the defendants in this case are mere sureties for their Treasurer; and are, therefore, entitled to the benefit of the law in favor of sureties. This is certainly an error. He is no more the principal debtor than the Comptroller of the State is the creditor. The Treasurer is the officer of the county; the supervisors appoint him; they take his sureties, and judge of their sufficiency; and the county is liable for his default and misconduct. But he is not in default, unless he receives the public money, and neglects to pay it over; or neglects the proper measures to compel its collection. From the facts stated in the case, there is no ground to impute anything like misconduct to the Treasurer. He satisfied the Comptroller that he had not received the money, and had performed his duty —else he would have been prosecuted. But it would be extraordinary indeed, to prosecute the Treasurer because the collectors had not paid to him the money collected by them; though sued for the purpose of recovering it; or which, perhaps, they had not collected, and could not collect; or, what is possible, which the supervisors had neglected to assess. If, however, the fault was in the Treasurer, the defendants have their remedy against his estate, and his sureties upon the bond taken when he was appointed.

It also urged that the defendants are not liable, because no notice was given to them of the arrears due. No other notice was necessary to be given than the one which was given to the Treasurer. All the correspondence as to the accounts between the State and county, on the subject of the payment of taxes, is carried on between the Comptroller of the State and the Treasurer of the County. It was the duty of the supervisors to have examined the books and vouchers of the Treasurer; and thus to have ascertained the true state of his accounts.

It has also been contended that the Act of 1822, sess. 45, ch. 127, sec. 5, has given a legislative exposition to the law on the question of interest. The truth is, that Act does not alter the question one way or the other. Balances had been for years accumulating on the **337***] books of the treasury. Payment *was delayed by some of the counties, under a misapprehension of the powers of their supervisors; and the Act was intended as declaratory of their powers and duties. This case was then the subjeet of discussion; and the proviso was inserted, expressly to prevent the Act having an operation upon it; but not as expressive of any doubt upon the propriety of the charge. The practice of charging interest on balances against counties, at the Comptroller's office, was well known; and the doubts expressed by some of the supervisors, as to raising balances, extended as well to the principal as the interest. The object of the Act was to secure prompt collections of balances due the State; and not to sanction doubtful charges, as has been supposed by the counsel for the defendants. No doubts of that kind were ever entertained at the office of the Comptroller.

There is no ground for the objection taken, that the plaintiff here seeks to recover interest after the principal has been paid. The fact is not so stated in the case; nor are we to presume the accounts kept in so skillful a manner as to present that question. For aught that appears, the payments were made and received, generally, on account; which account was composed of principal and interest. The payments exceeding the interest, that part of the account was extinguished. All we learn from the case is, that the sum now due is precisely equal to the amount of interest charged.

On the whole, therefore, I am of opinion that the plaintiffs are entitled to recover interest; and that thirty days from the time of rendering the account current is the proper time from which to calculate it; *and this is the opinion of the Court.*

Cited in—15 Wend., 80; 15 Hun, 361; 24 Hun, 638; 23 Barb., 346; 42 Barb., 57; 61 Barb., 189; 40 Mich., 6; 2 Am. Rep., 350 (32 Ind., 330).

---

*SOLOMON WRIGHT [*338
v.
WILLIAMS.

Avowry for a Distress for Rent—Defendant Must set forth his Title—If Less than the Fee, It must be Particularly Set Out—Executor Must show that the Rent Fell Due, Before Testator's Death—Pleading.

In avowry for a distress for rent, the defendant must set forth his title; but this rule does not mean that he must deduce it down from the remotest source. If he be seised in his *demense* as of fee, it is enough for him to say so generally; or if seised or possessed of an inferior estate, he must show the seisin in fee of the one under whom he claims; and then trace the title to himself particularly, down through its different stages. So if the demise was made by another, he must show the lessor's estate, and trace it particularly down to himself.

This rule fully illustrated by the cases collated by Sutherland, *J.*

In avowing an executor for a distress for rent, the avowant must show affirmatively that the rent fell due before his testator's death.

If it fall due after, it goes to the heir.

An avowant for a distress of cattle of a stranger, for rent, need not show that they were *levant et couchant* on the demised premises. It is enough to say they were there; and it lies with the plaintiff to plead that they were not *levant et couchant.*

Citations—Stat. 11, Geo. II., ch., 19, sec. 22; 2 Saund., 282, 284; *c, n.*, 3, 309; 2 Chit. Pl., 510, 512; 2 Salk., 562; 1 Ld. Raym., 173, 331; 2 Str., 796; 2 Wils., 258; 2 Bos. & P., 359, *n.* (*a*); 4 Bos. & P., 56; Willes, 429; 1 Johns., 380; 6 Bac. Abr., Replevin & Avowry, K, 80; 1 R. L., 439, sec. 18; Woodf., 600.

ON demurrer to the defendant's avowries. The action was replevin for two bay mares and a colt, commenced by plaint in the C. P. of Washington Co., and removed into this court by *certiorari.*

The defendant, among other matters of defense, interposed two avowries of the taking as a distress for rent.

The first was as executor of John Williams, deceased; and averred that the testator was, Jan. 13, 1804, lawfully possessed in his *demense* as of fee simple of certain premises, situated, &c.; and that one Samuel Wright enjoyed them by virtue of a certain demise to him, made by the testator, in his lifetime, under the yearly rent of $35, payable Apr. 1, in each year; and because $595, being rent for 17 years, ending Apr. 1, 1823, was in arrear and unpaid, either to the testator, in his lifetime, or the defendant as his executor, he, as executor, avowed the taking of the beasts on the demised premises, as a distress for that sum.

The second avowry was, that the defendant, Sept. 1, 1806, was lawfully possessed in his *demense* as of fee simple, of certain demised premises, situated, &c.; and being so possessed, one Samuel Wright, for 17 years before, and ending Apr. 1, 1823, and thence to the time when, &c., enjoyed them as tenant to the defendant, under and by virtue of a certain demise, &c., at the yearly rent of $35, payable Apr. 1, in each year; and because $595 for 17 years, ending Apr. 1, 1823, was due to the defendant, he avowed the taking of the beasts on the demised premises.

339*] *Demurrer to each avowry; assigning for cause that the defendant had not set forth, particularly, what estate he had in the premises.

Joinder in demurrer.

Mr. S. Stevens, in support of the demurrer:

1. The landlord who avows the taking as a distress for rent, must set forth his title particularly. *Scilly* v. *Dally*, 2 Salk., 561; 2 Wils., 261; 2 Bos. & P., 359; 2 Saund., 283, 284 *c*, *note* 3; *Id.*, 310; 314, *note* 13; Yelv., 148; 3 Lev., 193. He must show the commencement of his estate laying the fee in the person who granted the term; and deducing the title down to himself. (2 Saund., 384 *c*, *note* 3; 2 Salk., 562; 2 Str., 796.) It is not sufficient for him to say, generally, that he was seised in his *demesne* as of fee. He must show by what title he was seised; and what estate he has. (2 Bos. & P., 359; 1 Johns., 384, per Kent, *Ch. J.*) The strict common law rule, in this respect, has not been relaxed in this State, as it has in England, by the Statute 11 Geo. II., ch. 19, sec. 22 (1 Johns., 380); and the rule still remains in England as to a rent charge. (4 Bos. & P., 60; Willes, 429.) The defect, in this respect, is one of substance; 1 Johns., 380; *Bain* v. *Clark*, 10 *Id.*, 424; and it exists in both avowries.

2. The defendant could not distrain as executor for rent which fell due after the testator's death. This went to the heir. (Woodf., 391; Toll., 135; 2 Bac. Abr., 420, Ex'rs, &c., pl., 3; Cro. Car., 207; Bradby, 77, 81; 1 R. L., 439, sec. 18.) It follows that the avowry should allege positively and affirmatively, that the rent accrued and became due before his death. The first avowry is, clearly, defective on this ground.

3. The plaintiff is a stranger; not the tenant of the defendant; and it was, therefore, incumbent on the defendant to show that the beasts were *levant et couchant* upon the premises before he could distrain them. (Woodf., 388, ch. 13, sec. 1 tit. Remedy for Rent by Distress.) Both avowries are defective in this particular.

Mr. S. G. Huntington*, contra. True, **[*340 in *Harrison* v. *M'Intosh*, 1 Johns., 380, it was held that the avowant must set forth his title. That case puts us on common law ground; but it does not deny that the manner of setting forth the title in these avowries is sufficient. It lays down the rule, and stops there. We have complied with the rule. We allege a seisin in fee generally. In the first avowry it is in the ancestor; in the second, the defendant avows upon his own seisin. He need not go into all the *minutiæ* of his title, as to how it was acquired. The course is to go back to a seisin in fee, aver that generally, and bring down the title by *mesne* conveyances to the avowant. (2 Saund., 282, 284 *c*, *note* 3 *Id.*, 316, 416; 2 Chit. Pl., 200, *note c*; 1 *Id.*, 347; Com. Dig., Pleader, C, 35; Co. Litt., 17 *a*; Woodf., 600; 6 Bac., 82, K.

As to the second objection; all that is said in the first avowry about the defendant's being executor, may be rejected as surplusage; and the avowry be taken as his own right. (Woodf., 597; 6 Bac., 82, K.)

Levancy and couchancy need not be averred in an avowry. It is enough to prove it on the trial.

Curia, per SUTHERLAND, *J.* The Statute of 11 Geo. II., ch. 19, sec. 22, which authorizes defendants in replevin to avow or make conusance generally, that the plaintiff in replevin, or other tenant of the premises whereon the distress was made, enjoyed the same under a grant or demise at a certain rent, during the time wherein the rent distrained for accrued; and which was then, and still remains due, without further setting forth the title of the lessor or owner of the premises, has never been adopted in this State. We have, therefore, no relaxation of the common law rule, which requires the avowant to allege what estate he is seised of in order to show by what authority he distrains. That this is necessary at common law, there is no doubt. And the only question is as to the degree of particularity with which the title must be stated.

Mr. Sergeant Williams, in a note to *Pool* v. *Longuevill*, 2 Saund., 284 *c*, *note* 3, thus states the rule: it was necessary, *at com- **[*341** mon law, in the avowry or cognizance, to show that the defendant, or some person from whom the reversion came to him, was seised, and the quantity of estate which he was seised of; and that he made a lease to the plaintiff for life, or years, or at will, and the descent or grant of the reversion to him. So, if tenant for years had let the estate to another, for a less term, at a certain rent, and distrained for the rent, it was incumbent on him, in his avowry, to show the commencement of his estate, by laying the fee in some person who granted the term, and then deducing the title to it down to himself, from the grantee of the term; which (he remarks) was often a difficult and impracticable thing to be done, especially in long terms for years, which are generally assigned to a great number of persons." The title thus set forth, may be traversed by the plaintiff, and the defendant be compelled to prove it. (*Id.*, 284 *d*, *note* 3). If the landlord, who distrains, has a less estate in the premises than the fee, as if he be tenant for life or for years, he must show in his avowry who is the owner in fee, and how he became possessed of the term. He must support his particular estate by showing its commencement and connecting it with the fee. Or if the owner of the fee make a lease for life, or years, or at will, and then die, or grant the reversion, and the reversioner distrain, he must, in his avowry, allege the seisin in fee of the original lessor; and show how he became seised of the reversion; whether it was by descent or by purchase. But if the original lessor, being the owner in fee, distrain, a general averment in the avowry, that he was seised or possessed in his *demesne*, as of fee simple, of the premises, &c., is sufficient; and it is not necessary for him to show, in the avowry, how he acquired his title. This is very clear from an examination of the cases and precedents.

Thus, in the very case of *Poole* v. *Longuevill*, 2 Saund., 282, to which the note of Mr. Williams is attached, the avowry is general, "that before and at the time of the taking of the said cattle, &c., the said Sir Thomas Longuevill, in right of Mary, now his wife, was, and yet is **342***] seised of and *in a certain messuage, &c., whereof the said place called Parkes, in which the distress was made, was parcel, in his *demesne* as of fee;" and then states the demise from him to one Burdax for a year; that the rent was in arrear: and that he entered and distrained the cattle, &c., for said rent. The defense was that the cattle, not being those of the tenant, came on the premises, &c., through the defect of the fences, which the tenant was bound to repair, &c. But no exception was taken to the avowry as being too general. The avowry, too, was not under the statute, but at common law, being in the time of Car. 2, before the statute was passed.

So in *Bennet* v. *Holbech*, 2 Saund., 309, the defendant, Holbech, avowed and justified the taking for rent; and alleged that the place where, &c., was parcel of the manor of old Filloughley; and that long before the time when, &c., the mayor, bailiff and commonalty, of the City of Coventry and certain other feoffees, were seised of the manor aforesaid, whereof the place in which, &c., was parcel, in their *demesne* as of fee; and that they demised the same by indenture to one Thomas Bassnet, for the term of 21 years, reserving a certain rent; who entered, and was possessed thereof: and being so possessed, afterwards, &c., sold and assigned to the defendant the said indenture, and all his term remaining in the premises, &c., by force whereof the said defendant entered and was possessed thereof, for the residue of the term, &c.; and being so possessed, demised the *locus in quo* to the plaintiff from year to year at a fixed rent. By virtue whereof the plaintiff entered, &c., and occupied for two years, &c.; and because half a year's rent was in arrear to the defendant, he avowed the taking, &c. No exception was taken to this avowry on the point which we are now considering. This, also, was at common law, being in the time of Car. 2.

So in 2 Chit. Pl., 510, the avowry is, that one E. F. was seised of the *locus in quo*, in his *demesne* as of fee; and demised the same to the defendant for a term of years, who entered and was possessed thereof; and avows and justifies the taking of the cattle, &c., *damage feasant*. Avowries and cognizances for distresses *damage feasant* are not within the Statute, *11 Geo. II., ch. 19, sec. 22. They [***343** remain, therefore, as they were at common law, and are regulated by the same principles as avowries for distress for rent before the statute. (2 Saund., 284 *c*, *n*. 3.) The form of an avowry under the statute is given in 2 Chit. Pl., 512.

Nor is there anything in the cases cited by the plaintiff, which shows the avowry to be bad for the want of a more precise and particular description of the estate of the defendant. Thus in *Scilly* v. *Dally*, 2 Salk.; 562; S. C., 1 Ld. Raym., 331; the defendant made conusance, as bailiff to John Treaceagle; and said that July 31, 1645, Joseph Treaceagle, grandfather to John, was possessed of and in one messuage, for a certain term of years; and made a lease thereof for a less term to J. C. and R. C., rendering rent; that J. T. died, and the term came to the executor; and made conusance of the taking as bailiff to the executor, as a distress for rent in arrear. Upon demurrer, this conusance was held bad; because it did not show who was the lessor of J. T.; and as he had only a particular estate, it was necessary to show its commencement by connecting it with the primitive estate. This case is very fully reported in Ld. Raymond; and much of the learning upon this subject is to be found there.

In *Reynolds* v. *Thorpe*, 2 Str., 796; the defendant avowed for rent; and stated that A., having title, demised to him; and that he made an under lease to the plaintiff. Upon demurrer, this was held bad; it not appearing what the title or estate of A. was.

In *English* v. *Burnell*, 2 Wils., 258, the avowry was, that Burnell one of the defendants, was seised in fee, and in possession of a certain ancient messuage; and that Ingham, the other defendant, was tenant and occupier of another ancient messuage; and that they as owners and occupiers of said messuages, and all other occupiers of said messuages, have had time out of mind, &c., common of pasture in the *locus in quo;* and avowed that they took the cattle *damage feasant*. The plaintiff traversed the right of common; and upon that issue a verdict was found for the defendants. Upon a motion in arrest of judgment, the avowry was held bad, the prescription for right of common being laid in the occupiers *of the mes- [***344** suages only; whereas, such prescriptions can be made only by those who have a permanent interest. It was necessary for the avowry, therefore, to set forth the title of the occupiers, in order to show that it was of such a character as would support a prescription; and though the avowry, as to Burnell, might be good, yet being bad as to the other, the whole must fail. The general doctrine is here maintained, that in replevin the avowant must allege what estate he is seised of; and the allegation that they were occupiers, &c., was held not to be sufficient.

In *Hawkins* v. *Eckles*, 2 Bos. & P., 359, the defendants avowed and made conusance of the taking, for *damage feasant*, and alleged that Routh, one of the defendants, was seised in his *demesne* as of fee, of and in a certain messuage &c.; and that the said Routh, and all whose estate he now has, from time whereof, &c.,

have had, &c., common of pasture, in and throughout the *locus in quo*, for two cows, &c., as to the messuage, &c., belonging. There were two other pleas, or avowries, in which it was stated that Routh was possessed of a certain messuage, by virtue whereof, he was entitled to common in the *locus in quo*. Upon special demurrer, it was not objected to the 1st avowry, that Routh did not sufficiently set forth his estate or title; but the objection was, that the prescription for right of common was bad; because it did not aver a right of common at all times of the year; and that objection was sustained. The other avowries were clearly bad, as they merely alleged a possession in Routh, without stating any estate or title whatever. (*Vide note a*, at the end of that case.)

The case of *Bulpit* v. *Clarke*, 4 Bos. & P., 56, merely decides that a rent charge is not within the provisions of the Statute of 11 Geo. II., ch. 19, respecting avowries; and that in cases which are within that statute, the plaintiff cannot put the defendant upon proof of his title, by replying to the general avowry given by the statute, that the avowant, or those under whom he claims, were not seised, &c., in their *demesne* as of fee. *Linden* v. *Collins*, Willes, 429, S. P., as to a rent charge.

345*] *In *Harrison* v. *M'Intosh*, 1 Johns., 380, the defendant justified the taking, &c., on the ground that the plaintiff, for the purpose of defrauding the defendant, and to prevent him from distraining the goods for rent, did willfully aid and assist to carry them away from certain premises, before that time let by the defendant, as landlord to one Edmund King, to whom the defendant averred the goods belonged. This was the only allegation as to the defendant's title or estate; and Kent, *Ch. J.*, correctly says, the avowry is clearly bad. It was necessary for the avowant to have set forth his title, and to allege the estate of which he was seised.

In Woodfall, 600, it is said, if the defendant avows or makes conusance for *damage feasant*, he must show that the place where, &c., is his freehold, or that of B., under whom he makes conusance; and if he says that he himself or B. was seised, he must say of what estate, in fee, tail, or for life.

Again: the general rule in pleading is that where a title is made under a particular estate, the commencement of that estate must be shown; but that an estate in fee may be alleged generally. (6 Bac. Abr., Replevin and Avowry, K.)

The avowries demurred to, therefore, contain a sufficient specification of the estate or title of John Williams, the lessor; and so far as that exception is concerned, it is not well taken.

But I am inclined to think the first avowry is bad, in not averring that the rent, for which the distress was made, was due and behind at the death of the testator. It is for such arrearages only that the executor can distrain. (1 R. L., 439, sec. 18.) The subsequent rent goes not to the executor, but the heir. It was, therefore, a part of the defendant's title, and ought to have been stated. He avows as executor of John Williams, for 17 years rent in arrear; and yet he does not show when his testator died, or whether the rent accrued before or after his death. All the precedents, it is believed, state the rent as having accrued in the lifetime of the testator. And *vide Hool* v. *Bell*, 1 Ld. Raym., 173.

The second avowry, however, is not in the character of executor; but in the defendant's own right, and is, therefore, free from this objection.

*Nor was it necessary for the defendant to show in his avowry, that the cattle or horses in question (belonging to a stranger, and not to the tenant), were *levant et couchant*, before they were distrained; it is for the plaintiff to show that they were not. (6 Bac. Abr., 80; Woodf., 600.) [*346

The plaintiff, therefore, is entitled to judgment upon the demurrer to the first avowry, with leave to the defendant to amend; and judgment is for the defendant upon the demurrer to the second avowry.

Rule accordingly.

Cited in—4 Wend., 667; 8 Wend., 450; 9 Wend., 155.

JACKSON, ex dem. TEN EYCK ET AL., v. FROST.

Description of Land in Patent—Natural Objects Control Courses and Distances—Map by Proprietors Inadmissible Against Proprietors of Adjoining Patent—Legislature has no Power to Settle Rights of Parties to Land—Adverse Possession.

Natural objects control courses and distances, in the description of land in a patent.

The east line of the Halfmoon patent, running from the Mohawk to the Hudson River, should touch the source of Anthony's Kill.

The map of a patent made by the proprietors, is inadmissible as evidence against the proprietors of an adjoining patent.

The Legislature have not the power to determine the rights of parties to land, either by themselves or commissioners, without the consent of the parties.

To constitute such an adverse possession as will bar a right of entry, it must be accompanied with what the law will consider, *prima facie*, a good title.

Where one entered, and possessed land, claiming it as a gore between two patents; held, that this was not such an adverse possession as would bar the true owner's right of entry; though continued for more than 20 years before ejectment brought.

The declarations of a tenant, that he has a deed, are inadmissible, even to show in what character he claims; as whether adversely or not.

Citations—5 Cow., 135; 16 Johns., 301.

EJECTMENT for a lot of land in the Halfmoon patent, in the County of Saratoga, tried at the circuit in that county, Dec. 29, 1823, before Walworth, *Circuit J.*

At the trial, the plaintiff deduced a regular title under the Halfmoon patent, to Andreas Ten Eyck, who received a conveyance of the premises in question, Sept. 25, 1767, and died in Oct., 1802; having devised them to the lessors of the plaintiff.

The patent of Halfmoon was proved. It bore date May 30, 1687; and granted to Anthony Van Schaick in fee as follows: "a certain parcel or tract of land purchased of the

NOTE.—*Deed—Construction of—Natural objects control distances, &c.* See Doe v. Thompson, *post*, p. 371, *note*.

Indians, proprietors, by license from the Governor, lying and being to the north and above the Town of Albany; and is commonly called and known by the name of Halfmoon, which stretches up alongst the North River, from a certain place where are several streams of water, to a creek or kill, where there is a fall of water, which running into the land, hath 347*] *his course into the North River; the said creek or kill and fall, being by the Indians called Tienwenendahow (now Anthony's Kill); and from thence runs up the Maqueas Kill (now Mohawk River), westward to a place called Dowaelsoiaex; and so strikes presently eastward, up alongst by the said streams of water and then to the North River aforementioned; together with three small islands, lying in the said river, over against the tract or parcel of land called the Halfmoon aforesaid."

It appeared that a line from the mouth of Anthony's Kill, directly to the Dowaelsoiaex, as run by the commissioners hereinafter mentioned, would exclude the premises in question from the Halfmoon patent. But if run from the source of Anthony's Kill, it would include them. The defendant insisted on the first, as the true line, but the judge adopted the last.

The defendant then produced certain petitions to the Legislature, purporting to be signed by the porprietors of the patents of Halfmoon, Clifton Park and Kayaderosseras; and an Act of the Legislature pursuant to these petitions, passed in 1793 (noticed more at large in *Jackson* v. *Davis*, *ante*, 123), appointing commissioners to settle certain disputes about the boundary lines of these patents. The award of the commissioners was also produced, according to which the premises in question are not in the Halfmoon patent. It appeared, however, that Andreas Ten Eyck, did not sign the petitions, or either of them, on which the statute was founded; and that by a subsequent Act, in 1795 (*vide*, also, *Jackson* v. *Davis*, *ante*, 123), the Legislature declared that no person claiming title to land in these patents, by lease or purchase in fee simple, and who did not unite in the application for the appointment of commissioners, should be bound by their determination.

The defendant also offered in evidence a map of the patent of Kayaderosseras which joins Halfmoon patent dated Nov. 12, 1770, to show that the premises in question, were in Clifton Park patent, which was rejected by the judge.

The defendant then proved that one M'Alpin 348*] occupied *the premises in question in 1795, claiming them as his own, saying they were in a gore; which, therefore, belonged to the settlers; that M'Alpin was in possession 25 years before the trial, and more than 20 years before the suit was commenced; that about 25 years before the trial he exchanged farms with one Millier, now deceased.

The defendant offered to show, by Miller's declarations, that he had a deed from M'Alpin, which evidence was objected to and excluded by the judge.

The defendant then proved that Miller remained in possession 12 or 15 years, whence the possession passed through several hands down to the defendant.

The widow of Miller swore that when her husband exchanged with M'Alpin, he took a quitclaim deed from M'Alpin, who said he thought he had a good title; that no rent had been claimed or called for; and the premises in question were not included in any of the patents; that this was 27 years before the trial; that she could not read; did not see any deed executed; but M'Alpin agreed to give one, and her husband had a paper which he said was a deed from M'Alpin.

The judge charged that the plaintiff had made out a sufficient title and location; and that the defendant had failed in establishing a bar by adverse possession.

Verdict for the plaintiff.

Mr. J. L. Viele now moved for a new trial;

1. Because the premises in question were not situated within the Halfmoon patent.

2. Because the proof offered by the defendant was improperly rejected.

3. Because the defendant made out a sufficient adverse possession to bar the action.

4. Because the judge misdirected the jury.

5. Because the verdict was against law and evidence.

He cited 1 Johns., 163; Ballantine on Limitations, 19, 21; Esp. Ev., 195, 196; *Jackson* v. *Wheat*, 18 Johns., 40.

[*349 **Messrs. S. G. Huntington* and *A. Van Vechten*, contra, cited 2 Johns., 382; 3 *Id.*, 375; 4 *Id.*, 202; 6 *Id.*, 257; 7 *Id.*, 536; 10 *Id.*, 381; 18 *Id.*, 490; 2 *Id.*, 382; 15 Mass., 153; 3 Johns. Cas., 101; 1 Phil. Ev., 182, *note a*, and the cases there cited; 1 Johns., 159, 340; 4 *Id.*, 230; 6 *Id.*, 19; 10 *Id.*, 377; 2 Day, 127; 3 Cruise, 346, secs. 33–36; 5 *Id.*, 213, sec. 13; 1 Cow., 276; 9 Johns., 163.

Curia, per SAVAGE, *Ch. J.* The only difficulty in locating the patent, arises from the last course running from the Mohawk River to the Hudson. The commissioners ran a straight line to the Hudson, at the mouth of Anthony's Kill, by which they disregarded the course, "up alongst by the said streams of water, and thence" to the North River. It is perfectly well settled that natural objects must control courses and distances. Although, therefore, the course is, "and so strikes presently eastward;" yet, we must take the whole together, adding, "up alongst by the said streams of water." What streams? Not the Mohawk, for the course leaves it—not the Hudson, for it ends there, after passing "up alongst by the said streams." The only other stream is Anthony's Kill. I think, therefore, the plain location is as if the words "presently eastward" had been omitted. It would then be, "and so strikes up alongst the said streams of water, and thence to the North River." Had such been the language, it seems to me there would be no dispute about the location. The line must run to the source of Anthony's Kill. The premises in question are, of course, included.

The judge was correct in excluding the map of the Kayaderosseras patent. The introduction of it would only show that the proprietors of that patent claimed to the commissioners' line; and after the award in their favor, they were justified in so claiming, against all who entered into the submission; but surely not against such as never assented to it. The Legislature never intended that the award should be valid against those who held property in severalty, in the disputed tract, but had not signed the petition. *Jackson* v. *Davis*, 5 Cow., 135.

350*]. *But even had the Legislature undertaken to settle this controversy themselves, without any submission, it will not be contended that they had power to do so. If the grant conveyed to Halfmoon the territory in dispute, the proprietors had a vested interest, which the Legislature could not devest without their consent. If they had not this power as to the whole collectively, they had it not as against a single individual. The only object which the Legislature could have had, was to give their sanction to the acts of the parties. If they attempted anything more, they clearly were assuming powers which belonged to another branch of the government. If they converted themselves into a court of law, their acts, in that assumed capacity, were unauthorized by the Constitution, and of course not binding on the parties.

The lessors of the plaintiff, then, having shown the legal title to be in them, and having never consented that their right should be adjudicated upon, or interfered with, by the commissioners, or anybody else, come now to demand their property, as if no such proceedings had ever taken place; and they are entitled to have it restored, unless they are barred by the Statute of Limitations.

The defendant, and those under whom he claims, have had possession for a sufficient length of time. The only difficulty is as to the character of that possession. Was it adverse? M'Alpin was the first possessor; he claimed it as his own. Why? It was a gore; no rent had been demanded; and it, of course, belonged to the settlers. This amounts to saying that he claimed it because he had no title; for if it was a gore, then the land belonged to the State. The idea that rent could be demanded, presupposes a landlord and, of course, an owner. The deed to Miller was given with this parol abstract of the title; it was not that he owned the land, because the fee was vested in him by purchase, or descent; but it was his, because there was no other owner. This is no title on which to rest an adverse possession. The purchaser, who took such a deed, knew that what he purchased amounted to nothing; for he was bound to know it.

I am aware that it was said in the case of *Jackson* v. *Thomas*, 16 Johns., 301, that "if a **351***] man enters on land, *without claim or color of title, and no privity exists between him and the real owner, and such person afterwards acquires what he considers a good title, from that moment his possession becomes adverse." This doctrine must not be understood as authorizing the purchaser to consider a naked possession a good title. It must be, as I understand the law, such a title as the law will, *prima facie*, consider a good title. Otherwise, there would be no uniformity. The character of the possession might be made to depend upon the understanding of the tenant; and the same possession, which would be a good defense to one, would be worthless to another. And hence a possession under a French grant was held not to be adverse, because such a grant could not possibly be the source of a good title.

The possession of Miller, therefore, seems to me to be merely a continuation of M'Alpin's possession, with no greater rights, but precisely of the same character. Admitting, therefore, that the possession of Miller's grantee was adverse, the length of time is not sufficient to bar the plaintiff.

In my opinion the plaintiff is entitled to judgment.

Judgment for the plaintiff.

Cited in—7 Cow., 357; 5 Wend., 147, 534; 9 Wend., 517; 1 N. Y., 527; 44 Barb., 465; 5 Duer, 277; 5 Rob., 717; 2 Sweeny, 744; 4 McLean, 500; 33 Cal., 676; 20 Wis., 432.

MOODY *v.* BAKER.

Slander—Action Lies for Words not Actionable per se, *When Special Damage is Caused—As Breach of Marriage Contract—Excessive Damages—When New Trial Allowed—Evidence.*

An action of slander lies for words not actionable in themselves; in consequence of which, a marriage contract between the plaintiff and another, was violated by the latter, though the plaintiff had a remedy against the latter for a breach of the contract.

It seems that recovering satisfaction for the damage occasioned by the slander, would be a bar to an action for a breach of the marriage contract.

In such an action, a conversation between the one who contracted marriage with the plaintiff, and a third person, it not being offered to support the testimony of the former, who had been sworn as a witness, was held not admissible in evidence.

What shall be considered proof of special damage charged in such a case.

In slander a new trial will not be granted for excessive damages, if there is no grounds to believe the jury were influenced by passion, prejudice or partiality.

Citations—8 East, 1; 2 Bos. & P., 283, 284; 4 Co., 17; Cro. Car., 269, 322; Cro. Eliz., 787; 1 Com. Dig., A, p. 178, 37[illegible], C, 1; Co. Litt., 145 *a*; 3 Burr., 1346, 1354; 7 Bac., p. 98, 76, B; Aleyn, 3; 2 Ld. Raym., 1116; Cowp., 54; Reeve Dom. Rel., 376; 4 Bac., Abr., 593; 19 Johns., 228; 2 Leon, 111; Cro. Jac., 162, 163.

SLANDER. The declaration alleged a contract of marriage between the plaintiff and Parkman Baker; and that the defendant, to prevent the intended marriage, in a conversation with Parkman Baker declared that he had had *carnal intercourse with the plaintiff; [***352** by reason whereof Parkman Baker refused to marry her.

The cause was tried at the Cayuga Circuit, 1824, before Throop, *Circuit J.*

The verdict being for the plaintiff for $1,450 a motion was now made in arrest of judgment, on the ground of the insufficiency of the declaration, and for a new trial upon a case. The latter depended mainly upon the objection that the judge had, in the course of the trial, refused to allow Halsey Phelps, a witness for the defendant, to testify to a conversation between him and Parkman Baker, who had also been sworn as a witness. The offer of this evidence was made by the defendant with a

NOTE.—*Slander.* See, generally, Van Rensselaer v. Dole, 1 Johns. Cas., 279, *note*; Dole v. Van Rensselaer, 1 Johns. Cas., 330, *note*; Lewis v. Few, 5 Johns., 1, *note*; Thorn v. Blanchard, 5 Johns., 508, *note*; Foot v. Tracy, 1 Johns., 46, *note*; Hotchkiss v. Lathrop, 1 Johns., 286, *note*; Buys v. Gillespie, 2 Johns., 115, *note*; Tillotson v. Cheetham, 3 Johns., 56, *note*; Hopkins v. Beedle, 1 Cai., 347, *note*; Lyle v. Clason, 1 Cai, 581., *note*; Thomas v. Croswell, 7 Johns., 264, *note*; Foot v. Brown, 8 Johns., 64, *note*; Martin v. Stillwell, 13 Johns., 275, *note*.

view to show that Parkman Baker had not been influenced to break off the match by anything which the defendant had said.

The main question arose on the motion in arrest. The facts on which both motions rested are more particularly stated in the opinions of the judges.

Messrs. J. L. Richardson and *T. J. Oakly*, for the motion in arrest, cited 4 Rep., 17; Cro. Car., 269, 322; Cro. Eliz., 787; Cro. Jac., 484, 485; 2 Bulst. 267, 276, 277; Cro. Jac., 162, 422; Cro. Car., 404.

But they relied mainly on *Vicars* v. *Wilcocks*, 8 East, 1, as in point; and which was recognized in *Butler* v. *Kent*, 19 Johns., 228. Also, *Morris* v. *Langdale*, 2 Bos. & P., 284.

In support of the motion for a new trial they cited 10 Johns., 281; 15 *Id.*, 493; 1 Phil. Ev., 213.

Mr. A. Spencer, contra, cited 3 Rep., 16; Cro. Eliz., 787; Com. Dig., Action on the Case for Defamation, D, 30; 1 Roll. Abr., 35; 2 Esp. Dig., N. Y. ed., 87; Bull. *N. P.*, 7; 8 Wentw. Pl., 247-276; 3 Burr., 1345; 1 Phil. Ev., 230; 4 Cow., 356

Curia, per WOODWORTH, *J.* The words spoken are not in themselves actionable. If the action is sustainable, it must be on the ground of special damage.

It is contended on the part of the defendant that no action can be maintained on the facts
353*] alleged in the declaration. *The case of *Vicars* v. *Wilcocks*, 8 East, 1, is relied on as an authority in point. In that case it was held, that when special damage is necessary to sustain an action for slander, it is not sufficient to prove a mere wrongful act of a third person, induced by the slander; but the special damage must be a legal and natural consequence of the words spoken. It appeared, that in consequence of speaking the words, the plaintiff had been dismissed from his employment before the end of the term for which he had contracted. Ld. Ellenborough proceeded on the ground that this was an illegal consequence—a mere wrongful act of the master, for which the defendant was not answerable; and inquired whether any case could be mentioned, of an action of this sort, sustained by proof only of an inquiry by the tortious act of a third person. If the doctrine here advanced is well founded, it disposes of the case before us.

The learned judge does not refer to authority in support of the decision. In my view, it seems to be a departure from well established principles, applicable to this species of action. *Morris* v. *Langdale*, 2 Bos. & P., 284, was cited on the argument, as supporting the doctrine laid down by Ld. Ellenborough. The plaintiff in that case stated that he was a dealer in the funds and, as such, had been accustomed to contract: that the defendant said of him, as such dealer, he is a "lame duck;" in consequence of which divers persons refused to fulfill their contracts with him; and he was prevented from fulfilling his contracts with other persons. It was held that it did not sufficiently appear, either that the words were spoken of lawful contracts, or that the plaintiff was a lawful dealer in the funds; and that the declaration was, therefore, bad.

Part of the *gravamen* was, that divers persons refused to fulfill their contracts. If the test is, that the special damage must be the legal and natural consequence of the words spoken; and that the plaintiff is not entitled to recover because he had a right of action on his contract, it is surprising that this ground had not been taken by the counsel who argued. But it is not even suggested. The opinion of the *court also seems to be placed on [***354** other grounds. It is true Ld. Elden observed that a doubt had arisen in the mind of the court whether the special damage had been so laid as to support the action; and that if the plaintiff had sustained any damage in consequence of the refusal of any persons to perform their lawful contract with him, it is damage which may be compensated in actions brought by the plaintiff against those persons. These remarks were not necessary to the decision of the cause. Admitting them, however, to be correct, the case was not like the present. If persons had refused to fulfill their contracts with the plaintiff, he was entitled to recover damages. The court probably considered it substantially a contract for the payment of money; in which case the refusal to pay by the debtor, in consequence of the speaking of slanderons words, would not be a ground of special damage. Most, if not all the cases, for loss of marriage, to be met with in the books, allege a communication or treaty of marriage only; and that the marriage was lost by reason of speaking the words. (4 Co., 17; Cro. Car., 269, 322; Cro. Eliz., 787.)

By a communication, or treaty of marriage, must, I think, be understood, that the parties had contracted to marry each other. If this had not taken place, how can it be said correctly that a marriage was lost? In this case a valid contract of marriage is set out in the declaration. That the action can be maintained will not be questioned, if it be shown that the law has given this remedy in cases analogous and similar in principle.

It is a general rule, that where a man has a temporal loss or damage by the wrong of another, he may have an action on the case, to be repaired in damages. (1 Com. Dig., Action on the Case, A, p. 178.) If a party has several remedies for the same thing, he has an election to pursue either. (Co. Litt., 145 *a.*) But after having recovered satisfaction for the injury from one person, he cannot afterwards proceed against any other person for a further satisfaction. (3 Burr., 1354.)

*The case of *Bird* v. *Randall*, 3 Burr., [***355** 1345, was twice argued, and decided after great consideration. The principles recognized and acted on by the court, if sound, are, in by mind, decisive of the present question. It appeared that one Burford, by articles of agreement, covenanted to serve the plaintiff for five years as a journeyman, and bound himself in the penalty of £100. After continuing a part of the time, the defendant procured and enticed him to depart; which he accordingly did. The plaintiff sued Burford for the penalty, and recovered judgment against him; but the money was not actually paid, until after the commencement of the action against the defendant. The question was, whether it was maintainable. It is remarkable that the point, whether the action could be sustained (inasmuch as the plaintiff had a remedy on the contract), was not even hinted at by the court or counsel. It is manifest that no such notion of the law was then entertained; for Ld. Mansfield, who delivered the opinion of the court, observed that the case turned upon two points: 1. Whether the plaintiff could maintain the action, if the £100 recovered against the servant had been actually received before the commencement of the action; and 2d. If it could not, whether the receipt of the money subsequently, would vary the case. I cannot well conceive of a more perfect recognition, that the fact of an existing remedy on the contract formed no objection. All the reasoning of His Lordship goes clearly to prove this. The ground upon which he places the decision, is, that satisfaction had already been received; which implies that if it had not, there was no obstacle in the way. This case is very analogous to the one before us. In each there was a contract between the plaintiff and another person, and in each the attempt was to recover damages by proof of an injury sustained by the tortious act of a third person.

If, then, the principle recognized in *Bird* v. *Randall* would authorize a recovery, when there was a contract for service, upon which damages might be recovered, I think it will apply with greater force when there has been **356***] a contract *of marriage, and performance of it refused in consequence of the slander of the defendant. A contract of marriage looks principally to a specific execution. It is of a very different nature and character from the preventing of the fulfillment of a contract to pay a sum of money. In the latter case, the non-fulfillment of the contract by means of a third person, would have no effect on the ability of the contracting party; whereas, in a case of the specific execution of a contract to marry, its value does not depend on the ability of a person to pay damages. It is, indeed, a temporal loss, but of a character not capable of being wholly repaired by the payment of money—the only substitute the law has devised.

But there are other cases which rest on the same principle. If one slanders my title, whereby I am wrongfully disturbed in my possession, though I have a remedy against the disturber, yet I may have an action against him that caused the disturbance. (1 Bac., tit. Action on the Case, p. 98; Aleyn, 3.) This is equally against the doctrine of Ld. Ellenborough; for here damages are given, which were caused by the tortious act of a third person. Again; in the action for enticing away another's servant, the servant is always liable; and yet the law is well settled that the seducer is also liable. 2 Ld. Raym., 1116; *Hart* v. *Ald ridge*, Cowp., 54; Reeve Dom. Rel., 376; 4 Bac. Abr., 593.

The doctrine contended for strikes at the root of society; and in my view, overturns some of the well settled and revered principles of the common law. I cannot, therefore, doubt that the declaration contains a good cause of action, and that the motion in arrest of judgment should be denied.

The next question is, whether there is ground for a new trial. The plaintiff proved the speaking of the words; and there existed a contract of marriage between Parkman Baker and the plaintiff. This was proved by the admissions and confessions of the defendant. He confessed that the day had been fixed for their marriage. The marriage was broken off. It is proved that the defendant admitted he had told P. Baker these things (meaning his pretended illicit intercourse with the plaintiff), and that he had once prevented *their marriage; and [***357** wished yet to do so; and desired others to assist him in preventing it.

The inference from all this is, not only that he once prevented it by his slanders, which is enough to maintain the action, but that he entirely frustrated the marriage. The facts offered to be proved by Halsey Phelps, so far as respects Parkman Baker, were not offered as confirmatory of the evidence given by him; nor to show that he had made declarations consistent with what he had sworn. The offer was to prove a conversation between two persons not parties to the suit, to make out a fact; that P. Baker was not influenced by his father's slanders; but the offer went to what Phelps had told P. Baker, as well as what P. Baker had told the witness. As to the declarations of Phelps, they were clearly inadmissible. When the judge rejected the evidence offered as one connected proposition, if the defendant intended or wished to prove P. Baker's declarations to Phelps, as showing the consistency of his evidence, it was the duty of the counsel to offer it in that light, and with that view. The language of the judge must have been, that he could not admit a conversation between two persons, not parties to the action, to be given in evidence. It is manifest the defendant did not wish to give in evidence P. Baker's declarations unaccompanied with what Phelps told him. If the latter was not admissible, then the evidence offered was rightly rejected. The credibility of Parkman Baker was a question for the jury to decide. From the facts in the case, they were fully warranted in disregarding his testimony. The damages, although liberal, are not so extravagant as to require the interposition of the court. There are no grounds to believe the jury were influenced by passion, prejudice or partiality. The motion for a new trial must be denied.

SAVAGE, *Ch. J.*, dissenting. Two motions are made in this case: 1. In arrest. 2. For a new trial.

To determine the first question, we must examine the declaration, to ascertain whether it contains any cause of action. The first count states, that at and previous to the speaking of *the slanderous words, one Parkman [***358** Baker had paid his addresses to the plaintiff in the way of courtship, with a view of contracting matrimony with her; that an engagement was formed, and a contract entered into that they should be united by marriage. Yet the defendant, well knowing these facts, and with a view to prevent the marriage of the plaintiff with Parkman Baker, spoke the slanderous words in the declaration, charging the plaintiff with incontinence.

The second count is substantially like the first, varying the words.

The words spoken are not actionable in themselves, and it is only on account of the special damage that the plaintiff can expect to recover.

It is contended, that as she has averred a contract of marriage with Parkman Baker, her remedy is on that contract; that the injury complained of was the consequence of an illegal act of a third person, for which the defendant is not answerable.

To support this position, we are referred to several cases, some of which I will briefly state.

In the case of *Morris* v. *Langdale*, 2 Bos. & P., 283, the plaintiff being a dealer in stocks, the defendant said of him that he was a "lame duck," meaning that he had not fulfilled his contracts in respect of the stocks or funds. The special damage alleged was, that he lost great gains which he would have acquired by the fulfillment of his contracts; and others refused to fulfill their contracts with him, or to have any further dealings with him. Ld. Eldon, in giving the opinion of the court, says, "a great part of the special damage consists in an allegation that other persons did not perform their contracts with him. Now, if the plaintiff has sustained any damage in consequence of the refusal of any persons to perform their lawful contracts with him, it is damage which may be compensated in actions brought by the plaintiff against those persons; and the law supposes that in such actions the plaintiff would receive a full indemnity."

The case of *Vicars* v. *Wilcocks*, 8 East, 1, was an action of slander showing special dam-
359*] age. On the trial, it appeared *that the plaintiff was engaged for a year as a journeyman rope-maker, by J. O.; and that in consequence of the words spoken by the defendant (viz.: that the plaintiff had unlawfully cut some flocking cord of J. O.), the plaintiff was discharged by his master before the expiration of the year. Lawrence, *J.*, nonsuited the plaintiff, being of opinion that the discharge of the plaintiff by his master was not justified. It was, of course, wrongful, and he was answerable to the plaintiff. The supposed damage was the loss of those advantages which he was entitled to under his contract, which he could not be considered as having lost, as he had a right to claim them of his master. Upon a motion to set aside the nonsuit, Ld. Ellenborough said, that "the special damage must be the legal and natural consequence of the words spoken; otherwise, it did not sustain the declaration; and here it was an illegal consequence; a mere wrongful act of the master, for which the defendant was no more answerable than if, in consequence of the words, other persons had afterwards assembled and seized the plaintiff and thrown him into a horse-pond by way of punishment for his supposed transgression." This case seems to be recognized by this court, in *Butler* v. *Kent*, 19 Johns., 228.

Several cases are cited to show, that when the plaintiff has recovered for loss of marriage, no contract of marriage is stated, but merely a communication of marriage. Such is the report of *Anne Davis'* case, 4 Rep., 17. So, also, in *Holwood* v. *Hopkins*, Cro. Eliz., 787, though there the action did not lie, as the words were not spoken to the person who was in communication of marriage with the plaintiff, but to a third person; and so the damage was collateral; and no action would lie. *Williams* v. *Linford*, 2 Leon., 111, contra, as to slander of title. The same mode of stating the communication of the intended marriage is found in Cro. Jac., 162, 163, and Cro. Car., 269.

On the other side, the case of *Bird* v. *Randall*, 3 Burr., 1346, is relied on to show that a person who seduces another to violate his contract, is liable, unless he who has violated his contract has made compensation. In that case, Bird had covenanted with one Burford, by which Burford *was to serve as a jour- [***360**
neyman five years, and bound himself in a penalty of £100. The defendant enticed Burford to violate his engagement; and on being sued for that cause, judgment was given for him, on the ground that, before the trial, Burford had paid the penalty. Ld. Mansfield seemed to take it for granted that the defendant would have been liable if the servant had not paid the penalty. Sir Fletcher Norton, Solic.-Gen., in argument, cited the case of *Newman* v. *Zacharay*, Aleyn, 3, in which a case was put by Hale, of slander of title; where the person whose title is slandered shall have an action against him that caused the disturbance, though he has remedy against the trespasser. This last case is quoted by Bacon and Comyn, 1 Bac. Abr., 76, B; 1 Com. Dig., 370, C, 1.

The case itself is as follows: "Newman sued Zacharay, who was the plaintiff's shepherd, in an action on the case; for that two of his (the plaintiff's) sheep did estray, one of which, being found again, the defendant affirmed to be the plaintiff's; whereupon the plaintiff paid for the feeding of it, and caused it to be shorn and marked with his own mark; and yet, afterwards, the defendant contriving to disgrace the plaintiff, and knowing the said sheep to be the plaintiff's, falsely and fraudulently affirmed to the bailiff of the manor that had waifs and strays belonging to it, that this sheep was an estray; whereupon the bailiff seized it, to his damage, &c. And after verdict for plaintiff, Latch moved that there was no cause of action; for there is no breach of trust in the defendant, as shepherd; and his words cannot endamage the plaintiff; for he shall have his remedy against the bailiff of the manor that seized the sheep wrongfully. But it was adjudged that the action would lie; because the defendant, by his false practice, hath created a trouble, disgrace and damage to the plaintiff; and though the plaintiff have cause of action against the bailiff, yet this will not take off his action against the defendant in respect of the trouble and charge that he must undergo, in the recovery against the bailiff; and Hale said, that if one slander my title, whereby I am wrongfully disturbed in my possession, though I have remedy against the trespasser, I shall have an action against him that caused the disturbance."

*The principles established by these [***361**
different classes of cases are not to be reconciled. The cases of *Morris* v. *Langdale* and *Vicars* v. *Wilcocks* seem to establish the principle, that no action lies for inducing a third person to violate his contract; for if the damage must be the legal consequence of the words spoken, no action will lie for procuring another to do an illegal act. And the reason assigned in those cases is, that the plaintiff has

his remedy against the person violating his contract, or doing the illegal act.

The case of *Bird* v. *Randall* decides that the party inducing another to violate his engagement is responsible, in case the injured party has not already received satisfaction for the injury from the party breaking his engagement. The case of *Newman* v. *Zacharay* holds the person causing the illegal act responsible at all events.

I am inclined to follow the first two cases, as they were both actions for defamation, alleging special damage. The others were not, though they were all actions on the case sounding in tort. This court, too, in *Butler* v. *Kent*, adopt the principal of *Vicars* v. *Wilcocks*, so far as to decide, "that in cases of torts, it is necessary to show that the particular damage in respect of which the plaintiff proceeds, must be the legal and natural consequence of the wrongful acts imputed to the defendant."

The principle established by these cases seems to be this: that every one who enters into a contract with another looks to the responsibility of the contractor, to fulfill the contract, or pay the damages arising from a refusal to perform, and that no action lies against a third person, who, by slanderous words, not actionable in themselves, induces the contractor to violate his contract. If I am correct in this proposition, it necessarily follows that no action lies against a person for inducing another, by such means, to violate a marriage contract. Hence it results, that the declaration in this case, contains no cause of action; and the judgment must be arrested.

But as I may be incorrect in my notions on this point, I proceed to examine the other **362***] points in the case. And *first, I will inquire whether the plaintiff showed a cause of action by legal testimony; supposing the declaration to contain a good cause of action.

The first witness proves that the defendant said he had at a certain time prevented the marriage, but was apprehensive the plaintiff and his son had then gone off to get married; and wanted to find his son still, to prevent the marriage. He then gave, as a reason, the girl's depravity, which he personally knew. By this witness, it appeared the defendant was alarmed for the fate of his son, who was still a minor. He said he had told his son of his own familiarity with the girl.

The second witness, Sloan, testified to a conversation with Parkman Baker; and was permitted to relate what P. B. had told him as to the declarations of the defendant. This was clearly irregular and improper; but if to be considered evidence, shows that Parkman did not believe what his father had told him about the plaintiff; and he was still determined to marry her.

The defendant proved by P. B. that he was not prevented from marrying the plaintiff by anything the defendant had said, but because the plaintiff had confessed to him that she had been intimate with other men.

Parkman Baker was then attacked and supported by witnesses as to his general character; and it appeared that he had related the story differently, to other persons, from what he had testified.

The defendant then offered to prove what had passed between P. B. and one Halsey Phelps, to show that he (P. B.) did not break his engagement, in consequence of what his father had said. This was overruled, and I think properly.

In my opinion, however, a new trial should be granted, as the judge admitted improper testimony—the declarations of Parkman Baker, before he was sworn as a witness. These were given in evidence to support the action; not to impeach the witness. The damages are certainly excessive, but courts do not lightly interfere on that ground, in actions sounding in tort.

*I am of opinion, therefore, that [***363** judgment should be arrested; and also that there is sufficient ground for a new trial.

Motions denied.

Cited in—5 N. Y., 20; 12 Barb., 663; 1 Hall, 416; 4 Bos., 637; 3 Am. Rep., 521 (63 Penn., 46).

OVERSEERS OF THE TOWN OF GUILDERLAND
v.
OVERSEERS OF THE TOWN OF KNOX.

Practice—Notice of Appeal—Waiver of Objection as to Time of Service—Service of Order of Removal of Pauper—What Sufficient—Settlement of Pauper—Agreement as to Services of Apprentice.

It is too late for the respondents, on appeal to the sessions from an order of removal, to object that the notice of appeal was not in season, after they have appeared and prayed, and obtained time for a hearing upon it.

It seems that an order of removal may be served by the pauper himself, delivering it to the Overseers of the Poor of the town to which he is removed.

But the mere circumstance that the Overseers of the town found the order among the papers of their predecessors, is not sufficient proof of service.

The services of an indented apprentice may be assigned by the original master to another; and his service under such assignment, for two years, in a town distinct from that where the master resides, gains him a settlement in that town.

And it is enough that such service be by the privity and consent of the original master, though there be no written assignment.

An agreement, for consideration, that an apprentice shall serve another, is binding as between the parties.

Citations—1 R. L., 279; 12 Mod., 554; Burr. Set. Cas., Nos. 5, 91, 95, 133, 186; 1 Str., 10; 2 Str., 1001, 1115; 3 T. R., 607.

ON *certiorari* to the General Sessions of Albany. Two justices made an order, Oct. 19, 1822, removing Patience York, a free woman of color, and her children, from Knox to Guilderland, Albany Co., on which the paupers were delivered, Oct. 21, 1822. Guilderland, Dec. 14, 1821, gave notice of an appeal to the sessions, at their next term commencing the 2d Tuesday of Mar., 1823.

On the hearing at June Term, after the appellant had sworn several witnesses on the merits, the respondents objected that notice of the appeal should have been given for the December Term of the sessions preceding; as the order was served in Oct.; and the statute confined the right of appeal to the next sessions; and, because it did not appear from the minutes of the court that the appeal had been then entered and continued. But it appearing that the appeal was then filed, and that the respondents had come in and prayed time from March to June Term, the objection was overruled, although no entry of giving time was actually made by the clerk.

The appellants proved an order of removal of Patience and her children, made by two justices of Stephentown, Rensselaer Co., dated
364*] *July 18, 1811, adjudging her settlement in Berne, Albany Co., of which Knox was a part; and ordering her to be removed to that place. Patience swore that she and her children were conveyed on this warrant from constable to constable, &c., through several towns to a constable of Berne, who sent her with the warrant to one Wells, then an Overseer of the Poor of Berne, to whom she delivered it.

This was denied by Wells, called for the respondents, who swore that he had no recollection of seeing the order during the year in which Patience, the pauper, came to his house; but he had been informed by the respondents that the order was found among the Overseers' papers of their predecessors in office, among the town papers of the town of Berne.

The testimony of Patience was otherwise impeached.

The respondents also proved that, 13 years before the hearing, Patience was married to Ichabod, a black man, in the town of Berne, and lived with him there.

They also proved that Ichabod was bound by his father and mother to Eliakim Williams, by indenture, in Conn., about 30 years before the hearing; and he then removed with him to the town of Berne, Ichabod being about three years old. He kept Ichabod till 16 years old; when he assigned him, by delivering the indenture, for the consideration of $40, to John Howard, of Guilderland, with whom he served in that town till 21. Howard gave Williams a bond to perform his duty to Ichabod. It was agreed, that if the paupers were settled in or chargeable to Berne, they now belonged to Knox, which was formerly a part of Berne.

The sessions, at their September Term, 1823, adjudged that the order appealed from should be affirmed, and the appeal dismissed; upon which the appellants brought their *certiorari* to this court.

Messrs. J. M'Kown and *I. Hamilton*, for the plaintiffs in error. The appeal was regularly entered and noticed; and if not, the objection on this head came too late. It was waived. The whole proceeding was, in this respect, a mere matter of practice, and discretionary with the sessions. (1 R. L., 285, secs. 17, 19.)
365*] *The indentures of apprenticeship were void, the apprentice not being a party. (8 Johns., 328.)

The assignment was void. The master had no power to assign his apprentice; and he must be deemed to have served in Knox. The indenture is personal and fiduciary; and if it was a service at all, it was under the original master. (Burr. Set. Cas., 320; 1 Mass., 172; Reeve Dom. Rel., 344.) It was no more than a service for wages under the first indenture. (Cond. Gen. Poor, 356, Backus' ed. 1819, and the cases there cited.)

The Stephentown order was conclusive. It was enough that it came to the possession of the Overseers of Berne, so as to put them on inquiry. Patience, the pauper, and her children, were removed to that place. There is no need of the constable's delivering the order personally. It is not so much in the nature of process as to require the delivery by an officer in any way. The statute contemplates a voluntary removal; and it was only in default of the paupers, obeying the order themselves, that they could be sent by a constable. If paupers go voluntarily, and notice comes to the Overseers, they must appeal. It will be intended that the court below adjudged that it came to the hands of the Berne Overseers properly; and denied the legal effect to the proceeding.

Mr. Hamilton cited Burr. Sett. Cas., 664, No. 207; 2 Const' ed. of Bott's P. L., 74, 118, No. 801; Carth., 449; 18 Vin., 470, Removal, L, pl. 2; H, pl. 1; 3 T. R., 150; 7 *Id.*, 200; 1 R. L., 34, 47, 131, 135, secs. 2, 6, 8; 2 R. L., 203, secs. 5, 6; 2 Jones & V. ed. of L. N. Y., 197, secs. 2, 14; Burr. Sett. Cas., 272, 540; 4 T. R., 770; 2 Cow., 541; Burr. Sett. Cas., 656; 8 T. R., 379; 3 *Id.*, 380; 9 E., 295; 2 Str., 1172, 1173; 6 T. R., 615; 8 T. R., 620.

Mr. M. T. Reynolds contra. The sessions passed on the right of appeal, and the merits, at the same time; and this court will not separate them. It may fairly be presumed that they dismissed the appeal, affirmed or refused to interfere with the order (which are the same thing in effect), on the *ground that **[*366**
gross neglect had defeated all right of appeal. In this they decided correctly. (3 T. R., 504; *Id.*, 193.) The appeal was not even entered and continued.

The Stephentown order was not conclusive. Whether such an order is conclusive on any one, except the town procuring it, is still unsettled in the English courts. (1 Str., 1172; 6 T. R., 615; 1 *Id.*, 353; 4 *Id.*, 651.) Our statute, 1 R. L., 282, sec. 10, provides expressly that no one shall gain a settlement on an order of removal. There is no such provision in the English Acts.

But the order was never legally executed. The statute contemplates its execution by a constable; and it uniformly commands him to deliver the order, or a copy, to the Overseers. This accords with good sense. The 10th section (1 R. L., 282) imposes a penalty on the Overseers refusing to receive the paupers. Official notice should, therefore, be given. They would not be liable on an unofficial delivery. (Burr. Sett. Cas., 664.) In *Adams* v. *Foster*, 20 Johns., 452, 455, it was held that delivery of a copy was of no avail, unless accompanied with the delivery of the pauper. The Overseers could not, in this case, know how the pauper came. The order is *ex parte*. Strict notice should, therefore, be required, to give a full and fair chance of appeal.

It is well settled that the indentures of service were valid for the purpose of gaining a setlement to Ichabod, the husband, in the town of Guilderland. (Doug., 70; 1 Str., 10; 2 *Id.*, 1001, 1115; 3 T. R., 605.)

The original indenture was valid. (6 Mass., 278.)

Curia, per WOODWORTH, *J.* The objection that notice of appeal was not served before

December Term, came too late. The respondents appeared at March Term, and prayed that the appeal be continued. This was a waiver.

The order of Stephentown is not conclusive on Berne, because not regularly served. Patience York testified that she delivered the order the day after her arrival in Berne, to one of the Overseers of the Poor, who treated it as a valid service, and said he would give her a certificate. If this statement had not been materially impeached, perhaps the service would be deemed sufficient; as in that case there was 367*] *a reasonable time for the Town of Berne to appeal. Wells, the Overseer, denies the receipt of the order, or any knowledge of it during that year. Its discovery afterwards among the papers of his successors, is insufficient. When the order was received, is not shown. It may have been long after the time had elapsed for entering an appeal. It would be unsafe and unjust to conclude a town on such evidence.

The question then arises: Was the settlement in Guilderland? This will depend on the settlement of Ichabod, the husband. He was the apprentice of Williams, who lived in Berne. Williams gave the indenture to Howard, who lived in Guilderland, for $40; but made no assignment in writing. Howard gave a bond to indemnify Williams. In consequence of this agreement, the apprentice went to live with Howard, at the age of 16; and served with him the remainder of his term, being five years.

Although, in strictness, an apprentice is not assignable over; yet, where the master makes an agreement that another shall have the service of his apprentice, it is a valid contract between the parties, although it does not alter the legal interest of the apprentice. It seems to be well settled that the apprentice need not continue in the actual service of the first master during the whole term; but that if he be assigned over by the first master, and continue with his privity and consent, in the service of another person, he may gain a settlement by serving the second master.

In this case, the indenture was handed over to Howard. Williams received compensation for the residue of the term, and consented that Howard should have the benefit of the services. The apprentice was placed in a situation to gain a settlement in Guilderland, if he continued to serve the time required by the Statute, 1 R. L., 279. This doctrine is fully supported by adjudged cases. (12 Mod., 554; Burr. Sett. Cas., Nos. 5, 91, 95, 133, 186; 1 Str., 10; 2 Str., 1001, 1115; 3 T. R., 607.)

I am of opinion that the apprentice gained a settlement in Guilderland; and that the order of the sessions be affirmed.

Order affirmed.

368*] *J. WILLIAMS

v.

CRARY, Executor of M. WILLIAMS.

Pleading—Set-off—Cannot be Pleaded—Notice with General Issue—Legacy to Creditor—When a Satisfaction of Debt—Pleading of, as such.

A set-off cannot be pleaded. It must be by notice with the general issue.

A bond which has been canceled cannot be set off.

It is a general rule that a legacy, given by a debtor to his creditor, which is equal to, or greater than the debt, shall be considered as a satisfaction of it; but this does not apply to a debt existing in an open unliquidated account.

The plea of a legacy in satisfaction should always aver, either that the bequest was made in satisfaction of the debt, or was intended as such. Merely pleading the bequest, and showing it equal to, or greater than the debt, is bad as an argumentative plea.

Citations—10 Johns., 399; 13 Johns., 24; 2 Burr., 820; 4 Burr., 2214; Toller, 264; 1 P. Wms., 324, 409, *n.* 1; 2 P. Wms., 614; 2 Fonbl., 322, sec. 5, 323, *n. b.*

ON demurrer to the defendant's plea. The action was *assumpsit* for goods sold to, and work and labor, care and diligence done, performed and bestowed by the plaintiff and his servants, horses and carriages, in and about the business of the defendant's testatrix, in her lifetime, &c., with the money counts.

The defendant pleaded several pleas, the third of which was, that the plaintiff, in the lifetime of the defendant's testatrix, to wit: Aug. 6, 1806, made a bond and mortgage to the defendant's testatrix, conditioned for $1,000, annuity, to her during her natural life; that before Apr. 1, 1819, the testatrix was indebted, as set forth in the declaration, but in an amount $1,600 less than the plaintiff owed on his bond and mortgage; and being distant from the plaintiff, unable to account with him or ascertain the amount of his demand, and desirous that no more should be exacted of the plaintiff, she made her will on that day, ordering that when the plaintiff should pay that sum to her executors, they should cause satisfaction of the mortgage to be entered of record. That she died Aug. 19, 1819, when the plaintiff owed on the bond $4,000; more than sufficient to satisfy the plaintiff's demand, after the $1,600 were deducted. That the plaintiff afterwards paid the $1,600, Feb. 19, 1820; and satisfaction was entered according to the will; and the bond was canceled; but that the plaintiff is still indebted in $2,400, the balance, after deducting the $1,600; which $2,400 exceeded the damages due the plaintiff, for the causes set forth in his declaration; and this, the defendant, by his plea, offered to set off against the plaintiff's claim.

Demurrer and joinder.

Mr. S. Stevens, in support of the demurrer. The plea is of a set-off which can only come in by way of notice. (10 Johns., 396; 13 *Id.*, 9.)

*The legacy cannot be deemed a [*369 satisfaction. It is never so, though bequeathed by a debtor to his creditor, if the claim be unliquidated. (1 P. Wms., 299; Toll., 264, 265; 7 Bro. P. C., 12.) The plea, in truth, does not show any bequest to the plaintiff. It is to be intended that only $1,600 were due, which the plaintiff was required to pay. The debt claimed to be set off arose after the will. (3 P. Wms., 355; 1 *Id.*, 299; 2 Salk., 508; 2 P. Wms., 616.)

The plea sets out the evidence of the defense, whereas it should have stated the legal conclusion. If anything, the facts pleaded would make out payment, or accord and satisfaction, and should have been so pleaded.

At any rate, the matter pleaded is no defense at law. It is merely of equitable cognizance; and within the cases, it would be no defense even in chancery.

Mr. J. Crary, contra. The only question is, whether the bequest was intended as a satisfaction for the debt, and was accepted by the plaintiff as such. If this was so, it forms a good legal defense. "Where a legacy is given by a debtor, to his creditor, which is equal to, or greater than the debt, the former is presumed to be intended to be in satisfaction of the latter; though no notice is taken of the debt in the will." (Newl., Cont., 275, and the cases there cited.)

I am not aware that the form of introducing this set-off has ever been condemned. A plea of set-off is very common, as well as a notice.

Curia, per SUTHERLAND, *J*. The demurrer is well taken. The plea is bad both in form and substance. From the conclusion, it seems to be intended as a plea of set-off. In this respect it is bad; because a set-off under our statute cannot be specially pleaded, but must be taken advantage of under the general issue, by way of notice. *Alsop* v. *Caines*, 10 Johns., 399; 13 Johns., 24.

There is no right of set off at common law. It is a remedy given exclusively by statute. The mode in which the statute authorizes parties to avail themselves of it, is by a plea of the **370***] *general issue, and notice. This mode, therefore, must be pursued. The English Statutes of Set-off allow it either to be pleaded, or notice to be given with the general issue. (2 Burr., 820; 4 *Id.*, 2214.) Our statute allows only the latter mode.(*a*)

But if it could be pleaded, the plea in this case is bad; because it appears on the face of it, and, indeed, is expressly averred that the bond, which is sought to be set off, has been canceled by the defendant, and the accompanying mortgage satisfied of record. After canceling the bond, the defendant cannot avail himself of it, by way of set-off at law. If it was surrendered through mistake or misapprehension of his right, the defendant's remedy must be sought in a different way. But here it was canceled in obedience to the express directions of the testatrix in her will. It is admitted by the plea that the plaintiff paid the amount which the will directed should be received, in full satisfaction of the bond. It is not a case of set-off, therefore, in any form of pleading.

Nor can it be sustained as a plea of legacy, or bequest in satisfaction of the demand of the plaintiff. It is not pleaded as a legacy. And although it is a general rule that a legacy given by a debtor to his creditor, which is equal to or greater than the debt, shall be considered as a satisfaction of it; yet, where there are any circumstances in the case to repel the presumption that such was the intention of the testator, courts have always eagerly seized upon them to prevent the application of the rule. It has never been applied to the case of a debt existing in an open and unliquidated account; because the testator, in such a case, is not supposed to know how the balance stands, and whether the legatee is his creditor or not.

Here the plaintiff's demand consists entirely of an unliquidated account for board and lodging, care and diligence, and services rendered, &c.; and the plea expressly avers that the testatrix did not know the amount of the plaintiff's demand, and had no means of ascertaining it, when she made her will. (Toll., 264; 1 P. Wms., 324, 409, *note* 1, and cases *there [***371** cited. (2 *Id.*, 614; 2 Fonb., 322, sec. 5, particularly *note b*, 323.)

The plea is also argumentative. It contains no averment on which the plaintiff could have taken issue, which would have presented a material question for trial. It does not allege that the testatrix made a bequest to the plaintiff in satisfaction of his debt. Nor does the plea expressly aver that such was the intention of the testatrix, in directing the plaintiff's bond to be canceled upon his paying $1,600.

Judgment for the plaintiff.

Cited in—6 Cow., 750; 7 Cow., 452; 4 Wend., 447; 12 Wend., 68; 37 Am. Rep., 557 (82 N. Y., 103).

(*a*) See Wheeler v. Raymond, *ante*, 231.

DOE, ex dem. ARDEN ET AL.,
v.
THOMPSON.

THE SAME *v.* PARKER ET AL.

1. Disseisin — What Amounts to. 2. Descriptions in Deeds—Most Material and Most Certain Parts Control Those Which are Less so—Courses and Distances Yield to Natural and Ascertained Objects — Practical Location of Boundaries.

It is a rule of construction, as to the description of premises in a deed, that what is most material and most certain shall control that which is less material and less certain.

Courses and distances yield to natural, visible and ascertained objects.

Though an agreement by parol, as to locating or bounding land under a deed, will, it seems, bind the parties; yet the agreement of the remainder-man shall not control the owner of the particular estate, unless the former act by the authority of the latter.

To constitute a disseisin, upon which a descent may be cast, so as to toll the right of entry, it must be commenced by wrong, and founded in an ouster of the true owner. There must be a disseisin in fact; and the rightful owner must have been expelled, either by violence or by some act which the law regarded as equivalent in its effects.

A mere entry upon another is no disseisin, unless it be accompanied with expulsion.

An estate by disseisin is an estate gained by wrong and injury; and herein it differs from dispossession which may be by right or wrong.

NOTE.—*Deed — Construction of — Natural objects control distances, &c.*

As a general rule of construction, what is most material and certain controls that which is less so. Courses and distances yield to visible and ascertained objects. Jackson v. Moore, 6 Cow., 706; Jackson v. Camp, 1 Cow., 605; Jackson v. Frost, *ante*, 346; Jackson v. Ives, 9 Cow., 661; Jackson v. Widger, 7 Cow., 723; Jackson v. Britton, 4 Wend., 507; Wendall v. Jackson, 8 Wend., 183; Smith v. McAllister, 14 Barb., 434; Van Wyck v. Wright, 18 Wend., 157; Cudney v. Earley, 4 Paige, 209; Schoonmaker v. Davis, 44 Barb., 463; Raynor v. Timerson, 46 Barb., 518; Yates v. Van De Bogert, 56 N. Y., 526; Pernam v. Wead, 6 Mass., 131; Belden v. Seymour, 8 Conn., 19; Call v. Barker, 12 Me., 325; Riley v. Griffin, 16 Ga., 141; Moreland v. Page, 2 Iowa, 139; Newsom v. Pryor, 7 Wh., 10; McIvers v. Walker, 9 Cr., 173; Barclay v. Howell, 6 Pet., 498; Derr v. Wright, Pet. C. C., 64.

But this rule is not inflexible. For exceptions, see Seaman v. Hogeboom, 21 Barb., 398; Baldwin v. Brown, 16 N. Y., 359; Townsend v. Hoyt, 51 N. Y., 656; B. N. Y., &c., Ry. Co., v. Stigeler, 61 N. Y., 348; Younkin v. Cowan, 34 Pa. St., 198. See, generally, 3 Washb. Real Prop., 403; Mann v. Pearson, 2 Johns., 37, *note*.

To establish a disseisin, the party must show a tortious seisin affirmatively.

Entering on land apparently vacant, and inclosing it with a fence, will not, *per se*, furnish a presumption of wrong, so as to make out a disseisin.

Citations—1 Cow., 605, 612; 1 Cai., 493; 2 Johns., 37; 15 Johns., 471; 18 Johns., 81; 2 Mass., 380; 6 Mass., 131; 11 Mass., 193; 5 Cow., 221; 6 Johns., 197.

THESE actions were ejectment for land in the eighth ward of the City of N. Y., tried at the N. Y. Circuit, Mar. 25, 1825, before Betts, *Circuit J.*

Verdicts were taken for the plaintiff, upon the third count of the declaration in each cause, which was on the demise of Rachael Arden only. This was pursuant to the decision of the circuit judge upon various points, to which the counsel for the defendant excepted; and the causes now came before the court upon a case and bill of exceptions, and affidavits of newly discovered testimony. For every material purpose, the facts are sufficiently stated in the opinion of the court.

372*] **Mr. A. Burr*, for the defendants, cited 1 Phil. Ev., 74, 75; *Rex* v. *Hardwick*, 11 East, 578; *Brandt* v. *Cline*, 1 Phil. Ev., 126, 129, *note a*, 8th paragraph; *Jackson* v. *Demarest*, 2 Cai., 382; 1 R. L., 186, sec. 4.

Mr. J. Anthon, contra, cited 2 Mass., 380; 6 *Id.*, 131; 11 *Id.*, 183; 12 *Id.*, 469; Dy., 80; Shep. Touch, 100, 248; Com. Dig., Fait, 163; 1 Cai., 493; 2 Johns., 37; 15 *Id.*, 471; 18 *Id.*, 81; 5 East, 59, 79, 80; Johns. Dig., 348, New Trial, and the cases there cited; 6 Johns., 197; 8 *Id.*, 489.

Curia, per WOODWORTH, *J.* The plaintiffs gave in evidence a deed from Aaron Burr to Jacob I. Arden, dated Aug. 18, 1797, for 23 lots of ground, distinguished on a map annexed, by certain numbers. Seven of the lots bounded southerly by Arden St., notherly by land belonging to Aaron Burr; easterly by Bedford St.; and westerly by the division line of land belonging to the corporation of Trinity Church; each lot being 25 feet in front and rear, and 100 feet long, except lot 23, being one of the seven, which was less. The other 16 lots are described as lying in a block, adjoining each other, bounded southerly by Burton St.; easterly by Bedford St.; northerly by Arden St.; and westerly by the said division line; each lot being 25 feet in front and rear, and 90 feet long, except Nos. 24 and 71, which were less.

It was admitted that Burr was seised of the premises when he conveyed. Arden devised the lots to his wife during her widowhood, remainder to his son Jacob S. Arden. The declaration contained demises from both. The plaintiff proved that James Slater, 22 or 23 years ago, occupied the premises in question, as a pasture, under Rachel Arden.

The defendant proved that Joseph Watkins, upwards of 17 years ago, caused a fence to be made inclosing the premises in question. It has continued in fence since; that Loss, a surveyor, measured the ground, and pointed out the line where the fence was put; that Arden, the remainder-man, was present a great part of the time, when the fence was erected. He as- **373***] sisted *in measuring the ground and fencing the line of division. Watkins died May 19, 1817. His son John died Mar. 13, 1823; and Joseph, Sept. 20, 1823.

The facts in the second cause are the same, excepting that Watkins erected a house on the premises in the possession of the defendants in the last cause, in 1817.

It will be perceived, that although the deed gives the number of the lots, and their length and breadth, it is an estimate merely, founded on a calculation, that 23 lots, of the dimensions given, would include all the land between Bedford St. and the division line of Trinity Church. They were probably so laid down by the surveyor who made the map. It is now ascertained that the lots, as described, do not include all the land. The defendant contends that the plaintiff is restricted to the number of feet and inches. The construction to be given to the deed will not support this objection; because the whole parcel granted is expressly stated to be bounded westerly by the division line of Trinity Church. It was a visible line. A fence was, at that time, erected on it. This line has never been changed; it is a known line, and has been recognized by both parties. The present fence stands as in 1770. It is evident the parties intended the church line as a boundary; for the deed is express. It was, undoubtedly, believed that there would be no surplus, after measuring off the 23 lots; but whatever may have been the intent of the parties, it must be collected from the deed.

The rule of construction is this: what is most material and most certain, shall control that which is less material and less certain. Courses and distances yield to natural and ascertained objects. (1 Cow., 605.) It the present case, it can scarcely be said that the question is presented, whether the corporation line shall control the number of feet. If it is then according to the course of decisions, the line would control on the ground of being a known, visible, ascertained object. Here the number of feet is merely an inference, incorrectly drawn from the premises. It is like the case of a single lot, where courses and distances or natural objects *are given, and then [***374** saying "containing 100 acres." If the boundaries contain more, it passes; if less, the grantor is not liable for the deficiency. The following are authorities to establish the doctrine: 1 Cai., 493; 2 Johns., 37; 15 Johns., 471; 18 Johns., 81; 2 Mass., 380; 6 Mass., 131; 11 Mass., 193; 1 Cow., 612.

It does not appear that Mrs. Arden had any knowledge of the inclosure made by Watkins; or that Jacob S. Arden acted as her agent in making the measurement, before the fence was erected. Without proof, the law will not presume that he acted with her privity or consent. She had an estate for life, which could not be affected by any act of the remainder-man. In the case of *Jackson* v. *Luquere*, *ante* 221, it was held that the tenant for life could not bind those in remainder. In this case, it does not appear that Watkins had any title; for aught that appears, he was an intruder; and cannot avail himself of the rule, which applies where the owners of adjoining lands, not knowing their exact boundaries, agree upon a common division line. In such cases, neither of them will be allowed to question it.

It is further urged that here was a disseisin and descent cast, which tolled the right of en-

try. It has been decided in our courts that to constitute a disseisin, upon which a descent may be cast, it must be commenced by wrong and founded on an ouster of the true owner. There must be a disseisin in fact. The rightful owner must have been expelled, either by violence or by some act which the law regards as equivalent in its effects. A mere entry upon another is no disseisin, unless it be accompanied with expulsion. Disseisin is an estate gained by wrong and injury; and therein it differs from dispossession, which may be by right or wrong. The defendant was bound to show this tortious seisin affirmatively, which he has not done. Watkins inclosed the premises by a fence about 20 years ago, without opposition or objection. Arden, the remainderman, was present. His acquiescence may be inferred from his acts. Eldridge, the defendant's witness, says he did not discover any old fence when he put up Watkins' fence. It may have been pulled up. He saw the nursery fence only. From this it appears that Wat-
375*] kins *made a peaceable entry on land apparently vacant; which furnishes no presumption of wrong. The law on this point is fully recognized in *Smith* v. *Burtis*, 6 Johns., 197.

The verdict was taken on the count on the demise of Rachael Arden. There was no community of interest between her and the other lessors; and consequently, their admissions or acts are not within the rule which allows the declarations of one among several plaintiffs to be received as competent testimony against the residue.

The defendant also moves for a new trial, on the ground of newly discovered testimony. Slater, a witness for the plaintiff, among other things, testified that he was employed by Rachael Arden to dig sods on the premises, &c; that he dug close to the church line; that there was a sort of post and rail fence, a part of which was down. It was a ridge where he dug. The evidence produced since the trial goes to disprove some of the facts related by Slater. The plaintiff has presented a number of depositions to support his testimony. There seems to be no necessity for passing on this point. The view taken shows that Slater's evidence may be dispensed with altogether. The deed to Arden conveyed the title to the premises. It is not pretended there was an adverse possession at the time; and if not, the possession continued in him who had title, until the adverse possession commenced by Watkins, which is less than 20 years. It was not necessary for Arden to have actually entered on the premises as related by Slater. He had a legal possession without it, the land not being occupied.

On the whole, I am of opinion that the motion for a new trial be denied.

Motion denied.

Cited in 6 Cow., 717; 2 Wend., 203; 8 Wend., 190; 14 Wend., 690; 16 Wend., 311; 6 Hill, 457; 46 N. Y., 207; 73 N. Y., 209; 16 Barb., 437; 21 Barb., 408; 1 Pet., 572; 2 Wall., Jr., 308; Hemp., 635; 18 Minn., 104; 20 Wis., 432; 44 Mo., 335; 19 Am. Dec., 577; 20 Am. Dec., 582 (5 N. H., 280), 22 Am. Dec., 639.

376*] *TAYLOR *v.* BATES.

Assignee of Chose in Action takes Subject to Liens Against Assignor—Attorney, not Liable to Suit for Collections, till Demand Made—His Promise to Pay to an Assignee of Claim in His Hands, More than Amount Due Assignor, is Nudum Pactum *as to Excess—Parties.*

An attorney received an order for collection, in favor of B., who directed the attorney to retain out of the moneys to be collected, a debt due to him and another; afterwards, B. assigned the demand to T. to whom the attorney promised to pay the whole demand when collected; held, that the promise was *nudum pactum*, as to the sum which B. agreed he should retain, and that he was bound to pay no more than the balance after duducting that sum.

An assignee of a chose in action takes subject to all liens against the assignor.

T., an assiguee of a demand left with an attorney for collection, assigned it to another, excepting $50, of which the attorney had notice, and then received the money; held, that an action for money had and received would lie in the name of T. against the attorney for the $50, but no more; and his assignee must sue for the residue; that the money was received for the use of those who had right as assignees respectively, but that neither could sue till demand made of the attorney.

An attorney is not liable to a suit for money collected for another, till demand made, or directions to remit. He is not in default, till he receives orders from his principal.

Citations—10 Johns., 285.

ASSUMPSIT, tried at the Rensselaer Circuit, Nov. 1824, before Duer, *Circuit J.*

Verdict for the plaintiff, subject to the opinion of the court, on a case, which is fully stated in their opinion.

Mr. J. Paine, for the plaintiff, cited Cowen Treat., 68; 17 Johns., 248; 3 B. & A., 696; 6 Johns., Ch. 358.

Mr. E. Cowen, for the defendant, cited 13 Johns., 238.

Curia, per WOODWORTH, *J.* The declaration contains the usual money counts. It appeared in evidence that Calvin Barnes, Apr. 17, 1817, placed in the hands of the defendant, for collection, an order drawn on the Treasurer of Addison Co., Vt., for $203, which had been accepted Jan. 2, 1816. At the time Barnes left the order, he was a bankrupt; and indebted to the defendant and Daniel Chipman $120; and directed the defendant to retain that sum out of the money, when collected. June 26, 1822, the defendant received $252.41 on the order, and paid Chipman his share of the debt against Barnes, being $60.

It further appeared, that shortly before Dec. 3, 1817, Barnes assigned to the plaintiff the order; and Dec. 3 the defendant wrote to the plaintiff, saying that he might retain the defendant's receipt and *keep his let- [*377 ter as evidence of his engagement to pay the money to the plaintiff, when collected.

Aug. 26, 1819, the plaintiff assigned to Southwick, Cannon & Warren, all his claim to the money, when collected on the order, except $50, of which the defendant soon after had notice. He also delivered to them the receipt given by the defendant.

Immediately after the collection of the money, the defendant sent to Southwick, Cannon & Warren (who were authorized by the plaintiff to receive the whole amount of the order) $132.41, on account of the money for which this action is commenced; but they refused to receive it, because the whole $252.41 was not offered. By the assignment from Barnes to Taylor, the latter acquired no other or greater right than the former possessed. Barnes was entitled to all that remained, after deducting $120. The defendant probably wrote the letter to the plaintiff, not recollecting, at the moment, his right to retain a part. It undoubtedly implies that the whole amount of the order would be paid; and if this assumption is legally binding the defendant must submit to the loss. Whether Barnes stated to the plaintiff, at the time of the assignment, that the defendant had a lien does not appear. If it was intended to be a transfer of the whole sum, Barnes committed a fraud, which we cannot intend, unless the fact is clearly made out. All that is said is, that he assigned the order. In the absence of other proof, I understand this as a transfer of all the right of Barnes, or all that was due on the order. An assignment of the order merely, without stating the sum due or further explanation, is an assignment of no more than Barnes had a right to claim. This construction is warranted by the general terms of the assignment.

All this took place before the defendant wrote to the plaintiff. There is no proof that the defendant in any manner induced the plaintiff to take a transfer from Barnes; or that he had any knowledge of the transaction, previous to its taking place. The letter admits that the plaintiff had been at Middlebury; but whether he then saw, or conversed with 378*] *the defendant, does not appear. It also states that after the plaintiff left that place, the defendant informed Barnes that he should account with the plaintiff for the order.

Was this previous to the assignment? The case is silent as to that fact. If it was previous, what is the fair import of those expressions as between Barnes and the defendant? It will be remembered that this declaration was made to the man who had directed the defendant to retain his own debt, when speaking to him of accounting. I should consider it the same as engaging to pay what Barnes had a right to claim. Besides, was this assurance to Barnes, such as it is, communicated to the plaintiff before he accepted a transfer; and was he thereby induced to purchase? No such facts were given in evidence. The defendant, then, was under no legal or moral obligation to pay more than the balance remaining after satisfying himself. I admit he did promise to pay the plaintiff the whole; but where is the consideration for such a promise? I have not discovered any. There was no benefit to the defendant; and it is not shown that, in consequence of any act or thing done by the defendant, the plaintiff was injured. The promise was entirely gratuitous. But it is said the promise was a waiver of a lien. The same difficulties, however, lie in the plaintiff's way. He did not waive it before the assignment; and if after, there is no consideration for the agreement to waive the lien. It will not, I apprehend, be contended, that in this case there is any substantial difference between a promise to pay the face of the order, and a promise to waive the lien. The result would be the same. My opinion is that the promise, being a *nudum pactum*, the defendant was entitled, by law, to retain $120.

The next question is: Can the plaintiff sustain an action for that portion of the money assigned to Southwick, Cannon and Warren? It is to be observed that the action is not founded on any written contract or chose in action, where the right of the trustees to sue in his own name, for the benefit of the *cestui que trust*, is unquestionable; but it is an action for money had and received, founded on an implied promise. In this form of action, the plaintiff can only *recover what has [*379 been received for him. He is not connected with Southwick, Cannon & Warren. He reserves to himself, by the assignment, $50, and transfers to them the right of receiving the residue. Of this the defendant had notice before the money was received on the order, and became answerable to them for so much money as he received for their use. The two claims are distinct, and cannot be recovered in one suit. It has already been shown that the defendant was entitled to deduct $120; so that the claim of Taylor, the now plaintiff, was $132,41. After his assignment, it became the duty of the defendant to pay the plaintiff $50 when demanded, the defendant having notice that the transfers was made with this exception. The assignees were entitled to the residue only, being $80.41. I am of opinion that the defendant is liable to the plaintiff for $50, whenever the same is demanded, or if the defendant refuses to remit the same as the plaintiff shall direct.

The remaining inquiry is, whether the defendant is liable to this action for the $50. The defendant was the attorney or agent of the plaintiff, and held the money in that capacity. No laches are shown on the part of the defendant, or unwillingness to pay. It does not appear that the plaintiff ever demanded payment, or requested the money to be remitted. The offer to pay the balance to Southwick, Cannon & Warren immediately after it was due, shows a solicitude in the defendant to discharge himself from the trust. They were authorized to receive as well the plaintiff's share as their own, and refused to accept all that could be legally claimed. The defendant was not liable to an action. To support it would be in opposition to the nature of the trust the defendant had assumed as well as against justice and good faith, until he had refused to pay, or remit, according to instructions. This case is analogous to that of *Ferris* v. *Paris*, 10 Johns., 285, where it was held that a factor or consignee, apprising his principal of the sale of goods consigned to him, may wait to receive directions as to the mode of remitting the net proceeds; and is not liable to an action, until a default on his part in remitting or paying the proceeds, *according to the order of his princi- [*380 pal. I am of opinion that judgment of nonsuit be entered.

Rule accordingly.

Cited in—5 Wend., 347; 7 Wend., 321; 15 Wend., 305; 23 Wend., 531; 24 Wend., 205; 5 Hill, 397; 45 N. Y., 738; 76 N. Y., 356; 1 Keyes, 202; 2 Abb. App. Dec., 309; 14 Hun, 359; 36 Barb., 664; 2 Abb. Pr., 304; 4 Sand., 594; 4 E. D. S., 496; Hemp., 669; 56 Ill., 159; 5 Kan., 67; 48 Pa., 526; 40 Am. Dec., 360; 8 Am. Rep., 682 (56 Ill., 156); 38 Am. Rep., 426 (83 N. Y., 318).

THE GLOBE INSURANCE COMPANY
v.
LANSING.

Foreclosure and Sale of Mortgaged Premises, Extinguishes Debt only to extent of Amount Realized.

After a foreclosure and sale upon a mortgage, for a less sum than will satisfy the amount of the mortgage debt, the mortgagee may prosecute at law, on his bond, for the balance.

Citations—3 Johns. Ch., 331; 2 Dick. 551, 785; 2 Br. C. C., 125; 13 Ves., 204, 205; 2 Gall., 152; 3 Mass., 562.

ON demurrer to the plaintiff's replication. The declaration was in debt on bond; to which the defendant pleaded, that the bond was executed concurrently with and as collateral security to a mortgage; that the mortgage was foreclosed in chancery, and the mortgaged premises sold, whereby the debt was satisfied; and the plaintiff replied that the premises did not sell for sufficient to satisfy the bond and mortgage, and showed that more than $4,000 were unpaid by the sale or otherwise.

General demurrer and joinder.

Mr. J. Lansing, Jr., in support of the demurrer, said the question was, whether after a foreclosure and sale of mortgaged premises, the mortgagee could prosecute on the bond. I do not find any adjudged case upon this question; nor is it determined by any statute. At common law, if the money was not paid at or before the day, the mortgage estate become absolute. (Pow. on Mort., 7-10; *Id.*, 438.) This was esteemed a harsh consequence, and chancery interposed but the mortgage and bond being both executed at the same time, were deemed but one instrument; and all the mortgagee could do was to make his election, either to take the land, or proceed at law for the money. Chancery would not allow him to do both. The law would not allow this. If he took the land, it was a satisfaction; and if he obtained the money, it discharged the land. If he went to the land, he was bound to take the whole or none. The money was divisible, but not the land. This is the course of the court of chancery in England. (1 Eq. Cas. Abr., 317; 2 Br. C. C., 155, 156; *Id.*, 107; 13 Ves., 198, **381***] 200; 2 Dick., 551; *785; 8 Ves., 527.) The action there opens the foreclosure; but in this State it can do no such thing, after a sale upon the Statute. The estate is gone into the hands of a purchaser. The party has put it out of his power ever to restore it. The declaration of Kent, late *Chancellor* (3 Johns. Ch., 331), that the bond may be sued after foreclosure, was merely *obiter;* and Story's opinion there cited went much on the local law of Mass.

Mr. J. L. Wendell, contra, should rely upon the opinion of Kent, late *Chancellor*, and the authorities cited by him in *Dunkley* v. *Van Buren*, 3 Johns. Ch., 330. That opinion, he said, will be found to be very ably supported by Story *J.*, in *Hatch* v. *White*, 2 Gall., 152.

Curia, per SAVAGE, *Ch. J.* The question presented is, whether a foreclosure and sale of the premises mortgaged as a collateral security, is an extinguishment of the debt due on the bond. It most clearly is not, any further than to the extent of the money produced by the sale of the mortgaged premises. In the case of *Dunkley* v. *Van Buren*, 3 Johns. Ch., 331, the late *Chancellor* Kent says: "It seems to be generally admitted in the books that the mortgagee may proceed at law on his bond or covenant, at the same time that he is prosecuting on his mortgage in chancery; and that after foreclosure here, he may sue at law on his bond for the deficiency." He cites many of the cases cited at the bar; and those cases certainly support the doctrine.

In *Aylet* v. *Hill*, 2 Dick., 551, Ld. Thurlow held that a mortgagee might proceed on his bond, notwithstanding he had obtained a decree of foreclosure; and denied an injunction to stay proceedings at law. Afterwards in *Took* v. ———, *Id.*, 785, A. D. 1784, the same question came before him; and he decided that so long as the mortgagee, after foreclosure, remained in possession of the mortgaged premises, he must take the pledge as a satisfaction; but if he sold the estate fairly, and it did not produce sufficient to pay the debt, he had a right to bring an action against the mortgagor, to recover the deficiency. Two years afterwards, *he adhered to the same opinion [***382** in the case of *Tooke* v. *Hartley*, 2 Bro. C. C., 125. In the case of *Perry* v. *Barker*, 13 Ves., 204, 205, Ld. Erskine decreed a perpetual injunction, where a mortgagee had taken possession under a foreclosure, though he had afterwards sold the estate at auction, for less than the amount due. Yet he seems to admit that had the decree been for a sale instead of a foreclosure, as practiced in Ireland, the proper course would be, if the sale produced more than the debt, to decree the surplus to the mortgagor; and if less, then to allow the mortgagee to proceed on his bond for the difference.

The whole subject has been very fully and ably discussed by *Mr. Justice* Story, in the case of *Hatch* v. *White*, 2 Gall., 152, where the principle is established, that the mortgagee is entitled to recover, on the accompanying security, the deficiency of the mortgaged property to pay the debt, calculating its value at the time of the actual extinction of the equity of redemption. In that case, there had been no actual sale; but the creditor had taken possession. In *Amory* v. *Fairbanks*, 3 Mass., 562, the plaintiff had execution for the balance due on the bond, deducting the value of the land after foreclosure, according to appraisement.

The plaintiffs are entitled to judgment, with leave to the defendant to withdraw his demurrer, and rejoin in 20 days, on payment of costs.

SUTHERLAND, *J.*, being related to the defendant, gave no opinion.

Judgment for the plaintiffs.

Cited in—4 Wend., 384; 21 Wend., 276; 2 N. Y., 340; 39 Am. Dec., 348 (5 Ala., 787).

---

*JACKSON, ex dem. EDSON and COATES, [***383**
v.
GAGER.

1. Witnesses to Deed or Power of Attorney—Absence of all must be Accounted for. 2. Awards—Void, by Dissent of One Arbitrator—Dissent must be made when Award is Published.

Where there are several subscribing witnesses to a deed, or power of attorney, it is not enough to prove one of them dead, or out of the jurisdiction of the court, and then prove his handwriting, with that of the party; but the absence of all must be accounted for; as that they are dead, or out of the jurisdiction of the court, or, on diligent inquiry, cannot be found.

Semb. that an award, on parol submission, as to the boundaries or location under a deed of land is binding in an action of ejectment.

To avoid an award by dissent of one of the arbitrators, he must dissent when the award is published.

Citations—1 Phil. Ev., 169, 362; 7 T. R., 261, 262 *n. c*; 11 Johns., 64; 1 Bos. & P., 360; 2 East, 183; 3 Binn., 192; 2 Cai., 198; 3 East, 15; 15 East, 100; 4 Dall., 120; Add., 216, 219; Kyd. Aw., 106, 62 *n. d*; 15 Johns., 197, 497; 2 Cow., 650.

EJECTMENT, for land in Willsborough, Essex Co.; tried at the circuit in that county, June 30, 1824, before Nelson, *Circuit J.*

On the trial, it was admitted that one James Ross conveyed certain lands granted to him by a patent, including the premises in question, to John Goodrich and William Wilson, who made partition—Goodrich taking the west, and Wilson the east half, which east half contained the premises in question. The partition deeds contained this reservation: "and the said William Wilson, for himself, his heirs and assigns doth covenant, grant and agree with the said Goodrich, his heirs and assigns, by these presents, that the said William Wilson will leave out of his part of the tract of land which was granted by James Ross, as aforesaid, two hundred feet of land up the River Boquet, from the falls; and two hundred feet below the falls, and as many feet back from the said river as shall contain, in the whole, twenty acres of ground, to be in common for them, the said William Wilson and John Goodrich, and their heirs and assigns forever." The lessors of the plaintiff derived title to the west half from Goodrich; and Wilson conveyed the east half to Obadiah Thayer, under whom the defendant claimed to hold as lessee. The only question was, in what shape the common lot was to be located.

This depended much on a submission of these boundaries to arbitration, by Ralph Hascall, deceased, as attorney of Obadiah Thayer, by which the lessors of the plaintiff contended Thayer was concluded.

To prove the power, Henry H. Ross, the administrator of Hascall, was called as a witness; who swore that he found the power among the papers of Hascall; that he never saw the power before H's death. Nathl. T. Thayer and I. F. Thompson were the subscribing witnesses. David Thayer, a witness for the plaintiff, **384***] swore that he knew *Nathl. T. Thayer when alive, who lived and died in Boston; and proved his handwriting, and that of Obadiah Thayer, the principal, who was described in the power, as of Newton, in the County of Middlesex, and Commonwealth of Mass. No proof was adduced to prove the death, residence or handwriting of Thompson, the other subscribing witness.

The defendant's counsel objected to the power as not sufficiently proved, but it was admitted by the judge, and read in evidence.

A parol submission under it, was then offered to be proved by the plaintiff, to Reuben Whallon, Ezra C. Gross, and Thomas Stower, Esqrs. This was objected to, but admitted by the judge.

The award made, decided that the premises in question were within the common lot described in the partition deeds.

Stower did not dissent from the award at the time it was declared. He declared the award himself, but it was not remembered whether he declared it as the award of the majority or not.

The defendant offered to show that he dissented; but the judge overruled this, unless it could also be shown that he declared his dissent at the time when the award was published.

The judge expressed an opinion that the award was valid, though by parol; and the jury found for the plaintiff, for one undivided half of the premises in question.

Mr. S. A. Foot, for the defendant, moved for a new trial:

1. On the ground that the power was not legally proved. (2 Phil. Ev., 362; 2 East, 183.)

2. That the award not being in writing, and relating to lands, was not valid. (15 Johns., 197; *Id.*, 200, *note*, and the cases there cited.) To conclude as to lands, he said, an award must operate by estoppel; and all the cases where this is held, are of bonds under seal. A parol submission is within the Statute of Frauds, 1 R. L., 78. The effect contended for is the transfer of title in land—a possessory interest at least.

*3. The award being by only two of [***385** the arbitrators, without any agreement to this effect, is void.

Mr. Z. R. Shipherd, contra. The title was admitted by the parties; and in order to locate under it, they submitted to an arbitration. To be void within the statute, it must relate to the title. Any act of the parties, *in pais*, as a parol agreement, or making a fence, should conclude as to boundaries or location. A partition may be made by parol.

The power was made in Mass.; the party who executed it resided there; and it is fairly to be intended that both the witnesses resided there also. Thompson was a person wholly unknown to us; and under the circumstances, the evidence of the handwriting, both of the party and one of the witnesses should be received as satisfactory.

Stower's dissent was of no avail, unless declared at the time of publication.

Mr. Foot, in reply, said an actual assent of all the arbitrators should be shown. Mere silence at the time of publication is not enough. An award is not like the verdict of a jury delivered by the foreman. They are appointed, by the law, arbitrators by the parties.

Curia, per SUTHERLAND, *J.* The power of attorney from Obadiah Thayer to Ralph Hascall was not sufficiently proved. It was attested by two subscribing witnesses. The handwriting, of the party who executed the power and of one of the subscribing witnesses, was proved; they both being resident in the State of Mass. No account whatever was given of the other subscribing witness. This should have been done.

The general rule is, that where there are several witnesses to a deed, it may be proved by one of them. If none of them are in being, or from any other sufficient cause, cannot be produced, proof of the signature of one of them is sufficient. (1 Phil. Ev., 169.) But before evidence can be given of the handwriting of either of the witnesses, some account must be given of all of them; as that they are dead or beyond the jurisdiction of the court; or that **386***] upon diligent *inquiry, nothing can be heard of them; 7 T. R., 261, 262; though I admit the rule has been, under peculiar circumstances, somewhat relaxed, as in case of an ancient deed. *Jackson* v. *Burton*, 11 Johns., 64. In *Wallis* v. *Delancey*, 7 T. R., 262, *note c*, the action was brought on a bond, executed at N. Y. and attested by two witnesses, Rivington and Moreton. After the handwriting of the obligor and of Rivington had been proved, Ld. Kenyon held the proof deficient, unless some account was given of the other witness. It was then proved that there had been a man of the name of Moreton, a clerk in the store of Rivington, at N. Y. Ld. Kenyon held this sufficient, it being a foreign transaction. And *vide Adam* v. *Kers*, 1 Bos. & P., 360. In *Cunliffe* v. *Sefton*, 2 East, 183, proof of the handwriting of one of the subscribing witnesses was admitted, after it had been proved that, upon diligent inquiry, no trace of the other witness could be obtained. But without such evidence the proof would clearly have been held defective. And *vide Clark* v. *Anderson*, 3 Binn., 192; 1 Phil. Ev., 362, N. Y. ed. of 1816, and the cases there cited.

Here no inquiry was made for Thompson. For aught that appears, he may have been within the jurisdiction of the court, at the time of the trial; and his attendance might have been enforced by the ordinary process. A proper foundation, therefore, was not laid for the admission of secondary evidence.

I am inclined to think, without, however, intending to express a definitive opinion upon the subject, that the submission and award, though relating to real estate, and by parol, were valid, and not within the provisions of the Statute of Frauds.

The object of the submission was to ascertain and settle the true location of a particular lot, of which the parties to the submission were joint proprietors; the surrounding or adjoining lots, or some of them, belonging to them in severalty. It was, then, an agreement that the arbitrators named should determine the boundaries of the common lot, according to the description in the partition deed of the patent, under which both parties derived their **387***] title. The title to *the common lot was not in question. It was admitted to be in the parties jointly.

In *Jackson* v. *Dysling*, 2 Cai., 198, it was held that a parol agreement between the proprietors of two adjoining lots, to abide by a certain division line, though it did not pass the land, was sufficient to prevent either party from claiming in ejectment contrary to it; and that it was not within the Statute of Frauds.

Spencer, *J.*, says an agreement by parol to the settlement of a line appears to me effectual and not liable to any objection, on the score of the Statute of Frauds and perjuries. Thompson, *J.*, observes, the submission to two surveyors, and their decision thereupon, cannot be considered as extending to the title of the land, or to have the operation of a conveyance. The submission was of a mere matter of fact, to ascertain where the line would run on actual survey, beginning at a place agreed on between the parties. Livingston, *J.*, considered the agreement within the Statute of Frauds.

If a parol agreement between the parties, fixing the location or boundaries of a lot, is valid, a similar agreement, that certain persons, named by them, shall ascertain and determine the true location, would seem to be equally exempt from the operation of the Statute of Frauds.

An award, whether it relates to the title, the possession, or the location, or boundaries of land, has not the operation of a conveyance. But the parties are concluded by their agreement from disputing the location, or boundaries, or title, as settled by the arbitrators. Its operation is in the nature of an estoppel. *Doe* v. *Rosser*, 3 East, 15; *Hunter* v. *Rice*, 15 East, 100; *Calhoun's Lessee* v. *Dunning*, 4 Dall., 120; *Lessee of Dixon* v. *Morehead*, Add., 216, 219. The award in such cases is not offered as evidence of title; but to prevent either party to it from setting up a title, &c., which had been negotiated by the award. Kyd Aw., Phil. ed., 1808, 62, *note d*; *Sellick* v. *Addams*, 15 Johns., 197; *Shepard* v. *Ryers*, *Id.*, 497, and cases there cited; *Cox* v. *Jagger*, 2 Cow., 650.

The evidence, offered to show that Stower one of the arbitrators dissented from the award, was properly rejected. *It did not go [***388** to establish the fact that he did not unite in making the award, or that he dissented from it at that time, but merely that he differed in opinion with the other arbitrators.

It was clearly proved that he was present when the award was published, and I think the evidence warrants the belief that he pronounced the award as the decision of the arbitrators. This is sufficient to constitute it the award of all the arbitrators; Kyd on Aw., 106; which, on such a submission, is undoubtedly necessary.

But a new trial must be granted on the first ground.

New trial granted.

Cited in—12 Wend., 583; 13 Wend., 198; 32 N. Y., 568; 10 Barb., 346; 20 Barb., 489; 80 Ill., 30.

GILLIS, Widow, *Demandant*,
v.
BROWN, *Tenant.*

No Dower in Estate Per Auter Vie.

Dower cannot be had of an estate *pur auter vie.*

If not devised, such an estate goes to the executor, and is assets in his hands.

One buys land under an execution against tenant by the curtesy initiate; the former is tenant *per auter vie*; and his widow not dowable.

Citations—Stat., 29 Car. II., ch. 3, sec. 12; 4 T. R., 229; Act, 1 R. L., 365, sec. 4.

DOWER, of land in Argyle, Washington Co., tried at the Washington Circuit, Jan. 5, 1824, before Walworth, *Circuit J.*

At the trial, the demandant deduced a title to her husband, Archibald Gillis, in his lifetime, by a sheriff's sale and conveyance in fee, to him, under executions on judgments docketed Dec. 20, 1816, against Brown, the tenant; and rested.

The tenant then proved a deed from one Reed, Middleton and others to Duncan Campbell, in fee simple, including the premises in question. That Campbell died about 20 years before the trial, leaving Elizabeth and Nancy, his daughters, and heirs at law. That Nancy intermarried with Brown, the tenant, previous to 1816; and is still living, having several children by Brown. That he took possession, and claimed title to the premises in question, in right of his wife merely.

Verdict for the demandant, subject to the opinion of the court.

Messrs. D. Russell and *S. Stevens*, for the demandant. Archibald Gillis acquired an estate **389***] under the sheriff's sale, of *which his widow is dowable. (1 R. L., 56, sec. 1.) The deed was to him and his heirs, and the estate not having been devised, his heirs would take as special occupants. *Atkinson* v. *Baker*, 4 T. R., 229: *Doe* v *Luxton*, 6 *Id.*, 289. And when the heir, as such, is entitled to take, the widow is dowable.

Though he had a freehold defeasible, his wife shall take, till it be defeated. Vin. Abr., Dower, G, pl. 14; *Seymor's* case, 10 Rep., 95, 96; Plowd., 555, 557.

Mr. P. S. Parker, Mr. A. Spencer same side, contra. Brown was a mere tenant by the curtesy initiate; and at most, Gillis could acquire and hold no more than an estate *pur autre vie.* Clearly, at common law, the widow would not be dowable of such an estate (2 Saund, 46, *note* 5; Co. Litt., 32 *a;* 2 Bl. Com., 129; Litt., sec. 9; 3 P. Wms., 263; 1 R. L., 365, sec. 4); and the Statute, 1 R. L., 56, gives no greater right. It was passed merely with a view to the remedy, leaving the rights of the widow precisely as they were before.

Curia, per WOODWORTH, *J.* The husband of the demandant had not an estate that could descend to his heirs. It was *pur autre vie.* By the English Statute, 29 Car. 2, ch. 3, sec. 12, such an estate descends to the heir, if it comes to him as a special occupant. It was enacted to prevent the mischief, which previously existed, that where no special occupant was designated by the grant, it belonged to the person who first took possession. (4 T. R., 229.) This Act enables the proprietor to devise the estate; but when no devise is made, it is chargeable in the hands of the heir, if it comes to him by reason of a special occupancy as assets by descent, as in case of lands in fee simple; and if there be no special occupant, it shall go to the executor and be assets. Our Act, 1 R. L., 365, sec. 4, declares that estates of this description shall be devisable; and if no devise be made, they shall go the executor or administrator, to **390***] *be applied and distributed as part of the personal estate. The consequence is, the demandant is not entitled to dower; and the tenant is entitled to judgment.

Judgment for the tenant.

RUSSELL v. GIBBS.

Dormant Executions—Indulgence of Six Months, held not, per se, *Fraudulent—Plaintiff Purchaser on his own Execution—Not Bound to Pay Money.*

A levy on a *fi. fa.* by the deputy of a sheriff, is a constructive levy, on the same property, of a subsequent *fi. fa.* delivered to another deputy of the same sheriff. And this, though the property first levied upon be, afterwards, before the delivery of the second execution, removed into another State and remain there till after the return day of the second execution.

A *fi. fa.* does not become dormant or fraudulent, as to subsequent executions, by the mere indulgence or negligence of the sheriff to proceed and sell, without any act of the plaintiff.

A plaintiff bidding on his own execution is not bound to pay the money.

But if there be a dispute between him and other creditors, as to which execution the money is to apply, *semb.* the sheriff may refuse the plaintiff's bid; or refuse to deliver the property till the money be paid; and proceed to sell again if it be not paid according to the bid made.

But if he sell and deliver the property to the plaintiff he cannot maintain an action for the price bid.

Citations—2 Johns., 422; Prec. in Ch., 286, 287; 2 T. R., 596; 1 Vern., 245; 7 Mod., 37; 8 Johns., 20; 11 Johns., 112; 17 Johns., 274; 3 Cow., 279; 19 Johns., 92; 1 T. R., 729.

IN ERROR from the Washington C. P., Gibbs sued Russell, in a justice's court, for the price of a mare sold and delivered by Gibbs, as Sheriff of Washington Co., on an execution, to Russell, who bid off and received the mare. The justice having rendered judgment for Gibbs, Russell appealed to the Washington C. P., where the judgment was also for Gibbs; whence Russell brought error to this court upon a bill of exceptions, presenting the following facts:

Russell was the owner of a judgment rendered by the Washington C. P. in favor of Lane against Nichols. A *fi. fa.* on this judgment, tested in August Term, 1818, of the Washington C. P. and returnable in December Term of the same year, was levied on the mare in question, about the 5th of Sept., of the same year, by S., a deputy of Gibbs. Afterwards, M., another deputy of Gibbs, received another *fi. fa.* against Nichols in favor of Lacy, issued from the Washington C. P., tested Mar. 10, 1819, and returnable the last Tuesday of May, in the same year, which he levied on the personal property of Nichols, May 14, 1819; but did not find the mare; she having been, before the receipt of the execution by M., removed by Nichols into the State of Vt.; where she remained till June 20, 1819; *when she was brought back to Wash- [***391** ington Co., being after the return day of Lacy's execution. M. advertised Nichols' property to be sold June 21, 1819; and sold all he could find, except the mare, which he then caused to be set up. Russell then stated he should bid off the mare upon his own execution, in S.'s hands. M. replied, that all the property sold must be applied on Lacy's execution. Russell, however, purchased the mare at $45; but refused to pay the bid, insisting on the right to apply this sum on his own execution.

This case being made out in the C. P., Russell objected to Gibbs' recovering, on three grounds:

1. Because Russell's execution was entitled to be first satisfied.

2. Because Lacy's execution had never been levied; and the mare being out of the State, during the life of Lacy's execution, the previous levy by Stevens would not work an implied levy upon the second execution.

3. Because the mare could not be sold under Lacy's execution.

The C. P. overruled these objections; holding that whether Lacy or Russell was entitled to the money, the sheriff should recover it, and then pay it out as the law might require.

Mr. Russell excepted to this opinion, and brought error.

Mr. S. G. Huntington, for the plaintiff in error, cited 12 Johns., 403; 13 *Id.*, 255; 16 *Id.*, 287.

Mr. S. Stevens, contra. The question is, whether Russell's execution was not dormant from the great lapse of time, during which it lay without being enforced. For the purpose of having that question properly decided, the sheriff should hold the money, till appropriated by law.

The sheriff having before, by his deputy S., levied on the mare in question, she is to be considered all along in his custody; and the delivery of the second execution was a constructive levy. (17 Johns., 116.)

392*] *Russell's execution was a dormant one. (17 Johns., 274.)

Mr. D. Russell, in reply. *Doty* v. *Turner*, 8 Johns., 20, is a full answer to the objection of Russell's execution being dormant. The delay was not his fault. He never directed or countenanced it.

The right to retain the bid, depends on the question, where the money was to go. Russell's holding it would not prevent its application by the law. Lacy should have moved the court for direction on that head. *Nicholls* v. *Ketchum*, 19 Johns., 92, is in point, that a creditor bidding on his own execution need not pay the money.

Curia, per SAVAGE, *Ch. J.* The important question is, whether the first execution was dormant. If so, then it was as no execution, and the plaintiff below might sell the goods levied on under it; or they might be levied on by a second execution. But as no levy was actually made under the second execution, on the mare in question, till after the return day, the sheriff had no authority to sell, unless, indeed, she was in his possession by virtue of the levy under the first. But if she was so in his possession, then it seems to me to follow that the first execution was not dormant. If not so, it was of course entitled to be first paid by the sales of property levied on under it. Whether the plaintiff in that execution would be entitled to retain the money bid for property purchased by him, against the consent of the sheriff, is another question. If the first execution was dormant, it became so by lapse of time, or by leaving the property levied on in the hands of Nichols; for it does not appear that any instructions for delay were given to the sheriff by the plaintiff, or the assignee of that execution. Nor was there any agreement for delay between the parties.

It may be useful to review some of the cases, to ascertain whether the first execution was dormant. Our books are full of cases where the subject of dormant executions is discussed: but in most, if not all, there has been some instructions given the sheriff by the plaintiff to delay the collection of the money.

The first case in our own reports, in which I have observed this doctrine noticed, is that of **393***] *Whipple* v. *Foot*, 2 Johns., *422. An execution was levied on wheat growing, and remained in the sheriff's hands from Dec. 19, 1805, till the following Aug., when the wheat was harvested and sold. The court said the mere delay, in such a case, would not of itself amount to a fraud in law. Thompson, *J.*, in giving the opinion of the court, says, this could not be considered a dormant execution within the operation of the rule, "that if a creditor seize the goods of his debtor on execution, and suffer them to remain in his hands, the execution is deemed to be fraudulent and void against a subsequent execution." He cites Prec. in Ch., 286; 2 T. R., 596; 1 Vern., 245; and 7 Mod., 37, as containing this rule. In *Edwards* v. *Harben*, 2 T. R., 596, Buller, *J.*, refers to Pr. in Ch., 287; and says: "Sir E. Northey cited a case where a man took out execution against another; by agreement between them, the owner was to keep the possession of them upon certain terms; and afterwards another obtained judgment against the same man, and took the goods in execution; and it was held that he might, and that the first execution was fraudulent and void against any subsequent creditor, because there was no change of the possession, and so no alteration made of the property." I apprehend the true reason of this case was, that the possession continued in the defendant for an indefinite period, by an agreement with the plaintiff. The 1 Vern., 245, contains nothing on the subject; and the 7 Mod., 37, was this: "*Rice* v. *Sargeant*. A man has judgment for a just debt against A, and takes out a *fi. fa.*, and gets the sheriff to seize the goods; but would not let him proceed further, but suffered the goods to remain in the custody of the debtor. B, who has also a judgment against A for a just debt, takes out a *fi. fa.*; and the question was, whether he could seize upon the same goods. And, *per curiam*, he may; for the former was a fraudulent execution; and the sheriff might very well return *nulla bona* upon the first execution." Here, again, the conduct of the plaintiff raises the presumption of fraud. The sheriff wished to proceed, but the plaintiff would not let him. Not so in this case. No direction from the plaintiff appears. And the court in the last case say the sheriff *might have returned [***394** *nulla bona.* Could he have done so in this case? Clearly not; for, from the evidence, all the delay and all the indulgence to the defendant arose either from the favor or negligence of the sheriff.

The rule in England, then, I apprehend, is not so broad as it is laid down in *Whipple* v. *Foot*. But if it were, it has never been considered in this State, as I understand the law, that the plaintiff in an execution is to be charged with fraudulent conduct, without some act of his, other than delivering his execution to the sheriff to be served according to law.

In *Doty* v. *Turner*, 8 Johns., 20, the plaintiff's agent, when he gave the *fi. fa.* to the sheriff, told him to proceed, at the same time saying the plaintiff did not wish to distress the defendant, who was his father-in-law; and that the sheriff need not take a receipt for the property, as the defendant would not squander or conceal it. The sheriff levied, and did nothing more until a second execution came into his hands, when he sold on both; and the court decided that the plaintiff was entitled to the money. They say there was no instruction to delay. There was no agreement between the plaintiff and defendant that the execution should sleep. It is added: "If a long time had intervened between the one execution and the other, it would have been ground for the jury to have inferred the consent of the plaintiff to the delay, and might have established the legal presumption of fraud."

The case of *Storm* v. *Woods*, 11 Johns., 112, the court said, came within the principle established in the English courts. The facts were, that the plaintiff in the first execution delivered it to the sheriff June, 5, 1807. In Sept. after, he assigned it to A. & D. Lane. In May, 1808, the second execution came; but the proceedings on the first were stayed by directions in writing from the plaintiff's attorney, which were never countermanded until after the receipt of the second. And in Aug., 1808, A. & D. Lane directed the sheriff not to sell unless pressed by younger executions.

395*] *In the case of *Kellogg* v. *Griffin*, 17 Johns., 274, the plaintiffs delivered their execution Oct. 13, 1817; and instructed the sheriff to make a levy, and do nothing further until ordered, unless crowded by younger executions. They presented him with an inventory at the same time. A receipt was indorsed; and they told the defendant that if Evertson forced the sale, they would bid off the property, and leave it with him. May 5, following, Evertson's execution was delivered, on which the property was sold in July. The court say, "the evidence warrants the inference that the plaintiffs issued their execution, not with an absolute intention of collecting their debt, but partly, at least, with a view to cover the property of the debtor, for his use." Their execution was held fraudulent.

In all these cases, and in all the cases of this description, which I have seen, there has been some act of the plaintiff authorizing the delay. And the case of *Rew* v. *Barber*, 3 Cow., 279, distinctly makes this qualification to the rule as laid down in *Whipple* v. *Foot*. In *Rew* v. *Barber* we considered it an important circumstance that there was no direction to delay the execution, or liberty to the defendant in the execution to use the horse, though he was left with the defendant by the express direction of the owner of the execution.

There may be cases, undoubtedly, where an unreasonable delay, or omission to urge on the sheriff to do his duty, will be construed into a consent, on the part of the creditor, to the delay. That this is such a case, I am not prepared to say. The execution was tested in Aug., 1818, returnable in Dec. Until the return, the plaintiff could not rule the sheriff. He took no step to procure a return of his execution; at least none is shown, for six months, or from Dec. till June. Whether the other property levied on by the first execution had been sold, we are not informed. But to say that an implied indulgence of six months, when no other creditor was pressing, is such a culpable negligence as to become, *per se*, evidence of a fraudulent intent to cover the defendant's property,

396*] and to delay and hinder his *other creditors from collecting their just debts would be judging very harshly of the motives of our fellow citizens, and inculcating a degree of rigor which may become highly oppressive to unfortunate debtors.

In my opinion the first execution is not to be considered dormant. The sheriff, therefore, was s i in selling the mare under the second execution. But the first execution is entitled to be first paid. (1 T. R., 729.) And the property in question having been levied on under that execution, the plaintiff was entitled to receive the money.

The only remaining question is whether the sheriff is entitled to recover the value of the mare from the plaintiff in error, though the latter is entitled to receive the same money from the sheriff at the moment of its payment. The answer seems to be, *cui bono?* Since the plaintiff is entitled to the money, why compel him to pay it? Why should he do this, when he may turn round and sue the sheriff for it? The general rule undoubtedly is that the sheriff must sell for cash; but the court, in *Nichols* v. *Ketchum*, 19 Johns., 92, say, "it would be unreasonable and injurious to debtors, as well as creditors, to insist that the creditor on the execution should advance money on his bid, when the sole object of the sale is to put money in his pocket by paying a debt due to him."

But it may be urged that in case of contest it is proper for the sheriff to bring the money into court. It is so. And in such case it may be proper for the sheriff to refuse to deliver the property till he receives the money; and if the money is refused, he may resell the property. But if he delivers the article without receiving the money, and chooses to prosecute for it, is it not a good defense for the purchaser to show that the money belongs to him? And will not the court allow him to retain his own money in preference to paying it to the officer, and compelling him to sue for it?

In this case the purchaser asserted his right to bid on his own execution. The sheriff told him the money must be applied on the second execution. If the sheriff intended to insist on the money, he should not have received the bid, *or he should have resold on the [***397** purchaser's refusing to pay the money. But by delivering the mare, it seems to me, he conceded the point in dispute. By selling property which he could not have sold on any other principle than the force and effect of the plaintiff's execution, he admits his right to the money.

On every ground, therefore, I think the sheriff could not recover.

The judgment below must be reversed, and a *venire de novo* issue from that court.

Judgment reversed.

Cited in—4 Wend., 335; 11 Wend., 552; 4 Hill, 160; 1 Barb., 546; 5 Barb., 391; 13 Abb. Pr., 118; 2 Duer, 380; 12 Leg. Obs., 9; 11 Minn., 222; 39 Mo., 49; 55 Wis., 214; 27 Am. Dec., 102; 39 Am. Dec., 305 (4 Ala., 543); 44 Am. Dec., 529 (2 Eng. [Ark.], 28); 46 Am. Dec., 432 (3 Ga., 239).

JACKSON, ex dem. THE PEOPLE,

v.

LERVEY.

Slaves — Children of, Capable of Inheriting Lands Granted to Ancestors for Services in Revolutionary War—Statute of Feb. 17, 1809.

Legalizing Marriages and Births of Slaves, was Retrospective.

It seems that, at common law, a slave could not contract matrimony; and his right to marry in this State depends upon the Statute of Feb. 17, 1809, sess. 32, ch. 44, sec. 2; 5 W., 450; 2 R. L., 201. Hence the child of a slave could not inherit at common law.

At common law a slave was not capable of taking lands, either by descent or purchase.

But, by the resolutions and laws of this State, a slave might take lands granted to him for military services during the Revolutionary War.

The children of such a slave, though born of a slave with whom he had contracted marriage before the Statute of Feb. 17, 1809, sess. 32, ch. 44, sec. 2; 5 W., 450; 2 R. L., 201, may inherit.

That Act was retrospective, and legalized all marriages and births of slaves before, as well as after, its passage.

Citations—Act of 1790; Act of April 5, 1803; 20 Johns., 693; Taylor's Elements Civil Law, 429; Cooper's Justinian, 411, 420; Act Feb. 17, 1809.

EJECTMENT, to recover possession of 50 acres of land, being a part of lot number 26, in the Township of Locke, as escheated land.

The following facts were agreed upon by the Attorney-General and the attorney for the defendant:

Lot number 26, in the Township of Locke, was drawn by Peter Stringerland, a soldier in the Revolutionary War. Stringerland was a slave, and died during the war, leaving a child born of a woman, between whom and Stringerland the ceremony of marriage had taken place, previous to the birth of the child; and the defendant derived title, *bona fide*, from the child of Stringerland. The mother of the child was also a slave, and the child was born before the Revolutionary War.

Mr. John Porter, for the defendant. There is nothing in the common law which disquali-
398*] fies the child to take and hold *real estate as the heir of his father, who was also capable of taking, though a slave. By the civil law, it is true, all conveyances to slaves inured to the benefit of their masters; but the common law was never so strict. I find no case on the point in this country; but at common law villeins approached, in their character and capacity, the nearest to an American slave. The villein could always take and hold property in his own right. (Co. Litt., sec. 172; 2 Bl. Com., 93.)

At any rate, an implied capacity to take is conferred by statute, and results from the nature of the grant, both as to the grantee and his heirs. (See the resolutions and statutes cited by Kent, *Chancellor*, 20 Johns., 703, *et seq.*)

The marriage of Stringerland, though both parties were slaves, was valid. Though a slave be restricted as to some contracts, yet he may make such as do not interfere with his master's rights. No case denies the validity of a marriage contract between slaves. It was permitted between villeins. The books speak of the heirs of villeins; and even in Rome, where absolute slavery prevailed, cohabitation between slaves was permitted by the law. Slaves were there held as nothing beyond any article of personal property. Not so here. The marriage in question would have been lawful in this State. (2 R. L., 201, sec. 2.) This Act was merely declaratory of the common law. It is retrospective in its terms.

Mr. Talcott, Atty-Gen., contra. The slave could not enlist without his master's consent, which does not appear. If so, the commissioners have gone beyond their authority in allowing the patent to issue.

He could not take under the grant. The right and capacity of slaves are far different from those of English villeins. The former have no rights, except such as are given by statute. The civil law and the law of all countries where slavery prevails is so. A villein, as to every matter except where his lord was concerned, was a freeman. He might sue and be sued, even, by his lord, when he stood *en autre droit*. He might take land, though his lord could enter upon him. To find authorities applicable to this head we must avoid England, and go to countries where slavery is tolerated. *By the laws of [*399
the latter, slaves are not considered members of civil society to any purpose. Sidney, Gov., sec. 14; 2 Locke's Works, 181; 1 Harris & M'H., Md., 561, *et seq.*; *Cunningham* v. *Cunningham*, Cam. & Norw., N. C., 353; *Bynum* v. *Bostick*, 4 Des., S. C., 266; Bradford's ed. N. Y. L., 63.

But if the father could take, he could not transmit the land to his child. The marriage, being of slaves, was not so far valid as to legitimate the issue. Such a contract is incompatible with the duty of the slave to his master. This incapacity is clear at the civil law, by which the marriage of a slave conferred no civil rights. (*Grot. de Jur. Bel. et Pac. L.*, 3, ch. 7, sec. 5, *note* by Barb.; *Id.*, L, 2, ch. 5, sec. 15; Tayl. Civ. L., 429; 20 How. St. Tr., 27; Dom. Prel. Book, tit. 2, sec. 2; Puff., B, 3, ch. 7, sec. 11.) And it is equally clear with us. *Concklin* v. *Havens*, 12 Johns., 314. The child followed the condition of the mother. *Marbletown* v. *Kingston*, 20 *Id.*, 1.

The law will not do so idle a thing as to give the child an estate which he cannot hold. It is like the cause of an alien heir, upon whom the law will not cast land by descent for a moment. True, in *Jackson* v. *Goodell*, 20 Johns., 693, a different view was taken of a grant for military services by the late *Chancellor* Kent. But this view was not necessary to the decision of that cause; nor does it appear that the court proceeded upon it. If fully examined, I think it will be found a mistaken one. The people succeeded to the rights of the King, who could not make a valid grant of lands to an alien. (Jac. L. D., Alien, II.) These military grants are no more than a grant by the Crown. A legislative grant is direct, and operates, *per se*, as a naturalization for the purpose of holding. The statutes authorize the commissioners to grant, but create no new capacity. A grant of the Crown cannot make a new rule of inheritance. (Plowd., 335.)

But this is even stronger than the case of an alien, who may take and have heirs. A slave can do neither.

The Statute of this State, 2 R. L., 210, sec. 2, never meant to vary the rights growing out of slavery. They were vested, *and [*400
could not be reached by statute. But the very passage of that Act implies that, at common law, slaves could not contract marriage.

Mr. Porter, in reply. *Jackson* v. *Goodell*, 20 Johns., 693, is a decisive answer to the objection that the commissioners exceeded their authority. Consent of the master to his slave's enlistment will be inferred, till the contrary be shown.

The Roman law is cited. With the Romans, slaves were like cattle. It is not so with American slaves. That our slaves may acquire manumission, acknowledges that they have some capacity. They are not civilly dead.

Curia, per WOODWORTH, *J.* Peter Stringerland, a slave, was a soldier in the Revolutionary Army, and died during the war, leaving a child born of a woman, also a slave, to whom Stringerland had been married, before the birth of the child. From him the defendant is a *bona fide* purchaser. The lot in question was drawn by Stringerland.

The Act of 1790 directed the patents to issue in the names of the persons who had actually served, and to their heirs and assigns forever; and that the lands should be deemed to have vested in the grantees and their heirs, Mar. 27, 1783.

The Act of Apr. 5, 1803, declared that patents made to persons, who were dead in 1783, vested in those persons at the time of their deaths respectively.

In my opinion, the question here presented will depend on a just construction of the patent, and the several Acts of the Legislature; and not on the question, independent of those Acts, whether a slave has capacity to take hold or transmit to heirs by descent. Whatever may be the disabilities of a slave, in these respects, in ordinary cases, I am not disposed now to apply them, if it shall appear, that in so doing, the manifest intention of the Legislature would be defeated, and the objects of their bounty excluded. The circumstances of the case are peculiar, and require a liberal construction of the grant. The gratitude of the country was **401***] *due to the defenders of our rights in the Revolutionary struggle. It was directed to the men who had rendered the service, whether citizens, aliens, or slaves. It was not intended to discriminate. The benefits derived were the same, to whichever class the individual belonged. The remuneration was intended to apply equally to all. This is necessarily to be presumed. In coincidence with this intent we find the concurrent resolutions and Acts of the Legislature explicit and certain. The patents are to issue in the names of the persons who served, and to vest in them and their heirs. The Commissioners of the Land Office had no discretion on this subject. The law was mandatory. Can it be supposed that the party thus granting in express terms to the soldier and his heirs, intended to raise the question of disability arising from alienism or slavery? I apprehend not. The soldier being dead when the patent issued, it was, in effect, a grant to his heirs. What heirs were intended? I think, evidently, the persons who stood in such relation to him as would be entitled to inherit, provided the soldier had been a free man and citizen.

The case of *Goodell* v. *Jackson*, 20 Johns., 693, is, in some respects, analogous. The patent in that case issued in the name of an Oneida Indian who died in the war, leaving an only son. One question was, whether the heir could take. In the opinion delivered, the *Chancellor* observes: "Could the government of this State have meant any other than Indian heirs? If it was not intended for his Indian heirs, it was a void and absurd grant.' Can we believe that a specific grant in fee, made by due authority of government, to an individual Indian by name, was intended to be illusory and mean nothing? The government acted with knowledge and discretion on the occasion. They knew the character of the grantee, and they knew the services he had rendered. The honor and good faith of the State would seem to require that the grant should have a real and effectual operation; and be deemed to inure to the benefit of the only lawful issue of the patentee. Whether the Oneida Indians are to be regarded as aliens or citizens, *appears to be quite imma- [***402** terial in reference to the title of the heir." And again: "It is no matter in what civil or political relation the Indian heir stood in respect to the whites; he still took as heir, because the government was competent to vest him with that capacity; and the intention to do it is implied in the grant itself, which was issued by authority of law."

Applying the same principles of construction to the case under consideration, I think we are called on to decide that the disabilities of the patentee and the heir, arising from a state of slavery, are removed by the Acts authorizing the grant. Although the word "heirs," as applicable to slaves, is inoperative; and would so be considered in a conveyance from a freeman to a slave, it does not decide this question; for here, it is manifest to my mind, the Legislature intended to place every person who had served, and was entitled to a patent, in a capacity to take, hold and transmit the property acquired; and that by the word "heir," in the present case, is to be understood the lawful issue of the slave; and to confer on such issue the right of taking and alienating, with the like effect, as the heir of a freeman might do under any of these patents.

But it is contended that the marriage of a soldier had not been legalized, and consequently the child not legitimate.

By the civil law, slaves could not take by purchase or descent. They had no heirs and, therefore, could make no will. They were not entitled to the rights and considerations of matrimony; and therefore had no relief in case of adultery. Nor were they proper objects of cognation or affinity; but of *quasi* cognation only. (Taylor Elements Civ. L., 429; Cooper Justin., 411, 420.) Contubernium was the matrimony of slaves; a permitted cohabitation not partaking of lawful marriage, which they could not contract. The same disability, I apprehend, will apply in the case of slaves with us. The state of slavery in this country compares with that existing under the Roman law, in many respects. The progress of society in civilization, more correct notions on the subject of moral obligation, and above all, the benign influence of the Christian religion, have softened *many of the rigors attendant on slav- [***403** ery among the ancients. But the rights of the slave in respect of marriage and the acquisition and transmission of property by way of inheritance, remain substantially on the same ground.

Sound policy and a regard to the public morals, undoubtedly called the attention of the Legislature to this subject, and gave rise to the Act of Feb. 17, 1809. This Act was intended to be retrospective in its operation. By so considering it in the present case, I do not perceive any well founded objection. It is not relied on here to devest any estate acquired under the law, as it was supposed to exist before the passing of the Act. If, by the statute, the marriage is legalized, the effect of it is, that the State cannot resort to the doctrine of escheat, and reclaim the land granted, on the ground that the son was illegitimate and, consequently, that there was no heir to take. They had the right of disclaiming a forfeiture for want of heirs; and, in my view, they have done so.

The Act declares that all marriages contracted, or which may thereafter be contracted, wherein one of the parties was, or might be, slaves, shall be considered equally valid as though the parties thereunto were free, and the child or children of such marriages shall be deemed legitimate. The words are general, and extend to all marriages. Why should it be restricted to cases where the parties were then living? One object was to render the children legitimate. What superior claims had the children of parents then living to the interference of the Legislature, to those whose parents were dead when the statute was enacted? I perceive none. The words of the Act are sufficiently broad to include both; and ought so to be construed, to effectuate the intent. If I am right in this construction, then the child of the soldier was legitimate, and became the heir of the father; subject, however, to every disability attending on the issue of a slave. The validity of the marriage, and the legitimacy of the issue, did not confer a capacity to inherit and transmit, not enjoyed before; but it placed the issue in a state to be considered as the heirs of the deceased, provided the disability as to inheriting should also be re- **404***] moved. They became *heirs within the meaning of the term as used in the grant; and being such, the Legislature intended to remove the disabilities incident to slavery, so far as to permit the issue to take an estate of inheritance; and transmit it, in the same manner, as if no disability had existed.

I am of opinion that the defendant is entitled to judgment.

Judgment for the defendant.

Cited in—2 Wend., 134; 7 N. Y., 310; 28 N. Y., 40; 19 Barb., 555; 2 Redf., 295.

TOPPING *v.* ROOT.

Practice—Action for Non-Delivery of Goods—Plaintiff must Aver and Prove Readiness to Pay—Notice.

In an action for non-delivery of goods, to be paid for at the time of delivery, the plaintiff must not only aver that he was ready to pay at the time, but he must also prove that he was ready.

Till this be done, the defendant is not bound to show performance, or a readiness to perform on his part.

NOTE.—*Sales—Action for non-delivery of goods—Readiness to pay.* See Porter v. Rose, 12 Johns., 209, note.

Where R., Aug. 22, agreed to deliver a certain quantity of hops to T., between Oct. 1 and Dec. 1, to be paid for on delivery at a certain place, with liberty in T. to increase the quantity, on giving reasonable notice: in an action by T. for not delivering the increased quantity, held that he was bound to give the notice before Oct. 1, and prove that he was ready to pay for the increased quantity.

Citations—2 Johns., 207; 10 Johns., 266; 12 Johns., 209; 7 T. R., 125; 1 East, 203; 2 Bos. & P., 447; 1 Saund., 320, *n.* 4; 5 Johns., 179.

ASSUMPSIT, for non-delivery of hops, tried at the Rensselaer Circuit, Nov. 17, 1824, before Duer, *C. J.*

At the trial, it appeared that the defendant, by a note in writing, dated Aug. 22, 1823, contracted to deliver to the plaintiff, at his brewery, between Oct. 1 and Dec. 1, 1823, 8,000 lbs. of hops; the plaintiff having the liberty of extending the quantity to 10,000 lbs.; in such case reasonable notice to be given, and the defendant was to receive 13 cents for each pound of hops. Should it not be convenient for the plaintiff to pay all the money on delivery, his note for a part, say half, should be given at 60 or 90 days. About the middle of Oct., the defendant had delivered 7,933 lbs. and received payment, when the plaintiff gave him notice that he claimed the 10,000 lbs.; but no more were delivered. This suit was for the non-delivery of the 2,057 lbs.

The declaration averred a readiness on the part of the plaintiff to receive and pay for the hops; but no proof was given under this averment.

The defendant moved for a nonsuit on this ground, which was denied.

He also objected that the notice was not in proper season; that it should have been before Oct. 1. *This was also overruled; and [***405** a verdict was found for the plaintiff for $246.84 damages.

Mr. S. Stevens, for the defendant, now moved for a new trial, on the grounds taken at the circuit; and cited 2 Johns., 207; 10 *Id.*, 266; 12 *Id.*, 209; 1 Salk., 112; 7 T. R., 121. He said the promises were dependent.

Mr. S. A. Foot, contra, said the plaintiff need not prove readiness, when the defendant totally neglects any attempt to perform on his part. In *Porter* v. *Rose*, 12 Johns., 209, the defendant was ready, and pressed the performance, but the plaintiff was not ready. The defendant offered to deliver, but made a condition that the plaintiff should pay. The objection that the notice was not reasonable, was properly overruled, and submitted to the jury.

Curia, per SAVAGE, *Ch. J.* The defendant's counsel contends that the promises are dependent—one being to deliver, the other to pay; and that in such cases, the party complaining of the non-delivery, is bound not only to aver a readiness to pay, but also to prove that averment.

In the case of *Green* v. *Reynolds*, 2 Johns., 207, the action was covenant. The plaintiff covenanted to give a deed of land, and the defendant to pay $1,000. The plaintiff sued for the money, but did not aver a tender of the deed. The courts said the covenants were clearly dependent, and that the good sense of the contract was that the money was not to be paid till the deed was ready for delivery. In *Jones* v. *Gardner*, 10 Johns., 266, the contract was that the plaintiff should convey to the defendant a farm; the payments were specified; and whenever the defendant received a good and sufficient deed, he was to give a bond and mortgage for the purchase money. The plaintiff tendered a deed, but it did not include the whole farm; and on that ground the defendant had judgment. The court held the covenants to be dependent.

The case of *Porter* v. *Rose*, 12 Johns., 209, sustains this motion for a nonsuit. That was an **406***] action on a contract for *6,000 gallons of whisky, at 70 cents, to be delivered at Buffalo, and to be paid for on delivery. On the trial the defendant's counsel moved for a nonsuit, because the plaintiff had not shown a readiness to pay. The objection was overruled, on the ground that this was not necessary. Spencer, *J.*, in delivering the opinion of the court, says, "it is fully settled in a variety of modern cases, which have disregarded the artificial and subtile distinctions of former times; and looked to the real intention and meaning of the parties, that when two acts are to be done at the same time; as when the one agrees to sell and deliver, and the other agrees to receive and pay, an averment by the purchaser, in case he sues for the non-delivery, of a readiness and willingness to pay is indispensably necessary; and that, consequently, the readiness and willingness to pay is matter to be proved on his part—whether the other party was at the place ready to deliver the thing contracted for or not." And he cites many cases to prove the doctrine; 7 T. R., 125; 1 East, 203; 2 Bos. & P., 447; 1 Saund., 320, *note* 4; 5 Johns., 179; 2 *Id.*, 207; all which decide that a readiness must be averred; but none go so far as to say that actual proof of readiness must be given at the trial. It is, however, a general rule, that all material averments must be proved. And the case of *Porter* v. *Rose* is a direct application of the rule to the principal case.

Again; the notice was not reasonable. It should have been given a reasonable time before the 1st of Oct.; when the defendant was at liberty to deliver the whole quantity contained in the contract.

A new trial must be granted, with costs to abide the event.

New trial granted.

Cited in—15 Wend., 226; 1 Hill, 523; 3 Den., 367; 43 N. Y., 90; 45 N. Y., 836; 8 Barb., 331; 12 Barb., 507; 22 How. Pr., 197; 38 How. Pr., 448; 2 Sweeny, 463; 44 Ill., 174; 46 Pa., 293.

407*] *TERBOSS v. WILLIAMS.

Landlord and Tenant—Distress, after Removal of Tenant—Pleading.

A landlord cannot distrain goods for rent after the term has expired and the tenant has removed from the premises, and abandoned the possession, though 30 days after the goods are removed have not expired.

But during the term, the landlord may distrain the tenant's goods within 30 days after they are removed from the demised premises, though more than 30 days have elapsed between the rent falling due and the distress.

Where a plea simply denies certain facts set up in an avowry, introducing no new matter, it should conclude to the country; but if it conclude with a verification, it will be good on general demurrer.

A wrong conclusion of a plea in bar can be taken advantage of only by special demurrer.

Citations—3 Cow., 271; 2 Saund., 190, *n.* 5.

ON demurrer to one of the plaintiff's pleas to the defendant's avowry. The action was replevin for certain household furniture, alleged to have been taken May 29, 1823.

The defendant avowed the taking as a distress for rent, upon a demise from him to the plaintiff, of a certain hotel lot in Salem, Washington Co., at $450, annual rent; and averred that the plaintiff enjoyed the premises, under a demise from the defendant, from Feb. 1, 1816, until May 1, 1823; and from thence until, &c. That Feb. 1, 1823, $1,350 rent was due for three years; and that, on the day mentioned in the declaration, after that sum became due, the plaintiff fraudulently and clandestinely removed the goods from the demised premises; and within 30 days thereafter, the defendant distrained them for the $1,350 in arrear.

To this avowry the plaintiff interposed several pleas—one of which was, that all interest, title, term and estate which the plaintiff had by virtue of the demise, before the time when, &c., to wit: May 1, 1823, wholly ceased, determined and ended; and the plaintiff on that day wholly removed off, from and out of the possession of the premises; and had since never been in possession of the whole or any part, nor in any manner since that time been tenant to the defendant.

General demurrer and joinder.

Mr. D. Russell, in support of the demurrer.

Mr. S. Stevens, contra, cited *Burr* v. *Van Buskirk*, 3 Cow., 263, 269, 271; 1 R. L., 438, sec. 17; 5 Laws, 178 *b*, sec. *17; 1 R. L., [***408** 347; Bradb. on Distr., 127; *Pennant's* case, 3 Rep., 54; Co. Litt., 47 *b*; 2 Saund., 284 *b*, *note* 2.

Curia, per WOODWORTH, *J.* The avowry alleges a subsisting demise and possession by the plaintiff, when the defendant distrained the goods fraudulently removed. The avowry is, therefore, sufficient. The opinion expressed in *Burr* v. *Van Buskirk*, 3 Cow., 271, that a distress off the premises can only be made within thirty days after the rent fell due, was not necessary to the decision of that cause; and on more full consideration, must be overruled.(*a*)

The plea substantially takes issue on the material fact in the avowry; for if the plaintiff's interest ceased May 1, 1823, and he removed off the premises before the time, when, &c., it negatives the averment that the plaintiff was possessed, &c., as tenant to the defendant, at the time of making the distress. This fact being admitted by the demurrer, puts an end to the right of distress. It is said the plea ought to have concluded to the country. This is correct; but it is not cause for a general demurrer. (2 Saund., 190, *n.* 5.)

I am of opinion that the plaintiff is entitled to judgment, with leave to the defendant to amend.

Rule accordingly.

Affirmed, 2 Wend., 148.
Cited in—19 Wend., 555; 6 Hill, 499; 44 Ill., 525.

(*a*) *Vide* Reynolds v. Shuler, *ante*, 323.

LION v. BURTIS.

Action for Mesne *Profits—Recovery in Ejectment, Conclusive as to Title—Parties.*

A recovery of the *mesne* profits, intermediate the judgment in ejectment, and affirmance in the Court for the Correction of Errors, pursuant to 1 R. L., 144, is no bar to the common action for *mesne* profits for the residue of the time during which the defendant in the ejectment, was in possession.

In trespass for *mesne* profits, the recovery in ejectment is conclusive evidence of title against the defendant and his servants, from the time of the demise laid in the declaration.

The action for *mesne* profits may be sustained by the nominal or real plaintiff in the ejectment.

Citations—1 R. L., 144; 2 Bac. Abr., 437; Bull., *N. P.*, 87, 88; 4 Cow., 329.

TRESPASS, for *mesne* profits. Verdict for the plaintiff. The case is sufficiently stated in the opinion of the court.

409*] **Mr. M. Wilkins*, moved for a new trial.

Mr. A. Burr, contra.

Curia, per WOODWORTH, *J.* This is an action of trespass for *mesne* profits. It appeared in evidence that the plaintiff had recovered judgment in the Supreme Court, which was affirmed in the Court for the Correction of Errors. After the affirmance, a writ of inquiry was executed, in pursuance of the 3d section of the Act, 1 R. L., 144, to ascertain the damages, as well for the *mesne* profits, as for any waste committed after the first judgment. The damages thus assessed have been paid; and it is now contended that this recovery is a bar to the present action.

The Act was intended to give the plaintiff in ejectment compensation for the delay of execution, by reason of the writ of error, between the rendition and affirmance of judgment. It is a remedial statute, which affords a speedy and beneficial remedy for that portion of time; but does not, as I apprehend, in any way affect or impair the right of the plaintiff to damages prior to the judgment. The spirit and design of the Act seem to be at variance with the doctrine urged by the the defendant. There is a *dictum* in Bull. *N. P.*, 88, that "if the plaintiff were, upon the judgment in ejectment being affirmed in error, to have a writ of inquiry, it would, probably (if rightly pleaded), prevent his recovering anything in a subsequent action in trespass." I do not find any authority cited to support this position. It is not noticed by Bacon. The editor, however, has inserted the remarks of Buller in his notes. (2 Bac. Abr., 437.)

The other points raised by the defendant are, that the judge, at the trial, overruled the evidence offered, to show that the plaintiff had not title. In this action, the judgment recovered is conclusive upon the defendant, as to the question of title. The action may be sustained in the name of the nominal or real plaintiff. The record of recovery in ejectment is conclusive evidence of title in the lessor of the plaintiff, from the time of the demise laid, against the defendant and his servants; who cannot, therefore, in an action of *tres- [***410** pass, show title in another, after that time. (Bull. *N. P.*, 87; 4 Cow., 329.)

The plaintiff produced the judgment in ejectment, and the writ of possession executed, he proved the value of the profits; and was entitled to recover. I am of opinion that the motion for a new trial be denied.

New trial denied.

[END OF FEBRUARY TERM, 1826.]

CASES

ARGUED AND DETERMINED

IN THE

SUPREME COURT

OF THE

STATE OF NEW YORK,

IN

MAY TERM, 1826, IN THE FIFTIETH YEAR OF OUR INDEPENDENCE.

413*] *MOODY v. BAKER.

Practice—Contents of Notice of Bail.

Notice of bail in error must specify their names, additions, and places of residence.

They are liable to exception in the same manner as bail to the action.

JUDGMENT being for the plaintiff, on the last day of last February Term, the defendant's attorney sued out a writ of error; the defendant entered into the usual recognizance, with two sureties, conditioned to prosecute the writ of error, &c., before Throop, *Circuit J.* Apr. 4, last, the defendant's attorney served this notice on the plaintiff's attorney: "Elijah Baker ads. Parnell Moody, &c.: Sir, take notice that a writ of error has been duly filed, &c., and that a recognizance has been duly entered into, and acknowledged according to the form of the statute in such case made and provided, to be filed in the Supreme Court clerk's office, Albany."

The plaintiff's attorney disregarded this notice, and issued execution; which,

Mr. P. C. Van Wyck now moved to set aside, as irregular.

Mr. J. Platt, contra, objected that the notice was a unlity, in not naming the bail and giving their addition and residence. He said the same form should be pursued in this as in the ordinary case of special bail; for the defend-
414*] ant in error has *the same right to except. (2 Dunl. Pr., 1138, 1139; Tidd. Pr., 1087; Tidd. App., ch. 43, sec. 15, p. 350; 6 Mod., 24; Tidd. Pr., 222, 223; 11 Mod., 2, case 9.)

Mr. Van Wyck denied that this was so as to bail in error. He said it is necessary by the Statute, 1 R. L., 143, to put in bail by recognizance before the court which renders the judgment, and which passes judicially, at the time, on the competency of the bail. This is conclusive, and is always deemed so in practice. But,

Per Curiam. The defendant's notice was defective, in not setting forth the names, additions and places of residence of the bail. The defendant in error may guard against their incompetency or insolvency, by excepting and compelling them to justify, in the same manner as the plaintiff may do in case of bail to the action. For this purpose, he must have notice who they are. The plaintiff has, therefore, been regular; but as the proceeding to bring error, and put in bail, was in good faith, let the execution be set aside on payment of costs; and the bail justifying in the usual way, if required.

Rule accordingly.

Cited in—4 Bos., 637.

WOOD v. BISHOP AND BISHOP.

Practice—Change of Venue.

In a transitory action, the venue will not be changed from one county to another, on the ground of the number of witnesses, unless the number in the latter exceed those in the former. It is not enough that the number be equal.

IN *assumpsit.* On motion to change the venue from Ulster to Dutchess, the defendant swore to "10 or 12 material witnesses," &c., in the latter county; and the plaintiff to ten in the former.

Mr. L. Maison, for the motion.

Mr. A. D. Soper, contra.

Curia. The number of witnesses being equal, the motion must be denied.

Motion denied.

---

*THE PEOPLE, ex rel. HOLDEN, [*415

v.

BALL, late Sheriff of ORANGE.

Practice—Attachment Against One in Custody.

The defendant in an attachment being in custody on a *ca. sa.*, before the attachment was served; the court ordered that interrogatories should be administered at the jail by a commissioner.

BALL, being in custody of the now Sheriff of Orange, upon *ca. sa.*, an *alias* attach-

NOTE.—*Practice—Change of venue, to accommodate witnesses.* See Spencer v. Hurlbert, 2 Cai., 374, *note;* Bentley v. Weaver, 1 Johns. Cas., 240, *note;* Gourley v. Shoemaker, 1 Johns. Cas., 392, *note.*

ment was directed to him against Ball, returnable at the present term; and the sheriff now submitting to the court whether Ball could be brought up on the attachment without a *habeas corpus*, and fearing that a compliance with the attachment might subject him to an action for an escape,

The Court directed that interrogatories should be administered to Ball on the attachment, at the jail, by a commissioner in the County of Orange.

Mr. G. Waterman, for the sheriff.

Mr. D. Lord, Jr., for the relator.

CORLIES AND WIDDIFIELD v. CUMMINGS.

Practice.

Where the plaintiff took a bill of exceptions at the circuit, and afterwards made a case, the court made a rule that he should elect one; and that the other should be set aside.

Citation—1 Johns., 192, 195.

At the trial of this cause, the plaintiffs took a bill of exceptions on certain points of law; and afterwards made a case embracing the same points, and also bringing up the question as to the weight of evidence.

Mr. D. Lord, Jr., moved that the defendant should elect which he would abide by; and that if he should elect the one, the other should be set aside.

Mr. Fessenden, contra.

Curia. The defendant cannot pursue the bill and case both. He must elect. (1 Johns., 192, 195.)

Mr. Fessenden. We then waive the bill; and will proceed with the case.

Rule accordingly.

416*] ## *EX PARTE DENNISON.

Practice—Costs on Appeal.

On appeal to the C. P., and verdict for the defendant, the court may award double costs, within the Statute for the More Easy Pleading in Certain Suits, 1 Rt L., 155.

DENNISON sued W. & C. Babcock in trespass, for two cows, in a justice's court in the County of Madison, and the justice gave judgment for the defendants. Dennison appealed to the C. P. of Madison; and on the trial of the appeal, one of the appellees justified the taking as constable, under an execution. A verdict being found for the defendants, the C. P., by rule, allowed to them double costs.

Mr. J. A. Spencer, for Dennison, now moved for a *mandamus*, commanding the C. P. to vacate this rule, on the ground that the statute allowing the appeal (6 Laws N.Y., 296 c., sess. 47, ch. 238, secs. 39, 41), providing for costs in all cases, they must be regulated entirely by that Act; and were not within the "Act for the More Easy Pleading in Certain Suits," 1 R. L., 155. He said costs were a creature of the statute, must be expressly given, and nothing is to be implied. If no costs had been given by the Fifty Dollar Act, clearly none would have been recoverable under the Act giving double costs; and single costs being given they only can be recovered.

Mr. W. Crafts, contra.

Curia. The Statute for the More Easy Pleading in Certain Suits is general in its terms; and no doubt the defendants would have been entitled to their double costs before the justice. It follows that in a court of appellate jurisdiction, upon the same matter, the like judgment should be given. The C. P. were right, and the motion must be denied.

Motion denied.

---

*DORLAND v. DORLAND AND WILLETS. [*417

Practice—Second fi. fa.—*When Allowed.*

A second *fi. fa.* cannot issue until the first (if levied) be returned, unless it be to a county other than that to which the first issued.

THE judgment being for the plaintiff on confession upon bond and warrant of attorney, he issued a *fi. fa.* to the Sheriff of Onondaga, returnable in February Term last, which was levied on certain property of Willets. After the return day, but before the return of this *fi. fa.*, the plaintiff discovered other property of Willets not levied upon. Whereupon the plaintiff obtained a stipulation from Dorland, one of the defendants, that a second *fi. fa.* might issue to the sheriff of the same county, and that he would not move to set it aside. He then issued a second *fi. fa.* to the same sheriff, and caused it to be levied on Willet's property, so found, which,

Mr. J. A. Dunlap now moved to set aside as irregular.

Mr. W. Crafts, contra, cited 14 Johns., 330; 2 Cow., 405.

Curia. The second execution was irregular. The farthest we have gone, before the first execution returned, is, to allow another in a county different from the one to which the first issued. The consent of Dorland cannot affect the rights of Willets. The second *fi. fa.* and all subsequent proceedings upon it, must be set aside with costs on the defendant, Willets, stipulating to bring no action for the levy under it.

Rule accordingly.

---

*JACKSON, ex dem. SUTHERLAND ET AL., v. STILES, ARTHUR, Tenant. [*418

Practice—Ejectment—Discontinuance by Lessor—Surplusage, in Entry of Tenant's Default—Rights of Plaintiff, Under Writ of Possession.

In ejectment, where the rights of the defendant are not affected by the proceedings, or he consents, the name of a lessor may be stricken out on motion in his behalf at any stage of the proceedings, though he originally consented to its insertion, on paying his share of the costs to the plaintiff's attorney.

Inserting the word "judgment" in the entry of

the tenant's default for not appearing, &c., in an action of ejectment, will not alter the legal effect of the entry; but it will, notwithstanding, be good; and the word "judgment" may be rejected as surplusage.

Following this by a rule for judgment generally, without saying against whom; held, a good rule for judgment against the casual ejector.

Where the plaintiff on judgment by default, against the casual ejector, on a writ of possession, took possession of the whole premises, it appearing that he had no title to three sixths, he was ordered to restore so much to the defendant.

EJECTMENT. Dec. 16, 1825, the tenant having neglected to appear and enter into the consent rule, the plaintiff's attorney, on the usual affidavit of service, entered a rule in the common rule book that the tenant appear and enter into the consent rule in twenty days, or judgment against the casual ejector by default. This rule not being complied with, Jan. 24, 1826, he entered a rule for judgment against the casual ejector by default; and Feb. 27, thereafter, a rule for judgment generally without stating against whom. Previous to the judgment the defendant had extinguished all the rights of the various lessors except to three sixths of the premises in question; notwithstanding which, the plaintiff had perfected judgment for the whole, and taken possession generally by writ of possession. Sutherland now made an affidavit that he never had retained the attorney for the plaintiff to bring the action; but he was fully contradicted by affidavits on the part of the plaintiff.

On papers disclosing the above facts,

Mr. J. Story, in behalf of the tenant and Sutherland, now moved that the default, and all subsequent proceedings be set aside for irregularity; and that, at any rate, Sutherland's name should be stricken from the proceedings.

Messrs. M'Kissock and *T. J. Oakley*, contra.

Curia. Sutherland has a right to have his name stricken from the proceedings, on paying his proportion of the costs to the attorney for the plaintiff. A lessor in ejectment may discontinue in this way at any stage of the pro-
419*] ceedings *where the rights of the defendant to costs are not affected; or he consents, as here, that it may be done; although such lessors may have originally retained the attorney who brings the suit. It does not, in general, lie with his co-lessors to object.

There is no ground for setting aside the default and subsequent proceedings. Though the rules may not have been aptly or fully drawn, yet, looking to the nature and purpose of the action, and the times at which they were entered, their meaning cannot be mistaken. Inserting the word "judgment" in the rule for the default, will not vitiate it, or alter the legal effect. The word may be rejected as surplusage. Upon the same principle the words "against the casual ejector" may be supplied in the final rule, which orders judgment generally without saying against whom.

But the plaintiff has taken possession beyond his right. The execution of the writ of possession was unqualified; though, as appears fully from the papers, the right to three sixths of the premises in question was extinguished. Let the defendant be restored to so much. No costs are allowed on either side.

Rule accordingly.

Cited in—3 McLean, 413.

THE PRESIDENT, DIRECTORS AND COMPANY OF THE BANK OF UTICA, *v.* HILLARD.

Practice—Notice, to Adverse Party, to Produce Books, &c.—Subpœna Duces Tecum.

In an action where a bank is a party, the opposite party cannot compel the cashier to produce the books or papers, by a subpœna *duces tecum.*

Citations—1 Campb., 562; 1 Taunt., 167; 1 Anstr., 259; 2 Anstr., 547; 1 Phil. Ev., Am. ed., 1820, 11, 12, 335, 336.

THE cashier of the plaintiffs had been required by a subpœna *duces tecum*, sued out by the defendant, to produce, on the trial of this cause, certain books, &c., of the plaintiffs. Not having done so,

Mr. J. A. Spencer now moved for an attachment against him, and cited 5 Cow., 153; 1 Campb., 562; 1 Taunt., 167; 1 Anst., 259; 2 *Id.*, 547.

Curia. The motion must be denied. The course for proving the books or papers of the Bank, where it is the adverse party, is to give notice to produce them; and on its non-compliance, *to show the contents by infe- [*420
rior evidence as in other cases. The effect of this motion would be to compel a party to produce evidence against himself. True the books are ordinarily in the possession of the cashier. How? He holds them as the officer, the agent or servant of the Bank, in the same manner as an attorney holds the papers of his client. The cases in which the production of papers may be coerced by subpœna are where they are the property of a competent witness, or, at least, where they do not belong exclusively to the adverse party. When he can say "these are my papers," we will not compel one who happens to have the temporary possession of them, in the right of the party, to produce them on subpœna. The question is not now what order this court, or a judge of this court, might make upon the Bank, touching the production of these papers, within the cases cited from Campbell, Taunton and Anstruther. It relates to the effect of a subpœna *duces tecum;* and it is clear that by this a party cannot have his papers taken from his custody. (1 Phil. Ev., Am. ed., 1820; and the cases there cited at p. 11, 12, 335, 336.)

Motion denied.

Cited in—6 Cow., 62; 1 Blatchf., 240, 241.

WIGGINS *v.* WILSON, Impleaded with DOE, Manucaptors of BOARDMAN, ET AL.

Practice—Special Bail—Time.

The 8 days during which special bail may surrender *ex gratia*, are to be computed of those within the test and return days of process.

THE defendants were special bail for E. O. and D. Boardman, at the suit of Wiggins, who obtained judgment; and the *ca. sa.* was returned *non est inventus*, as to all the defendants. The bail, defendants in this suit, were

then sued by *capias ad respondendum*, returnable Mar. 4, 1826, the last return day of the term, though the court continued its session to the 25th. O. Boardman had been discharged Oct. 20, 1825, under the Insolvent Act of Apr. 7, 1819, "to Abolish Imprisonment for Debt in Certain Cases." Mar. 24, 1826, D. Boardman was surrendered to the
421*] Sheriff of Cortland; and *Apr. 22, E. Boardman was surrendered to the Sheriff of Albany, by the bail.

Mr. J. Hoyt now moved that an *exoneretur* be entered on the original bailpiece, upon payment of costs.

Mr. E. Paine, contra, insisted that the motion came too late. He said the term for the purposes of surrender, and, indeed, for all purposes, except the mere test and return of process, continued to the 25th of March; and so it is considered in practice. In this view, the 8 days in full term had elapsed before the surrender; and there being no adequate excuse for the delay, the bail were irrevocably fixed. *Thomas* v. *Bulkley*, 5 Cow., 25.

Curia. We are not aware what the practice has been; whether the 8 days have been considered as belonging to the first fortnight, or the term at large. Were we satisfied that the latter had been the case in general practice, we should probably follow it. But this is a motion in favor of bail, and counsel have acted under the idea that the time is to be taken according to the test and return days of process. We adopt this as the correct practice, and direct that it be followed in future.

Motion granted.

EX PARTE S. C. RAYMOND.

Commissioner, Who is Also Master, Cannot Take Acknowledgments.

A commissioner under the Act of Apr. 19, 1823, who is, at the same time, an acting master in chancery, cannot take the acknowledgment or proof of deeds.

Citations—Act Apr. 19, 1823 (sess. 46, ch. 197, sec., 4); Stat. March 24, 1818 (sess. 41, ch. 55, secs. 2, 4).

APR. 16, 1825, D. V. N. Radcliff, Esq., was appointed, by the judges and supervisors of Dutchess, a commissioner to take the proof and acknowledgment of deeds, &c. He took the oath of office, and acted as such till Apr. 17, 1826, when he was appointed and sworn in as master in chancery. After this, he took the acknowledgment of a deed as commissioner, but the clerk of Dutchess refused to record it, on the ground that he had no power to take the acknowledgment.

A motion was now made for a *mandamus*, commanding the clerk to record this deed.

422*] **Curia*. The motion is made on the idea that the Act of Apr. 19, 1823, sess. 46, ch. 197, sec. 4 makes no mention of masters in chancery; and that they are, therefore, not prohibited from taking acknowledgments and proofs of deeds, as they were by the Statute of Mar. 24, 1818, sess. 41, ch. 55, secs. 2, 4. True, they are not expressly so forbidden; but both Acts are in *pari materia;* and the Act of 1823 refers to and adopts the provisions of the former. To allow a commissioner, who is at the same time a master, to take acknowledgments, would be to violate the very words of the 4th section of the first Act. The motion must be denied.

Motion denied. (a)

(a) *Vide Ex parte* Calvin Goodell, 14 Johns., 325.

CASE v. BELKNAP.

Practice—Motion for Judgment, as in Case of Nonsuit—Costs.

On moving for judgment as in case of nonsuit, it is enough, *prima facie*, that the defendant's affidavit showed that the plaintiff had noticed the cause for trial at the circuit, where it is alleged, he omitted to try, without expressly stating that the venue was laid there.

To excuse from trial and costs, on account of the defendant's insolvency, the plaintiff must show that he was discharged under the Insolvent Act after suit brought, and move to discontinue without costs.

That the plaintiff was surprised with a defect of testimony which he could not supply at the circuit, allowed as an excuse from stipulating, but not from costs.

Citation—1 Cai., 93.

ASSUMPSIT. Grim moved for judgment as in case of nonsuit, on an affidavit that this cause was noticed for trial, by the plaintiff, for the last Orange Circuit, but not tried. The affidavit did not state where the venue was laid;

Mr. Ross objected to this as a defect, and cited 3 Cai., 128, 3 Johns., 446.

Per Curiam. The noticing of the cause for trial in Orange, is, at least, *prima facie* evidence, that the venue was laid there. In the cases cited, it does not appear that they had been noticed for trial.

Mr. Ross then read an affidavit to show that the defendant was insolvent, but not that he had been discharged under the Insolvent Act; and cited 1 Johns., 141, 143.

**Curia*. Had the defendant been [*423
discharged under the Insolvent Act, after suit brought, we should allow you to discontinue without costs. But we cannot try the fact of insolvency on this motion by mere affidavit. Besides, you do not seek to discontinue.

Mr. Ross then read an affidavit showing that, on coming to the circuit, the plaintiff was surprised by a defect of testimony, which he could not supply during the circuit, and cited 1 Johns. Cas., 30.

Curia. For this reason, we excuse you from stipulating, but not from costs. *Jackson* v. *Haight*, 2 Cai., 93.

Rule accordingly.

Cited in—45 Super., 514.

ANONYMOUS.

Practice—Notice for Trial—Reference.

The excuse for not noticing a motion for the first day of term need not be given in the affidavits served.

To warrant denying a reference on the ground that questions of law will arise, the court must be satisfied that they will be questions of real difficulty.

ASSUMPSIT. *Mr. Craig* moved for a reference, on a notice of motion for Friday, the second week in term.

Mr. T. A. Emmet, contra, objected that the notice should have been for the first day in term.

Mr. Craig read an affidavit showing an excuse for not noticing for an earlier day. This excuse, he said, was contained in the affidavit of service.

Mr. Emmet said the affidavit of excuse should have been served with the other papers, so that it might be denied.

Per Curiam. The constant practice is otherwise. The excuse is for the court, not for the party, and may be shown at the time of moving.

Mr. Emmet then read an affidavit, showing that certain questions of law would arise before the referees, specifying them. These would arise under the plea of the Statute of Limitations.

424*] **Curia.* The questions which you state are of easy solution. Questions of law may, and to a certain extent must, arise on every reference. We must be satisfied, however, that they are questions of real difficulty, to warrant our denying a reference on this ground. The doctrine of evidence upon the plea of the Statute of Limitations is, in general, very well settled.

Motion denied.

Cited in—10 How. Pr., 352; 13 How. Pr., 439; 39 Super., 416.

FAIRLIE ET AL., Com'rs of the Almshouse in the City of New York,

v.

LAWSON & STANBERRY.

Action on Penal Bond—Penalty the Extent of Recovery—Especially Against Surety—Interest—Costs.

Judgment for the plaintiff in an action on a penal bond is properly for the penalty, in all cases, except where the demand is reduced by a set-off, within the Statute, 1 R. L., 515, 16; and if the penalty exceed $250, the p ai iff is entitled to Supreme Court costs, though the damages recovered on an assignment of breaches be less than $250.

Interest cannot be taxed as costs, on recovery upon a bond, where its effect will be to compel the defendants to pay (one of them being a surety) beyond the penalty of the bond.

A s re y is not liable beyond the penalty of his bond.u t

Citations—1 R. L., 515, 516; 2 Cow., 412; 3 Cow., 151.

IN debt on bond, conditioned for the maintenance of a bastard child, in the penalty of $400, the plaintiffs assigned breaches according to the Statute, 1 R. L., 518. The defendants (one of whom was a surety) pleaded payment of $264.25, and *non damnificatus* beyond that sum. The defendants proving payment according to their plea, the court held that the plaintiffs could recover only $135.75, though they proved damages beyond this, over and above what had been paid.

Judge Irving taxed Supreme Court costs for the plaintiffs; who insisted that he should also tax interest on the verdict to the time of the judgment, which he refused.

It was now submitted, whether the costs should not have been taxed at the C. P. rate only, and whether interest should not have been taxed.

Mr. W. S. Johnson, for the plaintiffs.

Mr. W. A. Seely, for the defendants.

Curia. The taxing officer was right in both particulars. In case of an action on a bond, other than for the payment of money; and indeed, where it is for the payment of money, except where it is met by a set-off, in which case the *condition is to be the measure **[*425** of the judgment (1 R. L., 515, 516), the penalty is the criterion of cost. If that be more than $250, Supreme Court costs are allowed. (2 Cow., 412.)

Interest is not allowable, where it will swell the recovery to, or, in effect, compel the defendants to pay, in the whole, an amount beyond the penalty of a bond, especially against a surety. *Clark* v. *Bush*, 3 Cow., 151.

Taxation affirmed.

Cited in—6 Cow., 58, 64; 12 Wend., 141; 7 Barb., 583; 19 How. Pr., 388; 2 M'Lean, 587; 13 Mich., 202; 46 Mo., 381.

EX PARTE McKINNEY AND THOMPSON

v.

NEWCOMB.

Award—Motion to Set Aside—Merits Not Inquired Into.

On a motion to set aside an award which was agreed to be made a rule of court, the merits of the award are not inquirable into. It will not be set aside in a court of law, unless the arbitrators have acted dishonestly or corruptly.

Citations—2 Archb. Pr., 289; 2 Burr., 701; 1 Str., 301; 1 Saund., 327 *d*; 17 Johns., 410, 411.

THE parties had submitted to arbitration, and agreed that the submission should be made a rule of court. The award being for McKinney and Thompson, it was, early in this term, on motion, made a rule of court and performance demanded; and now two motions were made—one for an attachment against Newcomb for not performing the award, and another in behalf of Newcomb to set aside the award, on the ground that the arbitrators had rejected a material witness offered by Newcomb.

Mr. Lockwood, for Newcomb, cited 17 Johns., 410, 411; Kyd on Aw., 317; 1 Str., 695; 1 Burr., 278; 1 R. L., 125, 126.(*a*)

Mr. Anderson, for McKinney and Thompson.

NOTE.—*Principal and surety—Contract strictly construed.* See Ludlow v. Simond, 2 Cai. Cas., 1, *note*; Walsh v. Bailie, 10 Johns., 180, *note*; People v. Jansen, 7 Johns., 332, *note*; King v. Baldwin, 17 Johns., 384, *note*; Powell v. Waters, 17 Johns., 176, *note*; Pain v. Packard, 13 Johns., 174, *note*.

(*a*) He also objected that the submission could not be made a rule of court after the award, on the authority of Spettigue v. Carpenter, 3 P. Wms., 361; but the court did not hesitate to disallow this objection, as the contrary is clearly settled: Alardes v. Campbell, 1 Barnard, K. B., 152; Pownall v. King, 6 Ves., 10; Caldw. on Arb., Am. ed., 20; and it was so held lately, by this court, in *Ex parte Vasques*, *ante*, 29.

Curia. Here is no pretense of dishonesty or corruption in the arbitrators. We do not examine the merits on an application to set aside the award. (2 Archb. Pr., 289 ; 2 Burr., 701 ; 1 Str., 301 ; 1 Saund., 327 *d.*) A mere mistake **426***] *of the law is not a ground for our interference ; and that is all which is pretended. The case cited from the 17 Johns. was in a court of equity. The motion to set aside the award must be denied, and the attachment must go.

Rule accordingly.

Cited in—12 Wend., 583.

Ex parte ELIPHRAS HOLMES AND TEN OTHERS.

Practice—Notice under Statute—Service of—Counsel Appearing Deemed, Prima Facie, *Authorized to Appear—Corporation—Election of Directors—Trustee of Stock Cannot Vote on it—Powers of Company, as to Stock.*

Notice of a motion, under the Act to Facilitate Proceedings against Incorporated Companies, &c., sess. 48, ch. 325, sec. 9, which draws in question the election of Directors of a Company, is sufficient, if served on the Directors, whose election is questioned. It need not be served on the President, or the Directors whose seats are not questioned.

Nor need notice be given to persons whose right to vote is in question.

The counsel who appear in behalf of such an application, and the counsel who oppose, will be deemed by the court, *prima facie*, authorized thus to appear.

But anyone named as a relator may move to have his name stricken from the proceedings, if, in truth, he did not authorize the application.

The proceedings are, in the first instance, the same as upon an ordinary non-enumerated motion ; and counter affidavits need not be served.

One, in whose name stock stands on the books of an incorporated Company, as trustee, cannot vote on such stock. The right of voting belongs to his *cestui que trust.*

A Company cannot hold its own stock, so as to give its Directors or Trustees a right to vote upon it.

Yet it may take its own stock in pledge, or as security for a debt due to it, where this is necessary.

Rule setting aside an election of Directors, and ordering a new election, pursuant to the Statute, sess. 48, ch. 325, sec. 9.

Citations—Sess. 48, ch. 325, secs. 9, 11, Act, April 21, 1825.

MR. J. W. MULLIGAN moved for a rule to establish the election of Zebedee Ring, and 24 others, who, as he claimed, had been chosen Directors of the Tradesmen's Ins. Co. in the City of N. Y.

He read affidavits, stating that the Company had been incorporated by an Act of the Legislature passed Mar. 14, 1825 (see Laws, sess. 48, ch. 31) ; that they went into operation about Apr. 20, 1825 ; that Nov. 8 last, they passed a resolution that they would accept 1582 shares of their capital stock, then held by the New Jersey Manf'g and Banking Co., in part payment of funds on deposit in that Company, belonging to the Ins. Co.; and the latter appointed Z. Ring, A. M. Merchant, and W. P. Hallett, three of their Directors, trustees to receive and hold the stock in their behalf, subject to the direction of the Board of Directors. That Nov. 9 last the shares were transferred **427***] *accordingly ; and a check drawn by the Ins. Co., upon the N. J. Manf'g and B. Co., for $79,100 in full payment for the shares ; and the trustees executed a declaration of trust to the Ins. Co., declaring that the stock was held in trust for them, and that, when sold, the proceeds should be paid to them.

That by the Act of Incorporation, the stock, property affairs and concerns of the Corporation, were to be managed by 25 Directors, to be elected annually, on the first Monday in May ; the election to be holden under the inspection of three stockholders, not being Directors, to be appointed previously to every election by the Board of Directors.

That Apr. 26, last, a meeting was held, and Directors appointed, when it was resolved by the Directors that the 1,582 shares, held by the three trustees, should be voted upon at the (then) next election, by Z. Ring, chairman of the trust committee. That the whole number of the Company's shares is 4,000.

That at the next election (May 1, 1826), the vote was offered by Ring ; but objected to by Hallett, one of the trustees, who called for the transfer books. That these being produced, it was found that the stock stood in the names of "Zebedee Ring, Aaron H. Merchant and William P. Hallett, Trustees." That, notwithstanding this objection, the vote was received by the inspectors.

That, in consequence of this vote being received, John Leveridge, and ten others, were elected, and reported as duly elected by the inspectors.

The object of the present motion was to vacate the election of these eleven Directors ; and establish that of the eleven who were candidates against them. The candidates on both sides were named in the affidavits, and as to thirteen persons, there was no dispute but that they were duly elected.

The motion was founded on the Act entitled "An Act to Prevent Fraudulent Bankruptcies by Incorporated Companies; to Facilitate Proceedings against them, and for other purposes; *passed April 21, 1825," (sess. 48, ch. [***428** 325, and see a summary of this Act, 4 Cow., 123, 123, *note.*)

Messrs. J. Smith and *J. Platt,* contra, objected that notice of the motion should have been given, not only to the Directors whose seats were contested (which they admitted had been done), but to the President and the other Directors of the Company. They said, all the stockholders of the institution were interested in this proceeding, and entitled to be heard through the President and the other officers, whose election was confessedly legal.

Curia. The statute is, that notice shall be given to the adverse party, or to those who may be affected by the application. (Sess. 48, ch. 325, sec. 9.)

The Directors whose seats are sought to be vacated are, we think, the true parties, and the only persons to be affected within the meaning of the Act. The application comes in place, and is in nature of an information—in nature of a *quo warranto.* Had an information been filed, these Directors would be the proper, and the only proper defendants. Suppose we should order an information to be filed, as we may do, if the nature of the case require it ; clearly the process, in such a case, could go only against the Directors whose seats are questioned.

Mr. Platt. The three persons who were allowed to vote on the 1,582 shares are deeply interested in this question. Yet they have had no notice.

Curia. We think no notice was necessary to them.

Mr. Platt. We then deny the authority of the counsel who appear in behalf of the application; and we demand that before they be permitted to proceed, they prove their authority to this court. Here is no *lis pendens;* and, of course, the case is not within the rule which declares that the appearance of an attorney shall be good as to the court, without showing his warrant. The rule is confined to a suit brought. [And he offered affidavits to show that as to some of the applicants no authority whatever had been given.]

429*] **Curia.* It may be very proper to strike out the names of those who move that this should be done, on affidavit. The motion goes on upon the peril of costs; and like a lessor in ejectment, those named as applicants may see to it that their names are not used, so as to impose on them an unauthorized expense.

But we cannot consent, on a mere unsupported suggestion of want of authority, to require that the gentleman concerned should go into proof that they are properly here in the names of those whom they profess to represent. They come as officers of the court, whether to prosecute a suit or make a motion; and as to the court, they must be taken to have a warrant. They are amenable, as in other cases, should it turn out that they are not retained. Suppose it should be objected that the counsel who oppose are not armed with proper authority. This might as well be done; and thus, before we could go on to a hearing, we must appoint a day for proof that the officers of the court have a right to appear before it in their respective duties. *Prima facie,* we must take it that they act properly.

Mr. E. T. Pinckney, same side with *Messrs. Smith* and *Platt,* was then proceeding to read affidavits upon the merits; when,

Mr. Mulligan objected that the affidavits were in nature of pleadings, and that not only the affidavits for the motion, but against it, should be served; that the applicants had not been served with the affidavits now proposed to be read.

Curia. You must go on as in case of an ordinary non-enumerated motion. The counter affidavits not being served, is, in this view, no reason against their being read. Should we finally see that, in consequence of the omission, the applicants are surprised, it may be a reason to give further time, or award an issue.

Mr. Pinckney then proceeded to read various affidavits to show that the 1,582 shares upon which the trustees had voted, were owned by them in trust for the insurance company, *bona*
430*] **fide,* and that the stock had not been created in order to control the direction of the Company.

It appeared from these affidavits that seven persons, composing the finance committee of the Company, had, at its first organization, procured to themselves stock in the Company amounting at par to $113,300, a majority of the whole stock of the Company, which enabled them to control its concerns. Their mode of doing it was this: they deposited about $80,-000 received for stock in the N. J. Manf'g and Bk'g Co., at Hoboken of which one of that committee was President; and the further sum of $113,000 was placed in the books of the bank to the credit of the Tradesmen's Ins. Co., the whole bearing an interest of six *per cent. per annum.* And they hypothecated most or all of their stock to the bank. It also appeared that four of the committee had privately combined to leave the whole amount of the Ins. Co.'s capital in the possession of the bank for one year at least, and to apply to the Legislature for a bank; and then to withdraw the money for the use of the new bank. That in consequence, the Ins. Co. had been prevented from making various loans at seven *per cent.;* the bank, by direction of a majority of the finance committee, refusing to accept checks drawn by the Co. That the directors having discovered the situation of their funds, and fearing their loss, were induced to take a transfer of the stock of the Co. to the amount of $79,100 (the 1,582 shares in question) being the stock hypothecated to the bank in the manner above mentioned. That this was accepted in payment of so much; the bank owing the Co., in the whole, about $155,900; and agreeing to secure them for the balance in some other way. That the Directors thought it their duty to take the stock at par value, though it was then from five to ten *per cent.* below par in the market; and to pay the president of the bank $2,000. That, accordingly, the resolution of Nov. 8, last, mentioned in the depositions on the part of the applicants, was passed; and the check for the $79,100 drawn for the purpose of canceling so much of the debt then due from the bank; and not by *way [***431**
of payment for the stock so transferred. That there is still due from the bank to the Co. about $45,000 unsecured.

Mr. Mulligan, for the relators. Without inquiring whether one of several owners of stock, tenants in common or joint tenants, would have a right to vote, without the concurrence of his co-tenants, it is clear that one of several trustees for the Company cannot. They were not only joint tenants, but trustees. The trust was personal to themselves; and their united concurrence was necessary in this, as it must be in every act of trustees. No proxy was made. It was, in truth, a vote by the minority of the trustees. They stood like any other persons having a joint power. A single individual cannot execute it.

But suppose a majority could control in a purpose of the trust; they could not vote. The declaration of trust to which they were confined, contemplated no such power. It was merely to receive and pay over the money on sale of the stock.

They were not owners within the test given by the Act of Apr., 21, 1825, sess. 48, ch. 325, sec. 11; for the stock was not holden in their name, within the meaning of that Act. It stood in the name of the Directors, and the vote was their's.

The Directors had no right to use this stock for the purpose of controlling the election. When it came to the hands of the Company, it ceased to be stock. In their hands, it has no legal existence. It is only in the hands of the stockholders that it can be anything. The law cannot be evaded by placing it in the name of trustees for the use of the Company. It is still their property. They have a right to control it for all purposes; and if they are allowed to vote upon it, the consequence is that a majority of the Directors may maintain themselves in office, by the votes of stock in which they have no interest as individual stockholders.

Messrs. P. W. Radcliff and *J. Platt*, contra. There can be no doubt that the stock was prop-
432*] erly obtained; and properly *held by the trustees in their own names. The question is, what rights they acquired.

There is no statute or common law rule, which prohibits the vote of this stock. It is not necessary that voters should hold stock in their own right. The charter contemplates a vote upon stock by persons holding in the right of another.

The 5th section (sess. 48, ch. 31) requires that a Director shall hold in his own right; otherwise, he is not eligible. But no such distinction is made as to voters. For this purpose, it speaks of stockholders generally. And by the statute cited on the other side, the person or persons in whose name the stock stands, when they come to vote, are declared to be qualified. Now each person cannot vote, when several hold as co-tenants. There can be but one vote; and this may be given by a majority; or, indeed, the vote of one might be good, if there be no dissent of the others. If only two, the dissent of one might well neutralize the vote; but this would be unjust as to a majority. If it be so as to three persons, it would be the same of two hundred. We agree that the trustees are joint tenants; but they are trustees for an institution which acts throughout by majorities. They hold under the Board of Directors. These are the *cestuis que trust*, the parties concerned; and it does not lie with the relators to question the vote which accords with the views of the real parties in interest, on account of the form in which it was given. It is enough that they declared which of their trustees should vote for them. They had a right thus to constitute him their proxy. There is no particular form of making a proxy. It may as well be by a corporate resolution as in any other way. The power was, in some respects, of a general or public nature; in which view, it is clear that a majority may vote. Here a majority were actually assenting. If their trust was of a public nature, then there is no doubt the act was valid. (1 Bos. & P., 236, per Eyre, *Ch. J.*; 2 Atk., 212; 3 T. R., 592-595, per Ld. Kenyon, and Buller, *J.*; 16 Johns., 41; Cowp., 377; 6 T. R., 398.)

By the Act of Apr. 21, 1825, sec. 9, this court are to proceed in regard to these elections as right and justice may require. It is, *quoad hoc*,
433*] a court of chancery; and will *take a wide and equitable view. (10 Johns., 495.) A court of chancery may even change a trustee in order to promote the equity of the case. It will do this wherever he acts improperly or unreasonably. It will always prevent an abuse of trust.

Mr. T. A. Emmet, in reply. Certainly the Directors could not vote, yet it is said they could make a proxy, and that they had done so by their resolution. The law undoubtedly means to confine the right of voting, where stock is hypothecated, to the *cestui que trust*. The persons to whom it is hypothecated can have no control over the votes of the general owners.

It is not denied that if this stock had stood in the name of the Company, it would have been a diminution of so much of their stock capable of voting. It is not the same thing standing in the name of trustees. The stock is inactive. It produces nothing. It is held in trust for the Company. Is it more or less than the stock of the Company? They may take a pledge of stock from necessity; but they are bound to sell it the very first opportunity, and cannot keep it to vote upon. The sole purpose of the pledge is security. That is not increased by exercising the right to vote.

In this way, an irresistible power may be obtained by the Directors to control the election at any time, and bid defiance to the stockholders. No matter that they may have acted *bona fide* in receiving this pledge. There is no difference between buying stock for the purpose of voting and buying it for another purpose, but using it to control the election.

If we are so far wrong, a mere majority of the trustees could not vote. If the refusal of one to concur was a breach of trust, the Court of Chancery alone can give relief. Trustees are chosen for the benefit of all the *cestuis que trust*. Each trustee represents all. A minority of joint owners cannot control the rights of the whole unless it be so agreed. (4 Johns. Ch., 573.) Besides; the vote in question is not a compliance with the general Act, sess. 48, ch. 325, sec. 11, on the subject. This declares that stock standing in *the name of persons [***434**
shall be voted upon by themselves directly, or by proxy. This is the vote of only two out of three joint stockholders, one dissenting expressly.

Curia. The fact to facilitate proceeding against incorporated companies, &c. (sess. 48, ch. 325), upon which this motion is made, provides (sec. 11) that, "in all cases, where the right of voting upon any share or shares of the stock of any incorporated Company of this State, shall be questioned, it shall be the duty of the inspectors of the elections to require the transfer books of said Company, as evidence of stock held in the said Company; and all such shares as may appear standing thereon, in the name of any person or persons, shall be voted on by such person or persons, directly by themselves, or by proxy, subject to the provisions of the Act of Incorporation." There is nothing in the Act of Incorporation of the Tradesmen's Ins. Co. which interferes to prevent the application of this provision; and it is broad enough, literally to include all stockholders, whether in their own right, or as mere trustees for others.

But the question remains, whether the latter are to be deemed stockholders, within the spirit of the Act. True the stock on which they voted, in this case, stands in their name; but on the face of the entry they are declared to be mere nominal holders. The real owner of the stock should vote, especially where his name is truly expressed in the books; though it might be otherwise, if he choose to have the entry simply in the name of another, without expressing any trust. Now these three persons, a majority of whom claim a right to vote, are mere trustees; and they are trustees not for the directors; but the Co., the Corporation itself. If there could be a vote at all upon such stock, one would suppose that it must be by each stockholder of the Co., in proportion to his interest in it.

This brings us to the important difficulty in the case, which is, whether stock thus held can vote at all. And we think it is not to be considered as stock held by any one for the purpose of being voted upon. No doubt the Co. may, from necessity, as in this case, take **435*]** their own stock in *pledge or payment; and keep it outstanding in trustees, to prevent its merger; and convert it to their security. But it is not stock to be voted upon within the meaning of the charter, or the general Act upon which we are proceeding. It is not to be tolerated that a Company should procure stock, in any shape, which its officers may wield to the purposes of an election; thus securing themselves against the possibility of removal. The motion is accordingly granted; but as the question is a new one, this must be without costs.

The view which we have taken of the case precludes the necesssity of determining the other question raised at the bar, whether joint holders of stock must all concur in a vote; whether they must vote severally according to their several interests, or the vote be controlled by a majority.

We direct the following rule:

SUPREME COURT.

In the Matter of the Application of ELIPHRAS HOLMES, &c. (naming the other the other ten who applied).

On reading and filing a notice of motion for a rule, or order to confirm and establish the election of Zebedee Ring, &c. (naming 24 persons), as Directors of the Tradesmen's Ins. Co., in the City of N. Y.; and to make such order, and give such relief in the premises as right and justice might seem to require; and on reading and filing the depositions and proofs of the parties, as well in behalf of as against the said application; and after hearing counsel, as well on behalf of the said application as in opposition thereto, it is adjudged that the fifteen hundred and eighty two shares of stock mentioned in the said depositions of the said parties, as being held in trust for the benefit of the said Insurance Company, were illegally voted upon by the trustees holding said stock for the said Co.; the trustees not being stockholders within the provisions of the 11th section of the Act entitled, "An Act to Prevent Fraudulent Bankruptcies by Incorporated Companies, to Facili- **436*]** tate Proceedings *against them, and for other purposes, passed Apr. 21, 1825."

And it is, therefore, ordered that the election of the following persons, viz.: John Leveridge, &c. (naming the other ten whose election depended on the vote upon the 1582 shares), being eleven of the recently elected Directors, be set aside; on the ground that they were unduly elected by virtue of the vote given upon the said trust stock.

And it is further ordered that a new election of eleven Directors of the said Company, in the place of the persons last above mentioned, be held under the inspection of John Gray, James W. Pinckney and Micajah Reynolds, the inspectors heretofore appointed by the Board of Directors, of the said Company, and under whose direction the late election was held.

And it is further ordered that the officers of the said Company forthwith cause public notice of such new election to be given, for twenty days prior to the holding of the same, in such manner as is prescribed by the charter of said Company in cases of election.

Cited in—7 Cow., 411; 6 Wend., 510; 3 Sandf. Ch., 290; 15 Hun, 224; 63 Barb., 567; 6 How. Pr., 25; 1 Hall, 74; Co. R. N. S., 188; 37 Cal., 27; 22 Ohio, 369; 101 Mass., 403; 114 Mass., 43; 46 Am. Dec., 188 (3 Gratt., 19); 3 Am. Rep., 381 (101 Mass., 398).

THE PEOPLE, ex rel. THE NEW LOAN OFFICERS OF THE COUNTY OF ULSTER,

v.

THE SUPERVISORS OF THE COUNTY OF DELAWARE.

Mandamus—*Erection of New County—Duties of Loan Officers in Providing for Deficiencies.*

Delaware Co. was erected by an Act of Mar. 10, 1797, from Ulster and Otsego. The Act providing that deficiencies on mortgages to the new loan officers of Ulster, of lands situated in that part of Delaware taken from Ulster, should be paid by tax on the inhabitants of that part, &c.; held, that, to determine the deficiency, the loan officers of Ulster were not bound either to advertise or sell in Delaware, but might do both in Ulster.

Citations—3 Greenl., 396; Act, March 14, 1792; sess. 15, ch. 25, sec. 515; 2 Greenl., 406; Act, March 10, 1797.

BY the defendants' return to an alternative *mandamus*, requiring them to show cause why they should not raise certain moneys in arrear on a mortgage executed by John Moore, for $750, to the new loan officers of Ulster Co., May 5, 1795, on lands then in Ulster, but now in that part of Delaware Co. which was taken from Ulster, it appeared that the principal, and one year's interest, being due in May, 1823; and default being made in the payment of that *interest, the lands were advertised and **[*437** sold in Ulster Co., for $500. The new loan officers of Ulster certified the balance to the Supervisors of Delaware, who refused to levy it, on the ground that the proceedings of the new loan officers, as to the sale, were irregular.

The County of Delaware was erected from the Counties of Ulster and Otsego, by the Act of Mar. 10, 1797. (3 Greenl. L., 394, sess. 20, ch. 33.)

Messrs. L. Munson and *S. Sherwood*, for the defendants, insisted that the lands should have been advertised for sale in the County of Delaware, and cited the Statute, sess. 15, ch. 25, sec. 15, 2 Greenl. ed. L., 406, and *Denning* v. *Smith*, 3 Johns. Ch., 341.

Mr. C. H. Ruggles, for the plaintiffs, cited 2 Greenl. ed. L., 405, sec. 13, and *King* v. *Stow*, 6 Johns. Ch., 333.

Curia, per SAVAGE, *Ch. J.* The Act cited, setting off the County of Delaware from Ulster and Otsego, provides (3 Greenl., 396) that all losses which may arise from deficiencies on loans by the loan officers, made on lands mortgaged, and which are situated in the County of

Delaware shall be borne and paid in manner following; that is to say, such deficiency as shall arise from lands mortgaged while part of the County of Otsego, shall be borne by the inhabitants of that part of the County of Delaware taken from the County of Otsego; and the like rule shall prevail as to any deficiency which may arise on loans made by the loan officers of the County of Ulster. And the loan officers of Ulster and Otsego, respectively, were required to certify the deficiency to the Supervisors of Delaware, who were required to levy and collect it on the principle mentioned in the Act.

The Supervisors rest their objection on the fact that the sale was not advertised and made in Delaware Co.; and they relied on the Act of Mar. 14, 1792, sess. 15, ch. 25, sec. 15, 2 Greenl., 406, under which this loan was made; which requires the notice to be given, and the sale to be made in the county where the mortgaged premises are situated. But I apprehend this **438***] must be taken *in reference to the then organization of the counties. Several counties have been erected from parts of Ulster since this Act passed. The loan officers are required to advertise all sales for the same day; and surely it was not intended that they should advertise in each of those counties, and sell in each of them at the same time. Albany Co., now, has mortgages in Saratoga, Schenectady, Greene, Columbia and Rensselaer; and the sales are to be on the third Tuesday of Sep. in each year. It is impossible to comply with the construction contended for by Delaware. The Legislature did not intend that these loan officers should act out of their proper counties.

The loan officers are to proceed precisely as if no separation had taken place, until a deficiency happens. Then they are to certify the deficiency to the Supervisors of Delaware, who are to cause it to be raised according to the directions of the Act of 1797.

In this view, the loan officers have been regular. The return, therefore, showing no sufficient cause, a peremptory *mandamus* must be granted.

Rule accordingly.

Cited in—3 Paige, 397; 13 Barb., 448.

ROSEVELT
v.
FULTON, Surviving Executrix of FULTON.

Practice—Order to Stay Proceedings—Notice of Motion—Duty of Sheriff.

An order to stay proceedings with the view to a non-enumerated matter, is not operative unless accompanied with notice of a motion by the party or person obtaining it.

But though notice of motion be not given, if the order be served on the sheriff to stay his proceeding upon an execution it will be vacated, on motion, with costs; though he may, at his peril, disregard it.

Citations—3 Johns., 451; 1 Cai., 484, 485, 506; 3 Cai., 151, 152, 106; 4 Cow., 539.

THE last Febuary Term, judgment was given for the plaintiff, upon a bill of exeeptions taken by the defendant. The plaintiff was proceeding to sell the goods of the testator May 6, when an order of the Recorder of N. Y., dated May 5, was served on the sheriff, reciting that the defendant had lately died; that administration had not been granted, though application had been made therefor, and directing that proceedings be stayed upon the execution, till the last non-enumerated day of this term; and until the further order of this court. The order was not served on the plaintiff nor was it followed by any notice *of [***439** a motion, the sheriff declining to proceed in the sale,

Mr. J. I. Roosevelt, Jr., now moved to vacate the order.

Mr. C. D. Colden, contra, read an affidavit stating that the testator's children were infauts; that Dale, the husband of the defendant, who is now dead, had been appointed their guardian, and had applied for letters of administration, with the will annexed of the testator's estate, against which the plaintiff had entered a *caveat;* that Dale intended, on obtaining letters, to bring error; and the counsel moved for a rule to stay proceedings farther, in order that this might be done.

Curia. The motion to vacate the order must be granted. As to the plaintiff it was inoperative, both for want of being served, and because it was not followed with a notice of motion. It is well settled that in the case of an order to stay proceedings with the view to a non-enumerated motion, this must be aecompanied with a notice of the motion; otherwise, it does not stay the proceedings. (3 Johns., 451.) If this were not so, an order like the present would, in all cases, throw the burden of a motion upon the party against whom it is taken. There is much more reason for holding the party to his notice in this case, than in that of enumerated motions. In these, each party is considered an actor as to the motion, and may get rid of the order in several ways; as by noticing the motion, placing it on the calendar, and bringing it to a hearing; 1 Cai., 484, 485; 3 *Id.*, 151, 152; or by getting the judge to discharge it; 3 Caines, 106; or by appealing to the court. (4 Cow., 539.) Yet it has been holden that notice is necessary even in enumerated motions, within the 4th rule of January Term, 1799. (1 Cai., 506.)

But though the plaintiff might have disregarded the order, even if it had been served upon him, it is not so as to the sheriff. He cannot know whether the matter is properly put in train for a motion or not. He may disregard a naked order, if he will rely on the assurance of the party that no notice of motion is given, or he may be indemnified against proceeding; but the party should not be put to the embarrassment *of indemnifying [***440** him; nor should he be required to proceed in the face of an order to the contrary; which, for aught he knows, may be valid; and by violating which, he may be punished as for a contempt or a trespass.

The rule to vacate the order must be granted, with costs, to be paid by Dale, who obtained the order.

Rule accordingly.

Cited in—1 Den., 668; 3 How. Pr., 273; 7 How. Pr., 9; 8 How. Pr., 350.

NOTE.—*Officers—Ministerial—How far protected by process—Sheriff.* See Warner v. Shed, 10 Johns., 138, *note, and other notes there cited.*

SHOOKE
v.
JOHN PHILLIPS ET AL., Heirs and Devisees of WILLIAM PHILLIPS, Deceased.

ALLENDORF *v.* THE SAME.

Practice—Statute for Protection of Infants, Does not Protect Others Joined with Them.

Where judgment is obtained against heirs, or devisees, part of whom are infants, and part adults, execution may go against the latter immediately, the Statute, 1 R. L., 318, applying to the infant defendants only.

THE judgment was perfected against the defendants, as heirs and devisees, in February Term last. John Phillips was an adult; the other defendants were, and still are, infants. The plaintiff's attorney issued executions against all the defendants within the year, contrary to the Statute, sess. 36, ch. 93, sec. 6; 1 R. L., 318.

Thursday, Apr. 27, the defendants gave notice of a motion to set aside the executions.

On Thursday or Friday, the 27th or 28th of Apr., the plaintiff's attorney withdrew the executions from the hands of the sheriff, nothing having been done upon them; and altered them, so that they stood against John Phillips, the adult only; he (the attorney) having issued the executions by mistake, without adverting to the statute which requires a year's delay of execution against infant heirs. On the same day he gave notice of the alteration to *Mr. Wheeler*, the attorney of John Phillips, and guardian *ad litem* of the other defendants; and offered (by stipulation in writing) to pay the costs which had accrued about the motion.

Mr. J. W. Wheeler now moved to set aside the executions; and he insisted that executions could not go even against the adult, until after the year—the statute being, that no execution, in any cause, issue within one year after **441***] the rendition *of the judgment. The withdrawing of the executions extended only to the infants. They should also have been withdrawn as to the adult.

Mr. G. A. Shufeldt, contra.

Curia. The statute was clearly made for the protection of the infants only, not adults, whether joined with them or not. The motion must be denied.

RULE in each cause: that the motion be denied; that the plaintiff pay the costs of the defendants' motion up to the time when the offer to pay was made.

No costs of this motion.

MONELL *v.* SMITH AND JENKINS.

Practice—Rights and Powers of Surety, Under a Bond and Warrant, to Confess Judgment Against His Principal.

Where one becomes indorser or surety, and takes a bond and warrant to confess judgment from his principal, as counter security, he may enter judgment, and sue out execution for the sum for which he is liable as surety, the same being due, in part or in whole, before actual payment by him.

And this, though the bond be not for a specified sum, but conditioned to pay certain indorsements made and to be made by him for the obligors, and to indemnify against costs, &c.

And he may issue execution for the whole penalty without motion, subject to specific directions to the sheriff as to the amount to be levied, as soon as he can ascertain it.

If execution be issued for too much, the court will correct this on motion.

And they may also, on motion, make order for securing the sum to be levied, to the creditors to whom the surety is bound, if they see that this is necessary.

Citations—6 Johns., 266, 279-285; 18 Johns., 505.

DEC. 31 last, the defendants executed their bond and warrant of confession to the plaintiff, in the penalty of $25,000; conditioned, among other things, to pay all notes theretofore indorsed, or thereafter to be indorsed, by the plaintiff for the defendants, or either of them; and to indemnify the plaintiff against all costs, &c., by reason of or on account of such notes.

On this bond the plaintiff caused a judgment to be entered, and two executions to be issued; one to the Sheriff of Columbia and the other to the Sheriff of N. Y., for the $25,000; without any special directions as to the amount which they should levy. The Sheriff of Columbia was informed by the plaintiff's attorney that he would afterwards receive instructions on this head, so soon as the plaintiff could ascertain what should be levied; and he afterwards gave directions *to levy $14,- [***442** 549.14 of the joint or several property of the defendants; and $8,000 of Smith's individual property. The former was the amount to which the plaintiff had indorsed (by blank indorsements and otherwise) for the defendants jointly, and the latter the amount of his indorsements for Smith individually. He made no indorsements for Jenkins alone.

A small part of the $14,549.14 had fallen due on the notes indorsed, and the plaintiff was prosecuted for it, before the executions issued. A still larger amount was about falling due, and the whole was unprovided for by the defendants Apr. 11 last, when the executions issued. They were levied on property of the defendants, and of Jenkins individually, to the value of about $7,500.

The order of the *Chief Justice* being obtained by Jenkins, to stay proceedings, with a view to move the court upon the subject, Monell immediately offered Jenkins to give security, that all which should be raised by the executions out of the joint property of the defendants, or of Jenkins' individual property, should be applied in discharge of the indorsements on their joint account. Monell had then confessed a judgment to the Bank of Columbia, of about $7,629.60; being the amount of his indorsements for the defendants to that bank. The defendant, Jenkins, declined entering into any arrangement on the subject. Monell had become insolvent by these indorsements; and,

Messrs. D. B. Tallmadge and *T. J. Oakley* now moved to set aside the executions as irregular, and insisted that they could not issue till actual payment by the plaintiff. He may collect the money, and appropriate it to his own use, still leaving the defendants liable.

Upon a bond like this, where no sum is mentioned in the condition, the plaintiff should ap-

NOTE.—*Principal and surety—Remedies of surety.* See Pain v. Packard, 13 Johns., 174, *note*. See, generally, Fairlie v. Lawson, *ante*, p. 424, *note*, *and other notes there cited.*

ply to the court for leave to take out execution for what he claims to be due, on the usual notice to the defendant. This is the settled rule, even as to bonds for the payment of annuities, where part has been levied. (2 W. Bl., 843.)

The executions are irregular in any view, as they issued for $25,000.

443*] *At any rate, the court will provide some mode of securing the money to the creditors of Smith and Jenkins, the plaintiff being insolvent, and neither the creditors nor the defendants being secure, that the moneys to be raised will be properly applied. *Bank of Auburn* v. *Throop*, 18 Johns., 505. This court exercises an equitable jurisdiction over judgments upon bond and warrant. *Frasier* v. *Frasier*, 9 Johns., 80.

If insufficient to pay all the debts for which the plaintiff is bound, the money should be paid ratably among them. (4 Johns. Ch., 619, 648, 649, 687.) Why should the Bank of Columbia be preferred? They also cited 6 Johns., 283, 43, and 12 Johns., 350.

Messrs. C. Bushnell and *E. Williams*, contra. It will not be denied that several executions may run on the same judgment at the same time in different counties; 2 Cow., 456; and as to the sum to be levied, it was fixed as soon as the plaintiff could ascertain the amount of his liabilities. If not so, it may be corrected now. To delay him till he had ascertained the amount, or applied to this court on the subject, might defeat the very end of the security. In the meantime the defendant's property might have been placed beyond the reach of an execution.

A judgment for future responsibilities is good; 5 Johns. Ch., 326; and the surety may collect on such a judgment, though he has not paid the debt. (6 *Id.*, 281-288, and the cases there cited.) On a bond conditioned like this, an action lies without waiting to be damnified. (*Id.*, 2 T. R., 100; *Id.*, 640.) The plea of *non damnificatus* would be inapplicable to an action on this bond. The judgment was for the purpose of indemnity—which cannot be carried into effect, unless the plaintiff be allowed to levy before payment.

Curia. Where one becomes surety for another, for a certain sum or sums of money, and takes a bond and warrant from his principal in the usual form for a sum or sums corresponding in amount, or a bond and warrant conditioned to pay the specific sum or sums to 444*] the creditor; and *there is a partial or total default of payment by his principal, even though the whole money be not due, he may issue execution for the whole; and this, whether he has made payment or not. This position is warranted by the cases which are cited and considered by the late *Chancellor*, in *Roosevelt* v. *Mark*, 6 Johns. Ch., 266, 279-285. The decision of that cause follows the cases cited, and we think with good reason. The only question is, whether the same course may be pursued where the bond relates in general terms to liabilities as surety or indorser, past and prospective, without mentioning a sum certain; and we think it may. It is true the sum does not appear on the face of the bond, and there is no doubt that in an action on such a bond, breaches must be assigned. It would be the same, however, we think, as to a bond conditioned to pay specified sums to third persons. The certainty is the same in both cases. In both, we may be obliged to look beyond the face of the bond to see what is due. In a technical sense, that is certain which may be made certain. We all know the objects of the parties to these instruments. It is to afford the most prompt indemnity. This, many times, cannot be done, where the surety is first obliged to pay, and then resort to his execution. Such a course might ruin him. And even then there might be a dispute as to the propriety of his actual payments, as whether the principal may not have paid them before. Great caution is used in these cases to make the security perfectly adequate. The warrant of attorney, generally, contains a power to release all errors and irregularities; and if there be any abuse, it is perfectly competent for this court to afford equitable redress. If the amount due be doubtful, the defendant may have an issue. If the plaintiff is plainly seeking to levy more than is due, he may be restrained on motion. If there be danger of misapplication, this may be provided against by security or otherwise. *Bank of Auburn* v. *Throop*, 18 Johns., 505. In the present case, the only doubt with us was, whether, as the plaintiff is alleged to be insolvent, we ought not to direct the money which shall be levied to be brought into court, or otherwise secured *to the creditors of [*445 Smith and Jenkins. But it appears that the plaintiff has, in fact, extinguished a debt which he incurred as indorser to the Bank of Columbia, which more than covers the amount that he has levied upon; and there is nothing at present which induces us to believe that should he succeed in levying more, there will be any want of good faith in its application. Under these circumstances, we deny the motion.

Motion denied.

Cited in—1 Sandf. Ch., 45; 6 N. Y., 160; 22 N. Y., 383; 27 N. Y., 353; 6 Barb., 22, 347; 2 Leg. Obs., 251.

JACKSON, ex dem. COX, v. HAIGHT.

Practice—Jurisdiction of Supreme Court, as to Costs in Court of Errors.

The Supreme Court have not jurisdiction to order a retaxation of costs taxed by the *Chief Justice*, as judge of the Court of Errors.

Citation—16 Johns., 606.

THE plaintiff had, by writ of error, removed this cause from the Supreme Court into the Court for the Trial of Impeachments and the Correction of Errors, where the judgment was affirmed: and the defendant's costs were taxed by Savage, *Ch. J.*

A motion was now made to this court for a retaxation, on affidavits entitled "In the Court for the Trial of Impeachments and the Correction of Errors."

Messrs. King and *Randall*, for the motion.

Mr. A. Burr, contra.

Curia. The affidavit is entitled, and we think properly, in the Court of Errors. The taxation was upon a judgment of that court awarding costs, to be taxed; and was before the *Chief*

Justice, as a judge and taxing officer of that court, pursuant to their 17th general rule. (16 Johns., 606.) By that rule, the costs, when taxed, form a part of the *remittitur;* and if too high, should be reviewed there on a motion to retax and correct the *remittitur*. Though we are, by the rule cited, to collect these costs, we have no further control over them. To **446***] grant this motion, would be *to tax the costs of another court. It would be to correct what the Court of Errors have done on review of a judgment rendered by this court.

Motion denied.

THORP *v.* FOWLER.

Practice—Motion, to Set Aside Inquest After 7 Years, Denied—Attorneys—Second Execution.

Motion on affidavit of merits, to set aside an inquest regularly taken, after 7 years, denied, though the defendant and his attorney had reason to suppose the cause had never been tried.

An attorney other than the regular attorney in the cause, may issue execution in his own name without any formal substitution.

Testatum clause amended.

One execution being issued and returned, another may go, more than a year after, without a *sci. fa.*

Citations—Dunlap. 82, 675; 10 Johns., 486.

MOTION to set aside an inquest taken in this cause, at the Ontario Circuit, in 1818, with the execution. The cause was regularly noticed for trial at that circuit, by serving the notice on the defendant's attorney, who resided at Buffalo. He sent an affidavit to counsel at Canandaigua to put off the trial, and hearing nothing more of the cause till last Mar., when a *testatum fi. fa.* was levied on the defendant's property, both he and the defendant supposed that the suit was abandoned. There was an affidavit of merits—the defense lying in set-off alone. The judgment was perfected Sept. 5, 1818.

The venue was laid in Ontario, but the *testatum* clause in the execution was of Erie, and the direction to the Sheriff of Erie. There was also another mistake, the name of *Mr. Wilson* being on the execution as attorney, whereas *Mr. Spencer* was the attorney in the cause. A previous writ of *test. fi. fa.* to the Sheriff of Niagara Co., had been issued in the cause and returned *nulla bona*, Feb. 5, 1819.

Mr. T. Root, for the defendant.

Mr. J. C. Spencer, for the plaintiff.

Curia. The plaintiff moves to amend his execution, which is granted, though the motion was clearly not necessary as to the name of the attorney. An execution may issue in the name of another attorney without any formal substitution. (Dunl., 82.) The first execution will support the second without a *sci. fa.* The *testatum* clause may be amended, on payment of costs.

447*] *As to the motion to set aside this inquest, there has been a delay of more than seven years since it was regularly taken on notice to the defendant and his attorney. They were both put fully on inquiry; and the case is one of gross negligence. A stronger one can hardly be conceived. In the case of an irregular notice of trial, where it was received by the attorney; and he omitted to move to set aside an inquest taken under it, till after the term next succeeding the circuit, he was holden concluded; though he supposed that no inquest would be taken and, therefore, omitted to inquire. (10 Johns., 486; Dunl., 675.) True, this is not a mere case of irregularity, but the principle is much the same. The defendant, if we are to believe his affidavit of merits, has had the strongest motives for inquiry for more than seven years. He has manifested a most stupid and willful disregard of his rights.

Motion to set aside inquest denied, with costs. Motion to amend granted.

Cited in—26 Barb., 87; 4 How. Pr., 258; 13 How. Pr., 574; 4 Leg. Obs., 385; 9 Leg. Obs., 66; 9 Minn., 58.

JACKSON, ex dem. HOWLAND, *v.* STILES; SMITH, RANDOLPH and HAY, Tenants.

Practice—Motion to be Allowed to Defend as Landlord in Ejectment.

On motion to be received to defend as landlord in ejectment, it is competent for the plaintiff to show that the landlord had, after the lease, conveyed away all his interest in the premises in question.

Citation—10 Johns., 67.

MOTION, in ejectment, that Wightman be admitted to defend as the landlord of Smith.

Wightman's affidavit stated that Smith was his tenant, of about 300 acres of the premises in question, at the last February Term, when the declaration was served; that he entered under a lease from Wightman, made about July 1, 1825; that the term expired Apr. 1, last, when he had agreed with Wightman to surrender the possession to him; that he did not know of this action till about Mar. 18, last; and that Smith refused to defend the suit in any way. It also appeared that Smith had abandoned the possession about Apr. 1; and that a default for want of his appearance had been entered; that Wightman's attorney had proposed to the plaintiff's attorney *to [***448** enter into the consent rule in behalf of Wightman as landlord; but the proposal was declined.

The above facts were not denied, in any material part, by the plaintiff.

But it was shown very satisfactorily by a series of affidavits produced on the part of the plaintiff, that Mar. 14, last, Wightman, by a deed of conveyance, without any covenant, parted with all his interest in the premises to Henry and Everitts; directed Smith to surrender possession to them; and, that Apr. 1, last, possession was rendered to them accordingly.

Mr. Asgill Gibbs, for the motion.

Mr. S. Wood, contra,

Curia. That the landlord has parted with all his interest in the premises is, no doubt, a conclusive answer to the application. *Jackson* v. *Stiles*, 10 Johns., 67. The motion must be denied, with costs

Motion denied.

JACKSON, ex dem. NORTON, v. SHELDON.

Landlord and Tenant—Distress—Statute Concerning—Making Distraint Waives Forfeiture—Subsequent Ejectment, on Account of Same Rent, Does not Lie.

A lessor, after distraining for rent arrear though the distress be insufficient to satisfy it, cannot afterwards bring ejectment on account of the same rent upon the clause of re-entry under the 23d section of the Statute concerning Distresses, Rents and the Renewal of Leases. 1 R. L., 440, 441.

The act of distraining waives the forfeiture.

When a forfeiture has accrued upon a clause of re-entry for rent in arrear, the forfeiture will be waived if the landlord afterwards do any act which amounts to an acknowledgment of a subsisting tenancy; as if he receive rent due at a subsequent quarter, or distrain for that in respect of which the forfeiture accrued.

Citations—1 R. L., 440; 2 Geo. II., ch. 28; 1 Saund., 287, *n.* 16; 1 Burr., 619; Co. Litt., 201 *b*, and 211 *b*; 3 Co., 64; 3 Salk., 3; Adams, Ej., 160, 161; Woodf., 496; 1 H. Bl., 311; 6 T. R., 186, 220; E. 23 G, 3 B. R.; Cowp. 243; Stat. 4 Geo. II.; 2 D. & E. 425.

EJECTMENT for part of lot No. 69, Bedlingtou patent; tried at the Delaware Circuit, Sept., 1823, before Nelson, *Circuit Judge.*

The action was upon the 23d section of the Statute concerning Distresses, Rents and the Renewal of Leases (1 R. L., 440, 441).

On the trial, it was proved that John Lake, by indenture of lease, dated May 31, 1792, granted and demised in fee simple, certain land of which the premises in question are a part, **449***] *to William Cornell and others, at the annual rent of $118.75, payable May 30. The lease contained the usual clause authorizing the lessor to distrain ; and if no sufficient distress could be found, to re-enter. Lake, having devised all his interest in lot 69 to the lessor of the plaintiff, and there afterwards being in arrear $1,825.09 of rent, he, by his bailiff, Sept. 19, 1821, distrained, for that sum, all the goods and chattels to be found on the lot, the value of which distress was less than $1,000. Thus, not being able to find a sufficient distress, the bailiff afterwards, on the same day, served the declaration in this cause on the defendant, who was one of the tenants in possession, claiming under the lease.

The plaintiff resting here, the defendant's counsel moved for a nonsuit, on the ground that the distress was a waiver of the forfeiture for non-payment ; that the plaintiff could not both distrain and bring ejectment for the same rent. It being admitted that there was no forfeiture for non-payment subsequent to the distress, the judge nonsuited the plaintiff.

A motion being made, for the plaintiff, to set aside the nonsuit; the single point was, whether distraining for the rent waives the right to maintain ejectment under the statute.

This cause was twice argued—first at August Term last, and afterwards, by direction of the court, in February Term last.

Mr. S. Sherwood, for the plaintiff, agreed that at common law a distress would waive the forfeiture. He said the forfeiture there being absolute and final, the law seized on every pretense to do it away. But, under the statute, nothing short of actual payment should be allowed to have that effect. This action of ejectment is, in effect, a mere suit for the recovery of the rent—a mode pointed out by statute to compel its payment. For this purpose, it declares the forfeiture, and the extent of it. One half year's rent in arrear, a clause of re-entry, and no sufficient distress, are enough to maintain the action.

It is true that Woodfall, in his treatise on Landlord and Tenant, speaking of the Statute 4 Geo. II., ch. 28, sec. 2, from *which [***450** the statute in question was copied, says that distraining for rent will waive the forfeiture. He cites Cowp., 247, which certainly does not bear him out, and, perhaps, lays down the true rule on the subject. That was the case of a receipt of rent, and the question was whether this was not a waiver of the notice to quit. The court held that the question should be left to the jury to say with what intent the rent was received, and whether it was meant as a waiver or not. *Doe* v. *Batten*, Cowp., 243, &c.

A distress and action of debt, or *assumpsit*, for the rent, are concurrent. *Cornell* v. *Lamb*, 20 Johns., 407. Why not ejectment also, which is turned by the statute to the purpose of recovering the rent ? The cases go upon an intention to affirm the title or continue the tenancy, on the part of the landlord. This is plain from *Green's* case. Cro. Eliz., 3 ; S. C., 1 Leon, 262 ; S. C., 18 Vin. Abr., Rent, L, *b*.

A case in point was cited by Gibbs, *arguendo*, in *Goodright* v. *Cordwent*, 6 T. R., 220. It is that of *Brewer* v. *Eaton*, before Ld. Mansfield, in which he held expressly, that taking an insufficient distress was not a waiver of a previous re-entry. This case is cited and recognized as good law by Adams, Eject., 161, Am. ed. True this was not upon the statute, but the principle of the case applies. The forfeiture is now complete without any re-entry. The statute declares certain things shall be equivalent to that; and the right is as firmly fixed as if the formality of a common law entry had been resorted to.

Indeed, distress is but a mode (and it is many times a necessary mode) of determining whether there be enough property on the premises to countervail the arrears of rent. This may be determined with greater certainty by distress and sale, than by a mere estimate. There may be enough to pay a part of the rent. Till it is determined that the distress is insufficient, there can be no ejectment. The insufficiency must first be settled in some way. A distress would seem to be necessary, in order to entitle the landlord to bring the action. Till it is made, and has failed to produce enough, no forfeiture has arisen.

Mr. Talcott*, Atty-Gen., for the de- [*451** fendant. No doubt an action for rent and distress are concurrent remedies. Their object is the same. They both suppose the tenancy to continue, and concede that it may continue. But the question is very different in ejectment, which, in its nature, denies a subsisting tenancy. Suppose, as is contended on the other side, that this defendant's title had been devested by a common law re-entry, the subsequent receipt of rent would not revest the title. Suppose, also, that the proceedings under our statute come in place of the common law entry, it does not follow that here has been no waiver, but the contrary. When the entry was made at common law, the estate was gone ; but it is not so upon the statute. It continues. The statute re-entry is incomplete till after the trial. The rights of the landlord then, and not till then, become fixed as at common law. And it cannot be denied that an action or a distress for the rent, before the estate is vested in the landlord, will be a waiver of the action of ejectment.

The principle of the cases cited on the other side does not relate to the *quantum* of rent received—as whether it be the whole or only a part. They go upon the ground that a receipt of rent acknowledges the continuance of the tenancy. This is the same, whatever the sum which is received may be. A stronger acknowledgment of tenancy cannot be conceived than what arises from a distress. After such an act, the landlord cannot say that he has terminated the tenancy. He is estopped to hold such language. (Woodf. L. & T., 2 Lond. ed., 519; Bull. *N. P.*, 96; Cowp., 247; Woodf. L. & T., Am. ed., 161, 247, 248; Cro. Eliz., 3; 3 Salk., 3; 1 T. R., 386, 387.)

But suppose the want of a sufficient distress, &c., the case provided for by the statute, is, *per se*, a forfeiture, and vests the landlord with title like an entry at common law; the authorities are strong, especially in the case of a freehold lease, that the receipt of rent, or a distress, is a waiver of the ejectment, whether at common law or upon the statute. (Adams, Eject., Am. ed., 160, 161, and the cases there cited.)

452*] *The statute merely gives a new ground for a remedy on an old covenant or provision in leases; and if a distress waived the old ground, for the same reason, it waives the new one.

Mr. D. Cady, in reply. I will not deny that what would be a waiver at common law is so under the statute. It is enough that less will not be a waiver, in the latter than was necessary in the former case. Now, it is certainly clear, upon authority, that, at common law, the landlord might receive rent, and by parity of reason, distrain the next day after he had made a demand and technical entry; and yet, that this should not work a waiver of his entry. The 25th section of the statute expressly provides that if the rent be received or tendered after suit brought, it shall be a waiver. It follows that, in truth, the right which an entry at common law gave, does not arise under the statute till after the trial. At a certain point of the proceedings, payment is declared to be unavailable. There is no forfeiture, in this case, till after trial. Till that time payment may be made, whether the landlord consent or not. Thus, the statute does not merely provide a new remedy; it gives new rights to the tenant. At common law, if the estate was forfeited, the tenant was obliged to go directly to a court of equity. In this case he need not do so, provided he pay at any time before the trial. At any previous stage of the suit this court may interfere.

Here the distress was in the morning, and the ejectment in the afternoon of the same day. Suppose, at common law, the landlord goes the rent day of the second year, and distrains for the first year; and then, just before sundown, demands the second year's rent, and enters technically for its non-payment. The land is gone at law. The object of the proceeding was the land. Here it is the rent. The declaration in ejectment need not be served on the precise day of the rent becoming due. The service afterwards stands in stead of a re-entry. It takes effect from the time when the act is done, and does not relate to the common law day of entry. This produces the forfeiture. It comes *in place of the common law demand. [*453 The mere want of sufficient distress, is, in neither case, a forfeiture; and let it be granted, that in both cases, if the landlord receive the rent, the entry is waived; the ejectment is gone. Under the statute, the estate is not lost to the tenant, even at law till after the trial. It is not lost in equity till six months after execution executed.

No doubt the landlord might have sued upon the covenant. This, however, might or might not have proved efficacious, accordingly, as he was able or not to find out the assignees. Legislative provision was necessary for such a case. The statute declares when judgment shall be given. It follows on proof, that six month's rent is due; that there is a right of re-entry, and no sufficient distress. It was certainly competent for the Legislature to make this provision. In all cases, the landlord may reply that he distrained, and that the distress proved insufficient. (18 Vin., 553, Rent, C, *c*, pl. 1.) We have pursued the course marked out to us by the law. We had a right to distrain in the morning. We did not find enough to satisfy our rent, and we found nothing in the afternoon. We then brought our ejectment. We had a right to these various remedies. If the whole rent be not satisfied, the landlord may re-enter. (6 Bac. Abr., Am. ed., 38, tit. Rent; Cro. Jac., 511.) The forfeiture in this case, is made merely nominal by the statute, like the penalty of a bond, where we always look to the condition. In this case, our attention is confined to the rent. Why, then, all the strictness, which is contended for, when no more than equity is done to the claimant?

Curia, per WOODWORTH, *J.*, after stating the facts:

The question to be decided is, whether the plaintiff, after having distrained, can, under the statute, maintain this action.

It is material to inquire whether, as respects the point under consideration, the statutes, 1 R. L. 440, and 2 Geo. II., ch. 28, have changed the common law doctrine, as understood before the passing of those Acts. Where there is a *condition of re-entry reserved for [*454 non-payment of rent, to entitle a party to re-enter, the common law requires that a demand be made of the precise amount of rent due, on the day it is payable, at the most notorious place upon the land, and convenient time before sunset. (1 Saund., 287, *n.* 16, and the authorities there cited.) If all these steps were regularly pursued, and the landlord recovered, he still continued always liable to an nucertainty of possession, from its remaining in the power of the tenant to offer a compensation at any time, in order to found an application for relief in equity. The intention of the statute was to obviate the niceties before specified, and to limit and confine the tenant to six calendar months after execution executed, to make application for relief. (1 Burr., 619; 1 Saund., 287, *n.* 16.) As to every other point, not provided for by the statute, the law remains the same as before the passing of the Act. Whatever might be urged as sufficient to defeat the action, where the re-entry is under proceedings at the common law, must necessarily be so, when they are under the statute. The estate granted in this case was upon condition, and might be defeated if the condition was not performed. (Co. Litt., 201 *b.*) A re-entry for condition broken, can only be supported on the ground that the tenant's right is forfeited at law; but the right of forfeiture may be waived by the landlord, and whenever this is done, it follows that the action is gone. When a forfeiture has accrued upon a clause of re-entry for rent in arrear, the forfeiture will be waived, if the landlord do any act after the forfeiture, which amounts to an acknowledgment of a subsisting tenancy; as if he receives rent due at a subsequent quarter, or distrain for that, in respect of which the forfeiture accrued. In the case of a distress, the reason is given by Ld. Coke. "If the lessor distrains for the same rents, for which the demand was made, he had thereby affirmed the lease, for after the lease determined, he cannot distrain for the rent." *Pennant's* case, 3 Rep., 64; Adams Eject., 160; Co. Litt., 211 *b*, 3 Salk., 3; Woodf., 496; 1 Saund., 287, *n.* 16. This seems to be the established common law doctrine, and is decisive as to the case before us. If the plaintiff here **455***] is *entitled to recover, it must be on the ground of forfeiture; that the rent has not been paid according to the condition. If the tenancy still exist, there can be no foundation for the action. In this case there was no sufficient distress, and more than six months rent in arrear. By the terms of the lease it was voidable, at the election of the plaintiff. He elected to distrain, which he could not do at the common law, if the lease was determined. This shows that he intended to waive the forfeiture; at least so the law considers it. After this the remedy by re-entry, so far as respects the rents previously accrued, could not be enforced.

The doctrine thus laid down is supported in all the subsequent cases. Thus, in 1 H. Bl., 311, it was held that a distress taken for rent, accrued after the expiration of a notice to quit, is a waiver of the notice. Ld. Loughborough observed that the taking a distress was an express confirmation of the tenancy. On the same principle, it is held that the receipt of rent, as such, after the expiration of a notice to quit, in a waiver. (6 T. R., 220.)

The fact that an insufficient distress was taken, cannot vary the principle; for the tenancy is equally affirmed, whether the landlord finds goods and chattels to satisfy all the rent due, or a part only. It is the act of distraining that shows the intent to waive the forfeiture; not the amount that is recovered under that proceeding.

I have not discovered anything that seems to hold a different language, except the remarks in Adams on Eject., 161. He observes cautiously, that a landlord will not waive his right of re-entry for a forfeiture, incurred by non-payment of rent, by taking an insufficient distress for that rent. The case of *Goodright* v. *Cordwent*, 6 T. R., 220, is cited. The point there decided was that if a landlord receives rent, due after the expiration of a notice to quit, it is a waiver of that notice. But Gibbs, *arguendo*, referred to *Brewer* v. *Eaton*, E, 23, G, 3, B.R., where as he alleged, it was held that the lessor of the plaintiff had not waived his re-entry on a forfeiture incurred by non-payment of rent, by taking an insufficient distress for that rent; and that Ld. Mansfield said, "it is like the receipt of rent after *the demise, about [***456** which there was so long a puzzle. That is now finally settled to be no objection. It is receiving what the landlord might recover in an action for the *mesne* profits." I have not been able to find the report of this case. It seems to me, however, that if the action was to recover on the ground of a forfeiture, incurred for non-payment of rent, it is opposed to the whole current of authority on this subject; for it is not like the case of receiving rent after a forfeiture which accrued previously, and may be received without a waiver, because the landlord can recover it on the covenant to pay; but it is like the receipt of rent, as such, accrued subsequent to, and received after the forfeiture, which implies an affirmance of the lease; inasmuch as rent cannot accrue on an estate that is forfeited. The landlord, it is true, may recover damages in an action for the *mesne* profits, after the re-entry, by reason of the forfeiture, is perfected; but in that case the defendant is considered a trespasser. In *Cheney* v. *Batten*, Cowp., 243, it was held that the mere acceptance of rent by a landlord, for occupation subsequent to the time when the tenant ought to have quitted, according to the notice given to him for that purpose, is not, of itself, a waiver of the notice. Admitting this to be the law, where the tenant holds over, and has received a notice to quit, it does not prove that the same principle is to be applied, when the right of re-entry is founded on a forfeiture—which is in derogation of an existing estate. The distinction is taken by Aston, *J.*, in the case last cited, who observes that where an ejectment has been brought on the statute 4 Geo. II., for the forfeiture of a lease, there, acceptance of rent by the landlord has been held a waiver of the forfeiture; which might well be, for it is a penalty, and by accepting the rent, the party waived the penalty; but in the case of a notice, it was only a waiver of the right to double rent, and did not necesarily imply a consent that the tenancy should continue. The case of *Roe* v. *Harrison*, 2 T. R., 425, supports this distinction. It was an action to recover on the ground of forfeiture for assigning without leave in writing, which the proviso required. It was there held that receiving rent after the forfeiture was no waiver, *un-[***457** less the forfeiture were known at the time. Ashurst, *J.*, says, and the other judges concurred, that the receipt by the landlord of rent subsequent to the forfeiture, was, indeed, an acknowledgment of the tenancy, when he knows the act of forfeiture at the time; and in *Goodright* v. *Cordwent*, 6 T. R., 186, the case from Cowper was overruled, for there, even in the case of a notice to quit, it was held that if the landlord receive rent, due after the expiration of the notice, it is a waiver of that notice. Ld. Kenyon, who delivered the opinion of the court, in reference to the cases of *Doe* v. *Batten*, and *Brewer* v. *Eaton*, says: "I cannot assent to the doctrine laid down in these cases, that the receipt of rent, accruing after the expiration of the notice to quit, is not a waiver of it; for, according to that doctrine, the same person might stand in the relation of tenant and trespasser to his landlord at the same time. From this review, I think the case cited by Gibbs cannot be received as law; for whatever may be the effect of receiving rent after a notice to quit, making a distress after forfeiture, as had been shown, in a waiver; for it cannot rightfully be made, unless the lease is affirmed. The one is an unequivocal act of affirmance. The receipt of rent is not, in all cases, a waiver. Ld. Coke, in 3 Rep., 64, has stated the rule with precision: "If a man makes a lease for years, rendering rent, on condition that if the rent be behind, to re-enter, in that case, if the lessor demands, and it is not paid, and afterwards he accepts the rent at a day after (that is, rent that accrued subsequent to the demand) he hath dispensed with the condition; but although in such a case, he accepts the rent due at the day the demand was made, yet he may re-enter; for as well before as after his re-entry he may have an action of debt for the rent, on the contract between the lessor and lessee."

After a patient examination of the authorities, and attentive consideration of this cause, I am of opinion that the motion to set aside the nonsuit be denied.

Motion denied.

Cited in—1 Wend., 136; 9 Wend., 380; 19 Wend., 394; 21 Wend., 587; 11 Barb., 35; 3 Leg. Obs., 45; 25 Cal., 394; 41 Am. Dec., 116 (5 Ark., 595).

458*] *JACKSON, ex dem. ATWOOD ET AL.,
v.
DOUGLASS.

Date of Patent for Land, not Conclusive as to Time of Issue—Patent Issues when it Passes the Secretary's Office—Governor, as such, Has no Authority to Sell Public Lands.

A patent or grant of lands by the State, takes effect only from the time when it is approved by the Commissioners of the Land Office, and passes the Secretary's Office.

The date is not conclusive of the time of its issuing.

The Governor, as such, has no power to sell or contract for the sale of the unappropriated lands of the State. He has no more power than any other Commissioner of the Land Office.

His signature to a patent, therefore, under a certain date is no evidence of a contract at that time to sell the lands; nor that the patent issued at that time.

What is meant by a patent passing the Secretary's office.

Citations—1 R. L., 292; Greenl., 280; *12 Johns., 141; 3 Cow., 80.

EJECTMENT for the east half of lot 22, in Beekmantown, Clinton Co., tried at the circuit in that county, Jan. 21, 1825, before Walworth, *Circuit J.*

The lessors of the plaintiff claimed under a patent, including the premises in question, from the people to Zephaniah Platt, dated, and which passed the Secretary's office Feb. 28, 1787. And the defendant claimed under letters patent from the people, covering the same premises, to Simeon Metcalf, bearing date, and tested, and signed by the Governor, Aug. 14, 1786; but it did not pass the Secretary's office till July 27, 1790. The patent to Platt, thus having passed the Secretary's office before the patent to Metcalf, the judge directed the jury that the former took preference for this reason; and they found for the plaintiff. The respective times at which the patents passed the office of the Secretary, and were signed by the Governor, appeared on the face of them.

Mr. H. Bleecker, for the defendant, moved for a new trial. He said the note of the time when the patents passed the Secretary's office could not be regarded. The date must determine when they were to take effect.

But at any rate, the patent to Metcalf should be holden to relate to the time of its date, the Governor's signature being evidence of a contract to convey at that time. *Jackson* v. *Ramsay*, 3 Cow., 75; 18 Vin., Relation, E, p. 290; Cro. Jac., 512; 1 Johns. Cas., 81; 2 Inst., 674, 675; 2 Ves., Sr., 70; 13 Rep., 21. The grant by the commissioners was a mere technical consummation of the agreement. It must be presumed that the money was paid at the date; and that the patentee had done everything on his part to be performed. *Heath* v. *Ross*, 12 Johns., 140, is in point to this question of relation. The subsequent patentee is privy to the first grant, and thus stands in a situation to be affected by the relation.

*These patents being matters of rec- [*459 ord, nothing can be averred against the date. (18 Vin., 289, Relation, D; 2 Bl. Com., 346; 17 Vin., 166, Prerogative, &c., Y, ch. 2; Com. Dig., Patent, A; Co. Litt., 260 *a*.)

Mr. J. Platt, contra. There is no evidence that Metcalf paid the money, or did any other act entitling him to the grant before the patent issued; and it is begging the question to say there was a previous contract. As between individuals, the date of a deed is of no manner of importance. It is *prima facie* evidence, and no more. The doctrine contended for would be a strange anomaly. We deny that a record can have the relation contended for; much less is it to be conclusive. The case coming the nearest to the one before the court, is that of *Heath* v. *Ross*, 12 Johns., 140. But the question in that case was agreed to be the same as if it had stood between the government and the patentee. As between them, it was held that the patent related to the time of its date; but the express reservation is made in that case, that the effect given to the patent should not avail, so as to injure third persons, strangers to the grant; and as to them, the court declare, in terms, that the grant is to have effect only from the time when the Commissioners of the Land Office approve the conveyance. It is not pretended that Platt, the patentee, had any notice of Metcalf's proceedings. Where was the legal title during the three years that intervened between the passing of Platt's patent and that of Metcalf? Did it not vest in Platt as soon as the patent issued to him? No doubt it was indefeasibly in him, and the commissioners could not devest it; nor could the Governor and Secretary do this. If, as contended, a patent is to conclude by its date, the keepers of the great seal may devest rights when they please. All that is necessary would be to antedate a grant. No adjudged case is produced that even the King of England may do this. *Magna Charta* forbids it, and the English authorities forbid it. (Com. Dig., Patent,

E. F.) In England patents are granted by the King; here by the Commissioners of the Land Office. (1 Greenl. L., 280.) A patent signed **460***] by the Governor alone would be *void. From the time when the King or the Commissioners express their will, the land passes, and not before.

The case of *Jackson* v. *Ramsay*, cited from 3 Cow., was a sheriff's sale upon execution, and went on the ground of a previous lien by the judgment. Platt could not be privy to a patent which had no existence till three years after his own grant.

Curia, per SUTHERLAND, *J.* The Governor, as such, has no authority to sell, or contract for a sale, of the unappropriated lands of this State. That power is intrusted to the Commissioners of the Land Office. The person administering the government is, *ex officio*, one of those Commissioners; but he possesses no greater power than any other member of the Board. (1 R. L., 292; 1 Greenl., 280.) The Commissioners are authorized to direct the form of the patent to be issued. But whatever the form may be, the sale and the patent are efficacious, only as directed by, and emanating from the Commissioners. The mere signature of the Governor does not afford the requisite legal evidence that the patent is approved of by the Commissioners. The statute has not declared that such shall be its effect; and there is nothing to show that the Commissioners (admitting it was competent for them to do it) ever constituted the Governor their agent or representative for that purpose. Having no authority, therefore, to sign the patent to Metcalf, under whom the defendant claims, until it was approved of by the Commissioners; and it not appearing that it was so approved till July 27, 1790, when it passed the Secretary's office; it is immaterial whether it was, in fact, signed by the Governor when it bears date or not. But the legal presumption is, that his signature, and the affixing of the great seal to the patent (which I understand to be what is meant by passing the Secretary's office), were contemporaneous acts. This would also appear to have been the fact from inspection of the patent, if the signature and certificate in the original patent were placed as they are by the copy given in the case.

461*] *From what time, then, is this patent to Metcalf to take effect? From its date in Aug., 1786, or from the time when it actually issued or passed the Secretary's office, in July, 1790? It is said by the court, in *Heath* v. *Ross*, 12 Johns., 141, that, "according to the usage and practice of the Secretary's office, the patent is dated at the time when the grant is ordered by the Commissioner of the Land Office; and this must be taken to be the time when the contract for the grant was made." What the evidence of the usage was, in that case, does not appear. None is stated. I cannot suppose it to be so notorious that the court would take notice of it without proof. And, with great respect, I should have entertained very serious doubt, whether evidence of usage would have been admissible, if objected to. The deputy Secretary of State is, by law, declared to be clerk to the Commissioners of the Land Office; and it is expressly made his duty to enter the minutes of their proceedings, and to keep the same in the Secretary's office in proper order, with the papers and documents which may be presented to the Board. (1 R. L., 292, sec. 2.) The application for the patent, therefore, and the order of the Commissioners that it issue, must appear upon the minutes of their proceedings, on record in the Secretary's office. Those minutes certainly afford evidence of a higher character, as to the time when the patent was ordered to be issued, than the mere date of a patent, in a case in which it is admitted that it did not actually issue when it bears date. The date may have been erroneously inserted in the patent, either by accident or design. It may have been an error in transcribing, or have occurred in a variety of ways, each of which is more probable, than the supposition that it was intended to designate the time when the contract for the land was made.

The defendant, therefore, I apprehend, fails in laying a foundation for the doctrine of relation for which he contends. He does not show a previous contract to which the act that consummates his title is to relate, and from the date of which, it is, by relation, to take effect.

*I do not, therefore, deem it material [***462** to inquire whether Zephaniah Platt was a privy, so that the doctrine of relation would apply to this case, if there were no other objection to it. It is a fiction of law; and is never to be adopted when third persons, who are neither parties nor privies, are to be affected by it. (3 Cow., 80, and the cases there cited; 12 Johns., 141.)

I am, therefore, of opinion that the patent to Metcalf can take effect only from the time when it appear to have been approved of by the Commissioners and to have passed the Secretary's office; and consequently, that the motion for a new trial must be denied.

New trial denied.

Cited in—10 Wend., 658; 14 Mich., 208.

DUNHAM AND DANIELS
v.
THE TRUSTEES OF THE VILLAGE OF ROCHESTER.

By-Laws by Trustees of Village Corporation—Must be Reasonable—Generally Void, if in Restraint of Trade—Power of Corporation to Pass By-Laws, must Appear.

An Act Authorizing the Trustees of a Village Corporation to make By-laws Relative to Hucksters, and to pass such prudential by-laws for the good government of the village, &c., as they may deem necessary, not inconsistent with the laws of the State or U. S. (*e.g.*, the Act Incorporating Rochesterville, sess. 40, ch. 96), does not authorize them to pass a law that hucksters shall take and pay for a license of the trustees under a penalty, especially where it does not appear, expressly, that prudence required the by-law.

Such a law is in restraint of trade; and, as such, contrary to the general principles of the laws of the State.

NOTE.—*Municipal corporation—Power to make by-laws—Such by-laws must be reasonable, clearly within the authority of the corporation, and in accord with the laws of the State.* See Buffalo v. Webster, 10 Wend., 99, *note*.

Corporations must show their power to pass by-laws, and bring themselves by proof within that power.

A by-law, in restraint of trade, is, in general, void.

By-laws must be reasonable.

Citations—Sess. 40, ch. 96, sec. 5; 2 Kyd Corp., 107-109, 104-107, 118, 119, 122, 124, 125, 131.

THIS cause came from a justice's court of the County of Monroe. The action in the court below was debt by the trustees against D. and D. for keeping a huckster's shop and gin shop, in violation of the following by-laws of the village: "And be it enacted, that all petty grocers, hucksters and victualers (public innkeepers excepted), in said village, shall be licensed by the trustees of the same; and every person keeping a grocer's, huckster's or victualing shop without such license, shall, for each and every offense, forfeit and pay a fine of five dollars, for each and every day he, she or they shall keep such grocery, huckster or victualing shop; and each and every keeper **463***] or keepers of any petty *grocery, huckster or victualing shop, who shall sell any spiritous liquors, unless he, she or they have a town license, shall forfeit his, her, or their license." This by-law was passed in 1818.

The other by-law passed May 12, 1825, and is in the words following: "Resolved that grocers, keepers of victualing houses, gin shops and huckster's shops, and street pedlars, to be taxed for a license for the present year, from five to thirty dollars, at the discretion of the president, and enter into such bonds as the president shall deem sufficient." The plaintiffs claimed $50 for ten penalties.

It was admitted by the defendants, that they had kept, since the mouth of Apr., 1825, till the commencement of the suit, a shop in the village of Rochester, wherein they sold by retail, dried herring and all kinds of salt fish, pepper, allspice, sugar, coffee, tea, tobacco, cigars and snuff. They occasionally bought and sold butter, potatoes and cucumbers. They kept and sold liquors of all kinds, including beer by retail, for which they had a town license. They butchered and sold in the shop from 8 to 12 quarters of mutton and lamb daily. The value of the articles, exclusive of meat kept for sale in the store, varied from $100 to $200. The action before the justice was commenced July 1, 1825. He rendered judgment for the plaintiffs for $50. It was admitted that the defendants had never taken any license or given any bond, according to the requisition of the by-law.

Mr. V. Matthews, for the plaintiffs in error, cited 2 Com. Dig., 156, 159; 8 Rep., 126; 1 Ld. Raym., 498; 12 Johns., 122; Cowp., 640; 7 Johns., 134; 11 Rep., 53, 54; 2 Str., 1084, 1085; Skinn., 371; F. Moor, 403; Cro. Jac., 597; Rolle Abr., 364; 1 Burr., 12; 3 *Id.*, 1322; 8 T. R., 356; 2 Bos. & P., 35; 1 T. R., 118; T. Raym., 288, 289, 324; 3 Wheel. Cr. Cas, 69, 250; 3 Johns. Cas., 108; 1 Wood. Lect., 495; 3 Burr., 1832; Skinn., 380, 382; Cro. Jac., 555; T. Raym., 446; 1 Str., 675; 1 Burr., 127; 2 *Id.*, 892; Cowp., 269; 5 Rep., 63; Skinn., 378.

464*] **Mr. E. Griffin*, contra, cited 3 Burr., 1838; 1 Bl. Com., 59; 1 Show., 108; Hardr., 344; 1 Inst., 235; 2 *Id.*, 222, 306; 12 Rep., 130, 131; 1 Inst., 24; Plowd., 467; *Id.*, 109; 3 Rep., 7; Hob., 346; Plowd., 36, 59; 10 Mod., 117, 282, 341; 4 Wh., 660, 668; 18 Johns., 60; 1 Hamilton, Works, 118; 3 Wheel. Cr. Cas., 250; Salk., 193; 1 Kyd, Corp., 47; 3 Burr., 1847; 1 Ld. Raym., 113; 2 Com. Dig., 157, 158; 1 Cowp., 269; 1 Wheel. Cr. Cas., 29; 8 Johns., 418.

Curia. The question presented by this case is, whether the trustees of the village of Rochester had authority to pass the by-laws in question.

The 5th section of the Act incorporating the village of Rochesterville (sess. 40, ch. 96) provides that it shall be lawful for the trustees, &c., to make such prudential by-laws, rules and regulations as they, from time to time, may deem meet and proper; and such particularly as are relative to the public market, streets, alleys, highways, foot-walks, side-walks, slaughter-houses, houses of ill fame, and nuisances generally; relative to a village watch, and lighting the streets; to the restraining of dogs, swine, &c., and the better improvement of their common lands and real estate; relative to the inspection of weights and measures, and the assize of bread; to hay scales, public pumps, reservoirs, and for the extinguishment of fires, &c.; relative to establishing fire companies, &c.; and keeping chimneys clean and in good repair; "relative to taverns, gin shops, and huckster shops in said village;" and relative to anything whatever that may concern the good government of the said village. But no such by-law shall extend to the regulating or fixing of the prices of any commodities or articles of provisions, except the article of bread, that may be offered for sale; provided always, that such by-laws be not contrary to or inconsistent with the laws of this State or of the U. S.

The 19th section declares the Act to be a public Act, and that it shall be construed in all courts of justice, within this State, benignly and liberally, to effect every beneficial purpose therein mentioned and contained.

*The 6th section provides that the [***465** trustees may ordain such reasonable fines, &c., against the offenders of such by-laws, as they may deem proper, not exceeding $25 for any one offense.

The power conferred is to make such prudential by-laws, rules and regulations, &c., not contrary to or inconsistent with the laws of this State or of the U. S.

Admitting the power to limit, or prohibit altogether, the erection of huckster or gin shops, if required by prudence for the good of the Corporation; it is not shown how they could be an evil, if conducted under proper regulations; nor can we see judicially that any restriction was necessary.

The authority of the Corporation is a limited one. The trustees cannot arbitrarily pass what laws they please. Their laws are to be prudential, and aimed at the correction of some probable evil. This is also conformable to the general law of corporations, which demands that their by-laws should be reasonable. (2 Kyd, Corp., 107.) For all the purposes of jurisdiction, they are like the inferior courts, and must show the power given them in every case. If this be wanting, their proceedings must be holden void whenever they come in question even collaterally; for they are not judicial, and subject to direct review on *certio-*

rari. (2 Kyd, Corp., 104–107.) This view is not inconsistent with the provision of the charter, that it shall be construed benignly and liberally, to effect every beneficial purpose therein mentioned and contained. It must be shown, in proof, that the purpose is a beneficial one within the Act, before this duty of construction attaches. Nothing is to be intended in favor of jurisdiction.

But how do these by-laws stand with the general law of the State, or with the general principles of that law? By-laws must accord with both. (2 Kyd, Corp., 107, 109.) Hence, such by-laws as these, against trade, are said to be against the common law which favors trade, and are not allowed except by particular custom. (*Id.*, 118, 119, 122, 124, 125, 131.)

The defendant was carrying on the business of a retail dealer in various articles; and sup-
466*] pose, for the purposes of *the argument, that he was a huckster. He was also selling gin and other spirituous liquors under a town license, founded on a public law of the State. Perhaps the Corporation might do more towards regulating and restraining him from the abuse of his business to immoral, unsafe or unhealthy purposes, &c., than could be done under any general state law. A more efficient police on these subjects was, probably, aimed at by the charter than is given by the state law in the like cases. But it does not follow that any man is to depend, for the fair and innocent exercise of his business, on the will of the Corporation; that they have the power of licensing his trade, at their pleasure; prohibiting it altogether, or crippling it by heavy charges and grievous penalties.

Nor is the right to pass these by-laws derivable from the taxing power of the Corporation. This is conferred by another part of the charter, in definite and specific terms, which, it is not pretended, reach the present case.

This being our opinion, it is not necessary to look into the by-laws to ascertain whether they are good, in point of form. We are of opinion that they are void, both for want of jurisdiction and conformity to the general law.

Judgment reversed.

Cited in—9 Wend., 606; 10 Wend., 102; 12 Wend., 186; 57 N. Y., 596, 698; 59 N. Y., 102; 18 Hun, 478; 15 Barb., 435; 24 Barb., 577; 3 Duer, 149; 3 Rob., 97; 25 Minn., 252-255; 41 N. J. L., 79; 42 N. J. L., 369; 29 Wis., 315; 24 Am. Dec., 193; 36 Am. Dec., 445, 446 (3 Ala., 137); 8 Baxt., 228; 36 Am. Rep., 522 (13 Vroom., 364); 38 Am. Rep., 631 (54 Tex., 388); 42 Am. Rep., 52 (57 Iowa, 555).

COLLET *v.* FLINN.

Pleading—Plea in Trespass.

A plea, in trespass *quare clausum fregit* that a third person was seised in fee, and demised to the defendant for years, without giving express color, amounts to the general issue, and is bad on special demurrer.

Citation—1 Chit. Pl., 500.

ON ERROR from the C. P. of the City and County of N. Y. Flinn sued Collet in the court below in trespass for breaking and entering a stable, &c. The defendant below pleaded that one Hone was seised in fee of the stable, and demised it to the defendant for one year; that by virtue of this demise he entered, &c., concluding with a verification. The plaintiff below demurred specially to this plea as amounting to the general issue. The court allowed the demurrer, and rendered judgment for the plaintiff.

Mr. J. S. Mitchell*, for the plaintiff [*467**
in error, cited, 1 Chit. Pl., 494, 500, 503, 533, 566, 606; 2 *Id.*, 565, 600, 602; 6 Cal., 233; 3 Bl. Com., 311; 2 Bl., 1089.

Mr. W. Mulock, contra, cited 10 Johns., 289; 3 Salk., 272; Archb. Pl., 211; 10 Rep., 89; Doct. & Stud., 271; 3 Bl. Com., 309.

Curia, per SAVAGE, *Ch. J.* The doctrine contended for by the plaintiff in error is not denied—that when the declaration in trespass is general, the defendant may plead *liberum tenementum*, and drive the plaintiff to a new assignment. But it is denied that the plea demurred to is a plea of *liberum tenementum*. It shows a freehold in Hone, and only a possessory right in the defendant below; and, in such cases, the plea, not giving color to the plaintiff, amounts merely to the general issue.

It is laid down by Chitty, 1 Ch. Pl., 500, that in trespass to lands, the plea of *liberum tenementum* gives implied color; and if the defendant claim under a demise from the plaintiff, express color need not be given. "But when, from the nature of the defense, the plaintiff would have no implied color of action, the defendant cannot plead specially any matter which controverts what the plaintiff would, on the general issue, be bound to prove, without giving express color. Thus, in trespass to land, if the defendant plead a possessory title under a demise from a third person; this plea, showing that the right of possession is in the defendant, would, without giving express color, amount to the general issue." But giving color creates a question of law for the decision of the court, and prevents the plea from amounting to the general issue. This doctrine is supported by the adjudged cases cited in Chitty, and decides the plea to be bad. Such was the decision of the C. P.; and the judgment must be affirmed.

Judgment affirmed.

Cited in—13 Wend., 80; 1 Hill, 287.

*ELMENDORF ET AL., Executors [***468** &c., of VAN RENSSELAER,

v.

ABRAHAM G. LANSING, Impleaded with others.

Action, Against Surety on Bond—Bond, Given on Decretal Order, to Pay Over Part of an Estate Before Final Settlement—Held to be for Indemnity of Executors and not to Extend to Cestuis Que Trust.

The executors of V. divided certain moneys, stock and securities of their testator into two parts; and on petition of certain legatees claiming one part, the Court of Chancery made a decretal order in a suit wherein the executors, petitioners and others were parties, that the executors should assign that part to L. for the use of the legatees, L. first giving a bond with two sureties, that when required by order or decree, he should account for that part; and if that, or any portion of it, should be decreed to any parties other than the petitioners, or those whose interest they represented, he should pay what he might have received to such parties, &c., as should be designated by order or decree. Accordingly L., with two sureties, gave bond to the executors, which.

instead of being conditioned "to pay to such parties, &c., as should be designated by order or decree," was, "to pay to such person or persons as then were, or thereafter should be, designated by order or decree, &c., according to the true intent and meaning of the decretal order, or any other order or decree of the said court, touching or concerning the premises." The executors brought a suit upon this bond against one of the sureties, wherein it appeared, upon the pleadings, that an order of the Court of Chancery had been made that L. should pay a certain balance of the part assigned to him, to the register of the Court of Chancery, for the use of his *cestuis que trust*, and that he had not complied with this order. Held, that this was not a breach of the bond to the executors; that this bond was no wider than the decretal order under which it was executed; that it was intended merely to indemify the executors, not the *cestuis que trust*; and the former showing no damage to themselves, no action would lie.

DEBT on bond in the penalty of $54,832. The pleadings were conducted between the parties to a rebutter, to which the plaintiffs demurred generally, and the defendant, A. G. Lansing, joined in demurrer. For the purpose of the legal questions decided by the court, the pleadings and points are stated in their opinion.

Messrs. D. F. Butler and *S. A. Foot*, in support of the demurrer.

Mr. A. Van Vechten, contra.

Curia, per WOODWORTH, *J.* This action was commenced on a bond, given by the defendant as one of the sureties of Sanders Lansing.

The question to be decided is, whether, on the facts disclosed by the pleadings, the defendant is liable.

July 29, 1812, a decretal order of the Court of Chancery was entered, in a cause wherein Gerritt Y. Lansing and wife were complain-
469*] ants; and the now plaintiffs *and others, devisees and legatees of Jeremiah Van Rensselaer, deceased, were defendants.

The order was made on the petition of the plaintiffs and Sanders Lansing, and others, some of the defendants. The present plaintiffs, in their answer in that cause, alleged that, in pursuance of the will of the deceased, they had divided certain portions of his personal property into two equal parts, and had assigned one portion to Peter Van Rensselaer and others, and the other portion to Sanders Lansing and others.

The petitioners stated that the portion alleged to have been assigned to them had been retained in the hands of the executors; that they were willing, and then offered to accept the moneys, stock and securities alleged to have been assigned for their share; and to give such security as the court should deem reasonable; and prayed that the portion should be assigned and delivered to Sanders Lansing for their use, if they should be deemed, on the final hearing of the cause, entitled to it; and if not, to be accounted for and paid according to the decree. The *Chief Justice*, sitting as *Chancellor*, ordered the executors to make the assignment; but that Sanders Lansing should first give bond with two sureties, that he should, at all times, when thereunto required by any order or decree of the Court of Chancery, faithfully account for the money, stock and securities received by him; and if the same, or any part thereof, should be decreed to be paid to any other of the said parties than the petitioners, or those whose interest they represented, in every such case, he should pay such sum or sums received, or which might have been received without his willful default, to such of the said parties, or their representatives, as should be designated and appointed for that purpose by such order or decree.

In pursuance of this decree, the appointment was made; and the defendant, as one of the sureties of Sanders Lansing, executed the bond in question—the condition of which corresponds with the order of the court, excepting in this; instead of saying "to pay to such of the parties or their representatives as should be designated and appointed for that purpose, by such order or decree;" the condition is, "to *pay to such person or persons as then [*470
were or thereafter should be designated and appointed, by any order or decree of the Court of Chancery, according to the true intent and meaning of the decretal order, or any other order or decree of the said court touching or concerning the premises."

Although the conclusion is expressed in more general terms than the order which directed security to be given, yet it is evident that nothing more was or could be legally demanded of Sanders Lansing, than to satisfy the requirements of the decree. The bond and decree are in *pari materia*, and must be construed together. The petitioners stated that they were willing to give such security as the court should deem reasonable. The court has prescribed the form of the security. Unless, therefore, the expressions in the conclusion of the bond show clearly and distinctly that something more is provided for than the order directs, I think the construction ought to be controlled by the decretal order. It appears to me there is no difficulty in reconciling the one to the other. They speak the same language. When the bond requires Sanders Lansing to pay to such person or persons as then were or thereafter should be designated, it evidently refers to that part of the decree which provides for the payment of so much as should be decreed to be paid "to any other of the said parties than the petitioners, or those whose interest they represented." Such a construction is also required by the reference in the condition. After the specification of what is to be done, the whole is qualified, "according to the true intent and meaning of the said recited decretal order." It is true the words are added, "or any other order or decree of the said Court of Chancery touching or concerning the premises;" but they do not enlarge the liability. The words seem to be unnecessary, and are expletives merely. They cannot, I apprehend, intend that Sanders Lansing should pay to persons not contemplated by the parties, and not designated in the order. They can only refer to such orders as might be made, consistently with that directing the transfer, and the manner in which security should be given. Besides, it is a well established rule of construction, that after an enumeration of particulars, general words shall *be restrained and limited in their [*471
operation to the particulars specified.

The liability, then, of the defendant, will depend on the fact whether the condition required by the decretal order has been broken. In collecting the intent of the parties, it may be observed that the plaintiffs in this cause had no other interest or concern than for the protection of themselves. It was possible, that, eventually, there would be a deficiency of assets, to satisfy creditors and legatees, or the amount transferred might turn out to be more than the petitioners were entitled to under the will. It was, therefore, proper, and the case required, that security should be given to account with the executors and pay over what might be decreed by the court. But to whom? The decretal order answers the question. Sanders Lansing was to pay, if any part should be decreed to be paid to any other of the said parties than the petitioners. The allegation in the plea now in question is, that this has not been done. Until such decree is made, there is no liability on the bond. Neither the intent nor the words of the condition will warrant a different construction. The sole object of the petitioners seems have been to get the property out of the hands of the executors. They pray that it may be assigned to Sanders Lansing for their use, and offer to give such security as shall be deemed reasonable; which evidently means such security as would protect the executors, in case any claim should afterwards be established against them—not security that the trustee should be faithful to the individual interest of the petitioners. As far as that was concerned, they reposed themselves upon his fidelity. So we are bound to presume, for no intimation is given to the contrary. This must have been the light in which the court considered the application, for the security directed to be given is in coincidence with this intent. The executors have sustained no damages. Sanders Lansing was not their trustee. No decree has been made directing payment to any other parties, in the chancery cause, other than the petitioners. The allegation, therefore, in the plea is, in my opinion, a conclusive bar to the plaintiff's action.

472*] *The replication setting forth a decretal order of the Court of Chancery to pay to the register a balance of $10,268.29 due from Sanders Lansing to his *cestuis que trust*, which he had not obeyed, does not avoid or falsify the plea ; for, if the view taken of the nature and extent of the liability incurred be correct, it follows that the breaches assigned in the replication, which are mere breaches of trust as between Sanders Lansing and his *cestuis que trust*, are not within the condition of the bond.

The rejoinder fortifies and supports the plea by setting out, at length, the petition, decretal order, master's report and proceedings ; and concludes with an averment that the balance of $10,268.29, received by Sanders Lansing, hath not been decreed to any other parties to the suit mentioned in the decretal order than the petitioners.

The surrejoinder sets out new matter in support of the replication, viz.: that Sanders Lansing confessed a judgment in favor of John Lansing, Jr., one of the sureties ; and that in the specification one item set forth is, that the judgment was given, among other things, to secure J. Lansing, Jr., and Abraham G. Lansing, being sureties of Sanders Lansing, in the bond in question in this cause, conditioned for the faithful performance of a trust assumed by the said Sanders Lansing ; and that afterwards John Lansing, Jr., confessed a judgment in favor of Abraham G. Lansing ; and that in the specification filed it is set forth that a part of the consideration of the judgment is the equal moiety of the sum of $7,000, due on a joint bond executed by J. Lansing, Jr., and Abraham G. Lansing, to the plaintiffs, conditioned that Sanders Lansing should account for the proceeds of certain stock, securities and property of Van Rensselaer, the testator, which were placed in his hands for distribution.

This new matter does not change the complexion of the case. It was, perhaps, known that Sanders Lansing was in failing circumstances. His sureties might or might not become liable. It was a cautionary measure on their part—a transaction between sureties and principal. It neither diminished nor enlarged their responsibility to the plaintiffs ; for the plain reason that it was an arrangement with which *they had no concern. If it be [*473 conceded that the parties acted under an impression and belief that they were liable when, in judgment of law they were not, I am not acquainted with any principle which will admit a plaintiff to avail himself of such a recognition to extend the legal operation of a contract.

The rebutter sets out the specification *in hæc verba*, and concludes with a verification, to which the plaintiffs demur, and the defendant joins in demurrer.

My conclusion is, that no breach of the condition has been shown ; and, consequently, that the defendant is entitled to judgment.

Judgment for the defendant.

ROBERTSON v. LIVINGSTON.

Commission Merchant may Sell on Credit—Settlement of Account—Assumption of Vendee's Debt, by Commission Merchant.

Where a commission merchant sold goods on a credit, and then settled with his principal, giving him a note for the balance, which he stated was to accommodate him; and, for that reason, he made it payable a few days after the note of the vendee fell due; held, that this was not an assumption of the vendee's debt, but that to throw this upon the commission merchant, a clear intention to assume it should have been shown.

It seems that where a commission merchant is not restricted by instructions he may sell on a credit.

Citation—4 Cow., 250.

ASSUMPSIT, tried at the N. Y. Circuit, Mar. 26, 1825, before Betts, *Circuit J.*, when the following facts were shown in evidence :

Nov. 19, 1822, the plaintiff sold the defendant a lot of sheep for $292; and the defendant at the same time, left with the plaintiff wool, for sale on commission, which, Jan. 10, 1823, the plaintiff sold to Pearson & Co., of N. J., about 15 miles from the City of N. Y. (where the plaintiff traded), the vendees then being in good credit, for $385.44. The sale was on a credit of six months.

In Apr., 1823, Moses Robertson called on the plaintiff, with an order in writing from the defendant to the plaintiff, to settle with the bearer, M. R., for the wool which he left with the plaintiff the last fall for sale, and that should be his discharge for the same.

274*] *Apr. 29, 1823, the plaintiff settled with M. R., and gave him his note, payable to the defendant at three months, for $99.42, the sum due to the defendant, after giving him credit for the net proceeds of the wool, and $39.52, the net proceeds of another small lot of wool, and charging him with the sheep. The plaintiff, at the same time, stated an account upon the above principles, and informed M. R. that the note of Pearson & Co. had not become due; but in order to accommodate the defendant he agreed to give his note as above, payable, however, some few days after the note of Pearson & Co. would fall due. Pearson & Co. had failed.

The jury found for the plaintiff $187.75.

Mr. J. Crary, for the defendant, now moved for a new trial, on the ground that the settlement and voluntary payment of the balance, was an assumption of the debt due from Pearson and Co.; *Oakley* v. *Crenshaw*, 4 Cow., 250; and that the money paid as this was, with a full knowledge of all the facts, could not be recovered back. He also objected that the plaintiff had no right to sell on credit.

Mr. B. F. Butler, contra.

Curia, per SUTHERLAND, *J.* Robertson, as a general agent, unrestricted by instructions, was authorized to sell the wool of the defendant on a credit. That objection, however, was not taken at the trial and cannot be now raised. If the proposition be not true, in general, it may be the custom and usage of this branch of trade, which the plaintiff had no opportunity of proving, as the question was not raised before the jury.

The evidence clearly establishes that Pearson & Co., to whom the wool was sold, were in good credit at the time, and that the plaintiff acted in good faith, and with all the circumspection which his duty required in the transaction.

The circumstances attending the settlement of the account between the parties, and the giving of the note by the plaintiff for the balance, repel the presumption which might otherwise arise, that he intended to make himself 475*] absolutely *responsible for the payment. The agent of the defendant, with whom the settlement was made, was informed that the wool had been sold at six months' credit; and that the note given by the plaintiff would fall due a few days after that of Pearson & Co. The account delivered to the agent at the same time, showed that the sale was on a credit of six months, which would expire in July, about two months after the settlement. It is evident, therefore, that the settlement was nothing more than a liquidation of the account, and not an assumption on the part of the plaintiff, of any responsibility which he had not previously incurred in relation to the solvency of Pearson & Co. In the ease of *Oakley* v. *Crenshaw*, 4 Cow., 250, the agent in so many words, authorized his principal to draw for the whole amount of the balance due to him for the express purpose of finally closing the account; although he stated, at the time, that but a part of the money had been received by him. This was properly held a final settlement and assumption of the debt, because it was evident that such was, at the time, the intention of the agent and the understanding of the principal. There were, also, other circumstances which distinguished that case from the present. The motion for a new trial must be denied.

New trial denied.

Cited in—5 Am. Rep., 495 (43 Miss., 288).

POLLY HUNT v. A. PEAKE.

Breach of Promise of Marriage—Infant Not Liable to Action for—Action May be Maintained by Infant.

An infant under the age of 21 years, is not liable to an action for a breach of promise of marriage.

Semble, that such a contract is not void, but voidable at the election of the infant, who may maintain the action though he is not liable to it.

Citations—2 Str., 937; Com. Dig., Enfant, B, 6.

ACTION for breach of marriage promise. Plea infancy. General demurrer and joinder.

Mr. S. Starkweather, in support of the demurrer, said that infants may intermarry at the age of discretion, which is 14 in males, and it would seem to follow that a promise to do so is binding.

**Mr. L. Ford*, contra, cited *Holt* v. [*476 *Ward*, 2 Str., 937, and S. C., 15 Vin., Marriage, C. pl. 4, as in point against the action.

Curia, per SAVAGE, *Ch. J.* The general principle is against the liability of the infant, and I do not find that this case is an exception. In *Holt* v. *Ward*, 2 Str., 937, it was decided, after full argument and deliberation, that the contract to marry by an infant is not void, but voidable at the election of the infant; yet, as to the person of full age contracting with the infant, it absolutely binds. Hence, an infant may maintain this action against an adult, but an infant defendant is not liable. (Com. Dig., Enfant, B, 6.) The defendant is entitled to judgment.

Judgment for the defendant.

Cited in—7 Cow., 23; 21 Hun, 488; 26 Barb., 616; 6 Abb. Pr., 142; 13 Abb. N. S., 403, *n.*; 1 Park, 455; 31 Ohio, 522; 17 Am. Dec., 497; 27 Am. Rep., 524 (31 Ohio, 521).

PARSONS v. PARSONS ET AL.

Note Indorsed After Maker's Death—Indorsee May Sue Maker's Heirs in His Own Name—Construction of Remedial Statute, Liberal—Pleading.

An indorsee of a promissory note indorsed after the maker's death, may, in his own name, sue the maker's heirs, &c., under the Act, 1 R. L., 316.

Though a promissory note be indorsed long after it fall due, it may be declared on as indorsed when it was due.

A note being indorsed after the maker's death, the indorsee declared against the maker's heirs, and alleged that the intestate, in his lifetime, became liable to pay the plaintiff; and by reason of the premises an action accrued against the heirs. Plea, that the intestate did not owe the plaintiff in his lifetime. Held, that this was no variance; that the plea was vicious in denying a debt to the plaintiff during the intestate's lifetime, but that the defendants could not take advantage of the defect.

The defendant, the verdict being against him, cannot object that his own plea was vicious, as tendering an immaterial issue.

Citations—1 R. L., 316, 311, 312, 119; 5 Com. Dig., Pleader, E, 37.

DEBT against the defendants, as heirs of S. Parsons, Jr., deceased, tried Sept. 21, 1824, before Duer, *Circuit J.*

The declaration contained two counts. The first was on a promissory note made by S. Parsons, Jr., to Leggett, dated Apr. 9, 1819, for $200. payable to Legget or order, Dec. 1, 1820. The declaration stated that the note was, on the day of its date, indorsed by the payee to the plaintiff; and that S. Parsons, Jr., in his lifetime, had notice of the indorsement; and that by reason thereof, and by force of the statute, he, in his lifetime, became liable to pay
477*] *to the plaintiff the sum of money in the note mentioned; and that by reason of the premises, and by virtue of the Act for the Relief of Creditors against Heirs and Devisees, an action accrued to the plaintiff, to demand of the heirs at law, &c. The second count was for money lent by the plaintiff to S. Parsons, Jr. Breach to both counts, that S. Parsons, Jr., in his lifetime, and his heirs after his death, had not paid, &c.

The defendants pleaded, by their guardian, that S. Parsons, Jr., deceased, in his lifetime, did not owe to the plaintiff the several sums of money demanded by the declaration, nor any, nor either of them.

The plaintiff introduced, in evidence, the note set forth in the declaration; but it was proved that it had been indorsed to the plaintiff about two years after its date, and some time after the death of S. Parsons, Jr.

On the part of the defendants, it was objected that the plaintiff could not recover on the note: 1. Because the heirs at law were not liable by the Statute relating to Heirs and Devisees, except to a creditor of the deceased; and that the plaintiff never was his creditor. 2. Because the proof varied from the declaration, which stated the note to have been indorsed on the day of its date; that the deceased had notice of the indorsement; and that the deceased became liable to pay. 3. Because, by the plea, the issue to be tried was, whether the deceased was indebted to the plaintiff. The judge overruled these objections.

The plaintiff also gave in evidence the payment of $20 for S. Parsons, Jr., deceased, sometime in 1819.

The jury found for the plaintiff, on the first count of the declaration, the debt, $200, and damages, $47.46, being the interest on the note; and on the second count $27.84, being the $20 lent, and interest thereon, parcel of the debt in that count mentioned, and *nil debent* as to the residue.

A motion was now made, on the part of the defendants, for a new trial, on the grounds taken at the circuit.

Messrs. Van Dyck and *Bronk*, for the defendants.

478*] **Mr. A. Kirkland*, contra.

Curia, per WOODWORTH, *J.* The first question is: Was the plaintiff a creditor of the deceased?

By the 1st section of the Act, 1 R. L., 316, every creditor, whether by simple contract or specialty, may maintain his action against the heirs at law of any debtor.

At the common law, the heir was not liable on the simple contract of his ancestor; nor on a specialty, unless the heir was named. The intent of the statute was to enlarge the remedy. That is done in general terms, by saying every creditor may maintain his action. As this is a remedial statute, it should be construed liberally, so as to advance the remedy. Every person, who holds a demand arising on simple contract or specialty, seems to be within the meaning of this section. Such persons are certainly creditors within the general acceptation of the term, whether a right of action accrued in the lifetime of the deceased, or subsequently, by the transfer of negotiable paper. They would be recognized as such in a course of administration. There is nothing in the words of the section confining the remedy to persons who were creditors of the ancestor at the time of his death. If such be the construction, great conveniences would result. In the case of an assignment by an insolvent debtor, who was the payee of a note, if the assignee is not a creditor within the meaning of the Act, there is no remedy at law against the heir, for the insolvent cannot sue. So, also, the executors of a deceased payee of a note may not be creditors of the deceased maker in his lifetime; and yet it would not, I apprehend, be contended that they would be without the Act, because the maker happened to die before this testator.

My opinion is, that under this section the plaintiff may sustain the action.

But it is contended that the proviso, in the 3d section, is decisive of the question. This section declares that no judgment against any executor or administrator, for any debt, damages, or sum of money, in right of his testator or intestate, shall be adjudged a bar to any subsequent action against *the heirs; **[*479**
but that the heirs shall be liable as if no such judgment had been recovered; provided, that nothing therein contained shall be construed to make any heirs liable to any other person than a creditor of the deceased by simple contract or specialty, in like manner as is expressed in the 1st section of the Act, and not otherwise.

The enacting part of this section speaks of debts, damages, or sums of money, for which judgment may be recovered against the executor. Damages may be recovered against an executor or administrator, in trespass; 1 R. L., 311, 312; but no action lies against the heir. When it is declared, generally, that a recovery for any of the causes specified shall not be a bar to a subsequent action against the heir, it would seem to imply that an action would lie against the heir when the recovery has been against the executor for damages, although not arising on simple contract or specialty. I apprehend the proviso was intended to guard against such a construction, and explicitly to declare that the heir should not be liable except as specified in the 1st section. But the proviso does not profess to vary its operation. On the contrary, it expressly refers to it; and declares that the heir shall be liable in like manner as is expressed in that section, and not otherwise.

The variance between the declaration and proof is not material. The plaintiff may declare that an indorsement is made on the date of a note, although it is made afterwards.

It is also urged that the proof did not maintain the issue—which is, that the intestate did not owe the plaintiff. The allegation in this declaration is that the intestate, in his lifetime, became liable to pay the plaintiff; and by reason of the premises, an action accrued to the plaintiff to demand of the heirs at law. I consider the latter allegation as the substantial part. The other seems to be immaterial. If so, the defendants tendered an immaterial issue, by denying any indebtedness of S. Parsons, Jr., in his lifetime, to the plaintiff.

The defendants were called on to answer whether they were liable on this note. If they are, then it cannot be material to inquire, whether the plaintiff had any claim against the **480***] *intestate, in his lifetime. If the issue is misjoined, the objection is removed by the Statute of Joefails, 1 R. L., 119. It is a rule that where a defendant pleads an insufficient plea, whereon issue is joined, and a verdict for the plaintiff, no advantage shall be taken by the defendant of his own bad pleading. (5 Com. Dig. Pl., E, 37.)

I am of opinion that the plaintiff is entitled to retain his verdict on the first count, and that the motion for a new trial be denied.

New trial denied.

Cited in—47 Ind., 350.

TRONGOTT *v.* BYERS.

Slave—Prima Facie *Evidence that One is a Slave—Contract Amounting to Sale of—Action for Services of—Parol Agreement to Manumit, Void—Notice—Advances to Slave.*

That a negro works for and is claimed by one as a slave is, *prima facie*, evidence that he is a slave.

An agreement by the owner of a negro slave that the slave shall work for another during his life; provided, that if the vendee sell him within two years, he shall pay the vendor one half the purchase money is a sale of the slave; and though his term of slavery would be out in 1827, yet it passes all the interest of the owner.

The owner of a slave who deserts his master and works for another, need not give notice of his claim to entitle himself to an action for the slave's services.

Evidence of advances made to a slave while wrongfully in the service of another, are not, however necessary they were, a matter off-set against the owner, in an action for his slave's services.

A parol agreement with a slave to manumit him, is void.

Citations—6 Johns., 274; 7 Johns., 324; 9 Johns., 144; 14 Johns., 324.

ASSUMPSIT for the work and labor of the plaintiff by his slave. Plea, the general issue, and notice of setting off necessary articles furnished the plaintiff's slave, while at work with the defendant.

The cause was tried at the Montgomery Circuit, in May, 1824, before Nelson, *Circuit J.*

It was proved on the trial that Peter Gilbert, a black man (then about 30 years of age), previous to May 28, 1819, worked for one Paff, as a slave, and Paff claimed him as such, about 2½ years. That Paff then promised him that if he would stay and work on his farm (which he had then leased to the plaintiff) 5 years, he should be free. The lease of the farm contained an agreement between Paff and the plaintiff that Paff should leave Peter with the plaintiff during his natural life; and that if he should be sold in two years, one half the purchase money should be paid to Paff. The lease of the farm was for 2½ years. Peter worked on the farm for five years (in the service of the plaintiff, who *continued his posses- [***481** sion), as proposed by Paff, with a view to his freedom; but no written manumission was shown. After this, Peter left the plaintiff's service and worked for the defendant.

It was objected for the defendant that the lease, taken together, showed but a demise of Peter for 2½ years. That if the covenant was to be construed a sale, it was void; as being in contravention of the Statute Declaring all Slaves Free in 1827. Also that there was no sufficient evidence that Peter was a slave of Paff.

These objections being overruled, the defendant offered to prove that when Peter came to him, he was almost naked; and that he furnished him with necessary clothing; that during his service with him, he was sick; and he furnished him with medical attendance and necessaries in his sickness, which he offered to set off against Peter's wages.

This was objected to, and overruled.

It also appeared that Peter worked some time for the defendant before he had notice of the plaintiff's claim, and it was objected that the plaintiff should not recover for that time.

This objection was also overruled, the judge deciding that the defendant was liable for the whole time without deduction; and the jury found for the plaintiff, under a charge to that effect.

Mr. L. Ford, for the defendant, now moved for a new trial, on the grounds, 1. That there was no sufficient proof that Peter was the slave of Paff. 2. That there was no proof that Paff ever sold Peter to the plaintiff, as a slave. 3. That the agreement between Paff and Peter was valid, and operated as a manumission. 4. That the defendant should have been allowed to prove his set-off.

Mr. M. T. Reynolds, contra. The contract between Paff and the plaintiff passed the property in the slave. The sale was good, at least, for such interest as the vendor had. The matter of set-off would not have been a ground of action, and was inadmissible. The promise to Peter was void. At *common law, a [***482** promise to a slave would be void for want of consideration; and all agreements to manumit derive their force from the statute. (7 Johns., 354; 9 *Id.*, 144; 14 *Id.*, 324; 19 *Id.*, 53.) This requires that they should be in writing. At any rate, the promise was revocable, and was revoked by the sale. Notice to the defendant was not necessary. (6 Johns., 274; Co. Litt., 117 *a*, *note* 161, by Hargr.; 12 Johns., 136; 1 Com. on Cont., 224, 225; 1 Salk., 68; 1 Ves., Sr., 83.)

Curia, per SUTHERLAND, *J.* The evidence was, *prima facie*, sufficient to establish the fact that Peter was the slave of Paff. Peter, himself, testified that he lived with Paff, and worked with him on his farm as a slave; and that Paff claimed his services as a slave. This was sufficient, in the first instance, without tracing him back to his infancy, and showing that he was born a slave.

That the contract between Paff and the plaintiff amounted to a sale of the negro, there can be no doubt. The latter was to have the services of Peter during his natural life; but if he sold him within two years, he was to pay one half the amount received to Paff. The plaintiff did not sell him; and his interest became absolute and exclusive. The object of the condition, on the part of Paff, was, probably, to secure the labor of Peter upon the farm that he had leased to the plaintiff, by the same instrument which conveyed the slave for two and a half years.

Although Peter could not be held in slavery after 1827, still the sale was valid till that period, unless the plaintiff elected to avoid it on the ground of fraud or misrepresentation. It transferred all the interest of Paff, whatever that was.

The judge properly ruled that it was not necessary to show notice of the plaintiff's claim to the negro, in order to entitled him to recover.

Evidence of advances made to the negro, while in the defendant's service, was, also, properly excluded. The case of *James* v. *Le Roy*, 6 Johns., 274, is conclusive on both those points.
483*] *A slave stands on the footing of an apprentice, not of a hired servant.

The parol agreement of Paff, to manumit Peter, if he served faithfully for 5 years, was not a valid manumission. Such a manumission can only be in writing. *Kettletas* v. *Fleet*, 7 Johns., 324; *Wells* v. *Lane*, 9 Johns., 144; 14 *Id.*, 324. The motion must be denied.

New trial denied.

Cited in—6 Wend., 437.

JACKSON, ex dem. KROM, v. BRINK.

Possession of Tenant in Common, may become Adverse by some Notorious Act and Claim of Title—Such Act is the Hostile Inception Required to make the Possession Adverse—Hostile Inception does not Apply to the Entry.

Though a tenant in common enter, without claiming adversely to his co-tenants, yet his possession may afterwards become adverse, by some notorious act and claim of title; as if he purchase his co-tenant's interest under a deed from the sheriff; and this, though the deed be defective for want of a particular description of the land.

To constitute an adverse possession, it is not necessary that the deed, under which it is claimed, be valid.

The rule, that an adverse possession, to bar an action of ejectment, must be hostile in its inception, and continue so for 20 years, does not apply to the entry of the tenant, but to the act by which the possession becomes adverse.

Citations—13 Johns., 551,2; 5 Wh., 124; 7 Wh., 120, 121; 15 Johns., 501; 1 Johns., 156; 16 Johns., 301; 5 Cow., 74.

EJECTMENT, tried at the Ulster Circuit, Oct. 14, 1823, before Betts, *Circuit J.*

It appeared that Benjamin Krom, the father of the lessor of the plaintiff, died seised of the premises in question, a farm in Marbletown, Ulster Co., leaving a wife and four children, the lessor being the eldest, and a child of a former wife. The widow entered into possession with her children. In 1798, the right and title of the lessor to the real estate of which his father died seised in Marbletown, was sold by the sheriff on a warrant from the County Treasurer, against the lessor as a defaulting collector. The widow became the purchaser and received a deed from the sheriff, dated Nov. 28, 1800.

The judge decided that this deed passed no title for want of a particular description; and that, though the widow and the defendant who claimed under her had been in possession down to the commencement of the suit, he held that the entry and possession of Mrs. Krom, after her husband's death, being in common with the infant co-heirs of the lessor, was not hostile in its inception; and could not become so, as to the plaintiff, by her purchase at sheriff's sale; and the jury found for the plaintiff, under his direction, to that effect.

Mr. C. H. Ruggles, Mr J. Sudam*, [*484** same side, moved for a new trial, and cited 7 Wh., 120; Cowp., 217; 16 Johns., 301; 5 Cow., 74; 2 W. Bl., 692.

Mr. B. F. Butler, contra, cited 5 Wh., 116, 124; 4 *Id.*, 213; 9 Johns., 163.

Curia, per SAVAGE, *Ch. J.* Admitting the first point to be correctly decided according to *Jackson* v. *DeLancey*, 13 Johns., 551, 552, yet I think the judge erred on the other point. It is undoubtedly true that the possession of one tenant in common, in general, inures to the benefit of all. But it is equally true that one tenant in common may oust his co-tenant, and hold adversely to him. It will not be presumed from a sole possession, unless accompanied with some notorious act, or claim, which is sufficient to give character to the possession. (5 Wh., 124; 7 *Id.*, 120, 121; 15 Johns., 501.)

In this case, it seems to me there is abundant evidence of a public claim, made by the widow, to the individual ownership of the right of the lessor in the premises in question. The sheriff's deed is certainly evidence that she purchased something—some supposed right of the lessors to lands in Marbletown—which right she located upon the premises in question. Here was a public act. A sale at the court house, a purchase and payment of money; her declarations afterwards, that she owned land of her own, all go to mark the change in the character of the possession. It is not necessary that the deed should convey a good title. It is enough that it gives color to the claim of title set up under it.

The judge certainly misapplied the rule, that a possession, to be adverse, must be hostile in its inception. The rule is so laid down, *Brandt* v. *Ogden*, 1 Johns., 156, but has often been subsequently qualified, and is understood not to apply to the entry upon the premises; for it has often been decided that a possession taken under the true owner may, by a disclaimer of his title, subsequently become adverse. (16 Johns., 301; 5 Cow., 74.) It was certainly not necessary *to change the [***485** occupancy, in order to change the character of the tenancy or claim of title.

It seems to me that the defendant made out an adverse possession in himself, and the widow, under whom he claims, from the time of the sale in 1798, but clearly from 1800, the date of the deed.

NOTE.—*Adverse possession—What constitutes.* See Jackson v. Smith, 13 Johns., 406, *note, and other notes there cited*; Jackson v. Sharp, 9 Johns., 163, *note*; Brandt v. Ogden, 1 Johns., 156, *note*.

A new trial, therefore, should be granted, with costs to abide the event.

New trial granted.

Cited in—2 Wend., 368; 20 N. Y., 330; 47 N. Y., 256; 68 N. Y., 352; 16 Hun, 92; 41 N. J. L., 541; 28 Mich., 317.

JACKSON, ex dem. MONTGOMERY ET AL.,
v.
CHAPIN ET AL., Trustees of the First Presbyterian Society in Rochester.

Judgment, not a Lien on a Mere Equity—Acknowledgment may be taken by the First Judge of a County.

A judgment is not a lien upon a mere equity, and such an interest cannot be sold on execution.

Thus, where R. conveyed lands to B., who held as R's trustee, but under an equitable obligation to convey to another; held, that a judgment against R. was not a lien on his interest and that it could not be sold on execution.

A first judge of a county, being a counselor, &c., of the Supreme Court, may take acknowledgments of deeds which may be registered in any county in the State, without a certificate of the county clerk, that he is a first judge.

Parol evidence that a grantee in a deed of land acknowledged, that though the deed had been offered to him, he refused to accept the delivery, is inadmissible.

EJECTMENT for lot No. 61 and 62, and the north half of lot No. 63, in the Village of Rochester, in the County of Monroe, tried at the Monroe Circuit, Apr. 16, 1825, before Walworth, *Circuit J.*; when a verdict was taken for the plaintiff, subject to the opinion of this court upon a case; which is sufficiently stated in the opinion of the court.

Mr. J. A. Collier, for the plaintiff.

Mr. P. S. Parker, for the defendants.

Curia, per WOODWORTH, *J.* It appeared in evidence that Robb, who was the common source of title, executed a deed to Montgomery, June 12, 1818, which was recorded Mar. 25, 1825. The defendant proved that Montgomery said the deed had been offered to him; but he refused to receive it, because Robb's wife was not a party. This being parol evidence, tending to destroy the operation of the conveyance, was inadmissible.

486*] *The plaintiff also gave in evidence a contract from Robb to Montgomery, for the sale of the premises in question, dated June 12, 1817. Apr. 15, 1818, Robb assigned the contract to Bemis, subject to Montgomery's article of agreement, which Bemis was to perform, if Montgomery made payment agreeably to his covenant. On the same day he executed a deed to Bemis, with a proviso, subject to the article of agreement to Montgomery. The deed was recorded Mar. 5, 1822, on the certificate of N. W. Howell, First Judge of Ontario, a counselor of this court, which was sufficient, he being, *ex officio*, a commissioner to perform certain duties of a judge of the Supreme Court. No certificate of the clerk of Ontario was necessary to warrant the registry. At the time of receiving the assignment, Bemis executed a writing under seal to Robb, stating that the transfers were made to him as security; that he was to account for all money received of Montgomery, or on a resale, after satisfying his responsibilities; and if Robb should pay off the notes indorsed by Bemis, he would reconvey. Subsequently, Bemis was fully exonerated. July 12, 1818, Robb wrote to Bemis, to assign over and deliver the bond (meaning the contract) to Strong and Clark, which he accordingly did, July 14, 1818.

Clark assigned his interest, Dec. 23, 1818, to Fellows and McNab; Strong, about the same time, transferred his interest to the same persons; and the contract was delivered, but he did not make an assignment in writing until Apr. 1825. Strong testified that he received the assignment, in payment of a debt from Robb, as so much cash.

From the facts stated, it appears that Bemis, after he was relieved from his responsibility as surety, held the deed and contract as a trustee for Robb, and was bound to comply with the directions of his *cestui que trust.* He accordingly assigned the contract to Strong and Clark. They became entitled to all benefit to be derived from it; and although Bemis did not convey the land at the same time he was bound to do so, on request; for I consider Strong and Clark as acquiring all Robb's right and interest, and entitled to receive a deed also from Bemis; and thereby placed in a situation *to convey to Montgomery, provided [*487 he made payment. It seems, however, the legal title remained in Bemis until Fellows and McNab applied for a deed, they having succeeded to the rights of Strong and Clark. The letter of Robb to Bemis, Mar. 5, 1820, seems to warrant the inference that he was willing that Bemis should convey to Fellows, on his receiving the balance due to him from Robb. The letter is not explicit, but this is manifestly the intent. Why Robb interfered at all, after he had parted with his interest to Strong and Clark, does not appear. Bemis received $20 of Fellows, as a balance due from Robb to him, and conveyed to Fellows and McNab. They afterwards, Aug. 5, 1822, conveyed to Montgomery. Thus the legal estate, and for aught I perceive, the equitable also, is vested in Montgomery, one of the lessors of the plaintiff.

The defendant's title is under a judgment of Hale against Robb, which was docketed Aug. 30, 1819; by execution upon which, the premises in question were sold to Wadhams. Before that judgment was entered, the title had been conveyed to Bemis, who passed it to the plaintiff. Bemis, it is true, stood in the relation of a trustee to Robb; but that fact made out an equity merely. The judgment, in consequence of this, did not become a lien at law. Robb had neither the legal title nor possession. The judgment could not attach upon a mere equity. The sale under it conferred no title. The right of Robb was not a subject of sale. Wadhams, who purchased, was informed of the trust and took subject to it. When he conveyed to Scofield, the land was held adversely by Montgomery. I do not, however, deem it necessary to examine all the questions raised in this cause, inasmuch as the lessors of the plaintiff, some or one of them, have a legal seisin of the estate derived from Bemis. He was seised by virtue of a eouveyance from Robb, executed before the entry of Hale's judgment, under which the defendants claim. The deed to Bemis was recorded before the sheriff's deed to Wadhams; so that, whether the judgment was a lien or not,

488*] becomes immaterial,*the plaintiff still being first in point of time. The plaintiff is entitled to judgment.

Judgment for the plaintiff.

Criticised—46 Barb., 161.
Cited in—9 Cow., 81, 112; 11 Wend., 99; 3 Bank. Reg., 92.

MORE v. TRUMPBOUR.

Agreement, that one making Advances on a Judgment should be Interested in the Judgment as Security, Valid.

T. had a judgment against M., and both agreed that P. should advance $100 to M. to pay to T. on the judgment; and that the judgment, which was for about $380, should stand as security for the $100 to P. The advance was accordingly made, and the money paid to T., M. not having repaid the money to P.; held, that T. might levy the sum upon the property of M.; and that, when this was done, he held it in trust for P.

If one levy more upon a judgment than is due, the defendant may recover back the excess in an action.

ASSUMPSIT, for work, goods, &c. (with the money counts), tried at the Delaware Circuit, Dec. 23, 1823, before Nelson, *Circuit J.*; when it appeared, among other things, that the plaintiff had confessed a judgment in this court, January Term, 1816, in favor of the defendant and one Eligh, on a bond conditioned for about $380. That Oct. 31, 1820, one Palen advanced to the plaintiff $100, which was paid by him to, and receipted by the defendant on this judgment, upon an agreement between all three of them, that Palen should be interested in the judgment to the amount of the $100, as his security; and papers passed between the parties, showing that this was their understanding. In pursuance of this agreement, the defendant had levied the judgment of the plaintiff's real estate, by execution, without giving him credit for the $100, which (with two other small items) the plaintiff sought to recover of the defendant in this action. He attempted to show, at the trial, that, before the sale of his property, he had paid Palen the $100; and though the balance of evidence was against him on this point, the jury found for him for his whole claim, the judge having charged them that, at all events, and whether the plaintiff had paid Palen or not, the defendant had no right to collect the $100.

Now, therefore, on a motion for a new trial, one question was, whether Palen could be secured in the manner above stated, so as to entitle the defendant to sell and collect the money for him.

Mr. J. Van Orden, for the motion.

Mr. J. Sudam, contra.

489*] **Curia*, per SUTHERLAND, *J.* I am of opinion that the judge erred in his charge to the jury, concerning the $100 payment, and that the verdict on that point is, also, against the weight of evidence. There is no doubt that Palen was to be interested in the judgment to the amount of $100, by way of security for that sum, advanced by him to More, to pay to Trumpbour. The memorandum sent by Trumpbour to Palen, dated Oct. 30, 1820, and the receipt of More indorsed upon it, are conclusive evidence that the advance by Palen was upon the express condition that the judgment should be his security, and that both Trumpbour and More fully assented to it.

If More had paid the $100 to Palen before the sale on the execution, then he is undoubtedly entitled to recover back that amount with interest from Trumpbour; because he has in fact received $100 more than the amount of the judgment. But he received that excess as the agent, and for the benefit of Palen, to whom he is accountable for it. The money advanced by Palen was, in reality, advanced to Trumpbour, and not to More; and did not, nor was it intended by the parties to operate as a payment upon the judgment, until More had settled the amount with Palen. The weight of evidence is very decidedly against the fact of payment to Palen. The testimony of Burhans is conclusive on the point.

New trial granted.

Cited in—15 Wend., 323.

GRAM AND STEWART v. CADWELL.

Partnership—Dissolution—Agreement that one Partner shall Continue and settle the Business—The other cannot Subsequently Release Debt Due Firm—Nor at any time, in Consideration of Debt Due from Himself Individually.

An agreement between partners, on dissolution, that one shall have the settlement of their affairs, he continuing the business, and assuming all debts and accounts outstanding and due, with which the firm had connection, until they should be settled; and that all the moneys contributed by the outgoing partner, except what had been drawn out by him, should be paid back by the other within a limited time, creates a separate interest in the remaining partner; and the subsequent release of a debt by the outgoing partner, to a creditor having notice of the agreement, is void.

One partner cannot release a debt due to the firm, even during the partnership, in consideration of a debt due from him individually; and if such appear to be the fact, on the face of the release, it is void.

Citations—2 Stark., 50; 4 Binn., 375; 2 Campb., 561; 16 Johns., 34; 11 Johns., 47.

ON demurrer to the replication. The declaration was in *indebitatus assumpsit*, for goods sold, &c. Plea, a release; *which was [*490 set forth on oyer, as follows: "Jamesville, 20th September, 1824. In consideration of two hundred and eighty dollars and thirty-one cents, cash received from sales of ashes in June last, belonging to Matthew Cadwell (the defendant), and of the consignment to me by him of a lot of cherry boards, supposed to be about thirty-five thousand feet, I do hereby release and discharge the said Matthew Cadwell from all debts and demands due by him to the late firm of N. B. Gram & Stewart, supposed to be about six hundred and fifty dollars; as witness my hand and seal. F. A. Stewart (seal), one of the late

NOTE.—*Partnership—Release by one partner after dissolution—When binding.*

An agreement by partners, on dissolution, that one shall settle up the affairs and pay to the outgoing partner a certain sum, operates as an assignment of the debts due the firm to the remaining partner. A subsequent release, by the outgoing partner, of a debt due the firm, the creditor having notice of the agreement, is void. In addition to the above case of Gram v. Cadwell, see Lunt v. Stevens, 24 Me., 534. See, also, Robbins v. Fuller, 24 N. Y., 572; Hilton v. Vanderbilt, 82 N. Y., 591; Bank of Montreal v. Page, 98 Ill., 109. But see Gordon v. Freeman, 11 Ill., 14.

firm of N. B. Gram & Stewart." The plaintiff replied, that at the time of the dissolution of Gram & Stewart, by certain articles under their hands and seals, dated and executed May 1, 1824, it was agreed that Gram should have the settlement of the affairs of the firm; that their connection should be dissolved; that the business of the firm should be settled as soon as practicable to write up the books; that as N. B. Gram was in business previous to the connection, he should continue the business and the settlement thereof, assuming all debts and accounts outstanding and due, with which the firm had connection, until they should be settled; that all moneys put in and applied by F. A. Stewart should be paid back to him by N. B. Gram, within ten days from that time, excepting what might have been drawn out by him, as should appear from his individual accounts, of which the defendant, before the execution of the release, had notice.

General demurrer and joinder.

Mr. D. Lord, Jr., in support of the demurrer. The instrument set forth in the replication is not an assignment of the debt to Gram. The replication does not call it so. The whole was a mere temporary arrangement; and if Gram had just cause of complaint against the defendant, for taking the release, his remedy was in equity, as in *Legh* v. *Legh*, 1 Bos. & P., 447. If Stewart had any interest, his release bars the action. (4 Binn., 375.) The defendant is a debtor paying his debt in full. The authority conferred by the agreement was revocable; and counter-
491*]manded, *quoad hoc* by the release. **Bristow* v. *Taylor*, 2 Stark., 50; 3 Chit. Com. Law, 224, S. C.; *Salmon* v. *Davis*, 4 Binn., 375.

Mr. C. Walker, contra. The agreement at the time of the dissolution, was an assignment of the demand in question to Gram; or, what is equivalent, a power to collect the debt, coupled with interest. 1 Cai. Cas., 15; *Raymond* v. *Squire*, 11 Johns., 47. For this there is a valuable consideration. The plaintiff agreed to dissolve on certain terms—the continuation of the business, and settlement of the concern was left to Gram, who agreed to repay to Stewart his capital and pay all debts. These features of the case distinguish it from the authorities cited in support of the demurrer. This court will protect the assignee of a chose in action. (1 Mass., 117; 1 Johns. Cas., 411; 3 Johns., 425; 16 *Id.*, 51: 19 *Id.*, 95.)

That there may be a resulting interest to Stewart, does not affect the question. It is like an assignment to trustees, to pay creditors. The assignor's residuary interest there would not warrant his interference. (5 Johns., 336; 20 *Id.*, 142, 442; 12 *Id.*, 343.)

This case is precisely similar to *Henderson* v. *Wild*, 2 Camph., 561.

But the release was for the consideration of Stewart's individual debt, and is inoperative for this reason. *Dob* v. *Halsey*, 16 Johns., 34.

Curia, per SAVAGE, *Ch. J.* In June following the dissolution, Stewart received $280.31, from sales of Cadwell's ashes; and subsequently a consignment of 35,000 feet of cherry boards; in consideration of which he, Sept. 20, executed the release. This can be of no avail, unless Stewart had a right to execute it; and that right depends on the question whether he had assigned his interest in the partnership concerns. It has been often decided that this court will protect the rights of assignees; and if the article of dissolution amounts to an assignment of Stewart's interest, there is an end of the question.

The cases referred to do not seem to settle this definitively. *Bristow* v. *Taylor*, 2 Stark., 50, proves that when *two partners ap-[***492** point an agent to collect their debts, he has no interest in the debts to be collected; and either partner may revoke his authority, and receive payment himself. Without expressing any opinion, as to the soundness of this decision, it is only necessary to say that it does not control this case if the instrument in question conveyed an interest in the debts of the firm.

The case of *Salmon* v. *Davis*, 4 Binn., 375, was this: the plaintiffs had been partners, and on a dissolution gave notice that all persons indebted should pay to Salmon, who was authorized to receive. Salmon released the debt due from the defendant; and on a suit by Brown, for his own benefit, the plaintiffs were nonsuited; and the court refused to set aside the nonsuit, saying that Salmon had a right to release half the demand at any rate, and that was sufficient to defeat the action. To make that case analogous the release in this case should have been executed by Gram.

In *Henderson* v. *Wild*, 2 Camph., 561, after dissolution of the plaintiff's partnership, and notice in the gazette intimating that all debts due the firm should be paid to Henderson only; the defendant produced receipts, by Smith, of payment by his own private account; and it was held no defense. Ld. Kenyon seemed to think that such a payment, during the partnership, would have been valid; but it certainly would not here. *Dob* v. *Halsey*, 16 Johns., 34.

Raymond v. *Squire*, 11 Johns., 47, shows that a chose in action may be assigned and transferred, without using those words. In that case the right of action consisted in a breach of the covenant of seisin in a deed. The plaintiff conveyed to St. John, and gave him a letter of attorney to collect of the defendant all such sums of money, &c., for the use of St. John. Of this the defendant had notice; and a release afterward, by the plaintiff, was held inoperative and void, as the power of attorney, conveying an interest to St. John, was irrevocable.

In the present case, the plaintiff, Gram, wanted no authorization from Stewart to receive debts, by way of conferring power upon him.

*During the existence of the part- [***493** nership, each partner may receive the debts due, and give discharges. So after the partnership is dissolved, without some contract or conveyance by one to the other. Had there been no special stipulations between the plaintiffs, each would have had the same rights and authority over the partnership debts. The article of dissolution was intended, then, to have some effect, varying the rights of the parties as they existed before the execution of the instrument. They agree that Stewart shall retire from the concern, and Gram shall continue the business; further, that Stewart shall receive his whole capital in ten days, and that Gram shall assume all debts and accounts outstanding until they are settled. This language in an instrument signed by both, amounts, in my judgment, to an assignment. And that is all the security which Gram has for the advance he makes to Stewart; for, supposing the business not to have produced anything, how else could Gram be made whole but by receiving all the debts? How shall he assume but by consent of Stewart? And having signed and sealed the instrument, in which Gram covenants to assume the debts, it is a virtual conveyance to Gram of his interest. That Stewart may have an interest in those debts after settlement, I think does not vary the question.

But if this were otherwise, another question arises—whether the release on its face does not show that this partnership debt was not paid by a set-off of Stewart's own individual liability. He does not appear to have received the ashes, or the boards, in payment of the partnership demand; but he was liable in Sept. to the defendant for money received in June, to the defendant's use, for ashes sold by him, probably on commission; and other property was also committed to him for sale on the defendant's account. If this was not a receipt of the debt from the defendant, but a payment of Stewart's sole debt, by releasing the partnership demand, then it was void, even if no assignment had ever been made.

But on the ground that the article of dissolution conveyed all Stewart's interest in the debts **494***] and accounts, until settlement, *I think it clear that the release was void. I think, therefore, the plaintiff is entitled to judgment.

Judgment for the plaintiff.

Distinguished—82 N. Y., 596.

Cited in—4 Wend., 585; 7 Wend., 328; 9 Wend., 121; 24 N. Y., 574; 41 N. Y., 380; 32 Barb., 304; 45 How. Pr., 200, 205; 35 Super., 411; 26 Hun, 224; 43 Wis., 218; 29 Am. Dec., 658 (8 N. H., 238); 28 Am. Rep., 541 (43 Wis., 213).

FRELIGH *v.* PLATT.

Sale of Church Pew—Interest Usufructuary Merely—Failure to Convey—Remedy—Promissory Notes Cannot be Avoided, Because of.

A promissory note given in consideration of a sale of pews followed with possession in the vendee, cannot be avoided on the ground that the vendor refuses to convey. The remedy is by compelling a performance.

An order of the *Chancellor* is not necessary, to warrant a sale, by a religious incorporation of pews in their church; the case not being within the 11th section of the Act Relative to Religious Societies, 2 R. L., 216. That respects absolute sales only.

The interest in a church pew is limited and usufructuary merely.

Citations—Act, April 5, 1813; 14 East, 486; 3 Campb., 38; 2 R. L., 216.

ON demurrer to the rejoinder, the case was argued by,

Mr. J. L. Wendell, in support of the demurrer, who cited 6 Taunt., 209; and,

Mr. S. A. Foot, contra, who cited 11 Johns., 50.

The pleadings are sufficiently stated in the opinion of the court, which was delivered by,

WOODWORTH, *J.* The plaintiff declared on two promissory notes, payable to certain persons or bearer, in two and three years; that the payees, on the day of the date, assigned over, and delivered the notes to the plaintiff.

The second plea alleges that the notes were made to the Trustees of the First Presbyterian Congregation in Plattsburgh, in consideration of the sale of three pews in the meeting house, to the defendant, his heirs and assigns, forever; that the Trustees would not and never had conveyed to the defendant, whereby he hath any title; but have wholly refused; and so the consideration of the notes has failed. The plea also alleges that the notes remained in the hands of the payees until after due.

The third plea alleges a sale of the pews, as the consideration of the notes; that the Trustees delivered a pretended conveyance, without having obtained from the *Chancellor* any order for the sale, pursuant to the 11th section of the Act to Provide for the Incorporation of Religious Societies, passed Apr. 5, 1813; and without having any right to sell and convey them, whereby the conveyance was void, and so the consideration has failed; and that the notes were negotiated after due.

*The replication gives a history of [*495 the proceedings relative to the finishing of the meeting house, and sale of the pews; and contains much irrelevant matter. I do not think it necessary to analyze it for the purpose of deciding this cause, as my opinion is founded on the invalidity of the pleas.

The rejoinder reiterates the facts alleged in the pleas, with a traverse, which it is not necessary to consider.

The plaintiff demurs specially to the rejoinder.

As to the second plea, it rests on the fact that the Trustees have refused to execute a conveyance. This cannot be considered a failure of the consideration; for the defendant has his remedy against them, to compel a performance. It is admitted by the pleadings that he has had the undisturbed occupation of the pews ever since the purchase.

In the ease of *Moggridge* v. *Jones*, 14 East, 486, the action was brought by the plaintiff as drawer, against the defendant as acceptor, of a bill of exchange. The latter set up, by way of defense, that there was no consideration; for that the money, for which the bill was drawn, was agreed to be paid in consideration of the plaintiff's executing a lease of certain premises. The defendant was let into possession, after which the plaintiff refused to execute the lease. It was held that this was no defense to the action, the defendant's remedy being on his agreement. Ld. Ellenborough, in 3 Campb., 38, S.C., observed the consideration has not completely failed; as the defendant has continued in possession of the premises. The consideration was good; being the sale, and possession under it.

It may be further observed that the plea is defective in not alleging that there was any agreement or promise by the trustees to convey; and, admitting there had been, the defendant must proceed against them on their contract.

The third plea is, in my opinion, clearly bad. It admits a sale and conveyance, but alleges that no order of the *Chancellor* was obtained. It is nowhere alleged that the Trustees, by their contract, agreed to obtain such order. *Non constat*, but that the defendant agreed to take such conveyance *as they offered, and [*496 actually delivered. By the plea, it appears that the contract was executed; for the notes were given in consideration of a sale and conveyance of the pews made at the time. We cannot say the defendant was unwilling to give his notes for such a sale and conveyance. No fraud, concealment or misrepresentation are alleged. The allegation that the Trustees sold without possessing any right to sell and convey, is an inference only from the fact that no order was obtained from the *Chancellor*.

By the 11th section of the Act respecting Religious Societies, 2 R. L., 216, it is declared that the *Chancellor* may make an order for the sale of any real estates belonging to the Corporation. This, evidently, relates to a case where the absolute right and title to lands belonging to them are to be sold. Cases of this kind may and do occur. It is often necessary to sell a portion of the real estate, for the advancement of the residue. Sometimes it becomes necessary to sell the church and lot, when a new church is built and located at a different place. In all these cases, the purchasers acquire the absolute inheritance; and to such only, in my opinion, does the statute apply. A sale of real estate *ex vi termini*, means an absolute transfer of the property. But the sale of pews in a church is not a sale of real estate within the meaning of the Act. By the grant of a pew, the grantee acquires a limited usufructuary right only. He may use it as a pew in a house of religious worship; but has not an unlimited, absolute right. He cannot use it lawfully for purposes incompatible with its nature. The right, too, is limited as to time. If the house be burnt, or destroyed by time, the right is gone. An order of the *Chancellor* was not necessary. As the pleas cannot, in my opinion, be supported, the plaintiff is entitled to judgment.

Judgment for the plaintiff.

Cited in—15 Wend., 220; 2 Edw., 612; 3 Edw., 159; 18 N. Y., 405; 4 Hun, 461; 8 Barb., 148; 17 Barb., 108; 41 Barb., 431; 5 How. Pr., 71; 3 Daly, 7; 7 Daly, 39; 2 Rob., 141; 4 Bradf., 9; 7 Leg. Obs., 364; 66 Pa., 422; 5 Am. Rep., 382 (66 Pa., 411).

497*] *FROST AND SMITH *v.* EVERETT.

Simultaneous Parol Agreement, Inadmissible to Vary Written Contract—Pleading.

A parol agreement to enlarge the time of the delivery of articles, promised in writing to be delivered on demand, made at the time of or before executing the written contract, though repeated immediately afterwards, is no defense to an action on the contract brought before the time to which the parol agreement related. Such parol agreement is void, though for a valuable consideration.

A valid agreement to enlarge the time of performing a contract, may be given in evidence under the general issue.

But if a plea or notice were necessary, the defendant is not confined to the precise day at which he states the agreement to enlarge to have been made.

Citations—1 Johns. Cas., 22; 3 Johns., 528; 1 Cow., 250; 1 Chit. Pl., 258, 472; 13 Johns., 56; 15 Johns., 231; 4 Taunt., 163.

ASSUMPSIT on an agreement in writing, dated June 20, 1820, by which the defendant, for value received, promised to pay the plaintiffs, on demand, 448 gallons of whisky; tried at the Onondaga Circuit, July, 1823, before Throop, *Circuit J.*

The defendant set up, as a defense, and proved, though the evidence was objected to, that before the written agreement was executed, he had become surety with the plaintiffs for a considerable debt due by them in N. Y., which had since, and after the assignment of the agreement, been collected of him; that when the agreement was given, he objected, on account of his being holden to pay debts for the plaintiffs in N. Y.; but they both replied that they would not dispose of the agreement or call for the whisky, till the N. Y. debts were settled by them. The defendant then signed the agreement, and after signing it, they repeated the declaration; but afterwards, being insolvent, assigned the agreement to T. H. & A. Leggett, who demanded the whisky before the defendant had paid the plaintiffs' notes. The defendant had given notice with the general issue, that he would prove the agreement to enlarge the time, but stated that it was made on the 1st November, 1820, without a *videlicet*. The judge directed the jury to find for the defendant, on the ground of the parol agreement; which they did accordingly.

Mr. J. A. Collier moved for a new trial. He cited 4 Johns., 450, and *note* to the new ed.; 8 Johns., 189; 1 Phil. Ev., 433, 437; 1 Cow., 249.

Mr. D. Cady, contra, cited 20 Johns., 361; 1 Johns. Cas., 22; 3 Johns., 528, 287; 1 Cow., 250; 1 Chit. Pl., 258, 472; 2 Str., 806; 10 Mod., 313; 1 Cow., 674; 13 Johns., 56; 15 Johns., 231; 4 Taunt., 163.

**Curia*, per SUTHERLAND, *J.* The [*498 agreement on the part of the plaintiffs, not to dispose of or call for the payment of the note on which this suit was brought until the N. Y. debts, for the payment of which the defendant had become security for the plaintiffs, were settled, was made at the time of giving the note, It was not a subsequent agreement to enlarge the time of payment. The defendant objected to giving the note, on the ground that he was holden for the N. Y. debts; the plaintiffs then declared that they would not dispose of or call for the payment of this note until the N. Y. debts were settled; upon which the defendant signed the note; and after he had signed and delivered it, the plaintiffs reiterated the declaration that they would not dispose of or call for payment of the note. This was all one transaction. The agreement to enlarge the time of payment was, in fact, made before the vote was given. The subsequent declarations of the plaintiff, made during the same conversation, was merely an acknowledgment that such was the agreement made between the parties. The evidence should have been rejected. (1 Johns. Cas., 22; 3 Johns., 528; 1 Cow., 250, and the cases there cited.)

The defendant was not confined to the precise day stated in the notice. The day was not material, provided it was subsequent to the original contract. (1 Chit. Pl., 258.)

Evidence of an enlargement of the time of performance is admissible under the general issue. It shows that the plaintiffs, at the time of suit brought, had no cause of action. (1 Chit. Pl., 472; 13 Johns., 56; 15 Johns., 231; 4 Taunt., 163; 1 Johns. Cas., 22; 3 Johns., 528.)

A new trial must be granted on the first ground.

New trial granted.

Cited in—8 N. Y., 505; 20 Barb., 64; 5 Duer, 206; 66 Pa., 422; 37 Am. Dec., 157 (3 Mer., 412).

499*] *MATSON v. BUCK.

Slander—Mitigation of Damages.

In slander, for charging the plaintiff with a specific offense, the defendant cannot show, in mitigation of damages, or otherwise, that the charge was generally reported to be true.

Citations—1 Johns., 46; 2 Cow., 815; 6 Mass., 514.

SLANDER, tried at the Cayuga Circuit, Sep. 9, 1824, before Throop, *Circuit J.*

The action was for saying of the plaintiff, as a Superintendant and Collector of the Erie canal, "he has cheated the State; he has taken a receipt for ten dollars, and paid but one dollar; he has taken a receipt for thirteen dollars, and paid but six dollars."

The plea was the general issue with notice of justification. Failing to make out this on the trial, the defendant's counsel proposed to show that the plaintiff's general reputation as to his official conduct was bad; and that it was generally reported and believed in the neighborhood that he had, in several instances, defrauded the State by taking receipts unjustly, for larger sums than he had paid out, and by employing the canal workmen upon his own private concerns, fraudulently, at the expense of the State.

On objection, this evidence was rejected by the judge, and the jury found for the plaintiff $500 damages.

Mr. S. M. Hopkins, for the defendant, now moved for a new trial; and cited 1 Johns., 46; Bull. *N. P.*, 298; 2 Cow., 815; 3 Mass., 546; Wheat. Selw., 977, and the cases there cited; 1 Binn., 90, *note;* Peake Ev., 287; 2 Campb., 251, 253, 254.

Mr. John Porter, contra, cited 6 Mass., 514.

Curia, per SAVAGE, *Ch. J.* After the defendant had failed in proving specific charges, relating to the plaintiff's official conduct, which the former had put upon the record, he seeks to do indirectly what would be the same thing. He could not prove the truth of his slanderous charges, yet he wishes to save himself from damages, by showing that other people had said and believed what had turned out to be false. No offer was made to attack the plaintiff's general 500*] *character. Such evidence would have been proper under the decisions of this court. (1 Johns., 46; 2 Cow., 815.) But, in this case, particular charges are sought to be sustained by unfounded reports. They must be considered so; because the defendant had failed in proving them, though he had attempted to do so.

This precise question arose in *Wolcott* v. *Hall*, 6 Mass., 514. Parsons, *Ch. J.*, after stating that evidence of general character ought to be received, adds: "But evidence of the plaintiff's general character was not offered, but only an attempt to blast his reputation by particular reports, which he might not have it in his power to silence, but by commencing this prosecution. And if such reports could be given in evidence, the subject of them, however innocent, instead of seeking redress from the laws, had better sink privately under the weight of unmerited calumny; lest, by attempting his justification, he should give notoriety to slanders which had before been circulated only in whispers."

There is no doubt, the admission of such testimony would operate as a total denial of justice. These unfounded reports are the basis of charges made by the defendant; and when the plaintiff prosecutes, in order that their truth may be proved, the same slanderous reports are offered, to reduce the plaintiff's verdict to a nominal sum, which is equal to a verdict for the defendant. Thus they answer the same purpose as a justification. This is altogether insufferable.

The judge decided correctly; and a new trial should be denied.

New trial denied.

Cited in—7 Cow., 629; 4 Wend., 663; 8 Wend., 580, 608; 10 Wend., 121; 13 How. Pr., 101; 80 Pa., 514; 24 Am. Dec., 101; 25 Am. Dec., 469 (6 N. H., 413); 21 Am. Rep., 117 (80 Pa., 411).

---

*M. WRIGHT v. WILLIAMS. [*501

Landlord and Tenant—Rent Accruing After Lessor's Death Goes to Heir or Devisee—Executor Cannot Distrain for—Avowry—Replevin—Amendment.

The executor of a lessor, who was seised of the demised premises in fee, cannot distrain for rent (though due on a lease for years) which accrued subsequently to the testator's death.

Such rent goes to the heir or devisee.

How the heir or devisee should avow.

Where an executor avows for rent as due subsequently to his testator's death, he cannot show, in proof, rent due before.

The defendant in replevin must set out strictly and truly, in his avowry, his authority for making the distress.

In replevin, where the defendant was defeated at the trial for a technical defect in his avowry, which was as executor, when it should have been as heir or devisee, he was allowed to amend, on payment of all costs.

Citations—Cro. Car., 207; Toll., 135; 1 R. L., 439; 1 Chit. Pl., 304; 1 Johns., 384; Bos. & P., 243; 3 Taunt., 81.

REPLEVIN, tried at the Washington Circuit, Jan. 5, 1824, before Walworth, *Circuit J.*, when a verdict was found for the plaintiff, on the opinion of the judge, that the defendant had avowed in a wrong character.

A motion for a new trial was now made by, *Mr. S. G. Huntington*, for the defendant.

Mr. S. Stevens, contra.

The facts are sufficiently stated in the opinion of the court which was delivered by,

WOODWORTH, *J.* The defendant first avows the taking, as executor of John Williams, for $195 rent, in arrear for 13 years, ending May 1, 1820; that the testator being lawfully possessed in fee, Oct. 27, 1794, one Samuel Wright, for 13 years before, and ending May 1, 1820, enjoyed the premises by virtue of a demise to him, made by John Williams, in his lifetime, under the yearly rent of £6.

The plaintiff pleads a number of matters in bar to the avowry; and takes issue to the country.

It is not necessary to notice particularly the other avowries; because, if the evidence introduced at the trial does not make out a good defense under this issue, the defendant cannot prevail. The evidence offered is applicable to this avowry only.

In the second avowry, the defendant alleges that he leased the premises to Samuel Wright, at the rate of £10, &c., and distrained for rent in arrear.

In the third, the defendant avows as in the first, except stating the yearly rent to be £4 4s.

502*] *The fourth avowry does not vary materially from the second.

At the trial, the defendant gave in evidence, a lease in fee from John Williams to Samuel Wright, dated Oct. 27, 1794, reserving £6 rent annually. It appeared that the lessor died in July, 1806. This lease is not correctly described in the third and fourth avowries. No lease was ever executed by the defendant; and it does not appear that there ever was a lease reserving £4 4s. for annual rent.

The defendant was bound to show a legal authority for making the distress. He claimed a right to distrain, as executor, for thirteen years of rent, which accrued next preceding May 1, 1820. He alleges no right in any other character. All the rent, for which the distress was made, accrued subsequent to the death of the testator. It is well settled that an executor cannot distrain for rent accruing after the death of the testator, who was seised in fee, because it goes to the heir. (Cro. Car., 207; Toll., 135.) Our Statute, 1 R. L., 439, only authorizes executors to distrain for rent due at the death of the testator, and when he might have distrained before his death. If the defendant is heir or devisee of John Williams, he ought to have avowed as such, stating the lease from the ancestor to the tenant, the death of the ancestor, and the descent or devise of the premises, or the rent to the defendant. But *non constat*, from the pleadings that he is either. He rests his claim on his right as executor. The plaintiff went to trial to contest his right on that ground. The admission, at the trial, that the defendant was heir at law and devisee, is insufficient; for that fact was not admitted, or put in issue by the pleadings. The judge, therefore, decided correctly, that under the avowry as executor, the defendant could not show rent due previous to the death of the testator; nor was he entitled to distrain for rent accruing subsequently. The rule is, that a defendant must set out strictly and truly in his avowry, his authority for making the distress. (1 Chit. Pl., 304; 1 Johns., 384.)

As, however, the point upon which the defendant failed, was purely technical, and in

503*] consequence of erroneous *pleading, this is a proper case for the interference of the court, on terms, to the end that the avowries may be amended, if the defendant shall so elect.

I am of opinion that the verdict be set aside on payment of all costs accrued subsequent to the issues joined; and that the defendant have leave to amend his avowries on payment of costs. This course is in favor of the justice of the case, and is warranted by the practice of the court in another cause not reported.(a) A similar practice has obtained in England, as appears from Bos. & P., 243, and 3 Taunt., 81.

Rule accordingly.

Cited in—6 Hill, 284, 290.

(a) And *vide* Jackson v. Bailey, *ante*, 265, S. P.

GIBBS v. DEWEY.

Slander—Charge of Embracery is Slanderous—Delivery of Paper to Jury by Witness—Pleading—Arrest of Judgment.

To say of a man who was a witness, he handed papers to a juror, to influence the jury or to influence and bribe the jury, is slanderous, as amounting to a charge of embracery.

Embracery is an attempt by either party, or stranger, to corrupt or influence a jury, or to incline them to favor one side by gifts or promises, threats or persuasions, or by instructing them in the cause, or any other way, except by opening and enforcing the evidence by counsel at the trial, whether the jurors give a verdict or not, and whether the verdict be true or false.

On a general verdict for the plaintiff, if one count be bad, judgment will be arrested.

To render words actionable, they need not be stated with the same certainty as in an indictment. If the words stated import a crime in their natural and ordinary signification, it is enough.

Any attempt by a witness to influence a jury in any other way than by the open delivery of his testimony, is improper and, in judgment of law, corrupt.

A witness has no right to deliver a paper to the jury, without the direction of the court.

Citations—3 Bac. Abr., 785; 1 Hawk. P. C., ch. 85; Co. Litt., 369; 1 R. L., 174, 334; 4 Bl. Com., 140; 6 T. R., 691; 1 Cai., 347; 3 Cow., 231; 8 Johns., 74; 13 Johns., 48.

IN slander, the plaintiff declared, in the first count, that he was a witness for the prosecution upon a certain trial of an indictment against the defendant, who was acquitted; and that the defendant said of him: "I should have got clear of the charge without the jury's going out of the box, if old Gibbs (the plaintiff) had not handed papers to John Wilson (one of the jurors) to influence the jury; and he run away, or the judge would have shut him in prison, where he could not have got out in one week." In the 2d count the words were thus laid: "Gibbs handed papers to influence or bribe the jury." In the 5th: "He (the plaintiff) handed papers to influence or bribe the jury." In the 11th: "He (the plaintiff) *handed papers to influence or [*504 bribe the jury to bring him (the defendant) in guilty." In the 12th: "Gibbs handed papers to influence or bribe the jury."

A general verdict being for the plaintiff on these and other counts, confessedly g d, a motion was now made in arrest of judgment, on the ground that the words in the 1st count do not import any crime; and that those in the 3d, 5th, 11th and 12th counts do not positively impute any crime, but are in the disjunctive; "to influence or bribe the jury;" and, for ought that appears, the plaintiff might innocently have influenced the jury; that the charge of handing papers, as in the 11th and 12th counts, does not amount to the imputation of a crime. It is neither a charge of bribery nor of corrupt influence over, or a corrupt attempt to influence the jury.

Mr. S. Sherwood, for the defendant, cited 3 Bac. Abr., 384; Co. Litt., 369 *a*; 4 Bl. Com., 140; 1 Hawk. P. C., 548, ch. 85, sec. 1; 1 R. L., 334, sec. 26; 6 T. R., 691; 6 East, 427; 1 Cai., 347.

NOTE.—*Slander—What amounts to.* See, generally, Moody v. Baker, *ante*, p. 351, *note*, *and other notes there cited.*

Mr. L. Monson, contra, cited Starkie on Slander, 266; 4 Bl. Com., 140; 1 R. L., 174; Co. Litt., 369; Jac. L. Dict., 369; 1 Saund., 301, 302; 2 East, 14, 16; 5 Day, 272–274; 3 *Id.*, 309; 1 Russell, Crimes, 277; Hawk. P. C., ch. 85, sec. 2; 7 Johns., 360; 12 *Id.*, 240; 13 *Id.*, 48.

Curia, per SUTHERLAND, *J.* Embracery is defined to be an attempt by either party, or a stranger, to corrupt or influence a jury, or to incline them to favor one side by gifts or promises, threats or persuasions, or by instructing them in the cause, or any other way, except by opening and enforcing the evidence by counsel at the trial, whether the jurors give a verdict or not, and whether the verdict be true or false. (3 Bac. Abr., 785; 1 Hawk. P. C., ch. 85; Co. Litt., 369.) And it is an offense at common law, as well as by statute (*Id.*, 1 R. L., 174, 334; 4 Bl. Com., 140), and punishable by fine and imprisonment.

The *colloquium* shows that the plaintiff was a witness upon the trial of an indictment
505*] against the defendant; and that *the words alleged to have been spoken by the defendant were spoken of the plaintiff in relation to his conduct as a witness upon that trial.

The jury found a general verdict for the plaintiff; and if any of the counts are bad, the motion in arrest of judgment must prevail. (6 T. R., 691; 1 Cai., 347; 3 Cow., 231.)

It is not necessary, in order to render words actionable, that there should be the same certainty in stating the crime imputed as in an indictment for the crime. If the words spoken, in their natural and ordinary signification, import a criminal charge, it is sufficient to render them actionable. (8 Johns., 74; 13 *Id.*, 48.)

The substance of the first count is that the defendant charged the plaintiff with having handed papers to one of the jurors (on the trial alluded to in the *colloquium*) to influence the jury: and that he ran away, or the judge would have put him in prison for it. It is objected to this count that the attempt to influence the jury is not alleged to have been corrupt; and does not, therefore, amount to a crime punishable by indictment. Any attempt by a witness to influence a jury, in any other way than by the open delivery of his testimony, is improper; and, in judgment of law, corrupt. A witness has no right to deliver any paper to the jury, without the direction of the court. The act is as criminal in a witness as it would be in a bystander. There can be no doubt of the intention of the defendant to charge the plaintiff with the commission of a criminal act; and the terms used by him necessarily import a charge of that character.

The 3d, 5th, 11th and 12th counts are objected to, on the ground that they do not positively impute to the plaintiff the commission of any offense — the charge being that the plaintiff handed papers to the jury to influence or bribe them. It is evident that these terms were intended to convey the same idea. The connection shows it. To influence a jury, by handing them papers, and to bribe them, by handing them papers, are synonymous expressions, when applied to an individual who had no right to interfere with the jury at all.
506*] *The expression that a man bribed a jury by handing them papers, if standing alone, would not be understood as conveying a charge of bribery, in its ordinary signification; but simply as imputing to him the offense of improperly attempting to influence them, through the medium of the papers thus handed to them. It is, therefore, as here used, a species of tautology—a mere repetition, in terms perhaps somewhat stronger, of the previous charge. There is, then, no uncertainty in the charge contained in these counts; and the words are clearly actionable, for the reasons already assigned in relation to the 1st count. The motion in arrest must be denied.

Motion denied.

Cited in—3 Hill, 23; 3 Den., 54; 4 Barb., 511.

FRANCHOT *v.* LEACH.

Tender of Deed—When Unnecessary—Agreement as to Place—Fraud.

Where no place is mentioned for the delivery of the deed, in articles for the sale of land, though the vendor is bound to seek the vendee and tender a deed, yet the parties may, by parol, agree on a place of performance, after the execution of the articles; or the vendee may appoint a place, and if the vendor tender at the place, it is well.

Semb. if the vendee tell the vendor, before the day, that he will not perform, no tender is necessary.

Fraud, as to the consideration, cannot be set up to avoid an agreement under seal; but only fraud as to the execution.

Citations—13 Johns., 430; 2 Johns., 177.

COVENANT, tried at the Chenango Circuit, June 22, 1825, before Nelson, *Circuit J.*

The action was on an agreement dated Apr. 5, 1824, by which the plaintiff agreed to sell to the defendant a lot of land for $300; and to execute a deed by July 1 then next; in consideration whereof, the defendant agreed then to pay $100, and give a bond and mortgage for the balance. It was in evidence at the trial, that immediately, and within a few minutes after the execution of this agreement, the parties agreed by parol that the office of Birdsall &. Buttolph, in Norwich, Chenango Co., should be the place of performance; the plaintiff living in the town of Butternuts, Otsego Co., and the defendant in New Berlin, Chenango Co. In the latter part of June, 1824, the defendant was in Norwich, when the plaintiff's attorney, Mr. Buttolph, saw him, and told him that the plaintiff would attend July 1, to perform the agreement. The defendant replied, it would be of no use, for he should not fulfill; alleging that there was not water on the lot sufficient *for a dis- [*507
tillery. The plaintiff attended at the place, and on the day appointed, with a deed according to the parol agreement; but the defendant did not attend. A few days after the plaintiff's attorney offered the deed to the defendant, which he refused to receive; but blamed one Cook, for not attending to inform the plaintiff of the reason why he would not fulfill the agreement. The defendant took pos-

NOTE.—*Deed—Fraud as to consideration, does not avoid at law—Fraud as to execution, does avoid.* See Jackson v. Hills, 8 Cow., 290, *note*; Vrooman v. Phelps, 2 Johns., 177, *note*.

session of the lot soon after the agreement, and kept possession to the time of trial by Cook, his tenant.

The declaration set forth the parol agreement as to the place of delivery, and averred the attendance of the plaintiff accordingly; and that the defendant did not attend.

The evidence of this was objected to, but admitted by the judge. The defendant then offered to prove that he purchased the lot for the purposes of distilling and manufacturing; which the plaintiff knew, and represented that the stream of water, running through the lot, was sufficient for those purposes, well knowing, at the same time, the contrary.

The judge rejected this evidence; and the jury, under his direction, found for the plaintiff, the consideration money and interest.

Mr. J. Clapp, for the defendant, now moved for a new trial. He cited 1 Chit. Pl., 310; 1 Saund., 320; Co. Litt., 211 *a*; 2 Com. Dig., 452; Litt., sec. 340; Co. Litt., 210 *b*; 1 Bac. Abr., 429, old ed.; Poth. Obl., No. 513, p. 356, Ev. ed.; Chipm. Cont., 24, 28; 3 Johns. Cas., 250; 8 Johns., 476; 4 Cow., 452; 1 Phil. Ev., 424; 1 Cow., 250; 8 Johns., 192; 4 *Id.*, 288; 3 Barn. & Cress., 205; 1 Johns. Ch., 282; 5 Ves., 736; 13 *Id.*, 228; 1 Johns. Ch., 370; 1 Johns. Cas., 22; 3 Johns., 528; 1 Johns. Ch., 425, 343; 2 *Id.*, 554; 1 R. L., 78; 14 Johns., 32; 15 Johns., 204; 17 *Id.*, 437; Rob. Fraud. Conv., 522; 4 Johns., 412; 13 *Id.*, 327, 395; 4 Mass., 488; 1 Salk., 211; 2 Ld. Raym., 1118; 1 Sid., 146; 1 Ves., 127; 3 Atk., 383; 6 Mod., 34; 3 Johns., 71; 6 *Id.*, 182; and *notes* to Co. Litt., 384 *a*.

Mr. J. A. Collier, contra.

508*] **Curia* per SAVAGE, *Ch. J.* The delivery of the deed was, no doubt, a condition precedent to the payment of the money; and but for the parol agreement, the plaintiff must have sought the defendant, and offered him the deed. There can be no doubt that a written contract cannot be contradicted by parol; and that all which passes between parties previous to a writing is merged in the writing. But in this agreement no place was mentioned for the performance of it; and surely it was competent for the defendant, at any time after the execution of the agreement, to designate the place where it should be done. Besides, it is questionable whether any offer of a deed was necessary, as the defendant had told the plaintiff's agent that it was unnecessary; for he, the defendant should not perform the agreement. The defense offered was properly excluded. The case of *Dorr* v. *Munsell*, 13 Johns., 430, is in point. There the plea was, that the plaintiff obtained the bond fraudulently, by falsely representing himself as the inventor and patentee of an improvement, which it was averred was untrue. The court decide the plea is bad and cite 2 Johns., 177, where it is decided that a fraudulent representation of the quality and value of the thing sold, forms no defense to a suit on a specialty. The fraud which avoids a deed, is not a fraudulent representation as to the consideration, but a fraud relating to the execution of it—as a fraudulent misreading or obtaining such an instrument as the obligor did not intend to give.

The motion for a new trial must be denied.

New trial denied.

Cited in—8 Cow., 293; 9 Cow., 41; 8 Wend., 618; 9 Wend., 79; 17 Wend., 379; 21 Wend., 233, 638; 23 Wend., 70; 6 N. Y., 596; 44 N. Y., 623; 50 N. Y., 43; 55 N. Y., 484; 61 N. Y., 370 (19 Am. Rep., 290); 64 N. Y., 394; 69 N. Y., 293; 6 Barb., 151; 12 Barb., 370; 17 Barb., 265; 27 Barb., 77; 34 Barb., 387; 5 How. Pr., 45; 42 How. Pr., 60; 4 Abb. Pr., 470; 11 Abb. N. S., 495; 2 Hall, 447; 48 Super., 258; 1 E. D. S., 308; 1 Hilt., 289; 79 Ill., 97; 33 Mich., 327; 102 U. S., 571; 24 Am. Dec., 127; 44 Am. Dec., 544 (2 Eng., Ark., 153); 50 Am. Dec., 234 (10 Ark., 9).

---

*CHAMPION, Survivor of STORRS, [***509**

v.

WHITE.

Covenants, to Convey and Pay for Land, are Independent—Action for Purchase Money—Defendant Cannot show that Vendor owned only Part of the Land—Parol Evidence Inadmissible.

Where, in articles for the sale of land, the vendee covenanted to pay one sixth of the purchase money in one year and the residue in five equal annual installments; and the vendors covenanted, that on payment of the sums of money, and fulfillment of the agreements to be performed by the vendee, they would convey, &c.; held, that these covenants were independent.

The description of the land in the articles was, "all that certain piece or parcel of land in H., being all that part of lot 44, owned by them (the vendor) that lies south of the Watertown road, bounded easterly, southerly and westerly by the lines of the lot, as surveyed and established by R. M." Held, that the words "owned by them," were mere words of description, not of restriction; and would not confine the vendee to what the vendors owned, if this was less than the lines included; but he had a right to the whole according to the lines mentioned.

A covenant cannot be avoided in a court of law, on the ground of misrepresentation as to the consideration.

The construction of a written agreement to convey certain described land, cannot be varied by showing the intent of the parties, by parol.

Where the covenants, in articles to convey and pay for land, are independent, the vendee cannot show, in an action for the purchase money, that the vendor owned only a part of the land, the title to which he covenanted to convey.

Citations—4 Cow., 207; 5 Johns., 181; 2 Johns., 15, 130; 2 Burr., 1089; Cro. Eliz., 113; 15 East, 57.

COVENANT, tried at the Jefferson Circuit, June 21, 1825, before Williams, *Circuit J.* The cause came here, on a motion for a new trial upon a bill of exceptions. The verdict was for the plaintiff.

Mr. J. Butterfield, for the defendant.

Mr. M. Sterling, contra.

The facts are sufficiently detailed in the opinion of the court, which was delivered by,

WOODWORTH, J. The plaintiff declared on a covenant, that on payment of the sums of money, and fulfillment of the agreements to be performed by the defendant, he, with Storrs, would convey a title in fee simple to all that piece or parcel of land situated in the town of Hounsfield, &c., being all that part of lot 44, owned by them, that lay south of the Watertown road, bounded easterly, westerly and southerly, by the lines of the lot, and estimated to contain about 300 acres. The defendant covenanted to pay $5 for every acre of the premises—one sixth at the expiration of one year, and the residue in five equal annual installments. The articles were dated Nov. 25, 1816.

NOTE.—*Deed—Fraud as to consideration, does not avoid at law—Fraud as to execution, does avoid.* See Jackson v. Hills, 8 Cow., 290, *note*; Vrooman v. Phelps, 2 Johns., 177, *note.*

The pleas were, 1. *Non est factum.* 2. That the articles were obtained by fraud.

It appeared at the trial, that at the time of 510*] making the contract, *the vendors were not owners of all the lot on the south side of the road, about 22 acres having been previously conveyed. The plaintiff contended, that by the terms of the agreement, this parcel was excepted. Upon the supposition that this construction is correct, the question of fraud arises. In support of that issue, the defendant proved that the agent of the vendors, who made the contract, at that time affirmed and represented to the defendant that the vendors did own all the lot on the south side of the road; and that it was intended the contract should cover the whole. The agent, however, testified that he then believed the representation to be true. It further appeared that the part actually owned by the vendors was much less valuable than it would have been had it bounded on the road. By this proof, no fraud was established; for no act was done intentionally wrong; but there was an evident mistake, and erroneous representation of a material fact; for which, however, relief cannot be had in a court of law. The *gravamen* falls peculiarly within equity jurisdiction. Admitting that this related to the execution of the instrument, or the defendant's capacity to execute, and so could be noticed at all by us; (*a*) yet it is a well settled rule, that in a court of law, to avoid an instrument, the fraud must be clearly established. It is only in such cases that a court of equity and a court of law have concurrent jurisdiction. In a court of equity, relief may be had on an instrument unduly obtained, when a court of law could not enter into the question. This doctrine is examined and considered in *Jackson* v. *King*, 4 Cow., 207, and the cases there cited. The defendant cannot succeed on this issue.

The next question that arises is, whether the covenants are not independent; and if so, whether it is competent for the defendant, in this action, to object that the vendors were not seised of a part of the land they covenanted to convey.

Where the covenants are dependent, the conveyance of the land, and the payment of the money must be simultaneous. In this case, it appears to me they were mutual and independ-511*] ent. *The covenant is not, that on payment of the whole consideration money on a particular day, the vendors shall convey, but on the fulfillment of the agreements as specified. The money was payable by installments at different periods, which shows the order or precedency in which the acts are to be done. The decision was placed on this ground in *West* v. *Emmons*, 5 Johns., 181. By the terms of such a contract, it is evident the defendant was willing to part with his money, and rely on the vendor's covenant to compel the execution of a conveyance. The case of *Robb* v. *Montgomery*, 20 Johns., 15, is very analogous to the present. The defendant covenanted to pay $2,500 by installments, and in consideration of the payments being punctually made, at the times and in the manner specified, the plaintiff bound himself to convey. Spencer, *Ch. J.*, observed that the payments were to be made without reference to the conveyance, and the conveyance was not to be given until all the payments were made; that it was impossible for language to render covenants more independent than these. I do not perceive any substantial difference between the two cases. The same rule of construction ought to be applied. The conveyance and payments were not intended to be simultaneous acts, but the former were to precede the latter; and in such cases it is no excuse for non-payment, that there is not a capacity to convey a good title. The ease of *Parker* v. *Parmele*, 20 Johns., 130, is clearly distinguishable. The defendant agreed to pay the whole consideration money on a particular day, and the plaintiff covenanted, when performed, to execute a deed. The court held the covenants to be dependent—that the acts were to be concurrent—and that the fair intent and good sense of the contract was, that the money was not to be paid until the deed was ready to be delivered.

My conclusion is, that the defendant is liable in this action, although it be conceded that the plaintiff cannot give a good title to all that part of the lot on the south side of the Watertown road.

If, however, I am mistaken on this point, then the question arises as to the quantity of land covenanted to be conveyed. *This [*512 question is not free from difficulty. Parol evidence cannot be received to prove the intent, so as to vary the legal construction arising from the words used in the covenant. If there has been manifest mistake, it belongs to a court of equity to afford relief. Omitting the words "owned by them," the boundaries are definite and certain. They clearly include all the land on the south side of the road. The description is, "bounded easterly, southerly and westerly, by the lines of said lot, as surveyed and established by Robert M'Dowell." If a part of the lot only is bounded on the westerly line, it will not satisfy the description. If all the lot on the south side is to be conveyed, the western boundary, in the whole extent, must be on the west line. In order to support the construction contended for by the plaintiff, it must appear that the words "owned by them" are words of limitation and restriction; otherwise they cannot control the residue of the description, which is perfectly intelligible. The question is, are they to be considered as words of additional description? If they are, they will not vitiate anything sufficiently described before. In *Goodtitle* v. *Paul*, 2 Burr., 1089, the words of the devise were, "my farm at Bovington, in the tenure of John Smith." These latter words were intended to render the description more perfect. If John Smith had been in possession, effect would be given to the additional description; but as the farm was not in possession of Smith, the description was rejected as repugnant. So, in this case, it seems to me that the words "owned by them" are merely a further description of the thing to be conveyed. I consider the agreement as saying, the vendors will convey a parcel of land accurately bounded; and that their title is co-extensive with, and includes the premises covenanted to be conveyed. If this be correct, then the words are additional description only; and do not limit the defendant's right to claim the portion only to which the vendors had title.

(*a*) *Vide* the next preceding case.

In *Goodtitle* v. *Paul*, the description afforded the same ground of argument as here, but the words were considered as additional description merely. The same principle is recognized in Cro. Eliz., 113, and 11 East, 57.

513*] *In order to construe these words as restricting the quantity, it would be necessary to supply words which are not in the covenant. Instead of "all that parcel of land," we must substitute the words "so much of the lot as the plaintiff's title covers." I think this would be a departure from the intention of the parties, as derived from the agreement itself. The estimated quantity of land was conjectural. Neither party knew the number of acres. It was provided that a further survey be made. Whether the contents were more or less than 300 acres, cannot affect the question. The survey, to ascertain the number of acres, was not necessary to give the plaintiff a right of action. It was only essential to ascertain with accuracy the amount of damages.

The result of my opinion is, that the motion for a new trial be denied, on the ground that the covenants were independent. The defendant failed altogether on the issue of fraud.

New trial denied.

Cited in—8 Cow., 293; 8 Wend., 618; 1 N. Y., 574; 33 N. Y., 342; 5 Barb., 165; 7 Daly, 223; 2 Blatchf., 66; 43 Wis., 34; 37 Am. Dec., 165, 167; 28 Am. Rep., 533 (43 Wis., 23).

FOX v. VANDERBECK.

Slander—Charge of Perjury—Pleading—Words must be Substantially as Laid.

Where one interrupted another, who was giving his testimony, as a witness before a justice; required the justice to be particular in keeping minutes of the testimony; afterwards demanded the minutes of the justice, and said he wanted them to prosecute the witness for perjury; and on another occasion said the witness swore false, or to what was not true; and that he thought he should prosecute him for perjury; held, that these words were actionable as imputing the crime of perjury.

The witness brought an action for the above words; and declared in his first count, that the defendant said "you are perjured; and I will put you into the State Prison;" in the second, "he has sworn false, and perjured himself; and I will put him into the State Prison;" in another, "he swore to an absolute falsehood, and has perjured himself;" held, that the proof did not support either of these counts.

In slander, the words must be proved as laid, and it is not sufficient to prove equivalent words. Words to the same effect are not the same words.

The plaintiff need not prove all the words on the record, but he must prove so much of them as will be sufficient to sustain his cause of action.

The words in which the slander is conveyed, must be stated in the declaration and substantially proved.

Citations—9 East, 93; 3 Cow., 231; 8 Johns., 74; 2 Phil. Ev., 97; 2 East, 434, 438; Bull. *N. P.*, 5; 4 T. R., 218; 8 T. R., 150; 3 Maule & S., 110; 8 Johns., 75.

SLANDER, tried at the Cayuga Circuit, Sept. 9, 1824, before Throop, *Circuit J.*

On the trial, the plaintiff abandoned all the parts of his declaration, except those in which the defendant was alleged to have charged him with having committed perjury.

The words charged in the first count were, "you are perjured, *and I will put you [*514 into the State Prison;" in the second, "he has sworn false, and perjured himself, and I will put him into the State Prison;" in the fourth, "he swore to an absolute falsehood, and he has perjured himself."

The only proof of speaking the words was by E. Branch, a witness for the plaintiff, who testified that he was present at an examination for felony, before G. Morse, Esq., a justice, on which the plaintiff was sworn as a witness. That while testifying, the defendant interrupted and contradicted him, and told him it was not so. That the defendant was particular in requiring Morse to keep the minutes of the plaintiff's testimony, and demanded them afterwards. He thought the plaintiff said, he wanted them to prosecute for perjury; that it carried that idea to him. The witness afterwards had a conversation with the defendant, relative to the plaintiff's testimony, in which, he thought, the defendant told him, and that he thought he should prosecute the plaintiff for perjury.

Morse, the justice, was sworn for the plaintiff, and testified that the defendant called on him for his minutes, and said he wanted them to go to some lawyer, to prosecute the plaintiff.

The defendant moved for a nonsuit, on the ground that the declaration of the defendant, that he thought he should commence a suit for perjury, against the plaintiff, did not support the charge of perjury, or, at all events, that it did not support the charge as laid in the declaration. The judge overruled the motion and charged the jury, that if they were satisfied that the defendant said that he should commence a suit against the plaintiff for perjury, it amounted to a charge of perjury, and would entitle the plaintiff to recover. To this opinion and charge the defendant excepted. Verdict for the plaintiff.

A motion was now made, in behalf of the defendant, for a new trial.

Mr. F. G. Jewett, in support of the motion, cited Cro. Eliz., 279; 7 Taunt., 431; 3 Cow., 231; 1 Bulst., 40; Hob., *177; 4 Rep., [*515 15 *a*, to show that the words proved were not actionable; and to show that if actionable, they did not support the declaration, he cited 3 Maule & S., 110; 2 East, 434; 8 T. R., 150; 4 *Id.*, 217.

Mr. J. Hussey, contra, cited 8 Johns., 75.

Several points were also made by the defendant's counsel, which did not appear upon the bill of exceptions to have arisen at the trial.

Curia, per SUTHERLAND, *J.* The words proved are actionable. They are calculated to convey to the mind of an ordinary hearer, the imputation upon the plaintiff of the crime of perjury. In *Roberts* v. *Camden*, 9 East, 93, the words were, "he is under a charge of prosecution for perjury. G. Williams had the Atty-Gen.'s directions to prosecute for perjury." Upon a motion in arrest of judgment, these words were held to amount to a charge of perjury; that being the plain and popular sense in which the hearers would naturally understand them. All the cases are there considered. And *vide Goodrich* v. *Wolcott*, 3 Cow., 231, and the cases there cited; and *Miller* v. *Miller*, 8 Johns., 74.

NOTE.—*Slander—Charge of perjury—Words, charging an indictable offense, are actionable* per se. See Hopkins v. Beedle, 1 Cai., 347, *note*; Martin v. Stilwell, 13 Johns., 275, *note*. See, generally, Moody v. Baker, *ante*, p. 351, *note, and other notes there cited.*

But the words, as proved, do not support the declaration. They must be proved substantially as stated. All the words need not be proved; but it is enough to prove some material part of them. The rule is correctly stated in 2 Phil. Ev., 97: "The words which are proved, must be proved as laid; and it will not be sufficient to prove equivalent words of slander. Words to the same effect are not the same words. The plaintiff need not prove all the words on the record; yet he must prove so much of them as will be sufficient to sustain his cause of action." (2 East, 434. 438; Bull. *N. P.*, 5; 4 T. R., 218; 8 T. R., 150.) The words in which the slander was conveyed, must be stated in the declaration; and it must be substantially proved. *Cook* v. *Cox*, 3 Maule & S., 110. In *Miller* v. *Miller*, 8 Johns., 75, the court say, it is now sufficient to prove the substance of the word; **516***] and the sense as well as manner *must be the same. There the substantial words charged to have been spoken were proved, though not all the words charged.

The other points made by the defendant's counsel do not properly arise in this case. This is a bill of exceptions, simply presenting the question, whether the judge erred in refusing to nonsuit the plaintiff, and in his charge to the jury. I am of opinion that he did err in these respects, and that a new trial should be granted.

New trial granted.

Cited in—1 Wend., 509; 8 Wend., 577; 11 Wend., 39; 15 Wend., 329; 3 Barb., 633; 51 Barb., 394; Abb. Adm., 543; 55 Mo., 358; 24 Am. Dec., 98.

LOBDELL *v.* HOPKINS.

Note Payable in Specific Articles—Time and Place—Demand.

A note payable in specific articles, without mentioning day or place, is, in law, payable on demand; and a special demand is necessary.

A note thus payable in farm produce, should be demanded at the farm of the debtor.

A note thus payable in merchandise, or manufactures, should be demanded at the store of the merchant or the shop of the manufacturer.

Citations—1 Root, 209; 5 T. R., 409; 6 Mass., 310; Tayl. N. C., 149; Chipm. Tr., 49, 28, 29.

ON *certiorari*, from the Justices' Court of the City of Albany. Lobdell sued Hopkins in the court below, on the following instrument in writing, signed by the defendant: "Moscow, 29th August, 1817. I certify that on the settlement made with Amos H. Arnold, Noble Lobdell and Caleb Lobdell, on a contract with them, or some of them, for a job of clearing, there remained a balance due said Caleb Lobdell, of thirty-five dollars $\frac{95}{100}$, payable in farm produce, at the market price, according to said contract." The defendant, at the trial, admitted the execution of this paper; and the plaintiff admitted that the defendant at the time of the execution was a resident of Moscow, in Livingston Co.; and that he resided there until June, 1822, and owned a farm there. The court below gave judgment for the defendant.

The main question now raised was, whether it was necessary actually to demand the farm produce mentioned in the contract of the defendant, before bringing the action below; and,

Mr. J. T. B. Van Vechten, for the plaintiff in error, contended that it was not; and he cited 5 Johns., 119; 7 Johns., 461.

Mr. S. M. Hopkins, contra. It is admitted that if a man engage to deliver a horse, or other article worth so much, at *a given time [***517** and place, nothing is left to either party. Both parties are apprised, by the contract, of the time, place and manner of its execution. Each will be prepared accordingly. But if neither time, place, nothing is determinate, they remain to be fixed by the election of one party or the other; and the rights of each must be fixed with a due regard to the nature of the case. It may not, at the date of such a note as this, be the season to pay in farm produce. All such contracts are presumed to be in favor of the debtor. (Chip. Cont., 35, citing Poth. Ob., No. 497.) A contract payable in portable specific articles, at a day certain, not at any specified place, are payable at the creditor's residence; but "not so as to specific articles which cannot attend the person of the debtor. They are supposed to be at the debtor's place of residence; and the creditor must, therefore, demand the payment." (Chip. Cont., 25, 28.) In the case of a merchant or mechanic, who gives an engagement to pay in merchandise, or in his manufactures, the shop of the debtor is the place of payment. (*Id.*, 28–30.) And there must be a demand at his place of residence. (*Id.* 49.) By the French law, wherever anything indeterminate is promised, it must be demanded, and is deliverable at the domicil of the debtor. (Poth. Ob., pt. 3, ch. 1, No. 513.) At No. 512, Pothier puts the case of a determinate thing, payable at a fixed place, in which he says the thing is to be delivered at the place where it exists. He quotes the civil law to this effect; and, in giving an example, mentions a crop of wine in his repository. Now, farm produce is, presumptively, on a farm, and has locality attached to it, as well as the produce of a vintage.

Curia, per SAVAGE, *Ch. J.* On the merits, the only question is, was a demand necessary before action brought?

The note declared on refers to another contract, which, if produced, might have shown a time and place of payment and, perhaps, a specific mode; but the note, unexplained, amounts to a note payable in specific articles without time or place; and the want of time renders it payable on demand. On such a note a special demand is necessary. **Smith* v. *Leav-* [***518** *ensworth*, 1 Root, 209; *Bach* v. *Owen*, 5 T. R., 409; *Chandler* v. *Windship*, 6 Mass., 310; *Benners* v. *Ers. of Howard*, Tayl. N. C., 149.

The question has also been examined, by the counsel for the defendant, where this demand should be made. Mr. Chipman in his valuable treatise, says: "If the note be payable in specific articles, on demand, and no place of payment be designated, the debtor's place of residence is the place of payment, and the payment must be there demanded." (Chip. Tr., 49, and *vide Id.*, 28, 29.) This case is analagous to that of a due-bill without time or place, given by a merchant for goods, or a mechanic for work. Surely the goods must be demanded of the merchant at his store, or of the mechanic at his shop, before a suit can be sustained. The instrument in question is payable by a farmer in farm produce. Certainly there should have been a demand at the debtor's farm.

Judgment affirmed.(a)

Cited in—4 Wend., 528; 5 Wend., 190; 7 Wend., 313; 20 Wend., 197; 2 Den., 147; 5 Den., 452; 12 Barb., 158; 5 Daly, 76; 21 Am. Dec., 164, 212; 25 Am. Dec., 455 (6 N. H., 159); 35 Am. Dec., 494 (11 N. H., 256); 40 Am. Dec., 59; 22 Am. Rep., 332 (27 Ohio 484).

(a) Where a contract is made for the delivery of property, and the debtor has a known place of residence within the State, a demand of the property must be made there. Chambers v. Winn, Prin. Dec., Ky., 192. On contracts for the delivery of property, where no place is expressed, the usual residence of the obligor is the place of performance; and where no place is named, and the property is to be delivered on request, a special request at the obligor's residence must be averred. Wilmouth v. Patton, 2 Bibb. Ky., 280. Where one contracts to deliver specific articles on demand, he should be always ready at his dwelling-house or place of business. If he be absent, a demand of his wife has been held sufficient. Mason v. Briggs, 16 Mass., 453.

519*] *BEEKMAN AND ELMENDORF v. SATTERLEE.

Practice—Capias ad Respondendum *to save Statute of Limitations* — *Pleading* — *Variance* — *Amendments.*

A *capias ad respondendum* to save the Statute of Limitations is mere matter of form, and may be delivered to the sheriff with instructions to return it *non est.*

If it be, by mistake, issued in favor of the plaintiff, as executor, and the *pluries* be in the plaintiff's individual character, *semble*, this is no objection.

But if otherwise, the first *capias* may be amended, even after verdict.

The course at the circuit is for the jury to find the facts in issue; but where a party puts matter in issue which is not material, though the jury find against him, contrary to evidence, this is no ground for a new trial.

Citations—2 Saund., 63, *n.* 6; 2 Salk., 420; 8 T. R., 617; 12 Johns., 430; 8 T. R., 416; 5 T. R., 402; 3 Wils., 61, 141; 2 Bl., 722; 1 Bos. & P., 384.

ASSUMPSIT against the defendant as indorser of a promissory note to the plaintiffs, tried at the Albany Circuit, Oct. 11, 1823, before Duer, *Circuit J.*

The note was for $500, dated Aug. 29, 1815, and payable 6 months after date. The declaration also contained the money counts.

The plea was *non accrevit infra sex annos.* Replication, that within six years after the plaintiffs' causes of action accrued, viz.: Aug. 18, 1821, at, &c., the plaintiffs sued and prosecuted out of this court a certain writ called a *capias ad respondendum*, directed to the Sheriff of the City and County of Albany, by which he was commanded to take the defendant, if, &c., and him, &c. So that, &c., at the Academy in the Town of Utica, on the 3d Monday of Oct. then next, to answer unto the plaintiffs, executors of the last will and testament of Jeremiah Van Rensselaer, deceased, in a plea of trespass; and also to a bill of the plaintiffs against the defendant of $1,000, upon promises, according, &c., which writ, afterwards, and before the day of the return thereof, to wit: Oct. 10, 1821, at, &c., was delivered to the then Sheriff of the City and County of Albany, in due form of law to be executed; at which day, that is to say, on the 3d Monday of Oct., 1821, being the day of the return, before, &c., to wit: at the Academy, &c., came the plaintiffs, by B. F. B., their attorney, and offered themselves against the defendant; and the Sheriff of the City and County of Albany, to wit: C. V. A., Esq., at that day returned upon the writ, to the court, that the defendant was not found in his bailiwick; nor did the defendant come, or appear in the court, before, &c., according to the exigency of the writ; whereupon, the plaintiffs prayed another writ out of the same court, to be directed to the Sheriff of the City and County of Albany, in form aforesaid; and it was granted to them, returnable before the justices aforesaid, *at the same court, at the Capitol [*520 in the City of Albany, on the 1st Monday of Jan., then next, for the defendant to answer unto the plaintiffs, in the plea aforesaid, the same day was given to the defendant, there, &c.; at which day; that is to say, on the first Monday of Jan., being the day of the return, &c., before, &c., at, &c., and offered, &c., and the sheriff of, &c., did not send the last mentioned writ; nor did he do anything therein; nor did the defendant come or appear in the court, &c., before, &c., according, &c. Wherefore the plaintiffs prayed, &c. (And so pleading the *capias* continued through May Term, August Term, October Term, 1822, to the first Monday of January Term, 1823.) Whereupon the plaintiffs prayed another writ out of the same court to be directed to the Sheriff of the City, &c., of Albany, in form aforesaid; and it was granted to them, returnable, &c., on Saturday, Jan. 18, then, instant, for the defendant to answer, &c., the same day, &c. at which day; that is to say, Jan. 18, &c., being the return day, &c., at, &c.; and the defendant by H. B., his attorney, also came, according to the exigency of the last mentioned writ; and the plaintiffs offered themselves on the same day against the defendant in the plea aforesaid, as by the record and proceedings thereof, remaining in the same court, &c, before, &c., more fully, and at large appears. That these writs were so prosecuted, with intent to implead the defendant upon and for the causes of action in the declaration mentioned; and to cause him to appear in the said court here, and upon his appearance to declare against him, for the several causes of action, &c.; that according to that intent, they afterwards, to wit: in the Term of January, to wit: on Saturday, Jan. 18, 1823, exhibited their bill, and declared therein against the defendant as aforesaid, to wit: at, &c.; that the plaintiffs' causes of action in their declaration, &c., did accrue to the plaintiffs within six years next before the issuing of the first mentioned writ, &c., in manner and form, &c., and that the several causes of action in their declaration mentioned, and those for which the writs issued, were and are one and the same, and not other or divers; and that the parties are the same.

*Rejoinder, that the writ first men- [*521 tioned was not delivered to the sheriff to be executed in manner and form as the plaintiff alleged; and was not sued and prosecuted by the plaintiffs against the defendant, with intent to implead the defendant, upon and for the several supposed causes of action in the declaration mentioned, and to cause him to appear, and upon his appearance to declare against him for the said several supposed causes of actions, &c., in manner, &c.

On the trial, the plaintiffs produced the *capias* with the return set forth in the replication, and proved, by the plaintiffs' attorney, that it was issued on the note in question, for the purpose of saving the Statute of Limitations; and that it was returned and filed in the Albany clerk's office, Oct. 16, 1821.

The defendant's counsel objected, that it being issued by the plaintiffs in their representative character as executors, and this suit being in their own right, it would not support the subsequent process, so as to save them from the effect of the Statute of Limitations. This objection was overruled.

The defendant's counsel then moved for a nonsuit, on the ground that the plaintiffs had not made out the facts affirmed in the replication, and upon which issue was taken by the rejoinder. The judge overruled this objection, also, and decided that, from the facts proved, it was to be intended that the writ was issued with intent to be executed.

The defendant's counsel then offered to prove that the writ was not issued with intent that the same should be actually served on the defendant. This testimony was objected to by the plaintiff's counsel as immaterial and irrelevant, but was admitted by the court, subject to the exception.

The defendant then called J. Colvin, the under-sheriff of Albany, who swore that the writ was delivered to him at the time indorsed upon it, Oct. 10, 1821, by the attorney in his office, who said it was merely to save the statute, and he did not wish it served; and therefore the witness made no effort to serve it, and it was not served. The plaintiff's attorney requested him to return it not found, which was done, in consequence of these instructions.

522*] *It was admitted by the plaintiff's counsel that the defendant lived in Albany, and was at home while the writ was in the sheriff's hands. The defendant's counsel then contended that the defendant had fully proved what he had alleged in his rejoinder, and that on the second issue joined in the cause, the jury ought to find for the defendant. That if the rejoinder was bad, the plaintiff ought to have demurred. The question of law was not then to be decided; but the jury must find the facts put in issue.

The judge charged the jury, that the plaintiffs had maintained the second issue in the cause; that the facts proved by the defendant were immaterial, and they ought to find for the plaintiffs on both issues. The jury found accordingly $785.35 for the plaintiffs.

Exceptions were taken to the several opinions expressed by the judge; and it was agreed that either party might turn the case into a bill of exceptions.

Mr. H. Bleecker, for the defendant, now moved in arrest of judgment, or for a new trial. He said that process issuing in a special could not be pursued in a general character, so as to save the statute. (1 Chit. Pl., 254, 255; 1 Dunl. Pr., 239, 240; 1 Tidd, 403; 4 T. R., 402; 3 Wils., 61; 2 Saund., 63, 64, *note* 6.) The replication is, therefore, defective, and the judgment should be arrested. The same matter was urged at the circuit on the ground that, in point of evidence, the replication was not sustained. If the continuance be imperfect, we are entitled to relief in one view or the other.

The plaintiffs did not sustain the issues taken by the rejoinder. It lay with them to prove the intent with which the writ issued. They held the affirmative. But whether this be so not, the defendant negatived the intent in the very terms of the rejoinder; and the verdict is against evidence.

The intent was matter of substance. The statute requires that all actions should be commenced, and all process sued out within six years. Is suing out process, with intent not to have it served, the commencement of an action? The process should go with the opposite intent *with the view of bringing the defend- [*523 ant into court. What can the defendant otherwise know of it? What good does it do? What purpose does it effect? The statute is a dead letter, if it can be avoided in this way. If the suit be *bona fide*, it is an act of diligence, which we agree, should save the plaintiffs' rights. Quieting estates, and avoiding suits, are the objects of the statute. These objects are expressly recited in the English Act. Laws are made to subserve the vigilant; not the indolent.

The precedents all contain the averment that the writ was issued with intent to be served; and the cases hold that this should be so. (2 Burr., 950, 961; 2 Chit. Pl., 598, 606; 1 Wils., 141; 1 Lill. Ent., 32; 3 Went. Pl., 203; *Id.*, 178; 3 Johns. Cas., 145; 17 *Id.*, 65; 18 *Id.*, 14; 2 Sell., 343.) The case in Wilson was one of tender. Would this writ be an answer to a plea of tender? One of the cases cited is of an escape. Is the court prepared to overturn the whole doctrine on that subject?

Messrs. B. F. Butler and *S. A. Foot*, contra. The replication does not aver the intent, that the writ should be served. "To be executed in due form of law," refers to the manner of execution. The rejoinder goes beyond this, and denies the intent that it was to be served. This should be rejected, and the issue confined to the fact which the replication contained. Nothing more could be put in issue.

The variance was not material, even if it had been taken advantage of in season. (2 W. Bl., 1131-1133.) The court would not have set aside the proceedings, but only have discharged the defendant on common bail. (1 Archb. Pr., 59; Dunl. Pr., 239, 240, and *note*; Barn., 494; 2 W. Bl., 722; 4 Burr., 2417, 2418; 8 T. R., 416.) But it is now too late to take advantage of the defect, if it be one. (Dunl. Pr., 332 and *note*; 1 Sell., 100; 2 Johns., 365; 12 *Id.*, 430.) The words "executors, &c.," may be rejected as surplusage. The plaintiffs are not described as executors in the *ac etiam*, where the true cause of action is to be looked for. The first is mere form. (1 Dunl. Pr., 122; 1 Sell., 81, and the cases cited by these.) At any rate, the court will now amend the writ, ordering the representative *character to be stricken out, [*524 as they would in the first instance. (1 R. L., 117, sec. 6; 18 Johns., 513; 2 Dunl., 702, and the cases there cited; 2 W. Bl., 1133; 12 Johns., 430.

The writ was delivered to be executed. A delivery, for the purpose of having it returned

non est, is a delivery for the purpose of execution, within the words and meaning of the statute. It is enough that the writ is issued and returned to the proper office within the six years. Process, by which the statute is to be avoided, is to be considered in a two fold view. If only one *capias* is issued, which is served, it may be material to inquire into the intent with which it was delivered, provided it was issued before, but served after the lapse of the six years. It is material, in such a case, to see that it was delivered in good faith. Another case is, where a writ is delivered as a mere matter of form, to enable the party to go on at a subsequent period. There the intent to have it served is not material. (2 Sell., 343.) This should not startle because it is a fiction. Fictions are abundant in the law. Ejectment is a fiction throughout. Trover is another. In *sci. fa.* nothing is more usual than to procure returns of *nihil* upon express instruction. And the same thing may be said of a *capias* to avoid the statute. (Cowen Treat., 467; 3 T. R., 662; 6 *Id.*, 617; 7 Mod., 5.) It is evidence, according to the forms of law, that the plaintiff will not acquiesce in the barring of his debt. The *lis pendens* is notice to the defendant. This is the very common case of a *capias* returned *non est*, and a continuance by *vice comes non misit breve*—the whole of which is fiction and matter of form. The very existence of the intermediate process is mere fiction. The issue here presents the simple question, whether the process issued for the same cause of action is that mentioned in the declaration. If the argument against us is to prevail, the long settled practice will be overthrown, and important rights destroyed. The defendant cannot complain. Is there any doubt that a *capias* may go to a foreign county, where the defendant is a stranger? The plaintiff is not confined to one county more than another. Had we issued our process to Erie, with instructions to serve it, no one would pre-
525*] tend that we could *not have continued it. And what is the difference between preventing a service in that way and any other?

Mr. Bleecker, in reply. I did not suppose any human being could understand the words, "to be executed in due form of law," in any other sense than to be served—to be made effectual—to bring the party into court. The sheriff is bound, in the same sense, by oath, to execute all writs delivered to him for the purpose. With the same reason, it may be said he is, by oath, bound to return them *non est*.

We could not apply to set aside proceedings for the variance, when the declaration agreed with the writ which went immediately before it.

There is nothing in the distinction set up between a single *capias* served, and one or more returned *non est*, as to the form of the pleading. The precedent which I cited from Lill. Ent., 32, was of a plurality; yet the same form is pursued as in the case of a single process. Has it indeed come to this, that the Statute of Limitations is to be avoided by what gentlemen, and the reporter in his treatise cited by them, are pleased to call a mere ceremony?

Curia, per WOODWORTH, *J.* The rejoinder puts in issue two facts: 1. It denies that the writ was delivered to the sheriff to be executed. 2. That it was sued out with intent to implead the defendant upon the supposed causes of action.

As to the first, the evidence is express that the writ was not delivered to be executed; that is, to be actually served on the defendant. As to the second, although not intended to be served, it was, nevertheless, issued with intent to implead the defendant in the action. It was to save the Statute of Limitations, on the ground that process had been sued out before the statute attached; and being returned *non est*, might be continued down until the defendant appeared, and thus deprive him of the benefit of his plea, should it be interposed. The writ, then, although not delivered to be executed, must be considered as delivered with the intent to implead the defendant. And the question arises, whether *a delivery of the writ, [***526** with direction not to execute it, be a material fact. The usual course at the circuit is, for the jury to find the issue according to the evidence without regard to its materiality. If immaterial, the party against whom the verdict is found, would be entitled to an arrest or judgment *non obstante veredicto*. But, admitting that this issue should have been found for the defendant, there is no sufficient ground for the court to interfere and set it aside, provided it be immaterial; because the defendant would derive no benefit, if a new trial should be granted. If, however, the issue be material, a new trial should be granted.

I have not found any case, where the fact that the writ was delivered with directions not to execute it was the point in issue. The general doctrine seems to be this: the plaintiff may reply a *capias* sued out within time, and returned *non est inventus* by the sheriff; and show that the process was regularly continued by *vice comes non misit breve*, to the time of declaring. (2 Saund., 63, *note* 6; 2 Salk., 420; 6 T. R., 617.) This is considered a good commencement of the suit, for the purpose of defeating the operation of the statute; and if so, I do not perceive how the principle can be affected by giving the sheriff directions not to make personal service of the first writ. The defendant is not thereby deprived of any defense that he would have had, independent of such instructions given to the officer. The plaintiff may thereby be subjected to greater delay, but the defendant sustains no injury. To him this fact is not material. I am of opinion that the motion for a new trial be denied.

To support the motion in arrest, the defendant contends that the first *capias*, being issued by the plaintiffs in their representative character, cannot support the subsequent process and proceedings in their own right. The identity of the cause of action, and the issuing the first writ, are put in issue. It is true, in that writ the plaintiffs are described as executors, and declare in their own right. If this is irregular, after plea pleaded it was too late to take advantage of a variance between the declaration and the writ. (12 *Johns., 430.) [***527** The proper course is, to move the court that the defendant be discharged on common bail. (8 T. R., 416; 5 *Id.*, 402; 3 Wils., 61, 141; 2 Bl., 722; 1 Bos. & P., 384.)

From an examination of the authorities, I am inclined to the opinion that the variance did not entitle the defendant to anything more than to be relieved on filing common bail. If, however, the objection can now be properly urged, it is not too late, after trial, to allow an amendment, by striking out the description of the plaintiffs as executors. The doctrine laid down in *Lion* v. *Burtis*, 18 Johns., 512, is, that amendments, in furtherance of justice, ought to be made, even after trial, as to mere formal mistakes, arising from clerical errors, when the substantial rights of one party will be promoted by the amendment; and the other party is no otherwise prejudiced, than by depriving him of a formal objection. I am of opinion that the motion in arrest be denied.

Motions denied.

Criticised—14 Wend., 653.
Cited in—6 Cow., 473; 7 Wend., 124; 14 Wend., 84.

OVERSEERS OF THE TOWN OF OWASCO
v.
OVERSEERS OF THE TOWN OF OSWEGATCHIE.

Settlement of Child.

The binding of a child by its mother, living the father, he not dissenting, and the child serving two years according to the indenture, confers a settlement on the child.

Citation—31 Johns., 245.

ON *certiorari* from the General Sessions of the Peace of the County of St. Lawrence.

Two justices made an order for the removal of the children of Diana, a black woman, by her husband, Peters, from Oswegatchie to Owasco, in St. Lawrence Co. On appeal by the Overseers of Owasco, the General Sessions affirmed the order. It was admitted, on the hearing, that Peters had never gained any settlement in Owasco, or elsewhere in this State; that Diana, the mother, was born in Owasco, and the order of removal was made on this ground, as the residence of the children would follow that of the mother.

Daniel Kellogg was sworn at the hearing before the sessions, on the part of the appellants; **528***] and testified that in the *fall of 1804 or 1805, Diana, the mother, then single, came to reside with him at Marcellus, Onondaga Co., where he then and now resides. That there was a writing made between the witness and the mother of Diana, under which she served; but which he had lost, and could not find on diligent search. The writing was signed by the mother of Diana. She had, at that time, a husband living, who did not act in the contract. The witness did not remember whether the contract was signed by him or not.

The court below decided that this contract was not binding within the statute.

The appellants then offered to prove that the contract was in the usual form of an indenture of apprenticeship, and that Diana was bound by it to serve a term of more than two years. But the court refused to hear any parol evidence of the contents of the contract.

The witness then stated that he clothed and provided for Diana; and that she served the term specified in the contract; that Elizabeth was the reputed wife of one DeWitt; but that she had absconded, and lived with a black man called Cuff, sometime before the birth of Diana; that at the time of the binding, she lived with Cuff, who, though he knew of it, did not interfere with the contract; nor did any other person.

Mr. John Porter, for the plaintiffs in error.
Mr. B. Perkins, contra.

Curia, per SUTHERLAND, *J.* The court below clearly erred in rejecting the parol evidence offered, if a valid indenture was shown to have been given. The objection was, that it was executed by the mother and not by the father. It appears that at the birth of Diana (but how long before does not appear), the mother lived with a man who was not her husband, and continued to live with him when she bound the child to Kellogg. She served her time out with Kellogg, and the father does not appear ever to have interfered, or manifested any disapprobation of the binding. The case of *O. of Hudson* v. *O. of Taghkanac*, *13 Johns., [***529** 245, is precisely in point. The objection there was, that the binding was by the mother (the father being alive), but it was held that the indenture was only voidable at the instance of the father; and that a binding by a voidable indenture, and a service under it for two years, gives an apprentice a settlement in the town where he serves; and it is not competent for the town to object to the validity of the binding. Though Diana was born in Owasco, an offer was made of competent evidence, to show that she subsequently acquired a settlement in Marcellus. This having been rejected by the court below, their order must be reversed.

Order reversed.

Cited in—6 Cow., 659.

JACKSON, ex dem. HILL, *v.* STREETER.

Misrecital of Judgment in Sheriff's Deed, not Material—Defendant in Ejectment, cannot Question Common Source of Title.

The misrecital of the judgment in a sheriff's deed is not material, provided it appear, in fact, that the sale was under a subsisting judgment and execution.

A recital is no material part of a deed.

But if a recital of the judgment, in a sheriff's deed be necessary; and it be wrong as to the amount and date of the judgment, but right as to the court, the parties and the test, and return of the execution which agree with the judgment, this shows a sufficient authority for the sale.

Where one takes by descent as a co-heir and tenant in common, in ejectment by his co-heir, or one claiming under him, he cannot show that the ancestor had no title.

Citations—10 Johns., 381; 3 Ch. Cas., 101; 18 Johns., 7; 9 Johns., 90; Hob., 130; Co. Litt, 352 *b*.

EJECTMENT, tried at the Onondaga Circuit, Sept., 1825, to recover the possession of an equal undivided half part of 68 acres of land, in the southeast corner of lot No. 74, in Camillus.

The plaintiff proved a deed in fee for the premises in question, dated Sept. 28, 1798, from Josiah Buck to John Streeter; a quitclaim deed in fee from Amasa Spalding, Jr., and Sarah, his wife, dated Jan. 21, 1819, of all their right to the premises in question, to Joseph Streeter; that John Streeter died, seised of the premises in question, 19 or 20 years before the

trial, leaving Joseph Benjamin (the defendant), Sarah, the wife of Amasa Spalding, Jr., and Joanna, his children and heirs at law; that the defendant had since possessed the premises. He then proved a judgment against Joseph Streeter in a justice's court, rendered July 25, 1820, for, $28.69, which was transcribed, &c., and his interest in the premises in question sold on execution by the sheriff to one Lombard, Feb. 27, 1821, from whom the lessor of the plaintiff, redeeming as a junior
530*] judgment *creditor, received a deed of the sheriff, dated Feb. 17, 1823. This deed misrecited the day and amount of the judgment, viz.: that it was obtained July 20, 1820, and amounted to $29.72. But the magistrate was rightly named, and the parties, with the test and return of the execution, were rightly recited; and the judgment and execution, in fact, corresponded in all respects. It was objected that the variance was fatal, but the objection was overruled.

The defendant then offered in evidence the exemplification of a patent from the State for lot 74, in Camillus, to John Miles, dated July 9, 1790, which was objected to; and the judge decided that it was not, in itself, evidence of a title out of the lessor of the plaintiff. The defendant also offered to show that Josiah Buck never had any title, which was also overruled. Verdict for the plaintiff.

A motion was now made, in behalf to the defendant, for a new trial.

Mr. J. R. Lawrence, for the defendant.

Mr. H. F. Mather, contra.

Curia, per SUTHERLAND, *J.* A competent authority to make the sale appears, if it was, in fact, made under the judgment and execution. That it was so made, the evidence leaves no doubt. In *Jackson* v. *Pratt*, 10 Johns., 381, the execution was for £66 14*s*. 3*d*., and in the sheriff's deed it was recited as an execution for £66 14*s*. 3*d*., debt, and £1 14*s*. costs. The court say "the recital was no necessary part of the deed, and a variance would not be material, nor affect the validity of the sale, so long as there was existing a sufficient power to warrant the sale." (3 Ch. Cas., 101, per Holt, *Ch. J.*; 18 Johns., 7.) A mistake in the recital of a bond will not vitiate it. It is not an essential part of the bond. (9 Johns., 90; Hob., 130; 3 Ch. Cas., 101; Co. Litt., 352 *b*.)

I do not understand the judge as having excluded the patent to Miles; but only as deciding that the patent itself, without other evidence, would not show a subsisting title out of the lessor of the plaintiff. In this, I appre-
531*] hend, he *was correct. The plaintiff had shown a deed for the premises in question from Buck to John Streeter, in Sept., 1798; that Streeter went into possession under the deed, and continued in possession until his death, 19 or 20 years before the trial, leaving four children (the interest of two of them being owned by the lessor); and that the defendant, Benjamin, one of the children, has been in possession ever since. This was a good adverse possession against the patent granted in 1790.

The evidence that Buck, who gave the deed to John Streeter, had no title, was properly rejected on several grounds. John Streeter was the common source of title to both parties. His children, there being no will, are presumed to have taken the premises by descent, as tenants in common. It is not for the defendant to say that the common ancestor had no title, and that his possession is not as tenant in common, but in his own individual right.

New trial denied.

Cited in—7 Cow., 19; 9 Cow., 192; 4 Wend., 589; 8 Wend., 680; 11 Wend., 427; 25 Wend., 393; 10 N. Y., 535; 9 Barb., 227; 41 Barb., 81.

LIVINGSTON v. ACKESTON.

Promise to Pay for Services Rendered, not Implied, Where it was Understood no Compensation should be Given.

Where one purchased the time of a negro till he was 28, for a valuable and full consideration, both the negro and the vendee supposing that he was bound to serve that length of time though the negro was, in fact, a freeman, no action lies at his suit, against the vendee for his services.

Under such circumstances, the law will not imply a promise to pay for the services.

Where work is done by one for the benefit of another, with his knowledge and approbation, the law will imply a promise to pay for it, unless it appear that there was an understanding that no compensation should be given; but where there is such understanding, the law will not imply a promise.

Citations—3 Johns., 201; 3 Esp., 4; 1 Com. Cont., 227; 12 Johns., 188.

ON ERROR from the C. P. of Columbia. The action below was *assumpsit* for work and labor by Ackeston against Livingston; and the verdict and judgment was for the plaintiff, on the facts stated in the bill of exceptions, upon which the writ of error was founded. Those facts were, that Ackeston, a black man, worked for Livingston, from the spring of 1819 till June, 1820, when he sold him to one Benn. That Livingston had bought him of one Ham, as a slave or servant, at $200; and that he was to serve till he was 28 years old. That he became dissatisfied and procured Benn to purchase him of Livingston. That Ackeston was born of black parents, who kept house and acted for themselves as long ago as 1798, in which year he was born. The parents had before *been slaves to one Dings. Ham had [***532**
also bought Ackeston, as a servant, till he was 28. He was sold to Livingston at 16 years and 4 months old.

The counsel for the defendant below moved for a nonsuit, on the ground that there was no contract to pay wages, and none could be implied, between the parties. But the motion was overruled.

Mr. D. B. Tallmadge, for the plaintiff in error, cited 1 Com. Cont., 228, 229; *Alfred* v. *Marquis of Fitzjames*, 3 Esp., 3.

Mr. C. Bushnell, contra, cited *Oatfield* v. *Waring*, 14 Johns., 192; 4 L. N. Y., b. 136, secs. 5, 6; 4 Serg. & R., 426; 1 *Id.*, 23; 1 Dall., 469; 2 Greenl. ed. L. N. Y., 88; 9 Johns., 144; 1 Cow., 127; 1 R. L. of 1801, 613; *Jacobson* v. *Exrs. of Le Grange*, 3 Johns., 201; *Cook* v. *Husted*, 12 Johns., 188.

Curia, per SUTHERLAND, *J.* The plaintiff, upon the evidence in the case, must be considered as having been a freeman, during the period he was in the service of the defendant. But the defendant purchased him as a slave in perfect good faith, for a large and valuable consideration. The plaintiff supposed himself to have been a slave and, at his own request, was sold by the defendant to a person whom the plaintiff had induced and procured to purchase him. There is no pretense of an express promise, on the part of the defendant, to pay the plaintiff for his services; and the question is, whether, under the circumstances of this case, such a promise is to be implied. No doubt the services of the plaintiff, having been performed for the benefit of the defendant, with his knowledge and approbation, the law will imply a promise to pay for them, unless it appears they understood that no compensation was to be made. *Jacobson* v. *Exrs. of Le Grange*, 3 Johns., 201. In this case, it clearly appears that such was the understanding of the plaintiff, as well as the defendant. The plaintiff knew and admitted that the defendant had purchased his time until he was 28 years of age; that he paid **533***] $200 for it; *that he was entitled to his services. He procured another person to purchase the unexpired term of his services from the defendant—thereby admitting the defendant's right to sell it. The law, under such circumstances, cannot raise an implied *assumpsit*.

The case of *Alfred* v. *Fitz James*, 3 Esp., 4, is precisely in point. It appeared, in that case, that the plaintiff, a colored man, came over from Martinique with the Duchess of Fitz James, having been born a slave on an estate belonging to her in that Island. There was no contract of hiring for wages; but a witness said the Marquis had been heard to promise him wages. Ld. Kenyon ruled, that up to the time of the promise to pay wages, the plaintiff could not recover, as there was no original contract of service for wages. (And *vide* 1 Com. Cont., 227.)

The case of *Cook* v. *Husted*, 12 Johns., 188, has no analogy to this. There Cook purchased the time of a black girl from one Israel Pugsley. She did not, in fact, belong to Pugsley, but to Sarah Husted, the plaintiff; and the action was brought by her to recover the value of her services while she lived with the defendant. Having shown the slave to be hers, and to have performed services for the defendant, she was, of course, entitled to be paid for them, unless there was something to show the parties understood no compensation was to be made. There was nothing of that kind in that case, or from which it could be inferred.

Judgment reversed.

Cited in—14 Wend., 213; 2 Barb., 210; 12 Barb., 477; 13 Barb., 507; 20 Barb., 391; Tuck., 29; 22 Cal., 511; 39 Mich., 351; 33 Am. Rep., 399 (39 Mich., 345).

534*] *KELLEY AND CLAWSON *v.* HURLBURT AND STUART.

Dormant Partner—Not Liable for Purchases after Dissolution, though no Notice Given.

NOTE.—*Partnership—Dormant partner—Dissolution—Notice.*

Power of other partners to bind a dormant partner ceases with his retirement, though no notice of dissolution is given. Davis v. Allen, 3 N. Y., 168; Warren v. Ball, 37 Ill., 76; Scott v. Colmesriel, 7 J. J. Marsh., 416; Edwards v. McFall, 5 La. Ann., 167; Magill v. Merrie, 5 B. Mon., 168; Deford v. Reynolds, 36 Pa. St., 325; Carter v. Whalley, 1 B. & Ad., 11; Heath v. Sansom, 4 B. & Ad., 172.

Where two were concerned together as partners, but the business was done in the name of one, and it was not generally known that they were partners; held, that the other was a dormant partner.

And where the acting partner made a contract to pay for goods within the scope of their former partnership—this being after actual dissolution, though no public notice had been given of the dissolution; and it not appearing that the vendors ever had any dealings with the firm, and they never having heard of its existence; held, that the dormant partner was not liable.

Where a partnership is publicly and notoriously known, all the partners are responsible for the contracts of each, within the scope of the partnership, until public notice of the dissolution is given; but it is otherwise, of a dormant partner. Actual dissolution, without notice, will protect him.

Citations—4 Esp., 90; Doug., 371, 373; 2 Johns., 204; 6 Johns., 144.

ASSUMPSIT tried at the Cayuga Circuit, Sept. 10, 1824, before Throop, *Circuit J.*, when a verdict was taken for the plaintiffs, subject to the opinion of the court upon a case, and with leave to either party to turn it into a special verdict. The facts are stated in the opinion of the court.

Mr. D. Kellogg, for the plaintiffs.

Mr. S. Wood, contra, cited 4 Esp., 89, 91; Doug., 371.

Curia, per SUTHERLAND, *J.* The plaintiffs sold $652.61 worth of goods, wares and merchandises to Simeon Hurlburt, one of the defendants, in May, 1823. At the time of the sale, nothing was said about Hurlburt's having a partner, and the plaintiff being ignorant of that fact, took the individual note of Hurlburt for the amount of the goods sold, payable in six months. Hurlburt having failed, and the plaintiffs having learned that Stuart had been concerned with him in trade, they commenced their suit against them, as partners, for the goods sold to Hurlburt. On the trial, they produced the note given by Hurlburt and offered to cancel it.

The evidence clearly establishes the fact that a general partnership was formed between the defendants in 1815, and that no public notice of the dissolution of that partnership had ever been given. It was not limited in its duration, by the original terms of the agreement, except that, at the end of ten years, a division might be made, if the parties wished it.

One of the witnesses testified that the existence of the partnership was a matter of general notoriety since 1818; and repeated declarations of Stuart that he was interested *in the [***535** store, were proved, though the business was always conducted in the name of Hurlburt alone. Another witness testified that he had been a clerk in Hurlburt's store, and that though many persons knew of the partnership between the defendants, he did not believe that it was generally known. I think the weight of evidence is in favor of the opinion of this witness.

The dissolution of the partnership was alleged to have taken place in Nov., 1822; and although some of the evidence to establish that fact was improperly admitted (being the declarations of the defendants themselves, and objected to by the plaintiffs), still, I think, the fact that a dissolution did then take place, is satisfactorily made out by competent evidence; and it seems to have been as generally known, and as much the subject of conversation, and some of the witnesses say more so, than the partnership itself.

Upon this state of facts, the question arises, whether Stuart is responsible for the goods sold to Hurlburt after the partnership was dissolved —the plaintiffs never having had any previous dealings with the firm, and never having heard of its existence.

I am inclined to think that Stuart must be considered a dormant partner; and, as such, not liable for any debts contracted by Hurlburt after the partnership was dissolved, although no notice of the dissolution was published. The business was carried on in the name of Hurlburt alone; and although it was known to some and believed by others, that Stuart was concerned with him, that knowledge or belief was by no means general, even in their immediate neighborhood; and cannot reasonably be considered as laying a foundation for the presumption that the credit of Hurlburt was increased by it. It appears affirmatively in this case that the plaintiffs never knew or suspected that Hurlburt had any partner until long after the goods in question were sold to him.

Stuart undoubtedly is jointly liable with Hurlburt for all partnership debts contracted before the dissolution. He was entitled to a share of the profits, and is responsible for the debts. But he can be held responsible upon **536***] contracts *subsequently made by Hurlburt, only on the ground that he was guilty of an omission of duty, in neglecting to give notice of the dissolution. Now, if he was a dormant partner, his name not appearing in the firm, and not publicly known as concerned in the house, notice that the partnership was dissolved would seem to be a work of supererogation. The credit of the house was not increased by his connection with it, for it was not known. There is no room, therefore, for the presumption that the public was misled by the omission to give notice of the termination of the partnership.

In *Evans* v. *Drummond*, 4 Esp., 90, it was held by Ld. Kenyon that a partner, whose name does not appear in the firm, is only liable for goods furnished during the time he receives a share of the profits, unless he has been known to be a partner; in which case he shall be liable for subsequent contracts, unless he has given notice of his quitting the concern. The case was decided on another point; but Ld. Kenyon expressly ruled that it was incumbent on the plaintiff to show that Drummond, the dormant partner, was known publicly in the partnership, as (he remarked) there must be some publicity of his situation, to which the plaintiff might be presumed to trust; otherwise, he could only be charged during the time he was actually a partner, and was receiving the emoluments and profits of the business. (Doug., 371, 373.) In the case of a partnership publicly and notoriously known, all the partners are responsible for the contracts of each within the scope of the partnership, until public notice of the dissolution is given. (2 Johns., 304; 6 Johns., 144.) The reason of the distinction between the two classes of cases is obvious.

I am, therefore, of opinion that the defendants are entitled to judgment.

Judgment for the defendants.

Cited in—12 N. Y., 288; 30 N. Y., 330; 3 Hun, 145; 65 Barb., 575; 5 T. & C., 290; 5 Bos., 10.

---

*HUBERT v. WILLIAMS. [*537

Discharge of Debtor—Subsequent Promise to Pay Debt.

A subsequent promise to pay a debt, as to which the debtor has been discharged from imprisonment under the Act of 1819, sess. 42, ch. 101, will not take away the effect of such discharge.

Citations—Sess. 42, ch. 101, sec. 3; 3 M. & S., 595; 54 Geo. III., ch. 28, sec. 28; 14 Johns., 178.

ON demurrer to the replication. The declaration was in *assumpsit* on a promissory note made by the defendant, dated Dec. 2, 1822, to which he pleaded his discharge, under the Act to Abolish Imprisonment for Debt, granted Oct. 3, 1823. To this, the plaintiff replied that after the discharge, the defendant ratified, renewed and confirmed the promise set out in the declaration.

General demurrer and joinder.

Mr. E. Cowen, in support of the demurrer, cited Laws, sess. 42, ch. 101, sec. 3, and *Wilson* v. *Kemp*, 3 Maule & S. 595, and the cases there referred to.

Mr. W. L. F. Warren, contra, cited *Shippey* v. *Henderson*, 14 Johns., 178.

Curia, per SUTHERLAND, *J.* The demurrer is well taken. There was no new consideration for the subsequent acknowledgment, or promise to pay the debt. The action is not upon that, but the original promise; and the Statute of 1819, sess. 42, ch. 101, sec. 3, is express that the insolvent shall, forever after his discharge, be exempt from imprisonment for or by reason of any debt or debts due at the time of making the assignment.

The defendant was never discharged from the debt. The new promise, therefore, was nothing more than an acknowledgment of his existing liability; and would not be the foundation of a new action. It, in no respect, waived the pre-existing rights and liabilities of the parties.

In *Wilson* v. *Kemp*, 3 Maule & S., 595, it was held that an insolvent debtor, who had taken the benefit of the 54 Geo. III., ch. 28, was not liable to arrest on a subsequent promise to pay a debt contracted prior to the day prescribed in the Act. The 28th section of that Act is very similar in its terms to the 3d section of the Act of 1819. If a new promise will not authorize the defendant to be held to bail, *it surely will [***538** not subject his person to imprisonment upon final process. The case cited for the plaintiff, of *Shippey* v. *Henderson*, was one of an absolute discharge. But, in this case, I should question very much, whether even an express promise, by the defendant, not to avail himself of his discharge without any new consideration, would be binding. Judgment must be for the defendant, with leave for the plaintiff to amend, on payment of costs.

Judgment for the defendant.(a)

Cited in—27 Am. Dec., 284 (4 Rawle, 452).

(a) *Vide* Couch v. Ash, *ante*, 265, S. P.

THE CORPORATION OF THE BRICK PRESBYTERIAN CHURCH IN THE CITY OF NEW YORK

v.

THE MAYOR, ALDERMEN AND COMMONALTY OF THE CITY OF NEW YORK.

Sale of Land by Corporation of New York with Covenant for Quiet Enjoyment—Legislative Power of Corporation to Repeal Covenant.

The Corporation of the City of N. Y. conveyed lands for the purposes of a church and cemetery with a covenant for quiet enjoyment: and afterwards, pursuant to a power granted by the Legislature, passed a by-law prohibiting the use of these lands as a cemetery; held, that this was not a breach of the covenant, which entitled to damages, but it was a repeal of the covenant.

A corporation cannot, by contract, abridge their legislative power.

Where one covenants not to do a thing which it is lawful for him to do; and an Act of the Legislature comes after and compels him to do it; then the Act repeals the covenant, and *vice versa;* but when a man covenants to do a thing which was unlawful at the time of the covenant, and afterwards a statute makes it lawful it does not repeal the covenant.

Citations—4 Wh., 652; 3 Mod., 39; 1 Ld. Raym., 317, 321; 1 Salk., 198; 2 T. R., 769.

ON demurrer to the plea, in an action on the covenant for quiet enjoyment.

Messrs. H. Holden and *G. Griffin*, in support of the demurrer, cited *Holder* v. *Taylor*, Hob., 12; *M'Gooch* v. *M'Gooch*, 4 Mass., 348, 352; *Chisholm* v. *State of Ga.*, 2 Dall., 419; *Paradine* v. *Jane*, Aleyn, 26; *Brason* v. *Dean*, 3 Mod., 39; 12 Johns., 122, 125; 3 Johns., 471; Com. Dig., Covenant, D, 2 E, 1.

Messrs. P. A. Jay and *M. Ulshoeffer*, contra, cited *Norton* v. *Simmes*, Hod., 12; S. C., F. Moore, 856; *Brewster* v. *Kitchin*, 1 Ld. Raym., 317, per Holt; Com. Dig., Covenant, F; 2 Gwil. Bac., 80; 1 Kyd Corp., 271; Com. Dig., Covenant, A, 3; 1 Roll., 518; Cro. Eliz., 914; Noy., 50; 1 Lev., 94; Skinn., 344; Bendl., Pl., 110; Hardr., 132; 2 Saund., 180; 1 Sid., **539***] 466; 3 Mod., 135; 1 Lev., 301; 2 *Vent., 62; 3 Lev., 305, 325; 8 Rep., 91; 2 Mass., 437; Com. Dig., Pleader, C, 48; *Pomfret* v. *Rycroft*, 1 Vent., 44, per Twisden, *J.*; 1 Sid., 429; *Waldon* v. *M'Carty*, 3 Johns., 473, per Spencer, *J.*; 2 R. L., 445, sec. 267; *Mayor* v. *Ordrenau*, 12 Johns., 122; *Furman* v. *Knapp*, 19 Johns., 248; 1 Chit. Pl., 232–234; 4 Wh., 652, per Marshall, *Ch. J.*; *Watson* v. *The Master, &c.*, 14 Ves., 333; *Auburn Academy* v. *Strong*, Hopk. Ch., 278; *Commonwealth* v. *Bird*, 12 Mass., 442; *Gosler* v. *Georgetown*, 6 Wh., 597; 4 T. R., 794; *Fartitle* v. *Gilbert*, 2 T. R., 169; *Pendleton* v. *Dyett*, 4 Cow., 583; 10 Johns., 96; 11 *Id.*, 443, and the cases there cited.

The pleadings and points decided are stated in the opinion of the court; which was delivered by,

SAVAGE, *Ch. J.*:

This action is brought for an alleged breach of the covenant for quiet enjoyment.

Feb. 25, 1766, the defendants conveyed to those whom the plaintiffs represent, the premises on which the Brick Presbyterian Church now stands, in the City of N. Y. By the deed, the lessees covenanted for the payment of an annual rent, and also that, within ten years, the premises should be inclosed in a fenee; and that a church should be built thereon, or the premises should be used as a cemetery; and, also, that they should never be used for private secular uses.

The defendants then covenanted that the lessees and their assigns, paying the rent and performing the conditions, should quietly use, occupy and enjoy the premises, without any let or hindrance of the defendants or any other person, &c.

The plaintiffs aver performance on their part, and a breach of the covenant on the part of the defendants, by reason of their by-law of Oct. 27, 1823, prohibiting the use of the premises, as a cemetery, for the interment of the dead.

*The defendants, by plea, justify [***540** under their Charter of Incorporation, and the Act of the Legislature of the State, 2 R. L., 545, sec. 267; by which they have full power and authority to make and pass such by-laws and ordinances as they shall, from time to time, deem necessary and proper, "for regulating, or if they find it necessary, preventing the interment of the dead within the said city." To this plea the plaintiffs have demurred.

The principal question, and the only one which it is necessary to decide, is, whether the by-law of Oct., 1823, is, *per se*, a violation of the covenant for quiet enjoyment, contained in the deed of Feb. 25, 1766, for which the defendants are liable to pay damages.

The validity of the by-law is asserted by both parties. We are relieved, therefore, from any inquiry on that point.

The defendants are a Corporation, and in that capacity are authorized by their charter, and by law, to purchase and hold, sell and convey real estate, in the same manner as individuals. They are considered a person in law within the scope of their corporate powers, and are subjeet to the same liabilities, and entitled to the same remedies, for the violation of contracts, as natural persons. They are also clothed, as well by their charter as by subsequent statutes of the State, with legislative powers; and, in the capacity of a local Legislature, are partienlarly charged with the care of the public mor-

NOTE.—*Constitutional Law—Municipal corporations—Cannot surrender legislative powers.*

Municipal corporations hold their powers for public purposes. Legislative powers conferred upon them, can neither be delegated nor bargained away. They may make authorized contracts, but they are without power to make contracts which shall limit their legislative or governmental powers. In addition to the above leading case of Brick Pres. Church v. Mayor, see Stuyvesant v. Mayor, 7 Cow., 588; Mayor v. Britton, 12 Abb. Pr., 367, *note;* Davis v. Mayor, 14 N. Y., 506; Atty-Gen. v. Mayor, 3 Duer, 119; Costar v. Brush, 25 Wend., 628; N. Y. & H. Ry. Co. v. Mayor, 1 Hilt., 562; Milhau v. Sharp, 27 N. Y., 611; Martin v. Mayor, 1 Hill, 545; Mayor v. Second Av. Ry. Co., 32 N. Y., 261; *Ex parte* Mayor, 23 Wend., 277; Lyon v. Jerome, 26 Wend., 485; Davis v. Read, 65 N. Y., 566; Bryson v. Philadelphia, 47 Pa. St., 329; Kincaid's Appeal, 66 Pa. St., 411; 5 Am. Rep., 377; Johnson v. Philadelphia, 60 Pa. St., 445; State v. Cincinnati Gas Co., 18 Ohio St., 262; Oakland v. Carpenter, 13 Cal., 540; Jackson v. Bowman, 39 Miss., 671; State v. Graves, 19 Md., 351; Hamrick v. Rause, 17 Ga., 56; Morgan v. Smith, 4 Minn., 104; Supervisors v. Brush, 77 Ill., 59; Thomson v. Booneville, 61 Mo., 282. See, also, Dill. Mun. Corp., secs. 60, 61, and authorities there *cited;* Cooley Const. Lim., pp. 150, 249–251, 342, 343, and authorities there cited.

On the question of police powers, see Vanderbilt v. Adams, 7 Cow., 349, *note*.

als, and the public health within their own jurisdiction.

In ascertaining their rights and liabilities as a Corporation, or as an individual, we must not consider their legislative character. They had no power, as a party, to make a contract which should control or embarrass their legislative powers and duties. Their enactments, in their legislative capacity, are to have the same effect upon their individual acts, as upon those of any other persons, or the public at large, and no other effect.

The liability of the defendants, therefore, upon the covenant in question, must be the same as if it had been entered into by an individual; and the effect of the by-law upon it the same as if that by-law had been an Act of the

541*] State *Legislature. It is expressly authorized by the Legislature; and whether it be their Act or an Act of the local city Legislature, makes no difference. (4 Wh., 652.)

The plaintiffs, then, are entitled to the same remedy as if the premises had been conveyed to them by an individual, under the like conditions and covenants. This being so, the defendants' proposition is, that the Act of the Legislature rendering the covenant unlawful, the covenant itself becomes inoperative.

There are but few authorities on this question, and those few are at variance. The case of *Brason* v. *Dean*, 3 Mod., 39, decided in 1683, was covenant upon a charter-party for the freight of a ship. The defendant pleaded that the ship was loaded with French goods, prohibited, by law, to be imported. And upon demurrer, judgment was given for the plaintiff; for the court were all of opinion, that if the thing to be done was lawful at the time when the defendant entered into the covenant, though it was afterwards prohibited by Act of Parliament, yet the covenant was binding. But in the case of *Brewster* v. *Kitchin*, 1 Ld. Raym., 317, 321, A. D. 1698, a different and a more rational doctrine is established. It is there said, "for the difference when an Act of Parliament will amount to a repeal of a covenant, and when not, is this: when a man covenants not to do a thing which was lawful for him to do, and an Act of Parliament comes after, and compels him to do it, then the Act repeals the covenant, and *vice versa*. But when a man covenants not to do a thing which was unlawful at the time of the covenant, and afterwards an Act makes it lawful, the Act does not repeal the covenant."

In 1 Salk., 198, where the same case is reported, the proposition is thus stated: "Where H. covenants not to do an act or thing which was lawful to do, and an Act of Parliament comes after and compels him to do it, the statute repeals the covenant. So if H. covenants to do a thing which is lawful, and an Act of Parliament comes in and hinders him from doing it, the covenant is repealed. But if a man covenants not to do a thing which then was unlawful, and an Act comes and makes it lawful to do it, such Act of Parliament does not repeal the covenant."

*That such is the correct rule, as be- **[*542** tween individuals, seems to be admitted by the counsel for the plaintiffs. But it is contended that the rule is not applicable to a case where the same party makes the covenant, and afterwards makes the legislative Act, which abrogates the covenant. There is, indeed, a seeming inconsistency; but the solution has already been given, viz.: that the defendants had no power to limit their legislative discretion by covenant; and they are not estopped from giving this answer. (2 T. R., 169.)

The reasonableness of acting upon the rule, in this case, cannot be more strongly exemplified than by the case itself. Sixty years ago, when the lease was made, the premises were beyond the inhabited part of the city. They were a common, and bounded on one side by a vineyard. Now they are in the very heart of the city. When the defendants covenanted that the lessees might enjoy the premises for the purpose of burying their dead, it never entered into the contemplation of either party that the health of the city might require the suspension or abolition of that right. It would be unreasonable, in the extreme, to hold that the plaintiffs should be at liberty to endanger not only the lives of such as belong to the Corporation of the church, but also those of the citizens generally, because their lease contains a covenant for quiet enjoyment. Suppose these premises had been let for a certain purpose which is proper in itself, in a detached situation, but a nuisance in the city thickly inhabited—for instance, a slaughter house—could it be seriously contended, that when the use of the property in the way contemplated by the parties to the conveyance, was forbidden by the Legislature, an action would lie against the grantor? Such a rule, I apprehend, would be extremely oppressive and unjust, as to individuals; and equally so as to the defendants in this cause.

The defendants are entitled to judgment on the demurrer.

Judgment for the defendants.

Cited in—7 Cow., 604; 9 Wend., 598; 23 N. Y., 325; 27 N. Y., 622; 32 N. Y., 271; 72 N. Y., 7; 78 N. Y., 179, 237; 20 Hun, 235; 13 Barb., 39; 23 Barb., 58; 25 Barb., 643; 32 Barb., 113; 34 Barb., 44; 21 How. Pr., 256, 260, 270; 31 How. Pr., 342, *n.*; 49 How. Pr., 493; 58 How. Pr., 491; 5 Abb. Pr., 434; 6 Abb. Pr., 276; 12 Abb. Pr., 366; 12 Abb. N. S., 345; 3 Abb. N. C., 500; 6 Abb. N. C., 337, *n.*; 3 Duer, 147; 4 E. D. S., 608; 7 Daly, 546; 109 Mass., 215; 115 Mass., 155; 118 Mass., 362; 9 Minn., 89; 12 Minn., 49; 19 Mich., 282; 48 Sup. Ct., 498; 24 Am. Dec., 186; 2 Am. Rep., 91 (19 Mich., 259); 5 Am. Rep., 384 (66 Pa. St., 24); 7 Am. Rep., 725 (44 Miss., 513); 16 Am. Rep., 736, 3 S. C., 347); 20 Am. Rep., 601 (41 Iowa, 297).

[END OF MAY TERM, 1826.]

CASES ARGUED AND DETERMINED

IN THE

Court for the Trial of Impeachments

AND THE

CORRECTION OF ERRORS

OF THE

STATE OF NEW YORK,

IN DECEMBER, 1825.

547*] *WILLIAM MACKIE, ANDREW MILNE AND ANDREW LOCKHART, *Appellants,*

v.

WILLIAM CAIRNS, ROBERT SEDGWICK AND DANIEL LORD, *Junior, Respondents;* and

WILLIAM CAIRNS, ROBERT SEDGWICK AND DANIEL LORD, *Junior, Appellants,*

v.

WILLIAM MACKIE, ANDREW MILNE AND ANDREW LOCKHART, *Respondents.*

Assignments by Merchant, for Benefit of Creditors—Provision for Himself—Subsequent Confession of Judgment to Same Trustees for Same Purposes, Excepting Provision for Himself—Judgment to be Resorted to, only in Event of Assignments being Held Invalid—Assignments Held Void in toto, *being Void in Part, for Fraud—Judgment also Held Void, as a Fraud upon Creditors—Costs—Statute*—Lex Loci Contractus.

C., a merchant in failing circumstances, executed to trustees sundry deeds of assignment of his property, in trust to pay his creditors, who were thereby ranked into classes, and were to be paid in a certain order of priority. One of the deeds declared a trust to pay a certain sum annually, for a limited time, to C., the debtor; and all the assignments were subject to this trust. By another of the deeds, any creditor who should attach any of the debtor's property, was to be excluded from the benefit of the trusts; which last provision was subsequently annulled. Afterwards, fearing that the assignments might not prove valid, C. confessed a judgment to the same trustees, upon the same trusts for creditors, but without the reservation in his own favor; which judgment was intended to be resorted to, only in case the assignment should not be adjudged valid.
548*] *Held, that both the assignments and judgment were void *in toto*, being a fraud upon creditors.

An assignment in fraud of creditors, being valid, as between the parties, the assignee cannot take a judgment and execution, which shall bind the subject of the assignment, until this is annulled, released or abandoned, so as to revest the property in the assignor.

The intention to use a judgment confessed by a fraudulent assignor, to a fraudulent assignee, only in case the assignment should be adjudged invalid, connects the judgment, and infects it with the vices of the assignment.

An insolvent debtor may pay some creditors in preference to others; and may secure his preferred creditors by assignment or judgment in trust for such creditors; but he can make no assignment of any part of his property in trust for himself; and if the security for the benefit of his creditors contain any such provision, or be intended to come in aid of another security containing such provision, it is void, not only for the portion reserved, but for the whole—not only in equity but at law.

A deed or judgment void in part, as being a fraud on creditors, is void *in toto*.

A contract, or judgment, illegal and void in part, as being against the provisions of a positive statute, is illegal and void *in toto*.

The cases of Murray v. Riggs, 15 Johns., 571; S. C. 2 Johns., Ch., 565, 580; Estwick v. Caillaud, 5 T. R., 420; 2 Anst., 381, S. C., and Tarback v. Marbury, 2 Vern., 510, considered and explained, in reference to the question, whether an insolvent debtor may, in a deed of trust for the benefit of his creditors, reserve a provision for himself.

Incumbrancers brought in by a mortgagee on a bill to foreclose, and answering and disclaiming as to him, are entitled to the costs of appearing and answering, out of the mortgage fund; though they contest the right to the surplus, as between themselves.

Authorities, showing that they are generally entitled to these costs out of that fund, cited by Sutherland, J.

Decreed by the Court for the Correction of Errors, making various provisions as to costs, between such incumbrancers, relating to, and awarded by divers interlocutory and final orders and decrees of the Circuit Court, Court of Chancery, and Court for the Correction of Errors, in a cause which was commenced in the Circuit Court, and passed through the two latter courts by appeal, the cause having received different determinations on the merits in each court.

The decision of the Court for the Correction of Errors is binding till its doctrine be altered by the Legislation. Per Colden, *Senator.*

But Savage, *Ch. J.*, seems to question the decision of that court, in Murray v. Riggs, 15 Johns., 571.

The *lex loci contractus* governs as to the right of property in the garnishee under the foreign attachment law of the State of La. Chartres v. Cairns, Court of the E. D. of La., 1825. Note to the opinion of Colden, *Senator.*

An assignment, by an insolvent, of property in trust for his creditors, reserving a provision for himself, is void by the law of La. Chartres *v. [*549 Cairns, Court for the E. D. La., 1825. Note to the opinion of Colden, *Senator.*

The property of a debtor who fails, belongs in moral justice to his creditors. Per Savage, *Ch. J.*

Citations—2 Johns. Ch., 565, 580; 15 Johns., 571; 2 Vern., 510; 5 T. R., 420, 424; Rob. Fraud. Conv., 491, n. k; 20 Johns., 442, 447, 449; 4 East, 14; 1 Ves., Jr., 160; 14 Johns., 458, 465; 3 Johns. Ch., 61; 13 Ves., 370; 7 Ves., 583; 2 Madd., 554, 559; 1 R. L., 75, sec. 1, 2; 7 Johns., 161; 2 Anst., 381.

THESE were cross appeals from a decree of the Court of Chancery. The facts are stated in S. C., 1 Hopk. Ch., 373–386. The prominent facts of the case, will also be found stated in the opinions delivered by Sutherland, *J.*, and Colden, *Senator*, in this court.

SANFORD, *Chancellor*, now assigned his reasons for the decree, as in S. C., 1 Hopk. Ch., 393, to 408.

The decree appealed from was, in substance, that the judgment confessed by Cairns to Sedgwick and Lord was not fraudulent or void, as against Mackie, Milne and Lockhart, junior judgment creditors of Cairns, but that the assignment or conveyance by Cairns, to Sedgwick and Lord, in trust to pay certain creditors of Cairns, was void as against Mackie, Milne and Lockhart, by reason of the trust or provision for the benefit of Cairns; and it reversed the decree of the Circuit Court, awarding costs against Mackie, Milne and Lockhart, of their claim, interposed in that court, to the surplus fund arising from the sale of the mortgaged premises; and affirmed the decree that they should pay the costs of an application in that court, to examine Cairns, and to alter a previons order to decree in the cause. The decree then provided that the costs (excepting those of the applications in the Circuit Court, to be paid by Mackie, Milne and Lockhart) should be paid out of the surplus mortgage moneys in question; and that the residue should be paid to Sedgwick and Lord, as senior judgment creditors.

The alteration of the previous decree in the Circuit Court, was made by the circuit judge on petition, so as to charge Mackie, Milne and Lockhart with certain of the interlocutory costs, on the ground that this had been unadvisedly omitted in that decree. It did not explicitly appear, whether this amendment was before or after the final decree was enrolled.

Vide further as to the history of these costs, the opinion of Colden, *Senator*, *post.*

550*] *It is proper also to state here, that it appeared plainly, from the declarations of Sedgwick, and the course of conduct pursued by the trustees, that it was their intention to enforce their judgment, only in the event of the assignments being adjudged void; a circumstance alluded to by the *Chancellor*, 1 Hopk. Ch., 394. The facts connecting the judgment with the assignments will be found more particularly stated, in the opinion of Colden, *Senator*, *post.*

This cause was very fully argued. But as the reasoning and authorities applicable to the case were gone into in the court below, by the arguments of counsel, and the opinion of the *Chancellor*, and will now again be found in the opinions delivered here, I state little more of the arguments of counsel than the points made and the authorities cited by them.

Messrs. R. Sedgwick and *S. Jones*, for Cairns, Sedgwick and Lord. It was unequivocally decided by this court, in *Murray* v. *Riggs*, 15 Johns., 571, that a *bona fide* conveyance made by a debtor in insolvent circumstances, for the benefit of his creditors, should not be avoided by reason of its providing for the maintenance of the debtor or his family; and that if the creditors are dissatisfied, their remedy is in equity, to have the provision applied for their benefit. This decision was recognized, in the sense we ascribe to it, by *Austin* v. *Bell*, 20 Johns., 442; and accords with the general understanding of the legal profession. Many titles to property have doubtless been accepted upon the faith of these decisions, which should not be shaken, even if this court should think that they were originally erroneous. In *Wilkes* v. *Ferris*, 5 Johns., 335, a conveyance to the use of creditors, by general words which left a part to result to the assignor, was holden valid. *Murray* v. *Riggs* did not proceed upon the special circumstances of the case; but on the general ground that a provision like that in question was valid. The acquiescence of creditors, in that case, was relied on merely in respect to several assignments containing a power of revocation, confessedly void, made previously to that of the 31st of May, 1800, which was held good. As to the latter assignment, creditors *were prompt in manifesting their dis- [*551 satisfaction, and litigating it from the first moment.

But if the cases cited may be recanvassed, we insist they were rightly decided. They are directly supported by *Estwick* v. *Caillaud*, 5 T. R., 420. It does not follow, that because a deed is in part void by statute, it is, therefore, and of necessity, void *in toto*. This has been holden in several cases upon the very Statute of Fraudulent Conveyances. (Rob. on Fraud. Conv., 112; Sty., 428; 1 Ch. Cas., 243; 1 Vern., 285, 286; Lane, 22; 5 Johns., 335; 1 Johns. Ch., 482.) The best construction of a statute is that which comes nearest to the rule and reason of the common law. (Bac. Abr., Statute, I., pl., 4.) And it cannot be denied that a deed void in part by the common law, may yet be good for the residue. Here we have to rely on the construction which the common law itself fixes. The statute does not in terms declare that where the conveyance is partly void, it shall be so for the whole. This would many times be unjust, and work an injury to the innocent creditor. Can it be doubted that a bond and mortgage, in trust for several specified creditors, the debt to one turning out to be usurious or fictitious, would yet be valid as to all the rest?

Murray v. *Riggs* is decisive to show that the assignment of Apr. 18, 1823, was not void on account of the clause denying all interest in the trust to attaching creditors.

At any rate, the judgment confessed was not affected by any improper trusts. It cannot be rendered void by construction, but only by proof of actual fraud. And so of any judgment. It does not stand on a footing in this respect with matter *in pais*.

If the assigneees have not conformed to the law, this was the result of mistake, and should not prejudice the *cestui que trust*. They should be brought into court, and have an opportunity to rebut the charge of acquiescence.

A debtor has a right to secure one creditor in preference to another. *Ludlow* v. *Hurd*, 19 Johns., 218.

We were not bound to elect between the as-

signments and judgment. One stood merely as a collateral security to the other. The doctrine of election implies that one thing operates
552**] inconsistently with and excludes the use or necessity of the other. *Dillon* v. *Parker*, 1 Swans., 359; *Sanger* v. *Wood*, 3 Johns. Ch., 416. The party, too, must have a right to elect. It is denied that we have such a right because the assignments were void.

As to the alteration of the decree, by the Circuit Court, the counsel cited *Beekman* v. *Peck*, 3 Johns. Ch., 415, 416, and *Lawrence* v. *Cornell*, 4 *Id.*, 545. They insisted that the award of costs in that court upon interlocutory subjects, being a mere matter of discretion, this court would not interfere concerning them.

Mr. T. J. Oakley, for Mackie, Milne and Lockhart. The judgment confessed by Cairns was fraudulent and void. It was to be set up only in case the assignments should fail. This was a secret; and not expressed in the declaration of the trusts of the judgment. Fraud as to creditors avoids an assignment, though it be on full consideration. (Rob. on Fraud. Conv., 490; 1 Burr., 474, 475; Cowp., 431; 8 Johns., 452; 1 R. L., 75.) The evidence of the fraud is strengthened by the conduct of the assignees subsequent to the judgment, in relation to the execution issued by them. The judgment and assignments cannot both be valid. The latter were good between the parties; 8 Johns., 161; 1 Cow., 622; 4 Cruise Dig., 529; and the assignees being parties also to the judgment, and having with Cairns constantly maintained the validity of the assignments, are estopped to set up the judgment, and still treat the subject of the assignments as the property of Cairns. They were bound to elect between them; and the whole tenor of their conduct shows that they did elect the assignments.

If the judgment be not fraudulent, the trustees should not avail themselves of it without accounting for Cairns' personal estate.

The assignments are clearly void for the reasons stated by the *Chancellor*. The cases on this head are also fully considered in *Hyslop* v. *Clarke*, 14 Johns., 458.

Mackie, Milne and Lockhart ought to have their costs out of the fund, even if both the
553*] judgment and assignments should *be holden valid. They came into court as defendants, and merely claimed what they had reason to consider their just rights. As to the questions of costs in the cause, he cited 3 Johns. Ch., 61; 13 Ves., 370; 7 Ves., 583; 2 Madd. Ch., 554, 555, 2 ed.; 5 Ves., 117; 1 Sch. & L., 12; 4 Johns. Ch., 608; 3 Ves. & B., 143; 13 Ves., 87.

As to the right to alter the decree in the Circuit Court in respect to the costs, he cited Newl. Ch. Pr., 185, Alb. ed.; Harr. Pr., 322; 2 Madd. Ch., 488, 518, 2d ed.; 2 Johns. Ch., 205; 13 Ves., 394; 2 Madd. Ch., 39; 3 Johns. Ch., 415; 4 *Id.*, 545.

That a mistake of the law could not avail anything to the assignees, he cited 2 Johns. Ch., 51; 1 *Id.*, 512; 6 *Id.*, 166; 2 Cow., 678.

He said the objection as to a want of parties could not be made here, inasmuch as it was not urged in the court below. Had this been done, the defect might have been supplied. But the trustees represent the creditors, who are, therefore, virtually before the court. It is not necessary they should be actually brought in.

That a deed void in part by statute, is void for the whole, he cited 22 Vin. Abr., 13, pl. 8, and 14 Johns., 464–466.

SUTHERLAND, *J.* The *Chancellor*, by his decree of Mar. 9, 1825, decided that the general assignment or conveyance from Cairns, Sedgwick and Lord, made Apr. 18, 1823, was void in all its parts in consequence of the trust or provision contained in it, of $2,000 *per annum* for the benefit or support of the grantor. But he held the judgment confessed by Cairns to Sedgwick and Lord Aug. 1, 1823, to be valid; and that by reason of its priority to the judgment of Mackie and others against Cairns, Sedgwick and Lord were entitled to the fund in controversy. From the first part of the decree denying the validity of the assignment, Cairns, Sedgwick and Lord have appealed and Mackie and others have appealed from that part of the decree which establishes the validity of the judgment. If either the assignment or the judgment is sustained, it will entitle Sedgwick and Lord to the fund in controversy.

*I shall first consider the question as [*554
to the validity of the assignment. It is not attempted to be impeached on the ground of actual fraud. It is not pretended that the debts, which it was the primary object of the assignment to secure, were not justly due. Nor is the right of a debtor in failing or insolvent circumstances, to prefer one class of creditors to another, called in question. But the assignment is said to be void within the Statute of Frauds, as being made with the purpose and intent, in judgment of law, to delay, hinder and defraud creditors, in consequence of the trust which it contains in favor of the grantor. That trust is as follows: "In trust, nevertheless, that the said Robert Sedgwick and Daniel Lord, Jr., shall first pay to the said William Cairns, out of the proceeds of the assigned premises, from time to time, for the support of the said William Cairns and his family, after deducting all costs and reasonable charges of the said Robert Sedgwick and Daniel Lord, Jr., in and about the premises, at and after the rate of $2,000 *per annum*, until the said William Cairns shall be discharged from his debts under some insolvent or bankrupt law, or otherwise; provided, however, that such period of payment to the said William Cairns, shall not endure beyond the period of four years from the date hereof."

It is conceded that this is a trust which cannot be enforced if objected to by the creditors of the assignor, or any of them, provided the funds assigned are inadequate to the payment of their debts; and the only question is, whether the whole assignment is rendered void by the illegal trust. An assignment of property to a third person for the benefit of the assignor, is, as against his creditors, equally inefficacious at common law, as it is under the statute. Standing alone and unconnected with any other trust, it would be conclusive evidence of an actual fraudulent intent to put his property beyond the reach of his creditors. No other construction could be put upon the transaction; for, in the nature of things, it could originate in no other motive.

But a partial reservation for the benefit of

the assignor, out of a general assignment for the benefit of his creditors, although it might be avoided as being constructively fraudulent **555*]** *at common law, clearly would not vitiate the other trust and annul the whole deed.

But under the statute, it is contended, the result is different. In *Riggs* v. *Murray*, 2 Johns. Ch., 565, 580; S. C., 15 Johns., 571, on appeal, this question came before the late *Chancellor*. That was the cause of an assignment by an insolvent debtor of all his property upon certain specified trusts; reserving to the grantor the power to alter or revoke the trust and appointments at his pleasure. The assignment was made Mar. 23, 1798. On the 24th the grantors by deed declared certain other trusts, reserving as in the first deed, the power to alter or revoke the appointments within a year. Mar. 21, 1799, the grantors, by deed, revoked and annulled the appointments and trusts of the deed of Mar. 24, 1798; and declared certain other trusts, but still reserving the power to alter and revoke. Mar. 22, certain other trusts were declared, and the power to alter and revoke was still reserved. May 31, 1800, the grantors made a final and absolute declaration of the trusts, without any reservation of the power to revoke or make further appointments; and by this deed the trustees were directed, out of the proceeds of the property assigned, to pay: 1. All the expenses incurred. 2. A sum not exceeding $2,000 *per annum* for each of the grantors (four in number), towards their support from Mar. 28, 1798, until they should be respectively discharged from their debts, or until one year after they should be discharged by law.

June 15, 1801, a commission of bankruptcy was issued against Robert Murray; in July, 1801, an assignment of his property was made to the complainants in the suit, who were the assignees under the commission; and in 1802, they filed their bill against the trustees to annul and set aside the assignment. The bill alleged that the assignment was fraudulent and made to delay, hinder and defraud the creditors of the grantors. The fraud was denied in the answers of the assignees, and a reference was made to a master by consent, to ascertain the amount received by J. B. Murray, one of the assignees; and what sum he was entitled **556*]** *to under the deed of trust. Upon the report of the master, which found a large balance to be due to J. B. Murray, and upon the equity reserved, without any proofs having been taken before the master except as to the accounts, the cause came to a hearing before the *Chancellor*. And he held the assignment void, on account of the power of revocation which it reserved to the grantors. He considered all the deeds as parts of the same transaction, and constituting, in fact, but one act or deed; and although the last deed of the 31st of May, 1800, did not reserve the right to revoke or alter the trusts, in terms, still, as it referred to the deed of 1798, which did contain that power, he held that they must be considered and taken in connection with each other. He remarks: "It may, therefore, be assumed, as a clear and undisputed fact, that whether these deeds be viewed separately, or taken in connection as parts of one whole, and forming one entire act they were made subject to the future disposition and power of the grantors, as well in respect to the debts due to Clark and Murray (the trustees), as in respect to the debts of the other creditors alluded to in those deeds. This leads us (the *Chancellor* continues) to the consideration of the important question arising out of this case; whether such an assignment, by an insolvent debtor to a few select creditors, with such a power of revocation attached to it, can be deemed valid in law. The necessary inference seems to be, that it was made to 'delay, hinder or defraud creditors.' That such powers of revocation are fatal to the instrument and poison it throughout, appears to have been well established by authority."

He then comes to the consideration of that part of the case, which has an immediate bearing upon the one now under consideration. He says, "a reservation of a part of the interest to himself, as in *Tarback* v. *Marbury*, 2 Vern., 510, and in *Estwick* v. *Caillaud*, 5 T. R., 420, does not destroy the provision in respect to the residue; though if the part unreserved be deficient, the creditors might, perhaps, apply to a court of equity for the residue. But if the power enables the grantor to defeat the whole provision, all the cases concur in declaring it null and void.

*Here is a clear and explicit declara- **[*557** tion of the opinion of that learned judge, that a reservation of a part of the trust fund, for the benefit of the assignor, will not vitiate the other provisions in the deed. This was not an *obiter dictum*. It related to a point fairly presented in the cause, and on which the *Chancellor* could not well have avoided the expression of an opinion.

Upon an appeal brought to this court (*Murray* v. *Riggs*, 15 Johns., 571), the prevailing opinion was delivered by *Ch. J.* Thompson. And in relation to the reservation for the maintenance and support of the grantors, his opinion was in perfect coincidence with that of *Chancellor* Kent. He says: "The grantors having reserved to their own use, for their maintenance and support, a part of the property covered by this deed, forms no objection to the appropriation of the residue. This is fully established by the cases I have already referred to, and is indeed admitted by the *Chancellor* in the case before us; though in case of a deficiency to satisfy the creditors, they might apply to a court of equity for the appropriation of the property so reserved towards the payment of their demands." *Chancellor* Sanford considers this opinion of *Ch. J.* Thompson founded on the peculiar circumstances and equities of the case before him, and not as intended to sanction and establish the general proposition which, in terms, it seems to maintain. He says: "I cannot understand the decision of the Court of Errors, to legalize, by one universal rule, these reservations by an insolvent debtor for his own use. But I understand by their decision that in special cases of peculiar equity, the whole assignment shall not be subverted by this illegal trust." I cannot but think, with great deference and respect, that the *Chancellor* has misapprehended the scope and bearing of the opinion of the *Ch. J.* He was for reversing the decree below, principally on the ground that the deed of May 31, 1800, was absolute and irrevocable; and did

not, like the previous deeds, contain a reservation to the grantors of a power to revoke and alter the trusts; and that that deed, in connection with the original assignment of Mar. 23,
558*]1798, was sufficient to protect and *establish the appellants preference; and that the intermediate deeds or declarations of trust might be laid out of view. That as the title of the respondents as assignees of the bankrupt, did not accrue until June, 1801, they had no right to impeach the trust deeds on grounds which had been removed before they had any right or interest in the question. That the power of revocation did not render the deeds absolutely void and incapable of confirmation, as between the parties, before the rights of third persons intervened. Whatever, therefore, might have been the original character of the transaction, he held that every legal objection to it was removed, and the title of the appellants rendered perfect before the respondents had any interest in the funds in controversy. That Robert Murray himself, after the deed of May, 31, had no control over the trust fund; and that his assignees under the commission, could take nothing which the bankrupt had not a right to assign to them. He remarks, "there can be no doubt but at that time (May, 1800) an original assignment might have been legally made giving to John B. Murray all the claim now set up; if so, there could be no good reason against his then taking a ratification or confirmation of any prior defective assignment." He then proceeds: "Where the creditor is pursuing his debtor with a judgment and execution, or in any other manner, to enforce payment of his demand, an assignment of the debtor's property, containing a power of revocation, may very well be considered as made to 'delay, hinder or defraud creditors,' according to the language of the Statute of Frauds. But I do not see how it could, in any sense, be said to delay or hinder a creditor who was taking no measures to enforce payment of his demand as in the case now before us. For anything that appears, all the creditors of Robert Murray & Co. were satisfied with the assignment and the provision there made for the payment of their debts."

The *Chief Justice* is here considering the effect of the power of revocation in the deeds prior to that of May, 1800, and he admits, that that provision would clearly have rendered them void against any creditor, who, during
559*] their existence, *might have attempted to enforce payment of his demand. As against such a creditor, he concedes, they must have been considered as made with the intent to delay, hinder and defraud him. But his argument is, the respondents are not such creditors; they did not become creditors until after the power of revocation in those deeds had been abrogated by the deed of 1800; and they ought not now to be permitted to impeach the assignment on a ground which had ceased to exist before their title accrued; especially, when, for aught that appears, all the creditors of Robert Murray & Co. were satisfied with the assignments (containing the power of revocation) and the provision there made for the payment of their debts. The parties in interest, during the continuance of those assignments, never complained; and the representatives of those parties (the respondents, the assignees in bankruptcy) shall not now avail themselves of the objection. The whole argument relates exclusively to the power of revocation and the deeds in which it was contained; that is, the deeds prior to that of May, 1800. Now, none of those deeds contained the trust for the benefit of the grantors. That was contained in the deed of May 31, 1800, which did not reserve the power of revocation. The special circumstances, therefore, on which the *Ch. J.* dwelt, and which the *Chancellor* supposes influenced the judgment of the court, and distinguishes it from the case now before us, I humbly apprehend were urged exclusively in relation to the power of revocation, and had no reference to, or bearing upon, the reservation of a portion of the fund for the benefit of the grantors. The *Ch. J.* could not have intended to say, that, for anything that appeared in that case, the creditors of Robert Murray & Co. were satisfied with the assignment of May 31, 1800. He could not have intended to discriminate between the respondents, who were the representatives of the creditors, and the creditors themselves; and to intimate that the case would have been varied, if the assignment had then been impeached by a creditors instead of the assignees. The assignees succeeded to all the right of all the creditors; and their dissatisfaction with the assignment was conclusive evidence, in judgment of law, *that each individual creditor was dis- [***560**
satisfied. (*Vide* Rob. Fraud. Conv., 491, *note*, K.) Nor could he have intended to say that none but judgment creditors at the time of the assignment could impeach it. I repeat, therefore, that, in my humble apprehension, this court did not decide the case of *Murray* v. *Riggs*, upon any special circumstances, so far as the trust in favor of the grantors was concerned. But that they proceeded upon the broad principle that such a trust, in an assignment for the benefit of creditors, does not, *per se*, vitiate and destroy the whole deed. Nor do I perceive how the judgment in that case can be sustained on any other ground.

Such, too, was the view the Supreme Court took of that case in *Austin* v. *Bell*, 20 Johns., 447. The assignment in that case was impeached on the ground that it contained a reservation of a certain sum for the maintenance and support of the grantor and his family; and, also, because it provided, that if any of the creditors named in the assignment should not, within a limited time, assent to the assignment, then the trustees should pay to the grantors the proportion of the fund which would have belonged to such creditors. The assignment was held to be void on the latter ground. But in relation to the first objection, *Ch. J.* Spencer, in delivering the opinion of this court, remarks: "In the case of *Murray* v. *Riggs*, one of the appointments and reservations in the trust deed of the 31st of May, 1800, was that the trustees should pay out of the proceeds of the property assigned, towards the support of the grantors, a sum not exceeding $2,000 a year, for each of the grantors. As to this reservation, the *Chancellor* was of opinion, on the authority of *Estwick* v. *Caillaud*, 5 T. R., 420, that it did not destroy the provisions in respect to the residue; and he intimates an opinion that if

the part not reserved was deficient, the creditors might apply to a court of equity for the residue. In this part of the *Chancellor's* opinion," he observes, "*Ch. J.* Thompson, who delivered the opinion of the Court of Errors, concurred. This, then," he continues, "puts an end to the objection made to this assignment, as to a reservation out of the trust property, of a sup-
561*] port for *a limited time, for one of the assignors." The Supreme Court, therefore, considered the position upon this subject laid down by *Chancellor* Kent, and concurred in by this court, as a general proposition, and not founded upon the particular circumstances of that case; and as settling the question that a reservation out of the trust property, for the support of the grantor, for a limited time, did not, *per se*, vitiate and destroy the residue of the assignment. Coinciding fully, for the reasons which I have assigned, in this view of the case of *Murray* v. *Riggs*, I cannot consider that question as now open for discussion.

But if it were open, I think the decision on this point in *Murray* v. *Riggs*, fully supported by the case of *Estwick* v. *Caillaud*, 5 T. R., 420. In that case, Ld. Abingdon assigned a certain mansion house, with the park pleasure grounds, and personal chattels belonging to it, to one Estwick, for 99 years, in trust to receive the rents and profits, and pay one half of them to the grantor during his life; and the other moiety to certain creditors enumerated in a schedule attached to the deed. One Townsend, not being a favored creditor, obtained a judgment against Ld. Abingdon, and levied an execution on some of the property assigned; for which the assignee brought an action of trespass. Upon the trial, it was left to the jury to determine the actual intent of the transaction; and they found it to be fair, and gave a verdict for the plaintiff. Upon a motion for a new trial, it was contended that the deed was void, on the face of it, under the Statute of Frauds, 13 Eliz., on account of the reservation in favor of the grantor. But the court were unanimously of opinion that that did not destroy the deed. It was contended in *Austin* v. *Bell*, and also in this case, that *Estwick* v. *Caillaud* was decided on the ground, that it was a partial and not a general assignment of the property of the grantor; and that, for aught that appeared, enough was retained by him to pay the creditor who was then prosecuting. Spencer, *J.*, in *Austin* v. *Bell*, also remarks, "that the case of *Estwick* v. *Caillaud* was decided on the ground that Ld. Abingdon had not assigned all his property; but that he reserved enough to satisfy the particular creditor
562*] who *sought to set aside the assignment." Now, I humbly apprehend, that it does not appear that that was the ground of the decision, in any sense that affects the question of the reservation for the benefit of the grantor. The fact that it was a partial assignment, is inferred only from the circumstance that it did not appear on the face of the deed to be a general one; and this circumstance is alluded to by the judges, not intending to show that the deed was not fraudulent under the Statutes of Elizabeth, but that it did not come within the operation of the spirit of the Bankrupt Laws, as being a general assignment for the benefit of favored creditors. Ld. Kenyon says: "There was nothing fraudulent, either in the construction of the deed or in the manner of carrying it into execution. It was neither illegal or immoral to prefer one set of creditors to another. This case differs, in many respects, from the preference given by bankrupts. But it was never held, even in the case of a trader, that he could not give a preference in some respects, provided he did not exhaust his whole estate, or approach so near to a disposition of the whole, as that the exception was merely colorable. But as it does not appear that this was a conveyance of the whole of Ld. Abingdon's property, the case is delivered from the objection which asserts that the deed is fraudulent, because it was only intended as a provision for some of the creditors to the exclusion of the rest." The objection was, that the assignment was bad, because it was not for the benefit of all the creditors. Ld. Kenyon answers it by saying, it was a partial, not a general assignment, having no reference or allusion whatever to the reservation in favor of the grantor. *Mr. Justice* Ashurst says: "There is nothing illegal on the face of the deed; for a debtor may prefer one set of creditors to another, except in certain cases on the Bankrupt Laws. Where the Bankrupt Laws do not interfere, a debtor may give a preference to particular creditors. There appears," he continues, "no badge of fraud in any part of the transaction. All the legal property was transferred to the plaintiff for legal purposes. And though a part of the profit was reserved for Ld. Abingdon himself, that alone will not avoid the legal estate in the trustee for the benefit of *the schedule creditors. And when [***563**
those creditors are satisfied, the other creditors may apply to a court of equity for the residue." *Mr. Justice* Buller says: "If we are to decide on the face of the deed itself, that is a question of fraud in point of law. Now taking the deed by itself, not accompanied with the circumstance that there were other creditors of Ld. Abingdon, there is no pretense for the objection. Nor does the objection occur here, that this was a conveyance of the whole of Ld. Abingdon's property; for it is not so stated in the deed, and the contrary appears from the evidence;" alluding, evidently, to the objection which had been answered by Ld. Kenyon, that it was an assignment for the benefit of favored creditors; and therefore fraudulent within the spirit of the Bankrupt Laws. The fact that Ld. Abingdon had, previously to the assignment, offered Townsend the materials of another building in satisfaction of his demand, could not have affected the question of legal fraud appearing on the face of the deed, whatever influence it might have had on the question of actual intent. (*Vide*, also, 2 Vern., 510; 4 East, 14; 1 Ves., Jr., 160.)

Nor am I dissatisfied with the decision in *Murray* v. *Riggs*, upon principle. The question is not, whether a man can put his property beyond the reach of his creditors, by conveying it in trust for his own use—it is conceded that he cannot; but it is whether the reservation of a moderate portion of his property for the maintenance of his family, for a limited time, in a general assignment for the benefit of his creditors, shall, in all cases, be conclusive evidence, in judgment of law, of an

intent to delay, hinder and defraud his creditors, within the meaning of the Statute of Frauds, so as to vitiate and destroy the whole conveyance. I fully agree with the *Chancellor*, and with the decision in *Hyslop* v. *Clarke*, 14 Johns., 458, that if such a provision is to be considered conclusive evidence that the conveyances were made with an intent to delay and hinder creditors, it must avoid and destroy the whole assignment; because the statute has declared that all conveyances made with such intent, shall be absolutely void and of none effect. It is for that very reason, believing that cases may exist, in which such a provision would be
564*] *neither unjust nor improper, that I would hold it voidable only upon application to a court of equity, and not absolutely void within the statute.

The principle in relation to this point appears to me not to be stated with perfect accuracy by the learned judge who delivered the opinion of the court in *Hyslop* v. *Clarke*. He says (14 Johns., 465): "It appears to be an established rule that where a bond is void in part, as against the positive provisions of a statute, the whole bond is void." Now, I apprehend, that if a bond contains provisions which are declared illegal, or void by statute, and other provisions, which are legal, the whole bond will not be void, unless the statute expressly provides that those illegal provisions shall render the whole bond void. Suppose the Statute of Frauds had expressly declared that any provision, for the grantor, in an assignment for the benefit of creditors, should be considered fraudulent and void; would an assignment, unexceptionable in every other respect, but containing such a provision, be void throughout? I apprehend not. The statute having merely declared that such a provision should be void, without having declared what its effect should be upon the residue of the assignment, that effect would have been left to be ascertained and determined by the rules of the common law. But if the statute had declared, not only, that any such provision should be considered fraudulent, but also that any conveyance containing any such provision should be absolutely void, then the whole deed undoubtedly would be void; not because it was void in part, as against the positive provisions of a statute, but because the statute had declared, in terms, that being void in part, it should be void throughout. The provision for the benefit of the assignor in this case, may be set aside, without affecting the other provisions of the deed, and without conflicting with any of the cases which have been cited.

I am, therefore, of opinion that so much of the decree of the *Chancellor* as adjudges the assignment from Cairns to Sedgwick & Lord to be void, throughout, by reason of the trust or provision for the benefit of Cairns, should be reversed.

565*] *Holding the assignment to be good, there is no ground on which the judgment can be impeached as fradulent. It is a cumulative security only, for a justifiable object. But admitting the assignment to be fraudulent, I should still hold the judgment to be valid, for the reasons assigned by the *Chancellor*. The written declaration of trust accompanying the judgment, and which is testified by the oath of one of the assignees, shows that the judgment was confessed for the purpose of securing payment to certain creditors, and for that purpose only. There was no trust for the benefit of the insolvent. The judgment was not intended (nor could it possibly have the effect) to protect the annuity to Cairns. Sedgwick swears, expressly, that all the trusts were contained in the written declaration accompanying the judgment. But it is unnecessary to enlarge on this point. I think, as to judgment, the decree of the *Chancellor* should be affirmed.

I think both parties are entitled to the costs of their answers, as defendants to Mr. Hone's bill. They were subsequent incumbrancers; and were necessarily made parties. They both answered and disclaimed, as against Mr. Hone's prior lien and assented to the sale of the premises, reserving their respective claims to the surplus. There is nothing to except this case from the general rule, that, on a bill to foreclose a mortgage where subsequent mortgagees or judgment creditors, who are made defendants, answer and disclaim, they are entitled to their costs, to be paid out of the fund. (3 Johns. Ch., 61; 13 Ves., 370; 7 Ves., 583; 2 Madd., 554, 559.)

My opinion being in favor of the validity of the assignments and judgment, which it was the object of all the proceedings, subsequent to the decree of the 12th of January, 1824, to impeach, I think Cairns, Sedgwick and Lord are entitled to their costs, upon all those proceedings before the judge of the first circuit, except the proceedings upon the petition of Mackie, Milne and Lockhart, for the examination of Cairns, which the circuit judge disposed of by an interlocutory decree of May 26, 1824; and upon the petition of Cairns, Sedgwick and Lord for a modification of the decree of Jan. 12, 1824, which were also *dis- [***566**
posed of by an interlocutory decree of May 27, 1824. The costs of those motions having been disposed of by the circuit judge, I am of opinion his decision, in this respect, should not be disturbed. They are also entitled to all their costs of the proceedings upon appeal in the Court of Chancery—to be paid by Mackie, Milne and Lockhart.

WOODWORTH, *J.*, and Brayton and Redfield, *Senators*, concurred.

COLDEN, *Senator*. Will the law permit an insolvent debtor to assign his property, so that he may enjoy, against the will of his creditors, such part as he may choose to reserve for his own use?

However simple and disembarrassed this question may at first appear, it is one of those so elaborately argued before us, and which we have now to decide.

Mr. Cairns, being insolvent, assigned, by several instruments, all his property to Messrs. Sedgwick and Lord, in trust, that they should allow him out of the proceeds, or out of the rents and profits, $2,000 a year, till he should be discharged from his debts; but the allowance was not to extend beyond four years; and upon the further trust that the residue should be distributed among certain of his creditors.

Here, then, is a conveyance by which an insolvent debtor reserves to himself out of his property such revenue as he sees fit, for such time as he thinks will suit his convenience;

and when his creditors, who are not among those he has chosen to favor, and who are dissatisfied, obtain an execution against his estate, they find in their way a conveyance which not only hinders them from levying their debt; but secures the property, in part at least, to their debtor.

If there be such a thing as natural equity; if we may ever appeal to those perceptions of right and wrong which are independent of all learning, it seems to me that we may do so on this occasion; and cannot hesitate to decide that such a disposition of property is invalid.

We are not left, however, to the mere dictates of natural justice. The Legislature has **567***] thought proper to record its *precepts; and we have them in the Statute, 1 R. L., 75, which enacts that every conveyance which is devised or contrived with an intent to delay, hinder or defraud creditors, shall be clearly and utterly void, frustrate and of none effect; any pretense, color, feigned consideration, expressing of use, or any other matter or thing to the contrary notwithstanding. That the conveyance or assignment in question has delayed and hindered creditors, the testimony before us establishes. If to put property in such a situation that an insolvent may enjoy it in defiance of those to whom he is indebted, is to defraud them, the assignments in question will, if they stand, have that effect. Generally, and unless the contrary appears, we must infer that the consequences which naturally flow from the acts of a person were intended by him. This will lead us to the conclusion that the assignments not only did hinder and defraud creditors, but were intended so to do.

It is unnecessary, however, to resort to this reasoning to arrive at this conclusion. It is avowed that the assignment was intended to prevent certain of his creditors from touching the property, so that the insolvent might enjoy that benefit from it which he had thought proper to reserve for himself; and that the residue might be distributed among those he chose to favor. One would think, therefore, that this assignment was not only conscientious, but directly against the statute.

But we are referred from legislative enactments to judicial decisions; and told that we must receive these as the law, however they may be in collision with the letter of the statute. And yet, it would seem that the prescriptions of the judicial code must be contradictory, or liable to very different interpretations; for in this case many authorities have been cited by the counsel on each side, to maintain their respective and directly opposite propositions.

We are bound to pay great respect to the opinions of other tribunals. We owe obedience to the former judgments of this court. If this court has, heretofore, determined that an assignment like those now under consideration, made under the same circumstances, may be **568***] maintained, we ought to *consider this as the established law, however we might be disposed to decide otherwise if the question was now agitated here for the first time. An inferior tribunal is at liberty to change its decisions as the opinions of its members may alter; but if this court, of the last resort, were to exercise the same liberty, there would be no security for property. The members of this court are, in part, annually changed; and if those who compose it at any time should feel themselves unrestrained by the determinations of their predecessors, the rights of things and persons might vary as often as the court was in session; and we should be in that condition which one of our oldest writers says, marks a miserable people, "where the laws are vague and uncertain." If the law, as settled by this court, be inconvenient or wrong, it must be for the Legislature to change it. They can do it without disturbing dispositions of property which may have been made in accordance with the judgments of this court; whereas, a judgment here, in opposition to former decisions of this tribunal, unsettles all that may have been done pursuant to what the community had a right to consider as the established law.

With these views I shall, for a moment, advert to some of the cases which have been cited in support of the assignments. One class of them establish that a conveyance by an insolvent in favor of some creditors, to the exclusion of others, is not against the statute. But these cases are very different from one where an assignment reserves part of the estate to the assignor. In the former case, though one creditor may be hindered and even deprived of any share of his debtor's property, yet it cannot be said to hinder or delay creditors, when the whole property is immediately put out of the hands of the assignor, and the whole of it goes to creditors. In these two cases there is all the difference that there is between an assignment, the object of which is to prefer some creditors, and an assignment, the object of which, as to the part reserved, is not only to hinder but forever to defeat all creditors.

Ld. Abingdon's case, *Estwick* v. *Caillaud*, 5 T. R., 420; 2 Anst., 381, is one much relied upon; and I confess I find much difficulty in distinguishing that case, in principle, from the *one we are now considering. It ap- [***569** pears to me that the report of that case develops one of those contrivances by which the nobility of England put their estates at nurse; so that they may recruit without being harrassed by importunate creditors. How far the policy of protecting the wealth of the aristocracy of England may have influenced the jury and court in favor of Ld. Abingdon, I will not pretend to say. "The effect of that decision was to allow Ld. Abingdon to enjoy his mansion house, park and pleasure grounds;" to permit him to make presents of his deer, and run his horses at New Market, while his creditor, who had built his house, and whose debt had been due more than twenty years, was obliged to look on, with his execution in his hands. I will presume that this English case may be distinguished from that now before us by the circumstances which the *Chancellor* has noticed; but if it be not, I find nothing in this decision of the Court of K. B. that commands my respect; and I owe no obedience to it; because it was decided long subsequently to the Revolution.

It is not so with the case of *Murray* and *Riggs*, 15 Johns., 571; that being a judgment of this court, according to the principles which I have professed, I hold myself bound by the decision. Whenever another case occurs similar in all its circumstances, I will decide as this court has heretofore decided. But I think the court in that case carried its indulgence to the insolvent debtor to the very utmost length. I will not consent to go one step further in the same course. I think we cannot do so without trampling on the statute.

When, therefore, I am to determine whether an assignment made by partners of their partnership property only, which reserves out of the property assigned a sum for their support, be void; when the creditors have acquiesced in the assignment for several years, and till the assignees have distributed the money arising from the assets, among the creditors; where no creditor has been actually impeded in the pursuit of his remedy, and where at last the creditors themselves do not sue; but the assignment is questioned by assignees under a commission
570*] of bankruptcy, I shall give an *opinion in favor of such an assignment. But I shall not attempt to give any other reason for my opinion, than that, in the case of *Murray* and *Riggs*, this court has decided that such an assignment, under such circumstances, is good.

In the case of *Austin* and *Bell*, 20 Johns., 442, *Ch. J.* Spencer, after having applied his great and discriminating mind to the consideration of the case of *Murray* and *Riggs*, notwithstanding that case, says: "I am bound to say, that a deed which does not fairly devote the property of a person, overwhelmed with debt, to the payment of his creditors, but reserves a portion of it to himself, unless the creditors assent to such terms as he shall prescribe, is, in law, fraudulent and void, as against the Statute of Frauds, being made with intent to delay, hinder or defraud creditors of their just and legal actions." The assignments of Mr. Cairns have all these characters of the assignment of the Messrs. Secors, which induced the Supreme Court, unanimously, to pronounce that assignment void. Mr. Cairns was overwhelmed with debt. He reserved an annuity of $2,000 a year for four years, unless within that time his creditors would assent to his discharge.

The case before us presents none of the features which were peculiar to the case of *Murray* and *Riggs*. And I think we can not sanction this assignment of Mr. Cairns without so far repealing the Statute for the Prevention of Frauds; or give effect to any part of the assignments, without overruling the decisions of the Supreme Court in the cases of *Hyslop* v. *Clarke*, 14 Johns., 458, and *Austin* v. *Bell*, 20 Johns., 442.

If we decide that the assignments are invalid, we dispose of a large part of this case. The judgment confessed by Mr. Cairns remains to be considered. The language of the Statute in relation to Judgments and Executions is the same as in relation to Grants or Conveyances. It is declared that they shall be clearly and utterly void, and of no effect, if they be entered with intent to hinder or defraud creditors of their actions or just debts, or to hinder or let the due course and execution of law and justice. Though a judgment be fraudulent, this will never appear on the face of it. All judg-
571*] ments *are entered according to certain forms; and if these be duly observed, they are valid, unless they may be set aside by a court on grounds which do not appear on the record. Whether a judgment be void or not, under the statute, depends on the intent with which it was entered. The intent must be gathered from the acts and declarations of the parties in relation to it. If a judgment be intended to secure to a person a part of his property, so that he may enjoy it against the will of any one of his creditors, and if it will have that effect, it is void.

Messrs. Sedgwick and Lord, on the day the judgment was entered, executed a declaration that they held the judgment in trust for securing to the honorary and confidential creditors of Mr. Cairns, mentioned in a schedule to the declaration annexed, the payment of their debts, as in the schedule specified. Among these creditors, Mackie, Milne and Lockhart are not named.

There cannot be a doubt, that if the judgment and declaration were an independent transaction between the parties, the judgment would be valid. It would be a legal means of giving a preference to creditors, which the law allows.

I entirely concur with the *Chancellor* in the opinion he has expressed, that where a security is taken which is defective or questionable (and I will add fraudulent), a party may take a new security that may be exempt from all objection. But then he must abandon the objectionable or fraudulent security. He cannot hold the good security, and yet avail himself of that which is vicious. Much less can he make the new security a means of sustaining that which was illegal. The declaration of trust cannot be conclusive as to the intent of the parties. For as to the intent, as in relation to other instruments, we must look to acts and expressions.

Mr. Sedgwick, in his answer to the seventh interrogatory, says, that "the instruments and judgment are now held by defendant and Daniel Lord, Jr., upon the trusts declared as above stated, in relation to the same respectively." And in a further answer to the same interrogatory, he says, he "knows of no act or thing by which the trusts in the assignment of the 25th of March, or either of them, have been annulled *or abrogated, impaired or [***572**
modified, otherwise than by the operation of the other instruments of writing above mentioned." That is, by the subsequent assignments, and the declaration as to the judgment, all of which, except the last, refer to, and confirm the trusts expressed in the first assignment of March 25.

In a petition presented to the Circuit Court by Messrs. Cairns, Sedgwick and Lord, May 4, 1824, they say they "claim as assignees under certain trust deeds or assignments, and under a certain judgment confessed to them in trust for the benefit of the creditors of Cairns; the said deeds and last mentioned judgments being all prior to the said judgment of Mackie, Milne and Lockhart."

In answer to the fourth interrogatory before Master Bolton, Mr. Sedgwick answers, that he and Mr. Lord "have at all times, since the 18th of April, 1823, insisted upon the validity of the several assignments and conveyances."

This, as well as their answer to the bill, is sufficient to show that Messrs. Sedgwick and Lord never gave up the assignments; and there is abundant evidence that, in accordance with their opinion, they continued to act under them, long after the judgment was entered.

They sold the houses to Henry D. Sedgwick and Develin, Jan. 15, 1824, and they say they then considered themselves as holding under the assignments.

They had paid to Mr. Cairns, as they say, on account of the provision for his maintenance contained in the assignments, between $2,000 and $3,000. A great part of this was paid after the judgment was entered ; so that Mr. Cairns received, to his own use, this large amount of his property, while Mackie, Milne and Lockhart could receive nothing on account of their debt of $3,000, which sum they had paid to Mr. Cairns for a bill of exchange, only four days before he failed, and before he made his first assignment.

Add to this, that when the sheriff, who held the *fieri facias* issued on this judgment, applied to Mr. Sedgwick to show if there was any property of Mr. Cairns on which the execution might be levied, Mr. Sedgwick told him he 573*] knew *nothing about it; by which the witness understood he had no directions to give concerning it; and when the sheriff asked him if the property had not been assigned, he answered it had.

There seems no kind of question, then, that, after the judgment was entered, Messrs. Sedgwick and Lord continued not only to insist on the validity of the assignments, but to act under them.

That they availed themselves of the judgment to maintain the assignments appears from the testimony, which I shall now notice.

In his answer to the sixth interrogatory before Master Bolton, Mr. Sedgwick states that the assignees always maintained, that if the assignments and conveyances were not good and valid in law, then the judgment was valid and binding.

In another part of his testimony, he says the judgment was to be resorted to, only in case the assignments were not valid. And again, the *fieri facias*, he says, was intended to cover all property assigned, provided the same was subject thereto, notwithstanding the assignments.

Mr. Sedgwick repeatedly states that his intentions were fair and honorable; and that neither the assignments nor judgments were intended by him to have what he esteemed an undue or fraudulent operation. To this, no one will more readily assent than myself. But we cannot consider declarations of this nature from parties interested, made in exculpation of their conduct. We must interpret acts by their consequences; and must presume persons intended to produce the effects which naturally flow from their acts. We can not doubt that the assignees, Messrs. Sedgwick and Lord, intended to continue, and would have continued to pay Mr. Cairns his annuity, and to have executed their trust according to the assignments, if Mackie, Milne and Lockhart had not instituted a suit to avoid these assignments. In what situation, then, do the assignee place the creditors by means of the judgment? They hold to the creditors, in effect, this language: "We shall go on and execute the trust according to the assignments, whether they be good or bad. 574*] *If you institute a suit, and set the assignments aside, you can get nothing by it; because, then, we shall claim all the property under the judgment; and however this may benefit the favored creditors, mentioned in the schedule, yet it can be of no advantage to you." Indeed, this is exactly the operation of the judgment, if this court confirm the decree of the *Chancellor* as to the assignments. These will be declared fraudulent and void; and yet, if the judgment is permitted to stand, Mackie, Milne and Lockhart will have gained nothing by their suit; but, on the contrary, will have borne uselessly all this litigation. Mr. Cairns may yet receive his $2,000 a year, if the schedule creditors do not object; and the assignees will be perfectly secure that no other dissatisfied creditors, who may not be among those Mr. Cairns has thought proper to favor, will ever question their conduct. The judgment protects them, however illegal the assignments may be, under which, since the judgment was entered, they have acted, and may continue to act.

Let us suppose, for a moment, that the declaration executed when the judgment was entered, instead of being as it is, should have expressed trusts simular to those contained in the assignments; that is to say, that Mr. Cairns should receive out of his property $2,000 a year; provided that, if any creditor should be discontented, and should succeed in establishing, in a court of chancery, that this provision, was fraudulent and void, then the judgment should stand good for the benefit of certain favored creditors. I cannot think that we should hesitate, for a moment, to pronounce a judgment connected with such a declaration void. It can make no difference that the trusts, as to the judgment now in question, are not on the same paper with the declaration made when the judgment was entered.

I cannot concur in opinion with the *Chancellor*, that the judgment is a new security, unconnected with the assignments, and exempt from all the objections which apply to them. I think the facts, as they stand before the court, so far from not admitting, as the *Chancellor* supposes, a presumption that the judgment was given and taken upon the *trusts [*575 expressed in the antecedent assignments, prove incontestably that the judgment was so given and taken. The evidence that the assignees continued to act under the assignments; that they paid Mr. Cairns money according to the assignments, after they had obtained the judgment, and intended to continue to act under the assignments until they should be declared invalid, is as positive proof, it appears to me, as the nature of the case admits, that the judgment was confessed by Mr. Cairns with an intent that it should be used, if it could be so used, to support the assignments and deter dissatisfied creditors from questioning them, and for no other purpose.

I, therefore, think that this judgment was devised and contrived to delay creditors of their lawful actions and demands, to the hindrance of the due course of the execution of law and justice, and that so it is against the statute, and must be held utterly void.

There remains to be disposed of, the two interlocutory decrees of the Circuit Court, one of May 26, 1824, ordering Mackie, Milne and Lockhart to pay the cost of an unsuccessful application which they had made to have Mr.

Cairns examined before the master, and the other of the 27th of the same month, ordering the same parties to pay the costs of a successful application which Messrs. Cairns, Sedgwick and Lord had made to have the decree of the Circuit Court amended.

These decrees, in my opinion, were both erroneous. The only reason that we can find for the first decree, is suggested by Mr. Sedgwick in an affidavit which he made and read to oppose the application; which is, that the whole business having been conducted under his advice and agency, he was better acquainted with all the facts than Mr. Cairns; and he, Mr. Sedgwick, having been examined, it was unnecessary to examine Mr. Cairns.

But why were Mackie, Milne and Lockhart obliged to rest on the examination of one party? Had they not the same right to have Mr. Cairns examined that they had to have the testimony of Mr. Sedgwick? Possibly Mr.
576*] Cairns and *Mr. Sedgwick might not have agreed in their testimony. Possibly Mr. Cairns might not have given the same answers, as to the intent of the assignments and judgment, that Mr. Sedgwick had given. I can imagine no possible reason why this application should not have been granted. I think, therefore, that the Circuit Court not only erred in compelling Mackie, Milne and Lockhart to pay the costs of that application, but in refusing to let Mr. Cairns be examined.

May 27, the Circuit Court ordered that its own decree of Jan. 12, preceding, so far as it ordered costs out of the fund to Mackie, Milne and Lockhart, having been unadvisedly entered without the authority of the court, should be expunged. Now, if this decree had been wrongfully entered by Mackie, Milne and Lockhart, then they might have been justly chargeable with the costs of the application to set the decree right. But Messrs. Cairns, Sedgwick and Lord state in their petition to have the decree altered, that they were informed by the solicitor of Mackie, Milne and Co. that the order that they should have costs, was inserted by the solicitor of Philip Hone, the original complainant in the suit. There is nothing to contradict this information. Messrs. Sedgwick and Lord do not allege that is was incorrect; nor is there anything to show that Mackie, Milne & Co. had ever been requested to consent to an alteration of the order. I cannot conceive, therefore, why Mackie, Milne and Lockhart should be charged with the costs of correcting this mistake. In my opinion, the order of the Circuit Court should not have been affirmed by the *Chancellor*.

My opinion is, that the decree of the *Chancellor*, so far as it respects the assignment, be affirmed. That so far as respects the judgment, and the two interlocutory orders of the Circuit Court, it be reversed, and the judgment declared void. That the money which Mackie, Milne and Lockhart have paid under the two last mentioned decrees, be refunded to them by Cairns, Sedgwick and Lord; and that they pay to Mackie, Milne and Lockhart the costs of those applications. That so much of the money
577*] arising from the sale of *the premises mortgaged to Philip Hone as remains (after satisfying the mortgages to which the same premises were liable, and the costs of the mortgagees, or of those representing them), be paid to Mackie, Milne and Lockhart, on account of their judgment; and that Cairns, Sedgwick and Lord pay to Mackie, Milne and Lockhart, their cost incurred in the Circuit Court, the Court of Chancery and this court.

Since this cause was argued we have been furnished with a manuscript, purporting to be the report of a case decided in the Supreme Court of the State of La., sitting in the Eastern District (*Chartres* v. *Cairns et al.*, June Term, 1825, M. S.), by which it appears that one of the assignments of Mr. Cairns, now before this court, was by the judgment of the Court of La., declared to be valid. The judges of La. say that the decree of our *Chancellor*, avoiding the assignment, "is most clearly correct according to the laws of this State, on the subject of insolvencies." But the Court of La. consider that the *lex loci contractus* ought to govern. They, therefore, feel themselves constrained to ascertain what is our law; and come to the conclusion, that it is settled in favor of the assignments by the case of *Murray v. Riggs;* notwithstanding our *Chancellor's* opinion, that that case could not sustain the assignments of Mr. Cairns. I have already noticed the circumstances which, in my opinion, render the case of *Murray v. Riggs* different from that in which we are now rendering our judgment. I am entirely disposed to pay to the court of the State of La. all the respects that may be due to it; but when I am searching for an exposition of the decisions of our own tribunals, I think it safer to take as guides our own *Chancellor* and judges, than to follow those who, as they say themselves, probably have no practical, and may be supposed to have little, even theoretical, knowledge of our laws. In the cases of *Hyslop v. Clarke*, and of *Austin v. Bell*, our Supreme Court has given a different interpretation to the case of *Murray v. Riggs*, from that which has been adopted in La. I have already assigned my reasons for believing that the judgment of the Supreme *Court in these cases was [***578**
correct; and I find nothing in the report of the case from Louisiana(a) to change my opinion.

Clark, Lefferts, Lynde, Thorn and *Wilkeson, Senators*, concurred.

(a) The following is the report of that case as furnished.

Eastern District of the State of La.—June Term, 1825.

CHARTRES V. CAIRNS ET AL.

Appeal from the court of the first district.

MATHEWS, J., delivered the opinion of the court. In this case the plaintiff commenced his suit by attachment, which was levied on property and funds of the defendants, alleged to be in the hands of Thomas M. Rogers, who was summoned as garnishee; and, in the first instance, deposed that he had no property or funds in his possession belonging to the defendants; but afterwards, on further interrogatories, disclosed the whole of the facts relative to the property which he once held for said defendants, and which had been assigned by him to persons in trust in the City of N. Y., for the purpose of paying certain creditors designated by the deed of assignment, and for his own support, until he should be discharged in pursuance of some insolvent or bankrupt system; and of this assignment the garnishee had notice previous to laying the attachment, and agreed to hold the funds for the assignees.

Under these circumstances, the court below dismissed the attachment; and from that judgment the plaintiff appealed.

The correction of the judgment of the District Court depends on the validity of the deed of trust; and its validity depends on the law of the State of N. Y. as being *lex loci contractus*. Both parties.

579*] *SAVAGE, *Ch. J.*, after stating the facts. In my judgment, all depends upon the validity of the assignments, particularly the assignment of Apr. 18, 1823. It purports to be a conveyance of the very property out of which the fund in question arises. If it did convey the property, then, clearly, Cairns was not the owner Aug. 1, 1823, when Sedgwick & Lord's judgment was docketed. They were themselves the owners; and a judgment in their favor could not be a lien on their own property. If the assignment was fraudulent and void as to creditors, still it was valid as between the parties; and their rights, under it, will be the same as if it were valid against all the world. It does not lie in the mouths of the parties to the fraudulent conveyance, to say it is fraudulent. (7 Johns., 161.)

I lay the judgment entirely out of the question. Had the plaintiffs intended to rely upon it, they should have released to the defendant the property on which it was to become a lien. It is admitted that the judgment was intended to come in aid of the assignment; and hence the assignees have subsequently been executing the trusts of Mar. 25, and Apr. 18, 1823; particularly the first, which relates to the provision for the insolvent.

The question then recurs, were those assignments valid; or, if not, were they void in part, **580***] or *in toto?* Suppose the *debtor, finding himself in failing circumstances, had conveyed the whole of his property to assignees, in trust for himself; could there be a question on the subject? An insolvent will not be permitted thus to defraud his creditors and mock the insulted majesty of the laws. When a debtor fails, either from misfortune or folly, or from dishonest motives, his property, in moral justice, belongs to his creditors. He is permitted to prefer in payment such creditors as he pleases. This is giving him power enough; but when he appropriates the property to his own use, the act becomes fraudulent. Nor does it lie in his power to prescribe terms to his creditors. The law is open to them. They have a right to pursue their debtor in the mode pointed out by law, and any act which obstructs them in their pursuit is against law, and of course void, unless such act appropriates the property to the payment of debts.

Our Statute of Frauds, 1 R. L., 75, sec. 1, declares all conveyances of goods, to the use of the grantor, void and of none effect. The 2d section declares all conveyances of lands or goods, made with intent to delay, hinder or defraud creditors, utterly void, as against such creditors. This statute, as has often been said, is only in affirmance of the common law.

The trusts created by the assignments are good in part and bad in part, and the rule in such cases has been settled in the case of *Hyslop* v. *Clarke*, 14 Johns., 465. The court say: "It appears to be an established rule, that where a bond is void in part as against the positive provisions of a statute, the whole bond is void." This doctrine is recognized in *Austin* v. *Bell*, 20 Johns., 449, and is not controverted, in terms, in any subsequent case. How far it is impaired, if at all, by *Murray* v. *Riggs*, 15 Johns., 571, I will next consider.

When that case was discussed by the late *Chancellor*, he remarked, speaking of *Tarbuck* v. *Marbury*, 2 Vern., 510, that a reservation of part of the interest to himself, as in that case, and in the one of *Estwick* v. *Caillaud*, 5 T. R., 420, did not destroy the provision in respect to the residue; though, if the part unreserved was deficient, the creditors *might per- [***581** haps apply to a court of equity for the residue. But if the power enabled the grantor to defeat the whole provision, all the cases concurred in declaring it null and void. When that case came into this court, *Ch. J.* Thompson, who delivered the opinion of the court, says: "The grantors having reserved to their own use, for their maintenance and support, a part of the property covered by this deed, forms no objection to the appropriation of the residue. This is fully established by the cases I have already referred to; and is, indeed, admitted by the *Chancellor* in the case before us; though, in case of a deficiency to satisfy the creditors, they might apply to a court of equity for the appropriation of the property so reserved, towards the payment of their demands."

As the learned judge has cited no case immediately to this point, I have examined all the cases cited by him. In none of them does this feature exist, except the two cases cited by the *Chancellor* from 2 Vern., 510, *Tarbuck* v. *Marbury*, and 5 T. R., 424.

The first of these cases was as follows: Wm. Marbury, in 1672, made a conveyance to Brook and others, of his estate to the use of himself for life, with power to mortgage such part of the estate as he pleased, remainder to the trustees and their heirs, in trust to sell and pay all

plaintiff and defendants, interested in the event of the suit, are citizens of that State: so that whatever decision may be given, the citizens of our State will not be affected. The task which is often imposed on the courts of justice of the State of La., of deciding in controversies between citizens entirely of other States, in consequence of our Attachment Laws, is by no means pleasant to the tribunals, or useful to the community. With the best intentions to do right, it is with difficulty that error can be avoided in many cases arising under our own laws, of which the judges are presumed to have competent knowledge. What, then, must be the embarrassment and uncertainty in deciding an intricate and complicated case, which is governed wholly by foreign laws of which the court probably has no practical knowledge, and may be supposed to have little, even theoretical.

As evidence of the laws of N. Y., in relation to the present case we are referred to decisions of the Supreme Court of that State, and Court for the Correction of Errors, and also to decisions of the Court of Chancery, as reported by Johnson. They have been attentively examined by us; and it is believed that the judgment of the District Court is supported by them. In opposition to these decisions a decree is furnished, lately made by a Court of Chancery in that State, by which the same deed of trust, now under consideration, is declared null and void, by reason of the reservation or provision contained therein, for the benefit of the grantor or assignor. This decision is most clearly correct, according to the laws of this State on the subject of insolvencies; but it seems to be contrary to the principles recognized as prevailing in the State of N.Y., by the judgments of the Supreme Court and Court for the Correction of Errors, in the cases cited. Being a court of inferior jurisdiction, we cannot admit its decree has such force as to overturn those principles which seem to be established by the tribunal of highest authority. See Johns., Vol. XX., and the cases there referred to, p. 447, particularly Vol. XV. of these reports, p. 571.

It is, therefore, ordered, adjudged and decreed, that the judgment of the inferior court be affirmed with costs.

Mr. Livermore, for the plaintiff.
Mr. M'Caleb, for the defendant.

his debts. Mortgages were executed on all the estate. Debts were incurred by him, by judgments, statutes, bonds and simple contracts. The trustees having the legal estate, the creditors could not recover at law. The question in chancery was, whether the creditors by judgment and statute should be preferred to those by bond and simple contract; or whether they should take their average with the others. The court held the deed of trust fraudulent and void; and assigned two reasons: first, because Marbury continued in possession, and kept the deed in his custody, and the creditors had no notice of it; secondly, that having reserved a power to mortgage, he might have charged it to the full value; which amounted, in effect, to a power of revocation and, therefore, was fraudulent as against creditors by judgment and statute. If this case proves anything, as to the point now under consideration, it is this: that a convey-
582*] ance *to trustees to the use of the grantor, is void; and the creditors have the same remedies as if the conveyance had never been made. But it by no means shows that a reservation, in a deed, to the use of a grantor, is valid as against creditors. It does not appear, in this case, that Marbury was indebted to any great amount. Above all, it does not appear that he was insolvent when he executed the conveyance.

The only case which is left to support this doctrine is that of *Estwick* v. *Caillaud*, 5 T. R., 420.

In that case, it appeared that the defendant had levied on certain property, in possession of the plaintiff, by virtue of an execution against Ld. Abingdon, at the suit of one Townsend. Ld. Abingdon being indebted, but not insolvent (for that is not stated, nor is it inferrible), made a conveyance to the plaintiff, of part of his property, in trust to receive the profits, and pay one half to Ld. Abingdon, and the other half to his schedule creditors. On the trial, it was left to the jury to decide whether the deed was made to defraud Ld. Abingdon's creditors. It appeared that Townsend's debt was one of long standing; that his father, the original creditor, had never demanded the debt; the present Townsend had not sued, nor threatened to sue, when the deed was given; and some time before it was done, Ld. Abingdon had offered to pay Townsend, in the materials of a house. The debt arose originally by Townsend's father building a house for Ld. Abingdon. The jury found for the plaintiff, being of opinion that there was no intention of defrauding creditors. The court refused a new trial, saying that Ld. Abingdon had a right to prefer one set of creditors. Ashurst, *J.*, says, "though a part of the profits was reserved for Ld. Abingdon himself, that, alone, will not avoid the legal estate in the trustees, for the benefit of the scheduled creditors; and when those creditors are satisfied, the other creditors may apply to a court of equity for the residue." Buller, *J.*, said, taking the deed by itself, it did not appear to be fraudulent. It was not stated to be a conveyance of all the property of Ld. Abingdon; and the contrary appeared from the evidence, as Ld. Abingdon had offered payment out of other funds; which showed that
583*] *he had no intention of defrauding Townsend. He also adds: "As Ld. Abingdon assigned over more than would probably be sufficient to satisfy those creditors, it seems to me that it was a fair proposal on his part, that a certain portion of the rents and profits should be reserved for his own benefit in the meantime." This, however, had reference to the fairness of the transaction as between Ld. Abingdon and the scheduled creditors.

The plaintiff, in that case, being told that his remedy was in equity, filed his bill in the Exchequer, and obtained an injunction; and on a motion to continue it, that court considered the question of fraud as *res judicata*, having been decided in the K. B. And as to reaching property in the hands of a trustee, or stock in the funds, *Ch. B.* Macdonald said, "courts of equity have never granted an injunction in a similar case." (S. C., 2 Anstr., 381.)

If this, therefore, is to be considered a parallel case, and as controlling the present, it proves that both the *Chancellor* and *Ch. J.* Thompson were mistaken, in saying that a court of equity would direct the property reserved to be appropriated to the payment of the creditors not contained in the schedule. But, in truth, it is not analogous. Ld. Abingdon was not an insolvent debtor. Townsend was not a creditor pursuing his legal remedies when the deed was executed, nor for several years afterwards. Before the deed was given, Ld. Abingdon offered payment. He left part of his property unconveyed; and, as may be inferred from the remarks of Mr. *J.* Buller, sufficient to pay the debt in question. Such is the case from which the late *Chancellor* and *Ch. J.* Thompson drew the doctrine that, "the grantors having reserved to their own use, for their maintenance and support, a part of the property covered by the deed, forms no objection to the appropriation of the residue." It should be stated that this was not considered the principal point in the case they were deciding.

However unsupported this proposition may be, and I think I have shown that it has no adjudged case to support it; yet it seems to be distinctly asserted and assented to by this *court. The *Chancellor* thinks the case [*584 in which it was asserted not in point for the one we are considering. It is true that *Ch. J.* Thompson considered all the creditors of the insolvents as satisfied with the arrangements made by the assignments. He regards this as important. And if the facts are so to be understood, there can be no objection to it; nor would it be an authority for this case. Here the creditors, Mackie, Milne and Lockhart, have never assented to the assignment. They have lost no time in endeavoring to recover their just dues by legal process. Nor are laches of any kind imputable to them.

But if the case of *Murray* v. *Riggs* is to be considered as an authority in this case (and *Ch. J.* Spencer so considered it in the case of *Austin* and *Bell*, though he evidently denied its correctness), if it must be met, then I would ask in the very appropriate and forcible language of the present *Chancellor*: "Is it law that every insolvent debtor in this State may, by assigning all his property in trust, secure to himself an allowance of $2,000 a year, or any other sum from his own property?" And, I will add, is it not directly against the statute? Our laws have specified what property of a debtor the creditor shall not take from him. Any attempt of the debtor to set apart a fund for his own support must be fraudulent and void. If he may take to his own use $2,000 a year, why not $5,000? And if for four years, why not for ten, or even twenty, as in the case of *Murray* v. *Riggs*. To state such a proposition, is a sufficient refutation of it. It offends the moral sense; it shocks the conscience, and produces an exclamation. It is directly against the statute, and cannot stand before it.

But even should this assignment be considered a valid one, it is conceded that the amount appropriated to the grantor's use may be taken to satisfy creditors, by an application to a court of equity for that purpose. What, in substance, is the present application, but a contest for this very appropriation? The validity of this reservation does not arise collaterally; it is directly called in question. It is almost the only ground of contention. If, therefore, it is admitted that these creditors
585*] will be entitled to the reservation *in question by filing a bill expressly for that purpose; then, I would ask, why turn them out of court, when it is admitted, if they come in a different attitude, they will be entitled to what they ask? For whose benefit are we to direct all this circuity of action? Surely not for the benefit of the creditors; nor yet for the benefit of the insolvent.

On the whole, I am of opinion that the assignments are fraudulent and void, as against creditors pursuing their legal remedies, but valid as between the parties. That the judgment constitutes no lien on the property out of which the fund in question was raised; the equity of redemption having been previously conveyed by a deed which was valid as between Cairns and his assignees; and therefore, that Mackie, Milne and Lockhart are entitled to the fund in question, or so much thereof as will pay their judgment. Certain deductions, however, should be made from it. In my judgment, both these parties litigant should receive their costs for appearing as defendants at the suit of Philip Hone. But after the consent for this fund became a suit between them, costs should be awarded to the prevailing party.

I am of opinion, therefore, that so much of the decree of His Honor, the *Chancellor*, as awards the fund, in court, to Sedgwick & Lord should be reversed, with costs. And so much as affirms the decree of the circuit judge of May 27, altering the decree of Jan. 12, 1824, should also be reversed with costs; and the residue affirmed.

Burt, Cramer, Crary, Gardiner, Greenly, Haight, Lake, Mallory, McIntyre, Morgan, Nelson, Wooster and *Wright, Senators*, concurred,

For affirmance, *Bowman, Burrows, Dudley, Earll, Ellsworth* and *Keyes, Senators*.

A majority of the court concurring in the result of the opinions delivered by Savage, *Ch. J.*, and Colden, *Senator*, the following decree was thereupon entered:

DECREE: A majority of this court being of opinion that the assignment or conveyance
586*] made by the said William Cairns *to the said Robert Sedgwick & Daniel Lord, Jr., is void, by reason of the trust or provision contained therein for the benefit of the said William Cairns, it is adjudged and decreed, that so much of the aforesaid decree of the Court of Chancery, as relates to the said assignment or conveyance, be in all things affirmed.

And a majority of the court being also of opinion that the judgment confessed by the said William Cairns to the said Robert Sedgwick and Daniel Lord, Jr., is also void, it is adjudged and decreed that so much of the aforesaid decree of the Court of Chancery, as affirms the validity of the said judgment, be reversed.

And it is also adjudged and decreed that the surplus moneys arising from the sale of the mortgaged premises mentioned in the pleadings in this cause, and now remaining in the court of equity for the first circuit of this State, be applied as follows: first, to the payment of the amount due on the judgment in favor of the said William Mackie, Andrew Milne and Andrew Lockhart; next, to the payment of their costs as hereinafter decreed, and that the balance, if any, do remain in the said Circuit Court, subject to the order thereof.

And it is also adjudged and decreed, that the costs of the said William Mackie, Andrew Milne and Andrew Lockhart, in the Circuit Court and in the Court of Chancery, including their costs on the interlocutory decree of the Circuit Court, made on the twenty-sixth day of May, one thousand eight hundred and twenty-four, and on the interlocutory decree of the same court, made on the twenty-seventh day of that month, be paid to them out of the aforesaid surplus moneys, provided the said surplus moneys shall be sufficient for that purpose, after paying to the said William Mackie, Andrew Milne and Andrew Lockhart, the amount of their judgment as above directed; and in case the said surplus moneys shall not be sufficient, it is hereby adjudged and decreed that so much of the said costs as may have accrued since the making of the decretal order, made by the Circuit Court for the sale of the said mortgaged premises, be paid to the said William Mackie, Andrew Milne and Andrew Lockhart, by the *said William Cairns, Robert Sedgwick [***587**
and Daniel Lord, Jr.

And it is also adjudged and decreed that the said William Cairns, Robert Sedgwick and Daniel Lord, Jr., do refund to the said William Mackie, Andrew Milne and Andrew Lockhart, the amount of the costs paid by them to the said Cairns, Sedgwick and Lord, pursuant to the aforesaid interlocutory decrees of the twenty-sixth and twenty-seventh of May, one thousand eight hundred and twenty-four.

And it is also adjudged and decreed that so much of the aforesaid decree of the Court of Chancery, relating to the application of the surplus moneys arising from the sale of the mortgaged premises mentioned in the pleadings in this cause, and to the costs of this suit, as is inconsistent with the provisions of this decree, be reversed; and that this cause be remitted to the Court of Chancery, to the end that this decree may be carried into effect.

And it is also adjudged and decreed that the costs of the said William Mackie, Andrew Milne and Andrew Lockhart, upon the proceedings in this court, be paid to them out of the aforesaid surplus moneys, in case the same shall be sufficient for that purpose, after payment of the judgment and costs, hereinbefore mentioned; and if not, then by the said William Cairns, Robert Sedgwick and Daniel Lord, Jr.

S. C.—1 Hopk., 373.

Distinguished—2 Wend., 224; 36 Am. Rep., 565 (33 N. J. L., 298).

Cited in—6 Cow., 288; 7 Cow., 738; 8 Cow., 433; 9 Cow., 86, 725; 4 Wend., 112; 11 Wend., 118, 194, 258; 18 Wend., 363, 388; 1 Hill, 462; 4 Hill, 258, 475; 6 Hill, 439; 1 Den., 197; 1 Paige, 310; 2 Edw., 124, 292; 1 Sand. Ch., 10, 45, 138; 15 N. Y., 116; 36 N. Y., 539; 66 N. Y., 382; 3 Keyes., 401, 408; 3 Abb. App. Dec. 302; 2 Barb., 309; 4 Barb., 121; 12 Barb., 178; 17 Barb., 407; 19 Barb., 454; 20 Barb., 437; 23 Barb., 81; 24 Barb., 126; 47 Barb., 175; 13 How. Pr., 158; 25 How. Pr., 249; 46 How. Pr., 458; 3 Abb. Pr., 403; 5 Abb. N. S., 445; 2 Sand., 597; 2 Leg. Obs., 73, 251; 4 Leg. Obs., 425; 25 Ind., 542; 19 Am. Dec., 439, 440 (1 Paige, ch., 305); 23 Am. Dec., 70 (3 P. & W. 83); 25 Am. Dec., 478, 487, 627, 643, 645, 654 (1 Greenl. Law, 326); 26 Am. Dec., 246 (4 Yerg., 541); 33 Am. Dec., 382 (13 Conn., 75).

THE PRESIDENT, DIRECTORS AND COMPANY OF THE RENSSELAER GLASS FACTORY, *Plaintiffs in Error*, v. JANET REID, Administratrix, &c., of JOHN REID, Deceased, *Defendant in Error*.

Interest on Accounts—When Allowed—Criterion as to Allowance of—Generally Allowed on Cash Advances by One for Another, though Resting in a Mutual, Current, Unliquidated Account—Not on Unliquidated Account for Work and Labor—On Running Account Interest Allowed till Request Made to Make out Account, but not After, the Request not having been Complied with—Advances of Money—Salary—History of Interest—Referees—Common Law of England and Decisions of Neighboring States—How far Binding Here—Error Lies to Judgment based on Facts Found by Referees.

May 1, 1812, the president, &c., of the Rensselaer Glass Factory, a company engaged extensively in the manufacture of glass, entered into a partnership, for a year, with R. & A., two stockholders, in conducting the concern; R. & A. to make the necessary advances in money, and receive interest. May 1, 1813, the Co. appointed R. their general agent, large advances being necessary to carry on their business. No salary was agreed on; but a previous agent had 588*] received *a salary of $1,250 *per annum*; and this was no more than a reasonable compensation for R's services, while agent, until the factory was destroyed by fire May 3, 1815. R. continued agent from May 1, 1813, till his death, in Aug. 1821; residing in the vicinity of his principals, who occasionally met at his house. During the time of his agency, he made necessary cash advances, in and about carrying on the concerns of the Company, to more than $100,000, which he had charged in an account of more than 500 items: and had received in cash nearly the same amount, which he credited in the same book in upwards of 700 items. He never rendered any account to the Company: nor did he apprise them that they were in arrear, until Jan. 2, 1819, when he was requested, by one or more of the Directors, to present his account; which request was afterwards repeated, by one or more of the Directors, but never complied with. On his death, his personal representative claimed interest on the advances, as well as on the salary or compensation for his services; held, that she should recover interest upon the advances to Jan. 2, 1819, when he was requested to make out his account, but not after. Held, also, that she should not recover interest on the salary.

As a general rule, interest is allowable on cash advanced by one for another, though the advances rest in the form of a mutual, current and unliquidated account.

Interest is not allowable on an unliquidated account for work and labor.

The facts before referees, appointed by the court pursuant to the Statute, 1 R. L., 516, may, under the order of the court in which the cause is pending, be entered on the record, and the decision upon them reviewed on error.

Form of a judgment record, on reference pursuant to the Statute, 1 R. L., 516.

The word "account" has no definite legal meaning; and it seems that a demand lying in account, is not the criterion for determining whether it shall carry interest. The question is whether the demand itself be liquidated. Per Sanford, *Chancellor*.

How far the administration of justice is capable of being governed by positive rules. Per Colden, *Senator*.

Advances of money by one man for another, without an express or implied authority from the latter, will not bind him to pay. Per Colden, *Senator*.

Courts may compel referees to report the facts before them specially; and a review of their decision upon such a report, is preferable to one on motion founded upon affidavit. Per Spencer, *Senator*.

History of the law of interest. Per Spencer, *Senator*.

The authorities, requiring or authorizing the allowance of interest on a debt or demand, classified and arranged under their respective principles of, 1. An agreement expressed or implied; and the latter considered in reference, 1, to the usage of business; 2, to the case where the principal is to be paid at a specified time, and there is a default as to the payment; 3, an account liquidated, &c., 4, an account rendered, and not objected *to, &c.; 5, [*589 the giving of a void note or bill, or offering security, &c.; II. The allowance of interest by a jury, in their discretion, under the direction of the court. 1, in action arising *ex delicto*; 2, in actions arising *ex contractu*; with various instances and illustrations under each head; and remarks on the evidence applicable to some of the heads. Per Spencer, *Senator*.

How far the decisions of the neighboring States are authority here. Per Crary, *Senator*.

How far the common law of England is binding here; and what is the evidence of that law. Per Spencer and Crary, *Senators*.

There is no case to be found, where attorneys or solicitors have advanced money for their clients, allowing interest on their account before it is liquidated. Per Crary, *Senator*.

The legal security of capital is the strongest inducement to its accumulation. Per Crary, *Senator*.

A note payable on demand carries no interest, till a demand is made by suit, or otherwise. Per Spencer, *Senator*.

To what extent, the common law is flexible. Per Spencer, *Senator*.

Citations—3 Cow., 419 to 438; 6 Johns., 45, 283, 337; 12 Johns., 31, 64, 156; 3 Cai., 266; 1 Johns., 315; 15 East, 223, 226; 6 Johns. Ch., 21, 353; 1 Mass., 436; 9 Mass., 37; 12 Mass., 4; 1 Dall., 265, 313, 349, 50, 52; 13 Mass., 218, 232; 1 Conn., 32, 35; 1 Ves., Jr., 60; 1 Binn., 448, 494; 3 Cai., 226, 238; 2 Van Schaack's Colonial Laws, 517; 17 Johns., 484; 1 Campb. *N. P.*, 52, 53; 1 Hawk. Ch., 82; Hard., 420; Hume, Ch., 33; 1 Am. State Papers, 307; Stat. Hen. VIII., ch. 9; Doug., 375; 1 Starkie, 487; 2 Burr., 1085, 1088, 1806; 2 Br. C. C., 3; 2 Bos. & P., 219, 337; W. Bl., 761; 3 Wils., 205; 15 Johns., 424; 1 Dick., 428; 2 Salk., 623; 1 H. Bl., 303, 304; 2 Gall., 45; 1 P. Wms., 376; 7 Johns., 213; 2 Vern., 276; 2 Ves., 239; 2 Atk., 252; 1 Serg. & R., 179; 8 Johns., 446; 14 Johns., 128, 255, 273, 385; 3 Johns. Cas., 310; 2 Campb. *N. P.*, 426; 9 Johns., 71; 13 Johns., 255; 11 Mass., 501; 3 Binn., 123; 7 Mass., 14; 4 Dessaus., 110; 4 Vin. Abr., 458, pl. 10; Sel. Ch. Cas., 50; 2 Eq. Cas. Abr., 531, pl. 15; 1 Ves., Jr., 63; 20 Johns., 28, 603; 13 Ves., 53; 11 Ves., 359; 8 Ves., 363; 1 Jac. & Walk., 135; 4 Dall., 289.

ON ERROR from the Supreme Court. The same case in the court below is reported in 3 Cow., 392, 438.

SUTHERLAND, *J.*, and SAVAGE, *Ch. J.*, assigned the reasons in support of the judgment in the court below, as in 3 Cow., 419–438.

The case was argued by,

Mr. B. F. Butler, for the plaintiffs in error, and,

Mr. S. A. Foot, for the defendant in error, upon the points made, and authorities cited on their argument in the court below, which see 3 Cow., 399–419.

NOTE.—*Interest—When allowable on accounts.* For full discussion, see Newell v. Griswold, 6 Johns., 45, *note*.

Mr. Foot also raised the question here, whether a writ of error could be brought to review the decision of referees; which was discussed by the counsel much upon the same grounds as, in the court below on the motion for a rule requiring the plaintiff below to incorporate the facts of the case in the judgment record. The arguments of the same counsel, on that occasion, are reported in 3 Cow., 387-389, S. C.

The main facts in the case, both as to the preliminary point and the merits, will also be found stated or adverted to by the *Chancellor* and *Senators* in delivering their opinions in this court. In these, some circumstances will be **590***] *found stated, especially in the opinion of Spencer, *Senator*, not mentioned in the former report of the cause.

The record returned, which was admitted to be correct in form, and which was stated to be in due form by Colden, *Senator*, was thus:

Placita, of October Term, 1821; Warrants of attorney; Memorandum of October Term, 1821; Declaration; Plea of the general issue; which was followed with the usual general notice of set-off. The record then proceeded thus:

"Therefore," &c. (award of *venire*, returnable on the first Monday of January then next). "At which day, before, &c., at, &c., come the parties aforesaid, by their attorneys aforesaid, and the sheriff hath not sent the writ of the people, to him, in that behalf directed. And hereupon, the said Janet Reid, administratrix as aforesaid, gives the said court of the people, here, to understand and be informed, that the trial of the issue in this cause, will require the examination of a long account, on the part of her, the said Janet Reid, administratrix as aforesaid; and the said Janet Reid, administratrix, as aforesaid, according to the form of the statute in such case made and provided, prays the court of the people now here, by a rule in that behalf made, to refer this cause to referees, not being less than three persons, to be nominated by the said court of the people now here, to finally hear and examine the matters in controversy, in this cause. And because the said President and Directors of the Rensselaer Glass Factory do not deny the allegation aforesaid, but admit the same to be true; therefore, in pursuance of and according to the aforesaid statute, let it be, by rule for that purpose to be duly entered, referred to James Van Ingen, Gideon Hawley and Nicholas Bleecker, Jr., Esqrs., all of the City of Albany, as referees, to hear and examine the matters in controversy, between the said Janet Reid, administratrix, as aforesaid, and the President and Directors of the Rensselaer Glass Factory; and let the said referees, upon pain of contempt, report thereon to the said court of the people, before the aforesaid Justices thereof, at the City Hall of the City of New York, on the first Monday of May next. And the same day is given to the parties aforesaid, at the same place. At which day, before **591***] the said *Justices of the Supreme Court of Judicature aforesaid at the City Hall of the City of New York, come the parties aforesaid by their attorneys aforesaid; and the referees above mentioned, to wit: James Van Ingen, Gideon Hawley and Nicholas Bleecker, Jr., to whom it was referred to hear and examine the matters in controversy, between the said Janet Reid, administratrix as aforesaid, and the said President and Directors of the Rensselaer Glass Factory, and to report thereupon, now report, that they find there is due to the said Janet Reid, administratrix as aforesaid, from the President and Directors of the Rensselaer Glass Factory, the sum of twelve thousand two hundred and eighteen dollars and eighty four cents, besides her costs and charges, by her about her suit in this behalf expended." [The cause was then continued by *curia advisare vult*, to October Term, 1824.] "At which day, &c., at, &c., comes as well, &c., and thereupon, all and singular the premises being seen, &c., it is considered by the same court, that the said report do stand confirmed; and it is further considered, that, &c., do recover, &c., her said damages, by the referees aforesaid, in form aforesaid reported; and also, &c., for her said costs and charges, &c."

A rule of the Supreme Court was, on motion of the counsel for the defendants below, made by that court, and entered Nov. 13, 1824, in the words set forth in 3 Cow., 389, S. C., which was also certified with the record in this cause; and in obedience to which, the facts came before this court, being inserted in the record pursuant to the rule.

Further particulars, as to the manner in which the merits came here, will be found in the opinions of Colden and Spencer, *Senators*.

SANFORD, *Chancellor*. This case presents several important questions. A preliminary one raised by the counsel for the defendant in error, is, whether the merits of the cause come properly before the court. A motion was made in the court below to refer the cause; which was granted on the usual ground, that it involved the examination of long accounts. The referees heard and reported *upon the [***592** case; and the Supreme Court, on an examination of the report, after directing certain modifications to be made, rendered judgment for the plaintiff below. They afterwards directed the facts in proof before the referees, to be spread upon the record, so that the defendants below might have them reviewed by this court, in the same way as if they had been found by a special verdict, or stated in a bill of exceptions. It is now insisted, that not being legally upon the record, they must be disregarded by us, and the record passed upon as containing no more than the usual general history of the cause. I do not think so. The motion to refer in this State is founded on the statute. It is made on the affidavit of either party that the cause will involve the examination of a long account. It is not founded as in England, on the course and practice of the court. In such a case, I admit that this history of the facts might not be properly considered a part of the record. But I cannot believe that the Legislature, when they took the cause from a jury without the consent of the party, meant also to deprive him of his remedy by writ of error. Something more than mere implication is, I think, necessary to produce such a consequence; and I am not aware that the case could be brought before us in any other mode than the one adopted here. I, therefore, consider the merits properly on the record; and that it is our duty to pass upon them in the same manner as if they had come up in the more ordinary way of a special verdict, or bill of exceptions.

The *Chancellor* here stated the leading facts, as they appeared upon the report.

The question is, whether Reid, the intestate, was entitled to interest on his advances of money, as agent for the Company. The first inquiry relates to the character of his agency. His appointment was by a very short and general resolution, declaring him agent, and nothing more. No instructions were given; and we are left to infer his powers from the history of his acts, and the acts of the Company; whence it would seem, he was their general agent; being intrusted with all power necessary and
593*] proper for the successful *prosecution of their business. It was found to be a losing concern; but they, notwithstanding, resolved to continue it, and did continue it under his superintendence.

It is objected that the claim against the Company rested in an unliquidated account, which will not carry interest. True we have such expressions in the books, but they are very indefinite and unsatisfactory. Anything may enter into an account. The sum due on a boud of several years' standing, on which there have been various payments, may be said to rest in account, and to be unliquidated. An account is no more than a list or catalogue of items, whether of debts or credits. It seems to me there is no difference, whether the demand upon which interest is claimed lie in account or in anything else. This cannot be the criterion. If the demand itself be unliquidated, it cannot carry interest; and on the other hand, if it be liquidated it may. Have we any settled law upon this head of inquiry? I have looked into the cases cited, and I find them deplorably inconsistent. But it seems to me that the courts of Pa. have seized on the true principle. They appear to put the allowance of interest on the fault of the party who is to pay the money.

The difficulty in the case before us arises from the peculiar state of the facts. There is no reported case like it. It appears to me, however, that the advances of Reid were fairly within the scope of his agency. He was to keep the workmen together and manage the whole concern. In doing this, he was obliged to make heavy disbursements; and there is no pretense that he did not act in perfect good faith. If the advances were within the scope of his power, this was equivalent to an express authority to make them.

It is urged that he did not render an account; that he was negligent in keeping the Company advised as to the state of their business, in point of profit and loss. On this question the case is very obscure. Some of the Directors requested him to account, but there was no formal demand made. The Company understood it to be a losing concern. Was he bound to account without any request? I can see no legal duty on his part to furnish an account,
594*] any more than *on the part of the Company to demand one. So much confidence seems to have been reposed, that they did not think it necessary to call for any account.

With all the obscurity of the case, it is plain that he advanced his money for the use of the Company. He was deprived of the use of that money, and the Company had the benefit of it, under circumstances which, I think, are equivalent to a request on their part. Indeed, they do not pretend the contrary. To do so, would be to deny him the principal sum.

I do not intend to go over the cases cited. I have prepared no written opinion. The reasoning of *Ch. J.* Savage and *Mr. J.* Sutherland, is very able; and to my mind, most satisfactory and conclusive. I can add nothing to the view which they have taken of the subject; and it would be idle to say over again, what they have so well said already. Indeed, I do not wish to be considered as departing from the Supreme Court, in any one particular. I am entirely satisfied with the conclusion to which they came; and I hope their judgment will be affirmed.

COLDEN, *Senator*. The documents returned with the writ of error, are a regular record of a judgment of the Supreme Court, on which is entered a declaration in an action on the case, a plea and issue, with a notice of set-off; an order of reference, a report of the referees in favor of the plaintiff below for the sum of $12,-218.84; and a judgment of the court for that sum, with $2,547.87 costs.

It has not been, and could not be, suggested, that in this record there is any error.

But there is also returned, with the writ of error, another document, purporting to be a case, which presents a history of the proceedings of the Supreme Court in the same cause; by which it appears that, Nov 13, 1824, the Supreme Court made an order, that a statement of facts should be drawn up, under the direction of the *Ch. J.*, to be incorporated in the record in the cause, in order that the defendants below might be enabled to prosecute their writ of error, if advised so to do.

*In obedience to this rule (as is said in [***595**
the document annexed to the writ of error), a statement of facts, which are set forth in that document, was made; to be annexed to, and form part of the record in this cause.

From this statement, it appears that the cause was first referred in Jan., 1822; that, in Mar., 1824, the referees made a report in favor of the plaintiff below for the sum of $14,913.-46. That the defendants below were dissatisfied with this report, and made an application to the Supreme Court to set it aside; which application was made on a statement of the evidence before the referees, agreed upon by the attorneys for the respective parties, instead of being made on affidavits in the usual way.

The application to set aside the first report having been heard, the Supreme Court, in Aug., 1824, made an order that the report should be set aside, so far as it allowed interest to the plaintiffs below, after Jan. 2, 1819, and on the charges for salary. And further, that in pursuance of a stipulation of the parties, the cause should be again referred to the same referees; and that they should report the amount due to the plaintiff below for interest to the last mentioned date, in addition to the sum due for principal. In pursuance of this order, the referees, in Oct., 1824, reported that there was due to the plaintiff below, the sum of $4,565.38, for principal, and $7,653.46, for interest, making together, $12,218.84, for which sum, with costs, the judgment was entered in October Term, 1824.

The document returned with the writ of error, concludes with a certificate under the hand and seal of the *Ch. J.*, that the state of facts had been settled under his direction, and that he approved of the same.

Now, from what I have stated, it appears that the error in this case, if error there be, is not in rendering the final judgment upon the record as it is returned with the writ of error; but in the directions given by the interlocutory order of Aug. 20, 1824.

It seems to me we ought to be very cautious how we decide that a writ of error will lie on such matter so brought up. If a writ of error
596*] will reach this interlocutory order *and the affidavits or statement of facts on which it was founded, I do not see why we may not have a writ of error to bring up every rule for a new trial that is granted or refused, with the depositions on which the application for the rule may be founded. This is not, in my opinion, like the case of *Yates* v. *People*, 6 Johns., 337, or of *Clason* v. *Shotwell*, 12 Johns., 31, in both of which cases the writ of error was brought on the final judgment of the court.

But I do not find myself under the necessity of deciding whether the document returned with the writ of error, which is called the case, is properly before us or not. The record of the judgment is undoubtedly presented to us in proper form, and I am ready to decide that there is no error in that. And my opinion is the same whether I refer to the case or not.

With these views, I shall examine the cause as if the facts stated in the case transmitted with the judgment roll were properly before us.

As often as the question of interest has been before a court, the judges seem to have considered it as depending on general equitable principles; and, in most instances, to have decided each case in reference to its particular circumstances, without attempting to give any rule which might be generally applicable.

In the case of *Pease* v. *Barber*, 3 Cai., 266, which was an action for money had and received, *Ch. J.* Kent says, "there may be cases in which a defendant ought to refund the principal money only; and there may be other cases in which he ought, *ex equo et bono*, to refund the principal, with interest. Each case will depend on the justice and equity arising out of its particular circumstances."

So far have questions of interest been considered matters of equity, and not of strict law, that, as in the anonymous case in Johnson, 1 Johns., 315, they have been left for the jury to decide. In this case the court say, "jurors have, in many cases, a discretion to allow interest by way of damages, according to the circumstances of the case."
597*] *It was said, in the argument, that it was derogatory to our jurisprudence to admit that there are not established rules by which every question arising in the administration of justice may be decided; that discretion is the law of despots, and that the rights of individuals must be precarious where it may be exercised. But human institutions must partake of the imperfections of human nature; and it requires no great experience to learn how much it is beyond the capacity of man to prescribe laws which may be applied, without the exercise of any discretion in those who administer them, to all possible circumstances. Notwithstanding our statutes are so voluminous, are the work of so many ages and have been so repeatedly revised, our multiplied books of commentaries and reports, show how inadequate legislative enactments are to afford rules for all occasions; and how much, after all, must be left to the wisdom and discretion of judges and of jurors; "and to that moral sense of right and wrong, which, like the senses of tasting and feeling in every man, makes a part of his nature."

The question of interest, often depending so much upon considerations of equity growing out of the facts belonging to each particular case, the counsel, on either side, have not found it difficult to refer to innumerable cases, which, with the help of great ingenuity, and the liberty of reasoning from analogy, they have made to appear well calculated to support their respective pretensions.

It must be recollected that the question in this case arises on money advanced, by the intestate, for the use of the plaintiffs in error. However analogous this may seem to money lent, or to money had and received, the cases are not the same in principle.

Where money is lent by one to another, it is a transaction between the parties personally; and, as was said by Gross, *J.*, in the case of *Calton* v. *Bragg*, 15 East, 223, which was an action for money lent. "If there be no proof of a contract, it might be given against the intention of the parties at the time of the loan. If they did not then contract for interest, it shows that they did not mean to reserve it." But this reasoning will not apply, when money is advanced *by one, for the use of another, [***598**
under an implied contract, and where there was no special or express agreement between the parties.

I do not find that any one of the cases, cited from the English books or from our own reports, is a case where interest has been denied for money advanced. Nevertheless, it is certainly true that the judges often use expressions which would apply to such a case; but my meaning is, that the question whether interest was, or was not to be allowed on money advanced for the use of another, on an implied authority, has, in no case where there has been a decision against the allowance of interest, been the matter presented, by the facts, for the decision of the court.

It would be a tedious and irksome task to refer to all the English cases which have been quoted, in order to show that not one of them is inconsistent with this assertion. I shall content myself with remarking, that the case of *Calton* v. *Bragg*, which was so much relied upon in the argument, was an action for money lent.

But I will, as briefly as I possibly can, notice the cases in our own books to which we have been referred.

The counsel for the plaintiffs in error cited the case of *Campbell* v. *Mesier*, 6 Johns. Ch., 21, to show that there the *Chancellor* allowed interest for money advanced, from the time of demand and refusal only. The circumstances of that case were very peculiar. The defendant was liable to contribute to the rebuilding of a party wall. He not only refused to contribute, but forbid the prostration of the old wall. The complainant erected a new one, at a much greater expense than the re-establishment of the old one, required. It could not be ascertained till the new wall was appraised, and it was estimated what it would have cost to restore the old wall, how much the defendant ought to have paid. When this appraisement and estimate were made and the extent of the defendant's liability was thereby settled, the complainant demanded the amount. The *Chancellor* decided that the defendant should pay interest from that time. Here was a case very different from an advance of specific sums of money. It is true the demand is considered **599***] *in the Court of Chancery as a demand for money advanced; but it was more like a demand for unliquidated damages, which never carries interest. The defendant could not have discharged the principal till after the appraisement and estimate had settled how much he was liable to contribute to the party wall. But nevertheless the *Chancellor*, in giving his opinion, in that case, says, "it is the settled rule in the law of this State that interest is to be paid for money received, or advanced for the use of another, after a default in payment." Let it be remarked that the *Chancellor* does not say, after demand and refusal, but after default in payment. It is true that the decree is for interest from the time of the demand and refusal. But it appears that this was all that was asked by the counsel. They contended, as appears by the report of the case, for no more than that interest ought to be allowed from the time of the advance of the money for the building of the wall in 1803, and the demand, and refusal of payment. But I do not think this case of *Campbell* v. *Mesier* can be relied upon as establishing any general principle applicable to the case before us. The circumstances were very peculiar, and so different from those now under consideration, that I should not have noticed it so particularly, had not the counsel for the plaintiffs in error seemed to rely upon it as an authority much in their favor.

In the case of *Kane* v. *Smith*, 12 Johns., 156, the question as to interest turned upon the construction of a special agreement. The plaintiffs were to pay interest for so much as the wines shipped by the defendants might produce, more than sufficient to reimburse to them the value of the merchandise which they consigned to the defendants But there was no stipulation for interest in case, as it happened, the sales of the wines should not be equal to the value of the cargoes furnished by the Kanes. In the first place, it is to be remarked, that here was no advance of money, made by the plaintiffs, in virtue of an implied authority from the defendants. And the court would not construe the agreement to mean that the defendants should be liable for interest, for which there was no stipulation, if the result of the **600***] *adventure should leave them a sum to make the plaintiffs good.

In *Porter* v. *Bussey*, 1 Mass., 436, the Supreme Judicial Court of Mass. would only allow interest from the commencement of an action to recover a return premium.

In *Storer* v. *Storer*, 9 Mass., 37, the same court refused to allow an administrator interest on advances; because, as the court said, he might have put himself in cash from the estate.

The case of *Winthrop* v. *Carleton*, 12 Mass., 4, so far from showing that interest is not to be allowed on advances, is directly the reverse. The claim was for interest on money advanced by the plaintiff, as consignee of the defendant's ship. Parker, *Ch. J.*, says: "The defendant must be considered as indebted to the plaintiff, in Charleston, the moment the money was advanced; and he ought to pay the same interest which he would have paid, had he given his promissory note at the time." But, for some reason which is not apparent, (*a*) part of the interest to which the plaintiff was entitled, could not be allowed. For, the *Ch. J.* adds: "The plaintiff will lose the interest of his money, from the time of his advancing it to the commencement of the action, which, perhaps, he might have recovered, if it had been attended to in season."

In *Jacobs* v. *Adams*, 1 Dall., 52, the claim was for money paid to an executor, appointed by a will which was afterwards revoked. The court said, as the money was paid as well as received in mistake, and no fraud could be imputed to either party, interest was only payable from the time of demand.

*In *Williams* v. *Craig*, 1 Dall, 313, [***601** the court set aside the report of referees, because they had allowed interest upon an unsettled account. But it does not appear by this report, that the account was for money advanced. On the contrary, by a reference in that case to *Henry* v. *Risk*, 1 Dall., 265, as an authority, it would seem that the account in the former was for goods sold and delivered.

There were two other cases, one from 13 Mass. and another from 1 Conn., cited by the counsel for the plaintiffs in error, to show that interest had been denied on cash advances, which I have not had an opportunity of examining. I have not taken much pains to procure them; because, whatever they might decide, they could not control what I consider to be the whole current of authority on the subject. And unless these cases are to the contrary, I think I may repeat, what I said in the outset, that no one case, cited by the counsel for the plaintiffs in error, decides that interest is not to be allowed, on money advanced by one person for the use of another.

On the other hand, there are very many cases by which it has been decided that interest is to be allowed on such advances, from the time they are made. Of these cases I shall notice but two or three.

Craven v. *Tickell*, 1 Ves., Jr., 60, was a case of money expended by the complainant for the defendant, in building a house. *Ld. Chancellor* Thurlow says: "Interest must be given on the money expended, since it was laid out. Money paid to the workmen who were to be

(*a*) It seems, from the opinion of *Ch. J.* Parker, that the only question in relation to interest, in that case, was, whether S. C. interest, at the rate of seven *per cent*, was to be allowed, or Mass. interest, which was only six. By the report of the case, which is rather obscure, it does not appear that the interest which accrued prior to the commencement of the suit, was claimed at the trial. If it was not, the court could not allow it under the stipulation by which the cause was brought before them. It is probably this fact to which the *Chief Justice* alludes, when he intimates that such interest might have been recovered, and at the S. C. rate, if it had been attended to in season.

paid by the defendant, is money advanced for him."

In *Lessee of Dilworth* v. *Sinderling*, 1 Binn., 494, *Ch. J.* Tilghman says: "It may now be safely affirmed, that for a considerable time past, the settled law has been, that interest is recoverable for money lent and advanced." And interest was allowed from the time of the advances.

In *Liotard* v. *Graves*, 3 Cai., 238, Thompson, *J.*, says: "with respect to interest on the plaintiffs' account, I think they had a right to charge it on the money advanced, but not on the account, as it was unsettled; and therefore, interest ought not to be calculated, ex-
602*] cept on the money advanced." *In the same case, Livingston, *J.*, says: "Interest ought to be allowed on all moneys advanced from their respective payments." *Ch. J.* Kent says: "The account exhibited is but a naked account current; and interest is to be allowable only on such items in it as are for moneys advanced."

However, it may be, with respect to money lent, or as to money had and received, or in regard to merchandise sold and delivered; or, however it may be where advances are made in pursuance of an express agreement, in which nothing is said about interest, I think the above authorities will admit of no other conclusion than that it is now a well established general rule of law that where a person advances money for the use of another, under an implied authority, he who makes the advance, is entitled to interest from the time it was made.

That the advances were made, by the intestate, under an applied authority from the plaintiffs in error, it appears to me, is well established by the facts stated in the case. It is stated that when Reid assumed the agency of the factory, in 1813, it could not have been kept in operation without advances. It would be extending an indulgence to incorporated companies to which I do not think they are entitled, to presume that the plaintiffs in error were so ignorant of their affairs, as not to know that this was their condition. They afterwards found the factory proceeding. They must, therefore, have known that there were advances, without which it could not have been put in operation, or carried on; and they must have known that these advances could only have been made by their agent, Reid.

Again; when the factory was conducted by Reid & Alsop, in partnership with the plaintiffs in error, there was an express stipulation that Reid & Alsop should make the necessary advances, upon which interest should be allowed.

When Reid, as to the management of the concern, took the place of Reid & Alsop, and found that advances were yet necessary, and that the Company made no provision for them I think he had a right to presume that it was intended by the Company that he should make
603*] them; and that they *were to be made on the same terms in which they had been made by him, and his partner, Alsop; that is to say, that interest was to be allowed. But independent of all these circumstances, I think the report of the referees is conclusive, as to the advances having been made under the implied authority of the plaintiffs in error. There was no express agreement relative to advances; and unless the referees had found that the intestate had an implied authority from the Company to advance, they could not have reported anything to be due to the administratrix. It is not sufficient that advances are made for my use, to make me liable therefor. I must have authorized them, either expressly or impliedly; or given them my sanction after they were made. If a person volunteers a payment on my account, without any authority expressed or implied, I am not obliged to reimburse him.

It has been insisted that interest is not allowable on an open unliquidated running mutual account; and many authorities have been cited, which, I think, establish this as another general rule. But in the case of *Liotard* v. *Graves*, in which the claim for interest was on such an account, we see that the plaintiffs were allowed to select the items which were for money advanced; and to recover interest on these from the time of the advances, although it was disallowed on the general balance.

In the case before us, the account, on the one side, is wholly for cash advances made by the agent; and on the other, of cash received by him. It does not appear to me that this is a mutual, running account, in the sense of those terms as they are used in any of the cases which have been cited. If the agent would have been entitled to interest if he had advanced only one sum, and so could have made only a single charge, and could not, therefore, have exhibited a running account, I cannot conceive why, when repeated advances would oblige him to make an account of many items, he should not have the same claim for interest on each advance, that he would have had if his whole advance had been made at one time.

*I have said that it is a general rule [***604**
that interest shall be allowed on money advanced on an implied authority; but, like all other general rules, this may have its exceptions, growing out of circumstances connected with the transaction which may render the claim of interest inequitable. I find, however, no such circumstances in this case. On the contrary, it appears to me that it would be very unjust to allow the plaintiffs in error to have the benefit of the intestate's advances, without obliging them to make any compensation for those advances. I think that neither law, justice or policy would sanction such a decision.

I am in favor of affirming the judgment of the Supreme Court.

Bowman, Earll, Ellsworth, Haight, Keyes, Lake, Lefferts, Mallory, M'Intyre, M'Michael, Ogden, Redfield and *Thorn, Senators*, concurred in the result of these opinions.

SPENCER, *Senator*. A preliminary objection is made, that a writ of error does not lie upon the record in this cause, so as to bring up the case settled by the *Chief Justice*, and which has been substituted for the report of the referees. There certainly is great irregularity in the form in which the facts are presented. It was competent to the court below to compel a detailed report by the referees of all the testimony before them, which might have been amended on the motion of either party in the same manner as justice's returns to writs of *certiorari;* and the report thus perfected, being spread on the record, would present the case with all the precision and accuracy of a special verdict. When the beneficial operation of the Statute Authorizing References is considered, and the multitude of causes which, under the modern liberal practice, are determined by that method, it is desirable that the present loose mode of presenting the merits by affidavits, often contradictory and always obscure, should be superseded by the more technical and regular reports of referees, which will at least abbreviate the proceedings and save labor in the examination of **605***] a case. Had not *the counsel for both parties acquiesced in the manner in which the facts in this case should be settled and presented, I should, as one, refuse to consider them as any part of the record, upon the same principles that a case settled before a judge, in an ordinary trial at law, forms no part of the record of judgment, and is not brought up by a writ of error. But from the proceedings which have taken place in the court below, I consider both parties as having agreed that the case settled by the *Ch. J.* should be taken and received in place of the affidavits used in the Supreme Court. And then I apply to this case the remarks of Sandford, *Senator*, in *Clason* v. *Shotwell*, 12 Johns., 64, in which I entirely concur, that "whatever may be the mode of proceeding adopted by the Supreme Court, whether formal and usual, or extraordinary and summary (by which that court acquires jurisdiction), it can make no determination of the cause which will not be subject to the constitutional revision of this court." "All causes determined in the Supreme Court, whatever may be the course or mode of proceeding by which they may be conducted or determined, are subject to the appellate jurisdiction of this court."

Considering it in that light, and as a part of the record, it is to be treated as a special verdict presenting facts, and leaving questions of law for the determination of the court. This view removes the technical objections which were urged on the argument.

That it is a novelty, that a writ of error should be brought upon a judgment founded on the report of referees, furnishes no solid objection, when the same principles apply, and the same reasons exist for bringing it, which subject judgments upon special verdicts, and demurrers to evidence, to the same revisal. It strikes me as a monstrous proposition, to say that the right of trial by jury may be taken away by statute, and then, because it is taken away, the judgment which may be rendered, shall not be subject to the revision and appeal provided by the Constitution. If that were, indeed, its effect, I should say that the law itself, which provided such a mode of trial would be **606***] unconstitutional, and any *judgment rendered pursuant thereto, for that reason, erroneous. If we were to yield to the counsel for the defendant in error the force of his objection, that because this action had been referred, and judgment rendered upon the report of referees, therefore there could be no writ of error, the conclusion in my mind would be, that for that very cause the judgment should be reversed; for the same reasons that this court would reverse or revoke a judgment in an action of trespass where it appeared that the court below had refused a trial by jury. References having been authorized by the Colonial Laws (2 Van Schaick's ed., 517), they do not contravene the provisions of our Constitution. It is, therefore, a constitutional mode of trying certain questions. This cause has been tried in that manner, the Supreme Court has confirmed the report of the referees and rendered judgment thereon. The only question presented is, whether that judgment be a final determination of the cause.

It was remarked in the argument that the motion in the Supreme Court to set aside the report was in the nature of a motion for a new trial. This is true. Of the same character would be a motion to set aside a special verdict, and for a new *venire.* But the refusal in either case would be a confirmation of the report or verdict; and if followed by a judgment, would necessarily be final. The court having confirmed the report would no longer entertain any motion or other proceeding in the same court to revise their judgment. There can be no question, then, I apprehend, that this is, to all intents and purposes, and in the most technical sense, a "judgment of the Supreme Court."

It seems hardly necessary to refer to any case to decide whether a writ of error lies upon a final judgment; for if not in such a case it does not lie in any. The case of *Clason* v. *Shotwell*, 12 Johns., 31 turned, entirely, upon the question, whether the rule of the Supreme Court directing restitution of the possession of property, which had been taken under a forcible entry and detainer, was or was not a final judgment. It was conceded by counsel on both sides, is expressly admitted in the dissenting opinion of *Chancellor* Kent, and is the basis of that delivered by Sanford, **Senator*, [***607**
that if the cause be terminated in the Supreme Court; if there be a definitive judgment, which gives or concludes the right of the party, a writ of error lies. The case of *Brooks* v. *Hunt*, 17 Johns., 484, recognizes the same principles. The writ of error, in that case, was brought on the refusal of the Supreme Court to set aside an execution; and one of the reasons for quashing it was, that the rule denying the motion was not a judgment; and this court then decided that the writ would lie only upon a final judgment or determination of a cause. That this cause has terminated in the Supreme Court; that there is a definitive judgment concluding the rights of the parties, cannot admit of a question. And as that is the only test to determine whether a writ of error lies, I am of opinion it is well brought in this case.

In approaching the merits of this cause, the magnitude, importance and difficulty of the questions which it involves, will excite distrust in any conclusions to which the mind may arrive. But having the solemn duty to perform, of making up an opinion satisfactory to myself, and having bestowed all the time, labor and attention which it required, I have come to a conclusion which I am bound to express. Yet when the difficulties of the subject are considered, there will be little occasion for surprise, if differing views should be entertained.

An English reporter has remarked, that "it

would fortunately be a very difficult matter to fix upon another point of English law in which the authorities are so little in harmony with each other." (1 Campb. *N. P.*, 53.) And yet there are few branches of the law of more immediate, direct and practical importance, not only in our extensive commercial transactions, but in the everyday business of every man, in every station and condition of life. The cause of the contradiction of opinions and of the inconsistency of adjudged cases, on any subject, will be found always to be, the attempt to establish arbitrary rules without referring them to the reasons and principles on which they should be founded. Such has been the case with the law of interest. No elementary writer has ever attempted to annalyze the multitude of **608***] *cases and exhibit the principles which govern them. And although some judges have, in isolated cases, given the reason of the rules they prescribed, yet have these reasons been as various and discordant as the cases themselves; and have produced confusion instead of system.

The experience of ages demonstrates that the law can never be rendered clear, intelligible and permanent, without the reasons for its rules are understood, its leading principles settled, and the cases which arise under it founded upon those principles. In many of the branches of the law, we are indebted for the advances towards certainty which have been made, to the efforts of individuals to reduce the confused mass of cases into system, and extract from them the principles which can alone guide us in the decision of new questions as they arise. This cause presents such a question, and it appears to me that it cannot be satisfactorily determined without reference to the great principles of the law of interest, and to the reasons of the rules in analogous cases. The attempt, therefore, to reduce that branch of law into some kind of system, seems required by the necessity of the case, and however unsuccessful, still it may be useful in stimulating further exertions, and inducing others more competent, hereafter to accomplish it.

The cases to which we have been referred, and many others, have been examined, and an effort will be made to arrange them in appropriate classes, or divisions, in reference, solely, to the principles which it is supposed governed their decision. This will be done, to prove the principles themselves, to sustain and fortify them, and to show that these cases, with very few exceptions, do, in truth, proceed on a common reason, and may be brought into a harmonious system.

It seems to be the better opinion (Hawk., bk. 1, ch. 82) that, by the ancient common law, it was absolutely unlawful to take any kind of interest or usury, as it was then called for money. In an anonymous case in Hardus (Hard., 420), Ld. Hale is reported to have said that "Jewish usury was prohibited at common law, being £40 *per cent.* and more; but no other." But Hume, in his 33d chapter, says: "In 1546 a law was made for fixing the interest **609***] *of money at ten *per cent.* the first legal interest known in England. Formerly all loans of that nature were regarded as usurious. The preamble of this very law treats the interest of money as illegal and criminal." Mr. Jefferson, in a letter to Mr. Hammond, which will be found in the 1st vol. of American State Papers, 307, 1st ed., says, that "in England all interest was against law, until the Statute of 37 Hen. VIII., ch. 9," which is the statute referred to by Hume. And he furnishes the strongest reasons for confidence in his correctness, by the statement of a fact that interest is considered unlawful in all Roman Catholic countries. Until the time referred to, that was the established religion in England. This has appeared to be a starting point of some importance, as it has a considerable bearing in construing the statutes on the subject.

The Statute of Hen. VIII., referred to, simply provides that "none shall take, for the loan of any money or commodity, above the rate of ten pounds for one hundred pounds, for one whole year." All the statutes which have been passed in England and in this State are in the same language. They are negative, prohibitory of interest being taken above a certain rate; they are none of them affirmative; they do not declare in what eases interest shall be taken; much less do they in any case require it to be paid.

Since, then, neither by common law nor by statute, is a party in any case required to pay interest. It follows inevitably and irresistibly, upon the universal principle of all law, that a man cannot be made legally liable to pay interest, as such, without his own agreement to that effect. All liability must be created by law or by agreement. Some agreements are contrary to law. Such were contracts for the payment of interest, until the statute allowed them: such contracts for a higher rate than is allowed by statute are still contrary to law. These deductions seem obvious and familiar; but I apprehend they lie at the foundation of the questions in this cause. If correct, they establish a great principle in the law of interest, which will guide us through its labyrynths; that its allowance by the courts, as an incident to the debt, and invariably following it, is founded solely *upon the agreement of the par- [***610** ties. It is allowed, also, in another class of cases, by juries, as a measure of damages, under the advice of the court, but in their absolute discretion; which class must be carefully distinguished from that when it is allowed by the courts, as the judgment of law. The confusion and mingling of these classes has led to much of the difficulty which has arisen on this subject. They depend on principles entirely distinct, and do not furnish even an analogy to each other.

To sustain the above position, that whenever the courts allow interest as such, as incidental to the debt, and under rules precluding all discretion, they do so on the ground of the agreement of the parties, in addition to the reasoning founded upon the common law and the statutes, I refer to the case of *Calton* v. *Bragg*, 15 East, 226, as full and conclusive authority. Ld. Ellenborough says in that case, "Ld. Mansfield sat here for upwards of thirty years, Ld. Kenyon for above thirteen years, and I have now set here for more than nine years (a period of 52 years), and during this long course of time, no case has occurred where, upon a mere simple contract of lending, without an agreement for the payment of the principal at a certain time, or for interest to run immediately, or under special circumstances, from whence a contract for interest was to be inferred, has interest been ever given." I quote this, not as an opinion, but as evidence of a fact; and coming from such authority, conclusive proof of the law of England, at the time mentioned. The researches of counsel confirm the evidence, if it needed any; and it is strengthened by the opinion of Mr. Jefferson, in the letter to Mr. Hammond before referred to, and quoted by the counsel for the plaintiffs in error. These remarks are to be understood as applicable only to the first class of cases, where the court allow interest, and not to that class where juries in their discretion give it as damages; for Ld. Ellenborough, himself, frequently directed it in actions of trover and trespass for chattels, and in other actions of tort.

I consider it established, then, beyond all question or cavil, that the allowance of interest, by the court, as an incident to the debt, is always founded on the agreement of the par-
611*] ties. *It will be seen that most of the cases in England and in this country recognize this great principle, and that it is the only one upon which they can be reconciled and harmonized. It is one of plain common sense, easily applied, and which rejects all the artificial reasoning which has been sometimes employed.

This agreement may be expressed in writing or by words, or it may be implied.

First. If there be an agreement in the body of a note or other instrument, that interest shall run with the debt, it is invariably assessed. If there be a verbal agreement to pay it, that is equally binding: for there is no law requiring such a contract to be in writing.

Second. This agreement may be implied:

1st. From the custom or usage of the business in which the debt is contracted. When such custom is known to the parties, or may reasonably be presumed to have been known, it enters into the original contract, and forms a part of it. *Eddowes* v. *Hopkins*, 1 Doug., 375; *Selleck* v. *French*, 1 Con. N. S., 35. But there ought to be evidence that such custom was known. (1 Stark., 487.)

2d. Where the principal is to be paid at a specific time the law has always implied an agreement to make good the loss arising from a default, by the payment of interest. Per Ld. Mansfield, in *Robinson* v. *Bland*, 2 Burr., 1086. This proceeds entirely on the idea of a default, and it is a universal maxim, that where interest does not run with the principal none accrues until a default is made in payment.

This is illustrated by the familiar case of a note p y on demand, when it is never allowed but from the time of demand made by suit or otherwise.(a) When a default of payment is made, then interest attaches. "All contracts to pay, undoubtedly give a right to interest from the time when the principal ought to be paid," is the remark of Ld. Thurlow, in 2 Bro. C. C., 3. The same principle is admitted by Ld. Ellenborough in *Callon* v. *Bragg*, before cited; and in *Mountford* v. *Willes*, 2 Bos. & P., 337.

Interest is allowable on money lent, from the time it was agreed to be paid. This was the decision in *Robinson* v. **Bland*, 2 Burr., [***612**
1085; and this must be the meaning of the judges in *Blaney* v. *Hendricks*, W. Bl., 761, where they say, simply, that interest is allowable on money lent. The case of *Robinson* v. *Bland* was referred to, and would appear to be the authority for their decision. And so Kent, *Ch. J.*, in *Day* v. *Brett*, 6 Johns., 24, says, "money received or advanced for another, carries interest after a default in payment." But there cannot be a default unless there was a specified time for payment, or there has been a demand or something equivalent.

3d. Where an account has been liquidated by both parties, and the debt, therefore, becomes due and payable, it carries interest on the same ground of a debt payable at a specific time; that there is an implied contract to pay. This reason is given in *Boddam* v. *Ryley*, 2 Bro. C. C., 3. The rule is settled by other cases. (2 W. Bl., 761; 3 Wils., 205, and 15 Johns., 424.) It is also recognized by those cases, which decide that upon an open account, where mutual credits exist, interest is not allowable until a liquidation; 1 Dick., 428; 6 Johns., 45; 1 Johns., 315; and by those cases where it is held that interest is not allowable on unliquidated accounts. (2 Salk., 623; 1 H. Bl., 303; 2 Bos. & P., 219; 2 Gall., 45; 1 P. Wms., 376; 7 Johns., 213.)

Where a demand is liquidated by a judgment, the right to recover interest in a new action, is founded on the same principle. (6 Johns., 283.)

4th. Where an account has been rendered, and the debtor, during a reasonable time for that purpose, makes no objection, it may fairly be presumed that he has acquiesced in it. It then becomes a liquidated account, and carries interest, upon the same principle, from the time of such presumed liquidation. (2 Vern., 276; 2 Ves., Sr., 239; 2 Atk., 252; 15 Johns., 424.)

For the same reason, a demand of payment of an unsettled claim for wages, being equivalent to the rendering of an account, entitles to interest for such demand; as then the debt is liquidated, due and payable. (2 Gall., 45.)

*And this, I apprehend, to be the [***613**
principle which governed the decision of the Supreme Court, in the case of *Kane* v. *Smith*, 12 Johns., 156. The defendants were charged with interest from the time the deficiency in the funds provided by them was ascertained, and they were notified of the balance; for until then, the court say, the defendants could not be deemed in default. So, the case of *Brown* v. *Campbell*, 1 Serg. & R., 179, upon notice that the plaintiff's money was applied to his use, the defendant was in default, in withholding payment.

5th. Upon the same principle, there may be various other circumstances in the transactions between the parties, which furnish evidence of an intention by the debtor to pay interest. The giving a note or bill of exchange, which is void or turns out to have been of no value at the time, or the offering to give a written security for the debt, has justly been considered evidence that the debtor considered the debt to be due and payable, and carrying interest on the same ground, as where it was payable at a specific time. Such an instance

(a) *Vide* Jacobs v. Adams, 1 Dall., 52, per M'Kean, *C. J.*

is furnished by the case of *Robinson* v. *Bland*, 2 Burr., 1088.

The rendering an account, containing a charge of interest on particular items, and that account being liquidated by the debtor, is evidence of an agreement to pay the interest thus charged; and is so held by Ld. Ellenborough, in the case of *Calton* v. *Bragg*, before cited.

So, such an account being acquiesced in by the debtor's omitting to object to it within a reasonable time, furnishes the same evidence of an agreement to pay the interest charged, as was held by Livingston, *J.*, in *Liotard* v. *Graves*, 3 Cai., 226.

And in subsequent dealings between the same parties, of the like nature, the liquidation of such a former account, there being no new agreement and no new circumstances to vary the case, would furnish sufficient ground to imply an agreement to pay the like interest in those subsequent dealings. Such was the case of *Nichol* v. *Thompson*, 1 Campb. *N. P.*, 52.

614*] *And on the same principle, where interest has, under like circumstances, been allowed by the debtor to other creditors, the knowledge of which comes to the creditor in the given case, and he acts in expectation of a similar allowance, there would be good ground to presume an agreement to pay interest also to the new creditor. This would be in analogy to the rule which exists where there is a custom or usage of trade. I find no adjudged case which precisely determines such a rule, although there are many analogous. It is certainly as broad and liberal as the most strenuous advocates for the allowance of interest could require, and is more nearly applicable to the present case than any other.

It is believed that these classes comprehend all the cases of implied agreements that have been cited, excepting those of *Liotard* v. *Graves*, 3 Cai., 226, and *Dilworth* v. *Sinderling*, 1 Binn., 494. In most of them, the question whether there was an agreement to allow interest is one of fact, which should be left to a jury; and that fact once ascertained, the rule of law applies. A great share of the difficulty on this subject has arisen from the court's undertaking to draw a rule from the facts of each case, by which it is made fluctuating and uncertain.

In these classes which have been enumerated, the interest is considered a necessary incident to the debt, following it, as is said in one of the cases, like a shadow following its body.

But there is another class of cases, already alluded to, in which interest may be allowed by a jury, under the advice of the court, in their discretion, and which, when fairly exercised, the courts will not disturb.

This second class comprehends those cases only where interest is not a necessary incident to the debt, but may be allowed under circumstances, by way of mulct or punishment for some fraud, delinquency or injustice of the debtor, or for some injury done by him to the creditor; and in such cases the legal rate of interest is assumed as the measure of damages. This is done,

1st. In actions of tort, technically so called, as in trover, or in trespass for taking chattels. (8 Johns., 446; 14 Johns., 128, 273, 385.)

*The application of the rule, in these [*615 cases, may sometimes be capricious; but the rule itself is as certain as any other which allows damages in any case. The judgment of twelve indifferent men, is the best criterion that can be established.

2d. In actions upon contracts. Thus, Radcliff, *J.*, in his opinion, which was sustained by this court, in the case of *Lynch* v. *De Viar*, 3 Johns. Cas., 310, says: "It is a settled rule that money received to the use of another and improperly retained always carries interest." In that case, the party had expressly promised to pay the money when received, and withheld it under frivolous and unjust pretexts. The contrary doctrine which was laid down in *De Bernales* v. *Fuller*, 2 Campb. *N. P.*, 426, must have arisen from not sufficiently distinguishing between the cases where a jury, may, allow interest and those in which the court must, allow it. It seems to have been confounded with the latter class. It is contradicted by the decision of this court already referred to; by the Supreme Court of this State, in *People* v. *Gasherie*, 9 Johns., 71, and *Slingerland* v *Swart*, 13 Johns., 255; by the Supreme Court of Mass., in *Wood* v. *Robbins*, 11 Mass., 504, and *Wyman* v. *Hubbard*, 13 Mass., 232; by the Supreme Court of Pa., in *Crawford* v. *Willing*, 4 Dall., 286, 289; *Commonwealth* v. *Crevor*, 3 Binn., 123, and *Brown* v. *Campbell*, 1 Serg. & R., 179. All these cases allow interest where there has been fraud, injustice or delinquency; and none of them put the allowance of it on the ground of gain or benefit to the debtor from the use of the money alone. The case of *De Bernales* v. *Fuller* is opposed also to the most respectable English authorities. Ld. Mansfield, 1 Doug., 375, says: "In cases of long delay under vexatious and oppressive circumstances, interest may be recovered, if a jury, in their discretion, think fit to allow it." This remark is the more valuable, as showing the correctness of the distinction between the allowance of interest by the court and by the jury.

In the case of *Trelawney* v. *Thomas*, 1 H. Bl., 304, cited and much commented on in the argument, the defendant had engaged the plaintiff to advance money in order to carry on an election, which he had done according to the request; *and in an action [*616 brought to recover the money thus expended, the jury allowed the plaintiff interest, which the court confirmed. This case is to be referred either to the second head of implied agreements, that money received or advanced for another carries interest after a default in payment, upon the ground that being advanced on request, it was payable immediately, and the default arose on the first neglect, which would be sufficient to sustain the decision; or it may be considered as proving such delinquency and injustice in the debtor, as to furnish sufficient ground for a jury to punish him by giving interest as damages. There may in many cases be such a complication of circumstances as would justify the allowance of interest on more than one ground; and such is this case of *Trelawney* v. *Thomas*.

Probably the rule of easiest application would be this: where money has been lent, advanced or expended by request, and under an agreement to pay at a specific time, or where it has been had and received under a like agreement, then the allowance of interest may be safely referred to the principle of an implied contract to pay interest on default; and so, also, where the money is not to be refunded at a particular time, but a default arises from a demand or notice, the same principle will apply. But where no time of payment is fixed, and where the duty to pay arises from the relative situation of the parties, it seems that it should be referred to a jury to determine whether damages shall be given, by an allowance of interest. Thus, sheriffs and other public officers are required to pay interest on moneys received by them, which it was their duty to pay over immediately. *People* v. *Gasherie*, 9 Johns., 71; 14 Johns., 255; 7 Mass., 14. So a private agent, not applying money as directed, is chargeable with interest. (4 Dessau., 110.) But we also find it settled in *Williams* v. *Storrs*, 6 Johns. Ch., 353, that where an agent is ready to pay over money received by him to the party entitled to it, he is not in default and shall not be chargeable with interest, unless he has employed the money for the purposes of gain. These are equitable considerations that must be left to a jury, and which a court ought not attempt to estimate. All that a court should **617***] *do is to instruct a jury that if there be fraud, injustice, delinquency or default, they may allow interest. This doctrine is recognized by the Supreme Court in an *Anonymous* case, 1 Johns., 315.

With respect to the allowance of interest to an agent for moneys advanced by him, there is nothing in his character of agent to entitle him to it. He must receive it upon the same principles which would give it to any other creditor. Indeed, the general policy of the law is adverse to the allowance of interest to an agent or trustee for advances; it is presumed, for the purpose of withholding any temptation to speculate on the funds of his principal. (1 P. Wms., 376; 14 Vin. Abr., 458, pl. 10; Select Cas. in Ch., 50; 2 Eq. Cas. Abr., 531, pl. 15.) So in the case of an administrator, the Supreme Court of Mass. refused interest on advances. (9 Mass., 37.)

But where an agent has expended money by the directions of his principal, there can be no reason for distinguishing it, from the case of money lent or advanced by any other person. An instance of its allowance in such a case is found in *Craven* v. *Tickell*, 1 Ves., Jr., 63, which refers to the distinction between allowing interest on the contract, or by way of damages.

So, if advances are made by an agent with the knowledge and acquiescence of the principal, it is but advancing a single step in the same train of reasoning, to presume a request. And if a request, an implied agreement to pay; and on a default in payment, the like agreement as in all other cases of default, to pay interest.

So, in an advance of a single sum, on a particular occasion, or a few sums may, from the circumstances, furnish ground for presuming knowledge in the principal, acquiescence by him, and an implied promise to pay immediately, which, as we have seen, carries interest from the time of default.

All these are cases of advances on the one side, and depend upon the same principles which would regulate the allowance of interest to any creditor not an agent.

The same principles will be found applicable to the case of mutual credits between an agent and his principal. There *must be a [***618** knowledge by the principal that the advances are making for him, and an acquiescence, to supply the want of a request. There must be a default on his part before he can be charged with interest; for the citation of cases already made must have been to very little purpose if they have not established the universal maxim that there can be no interest without default, where, by the contract, it does not run with the principal. But to cause a default, there must be knowledge of a debt.

In the case of single advances, or where they are made only on one side, that knowledge is implied necessarily from the fact of knowing that such advances are made. In the case of mutual credits, that inference does not follow; for the credits may be equal to, or overbalance the advances. Hence it seems to be an irresistible consequence that in the case of mutual credits, there cannot be a default without the knowledge of a balance to be paid. The same principles which govern the laws of interest in all the other cases stated, ought to control here. If it is to be charged on the ground of an implied agreement, then there should certainly be a request to advance the money or something tantamount, as knowledge and acquiescence, and a default upon which the implied agreement to pay interest arises. If it is to be charged upon the ground of delinquency in not paying, there must be knowledge of the fact on which the delinquency arises, before it can exist. That fact is the existence of a balance. These deductions seem to flow plainly from the principles which have been extracted from all the cases; and which an effort has been made to arrange. And they are consonant to the first dictates of common sense and common justice; that no man should be held liable to pay interest for moneys advanced, not only without his request or consent, but without his knowledge; that he should not pay it where there was no default on his part, and where there could be none.

The distinction between the case of an account containing items only on one side, and that where there are mutual dealings and mutual credits, is exemplified by the different rule which is applied to those cases under the Statute of Limitations. *It was decided by [***619** this court in *Murray* v. *Coster*, 20 Johns., 603, that the exception of merchants accounts in that statute, from its operation, applied not to the first case of items on the one side only, but did apply to the second case of mutual credits; that is, that an action for the balance of an account founded on mutual credits, was not barred by the statute. Upon what other principle can this distinction possibly proceed but this; that in the first case, the debt was due and payable from the time it was incurred, or might have been demanded; and in the second case, that of mutual credits, a liquidation by the parties or by suit was necessary. This distinction under the statute is applicable as well to an account for money advanced as to one for work and labor; it is applied without reference to the character of the items, and depends simply on the fact whether there were mutual credits or not. It appears to me that the symmetry of the law would be marred by amalgamating and confounding cases in the law of interest, which are distinct in the law of prescription; and that to preserve the harmony of the system and the mutual dependence of the different parts, we should hold that a debt which is not considered due and payable by the law of limitation, shall also not be considered due and payable under the law of interest. And we shall thus pursue and preserve the policy which punishes neglect in demanding payment by refusing an action after a certain period, and shall stimulate and reward vigilence by giving interest where it is earned by promptness in liquidating accounts; and we shall thus prevent the unwary debtor, from becoming the victim of either the intentional, or the negligent, delay of his creditor.

These principles are believed to be in accordance with the opinions expressed by the judges of the Supreme Court in this cause, or to be legitimate conclusions from them, and from the numerous cases on the subject. But there is one ground for the allowance of interest, intimated by one of the judges to which, as I understand it, I cannot subscribe. It is, that a "universal obligation rest upon every man to render a just equivalent for the use of that which does not belong to him." This is unquestionably true, if that beneficial use has been
620*] *at his instance. But my researches have not enabled me to discover a case, and certain I am that none has been cited, that a man is bound to pay for the use of money or other property which has been applied to his benefit without his consent. The case of *Bartholomew* v. *Jackson*, 20 Johns., 28, is one like, perhaps, hundreds which may be found in the books establishing a contrary doctrine. In that case it was held, that labor voluntarily performed by the plaintiff for the defendant, without his privity or request, however meritorious and beneficial it may be to the defendant, as in saving his property from destruction by fire, affords no ground of action. A claim for compensation or damages in the shape of interest, for money applied to the benefit of another, without his privity or request, must rest on the same foundation with any other service. The benefit received is not the test. It must be requested, or agreed, to be received. Every man is permitted to regulate his own affairs in his own way, and he is the best judge when and where he will have services performed or money advanced for him. There is no equity in making him pay for the use of money, although employed for his benefit, without his request.

I proceed to apply the principles thus deduced to the present case.

First. It is not pretended that there has been an express agreement by the plaintiffs in error to pay interest on the moneys advanced by Reid. Second. Is there any evidence of an implied agreement to that effect?

1st. There is no usage or custom known to the parties, set up. 2d. There was no specific time of payment agreed on. 3d. The account has never been liquidated. 4th. No account was ever rendered by Reid. *Ch. J.* Savage, in the opinion delivered by him in the Supreme Court, says: "There certainly appears to have been a culpable negligence on both sides;" in Reid, in not rendering his account, and in the plaintiffs in error, in not requiring them. Upon the principles which have been stated, as Reid or his representative holds the affirmative, and is bound to show the circumstance or fact which evinces an agreement to pay interest, *the admission of a culpable neg- [*621
ligence on his part in omitting to do that which would apprise the adverse party of the state of affairs, and which would furnish him a claim to interest is, in itself, a strong circumstance against him. The plaintiffs in error then were, and still are, on the defensive. Generally speaking, it is not the business of one who does not know the state of the accounts, and who turns out to be the debtor, to inquire into them; on the contrary, it is the duty of the creditor to apprise his ignorant debtor of the existence of the claim. And most clearly, I apprehend, is this the law with respect to agents. In the case of *Lady Ormond* v. *Hutchinson*, 13 Ves., 53, Ld. Eldon says, with respect to the steward of an estate, that "it is not necessary to call for an account from him. His duty requires him to render accounts periodically, and if from negligence or any other cause he fails in that, he cannot make the obscurity occasioned by that omission, a cover to him." The similarity of the case of a steward and that of an agent for a manufacturing company is evident; and the difference, if any, is in favor of holding the latter to a more strict accountability. It appears to me, upon general principles of policy, that no agent ought to be permitted to found a claim of any kind, either for interest or salary, upon his own culpable negligence.

Conceding, then, that the plaintiffs in error were equally culpable, in their neglect to require an account, but which is not admitted, the precise case is presented where the maxim applies, contained in Jenkins: "Where neither party has any right, the condition of the possessor is the best." The case of *Beaumont* v. *Boultbee*, 11 Ves., 359, decides, that where there had been such a mutual acquiescence and negligence on both sides, very similar to the present case, the agent should not be allowed interest until after the bill filed. The cases of *White* v. *Lincoln*, 8 Ves., 363, and *Pearse* v. *Green*, 1 Jac. & Walk., 135, cited on the argument on the part of the plaintiffs in error, together with various others in the equity reports, show the vigilence of the chancery courts in preventing an agent from deriving any advantage *from his own laches; and es- [*622
tablished the broad doctrine that where he has been guilty of it in rendering his accounts or any other neglect, he shall not recover interest, and in many cases he is deprived of his commission. All business men will probably subscribe to the justice and policy of this rule. I am not aware of its having ever been questioned; and unless there be some other grounds in the case to sustain the claim of the defendant in error, the culpable negligence of Reid in this respect, furnishes, in itself, a complete bar to the recovery of any interest. I cannot consider his negligence in any way excused or mitigated by that of his principals, nor is the rule

referred to, affected by any such circumstance. Under this head, therefore, no ground to claim interest is afforded by the rendition of an account; and on the contrary, the omission to render it for more than six years, ought to be a bar.

Under the fifth head, as I have arranged it, of implied agreements to allow interest, we are to inquire whether there are any facts or circumstances in the transactions between the parties, either in the same or in any former business of the like nature, where interest has been allowed, or an intention to allow it has been evinced. It is not pretended, nor would the case warrant it, that there are any such circumstances in the transactions between the parties themselves, as evince an agreement to allow interest. But it is suggested in the opinion of the *Ch. J.*, that the defendants having agreed to pay interest on the advances made by Reid & Alsop, the year preceding, furnishes some ground for charging the plaintiffs in error with it in this case. It is due to the *Ch. J.* to observe that this does not appear to be much relied on by him; but as it was thrown out by him, and has been urged with much force by the counsel for the defendant in error, it ought to be briefly examined. In the first place, it was not a transaction between these parties; and the fact that the Company had made a particular agreement with one agent to allow interest, and had subsequently made another agreement with another agent, in which nothing was said about interest, would furnish, at least, as strong reason for saying that the one **623***] did not mean to pay it, *as that the agent meant to receive it. But, secondly, it was not a business of the like nature. Reid & Alsop entered into partnership with the Company, and were to advance the necessary funds; and the stipulation always made in such cases, was made in this; that the partner advancing capital was to be allowed interest thereon, before a division of profits should be made. But on the termination of this contract, Reid was appointed agent, and is allowed a salary as such, and never was a partner; and in his new capacity his connection with the Company was of a character entirely different, and involving new rights and duties wholly distinct from the former. Indeed, the argument is very strong against its being considered the intention of the parties that Reid should make advances, from the very fact that when these new arrangements were making, no stipulation to that effeet was entered into, although it had been so so carefully provided for in the agreement with Alsop & Reid.

I conclude, then, that there is nothing in the agreement with Reid & Alsop, which can show the nature and terms of the subsequent agreement with Reid alone; and I consider that there is nothing in this case to establish an express or implied agreement to pay interest, which would oblige the court to allow it, as a rule of law.

Is it, then, a case included under the second general head, where a jury might, in their discretion, allow interest? It certainly is not one of those actions for wrongs, where such a discretion exists. Does it come under the second subdivision of this head? And is it a case where, upon natural principles of equity, the debtor ought to pay interest in consequence of any fraud, delinquency or injustice? The difficulty of arriving at precise and definite rules to govern this class of cases, has already been mentioned, and the causes of it explained. But I think I have shown that the general rule being, that an agent is not to be allowed interest, unless there be evidence of an agreement to pay it, or a delinquency, the burden is on the agent claiming it, to establish the agreement or the delinquency; and that he must at least prove a knowledge on the part of his principal, that advances were making, and an acquiescence in their being made, *before he [***624** can claim, upon equitable principles, any interest on those advances. Indeed, I understand this principle to be tacitly admitted by the *Ch. J.*, and he seems to endeavor to bring the case within it by these remarks: "On the whole, I am of opinion that from the manner in which the business had been done the year next previous to the appointment of Reid as agent; from this being done with a full knowledge, on both sides, that large advances were necessary, if the defendants did not mean to pay interest, they ought so to have informed Reid, that he might not be using a large capital in their service when it was to be wholly unproductive to him." It will be perceived, that admitting the whole of this statement, it does not come up to the point of establishing a knowledge on the part of the Company, or the directors, that Reid was actually making advances for them. There could be no default on their part without a knowledge of their being indebted to Reid; and that, they could not possess, until the fact that he was making advances, was brought home to them. The remark of *Ch. J.* Tilghman, in *Brown* v. *Campbell*, 1 Serg. & R., 179, contains not only the law on this subject, but the reason and principle of it, such as I have been endeavoring to show, "that until the defendant was informed that the plaintiff's money was applied to his use, he was in no default and, therefore, ought not to pay interest; but being informed, he became a wrong-doer in withholding payment and, therefore, should pay interest." Let it be observed, this is not a claim for the principal, but for the interest of the advances; and it proceeds entirely on the ground of a default in the debtor; for, as has been before remarked, it is a universal maxim, that there never can be interest where there is no agreement that it shall run with the principal, without a default. The knowledge that advances were necessary at the time Reid & Alsop took charge of the concern, is no evidence whatever of the same knowledge existing when Reid was appointed. But admitting, for the sake of the argument, that it did exist at that time, it was accompanied by a knowledge that he would be in the receipt of heavy sums from the establishment, from which he could refund himself; *and it, therefore, did not amount to [***625** knowledge or notice that there was a balance of those advances against the Company, without which there could be no default. This is the peculiarity attending the case of mutual credits, as has been before explained; that a knowledge of advances being made does not imply a knowledge that a balance was accumulating against them. It is different from the case where the advances are all on one side. There the mere fact of knowledge of such advances and acquiescence in them, might be sufficient to imply an agreement to pay at once; and there being a default, entitle to interest; but the same principle requires us, in the case of mutual credits, to go a step further, and demand proof of knowledge of an accumulating balance, and an acquiescence in that; for, until there be such an accumulation, there is no debt. The knowledge of a debt must precede the idea of a default in not paying it. This view is further confirmed by the subsequent remark of the *Ch. J.*, that the Company ought to have given Reid notice, "that he might not be using a large capital in their service." But how could they give the notice if they did not know the fact? For Reid could not be using his capital unless his advances exceeded his receipts; and they of course could not know it, until he informed them such was the fact; that is, that a balance was accumulating against them. It is with great deference, but with considerable confidence, that I consider the remark of the *Ch. J.* as not applicable to the case of mutual credits, although sound and correct when applied to cash advances, altogether on one side.

The facts in this very case illustrate the principle. By the schedule A, referred to in the case and printed with it, it will be seen that the balances fluctuated, and that of those stated by the referees, ten were in favor of Reid and thirty in favor of the Company. Is it reasonable, in such a state of things, to require of the Company knowledge, or even reason to presume that there was an ultimate balance against them?

Again; by the resolution of June 15, 1813, the agent was directed to furnish an estimate **626***] of the funds necessary for *carrying on the works for the ensuing year; but this direction appears never to have been complied with. If advances were necessary, was it not emphatically the duty of the agent, after this special injunction, to inform the Company? And shall he be permitted, in neglect of that duty, to proceed without their knowledge, to make those advances, and then claim compensation by way of interest? It is wholly immaterial whether the Company derived benefit from those advances or not. They had a right to know what amount of funds would be necessary, and to provide their own means of raising them. By this culpable negligence of their agent, they are deprived of the opportunity of doing so, and are made to borrow money of him to an indefinite amount, without their privity or request, and are then called upon to pay interest, not only for the time the money was used in their service, but for as long a period afterwards as the agent chooses to conceal from them a knowledge of the fact of their being his debtors. I can never subscribe to such consequences. And if this case is to be determined upon equitable considerations, this one fact shows conclusively, to my mind, that all equity and natural justice are against the defendant in error.

How can it be said that the Company should have given Reid notice that they did not mean to pay interest on the balance of his advances, when they were kept ignorant by him of the fact of his making them; and when, from the nature of the business, they could not know that there was or would be such a balance? And is it correct, in any case, to require a party to give notice that he will not be accountable? Is it not incumbent on the plaintiff to show a liability, affirmatively, and can he be permitted to say that it exists, because a defendant has said and done nothing about it, either to create or acknowledge it, or to deny it?

Thus far, this case has been considered strictly in reference to those general principles of the law of interest, which have been stated in the former part of these remarks. It is believed that every case which has been cited is comprehended in that arrangement, and classed in one or other of the divisions, excepting only two, which have been much relied upon in the *argument. Perhaps the very fact, [***627** that these two cases, as they seem to be understood, cannot be classed with any others in the books, and that they are contrary to the analogy to the law of interest, in all the other cases, furnishes some proof that they are themselves anomalous and erratic. But as one of the judges appears to place his opinion chiefly on the ground of their authority, it becomes a duty to examine them carefully, and as briefly as possible.

The cases alluded to, are those of *Liotard* v. *Graves*, 3 Cai., 226, in the Supreme Court of this State, and *The Lessees of Dilworth* v. *Sinderling*, 1 Serg. & R., 179, in Pa. They are supposed to decide that interest is allowable on cash advances, whether on one side only, or in the case of mutual credits, without the account being liquidated, and without any other evidence or circumstance, to infer an agreement for the payment of interest. It will strike every one that such a rule founded on and resulting from a particular case, instead of being deduced from general principles, must necessarily be arbitrary, fluctuating and capricious. To whatever extent the Supreme Court may have felt itself bound by a prior decision of the same court, it is proper to observe, that in this court that decision is no authority. We are as much bound to revise it as the one brought up by this writ of error. The decisions, in both cases, are upon the same footing, and are entitled to regard, not for the names and stations of the judges, but for the principles and reasons on which they are founded, and which they contain. With respect to that of *Liotard* v. *Graves*, truth compels me to say that there are no principles to be extracted from it. Livingston, *J.*, allows the claim of interest, expressly on the ground that "an account was rendered as early as 1797, in which interest is calculated, and yet no objection to it was made, in the succeeding correspondence, from which, I conclude, such charge consisted with the understanding of the parties." This is sound and intelligible. The principle of an implied agreement is recognized, and properly applied. Had this been the only opinion delivered, there would have been no difficulty. But those of the other judges state the rule of law absolutely to be, that interest is legally demandable *on money advanced. They [***628** furnish no reasons; they advert to no principle, but content themselves with the simple declaration of the rule. Now the cases which have been adduced at the bar, and in the opinions of the judges, must have satisfied every one, that in 1805, when that cause was decided, there was no such settled rule; that up to the period of our Revolution, the rule was directly the contrary; and that the whole current of authority, and the conclusive testimony of L'd. Ellenborough, before quoted, establish as firmly as any rule of law can possibly be established by decisions, that interest is not allowable in such a case. In the quotations which we have heard from the Pa. Reports, it is distinctly admitted that the law was so settled, but that a change had taken place in it. By what authority? No legislative sanction is pretended. As one, I am not prepared to admit or yield to judicial legislation, in a question so extensively affecting not only the commercial part of community, but every other.

I admire that principle of flexibility in the common law, which enables it to be adapted to the ever-varying condition of human society; and it is in that respect, unquestionably, altogether superior to any written code. But I understand that flexibility to consist, not in the change of great and essential principles, but in the application of old principles to new cases, and in the modification of the rules flowing from them, to such cases as they arise, so as to presume the reason of the rules and the spirit of the law.

Such, however, does not appear to be the case with the decision in *Liotard* v. *Graves*, if it be correctly understood by the judges of the Supreme Court; for, unless it is put upon the ground assumed by Livingston, *J.*, it departs from the spirit of the law of interest, and from the reason of all its rules in other cases. Admitting it, then, to be as supposed, it is not entitled to be regarded as evidence of the law.

But the *dicta* of the other three judges (for really they can be called nothing else, in that case) do not come up to the present. They say interest is to be allowed on money advanced; but whether, in a case where the advances are all on one side, or in a case of mutual credits, **629***] they do not *say; nor do they say whether a request to make those advances, or something tantamount, shall or shall not be required to entitle to interest. It will be perceived at once, that these are the two hinges on which this case turns; and the decision in *Liotard* v. *Graves* is, therefore, really not applicable to it.

If, in considering that case, we are to be governed by the usual rules of construction, and confine the remarks of the judges to the case before them, the fair import of their decision will be found to be, that in a case where the advances are all on one side, and are made at the request of the principal, interest is allowable. The claim to interest, in that case, was upon the charges for advances to Weeks, the captain of the vessel, and for other disbursements in London, while prosecuting the claim and appeal there. These advances were made by the express order of the defendant; and I cannot discover in the case the least evidence that the plaintiffs had received moneys belonging to Graves. In such a state of things, the decision in that case would be perfectly correct, and in conformity to the principles I have endeavored to establish; but is, obviously, wholly inapplicable to the present case, where moneys were received and paid out, and mutual credits existed; and where there is no evidence of a request or even knowledge of advances being made. From the cases cited, subsequently decided by the same judges, it would seem to me that they did not intend to establish a general rule, by the decision in that case, but were governed by its peculiar circumstances. With regard to this case then, I consider, firstly, that it does not establish the rule contended for, and is inapplicable to this case; and secondly, that if it did, it would be contrary to the whole current of authority, in England, and in this country, at the time of our Revolution and long after, and unsupported by the principles of analogous cases, and ought not to be regarded as authority in changing the law.

The other case relied on as an authority to sustain the judgment of the Supreme Court, is that of *Dilworth's Lessees* v. *Sinderling*, 1 Binn., 448. That was, indeed, a most extraordinary case, in all its features. It was an action of *ejectment, brought by the *cestuis* [***630** *que trust*, claiming an equitable interest, against the executor and devisee, having the legal interest—to us, and according to our ideas of law, a perfect monster. But the recovery of the possession of land was to be subject to certain deductions, for advances made in a long series of years, and which were indispensable, for the repair of the premises. Upon whom these deductions were to be apportioned, and how collected by a defendant in an action of ejectment, we are uninformed. But so it was, and the court was called upon to say whether interest should be allowed on those advances. It is to be observed that the persons interested in the estate were infants, and incapable of making any request for advances; but these being indispensable for the preservation of the property, and there being, in fact, no principals to notify, those advances may well be considered as having been done upon request, or something tantamount, or even superior—so as to entitle the trustee equitably to interest. This will, probably, distinguish it from the present case, where no such necessity existed for making advances without the knowledge of the principals. Again; it was obviously an equity case; the courts of common law in that State being obliged to strain their jurisdiction to cover such cases, from there being no court of chancery established there; a very hazardous guide to us, in a court of law, at least; and when in opposition to almost every other case in the books, one not to be trusted. But taking it as it is, there is a fact stated in the opinion of *Ch. J.* Tilghman, and to which he seems to give weight, which clearly distinguishes that case from the present. Fuller, the person who made the advances, did not charge and was not allowed any commissions or salary, or any compensation in any other shape than by way of interest. Here Reid has been allowed a salary of $1,250 for two years and six months, embracing a portion of time somewhat greater than he was actually employed. Considered as a case in equity, this circumstance would be entitled to weight, in determining the allowance of interest, whatever may be its effect on the rule of law. But the greatest objection to this case is, that the decision is averred by the judges who 631*] made it, to be *contrary to the former rule, and to be founded on more mature reflection, which has "settled the law for a considerable time past, that interest is recoverable for money lent and advanced." The earliest case cited by the counsel in that cause, showing such a rule even in Pa., occurred in 1803, 4 Dall., 289, only five years before *Dilworth* v. *Sinderling*. It was upon a settled and liquidated account and, therefore, not applicable. Now, whatever authority the judges in Pa. may have, to overthrow a settled and acknowledged rule of law, their decisions cannot be received here for that purpose. Reported cases are only evidence of the law, not the law itself; and like all other evidence, it must be sifted and examined, to be understood. Were a witness to declare that he appeared, not to testify to a fact, but to something directly the contrary, which he believed would promote justice, he would not be heard. So, when a case admits that it overthrows the law, it should cease to be regarded as evidence of that law. For these reasons, I refuse any weight to the case of *Dilworth's Lessees* v. *Sinderling*.

But, if we may look abroad for cases, to sustain and fortify our conclusions, there are two, proceeding from the very respectable Supreme Courts of Mass. and Conn.; which are worthy of our attention, not only on account of the sources from which they emanate, but from their harmony with the other cases and with analogous principles. That of *Winthrop* v. *Carleton*, 12 Mass., 4, is precisely like that of *Liotard* v. *Graves*, as it seems to be understood by three of the judges who decided it. The Supreme Court of Mass. refused interest on such advances except from the time of the commencement of the suit, because there had been no liquidation of the accounts, and no demand made.(a) In *Selleck* v. *French*, 1 Conn. N. S., 32, the same principle is decided, that unless there be some promise or usage, interest cannot be allowed in a case of mutual accounts founded on mutual dealings, and where there has been no liquidation. In point of authority, these cases would seem entitled to more regard than the one in Pa.

632*] *Having finished the examination of the only two cases which are relied on to sustain the position that interest is allowable on money lent or advanced without any agreement express or implied for the payment of interest, and without any liquidation of the account, or any other circumstance to show a default in the debtor, I am brought to a point in this cause where firm ground is felt, and where we are relieved from the obscurity and inconsistency of the modern cases. It has already been alluded to incidentally. The common law of England, as it stood Apr. 19, 1775, in relation to the allowance of interest on money advanced in the case of mutual credits, without liquidation of the account, has not been denied or questioned. In such a case interest was not allowable. The testimony of Ld. Ellenborough and Mr. Jefferson, the chronological arrangement of the cases in the opinion of *Ch. J.* Savage, and the citations of the counsel on both sides, establish this position beyond all controversy. The Constitution declares that it "shall be and continue the law of this State, subject to such alterations as the Legislature shall make concerning the same." The Legislature has made no alterations in the law now under consideration. I feel myself as much bound to adhere to that law, as if it were engrafted in the Constitution in so many words; and I can no more depart from it than I can from any other principle of the common law. I mean not to be understood that when the judges of England have applied the principle of the common law erroneously, we are not at liberty to correct the application, and restore those principles to their original purity. But it should be a clear and unequivocal case of erroneous application; and even then, we should not lightly disturb a rule settled for a century.

It has been one object of the review and arrangement of the cases which has now been made, to show that the courts in England have correctly applied the principles of the law of interest in all other cases to that of mutual accounts for money advanced and received; and that they pursue the analogy of those cases and follow the reason of them, when they require an agreement, express or implied, to pay interest, *to be inferred from the liqui- [*633 dation of an account, or some other circumstance; or such a delinquency in the debtor as justifies punishment by charging him with interest in the shape of damages. This case does not furnish evidence of such an agreement. It is deficient, in not presenting liquidated accounts, custom, former transactions, specified time of payment, or any other ground to imply one. Nor does it furnish any evidence of a knowledge by the debtors of the existence of a claim against them—which knowledge must necessarily precede the idea of a delinquency. It is satisfactory to be able to repose at once upon a clear and acknowledged rule which has never been abrogated by any competent authority, and upon a series of admitted principles in analogous cases, exhibiting the reason and propriety of that rule, and explaining, sustaining and confirming it.

The result of my opinion is, that this being a case of mutual credits, where the account was never liquidated, there being no evidence of any agreement to pay interest; and there being no default in the plaintiffs in error for not paying a balance of the existence of which they were ignorant, interest ought not to be allowed on any of the items. And if, in any case of mutual credits without a liquidated account, it could be allowed, I am of opinion that the culpable negligence of Reed, in omitting to furnish an estimate of the necessary funds as directed, and in omitting to render his accounts, for more than six years after the balance accrued to him, ought to preclude him or his representative from the recovery of any interest, but from the time when he made a demand of that balance by suit.

I am, therefore, for reversing so much of the judgment of the Supreme Court as allows the defendant in error any interest before the commencement of the action.

CRARY, *Senator* · May, 1, 1813, all the materials and stock then owned by the Directors amounted to $13,186.58. The intestate then took the active agency of the factory. The stock, materials and funds of the Directors

(a) But see *note*, *ante* p. 600.

were insufficient to keep the factory in operation, and large advances were required for that 634*] purpose. The proceeds of *all glass manufactured after May 1, 1813, were received exclusively by the intestate; all the accounts of the Corporation and the book of minutes were kept by the intestate. The factory was in actual operation from May 1, 1813, to May 3, 1815, when it was destroyed by fire; and afterwards no glass was manufactured. It was admitted that, on Jan. 2, 1819, when there was a meeting of the Directors at his house, the intestate said to the Directors that there was a balance due to him from them. Then one or more of the Directors desired him to make out his account, and after that time the request to do it, was repeated. But the account was not made out until after the death of the intestate, owing to his habits.

Oct. 12, 1821, the general account current was rendered to the Directors. The debit side of the account contained 527 items, each of which was for cash advanced or paid out by the intestate for the purpose of keeping the factory in operation. The credit side of the account contained 787 items, each of which was for cash received by the intestate for the glass made at the factory, and for other property of the Directors, sold by the intestate. The whole amount of cash advanced and paid by the intestate for the Directors, between May 1, 1813, and the time of his death, was $107,579.74. The amount received by him during the same time, and credited to the Directors, was $100,-099.88.

The referees were unanimous in opinion that there was due to the intestate Mar. 21, 1822, for principal, the sum of $6,882.91; but they differed in their opinion on the subject of interest, the referees dissenting from the report, being of opinion that interest ought to be calculated only to Jan. 1, 1816, and the two referees making the report, being of opinion that it should be calculated to the 4th day of May Term, 1822.

635*] *The Supreme Court set aside the report, so far as it allowed interest after Jan. 2, 1819; and also on the charges for the salary of the intestate; and allowed interest on the receipts and advances of cash from the time of making or receiving it, to Jan. 2, 1819. In coming to this decision, the court have commented upon most of the English and American decisions on the subject of interest, but have conceded that no case is to be found precisely parallel with the present. The decisions of the courts of other States, are not obligatory upon the courts of this; but are entitled to great respect, as the opinions of learned men and able jurists. While the common law of England, as it existed in 1775, is adopted by the Constitution of this State and, therefore, obligatory on every court in it; this adoption, however, must be understood so far only, as the common law of England is applicable to our system. On the question of interest, it is not pretended there is any difference in principle. In point of fact, the rate of interest is two *per cent.* less there than here. If, then, the same law is to govern, and interest cannot be recovered in England at five *per cent.*, can it be recovered here at seven? That is the question.

Mr. J. Sutherland, in giving his opinion in this cause, says: "It may now be considered as settled, in England, that no interest is recoverable upon money lent, money had and received or paid, laid out and expended, without an express contract for its payment, or proof that the money has actually been used by the defendant, or of special circumstances, from which an agreement to pay interest may be inferred.

Mr. Ch. J. Savage, in giving his opinion, does not controvert this position. These are the only opinions delivered in this cause. Yet the conclusion in both is to allow interest.

Mr. J. Sutherland speaks of the present time, "now settled in England," as if it had not been long settled. How then is the fact? *Mr. Ch. J.* Savage says, that in *Calton* v. *Bragg*, 15 East, 223, Ld. Ellenborough said that Ld. Mansfield had sat in the K. B. for *upwards of 30 [*636 years, and Ld. Kenyon for more than 13 years; that he had been there above 9 years: and during all that time no case had occurred where interest had been allowed upon money lent, without an agreement for it, or for the payment of the principal, at a certain time, or under special circumstances, from which a contract might be inferred.

Here, then, is the declaration of Ld. Ellenborough, as to the uniformity of the decisions on the question of interest, in England, for more than half a century—carrying us back beyond a period of our Revolution, and the adoption of our Constitution. And when, in point of fact, he is not shown to be mistaken, how can we conclude that he is so? It is an official declaration, made in the decision of a cause, in which the length of time that the rule had been settled is assigned as a reason for not altering it. It is to be supposed that this declaration, made by the *Ld. Ch. J.* of England, in the face of that nation and of the world, is not true? And, if it is true, it appears to me there is an end to this question. For no one will pretend that we are not bound, in the decision of this cause, by that rule of law which is recognized as part of the Constitution of the State. If I am correct in this application of the Constitution and the law, though I have other reasons, it could not be necessary to state them. But as my application may be questioned, and my opinion is founded as well upon equity and justice, as upon what I conceive to be the Constitution and the law, I shall proceed to examine the law on other grounds.

It is not pretended that interest is recoverable on an unliquidated account for work and labor, or goods sold and delivered, unless the work is done, or the goods delivered, in pursuance of an agreement to pay interest.

The reason for an exception in favor of cash accounts, I have never been able to discover, or in what particular an unliquidated cash account is different from any other unliquidated account.

The liquidation of accounts, whether for labor, goods or money, is matter of fact for the consideration of a jury, without regard to the nature of the items of which the account is *composed: until the facts are ascer- [*637 tained there is no demand on which interest can be calculated.

Interest must be computed on a certain sum; and so long as the amount is uncertain, it forms no criterion for the computation of interest; consequently, interest can never form any part of an unliquidated account of any description. It is no part of the amount due, and can only be computed on the amount when ascertained.

There is nothing in money, that makes it better than labor or goods. The chief use of money is to purchase labor and goods. Money is only the means of facilitating exchange; and whenever used, the commodity purchased is paid for, and no account is necessary to be kept against the purchaser. It is only when business is done on credit, that accounts are necessary to be kept, and that necessity must be limited to the commodities purchased and sold—such as labor and goods, and can never, on principle, be extended to money. But if cash accounts are kept, and are unliquidated, they must be placed upon the same footing of other unliquidated accounts.

Whenever items for cash have appeared in unliquidated accounts for other things, the items of cash have been considered by the Supreme Court as if they were different from other items in the same account. But I know of no case where any reason is assigned for that difference. The liability of the defendant to pay interest cannot depend upon the nature of the consideration for which he is indebted, whether that consideration is for labor, goods or money; for that would be making a distinction where there is no difference. Whenever the amount due is ascertained, it must be done in the money of account of the U. S., which is dollars and cents; and whether those dollars and cents are for husks or pearls, it can make no possible difference. "Things equal to one and the same thing, must be equal to one another."

In practice, money to any very considerable amount is never lent or advanced, unless the terms upon which it is done are agreed upon between the parties. If it is agreed that interest should be paid, the rate is fixed by the stat-**638***] ute; but *not so where interest is not specified in the agreement. The statute makes void any agreement for more than seven *per cent.*, but gives effect to agreements for interest to that amount. Suppose no statute on the subject, will it be pretended that interest could be recovered? And if not, on what principle can it be done, where there is no agreement within the statute?

It is the difference between the party who has secured interest by agreement and the party who has neglected to do it, that has given rise to all the devices used to recover it. If this difference is a sufficient consideration, it would, on the same principle, and for the same reason, justify the court in altering every contract complained of by either party, as unequal or disadvantageous; and thus make the measure of justice, in every case, depend upon the whim of the court, and not upon the agreement of the parties.

But there is another view of this subject. The intestate was one of the principal stockholders, and most intimately acquainted with the business of manufacturing glass; and well knew whether it was profitable or otherwise. He had been concerned as a copartner the year preceding the commencement of his agency. With his interest, then, as a stockholder, and his experience and knowledge as an individual, he advanced and paid for the Directors between May 1, 1813, and the time of his death Aug., 1821, $107,579.74. If the intestate had not been reimbursed, during the same period, any part of that sum, or had not been reimbursed the greatest part of it, by the Directors, the inference made by the Supreme Court, that it must be intended that the intestate should make the advances on the credit of the Directors, might be correct. But when it is considered, that during the same period, the intestate received for glass made at the factory, and other property of the Directors sold by him, $100,199.88, and never informed them that there was any deficiency, or called upon the Directors for any advances, is it not a more rational inference that the *intestate [***639** looked to the proceeds of the sales of glass and other property of the stockholders, as the means of reimbursement, at least, so far as not to make calls upon the Directors for advances, until those means were exhausted?

If the Directors put into the hands of the intestate the means of creating a fund, and he looked to those means and that fund for reimbursement, and made the advances upon the credit of the fund, which he thus had the power of creating, and has never been deprived of that power, and has always had the benefit of that fund, his expectations are as fully realized, as if he had the bond of the Directors, under their corporate seal, and they had tendered to him a full and complete performance of it; for the best and most satisfactory perfomance is that which equals the expectations of the parties. "Whatever is expected by one side, and known to be so expected by the other, is to be deemed a part or condition of the contract;" and that is a principle of universal law.

The chief business of the intestate, as agent, had ceased May 3, 1815, when the factory was destroyed by fire. From the account of the intestate as exhibited after his death, the balance of principal claimed was $7,379.86. It does not appear that the intestate had even intimated that a balance was due to him, until Jan. 2, 1819; and that is the day to which the Supreme Court allow interest to be computed. But the reason for resting on that particular day does not appear. It is assumed, however, that it must be on account of the intimation of the intestate to the Directors, that a balance was due at that time. If the intestate had, at the same time, exhibited his account, and such account had not been objected against, it might have been considered as liquidated, and such liquidation might have warranted the allowance of interest after that time. But on what principle an intimation that a balance was due, followed by a request to make out the account, which was not done, should have the effect of giving interest to that time, and of preventing the accumulation of it thereafter, is inconceivable to me. And it is equally difficult for me to conceive how such intimation and request, *so long as the account [***640** was not exhibited, should have any operation or effect upon the rights of the parties.

In giving the opinion of the Supreme Court, it is said to be "stated in the case, that when the intestate was appointed agent in 1813, the stock, materials and funds of the Directors were insufficient to keep the factory in operation, and large advances were required for that purpose." It is then asked, "what, then, was the understanding of the parties as to the manner of carrying on the business? How were those advances to be made, and by whom? And on what terms? Without funds the business could not be prosecuted. Had the Directors intended to furnish the necessary funds themselves, they would have made a further call upon the stockholders. Not having done so, they must have intended that the advances should be procured in some other way; and of course, by the agent, as he was the only active person engaged in the business, and had, the preceding year, made the advances in the same business." This is assuming facts that do not appear, and then reasoning from them, as if they existed. The preceding year, the intestate, Robert Alsop, and the Directors, entered into a copartnership, under the name of John Reid & Co., for the purpose of manufacturing glass; and by the articles of copartnership, it was stipulated what each one should do; but at the end of the year, when the intestate took charge of the business as agent of the Directors, no such stipulation was entered into between the parties; and that is one point of difference between the two cases. Another is, the parties are not the same. If there is any implication of law as applicable to a tenant holding over, it can only exist as between the parties; but the application of such a rule to this case might be questioned on other grounds. The interrogations are also made upon a misapprehension of facts. It now appears that the stock, materials and funds, were insufficient to keep the factory in operation. But did it appear before the advances were made? And if so, who knew it? The intestate was the only person who had charge of the business; and, consequently, the only person to whom the fact could be known. It is true, it was his business 641*] to know it, *and his duty to communicate it. But it was not done. And that is the reason, calls were not made, and could not be made, by the Directors, upon the stockholders. On such a state of facts, how can it rationally be supposed, that the Directors expected that the intestate should make the advances, merely because the Directors did not make the calls when, without notice from the intestate, they did not, nor could they, know that any sum was required.

The sense of the parties, as indicated by their acts, evidently is, that the proceeds of the sales of glass, and other property of the Directors, should be disbursed by the intestate as their agent, if necessary, in carrying on the business and keeping the factory in operation. And if such p ce ds were not sufficient, it was expected the intestate would notify the Directors, which he did not do; but proceeded to make the advances without giving such notice—thus, not only neglecting his duty, but transcending his authority as an agent. It follows, therefore, that the intestate was the delinquent, and the court are now called upon to reward his delinquency, not merely by reimbursing the money advanced, but to do it with interest.

If the above reasoning is correct, it would go to preclude any recovery for either principal or interest. But there is no question as to the principal. If, however, it was in question, and could not be recovered, can any recovery be had for the interest? If the Directors had received any profits from the use of the money advanced by the intestate, it would be just and equitable that they should be charged with the interest to the amount of such profits; or, had the money been advanced at the request of the Directors, they would then have assumed the risk, and without regard to the profits, been justly chargeable with the interest. But when we consider the money voluntarily advanced, not on the credit of the Directors, but on the credit of the business, a business conducted solely by the intestate, why should the failure of the business give him a claim upon the Directors for interest? Had the Directors known, as the intestate must have done, that manufacturing glass was a losing business, it is not to be supposed they would have continued it. *This information they had a right to [*642 expect from the intestate, but did not receive. And is it just or reasonable that he should profit by his neglect, when that profit must be at the expense of the Directors? What have the Directors done that they should be visited with such penalties? At the commencement of the intestate's agency, the stock and materials of the Directors amounted to more than $13,000. During the continuance of that agency, that stock and those materials were swallowed up and lost. No dividends have been declared or received; and the Directors are now called upon for more than $12,000. These suggestions of hardship ought not to have any influenee in deciding upon the rights of the parties; and would not be mentioned by me, if I could perceive that the intestate had any legal or equitable claim to interest.

It is conceded by the Supreme Court, in giving their opinion, that there is no case parallel with the present. If this concession is true, it may be questionable whether it ought not to be sufficient to reverse this judgment. I have always considered justice best administered, when the court pronounced the law as it was at the time of the decision. The legitimate power of the court is limited by the law of the land; if not exercised according to that law, it is done against right and is a usurpation. New rules of property should be established from the principles deduced from analogous cases, and the fitness of things; but old rules should never be altered for such causes. The community suffer less from the number of new rules than from the alteration of old ones. The ends of justice require that the law should be certain. If the facts presented in the present case had never before existed in any other, the decision of the Supreme Court would not be complained of as erroneous. But, in practice, the same facts must have frequently occurred. The disbursements of agents, in conducting the business of their principals, of attorneys and solicitors, in the progress of their client's causes, are every day cases, that happen as often as agents are appointed and attorneys and solicitors retained. Yet no case is to be found where interest *was ever allowed for [*643 such disbursements, until after the liquidation of the account. This is the simple case of an agent, possessing unlimited power over a particular business of his principals, voluntarily making advances in a losing business, known only to himself, and charging interest on such advances; yet omitting, for more than six years after the chief business of his agency had terminated, to furnish his account, and then claiming interest from the time the advances were made.

The security for capital, that is given by the government and laws of any country, is the strongest inducement to the accumulation of it. And in a nation like this, where so much capital is employed in the hands of agents, I should shudder at a decision giving to the agent the right of swallowing up that capital, by interest on advances of his own, voluntarily made, in a losing business, known only to himself, and not disclosed to his employers. The force of principle might compel me to yield to such a rule, if settled as the law of the land; but I cannot do it on the score of comity. And I must say, I should mourn over that land, were I an inhabitant of it, where such a rule prevailed.

If this had been an ordinary case, I should have contented myself with giving my opinion without my reasons. But viewing the decision of the Supreme Court as I do, not only erroneous in principle, but fraught with incalculable mischief to the community, I have taken the liberty of troubling the court with these reasons; and such is my apology, if any is necessary, for doing it.

Burt, Clark, Dudley, Gardiner, Lynde, Wilkeson, Wooster and *Wright, Senators*, concurred in the result of these opinions.

But a majority of *The Court* concurring in the result of the opinions delivered by Sanford, *Chancellor*, and Colden, *Senator*,

It was thereupon ordered, adjudged and decreed that the judgment of the Supreme Court be, in all things, affirmed, &c., and that the record and proceedings be remitted, &c.

Affirming—3 Cow., 393.
Criticised—11 N. Y., 407.
Cited in—11 Wend., 481; 16 Wend., 27; 18 Wend., 575; 5 Denio, 57, 137; 2 Sand. Ch., 127, 277; 3 N. Y., 504; 8 N. Y., 157; 15 N. Y., 399; 39 N. Y., 504; 19 Hun, 598; 2 Barb., 666; 17 Barb., 456; 23 Barb., 604; 41 Barb., 22; 42 Barb., 57; 26 How. Pr., 237; 37 How. Pr., 359; 58 How. Pr., 324; 19 Abb. Pr., 409; 6 Abb. N. S., 381; 12 Abb. N. S., 242; 1 Rob., 657; 4 Rob., 361; 1 Sweeny, 202; 1 Bradf., 234; 1 Daly, 157.

644*] *THOMAS GOURLEY AND ABEL WOOD, *Plaintiffs in Error*,

v.

ABRAHAM ALLEN AND ARCHIBALD M'ALLISTER, *Defendants in Error*.

Overseers of Poor not Liable for Medical Services to Pauper, in Absence of Express Promise to Pay—Powers of Overseers—Statutes.

No action lies by a physician or surgeon, against Overseers of the Poor, for services in attending upon a pauper, though upon the most pressing necessity; these services not being done at the request of the Overseers, and they not having promised to pay.

Overseers have no right to appropriate the public moneys, &c., for the support of the poor in any case without a previous order of a justice or justices of the peace.

The English and N.Y. Statutes and decisions touching the relief of casual poor, considered. Per Colden, *Senator*.

The N. Y. Statute and decisions on the same subject commented upon. Per Spencer, *Senator*.

Citations—3 Bos. & P., 247, 250, 253; Poth. on Ob., pt. 4, ch. 1, sec. 2; 3 Esp., 91; Bull. *N. P.*, 147; Stat., 4 Eliz. Ch., 2; Ld. Raym., 1013; 2 Salk., 531; 1 R. L., 287, sec. 23, and 287, 288, sec. 25, and 289, sec. 28, and 284, 285, 286, secs. 16, 25; 3 W. & M., ch. 11, sec. 11, and 9 Geo. I., ch. 7, secs. 1, 2; 8 Johns., 323, 326; 12 Johns., 352; 19 Johns., 256, 260; 1 Cow., 260; 7 Johns., 89; 4 Cow., 139.

ON ERROR from the Supreme Court. The cause was originally commenced Nov. 18, 1818, before a justice of the Peace of Washington Co. In that court, Allen & M'Allister, plaintiffs, sued Gourley & Wood, defendants, who were both served with a summons, returnable the 20th (then) inst. The plaintiffs in that court then declared against the defendants, as Overseers of the Poor of the Town of Hebron, for $50 or under, for work and labor, as surgeons and physicians, for a pauper, chargeable to the Town of Hebron, which the defendants had promised to pay. Plea, the general issue.

The cause was tried Nov. 27, 1818.

Samuel Livingston, a witness for the plaintiffs, testified that in 1817 he was one of the Overseers of the Poor of the Town of Hebron and understood from David Wheeler, the other Overseer for that year, that there was a child at the widow Roache's, chargeable to that town; but the witness did not see the child. That in the spring of 1816 or 1817, the town agreed to vendue the poor; and the child was put up and bid off by one Russell Rotch, at $59.75; and Rotch was to indemnify the town against the maintenance of the *child; [***645** that soon after, Rotch brought to the witness a note for $59.75, signed by David Wheeler, which the witness also signed; that, at the same time Rotch brought indentures to the witness, binding the child to Rotch. The witness signed the indentures; they were approved by two justices, but never executed by Wheeler. That, in the latter part of 1817, or the beginning of the spring of 1818, there was a child left at the house of the witness, in Hebron, he still being one of the Overseers of the Poor of that town, which he supposed to be the child that Rotch had bid off. The child was called Major Dutcher. That the witness paid the note, before given, as Overseer.

Peter Dutcher, a witness for the plaintiffs, testified that he knew the child. That he was hurt in the street, by a wagon running over his foot, near the plaintiff's shop, in Sept., 1817. He saw the child in the plaintiff's shop soon after it was hurt; and they were then dressing the child's foot which was mashed by the wagon. That the plaintiffs continued to attend the child till in the winter following. That the injury took place in the Village of Salem, where Rotch then lived. That Rotch had then become poor and been on the jail limits; and he, his family and the child, suffered for want of the necessaries of life. That the child needed the assistance bestowed by the plaintiffs.

NOTE.—*Paupers—Liability of overseers, for supplies furnished to the poor.*

Overseers are not liable for supplies furnished to the poor, without their request or subsequent promise to pay. There is no implied promise however necessary the supplies furnished or services rendered.. Flower v. Allen, *post*, p. 654; Everts v. Adams, 12 Johns., 352. See statutes in the various states. See, also, Calkins v. Joslin, 8 Weekly Dig., 375.

It further appeared in evidence, that soon after the child was hurt, the plaintiffs sent verbal notice of the fact to one of the Overseers of Hebron.

The plaintiffs' account was $17.18. The defendants admitted that services to that amount had been performed as charged, but denied their liability to pay all or any part.

Dec. 1, 1818, judgment for the plaintiffs for $17.18 damages, and $1.17 costs — $18.35.

The defendants removed the cause by *certiorari* to the Supreme Court, which, in October Term, 1821, affirmed the judgment of the justice, upon a return of the above facts; and the defendants brought error to this court.

Mr. J. Crary, for the plaintiffs in error. The action was *assumpsit* against the plaintiffs in **646***] error, as Overseers *of the Poor. To sustain this action against Overseers of the Poor, a request, or an express promise on their part, must be shown in evidence. *Everts* v. *Adams*, 12 Johns., 352. The law imposes no obligation upon them, to relieve either a resident, or casual pauper, without the order of a justice, in the first case (*Ib.*); or the previous adjudication of two justices in the last. *Voorhis* v. *Whipple*, 7 Johns., 89; *Hull* v. *Supervisors*, 19 *Id.* 259. The office of Overseer is created, and its duties prescribed, by statute. The plaintiffs in error have neither done nor omitted anything prescribed by the Act.

Again; they were not Overseers when the cause of action accrued; and according to the established rule of law, are not liable for any neglect of their predecessors.

Mr. S. Stevens, contra. Although the office of Overseer of the Poor is created by the statute, it is far from prescribing their whole duty. This is general — to provide for and render every necessary relief to paupers. In many cases should the Overseers wait for an order of a justice, or an adjudication of justices, the death of the pauper would be the consequence. They must, then, render assistance without an order, and the town is bound to reimburse them. And if a third person relieve, on their default, he may sue them, and recover a just compensation.

The action properly lies against their successors in office. *Todd* v. *Birdsall*, 1 Cow., 260.

COLDEN, *Senator*, after stating the facts. When this case was opened at our bar, few of us, I believe, considered it of any very great importance. Nor is it so, as to the amount which was originally in question. But it is a case which concerns the poor. It is, therefore, of great interest. It also regards the liability of public officers, who take upon themselves, almost gratuitously, very benevolent and onerous duties. On these accounts, it is no less de- **647***] serving careful *examination, and attentive consideration, than any other case.

As the defendants in error were not employed by the plaintiffs, and as they made no express promise to pay for the services which were rendered to the pauper, if they are liable, it must be in virtue of an implied promise.

The only foundation on which an implied promise can be raised, is a legal obligation to perform that which is presumed to have been promised. (3 Bos. & P., 250, *note a.*) An implied promise is the *quasi contractus* of the civil law, which allowed it to be presumed that a party had contracted to perform that which the law exacted of him. (Poth. Ob., pt. 1, ch. 1, sec. 2.) If the Overseers were, by law, bound to pay for the services which were rendered to the pauper, then the judgment in favor of the defendants in error ought to be maintained.

Were the Overseers of the Poor, with us, precisely in the place of parish officers in England, we should have no difficulty in deciding this case, if we chose to abide by English authority.

The cases of *Simmons* v. *Wilmot, etc.*, 3 Esp., 91, of *Watson* v. *Turner*, Bull, *N. P.*, 147, and of *Wennall* v. *Adney*, 3 Bos. & P., 247, 253, very conclusively establish, that the church-wardens and Overseers of the Poor would, in England, be liable in a case like that we are now considering. In the last case, Ld. Alvanley, *Ch. J.*, says: "I have no doubt, whatever, that parish officers are bound to assist where such accidents as these take place; and that the law will so far raise an implied contract against them, as to enable any person, who affords that immediate assistance which the necessity of the case usually requires, to recover against them."

But we cannot take English authorities for our guide in this case; because the office and duties of our Overseers of the Poor are very different from the office and duties of the parish officers of England.

The former, as well as the latter, are created by and derive all their powers and authority from statute. It is only *to compare [***648** our own law with the Act of Parliament, to see that the powers and obligations of the English parish officers and our Overseers of the Poor are not alike.

The English parish officers are appointed pursuant to the Statute of the 43 Eliz., ch. 2, and their powers and duties are prescribed by the same statute. They are, from time to time, to raise, weekly or otherwise, in their respective parishes, competent sums to relieve the old, blind, lame and indigent; and they, independently of any other authority, may apply, according to their own discretion, the relief which may appear to them to be requisite; so that whatever sums they may rightfully pay or expend, they can always, as is said in *Tawney* v. *Case*, Ld. Raym., 1013; 2 Salk., 531, reimburse themselves by "making a rate" on the parishioners. They can never, therefore, allege a want of power or means to afford the required relief. The law may, consequently, well raise an implied promise against them, in favor of one who shall have supplied the relief a pauper required and which the church-wardens and Overseers neglected or refused to afford.

But our Overseers are in a very different situation. Our statute has not authorized them to levy money, nor trusted to their discretion to apply any part of that which is raised in the respective towns.

By our Act, 1 R. L., 287, sec. 23, the sum requisite for maintaining the poor, is to be determined by the inhabitants in town meeting, and is to be raised in each town by the authority of the supervisors of the county.

The Overseers can make no appropriation for the relief of a pauper, without an order of a justice of the peace, made in writing; and "the Overseer is to make no other, or further allowance than what by the order shall be directed." (*Id.*, 287, 288, sec. 25.)

So cautious has our Legislature been, to prevent Overseers from exercising a discretion in relieving paupers, that our Act (*Id.*, 289, sec. 28,) provides, "that if any Overseer shall relieve any poor person without such order, he shall forfeit and lose all such money and goods **649***] paid and distributed to *such poor person; nor shall any allowance be made to him for the same, in passing his accounts."

There is a provision in the English law, frequently referred to in the reports (3 W. & M., ch. 11, sec. 11, and 9 Geo. I., ch. 7, secs. 1, 2), for what are commonly called casual poor; that is, paupers who are taken sick, or meet with an accident, and are not on the collection books of the Overseers. These a justice may make an order to relieve, where the Overseers refuse or neglect to do it.

Our Statute, 1 R. L., 284-286, secs. 16, 25, makes provision for the same objects; but however urgent a case may be, the Overseers can afford no relief from the public purse, without an order from a justice of the peace.

In all the cases which have heretofore been decided by the Supreme Court on this subject, these limitations of the powers of Overseers of the Poor have been recognized.

In the case of *Adams* v. *Supervisors*, 8 Johns., 323, 326, the court decided that, after justices had made an order for the relief of a casual pauper, the Overseers were liable to the physician who had attended him, for the sum which the order directed to be paid.

In *Everts* v. *Adams*, 12 Johns., 352, two justices made an order that a pauper should be furnished with medical aid, to be administered by Dr. Malcom. The defendant in error, Adams, attended, but it was not proved that he did so at the request of the Overseers of the Poor. The court say, that if the Overseers had paid Adams, it would have been directly in face of the order, which was, that Malcom should be employed; and they question whether the Overseers would have been allowed a payment to Adams, in passing their account. And the court decided expressly that the Overseers were not liable; because they had, in no way, sanctioned Adams' demand, or engaged to pay it; and had not in any manner employed him to perform the service. "There is no obligation," says the court, "to pay, unless it be implied by law; and the law will create no such liability; especially as it would be directly in face of the order." *A fortiori*, there can be no liability where there is no order.

650*] *In the case of *Hull* v. *Supervisors*, 19 Johns., 259, Platt, *J.*, in delivering the opinion of the court, says: "The extraordinary expenses of a surgical operation cannot be legally imposed on the public (although proper and necessary), without an express previous order of the justice, on the application of the Overseers; or, at least, a subsequent ratification and sanction by the justices and Overseers." And he says (as must be said in the case we are now deciding): "Here was no such previous order, nor any subsequent adoption of the claim. We are, therefore, constrained to say, that, in rendering the service, the relator" (*i. e.*, the physician) "must be deemed to have acted gratuitously; or to have relied upon individual responsibility for his reward."

Now if the Overseers had not funds at their disposal for the relief of the pauper; if they could give him no relief without an order of a justice; how can we say that they were under a legal obligation to pay the defendants in error?

Possibly no justice in the county would give the order required by law, under a belief that the child, after he had been illegally and barbarously vendued, as it is called, and after Rotch had been paid for maintaining him, was not entitled to relief.

If the plaintiffs in error had paid the doctors, they must have done it out of their own pockets. This, I am persuaded, they were under no legal obligation to do; and, therefore, the law raises no implied promise against them.

If the question were, what the law ought to be, humanity would seem to plead powerfully in favor of a provision for immediate relief in a case like that which we are now considering. The question, however, is not, what the law ought to be, but what it is. The Legislature may have thought that doctors had as much benevolence as the rest of their species; and that no human being would stop to inquire how he was to be paid before he rendered the first assistance which such a casualty might require. It might have been considered that the sympathies of our nature would afford all the succor that could be necessary, in a case of emergency, till more permanent relief might be obtained, with the precautions which the law has thought proper to prescribe. *But [***651** whatever may have been the motives of the Legislature, it appears to me that it has not intrusted to Overseers of the Poor power to dispose of the public funds for the relief of paupers in any case; and I do not think they can be made to give such relief at their own expense; which would be the effect of suffering the defendants in error to retain the judgment which had been rendered in their favor in the court below. For it is to be recollected, that if that judgment is maintained, an execution may be issued for the sum recovered, and the costs against the defendants below. And when the amount has been levied by a sale of their property, how are they to be repaid? The law has made no provision by which they can compel a reimbursement. It is not with them as it is with the parish officers in England. They, under such circumstances, would indemnify themselves by a competent rate on the parishioners. (*Tawney's* case, 2 Salk., 531.)

We are unfortunate in not having the reasons which the Supreme Court assigned, upon giving their judgment in favor of the defendants in error. For want of these, I have referred to their decisions in former cases, and I acknowledge that I find myself incapable of reconciling them with that now before us, which I think ought to be reversed.

I have considered this case, as if the defendants below had been the Overseers of the Poor at the time the services were rendered. They were not so. Therefore, though the former Overseers were liable, another question would be, whether that liability was transferred to the plaintiffs in error, who were not in office till at a subsequent period. But if the original Overseers were not responsible, certainly their successors could not be. In my view of the case, therefore, it is unnecessary to give any opinion on this last point.

I am in favor of reversing the opinion of the Supreme Court.

SANFORD *Chancellor*, concurred. He said he had not written an opinion in the cause, and should not go over the ground examined by *Mr. Colden;* but would notice one point 652*] *which *Mr. C.* had deemed it unnecessary to discuss. As had been observed by *Mr. C.*, the action was brought in the court below, not against those gentlemen who were Overseers of Hebron, when the services in question were performed, but their successors in office. In view to this point, the court were referred, on the argument, to *Todd* v. *Birdsall*, 1 Cow., 260; and he admitted, with the case cited, that for a clear debt, the successors would be liable. The claim in that case was confessedly upon a promise legally binding on the predecessor. That is denied in the present case; and he thought correctly, for the reasons assigned in the opinion of *Mr. Colden. Todd* v. *Birdsall* does not profess to determine what shall constitute the debt, for which the successor is liable; and has, therefore, no application, beyond the question of parties.

SPENCER, *Senator*. The first question presented is, whether the Overseers of the Poor of a town are liable to be prosecuted for medical services rendered to a pauper, without a previous order of a justice, directing disbursements for such a purpose. It appears that, in the year 1817, when the services were rendered, the pauper was admitted to belong to the Town Hebron, and provision was made by that town for his sustenance. The present seems, then, to present the same case, precisely, as that of *Hull* v. *Supervisors*, 19 Johns., 260, in which it was decided that an order for the sustenance of a pauper, was not sufficient authority to justify the extraordinary charges for amputating a leg, and other surgical attendance; and that an order for that express purpose was necessary. In that case, as in this, the services were rendered on the emergency, without any application by the Overseers, and without any order of a justice; and the Supreme Court refused a *mandamus* to compel the supervisors to allow the account. Unless the reasons for the determination in that case are unsound, it is decisive of the present: for if a county or town is not liable without such order, the officers of the town cannot be made responsible.

For myself, I consider that decision in perfect accordance with the policy of the statute 653*] which requires that, before *towns shall be charged with any expenses, they shall be authorized by a justice of the peace. Such are the positive provisions of the 28th section of the Act for the Relief and Settlement of the Poor; and such have been the uniform and invariable decisions of the Supreme Court. The cases of *Voorhis* v. *Whipple*, 7 Johns., 89; *Everts* v. *Adams*, 12 Johns., 352; *Ex parte Dow*, 1 Cow., 205, and *Ex parte Overseers of Gates*, 4 Cow., 139, all expressly decide, or recognize the principle, that a previous order is indispensable. I see no reason for overturning them, nor any authority for repealing the statute.

The case of *Todd* v. *Birdsall*, 1 Cow., 260, was cited by the counsel for the defendants in error, to show that the defendants, as successors in the office of Overseers of the Poor, might be prosecuted for a debt contracted by their predecessors. Without assenting to the principle of that decision, which considers those officers a corporation, or *quasi* a corporation, it is sufficient to observe, that it is not applicable here, as the predecessors of these defendants never did contract this debt; and they were never legally liable to pay it, if the previous order of a justice was necessary.

I confess my surprise, that the decision of the justice was affirmed by the Supreme Court; and as we have not been furnished with the reasons of that judgment, I have been at a loss to discover them.

In my opinion, the judgment of the Supreme court should be wholly reversed, for the reasons given by Colden, *Senator*, Sanford *Chancellor*, and Spencer, *Senator*.

Per totam Curiam.

Judgment reversed.

Cited in—3 Wend., 198; 9 Barb., 264; 66 Barb., 71; 84 Ill., 307; 58 How Pr., 324; 25 Am. Rep., 465 (84 Ill., 303).

---

*ROSWELL FLOWER, LEVI [*654 JOHNSON, GROVE MOORE, THOMAS SHELDEN AND SILAS HARWOOD, *Plaintiffs in Error*,

v.

ABRAHAM ALLEN AND ARCHIBALD M'ALLISTER, *Defendants in Error.*

Personal and Corporate Liability of Overseers of Poor—Not Liable for Medical Services to Pauper, in Absence of Express Promise—Parties Plaintiff in Actions against Court of Errors—Powers of, over Judgments of Supreme Court—Not Error, Under Statute, for C. P. to try the Cause without a Jury, a Jury Trial not having been Demanded.

On appeal under the late Act, sess. 41, ch. 94, it was not error for the C. P. to try without a jury, when none was demanded by either party.

Overseers of the Poor are not liable for medical or other services rendered to a pauper, without their request, or express promise to pay.

These officers have no right to appropriate the moneys of their town, in any case, without the previous order of a justice of the peace.

Upon error brought, and the judgment of the court below being reversed, for a defect of form, as the want of a *venire*, the merits being with the defendant in error, the proper course is to award a *venire* to the court below, that the cause may be tried in due form, and a verdict and judgment rendered accordingly.

Whether Overseers of the Poor are ever liable in their corporate capacity, *quære*. Per Spencer, *Senator*.

And, per Tallmadge, *President*, they are.

Whether the select men of another State are liable to an action here for neglect of official duty, *quære*. Per Spencer, *Senator*.

And, per Tallmadge, *President*, they are not.

A pauper may, under certain circumstances, sue the Overseers of the Poor, for a total neglect of duty; but third persons, not interested, cannot do this. Per Spencer, *Senator*.

The Court of Errors may reverse a judgment of the Supreme Court in part, and affirm it in part.

Overseers of the Poor are liable, sometimes in their corporate, and sometimes in a personal capacity. In the former case, their persons or property are not affected by the judgment; but only the cor-

---

NOTE.—*Paupers—Liability of overseers, for supplies furnished to the poor.* See Gourley v. Allen, *ante*, p. 644, *note*.

porate property. Otherwise, where they are liable personally. Per Tallmadge, *President.*

Citations—Act, sess. 41, ch. 94; sess. 36, ch. 53, sec. 17; 20 Johns., 280; sess. 47, ch. 238, sec. 38; 3 Esp., 91; 3 Bos. & P., 253; 4 M. & S., 275; Bull. *N. P.*, 147; 2 East, 505; 12 Johns., 352; 15 Johns., 281; 1 Cow., 260; Doug., 722; Cowp., 89; 2 T. R., 125; 1 Cai., 587; 3 Johns., 443; 8 Johns., 79, 82, 116.

ON ERROR to the Supreme Court. This cause began in a justice's court, of Washington Co., in which the defendants in error sued the plaintiffs in error, for care, medicine, attendance, services rendered, &c., as surgeons and physicians, done and performed for one Wilkins, a pauper, in 1817, in the town of Rupert, in the State of Vt., the plaintiffs in error then being selectmen of that town, and by virtue of that office, Overseers of the Poor; which services, &c., as the plaintiffs before the justice **655***] alleged, were *done at the request of the defendants, and for which they promised payment, &c., to the damage of the plaintiffs of $50, &c. Plea the general issue. The cause was tried before the justice, without a jury, May 22, 1820; and a judgment rendered for the plaintiffs below for $52.98, damages and costs. From this judgment, the present plaintiffs in error appealed to the Court of C. P. of the County of Washington; where the cause was tried at December Term, 1820; and that court reversed the judgment of the justice. From this reversal, the present defendants in error brought error to the Supreme Court. With this writ, the C. P. returned a record, with a *placita*, in May Term, of the C. P., 1820, &c., and after setting forth the return of the justice, it then stated an issue in the usual form of an assignment of errors, by the present plaintiffs in error and a joinder in error by the other side; continuances by *curia advisare vult.* And at December Term, 1820, a judgment of reversal by the C. P., in the usual style of a court of error; which was stated to be upon the examination, by the court, of the witnesses named in the justice's return, &c., mature deliberation, &c., omitting all mention of any jury; and without any continuance by *vicecomes non misit breve.*

They also returned a bill of exceptions taken before them, on the hearing of the cause, by the present defendants in error.

By this, it appeared that on the hearing, evidence was given that in 1817 the plaintiffs in error, being selectmen and Overseers of the Poor of the Town of Rupert, as stated in the declaration, the defendants in error, in the same year, being surgeons and physicians in the Town of Salem, Washington Co., performed the services, compensation for which was claimed. That these services were the amputation of Wilkins' leg, who was a pauper, in Rupert; and the operation was necessary to save his life. It did not appear that Wilkins had any settlement in Rupert; but a justice of the peace had, previous to the amputation, by order, made an appropriation of $20, which had been applied in procuring medical care of the pauper, who resided in Rupert—$12, part **656***] *of it, being paid to the defendants in error, towards their services, and receipted by them in part payment. That they refused to receipt their demand in full; and this was all the plaintiffs in error were authorized by the town to pay them. That eight or ten days before the amputation, a complaint in writing was made to one of the plaintiffs in error, stating Wilkins' situation, &c., upon which the order for relief was made. But the defendants in error were called to Wilkins by his father; and there was no evidence that the plaintiffs in error had requested the services of the defendants in error, or ever expressly promised to pay for them.

At August Term, 1824, the Supreme Court reversed the judgment of the C. P., generally, with costs; and did not direct a *venire de novo* to issue.

Mr. J. Crary, for the plaintiffs in error:

1. The judgment of the C. P. should not have been reversed by the Supreme Court for error in the record. The Statute, sess. 41, ch. 94, gave the C. P. jurisdiction of the cause. This includes the power of deciding it. The manner is merely incidental. Judgment may be given on demurrer, by default, on confession, or the cause may be decided by the court on the facts, with the consent of the parties, and without a jury.

2. There is nothing in the nature and duty of the office of Overseers of the Poor which renders them liable to an action for services rendered to paupers, without their request or express promise; and neither of these were proved in the court below. At common law, the poor depended for support upon the charity of private individuals. (1 Bl. Com., 359.) But if the defendants in error are allowed a resort to the Statutes of Vt., these will not aid them. As to the support of the poor, they will be found the same as our own; according to which the Overseers of the Poor have not in themselves the power to appropriate the public moneys to the support of paupers. In the present case, there is proof that they had exhausted the means conferred on them by the town. The $12 was all they could control. This has been paid to the defendants in error. The law will not imply a promise from the facts in this case. The office of Overseer *is created, and [***657** the duties prescribed, by statute, and the plaintiffs in error have not been proved liable within its provisions.

Mr. S. Stevens, for the defendants in error:

1. The Supreme Court were right in reversing the proceedings of the C. P. for error in their proceedings. They should have tried the cause by a jury, upon a proper issue of fact. The cause should have been continued by *vicecomes non misit breve* (1 Dunl. Pr., 594; Gilb. C. P., 79, 83); not, as here, by *curia advisare vult.* The C. P. erected themselves into a court of error; and proceeded upon an assignment of errors and joinder to a judgment of reversal; whereas, they should have tried the cause *de novo*, upon the issue joined before the justice. *Cowen* v. *Bush*, 3 Cow., 343; *Breese* v. *Thompson*, 20 Johns., 280. If this court sustain such a judgment as that of the C. P., there is an end of all form. A party may make up anything and call it a record.

2. The plaintiffs in error, as Overseers of Rupert, being bound to provide for Wilkins, the pauper; and the services of the defendants in error being rendered in a case of urgent necessity, with the knowledge of the plaintiffs in error, they are liable without any express promise. The law raises a promise. *Simmons* v. *Wilmot*, 3 Esp., 91; *Wennall* v. *Adney*, 3 Bos. &

P., 247, 253; *Lamb* v. *Bunce*, 4 Maule & S., 275. The plaintiffs in error were liable personally for a neglect of their duty as Overseers.

Mr. Crary, in reply. As to the formal objection, it was held by the late Supreme Court that the issue in the C. P. must, under the Act in question, have been the same as before the justice. *Rawson* v. *Adams*, 17 Johns., 132. The C. P. were to proceed as the very right of the case should appear, upon the same issue and the same witnesses with those before the justice. *Id.*, *M'Chesney* v. *Lansing*, 18 Johns., 388. Now, it is optional with a party, whether his cause shall be tried by a justice or by a jury. Neither party demanded a jury before **658***] the justice. The C. *P. come in the place of the justice; and no *venire* is demanded there.

Whose business was it to issue the *venire?* Not ours, but the appellees', the plaintiffs in the C. P. Then it does not lie with them to come and object to this irregularity of their own. They went on and took a bill of exceptions. This step was a waiver of the irregularity. (Johns. Dig., Practice, XXXVIII., and the cases there cited.) Nor was it competent for the party to object in the Supreme Court for the first time. He should have done so in the C. P.; where the difficulty might have been obviated, in the first instance, or a *venire de novo* have been issued. *Beeckman* v. *Frost*, 18 Johns., 544, 558.

There was no need of any issue in the Court of C. P. The cause stood ready for trial upon the issue returned by the justice; and the new one of *in nullo est erratum*, may be rejected as surplusage.

As to the merits, the English cases do not apply to this State or Vt. The English Statutes, concerning casual poor, are different both from ours and those of Vt. That these Overseers would not be liable, upon the case made out, in this State is well settled. *Everts* v. *Adams*, 12 Johns., 352; *Hull* v. *Supervisors*, 19 Johns., 259, 260. They cannot be compelled to pay beyond the funds provided by law. *Bartlet* v. *Crozier*, 17 Johns., 439.

Nor has the rule contended for upon the other side passed without question, even in England. *Atkins* v. *Barnwell*, 2 East, 505, 506. *Everts* v. *Adams*, adopts the principle of this case; and *Olney* v. *Wickes*, 18 Johns., 122, goes further. It holds that an Overseer is not liable even on an express request. *O. of Pittstown* v. *O. of Plattsburgh*, 18 Johns., 407, 418, held that Overseers might be sued as a corporation; but that was upon a point of nonfeasance.

SANFORD, *Chancellor*, in delivering his opinion, after stating the case, spoke nearly as follows:

1. Were the Court of C. P. right in proceeding to try the cause without a jury?

659*] *It will be recollected that this appeal was made under the Act of 1818, sess. 41, ch. 94. A trial by jury was not demanded, either before the justice, or the Court of C. P.; and the statute in question did not, in terms, require the court to proceed by jury. Before the justice no jury was necessary, without a demand of one; and if the Court of C. P. are to be considered as taking the place of the justice, in this respect (and I should say the good sense of the statute would not require more of them), the party cannot complain that the cause proceeded without a jury, till he shows us that he required one.

But there is another answer to the question. By the 19th section, when the Court of C. P. became possessed of the cause, they were required to proceed and give judgment, according as the very right of the case should appear, without regard to the previous trial. I cannot but think that the object of this provision was, to put the Court of C. P. as near as might be, in the place where the Supreme Court formerly stood, under the old system of proceeding by *certiorari;* in relation to a decision upon which, it is remarkable that the same words were used by the Statute. (Sess. 36, ch. 53, sec. 17; 1 R. L., 397.) At any rate, I do not believe the Legislature ever intended that the party should have an absolute right to a trial by jury, without demand. It is highly probable that the Supreme Court reversed the judgment of the Court of C. P., upon the ground that there was no jury; for I perceive that, in a previous case, *Breese* v. *Thompson*, 20 Johns., 280, they asserted that all issues of fact should be tried, on appeal, by a jury. To this doctrine I cannot assent. There is nothing to warrant it in the words of the Statute under which the Court of C. P. acted; and if there be such a doctrine, it must arise from inference. I cannot but think that the omission to require a jury expressly was intentional; and this is rendered the more probable, from the circumstance that the Act of 1824, now in force, upon the same subject (sess. 47, ch. 238, sec. 38), does, in its terms, require a jury. If, therefore, the Supreme Court reversed the judgment of the Court of C. P. on the ground *of a formal defect in their pro- [***660** ceedings, my opinion is that they erred.

2. As to the merits. The declaration avers a promise to pay; but the evidence, as detailed in the bill of exceptions, is far from making it out. It does not appear that the plaintiffs in error ever retained the defendants in error to do the services which were the subject of the suit. If there be any promise in the case, it must have been implied by law. If we are permitted to look into the printed Statutes of Vt. (which, by the by, were not in evidence), it will be perceived that they do not vary materially from our own; according to which, the Overseer of the Poor is controlled in every appropriation of the public money by the order of a justice. In the case before us, an inquiry took place; provision was made for raising $20 which had been appropriated before the suit was brought. Here was a compliance with all that the law required of the plaintiffs in error. This was not enough, it seems, to pay off the physicians; but I can see no legal obligation on the Overseers of the Poor to pay any more. That a sufficiency was not provided, was not their fault. They were bound to lay open the circumstances to the magistrate, and abide his decision upon the case.

It follows that the judgment should be reversed.

3. Suppose the Supreme Court were right in reversing upon the objection of form, it did not follow that a general judgment of reversal should be given; and that this should end the matter. By reversing the judgment of the Court of C. P., generally, they restored that of the

justice, which went to charge the plaintiffs in error personally. This consequence would not legally follow the error of the C. P. in mere matter of form. The proper course in such cases is, to follow up the reversal with the award of a *venire*—that all may be set right by a new trial in proper form.

My opinion is, that the judgment of the Supreme Court should be wholly reversed, on the ground that the judgment of the Court of C. P. was right both in form and substance; but should this court hold the latter only, then I **661***] *am for awarding a *venire* to the Court of C. P., to the end that the plaintiffs in error may protect themselves by a valid trial, verdict and judgment in their favor.

COLDEN, *Senator*. The liability of the plaintiffs in error must be determined by ascertaining what are the duties of the selectmen of the towns in Vt., under the laws of that State, to which I have not had access.

I shall take for granted that they are, as has been stated by counsel on the argument, and now by His Honor, the *Chancellor*, the same as are prescribed for Overseers, by our Statute for the Relief and Settlement of the Poor. If they be so, I am of opinion that the plaintiffs in the justices' court had no right to recover against the defendants. My reasons, in support of this opinion, I have already assigned in the case of *Gourley* v. *Wood* against the same defendants in error.

But, in this case, there are circumstances which render it, in my opinion, stronger against the defendants in error than that case. Here was no sudden emergency; the pauper had no settlement in Rupert; $20 were actually raised and appropriated by legal authority to the payment of physician's bills, and a portion of that sum was paid to the defendants in error, &c.

The plaintiffs in error having faithfully applied all the money that was allowed by the town to the relief of the pauper, I think they very properly insisted that they were not liable any further. It would, in my opinion, be the height of injustice to oblige them to pay anything beyond what they were by law allowed to expend. Whatever should be levied against them, upon an execution in this suit, must be paid out of their private property, without its being in their power to compel either the town or any person to reimburse them.

Were we to permit recoveries under such circumstances, all the precautions of the law to prevent unauthorized expenditures for the relief of the poor would be frustrated. Every person might relieve a pauper, when he pleased, and as he pleased; and make the Overseers of **662***] the town, *where the pauper happened to be found, without any regard to his place of settlement, liable for services, or for what articles might be furnished. It would be better to repeal our existing law at once, and to declare that any doctor who got a pauper into his hands should, as to that pauper, be justice of the peace and Overseer of the Poor, and should have a right to levy his bill on the inhabitants of the town.

I am persuaded that the defendants in error ought not to have prevailed in the suit before the justice; and I am, therefore, of opinion that the judgment of the Supreme Court should be reversed.

I have not examined the question raised upon the form of proceeding in the Court of C. P.; but am convinced, from the reasoning of His Honor, the *Chancellor*, that, at least, the defendants in error could not object to this, in the Supreme Court, after having stood by and silently acquiesced in the C. P.

Burt, Clark, Dudley, Ellsworth, Gardiner, Haight, Lake, Lefferts, Lynde, M'Intyre, M'Michael and *Wooster, Senators*, also concurred with the *Chancellor*.

SPENCER, *Senator*. Upon the merits of this case, there can be little difficulty. The plaintiffs in error, defendants below, as Overseers of the Poor of the Town of Rupert, in Vt., were prosecuted for the amount of a bill for medical services, rendered in that State, to a pauper who was not settled in that town, without any request by the defendants below, and who never made any promise to pay.

It is contended that the defendants below were liable at common law, as public officers, to provide for casual poor; and the service having been rendered, they ought to remunerate the plaintiffs below for it, and some cases have been cited, to show that such is the common law. The case of *Simmons* v. *Wilmot*, 3 Esp., 91, was an action against church-wardens and Overseers of the Poor for medicine and attendance, &c., furnished a pauper upon an emergency occasioned by a sudden accident. Ld. Eldon, before whom the cause was tried, observed that the case was new to him; but held that parish officers were bound to take care of casual *poor; and if a common [***663** person took care of the pauper, on the liability of the parish officers, that he had a right to recover. What became of the cause, does not appear. Much weight certainly ought not to be given to a *Nisi Prius* opinion, expressed as this was, with hesitation, upon a question which must be of every day's occurrence in England; and which was unsupported by any adjudged case upon the point.

In *Wennall* v. *Adney*, 3 Bos. & P., 253, referred to by counsel, the action was against the master for medical services rendered to his servant, also upon an emergency occasioned by an accident. The court held the action would not lie; and Ld. Alvanley, *Ch. J.*, says: "I have no doubt, whatever, that parish officers are bound to assist when such accidents as these take place, and that the law will so far raise an implied contract against them, as to enable any person who affords that immediate assistance which the necessity of the case usually requires, to recover against them the amount of money expended." There, the rule is confined to cases of necessity.

In the case of *Lamb* v. *Bunce*, 4 Maule & S., 275, also referred to by counsel, an action was brought for a surgeon's bill against the Overseer of a parish, and Ld. Ellenborough, *Ch. J.*, held that, where "there is not time for procuring an order of justices, the law raises an obligation against the parish where the pauper lies sick as casual poor, to look to the supply of his necessities; and if a parish officer stands by and sees that obligation performed, by those who are fit and competent to perform it, and does not object, the law will raise a promise on his part to pay for the performance." The defendant was held liable in that case, on the ground of an implied promise arising from the circumstances.

In *Watson* v. *Turner*, Bull. *N. P.*, 147, which was not cited on the argument, where a pauper was suddenly taken ill, and an apothecary attended her without the previous request of the Overseers, and afterwards they promised payment, it was holden good; for they were under a moral obligation to provide for the poor.

From these cases I extract the following principles: 1. That Overseers of the Poor **664***] are bound to provide for casual *poor; 2. That as they have the duty to perform, they have a right to exercise their discretion as to the persons to be employed, the terms, time and extent of relief; 3. That if the emergency be such as not to allow time for an application to them, or for an order of justices, any person may afford such relief as the necessity of the case requires, and look to those officers for remuneration; and 4. That if there be an express promise to pay, or one may be implied from the circumstances, they will be liable.

The case of *Atkins* v. *Banwell*, 2 East, 505, is directly contrary to the third of these principles; for in that case it was decided by Ld. Ellenborough, *J.*, Le Blanc, *J.*, and the whole court, that the law will not raise an implied promise in parish officers to pay for necessary medical attendance on a pauper suddenly attacked with a dangerous illness, which prevented his being removed to the place of his settlement—where there were no circumstances from which to infer a promise. And Ld. Ellenborough uses this very strong language: "There is no precedent, principle or color for maintaining this action."

This case is referred to by the Supreme Court in *Everts* v. *Adams*, 12 Johns., 352, and its principle recognized. The court there say, "there is, therefore, no obligation to pay (there being no request or promise by the defendant), unless it be implied by law, and the law will create no such liability."

Nor does the case of *King* v. *Butler*, 15 Johns., 281, in the least infringe upon this principle. There, the Overseer expressly directed the attendance, and promised to pay for it; and the court very properly held that it was his business to see that he was duly authorized.

So the case of *Todd* v. *Birdsall*, 1 Cow., 260, proceeds upon the fact of a written order by the Overseer, for the payment of money to a pauper.

It will be seen from this review, that it is, at least, very doubtful whether, in England, parish officers are, in any event, or in any emergeney, liable for supplies furnished to a pauper without their request, and without any subsequent promise to pay; and that, in this **665***] State, the law has uniformly *been held to be, that Overseers of the Poor are not liable in such a case. This presents a formidable obstacle to any recovery by the defendants in error.

But admitting the law to be as contended, to the whole extent of the authorities cited in the English courts, this case does not come up to them. Here was no exercise of the discretion of the Overseers, although there was abundant opportunity for it, as to the persons to be employed, the terms or the extent of the relief. It was not a case of emergency; another physician had been employed sometime before; and eight or ten days before the services were rendered by the defendants in error, a complaint was made to the select men, the plaintiffs in error; and an order was made for a specific sum to be applied to the relief of the pauper. Under these circumstances, the defendants in error were volunteers, and had not the shadow of a claim against the Overseers, whose consent was never solicited, although there was abundant time for it.

There are various other questions founded on the merits, which would be interesting, but which it is not necessary to decide. Thus, whether Overseers are liable, in any event, or under any circumstances, to an action against them in their official character, is a point which will deserve the serious consideration of this court, whenever it becomes necessary to determine it. And if it should be held that the Overseers of the Poor in this State are so far to be regarded as a corporation, as to be liable to an action, another, and still more difficult question, is, whether the selectmen of another State are to be thus regarded. And whether it would be consistent with the general principles of the law of nations, and with those peculiar principles which regulate the Confederacy of the U. S., for the courts of N. Y. to entertain jurisdiction of an action against the public officers of another State in their official character, for services rendered in that State, and the remuneration for which, depends, upon the laws of that State. The view which I have taken of this cause, avoids all these questions, and enables me to dispose of it on the gratuitous concession that an action would lie against them.

*It was remarked by the counsel for [***666** the defendants in error, that the selectmen were not sued officially, but personally, for a neglect of official duty. Granting, that public officers may be thus prosecuted, the much more difficult question is again presented, whether the courts of one State will entertain suits for the official misconduct of officers of another State. If such action could be maintained, it must certainly be brought by the party grieved by such misconduct. If the Overseers had wholly neglected their duty in providing for the pauper, I have no doubt he might, under circumstances, maintain an action for the injury sustained by such neglect. But this would give no right to third persons to prosecute. The physicians, in this case, cannot say that the selectmen have neglected their duty, in omitting to pay them for their services, until they establish that it was their duty, and that they had the means of doing it. But if the view taken be correct, it was not their duty to pay the defendants in error; there was no legal obligation on the town or its officers; and so far from the selectmen having the means to pay, it appears expressly from the case, that they had expended the sum allowed for this purpose.

Upon the merits of this cause, then, I apprehend there can be no difficulty in determining that the physicians, the defendants in error, had no cause of action whatever against the plaintiffs in error.

The justice before whom the action was brought, rendered judgment in favor of the physicians for $50. On an appeal to the Court of C. P. of Washington Co., that court reversed the judgment of the justice. So far as the merits of the cause are concerned, that reversal was correct. But in that proceeding, it is alleged, the Court of C. P. committed an error in trying the cause, without the intervention of a jury; and for that error, the judgment rendered was reversed by the Supreme Court, and the plaintiffs before the justice, were restored to all things they had lost.

In my opinion, the Supreme Court was correct in reversing the judgment of the C. P. The Court of C. P. seem to have considered **667***] the proceeding before *them, in the same light as one upon *certiorari*, and to have reversed the judgment as if it were before them by writ of error. This appears to me entirely erroneous. The appeal to the C. P. is a proceeding unknown to the common law. It opens the whole case, and presents it for a new trial upon the examination of witnesses, in open court, and a new judgment must be rendered; whereas, the writ of *certiorari* brings up the history of the proceedings before the justice; and for errors in those proceedings, the judgment is reversed, or if they are correct, it is affirmed. The writ of *certiorari* is thus, in effect, a writ of error. No two things, it appears to me, can be more dissimilar than the remedy by appeal, and that by *certiorari*. In the one case, there is a new trial; in the other, there is no trial whatever. The practice of the Supreme Court on *certiorari*, therefore, furnishes no analogy for proceedings on appeal.

The Court of C. P., being required to proceed and try the cause, it must do so according to the course of the common law. The Constitution (old Const., art. 41) provides that trial by jury as it hath heretofore been used in the Colony of N. Y., shall remain inviolate forever. This provision was in force at the time this cause was heard in the C. P. of Washington Co. The trial by jury had always been preserved in the Colony and State, where the demand exceeded $25; and it would have been unconstitutional for the Legislature to have authorized the trial of an issue of fact in any other way. The Legislature has not done so. I agree with the Supreme Court in the case cited by the counsel on the argument, from 20 Johns., 280, that it is fairly to be inferred from the Act of 1818, authorizing appeals, that the courts of C. P. are to proceed on them in the same manner as if the cause had been originally instituted in those courts. But admitting that the statute does not explicitly point out the mode of trial, the Constitution did; and I cannot indulge any refined reasoning from analogy, to abridge the right of trial by jury in any case; and much less where it is positively enjoined by the Constitution. I cannot **668***] entertain a doubt, therefore, *that the proceedings of the C. P., in reversing the judgment of the justice, as if it were before that court by writ of error, were erroneous, and that they were unconstitutional in determining the cause without a trial by jury.

But it would be a lamentable consequence, and an aspersion on the administration of justice, that the reversal of the judgment of the C. P. for such errors in its proceedings, should have the effect of confirming the original judgment of the justice. Yet such is the effect of the judgment of the Supreme Court; and if it should be affirmed by this court wholly, the original plaintiffs would recover their demand —not on account of its justice, but because the Court of C. P. committed an error in the mode which it adopted of revising the judgment of the justice; and because that court had, in truth, never legally tried the cause. Yet the judgment of the Supreme Court is correct in reversing that of the C. P. In this dilemma, there was a course which would have removed all difficulties, which was within the power of the Supreme Court, and which would undoubtedly have been adopted, if requested by the counsel for the present plaintiffs in error. It was to direct the Court of C. P. to issue a *venire*, and proceed to the trial of the cause according to law, or to have awarded a *venire* out of the Supreme Court.

The cases of *Grant* v. *Astle*, Doug., 722; *Harwood* v. *Goodright*, Cowp., 89; *Davies* v. *Pierce*, 2 T. R., 125; *Brown* v. *Clark*, 3 Johns., 443, and *Arnold* v. *Crane*, 8 *Id.*, 79, 82, establish, beyond all question, that whenever a judgment is reversed upon some ground which does not involve the merits of the cause, a *venire de novo* is awarded, of course, to try those merits. It appears from the report of the case of *Livingston* v. *Rogers*, 1 Cai., 587, that this court on reversing a judgment of the Supreme Court, in that cause, ordered a *venire de novo*, to be issued by the Supreme Court. The correctness of this practice is vindicated by Kent, *J.*, and abundantly sustained by the authorities cited by him.

*Nor can there be any doubt of the [***669** authority of this court to reverse in part, and affirm in part. (Str., 188; Ld. Raym., 894, 1534.) And as that is the only possible mode by which justice in this cause can be attained, and a trial had according to law, I am of opinion that so much of the judgment of the Supreme Court as reverses the judgment of the Court of C. P. of Washington Co., be affirmed; that the residue of the judgment in the Supreme Court be reversed; that the record be remitted to the Supreme Court, with directions either to issue a *venire* and try the cause in that court, or to remit the record to the Court of C. P. of Washington Co., with similar directions to issue a *venire* and proceed to the trial of the appeal; and that neither party be entitled to any costs upon the writ of error.. *Cole* v. *Wendell*, 8 Johns., 116.

Bowman, *Earll*, *Greenly*, *Keyes*, *Ogden*, *Redfield*, *Thorn*, *Wilkeson* and *Wright*, *Senators*, concurred with Spencer, *Senator*.

TALLMADGE, *President*, said his opinion accorded with that of the *Chancellor* and of Colden, *Senator*, that the judgment of the Supreme Court should be reversed upon the merits. There was no sufficient promise to sustain the action. According to the laws of Vt., there was no omission of official duty, and no cause of action on this ground. But I would not put the decision on the latter point; because it would imply the right of the courts of this state to inquire into the official conduct of the officers of another state. This court cannot entertain the question. It is within the reason of the cases which hold that the courts of one State cannot enforce the penal or local laws of another. The performance of official duties imposed by the laws upon the officers of another

State cannot be enforced, or the omission punished, by the laws of this State; though it is otherwise as to contracts made in other States. The action can be sustained on the ground of contract only; and in this respect the proof is deficient.

670*] *Overseers of the Poor must be proceeded against like officers of other incorporations. They must be made liable in their official or corporate capacity, or be charged as individuals. The action must be shaped accordingly, and be supported by sufficient proof. For official neglect or misconduct, they may be indicted; but they can never be prosecuted for official liabilities, and be rendered individually responsible for the judgment, in their property and persons. This distinction between individual and official liability must be regarded; and will regulate the form of the proceedings, and the proof necessary to sustain the action. The judgment in the one case is against them as individuals, and becomes a lien on their property; in the other it is against them as a corporation, and only binds their corporate property. The Corporation which the plaintiffs in error are said to represent, cannot be prosecuted in this State. The action was against them as individuals; and in that view the proof was wholly insufficient to charge them.

Should the court, however, think differently, and hold that there was a sufficient cause of action, then I should agree with Spencer, *Senator*, that the facts should have been tried by a jury; and that, for this purpose, the judgment should be reversed, without costs on either side; and that the cause be sent to trial upon a *venire*.

The court, on a division, being in favor of a total or general reversal, according to the result of the opinions delivered by Sanford, *Chancellor*, Colden, *Senator*, and Tallmadge, *President* —12 *Senators* concurring generally with the *Chancellor*, and 9 *Senators* concurring generally with Spencer, *Senator*—the following rule was thereupon entered with the clerk:

"Counsel having been heard in this cause, and due deliberation being thereupon had, it is ordered, adjudged and decreed that the judgment of the Supreme Court in this cause be reversed, with costs to be taxed. And it is further ordered that the record be remitted, &c."

Cited in—3 Wend., 198; 9 Wend., 676; 8 Paige, 410; 9 Barb., 264; 66 Barb., 71; 31 N. J. L., 311.

671*] *URIAH MARVIN AND LEWIS BENEDICT, who are Impleaded with GEORGE COOPER, *Appellants*,

v.

JOHN VEDDER, *Respondent*.

Delivery of Money by Mortgagor to Mortgagee Operates as Payment, whether Indorsed on Mortgage or Collateral Security or not—Subsequent Loan of the Money to Mortgagor, not secured by the Mortgage.

A delivery of money due from a mortgagor to a mortgagee, with an intention to pay, operates as a payment, without a receipt, or an indorsement on the mortgage, or on the collateral security. And if the money be afterwards delivered back by the mortgagee to the mortgagor, this shall be construed a loan on the personal credit of the mortgagor. And the lien by the mortgage, as to the sum paid, cannot be revived by the agreement of the mortgagor and mortgagee, as to third persons who hold *bona fide* incumbrances upon the mortgaged premises.

A delivery of money due from a mortgagor to a mortgagee is, of itself, *prima facie*, evidence of payment to the extent of the sum so delivered, without the payment being indorsed, or a receipt given. Per Colden, *Senator*.

When a debtor advances money to his creditor, which is intended, by both parties, to be applied on the debt due, it is but another name for payment. Per Savage, *Ch. J.*

NOTE.—*Mortgage—Payment—Refunding payment—Payment discharges the lien, to the extent of such payment.* Subsequent refunding of the money does not restore the lien as to third persons. In connection with above case of Marvin v. Vedder, consult De La Vergne v. Evertson, 1 Paige, 181. See, also, Niagara Bank v. Rosevelt, 9 Cow., 409.

ON appeal from the Court of Chancery. The respondent, July 7, 1818, filed his bill against the appellants and George Cooper, for the foreclosure of a mortgage executed by Cooper to the respondent, June 20, 1814, of certain lands in Palatine, Montgomery Co., which, with a bond as collateral security, was conditioned to pay $1,000, on or before June 1, 1815; and $1,000, on or before June 1, 1816, with interest.

The appellants were made parties, as being creditors of Cooper by a judgment confessed, docketed Jan. 18, 1815.

The main question was whether Cooper had paid the first installment.

In relation to this, the bill charged, that on or about June 1, 1815, Cooper advanced to the respondent $1,000, which was intended, at the time of such advance, to have been applied to satisfy the first installment of the mortgage money; but that, within a very few days thereafter, and before *this sum was credited [***672** on the bond and mortgage, Cooper applied to the respondent to take back the advance, and for an extension of the time to pay the first installment; and that the respondent thereupon returned the $1,000 to Cooper, and agreed to wait for the first installment some time longer; and until the respondent should demand it.

Dec. 15, 1818, the appellants answered, that on or about June 1, 1815, Cooper actually paid the $1,000 to the respondent, being the first installment of principal then due; and that the payment was absolute and unqualified; that it might be true, that Cooper, a few days after the payment, applied to the respondent to get back the $1,000, and for an extension of time to pay the first installment; and that the respondent might thereupon have returned the $1,000 to Cooper, and agreed to wait for the first installment some time longer, and until the respondent should demand the same; but the appellants had no knowledge of the facts; and therefore left the respondent to make proof thereof as he should be advised.

On replication and issue, Edward Burdick, a witness for the appellants, examined Aug. 23, 1821, testified, that in Feb. or Mar., 1818, the respondent stated in conversation with one Snell, that he had received the first installment of $1,000 that had become due on the mortgage from Cooper; but had not indorsed it on the bond and mortgage; and that he had let Cooper have the money again shortly afterwards. And again, in June or July, 1818, after Cooper had been reputed insolvent, he inquired of the respondent whether he had a prospect of getting the $1,000 he had let Cooper have? The respondent replied that the money had been in his house but about three days when Cooper got it again; and that he thought the mortgage stood good for the whole. Witness had heard the respondent say he had reloaned the $1,000, being the first installment due on the bond and mortgage, to Cooper; that he was to have had the payment indorsed on the mortgage; and intended to get Jacob Snell to make the indorsement; but the indorsement 673*] was *not made when Cooper called for the money; and then he did not have it made.

Jacob Snell, a witness for the appellants, examined Sept. 6, 1821, testified that about 4 years ago he heard the respondent admit that he had received $1,000 of Cooper; but that in a few days Cooper got it from him again; and the witness understood that the money was received on the mortgage; because the respondent remarked, at the time, that it had not been indorsed on the mortgage.

The mortgage and bond being produced, on the former there was no indorsement; but on the bond were indorsed payment as follows: Interest in full to June 1, 1816; and Aug. 17, 1816, $200; June 20, 1817, $500 (paid by Benedict, one of the appellants); Oct.—1817, $120.

Frederick I. Dockstader, a witness for the respondent, examined Jan. 30, 1821, testified, that the latter part of Dec. 1818, he heard the respondent ask Benedict, one of the appellants, to let him have $500, on the mortgage of Cooper. Bendict said this was inconvenient at the time; but he would pay that sum to the respondent in two or three months. At the same time he told the respondent he was safe; for Cooper had sufficient property to pay double the sum he owed the respondent.

Harman Vedder, a witness for the respondent, examined Jan. 3, 1821, testified, that in the latter part of July, 1815, in the witness' field, Cooper requested the respondent to let him keep the first installment of $1,000, due on the mortgage; and gave as a reason that the respondent did not want the money; if he kept it, would have to put it out in small sums, &c.; that the money was safe; and the security better at that time than when it was taken. The respondent told Cooper he might retain the first installment if he would pay the interest then due upon that installment; that if he would call in the evening at the respondent's dwelling house, they would then arrange the business, so as to let Cooper retain the $1,000, to which Cooper assented.

May 5, 1823, the late *Chancellor* Kent made a decree, declaring that the $1,000, admitted in the bill to have been advanced, and stated in the 674*] answer to have been *paid, &c., were not paid to, received or applied by the respondent, as a payment on the bond and mortgage; but were merely deposited by Cooper with the respondent for a short time; and taken back at the request of Cooper, with the consent of the complainant, without being intended, or understood by either party to be taken and applied as such payment. He, therefore, decreed a reference to a master, to take an account upon this principle, and a sale, &c.

From this decree Marvin & Benedict appealed to this court.

KENT, late *Chancellor*, assigned no reasons for the decree beyond the above, which were contained in the decree itself.

Mr. J. V. Henry, for the appellants.

Mr. H. Bleecker, for the respondent.

SAVAGE, *Ch. J.*, after entering at large into the facts. There is no question of law in dispute; and but one of fact—and that seems to me to have been virtually conceded by the respondent in his bill. He admits the money was advanced to him, and was to have been applied on the mortgage. Now, when a debtor advances money to his creditor, which is intended to be applied upon the debt due, and is so received by the creditor, it is but another name for payment. An advance presupposes that the money is not payable at the time; but in this case it was due. The idea of a deposit, under such circumstances, seems to me extraordinary. The only answer to the admission on the record, and the declarations made to Burdick and Snell, is a promise to pay $500 on the mortgage, made under a belief, as it appears that Cooper had property sufficient to pay the whole demand. This proves nothing as to the fact in dispute.

The money was clearly delivered in payment; and afterwards reloaned; and however just it may be, that the lien should be revived as between mortgagor and mortgagee, the *bona fide* creditors of the mortgagor ought not to lose the benefit of their security, by the indulgence or negligence of the mortgagee.

*I am clearly of opinion that the de- [*675 cree of His Honor, the late *Chancellor*, be reversed.

SUTHERLAND, *J.*, concurred.

WOODWORTH, *J.*, not having heard the argument, gave no opinion.

COLDEN, *Senator*, delivered his opinion, substantially as follows: I should entirely concur in the decree of the late *Chancellor*, could I agree with him as to the proofs, that the $1,000 was not received or applied by Vedder as payment, but merely deposited for a short time, and taken back by Cooper with Vedder's consent.

The *Chancellor* must be understood to speak of the time when Vedder received the money; and, unquestionably, we must refer to that time for the character of the transaction. If the $1,000 were given to Vedder, and received by him as an absolute payment in the first instance, it is of no consequence whether it was afterwards taken back by Cooper, with Vedder's consent; or whether they, or either of them, when it was so taken back, intended and understood that it should not be applied as a payment.

[Here *Mr. C.* examined the pleadings and evidence.] I cannot find a single word that appears to me to warrant the conclusion that the money was deposited, for a short time, and not received by Vedder as a payment. On the contrary, the proofs, arising either from the pleadings or the examinations, appear to me to be full and positive, that neither of the parties had any other idea than that the payment was absolute. The respondent's bill does not pretend that he received the money as a deposit; and the answer expressly and unequivocally denies that it was so received, and insists upon a payment.

Independent of all testimony, how can we

suppose that the $1,000 were intended by Cooper, or considered by Vedder as a deposit. The amount was due at the time; and unless an agreement between the parties that it should be considered a deposit, be expressly proved, we must consider it a payment. It is very dif-
676*] ficult to suppose *that any good and honest reason should have existed why this money should have been held by Vedder as a deposit. If there was, in truth, any motive for leaving it in his hands, for any purpose other than that of payment, it was incumbent on the respondent to have shown this.

Then the question which presents itself for our decision is, whether a mortgagee, who receives a payment on his mortgage, by which his lien on the mortgaged premises is diminished to the amount of the payment, can, at any time afterwards, at his pleasure, revive his lien for the previous amount, by a reloan to the mortgagor, to the prejudice of a *bona fide* incumbrancer, whose incumbrance is subsequent to the mortgage, but prior to the reloan.

I think a mortgagee has no power to do this; and I understand the late *Chancellor* to be of the same opinion. He assumes the fact that the $1,000 was intended by the parties merely as a deposit, while, as it appears to me, it is very fully proved to have been an absolute payment.

There seems to me no doubt, therefore, as to the law; and so far were the counsel for the respective parties agreed on this subject, that not a single authority was cited, at the bar, on either side.

If Vedder was at liberty to re-establish his lien by giving back the money to the mortgagor at the end of two or three days, he might have done so at the end of two or three years. This would hardly be contended; and yet I cannot perceive that the lapse of more or less time could make any difference as to the principle; nor can it make any difference whether the receipt of the money was indorsed, or not.

I shall forbear, at this time, and on future occasions, to repeat expressions of the feelings of respect and deference, with which I differ from the late *Chancellor*. No man more highly appreciates his learning and abilities than I do. But these are sentiments to which I am not at liberty, in my present situation, to sacrifice the convictions of my understanding. But in this case I have the less reluctance in giving an opinion in opposition to the decree; because, in doing so, I do not differ from the court below on any law point. The case turns entirely upon the proofs; and requires but
677*] *very humble talents to examine these with an attention which a press of business or other causes, might have rendered it impossible for the *Chancellor* to bestow.

My opinion is, that the *Chancellor's* decree be reversed; and that the record be remitted, with instructions that the court below shall permit the appellants to redeem on payment of what may be due, after crediting the $1,000 as paid on the first of June, 1815; and that they be allowed their costs.

Bowman, Brayton, Burrows, Clarke, Cramer, Dudley, Ellsworth, Gardiner, Greenly, Haight, Keyes, M'Intyre, Morgan and *Wilkeson, Senators*, concurred in the result of the opinions delivered by the *Chief Justice*, and Colden, *Senator*.

For affirmance—*Earll, Lefferts, Lynde, Mallory, M'Michael, Redfield, Wooster* and *Wright, Senators.*

A majority being for a reversal, it was, thereupon, ordered, adjudged and decreed that the decree of the late *Chancellor* should be and the same was thereby reversed. And it was further ordered, adjudged and decreed that the appellant should be permitted to redeem the mortgaged premises, upon payment of what was due to the respondent, for principal and interest, on the 12th day of November, 1819, giving credit for the sum of $1,000, mentioned in the decree, and upon payment of the respondent's costs in the court below, until the coming in of the appellants' answer. And further, that the respondent should pay to the appellants their costs in the said court, to be taxed, subsequent to the filing of their answer; and that the record, &c., should be remitted, &c.

Cited in—1 Wend., 436; 1 Paige, 182; 1 Sandf. Ch., 386; 2 Lans., 380; 6 Barb., 22; 12 Barb., 583; 34 Barb., 543; 36 Barb., 521; 38 Barb., 428; 42 How. Pr., 89; 11 Abb. N. S., 198; 39 Wis., 650; 19 Am. Dec., 412 (1 Paige, ch., 181).

---

*EBEN WARREN AND JAMES R. NORTON, *Plaintiffs in Error*, [*678

v.

ORMUS DOOLITTLE AND RUBEN DOOLITTLE, JR., *Defendants in Error.*

Act Concerning Distresses, Rents and Renewal of Leases—Recovery of only one Penalty, Against Two or More Jointly—Damages—Pleading.

An action, upon the 14th section of the Statute concerning Distresses, Rents and the Renewal of Leases, 1 R. L., 437, 438, for aiding and assisting a tenant to remove goods from the demised premises, &c., lies against two or more jointly, the offense being in its nature one and inseparable. But only one penalty follows, and is imposed on all the defendants; not on each and every of them.

Where a statute declares that "any person" doing a certain act offends, and that every person so offending shall forfeit and pay, &c., it depends on the nature of the offense, as being entire or several, whether several persons jointly and simultaneously committing it are to be subjected, the whole to but one pe[illegible]y, or each to the whole penalty.

When a statute gives double the value of goods, by way of penalty, to be recovered in debt, the jury may find the value of the goods, and the court double the value in their judgment; and it is sufficient that the verdict say the value of the goods. This shall be intended the single, not the double value; and the verdict need not say single value, in terms.

In such case, if the declaration claim a certain sum, in conclusion referring to the statute by its title and date, or generally, "contrary to the form of the statute, &c.", and the jury find the value; this is sufficiently specific, to warrant the court in doubling the value.

It is not necessary in actions of debt for penalties of uncertain amounts, depending, for instance, on the value of goods, that the plaintiff should recover the precise amount laid in the declaration.

Under the Statute, 1 R. L., 437, 438, the landlord can recover but one penalty either in a joint or separate action against several persons jointly concerned in aiding, &c., to carry away the goods. Per Colden, *Senator*.

The practice of the courts of law, in doubling or trebling damages, or value, upon statutes, on verdict, finding single damages or value, approved. Per Sanford, *Chancellor*, and Colden, *Senator*.

Citations—Cro. Eliz., 480; Moore, 453; Noy., 52, 62; Cowp., 610; 8 Geo. 1, ch. 18, sec. 25; 1 & 2 Ph. & Mar., ch. 12; 8 Johns., 345; Act, April, 5, 1813; 1 H. Bl., 149; 1 Gall., 26; 2 East, 570.

ON ERROR to Supreme Court. The action was debt, originally brought by the defendants, against the plaintiffs in error, in the Court of C.P. of the County of Washington, in March Term, 1817.

The declaration was in debt for $100; for that whereas the plaintiffs below, being seised, &c., of a lot in Hampton, Washington Co., demised it to Leeland, for one year, at $35 rent, **679***] *who entered and held till the rent was due; when divers goods and chattels, to wit: one &c., of the value of &c. (setting forth the goods and their value), amounting in the whole to the value of $100, then being on the demised premises, Leeland and the defendants, well knowing the premises, and intending to cheat and defraud the plaintiffs of the rent, and prevent them from distraining the goods, &c., the defendants willfully and knowingly did aid and assist Leeland, being tenant, &c., in conveying and carrying off the demised premises, the goods and chattels specified, leaving the $35 rent unpaid, contrary to the statute in such case made and provided. And the plaintiffs averred, that neither when the rent became due, nor afterwards, &c., were there goods and chattels on the demised premises, sufficient to have satisfied the rent by distress, or any part thereof, &c., whereby an action had accrued, &c., to demand and have of the defendants the $100 demanded, according to the form of the statute in such case made and provided, entitled "An Act concerning Distresses, Rents and the Renewal of Leases," passed Apr. 5, 1813. Nevertheless, &c.

There was a second count to the same effect, in substance for the purpose of the several questions raised in this court. But it concluded "contrary to the form of the statute in such case made and provided:" without referring to any statute more particularly. Plea, *nil debent.*

The cause was continued on the record to March Term, 1818, when it was tried; and the jury found a general verdict upon the whole declaration, that the defendants were guilty of the premises in manner and form, &c., and they also found that the value of the goods and chattels conveyed away was $29; whereupon, upon the prayer of the plaintiffs, the C.P. gave judgment for them to $58, double the value found by the jury, and the costs.

Error was brought by Warren & Norton to the Supreme Court, who, in May Term, 1820, affirmed the judgment.

A bill of exceptions was taken in the C. P.: but as this court were of opinion that it presented no point of law, upon the merits, I do not set it forth.

680*] **Mr. J. Crary*, for the plaintiffs, in error, said the offense for which the action was brought, was created by statute, (1 R. L., 437, 438, sec. 14.) By that statute, the offense is laid on "any person so offending," not persons, and the suit should not have been brought against two. The offense of one is not the offense of another. *Barnard* v. *Gostling*, 4 Bos. & P., 245; Esp. on Pen. Act., 69, S. C.; *Rex* v. *Clarke*, Cowp., 610.

The penalty, that is double the value of the goods, is not claimed in the declaration. (7 Wentw. Pl., 161, 162; Esp. Pen. Act., 118, 119; Bull. *N. P.*, 196.)

The Court of C. P. did not give judgment on the verdict, which was $29, but for $58; on the ground that they had a right to double the value found by the jury. They had no right to do this. Enough did not appear upon the record to warrant it; which is essential, according to *Newcomb* v. *Butterfield*, 8 Johns., 342, a reference to the statute generally, is no guide. The particular section should be mentioned. It is settled in England, that the court cannot alter the verdict. *Spencer* v. *Goter*, 1 H. Bl., 78; *Jackson* v. *Williamson*, 2 T. R., 281. The declaration should have claimed double the value expressly. Not having done so, the plaintiffs below could not avail themselves of the statute. Essential matter, not averred, cannot be proved. *Lane* v. *Hitchcock*, 14 Johns., 218. The title of the plaintiffs below, as set out, was defective, and is not cured by the verdict. (1 Saund., 228 *c*, *note* 1).

Mr. S. M. Hopkins, for the defendants in error, said the question of joinder depended upon the nature of the offense. If it was such as could be committed jointly, the action lay against more than one; otherwise, if that was impossible. A joining, in such an offense as is here charged, is not only possible, but extremely natural. The double value can be recovered but once. The result of all the cases is that where the act punished is, in its nature, necessarily confined to one there the action must be several. It can be committed by one only, and the action must be confined to him, otherwise, if many may be concerned. *Rex* v. *Bleasdale*, *4 T. R., 809; *Partridge* v. *Naylor*, [***681** Cro. Eliz., 480; Moore, 453, S. C.; Noy, 52, S. C., *Id.*, 62, S. C., by the title of *Patridge* v. *Emson;* Hardyman and Whitaker, 2 East, 573, *note a*; *Collins* v. *Morgan*, 1 H. Bl., 244; *Rex* v. *Clark, et al.*, 1 Cowp., 610.

It is not necessary that the declaration should, in terms, claim double the value. It is enough that it define the offense and claim a round sum, sufficient to cover the double value. In debt for the value of goods upon a statute, it is impossible to fix the precise worth of them in pleading and, therefore, it is never required. *Pemberton* v. *Shelton*, Cro. Jac., 498.

The jury find the value expressly; and it is well settled, that where this is done, the court may double it. The principle of the cases allowing damages to be doubled or trebled by the court, applies to a penalty.

SANFORD *Chancellor*, after stating the case, delivered his opinion to the following effect: The first point made by the plaintiffs in error is, that the action will not lie against two defendants jointly. I cannot recognize this objection. The words of the statute in question are, "if any person shall willfully and knowingly aid or assist any such tenant or lessee in such conveying away or carrying off any part of his goods or chattels, or in concealing the same, every person so offending, shall forfeit and pay, &c., double the value of the goods by him carried off, or concealed, as aforesaid, to be recovered by an action of debt," &c. I cannot bring myself to doubt, that where two or more persons concur in the act of conveying away or concealing the goods, but one penalty attaches; and they may be sued jointly. I understand the rule to be, that where the offense is, in its nature, one and entire, the penalty is one. Several penalties cannot be imposed upon the several offenders. This is so in the nature of things, and is abundantly settled by authority.

The true inquiry is, can the single offense created by the act be committed by several persons? If this question may be answered in the affirmative, though the offense is, in fact, committed by several, but one penalty follows; **682***] and it may *be recovered by a single action, against all the offenders jointly. The offense is then, in its nature, single and cannot be severed. This is the ancient and well established distinction. It never has been questioned with success, since the leading case of *Patridge* v. *Naylor*, in 38 Eliz., on error in the K. B., which is reported in several books cited at the bar. By consulting the report in Cro. Eliz., 480, and F. Moore, 453, it will be found fully to the point. The action was in C. B. upon the 1 and 2 Ph. & M., ch. 12, against three, for impounding a distress in several pounds, in three several hundreds. The case was, that three distrained a flock of sheep; and severally impounded them in three several pounds in several hundreds. The clause of the statute in question is set forth in Moore, *verbatim*. It was, that no cattle taken by distress at one time, should be impounded in several places, upon pain that every person offending contrary to the Act, should forfeit to the party greived £5 and treble damages. Upon a verdict of guilty, damages were assessed by the jury, at 40*s*.; and judgment entered that every of the defendants should forfeit £5, and the treble of 40*s*. It was assigned for error, that there should have been but one £5 against all; and one trebling of the 40*s*. against all; for it was but one distress, and one offense, in them all, against the statute. After several arguments, the K. B. held the judgment to be erroneous; and the following pertinent reasons were given by the court, according to the report in Moore; because the words "every person offending" did not refer to severalty of persons, but offenses; and because all three offended in a joint fact, they should forfeit but one £5.

Rex v. *Clark*, Cowp., 610, illustrates the other side of the question. An information was filed against three persons, upon the Statute, 8 Geo. I., ch. 18, sec. 25, for assaulting and resisting certain custom-house officers, concluding that by reason thereof, they had severally forfeited £40 a piece. There was a second count for a rescue, which concluded in the same manner. Upon not guilt pleaded, the jury found the defendants severally guilty. **683***] There was a motion in arrest, *on this ground. The motion was denied; but the Court of K. B. and Ld. Mansfield at their head, recognize the case of *Patridge* v. *Naylor*. Ld. Mansfield states the distinction which runs through the cases. He says, "where the offense is, in its nature, single, and cannot be severed, there the penalty shall be single; because, though several persons may join in committing it, it still constitutes but one offense. But where the offense is, in its nature, several, and where every person concerned may be separately guilty of it, there each offender is separately liable to the penalty; because the crime of each is distinct from the offense of the others; and each is punishable for his own crime. For instance; the offense created by the 1 & 2 Ph. & M., ch. 12, is, the impounding a distress in the wrong place. One, two, three or four may impound it wrongfully. It is but one act of impounding. It cannot be severed. It is but one offense, and therefore, shall be satisfied by one forfeiture. So under the Statute 5 Anne, ch. 14, for the preservation of game; killing a hare is but one offense in its nature, whether one or twenty kill it; it cannot be killed more than once. If partridges are netted by night, two, three or more may draw the net, but still it constitutes but one offense. But this statute relates to an offense in its nature several; a several offense at common law; and the statute adds a further sanction against that, which each man must commit severally. One may resist, another molest, another run away with the goods; one may break the officer's arm; another put out his eye. All these are distinct acts; and every one's offense is entire and complete in its nature. Therefore, each person is liable to the penalty for his own separate offense.

Now here, two several persons are implicated, by this verdict, in the fact or offense of jointly and simultaneously carrying off the goods. The injury resulting therefrom is, in its nature, single and inseparable, as much so as the impounding a distress in several places, killing a hare or netting a partridge; though the defendants contributed to that result by different acts. Being governed, therefore, by the nature of the offense, as I think we must be, upon unquestionable *authority, [***684** there cannot be a doubt that the action was, in this instance, well brought against both of the defendants below.

Another objection is, to the form in which the sum found by the jury was doubled. It cannot be pretended that this should not have been doubled in some form. In principle it is wholly immaterial, whether it be done by the court or jury. The practice, in similar cases, seems to be well settled. Where double or treble value is given in damages by statute, the courts are in the habit of instructing the jury to find the single value, and afterwards doubling or trebling that value by judgment. The whole matter is thus fairly spread upon the record, and I can conceive no objection to this course.

The facts constituting the offense were set forth with sufficient precision to show a violation of the statute, which is expressly referred to by the declaration. There was, therefore, no want of authority, upon the record, for awarding the double value.

The *Chancellor* also examined the objections made upon the bill of exceptions, which he considered untenable; and concluded that the judgment should be affirmed.

Colden, *Senator*, after considering, and expressing his opinion against the objections raised upon the bill of exceptions. It is contended that there is error in the judgment, because it is against two defendants; whereas, the statute is in the singular, and applies to one person only; its words being, "if any person" shall aid a tenant, &c.

We must interpret this statute according to its obvious meaning. It undoubtedly intended that all persons who should assist a tenant to defraud his landlord should be punished. It is not unusual in enactments of this kind to use the singular number, not in a numerical sense, but as designating a whole species. So in the decalogue, we are commanded not to covet our neighbor's wife, or his ox, or his ass, or his house. It has never been thought, I believe, that this precept was confined to one of these objects; and that if our neighbor has two wives, two oxen, two asses, or two houses, we **685***] *may covet one of them. We must read the statute, in my opinion, as if it had said, "all persons" who shall unlawfully assist a tenant to remove his goods, shall pay to the landlord double the value.

Then the question is, whether the defendants, having been engaged in the same prohibited act, are each liable for the whole penalty in separate actions; or whether they are jointly liable for a single penalty in one action. It is very certain that the statute will permit the landlord to recover the double value of the goods but once; so that unless those who were concerned in the transgression, and were equally guilty, are jointly liable, but one of them can be punished. This we cannot presume was the intent of the Legislature. We should not give the statute a construction which would be so at variance with common sense and common justice. If an authority be necessary to show that this objection to the judgment ought not to prevail, it will be found in the case of *Barnard* v. *Gostling*, 2 East, 570, in which the English court decided that upon their statute, which prohibits an unqualified person from using a greyhound, under a penalty of £5, two might be convicted in one penalty, though they could not each be charged with £5 for the same act.

This objection comes rather awkardly from the defendants below, because it is insisting on an error, which if it be one, is in their favor. Each insists that the judgment ought to be reversed, because he has been rendered liable for the penalty, together with his co-defendant; whereas, each should be charged, as they contend, with the whole of the double value of the goods. I think the case will not permit us to indulge the plaintiffs in error by pronouncing that they are liable so far beyond the present recovery.

It is insisted that the action is wrong, because it is not for the double value, and that nothing is said of the double value in the declaration.

I do not think this is so. The action is in a plea of debt for $100. The first count concludes with an averment that "an action had **686***] accrued to the plaintiffs to *have from the defendants the said sum of $100, according to the form of the statute in such case made and provided, entitled An Act concerning Distresses, Rents and the Renewal of Leases, passed Apr. 5, 1813;" and the second count avers that the defendants below assisted the tenant to remove his goods, "contrary to the form of the statute in such case made and provided." In the case of *Newcomb* v. *Butterfield*, 8 Johns., 345, in which the plaintiff attempted to recover treble damages for a trespass, the Supreme Court say, "the declaration should refer to the act, so that the defendant may be apprised of the extent of the demand." In the case we are now considering, the declaration does, as we have seen, refer to the statute very particularly. It gave the parties and the court sufficiently to understand that the action was for the double value. The declaration states the value of the goods, and the jury has found that they were worth $29; which, when doubled, is $58, for which the judgment is rendered.

The plaintiffs below do not recover more than they have demanded. In actions for penalties, where they depend on uncertain values, the plaintiff may recover less than he counts for. The rule, that in an action of debt, a plaintiff must recover according to his count, has been relaxed in a thousand instances, as in *M'Quillin* v. *Cox*, 1 H. Bl., 149; and if the old rule were still adhered to, in actions of this nature, it would render all penal statutes nugatory which provide that value shall be the measure of a penalty. It would be equally absurd to say that a party must, at his peril, fix the value at neither more nor less than a jury may think right. If this were required, it is hardly possible that a penalty of this nature could ever be recovered.

The third point of the plaintiffs in error is, that the court below, "under pretense that the jury had given a verdict for the value of the goods only," instead of giving judgment on that verdict, gave judgment for double the amount of it, without regard to the finding of the jury.

So far as this point refers to facts, it is not supported by the record. For certainly the jury did find specially the *value of the [***687** goods; and so far from the court's not having regarded the verdict, the record states, that "thereupon, according to the form of the statute, the court gave judgment for $58, being double the value of the goods and chattels so as aforesaid, by the jury aforesaid, found."

But it was contended that the double value ought to have been found by the jury, and could not be assessed by the court. Where double damages are given, they are constantly doubled by the court, and there seems to be no reason why the same course may not be pursued where a party is entitled to a double value by way of penalty.

Penalties are frequently given in this form, under the Acts of Congress, and the question now under consideration has often been presented in the courts of the U. S.

In the case of *Cross* v. *U. S.*, 1 Gall., 26, the court say: "In looking into precedents on informations for breaches of the revenue laws, we find, that in general, the verdict is for the single value. But in such precedents, the issue is not found to be *nil debet*, but is a special issue; and the single value of the property is assessed by the jury, to enable the court to impose the penalty as well as to decree the forfeiture of the goods." In the case before us, by finding for the plaintiffs upon the general issue, and finding the value of the goods, the jury found all the facts necessary to enable the court to see that the case was one in which the plaintiffs below were entitled to the double value of the goods, to assess such value, and to render their judgment accordingly.

In my opinion the judgment of the Supreme Court must be affirmed, with costs.

Per totam Curiam.

Judgment affirmed.

Cited i —1 Den., 232; 4 Den., 379; 3 Allen, 192; 20 Am. Dec., 619.

688*] *PETER SMITH, PETER SKEN. SMITH, ABRAHAM TURCK, JONATHAN TURCK, WILLIAM SOULDEN AND ABRAHAM VAN SANTVOORD, *Plaintiffs in Error*,

v.

ERI LUSHER AND RICHARD McMICHAEL, *Defendants in Error.*

Partners—Partnership May Bind Themselves by Note, to a Member of Firm—Action on Such Note, by Indorsees, Lies—Payee's Remedy on in Equity—Pleading.

S. and V., being partners in trade with Smith and three others, under the firm of S. & Co., S. made a promisory note, payable to V., to secure an alleged balance due from the firm to V., without the knowledge or consent of Smith; which note was, before it became due, indorsed by V. to L. and M., who had notice of the firm, and that V. and S. were members of the firm, and of the consideration for which the note was given. In an action by the indorsees against the firm, as makers, including V., these facts were pleaded by Smith: but he did not aver that the alleged debt was not in fact due, nor that the note was given in fraud of the firm; held that though no action would have lain by V., he being both maker and payee, yet the indorsees might bring an action against the firm, and declare on the note as payable by the firm to V., and indorsed by V. to them, and recover in that form.

Held, also, that the plea of want of knowledge and consent in Smith, did not amount to the general issue, but was merely a denial of actual knowledge or consent in the particular transaction, and left legal knowledge and consent to be implied, from the nature of the connection between the partners, and from the law merchant.

But had the execution of the note been a fraud upon the firm, or the debt for which it was given depended on the adjustment of an account between the members of the firm, this would have constituted a defense at law or in equity. Per Sanford, *Chancellor*.

It is the constant practice for one partner to draw bills, or make notes in the name of the firm, without the knowledge or assent of his copartners. Per Colden, *Senator*.

So for partners to make a firm note payable to, or to draw a bill on, one of the partners; and it seems not to have been questioned, that an indorsee may recover upon these, unless they originated in a matter not concerning the partnership; and that known to the indorsee at the time of the indorsement. Per Colden, *Senator*.

If payment of a firm note be resisted, as being in fraud of the partnership with the knowledge of the holder, the defendant, or defendants, must plead and prove these facts. Per Colden, *Senator*.

A man cannot be bound to himself; and it seems that a bond, &c., by three persons to one of the three, could not be enforced at law. Per Colden, *Senator*.

In general, one man cannot bind another without his consent. Per Colden, *Senator*.

689*] *The power of one partner, to bind another without his knowledge or consent, results from the nature of a partnership, and from the law merchant. Per Colden, *Senator*.

Whether a note made by one partner in the name of the firm, for a debt of the firm, could be impeached on the ground that it was made against the will of the other partners, and that known to the indorsee, *quære*. Per Colden, *Senator*.

A *bona fide* note, made by a partnership, payable to one of the firm, though it cannot, in the hands and name of the payee, be enforced at law, yet he may have relief in equity. Agreed, Per Sanford, *Chancellor*, and Colden, *Senator*.

For a partnership may be indebted to one of the firm, and bind themselves, by note, to him. How this may be. Per Colden, *Senator*.

Various cases of commercial paper, which, though it cannot be enforced at law between the original parties, yet may be after being negotiated. Per Colden, *Senator*.

Citation—1 R. L., 151.

ON ERROR from the Supreme Court. The action in the court below was *assumpsit* by the defendants in error, against the plaintiffs in error, as makers of a promissory note. The declaration was of August Term, 1820, against P. Smith and Soulden, being in custody, &c., and Van Santvoord, P. Sken. Smith and the Turcks, returned by the sheriff not found; and the first count was, for that whereas, the defendants below, being merchants and copartners in trade and merchandise, and the business of merchants and traders exercising and carrying on, under the name, style and firm of William Soulden & Co. at, &c., Mar. 15, 1816, under their name, style, firm and description of William Soulden & Co., made a certain note, &c., bearing date that day; and then and there delivered it to Abraham Van Santvoord, by which the defendants promised to pay him or order, $5,000, with interest, six months after date. And Abraham Van Santvoord, before payment, or the day fixed for the payment, to wit: on the day of the date, indorsed the note to the plaintiffs; and thereby ordered and appointed the contents of the note to be paid to the plaintiffs, or order, &c.; of which indorsement the defendants, on the same day of the date, had notice, &c. This was followed by the usual money counts, a count for goods sold, &c., and the count on an *insimul computassent*.

P. Smith and Soulden imparled from term to term till October Term, 1821, when P. Smith pleaded several pleas. *The first and [*690 second pleas were to the count on the note. The third plea was the general issue to the other counts, except as to so much of them as the plaintiffs claimed to apply to the note; and as to this, special matter.

The fourth plea was as follows: As to the promise mentioned in the plaintiffs' declaration, and supposed to have been made for goods, wares and merchandise, alleged to have been sold and delivered by the plaintiffs to the defendants, that he did not, with Van Santvoord, &c., undertake and promise in manner and form, &c.; concluding to the country.

"And as to all the other several supposed promises and undertakings, in the plaintiffs' declaration mentioned, &c., that they are for one and the same cause of action, which is set out in the first count of the plaintiffs' declaration, and not for different and distinct causes of action. And as to all such other supposed promises and undertakings, &c., that the said Abraham Van Santvoord, named as payee in the said note mentioned in the plaintiffs' declaration, is the same Abraham Van Santvoord, who is one of the defendants in this cause, and was a partner in the said firm of William Soulden & Co. at the time the said note is alleged to have been made; and that the said note was made by the said William Soulden, in the name of the said firm, to the said Abraham Van Santvoord, without the knowledge or consent of the said Peter Smith, for an account then alleged by the said Abraham Van Santvoord to be due from the firm to him. That the plaintiffs, at the time the said note was indorsed to them by the said Abraham Van Santvoord, had notice that the said note was made by the said William Soulden, in the name of the said firm, payable to the said Abraham Van Santvoord, a partner in the said firm; and for what consideration the said note was made. And this," &c.

In reply to this last plea, as to all except the first count of their declaration, the plaintiffs entered a *nolle prosequi;* and for replication, so far as it related to the first count, said, "that although true it is, that the said note was made by the said William Soulden, in the name of the said firm of William Soulden & Co.; and 691*]that the said Abraham Van *Santvoord, named as payee in the said note mentioned in the plaintiffs' declaration, is the same Abraham Van Santvoord who is one of the defendants in this cause, and was a partner in the said firm of William Soulden & Co. at the time the said note was made; yet, &c., that, at the time the said note was indorsed, &c., as in the declaration is alleged, they had not notice that the said note was made by the said William Soulden, to the said Abraham Van Santvoord, without the knowledge or consent of the said Peter Smith, for an account then alleged by the said Abraham Van Santvoord to be due from the said firm to him; and for what consideration the said note was made; and this," &c., concluding to the country.

Special demurrer, assigning for cause, that the replication concluded to the country; whereas it should have concluded with a verification; inasmuch as the plea averred, "that the said note was made by the said William Soulden, in the name of the said firm, to the said Abraham Van Santvoord, without the knowledge or consent of the said Peter Smith:" and the plaintiffs, in their replication, instead of taking issue on that fact, said, by way of avoidance, that, at the time the note was indorsed, &c., they had not notice that it was made by Soulden to Van Santvoord, without the knowledge or consent of the said Peter Smith; also, that the replication was informal and uncertain in this: the plea averred that the plaintiffs at the time, &c., had notice that the note was made by Soulden, in the name of the firm, payable to Van Santvoord, a partner in the firm; and the plaintiffs, instead of admitting or denying such notice, say, that at the time, &c., they had not notice that the note was made by Soulden to Van Santvoord, without the knowledge or consent of Peter Smith, for an account then alleged by Van Santvoord to be due from the firm to him; thus seeking to put in issue matter not expressly alleged in the plea; and leaving it uncertain and doubtful, whether the plaintiffs intended, by the replication, to admit or deny the notice averred in the plea, &c.

Joinder in demurrer.

692*] *Soulden appeared and confessed the action; and the cause was continued upon the demurrer by *curia advisare vult,* to August Term, 1824, when the Supreme Court gave judgment for the plaintiffs. The cause was then continued by *vice, comes non misit breve,* to February Term, 1825, when final judgment was rendered for the plaintiffs; whereupon the defendant below brought error to this court.

The reasons for the judgment on the demurrer were assigned by that court as follows:

The plea consists of two parts:

First. That Abraham Van Santvoord, named as payee in the note, is the same Abraham Van Santvoord who is one of the defendants, and was a partner in the firm when the note was made; and that the note was made by Soulden, in the name of the firm, without the knowledge or consent of Smith, for an account alleged to be due from the firm to Van Santvoord.

Second. That the plaintiffs, at the time the note was indorsed to them by Van Santvoord, had notice that the note was made by Soulden in the name of the firm, payable to Van Santvoord, a partner in the firm, and for what consideration.

There is no averment in the plea that the plaintiffs had notice that the note was made without the knowledge of Smith. The fact of its having been so made, is averred in the first part of the plea. But the notice which the plaintiffs are alleged to have had in the second part of the plea, is merely that Soulden made the note in the name of the firm, payable to Van Santvoord, a partner in the firm.

The fact, therefore, alleged in the replication, that the plaintiffs had not notice that the note was made without the knowledge of Smith, &c., is no answer to the averment in the plea; but is new matter, set up by way of avoidance: and it is an invariable rule in pleading, that whenever new matter is introduced, the pleadings must conclude with a verification, in order to give the opposite party an opportunity of answering it. (1 Chit. 5, 38; Com. Dig., Pl., E, 33; 1 Saund., 103, *note,* and cases there cited.) The replication takes issue upon a fact not previously averred. The special causes of demurrer, therefore, are well taken.

*But the material inquiry is whether [*693 the replication be good in substance—as leave will, of course, be granted to the plaintiffs, to amend it in point of form; and whether it be good or not, depends upon the fact, whether the matters set forth in the plea amount to a good bar of the plaintiffs' action. If they do, the plaintiffs, by not answering, have admitted them; for whatever is material, and is not traversed, is, in effect, admitted. (1 Chit. Pl., 591.)

The point presented by the plea is this—whether a promissory note, made by one of six members of a firm to another member, in the partnership name, without the knowledge or consent of the other members of the firm, though for a debt due from the firm to the payee of the note, is valid and effectual in the hands of an indorsee, with notice that it was made by one of several partners to another, for a partnership debt due to him, but without notice that it was made without the knowledge or consent of the other partners.

We perceive no legal objection to one of several partners becoming the creditor of the firm, and taking a promissory note in the name of the firm as evidence of his debt. It is true he cannot maintain an action at law upon the note; because, being one of the makers, he cannot sue himself. *Mainwaring* v. *Newman,* 2 Bos. & P., 124; and *Moffat* v. *Van Millingen,* cited in note to last case. But that circumstance will not prevent the instrument from being valid as a promissory note, in the hands of an indorsee. It is an absolute promise on the part of A, B and C to pay to A, or order, a certain sum of money. A, B and C are not the same persons with A. It is, therefore, a promise from one person to pay to another. The payment is not to be made out of a particular fund, nor does it depend upon any contingency.

A bill of exchange is defined to be an open letter of request from one person to another, desiring him to pay a sum named therein to a third person on his account. (2 Bl. Com., 466;

Chit. Bills, 1.) But who ever doubted the validity of a bill, because it was drawn by one member of a firm upon the partnership, or by the firm upon an individual member?

694*] *It is conceded, that if this had been an accommodation note, made for the purpose of raising money for the benefit of the firm, it would have been valid in the hands of an indorsee as a promissory note. But we apprehend the object with which an instrument is made, can have no influence in determining whether it be a promissory note, or not, within the statute. That must depend upon the face of the instrument itself. Whether it can be enforced, as between the parties litigant, admitting it to be a note within the statute, is a distinct question.

It is admitted, by the pleadings, that the note was given for a partnership debt due to Abraham Van Santvoord, and not for the individual debt of Soulden, who drew the note. Now, each partner has an implied authority to give the partnership security for the debt of the firm; and we have not felt the force of the considerations which were urged by the defendant's counsel, to show that debts due to the individual members of the firm were excepted from the operation of this general authority.

It is said, that although, as between a creditor and the firm, all the parties are liable for the whole debt, yet, as between themselves, each is answerable only for his respective share; so that one partner can have no right against his copartner, in capacity of partner, but to what is due to him out of the joint stock, after making all just allowances; 1 East, 30; Watson Part., 18, 34; that Peter Smith, therefore, is liable only for one sixth of the original debt for which this note was given; whereas, it is now sought to charge him with the whole.

It will at once be perceived, that this doctrine has no application to a case where the partnership funds are sufficient to pay all the debts of the firm. It can only apply, where, in consequence of a deficiency in the partnership property, an individual partner has been compelled to pay a debt of the firm, and calls on his associates for contribution. Then each is responsible only for his individual share. Now, in this case, as in every other, we are to intend that there was sufficient partnership property to pay all the debts, unless the contrary be shown; and there is no averment that there was any deficiency.

695*] *This, then, being a debt due from the firm, for which each partner had an implied authority to give the partnership paper, the averment in the plea, that the note was given without the knowledge or consent of Peter Smith, is immaterial. If it had been the individual debt of William Soulden, then the transaction, not being within the partnership business, it would have been incumbent on the plaintiffs, before they could have recovered, to show the individual consent of each partner to the giving of the note. This doctrine is perfectly settled in this court. *Dob* v. *Halsey*, 16 Johns., 38; *Foot* v. *Sabin*, 19 Johns., 157. But in a transaction within the scope of the partnership, the acts of each partner are legally binding on the whole, though done without their knowledge and consent.

Suppose one of six partners should object to the giving of the partnership paper, for a preexisting debt of the firm, for which they were unquestionably liable—and at the time of giving it, should give notice to the creditor that it was against his consent—would that invalidate the security? Or, in an action against the firm, upon the note, would it afford any defense to the dissenting partner if he set it forth by way of plea? The conclusive answer is, "your individual consent was not necessary to the validity of the instrument, but only the assent of the firm." And the averment in the plea is perfectly consistent with the allegation in the declaration, that the defendants, in their partnership character, made the note in question.

A plea like this, in an action against a *sole* defendant, might amount to the general issue; and, in such a case, the doctrine of the defendant's counsel, in relation to express and implied contracts, might have some application. (Lawes, 87.)

We are, on the whole, of opinion that the plea is bad; and that the plaintiffs are entitled to judgment upon the demurrer.

Mr. D. Cady, for the plaintiffs in error. The replication is bad both in form and substance. This was conceded by the court below. But we contend that they erred in overruling the plea.

*The averment that the note was **[*696** made without the knowledge or consent of Peter Smith, was material, and negated both implied and express consent; and the defendants in error were bound, either to have taken issue upon it, or to have demurred specially, on the ground that it amounted to the general issue. That averment being admitted, in its broadest sense, shows the declaration to be bad. The defendants in error cannot now be permitted to urge that the note was made with the implied consent of Peter Smith. A man cannot be bound without his consent. Saying such a thing was done without consent, in fair construction, negatives consent either express or implied. Can the law imply a promise where it cannot imply consent? On the general issue, there is no doubt that consent, either express or implied, must have been proved. One or the other enter into the essence of every contract. Pow. Cont., 9; Com. Cont., 3; *Fenn* v. *Harrison*, 3 T. R., 757; *Sheriff* v. *Wilkes*, 1 East, 48; 2 Mont. Part., 145. A partner is but the agent of his firm. Suppose the master of a ship to contract for his owner, as in *King* v. *Lenox*, 19 Johns., 236, or a merchant's clerk for his principal, or a wife for her husband; and suppose, in each case, a note be given in the name of the principal; is there a doubt that, on the general issue, an express or implied authority must be shown? The Supreme Court have decided that a partner is bound, notwithstanding his express dissent. Suppose, to an action on a note given by the wife in the name of the husband, he should plead that he never consented, and the plaintiff should admit this in his replication, can it be pretended that the action would lie?

One partner has no authority to make a promissory note in the name of the firm, to one of the partners, without the express consent of all the partners; and the note is, therefore, fraudulent and void against all the partners who did not consent to its being made. There is a great difference between a debt due to a third person, and one due from the firm to an individual member of it. The former is one for which they are all jointly liable. The creditor must sue them jointly; and he may then take their **697***] joint or separate *property or persons. No case can be found, where a partner was held able to bind the firm by a note, from the firm to himself, or another member of the firm. The claim in *Foot* v. *Sabin*, cited by the Supreme Court, was due to a third person; and such was also *Sheriff* v. *Wilkes*, 1 East, 48. All the members of a firm cannot be jointly indebted to one. (1 East, 20.) The law presumes that each put into the partnership stock equal sums, to be managed for the mutual benefit of all the partners, and to be divided equally. (Law of Part., 34.) Here the partnership is admitted in general terms. The balance is the partnership fund. As between the partners, nothing can be claimed except the balance, after making all just allowances. (Watson Law Part., 18; 1 East 20; Cowp., 445, 449.) There is no personal claim by one member of the firm against the others, except for misconduct, waste or squandering the partnership effects; and this, only after a balance struck, or an adjustment by a court of equity. No action at law will lie till a balance struck. (12 Johns., 401, 402; 14 *Id.*, 318, 322; 4 Dall, 434, 435; 13 East, 7; 1 Mont. Part., 63.) Can a member of the firm, by this indirect proceeding, take the remedy into his own hands? Can he thus superadd the personal responsibility of the partners? The partners cannot be deprived of the ordinary remedy between themselves, without their consent. (4 Dall., 435.) A partner never acts by the authority of his firm, except when he acts with third persons; and, in that case, the express dissent of one partner, and notice to the creditor, will take away the binding effect of a note given by the other even for a previous partnership debt. *Ld. Viscount Galloway* v. *Mathew*, 10 East, 264. Nor is the firm liable, if, in fact, the note was given for an individual debt. *Dob* v. *Halsey*, 16 Johns., 34, 38; *Livingston* v. *Hastie*, 2 Cai., 246, 249; *Lansing* v. *Gaine*, 2 Johns., 300; *Livingston* v. *Roosevelt*, 4 *Id.*, 251; *Sheriff* v. *Wilkes*, 1 East, 48. These cases all go on the ground that you cannot, without consent, express or implied, subject those members of the firm, who are, in fact, strangers to the transaction, and not in duty bound to pay **698***] the debt created. *If a sufficiency of funds was in question, it lay with the plaintiffs below to aver and prove this. But, in truth, it makes no difference whether the firm have funds or not. If there be sufficient, it is the best of all possible reasons why their persons should not be bound; but the fund alone, looked to. In *Mainwaring* v. *Newman*, 2 Bos. & P., 120, and see the notes to that case, *Id.*, 124, great doubts were entertained whether the note was good. But admitting that case to be law, we do not see the bearing of it. The question was not one of consent. A man cannot, with others, promise to himself at all, so as to bind him in law; but he must go into equity for his remedy. *Bosanquet* v. *Wray*, 6 Taunt., 597, 605. It should be borne in mind that this is not the case of a bill of exchange, drawn by the firm on one of the partners, or *é converso*, in favor of a third person. But even then, the claim would not be bettered if the third person had knowledge of the facts. Here, the plaintiffs below must have recovered upon this paper, technically, as a promissory note, or not at all.

The facts in the plea, showing that the note was fraudulently made and put in circulation, the plaintiffs below should have averred that it was indorsed to them for a valuable consideration. (10 Johns., 231; 1 Camph., 100; 2 *Id.*, 574.)

The defendants in error took the note, subject to every objection which the partners who did not consent to its being made might have urged against it in a court of equity, while it remained in the hands of the payee. They knew the parties and knew the firm, and were bound to know all the peculiar circumstances and, therefore, acted against good faith. They cannot allege ignorance of the law, that Soulden could not make the note. Whatever Van Santvoord must have shown in a suit by him, the indorsees were bound to show. (12 Johns., 161; 4 Dall., 370.) To bind Smith, either at law or in equity, he must have been shown to have consented.

The plea does not admit, as supposed by the Supreme Court, that the firm owed Van Santvoord. The language is, that the note was given for a debt alleged by himself to be due to him. He might admit a debt due from the firm to *third persons (1 Phil. Ev., 73, and [***699** the cases there cited), but not to himself.

The note was not originally a note within the statute; nor could it be made so by any subsequent event, nor be declared on as such. If it be considered as a note made by the partnership, payable to one of the partners, it was, according to its legal effect, payable out of the partnership funds; and if so, in the hands of the payee it did not cease to be so payable, by being indorsed to the defendants in error. (Willes, 393, 399; 12 Johns., 159.) The character of this paper must be looked to, while it was in the hands of Van Santvoord. It was a nullity when there.

[COLDEN, *Senator*. What would you do with a note or bill drawn by yourself and payable to yourself?]

It would be waste paper.

[COLDEN, *Senator*. But you pass it away.]

Still it could not be declared on as a note payable to me. It must be brought forward in some other character. Here the note is, not only in fact payable by one to himself, but it is declared on as such by the plaintiffs. The declaration is *felo de se*.

Mr. J. V. Henry, for the defendants in error. This case has been reviewed wrongly by the gentleman from the outset. He has treated it both in the court below, and now again in this court, as a question between partners. This is the grand mistake. It is not so. Is it to be endured that a bill drawn by a partner on his firm, or *e converso*, and indorsed by the payee, shall be void, because on or by a house of which the drawer or acceptor is a member? Or, as seemed to be insisted by the gentleman, in reply to the inquiry of an honorable member of the court, that a note made by a firm payable to itself, or the order of itself, and indorsed by the firm, would be a nullity? The whole of the argument against us is founded on this fallacy. If consent is necessary, what becomes of a partnership where many members of the firm reside at such distances as to preclude the inference, **700***] that *consent is in fact given? They are bound, though entirely ignorant of the contract.

I shall not attempt to vindicate the replication against the special demurrer. I grant that, having replied new matter, we should not have concluded to the country. We object to the plea. We come as *bona fide* indorsees, in the fair course of trade. Being so, can Peter Smith defend on the ground that there was, in him, a want of knowledge or consent?

If the firm did not owe Van Santvoord, Smith should have said so in his plea. The indebtedness not being denied, shall be intended in support of the note, and constitutes a valid consideration. Suppose Van Santvoord had loaned $5,000 to the firm; is it to be doubted that the sum might have been secured in the form now in question? A debt from the firm to the individual member, would be created by the loan; and being created, could not the same member who negotiated the loan, furnish evidence of the debt? And could not a note, given in security, be transferred for a valuable consideration? In such a case, the note is signed without, but not against, the consent or will of the other partners. Nothing is said, that the firm were, in this case, unable to pay. So much, supposing we took with full notice of everything.

But as the case stands, if there was not a cent due, the firm are holden, because we took the note in good faith. The sum was alleged to be due; and we believed and trusted to the allegation. Such is the substantial language of the plea. Can this be made to mean, as now contended, that in truth no debt whatever was due? The plea does not pretend that we had notice of the alleged want of knowledge or consent.

The power of one partner to contract and give notes for firm debts, without the consent of the other members of the firm, is well settled by authority. Bac. Abr., Merchant and Merchandise, C; *Livingston* v. *Hastie*, 2 Cai., 246; *Lansing* v. *Gaine*, 2 Johns., 300; *Swan* v. *Steele*, 7 East, 210; Chit. Bills, 5th ed., 39, and the cases there cited, particularly in *note c;* **701***] *Livingston* v. **Roosevelt*, 4 Johns., 251, 269. In this last case, at page 265, Van Ness, *J.*, admits the general rule, in terms, as we have presented it upon these pleadings. He says that the rule applicable both to general and special partners is, that in transactions relating to the joint concern, one of several partners may bind the rest; that he may sign notes, indorse, or accept bills for the common benefit, &c., without applying to the rest in every particular case. In the same case (p. 270) Spencer, *J.*, recognizes the case of *Swan* v. *Steele*, 7 East, 210, as sound law.

The breach of confidence among partners cannot affect third persons. The power of one takes in and binds the whole firm, and every individual member of it, to the same extent as himself. (Chit. Bills, 5th ed., 39–41, and the cases there cited, particularly in *note e.*) *Lane* v. *Williams*, 2 Vern., 277, is a very strong case to this point. The partner was there holden bound in equity by a note of his copartner, for money which was never applied to the common business.

The note in question was originally good within the Statute of Anne, 1 R. L., 151. It was not payable out of a particular fund; and especially, after it was indorsed, it became a perfect note within the statute, being the same in both form and effect as an inland bill of exchange. Chit. Bills, 421, 5th ed., and the cases there cited; *Heylin* v. *Adamson*, 2 Burr., 669, 676; *Brown* v. *Harraden*, 4 T. R., 148. It may, therefore, be treated as a valid promissory note in every shape. Even if it took its existence as a promissory note only after indorsement, it may be called by that name throughout, upon the doctrine of relation. A note payable to a man's own order is good. A promise by a partnership to pay one of the firm, is like a promise in a corporate capacity to pay an individual member of the corporation. *Ridley* v. *Taylor*, 13 East, 175, is a complete illustration of this position. (Chit. Bills, 5th ed., 44, *note c*, S. C.) This, it is true, was the case of a bill; but we have seen that a note has the same effect, under the Statute of Anne. The doubt expressed by Ld. Eldon, in *Mainwaring* v. *Newman*, 2 Bos. & P., 120, went on the effect of a dissolution *before the [***702** note was negotiated (*Id.*, 125); and the *notes* to that case, p. 124, go no farther.

We have seen that if this note were an inland bill of exchange, we might clearly have recovered upon it. (Chit. Bills, 5th ed., 44.) We have also seen, that it is so in effect. It is now said, however, that we cannot go upon it as such, because we have miscalled it a promissory note. But this makes no difference. If our declaration makes out a title, and shows the essentials of a bill of exchange, this is enough. It is substantially a declaration on an inland bill.

It is not necessary to make out a *bona fide* indorsement and holding, that we should aver value received. This averment is unusual and, indeed, inapplicable to indorsements; and the omission was never holden to discredit a note in the hands of an indorsee. (Chit. Bills, 5th ed., 461, and the cases there cited.) The defendants below must, by pleading or proof, have cast suspicion upon the fairness of the transaction, before the plaintiffs could be called on to show a consideration paid. (*Id.*, 511, and the cases there cited.) And with this doctrine agree the cases cited to this point on the other side. *Brown* v. *Mott*, 7 Johns., 361; *Paterson* v. *Hardacre*, 4 Taunt., 114, S. P.

A bill is never taken by a third person, on the credit of the partnership fund merely, but of the individuals also; and if otherwise, it is no objection to the note being within the statute. No matter if the fund was looked to as the sole source of payment, so long as this does not appear on the face of the note.

No equity is shown which could defeat the note, even on a bill filed, between the original parties. The equitable rule contended for, even if applicable, fails here, because it is not sustained by the facts. But to the great number of cases cited on the other side, the general answer with which I set out will apply; that they, almost without exception, relate to the question between the partners themselves, and not to third persons.

Mr. Cady, in reply. This case presents a new and important question—one never before pre-

703*] sented in a court of justice. *Not one case has, or can be produced, where an assignee was ever allowed to recover, on a contract void from the beginning. *Livingston* v. *Roosevelt*, 4 Johns., 251, was the case of an action by an indorsee against indorsers, who are liable even though the note be a forgery. The question related merely to the validity of the indorsement, and this was holden void, because the partner had no authority to indorse for his individual debt; and so far supports the doctrine for which we contend here—that the debt should have been due from all the partners. *Mainwaring* v. *Newman*, 2 Bos. & P., 120, 124, cited by the Supreme Court, will be found to be a two-edged sword. Why was not Brander sued there alone as maker, if one partner can give a note from himself to the firm? This not being done, am I not justified in saying that it was not believed to be a valid note, as between the maker and payees. Not a single case can be produced, of an action by a payee, who was one of the firm that made the note. All the cases are of indorsers, whose liability depends on a distinct principle. Indorsement creates a new contract. It assigns all the interest of the indorser, and superadds an agreement to pay in default of the maker. Had Van Santvoord any legal rights? None. He could, therefore, transfer none. If he had been sued as indorser, then the case, I admit, would have been parallel with Roosevelt's; not otherwise. A man may be drawer, payee and acceptor, it is true, in form; but no action can lie in this shape. The paper is good for nothing till indorsed, and then you cannot treat or declare on the bill as valid in its original shape; but you must go against the party as indorser. He is liable independent of the original goodness of the paper, and his responsibility alone is to be looked to. As indorser, he is liable though the note be void. (Chit. Bills, 156; 3 Day Cas., 12; 2 Camph., 182; Doug., 633, 634.)

This declaration cannot be so modified as to meet a bill of exchange. If it were a bill, drawn by Van Santvoord, the payee, he and his firm would have been acceptors, and must have been declared against as such; not as makers of a promissory note. The plaintiffs below could not declare in that form, and now be allowed to amend their declaration, and fit 704*] *it to a bill of exchange. The note may have been good against Soulden, and as between him and Van Santvoord; but not beyond these. If it created but an equity against the firm, then the indorsees are the mere assignees of an equity.

The plea clearly amounts to the general issue; and by admitting its truth, the plaintiffs below admitted away their cause of action. Averring that the note was made without the knowledge or consent of Smith, is equivalent precisely to a denial of the promise alleged. If a man acts by my authority, it is by my consent; hence, by denying consent, we deny all authority. This fact is granted by the replication, which does not insist upon consent or knowledge.

The defendants in error are not *bona fide* assignees. They knew for what the note was given. They knew it was made by Soulden to Van Santvoord. They were fairly put on inquiry, and were bound to ascertain all the circumstances. (Doug., 654; 12 Johns., 343; 3 Dall., 384; 4 *Id.*, 370, 371.)

I deny that a partner can make a loan of $5,000 to the firm, and afterwards pledge their responsibility, or alter the implied, to an express contract, by giving a note or drawing a bill. He must rely on the funds of the concern, and cannot go to their persons. The contrary argument is saying to every man, "If you have a debt due to you from another, do not hesitate to make a note to yourself."

Lawes' Plead., 87, cited by the Supreme Court, does not apply, unless, as they seem to suppose, there is a distinction between the one partner and his firm, and the consent of all is not necessary to bind them. The court wrongly suppose that the consent may exist as to the firm, without the consent of each member of the firm. In *Dob* v. *Halsey*, 16 Johns., 34, which they also cite, the difference will be found between the law, as settled upon this head by the K. B., and the Supreme Court of this State. Here, when a creditor sues a firm upon a note or bill, the *onus* of showing the consent lies with him; in England, it will be presumed, till the firm show the contrary. In this State the authority of one to bind the other members of a firm must be proved in the first instance by the one who *seeks [*705 to charge them; in England they stand charged till they have disproved the authority. The English rule is an anomaly in their law of evidence.

I admit this case would have presented a different aspect if the paper had come to the hands of a *bona fide* holder for valuable consideration. In *Swan* v. *Steele*, 7 East, 210, cited by the counsel for the defendants in error, the holders were ignorant of the circumstances under which the note was given.

THE CHANCELLOR. Many parts of this record are not here in question; and the cause is now to be determined upon those pleadings of the parties, which terminated in a demurrer. In considering the questions before the court, I shall apply the terms, plaintiffs and defendants, to the parties as they stood before the Supreme Court.

The declaration alleges that the defendants were partners in trade, under the firm of William Soulden & Co.; that, as partners, they made a promissory note payable to Abraham Van Santvoord; and that Van Santvoord indorsed the note to the plaintiffs.

The special plea of the defendant Peter Smith, which is now in question, avers that Van Santvoord, to whom the note was made payable, and who is one of the defendants, was a partner of the firm of William Soulden & Co. when the note was made: that the note was made by William Soulden, in the name of the firm, to Van Santvoord without the knowledge or consent of Peter Smith, for an account alleged by Van Santvoord to be due from the firm to him; and that the plaintiffs, when the note was indorsed to them by Van Santvoord, had notice that the note was made by Soulden, in the name of the firm, payable to Van Santvoord, one of the partners, and for what consideration the note was made.

Is this plea a sufficient answer to the declaration?

The declaration states the partnership of the defendants in the usual form; the plea admits that they were partners, and upon these allegations it must be understood that the defendants were general partners in trade. I 706*] use the expression *general partners to convey the idea of an ordinary mercantile partnership, in distinction from special cases of limited partnership.

The plea states that the note was given for an account alleged by Van Santvoord to be due to him from the firm. An indefinite phrase is here presented, by the terms, an account alleged to be due from the firm; but this is the statement of the defendant, and he does not controvert the allegation which he thus states to have been made by Van Santvoord. The most obvious sense of this part of the plea is, that the partners of Van Santvoord were indebted to him, and that Soulden gave the note in question for that debt; and so the plea must be understood.

The origin and nature of this debt, from the partners of Van Santvoord to him, do not appear. As nothing peculiar concerning this debt is stated, it must be understood to have been a just debt to Van Santvoord from his five partners, which they were bound to pay, and for which they were fully and personally responsible. Van Santvoord might, then, have recovered this debt by a suit; he might have assigned it to another person; and any one of the debtors, acting for himself and his indebted partners, might have paid it, on behalf of all the debtors.

For this debt, Soulden, one of the partners, made this promissory note, in the name of the firm, to Van Santvoord. I do not perceive that this transaction was either a fraud or illegal in itself. No fictitious or new debt was created by Soulden; but for an existing debt he gave the promissory note of the partnership. Van Santvoord could not, indeed, be both debtor and creditor in the same transaction; and as he could not maintain a suit against himself, it is urged that this note was totally void. But why should this consequence follow? If the note did not bind Van Santvoord, why should it not bind the other partners? If Van Santvoord could not maintain a suit against himself, how does that principle produce a penal consequence that he loses his rights or remedies against others? If the note was void against Van Santvoord, it was so merely by force of the principle that he could not be bound as a debtor where he 707*] *was the creditor; but this principle has no application to the other partners. As this objection to the note relates to Van Santvoord alone, it is reasonable that the effect of the objection should be confined to him; and that, though the note may be void or ineffectual against Van Santvoord, it is not void against the other partners. To consider the note as wholly void, merely because Van Santvoord could have no remedy against himself, would defeat the intention of the Act and the justice of the case, when such a decision is not required by any principle of law. To consider the note as binding all the partners excepting Van Santvoord is to pursue the truth and justice of the transaction, and to charge the real debtors with their debt to the real creditor. This transaction, as it is stated, was free from all fraud; and the fact that Van Santvoord was one of the partners whose firm was used in giving the note, does not, in my opinion, invalidate the note against the other partners.

The plea states that when Van Santvoord indorsed the note to the plaintiffs, they had notice that the note was made by Soulden in the name of the firm, payable to Van Santvoord, one of the partners, and of the consideration for which the note was made. As the facts of which the plaintiffs thus had notice did not invalidate the note against Van Santvoord's partners, the knowledge of those facts cannot affect the claim of the plaintiffs against Peter Smith.

The plea of Peter Smith avers that this note was made in the name of the firm without his knowledge or consent. Peter Smith might be bound without his knowledge of the making of the note, and without his consent to the act. He was one of six partners; each of them had power to act for all the partners; and each partner might bind all, without the knowledge or consent of his associates. This averment is not a denial of the partnership of the defendants, or of the authority of Soulden to act as one of the partners. The sense of the averment is that Peter Smith was ignorant of the making of the note, and that he gave no consent to that act. But this general partnership was then in full force; and Soulden, the partner who made the note, had power to bind Peter Smith without his knowledge and without his *consent to the particular [*708 act. This averment, therefore, presents an immaterial fact.

If the execution of this note had been a fraud between Soulden and Van Santvoord, or if the justice of this claim depended upon an adjustment of accounts between the partners or against them, a legal or equitable defense would arise from such facts. But no such fact is alleged. This plea advances no matter of equitable defense against this action; and the matters alleged in the plea, whether considered separately or taken collectively, afford, in my opinion, no legal defense to the cause of action stated in the declaration. It is, therefore, unnecessary to examine the replication, which was the immediate subject of the demurrer. The plea being insufficient in substance, the plaintiffs are entitled to judgment on the demurrer; and so the Supreme Court have decided.

COLDEN, *Senator*. The demurrer of the defendant below refers us to his plea, and we are to determine whether that be a sufficient bar to the action.

From the declaration and plea, we may assume the following facts: the defendants in error are *bona fide* indorsees of a promissory note, made by one of several copartners under their mercantile firm, without the consent and knowledge of Peter Smith, the plaintiff in error, who was one of the partners, payable to one of the firm or to his order. It is not alleged that the note was not given for a matter which concerned the partnership.

It was indorsed by the payee to the holders before it became due.

The plaintiff in error, Peter Smith, contends

that, under these circumstances, the indorsees ought not to recover on the note.

If he be right, mercantile operations have been conducted under wrong notions a great length of time; and if we reverse the judgment on the principles which the plaintiff in error has attempted to maintain, we shall affect and render nugatory a very large portion of the **709*]** mercantile securities *which are now afloat. For it long has been, and now is, the constant practice for one of a copartnership to draw a bill or make a note in the name of a firm, without the consent or knowledge of one or more of the partners. It often happens that the business of a mercantile concern is conducted by one partner while his copartners are in different quarters of the world, and could have no knowledge of the transaction. It is, also, every day's practice for partners to make a note under their firm, payable to, or to draw a bill on one of the copartners; and I believe it has never heretofore been questioned but that a *bona fide* indorsee might recover against all the copartners on such a bill or note, unless it were given for a matter which did not concern the partnership, and that fact was known to the holder at the time of the indorsement.

Where the payment of a bill or note, made in the name of a partnership, is resisted on the ground that it was given in fraud of the partnership, with the knowledge of the holder, it is incumbent on the defendant to plead and prove these facts. There being no averments to this effect in the plea under consideration, we are to presume, as the indorsees had a right to presume, that the note was given for a matter which concerned the partnership.

It appears to me that in the argument of this case there has been a mistake, in not distinguishing between simple contracts made by a partnership, and other contracts and obligations purporting to be made by several persons.

It is certainly true, as has been insisted, that a man cannot be bound to himself. If three persons were to enter into a bond or covenant to pay to one of the three, I presume no action at law could be maintained on such a specialty. And it is, no doubt, generally true that one person cannot bind another without his consent; but this general rule does not apply to mercantile concerns.

Promissory notes are on a different footing from other contracts. They are made negotiable by, and when negotiated, derive their force and effect from statute. The question then is, whether in virtue of the Act concerning **710*]** Promissory *Notes, 1 R. L., 151, and the law merchant, the defendants in error are not entitled to recover as indorsees of the note described, in the declaration, notwithstanding anything alleged in the plea.

First, as to the power which the other partners had to make the note, without the knowledge or consent of Peter Smith.

When Peter Smith entered into partnership he gave each of his copartners power to bind him by any promise or agreement which related to the partnership concerns. I do not mean to say that the power of partners does not extend further, and that all the members of a firm may not be bound by a bill or note given by one partner, in the name of all, although it may not have been for a debt of the firm, if an indorsee takes such a note without knowing for what consideration it was made. But it is unnecessary to give any opinion on this point at present.

If it be asked from whence partners derive their power to bind each other, the answer is, it results from the nature of partnerships and from the law merchant applicable to them. It is no defense for one of the several partners to say he did not assent to the contract, or that it was made without his knowledge. If he expressly dissented, it certainly would not avail, if the party claiming the benefit of the contract did not know that he had dissented. And if the transaction was *bona fide*, and concerned matters which were within the scope, and accustomed dealings of the partnership, I doubt whether a plea by one partner, that the indorsee knew when he took a note that it was given against the will of one of the partners, would be a bar to an action on the note.

It seems to me, therefore, that it cannot be questioned but that Peter Smith's partners and each of them, had power to bind him by the note in question, although he never assented to the note's being made, and though it was given without his knowledge. So that if the note had been payable to any other person than to one of the firm, undoubtedly, it would have bound all the partners.

But it was payable to Van Santvoord, one of the firm; and the remaining question is, whether that circumstance should pre- **[*711** vent the defendants in error, who are his indorsees, from recovering.

If the note had remained in the hands of Van Santvoord, he could not have sustained any suit upon it. For either he must have sued all the partners, and then it would have been a suit by a man against himself, or he must have sued his copartners only, and then the note would not have supported his declaration, in which he must have averred that the defendants promised; whereas, the note would show that the promise was by all the partners. These would be technical objections, which would be fatal in a suit at common law in the name of the payee. Yet there can be no doubt that a partner might have relief in a court of chancery on a note given to him by his copartners. For certainly a partnership may become indebted to one of the firm; as if there should be a copartnership for manufacturing and vending linens, and one of the partners should be a farmer. The partnership might well become indebted to him for the raw material, and might bind the firm by a note given for the article furnished. Though the farmer might not be able to maintain his suit at law, he could recover in a court of equity. Such a note in the hands of one of a firm the world has a right to regard as an evidence of a debt due from the firm to the partner, to whom it is given. The indorsee is, therefore, justifiable in taking the note, although he may know and see upon its face that his indorser is one of the firm; and when the indorsee brings the action, there are no technical obstacles to his recovery. The suit is not, then, by a person against himself; and his demand is pursuant to the contract by which all who compose the firm are bound, and against these his action is brought.

That because a suit at common law cannot

be supported against the makers of a note, previously to its being negotiated; therefore, no suit can be maintained by the *bona fide* holder, after it is indorsed, is a proposition that cannot be sustained. Nothing is more common than for partners to draw a bill payable to one of the firm. Often bills are made payable to, and drawn upon the makers themselves; and very often bills are made payable to fictitious pay-
712*] ees. *These bills may he mere waste paper, until they are negotiated; but the moment they are indorsed, they become efficient securities in the hands of the indorsees. If it be asked, by what law do they become so, the answer is, it is by the *lex mercatoria*, the evidence of which is long, constant and continued usage. This is the law merchant with respect to bills of exchange; and by the statute it is provided that promissory notes "shall have the same effect, and be negotiable in like manner, as inland bills of exchange according to the custom of merchants." Since promissory notes have been put on the footing of bills of exchange they have, like them, been made payable to the order of one of the makers, or to the maker's own order. Our bank notes are very generally made payable to fictitious payees. There is no instance of an objection to the right of *bona fide* indorsees or holders, to recover on such notes. On the contrary, the cases cited by the counsel for the plaintiffs below, show that suits have been maintained on notes so made and indorsed.

I think the law well settled. The plea of the defendant below, in my opinion, is no bar. I am, therefore, in favor of affirming the judgment of the Supreme Court.

Per totam Curiam.

Judgment affirmed.

Distinguished—54 N. Y., 538.

Cited in—3 Wend., 417; 17 Wend., 49, 223; 3 Hill, 110; 1 Edw., 111; 36 Barb., 284; 43 Barb., 391; 44 Barb., 421; 57 Barb., 112; 66 Barb., 193; 23 How. Pr., 545; 1 Bos., 205; 4 How. (U. S.), 416, 588; 1 Wood. & M., 119; 3 McLean, 174; 66 Ill., 463; 21 Ohio St., 484; 30 Wis., 543; 45 Am. Dec., 279 (6 Smed. & M., 212).

THE AMERICAN INSURANCE COMPANY OF NEW YORK, *Plaintiffs in Error*,

v.

STEPHEN WHITNEY, *Defendant in Error.*

Marine Insurance—Valued Policy.

Of the extent of liability on a valued policy of insurance.

An insurance by a valued policy on a cargo out and return home, embraces goods procured by an hypothecation of the outward cargo, to its full value.

ON ERROR from the Supreme Court. The action in that court was *assumpsit*, by the present defendant, against the present plaintiffs in error. Judgment was for the plaintiff
713*] *below upon the case, and for the reasons given by the Supreme Court, as reported in 3 Cow., 210–220.

Messrs. J. Duer and *D. B. Ogden*, for the plaintiffs in error.

NOTE.—*Marine insurance—Valued policy—Extent of liability on.* See the above case of American Ins. Co. v. Whitney, as reported in 3 Cow., 210, *note, and other notes there cited.*

Messrs. G. Griffin and *J. O. Hoffman*, for the defendant in error.

SANFORD, *Chancellor*, and Colden, *Senator*, delivered opinions, in which they examined and vindicated at large the points decided by the Supreme Court, fully agreeing with that court—and in these opinions, this court unanimously concurred. Accordingly,

Per totam Curiam.

Judgment affirmed.

PHILIP FORGEY, *Plaintiff in Error*,

v.

SARAH SUTLIFF, *Defendant in Error*

Dower—Widow of Alien Purchaser.

The widow of an alien purchaser, under the Statute, 2 R. L., 542, takes her dower as purchaser, within the meaning of that Act, according to Sutliff v. Forgey, 1 Cow., 89–97.

ON ERROR from the Supreme Court. The action in that court was dower *unde nihil habet* by the present defendant against the plaintiff in error. And judgment was there for the demandant upon the case, and for the reasons given by the Supreme Court, as reported in 1 Cow., 89–97.

Mr. S. Stevens, for the plaintiff in error.

Mr. J. Crary, for the defendant in error.

SANFORD, *Chancellor*, and Colden, *Senator*, delivered opinions here, in which they concurred with the court below, that the demandant took her dower as purchaser within the meaning and construction of the Act of 1802, 2 R. L., 542. And the judgment of the Supreme Court was affirmed by the whole court, except Lynde and Redfield, *Senators*, who were for reversal.

Judgment affirmed.

Affirming—1 Cow., 89.

Cited in—12 Wend., 66; 16 Wend., 620; 20 Wend., 349, 356; 21 Wend., 61; 1 Hill, 463; 3 Den., 232; 2 N. Y., 251; 20 N. Y., 328; 1 Abb. App. Dec., 275.

See 1 Keyes, 359.

---

*CHARLES WOOLCOTT, *Plaintiff* [***714**
in Error,

v.

ISSACHAR H. GOODRICH, *Defendant in Error.*

Slander—Charge of Crime Against Nature.

To say of one, "He has been with a sow," holden legal slander; the declaration, averring that the defendant intended to charge the plaintiff with the crime against nature.

ON ERROR from the Supreme Court. The action in the court below was by Goodrich against Woolcott, for slander in saying of the plaintiff (as charged in the 4th count): "He has been with a sow." The Supreme Court gave judgment for the plaintiff upon the case, and for the reasons as reported in 3 Cow., 231–240. SUTHERLAND, *J.*, delivering the opinion of the court.

NOTE.—*Slander—What constitutes.* See Moody v. Baker, *ante*, p. 351, *note, and other notes there cited.*

SAVAGE, *Ch. J.*, now assigned the reasons for the judgment below.

Mr. D. Selden, for the plaintiff in error.

Mr. S. M. Hopkins, for the defendant in error.

SANFORD, *Chancellor*, delivered his opinion at length in support of the judgment below, upon the grounds stated in the former report of the case above cited; and,

Per totam Curiam.

Judgment affirmed.

Affirming—3 Cow., 231.
Cited in—19 Wend., 298; 25 Wend., 201; 6 Barb., 47; 5 How. Pr., 176; Edm., 229; 3 Rob., 294.

MARY JANE DELANCY ET AL., *Appellants*,
v.
WILLIAM SEYMOUR, *Respondent.*

Specific Performance—Evidence—Case for Issue At Law.

Upon a bill for the specific performance of a contract for the sale of lands, and upon exceptions to the master's report in favor of the title, it appeared that one link in the chain was a deed from L. found among the title papers accompanying the possession, but with respect to which the weight of evidence was that the deed was not genuine. By ex-
715*] cluding *that deed, the complainant would be reduced to rely upon adverse possession, which was less than twenty-five years. There was slight evidence that L. was an alien; and if not so, there was no account of his heirs or devisees.

Held, to be a proper case for an issue at law.

ON appeal from the Court of Chancery.

SANFORD, *Chancellor*, assigned the reasons for the decretal order of the court below, awarding an issue upon the title of the respondent, as in 1 Hopk. Ch., S. C. See that book, p. 436–450, for the report of this case in the court below, which presents the same points now passed upon by this court.

The cause was argued here by,

Mr. Talcott, Atty-Gen., and *Mr. S. Jones*, for the appellants, and,

Messrs. J. Duer and *J. V. Henry*, for the respondent.

WOODWORTH, *J.*, SAVAGE, *Ch. J.*, and COLDEN, *Senator*, afterwards discussed the questions argued by counsel, giving their reasons at large to the court for the opinions they had respectively formed. They all three differed from the *Chancellor*, and were for a reversal of the decree; WOODWORTH, *J.*, and COLDEN, *Senator*, thinking the title, as reported by the master in the court below, sufficient; and that, therefore, there should be a decree for specific performance; and SAVAGE, *Ch. J.*, holding the title so doubtful, that the appellants ought not to be compelled to accept it, even though a jury should think it good.

Whereupon a majority of *the Court* were for affirming the order of the *Chancellor;* and it was thereupon,

Ordered, adjudged and decreed that the decretal order appealed from, be, &c., affirmed; that the appellants pay to the respondent his costs in this court, to be taxed; and that the record be remitted to the Court of Chancery, to the end that the decree might be carried into execution.

[END OF DECEMBER TERM, 1825.]

CASES ARGUED AND DETERMINED

IN THE

Court for the Trial of Impeachments

AND THE

CORRECTION OF ERRORS

OF THE

STATE OF NEW YORK,

IN JANUARY, 1826.

719*] *JAMES REID, *Appellant.*

v.

JOHN G. VANDERHEYDEN, *Respondent.*

Parties—One Having no Interest Cannot be a Party—If His Interest Ceases after Commencement of Suit, His Right to Prosecute or to Appeal also Ceases—Interest in Costs—Wills— Caveat *against Proof of—Practice.*

J. G. V., a brother of the half blood to S. V., who died without issue, leaving his wife *enceinte*, filed a *caveat* against the proof of the will of the deceased. Whereupon the surrogate caused the parties interested, to be cited; proceeded to take proofs, and four days after the birth of the child, made a decree establishing the will. J. G. V. appealed to the *Chancellor*, before whom a motion was made to quash the appeal, on the ground that his interest having ceased, he was no longer a proper party in the cause. This motion was overruled: and the *Chancellor* afterwards awarded an issue to try the sanity of the testator, more than 15 days having elapsed from the time of making the first order. On appeal to the Court of Errors from the last order,

Held, that the first order being connected with it, was examinable by that court, notwithstanding the lapse of time.

Held, also, that the *Chancellor* should have quashed the appeal.

A person having no interest in the subject-matter of a suit, cannot be a party in any court.

If he have an interest at the commencement of a suit, and that interest ceases, the right to prosecute the suit, or to appeal, also ceases.

The declaration or order of a surrogate, on making a decree establishing a will, that each party shall pay his own costs, is not the subject of an appeal: 1. Because this is not a decree in form. 2. Because a surrogate having no power in such case to award costs, a decree in form for costs, is *coram non judice*, and void, without reversal by appeal.

720*] *It seems that a mere stranger may file a *caveat* against the proof of a will, but this act is merely advisory, and he has no power to litigate concerning the will.

A mere interest in the costs, gives no right of appeal in respect to any other matter.

Citations—1 Hopkins Ch., 409-415; Com., 590; 2 Madd. Ch., 1 ed., 400; 2 Vern., 548, 632; 1 Johns. Cas., 498; 17 Johns., 548.

ON appeal from a decretal order of the Court of Chancery, sitting as a court of probate, in a testamentary cause on appeal from a decree of the Surrogate of the County of Rensselaer.

The order appealed from, awarded an issue upon the will of Samuel Vanderheyden.

The facts, so far as they related to the points of discussion in the Court of Chancery, on the merits, are stated in 1 Hopk. Ch., 408, 409, S. C. But the cause going off in this court upon an objection for want of parties, not notified in that report, a supplemental statement of facts becomes necessary.

Samuel Vanderheyden, of the County of Rensselaer, died Nov. 27, 1823, leaving a large real and personal estate, and having first executed a paper writing, dated Nov. 14, 1823, purporting to be his last will and testament, and which was the paper in question in the cause.

Dec. 10, 1823, James Reid, by his counsel, appeared before the surrogate, presented this paper, and prayed that it should be allowed, and proved by the surrogate, as the last will and testament of the deceased. A *caveat* had previously been entered by the respondent against proving the will.

Citations were, therefore, issued by the surrogate, directed to the respondent, who was a brother of the deceased, and to others the next of kin, to show cause against the allowance of the will.

On the return of the citations, the parties appeared and the cause was contested. The objection to the paper in question was, that at the time of its alleged execution, the deceased was not of sound and disposing mind and memory. On this question of fact, many witnesses were examined; and Apr. 20, 1824, the surrogate made a decree that the paper writing was duly proved as such will, *and was valid and **[*721** effectual in law. From that decree, an appeal was prosecuted by the respondent to the *Chancellor*, who, in March Term, 1825, awarded an issue upon the will; whence the present appeal was prosecuted to this court.

The surrogate's return to the *Chancellor* contained a concise history of the proceedings, with which was transmitted a copy of the will, and the testimony of witnesses, which had been reduced to writing, in the form of depositions.

The above facts appear from the report of Mr. Hopkins.

The surrogate decreed, substantially, that

each party should pay his own costs. It appeared before the *Chancellor* that the deceased died, leaving his wife, Eliza Ann Vanderheyden, *enceinte* of a male child, who was born Apr. 16, 1824, and who was living at the time of the appeal to him, being the only child of the deceased. That the deceased left one brother and two sisters of the whole blood, the respondent being a brother of the half-blood, by a different mother; but he left no father or mother living. The will in question disposed of all the property of the deceased to persons other than the respondent, viz.: to the wife and child; and in the event of the marriage of the former and death of the latter, then to the two sisters. The will also appointed the respondent, the appellant, and J. R., guardians of the child and executors of the will; directing, however, that the mother should have the sole control of the child till 10 years of age, unless she should marry before that time.

These facts appeared in the Court of Chancery on petition to quash the appeal, presented by the appellant, accompanied with affidavits duly verifying them. But the prayer of the petition was denied by the *Chancellor*, July 28, 1824.

The present being, in terms, an appeal from the decretal order awarding an issue which was made afterwards, Apr. 29, 1825; when no objection for want of parties was taken.

SANFORD, *Chancellor*, assigned the reasons in support of this decretal order, as in 1 Hopk. Ch., 409–415.

722*] **Mr. J. Radcliff*, for the appellant, now insisted that the appeal from the surrogate's decree should have been dismissed by the *Chancellor*, on the ground that the respondent, after the birth of the posthumous son, had no right by law to appeal. The respondent was not aggrieved. True, before the birth of the child, being then one of the next of kin, he had an interest, as distributee, to set aside the will. He was also one of the heirs, but all interest ceased with the birth of the child. There was not even a contingent interest, left in him. The property vested in the child, and the respondent c d not claim even on the death of the childoul

It is no answer that the respondent had an interest when he instituted his proceedings before the surrogate. There are many instances in which a change of interest will be regarded in the prosecution of a suit both at law and in equity. (2 Tidd, 1096; 2 Str., 880, 1015; Coop. Eq. Pl., 63; 4 Ves., 387; 18 *Id.*, 426.) This very point was decided in *Downing* v. *Porter*, 9 Mass., 386. That case decides that a contingent interest is not sufficient to entitle a party to appeal; but it must be by the person holding the immediate interest.

It may be said the respondent was interested in the decree, at least so far as the question of costs was concerned. The surrogate's decree was undoubtedly right in this respect. He had no power to award costs to either party as against the other; and could only leave them, as he has done, each to pay his own costs. As against the failing party, costs depend on the Statute, 2 Inst., 288; which is silent as to costs in this case. (1 R. L., 446, 447, sec. 9.) The legal consequence is, that each must pay his own costs. The respondent is the last person who should complain of the costs; for he having failed before the surrogate, any modification of the decree in this respect must be against him.

But an appeal will not lie from a decree for costs only, 1 Ves., Sr., 250; 10 Ves., 572; *Travis* v. *Waters*, 12 Johns., 500.

That an appeal from the last decree brings up the former orders in the cause, he cited 1 Johns. Cas., 436; 12 Johns., 500; 2 Cow., 195.

*As this was a preliminary point, *the* [***723** *Court* directed the counsel on both sides to be heard upon it before going into the merits—inasmuch as if they should be with the appellant upon this, it would dispose of the cause, without discussion on the points involved in the merits.

Messrs. D. Buel and *J. P. Cushman*, for the respondent. There is no pretense for going back to the order of July, 1824. We supposed, that when the appellants passed by the 15 days to which the Statute, 1 R. L., 134, sec. 9, limits an appeal, it was a tacit admission that he was unwilling to stand or fall by it. This order relates to a mere question of technical form. It is not material to the event of this suit, who is the party. Here he is the oldest uncle of the half-blood, who, by the common law, next to the mother, would be guardian in socage to the infant, if the land should descend.

But the appeal from this interlocutory order should have been prosecuted within 15 days. (1 R. L., 134.)

Again; it was an order relating to the mere practice of the court. Such an order is not the subject of an appeal. (9 Johns., 443, 444, 489, per Spencer, *J.*) It related to the form of the proceeding only. The respondent is named as a party in the decree of the surrogate, made after the fact had transpired, which, it is now contended, disqualified him from being a party to the *caveat*. The appellant had passed the time for objecting to a matter of form. The objection should have been made before the surrogate. Not being made there, it could not be heard by the *Chancellor*, on appeal; nor will it be noticed by this court.

It is difficult to define who is a proper party in a surrogate's court.

It is, perhaps, true, as a general rule, that an appeal from a final decree shall open the previous orders in a cause. But this case does not come within the rule. The decree appealed from is plainly not a final decree. All the books agree in calling an order for an issue interlocutory. *Le Guen* v. *Gouverneur*, 1 Johns. Cas., 436, confines the rule, that you may go back on an appeal from an interlocutory decree, to the previous orders, to cases where the merits *are fully before this court, so as to [***724** warrant a final decree here. *Jaques* v. *M. E. Church*, 17 Johns., 548, requires that the previous order should be connected with the merits of the cause.

But the party should never be allowed to question on the argument, an order which he has not mentioned or even alluded to in his petition of appeal. It is a rule of practice that he must, in the appeal, specify particularly what he appeals from, and file his appeal with the register of the court. (Blake Ch. Pr., 2d ed., 172, 465, 7 and 8 Gen. Rule of this court.) Nothing can be put in the petition of appeal except what is put in the appeal itself; and the court will pass on those parts of the decree only which are mentioned in the petition. *Sands* v. *Codwise*, 4 Johns., 536.

On the face of this case, it came here by an appeal from the decree of March Term, 1825. The Constitution requires that the *Chancellor* shall assign his reasons. This is not done as to the previous order. That order is not alluded to in the opinion. Mentioning it in the petition was evidently the result of an after-thought. There being no regular appeal from that order, the *Chancellor* was not required to assign his reasons for it.

The right to object now is waived on another ground. The appellant passed over the previous order, and proceeded to an argument on the merits. Even as to the court below, and especially as to this court, he had waived the objection. *Atkinson* v. *Manks*, 1 Cow., 691, 709, per Sutherland, *J.* In the very case cited on the other side, of *Travis* v. *Waters*, 12 Johns., 511, the same doctrine is laid down. That case decides that a delay to apply on the subject of costs, was a waiver of all objection. The doctrine proceeded on the ground of laches—not that there was no right to appeal from a decree concerning costs.

But supposing the objection to be in season, the decision of the *Chancellor* denying the prayer of the respondent to quash the appeal for want of parties, was correct in principle. There can be no doubt that the respondent was competent to file a *caveat*. The books which relate to the ecclesiastical courts, are on most **725***]subjects meager and unsatisfactory;*but they are full and clear as to the party who may enter a *caveat*. So far from being confined to the person in interest, it may be entered by a mere stranger. (Toll., 72, 73, ch. 2, sec. 9; Bac. Abr., Ex'rs and Adm'rs, E, pl. 8, p. 41; *Hutchins* v. *Glover*, Cro. Jac., 463, 464; *Manning* v. *Napp*, 1 Salk., 37.) In some of these authorities, the effect of a *caveat* is considered, as to a court of common law; and it is doubted whether it shall have any effect. But we are here proceeding according to the canon law. In 1 Burns' Eccl. Law, a *caveat* is defined thus: "a caution entered in the spiritual court, to stop probates, administrations, licenses, dispensations, faculties, institutions and such like, from being granted without the knowledge of the party that enters it." Has a *caveat* in our law any different effect as to the court of the surrogate? It is plainly admissible, being expressly recognized by our Statute, 1 R. L., 446, 447, sec. 9. On entering it, the judge of probate, or surrogate, is to cause the parties to appear before him, and hear and determine the matter in controversy. The right to enter it is not confined by the statute to the party in interest. It is granted in general terms. The Legislature doubtless had some idea of what the law was in England. If they had an objection to this right being exercised by a stranger, why not say so?

But at what stage did the proceeding become irregular? The original decree was entered Apr. 20, 1824. The child was born on the 16th, 4 days previous to the decree. If there was any irregularity, it happened before the surrogate; and how is that to be got rid of, but by an appeal to the Court of Chancery for that very cause? It should, then, appear upon the return that the objection was taken. It could not be made on petition or motion, being upon a matter which arose before the decree by the surrogate.

There is good reason why a stranger should be allowed to enter a *caveat*. Its propriety is eminently illustrated in this case. A will is obtained by the greatest fraud, and the most odious conspiracy. The only one in immediate interest *is a child. The rule is highly [***726** reasonable that any responsible person may interpose. The court can settle the question of costs. Admit that the party here cannot, by any possibility, have a claim to the subject of controversy; he is near of kin, and for the very reason that he cannot inherit the real estate, he may be guardian in socage (1 Bl. Com., 488); and is esteemed in law and equity the most proper person to take charge of the infant's person and rights. The same principle is adopted in appointing committees of lunatics. The court have a right to be satisfied that he is actuated with a single view to the interest of the child.

Downing v. *Porter*, 9 Mass., 386, cited on the other side, is a case which can make nothing for or against us. The proceeding was probably based on some statute of Mass. It was not the case of a *caveat*. Administration had been granted. The question of parties is peculiarly proper to be left as a matter of discretion to the court where the proceeding happens to be pending. In this case, if the child dies, living the mother, she will be the next of kin, and take the personal property from him. (1 P. Wms., 48, 49.) It then goes to her connections, on her dying, and not to the respondent. In the eye of the law, then, the respondent is the proper person to be guardian to the infant—as having no expectation, or a very remote one at least, from his death.

It is not denied that the *caveat* was valid. Does it not follow that the right to appeal exists? Costs are given by the decree against us. May we not appeal from the decree, on the ground that the costs should have been awarded, wholly against the opposite party? That an unjust burden was left upon us by the surrogate? By the Statutes, 1 R. L., 454, sec. 32, and Laws, sess. 46, ch. 70, sec. 3, p. 63, any person claiming to be aggrieved may appeal. The respondent claims to be aggrieved, and he shows himself to be aggrieved in the article of costs. This is said to be such a distribution of costs as would be made by operation of law. Be it so, for the purposes of the argument. This can make no difference as to the right of appealing. We are now on the preliminary question. The doubt started is, whether we have such an interest as warrants our being a party. We do *not concede that the decree has no [***727** operation beyond the law. We have a right to say that we are aggrieved, and to appeal. It is admitted that there is no statute authorizing the surrogate to decree costs in this case, and that none can be given by the common law.

If there was originally a right of appeal, there has been nothing to change it. In the eye of the law, the interest of the respondent is the same now as when he entered a *caveat*. The rights of the child are the same. The rights of an infant, *en ventre sa mere*, are the same as if born. (1 R. L., 54, sec. 5; 1 Bl. Com., 129, and Christian's *note*.) These rights might, then, have been the subject of an appeal in chancery.

The cases are against the reversal of decrees upon the mere want of proper parties. Neither bills nor appeals are dismissed on that ground. *Wharton* v. *Squire*, Colles, 270. Proper parties may be added; and interest in a party is not always required, even in a court of law. *Raymond* v. *Johnson*, 11 Johns., 488. The whole is mere arbitrary matter of practice, belonging exclusively to the court below. Even in a court of law, bankruptcy, during the pendency of a suit, is no abatement. (*Ib.*) In a court of chancery, it merely stays the proceedings till the assignees are brought in. There is no strict rule on this subject, as to *caveats*. The law, we have seen, is less rigid on this head than any other.

As to the objection, that costs alone are not the subject of an appeal, the rule is unsettled. Platt and Spencer, *JJ.*, differed on the point, in *Travis* v. *Waters*, 12 Johns., 500. An appeal is denied in England, because chancery has a perfect discretion on the subject. But it would be error in a court of law to give costs where none are allowed, and it is so in the Ecclesiastical Court. The cases of appeals from chancery do not apply to a testamentary case.

The interest, even of an immediate distributee, is always somewhat contingent. It depends on the question whether there will be a surplus beyond the payment of debts. We never had any absolute interest. Yet it is granted that we were right in the beginning. The **728***] Court of Probates being *formed on the model of the English prerogative court, we must take the law as it stands in relation to that court; and if a stranger may enter a *caveat* and proceed in an appeal there, he may do so here.

Even in the case of a writ of error, the suit does not abate by the death of the defendant; and after an assignment of errors, does not abate by the death of the plaintiff, but it goes on for the benefit of the persons interested. All this, and the like doctrine, is technical. The death of the *Ch. J.* before the return is signed, formerly rendered the writ of error ineffectual; and the prorogation of Parliament discontinued its proceedings. If a suit may be carried on in the name of a party who becomes bankrupt, for the benefit of his assignees, on the same principle it may go on in this case for the benefit of the child. No rights of the child can be lost, and they may be benefited. The object is the furtherance of justice. There can be no ultimate proceeding by execution; but the court are to pass upon the mere question: is this the will of the deceased?

Mr. A. Van Vechten, in reply. The decision of this cause cannot bind the respondent, for he has no interest which it can affect. It cannot bind the infant who is not a party. If it cannot bind the respondent, of course it will not affect the infant, for it should be mutually binding.

The previous order is as much in question as if there had been a direct appeal from it, and it is a sufficient objection that the respondent had no interest. He does not appear as guardian to the child, and is to be deemed a mere intruder. The right to enter a *caveat* is not followed by the power to become a party, and litigate the will. It is conceded to be a mere caution which a stranger may give. Being merely cautionary, it is not an act of litigation. It is like the act of a counselor rising in court and advising *ut amicus curiæ*. When the *caveat* is entered by the stranger, all is done which he has power to do. We could not apply to quash the *caveat*, which was a mere notice. There was nothing to aggrieve the respondent, because he had no rights. True the statue gives the right of appeal to the party claiming to be aggrieved; but there must be some foundation for the *claim. [***729** How can he be said to be aggrieved when he has no interest to be affected? This has been treated as a chancery proceeding; but in that court the cause is never suffered to proceed on a change of interest appearing, without the proper parties being brought in. If a stranger of wealth may come in and litigate the will, a man of straw may do the same, and there will be no end to the number of parties. Nor can the court ever require security for costs of a resident citizen. A man of property might sacrifice the whole estate by a *caveat* and appeal and that, too, with impunity; for it is not pretended that costs can be given against him. They are unauthorized by the statute.

The decree for costs is no more than saying each party shall pay his own costs, and it does not seem to be denied that this is precisely what the law would imply. No sum is specified, and there was no taxation. The decree for costs could have no effect. It could not be enforced by execution. The persons who performed the services for which costs were due, must, notwithstanding, bring their action to collect them; and declare on a *quantum meruit*, and show in proof what the law entitled them to. Ample relief might have been obtained short of this court of *dernier resort*. It is a trifling subject, and not worthy the strength of Hercules.

But if these costs are the subject of an appeal, it does not follow that there is a right of appeal as to the merits. These are not affected by the question of costs.

The objection that the order of July, 1824, is not appealed from, is strict and technical. The merits are all before the court; and we are, in effect, discussing the power of a judge of probate—not a proceeding in the Court of Chancery under its general powers. An issue has been awarded; and the very question is, whether the respondent can come to the *Chancellor*, and go down on an issue to try rights which he confessedly does not possess. The decision of the jury will be of no effect. It can operate on the rights of no one, and all this round of litigation is idle—a mere course of speculation upon an abstract right.

The question of proper parties is always important; and the want of them cause for appeal. It is essential that they *should [***730** have an immediate interest. *Hickcock* v. *Scribner*, 3 Johns. Cas., 315; *Grant* v. *Duane*, 9 Johns., 611, 612.

The respondent is neither interested, nor does he appear *pro forma*, for the benefit of any party in interest. If he comes in the character of guardian, or in any way representing the rights of others, this should be stated on the record.

The objection as to parties might have been made at the hearing; but this was not necessary to save our rights of appeal. It is surely sufficient that we raised it *in limine;* 9 Johns., 612; and it would have been indecorous to mention it again before the *Chancellor*, after we had been overruled. A court of appeal may examine all the errors of the court below, as well those of omission, as of commission. *Bush* v. *Livingston*, 2 Cai. Cas., 66.

All the parties in interest acquiesce. Not a word of complaint is heard from any one having a right to complain.

In *Buel* v. *Street*, 9 Johns., 443, the appeal was dismissed, because it related to a mere question of practice in the court below, not at all connected with the merits of the case. The order in question related directly to the merits; and being connected with the last decretal order, it is opened by the appeal. *Jaques* v. *M. E. Church*, 17 Johns., 548. The case cited was an appeal from a final decree. The decree appealed from in this case is either final as affecting the merits, or it should have been so. If not, then, in itself, is a cause of appeal. The cause should have been dismissed by the *Chancellor*. That would have been final. *Sands* v. *Codwise*, 4 Johns., 536, cited against us, was the case of several distinct, disconnected and independent decrees. Where they are so, it is true, each should be made the ground of a distinct and specific appeal. But when the error of the first runs on into the order appealed from, if the latter is erroneous because the first was so, all the orders present the same point. They differ merely in the order of time, and the error exists as much in the last as in the first. The want of parties in this case is the single point. It is a whole, and cannot be divided. Being so, the appeal from the last
731*] embraces *both orders. In *Atkinson* v. *Manks*, 1 Cow., 709, the decree was entered by the consent of both parties; and for that reason alone was the appeal held to come short of it.

The authorities cited to show the effect of a *caveat*, merely show how it is regarded in the eye of the ecclesiastical law. *Manning* v. *Napp*, cited by the counsel from 1 Salk., 37, allows that the *caveat* was *damnum absque injuria;* "for the property of the goods till administration, was in the ordinary; and the plaintiff had neither *jus in re nec jus ad rem:*" thus sanctioning the principle that a *caveat* is unknown to the common law. Are we governed by the ecclesiastical law? The surrogate derives his authority from the statute. His powers are defined and limited by it. The will is to be proved before him. A *caveat* may be entered, when there is a dispute; and he is then to cause the parties to appear before him and hear and determine the matter in controversy (1 R. L., 446, 447, sec. 9.) Who are these parties thus to be cited? Certainly those interested merely. None others have a right to be heard. Suppose they all come and concur in the proof of the will, can they be kept at bay by this *caveat* entered by a stranger? Can he drive them to a course of litigation? If they do not come, the legal conclusion is that they acquiesce; that they are opposed to any controversy which the intruder wishes to involve them in. Would the surrogate be bound in such a case to wait during the three months, the time which the cases allow to the operation of the *caveat?* The duties of all concerned in managing the estate, are to be performed according to the course of the common law. "A *caveat* is of such validity by the canon law, that if an institution, administration or the like be granted pending such *caveat*, the same is void. But not so by the common law. For, by the common law, an admission, institution, probate, administration or the like, contrary to a *caveat* entered, shall stand good; in the eye of which law, the *caveat* is said to be only a caution for the information of the court, &c., but that it doth not preserve the right untouched, so as to null all subsequent proceedings, because it doth not come, nor hath it ever been determined, that a bishop became a disturber, by giving institution *without [***732** regard to a *caveat;* on the contrary, it was said by Coke and Doderidge in the case of *Hutchins* v. *Glover*, H. 14 Ja., that they have nothing to do with a *caveat* in the common law." (1 Burn Eccl. Law, 207, 208.)

If the statute had said a notice in writing instead of a *caveat*, it would have been the same thing.

The notion which the gentlemen advance as to the common law guardian in socage, is entirely correct. He is one to whom the inheritance cannot possibly descend. Where there are several of this class in equal degree, an appointment is to be made. But here the mother is guardian in socage; and in default of her, the uncle on the mother's side. (1 Bl. Com., 488.) The respondent cannot be recognized as guardian till he is appointed to that office. He did not enter the *caveat* as guardian.

A contingent or expectant interest must rest on some present vested right to support it; otherwise, where are we to stop? We know not who may finally be interested. If it can be demanded that we should litigate with all who may possibly have an interest, we may be driven to enter the lists with every one of the family with which we are connected immediately or remotely.

[The counsel were heard during the short intervals from legislative business, on the 9th and 11th of Jan.

And now, after several members of *the Court* had expressed their opinions, and adverted with more or less particularity to the reasons upon which they should vote, the question was taken, Sutherland, *J.*, being absent.]

WOODWORTH, *J.* I have not been able, in the short space of time allowed for considering the point presented and the arguments and authorities on which it depends, to reduce my opinion to writing. Aided, however, by the very full and learned discussions of counsel, presenting the case in almost every possible point of view, I have come to a conclusion perfectly satisfactory to myself; which, with the considerations upon which it has proceeded, I will briefly state to the court.

*The question presented for our de- [***733** termination is, whether the respondent, John G. Vanderheyden, was properly made a party to the appeal from the surrogate. If he was, the argument must then proceed on the merits; if not, there is an end of this cause.

It is an elementary principle, recognized in all the books, that a person having no interest in the subject of dispute, cannot be a party litigant; and I am not aware of a single exception in any one of our courts, whether proceeding according to the course of the common, civil or canon law. To show the nature and universality of the rule, and illustrate and enforce it, we need only go to the doctrines of a court of equity, where the greatest possible latitude as to parties is indulged. There, not only must the original parties have an interest, but that interest is followed in all its changes. Although an action may proceed in some cases in the name of the original plaintiff, in trust for others, on whom the interest is cast by operation of law; 11 Johns., 488; yet, in equity, even in cases of change by bankruptcy or insolvency, a bill must be filed in nature of a bill or revivor. Thus, where B filed his bill; and after answer, was discharged under the Act for the Relief of Insolvent Debtors; and his effects were assigned to B, who assigned to C, it was held that a bill was necessary. to bring in the new parties in interest. *Harrison* v. *Ridley*, Com., 590, and *vide* 2 Madd. Ch., 1st ed., 400; 2 Vern., 548, 632. The case in Comyn examines the subject, and shows the ground and necessity of adhering to interest as the criterion of parties. Indeed, the contrary rule would produce a very singular state of things. Any stranger would be enabled to crowd our courts with business, as his curiosity, his revenge or the spirit of litigation or gain might prompt him; and that, too, without settling any right, without the court being able to do a single act personally binding on anybody beyond the mere question of costs.

It is not necessary to controvert the proposition so much dwelt upon at the bar that any one may enter a *caveat* against the proof of a will. Admitting this to be so, I do not see that **734***] *the consequences, sought to be deduced, would at all follow. This *caveat* is a mere monitory act. It requires the surrogate to advise the parties in interest, who will then govern themselves accordingly. They are the only persons who can interfere beyond the *caveat*. The power of the stranger is limited to the act of entering it. Admitting the contrary doctrine, would result in a very strange absurdity. Suppose all the parties interested, to come in and declare themselves satisfied that the will is genuine; is it to be tolerated that a mere stranger may drive them to the delay, vexation and expense of litigating those very rights to which no one pretends any claim, and which never can be asserted against them? The neglect to appear and contest the will, on being duly served with a citation, work the same consequence in construction of law. It is equivalent to a confession. It appears to me that the mere stating of the doctrine contended for by the respondent, in all its extent, is enough to show its utter inadmissibility; and the only question must be, whether the respondent had an interest at the time of the appeal.

I do not deem it necessary to inquire whether he had such an interest as would warrant his being a party when he commenced his proceedings in the court of the surrogate. Admitting him to have been one of the distributees of the estate at that time (and I think he was to be so regarded), that interest was defeasible; and was, in truth, defeated by the birth of a posthumous child on the 16th of Apr., four days before the decree of the surrogate was pronounced. This event changed the rights of the parties altogether. It not only devested the respondent's right as distributee; but it appears to me it took away all possibility of interest, all expectancy, unless it be a very remote one indeed. The will being out of question, all the estate, real and personal, vested in the child. To the real estate, the respondent plainly never could succeed, even on the death of the child, being an uncle of the half-blood. But the real estate is not in question. The personal estate, if any, beyond the payment of debts, would pass to the next of kin. This is the mother; and on her death, it would pass to her next of kin. Her *death before [***735** that of the child, would still leave the respondent's right of succession doubtful in law. For the purposes of this question, then, he was, at the time of pronouncing the decree by the surrogate, a mere stranger. When his interest ceased, his right further to litigate ceased with it. All power of appeal was, therefore, gone.

Is the respondent a proper party *pro forma*, to vindicate the rights of others? No such thing appears upon the record, or in any other way. It is not pretended that he is guardian to the infant, either *ad litem* or otherwise. He has neither the custody nor protection of the child; and there is no rule in the books giving him a right to claim the guardianship. The uncle of the mother's side would, doubtless, be preferred. Why allow the respondent to litigate under pretense of benefiting persons who have a real interest? Are we to presume them inattentive to their rights and that the infant will be injured by their neglect? If this be so, I repeat, what right has a stranger to interfere? The infant must seek his remedy on coming of age.

I think it follows, conclusively, that the appeal should have been quashed by the Court of Chancery when the motion was made for that purpose.

It was strenuously urged, however, by the counsel for the respondent, that it is now too late for the appellant to question the order then made; because, being interlocutory, he suffered the limitation of 15 days to pass before his appeal was entered. This raises the question whether the appeal taken from the order awarding an issue involves and brings up the previous one. It seems to me that that order is necessarily drawn in question. The inquiry, whether there be proper parties to the litigation, runs through the whole proceeding. Not a step is to be taken without them. The award of an issue, or any other order, is nugatory. They are essential to the form and constitution of the suit. This being so, the general principle was laid down in *Le Guen* v. *Gouverneur*, 1 Johns. Cas., 498, and is now well established, that "by an appeal from any interlocutory or final decree, all the proceedings in the cause anterior to the decree are necessary to be presented to the court; and proper for *its determination. It may fre- [***736** quently become indispensable to reverse, alter or modify the previous proceedings, in order to make them consistent with the decree to be pronounced."

The rule thus laid down is forcibly illustrated by the principal case. In deciding the question, whether there should have been an issue, we must look at the whole of it; and any ground which shows that there should not have been one may be urged. Whether the proof was satisfactory upon the depositions, is one question; and above all, whether there are any rights to be determined. The two orders appear to me to be so essentially connected, that justice cannot be done, otherwise than by considering them in one view. The doctrine on this subject was also advanced in general terms in *Jaques* v. *M. E. Church*, 17 Johns., 548. The importance of adhering to the rule may be illustrated in a variety of ways. Cases may be supposed where it is vitally essential to the administration of justice. Suppose a party should file his bill to be relieved against proceedings at law, and obtain an injunction, which is dissolved on the coming in of the answer. The case, however, eventually turns out to be a doubtful one at the hearing, as depending on a variety of facts and an issue is awarded. From this there is an appeal, and the issue is confirmed. Would not this court look back, and see whether the injunction was properly dissolved; and if not reverse the order of dissolution, and direct it to be renewed by the *Chancellor*, in order to save the party against being stripped of the fruits of his litigation by the judgment and execution at law?

The only remaining question respects the costs before the surrogate. It is said the respondent has such an interest in these as entitles him to an appeal. If this be admitted, it by no means follows that we can consider the merits of the case, further than they are connected with the question of costs. On seeing that they were improperly awarded, the decree may be reversed *pro tanto*. This, however, gives no right to the respondent upon the other branch of the subject.

737*] *But, I confess, I can see no possible ground of objection to the decree, so far as it relates to the costs. Indeed, it cannot be called a decree affecting costs. It leaves the parties precisely as they would have stood had there been no decree; to the question between them respectively and the surrogate, as to what they shall pay him for his services. There is no formal decree for costs: nothing which can be enforced by execution. The surrogate, being satisfied, probably, that he had no power to award costs, did not intend to make any decree respecting them; and what he said in the decree was his mere *ipse dixit* as to his own claim. It had no more effect than if he had pronounced it on any other occasion. It is not possible to make it out a decree within the meaning of the law.

At any rate, if it be a decree in form, it cannot affect the party. The surrogate had no authority to award costs. There being a want of jurisdiction, the decree was, for so much, *coram non judice*, and void. It could never have been enforced.

On the whole, I am of opinion that the decree of the Court of Chancery should be reversed; and that the proceedings be remitted, to the end that the appeal from the surrogate be dismissed from the Court of Chancery.

SAVAGE, *Ch. J.* I concur in the opinion delivered by *Mr. Justice* Woodworth. The cases cited by him show clearly that we may go back from an interlocutory order mentioned in the appeal to another and previous order connected with it, though the latter was made more than 15 days anterior to the appeal. I cannot entertain a doubt of our right to do so in this case.

The respondent appears to me to have no rights, either in the real or personal property, which warranted his being made a party to the appeal. They ceased with the birth of the child; and he does not pretend to be pursuing this litigation in any other right than his own. It is remarkable, that when the petition was presented, and the motion made before the *Chancellor* to quash the appeal, the respondent himself, under oath, disclaimed all interest whatever in the subject of the controversy.

*The question of costs is clearly a **[*738** matter between the respondent and the surrogate, and is untouched by the decree.

On the whole, who and what does this proceeding by appeal conclude? No one, in any single particular. After the infant comes of age; or when any other person duly representing him, comes before the proper tribunal, the whole ground must be gone over again, even if we interfere now, and either reverse or affirm the decree on the merits.

I am in favor of a reversal, for the want of parties.

COLDEN, *Senator*. I confess I felt myself unprepared to decide this cause. when the court took a resolution to pass upon it. I could readily concur in the general principle, that the party instituting a suit must have an interest. And there is another general principle, that when the interest ceases, the right to prosecute ceases. It is not necessary, then, to look back beyond the birth of the child; for the question comes to this: did the interest cease when the child was born, so absolutely as to take away all right to continue the suit?

I have listened with great attention to the reasoning in support of this order, particularly to that part of the reasoning which was intended to show that the respondent had an interest in some shape, either in his own right, or as representing others, which warranted the order of the *Chancellor* refusing to quash the appeal. And this is a question which I would willingly have looked farther into, as it appeared to me to be the turning point in the cause. But I confess the reasoning of *Mr. Justice* Woodworth seems to place the matter in a very clear light. It has convinced me that the respondent had no right whatever to prosecute the appeal. To adopt the language of the question, which we put to a witness as the test of his competency, it seems to me the respondent can "neither gain nor lose in the event of this suit," so far as the subject-matter is concerned. Nor will an interest, merely contingent, vary the case, though I confess I cannot see that the respondent has any such. An interest strictly contingent will not even disqualify a witness. A rule which should receive a party upon the footing of *such an interest would lead **[*739** to very great litigation and vexation. Here, two deaths certainly must intervene, as I understand to be admitted by the respondent's own counsel, before he can claim any vested interest. By the same rule, we might let in a relation in the 20th degree to litigate the question; nor do I well see that we can stop anywhere.

As to the objection which goes upon the Statute of Limitation; the rule is that all interlocutory orders connected with the decree appealed from are brought up with it. I understand this to mean that the orders are essentially connected, so that you cannot dispose of the one appealed from, according to the justice of the case, without interfering with the former orders, some or one of them. It is only necessary to see, in this case, that the appeal brings up the question of proper parties, to warrant our looking into the previous order. Now I understand the question of parties to be always connected with a decree touching the merits. Suppose this cause had gone to a final hearing and decree, is there a doubt that an appeal would then have brought up this question? I think not. If so, an appeal from an interlocutory decree relating to the merits, ought, *a fortiori*, to have the same effect. Whether a court be one of original jurisdiction or appeal, it is always proper that it should look and see if the parties before it are such whose interests and rights are to be concluded. This is always a question on the final hearing of a cause. Suppose this were the first moment of presenting the question in the whole course of the cause, I do not think we should hesitate to interfere.

On the question of costs, I concur with *Mr. Justice* Woodworth.

VIELE, *Senator*. I am in favor of hearing the argument upon the merits before giving any opinion. For that reason I shall vote against the dismission of the appeal by the *Chancellor*.

SPENCER, *Senator*. I concur with *Mr. Justice* Woodworth and the *Chief Justice*. As to the right of going back to and looking into the previous order, there is a great similarity between the principal case and that of *Le Guen* **740***] *v. *Gouverneur*, cited by *Mr. Justice* Woodworth. In that case a bill was filed to overhaul a judgment at law, obtained, as was alleged, against the respondent, notwithstanding he had a good defense, on the ground of fraud. It was objected that such a bill would not lie; that the defense should have been insisted on at law. But the *Chancellor* overruled the objection, and awarded a feigned issue to try the question of fraud. Both the order overruling the objection, and that awarding an issue, were interlocutory; yet an appeal from the latter (an order for an issue, as in this case) was held to reach the former.

I must say I think, with *Mr. Colden*, that if the objection for want of parties were now made for the first time, we ought to listen to it.

On the question whether there be any interest in fact in the respondent, I have nothing to add to what has been said already. But there was one thing on this head which drew my attention particularly, as I now learn it did that of the *Chief Justice*. It is, that the respondent (the appellant in the Court of Chancery) came into that court with a sworn disclaimer of all interest. I will read an extract from his affidavit, made and read in opposition to the motion to quash the appeal on the ground that he had no interest: "And this deponent further saith, that in objection to the proof of said paper (the will in question), and filing a *caveat*, and in appealing from the decree of the said surrogate, this deponent hath not been actuated by the hope or expectation of benefitting himself by acquiring any part of the estate of the said Samuel; but on the contrary, this deponent hath often stated to his counsel, and to others, that he did not intend to participate in the estate of the said Samuel in any event; and hath declared it to be his intention to release all claim which he might make thereto."

Here is as strong a disclaimer as can be stated on any record. A decree should always be final. It cannot be so unless the party upon whom it is to operate have an interest in the subject of it. I want no authority to show that a party must always be thus interested.

*GARDINER, *Senator*, stated that, not [***741** having had time to examine the question, he was not satisfied how it should be decided; and, therefore, declined giving any opinion.

WRIGHT, *Senator*. I understand the object of the issue was to ascertain the single fact, whether the deceased was or was not of sound mind and memory when he executed his will. I confess I am not at this moment prepared to deny that truth may be elicited in this form: although the party to the issue may not be technically interested in the subject bequeathed. Further reflection might convince me that this is so; but not being prepared at present to join in such a decision, I must vote against the dismissal of the appeal by the *Chancellor*.

ELLSWORTH and MALLORY, Senators, concurred with *Mr. Wright*, that the appeal should not be dismissed, the rest of the court concurring with *Mr. Justice* Woodworth.

It was thereupon ordered, adjudged and decreed, that the order or decree of the Court of Chancery, of the 29th day of April, 1825, directing a feigned issue to be made up and tried between the above named parties, be, &c., reversed and vacated; that the Court of Chancery do dismiss and quash the appeal brought by the said John G. Vanderheyden, in the said Court of Chancery, from the order or decree of the Surrogate of the County of Rensselaer, and all proceedings had thereon, without costs below to either party; and that the record and proceedings be remitted to the Court of Chancery, that the decree might be executed.

Reversing—1 Hopk., 408.
Overruled—1 Hill, 463; 20 Wend., 338.
Cited in—11 Wend., 237; 1 Paige, 95; 2 Paige, 81: 3 Paige, 185; 1 Edw., 270; 26 N. Y., 449; 40 N. Y., 583; 78 N. Y., 309; 10 Hun, 291; 25 How. Pr., 8: 39 How. Pr., 182; 53 How. Pr., 11; 3 Daly, 192; 1 Bradf., 37: 2 Bradf., 183; 2 Redf., 146, 229; 22 Wall., 336; 8 W. Dig., 545.

[END OF JANUARY TERM, 1826.]

REPORTS OF CASES

ARGUED AND DETERMINED

IN THE

SUPREME COURT,

AND IN THE

COURT FOR THE TRIAL OF IMPEACHMENTS

AND

THE CORRECTION OF ERRORS,

IN THE

STATE OF NEW YORK.

BY ESEK COWEN,

COUNSELOR AT LAW.

VOL. VI.

1837.

JUDGES

OF THE

SUPREME COURT

OF THE

STATE OF NEW YORK,

DURING THE PERIOD OF THESE REPORTS.

JOHN SAVAGE, *Chief Justice.*

JACOB SUTHERLAND, *Associate Justice.*

JOHN WOODWORTH, *Associate Justice.*

CIRCUIT JUDGES.

FIRST CIRCUIT.

OGDEN EDWARDS.

SECOND CIRCUIT.

SAMUEL R. BETTS.*

THIRD CIRCUIT.

WILLIAM A. DUER.

FOURTH CIRCUIT.

R. HYDE WALWORTH.

FIFTH CIRCUIT.

NATHAN WILLIAMS

SIXTH CIRCUIT.

SAMUEL NELSON.

SEVENTH CIRCUIT

ENOS T. THROOP.

EIGHTH CIRCUIT

JOHN BIRDSALL.

SAMUEL A. TALCOTT, *Attorney-General.*

* MEMORANDUM.—On the 20th of February, 1827, James Emott was, on the nomination of the Governor, and with the consent of the Senate, appointed a Circuit Judge of the Second Circuit, in the place of Samuel R. Betts, who had resigned that office, in consequence of being appointed District Judge of the United States for the Southern District of this State. The commission of Judge Emott bears date the 21st of February, 1827. On the 27th of the same month he took the oath of office.

CASES

ARGUED AND DETERMINED

IN THE

SUPREME COURT

OF THE

STATE OF NEW YORK,

IN

AUGUST TERM, 1826, IN THE FIFTY-FIRST YEAR OF OUR INDEPENDENCE.

FULLER
v.
HUBBARD AND WILLIAMS, Adms. of SMITH, Deceased.(*a*)

Contract to Convey Land—Payment of Purchase Money—Action, by Vendee to Recover the Money Paid, does not Lie—Remedy is on the Contract—No Right in Vendee to Rescind—He Should Demand a Conveyance.

Where, on a contract to pay for, and receive a conveyance of land, the money has been paid, though a conveyance has not been given, the vendee cannot rescind the contract and sue for the purchase money and interest; but must bring his action on the contract as one still subsisting.

Where one agrees to convey land, on the payment of money, the vendee must not only tender or pay the money, but he must demand a conveyance; and after waiting a reasonable time for it to be made out, must present himself to receive it.

Where the agreement is to convey land in fee simple, a judgment against the vendor will not, at law, authorize the vendee to rescind the contract. A conveyance without covenants would satisfy such an agreement.

Citations—14 Johns., 326; Forrest's Exch., 61, 62; 1 Esp. *N. P.*, 190; Sugd. L. V., 181, 182, Am. ed., 1820; 20 Johns., 27, 133; 5 Johns., 58; 7 Johns., 380; 13 Johns., 363; 12 Johns., 443; 9 Johns., 126.

ASSUMPSIT, commenced in August Term, 1821, and tried at the Chenango Circuit, Aug. 26, 1823, before Nelson, *Circuit J.*

The declaration was on the special contract of Fuller and Smith, as proved upon the trial; and also contained the money counts.

The following facts were in evidence at the circuit: May 15, 1812, Smith, the intestate, by a memorandum in writing, signed by both parties, agreed to sell Fuller 100 acres of land, in Lisle, Broome Co., for $600, in consideration of $100 then received in part payment. Fuller agreed to pay the residue in three yearly installments, with interest. And upon pay- 14*] ment of *these sums, at the times mentioned, Smith agreed to convey to Fuller in fee simple. It was further agreed that if the payments were not made at the day, Smith might elect to go on with the contract or not. Payments were made by Fuller from time to time, to the intestate and the plaintiffs, to the amount of the whole conisderation money and interest; the last payment being made to the plaintiffs, May 12, 1819.

The defendants objected that the plaintiff could not recover on the general counts for money had and received; but the objection was overruled.

They also objected that the plaintiff could not recover till he had shown a deed prepared by him, and tendered to the heirs of Smith; and that they had neglected or refused to execute it; or, at least, that a conveyance had been demanded of them, and refused. This objection was overruled.

They also proposed to show that the plaintiff had been in possession of the land since the contract, and had cut and sold timber to a large amount, which, they insisted, should be deducted from the claim of the plaintiff. This was also overruled; and the jury, under the direction of the judge, found for the plaintiff the amount of the consideration money and interest.

The defendants had pleaded a judgment of $7,000, outstanding against the intestate, recovered in 1815, with a debt upon bond and award, against him; and *plene administravit* except $1. To this plea, the plaintiff had replied, praying judgment of assets *quando acciderent.*

Mr. G. C. Bronson, for the defendants, moved for a new trial, on the grounds:

1. That the plaintiff could not recover on the general counts, but was confined to the special agreement. *Raymond* v. *Bearnard*, 12 Johns., 274; *Clark* v. *Smith*, 14 Johns., 326; 1 Chit. Pl., 342; *Towers* v. *Barrett*, 1 T. R., 133; *Power* v. *Wells*, Cowp., 818; 4 Mass., 504; *Weston* v. *Downes*, Doug., 23; *Hunt* v. *Silk*, 5 East, 449; *Caswell* v. *Black River Man'fg. Co.*, 14 Johns., 453; *Taylor* v. *Hare*, 4 Bos. & P., 260; *2 [15 Phil. Ev., 64; 1 Wh. Selw., 79; 2 Com. Cont., 56; Sugd. L. V., 206. He should have elected one, and cannot go on both. 7 T. R., 181; *Linningdale* v. *Livingston*, 10 Johns., 36.

2. He could not sustain an action, without having first tendered a deed for execution, or at least having demanded a deed from the heirs. Sugd. L. V., 182, 296, Phil. ed., 1820; *Parker* v. *Parmele*, 20 Johns., 130; *Phillips* v.

(*a*) This cause was decided in October Term, 1825.

Fielding, 2 H. Bl., 123; *Greenby* v. *Cheevers*, 9 Johns., 126.

3. The judge adopted an improper rule of damages, and rejected proper evidence affecting this question. 4 Bos. & P., 262, per Heath, *J.*; 1 T. R., 136, per Buller, *J.*; *Hopkins* v. *Lee*, 6 Wh., 109; 19 Ves., 510, 511, per Mast. Rolls, in *Dyer* v. *Hargrave*.

Mr. J. A. Collier, contra. The contract on the part of the plaintiff was fully performed. After the money was paid, he was, by the terms of his contract, entitled to a deed; and no demand was necessary. *Shackleford* v. *Barrow*, 2 Bay N. C., 91; *Baker* v. *Bulstrode*, 1 Mod., 104: *Pincke* v. *Curteis*, 4 Bro. Ch., 332; *Heard* v. *Wadham*, 1 East, 627, Abbott, *arg.*; *Sweitzer* v. *Hummell*, 3 Serg. & R., 228; Lawes Pl. in *Assumpsit*, 246; Com. Dig., Pleader, C, 75; *Utica Bank* v. *Van Gieson*, 18 Johns., 485.

A large class of authorities establish the distinction between cases where the conveyance and the payment are to be simultaneous; or, in other words, where the covenants are dependent; and where they are independent. *Green* v. *Reynolds*, 2 Johns., 207; *Jones* v. *Gardner*, 10 Johns., 266; *Parker* v. *Parmele*, 20 Johns., 130-135; *Heard* v. *Watts*, 1 East, 619; 1 Saund., 320 *c*; *M'Crady's Exrs.* v. *Brisbane*, 1 Nott & M'C., 104. But even in these cases no demand has been held necessary. A performance, or offer to perform, by the vendee, is enough. The late case of *Fairfax* v. *Lewis*, 2 Rand. Va., 20, 35, will be found to sustain us throughout.

16*] *We submit whether the payment was not a sufficient demand; and whether this, and waiting a reasonable time, would not satisfy the rule, if a demand was necessary.

But if the demand be necessary of the promisor, it is not so of his heirs. The law will not require us to know who they are, or to find them out. There is a privity between them and the administrators, and payment or notice to the latter is equivalent to a payment and notice to the former.

But the property was incumbered with a judgment of $70. This disqualified the promisor and his heirs from conveying, and dispensed with the necessity of a demand, if it had otherwise been necessary. *Seaward* v. *Willock*, 5 East, 198, 202; Sugd. L. V., 164, 165, Am. ed., 1820; *Greenby* v. *Cheever*, 9 Johns., 126; *Gillet* v. *Maynard*, 5 Johns., 87, 88; *Judson* v. *Wass*, 11 Johns., 527; *Tucker* v. *Woods*, 12 *Id.*, 190; *Duke of St. Albans* v. *Shore*, 1 H. Bl., 279; *Gazley* v. *Price*, 16 Johns., 269; *Ketchum* v. *Evertson*, 13 *Id.*, 364; 2 Chit. Pl., 125, *note i.*

If there could be no performance, the plaintiff had a right to rescind the contract, and recover back the money on the general counts for money had and received.

The offer to show the cutting and conversion of timber was a mere offer to set off damages done by a trespass. We had no right even to enter, till a conveyance; nor, if we had the vendor's consent to enter, could we have cut timber. Our liability sounds in tort. A claim of this sort cannot be set off. *Duncan* v. *Lyon*, 3 Johns. Ch., 358, and the cases there cited; *Livingston* v. *Livingston*, 4 *Id.*, 292. An action for use and occupation would not lie. *Smith* v. *Stewart*, 6 Johns., 46.

Staats v. *Ten Eyck's Exrs.*, 3 Cai., 111, 114, lays down the true rule, as to the measure of damages. It should be the same as if we had received a conveyance, with covenants, and been ejected for defect of the vendor's title. The measure, then, is the consideration paid, with interest. The cases on this head will be found collected in 2 Wh., 63-65, *note*.

We are liable to be ejected by the heirs. Then is the time to liquidate the claim for the *mesne* profits of the estate. *Murray* v. *Gouverneur*, 2 Johns. Cas., 438.

**Mr. Bronson*, in reply. The objec- [*17 tion as to the outstanding judgment was not made at the trial. But it cannot be sustained, it it had been made in season. The promise is to give a deed good in form, and the vendee cannot object a mere incumbrance. *Van Eps* v. *Mayor, &c.*, 12 Johns., 436; *Nixon* v. *Hyserott*, 5 Johns., 58; *Sedgwick* v. *Hollenback*, 7 Johns., 376; *Stanard* v. *Eldridge*, 16 Johns., 254.

Curia, per WOODWORTH, *J.* The plaintiff was not entitled to recover under the general counts. The special contract is still subsisting, and the remedy of the plaintiff is on the contract. *Clark* v. *Smith*, 14 Johns., 326. That the plaintiff had no right to rescind, follows from the conclusion (which we have come to on another point in the cause), that the outstanding judgment admitted by the pleadings, was no obstacle in the way of performing the promise to convey according to its terms. The payments were made by the plaintiff upon the foot of the special contract. Everything has gone on, for a series of years, upon the supposition that the agreement was valid and subsisting.

It is unnecessary to consider the question of damages; as we think the action cannot be sustained on the contract, the purchaser not having put the vendor or his heirs in default.

In this case, it was necessary for the plaintiff to show, at least, that he had demanded a conveyance from the heirs of Smith, the intestate; and that, then after waiting a reasonable time for making out and executing it, he had offered to receive it. The English law is peculiarly strict. By this, it seems, the vendee, who sues for a breach of the contract to convey, is required, not merely to show payment of the purchase money; he must also prove the preparation and tender of a conveyance ready for execution. Till this is done, the vendor is not put in default. In *Baxter* v. *Lewis*, Forrest Exch., 61, 62, on a bill filed by the vendor of land against the purchaser, for a specific performance, the defendant was decreed to pay the purchase money. He neglected to do so, and was attached. A motion being made to set aside *the attachment [*18 on the ground that, as the vendor had not prepared and tendered a conveyance, the defendant was not bound to pay, and the attachment was, therefore, premature. Mr. Pemberton, for the plaintiff, said: "It is the duty of the purchaser to make and tender a conveyance. The vendor is never called upon to do so." The court denied the motion, thinking it was incumbent on the defendant "to prepare and tender the conveyance, and pay the purchase money." In *Knight* v. *Crockford*, 1 Esp. *N. P.*, 190, on an objection by Adair, Sergeant, that the plaintiff, a purchaser, could not recover on the contract in question (which consisted of a promise by the plaintiff to pay for, and of the defendant to convey real estate), because he had not shown the preparation and tender of a conveyance to the defendant; *Eyre, Ch. J.*, did not question that the objection was according to the general rule; but distinguished the case, saying the defendant had incapacitated himself to convey by selling to another, which rendered a strict performance on the part of the plaintiff unnecessary.

Mr. Sugden declares the rule of *Baxter* v. *Lewis* to be the settled rule of the profession in England; and notwithstanding some *dicta* which he mentions to the contrary, he still infers that the purchaser, and not the vendor, ought to prepare and tender the conveyance. (Sugd. L. V., 181, 182, Am. ed., 1820.) Sugden agrees that the contrary was the general rule when the simplicity of the common law reigned, and possession was the best evidence of title; but upon the modifications of estates, unknown to the common law, which resulted in the difficulties surrounding modern titles, the more convenient rule which he mentions had grown up among the conveyancers. This
19*] doctrine *of Sugden is mentioned with approbation by the late *Ch. J.* Spencer, in *Hudson* v. *Swift*, 20 Johns., 27; and the court decide in that case, that, to put the vendor in default, and entitle the vendee to recover back
20*] part of the *purchase money, which he had paid in advance, he must tender the residue, and demand a conveyance. There is, then, something more to be done than the simple payment, or the tender of the purchase money.
21*] A conveyance must *be demanded. Nor would this alone appear to satisfy the principle of the rule. A reasonable time should be allowed to the vendor to prepare the conveyance. The purchaser not having himself pre-
22*] pared it (which he may do), *he shall not be allowed to retire immediately, and bring his action; but should present himself to receive the conveyance, which he has thus required to be furnished. Deliberation and advice of counsel may be necessary in settling its terms. The framing and execution of modern conveyances, even with us, where the titles to real estate are much less complicated than in England, are not like the payment of money, or the delivery of a chattel. I admit the general rule to be, as contended by the counsel for the plaintiff; that where a party engages to do any act, and a demand is not a part of the contract, the bringing of the action is, in itself, a sufficient demand. Such an important transaction, however, as the assuring of a title to real estate, under the modern system of conveyancing, is an exception to that rule.

Clearly, the judgment recovered against Smith is no ground, in a court of law, for rescinding the contract. The agreement was to convey in fee simple. A conveyance is good and perfect, without warranty or personal covenants. Such a conveyance will satisfy the terms of this contract. The judgment is, of itself, no transfer of title. It does not destroy the seisin of Smith or his heirs, nor take away the capacity to convey. (5 Johns., 58; 7 *Id.*, 380; 13 *Id.*, 363; 20 *Id.*, 133; 12 *Id.*, 443; 9 *Id.*, 126.)

A new trial must be granted, with costs to abide the event.

New trial granted.

Overruled—62 Barb., 591.

Cited in—7 Cow., 54; 3 Wend., 250; 7 Wend., 131; 8 Wend., 619; 1 Den., 60, 546; 5 Den., 164; 2 Edw., 81; 25 N. Y., 197; 50 N. Y., 43; 59 N. Y., 373; 4 Barb., 358; 6 Barb., 149, 648; 11 Barb., 553; 12 Barb., 516; 14 Barb., 569; 15 Barb., 364; 17 Barb., 409; 48 How. Pr., 346; 3 Bos., 59; 2 Rob., 68, 174; 25 Cal., 279; 34 Am. Dec., 521 (4 Whart., 482); 44 Am. Dec., 542, 544 (2 Eng., Ark., 153); 49 Am. Dec., 767 (20 Vt., 118); 50 Am. Dec., 283 (2 Fla., 403).

---

*THE TRUSTEES OF VERNON SOCIETY [*23

v.

JESSE HILLS.(*a*)

Forfeiture of Corporate Rights—Cannot be Taken Advantage of in a Collateral Proceeding—Religious Society.

In an action by the trustees of a religious society regularly incorporated under the Act of 1813, 2 R. L., 212, 214, the defendant cannot show that they have forfeited their corporate rights by misuser or nonuser. The forfeiture can be taken advantage of in no other way than by a suit in behalf of the people. And till it has been judicially declared in this form, individuals cannot avail themselves of it.

A religious incorporation stands, in this respect, on the same footing with any other incorporation.

The trustees, *de facto*, of a religious society, though they were irregularly elected, yet are in, *colore officii*; and their proceedings are valid till they are ousted by judgment at the suit of the people.

Citations—8 Johns., 378; 14 Johns., 245, 6; 9 Johns., 147, 149, 159; 10 Mod., 146; Str., 625; 5 Johns. Ch., 379, 381.

ON *certiorari* from a justice's court. The plaintiffs sued the defendant before the justice, on a subscription, dated Sep. 25, 1817, by which the defendant obligated himself to pay the plaintiffs $6 annually, in semi-annual payments, so long as the Rev. Orange Lyman should continue to administer the gospel, &c. Plea, the general issue.

The only question before the justice was, whether the plaintiffs were a corporation when the suit was brought. The original certificate of their proceedings to organize as a Corporation, in 1803, was, by counsel here, admitted to be sufficient; and they were regularly incorporated under the 3d section of the Act of 1801, 1 K. & R., 336, &c., and that all irregularities in their proceedings previous to Apr. 5, 1813, were cured by the statute then passed, re-enacting the Statute of 1801, and expressly confirming former incorporations. (2 R. L., 212, 218.) But it appeared before the justice, that at the annual elections subsequent to that period, only one person presided; whereas the Statute, 2 R. L., 214, sec. 36, requires two; that at such elections no certificate of the result was given as required by the 6th section of the Statute, 2 R. L., 216; that the regular annual meetings of the society were the first Tuesday of May, in each year; yet there was no record of any meeting in 1818; and no evidence of any meeting in that year, except the record of a resolution in 1820, reciting that the record of 1818 was lost, and directing the clerk to record the election of the trustees of that year It appeared by the plaintiff's book of minutes, first introduced by them, but afterwards used by the defendant, that the persons prosecut-

(*a*) This cause was decided in October Term, 1824.

24*] ing in the court below *were Trustees of Vernon Society; but they produced no certificate of their having been regularly elected.

On this evidence, the justice gave judgment for the defendant below.

Mr. G. C. Bronson, for the plaintiffs in error, insisted that none of the irregularities presented by the justice's return, were such a misuser or nonuser as would work a dissolution of the Corporation. But if otherwise, it is clear that it did not lie with the defendant to make the objection in the suit before the justice. Though a corporation may forfeit its charter by an abuse or neglect of its franchises, the forfeiture must be ascertained and declared by regular process and judgment of law, before its powers can be taken away, or the corporation be considered as dissolved. The remedy is by *sci. fa.* prosecuted at the instance, and on behalf of the government, or by an information in nature of a *quo warranto.* 1 Bl. Com., 485; *Slee* v. *Bloom*, 5 Johns. Ch., 366, and the cases there cited; S. C., 19 Johns., 456, 474. The cases cited show the rule and its exceptions; and, indeed, are perfectly conclusive.

The trustees who are duly elected, hold over till others are chosen in their place. (9 Johns., 147.)

Besides, the defendant contracted with the plaintiffs as a Corporation, and by their corporate name, and he is precluded from objecting that they are not a Corporation. (14 Johns., 245.)

Mr. J. A. Spencer, contra, cited 8 Johns., 378, to show that the plaintiffs must prove themselves a corporation upon the general issue. He said, no election had been legally conducted. Only one person had presided at any of them. This was the same as if no election had taken place. The whole was void; and the plaintiffs not authorized to sue as trustees. (2 R. L., 216, secs. 3, 6.)

There is no need of a *sci. fa.* or *quo warranto*, to try the question of dissolution, in the case of a religious incorporation under the statute. It must, at all times and in all suits, be prepared to show its continuance as a corporation, 25*] *as well as its original formation. Here is not only an irregularity in the election for a single year but it was continued for a series of years. The 9 Johns., 147, therefore, is not applicable; nor will the 14 Johns., 245, be found to help the plaintiffs.

Curia, per SAVAGE, *Ch. J.* It is settled by the repeated decisions of this court, that when a corporation sues, they are bound, on the general issue, to prove that they are a corporation. (8 Johns., 378; 14 *Id.*, 245, 246.)

Had the irregularities complained of, been confined to a single year, they would have had no effect upon the plaintiffs' rights, according to the decision in *People* v. *Runkle*, 9 Johns., 147, 149. It was conceded by the court, in that case, that the trustees, chosen under the Act in question, and who go out of office at the end of the year, hold over till others are elected. The question there was, whether an election after the day was good. The court said, "perhaps the language of the statute is too peremptory, that the seats of one third are to be vacated at the expiration of every year; but the Corporation is not thereby dissolved; for two thirds of the trustees continue in office." There are cases which hold that where an officer is to be chosen annually, he may hold over after the year until another is chosen (10 Mod., 146; Str., 265); and in *People* v. *Runkle*, the court said that trustees elected after the day would be in by color of office; that the election would not be void and their acts would be good; that the Corporation would still remain; and the irregularity, if any, would cure itself in a subsequent year. That reasoning, however, is not applicable to this case. The persons claiming to be a Corporation in 1817, when the contract was made with them as such, came into office, if at all, since that period. The same irregularity was continued for three years in succession; and if it renders the election void, the Corporation was dissolved; or in a situation to be dissolved by appropriate judicial proceedings. For the same reason, the defendant is not estopped to question the plaintiffs' being a Corporation by reason of *his contract with them as such. [*26 The estoppel, if any, relates to the time of entering into the contract; and does not admit that there cannot be a dissolution.

This view of the subject renders it necessary to inquire whether such a nonuser or misuser as is a sufficient ground to produce a forfeiture of corporate rights, can be taken advantage of in this collateral way; or whether the forfeiture must not first be judicially declared in a direct proceeding by the people.

This point is, I think, settled by the decisions of our own, as well as those of the English courts. In *Slee* v. *Bloom*, 5 Johns. Ch., 379, 381, *Chancellor* Kent held that the forfeiture of corporate rights must be judicially ascertained and declared; and that corporate power which may have been abused or abandoned, cannot be taken away but by regular process. He considers the cases, and expresses a belief that there is no instance of calling in question the rights of a corporation, as a body, for the purpose of declaring its franchises forfeited and lost, but at the instance and on behalf of the government.

The decree in *Slee* v. *Bloom* was reversed in the Court for the Correction of Errors: not, however, on the ground that the *Chancellor's* position, so far as it related to acts of nonuser or misuser, was incorrect. Spencer, *Ch. J.*, who gave the unanimous opinion of the court, said: "Upon the authorities and for the reasons given by the *Chancellor*, misuser or nonuser cannot be relied on as a substantive and specific ground of dissolution." *Silver Lake Bank* v. *North*, 4 Johns. Ch., 373. But the reversal proceeded upon the fact that the Corporation in question had surrendered, or done what was equivalent to a surrender of, their corporate rights.

These cases seem to me conclusive against allowing the objection, coming, as it does, collaterally, that this Corporation was dissolved. There is nothing in the statute showing that the Legislature considered religious incorporations as standing on a different footing in this respect from other corporate bodies.

*The plaintiffs have acted as trustees [*27 upon the matter in question, and in bringing their suit, *colore officii;* and before an objection to their right can be sustained by the defendant, on the ground that they were not regularly elected, he must show that proceedings have been instituted against them by the government, and carried on to a judgment of ouster. (9 Johns., 159.)

In my opinion, the judgment below was erroneous, and should be reversed.

Judgment reversed.

Cited in—7 Wend., 553; 11 Wend., 611; 19 Wend., 145; 23 Wend., 590; 5 Hill, 630; 1 Paige, 594; 3 Sandf. Ch., 653; 4 Sandf. Ch., 758; 17 N. Y., 99; 19 N. Y., 485; 7 Hun, 333; 24 Barb., 399; 37 Barb., 606; 52 Barb., 236; 58 Barb., 489; 49 How. Pr., 22; 19 Abb. Pr., 433; 1 Hall, 198; 1 Rob., 147; 33 N. J. L., 202; 35 Mo., 28; 20 Am. Dec., 122 (2 Blackf., 367); 27 Am. Dec., 109; 33 Am. Dec., 660 (16 Me., 224); 41 Am. Dec., 692 (15 N. H., 162); 43 Am. Dec., 464 (2 Doug. Mich., 124); 30 Am. Dec., 111 (9 Gill. & J., 365); 39 Am. Dec., 354 (5 Ala., 787); 44 Am. Dec., 578 (17 Conn., 585); 41 Am. Dec., 117 (5 Ark., 595).

THE PEOPLE v. DEAN.

Witness — One Whose Name has been Forged, Competent on Trial of Forger.

A witness whose name has been forged, is a competent witness, on the trial of an indictment, to prove the forgery.

Citations—4 Johns., 302; 4 East, 582.

THE defendant was convicted at the last Oyer and Terminer of Washington Co., of forging a promissory note for the payment of money, purporting to be signed by Solomon Dean, payable to Gerrit Wendell, or order, at the Bank of Lansingburgh, with intent to defraud Wendell. On the trial, Solomon Dean was offered as a witness for the people; but he admitting that he had not paid the note, was objected to by the defendant's counsel as incompetent. The objection was overruled by the judges, and he was sworn and testified in the cause.

Judgment was suspended in the court below, for the purpose of taking the opinion of this court upon the above point; and the record removed here by *certiorari*, accompanied with a case presenting the point.

The prisoner now being brought up by *habeas corpus*,

Mr. S. Stevens, his counsel, said it was well settled by an unbroken series of English decisions, both before and since the Revolution, that the person whose name had been forged to a contract, cannot be a witness, on the trial of an indictment, to prove the forgery. Hardr., 331; 3 Salk., 172; 2 Str., 728; 1 Leach, 8, 155, 214; 2 East P. C., 993–995; 5 Bos. & P., 87; 2 East P. C., 996; *Robert Rhode's* case, 1 Leach, **28***] 31; McNally Ev., 141, 143. *Chitty and Phillips lay down the same doctrine. The same thing was held by this court in 1794. The decision is mentioned by Kent, *Ch. J.*, in *People* v. *Howell*, 4 Johns., 296, 302. The *Ch. J.* there questions the soundness of the rule, but declares there was no necessity for interfering with it in that case, and that the court did not interfere with it.

I am aware that the rule has been questioned and, indeed, overruled in other States, but those decisions are not binding here. The question with us should be, what is the common law of England. Our Constitution has expressly adopted that law. It is as binding upon the court, as if the Legislature had passed an Act, declaring that the English rule in this particular case, should be our rule. The highest evidence of the common law is the English cases.

I know the reason of the rule may be questioned. English judges themselves have admitted it to be an anomaly in the law of evidence, but it is enough for us in a criminal case to show what the rule is. It must continue till altered by the Legislature.

Nor is it entirely destitute of reason. Suppose a trial of an indictment for the forgery of the maker's name to a note, which is believed by all the witnesses, except the maker, to be genuine. He is then called. If he admits its genuineness, what he says would be evidence against him, on a private suit for the money. In this view, he would be interested to deny his signature, in order to escape the effect of swearing true. It is well, where crimes of this high nature are in question, to avoid even a temptation to perjury against the criminal.

Mr. Talcott, Atty-Gen., contra. There was a time when the rules of evidence were so strict that the person sought to be injured either by usury, perjury or forgery, was an incompetent witness to prove the crime. This arose from confounding an interest in the question, with an interest in the event of the cause. The cases of *Bent* v. *Baker*, 3 T. R., 27, and *Abrahams* v. *Bunn*, 4 Burr, 2251, placed the doctrine of interest on its true footing; and since *that [***29** time, to exclude a witness for this cause, he must be interested in the event of the suit. In general, to exclude him, it must appear that the record in the suit wherein he is called to testify will be evidence for, or against him; otherwise, he neither gains nor loses anything by the event. After this rule was established, it was, as remarked by the prisoner's counsel, agreed by English judges that the doctrine which he contends for was an anomaly, not justified by principle, yet it was obstinately adhered to. But if all the cases, except those relating to the point before the court, have been made to square with the more enlightened rule; if all cases to the contrary, except those now in question, have been overruled (see 4 Burr., 2251; 4 East, 572), why not overrule these also? Such a step is justified by the same reasons upon which the other cases were disregarded, and considered no longer binding.

There may be one reason for the exception in England, which has no existence here. In many cases, the instrument forged is forfeited to the Crown; the party who would otherwise be benefited by it loses all interest; nor can the Crown sue upon it, because the very record through which it must derive its interest shows the forgery. In all other cases the instrument is impounded by the court, and the party cannot reach it. (2 East P. C., 994.) Evans remarks, in his commentary on Pothier: "I have heard a learned judge assign a reason for not admitting a person whose name is forged to an instrument, purporting to subject him to an obligation, viz.: that though the Crown acquires a right, by forfeiture, to the goods of the offender, it may not be allowed to set up such a right in respect of the particular obligation, which, by the same record that is necessary to the title, is found to be a forgery." (2 Ev. Poth.,

316.) In *Commonwealth* v. *Snell*, 3 Mass., 82, the English cases have been overruled. Parsons, *Ch. J.*, said in that case, that "formerly, both in civil and criminal prosecutions, the witness was held to be incompetent, if he was interested in the question; that in England, since *Ld. Ch. J.* Parker's time, the rule had been altered; and no witness was now excluded from **30***] *testifying by reason of any supposed interest, unless he was interested in the event of the suit, or unless the verdict in the cause, whichever way it may be found, could be given in evidence in any other action, in which he was a party; that in England, the party whose name is said to be forged cannot now be a witness, for he is considered as interested; because, if the instrument is found by the verdict to be a forgery, it is impounded by the court, so that it cannot again be used as evidence." (*Id.*, 84.) The courts in Pa. hold the same doctrine. *Respublica* v. *Ross*, 2 Dall., 239.

True in 1794 this court did hold with the English cases, but that decision was afterwards questioned by Kent, *Ch. J.*, in *People* v. *Howell*, 4 Johns., 302; and the courts of oyer and terminer have since been in the uniform practice, I understand, of admitting the witness whose name has been forged.

[WOODWORTH, J. I have known this to be so in several cases at the Oyer and Terminer, and its propriety was not drawn in question.]

As to the temptation to perjury, from fear that an admission of the handwriting may be given in evidence against the witness in a private prosecution, the argument proves too much. It would go to render witnesses incompetent in thousands of cases, where their competency was never thought of being questioned.

So far as the true principles of evidence are in question, there is no doubt. That principle is sanctioned by many cases and, indeed, is not denied; and it will be always found that one good principle is worth a hundred precedents. The court are called on, not to overrule, but return to the law. I should be sorry to suppose there is anything either in the Constitution or common law which will prevent their doing so.

Mr. Stevens, in reply, said he was not aware that in England the forged instrument was ever considered as forfeited to the King. He did not believe that it came within the doctrine of **31***] *deodands. If this be so, why did the learned men of that country agree in styling the doctrine for which he contended an anomaly? In truth, if this were as contended by the Atty-Gen., the witness would have the highest interest. To impound the instrument was also a very ancient practice, and has not prevailed in England for many years. The question has been considered entirely unembarrassed with either of these difficulties. The reason of the rule is the same on both sides of the Atlantic.

Curia, per SAVAGE, *Ch. J.* There has been a difference upon the point presented by this case between the English and American decisions—the former holding that the party whose name has been forged to an instrument cannot be a witness against the offender, and the latter that he may. Although this court, in 1794, decided according to the English cases, yet the reasoning of Kent, *Ch. J.*, in *People* v. *Howell*, has generally been considered by the profession as satisfactory; and it has, as far as we can learn, been followed in practice, at the courts of oyer and terminer. Besides, if we pass from the conflict of decision and practice on the subject, we find a principle long and well established, and so fully embracing the point, that the English judges, when this question has come before them, acknowledge their own course to be a mere anomaly in the law of evidence. (4 East, 582.) That principle is, that whenever the witness cannot possibly derive any benefit or sustain any loss from the event of the cause, he is competent. To this rule, even in England, the point in question forms a solitary exception, for which no reason can be given. (*Vide* 4 East, 582.) Why every other case should have been brought to that test, and this alone form an exception, is not explained, except upon the foundation of precedent. Yet the precedents are not so old as to deny us the power of seeing how they arose, or that their reason and foundation have been overruled.

These passing away, it is certainly warrantable to dismiss the superstructure with them.

*We are, accordingly, of opinion that [***32** the court below decided correctly.

The prisoner was sentenced to the Auburn State Prison for 10 years.

Rule accordingly. (*a*)

Cited in—19 Wend., 341.

(*a*) The English doctrine seems to prevail in Vt., State v. A. W., 1 Tyler 280, and Conn., State v. Brunson, 1 Root, 307; *Id.* v. Howard, *Id.*, 308; *Id.* v. Blodget, *Id.*, 534.

ALLEN *v.* CALHOUN ET AL.

Supreme Court will not Correct Circuit Calendar.

The Supreme Court will not interfere with the practice of the circuit judge, as to the correction of his calendar.

It seems a cause should be placed there, according to the date of the oldest issue in it.

Citation—3 Cow., 16.

MR. L. BEARDSLEY moved to set aside the inquest taken against the defendants, at the last Otsego Circuit, on the ground, among others, that though the notice of trial for the circuit was not for an inquest; yet an inquest was taken by the plaintiff out of its order on the calendar. There were issues of different dates in the cause—the first was the general issue, and the others were joined, at a later period, by replication to the defendant's special pleas. The cause stood on the calendar as of the last date; but on motion of the plaintiff's counsel on the third day of the circuit, it was raised to the date of the first, by order of the circuit judge; called as of that date, and an inquest taken.

Messrs. J. Brackett and *A. Stewart*, contra.

Curia. The correction of the circuit calendar belongs exclusively to the judge; nor will we interfere with his rules of practice on this head. Besides, he proceeded on the same principle which we have adopted in the correction of our own calendar. *Griswold* v. *Stewart*, 3 Cow., 16. There is, however, an affidavit of merits; and the defendants may take their motion on payment of costs, they having accounted for not appearing at the trial.

Rule accordingly.

33*] *SATTERLEE v. GROOT.

Change of Venue—Contents of Affidavit.

The affidavit for a change of venue, should state that the witnesses, on account of whose place of residence the venue is sought to be changed, are such that, under the advice of counsel, the party cannot safely proceed to trial without them.

MR. S. W. JONES, for the defendant, moved to change the venue from Albany to Schenectady.

He read an affidavit of the defendant, that he had thirteen witnesses residing in Schenectady, whose testimony, as he was advised by counsel and verily believed, would be material to his defense; but he did not add that, as he was advised by counsel and believed, he could not safely proceed to trial without their testimony; and therefore,

Mr. J. L. Wendell, contra, objected that the affidavit was defective.

Curia. The point has not been before raised, and the practice has been different. There is often a very great laxity of swearing upon these motions, and the party should certainly be holden to express himself clearly. That the witnesses are material, implies perhaps that the party cannot safely proceed without them, but the expression may be considered equivocal by the party. That witnesses residing in the county to which the venue is sought to be changed, know of a material fact, is not enough. A dozen witnesses, residing in the county where the venue is laid, may know the same thing, and be more easily reached than those in the other county; and yet, in one sense, the testimony of these may be said to be material. But it would be no ground for a change of venue. The witnesses intended are such that the party cannot safely go to trial without their testimony, and he should swear to this under the advice of counsel. The motion must, therefore, be denied, for the defect of the affidavit; but as the point has not been before decided, this must be without costs.

Motion denied.

34*] *BREWSTER AND BOSTWICK
v.
HALL ET AL.

When Special Plea, set Aside on Motion.

A special plea, under the Statute of Double Pleading, though it be an ordinary plea, and good on its face; if it be sworn to be altogether false, in fact, by the plaintiff and not pretended to be true, by the defendant or his attorney, will be set aside on motion, even after replication, demurrer and joinder; and after the plaintiff's attorney has placed it on the calendar for argument; and even after the cause has been tried upon the general issue.

Citations—2 Cow., 287-8, *n. a*, 634, 637; 1 Bing., 380; 4 Cow., 634; 2 B. &. A., 197, 199; 2 Barn. & C., 81, 286; 5 B. & A., 750, *n. a*; 1 R. L., 519, sec. 10.

IN *assumpsit*. *Mr. J. Dickson*, for the plaintiffs, moved to set aside, three special pleas interposed by the defendants. The first was a plea of accord and satisfaction, in nearly the common form. The second was, that the parties had stated an account, when a balance was found for the plaintiffs of $700.99, for which the defendants gave their bond, as security; that the plaintiffs had recovered judgment thereon; that one of the defendants paid the judgment in full, &c. These fact were pleaded with great particularity of day, place and circumstance. The third plea was a very formal plea; first of a special accord between the parties, and a formal and particular satisfaction in pursuance of it.

These had been pleaded, according to the statute, &c., with the general issue. The plaintiffs had replied to the special pleas, taking issue to the country, and the defendants had demurred to the replication; and the plaintiffs joined in demurrer. At the last Monroe Circuit, the plaintiffs took an inquest, pursuant to notice for that purpose, no affidavit of merits having been filed by the defendants.

The plaintiffs' attorney had also placed the demurrers on the calendar of the present term for argument.

The counsel read an affidavit, of one of the plaintiffs, showing the falsity of the special pleas in point of fact; and this was not denied in any way by the defendants, or their attorney. He cited 2 B. & A., 197, 199; 5 *Id.*, 750; 2 Cow., 634, 637, *note a.*

Messrs. R. M. Morrison and *G. C. Bronson*, contra, said the court would not interfere in this form, merely because the pleas were untrue in point of fact. (4 Cow., 47, 48, and *note*.) Besides, it is now too late to move; the plaintiffs having replied to the pleas, and joined in demurrer to the replications. They must now be argued.

**Mr. Dickson*, in reply, relied on *Corbet* [*35 v. *Powell*, *note* to *Shadwell* v. *Berthoud*, 5 B. & A., 750, to show that he was not too late with his motion. In the case cited the plaintiffs had replied, and there was a demurrer to the replication, yet the plea was stricken out, on motion, as false.

Curia, per SAVAGE, *Ch. J.* The defendants have pleaded a series of sham pleas, without a pretense of merits in their cause, or that the pleas are true in a single particular; and demurrers growing out of them are now gravely placed upon the calendar of the present term for argument. The question is, whether we are bound to sit in judgment upon such a case, or summarily dispose of it upon non-enumerated motion. This subject has lately been twice before us. First, in *Steward* v. *Hotchkiss*, 2 Cow., 634, when we set aside the plea, it being false in fact, and of somewhat a doubtful character in law; secondly, in *Tucker* v. *Ladd*, 4 Cow., 47. In the last case all the material allegations of the plea were verified by affidavit, and, of course, we refused to set it aside. We also intimated, although this was not necessary to the decision of the cause, that to warrant our interference on a motion to set aside the plea, it must appear not only to be false but of a doubtful character, and calling for a course of special pleading which might compromit the rights of the parties; and *Young* v. *Gadderer*, 1 Bing., 380, appended to that case in a note by the reporter, holds a similar doctrine. That case reviews the previous course of decision in the K. B. There a plea had once been set aside because it raised different issues, requiring different modes of trial, and imposed on the plaintiff an improper difficulty. *Thomas* v. *Vandermoolen*, 2 B. & A., 197. In *Bartley*

v. *Godslake*, 2 B. & A., 199, the court interposed on the ground that the plea was ingenious, and would put the defendant's attorney to the necessity of consulting counsel upon it; and thereby occasion delay and expense. And in *Richley* v. *Proone*, 2 B. & C., 286; 2 Cow., 287,
36*] 288, *note a*, S. C., the K. B. set *aside an ordinary plea of accord and satisfaction, it appearing plainly to be false. The earlier cases were cited by *Judge* Platt, the counsel who moved in *Steward* v. *Hotchkiss*, 2 Cow., 637. The following cases upon this point are reported in 5 B. & A., 750 and *note a*. In *Shadwell* v. *Berthoud*, to an action on a bill of exchange, the defendant pleaded that the plaintiff was indebted to him in a large sum, on a recognizance in the Exchequer; and the court ordered it stricken out, on the ground that it was obviously intended to gain time and the attorney would be obliged to consult counsel. In *Body* v. *Johnson* the defendant pleaded as to one third of the plaintiff's demand, a bond to another; a set-off to one third and to the residue that he had given a promissory note; and the plaintiff had judgment as for want of a plea. *Corbet* v. *Powell* was debt by an executor on a bond. Plea, that the bond had been assigned and paid to the assignee; replication and issue. The defendant struck out the *similiter* and demurred to the replication. The court interfered even at this late stage of the pleadings, and gave judgment as for want of a plea.

The last case furnishes an answer to the objection that taking issue on the plea is a waiver of the motion to strike out. We think this may be done at any time, before the plea is disposed of in the ordinary way, by trial or on demurrer.

In *Merrington* v. *Becket*, 2 B. & C., 81, the authority of *Richley* v. *Proone* is questioned; and the court refused to set aside the plea. It does not appear what it was.

Thus it will be seen that the English cases do not entirely agree, as to the kind of pleas which the court will strike out. They do all agree, that the plea must be without pretense in point of fact; but when we come to its legal nature, we find precedents for setting aside both those which are plainly good, and others of a doubtful validity. Sometimes the criterion is delay and expense, and sometimes ingenuity and delusion. In truth, perhaps, no general rule can be laid down on the subject.
37*] Courts have never yet *set aside the general issue; but beyond that, it seems to me, the matter must, in a great measure, rest in sound discretion. The power to set aside sham pleas is now well established. The great object is to prevent delay and expense to the plaintiff, and consuming the time of the courts in passing upon pleas which are a mere fiction, and an unseemly and expensive incumbrance upon the record, and a fraud upon the rule which allows double pleading. Double pleas are made by the Statute, 1 R. L., 519, sec. 10, dependent on the leave of the court. To be sure, both in England and this State, they are generally pleadable without actual leave. In England, I believe, a rule is still taken out for the purpose, but it is of course. It has been found more convenient to let the party take his own head, and look to the question of right afterwards. This is even doing less than the statute authorizes, for an affidavit of the probable truth of the plea might be required in the first instance. The statute would hardly be satisfied without some sort of restraint. And where it is admitted, as in the case before us, that the pleas are without color of truth for their support; where we cannot but see that they are intended as a mere instrument of delay, whatever be their legal merit (and we admit that one of these pleas is of a very familiar and ordinary character, and unquestionably good upon its face), we cannot sit here to pass upon them or any question growing out of them; nor should they be retained upon the record.

In this view, the motion must be granted, with costs; and the cause, which is on the calendar upon the demurrer, must be stricken off, with costs of this motion, and the costs of the plaintiffs, incurred in following up these pleas with a replication, joinder in demurrer, preparation and attendance for argument.

Rule accordingly.

Cited in—10 Wend., 624; 18 Wend., 566; 18 N. Y., 321; 15 Barb., 16; 5 How. Pr., 248; 6 How. Pr., 356; 7 How. Pr., 483; 8 How. Pr., 485; 48 How. Pr., 82; 7 Rob., 437; 38 Super., 139; 1 Daly, 390; 3 Co. R., 242; 35 N. J. L., 263.

---

*JACKSON, ex dem. ABEL, [*38
v.
MILLER.

Settlement of Testimony by Circuit Judge.

The Supreme Court will not order a case to be referred to a circuit judge, for settlement, as to the evidence, where it has been settled by him according to the practice of the court, unless there be a very plain mistake.

MR. J. L. VIELE, for the defendant, moved that a case be made for the purpose of moving for a new trial in this cause, and which had been settled by the circuit judge who tried the cause, be again referred to him for re-settlement. The motion was founded on affidavits of the defendant's counsel, and of witnesses sworn at the trial, that, according to their recollection, some of the testimony given at the trial had been mistaken by the judge.

Mr. E. Cowen, contra, produced affidavits of the plaintiff's counsel, that, according to their recollection, the evidence was correctly stated by the judge.

Curia. Where the testimony in a case has been settled by a circuit judge, according to the practice of this court, we will not examine its accuracy on affidavit, and order it referred for correction, unless there be a very plain mistake. He hears witnesses and takes minutes of their testimony, which he has before him, and is, therefore, more competent to settle the testimony than this court. The motion must be denied.

Motion denied.

JACKSON, ex dem. DEMONT,
v.
SACKETT AND DAVIS.

Attachment for not Paying Costs.

To warrant an attachment for not paying costs pursuant to a rule of court, where the costs are not demanded by the party entitled to them, or his attorney, the power to demand them, should be exhibited to the party of whom they are demanded.

MR. T. MUMFORD moved for an attachment against the defendants for not paying costs, pursuant to a rule of this court. The costs had been demanded of the defendants by Mr. C., pursuant to a power of attorney from Mr. M., the attorney for the plaintiff; but it did not appear in the affidavit for the motion 39*] that Mr. C. had exhibited his power *to the defendants, to make the demand; and, on this ground,

Mr. L. F. Stevens, opposed the motion.

Mr. Mumford, said it lay with the defendants to object the want of a power at the time, and demand and exhibition of it: otherwise, they waived its production.

Curia. We think otherwise. You must show the defendants to be in contempt. For this purpose you are required to exhibit the original rule. It is still more important that the power should be shown. In most cases, parties have knowledge of the rule taken against them; or may, at least, obtain knowledge of it by searching the minutes of court. The power is a private document, the knowledge of which lies between the attorney and his agent. The uniform practice has been to require its exhibition. The motion must be denied.

Motion denied.

Cited in—58 How. Pr., 228.

JACKSON, ex dem. ABBY, v. SMITH.

Leave to Amend Declaration in Ejectment.

Leave to amend a declaration in ejectment, by adding a new demise, will not be given on a mere notice of motion, without any cause shown by affidavit.

Citations—4 Johns., 483; 1 Cow., 156.

UPON a mere notice, unfounded on any affidavit, or other papers, a motion was made to amend the declaration by adding a new demise particularly specified in the notice; and *Anonymous*, 2 Cai., 261, was cited.

Mr. W. D. Ford, for the motion.

Mr. E. C. Reed, contra.

Curia. The motion must be denied. The case cited from Caines has not been followed in practice. Without proof of the fact, we cannot see the necessity of the amendment; nor even that there is any action pending. Great liberality prevails in allowing these amendments, but they are not merely of course. If so, why not enter a common rule? Some reason for applying to the court should be shown 40*] *by affidavit, or otherwise. The question of amendment is one of discretion, depending on various circumstances. That the person from whom the demise is sought to be added, has a subsisting claim to the premises, or some other substantial reason, is usually required to be shown; and there are several cases in which we have refused the amendment for want of this. *Jackson* v. *Richmond*, 4 Johns., 483; *Jackson* v. *Murray*, 1 Cow., 156. The motion must be denied.

Motion denied.

SEEBER v. YATES.

Judgment by Default, on Note with Money Counts —Amendment—Costs.

Where, on a judgment by default, on a declaration upon a promissory note, with the money counts, the plaintiff had caused the damages to be assessed by the clerk, and taken final judgment without entering a *nolle prosequi* as to the money counts; on a motion to set aside the judgment and subsequent proceedings, he was allowed to amend on payment of costs, by then entering a *nolle prosequi*; and the motion to set aside the judgment was denied.

THE declaration, containing the money counts, with a count on a promissory note, the plaintiff's attorney had, after a judgment by default, inadvertently caused the damages to be assessed by the clerk on the note without first entering a *nolle prosequi* as to the money counts, and taken his final judgment and execution.

On this ground, it was now moved, in behalf of the defendant, that the judgment and subsequent proceedings should be set aside for irregularity.

For the plaintiff, it was moved that he might now enter a *nolle prosequi* as to the money counts; and having thus amended, retain his judgment and execution.

Mr. D. Eacker, for the motion.

Mr. N. N. Van Alstine, contra.

Curia. The plaintiff may amend, on paying the costs of the defendant's motion, upon which his motion shall be refused.

Rule accordingly.

---

*ANONYMOUS.]*41

Preference of Suits Under Statute.

A suit on a policy against an incorporated insurance company, not entitled to preference, within the Statute, sess. 48, ch. 325, sec. 4.

Citation—Act, April 21, 1825, sess. 48, ch. 325.

ON motion that an argument, takes preference on the calendar:

The Court decided that a suit upon a policy of insurance against an incorporated insurance company, was not entitled to preference within the 4th section of the "Act to Prevent Fraudulent Bankruptcies by Incorporated Companies," &c., passed Apr. 21, 1825, sess. 48, ch. 325; a policy not being a contract, note or other evidence of debt, within the meaning of the statute. They said it meant some instrument which is, in itself, evidence of debt, as a note, bill of exchange or bond, &c.

Cited in—25 Hun, 584.

THE PEOPLE v. BROWN, late Sheriff of SCHOHARIE.

Amendment of Interrogatories—Liability of Sheriff.

Interrogatories, filed on the return of an attachment, amended by inserting an additional interrogatory.

The sheriff is liable to an attachment for not returning process pursuant to a rule, though it never came to his own hands, but only to the hands of his deputy.

Citations—7 Johns., 555; 1 Johns. Cas., 137; Col. Cas., 76.

THE defendant being brought up on attachment for not returning a *fi. fa.*, in answer to the interrogatories filed, said that the *fi. fa.* had been received by his under-sheriff, and that the money had been collected; and that he had not returned the execution; but did not say whether he had received notice of a rule to make the return; and the attorney for the plaintiffs had inadvertently omitted an interrogatory to that point.

Mr. James Edwards, for the plaintiffs, moved to amend by inserting this interrogatory.

Mr. M. T Reynolds, contra, insisted that the amendment was not admissible; but,

The Court allowed it.

This being made, the defendant admitted notice of a rule to return the *fi. fa.* But then,

42*] **Mr. Reynolds* submitted whether he should not be discharged, on the ground that the execution and the money collected had not come to his own hands, but the hands of his under-sheriff. And he cited *People* v. *Waters*, 1 Johns. Cas., 137; *People* v. *Gilliland*, 7 Johns., 555. But,

The Court agreed that this was no objection. They said the remedy by attachment, although in form a criminal, was in truth but a civil proceeding; and the sheriff was liable for the act of his deputy, the same as in a civil action; that *People* v. *Gilliland* went upon the very great delay, and the death of the deputy. The case cited from *Johnson's* and *Coleman's* cases has not been followed. The court look to the sheriff. They do not know the deputy in this and the like proceedings. The sheriff must stand committed till the money and costs are paid.

Rule accordingly.

Cited in—2 Wend., 281; 31 Barb., 443; Abb. Adm., 514, 518.

JACKSON, ex. dem. WELLS ET AL., v. BREESE.

Practice—Costs.

Where a cause goes off at the circuit, because the plaintiff is not ready, he cannot recover the costs of that circuit, though he finally succeed in the cause.

EJECTMENT. Verdict and judgment for the plaintiff. The cause had been noticed for trial twice. On the first notice, the plaintiff not being ready at the circuit, the cause went off for that reason. The plaintiff's attorney insisted on having his costs of that circuit taxed in the final bill, and that they should make a part of the judgment; but,

Mr. Storrs, first judge of Oneida, before whom the taxation took place, excluded them.

Mr. T. E. Clarke, therefore, moved for a retaxation.

Mr. J. Platt, contra.

Curia. Judge Storrs was right in disallowing these costs. Where a cause goes off at the

43*] circuit, because the *plaintiff is not ready, he cannot recover his costs of that circuit, though he is finally successful; and so we have often decided.

Motion denied.

Cited in—6 Wend., 525; 2 How. Pr., 11.

EX PARTE FORT.

Non Pros. *in Replevin—Defendant's Rights—Costs*—Mandamus.

The defendant may *non pros.* the plaintiff in replevin, though the plaint has not been returned, especially where it is withdrawn by the plaintiff from the sheriff's hands.

And to support the proceedings, even after error brought, the court may allow the defendant to file a plaint *nunc pro tunc.*

Citation—1 R. L., 91, sec. 1.

MR. J. A. Spencer, moved for a *mandamus* to the C. P. of Madison Co., commanding them to vacate a rule allowing Ratmour and Smalley, defendants in replevin, in that court, at the suit of Fort, to file a plaint *nunc pro tunc.* The facts were, that the clerk of Fort's attorney had made out and delivered, a plaint in replevin to the Sheriff of Madison, against Ratmour and Smalley, which was executed. But the attorney, on the fact coming to his knowledge, being satisfied that the action would not lie, withdrew the plaint; and it was never returned. The attorney for Ratmour and Smalley, however, entered their appearance and proceeded to *non pros.* the plaintiff. Whereupon Fort brought error to this court, and assigned, among other errors, diminution in the want of a plaint in the C. P. The attorney of Ratmour and Smalley applied to the C. P., who granted them leave to file a proper plaint *nunc pro tunc*; so that Fort's writ of error would be defeated in this respect.

Mr. Spencer insisted that the plaintiff had a right to withdraw the plaint. The only consequence was that he forfeited the bond, which he had given to prosecute the suit with effect. Until the plaint was returned, and the plaintiff appeared, the defendants could not *non pros.* him, but should have taken their remedy upon the bond. (2 Archb. Pr., 64; 1 Bos. & P., 410.) The right to *non pros.*, both in England and this State, depends on statute—in England, on 13 Car. 2, St. 2, ch. 2, sec. 3. (1 Tidd, 412.) Under that statute, the defendant may appear and *non pros.* the *plaintiff, though the [*44 process be not returned. (*Id.*, 413; 7 Mod., 32.) But it will be seen that our statute on the same subject, 1 R. L., 345, sec. 11, differs from the English. It requires the return of the process.

Messrs. S. Chapman and *A. Stewart*, contra, cited Col. and Cai. Cas., 61; 1 Archb. Pr., 228, 229.

Curia. The Statute, 1 R. L., 91, sec. 1, makes it the duty of the sheriff to return the plaint, to the next Court of C. P. It is, in this respect, like any other process in his hands. Now, whether the plaintiff had a right, in this case, to withdraw the process or not, we think the C. P. were correct in the rule which they made. The defendant should not be deprived of his *nonpros.* by the act of the plaintiff in withdrawing the process. It is served. The defendant's duty to himself requires that he should defend his rights. He retains an attorney, incurs expense, and his only remedy for his costs, in ordinary cases, is by *non pros.* He has, we think, the same remedy in replevin. If, as insisted by the counsel for the relator, it is necessary that the process be actually returned, to warrant the *non pros.*, this, of itself, shows the importance of allowing process to be filed *nunc pro tunc*, in order that the proceedings may be sustained in point of form. And more especially, where the process is withheld from the files by the plaintiff.

The motion must be denied.

Motion denied.

Cited in—6 How. Pr., 51.

EX PARTE STAFFORD.

Practice—Appeal.

An appeal lies from the judgment of a justice in favor of the plaintiff, where an issue is joined; though the defendant do not appear, and take no part in the trial.

STAFFORD sued Faniham before a justice of Madison Co. He declared, and Faniham pleaded the general issue. The cause was then **45***] adjourned. The defendant *did not appear at the adjourned day, when the justice heard the cause and gave judgment for Stafford. Faniham appealed to the Madison C. P. On a motion before them, in behalf of Stafford, to quash the appeal, on the ground that, there having been no trial before the justice, a *certiorari*, not an appeal, was the proper remedy, they denied the motion.

Mr. J. A. Spencer, now moved, *ex parte*, for an alternative *mandamus*, commanding them to quash the appeal, and cited laws of 1824, sess. 47, ch. 238, p. 294, sec. 36, and *Harwood* v. *French*, 4 Cow., 501.

The motion was not opposed; but,

Per Curiam. The case cited was one in which no issue was joined. If an issue is joined, there must be a trial before judgment can be rendered for the plaintiff; though it may be *ex parte*, and like an inquest at the circuit. It is not the less a trial of the cause, within the words of the statute, because it is not actually contested, and witnesses sworn on both sides. It does not alter its character, whether the defendant be present or absent.

The motion must be denied.

Motion denied.

PRESCOTT
v.
ROBERTS, Impleaded with HIBBARD.

One Affidavit of Merits to Prevent Inquest, Sufficient.

One affidavit of merits to prevent an inquest is sufficient, though the cause be several times noticed for trial and inquest.

And if filed and served on the plaintiff's attorney, for a circuit in one county, it is sufficient, though the venue be afterwards changed to another county, and the cause be tried in the latter.

Citation—4 Cow., 540.

THE venue, in this cause, was at first laid in the County of Onondaga, and was noticed for trial and inquest there, at the last March Circuit. To prevent an inquest, and put the plaintiff to the regular course of the calendar, the defendant filed with the circuit clerk the usual affidavit of merits, and served a copy on the plaintiff's attorney. The cause not being then tried, the venue was changed to the County of Rensselaer, by stipulation between the parties. *The plaintiff then noticed the [***46** cause for trial and inquest, at the last June Circuit in Rensselaer, when an inquest was taken against the defendant in the cause out of its order on the calendar—no new affidavit of merits being filed and served by the defendant, in order to prevent this.

A motion was now made, on the part of the defendant, to set aside that inquest, and all subsequent proceedings, for irregularity; and 6 Johns., 19; 2 Dunl. Pr., 686, and 4 Cow., 539, 540, were cited in support of the motion.

Mr. J. Watson, for the motion.

Mr. J. Fleming, Jr., contra.

Curia. We held (4 Cow., 540) that a single affidavit of merits extends throughout the whole progress of the cause; that there is no need of one at every circuit at which the cause may be noticed. This was, however, of a cause where there had been no change of venue. The affidavit filed at Onondaga was not notice to the circuit judge at Rensselaer, but it was notice to the attorney for the plaintiff. This was enough. A change of venue does not vary the principle. The motion must be granted. But as the precise point has not before been decided, we grant the motion without costs.

Motion granted.

Cited in—6 How. Pr., 105.

THE PRESIDENT, DIRECTORS AND COMPANY OF THE NEW JERSEY PROTECTION AND LOMBARD BANK
v.
THORP.

Parties—Foreign Corporation—May Sue in this Court—Substitution of Trustees.

A foreign corporation may sue in this court.

And where, after suit commenced, the Act of Incorporation was repealed, and the property of the Corporation vested in trustees, who were authorized to sue, and be substituted for the Corporation in suits brought; on motion, the trustees were made parties to the suit, instead of the Corporation.

Citation—4 Cow., 529, *n.*, 530, *n.*

THE plaintiffs were incorporated by an Act of the Legislature of N. J., reserving the right to appeal or *modify the Act, at [***47** any time. The plaintiffs sued in this court for a debt due to them. Afterwards the Legislature of N. J. repealed their charter, and passed a law vesting all the property of the Corporation in three trustees. This last Act was passed Nov. 23, 1825; and afterwards in Dec. of the same year, the Legislature passed a supplemental Act, authorizing the trustees to maintain suits in their own names as trustees; and providing that they should be substituted for the plaintiffs, in suits before commenced in the name of the plaintiffs.

NOTE.—*Corporations—Foreign—May sue and be sued out of the jurisdiction creating them.*

A Corporation created in one State has, strictly speaking, no extra territorial life or authority. Generally, however, its existence is recognized in other states, and its operations are permitted where such operations do not come in contact with their own laws. Merrick v. Van Santvoord, 34 N. Y., 208; Mumford v. Am. Life Ins. Co., 4 N. Y., 463; Bard v. Poole, 12 N. Y., 495; Stoney v. Am. Life Ins. Co., 11 Paige Ch., 635; Silver Lake Bank v. North, 4 Johns.

Mr. P. W. Radcliff moved that these trustees be substituted in this suit accordingly. He cited 4 Johns. Ch., 370, 372, and the cases there cited.

Mr. D. Selden, contra, cited 1 Bl. Com., 512; *Id.*, 311; 2 Kyd, Corp., 516; 3 Ves., 429, 435; 10 Ves., 352; 8 Wh., 488; 3 T. R., 727; 1 H. Bl., 123; 3 Cr., 319.

Curia. It was very properly conceded on the argument, by the counsel for the defendant, that foreign corporations may sue here. Nothing is better settled. (4 Cow., 529, *note*, and cases there cited.) Is this case, then, distinguishable in principle? We think not. The Act does not interfere with an existing remedy of our own. It was likened to the case of the assignees of foreign bankrupts, who, as it is held by some cases, cannot sue here. (*Vide* 4 Cow., 530, *note*, and cases there cited.) But the cases are not similar. Though bankrupt assignments are sanctioned by statute, they have been regarded in the light of voluntary assignments; and when they relate to choses in action, we may apply our own remedies—holding that the suit must still be in the name of the original creditor. These trustees are a *quasi* Corporation, and come directly within the rule which gives an action here in favor of a foreign corporation.

Motion granted.

Cited in—5 Wend., 482; 5 N. Y., 341; 6 Lans., 28; 29 Barb., 587; 10 How. Pr., 7; 57 How. Pr., 15; 14 Abb. Pr., 120; 36 Super., 187; 2 Leg. Obs., 274.

48*] *ROOSEVELT
v.
FULTON ET AL., Heirs of FULTON.

Venire—*Non-Enumerated Motion.*

Matters properly inserted in a bill of exceptions cannot be heard on non-enumerated motion: *e. g.*, an objection that the plaintiff was proceeding in defiance of an injunction from the court of chancery.

On a plea of *riens per descent*, the *venire* need not be special.

Though there be several issues of fact the *venire* need not be special.

The *venire tam quam* applies only where there is a demurrer or default, as well as an issue of fact.

IN covenant against the defendants, they pleaded *non infregit conventionem*, and *riens per descent*. To the latter plea the plaintiff replied, that the defendants had sufficient lands by descent, &c., and issue. The award of the *venire* on the roll was in the common general form, and the *venire* itself was in the same form—commanding the sheriff to summon 12, &c., to make a jury, &c., between the parties in a plea of covenant, &c., without referring to the plea of *riens per descent*, or expressing the purpose to inquire into the value of the lands descended, according to the Statute, 1 R. L., 317, sec. 4. An objection was made to the *venire* at the circuit, as irregular on that account; but the judge overruled the objection; nor was the value of the lands inquired of by the jury.

Several other objections were made by the defendant in the course of the trial, and among others, that the plaintiff was going on with the trial in violation of an injunction which had issued from the Court of Chancery, enjoining him not to proceed against the defendants as to part of the moneys which he claimed in this suit; and it was insisted that the plaintiff should not be allowed to claim before the jury, the moneys thus enjoined; but the judge overruled the objections, and the defendants excepted. The bill of exceptions was settled, and the cause placed upon the calendar for argument upon that bill.

Mr. C. Graham now moved to set aside the verdict for irregularity, and cited 1 Archb. Pr., 156, 159; 1 R. L., 317; 2 Archb. Pr., 136, 137; 1 Wentw. Pl., 43; 2 Saund., 7, *note.*

Mr. J. I. Roosevelt, contra, cited Mitf., 208; 2 Johns., 24, 181; Phil. Ev., 226; 1 Munf., 437; 3 Cow., 622; Coop. Pl., 269; Mitf., 194; 1 Johns., 287; Gilb. Ev., 28; Bull. *N. P.*, 232; 1 Munf., 394, 403; Phil. Ev., 231; Hardr., 472; Rep. *t.* Holt, 134; 3 Mod., 141; 3 *East, 365; 18 Johns., [*49 352; 5 Mass., 181, 182; Mitf., 193; 1 Esp., 43; 4 Johns. Ch., 619; 1 Ch. Pl., 459; 7 East, 153; 8 *Id.*, 344; 10 *Id.*, 377; 2 *Id.*, 442; 4 *Id.*, 311; Tidd, 1022; 2 Camph., 396; 10 East, 38; 16 *Id.*, 39; 1 Phil. Ev., 237; 13 Johns., 139; 1 Johns. Cas., 436; 4 Johns., 510; 1 Archb., 159.

Curia. The questions properly in the bill of exceptions cannot be heard now. The only point which we can decide on non-enumerated motion is, whether the *venire* was regular, being in the general form; and we think it was. Because a jury are required by law to find any matter specially, it does not follow that the *venire* should contain that matter. Wherever there is an issue or issues of fact, the *venire* is general, "to make a jury between the parties, in such a plea, because they have put themselves upon that jury." This reaches every case except the single one cited from Archbold by the counsel, where there is a demurrer or default as well as an issue of fact. There the *venire* cannot say, generally, the parties have put themselves on a jury. This is only true of part. Hence the *venire tam quam*, which is almost the only exception. There are many other cases in which the jury are required to

---

Ch., 370; Jessup v. Carnegie, 80 N. Y., 441; Lumbard v. Aldrich, 8 N. H., 31; National Trust Co. v. Murphey, 30 N. J. Eq., 408; Lathrop v. Commercial Bank, 8 Dana, 114; Bateman v. Service, 6 App. Cas., 386; Bank of Augusta v. Earle, 13 Pet., 519; Covoell v. Springs Co., 100 U. S., 55; Christian Union v. Yount, 101 U. S., 352. See, also, Kennebec Co. v. Augusta Ins. Co., 72 Mass. (6 Gray), 204; Newburg Petroleum Co. v. Weare, 27 Ohio St., 343; Bank of Cincinnati v. Hall, 35 Ohio St., 158; Howe Machine Co. v. Walker, 35 U. C. Q. B., 37; Runyan v. Coster, 14 Pet., 122; Williams v. Creswell, 51 Miss., 817.

But it cannot exercise greater powers elsewhere than are allowed to it by law where created. Kerr v. Dougherty, 79 N. Y., 327; Thompson v. Waters, 25 Mich., 214; Starkweather v. Bible Society, 72 Ill., 50; S. C. 22 Am. Rep., 133.

A corporation created in one state or country may, generally, sue and be sued in the courts of another on compliance with the conditions imposed as to costs, service of process, &c. Cunningham v. Pell, 5 Paige, 607; N. Y. Floating Derrick Co. v. N. J. Oil Co., 3 Duer, 648; Mutual Benefit Life Ins. Co. v. Davis, 12 N. Y., 569; Silver Lake Bank v. North, 4 Johns. Ch., 370; Bank of Commerce v. Rutland & C. Ry. Co., 10 How. Pr., 1; Elizabethport Mfg. Co. v. Campbell, 13 Abb. Pr., 86; Fisk v. Chicago & C. Ry. Co., 4 Abb. Pr. N. S., 378; Paper Works v. Willett, 14 Abb. Pr., 119; British Am. Land Co. v. Ames, 47 Mass. (6 Met.), 391; American Ins. Co. v. Owen, 81 Mass. (15 Gray), 493; Runyan v. Coster, 14 Pet., 122; Society &c. v. Wheeler, 2 Gall., 105; Bank of Augusta v. Earle, 13 Pet., 519, 588, 589; Berne v. Bank of England, 9 Ves., 347.

find specially, without any special *venire*. In replevin, they are required, if the distress was for rent, to inquire of two things—the amount in arrear, and the value of the goods distrained. This, too, is by statute; but a special *venire* was, we presume, never thought of in such a case.

Motion denied.

Cited in—3 Wend., 262.

50*] *VAN DEUSEN
v.
A. BROWER, J. BROWER, P. BROWER AND C. M. BROWER.

Failure of Infant, to Appear in Non-Bailable Action—Appointment of Nominal Guardian—Execution—Amendment.

In a non-bailable action against infants, the plaintiff may take a rule that they appear in 20 days after personal service of the rule; or that the plaintiff's attorney have leave to appoint John Doe, a nominal person, for their guardian, and enter their appearance.

On filing an affidavit of the service, the plaintiff may enter a rule of course for the appointment of John Doe as guardian.

In an action against heirs, if they will show nothing by descent, or insufficient assets by descent, they must plead, or give notice of this specially; and cannot show it upon the general issue.

The rules of pleading are the same in this respect, in the case of heirs, as of personal representatives.

If they do not so plead, the plaintiff may take judgment, either generally, or of assets descended, at his election.

Execution against infant heirs, cannot issue till a year after judgment.

But where some of the heirs are adults, it may issue against them short of the year.

If issued against both short of the year, it may be so amended as to affeet only the adults.

Where the plaintiff appears for infants, by a nominal guardian, the court will, at any time before the judgment is finally executed, let them in to plead, the judgment standing as security.

Execution amended as to the return day.

Citations—2 Sellon, 68; 2 Archb. Pr., 145, 137-8.

THIS action was *assumpsit* against the defendants, as heirs at law of Aaron Brower, deceased. The *capias ad respondendum* was returned served on all the defendants, in August Term, 1820. A. and J. Brower, being adults, appeared and pleaded the general issue. The other two defendants, being then and still infants, the plaintiff, at the October Term, 1820, obtained a rule that they appear by some guardian, in 20 days after personal service of the rule; or that the plaintiff's attorney should have leave to appoint John Doe for their guardian, and enter their appearance. Service of the rule being made accordingly, and they not appearing, on filing an affidavit of the service, the plaintiff entered his rule for the appointment of John Doe, a nominal guardian, having no real existence.

The cause was afterwards tried on the general issue as to the other defendants, and no defense of *riens per descent* was interposed. In February Term, 1825, the plaintiff entered a judgment for the plaintiff generally against all the defendants, upon the verdict against the adults, on on *nil dicet*, as to the infants.

A *fi. fa.* was issued against and levied on the property of all the defendants before one year had elapsed after the judgment. No return day was mentioned in this execution.

Mr. J. A. Spencer moved to set aside the judgment, and all subsequent proceedings. He cited 2 Tidd, 854; 13 Johns., *97; 1 R. [*51 L., 515; 14 Johns., 417; 12 Johns., 434; Bac. Abr., Error, M; 1 R. L., 318, sec. 6; 41 Johns., 424; *Simonds* v. *Catlin*, 2 Cai., 61; 2 Str., 1076; 2 Wils., 50; 2 Johns. Dig., 20, Infant, III.; 2 Johns., 192; 2 Cow., 430.

Mr. Jas. Edwards, contra, cited 2 Sell. Pr., 67, 68; 2 Archb. Pr., 145; Bac. Abr., Heir and Ancestor, H; Plowd., 440; 20 Johns., 414; 1 R. L., 316, sec. 4; 2 Cow., 619.

Curia. In the English courts, if an infant do not appear in a non-bailable action, the plaintiff obtains an order from a judge, which is, of course, that unless the infant appear in six days after personal service of the order, the plaintiff may assign John Doe for his guardian, and file common bail for him. This has long been the settled practice. (2 Sell., 68; 2 Archb. Pr., 145.) Of course, it is the practice of this court, except that the six days are changed to 20. The judgment is, therefore, regular against all the defendants, unless the exceptions to its form be well taken.

The principles of pleading seem to be the same, both as to the real and personal representative. If the latter mean to protect himself from personal liability, he must do so by showing the state of the assets, if he cannot succeed in defeating the action upon the merits. So the former must plead *riens per descent*, or other plea adapted to try the amount of assets descended. If he omit to do so, the plaintiff may, in his election, take judgment of the assets; or proceed as he has done here, to a judgment generally, the same as if the action had been for the defendant's own debt. A summary of the authorities on this head is given in 2 Archb. Pr., 137, 138.

The execution is irregular as to the infants, but not so as to the adults. *Shooke* v. *Phillips*, 5 Cow., 440. As to the former, it must be set aside; but the plaintiff may so amend that it shall command the sheriff to levy of the property of the latter. He may also amend by inserting a return day.

*But no laches can be imputed to the [*52 infants, and if any one will put in an advantageous plea for them, it should be received. Let the default as to them be set aside, provided they appear by guardian in two months—the present judgment, however, to stand as security.

No costs are allowed on either side.

RULE: That the motion to set aside the judgment and execution be denied as to Aaron and John Brower, but granted as to the other defendants; that the plaintiff have leave to amend his execution by inserting a return day; and so that it shall be operative against the estates of Aaron and John Brower only; that the default against the other defendants be set aside, provided they appear in two months by a real guardian, the present judgment standing as security; and no costs of this motion to be allowed on either side.

Cited in—10 Barb., 353.

W. GOULD, BANKS AND S. GOULD v. OGDEN.

Question of Law Before Referees.

Where a question of law arises before referees, which is brought before the Supreme Court and decided, they will order a special entry on the record, so as to present the same question to the Court of Errors.

Citation—3 Cow., 389.

ASSUMPSIT for goods sold, &c., with the other common counts. Plea, *non assumpsit*, with other pleas, and a notice of set-off.

The cause was referred on the defendant's motion; and the question before the referees was, whether certain payments made by the defendant to and receipted by S. Gould, should be applied to the demand in favor of the plaintiffs. The referees allowed the payment and reported only $3.70 in favor of the plaintiffs. The report was signed Nov. 20, 1823; and being filed, notice was given of a motion to set it aside on the merits, at February Term, 1824. In February Term, 1825, the motion was denied. The defendant, Apr. 29 last, gave notice of taxing his costs.

The motion to set aside the report was founded on the sole affidavit of the counsel for the plaintiffs; and,

53*] *Mr. *J. Hoyt* now moved that the defendant be required to incorporate that affidavit in his judgment record, so as to enable the plaintiffs to bring error upon the decision of the referees; and cited *Reid* v. *Renss. Glass Factory*, 3 Cow., 387.

Mr. J. Platt, contra.

Curia. Take a similar rule to the one granted in *Reid* v. *Renss. Glass Factory*, 3 Cow., 389.(*a*)

Rule accordingly.

(*a*) *Vide* S.C., on error, 5 Cow., 587, where the practice adopted by the Supreme Court was sanctioned.

EX PARTE CAYKENDOLL.

Jurors—When Affidavits of to Show Mistake, not Received.

The affidavits of jurors cannot be received to show a mistake in making up their verdict, unless the mistake is produced by circumstances passing at the trial, which are equivalent to a misdirection of the judge.

Citation—5 Cow., 106.

IN December Term, 1825, of the Orange C. P., a cause was tried between Caykendoll, plaintiff, and Van Bomel, defendant. The action was *assumpsit*, and the jury found for the plaintiff $60 damages.

Afterwards, three of the jurors made affidavit that the action was brought on a written agreement for drawing, rafting and running boards, by the plaintiff for the defendant; that the price fixed by the contract was 9*s* per 1,000 for drawing, and 10*s*. for rafting and running; and that, in calculating the sum to be allowed the plaintiff, the jury multiplied the number of boards drawn by 19, instead of 9, which made about $60. That the jury intended to allow for the drawing only; and the deponents believed that the mistake arose from the jury reading 19 for 9, in the agreement (which was delivered to the jury), and supposing this was the sum fixed for drawing only; that they did not discover their mistake till the day after the verdict, when it became a subject of anxious inquiry among them how the mistake should be rectified.

On these affidavits, the C. P. granted a new trial.

*A motion was now made for a *mandamus* commanding the C. P. to vacate their rule for a new trial, and give judgment according to the verdict. [*54

Mr. C. Monell, for the motion, cited 2 T. R., 281; 5 Burr., 2667.

Curia, per SUTHERLAND, *J.* The decision of the Court of C. P. cannot be sustained. It is certainly well settled, that the affidavits of jurors cannot be received, to show a mistake in making up their verdict; and we never intended to detract from that rule in *Sargeant* v. ———, 5 Cow., 106. In that case, the counsel advanced an erroneous rule of damages to the jury, which was not corrected in the charge of the judge. The jury were in this way led to adopt the rule. We considered these circumstances equivalent to a positive misdirection of the judge; and allowed the affidavits of jurors to be read, showing that they were, in fact, misled. It was impossible to make out what, in truth, operated as a misdirection of the judge, in any other way. Misdirection is a very usual ground for granting a new trial; and the case cited establishes merely, that a set of circumstances may amount to the same thing; and may be shown by the affidavits of jurors. Further we did not mean to go; and we expressly disclaimed the idea of trenching on any of the cases which had refused to hear the affidavits of jurors. The motion must be granted.

Rule for an alternative mandamus.

Cited in—5 Den., 369; 63 N. Y., 363; 25 Cal., 400; 40 Am. Dec., 166 (13 N. H., 462); 20 Am. Rep., 546 (63 N. Y., 361).

JOHNSON v. GAY.

Order of Referees as to Costs.

An order of referees as to the costs, on postponing the hearing before them, is not a foundation for a rule on the subject, in the Supreme Court;

Whether they may impose costs as the condition of adjourning, *quære*.

THIS cause being referred, and the referees having convened to hear it, the defendant's counsel moved, on the affidavit of the absence of a material witness, to put off the hearing. *This was objected to by the plaintiff's [*55 counsel, unless the plaintiff's costs of preparing for the hearing were first paid. But the referees, doubting their power to impose this condition, though they agreed that the costs should be paid, adjourned unconditionally.

Mr. W. H. Maynard now moved for a rule against the defendant, that he pay the costs, which had been taxed, or that an attachment issue.

Mr. C. P. Kirkland, contra, cited 1 R. L., 516, sec. 2; Jac. Law Dict., Attachment.

Curia. Any order or direction as to costs, which referees may make, is no foundation for our interference by attachment. Nor is it necessary, in this case, for us to say whether they have power to impose the payment of costs, as the condition of an adjournment.

Motion denied.

Cited in—9 Wend., 253; 5 Hill, 375; 15 Abb. N. S. 220.

DOE v. ROE.

New Trial—Motion.

The Supreme Court will not, in general, hear a motion for a new trial, on a case made upon the trial of a feigned issue, ordered by a circuit court of equity.

The proper course is, to move in the court which ordered the issue.

THIS was a case made on trial of a feigned issue of *devisavit vel non*, directed by the judge of the 6th circuit, sitting in equity.

The judge of that circuit tried the cause at law. The cause being on the calendar of the present term for argument upon the case,

Mr. J. Platt moved, on the authority of *Doe* v. *Roe*, 1 Cow., 216, to strike it off.

Mr. J. A. Spencer said that case was distinguishable from this—not only as being an issue on a bill filed for a divorce, but also as arising under the old organization of the judiciary, when the judge who held the circuit had no chancery powers. Here the very judge who orders the issue tries the cause at the circuit, and reviews it on a motion for a new trial.

56*] **Curia.* We do not mean to say that we have not power to hear the case, but we think the most proper course is to move in the court of equity.

Motion granted.

ADAMS v. MINTON.

Time of Service of Plea.

A plea served before special bail is perfected, in a bailable action, is a nullity, and does not become good by a subsequent justification, unless it was received *de bene esse*, and notice of this given to the defendant.

Citations—2 Cow., 622; 1 Cow., 54, 60, 226; 1 Archb., 112; 4 T. R., 578; 2 East., 406.

MOTION, by the defendant, to set aside the plaintiff's verdict for irregularity.

The action was a bailable one. The defendant put in R. Farr and John Doe as bail, and sent a plea of the general issue to the plaintiff, Apr. 24, last. On the 30th, the plaintiff gave notice of exception to the bail. The defendant then gave notice of moving for an order to mitigate bail, and that two substantial persons would justify as such, May 20. On that day the amount of bail was fixed by the commissioner, and a justification took place accordingly; whereupon, without waiting for a new plea, the plaintiff immediately, on the same day, served notice of trial for the following June Circuit, when he took an inquest. This was on June 9. June 30, the plaintiff was served by the defendant with a copy of the former plea.

Mr. J. H. Ostram, for the defendant, now insisted that the first plea was a nullity, on the ground that the bail had not become perfect when it was served.

Mr. A. Dana, contra.

Curia. It is impossible to sustain this proceeding. Here was no bail, for any substantial purpose, when the first plea was served. This has been decided over and over. (2 Cow., 622; 1 *Id.*, 54, 60, 226.) In the last two cases, the plaintiff's attorney returned the pleas, on the ground that bail was not perfect; but there is no need of this ceremony. Whether he do it or not, the plea must *be regarded as a [*57 mere nullity; and the plaintiff may take his default, even after the bail have justified (1 Archb., 112; 4 T. R., 578), except in the case of a plea in abatement. (1 Archb., 112; 2 East, 406.) The justification does not make the plea good in the plaintiff's hands; nor will his filing common bail have that effect, after he has refused a plea for want of special bail. (1 Cow., 226.) The course of the plaintiff was to wait the four days after justification; and then take his default for want of a plea, according to the 7th Gen. Rule of April Term, 1796. This case is the stronger, inasmuch as the plaintiff virtually declined the plea, by excepting to the bail. If he had intended that it should become good without any new service, he should have received it specially, and given notice of this to the defendant's attorney.

Motion granted, with costs.

Cited in—7 Cow., 509.

HARVEY AND WALKER v. BARDWELL ET. AL.

Action on Penal Bond—Penalty, Proper Measure as to Costs—Exception in case of Set-Off.

In an action on a penal bond, or of debt on the penalty in articles of agreement, the judgment is properly for the penalty in all cases, except where the sum is reduced by set-off under the Stat. 1 R. L., 515, 516.

And where the penalty of articles was $500, though the money due was only $14; held, that the plaintiff recovering, should have full costs.

Citations—13 Johns., 345; 1 R. L., 515, 516; 2 Johns. Cas., 406; 10 Johns., 219; 5 Cow., 424; 2 Cai., 107; 2 Cow., 412.

A MOTION was made in behalf of the defendants, that the judgment for the plaintiffs, as to costs, be set aside, and that the defendants be allowed their costs.

The action was debt for the penalty of $500, on sealed articles between the parties, by which the defendants, among other things, agreed to pay certain moneys to the plaintiffs. The breaches assigned were the non-payment of the moneys. The same articles contained various covenants on the part of the plaintiffs to the defendants. On the penalty for the non-performance of these covenants, the defendants had, shortly after the commencement of this suit, brought their action against the plaintiffs, and obtained judgment, with full costs. In the suit brought by the defendants there was a reference; and all matters of dispute arising under the articles, except the subject-matter of this suit, were heard and passed upon by the referees, who reported for the defendants $16 ; so that the question in this suit was confined merely to the amount of moneys **58***] *due to the plaintiffs. This cause was also referred, and the referees passed upon the claim of the plaintiffs, reporting $14 in their favor. They entered up judgment for the penalty, with full costs.

Mr. J. Dickson, for the motion.

Mr. C. Perkins, contra.

Curia. The demand of the plaintiffs having been narrowed down to a money claim ; and there being no need of the penalty to secure further breaches, and the damages reported being only $14, and below what, in a judgment, would carry costs, the question is, whether the penalty or the damages were the proper measure of the judgment. When that is ascertained, we have a test for the costs. (13 Johns., 345.)

The case of *Alendorf* v. *Stickle*, 2 Cow., 412, was one of set-off, within the Statute 1 R. L., 515, 516. It was this which led to the distinction mentioned by the court, between bonds for performance of covenants, and money bonds. Where the latter are in question upon a set-off, the sum really due is the debt ; and the judgment goes accordingly, either for plaintiff or defendant. Except in the single case of set-off, all bonds and agreements secured by a penalty stand on the same footing, and the plaintiff recovers costs according to the penalty. The case of set-off is *sui generis*, and stands upon the statute providing for that alone. *Vide* 2 Johns. Cas., 406 ; 10 Johns., 219 ; 13 *Id.*, 345 ; 5 Cow., 424 ; 2 Cai., 107.

The motion must be denied, with costs.

Motion denied.

Cited in—12 Wend., 141; 19 How. Pr., 388.

59*] *CLARKE *v.* SPENCER.

Power of Judge at Chambers.

A judge at chambers, has no power to order a party to furnish copies of papers, which are evidence in the cause, to his adversary.

Citation—19 Johns., 268.

GENERAL *indebitatus assumpsit.* On the application of the defendant's attorney to a commissioner, having power to do chamber business of a judge of this court, he made an order, "that the plaintiff's attorney deliver to the defendant's attorney a copy of the receipt, which is the evidence of the payment of the money for which this suit is brought ;" and, in the meantime, that all proceedings in the suit be stayed.

A motion was now made to set aside this order, on the ground that the commissioner had exceeded his powers.

Mr. H. Welles, for the motion, cited 19 Johns., 268 ; 1 Cow., 574.

Mr. B. D. Noxon, contra, cited 1 Cow., 571; 2 Archb. Pr., 197, 198.

Curia. In *Willis* v. *Bailey*, 19 Johns., 268, this court declared they had not adopted the English practice of allowing these orders at chambers. Aside, therefore, from the question, whether even this court would order copies of papers, which are not the direct foundation of the suit or defense, to be furnished, the motion must be granted.

Motion granted.

Cited in—12 Leg. Obs., 139.

EX PARTE DECKER.

Appeal Bond Executed in Blank—Agent Cannot Change, After Delivery to Justice.

An appeal bond executed in blank, and delivered to an agent, to fill up and make perfect, cannot be altered by him, after he has filled the blanks, and delivered the bond to the justice.

Whether a parol power to fill the blanks and perfect the bond, was valid, *quære*.

BAKER recovered judgment against Decker, in a justice's court of the County of Steuben, whence Decker sought to appeal. For this purpose, within the time limited for appealing, the requisite bond was prepared, with a blank *for the penalty and the amount [***60** of the judgment, and executed by Decker and a surety. This they delivered to the subscribing witness, with oral power to fill up the blanks according to the judgment, and also to make any other alterations necessary to render it valid according to the statute. The witness carried the bond to the justice, and on learning the amount of the judgment, filled up the bond. Afterwards, and still within the time for appealing, supposing the bond to be defective in other particulars, the witness requested the bond of the justice, for the purpose of making it perfect. The justice refused his consent to the alteration, declaring that he did not think it proper. But the witness took the bond, and added the clause, obliging the obligors to pay the judgment before the justice, with interest and costs of the appeal, &c.

The justice made the proper return ; but the C. P. dismissed the appeal, on the ground that the authority of the witness was by parol.

Mr. Wm. M. Oliver, now moved for a *mandamus* commanding the court to proceed in the cause. And he relied mainly on *Texira* v. *Evans*, cited in *Master* v. *Miller*, 1 Anst., 228, which was the case of a bond executed with blanks for the name of the obligee and sum, and delivered by the obligor to an agent, for the purpose of raising money. The plaintiff lent money, and the agent filled the blanks accordingly, and delivered the bond to the plaintiff. On *non est factum*, the bond was held good.

He also cited 11 Johns., 169 ; 4 *Id.*, 54 ; 18 *Id.*, 499.

The motion was not opposed ; but,

Per Curiam. The C. P. decided correctly. Though the agent might have had power to correct the bond on its delivery (a point which it is not necessary to decide), he certainly had no right to tamper with the bond in this way. He could not alter it again, and again, at his discretion. Such a general power cannot extend beyond the time of delivery. Its force was spent on filling up the blank.

Motion denied.

Cited in—13 Wend., 590; 22 Wend., 365; 24 N. Y., 387.

61*] *EX PARTE LA FARGE.

Mandamus—*Appeal from Justice Court—Costs.*

On motion for a *mandamus*, heading the affidavit, "Sup. Court. In the matter of J. L., against the judges, &c," is not such an entitling, as to prevent its being read.

To warrant an appeal from a justice's court, the costs must be actually paid. It is not in the power of the justice to waive the payment, by charging them in account against the party.

MR. G. C. BRONSON moved for a *mandamus* to the judges of the C. P. of Jefferson Co., commanding them to vacate a rule quashing an appeal, by La Farge, from a judgment before a justice against him, at the suit of Fuller and Everts.

No costs were actually paid to the justice, on serving the notice of appeal; but La Farge directed him, in writing, to charge the costs in account against him, which the justice did; and made an affidavit, which was read in the C. P. on the motion to quash the appeal for this cause, that he accepted this direction for the costs.

Mr. J. A. Spencer, contra, objected to the reading of the affidavit on which the present motion was founded, on the ground that it was entitled, "Sup. Court. In the matter of *John La Farge* against the judges of the Court of Common Pleas of Jefferson County."

Curia. This is not such an entitling of the affidavit, as comes within the rule relied on, that an affidavit entitled cannot be read. It is is not entitled in any cause, as pending in this court.

As to the merits of the motion, however, clearly there was no payment. The writing was a mere acknowledgment that La Farge owed the costs, and a request that they should be charged to him. To entitle him to an appeal, the party must comply strictly with the terms of the statute. The money must be actually paid.

Motion denied.

Cited in—1 Wend., 282; 4 Wend., 202; 18 Hun, 483; 10 Minn., 223.

62*] *THE PRESIDENT, DIRECTORS AND COMPANY OF THE BANK OF UTICA

v.

HILLARD.

Practice—Evidence—Denial of Motion to Inspect Books of Bank, or Allow Copies.

The English practice of ordering a party to furnish papers, or allow copies to be taken, thus furnishing evidence against himself, has not been adopted by the Supreme Court, except where the paper is the immediate foundation of the action; and in a few other cases depending on peculiar circumstances.

Motion to inspect the books of a bank, or compel them to allow copies to be taken, denied.

Citation—19 Johns., 286, 289.

MR. J. A. SPENCER, for the defendant, moved for a rule upon the plaintiffs, that they furnish to the defendant's attorney, copies of certain entries made in their books, relating to the note which they had declared on in this cause, or allow some proper person, to inspect and take copies of their books.

He cited *Clifford* v. *Taylor*, 1 Taunt., 167; *Goldschmidt* v. *Marryat*, 1 Camph., 561, 562; *Potts* v. *Adair*, 1 Anst., 259, and *Gabbit* v. *Cavendish*, 2 Anst., 547.

Mr. S. Beardsley, contra. This is not a motion by corporators, who have an interest in the books sought to be inspected, but by a mere stranger, who has no right to look into the private account books of his adversary. There is no difference, in this respect, between a corporation and a private person. When the writing, sought to be examined, does not constitute the immediate foundation of the action or defense, the court will not order an inspection, or a copy to be delivered, except in cases where forgery is alleged, or in actions on policies of insurance.

Curia. It seems by one of the cases cited in support of this motion, that the English courts go great lengths in granting the description of order applied for. It is granted by a judge at chambers, and the party is compelled to furnish evidence to the full extent of what he would be bound to do on a bill of discovery. This practice is of recent origin in England. It has not been adopted by this court; and we have often declined to follow it, on motion to compel the party to furnish evidence in this way against himself, except in certain cases; as where the instrument to be inspected or copied, is the immediate foundation of the action; and in a few other cases, depending on peculiar circumstances. *Willis* v. *Bailey*, 19 Johns., 268, 269.

*We see no reason, in the instance be- [*63 fore us, for going farther.

Motion denied.(a)

Cited in—25 How. Pr., 528; 1 Rob., 686; 12 Leg. Obs., 139.

(a) *Vide* 5 Cow., 419, S. C., and Clark v. Spencer, *ante*, 59.

OSHIEL

v.

DE GRAW, Impleaded with ROGERS and ROGERS.

Insufficient Service of Paper on Attorney—Stay of Proceedings.

Service of a paper on an attorney, in the city of N. Y., by affixing it on the door of the office, no one being at the office, and the door locked, before 9 A. M., is not good service.

Service of papers at the office of an attorney, in the City of N. Y., should be within office hours, which do not commence before 9 A. M.

Proceedings ordered to be stayed, in an action against the surety in a bond given on appeal from a justice's court, on his paying the amount of the penalty into court, with costs.

COVENANT, on a bond given by De Graw, as surety, under the Statute authorizing an appeal from a justice's court, conditioned to prosecute the appeal, &c.

Mr. Jas. Edwards, for the defendant, moved to set aside a default for not pleading; and that, on the defendant's paying the penalty of the bond, which was $100, with costs, into court, all further proceedings be stayed, &c.

Mr. W. Mulock, contra.

The facts are stated by the court.

Curia. The motion to set aside the default must be granted, if the service of an order to stay proceedings on the plaintiff's attorney was regularly made before the default was entered. The service was between 7 and 8 A. M., by affixing the paper on the office door, in the City of N. Y., no one being within. The default was entered after 9 A. M. of the same day, by the plaintiff's attorney, on his way to the office, without his knowing anything of the order. His office was in Pine St. and his residence in Spring St.; both facts being known to the defendant's attorney.

In serving a paper, everything should be done, which ordinary diligence requires, to bring a knowledge of it home to the attorney in proper season. The service here was at an hour of the morning before the offices are usually open in N. Y., with a knowledge that the attorney resided in the same city, and **64***] after the expiration of a previous *order enlarging the time to plead. On finding the attorney and his clerk both absent from the office, which was naturally to have been expected, the obvious course was to search for him at his residence. Allowing this very loose manner of service, is certainly calculated to entrap the opposite attorney, though he may proceed with the greatest caution. No case has gone so far, where it appears, as it does here, that the paper was not actually received. Services at the office, in the City of N. Y., should be within office hours, which do not commence before 9 A. M. There is no affidavit of merits; though, it seems, an important question of law exists as to the amount which the plaintiff claims against the defendant.

We think the service was irregular.

Still there can be no objection to the other branch of the defendant's motion, if this be a case in which the plaintiff is plainly entitled to no more than the penalty of the bond. The amount of the penalty, with the costs, have been tendered to his attorney. Money has been paid into court after a verdict in slander, with a view to save further costs. *Hatfield* v. *Baldwin*, 1 Johns., 506. And staying proceedings in an action on a bond for the performance of covenants, and the like, on payment of the penalty and costs, is a very usual exercise of power. (1 Dunl. Pr., 338, and the cases there cited.) It is now well settled by a series of decisions, that a surety is never liable on a bond beyond the penalty. *Clark* v. *Bush*, 3 Cow., 151; *Fairlie* v. *Lawson*, 5 *Id.*, 424. And there can be no objection, therefore, on the ground that the sum is unliquidated, where the proposition is to pay to that extent. This being the undoubted rule, as to bonds in the course of private business, is the case of a bond, given by a surety pursuant to a statute, an exception? *Fairlie* v. *Lawson* presents such a case, but the point was not raised. Why is the penalty limited by the statute, unless for the protection of the sureties?

We are not aware that statute sureties, such as bail to the sheriff, bail in error, &c., who **65***] give a bond or recognizance *with a penalty, have ever been holden liable beyond that penalty. And in *Hefford* v. *Alger*, 1 Taunt., 218, the C. P. held the two sureties in a replevin bond, together liable only for the penalty and costs.

True, on appeal, the security may, in this view, be many times very inadequate. Being regulated by the amount of the judgment below, it may sometimes be merely nominal. But this evil can be remedied by the Legislature only.

The appellee must look to the party, for all beyond the penalty.

This branch of the motion is, therefore, granted.

Rule accordingly.

SHARP AND TUTTLE *v.* CASWELL.

Practice—Second Execution on Ground of Escape—Sci. fa. the Proper Remedy.

It seems that a second execution, cannot be issued within the Statute, 1 R. L., 426, sec. 24, on the ground that the defendant has escaped, unless the escape continue, till the time of its issuing.

The escape must be such as will charge the sheriff.

At any rate, on so grave a question, the plaintiff should proceed by *sci. fa.*

Citations—1 Johns., 506; 1 Dunl. Pr., 338; 3 Cow., 151; 5 Cow., 424; 1 Taunt., 218.

MR. L. FORD, for the defendant, moved to set aside the *testatum fieri facias*, issued in this cause against the defendant, for irregularity.

He read an affidavit, showing that a judgment was perfected in favor of the plaintiffs against the defendant, for $442.96, in Oct., 1817. That soon afterwards, a *testatum capias ad satisfaciendum* was issued on the judgment, upon which the defendant was imprisoned in the common jail of Herkimer Co.; and having procured bail for the jail liberties, had continued a prisoner upon the liberties from that time to the present, upon the *ca. sa.* That Feb. 3 last a *testatum fieri facias* was issued upon the judgment, and placed in the hands of the present Sheriff of Herkimer, by virtue whereof, he had levied on a large amount of personal property owned by the defendant.

Mr. M. Hoffman, contra, read various affidavits, showing that the defendant had made frequent escapes from the liberties since he was committed, and before the issuing of the *fi. fa.*; and claimed that it issued properly within *the Statute, 1 R. L., 426, sec. 24, [***66** which provides, "that if any person who shall be taken on any execution, or committed thereon to any prison, shall escape by any ways or means howsoever, the creditor, at whose suit such prisoner was taken or charged in execution, may retake such prisoner by any new *capias ad satisfaciendum*, or sue forth any other kind of execution on the judgment, as if the body of such prisoner had never been taken in execution."

But it appeared that these escapes were principally on Sunday, and that when the *fi. fa.* issued, the defendant had returned, and was within the jail liberties.

Mr. Ford insisted that the statute did not apply to a temporary escape, from which the prisoner has returned and is in custody at the time of the second execution. The escape intended is a permanent one—such an escape as will work a forfeiture of the jail bond.

Mr. M. Hoffman, contra. Departing from the jail on Sunday was an escape. This was held, in *Tillman* v. *Lansing*, 4 Johns., 45. *Jansen* v. *Hilton*, 10 Johns., 549, supports the same position. The escape being on Sunday, goes only to the remedy. Process cannot be served if there be a return before the day closes. (1 R. L., 163, sec. 5.) Formerly even this was otherwise. (Com. Dig. *t.* B., 3.) Every going at large is an escape, unless it be on *habeas corpus* or rule of court. (1 R. L., 426, sec. 21.) The condition of the limit bond is, that the person arrested on the *ca. sa.* shall remain a true and faithful prisoner, and shall not, at any time, &c., escape. The recaption or return is matter of defense to an action ; *Id.*, and 3 Salk., 150, case 5 ; and it must be pleaded. (1 R. L., 426, sec. 23.)

If this be an escape, the condition arises within the statute, upon which a second execution may be issued. This was held in the late case of *Mumford* v. *Armstrong*, 4 Cow., 553.

67*] *The statute upon which we issued the second execution is remedial of a defect in the common law, which considered the body a satisfaction. It should, therefore, be construed liberally in favor of the plaintiff's right.

It has never been held necessary to issue a *sci. fa.* or resort to a motion in such a case. The execution may go of course.

By issuing the second execution, we elect to pursue the property and discharge the body. But if otherwise, there can be no objection to this course. In *Jackson* v. *Bartlett*, 8 Johns., 361, the *fi. fa.* and an action for the escape, were both held to be consistent remedies, and that they might both be pursued at the same time.

At any rate, a motion is not the proper course for relief. If we have proceeded irregularly, let the defendant bring his action against us.

Mr. J. Platt, in reply. This motion goes the length of saying, that though we had escaped but for a moment, just after our first imprisonment, the plaintiffs may lie by for years, acquiesce in our imprisonment, and then pursue us by a *fi. fa.* The escape complained of is the mere going off and returning to the limits on Sunday, before any suit brought or execution issued. This is certainly very bold and novel practice. Such a case was never before heard of, though the statute is a very ancient one, and has existed for a long time in England. In *Mumford* v. *Armstrong*, 4 Cow., 553, there was no pretense of a return. At common law, an imprisonment and escape were a satisfaction ; but the sheriff may be insolvent, and hence this remedy of a second execution was provided. It comes in the place of such an escape as will make the sheriff liable. An escape and return on Sunday, therefore, or on any other day before suit brought, is not within the Act. An execution can go only where an action will lie against the sheriff. It must be issued before the escape is purged. An escape works no injury to any one, if there be a return before it is availed of. The words relied on, "if he shall at any time escape," must be taken subject to **68***] *this qualification. All the statutes declaring the effect of an escape, must be taken in the same way.

But, at any rate, on a grave question of this kind, the plaintiff should be put to his *sci. fa* or motion, before he is permitted to take a second execution. The former should be preferred, because it will enable the party to pursue fully what he conceives to be his right, should the opinion of this court be against him. To turn us round to an action would be no remedy, for the process will protect the sheriff and the party, if suffered to stand.

Curia. We are inclined to think the true construction of the statute is as contended for by the counsel for the defendant—that this remedy by a second execution cannot be taken, except is a case where the sheriff might be charged for the escape ; and that, at any rate, it must be issued before the escape is purged by the return. This construction is strengthened by the phraseology of the statute in relation to a second *ca. sa.* It is, that the plaintiff may retake the defendant by a new *ca. sa.*, or sue forth any other kind of execution. Now, how can he retake the defendant when he has already returned into custody and remains there ? This can only be where there is a continued escape, and we think a remedy by any kind of execution must depend on the same condition. There is nothing in the statute making a distinction, and giving a *fi. fa.* where a second *ca. sa.* would not lie.

We do not mean, however, to be understood as finally determining the question. The party may still go to his *sci. fa.*, if he chooses ; and we do mean to say, that on a question so important that is the proper course.

The motion must be granted, without costs.

Rule accordingly.

WOODWORTH, *J.*, was absent.

---

*EX PARTE STEPHENS. [*69

Practice—Appeal from judgment of Justice—Costs to be Paid.

To entitle a party to appeal from the decision of a justice under the Fifty Dollar Act, he must pay, not only the 75 cents for making and filing the return, but the costs to the justice. Paying the 75 cents to the justice, and the costs to the opposite party, will not satisfy the words of the Act, which are to be taken strictly against the party seeking to appeal.

Citation—Act, sess. 47, ch. 238, sec. 36, p. 295.

JUDGMENT was recovered against Stephens by Phillips, before a justice of Onondaga, and execution issued, upon which Stephens, being imprisoned, paid the judgment to the plaintiff and took his receipt. Being discharged, he attempted to appeal to the Onondaga C. P., and paid 75 cents to the justice, but did not pay him the costs of the suit, supposing that the payment to the plaintiff was the same thing. The justice making no return, the C. P. granted a rule that he return, or show cause, &c., which they afterwards discharged, on the ground that the costs were not paid to the justice.

A motion was now made for a *mandamus* commanding the C. P. to proceed, and compel a return.

Mr. G. Lawrence for the motion.

It was not opposed ; but,

Per Curiam. The Act is very strictly construed. To entitle the party to appeal, he must follow up the requisites prescribed to him with great exactness. Such appears to have been the intention of the Legislature, and with this accords the current of decision. The Statute, sess. 47, ch. 238, sec. 36, p. 295, is, that the party appealing shall pay to the justice the costs of the suit, and also the sum of 75 cents for making and filing the return. The words have not been complied with. The 75 cents, but not the costs, were paid to the justice. The motion must be denied.

Motion denied.

Cited in—1 Wend., 282; 18 Hun, 483; 10 Minn., 223.

70*] *BALL

v.

THE PRESIDENT, DIRECTORS AND COMPANY OF THE BANK OF UTICA.

Pleading—Variance.

A declaration will not be set aside on the ground that it varies from the original writ, though that original, be a special one.

Citations—1 Chit. Pl., 246, 249; 1 Saund., 318 *a*, *n.* 3; 6 T. R., 363.

MR. G. C. BRONSON moved to set aside the amended declaration, on the ground of variance from the special original. The writ was in *assumpsit*, and had four counts on special agreement. The first declaration followed the writ; but the plaintiff amended of course, omitting all the special counts of the writ, and inserting the general ones in *assumpsit*.

Mr. D. B. Noxon, contra, relied on 1 Saund., 318 *a*, *note* 3, and the cases there cited; with what this court said in *Rogers* v. *Rogers*, 4 Johns., 485, and the cases there cited.

Mr. Bronson, in reply, said these authorities sanctioned the variance only in cases of general originals; as the original *quare clausum fregit*, which is used in the English C. P.

Curia. This does not appear to be the distinction. In general, now, variance from the original cannot be pleaded in abatement, whether the original be general or special. There is hardly an exception to this rule. Even on error for the variance, this court will suffer the plaintiff to amend the original, so as to conform to the declaration; and that may be done at any time in this case, provided it becomes necessary. (1 Chit. Pl., 246, 249.)

Then the defendant shall not be permitted to do that by motion to set aside the proceedings, which he could not do in any other way. We will not look into the original to sustain such a motion. (1 Saund., 318 *a*, *note* 3.)

Spaulding v. *Mure*, 6 T. R., 363, is in point. That was a special original with four counts in *assumpsit*, two against the defendants as surviving partners; the others in their own right. They having given bail, the plaintiff declared against them in their own right only.

71*] The court agreed *that this was a variance in substance; and they discharged the bail. But they refused to set aside the declaration.

Motion denied.

Cited in—17 Wend., 442; 22 Wis., 254.

FORD *v.* CRANE AND CANFIELD, Executors of WARING.

Plea by Executors—Omission of Plaintiff to Reply.

Where the defendants, being executors, pleaded the general issue, with an outstanding judgment, and *plene administravit præter;* and ruled the plaintiff to reply to the last plea, which he omitted; held, that the only effect of the default would be, judgment for the defendant, with the costs on that branch of the defense founded on the special plea; but the plaintiff might still go to trial on the issue; and if he succeeded, take his judgment *quando acciderint;* and the judgment could not be perfected for the defendant till the issue was disposed of.

Citations—2 Saund., 226; 19 Johns., 266.

MOTION to set aside the *non pros.* of the plaintiff, for not replying, with all subsequent proceedings.

The action was *assumpsit* against the defendants as executors. They pleaded: 1st, *non assumpsit;* and 2d, an outstanding judgment and *plene administravit præter.* The defendants ruled the plaintiff to reply to the last plea; which not being done within the 20 days, they entered the plaintiff's default; and were now proceeding on a rule for judgment of *non pros.* to perfect a judgment, with costs against the plaintiff.

It was conceded that the default was regular; and the only question was, what judgment should follow.

For the plaintiff, it was insisted that it should be the same as if he had replied, admitting the plea, and praying judgment *quando*, &c.

Mr. L. Ford, for the plaintiff, cited 2 Saund., 226.

Mr. J. Butterfield, contra.

Curia. There is no doubt of the plaintiff's right so to reply, and take judgment of assets *in futuro*. This is all which is proved by *Noel* v. *Nelson*, cited for the plaintiff from 2 Saund., 226. But he might also have replied *nul tiel record*, or taken issue on the question of assets *præter;* and so have sought to oust the defendants of their defense. It was impossible for them to say which course the plaintiff would pursue. If he had taken the latter, and failed in maintaining his issue at the trial, the judgment *would have been for the defend- [*72 ant, that he recover his costs, even though he might have failed on the general issue. *Osterhout* v. *Hardenbergh*, 19 Johns., 266. According to this case, the plaintiff may still go on upon the general issue, and recover his judgment of assets *quando acciderint*, if he succeed upon that issue. But that is no reason why the defendants should not take their *non pros.* with costs. It does not finally dispose of the cause; but it does dispose of this particular plea of *plene administravit præter*, the same as if it had been found for the defendants on an issue. It carries their costs. The error of the plaintiff lies in his supposing that the defendants are bound to know what he would reply. It is not so. He should elect. Not doing so, the defendants may take the most from their plea. The *non pros.* is qualified according to the nature of the plea, which, though true, is not a perfect bar; and, for that reason, if false, will not subject the defendants to judgment *de bonis propriis.* (*Id.*)

But the judgment for the defendant cannot be perfected, till the other issue is disposed of.

We order the rule for judgment of *non pros.* to be set aside. This leaves the default standing; and what is to be finally done, must await the result upon the other issue.

Rule accordingly.

Cited in—1 Wend., 31; 6 How. Pr., 114.

THE PEOPLE *v.* GEORGE PEACOCK.

Indictment — Forgery — Obtaining Advance on Coal Consigned to Another of Same Name.

Certain coal being consigned to P., of N. Y., arrived there, and was claimed by another of the name of P., who resided in the same city, but was not the true assignee; and he, knowing this, obtained an advance of money, on indorsing the permit for the delivery of the coal with his own proper name. Held, that this was forgery, and not the merely obtaining of goods upon false pretenses.

Citation—4 T. R., 28.

THE defendant was convicted of forgery at the last Court of Oyer and Terminer in the City and County of N. Y., and now stood committed for sentence, upon the following facts:

May 8, 1826, the brig Rival arrived from New Castle, in the City of N. Y., with a quantity of coal consigned to George Peacock, there 73*] being two persons *of that name residing in different streets in the city. The consignment was, in truth, intended, not to the prisoner, but the other person of the same name, and this was known to the prisoner. He, however, claimed the coal, and went to Mr. Masters, the consignee of the ship, and told him that the coal belonged to him (the prisoner). He then went to Mr. Pell, said he had a quantity of coal, and wanted an advance. Pell made an advance of $450, on the defendant signing over to him the permit for the delivery of the coal. There was some slight proof, at the trial, that the prisoner's name was George W. Peacock; but he had always been known and called in the city, where he had been in trade, by the name of George Peacock. He did not imitate the handwriting of any other person upon the permit, and did not represent himself as residing at any particular place.

On application of the prisoner's counsel, the Oyer and Terminer suspended the sentence till the opinion of this court could be taken, whether the above facts warranted the verdict.

Mr. J. D. Wheeler, for the prisoner. The prisoner represented himself to be the owner or consignee of the coal, and the person named in the bill of lading, and indorsed his own name in his own proper hand.

Offenses should be kept distinct, and not suffered to run into each other. Now, though this may be a fraud, indictable under the Statute, 1 R. L., 410, sec. 13, as an obtaining of money upon false pretenses, it is not a forgery. The latter is defined to be "the fraudulent making, or alteration of a writing to the prejudice of another man's right." (4 Bl. Com., 247.) The definitions in the other books are substantially the same (2 Ch. C. L., 1023; Stark. Cr. Pl., 449; East P. C., 853; 2 Leach C. L., 898, per Grose, *J.*); and all the precedents of indictments, whether at the common law, or on English or American statutes, contain this allegation: "did falsely make, forge and counterfeit." (2 Ch. C. L., 1053.) What is falsely forging? *In common mean- [*74 ing it is a lie. But in the law it has a technical and confined meaning; and if one make a false coin or writing, it is a forgery. But if one puts his true name to a writing, how can that be called false? The representation that he is the very man may be false, but not so as to the signature. That is true, and the averment of falsehood is not made out. Counterfeit implies imitation, or the use of a name not in existence or not known, and in either case this must be by writing. *Rex* v. *Parkes*, 2 Leach, 775, does not come up to this case. Parkes wrote the note and signed Brown's name, and Brown was convicted of passing it as the note of another. Parkes was found not guilty. I admit the signing of a fictitious name is forgery. *Rex* v. *Dunn*, 1 Leach, 57; *Rex* v. *Taylor*, *Id.*, 257; *Rex* v. *Taft*, *Id.*, 172; *People* v. *Grant*, 3 C. H. Recorder, 143, *Mead* v. *Young*, 4 T. R., 28, was a civil action. The court were not called on to determine what shall constitute forgery, nor could they do so in that action. Fraud would vitiate the indorsment as well as forgery, and there was a plain fraud in the case. The court chose to call it a forgery, but it does not follow that it was indictable as such. That, it is true, was the case of a man's indorsing his own name as payee of a bill, representing himself to be another person intended by the drawer. In *Aickles'* case, 1 Leach, 438, this very question arose in principle. One who claimed the same name, signed, representing himself to be another; and it was held not to be forgery. This doctrine was much discussed in *Putnam* v. *Sullivan*, 4 Mass., 45, by Parsons, *Ch. J.* One obtained notes indorsed in blank, by false pretenses, and afterwards filled them up differently from what was intended by the indorser. Yet this was held not to be forgery.

The offense in this case is, in truth, merely that of falsely personating another, for which the defendant may be indicted at the common law; and various statutes have been made in England against personating in certain cases. (2 Chit. C. L., 1081.) The doubt really is, whether the *crime be false personating, [*75 or obtaining goods under false pretenses; not whether it be forgery.

Mr. Talcott, Atty-Gen., contra. The name of the defendant was not literally indorsed. It appears by the case that George W. Peacock is convicted of indorsing the name of George Peacock, the name of another person, not his own name. The doctrine in *Franklin* v. *Tallmadge*, 5 Johns., 84, that the law knows of but one Christian name, and the omission of the middle letter was, therefore, immaterial, is not borne out by the authorities, in the full extent to which it is laid down. A man may not have more than one name of baptism. This was the ancient rule, and the case cited makes a wrong application of it. It does not follow that a man cannot have two names.

But if the defendant has signed his own name, still there is no difficulty in the case. The circumstance that he omitted to mention a place of residence, is only matter of evidence. Had he mentioned one, the falsehood might have been clearly made out from that circumstance. But when he says directly that he is the owner of the coal, which is as directly contradicted, it amounts to the same thing, and there is no want of evidence.

In East C. L., 969, a corrected account is given of *Aickles'* case, cited by the counsel from Leach. It is there put on the fraud or intent to deceive, and holden forgery, by East; but, in truth, the case never was decided.

The credit in the principal case was not given to the person, but to the permit, which it was supposed gave a legal right to demand the coal. *Shepherd's* case, East C. L., 967, taken in connection with the case of *Aickles*, will show the force of this distinction. If the credit be given to the paper, it is beyond doubt a forgery. *Rex* v. *Parkes* was the same thing as if Brown had himself signed the note. It was signed by the name of a T. Brown, not by the name of the T. Brown. This was held to constitute the offense. *Mead* v. *Young*, cited by the counsel for the prisoner, involved the very question in dispute.

76*] *There the indorser put his own name, pretending to be the true payee, when in fact he was not; and the court unhesitatingly pronounced it a forgery. (2 Russ Crimes, 1416; East C. L., 962, 966, 856, S. P.)

The Court intimated a strong inclination against the prisoner in the course of the argument, relying much on the authority of *Mead* v. *Young;* and at another day,

The *Chief Justice* said they had considered the case, and were satisfied that the indictment for a forgery was sustainable; and they, accordingly, advised the Oyer and Terminer to pass sentence upon the prisoner.

Cited in—1 Wend., 201; 15 Hun, 160; 19 Am. Dec., 479.

DEMAREST v. HARING.

Slander — On Motion in Arrest of Judgment, Words Taken to Have Been Proved as Laid— Words Actionable per se*— Words Spoken of Persons in Particular Calling or Profession —Charge of Inconstancy Against Clergyman — Words to be Given their Plain and Natural Import—Jury to Determine Which of Two Senses in Cases of Doubt.*

In slander, on a motion in arrest of judgment, because the words are not actionable, they must be taken to have been proved as laid, and with the intention imputed by the declaration.

In slander, words are to be understood, by courts and juries, according to their plain and natural import—according to the ideas they are calculated to convey to those to whom they are addressed.

When doubts arise, the jury are to decide whether the words are used maliciously and with a view to defame; this being a question of fact, to be collected from all the concomitant circumstances; and the court are to determine whether such words, taken in the malicious sense imputed to them, can alone, or by the aid of the circumstances, stated upon the record, form the legal basis of an action.

Courts and juries will understand the words in the same way other people would.

Words charging the plaintiff with being the father of a bastard child by his sister-in-law, of which she was pregnant, and that he wished the defendant to make away with it, are actionable in themselves, as importing a wish that the defendant should destroy the child as soon as born. It imports that the plaintiff applied to him to commit murder.

To be actionable in themselves, words must impute some act constituting a crime or misdemeanor, for which corporal punishment may be inflicted in a temporal court.

It is a high misdemeanor for one person to apply to another, and solicit him to commit murder.

Words not actionable in themselves, become so, by being spoken of persons in a particular calling or profession; and *semble*, in any lawful employment by which they may gain a livelihood.

Words imputing incontinency to a clergyman are within this rule.

Where words may be understood in two different senses, one as imputing a crime, and the other not, it is proper to submit the question how they were understood, to the jury.

Semb. That setting forth the plaintiff's character in slander, as that he is a clergyman; and then a slander affecting him in that character, is sufficient, without saying the slander was spoken of him, in relation to that character. And *vide* the cases cited by Emmet and Oakley, *arguendo*, last paragraph of their argument, S. P.

Citations—3 Cow., 239, 240; Starkie Tr., Slander, 41, 44, 108, 107; 7 Serg. & R., 451; Cro. Eliz., 747, 808; Aleyn, 63; Comb., 253; Str., 946; Hammond Tr. *N. P.*, 300; 1 Binn., 184.

SLANDER, tried at the N. Y. Circuit, Dec. 8, 1824, before Edwards, *Circuit J.*

*The first count of the declaration **[*77** stated that the plaintiff was a minister of the gospel of the Reformed Dutch Church, ordained and duly installed as the clergyman of the Reformed Dutch Church, at Kakiat, in the Town of Hempstead, in the County of Rockland, at a certain yearly salary. That he faithfully performed his duty as such. That the defendant, wickedly and maliciously intending to injure the plaintiff in his good name, fame, &c., and in order to disgrace him, and to cause it to be believed that he was guilty of felony, adultery and lewdness, &c., Aug. 8, 1823, at, &c., spoke and published certain Dutch words of the plaintiff, setting them forth, of the same signification and meaning with these English words: "That his (the defendant's) sister Peggy (Margaret Haring meaning) had been delivered of a child (meaning an illegitimate child); and that the *domine* (meaning the plaintiff) was the father of the said child; and that he (the plaintiff) had laid it upon Timothy (meaning one Timothy Secor) to clear himself. But he (the defendant) believed it was the *domine's* (meaning the plaintiff), and that the *domine* had desired him to make away with it" (meaning that the plaintiff attempted to procure and induce the defendant, feloniously to kill and murder the child).

The second count was substantially the same, slightly varying the words.

The third count was the same with the first, as to the words, except that, in conclusion, it charged the defendant with saying of the plaintiff, that he had desired the defendant and his wife to make the child out of the way; imputing by *innuendo* the intent, as expressed in the first count, to induce the defendant and his wife feloniously to kill and murder the child.

The declaration then concluded thus: "by means of the committing of which said several grievances, &c., the said plaintiff hath been and is greatly injured in his said good name, &c.; and brought into public scandal, &c., amongst all his neighbors; and the persons composing his *said congregation, &c., **[*78** insomuch that divers, &c., suspected, &c., the

NOTE.—*Slander*—See Moody v. Baker, 5 Cow. 351, *note, and other notes there cited.*

said plaintiff to have been, &c., a person guilty of felony, adultery and lewdness; and have, by reason, &c., refused, &c., to have any transaction, acquaintance or discourse with him, &c. And the said plaintiff hath been obliged to expend great sums of money, &c., to make manifest his innocence, &c. And a certain Samuel Helmes and Henry Van Houten, and divers other members of his said congregation, who, before the speaking and publishing the aforesaid false and scandalous words, by the said defendant, of and concerning the said plaintiff, had been and continued members of the Reformed Dutch congregation, to wit: at Kakiat, in the Town of Hempstead, in the County of Rockland, and then were yearly subscribers of a large sum of money, to wit: ten dollars yearly, to the support and maintenance of the said plaintiff and his family, have refrained from attending divine service under the ministry of the said plaintiff, and have withdrawn themselves from his said congregation; and have refused any longer to pay their yearly subscriptions aforesaid, for the support of the said plaintiff and his family, and still do refuse; all which is to the damage of the said plaintiff, &c.; and therefore, &c."

Plea, the general issue.

On the trial, the plaintiff proved by J. S. that the defendant had spoken of the plaintiff at two different conversations, a set of words in the low Dutch language, which were taken down in writing, as stated by the witness, by the Reverend C. T. Demarest and the Reverend W. Eltinge.

The Rev. C. T. Damarest, having been sworn as an interpreter, translated the words as follows: "There was confusion by Secor's respecting that child. Witness asked him whose child? He, defendant, said his sister Peggy's. He, the defendant, said the *domine* would have that I and my wife Caty should make that child away, or out of the way. (The witness said the import of the Dutch words, here used, would be either to conceal, hide or destroy; and he should think, in connection with what was said **79***] *about the soul, it should be rendered destroy.) He (defendant) said he could not do so, as it had a soul to answer for as well as I; and he (defendant) said that the *domine* had laid it upon Tim, to clear himself; but he believed it was the *domine's*. Defendant said then, he (the *domine*) would have it put upon the stoop, or on the street; but the defendant would not have that. Then the *domine* would bring it to the blacks; but he, the defendant, would not have that either. The *domine* took the child away by force from its mother, and brought it to bad people (or persons of no great repute), and the child had suffered there till it died. He (the defendant) said something about complaining to the grand jury; but he did not remember whether defendant said he would do that or that it ought to be done."

The second conversation was an explanation of the former, and a mere expression of a belief, by the defendant, that the plaintiff was the father of the child.

Witness (J. S.) further said, he thought, at the time, that the defendant intended to be understood as saying that the *domine* wanted him and his wife to murder the child; and he was shocked and scared when he said it; and he thought, if it was true, the *domine* was no preacher for him.

The witness (J. S.) was then cross-examined, and stated that the first conversation was after the defendant had been elected an elder in the church, and about the time they were to elect deacons and elders. Before the conversation, the *domine* had refused to call off the defendant a third time, which was necessary to warrant his ordination. The conversation was after the death of the child. The expression, "make it away," or "put it away," is the same in Dutch. Peggy had been living off and on at the *domine's* a long time. She was his wife's sister. The plaintiff had told the witness that the child was born at Newark, and he understood the plaintiff that he went down to Newark with the girl; and that the plaintiff and defendant went down after the child was born. At a trial *before the consistory, the plaintiff [***80** acknowledged that he and Lansing Haring had agreed to keep the matter concealed. The plaintiff said many plans were laid between them, but the last was adopted. The plans were, that the child was to be laid on the stoop; put on the street; put by blacks; and in the poor-house. All the plans were talked of before the child was born. The *domine* admitted that the plan of going to Newark was laid by him, and adopted; and that the child, after it was born, was to be put out, and the mother was to return home. In connection with the plan of the child going to the poor-house, the plaintiff was to take the child at two years old.

The Rev. W. Eltinge, being sworn as an interpreter on the part of the defendant, translated the words relied upon by the plaintiff, as importing a wish to induce the defendant to kill or murder the child, as follows: "and then the *domine* would have (or willed) that the child should be made aside (or out of the way), the *domine* would have (or willed) that Haring and his wife should make that child aside (or out of the way"). He testified that the meaning of these words as used by J. S., and taken in connection with the context, was no other than to make aside; to put out of the way; to secrete the child so as to hide the shame of the family; and if any other meaning should be attached to them, it would be a forced one; an indirect meaning; but the meaning is the same as the English words "put out of the way," or "make away with;" and must depend on circumstances. And the witness gave several illustrations of the meaning when applied to different circumstances.

The plaintiff then proved two other conversations with two different witnesses, the words of which were the same, as to making away with the child, as stated by the first witness; and one of the last two witnesses understood it to mean the same as the first.

To prove the special damages, the plaintiff then called J. A. Johnson, and asked him whether divers persons had not left the congregation in consequence of the reports against the plaintiff's character.

*To this question the defendant's coun- [***81** sel objected: 1. Because the plaintiff had not supported the averments in his declaration, that he was a clergyman, established, &c., over the church, as alleged; and had not made title to any income from that society; and 2. That he was confined in his proof to the damages specifically laid; and could not introduce proof, in support of the allegation, that divers other persons had refused to pay.

The judge decided that the plaintiff had proved enough as to his special character, to warrant the proof, and that it was admissible under the allegation in the declaration; and the counsel for the defendant excepted.

The plaintiff then proved that he was duly licensed and ordained. His license was produced and read. He also proved his call from the church of West New Hampstead and Ramapo, an incorporated religious society, dated Nov. 16, 1808, at a certain salary and privileges; which call was accepted, and he regularly installed, pursuant to the call.

Johnson was again called, but did not state any special damage.

The plaintiff, however, rested; and,

The defendant's counsel insisted that the plaintiff should be called, inasmuch as no special damages had been proved, and the words were not actionable in themselves.

The plaintiff's counsel insisted that the words were actionable in themselves, even if spoken of an ordinary person; and especially so, when spoken of a clergyman as such.

The judge decided that the words imputing a want of chastity, or charging him with committing fornication, were not actionable, *per se;*

That there was no evidence of special damage;

But that the charge, made by the defendant, that the plaintiff desired him "to make away with the child," or "make the child away," or "make the child out of the way," if made in the sense charged in the declaration, were actionable in themselves; that the sense or meaning in which those words were used by the de-
82*] fendant, was proper *matter to be submitted to the jury; and that there was sufficient evidence to carry the cause to the jury upon this point. That whether the *innuendoes* were well laid, was matter appearing upon the face of the record; and it was not competent for him to pass upon it. But there was sufficient evidence of their truth to carry the cause to the jury, upon that point also.

He, therefore, refused to nonsuit the plaintiff; and the defendant's counsel excepted.

Verdict for the plaintiff.

Mr. E. Williams, for the defendant, now moved in arrest of judgment, or for a new trial on the bill of exceptions.

In arrest, he took the following grounds:

1. That the words laid are not actionable in themselves.

2. They are not alleged to have been spoken of the plaintiff, in relation to his profession, trade or calling.

3. The *innuendoes* are not justified by the words as laid.

4. The first and second counts contain no allegation of special damages; and the verdict being general, the judgment must be arrested.

He observed that the words could not be enlarged by the *innuendo* (1 Saund., 343, *note* 4; 8 Johns., 109; Stark. Slander, 302, Am. ed.; 1 Chit. Pl., 383), and there is no *colloquium,* nor any averment that a child had been born, or murdered or killed; or that there had been any attempt to kill a child. The illegitimacy of the child is not averred; nor whether the girl was married or single. The words, "that the *domine* had desired the defendant to make away with the child," are, without any authority, made by the *innuendo* an attempt to procure the defendant to murder it. The defects should have been supplied by proper averments. (Stark. Slander, Am. ed., 302, 304.)

In support of the motion for a new trial, he made these points:

1. The words in the declaration are not proved.

2. The averment that the plaintiff was installed the clergyman of the congregation at Kakiat, was not supported by the proof; and the evidence of damage, in that character and *office, was improperly admitted. *Herrick* v. *Lapham,* 10 Johns., 281. [*83

3. The words proved, are not actionable in themselves, taken in their ordinary acceptation, as they must be. (9 East, 93.)

4. The *innuendoes* are not justified by the words laid or proved; and the point, whether they were proved, should not have been submitted to the jury.

He observed that instead of one, the plaintiff is proved to have been the settled minister of two churches—neither of them, the church stated in the declaration. And though he failed as to special damages, he had the full benefit of this evidence, with the jury. It varied from the declaration, which avers a settlement over one church only, naming it.

Then it comes to this: does the slander import a crime punishable as a felony? It charges a mere wish to destroy the unborn infant, or a desire that it should be destroyed; certainly nothing beyond this. No overt act is charged. (Stark. Slander, Am. ed., 89.) A mere wish to commit a felony will not sustain an indictment; nor would a request. (Stark. Slander, Am. ed., 89, 21, 22, 23, 66, 67.)

It cannot be pretended that the words as laid, imported anything more than a wish to hide or secrete the child. The words, according to the construction of them, proved, or sought to be proved at the trial, imported a wish to kill or murder. This was one variance.

If there are any material words proved, in order to make out the charge, beyond what the declaration contains, this is a variance. The declaration should have stated them by way of *colloquium* or otherwise. (Stark. Slander, Am. ed., 302, 304.) If the words, "the child has a soul to gain or lose," be material to make out the sense contended for, they should have been stated.

Messrs. T. J. Oakley and *T. A. Emmet,* contra, made the following points.

*1. The words laid are actionable in themselves. After verdict, they must be taken to have been spoken in the sense alleged in the declaration. [*84

2. They are actionable on account of the professional character of the plaintiff.

3. They are actionable on the ground of the special damage alleged, which, on the motion in arrest, must be taken to have been proved. *Harley* v. *Herring,* 8 T. R., 130; Stark. Slander, Lond. ed., 191.

4. The *innuendoes* laid cannot vitiate. They may be rejected as surplusage, if not necessary to support the action. *Smith* v. *Cooker,* Cro. Car., 512; *Lindsey* v. *Smith,* 7 Johns., 359.

They insisted that the allegation of special damage must be taken to apply to all the counts. It does so in terms, though it comes in at the conclusion. It was not necessary to repeat it at the close of each count.

When words are equivocal in themselves, an *innuendo* is proper to fix the criminal meaning. *Wilner* v. *Hold*, Cro. Car., 489; Stark. Slander, 339, 341. The words, "to make away," are of that character, and may be thus explained. They are not necessarily innocent on their face. They are, in English, understood to mean killing or murder, when applied to a child, oftener than anything else. And in *Falkner* v. *Cooper*, Carter, 55, 56, these very words were held actionable. At any rate, the words cannot always mean the mere act of secreting. If the words may import criminality, then the verdict fixes the intent, and must be sustained. The jury have found the meaning. After a verdict for the plaintiff, the words shall be taken in their worst sense. Stark. Slander, Lond. ed., 65.

Words importing a solicitation to commit a felony are actionable. "He wished me to make away with the child," is, in one sense, the charge of solicitation to do it. For this the plaintiff, beyond all doubt, would be punishable in the temporal courts. *Passie* v. *Mondford*, Cro. Eliz., 747; *Preston* v. *Pinder*, *Id.*,
85*] 308; 2 Chit. Cr. L., 117, **note y; Id.*, 50, 993; *Mayne* v. *Digle*, Freem., 46; Ham. *N. P.*, 300, 301.

Taken together, the language charged plainly imports that the child was illegitimate, and imputes to the plaintiff a want of chastity—a lewdness which unfits him for his duties as a clergyman—and destroys his professional character. Words to this effect, spoken of a clergyman, were held actionable in *Dod* v. *Robinson*, Aleyn, 63. They are, then, actionable on the principle which makes any words so, as affecting a man in his particular profession or calling. The example usually put is, that of charging a lawyer with being a knave. To charge a blacksmith with keeping false books would be actionable for the same reason. To say of a clergyman, he is a drunkard, is actionable. *M'Millan* v. *Birch*, 1 Binn., 178; *Chaddock* v. *Briggs*, 13 Mass., 249, S. P. The court cannot but see that a charge of incontinency would affect a clergyman in his profession, though it would not have that effect when made against an ordinary person. In this country clergymen of all denominations have the same right to protection as the established clergy in England. (1 Binn., 184, 185; Stark. Slander, Am. ed., 107.)

Where words are equivocal, it is sufficient to state them in the declaration, point them with an *innuendo;* and then prove the truth of the *innuendo* by circumstances. Nothing is more common than to prove words not laid, in order to show the sense in which those which are laid, were spoken. The declaration need not be loaded with the particulars. Words are always to be taken as they are understood by the hearers. *Cooper* v. *Smith*, Bridgm., 60.

After proof of special damages had failed, further proof was admitted. This was not objected to at the trial, and its admissibility cannot be questioned here. The proof of settlement over two churches instead of one, as alleged in the declaration, was a part of this unquestioned proof. The court will intend that the two churches spoken of are in truth but one, and that this is the same church mentioned in the declaration. This might have been shown, if there *had been an ob- [***86** jection at the trial. The defendants' counsel should have put his finger upon the variance.

There was no ground for a nonsuit. The words alleged were substantially proved. This is sufficient. The proof need not literally correspond with the words set forth in the declaration. It was sufficient to carry the cause to the jury, that some of the witnesses understood the words to import criminality. The jury were to determine the sense of the words. They are always to do this, if there be any ground for doubt. *Dexter* v. *Taber*, 12 Johns., 239; *Ex parte Baily*, 2 Cow., 479, 482; *Goodrich* v. *Woolcott*, 3 Cow., 231, 239, 240.

That the *colloquium* in the declaration need not apply the words spoken particularly to the professional character of the plaintiff; but that it is sufficient to apply them in proof, the counsel cited *Stanton* v. *Smith*, Ld. Raym., 1480; *Reeve* v. *Holgate*, 2 Lev., 62; *Sir John Isham* v. *York*, Cro. Car., 15; *Taylor* v. *Starkey*, *Id.*, 192; *Webb* v. *Nicholls*, *Id.*, 459; *Fleetwood* v. *Curle*, Cro. Jac., 557; *Carn* v. *Osgood*, 1 Lev., 280; *Goodyear* v. *Bishop*, Cro. Car., 265; *Cawdry* v. *Highley*, *Id.*, 270; *Fowle* v. *Robbins*, 12 Mass., 498, and *Chaddock* v. *Briggs*, 13 *Id.*, 249.

Mr. Williams, in reply. The first and second counts are complete in form, and profess to rely on themselves. The allegation of special damage, at the conclusion of the declaration, cannot be attached to them. If it was intended to support them on that ground, they should each have charged the special damage individually and distinctly. As inserted, it cannot aid any beside the third and last count. If this be not so, where do these counts begin? Where do they end?

We deny that doubtful words can be helped by an *innuendo*. This can be done only by a *colloquium*. (Stark. Slander, Am. ed., 302.)

The authorities cited to show that the act of solicitation is legally criminal, do not apply to a case of this kind. A solicitation to kill, in order to be criminal, must relate to a living *person. The declaration does not aver [***87** that the child was born, or had even quickened in the womb. The wish, or request, or solicitation insisted on, therefore, could not relate to a felonious killing. It could be no more than a request to commit a misdemeanor. This is not an offense indictable at all.

There is no more reason why words, importing a want of chastity, should be deemed actionable, when spoken of a clergyman, than of the advocate, the judge or the physiclau. In neither case are they actionable. Even the female is not protected by the law against such an imputation, though no one is so much injured by it.

Curia, per SAVAGE, *Ch. J.*, after stating the facts. With regard to the motion in arrest, the inquiry is, whether the words, as laid, are actionable; for, on this motion, we are to take it for granted that they were proved as laid, and with the intention imputed.

The doctrine of construing words in *mitiori sensu* has been exploded, and a more rational rule now prevails—that words are to be understood according to their plain and natural import, according to the ideas they are calculated to convey to those to whom they are addressed. *Goodrich* v. *Woolcott*, 3 Cow., 239, 240, and cases there cited. Mr. Starkie, in his valuable Treatise on Slander (p. 44), states the rule as follows: "Both judges and jurors shall understand words in that sense which the author intended to convey to the minds of the hearers, as evinced by the whole circumstances of the case. It is the province of the jury, where doubts arise, to decide whether the words were used maliciously and with a view to defame, such being matter of fact, to be collected from all concomitant circumstances; and for the court to determine, whether such words, taken in the malicious sense imputed to them, can alone, or by the aid of the circumstances stated upon the record, form the legal baisis of an action." Courts and juries will understand them in the same way that other people would. *Walton* v. *Singleton*, 7 Serg. & R., 451.

88*] *The jury have found that the words were spoken maliciously, and with a view to defame and injure the plaintiff, as laid in the declaration. If they had been spoken otherwise, the verdict would have been different.

What idea, then, do we, and all persons of common understanding, receive from the charge, that the plaintiff wished the defendant to make away with a bastard child, of which he was the father, and standing in the relation of brother-in-law to the mother? What must have been his motive, but to prevent entirely, and in the most effectual manner, a public exposure of his misconduct, that he might avert disgrace and infamy? I apprehend the plain meaning is, that the plaintiff wanted the defendant to destroy this infant child as soon as born. Does this charge, then, amount to an offense which is punishable, and one involving moral turpitude? It is not necessary, here, to say whether it be actionable, in general, to impute evil inclinations or wishes. It is sufficient to take the rule as established, that the charge must impute some act constituting a crime or misdemeanor, for which corporal punishment may be inflicted in a temporal court. (Stark. Slander, 41.)

Is it not a high misdemeanor for one person to apply to another and solicit him to commit murder? There is, in such an act, something more than wickedness of intention. There is an act tending to carry such evil intention into effect. *Passie* v. *Mondford*, Cro. Eliz., 747; *Preston* v. *Pinder*, *Id.*, 308.

According to my understanding of this charge, in the declaration, the words are actionable in themselves, whether spoken of a clergyman or any other person.

There are other words, however, laid, which, spoken of individuals in general, would not be actionable; and it is objected that they are not so when spoken of a clergyman.

The words convey a direct charge of incontinency.

It is familiar to all, that words not actionable in themselves, become so by being spoken of persons engaged in a particular calling or profession. Thus, to call a lawyer a knave, or a physician a quack, is actionable. So, also, to *call a merchant a bankrupt. And the [***89** action seems to extend to words spoken of a person in any lawful employment, by which he may gain his livelihood. (Stark. Slander, 108.)

It has been contended that this rule does not extend to clergymen, and there are some cases which look that way; but there are also cases and *dicta* of learned men in favor of the action.

The oldest case to which we have been referred, is *Dod* v. *Robinson*, Aleyn, 63, in which it was held that to say of a clergyman "he is a drunkard" was actionable: drunkenness, being an offense for which a clergyman is liable to be deprived of his preferment. So, he is a rogue and a dog. *Pocock* v. *Nash*, Comb., 253. So, he is a rogue and a contemptible fellow. *Musgrave* v. *Bovey*, Str., 946. These cases are cited by Starkie, in his Treatise on Slander, 107. Hammond, in his Treatise on the Law of *Nisi Prius*, p. 300, says: To charge a man with seduction, adultery and such like, or to impute to him criminal inclinations, is not defamatory, and the reason assigned is, because he is not thereby exposed to the vengeance of the law. He further states, that words actionable in relation to one's profession or trade, are such as impute to him the want of those qualifications which are essential; as to attribute knavery to a lawyer, ignorance to a physician, profligacy to a divine, cowardice to a soldier or dishonesty to a tradesman. In *M'Millan* v. *Birch*, 1 Binn., 184, Tilghman, *Ch. J.*, says: "The reason why certain expressions are actionable, when applied to persons of certain professions, is this: that from the nature of the case, it is evident that damage must ensue. So, to say of a clergyman, that he is a drunkard; because these words, if believed, must deprive him of that respect, veneration and confidence, without which he can expect no hearers as a minister of the gospel." The temporal damage arising from a loss of reputation for moral rectitude, in his profession, is as great to the clergyman as to a lawyer. Then, why is it that the former should not be equally protected in his *character with the latter? Finding [***90** such respectable authority for the position, I am decidedly in favor of holding words, importing a charge of incontinency against a clergyman, actionable.

Being of opinion that the words are action able, a part in themselves, and a part in respect to the plaintiff's profession, it is useless to consider the nature and office of an *innuendo*, or to inquire whether special damages are laid as to more than one count.

The judge correctly decided that the sense in which the words were used was proper to be determined by the jury.

In my judgment, both the motion in arrest and for a new trial must be denied.

Motions denied.

Cited in—3 Wend., 395; 8 Wend., 577; 19 Wend., 300; 16 N. Y., 376; 3 Barb., 633; 4 Barb., 511; 6 Barb., 47; 22 Barb., 397; 33 Barb., 618; 23 Ind., 270; 27 O., 295; 24 Am. Dec., 98; 22 Am. Rep., 304 (27 Ohio, 292).

THALLHIMER v. BRINCKERHOFF, Gentleman, one, &c.

Agreement to Furnish Pecuniary Aid to Recover Possession of Land for Part thereof—Compromise—Action for Money had and Received Lies for Part of Money Paid on the Compromise—Evidence of Payment of Consideration—Deeds by Agent Prima Facie *Evidence, of Receipt of Money—Accounts, Drafts, &c., of Agent, Competent as Part of the* Res Gestæ—*Notice to Produce Letter—Proof of Mailing—Letter-Book Copy Admitted.*

T., having title to land held in possession by others, made an agreement, not void, for champerty or maintenance, in consideration of Th.'s agreeing to furnish pecuniary assistance about recovering the land, that he would convey one fourth of the land which should be recovered, to Th. T. appointed B. his attorney to conduct suits for the recovery of the land. The suits were finally compromised by T., who conveyed to the possessors by various deeds executed by B., as his attorney, which deeds acknowledged the receipt of the consideration money.

Held, that an action for money had and received, would lie against T. if he had received the money, in behalf of Th., for one fourth of the money so received by T. But B. having received the money, held, that the action lay against him,

Held, also, that the deeds executed by B., as attorney for T., were, *prima facie*, evidence that B. had received the money.

What is sufficient evidence, that B. knew of Th.'s claim under the contract.

What is sufficient evidence, that Th. knew of B.'s paying over the whole proceeds of the compromise to T.; and that he (Th.) acknowledged T. as his agent to receive the proceeds; and looked to him for his, Th.'s share of them, and not to B.

Where an agent is authorized to receive money, for his principal, or do any other thing, his drafts, receipts, account stated, or admissions relative to the subject of his agency, and especially when all these are offered in connection, constitute a part of the *res gesta*; and are competent, though not conclusive evidence, against the principal.

Due notice being given to produce a letter, written by one party to another, and the latter refusing to produce the letter, the former offered to prove by his clerk that he copied the letter into a letter-book, and that it was his invariable custom to carry letters, thus copied, to the postoffice, and seldom handed them back; held, that this was sufficient evidence of sending the letter, though the clerk could not recollect that he sent the particular letter, and that a copy was admissible in evidence.

Where letters are written in the course of business or negotiation, by an agent, they are evidence against his principal, so far as they relate to the subject of his agency, but no farther.

Where mortgages are assigned, or conveyances executed, acknowledging the receipt of the consideration by the assignor or grantor, this is, *prima facie*, evidence that the consideration was actually paid, as expressed; and this, too, although the assignor or grantor was at the time indebted to the assignee or grantee, to the amount of the consideration expressed. The assignments or conveyances shall not, for that reason, be taken to have been in satisfaction of the debt.

Citations—1 R. L., 172; 20 Johns., 386; 3 Cow., 623, 649; 3 T. R., 454; 7 T. R., 665; 1 Esp., 375; 4 Taunt., 511, 565, 663; 10 Ves., 125, 128; 10 Johns., 44; 5 Esp., 74, 135; 2 Esp., 511, *n.*; 2 Campb., 555; 1 Phil. Ev., 77; 2 Wh., 380; 4 Campb., 193; 5 Johns., 375; 3 Campb., 305, 379; 2 Phil. Ev., 20, *n.*

ASSUMPSIT for money had and received, tried at the N. Y. Circuit, Oct. 5, 1824, before Edwards, *Circuit J.*

91*] *At the trial an agreement was given in evidence between the plaintiff and one Heury R. Teller, dated Apr. 10, 1807. This agreement recited a claim to certain lands by Teller, to whom the plaintiff was related; and provided, that on its recovery the former would convey to the plaintiff one fourth of it. Teller made the defendant his attorney, for the purpose of recovering the land; but instead of actually taking possession of it, the claim was compromised between Teller and the possessors, who paid a large sum of money, which came to the hands of the defendant, and for one fourth of which this suit was brought. (See the agreement more at large, 20 Johns., 386, where its legality came in question. It was adjudged legal, 3 Cow., 623, S. C., on error.)

On the compromise, various deeds were executed, by the defendant, as the attorney of Teller, of different parts of the land, expressing the consideration received in money; and these were offered by the plaintiff, and admitted (though objected to) as evidence, *prima facie*, that the defendant had received the money.

The judge overruled a motion for a nonsuit, made on the ground that the action for money had and received would not lie at the suit of the plaintiff.

The defendant set up, in his defense, that he knew nothing of the agreement between the plaintiff and Teller until after he had paid to or for Teller, and the latter had discharged him from all the moneys he had received; and that Teller was, in truth, the agent of the plaintiff to receive the money, or otherwise discharge the claim for it. Among other evidence to show this, he offered to prove *a correspond- [***92**
ence between himself and the son of the plaintiff, Barent Thallhimer, who, he insisted, was the agent of the plaintiff. This correspondence was offered, particularly, to show that long after the defendant had received the money, this being known to the plaintiff, he had acknowledged himself indebted to the defendant on mortgage, and had set up no claim for the moneys in question. Notice had been given to the plaintiff, to produce the letters written by the defendant, but the judge rejected his letter-book as evidence, though the plaintiff declined to produce the letters called for by the notice. The offer of the letter-book was accompanied with evidence which will be found detailed in the opinion of the court.

Various mortgages taken by the defendant on the sale of the real estate, payable to Teller, had been assigned by the latter to the defendant, for a consideration expressed in the assignment to have been received by Teller. The registry of these assignments was offered in evidence against the defendant, but rejected.

The judge admitted in evidence, though objected to by the defendant, certain conveyances of land from Teller to the defendant, in which a consideration was expressed to have been received by Teller.

The defendant offered in evidence certain receipts, drafts and an account stated by Teller, showing the receipt of and final settlement for the money in question, which were rejected by the judge.

The defendant excepted to the various decisions of the judge, which were against him.

The verdict was for the plaintiff, for upwards of $13,500; and the cause now came here on motion by the defendant for a new trial, on the bill of exceptions; and also on a case made.

The above is a very slight outline of the facts to which the points of law decided by the court relate.

NOTE.—*Champerty and maintenance*—See Van Dyck v. Van Beuren, 1 Johns., 345, *note*.

. To say more of the facts here is deemed unnecessary, as they will be found sufficiently stated in the opinion of the court.

93*] *Mr. G. Brinckerhoff, for the defendant, said an action for money had and received, would not lie. The plaintiff being liable to one half or one fourth of all the expenses incurred in the recovery of the land, the accounts of the parties cannot be adjusted in this suit. The plaintiff considered Teller alone as accountable to him; and the defendant was accountable to Teller only. The plaintiff never gave the defendant notice to retain the money; and made no demand till after the defendant had paid over the money to Teller. (3 Johns. Ch., 473, and the cases there cited.) The decision of the Court of Errors, in *Thallhimer* v. *Brinckerhoff*, 3 Cow., 623, so far as it relates to the form of the action, and the nonjoinder of Teller, is out of the case and not binding. (13 Johns., 577; 1 Hopk., 77, 78, 290; 7 Johns. Ch., 305, 310; 16 Johns., 233.) The letter-book,and the parts of letters rejected by the judge should have been received. (4 Campb., 193; 3 *Id.*, 379, 305; 2 Phil. Ev., 20, *note a.*) He examined at large the various decisions of the judge,noticed hereafter in the opinion of the court, and insisted that they were erroneous.

Mr. S. G. Huntington, contra, examined the decision in *Thallhimer* v. *Brinckerhoff*, 3 Cow., 623, and insisted that this case settled the form of the action; and that it was correctly brought in the name of Thallhimer alone. The judge was, therefore, right in denying the motion for a nonsuit. He argued at length in support of the other decisions of the judge at *Nisi Prius*.

A full history of the arguments is not given, because they would not be intelligible without a very long detail of facts, not deemed material to the law of the case.

Curia, per SUTHERLAND, *J.* The first question which arises is, whether, under the circumstances of this case, an action for money had and received can be sustained by the plaintiff. His rights all grow out of the agreement between him and Henry R. Teller, of Apr. 10, 1807. That agreement was originally held by 94*]this court, *to be void as against the Act, 1 R. L., 172, to prevent champerty and maintenance. (20 Johns., 386.) But the Court of Errors reversed that judgment and established the validity of the contract. (3 Cow., 623.) Whether that agreement was void or not, was the only point which strictly and properly arose upon the bill of exceptions. But the counsel discussed and the Court of Errors expressed an opinion upon the question, whether, admitting the agreement to be valid, an action for money had and received could be sustained by the plaintiff. And although that opinion cannot be considered as settling the point on the ground of authority, it is entitled to great weight in the consideration of the question.

It was obviously the intention of Teller to give to Thallhimer a right to one fourth part of whatever might be recovered in the suits, which the agreement recites he was about to commence. The inducement to the agreement was not only a natural and meritorious one, but the consideration on which it was founded was valuable, and such as, under all the circumstances of the case, made the arrangement an act of prudence and discretion on the part of Teller. It was foreseen that the controversy would be protracted and expensive. Its results could not be anticipated with certainty, and Teller knew, if he should fail to recover, that the costs and expense of the controversy would be enormous. He acted wisely, therefore, in guarding against a result that would have been so ruinous, by the agreement which he made with the plaintiff. If the suits had proceeded to judgment, and the land had been recovered, Teller was expressly bound by his covenant to convey one fourth part of the property to the plaintiff. The agreement made no express provision for the case of a compromise. But the legal title being admitted to be in Teller, he had a clear right to discontinue or settle the suit, on such terms as he pleased; and if he acted with good faith, and under the advice of counsel, all that the plaintiff could require would be to participate in the fruits of the compromise, in the same proportion to which he would have been entitled if the land itself had been recovered. *If the money had been paid [*95 to Teller upon the compromise, whether he had a right to compromise or not, there can be no doubt that Thallhimer might have affirmed the settlement, and recovered from him one fourth of the amount. It would work the grossest injustice to give to the agreement a construction which would enable Teller to defeat its beneficial operation, so far as the plaintiff is concerned, by a settlement, and then to answer the plaintiff's claim by saying that his contract bound him only to convey one fourth of the land recovered, and not to pay one fourth of the money received in lieu of the land. The sense of the contract evidently is, as remarked by the *Chancellor* (3 Cow., 649), that in the event of success, Thallhimer shall have one fourth part of the property, whether the fruits of the claim shall be realized in land or money.

If an action for money had and received, could have been sustained by the plaintiff against Teller, on the money being paid to him, I perceive no reason why it cannot against the present defendant, admitting the money still to be in his hands, or to have been paid over to Teller without the authority of the plaintiff, either express or implied. It is no objection to the action that Thallhimer was to bear a proportion of the expenses of the controversy. It may be questioned whether, according to the true construction of the contract, he was to pay anything before the termination of the suit; for the agreement provides that if the suits should be unsuccessful he should pay half the expenses, but if Teller should recover,then only one fourth of them. Pending the controversy, therefore, what proportion was he to advance? The testimony of Mr. Emmet renders it probable that when this agreement was made, it was understood between the parties and their counsel that a very small proportion, if any,of the costs, were to be paid, until the final termination of the suits. He expressly says that such was the agreement in relation to the counsel fees, and that they were not paid until after the compromise. The attorney's fees, it is evident, were *not advanced by Teller, for [*96 Brinckerhoff now claims the $15,000 at which they were liquidated,and paid by the defendants in the suits. But if they had been previously paid by Teller, that amount would belong to him, and not to Brinckerhoff. It is clear, therefore, that little or nothing was paid by Teller or Thallhimer while the suits were pending; and that there can be no account between them in relation to the costs, to be liquidated and adjusted. The costs are to be deducted from the $75,000 agreed to be paid by way of compromise, and the plaintiff is entitled to one fourth of the balance, either from Teller or the defendant.

I think the evidence warrants the conclusion that the agreement between Teller and Thallhimer was known to the defendant. It was in the handwriting of his clerk and witnessed by him and the defendant. The parties, therefore, were probably together in his office; and it is irrational to suppose that an arrangement in which the defendant might eventually have so deep an interest, and which there was no possible reason for concealing, was not communicated to him. He was, probably, at that time, if he had not previously been, retained as attorney in the suits, which the agreement recites it was the intention of the parties to commence. A contract of so much importance must have been a matter of conversation and discussion between the parties, at least, before it was finally concluded; and under all the circumstances of the case, the fair, and I think, the irresistible presumption is, that the defendant was fully apprised of all its provisions.

The next inquiry is, whether Teller was authorized by the plaintiff to settle with the defendant for his share of the recovery (assuming for the present that such settlement has in fact been made). It is not necessary that there should have been an express authority for the purpose. If the plaintiff has subsequently recognized or ratified the acts of Teller in that respect, it is equivalent to an original express power to perform those acts.

The power of attorney from Teller to the defendant, under which the suits were compro-
97*] mised, bears date *Dec. 22, 1813; and the compromise itself took place in the following month. The deeds which are proved to have been given, bear date from Dec., 1813, to the following Apr. Independent of all evidence, it is incredible that Thallhimer should not have known of the settlement in which he had so deep an interest. It was a matter of general notoriety. The suits affected a large number of individuals, and we have had very few controversies in our courts, the progress and termination of which were more generally known. It is not to be believed that the plaintiff, who resided within twelve miles of the City of Albany, where he had a son engaged in active business, and much nearer to Schenectady, where Teller, his brother-in-law, appears to have lived, was not informed both of the fact and the terms of the settlement, about the time when it was effected And yet no application is made by him to the defendant for his share of the proceeds of the settlement, nor any intimation given him of his intention to call him to an account, until 1821, when this suit was commenced. How is this to be accounted for, except upon the supposition that the plaintiff considered and acknowledged Teller as his agent, and was content to leave the final settlement, as he appears to have done the previous measures, to his judgment and discretion, and to look to him, and not to the defendant, for his share of the proceeds?

This view of the case derives strong confirmation from the circumstances attending the foreclosure of Brinckerhoff's mortgage against the plaintiff. The mortgage was foreclosed in 1816, for the non-payment of the interest. Many letters passed between the parties, from 1816 to 1818, pressing for payment on the one side, and begging indulgence on the other; but not an intimation is to be found of any claim on the part of the plaintiff against the defendant, in relation to the Teller property. Among the various suggestions made by the plaintiff, to avoid the ruinous consequences which he apprehended from a foreclosure of the mortgage, no allusion whatever is made to the fund in question, as laying the foundation either of a *legal or equitable claim against the [*98
defendant. The correspondence, from the first to the last, admits the justice of the demands and entreats only for forbearance.

Assuming (what I have endeavored to show must have been the fact) that the plaintiff knew of the compromise at the time it was made, is it credible that he remained uninformed and ignorant of the subsequent transactions between Teller and Brinckerhoff? He must have known (if such was the fact) that Teller was assuming to act for him, as well as for himself, in the settlement with Brinckerhoff; and, considering the origin of the plaintiff's interest in the fund, that it grew out of the voluntary act of Teller, who alone appears to have taken any part in the management or direction of the controversy, nothing was more natural than that Brinckerhoff should have supposed that Teller possessed the authority which he assumed, to settle the whole claim. And the plaintiff must, under all the circumstances of the case, be considered as having subsequently affirmed, if he did not originally authorize, his acts.

It was suggested, on the argument, that the reason of the plaintiff's omission to assert his claim against Brinckerhoff was, his being advised by counsel that the agreement between him and Teller, out of which his rights grew, was illegal and void. Admitting the fact, of which there is no evidence, it does not vary the case. It is immaterial to the defendant what were the plaintiff's reasons for permitting Teller to assume the character and power of an agent. He did permit it; and upon him, and not upon the defendant, must the disastrous consequences, if any have ensued, be visited.

If Brinckerhoff, therefore, has fully settled with Teller, and paid over to him the whole amount received upon the compromise of the suits, it ought, upon every principle of law and justice, to be a bar to the plaintiff's claim.

Whether the evidence in the case shows such settlement and payment, is a question which I do not intend to examine; as I have come to the conclusion that some material evidence, offered by the defendant upon this, as well as *other points, was improperly rejected; [*99
and that a new trial must be granted. I deem it, therefore, not only unnecessary, but improper, to discuss a pure question of fact which must again, upon additional evidence, be submitted to the consideration of a jury.

The learned judge who tried the cause decided that the defendant might show that he had accounted with and paid over all the money to Teller, on the ground that the plaintiff had acquiesced in such payment, and thereby admitted the authority of Teller to act in his behalf. Under this decision the defendant offered to prove, by the receipts and drafts of Teller, that he had fully settled his accounts with him, and paid over to him all the money which he had received for and on account of the settlement. He, also, for the same purpose, offered in evidence a stated account between him and Teller; and that Teller, Mar. 26, 1818, twenty months before the commencement of this action, had finally settled with the defendant in relation to the fund in question, and admitted a balance of upwards of $3,000 to be due to him. The whole of this evidence was objected to by the plaintiff's counsel, and rejected by the judge. The ground of the objection, or of the decision, is not stated in the case.

I see no legal objection, in point of competency, to any part of this evidence.

If Teller was the authorized agent of the plaintiff, for the purpose of receiving his share of the money (and it is only upon this supposition that proof of payment to the former is admissible at all), then his receipts or drafts for the money, or his admissions that it has been paid, are competent evidence of that fact. The agent in such a case need not be called personally to prove the payment, but it may be established by other evidence. I am not aware that this position has ever been questioned, where the receipt is given or admission made at the time of the payment of the money or delivery of the goods, or other thing which the evidence is designed to establish. So, where an agency is established, what the agent says or does in making a contract **100***] becomes part of the contract or **res gesta*, and is admissible in evidence against the principal. (3 T. R., 454; 7 *Id.*, 665; 1 Esp., 375; 4 Taunt., 511, 565, 663; 10 Ves., 128; 10 Johns., 44; 5 Esp., 74, 135; 2 *Id.*, 511, *note;* 2 Campb., 555; 1 Phil. Ev., 77; 2 Wh., 380.)

In this case we are to presume that it would have appeared from the receipts and drafts themselves, or been otherwise shown, that they related to the fund in question. The account I understand to have been offered in connection with the drafts and receipts, and not as an independent piece of evidence; and that the admission of a balance due to the defendant was made at the time of the settlement of the account. They all related to and were parts of the *res gesta* to which the agency of Teller extended.

This evidence, therefore, I think ought to have been submitted to the jury. It was competent, but not conclusive against the plaintiff. He might have impeached it, by showing either fraud or mistake on the part of Teller in making the settlement. What weight the evidence was entitled to with the jury is an entirely distinct question.

I do not understand the defendant to have offered his own answer to a bill in chancery in evidence. The case states that he offered to read in evidence the account, copies of which are annexed to an answer of the defendant to a bill filed against him, &c. Neither the answer nor the copies of the accounts were offered in evidence. Why any allusion was made in the case to the answer or the copies does not satisfactorily appear. Perhaps the phraseology of the case is inaccurate, and the answer was in fact offered in evidence. If so, it was properly rejected.

The copies of the letters from the defendant to the plaintiff, contained in what is called the defendant's second letter-book, should have been permitted to be read. The objection made to them was that it was not sufficiently proved that the original letters were sent according to their direction. Westuvelt, the defendant's clerk, testified that the letters in the second book were in his handwriting. That it was his invariable practice to carry the original *letters to the postoffice as soon [***101** as he had copied them in that letter-book. That he very seldom handed them back. The accuracy of the copy was not questioned. The only objection was that the evidence did not make out the fact that the original was sent. It comes fully up to what Ld. Ellenborough, in *Hetherington* v. *Kemp*, 4 Campb., 193, held would be sufficient. There the fact to be established was notice of the dishonor of a bill; and the plaintiff proved that he wrote a letter to the defendant containing such notice; that the letter was put on a table where, according to the usage of his counting-house, letters for the post were always deposited, and that a porter carried them thence to the postoffice. But the porter was not called, and there was no evidence as to what had become of the letter after it was put down on the table. Ld. Ellenborough held this insufficient. But he remarked, "had you called the porter, and he had said that, although he had no recollection of the letter in question, he invariably carried to the postoffice all the letters found upon the table, this might have done." Now the clerk, in this case, does swear that it was his invariable custom to carry to the postoffice the original of all the letters copied by him. In *Miller* v. *Hackley*, 5 Johns., 375, the notary testified that it was usual for him, where the drawer or indorsers lived at a distance, to send a written notice of the dishonor of the bill to them by post on the evening of the same day, and that he believed he had sent such notice in that way in the present case. This was held sufficient in the first instance. In such cases, too, strict proof is always required. (3 Campb., 305, 379; 2 Phil. Ev., 20, *note.*)

It was satisfactorily proved that Barent Thallhimer acted as the agent, and with the knowledge and approbation of his father, in his negotiations and correspondence with the defendant upon the subject of his mortgage. So far, therefore, as his letters strictly relate to that topic, they are competent evidence against the plaintiff: no farther. The letters of Jan. 5 and Feb. 6, *1816, are not of [***102** this description, and were properly excluded by the judge. The plaintiff's claims against Teller had no connection with Brinckerhoff's mortgage, and an authority to his son to correspond with the plaintiff in relation to the mortgage conferred no power upon him to bind or commit him by any representations or declarations that he might make in relation to other topics. There is no proof that he was the authorized agent of his father in the settlement of his demands against Teller. When he says, therefore, in his letter of Jan. 5, that in his opinion $2,000 will balance accounts between Teller and his father, he speaks without authority, and of course without effect. The same observations apply to the letter of Feb. 6. The opinion of the Master of the Rolls, in *Fairlie* v. *Hastings*, 10 Ves., 125, is very clear and explicit on this point. And all the cases already cited upon the authority of agents to bind their principals, by their acts or declarations, are applicable here.

The acknowledgment contained in the deeds executed by Brinckerhoff, as attorney for Teller, that the consideration money expressed therein had been paid, was correctly held by the judge to be, *prima facie*, evidence that the money was actually paid to him. If such was not the fact, he had it in his power to show to whom it was paid, by calling the different grantees as witnesses. Brinckerhoff was properly allowed credit for all the mortgages given directly to Teller.

If the acknowledgment of the receipt of the consideration money in the deeds executed by Brinckerhoff, as attorney, is evidence of the payment of the money to him, then, upon the same principle, the consideration money of the mortgages assigned by Teller to Brinckerhoff, and for the different lots conveyed to him, must be presumed to have been paid by Brinckerhoff to Teller, as all those instruments contain a similar acknowledgment. There is nothing to show that those assignments and conveyances were made in part payment of Brinckerhoff's debt; and were not, as they purport, distinct and independent purchases. He **103***] cannot, therefore, be charged *with those sums. A case, however, involving so large an amount of property, ought not to be decided upon such slight presumptions, where evidence of a much more satisfactory character, must be in the power of the parties.

I am not aware of any other point, upon which it is important for the court to express an opinion.

New trial granted.

S. C.—20 Johns., 386; 3 Cow., 623.

Cited in—7 Cow., 362; 4 Wend., 396; 10 N. Y., 528; 47 Barb., 502; 3 Wood. & M., 478; 17 Am. Dec., 522; 19 Am. Rep., 524 (41 Conn., 421).

PETERS v. NEWKIRK.

Award—Parties Entitled to Notice of Making—Distraint—Statute—Surrender of Part of Premises—Time to Distrain.

An award made, without giving notice to the parties, so that they can be heard before the arbitrator, is a nullity.

An action does not lie on the Statute, 1 R. L., 436, sec. 9, for double value of goods, &c., for distraining for more rent than is due, or for distraining for rent for which there is no right to distrain; but only for distraining where no rent whatever is due. If there be any, the least rent due, it protects the distrainor, though he may be liable in some other form.

Where a lease is surrendered as to part of the premises, the right to distrain continues as to the residue.

Where rent is agreed to be paid at the end of the year; but before that time the tenant surrenders part of the premises, giving a due-bill for the rent, payable presently; held, that the landlord may distrain for the rent immediately.

Rent may be payable in advance, and may, in such case, be distrained for when due.

Citations—4 Dall., 232; 1 R. L., 436; Gilb. on Rents, 25; 2 T. R., 600; 4 Cow., 576; 2 Cow., 652; 10 Johns., 432.

CASE, for distraining the plaintiff's goods, when no rent was in arrear, under the Act, 1 R. L., 436, sec. 9, tried at the Ulster Circuit, Oct. 14, 1823, before Betts, *Circuit J.*

Plea, the general issue.

It appeared, at the trial, that Newkirk, the defendant, had demised certain premises, being a grist-mill, fulling-mill, house, &c., to the plaintiff, for three years from May 20, 1822, at $300 rent *per annum*, payable out of the carding or fulling-book; the defendant to have the privilege of taking the accounts as they stood, beginning either at the top or bottom. The lease provided that either party might determine it, on three months' notice previous to the end of the year. The witness who proved this lease, did not recollect distinctly when the rent was payable, though he thought it was at the end of the year.

Feb. 3, 1823, the parties agreed to destroy the lease, and it was accordingly destroyed; and *they struck a balance of the rent. [***104** Newkirk agreed to give off and deduct $60; and it was agreed in writing, that Peters should give up the possession of the grist-mill immediately, and retain possession of the house and barn, with the privileges under the first lease, till May 1, 1823, and then leave possession; and that he might finish his cloth in the shop. The balance of rent due to Newkirk was agreed to be $87.75, for which Peters gave his due bill in these words: "Due, this 3d day of February, 1823, to Christopher Newkirk on a settlement for rent of the mill, fulling-mill, &c., the sum of eighty seven dollars seventy five cents, &c." It was also agreed that Newkirk should take a shearing machine to be appraised by C. Sturges, in part pay of the due-bill; and to be indorsed upon it; and Feb. 10, 1823, he made the appraisement at $85, at the request of the plaintiff, and in the absence of the defendant, who was not notified.

The defendant offered to show by Sturges, that in making the appraisal, he took the first cost of the machine, and deducted the damage occasioned by its use; but that, in his opinion, the real value, to a man engaged in the clothing business, was not more than $25. The evidence was objected to, and overruled by the judge.

The distress was made Feb. 6, 1823, for the $87.75, and on the 12th, after the appraisal of the machine, the plaintiff caused to be served on the defendant a copy of the appraisal, tendered him $7, and demanded a return of the goods distrained. The defendant refused to return the goods, but proceeded to sell them.

The judge decided and charged the jury, that, to protect the defendant, it must appear, not only that rent was due, but that it was due with right of distress. That the jury must be satisfied that the due-bill was given for the rent then in arrear, or made payable in advance by express agreement. That if the $85 discharged all the rent due Feb. 3, the plaintiff was entitled to recover; *but if, un- [***105** der the agreement of the parties, any rent was then due and in arrear, they should find for the defendant.

Verdict for the plaintiff $92, single damages, the value of the goods distrained.

Mr. C. H. Ruggles, for the defendant, now moved for a new trial. He said that even if the $85 was to be applied as of Feb. 3, there was still $2.75 yet due, for which the defendant might distrain, and which would protect him from the penalty imposed by the Statute, 1 R. L., 436, sec. 9. There is an adequate remedy for an unreasonable distress. The statute gives the treble damages, only in a case where no rent whatever is due. Although the first agreement was uncertain, as to the time of payment, the second one changed it, and fixed the time at Feb. 3, the date of the due-bill.

If the rent was in fact due, this was enough, whether there was a right to distrain or not. The statute applies to a case where no rent is due; not where the party mistakes his remedy. (Woodf. L. & T., 258, Am. ed.; *Id.*, 395, Lond. ed.)

But the whole $87.75 was due. The award or appraisal of Sturges was void for want of notice to the defendant. (4 Dall., 232.) At any rate, evidence should have been received to show the false basis on which the arbitrator made his appraisal.

Mr. J. Sudam, contra. The rent, as originally reserved, was not of a nature to be the subject of a distress. The reservation was void. (Shep. Touch., 80.) But if otherwise, here was no rent in arrear when the distress was made. The original rent had not yet fallen due; and the mere act of giving the due-bill did not change the time of payment. But if it did work a change as to the time, we say the situation of the parties was changed by the new agreement. The relation of landlord and tenant ceased for the purposes of a distress. 1 T. R., 441; *Bain* v. *Clark*, 10 Johns., 424. And there was no new agreement which gave a **106***] *right to distrain. It was left to the jury upon this question; and they found there had been no change as to the time. In this view, it was immaterial whether the appraisal by Sturges was valid or not.

Mr. Ruggles, in reply. *Bain* v. *Clark* was the case of a distress after a total surrender of the lease. Here a new lease was substituted, and the rent was payable immediately.

Curia, per WOODWORTH, *J.* The evidence as to the basis of Sturges' appraisal should have been received. The appraisal was irregular, and not conclusive on the defendant. Both parties should have had notice, so that an opportunity might be afforded to submit their remarks to the appraiser, and adduce proof, if deemed necessary. (4 Dall., 232.) The plainest dictates of natural justice require that no man shall be condemned unheard. The right to notice was implied in the agreement to submit. As the appraisment was, in my view, a nullity, the value of the machine was a proper subject of inquiry at the trial, in order to decide whether any rent was due.

If, however, the appraisement be allowed, there remained a small balance due. The question in this case seems to be, not whether the defendant took an unreasonable distress, but simply whether any rent was due. The count on which the plaintiff recovered is clearly founded on the 9th section of the "Act concerning Distresses," &c., 1 R. L., 436, which provides that whenever a distress and sale shall be made by color of the Act, for rent pretended to be in arrear, when in truth "no rent is in arrear or due," the party shall render double the value of the goods. The fact being conceded that some rent was due, this action cannot be sustained, unless the charge of the judge be correct, that there must also be a right of distress.

If it be admitted that the defendant had no right to distrain, the answer is, the plaintiff does not claim to recover on that ground. The statute remedy is relied on. If the case is brought within the statute, the damages are regulated. *The plaintiff shall recover [***107** double the value of the goods. A case cannot be within the statute, if rent is actually due, let the right to distrain be as it may. If the defendant had no authority to distrain, he is answerable in a different form of action; but then he is not liable to double damages. The plaintiff must show a right to double damages, or this action fails. There is no discretion given in the assessment. It seems, therefore, to follow as a necessary consequence, that, whether the defendant had the right to distrain or not, is an immaterial inquiry under the pleadings before us.

But I am of opinion that the defendant had a right to distrain, although the original lease was surrendered and destroyed. The relation of landlord and tenant existed; for Feb. 3, 1823, the date of the due-bill at the time it was given, and as part of the arrangement then made, there was another writing between the parties, by which, among other things, the plaintiff was permitted to remain in the house until the 1st of May then ensuing, and have the privilege he had had in the same, and in the barn; and to finish his cloth in the shop. The effect of the arrangement was, that the plaintiff gave up a part of the premises, and retained the residue to the end of the year. The due-bill is stated to be a sttlement up to May 1; so that it included all the rent claimed for the year; as well the rent on the premises retained by the plaintiff to May 1, as the rent which had accrued when this agreement was made.

The operation of the settlement was, to make a part of the rent payable in advance. This is no objection to the right of distraining. (Gilb. Rents, 25; 2 T. R., 600; 4 Cow., 576.)

If it be urged that the due-bill also included the rent, accrued on the original lease, prior to its surrender, and as to that there could not be a distress; it only proves that the distress may have been unreasonable, the defendant having distrained for the whole; but it does not destroy the right altogether.

*I perceive, therefore, no ground to [***108** question the authority to distrain. *Cornell* v. *Lamb*, 2 Cow., 652.

This case is clearly distinguishable from *Bain* v. *Clark*, 10 Johns., 432. There the tenant surrendered the lease and quit the premises. The relation of landlord and tenant having ceased, the personal responsibility of the tenant, on his agreement to pay, alone remained.

The verdict must be set aside, and a new trial granted, with costs to abide the event.

New trial granted.

Denied—35 Am. Rep., 176 (95 Ill., 540, 546).

Cited in—5 Wend., 520; 23 Wend., 632; 35 N. Y., 310; 20 Barb., 413; 61 Barb., 279; 9 How. Pr., 72; 38 Mich., 60; 37 N. J. L., 94; 35 Am. Dec., 589.

COOK v. SATTERLEE AND SATTERLEE.

Bills and Notes—Essential Qualities of—Must be Payable Absolutely, and in Money Only.

The essential qualities of a bill of exchange, or promissory note, are, that it be payable at all events, not dependent on any contingency, nor payable out of a particular fund; and that it be for the payment of money only; and not for the performance of any other act, or in the alternative.

An instrument in writing, by which A directs B to pay C, or bearer, $400, and take up A's note of that amount, though the instrument be accepted by B, is not a bill of exchange.

Citation—Chit. Bills, 55.

ON demurrer to the declaration. The plaintiff declared in *assumpsit*, that July 25, 1825, W. F. and C. E. Clarke, according to the usage and custom of merchants, &c., made their certain bill of exchange, &c., dated on that day, directed to the defendants, by which they requested the defendants, 90 days after date, to pay to the plaintiff, or bearer, $400, and take up their note given to William and Henry B. Cook for that amount, dated Apr. 19, 1825; which bill the defendants on the same day accepted, according to the usage, &c.

General demurrer and joinder.

Mr. E. Cowen, in support of the demurrer, insisted that the instrument set forth was not a bill of exchange. That the object was special; and an acceptance imposed not only the obligation to pay the money, but do a further act—the taking up of the note. Nor was it for the absolute payment of money. The acceptors might exact the note, before they would be obliged to pay the money.

Mr. E. Griffin, contra, cited Chit. Bills, 41, 61; 1 Str., 706; Bull. *N. P.*, 270, and 8 Johns., 485.

Curia, per SAVAGE, *Ch. J.* The essential qualities of a bill or note, are, 1. That it be payable at all events; not *dependent [*109 on any contingency, nor payable out of a particular fund; and 2. That it be for the payment of money only, and not for the performance of some other act, or in the alternative. (Chit. Bills, 55.)

Is not the instrument declared on payable upon a contingency? From the face of the instrument itself, it appears that the drawers had, Apr. 19, preceding its date, given their note for $400, to Wm. and H. B. Cook; and the object of drawing the instrument in question was to take up that note. The engagement of the acceptors must be construed according to what is required of them by the drawers. The note was supposed to be in possession of the payee or holder of the bill, and the payment of the money and taking up the note of the drawers, must be simultaneous acts. The acceptors could not take up the note till it was presented; nor were they bound to pay the money till the plaintiff was ready, and offered to enable them to take up the note. It seems to me, therefore, that, substantially, this instrument is payable upon a contingency; and is the same as if it had said, "Pay W. C. $400, on his giving up our note," &c. Had such been the form, it would clearly not be technically a bill of exchange. The holder, in declaring upon it, should aver his readiness to deliver up the note. Upon a contrary doctrine, the defendants may be compelled to pay the bill; and the drawers to pay the note, provided it has been transferred before due.

The defendants are entitled to judgment, with leave to amend on the usual terms.

Rule accordingly.

Cited in—1 Wend., 523; 23 Wend., 74; 2 N. Y., 543; 39 N. Y., 101; 57 N. Y., 578; 15 Am. Rep., 537; 61 N. Y., 257; 6 Trans. App., 260; 33 Barb., 639; 5 Duer, 213; 31 Ill., 528; 51 Ind., 394; 1 Kan., 36; 33 Mich., 34; 35 Am. Dec., 547; 30 Am. Rep., 768 (45 Wis., 403).

NOTE.—*Negotiable paper—Essential qualities of notes and bills of exchange.*

"*The essential qualities of a bill or note are*, that it be payable at all events, not dependent on any contingency, nor payable out of any particular fund, and that it be for the payment of money only, and not for the performance of some other act or in the alternative." Above case of Cook v. Satterlee. See also, Wait Act. & Def. vol. 1, p. 548; Atkinson v. Manks, 1 Cow., 691; Hinnemann v. Rosenback, 39 N. Y., 98; Luff v. Pope, 5 Hill, 413; Pope v. Luff, 7 Hill, 577; Gillilan v. Myers, 31 Ill., 525; Bunker v. Athearn, 35 Me., 364; Hays v. Gwin, 19 Ind., 19; Brooks v. Hargreaves, 21 Mich., 254; Marret v. Equitable Ins. Co., 54 Me., 537; Tucker v. Maxwell, 11 Mass., 143; Smurr v. Foreman, 1 Ohio, 272; Wooley v. Sergeant, 8 N. J. L., 262; Carlos v. Fancourt, 5 T. R., 482; Alexander v. Thomas, 16 Adol. & Ell. (N. S.), 333; Pars. Notes and B., ch. III, pp. 30-51, and numerous authorities there cited.

"The paper must carry its full history on its face, and embrace the following requisites: First—It must be open, that is, unsealed. Second—The engagement to pay must be certain. Third—The fact of payment must be certain. Fourth—The amount to be paid must be certain. Fifth—The medium of payment must be money. Sixth—The contract must be only for the payment of money. And Seventh—It is also essential to the operation of the instrument that it should be delivered." 1 Dan. Neg. Inst., secs. 30-71, and numerous authorities there cited.

As to medium of payment, see Saxton v. Johnson, 10 Johns., 418, *note*.

---

*CHAPMAN AND SCHOOLCRAFT [*110 v. LATHROP.

Sales—When for Cash, Delivery and Payment, Simultaneous Acts—Vendor, may Refuse to Deliver without Payment—Delivery Waives Condition, and Property Passes—Set-Off—Stoppage in Transitu.

Where goods are sold, to be paid for in cash, no time being agreed on for the payment, both the delivery and payment are simultaneous acts; and the vendor may refuse to deliver without actual payment, the latter being a condition of the sale.

But if he deliver without payment, the property passes, and the condition is waived; and though the vendee afterwards refused to pay, trover will not lie for the goods.

Otherwise, it seems, where they are obtained by the fraudulent contrivance of the vendee.

NOTE.—*Sales—Payment and delivery, as mutual and concurrent conditions precedent.*

As a general rule, in executory agreements for the sale of goods, payment and delivery are mutual and concurrent conditions precedent. Neither party can enforce the agreement without showing performance, offer to perform, or readiness to perform. Porter v. Rose, 12 Johns., 209, *note*; Topping v. Root, 5 Cow., 404; Coonley v. Anderson, 1 Hill, 519; Bronson v. Wiman, 8 N. Y., 182; N. Y. &c. Ins. Co. v. De Wolf, 2 Cow., 56; Davis v. Adams, 18 Ala., 264 Coll v. Willis, 18 Ohio, 28; Colo v. Swanston, 1 Cal., 51 Johnson v. Powell, 9 Ind., 566; Houdlette v. Tall-

If the goods be delivered without payment, the vendee may avail himself of a set-off against the vendor. Per Savage, *Ch. J.*, delivering the opinion of the court.

If the vendee become bankrupt, the vendor may stop the goods *in transitu*. Per Savage, *Ch. J.*, delivering the opinion of the court.

Citations—Com. Cont., 221; Cook Bankr. Law, ch. 8, sec. 17, 18; 4 Mass., 405; 12 Johns., 348; 5 T. R., 231; 13 Johns., 434.

TROVER for a hogshead of rum, a hogshead of sugar, and a box of raisins, tried at the Albany Circnit, Sept. 15, 1824, before Duer, *Circuit J.*

The following facts appeared at the trial: May 6, 1824, the defendant called at the plaintiffs' store, and inquired for the articles in question. Being informed by Schoolcraft, one of the plaintiffs, that he had them, the defendant told him to put them as low as he could and he, the defendant, would pay for them in cash, or current bills. Schoolcraft replied that, on those conditions, he would sell them as low as he could. On the same day the goods were delivered to the defendant, who took them to his store on carts. The next day the defendant's clerk called on the plaintiffs to pay for them, and offered a note which had been indorsed by the plaintiffs, and regularly protested, proposing to pay the balance in cash. The plaintiffs refused to receive the note, and about a fortnight after demanded the property of the defendant, which he refused to deliver.

The note had been drawn by one Northrop payable to the plaintiffs, or order; and was indorsed by them to Isaiah Shaw. It was given for horses purchased of Shaw, which Northrop took to Boston, and there delivered them to one of the plaintiffs. The note had been discounted at the Albany Bank, and taken up by Shaw after protest.

The defendant offered to prove that the plaintiffs had indorsed notes to a large amount for Northrop, had received from him the property purchased with those notes, and then stopped payment, with the avowed intention of preventing the holders from collecting them.

This testimony was objected to and overruled.

111*] *The judge left two questions to the jury: 1. Whether the goods in question were sold on the understanding that they were to be paid for in cash or current bank bills. 2. Whether the plaintiffs were induced to part with the goods on the misrepresentations or deceptions of the defendant; and under circumstances against which common prudence could not guard; and that in either case the plaintiffs were entitled to a verdict. To this charge the defendant excepted.

Verdict for the plaintiffs for $213.97, the value of the goods, with interest.

Mr. I. Hamilton, now moved for a new trial. He insisted that the goods were delivered pursuant to a fair contract, and that *assumpsit* should have have been brought. The delivery vested the property. (Bro. Cont., pl. 26; Shep. Touch., 224; Noy Max., 88; 1 Salk., 113; 7 East, 558, 571; 14 Johns., 167; 2 Com. Cont., 210, 212, 221, 231-233; 3 Bos. & P., 584.) If the opposite doctrine be allowed, which seeks to avoid all cash sales, followed by delivery, where the money is not paid, the situation of purchasers must be very insecure. If void as to the immediate vendee, it is so as to the most remote. The delivery without payment gave a credit to the vendee. (4 Rep., 119 *b;* Cooke B. L., 447, ch. 8, sec. 18; 5 T.R., 231; 3 Cow., 84.) It was a waiver of the cash payment. (1 East, 375.) To save the lien, the delivery itself should have been conditional, as in *Hussey* v. *Thornton*, 4 Mass., 405. Security might have been demanded at the time. There are not only many direct authorities; but the whole doctrine of stoppage *in transitu* shows that the very moment goods reach the hands of the vendee, or his agent, the right to reclaim them is gone. (3 Bos. & P., 584; Cowp., 294; 8 T. R., 330; 3 P. Wms., 186; 12 Johns., 348.) The cases which have gone to the jury upon the validity of the sale, are all cases of fraud. Such was *Hollingworth* v. *Napier*, 3 Cai., 183; *Hunn* v. *Bowne*, 2 *Id.*, 38, and *Allison* v. *Matthieu*, 3 Johns., 235.

*The testimony offered by the defend- [*112
ant and overruled should have been received. It went to show that the plaintiff had not been damnified. The measure of damages in trover is not always the value of the goods. (5 Mass., 104-106.) The note of the party was equivalent to cash, and better than bank bills. (5 Mass., 299.) An individual as well as a bank is bound to take his own notes in payment. Promissory notes are often considered as cash. (8 Johns., 206; 11 *Id.*, 468.)

Demand and refusal is no evidence of a conversion, where there is a good excuse for not complying with the demand. (5 Burr., 2826.)

Mr. S. S. Lush, contra, cited *Allison* v. *Matthieu*, 3 Johns., 235; *Murray* v. *Burling*, 10 *Id.*, 172; *Hunn* v. *Bowne*, 2 Cai., 38, and *Van Cleef* v. *Fleet*, 15 Johns., 147.

He said these cases, together with that of *Woodworth* v. *Kissam*, 15 Johns., 186, establish, beyond all doubt, that where the creditor obtains possession of his debtor's goods by fraud, the property is not changed, and the debtor may maintain trover for them; and that what circumstances are necessary to make out the deception are matter for the jury. He also cited *Parker* v. *Norton*, 6 T. R., 695.

In *Palmer* v. *Hand*, 13 Johns., 434, the doctrine is explicitly laid down that where goods are to be paid for on delivery the vendor has a lien; so that if they be actually delivered to the vendee and, on demand, he refuses to pay, the property is not changed, the delivery being conditional.

---

man, 14 Me., 400; Summers v. Sleeth, 45 Ind., 598; Phelps v. Hubbard, 51 Vt., 489; Jones v. Marsh, 22 Vt., 144; Cleveland v. Sterrett, 70 Pa. St., 204; Posey v. Scales, 55 Ind., 282; Stoolfire v. Rayse, 71 Ill., 223; Morton v. Lamb, 7 T. R., 125; Rawson v. Johnson, 1 East, 203; Jackson v. Allaway, 6 Man. & G., 942; Boyd v. Lett, 1 C. B., 222. But see Hapgood v. Shaw, 105 Mass., 276; Barr v. Myres, 3 Watts & S., 298; Allen v. Woods, 24 Pa. St., 76.

Though to be paid for on delivery, if goods are delivered without payment, the title passes. Such delivery is a waiver of condition. Lupin v. Marie, 6 Wend., 77; Hennequin v. Sands, 25 Wend., 640; Smith v. Lynes, 5 N. Y., 41; Ives v. Humphreys, 1 E. D. Smith, 196; Conway v. Bush, 4 Barb., 564; Husted v. Ingraham, 75 N. Y., 251; Meeder v. Cook, 31 Me., 340; Bowen v. Burk, 13 Pa. St., 146; Smith v. Dennie, 23 Mass. (6 Pick.), 262; Farlow v. Ellis, 81 Mass. (15 Gray), 229; Pitts v. Owen, 9 Wis., 152.

Where the sale is of a large quantity of merchandise, which will require some time in the delivery, payment and delivery are not regarded as simultaneous acts. Lees v. Richardson, 2 Hilt., 164; Baker v. Higgins, 21 N. Y., 397.

The testimony offered by the defendant and rejected by the judge, was irrelevant.

Mr. Hamilton, in reply, said that *Palmer* v. *Hand* was a case of gross fraud, and there was no actual delivery or acquiescence by the vendor, as in the case before the court.

Curia, per SAVAGE, *Ch. J.* The principal question is, whether trover will lie upon the facts proved.

113*] *If there was a fair contract for the goods, and they were delivered to the purchaser without any fraudulent contrivance on his part to obtain possession, the property passed, and the plaintiff's remedy is by a different action.

It is conceded that the plaintiffs were entitled to pay for the goods upon delivery. They might have refused to part with the goods until payment. Where no time is agreed on for payment, the delivery and payment are to be simultaneous acts. But if the vendor delivers the goods to the vendee, and the latter omits to pay, the property of the goods is changed. If the vendee becomes bankrupt while the goods are on their passage, but before actual delivery, the vendor may stop them *in transitu*. (2 Com. Cont., 221; Cooke Bank. L., ch. 8 secs. 17, 18.)

In case of an agreement to pay down for goods, if the vendor deliver the goods without actual payment, the vendee may avail himself of any legal set-off, notwithstanding the agreement to pay ready money. (*Ibid.*, 1 East, 375.)

In *Hussey* v. *Thornton*, 4 Mass., 405, the plaintiffs had agreed to sell a quantity of candles to T. & W. on credit, and on their giving security. The agent of T. & W. received the candles on board a vessel through the hands of cartmen sent by him. While part of the candles were on the wharf and part on board the vessel, one of the plaintiffs appeared and said he should consider the candles the property of the plaintiffs until security was given, to which the agent assented. These candles were attached by the defendants as the property of T. & W.; and the question was, whether they were so. Parsons, *Ch. J.*, states the inquiry to be, whether this was an absolute delivery, not revocable; or, if revocable, yet not revoked. "We think," said he, "they (the plaintiffs) were bound to recollect the condition they had themselves made, and not to have delivered the candles until it had been complied with." The court, however, decided the cause, on the ground that the agent had accepted of a conditional delivery and, therefore, the property remained in the vendors. But the decision 114*] would have been different *if the goods had been sold or attached while in the possession of T. & W. According to the doctrine of this case, the absolute delivery of the property is a waiver of any condition antecedently made.

In *M'Carty* v. *Vickery*, 12 Johns., 348, this court decided that trespass would not lie where the vendor had parted with the possession, even though by fraud. They add, the property was changed by the delivery.

In 5 T. R., 231, *Mr. J.* Buller cites the case of *Haswell* v. *Hunt*, where Lacey in the morning, purchased some tobacco of the plaintiffs, to be paid for in cash, and then went off to France to absent himself from his creditors. The tobacco was delivered by the plaintiffs' servants at Lacey's house, without demanding the money or having any orders to do it. Eyre, *Ch. J.*, held that the sale was made complete by the act of the plaintiffs; that by delivering the goods, without demanding the money, the property was vested in Lacey as upon a complete sale *ab inito*, without ready money. That was a much stronger case than the present.

Suppose the plaintiffs' note had never been presented, but that after a fortnight had elapsed they had sent a bill of the goods, and the defendant had omitted to pay; could it be pretended that trover would lie? If so, the vendor has only to make his contract for cash, and may then pursue the property, whose hands soever it may reach, at any length of time not barring an action upon the Statute of Limitations. The proposition is monstrous.

As to fraud, it seems to me, if there be any in the case, it is on the side of the plaintiffs. The judge admitted that the defendant acted under an erroneous opinion of his rights, and yet charged the jury that his conduct might be fraudulent. The fraud, I presume, was that of paying the plaintiffs with their own paper. If that be fraudulent, it must be admitted that the defendant is guilty. But there is no evidence in the case showing that he contemplated making such a payment when he purchased the goods, or when he received them.

*The case of *Palmer v. Hand*, is not [*115 in point. The purchaser in that case never received the delivery of the lumber; but while the hands were piling it, he defrauded the defendant of nearly the value of it, and absconded.

I find no case which will warrant a recovery in this action; nor is it sustainable upon any principle of law.

I think the judge erred; and there must be a new trial, with costs to abide the event.

New trial granted.(a)

Cited in—6 Wend., 81, 157; 7 Wend., 406; 8 Wend., 263; 14 Wend., 565; 15 Wend., 225; 22 Wend., 664; 24 Wend., 460; 1 Den., 51; 2 Paige, 172; 1 Edw., 145; 5 N. Y., 44; 18 N. Y., 311; 4 Barb., 565; 12 Barb., 280; 20 Barb., 61; 66 Barb., 38; 37 How. Pr., 353; 6 Abb. N. S., 375; 3 Sand., 208; 3 Duer, 316; 38 Super., 151; 1 Sweeny, 196; 1 E. D. S., 199; 2 Hilt., 173; 1 Daly, 27; 21 Am. Dec., 258; 28 Am. Dec., 541, 543.

(a) There is no doubt that the strong general proposition laid down by Platt, J., in Palmer v. Hand, 13 Johns., 434, joined with the subsequent case of Haggerty v. Palmer, 6 Johns., Ch., 437, decided by Kent, late *Chancellor*, have led the profession generally to an adoption of the doctrine as stated in Mr. Johnson's marginal note to the former case; that "where goods are sold, to be paid for on delivery, if on the delivery being completed, the vendee refuses to pay for them, the vendor has a lien for the price, and may resume the possession of the goods." This case was at law. Haggerty v. Palmer, in equity, goes about the same length, as between vendor and vendee, and where no *bona fide* purchaser intervenes. No case is cited in support of either the *dictum* of Platt, *J.*, or the decision of Kent, *Chancellor*. But they were very learned and able judges. And as the *dictum* cited is certainly at war with the decision in the principal case, whatever may be said of Haggerty v. Palmer; and as it is important that a principle of such extensive practical application be as firmly settled as possible, I give below the decision of Story, *J.*, in Conyers v. Ennis, 2 Mas., 236. This case declares the law, as I believe it was held by the profession, till the two decisions cited from Johnson, viz.: that a fair sale for cash, or a bill, or other mode of payment at the time; and a delivery, though without payment, passes the property of the goods absolutely, both at law and in equity, even as between vendor and vendee; and that no lien remains for the price. This, I am sure, was the conceded and well established doctrine, at least, in a court of law; and I am not aware that even in equity, after *transitus* determined, the doctrine of lien for the price was ever applied, till the case of Haggerty v. Palmer. The question was much discussed in Warren v. Sproule, 2 Marsh, Ky., 528, and at p. 536, *Judge* Owsley, who delivered the opinion of the court, asserts in terms, and as the clear and settled doctrine, that it is only while the goods are *in transitu*, that the consignor can retake them, even though the consignee be insolvent; and he denies that the consignor can, after the delivery, have any lien in such a case for the price. The question there was in equity. The case, however, does not determine the point as between vendor and vendee; for the latter had sold to another, who purchased *bona fide*, and would be protected even within the doctrine of Haggerty v. Palmer.

116*] *CONYERS ET AL. *v.* WILLIAM ENNIS ET AL., Administrators of LEWIS ROUSMANIERE.

A BILL in equity which was set down by consent for a hearing upon the bill and answer. It was argued by *Mr. Hunter*, for the plaintiff, and by *Mr. Randolph*, for the respondents, upon the point stated in the opinion of the court.

STORY, J. This is a case of extreme hardship, and such as might well induce a court to strain after some mode of redress. The cause has come on upon the bill and answer, and the material facts are these: The intestate, Lewis Rousmaniere, a merchant of Newport, being deeply and fraudulently insolvent, May 4, 1820, wrote a letter to the plaintiffs, who are merchants in Charleston, S. C., and with whom he had previously done business, containing an order for the purchase and shipment of 30 casks of rice on his own account, from Charleston to Newport. May 6, the intestate, in consequence of the discovery of his frauds, committed suicide. The letter of May 4, duly reached the plaintiffs, who, May 16, shipped the 30 casks of rice consigned to the intestate on his own account and risk, and drew a bill on the intestate for the amount, in $500.73, payable at 30 days sight. The rice duly arrived at Newport, May 24, and was received and freight and charges paid by the defendants, who had previously taken administration on the estate of Rousmaniere, and represented it insolvent, according to the laws of R. I. On the evening of the day in which the rice was received by the defendants, a letter arrived by the mail, from the plaintiffs, containing an invoice of the rice, and advising of the draft drawn for payment. Upon the presentment of the draft, the defendants refused payment, and it was duly protested. The rice was sold by the defendants, and the present bill is brought to obtain payment of the cost of the rice, out of the proceeds in the hands of the defendants. The defendants' answer admits that at the time of the order, the intestate must have been insolvent, but that whether that fact was then known to him, they are unable to say; and it states that the defendants are ignorant of any representations made by the intestate to the plaintiffs of his ability to comply with his engagements, and if he made any, whether he made them being himself deceived as to his pecuniary circumstances, or with a view to deceive the plaintiffs. It further states that the intestate, to the day of his death, was actually engaged in business, and was in the daily receipt and payment of considerable sums of money.

The principal point which, under these circumstances, has been pressed at the bar is, that the right of a consignor to stop property in cases of insolvency, ought not to be confined to stoppage *in transitu*, but in equity should extend to all cases where the property is not paid for, and remains in the hands of the consignee. It is admitted that the decisions in England have confined the right of stoppage to cases where the property is in its transit. But it is suggested that the point has not been solemnly adjudged in the U. S., and that it is open for the court to adopt the more enlarged rule, hinted at by Ld. Hardwicke, in Snee v. Prescott, 1 Atk., 245.

117*] *His Lordship there says: "Though goods are even delivered to the principal, I could never see any substantial reason why the original proprietor, who never received a farthing, should be obliged to quit all claim to them and come in as a creditor only, for a shilling perhaps in the pound, unless the law goes upon the general credit the bankrupt has gained, by having them in his custody." The reasoning, too, of Ld. Loughborough, in Lickbarrow v. Mason, 1 H. Bl., 357, is brought in aid of the same doctrine.

All argument of this sort is addressed in vain to this court. I do not sit here to revise the general judgments of the common law, or to establish new doctrines, merely because they seem to me more convenient or equitable. My duty is to administer the law as I find it, and I have not the rashness to attempt more than this humble discharge of duty. Nothing is better settled, if an uninterrupted series of authorities can settle the law, than the doctrine, that the vendor, in cases of insolvency, can stop the property only while it is in its transit. If it has once reached the consignee, there is an end of all right to reclaim it as a pledge for the payment of the purchase money. If the doctrine were to go the length now contended for, it is far from certain that it would promote public convenience or policy. Where could we stop? Could it be applied with safety to purchases made at at any distance of time, if it should turn out in the event that the buyer was then insolvent? It is very true, as has been stated at the bar, that our law respecting the distribution of the estates of persons dying insolvent differs from that of England, where the assets are marshaled, and payment goes according to the dignity of the debt. Here, all debts are paid *pari passu*. This, however, affords no ground to change the general rights and duties of vendor or vendee, or to create relations between debtor and creditor hitherto unknown to the law. The cases arising under the Bankrupt Laws are not, in principle, unlike those which arise here under insolvencies. And the Bankrupt Laws furnish no instance of an attempt to establish any doctrine like that now sought from the court. It is sufficient for me to stand upon the law, as it is now universally received. If there are public mischiefs growing out of its principles, let them be remedied by the Legislature.

The only point of view, in which it seemed possible to sustain the plaintiff's bill, struck me at the argument to be, that there was a meditated fraud and concealment practiced on them by Rousmaniere. If the latter had, by false affirmations and contrivances, imposed upon the plaintiffs, and induced them to send him the property, there might be reason to say that the contract was *ab origine* void for fraud. And the question then would be, whether the *suppressio veri*, under the strong circumstances of the present case, was not equivalent to the *allegatio falsi*, since the imposition as to the intestate's insolvency was complete. If a man, knowing his own insolvency and utter incapacity to make payment, purchases goods of another, who is ignorant of any change of his circumstances, and sells them under the most implicit belief of the good faith and solvency of the buyer, in what respect does the transaction differ from a direct affirmation by the buyer of his own good faith and solvency? If the buyer conceals a fact, that is vital to the *con- [*118 tract, knowing that the other party acts upon the presumption that no such fact exists, is it not as much a fraud as if the existence of such fact were expressly denied, or the reverse of it expressly stated?

Upon looking more attentively to the facts of this case, strong as at first blush they seem to be, I do not think they establish a case of meditated fraud. The intestate was in full business as a merchant, and there is no reason to suppose that he did not expect, still to keep on in business. It is admitted at the bar that the accidental discovery of his fraudulent conduct led to the unhappy catastrophe which terminated his life, and he might have been able and have intended fairly to pay for the rice in question, at the time when payment should become due. The sum was not so large as not to be completely within the ordinary means of a merchant. At all events, the bill does not pointedly put the case as one of meditated fraud and imposition; and so far as any conclusion to this effect might be drawn from the facts, it is repelled by the answer.

I do not say that the *suppressio veri*, if made out in this case, would have sustained the plaintiff's bill, even if it were a concealment of positive and deep insolvency, no device or contrivance having been made use of to deceive the plaintiffs. That is a question with which we need not at present intermeddle; and sufficient unto the day is the evil thereof. In the case now before the court, there is no pointed averment of such fraudulent concealment to cheat the plaintiffs; and if it had been averred, no attempt has been made to sustain it by proof; and without proof no court of justice ought to presume it, unless the presumption from the other facts, be direct and irresistible.

Let the bill be dismissed, with costs.

MARY WOODBECK, an Infant, by C. I. L., her Guardian,
v.
KELLER.

Slander—Charge of Perjury—Evidence of Proof of Charge Must be Sufficient to Convict on Criminal Prosecution—Two Witnesses—Notice of Justification—New Trial.

In slander for charging the plaintiff with perjury; the defendant, in order to justify by proving the truth of the charge, must give evidence of the same strength as would be necessary to convict of perjury on a criminal prosecution.

Accordingly, one witness alone is not sufficient to sustain the justification. His testimony must, at least, be corroborated by independent circumstances.

In neither case, is it precisely accurate to say that the charge must be made out by two witnesses swearing positively, or by circumstances equivalent to a second witness. If there be only one witness, circumstances strongly corroborative are enough, although not, of themselves and uncontradicted, sufficient to prove a fact.

In an action of slander there were four witnesses against two as to one fact, and the judge charged the jury not to believe the two. On moving for a new trial, upon the ground that the judge should have left the evidence to the jury, held that he should have done so; but as it was plain, from the case, that they ought to have come to that conclusion, a new trial should not, for that reason, be granted.

A notice of justification in slander should be proved with great particularity.

Citations—1 Phil. Ev., 112, 113; 1 Chit. L. C., 112, 113, 563; 4 Bl. Com., 357; 2 Str., 1230; Peake, Ev., 9, 10; Stat. 1 Edw. 6, ch. 12, sec. 22; 1 McNally, 31; 20 Johns., 357; Starkie on Slander, 179; 11 Johns., 38; 8 Johns., 369; 9 Johns., 264.

SLANDER, for accusing the plaintiff of perjury, tried at the Montgomery Circuit, in Dec. 1825, before Williams, *Circuit J.*

119*] *The defendant gave a notice that he would prove special matter on the trial in justification of the slander, setting forth in his notice that the plaintiff had prejured herself, in falsely swearing to certain facts on a trial between her father and one Vrooman. On the trial, he proceeded to the proof in justification; and one question was, whether there was not a variance between the proof and the notice. Another question was, whether the same testimony was necessary, to prove the truth of the slander, as to sustain a criminal prosecution for the perjury. There was also conflicting testimony as to what the plaintiff had sworn, the witnesses standing four for the plaintiff and two for the defendant on this point.

The judge charged the jury, that the two witnesses for the defendant, being contradicted by four witnesses on the part of the plaintiff, as to what she did swear, the former were not to be believed.

Also, that it is the settled law, that to sustain the justification, the defendant must prove the perjury by two witnesses; or by one witness, and circumstances tantamount to another witness. And that one of the facts sworn to by the plaintiff, being disproved by only one witness, this was not sufficient to sustain the justification in that respect.

Verdict for the plaintiff for $200 damages.

The remaining facts in the case are sufficiently stated in the opinion of the court.

Mr. M. T. Reynolds, for the defendant, now moved for a new trial.

Mr. D. Cady, contra, cited 20 Johns., 351; 9 *Id.*, 264; 3 *Id.*, 170.; 8 *Id.*, 369.

Curia, per SUTHERLAND, *J.* I understand the rule to be, as laid down by the judge, that where, in an action of slander, a defendant justifies a charge of perjury, one witness is not sufficient to prove the truth of the charge and sustain the justification. The evidence must be the same as required to convict a defendant on an indictment for *perjury. There [*120 must be either two witnesses, or one witness corroborated by material and independent circumstances. Upon an indictment, the rule is well established and undisputed; 1 Phil. Ev., 112; 1 Chit. L. C., 563; 4 Bl. Com., 357; 2 Str., 1230; Peake Ev., 9 10; and no ground of distinction is perceived between the two cases. The defendant must affirmatively make out the fact of willful and corrupt falsehood, as the public prosecutor must upon an indictment. And if, in the latter case, the oath of the defendant is to be considered equivalent to the oath of a witness, why should not a like effect be given to it in a civil prosecution? The general rules of evidence are the same in both cases; and no principle is perceived which requires the adoption of a different rule in this case.

It was asked upon the argument, whether two witnesses would be required to justify a charge of treason? Unquestionably not. At common law, one witness was sufficient to convict of that offense. The Statute of 1 Edw. VI., ch. 12, sec. 22, was the first which required two witnesses to indict or convict of treason; and that statute, not having been enacted in Ireland, the common law rule was enforced, and convictions for treason were held upon the testimony of a single witness, after the passing of that Act. (1 M'N., 31; 1 Chit. C. L., 112, 113.)

The reason of the rule in cases of perjury does not apply to treason. In the latter case there is no oath against oath. The true reason, as remarked by Mr. Peake, in his Treatise on Evidence, p. 10, which induced the Legislature to require two witnesses in such cases, undoubtedly was, "a due regard to the lives and liberties of men, which, in heated and intemperate times, would be much more liable to danger, from pretended plots and conspiracies, if one witness was permitted to convict them of such offenses."

There is no analogy, in point of principle between the two cases.

It is not, perhaps, precisely accurate to say, that the circumstances required, in addition to the oath of a single *witness, in order [*121 to convict on an indictment for perjury, or to sustain a justification of that charge in an action of slander, must be tantamount to another

NOTE.—*Slander—Charge of perjury—Justification by proving the truth of the charge—Evidence necessary.*

The evidence to sustain the truth of the charge of perjury, as a justification in an action of slander, must be such as would be necessary to convict of perjury on a criminal prosecution. In connection with the above case of Woodbeck v. Keller, consult Willmett v. Harsner, 8 Car. & P., 695.

But the plaintiff need not be proved guilty beyond a reasonable doubt. Kincade v. Bradshaw, 3 Hawks. 63; Spruil v. Cooper, 16 Ala., 791. See generally on charge of perjury as slander, Hopkins v. Beedle, 1 Cai., 347, *note*: Martin v. Stillwell, 13 Johns., 275, *note*.

witness. The same effect is to be given to the oath of the party, as though it were the oath of a disinterested witness. It is, therefore, witness against witness. The scale of evidence is poised; and the equilibrium must be destroyed, by material and independent circumstances, before the defendant can be convicted, or the justification sustained. But the circumstantial evidence need not be such as would, standing by itself, justify a conviction, or sustain a justification, in a case where the testimony of a single witness would be sufficient. It must be corroborative, and strongly corroborative, of the testimony of the accusing witness. This is all that is required.

This rule is distinctly recognized by Mr. Phillips. He says, it does not appear to have been laid down that two witnesses are necessary to dispose the fact sworn to by the defendants; nor does that seem to be absolutely requisite; but at least one witness is not sufficient; and in addition to his testimony, some other independent evidence ought to be adduced. (1 Phil. Ev., 113.)

Although this question was raised in *M'Kinley* v. *Rob*, 20 Johns., 351, it was not adverted to in the opinion of the court, the case turning on other points.

The charge of the judge, therefore, in this case, upon the principle of evidence applicable to it, was substantially correct.

The justification was not sustained in relation to the pulling of the flax, and the number of bills paid to Vrooman. The plaintiff's oath in relation to those points was contradicted only by a single witness, uncorroborated by circumstances.

In relation to working in the oats, two witnesses, Vrooman and Magely, testified that the plaintiff swore that she had worked half a day for the witness, raking oats. That she commenced a little after dinner, and worked an hour or two after dark. If she swore to this, the testimony is abundant to show that she swore falsely.

122*] *But the judge charged the y, that Vrooman and Magely were contradicted by four witnesses, as to the evidence given by the plaintiff, in relation to working in the oats, and ought not, therefore, to be believed.

John Cranker testified that she swore "that she thought she had worked late enough, after it was time to quit, to make up half a day."

James Pettit—that she swore "that it was some time in the afternoon when she came to bind oats; and that she worked till late in the evening; and that she worked enough, after it was time to quit, to make up half a day."

Cornelius Bennett—"that she came to work at the oats a little after noon; she went home for a rake; and she worked long enough, after it was time to quit, to make half a day."

Henry Woodbeck—"that she went to work a little after noon, and worked faithfully without going to tea, and thought she had worked a good half day."

Not one of these witnesses heard her swear that she had worked an hour or two after dark, but only that she thought she had worked enough after it was time to quit, to make half a day—that she worked till late in the evening.

This is essentially different from a positive oath—that she worked one or two hours after dark. As to the latter fact, she could not have been mistaken. If it was not true, it was willfully false.

But according to the other witnesses, what she swore to was expressed as an opinion, or in the vague terms of late in the evening—certainly leaving a much wider field for the belief of unintentional mistake or error than in the other case.

The notice of justification states that she swore, in substance, and to the effect following: "That she had bound oats half a day at one time for the said John S. Vrooman, under her father, some time in August, 1832. That she had worked, on that occasion, an hour or two after dark, so as to make up half a day."

A justification must be proved with great particularity. (Stark, Slander, 179; 11 Johns., 38, and the cases there cited.)

*The judge ought to have left it to **[*123** the jury to decide between the witnesses. But if the jury ought to have come to the same conclusion, the strong charge of the judge, in an action of this description, is not sufficient cause for granting a new trial. (8 Johns., 369; 9 Johns., 264.)

On the whole, I am of opinion that a new trial should be denied.

New trial denied.

Cited in—16 Wend., 603; 25 Hun, 253; 3 Barb., 601; 45 Barb., 180; 2 Hilt., 356; 14 Pet., 447; 2 Wood. & M., 154; 35 Ind., 59; 32 Am. Dec., 42 (4 Blackf., 460); 41 Am. Dec., 214 (7 Blackf., 83); 20 Am. Rep., 414 (9 Vroom., 441); 40 Am. Rep., 7 (4 Lea, 233).

TOWNSEND

v.

MORRIS AND VAN COURTLANDT, Executors of VAN COURTLANDT.

Covenant of Warranty—Eviction, Breach of—Pleading—Damages for Eviction, Personal—Survivor of Tenants in Common may Sustain Action for.

A warranty of lands, in a deed in fee, is the subject of a personal action of covenant against the executors of the warrantor; and the grantee is not confined to his voucher or *warrantia chartæ*, as it seems he was anciently.

It is sufficient, in declaring upon this covenant, to aver, generally, that the grantee was evicted of a part or the whole of the granted premises by lawful right and title of a stranger, without setting forth the title or manner of eviction more particularly, especially on general demurrer.

The damages for an eviction of two tenants in common, to whom lands are granted with warranty, are personal, and an action will lie for them by the survivor.

Citations—7 Johns., 258; 5 Cow., 137; 2 Bl. Com., 301, 202; Co. Litt., 365 *a*, *note* 315; 3 Mass., 544; 1 Brownl., 21; 2 Brownl., 164, 165; 2 Mass., 438.

ON demurrer to the declaration in covenant. The action was upon a covenant in a conveyance by way of lease and release, of certain land at Goshen, in Orange Co., and set forth that the testator thereby conveyed the land in fee to the plaintiff and one S. Townsend, now deceased, on the 12th and 13th days of Oct., 1788; and thereby, for himself and his heirs, did warrant and engage to defend to the plaintiff and S. Townsend, now deceased, and their heirs and assigns forever, the land so conveyed. The declaration then averred that the people of the State of N. Y. had before, and at the time of, and since the conveyance, a title to a certain part of the premises; and afterwards entered and ejected, expelled and amoved the plaintiffs from that part, in S. Townsend's lifetime.

The defendants craved oyer, and demurred generally, the plaintiff joining in demurrer.

Mr. P. A. Jay, in support of the demurrer. This is a covenant real, and not binding on the personal representatives of the warrantor. The only remedy is by voucher or *warrantia chartæ*. *Rudy* v. *Pincombe*, 1 Roll., 25, 26; S. C., Hob., **124***] 3, 4; 3 Bl. Com., 300; Rast. Ent., *396, *Garrantie de Charters; Sir Henry Roll* v. *Sir Robert Osborn*, Hob. 20; Hale Anal., 33; Shep. Touch., 182–184; Co. Litt., 389 *a*.

Neither the right and title of the people, nor the eviction, are set forth in the declaration with sufficient certainty.

The plaintiff is only a tenant in common, and yet claims the whole damages as survivor. This is inadmissible.

Mr. R. Manning, contra. The warranty is a covenant. An action of covenant will lie upon every agreement under seal, and the covenantor is personally bound. This rule has been repeatedly applied to actions upon covenants of warranty in relation to lands, and that, too, without question. *Withy* v. *Mumford*, 5 Cow., 137, and the note to that case, at p. 143; 1 Mass., 464; 8 *Id.*, 162; 7 Johns., 258. *Warrantia chartæ* and voucher are mere supplemental remedies, and the latter cannot be used by the grantee, except as tenant in a real action. Nor can he resort to the writ of *warrantia chartæ*, with a view to any other estate than the real. Both operate upon the real estate only of the grantor, leaving his person and his personal property untouched.

As to the breach, it is sufficient to show that a right existed in a stranger, before and at the time of the grant, under which right we were evicted. It is not necessary to say that it is a right in fee. It is enough that it be for life. (2 Saund., 181 *a*, *note* 10.) It is not necessary to show what the title is. That may be impossible, for the claim is by a stranger. Nor is it necessary to aver an eviction by process of law, nor show by what agents the eviction was effected. (1 T. R., 671.)

The eviction took place when all parties were alive, since which one of the grantees has died. By the breach, the right to damages became a chose in action (2 Johns., 1), and survived. The action is, therefore, properly brought in the name of the survivor. The covenant being **125***]*personal as well as real, the action was properly brought against the executors. (1 Chit. Pl., 37; 3 Wils., 29; Cro. Eliz., 553; Com. Dig., Covenant, C, 1; 2 Johns., 1.)

Mr. Jay, in reply. The question whether the covenant was real or personal, was not raised in the cases cited from 5 Cowen. No doubt the warranty is a covenant; but the question is, for what purpose? Not for a personal purpose. The words *dedi et concessi* sometimes imply a covenant of warranty, yet a personal action will not lie. *Soper* v. *Morgan*, 1 Keb., 821. And the rule holds mutually. The heir alone can bring the action, and it should have been brought in his name. He may have *warrantia chartæ*, but he cannot bring a personal action of covenant. This is the ground of our objection that the action cannot be maintained by the surviving tenant. The right is real property, not personal. The action must be brought by the heir of the deceased grantee, against the heir of the deceased grantor. The recovery is of land.

There is, perhaps, no ground for our objection that the action is brought by the surviving grantee, if the claim be, in truth, a personal one, which would pass to an executor on one side; and can be enforced against him on the other.

Nor do I, upon this general demurrer, feel any great confidence in the objection to the manner of setting forth the title of and eviction by the people.

Curia, per WOODWORTH, *J.* It is contended that the action cannot be sustained upon the warranty—it being a covenant real, and not binding on the personal representatives of the testator.

I am not aware that this question has been expressly decided in our courts. Actions have been sustained on the covenant of warranty, but this point seems not to have been raised, or noticed by the court or counsel. The causes were disposed of on other grounds.

*Thus, in *Kent* v. *Welch*, 7 Johns., [***126** 258, the plaintiff declared on a deed, whereby the defendant gave, granted, bargained and sold a tract of land, and engaged to warrant and defend; it was held that no action could be maintained, either on the implied or express covenant, without alleging and proving an eviction; and that the express warranty qualified and restrained any implied covenant of seisin, arising from the word "give." From this case it may be inferred that the form of action was not considered objectionable, or it would have been suggested, inasmuch as the evidence there required, would, under any form of pleading, have been unavailing, if the objection now taken is well founded. So also in *Withy* v. *Mumford*, 5 Cow., 137, the action was covenant for breach of a warranty. The defendant demurred, on the ground that his grantee conveyed to the plaintiff with warranty. It seems to have been taken for granted that a personal action was sustainable, for the point was not even discussed.

As this is a fit occasion, I will briefly state my views on the question.

At common law, a warranty was the foundation of a voucher, by the tenant, when impleaded; and if he lost the land, he might have judgment to recover of the warrantor other lands to the value. It is of feudal origin. According to 2 Bl. Com., 301, warranties were introduced in order to evade the strictness of the feudal doctrine of nonalienation without the consent of the heir. Butler, in his *note*, 315, to Co. Litt., 365 *a*, observes of the doctrine of warranty, that "the effect and operation of warranties having, by repeated Acts of the Legislature, been reduced to a very narrow compass, it is become, in most respects, a matter of speculation, rather than of use." The use of this covenant is superseded by the introduction of other personal covenants. In many, if not in most cases, there is no occasion for resorting to the covenant of warranty. In some, however, it is the only express covenant inserted. With us the remedy by *warrantia chartæ*, or voucher, may be considered obsolete. No case 127*] of the kind has *been reported in this State, if any ever existed. The reasons upon which it is founded in England do not apply here, our tenures being allodial, not feudal. The term "warrant," as applied to real estate in that country, having obtained a technical and legal signification derived from feudal principles, I do not perceive the necessity, so far as regards the remedy or form of action, of understanding the term in the same sense, when used here. If effect is given to such a covenant by action to recover damages, as on a warranty of things personal, I apprehend no principle of law will be violated. Such a construction will, no doubt, correspond with the intention of the parties; while the ancient remedy is inconsistent with what must be supposed to be the intent. That remedy may frequently become illusory, as where the proceeding is against the heir; the obligation to yield other lands is only on condition that he had other sufficient lands by descent from the warranting ancestor. (2 Bl. Com., 302.) As the right to bring a personal action seems never to have been made a question in our courts, from the inadequacy of the remedy by *warrantia chartæ;* from the fact that the covenant of warranty singly, has been generally deemed sufficient, and as giving a remedy by personal action; and more especially as the reason of the doctrine is foreign to our institutions and laws, I think it may safely be concluded that an action of covenant is sustainable on a deed with warranty.

In Mass. the law has been so considered. In *Gore* v. *Brazier*, 3 Mass., 544, *Ch. J.* Parsons, in commenting on this subject, observed that "the remedy to recover a recompense in other lands, to the value, existed very anciently, when the principal consideration received on the alienation was the services to be performed by the tenant. But when lands were aliened for money, and when the alienor might have no other lands to render a recompense in value, it became expedient that another remedy for the purchaser on eviction should be allowed." He further adds: "It is certain, that before the emigration of our ancestors, the tenant on being lawfully ousted by a title paramount, 128*] might maintain a personal action *of covenant broken, on a real covenant of warranty." 1 Brownl., 21, and 2 Brownl., 164, 165, are cited.(a) The same doctrine is laid down in *Marston* v. *Hobbs*, 2 Mass., 438. If this position be correct, then even according to the English law, this action may be maintained—the grantees having been expelled by lawful right and title.

It follows that if the covenant is personal, the representatives are liable; and the grant being to two, who were evicted in their lifetime, the action is well brought by the survivor.

(a) Waters v. The Dean, etc., 9 & 10 Jac., in a personal action of covenant; on a covenant in a lease by the defendants to the plaintiff for three lives. The covenant was to acquit and serve the lessee harmless, during the term, against any previous lease by the lessors or their predecessors. (*Vide* 2 Brownl., 158.) The main question was, whether the covenant was binding, the lease being voidable; and held that it was; and judgment for the plaintiff.

Judgment must be rendered for the plaintiff with leave to the defendants to amend.

Judgment for the plaintiff.

Cited in—21 Wend., 249; 41 Am. Dec., 37 (6 Ala., 60).

BELL ET AL.
v.
PALMER AND HAMILTON.

Consignee or Factor—Advances to Principal, on Consignment by—Still Bound to Obey Instructions as to Time of Sale.

A consignee, or factor, making advances on the goods of his consignor or principal, to an amount even beyond their value, is yet bound to obey the instructions of the latter as to the time of sale, though there be no agreement to that effect. And if, being instructed to sell immediately, he refuse the first offer, in expectation of a more favorable market, and afterwards sell at less than the offer, he is liable, though he act in perfect good faith.

Citations—Cowp., 256; 3 Johns. Cas., 37; 2 Gall., 13; 1 Johns. Cas., 178, 9; 13 Johns., 333, 334; Yeates, 487; 4 Binn., 361.

ASSUMPSIT, tried at the N. Y. Circuit, Dec. 3, 1823, before Edwards, *Circuit J.*, when the following facts appeared:

The defendants, at N. Y., having on hand a quantity of cocoa consigned to them by D'Arcy & Dedier, of Baltimore, at the request of Darby, one of the plaintiffs, consigned to their house of trade at Leghorn, Italy, a part of this cocoa in two parcels on an advance by the plaintiffs of £2,100 sterling, the defendants agreeing to be personally liable for the advance. The consignment to the plaintiffs was by the ship Minerva Smith, which arrived at *Leghorn, Sept. 1, 1819. The consign- [*129 ment was accompanied with the defendants' letter of instructions as to the principal parcel, dated June 23 previous, in which they said, "we inclose invoice and bill of lading for 910 bags of Guayaquil cocoa, for a very superior quality; amounting per invoice to $13,660. It is our wish that an immediate sale be made of this shipment on its arrival; and Mr. Darby gives us assurances of a favorable result, judging from quotations of the article at your port." A subsequent letter as to the smaller parcel referred to the former letter for instructions. The article was ready for sale at Leghorn Sept. 20. Between that day and the 28th of the same month, the plaintiffs had an offer of 12¾ pesos per cwt. which they declined, on the ground that it would not cover anticipations, freight, insurance and charges; and was finally not sold, till June, 1820, at $11 per cwt. In the meantime, they had made various attempts to sell at a greater advantage. Aug. 9, 1820, the plaintiffs sent to the defendants their account of sales and account cur-

NOTE.—*Factors and agents—Bound to obey instructions of principals.*

Factors and agents are bound to follow instructions of their principals strictly. Blot v. Boiceau, 3 N. Y., 78; Marfield v. Goodhue, 3 N. Y., 62; Evans v. Root, 7 N. Y., 186; Jervis v. Hoyt, 2 Hun, 637; Johnson v. N. Y. C. R. R. Co., 33 N. Y., 610; Scott v. Rogers, 31 N. Y., 676; Wilson v. Wilson, 26 Pa. St., 393; Rechtscherd v. Accommodation Bank, 47 Mo., 181; Williams v. Higgins, 30 Md., 404; Brown v. McGran, 39 U. S. (14 Pet.), 479; Whitney v. Merchants' Union

rent, showing a balance in their favor of $2,565.52, for which this action was brought. The defendants refused to pay that sum; but on Apr. 1, 1822, they paid the plaintiffs $600.26, which would be 20 cents more than the balance due the plaintiffs, if they had taken the offer of 12¾ pesos.

Evidence was given at the trial upon the question whether the plaintiffs had conformed to the spirit of their instructions, and whether the defendant had acquiesced in their proceedings. But it is not necessary to state this, as the case here turned on the charge of the judge upon the effect of the instructions.

In his charge he stated the rule of law to be, that (unless a special agreement exists) consignors, by receiving an advance upon property shipped, subject it to the power of the consignees, and part with their right to control the disposition of it; so far as to enable the consignees to hold it a reasonable time to con- **130***] sult the market, and to adopt *such reasonable measures, as may be necessary to enable them to reimburse themselves. The letter of instructions he considered immaterial, for if there was no special agreement, the instructions could be of no avail, against the lien of the plaintiffs.

The jury finding difficulty on the question of the agreement, the judge further charged them, that in order to hold the plaintiffs liable, they ought to find that there was an express agreement that the goods should be sold immediately on their arrival. That if there was not an agreement to that effect, the letters of instructions were of no importance, and ought to be laid out of the question; and that it lay with the defendants to establish the agreement.

The jury found for the plaintiffs $2,514.02.

Mr. J. Duer now moved for a new trial, on this ground, among others, that the plaintiffs were bound by the defendants' instructions to sell the cocoa immediately on its arrival, and the judge erred in charging the jury that the letters of instruction were of no importance and that there must have been an express agreement. (1 Johns. Cas., 436, 437, 462–467, *note*; 4 Johns., 103; 13 *Id.*, 332.) He agreed that the plaintiffs had acted in good faith, but this was not enough. They should have accepted the first offer of 12¾ pesos per cwt. He denied that there was any authority for requiring a special agreement, and insisted that the right and duty of the consignees were not varied by the advance. True, he said, the consignee has a lien, in such a case, but he has no right to sell in virtue of his lien merely. Before that can be done, the pledgor must be formally called on to redeem.

The instructions in this case are sufficiently explicit. A request by one having a right to command, is always construed imperatively. No discretion was allowed, and the parties must have so understood the letter.

It was a condition that we should not be liable unless there was an immediate sale. This should have been strictly performed. Where *one is under an obligation to sell, if [***131** he lets an opportunity to sell to advantage pass, and afterwards sells at a less advantage, he must abide the loss. *Curry* v. *Edensor*, 3 T. R., 524.

Messrs. P. W. Radcliff and *T. A. Emmet*, contra. The letters of the defendants do not import an absolute order to sell immediately, and, at all events, whatever might be the state of the market. They must be understood as meaning a sale which should not be injurious to the consignor. If otherwise, the order was not obligatory. It was not competent to the defendants, after receiving an advance on the credit of the cocoa, to compel a sale which would not cover advances and charges, unless there was a special agreement at the time, authorizing such an order. Otherwise, the consignor may defeat the object of the consignment, which is security for the advance. Whether there was such an agreement, is a question of fact, and was properly put to the jury.

It is conceded that we acted in good faith. This was sufficient under the circumstances. (3 Cow., 281.) We were not bound literally to follow instructions, at whatever sacrifice. (1 Johns. Cas., 174; 3 *Id.*, 311; 4 Binn., 361; 1 Yeates, 486; *Id.*, 409; 1 Liv. Agency, 369.) If we had sold and the market had afterwards risen, the case would have been stronger against us.

The lien gives a right to hold the goods, if not to sell them. There was no need of calling on the defendants to redeem. There was authority to sell, though not positive and effectual instructions to sell immediately.

All we contend for is, that the consignee should have a reasonable time to look to the market.

This is not the case of a will, in which we admit that the mere expression of a wish is to be construed imperatively.

But when one parts with an interest in property, he parts *pro tanto* with the control of it. He cannot diminish its value by hastening the sale, whether it be the sole *security or [***132** not. He can no more do this than a mortgagor of real estate, who is always bound personally.

The counsel also cited 2 Gall., 13.

Mr. J. O. Hoffman, in reply. The judge finally excluded from the jury everything except the question whether there was an express agreement. He did not even leave room for

---

Ex. Co., 104 Mass., 152; S. C., 6 Am. Rep., 207; Hall v. Storrs, 7 Wis., 253; Courcier v. Ritter, 4 Wash. C. C., 549; S. C., 1 Smith L. C., 828.

Even where a factor has made advances on the goods to an amount beyond their value, he must obey the instructions of his principal. See above case of Bell v. Palmer. See, also, La Farge v. Kneeland, 7 Cow., 456; Marfield v. Goodhue, 3 N. Y., 62; Blot v. Boiceau, 3 N. Y., 78; Hidden v. Waldo, 55 N. Y., 294; Wicks v. Hatch, 62 N. Y., 535; Hilton v. Vanderbilt, 82 N. Y., 591; Frothingham v. Everton, 12 N. H., 239.

But the Supreme Court of the United States holds a somewhat different doctrine. "It is true that factors are generally bound to obey all orders of their principals respecting the time and mode of sale, yet when they have made large advances or incurred expenses on account of the consignment, the principal cannot, by any subsequent orders, control their right to sell at such time, as, in the exercise of a sound discretion and in accordance with the usage of trade, they may deem best to secure indemnity to themselves, and to promote the interests of the consignor. Of course they must act in good faith and with reasonable skill." Feild v. Farrington, 77 U. S. (10 Wall.), 149; Brown v. McGran, 39 U. S. (14 Pet.), 479, *note in Law. ed.*

See generally, Le Guen v. Gouverneur, 1 Johns. Cas., 437, *note*; Urquhart v. M'Iver, 4 Johns., 103.

them to find an implied agreement. No authority has been, or can be cited, showing the necessity of any agreement to secure the control of the consignors.

The lien was merely on the proceeds of the goods, not on the goods themselves. These were to be sold and so both parties understood. The instructions of the principal must be obeyed. The plaintiffs were the mere agents or factors of the defendants. And the lien for advances was never held to give the factor a control beyond what he would otherwise have. The principal may order a sale when he pleases and require his factor to rely on his personal security for the balance of the advance, if it exceeds the amount of sales. The consignee always agrees to this. It is implied from the nature of the transaction.

In good sense, these instructions were to sell at the market price on the first offer.

Curia, per SAVAGE, *Ch. J.* There is no dispute but the advance on the goods exceeded their value, and the defendants admit their liability to refund the difference between the money loaned, and the value of the cocoa at 12¾ pesos. But they contend that the plaintiffs, not having taken that price when offered, and having subsequently sold for eleven, must bear the loss. Whether the plaintiffs were bound to have taken that offer, and to have sold immediately on the arrival of the cocoa; or, whether they were justified in holding it longer, to try the market, is the only question.

The judge, at the trial, charged the jury that the letters of instruction were to be laid out of the question, unless there was an express agree- **133***] ment to sell immediately. In *this I apprehend there was an error. The plaintiffs, by their representative, Darby, had refused to purchase, but solicited the consignment of the cocoa. They received it as factors and, of course, under the rights and duties which exist by law between principal and agent. The plaintiffs having advanced money upon the goods, gave them a lien for the amount of their advance; but I do not find any authority for saying that the lien thus created alters the rights of the parties in any respect, so far as relates to the duty of the factor in making sale of the goods. Nor is there any reason why it should. The principals are liable for the money advanced; and the goods being at their risk, are subject to their order and control, in every respect, not inconsistent with the lien of the factor.

The factor's lien is upon the goods, and upon the proceeds. (Cowp., 256.) The most advantageous sale should be made, that the balance, if in favor of the principal, may be as large as possible; and, if against him, as small as possible. It is the duty of the factor to manage the affairs of his principal in the same manner, and with that care and diligence, which a prudent and discreet merchant would exercise in relation to his own affairs. But he must still obey his instructions, because it is the principal who bears the loss. The factor must, for that reason, be liable for negligence or for departure from instructions in the same manner as in ordinary consignments.

It was said by this court, in *Rundle* v. *Moore*, 3 Johns. Cas., 37, that agents or factors who disobey their instructions through mistake or design, are undoubtedly responsible. In *Evans* v. *Potter*, 2 Gall., 13, Story, *J.*, says, "a factor is bound to ordinary diligence in relation to the property confided to him. Where the orders leave the management of the property to his discretion, he is bound only to good faith and reasonable conduct." "If he can advantageously sell the property, and neglect so to do, he must answer in damages. But if the markets are low or unusually crowded, if new and unexpected difficulties arise, he is not obliged to sell at all events, and under every disadvantage." The same doctrine of *the lia- [***134** bility of the factor for ordinary negligence, is found in the Treatises on Agency, by Paley and Livermore, and cases cited by them. See, also, 1 Johns. Cas., 178, 179. But the consignee must obey his instructions. If he sell under the given price, though from good motives, he is bound to make good the loss. *Guy* v. *Oakley*, 13 Johns., 333, 334.

If the principal give orders to his factor, they must be pursued, or he becomes liable. If none are given, or they are not clear and explicit, the factor is allowed to use his best discretion according to the usage of trade. *Geyer* v. *Decker*, 1 Yeates, 487. This case was cited to show that orders to sell on arrival, were complied with, if a sale was made within six months. But the time was not made a point in the cause. The breach, it was contended, consisted in selling on credit, when the orders were for cash; the language being to sell on arrival, and remit the produce by the same vessel, or any other vessel, to Philadelphia, in bank notes. The court held that was no direction to sell for cash only. They also say there was strong proof of acquiescence.

The case of *Dusar* v. *Perit*, 4 Binn., 361, maintains the proposition, that a departure from instructions may be excused by an event not contemplated at the time the instructions were given. The supercargo, in that case, was compelled to go to the Havana to repair his vessel, in consequence of an accident. He sold the vessel and part of the flour, at the limited price. The residue of the flour was sold at less than the price fixed by his instructions, in consequence of the arrival of other cargoes. The general principle, of the liability of agents in case of deviation from instructions, is not at all impugned by this case. Yeates, *J.*, says: "I think it a matter of great moment in commercial transactions, that agents should be strictly held to execute the orders of their principals; but I do not think this such a case as demands the court's interposition in order to guard that principle."

In none of the cases cited, nor in any which I can find, is the distinction taken which was relied on by the judge; *to wit: that [***135** in cases where advances are made on goods consigned, the consignee is not bound to obey the instructions of the consignor.

The analogy between consignor and consignee, and mortgagor and mortgagee, does not strike me as very forcible, except it be that the mortgagee, in the act of foreclosing his mortgage by sale, resembles the consignee in selling goods upon which he has made advances. In such case, should the mortgagee refuse a higher price, and afterwards take less, ought be not to account to the mortgagor for the highest price offered ?

I do not wish, however, to be understood as now expressing an opinion upon what I conceive to be the question hereafter to be tried, to wit: whether the plaintiffs were guilty of negligence by disregarding their instructions. This is a question of fact, which should have been submitted to the jury.

A new trial must be granted, the costs to abide the event.

New trial granted.

Cited in—7 Cow., 459; 3 N. Y., 74; 7 N. Y., 190; 1 Sand., 122; 8 Leg. Obs., 120; 1 Blatchf., 294, 295.

JACKSON, ex dem. LOOP and Others, v. HARRINGTON.(a)

Two Successive Conveyances of Military Lots—Failure to Register Under Statute—Second Deed has the Preference—Subsequent Sale by Patentee, Valid if Without Notice.

Where two successive conveyances of military lots were made by the patentee before the Statute of Jan. 8th, 1794, 1 R. L., 209, neither of which were deposited in the clerk's office of Albany, pursuant to that Act; held, that the deed last executed took preference.

Held, also, that a conveyance by the patentee for a valuable consideration, subsequent to the second, should take preference of that; but it appearing that it was executed pending an ejectment by those claiming under the second conveyance, to a grantee who had notice of that conveyance, and actual knowledge of the first; held, that it lay with the defendant to show, otherwise than by the last conveyance, that a valuable consideration was in fact paid.

Whether a subsequent conveyance for valuable consideration, with notice of a prior deed, comes within the protection of the Statute, 1 R. L., 209, or it must be *bona fide* in the full sense of the terms, *quære*.

Citations—1 R. L., 209, 211; 1 Cai., 82.

EJECTMENT for part of military lot No. 43, in Sempronius, in the County of Cayuga, tried at the circuit in that county, Sept. 8, 1824, before Throop, *Circuit J.*

At the trial, the plaintiff proved the patent of the lot to Schreider the soldier, dated July 8, 1790; and a conveyance of all his expected
136*] military bounty land from him to *C. Loop, the deceased father of the lessors of the plaintiff, and under whom they claimed as heirs, dated in the spring or summer of 1784. It appeared that this deed was lost or destroyed by accident, in 1796 or 1797; and was, therefore, never delivered to, or deposited with the clerk of the City and County of Albany, according to the Statute, 1 R. L., 209.

The defendant produced and proved a conveyance from Schreider to F. Carbine, now deceased, dated Aug. 7, 1783, of all his (S.'s) expected military bounty lands. This conveyance had never been filed according to the statute; but was recorded in the clerk's office in the County of Cayuga, Sept. 7, 1824. It was proved that the defendant held as a tenant under the Carbine title.

(a) This case was decided in February Term, 1826.

NOTE.—*Registration of Deeds—Subsequent purchase without notice of prior unrecorded deed.* See Jackson v. Sharp, 9 Johns., 163, *note.*

This suit was commenced in May Term, 1823; and it further appeared at the trial, that after it was so commenced, Schreider, the soldier, conveyed the whole lot to E. Z. Carbine, a grandchild of F. Carbine, and one of the heirs of the old title to F. Carbine. This deed was dated Sept. 29, 1823; and purported to be for the consideration of $3,000; and was acknowledged and recorded Oct. 9, 1823. E. Z. Carbine made this purchase with notice of the claim by the lessors of the plaintiff, and of the title under which they claimed.

Verdict for the defendant, with leave to move for for a new trial.

Mr. J. A. Collier, for the plaintiff. Neither conveyance having been deposited, the question is, which shall be preferred. The Act, 1 R. L., 209, does not declare that a deed not deposited shall be deemed void, except as to subsequent purchasers. The Act means the last purchaser prior to Jan. 8, 1794.

If there be several conveyances, and none filed, the last is to be preferred. *Jackson* v. *Hubbard*, 1 Cai., 82, amounts to this. Though the subsequent deed was recorded in that case, such a circumstance can make no difference. It was good without being filed or recorded, as to all former deeds not filed. (19 Johns., 281.)

*E. Z. Carbine was not a *bona fide* [*137 purchaser, but took with full notice. Beside, the conveyance was for land in suit, and the sale, therefore, void.

Mr. D. Kellogg, contra. Neither deed being filed, the question remains as at common law, and the Carbine deed being oldest, takes preference.

It is no objection to the deed of Sept., 1823, that the grantee, E. Z. Carbine, had notice. The object of the statute in question is more than the common Registry Acts. The deeds are required to be deposited, in order to enable subsequent grantees to detect forgeries. If such grantees have paid a valuable consideration, it is enough, whether they have notice or not. And so are the words of the Act.

Curia, per SAVAGE, *Ch. J.* Were this question to be determined by the common law, undoubtedly the first deed would be operative, and the second void. But the Legislature, Jan. 8, 1794, R. L., 209, passed "An Act for Registering Deeds and Conveyances Relating to the Military Bounty Lands;" reciting that many frauds had been committed respecting the titles to those lands, by forging and antedating conveyances; and by conveying to different persons, and by various other contrivances, so that it had become very difficult to discover in whom the legal title to some of the lands was vested. For remedy whereof, and in order to detect these frauds, and to prevent the like frauds in future, it was enacted, that all deeds and conveyances theretofore made and executed, or pretended so to be, of such lands, should be deposited with the clerk of the City and County of Albany, on or before May 1, 1794; and that all deeds and conveyances of military bounty lands, "which shall not be delivered to, and deposited with the said clerk, on or before the said May 1, aforesaid, shall be adjudged fraudulent and void against the subsequent purchaser or mortgagee for valuable consideration." By an Act of Mar. 27, 1794, 1

138*] R. L., 211, the time *of depositing such deeds was extended to May 1, 1795. These deeds were to be kept in bundles alphabetically; and a register made of the names of the parties, for the purpose of inspection. They were, after a certain time, to be delivered to the clerk of the county in which the lands lay, there to remain for the benefit of all persons interested. It was also enacted that all conveyances, to be executed after Jan. 8, 1794, should be recorded; and that the deed first recorded should be operative. These deeds were to be acknowledged or proved. Not so of those executed prior to the passing of the Act. It is contended for the plaintiff, that every deed is to be tested by the statute; and if not deposited as the statute directs, is fraudulent and void against the subsequent purchaser; and, of course, the deed of Carbine, dated in 1783, not being deposited, must be adjudged fraudulent and void as against the Loop deed, executed in 1784.

Each of the deeds is valid as between the parties, and as to all the world, except subsequent purchasers or mortgagees. It follows that the deed of 1783 is void as to the deed of 1784, and that would also be void as to a subsequent one, had there been such an one before the passing of the Act of Jan. 8, 1794.

The argument on the other side is, that both being *in pari delictu*, the question is left as at common law, and the elder title must prevail.

Jackson v. *Hubbard*, 1 Cai., 82, was cited by the counsel for the plaintiff. In that case, the patentee of a military lot sold it in 1783. The deed was recorded in the Secretary's office, but was not deposited in the clerk's office according to the statute. Oct. 1, 1788, the patentee executed a power of attorney, by virtue of which the lot was conveyed by the attorney, Aug. 14, 1795, and the deed was duly recorded in Onondaga Co. The court decided, that though the first deed was recorded, yet that did not satisfy the Act, as the object was declared to be the pre- **139*]** vention of frauds *by facilitating the means of discovering forgeries. And the junior title prevailed. In that case, the power of attorney under which the junior deed was executed, was not deposited, though executed prior to passing the Act. Possibly the court considered simply the execution of the deed, which was after the time limited for depositing deeds, and gave it the same efficacy as if executed at its date by the patentee himself, laying out of view the date of the power of attorney. If this was so, the case is not an authority for preferring the last of two deeds executed before the Act, and not deposited; though if it was considered material that the power should be deposited, the authority of that case is in favor of the junior title in this.

But independent of authority, it seems impossible to sustain the elder deed here, consistently with the statute; and if no further facts appeared, the plaintiff would be entitled to recover.

On the trial, the defendant produced a deed from the patentee to E. Z. Carbine for the whole lot, purporting to be in consideration of $3,000, dated Sept. 29, 1823, and recorded Oct. 9, 1823; after this cause had been noticed once for trial, and the grantee had notice of the suit, and of the title under which the lessors claim.

According to the construction which I have given to the Act, and according to the case of *Jackson* v. *Hubbard*, E. Z. Carbine must hold in preference to either of the deeds of 1783 and 1784, provided he can be considered, in the language of the Act, a subsequent purchaser for valuable consideration. He certainly knew that he was purchasing what he before claimed under the deed of 1783, and he knew also that he was purchasing a disputed title. The act of purchasing in 1823, the same lot which his grandfather purchased in 1783, forty years previous, was an admission that he did not choose to rely on the old deed. Clearly he was not a *bona fide* purchaser, within the full meaning of the phrase, for he had notice.

*Is E. Z. Carbine, then, to be consid- **[*140** ered a purchaser for a valuable consideration, supposing this to be sufficient? Had we heard nothing of this purchase but what appears on the face of the deed, we should be bound to receive it as, *prima facie*, evidence of a valuable consideration. The circumstances are, however, peculiar; and I think call for further proof that a valuable consideration was paid. The soldier had notoriously given conveyances valid as to himself in two successive instances —one of these was well known to E. Z. Carbine when he purchased; and of the other he had notice, and, at least, must have entertained a strong suspicion. Is it natural, that dealing with the soldier under such circumstances, he should neither exact, nor Carbine pay him a valuable consideration? Is it not probable that the consideration was merely nominal, paid to and received by the soldier, not as the value or price of the land, but colorably, and in fraud of the suit then pending? Without saying whether the deed was void as being for a thing in action, we think the circumstances of the case required proof by witnesses, or in some way independent of the deed, that a valuable consideration was in fact paid.

A new trial must, therefore, be granted.

New trial granted.

Cited in—5 N. Y., 429.

---

*JACKSON, ex dem. SPRAGUE ET AL., **[*141**

v.

BOWEN.(a)

Registration of Deeds Under Act of 1794—Power of Atty. as well as Deed to be Deposited.

To render the conveyance of a military lot, executed before Jan. 8, 1794, valid as against a subsequent purchaser; not only the immediate deed must have been deposited, pursuant to the Act of 1794, 1 R. L., 209, 211, but also the power of attorney under which it was executed.

Citations—Act, Jan. 8, 1794; 1 Cai., 82; 10 Johns., 374; 5 Johns. Ch., 229; 20 Johns., 659.

EJECTMENT for a part of lot No. 5, in Lysander, tried at the Oswego Circuit, in Dec. 1824, before Throop, *Circuit J.*

At the trial, the plaintiff insisted that the defendant had entered upon the premises in question, under a contract to purchase them of the lessors of the plaintiff. A contract of purchase was accordingly given in evidence, but the testimony was conflicting upon the question,

(a) This cause was decided at May Term, 1826.

whether the defendant in fact entered under it, he insisted that he entered and held possession under a contract with one Camp, whose claim was adverse to that of the lessors.

The plaintiff then went to his title, and proved letters patent for lot No. 5 to Godfrey Byerd, a soldier, for Revolutionary services, which passed the Secretary's office Aug. 7, 1790. He then proved a conveyance of the lot in fee from Byerd to Reuben Murray, dated June 9, 1792, which was duly deposited in the Albany clerk's office according to the Acts of Jan. 8, and Mar. 27, 1794. (1 R. L., 209, 211.) From Murray he deduced title in fee to the lessors of the plaintiff.

The defense was a deed from the soldier to Edward Cumpston, dated Nov. 5, 1783. This deed conveyed all the soldier's expected bounty lands in fee to Cumpston, with a power of attorney to Jeremiah Van Rensselaer and Abraham Ten Eyck, to convey to Cumpston in fee, and a covenant that when a patent should issue for the soldier's lands, they (his attorneys) should convey them in fee simple to Cumpston. The defendant then proved a deed executed by the attorneys, reciting the power, and dated Sept. 23, 1790, from the soldier to Cumpston in fee. This deed, executed by the attorneys, was deposited pursuant to the statutes before cited, but the deed constituting them attorneys **142***] was not. *The defendant claimed under the Cumpston title, showing several intermediate conveyances of title from him to one Leffingwell, with whom Camp contracted to purchase, and under whom the defendant, as before mentioned, claimed to have taken possession.

The judge directed the jury to find for the plaintiff, if they believed that the defendant took possession under the lessors; but if they believed that he took possession under Camp, and found the deed to Cumpston to be genuine, they should then bring in their verdict for the defendant; it not being necessary that the deed containing the power should be deposited.

Verdict for the defendant.

A case was made, and it was agreed that it might be turned by either party into a special verdict; and that if this court should be of opinion that the deed to Cumpston containing the power, was void as to the deed of June 9, 1792, by reason of not being deposited, that then the judgment should be for the plaintiff.

But if the court should be with the plaintiff on any other ground, a new trial to be granted.

If they should be with the defendant on all the grounds, then judgment to be entered for the defendant.

Mr. J. Platt, for the plaintiff. The deed from the soldier, containing the power of attorney, not having been deposited, was void; and all the title derived from it was inoperative as against the lessors of the plaintiff, who claimed under a subsequent deed from the soldier.

If notice only had been designed by the Statute, 1 R. L., 209, a mere registry would have been enough. The Legislature had a further object. That was to detect frauds, and they required the original instrument to be deposited with that view. The mischief could not be reached without this being done. Indeed the detection of frauds was the declared object of the statute.

The deed from the attorneys was an act of supererogation. The whole title depends on the original deed to Cumpston. It passed the estate under the Statute, sess. 13, ch. 59, sec. 5; 2 Greenl., 333. That Act was remedial, and *should be construed liberally. The [***143** original deed, then, is not to be regarded as a mere power of attorney, but as a conveyance in itself. It became valid, as such, by the Act last cited; and when the Act of 1794 passed, requiring the deposit of military deeds, it extended to the deed containing the power. In this view, *Jackson* v. *Neely*, 10 Johns., 374, on which the circuit judge relied, does not dispose of the question. That was the case of a naked power. But how stands the authority of that case? *Jackson* v. *Hubbard*, 1 Cai., 82, is directly opposite in principle. The former regards the Statute as a mere registering Act; the latter declares its object to be the detection of frauds and forgeries. *Jackson* v. *Hubbard* was entirely overlooked in *Jackson* v. *Neely*, although the former was much more fully considered. Even a naked power is plainly within the spirit and intention of the statute. It is a matter which affects the title, and any paper having this effect must be deposited. *Jackson* v. *Neely* was virtually overruled by the Court of Errors in *Wendell* v. *Wadsworth*, 20 Johns., 659.

Mr. A. Van Vechten, contra. The original deed to Cumpston not being able to reach the soldier's land by any definite description, provided for this defect, by a power to convey when the patent to the grantor should be executed. The defendant's claim is, therefore, under the subsequent deed, given in virtue of the power. Whether the first deed passed the title or not, there is nothing to prevent the soldier giving a second; and both are prior to the deed under which the plaintiff claims; so that the only question on the merits is, whether the power should have been deposited. A power of attorney is no part of the conveyance, but a mere authority to convey. One object of the Legislature must have been notice. The deed of 1790 contains all that is necessary, to enable the party to look into the power of attorney. The power and all the particulars are recited, and names are given. *Jackson* v. *Neely* is full to this point. *Wendell* v. *Wadsworth* did not mean to overrule *Jackson* v. *Neely*. So far *from it, this case is not mentioned in [***144** *Wendell* v. *Wadsworth*.

Curia, per SAVAGE, *Ch. J.* The doctrine that he who enters under the title of the lessor of the plaintiff cannot afterwards dispute it, is not controverted in this case, but the fact is denied that the defendant did so enter. The jury, by their verdict, have found that the defendant entered under Camp. On that fact the evidence was contradictory, and the verdict should not be disturbed in this respect.

The important question is, whether the power of attorney from Byerd to Van Rensselaer and Ten Eyck should have been deposited.

The object of the Legislature, in passing the Depositing Acts of 1794, as declared in the preamble to the Act of Jan. 8, 1794, was to afford every possible facility to the detection of forgeries. It was notorious that many spurious deeds were in circulation, purporting to convey those lands, which were then becoming valuable, and had been, since the Revolutionary War, the subject of much speculation. To prevent litigation, and to enable claimants not only to know what elder titles were in existence, but to ascertain their genuineness by actual inspection, were the objects of the Act. If I am right in this, it would seem to follow that a deposit of a deed, executed by power of attorney, without the power of attorney itself, would be insufficient. One object was to ascertain the genuineness of the signature of the soldier. How is that accomplished by depositing his signature avowedly written by another? As a conveyance, the deed of 1783 is clearly void for not being deposited; and if, as a power of attorney, it need not be deposited, the object of the Legislature is frustrated. A deed, executed under a forged power of attorney, gave as much notice of the claim as if the power of attorney had been genuine; and depositing such a deed has the same effect as if supported by a true power. This construction of the Act may be consistent with the idea that the intention was **145***] *merely to give notice; but totally repugnant to the declared object, which was to detect frauds and forgeries.

When this court was first called upon to give a construction to the Depositing Acts, in *Jackson* v. *Hubbard*, 1 Cai., 82, it was expressly declared that the object of the Acts was the prevention of frauds, by facilitating the means of discovering forgeries. And it was then decided, that though a deed was recorded in the Secretary's office, and the clerk's office in Onondaga Co., if not deposited according to the Acts of 1794, it was void and inoperative against a subsequent purchaser. It was remarked that the examination of a mere record could not answer the object of the Act; and yet an inspection of a record is quite as useful to ascertain the genuineness of the original as the examination of a deed by an attorney, to ascertain the genuineness of his power, when that power is not produced. The court there say, "nothing short of an inspection would, in many cases, answer the purpose;" and it might with equal propriety have been said, in all cases, nothing but actual inspection would answer.

The next case is *Jackson* v. *Neely*, 10 Johns., 374, where this precise question came before the court. They say, however, it is unnecessary to decide, whether the power should have been deposited; "for admitting it to have been requisite to deposit the letter of attorney with the conveyance, yet, as the conveyance was duly deposited, and as it recited the letter of attorney by virtue of which the conveyance was made, the subsequent purchaser had notice of the power by means of the recital, and is affected equally, as if the power itself had been deposited." This decision was made in Oct., 1813. The case of *Jackson* v. *Hubbard*, decided in May, 1803, was not referred to by either the counsel or the court, and it is manifest that the two cases are at variance with each other—the one proceeding on the principle that the object of the deposit was to detect frauds and forgeries; the other, that it was merely to give notice, which a record or registry would have done as well. That the **146***] latter was the principle *upon which the court acted in *Jackson* v. *Neely*, is manifest from what is said by *Chancellor* Kent, in *Wadsworth* v. *Wendell*, 5 Johns. Ch., 229. He presided in this court when *Jackson* v. *Neely* was decided, and acting upon the same principle in *Wadsworth* v. *Wendell*, he says, "the deposit of these conveyances was intended by the Legislature to be notice to all subsequent purchasers, of their existence and contents; and the deposit of them would have been in a degree useless, if it was not intended to operate as notice." He adds, that the deposit was a substitute for registry and equivalent to recording. This doctrine was overruled by the unanimous opinion of the Court for the Correction of Errors in the same case, when carried up on appeal. Spencer, *Ch. J.*, who delivered the only opinion, says, "the construction put upon this statute by the *Chancellor* is such as was never anticipated by the profession, nor imagined by the Legislature; and with the utmost deference, I must say, that in my judgment, it cannot be supported." He subsequently adds, "when, therefore, the Legislature required these unauthenticated, unacknowledged, unproved and unrecorded deeds, to be deposited by a fixed day; and declared that if they were not thus deposited, they should be adjudged fraudulent and void against subsequent purchasers for valuable consideration, they could not have intended to give greater effect to them than they had before," &c., or to require subsequent purchasers to take notice of them.

This case is no otherwise applicable here, than as it decides, expressly, that the object of the Legislature was not to make the deposit a notice to subsequent purchasers, but merely to enable those interested to prevent frauds and detect forgeries.

Such being the object, as declared by the Legislature, and adjudicated by our highest court, the case of *Jackson* v. *Neely* is virtually overruled.'

The object of the Depositing Acts, then, being an inspection of the original deeds and signatures, of those who had drawn these lands, and of whose signatures it was alleged there were many forgeries, the depositing of the *deed executed by attorney was not a [***147** compliance with the Act. The power of attorney being void by force of the Acts of 1794, the deed founded upon it falls; and with it, all pretense of title in the defendant, or out of the lessors. They are, therefore, entitled to judgment.

Judgment for the plaintiff.

Cited in—8 Wend., 624.

V. DICKENSON
v.
JACKSON, ex dem. CALDWELL.(a)

Pleading—Ejectment—Demise—How Laid.

The demise in a declaration in ejectment, must be laid as of a day subsequent to that when the lessor's right of entry accrued.

In ejectment by the mortgagee against the mortgagor, or those claiming under him, the demise must be laid as of a day subsequent to a default in payment; and subsequent to a dissolution of the tenancy by notice to quit, or otherwise.

Citations—6 Johns., 273; 18 Johns., 488; 11 Johns., 538; 19 Johns., 326; 4 T. R., 680.

(a) This cause was decided at a previous term.

ON ERROR from the Warren C. P. The action in the court below was ejectment on the demise of Caldwell against Dickenson, tried in the court below at its January Term, 1823. The declaration was returnable at its May Term, 1821. It contained but one count, and one demise, which was laid Sept. 8, 1817.

At the trial, the plaintiff below claimed to recover the premises in question under a mortgage of them, dated Sept. 8, 1817 (the day of the demise), executed by one G. Dickenson, to the lessor of the plaintiff. G. Dickenson, before the commencement of the ejectment, conveyed the premises in question to the defendant below by deed, in fee simple absolute, without any allusion to the mortgage. This deed was dated July 5, 1819, and on the same day the defendant below entered and took possession under the deed.

The amount secured by the mortgage was $400, payable on or before Sept. 8, 1821, with interest Sept. 8, in each and every intervening year. One year's interest, and no more, had been paid by G. Dickenson, and none of the principal, when the suit was commenced.

The above facts were mutually admitted on the trial.

The defendant below objected to the plaintiff's recovery, and moved for a nonsuit, on the ground that he had shown neither a right of entry in himself, nor possession of the defendant below, on the day of the demise laid in the declaration, nor any notice to quit.

148*] *The objection and motion were overruled by the court below, and the defendant excepted.

The verdict and judgment being for the plaintiff below, the cause now came here by writ of error on the record and bill of exceptions.

Mr. W. Hay, Jr., for the plaintiff in error. The plaintiff below was bound to show a complete right of possession prior to the day of the demise. *Jackson* v. *Wheeler*, 6 Johns., 272. The demise should always be laid subsequent to the day when the right of entry accrued. (Runn. Ej., 87; 2 Chit. Pl., 444, *note;* Wheat. Selw., 553, 534.) The reason is, because the law rejects fractions of a day. (2 Bl. Com., 41.)

The demise should have been subsequent to the forfeiture. In ejectment on a mortgage, it is always deemed material to show the money due, in order to establish the right of entry. *Jackson* v. *Fuller*, 4 Johns., 215; *Jackson* v. *Hopkins*, 18 *Id.*, 487; *Jackson* v. *Dubois*, 4 *Id.*, 221; *Jackson* v. *Hull*, 10 *Id.*, 482; *Peterson* v. *Clark*, 15 *Id.*, 205; *Jackson* v. *Bronson*, 19 *Id.*, 325; *Ives* v. *Ives*, 13 *Id.*, 235; *Runyan* v. *Mersereau*, 11 *Id.*, 534; *Peterson* v. *Clark*, 15 *Id.*, 205; *Jones* v. *Clark*, 20 *Id.*, 61. In all these cases, the money being due is treated as a material fact.

One year's interest is received. By allowing the mortgagee to lay his demise at the date of the mortgage, we allow him to collect *mesne* profits from that time. *Jackson* v. *Randall*, 11 Johns., 405; *Benson* v. *Matsdorf*, 2 *Id.*, 369; *Van Alen* v. *Rogers*, 1 Johns. Cas., 281.

[The counsel took other grounds, but as the decision turned on the day of the demise, it is not material to pursue the argument further.]

To show the power, and duty of the court below to nonsuit, he cited *Foot* v. *Sabin*, 19 Johns., 154.

Mr. S. C. Baldwin, contra. The English common law doctrine places the legal estate in the mortgagee. *Moss* v. *Gallimore*, Doug., 279; 2 Bl. Com., 159. The mortgagor *in [***149** possession is considered the lessee of the mortgagee. *Runyan* v. *Mersereau*, 11 Johns., 534, citing *The King* v. *St. Michaels*, Doug., 630, 632. The English rule has been fully adopted by this court. *Johnson* v. *Hart*, 3 Johns. Cas., 326; *Jackson* v. *Dubois*, 4 Johns., 216; *Hitchcock* v. *Harrington*, 6 *Id.*, 290; *Jackson* v. *Hopkins*, 18 *Id.*, 488. The only question is, when does the legal estate commence? Common sense would say, when it passes to the mortgagee. At that time the right of entry and possession commences. As between third persons, perhaps the title may be differently regarded; but all the authorities agree, that, as between mortgagor and those claiming under him, and mortgagee, the legal title and present right of entry are in the latter.

Curia, per SAVAGE, *Ch. J.* The rule is well established, that the demise in the declaration must be laid after the lessor's title and right of entry accrue. (6 Johns., 273.) This rule is not disputed; but the question is, when did the lessor's right of entry accrue in the case before us? This is the only real question in the cause; as the defendant, having taken an absolute conveyance, not acknowledging the mortgage, was not entitled to notice to quit, the sale itself being an act of disloyalty. (18 Johns., 488.)

"It has repeatedly been decided in this court, that, as between the mortgagor and mortgagee, the former is to be regarded as a tenant at will by implication, and is entitled to notice (by which is meant six months' notice) to quit." (18 Johns., 488.) The mortgagor is entitled to the possession; and, so far from being treated as a trespasser before notice to quit, this court has held that he may maintain trespass against the mortgagee. (11 Johns., 538.) And in *Jackson* v. *Bronson*, 19 Johns., 326, it was decided that the mortgagor might maintain ejectment against the grantee of the mortgagee, who was not also assignee of the debt.

In *Goodtitle* v. *Herbert*, 4 T. R., 680, it was decided that a tenant at will is not a trespasser. In that case, the *demise was laid Oct. [***150** 1, and the demand of possession, which was tantamount to notice to quit, was made on the 5th of the same month. The demand in that case terminated the tenancy, which, not being until after the day of the demise in the declaration, the defendant had judgment.

The mortgagor, in this case, was *quasi* tenant at will; and had he continued in possession, that tenancy must have been terminated by a notice to quit. And until such termination, the mortgagee had no right of entry. The mortgagor, however, chose to terminate the tenancy July 5, 1819, by giving a conveyance in fee absolutely. The first default happened Sept. 8, 1819. Then the mortgagee's right of entry accrued, the tenancy having been previously terminated. But the demise was laid long anterior, to wit: at the date of the mortgage, before the lessor had any right of entry—the mortgage then being a mere chattel, a security for money. To give the mortgagee a right of entry, two thing are necessary: 1. Default of payment, in whole or in part. 2. A termination of the tenancy—neither of which had happened at the time of the demise, as laid in the declaration.

The plaintiff below had no right to recover. The court below, therefore, erred. The judgment must be reversed; and a *venire de novo* awarded from Warren C. P.

Judgment reversed.

Cited in—5 Wend., 616; 8 Wend., 586; 9 Wend., 232 14 Wend., 66; 26 Barb., 406; 2 Bos., 529; 24 Am. Dec., 107.

151*] *B. & A. DE FORREST v. FRARY.

Pleading—Action by Assignee of Non-negotiable Draft or Order—Consideration may be set Forth Fully—Where Order is Payable to Two, One Cannot Assign it—Order Payable on the sale of Certain Carriages, is not Negotiable.

In an action by the assignee of an order or draft, not negotiable, in the name of the assignee against the acceptor, on an express promise by the latter to pay, it is proper to set forth all the circumstances which go to form the consideration of the order.

Where such an order is payable to two persons for a debt due to them from the drawer, one alone cannot assign the order, they being tenants in common of the debt due on the order. And in declaring on an assignment by one, it must be shown that he was a partner with the other, or in some other way had authority to assign, or the declaration will be bad; and this, even though the draft be drawn payable to the order of either of the payees.

An order payable on the sale of certain carriages is not negotiable as an inland bill of exchange, though it be in terms made payable to the order of the payee.

It seems that in pleading an unsealed assignment of a chose in action, the consideration for such assignment must be set forth at large. It is not sufficient to aver generally, that the assignment was for a valuable consideration paid by the assignee to the assignor.

Citations—Lawes' Pl., in *Assumpsit*, 31, 49; 1 Chit. Pl., 295, 296; 1 Mass., 117; 17 Johns., 292.

ON demurrer to the first and second counts of the declaration.

The first count stated, that on Dec. 7, 1822, in consideration that one Wm. Woodworth was then indebted to T. Kellogg and L. R. Meller, in the sum of $200; and that Woodworth, having carriages worth $1,000, would and did, at the request and for the benefit of Kellogg and Meller, for the security and payment of his (W's.) debt to them, deliver the carriages to the defendant, to be disposed of by him, and out of the avails to pay K. and M. their debt; and in consideration that W. then, as a part of the same transaction, drew his order in writing, upon the defendant, and thereby requested him to pay to the order of "T. Kellogg or L. R. Meller," $200, whenever the defendant had sold of the carriages to the amount of the order; he, the defendant, accepted the carriages, and took possession of them for the purposes aforesaid; and in consideration of the premises, then agreed to pay the $200 to the order of "T. Kellogg or L. R. Meller," whenever he had sold of the carriages to that amount; and in pursuance of the agreement, and as part of the same transaction, for the consideration aforesaid, accepted the order, his own proper handwriting being thereunto subscribed by him, for the purposes aforesaid; which order was then delivered to Kellogg. That Kellogg, for himself and Meller, to the order of either of whom the $200 were made payable, on the same day when it was given, for a valuable consideration paid him by the plaintiffs, transferred, indorsed and delivered the order with the acceptance to the plaintiffs; and thereby ordered and *appointed [*152 the $200 to be paid to them, and authorized them to demand and receive that sum according to the terms of the defendant's agreement and acceptance. And the defendant, knowing the premises, at the request of the plaintiffs, then promised to pay them the $200, according to the tenor and effect of the order, &c.

This count then averred, that after these transactions, the defendant did sell and dispose of the carriages to the amount of $1,000.

The second count stated that Dec. 7, 1822, Woodworth was indebted to Kellogg and Meller, in $200; and that in consideration of this debt, and that they then agreed to wait on W. for a still longer time for payment, W. agreed with them and the defendant, that he would deliver, and he did deliver accordingly, a quantity of carriages to the defendant, worth $1,000, to be sold by him to pay the debt to K. and M. or their order, when he should have sold to that amount. That W. drew his order in writing on the defendant, by which he requested him to pay to the order of "T. Kellogg and L. R. Meller," $200 (as in the first count). That in consideration of the premises, the defendant accepted this order, which was delivered to Kellogg. That the defendant sold the carriages, &c. (as in the first count). This second count then averred an assignment of the order to the plaintiffs in the same manner as in the first count; and that the defendant, with knowledge, and in consideration of the premises, promised as in the first count.

Demurrer, assigning for cause: 1. That the two counts set out the consideration of the order as between Woodworth and the payees, to which the plaintiffs were not privy; and the statement did not, therefore, aid the plaintiffs' claim. 2. That these counts set out the consideration on which the order was accepted, to which the plaintiffs were not privy, and their claim not aided by the statement. 3. That setting out the indebtedness of Woodworth to Kellogg and Meller did not aid the plaintiffs' claim, they not being privy to it. 4. But if it was proper to state such indebtedness, the consideration should *have been stated. [*153 5. That the plaintiffs were not privy to the pledge of the carriages, and their claim not strengthened by that fact. 6. That the parol negotiations and agreements were set forth, which were extinguished by the making and acceptance of the order. And such negotiations or agreements could not aid the plaintiffs' right. 7. That the first count avers that the transfer and delivery of the order authorized the plaintiffs to demand and receive the $200, according to the defendant's agreement and acceptance; whereas the plaintiffs could acquire no right independent of the order and acceptance. 8. As to the second count, that the plaintiffs were not privy to the agreement for delaying payment of the debt due from Woodworth

---

NOTE.—*Negotiable paper—Essential qualities of.* See Cook v. Satterlee, *ante*, p. 108, *note*; Saxton v. Johnson, 10 Johns., 418, *note*.

to Kellogg & Meller, mentioned in the second count, and the plaintiffs' claim not aided by that circumstance. 9. As to the second count, that the plaintiffs were not privy to the indebtedness of Woodworth to Kellogg & Meller, or any agreement concerning the indebtedness, and the indebtedness or agreement to pay out of the carriages, did not aid the plaintiffs' claim. 10. The tenth cause was inferential from the former causes, that the two counts contained irrelevant and unnecessary matter.

Joinder in demurrer.

Mr. D. B. Tallmadge, in support of the demurrer. The order was clearly not negotiable, the time of payment being uncertain, and the payment itself depending on a contingency. No action, then, lies upon the order as an inland bill. The plaintiffs must show a complete title by assignment, before the defendant received the money, in order to entitle them to an action for that money. This they have not done. They should have set forth particularly the consideration of the assignment. An averment generally, for a valuable consideration, is not sufficient. *Andrews* v. *Beecker*, 1 Johns. Cas., 411; *Littlefield* v. *Storey*, 3 Johns., 425, and *Compton* v. *Jones*, 4 Cow., 13, merely recognize the assignments of choses in action, and declare **154***] that the court will protect them; *but the manner of pleading the assignment was not drawn in question. In the last case, it is true, the manner is shown. It was general as here. But the point not being made, the case is not an authority in this respect. All the court decide is, that *assumpsit* will lie on a promise to pay the assignee of a specialty. *Perkins* v. *Parker*, 1 Mass., 117, however, raises and decides the point that the assignee must show the consideration in his pleadings. That case is recognized as authority in *Prescott* v. *Hull*, 17 Johns., 292.

Again; the assignment of the order was not made by both Kellogg and Meller, the payees. The second count states it as payable to the order of both. They were tenants in common, and one could not devest the title of the other without his consent. *Sanford* v. *Mickles*, 4 Johns., 224. The plaintiffs, by the assignment, became tenants in common with one of the payees, Meller, who did not assign; and the action should have been in his name, joined with the plaintiffs. There is, then, a plain nonjoinder, which is always fatal to the plaintiff, in an action arising *ex contractu*. It need not be pleaded in abatement. Would Meller be liable as a warrantor of this order in any respect, provided it should prove bad in the hands of the assignees?

The special causes of demurrer are well taken.

Mr. C. Bushnell, contra. The matters objected to by the special causes of demurrer, are all parts of the circumstances, which together form the consideration of the original order of Woodworth, and the acceptance and agreement of the defendant. All these should be set forth. (Lawes Pl., in *assumpsit*, 31, 49-54; 1 Chit. Pl., 295, 296; 6 East, 569, 570; 2 Chit. Pl., 10, &c., in the precedents; Com. Dig., Action on the Case upon *Assumpsit*, H, 3.)

The declaration avers an assignment for a valuable consideration paid by the plaintiffs to Kellogg. This is the same as if it had said money paid. All the precedents, and all the books of reports, agree that this general averment is enough.

*The draft was payable, in terms, to [***155** the order of Kellogg or Mellor, in the disjunctive. This is equivalent to saying, the assignee of either of them. It authorized Kellogg, to whom alone it was delivered, to assign it for a valuable consideration.

Both counts aver that the defendant, with full knowledge of all the circumstances, expressly promised to pay the plaintiffs. On this promise, the action can be sustained.

If either of these counts be good, the demurrer being to both, must fail. *Mumford* v. *Fitzhugh*, 18 Johns., 457.

Curia, per SUTHERLAND, *J.* It is a fatal objection to both counts that they aver the assignment of the order, which is the foundation of the plaintiffs' action, to have been made by Kellogg alone, for himself and Meller, without averring that they were partners, or showing, in any other way, the authority of Kellogg for that purpose. This draft was payable to the order of Kellogg or Meller, in the disjunctive, as stated in the first count, out of the proceeds of certain carriages, whenever they should be sold. It was, therefore, not negotiable; and its legal effect is the same as though the word "order" had been omitted. Both counts aver that the consideration of the order, was a debt due from Woodworth to Kellogg and Meller. They were tenants in common, therefore; and neither had a right to assign, without the express authority of the other. The second count avers that the draft was payable to the order of both. We cannot presume a partnership. It should be averred, so that the defendant may have an opportunity of contesting it.

The plaintiffs having failed to show a legal title to the order, the consideration for the defendant's promise fails, and the plaintiffs cannot recover.

The special causes of demurrer are not well taken. It was necessary for the plaintiffs to show the original consideration of the order and acceptance, and the matters objected to all go to form that consideration. (Lawes Pl., in *assumpsit*, 31, 49; 1 Chit. Pl., 295, 296.)

*I am inclined to think the general [***156** averment, that the assignment was for a valuable consideration, is not sufficient. The consideration should have been stated at large. (1 Mass., 117; 17 Johns., 292.) On this latter point, however, it is not necessary to express a definitive opinion.

The defendant must have judgment, with leave to the plaintiffs to amend on the usual terms.

Rule accordingly.

Cited in—2 Wend., 422; 23 Barb., 144; 20 Am. Dec., 634.

HOMER v. MARTIN AND GILMAN.

Practice—Depositions under Statute—Signature of Counsel to Interrogatories—Form of Direction.

The interrogatories under a commission to examine witnesses, issued pursuant to the Act, sess. 36, ch. 56, sec. 11; 1 R. L., 519, 520, may be signed by counsel, without the addition of his character to the signature. Is is enough that he is, in truth, a counselor.

A judge of the C. P. of the degree of counsel in the Supreme Court, may direct as to the return of a commission, within the Act, sess. 45, ch. 217, sec. 2.

So the first judge of the C. P. of N. Y.

Form of the direction.

A direction to return the commission by mail, directed to one of the clerks of the Supreme Court, is complied with, if the commission be delivered from the postoffice to the clerk, by any of the ordinary means, as by a messenger, the penny-post, &c. Nor is it any objection that it be delivered by the attorney for one of the parties. The true question is, was it delivered to the clerk in an unaltered state. If the court be satisfied there has been no abuse, it may be received in evidence.

Citation—Stat., sess. 45, ch. 217, secs. 1, 2.

ASSUMPSIT, tried at the N. Y. Circuit, Jan. 20, 1826, before Edwards, *Circuit J.*

At the trial, the plaintiff had no evidence to sustain his action except what was derivable from a commission issued in his behalf, and executed in the cause at the City of Boston. The direct interrogatories, administered under this commission, were signed by the attorneys for the plaintiff, thus: "*Ward* and *Hoyt*, Atts. for Pltff." They were, in truth, at the time of signing, counselors of this court; but no addition to that effect was made to their signature. The interrogatories were allowed by the first judge of the C. P. of N. Y. by an indorsement thus: "allowed this 6th day of May, 1825, Jno. T. Irving."

May 6, 1825, before the commission was sealed up, *Judge* Irving indorsed the following order on the back thereof: "After this commission shall have been executed agreeably to the instructions annexed, let one of the commissioners put the sealed packet into the postoffice at Boston, stating on the back that the **157***] same *had been so put into said office by him, and signing his name to said indorsement. The packet, when sealed up by the commissioner, will be addressed to the clerk of the Supreme Court at the City of N. Y. May 6th, 1825. JOHN T. IRVING."

It appeared by the post-mark and certificate that the packet was mailed at Boston, June 3, 1825, and was indorsed by the deputy-clerk of this court at N. Y., on the 6th of the same month, "received and filed;" but that previous to so indorsing or filing the commission, the penny-post had carried the packet to the deputy-clerk at the office, who refused to pay the postage; wherefore, the penny-post took the packet down to the office of the plaintiff's attorneys to get the postage. They received the commission and paid the postage. One of the plaintiff's attorneys then took the packet to the office of the defendant's attorney, who objected to the irregularity of its being in the plaintiff's attorneys' possession. He, the plaintiff's attorney, then took it to the clerk's office, where it was filed and indorsed.

The direction on the cover of the commission was thus:

"NEW YORK, SUPREME COURT.

FITZHENRY HOMER
v.
ALEXANDER MARTIN and ROBERT GILMAN. } Ward and Hoyt, Attys. for Pltff.

To James Farley, Esquire, clerk of the Supreme Court, City Hall, City of New York."

It was also indorsed: "Put into the postoffice in the City of Boston, this 3d day of June, 1825, by Josiah P. Cook, Commissioner."

The defendant's counsel objected that the depositions taken under the commission should not be read: 1. Because of the irregular manner in which the return came to the clerk's office; but the judge overruled the objection. 2. Because *Judge* Irving had no authority to make the order as to the mode of return. This objection was also overruled. 3. That the direct interrogatories were not signed by counsel; *whereupon proof was offered that [***158** Ward and Hoyt were in fact counsel, at the time of signing. The judge rejected this proof, and with it the commission and return, and the plaintiff was nonsuited.

Mr. J. Hoyt, for the plaintiff, now moved to set aside the nonsuit, and for a new trial. He cited the Statutes, sess. 36, ch. 56, sec. 11; 1 R. L., 519, 20; sess. 45, ch. 217, sec. 2, p. 226, to show the manner in which commissions may be executed and directed to be returned. The section last cited, he said, confides the direction to a commissioner of the court; and the Statute, sess. 36, ch. 16, sec. 1; 1 R. L., 322, authorizes the appointment of commissioners for Oneida and Ontario, declaring their powers, and conferring on them the same authority at chambers as a judge of this court possessed.

Then came the Statutes, sess. 41, ch. 195, sec. 1, p. 173, and sess. 44, ch. 72, p. 64—the former extending the powers of commissioners to judges of the C. P. who are counselors of this court, and the latter erecting the C. P. of N. Y., requiring the first judge to be of the degree of counsel, and the 12th section restraining the application of the Act, sess, 41, ch. 195, to the first judge of that court. The 3d section of the Act, sess. 44, ch. 72, gives the same power to the C. P. as then belonged to the Mayor's Court of that city.

Mr. Talcott, Atty-Gen., contra. The Statute, sess. 36, ch. 56, sec. 11, directs the interrogatories to be signed by the party or his counsel. This statute being in derogation of the common law, must be strictly followed. (20 Johns., 361.) It is not enough that the person signing is in fact counsel. He should appear to be so on the face of the proceedings. They should speak their own regularity. This is always so in relation to the signature to special pleas; *Dubois* v. *Dubois*, 5 Johns., 235, 236; and *a fortiori*, as to interrogatories under a commission.

The order was to deliver the commission to the clerk. This court can make no new order. Suppose the penny-post had delivered the commission to A and he to B; and *it had [***159** thus passed round through half the city to the hands of the attorney; it must be received, within the doctrine contended for on the other side. Is there any safety in such a practice?

But the judge had no authority to make the order. The Statute of 1818, sess. 41, ch. 195, sec. 1, did not mean to confer on the judges of the C. P. all the powers which might thereafter be given to commissioners appointed under the Act of 1813, sess. 36, ch. 16, sec. 1. The words of the Act of 1818 are, "to do all the duties, and exercise all the powers which are given to such commissioners by any subsequent Acts of the Legislature;" not which shall be so given. The power conferred by the subsequent Statute of 1822, sess. 45, ch. 217, sec. 2, p. 226, is confined in terms to a judge of this court or commissioner. There being no prospective words in the Act of 1818, judges of the C. P. take no power under the Statute of 1822. This construction is warranted by *Jones* v. *Reed*, 1 Johns. Cas., 20. Judges being an inferior jurisdiction, can take nothing by implication. The Statute, sess. 44, ch. 72, confers no power on the first judge of the C. P. of the City of N. Y. to make this direction. Suppose his powers to be the same with those of the judges of the Mayor's Court under the Statute relating to the Mayor's Court of N.Y., sess. 36, ch. 85; 2 R. L., 501; no such power as is here exercised will be found there. But if it was conferred by that Act, it is not adopted by the Act organizing the C. P., sess. 44, ch. 72. The 3d section of the last Act refers merely to the power of the former Mayor's Court considered collectively; and the 12th section is restrictive merely. The creation of a new Court of C. P. will not give this power to its judges. The Act of 1822 did not mean that any C. P. judge, in any part of the State, of the degree of counsel, should have power to give these directions. It is even a greater power than this court itself possesses, who can only direct a return by mail. (Sess. 45, ch. 217, sec. 1.) The consequences of the construction contended for should be looked to. (Bac. Abr., Statute I., pl. 10.)

160*] **Mr. Hoyt*, in reply. Most likely the direction in this case was literally complied with: the clerk had the commission in his hands before he looked at the amount of postage. Neither the statute nor order provides negatively that the commission shall not come to the hands of the attorney. The accident of its coming there is matter of regularity; and the effect of this accident must be declared by the court upon their rules of practice. No one has been injured. It was not five minutes with the attorney. It was usual formerly to deliver the commission to the attorney in the first instance, though not perhaps strictly justifiable within the Act. (Cai. Pr., 426.) The commission being delivered back by the clerk to the penny-post, he may be considered the agent of the clerk.

We submit to the examination of the court, the various statutes on which the powers of *Judge* Irving must rest. The practice has been to consider judges of the C. P., of the degree of counsel, commissioners within the Act of 1822.

Curia, per WOODWORTH, *J.* The statute direct that the interrogatories be signed by the parties, or their counsel. They were signed by Ward and Hoyt, attorneys for the plaintiff; and approved by the judge. Proof was offered that Ward and Hoyt were counsel. I think this sufficient. The fact that they were counsel was a compliance with the Act, although they were not described as such. The strictness applicable to special pleas was, as apprehended, never intended. This is evident from the statute allowing the party as well as his counsel to sign. No good reason can, in my view, be assigned for rejecting the evidence, because the names were not followed by the addition of counsel.

The Statute, sess. 45, ch. 217, sec. 1, authorizes the judges to prescribe a return of the commission by mail, to be directed to one of the clerks of this court, and to be by him opened and filed in his office. This duty may be performed by a single judge. (*Id.*, sec. 2.) The power was rightfully exercised by *Judge* Irving, who has the power of a judge of this court in vacation.

*There is no express provision as to [***161** the manner of conveying the commission from the postoffice to the clerk's office. I think it may safely be concluded that the Legislature were satisfied to leave the transmission from the one office to the other, to the usual course, and the vigilance and care the court would exercise when there was any suspicion of unfairness and fraud. The manner letters are taken from a postoffice was undoubtedly known.

Sometimes the person to whom the letters are addressed calls and receives them. Perhaps more frequently they are sent for by a messenger. At other times they may be delivered by a penny-post. A delivery in either way is sufficient. It will not be pretended that the clerk must attend personally and receive the commission from the office. If that ground be abandoned, it follows that a delivery to any person is allowable.

The only question would seem to be, was the commission delivered to the clerk, in the same state as when received from the postoffice. The attorney of the party is not disqualified from being the medium of conveyance. If he has discharged the duty faithfully, the commission should be received; and is no more objectionable on that ground than if the penny-post or the clerk's messenger had been the carrier. The commission has been opened by the clerk and filed in the office. There is not a suggestion that it was opened by any other person. The nonsuit must be set aside, and a new trial granted.

New trial granted.

---

*WILBUR, Survivor of DOREMUS, [***162**

v.

SELDEN, Impleaded with RICHARDS, Survivors of OGDEN.

Negotiable Paper—Action by Intermediate Indorser of Note against Prior Indorser, for Money Paid to Subsequent Indorsee—Proof of Demand and Notice to Defendant Necessary—Evidence Taken at Former Trial—When Admissible—Register of Deceased Notary Inadmissible where Entries were Made by Clerk.

An intermediate indorser of a promissory note, though he did not hold the note when it became due, yet must, in an action against a prior indorser, for the money paid by him (the intermediate indorser), to a subsequent indorsee, to take up the note, prove a regular demand of payment and notice to the defendant, the same as in an ordinary action against an indorser.

NOTE.—*Evidence—Testimony of deceased witness at a former trial—When admissible.*

The testimony of a deceased witness, given at a former trial, between the same parties, is admissible for the same purpose. Jackson v. Bailey, 2 Johns., 17; Beals v. Guernsey, 8 Johns., 446; White v. Kibling, 11 Johns., 128; Jackson v. Lawson, 15 Johns., 539; Crary v. Sprague, 12 Wend., 41; Powell v. Waters, 17 Johns., 176; Osborn v. Bell, 5 Den., 370; Cleavland v. Huey, 18 Ala., 343; Lane v. Brainard, 30 Conn., 565; Litcher v. Norton, 5 Ill., 575; Jaccard v. Anderson, 37 Mo., 91; Conway v. Erwin, 1 La. Ann., 391;

The register of a deceased notary is not evidence of demand and notice on a promissory note, where the entries were made by his clerk, who is still alive, though he be gone out of the jurisdietion of the court, and cannot be found on diligent inquiry.

What one swore on a former trial cannot be given in evidence unless he be dead. That he is beyond reach of process of subpœna, and cannot be found on diligent inquiry, will not render such proof admissible.

To render what a witness swore on a former trial admissible, it must have been between the same parties, and the point in issue the same.

The words of the witness must be given, not what is supposed to be the substance of his testimony.

Citations—20 Johns., 172, 173; 1 Phil. Ev., 215; Bull. *N. P.*, 243; 4 T. R., 290; 14 Mass., 36, 234; 4 Serg. & R., 203; 5 Cr., 13; 3 Binn., 192; 4 Johns., 467; 3 Taunt., 261.

ASSUMPSIT by the plaintiff, an indorsee, against the defendants, indorsers of a promissory note. The declaration stated that the note was for $800, payable to Canfield & Co.; by them indorsed to the defendants; by them to Doremus & Wilbur (the latter of whom, as survivor of Doremus, is the plaintiff); by them to Bostwick & Sterling; and by them to the Bank of N. Y. It then averred a demand of the makers, and notice of non-payment to all the indorsers, and a payment by the indorsers respectively, who were subsequent to the defendants.

The cause was tried at the N. Y. Circuit, Mar. 30, 1824, before Edwards, *Circuit J.*; when, after proving the note paid and taken up as averred, one question was, whether demand of payment had been made, and notice given to the defendants.

To prove this, the notarial register of John Wilkes, the notary of the Bank, was offered in evidence by the plaintiffs. All the entries in this book were in the handwriting of one Scott, Wilkes' clerk, who transacted his business, and who had left the City of N. Y., declaring that he was going to the back parts of Pa., and could not be found on diligent inquiry. The register was rejected by the judge.

The plaintiff then offered to prove what Scott had sworn to on the trial of an action before brought by Doremus & Wilbur against Selden, Richards and Ogden, to recover the sums which the former had paid to the holders of the note in question, in satisfaction of their **163***] liability as indorsers, *and one of which sums was the amount now claimed. This evidence was objected to, but admitted by the judge.

Mr. H. D. Sedgwick, one of the counsel in the former cause, was then sworn for the plaintiff, and said he could not state with precision what Scott swore to, and could not recollect the phraseology of the witness. His testimony was, therefore, objected to; but the judge allowed him to state his recollection of the substance of what Scott swore to; and he produced his notes of Scott's testimony, but did not pretend that they contained Scott's exact words or phraseology.

The defendants excepted upon the above points; and the verdict being for the plaintiff, he now moved for a new trial.

Mr. G. Griffin, for the defendant. The testimony of Mr. Sedgwick should not have been received. The former trial was not between the same parties, or for the same cause of action, and it did not appear that Scott was dead. Nor could Mr. Sedgwick repeat the words or phraseology of Scott. 1 Phil. Ev., last Am. ed., 199, 200, and *note;* 17 Johns., 179; *Le Baron* v. *Crombie*, 14 Mass., 234; Bull. *N. P.*, 243; 4 T. R., 290, per Ld. Kenyon, *Ch. J.; Lightner* v. *Wike*, 4 Serg. & R., 203.

Messrs. R. Sedgwick and *H. D. Sedgwick*, contra, denied that the plaintiff, being a subsequent indorser, and holding the note when it fell due, was bound to show a regular demand of payment and notice to a prior indorser. They said the most that can be required is, that he should show notice to the party he means to charge, of having actually paid and taken up the note, within a reasonable time after so doing. In this case, the plaintiff seeking to recover only what he has paid, no notice whatever was necessary.

[They were proceeding to argue in support of these propositions; but *the Court* told them the law was so well settled against them, that they could not sit to hear the argument.]

*In support of the proposition that [***164** the evidence of what Scott had sworn was admissible, especially in connection with the record made by him in the notarial register, they cited *Sluby* v. *Champlin*, 4 Johns., 461; *Cooke* v. *Woodrow*, 5 Cr., 13; *Clark* v. *Sanderson*, 3 Binn., 192; *Jackson* v. *Gager*, 5 Cow., 383; *Welch* v. *Barrett*, 15 Mass., 380; *Halliday* v. *Martinet*, 20 Johns., 168, and *Doncaster* v. *Day*, 3 Taunt., 261.

Curia, per SAVAGE, *Ch. J.* The only question is as to the competency of the testimony objected to.

The books of a deceased notary have been received in evidence when the entries were made by the notary himself, but when they are made by a clerk, the notary does not attest to them; and in that case the evidence of the clerk is higher. And, indeed, the book, unaccompanied by his testimony, would prove nothing. (20 Johns., 172, 173, and the cases there cited.)

The rule as to admitting what a witness swore upon a former trial, is supposed to be this: that to render such testimony admissible, it must be between the same parties, and

Harper v. Burrow, 6 Ired., 30; Ephraims v. Murdock, 7 Blackf., 10; Mathewson v. Sargent, 36 Vt., 142; Bailey v. Woods, 17 N. H. 365.

The death of the witness must be proved. Powell v. Waters, 17 Johns., 176; Weeks v. Lowerre, 8 Barb., 530; Crary v. Sprague, 12 Wend., 41; Le Baron v. Crombie, 14 Mass., 234.

The parties must be the same. Jackson v. Crissey, 3 Wend., 251.

The witness, called to prove what a deceased witness testified, was formerly required to give his precise words. U. S. v. Wood, 3 Wash., 440; Ephraims v. Murdock, 7 Blackf., 10; Foster v. Shaw, 7 Serg. & R., 163; 4 T. R., 290; Commonwealth v. Richards, 18 Pick., 434.

The substance of all that was said by the deceased witness on the former trial is now generally held sufficient. Clark v. Vorce, 15 Wend., 193; Crawford v. Loper, 25 Barb., 449; Van Buren v. Cockburn, 14 Barb., 118; Huff v. Bennett, 6 N. Y., 337; Home v. Williams, 23 Ind., 37; Wagers v. Dickey, 17 Ohio, 439; Thurmond v. Tramnell, 28 Tex., 371; Trammell v. Hemphill, 27 Ga., 525; Emery v. Fowler, 39 Me., 326; Lime Rock Bank v. Hewett, 52 Me., 531; Young v. Dearborn, 22 N. H., 372; Cornell v. Green, 10 Serg. & R., 14, 16; Chess v. Chess, 17 Serg & R., 409, 411; Williams v. Willard, 23 Vt., 369; Brown v. Commonwealth, 73 Pa. St., 321; U. S. v. Macomb, 5 McLean, 286; Greenl. Ev., Vol. I., secs. 163-167, *and authorities there cited.*

the point in issue the same; and the words of the witness must be given, not what is supposed to be the substance of his testimony. The witness must also be dead. (1 Phil. Ev., 215; Bull. *N. P.*, 243; 4 T. R., 290; 14 Mass., 234; 4 Serg. & R., 203.)

In this case the parties are substantially the same, the cause of action is the same, and the point in issue the same. But the witness, Scott, is not dead. He is absent, in the State of Pa.; and, possibly, upon inquiry there, he may be found, and examined upon commission.

It is urged by the plaintiff's counsel that the case is analogous to one of a subscribing witness to a bond, whose signature may be proved, if he be absent; and the proof of which establishes the execution of the bond, without proof of the signature of the obligor. That rule rests upon the presumption that the parties have selected the witness to testify to **165***] *the execution and, therefore, proof of his signature, is proof that the bond was executed in his presence. The rule is certainly a very dangerous one, but too well established to be now controverted. (5 Cr., 13; 3 Binn., 192; 4 Johns., 467.) It is not, however, at all analogous in principle to the one contended for in this case. No special confidence can be charged upon the defendants. They could not control the Bank in the selection of its notary, nor the notary in the selection of his clerks. The witness, Scott, was never selected by the parties to testify between them; nor was he called to testify to their acts, but his own.

In *Le Baron* v. *Crombie*, 14 Mass., 236, the Supreme Court of Mass. refused to hear what had been sworn to by a witness who, though naturally alive, was civilly dead, having been convicted of felony. They say the rule in England is limited to the case where the principal witness is dead. If, however, the death of the witness were not an indispensable circumstance, there is yet another difficulty. Mr. Sedgwick could not state the words of the absent witness, but only the substance of his testimony. He produced the notes which he took as counsel on the former trial; but whether he testified from these or from recollection, does not appear in the case. The rule laid down by Ld. Kenyon, 4 T. R., 290, is, that the words must be given, and not the effect of them; and the reason is, because the jury are to judge of the effect of the testimony, and not the witness. In *Lightner* v. *Wike*, 4 Serg. & R., 203, *Ch. J.* Tilghman shows, very satisfactorily, the reason of the rule; and also that notes of counsel should not be relied on, as it is not their practice to take the words, but the substance, as they understand it. And he remarks, that during a trial, the ideas of counsel pass through a medium which diverts them from a right line.

The case of *Doncaster* v. *Day*, 3 Taunt., 261, does not contradict the rule, that the words must be given, but holds that they may be given from notes or memory, provided the accuracy be sworn to.

166*] *I am of opinion that this evidence was improperly admitted, and that a new trial should be granted.

New trial granted.

Criticised--12 Wend., 45.

Cited in—15 Wend., 196; 16 Wend., 595; 20 Wend., 85; 2 Hill, 538; 5 Hill, 296; 8 Barb., 533; 46 How. Pr., 254; 2 Abb. N. S., 189; 15 Abb., N. S., 449; 1 Rob., 411; 38 Super., 271; 2 McLean, 472; 5 McLean, 294, 295; 27 Am. Dec., 113; 29 Am. Dec., 611 (18 Pick., 434); 30 Am. Dec., 53.

WILLIAMS v. SMITH.

Action against Toll-gatherer of Turnpike Company, under Statute—Stockholder Competent Juror—Certificate of Commissioner of Highways.

In debt against the toll-gatherer of a turnpike company for the penalty imposed by the 16th section of the Act relative to Turnpike Companies, 1 R. L., 236, for shutting the gate and taking or demanding toll, after the commissioners of inspection have ordered it to be opened: it is not a principal cause of challenge to a juror, that he is a stockholder of the Company.

The Company are not accountable, in any event, on account of the recovery; though otherwise as to a recovery upon the 9th section.

After a turnpike gate has once been opened by order of the commissioners of inspection, because the road is out of repair, it cannot be lawfully shut, and toll demanded, until one of the commissioners certifies that the road is in sufficient repair. And where the certificate stated that the road was still out of repair, but that the contractors had given assurances that it should be repaired, and directed the gate-keeper to shut the gate; and he did so, and demanded and received toll: held, that he was liable to the penalty of $10 within the 16th section of the Act relative to Turnpike Companies, 1 R. L., 236.

The certificate of a commissioner in due form, is conclusive; and will protect the toll-gatherer.

Citation—1 R. L., 236.

ON ERROR from the C. P. of Tioga. The cause came to that court by appeal from a justice's court. The action was by Williams against Smith, for $10 debt, for the defendant's unlawfully demanding and taking toll of the plaintiff at the middle gate on the Ithaca and Owego Turnpike Road. In the C. P., Charles Pumpelly, a stockholder of the Corporation who owned the road, was drawn as a juror. He was challenged, therefore, by the plaintiff, who at the same time admitted that the defendant was able to pay the judgment claimed against him. The court overruled the challenge, and the juror was sworn and sat and tried the cause.

It was admitted by the parties at the trial, that the road being completed, and officers appointed according to the Act of Mar. 13, 1807, and the other Acts, &c.; afterwards, July 23, 1824, the commissioners of inspection certified that the road was out of repair; and ordered the middle gate to be opened till further orders. Afterwards, Sept. 23, 1824, two of the commissioners certified that they had viewed the road, found considerable repairs made, and that some remained to be done, specifying what and where, and how they should be done; and from the assurances given *by the con- [***167** tractors that the repairs would be done, they directed the keeper of the middle gate to shut it and keep it shut till further orders. After this certificate was given, to wit: in the spring of 1825, the plaintiff passing the gate with a wagon and two spans of horses, the defendant demanded, and the plaintiff paid 75 cents, which was according to the legal rate of toll.

The plaintiff objected that the last certificate was insufficient. The court below overruled the objection, and charged the jury in favor of the defendant. The plaintiff excepted. Verdict and judgment for the defendant.

The statute in question is the general Act relative to Turnpike Companies, passed Mar. 13, 1807, sess. 30, ch. 38; 1 R. L., 228.

Mr. E. Griffin, for the plaintiff in error, contended that Pumpelly was not an impartial juror, and that the defendant had no right, under the statute, to shut the gate, till the commissioners should certify that the road was in sufficient repair.

Mr. H. Bleecker, contra, cited 2 Cow., 551; 2 Cai., 179, and 1 Cow., 251.

Curia, per SUTHERLAND, *J.* Pumpelly was a competent juror. The Company of which he was a stockholder are not responsible, in any event, on account of a recovery against the toll-gatherer, for a violation of the 16th section of the Statute under which this action was brought 1 R. L., 236. For delay or extortion by the toll-gatherer, under the 9th section, the Company are responsible, if the penalty cannot be collected from the goods and chattels of the defendant. That provision is not incorporated into the 16th section. The toll-gatherer may be imprisoned on any judgment upon the 16th section, but not under the 9th.

The certificate of Sept. 23, 1824, did not authorize the toll-gatherer to shut the gate and demand toll. The 16th section directs, that when a gate shall be opened, by order of the commissioners, &c., it shall be opened, "and **168***] *shall remain open, and no toll shall be demanded in passing the same, until a certificate is received by the person keeping such gate, under the hand of one of the commissioners aforesaid, that such road is in sufficient repair, and granting permission to shut such gate." The certificate must not only contain a permission to shut the gate, but it must also declare the road to be in sufficient repair. When a gate is once opened by order of the commissioners, it cannot be shut again until the road is put in sufficient repair. Whether it is in sufficient repair or not, it is undoubtedly the province of the commissioner to determine; and if he will certify that it is, and order the gate to be shut, the toll-gatherer incurs no hazard in obeying the order. But if, as in this case, it appears on the face of the certificate that the road is not in repair, and the order to shut the gate is founded on the alleged expectation that the road will be repaired, and not on the fact that it has been, the toll-gatherer is bound to know that the order is unauthorized; and he obeys it at his peril. There is no hardship in this. He is not responsible for the truth or falsehood of the certificate. All he has to do, is to see that it assert the fact that the road is repaired; and, on that ground, permits or orders him to shut the gate.

The judgment below must be reversed; and a *venire de novo* awarded by the Broome C. P.

Judgment reversed.

169*] *THE MAYOR, ALDERMEN AND COMMONALTY OF THE CITY OF NEW YORK

v.

STAPLES.

Construction of Statute Requiring Masters of Ships to Give Bonds for Passengers Imported.

If a master of a ship, or other vessel, arriving from a foreign country, or any other of the U. S., who shall enter his vessel at the custom-house in the City of N. Y., suffer an alien passenger to land there, without giving, if required, pursuant to the Statute, sess. 36, ch. 86, sec. 252; 2 R. L., 441, such bond as is required by that section, or without such permission in writing as is required by that section, unless it be refused on demand, he incurs the penalty of $500, mentioned in that section.

The course to be pursued under the 251st and 252d sections of that Act, as to an alien passenger, is, on report by the master, for the Mayor or Recorder to require a bond; when it must be given. If not required, or if required and given, the master must then demand a permission in writing from the Mayor or Recorder, to land his passenger; when, if it be granted or refused, he may land. But a permission, or demand and refusal, is essential to the right. A bond only, or neglect to demand one, is not enough.

The Statute is not, in this respect, void, as being contrary to the Constitution of the U. S.

Citation—2 R. L., 440, secs. 251, 252.

ON demurrer to the defendant's second plea.

The action was debt for $500, under the 252d section of the Act to Reduce the Several Laws, relating particularly to the City of N. Y., into One Act, 2 R. L., 441. The declaration recited the 251st, 252d and 255th sections of that Act, together with the 1st and 4th sections of the Statute, sess. 43, ch. 222; and averred that the defendant was master of the schooner Penobscot Packet; and July 1, 1823, he arrived in the port of N. Y. from Halifax, and entered the schooner at the custom-house. That a certain alien was brought in the schooner, and suffered to land before any bond had been given, as required by the 252d section, though it was required by the Mayor, in the penalty of $300; and without any permission in writing from the Mayor or Recorder as required by that section.

The second plea was, that neither the Mayor nor Recorder of N. Y. ever required the bond from the defendant, concluding with a verification.

Demurrer and joinder.

Mr. M. Ulshoeffer, in support of the demurrer. The master had no right to land an alien passenger, without both a bond and permission in writing under the 252d section. The permission is the only evidence that the bond is dispensed with. The plea is also bad, because it justifies, without confessing the landing. If we were bound, in assigning the breach, to negative both bond and permission, *the plea must be equally broad. [***170** (1 Chit. Pl., 327; *Id.*, 509; 26 Johns., 206; 18 *Id.*, 30.) As a plea to the whole declaration, we could not traverse it. Unless the negative to a permission is mere surplusage, it should be met. (3 Johns., 206; 2 East, 452.) The defendant, at least, should have shown by his plea, that he applied to the Mayor or Recorder for a permission. Till that is done, they know nothing of the landing. The statute should be construed according to the reason of the case. (3 Cow., 89.) The excuse must be fully shown. (1 Gall., 157.) A permission, if granted, should have been pleaded in the very words of the statute. (6 T. R., 720.)

Messrs R. Sedgwick and *H. D. Sedgwick*, contra. If the master reports his passengers, and the Mayor and Recorder neglect to require a bond, the penalty does not attach. A permission is never required after the master has reported his passengers, unless a bond is first required by the Mayor or Recorder, and the penalty is named, and the master delays or neglects to give the bond. The naming of the penalty, and requiring the bond, should precede the action for the penalty of the statute. This being denied by the plea, it is sufficient. They cited Bac. Abr., Statute, I, pl. 10.

They also contended that the statute is unconstitutional and void. *Gibbons* v. *Ogden*, 9 Wh., 1.

Curia, per WOODWORTH, *J*. The Act relative to the City of N. Y., 2 R. L. 440, sec. 251, declares, that every master or commander of any ship,or other vessel, arriving from a foreign country, or from any other of the U. S., shall, in the manner specified by that section, make a report of every person who shall have been brought as a passenger. The 252d section declares that the Mayor, or, in case of his sickness or absence, the Recorder, may require every such master to be bound with sureties, in a sum not exceeding $300 for each passenger, to indemnify and save harmless the plaintiffs from all expenses and charge which may be

171*] incurred for the maintenance and *support of the person imported, in case such person shall, within two years, become chargeable; and if any such person, so brought, and not being a citizen of the U. S., shall be permitted or suffered to land within the city, from any such ship or vessel, before such bond shall have been given, and without a permission in writing, from the Mayor or Recorder, the master or commander shall be subject to the penalty of $500.

The declaration alleges that the defendant was master of a schooner; that he arrived at N. Y. from Halifax, and brought an alien passenger, who was permitted to land before such bond was given, although it was required, and without a permission in writing from the Mayor or Recorder.

The defendant pleads that neither the Mayor nor Recorder ever required the bond. To this plea there is a demurrer.

The decision of this cause depends on the construction to be given to the Act. The course contemplated by the statute to be pursued, appears to be this: on making the report by the master, the Mayor or Recorder should require a bond to be given, in a sum not exceeding $300. As the penalty rests, in part, in their discretion, it is necessary that the master be informed in what sum he is required to be bound, before he can comply with the law. This part of the Act relates to the duty imposed on the Mayor or Recorder. By the demurrer, it is conceded they have neglected the duty. Consequently, the defendant had not the information, requisite to enable him to execute such a bond as the statute requires.

If the Act had merely directed the master to execute the bond, on being required, the defense would be complete. But the Act goes further, and makes the master liable, if the passenger is suffered to land without a permission in writing. There must be a bond, and also a permission in writing. The Act is not in the alternative. Both requisitions must be complied with. If the Mayor or Recorder neglect to require a bond, or dispense

172*] with it, that is a *sufficient excuse for the master, so far as respects the bond; on the principle, that if he who is to do the first act, prevents the act which is to follow on the other side, or is the cause of its non-performance, he shall never urge the omission as a breach. The liability then, if any, arises on the want of a permission in writing. The Legislature have thought proper to require it in express terms. Whether it has the appearance of unnecessary strictness, we do not stop to inquire. It was, undoubtedly, considered as an additional precaution, adapted to the exigency of the case. After giving the bond, or after a neglect to require it, the master would have a right to demand the written permission. If it should be withheld, and if the refusal should be persisted in, he would then be justified in landing his passengers, on the ground that the plaintiffs having refused a permission, which it was their duty to grant, and the master having done everything on his part required to be done, according to the intent and spirit of the Act, the forfeiture is not incurred. The defendant here has not placed his defense on this ground. The plea concedes there was no permission to land given: whether, by reason of a refusal to grant it, on request, or the omission of the defendant to make the request, does not appear. No cause is assigned. The plea, therefore, is defective in substance.

Judgment must be entered for the plaintiffs, with leave to the defendant to amend, on payment of costs.

Judgment for the plaintiffs.

---

*WARD & WARD *v.* GREEN. [*173

Admiralty—Agency of Master—Owners Bound by His Acts, Unless on Board and Attending to Business of the Ship Exclusively Themselves—General Ship.

The master of a vessel, when abroad, is the agent of the owners, and has power to make contracts in relation to freight, which are binding upon the owners. When an owner is on board, and exclusively attending to the shipment of the cargo, he is not bound by the master's contract. But, to relieve himself from liability, he must show the fact that he was exclusively attending to the shipment of the cargo. And he must show the same thing, though he was on board as supercargo.

It is not enough that one of the owners is on board as a supercargo; and where this was the case, and the master of a general ship receipted dollars for transportation, without the knowledge of the owners, and which were not put in the freight list, the money being stolen on the voyage; held, that the owners were liable.

What shall be deemed a general ship.

Citations—Abbott, part 2, ch. 2, secs. 2, 3, 4; Rep. t. Hardw., 83, 183; Abb. Ship., 119; 19 Johns., 236; 11 Mass., 99.

ON ERROR from the C. P. of N. Y. The action below was *assumpsit*, by Green against the Wards. The declaration contained the common money counts.

On the trial, it appeared that the defendants were, June 27, 1825, the owners of the ship Morgiana, James Allen master. The plaintiff below gave in evidence the following receipt, signed by the master: "Received of Benjamin Green (the plaintiff below) two hundred and seventy Spanish dollars, deliverable at New York, dangers of the seas excepted, unto the said Benjamin Green, one ½ *per cent.* primage.

New Orleans, the 27th of June, 1825." On this testimony the plaintiff below rested.

The defendants below then gave in evidence the freight list of the ship, dated June 28, 1825, containing various articles, in the name of various shippers, on various consignments, which did not include the dollars. Also a receipt signed by one of the defendants, Henry Ward, of even date with the above receipt, acknowledging the receipt of $15 of the plaintiff, as his, the plaintiff's passage money to N. Y. in the steerage. They further proved that the plaintiff below was a passenger in the ship to N. Y., and that Henry Ward sailed as supercargo. And it was admitted by the parties that the contract to transport the specie was made with the master without the knowledge of Henry Ward, the part owner and supercargo, and that he knew nothing of the contract till after the master alleged that the specie had been stolen.

The court below charged that the master of a vessel is, when abroad, generally the agent of the owners, and is, from his station in the vessel, empowered to attend to the shipment of the cargo, and make contracts in relation to **174***] *the freight, which are binding upon the owners. That when an owner is on board, and exclusively attending to the shipment of the cargo abroad, and to making contracts in relation to the freight, the owners are not bound by any contract of the master in relation to the freight. But it is incumbent on the owner to show, in order not to be affected by the engagements of the master, that he was thus exclusively attending to the shipments and the making of contracts; and that, although by an arrangement between one of the defendants and his copartner, the other defendant, the latter was made the supercargo of the vessel, yet, being at the same time owner, the same proof that he was exclusively attending to the shipment and the making of contracts was necessary. Otherwise, the contracts of the master are binding. Under this direction, the jury found for the plaintiff below; and the defendants below excepted to the charge, and prosecuted their writ of error, on the judgment and a bill of exceptions.

Mr. J. L. Graham, for the plaintiffs in error. The owner being present at the time of the theft, the carrier is not liable. (2 Com. Cont., 330.) To make the owner liable, the property should have been mentioned in the freight list. That the whole was a matter between the bailor and the master, is evident from the payment of primage, which is defined to be a duty at the water side, payable to the master and mariners. (Jac. L. Dict., Primage.) The payment of passage money by Green to Henry Ward, one of the defendants below, shows that the former knew in what character the latter was acting. The defendants below were not bound to show that the supercargo and part owner attended exclusively to the shipments. *Walter* v. *Brewer*, 11 Mass., 99, is in point for the plaintiffs in error. See, also, *Boucher* v. *Lawson*, Rep., *t.* Hardw., 83; *Id.*, 183; Poth. Mar. Cont., Cushing ed., 27. The owners can only be chargeable on a bill of lading, to which the receipt was not equivalent. It does not mention the name of the vessel. Allen did not sign as master, and no freight is specified.

Mr. P. W. Radcliff, contra. Any [***175** objection not taken at the trial cannot be raised here. (15 Johns., 338.) The owner of the property being present, the rate of primage, and receipt not amounting to a bill of lading, are out of the question. So, whether the verdict be against evidence. The argument is confined to the point in the bill of exceptions. (14 Johns., 304; 2 Cai., 168; 8 Johns., 495.) Of course, the court have nothing to do with the objection that the property was not mentioned in the freight list.

The only question really presented by the bill of exceptions is, whether the master's contract, under the circumstances of the case, was obligatory upon the owners. He may bind his owner for the carriage of goods within the ship's usual employment. (Abb. Ship., pt. 2, ch. 2, secs. 2-4.) The owner was on board as supercargo only; having nothing to do with the employment of the ship or procuring of freight. She was a general ship for the carriage of merchandise, not sent out for a special purpose, or intended exclusively, or at all, for the owner's use. This appears from the freight list. *King* v. *Lenox*, 19 Johns., 235, shows the true rule and its exceptions. So, also, *Walter* v. *Brewer*, 11 Mass., 99, cited on the other side. The court below laid down the law correctly.

Curia, per SAVAGE, *Ch. J.* Abbott on Shipping, in treating of the liability of the owners, on the contracts of the master, states that the owners are bound to the performance of every lawful contract made by the master, relative to the usual employment of the ship. The master is the confidential agent of the owners at large, and is intrusted with the conduct and management of the ship. It often happens that no contract can be made with the owners personally, as where the ship is in a place distant from their residence. But even when the ship is at the place of their residence, and is intended to be employed as a general ship, it rarely happens that the owners interfere with the receipt of the cargo; and without doubt they are legally bound to perform every contract made by the *master relative to the usual [***176** employment of such a ship. (Abb., part 2, ch. 2, secs. 2-4.)

A general ship is defined to be one in which the master or owners engage separately with a number of persons, unconnected with each other, to convey their respective goods to the place of the ship's destination.

There can be no doubt that, in this case, the ship was a general one, and the owners are liable for the performance of the master's contract, unless they are discharged by reason of one of the owners being present at New Orleans, and acting as supercargo.

The case of *Boucher* v. *Lawson*, Rep. *t.* Hardw., 83, 183; S. C., Abb. Ship., 119, was an action against the owner, to recover the value of Portugal coin, delivered to the master at Lisbon, to be conveyed to London; and of which, by the usage of that particular trade, the master was to receive the freight to his own use—and which he had embezzled. The court held, that if it had appeared that the ship was employed in carrying goods for hire, the owner would have been answerable for the loss. But as that did not appear, and possibly the ship might have been sent for a special purpose, the master could not charge the owners, by taking in goods contrary to his duty.

In the case of *King* v. *Lenox*, 19 Johns., 236, the general liability of the owner is asserted as I have before stated it, but in that case the owner was held not responsible, because the ship was freighted wholly by him. The master, therefore, had no authority to receive goods on freight. The contract was, consequently, deemed to be made with the master in his individual capacity, and not as agent of the owners. In the case of *Walter* v. *Brewer*, 11 Mass., 99, the owner went in the ship, intending to freight her himself. The ship was not advertised for freight, nor did she bring any from Montevideo; but the cargo belonged to the owner; except the bales of skins which the master received from the plaintiff, and stowed away secretly. The judge instructed the jury that the owners were generally liable on the **177***] contracts of *the masters abroad on the voyage; but as the owner had gone in the ship to procure a cargo, as the ship was not put up for freight, and as the defendant was not consulted, but the goods were taken on board without his knowledge, he was not liable. But had the owner known of the shipment of the goods before he left Montevideo, he would have been accountable.

On a motion for a new trial, the court concurred generally in the doctrine pronounced at the trial—that the owner is not liable for goods clandestinely taken on board by the master, the former being present, and having the management of the voyage himself, leaving nothing to the master but the care of sailing and directing the ship, especially when the ship is not a freighting ship. But, even under such circumstances, the court declared they would hold the owner liable, if he knew the goods were received on board upon freight. And the judge delivering the opinion of the court, concurs with the doctrine of *King* v. *Lenox*, that in such a case it is reasonable that the owner of goods, who avails himself of the master's privilege, should be holden to trust to his individual responsibility.

In neither of these cases was the ship a general one; and Abbott thinks it makes no difference that the goods are taken as part of the master's privilege, because it is immaterial whether he is paid by a privilege or by wages.

The case under consideration is not like either of those cited. Here the ship was a general one. She was freighted by sundry persons. The cargo did not belong to the owner. The master, therefore, had authority to receive goods on freight, unless he was prohibited by the owner's presence.

I can see no error in the opinion of the judge who delivered the charge in the court below. He stated that the master of a vessel, when abroad, is the agent of the owners, and has power to make contracts in relation to freight, which are binding upon the owners; that when an owner is on board, and exclusively attending to the shipment of the cargo, he is not bound by the master's contract. But to relieve himself from liability, he must show the fact **178***] *that he was exclusively attending to the shipment of the cargo. This doctrine seems to me to be supported by the authorities referred to, and is reasonable in itself. If the jury did not correctly apply the law to the facts of the case, the remedy is not by bill of exceptions and writ of error.

I am of opinion that the judgment of the court below should be affirmed.

Judgment affirmed.

Cited in—1 Daly, 2; 2 Wood & M., 316, 318.

JACKSON, ex dem. LEAH HENRY,
v.
THOMPSON.

Wills—Devise to "Children"—Survivors Take in Exclusion of Grandchildren.

B. devised his real estate to his four children, in fee, in four separate parcels; and provided that if any of them should die without issue of their body or bodies, lawfully begotten, the share of the deceased should be equally divided between the survivors. Two having died with, and one without issue, leaving one surviving, held, that the latter took the whole of the deceased child's share in exclusion of the grandchildren of the testator.

Such a limitation is good by way of executory devise.

Proof by a subscribing witness that he, with two others, saw executed, and that they witnessed a will of land which he had seen in the surrogate's office, which was identified with the one produced on the trial: though the witness was too dim of sight to see it at the trial; held, sufficient proof of the will on a trial at law.

A will of lands, with a corresponding possession of 40 years under it, need not be proved by the subscribing witness. It is proper evidence as an ancient deed.

One claiming through deeds which recite a will, is estopped to question its genuineness.

Citations—1 Phil. Ev., 404; 3 Johns., 292, 297; 3 Johns. Cas., 283; 17 Johns., 161; 14 Johns., 224; 16 Johns., 382; 20 Johns., 483; 2 Cow., 333; 11 Johns., 246.

EJECTMENT, for a lot of ground in Oak St., in the 4th ward of the City of N. Y., tried at the N. Y. Circuit, Jan. 19, 1826, before Edwards, *Circuit J.*, when a verdict was taken for the plaintiff, subject to the opinion of the court.

The lessor of the plaintiff claimed under the will of Elias Brevoort, her father, deceased.

The facts are sufficiently stated in the opinion of the court.

For the plaintiff, to show that the will was duly proved, or receivable as an ancient will, were cited 3 Johns., 292; 3 Johns. Cas., 283; Phil. Ev., 349; *Id.*, 385, *note;* 4 T. R., 707. That the defendant's title deeds, referring to and reciting the will as the source of title, estopped him to question it, were cited 14 Johns., 224; 17 *Id.*, 161; 3 Johns. Cas., 174. That on the death of John Brevoort, the premises in question vested in the lessor of the plaintiff, as the sole surviving child of the devisor, were

---

NOTE.—*Wills—Construction of the word "children" —Executory devises.*

The word "children" does not, prima facie, *include grandchildren or other remoter offspring.* Jackson v. Staats, 11 Johns., 337; Sherman v. Sherman, 3 Barb., 385; Tier v. Pennell, 1 Edw. Ch., 354; Mowatt v. Carow, 7 Paige, 328; Hone v. Van Schaick, 3 N. Y., 538; Low v. Harmony, 72 N. Y., 408; Palmer v. Horn, 84 N. Y., 516; Walker v. Williamson, 25 Ga., 549; Hopson v. Skipp, 7 Bush, 644; Moors v. Stone, 19 Gratt., 130; Denny v. Closs, 4 Ired. Eq., 102; Feit v. Vanatta, 21 N. J. Eq., 84; Turner v. Withers, 23 Md., 18; Osgood v. Lovering, 33 Me., 464; Tillinghast v. DeWolf, 8 R. I., 69; Gable's Appeal, 40 Pa. St., 231; Castner's Appeal, 88 Pa. St., 478; Thomson v. Ludington, 104 Mass., 193. See, also, Crooke v. Brooke-

cited 16 Johns., 382; 2 *Id.*, 483; 2 Cow., 333; **179***] *3 Johns., 292; 11 *Id.*, 337. That the lessor's death, since the commencement of this suit, did not abate it, was cited 8 Johns., 495.

Mr. H. S. Mackey, for the plaintiff.

Mr. J. Dill, contra.

Curia, per SUTHERLAND, *J.* The lessor of the plaintiff, Leah Henry, was the only surviving child of Elias Brevoort, when this suit was commenced. She has since died, but the defendant expressly waives all question as to the effect of her death upon this suit.

Elias Brevoort died prior to Apr. 27, 1777, leaving four children—Henry, John, Jacomentye and Leah. By his will, he made a specific distribution of his real estate, in fee, among his children, in nearly equal proportions, and at the end of his will inserted this provision: "It is my mind and will, that if any of my children shall depart this life, without issue of their body, or bodies, lawfully begotten, that the share or portion of such, so departing this life, shall be equally divided, share and share alike, between the surviving ones." Henry and Jacomentye died leaving issue. John died in Sept., 1825, without children, leaving his sister, Leah, the lessor of the plaintiff, the sole survivor of the four children of her father, Elias Brevoort. As such survivor, she claims John's share of her father's estate under the clause in the will, which I have stated.

1. The will was properly admitted in evidence. Its execution was sufficiently proved by Richardson, one of the subscribing witnesses. He testified, positively and distinctly, to every fact necessary to show a valid execution of the will. His recollection, as to every circumstance, was clear. Being more than ninety years of age, he could not see to read and, therefore, could not testify upon the trial to his signature as a witness. But he swore that he had seen the will in the surrogate's office and that he then read and recognized his signature as genuine. As to the identity of the will produced **180***] on the *trial, and that which the witness had seen in the surrogate's office, there was no dispute.

2. But the will required no proof by a subscribing witness. It was made in 1774; and the testator died prior to Apr. 27, 1777; for, on that day, probate of the will was made before Carey Ludlow, the then surrogate of N. Y.; and, at the trial, possession was shown to have been in conformity to the will, from the death of the testator. Here, then, is a will and a corresponding possession, of more than 40 years. Under such circumstances, no proof by subscribing witnesses was necessary. 1 Phil. Ev., 404, Gould ed., 1823, *note a; Jackson* v. *Blanshan*, 3 Johns., 292; *Jackson* v. *Laroway*, 3 Johns. Cas., 283.

3. The deeds under which the defendant claims the premises in question, refer to the will of Elias Brevoort, as the source of title. The defendant may, therefore, be considered as estopped from denying the genuineness and validity of the will. (17 Johns., 161; 14 *Id.*, 224.)

That John's share of his father's estate, upon the death of the former without issue, vested in the lessor of the plaintiff in fee simple, as the sole survivor of the four children of the testator, is clearly established by the cases which have given a construction to the will of Medcef Eden. *Jackson* v. *Anderson*, 16 Johns., 382; *Lion* v. *Burtis*, 20 *Id.*, 483; *Wilkes* v. *Lion*, 2 Cow., 333. The terms used are the same in both wills, and it is impossible to distinguish this case from those cited. The limitation over was good as an executory devise.

The grandchildren of the testator, the children of Henry and Jacomentye, are not surviving children within the intention of the testator. *Jackson* v. *Blanshan*, 3 Johns., 297, per Spencer *J.; Jackson* v. *Staats*, 11 *Id.*, 337.

The plaintiff is entitled to judgment.

Judgment for the plaintiff.

Cited in—3 Wend., 225; 4 Wend., 282; 1 Barb., 580; 32 Barb., 333; 20 How. Pr., 45.

---

*CORLIES AND WIDDIFIELD [*181
v.
CUMMING.

Factors—Advances on Goods—Remedy for Reimbursement—Note taken by Factor for Sale of Several Parcels of Goods Belonging to Several of his Principals—Remedy of Principals.

The sale of several parcels of goods by a factor, belonging to several of his principals respectively, on a credit, to one person, and taking one note from the vendee for the whole, payable to himself, will not, *per se*, render him liable to his principals. The note does not extinguish the demand for goods sold, but leaves each principal to his usual remedy.

Nor will the factor's giving up the note, and taking others, payable earlier, or at the same time with the first, render him liable, provided he still retain the name of the vendee, either as maker or indorser.

A factor advancing money, and having goods in his hands, is not confined in his remedy for his advances to the mere fund deposited, but gives a joint credit to the fund and the person of his principal; yet, from the nature of the contract, resort must first be had to the fund, if it can be made available.

Citations—1 Gall., 360; Cowp., 255; 6 Johns., 69; 5 Johns., 68; 7 Mass., 36.

ASSUMPSIT, tried at the N. Y. Circuit, June 24, 1824, before Edwards, *Circuit J.*

---

ing, 2 Vern., 106; Reeves v. Brynser, 4 Ves., 698; Rayle v. Hamilton, 4 Ves., 439; Earl of Orford v. Churchill, 3 V. & B., 59.

Nor does the word "children" include either step-children or adopted children. Cromer v. Pinckney, 3 Barb. Ch., 466; Barnes v. Greenzebach, 1 Edw., Ch., 41; *In re* Hallet, 8 Paige, 375; Cutter v. Doughty, 23 Wend., 513; Sydnor v. Palmer, 29 Wis., 226; Schafer v. Eneu, 54 Pa. St., 304; Johnson's Appeal, 88 Pa. St., 346. See, also, Kimball v. Story, 108 Mass., 382.

In the absence of children, and for other reasons, the word is sometimes held to include grandchildren. This construction is generally applied where the will would otherwise be inoperative and where the intent is clear. Mowatt v. Carow, 7 Paige, 328; Tier v. Pennell, 1 Edw. Ch., 354; Marsh v. Hague, 1 Edw., 174; Cromer v. Pinckney, 3 Barb. Ch., 466; Prowitt v. Rodman, 37 N. Y., 42; Houghton v. Kendall, 89 Mass. (7 Allen), 72; Sorver v. Berndt, 10 Pa. St., 213; Whitehead v. Lassiter, 4 Jones Eq., 79; Hughes v. Hughes, 12 B. Mon., 115; Smith v. Case, 2 Desaus. Eq., 123. Compare Hone v. Van Schaick, 3 N. Y., 538.

It may include descendants however remote. Prowitt v. Rodman, 37 N. Y., 42.

The word "children" does not include illegitimate children. Gardner v. Heyer, 2 Paige, 11.

See, generally, 2 Jarm. Wills, 147-150, and authorities there cited.

Executory devises. See Moffat v. Strong, 10 Johns., 12, *note;* Jackson v. Bull, 10 Johns., 19, *note;* Fosdick v. Cornell, 1 Johns., 440, *cases cited.*

At the trial the following facts appeared: The plaintiffs being commission merchants in Philadelphia, the defendant left with them in the autumn of 1820 and winter of 1820 and 1821, a quantity of cheese to sell on commission. In Dec., 1820, the plaintiffs advanced to the defendant $900 upon the cheese, for a balance of between $300 and $400 of which this action was brought. The plaintiffs made various sales of the cheese, and, among others, Mar. 9, 1821, sales to one Kellogg, on a credit of 90 days, to the amount of $799.53. They, at the same time, sold him other cheese, belonging to another of their principals, one Brown, and took from Kellogg one note, payable to themselves, for both. After the sale the plaintiffs changed the first note for two notes drawn by one Dickson, and indorsed by Kellogg, for part of the sum due to the defendant, and Kellogg's sole note for the residue. But all these notes were payable a few days earlier than the note given upon the sale. The testimony was somewhat doubtful as to the fact of the price for Brown's cheese being included in the first note. The judge charged the jury that if they believed this to be the fact, they should find for the defendant; and they found for him accordingly, stating this to be the ground of their verdict.

Various other evidence was given, and questions raised upon the trial, and included in the case made by the plaintiffs, on which a motion was now made for a new trial. But, as the above, with those which are stated in the opin-
182*] ion *of the court, are the only facts material to the law of the case, it is not ueeessary to give any others.

The principal points now argued were whether the defendant was entitled to his verdict on either of the grounds above stated, viz.: the joining of the demand against Kellogg in the same note with that against Brown, or the subsequent change of security.

Messrs. Ketchum and *Fessenden*, for the plaintiffs, insisted that he was not, and that the plaintiffs' liability should stand on the ordinary question between factor and principal; that is, whether the factor has discharged his duty with becoming vigilance and fidelity, or whether he has been guilty of fraud or gross negligence. 3 Cai., 226; Pal. Ag., 26; *M'Kinstry* v. *Pearsall*, 3 Johns., 319, 321; *Ingraham* v. *Gibbs*, 2 Dall., 136, *note;* 4, Dall., 136, S. C.; *Goodenow* v. *Tyler*, 7 Mass., 36; 1 Liv. Ag., 85; Willes, 400; *Favenc* v. *Bennett*, 11 East, 36; 5 Com. Dig., Merchant, p. 76, new ed.; 15 Ves., 439; 2 Bl. Com., 405; 4 Cow., 205; 1 Cai., 43; 6 Johns., 69; *Russell* v. *Hankey*, 6 T. R., 12; 1 Pick., 343; *Burrill* v. *Phillips*, 1 Gall., 360. That an action will lie, without first resorting to the fund pledged, they cited 1 Str., 919, and 1 Gall., 362, 363.

Mr. D. Lord, Jr., contra. The plaintiffs cannot maintain this action till they show that the fund has failed them without their fault. (17 Johns., 38.)

Blending in one security the sales of the defendant's property with those of another made the plaintiffs accountable for the amount of the sale. By changing the securities the plaintiffs made themselves accountable. These are rules of law. Toll. L. E., 425, tit. *Devastavit; Wall* v. *Buckley*, 2 Ch. Rep., 97; *Floyd* v. *Day*, 3 Mass., 403; *Wren* v. *Kirton*, 11 Ves., 377; *Massey* v. *Banner*, 1 Jac. & W., 241. In *Jackson* v. *Baker*, C. C. U. S., Apr., 1806, M. S., a note of which is furnished in Whart. Pa. Dig., Agent, 28, it was decided that if a factor *sell on credit, and take a bond for the [***183**
amount, blending with it another sum due to himself, the principal is not obliged to wait till the factor has recovered the money, but may sue the factor at once.(*a*)

Curia*, per WOODWORTH, *J.* The [*184**
defendant deposited a quantity of cheese with the plaintiffs, as factors, upon which they made an advance of $900. Whether the plaintiffs can sustain an action to recover back the advance, before any attempt is made to reimburse themselves by a sale, it is not material to decide. If it be admitted they can, the question arises,

(*a*) The following note of this case has been furnished to the counsel by the Hon. Richard Peters, and was produced on the argument of the principal case:

JACKSON v. BAKER. } Circuit Court of the United States; Pennsylvania District, April, 1806.

The plaintiff consigned a number of boxes of hats to the defendant to sell. The only question in dispute was as to one box which the defendant sold on credit for $211, the amount of which he included in a bond taken to himself from the purchaser for a much larger sum due to the defendant personally.

Mr. Hallowell, for the defendant, insisted that the plaintiff ought not to recover the $211, as he had not yet received it from the person who purchased, and that his taking a bond for the amount made no difference. Price v. Ralston, 2 Dall., 60.

The Court stopped *Mr. Meredith*, who was for the plaintiff, and informed the jury that the defendant ought either to have paid this money to the plaintiff, or enable him to look to the purehaser; but that he had not done the former, and had disabled himself from doing the latter. That the plaintiff could not have sued the purchaser, because the simple contract debt was extinguished by the bond; and the defendant, having mixed the debt due to himself and to the plaintiff in one bond taken in his own name, that the plaintiff had no remedy on the bond: and it does not appear that any offer was made to assign the bond. If the plaintiff cannot recover from the defendant now, when can he recover? Sue him when he pleases, the defendant may keep him at arm's length by saying, "I have not yet collected the money;" whereas, the debt having been originally due to the plaintiff, he might have sued for it at any time in his own name, if he had not been prevented by the conduct of the defendant, who, if he is the cause why the plaintiff cannot sue the real debtor, makes himself the debtor.

The jury found, accordingly, for the whole sum.

JACKSON v. BAKER.

Rule for a new trial: 1st. Because the defendant was not answerable until he should have received the money. 2 Dall., 60.

2. That *indebitatus assumpsit*, for money had and received, will not lie in this case.

On the first point, I repeated what was stated in the charge to the jury.* 2d. That by the conduct of the defendant, in extinguishing the original debt and destroying all privity between the plaintiff and the person to whom the goods were sold, he is to be considered as a receiver of that debt to the use of the plaintiff, as much so as if he had released the debt.

Rule discharged.

* The principal ground used on the argument for a new trial was that the plaintiff ought to have demanded the bond before he brought the suit. The court, in answer, observed that if a bond had been taken for this debt alone, the argument might have weight in it. But, as it was mixed with the defendant's money, such demand was unnecessary, because the plaintiff could not have compelled the defendant to deliver the evidence of a debt due to the defendant, though, in part, it contained money due to the plaintiff.

have they made themselves liable for the cheese sold? If they have, it becomes a subject of set-off, which more than satisfies their claim.

As to the law on this point, I entirely concur in the principle laid down by *Mr. J.* Story, in *Burrill* v. *Phillips*, 1 Gall., 360; that the mere relation of principal and factor does not confine the rights of the latter to recover for advances, to the mere fund deposited; but that such advances are made on the joint credit of the fund and the person—to which I would add this qualification, that from the nature of the contract, resort must first be had to the fund, if it can be made available, before the principal is liable.

There does not appear to be any sufficient ground, from the evidence, for charging the plaintiffs with negligence, or the want of reasonable care and prudence, in making the sale to Kellogg. The cause was fairly submitted to the jury; who, by their verdict, have, in this respect, approved the plaintiff's conduct.
185*] *The judge, in his charge, submitted to the jury a question of fact, upon which he expressed an opinion, that if the plaintiffs did, in the first instance, include the amount of the defendant's cheese, with that of another person, in the same note, they ought to find for the defendant. They found for the defendant, and stated the ground of their verdict to be, that the plaintiffs took from Kellogg one note, for the amount of the defendant's and Brown's cheese.

On this statement two questions arise: 1. Whether the verdict is against the weight of evidence. 2. If it is not, whether the law was correctly laid down by the judge.

Before I consider these questions, I will dispose of that part of the case, in which it appears that, a considerable time after the sale to Kellogg, the plaintiff, for reasons not stated, changed the notes originally taken, and accepted in their stead notes drawn by Dickson and indorsed by Kellogg, and one note drawn by the latter. These notes were all payable a few days before the expiration of the 90 days, the credit originally given to the purchaser. It is probable the exchange was made to improve the security. It might have been beneficial, but could not be prejudicial. Whether drawer or indorser, Kellogg was still holden. The time of payment was not extended, and the securities were equally available to the defendant, with that taken in the first instance. The plaintiffs did not, by this act, therefore, make themselves liable for the loss.

As to the question of fact, Meade testified, in answer to the sixth interrogatory, that the plaintiff sold to Kellogg a quantity of cheese belonging to one Brown, the amount of which was included in the same note with the defendant's, and that the plaintiffs guarantied to Brown his share of the note. This witness was a clerk of the plaintiffs, at the time of the sale, and so continued until 1823. He did not know what became of the note, nor did he recollect the date or amount, but he believed it had 90 days to run. As to this witness, it may be observed that, from his situation, correct infor-
186*] mation as to the manner *of taking the note was to be expected. Kellogg, the purchaser, swears that he gave his note to the plaintiffs for a quantity of cheese, the amount a few cents short of $800; that about the same time, and a little before, he purchased another parcel to upwards of $800, and gave his note to the plaintiffs. That after the notes became due, and in the summer following, he made an exchange, by giving Dickson's note and his own note for a part, payable to a clerk of the plaintiffs, on demand. This evidence is certainly contradictory to Meade's. The jury have passed on their relative credibility. There is ground to question the accuracy of Kellogg's recollection. I think it evident he was mistaken in supposing he gave a note, on the exchange, to the plaintiffs' clerk, or that it was payable on demand. The notes exhibited to Meade, on his examination, were Dickson's notes to Kellogg, and Kellogg's note to the plaintiffs, each at 90 days. They correspond in amount with the sales, and are presumed to be the notes referred to. It is, therefore, apparent that perfect reliance cannot be placed on Kellogg's recollection. The jury reposed more confidence in Meade's testimony. It was within their province. I cannot say that the verdict was not warranted by the evidence.

As to the next question, I am inclined to think the plaintiffs are not liable by reason of including the two demands in one note. A factor is not obliged to disclose to his purchaser the name of his principal, or that he sells as factor. He may or may not take an instrument in writing as evidence of the debt. He may maintain an action in his own name for the price of the goods, and give a valid discharge. (Cowp., 255.) It is equally certain that the principal may come forward at any time before payment to the factor, and arrest his right. An action may be supported against the vendee in his (the principal's) name. (*Id.*) The factor has authority to sell on credit, for the period usual in the market, unless prohibited by his instructions (6 Johns., 69), and will not be responsible, if he appear to have acted with reasonable care and prudence, *and has not been guilty of breach of [***187**
orders, negligence or fraud.

Now, then, can the fact that a note was taken for two demands be material, unless the principal has been injured by this? If the factor had omitted to take any note, he would not, for that omission, be responsible. The sale in that case would have been charged in his books; the principal might sustain an action on it in his own name, or give information to the purchaser and forbid payment to the factor. All these rights remained after the note was given. It is well settled that giving a promissory note for goods sold is not a payment or extinguishment of the demand, unless such was the agreement of the parties. (5 Johns., 68.) The defendant then, had, notwithstanding the note, a remedy against Kellogg by action. Why should the taking of a note, which the factor might justifiably have omitted, be considered an act absolutely charging the factor? All the remedy the principal had a right to claim still remained. If it had appeared that the principal had demanded the note taken for his goods and the factor had refused to assign it, or to allow the principal the benefit of it, that would present a different question. Then, indeed, the imprudence of having taken but one note for several demands, would be manifest, inas-

much as the factor thus put it out of his power to assign to each of his principals. By pursuing such a course, he incurred the risk of not being able to perform what his principals had a right to demand. Although not required to take a note in the first instance, yet having taken it, the principal would be entitled to the security, so as to enable him to pursue the course deemed advisable. But that case never occurred. Kellogg became insolvent. He was unable to pay anything. Whether prosecuted on the note, or for goods sold, the result would be the same. The defendant never requested an assignment. The note was of no value. From the evidence, it is clear that the defendant has not sustained, nor was it possible that he could sustain, any injury by this act of the factor. He has never demanded the note or intimated a desire to obtain an assign-
188*] ment. *He has not put the factor in default by a refusal. His claim rest singly on this—that the amount of the defendant's sales was included in one note with Brown's demand. I apprehend the principle contended for by the counsel for the defendant cannot be supported, either on the ground of expediency, policy or justice. I am not aware that in a case like the present, it has ever been recognized.

In the case of *Goodenow* v. *Tyler*, 7 Mass., 36, the factor took a note payable to himself. By the laws of Mass., where a negotiable note is taken to secure the payment of money due by simple contract, it is merged in the note. Yet it was held that the factor was not answerable to his principal for the value of the goods; that although the remedy against the purchaser was changed, yet the relation between principal and factor was not affected.

My opinion is, that, independent of usage, the plaintiffs did not, by taking the note, make themselves liable. A new trial must be granted, with costs to abide the event.

New trial granted.

Cited in—5 Barb., 338; 8 Barb., 339; 14 Barb., 606; 1 Sweeny, 632; 129 Mass., 303; 46 Sup. Ct., 534, 535; 33 Wis., 502; 5 Am. Rep., 495 (43 Miss., 288); 37 Am. Rep., 358 (129 Mass., 301).

189*] *HARLOW *v.* HUMISTON.

Bill of Exceptions—What Sufficient—Presumption of Regularity—Highways—Width of—Obstruction of by Servant.

Where a bill of exceptions, taken in the C. P., stated the charge of the court upon points of law, and that the jury found a verdict and that the party excepted; held, that the bill was sufficiently pointed to bring the charge in question on error; and though, in the order of statement, the exception appeared to be subsequent to the verdict, yet held, that it should be intended that the exception was taken at the proper time; otherwise, the judges, it is to be presumed, would not have signed it.

Though the Statute, 2 R. L., 277, requires public roads to be laid out four rods wide, and where they are laid out under the statute they are to be deemed of that width; yet, where they are claimed not as being laid out under the statute, but by reason of a user for twenty years or more, they may be less than four rods wide.

And in trespass, for laying wood in a highway of the latter sort, by which the plaintiff's horse, being frightened, ran upon it and was killed, the road, in fact, being but 2 and 2½ rods wide; and it being questionable on the evidence whether the wood was laid within the road as established by use; though it lay within the road fence on the land of the defendant; held, that it should have been left to the jury to find whether the wood was in the highway.

All the land within a highway fence is not necessarily subject to the right of way, and if not, it may be occupied by the owner. And if he place an obstruction there and another be injured by it, he is not, therefore, liable.

And though such obstruction be within the highway he is not liable, unless the person injured exercise ordinary diligence to avoid it.

If a man's servant, in the ordinary course of his business, obstruct the highway, from which a traveler receives special injury, the master is liable.

The question seems to be, whether the act be such that he can justify himself to his master; if he may it shall be deemed in the course of his business as a servant, and the master is liable.

Thus, where the master had been accustomed to lay his wood in a certain place for several years, and his servant laid the master's wood in the same place, while the latter was sick, and without his knowledge; held, that it was an act in the course of his business as a servant.

Citations—19 Johns., 385; 11 East, 60, 61.

ON ERROR from the Washington C. P., where the cause was tried on appeal from a justice's court.

The action was case, by Humiston against Harlow, for a nuisance in wrongfully placing logs and tree-tops in the public highway, by means of which, the plaintiff's horse, being frightened, ran upon a tree-top and was killed.

On the trial, it appeared that the tree-top was laid by the servant of the defendant below, during the defendant's sickness, and without his knowledge, in a place claimed by the plaintiff below to be in the public highway. It had, however, long been occupied by the defendant himself, as a place for laying his wood, and the supposed road ran through his land. The defendant below contended that, though within the road fence, the tree-top was not within the bounds of the public highway. Evidence was given upon this point, and as to the manner in which the injury *to [*190 the horse was occasioned, while the plaintiff's servant was riding him; but as the cause here turned on the question, whether the charge given by the court below was correct in point of law, it is not necessary to notice the evidence further than it appears in the opinion of the court.

The court below charged the jury that all the land not fenced in was a public highway, and if it had been ten rods wide, the defendant had no right to any part of it; but had always been a trespasser upon the public, in laying his wood within the highway fence, though he had ocenpied the place for 38 years; and it made no difference that the width was greater from the tree top than the ordinary width. They also charged that, though the defendant was sick, and knew nothing of the act of his servant in laying the tree-top there, he was accountable.

The defendant below took exception to the charge; and the bill of exceptions, after detailing the evidence and the charge of the court, concluded thus: the jury retired and returned, and delivered their verdict in favor of the plaintiff for $50 damages; to all which charge the counsel for the appellant (the defendant below) excepted.

Judgment for the plaintiff below.

M. Z. R. Shipherd, for the plaintiff in error, cited Vin. Abr., Actions, Nuisance, N. *b*, pl. 4; *Blyth* v. *Topham*, Cro. Jac., 158; 2 R. L., 277; Bac. Abr., Nuisances, A; 2 Esp. *N. P.*,

Gould ed., 268, and *Butterfield* v. *Forrester*, 11 East, 60, 61.

Mr. B. Russell, contra, insisted that the bill of exceptions was too general and, therefore, went for nothing. A party cannot except to a charge, without saying in what particular. He should specify his ground of objection. (8 Johns., 495 ; 20 *Id.*, 357.) Besides, the exception was taken too late. On the face of the bill, it appears to have been after verdict. (10 Johns., 312.)

On the merits, he cited the Statute, sess. 40, ch. 43, sec. 3 ; 17 Johns., 280 ; 1 Cow., 78 ; 1 **191***] Stark., 285 ; Bac. *Abr., Actions on the Case, F; 2 Esp. *N. P.*, Gould ed., 217 ; and 1 Binn., 463.

Curia, per SAVAGE, *Ch. J.* It is objected that the exception came too late, and that it is too general. We must presume it was taken in time; otherwise, the court would not have allowed it. As to the generality of the exception, the objection cannot prevail. Take it in connection with the charge, and the points are sufficiently specific.

The court certainly erred in charging that all the land not inclosed in fence was a public highway, though it be ten rods wide. The public is entitled to the use of four rods only, at most, and a man may occupy his land without fencing it, if he chooses to do so. It would certainly be very bad husbandry, but he may plant and sow his grounds uninclosed, and may maintain trespass, too, against the owners of cattle which may injure him, unless there is some town regulation permitting cattle to run at large. (19 Johns., 385.)

It is no doubt a nuisance to dig a ditch or lay logs in the highway, and whoever sustains an injury from such a cause, without any fault of his own, may maintain an action against the author of it.

In the case of *Butterfield* v. *Forrester*, 11 East, 60, 61, the defendant had obstructed the street of Derby, to make some repairs to his house. The plaintiff rode furiously against the obstruction, when, with ordinary care, he might have avoided it ; and the court held that no action lay. Ld. Ellenborough remarks : "Two things must concur, to support this action—an obstruction in the road, by the fault of the defendant, and no want of ordinary care to avoid it on the part of the plaintiff." And he instances the case of persons traveling upon what is considered the wrong side of the road, which will not authorize another purposely to ride against them.

Negligence by the defendant, and ordinary care by the plaintiff, are necessary to sustain the action.

In this case, there was no want of care by the servant of the plaintiff below. The only **192***] question is, was there negligence *in the defendant below ? And this depends on the fact of the tree being in the road or not. The evidence, I think, shows it was not. The road appears to be but two and two and a half rods wide. Though the statute directs all roads thereafter laid out to be four rods wide, yet it does not appear that this road was ever laid out under that statute. This is probably a public road, from having been so used for more than 20 years.

The court below should have charged the jury to inquire whether the tree lay in the highway. If so, then the plaintiff below was entitled to recover. But if it was not within the highway, the verdict should have been for the defendant below. Though it may have been an act of carelessness in him to leave the tree so near the highway, yet, as the public have no right beyond the highway, whether inclosed or not, and as the defendant below had a right to use his land in any way not injurious to his neighbors or the public; and had used the place in question for a woodyard for near 40 years, he ought not to be responsible, though the plaintiff below may have unfortunately suffered.

If there was culpable negligence in this case, I consider the defendant below responsible. The master is accountable for the acts of his servant in and about his ordinary business. The servant, in this case, placed the wood where the defendant below, himself, had been accustomed to place his wood for near forty years. This was sufficient to justify the servant to the defendant below ; and, in my judgment, sufficient to render the latter responsible, if the act itself was reprehensible. I am of opinion that the judgment be reversed, and a *venire de novo* awarded by the court below.

Judgment reversed.

Cited in—23 Wend., 319, 447 ; 18 N. Y., 251 ; 20 N. Y., 52 ; 5 Barb., 338 ; 21 Barb., 79 ; 33 Barb., 416 ; 37 Barb., 405 ; 40 Barb., 382 ; 55 Barb., 246 ; 7 Bos., 135 ; 5 Duer, 25 ; 7 Rob., 422 ; 2 Hilt., 38 ; 5 Kan., 187 ; 38 Cal., 634 ; 40 Ill., 433 ; 35 Am. Dec., 577 ; 43 Am. Dec., 252 (25 Me., 39) ; 28 Am. Rep., 563 (43 Wis., 513).

---

*TUCKER *v.* IVES. [*193

Statute of Limitations—Interest not Allowed on Unliquidated Account—Money had and Received.

Where I. sold a note to T. and guarantied the payment, the note to be sued in the name of the payee, one O. T., who died, and I. became his administrator; and T., in I.'s name, sued on the note, obtained judgment against, and imprisoned the maker; and then I. compromised with him, taking notes with good sureties, and discharging him from imprisonment; and then I. received the money on the last notes; all which, except receiving the money, was more than six years before suit; but the money was received within six years; held, that I. was liable to T., as for money had and received, and that the claim was not barred by the Statute of Limitations.

Interest is not allowable on an unliquidated account for goods sold and delivered, where no time is fixed for payment; and there is no agreement to allow interest, express or implied.

An account, many items of which arose within six years before suit, is not barred by the Statute of Limitations as to those items which arose more than six years before suit. And this rule extends as well to the defendant's account, introduced by way of set-off, as to the plaintiff's.

Citations—3 Cow., 393; 4 Cow., 496.

ON motion, by the defendant, to set aside the report of referees, which was in favor of the plaintiff. The facts are stated in the opinion of the court.

Mr. W. H. Maynard, for the motion.

Messrs. F. C. White and *H. R. Storrs*, contra.

NOTE.—*Interest—When allowed on accounts.* For a full discussion, see Newell v. Griswold, 6 Johns., 45, *note.*

Curia, per SUTHERLAND, *J.* The application is founded principally upon the allegation that the whole of the plaintiff's demand, amounting to between $700 and $800, was barred by the Statute of Limitations, and ought not to have been allowed by the referees.

That demand originated as follows: Feb. 11, 1809, the defendant, Ives, sold and transferred to the plaintiff, a note made by one George Stowbridge to one Oliver Tuttle, for $291. Ives, at the same time, agreed to be responsible to Tucker for the amount of the note, if Stowbridge, the maker, should fail to pay it. He, at the same time, gave Tucker a memorandum, stating the transfer of the note, and his agreement to be responsible for the amount; and it was also stipulated, that if the note should be sued, it should be in the name of Tuttle, the payee. Tuttle died, and Ives, the defendant, became his administrator. In August Term of this court, 1810, Tucker recovered a judgment against Stowbridge upon the note, in the name of Ives, administrator, and issued a *ca. sa.* upon which Stowbridge was taken and imprisoned.

194*] *In June, 1811, while Stowbridge was still in custody on the *ca. sa.*, Ives made a compromise with him of this and other demands, amounting to about $700; took his notes with good sureties for the amount, and discharged him from his imprisonment. Those notes were subsequently prosecuted by Ives, and the whole amount has been collected and received by him within six years before this suit was commenced.

The question is, whether enough of this money to cover the judgment obtained by Tucker, in the name of Ives against Stowbridge, is not, in judgment of law, to be considered as received by Ives to the use of Tucker. The referees held that it was; and in this, I think, they were correct.

There is nothing in the case to show whether Tucker did or did not assent to the discharge of Stowbridge, and the new arrangement with him by Ives. But if it were necessary, in order to sustain a demand so obviously just, I think we should have a right to presume that Ives acted as the agent of Tucker, so far as his judgment was concerned; and that the security taken was, *pro tanto*, for his benefit, and taken with his knowledge and consent. If so, then Tucker had no cause of action against Ives, until he collected the money, or made himself responsible by some new promise, or some neglect of duty in enforcing the new securities obtained.

The fact that Tucker never enforced the guaranty of Stowbridge's note, given to Ives, strengthens the presumption that he assented to the arrangement made by Ives, and looked to the new security obtained, in the first instance.

Interest upon the judgment was properly allowed, from the time when it was obtained, although judgments did not carry interest until 1813. Stowbridge, who was examined as a witness, states that he gave his notes with two sureties to Ives, for the whole amount of Ives' claim against him. Although the judgment did not carry interest, it was perfectly just and proper that Stowbridge should have paid it; **195***] *and it is fairly to be presumed that it was claimed and allowed in the settlement.

The referees have obviously made a mistake in the amount of the receipt for the note of Ambrose Cone, of Aug. 1816. They read the receipt as for $24.35; whereas, it is clearly shown that it was for $74.35. There was no dispute as to this item, and the error originated in the obscurity of the writing. It would make a difference of $50, with interest from 1816, in favor of the defendant, and would have entitled him to a report in his favor; the report, as it now stands, being only $44 in favor of the plaintiff.

But I think the referees erred in allowing the defendant interest upon a portion of the account exhibited by way of set-off. If the orders mentioned in the account were for money, they would carry interest. But so far as the account consists of charges for goods, provisions and other articles sold to the plaintiff, I know no principle on which interest is allowable; there never having been a liquidation of the account, and there being no evidence of an agreement, expressed or implied, to pay it. (3 Cow., 393; 4 *Id.*, 496.) No time of payment appears to have been fixed, and there is no evidence of the credit usually given at the defendant's store, if he kept one, which does not affirmatively appear.

Many items of the account being within six years, the whole account is thus taken out of the Statute of Limitations, and the defendant is entitled to the allowance of it, with the above exception in relation to interest.

On the whole, I thing the report should be set aside, and the cause be again referred to the same referees.

Motion granted.

Cited in—7 Wend., 325; 79 N. Y., 7; 6 Hun, 81; 4 Barb., 47.

---

*THE PEOPLE OF THE STATE [*196 OF NEW YORK

v.

THE PRESIDENT, DIRECTORS AND COMPANY OF THE BANK OF NIAGARA.

Corporations—Quo Warranto *Lies against Corporation for Forfeiture of Franchises—Pleading—Forfeiture of Charter under Statute—Act of April 21, 1825, not Retroactive.*

Forms: of information in nature of a *quo warranto* against an incorporated bank, for exercising banking privileges without warrant;

Of plea, setting forth its Act of Incorporation, and organization under it;

Of three several replications: 1. That on, &c., the debts due by the Bank, over and above the amount of their specie deposits, exceeded three times the sum of the capital stock subscribed and paid in; rejoinder and issue thereon. 2. That they refused to redeem, &c., in specie, &c.; and yet not wholly discontinue their banking operations; rejoinder and issue thereon. 3. That they became insolvent, by the fraud, neglect or mismanagement of them, or of some or all of their officers or agents; stopped payment, and discontinued and closed their banking operations, for several years. Rejoinder to the last

---

NOTE.—Quo warranto *against corporation—Against usurper of a public office.*

An information, in the nature of a quo warranto, *lies against a corporation* for usurping a public franchise. See People v. Utica Ins. Co., 15 Johns., 358, *notes*; People v. Tibbets, 4 Cow., 358, 384, *notes*.

Against usurper of a public office. See People v. Van Slyck, 4 Cow., 297, *note*.

replication, admitting its truth, but saying that the Bank, on, &c., resumed payment, and continued it ever since that time. Demurrer and joinder.

Held, that the rejoinder was sufficient.

Under the Act incorporating the Bank of Niagara, sess. 39, ch. 167, the Bank did not forfeit its charter by insolvency and closing their banking operations, if, before they were prosecuted by the people, they resumed the payment of their debts.

Otherwise, if the prosecution had been commenced before they resumed payment.

The Statute, sess. 48, ch. 325, sec. 6, passed Apr. 21, 1825, limited such insolvency to one year. If it exceed that term, the Bank forfeits it charter. But this Act does not extend to cases of forfeiture happening before it passed.

An information in nature of a *quo warranto* against a corporation, for a forfeiture of its franchises, may be filed against it by its corporate name —may charge it generally with usurpation: and on the defendants' setting forth the Act of Incorporation, and justifying under it, the Attorney-General may reply the causes of forfeiture specially.

Such a replication is not a departure.

Citations—3 Harg. St. Tr., 545; 2 T. R., 575; Act, April 21, 1825, sess. 48, ch. 325, sec. 6.

ON information in nature of a *quo warranto*. The pleadings were as follows.

Albany County, *ss*: Samuel A. Talcott, Attorney-General of the people of the State of New-York, who sues for the said people in this behalf, comes here before the justices of the people of the State of New York of the Supreme Court of Judicature, of the same people, on the 8th day of March, 1825, in this same term of February; and for the said people, gives the said court here to understand and be informed, that the President, Directors and Company of the Bank of Niagara, at Buffalo, to wit: at Albany, in the County of Albany, for the space of six months now last past, and upwards, have used, and still do use, without any warrant, grant or charter, the following liberties, privileges and franchises, to wit: that of being a body politic and corporate in law, fact and name, by the name of the President, Directors and Company of the Bank of Niagara, and by the same name to plead and be impleaded, answered and be answered unto; and **197***] also the *following liberties, privileges and franchises, to wit: that of being or becoming proprietors of a bank or fund for the purpose of issuing notes, receiving deposits, making discounts and transacting other business which incorporated banks may lawfully transact by virtue of their respective Acts of Incorporation; and also, that of actually issuing notes, receiving deposits, making discounts, and carrying on banking operations and other moneyed transactions which are usually performed by incorporated banks, and which they alone have a right to do—all which said liberties, privileges and franchises the President, &c., aforesaid, during all the time aforesaid, have usurped, and still do usurp upon the said people, to their great damage and prejudice; whereupon, the said Attorney-General prays the advice of the said court in the premises, and due process of law against the President, Directors and Company of the Bank of Niagara, aforesaid, in this behalf, to be made, to answer to the said people, by what warrant they claim to have, use and enjoy the liberties, privileges and franchises aforesaid.

And now at this day, &c. (imparlance to August Term, 1825, and appearance of the defendants, by *Messrs. T. Van Vechten* and *E. Baldwin*, their attorneys).

And the said President, Directors and Company of the Bank of Niagara, having heard the said information read, complain that, under color of the premises in the said information contained, they are greatly vexed and disquieted; and this by no means justly; because, protesting that the said information and the matters therein contained, are insufficient in law, and that they need not, nor are they obliged, by the law of the land, to answer thereto: yet, for plea in this behalf, the said President, &c., say, that by a certain Act of the Legislature of the people of this State, passed on the 17th day of April, A. D. 1816, entitled "An Act to Incorporate the Bank of Niagara," they, the said President, &c., were ordained, constituted and declared to be, from time to time, and until the 1st day of January, A. D. 1832, a body corporate and politic, in fact *and in name, [***198** by the name of The President, Directors and Company of the Bank of Niagara; and by that name, it is enacted and declared, in and by the said Act, that they, the said President, &c., and their successors, until the said 1st day of January, A. D. 1832, may, and shall have succession; and shall be, in law, persons capable of suing and being sued, pleading and being impleaded, answering and being answered unto, defending and being defended, in all courts and places whatsoever, and in all manner of actions, suits complaints, matters and causes whatsoever; as by the said Act of the Legislature of the people of the State of New York, reference being thereunto had, will, among other things, more fully and at large appear. And the said President, &c., further say, that by the force of the said Act of the Legislature, and of the provisions thereof, they were created and constituted, and still continue to be, and are a body politic and corporate in fact and in name, and are entitled to do all lawful acts, and to have use and enjoy all the rights, liberties, privileges, franchises and immunities granted to them, and conferred upon them, by the said Act and by the law of the land; by virtue whereof, they, the said President, &c., for all the time in the said information in that behalf mentioned, have used and exercised and still do use and exercise, the liberties, privileges and franchises of a body politic and corporate, in law, fact and name, by the name of The President, Directors and Company of the Bank of Niagara; and by the same name, suing and being sued, pleading and being impleaded defending and being defended, answering and being answered unto, in all courts and places whatsoever, and also the liberties, privileges and franchises of being and becoming proprietors of a bank or fund, for the purpose of issuing notes, receiving deposits, making discounts and transacting other business which incorporated banks may lawfully transact, by virtue of their respective Acts of Incorporation; and of actually issuing notes, receiving deposits, making discounts and carrying on banking operations, and other moneyed transactions which are usually performed by incorporated *banks. And the said President, &c., [***199** have claimed, and used and enjoyed, and yet do claim to have, use and enjoy, all the liberties, privileges and franchises allowed to and conferred on them, in and by the aforesaid Act of the said Legislature, as it was and is lawful for them to do. Without this, that the said President, &c., during all or any part of the time mentioned in said information, have usurped or do still usurp the said liberties, privileges and franchises, mentioned in the said information, or any of them, upon the said people of the State of New York, in manner and form, as by the said information is above supposed; all which several matters and things, they, the said President, &c., are ready to verify, &c. Whereupon, they pray judgment, and that the aforesaid liberties, privileges and franchises, by them, claimed in manner aforesaid, may be allowed and adjudged to them, the said President, Directors and Company of the Bank of Niagara; and that they may be dismissed and discharged by the court here, of and from the premises above charged upon them, &c.

And the said Samuel A. Talcott, Attorney-General, having heard the said plea of the said President, &c., for the said people, &c., saith, that the said people ought not to be barred from having their aforesaid information against the said President, &c., because, he says, that the said President, &c., after their incorporation, did willfully, or negligently, so transact and manage the affairs of the said Corporation, that, afterwards, to wit: on the first day of January, 1818, the total amount of debts due by the said Corporation, over and above the specie, then actually deposited in the Bank, did exceed three times the sum of the capital stock, subscribed and actually paid into said Bank; and this, &c.

And the said Attorney-General further saith that the said people ought not to be barred, &c.; because, he says, that after the passing of the Act of Incorporation, in the plea of the said President, &c., mentioned, to wit: on the said 1st day of July, 1819, they, the said President, &c., did refuse, on demand being made at their **200***] banking house, *during the regular hours of doing business, to redeem in specie or other lawful money of the United States, the bills, notes and evidences of debt issued by the said President, &c.; and the said President, &c., did not thereupon wholly discontinue and close their banking operations, by way of discount and otherwise, until such time as the said President, &c., did resume the redemption of their bills, notes, and other evidences of debt; but on the contrary thereof, after such refusal to redeem their said bills, notes, and other evidences of debt, and before they resume the redemption thereof, to wit: on the 2d day July, in the year aforesaid, and at divers other days and times, the said President, &c., did receive deposits, discount notes, and issue promissory notes of the said President, &c.; and this, &c.

And the said Attorney-General further saith, that the said people ought not, &c.; because, he says, that after the passing of the said Act of Incorporation, in the said plea mentioned, and after the said President, &c., had entered upon the business of banking, to wit: on the 2d day of July, 1819, large amounts of the bills, notes and evidences of debt of the said President, &c., had been put into circulation by the said President, &c., and then were in circulation; and that while the said bills, notes and evidences of debt were in circulation, to wit: on the day and year last aforesaid, the said President, &c., by the fraud, neglect or mismanagement of them, or of some or all of their officers or agents, became wholly insolvent and unable to redeem the said bills, notes and evidences of debt, so in circulation, in specie or other lawful money of the United States; whereupon, the said President, &c., to wit: on the day last aforesaid, discontinued, ceased and closed their banking operations, and from that time afterwards, to wit: until the 1st day of October, 1824, neglected to resume their banking operations, either by way of discount or otherwise; and this, &c.

And the said defendants, as to the said plea of the said Samuel A. Talcott, Attorney-General, first above pleaded, &c., in reply to the aforesaid plea of them, the said defendants, *protesting that the same replication, [***201** and the matters therein contained are not sufficient, in law, to convict them, the said defendants, of the premises in the said information above charged upon them, nor to remove them from the liberties, privileges and franchises aforesaid, and that they need not, nor are they bound by the law of the land, to answer thereto; yet, for a rejoinder in this behalf, the said defendants say, that they, the said President, &c., did not, after their incorporation, willfully or negligently so transact and manage the affairs of the said Corporation, that on the 1st day of January, 1818, or at any time before or after the said day, the total amount of debts due by the said Corporation, over and above the specie then actually deposited in the Bank, did exceed three times the sum of the capital stock subscribed and actually paid into said Bank, in manner and form as the said Attorney-General hath, for the people, &c., above in his said replication, in that behalf alleged; and of this they, the said defendants, put themselves upon the country, &c.

And the said defendants, as to the said plea, &c., secondly above pleaded, &c., in reply, &c., say, that the said people, &c., ought not, &c., because they say, that though true it is, that after the passing of the Act of Incorporation, in the plea of them, the said defendants, mentioned, to wit: on the day in the said replication mentioned, they, the said defendants, did refuse, on demand being made at their banking house, during the regular hours of doing business, to redeem in specie, or other lawful money of the United States, the bills, notes and evidences of debt issued by them, the said defendants, as in the said replication is alleged; yet the said defendants, in fact, say, that they did themselves wholly discontinue and close their banking operations, by way of discount and otherwise, until such time as they, the said defendants, did resume the redemption of their bills, notes and other evidences of debt; without this, that after such refusal to redeem their said bills, notes and other evidences of debt, and before they resumed the redemption thereof, at the time mentioned in said replication in that behalf, or at other days or times, they, *the said defendants, [***202** received deposits, discounted notes, and issued promissory notes of them the said President, &c., and of this, they the said defendants put themselves upon the country, &c.

And the said defendants as to the said plea, &c., thirdly above pleaded, &c., in reply, &c.

(protesting that it is insufficient in law, &c., and that they did not become insolvent as therein alleged); yet for a rejoinder, &c., the said defendants say, that though true it is, that after the passing of the said Act of Incorporation, in the said plea mentioned, and after they, the said defendants, had entered upon the business of banking, to wit: on the day mentioned in the said replication in that behalf, large amounts of the bills, notes and evidences of debt, of them, the said defendants, had been put into circulation by them, the said defendants, and then were in circulation, and that while the said bills, notes and evidences of debt were in circulation, to wit: on the day and year mentioned in the said replication in that behalf, they, the said defendants, became unable to redeem the said bills, notes and evidences of debt, so in circulation, in specie or other lawful money of the United States; and that, thereupon, the said defendants, on the day in the said replication in that behalf mentioned, discontinued, ceased and closed their banking operations; and from that time, for a long time afterwards, to wit: until the day and year, in the said replication in that behalf mentioned, neglected to resume their banking operations, either by way of discount or otherwise, as in the said replication is alleged; yet, the said defendants, in fact, say, that in and by the Act of the Legislature of the people of this State, in the plea of the defendants above mentioned, wherein and whereby they, the said defendants, were ordained, constituted and declared to be a body corporate and politic, in fact and in name, in the manner set forth in said plea, it was, among other things, enacted, that if, at any time after the passing of said Act, the said President, Directors and Company should refuse, on demand being made at their banking house, during the regular hours of doing business, to redeem in specie or other lawful money of the United States, 203*]*their said bills, notes or other evidences of debt issued by the said Company, the said President, Directors and Company should, on pain of forfeiture of their charter, wholly discontinue and close their said banking operations, either by way of discount or otherwise, until such time as the said President, Directors and Company should resume the redemption of their bills, notes or other evidences of debt, in specie or other lawful money of the United States, as by the said Act of the Legislature of the people of the State of New York, reference being thereunto had, will, among other things, more fully and at large appear.

And the defendants aver that, at the time of their refusal to redeem in specie, or other lawful money of the United States, their said bills, notes and other evidences of debt, as hereinbefore stated, and until the 28th day of May, A. D. 1825, they wholly discontinued and closed their said banking operations; and that on the said 28th day of May, &c., they resumed the redemption of their bills, notes or other evidences of debt, in specie or other lawful money of the United States; and have, ever since that time, and still do continue to redeem the same, in manner aforesaid; and this, they, the said defendants, are ready to verify, &c., wherefore, &c. (as in the plea).

Issue to the country on the 1st and 2d rejoinders, and general demurrer to the 3d and last. The defendants joined in demurrer.

Mr. Talcott, Atty-Gen., in support of the demurrer, made the following points: 1. The information is correctly brought against the defendants, by their corporate style, for the purpose of obtaining judgment of ouster, or of seisin of their franchise of being a corporation, for neglect or misuser. 2. *Non constat*, upon the information, that those who have assumed to act as such Corporation under the name mentioned, ever were a Corporation. 3. The information is good at all events, for the undue exercise of the other franchises enumerated, even if it should be deemed objectionable to bring it against the Corporation by its corporate *name, for usurping the franchise [*204 of being a Corporation. And since there have been pleadings over, and a demurrer, if the information is, on the face of it, good for any part, it cannot now be objected to. It is like the case of a general demurrer to a whole declaration consisting of several counts, one count being good. 4. The replication sets forth sufficient causes of forfeiture; and by pleading over, if there are any defects in the replication, they are cured. 5. The rejoinder, as far as embraced by the demurrer, admits enough to forfeit the charter.

Mr. A. Van Vechten, contra, stated these points: 1. The information against the defendants as a Corporation is bad; because it does not state any cause of forfeiture. 2. This defect cannot be supplied by the replication; but if it can, then, 3. The replication is bad for uncertainty.

He said, so far as the information seeks a forfeiture, and a fine for the usurpation, this proceeding is the nature of a criminal prosecution. The plea is a direct answer. It sets forth the statute, and that the defendants organized a Bank under it, which are admitted by the replication. This destroys the *gravamen* of the information. If so, what becomes of the charge that the defendants exercised banking operations, without warranty or authority? Has the Attorney-General a right to say, in his replication, for the first time, "though you had such warrant, you have forfeited it?" A forfeiture is not to be presumed; and it must be made a substantive ground of attack in the information. It must be expressly charged in the first instance. The defendants are not bound to set out their title, and negative a forfeiture, which has not been charged upon them. The information alleges a usurpation only. It is good for so much, and no more. This being met, the whole is answered. If it was intended to go for the forfeiture, the precise ground should have been stated, with time, place and circumstance. *Commonwealth* v. *Un. F. Ins. Co.*, 5 Mass., 230. This case shows a plain distinction in the proceedings and judgment, between the two cases of usurpation and forfeiture. In the *former, there is a judgment of ouster; [*205 in the latter, of seizure. If there be a difference in the judgment, with what propriety can it be pretended there should be no distinction in the information? It is said that all may come out in the course of the pleadings. But suppose the defendants do not choose that this should be so—suppose they insist on having the true cause spread upon the information—have they not a right to do so? In England, the charters of incorporation are deemed mere private grants, and the Attorney-General is not presumed to know either of the grant or its extent. Not so of the Corporation in question. It is created by a public Act. Let the Attorney-General, then, state precisely the nature of the act which has produced a forfeiture. There being no such act stated, is the replication consistent with the information? No. It is a departure. The information admits the corporate existence of the defendants. The replication insists on a forfeiture. This order makes the latter the expositor of the charge, instead of the information. If it be insisted that the Act of 1825, sess. 48, ch. 325, sec. 7, gives a *scire facias*, or *quo warranto*, in this case, the answer is, it has not prescribed the form. This must be according to the common law. Did not the Legislature mean that the Attorney-General should proceed for the forfeiture itself? And could it have intended that he may do this without saying so in the information? Suppose a default for want of a plea: could the Attorney-General have taken such a judgment upon this information as the statute directs? No. He could only have judgment of ouster for the usurpation.

As to the effect of pleading over, we deny usurpation; and then the Attorney-General comes and shows a case of forfeiture, to which we rejoin. We say this is a departure, which, it will not be denied, is matter of substance, and bad on general demurrer. And it follows, that it is bad after pleading over.

The replication is defective in itself, independent of the departure. It relies upon the 206*] fraud, &c., of the defendants, *or their officers. Admit the fraud of the officers; the defendants do not admit their own fraud. The fraud, or other acts charged upon the officers, will not work a forfeiture. What these acts are, does not appear. No single act is pointed out. Still, the defendants may show it was not their own fraud.

There is a total want of certainty and precision. It is not stated whether there was fraud, or mismanagement, or neglect. The allegation is in the alternative. We certainly admit, by pleading over, no more than is alleged. It is not said whether the fraud was willful and actual, or merely constructive. Which of these alternative particulars may be a ground of forfeiture, it is not said. It may be this, that or the other. It is also defective in not specifying the particular acts of violation or omission. To say fraud or mismanagement, is not enough. The cause of forfeiture does not consist in the sound, but in the act.

But the replication is answered by the rejoinder. The ground of forfeiture is the defendants continuing their operations after they ceased to redeem their bills, and before they resumed specie payments. In such a case, the Act declares the forfeiture of the charter to be the consequence. This provision is, in substance, an express authority to resume their banking operations whenever they resume their payments. The object was to prevent further issues of paper while they were unable to redeem it; and it is always a good answer, that they have followed the directions of the Act. If there be a limit to the time during which they may forbear business and forbear payment, who is to judge of it? There is a period beyond which the charter cannot endure. But till that time arrive, the Legislature have not only sanctioned but they have enjoined a cessation of all banking operations under given circumstances. The general Act of 1825, before cited (sec. 6), has limited the period to one year. If the court may judge of the time, where was the necessity of this legislative interference?

At any rate, the Legislature may do an act which amounts to a waiver of any forfeiture of this kind already incurred. *And have [*207 they not done so by passing a statute which declares there shall be a forfeiture by certain acts, after its passage? They recognize all corporations as operative, and as not forfeited by any acts of omission or nonuser as to which there was no limitation of time before the Act passed.

Indeed, is not the acquiescence of the State for this length of time without any prosecution, in itself, a sanction to the Bank, in the resumption of their banking business.

Mr. Talcott, in reply. The replication does not depart form the information. The latter is not inconsistent with the former. True, we admit the Corporation to have existed; that it once had the privilege of banking. Neither the information nor replication deny this. But in the replication we follow out the subject and allege a forfeiture. Having forfeited them, their exercise is the usurpation of which the information complains. Thus the case goes on according to the course of pleading in *quo warranto*. The information asks, by what authority do you exercise these privileges? They say we should ask in a different form: why do you continue to exercise them? Where is the material difference? The judgment follows the nature of the case as it appears upon the pleadings, whether there be a default or verdict. A default upon the information would have admitted the usurpation; though not perhaps the reason and nature of it, so particularly as after it was explained by the replication. The Statute of 1825, sec. 7, is positive that the Corporation shall be prosecuted by *sci. fa.* or information, &c., and that, too, in cases of forfeiture. This information follows the express provisions of the Act. We cannot sue a corporation, unless by its corporate name. An action against the individuals would not be an action against the Corporation. The objection that there is a departure, would apply to every proceeding by information in England. There is no difference in the mode of setting forth a usurpation, by pleading, whether it arise from the provisions of a private charter, or a public Act of the Legislature. In every case where the information *was general, and the de- [*208 fendant justified (and it is so in every English case), the courts must have sustained the proceeding on grounds which are applicable here.

The authorities, however, are abundant that the defects of the informtion, if there be any, are cured by the defendant's pleading over. 8 Johns., 110; Cro. Car. 288; *Frith's* case, Cro. Eliz., 68; 12 Mod., 459, 466, per Holt, *Ch. J.*

True, the replication is in general terms; but it may be added that the rejoinder admits all that is stated by it—thus presenting the question, whether a disability to pay arising from the fraud, mismanagement, or neglect of the corporation, or its agents, is a ground of forfeiture. It admits a case which never could arise from honest inability.

It is said the acts charged may not be those of the whole Company. I will not stop to inquire what the act of the Company is, if it be not the act of their agent; nor whether the Company would be liable, as such, on a note made by their agent. If the act of the agent is not to be considered cause of forfeiture, it is difficult to see how the charter can be forfeited, either by nonuser or misuser; cases provided for, both by common law and by the Statute of 1825. Where is the case in which the fraud, mismanagement or neglect has been the act of all the individuals of a banking Company? If this be necessary, when shall we find a case in which the charter can be forfeited? Wherever an agent acts within his powers, his is the Act of the Company, and may be treated as such to all intents and purposes; and this, whether it be in carrying on their business, or entirely desisting.

The Company contend for allowing them time to lie by, in a dormant state. This, it is said, they have a right to, under the 10th section of the Act of Incorporation. (*Vide* sess. 39, ch. 167, secs. 10, 13.) But the 13th section contains the only provision for nonuser with impunity, and this restrains the right to Jan. 1, 1817. But what does the 10th section grant? That the defendants may lie still as long as **209***] they please? No such thing. *But if they do stop payment, they shall not issue paper before resuming payment, upon pain of forfeiture. The Legislature say, "remain dormant as long as you dare, without resuming payments, and we leave the general law to take hold of you." That law declares nonuser to be a cause of forfeiture. The Legislature add another cause to the list misuser. Does it follow that they intend to sanction a misuser to an unlimited extent?

The rejoinder denies insolvency, but admits a temporary inability to pay debts. What is this but insolvency? Whenever one becomes unable to pay his debts according to the ordinary course of business, he is insolvent. Here the defendants admit, in terms, that they were totally insolvent, for a long time. If the mere act of making payment is an answer, the defendants may defeat any proceeding against them by information or otherwise, very easily. All they have to do, is to pay a trifle at their counter; and plead it, either as a general bar, or *puis darrein continuance*, according to the time of payment.

Curia, per SAVAGE, *Ch. J.*, after stating the pleadings. The first questions respects the sufficiency of the information. Upon this, I shall only remark that the form adopted here, is the same which was used in the celebrated case of *The City of London*, 3 Hargr. St. Tr., 545, and which was there adjudged sufficient. A like precedent is given in *Rex* v. *Amery*, 2 T. R., 515.

I am perfectly satisfied, therefore, with the form of the pleadings; and shall only examine the question presented by the demurrer, on the merits of the case; that is, whether the Bank, having become insolvent and unable to redeem its paper, and having stopped business from July 2, 1819, till Oct. 1, 1824, when it resumed the redemption of its bills, has, thereby, forfeited its charter.

I have not been able to find any adjudication which defines what nonuser shall amount to a forfeiture. Nor is it very important in this case, as it must be decided upon the statute granting the incorporation.

*The 10th section enacts, "that, if [***210** at any time after the passing of this Act, the said President, Directors and Company shall refuse, on demand being made at their banking house, during the regular hours of doing business, to redeem in specie, or other lawful money of the United States, their said bills, notes, or other evidences of debt, issued by the said Company, the said President, Directors and Company shall, on pain of forfeiture of their charter, wholly discontinue and close their said banking operations, either by way of discount or otherwise, until such time as the said President, Directors and Company shall resume the redemption of their bills, notes, or other evidences of debt, in specie or other lawful money of the United States. And in case the said President, Directors and Company shall, at any time hereafter, offend against either of the provisions of this Act, it shall be the duty of the Attorney-General of this State, by information or otherwise, to prosecute the said Company for such offense; and on conviction thereof, their charter shall be deemed void."

It seems the Legislature anticipated the insolvency of this Bank, and provided, that while insolvent and unable to pay, it should cease doing business as a Bank, until it should be able to redeem its paper, or, in other words, become solvent. The Bank did, as the Legislature expected, become insolvent and, according to its charter, stopped business until it became solvent again. At the commencement of this prosecution, it was solvent, doing ordinary business and redeeming its bills. The Legislature had not then declared how long the Bank might suspend business. They have since (sess. 48, ch. 325, sec. 6, Apr. 21, 1825) limited that indulgence to one year; but that Act can have no effect in deciding this case.

It seems to me that under the Acts in force when this information was filed, it is a sufficient answer to say that the Bank is now doing business and redeeming its bills; that it had a right, recognized by its charter, to suspend business, to become insolvent, or unable to pay; and that *if proceedings were not insti- [***211** tuted against it till it became solvent, the right to prosecute for a forfeiture had ceased.

Had the insolvency continued till the prosecution was commenced, the forfeiture would have been irremediable; but the defendants, having resumed the redemption of their bills, and thereby shown their solvency; and having, in the meantime, complied with their charter, by discontinuing banking operations, it is now too late to complain of an insolvency which no longer exists.

The defendants are entitled to judgment on the demurrer.

Judgment for the defendants.

N. B. WOODWORTH, *J.*, did not give any opinion as to the effect of filing an information before the resumption of payment. And see the next case, where he delivers an opinion upon a similar replication, but does not recognize the doctrine that filing an information would take away the right of the Bank to resume payment. He there says, there must be something more than mere insolvency; that there must be a total nonuser to work a forfeiture. And he repeats and enforces the same proposition in the next case, *People* v. *Bank of Hudson*.

Cited in—4 Wend., 282; 9 Wend., 377; 15 Wend., 126; 21 Wend., 249; 23 Wend., 235, 258, 569, 573; 103 Ill., 511; 12 Mich., 538; 30 Am. Dec., 35, 36.

THE PEOPLE OF THE STATE OF NEW YORK

v.

THE PRESIDENT, DIRECTORS AND COMPANY OF THE BANK OF WASHINGTON AND WARREN.

Quo Warranto—*Insolvency and Refusal to Pay Bills, Not Sufficient Ground for Information Under Act of April 7, 1817—Total Non-user Necessary—Pleading.*

Insolvency and refusal to pay bills, &c., in specie or other lawful money, on demand, &c., are not, of themselves, within the Act, sess. 40, ch. 185, incorporating The President, Directors and Company of the Washington and Warren Bank, a ground for an information in nature of a *quo warranto*, or other proceeding, to oust them of their corporate rights.

To work such forfeiture, there must be a total nonuser. Per Woodworth, *J.*

The Statute, sess. 48, ch. 325, sec. 6, passed Apr. 21, 1825, is prospective in its operation as to the causes of forfeiture, but not exclusively so as to the remedy.

Citations—Act, April 21, 1825; Act, April 7, 1817, sess. 40, ch. 185; 5 Cow., 161; 19 Johns., 456; 4 Mod., 58; 12 Mod., 19; 4 Com. Dig., 272, Franchises, G, 3.

ON information in the nature of a *quo warranto*. The pleadings were nearly the same in this as in the preceding case of *People* v. *Bank of Niagara*, *ante*, 196. The information was filed in both cases at the same time, and the difference in the pleadings will appear by a summary of them given in the opinion of the court.

212*] **Mr. Talcott*, Atty-Gen., in support of the demurrer, made the same points as in *People* v. *Bank of Niagara*, and also insisted on the special causes of demurrer mentioned by the court. He cited 5 Mass., 230; 12 Mod., 19; 19 Johns., 456; 4 Mod., 58; 2 Show., 278, 279; Skinn., 310; Com. Dig., Franchises, G, 3; Laws N. Y., sess. 40, ch. 185, sec. 5; 4 Johns., 457, 460; 1 Phil. Ev., 163, and cases there cited in the *notes*, ed. of 1820; 6 T. R., 265; 2 Saund., 291 *a*, and 2 Kyd, Corp., 497.

Messrs. B. F. Butler and *A. Spencer*, contra, cited 19 Johns., 349; Laws N. Y., sess. 40, ch. 185, sec. 10; 1 Hopk. Ch., 354, 360; 5 Johns. Ch., 366; 19 Johns., 456, 474; 20 Johns., 404; 1 Chit. Pl., 586.

One question made by the defendants, in addition to those which were raised in *People* v. *Bank of Niagara*, was, whether the remedy should not have been by a *sci. fa.* instead of an information in the nature of a *quo warranto*.

NOTE.—Quo warranto *against corporation*—*Against usurper of a public office.*

An information, in the nature of a quo warranto, *lies against a corporation* for usurping a public franchise. See People v. Utica Ins. Co., 15 Johns., 358, *note*; People v. Tibbets, 4 Cow., 358, 384, *notes*.

Against usurper of a public office. See People v. Van Slyck, 4 Cow., 297, *note*.

Curia, per WOODWORTH, *J.* This is an information filed by the Atty-Gen., alleging that the President, Directors and Company of the Bank of Washington and Warren, without any warrant, grant or charter, have, for more than six months, used, and still do use, certain liberties, privileges and franchises, in the information set forth; and praying that process may be had against them, to answer by what warrant they claim to use and enjoy these privileges, &c.

The defendants plead, that Apr. 7, 1817, by an Act of the Legislature, they were constituted a body politic, by the title mentioned in the information, to continue until Jan. 1, 1832; that by the provisions of the Act, they continue to be a body politic and corporate, and are entitled to use all the rights, privileges and franchises allowed to them by the Act; by virtue of which, for all the time in the information mentioned, they have used, and still do use, the liberties, privileges and franchises of being proprietors of a bank, for the purpose of issuing *notes, receiving deposits, mak- [*213 ing discounts and transacting other business which incorporated banks may lawfully transact, by virtue of their respective Acts of Incorporation; and also of actually issuing notes, receiving deposits, making discounts and carrying on banking operations and other moneyed transactions, which are usually performed by incorporated banks; and claim the right conferred on them by the Act to have and use all these privileges, &c.; concluding with a traverse.

The plaintiffs replied, by separate replications, several distinct matters.

First, that the defendants did willfully and negligently so transact the affairs of the Corporation, that Jan. 1, 1818, the total amount of debts due by the Corporation, over and above the specie deposited in the Bank, did exceed three times the sum of the capital stock subscribed and actually paid in.

Secondly, that the defendants refused, on demand, to redeem in specie, or other lawful money, the bills, notes and evidences of debt issued by them; and that they did not wholly discontinue and close their banking operations, until such time as they resumed the redemption of their bills, notes and other evidences of debt; and before they resumed the redemption of them, they received deposits, discounted notes, and issued promissory notes.

On these replications, issues are joined to the country.

Thirdly, the plaintiffs reply, that after the defendants had entered on the business of banking, to wit: May, 2, 1818, large amounts of their bills, notes and other evidences of debt, had been put, and then were in circulation; and while so in circulation, by the fraud, neglect or mismanagement of the defendants, or of some or all of their officers or agents, they became wholly insolvent, and unable to redeem their bills in specie or other lawful money; and on that day discontinued and closed their banking operations; and from that time, until July 1, 1824, neglected to resume their business, by way of discount or otherwise.

*The defendants rejoin, admitting [*214 their inability to redeem their notes in circulation, and that they discontinued and closed their banking operations, as alleged in the last replication; and they then plead that they did not, by the fraud, neglect or mismanagement of the defendants, or of some, or all, or any of their officers or agents, become wholly insolvent, or unable to redeem their bills, &c., in circulation, in specie or other lawful money.

To this rejoinder the plaintiffs demur, and assign for cause:

1. That it attempts to put in issue an immaterial question, to wit: whether they became insolvent by reason of the fraud, &c., set forth; whereas, it is immaterial whether the insolvency was occasioned by fraud or not.

2. Because the rejoinder is a negative pregnant—as by averring that the insolvency was not by reason of such fraud, &c., it admits they did become insolvent, and unable to redeem, for some other reason.

The defendants join in demurrer.

It was stated on the argument, by the defendants' counsel, that no objection would be taken to the form of the information.

If the replication is good, independent of the causes which it assigns for the insolvency, the rejoinder is then bad, for the reasons given by the special causes of demurrer. If the allegation that the insolvency was occasioned by fraud, &c., is immaterial, the averment of the existence of such insolvency, and not the cause thereof, was what the defendants were bound to answer; and on this ground the rejoinder is bad. If, however, it was material to allege in the replication, that the insolvency was produced by fraud, &c., then the rejoinder is good; for it negatives material facts, to wit: the causes of insolvency; and on this ground cannot be considered a negative pregnant, although it implies that the insolvency was owing to other causes.

The material question is, whether the replication be good in substance.

The Act to Prevent Fraudulent Bankruptcies, passed Apr. 21, 1825, is prospective in its 215*] operation. Its effect, *in this case, is on the form of the remedy merely. The grounds of forfeiture contained in the Act apply to cases thereafter to arise.

The facts stated by the replication are not a cause of forfeiture in the Act of Apr. 7, 1817, by which the defendants were incorporated. (*Vide* sess. 40, ch. 185.) The 10th section declares, that on refusal to redeem in specie, the defendants should, on pain of forfeiture, discontinue and close their banking operations, until such time as they should resume the redemption of their bills. It further allows 10 *per cent.* damages on all notes, which shall have been demanded and not paid. It has been adjudged that the damages thus given are exclusive of legal interest. *Wendell* v. *Bank*, 5 Cow., 161.

It will be seen, by this specification, that the time for resuming operations is not limited in terms, nor was it intended to be. I think it manifest the Legislature did not intend that the refusal to pay on demand should be a ground of forfeiture, whatever may have been the cause of refusal; but on the contrary, they intended that the business of the Bank might be again commenced at an indefinite period, whenever the defendants should resume the payment of their bills. If this be the construction of which I have no doubt, it follows, that whether the suspension was six months or six years, there was no cause of forfeiture. It was considered that 10 *per cent.* damages, beyond legal interest, would be a sufficient impulse to resume business at an early day, without specifying, as in the Act of Apr. 21, 1825, that insolvency, neglect to redeem, or suspension of business for one year, should be deemed and adjudged a surrender of their rights. It seems to me, then, that the facts admitted by these pleadings, to wit: an insolvency at a particular time, a suspension of business from that to another period, and then the resumption of banking operations, present a case contemplated by the Act, and by it protected against forfeiture.

It does not become necessary, in the view I have taken, to consider whether the facts here presented would have *been sufficient [*216 cause for dissolving the Corporation, had the 10th section in the Act of Incorporation been omitted. I entirely subscribe to the doctrine in *Slee* v. *Bloom*, 19 Johns., 456. Suffering an act to be done which destroys the end and object for which a corporation is instituted, must be regarded as equivalent to a direct surrender. It cannot then answer the end of its institution, and is thereby dissolved. (4 Mod., 58; 12 Mod., 19; 4 Com. Dig., 272, Franchises, G, 3.) In *Slee* v. *Bloom* considerable stress is laid on the fact that it was not pretended the Corporation hoped or expected to resume its functions. In this case, the operations of the Bank were discontinued for a time, and again commenced, before the filing of the information. Insolvency is admitted on May 2, 1818, but it nowhere appears how long it continued. It does not necessarily follow that the insolvency continued six years, or even one year. Much would depend on the ability of the debtors to the Bank. They might, on a particular day, be unable to take up their paper, or even be wholly insolvent; and yet, within six months or a year thereafter retrieve their circumstances and meet their engagement at the Bank. Such an occurrence might restore the Bank to solvency. I cannot, therefore, assent to the proposition that insolvency merely, at a particular time, however produced, is good cause for dissolving the Corporation. Its continuance must be such as to afford substantial ground to consider the object for which the institution was created, as defeated.

Waiving, however, the question, how long the insolvency must have continued to work a dissolution, the answer here is, that its continuance is not alleged. The refusal to pay, unless arising from continued insolvency, is, in my apprehension, no ground of forfeiture. The remedy of the creditors would seem to be by action. As to suspending operations, that may, in some cases, be a prudent and justifiable measure, and consistent with the ultimate solvency of the Bank. There must be a total nonuser, to be a ground of forfeiture. For aught that appears, *this Corporation may [*217 have continued to sue for debts and elect their officers.

Whether an information is the proper remedy, it is unnecessary to inquire, *the Court* being of opinion that no cause of forfeiture appears on these pleadings, and, consequently, that the defendants are entitled to judgment on the demurrer, for that cause.

Judgment for the defendants.

Cited in—6 Cow., 219; 21 Wend., 249; 23 Wend., 237.

THE PEOPLE OF THE STATE OF NEW YORK
v.
THE PRESIDENT, DIRECTORS AND COMPANY OF THE BANK OF HUDSON.

Quo Warranto *Against Corporation for Forfeiture of Franchises—May be Against Company in Corporate Names—Judgment is One of Seizure—Franchises Forfeited by Misuser or Nonuser Pleading.*

An information, in nature of a *quo warranto* against an incorporated company, seeking to deprive it of its franchises, on the ground of forfeiture by nonuser, &c., may be against the Company in its corporate name.

The judgment is a judgment of seizure.

Corporate rights may be forfeited by nonuser or misuser.

Suffering an act to be done which destroys the end and object for which a corporation was instituted, is equivalent to a surrender of its corporate rights.

As where an incorporated bank becomes insolvent, and assigns so much of its property to trustees for the purpose of paying its debts, as to prevent its resumption of banking business.

And the Attorney-General may, on an information in nature of a *quo warranto*, reply such assignment in general terms, without saying, in partienlar, how much was assigned, or its value; or how much or what value was necessary to disable the Bank from resuming its operations.

Citations—Act, March 25, 1808; 5 Cow., 161; 9 Cr., 51; 19 Johns., 456.

ON information in nature of a *quo warranto.* The information was filed at the same time, and was in the same words, *mutatis mutandis*, as those in the two preceding cases of *People* v. *Bank of Niagara*, and *Same* v. *Bank of W. & W., ante*, 196, 211. The particulars, in which the subsequent pleadings differ, will be found stated in the opinion of the court, where a summary of all the pleadings is given, sufficiently full to render any statement of them here unnecessary.

It will be there seen that the defendants demurred specially to one of the replications interposed by the Attorney-General.

The plaintiffs joined in demurrer.

Mr. C. Bushnell, in support of the demurrer.

Mr. Talcott, Atty-Gen., contra.

218*] **Curia*, per WOODWORTH, *J.* This is an information in nature of a *quo warranto.* The defendants plead, that by an Act passed Mar. 25, 1808, they were incorporated as a Bank; which Act was subsequently continued in force until the first Tuesday of June, 1832; that by virtue of these Acts, they are a body corporate, and entitled to do all lawful acts allowed by the Statutes of Incorporation; concluding with a traverse of the usurpation alleged in the information.

The plaintiffs reply, that Aug. 1, 1819, the debts of the Corporation, over and above the specie then actually deposited, exceeded three times the sum of the capital stock subscribed. On this the defendants have taken issue to the country.

The plaintiffs reply, secondly, that Aug. 21, 1819, large amounts of bills, notes and evidences of debt of the defendants, had been put in circulation. And on the day last mentioned, the defendants, by the fraud, neglect or mismanagement of them, or some, or all of their officers or agents, become wholly insolvent, and unable to redeem their bills, &c.; whereupon the defendants discontinued their banking operations, either by way of discount or otherwise; and on the day and year last aforesaid, assigned and transferred so much of their property to trustees, in trust for the payment of their debts, as to render themselves incapable of continuing their banking operations, according to the intent of the Statutes of Incorporation.

To this replication, the defendants have demurred, and assign several special causes of demurrer.

It is objected, in the first place, that the information being against the defendants by their corporate name, is bad. To this it may be answered, the information is merely descriptive. It is not an affirmation that the defendants are a Corporation; but that, by the name of The President, Directors and Company of the Bank of Hudson, or using that name, they have done the acts in the information alleged. And it then calls on them to answer, by what authority. Besides, the statute authorizes proceedings against the Corporation. The judgment *must be against the corporate name. [***219**

A corporation, created by the Legislature, may lose its franchises by a misuser or a nonuser of them. They may be resumed by the government under a judgment upon a *quo warranto*, to ascertain and enforce the forfeiture. (9 Cr., 51.) The judgment to be given is a judgment of seizure, which produces a dissolution of the corporation.

I perceive no substantial difficulties in the plaintiffs' way as to form. The material question is, whether the replication is good in substance For the reasons given in *People* v. *Bank of W. & W.* I am of opinion that the mere fact of insolvency at a particular time, however produced, is insufficient. For aught that appears, if the pleadings go no further, the Bank may have subsequently become solvent. It ought to appear affirmatively that the insolvency continued; or if it did not continue, then that the defendants subsequently became solvent, and notwithstanding, ceased to exercise the franchises granted. So, also, with respect to the fact that the defendants ceased to exercise banking operations, for the time in the replication stated. Enough is not shown, to the statement of that fact, to warrant a judgment that the Corporation is dissolved. We cannot say that the discontinuance was not justifiable. It may have been a prudent and necessary measure. The Bank, subsequently to Aug., 1819, may have become solvent. The state of the funds may have been so disposed as to be incapable of being realized, and not to have permitted the defendants with safety

---

NOTE.—Quo warranto *against corporation—Against usurper of a public office.*

An information, in the nature of a quo warranto, *lies against a corporation* for usurping a public franchise. See People v. Utica Ins. Co., 15 Johns., 358, *note*; People v. Tibbets, 4 Cow., 358, 384, *notes*.

Against usurper of a public office. See People v. Van Slyck, 4 Cow., 297, *note*.

to resume their business. If, indeed, the suspension was the consequence of continued insolvency; or, afterwards, on becoming solvent, if the defendants had still continued to suspend banking operations, I apprehend the right to dissolve the Corporation would be established.

There is, however, another fact alleged, which, if well pleaded, will sustain the prosecution. It is this: that the defendants assigned and transferred so much of their property to trustees as to render themselves incapable of **220***] continuing *their banking operations. This fact, if conceded, presents a case falling within the general principle laid down in *Slee* v. *Bloom*, 19 Johns., 456; that the suffering an act to be done, which destroys the end and object for which the Corporation was instituted, must be regarded as equivalent to a direct surrender.

But it is contended that this part of the replication presents a question of law, as to how much property must be assigned in order to incapacitate the defendants from continuing their banking business; and upon this the jury would have to pass, if issue were taken on the allegation thus stated.

The answer to the objection seems to be that the plaintiffs are not presumed to know the exact amount of property assigned. It is a fact resting in the knowledge of the defendants. It was competent for them to rejoin that no assignment was made, or that the assignment did not exceed a certain specified amount, upon which issue might be taken.

We are of opinion that the plaintiffs are entitled to judgment on the demurrer, with leave to the defendants to withdraw the demurrer and rejoin.

Judgment accordingly.

Cited in—9 Wend., 377; 21 Wend., 249; 23 Wend., 237; 12 Hun, 266; 20 Barb., 526; 103 Mass., 140; 12 Mich., 395; 23 O., 127; 41 Am. Dec., 119 (5 Ark., 595).

221*] *DAKIN

v.

HUDSON, Sheriff of COLUMBIA.

Pleading—Declaration in Debt for an Escape—Material Averments—Facts to show Jurisdiction of Inferior Courts—Repugnancy between Counts—Defects in Proceedings, no Excuse to Sheriff for Escape.

Form of declaration in debt, against the sheriff for suffering an escape from execution on a surrogate's decree for distribution.

Such a declaration must aver that the surrogate's court, which made the decree, granted the administration.

For otherwise, it has no jurisdiction to decree distribution.

In pleading a proceeding of an inferior jurisdiction, the facts necessary to give it jurisdiction, must be set forth, and then the pleader may say *taliter processum fuit.*

The surrogate's court is a creature of the statute; and in pleading its decree, it must be shown, affirmatively, that the facts upon which it acted gave jurisdiction of the subject-matter and the persons.

In a declaration against the sheriff, for suffering an escape from execution, it is not good cause of demurrer, that the judgment appears to be against A. and his wife, and the execution against A. only; nor that the execution appears to have been indorsed with a direction to receive interest when no interest runs on the judgment; nor that the judgment and execution appears to be in favor of D. and others, without saying what others.

Any or all of these defects in the proceedings, are no excuse to the sheriff who suffers the escape.

Such a declaration must describe the record and proceedings correctly; and if, when produced on the trial, they do not correspond, the objection may then be made on the ground of variance.

Such a declaration, set out in the first count a surrogate's decree, execution to the sheriff, and a voluntary escape. The second count set out a similar decree, execution, &c., and an involuntary escape. In setting out the decree, this second count said a certain other judgment or decree, but then dropped the word "other," and referred to the judgment, &c., by the word "said." It set forth the execution as issued on the last mentioned judgment, &c.; but afterwards referred to this execution by the word "said," on general demurrer to the whole declaration, held well, and that there was no repugnancy between the two counts.

Citations—Act, 1 R. L., 448, sec. 11, 12; 4 Johns. Ch., 410, 411.

ON demurrer to the declaration. The first count was in debt for $200. "For that whereas, by a certain final judgment or decree, made before Abraham A. Van Buren, Esq., Surrogate of the County of Columbia aforesaid, in a certain matter depending before said Abraham A. Van Buren, Surrogate of the county aforesaid, wherein Anson Dakin and others, heirs at law of Joshua Dakin, deceased, were plaintiffs, and Abner Bristol and Lydia Bristol, his wife, administrator and administratrix of the estate of the said Joshua Dakin, deceased, were defendants, concerning the administration and distribution of the estate of the said Joshua Dakin, deceased, it was, among other things, heretofore, to wit: on the 9th of November, A. D. 1823, in due form of law, ordered, adjudged and decreed by the said surrogate, that the said Abner Bristol and Lydia Bristol, his wife, administrator and administratrix as aforesaid, pay to the said Anson Dakin, the sum of $78.64, as by the said decree remaining as of *record in the office of [***222** the said surrogate, doth and may more fully appear. And whereas the said Abner and Lydia, having neglected and refused to perform the said order and decree, and to pay the sum thereby adjudged to the said plaintiff, and the said judgment, order and decree remaining in full force, not annulled or reversed in any way, the said plaintiff, for having execution of the said order, judgment and decree, afterwards, to wit: on the 8th day of November, A. D. 1824, sued and prosecuted out of the said court of the said surrogate, before the said surrogate, according to the form of the statute in such case made and provided, a certain process or execution upon the said judgment and decree, against the said Abner Bristol, directed to the Sheriff of the County of Columbia, by which said writ or process, the said sheriff was commanded to take the said Abner Bristol, if he should be found in his bailiwick, and him safely imprison, until he should perform the said sentence and decree, or until he should be delivered by due course of law. Which said writ, afterwards, and before the delivery to the said Sheriff of the County of Columbia, aforesaid, to be executed as hereinafter mentioned, was duly indorsed, with a direction to the said sheriff, requiring him to receive $78.64, and interest, from the 9th of November, 1823, and $2.13, surrogate's fees of the said attachment or process, besides sheriff's fees, and which said writ or process, so indorsed as aforesaid, afterwards, to wit: on the 10th day of Novem-

ber, 1824, to wit: at Hudson, in the county aforesaid, was delivered to the said Samuel E. Hudson, who then was, and still is, sheriff of the County of Columbia, aforesaid, to be executed in due form of law. By virtue of which said writ or process, and of the said indorsement so made thereon as aforesaid, the said Samuel E. Hudson, so being Sheriff of the County of Columbia, aforesaid, afterwards, to wit: on the 18th day of December, A. D. 1824, and within the bailiwick of the said Sheriff of the County of Columbia, aforesaid, to wit: at Hillsdale, in the said county, took and arrested the said Abner Bris-
223*] tol, by his body, *and then and there, by virtue of the said process, and of the said indorsement so made thereon, as aforesaid, had and detained him in his custody for the said sum of $78.64, and interest from the 9th of Nov., 1823, and $2.13, surrogate's fees of the said attachment or process, besides sheriff's fees, so indorsed on the said writ or process, as aforesaid, and kept and detained him in his custody, from thence, until the said defendant, so being Sheriff of the County of Columbia, as aforesaid, afterwards, to wit: on the said 18th day of December, A. D. 1824, at the City of Hudson, in the county aforesaid, without the leave or license, and against the will of the said plaintiff, voluntarily suffered and permitted the said Abner Bristol to escape and go at large. And the said Abner Bristol did then and there escape and go at large, wheresoever he would, out of the custody of him, the said defendant; he, the said defendant, so then being Sheriff of the County of Columbia, aforesaid; and the said sum of $78.64, with interest from the 9th of November, 1823, and the said sum of $2.13, surrogate's fees of the said process, so indorsed on the said writ or process as aforesaid, being then and still wholly unpaid and unsatisfied to the said plaintiff, to wit: at Hillsdale, in the County of Columbia, aforesaid, whereby," &c.

The second count was substantially the same, except that it was for an involuntary escape. It set forth a certain judgment or decree, &c., as a certain other judgment or decree, but then dropped the word "other," and referred to this judgment or decree by the word "said." It mentioned the execution as one upon the said last mentioned judgment, &c., and then referred to the execution by the word "said."

General demurrer and joinder.

Mr. D. B. Tallmadge, in support of the demurrer, took five exceptions:

1. That the execution should have issued, both against administrator and administratrix.
224*] *2. Interest is not collectable upon the decree of a surrogate.
3. The declaration describing the decree or judgment, as between "John Dakin and others," plaintiffs, &c., it is bad. (1 Saund., 37; 11 East, 516; 1 Chit. Pl., 355; 2 *Id.*, 147; Com. Dig. Pl., 2 W, 12.)
4. The declaration does not give jurisdiction to the surrogate. (Archb. Pl., 162; 1 Saund., 92, *n.* 2; 3 Cow., 206.)
5. The counts are repugnant to, and inconsistent with each other. (Bac. Abr., Pleas and Pleading, B, 1; 1 Chit. Pl., 397; 1 Salk., 213; 2 Ld. Raym., 842.)

Mr. C. Bushnell, contra, cited *Seymour* v. *Seymour*, 4 Johns. Ch., 409.

Curia, per SAVAGE, *Ch. J.* The defendant makes five objections to the sufficiency of the declaration.

First, it is said the execution should have been issued against Bristol and wife; and secondly, that interest is not recoverable. If these objections were well founded, the sheriff would not, therefore, be at liberty to suffer an escape; nor would he, if the third point be tenable. The declaration must describe correctly the record and proceedings it purports to set out; and if the record or proceedings produced on trial do not correspond with the description, the objection may be taken for the variance.

But it is objected, fourthly, that the declaration does not give jurisdiction to the surrogate; and it seems to me that this objection is unanswerable. The construction given to the Act, 1 R. L., 448, secs. 11, 12, by the late *Chancellor* Kent, 4 Johns. Ch., 410, 411 is, that the surrogate granting administration has power to call the administrator to account. I think jurisdiction belongs to that surrogate's court alone which granted the administration. It is not averred in this declaration, either that the Surrogate of Columbia Co. granted administration, or that he had jurisdiction, of the matter.

The rule is, that the pleading, relying on a proceeding of an inferior jurisdiction, must set forth the facts necessary *to give juris-]***225**
diction; and it may then say, *taliter processum fuit, &c.* Such summary proceedings are contrary to the course of the common law. The surrogate's court is entirely a creature of the statute. It should be shown to the court affirmatively, therefore, that the surrogate had power to make the decree; that the facts upon which he acted gave him jurisdiction of the subject-matter, and of the persons before him.

There is nothing in the last objection that the counts of the declaration are repugnant.

The defendant is entitled to judgment on the demurrer, with leave to the plaintiff to amend, on payment of costs.

Judgment for the defendant.

Cited in—8 Cow., 308; 12 Wend., 104; 16 Wend., 39; 1 Hill, 139; 7 Hill, 41; 3 Den., 572; 5 N. Y., 511; 56 N. Y., 386; 3 Barb., 343, 606; 10 Abb. Pr., 437; 14 Abb. Pr., 150; 15 Abb. Pr., 29; 9 Bos., 588; 10 Bos., 305; 2 Sweeny, 580; 1 Bradf., 185; 33 Cal., 536; 60 Ill., 336; 30 Mich., 219; 17 Wis., 202; 37 Am. Dec., 305.

HALE *v.* ANDRUS.

Promise to Indemnify Surety—Promisor, Liable for Money Expended by Surety in Defending Suits Against Him as Surety—Pleading—Statute of Limitations.

H. and others became sureties for B., a deputy-sheriff, to A., the sheriff; and then A. promised H., that if he would become surety for him, A., as sheriff, he would indemnify H. against his suretyship for B. H. accordingly became surety for A. A. was afterwards sued for B.'s wrongfully taking the goods of one, on a *fi. fa.* against another; and H. and his co-sureties for B., with A.'s knowledge, defended the suit, brought a writ of error, and reversed one judgment against A.; defended another suit against A. for the same cause; brought error; but the judgment was affirmed; and all this with A.'s knowledge; in which H. expended moneys in retaining an attorney and defending the suit, and prosecuting the writ of error; in an action by H. against A. on his promise of indemnity; held, that he might recover the moneys thus expended; for A.'s consent to the expenditure might, under the circumstances, be presumed.

The declaration was, that, in consideration that H. would become surety for A., he (A.) would indemnify H. against being surety for B.; and averred that H. did become surety for A.: the proof was that A. said to one witness that he had agreed to indemnify H. in consideration of his becoming bail; and to another witness, and at another time, that in consideration that H. had become bail for him, he had agreed to indemnify H. as bail for B.; held, that the first admission supported the declaration; and though both witnesses were H.'s, he might reject the second admission, and rely on the first: and that A. could not avail himself of his own admission to the second witness, to contradict the admission to the first.

To a declaration on promises of indemnity, the defendant pleaded a former recovery on the same promises; the plaintiff replied that the recovery was on other and different promises, and prayed judgment, because the defendant had not answered the promises thus newly assigned: the defendant rejoined *non assumpsit* to the promises so newly assigned; and on the trial no record of the former recovery was produced: and objection was taken that the *onus* lay on the plaintiff, to avoid the plea by sustaining the replication; on verdict at the circuit for the plaintiff, subject to the opinion of the Supreme Court, on this, among other points, that court, being with the plaintiff on the other points, held, that the issue on this plea was informal, but amendable after verdict; that the replication admitted the former recovery; that the *onus* of proving that the former and present cause of action were not the same, lay on the plaintiff; and that unless the defendant would relinquish his plea, there should be a new trial to enable the plaintiff to give the requisite proof.

Held, also, the proper replication would be that the former and present cause of action are not the same, and a direct issue to the country.

Non Assumpsit infra sex annos, to a declaration on a promise of indemnity, is bad in substance; and though issue be taken thereon, and there be a verdict found for the plaintiff subject to the opinion of the court; and the evidence be plainly against the plaintiff upon the issue; if the cause be in other respects with him, he shall have judgment; and although such an issue be found for the defendant, the plaintiff shall have judgment *non obstante veredicto*.

Semble, that on a promise to indemnify, one action may be brought, and a recovery had for a breach or breaches; and then a subsequent action on the same promise for another breach or breaches, happening after the first recovery, &c.

Citations—16 Johns., 136; 7 Johns., 87; 18 Johns., 455; 1 Chit., 297.

ASSUMPSIT on a parol promise of indemnity, tried at the Jefferson Circuit, Dec. **226***] 20, 1825, before Williams, **Circuit J.*, when a verdict was taken for the plaintiff, subject to the opinion of this court.

The declaration contained two counts. The first count was, that Mar. 18, 1816, the plaintiff having, with others, become surety by bond to the defendant, then Sheriff of Jefferson Co., for one Bealls, his deputy; afterwards, Sept. 6, 1817, the defendant, in consideration that the plaintiff would then become surety by bond for the defendant, as sheriff, promised the plaintiff to indemnify and save him harmless against all damages, &c., which he might pay or become liable to pay, in consequence of having executed the bond as surety for Bealls. That the plaintiff had paid, and become liable to pay large sums of money, specifying the particulars, to wit: that the defendant recovered judgment for the penalty of the bond given by the sureties of Bealls, in the Supreme Court, in January Term, 1819, and certain damages were assessed thereon; and afterwards, in May Term, 1823, recovered a judgment of damages for further and other breaches, against the sureties, by *sci. fa.* on the record of the first recovery, upon which last recovery by *sci. fa.*, the plaintiff paid $250, including the costs of defending. And further, that one Eliakim Barney, in Oct., 1819, recovered judgment against the defendant in trover for a yoke of oxen, which Bealls had taken as deputy on a *fi. fa.*, which judgment was afterwards reversed on error, which action was defended, and writ of error prosecuted by the obligors in the bond of surety for Bealls. And a like action was prosecuted, and a like recovery had for the oxen, *in Dec., 1821, which, on error, [***227** was affirmed; which action was defended, and a writ of error prosecuted by the obligors in the bond of surety for Bealls; and on account of which actions and writs of error, the plaintiff had paid $120.

The second count was substantially the same. The declaration was entitled of May Term, 1825.

The defendant pleaded, 1. *Non assumpsit*. 2. *Non assumpsit infra sex annos*. 3. *Non accrevit infra sex annos*; to which 2d and 3d pleas the plaintiff replied, *assumpsit, et accrevit, infra sex annos*; on which issue was joined.

The defendant pleaded, fourthly, that in the Term of January, 1823, the plaintiff impleaded the defendant in this court for not performing the same identical promises and undertakings mentioned in the declaration; and in February Term, 1824, recovered judgment for $1,745.06; to which the plaintiff replied that he brought the action pleaded, not for the non-performance of the promises and undertakings in the plea mentioned, but for the non-performance of other and different promises and undertakings, concluding with a verification; and praying judgment, because the defendant had not answered the complaint of the plaintiff, as to the breach of the promises in the declaration mentioned and so newly assigned in the replication. To this the defendant rejoined, that as to the supposed promises newly assigned, he did not undertake and promise, &c. Upon this, issue was joined.

On the trial, the breaches mentioned in the declaration were proved, and that the cause of action arose within six years before suit brought.

No proof was given touching the former recovery, and the defendant objected that it lay with the plaintiff to establish his replication to the fourth plea, by proof.

The additional facts of the case, so far as they are material, will be found stated in the opinion of the court.

Mr. D. Tillinghast, for the plaintiff, argued the cause upon the following points, among others: 1. That the promise of indemnity was proved as laid in the declaration. *(1 [***228** Phil. Ev., 163, 222, 3d ed., 1820; 14 Johns., 215; 15 *Id.*, 409; 11 Hargr. St. Tr., 261; Com. Dig., Estoppel, A, 1; 3 Cow., 120; 4 *Id.*, 559.)

2. The Statute of Limitations is no bar. (2 Chit. Pl., 449, *note e*; *Id.* 450, *note f*; 18 Johns., 14.)

3. The plea of a former recovery is no defense.

4. The plaintiff had sustained damages to the full amount of the verdict. (12 Johns., 207; 2 Ld. Raym., 1072; Cro. Eliz., 237; 4 Cow., 417; 8 Johns., 249; 5 Johns., 168.)

5. The issue on the replication to the fourth plea is, at most, informal, and cured after verdict.

A question was made on the argument, whether, admitting the plaintiff had once before recovered on the same promise now in question, though for former breaches, this recovery was not a bar to any further recovery for a breach or breaches subsequent to the former recovery. As to this,

Mr. Tillinghast, said the true test always is, whether the same evidence will support both actions. *Kitchen* v. *Campbell*, 3 Wils., 308; *Rice* v. *King*, 7 Johns., 20. *Johnson* v. *Smith*, 8 *Id.*, 383. Even though the plaintiff declare in both actions for the same cause, if he gave no evidence in the first, touching the ground of action in the second, it is not barred. *Seddon* v. *Tutop*, 6 T. R., 607. It is enough that the present demand has not been satisfied, and never submitted to the consideration of a jury. *Snider* v. *Croy*, 2 Johns., 227. Where the debt or duty is to arise from several acts to be performed at different times, each performance is a distinct duty, for which a separate action lies. *Barker* v. *Sutton*, *Norfolk Ass.* 1662, per Hale, Tr. *per Pais* 186; 1 Esp. *N. P.*, Gould's ed., pt. 1, 247, S. C. In *Swann's* case, Cro. Eliz., 3, it was said to be adjudged, that in covenants perpetual, if they be once broken, and an action of covenant brought, and a recovery upon it, if they be afterwards broken, a *scire facias* shall be had upon the judgment, and the party need not bring a new writ of cove-**229***] nant. This case clearly *recognizes a new remedy for every new breach; and although a *sci. fa.* lies, at the election of the covenantee, this does not preclude a new action.

Mr. Talcott, Atty-Gen., contra. Though the plea of *non assumpsit infra sex annos* may be defective, yet it is true, and entitles us to judgment on the case.

The issue on the replication to the fourth plea, substantially presents the question, whether there had been a former recovery on the very promise now in question. The informality is not material after verdict. (1 Chit. Pl., 402, 507.) The plaintiff did not reply, as he might have done, that this is a suit for a subsequent cause of action upon the same promise. Had he done so, then I agree that the action would lie. But the new breach should have been replied distinctly. That is the only mode in which he can avail himself of it. It would not have been a departure. (14 Johns., 178.) The pleadings are conclusive that both actions were on the same promise. At least, it lay with the plaintiff to show they were not.

The defendant is not liable for the costs of the case in which the plaintiff improperly brought a writ of error, and in which the judgment was, therefore, affirmed.

As to the variance, the contract consists both of consideration and promise. Both must be proved as laid. The declaration alleges an executory consideration. The consideration in proof is executed, and the variance is fatal to the plaintiff's action. (18 Johns., 455.)

Mr. Tillinghast, in reply, said where a plea is bad in substance, the plaintiff may either demur or take issue, and if the issue be found against him, he may then move for judgment *non obstante veredicto*. And though the court see, on a case made, that the plea of *non assumpsit infra sex annos* is true, they will not give effect to it.

The new breach of the old promise, on which the plaintiff had before recovered, created a distinct duty—to perform which, the law would imply a new promise in the *terms of [***230** the original engagement. This satisfies the replication and falsifies the rejoinder. The case is like a single promise to pay by installments. There each installment is considered the subject of a separate promise, on which an action lies. The declaration may be simply on the promise to pay the last installment, without any allusion to the first.

It will be intended, in this case, that the damages in the first action were given for the breaches there in question, and for nothing more. The objection here goes, therefore, merely to the measure of damages. *Milles* v. *Milles*, Cro. Car., 241. In this view, there was no need of replying the new breaches.

Curia, per WOODWORTH, *J.*, after stating the pleadings. The pleas of the Statute of Limitations are no bar. As to the plea of *non accrevit*, it appears from the evidence that the *gravamen*, upon which the plaintiff relies to recover, is within six years. The plea of *non assumpsit infra sex annos* does not apply to the case. The promise was made more than six years before suit brought, but it was a promise to indemnify against liabilities on the bond executed by the sureties of Bealls. The statute did not begin to run from the time of making the promise, but from the time damages were sustained. The plea, therefore, was bad in substance, and is not cured by the replication. The issue was immaterial, and interposes no obstacle in the plaintiff's way. If the issue had been found for the defendant, the result would have been the same. In that case the plaintiff would be entitled to judgment, notwithstanding the verdict.

The issue joined on the fourth plea is informal, but is amendable after verdict. The question is, which party held the affirmative? It was undoubtedly the plaintiff. He alleges that he brought the action for the non-performance of other, and different undertakings, on which the defendant takes issue. The recovery of the judgment set out in the plea seems to be admitted. In the case of **Phillips* v. [***231** *Berick*, 16 Johns., 136, this question was considered. It was there held that the record of a former recovery, apparently for the same cause of action as that which is the foundation of the subsequent suit, is *prima facie* evidence only; and the plaintiff may repel it by showing that it was for a distinct demand. Spencer, *J.*, observes, that "if the defendant had pleaded specially, he must have stated a former recovery for damages, by means of not performing the same identical promises. The replication would be, that the promises in that action were not the same identical promises. This would have formed an issue to the country; and the inquiry *in pais* would be, whether the former recovery included the demand then in contest, and the burden of the proof would be thrown on the plaintiff."

According to this rule, the defendant was entitled to a verdict on the issue upon the replication, as the plaintiff offered no evidence in support of it. It is more than probable that this arose from misapprehension as to the point whether he held the affirmative. Had it been deemed necessary, it may be presumed he would have attempted to support the issue. If the former recovery was not for this specific demand, it was easily susceptible of proof. Surprise, or inadvertence, may have been the cause that the plaintiff directed his attention, exclusively, to establish a good cause of action, without adverting to the effect of the defendant's plea. As the case, therefore, stands, the defendant will be entitled to judgment, although the plaintiff, in every other respect, may have shown a right to recover, unless the court award a new trial to enable him to supply the omission. As this seems to have been a fact really in controversy, the justice of the case requires, that after a trial on the merits, the plaintiff should be relieved, if, in other respects, his action is sustained.

I will, therefore, proceed to examine the only remaining question, which is, did the evidence support the declaration ?

232*] *Keyes, a witness for the plaintiff, testified that the defendant admitted to him that he had agreed to indemnify the plaintiff, in consideration of his becoming bail for him as Sheriff of Jefferson Co.

Wardwell, another witness for the plaintiff, testified that the defendant said, in consideration that Hale had become bail for him as sheriff, he had agreed to indemnify him on the bond he had given as bail for Bealls.

It will be observed that the consideration stated in the declaration is executory, to wit: if the plaintiff would become bail for the defendant. Proof of a past consideration will not support the averment. The variance would be fatal. In the first, the performance of the consideration, on the part of the plaintiff, constitutes a condition precedent. But a past consideration may be traversed, and cannot be enforced unless laid to have been done upon request; or, at least, it must appear that the party promising was under a moral obligation to do the act. (7 Johns., 87; 18 Johns., 455; 1 Chit., 297.) It is very clear, the defendant has a right to insist on the variance, if it exists, for the distinction between the two cases is well settled and is material.

The only evidence of the agreement is derived from the admissions to the two witnesses, Keyes and Wardwell, at different times. Whether the contract to indemnify was before or after the plaintiff became bail for the defendant, does not distinctly appear. The expressions, as stated by Wardwell, seem to imply that the bond had been given before the promise was made; and yet, as the defendant was not speaking with an eye to what form of words might render him liable, it may have been intended to state merely, that the consideration to become bail was the promise to indemnify. It is more probable that the promise was the inducement to become security, than that subsequently, as a distinct transaction, the defendant should gratuitously make a promise to indemnify. The one is a very natural proceeding; the other, out of the ordinary course. If, then, from the evidence, we are to draw an inference as to the time this contract was made, I incline *to think [*233 the conclusion warranted, that the contract was executory.

But admitting Wardwell's testimony varies from the declaration; the only effect is, that the plaintiff must resort to other proof, or fail. Although it does not support the declaration as framed, it cannot be used as evidence that the contract was different. The defendant cannot avail himself of his own admissions.

The evidence of Keyes places this fact beyond reasonable doubt. If his testimony, singly, makes out the plaintiff's case, it cannot be impaired by a different confession of the defendant, to another witness, and at another time. When the defendant says that he had agreed to indemnify in consideration of the plaintiff's becoming bail, I understand him as saying that he was to indemnify if the plaintiff became his surety. He does not speak in the past tense. It evidently implies that one was the consideration of the other. In my opinion, the witness substantially supports the consideration as laid in the declaration.

The damages found are $150.87. There can be no good objection to the claim of one third of the execution levied on the plaintiff's property, nor for one third of the costs for which the plaintiff gave a note to his attorney. If the plaintiff had not defended the suits commenced by Barney against the defendant, for the default of Bealls, the defendant might have defended, and claim his costs on the bond. As the plaintiff would have been ultimately liable, and as the defense by the bail was with the knowledge of the defendant, under the circumstances, his assent may be presumed. These two items amount to the verdict.

The result of my opinion is, that a new trial be granted, with costs to abide the event, unless the defendant, within 20 days, shall deliver to the plaintiff's attorney a waiver in writing of the benefit of his fourth plea; and if such waiver shall be delivered, then, that judgment be entered for the plaintiff.

Rule accordingly.

Cited in—2 Wend., 375; 53 N. Y., 624; 1 Daly, 451.

---

*BOWMAN v. RUSS AND COLTON. [*234

Pleading—Facts Showing Jurisdiction of Inferior Courts, Must Appear—Plea of Justification by Overseers of Poor, for Seizing Plaintiff's Property.

In trespass, a plea of justification, by Overseers of the Poor, that they seized the plaintiff's property by virtue of a warrant of two justices, issued for that purpose, on the defendant's application, upon the ground that the plaintiff had left his wife and children a charge to the town, pursuant to the 22d section of the Act for the Relief and Settlement of the Poor, 1 R. L., 286, 287, which proceeding was afterwards affirmed by the General Sessions, must state, affirmatively and expressly, that the plaintiff had left his wife and children a charge, &c.

This is necessary to give the justices jurisdiction, and it may be traversed by the replication.

A party is not estopped, by the proceedings and judgment of a court of inferior jurisdiction, to question its jurisdiction, and enough must be stated by the party who would avail himself of such proceedings and judgment, to show that it had jurisdiction.

Citations—7 Johns., 75; 10 Johns., 161; 1 Cow., 316.

TRESPASS. The declaration contained four counts. The first was of trespass *quare donum fregit, et de bonis*, &c. ; the second of trespass *quare clausum fregit, et de bonis*, &c. ; the third of trespass *quare clausum fregit*, and the fourth of trespass *de bonis asportatis*.

To the 1st count, the defendants pleaded, in justification of breaking and entering the house, and taking and carrying away the goods, that long before, and at, and after the time when, &c., they were Overseers of the Poor of the Town of York, in the County of Livingston ; and as such Overseers, before the time when, &c., to wit : July 7, 1823, made application to Paul Goddard and Apollos Long, Esquires, two of the justices of the peace of the County of Livingston, under and by virtue of the 22d section of the Act for the Relief and Settlement of the Poor, setting forth that the plaintiff had absented himself from his wife and children, and left them a charge to the Town of York, and was possessed of real and personal estate lying and being in the County of Livingston, which justices afterwards, and before the time when, &c., to wit : July 7, 1823, upon due proof of the facts in the application set forth, issued their warrant under their hands and seals, directed to the Overseers of the Poor of the Town of York, commanding them to take and seize the goods and chattels of the plaintiff, and to let out and receive the annual rents and profits of the lands and tenements of the plaintiff in the County of Livingston, for and towards the maintaining, bringing up and providing for his wife and children, so left a charge, &c. ; whereupon the defendants, as such Overseers, by virtue of the warrant, &c., peaceably and quietly entered, &c., and seized and took, &c., as they lawfully might, &c. ; **235***] and that afterwards, *to wit : at the then next term of the General Sessions of the Peace of the County of Livingston, to wit : at, &c., they made application to that court, for the confirmation of the seizure, &c. ; that the court, by consent of both parties, postponed the hearing till their next January Term, when, after hearing the proofs and allegations of the parties, they ordered and adjudged that the seizure should be, in all things, confirmed ; which are the same trespasses, &c.

The pleas to the 2d and 4th counts were substantially the same.

To the 3d count the defendants pleaded severally, *liberum tenementum*.

The plaintiff replied to the pleas to the 1st, 2d and 4th counts, that at the several times when, &c., in those counts mentioned, he had not left his wife and children, or any or either of them, a charge to the Town of York ; nor had his wife, or any or either of his children, at any time previous to the several times when, &c., been a charge to the Town of York ; but, on the contrary, ever and until, and at and after the several times, when, &c., he did continue to provide them with an abundant supply of every necessary for their support and maintenance, wherefore, &c.

To the pleas to the 3d count, the plaintiff new assigned, more particularly describing the *locus in quo* ; and the defendants justified, as in their pleas in the 1st, 2d and 4th counts.

The defendants demurred to the plaintiff's replication to the pleas to the 1st, 2d and 4th counts, and the plaintiff joined in demurrer.

The plaintiff demurred to the rejoinder of the defendants, and the latter joined in demurrer.

Mr. Hastings, for the defendants. The plaintiff is concluded by the proceedings before the justices, and the subsequent confirmation by the sessions. The justices acted judicially. This was holden of a justice who acts under the 16th section of the Act in question, 1 R. L., 284, in **Adams* v. *Oaks*, 20 Johns., 282, [***236** which section confers the power in substantially the same words as the 22d section, 1 R. L., 286, 287. Being a judicial act, the plaintiff is concluded from questioning it in this collateral way, until reversed. The decision of the justices, and the confirmation of the Court of Sessions, are conclusive on the plaintiff, as well in relation to jurisdiction, as in all other respects. He appeared before the sessions, and litigated the questions in the cause, one of which was, whether the court had jurisdiction. The question on the merits was, whether he had deserted his family. This has been tried and determined against him. He is estopped to question the fact in this form.

Mr. F. Tracy, contra. The pleas are clearly bad, for not averring the fact, that at the time of issuing the warrant, Bowman had left his family a charge to the Town of York. This fact was necessary to give the justices jurisdiction, and must, therefore, be pleaded, and may be tried as a matter *in pais*. The authorities are full to this point. *Adkins* v. *Brewer*, 3 Cow., 206 ; *M'Clung* v. *Ross*, 5 Wh., 116; *Morgan* v. *Dyer*, 10 Johns., 161 ; *Mills* v. *Martin*, 19 *Id.*, 33 ; *Borden* v. *Fitch*, 15 *Id.*, 141 ; *Perkins* v. *Proctor*, 2 Wils., 382.

Curia, per SAVAGE, *Ch. J.* The question is, whether the warrant of two justices to seize the property of a man, for leaving his wife and children a charge upon the town, is a good justification in an action of trespass, where it is admitted upon the record that he had not left his wife and children such charge.

In pleading the proceedings of an inferior court, it is necessary to state sufficient to give jurisdiction to the court, and then the plea may say, such proceedings were had, &c.; but here, it is not averred that the plaintiff had absented himself, &c.—the very fact upon which alone the justices had power to proceed. According to the point insisted on by the defendants, the justices may proceed against any man, and take from his own possession the very property *with which he is contributing to [***237** the support of his family.

In the case of *Frary* v. *Dakin*, 7 Johns., 75, the plea of an insolvent discharge was held ill, because it did not state that three fourths of the creditors had signed the petition, which was necessary to give jurisdiction. In *Morgan* v. *Dyer*, 10 Johns., 161, the plea omitted to state that the defendant had been an inhabitant of the county for three months before presenting the petition, or was in prison—one of which is necessary to give jurisdiction under the Act of 1811 ; and the plea was held ill for that reason. In *Wyman* v. *Mitchell*, 1 Cow., 316, it was not stated in the plea that the defendant was an inhabitant of the county when he made his application, although it stated that, at, &c., within the county, he was an insolvent debtor within the meaning of the Act, yet, being an inhabitant was necessary to give jurisdiction, and the plea was held ill.

According to these decisions, the pleas in question are clearly bad. Suppose the plea in *Wyman v. Mitchell* had not been demurred to, but the plaintiff had replied that the defendant, when he applied to the first judge of Albany, was not an inhabitant of the county; surely that fact admitted, would put an end to all pretense that the discharge was valid. So here, as to the pleas to the 1st, 2d and 4th counts, the fact being admitted, that when these proceedings were had against the plaintiff, he had not been guilty of the misconduct which alone gives to the justices power to proceed against him, it clearly follows that their proceedings were *coram non judice* and void.

If I am right, judgment must be given for the plaintiff on both demurrers. The justifications are all defective in themselves.

Judgment for the plaintiff.

S. C.—14 Abb. Pr., 150.
Cited in—12 Wend., 104; 13 Wend., 48; 32 N. Y., 137; 6 Lans., 287; 3 Barb., 188; 6 Barb., 623; 14 Barb., 99; 14 Abb. Pr., 150; 9 Bos., 588.

238*] *THE PRESIDENT, DIRECTORS AND COMPANY OF THE BANK OF UTICA

v.

CHILDS.

Failure of Bank Notary to Give Notice to Prior Indorsers of Note Held by the Bank for Collection—Payment of Damages by Bank—Suit by Bank Against Notary, Barred by Statute of Limitations—Cause of Action Arose on Omission of Notary—Notary not Affected by Former Suit Against Bank.

Where a note was indorsed by the holders, to a Bank for collection, whose notary negligently omitted to charge a prior indorser by giving notice of non-payment; and the Bank was sued by their indorsers for neglect, and compelled to pay damages; in an action of *assumpsit* against the notary, held, that the cause of action arose immediately on the omission; and the Bank, not having sued till more than six years after, were barred by the Statute of Limitations.

And this, though the former suit, and recovery thereon against, and payment of damages by the Bank to, the holders, were all within six years of the suit against the notary.

Held, also, that the notary, not having notice of the former suit, could in no way be affected by it, even as to the amount of damages.

Semble, it would be otherwise as to the mere amount of damages, if he had had notice; but still that he must have been sued within six years from his omission.

Citations—16 Mass., 456; 3 B. & A., 288, 626.

ON demurrer to the plaintiffs' replication. The 1st count of the declaration stated, that Feb. 14, 1818, and for a long time before and after, the defendant was a public notary of this State, &c.; and in consideration of certain reasonable fees and reward, to be paid to him by the plaintiffs, he then undertook and promised to give due notice to John C. Spencer, of the non-payment of a certain promissory note, dated Aug. 12, 1817, payable to Spencer, or order, 6 months after date, for $1,237, with interest, at the Utica Branch Bank, indorsed by Spencer to Smedes & Canfield, and left at the plaintiffs' banking house there for collection, by the holders (S. & C.), Feb. 10, 1818; and which was not paid when due, Feb. 14, 1818. Yet the defendant did not give notice of the non-payment, nor cause it to be given to Spencer; by reason whereof, the plaintiffs had been compelled to pay the holders the amount of the note with interest, and costs of prosecuting and defending a suit in this court, and in the Court for the Correction of Errors.

The 2d count was in substance the same.

The defendant pleaded, thirdly, not guilty of all or any of the grievances alleged within six years next before the commencement of the suit.

The plaintiffs replied, that within six years next before this suit was commenced, and Jan. 1, 1821, the holders sued the present plaintiffs at law, for the neglect of giving notice as alleged in the declaration, which suit the present plaintiffs defended; that in January Term, 1823, the holders recovered judgment for $1,804.37, which was affirmed by the Court for the Correction of Errors in *1824; and that [*239 May 20, 1824, the plaintiffs paid the holders $2,206.92, in full of the judgment so affirmed.

General demurrer and joinder.

Mr. S. A. Foot, in support of the demurrer. The *gravamen* rests on the negligence of the defendant; not the recovery against the plaintiffs. The history of that recovery will be found in 20 Johns., 372, and 3 Cow., 662. The replication, avers the recovery as a consequence of the negligence, for which negligence an action on the case is brought. The grievance alleged is the omission to give notice to Spencer. This omission is the ground of the action; and the statute, as pleaded, relates to the time of the omission. The answer given by the replication is, "we have been obliged to pay money by reason of the negligence, a long time after it happened; and, therefore, you are guilty within six years." Is not this a very illogical conclusion? Suppose the holders had not prosecuted the Bank within ten years, and the Bank had omitted to interpose the Statute of Limitations; would Childs be liable over? Shall he be put in the power of the Bank in this way, they paying when they please, and then calling on him? The Bank would be under no obligation to plead the statute. (3 Cow., 330, 331, &c.) Suppose deceit in the sale of a horse; but the defect concealed does not show itself till six years after the sale. No damage results till that time. Could this be replied in answer to the statute, pleaded to an action brought after the six years? So of a warranty, and a suit against the last vendor, who is thrown in damages, and then sues his vendor, more than six years from the sale to him, but a few days after he has paid the money. Would it be competent to reply the recovery? The answer that he did not before know of the defect, would not avail the vendee, in either the case of the deceit, or warranty. *Troup v. Smith's Exrs.*, 20 Johns., 33. The fraud or breach of warranty was consummate at the sale. *Oothout v. Thompson*, 20 Johns., 279. The turn of reasoning in the last case goes to illustrate what we contend *for; that a distinction should be kept [*240 up between torts and their consequences; that it is the act which must control, and not the consequences which flow from it. In both the cases cited the actual damages arose within six years of the action, yet this was not made a point.

The bank had an immediate cause of action on the omission taking place. If so, the statute began to run immediately. (12 Mod., 111; 1 Sid., 95; T. Raym., 61.) A liability to pay damages was enough to sustain the suit. As between the plaintiffs and defendant, the former were the holders of the note. Suppose a clerk of a county omits to record a deed, by which a title is defeated, must the party injured wait till eviction, before he can sue for damages, thus running the risk of the death of witnesses and other losses of testimony? The right of action dates from the wrong committed. *Read* v. *Markle*, 3 Johns., 523. This is so of a misfeasance; Com. Dig. Pl., 2, O.; Cro. Jac., 255; and the same reason applies to a nonfeasance. In *Godin* v. *Ferris*, 2 H. Bl., 14, it was held that custom-house officers must be sued within the three months' limitation, after actual seizure of goods; though a question upon the condemnation had been, during the whole time, in the Exchequer, on a suit there, which was pending at the expiration of the three months. *Saunders* v. *Saunders*, 2 East, 251, S. P.

The former suits cannot affect the defendant. He was not a party to them, nor does it appear that he had notice.

Mr. J. Platt, contra. When was the right of action complete? Against torts, which, *per se*, give a right of action, as trespass, trover and slander, by words actionable without special damages, we concede that the statute begins to run immediately, on the wrong being committed. But where the injury is consequential, and where the action does not lie immediately, the statute runs only from the time of the injury being complete. This cannot be said till the consequences are unfolded. There must be *damnum et injuria*. In this case, the neglect was *damnum;* but there was no *injuria*, till **241***] the damages fell upon the *plaintiffs. Till this happened, it was entirely contingent whether they would ever sustain any damage. The note might have been recovered of the makers. The indorser might have been indemnified, and thus notice out of the question; and he might consequently have been reached in a court of equity. The plaintiffs might have obtained the money in a variety of ways, or the holders might have sued Childs directly, as the sub-agent. By a suit, they might have made him their immediate agent, adopted his acts, and thus have recovered against him. The action upon this very note, reported in 20 Johns., 372, and 3 Cow., 662, regards the relation between them in this light. Where the holders might go was uncertain. If the Bank had paid the money in advance, this would have been in their own wrong and a good defense to Childs. But the payment was by compulsion in its most rigid form. The claim was litigated to the last, and ended in a court of *dernier resort*.

As to the class of torts which become actionable by reason of consequential damages, the plea of the statute must always say *non accrevit*. (3 Burr., 1281; Bac. Abr., Limitation of Actions, D, pl. 3; 2 Salk., 421, 422; 1 Saund., 38, *note* 2; 2 *Id.*, 63, *note* 6.) The commencement of a suit against the plaintiffs, and driving them to incur expenses, was the point of time when the cause of action arose in this case. They were not damnified till the suit was brought against them.

SUTHERLAND, *J*. Suppose a potion unskillfully administered by a physician, from which the patient sustains damages.

Mr. Platt. If it was a slow poison, and not operative till a year after, the action would not lie till that time. Suppose it administered to your honor's servant, and the consequences are not felt by you till after the year; you could not maintain your action before that time.

Childs served as a deputy of the plaintiffs, and was bound to indemnify them, the same as a deputy-sheriff is *his principal, [***242** the sheriff. A promise of indemnity is implied from Childs' relation to the Bank. If so, then *non damnificatus* would be a proper plea to this action. It is the same case as a covenant of simple indemnity. In the case supposed, of a clerk's omitting to register a deed, I deny that the statute would begin to run at the time of the omission, or from the time of an eviction, but from the intermediate time, whenever the party can show that he has lost his right. The omission may or may not prove injurious. The loss is potential, contingent. In this case, the holders had a right to sue immediately; but not so with us. We were obliged to wait till we saw where they would go. As I have shown in the case of the physician, there is a difference between the right of the servant and the right of the master. As to the former, the action may be brought instantly. As to the latter, not till the consequences are felt by the master. In the case of the former, the act may be injurious *per se;* in the latter, only by consequence. Suppose a stage driver carelessly overturns the coach and breaks a man's arm; the latter has his election, either to sue the driver or the proprietors of the line; but he omits to sue at all for three years—clearly the owners could have no action over, for they have no claim against the driver for breaking the arm, till damages are recovered of them, or, at any rate, till they are sued and put to expense. So here, Childs, the servant, was the immediate instrument of the injury, and is answerable on the same terms. Suppose seven years ago, one dug a pit in the highway, and five years after a traveler falls into it, and breaks his leg—clearly he could not sue till the consequential injury happen; and till then there is no right of action on which the statute can operate. The misfeasance was complete five years before, but the consequences are not felt till five years after, and from this time the statute begins to run.

We admit that Childs is not concluded by the former recovery. We had the choice to give him notice, and make him a party, thereby concluding him; or to defend without him. But this does not vary the truth of the case, *though it varies the mode of proof. [***243** We were, however, bound to plead the former suits, and the consequent recovery, to complete our right. (3 Cow., 330, 331, &c.) *Ash* v *Bushnell*, cited on the other side, from Cro. Jac., 255, was after verdict. But clearly the declaration would have been held bad if the defendant had demurred.

While arguing, Manning's Dig. had been put into my hands, containing (Limitation of Actions, A *a*, pl. 2) the following note of *Compton* v. *Chandless*, 4 Esp., 18, which I had not seen: "If the statute be pleaded to an action against an attorney for negligence, *semble* that the six years must be reckoned from the period at which the plaintiff was damnified; not from the time when the blunder was committed." (Kenyon, *Ch. J.*) Several cases will be found cited at the end of that note in support of the doctrine from Espinasse. *Peake* v. *Ambler*, W. Jones, 329 (*a*); Cro. Car., 359, S. C.; *Shutfen* v. *Penow*, *Ibid.*, 138; *Hughes* v. *Thomas*, 13 East, 474; *Littleboy* v. *Wright* (*b*); 1 Lev., 69; *Hickman* v. *Walker*, Willes, 27.

Mr. Foot, in reply. The gentleman's illustration by the case of a pit dug seven years ago, is inapposite. The digging does not occasion the injury, but the falling in. The hypothesis of the stage driver is certainly apposite, if followed up with the addition that the owner of the line is a passenger in the stage. Short of this, it is not; for the proprietors do not own the arm of a stranger passenger. Here the plaintiffs were the passenger; or, to drop the simile, the were the holders of the note; not, as is supposed, the persons who indorsed **244***] it for collection. The plaintiffs *were treated and considered as the holders, in the former suits. The note was protested in their names; and notice, should have been given in their names. Their indorsers had no right to an action against Childs. But I deny that in the case supposed, of the stage driver, his master's action depends on the suit by the injured party. Suppose he break seven arms of seven different passengers by the accident, may the master wait and have seven separate actions against his servant at twelve years distance of time, or more, according to the date of the several suits and recoveries against the former?

No decision can be found, recognizing the distinction advanced, between pleading the statute in answer to immediate and consequential injuries. There is such a distinction in reference to the nature of the action, as whether it shall be trespass or case; but this is the first time I have heard it applied to the Statute of Limitations. If it be held in a case of damages remote, the next must be those more immediate, and thus we may go on to all the actions upon the case. In legal language and contemplation, the damages were not contingent in the principal case. If Childs was amenable to the indorsers of the Bank, and the former had sued him, this would not prevent their suing the Bank. But if there was this contingency of election, its consequence is mistaken. The right to demur does not follow; but the gentleman should have taken issue on our plea of the statute, and given the matter in evidence at the trial, or he should have replied this fact specially.

(*a*) The 3d res. in Jones, 330, is in these words: "If an *assumpsit* be, and the damnification accrue, not at one time, but parcel at one time, and parcel at several times after, as in this case, he may have entire action after the last time of damnification; and though parcel of the damnification was before six years of the action brought, and parcel within six years, yet the action well lies, notwithstanding the statute of 21 Jac." The action was on a promise of indemnity. The report in Cro. Car., 349, by the title of Peck v. Ambler, does not recite this general resolution in so many words; but the case is to the same effect.

(*b*) Slander, *per quod*, &c. Held, that the statute ran from the time of the special damage, which is the cause of the action.

It is admitted that the moment one cent of damages accrued to the plaintiffs, their right of action arose. This admits that the recovery did not give the cause of action, but only determines the amount of damages. A contingency is a matter which no one can control. The case of a promissory note, payable on demand, is stronger than the one put by Ld. Mansfield, in 3 Burr., 1281, and cited against us; yet the statute runs from the date.

In the case put, of the injury to the servant, *per quod servitium amisit*, it is the loss of service, not the injury, which gives the right of action to the master.

*This is not a technical contract of [***245** indemnity, but a promise to do a certain act. When a contract of indemnity is shown, we shall be ready to meet the question of the statute in relation to that. The present is a case of tort, and not of indemnity. It is admitted, as to the case put, of a clerk of the county, who omits to record a deed, a fixed liability to eviction, without eviction itself, is enough to constitute a ground of action. This admission, alone, gives us the cause.

Curia, per WOODWORTH, *J.*, after stating the pleadings. The question to be decided is, whether the Statute of Limitations began to run from the time when the note fell due, since which more than six years elapsed before the present suit was commenced, or from the time of the recovery against the plaintiffs, which was within six years.

It is contended that the cause of action was not complete until the plaintiffs sustained damages. I apprehend this cannot be the test. On the principle assumed, the defendant's liability might continue indefinitely, when, from the nature of the case, there is no such necessity. He was liable to be prosecuted by the plaintiffs, immediately after his default. He was their agent. In such an action, it is true, a question might be, what damages have the plaintiffs sustained. That would depend on the insolvency, or probable extent of the insolvency of the makers. To that extent, the plaintiffs were answerable to Smedes & Canfield, the holders of the note. The defendant could not object that Smedes & Canfield had not recovered of the plaintiffs. It would be a sufficient answer, that they were liable to the same measure of damages claimed from the defendant. To that amount, a loss had arisen, which the defendant ought to pay. He had no concern with the inquiry, whether the holders of the note would or would not, at a future period, call on the plaintiffs for the loss. I consider the cause of action against the defendant, to rest on that default in not giving notice; *and as arising immediately [***246** on the happening of the default. And if so, the statute began to run from that time. The case of *Miller* v. *Adams*, 16 Mass., 456, contains a recognition of the principle. The former brought an action against the latter, a deputy-sheriff, for making a defective return to an original writ, sued out against several defendants. The omission was, to return a summons as to two of the defendants; for which cause, the judgment obtained against them was reversed. Adams pleaded the Statute of Limitations, upon which the question was, whether it ran from the time when Miller was actually damnified by the reversal, or when the return was made; and held the latter. The court say, the judgment being then liable to reversal, the plaintiff might have immediately brought his action, and would have been entitled to his damages. A like principle will be found in two late cases, decided by the English K. B. *Batley* v. *Faulkner*, 3 B. & A., 288, and *Short* v. *M'Carthy*, *Id.*, 626. In the last the plaintiff, as here, declared in *assumpsit*, and stated, as a breach, that the defendant did not diligently and sufficiently make search at the Bank of England, to ascertain whether certain stock was standing in the names of certain persons, the defendant having been employed as an attorney so to do. The omission to search took place more than six years before action brought. The court held the omission to search was the cause of action, from the time of which the statute ran.

The recovery in the former case cannot be the measure of damages, because there is no averment that the defendant had notice; and consequently, for aught that appears, he had no chance of defending, as to the material point. What has been lost by the neglect? It will scarcely be contended, that if, notwithstanding the omission to charge the indorser, the makers of the note were unquestionably responsible, and of undoubted credit, the holders were entitled to recover the whole amount of the note. The defendant is not to be charged with the amount of the judgment when he has not been heard. If, indeed, the plaintiffs have given notice to the defendant **247***] of the suit *commenced against them, and required him to defend, I incline to think he would be concluded as to the damages. But even then, it must appear that the action was commenced against the defendant within six years; for the right of action was complete the moment after the neglect. If the plaintiffs omitted to prosecute till after a recovery against them, and that was after six years, the remedy would be barred by the statute.

If the view I have taken be correct, it follows that the plaintiffs might have sustained their action, without waiting to be prosecuted, or paying damages to the holders. If, however, it were otherwise, I think payment of the damages by the plaintiffs, without suit, would not have been in their own wrong; although it would be attended with risk in this respect. If they could not show that the damages sustained by the defendant's default was equal to the sum paid in satisfaction to the holders, they would incur a loss *pro tanto*. The defendant would be bound to indemnify for the amount paid, provided it did not exceed the injury proved at the trial. Beyond this, he would not be holden. If it be necessary to have paid the damages in the first instauce, I do not see how the plaintiffs, under the circumstances in which they were placed, could avoid this risk.

On the argument, this action was likened to the action for an injury to a servant, *per quod servitium amisit*; and the case of digging a pit in the highway seven years ago, in which the plaintiff's leg was broken five years afterwards, and several like cases. The difference between the two cases mentioned and the present case is this: here the damages accrued at the time of the defendant's default. In the cases mentioned, and supposed to be analogous, no damages accrued (except perhaps nominal in the case of the servant), until the loss of service took place, or the limb was broken. The same answer may be given to several other cases put upon the argument.

I am of opinion that the defendant is entitled to judgment; but the plaintiff may amend on payment of costs.

Judgment for the defendant.

Cited in—6 Cow., 491; 5 Barb., 396; 40 Barb., 241; 61 Barb., 142; 1 Sandf., 103; 97 Pa. St., 54; 39 Am. Rep., 795 (97 Pa., 47).

---

*JACKSON, ex dem. HOGARTH ET UX., v. NELSON. [*248

Ejectment—Witnesses—Competency of.

In ejectment by the heir at law, against a devisee, a co-devisee, and tenant in common with the defendant, not in actual possession, may be a witness for the defendant

And this, especially, if he say, on his *voire dire*, that he does not know that he is interested.

Citations—1 Johns. Cas., 275; 3 Johns. Cas., 234; 4 Johns., 232; 5 Johns., 158; 10 Johns., 21.

EJECTMENT, tried at the Putnam Circuit, Oct., 1824, before Williams, *Circuit J.*

At the trial, the following facts appeared: Joshua Nelson died in 1817, seised in fee of the premises in question; and the wife of the lessor of the plaintiff was a granddaughter of the deceased and, as one of his heirs, entitled to one third of the premises in question.

The defendant set up a devise from Joshua Nelson, of his land, including the premises in question, to his only son, Jacob Nelson, for life; remainder to the children of the latter, viz.: Cornelius (the defendant), Samuel C., Jacob, Joshua and James M., &c., in fee. Jacob, their father, died in 1811, leaving his five sons living at his death, and three daughters.

The plaintiff alleged that the ancestor, Joshua Nelson, burnt the will in Oct., 1813; and the defendant, that at the time of burning the testator was not of sound mind. And this was the question at the trial.

Samuel C. Nelson, one of the devisees (but who was not in actual possession as such), was offered as a witness for the defendant; and though objected to (being sworn on his *voire dire*, and stating that he did not know that he had any interest), was admitted by the judge, and sworn.

Verdict for the defendant.

Mr. T. J. Oakley, for the plaintiff, moved for a new trial. He relied on *Brant* v. *Dyckman*, 1 Johns. Cas., 275, as decisive against the admissibility of the witness. There, he said, the witness was not allowed to prove himself even in possession. Here the witness was allowed to protect both his interest and possession. The possession of his co-tenant was his.

Mr. W. Nelson, contra, cited *Van Nuys* v. *Terhune*, 3 Johns. Cas., 82, that a mere interest in the question, is no objection; but it must be an interest in the event. Here the

249*] *witness was not in possession, and the verdict could never affect him. It follows that he was competent. *Jackson* v. *Rumsey*, 3 Johns. Cas., 234; *Jackson* v. *Bard*, 4 Johns., 230; *Jackson* v. *Van Duzen*, 5 *Id.*, 144; *Stockham* v. *Jones*, 10 *Id.*, 21.

Curia, per SUTHERLAND, *J.*, after stating the facts. In *Brant* v. *Dyckman* the defendant denied that he was in possession when the action was commenced, and called one Vredenberg, to prove that he, Vredenberg, at the commencement of the suit, was, and then still continued to be, in possession; and not the defendant. He was excluded by the judge, and the Supreme Court held him incompetent. They say, "if he was in possession, he had an immediate interest to protect that possession and prevent a recovery." "Whether this be considered," they continue, "an interest in the event of the suit, or in the question between the parties merely, it is one of those cases in which the reason and policy of the law ought to exclude a witness. His interest in the question of possession, is almost the same as that of the defendant himself."

Admitting this decision to be sound, I think the present case is distinguishable from it. The witness was there called to support his own actual possession. A verdict against the defendant would have resulted in a judgment and execution, by which the witness would inevitably have been turned out of possession. But in this case, the possession of the witness is constructive merely, not actual. The effect of a recovery on the part of the plaintiff cannot be to turn him out of actual possession, nor can the verdict be evidence for or against him in any other suit. It is an interest in the question merely, and not in the event of the suit. (3 Johns., Cas., 234; 4 Johns., 232; 5 *Id.*, 158; 10 *Id.*, 21.)

Besides, the witness was sworn on his *voire dire*, and testified that he did not reside on the premises in question, and had no interest in them that he knew of. There may have been a partition.

Motion for a new trial denied.

250*] *RAPELYE AND SMITH, Survivors of LAWRENCE,

v.

MACKIE ET AL.

Sales—Delivery—Property does not Pass till Delivery—No Delivery where Something Remains to be Done to Ascertain Quantity or Price, even where there is a Part Delivery.

The plaintiffs, having cotton at three stores, in Brooklyn, 69 bales, marked G. G. & Co. at the store of B., and 30 of the same mark, at the store of M. & W., sold 66 bales marked G. G. & Co. to the defendants, delivering them a *pro forma* bill of parcels, thus: "66 bales, say 19,800 lbs., $12 per cwt., 1 *per cent.* off;" the defendants paying at the time, $1,800, in part for the whole. Then the cotton in M. & W.'s store was destroyed by fire, and the defendants demanded of the plaintiffs an order for the 66 bales, which was refused; but the plaintiffs gave an order for 36 bales. These were then weighed by the plaintiffs; and another bill of parcels delivered to the defendants, including the 36 bales, according to the weighmaster's bill; and the 30 bales at a certain weight each, with the remark, "deduct, for supposed loss, 150." The 36 bales were delivered at the time of weighing.

Held, that the property of the 30 bales did not vest in the defendants, and that, therefore, the plaintiffs could not recover the price.

The 30 bales not being identified in the contract, and specifically sold, the contract might have been satisfied by a delivery of 30 bales with the mark mentioned, from any other place beside Brooklyn; or if the contract related to Brooklyn, then out of any other store there, beside M. & W.'s; or if the contract had been to sell the 30 bales at M. & W.'s, yet they not being weighed, did not pass.

When something remains yet to be done, as between buyer and seller, or for the purpose of ascertaining either the quantity or price of the articles sold, there is no delivery; and the property does not pass, though the price be in part paid.

And so, if there be a part delivery, the other part not yet ascertained will not pass.

And there need not be an express agreement, that something farther shall be done. It is enough that it appear, from the circumstances of the case, to be necessary.

Citations 15 Johns., 349; 6 East, 614; 11 East, 210, 522; 12 East, 614; 2 Maule & S., 397; 4 Campb., 237.

ASSUMPSIT for goods sold and delivered, and goods bargained and sold, tried at an adjourned circuit in the City and County of N. Y., Jan. 30, 1824, before Edwards, *Circuit J.*, when the jury found a verdict for the plaintiffs, for $471.90, being the price, with interest, of 66 bales of cotton (after deducting $1,800 paid by the defendants), which the plaintiffs claimed on the trial to have sold and delivered to the defendants.

The facts proved at the trial are sufficiently stated in the opinion of the court.

Mr. J. Duer, for the defendants, moved for a new trial. He made the following points, and cited the authorities which follow, in support of them.

1. Where goods sold, are parcel of a large quantity, the property does not vest absolutely in the vendee, so long as there is no selection or designation of the part sold, or separation of it from the part unsold. (2 Johns., 16; 14 *Id.*, 167; 7 East, 558; Shep. Touch., 224; Long, Sales, 149.

2. Where any act of the seller, such as counting, weighing, &c., remains to be done, to ascertain the exact quantity sold, the property does not vest absolutely in the *vendee; [*251 but until such act is done, remains at the risk of the vendor. (2 H. Bl., 123; Bull. *N.P.*, 50; 12 Johns., 165; 13 *Id.*, 53; Long, Sales, 154–157; 5 Taunt., 617; 2 Maule & S., 397; 15 Johns., 349; 2 Campb., 240; Ross, Vendors and Purchasers, 28.)

3. In the present case, there was neither an actual nor constructive delivery to the defendants, of the 30 bales of cotton that were burnt in the store of Merry & Waite. (2 N. R., 61.)

4. That the payment of part of the price, does not, of itself, alter the property in the thing sold, but only binds the bargain. (2 Bl. Com., 448.)

Mr. G. Griffin, contra, insisted on the following points, among others, and cited the authorities which follow, in support of them:

1. There was a complete sale by the plaintiffs to the defendants, on or before Aug. 21, 1822, of the 30 bales of cotton consumed by fire in the store of Merry & Waite. (11 East, 211; *Id.*, 219, per Bayley, *J.*; *Id.*, 210; 2 H. Bl., 504; 4 Bos. & P., 69; 6 East, 614; 14 *Id.*, 614; 4 Campb., 237; 13 East, 522; 4 Taunt., 644; 5 *Id.*, 176; *Id.*, 617; 2 Maule & S., 397; 7 East, 558; 1 Pick., 476; Noy Max., 88; 2 Bl. Com., 448.)

2. The contract of sale was entire; and by accepting the two parcels that remained, after the fire, the defendants recognized and ratified the contract *in toto*.

Curia, per WOODWORTH, *J*. Aug. 21,1822, the plaintiffs sold to the defendants 66 bales of cotton, marked G. G. & Co. As evidence of the sale, the bill of parcels delivered to the defendants was produced, on which the charge is made thus: "66 bales, say 19,800 lbs., $12 per hundred, $2,376, 1 *per cent.* off." The defendants paid at the time, $1,800.

The plaintiffs' cotton was in three stores at Brooklyn; one kept by Van Bokkelen, another by Caze & Richaud, and the third by Merry & Waite. There were 69 bales, of the mark sold, in the store of Van Bokkelen, and 30 bales in the store of Merry &Waite. A night or two after **252***] *the delivery of the bill of parcels, the 30 bales were burnt. They had been weighed about the 16th or 17th of July. No order for delivery was given. The bill was a *pro forma* bill,the weight not being precisely ascertained. The plaintiffs' witness testified that he presumed the word "say" denoted that the estimate was made from the invoices; that had the weight been actually ascertained, and the cotton delivered,the deduction of 1 *per cent.* would have been carried out on the bill of parcels.

On Sept. 5, another bill was delivered to the defendants, charging the 36 bales according to the weigh-master's bill, which was produced. The 30 bales were inserted at a certain weight each, with a remark, "deduct for supposed loss, 150." The 36 bales were weighed at the request of the plaintiffs, as the witness supposed, at the time of delivery to the defendants, and subsequent to the fire; and if the sale had been made by the original invoice, the cotton would not have been reweighed, according to the usual course of business. After the fire, the defendants called for an order for 66 bales, which was refused; but an order for 36 was given.

On this statement, I am of opinion the plaintiffs are not entitled to recover for more than 36 bales.

The ground upon which the defense rests is, that, as to the 30 bales, burnt in the store of Merry & Waite,there never was a delivery. This is apparent from the fact that there was no proof as to the identity of this parcel. It would have been competent for the plaintiffs to deliver the number of bales sold,from any parcel, whether stored at Brooklyn, or in the City of N. Y.; and such a delivery would have satisfied the contract. The bill of parcels is general. There is no specification of the particular bales, or the place where stored. A number of bales, containing the quantity, is all that appears to have been required. The defendants could not insist on receiving the specific quantity at Merry & Waite's; and unless they had this right, I do not perceive on what ground they are to be subjected to the loss. The principle would render them liable for property which the plaintiffs **253***] might or might not *have elected to deliver, in satisfaction of the purchase. The case presented is one where a smaller parcel is sold out of a larger, without any designation. Had there been, it may be presumed the plaintiffs would have produced proof of it. The broker who made the contract was in court, and not called.

But if it be admitted that the purchase was of cotton stored at Brooklyn, the only specification is, that the bales were marked "G. G. & Co." No reference is had to Merry & Waite's store in particular. At that very time the plaintiffs had 69 bales of this description at Van Bokkelen's. Will it be pretended that a delivery of 66 bales of this parcel would not have satisfied the purchase? If it would,then it may be asked, where is the proof that the defendants had acquired an absolute right to the 30 bales burnt?

There is another conclusive objection against a recovery. The cotton was to be weighed before the delivery was complete. It is not necessary there should appear an express agreement was made to that effect. The first bill of parcels was well described by the plaintiff's clerk, as a *pro forma* bill. It was conjectural as to the quantity. The one *per cent.* was not carried out for that reason. The subsequent act of weighing was indispensable, unless the defendants had agreed to accept the cotton according to the estimate made. The plaintiffs must have so considered it. It was reweighed at their request. Then, for the first time, the one *per cent.* was deducted. It was then ascertained that the quantity was less than originally calculated. These facts show very satisfactorily, that the delivery was not complete when the 30 bales were burnt. Indeed, it is difficult to conceive upon what principle the seller would consider that there was a delivery,when it was not ascertained how much was sold, or the amount to be received. The principle that runs through all the cases is, that when something remains to be done, as between buyer and seller, or for the purpose of ascertaining either the quantity or price, there is no delivery. Whether the *question [***254** arises where the property is destroyed or where the right of stopping *in transitu* is drawn in question, cannot make a difference. If a delivery has been made, the goods are at the risk of the purchaser; and the seller's right of stopping *in transitu* ceases.

The delivery of the 36 bales, after the fire, was not a recognition of the right to claim for the residue. The defendants demanded and were entitled to 66 bales. The acceptance of a part is in exoneration of the plaintiffs, *pro tanto*, leaving the question, respecting the residue, as it was before that delivery.

The following authorities will be found to support the doctrine upon which we rest the decision of this cause: 15 Johns., 349; 6 East, 614; 11 East, 210; 12 East, 614; 11 East, 522; 2 Maule & S., 397; 4 Camph., 237.

There must be a new trial, with costs to abide the event.

New trial granted.

Cited in—3 Wend., 118; 8 Wend., 260; 15 Wend., 222; 1 Den., 52; 5 Den., 381; H. & D., 420; 8 N. Y., 297; 9 N. Y., 217; 19 Barb., 427; 62 Barb., 262; 64 Barb., 268; 10 Abb. N. S., 94; 3 Sandf., 619; 3 Duer, 233, 316; 4 Rob., 32; 2 Daly, 513; 9 Minn., 146; 20 Am. Dec., 671; 12 Am. Rep., 63 (51 N. H., 94).

SOUTHARD *v.* REXFORD.

1. Witness need not Criminate Himself—Personal Privilege—Questions Tending to Criminate may be Asked and Answered. 2. Action for Breach of Promise—Evidence of Promise—Breach of—Damages—Aggravation of—Discretion of Jury.

A witness may be asked a question, the answer to which will criminate him; and if he has no objection, may answer it.

His privilege is personal only; but it is the duty of the court to apprise him of it.

And where, in an action for breach of promise of marriage, the defendant asked his witness if he ever knew of any person having criminal connection with the plaintiff, and the judge would not suffer the question to be put; but himself told the witness he might, if he pleased, state any improper intercourse, if there had been any, between the plaintiff and him; held, that this was not a violation of the rule.

A jury may infer mutual promises of marriage from the defendant's visits to the plaintiff as a suitor, and his declarations that he had promised to marry the plaintiff.

After a defendant has once broken a promise of marriage, his offer to renew it is no defense to an action for the breach.

In an action for breach of promise of marriage, if the defendant give notice with his plea, that he will prove that the plaintiff has been guilty of fornication; but fail entirely to show it on the trial, the jury may consider this in aggravation of damages.

The damages in this action are in the sound discretion of the jury, under the circumstances of each particular case.

Citations—1 Phil. Ev., 222; 3 Campb., 210, 519; 3 Taunt., 424; 13 East, 58 *n*; 4 Day, 123; 2 Esp. Dig., 40; 13 Johns., 82, 229; 4 Esp., 243; Peake Ev., 129.

ASSUMPSIT, for breach of promise of marriage, tried at the Saratoga Circuit, June, 1825, before Walworth, *Circuit J.*

The plea was the general issue, with notice that the defendant would prove, in his defense, **255***] that the plaintiff *had, at various times, and with various persons, specifying them, committed fornication after the alleged promise.

The defendant attempted, at the trial, to prove this branch of his defense by one Stephen Aylesworth and others, but failed.

When Aylesworth was upon the stand, the counsel for the defendant asked him if he ever knew of any person having criminal connection with the plaintiff?

The judge told the witness he need not consider that question as including himself; that he was not bound to say anything respecting himself. That if he said he did know of any person, the plaintiff's counsel must be permitted to inquire who it was, in order to test his credibility, or for the purpose of enabling him to call witnesses to disprove it.

The witness then answered the question in the negative.

The defendant's counsel then claimed the right of putting the question in such manner as to include the witness in the answer to be given, leaving it to him to make the objection to answering it, if he thought proper.

The judge decided that it was improper to put a question to a witness, when it clearly appeared he was not bound to answer it. That the right of the witness to be exempt from declaring his own infamy or guilt was perfect, and must be preserved to its fullest extent. That it is the province of the court to decide, whether a direct answer to the question proposed will furnish evidence against the witness. In such cases the witness is not bound to answer the question either way, although the truth may not criminate him; and in all such cases it is the duty of the court to interfere, and prevent the question from being put to the witness, and not compel him to claim an exemption from answering, on the ground that it would criminate himself; because the very claim of exemption would cast a suspicion on him. Neither would the judge permit the counsel for the defendant to cast a suspicion upon the character of the plaintiff, by asking their own witness a question which she might refuse to answer, for the purpose of creating such a suspicion. That when the answer to a question cannot directly implicate *the [***256** character of the witness, but may do it collaterally; then the question may be put, and the witness must claim his exemption, and show how it may implicate him. And he must, in addition to that, on his oath, declare that his answer will, in his opinion, have that tendency.

The judge, therefore, refused to allow the question to be put in the form proposed, but told the witness that he was at liberty to state any improper intercourse, if there was any such, between the plaintiff and him.

Other questions upon the trial were, whether a valid promise of marriage was proved, and whether, if proved, it had been rescinded—both of which the judge left to the jury upon the evidence. Another question was, whether an offer by the defendant to renew his promise of marriage, and a refusal by the plaintiff, was a defense; as to which the judge charged, that if the defendant had violated his agreement and, in cousequence, the connection between the parties had been broken off, the offer and refusal were no defense.

As to the damages, he charged, "that in cases of this kind, the damages are always in the discretion of the jury; and in fixing the amount, they have a right to take into consideration the nature of the defense set up by the defendant. That in his defense, he had attempted to excuse his abandonment of the plaintiff, on the ground that she was unchaste, and had committed fornication with different individuals. But it appeared from the testimony of his own witnesses, that her character in that respect had not been tarnished even by the breath of suspicion. That with such a defense on the record, a verdict for nominal or trifling damages might be worse for her reputation than a general verdict for the defendant. That if the defendant had won her affections, and promised her marriage; and had not only deserted her without cause, but had also spread this defense upon the record, for the purpose of destroying her character, the jury would be justified in giving exemplary damages."

The judge also commented at length upon the testimony; and expressed to the jury a decided opinion in favor *of the plaint- [***257** iff on all the questions of fact submitted to their decision.

The other facts are stated in the opinion of the court.

Verdict for the plaintiff for $750.

Mr. A. C. Paige, for the defendant, moved for a new trial. He insisted there were no mutual promises of marriage proved; the promise of the defendant, therefore, was without consideration. But if there was a binding promise, the plaintiff's second engagement of marriage with another was a rescission of that with the defendant. (Holt *N. P.*, 151; 3 Mass., 189.) Besides, the defendant was discharged from his contract by his offer to perform, and the plaintiff's refusal. (17 Johns., 175; 1 Chit. Pl., 318.) Her refusal to receive the defendant's visits, and receiving those of others, were a breach of the contract on her part, and discharged the defendant.

The judge erred in overruling the question proposed to be put to the witness. (3 Taunt., 424; 1 Phil. Ev., 205, 206, and the cases there cited, ed. 1820; 3 Campb., 210, 519; 4 Esp., 226.)

The judge erred in charging that if the contract had been broken off without the plaintiff's fault, she was not bound afterwards to receive the defendant's addresses.

He also erred in charging that the damages were in the discretion of the jury, and that the defense interposed should aggravate the damages. (15 Mass., 48; 2 Phil. Ev., 103, 106, 107; 3 Johns., 62, 64, 65; 9 *Id.*, 51.)

Mr. S. G. Huntington, contra, cited 3 Campb., 519; 4 Esp., 225, 242; 1 Phil. Ev., 206, ed. of 1820; 2 Esp. Dig., Gould ed., 405, per Marshall, *Ch. J.*, in *U. S.* v. *Burr;* 2 Com. Cont., 410.

Curia, per SUTHERLAND, *J.* Whether there were mutual promises of marriage between the parties or not was properly left by the judge to the jury, as a question of fact. The evidence abundantly supports the verdict upon this point. The promise on the part of the defendant was clearly proved. In Jan., 1819, **258***] he admitted to an Eliza *Peck that he had promised to marry the plaintiff, and intended to fulfill his engagement. About the same time he told the brother of the plaintiff that he intended soon to marry her. A number of witnesses testified that from June, 1818, to 1823, the defendant visited the plaintiff as a suitor, and was apparently well received by her; and it was matter of public notoriety that he was courting her. The fact of an engagement of marriage between the parties—of a promise on the part of the plaintiff as well as of the defendant—is necessarily to be inferred from this evidence.

It was also correctly submitted to the jury, to determine as a question of fact upon the evidence, whether the engagement had been rescinded by mutual consent or had been broken off by the plaintiff before any breach on the part of the defendant. It was contended that the contract was broken by a subsequent engagement of the defendant to one Stephen Aylesworth in the spring of 1819. On this point the evidence, on the part of the defendant, was of a very doubtful and suspicious character. The case states that Stephen Aylesworth, who swore to the engagement, upon cross-examination by the court, repeatedly contradicted his previous statements, and told several different stories as to the time when the agreement to be married was made between him and the plaintiff. The testimony of Abel Aylesworth and Samuel Peterson as to the confessions of the plaintiff that she was engaged to be married to Stephen Aylesworth were not free from just grounds of suspicion. The jury, without doubt, entirely disregarded the testimony of Stephen Aylesworth; and if they believed the other two witnesses, they probably supposed the declarations of the plaintiff were not made in earnest, as all the testimony shows that, at this very period, the defendant was constant in his attention to her, and was publicly considered as her suitor, and received by her in that character.

The offer made by the defendant a short time previous to his marriage to renew his attentions to the plaintiff, and her refusal to receive them, afford him no defense against this *action. The only evidence upon this [***259** point is derived from the confessions of the plaintiff to Olive and Peter Tarpenny. She stated that a short time before the defendant courted his present wife, he came to her and wanted to be friendly again. She told him he had deceived and disappointed her so often that she could have no confidence in him. That the defendant then told her he was determined to get married, and that unless she received his visits he would go somewhere else. She then replied that he might go, for what she cared. The fair construction of this conversation is that the defendant had previously violated his engagement; that the plaintiff considered him so faithless that no reliance could be placed upon his promises, and she, therefore, refused to permit him to renew his visits. It is to be remarked that the defendant does not, on this occasion, offer to marry the plaintiff, but only to renew his addresses. She chose to consider the connection between them as at an end, and not subject herself to the pain and mortification of being again deceived. The defendant's offer is not to consummate the original contract, but to make a new one. Then she had a right to decline.

I think the judge erred in preventing the defendant from asking the witness (Stephen Aylesworth), in general terms, if he ever knew of any person having criminal connection with the plaintiff. The witness was not bound to answer the question, so far as the answer would criminate himself; and it was the duty of the court to apprise him of his right in that respect. But if a witness, under such circumstances, thinks proper to waive his privilege, I do not understand it to be either the duty or the right of the court to force it upon him, and to deprive the party of the benefit of such disclosures as he may voluntarily make. It is a personal privilege only. The fact that the witness had criminal intercourse with the plaintiff, the defendant had an undoubted right to establish. The witness was entirely disinterested and as competent to testify to that fact as any other. No man shall be compelled to criminate himself; but if, from a sense of justice or any other consideration, *he is willing to make disclosures [***260** which involve his own character, and may expose him to punishment, I know no reason, either of law or policy, which should prevent him.

If a question of this description cannot be put in general terms, how is a *particeps criminis* ever to testify against his associates?

In Phillips the rule is thus stated: "A witness cannot be compelled to answer any question which has a tendency to expose him to penalties or to any kind of punishment;" 1 Phil. Ev., 222; and I have found no case where the object of the question was to establish a fact material in the cause, and not directly to impeach the character of the witness and render him incompetent, in which the court have ever interfered, except upon the application of the witness. 3 Campb., 210, 519; 3 Taunt., 424; 13 East, 58, *note;* 4 Day,

123; *U. S.* v. *Burr*, 2 Esp. Dig., 405, per Marshall, *Ch. J.;* 13 Johns., 82, 229. The language of the judges, in all the cases is, that the witness is not bound to answer a question, the object of which is to criminate or render him infamous. In *Rex* v. *Lewis*, 4 Esp., 225, the witness, on his cross-examination, was asked "if he had not been in the House of Correction in Sussex." Ld. Ellenborough interposed, and said the question should not be asked. So in *M'Bride* v. *M'Bride*, 4 Esp., 243, Ld. Alvanley would not permit a witness to be asked "whether she lived in a state of concubinage with the plaintiff." In both these cases the questions were put on the cross-examination, and with the sole view of directly impeaching the witnesses. They cannot be supposed to have been willing to answer them; and though it does not affirmatively appear that they objected, yet, from the very nature of the case, such undoubtedly was the fact. (Peak. Ev., 129, *et seq.*)

But although the judge refused to permit the defendant's counsel to put the question generally to the witness, so as to include himself as well as others, in which I think he erred; still, he informed the witness that he was at liberty to state any improper intercourse, if **261***] there had been any, *between him and the plaintiff. The witness, therefore, was not prevented from making a full disclosure; and though, perhaps, he would be less likely to do it under such circumstances, still I do not think it a sufficient cause for setting aside the verdict.

Upon the question of damages, the charge of the judge appears to me to be unexceptionable. There can be no settled rule by which they are, in every case, to be regulated. They rest in the sound discretion of the jury, under the circumstances of each particular case; and where the defendant attempts to justify his breach of promise of marriage, by stating upon the record as the cause of his desertion of the plaintiff, that she had repeatedly had criminal intercourse with various persons, and fails entirely in proving it, this is a circumstance which ought to aggravate the damages. A verdict for nominal or trifling damages, under such circumstances, would be fatal to the character of the plaintiff; and it would be matter of regret, indeed, if a check upon a license of this description did not exist, in the power of the jury to take it into consideration in aggravation of damages.

The damages do not appear to be excessive.

New trial denied.

Witness' privilege of refusing to answer criminating question, is personal. Cited in—19 Wend., 195; 3 Hill, 566; 32 N. Y., 137; 72 N. Y., 573; 28 Am. Rep., 184; 33 How. Pr., 73; 39 How. Pr., 157; 4 Park., 181; 6 Park., 390; 18 Mich., 271; 21 Am. Dec., 55 (7 Hals., 42).

Breach of promise of marriage—Damages. Cited in—24 N. Y., 257; 42 N. Y., 475 (1 Am. Rep., 562, 566).

Justification. Cited in—30 N. Y., 291; 45 Cal., 115; 47 Cal., 202.

Offer to marry after action brought no defense. Cited in—44 Am. Dec., 443 (9 Ala., 325); 40 Am. Rep., 277 (76 Ind., 596).

Also cited in—38 Barb., 121; 8 Abb. Pr., 303; 9 Abb. Pr., 180; 2 Hilt., 512; 2 Wood & M., 22.

WOLFE *v.* WASHBURN AND HAM.

1. Covenant to Pay One Money Due Another—Covenantee may Sue on. 2. Set-off—When Allowed. 3. Contents of Certificate of Justice—When Extrajudicial, not Conclusive, and Subject to Contradiction by Parol Evidence.

A covenant to pay one money which belongs to another, and so appears on the face of the covenant, may be sued for and recovered in the name of the covenantee; and it does not lie with the covenantor to object that the suit is not sanctioned by the *cestui que trust*.

To warrant a set-off, there must be a subsisting debt due *in præsenti*, and it must be due from the plaintiff to the defendant; and if it be due from the plaintiff and another to only one of the defendants, it is not admissible as a set-off; and though it be claimed by the defendants, and allowed by the jury as a set-off, the claim being, in fact, due to but one defendant, and not payable at the time, this is no bar to a subsequent action for the same demand when it becomes payable, in favor of the defendant to whom it is really due.

The certificate of a justice, that a certain demand was claimed before him by the defendant as a set-off, is extrajudicial and, therefore, not conclusive, and may be contradicted by parol evidence, showing that the demand was not so claimed.

The official certificate of a justice within the Statute, sess. 47, ch. 138, sec. 29, can regularly contain no more than the process, pleadings, evidence, verdict and judgment; not what was stated before him by way of argument.

COVENANT on a sealed agreement, dated Aug. 14, 1824, reciting that Washburn had occupied, for three years, *certain land [***262** of which one Hallenbeck died seised; and that Washburn also occupied it at the date of the agreement, at $58 rent for the first, and $65 for the last two years; that half this rent was claimed by one More; that Hallenbeck left an infant son and a widow, who married the plaintiff. The defendants then covenanted by this agreement with the plaintiff, as well on behalf of the heir at law and the widow, his wife, as in his own behalf, that within six months from the date they would pay him the rent recited, or so much as still remained due and ought to be accounted for and paid to the heir at law, or widow, or any other representative of the rights and interests of H., the ancestor.

Plea: 1st. *Non est factum;* and 2d. That on Jan. 14, 1825, Washburn (one of the defendants) impleaded the plaintiff and his wife in *assumpsit*, before J. A. Showerman, a justice; and that on the trial, Feb. 7, 1825, the plaintiff and his wife gave in evidence, in support of their defense, the covenant declared on; and the jury allowed and set off the money due and owing for the rent secured to be paid by the covenant, against Washburn's claim, and rendered a verdict for him, which was followed by a judgment.

The defendants also gave notice, with these pleas, that they would prove in their defense, that after the execution of the covenant in question, and before this suit was commenced, Thaddeus Reid was, by the Surrogate of Columbia, appointed guardian of the infant, and that this suit was prosecuted by the plaintiff for his own benefit, without the authority or direction of the guardian.

The plaintiff replied to the 2d plea, that he did not give in evidence, or claim the covenant in question as a set-off on the trial in that plea mentioned; and that he did not claim the money secured by the covenant as a set-off, and did not consent to a set-off.

The cause was tried at the Columbia Circuit, Sept., 1825.

On the trial, the execution of the covenant being admitted, the defendants proved the facts stated in their notice, and then moved for a nonsuit, which was overruled.

263*] *The defendant then gave in evidence the certificate of J. A. Showerman, the justice, to prove the facts pleaded in the second plea. The certificate stated that the plaintiff's account before him was more than $100; that the covenant, now in question, was given in evidence by the defendants, who claimed to have the rent allowed them by the jury; that the jury, after being out a short time, sent for the covenant; that they found for the plaintiff $7.75. This certificate was drawn up by the defendants' attorney, under the direction of the justice, during the circuit. It was authenticated by the certificate of the county clerk, in the usual form; the certificate of the justice being dated the 27th, and that of the clerk Sept. 30, 1825.

The certificate of the justice was objected to as evidence, on account of the manner in which it was drawn up; but was received.

Several of the jurors before the justice were then sworn as witnesses for the present defendants, and stated that they allowed the rent, or a part of it, to the defendants, on the trial before the justice.

The plaintiff then offered in evidence a copy of the minutes of the justice, taken at the trial, verified by the official certificate of the justice, who was in court, and there fixed his seal, to contradict his first certificate. This was objected to, but received; and the balance of proof was, that though the jury allowed the rent to the defendants, yet it was not claimed by them as a set-off; but the covenant was given in evidence by them, to show that the payment of the plaintiff's demand had been by the agreement of the parties postponed, and that the suit was prematurely brought; that a part of the plaintiff's demand was for the rent of a room and pasture; and the covenant was mentioned by the defendants on the trial in reference to those charges; that the plaintiff, however, told the jury that they should allow the rent as a set-off.

Verdict for the plaintiff for $10.05, subject to the opinion of the court on a case containing the facts.

264*] *Other particulars will be found stated in the opinion of the court.

Mr. C. Bushnell, for the plaintiff. The action was rightly brought in the name of Wolfe. (11 Johns., 91.)

The judge properly admitted the evidence in contradiction of the justice's certificate. (3 Cow., 126; 18 Johns., 354; 4 Cow., 458; Com. Dig., Action, L., 4, new ed.; 16 Johns., 136.) So far as it related to the fact of set-off, it was extrajudicial. (Laws N.Y., sess. 47, ch. 238, sec. 29.)

The covenant was not admissible as a set-off before the justice. (11 Johns., 91; 12 *Id.*, 343; 4 Johns. Ch., 136; 4 Johns., 510.) And if received as such, it cannot affect the plaintiff's claim.

The proceedings in the former suit were not between these parties; nor was the demand on the covenant between the parties in that suit. It was inadmissible as a set-off in any view.

Mr. D. B. Tallmadge, contra. No doubt this rent has once before been recovered, and that, too, by persons authorized to receive it—one of them being this very plaintiff. (5 Johns., 66.) But the plaintiff has no rights. They passed to Reid, the guardian, on his appointment. He cannot be deprived of them by the plaintiff's act, who was a mere trustee for the infant, or the infant's guardian. The debt being, in truth, due to the guardian, he has a right to control it, though the plaintiff is the nominal creditor. (1 Johns. Cas., 411; 11 Johns., 47; 3 *Id.*, 425; 12 *Id.*, 343.)

At any rate, the former suit was a bar, if the plaintiff has the right. He had the same rights at the former trial, and they were set off and allowed. (5 Johns., 129.)

Parol evidence was not admissible to contradict the justice's certificate. (5 Johns., 351.)

Curia per WOODWORTH, *J.*, after stating the facts. It is urged that, as a guardian had been appointed for the heir of Hallenbeck, the plaintiff cannot sustain the action. The plaintiff stands in the relation of trustee, and must, undoubtedly, account with the guardian; but with this, *I apprehend, the defendants [***265** have no concern. They are bound to pay the plaintiff in the terms of their covenant.

In point of fact, it appears from the evidence, that the jury did allow, as a set-off to the defendants before the justice, the rent, or a part of the rent, secured by the covenant. But it also appears, very satisfactorily, that the covenant was not offered on that trial as a set-off, but to show that Washburn could not sustain an action on his account, inasmuch as the rent was not then payable, and that the claims of the parties against each other were suspended until the rent became due. The counsel for the defendants, before the justice, moved for a nonsuit, which was denied. After this the counsel put the covenant in his pocket. The jury retired, and at the request of the justice, he delivered the bond to the constable, who carried it to the jury.

The covenant was not the subject of set-off at law, it not being between the same parties to the suit before the justice. Besides, it was not then broken. The trial was Feb. 7, 1825, and the rent did not fall due till the 14th. And the weight of evidence is, that it was not offered as a set-off. If, notwithstanding this, the jury have arbitrarily allowed it, they have done Washburn an injustice; but that is no cause for depriving the plaintiff of his right.

The certificate of the justice states that the defendants, on the trial, claimed to have the rent secured by the covenant allowed to them by the jury in making up their verdict. The defendants in this cause objected to evidence contradicting the certificate in this respect. But it seems to have been admitted, as there is no mention in the case, that the judge allowed the objection.

I incline to think that the fact stated by the justice, to wit: that the defendants claimed to have the rent allowed them by the jury, is extrajudicial, and regularly no part of his record. It is not the statement of a proceeding, or the evidence; but rather that the defendants urged, by way of argument, that the rent should be allowed. The certificate of a justice must contain the process, pleadings, *evidence, [***266** verdict and judgment. Beyond these, he is not called on to certify. If he goes further, his statements conclude no one.

But, on general principles, a legal demand cannot be extinguished in this manner. The defendants might, on the ground now relied upon, have requested the jury to allow them money due on a bond, payable ten years after the trial; and if, unadvisedly, the jury had done so, it would undoubtedly have been good cause to reverse the judgment; but would not bar them of their remedy by action for the same claim, when it should become due. This is founded on the plain principles of reason, and of law. An allowance to a party, by way of set-off, is always founded on an existing demand *in præsenti*, and not one that may be claimed *in futuro*.

So far as respects the present action, the recovery before the justice has no operation.

I am, therefore, of opinion that the plaintiff is entitled to judgment.

Judgment for the plaintiff.

Cited in—3 Wend., 402; 5 Wend., 245; 12 Wend., 506; H. & D., 206; 25 N. Y., 616; 6 Barb., 33; 13 Barb., 160; 14 Barb., 288; 15 Barb., 26; 27 Am. Dec., 151.

AYMAR AND AYMAR *v.* ASTOR.

Common Carriers—Masters and Owners of Vessel, not—Damage to Freight by Rats—Evidence of Commercial Usage.

Bear skins were received by the master of a vessel to transport from New Orleans to N. Y., and there to be delivered in good order and condition, dangers of the seas excepted. The skins being damaged by rats, in an action against the owners of the vessel upon the undertaking: held, that evidence of mercantile usage and understanding, at New Orleans and N. Y., that injuries by rats are considered and treated as perils of the sea, was inadmissible.

The master or owners of a vessel transporting goods on the high seas, are not common carriers, within the meaning of the rule, subjecting the latter to all losses or injuries, which arise from any other cause than the act of God, or the enemies of the country. And in an action against the master or owners for loss or damage of goods from any other cause, it should be submitted to the jury, upon the evidence, whether they used ordinary care and diligence.

Citations—2 B. & P., 164; 5 B. & P., 213; 7 Johns., 389; 2 Johns., 335; 4 Campb., 203; Phil. Ins., 250; Abb. Ship., pt. 3, ch. 3, s. 9; 1 Wils., 281; Jones Tr. on Bail, 106, 103.

ON ERROR from the C. P. of N. Y. Astor brought *assumpsit* against Aymar and Aymar, in the court below, for the value of certain bear skins, shipped on board the defendant's vessel at New Orleans for N. Y., but which were destroyed by rats on the voyage.

By the bill of lading, signed by the master, the receipt of the bear skins was acknowledged, **267***] to be delivered in *good order and well conditioned to the plaintiff in N. Y., the dangers of the seas and of capture excepted.

When they were delivered in N. Y., they were damaged by rats, and the parties went into evidence in the court below upon the question whether the vessel was prudently managed for the avoiding of rats, or whether the master had been negligent in that respect.

The defendants offered to prove that both at New Orleans and N. Y. damage by rats was considered and treated by the usage of trade and merchants as a peril of the sea. The court below excluded the evidence, and the defendants excepted.

The court charged the jury that the defendants were common carriers, and liable as such for damage done, unless by the act of God, or the perils of the sea, excepted in the bill of lading. That damage by rats was not a peril of the sea. And the defendants excepted.

Verdict and judgment for the plaintiff below.

Mr. D. Lord, Jr., for the plaintiffs in error. The evidence of the merchantile meaning of the words "perils of the sea" should have been received. (4 East, 130; 2 Johns., 335, 549; 7 *Id.*, 385; 5 Bos. & P., 213; Park Ins., 44, *et seq.*; Abb. Sh., pt. 3, ch. 4, sec. 2.)

It is true *Hunter* v. *Potts*, 4 Camph., 203, held that a loss by rats was not a peril of the sea, but that case went on *Rohl* v. *Parr*, 1 Esp., 445, which presented a question of fact, and was decided by a jury. *Dale* v. *Hall*, 1 Wils., 281, is directly opposed to *Ganiques* v. *Cox*, 1 Binn., 592, 598.

At any rate, the liability of the defendants below should have been put to the jury upon the question of actual negligence.

Mr. D. B. Ogden, contra, relied on *Rohl* v. *Parr*, 1 Esp., 445; *Hunter* v. *Potts*, 4 Campb., 203, *Dale* v. *Hall*, 1 Wils., 281, as in point for the defendant in error. He also cited Phil. Ins., 251; Abb. Sh., pt. 3, ch. 3, sec. 9.

*SAVAGE, *Ch. J.*, said he thought [***268** the evidence of mercantile understanding and usage as to the meaning of the words "perils of the sea," should have been received. And he cited and commented upon various authorities as warranting this. *Anderson* v. *Pitcher*, 2 Bos. & P., 164; *Scott* v. *Bowdillion*, 5 *Id.*, 213; *Coit* v. *Com. Ins. Co.*, 7 Johns., 389; *Frith* v. *Barker*, 2 *Id.*, 335.

As to the question of liability, independent of the evidence offered, he said the terms "perils of the sea," as used in contracts of insurance, do not include those losses which may be prevented by proper care. In a late case, *Hunter* v. *Potts*, 4 Campb., 203, Ld. Ellenborough decided that a loss arising from rats eating holes in the ship's bottom is not within the perils insured against by the common form of a policy.

The cases decided against common carriers, are said by Mr. Phillips (Tr. on Ins., 250) not to be applicable in actions depending on the law of marine insurance. The master of a vessel at sea, he does not consider within the term common carrier.

It is the duty of the master to take all possible care of the goods on board; and though the master or owners are not liable for injury by a leak in the ship, by tempests, or other accident (Abb. Sh., pt. 3, ch. 3, sec. 9), yet they are liable if the leak be occasioned by rats. It was so decided in *Dale* v. *Hall*, 1 Wils., 281, which was an action against a hoyman, for so negligently carrying goods that they were spoiled. It was shown that the injury was occasioned by rats eating a hole in the vessel, and the defendant had a verdict, which the court set aside; Lee, *Ch. J.*, saying, "everything is neg-

NOTE.—*Masters and owners of vessels, as common carriers.*

Masters and owners of vessels, who undertake to carry for hire, are common carriers. There is no distinction between carriers by water and carriers by land. The above case of Aymar v. Astor is not sustained by the authorities. See Allen v. Sewall, 2 Wend., 327; Elliott v. Rossell, 10 Johns., 1, *note.*

ligence in a carrier, which the law does not excuse; and he is answerable for goods the instant he receives them into his custody; and in all events, except they happen to be damaged by the act of God, or the King's enemies, and a promise to carry safely, is a promise to keep safely." Sir William Jones says (Tr. on Bail., 105), "but the true reason of this decision is not mentioned by the reporter. It was, in fact, **269***] *at least ordinary negligence to let a rat do such mischief in the vessel."

This case is not supposed by Phillips or Abbott (Tr. on Sh., part 3, ch. 3, sec. 9) to be inconsistent with the ancient rule, that the master is not liable for such an injury, if he provides against it by taking a cat on board at the commencement of the voyage.

The master of a vessel, I apprehend, is not responsible, like a common carrier, for all losses, except they happen by the act of God or the enemies of the country.

A carrier for hire, ought, by the general rule, to be responsible only for ordinary neglect. (Jones, Bail., 103.) The liability did not exist formerly for robbery. That became necessary, to guard against collusion, by the carrier, with robbers. If the same liability attached to the master and owners of a vessel, it was useless to inquire (as was done in this case in the court below) whether it was proper for the master to smoke his vessel to destroy vermin.

The true question to be submitted to the jury was, whether the master had used ordinary care and diligence in carrying the goods in question. Whether a cat is a sufficient precaution against rats, or whether smoking the vessel is the proper and more efficacious remedy against this evil, is a proper subject for the consideration of the jury. Formerly, taking a cat on board was accounted ordinary diligence, and excused from damages. If subsequent experience has shown a better remedy, it is the duty of masters and owners to adopt it.

WOODWORTH and SUTHERLAND, *JJ.*, were of the opinion that the evidence of mercantile usage and understanding, was properly overruled by the court below; but they agreed with the *Ch. J.* in his opinion upon the other point.

The judgment was, therefore, reversed, on the ground that the court erred in charging the jury that the defendants below were common carriers, and liable as such.

Judgment reversed.

Overruled—2 Wend., 327; 6 Wend., 335; 21 Wend., 193.

Cited in—1 Wend., 37; 37 N. Y., 397; 75 N. Y., 77; 44 Barb., 488; 9 How. Pr., 227: Abb. Adm., 352; 4 Trans. App., 465; 24 Am. Dec., 738 (3 S. & P., 135); 31 Am. Dec 747 (12 Conn., 410); 39 Am. Dec., 400 (15 Conn., 539); 46 Am. Dec., 591 (27 Me., 132).

270*] *TREADWELL AND THORNE
v.
THE UNION INSURANCE COMPANY.

Marine Insurance—Underwriters may Show Incompetency of Crew—When Vessel is Disabled, Master should Procure Another—Exceptions—Seaworthiness at a Given Time.

In an action on a policy of insurance upon a cargo, the underwriters may show, in their defense, that the vessel had not a competent crew, or a captain or pilot of competent skill. But this is a question of fact to be submitted to a jury, upon the nature of the voyage, &c.

If the vessel become disabled, in such case the underwriters have a right to claim that the master should procure another vessel to forward the cargo, if in his power. The rule on this subject is, that if there be a vessel in the port of distress, or in a contiguous port, the master should procure it.

But where it appeared that resort must have been had to distant places and, independent of procuring a vessel, there were further serious impediments in the way of putting the cargo on board; held, that the rule was not obligatory.

A cargo was insured at and from N. C. to N. Y.; held, that if the vessel was seaworthy when she passed the boundary line of N.C., this was sufficient; and her unseaworthiness, previous to that point of time, would be no defense in an action against the underwriters for a loss.

Citations—1 Cai., 45; 7 T. R., 160; 12 Johns., 107.

ASSUMPSIT upon a valued policy of insurance, dated Sept. 22, 1823, on part of 800 bushels of wheat, on board the schooner Lodge Farrow, master, on a voyage at and from North Carolina to N. Y., containing the clause, "the captain at liberty to act as pilot," and the common memorandum, by which, among other things, grain of all kinds is warranted free from average, unless general.

The cause was tried at the N. Y. Circuit, Jan. 31, 1825, before Edwards, *Circuit J.*

On the trial, the plaintiffs proved that Sept. 13, 1823, the schooner sailed with the wheat on board, from Perquimions River, at or near the town of Hertford, in the State of N. C., on her voyage for N. Y.; and after experieueing a series of head winds, and, at last, very tempestuous weather, until Nov. 8, she was run on shore upon Cape Hatteras Banks, about 18 miles north of Cape Hatteras Light-House—this being deemed necessary by the master and crew, to save the vessel and cargo from total destruotion, and preserve the lives of the crew. In the act of running her on shore, she was so much injured as to be incapable of proceeding on her voyage, and was afterwards sold. The wheat was, in the end, so intermixed with sand and water, as, in the opinion of the master, to be unfit *for transportation, and was sold [***271** at public auction, after full notice by advertisement, for $70.55½; which, after defraying commissions, expenses, &c., left $22, afterwards paid to the consignees.

Verdict for the plaintiffs for the sum insured, with interest, as for a total loss, deducting the net proceeds of the salvage.

A motion was now made, in behalf of the defendants, for a new trial, grounded on a very voluminous case, containing the evidence at large, which, so far as it is material, beyond what is above given, will be found stated in the opinion of the court.

Mr. T. A. Emmet, for the motion insisted:

1. That the vessel was not seaworthy, either at the commencement of the risk or any other time. (1 Cai., 32; Marsh. Ins., Condv ed., 154, 155, 165 *a*, *n.* 16; *Id.*, 165 *b*, *n.* 17; *Id.*, 166, *n.* 18; 1 Johns. Cas., 184; 1 Mass., 436; Phil. Ins., 114, 117; Selw. *N. P.*, 4th ed., 954, *n.* 53.)

2. That the master was guilty of so many and great delays in the prosecution of the voyage, as amounted to a deviation.

3. That the voyage was broken up on account of the sale of the cargo, and not from the impossibility of procuring another vessel to send on the cargo to N. Y.; and that such a

vessel could easily have been procured. (18 Johns., 210, 211; 14 Johns., 138; 1 Cai., 196; 3 Cai., 108; 1 Johns. Cas., 226; Condy Marsh., 221, 224, 233; 1 Wh., 224; 7 East, 38.)

Mr. G. Griffin, contra:

1. The crew of the vessel was competent for the voyage. (Park Ins., 299, *note a*; 2 Camph., 235; 3 Taunt., 299; 2 B. & A., 320; 1 Cai., 217.)

2. There was no deviation, or unnecessary delay. (4 Esp., 25; 2 Condy Marsh., 840, 841, *note*; 2 Taunt., 301.)

3. It was not, under the circumstances, the duty of the master to attempt to forward the cargo to its port of destination in another ves- 272*] sel; and there was, therefore, *a loss of the voyage by a peril insured against. (Park. Ins., 152, 153, 221; Phil. Ins., 489, 490, and the cases there cited; 12 Johns., 107; 18 Johns., 208.)

Curia, per WOODWORTH, *J.* Three points are raised by the defendants:

1. That the vessel was not seaworthy.
2. That the master was guilty of so many and great delays, as amounted to a deviation.
3. That the voyage was broken up, on account of the state of the cargo, and not from the impossibility of procuring another vessel, to send on the cargo to N. Y.

As to the vessel, it is satisfactorily made out, that she was tight, stanch and strong, Sept. 13, 1823. Having received her cargo on board, she sailed on her voyage to N. Y., down Perquimions River, from a place at or near Hertford, in the State of N. C. The crew consisted of the captain, and one hand. Sept. 16, and while the vessel lay in Cape Hatteras channel, detained by head winds, the master shipped another hand. It satisfactorily appears that the crew previously on board was competent for river and sound navigation. The weight of evidence is, that three hands were a competent number for the residue of the voyage. Owing to adverse winds, there was great delay and little progress made; but there is no ground for believing that reasonable diligence was not used in the prosecution of the voyage. The risk commenced at and from N. C. If the vessel was seaworthy at the time she passed the boundary line of that State, it is sufficient. The insurers not being responsible for a loss happening previous to her arrival at the point of departure, the inquiry as to her previous seaworthiness, I apprehend, becomes immaterial.

But it is contended that there was not a competent crew, because the master was not acquainted with the science of navigation. This question was not raised at the trial. The attention of neither the judge nor jury was called to the point. It was a question of fact, whether 273*] the coasting *trade could be pursued with safety, without having on board a navigator capable of making an observation to find the latitude. From the finding of the jury, it may be presumed they considered it unnecessary. Had the question been raised at the trial, we cannot say that the plaintiffs might not have given further evidence, and shown that, from the nature of this navigation, the proximity to land, the number of harbors, as well as from other facts, it was consistent with prudence and safety to dispense with a scientific navigator. It is not, therefore, admissible to allow the defendants the benefit of this exception now. It should have been made at the trial. Berrian testified that not more than one fourth of the masters of vessels, of the size of The Lodge, engaged in this trade, understand the science of navigation; and that that fact is generally known in N. Y. This, it is true, does not prove a usage, sanctioned by the practice of the community generally; but it goes far to show in what light the practice is considered by mariners and navigators of vessels. That proof of general usage would have been admissible, I think undeniable, provided it had been made out according to the rule in *Smith* v. *Wright*, 1 Cai., 45. It is there observed, "the true test of commercial usage is, its having existed a sufficient length of time to have become generally known, and to warrant a presumption that contracts are made in reference to it."

If this view be correct, it follows that a new trial should not be granted, on the ground of an incompetent crew.

But the objection, if made in season, cannot avail. The assured, it is true, cannot recover, unless there be a sufficient crew, and a captain and pilot of competent skill. (7 T. R., 160.) But the plaintiffs have very satisfactorily proved the general competency of the master. Several witnesses speak of him as entirely competent for the voyage. If the alleged incompetency is founded on the fact that he was ignorant of navigation, it was incumbent on the defendants to have shown that such ignorance was a disqualification; that it was not considered safe to make the voyage, without having a scientific navigator. No *such testimony was [*274 given. The defendants' witnesses do not give an opinion on this point. They say, they have taken a navigator; but they do not say, it might not be safely dispensed with.

I should not, therefore, be disposed to disturb the verdict, on the evidence stated in the case relative to this ground of the motion.

As to the third question, the general rule is, that when a ship becomes disabled, it is the duty of the master to procure another vessel, if it is in his power; and the insurer is not answerable for his voluntary neglect so to do, unless such neglect is caused by an act of barratry. (9 Johns., 21.) What may be done, ought to be done, when the rights of third persons are essentially concerned in the act. This general rule, however, is restricted to reasonable limits. The circumstances of each particular case must be considered. From them it must be determined, whether the difficulties in the way were so great as to form an excuse for not sending on the cargo. In the case of *Saltus* v. *Ocean Ins. Co.*, 12 Johns., 107, it was decided that the master was not bound to seek a vessel, out of the port of distress, or out of a port immediately contiguous. In that case, there were a number of vessels at Cork, 16 miles distant, which the master supposed might have been obtained; but he made no attempt to procure them. The question revolves itself into this; not whether a master, by going to a distant port or place, might have procured another vessel; nor, whether by first conveying the cargo some distance over land, it was possible to effect a reshipment; but whether, under the circumstances in which he was placed, the law required him to make the attempt. Some certain rule, to govern the discretion of the mas-

ter, is desirable, wherever practicable. Although no general rule will govern every case, the approach to certainty will be considered beneficial to all parties. I think, then, the rule laid down in the last case is at once safe and reasonable. If there be a vessel in the same port, or a contiguous port, which is substan-
275*] tially *the same thing, his duty is clear. The rule is imperative. But where resort must be had to distant places and, independent of procuring a vessel, there are further serious impediments in the way of putting the cargo on board, the rule is not obligatory.

In the present instance, the vessel was wrecked and lying on the beach. There was no port within a number of miles. A vessel could not come along side for the purpose of reshipment. In the first place, the wheat must have been carted across the beach. After that had been done, it appears from the evidence, boats would have been necessary to carry it to the vessel, a distance of several miles, it not being practicable to approach the shore. The conveyance in boats would have been attended with danger; in a calm, with but little; but if a gale had come on, with almost certain destruction. Must this labor and hazard be incurred to make the underwriter liable? The master was not bound to transport the wheat by land, and then incur the risk of sending it in boats to the vessel. I think the application of so severe a principle unreasonable in itself, and not called for in order to enforce, in good faith, the execution of the contract. The master, under the circumstances, was justified in not making an attempt to procure a vessel. The insurer has no cause for complaint. An event happened beyond the control of all parties, which, in the given case, denies to the defendants the right of insisting on a reshipment.

I am of opinion that the motion for a new trial be denied.

New trial denied.

Cited in—32 N. Y., 431; 3 Bos., 367; 3 Daly, 144; 2 How. (U. S.), 609; 44 Am. Rep., 66 (60 Cal., 467).

276*] *MINKLAER
v.
ROCKFELLER AND FELLER.

Action will not Lie Against Overseers of Poor for Failure to Care for Pauper, by One who has Furnished Supplies—Mandamus *the Appropriate Remedy—Action in Name of Pauper.*

An action will not lie against Overseers of the Poor, for omitting to apply to a justice, to obtain an order for the relief of a pauper settled in their town, at the suit of one who, after giving them notice, and requiring them to provide for the pauper, supports him at his own expense, voluntarily, and without request from the Overseers of the Poor.

The appropriate remedy is by *mandamus*, in behalf of the pauper, to compel the Overseers to apply to a justice, and cause the case to be considered.

Semble, that, if an action would lie, it must be in the name of the pauper.

In an action against public officers for a nonfeasance, the plaintiff must show the neglect of duty, by proof on his part; and if an action would lie against Overseers of the Poor, for not taking the proper steps to obtain an order for the relief of a pauper, the *onus* of showing the neglect lies with the plaintiff. It is not enough that he shows it to be their duty; but he must show the negative, that they did not do their duty.

Citations—11 Johns., 114; 2 Mass., 243; 3 Cas., 317; 15 Johns., 281; 18 Johns., 122.

ON ERROR from the C. P. of Columbia.

Minklaer sued R. and F. before a justice, in case, for neglect of duty as Overseers of the Poor of the Town of Clermont, in not providing for John M'Gill and his wife, two paupers belonging to that town. The cause went to the C. P. by appeal, who nonsuited the plaintiff upon the following proof:

Jan. 25, 1823, the plaintiff served a written notice, signed by himself, on the defendants, that John M'Gill and his wife were at his house, wholly unable to provide for and maintain themselves; and requiring the defendants to make provision for them. The defendants said they could do nothing about it till they saw Mr. Edward P. Livingston. They admitted that they were then, and still continued to be, at the time of the trial in the C. P., Overseers of the Poor of the Town of Clermont; and that M'Gill and his wife were legally settled in the town. They were poor and helpless. The plaintiff had supported the paupers for a considerable time after the notice, and had incurred trouble and expense on their account. Further particulars will be found stated in the opinion of the court.

To the opinion of the C. P., nonsuiting the plaintiff, he excepted.

Mr. K. Miller, for the plaintiff in error. The defendants had omitted to perform a known official duty, and were, therefore, liable to a special action on the case. They *were [*277 under both a legal and moral obligation to support the paupers. It was their duty to inquire into the matter, and furnish relief according to the Statute, 1 R. L., 287, 288, sec. 25. This was held in *King* v. *Butler*, 15 Johns., 281, 282. The statute requires that when application is made to the Overseers, they shall make application to a justice, and with him inquire into the state and circumstances of the pauper; and the justice is to make an order for relief, if it shall appear to be necessary. The case cited, holds that this application for an order is merely to protect or indemnify the Overseer against the advance of money for relief. Platt, *J.*, in *Olney* v. *Wickes*, 18 Johns., 126, entertains this view of it.

An action is the only possible remedy which the plaintiff can have for the injury. A motion might, in the first instance, have been made for a *mandamus;* but that will not now reach the injury which has happened. He could not go to the sessions by appeal, because the Overseers refused to apply for the order of a magistrate. Without his application, no order could be made, one way or the other. A *mandamus* could not have been obtained till the term next after notice to the defendants; and we should, of necessity, have been put to this remedy for our damages in the meantime.

Mr. J. W. Wheeler, contra. This case does not come within the authorities or the principle relied on. Overseers have never been hold-

NOTE.—*Pauper—Liability of overseers for supplies furnished.*

Overseers of the Poor are not liable for supplies furnished to the poor, without their request or subsequent promise to pay. Gourley v. Allen, 5 Cow., 644, *note.*

en liable without an express promise, or an order of a magistrate previously obtained. Till one or the other takes place, there is no legal duty for the Overseer to perform. No action lies, therefore, either at the common law or upon the statute. Is it to be tolerated, that persons holding the office of Overseers of the Poor shall be bound to accept a pauper upon the complaint of anyone who may choose to interfere; and that, too, upon the penalty of answering to him in a suit, the sums he may think proper to expend for maintenance, in case of refusal? The plaintiff had no rights. But if his right was perfect, the proof of mis-
278*] conduct was altogether deficient. It *is not enough to show a mere omission of duty. It should be accompanied with an intention to harrass and vex the plaintiff. *Rogers* v. *Brewster*, 5 Johns., 125. Malice or corruption should have been shown. *Jenkins* v. *Waldron*, 11 Johns., 114. The statute points out the duty of the Overseer, but gives no remedy. The only remedy is by *mandamus;* or, in case of a corrupt refusal, an indictment. Overseers are a *quasi* corporation. *Todd* v. *Birdsall*, 1 Cow., 260. As such, they are not liable, except where the statute has made them so. They cannot act independent of the magistrate; and whether they will act with him, is a matter in their discretion. It would be singular that they should be made liable for a mere error in judgment. *Seamen* v. *Patten*, 2 Cai., 312; *Harman* v. *Tappenden*, 1 East, 561.

Mr. Miller, in reply, denied that Overseers have a discretion upon the question of acting. The statute is peremptory that they shall apply to a magistrate. So far their duty is ministerial. The judgment which they give with the magistrate, is another consideration. The cases cited against the plaintiff are of officers having discretion. The defendants should have shown they had done their duty as far as they could.

Curia, per SUTHERLAND, *J.* The bill of exceptions presents the question, whether an action on the case will lie against Overseers of the Poor, for omitting or refusing to take the necessary measures to provide for paupers, in favor of an individual who, from motives of humanity, furnishes them with the sustenance and attention, which their situation absolutely requires.

The declaration does not aver that the defendants acted fraudulently or maliciously; and their is no evidence that their neglect was willful, and without reasonable excuse, except what is to be inferred from their admission, that M'Gill and his wife were paupers, legally settled in the Town of Clermont. The evidence before the justice consisted principally of the admissions of the parties; and his return
279*] *is not sufficiently full and explicit to show the bearing and pertinency of much of the evidence. But I think it is fairly to be inferred, from the whole evidence, that the defendants did not intend to admit that the Town of Clermont was bound to maintain these paupers. When the notice was served on them, they said they could do nothing about it, until they saw Mr. Edward P. Livingston; and the return states that the defendants introduced and proved two written agreements between E. P. Livingston and his wife, and Adam Minklaer, Jr.; and also a bill of sale or agreement between John M'Gill and the plaintiff. The plaintiff introduced and proved three receipts given by E. P. Livingston—two to the plaintiff, and one to John M'Gill. The defendants proved an assignment or surrender, under seal, from John M'Gill to E. P. Livingston.

From this evidence, it is probable that M'Gill had been a slave; and that in the opinion of the Overseers, it was doubtful whether he had been so manumitted as to exonerate his master from the responsibility of maintaining him. This, however, is mere conjecture; and none of this evidence was given in the court of C. P. All the evidence there, consisted in proof of the notice given to the defendants; their declaration that they could do nothing about it until they saw Mr. Livingston; their admission that they were Overseers of the Poor of Clermont; that M'Gill and his wife were legally settled in Clermont; and proof that they were unable to maintain themselves; that the plaintiff had provided for, and kept them; and the value of the services, &c., rendered by him.

This evidence was clearly insufficient to entitle the plaintiff to recover. The defendants were not bound, nor had they any authority to make provision for the paupers in the first instance. All they could do, was, to apply to a justice of the peace and, together with him, inquire into the state and circumstances of the persons asking relief; and if it should appear that they were in such indigent circumstances as to require the relief sought, then the justice was bound to give an order in writing to provide for them. *Until such order was [***280**
given, the defendants had no authority to make any provision.

If they were guilty of any omission of duty, it was in not making the application to a justice and, together with him, making the necessary inquiry.

But, for aught that appears, all this may have been done: and the justice may have refused an order. When the plaintiff seeks to charge the defendants as public officers, for an omission of duty, he is bound to prove it affirmatively and clearly. (11 Johns., 114; 2 Mass., 243; 3 Cai., 317, per Livingston, *J.*) That, I think, in this instance, has not been done.

But, admitting that the defendants refused to take the necessary measures to obtain the order, are they responsible to the plaintiff, in an action on the case, for the trouble and expense of supporting and taking care of the paupers while they remained in his house?

I do not see on what legal principle the action can be sustained. The plaintiff was under no legal obligation to take care of the paupers. It was a commendable humane act, undoubtedly; but it must be considered voluntary on his part, and cannot lay the foundation of an action against the Overseers of the Poor. Damage to the plaintiff was not the necessary or legal consequence of the nonfeasance of the defendants; the proper, and for aught that I perceive, the only course to be pursued, when the Overseer refuses to act in a case like this, is, to apply to this court in behalf of the paupers for a *mandamus*. It is true that the paupers must be supported by some one pending the application, and that the *mandamus* would afford no means of reimbursement. I see no remedy for this, unless the Legislature should think proper to interfere, and make the Overseers responsible upon an implied *assumpsit* for necessary expenditures in support of paupers, chargeable upon their respective towns. It appears to me, that if an action would lie at all, it must be in the name of the paupers themselves.

King v. *Butler*, 15 Johns., 281, and *Olney* v. *Wickes*, 18 Johns., 122, have no application to **281***] this case. They *merely decide that an overseer of the poor may bind himself, in his individual capacity, by an express promise to pay for the maintenance of a pauper.

Judgment affirmed.

Cited in—8 Cow., 668; 3 Wend., 199; 2 Barb., 17; 14 Barb., 231; Edm., 551; 6 Leg. Obs., 65.

JACKSON, ex dem. SMITH, v. MARSH.

Patent of Lands—Issue Presumed Regular—A General Rule Cannot be Attached Collaterally —Surplusage..

A patent of lands, by the State, shall be presumed to have issued regularly; and, if it be not void on its face, cannot be avoided collaterally, in a suit between individuals, unless it issued without authority, or against the prohibition of a statute. Thus, where a patent issued in 1823, for lands which were occupied and improved, to the value of $25, Feb. 17, 1809; held, that it should be presumed that satisfactory proof was produced to the Commissioners of the Land Office, that the occupant had been satisfied for his improvements, previous to the date of the patent, pursuant to the Statute 1 R.L., 296, 297, sec. 17.

A patent was granted of subdivision No. 2, beginning at the southeast corner of the survey 50 acres; and then giving courses and distances which would not include subdivision No. 2, but the whole, or greater part of subdivision No. 4; whereas, had it begun at the northeast corner of the survey 50 acres, the same courses and distances would have included subdivision No. 2. The subdivisions had, before the grant, been surveyed, and a map made, and filed in the office of the Surveyor-General; according to which, subdivision No. 2 began at the northeast corner of the survey 50 acres, whence the courses and distances mentioned in the patent, were laid down, and would include subdivision No. 2. Held, that the word "southeast" should be rejected as surplusage, and that the location upon the map should control.

If there are certain particulars sufficiently ascertained in the description of parcels, in a patent or deed, which designate the thing intended to be granted, the addition of circumstances, false or mistaken, will not frustrate the grant.

Citations—1 R. L., 296, sec. 17; 10 Johns., 23; 7 Johns., 223; 18 Johns., 81; 19 Johns., 449; 4 Mass., 196.

EJECTMENT, tried at the Cayuga Circuit, Mar. 10, 1825, before Throop, *Circuit J.*, when a verdict was taken for the plaintiff, subject to the opinion of the court.

Mr. D. Cady, for the plaintiff.

Mr. B. F. Butler, for the defendant.

Curia, per WOODWORTH, *J.* The plaintiff gave in evidence at the trial, a patent to the lessor of the plaintiff, dated June 16, 1823, for subdivision No. 2; beginning at the southeast corner of the survey 50 acres; from thence giving certain courses and distances, and including 135 acres.

The case states, that the action was brought to recover subdivision No. 2, in lot No. 50, in **282***] the Township of Sempronius; *and that the defendant was in possession. It appeared by a map and certificate of the Surveyor-General, admitted as evidence, that lot No. 50 had been subdivided into several lots, of which lot No. 2 was one; that the map had been filed in his office; and that subdivision No. 2, as represented on the map, was, Mar. 23, 1818, sold to the lessor by the Surveyor-General, acting on behalf of the State.

By the Act of 1813, concerning the Commissioners of the Land Office, 1 R. L., 296, sec. 17, it is declared, that if any tract of land sold under the Act, was occupied and improved Feb. 17, 1809, to the value of $25, the occupant of such improvement shall be entitled to recover the value thereof from the purchaser; and the Commissioners of the Land Office are inhibited from causing letters patent to be issued, until satisfactory proof be produced, that the purchaser has satisfied the occupant for his improvements.

In this case, it appears that a contract, under which the defendant claims, was given for 50 acres, being a part of subdivision No. 2; and that before Feb. 17, 1809, 15 acres of the 50 were cleared, and 6 acres chopped, the value of such improvements exceeding $25.

The patent is evidence of the plaintiff's right, until set aside or vacated. The inhibition in the Act is not against the issuing of any patent; but against issuing until satisfactory proof be produced, that the purchaser has satisfied the occupant. We are authorized to presume, *omnia solemniter acta*, that public officers, to whom the government committed important trusts, had discharged their duty faithfully, and received the necessary proof, before the patent issued. No evidence was offered that the requisite proof was not produced to the Commissioners. The question is, therefore, not raised, whether, an inquiry of this kind was admissible on the trial. But if the question had been presented, I think the doctrine contained in the case of *Jackson* v. *Lawton*, 10 Johns., 23, decisive: "If the patent was issued by mistake, or upon false suggestion, it is voidable only; and unless letters patent are absolutely void on *the face of them; or the issuing of [***283** them was without authority, or prohibited by statute, they can only be avoided in a regular course of pleading." And again: "When the defect arises on circumstances *dehors* the grant, the grant is voidable only by suit. It would be against precedent, and of dangerous consequence, to permit letters patent to be impeached collaterally."

The material question is, whether the letters patent include lot No. 2. This is an evident mistake in the boundaries. Lot No. 2 begins at the northeast corner of the survey 50 acres. The description in the patent is, "beginning at the southeast corner."

If the map is rejected, as the counsel for the defendant contends, there is no difficulty in the case; for then it would not appear there was any misdescription. It would be intended that the boundaries in the patent were a correct description of No. 2. But the map, by agreement, forms part of the case. By that, it appears that lot No. 2 begins at the northeast corner of the 50 acre survey. The residue of the boundaries correspond with the description in the patent. By beginning at the southeast corner, lot No. 2 will not be included, but the whole or greater part of lot No. 4. The location of No. 2 is equally certain, as the southeast corner of survey 50 acres. Both are established by the production of the map. It is, therefore, doing no violence, to reject that part of the description, which commences at the southeast corner, and give effect to another part, to which equal certainty is attached; when it is manifest by so doing, full and fair effect is given to the intention of the parties. In truth, here is a direct contradiction. When the patent grants subdivision No. 2, it conveys that lot according to its real boundaries. By the map, it appears that the place of beginning is at the northeast corner of the survey 50. From the patent and the map, taken together, it may be affirmed that No. 2 begins at the northeast corner. After this, [follow the boundaries of No. 2, as described in the patent, which makes the place of beginning the southeast corner. The rule to be applied is, "if there are certain particulars **284***] sufficiently *ascertained, which designate the thing intended to be granted, the addition of a circumstance, false or mistaken, will not frustrate the grant." *Jackson* v. *Clark*, 7 Johns., 223. From the principles adverted to, I think the place of beginning, as described in the patent, may be rejected as surplusage—the description of the premises being sufficiently certain without those words. This was done in *Jackson* v. *Loomis*, 18 Johns., 81, afterwards affirmed on error. (19 Johns., 449.) In the case of *Worthington* v. *Hylyer*, 4 Mass., 196, the same doctrine is laid down by Parsons, *Ch. J.*, who observed that "if the description be sufficient to ascertain the estate intended to be conveyed, although the estate did not agree to some particulars in the description, yet it shall pass by the conveyance that the intent of the parties may be effected."

My opinion is that the plaintiff is entitled to judgment.

Judgment for the plaintiff.

Cited in—4 Wend., 105; 8 Wend., 190; 25 Wend., 404; 5 Den., 398; 9 N. Y., 320; 10 N. Y., 532; 16 N. Y., 272; 5 Lans., 368; 13 Hun, 20; 7 Barb., 622; 8 Barb., 287; 36 Barb., 539; 46 Barb., 525; 1 Abb. N. S., 88; 4 Sandf., 287; 1 Rob., 445; 36 Mich., 82; 20 Am. Dec., 581 (5 N. H., 280); 22 Am. Dec., 638; 40 Am. Dec., 109 (1 L. & M., 49).

WILDER AND HASTINGS, qui tam, &c., *v.* WINNE AND I. FONDEY.

Issue of Execution on Valid Judgment, to Defeat other Creditors, does not bring it Within the Act for Prevention of Frauds—Debtor in Failing Circumstances may Prefer Creditors.

If a judgment be valid in its concoction; *i. e. bona fide*, and upon sufficient consideration, though execution be taken out and enforced with a view to delay and hinder creditors, and it have that effect, yet it not fraudulent within the Statute for the Prevention of Frauds, sess. 10, ch. 44: 1 R. L., 75, and the plaintiff is not, therefore, liable to the penalty imposed by the 4th section of that Statute, 1 R. L., 76, 77.

It is lawful for a debtor in failing circumstances. to prefer one creditor to another, or to prefer one set of creditors, by confessing a judgment, &c., or otherwise.

Citations—Stat. 13 Eliz. ch. 5; 5 T. R., 235, 425, 530; 8 T. R., 528; 2 Johns. Ch., 306, 307; 5 Cow., 547; 4 East, 1; 1 R. L., 76, sec. 4.

DEBT, for the penalty of $12,000, upon the 4th section of the Statute for the Prevention of Frauds, sess. 10, ch. 44; 1 R. L., 76, tried at the Albany Circuit, in Sept., 1825, before Duer, *Circuit J.*

The declaration stated that the plaintiffs sued one Stephen Fondey, for a debt due to them, on Oct. 15, 1823, in this court; and at February Term, 1824, obtained judgment for $542.97. That at the time of commencing the suit, and until Feb. 3, 1824, S. Fondey possessed and owned divers goods and chattels of different kinds, specifying them, at Geneva, of the value of $6,000, which were liable to the plaintiffs' execution. *But that in the previous [***285** term of Oct., 1823, the defendants entered up a judgment, by confession, in this court against S. Fondey for $12,014.45, debt and costs.

The first count then charged that this last judgment was devised, &c., between the parties, of fraud, &c., to delay, hinder and defraud the plaintiffs of their action, demand and damages, &c.; and that the defendants, on Jan. 3, 1824, &c., put in use the judgment, as true and simple, &c.

The second count was the same in substance, with the addition that the defendants, Nov. 1, 1823, sued out a *test. fi. fa.* on their judgment, indorsed for $6,017.48, with interest, &c.; that Jan. 23, 1824, the sheriff seized the goods of S. Fondey and sold them at auction; and that this execution was devised and contrived, &c., and put in use, &c. (as before of the judgment).

The judgments, the execution and levy, as set forth in the declaration, were proved on the trial; and it appeared that the defendants' exetion, having a preference over one issued on the plaintiffs' judgment, the latter was returned *nulla bona*. It also appeared that the defendants' judgment was entered after S. Fondey had become insolvent.

The evidence was very satisfactory that the judgment of the defendants was *bona fide*, and that no part of it was paid when the execution issued.

It further appeared that the sale of S. Fondey's goods, on the execution, which was made at Geneva, Ontario Co., Jan. 30, 1824, amounted to about $980; the property being chiefly bid in for the defendants. That after this sale, the defendants, by a resale of the goods and otherwise, received enough and more than enough of S. Fondey to satisfy their judgment; while the other creditors of S. Fondey got nothing. That the goods purchased in by the defendants at Geneva, were sent to Albany, and on a resale at auction brought $1,573.45. That a small part of the defendants' judgment was to secure future advances.

*Various circumstances were given [***286** in evidence as to the manner in which the sale was conducted, and how the defendants afterwards obtained satisfaction of their judgment, which it is not material to state, as the decision of the cause here turned on the charge of the judge.

He recapitulated the evidence to the jury, and charged strongly in favor of the *bona fides* of the defendants' judgment. He told the jury that the object of the statute was to punish frauds, committed to delay and hinder creditors' recovering their just debts, and that such fraud might have been committed by a fraudulent use of the defendants' judgment against S. Fondey, to delay and hinder creditors, &c., admitting the judgment was legal. Hence, the intent of the defendants in enforcing their judgment, was a material question to be decided by the jury; for their liability depended on the fact of their being actuated by a fraudulent intent. This was required to be satisfactorily made out, before the defendants could be charged with the heavy penalty demanded of them. That if the jury thought there was room for a reasonable doubt whether the defendants intended to commit a fraud against the creditors of S. Fondey, they ought to find a verdict in their favor; but if they were satisfied that the defendants did intend to commit such fraud, they should find for the plaintiffs.

The jury found for the plaintiffs.

Mr. A. Van Vechten, for the defendants, now moved for a new trial, on the ground, among others, that the judge misdirected the jury.

Mr. S. A. Foot, contra.

Curia, per SAVAGE, *Ch. J.* It is contended that the judge erred in stating to the jury that the defendants could commit a fraud upon the creditors of S. Fondey, although their judgment was legal; and that the statute is applicable to those bonds, judgments, &c., only, which were fraudulent in their original concoction.

I cannot find any adjudged case in this court, where the subject in question has been consid-
287*] ered or decided. The *English Statute of 13 Eliz., ch. 5, is substantially like ours. That Act was passed for the avoiding of feigned, covinous and fraudulent feoffments, gifts, grants, alienations, conveyances, bonds, suits, judgments and executions, devised to the intent to hinder, delay or defraud creditors and others of their just and lawful actions; and enacts that all and every feoffment, &c., and every bond, suit, judgment and execution, for any intent or purpose before declared, shall be utterly void. It also, like our statute, gives an action *qui tam*. The same principles must, of course, be applicable to both statutes.

The case of *Holbird* v. *Anderson*, 5 T. R., 235, was not an action for a penalty, but it involved the inquiry as to what acts are void as being fraudulent within the 13 Eliz. The facts were, that one Shepherd had a judgment against Charter, who was also indebted to Holbird, the plaintiff. Charter, knowing that execution was about to issue on Shepherd's judgment, confessed a judgment to the plaintiff, on which execution was delivered to the sheriff two hours before Shepherd's. The sheriff levied upon Shepherd's execution, and returned the plaintiff's *nulla bona*; upon which he brought an action for a false return. It was contended for the defendant, that the warrant of attorney to confess judgment was void by the statute, being with intent to hinder or delay Shepherd's execution. Ld. Kenyon said there was no fraud in the case. The plaintiff was preferred by his debtor, not to benefit the latter, but to secure the payment of a just debt, in which he could see no illegality or injustice. The warrant of attorney, he adds, was given upon good consideration; and the words *bona fide*, in the Act, only apply to cases where possession is not delivered, or where it is merely colorable. Buller, *J.*, alluded to the case of executors, who confess judgments to some creditors, after suits against them by others, and which judgments cover all the assets.

It is perfectly well settled in this State, as it is also in England, in cases not coming within the Bankrupt Acts of that country, that a debtor, in failing circumstances, may prefer one creditor or set of creditors; and this may be *done by assignment, judgment or [*288
otherwise; and such assignment or judgment is not fraudulent, unless it be intended, in whole or in part, for the future benefit of the debtor. (5 T. R., 235, 424, 530; 8 *Id.*, 528; 2 Johns. Ch., 307, 306; 3 *Id.*, 446, 453.) In the late case of *Mackie* v. *Cairns*, 5 Cow., 547, in the Court for the Correction of Errors, this doctrine was fully considered and recognized. The authorities cited from the English Term Reports, and Johnson's Chancery Reports, also show that a security to indemnify for future advances is valid.

If, therefore, the fact be admitted, that the bond on which the judgment of the defendants was entered, was executed as a collateral security for goods, for liabilities, and for contemplated future advances, surely it was free from any suspicion of fraud. The judgment was entered after the failure of S. Fondey was known; and the execution was issued purposely to obtain payment in preference to other creditors. Undoubtedly, it had the effect to delay or hinder the plaintiffs in the collection of their demand. Every assignment or preference given by a failing debtor has that effect as to the creditors who are not preferred.

It, then, becomes necessary to inquire whether the issuing of an execution upon a valid judgment, done to defeat other creditors, renders the plaintiffs in the judgment liable to the penalty in the 4th section of the Statute for the Prevention of Frauds. The case of *Meux* v. *Howell*, 4 East, 1, is full to this point. That was an action on the Statute, 13 Eliz., ch. 5, sec. 3, from which our 4th section, 1 R. L., 76, was, in substance, taken. Many of the expressions are precisely the same in both. The declaration charged the defendants with putting in use a fraudulent judgment against J. Norton, the plaintiffs being his creditors, *contra formam statuti*. The plaintiffs were landlords of Norton, and had distrained for rent. They had also an account against him for beer. The defendants, being also his creditors, sued him, and he was surrendered by his bail. They finally took from him a judgment for the benefit of all the creditors. Execution *was [*289
issued, and Norton's goods sold. A tender was made to the plaintiffs as for their rent; but they would not receive it, being less than the rent distrained for. The question upon the argument was, whether the judgment against Norton was not, under these circumstances, fraudulent within the statute. Ld. Ellenborough said, "it is not every feoffment, judgment, &c., which will have the effect of delaying or hindering creditors of their debts, that is, therefore, fraudulent within the statute; for such is the effect, *pro tanto*, of every assignment that can be made by any one who has creditors. Every assignment of a man's property, however good and honest the consideration, must diminish the fund out of which satisfaction is to be made to his creditors. But the feoffment, judgment, &c., must be devised of malice, fraud &c." In conclusion, he said, "unless we were to go the length of saying, that every assign-

ment to a creditor is fraudulent as to the rest of his creditors, and prohibited to be made, this was not fraudulent. It has none of the qualities of fraud within the Act, which was meant to prevent deeds, &c., fraudulent in their concoction, and not merely such as in their effect might delay or hinder other creditors." Grose, J., remarked, if the judgment be given *bona fide*, and upon good consideration, it is not within the Act.

In that case it was admitted that the distress was not affected by the execution, and Ld. Ellenborough observed, that, as to the plaintiffs' book debt, they had taken no inchoate steps to recover it. In that respect, the case now before the court, differs from *Meux* v. *Howell*. So far, the claim of Meux was weaker than that of the present plaintiffs. But, in this very particular, the case of *Holbird* v. *Anderson* was much stronger with the plaintiff than the present.

After a full examination of this case, I am satisfied of the correctness of the general proposition, that if a judgment &c., be *bona fide* in its concoction, and upon good consideration, it is not within the Act for the Prevention of Frauds.

We are not called upon to say what remedy the plaintiffs may have against the defendants, **290***] for the property or *money in their hands belonging to S. Fondey. It is sufficient for us to say that, in our opinion, the defendants are not liable in this action, if the judgment was *bona fide*, and upon good consideration. If the facts stated in the case be undisputed; that it was given to secure a debt due to the defendants, and to indemnify them against their advances and liabilities, the judgment was not fraudulent. There are good and legal considerations to support it.

I may be allowed to express my regret, with the late *Chancellor* Kent, that such preferences are allowed to failing debtors; but the law is too well settled to be altered by anything but legislative enactment.

In my opinion it was incorrect to leave to the jury to decide upon the intent with which the execution was issued. It must, necessarily, have been to delay the plaintiffs; the property not being sufficient to pay both.

A new trial should, therefore, be granted, with costs to abide the event.

New trial granted.

Affirmed—4 Wend., 105.
Cited in—18 Wend., 363; 4 Sandf., 287; 9 Leg. Obs., 119.

THE PEOPLE v. BARTOW.

Construction of Act Against Unlicensed Bankers —Pleading—Demurrer.

In declaring on the 1st and 2d sections of the Statute, sess. 41, ch. 236, against unlicensed bankers, it is sufficient to set forth the Act so far as it relates to the offense charged, and then to describe the offense according to the statute, averring that, by force of the statute, the defendant forfeited, &c., and an action arose, &c., without saying, "contrary to the form of the statute."

An individual keeping an office of deposit for the purpose of discounting notes, is an offender within the Act, though the office be not for the purpose of any other banking operation.

An individual, keeping an office for carrying on any single banking operation, is within the Act. It is not necessary to subject him to the penalty, that it should be for carrying on banking business generally, or in more than one branch.

A declaration under the Act, that the defendant kept an office of deposit for the purpose of carrying on banking business and operations, without saying what, is not too general, as it follows the words of the statute.

A declaration on a penal statute creating an offense unknown to the common law, and giving an action, should, in some way, show an offense against the statute; but it is not always necessary to say *contra formam statuti*. It is enough that the offense appear to be, in truth, against the statute.

On a demurrer to the whole declaration, if either count be good, judgment will be for the plaintiff on that count, though the other counts be bad.

Citations—6 Bac. Abr., 391; 2 East, 333; 1 Chit. Pl., 353, 643; 2 Salk., 505; Holt, 632, 635; Fortes., 225; 1 Saund., 286, n. (9); 2 Saund., 379, n. (14).

ON demurrer to the declaration: This was in debt for $2,000. The first count recited the Statute passed Apr. 21, 1818, which enacted that it should not be lawful for any person, association of persons, or body corporate, from *and after Aug. 1, then next, to keep [***291** any office of deposit for the purpose of discounting promissory notes, or for carrying on any kind of banking business or operations, which incorporated banks are authorized by law to carry on; unless thereunto specially authorized by law. And that in case any person, or persons, or body corporate, should contravene the foregoing provisions, every such person or persons, and the members of every such corporation, who should, either directly or indirectly, assent thereto, should for every offense, forfeit the sum of $1,000, to be sued for, &c., and recovered in an action of debt, in the name of the people. This count then alleged that the defendant, not regarding the Act, nor the provisions therein contained, after, &c., to wit: on Apr. 1, 1825, at, &c., did keep an office of deposit, for the purpose of discounting promissory notes, he not being thereunto specially authorized by law; whereby, &c., by force of the statute in this case made and provided, the defendant forfeited $1,000; and, by force of the statute, an action hath accrued, &c.

The second count stated, that after, &c., to wit: Apr. 1, 1825, at, &c., the defendant, not regarding the Act, nor the provisions therein contained, did keep an office of deposit, for the purpose of carrying on banking business and operations, which incorporated banks are authorized by law to carry on, he not being thereunto specially authorized by law. Whereby, &c. (as before).

General demurrer and joinder.

Mr. S. A. Foot, in support of the demurrer. The 1st count is defective, in not alleging that the defendant has contravened all the provisions contained in the 1st section of the Act, sess. 41, ch. 236, sec. 1, 2. The same objection applies to the 2d count. The words in the 2d section are not the foregoing provisions, or any of them. The crime charged, is keeping an office only. To warrant the action, all the provisions, and each of them, must be violated. Otherwise the Act must be extended by construction which cannot be of a penal statute. Any man has a right *to keep an office of dis- [***292** count and deposit. The only object of the Act was to restrain companies not incorporated, from carrying on banking operations.

The offense is not alleged in either count, to have been committed against the form of the

Statute. Such an averment is material in an action for a penalty given by statute. A general demurrer is sufficient to reach this defect. In a penal action, a general demurrer is equivalent to a special one in any other. The defect is fatal even after verdict. 1 Chit. Pl., 358; *Lee* v. *Clarke*, 2 East, 353.

The 2d count is also bad for want of sufficient precision and certainty. It does not specify what kind of banking business or operations it was the purpose of the defendant to carry on.

Mr. Talcott, Atty-Gen., contra. The language of the statute is too plain to be mistaken. An individual can carry on no kind of banking business or operations. According to the construction contended for on the other side, any kind of banking business may be carried on, if all are not joined, and this too by a company. The object was to prevent every species of imposition which had so long been practiced upon the community by private banks. Yet, within the rule set up against us, three individuals, by dividing their operations, may violate all the provisions of the statute. If they do not go to work as a company, it is enough. They escape. One may keep an office of deposit; another issue notes; and a third discount. No. The true sense of the Act is distributive. It reaches any separate kind of banking business. The intention of the Legislature should be consulted. (Bac. Abr., Statute, I., pl. 9, and the cases there cited.)

As to the formal objection, *Lee* v. *Clarke*, is itself against the plaintiff. The only difficulty in that case, arose from the circumstance that there were two different statutes. This will be seen by adverting to the opinion of the court, and the cases cited in the course of the discussion.

The Atty-Gen. also cited to this point, Esp. on Penal Actions, 107, 108; 2 Salk., 504, and **293***] *Reynolds* v. **Smith*, 2 Browne (Penn.), 257, 260, which was a much stronger case for the defendant than the present one, the statute neither being recited in the declaration, nor the general conclusion inserted, *contra formam*, &c. Yet a motion in arrest was denied. It was held enough that the declaration brought the defendant within the Act by the description of the offense.

Mr. Foot, in reply, said if the construction contended for by the Atty-Gen., was the correct one, the statute might be extended to 20 or 30 different branches of business, very usually and generally carried on in community by individuals and mercantile houses. The words, "any kind of banking business or operations." would reach almost the whole of the commercial world.

Curia, per WOODWORTH, *J.* It is objected that the 1st count is defective, for two reasons: 1. Because it does not appear that the defendant has contravened all the provisions in the 1st section of the Act. 2. Because the offense charged is not alleged to have been committed against the form of the statute.

As to the first, it may be observed, that although a penal statute is to be construed strictly, the court are not to disregard the plain intent of the Legislature. Among other things, it is well settled, that a statute which is made for the good of the public, ought, although it be penal, to receive an equitable construction. (6 Bac. Abr., 391.) When it is considered that this statute was intended to strike at an existing evil, deemed to be of serious injury to the community, it cannot well be doubted that its enactment was to promote the public good.

Applying these rules to the construction of the Act, I apprehend the intention not to be mistaken. It is evident, from the first part of the section, that all banking operations are prohibited. To keep an office of deposits, for the purpose of discounting notes, is a specific violation of the statute. It next forbids the carrying on of any kind of banking business. The latter may include, but is *certainly [***294** more extensive than the former. There are operations of a bank other than the mere discounting of notes. The penalty attaches upon every person who contravenes the foregoing provisions. To allow the construction contended for by the defendant, would be to render the statute a dead letter. The discounting of notes, is, undoubtedly, the principal business of a banking institution. If, in addition to this, it must be shown that the defendant has conducted other and further operations incident to banking, before he is liable to the penalty, the Act becomes nugatory and inoperative. On this ground, it is only necessary for a party to confine himself strictly to the keeping of an office for discounting notes, the great evil intended to be remedied, and he is sure then not to be reached. He is excused, because he has not also conducted some of the minor operations of a bank, distinct from the discounting of notes. The statute speaks a different language. It must, I think, be understood to attach, whenever either of the prohibitions have been violated. This is the manifest construction, although the words, "or either of them," are omitted.

As to the second objection, it seems to be generally necessary, in an action on a penal statute, where the act prohibited was not an offense at the common law, to allege in the declaration, that it was done "against the form of the statute." Stating merely, that by force of the statute, an action accrued, is not sufficient. *Lee* v. *Clarke*, 2 East, 333; 1 Chit. Pl., 353. In *Lee* v. *Clarke*, the action was debt for a penalty on the game laws. The declaration did not set out the statute, or show that the acts done were prohibited by it, otherwise than by averring that the defendant had not lawful authority; whereby, and by force of the statute, an action accrued. It was held that the omission to say, against the form of the statute, was fatal. But the same case seems to admit, that the omission of these words may be supplied. Ld. Ellenborough observed, "the fact must be alleged to be done against the form of the statute. I do not see such circumstances stated, as brings the case within any of them, without *alleging it to be against the form of [***295** the statute." Lawrence, *J.*, inclined to the sufficiency of an allegation, "by force of the statute, an action hath accrued." On a subsequent day, the court commented on the case of *Coundell* or *Kendall* v. *John*, 2 Salk., 505; S. C., Holt, 632, 635; Fortes., 225, which was supposed by the counsel to decide that such an averment was unnecessary. Ld. Ellenborough remarked, that upon comparing the ease with other authorities, there did not appear to be that incongruity which the court at first apprehended. That the different reports of that case concur substantially in this: that it is not necessary to conclude *contra formam statuti;* but, in the language of Holt, *Ch. J.*, "you must bring yourself within the description of it." I think it appears that the court, in *Lee* v. *Clarke*, acquiesced in this distinction. It was observed by Ld. Ellenborough, with respect to the case of *Kendall* v. *John*, that the ultimate opinion of the court was, that in all actions founded on a statute, it is necessary, in some manner, to show that the offense on which you proceed, is an offense against the statute. This principle, which I think sound, disposes of the objection; for here it is clearly shown that the statute prohibits the keeping of an office for discounting notes, and that the defendant did keep such office. Independent, therefore, of the words insisted on as necessary, the offense appears to be against the statute.

The plaintiffs are, therefore entitled to judgment, even if the second count be defective, the demurrer being general to the whole declaration. On such a demurrer, if either count be sufficient, the plaintiff will be entitled to judgment upon it. (1 Chit. Pl., 643; 1 Saund., 286, *n.* 9; 2 *Id.*, 379, *n.* 14.)

But I think the second count also good. It is contended that this count does not specify what kind of banking business the defendant intended to carry on. The declaration alleges that an office of deposit was kept for the purpose of carrying on such business. The penalty is incurred, if an office of deposit is kept, and the purpose, or intent, be made out. The de- **296***] fendant must come prepared *to defend himself against the intent of doing any act, which may be considered as constituting banking business. The statute does not require a specification. The allegation, although general, is not more so than the statute.

The demurrer not being well taken to either count, the plaintiffs are entitled to judgment. But the defendant may withdraw his demurrer, and plead, on payment of costs.

Rule accordingly.

Cited in—4 Wend., 501; 17 Wend., 174; 8 B., 202; 1 Hall., 556; 2 Leg. Obs., 298.

NORTHRUP v. NORTHRUP.

Mutual Covenants—Performance—Pleading.

Where the defendant covenanted with the plaintiff to pay certain money to T. on a certain day; and the plaintiff covenanted that on the defendant's so paying, he, the plaintiff, would give up and discharge a certain bond and mortgage: held, that the payment was a condition precedent to the performance on the part of the plaintiff; who might sue for the non-payment without showing a performance, or offer to perform on his part; nor could the defendant plead the want of such performance or offer to perform.

Citation—Doug., 690.

ON demurrer to the defendant's plea. The plaintiff declared on a covenant, which, on oyer, was as follows: The defendant covenanted to pay certain rent due and in arrear, to one D. Tomlinson, on a certain farm, and all which should become due on Mar. 25, 1825; the whole to be paid on that day, and the plaintiff covenanted that on the defendant's so paying the rent, he, the plaintiff, would give up and discharge a certain bond and mortgage. The action was for not paying the rent at the day.

Plea, that the plaintiff did not, on the 25th day of March, 1824, give up and discharge the bond and mortgage, nor tender, nor offer to do so, on that day, or before or since.

General demurrer and joinder.

Mr. M. T. Reynolds, in support of the demurrer.

Mr. A. L. Jordan, contra, cited *Parker* v. *Parmele*, 20 Johns., 130, and the cases there referred to.

Curia, per SAVAGE, *Ch. J.* The plea is bad. The payment of the money to Tomlinson, on the day specified, is clearly a condition precedent. The performance by the plaintiff of his part of the agreement is not necessarily simultaneous, but was naturally to be subsequent. A general averment of his readiness to perform is all that *can be necessary or [***297** proper. To aver a tender was certainly not necessary.

Ld. Mansfield, in *Jones* v. *Barkley*, Doug. 690, makes three classes of covenants: 1. Such as are mutual and independent, where separate actions lie for breaches on either side. 2. Covenants which are conditions, and dependent on each other, in which the performance of one depends on the prior performance of the other. 3. Covenants which are mutual conditions to be performed at the same time, as to which the party who would maintain an action must, in general, offer or tender performance. I consider the plaintiff's covenant as clearly belonging to the second class. The defendant's covenant was absolute. The cases cited by the defendant's counsel relate to the third class.

The plaintiff must have judgment, with leave to the defendant to amend, on payment of costs.

Judgment for the plaintiff.

Cited in—7 Wend., 114; 8 Wend., 619; 11 Wend., 50; 1 Den., 60; 4 Am. Dec., 772 (5 S. & P., 119).

CLARK AND CLARK v. PINNEY.

Reversal of Judgment after Payment—Action of Indebitatus Assumpsit *Lies to Recover Back the Money—Writ of Restitution—Remedy by* Scire Facias—*Payment of Judgment by Note.*

Where the money was paid on a judgment of a Court of C. P., which was afterwards reversed on error; held, that it might be recovered back in an action of *indebitatus assumpsit* for money had and received.

The court would not turn the party round to the antiquated remedy by *scire facias*, though they agreed that this would lie: and that where it appears on the face of the record, that the money had been paid, a writ of restitution may issue, even without a *scire facias*.

Taking a promissory note as payment on an execution, and indorsing it satisfied, with the consent of the plaintiff, is equivalent to the payment of money, though the note be not negotiable. And the amount of such a note will be regarded as money, in an action for money had and received, on a reversal of the judgment upon which the execution issued.

Citations—1 Har. & Johns., 405; 2 Mumf., 272; Lofft., 207; 1 Bac. Abr., 261; 1 Ld. Raym., 742; Com. Dig. (3 B, 20); Cro. Car., 699; 2 Salk., 588.

ASSUMPSIT for money had and received, tried at the Onondaga Circuit, Sept., 1825, before Throop, *Circuit J.*

It appeared by the *N. P.* record, that the suit was commenced as early as February Term, 1825. The declaration contained the usual money counts. Plea, *non assumpsit*, with notice of set-off.

On the trial, the plaintiffs' counsel offered in evidence, the record of a judgment in the Onondaga C. P. of the Term of February, 1822, **298***] in favor of the defendant against *the plaintiffs, for $193.11; a *fi, fa.* indorsed satisfied by the sheriff, June 21, 1822, except sheriff's fees; that the execution was paid by a note of Walker & Clark, by which they promised the defendant to pay him $181.27, Feb. 1, 1823, with interest, provided the judgment in the C. P. should not be reversed before that day. That this was received as and towards payment of the judgment by Pinney and his attorney. The counsel also offered the record of a judgment for $216.73, in the Onondaga C. P. on this note, recovered at May Term, 1823, and an execution returnable at the next August Term, which had been paid before the return day, and was returned by the sheriff satisfied. They also offered an exemplification of a judgment record in the Supreme Court, in favor of the present plaintiffs against the present defendant, whereby it appeared, that the judgment first above mentioned had been reversed on a writ of error, at the October Term, 1824. All these facts were admitted by the defendant's counsel, on whose motion the judge nonsuited the plaintiffs, with leave to move to set aside the nonsuit, and for a new trial.

Mr. E. Griffin, for the plaintiffs, now moved accordingly; and the question was, whether an action for money had and received would lie in this case, or whether the plaintiffs should be put to their remedy by *scire facias*, or otherwise, on the judgment of reversal.

Mr. Griffin cited Cow. Tr., 69; Bull. *N. P.*, 131; Cowp., 419.

And that the note was equivalent to the payment of money, he cited 2 Esp., 571; 8 Johns., 202; 11 *Id.*, 464.

Mr. S. M. Hopkins, contra. That the action for money had and received is not the proper remedy, he cited 3 T. R., 125; 7 *Id.*, 269; 2 H. Bl., 416; 2 Com. Cont., 46, *note*; 1 Ld. Raym., 742; Com. Dig., Pleader, 3 B, 20; Cro. Jac., 698; Cowp., 417–419.

That giving the note, though it was accepted in payment, was not equivalent to money, it not being negotiable, he cited 3 East, 169.

299*] *That the money was recovered by judgment on the note given, and cannot be recovered back till that judgment is reversed, or, in some manner, out of the way, he cited 4 Johns., 240; 2 *Id.*, 157; 2 Com. Cont., 40, 41, and the cases there cited; 1 Esp, 84.

Curia, per SAVAGE, *Ch. J.* The important question in this case is, whether *indebitatus assumpsit* for money had and received, lies to recover money paid on an execution upon a judgment, which was afterwards reversed.

The general proposition is, that this action lies in all cases where the defendant has in his hands money which, *ex equo et bono*, belongs to the plaintiff. When money is collected upon an erroneous judgment, which, subsequent to the payment of the money, is reversed, the legal conclusion is irresistible, that the money belongs to the person from whom it was collected. Of course, he is entitled to have it returned to him. The only question is, whether this be the proper remedy.

The cases referred to by counsel do not fully decide the point; nor have I found any case where this very point has been decided, except *Green* v. *Stone*, 1 Har. & J., 405. It was raised in *Isom* v. *Johns*, 2 Munf., 272. There the defendant had been plaintiff in a former action; recovered judgment, and issued execution, upon which the defendant's property was sold by the sheriff. On the argument, most of the English cases which are now cited were referred to. The court decided against the plaintiff, on the ground that the money did not appear to have come to the defendant's use; not denying the doctrine, however, that, if the defendant had received the money, the plaintiff might recover it in this action.

In *Green* v. *Stone* this very point was decided in favor of the plaintiffs.

The principle in question is supposed to have been acted on in *Feltham* v. *Terry*, Lofft. 207, which was an action for money had and received by the church-wardens against the overseers of the poor, for money levied by the latter, *on a conviction of one of the [***300** former, which was subsequently quashed. The court held the plaintiff might sue for the money collected by a sale of the property; or, by bringing trespass, he might have recovered the value of the property. This conviction, I apprehend, must have been irregular; otherwise, the court would not have said trespass might have been brought. Trespass surely would not lie for collecting the amount of a judgment which was merely erroneous. In that case, therefore, the court must have acted on the principle, that the money was collected by a void authority. The authorities are clear and abundant that, in such a case, *indebitatus assumpsit* lies. 1 Bac. Abr., 261; *Newdigate* v. *Davy*, 1 Ld. Raym., 742.

In the case of *Mead* v. *Death*, 1 L. Raym., 742, it was decided, that money paid upon an order of the Quarter Sessions could not be, recovered back, though the order had been quashed on *certiorari*. And Tracy, Baron, before whom the cause was tried, compared it to the case where money is paid upon a judgment which is afterwards reversed for error, in which case *indebitatus assumpsit* will not lie. No reason is given why this action will not lie; nor is any case referred to in support of the *dictum*. It is shown, however, that, in the English courts, the proper remedy, upon the reversal of a judgment, is a *scire facias*, *quare restitutionem non*, upon which the party recovers all that he has lost by reason of the judgment. (Com. Dig., 3 B, 20; Cro. Car., 699.) And if it appear on the record that the money is paid, restitution will be awarded without a *scire facias*. (2 Salk., 588.)

Cases have been cited in which it is said, that

this action does not lie to recover money collected under legal process afterwards vacated, which is true as applied to those cases; but the principle is not applicable in this case.

Upon the whole, my view of the question is this: the general principle is, undoubtedly, in favor of sustaining the action. *Isom* v. *Johns*, decided by the Court of Appeals of Va., is a plain recognition of the principle as governing this very case; and *Green* v. *Stone* is an authority in point. These are opposed only by a **301***] *Nisi Prius* decision, at a time *when the action for money had and received had not come into general use. I am inclined to sustain the action. The inclination of courts is to extend the action for money had and received. It is not denied that the plaintiff is entitled to some remedy for the money, though it was taken from him by process erroneous merely. Then, why turn him round from this simple action to the antiquated remedy by *scire facias?* I do not think the purposes of justice require it.

It is also contended that the facts in this case do not amount to a payment of money to the defendant. A note was received by the sheriff as payment of the execution, by the direction of the plaintiff and his attorney. And the execution was returned satisfied. Nay, more; a judgment has been obtained, and the money actually paid upon that note. To what would the plaintiffs be restored on a *sci. fa.?* To the money paid by the note, as money. Restitution could be of nothing else. The difficulty in *Isom* v. *Johns* was, that the sheriff could not be held the plaintiff's agent. The facts show him to be so in this case.

In my opinion there should be a new trial.

New trial granted.

Cited in—1 Wend., 430; 3 Wend., 82; 10 Wend., 354, 501; 24 Wend., 33; 70 N. Y., 500; 72 N. Y., 582; 4 Trans. App., 251; 3 Lans., 56; 5 Barb., 155; 45 Barb., 617; 1 Park., 377; 1 Sand., 212; 1 Hilt., 362; 6 Pet., 17.

S. C.—37 N. Y., 299; 103 Ill., 407; 39 N. J. L., 558; 41 Mo., 420; 83 Ind., 87; 35 O., 646; 19 Am. Dec., 532; 26 Am. Rep., 625 (70 N. Y., 497); 43 Am. Rep., 62 (83 Ind., 86).

302*] *LAMETTI ET AL., Executrix and Executors of LAMETTI,

v.

ANDERSON.

Demise of Lot for Term of Years—Covenant to Surrender at End of Term with Improvements —Compensation to be Allowed for Improvements Authorized to be Made—Neither Building nor Repairing Lease—Covenant to Pay for Improvements Ran with the Land.

A., by indenture, demised a building lot in the City of N. Y., with a dwelling-house and shop thereon, to W. for 21 years, at a rent of $165. W. covenanted that he, his executors, &c., or assigns, would, at the end of the term, surrender the demised lot, with all such buildings and improvements as might be then remaining thereon, A. paying for such of the buildings and improvements as might be erected and made thereon by W. his executors, &c., or assigns. The parties agreed that W. his executors, &c., or assigns, at his and their proper costs and charges, during the term, might take down the dwelling-house, and erect such other buildings, as he, his executors, &c., or assigns might think proper; and that all such buildings and improvements, as should be so erected, and made, and remaining on the demised lot at the end of the term, should be valued (in a manner specified). And A. should pay W., his executors, &c., or assigns, the amount of the valuation, not exceeding $1,500.

Held, that this was neither a building nor repairing lease; that the covenant to pay extended to a new building, to be erected at the option of the tenant; but that though the old house was not torn down, and a new one erected; yet the lessor was liable to pay for such additions to, and alterations of the old house, as amounted to improvements; not, however, for ordinary repairs, such as new roofing the old house or rebuilding the chimney.

The term being passed by *mesne* assignments to L., though the improvements were not made by him, but mainly by the lessee, before assignment; in an action by the executors of L. on the covenant to pay for the improvements; held, that this covenant ran with the terms, which having passed to L. by assignment, before the covenant was broken, carried the covenant to L., who, or whose executors, might maintain an action upon it, in his or their own names.

Citations—5 Co., 17, 18; Com. Dig., Covenant, (B. 3); 3 Atk., 512.

COVENANT, tried Jan. 23, 1824, at the N. Y., Circuit, before Edwards, *Circuit J.*

The action was on an indenture of lease, dated Feb. 4, 1799, between the defendant as lessor, and one Warner, as lessee of a dwelling-house and lot, in the City of N. Y., *habendum*, to Warner and his executors, &c., and assigns, from May 1, then next, for, &c., 21 years, at a rent of $165.

Warner thereby covenanted that he, his executors, &c., or assigns, should peaceably, &c., at the determination of the term, surrender into the hands and possession of the defendant, his heirs or assigns, the demised lot, together with all such buildings and improvements, as might be then remaining thereon, the defendant, his, &c., paying for such of the said buildings and improvements, as might be erected and made thereon by Warner, his executors, &c., or assigns, in the manner thereinafter mentioned. The parties then mutually covenanted and agreed, for themselves, severally, and for their several and respective heirs, executors, &c., and assigns, that it should be lawful for Warner, his executors, &c., or assigns, at his and their proper costs and charges, during the term, to take down the dwelling-house, standing on the demised lot at the date of the lease, and erect thereon such buildings as he, *his executors, &c., or assigns, [***303** might think proper; that all such buildings and improvements as should be so erected and made, and remaining on the demised lot, at the end of the term, should then be valued and appraised by indifferent persons, one of whom should be chosen by each of the parties, or by their respective legal representatives; and in case the two persons could not agree in the appraisement, then they should choose a third indifferent person; and such three persons, or any two of them, should make the appraisement in writing, under their hands and seals; and that, thereupon, the defendant, his heirs or assigns, should pay to Warner, his executors, &c., or assigns, the amount of the valuation, provided that such amount should not, on any account, exceed $1,500.

The term yet to come of this lease was assigned by Warner, under his hand and seal, to Pell, Feb. 23, 1807; and Jan. 13, 1814, in the same form reassigned by Pell to Warner; and so by Warner, the same Jan. 14, to Lametti, the testator.

The above particulars appeared upon the declaration (which went upon the covenant to pay) and oyer, and were admitted upon the trial.

The plaintiffs then produced on the trial, an appraisement; but, on the defendant's objecting to it, on account of certain formal defects, withdrew it; and the defendant then agreed to try the cause on its merits, reserving all rights he might have upon the state of the pleadings —and particularly the right to object, that the plaintiffs could not maintain the action in their own names.

The plaintiffs then proved that the dwelling-house standing on the demised premises at the date of the lease, had never been taken down. They then offered to prove that material alterations of, and additions to the dwelling-house, had been made by Warner, to wit: an entire new story underneath, which was rendered necessary, in consequence of the street in front having been lowered 8 feet; an addition to the rear of the house, and rebuilding the chimney, and altering the staircases; and the plaintiffs **304***] *claimed the value of the whole. The defendant objected that the plaintiffs were not entitled to recover, unless the dwelling-house had been taken down, and improvements made by putting a new building or buildings on the lot. The judge decided that the plaintiffs might prove any alterations or additions to the house, or adjoining building on the lot, made during the term, and remaining at its expiration. The defendant excepted to this opinion.

The plaintiffs then gave the proof offered, and that a new roof was put on the house, and that various additions to, and alterations of a shop, standing on the demised premises at the commencement of the term, were made. That it was then a mere harness maker's shop, weather boarded, and there was a large gangway between that and the house. That during the term this shop had been converted into a dwelling-house, and extended over the gangway so as to join the other house; a chimney was built in it, and two convenient stories made in that part which formed the first story. That a wall worth $70 had been made by the lessee to keep the ground of the adjoining lot from falling on the demised lot; and that the whole of the additions and alterations made during the term, were worth, including the wall, about $2,300.

The judge charged the jury, that all alterations and additions made to the house or shop, during the term, and remaining at its expiration, should be allowed, if they amounted to improvements of the house or shop, to be valued at their worth when the term expired.

The defendant excepted to this charge.

The jury found for the plaintiffs.

The case came here on the bill of exceptions.

Mr. J. I. Drake, for the defendant, moved for a new trial. He said the plaintiffs were not entitled to recover anything. In true construction, the covenant does not cover either repairs or improvements. The $1,500 were intended to pay for a new house, to be erected in place of the old one, and nothing more. This is a building lease, not a lease for repairs. Improve- **305***] ments in the lease, do not *mean repairs, or alterations, but new erections only. The intent of the parties is to be regarded. An indenture is the language of both parties. There is not one word concerning repairs in the lease. The first clause is a building clause, and the word "improvements," afterwards added, is a mere expletive. The words "manner hereinafter mentioned," refer to the mode of payment or appraisal merely. The object was to secure a good building at the end of the term. *Lant* v. *Norris*, 1 Burr., 287. Additions and repairs to a house, are not equivalent to rebuilding. (3 Atk., 512.)

But the plaintiffs cannot recover in their own names, if entitled to recover at all; the subject of the covenant, as I have shown, not being *in esse* at the date of the lease; and so is *Spencer's* case, 5 Rep., 16, 17, 1st res. The second resolution in that case, is, that though the covenant be to make a new erection, yet if the word "assigns" be used, it shall then bind the assignee. But here the word "assigns" is not used throughout. It does not occur in the covenant touching the mode in which the appraisement is to be made. The words here are the parties, or their legal representatives, which do not include assigns. A covenant in a lease, relative to things merely personal, demised with the land, does not run with the term. (*Id.*, 17, 3d res.) The reason is, that the rent arises out of the land, and it is not certain that the chattels will go to the assignee. Here the thing never has come to the assignee; for it never has been built. Privity, both of estate and contract, must be shown by the plaintiffs. (Shep. Touch., 176; 1 Saund., 241, and *notes;* 2 Selw. *N. P.*, 426, and the cases there cited.) Here there is no privity, not even to support a right of distress—the term having expired, and the premises being surrendered. (5 Cow., 407; 10 Johns., 424.)

Mr. P. W. Radcliff, contra. The only question, aside from that of parties, is, whether the covenant extends beyond taking down the buildings and erecting new ones. If there be a doubt on this head, that doubt should be turned *against the covenantor. This [***306** rule applies alike to indentures and deeds poll. (1 Esp. Dig., 271.) The only question is, for whose benefit was the covenant intended? And if one will make an ambiguous covenant to another, the construction shall be most favorable for the latter. But we do not need the aid of this rule. The judge who tried this cause, gave to the covenant its strict legal and grammatical construction. "Buildings erected and improvements made," is the sensible distribution of the words. If the phrase, "in the manner hereinafter mentioned," does not refer to the mode of appraisal, it must refer to buildings and improvements made at the expense of the lessee. If it be doubtful, we have seen that it should receive the latter construction. The dwelling-house could not be taken down without the consent of the lessor. Such an act would have been waste, and the testator would not only have been liable to an action; 13 Johns., 31; but he would have forfeited his term. Hence the license to take down was inserted. But it is a mere license, of which the lessee might or might not avail himself. at his election.

As to the plaintiffs' right of suing in their own names, the counsel for the defendant treats this covenant as a chose in action, in itself not assignable. But it was not so. It was no more a chose in action, than rent yet to fall due upon a lease. It was an unbroken covenant, which ran with the term, and passed to the assignee. The one who held the lease at the expiration of the term, had the right, and the sole right, to sue upon it. If these plaintiffs cannot maintain an action upon it, no one can. Will it be pretended that each of the three different persons who held this lease, shall each have an action in respect to the different stages of building or improvements during their several tenancies? Till the end of the lease, it was not known that the lessor would be liable to pay anything to anybody. All rights passed to the assignees. The improvements belonged to the last assignee, who was entitled to the value. Then for the first time, a cause of ac- **307***] tion *arose. Then this covenant did become a chose in action.

Mr. P. C. Van Wyck, in reply. Neither the word "repairs" nor "alterations" is contained in the lease, and they are very properly omitted in the pleadings. Repairs are certainly out of the case; and a sum in gross was given for a particular object, which was building. All the lessor gets, is an old house repaired and kept in order, against 21 years deterioration on it. This is no more than the tenant was bound to return to him, without one word being said in the lease on the subject. The very relation of landlord and tenant implies that the latter should repair. But all the repairs in the world cannot satisfy the covenant in a building lease. *City of London* v. *Nash*, 3 Atk., 512. It was not intended that the old house should be retained and surrendered up, nor its necessary repairs paid for. There is but one place for building on the city lots of the class to which this belongs. If there be a house already, it must, therefore, be torn down before another can be erected. The word "repairs" is well understood, and if that be omitted, no word can supply its place. The word "improvement" means something new. Both the pleadings and proof should have shown that the old house was demolished.

Curia, per SAVAGE, *Ch. J.* There are but two points in this case of much importance:

1. Can the plaintiffs sustain the action in their own names?

2. Is the defendant liable for any additions, &c., unless the old house was taken down, and a new one erected?

The objection under the first point is, that the covenant does not run with the land; and the assignee cannot, therefore, prosecute for a breach—and *Spencer's* case, 5 Co., 17, is supposed to sustain the proposition. That case is not in point. The action was brought against an assignee of the term, upon a covenant by the lessee to build a wall on the demised premises; and the court held him not liable, because not named. In such cases, they held the **308***] *rule to be, that the covenant was binding upon the assignee, when it related to something *in esse*, parcel of the demised premises, to repair, for instance; but not when it concerned something to be built thereafter. Yet it was held, that even the latter covenant would be obligatory upon the assignee, if named. The sixth resolution in that case is, "if lessee for years covenants to repair the houses during the term, it shall bind all others, as a thing which is appurtenant, and goeth with the land, in whose hands soever the term shall come." It is further resolved, seventhly, that the assignee, or his executor, should have covenant. (*Ib.*, 18.)

According to this case, had the lessee, Warner, covenanted to erect buildings upon the demised lot; not only the lessee, but the assignee, and the executors of the assignee, would have been liable in this action for a breach of the covenant. The same doctrine is found in the other authorities cited by the counsel on this point; and in Com. Dig., Covenant, B. 3.) If the assignee would be liable on such a covenant, surely he must have a right of action, for the violation of a corresponding covenant on the part of the lessor.

The plaintiffs have an undoubted right to maintain the action in their own names, if they have succeeded in showing a right to recover at all.

I do not consider this either a building or a repairing lease. Those terms are peculiarly applicable to cases where the tenant pays no rent; but enjoys the premises a sufficient length of time to compensate him either for building or repairing, according to his contract. *The City of London* v. *Nash*, 3 Atk., 512, was a case where the lessee undertook to rebuild certain houses. He had a lease of them for sixty years. He, or rather his assignee, did not rebuild all, but repaired some of the houses. This was held to be a breach of the covenant.

Here the lessor grants a house and lot for a certain term, at a certain rent. The lessee was not bound to repair any further than so as, at the end of his term, to return the premises in good tenantable condition; unless the covenant *in the lease was compulsory upon [***309** him to build. The first covenant is, that the lessee shall surrender at the end of the term, the "lot of ground, with all such buildings and improvements as may be then remaining thereon, he the said Charles Anderson, his heirs or assigns, paying for such of the said buildings and improvements as may be erected and made thereon, by the said Jacob Warner, his executors, administrators or assigns, in manner hereinafter mentioned." Here it is observable, that the lot was to be surrendered, with all the buildings and improvements then remaining. But Anderson was to pay for such only as may be erected and made by Warner. Now, if it was intended to pull down the old house at all events, this discrimination between the buildings to be surrendered, and those to be paid for, was idle and unmeaning. The next covenant, however, proceeds: "and it is mutually covenanted and agreed, by and between the parties, &c., that it shall and may be lawful for the said Jacob Warner, his heirs, &c., at any time during the said term hereby granted, at his and their own proper costs and charges, to take down the said dwelling-house, now standing on the said hereby demised lot of ground, and to erect thereon such buildings as he, the said Jacob Warner, &c., may think proper; and all such buildings and improvements as shall be so erected and made, and remaining on the said lot hereby demised, at the end of the said term, shall then be valued," &c.; the money to be paid, not to exceed $1,-500. The true construction of this covenant, seems to me to be this: that the lessee might make any alterations which he pleased ; and it should be optional with him to take down the old house, and build a new one, or make any other erections which he should think proper; provided the lessor should only pay for such as the lessee left at the end of the term, and which should be improvements to the amount of $1,500.

I apprehend, however, that a fair construction of the lease does not authorize a recovery for ordinary repairs. Is was improper, therefore, to receive evidence of these ; such as new covering the old house, or rebuilding the chim-
310*] ney. *The lease does not speak of repairs, but buildings and improvements. That must mean new buildings or such alterations in the old one as to make it more convenient.

The charge of the judge was correct ; but as improper testimony was received, a new trial should be granted, the costs to abide the event.

New trial granted.

Affirmed—6 Wend.. 326.
Cited in—8 Cow., 276 ; 6 Wend., 326 ; 1 Paige, 414 ; 4 N. Y., 137 ; 2 Rob., 68 ; 8 Daly, 204 ; 1 Bradf., 59.

DICKEY v. GRANT ET AL.

Execution of an Order for Shipment of Hats by Merchants—Liable for Damages Resulting for Execution in other than Customary Manner.

An order was directed by a merchant at Boston to merchants at Leghorn, for 5 cases of Leghorn hats, without any directions as to the manner of packing or securing them. The Leghorn merchants, in executing this order, shipped the hats for Boston in a vessel which they knew was to touch at Palermo for a cargo of oranges and lemons; and yet neglected to secure the hats in the usual and customary manner; by reason whereof, they being placed in the hold on the boxes of fruit, were much injured, and sold at auction for less than the invoice price; held, that the Leghorn merchants, having undertaken to execute the order, were bound to do so in the customary manner; and not having done so, by reason whereof the purchaser sustained an injury, they were liable to him in an action for the damage.

THIS was an action to recover damages, for the injury to or loss sustained on 5 cases of Leghorn hats, shipped by order, and for account of the plaintiff by the defendants, resident merchants at Leghorn, on board of the schooner Penguin, bound from Leghorn to Palermo, in the Island of Sicily, and thence to Boston.

The cause was tried at the N. Y. Circuit, July 17, 1824, before Betts, *Circuit J.;* when a verdict was found for the plaintiff for $3, 277.24 damages.

Mr. G. Brinckerhoff now moved for a new trial.

Mr. T. J. Oakley, contra.

The facts are sufficiently stated in the opinion of the court, which was delivered by,

WOODWORTH, *J.* The question arising in this case is, whether the defendants are liable on the ground of negligence, for a loss sustained on 5 cases of Leghorn hats. The defendants are merchants residing at Leghorn. Dec. 8, 1817, the plaintiff sent an order for the hats, requesting to have them sent with the least possible delay, to be here early in the spring ; and if all were not ready when an opportunity
311*] offered, to divide the shipment. *Five cases were shipped in Mar., 1818, on board a vessel for Boston, to touch at Palermo, to take in a cargo of oranges and lemons, which was known to the defendants. The fruit was taken in at Palermo, and the cases containing the hats placed in the hold on the boxes of fruit, without any precaution taken to prevent injury from the heat and steam proceeding from them. This the plaintiff contends might have been prevented, had the cases been secured when put on board, according to the usual practice and custom in such cases. The goods were afterward sold at auction, for considerable less than the invoice price.

From the instructions given, it is plain that the plaintiff trusted to the care and diligence of the defendants only ; for although the order speaks of Benini, it has no reference to the manner of securing the goods when shipped ; nor is it a direction to the defendants to employ him. But on the supposition that the defendants would employ him, the plaintiff wished him to understand, that future orders going to him would depend on his executing this with care.

The judge stated to the jury that the defendants, having undertaken to execute the order, were bound to do it in the usual manner; and if there was an established custom relative to the manner of packing or preparing such articles for shipment, the defendants were bound to conform to it. He further stated that it did appear there was an established usage or custom in packing, or securing Leghorn hats ; which was, to put them in boxes, to cover the box with a tarred or waxed linen cloth, over that to put hay or straw, and then a coarse covering or wrapper over the whole. That if the defendants had varied from that manner of packing, without the plaintiff's original directions, or subsequent ratification, they would be liable for the damage. And he submitted to the jury, to determine whether the hats were secured according to the usage. The judge also expressed an opinion that the plaintiff had done no act which, in judgment of law, would amount to a ratification.

*I am inclined to think the charge was [***312**
substantially correct.

In the instructions to ship the hats no directions are given as to the manner of securing them. An earnest desire is expressed to forward them as early as practicable. But the duty of exercising proper care and diligence, necessarily devolved on the defendants The plaintiff had no other agents. There is evidently no subsequent ratification of the defendants' acts by the plaintiff. It it is true that in one of the plaintiff's letters he speaks of the liability of the underwriters. He entertained an erroneous opinion on this subject. But because he did so, it affords no ground to exonerate the defendants, if they are otherwise liable. There was no ratification subsequently and, consequently, the question of negligence is alone presented.

Without analyzing the testimony, I think it well established, that there was a general usage to pack and secure articles of this description, in a particular manner, which was not pursued in this instance. The practice appears to have been as stated by the judge to the jury. The defendants, in their letters to Langdon, seem to admit this to have been the manner of packing, but which had been departed from in several instances on the ground of economy, and at the suggestion of supercargoes. The articles shipped were or a delicate texture, and easily injured. The defendants had no authority to relax or depart from the course which prudent caution had pointed out, and experience sanctioned as necessary. The reasons were peculiarly strong in this case. The defendants knew that a cargo of fruit was to be taken in at Palermo, and ought to have anticipated the increased risk on that account. The steam and vapor arising from decayed fruit stained the hats. They became mouldy and deteriorated in value. If the cases had been secured in the usual manner, the witnesses are of opinion the loss would not have happened.

On the whole, I consider this a case of culpable negligence. The verdict is not against the weight of evidence, and the motion for a new trial must be denied.

New trial denied.

313*] *BOHUN
v.
TAYLOR AND COLLINS.

Witnesses—One of two Joint Defendants in Trespass, though he has Allowed Judgment by Default, Incompetent for the Other—Contra when—Damages Jointly Assessed—Mitigation of Damages.

One of two defendants, sued jointly for the same trespass, though he suffer judgment to pass against him by default, cannot be a witness for his co-defendant. Otherwise, if he plead, and there be no evidence against him.

In trespass against several persons jointly, fer the same act, the damages must be jointly assessed, though they sever in pleading; or one suffer judgment by default, and the trial proceed upon a *tam quam.*

In trespass *quare domum fregit,* held, that the defendants might show, in mitigation of damages, their motives and inducements to enter the house, as that it was to search for furniture which they had been informed was missing.

Wara v. Haydon, 2 Esp., 552, overruled.

Citations—1 Phil. Ev., 62; 10 Johns., 95; 2 Esp., 552; 2 Campb., 333; 1 Saund., 207 *a, n.* (2); 5 Burr., 2790-2792; 1 Archb. Pr., 195; Cro. Eliz., 860; 6 Binn., 316, 319; 1 Day, 34; 10 Johns., 21.

ON ERROR from the N. Y. C. P. The action in the court below was trespass against the defendants, for entering the plaintiff's house in the evening, without leave. Collins suffered judgment by default, and Taylor pleaded the general issue. Upon the trial of both upon a *venire tam quam,* the trespass being proved upon both, Taylor offered Collins as a witness for him. It was objected that he was incompetent, but he was admited and sworn. He was asked as to the motives and inducements the defendants had to enter the house, and how they came to be admitted. This was objected to, as no special plea in bar, or notice embracing the matter had been interposed. But the objection was overruled, and the counsel excepted to the decision of the court on both points. C. then swore that Taylor found him some furniture of one F. was missing, and C. being a city marshal, they went in search of it; found the outer door open, and went into the house, and looked at the furniture, to see if it was F's., &c.

The jury found for the plaintiff 6 cents damages.

Mr. D. Graham, for the plaintiff in error, cited 1 Phil. Ev., 53, 57, 61; 10 Johns., 21, 95; 14 *Id.*, 119; 1 Str., 633; 11 Johns., 57; 1 Lawy. Mag., 197; 1 Archb. Pr., 195; 1 R. L., 344, sec. 5; 2 Tidd, 902, 7th Lond. ed.; Cro. Eliz., 860; 11 Co., 6 *a*, 7 *a*; 6 Binn., 316, 319; 1 Day, 33; Bull, *N. P.*, 285; 2 Cowp., 333, *n.*; 13 Johns., 350; 2 Wash., 276; 1 Munf., 291; 16 Johns., 89.

Mr. J. Anthon, contra, cited 2 Esp., 552; 7 East, 108; 2 Camp., 638.

**Curia,* per SAVAGE, *Ch. J.* The [*314 questions are, 1st as to the competency of Collins, the witness; and 2d, the competency of his testimony, under the pleadings.

A defendant cannot regularly be a witness for co-defendants; but if no evidence has been produced against him, he is entitled to his discharge as soon as the plaintiff has closed his case, and may then give evidence for the others. But if there is any evidence against him, however slight, he cannot be discharged before the rest, and the case must go altogether to the jury. (1 Phil. Ev., 61, 62.)

A case is stated by *Baron* Gilbert, of trespass against two, for two trespasses, and the question was, if one might be a witness for the other. And he says, it seems that if it were the same fact, and the trespass committed at the same time and place, he may not be a witness, because he swears to discharge himself. But if it were not the same fact, or at the same time and place, the oath of one has no influence on the fact that laid to his charge, but merely goes in discharge of the other.

The reasoning of Gilbert is applicable to this case. There was but one joint trespass committed by both defendants; one fact, one time and place; and the testimony given by Collins was equally applicable to the assessment of damages against himself as against Taylor. Even by his own testimony, the trespass is proved.

So a co-defendant in an indictment, who suffers judgment by default, cannot be a witness, either for or against the other defendants. (1 Phil. Ev., 62.) And though they plead separately, and are tried separately, the rule is the same. They are parties to the record, and one is an incompetent witness for the other, until acquittal or conviction—the matter then being at an end as to him. (10 Johns., 95.)

It is contended, however, that the suffering of judgment to pass by default, against the witness, Collins, rendered him competent, as his liability was fixed by the default; and his testimony was applicable to the case of his co-defendant, Taylor. The case of *Wara* v. *Haydon,* 2 Esp., 552, is cited to support the proposition. *There, in an action of trover for [*315 goods wrongfully distrained, one defendant suffered judgment by default; and he was admitted by Ld. Kenyon, to prove that the other defendant had no agency in the transaction, except making an inventory of the goods. His Lordship held that the witness was not interested, as he was not liable for the costs of the other defendant.

In a subsequent case (*Chapman* v. *Graves,* 2 Campb., 333, *note*), before LeBlanc, *J.*, the same thing was offered, except that the witness was called by the plaintiff against the witness' co-trespassers; and he was rejected, the judge saying, that in the former case he had no interest to charge his co-defendants, as he was called to exculpate them, whereas he was now called to inculpate them. On the other hand, it is contended that the interest of the witness is direct, as the jury may assess joint damages against both defendants; and where there is but one trespass, and both are found guilty of the whole trespass, there the damages must be entire, though the defendants sever, and one suffer judgment by default. Such is the settled law in England. 1 Saund., 207 *a, note* 2; *Hill* v. *Goodchild*, 5 Burr., 2790–2792, and the cases there cited; 1 Archb. Pr., 195; *Austen* v. *Willward*, Cro. Eliz., 860. The same is established in Pa. *Wakeley* v. *Hart*, 6 Binn., 416, 319, and also in Conn., *Bostwick* v. *Lewis*, 1 Day, 34.

In this court, it has been held, that a joint trespasser, not taken, though named as a defendant in the *capias*, was a competent witness, as he had no legal fixed interest. *Stockham* v. *Jones*, 10 Johns., 21. (*a*).

But in this case, the interest of the witness was direct. He was testifying to reduce the damages against himself; for, as the act complained of was one entire act, the damages against both, even if not joint, must be the same. It is certainly dangerous to admit witnesses under such circumstances.

316*] *To the testimony itself, I can see no objection. The object was merely to mitigate damages, not to justify or excuse the trespass.

I am of opinion that the judgment be reversed, and a *venire de novo* awarded from the N. Y. C. P.

Judgment reversed.

Cited in—8 Barb., 663; 12 Barb., 365; 5 How. Pr., 9; 8 Abb. Pr., 72.

S. C.—1 Duer, 644; 4 Bos., 124; 4 E. D. S., 250.

See, 1 Kern., 428.

(*a*) Not being taken, he was not a party for any purpose. Rose v. Oliver, 2 Johns., 365.

JACKSON, ex dem. BRUYN ET AL., v. DEWITT.

Release of Equity of Redemption by Mortgagor Extinguishes Mortgage—Dower—Proceedings to Set Out not Conclusive as to Title in Widow.

D. took a deed in fee, of land, from B.; at the same time giving the latter a mortgage to secure the purchase money. D. then intermarried with M.; and then released his equity of redemption to B., and died, M. surviving. Held, that M., his widow, was not entitled to dower.

The proceedings before a surrogate, to admeasure and set off dower, are no evidence of title in the widow.

A release, or conveyance of the equity of redemption by the mortgagor to the mortgagee, extinguishes the mortgage.

Citations—5 Cow., 168; 17 Johns., 123; 2 Cow., 284; 6 Johns., 290, 294; 7 Johns., 278; 15 Johns., 458.

EJECTMENT, tried at the Ulster Circuit, Oct., 1823, before Betts, *Circuit J.*, when the following facts were admitted:

Bruyn, being seised in fee of a farm, Sept. 12, 1783, conveyed it in fee to Depuy, in consideration of £800, and on the same day Depuy executed to Bruyn a mortgage for the purchase money. Depuy, being in possession under his purchase, married Catherine Bevier. Apr. 8, 1793, the mortgage money being due, Depuy reconveyed to Bruyn, for the moneys due on the mortgage; and continued in possession, as tenant, two or three years, under Bruyn. The lessor of the plaintiff, Hixon, derived title by several *mesne* conveyances from Bruyn, for valuable consideration, all subsequent to the reconveyance. Depuy died several years since, and his widow intermarried with Miller. In 1817, her dower was admeasured and set off on application to the surrogate, and the admeasurement affirmed on appeal to this court. She recovered possession of her dower, by verdict, judgment and execution, in ejectment brought in this court, against Hixon, the lessor. (See the case, 17 Johns., 123.) Dewitt, at the commencement of this suit, held as her tenant.

Verdict for the plaintiff, subject to the opinion of the court.

Mr. J. Sudam, for the plaintiff, cited 15 Johns., 458; 4 Mass., 566; 1 Cow., 479.

Mr. B. F. Butler*, contra, cited 5 **[*317 Cow., 168; 2 *Id.*, 246, 286.

Curia, per WOODWORTH, *J.* The admeasurement of dower is not conclusive. When the widow brings ejectment, she must, as in other cases, make out a title. (5 Cow., 168.)

In this case, the defendant holds under the widow, who in a former ejectment recovered. (17 Johns., 123.) The question now raised was not then before the court.

If the mortgage given by Depuy had been foreclosed, it is conceded that the widow would not be entitled to dower; and it is contended that the release of the equity of redemption is to be considered the same as a foreclosure. On the other hand, it is urged, that on the execution of the release there was a merger, by uniting the equitable and legal estates in the same person, which precludes the mortgagee from setting up the mortgages as a subsisting security. (2 Cow., 284.) It is, undoubtedly, sound that the mortgage cannot be set up. But the question is, did the right of dower attach? The cases of *Hitchcock* v. *Harrington*, 6 Johns., 290, and *Collins* v. *Tracy*, 7 Johns., 278, decide that the widow may recover her dower out of the land mortgaged, against the tenant deriving title by *mesne* conveyance from the husband of the demandant; that the tenant cannot deny the seisin of the husband; nor set up the mortgage as a subsisting title, when there has been no foreclosure, or entry by the mortgagee. In this cause, the plaintiff's title is not derived from the husband of the widow; but from Bruyn, the mortgagee, who accepted a release of the equity of redemption. The plaintiff may, therefore, set up any matter that Bruyn, the mortgagee, might have set up, had Mrs. Miller brought an ejectment against him to recover the land set apart for her dower. From the case of *Stow* v. *Tift*, 15 Johns., 458, it is evident that up to the time that Depuy released, his wife could have no claim of dower; for the husband had an instantaneous seisin only. If the release operated as a discharge of the mortgage merely, *the **[*318** widow became entitled to dower—the husband being considered as having been seised *ab initio*.

(6 Johns., 294.) But there was no actual payment of the mortgage, leaving the husband seised. There was a merger, by which, it is true, the mortgage was satisfied; but the same act annihilated the mortgagor's title. There was not a moment of time between the discharge of the mortgage, and the vesting of the title in the mortgagee. It was all done *uno flatu*. If, then, no right of dower existed, the moment previous to the merger (and clearly there did not), and if the release extinguished all the title the mortgagor ever had, it follows that there never was an instant of time in which the widow was entitled to dower. I am of opinion that the plaintiff is entitled to judgment.

Judgment for the plaintiff.

Cited in—19 Wend., 173; 3 Hill, 103; 1 Sand. Ch., 80; 10 Page, 57; 1 Barb., 406; 23 Barb., 132; 42 Barb., 366; 13 How. Pr., 293; Edm., 283; 2 Bos., 529; 3 Leg. Obs., 127; 28 Hun., 237, 239; 65 Ill., 148.

BUCHANAN
v.
THE OCEAN INSURANCE COMPANY.

Voluntary Repairs of Vessel, by Owner of Cargo, does not Give Him an Insurable Interest—Total Loss—Pleading.

The owner of the cargo, without request from the owner of the vessel, repaired her on the voyage, and effected an insurance in his own name, on his expenditures for repairs. Held, that he had not an insurable interest; that the repairs being voluntarily bestowed, belonged to the vessel, and the property of them vested in the owner.

The insurance was by a wagering policy, and against total loss only. The owner of the vessel had previously insured her; and after she had arrived at her port of destination, she was abandoned as for a technical total loss, by the owner, to his underwriters; and sold with their consent, and for their account. The owner of the cargo, who had made the repairs, then abandoned to his underwriters. Held, that this was not such a total loss as came within the policy; that a constructive total loss of the subject was not enough. But the loss must be absolutely and finally total.

The provision in a policy of insurance that the risk is against total loss only, means an absolute, not a mere technical total loss, whether the policy be a wagering policy or not.

A declaration on a policy of insurance upon a vessel, need not aver any interest in the assured; and if interest be averred, this may be rejected as surplusage.

Citations—12 East, 655; 4 Cow., 222; 5 Cow., 63; S. P. Phil. Ins., 57; 1 Marsh Ins., 104; Park Ins., 374; 6 Mass., 465; 3 Cai., 108, 110, 141; 14 Johns., 138; Doug., 470; 2 Johns. Cas., 333; 2 East, 392.

ASSUMPSIT, for a total loss on a policy of insurance: tried at the N. Y. Circuit, in Jan., 1824, before Edwards, *Circuit J.*

At the trial, the policy was produced, bearing date Mar. 15, 1821; and was in the usual form of policies on vessels, commonly used by the insurance companies in the City of N. Y., partly printed and partly written. The first part was as follows: "Vessel. By *The [*319 Ocean Insurance Company. A. C. Buchanan" (the plaintiff). "On account of whom it may concern, in case of loss payable to A. C. B., do make insurance, and cause to be insured, lost or not lost, at and from Newport to Londonderry, upon the body, tackle, apparel and other furniture of the good ship called The William and Jane." It was what is called an open policy, the usual blank for the valuation not being filled with anything; this cause in the policy standing thus: "The said vessel, tackle, &c., hereby insured, are valued at , without any further account to be given by the assured, or any of them for the same." The premium was one *per cent.* The clause relative to the payment of loss and proof of interest, was in blank as to the person in whom the interest was to be proved; and was as follows: "In case of loss, such loss to be paid in 30 days, after proof of loss and proof of interest in the said ; the amount of the note given for the premium, if unpaid, being first deducted." The policy contained the usual printed clauses as to other insurance, &c., and was underwritten as follows: "$6,500. Six thousand five hundred dollars. The above insurance is hereby declared to be on amount disbursed for repairs of the said vessel at Newport, to which place she returned in distress, and is against total loss only." (Signed by the President, &c.) On the margin of the policy was written as follows: "It is hereby agreed to take the additional sum of two thousand dollars, on this risk, at the same rate of premium, being also on amount of repairs disbursed at Newport. New York, 19th, March, 1821." (Signed by the President and attested by the Secretary.)

The policy being admitted, the plaintiff read, as preliminary proof, an abandonment by the plaintiff as for a total loss, previous to the vessel's arrival at Londonderry, dated Aug. 25, 1821, an affidavit and statement showing the amount of repairs at Newport, &c., &c., which were admitted to have been duly furnished.

The following are the other material facts, as they appeared at the trial: the vessel, Wm. W. Polke, owner, sailed originally, Dec. 24, 1820, John *Brown master, from N.Y. [*320 for Londonderry, laden with a cargo of flax seed, belonging to the plaintiff; naval stores, staves and other articles. Dec. 25, she encountered severe weather, and was finally obliged to put into Newport in distress, where she arrived Jan. 2, 1821. Here she underwent the usual surveys and repairs, which were completed Mar. 1, 1821. The repairs amounted to $9,005.30, which sum was paid by the plaintiff's agent. Mar. 7, the vessel sailed from Newport. She arrived on the Irish coast the 27th, and took a pilot, and came to at Quigley Point, Loughfoyle; and after part of the cargo was taken out by lighters, in attempting to go up to the quay of Londonderry, she ran aground on the south side of Tuor Pateh, and was not got off and brought to the quay till Apr. 12. She was there, on survey, found to be much

---

NOTE.—*Marine Insurance.* 1. *Insurable interest* 2. *Wager* Policies.

1. *Insurable interest, necessary.* See, generally, Lawrence v. Van Horne, 1 Cai., 276, *note*; Smith v. Williams, 2 Cai. Cas., 110, *note*; Kenny v. Clarkson, 1 Johns., 385, *note*; Abbott v. Sebor, 3 Johns. Cas., 37, *note*.

2. *Wager policies are valid at common law.* Abbott v. Sebor, 3 Johns. Cas., 39; Juhel v. Church, 2 Johns. Cas., 333; Miller v. Eagle, &c., Ins. Co., 2 E. D. Smith, 268; St. John v. American Mutual Life Ins. Co., 2 Duer, 419; St. John v. Ins. Co., 13 N. Y., 31; Clendining v. Church, 3 Cai., 141, *note*.

Contra as to fire insurance policies. Freeman v. Fulton Fire Ins. Co., 14 Abb. Pr., 398; S. C., 38 Barb., 247.

injured, and incapable of repair, at Londonderry, for want of a dry dock. Nor could she be hove out; and it was extremely hazardous to send her to Glasgow or Liverpool. It was the opinion of the surveyors that she should be sold at Londonderry. She was accordingly sold for account, and with the consent of the agent of the London insurers, on the 18th or 19th of June; and purchased by the captain as agent for the owner, Polke, for £550—$2,200, or thereabouts. The plaintiff arrived at Londonderry after the sale. The captain knew nothing of the plaintiff's insurance at the time of the sale, though he knew the vessel was insured at Lloyd's. She could not have been repaired at Londonderry for less than £2,100—$8,200. July 8 she sailed for Liverpool, the plaintiff sailing there with her, where she arrived July 10, 1821. There she went into dry dock, and was repaired in 12 or 14 days. About Aug. 18, the captain chartered her for Philadelphia. The expense of the repairs at Liverpool was not precisely ascertained, but the captain thought they could not be less than $3,500; and that after being repaired, she might have been worth from $8,000 to $10,000. After the vessel returned to Philadelphia, she 321*] was sold and sent to the *East Indies. The owner had, before the insurance in question was made, insured the vessel at Lloyd's, London, for £3,000 sterling—$13,320; and he had been paid as for a total loss by the underwriters there, deducting the £550, for which the vessel sold; and when the defendants made insurance, they knew of the one made at London, which was from N. Y. to Londonderry. The plaintiff admitted himself, at Liverpool, to be the agent of Polke. The former had no interest in the ship, nor was he a member of the firm of Wm. Buchanan & Co., the consignees at Londonderry, of both vessel and cargo. The plaintiff abandoned, as before mentioned, Aug. 25, 1821.

Verdict, by consent, for the plaintiff, for $9,901.37, subject to the opinion of the court on a case, and with liberty to either party to turn the case into a bill of exceptions or special verdict.

The following points were now made for the plaintiff:

1. Such a loss as authorized an abandonment to the underwriters on the vessel, authorized an abandonment on the policy on the disbursements.

2. There was a technical total loss of the vessel.

3. Though there was a prior insurance on the vessel to her full value, yet this insurance is valid.

4. No interest in the vessel was necessary.

5. Though the vessel was restored when the abandonment was made, this did not destroy the right to abandon; for the subject continued to be totally lost.

Mr. C. D. Colden, for the plaintiff. This is the common form of a policy, when it is intended to insure something collateral to the body of the vessel or property, and the points all hang on the question, whether there was a total loss. This depends on the facts. The loss of the vessel was necessarily a loss of the repairs. The Company knew that the plaintiff had no interest in the vessel, and that they were insuring something distinct from the body of it. They insure disbursements for repairs expressly; and it is evident from the case, that they perfectly understood *what they [*322 were insuring. They knew that a loss which should transfer the whole subject-matter would be the ground of an action on the policy. An abandonment of the vessel passed the repairs insured to the underwriters at Lloyd's. The owner was not bound to forbear the abandonment on his part for the benefit of the plaintiff. The provision in the policy, that it should extend only to a total loss, must be construed to mean, as in other cases, either a physical or technical total loss. The meaning is the same in this as in any other policy. The only difficulty with which we can be met on the nature of the loss is that the vessel arrived at her port of destination. But it is not well settled that this will not prevent the loss being total. (Beawes' Lex. Merc., 298, 311, 4th ed., cited 1 T. R. 189; Phil. Ins., 400; 11 Johns., 295.) We do not deny that if the subject was restored when the abandonment was made, all right had gone. It was not so. It was totally lost; and never was restored to the plaintiff. It could not be; for it had passed to the other underwriters, and then, by the sale, to the purchaser. Indeed, an abandonment in the plaintiff's case was not necessary. It is never necessary, where you can claim nothing from it. It does not affect the rights of the parties. (8 Johns., 246; 2 *Id.*, 155; Phil. Ins., 382.) The plaintiff had nothing which he could abandon. It might have been a technical total loss as to the vessel, but it was physically total as to the plaintiff. (3 Johns. Cas., 34.) A party insuring profits, may recover, on proof that the cargo is lost. Here the incidental loss is equally certain. This is precisely like the case of an insurance of profits against a total loss only. (1 Johns., 435, 439.)

No doubt the vessel was insured by the London policy; but the defendants knew this; and the insurance in question is good, unless the London policy covered the repairs. The one who has insured the vessel is never received as an insurer on the profits also. The clause in the policy relating to other insurances, can only apply to the very subject insured at the time.

*The plaintiff clearly had an insura- [*323 ble interest. His interest was to have the voyage go on.

But the words of the policy dispense with the necessity of showing interest. If it were a mere wagering policy, it is not void according to our law. But it is not a wagering policy. The plaintiff had expended every cent he got insured.

Mr. T. A. Emmet, same side, cited 1 Bos. & P., 316; 1 Burr., 489; Marsh. Ins., 150; Park Ins., 374; Ph. Ins., 490, 491; 1 Wh., 219; 6 Mass., 119, 318; 1 Johns. Cas., 226; 4 Binn., 386; 15 Mass., 341; 3 Bos. & P., 308; 4 Dall., 421; 3 Rob. Adm., 288; 1 Peters Adm., 223; 4 Binn., 539, per Tilghman, Ch. J.; 5 Serg. & R., 473; 12 Mass., 214; 11 Johns., 223; 1 *Id.*, 249.

Mr. G. Griffin, contra. The clauses relied on as peculiar, by the other side, are now very common. If it be admitted, as it must be, that the London policy covered the vessel, then it follows that it cannot be covered by this, which provides in terms against such a case. Not

only the value of the vessel when she sails, but all subsequent repairs, are covered by an insurance on the vessel. By the settled rule of the English law, the whole would be covered. (12 East, 655, per Ld. Ellenborough, *Ch. J.*; 4 Taunt., 367.) Suppose a wagering policy to be good; this is not one. (1 Condy Marsh., 121; 1 T. R., 304; 3 Cai., 141.) The declaration avers interest in the plaintiff. This he must establish or fail for the variance. This is not a mere matter of form. It is the very gist of the case. The payment made for repairs was made by the plaintiff, as agent for Polke, the owner, who, for aught that appears, has reimbursed him. An insurable interest always involves the right to abandon. Here was no such right. The nature of the interest should have been specified in the policy. Clearly the plaintiff had nothing which was insurable, without being so specified. (2 Johns. Cas., 250; 2
324*] Johns., 346; 7 *Id.*, 522; 4 B. &*A., 582.) The policy mentions repairs. But it does not mention who the owner was, and could we dream that the plaintiff would insure repairs on another's vessel? It is wrong to consider this an insurance on profits. If it be so, where is the total loss against which we are to insure?

The words "total loss" mean an actual or physical total loss. This is clearly so, if, as contended for the plaintiff, the policy is a wagering one. (3 Cai., 141.) The words, providing against anything short of a total loss, mean the same thing as these words, "warranted free from average, unless general." That clause, like the one in question, has been construed to exclude a technical total loss. (Phil. Ins., 489; 6 Mass., 471, &c.; per Sewall, *J.*; 1 Condy Marsh., 227; 16 East, 214; 7 Taunt., 154; 2 Maule & S., 371; 1 Wh., 219, 224; 1 Johns. Cas., 226; 1 Cai., 196, 212; 3 Cai., 108; 14 Johns., 138.)

Here was neither a technical nor physical total loss. There was no loss of voyage, either as to vessel or cargo. The vessel remained, as a vessel. Suppose the plaintiff had an election to abandon, he was not bound to do it. And not doing so, it would certainly have been a partial loss only. There is no evidence, whatever, that the repairs at Liverpool amounted to 50 *per cent.* This being so, there was no right to abandon. It lay with the assured to show the extent of the loss. (3 Cai., 149.) Taking all the evidence, there is nothing like a loss to 50 *per cent.*, after deducting one third new for old.

But the subject was completely restored before abandonment. This is conclusive. (4 Cow., 222; 5 *Id.*, 63.) The repairs never could come to the hands of the insured. When the vessel was restored, the repairs were restored. They are a part of the vessel.

We are aware of the rule of law, that different individuals may be insured, as to different interests in the same subject. Thus, a lien may be insured; bottomry may be insured, &c., &c. But the plaintiff had no lien; or if he once had a lien, he parted with it, when he parted with the possession of the vessel. But he proved no lien at any time.

325*] **Mr. D. B. Ogden*, same side. There cannot, in the nature of things, be any loss without interest, without something to lose. And in such a case the assured cannot recover except on a wager policy. (Park Ins., 359.) Wager policies were bad at the common law. (*Id.*, 346; 1 Burr., 492.) It will be seen by examining the authorities, that, as the common law stood before our Revolution, there can be no doubt on the subject; and one question is, whether we are bound to follow the English courts in their adoption of a different rule afterwards. Before 1775, these wagering policies were unknown to the law of this State. Two cases have been before this court, *Juhel* v. *Church*, 2 Johns. Cas., 333, and *Clendining* v. *Church*, 3 Cai., 141, relative to these policies; and by neither was their validity sanctioned. Neither case passed upon the question of their validity; though, it is true, that in the last, a wagering policy was admitted to be good by counsel. *Bunn* v. *Riker*, 4 Johns., 426; *Mount* v. *Waite*, 7 Johns., 434, and *Campbell* v. *Richardson*, 10 Johns., 406, decided that wagers at common law are valid. But all these cases agree in the qualification, that if they are against public policy they are utterly void. Wager policies are clearly against public policy. At any rate, there can be no doubt of this as to the policy in question. To be consistent with sound policy, the contract of insurance should never be more than a contract of indemnity. If it be more, it is a departure from the first principles of insurance law. This was so held expressly, and on the single point being presented, in *Amory* v. *Gilman*, 2 Mass., 1. In that case, it was decided, in so many words, that "a wager policy is not a valid contract." The practice of making wagering policies was finally found to be so great an evil in England, that it was abolished by the 19 Geo. II., which brands it in the preamble as pernicious.

But why should we contend the point here? The variance is fatal. An interest is averred, but not proved. The insurance is not on repairs; but on the money expended for repairs. Suppose there had been a bottomry bond for the money: the insurance would not operate upon that, *because it is not [***326**
named. So of the repairs. These not being named, the insurance cannot reach them.

Suppose the plaintiff had a lien; he was bound to enforce it at Londonderry in a court of admiralty, where he would have got his money. His omission to do so, authorizes us to infer that his money has been paid to him. At any rate, the omission was his own fault. There could have been no loss without that fault; and for this we are not amenable. The obligation of the underwriters is entirely complied with.

But the object of repairing had been answered. The vessel reached her port of destination, and the risk then ended. The vessel was not irreparable, but was repaired, without expending one half her value. (4 Binn., 386.) Here was no right of abandonment. (10 Johns., 177.) There can be no such thing as a sale where there is but one man to be both vendor and vendee.

Mr. T. A. Emmet, in reply. If the insurance upon repairs is kept distinct from that upon the vessel, and Buchanan from Polke, much of the apparent difficulty of the case will be removed. If the plaintiff had an insurable interest, it is no matter whether it was covered by the English policy or not, so long as Polke is considered the owner, as he must be upon the case. The English insurance was not for the benefit of the plaintiff. With him, therefore, there is no double insurance.

But we deny that double insurance is contrary to commercial law. It is only contrary to the special contract of the parties. The effect upon the assured is, that he can receive but one indemnity, whatever be the number of insurances he may have effected. Out of these he may elect which; and this may come upon the others for contribution. This was never said to be against commercial policy. It cannot be that the London underwriters must pay for a partial loss on repairs, and then a total loss on the ship.

The subject is truly specified in the policy. It is the repairs in which the plaintiff had an **327***] interest. This was *enough. It was not necessary he should have an interest in the ship. He stood in a relation to the repairs from which he had a right to expect the worth of them. He had no personal remedy for his expenditures against Polke; nor does it appear that the repairs came within the English policy. They were put on the ship without the consent of Polke, who was probably unable to advance the amount. He might, therefore, refuse to pay. The whole was voluntary with the plaintiff.

The plaintiff is, in conscience, entitled to redress, and the court will, in order to promote justice, sustain a wagering policy. They will do this, at least, where they see no other remedy can be had.

But the interest is an insurable one. Payment for the repairs is, at all events, to be made to Buchanan; in justice, if the repairs were voluntary; in law, too, if they were made at the request of Polke. No matter who owned the ship. The value of the repairs was due to Buchanan. Suppose this to be a wagering policy because there was no technical legal interest, there is enough to sustain it as a wagering policy. *Kulen Kemp* v. *Vigne*, 1 T. R., 304, was much such a case as this. There the action would have been sustained, had there been a total loss. The validity of wagering policies has been repeatedly acknowledged by this court. When we allow an insurance on profits, we admit what comes very near a wagering policy, as in *Juhel* v. *Church*, 2 Johns. Cas., 333. But several of the cases which I cited on the opening show that the plaintiff had a lien for the price of the repairs, and such an one as might have been enforced by a court of admiralty. Less than this will give an insurable interest. (Phil. Ins., 27; 5 Bos. & P., 269; 1 Marsh. Ins., 105; 1 Bos. & P., 316.) It makes no difference, according to these authorities, whether the plaintiff could have paid himself by virtue of the English insurance, or not. The original interest cannot be affected by this consideration. But he could not recover upon the English policy. The whole went with the abandonment to the English underwriters, including the repairs. (Phil. **328***] *Ins., 477.) He could not go against them unless he was the owner. Each person interested may insure his own interest. (Phil. Ins., 41; Marsh. Ins., 105; Park. Ins., 374.)

No doubt the provision in the policy excludes an average loss. But I deny its application to this case. It does not apply when the subject itself is lost. Physical loss is not necessary to be shown. It may be by capture. (Phil. Ins., 488, 490, 491; 6 Mass., 318.) Such a loss would be within this policy. Anything creating a total loss, without a mere depreciation of the property, is within the policy. The technical total loss of the ship, resulted in the actual total loss of the incidental subject-matter, the repairs, and the remedy for their value. The lien was gone by the sale. The purchaser came in under a different and paramount right, a new title. The London underwriters directed the sale. The title was in them, and the repurchase did not revest the lien. The owner had a right to abandon; 11 Johns., 295; Phil. Ins., 400; 4 Binn., 386; 15 Mass., 341; 3 Johns. Cas., 34; and the underwriters at Lloyd's to accept the abandonment. The plaintiff had no control over the right. He had no hold on the ship at the time of the abandonment, by which he could secure his li n. At least, there is no evidence that he had.

The amount of repairs at Liverpool had nothing to do with the right of the owner to abandon. The ship had been damaged more than 50 *per cent.* on her voyage. And it is her state at the place of destination, where she was abandoned and sold, which is to determine the right. We go upon the abandonment, and acceptance in good faith, as taking away all our right.

It was not necessary for us to abandon. There could be no salvage. (4 Dall., 421; 5 Bos. & P., 310; 1 Johns., 433.) It was an idle ceremony. Nothing could pass by it. We did, however, abandon.

Curia, per SAVAGE, *Ch. J.* The question first in order is, had the plaintiff any insurable interest in the vessel? *The insur- [***329** ance is upon the body, tackle, apparel and other furniture of the good ship called The William and Jane. Afterwards is the following clause: "The above insurance is hereby declared to be on amount disbursed for repairs of the said vessel at Newport; to which place she returned in distress, and is against total loss only."

The plaintiff expended in repairs at Newport, $8,500; (*a*) at whose request, or by what authority, the case does not state. The owner of the cargo, not being the owner of the vessel, is not bound to repair. It is the duty of the owner of the ship, or his agent, the master, to see the vessel repaired, when necessary. The plaintiff told the captain at Liverpool, that he acted as agent of Polke, the owner. Whether he acted as agent of the owner at Newport, does not appear. If he did, then the repairs at that place were properly recoverable of the London insurers. (12 East, 655.) Ld. Ellenborough there says, "there may be cases in which, though a prior damage be followed by a total loss, the assured may nevertheless have rights or claims in respect of that prior loss, which may not be extinguished by the subsequent total loss. Actual disbursements for repairs, in fact made, in consequence of injuries, by perils of the seas, prior

(*a*) The amount stated *ante*, 320, includes some items of disbursement at Newport beside repairs.

to the happening of the total loss, are of this description. The vessel was insured in London, by Polke, the owner. If he paid for the repairs at Newport, he had a claim for those repairs upon the London underwriters. They were covered with the London policy, whether the policy by the defendants be a double insurance or not. If the plaintiff was not the agent of the owner at Newport, what interest did he acquire by making the repairs voluntarily? He took no bottomry or other security upon the vessel, which the master was authorized to give; nor did he receive any security from the owner. Did he then acquire any lien upon the vessel? It is conceded the plaintiff had no interest in the vessel. What interest had he? The cases cited show that a lender on bottomry may insure his interest; but it must be by name, and not an insurance on **330***] the ship. A *consignee of the cargo, and an assignee, may insure. Any one, in short, who has a lien on the ship or cargo, may insure the property on which his lien attaches. How could the plaintiff have proceeded to enforce his lien, if he had one upon the ship? He had, indeed, paid money in repairing the ship, which he was not bound to pay; and I am now supposing the money paid voluntarily. I know of no proceeding which he could have had, *in rem*, to have sold the vessel to reimburse himself. The money was paid for the benefit of the owner; but he might have preferred to have the captain raise the funds with those means which were authorized by law. The captain might have borrowed money. He might, under certain circumstances, have sold or hypothecated the cargo. In the case of *Dickey* v. *N. Y. Ins. Co.*, 4 Cow., 222; 5 Cow., 66, S. P., the captain did sell part of the cargo, and hypothecate part of it; and though it was strongly urged that the ship was bound to the cargo, as the moneys thus raised were expended in repairs, yet this court said there was no lien on the vessel, as it was not pledged for the payment. The present case is certainly not stronger. The captain, I will suppose, might have sold or hypothecated the plaintiff's flax seed, for the $8,500, expended in the repairs. According to *Dickey's* case, the lender on *respondentia* would have had no lien on the vessel. Here the owner of the cargo, being present, prefers to raise the money rather than have his property sold or hypothecated for that purpose. Can he be in a better situation than one who should advance his money? Whatever remedy the plaintiff in this case may have, I am not authorized to say that he had a lien on the vessel. No analogous case has been cited. I am well warranted, therefore, in saying none can be found. Nor do the writers on insurance enumerate any such demand as an insurable interest. (Phil. Ins., 57; 1 Marsh. Ins., 104; Park. Ins., 374.)

I am bound, therefore, to conclude, that the plaintiff had no insurable interest in the vessel. The repairs had become part of the vessel; and having no lien for the money expended, he had no insurable interest in that.

331*] *But suppose it were otherwise, and his interest were admitted: it is contended the defendants are not liable, the insurance being against total loss only.

In the case of *Murray* v. *Hatch*, 6 Mass., 465, the policy was in the usual form, except that at the bottom was a memorandum in these words: This risk is against a total loss only. The vessel was cast ashore, and though she might have been got off, and repaired for less than half her value, the master, having no funds, sold her. It was held that the insurer was not liable. Sewall, *J.*, who delivered the opinion of the court, considered this memorandum a restriction to some purpose. It was considered as having the same effect as exceptions and warranties against particular averages and partial losses, in what is called the common memorandum. The general principle in cases on such exceptions and warranties is, that the insurer is liable as for a total loss, when the subject-matter is destroyed, or when the voyage is defeated and lost. In *Nelson* v. *Col. Ins. Co.*, 3 Cai., 108, 110, the insurance was on corn, with the usual memorandum. The court say, so long as the corn physically existed, there could not be a total loss. See, also, 14 Johns., 138.

Whether there was, in this case, a technical total loss; whether an abandonment was necessary; or if so, whether it was made in due season, are questions not necessary to be discussed, upon the view which I have taken.

The only remaining question is, whether the plaintiff is entitled to recover as upon a wager policy? In these policies, the person insured is not required to have any interest in the thing insured. Wagering policies are mere games of hazard, like the casting of a die. (Doug., 470.) It is to be regretted that wagers ever were allowed to be the subject of an action. Wagering policies were, however, lawful in England, before they were prohibited by statute. They are unlawful in Mass. But they have been recognized by this court.

In the case of *Juhel* v. *Church*, 2 Johns. Cas., 333, in the body of the policy, $12,000 were insured on goods for *the voyage; but by [***332** a memorandum in writing, it was declared to be on profits. No proof of interest was to be required, and the goods were warranted free from average and without benefit of salvage. The ship returned to N. Y. in ballast, finding no goods on the Spanish Main, whither, and back, she was insured. Kent, *J.*, says: "I consider this as a wager policy. It was betting on the return of the ship." In that case, it was made a point, whether a wager policy was void. Kent, *J.*, says: "But supposing the policy to be good (and I wish not to be understood as intimating any opinion to the contrary), I am equally of opinion that the plaintiffs are not entitled to recover." In *Clendining* v. *Church*, 3 Cai., 141, the court considered the policy in the light of a wager policy.

The averment of interest is not necessary, in a wager policy, nor in a policy upon interest (2 East, 392), and may, therefore, be considered surplusage.

It is then settled, that a wager policy is a bet upon the arrival of the ship. The perils which happened during the voyage are immaterial. Her arrival determines the bet. Kent, *J.*, in giving the opinion of the court, in *Clendining* v. *Church*, says: "In wager policies, the loss should be absolutely and finally total; for otherwise, a temporary embargo of only one day, without any other interruption of the voyage, would be a total loss, although the vessel should have arrived in safety."

In whatever light, therefore, this case is considered, it seems to me the plaintiff cannot recover.

I am of opinion that judgment be given for the defendants.

Judgment for the defendants.

Cited in—13 Wend., 520; 23 N. Y., 523; 26 N. Y., 425; 9 Hun, 384; 23 Barb., 150; 38 Barb., 258; 9 How. Pr., 369; 14 Abb. Pr., 404; 2 E. D. S., 290; 7 Daly, 375; 46 Ind., 322; 28 Am. Dec., 478.

333*] *TOLE ET UX. v. HARDY.

Will—When Personal Action Lies Against Devisee—Legacy Charged on Land Devised—Evidence—Latent Ambiguity—Jurisdiction of Action to Enforce Payment of Legacy Charged on Land Devised.

An action of *assumpsit* lies, against a devisee, for a legacy charged exclusively on the land devised, or on his person in respect to the land if he enter, and promise to pay. But the aid of the personal estate must be excluded expressly, or by necessary implication, on the face of the will.

Evidence that a third person was in possession of the land, to whom the devisee, before his promise, gave directions as to remaining and quitting the possession, is sufficient evidence of the entry and possession of the latter to sustain an allegation to that effect in the declaration, and support a promise to pay the legacy charged; especially where, after the promise, the devisee took actual possession.

The assent of the executor is not necessary to a legacy charged on land.

Where the testator, having real and personal estate, by his will, provided a support for his wife, out of his estate, requiring her to pay his debts; and then bequeathed certain specific legacies; then devised his farm to his son, and directed, in terms, that he should pay certain pecuniary legacies to other children: and the will then said, "also, J. H. is to have $250; also to F. H. $100," and appointed the devisee of the farm one of the executors: held, that the direction to the devisee to pay, applied to all the legacies, and charged the land; but not so as to exclude the aid of the personal estate, it not appearing on the face of the will that all the personal estate had been bequeathed; and though this might have, in fact, been so, yet parol evidence could not be received to vary the construction as it stood on the face of the will, there being no latent ambiguity.

A latent ambiguity is that which arises from evidence, *dehors* the instrument. It may then be explained by such evidence.

A court of law has no jurisdiction of an action to enforce payment of a legacy charged on land devised, or on the devisee in respect of the land, though he may have entered and promised to pay, unless the land be exclusively charged. Where this is not so, jurisdiction belongs to a court of equity.

Though a legacy be charged upon land devised, or on a devisee in respect of the land, yet this does not exclude the aid of the personal estate from the payment. This is always the primary fund for the payment of legacies, unless it be excluded by express words in, or necessary implication, to be derived from the will itself on its face. Such a construction cannot be established by matter *dehors* the will.

What is sufficient proof of assent to a legacy by an executor?

In an action on a promise by a devisee, to pay a legacy charged on the land, or on the devisee in respect of the land, the value of the land is immaterial, and cannot be inquired of at the trial.

Citations—4 Mass., 64; Co. Litt., 211 *a*; 1 Saund., 278, *n*. 5; 3 Cow., 135; 3 Johns. Ch., 319; 8 Ves., 22; 18 Ves., 466; 1 Ball & Beat., 543; 1 Mer., 194; 3 Mer., 316.

ASSUMPSIT for $100, a legacy bequeathed to Mrs. Tole, one of the plaintiffs, by the will of her late father, William Hardy, deceased, tried at the Montgomery Circuit, June 9, 1825, before Walworth, *Circuit J.*

The declaration was of Saturday, Mar. 5, 1825; and alleged, that May 4, 1824, the testator, being seised in fee of a farm in Springfield, Otsego Co., devised it to the defendant in fee, subject (*inter alia*) to the legacy claimed; that the testator died June 12, thereafter; that the defendant entered into *possession, [*334 and in consideration of the premises, before suit brought, promised the plaintiffs to pay, &c. Plea, the general issue.

At the trial, the will was given in evidence; which was as follows: "And touching such worldly estate wherewith it hath pleased God to bless me, I will and bequeath in the following manner and form: It is my will, that my, &c., wife M. H. be maintained out of my estate as long as she lives, and she is to have a cow and four sheep, and a hog kept over and above per year; also, she is to have all the household furniture and household stuffs whatever; and also, she is to have all the grain that is in the chamber, and in the barn, and on the land at my death; and she is to have the old mare and feathered fowls, and pay all the debts; and she is to have all the cattle, sheep and hogs at her own disposal. Also, I give to my son, William Hardy (the defendant) all my estate that I now live on, which shall be his forever; and he is to pay as follows: that is, to my son J. H. $250; to my son C. $250; also to my son D. $250; to my son J. $200; also to my son Jer. $250; also Jas. is to have $250 and the Canada mare, and all the farming utensils, such as wagons, sleighs, &c.; the farming-mill and cider-mill is to remain on the farm. Also, my daughter Margaret is to have $100; also my daughter Mary $100; also to E. $100; also to F. H. (the plaintiff's wife) $100." The will appointed the widow executrix and the defendant executor, and was dated May 4, 1824, and duly attested by three witnesses. By a codicil, attested by two witnesses, the testator declared that his will should not take place till six months after his death.

It appeared that the testator died June 12, 1824, and the defendant moved on to the farm devised to him in Feb., 1825. The widow, a witness for the plaintiffs, swore that the defendant said, about six months after the testator's death, he would pay the legacies in the will, if she would release her dower, maintenance, &c. She did so, and the defendant then said he would go on and take the farm, and pay the heirs.

*On objection, the evidence of the [*335 release of dower was rejected by the judge. He also excluded evidence as to the value of the farm devised to the defendant.

The witness then testified that the testator's debts did not exceed $30 in the whole, and that they were all paid or assumed by her. Direct promises by the defendant, to pay the legacy due to the plaintiffs, was also proved to have been made in Jan. and Feb., 1825. But he finally refused to pay, unless a bond with sureties was given. It appeared that he afterwards claimed the farm by virtue of the will. It also appeared that the testator died in possession of the farm.

The plaintiffs having rested, the defendant

NOTE.—*Evidence—Parol—Admissibility of.* See Jackson v. Bowen, 1 Cai., 358, *note*; M'Kinstry v. Pearsall, 3 Johns., 319, *note*.

moved for a nonsuit, on the ground : 1. That the declaration stated the testator died seised in fee. This was overruled, the judge holding that his possession was, *prima facie*, evidence of the seisin in fee. 2. That no assent to the legacy by the executor and executrix was proved. The judge decided that this was not necessary. 3. That the promise was before the defendant entered, though the declaration alleged, as a part of the consideration, his previous entry. The judge decided that the defendant's election to take was enough; and the land, being devised to him and charged with the legacy, were the only real and legal considerations ; and if further evidence of taking possession was necessary, it might be given. 4. That the legacy was not charged upon the land, or upon the person of the defendant, in respect of the land, and was only chargeable upon the personal estate. The judge reserved this question.

The plaintiffs then proved that the will disposed of all the testator's personal estate, except a pew in the church, and one or two small notes, either of which articles were of but little or no value. That the whole of the testator's personal property was of about $500 in value, and his debts very trifling ; that the defendant had paid some of the heirs in part.

The evidence that there was no personal estate beyond what was mentioned in the will, and specifically devised, was objected to ; be-
336*] cause, to give a construction to *the will this should appear on the will itself. But the judge received the evidence, subject to the opinion of the court.

The plaintiffs also proved, that in Dec. 1824, the defendant gave James Hardy liberty to continue on the farm devised till May following ; and that the defendant, at the time of giving liberty, claimed the farm under the will, and said he would take possession and pay the legacies. That the defendant, shortly after, told James Hardy he wanted he should go off the farm sooner than he at first directed.

Farther particulars will be found stated in the opinion of the court.

Verdict for the plaintiff, subject to the opinion of the court on all the questions arising in the cause.

Mr. B. F. Butler, for the plaintiffs. 1. The seisin of the testator was proved, by showing him possessed of the premises at the time of his death. 2. *Assumpsit* will lie against a devisee of land, or on a devise of a legacy in respect of the land, whether expressly charged, or clearly so by implication. 3. The assent of the executor to a legacy is not necessary, when it is charged on the land. (Toll. L. E., 306, 2d ed.) 4. The defendant's accepting of the devise, promising to pay, and agreeing with James to continue in possession, before the promise, was a sufficient entry to support the declaration. The devise to the defendant is, in fact, the only true and legal consideration for the promise. (1 Chit. Pl., 295; 2 East, 452; 4 Mass., 64.) 5. The legacy bequeathed to the plaintiff's (Tole's) wife is, by the will, charged on the land devised to the defendant, or on the devisee in respect to the land, and not on the personal property. (3 Cow., 133.) 6. Parol evidence is admissible to show the situation of the testator, and his property, children, &c., at the time of his death, to aid the court and jury in arriving at his intention, and to give a proper construction to the will. (2 Ves., Sr., 216; 4 Johns., 63; 6 T. R., 676; Rob. on Frauds, 13, 14.)

Mr. I. Selye, contra:

1. Parol evidence cannot be admitted to explain a will, unless there be a latent ambiguity. (1 *Madd. Ch., 554; 2 Bro. Ch. Cas., [***337**
303.)

2. The defendant was not in possession when he promised. If not, there is a variance between the declaration and proof. The consideration must be proved as laid. (7 Johns., 321, and the cases there cited.)

3. A devisee of real estate is not bound to take it *cum onere*. And the evidence of an election to do so is, in this case, insufficient. In all the cases where a recovery has been had, of a legacy against a devisee, it appeared that the devisee had gone into possession under the will, and had, in consideration, made an express promise, or what was equivalent. (3 Johns., 189 ; 7 *Id.*, 99 ; 10 *Id.*, 30 ; 18 *Id.*, 428 ; 3 Cow., 133.)

4. The assent of the executor and executrix to the legacy should have been proved. This was stated in *Beecker* v. *Beecker*, 7 Johns., 99.

5. The value of the land was a proper subject of inquiry. The judge held this immaterial, on the offer of the plaintiff to prove it. That decision was without objection by the defendant, but it shut him out from similar proof on his part. He ought not to pay beyond the value of the land.

6. The legacy is not charged upon the real estate, either expressly, or by necessary implication. It is to be paid out of the testator's estate generally, and the personal estate is the first fund to be applied. On this point, I refer particularly to *Kelsey* v. *Deyo*, 3 Cow., 133. That case and the present are much alike in many features, but there is one striking difference. In that case, it appeared, from the will itself, that all the testator's personal property was disposed of ; here, only some specific articles. There is no disposition of the testator's general fund of personal property, unless the parol evidence is allowed to give a construction to the will. Even that testimony does not show the situation of the testator's personal property at the time of making the will. Its situation at any other time is of no consequence.

7. The plaintiffs' only remedy is in a court of equity.

Curia, per WOODWORTH, *J.* If this action can be sustained, it must be on the ground that the legacy claimed *is charged on the [***338**
estate devised, or on the defendant in respect to the estate; that the defendant became seised, entered on the premises, and thereupon promised to pay.

In the declaration, it is alleged that the defendant entered under the will, and thereby became liable to pay and, being so in possession, promised.

It is contended that the defendant had not taken possession when the promise was made. The evedence is, that James Hardy, being in possession about six months after the testator's death, the defendant gave him permission to remain on the farm devised, until the month of May following; that the defendant then claimed the farm by virtue of the will, and said he would take the land, and pay the legacies; that about a week or two afterwards, the defendant requested him to leave the farm, the then next week. The promises were made in Jan. and the beginning of Feb. The defendant actually took possession about Feb. 15.

If possession be necessary to be proved, as well as the election of the defendant to take, I think that fact sufficiently made out. James Hardy, also a son of the testator, was in the actual occupancy, not holding adversely. In law, it must be considered as the possession of him in whom the title was vested. It further appears that the defendant considered the possession as at his disposal, and that James held subject to his control. The defendant gave him permission to remain on the farm until May. That James acquiesced, is fairly to be presumed, as no objection was made on his part to the right assumed to control the possession. Afterwards, and before the promise, James is directed to quit. It is matter of inference that he did quit, as the defendant entered in Feb. These facts, taken in connection, show, very satisfactorily, that the defendant had possession, by his tenant, or by a person occupying subject to his direction or control.

I incline to the opinion that this testimony supported the promise as stated in the declaration. The case of *Wells* v. *Prince*, 4 Mass., 64, decides, that if a stranger is in possession, un-
339*] der, or acknowledging the title *of the devisee or remainder-man, it is equivalent to an actual entry. Parsons, *Ch. J.*, observed: "It is a general rule of law, that on the death of the devisor, dying seised, the devisee is not seised until entry be made for his use, or some other act done which in law is considered as having the effect of an entry." From what has been already stated, it will be perceived that the case before the court comes within the rule laid down. James Hardy must be considered as having been in possession under the defendant; and acknowledging his title.

If it was necessary to prove the assent of the executor and executrix to the legacy, enough was shown to establish that fact. On this point, the release of dower by Margaret Hardy, the executrix, to the defendant, who was the executor, may be noticed. She states that the defendant applied to her and said, if she would sign off her right, he would go on and pay the heirs. She complied; upon which he said he would then go on and take the farm. This act is a clear manifestation of assent.

But it was not necessary to prove the assent of the personal representatives. It is true that, if a man bequeaths his chattels real or personal, or gives any specific legacy, the legatee cannot enter, or take the legacy, without the consent of the executor. The reason is, because the personal estate is liable in the hands of the executor to the payment of the testator's debts. He must take care to satisfy debts before legacies. But when a man seised in fee devises, the devisee may enter without the assent of the executor; because the latter has nothing to do with the real estate. (Co. Litt., 111 *a;* 1 Saund., 278, *n.* 5.) This is the law in England; and the law is the same here, except that a power is given by statute, on the application of an executor, to sell lands for the payment of debts. The executor has no other control over them. He has no authority to take possession of, or hold the inheritance. Consequently the devisee need not prove his assent. Besides, in this case it appears that the debts did not exceed $30, and the personal estate was equal to $500. There could be no resort to the land.

*According to the principle upon [***340** which the liability of the defendant rests, the value of the farm is an immaterial inquiry, if the defendant elected to take it *cum onere*, entered into possession, and promised to pay.

The material question is, whether the legacy was charged on the land, in exoneration of the personal estate, by express words, or a plain intent of the testator.

This case bears some resemblance to that of *Kelsey* v. *Deyo*, 3 Cow., 133. Here, as in that case, the debts are directed to be paid out of the personal estate. This, I think, is manifest; as no real estate is devised to the wife of the testator, and she is directed to pay the debts. The farm is devised to the defendant; and pecuniary legacies to other children, of whom the wife (plaintiff) is one. The will says the defendant is to pay as follows, naming five of the children. It then proceeds, "also James Hardy is to have $250; also to Fidelia Hardy (the wife, plaintiff) $100." In my opinion the testator intended, and so the will is to be construed, that the defendant should pay the legacies. The direction at the beginning of the bequests undoubtedly applies to all, and shows pretty clearly that it was intended to charge the real estate. But it by no means proves that the personal estate was not first to be called in aid of the real. Several specific legacies of personal property are given in the will, but it nowhere appears that they included all the testator's personal estate. There is no bequest of the whole; and herein the case materially differs from *Kelsey* v. *Deyo*. The argument cannot be urged, that it is apparent the testator intended to charge the real estate exclusively, from the fact that all his personal property was given to others.

If, then, there is not enough on the face of this will to make the legacy a specific charge on the farm, or, in other words, to exclude the personal estate from coming in aid of the real; the cause belongs to a court of chancery. A court of common law has not jurisdiction. In *Livingston* v. *Newkirk*, 3 Johns. Ch., 319, this doctrine is fully examined. The *Chancellor* observed: "It is to well settled to be questioned, that the personal estate is to be *first [***341** applied to the payment of debts and legacies; and that a mere charge on the land will not exonerate the personal estate; nor anything short of express words, or plain intent in the will of the testator."

If such be the legal construction of this will, parol evidence cannot be resorted to, for the purpose of showing a different intent. There is no latent ambiguity. That is made out by proof of extrinsic facts, and may be removed by parol. Here the fact that the testator had no other personal property, raises no ambiguity; but, if admissible, it is to give a construction that the farm is exclusively to be charged; for so I am inclined to think would be the result, had the facts clearly appeared in the will. That such evidence must be rejected, is in accordance with the general current of authority. I need only mention a few cases, where it has been held that parol evidence is not admissible to show the intention of the testator, against the construction on the face of the will, and that the state of his property cannot be resorted to as a criterion to explain it; and that, generally, the will is not to be construed by anything *dehors*, where there is no latent ambiguity. (8 Ves., 22; 18 *Id.*, 466; 1 Ball & B., 543; 1 Mer., 194; 3 *Id.*, 316.)

It is evident, then, from the rules of evidence applicable to the construction of wills, that if, on the face of this will, it cannot be collected that the charge is exclusively on the land, evidence of the state of the testator's property cannot be called to its aid. The law, in its wisdom, has established certain land marks by which we are to be governed. The security of property depends on adhering to them. We are not permitted to lay hold of parts of a will which indicate a probable intent, and determine according to impressions thus derived. It is necessary that the will itself should contain what the law has adjudged competent evidence of intent. In this case, it is probable the testator may have intended to exonerate the personal property; but this intent is nowhere expressed; nor can it necessarily be inferred. So, also, the testator may not have possessed any personal property, other than that be- **342***] queathed. *His will is silent in this respect. There is, therefore, the omission of a material fact, without which, or without some other clear indication, not contained in the will, the law adjudges that the legacy is not a charge on the land exclusively.

I am of opinion that the defendant is entitled to judgment.

Judgment for the defendant.

Cited in—1 Barb. Ch., 401; 4 Edw., 739; 1 N. Y., 122; 2 N. Y., 507; 24 N. Y., 134; 5 Barb., 411; 26 Barb., 360; 33 Barb., 253; 8 Bos., 394; 60 How. Pr., 423.

J. ANN M'ALLISTER, by her next friend BULGER,
v.
HAMMOND.

When Either Case or Trespass Lies.

Where an injury done to another by negligence, is both direct or immediate, and consequential, the party injured has an election either to bring case or trespass.

Thus, where the defendant so carelessly drove his horse and gig, as to run against the plaintiff, in the street, and knock her down; whereby she was injured, and became permanently lame; held, that case was a proper action.

Citations—18 Johns., 283; 14 Johns., 432; 5 Bos & P., 446, *n*; 1 Com. Dig., 234, 244; 3 Campb., 188; 3 Wils., 336.

CASE, for driving a horse and gig so negligently and unskillfully, and so ignorantly and carelessly governing and guiding the horse and gig, as to run against the plaintiff, knock her down and injure her; by means whereof she was rendered sick and lame, and put to a great expense in procuring surgical and other aid and assistance. Plea, not guilty.

The cause was tried at the N. Y. Circuit, Feb. 13, 1824, before Edwards, *Circuit J.*

It appeared at the trial, that the defendant was driving a gig through one of the public streets of the City of N. Y. very fast. That the plaintiff, a child under two years of age, ran into the street after some pigs, which were running to the opposite side of the street, and was observed by a woman at the window, who, seeing the gig approach, called to the defendant to stop; which he did not do until after the child was knocked down by the horse or wheel of the gig; and that then the mother of the child raised the wheel with her shoulder, and rescued the child, and carried it into the house, whither she was followed by the defendant, who said he took it for a pig, and if he had killed it, he could have paid for it. He regretted the accident, desired that a doctor might be sent for, and promised to pay all expenses. He called the next day, but not afterwards. The child's knee was badly injured; *and notwithstanding the attendance [***343** of physicians, and careful nursing to the time of the trial, had assumed the form of a white swelling. The bones of the knee had united, the use of the joint was lost, the leg withered, and the child had become incurably lame.

The plaintiff's counsel disclaimed all attempts to fix an imputation of willfulness on the defendant, whose counsel moved for a nonsuit, on the ground that the action should have been trespass.

Verdict for the plaintiff for $700, subject to the opinion of the court, on the point made by the defendant's counsel, which was reserved by the judge.

Mr. D. Graham, for the plaintiff, said there is one distinction which has never been departed from by any of the cases; this is, that where the injury is immediately consequential, trespass should be brought: but where it is remotely so, case is the proper remedy. The doubt has been, where the damages are both immediate and consequential. In relation to such a state of facts, the cases are various. Sometimes they go on the intention with which the act is done; at other times, on the force; and again, on the question whether the defendant was personally engaged in it. *Huggett* v. *Montgomerg*, 5 Bos. & P., 446, and note to that case in late ed.; *Rogers* v. *Imbleton*, 5 Bos. & P., 117; *Ogle* v. *Barnes*, 8 T. R., 188; *Turner* v. *Hawkins*, 1 Bos. & P., 472. Where the consequential injury has been a sore, or wound, an action on the case has been allowed both in England and this country. *Slater* v. *Baker*, 2 Wils., 359; *Adams* v. *Hemmenway*, 1 Mass., 145. And it seems now to be settled in this court, indeed more clearly so than in any other that where immediate and consequential damage both result from the injury, the party may elect to bring either trespass or case. *Blin* v. *Campbell*, 14 Johns., 432; *Moran* v. *Dawes*, 4 Cow., 412. The plaintiff may waive the immediate, and go for the consequential injury: *Id.*, Cro. Jac., 122; making the latter the sole cause of *action. (9 Rep., 50.) This doctrine [***344** is too well established by precedent to be now questioned. (4 Rep., 94.)

Mr. D. B. Ogden, contra, said he should not go into the cases on this subject. They are all cited in *Percival* v. *Hickey*, 18 Johns., 257, where the court held that though the injury was the result of negligence merely, yet, being immediate, the action should be trespass, not case. The only decision to the contrary is *Blin* v. *Campbell.* That case was cited in *Percival* v. *Hickey*, but it was not followed. It was decided without argument, on *certiorari* from a justice's court, and evidently underwent much less consideration than the more important case of *Percival* v. *Hickey*. If that case be law, we contend that it settles the question. This action cannot be sustained.

Mr. Graham, in reply, denied that *Percival* v. *Hickey* settled the question. This court merely decided, in that cause, that trespass was preferable. It does not necessarily follow that case would not lie. Beside, in that case, and the cases relied upon to exclude an action on the case, the whole damage was immediate. Consequential damage was out of the question.

Curia, per SAVAGE, *Ch. J.* It was once important to ascertain whether trespass or case was the proper action. Originally, actions of trespass involved a breach of the peace; and besides damages to the party, judgment of *capiatur* was entered, upon which the defendant was taken, a fine was imposed, and he was imprisoned till he paid both the fine and the damages.

It is still important to preserve the distinction between the actions, on account of the costs and the pleadings.

Whether the one or the other action is proper, has been often a puzzling question; and decisions have not been uniform. The cases were principally reviewed by *Ch. J.* Spencer, in *Percival* v. *Hickey*, 18 Johns., 283. In conclusion he remarks: "I am perfectly satisfied, from a review of the cases that if the defendant is liable at all, this action is appropriate; and that **345***] it ought to have been *trespass rather than case, as the injury was immediate, and from gross negligence."

The general principle established by this case is, that whether trespass or case is the proper action, depends on the fact whether the injury was immediate or consequential. Another principle is also recognized—that if the injury is attributable to negligence, though it were immediate, the party injured has his election, either to treat the negligence of the defendant as the cause of action, and declare in case, or to consider the act itself as the injury, and to declare in trespass, as in *Blin* v. *Campbell*, 14 Johns., 432. There this court held case the proper action for carelessly firing a pistol, and wounding the plaintiff's leg. And had trespass been brought in that case, the court say they would also have considered it appropriate.

In some cases either action may be maintained, as where there is both an immediate and also a consequential injury.

Whether the act complained of was accompanied with force; whether it was willfully done; whether by the defendant himself, or through the agency of another; whether the act done was lawful; these have all been attempted as *criteria* by which to determine the form of the action; but have all been abandoned. (5 Bos. & P., *note;* 1 Com. Dig., Day ed., 234, where all the learning and all the cases on this question are collected.) There is, in the last book, at page 244, an ingenious argument in favor of the indifferent use of the two actions at all events. We have the authority of Ld. Ellenborough, for saying: "It may likewise be worthy of consideration, whether in those instances where trespass may be maintained, the party may not waive the trespass, and proceed for the tort" (3 Campb., 188), as you may bring trover for goods taken tortiously. (3 Wils., 336.)

In this case the injury was occasioned by the negligence of the defendant. The damages were partly immediate, but principally consequential.

I consider the case of *Blin* v. *Campbell*, as recognized and established by *Percival* v. *Hickey;* although in the latter *case, trespass [***346** was adjudged the proper action rather than case The courts of K. B. and C. P. in England, certainly do not think alike on that point, but in the decisions of this court there is no discrepancy. In *Percival* v. *Hickey* the whole injury was immediate—the destruction of the plaintiff's vessel. In the case of *Blin* v. *Campbell* it was, as in this case, partly immediate and partly consequential.

Besides, the action on the case is altogether the most favorable to the defendant. He can make any defense, without the technicality of special pleading, and the plaintiff must recover a larger sum than in trespass, in order to carry costs. She has, therefore, in this instance, selected that form of action most unfavorable to herself; and there cannot be a doubt but this recovery may be pleaded in bar to an action of trespass, should it be hereafter brought for the same injury.

In my opinion, the plaintiff is entitled to judgment.

Judgment for the plaintiff.

Cited in—21 Wend., 618; 3 Barb., 49; 47 Mich., 392; 34 Am. Dec., 274; 9 Am. Rep., 270 (50 N. H., 420).

GALLAGER AND MASON *v.* BRUNEL.

An Action Lies for False Representations of Present Facts as to Credit of Third Person, whereby Plaintiff is Induced to Extend Credit to such Person—Promise to Indorse Note of Third Person—Pleading.

An action lies for a false affirmation as to the credit of a third person, by which the plaintiff is induced to sell him goods, and is thereby injured, but not on the ground of a parol promise to indorse for the third person, by which the plaintiff is led to the sale; though the defendant know that such third person is insolvent at the time.

To warrant an action for a deceitful representation, it must assert a fact or facts as existing in the present tense. A promise to pay, though accompauied, at the time, with an intention not to perform, is not such a representation as can be made the ground of an action at law. The party should sue upon the promise; and if this be void, he has no remedy.

In *assumpsit* on a promise to indorse the note of another, the declaration should aver that a note was drawn and tendered for indorsement.

A sale of goods to A, on the request of B, is a good consideration for B's promise to pay for them. But the promise being collateral, should be in writing; otherwise, it is void by the Statute of Frauds.

Citations—3 T. & R., 51; 1 Campb., 4; 1 East, 318; 2 East, 92; 13 Ves., 131; 6 Johns., 181; 13 Johns., 224, 325, 395.

ON demurrer to the declaration. The first count stated that Apr. 9, 1823, Castro & Henriques proposed to purchase of the plaintiffs a quantity of cotton, at a certain price; part to be paid in cash, and part to be secured by the promissory note of the purchasers indorsed by

the defendant, at 4 months; that C. & H. were then unable to pay for the cotton; and the plaint-
347*] iffs therefore *unwilling to sell all, or any part, on their sole credit; and the defendant knew this. Yet, contriving and intending to injure and defraud the plaintiffs, and to induce them to sell and deliver the cotton to C. & H., and thereby subject the plaintiffs to the loss of the balance due after the cash payment, the defendant falsely and deceitfully represented and held out to the plaintiffs that he, the defendant, was willing to indorse the proposed note; and with the like intent, &c., falsely, fraudulently and deceitfully encouraged and induced the plaintiffs to sell and deliver the cotton. That they did sell and deliver it, in confidence of such false, frudulent and deceitful representation, &c.; when, in truth, the defendant was then not willing, and did not mean or intend to indorse the note, or make himself responsible; nor did he then, nor had he at any time since indorsed, or made himself legally responsible. By means whereof the plaintiffs lost the cotton and the price.

The second count averred that C. & H. were in bad credit and unfit to be trusted at the time of the sale. But the defendant, well knowing this, and contriving and intending to defraud and injure the plaintiffs, and wrongfully and deceitfully to enable C. & H. to obtain the possession of the cotton, and convert it to their own use, without paying the plaintiffs for it; falsely, fraudulently and deceitfully represented to the plaintiffs, and gave them to understand and believe, that, in case they would sell the cotton to C. & H., the defendant would become answerable to the plaintiffs, for so much as should be unpaid, by indorsing the note or notes of C. & H., &c.; that without such representation, they would not have sold the cotton, &c. (In other respects, this count was substantially the same as the first.)

General demurrer and joinder.

Mr. C. D. Colden, in support of the demurrer. There is no averment that the defendant was ever required to perform, Even admitting him to be bound, his obligation was conditional; and he cannot be made liable, till a note was drawn and tendered for indorsement.
348*] *There was no consideration for the promise of the defendant: and if otherwise, it is a fatal objection that there was no note in writing, to take the case out of the Statute of Frauds. The declaration is on an *assumpsit*; and it is evident, from its language taken together, that there was no note in writing; because it complains that the defendant never would render himself responsible in any way. This promise was collateral, and it is directly within the first class of promises enumerated by Kent, *Ch. J.*, in *Leonard* v. *Vredenburgh*, 8 Johns., 39, which have always been holden to be within the Statute of Frauds, and void.

The action cannot be sustained as one in nature of an action of deceit. I am aware that actions have been sanctioned on fraudulent misrepresentations as to the credit of another, by which vendors have suffered an injury. But these representations were always of an existing fact—that the vendee is worthy to be trusted—not a mere promise to pay, grounded on that fact. Besides, two things must concur to maintain the action. The defendant must not only know, or have strong reason to believe, that what he says is false; but the plaintiff must be ignorant that the vendee is unworthy of credit. Here the plaintiffs themselves aver that they knew the vendee was not worthy to be trusted, and reposed on the promise of the defendant. They could not be deceived. They do not pretend to have been deceived.

Messrs. P. W. Radcliff and *G. Griffin*, contra. The action is for the deceit, and no averment of consideration is necessary. But for the fraud, no sale at all would have been made. The principle of the action is well established. (6 Johns., 181; 13 *Id.*, 224; *Id.*, 325, 395; 1 *Id.*, 414; 3 Ld. Raym., 31; 1 Campb., 4; 3 T. R., 51; 3 Bulstr., 95; Com. Dig., Action on the Case for Deceit, A, 1; 13 Ves., 134; 3 Ves. & B., 112.)

But we are told the representation here was promissory; that it was in the future tense. Now, is there any difference between a false representation and a false promise? The moral *demerit is the same. Knowing that [*349
A is not trustworthy, we, with intention to decoy our neighbor into false confidence, say "we will indorse his note." Is not this the strongest representation? Is it not more likely to deceive than any other mode of representation? Can any man cheat with impunity, because he does not do it in writing? If a man make an honest promise, that is quite another affair.

But if here be a promise alleged, the court are to suppose that it was in writing. The objection must be made on the trial. It cannot arise upon demurrer. (1 Saund., 276 *a*, *note* 2; 15 Johns., 426, per Spencer, *J.*)

Mr. Colden, in reply. The plaintiff cannot be permitted, in this way, to turn a mere promise into a tort. The proposition laid down in the opening, that to warrant an action, the deceit must refer to present existing circumstances, is not answered by a single authority cited; nor can it be answered by authority or principle. We are referred to the old case of *Pasley* v. *Freeman*, 3 T. R., 51. There it was, at first, very seriously doubted whether fraudulent words of the present tense, asserting an existing fact, would sustain the action. And it has not been, without a great and constant struggle, that even this case has been sustained. The case may be likened to one in the criminal law, relative to obtaining goods upon false pretenses. A mere promise was never held to sustain an indictment. The pretense must be of an existing fact. It may as well be averred that a parol promise, by an executor, to pay his testator's debt, is a false affirmation; and that, therefore, he should be answerable for a deceit. Is it competent to say, that at the time of the promise the defendant did not mean to perform?

No man reading this declaration can doubt that this promise was by parol. The language of pleading must be understood in the same sense as that used in common conversation, where no technical words are in question.

But, if the court are to suppose the contract was in writing, we then ask, where is the consideration for the promise? *That [*350
should have been shown in pleading. (Rob. Frauds, 207, 208, ch. 3, pt. 6.)

Curia, per WOODWORTH, *J.* The ground of complaint is, that the defendant fraudulently and deceitfully represented and held out to the plaintiffs, that the defendant was willing to and would indorse the note of Castro & Henriques, in case the plaintiffs should sell and deliver the cotton; but that, in fact, he was not willing, and did not intend, nor has he indorsed the note, whereby the plaintiffs are injured. The second count alleges that Castro & Henriques were, at the time of the purchase, in bad credit, which the defendant knew; that intending to defraud the plaintiffs, and enable Castro & Henriques to obtain possession of the cotton, he represented, that if the plaintiffs would sell and deliver, he would become answerable by indorsing for the purchasers; that the plaintiffs did sell and deliver the cotton; that the defendant did not intend, nor has he made himself answerable or paid; nor has any other person paid and satisfied the plaintiffs, whereby they were deceived and have sustained damage.

The declaration is bad in substance, because it does not aver that Castro & Henriques ever made a note, which the defendant was required to indorse. The security to be given was the defendant's indorsement. The unwillingness to indorse refers to the time the assurance was made. If, however, it continued, it does not prove the essential fact, that he actually refused when required. As to the allegation that he never has indorsed; *non constat* that a note was ever presented for that purpose.

But as a decision upon this point, alone, would be merely a postponement of the important question arising in this cause, I will consider that also.

The attempt here is, to sustain the action, not on a contract, which, if in writing, might perhaps be obligatory; but on a deceitful representation. If the promise was in writing, I perceive no objection to its validity, inasmuch as a good consideration is stated, viz.: that if the plaintiffs would sell and deliver, the de-
351*] fendant would indorse. If, *then, there is a binding contract existing between the parties, and on which the defendant is liable, I apprehend it is not competent for the plaintiffs to say they have an election to turn this into an action for deceit, and recover in that form, unless the case is such as to render the party liable, not only on the contract; but, in addition, contains facts sufficient to sustain an action for deceit. For example, suppose A represents B to be solvent, knowing it to be false, whereby B obtains credit; but notwithstanding this representation, the seller takes from A his written stipulation to guaranty the payment. In this case I perceive no objection to a creditor's election of the remedy. The fraudulent representation of solvency would sustain the action for deceit. The written guaranty would support an action on the contract. It seems, therefore, immaterial here, whether the plaintiffs have or have not a demand which may be enforced in a different form. The question is: will the facts stated sustain an action for deceit?

After attentive consideration, I am inclined to think the plaintiffs are not entitled to recover. However reprehensible the conduct of the defendant may appear in a moral point of view, we cannot deny to him the protection of the common law, which does not reach cases of imperfect obligation. If this be an attempt on the part of the plaintiffs to get rid of the Statute of Frauds, I can only say, the occasion justified the experiment, and calls for a patient and critical examination.

If this case is stripped of the general allegations in the declaration, of fraud and deceit, it appears to me that the *gravamen* is nothing more than that the defendant encouraged the plaintiffs to sell to Castro & Henriques; and as surety, promised to indorse their notes. The intention of the party not to fulfill, has not, I believe, ever been considered among the fraudulent acts, which, in judgment of law, render a party liable. The maker of the promissory note may not, at the time, intend to make payment. On this note, the plaintiff may declare that the defendant intended to deceive and de fraud; but it is mere matter of form, sanctioned by the precedent in pleading. The maker may
*go further, and on the strength of as- [*352
surances to pay punctually, never intended to be performed, induce the lender to part with his money, and accept the borrower's note. All this is immoral. Still the remedy is on the contract. The law has not recognized it as the substantive ground for fraud. That no cases are to be met with in the books going the length contended for, is good evidence that the doctrine is novel, and has never been acted upon.

The general ground of liability seems to rest on the affirmation of a fact as true, which, at the time, is known to be false; and by means whereof, credit is obtained. The seller, in most cases, has not the means of ascertaining the truth at the moment. He must repose on the representation, or refuse the credit. Not so here. There was no necessity of relying on the defendant's representations, or his promise. Caution required the plaintiffs to pursue a different course—to insist that the note be drawn and indorsed *pari passu* with the delivery of the goods. By dispensing with this, they omitted that prudence and care which the law presumes every man will exercise in conducting his affairs. If the plaintiffs suffer, it is owing to their negligence and misplaced confidence, for which the law has not provided a remedy.

The general principles which govern this species of action, were ably examined in *Pasley* v. *Freeman*, 3 T. R., 51. In that case, the defendant encouraged the plaintiff to sell goods, and fraudulently affirmed that the purchaser was a person safely to be trusted. The *gravamen* was the false affirmation of an existing fact—not a promise to do a future act, at the time not intended to be performed; and which, notwithstanding the intent, might or might not be performed. Buller, *J.*, observed, "the foundation of the action is fraud and deceit in the defendant, and damage to the plaintiffs. Every deceit comprehends a lie; but a deceit is more than a lie, on account of the view with which it is practiced, its being coupled with some dealing, and the injury which it is calculated to occasion to another person." It is evident what must be the species *of [*353
fraud, for which the law gives redress; falsehood as to an existing fact. If, as Buller, *J.*, observes, every deceit includes a lie, it follows

that the representation and promise of the defendant are not comprised within the legal acceptation of that term. The test of a lie is, that the fact asserted is not true at the time, which cannot be predicated of the facts in this case; for, although the defendant promised with the intent not to perform, it was not then false, nor could it be. It referred to an act to be done *in futuro*. Until the defendant had refused to indorse, it could not be said he had violated his promise.

The case of *Thompson* v. *Bond*, 1 Campb., 4, was this: the plaintiff attempted to recover in *assumpsit*, for services rendered to a third person. It was not denied that the defendant had solicited the plaintiff, and promised to see him paid; but it was a collateral undertaking, and not in writing. It was held that the action could not be sustained on this ground. But, as the defendant had made a representation to the plaintiff, that he had authority from Mr. Sheridan's committee, which turned out to be false, Ld. Ellenborough observed that an action might be brought for the deceitful representation. This remark proceeded on the same ground as *Pasley* v. *Freeman*—that there was a false representation of a fact.

The case of *Eyre* v. *Dunsford*, 1 East, 318, cited by the plaintiffs' counsel, was decided on the same ground. There was a material suppression of the truth; for which the defendant was held liable. The case of *Haycraft* v. *Creasy*, 2 East, 92, turned on the ground that the representation was made *bona fide*, and with the belief of its truth. It has no bearing on this cause. In *Clifford* v. *Brooke*, 13 Ves., 131, the *Lord Chancellor* puts the right to recover for a deceit, expressly on the falsehood of the fact alleged. He observes, "there must be knowledge at the time. That is the sound principle; that the defendant knowing the person to be dishonest, insolvent and unworthy of trust, made the representation; and that is the subject of an action, or a bill in equity." In the case of *Upton* v. *Vail*, 6 Johus., 181, there was also **354***] a *recommendation of a person, as good, when the defendant knew he was insolvent. The doctrine of *Pasley* v. *Freeman* was approved, without a suggestion that the action could be maintained, when there was not knowledge of the falsehood at the time. The cases in 13 Johns., 224, 325, 395, hold the same doctrine.

I am of opinion that the defendant is entitled to judgment.

Judgment for the defendant.

Cited in—2 Wend., 389; 7 Wend., 22; 11 Wend., 409; 12 Wend., 521; 5 Hill, 487; 22 Barb., 654; 38 Barb., 212; 4 Bos., 572; 68 Ill., 616; 51 Ind., 136; 45 Wis., 305; 20 Am. Dec., 625; 40 Am. Dec., 367.

ANDREWS v. KNEELAND.

Sales by Sample—Goods Must Equal Sample in Quality—Authority of Broker or Agent to Sell by Sample or Warranty.

On a sale by sample, the vendor is responsible that the bulk of the commodity shall be equal in quality to the sample.

An agent or broker having power to sell goods, without any express restriction as to the mode, may sell by sample or with warranty.

And it makes no difference with his authority, whether the principal reside in the same city with him, or reside abroad.

The authority of a broker is not always confined to the power which the principal intends to confer on him, but may extend to that with which he is apparently clothed in respect to the subject-matter of the sale.

The principal is bound by the acts of the general agent, provided they are within the scope of his authority. But an agent constituted for a particular purpose, and under a limited and circumscribed power, cannot bind his principal by an act beyond his authority.

Where an agent, for the purpose of a single act, is not limited as to the manner of doing it, the principal may be bound by his acts, though exceeding the authority intended to be given.

Citations—4 Cow., 440; 1 Liv., 107, 108; 2 Johns., 48; 3 T. & R., 757; 4 T. & R., 177; Long on Sales, 233; 15 East, 38; 9 Wh., 644; 5 Johns., 58; 7 Johns., 393.

ASSUMPSIT on a warranty, that certain cotton, sold by the defendant to the plaintiff, should be of like goodness and quality with certain samples exhibited; tried at the N. Y. Circuit, Jan. 7, 1824, before Edwards, *Circuit J.*

At the trial, it was proved that the plaintiff, who was a merchant residing in Boston, Sept. 20, 1821, purchased of Smidt, the defendant's broker, 124 square bales of cotton, by sample, the defendant and the broker residing in the City of N. Y., where the sale took place. That the defendant consummated the sale by taking a note, in person, at his store in the city. The broker swore that he had no authority to warrant, but acted as broker for the defendant in selling a large quantity of cotton, of which the cotton in question was a part.

It appeared not to be the general practice, in the City of N. Y., to sell cotton by sample, though this was sometimes done.

*The cotton turned out to be much in- [***355** ferior to the samples.

The judge charged the jury, that the question whether there had been a warranty, depended not only on whether Smidt had made a warranty, but whether he had any authority to make one. That unless the defendant had in some way delegated that authority to the broker, the defendant could not be responsible. That if the practice in N. Y. for cotton brokers to warrant on their sales were universal, authority to warrant might be implied from this circumstance. He drew a distinction between general agents who may bind their principals by warranty without express authority, and special agents who have not this power; also between agents residing abroad, or near their principal; and charged that Smidt, living near his principal, was to be deemed a special agent; and had no authority to warrant, unless expressly delegated; that a power to sell did not imply a power to warrant; and that the defendant was not bound by a sale by sample, unless he knew that the sale was thus made when it was consummated by his acceptance of the plaintiff's note.

The plaintiff excepted to this charge. The jury found for the plaintiff six cents damages.

A motion was now made, in behalf of the plaintiff, for a new trial. The motion was founded on the bill of exceptions.

Mr. G. Griffin, for the plaintiff. Every sale by sample is a warranty that the bulk shall correspond with the specimen exhibited. *Oneida Manuf. So.* v. *Lawrence*, 4 Cow., 440. A power of sale implies a power to warrant.

(Pal. Ag., 161; 3 T. R., 757; 4 *Id.*, 177; 5 Esp., 75; 2 Campb., 55.) This is uniformly so, except in the sale of land, where there must be a written power produced; 5 Johns., 58; or where there was a fraudulent misrepresentation, which is *dehors* the authority. (7 *Id.*, 390.) I am not aware of any distinction between domestic and foreign principals; nor do I find any authority to support the judge in saying that an express delegation of authority **356***] *was necessary in this case. *Colden, Senator*, in *Perkins* v. *The Wash. Ins. Co.*, 4 Cow., 660, &c.; *Runquist* v. *Ditchell*, 3 Esp., 64, and Thompson, *J.*, in *Monte Allegre*, 9 Wh., 644, will be found to have laid down the true doctrine on the subject.

Mr. H. W. Warner, contra. The distinction drawn by the judge between a general and special agent, was clearly law; and what he said about the difference between domestic and foreign principals, was altogether unnecessary to the case; because, let the principal reside where he would, here was no more than a special agency. The judge did not charge that there must be an express delegation of authority. He admitted that an implied one was sufficient. We, however, insist that express authority was necessary, Smidt being a special agent. Where an agent is employed in business of a particular kind, with power to transact the whole, it is evidence that the principal is willing he should do everything ordinarily incidental to that branch of business. But it is far otherwise as to a special agency. This is admitted as to lands, and the same reason exists in the case of goods. In both cases the vendee must derive his title under the power. It is in business as in logic; a general agent gives you a general result. A series of instances is a good indication of his power. This may be trusted to; and what is apparently co-extensive with his power shall not be deemed to go beyond it. Not so of a single instance. There the evidence of the power must be special. It does not follow as an inference. But in the case of a general agent, no further evidence need be given than the fact of the general power. (Pal. Ag. 162, 164, 166; 15 East, 408.) The cases cited against us are either exceptions to the rule that the power of a special agent must be shown, founded on usage, as in the instance of a servant selling a horse in 2 Campb., 55; or where a knowledge or recognition of the act by the principal was to be inferred. Such is the case of *Runquist* v. *Ditchell*.

357*] **Mr. B. D. Ogden*, in reply, said a man is to be deemed a special agent only when a power is given, and he is restricted to exercise it in a particular way. But if a power be given, as in this case, to sell generally, and there be no express prohibition against a warranty, the agency is to be deemed general. This is the import of the English cases cited. And this distinction is expressly sanctioned in *Hicks* v *Hankin*, 4 Esp., 114. That case turned upon the distinction. The character of a special agent does not depend on the number of acts he has power to do.

Usage has nothing to do with the question.

Curia, per SAVAGE, *Ch. J.* The sale in this case was clearly a sale by sample. There could be no other, according to the weight of the testimony. That, however, is a question of fact.

It has been deliberately settled by this court in the case of *Oneida Manuf. So.* v. *Lawrence*, 4 Cow., 440, that in case of sale by sample the vendor is responsible that the bulk of the commodity shall be equal in quality to the sample.

It is only necessary to inquire whether the judge correctly charged the jury as to the power of the agent.

The difference between a general and a special agent is well understood. The principal is bound by the acts of a general agent, provided they are within the scope of his authority. But an agent constituted for a particular purpose and under a limited and circumscribed power, cannot bind his principal by any act beyond his authority. (1 Liverm., 107, 108.) Thus in *Batty* v. *Carswell*, 2 Johns., 48, the authority was limited to a single act, to be performed in a particular manner. The authority was was to execute a note for $250, payable in six months. The agent gave a note payable in 60 days. This court held the principal not bound. But where the agent is not limited as to the manner of doing a particular act, the principal may be bound by his acts, though exceeding the authority intended to be given to him. Thus, in the case of *Fenn* v. *Harrison*, 3 T. R., 757; 4 *Id.*, 177, the fact at first appeared to be *that the defendants had instructed [***358** their agent to get the bill discounted, but charged him not to indorse it. He, however, did indorse it; and though Ld. Kenyon was inclined to hold the defendants responsible, yet the rest of the court ruled otherwise, and granted a new trial. Upon the next trial it appeared that the defendants desired their special agent to get the bill discounted without restricting his power to indorse. The plaintiff had a verdict, which the court refused to set aside, on the ground that, as the defendants had authorized the agent to get the bill discounted without restraining his authority as to the mode of doing it, they were bound by his acts.

The authority of a broker to bind his principal is not, in all cases, confined to the power which the principal intended to confer on him. The interests of the mercantile world require that he should bind his principal within the limits of the authority with which he has been apparently clothed in respect to the subject matter of the sale. (Long, Sales, 233; 15 East, 38.)

In the case of *The Monte Allegre*, 9 Wh., 644, Thompson, *J.*, says: "A merchant who employs a broker to sell his goods, knows, or is presumed to know, the state and condition of the article he offers for sale. And if the nature or situation of the property is such that it cannot be conveniently examined in bulk, he has a right, and it is for the convenience of trade, that he should be permitted to select a portion, and exhibit it as a specimen, or sample of the whole; and that he should be held responsible for the truth of such representation. The broker is his special agent, for this purpose, and goes into the market clothed with authority to bind his principal. In such cases, if the article does not correspond with the sample, the injured purchaser knows where to look for redress; and the owner is justly chargeable with the loss, as he was bound to know the condition of his own property, and to send out a fair sample, if he undertook to sell in that way." This doctrine is supported by abundant authority, and decides that the broker had power **359*]** to sell *by sample; and that a sale by sample is a warranty that the bulk shall correspond with the sample.

In this case it is not denied that the defendant employed the broker to sell the cotton in question. His employment was a general one. There was no restriction as to the mode of sale, whether by sample or otherwise. He had authority to sell as cotton was sold in the due course of business. It appears that the most usual sales of cotton were by inspecting the bulk, but that it was unusual to sell by sample. The broker, no doubt, however, had authority to sell by sample, if he thought proper; and, as a sale by sample is of itself a warranty that the bulk corresponds with the sample, he was authorized, by virtue of his employment, unrestricted in the mode to be adopted by him, to bind his principal by such a sale.

Whether the principal and broker reside near each other, or far distant, seems to me not material; as, in this case, there was no reference to the principal, except as to the mode of payment.

The cases of *Nixon* v. *Hyserott*, 5 Johns., 58, and *Gibson* v. *Colt*, 7 *Id.*, 393, contain nothing opposed to the principles I have advanced. Here there were no written instructions communicated to the party, nor any fraud.

A new trial must be granted.

New trial granted.

Sales by sample—By warranty. Cited in—9 Wend., 26; 12 Wend., 418; 17 Wend., 271; 18 Wend., 440; 5 N. Y., 87, 99; 37 Am. Dec., 134.

Agents power to bind principal. Cited in—13 Wend., 520; 23 Wend., 268; 3 Hill., 270; Hoffm., 364; 28 N. Y., 289; 72 N. Y., 114; 23 Am. Dec., 89 (3 Rawle, 23); 37 Am. Rep., 829 (51 Wis., 331).

Broker having power to sell may sell with warranty or by sample. Cited in—5 Wend., 35; 6 Land., 232; 9 Hun, 266; 35 Barb., 441; 4 Daly, 285; 41 N. Y. L., 325; 32 Am. R., 213 (12 Vroom., 322).

360*] *EVERY v. MERWIN.

Evidence in Action of Covenant—Covenant Admitted, though Mutilated as to Signatures—Possession of Notes by Maker, Prima Facie *Evidence of Payment—Pleading—Variance.*

Sealed articles, declared on with profert, allowed in evidence, though the defendant's name and seal were torn off; it appearing probable that this was done before the plaintiff had declared; and the mutilation not being with the plaintiff's consent.

The copy of the declaration served was, in consideration that the plaintiff, by articles of agreement, granted to the defendant, the immediate, &c., possession of certain premises, together with one half of the yearly rent, then become due. The articles recited, that the plaintiff conveyed, relinquished and gave up the premises; and then proceeded, "all of which premises the said defendant is to have the immediate, &c., possession of, together with the yearly rent; or, that is to say, the half of the rent to become due, &c." The draft of the declaration and the oyer were right, as to the time of the rent becoming due; and the variance in the copy was a clerical mistake. The cause being referred, and the articles, though objected to, being received in evidence; held, that there was no variance in describing the possession as granted; and that as to the allegation of the time when the rent became due, it not appearing that any injustice had been in fact done by the referees, the plaintiff might amend, even after a motion by the defendant to set aside the report of the referees on the ground of this variance, on payment of costs; and that the report should then be confirmed.

Whether such an amendment may be granted by a judge on the trial, *quære.*

The amendment was granted by the court, on paying the same costs as if it had been made on motion, previous to the cause being heard before the referees.

Declaration on a covenant, in articles of agreement, that the defendant, after the plaintiff had deducted what he owed the defendant, and what the plaintiff owed one S., if S. would transfer the debt, would pay the remainder of a sum of $1,500, in three equal annual payments from the date of the articles. The covenant was to pay the remainder of the $1,500 after the deductions—to be paid in three equal annual payments, without saying from the date. Held, no variance; the covenant meaning that the time should run from the date; and being, therefore, set forth according to its legal effect.

The defendant covenanted to pay the plaintiff the remainder of $1,500, after deducting what the plaintiff owed him, &c. In an action on the covenant, the defendant claimed that plaintiff owed him, $106, money advanced. The plaintiff was allowed to give in evidence against the defendant, a receipt by him of a note of $325 from the plaintiff, for collection on which the $106 were indorsed; and it appearing that the defendant had collected the whole $325; held, that the plaintiff should be allowed the balance in the adjustment of accounts, not as a technical set-off against the defendant's claim, but as coming within the provisions of the covenant.

The fact that a promissory note was seen in the hands of the maker, is *prima facie* sufficient, to charge one who has receipted it for collection, with the amount.

Clerical mistakes in the pleadings, may be amended, even after trial, where the party objecting to the mistake will not be injured.

And the court have strongly inclined, that a single judge may allow the amendment at the trial.

The rules of evidence are the same before referees, as before a jury. Per Woodworth and Sutherland, *JJ.*, interrupting *Mr. Hobbie, arguendo.*

Citations—3 Taunt., 81; 18 Johns., 510; 1 Cow., 670.

ON motion to set aside the report of referees. The copy of the declaration served on the defendant's attorneys was in covenant on articles of agreement executed by the parties, dated Mar. 18, 1818 (with profert), by which, in consideration that the plaintiff (*inter alia*) had thereby granted to the defendant the immediate, quiet and peaceable possession of certain premises therein mentioned, together with the yearly rent; that is to say, one half of the rent then become due, for the privileges of a fulling-mill and pond, &c., the defendant did covenant, &c, with *the plaintiff, to **[*361** pay him the sum of $1,500 in the following manner; that is to say (after deducting what the plaintiff then owed the defendant, and a certain debt which the plaintiff then owed to Samuel Scouten, in case Scouten should transfer the same to the defendant), the defendant to pay the remainder of the said sum of $1,500 in three equal annual payments from the date of the said articles of agreement. Yet the defendant had not paid, &c.

By the oyer of the articles served with the declaration, it appeared that the plaintiff conveyed, relinquished and gave up the premises mentioned in the declaration; and the articles then proceeded: "all of which premises the said Merwin (the defendant) is to have the immediate, quiet and peaceable possession of, together with the yearly rent; or, that is to say, the half of the rent to become due, &c., which said rent is due for the privilege of a fulling-mill and pond," &c.; and then proceeded: "the said Merwin (the defendant) to pay the before mentioned $1,500, in manner following, to wit: in the first place, &c. (deductions as in the declaration), and then the remainder to be paid in three equal annual payments."

The cause was referred on the motion of the defendant.

The articles given in evidence before the referees, agreed with the oyer, except that in describing one parcel of the premises conveyed, &c., the oyer was, "bounded on the northeast;" and the articles, "on the east."

The variance, as to the consideration in respect to the rent, between the copy of the declaration served, and the articles; and the variance between the oyer and the articles as to the boundary, arose from a mistake of the clerk of the plaintiff's attorneys in copying; the draft of the declaration and a *Nisi Prius* record made out before the cause was referred, and the copy of the articles first made by the plaintiff's attorneys being correct.

On objection taken for the variance, by the defendant, before the referees, these facts were offered by the plaintiff in proof; but they refused to hear them, because they deemed the variance immaterial.

362*] *The defendant also objected to the variance between the defendant's covenant as set forth, and as contained in the articles, in respect to the time when the installments were to become due.

The articles being produced before the referees as evidence, it appeared that the name and seal of the defendant, and names of the witnesses, were wanting. But the plaintiff proved that when the suit was brought, the name and seal of the defendant, and the names of the witnesses, were to the instrument. Evidence was also offered as to the manner in which it was mutilated; which, with the proof of its execution, is sufficiently stated in the opinion of the court, together with such further facts as are material.

The referees reported a balance of $557.05, for the plaintiff.

Mr. S. Sherwood, for the defendant. The execution of the contract was not sufficiently proved; but, if otherwise, the several variances are fatal. 1 Chit. P. L., 304, 305; *Pitt* v. *Green*, 9 East, 188; *Bowditch* v. *Mawley*, 1 Campb., 195; *Hoar* v. *Hill*, 4 Maule & S., 470; *Saxton* v. *Johnson*, 10 Johns., 418; *Bristow* v. *Wright*, Doug., 664. In these cases the variances were more slight than those now objected; yet the plaintiffs were defeated by them.

The amount of the receipt claimed by the defendant was improperly allowed.

Mr. S. R. Hobbie, contra. The objections for variance are merely technical, and should not be listened to if inconsistent with the merits. Some of the cases have gone upon very nice grounds, especially that of *Bristow* v. *Wright*, the authority of which was long doubted. It was, however, finally confirmed in *Peppin* v. *Solomons*, 5 T. R., 496, and let it be taken for law. It has no application to this case. There the variance was as to the time of paying the rent, but the lease was a necessary part of the declaration. Here it was not so. The variance as to the time when the rent was payable is in the recital of the consideration for the defendant's covenant. This recital is but matter of inducement. Indeed,
363*] stating any consideration *was not necessary. The defendant's covenant was independent. It does not profess to be upon any consideration. A covenant under seal imports a consideration in itself; and the declaration would have been good if it had merely set forth the covenant, without allusion to any consideration whatever. The books all agree that where the words of any pleading are such mere surplusage that they may be expunged without vitiating; where they are not matter of description, and where they need not be proved, a variance will not injure. Here, all that is said about the consideration may be stricken out without destroying the plaintiff's right of action. If so, clearly the variance is immaterial. 1 Chit. Pl., 307; *Peppin* v. *Solomons*, 5 T. R., 496; *Hamborough* v. *Wilkie*, cited by Gaselee, *arg.*, 4 Maule & S., 471; *Welch* v. *Fisher*, 8 Taunt., 338; S. C., 2 Moore, 378; *Jansen* v. *Ostrander*, 1 Cow., 671. The case of *Wroe* v. *Washington*, 1 Wash., 357, is this very case; and the variance was held immaterial.

These observations and authorities apply to all the variances concerning the consideration. The legal effect of the words "is to have," in the agreement, is comprehended in the word "grant." In this respect there is no variance.

Again; it appears by the affidavits that the mistake in reciting the consideration as to the time of the rent being payable, as well as that in the oyer, were merely clerical. Proof of this was offered to the referees; and the whole may be now amended. *Jansen* v. *Ostrander*, 1 Cow., 670. A trifling mistake in the oyer will not injure. *Henry* v. *Brown*, 19 Johns., 49. The party could not be surprised. The courts incline strongly to overlook slight verbal variances, when they see no evil can arise from them. *Cockell* v. *Gray*, 3 Ball & B., 177; *Arnold* v. *Revoult*, 1 Ball & B., 443; *Gladstone* v. *Neale*, 13 East, 410; Munf., Index, 565, and the cases there cited.

The authorities cited also apply to the variance between the declaration and agreement, as to the time when the installments became due. But there is, in this respect, no substantial variance. The agreement is set forth according *to its legal effect. The ques- [***364**
tion is, what construction should be put upon it. Good sense would say the time should run from its date, and so the referees decided. Was it to be supposed that the payment might be postponed at the will of the plaintiff? That he might take his own time to make the deduction, and then compute the time from this act? If the language be ambiguous, the construction is to be taken most strongly against the covenantor. It is enough, however, to say that the agreement was set forth on oyer, which is to be deemed a part of the declaration. If there was a variance, the defendant should have demurred. It is cured by the report, which is equivalent to a verdict. (1 Chit. Pl., 328.)

There is another answer to all these objections for variance. The cause was referred on the motion of the defendant. I would submit whether objections of this nature can be raised by a party before referees appointed on his own motion.

[WOODWORTH, *J.* The referees must be governed by legal rules in the admission of evidence. They come in the place of a jury; and we must be satisfied that improper testimony has not been heard by them, the same as of a jury at the circuit. In this remark Sutherland, *J.*, concurred.]

I submit, then, whether in any case a party may take a subsequent step, by pleading over, after a formal variance, going to trial, and then, for the first time, raising the objection. He should have raised it by demurrer in the first instance. The whole case was before him on the declaration and oyer. It was a proper case for a demurrer, if the variances were material; and that was the only way in which he could take the objection. *James* v. *Walruth*, 8 Johns., 410; *Douglass* v. *Beam*, 2 Binn., 76. I may say this especially of a reference. The law does not consider referees, a proper tribunal for the decision of legal questions. If it be seen by the court that such questions will arise before them, the uniform course is to deny a reference.

365*] **Curia*, per WOODWORTH, *J.* The first objection is that the covenant declared on was not sufficiently proved. When produced, it appeared that the names of the defendant and the subscribing witnesses had been broken off. The plaintiff proved that it was entire when the suit was commenced. It had been delivered to his attorneys, who made a copy, and returned the original to the person with whom it had been deposited for safe keeping. The depositary afterwards delivered it to the defendant, where it remained a long time. After it was returned, he discovered that the names of the defendant and witnesses were missing. The execution was fully proved. For aught that appears the mutilation may have taken place after issue joined. From the facts stated the presumption is that it was after the plaintiff had declared. The objection was properly overruled.

It was then contended that there was a variance between the contract produced and the declaration. The latter sets out, in consideration that the plaintiff had, by the agreement, granted to the defendant, the immediate, quiet and peaceable possession of the premises, together with the yearly rent; that is to say, the one half of the rent then become due, for the privileges of a fulling-mill and pond, &c. The covenant is in these words: "All of which premises the defendant is to have the immediate possession of, together with the yearly rent; or, that is to say, the half of the rent to become due, on the premises bargained to be conveyed to Colwell and Scott, which said rent is due for the privilege of a fulling-mill and pond." The word "granted," in the declaration, is intended to describe the consideration for the defendant's covenant. It will be seen, by looking at a previous part of the covenant, that it contains the following clause: "The said Richard (the plaintiff) doth convey, relinquish, and give up," &c. This applies to all the premises contracted for by the defendant. Subsequently follows the clause that the defendant is to have the immediate possession, &c. I think the word "granted," as used in the declaration, is to be understood in a popu-
366*] lar *sense, and not according to the strict technical meaning of the term when used in a deed. It is an allegation that the plaintiff had parted with his right. But even on a strict construction, the declaration is warranted by the covenant. If the plaintiff actually conveyed the premises, as the covenant states, and further added that the defendant was to have immediate possession, he has done enough to allow the pleader, when describing the transaction, to say, "the plaintiff granted the immediate possession."

With respect to the clause relating to the rent, there is a variance. By the declartion, it would seem that the defendant was entitled to one half the rent that had become due when the covenant was executed. The instrument itself says, "rent to become due," having reference to subsequently accruing rent only. The oyer served on the defendant's attorney, is correct in this particular. The plaintiff's attorney testifies that the variance was a clerical mistake in copying; that the draft of the declaration and the *Nisi Prius* record (this cause having been noticed for trial at the circuit before it was referred) describe the rent as in the covenant. My construction of the instrument is, that the defendant was to have one half of the rent that should thereafter accrue on the premises which had been bargained to be conveyed to Colwell and Scott. What was the yearly rent, or at what time it commenced, does not appear. The defendant states the difference in amount, between a calculation on the basis of the rent as then due and the rent to become due; but it is not stated how much was allowed on this account. We cannot, therefore, determine whether injustice has been done by the referees. The objection, then, is merely technical. The defendant has not been surprised. The oyer was a true copy of the covenant, which was given in evidence. On that, the plaintiff relied as the ground for a recovery. It is now the well settled practice, that the court will not allow a formal objection to defeat an action, but will suffer the party to amend in any stage of the cause. The inclination of the court has been to allow the judge at the trial to *amend the pleading objected to, when **[*367**
it was evident that no injury would be sustained by the party making the objection, other than the depriving him of the mere formal advantage. Such a course is approved by Bayley, *J.*, in *Halhead* v. *Abrahams*, 3 Taunt., 81. We have not found it necessary that a single judge should exercise this power. We will apply the remedy even after trial, by allowing amendments in furtherance of justice, as to mistakes arising from clerical errors; provided, however, that no injury is thereby sustained by the party opposing the amendment. This doctrine is settled by the cases of *Lion* v. *Burtis*, 18 Johns., 510; and *Jansen* v. *Ostrander*, 1 Cow., 670; and in other cases not reported. In this case, the principle should be applied, as the defendant has not been deprived of any defense on the merits.

The variance between the oyer and covenant, by inserting "northeast," in the former, instead of "east" as in the original, is not available; nor was it urged on the argument.

The next variance alleged is, that by the covenant, the defendant was to pay the $1,500 in manner following: in the first place to deduct what the plaintiff owed to the defendant, and the debt the plaintiff owed S. Scouten, provided he should transfer it; and then the remainder, in three equal annual payments. Upon a close examination of the declaration, I do not find the objection well founded in point of fact. I think it describes the manner of payment substantially and, indeed, almost literally, as in the covenant. If it were otherwise, the only effect would be to impose on the plaintiff the costs of the amendment.

There is another objection for variance, set out in the affidavit of Mr. Parker, one of the attorneys for the defendant; but as it was not made a point on the argument, I presume it is not relied on.

The last objection is on the merits. In the defendant's accounts, offered by way of set-off, there is a charge of $106, advanced Aug. 19, 1818. In explanation of this charge, the plaint-
368*] iff produced and proved *a receipt, given by the defendant to the plaintiff, for a note or obligation against Abraham R. Knapp, for $325, to collect and account for. Upon the receipt was indorsed the sum of $106 received by the plaintiff. It appeared that this was the money charged in the account. For the purpose of showing that the charge was paid, and reducing the balance claimed by the defendant as a set-off, the plaintiff proved that Knapp had given six notes to six heirs, of whom the plaintiff was one. The witness testified that he had seen all the notes in the possession of Knapp, the maker, and understood the concern was settled. This was certainly, *prima facie*, evidence that the defendant had collected, or parted with the note. Nothing appears to have been offered by the defendant to resist this inference. In adjusting the account the referees properly allowed the amount of the receipt as a credit to the plaintiff.

My conclusion is, that, as to the objection well taken for variance, the plaintiff be permitted to amend, on payment of the same costs as if the amendment had been made previous to the hearing of the cause before the referees; and that the motion to set aside the report of the referees, be denied.

Rule accordingly.

Cited in—4 Duer, 230; 22 Am. Dec., 506 (1 Green, 23).

369*] *GOULD v. JAMES.

Trespass for Taking Oysters—Exclusive Right of Fishery, in Arm of the Sea—Prescription Must be Clearly Proved—Witnesses—Commoner, Incompetent as to Right of Fellow Commoner—Those having Interest in the Question but not in the Suit, Competent—Award as Evidence.

The inhabitants of Lloyd's Neck claimed by prescription, an exclusive right of fishing for oysters, opposite their respective farms, in an arm of the sea. In an action of trespass, by one of them, for a violation of this claim, another, interested as a remainder-man in a farm adjoining the *locus in quo* at Lloyd's Neck, was offered as a witness for the plaintiff; held, that he was admissible.

The inhabitants of H. claimed that the *locus in quo* was a free fishery for them. The defendant, however, an inhabitant of H., justified by plea, on the ground that it was a free fishery for all the citizens of this State. Held, that other inhabitants of H. were competent witnesses; and that too, though they had fished at Lloyd's Neck; and were liable to an action, if the plaintiff should succeed in establishing his right.

These witnesses had an interest in the question merely; not in the event of the cause.

A commoner cannot be a witness to support the right of his fellow commoner; but one may be a witness to support a right by prescription, in respect to another's estate, though the witness claim to prescribe in respect to his own estate, upon the same facts he is called to establish.

One may prescribe for an exclusive right of fishery in an arm of the sea, where the tide ebbs and flows. But such prescription must be clearly proved. Every presumption is against it.

A citizen of this State, is a competent witness to establish a public right of fishery, in all the citizens of the State.

An award of arbitrators was made between the owner of lands called L., adjoining to and bounded on an arm of the sea, where the tide ebbs and flows, on one part; and the trustees of the town of H. in this State, lying on the opposite side of the arm, of the other part; which award established certain boundaries between the parties, and decided that certain fishing ground lay within the boundaries of L. In trespass by the lessee of a part of the fishing ground, who claimed a right of several fishery therein by prescription, against an inhabitant of H., for taking fish on the demised premises; the latter justifying on the ground that the fishery was free to any citizen of this State; the plaintiff offered the award in evidence. Held, that it should not be received; that it determined nothing as to the rights claimed by the respective parties, and was, therefore, immaterial.

An inhabitant of a particular place, cannot be a witness, to prove a prescriptive right, common to all the inhabitants of that place.

A several fishery, in an arm of the sea, where the tide ebbs and flows, may be derived from a grant or prescription.

In trespass *quare clausum fregit*, against one, other trespassers on the *locus in quo*, or in other places, the title to which depends on the same question as that to the *locus in quo*, may be witnesses for the defendant; for the verdict will not be evidence for, or against them.

Citations—1 Phil. Ev., 47, 247; 1 T. R., 302, 303; 1 Ld. Raym., 731; Doug., 374; 1 East, 357; 2 Johns., 175; 14 Johns., 80, 81; 4 Burr., 2164; 3 Cai., 318; 10 Johns., 236; 17 Johns., 210; 20 Johns., 98; 1 Com. N. S., 384; 2 Com. N. S., 483.

ON ERROR from Queens Co. C. P. The action in the court below was trespass, by Gould against James, for entering the close of the former at Lloyd's Neck, in the Town of Oyster Bay, Queens Co., and catching, taking and carrying away oysters. Plea, that the *locus in quo* was, at the time when, &c., a navigable river, or arm of the sea; and a free fishery for any of the citizens of this State. The replication took issue on this fact.

At the trial, Nov. 30, 1822, the plaintiff claimed the *locus in quo*, as belonging in fee simple to inhabitants of Lloyd's Neck, and proved that the plaintiff held exclusive possession of a farm under a lease from a tenant by *the curtesy, in which the plaintiff [***370** covenanted to protect the shell-fish on the premises. That the farm was on Lloyd's Neck, and adjoining Lloyd's Harbor. That the fences on both sides, extended from the upland to the mud, at or near low water mark. That the flats between high and low water mark abound with oysters; of which the defendant, though forbidden by Mr. Lloyd, carried away several bushels. That the defendant said he would admit the right to the oysters to be in the proprietors of the upland, if they would permit him to take them away. It was also proved, that the right to the oysters had been claimed by the proprietors of the upland at Lloyd's Neck, as belonging exclusively to them, in front of their respective farms. That people generally asked for them; and those who did not, were commonly prosecuted. This exclusive right had been exercised, as one witness for the plaintiff said, 13 years to his knowledge; and another said 38 years.

John L. Cogswell, who was entitled to a right in remainder in a farm at Lloyd's Neck, adjoining the one possessed by the plaintiff, was called by the plaintiff as a witness. The defendant objected to his admission on the ground of interest. He was rejected by the court below as incompetent; and the plaintiff excepted.

The defendant offered four witnesses, citizens of this State, and inhabitants of the Town of Huntington; which lies on the west side of the neck opposite Lloyd's Harbor. This harbor was proved to be 70 or 80 rods wide; and it appeared that the shores on the west neck side, were within the town of Huntington; and free for all the inhabitants of that town. These witnesses had themselves taken oysters at Lloyd's Neck. They were objected to, by the plaintiff, as interested; but were received by the court below; and the plaintiff excepted. They testified as to the situation of the harbor, fences, &c., and to interruptions of the right claimed by the proprietors on Lloyd's Neck side.

The plaintiff then offered in evidence an award of arbitrators, made May 30, 1784, upon **371***] a submission between *Henry Lloyd, then proprietor of Lloyd's Neck, and the trustees of the Town of Huntington, by which certain boundaries were established, including the *locus in quo* in Lloyd's Neck. This was objected to, and being rejected by the court below, the plaintiff excepted.

Mr. W. T. M'Coun, for the plaintiff in error. Cogswell, the plaintiff's witness, was improperly rejected. He was, at most, interested in the question, not in the event of the cause. (1 T. R., 302.) The record in this cause would be evidence neither for nor against him. The prescription set up, and sought to be proved, is in the plaintiff and his reversioner, exclusive of all other persons. It is annexed to the *locus in quo*. It is not a prescription in favor of all the inhabitants of Lloyd's Neck in common. Hence, proof of a prescription in right of the plaintiff's close, can have no influence on the witness' claim. *Hockley* v. *Lamb*, 1 Ld. Raym., 731, is in point. It is not the case of commoners, in which, I admit, a witness, being a fellow commoner himself, could not testify. (1 T. R., 302.)

The defendant's four witnesses ought to have been rejected as incompetent. They were inhabitants of Huntington, who claimed in common against the plaintiff. (1 T. R., 302; 1 Ld. Raym., 731; *Carpenters* v. *Hayward*, Doug., 374.) The verdict in this case, if for the plaintiff, would be evidence against these witnesses, as in *Reed* v. *Jackson*, 1 East, 355, where the competency of a verdict against one parishioner, on the question of a common right of way for his parish, was received in evidence against another. Upon this principle, in trespass for fishing, against an inhabitant of Staten Island, an inhabitant of that place was holden an incompetent witness, to prove a common right of fishery in all the inhabitants. *Jacobson* v. *Fountain*, 2 Johns., 170.

The award offered in evidence was admissible. 15 Johns., 197; 1 Cow., 117; 2 Cow., 638; *Card* v. *Jeans*, Mann. Dig., Witness, *c*, *k*; Privies in Estate, p. 463.

Mr. R. Bogardus*, contra. The de- [372** fendant was entitled to a verdict on the plaintiff's own proof. The *locus in quo* being an arm of the sea where the tide ebbs and flows, the right of fishing was common to all. *Hooker* v. *Cumming*, 20 Johns., 90, and the cases there cited. If this be so, it is immaterial whether the witnesses, whose competency are in question, were received or not. Their testimony was offered with a view to the plaintiff's exclusive right; whereas, it is evident he could not have any. Neither the King nor the Legislature can grant away a public fishery. *Arnold* v. *Mundy*, 1 Halst., 1.

But Cogswell was properly rejected. Being a remainder-man of the farm adjoining the plaintiffs, the proprietors of which claimed the same exclusive right as the plaintiff and his lessor, he had a strong interest. Not so of the defendant's witnesses. They were not offered, as supposed on the other side, to establish a common right in a particular town, district or corporation to which they belonged; but to prove a right in the people of the State at large. Surely, it will not be contended that every man in the State is disqualified to be a witness upon such a question. The doctrine of interest has never been extended so far. Neither *Reed* v. *Jackson* nor *Jacobson* v. *Fountain* advance such a sweeping doctrine. They relate to common rights of way or fishery in the inhabitants of particular places. In trespass for traveling on ground claimed as a public highway, was it ever heard that the whole State shall be shut out from being witnesses?

Nor was the award admissible. The defendant was not a party to it; nor did it relate at all to the subject now in controversy.

Mr. M'Coun, in reply. It is true, that where the tide ebbs and flows, the right of fishing is, *prima facie*, in the citizens of this State. But we introduced evidence to show an exclusive right in the inhabitants of Lloyd's Neck. The circumstance that the tide ebbs and flows, is not conclusive for the people. A prescriptive right may still exist in private persons. Harg. L. Tr., part 1, ch. *5. p. 17, contains [***373** the whole doctrine on the subject. By this it will be seen that a subject may acquire an exclusive right of fishery in an arm of the sea, by grant from the King, by custom, or prescription. *Carter* v. *Murcot*, 4 *Burr.*, 2162–2165, and the cases there cited, contain the same doctrine. Several adjudications in this country have adopted the English doctrine. *Adams* v. *Pease*, 1 Conn. N. S., 481; *Coolidge* v. *Williams*, 4 Mass., 140. An exclusive right will be presumed, if it have been exercised for the length of time required by statute, to bar a right of entry. *Ingraham* v. *Hutchinson*, 2 Conn. N. S., 584; *Shaw* v. *Crawford*, 10 Johns., 236; *Bealy* v. *Shaw*, 6 East, 208; *Balston* v. *Bensted*, 1 Campb., 463; *Chalker* v. *Dickenson*, 1 Conn. N. S., 582. *Arnold* v. *Mundy*, it is true, denies the right of the King to grant, but admits a power in the Legislature. That case does not at all interfere with prescriptive rights.

As to the defendant's witnesses, if all the citizens of the State are interested, it is not the plaintiff's fault; nor can this court grant a remedy. The defendant should go to the Legislature.

Curia, per SAVAGE, *Ch. J.* The first question is as to the competency of Cogswell. Courts have lately inclined strongly to the rule that nothing but an interest in the event of a cause, shall disqualify a witness as interested. Phillips, in his Treatise on Evidence, Vol. I., 47, says, when the issue does not affect any common right; but is merely on a right of common, claimed by prescription, as belonging to the estate of A, one who claims a prescriptive right of common in right of his own estate, may be a witness; for though A may have such a right of common, it does not follow that B has; nor would the verdict in the action of A be evidence in B's action. And Buller, *J.*, in *Walton* v. *Shelly*, 1 T. R., 302, 303, says, if the issue be on a right of common, which depends on a custom pervading the whole manor, the evidence of a commoner, is not admissible; because, as it depends upon a custom, the record in that action would be evidence in a subse-
374*] quent *action brought by that very witness to try the same right; therefore, there is a good reason for not receiving his testimony in such a case. But the same reason does not hold, where common is claimed by prescription in right of a particular estate; because it does not follow, if A has a prescriptive right of common belonging to his estate, that B, who has another estate in the same manor, must have the same right. Neither would the judgment for A be evidence for B; and yet there are cases which lay it down as a general rule, that one commoner is, in no case, a witness for another. This *dictum* of *Mr. J.* Buller is not exactly applicable to the question upon Cogswell's competency. Here is no right of common, in controversy; but a claim by prescription is made by the plaintiff, of a right as belonging to him in common with the inhabitants, or rather proprietors of Lloyd's Neck. The witness is, therefore, interested in the question, but not in the event of the suit. He is interested in establishing the prescription; but this may be proved as to the plaintiff, and perhaps not as to any other proprietor of Lloyd's Neck, in the Town of Oyster Bay. A verdict for the plaintiff, therefore, could not be used by the witness, in a suit which he might afterwards bring, for a similar trespass upon his fishery.

I think the court below erred in rejecting this witness.

Did they err, also, in receiving the defendant's witnesses? The objection to those witnesses was that they were brought to establish a right of fishery in the inhabitants of Huntington, they being themselves inhabitants of that town. The rule seems to be well established, that an inhabitant of a particular place cannot be sworn to prove a prescriptive right in all the inhabitants, because that would be swearing to give himself a right there. (1 Ld. Raym., 731; Doug., 374; 1 East, 357.) In the case of *Jacobson* v. *Fountain*, 2 Johns., 175, Thompson, *J.*, who delivered the opinion of the court, lays down the rule with great precision. "A commoner," says he, "is inadmissible to prove a right of common, unless the common be claimed by prescription in right of a particular estate." *In that case, [***375** the witnesses were excluded, because the right or fishing was claimed by them, not in their individual capacity, but as inhabitants of Staten Island. The right set up by the defendants, if it existed at all, depended on residence exclusively. And hence the distinction between all the cases cited, and this case. There is here no right of common, no right of fishery in the inhabitants of Huntington, any more than those of any other town in the State. The right set up by the defendant is claimed by him in his individual capacity. It does not depend at all on residence. These witnesses were no more interested than any other citizens of the State, or of the U. S. So far, then, the court below was correct in admitting them.

But were they not interested to defeat the plaintiff's action; as, by their own testimony, it appears they were liable to an action themselves, if the plaintiff's right should be established? They would then come within the case of *Carpenters* v. *Hayward*, Doug., 374, where several persons were introduced to disprove the existence of a custom, in favor of the plaintiffs, that none but the members of their company should work in Shrewsbury, by showing that the witnesses had worked there as carpenters, without the company's license. Ld. Mansfield said, "if the company had failed in establishing the custom, they would have been discharged from actions to which they were liable for the breach of it." The most forcible objection to these witnesses is that they were interested to discharge themselves from actions to which they were liable as trespassers, if the plaintiff's right was established; and yet the verdict against the defendant could not be used in an action against the witnesses. The general rule is, that a verdict cannot be evidence for either party, in an action against one who was a stranger to it; who had no opportunity to examine witnesses, or to defend himself, or to appeal against the judgment. (1 Phil. Ev., 247; 14 Johns., 80, 81.) I think this case is not an exception to that rule.

*The witnesses were, therefore, no [***376** otherwise interested than any other persons, in the event of the suit; and, of course, were competent.

The award, I think, was properly excluded as irrelevant. It purported merely to establish the line between Lloyd's Neck and Huntington, which, in my judgment, was immaterial.

The court below having erred in rejecting the testimony of Cogswell, the judgment must be reversed; and a new trial granted; unless, indeed, as it is contended for the defendant, the plaintiff, from his own showing, cannot recover upon a further trial. It is urged by him that the plaintiff cannot recover, because the *locus in quo* is an arm of the sea, where the tide regularly ebbs and flows; and because, in such case, the right of fishing is common to all. The law on this subject, is truly laid down by Ld. Mansfield, in *Carter* v. *Murcot*, 4 Burr., 2164. "In rivers not navigable, the proprietors of the land have the right of fishery on their respective sides; and it generally extends *ad filum medium aquæ*. But in navigable rivers, the proprietors of the land on each side, have it not; the fishery is common; it is, *prima facie*, in the King, and is public. If any one claims it exclusively, he must show a right. If he can show a right by prescription, he may then exercise an exclusive right, though the presumption is against him, unless he can prove such a prescriptive right." This is the acknowledged law of Great Britain, and of this State. (3 Cai., 318; 2 Johns., 175; 10 *Id.*, 236; 17 *Id.*, 210; 20 *Id.*, 98.) So in Conn. (1 Conn. N. S., 384; 2 *Id.*, 483.)

The case of *Jacobson* v. *Fountain* is an instance, in which the plaintiff proved a prescriptive right to the fishery opposite his soil. Such a fishery may be the subject of a grant. Of course, it may be claimed by prescription.

The plaintiff is bound, in such case, to make out his right. Every presumption is against him. He must, therefore, establish his prescriptive right by satisfactory proof, before he can recover.

Judgment reversed, and a venire de novo *awarded.*

Cited in—1 Wend., 255; 14 Wend., 45; 60 N. Y., 65; 1 T. & C., 416; 11 Barb., 251; 15 Barb., 589; 19 Barb., 554; 16 Pet., 426; Olcott, 22; 19 Am., Dec., 496, 500.

377*] *JACKSON, ex dem. J. S. & W. BROWN,

v.

BETTS.(a)

Evidence—Wills—Not Produced—Parol Evidence of Existence and Contents—Diligent Search must be Shown—Declarations of Testator Incompetent—Party Competent to Show Loss—Name of Third Witness not Essential.

In ejectment, the plaintiff claimed under a will which could not be found. He proved that the testator made a will, several years before his death; and deposited it with M. for safe keeping. The testator afterwards took it back, for the avowed purpose of adding a codicil; which he did about July 7, 1821. March 1, 1822, his daughter saw a a paper in his desk drawer, which she had no doubt was his will. Between that day and his going a journey to visit his son, which was in the Apr. next following, she saw him take some papers from the desk and burn them, but did not know, and could not say they resembled the will. She saw him also several times engaged at the desk in arranging his papers, a bundle of which he placed in his trunk. She perused the paper but partially and hastily, &c. She was, however, satisfied that it was her father's will, and stated several circumstances calculated to identify it with the will and codicil proved to have been executed; and she stated other circumstances which had a contrary tendency. The testator died in May, 1822. The judge, at the trial, deeming it necessary to show the existence of the will subsequent to the execution of the codicil; and that this was not satisfactorily done by the daughter's testimony, nonsuited the plaintiff.

Held (without deciding whether the judge was correct in holding it necessary to show the existence of the will at any time after adding the codicil), that there was sufficient evidence upon this point to go to the jury; and that it should have been submitted to them, as well upon this question, as that of revocation; that the plaintiff, therefore, should not have been nonsuited.

(a)This cause was decided in May Term last.

NOTE.—*Evidence—Admissibility of secondary; of contents of will—Devisee as witness.* See Jackson v. Hasbrouck, 12 Johns., 192, *note*.

A devisee is competent to show loss of will, to let in secondary evidence of contents, in a suit to which he is a party. Above case of Jackson v. Betts. See, also, Dan v. Brown, 4 Cow., 483.

The declarations of a testator, as to the existence of his will, and the place where it may be found, are inadmissible in evidence, though made *in articulo mortis*.

A party in a cause (*e. g.*, a lessor in ejectment) is admissible as a witness, to show the loss of a will under which he claims, in order to let in secondary evidence of its contents.

If a subscribing witness to a will, show it duly executed, though he has forgotten who one of the witnesses was, this is sufficient proof of the execution.

Diligent search for a will at the last place of abode of a testator, in a desk where he usually kept his papers, and failure to find his will there, held, a sufficient ground for letting in parol proof of its contents, though he died abroad.

Citations—4 Cow., 490, 491; 3 Barn. & Ald., 489; 2 Johns., 31; 2 Phil. Ev., 197; 12 Johns., 192.

EJECTMENT for lands in the Town of Brunswick, Rensselaer Co., on a joint and several demise, from all and each of the three lessors; tried at the Rensselaer Circuit, July 9, 1824, before Betts, *Circuit J.*

On the trial, the lessors claimed as devisees, not as heirs of Benajah Brown, deceased; and the defendant admitted, that the lessors were the children of Benajah Brown, who died seised of the premises in question, in May, 1822.

The plaintiff then called James Mallory, who swore that Nov. 9, 1816, he received from Benajah Brown his will to keep for him, &c.

*The plaintiff having given notice [*378 to the defendant, to produce the will and codicil of Benajah Brown, which he did not do, next proceeded to the proof of their loss. For this purpose, J. Brown, one of the lessors, was sworn; and testified that about a week after Benajah Brown's decease, he went to his house in Brunswick, where he had last and for many years resided, to obtain possession of the will. That the witness made search for it, in the desk where his father said he had left it, but could not find it. He found the key of the desk. It was locked, but in such a situation, that it could be opened with other keys. His father died at the witness' house in Poundridge, Westchester Co., about 130 miles from Brunswick. Nancy Ayres, a daughter of Benajah Brown, was then sworn as a witness for the plaintiff, and testified that she lived with her father when he went from Brunswick to Poundridge, which was in Apr., 1822. On the 1st day of the next preceding Mar., she saw an article in a small drawer in the desk of her father, at his house in Brunswick, purporting to be his will; and had no doubt it was his will; read enough of it to see, how the daughters were provided for. After that, and a few days before he went from home, she saw him take some papers out of the desk and burn them, but did not know and could not say they resembled the will. She never examined the desk afterwards. Intermediate her seeing the will and his going away, she saw him several times engaged arranging his papers at that desk; whence he took a considerable bundle of papers, and put into his trunk. Mr. Mallory, called again, swore that he was one of the subscribing witnesses to the will, and Wm. L. Marcy, Esq., was another. Mr. Mallory swore to the due execution of the will, but could not remember who was the third witness. That some years after the will was executed, the deceased called for; and took it, stating that he was going to son James', and was about to make some alterations, or make a codicil to his will. The will was written on one sheet of letter paper, and the witness thought it was not slit.

379*] *The plaintiff then offered parol evidence of the contents of the will. This was objected to, because sufficient proof had not been given of its existence at the time of the testator's death. The judge said his opinion was, that if the will had been destroyed before the testator's death, though without his knowledge, it was not a valid will. But, on this point, the verdict had better be taken subject to the opinion of the court. That he thought the testimony too slight to repel the presumption that the testator destroyed the will. But for the purpose of bringing the whole matter in dispute before the Supreme Court, he would receive the testimony subject to the opinion of that court. The defendant then objected to the proposed testimony, on the ground that the execution of the will was not sufficiently proved, till the names of all three of the subscribing witnesses should be disclosed.

Ezra Lockwood was then called, who testified that about July 7, 1821, the deceased brought to the witness' dwelling-house, in Poundridge, a paper purporting to be his last will, on one sheet of letter paper, not slit or cut open, witnessed by Mr Mallory, Mr. Marcy, and another whose name he did not recollect; and requested the witness to write and add a codicil, which he did; and his impression was, that it was attached to the will by a seal. The codicil was properly attested to pass real estate. The witness then sealed up the will and codicil, and gave them back to the deceased. The codicil altered the will, merely by placing some of the devisees under the care of a trustee. Nancy Ayers, again called, did not recollect there was more than one paper; saw the seal of the wrapper was broken open; opened it, and saw the will; there might have been an article attached to it; presumed there was more than one sheet of the will; but whether it was attached together, she could not say. James Brown was named executor. She did not read the will through. Mr. Marcy swore to substantially the same facts as Mr. Mallory. The former drew the will. Mr. Lockwood, called again, said he thought the codicil was 380*] written on one page *of half a sheet; and it was his impression, that it was written to read by turning over the leaf.

The plaintiff then offered an authenticated record of the will of the deceased, exemplified under the seal of the Surrogate of Rensselaer Co. The judge rejected the evidence.

Nancy Ayers, called again, stated that there was no whole sheet of paper of the will. The paper was held or attached together at the top by something. Did not know how far she read the paper; and had no recollection that she turned over and examined the second page; believed she examined it carelessly; and looked it through; but has no recollection that she did. If her father's name was to the paper, she probably saw it; but has no recollection that she did. She might have had it in her hand a minute; but did not know; thought there was written on the cover, "The last will and testament of Benajah Brown." Did not know how many folds or pieces of paper the will consisted of.

The judge then ruled that the testimony failed to show, satisfactorily, that the paper seen by Mrs. Ayers, Mar. 1, 1822, was the will spoken of by Messrs. Mallory, Marcy and Lockwood; and that if proof of the codicil was to be considered proof of the execution of the will, yet the plaintiff could not be permitted to show the contents of the latter, without first giving evidence of its existence, after it was delivered by Mr. Lockwood to the deceased in July, 1821.

The plaintiff then offered to prove the declarations of the deceased, made on the day he was taken ill, before his last sickness, that in Apr., 1822, when he left his house in Brunswick, he left his will and codicil mentioned by Mr. Lockwood in the drawer mentioned by Mrs. Ayers. That in Apr., 1822, he applied to Mr. Lockwood to write another codicil, of the description mentioned by Mr. Lockwood. That the deceased repeatedly declared, during his last illness, and *in articulo mortis*, to Brown, the executor, that he had left his will and codicil *in his desk at Brunswick; and [*381 stated where the key was left.

This evidence being objected to, was overruled by the judge, who directed a nonsuit to be entered, the plaintiff having no further evidence.

Mr. J. P. Cushman, for the plaintiff, moved to set aside the nonsuit, and for a new trial. He said the execution of the will was sufficiently proved, and there is no sufficient evidence of its revocation. *Dan* v. *Brown*, 4 Cow., 490; 4 Burr., 2514. James Brown was a competent witness to prove the loss, and this was sufficiently established by his testimony. (4 Cow., 491.) Search was made in the place where the will was, most probably, to be found; *Jackson* v. *Hasbrouck*, 12 Johns., 192; and whether a bundle of papers was or was not in the trunk at some time, cannot be material. If reasonable diligence be shown, it is enough. (*Id.*) The judge erred in excluding proof of the contents of the will. It was not necessary to prove, that it had been seen after it was handed by Lockwood to the testator. But if otherwise, it should have been put to the jury to judge of the weight of Mrs. Ayres' evidence, as to the identity of the paper she examined. It was a question of fact. The judge also erred in requiring proof of the third witness. (*Id.*)

Mr. J. Paine, contra. The evidence shows that the deceased destroyed his will, if he ever made one. But if otherwise, the search proved was not sufficient to warrant a presumption of loss. Search should have been made in the testator's trunk, as well as in his desk. The declarations of the deceased were properly excluded. *Dan* v. *Brown*, 4 Cow., 490. Notice to the defendant to produce the will and codicil could have no effect. There was no evidence that he ever had them in his possession. The exemplification from the surrogate's office was properly rejected. (1 Phil. Ev., 433, 1 Am. ed.) The plaintiff was not prejudiced by the decision, that the third witness must be *disclosed. The defect was afterwards [*382 supplied; the decision went for nothing, therefore, and can be no reason for setting aside the nonsuit. (3 Johns., 528; 10 *Id.*, 447.) The mere facts that the testator made a will, which could not be found after his death, are not sufficient to establish it. The legal inference is, that the testator destroyed it himself.

Curia, per SUTHERLAND, *J.* The judge nonsuited the plaintiff, on the ground that there was not sufficient evidence of the identity of the will drawn by Marcy in 1816, and proved by him and Mallory and Lockwood, and that seen by Mrs. Ayres in the desk of the testator, in Mar., 1822; that parol evidence of the contents of the will drawn by Marcy could not be received, inasmuch as there was no evidence of its existence subsequent to July, 1821, when Lockwood drew a codicil for the testator, which, after it was duly executed, was attached to the will, and both delivered by him to the testator.

There certainly was evidence enough upon this point to go to the jury, and I think the learned judge erred, in not submitting it to their determination. It was a question of fact, which it was their particular province to decide.

Whether the will of the testator was among the papers which Mrs. Ayres testified that her father burned in Mar., 1822, before he went to Westchester, should also, I think, have been submitted to the jury. The evidence upon that point is of such a character, that we should not disturb any conclusion to which the jury might have come.

The declarations of the testator during his last sickness, as to the existence of his will, and the place where it would be found, were incompetent evidence, and were properly rejected by the judge. This point was decided in *Dan* v. *Brown*, 4 Cow., 490, in relation to this very will. (*Vide* 3 Barn. & Ald., 489; 2 Johns., 31; 2 Phil. Ev., 197, and the cases there cited.)

It was also decided in *Dan* v. *Brown*, that it was not essential to the due proof of the will, that the name of the third witness should be ascertained: the fact that it was attested by three witnesses, having been established.

*Assuming the execution of the will, [*383 and its existence at the time of the testator's death to have been established, the evidence of its subsequent loss, or destruction, was sufficient to let in parol proof of its contents. Diligent search was shown to have been made, where it was most likely to be found—in the desk of the testator, where he kept his papers, at his usual place of residence. This was, *prima facie*, sufficient. (4 Cow., 491; 12 Johns., 192.)

On these grounds, a new trial must be granted, with costs to abide the event.

New trial granted.

Reversed—6 Wend., 173.
Cited in—9 Cow., 220; 6 Wend., 187, 200; 1 Sandf. Ch., 237; 11 N. Y., 162; 26 N. Y., 437; 1 Lans., 159; 5 How. Pr., 285; 10 Leg. Obs., 59.

[END OF AUGUST TERM, 1826.]

CASES

ARGUED AND DETERMINED

IN THE

SUPREME COURT

OF THE

STATE OF NEW YORK,

IN

OCTOBER TERM, 1826, IN THE FIFTY-FIRST YEAR OF OUR INDEPENDENCE.

GAILLARD AND GRAVILLON *v.* SMART.

Attorney—May Discontinue a Suit—Failure to Enter Discontinuance.

An attorney may discontinue a suit, in virtue of his general power as attorney on record.

The attorney for the plaintiffs told the attorney for the defendant that the cause was discontinued; and being requested by the latter to enter a rule to discontinue, said this was not necessary; and in consequence, the defendant, with the consent of his special bail, went to Europe; whereupon, no rule being entered, the plaintiffs afterwards proceeded with the cause. On motion, the court ordered a discontinuance to be entered.

Citation—6 Johns., 296.

THE plaintiffs having sued the defendant for a large sum of money in *assumpsit*, and holden him to special bail, one of their attorneys afterwards gave parol notice to the clerk of the attorneys for the defendant that the suit had been discontinued, and offered to pay the costs. The clerk requested a formal discontinuance, but the attorneys for the plaintiffs told him this was not necessary. The costs were never demanded of the plaintiffs, but the defendant paid them to his attorneys; and, with the consent of the special bail, went to Europe, where he still continues. The plaintiffs afterwards proceeded with the suit, no rule for discontinuance having been entered.

Mr. H. Bleecker moved for a rule that the cause be discontinued, or, at least, that an *exoneretur* should be entered on the bailpiece.

Mr. S. A. Foot, contra, read an affidavit of one of the plaintiffs, that their attorneys had **386***] acted without their authority; *that he (the deponent) had merely given the defendant leave to go to France, on his encouragement that this would enable him to make a satisfactory arrangement of the plaintiffs' demand; and that the deponent had instructed his attorneys to suspend the suit; not to discontinue it. And that it was never the intention of either of the plaintiffs that the suit should be discontinued.

He contended that the attorneys could not discontinue without a special authority for that purpose. In this case it operated to destroy the remedy, which is a part of the contract. It is equivalent to a release or *retraxit*, a receipt or entry of satisfaction: neither of which are acts which an attorney can do, without special authority, unless the money be, in truth, paid to him. *Kellogg* v. *Gilbert*, 10 Johns., 220–222, and the cases there cited. Nor can he give a *cognovit*, without authority. *Denton* v. *Noyes*, 6 Johns., 296.

[WOODWORTH, *J.* The cases which you mention are those in which the right would be concluded. This is a mere discontinuance. Another suit may be commenced.]

In effect, the right is concluded. The defendant is beyond the reach of process. The Statute of Limitations has begun to run, and will continue till the debt is discharged, notwithstanding the defendant is abroad.

As to the bail, they took the risk of the defendant's going abroad; and if they will trust to a discontinuance without authority, they should take the consequence; not the plaintiffs. Besides, their application is premature. They should have waited to see if there will be a judgment.

Mr. Bleecker, in reply. The question is, whether the clients of the attorney are to abide the consequence of his unauthorized acts, or whether they shall be visited on the opposite party. Here is no discharge of the cause of action, but a step in the ordinary course of practice. Suppose an attorney suffers a nonsuit, or puts in a plea not adapted to his client's defense; clearly, the latter must be concluded. A discontinuance is no more; and indeed not *so much. An attorney may, under [***387** his general power, in a variety of ways, absolutely conclude the rights of his client. Are we to suffer because no rule was actually entered? That it was not, is the fault of the plaintiffs' attorneys. This is not the case of an agreement, which must be in writing by the 12th rule of April Term, 1796. It is the case of a notice that the suit was discontinued, and a waiver of the rule, or formality of actual discontinuance.

This is a totally different case from a *retraxit* or release, as remarked by His Honor, *Judge* Woodworth.

At any rate, the bail must be discharged on the plaintiff's own showing. They have licensed the principal to go beyond the reach of his bail.

Curia, per SAVAGE, *Ch. J.* It is worthy of remark, that only one of the plaintiffs makes an affidavit, denying any special authority in their attorneys to discontinue; and if this were the question, I think we ought, at least, to intend that the attorney would not act without such an authority, till the contrary is clearly shown by both.

But I do not think a special authority was necessary. *Denton* v. *Noyes* is relied on; but, as I understand that case, it is an authority in favor of the right to discontinue under the general power of the attorney. It was there held, that a judgment confessed by an attorney of this court, without process, was regular; and the court said the defendant must look to the attorney for his damages, if he had sustained any. It is true, this being such a strong act of the attorney, the court allowed the party to come in and plead; the judgment standing as security. They cite various cases, showing that, usually, if the client is prejudiced by the misconduct of his attorney in the course of the suit, he must take his remedy against the attorney. Van Ness, *J.*, who dissented, conceded that if a suit had been regularly commenced, the confession would have been conclusive, unless the attorney had been insolvent. Taking the rule as laid down by him, which is certainly **388***] the most favorable to the plaintiffs; *and still we must hold the discontinuance regular, if it had been actually entered. What has been done, is clearly equivalent to an actual discontinuance. The defendant's attorneys requested a rule to be entered, but the formality was waived. This is not the case of an agreement within the rule which requires a writing between the attorneys. Where an attorney is retained, we will not look for a special authority to do so ordinary an act of practice as the discontinuance of the cause. True, his general power does not extend to a *retraxit* or release; because they relate to the cause of action itself; not merely to the remedy which he is retained to conduct. But he may do all ordinary acts in the prosecution of the suit, or the final disposition of it.

Besides, here were instructions given to the attorney to suspend the suit. This is admitted by the plaintiffs. If these instructions have been misconstrued by the attorneys, it is better that their clients should suffer than the opposite party.

On the whole, we think a rule to discontinue must be granted; and this precludes the question as to the *exoneretur*. The bail are relieved, as a consequence.

Rule to discontinue granted.

Cited in—7 Wend., 515; 28 N. Y., 293; 45 N. Y., 635; 52 N. Y., 311; 63 N. Y., 419; 6 How. Pr., 328; 36 How. Pr., 380; 5 Abb. N. S., 283; 9 Bos., 550; 7 Rob., 540; 2 Sawy., 341; 42 Am. Dec., 653 (8 Ala., 590).

ANONYMOUS.

Affidavit on Which to Move Nonsuit—Contents of.

The affidavit upon which to move for judgment as in case of nonsuit, must show there has been a circuit at which the plaintiff might have tried his cause.

The court will not take judicial notice that there has been such a circuit.

MR. W. MULOCK moved for judgment as in case of nonsuit, for not proceeding to trial at the last circuit in the County of Delaware.

Mr. J. L. Tillinghast objected that it did not appear by the affidavit on which the motion was founded, that there had been any circuit in Delaware since the cause was put at issue.

Mr. Mulock suggested that the court would take judicial notice that there had been such a circuit.

**Curia.* We have often held other- [*389 wise. Before you can move for judgment as in case of nonsuit, you must show by your affidavit, affirmatively, that there has been a circuit at which the plaintiff might have tried his cause. Till this is shown, it does not appear that he was in default.

Motion denied.

ANONYMOUS.

Change of Venue—Contents of Affidavit.

The affidavit for a motion to change the venue, must state the names of the witnesses.

And also, that, as the party is advised by counsel, and believes he cannot safely proceed to trial without the testimony of each of them.

MR. J. A. COLLIER, for the defendant, moved to change the venue in this cause, on the ground that a greater number of witnesses resided in the county to which he sought to change it than in the county where the venue was laid.

Mr. H. Stephens, contra, objected that the affidavit upon which the motion was founded did not name the witnesses; nor state that, as the defendant was advised by counsel, and believed, he could not proceed to trial without their testimony.

Curia. For both reasons, the motion must be denied. Owing to the looseness of the practice in these respects, heretofore, parties have taken very great latitude in stating the number of witnesses on both sides. We think it proper to require that they should not only name their witnesses; but we now require them to swear that, as they are advised by counsel, and believe they cannot safely proceed to trial, without each of the witnesses named.

Motion denied, with costs.

---

*ANONYMOUS. [*390

Default Set Aside—Judgment Allowed to Stand as Security—Costs.

On setting aside a default for want of a plea, on the ground of merits, if it appear probable that the plaintiff may lose his demand by reason of the defendant's being in doubtful circumstances, the court will order the judgment to stand as security; and grant a rule that the defendant may plead and go to trial on payment of costs.

This means not only the costs of resisting the motion, but also of the default, and all subsequent proceedings.

MR. J. A. COLLIER, for the defendant, moved to set aside a default for want of a plea, on the ground of merits.

Mr. H. P. Hunt, contra, read an affidavit showing that, by reason of the defendant's doubtful circumstances, the plaintiff would be in danger of losing his debt, unless the judgment was suffered to stand as security.

Curia. Let the defendant plead and go to trial on payment of costs, the judgment to remain as security.

Collier. Do the court mean the costs of resisting the motion merely, or the costs of the default and subsequent proceedings also?

Curia. Both must be paid. The plaintiff is entitled to them as a consequence of the default, and at all events. Were this otherwise, the plaintiff would lose these costs altogether if he should not succeed. We do not mean his obtaining them should in any way depend on the event of the suit.

Rule accordingly.

Cited in—38 N. Y., 20; 4 Trans. App., 293; 35 How. Pr., 335; 4 Abb. N. S., 273.

COBB AND MORRIS v. DARROW.

Notice from Attorney—Right to Act on.

The plaintiff has a right to act on a notice of bail, received from an attorney of this court, though he may not have been retained; and though bail may not be in as stated in the notice.

AN attorney, without any authority from the defendant, gave notice to the attorneys for the plaintiff that special bail was in for the defendant. On this notice, and four days after, the plaintiff's attorneys entered the defendant's default.

And though no bail was, in fact, in, as the notice stated, and was not filed till some time after, and by another attorney;

391*] **The Court* refused to set aside the proceedings for irregularity, saying the plaintiffs had a right to act upon the notice.

Mr. D. Cady, for the motion.

Mr. H. P. Hunt, contra.

JONES v. SPICER.

Habeas Corpus—*Rule to Appear.*

A rule to appear upon a *habeas corpus*, cannot be taken before the return day, though the writ be actually returned when the rule is entered.

THIS cause was removed by *habeas corpus*, returnable Aug. 19, last. The writ being returned and filed Aug. 7, before the return day, the plaintiff took the usual rule to appear, and gave notice. The defendant not appearing pursuant to the rule, the plaintiff entered a rule for a *procedendo;* which,

Mr. W. Mulock now moved to set aside as irregular.

Mr. M. Ulshoeffer, contra.

Curia. The plaintiff has proceeded irregularly. A rule cannot be taken upon process till the return day. It is so of rules to bring in the body on writs of *capias;* and the same of *habeas corpus*.

Motion granted.

JACKSON, ex dem. FARMERS' TURNPIKE CO., v. STILES, WILD, Tenant.

Motion for Leave to Enter Into Consent Rule.

An affidavit that the tenant "claims as tenant in common with the lessors of the plaintiff; and that, as he is advised by counsel, and believes, he is tenant in common" with them, is sufficient to entitle him to enter into the consent rule specially.

MR. A. L. JORDAN, for the tenant, moved for leave to enter into the consent rule specially, on his affidavit, "that he, this deponent, claims as tenant in common; and that he is advised by counsel, and believes, that he is tenant in common with the lessors of the plaintiff."

He cited *Jackson* v. *Stiles*, 2 Cow., 585.

**Mr. W. Fraser*, contra, objected, [*392 among other things, that the affidavit was too loose and general.

Curia. We think it is sufficient. The form agrees with that required in the case cited.

Motion granted.

JACKSON, ex dem. VROMAN, v. VROMAN.

Practice—Notice of Motion for Judgment as in Case of Nonsuit.

Notice of motion for judgment as in case of nonsuit, cannot be given till after the circuit at which the plaintiff is bound to try has passed, though he entirely omit to notice his cause.

MR. C. Y. LANSING, for the defendant, moved for judgment as in case of nonsuit, for not going to trial at the last Schoharie Circuit, pursuant to stipulation. He read an affidavit, the *jurat* of which was dated Oct. 16, stating that no notice of trial was, on that day, at the time of making the affidavit, received for the circuit, which was to be holden Oct. 23. And he said the plaintiff was in default. He had let the time pass for noticing. It was impossible for him to try, and should be considered in the same light as if a circuit had passed, and the cause in fact not tried, through the plaintiff's fault.

Mr. I. Seelye, contra, said the application was premature. The cause might yet have been tried by arrangement between the parties, or the circuit might have fallen through. The plaintiff is not completely in default till his cause has been, or might be, called on the calendar.

And of this opinion was *the Court*.

Motion denied.

Cited in—1 Wend, 281; 7 Wend, 515; 8 How. Pr., 98.

Ex PARTE BACON AND LYON.

Practice—Discretion of C. P. as to Setting Aside Nonsuit.

Setting aside a judgment, by default, in a court of C. P., is matter of discretion with that court.

And this court will not interfere on such a subject by *mandamus*.

NOTE.—Mandamus—*Control of inferior court—Discretion.*

A mandamus *will not be issued to control the discretion of inferior courts.* See Hull v. The Supervisors of the County of Oneida, 19 Johns., 259, *note*.

THE C. P. of St. Lawrence Co. had set aside a regular judgment by default against the defendant, in a cause wherein the relators were 393*] plaintiffs, and one *Taylor, defendant, on the ground of merits, on payment of costs.

And this court were now moved that a *mandamus* issue, commanding the C. P. to vacate that rule.

Mr. B. S. Doty, for the relators.

The motion was not opposed; but,

Per Curiam. The C. P. must be their own judges, upon the circumstances before them, whether they will set aside a default upon the merits. This is so much a matter of discretion that we will not interfere by *mandamus*. The granting or refusal of such an application is governed by no fixed principles. No positive rule of law has been violated by the court below; nor can we fix bounds to their discretion upon this subject.

Besides, upon the circumstances disclosed here, we rather think we should have set aside the default in question on our own rules of practice. But upon this we give no opinion.

Motion denied.

Cited in—7 Cow., 364; 5 Wend., 123; 16 Wend., 378; 18 Wend., 96.

BENNETT *v.* W. M. DAVIS AND N. DAVIS.

Infants—Warrant of Attorney by, to Confess Judgment, Void.

A warrant of attorney by an infant, to confess judgment is void; and a judgment entered in virtue of it will be set aside on motion.

JUDGMENT for the plaintiff was rendered against both the defendants, on bond and warrant of attorney. At a previous term, the judgment had been set aside as to N. Davis, for irregularity in its entry, on grounds mentioned in the report of the same case, in 3 Cow., 68.

And now it was moved that the judgment be also set aside as to W. M. Davis, on the ground that he was an infant when the bond and warrant of attorney were executed.

Mr. W. H. Maynard, for the motion, cited 1 H. Bl., 75; Dunl. Pr., 359; W. Bl., 1133; Bing., Judg., 42; 1 Dall., 122.

394*] **Mr. G. C. Bronson*, contra.

Curia. The warrant of attorney was void as to the infant, and the judgment must, therefore, be set aside.

Motion granted.

Cited in—6 Hill, 242; 8 Abb. N. S., 466; 57 Barb., 175; 37 Mich., 239.

LOWN *v.* ROOSE.

Stipulation—Judgment of Nonsuit.

On a rule for a "judgment as in case of a nonsuit, unless the plaintiff shall stipulate and pay costs," the plaintiff must stipulate *instanter*, or at least within 20 days; or the defendant may perfect his judgment without demanding costs.

IN May Term, May 26, last, a rule was moved for, and taken against the plaintiff, for "judgment as in case of nonsuit, unless the plaintiff shall stipulate and pay costs." But no stipulation was served by the defendant's attorney till June 16, thereafter.

The defendant's attorney having taken judgment as in case of nonsuit against the plaintiff,

A motion was now made, in behalf of the plaintiff, to set it aside; and one question was, whether the stipulation was in sufficient season to comply with the rule. No demand of the costs by the defendant's attorney had been made.

Mr. J. W. Wheeler, for the motion.

Messrs. J. L. Wendell and *G. A. Shufeldt*, contra.

Curia. The obligation to demand costs on the rule *nisi* for judgment, as in case of nonsuit, does not attach till a stipulation be actually given. Here was a delay of more than 20 days to give the stipulation. On a rule of this kind, the stipulation must be given, at least, within 20 days from the rule, and we think *instanter;* or the defendant may proceed and perfect his judgment of nonsuit. The motion must be denied.

Motion denied.

---

*THE PRESIDENT, DIRECTORS AND COMPANY OF THE ONTARIO BANK [*395

v.

BAXTER.

THE SAME

v.

THREE OTHERS, in three several causes.

Several Suits on Same Note—Costs—Statute.

The Statute, sess. 41, ch. 259, sec. 6, regulating the costs in several suits on the same note, &c., applies to the general, not the interlocutory costs of the cause; *e. g.*, the costs of putting off a cause at the circuit.

Where several suits are brought against the maker and indorsers of the note, an affidavit of merits to set aside an inquest in all the causes, may be made by the maker; he being acquainted with the facts, and the defense being the same in all the causes.

Citations—Stat., sess. 41, ch. 259, sec. 6.

THESE were separate actions on the same promissory note, against the several defendants, as maker and separate indorsers.

All the causes being noticed for trial at the last Oneida Circuit, they were ordered by the circuit judge to be put off, on payment of costs. These were taxed at the full costs of the circuit in each cause. The defendant refused to pay according to the taxation, insisting that he was bound to pay full costs in only one of the causes, and disbursements only in the others, and claiming that the Statute of Apr. 21, 1818, sess. 41, ch. 259, sec. 6, extended to the case. He accordingly tendered this amount to the plaintiffs' attorney. The latter, claiming the full costs in all the causes, moved the three for trial, in which disbursements only were tendered, and took inquests.

An objection to this course was made to the circuit judge, and he was moved to order a retaxation. He replied, that the costs having been taxed by a competent officer, must be paid; that he had nothing to do with the taxation and the Supreme Court, only, could afford relief on this head. He, accordingly, suffered the inquests to be taken.

An affidavit of merits was now made by the maker, in the three causes, which were against the indorsers. He swore that he was acquainted with the defense in each cause, and that it was the same in each of the four causes.

On these facts,

A motion was made to set aside the inquests for irregularity, and that the costs be retaxed.

Mr. R. Cossett, for the motion.

Mr. C. P. Kirkland, contra.

396*] **Curia*. This motion cannot be granted, on the ground of irregularity. The Statute, sess. 41, ch. 259, sec. 6, regulating the costs of several suits on the same instrument or note, &c., against maker and indorsers, &c., applies only to the general, not to the interlocutory costs of the cause.

But there is an affidavit of merits. It is objected that this is made by the maker, who is not the nominal defendant in the three causes. He is, however, a party to the instrument, and asserts his acquaintance with the facts in each cause; and that the defense is the same in all. We think this sufficient, and grant the motion to set aside the inquests, on payment of all the costs.

The motion to retax is denied.

Rule accordingly.

Cited in—19 Wend., 126; 15 How. Pr., 201.

MUNRO *v.* BAKER ET AL.

Cause for Certiorari *Must be Shown—Exception.*

Cause must be shown for a *certiorari*, in all cases where it is to review the proceedings of an inferior jurisdiction for error, except where the writ is sued out by the people.

A WRIT of *certiorari* had issued in this cause, in behalf of Munro, to remove into this court the assessment list of highway work made by the Commissioners of Highways of the Town of Mamaroneck, in the County of Westchester, with their proceedings, and the determination of the Commissioners in affixing the names of persons mentioned in the list; and the number of days which they determined each person should work for the year; among whom they named Munro. The *certiorari* recited his complaint, that manifest error had intervened in the list and proceedings of the Commissioners; and the writ was allowed by the Recorder of N. Y., without any cause shown by affidavit, or otherwise.

Mr. S. S. Lush now moved to set aside the writ as irregular. He insisted that, at common law, it could be allowed only in open court; 2 T. R., 89, and the Statute, 1 R. L., 140, does not extend to the case.

397*] *At any rate, cause should have been shown by affidavit; for there are certain cases in which the court, from a regard to public convenience, will refuse to allow a *certiorari*. (2 Cai., 181, 182; 20 Johns., 84; 2 T. R., 234.)

Mr. S. M. Hopkins, contra, said the writ of issues, of course, unless restrained by the Legislature. This is proved by our various statutes on the subject. And see, also, Com. Dig., *Certiorari*, B. *Pro rege*, the writ issues, of course, even where it is forbidden by the general words of a statute.

Curia. Without saying whether an application should have been made to the court, we are clear that cause must be shown in all cases where a *certiorari* is brought to review the proceedings of an inferior jurisdiction for error. It is never of course, except where it is sued out by the people. If it were otherwise we might have every petty judicial controversy in the State before us.

Motion granted.

Cited in—20 How. Pr., 172; 11 Abb. Pr., 402; 88 Ill., 101.

GOODRICH, Administrator of GOODRICH, *v.* COLVIN AND LEIBER.

Debt on Judgment—Not a Local Action—Venue.

Debt on judgment is not a local action; and the venue may be laid in any county in the State, without regard to the place of filing the record or the venue in the original cause.

MR. J. M'KOWN, for the defendants, moved to change the venue in this cause from the County of Steuben to the County of Oneida, on the ground that the action was debt on a judgment of this court; and the venue in the original cause was laid in the County of Oneida; and the record of judgment filed in the office of the clerk of this court at Utica, in the County of Oneida.

He said the action of a debt on judgment is local, and the venue is confined to the place of filing the record and original venue. (1 Chit. Pl., 272; 2 Tidd Pr., 1035; 2 Johns. Cas., 381; 9 Johns., 259.)

Mr. J. M. Tillinghast*, contra. The [*398** case cited from 2 Johns. Cas., 381, was debt on a judgment of the Court of C.P. The reason of the English practice does not apply here. There, records are always filed at Westminster; and the object of confining the venue to that place is, that the record may be the more conveniently inspected. No such purpose is answered here, where we have three clerks' offices in three different parts of the State. The place of trial cannot follow the venue.

Curia. Admitting the English practice to be as stated, there is no reason why we should follow it. The main object of a venue is to facilitate the obtaining and introduction of testimony at the trial. These trials in debt on judgment, when by record, are in term time, by the record itself, without regard to the place where it may be filed. And if there be any other plea or issue than *nul tiel record*, the venue may be changed, to subserve the convenience of witnesses, as in ordinary cases. There is nothing in the nature of debt on judgment which makes it local.

Motion denied.

BURTCH, *Demandant*, *v.* HOAG, *Tenant.*

Practice in Supreme Court—Relief Against Defaults.

The Supreme Court are governed by the same rules in relieving against defaults in real, as in personal actions.

And default for not pleading, will, at the same term when taken, the counsel who took it being present in court, be opened of course.

AN imparlance had been granted to the first day of the present term, for the tenant to plead, which he omitted; and his default was entered.

After the *quarto die post*,

Mr. E. Cowen moved that the default be opened and the tenant received to plead, the counsel who took the default being in court. He said he supposed the motion for the default stood on the footing of any ordinary non-enumerated motion, which, under the like circumstances, would be opened during the term at which it was granted.

Mr. J. L. Tillinghast, contra, relied on the greater strictness which prevails as to real actions, and cited 2 Dunl. Pr., 912.

399*] **Curia.* The strictness contended for has been much relaxed; and, in real actions, we are now governed in granting relief against defaults by the same rules which prevail in personal actions.

Motion granted.

EX PARTE WRIGHT.

General Submission of Cause to Arbitration Operates as a Discontinuance—Exception.

A general submission of a cause to arbitration is a discontinuance: but not where the parties agree that a judgment may be entered on the report.

And in such a case, if the submission be revoked, the court may proceed with the cause to trial, notwithstanding the submission.

RICHARDSON sued Wright in the Oneida C. P. for assault and battery. Issue being joined, the parties stipulated in writing to refer the cause to three persons; that they should hear it on the pleadings; and that a judgment should be entered on their report. Afterwards, the defendant revoked the submission; but the referees, notwithstanding, proceeded to a hearing, and reported for the plaintiff. Then, the defendant having threatened to move to set aside any judgment entered on the report, the plaintiff noticed his cause for trial at the last September Term of the Oneida C. P. The defendant moved to strike the cause from the calendar on the ground of the above proceedings. The C. P. made a rule denying the motion.

A motion was now made for a *mandamus*, commanding them to vacate that rule. And 18 Johns., 22, and 1 *Id.*, 315, were cited in support of the motion.

It was insisted that the submission to arbitration was a discontinuance of the cause in the C. P.

Mr. T. Jenkins, for the relator.

The motion was not opposed; but,

Per Curiam. The court below were right. A general submission to arbitration is a discontinuance. Not so of a submission where a judgment on the report, or a *cognovit*, is to follow. By the very terms of the submission, the cause is to be continued in court. The motion must be denied.

Motion denied.

Cited in—1 Wend., 315; 2 Wend., 506; 13 Wend., 295; 15 Wend., 105; 19 Wend., 112; 27 N. Y., 232; 4 Barb., 544; 22 How. Pr., 343; 6 Rob., 495; 21 Wis., 296.

*EX PARTE LAMPMAN. [*400

Reduction of Judgment on Appeal—Discretionary Power of C. P. to Reduce Costs.

The plaintiff in a justice's court recovered $40; and, on appeal his recovery was reduced to $3.12½; held, that he was entitled to $7 costs with disbursements; and that the C. P. had no discretion to reduce the costs.

That discretion exists in those cases only, where the appellee recovers less in the C. P. than in the justice's court, but still more than $25.

Citations—Act, sess. 47, ch. 238, secs. 39, 41.

LAMPMAN sued Bennett and others in a justice's court of the County of Oneida, and recovered judgment for $40. The defendants appealed to the C. P. of that county; and a verdict was rendered for the plaintiff, on trial there, for $3.12½. The court held that this was a case in which they might exercise a discretion as to costs, within the 41st section of the Fifty Dollar Act, sess. 47, ch. 238, p. 296; and awarded the plaintiff $1, costs, only.

It was now submitted, by consent, to this court, whether the C. P. were correct in their construction of the Act.

Messrs. Allen and *Collins*, for the appellee.

Mr. A. Bennett, contra.

Curia. By the proviso to the 39th section of the Statute in question, in all cases of appeal, if either party recover a sum not exceeding $25, his costs are not to exceed $7 beside disbursements.

The case is, therefore, provided for by that section, and the court below erred in not awarding the $7 and disbursements.

The discretionary power of reducing the costs; is given by the 41st section, and is in cases not otherwise provided for. It can apply only to a case where the recovery in the C. P. is reduced below the recovery before the justice, but still exceeds $25.

ALLEN ET AL. v. HENDREE.

Affidavit for Commission.

An affidavit for a commission must show that issue is joined in the cause, or some reason for applying before.

MR. J. T. B. VAN VECHTEN moved for a commission to take the examination of witnesses; but the affidavit for the motion did not state that issue was joined in the cause; nor did it assign any special circumstances, showing the *necessity or propriety of [*401 a commission, before issue in the cause.

Mr. J. E. Lovett objected that the affidavit was defective. It should have stated that issue was joined in the cause. (2 Johns., 478; 3 *Id.*, 259.)

And of this opinion was *the Court*, and they denied the motion.

Motion denied.

JACKSON, ex dem. MARVIN ET AL. v. S. HOTCHKISS.

Entry on Lands Under Contract to Purchase—Failure to Pay Purchase Money—Estopped to Deny Vendor's Title even after 20 Years—

Presumption of Payment on Contract Under Seal, after 20 Years—May be Repelled.

Where one enters on land under a contract to purchase, but neglects to pay the consideration money, he and those claiming under him are estopped to question the title of the vendor, or his heirs; though more than 20 years have elapsed from the time when the last payment became due; though the vendee, and those claiming under him, have made permanent and valuable improvements, defended several actions of ejectment, and not been called on by the vendor to pay, and have even acquired title by conveyance from a third person.

A delay of twenty years to demand the money, or bring a suit upon a contract under seal, will raise a presumption of payment; but this may be repelled by showing that the covenantee died after the money fell due, leaving the contract in the hands of his attorney, who did not deliver it to the administrators, or place it within their control, till a number of years after the covenantee's death, it not appearing that they had any knowledge of the contract at the time of making out the inventory of their intestate's estate.

EJECTMENT, to recover part of military lot No. 44, in Homer, Cortland Co., tried at the circuit in that county, Jan. 25, 1825, before Throop, *Circuit J.*, when the following facts appeared:

The defendant came into possession of the premises in question, by agreement with Daniel Hoar and Abner Hotchkiss, who took possession under a written and sealed contract to purchase of Anthony Marvin, who died in 1811 (and of whom the lessors of the plaintiff are the children and heirs at law). This contract of purchase was dated Oct. 19, 1797, about which time the vendees took possession. The last payment was to have been made in Mar., 1799. Two payments of part of the purchase money were indorsed on the contract—the last, of $60, as of Feb. 14, 1798. The present action was commenced in 1824. The vendees and the defendant had continued in possession of the premises in question from the time of the contract of purchase, and made permanent and 402*] *valuable improvements; and the defendant had successfully defended several actions of ejectment for the same premises.

The defendant then offered in evidence a conveyance in fee of the premises in question, to himself from Henry I. Stewart, dated Nov. 6, 1806; a deed of the same premises from Henry Ennis to Stewart, dated July 29, 1806, in which Ennis was described as the heir at law of David Ennis, a dead soldier, to whom lot 44 was patented; and also the ballot-book and dead soldier list, by which it appeared that the lot was patented to David Ennis.

The whole of this evidence was objected to on two grounds: 1. That the defendant was concluded, having taken possession under the ancestor of the lessors. 2. That the conveyance from Ennis to Stewart was void, the lot being then in the adverse possession of the defendant.

The counsel for the plaintiff disclaimed producing the evidence offered for the purpose of setting up title against the lessors of the plaintiff or their ancestor, unless the jury should believe, under all the circumstances of the case, that the contract with the ancestor of the lessors had been rescinded.

In this view, the judge admitted the evidence; which was followed on the part of the defendant by evidence (this also being objected to), that the debt due to the ancestor of the lessors, on the contract of purchase, had not been inventoried by his administrators, in their inventory of his estate. This was met by the plaintiff with explanatory evidence, that the contract was, at the ancestor's death, and long before and after, in the hands of his attorney; and the judge putting the cause to the jury, upon the question of fact, whether the contract of purchase had not been abandoned, rescinded or in some way extinguished by the parties, the jury found the defendant.

Mr. S. Sherwood, for the plaintiff, now moved for a new trial, on the grounds that the judge had admitted improper evidence, and erred in submitting the question of abandonment to the jury. He cited Cowp., 214.

**Mr. J. A. Collier*, contra, cited 1 [*403 Johns. Ch., 354, and the case there cited; 1 Esp., 366; 3 Johns., 283, 290, 291; 5 Johns. Ch., 188; 3 Johns. Cas., 60; 6 Johns. Ch., 168; 1 R.L., 304.

Curia, per WOODWORTH, *J.* The evidence introduced at the trial, to show that the contract had been rescinded, was irrelevant and improper. The fact, that the defendant, in 1806, took a deed of the premises from Stewart, is no defense; the defendant being estopped from setting up a title against Marvin, under whom he held. It was an act done, for aught that appears, without Marvin's knowledge; and neither he nor his heirs can be affected by it, in an action of ejectment against the present defendant.

So, also, the evidence, that actions of ejectment had been commenced against the defendant and successfully defended by him, was wholly immaterial. It is not pretended that Marvin ever had notice of those suits. If he had, the question of rescinding his contract had no connection with that proceeding.

In judgment of law, there is no sufficient evidence to raise the question whether the contract was rescinded; and, consequently, it should not have been submitted to the jury.

More than twenty years had elapsed, between the time the last payment was to have been made, and the commencement of this action. Unexplained, I apprehend, the presumption of payment is made out. That presumption is, however, sufficiently repelled. Marvin died after the money became due. His papers relating to lot 44, appear to have been in the possession of Mr. Sherwood, his attorney, from 1807 to 1821. This sufficiently explains the omission of the contract in the inventory, filed by the administrators. At the time of making out the inventory, they probably had no knowledge that the contract existed. It is not urged that payment was ever made to Sherwood.

On the case before us, the plaintiff was entitled to recover.

*The verdict must be set aside, and [*404 a new trial granted, with costs to abide the event.

New trial granted.

Cited in—48 N. Y., 272; 3 Barb., 368; 14 Barb., 455; 18 Barb., 404.

FRANCIS
v.
THE OCEAN INSURANCE COMPANY.

Marine Insurance—Foreign Sentence of Condemnation, on Seizure for Illicit Trade—Right to Seize—Illicit Trade, how Proved—Preliminary Proofs, Waiver of Defects in Foreign Citizen not Bound by Decision of Court of His own Country—Interrogatories, Objections to.

In an action on a policy of insurance, upon a British ship, by an American underwriter, with a warranty against seizure for illicit trade, the defense was, that she was seized in a British port, and condemned by a court of admiralty there, for illicit trade; held, that the condemnation was not conclusive against the assured.

A citizen or subject of a country is not to be deemed a party to a sentence of confiscation in its courts; and, therefore, concluded by it as his own act.

And so, it seems, of a statute, or any other public authoritative Act of his government, as an embargo.

It seems that a foreign sentence of condemnation is, *prima facie*, evidence that the causes of condemnation mentioned in it exist, and of the authority of the court to pronounce sentence; and throws it upon the party who denies the existence of the causes or the jurisdiction of the court, to do them away by evidence on his part.

So of the regularity of the proceedings.

Any government may lawfully provide for the seizure of vessels, or property belonging to its own subjects, for a breach of its municipal regulations, either on the high seas or within its own territorial limits. And so of their subjects themselves.

And so, it seems, of vessels belonging to foreigners.

Where a seizure and condemnation was, in terms, for breach of some or one of the British laws relating to trade and navigation; held, that the party who would avail himself of the sentence, must not only show the proceedings of the court, but the existence of the law, under which the condemnation took place, by the usual evidence.

The libel and sentence are not evidence of the statute law upon which it is founded.

Proof that a ship's papers were seized with her, and delivered into the court where she was condemned, but that a certain paper belonging to her, could not be found there on search, is sufficient evidence of loss, to warrant parol evidence of its contents.

By a statute of England, a certain amount of repairs in a foreign port takes away the national character of the vessel. Held, that repairs being made to less than that amount, did not render it necessary to sail with evidence of the true amount of repairs, as part of the ship's papers.

If it be the duty of the master or supercargo, in behalf of the assured, to appear and put in a claim to a vessel insured, and improperly seized under pretense of carrying on illicit trade (of which *quære*), the omission of this duty may be excused by irregularity in the court where the suit is pending; as where process of monition is returnable at one place, and the cause heard, and the vessel condemed at another, unknown to the supercargo.

The assured, in a policy upon a ship, who sustains a total loss by seizure, &c., is entitled to recover all expenses fairly incurred in obtaining a restoration of the proceeds of the ship, on condemnation and sale.

In an action on a policy of insurance upon a ship, it appeared that when the underwriters were applied to for payment for a total loss, they replied that they would not settle the claim in any way. Held, that this was a waiver of preliminary proof of interest in the assured.

Answers to interrogatories upon a commission cannot be objected to, at the trial, as incompetent evidence, provided they are fairly within the scope of the interrogatories.

The proper time to object is, when the interrogatories are settled.

But the answers must be restrained in their effect to matters of fact, and cannot be received to establish a matter of law; as where a master of a vessel answered that the voyage was fair and lawful, &c. This was held inadmissible, beyond showing the *bona fides* with which he acted.

Citations—9 Johns., 192; 7 Johns., 57, 315, 425, 426, 514; 8 Johns., 307; 1 Dunl. Pr., 546; 3 Bos. & P., 291; 8 T. & R., 259; 10 East, 536 to 549; 15 East, 477, 525; 5 Taunt., 824, 674; 2 M. & S., 94; 2 Johns. Cas., 287, 481, 485; 4 Cr., 279; 6 Cr., 283; 2 Cr., 187, 234, 235, 236; 1 Cai. Cas. Err., xxix, 215; 1 Marsh., 347, *n.*; 3 Serg. & R., 74; 2 Marsh., 709, *a*, *n.* 713; 2 Cai., 155, 163; 3 Johns., 105, 310; 1 P. Wms., 431; Peak. *N. P.*, 18; 3 Esp., 58; 4 Esp., 79; 5 Johns., 298; 13 East, 332.

ASSUMPSIT for a total loss on a valued policy of insurance, on the British brig Francis, tried at the adjourned *N. Y. Circuit, Jan. 10, 1824, before Edwards, *Circuit J.* [*405

The policy was dated Nov. 15, 1817, and was at and from Middletown, in Conn. to one or more islands in the West Indies, &c.; and contained the usual risks of the seas, &c., takings at sea, restraints, &c., of all kings, princes or people, with a clause, that in case of any loss or misfortune, it should be lawful and necessary, for the assured to work, labor and travel, for, in and about the safeguard and recovery of the vessel; to the charges whereof, the defendants would contribute, &c., warranted free from any damage or loss which might arise in consequence of a seizure or detention, for, or on account of any illicit or prohibited trade, &c. The policy provided for payment within 30 days after proof of loss.

On the trial, the plaintiff admitted that no preliminary proof of interest in the assured had been furnished to the defendants. But he showed, that on producing the other preliminary proof to the defendants (Aug. 9, 1821), they answered that they would not settle the claim in any way. It appeared that the ship was owned by the plaintiff, a British subject, on whose account she was insured. She sailed on the voyage insured in Dec., 1816, under the British flag, Robert Garrick, a British subject, master. At the time he took charge of her (Sept. 21, 1816), the crew were all English, 8 in number. The ship was 147 tons, and had an English register, the last he saw of which, was in Dec., 1817. She had undergone repairs at Middletown; but to an amount less than 15*s.* for each ton. But there was no proof of this among the ship's papers. Garrick, the master, was examined for the plaintiff, on commission under the Statute, 1 R. L., 519, 520, and answered to the 11th and 12th interrogatories of the plaintiff, that the voyage, as far as he knew, was fair and lawful; that the vessel was regularly cleared out at Middletown; and he knew nothing of any illicit transactions on the voyage; and that she was not engaged in any illicit trade while he commanded her (which was during the voyage), with any power or powers. About *Dec. 25, 1817, Thomas Francis, a British subject, being then supercargo, the ship while standing off and on the port of St. Johns, in Antigua, to try the market, was seized and taken posseision of, with all her papers, by His Britannic Majesty's ship Antelope; in consequence of which, the voyage was broken up, and the ship and cargo lost to the plaintiff. The vessel being libeled in the Court of Vice-Admiralty at Antigua, the supercargo intended to make a defense; but being misinformed as to the time and place of hearing, the attempt failed. He went to the Court House; but was told on his arrival, that the vessel had already been condemned at the judge's chambers. [*406

The answers to the 11th and 12th interrogatories, were objected to as inadmissible; but the objection was overruled, and the defendants excepted.

Among the ship's papers was a license to the master, obtained from the British Consul at N. Y., to complete the crew by seamen not British. All the papers having been filed in the Vice-Admiralty; and no account being given of this paper by the registrar of that court, who was examined on commission, the plaintiff (though this was objected to) was allowed to give parol evidence of its contents.

The libel and sentence of the Vice-Admiralty were proved by the defendants under a commission. By these it appeared that the ship was captured on the high seas; that she was libeled, 1. As importing goods, &c., not being a British vessel, and manned with a crew three fourths British, against the form of the British Statute. 2. As importing goods prohibited by British Statute. 3. As having been repaired, when this was not necessary, &c., at Middletown, to the amount of more than 15*s* per ton, and yet importing, &c., contrary to a British Statute. 4. As importing prohibited articles from the U. S., contrary to a British Statute. The process of monition was to appear Jan. 21, between 9 and 12 A. M., at the St. Johns. Court House. It was served by being fixed on the Court House door. Here, as before men- **407***] tioned, the *supercargo appeared; but the condemnation was at the judge's chambers. The decree recited that no claim had been interposed, and condemned the vessel and cargo as forfeited, "for a breach of some or one of the laws relating to trade and navigation."

Considerable expense was afterwards incurred by the plaintiff, in prosecuting, by his agent the supercargo, a claim before the Lords Commissioners of the British Treasury, London, for the proceeds of the ship, by whom an order was made to restore the net proceeds.

Verdict for the plaintiff for $8,000, subject to the opinion of the court, &c., on a case, with liberty to either party to turn it into a special verdict or bill of exceptions.

Mr. J. Duer, for the plaintiff:

1. The preliminary proof was sufficient, the necessity of making proof of interest being waived by the conduct of the defendants. The refusal to pay was general. Had they intended to make an objection on the ground of a defect in the preliminary proof, they should have said so. *Vos* v. *Robinson*, 9 Johns., 192.

2. The defendants failed to prove that the vessel was seized and condemned on account of an illicit and prohibited trade. This was matter of defense. The warranty was not affirmative—as that a certain course of conduct should be pursued. In such a case, I agree that compliance must be shown by the assured. It is a condition precedent. (Condy, Marsh., 346, 347; 7 Johns., 47; 2 Serg. & R., 119.) In this case, however, the *onus* lies on the underwriters. What is the meaning of this clause of warranty? I agree that the cases in Mass. would seem to give effect to a sentence founded on a mere pretense of illicit trade, but they are in opposition to the decisions of both our own courts and those of England. These require that the underwriters should show a lawful authority, in fact, to seize and condemn; not merely a seizure and condemnation on the ground of illicit trade; but that the trade was, in fact, prohibited; that an offense was, in truth, committed, which formed a legal foundation *for the forfeiture. *Johnson* v. *Ludlow*, [***408** 2 Johns. Cas., 481; S. C., 1 Cai. Cas., xxix. So in the Supreme Court of the U. S.: *Church* v. *Hubbart*, 2 Cr., 187; Condy, Marsh., 346, *note* 55. So in Pennsylvania. *Smith* v. *Del. Ins. Co.*, 3 Serg. & R., 74, 82. The seizure in question was made on the ground of a violation of the municipal regulations of England; and though, if it had been for a violation of the law of war, the court would not require proof of the authority of a public armed vessel; yet they will require it in a case which does not rest on the law of nations. They cannot take judicial notice of the local municipal regulations of foreign countries.

But, if this is to be taken as a legal condem-Nation as between the owner and the British nation, yet it is an event against which we did not warrant. The vessel was seized on the high seas by a public ship. No nation has power to pass a law giving such an authority. The plaintiff's vessel was without the jurisdiction of municipal law; and subject only to the law of nations. There being a defect in the jurisdiction of the court at Antigua, the sentence was inoperative and void. *Rose* v. *Himely*, 4 Cr., 241, 268. The only evidence of condemnation on the ground of illicit trade is the record; and in no case should this be received, even as *primâ facie* evidence, without proof that the court had jurisdiction. There is no pretense that the Court of Vice-Admiralty acted under the law of nations. The subject was not within its ordinary powers, and this court cannot see that it had jurisdiction. As a court of admiralty, it had no power to enforce a municipal regulation. Its power must depend on some local statute. None is shown. In *Rose* v. *Himely* it was deemed necessary to show the authority of the court affirmatively, to punish infractions of the municipal law. It was conceded that it could not do this as a court of admiralty; but only in the character, of an instance court; and acting in the latter character, upon pretense of a municipal offense which did not exist, the property being seized on the high seas, the condemnation was holden void. The *rec- [***409** ord is proof of what appears upon its face, not of jurisdiction. And though there be jurisdiction, if the facts set forth do not warrant a condemnation, the record cannot be received to prove a breach of the warranty. 1 Johns., 485; 2 Cr., 187; 4 *Id.*, 241; *Fitzsimmons* v. *Newport Ins. Co.*, 4 Cr., 185; Doug., 574; Condy, Marsh., 397. Where it is seen that the foreign court acts properly nothing more is required, either to show jurisdiction or the cause of condemnation. But what means have this court of inquiring into and determining a question arising out of the municipal law of another nation? In every case in the courts of the U. S., the propriety and necessity of this inquiry into jurisdiction, and the original law conferring that jurisdiction, has been admitted. (4 Cr., 268; 2 *Id.*, 189.

But suppose the court had jurisdiction both of the place and subject-matter; still we say this sentence is void for defects apparent on the face of the proceedings.

It is void for uncertainty. It does not appear what law was violated. The cause of condemnation must be substantially shown, or the sentence is not evidence. To say the contrary, would make it conclusive—an effect which all the cases in this State deny to it. If we cannot avail ourselves of the uncertainty, there is nothing which we can deny. No time is mentioned; nor does it appear that the alleged violations had any connection with the trade in which the vessel was engaged. In truth, no cause of condemnation appears upon the face of the sentence, except the default of the master to interpose a claim. The sentence passed by default. There was no trial. Such a cause is altogether inadequate. The master was not bound to interpose a claim. *Gardere* v. *Col. Ins. Co.*, 7 Johns., 514. Besides, the proceedings are, on their face, fraudulent. The parties to be affected, had neither actual nor constructive notice. I admit, that where proceedings are *in rem*, as in admiralty and revenue cases, personal notice is not necessary; but the usual course is to proceed by attachment; or at least a monition must go. This is required by the law of nations. (*Vide* Hall, Adm. Pr., **410***] *132, 133. It does not appear here that the parties had or could have had any notice. The notice which was given, was calculated and probably intended to mislead. It was to appear and show cause at the Court House, at the very hour when the vessel was condemned at the judge's chambers.

Again; all the causes of condemnation alluded to by the libel are disproved. They rest on the single fact of importation, which means bringing to some port for the purposes of sale by way of commerce. The vessel had not reached the port when she was seized.

3. In addition to a total loss, the plaintiff is entitled to recover the moneys fairly expended in suing for, and obtaining a restoration of the proceeds of the vessel. (1 Johns., 412; 7 *Id.*, 57, 412.) We do not seek to recover what was properly chargeable on the cargo.

Messrs. G. Griffin and *B. D. Ogden*, contra:

1. There was no sufficient preliminary proof of interest. We leave it to the court to say, whether the plaintiff has brought himself, on this point, within *Vos* v. *Robinson*, which he relies upon.

2. The answers of Garrick to the 11th and 12th interrogatories, should not have been admitted. These answers were general, and went both to the law and the fact. Perjury could not be assigned of them. Aside from these answers, there is no evidence against the fact of illicit trade.

3. Parol evidence ought not to have been admitted of the contents of the paper obtained from the British Consul at N. Y. The registrar should have been interrogated on the subject particularly, or an authenticated copy should have been produced.

4. The assured being a British subject, cannot recover for any act done by or under the authority of his own State. The sentence was conclusive against the whole world. Here was no want of jurisdiction in the British Government, merely because the seizure was on the high seas. A nation may enforce its municipal regulations against its own subjects, either on the high seas or within its jurisdictional limits. **411***] *The plaintiff was a British subject; the vessel insured was British: both, therefore, subject to British laws; and the vessel, sailing under a British flag, was condemned by a British court for violating those laws. A public ship has jurisdiction everywhere over the subjects and vessels of its own nation, whether out at sea or in the harbor. There is no case limiting this authority, except as to other nations; and even as to these, it may extend beyond their immediate jurisdiction. (2 Cr., 234.) The court having jurisdiction, the plaintiff cannot question its proceedings. He was a British subject, and a party to those proceedings. They are to be deemed his own act. This has repeatedly been holden of the legislative Acts and public ordinances of a government. *Conway* v. *Gray*, 10 East, 536; *Same* v. *Forbes*, *Id.*, 539; *Murray* v. *Shedden*, *Id.*, 540; *Touteng* v. *Hubbard*, 3 Bos. & P., 291, 302. He is equally a party to the judicial acts of his own government. *Mennett* v. *Bonham*, 15 East, 477; *Flindt* v. *Scott*, *Id.*, 525; *Simeon* v. *Bazett*, 2 Maule & S., 94; *Bazett* v. *Meyer*, 5 Taunt., 824; *Flindt* v. *Scott*, *Id.*, 674; *Power* v. *Whitmore*, 4 Maule & S., 141. A condemnation by one of the assured's own tribunals, is like the interruption of a voyage by his own act. It is a general rule that the act of a government is the act of each individual of that government (7 Johns., 308, 309); except where both parties litigant are subjects of the government which does the act. (*Id.*, 318.) There the rule, which is a political one relating to foreign governments, does not apply.

5. There is no evidence that the vessel had not, in fact, been guilty of the infractions of the British laws relative to trade and navigation, charged in the libel. There can be no doubt that the sentence is, *prima facie*, evidence of the facts contained in the record. (2 Johns. Cas., 457, 467; 2 Cai. Cas., 217.) These are negatived, we have seen, by nothing but the oath of the captain. But in this case, the sentence is more than *prima facie* evidence. It is conclusive upon the plaintiff, because he was a British subject. The decisions cited, holding these sentences *to be only *prima facie* [***412** evidence, do not apply to a condemnation against one who is a subject of the State which condemns. They are founded on the danger of improper influence over foreign tribunals.

Again; it is not a compliance with the warranty that the trade was not illegal; it is equally violated, if the vessel be not navigated according to law, having all necessary papers to maintain its character. *Cleveland* v. *Un. Ins. Co.*, 8 Mass., 308, 320; *Oswell* v. *Vigne*, 15 East, 70. The warranty extends to the particular adventure. *Duguet* v. *Rhinelander*, 1 Johns. Cas., 360; *Miller*, *Ins.*, 496.

The sentence is certain enough. In law, that is certain which may be made so. Take the sentence in connection with the libel, and there is sufficient cause of condemnation apparent. How far from Antigua the vessel was when seized does not appear. If she was in the limits of the port, this amounted to an importation. *Leaver* v. *Smith*, Bunb., 79; 1 Chit. Com. Law, 244, 246. But we will not insist that here was an importation in fact. It is enough that the condemnation assigns this for cause. It is conclusive upon the plaintiff, who was a party to the proceeding.

6. There was a breach of the implied war-

ranty that the vessel should be navigated and documented as a British vessel. Being described as a British ship in the policy, this amounts to a warranty of her character; and she was bound to sail, and be furnished as such in all respects, so as to maintain her character. *Goix* v. *Low*, 1 Johns. Cas., 341; *Murray* v. *U. Ins. Co.*, 2 *Id.*, 163; *Barker* v. *Phœnix Ins. Co.*, 8 Johns., 307; *Blagg* v. *N. Y. Ins. Co.*, 1 Cai., 549. Three fourths of the seamen should have been British. The excuse for having a less number was not properly certified. (1 Chit. Com. Law, 256, 257.) Nor had the vessel any papers showing her repairs to be less than 15*s* on each ton. Here are two warranties—one express, the other implied; and if they be not both complied with, the underwriters are not accountable for the loss, let **413***] it happen from what cause *it would. (Phil. Ins., 127, and the cases there cited; Park, 287.)

We have a right now to show what are the British Navigation Laws, and may use Chitty's Commercial Law as evidence. (3 Johns., 107.)

[The counsel also cited different parts of Holt's Law of Shipping, to show that the British Navigation Laws had been violated by the vessel in question.]

7. No answer or claim was put in, or defense made to the libel. The master was bound to defend. All being British, and no successful defense being made, we are bound to infer that none could have been made, through some defect in the papers. Here being no immediate right to abandon, the master was the agent of the assured only. He continued so till after the condemnation. The claim might have been interposed before the monition was returnable. It is very usual in courts of admiralty to disregard the place of return, where no claim is interposed; and though the process mention one place, to condemn at another, where the judge happens to be at the time. They do this because no opposition appears. No fraud is, therefore, imputable on that ground. It is a common thing with our own courts of admiralty.

Mr. T. A. Emmet, in reply. The Lords Commissioners restored the proceeds of the vessel. This appears by the preliminary proof, and established the national character of the vessel and the interest of the assured, for the purpose of preliminary proof. But it is evident the defendants did not mean to question the plaintiff's interest, by the general ground which they took on the demand of payment

As to the answers of Capt. Garrick, illicit trade is what every navigator is bound to know. It was right, therefore, for him to answer generally; and if gentlemen desired him to be more particular, they should have cross-examined him. This is every day's p[illegible]c[illegible]ic[illegible], where the question relates to one's ordinary and daily oc- **414***] cupations, mixed up of *law and fact. If the answers were false, they were a fair subject of indictment for perjury.

But the objection came too late. It should have been made to the interrogatories when they were settled by the judge.

The loss of the paper received from the British Consul was sufficiently shown to warrant the parol evidence. All the papers went into the Court of Vice-Admiralty; and it was the duty of the registrar, when examined on commission, to annex it to the interrogatories, if it continued with him. Not having done so, the presumption is, that it was not to be found.

As to jurisdiction; the record speaks of the high seas as the place of seizure, and the evidence is inconsistent with the case being within the jurisdiction of a municipal court.

I yet want to see the law which says that the sentence of a court is more conclusive on the subject of the country to which the court belongs, than a foreigner. Whatever a sentence *in rem* may be, it is the same as against all the world. Its effect is not tried by the parties. If conclusive against one, it must be so as to all. But suppose this to be its effect; upon what is the sentence before the court conclusive? The libel states four different causes of condemnation, all under the Navigation Laws. The sentence does not establish all or either of them. I admit, that if this had referred to the libel, it would give certainty; but it does not.

If every citizen is to be deemed a party to the acts of his own government, it does not follow that he is a party to the proceedings of all its courts. The cases cited against the plaintiff on this head, do not go beyond laws and public acts of the government itself; and, in this respect, it will be found on examining them, that they are by no means uniform; and the higher and better authority in England, is now against the doctrine even to this extent.

A judgment by default may carry the consequences of a condemnation; but it establishes no fact. (13 Johns., 205.) No monition was served, except by affixing on the door of the *Court House. There was nothing done [***415** on board the ship to bring the notice home to the master or supercargo.

Illicit trade is municipal trade; and it is not enough that there has been a condemnation for that cause; but it must be shown that there was in fact an illicit trade. The law by which the trade was prohibited, must be proved as a fact before the jury. (My argument in *Smith* v. *Elder*, 3 Johns., 109.) A foreign law is traversable, and must always be proved, just like any other fact.

We were not bound to carry about the ship, proof as to the amount of repairs. Originally, she was a British ship. *Prima facie*, she was to be deemed so in all courts, she having her register about her; and it lay with the opposite party to justify the seizure, by proving that the amount of repairs had taken away her national character. (Abb., pt. 1, ch. 2.)

There is no decision that you may not abandon immediately, on a seizure under pretense of a violation of municipal laws.

Curia, per SUTHERLAND, *J.* The defendants waived whatever imperfection there may have been in the preliminary proofs of the plaintiff's interest in the subject insured, by not putting their refusal to pay upon that ground. They declared, "that they would not settle the claim in any way;" putting their objection to pay on the merits of the case, and not any defect in the proof of the plaintiff's interest. If that ground had been taken, the defect might, and undoubtedly would have been supplied. (9 Johns., 192; 7 Johns., 315; 8 Johns., 307.)

But this point was not much insisted upon by the defendant's counsel, and is clearly incapable of being supported.

It is objected, 2d: That the answers of Capt. Garrick to the 11th and 12th interrogatories, ought not to have been admitted in evidence. The interrogatories do not form a part of the case; but it must be assumed that the answers are responsive to them; not going essentially beyond the scope of the inquiries made. If so, **416***] it appears to me the *objection comes too late. It should have been made to the interrogatories. They are settled by a judge or other officer possessing the powers of a judge, upon due notice, after a copy has been served upon the opposite party. If improper, they may be excepted to, and the exception will either be sustained or overruled by the judge; and the interrogatories modified or established accordingly. (1 Dunl. Pr., 546.) If no objection is made to the interrogatories, the information sought by them is admitted to be proper, and the answers must be considered as competent evidence by the admissions of the parties.

Even in oral examinations at *Nisi Prius*, if a party will permit questions to be put to a witness without objection, and take his chance for a favorable answer; when that answer is given, and proves adverse to his wishes, it is too late for him to object that the question ought not to have been put.

But although the answers are not to be struck out of the case as incompetent evidence, they are to be restrained in their effect to matters of fact, and not to settle questions of law. When the witness says that the voyage, as far as his knowledge went, was a fair and lawful voyage; that the vessel was regularly cleared out from Middletown; and he knew nothing of any illicit transactions on the voyage; and that she was not engaged in any illicit trade while he commanded her; he must be understood as speaking merely to the *bona fides* of the object of the voyage, and the conduct of the master; and not as determining or attempting to determine, whether the transactions which are proved to have taken place, did, in judgment of law, amount to an illicit trade, or an attempt to carry on an illicit or prohibited trade or not.

It is objected, in the 3d place, that parol evidence ought not to have been admitted of the contents of the paper obtained from the British Consul at N. Y., allowing the master to complete his crew from foreign seamen, as a sufficient number of British not being obtainable. This objection is unfounded. The paper is shown, by the testimony of Charles Francis, **417***] to have been delivered to his *brother Thomas, the supercargo of the vessel (who died in 1821), immediately before she sailed. He further testifies that the vessel sailed with it, and that it was taken possession of by the captors. The affidavit of Sayre, the seizing officer, shows that all the papers taken from the vessel were delivered to the Court of Vice-Admiralty at Antigua; and the sworn certificate of Wm. Ramsay, the registrar of that court, shows that he has returned certified copies of the papers and proceedings in that court. The paper in question not being among them, the presumption is, that it is not in the office at Antigua. This is sufficient evidence of its loss to admit parol proof of its contents.

These, however, are very subordinate points. Having disposed of them, we now proceed to the consideration of the important questions presented by the case. And, 1. It is contended that the assured, being a British subject, and his vessel having been condemned by a British court, cannot recover for an act done by or under the authority of his own State. There is a class of English cases, which hold this doctrine in relation to the legislative Acts of a government; but no case has been furnished by the counsel, and no case has been found by the court, in which the principle has been extended to the decisions of courts of justice.

In *Touteng* v. *Hubbard*, 3 Bos. & P., 291, the plaintiffs, being Swedes, and owners of a Swedish vessel, in Dec., 1800, agreed with the defendant, a British merchant, that the vessel should, with all convenient speed, sail and proceed to the Island of St. Michaels; and there receive from the agents of the defendant a cargo of fruit in boxes, return with the same to the port of London, and there deliver her cargo, at a stipulated price per box. After the vessel had proceeded from London to Ramsgate harbor, and before she could be got to sea, to wit: Jan. 15, 1801, an embargo was laid by the British Government upon all Swedish vessels; by which she was detained in port until June 19 following, when the season for shipping fruit at St. Michaels *was over. [***418**
The defendant gave notice to the plaintiffs that they need not then proceed on the voyage, as no cargo would be furnished at St. Michaels. The action was to recover damages from the defendant, for not employing the vessel according to his agreement. And it was held by the court that the action could not be sustained. Ld. Alvanley, in delivering the opinion of the court, says, the ground on which the court decide this case is, that a British merchant is not liable to answer for any damages, which the owner of a foreign vessel may sustain, from an embargo laid by the British Government on foreign ships, in the nature of reprisals and partial hostility. He concedes that a common embargo does not put an end to any contract between the parties, but is to be considered as a temporary suspension of the contract only; and admits the principle of the case of *Hadley* v. *Clarke*, 8 T. R., 259, that a general embargo is a circumstance against which it is equally competent for the parties to provide, as against the dangers of the seas; and if they do not provide for it, they must abide by the consequences of their contract. But he takes a distinction between an embargo imposed for general purposes, and an embargo directed against the vessels of a particular nation, in the nature of partial hostilities; and he says, this embargo not only partook of the nature of hostility, but it was in the nature of hostility by the Government of Great Britain, of which the defendant is a subject, where the charter-party was entered into, and in the courts of which the Swedish captain now seeks compensation. And he held that it would be defeating the object of the government, which was a species of reprisal on Sweden, to compel a British subject to indemnify a Swede against the Acts of the British Government, intended to resist the injustice of the Swedish court; and would be enabling a foreigner to defeat all the effects of the British embargo, and throw the burden

upon a British subject. In the conclusion of his opinion, he says all the cases admit, that where a party has been disabled from performing his contract by his own default, it is not competent for him to allege the circumstances **419***] by which he *was prevented, as an excuse for his omission; and he asks, may not the loss which the present plaintiffs have sustained, be considered in a political point of view, as arising from their own default? Must not every subject of the Swedish State be answerable for what we must consider an act of aggression on the part of his sovereign? Here the voyage has been defeated by an act of the British State, to which all His Majesty's subjects are parties, occasioned by an act of the Swedish court, to which all the subjects of Sweden are parties.

In *Conway* v. *Gray*, and several other cases substantially like it (10 East, 536–549), the question came before the Court of K. B., how far the citizens of a country are to be considered as participating in, and assenting to the Acts of their government, where those Acts are brought to bear upon individual contracts. They were cases arising under our embargo law of Dec. 22, 1807. Conway & Davidson, the plaintiffs in the principal case, were the consignees of J. Townsend, a merchant in N. Y., who, Dec. 23, 1807, shipped on board a vessel a quantity of wheat and peas, consigned to Conway & Davidson, at Liverpool. The embargo was first known in N. Y. Dec. 25, before the vessel sailed, by which the voyage was, of course, broken up. The plaintiffs having been advised by Townsend of the intended shipment Jan. 25, 1808, effected an insurance upon it, with the defendant, and charged the premium to the account of Townsend. As soon as the plaintiffs heard of the detention, they abandoned to the underwriters and brought their action; and the principal question was, whether the American embargo would warrant an abandonment by or on behalf of an American subject against an English underwriter. The Court of K. B. held that the plaintiffs could not recover; and Ld. Ellenborough, in delivering the opinion of the court, remarks that "in all questions arising between the subjects of different States, each is a party to the public, authoritative Acts of its own government; and on that account, a for- **420***] eign subject is as *much incapacitated from making the consequences of an Act of his own State the foundation of a claim to indemnity upon a British subject, in a British court of justice, as he would be, if such act had been done immediately and individually by such foreign subject himself. In these cases," he continues, "the foundation of the abandonment is an act of the American government. Every American subject is to be considered as a party to that act. It has virtually the concurrence and consent of all; amongst the rest, the concurrence and consent of the assured in these cases. They have, therefore, joined in a resolution, that the ship in question shall not be allowed to sail, but shall remain in their port; and is it possible for them, afterwards, to make their not sailing the foundation of an action? The party who, himself, prevents the act from being done, has no right to call upon the underwriters to indemnify him against the loss he may sustain from such act not being done."

This doctrine was reiterated in a series of cases which arose in 1812, under the system then pursued by the British Government, of granting licenses to trade with the continental powers, with most of whom they were at war.

In *Mennett* v. *Bonham*, 15 East, 477, and *Flindt* v. *Scott*, 15 East, 525, the licenses were granted to British merchants, on behalf of themselves and others. The real parties for whose benefit they were obtained, were Russian subjects, and alien enemies residing in Russia. The goods were insured in England. They were seized and condemned in a Russian port, by the Russian Government; and it was held that the Russian assured, notwithstanding the license, could not recover from a British underwriter a loss occasioned by the act of his own government; on the ground that, in judgment of law, he was a party to that act. The latter case, of *Flindt* v. *Scott*, was subsequently reversed in the Exchequer Chamber; 5 Taunt., 674; and though the doctrine which we are now considering was not formally overturned, it was spoken of by the only baron who delivered an opinion (*Baron* Thompson), in terms, which show that he did *not [***421** consider it as settled; and that it by no means received his approbation. He says, "the second objection made to the plaintiff's recovering in this case, was, that the underwriters were not answerable for this loss, because it was occasioned by the Act of the Russian Government, to which the persons interested must be supposed to have given their assent, being Russians; and in support of that position," he continues, "two cases were cited, *Touteng* v. *Hubbard* and *Conway* v. *Gray*." And after stating the circumstances of the first case, and that the question which it presented was, whether the Swedish owner acquired a right by proceeding on the voyage after the embargo was taken off, to recover the freight against a British merchant, he says, "the court determined that he had no such right; and they went further and determined, what was not then a question before them, that an insurance upon the property of a foreigner, against a loss remotely occasioned by an Act of his own State, would be illegal. It was not the main question in that case, though certainly it was so decided. The case of *Conway* v. *Gray*, proceeded, in a degree, on the authority of *Touteng* v. *Hubbard*. But these decisions," he remarks, "even supposing them to be correct, as applied to the cases in which they were made, do not affect the present case." No doubt can be entertained from these expressions, that the *Ch. Baron* meant to be understood as questioning the correctness of those decisions; and that if they had stood in the way of a reversal of the judgment then under consideration, they would have been overturned. He adverts with approbation, to the more liberal doctrine held by Ld. Ellenborough in *Usparicha* v. *Noble*, 13 East, 332.

Ld. Ellenborough himself, in the more recent case of *Simeon* v. *Bazett*, 2 Maule & S., 94, seems to have been anxious to get around, without directly subverting his previous decisions upon this point. That was the case of an insurance effected in London, upon the ship

Sophia, at and from London to any port or ports in the Baltic or Gulf of Finland, &c. 422*] The insurance was made *by the order, and on the account and risk of certain Prussian subjects, resident at Colberg, in Prussia, who were avowed to be the parties in interest. The ship sailed from London to Colberg, carrying simulated papers, as was the custom of the trade, and bearing the Swedish flag. The ship and cargo having arrived near Colberg, were seized by certain persons exercising the powers of government in Prussia, and were finally confiscated by order of the Prussian Government. Prussia had, at that time, acceded to the continental system of the Emperor of France, but was at peace with England. One would think that no case could well have been presented, which would call more loudly upon a British court for the application of the doctrine that every citizen or subject must be considered a party to the authoritative acts of his government; and that the Prussian assured, residing in the very place where the seizure and confiscation were made, would not have been permitted to make his own wrongful act, if the act of his government be his, the foundation of a claim against a British underwriter in a British court. But Ld. Ellenborough held that he was entitled to recover, on the ground that, from the well known course of the Baltic trade (all direct intercourse between those ports and Great Britain being prohibited), the peril in question must have been within the contemplation and meaning of the parties. And he thus qualifies the doctrine of the previous cases: "The exclusion of risk occasioned by the act of the assured's own government, is only an implied exclusion from the reason and fitness of the thing; which, however, may be rebutted by circumstances. As the perils occasioned by the act of the party's own government, are held to be excluded on the reason of the thing, so they may be held to be included whenever the reason of the thing requires it." If I understand this gloss, it is neither more nor less than that there is no settled rule of law upon this subject; but that each case must be decided according to the view which the court may take of its intrinsic equities. In determining the equity of such a law, I pre- 423*] sume His Lordship would *have given no weight to the circumstance that the assured, when the act of his government which is complained of took place, was in another hemisphere; or if at home, that he solemnly protested against it. This case also came before the Exchequer Chamber, upon a writ of error. (5 Taunt., 824.) The judgment was affirmed on the broad ground that it was no objection to the plaintiff's recovery that the loss happened by the act of the country of the assured. And *Ch. B.* Thomson, who again delivered the opinion of the court, pointedly disclaims being governed by the distinctions taken by Ld. Ellenborough, and explodes the whole doctrine in this emphatic manner: "This was precisely one of the points disposed of in the case of *Flindt* v. *Scott*—that the loss was by the act of the country of the assured. I very imperfectly expressed myself in that judgment, if I did not express that which the whole court certainly decided, unless I misunderstood them, that it was no objection to the plaintiff's recovery, that the loss happened by the act of the country of the assured. It was argued on, and the court certainly took it into their consideration, and we cannot hear it argued again now. It may have happened that the Court of K. B. have given judgment below for the plaintiff in this action, on a different ground; but the facts support the judgment upon our reasons."

The contract of insurance is peculiarly one of equity and good faith; and I should regret to see it subjected to so technical and fanciful a rule of construction as that which we have been considering. All the cases admit that detention by an embargo, or other act of any other government than that of the assured, is one of the perils covered by the ordinary policy, and is good ground of abandonment. That an embargo by the government of the assured is as much within the actual contemplation of the parties, as an embargo by any other government, cannot be questioned; nor that the citizens of a country have no actual participation in the acts of the government, in any sense which would make it a violation of good faith to permit them to make those acts the foundation of a claim *against a [*424 foreign underwriter. It strikes me as unworthy of the advanced intelligence of the age, and of the enlightened condition of its jurisprudence, to suffer the symmetry of so important a department of the commercial law, to be broken in upon, on the strength of a notion so purely theoretical. This is the first time, I believe, in which this question has come before an American court; and I have, for that reason, dwelt upon it longer than was necessary, for the purposes of the case which we are now deciding.

But, admitting the doctrine of Ld. Ellenborough to be sound, I am not aware that it has ever before been contended, even in argument, that every citizen of a country is a party to all the judgments pronounced by its courts. The principle has never been attempted to be extended to any other than legislative Acts, or Acts of state; such as embargoes or confiscation founded upon state ordinances.

The assured, therefore, is not so far a party to the proceedings of the court at Antigua, as to preclude him from making those proceedings, if unauthorized and illegal, the foundation of a recovery against the defendant.

I do not deem it material to determine, whether it is incumbent on the plaintiff, in the first instance, to impeach the judgment and proceedings of the court at Antigua; or whether the burden of sustaining them is imposed upon the defendants. The evidence on both sides is before the court. I apprehend, however, that the sentence of condemnation, with the accompanying proceedings, so far as they disclose the causes of condemnation, are, *prima facie*, evidence of the existence of those causes, as well as of the authority of the court to pronounce the sentence; and impose the *onus* of impeaching, either the jurisdiction of the court, or the regularity of its proceedings, or the existence of the facts upon the assumption of which the decree has been pronounced upon the opposite party.

In *Church* v. *Hubbart*, 2 Cr., 187, the policy contained a condition similar to the one in this

case, that the insurers were not to be liable for seizure by the Portuguese for illicit trade. The vessel was seized and condemned by the Goveruor of Para, professing to exercise the pow-
425*] ers *of a court of admiralty, for an attempt to carry on an illicit trade with that port; that is, for a violation of its municipal laws. The defendant there produced the decree, as evidence that the condemnation was for the cause excepted from the policy. The objection was, that the decree was not properly authenticated; and that objection was sustained by the court. But it was not denied that the decree, if properly proved, would have been evidence of the grounds of condemnation, so far as they appeared on the face of the decree. The sentences of foreign admiralty courts have always been received in our courts as *prima facie* evidence against the assured. (2 Johns. Cas., 287, 481–485.)

But the condemnation, in this case, is impeached by the plaintiff on several grounds; and,

1. It is contended that it appears from the libel that the seizure was made upon the high seas; not as prize of war, but for a violation of the Municipal Laws of Great Britain; and that the right to seize for a violation of those laws, is confined to the territorial dominions of the government making it. This opinion was expressed by *Ch. J.* Marshall; and, as he supposed, it was concurred in by a majority of the court, in *Rose* v. *Himely*, 4 Cr., 279. But the contrary doctrine was finally established by the Supreme Court of the U. S., in *Hudson* v. *Guestier*, 6 Cr., 283. The seizure was there made for a violation of a municipal regulation in relation to the Island of St. Domingo at the distance of six leagues from the island; and confessedly, of course, beyond its territorial limits or jurisdiction. The only question in the case was, whether the seizure was warranted by the law of nations; and the whole court (with the exception of the *Ch. J.*) held that it was, and overruled the case of *Rose* v. *Himely*, so far as it conflicted with that opinion. The same doctrine had been previously advanced by that court, in *Church* v. *Hubbart*, 2 Cr., 234–236, where the seizure was made five leagues from land. These authorities dispose of this objection.

426*] *But admitting the general rule to be as contended by the counsel for the plaintiff—that a seizure either of persons or property, for a breach of a municipal regulation, cannot be made beyond the territorial limits of the government making it; it applies only to persons, not citizens or subjects, and property not belonging to citizens or subjects of that government. That it is competent for the sovereign authority of a country to authorize the seizure of its citizens, or of their property, for a violation of its laws, wherever they can be found, provided the jurisdiction of other nations is not interfered with, is a proposition too clear to require support or illustration. The high seas are the common property of all nations, where each has concurrent, and none exclusive jurisdiction. The sovereign authority of any country, therefore, may arrest its own subjects, or seize their property upon the high seas, without infringing the jurisdiction, or interfering with the rights of any other country. The seizure in this case was of a British vessel, sailing under a British flag, belonging to a British subject, for a violation of British municipal regulations or Navigation Laws.

Upon either of these grounds, this objection cannot be sustained.

But it is contended, secondly, that admitting the legality of the seizure, there is no sufficient evidence that the vessel had been engaged in an illicit trade; that the court, in making the condemnation, did not act in the capacity of a court of admiralty under the laws of nations; nor was the condemnation for any violation of that law; but for a breach of the statute law of Great Britain; "of some or one of the laws relating to trade and navigation," as it is expressed in the decree of the court. That it was incumbent on the defendant, therefore, in order to sustain the decree, to prove the existence of a law condemning the trade. This objection, as far as it goes, appears to me unanswerable. The warranty in the policy, against any "damage, charge or loss which may arise in consequence of a seizure or detention for, or on account of any illicit or prohibited trade," extends only to that risk to which *such [*427
trade is by law exposed. To constitute a breach of such warranty, the seizure must be for an actual, illicit and prohibited trade. A seizure and condemnation under pretext of such trade, is not sufficient, if the trade is not, in fact, illicit. Both a seizure and illicit trade must concur; and the illicit character of the trade is not proved merely by the fact of the seizure. *Johnson* v. *Ludlow*, 1 Cai. Cas. Err., xxix.; *Graham* v. *Penna. Ins. Co.*, 1 Marsh., 347, *note*.

In *Smith* v. *Del. Ins. Co.*, 3 Serg. & R., 74, the action was upon a policy containing a warranty or exception similar to this. The vessel was seized and condemned, for a cause, as it was contended by the defendants, within the warranty or exception. *Ch. J.* Tilghman (p. 82), remarks, "to bring the case within the warranty, there must be both a seizure and an illicit or prohibited trade. It is not enough that a seizure is made on an allegation of prohibited trade. It must be proved that there was a prohibition, and that the case is within it. So in *Church* v. *Hubbart*, 2 Cr., 236, *Ch. J.* Marshall, in speaking of this warranty, says, "that the exclusion from the insurance, of the risk of illicit trade, is an exclusion only of that risk to which such trade is by law exposed, will be readily conceded. It is unquestionably limited and restrained by the terms 'illicit trade.' No seizure not justifiable under the laws and regulations established by the Crown of Portugal, for the restriction of foreign commerce, with its dependencies, can come within this part of the contract. And every seizure which is justifiable by those laws and regulations, must be deemed within it." In *Smith* v. *Del. Ins. Co.*, the condemnation was alleged to have been for a breach of the 3d and 4th articles of a decree of the Emperor Napoleon, of Aug. 6, 1807. Those articles were accordingly read upon the trial, on the part of the defendants. Whether they were read by consent, without proof, or how they were proved, does not appear; nor is it material. The material fact is, that it was deemed necessary to produce upon the trial the law under which the condemnation was made; that the *court might judge whether [*428
it authorized the condemnation or not; and they

held that it did not. In the case of *Church* v. *Hubbart*, the same course was pursued. The case states, "that the defendants, to prove that the trade was illicit, offered a copy of a law of Portugal, entitled, &c.; and to prove that the vessel was seized for illicit trade, the defendant produced a paper purporting to be a copy of the sentence of the Governor of Para, on the brig Aurora." *Ch. J.* Marshall thus states this part of that case: "To prove that The Aurora and her cargo were sequestered at Para; in conformity with the laws of Portugal, two edicts and the judgment of sequestration have been produced by the defendant in the Circuit Court." And the judgment in that case was reversed solely on the ground that those edicts and that judgment were not properly proved.

These cases seem fully to establish: 1. That to show any particular trade to be illicit, under municipal regulation, the law by which it is prohibited must be produced and proved; and 2. That it is the business of the defendant to sustain the sentence by proving the law.

In the case at bar, there was no attempt to prove any law of Great Britain prohibiting the trade in which the ship Francis was engaged when seized at Antigua. So far, therefore, as the sentence of condemnation proceeds on the ground of illicit trade, it must be deemed to have been unauthorized and illegal.

The decree itself does not specify the grounds on which the condemnation is pronounced. It merely alleges that "it is for a breach of some, or one of the laws of navigation."

The libel states four grounds on which the seizure was made: 1. For importing goods, &c., on board the vessel, she not being wholly owned by a subject of Great Britain, and navigated by a British master and three fourths British mariners. 2. For importing into Antigua certain prohibited goods, &c., of the growth, production and manufacture of Europe, &c. 3. That the ship had undergone repairs in the U.S., not necessary, by reason of extraordinary damage,
429*] &c., *exceeding 15*s.* for every ton; whereby she became an alien vessel; and being such alien vessel, imported the goods, &c., being prohibited, &c. 4. That certain enumerated articles particularly named, were imported in the vessel by way of merchandises, from one of the ports of the U. S. of A., against the form of the statute, &c.

Upon which of these causes the condemnation proceeded, it is impossible to determine. If but one cause had been alleged in the libel, the decree might be supposed to have intended to adopt and verify that. The causes assigned are, however, not only various but inconsistent. The remark is alike applicable to them all, that they make the cause of seizure a violation of some British statute; and the fact of condemnation is the only evidence, not only of the breach, but of the existence of such statutes. *Ch. J.* Marshall, in *Church* v. *Hubbart*, 2 Cr., 236, in discussing this subject, remarks, that foreign laws are well understood to be facts, which must, like other facts, be proved to exist, before they can be received in a court of justice. The principle, that the best testimony shall be required which the nature of the thing admits of; or, in other words, that no testimony shall be received which presupposes better testimony attainable by the party who offers it, applies to foreign laws, as it does to all other facts. The sanction of an oath is required for their establishment, unless they can be verified by some other such high authority, that the law respects it not less than the oath of an individual. In *Robinson* v. *Clifford*, 2 Marsh., 706 *a*, *note*, it is said: "The statute or written law of foreign countries, should be proved by the law itself. The unwritten law may be proved by witnesses." 2 Cai., 155, 163; *Delafield* v. *Hand*, 3 Johns., 310; *Smith* v. *Elder*, 3 Johns., 105; 1 P. Wms., 431; Peak, *N. P.* Cas., 18; 3 Esp., 58; 4 *Id.*, 79. This evidence is adressed to the jury, and should be given upon the trial, and not at bar.

But it is said that the description of the vessel in the policy, as the British brig, &c., is an implied warranty that *she was a British **[*430** vessel, and should carry with her the documents necessary to establish that character; and that if the warranty is false, the plaintiff cannot recover, whether that was the cause of condemnation or not.

Admitting that a description which, in time of war, will amount to a warranty of the national character of a vessel, will in time of peace amount to a warranty of her commercial character (which may admit of very serious discussion), it is a sufficient answer, that the evidence in the case clearly establishes a compliance with this implied warranty. The testimony of Charles Francis shows that the vessel, at the time of her sailing, had on board a certificate or document from the British Consul at N. Y., dispensing with the usual proportion of British seamen. This document, undoubtedly, went into the possession of the captors, with the register and other papers belonging to the ship; and removes all objection to the character of the vessel, growing out of her deficiency in British seamen.

The evidence in the case also shows that the repairs put upon the hull of the vessel at Middletown cost less than 15*s.* for each ton.

It cannot be necessary for the master of a vessel to carry with him the evidence of the amount expended upon his vessel. If the fact be, that the repairs cost less than 15*s.* per ton, he has a right to rely upon the knowledge of that fact, and to presume her national character will not be impeached, without some evidence that she has violated the Navigation Laws in that respect.

Admitting it to have been the duty of the supercargo to have appeared and interposed a claim to the vessel, his omission to do it is sufficiently accounted for. It is shown to have been owing to the irregular proceedings of the court, and not to any culpable omission on his part. He attended at the time and place appointed for trial, and was informed that the vessel had already been condemned at the judge's chambers. (7 Johns., 426, 514.)

I am, therefore, of opinion that the plaintiff is entitled to recover as for a total loss. The cases of *Watson* v. *Mar. Ins. Co.*, 7 Johns., 57; *Maggrath* v. *Church*, *1 Cai., 215; **[*431** *Jumel* v. *Mar. Ins. Co.*, 7 Johns., 425, and *M'Bride* v. *Mar. Ins. Co.*, 5 Johns., 298, seem to show that he is entitled to recover all the expenses fairly incurred in obtaining a restoration of the proceeds of the vessel, unless the freight and cargo also belonged to him; in which case those expenses would be the subject of general average in the first instance. (7 Johns., 425.)

Judgment for the plaintiff.

Affirmed—2 Wend., 64.

Insurance—Proofs of loss—Denial of liability, under policy—Waiver of defects in. Cited in—6 Paige, 585; 3 N. Y., 128; 2 Hun, 361; 16 Barb., 255; 4 T. & C., 505; 8 Daly, 423; 2 E. D. Smith, 286; 9 How. (U. S.), 405; 6 Blatchf., 249; 4 Biss., 361; 12 Allen, 394; 13 Am. Rep., 412 (36 N. J. L., 37).

Foreign laws—How proved. Cited in—6 Wend., 482; 2 Am. Rep., 209 (48 N. H., 133).

Where interrogatories not objected to, answers competent. Cited in—14 Wend., 630; 11 Barb., 107; 28 Am. Dec., 558.

Also cited in—50 N. Y., 621 (10 Am. Rep., 531); 42 N. J. L., 457.

BURT *v.* PLACE.

Maintenance—Agreement to Aid One not an Attorney, in Defending Suit, Void—Money Paid or Received on Illegal Contract Cannot be Recovered.

An agreement to aid in defending a suit, with one who is not licensed as attorney or counsel, is illegal and void for maintenance.

And where B. sold and conveyed land to P., who was not of the legal p f ssi , upon an agreement that the latter should pay part in specific articles, and part in defending a law suit before a justice; held, that the whole agreement was illegal and void; and though the latter had sold the land, and received the money for it, the former could recover nothing.

Where money, &c., is received upon, or in consequence of, an illegal contract, both parties being *in pari delicto*, it cannot be recovered back.

Citations—1 R. L., 173-4; 1 Leon., 179-80; Dy., 355 *b*; Doug., 467, 696, *n.*; 8 T. R., 575; 5 Johns., 334; 7 Johns., 440.

ASSUMPSIT for land sold, money had and received, &c., tried at the Oneida Circuit, in March, 1826, before Williams, *Circuit J.*; when a verdict was taken for the plaintiff for $296.30, subject to the opinion of this court.

At the trial it appeared that the plaintiff had, in Apr., 1822, conveyed a small parcel of land to the defendant, by deed acknowledging the receipt of $300, consideration money. But $10 were, however, in fact paid. The defendant agreed to pay the residue in specific articles, excepting $50, which he was to retain for assisting the plaintiff in defending a law suit, pending before a justice. The defendant afterwards sold the land to one Addington by deed, acknowledging the receipt of $250, as the consideration. He assisted the plaintiff in defending the suit, but was not licensed as attorney or counsel.

Several objections to the plaintiff's recovery were taken at the trial; but the only one passed upon by this court was, that the transaction was illegal; that the plaintiff's claim for either the value of the land, or the money which the defendant had received for it, was founded on an illegal agreement between the parties, a part of the consideration being for maintenance. That this vitiated the whole transaction, and the parties being *in pari delicto*, the plaintiff could not recover.

432*] **Mr. Edw. Allen*, for the plaintiff, cited Bac. Abr., Maintenance, A; 3 Cow., 649; 20 Johns., 403; 5 Johns., 489, 500; 10 Johns., 185.

Mr. S. Beardsley, contra, cited 2 Chit. Cr. Law, 234, *note, a*; 4 Bl. Com., 134, 135; *Id.*, 125; Co. Litt., 368, *b*; 5 Johns., 334; 3 T. R., 23, 456; Cowp., 200, and several other cases, going to illustrate the distinctions laid down in Cowp., 200, by Ld. Mansfield.

Curia, per SAVAGE, *Ch. J.* Maintenance being prohibited by Statute, 1 R. L., 173, 174, and a part of the consideration being, therefore, illegal; this was sufficient to vitiate the contract. (1 Leon., 170, 180; Dy., 355 *b*.)

The main question then is, can money paid or received upon an illegal contract be recovered back.

The general rule of law is, that it cannot, when it is paid upon an illegal consideration, and both parties are equally criminal. This was so laid down by Ld. Mansfield in *Smith* v. *Bromley*, Doug., 696, *note*. His language is, "if the fact is, of itself, immoral, or a violation of the general laws of public policy there, the party paying shall not have this action; for where both parties are equally criminal against such general laws the rule is, *potior est conditio defendentis*." In *Lowry* v. *Bourdieu*, Doug., 467, he said he desired it might be understood that the court held that, in all cases where money has been paid on an illegal consideration, it cannot be recovered back; except in cases of oppression, where the parties are not *in pari delicto*. In *Howson* v. *Hancock*, 8 T. R., 575, Ld. Kenyon says, "there is no case to be found where, when money has been actually paid by one of two parties to the other, upon an illegal contract, both being *participes criminis*, an action has been maintained to recover it back." This doctrine has been since repeatedly recognized; and I know of no case containing a contrary doctrine. In *Lowry* v. *Bourdieu*, Buller, *J.*, says, "there is a sound distinction between contracts executed and executory; and if an action be brought with a view *to rescind a contract, you must **[*433** do it while the contract continues executory; and then it can only be done on the terms of restoring the other party to his original situation."

In *Hunt* v. *Knickerbacker*, 5 Johns., 334, Thompson, *J.*, says, "it is a general rule of law that all contracts or agreements which have for their object, anything which is repugnant to the general policy of the common law, or contrary to the provisions of any statute, are void, and are not to be enforced." In *Mount* v. *Waite*, 7 Johns., 440, the plaintiffs were allowed to recover back a premium paid upon the insurance of lottery tickets; but Kent, *Ch. J.*, who delivered the opinion of the court, put it expressly on the ground that they committed no crime in making the contract. They violated no statute nor was the contract *malum in se*. Not so in this case. The contract was both *malum in se*, and prohibited by statute; and although it is against conscience for the defendant to keep the plaintiff's money, the court will not lend its aid to enable the latter to recover back money thus illegally paid.

It is unnecessary, therefore, to decide whether the acknowledgment by the defendant in the deed to Addington, of having received the consideration of him, is evidence of the payment of the money to him.(a)

(a) *Semb.* that it is. Thallhimer v. Brinckerhoff, *ante*, 90.

The defendant is entitled to judgment.

Judgment for the defendant.

Cited in—15 Wend., 414; Hoffm., 483; 57 N.Y., 532; 14 Barb., 450; 17 Barb., 407; 20 Barb., 437; 63 Barb., 404; 30 How. Pr., 143; 9 Bos., 127. See 2 Wend., 319; 41 Am. Dec., 584 (1 Doug. Mich., 401); 36 Am. Rep., 211 (53 Iowa, 126).

THE OVERSEERS OF THE TOWN OF BERN

v.

THE OVERSEERS OF THE TOWN OF KNOX.

Pauper—Settlement of Child.

The settlement of the child follows that of the father, if he appear to have any. If not, it follows that of the mother.

The place of a child's birth is, *prima facie*, the place of its settlement; but the presumption is done away by proof that its mother had a settlement elsewhere.

Citations—Burr. Sett. Cas., 482, No. 153; 2 Cow., 537.

ON *certiorari* from the General Sessions of the Peace of the County of Albany.

434*] *Two justices made an order removing Hannah Cotton, a pauper, from the Town of Bern, Albany Co., to the Town of Knox, in the same county; and on appeal by Knox, to the General Sessions of Albany Co., that court quashed the order; on which the Overseers of Bern brought the present *certiorari*.

On the hearing before the sessions, the Overseers of Knox (the appellants) proved that Ephraim Palmer, the pauper's maternal grandfather, was in possession of a valuable farm of about 100 acres in the the Town of Washington, Dutchess Co., about forty-nine years before the hearing. He was reputed to be the owner, and devised the land, which was worth, in his lifetime, $25 per acre. He died about the close of the Revolutionary War; had a daughter Joannah, the mother of the pauper, who married John Cotton, who, with Joannah, his wife, after her father's death, removed to, and resided in Pittstown, Rensselaer Co., about a year; and thence to Bern, in Albany Co. They lived on a farm there, where the pauper, their daughter, was born, in that part of the town which is now Knox.

Mr. P. S. Parker, for the plaintiffs in error.

Mr. J. L. Wendell, contra.

Curia, per WOODWORTH, *J.* It appears that the mother of the pauper had a settlement in Dutchess Co., in right of her father; consequently the pauper had a settlement there in right of her mother.

It is not shown that the pauper's father had any settlement. The rule is, that the settlement of the child follows that of the father, if he has any; if not, the settlement of the mother. (Burr. Sett. Cas., 482, No. 153; 2 Cow., 537.)

It is stated in the case, that Cotton, the father, lived on a farm in that part of the Town of Bern now Knox, and that the pauper was born there. These facts are of no avail; for, although the place of birth is, *prima facie*, the place of settlement, it is only so, when the settlement 435*] of *the parents is not ascertained. Here the settlement of the pauper's mother is established. It not appearing that the father had any settlement, the pauper's settlement follows that of the mother. If, indeed, the Town of Knox had failed in proving a settlement gained by either parent, the charge would have been thrown on that town, by reason of the birth.

I am of opinion that the order of the sessions be affirmed.

Order of Sessions affirmed.

THE PRESIDENT, DIRECTORS AND COMPANY OF THE BANK OF CAPE FEAR

v.

GOMEZ, Impleaded with Others.

Power of Attorney to Add One's Name, as Surety, to Pre-existing Note—Description of Note—What Sufficient.

A power of attorney to add one's name, as surety, to a pre-existing note, describing the note correctly as to the parties, the sum, and the time when payable, though it omit to mention that the note bears interest before due, is sufficient to sustain a verdict upon it against the one whose name was put there under the power. The question whether the particular note was intended, is one of identity; and may properly be submitted for determination, to the jury.

ASSUMPSIT, on a promissory note, dated Wilmn., N. C., Dec. 1819, by which one B., as principal, and the defendant and others as securities, promised to pay to the order of the plaintiffs, on or before Jan. 1, 1821, $5,000, value received, payable and negotiable at the Bank of the plaintiffs, with interest from Jan. 1, 1820. This note was signed thus: "A. L. Gomez, (the defendant) by Lewis Gomez, atty," after the other makers in their own hand.

Gomez, the defendant, alone, was arrested, and appeared in this suit.

Plea, *non assumpsit.*

The cause was tried at the N. Y. Circuit, July 1, 1824, before Edwards, *Circuit J.*

At the trial, the plaintiffs proved a power of attorney, dated Feb. 22, 1820, signed and sealed by the defendant, authorizing his brother, L. Gomez, "to sign a note for five thousand dollars ($5,000), payable to the President, Directors and Company of the Bank of Cape Fear, of which J. F. B., &c. (naming the makers not arrested), are joint makers or drawers; also another note for five thousand five hundred dollars ($5,500), payable as above, and of which, J. F. B., &c. (other persons), are joint makers, *both of said notes payable on the [*436 1st day of January, 1821;" and that the defendant's name was subscribed to the note, sometime between Feb. 22, 1820, and Mar. 8, of the same year.

The plaintiffs then admitting a payment of $2,000, rested their cause.

The defendant moved for a nonsuit, because the note was signed by the attorney of the defendant; whereas, the power produced did not authorize such signature; that the power was simply to sign a note for $5,000, &c., without saying that it bore interest before due; whereas, the note signed bore interest from Jan. 1, 1820. The note in question was, therefore, not the one intended by the power.

The judge overruled the motion, and left it to the jury to say whether the note in evidence was the one intended by the power. The defendant excepted. The jury found for the plaintiffs.

In behalf of the defendant, a motion was now made for a new trial, on the ground that the power did not warrant the signature, and that the question submitted to the jury was improper for them.

Mr. J. Oakley, Jr., for the defendant. The attorney acted under a special and limited power; Paley, Ag., 2; and could not bind his principal by any act beyond the scope of his authority. *Fenn* v. *Harrison*, 3 T. R., 757; S. C. 4 *Id.*, 177. In pursuance of this principle, it has been decided, that a power to act for one as executrix, will not authorize the acceptance of bills to charge her in her own right, though for debts due from her testator. *Gardiner* v. *Baille*, 6 T. R., 591. An authority to sign a note payable at 6 months, will not extend to a note for 60 days. *Batty* v. *Carswell*, 2 Johns., 48. The same principle has been repeatedly recognized by this court. (7 Johns., 394; 15 *Id.*, 54.) And where an agent exceeds his power in any one particular, his acts are wholly void. They shall not bind the principal *pro tanto*. *Roe* v. *Prideaux*, 10 East, 158; *Jackson* v. *Huntley*, 5 Johns., 59, per *Cur.*, S. P.

437*] *This strictness of construction is, especially, applicable in favor of sureties. A bond that a clerk shall serve faithfully, and account for all money, &c., to the obligee and his executors, does not extend to money received by the clerk while in the employment of the executors, who continued the very business of their testator. *Barker* v. *Parker*, 1 T. R., 287. A promise to a house in trade, consisting of three, to pay for goods to be furnished to another, is confined to the very promisees; and cannot be enforced for goods furnished after one has withdrawn from the firm. *Myers* v. *Edge*, 7 T. R., 250. Nor will a promise to pay one for goods, bind the promisor to pay him for goods furnished by another on the promisee's request, and on his responsibility. *Walsh* v. *Bailie*, 10 Johns., 180.

The jury had nothing to do with the question. The objection raised related to the execution of a special power; and involved a point of law merely.

Messrs. D. B. Ogden and *J. O. Hoffman*, contra. We do not deny the general principle of law, that a special power must be strictly followed. But we do deny that either the general principle, or the authorities by which the counsel for the defendant has illustrated it, are applicable to the case before the court. This is not a power to execute a new note; but to sign one already in existence; and the only question which could arise was, whether the note in question was the one intended by the power. In other words, it was a mere question of identity; of correspondence in certain points of fact, or description; and being so, the judge had nothing to do with it, except to submit it, as he did, to the jury. The defendant took on himself a knowledge of all the circumstances in relation to the note. There was no other note in existence which corresponded in any one particular; nor was this pretended.

Mr. T. J. Oakley, in reply. There was nothing in evidence beside the power and the note. Their existence was not questioned; and there

438*] was, therefore, not a single fact to *be passed upon by the jury. The whole was a question of construction upon two written instruments. True, in all cases of the execution of a power, the question is, in a measure, one of identity, between the act intended and the act done; but it ceases to be a question for the jury, when every fact is conceded. The intent must be drawn from the written power. This is purely a question of law. There was a plain variance, and a substantial one, between the note and the power; and if a court of law are satisfied that the note in question was intended, they can give no relief. Such a mistake cannot be rectified short of a court of chancery.

Curia, per SUTHERLAND, *J.* The judge properly refused to nonsuit the plaintiffs. It is apparent, on the face of the power of attorney from the defendant to his brother Lewis, that he intended to authorize him to sign his name to a pre-existing note. It is, "to sign a note for $5,000, payable to the President, Directors and Company of the Bank of Cape Fear, of which J. T. B., and others, are joint makers or drawers, payable on the 1st day of January, 1821." The note is not to be made payable; but it is payable. J. T. B. and others are not to be joint makers, or drawers; but they are joint makers, or drawers. The note is not to be made payable on the 1st of January, 1821; but it is payable on that day. This is evidently intended as a general description or designation of a note, which the defendant knew to have been drawn; and to require only the signature of his name to render it perfect. He must, therefore, have been presumed to know the contents of the note; and to have described its several characteristics by way of designation only. The description is accurate, as far as it goes. It seems to me, then, to have been a question of identity merely, as to the note intended; and that was a question of fact exclusively for the jury. Whether the power of attorney would have authorized the making of a new note, like the one on which this suit is brought, is a distinct question, which I conceive does not arise in the ease. The jury have found that this *was the note intended by the [*439 power; and I think the evidence justifies their conclusion. But whether it does or not, is not material upon this application. It is founded on an exception to the opinion of the judge, in refusing to nonsuit the plaintiffs; and not on the ground that the verdict is against evidence. A new trial must be denied.

New trial denied.

FORT *v.* SMALLEY AND RATMOUR.

Practice—Replevin—Non Pros.

A defendant in replevin, whether sued by plaint or writ, may *non pros.* the plaintiff.

But it is error, if it appear on the record, that the *non pros.* was of the same term with the return of the process.

Citations—1 R. L., 91, 345; 2 Archb. Pr., 68.

ON ERROR from the Madison C. P. The action below was replevin by Fort against Smalley and Ratmour.

The proceedings were by plaint. The record contained a *placita* of June 15, 1824. It then stated that Smalley and Ratmour were summoned to appear, and did appear in the C. P. on the same June 15; and that "Fort does not further prosecute his bill or action of replevin," &c. Then judgment for the defendants for costs. The record was signed Oct. 16, 1824.

Mr. J. A. Spencer, for the plaintiff in error.

Mr. G. C. Bronson, contra.

Curia, per SAVAGE, *Ch. J.* There are two questions to be decided: 1. Can a plaintiff in replevin be *non prossed?* 2. If he can, is not the judgment premature, being on the return of the plaint?

The first point was considered at the last term (*vide ante*, 43), on a motion for a *mandamus* to vacate a rule made by the court below in this cause; and we see no reason to change the opinion we then expressed. By the Statute, 1 R. L., 91, two modes of proceeding, by writ and by p[illegible], are authorized: the plaint to be returned to the next C. P.; "and the like proceedings shall thereupon be had, in the same court, as may, or ought to be had upon a writ of replevin."

440*] *The 11th section of the Act concerning Costs, 1 R. L., 345, provides, that where any person shall sue out of any court, any process against any person, who shall be imprisoned on the same, or put in bail, or cause his appearance to be entered, if the plaintiff shall not declare before the end of the next term, the court may adjudge costs to the defendant. The judgment of *non pros.* is not mentioned by name; but, by the practice of the courts, that judgment is rendered for not declaring; and if a plaint is to be considered process within the meaning of the Act, costs may be awarded in that case. If a plaint is not technically process, still the same result will follow, as, by the Act concerning Replevin, the same proceedings are to be had upon a plaint, as upon a writ of replevin.

According to the English practice, the action is commenced either by writ or plaint, as with us. There, if the defendant wish to expedite the plaintiff, he must enter his appearance and rule the plaintiff to declare. If he do not, the defendant may sign judgment of *non pros.* (2 Archb. Pr., 68.) No distinction is made, whether the suit be commenced by writ or by plaint. There too, as here, the plaintiff, before he executes a plaint, takes a bond with sureties. But that makes no difference as to the mode of conducting the suit.

Whether, therefore, we follow the English practice, or look solely at our own statute, I think it is regular to enter a judgment of *non pros.*, in replevin, as in other actions. But, by the record in this case, the judgment seems to be entered at the return of the process. This is premature and erroneous, and the judgment must be reversed for this cause.

Judgment reversed.

Cited in—6 How. Pr., 51.

441*] *MURRAY *v.* MUMFORD.

Partnership—Right of Surviving Partner to Debts, Choses, Books and Other Evidences of Debt—Also in Case of Dissolution in Lifetime of Deceased Partner—Surviving Partner Liable to Account—Effect of Dissolution Generally.

On the death of one partner, all the debts, and other choses in action, with the books and evidences of debt, as incidents, survive, and belong exclusively to the surviving partner, who must collect debts, and is liable to suits for debts in his own name alone; subject, however, to account for the partnership property to the representatives of the deceased partner.

And so, though the partnership be dissolved by mutual consent, during the lifetime of the deceased partner.

And, in either case, the survivor may maintain detinue against the representatives of the deceased partner, for the books of account, and other evidences of debt.

The dissolution of a partnership by mutual consent, does not, *ipso facto*, render the partners mere tenants in common of the books and other choses in action belonging to the firm.

The partnership still continues, for the purpose of collecting and paying debts, with all the incidents belonging to that relation.

Citations—11 Ves., 5; 16 Ves., 57; 1 Swanston, 480, 507, *n. a;* 15 Ves., 227; 1 Taunt., 104; 1 East, 368; 1 Mont. on Partn., 17, *n.;* Gow. on Partn., 285, 157; 7 Mass., 257; 1 Dall., 248; 2 Dall., 65; 5 Serg. & R., 86; 1 Ld. Raym., 340; Johns. Dig. Partn., IV.; Watson on Partn., 364; Salk., 444.

DETINUE, for certain books of account; tried at the N. Y. Circuit, Apr. 15, 1824, before Edwards, *Circuit J.*,

When it appeared that Murray, the plaintiff, and one J.P. Mumford, were partners in trade, under the firm of Murray & Mumford. That their partnership was dissolved in 1806, by mutual consent, Mumford retaining possession of the books of account and choses in action belonging to the firm, for the purpose of settling the partnership concerns. He subsequently died, and this action was brought by the plaintiff, as surviving partner, to recover possession of the books belonging to the firm. They were admitted at the trial, to be in possession of the defendant, the administrator of J. P. Mumford; but,

The judge nonsuited the plaintiff, on the ground that, by the dissolution of the partnership, before the death of Mumford, the partners became tenants in common of the books; and that, therefore, the plaintiff was not entitled, as survivor, to the exclusive possession of them.

The plaintiff excepted; and a motion was now made, on the bill of exceptions, to set aside the nonsuit, and for a new trial.

Messrs. H. D. Sedgwick and *R. Sedgwick*, for the plaintiff, cited *Wallace* v. *Fitzsimmons*, 1 Dal., 248, 250; *M'Cartey* v. *Nixon*, 2 Dall., 65, *note*, and Gow. Part., Am. ed., 312.

Mr. J. Bulkley, contra, cited 1 East, 367; *Id.*, 366, *note;* 1 Ld. Raym., 340; 1 Madd. Ch., 177; 1 Ves., Sr., 242, 243; 5 Ves., Jr., 539; 8 Vin. Abr., 25.

Curia*, per SUTHERLAND, *J.* A dis- [*442** solution of a partnership does not, I apprehend, *ipso facto*, destroy the joint tenancy of the partners in the partnership property, and create a tenancy in common. They are still partners, for the purpose of settling the partnership concerns; and until that is effected. For that purpose, the partnership may be said still to continue, with all the incidents belonging to that relation. (11 Ves., 5; 16 Ves., 57; 1 Swanston, 480, 507, *note a;* 15 Ves., 227.) In *Wood* v. *Braddick*, 1 Taunt., 104, Heath, *J.*, says: "It is a very clear proposition, that when a partnership is dissolved, it is not dissolved with regard to things past, but only with regard to things future."

Suppose, which is alleged to be the case, that

at the time of Mumford's death, there were still debts due to and from the firm; could the representatives of Mumford sue, or be sued with the surviving partner for those debts? Most clearly not. The action must be brought by and against the surviving partner alone. The case of *Smith* v. *Stokes*, 1 East, 363, relied on by the defendant's counsel, is entirely different from this, and depending upon a different principle. That was an action of trover brought by the plaintiffs, as assignees of one Richardson, a bankrupt. Richardson and one Strickland were partners in trade. Jan. 29, 1800, Richardson committed an act of bankruptcy. On the 31st of the same month, the goods for which the action was brought, being partnership property, were received by the defendant, Stokes. Feb. 8, a commission of bankruptcy issued against Richardson. On the 14th of the same month, Strickland, the other partner, died, making Stokes, the defendant, his executor. Mar. 7, the commissioners, under the commission of bankruptcy against Richardson, executed an assignment of his effects to the plaintiffs, who brought the action against the executor of the deceased partner. It was held that the action would not lie: that though the assignment under the commission was not made until after the death of Strickland; yet, when **443***] made, it took effect *by relation, from the time of the act of bankruptcy of Richardson, which was before Strickland's death; that the assignees, of course, became tenants in common by relation from that time with Strickland, in his lifetime, and, since his decease, with his representatives, of whom the defendant was one. Then the familiar principle, that one tenant in common cannot (except under special circumstances) sustain trover against another, applied. The partnership was dissolved by the act of bankruptcy, and the assignees became not partners, but tenants in common with the other partner, in the partnership property. It was the same as if the interest of the bankrupt partner had been sold upon execution, and purchased by the plaintiffs. The sale would have produced a termination of the partnership as to him, and the vendee would not have become a partner, but a tenant in common with the other partner. *Sayer* v. *Bennett*, 1 Mont. Partn., 17 *notes*; Gow Partn., 285.

This case, therefore, stands precisely as it would have done, if the partnership of Murray & Mumford had continued until Mumford's death; and it is unnecessary to cite authorities, to show that, in such a case, the surviving partner is entitled to all the choses in action, and other evidences of debt belonging to the firm. They must be collected in his name, and he is entitled to the exclusive custody and control of them. The books of account are incidents to the debts or choses in action; and whoever is entitled to the one is, of course, to the other. The right of action, in relation to all partnership demands, is transferred to the surviving partner. But he is liable to account to the representatives of the deceased partner, for his share of the partnership property. (Gow, 157; 7 Mass., 257; 1 Dall., 248; 2 Dall., 65; 5 Sergt. & R., 86; 1 Ld. Raym., 340; Johns. Dig., Partn., iv.; Watson Partn., 364; Salk., 444.)

The nonsuit must, therefore, be set aside, and a new trial be granted.

New trial granted.

Reversing—Auth. *N. P.*, 294.

Cited in—25 Wend., 357; 13 N. Y., 337; 15 N. Y., 475; 24 N. Y., 110, 574; 45 N. Y., 789; 2 Barb., 629; 4 Barb., 536; 11 Barb., 76; 25 Barb., 133; 32 Barb., 303; 1 Redf., 207; 28 Hun, 90.

---

*JACKSON, ex dem. WOODRUFF [*444 ET AL.,
v.
SHEPHERD.

Exhibits to be Attached to and Returned with Commission—Exception.

A deed, or other exhibit, proved under a commission, must, in general, be annexed to, and returned with the commission.

But where it is in the custody of the law; *e. g.*, being a deed of a military lot, deposited with the clerk of the County of Cayuga, and forming part of the records of that county; annexing a copy is sufficient, and the exhibit may be produced on the trial, separate from the commission.

Citations—1 R. L., 520, sec. 11; 20 Johns., 361.

EJECTMENT, for part of a military lot, in Cicero, Onondaga Co.; tried at the circuit in that county, Mar. 1826, before Throop, *Circuit J.*

At the trial, in the course of the plaintiff's evidence, it became necessary for him to prove a deed deposited in, and belonging to the clerk's office of the County of Cayuga, pursuant to statute. The execution of this deed was proved under a commission executed in Conn. The clerk of Cayuga attended with, and exhibited the deed before the commissioners; and a copy of the deed was annexed to the commission, but not the original. The latter was, however, produced at the trial.

But because the original was not annexed, the judge, at the circuit, rejected the evidence of its execution; and the plaintiff was nonsuited, for the defect which such want of proof occasioned in his chain of title.

A motion was now made, in behalf of the plaintiff, to set aside the nonsuit, and for a new trial.

Mr. G. C. Bronson, for the motion.

Mr. C. P. Kirkland, contra.

Curia, per SAVAGE, *Ch. J.* The Act regulating the Execution of Commissions, 1 R. L., 520, sec. 11, requires that all exhibits produced to the commissioners, and proved by any witness, shall be annexed to the commission, and returned to the court, closed up and under the seals of two or more of the commissioners. In *Jackson* v. *Hobby*, 20 Johns., 361, Platt, *J.*, who delivered the opinion of the court, says of this Act, "when a statute makes innovations on the common law rules of evidence, its positive requirements must be strictly complied with." But in this case, a literal compliance was impossible. The exhibit produced, was a record of Cayuga Co.; not *subject to the con- [*445 trol of the party or commissioners. Everything possible was done to identify the paper; and no doubt can exist that the same deed was produced in court, which was proved before the commissioners. We think the peculiar circumstances of this case form an exception to the rule, as laid down in *Jackson* v. *Hobby*. The nonsuit must, therefore, be set aside; and a new trial granted.

New trial granted.

Cited in—9 Bos., 647.

GALE v. NIXON AND NIXON.

Assumpsit—*When it Lies on Contract for Sale of Lands—Written Recognition of Contract, Void Under Statute of Frauds, Makes it Binding—Performance—Tender of Deed.*

Semble, that a contract for the sale of lands, signed and sealed by the vendor only, and delivered to, and accepted by the vendee; and which purports to contain, on the part of the latter, a covenant to pay the consideration money, may be enforced against the latter by an action of *assumpsit*.

And where such a contract was recognized and ratified on the part of the vendees, by an indorsement under their hands and seals; held, that this was a sufficient signing to take the case out of the Statute of Frauds.

The indorsement not containing, in itself, or amounting, when taken in connection with the original contract, to a covenant to pay, and the vendor having tendered a conveyance; held, that he might maintain *indebitatus assumpsit* for the consideration money.

But if the indorsement had amounted to a covenant to pay, the action must have been covenant or debt.

The covenant by the vendor, was to convey within two years from the date; and the contract purported to contain a covenant, on the part of the vendees, to pay on receiving the conveyance. The latter took immediate possession, pursuant to another covenant in the contract on the part of the vendor; and by an arrangement between the parties and A., part of the premises were conveyed to the vendees by A., within the two years, A. having title; but the time had elapsed when the conveyance for the residue was tendered; and for that reason the vendee refused to receive the conveyance; yet, held, that the contract was not rescinded; and that the vendees were liable in *indebitatus assumpsit* for the consideration money.

To avoid this, the vendees should have redelivered possession, and rescinded the contract *in toto*.

To warrant an action of covenant, the contract must be sealed by the party or his attorney. A mere recognition of the contract, though under seal, will not sustain the action.

A written recognition of a contract, void by the Statute of Frauds, though after it is entered into, will make it binding.

Citations—1 Eq. Cas. Abr., 21, pl. 10; 1 Powell on Cont., 286; 3 Johns. Cas., 60; 2 Cai., 120; 1 Fonbl., 165, 166; Rob. on Frauds, 121; 3 Atk., 503; 3 Bro. Ch., 318; 1 Ves., 6; 9 Ves., 355; 1 Com. on Cont., 109, 110.

ON error from the C. P. of Tioga. The action in the court below was *indebitatus assumpsit* by the plaintiff against the defendants. The declaration contained counts for lands bargained, and sold; for lands bargained and sold and possession given; and lands sold and conveyed; with the money counts. Plea, the general issue.

On the trial in the court below, the plaintiff relied on articles of agreement signed and sealed by the plaintiff only, and delivered to, and accepted by the defendants, dated Apr. 14, 1821. These articles purported to be by **446***] *both parties; naming the plaintiff as of one part; and the defendants, W. & G. Nixon, as of the other. The plaintiff, for the consideration of $300 to him paid, and of $500 to be paid, as thereinafter mentioned, covenanted to convey, within two years, at his own costs and charges, two described parcels of land, of 60 and 80 acres, to the defendants in fee; and the defendants covenanted to pay the plaintiff, on the execution of the conveyance, $500. It was also agreed, that the defendants might take immediate possession of the premises, and continue so in possession, taking the profits, till the conveyance should be executed. On the articles, was an indorsement dated May 31, 1822, under the hand and seal of J. & W. Nixon, stating that they had, on the part of W. & G. Nixon, the defendants, with the consent of the plaintiff, entered into an arrangement with T. Astley, for the purchase of one of the described parcels (the 80 acre lot), and given their bond to Astley, for the balance on that lot, $391.42; and that they had taken Astley's bond to them for a deed; and that they did thereby discharge the plaintiff from so much of his agreement as bound him to convey this described parcel. Afterwards, the defendants paid this balance to Astley, who owned the 80 acre lot, and took a deed of him, within two years from the date of the articles. The payment to and conveyance by Astley, were pursuant to the agreement and understanding of both the parties to this suit, who agreed that the payment of the $391.42 should apply on the articles between them. A few weeks after the date of the articles, the defendants took possession of both parcels, and remained in possession up to the time of the trial. The plaintiff had caused a deed with warranty to be tendered to the defendants, for the 60 acre lot, before suit brought in the court below, but more than two years from the date of the articles. This deed was produced ready for them, at the trial.

The defendants moved the court below for a nonsuit, on these grounds: 1. That the articles were not signed by the defendants. 2. They being sealed, the action should have been covenant. The contract of the plaintiff, *not having been fulfilled, there was [***447** no express or implied promise to pay. 3. For the 80 acres, a deed was received from Astley, before the contract expired; and the deed for the 60 acre lot was not tendered till after the contract had expired.

The motion was granted, and the plaintiff excepted.

Mr. E. Dana, for the plaintiff in error. 1. Part performance, as payment, and taking possession, removes the objection arising from the Statute of Frauds, though the vendor only sign the contract, if it be delivered to the purchaser. (Str., 783; 1 Com. Cont., 80; 3 Johns. Cas., 65; 2 Cai., 120.) 2. The defendants, by the indorsement, ratified the original agreement. It is equivalent to signing. Yet, as it contained no express covenant to pay, covenant will not lie. *Assumpsit* is the proper action. 3. If the defendants had a right to rescind, they have not exercised that right. To do so, they should have offered to reinstate the plaintiff by a surrender of possession, and a conveyance of the 80 acres.

The plaintiff is without remedy, unless he can recover in this form of action. He cannot recover back the land conveyed.

Mr. A. Collins, contra. The contract was within the Statute of Frauds, 1 R. L., 78, sec. 10. The signature indorsed was long after the date of the articles. If any action will lie, it is covenant. The covenant to pay was dependent. (10 Johns., 266.) The tender of the deed at the day was a condition precedent, and the time having elapsed before the tender, all remedy was forfeited. The declaration was for lands sold and conveyed, but the defendant never accepted a conveyance. There was, then, a variance between the declaration and proof. Acceptance of a deed is essential to its validity. (1 Johns. Cas., 114 ; 12 Johns., 418.) No title having vested, there was nothing to raise an implied *assumpsit* as for land sold. *Assumpsit* will not lie for lands bargained and sold, but not conveyed. The plaintiff's remedy is, to recover back the land.

448*] **Curia*, per SUTHERLAND, *J.* The plaintiff was nonsuited at the trial, his right to recover being objected to on three grounds:

1. That the contract was within the Statute of Frauds, not being signed by the defendants.
2. That if it was a valid contract, it being sealed, the action should have been covenant.
3. That the deed not having been tendered by the plaintiff, until after the time stipulated, and the contract, therefore, not having been fulfilled on his part, there could be no implied promise, on the part of the defendants, to pay.

The article of agreement contains a perfect contract between the parties. It specified particularly what was to be done by each party. It was sealed by the plaintiff, and delivered to the defendants, who took possession of the land under it ; and the only objection to it is, that it was not signed by the defendants.

It is not necessary, in this case, to decide whether the action could be sustained merely upon the signature of the plaintiff to the contract, and the acceptance of it, together with the possession of the land, by the defendants, though I am inclined to think that it could. 1 Eq. Cas. Abr., 21, pl. 10 ; 1 Pow. Cont., 286 ; *Ballard* v. *Walker*, 3 Johns. Cas., 60 ; *Roget* v. *Merritt*, 2 Cai., 120, per Spencer, *J.;* 1 Foubl., 165, 166.

But the indorsement on the back of the contract, signed by both of the defendants, is clearly sufficient to take the case out of the statute, although made at a subsequent period. It is a full and complete recognition of the contract. It releases the plaintiff from the performance of one part of it. It is not necessary that the identical agreement should be signed ; but if it is acknowledged by any other instrument duly signed, it is sufficient. Rob. Frauds, 121 ; *Welford* v. *Beazly*, 3 Atk., 503 ; 3 Bro. Ch., 318 ; 1 Ves., 6 ; 9 Ves., 355 ; 1 Com. Cont., 109, 110.

Assumpsit was the proper form of action. Covenant will lie only where the instrument is actually signed and sealed by the party, **449***] or by his authority. A recognition *of the contract, though in writing and under seal, will not make it a covenant. If the instrument by which the original contract is admitted, contain, in itself, a specification of the terms, and consideration of the contract, an action perhaps might be sustained upon that ; and in such case, if it was under seal, the action must be either debt or covenant.

Under the circumstances of this case, it is not material that the deed was not tendered on the day fixed by the contract. The defendants were in possession of the land. They had, by a mutual arrangement between the parties, taken a deed from Astley for the largest parcel. They do not offer to deliver up possession of the land, and rescind the contract ; but seek to retain the land, and avoid paying the stipulated price. This they cannot do. They must either avoid the contract *in toto*, or else perform.

The plaintiff was improperly nonsuited, and the judgment must be reversed.

Judgment reversed.

Cited in—9 Wend., 618 ; 5 N. Y., 245 ; 28 N. Y., 355 ; 34 N. Y., 109 ; 1 Lans., 211 ; 1 Hun, 248 ; 4 T. & C., 32, *n.* ; 30 Barb., 223 ; 35 Barb., 78 ; 52 Barb., 486 ; 4 T. & C., 32, 33 ; 8 Abb. N. S., 424 ; 4 Rob., 255, 404 ; 12 How. U. S., 207 ; 14 How. U. S., 456 ; 22 Am. Rep., 579 (66 Me., 337) ; 49 Am. Dec., 767 (20 Vt., 118).

NORRIS *v.* BADGER & CALDWELL.

Action by Indorsee Against Indorsers—Intermediate Indorser May Sue Prior Indorser Without Showing Payment — Possession of Note Prima Facie *Evidence of Payment—Pleading—Evidence of Previous Incumbrances Admitted on Issue as to Sufficiency of Certain Property to Satisfy a Judgment—Parol—Variance.*

In a suit by indorsee against indorsers, the bill of particulars stated the indorsement in blank. This was filled up on the trial. Held, no variance.

One issue was on the sufficiency of G.'s property to satisfy a certain judgment and execution. Held, that the amount of previous incumbrances on the same property, was within the issue, and might be inquired of on the trial.

The party interested to show the insufficiency of the property was allowed to give parol evidence of judgments, &c., on cross-examining a witness introdueed by the opposite party, though the latter objected to this, and excepted, taking a bill of exceptions. The same bill stated that previous incumbrances, sufficient to reduce the value of the property to nothing, were afterwards duly proved by documental evidence. Held, on motion for a new trial, that though the parol evidence was improper, a new trial should not be granted ; that the jury could not have been misled by that evidence ; that, by the party going into documental evidence, he waived that by parol ; and, therefore, no error.

Semb. it would be otherwise, where the parol evidence might possibly have misled the jury, and had not been waived.

NOTE.—*Negotiable paper.* 1. *Presumption of payment.* 2. *Filling of blank indorsement.* 3. *Striking out special indorsement.*

1. *The possession of negotiable paper, by one bound to pay it*, is presumptive evidence of payment by him. Dugan v. U. S., 3 Wheat., 172 ; Mauran v. Lamb, 7 Cow., 174 ; Dollfus v. Frosch, 1 Den., 367 ; Dean v. Hewit, 5 Wend., 257 ; Baring v. Clark, 19 Pick., 220 ; Northampton Bank v. Pepoon, 11 Mass., 288 ; Green v. Jackson, 15 Me., 136 ; Brinkley v. Going, 1 Breese, 288 ; Campbell v. Humphries, 2 Scam., 478 ; Hunter v. Kibbe, 5 McLean, 279 ; Bank of U. S., v. U. S., 2 How., 711; Pfiel v. Vanbatenberg, 2 Camp., 439 ; Brembridge v. Osborne, 1 Stark., 374 ; Egg v. Barnett, 3 Esp., 196 ; see, also, Fellows v. Kress, 5 Blackf., 536 ; 2 Pars. Notes & B., 220 ; 2 Dan. Neg. Inst., sec. 1227 ; Story on Bills Sec., 452.

2. *Under an indorsement in blank*, the holder may fill in his own name before bringing suit, or at the trial. Lovell v. Evertson, 11 Johns., 52 ; Olcott v. Rathbone, 5 Wend., 490 ; Pickett v. Stewart, 12 Ala., 202 ; Cope v. Daniel, 9 Dana, 415 ; Fairfield v. Adams, 16 Pick., 381 ; Hance v. Miller, 21 Ill., 636 ; Croskey v. Skinner, 44 Ill., 321 ; Kiersted v. Rogers, 6 Harr. & J., 282 ; Whitten v. Hayden, 91 Mass. (9 Allen), 408.

The filling of the blank is unnecessary, however. Poorman v. Mills, 35 Cal., 118 ; Habersham v. Lehman, 63 Ga., 383.

3. *Striking out special indorsement.* In an action on negotiable paper a special indorsement may be stricken out. Bank of Utica v. Smith, 18 Johns., 230, *note* ; Mottram v. Mills, 1 Sandf., 37, and authorities cited ; Hagrous v. Lahens, 3 Sandf., 213 ; Manhattan Co. v. Reynolds, 2 Hill, 140.

An intermediate indorser of a note may sue a previous indorser, without showing actual payment by such intermediate indorser, to any subsequent indorsee, by a receipt; and without showing an indorsement back to such intermediate indorser. Possession of the note, and producing it in court, are, *prima facie*, sufficient evidence of payment, and he may recover, though his name still remain on the note.

Citations—1 Ld. Raym., 742; 7 Cr., 159; 3 Wh., 173, 183; 3 Johns. Cas., 263; 11 Johns., 53; 16 Johns. 73, 92; 1 Cow., 387; 17 Mass., 618; Chit. Bills, 190; 3 Cow., 621.

ASSUMPSIT; tried at the Onandaga Circuit, Mar. 20th, 1826, before Throop, *Circuit J.*

The declaration was against the defendants as joint indorsers to the plaintiff of a promis-
450*] sory note, also indorsed *by the plaintiff to the Utica Bank, made by one Elias Gumaer, dated Nov. 23, 1821, payable to the order of the defendants at the Utica Bank, 90 days after date, for $3,000. It also contained the money counts.

Plea: 1st, the general issue; and 3d, a judgment of $3,000 confessed by Gumaer to Norris, and Badger, one of the defendants, as security and indemnity to the indorsers, Feb. 18, 1822, and Oct. 27, 1823, execution issued and delivered to the sheriff, at the instance, and under the sole direction and management of the plaintiff, Norris—Gumaer then having property, which was bound and levied on, enough to satisfy it, but which was dissipated, and the debt lost through the delay and negligence of the plaintiff. Replication: that Badger, not the plaintiff, took control of the execution; that the debt was not lost by the plaintiff's negligence, &c.; that Gumaer had not sufficient property, &c., and collection could not be enforced, &c. Issue to the country.

On the usual order for a bill of particulars, the plaintiff furnished one, in which he set forth the note verbatim, as with a blank indorsement by the defendants.

On the trial, the defendants objected, that a mere blank indorsement would not carry the interest to the plaintiff; on which he filled up the indorsement in the usual form. The defendants then objected that it varied from the bill of particulars, but the objection was overruled.

The defendants then proved that the note was indorsed by both plaintiff and defendants, for the benefit of Gumaer; that the money was obtained thereon at the Bank, and applied to his use. The maker was himself sworn as a witness for the defendants; and testified, that from Oct. 27, 1823, to the Jan. next following, he had in his possession personal property to $800, and real estate worth $7,000. The plaintiff then asked him if there were not incumbrances or liens, previous to the judgment confessed. This question was objected to as improper, under the pleadings, or if admissible, that the facts inquired of, could not be established by parol. The judge overruled the objection; and the witness was allowed to
451*] *state large previous incumbrances by mortgage and judgment, and sales thereon.

The plaintiff then offered to show regularly, by records and executions, incumbrances having preference to the judgment and execution mentioned in the defendant's plea, sufficient to exhaust Gumaer's property. This was objected to, as not admissible under the pleadings; but the proof was received, and the facts proposed to be shown were fully established by exemplifications, executions, &c.

The defendants then objected that the note being an accommodation note, the plaintiff could not recover till he showed actual payment of the money by him; that showing himself in possession of the note was not enough, without having paid the money to the Bank. This objection was overruled, the judge charging that the evidence was, *prima facie*, sufficient to sustain the action. The defendants excepted to the several decisions of the judge.

Verdict for the plaintiff for $3,318.70.

Mr. N. P. Randall, for the defendants, now moved for a new trial. He said the note given in evidence was inadmissible under the bill of particulars. (1 Chit. Pl., 382.) But if admissible, being an accommodation note, the plaintiff, an intermediate indorsee, could not recover, before actual payment to the subsequent holder, the Bank. Indorsers on accommodation paper, are sureties; 16 Johns., 70; who cannot recover till they have incurred actual expenses. (8 East, 593.) The liability of the plaintiff was no more than that of the defendants, who indorsed before him. The Bank may still sue the latter. In ordinary cases, where the note is voidable for want of consideration or otherwise, the indorsee must show that he took it in the fair course of trade, and paid a valuable consideration. (1 Campb., 100.) That is not done in this case. It is not pretended that this is a note taken in the course of trade. But even if it was so taken, the plaintiff must show payment to the Bank, his indorsee, or some indorsee subsequent to him. (1 Ld. Raym., 742; 4 T. R., 714.) And this is especially so of accommodation paper. (3 Wils., *13, 346; 1 [*452
H. Bl., 640; 1 Cow., 394, per Woodworth, *J.*) When the indorser pays, he is remitted to his original rights of holder; and not till then. Before this, he is not in a situation to maintain an action. Possession of the note by the plaintiff, is not, in the case of accommodation paper, *prima facie*, evidence of payment. Indeed, it is not so in any case. *Welch* v. *Lindo*, 7 Cr., 159; *Gorgerat* v. *M'Carty*, 1 Yeates, 94.

Proof of incumbrances was inadmissible under the pleadings. The issue was on the amount of property bound by the execution; not whether there were incumbrances. The evidence offered admits the amount of property, but seeks to avoid the consequences by showing incumbrances. The replication is like one to a plea of an outstanding judgment, by an executor. Admitting the judgment, execution and lien, it should have replied the previous incumbrances specially, or any other matter in avoidance. Evidence cannot be given of matters out of the issue. (1 Phil. Ev., 131; 3 Mass., 552; 11 *Id.*, 313).

But if this evidence was admissible, there can be no doubt that the manner in which it was given, in the first place, was improper. The record evidence alone should have been received. Parol proof was clearly inadmissible. (Bull. *N. P.*, 293.)

There can be no doubt, that, if the plaintiff has lost the benefit of the judgment by his laches, this deprives him of all right to recover.

(2 Phil. Ev., 21, *note;* 7 Johns., 332; 1 Bos. & P., 422.)

Messrs. J. L. Edwards and *S. Beardsley*, contra. The variance from the bill of particulars was produced by the filling up of the blank indorsement on the trial, which is mere matter of form. It was substantially the same before, and a literal correspondence was not necessary.

The possession of the note, and its production on the trial, were *prima facie* evidence that it had been paid, if such proof was necessary. There being nothing to rebut it, the note must be taken to have been paid. (3 Johns. Cas., 5, 453*]*260, 263; Doug., 636; Chit. Bills, ed., 1821, p. 14, *note* 1, and cases cited; 3 Wh., 182, 183; 2 Dall., 147; 15 Mass., 436; 11 Johns., 53.) If the defendants had any objection founded on the original consideration, the *onus* lay with them. (Chit. Bills, old ed., 86; 2 Campb., 439, 440.) The only question is, what shall be evidence of payment? We admit, with the cases cited on the other side, that when one has indorsed a bill, and he would then sue upon a previous indorsement to himself, he must show payment. But those cases do not go to the evidence. The mere want of consideration between the original parties, is no answer. Holding the note, the plaintiff may fill up the indorsement to himself; and it does not lie with the defendants to object, though he was a mere trustee for the bank. (7 Johns., 361; 2 Campb., 339, 340; *Id.*, 5, 574; 1 Bos. & P., 648; 4 Esp., 56.)

The proof of previous liens was clearly admissible. Admit the issue to have been on the sufficiency of the property bound by the judgment or execution mentioned in the plea, how could that be determined, without looking to the amount of the previous charges on the property, which reduced it to nothing, and less than nothing?

The proof by parol was proper. It was like asking a man, "what are you worth?" In answer, he is bound to state incumbrances. But whether proper or not, was immaterial, for the defendants could not succeed in any view. They failed altogether to show any exclusive control over, or neglect concerning the execution on the plaintiff's part. Beside, the parol evidence came out collaterally, on cross-examination of the defendant's witness. It was proper, with a view to test his accuracy or credibility. If proper in any view, a new trial should not be granted; and the court will not incline to a new trial, especially when they see that the very facts inquired of from the witness were most abundantly established by documentary evidence. Indeed, this, alone, is a full answer to the point arising upon the parol evidence.

454*] *Again; the judgment confessed was a mere collateral security; and whether the plaintiff was negligent or not, makes no difference with his rights. He might entirely disregard it, and look to his indorsers in the first instance. Badger should have seen to his rights, and gone on, and collected himself.

Mr. Randall, in reply. Gentlemen argue as if this were a case upon the weight of evidence before the jury. On a bill of exceptions, we cannot look beyond the very points taken. If the parol evidence was, *per se*, improper, we must stop there; and cannot excuse its admission by other matter afterwards supplied, as may be done on a case, where the court have a discretion. That Gumaer was the defendant's witness, is no excuse for the plaintiff's proving by him what he should have shown by documents. When he takes the witness on cross-examination to an independent fact, he makes him *quoad hoc* his own witness.

Curia, per SAVAGE, *Ch. J.* The variance between the indorsement stated in the bill of particulars, and that filled up and used on the trial, was immaterial. The blank indorsement, mentioned in the bill, imported as much as if the formal words had been written over it. It is enough, that the bill and the proof agreed in substance. Beside, the note and indorsement were specially set forth in the declaration. There was no need of particulars as to these. It was necessary under the money counts only, which may be laid out of view.

There is no doubt the evidence of incumbrances was admissible. It went directly to the sufficiency of the property to satisfy the judgment.

The principal question is, whether the plaintiff was bound to show actual payment of the note, beside what was to be inferred from the fact of its being in his possession. In *Mendez* v. *Carreroon*, 1 Ld. Raym., 742, it was decided, that in an action on a bill of exchange, brought by an indorser who had been sued upon it, against the acceptor, the plaintiff must prove that he had paid the party who sued him.

*In *Welch* v. *Lindo*, 7 Cr., 159, it was [*455 held that the mere possession of a promissory note, by an indorsee who had indorsed it to another, is not sufficient evidence of his right of action against his indorser, without a reassignment or receipt from the last indorsee. But the same court who decided this case, afterwards, in *Dugan* v. *U. States*, 3 Wh., 173, 183, held, that "if a person who indorses a bill to another, whether for value or for the purpose of collection, comes again to the possession thereof, he is to be regarded, unless the contrary appears in evidence, as the *bona fide* holder and proprietor of such bill; and shall be entitled to recover thereon, notwithstanding there may be on it one or more indorsements in full, subsequent to the indorsement to him, without producing any receipt or indorsement back to him from either of such indorsees, whose names he may strike from the bill or not, as he thinks proper." The principle of this case is so precisely applicable, that I need cite no other, if it is to be received as authority. The same principle will be found running through a series of decisions in this court. (3 Johns. Cas., 263; 11 Johns., 53; 16 *Id.*, 73; 1 Cow., 387; *vide*, also, 17 Mass., 618; Chit. Bills., 190, Phil. ed., 1821.

The judge erred in receiving parol evidence of the amount of incumbrances; and this would be cause for a new trial, had it not been immediately shown by proper documentary evidence, viz.: exemplifications, &c., that the older liens on Gumaer's property greatly exceeded its value. The parol evidence was unnecessary, therefore. The verdict was fully sustained without it. Its admission might be error, had it been possible that the jury placed

any reliance upon it, or could have been misled by it; 16 Johns., 92; 3 Cow., 621; and then, this being on bill of exceptions, there should be a new trial, because the judgment we render might be reversed on error, which it is the object of this motion to guard against. Going into the documental proof, was equivalent to a waiver of the parol evidence, which takes away the error. (16 Johns., 92.) It could
456*] not possibly *have any effect; and the point, we think, cannot be regarded on writ of error. The motion for a new trial must, therefore, be denied.

New trial denied.

Cited in—1 Wend., 49; 16 Wend., 666; 21 Wend., 481; 7 Barb., 587; 1 Sandf., 42; 3 Co. R., 245; 36 Am. Dec., 119 (9 Watts, 273); 35 Am. Dec., 216 (16 La., 213).

DANIEL S. GRISWOLD
v.
SEDGWICK ET AL.

False Imprisonment—Marshal not Protected by Process, which does not, on its Face, Authorize the Arrest—Misnomer—Presumption of Continuance of Term of the U. S. Circuit Court—No Interference by Superior Courts of Law or Equity, with each other's Proceedings, because of Irregularity.

If process against the body, out of any court, do not, on its face, authorize an arrest, it is void, and will not protect any person concerned in the arrest; even the officer to whom directed.

Where Daniel S. Griswold was arrested on process of attachment, issued out of the equity side of the Circuit Court of the U. S., against Samuel S. Griswold; held, that an action of false imprisonment, lay by Daniel S. Griswold against the marshal, his deputy, and the solicitors concerned in the arrest; and this, although Daniel S. Griswold was the person intended.

Otherwise, of an execution against one by a wrong name, who appears in the suit, and omits to plead the misnomer in abatement; or, it seems, where he is known as well by the one name as the other.

It is no objection to process issued to enforce an order of the Circuit Court of the U. S., that it recites the order as having been made, on some day not appearing necessarily to be within the statute term of the court. It will be intended that the term continued to that day, unless the contrary appear, the duration of the term not being limited by statute.

Whether process issuing out of a court of equity be according to the course and practice of that court, is a question which cannot be tried collaterally, in an action at law. If it be irregular, the proper course is to move the court out of which it issued, to set it aside.

Superior courts, either of law or equity, will not interfere with each other's proceedings on the ground of irregularity.

Citations—6 T. R., 234; 8 East, 328; 2 Taunt., 400; 2 Campb., 270; 1 B. & A., 647; 1 Mass., 76; 3 Cai., 267; 3 Johns. Ch., 275; 1 Vern., 269; 1 Jac. & Walk., 636; 2 Dick., 619; 2 Str., 1218.

TRESPASS, for false imprisonment; tried at the N. Y. Circuit, Mar. 15, 1826, before Duer *Circuit J.*, when the following facts appeared:

The plaintiff, Daniel S. Griswold, was arrested under process, purporting to have been issued out of the equity side of the U. S. Circuit Court for the Southern District of N. Y., directed to the marshal of that district, commanding him to take the body of Samuel S. Griswold. The process was issued by the Messrs. Sedgwicks, two of the defendants in this suit, as solicitors and counsel for Samuel Hill; and the arrest was made by Reid, as deputy of Morris, the marshal—these latter being also defendants in this suit. As soon as the marshal discovered the mistake in the name, and before Griswold was taken to prison, he sent for the Messrs. Sedgwicks, who immediately assented to the discharge of the plaintiff, he being then present, although it was understood and admitted *that he was the [*457
person intended to be arrested on the writ or process. He was accordingly discharged; and this suit was against the defendants, the Messrs. Sedgwicks, Morris and Reid, all the parties instrumental in his arrest.

The process recited that Feb. 21, 1824, by an order made in the Circuit Court, by Wm. P. Van Ness, one of the judges of that court, in a cause there between Daniel S. Griswold, complainant, and Hill, defendant, that Griswold pay to the clerk of that court $1,200, in 10 days after notice of the order; and "whereas the said Samuel S. Griswold" had neglected to comply with the order, though more than 10 days had elapsed, it commanded the marshal to take the said Samuel S. Griswold, &c., and keep him in custody, till he should perform the order, or until the court should make order to the contrary. The process was tested Feb. 2, 1824, and returnable the first Monday of March. The plaintiff was arrested, discharged as before mentioned; and the process returned by the marshal *non est*, &c.

On this evidence, the counsel for the defendants moved for a nonsuit, which was granted by the judge, and the plaintiff excepted.

On the bill of exceptions,

Mr. H. W. Warner, for the plaintiff, now moved to set aside the nonsuit, and for a new trial. He said the plaintiff is not the person named in the precept of the writ. It is not sufficient that he was the person intended. (6 T. R., 234; 8 East, 328; 2 Taunt., 399; 2 Campb., 270; Doug., 40; 1 B. & A., 642.)

But if the plaintiff had been rightly named, it appears by the writ itself, that he was in no default under the order recited. No notice of the order is mentioned. And the writ is tested Feb. 2, at a time before the order was made. The *teste* is out of term; and the writ thus being irregular on its face, will not protect the officer, or any one concerned in its execution. Taken as a whole, the writ is unknown to the law of the land and, obviously, not necessary *for enforcing the order. The [*458
court will take notice of the practice of the Court of Chancery. (1 Chit. Pl., 224; 2 Co., 18; 15 East, 39.) This was neither an attachment nor execution. The plaintiff could not have had any sufficient notice of the order, and the court was entirely without jurisdiction. The course of proceeding on the equity side, is regulated by rules of the U. S. Supreme Court, pursuant to statute. (See Rules, 7 Wh., v—xiii.) By rule 33, where they do not apply, the English practice governs. (And *vide* 3 Wh., 213.) That practice will be found in Newland's Treatise, under the head Execution of Decrees. The parties should show the proceed-

NOTE.—*Ministerial officers*—How far protected by process. See Warner v. Shed, 10 Johns., 138, *note.* On the general subject, see Henderson v. Brown, 1 Cai., 92, *note;* Seaman v. Patten, 2 Cai., 312, *note;* Wallsworth v. M'Cullough, 10 Johns., 93, *note.*

ings to be regular, and according to the course of the court. (2 Wils,, 224.) Though it may be otherwise, where the defendant has appeared, and had a chance of defense. There, even a misnomer in the execution, will not subject the plaintiff to an action, if it follow the name in the record. (2 Str., 1218.) It will be seen by Newland, already cited, that this process could not be regular as an execution. It was equally irregular as an attachment. (1 Jac. & W., 637.) It is not an order of a circuit court. This requires the concurrence of a circuit and district judge. It was a mere order of *Judge* Van Ness, at his chambers in vacation. It does not appear for whose benefit the money was to be paid into court. The court is of a limited and special jurisdiction (5 Cr., 185), and should show their authority clearly, to issue such a writ. The jurisdiction of every court may be inquired into and impeached. (4 Cow., 294, 295.) If there be a want of jurisdiction, the process will protect nobody.

Messrs. R. Sedgwick and *Sullivan*, contra. The writ was founded upon, and authorized by the order. The plaintiff was, at first, rightly named; and the wrong name afterwards may be rejected as surplusage. On the whole face of the process, the court can see that the right man has been taken. It recites the contempt: and the *teste* is obviously a mere clerical mistake, as **459***] the court cannot help seeing. *It is plain from the writ itself. It recites that more than 10 days had elapsed from the making of the order.

As to the misnomer; admitting it to be a fatal one, the cases cited to show that false imprisonment will lie, are of *mesne* process: and even in respect to this, they are not without qualification. Suppose the defendant being misnamed, appears by his right name, as he may do (1 Bos. & P., 645), the suit may go on against him, by his true name, to judgment and execution. So, if he appear in any way, and do not plead the misnomer in abatement. (2 Str., 1218.) Clearly, in neither of these cases would false imprisonment lie. The proceedings become good *ab initio;* and in the latter case, it is settled that execution may go by the wrong name. (*Ib.*) In general, the distinction is between *mesne* and final process. A misnomer in the latter will not subject to an action for the arrest. (*Id.*, 1 Mass., 76.) The mistake is amendable. (1 Brod. & B., 188.) The process is not merely void. The U. S. Statute of Jeofails, is even broader than our own or the English. (Ing. Dig., Abatement.) If this court are, as contended, to look into the practice of the Circuit Court of the U. S., it will be seen that the writ would have been at once amended on motion there.

But this court will not look into the proceedings, with a view to see whether they were regular or irregular, void or voidable. The Circuit Court might have been continued by adjournment from its term to the *teste* day, and to a time long after the order and arrest were made. Jurisdiction will be intended till the contrary is shown. A court of equity is always open. It is not confined to particular terms, aud it has power to modify its process to suit the exigencies of each case. How is this court to know what process is held to be proper there? It is only in the absence of any practice of their own, that the English practice is to govern. How is this court to know that the English practice is not abolished in any particular case, and a new substituted? If this process had issued out of the Court of Chancery of this State, the present suit would have been arrested by injunction; upon the principle *that [***460** another have a right to, and will protect all those who act under its process; or will, at least, take the supervision of its own process, and the conduct of those who act under it, to itself. (Eden, Inj., 27; Dick., 619; 1 Jac. & W., 638.) This is right, and what every superior court insists upon. It is well settled in this court, that no suit will lie, grounded on the irregularity of process, until it is set aside on motion. *Reynolds* v. *Corp*, 3 Cai., 267. On application to set aside writs for any defect, nothing is more usual than for the court to order an amendment, without any formal cross motion for the purpose; or, if the motion be for irregularity, they will require the party moving, to stipulate that he will not bring any action. One court cannot decide on the regularity of process issuing from another court, over which it has no control, until that process is set aside. The defendants are officers; and are justified by the process. At any rate, it being in existence, never set aside or avoided in any way, they are protected against an action of false imprisonment. If liable to any action, it must be founded on an abuse of the process and should have been case, not trespass.

Curia, per SUTHERLAND, *J.* If the process, on the face of it, did not authorize the arrest of the plaintiff, then it was irregular and void as against him, and can afford no justification to any of the parties concerned in the issuing or execution of it. In such a case, it is not necessary that the process should be set aside before an action can be sustained; nor is it material out of what jurisdiction it purports to have been issued. The defendants justify the arrest of Daniel S. Griswold under an execution against Samuel S. Griswold. The execution itself may be regular; there may be no ground for setting it aside. A is arrested by the defendants, and calls upon them to show their authority for the arrest. They produce as their authority an execution, against B, issued out of the Circuit Court of the U. S. for the Southern District of N. Y. We do not question the jurisdiction of that court, nor the validity *or regularity of any of its pro- [***461** ceedings, when we decide that this is no justification for the arrest.

It is settled, by repeated adjudications, that an officer cannot justify the taking of the goods (much more the person) of A, under process against B, although it be averred that A and B are the same person, unless the party appeared and had an opportunity of pleading the misnomer in abatement; but omitted to do it. Thus in *Cole* v. *Hindson* 6 T. R., 234, the goods of Aquila Cole were taken under a *distringas* against Richard Cole. To an action of trespass brought for the taking, the defendants pleaded that the plaintiff, Aquila Cole, being indebted to two of them, they sued out against the said Aquila, by the name of Richard, a writ; and the said Aquila not appearing, &c., a *distringas* was issued, commanding the sheriff to distrain Richard Cole, meaning the said Aquila Cole,&c. Upon demurrer, the plea was held to be bad. And Ld. Kenyon remarked, the defendants were not justified in seizing the goods of Aquila Cole, under a *distringas* against Richard Cole, and that the averment in the plea, that Aquila and Richard are the same person, did not assist them, as they had not also averred that the plaintiff was known as well by one name as by the other.

So in *Shadgett* v. *Clipson*, 8 East, 328, Josiah Shadgett, the plaintiff, was arrested upon a *latitat* issued against him, wherein he was called by the name of John Shadgett. The plea averred that the writ was issued against Josiah by the name of John. This was held to be no justification to the officer who made the arrest, in an action for false imprisonment. Ld. Ellenborough says, process ought regularly to describe the party against whom it is meant to be issued; and the arrest of one person cannot be justified under a writ sued out against another.

In *Wilkes* v. *Lorck*, 2 Taunt., 400, it was held by Lawrence, *J.*, that the sheriff was liable to an action of false imprisonment, for arresting a defendant by a wrong Christian name.

462*] **Scandover* v. *Warne*, 2 Campb., 270, and *Morgans* v. *Bridges*, 1 B. & A., 647, are to the same effect.

In *Crawford* v. *Satchwell*, 2 Str., 1218, it was held that if a person sued by a wrong Christian name, omits to take advantage of the misnomer, by a plea in abatement, but suffers judgment to be entered, he shall not have an action of false imprisonment against the sheriff, for arresting him upon a *capias ad satisfaciendum*, issued upon the judgment. Ld. Kenyon, in *Cole* v. *Hindson*, already cited, adverts to this case, and says, the party had appeared in the original action, and done an act to avow that he was sued by the right name. That was also the case in *Smith* v. *Bowker*, 1 Mass., 76.

No distinction is taken, in these cases, between an arrest upon *mesne* and final process, and none is perceived by the court. In this case, the process was in the nature of an attachment, and the plaintiff has had no opportunity of taking advantage of the misnomer, by plea in abatement.

The case of *Reynolds* v. *Corp*, 3 Cai., 267, is not in collision with the cases already adverted to. Reynolds had been surrendered by his bail, and was subsequently discharged by a *supersedeas*, for want of being charged in execution in due time. A *ca. sa.* was afterwards issued upon the judgment, on which he was taken and imprisoned; for which he brought an action of false imprisonment against the plaintiff in the execution and the attorney who issued it. It was held that the action would not lie; the judgment remaining valid, and nothing appearing on the record to show that a *ca. sa.* could not regularly be issued. The court say, the process was voidable only, and not void; and nothing appearing on the face of the record or of the execution, to show that it had been issued irregularly, the plaintiff should have applied to the court, and had the writ set aside before he brought his action; that they would not decide upon its validity in that collateral way. (Per Kent, *Ch. J.*)

Thompson, *J.*, says: "I am inclined to think the execution is voidable only. It appears regular, upon the face of it; it is warranted by the judgment, and is to be avoided *by [*463 some matter *dehors* the record, and which, I think, cannot be taken advantage of in this collateral way."

In the case now before us, it is apparent on the face of the process, that it did not authorize the arrest of Daniel S. Griswold, the present plaintiff. There is no necessity, therefore, for any inquiry *dehors* the writ itself; and an action may be sustained by the plaintiff for the arrest, without having procured the writ to be set aside.

But it was also contended by the plaintiff's counsel that the order itself, in obedience to which the writ purports to have been issued and which is recited in it, was absolutely void; 1. As having been made at the chambers of the judge in vacation; and 2. As being against the settled and established mode of proceeding in such cases in the English Court of Chancery.

The first objection seems to have no foundation in fact. There is nothing on the face of the order, as recited in the writ, which shows where it was made; and it is expressly recited to have been made in the Circuit Court for the Southern District of N. Y.

But it is said that Feb. 21, when the order was made, was not a day in term, and it must, therefore, have been made at chambers. The time for the commencement of the terms of that court is fixed by law; but I am not aware that the duration of the terms is limited. Feb. 21, may, therefore, have been a day in term.

As to the other ground of objection, that the order is not in conformity to the established mode of proceeding in courts of equity, it is a sufficient answer, to say that that is a question not to be tried collaterally in an action at law. If the order was unadvisedly made, against the established practice, not only of the courts of equity in England, but of the very court in which it was made, as the objection seems to assume, application should have been made to that court, to vacate or set it aside.

The court had jurisdiction of the person of the plaintiff, and of the subject-matter in relation to which the order was made; for it was made in relation to a suit pending in that *court, in which the plaintiff was a [*464 party. The regularity of the order is not to be tried or inquired into in this court. Superior courts, either of law or equity, will not interfere with each other's proceedings, on the ground of irregularity. (3 Johns. Ch., 275.) And cases are to be found, in which courts of equity have enjoined suits at law, brought for executing the process of those courts irregularly issued. *Bailey* v. *Devereux*, 1 Vern., 269. In *Frowd* v. *Lawrence*, 1 Jac. & W., 636, an attachment had been irregularly issued, upon which the defendant was arrested. He applied to the Court of Chancery, and procured it to be set aside; and then brought his action at law for the false imprisonment. The Court of Chancery, after much deliberation and inquiry, stayed the suit at law; holding, that though the party might be entitled to compensation for the arrest, he must seek it by application to that court, and not by suit at law. The case in 1 Vern., 269, and also *May* v. *Hook*, before Ld. Bathurst, cited in *Dove* v. *Dove*, 2 Dick., 619, were relied upon as authorities for this decision. It is not necessary for us to express an opinion upon the principle assumed in these cases. They are cited merely for the purpose of showing the extent to which courts have gone, in denying the right or propriety of one court to inquire into or try the regularity of the process or proceedings of another court of equal dignity.

The process in this case was undoubtedly intended as an attachment for a contempt in disobeying a previous order of the court. It recites that previous order, and that the plaintiff had neglected to comply with it; and, therefore, commands the marshal to take his body, &c. It may not be formal. The court out of which it issued, might, upon application, vacate or modify the order or the attachment. But I see no ground for saying that either the one or the other is absolutely void.

The attachment, on the face of it, did not authorize the arrest of the plaintiff; and on that ground, and that alone, I think the action was technically sustained; and that the plaintiff ought not to have been nonsuited.

Nonsuit set aside.

Cited in—7 Cow., 333; 1 Wend., 182; 4 Wend., 557; 9 Wend., 320; 10 Wend., 347; H. & D., 92; 27 N. Y., 65; 28 Barb., 631; 32 Barb., 279; 67 Barb., 445; 52 How. Pr., 500; 18 Abb. Pr., 78; 2 Hilt, 575; 7 Kan., 455; 29 Wis., 588.

465*] *ARMSTRONG

v.

GARROW, Sheriff of CAYUGA.

Sheriff—Action Lies Against for Money Collected on Execution—Return of CA. Sa. "*Satisfied,*" *Evidence of Receipt of Money Before Return Day—Effect of the Taking of Promissory Note by Sheriff, on a* Ca. Sa.—*Interference by Plaintiff in Collection of Execution, Discharges Sheriff—Pleading.*

The return of a sheriff to a *ca. sa.* "satisfied," is evidence that he had received the money before the return day, though the *ca. sa.* be not, in fact, returned and filed till after the return day.

An action for money had and received lies against a sheriff, by one for whom he has collected money on execution.

It need not be averred in the declaration, specially, that he received the money as sheriff.

If the sheriff take a promissory note in satisfaction of a *ca. sa.*, and discharge the defendant, without the authority of the plaintiff, it is void as between the sheriff and the maker; and the plaintiff may sue the sheriff for an escape, or take a new execution. But if the plaintiff ratify the transaction, he may charge the sheriff as for money had and received, with interest on the amount from the return day of the *ca. sa.*; and then, *semble*, the note becomes valid as between the sheriff and the maker.

Where the plaintiff interferes, and directs a deputy-sheriff to take a course in the collection of an execution, out of the line required by law, as by giving a credit; selling land for less than the execution; and withholding a deed until the whole shall be paid, &c., he thereby makes the deputy his private special agent, and discharges the sheriff. Gorham v. Gale, *note a* to this case.

Citations—6 Cow., 467, *n. a*; 4 Cow., 553; 1 Cow., 46; 7 Johns., 159, 319; 8 Johns., 98, 206; Stat. 23 Hen. VI.; 2 Bos. & P., 151; 4 Campb., 46; 15 Mass., 534; 9 Johns., 98; 11 Johns., 518, 468; Auth. *N. P.*, 131; 3 Mass., 403.

ASSUMPSIT, tried at the Cayuga Circuit, Mar., 1826, before Throop, *Circuit J.*

The *capias* was returnable the 3d Monday of October, 1825. The declaration was against the defendant, describing him as Sheriff of Cayuga, and contained the common counts for money had and received, &c.

At the trial, the plaintiff proved a judgment in his favor against T. Mumford, for $436.50, in this court; a *ca. sa.* tested May Term, 1825, returnable August Term, 1825, indorsed, "receive $436.50, and discharge the defendant;" which, it appeared, was returned and filed by the present defendant, Nov. 26, 1825, "satisfied in full."

Here the plaintiff rested. The defendant then objected that the declaration should have been special, and charged that the defendant received the money as sheriff. The judge overruled the objection. The defendant then objected that the action was premature, having been commenced before the actual return of the *ca. sa.* satisfied. The judge sustained this objection, holding that the return was no evidence that the money was received before the *ca. sa.* was returned and filed.

The plaintiff then proved that, about Sept. 1, 1825, the deputy who held the *ca. sa.* admitted that he had not, in fact, received the money; but had taken J. P.'s note for the amount of the execution, and permitted the defendant to go at large. That the plaintiff's agent then demanded the note of the deputy, which was refused by him. That the *capias* in this suit was made out the same day, but not till after the demand. The defendant objected *that the taking of the note [*466 would not support the addition for money had and received.

Verdict for the plaintiff, for the amount of the judgment and interest from the return day of the *ca. sa.*, subject to the opinion of this court.

Mr. L. F. Stevens, for the plaintiff. The action was properly brought for money had and received; 2 Saund., 122, *note* 2; and a declaration in the general form is enough. The special character in which the money was received, need not be alleged. The insufficiency of the declaration cannot be urged on a motion for a new trial, but only on demurrer or motion in arrest. (4 Johns., 403.) The sheriff is estopped, by his return, to deny the receipt of the money: and the return relates to the return day of the writ, whether actually filed on that day or not. (13 Johns., 530; 14 *Id.*, 457; 9 *Id.*, 96.) Receiving the note was a payment of the debt, as to the sheriff. (11 Johns., 469; 3 Mass., 403; 8 Johns., 20; 3 *Id.*, 464; 1 Cow., 359; 3 Cow., 272.)

Mr. G. C. Bronson, contra, cited 3 Johns., 183; 8 Johns., 98; 7 *Id.*, 159, 319; 4 Cow., 553.

Curia, per SAVAGE, *Ch. J.* The general principle is not denied, that this action lies in all cases where any one has received the money of another, and refuses to pay it over. I can see no reason why an officer who has collected money on an execution, and refuses to pay it to the owner, should not be liable as for money had and received. The action is recommended by its simplicity, and should be encouraged where the defendant is in no danger of being misled or taken by surprise, which cannot be pretended in this case. The sheriff has received money for the plaintiff's use and, having refused to pay it, is rightly prosecuted.

I am of opinion, also, that the sheriff, having returned the execution satisfied, thereby admits the receipt of the money which he was directed to receive. This admission may well relate to the return day. The sheriff, by re- **467***] turning *the execution satisfied, admits that he executed the writ. He must have done so before the return day; as he could not, in his official character, enforce payment afterwards: and had he executed the writ by arresting the defendant, the return would have been different.

I shall, however, inquire, whether the sheriff is liable in this action, in consequence of his deputy's taking the note of a third person. The acts of the deputy are the acts of the sheriff, unless the plaintiff has, by his conduct, constituted the deputy his special agent, as in the case of *Gorham* v. *Gale*, decided February Term, 1826.(a)

468*] *It is contended by the defendant that he acted without authority in taking the note and discharging Mumford on the *ca. sa.;* and, therefore, though he may be liable for an escape, yet he cannot be charged in this action.

Such an objection comes with an ill grace from the defendant, who thus sets up his own misfeasance in his own discharge.

It is true that the sheriff violated his duty in discharging Mumford, without receiving the money contained in the direction on the back of the *ca. sa.* This was so decided in *Mumford* v. *Armstrong*, 4 Cow., 553, where the sheriff received a draft for the money, and discharged the plaintiff. We held the taking of the draft to be unauthorized, and not a payment; and *Bank of O.* v. *Wakeman*, 1 Cow., 46, was referred to, where a similar decision was made upon the sheriff's taking a promissory note for the amount of a *fi. fa.* in his hands, and discharging it. But those cases were between the original parties; and it was held that the party for whose benefit the execution was issued, should not be prejudiced, by the improper and unauthorized acts of the officer. The question whether the officer himself would be liable, was not determined.

There is no doubt that the plaintiff in this case, Armstrong, might have considered the enlargement of Mumford as an escape, and taken a new execution, or prosecuted the sheriff. But is he obliged to do so? May he not affirm the acts of the sheriff, consider the execution paid, and call on him for the money? Undoubtedly he may.

It is said the note is a nullity; and we are referred to several decisions where securities taken by sheriffs improperly, were held void, as taken for ease and favor.

In *Love* v. *Palmer*, 7 Johns., 159, the plaintiff, a deputy-sheriff, took a bond of indemnity in contemplation of an escape, which was held void both at common law and by statute, being for ease and favor, and by color of his office.

In *Richmond* v. *Roberts*, 7 Johns., 319, the plaintiff was jailer, and as such, took a bond and warrant on which *judgment was [***469** entered, and discharged the prisoner. The court set aside the judgment and warrant, on the ground that such a practice would lead to oppression. They also intimated an opinion that such a bond is against the statute, being for ease and favor.

In *Strong* v. *Tompkins*, 8 Johns., 98, the plaintiff, a deputy-sheriff, instead of taking a bail-bond on serving a *capias ad respondendum*, took a note as his indemnity, which he afterwards sued as indorsee, and was nonsuited. The court held the note void by our statute, which is a copy of the Statute 23 of Hen. VI.

In all these cases the security was taken by the sheriff, and prosecuted by him; and the decisions are all against the sheriff. The securities are said to be void. But it by no means follows that he would not have been held liable as for money had and received, had he taken a note instead of a bond, in the cases of *Love* v. *Palmer* and *Richmond* v. *Roberts*.

In England, where the Statute concerning Sheriffs is the same as ours, such securities are considered valid. In *Pilkington* v. *Green*, 2 Bos. & P., 151, the defendant being arrested on a warrant from the commissioners of excise, which was in nature of a *ca. sa.*, the officer took notes, and discharged him. The notes were accepted by those interested, and prosecuted. The defendant's counsel likened it to the case of a *ca. sa.;* and argued that if the discharge was without consideration, the notes were void. Ld. Eldon said, "we are of opinion that, under the circumstances of this case, the note having been accepted by those who were interested in it, has a sufficient consideration to support it." The case of *Sugars* v. *Brinkworth*, 4 Camph., 46, was similar, except that the warrant was in nature of a *fi. fa.* The note taken was held a valid security. In *Bowman* v. *Wood*, 15 Mass., 534, the plaintiff, a deputy-sheriff, received a negotiable note as collateral security, in discharge of an execution, and was allowed to recover upon it.

(a) GORHAM *v.* GALE.

Action for money had and received. The plaintiff proved a *fi. fa.* tested May 18, 1822, returnable the 1st Monday of Aug., 1822, for $276.03 in favor of the plaintiff against J. & W. Getty. This was delivered to Stevens, a deputy of the defendant, who was then sheriff of the County of Washington.

By the plaintiff's order, his attorney, Aug. 20, 1822, wrote to Stevens, the deputy, that J. Getty had proposed to the plaintiff to bid off the land belonging to W. Getty, for the amount due on the judgment, and costs; to pay $200 down, and the residue in 6 months. That if Mr. Getty paid the $200 on the sale, or in the week following, the deputy would give him a receipt for that sum, to be credited when the residue was paid and, on payment of the balance, give him a certificate, that is to say, to be no sale completed until the whole amount was paid. That the terms of sale should be for cash down and, of course, the bargain not to be completed till the whole amount should be paid. That Gorham did not wish to discharge the judgment, and take any new security, on the payment of $200; but to have it stand in force until the whole was satisfied; but was willing that Getty should have 6 months to pay the balance over $200.

W. Getty's property sold for more than $200 to J. Getty, who paid the $200. No deed had ever been executed. Sept. 17, 1823, the deputy stated an account, by which it appeared that $104 were still due on the execution, including all interest and costs.

The cause was tried Jan. 7, 1824, at the Washington Circuit, before Walworth, *Circuit J.;* who directed a verdict for the plaintiff for the $200, and interest, with leave for the defendant to move for a new trial on a case.

Messrs. J. B. Gibson and *S. Stevens*, for the defendant

Mr. W. Raleigh, for the plaintiff.

The Supreme Court granted a new trial, on the ground that the plaintiff had made the deputy his private agent, to whom he must look for the money, and the sheriff was not liable.

Cited in—59 Barb., 102.

According to these cases, Porter's note would have been recoverable by Armstrong, had the 470*] defendant passed it to *him when requested to do so. The party interested in the execution, having accepted of, and ratified the acts of the sheriff, there is a sufficient consideration for the note.

The only question remaining is, whether the taking of a promissory note is to be considered the receiving of money, so as to sustain this action. The case of *Denton* v. *Livingston*, 9 Johns., 98, shows that a sheriff is responsible for property sold, whether he receives the money or not; but proves nothing as to the right of action for money had and received.

In *Witherby* v. *Mann*, 11 Johns., 518, it was held that a promissory negotiable note, given and accepted as payment of a judgment, was an extinguishment of the judgment, being, in such case, equivalent to the payment of money.

In the case of *Beardsley* v. *Root*, 11 Johns., 468, Van Ness, *J.*, in giving the opinion of the court, says, "the general rule, indisputably, is that the action for money had and received cannot be supported, unless the defendant actually has received money. It has, however, been held in the English courts that taking negotiable paper is equivalent to the receipt of money; and although we have never sanctioned that doctrine by an express decision, yet, in the case of *Cumming* v. *Hackley*, 8 Johns., 206, the court seem to intimate their approbation of it."

In *Douglass* v. *Waer*, Auth. *N. P.*, 131, Spencer, *J.*, decided that the plaintiff having given a promissory note for the defendant's use entitled him to recover as for money paid, though the note was not paid, in fact, it having been accepted by the defendant's creditor in satisfaction of his debt. So, too, in *Beardsley* v. *Root*, no money was in fact received; but the defendant having discharged the plaintiff's debt, the action was held to lie. In that case *Floyd* v. *Day*, 3 Mass., 403, is cited with approbation; the principle of which is, that an agent who discharges a debt of his principal, by receiving a negotiable note, becomes accountable to the latter, as for so much money received.

471*] *In these cases the agent had discharged the debt of his principal. In the case under consideration the taking of the note in question did not, *per se*, discharge Mumford. The plaintiff might have taken another execution against him. But having subsequently ratified the act of the sheriff, by considering the transaction as a payment, and demanding the money or the note, I apprehend his remedy against Mumford no longer exists. If this be so, then this case is directly within the cases referred to between principal and agent; and the plaintiff is entitled to recover.

Interest was cast from the return day of the execution. If the plaintiff is entitled to recover at all, he is entitled to interest from that time.

Judgment for the plaintiff.

Cited in—1 Wend., 430, 541; 3 Wend., 82, 488; 5 Wend., 210; 6 Wend., 612; 7 Wend., 282; 10 Wend., 501; 13 Wend., 38; 15 Wend., 580; 19 Wend., 192; 22 Wend., 568; 7 Hill, 200; 1 N. Y., 445; 7 N. Y., 458; 10 N. Y., 401; 16 N. Y., 447; 77 N. Y., 471; 80 N. Y., 211; 9 Barb., 31; 17 Barb., 144; 29 Barb., 66; 2 How. Pr., 258; 8 How. Pr., 355; 2 E. D. S., 511; Hemp., 463; 13 Kan., 59; 19 Am. Dec., 532; 32 Am. Dec., 447.

BASKINS *v.* WILSON.

Statute of Limitations—Saving, on Ground of Unexecuted Process—What must be Shown—Witnesses—Indorser Incompetent for Indorsee in Suit against Maker—Exception.

To save the Statute of Limitations, on the ground of unexecuted process, within the six years, the plaintiff must reply that process was sued out and returned *non est inventus*; and connect it, by continuances, with the immediate process on which the defendant was arrested. And this replication must be sustained by evidence.

It is not enough to show that process was sued out, without being delivered to the sheriff, or returned.

The continuances may be entered at any time.

An indorser is an incompetent witness for the indorsee in a suit by him against the maker, even to prove the defendant's confession of the debt, so as to take it out of the Statute of Limitations, after the maker's signing has been proved by another. And where the indorser deposed that he had disposed of all his interest in the note, and believed that he had not been made responsible; held that this was not sufficient to do away the presumption of law that he was interested.

But, *semble*, that if he be not responsible as indorser, he would not be so far interested, by reason of an implied warranty of the genuineness of the note, as to preclude his being a witness to show the maker's confession, so as to take the note out of the Statute of Limitations, after the maker's signature had been proved by another.

Citations—1 Dunl. Pr., 57, 124; 5 Cow., 519; 15 Johns., 240; 16 Johns., 201.

ASSUMPSIT; tried at the Steuben Circuit, June, 1826, before Nelson, *Circuit J.*

The declaration was entitled of August Term, 1823, and contained the common money counts, to which the defendant pleaded *non assumpsit* and *non assumpsit infra sex annos*. Replication to the last plea, that the defendant did assume, &c., within six years, &c., and issue.

*At the trial the plaintiff introduced [*472 a promissory note for $164.50, dated Aug. 31, 1816, payable 90 days after date, made by the defendant, payable to George Minier or order, by whom it was indorsed. The maker's hand was then proved by H. Wells, Esq., and the indorsement by J. E. Jones.

To support the replication, the plaintiff then called G. C. Edwards, Esq., who testified that he and William B. Rochester, Esq., were partners as attorneys, in 1822; that Oct. 9, in that year, a *capias ad respondendum* was made out in this cause, with the *bona fide* intention of having it served; that it was taken by Mr. Rochester to Alleghany Co., where the defendant then resided; but he did not know that it had ever been delivered to an officer, or that it had ever been returned.

The plaintiff next offered the deposition of Minier, the payee and indorser, taken under a commission for the purpose of proving an acknowledgment of the note by the defendant within six years. In the course of this deposition, he stated that he had disposed of all his interest in the note, and was not made responsible, as he believed, on the indorsement. The deposition was, notwithstanding, objected to and excluded, on the ground that the witness was interested.

The judge nonsuited the plaintiff, on the ground that neither branch of his proof sustained his replication.

Mr. Z. A. Leland, for the plaintiff, moved to set aside the nonsuit for a new trial. He said Minier was competent to prove the mere acknowledgment of the defendant, after his handwriting had been established by another witness. (Chit. Bills, Phil. ed., 531, 532; 2 Camph., 332; 12 East, 38; 1 Camph., 407; 17 Johns., 176; 2 East, 458; 5 Taunt., 183.) If not, there was evidence of a suit commenced before the Statute of Limitations had attached. It is not necessary to continue the process to the time of filing the declaration. (18 Johns., 14, 494; 1 Cai., 69; 1 Chit. Pl., 554; 15 Johns., 326; 12 *Id.*, 430.)

473*] **Mr. H. Welles*, contra. Minier was incompetent by reason of interest. (2 Johns. Dig., 593; Evidence, pl., 280; 1 Phil. Ev., 53, 54.) His general assertion of not having been made responsible, does not amount to a direct and full denial of his liability as indorser. But if he was discharged in that respect, he is still liable on the implied warranty that the note was genuine. (15 Johns., 240; 16 *Id.*, 201.)

The plaintiff wholly failed to show the commencement of this suit within the six years. (1 Dunl. Pr., 57, 124, and cases cited; 6 T.R., 617.)

Curia, per SUTHERLAND, *J.* The title of the declaration is of August Term, 1823. The writ issued in Oct. 1822, is not the writ then, on which the defendant was arrested; nor does the *capias* on which he was arrested appear to have been an *alias* or *pluries*. No connection is shown between the two, and that issued in Oct., 1822, is totally unavailing. In order to render it availing, the plaintiff should have shown in his replication that it had been actually returned by the sheriff, *non est inventus*, and regularly continued on the roll from term to term down to the time of suing out the process on which the defendant was finally arrested. It is indispensable, for the purpose of saving the Statute, that the writ should be returned. The continuances may be entered at any time. (1 Dunl. Pr., 57, 124; *Beekman* v. *Satterlee*, 5 Cow., 519, and cases cited.) The evidence was not admissible under the pleadings.

The only question then, is, whether Minier was competent to prove an acknowledgment of the debt by the defendant within six years. The acknowledgment was sufficient to take the case out of the Statute, if it was proved by competent evidence.

The objection, on the trial, to Minier's deposition, was on the ground of his interest generally. The only evidence to show that he is not liable as indorser, is what he himself says in his deposition; "that he has disposed of all his interest in the said note; and that he is not made responsible, as he believes, on the said **474***] indorsement." This *appears to me altogether insufficient. The presumption of law is, that he has been regularly charged as indorser; and this presumption is rebutted only by the belief of the indorser, that he has not been made responsible. Upon what that belief is founded, does not appear. Whether he is liable or not, is a mixed question of law and fact. He may not have received actual notice of the dishonor of the note by the maker, and found his belief upon that circumstance. But if notice was actually sent to him he is charged although he may never have received it. The notice may, in his opinion, have been given too late; but whether it was or not, is a question of law, which he cannot be permitted to decide for the purpose of rendering himself a competent witness. He does not pretend that the note was taken by the indorsee upon the credit of the maker only, and under an agreement not to look to him as indorser. Such was the evidence in *Herrick* v. *Whitney*, 15 Johns., 240, and in *Shaver* v. *Ehle*, 16 Johns., 201. He must, then, be considered as indorser, liable to pay the note if it should be recovered from the defendant. He had, therefore, a direct interest in producing a recovery in this suit. On this ground, he was incompetent.

If he had not been responsible as indorser, I am inclined to think that his liability upon the implied warranty of the genuineness of the note, would not have disqualified him for the purpose for which he was offered.

The genuineness of the note had been previously established by proof of the handwriting of the maker; and although the testimony of the witness, as to the admission of the debt by the defendant, might tend to corroborate the previous testimony, it was not offered for that purpose; nor was such its natural legal effect. The rule upon this subject, as recognized in *Herrick* v. *Whitney* and *Shaver* v. *Ehle*, has always appeared to me to be founded on considerations extremely refined and artificial. It is, at all events, not to be extended.

The motion must be denied.

Motion denied.

Cited in—14 Wend., 84; 5 Hill, 477.

---

*MUMFORD *v.* BROWN. [*475

Landlord and Tenant—Repairs by Tenant—Tenants in Common—Assumpsit *for Necessary Repairs Made by One, when it Lies.*

A tenant cannot recover of his landlord, for repairs done by the former to the demised premises, unless there be a special agreement by the latter to pay for them.

Assumpsit will not lie by one tenant in common against another, for repairs to the land, though they be p pe or necessary, without a previous request to join in the repairs made, and a refusal by the latter. Whether, even then, *assumpsit* be the proper remedy, *quære*.

Citations—12 Mass., 65; 4 Mass., 275.

ON ERROR from the Seneca C. P. Brown sued Mumford before a justice, for money paid and work done, in repairing certain premises of which the parties were tenants in common. The former recovered, and the latter appealed to the C. P. where the former also recovered; on this state of facts, presented upon bill of exceptions, the parties being tenants in common of a lot, the plaintiff below made a board fence on the rear, where an old fence had rotted down. The new fence was a substantial benefit, and the lot would produce as much additional rent, as would pay for the repairs. When the plaintiff made the repairs, he was in actual possession of the lot, under a lease for one year from the defendant, of his half, at a stipulated rent. The defendant lived about three miles distance from the premises, and was often in the village where they lay. No express request for, assent to, or promise to pay for the repairs on the part of the defendant was proved; nor did it appear that, before making the repairs, the plaintiff had requested the defendant to make his share of them. The plaintiff claimed to recover one half the value of the repairs. The defendant moved the C. P. for a nonsuit, which they denied. Verdict and judgment for the plaintiff below.

Mr. Talcott, Atty-Gen., for the plaintiff in error. The building of the fence was, for aught that appears, without the knowledge and against the will of Mumford. Clearly, he is not accountable as landlord to his tenant for these repairs. (1 T. R., 20; 20 Johns., 28.)

Mr. L. F. Stevens, contra. The landlord is liable for such repairs as are necessary to preserve the premises from dilapidation.

At any rate, a tenant in common is liable for such repairs to his co-tenant. (F. N. B., 295, **476***] Writ *de reparatione *facienda; Id.*, 378; Writ of Contribution.) The action of *assumpsit* has taken the place of the ancient remedy. (9 Mass., 540.)

Mr. Talcott, in reply, said that no liability for repairs attached to the co-tenant till after demand and refusal.

Curia, per Savage, *Ch. J.* Clearly, the defendant below was not liable as landlord. It is not in the power of a tenant to make repairs at the expense of his landlord, unless there be a special agreement between them, authorizing him to do this. The tenant takes the premises for better and for worse; and cannot involve his landlord in expense for repairs, without his consent.

It is, however, a different question, whether the defendant below was not liable as tenant in common, for such repairs as were necessary to preserve the property.

The ancient mode of proceeding, by one tenant in common against his co-tenant, who refused to repair, was by writ, *de reparatione facienda*, a remedy which, probably, still exists. A recovery could not be had by this writ only in case of refusal to repair; and admitting that the action of *assumpsit* has superseded the ancient proceeding, should not the plaintiff below have shown a request and refusal? In *Doane* v. *Badger*, 12 Mass., 65, it was decided that one claiming a privilege in a well and pump, situate in the land of another, each being bound to contribute to the repairs, can have no action for repairs against him whose land the well is in, until after a request and refusal to repair. Jackson, *J.*, who delivered the unanimous opinion of the court, said, that considering the parties as tenants in common, with no prescription, or special contract as to repairs, it was clear the action could not be sustained, without a request by the plaintiff to the defendant to join in making the repairs. He says the action on the case seems to be a substitute for the old writ *de reparatione facienda*. But he adds, "if two co-tenants tacitly agree, or permit the house or its appurtenances to go to decay, neither can complain of the other, until after a request and refusal to join in making the repairs." The **477***] reason *upon which he founds this position, seems to be conclusive. It is, that, till such request and refusal, both tenants are in equal fault, one having as much reason to complain as the other.

In *Loring* v. *Bacon*, 4 Mass., 275, it appeared that the plaintiff owned the upper, and the defendant the lower story of a house. The plaintiff repaired the roof, after requesting the defendant to join in the repairs, and then sued to recover the defendant's alleged proportion. The court held that the plaintiff could not recover. The parties were considered, not as tenants in common but owners in severalty of the parts occupied by each. But the principle was recognized, that tenants in common may be compelled to repair by the writ *de reparatione facienda;* and also, that if one suffer his separate property to go to decay to the injury of another, a writ may be obtained to compel him to repair it; and that after an injury sustained, an action on the case lies. That case was very different from this; and no inference can be drawn from it, affecting the question now before the court.

I know of no adjudication or principle by which one shall be compelled to pay another for services rendered without request or assent, express or implied.

The plaintiff in error is not liable on the count for money paid, because it was without his assent; nor is he liable as co-tenant, because he was not in fault, having never been requested to make the repairs. That the repairs were proper and necessary, does not alter the case.

The judgment must be reversed.

Judgment reversed.

Distinguished—3 T. & C., 300.

Cited in—7 Hill, 90; 4 Paige, 343; 52 N.Y., 514; 57 N.Y., 220; 1 Barb., 507; 10 Barb., 590, 62?; 29 How. Pr., 262; 37 Super., 76; 1 Daly, 182, 486; 2 Hilt., 235, 344; 7 Wall., 423; 49 Ind., 198; 99 Mass., 77; 42 Am. Dec., 507 (16 Vt., 169); 15 Am. Rep., 484 (57 N.Y., 209).

---

*SPAFFORD *v.* HOOD. [*478

Construction of the 22d Section of the Act for Support of Common Schools—Does not Apply to Defective Performance or Omission of Particular Act by Clerk.

The penalty imposed by the latter part of the 22d section of the Act for the Support of Common Schools, sess. 42, ch. 161, upon the clerks, &c., of school districts, for the non-performance of their duties, does not extend to the defective performance, or omission of a particular act, but only to a general non-performance of the duties of their offices.

Accordingly, it does not attach for the omission of the clerk to warn a part of the taxable inhabitants of a school district to attend a special meeting ordered by the trustees.

The object of this section was to compel a *bona fide* acceptance of the offices which it enumerates.

A similar construction applies to the 5th section of the Act for the Assessment and Collection of Taxes, 2 R. L., 512, which imposes a penalty upon assessors. Per Sutherland, *J.*, delivering the opinion of the court.

Where it is the intention of the Legislature to impose a penalty on an officer, for the omission of any particular duty, they use language which is clear and explicit; *e. g.*, 2 R. L., 274, imposing $10 on Overseers of Highways for not warning people assessed to work, &c. Per Sutherland, *J.*, delivering the opinion of the court.

Citations—Act, April 12, 1819 (sess. 42, ch. 161); 2 R. L., 512, 129, 274, sec. 14.

ON ERROR from the C. P. of Orleans Co. The cause came into that court by appeal from a justice's court. The action was debt, by Spafford against Hood, for $10, the penalty mentioned in the 22d section of the Act for the support of Common Schools, passed Apr. 12, 1819. (Sess. 42, ch. 161, p. 187.) The declaration was for neglect of the duties imposed on the defendant, as district clerk of school district No. 8, in the Towns of Murray and Clarendon, in the County of Orleans.

At the trial, in the C. P., the plaintiff proved that the defendant was clerk for the district mentioned in the declaration, and that he acted as such in 1824; and that, as such clerk, he was ordered by the trustees of the district, in Dec., 1824, to call a special meeting for the 24th of that month. That he was ordered to do this more than five days previous to the meeting; but that he neglected to warn and notify certain individuals, taxable inhabitants, who resided in the boundaries of the district.

The court below deciding that, to warrant a recovery of the penalty, the omission of the defendant must be shown to have been willful and designed, evidence was given upon this point. The court also charged the jury that the omission must have been willful and designed; and the plaintiff excepted upon this, and other points which it is not necessary to notice. Verdict and judgment for the defendant.

Mr. L. B. Jewett, for the plaintiff in error.

479*] **Mr. R. Bryant*, contra.

Curia, per SUTHERLAND, *J.* The latter part of the 22d section of the "Act for the Support of Common Schools,' imposes the penalty of $10 upon the clerk, trustees and collector of each school district, who shall neglect the performance of the duties of his office. This section provides, in the first place, "that every person who shall be duly chosen, or appointed to either of said offices, and shall refuse to serve therein, shall forfeit and pay the sum of $5, &c.; and every person, who being duly chosen or appointed as aforesaid, to serve in any such office, and having accepted thereof, or not declared his refusal to accept, shall neglect the performance of the duties of such office, shall forfeit and pay the sum of $10; to be recovered, &c." The defendant was elected clerk of the school district in which he resided, and accepted the office; and for aught that appears, performed its duties generally in a faithful and satisfactory manner. But it appeared that in the month of Dec. 1824, he was directed by the trustees to call a special meeting of the district. That on such occasion he omitted to give notice of the time and place of the meeting, to two or three of the taxable inhabitants of the district; and that omission is the foundation of this action.

The plaintiff took several exceptions to the opinions expressed by the court below, which it is not necessary particularly to consider, as we are clearly of opinion that it is not a case to which the penalty given by the section in question was intended to apply.

It is apparent that the sole object of the 22d section of this Act, is to compel the individuals who may be elected, or appointed to the offices of clerk or trustees, or collector of any school district, to accept the appointment. It is accordingly provided in the first instance that any individual who, after having been duly elected or appointed to either of those offices, shall refuse to serve therein, shall forfeit and pay the sum of $5. But it was forseen that this provision might be evaded, by a nom-**480***] inal acceptance *of the offices, and an entire neglect or omission to perform any of their duties: and it was to guard against such an evasion, that the latter clause of the section was inserted. It is applicable only to cases where the acceptance of the office is colorable merely, without any *bona fide* intention, at the time of accepting it, of discharging its duties; and not to cases where the person elected or chosen, enters upon, and performs the general duties of the office; but is guilty in an individual instance, of a negligent, or even a willful omission of his duty. The duties of these officers are various and minute—some of a merely ministerial character, as calling meetings, giving notices, &c.; others of a more important and responsible description; and the performance of the latter is generally enforced, either by requiring security to be given, or imposing a specific penalty for the omission. Thus, by the 24th section, the collector of the district is required to give security in double the amount of the taxes, or other moneys to be collected by him; and by the 28th section, a penalty of $25 is imposed upon the trustees, or any one of them, who shall make a false report to the Commissioners of Common Schools for their town; by means whereof any moneys shall be fraudulently obtained from the Commissioners, or unjustly apportioned by them. And the 30th section imposes a similar penalty upon any trustee, who shall refuse or neglect to render an account of all the money received by him, or to pay over any balance which may be found in his hands. The discharge of the important duties of these officers being thus provided for, it is not reasonable to suppose that the Legislature intended to impose a penalty upon them, for an omission to perform each and every subordinate act appertaining to their offices. It is not usual with us to enforce the performance of the duties of our officers by penalties, except where, from the nature of the duty, there is peculiar danger of malfeasance.

The 5th section of the Act for the Assessment and Collection of Taxes, 2 R. L., 512, contains a provision very similar to that which we are now considering. It is, that if any assessor shall refuse, or, without being prevented *by sickness, neglect to perform the [***481** duties required of him by this Act, he shall forfeit and pay to the people of this State the sum of $50. There can be no doubt, I apprehend, that the neglect here spoken of and intended, is a total neglect, equivalent to a refusal to take upon himself the office, and not the omission of a single act.

The 9th section of the Act relative to the Duties and Privileges of Towns, 2 R. L., 129, contains a similar provision in relation to the town officers.

Where it is the intention of the Legislature to impose a penalty on an officer for the omission of any particular duty, they use language which is clear and explicit. Thus, in relation to the Overseers of Highways, 2 R. L., 274, sec. 14, it is provided, "that every Overseer of Highways, who shall neglect or to refuse to warn the people assessed, to work on the highways, &c., or to collect the moneys that may arise from fines or commutations, or to perform any of the duties and services required by the Act, or which may be enjoined on him by the commissioners, &c., shall forfeit for every such neglect or refusual, the sum of $10," &c. The difference in the phraseology of these Acts is very striking and, in my judgment, affords strong confirmation of the correctness of the construction we have given to the section of the School Act under consideration. The judgment of the court below must be affirmed.

Judgment affirmed.

Cited in—13 Wend., 68; 38 Barb., 41; 19 Am. Rep., 27 (50 Miss., 429).

BUTTERFIELD *v.* COOPER.

Agreement to Convey Certain Place, " Containing 100 Acres"—Quantity, Surplusage.

An agreement was, to convey "the Hawkins place containing 100 acres;" held, that the clause, "containing 100 acres," should be rejected as surplusage; and that the contract covered the whole lot surveyed and set off to Hawkins, and upon which he entered, improving part, under a parol contract of purchase; though it, in fact, contained 106 acres.

Citation—2 Johns., 37.

ASSUMPSIT; tried at the Jefferson Circuit Dec. 24, 1826, before Williams, *Circuit J.*

The action was, to recover back about $700, the consideration money paid by the plaintiff to the defendant, on a contract to purchase of the latter a lot of ground called the Hawkins lot.

482*] *The facts, as proved at the trial, were; that Mar. 10, 1824, the plaintiff agreed to pay the consideration; and the defendant to convey at the time, and in the manner specified in certain memoranda of the agreement, drawn up and signed by the parties on that day, one of which was retained by each. There was no question that the consideration had been paid; but the parties disagreed in the construction of these memoranda in the description of parcels. The memorandum signed by the defendant, and kept by the plaintiff, mentioned these as the Hawkins place. That signed by the plaintiff, and kept by the defendant mentioned them as the Hawkins place, containing 100 acres, lying partly opposite to H. Hilyerd's farm.

Before entering into the agreement in question, the defendant, owning a large tract of land, had contracted verbally with one Hawkins, to sell him 100 acres. A surveyor went with Hawkins and the defendant, to locate the purchase; and they commenced on one Conklin's east line, on the Quaker road, and ran easterly on that road 81 rods, where the surveyor stuck a stake. Thence they ran back from the road towards one Parish's land; but on account of an intervening swamp, they could not complete this, nor the other two lines. They were intended, however, to run along Parish's line to Conklin's, and thence along Conklin's to the place of beginning. The surveyor told the defendant he thought these lines would include more than 100 acres. Hawkins took possession of the premises, and cleared as far east as the stake, and back to Parish's land; his whole clearing, which he occupied, amounted to 31 acres. This purchase of Hawkins was called 100 acres, and Hawkins was not to have any more; but it, in truth, amounted to 106 acres. When the plaintiff and defendant came to arrange the draft and execution of the conveyance under their contract, the former was willing to take a conveyance of 100 acres only, but claimed to have the whole length on the road to the stake. The defendant insisted on conveying no farther east on the road than to include 100 acres between *Conklin's and Parish's land. The [***483** whole difficulty was about the 6 acres. The plaintiff was willing that the defendant should take out 6 acres back, so as not to take any of the improved land; but the defendant claimed to take part of this. Finally, the plaintiff demanded a deed of the Hawkins lot, or the 106 acres, which the defendant refused to give. The plaintiff then demanded the consideration paid. The defendant did not comply with this demand. He afterwards made out a deed, excluding a part of the improvements, so as to include 100 acres only. But this was never tendered to the plaintiff.

The judge charged the jury, that the plaintiff was entitled to the whole 106 acres, as at first marked out; and they found for the plaintiff $740.83 damages.

A motion was now made, in behalf of the defendant, for a new trial.

Messrs. E. Fowler and *M. Sterling*, for the motion.

Messrs. G. C. Sherman and *D. W. Bucklin*, contra.

Curia, per SAVAGE, *Ch. J.* Taking the two memoranda together, the agreement was, that the defendant should convey "the Hawkins place," as expressed in the memorandum signed by the defendant. According to the memorandum signed by the plaintiff, the agreement was for the purchase of "the Hawkins place, containing one hundred acres." Suppose the defendant had executed a deed in the language of the agreement, "the Hawkins place, containing one hundred acres;" how much would the purchaser have taken? The Hawkins place was a piece of ground, known by that name, because Hawkins had occupied it, and it was set off to him by the defendant in person. I apprehend that such a conveyance would authorize the grantee to hold all that was actually laid off to Hawkins, as far east as the stake stuck by the surveyor in the presence of the defendant and Hawkins, without regard to the quantity of acres. The words, "one hundred acres," were matter of description. It seems to me similar to conveying a lot by its number, containing 600 *acres. The purchaser [***484** takes the lot, whether it contains more or less than the specified quantity. This is like the case of *Mann* v. *Pierson*, 2 Johns., 37, where, in a deed of lot 74, Lysander, containing 600 acres, the contents were said to be matter of description merely. The court considered the number of the lot as a reference to the metes and bounds. In this case, the description of "the Hawkins place," referred to the actual location of the lot, as possessed by Hawkins.

I am of opinion the judge decided correctly, and that a new trial should be denied.

New trial denied.

Cited in—10 Barb., 422.

MURRAY AND MURRAY v. JUDAH.

Negotiable Paper—Checks—Demand Must be Made on Drawee Before Suit Against Drawer—Within a Reasonable Time—Warranty, of Title or Genuineness by one who Transfers Negotiable Paper, is Broken the Instant of Transfer—Subsequent Discharge, as Insolvent, Releases the One Making Transfer—He is then a Competent Witness for Holder—Accommodation Checks—Acceptor is the Principal Debtor, the Drawer, the Surety—Check as Evidence.

Demand of a check must be made of the drawee, before the holder can sue the drawer.

No particular time for demand is fixed. It is enough that it be within a reasonable time; and it does not lie with the drawer to object that the demand is too late, unless he has been injured by the delay.

One who has transferred a check or note, is an incompetent witness for the holder, in an action upon it, on the ground that he impliedly warrants his title and the genuineness of the paper; but if he be discharged from his debts under the Insolvent Act, subsequent to the transfer, this renders him competent.

Whether he be not a competent witness, where the genuineness of the paper is first established by other evidence, and there is no pretense that he wanted title to the paper, *quære*.

A warranty of title or genuineness by one who transfers negotiable paper, if it turn out to be false, is broken the instant of the transfer; and his liability is taken away by a discharge under the Insolvent Act, after the transfer, though before the want of title or genuineness be detected.

The drawer of a check is not a surety for the payee, though it be lent to or drawn for the accommodation of the latter. And therefore, though a subsequent holder give time to the payee to make payment, he being bound to pay such holder, this will not discharge the drawer, even though such holder know the check was for the payee's accommodation. As between the drawer and the payee and subsequent holder, the drawer is the principal, and the payee the surety.

Though a check be transferred as two, as collateral security for two several debts due to them respectively, yet one alone may sue upon it, and possession by him is, *prima facie*, evidence that the other has sold his interest to him.

In an action for money paid, &c., or money had and received, by the holder of a check against the drawer, the check is, *per se*, conclusive evidence; and the drawer cannot show, in his defense, that money was not had and received by or paid for him.

A check was transferred by the holder as collateral security for an antecedent debt. Afterwards, the drawer failing, it was appraised, and the creditor took it absolutely, at a sum less than its face, giving the holder credit at the amount of the appraisal. Held, that in an action by the creditor against the drawer, this circumstance could not be evidence to diminish the amount of the recovery; that, though the creditor gave less, yet he was entitled to recover according to the face of the check.

Citations—3 Johns. Cas., 5, 259; 15 Johns., 240; 16 Johns., 201; 6 Johns., 5; 6 Cow., 238; 11 Johns., 57; 3 Cow., 252; 2 Campb., 185; 3 Campb., 281, 362; 5 Taunt., 192, 551; 4 M. & S., 226, 232, 233; 17 Johns., 169; 12 Johns., 90.

ASSUMPSIT; tried at the N. Y. Circuit, Jan. 20, 1825, before Edwards, *Circuit J.*

485*] *The action was to recover the amount of a check, of which the plaintiffs were holders, drawn by the defendant on the Phœnix Bank, payable to bearer, drawn the 8th, but post-dated May 15, 1818, for $5,000. The declaration contained the common money counts only.

It appeared at the trial that the cheek had been duly executed. That at the date of the check, the defendant had in the Bank a little more than $500; and that Jan. 23, 1820, his account with the Bank was closed, and he drew for the balance. He had a considerable running account at the Bank, and often had large balances due to him; and from June 15 to 18, 1818, he had there $5,126.82; and if the check had been presented at its date, or within several months afterwards, it would have been paid. The defendant was in good credit till his failure, which was in July, 1819.

The defendant moved for a nonsuit, on the ground that no demand of payment was shown, by the plaintiffs, to have been made at the Bank. The judge overruled the motion, and decided that the plaintiffs were entitled to recover the amount which the defendant had in the Bank at the date of the check, this operating as a special assignment of that amount to any future holder of the check; and the withdrawal of the funds was money had and received for the use of the holder. The defendant excepted.

The judge refusing to declare that any future funds, deposited by the defendant in, and drawn from the Bank, were, in like manner, money had and received for the holder's use, the plaintiffs excepted.

The plaintiffs then called I. Foote as a witness. Foote had, May 10, 1819, passed the check to the plaintiffs and one Thomas, as security for a debt previously due to them respectively, of more than $1,200. But he had been discharged in 1821, under the Insolvent Act of Apr. 12, 1813. Proof of these facts were followed up by the production of the discharge and the proceedings to obtain it. The defendant objected that the witness was incompetent, as he might be liable, notwithstanding his discharge, *in case the check should prove [***486** invalid or ineffectual against Judah. The objection was overruled, and the witness sworn. The defendant excepted.

Foote then testified, that May 11, 1818, he gave his check on the Manhattan Co., for $5,000, to one Weston who obtained the money, in exchange for the check in question. That his check to Weston was a loan, upon the understanding that Weston should loan the witness a like sum, for the same length of time. On the day the check in question was due (it having been post-dated May 15), Weston requested the witness not to present it to the Bank, which the witness agreed to. He saw Judah within about 6 months after the check was due, and on his (J.'s) request, promised not to present the check, without letting him know it. There was a general understanding between the witness and Weston that the witness should not present the check. The witness also stated, that when he passed the check to the plaintiffs and Thomas, he did not know that it was a lent check. That the defendant promised the witness that the check should be paid, both before and after the transfer, and after the defendant knew of the transfer to the plaintiffs and Thomas. After the defendant's failure, and he believed after the commencement of this suit, the witness went to the Phœnix Bank, to inquire if there were any funds there, and had the check with him, having procured it from Mr. Murray for the purpose.

On cross-examination, he admitted that before he passed the check he heard both from Weston and the defendant that the check had been loaned to Weston for his accommodation.

Another check of the defendant for $5,000, dated in Apr., 1818, and negotiated by Weston with the witness, had also, at the same time, been transferred to the plaintiffs and Thomas; and when the defendant conversed with the witness, he spoke of both checks. Feb. 29, 1820, the witness received a deed from Weston of land in Madison Co., and, with the plaintiffs' and Thomas' consent, gave up the check dated in Apr., to be canceled. The land was **487***] conveyed for their *benefit. He, at the same time, with the consent of the plaintiffs and Thomas and as part of the arrangement, agreed, under seal with Weston, that on his paying $2,500, with interest thereon, after the lapse of six months, it should be in full of all claims which the witness then had against Weston; and that he would give up to Weston the check in question. This agreement was produced on the trial. The witness said he understood that if the $2,500 was not paid in six months, the check would be good for the whole amount.

The witness further testified that Mar. 31, 1821, the check in question, with certain other property, were appraised at $1,250, by agreement between the witness and the plaintiffs and Thomas, and that sum placed absolutely to the credit of the witness. That the plaintiffs and Thomas then became petitioning creditors for the witness' discharge, to the amount of the balance due after such credit.

He further stated that he did not inform the plaintiffs, at the time of his passing the check, that the money was raised for Weston, or the check for his accommodation.

The defendant now again moved for a nonsuit, on the ground that Thomas should have been a party plaintiff with the Murrays; and that the check having been lent to Weston by the defendant, the general money counts would not reach the case. The judge overruled the motion, on the grounds that the possession of the check by the plaintiffs was, *prima facie*, evidence that Thomas had transferred it to them; and that the plaintiffs might recover on the money counts, in the same manner as if they had declared upon the check. The defendant excepted on both points.

Weston, who had been discharged under the Insolvent Act, was then sworn for the defendant, and stated that he borrowed the check in question, May 11, 1818, it being post-dated the 15th. The check was borrowed for witness' exclusive use, and he so told Foote when he received it. Judah refused to consent to any **488***] arrangement, *except on the basis of giving up both checks, which the witness repeatedly told Foote.

The defendant then offered to prove, by this witness, that the deed of conveyance to Foote was in payment of both checks. To this the plaintiffs objected; but the evidence was received, and the plaintiffs excepted.

The witness then swore that the check in question was liquidated at $2,500, and that it was agreed that the residue of the check should be paid by the conveyance; and it was paid accordingly. On cross-examination, however, he admitted the whole agreement was contained in the writings.

Another witness for the defendant testified to the like effect.

Foote being again called, after a recess of the court, stated that, on further reflection, he recollected that he had obtained the check in question from Mr. Murray, and presented it before the commencement of this suit.

Considerable contradictory evidence was then given upon the question, whether the check had been originally given on an usurious consideration.

The judge charged that the legal presumption was, that the money for which the check was given had been paid for the defendant's use, or had and received by him; and that, in this case, he could not be permitted to show the contrary. That, to constitute usury, there must have been a corrupt agreement to pay more than legal interest for the check, and that both parties must have agreed to the corruption; that the plaintiffs were entitled to recover on the common money counts; that the defendant could not be considered in the light of a surety, though the check was loaned to Weston, and though Foote knew this when he took it; that the submission to arbitration, between the plaintiffs, Thomas and Foote, and the award thereon, were no obstacle to the plaintiffs' recovering the same amount as if the award had not been made; that no demand to fulfill the agreement concerning the check made in Feb., 1820, was necessary previous to the commencement of this suit. The defendant excepted upon *all the above points [***489** in the charge. The judge also charged that the agreement of Feb., 1820, was no bar to the plaintiffs' recovery; and left it to the jury to pass upon the contradictory evidence concerning the usury.

Verdict for the plaintiffs for $3,207.29.

Mr. J. O. Hoffman, for the defendant, moved for a new trial. He said the plaintiffs ought to have been nonsuited at the close of their testimony, no presentation of the check having been proved. (3 Johns. Cas., 5, 260; 12 East, 170; 7 East, 359; 15 East, 220.) By the authorities cited, it will be seen that a check is considered a bill of exchange; and that both demand and refusal of payment, and notice of these to the drawer, are necessary, before a suit can be sustained against him, unless there be a total want of funds in the hands of the drawee.

Foote was not a competent witness. (1 Phil. Ev., 47, 53; 6 Johns., 5; 11 Johns., 57.) He was a warrantor of the genuineness and validity of the check in the hands of the plaintiffs; who, on failing in this suit, may go against him; and the very record here will be evidence. The discharge does not destroy his interest, for his liability was contingent at the time when that discharge was obtained.

Any defense which might have been made against Foote, is equally available against the present plaintiffs; and any defense of Weston is equally the right of the defendant.

If the plaintiffs are entitled to recover at all, it can only be to the amount which they paid for the check.

Thomas should have been a party. The suit is not on the check, but for money had and received; and the check was transferred for the joint benefit of the plaintiffs and Thomas.

The check was an accommodation check, and so known to be. The defendant, then, was only a surety; and the extension of credit released his responsibility. The defendant never assented to the giving of credit.

The plaintiffs having taken the check merely as collateral security, cannot be deemed *bona fide* holders in the fair course of trade. (5 Johns. Ch., 54.)

490*] **Messrs. H. D.* and *R. Sedgwick*, contra. The general counts are always sufficient against any party to negotiable paper. (12 Johns., 90.) And the holder of such paper is always, *prima facie*, the owner. (11 Johns., 52; 3 Cow., 260.) The defendant signed the check as a principal; and this act estops him from now setting up the fact that he was surety merely—especially as to third persons, holding the security which he has put afloat. (17 Johns., 169.) But he has not shown himself to be a surety. If he is to be regarded as the drawer for the accommodation of Weston, the giving of time will not discharge him. This was directly decided in *Fentum* v. *Pocock*, 5 Taunt., 192. True, that case was decided of an acceptor for accommodation; but the principle is the same. *Carstairs* v. *Rolleston, Id.*, 551, was a still stronger case. There, a maker of a note for the indorser's accommodation, was held not to be discharged by a release of the indorser. The rights of parties must always be taken as they appear upon the written contract they have formed.

All Foote's liabilitity, as warrantor, or otherwise, was gone by the discharge.

Curia, per SUTHERLAND, *J.* The first point, made on the part of the defendant, is, that the motion for a nonsuit ought to have been granted, no demand of payment of the check at the Bank having been proved.

It is a sufficient answer to this point, that a demand was subsequently proved. That such demand was necessary to entitle the plaintiffs to recover from the drawer, is well established. A check is, in form and effect, a bill of exchange. It is not a direct promise by the drawer to pay money; but it is an undertaking, on his part, that the drawee shall accept and pay; and the drawer is answerable, only in the event of the failure of the drawee to pay. As a general rule, therefore, a check is not due from the drawer, until payment has been demanded from the drawee, and refused by him. As between the holder of a check and indorser, or third persons, payment must be demanded within a reasonable time. But as between the holder and the maker or drawer, a demand at

491*] any time *before suit brought is sufficient, unless it appear that the drawee has failed, or the drawer has, in some other manner, sustained injury by the delay. These principles are recognized and established by this court, in *Cruger* v. *Armstrong*, 3 Johns., Cas., 5, and *Conroy* v. *Warren, Id.*, 259.

2. Foote was a competent witness. The regularity and validity of his discharge as an insolvent were not questioned. That discharge took place in 1821, and he passed the check in question to the plaintiffs in 1819. The objection seems to be, that Foote was responsible upon the implied warranty of the genuineness of the check and of his own title to it which, it has repeatedly been held, accompanies the transfer of all negotiable paper. *Herrick* v. *Whitney*, 15 Johns., 240; *Shaver* v. *Ehle*, 16 Johns., 201; 6 Johns., 5. But I am inclined to think, that any cause of action arising from the forgery of the check, if it should prove to be forged, must be considered as having accrued to the plaintiffs at the time when they received the check, and not when the forgery might be detected. *Utica Bank* v. *Childs, ante*, 238. If this is so, then the discharge terminated all interest on the part of Foote.

But it is to be remarked that Foote was not called to prove the execution of the note. That had been previously established; and, in this respect, the case is distinguishable from those of *Herrick* v. *Whitney* and *Shaver* v. *Ehle*, where the witnesses were called to prove the exeention of the instruments which they had transferred and, by implication of law, warranted. The principle itself is a strictly technical one, and not to be extended to cases which do not fall within the reason on which it has been adopted. I am aware of the general rule, that where a witness has a direct interest in the event of a cause, he cannot be admitted to testify as to any matter on which the jury are to pass, in favor of such interest. *Butler* v. *Warren*, 11 Johns., 57. But it appears to me to be worthy of consideration, whether the class of cases which we are now considering ought not to be considered an exception to this rule; and whether a party who has transferred a negotiable instrument, *after its execution [*492 and genuineness have been established, and there is no pretense that he had not a right to transfer it, ought not to be considered a competent witness for every other purpose. *Williams* v. *Matthews*, 3 Cow., 252. I do not, however, intend to put the competency of the witness on that ground, but on the ground that his discharge terminated his interest.

3. It is contended that Foote knew this to be an accommodation check when he took it; that the defendant, therefore, stands in the light of a surety, and is discharged by the extension of credit given to Weston, and by the arrangement of Feb. 29, 1820, made between him and Foote. The judge decided that it was immaterial whether Foote knew it to be an accommodation check, or not. If he did, it would not entitle Judah to the privileges of a surety.

The acceptor of a bill of exchange is, undoubtedly, the principal debtor, and the drawer the surety, though it be accepted without consideration, and for the sole accommodation of the drawer; and nothing will discharge the acceptor but payment or a release. Ld. Ellenborough certainly fell into an error, when he held a contrary doctrine in *Laxton* v. *Peat*, 2 Camph., 185, and *Collott* v. *Haigh*, 3 Campb., 281. These cases were subsequently overruled by Gibbs, *J.*, in *Kerrison* v. *Cooke*, 3 Campb., 362, and by Mansfield, *Ch. J.*, in *Fentum* v. *Pocock*, 5 Taunt., 192, and *Carstairs* v. *Rolleston*, 5 Taunt., 551.

But here the drawer complains that time was given, not to the drawee, but to Weston, the payee of the bill. Now, that was an act by which the defendant could not possibly be injured; for he could never have a right of action upon this check against Weston. I know no case in which it has ever been held, that giving time to the payee or indorser, even of an accommodation bill will discharge the drawer. As between the drawer, the payee and the holder, the drawer is unquestionably the principal, and the payee the surety. *Claridge* v. *Dalton*, 4 Maule & S., 226, 232, 233, per Bayley, *J.*, and see *Seymour* v. *Minturn*, 17 Johns., **493***] *169. The opinion of the judge, therefore, upon this point was correct.

4. The judge was correct in holding that the possession of the check by the plaintiffs, was evidence that Thomas had transferred to them whatever interest he had in it. The check was also evidence of money had and received by the drawer to the use of the holder, and of money paid by the holder to the use of the maker. Both these points are fully considered and settled in *Pierce* v. *Crafts*, 12 Johns., 90.

5. The award as to the value of the check between the plaintiffs and Foote, did not affect their right to recover against the defendant. It was merely a mode of ascertaining its value, for the purpose of enabling the plaintiffs to become petitioners for Foote for the balance. It was a transaction with which the defendant has no concern. It was not an agreement on the part of the plaintiffs to collect no more than the amount at which the check was appraised from Judah. It was merely evidence satisfactory for the object in view—that that was the whole amount which probably could be collected.

From the amount of the verdict, I presume the plaintiffs recovered upon the basis that, by the arrangement of Feb. 29, 1820, $2,500 of the check were absolutely paid. It is unnecessary, therefore, to consider whether the parol evidence in relation to that settlement was properly admitted, as the defendant has had the benefit of it, and the plaintiffs do not ask for a new trial.

On the whole, I think the motion for a new trial must be denied.

New trial denied.

Explained—71 N. Y., 329 (27 Am. Rep., 57).

Cited in—1 Wend., 49; 6 Wend., 445; 10 Wend., 306; 13 Wend., 553; 16 Wend., 666; 19 Wend., 562; 21 Wend., 373, 481; 1 Hill, 507; 2 Hill, 427; 53 N. Y., 312; 71 N. Y., 440 (27 Am. Rep., 72); 87 N. Y., 122 (41 Am. Rep., 358); 3 Lans., 32; 11 Hun, 485; 10 Barb., 422; 1 Abb. Pr., 149; 12 Abb. Pr., 141; 2 Hall, 463; 6 Bos., 288; 9 Bos., 576; 4 Duer, 129, 130; 1 Sheld., 395; 38 Super., 195; 1 E. D. S., 402, 511; 3 E. D. S., 549; 2 Story, 517; 3 Allen, 259; 30 Ill., 403; 42 Ill., 242; 55 Ind., 273; 30 N. J. L., 293; 42 Am. Dec., 400 (2 Spear., 747).

494*] *H. DUBOIS *v.* J. DUBOIS.

Debt Lies on Decree of Surrogate for Payment of Money—Effect of Decree—Payment of Money Into Court—Set-Off.

Debt lies, on the decree of a surrogate, for the payment of money.

Such a decree, against an executor for the payment of a legacy, changes the character of the claim into one against the defendant, personally.

Hence, in an action of debt on the decree, by the legatee against the executor, the former may declare against, and charge the latter in his own right; and no security need be filed pursuant to the Statute, 1 R. L., 314, 15, sec. 19.

And the latter may set off a demand due to him, in his own right, from the plaintiff in his own right.

The surrogate has no authority, as agent for a party, to receive money which he has decreed that another should pay to the party.

Therefore, where the surrogate decreed that A should pay to B a sum of money; and A laid it down on the surrogate's table, who took out a part; and the residue was attached by a constable under process in favor of A against B; held, that this was not such a payment as would vest the money specifically in B; and that, therefore, it was not the subject of a levy on an attachment against him.

Held, that it was like money collected on execution by an officer, which cannot be levied on by process against the one at whose suit it was collected.

Held, also, that the surrogate, having no authority to receive the money, the payment did not satisfy the decree; but an action would still lie upon it.

In debt, on the decree of a surrogate against the defendant, requiring him to pay a legacy, such decree is, in itself, evidence that there was a will; and that the defendant was executor; and, therefore, neither of these facts need be shown by the plaintiff on the trial.

Citations—1 R. L., 448, sec. 11; 3 Cai., 22.

DEBT on the decree of a surrogate; tried at the Saratoga Circuit, June 8, 1824, before Nelson, *Circuit J.*

The declaration was, that Apr. 9, 1823, the plaintiff, by the consideration, judgment, order and decree of George Palmer, Esq., Surrogate of the County of Saratoga, upon and for a certain subject-matter within the jurisdiction of the surrogate's court of that county, recovered against the defendant $101.77, for and on account of a certain legacy bequeathed to the plaintiff by the last will and testament of G. Dubois, &c. Plea, *nil debet*, with notice of setting off a claim due from the plaintiff in his own right, to the defendant in his own right.

At the trial, the plaintiff proved a decree, reciting that the plaintiff and defendant were acting co-executors of G. Dubois, who had bequeathed a legacy to the plaintiff of $250, which decree ordered that the balance of $101.77 unpaid, should be paid by the defendant to the plaintiff, on the ground that assets had come to the hands of the former for that purpose. $23.61 was paid upon the decree, leaving still due $85.45, with interest.

The defendant then moved for a nonsuit: 1. Because the defendant was not named as executor. 2. Because the surrogate was not shown to have had jurisdiction. 3. Because no security to refund was filed. 4. Because no will was proved showing the defendant to have been executor. 5. *If he was proved to be [*495 executor, this was a variance from the declaration, which charged him in his own right. 6. That debt would not lie. 7. That no jurisdiction was shown by the declaration.

The motion being overruled, the defendant then proved that he put the money due on the decree, upon the table of the surrogate; but after the surrogate had taken out $23.61, the defendant caused a constable to take the residue on two attachments issued by a justice of the peace, in favor of the defendant, against the plaintiff, for debts due from the plaintiff, to the defendant. He also offered to prove that the plaintiff was indebted to him, in his own right, on promissory notes to an amount exceeding the balance due upon the decree, and to set off this demand. On objection, the judge overruled the evidence of set-off, on the ground that the suit was against the defendant as executor.

Verdict for the plaintiff, subject to the opinion of this court.

Mr. J. L. Viele, for the plaintiff, cited 3 Cai., 22; 1 Campb., 253; 17 Johns., 68, 301; 1 Esp., Dig., 78; 6 Bac. Abr., 136, Set-off, C; 1 Wash., 79; 1 Hen. & Munf., 176; Mont. on Set-off, 13, 19; 2 Johns., 155; 1 R. L., 314.

He suggested that, if the court should be against the plaintiff on the question of set-off, there should be a new trial, as there was other matter of defense against the set-off, not appearing in the case.

Mr. E. Cowen, contra, cited 1 R. L., 314, 315, sec. 19; 5 Serg. & R., 468; 18 Johns., 122; 1 Vern., 93; 1 Atk., 491; 6 Munf., 157, and cases cited; 2 Johns., 243; Swinb., 621, part 4, sec. 20, 7th ed.; Toll., 282, 283, old ed.; *Id.*, 230.

Curia, per SAVAGE, *Ch. J.* The objections to the proceedings before the surrogate came too late. They should have been taken before the surrogate. His decree sets out the proper citation and proceedings at length; and shows
496*] *a case in which he had jurisdiction. By the Statute, 1 R. L., 448, sec. 11, he is "to hear and determine all cases touching any legacy, or bequest in any last will and testament, payable, or coming out of the personal estate of the testator; and to decree and compel payment thereof; saving to every one the right of appeal."

The principal question raised is, whether debt will lie. On this point, we are without any direct authority. The general rule is, that this form of action is proper for any debt of record, or by specialty, or any sum certain. It has been decided, that debt lies upon a decree for the payment of money, made by a court of chancery of another State; *Post* v. *Neafie*, 3 Cai., 22; and no doubt the action will lie upon such a decree in our domestic courts of equity. The decree of the surrogate, unappealed from, is conclusive, and determines forever the rights of the parties. It may be enforced by imprisonment, and is certainly evidence of a debt due. Whether a surrogate's court is a court of record, need not be decided. It has often been said that a court of chancery is not a court of record. It is sufficient that a decree in either court, unappealed from, is final. Debt will lie.

It was also objected that the declaration does not describe the defendant as executor; but the proceedings before the surrogate were against him in that capacity. It is true the suit was for a legacy. But the surrogate, we must intend, had the proper evidence to justify a decree, whereby the defendant was to be made personally liable for a demand, which previously existed against him in his representative capacity only. By the decree, it became a personal matter. The judgment in this suit cannot be of the goods of the testator. Execution must go against the defendant personally, as for his private debt. I infer, therefore, that the character of the claim is changed by the decree; so that in prosecuting upon it, there can be no necessity to describe the defendant as an executor.

Other questions, however, arise out of the case made out and offered to be made out, on the part of the defendant.

1. Ought not the set-off to have been al-
497*] lowed? 2. Had *not the officer a right to levy on the money? 3. Was not the payment of the money a discharge of the defendant?

Without discussing these questions at much length, it seems to me, that the payment of the money into court was no compliance with the decree—which was, that the defendant should pay it to the plaintiff. If the payment into court was not a discharge, it seems to follow, that the levy by the constable was void. We have decided that a levy upon money collected by, and in the hands of an officer on execution, was not a levy upon the goods and chattels of the person for whom it was collected; because the identical pieces of money collected are not necessarily to be paid over to him. The money is not strictly his till actually paid over. Until that be done, his right is a chose in action. If, therefore, the surrogate had received the money for the plaintiff, it would not vest specifically in him, till paid over to him or his authorized agent.

But if I am right in supposing that the defendant became personally liable by virtue of the decree, then it follows that the set-off was a good defense, and should have been received.

A new trial must, therefore, be awarded, as it is suggested that the plaintiff can rebut the set-off, the costs to abide the event.

New trial granted.

Cited in—2 Wend., 418; 16 Wend., 363; 41 N. Y., 216; 11 Barb., 347; 15 Barb., 457; 40 Barb., 224; 64 Barb., 31; 13 How. Pr., 339; 14 How. Pr., 479; 5 Sand., 392; 1 Bradf., 4; 16 How. (U. S.), 77, 78; 24 Cal., 166; 33 Ill., 516; 47 Am. Dec., 71 (2 Doug., 433); 50 Am. Dec., 411; 28 Am. Rep., 35 (68 Me., 195).

JAQUES ET AL., Assignees of BUSSING, an Insolvent Debtor,

v.

MARQUAND.

1. *Witnesses—Insolvent, who has Released Claim to Surplus, Competent for Assignees.* 2. *Partnership—Use, in Partnership Business, of Money held in Trust or Borrowed by One Partner.* 3. *Discharge, under Insolvent Act, Constitutional as to Debts Contracted After the Act.*

An insolvent debtor, who has released all claim to a surplus, is a competent witness for his assignees.

A partner, who holds money in his individual right, in trust for another, cannot subject the firm to an action for the money, by applying it to the use of the firm, without the knowledge or privity of the other member or members of his firm. Otherwise, where it is applied with their knowledge or privity.

Where a partner borrows money on his individual credit, and afterwards applies it to the payment of partnership debts, or lends it to the firm, this does not make the original lender a creditor of the firm.

But where a partner borrows money generally, without saying for whom, the fact of its being used in the business of the partnership, is, *prima facie*, evidence to sustain an action against the firm.

An insolvent discharge, under the Act of 1813, is constitutional as to debts contracted after the Act.

Citations—5 T. R., 601; 1 Br. Ch., 68; 2 Br. Ch., 595; 2 Ves. & Beaw., 414; 3 Br. Ch., 112; 1 Atk., 223; 3 Esp., 250; 8 Ves., 549; Gow. Partn., 343-349; 15 Mass., 75, 331.

ASSUMPSIT; tried at the N. Y. Circuit, Feb. 5 and 6, 1824, before Edwards, *Circuit J.*

*The declaration contained the com- [***498**
mon money counts only, laying a promise by the defendant to Bussing, the insolvent; and also to his assignees, under the Act for Giving Relief in Cases of Insolvency.

Plea in abatement, that the promises laid, if any, were made by the defendant and one Cornelius Paulding, jointly, &c., and issue.

The plaintiffs, at the trial, offered Bussing as a witness, who had released all his interest in his estate assigned.

The defendant objected that the plaintiffs were first bound to prove the assignment, before they could proceed. This objection was overruled, on the ground that the plea admitted the assignment. The defendant then objected to the competency of Bussing, on the ground that his discharge, which was under the Act of 1813, was void by the Constitution of the U. S.; and he is still liable, therefore, to pay his debts. He stated on his *voire dire* that all the debts which he owed had been contracted since the passage of the Act under which he was discharged; and the judge admitted him to testify.

The plaintiff then produced an instrument in writing, dated Dec. 20, 1816, signed by the defendant alone, certifying that Apr. 12, 1814, one Crump, on the recommendation, and through the agency of the defendant, borrowed and received of Bussing 200 shares of the capital stock of the N. Y. Mfg. Co., which the defendant engaged to have returned and reconveyed to Bussing, within 30 days from the time of the loan; that default having been made in the return and reconveyance, Crump, at or about the expiration of the 30 days, placed in the defendant's hands sufficient property to indemnify Bussing, the proceeds of which the defendant was to have applied to that object; but that he had converted the property into cash and appropriated the proceeds to the use and business of the firm of Marquand & Paulding. That there was, at the date, due to Bussing on the account aforesaid, $7,763.89. (Signed) Isaac Marquand.

Bussing swore that this certificate was given to him by the defendant, and signed by his own proper hand and name.

499*] *The defendant then moved for a nonsuit, on the ground that the certificate was no evidence of money for the sole use of Bussing, or his assignees. The judge overruled the motion.

The parties then went into further evidence, upon the question, whether the transaction out of which the above certificate arose, was one of Marquand & Paulding, the latter of whom was the Cornelius Paulding mentioned in the plea, or whether it was an individual concern of the defendant. This evidence is sufficiently stated in the opinion of the court.

Bussing had, by mistake, as he swore, in his proceedings to obtain his discharge, inventoried the debt in question as due from the firm of Marquand & Paulding.

The judge charged the jury, that notwithstanding the debt being so inventoried, still, if it was, in fact, due from the defendant alone, the plaintiffs were entitled to recover; and that even if the proceeds of the property in question were originally received by Marquand & Paulding, and applied to their use, still if the property was assigned for the satisfaction of Bussing's claim against Marquand, the plaintiffs were entitled to recover from Marquand solely.

The defendant excepted to this charge, and the jury found for the plaintiffs $11,656.76.

The parties made a case, agreeing that it might be turned by either into a special verdict or bill of exceptions, so far as respects the exceptions to the opinions and charge of the judge.

A motion was now made for a new trial, on behalf of the defendant, on three grounds: 1. That Bussing was not a competent witness. 2. That the defendant never was individually responsible, but that Marquand & Paulding were liable. 3. That the charge of the judge was incorrect.

Messrs. H. D. and *R. Sedgwick* for the motion, cited 15 Mass., 75, 331.

Mr. G. Griffin, contra, cited 1 Mont. Partn., 198, 199; Gow. Partn., 344, 348.

*Curia, per SUTHERLAND, *J.* Bussing was a competent witness. He was discharged from all his debts Sept. 30, 1822, under the Act of 1813; and it appeared that all the debts, which he owed at the time of his discharge, had been contracted since the passage of that Act. According to the repeated decisions of this court, that discharge was valid, not only as to the person of the insolvent, but as to his future acquisitions. Those decisions, it is true, have been questioned, and cases are now understood to be pending in the Supreme Court of the U. S., in which the unconstitutionality of the whole series of our Insolvent Laws is broadly maintained. What the decision of that court will be, it is not for us to anticipate; but until its judgment is pronounced, we are not only authorized but bound to presume that it will be in accordance with our own. [***500**

Bussing released to the plaintiffs all his interest in the surplus of the property assigned, &c. He was properly admitted as a witness.

The instrument of Dec. 20, 1816, signed by the defendant, contained sufficient evidence of money had and received by him solely, to the use of the plaintiffs, to entitle them to recover. He acknowledged by that instrument, that Crump placed in his hands sufficient property for the indemnification of Bussing, which he was to have applied to that object. But that, instead of this, he converted the property into cash, and appropriated the proceeds to the use and business of the firm of Marquand & Paulding. He also admits, by that instrument, that there is now due to Bussing the sum of $7,763.89.

The firm of Marquand & Paulding had two houses—one at N. Y., where Marquand resided, and carried on business; the other New Orleans, under the direction of Paulding, who resided there. Paulding had no knowledge of any part of the transaction in question. It originated as follows: Reuben Crump, of the firm of Kelso & Crump, Apr. 12, 1814, borrowed of Bussing, upon the recommendation, and through the agency of the defendant, 200 shares of the capital stock *of the N. Y. Mfg. Co. Crump gave the following note, for the 200 shares: "Within 30 days from date, I promise to transfer to Mr. Isaac Marquand, or order, two hundred shares of the N. York Manufacturing Company stock, for the same number transferred to me by Mr. Abm. Bussing. REUBEN CRUMP. [***501**

New York, 12th April, 1814."

Indorsed thus: "Transfer the within shares to Mr. Abm. Bussing. ISAAC MARQUAND."

Crump having failed to pay this note, at or about the time when it fell due, gave Marquand an order for a quantity of cotton, sufficient to pay it. He acknowledges that he received it for that purpose, realized the money, and applied it to the use and business of the firm of Marquand & Paulding. The order for the cotton was in favor of Marquand & Paudling. It was sent to auction in their names, sold on their account, and the proceeds applied to their benefit. But it was all done by Marquand, and under his exclusive direction; Paulding being in New Orleans, and knowing nothing of the transaction. The question is, whether Marquand is individually responsible for the amount, which he acknowledges has been received for the benefit of Bussing, or whether the action should have been brought against the firm of Marquand & Paulding.

There can be no doubt, that in the origin of this transaction, when Marquand became security to Bussing for the return of the stock borrowed by Crump, he acted in his individual capacity, and not on behalf of the firm. Crump's note was payable to him individually, and by him individually indorsed or transferred to Bussing. If an action could have been sustained at all upon this guaranty, it must undoubtedly have been brought against Marquand individually, and not against the firm. Crump testifies that when he received the transfer of the stock from Bussing, the defendant alone became security for the transfer of it; and that the giving of such security was the individual transaction of the defendant. Bussing also testified that he considered the transaction as with Marquand, the defendant, and not with Marquand & Paulding.

502*] *Every presumption, therefore, is in favor of the supposition that the cotton which Crump delivered to Marquand in trust for Bussing, and by way of indemnity against his guaranty of the delivery of the stock, was delivered to him in the same character in which his responsibility was incurred. It must be borne in mind that the order for the cotton, though in favor of the firm of Marquand & Paulding, was, in fact, delivered to Marquand, who was the sole partner in N. Y. Marquand alone directed it to be sold, and he alone, in fact, received the proceeds. If he applied them to the purposes of the firm, which he seems to have done, it was without the knowledge or privity of his copartner. It is, then, the case of one partner being a trustee, bringing trust money into the firm, without a knowledge or privity on the part of his copartner, of its being trust money; and it has been repeatedly held, in such cases, that it does not create a joint debt on the part of the firm, which can be proved against their joint estate. For, although the partner abuses his trust, and advances the money to the partnership, it will not raise a contract between the firm and the *cestui que trust*, nor convert the innocent partners into implied trustees. In *Ex parte Apsey*, 3 Bro. Ch. Cas., 265, the case was this: Edward Allen, of the firm of Edward & James Allen, was assignee, together with the petitioner, Apsey, under a commission of bankruptcy, issued against one William Tory. As such assignee, he received between 400 and 500 pounds, belonging to the estate, and applied it in discharging the debts, and in other purposes of the firm. The Allens afterwards became bankrupts, and Apsey, the co-assignee of Edward Allen, petitioned the *Chancellor* (on appeal from the decision of the commissioners), for leave to prove the sum received by his co-assignee, and applied to the payment of the partnership debts, under the joint commission against the partnership. But *Ld. Chancellor* Thurlow refused the petition; and remarked: "here one, by abusing his trust, advances trust money to the partnership; that will not raise a contract between the partnership, and the *person [***503** whose money it is. But where the application of the trust money to the purposes of the firm, is made with the knowledge and privity of the other partners, they are all jointly liable. *Smith* v. *Jameson*, 5 T. R., 601; *Boardman* v. *Mosman*, 1 Bro. Ch. Cas., 68; *Ex parte Clowes*, 2 *Id.*, 595; *Ex parte Watson*, 2 Ves. & B., 414; 3 Bro. Ch. Cas., 112.

Where one partner borrows money on his individual credit, and afterwards applies it to the payment of partnership debts, or loans it to the firm, it does not entitle the original lender to consider himself a creditor of the firm, and to enforce payment against them. *Ex parte Hunter*, 1 Atk., 223; *Parkin* v. *Carruthers*, 3 Esp., 250, per Le Blanc, *J.*

Where one of a firm borrows money, the fact of its being used in the business of the partnership, is, *prima facie*, evidence that the debt is joint, where no express separate contract was made with the individual partner. (8 Ves., 540; Gow, Partn., 343-349.)

I do not consider this case as at all varied by the circumstance, that the order for the cotton was drawn by Crump in the favor of the firm, instead of Marquand alone. The consideration for the order, the whole transaction out of which it grew, was an individual one, on the part of Marquand, in which he did not profess and, indeed, had no authority to act for the firm; and it is worthy of remark, that it is Marquand himself, who denies his individual responsibility, and not the partnership, seeking to get rid of a claim which might, with some plausibility, have been preferred against them.

The application of the cases cited by the defendant's counsel, from 15 Mass., 75, 331, is not perceived. In those cases the question was, whether Gore was liable as one of the firm of Gore & Grafton, in an action for money had and received under the following circumstances: They were general partners, and Grafton made a note in the partnership name, payable to Thomas Cushing, or order; and forged the indorsement of Cushing, and raised money upon it. The indorsee brought an action *on [***504** the note, the declaration also containing the general counts. The court held that he was entitled to recover under the general counts, though there was no evidence that the money was actually applied to the purposes of the firm; because Grafton had an authority to raise money upon the credit of the house. Gore had reposed that confidence in him, and ought to suffer the consequences.

The exceptions to the charge of the judge are not well taken, and the motion for a new trial must be denied.

New trial denied.

Overruled—8 Wend., 490.

Criticised—16 Wend., 508.
Distinguished and explained—48 N. Y., 551.
Cited in—11 Wend., 76; 17 Wend., 48; 7 Paige, 33; Hoffm., 543; 45 N. Y., 183; 47 N. Y., 20; 13 Barb., 233; 17 Abb. Pr., 155; 2 Bos., 192; 44 Super, 115; 18 Mich., 120; 32 Ohio, 379; 89 Pa., 172; 30 Am. Rep., 609 (32 Ohio, 374).

WELCH *v.* HICKS.

Admiralty—Where Vessel is Disabled and Owner Receives Goods at Intermediate Port, He is Liable for Freight Pro Rata—*Acceptance must be Voluntary—Refusal of Master to Repair—Promise to do so, Doubtful.*

Where a ship is disabled from prosecuting her voyage by the perils of the sea, and puts into an intermediate port, and the goods are received there by their owner, he is liable for freight *pro rata itineris.*

But in such a case, where the master, without sufficient cause, refuses to repair his ship and send on the goods, and to procure other vessels for the purpose, the owner may immediately demand his goods, and shall be discharged from freight, both full and *pro rata.*

To entitle to *pro rata* freight, the acceptance must be voluntary.

And where the master, having thus put into an intermediate port, at first refused to repair and proceed, and to procure other vessels and send on the goods, though one might have been done; and the owner negotiated several days with him, in order to induce him to do the one or the other; and, at last, the master made an offer to repair and proceed, under circumstances calculated to excite doubt of his sincerity; whereupon the owner demanded and received the goods and transported them in vessels in his own procuring in an action for freight; held, that it should have been left to the jury to say whether the proposition to repair, &c., was made *bona fide*; and whether the acceptance was voluntary, so as to entitle the ship owner to *pro rata* freight.

Citations—2 Cai., 21; 1 Johns., 27; 2 Johns., 323, 336; 9 Johns., 19, 20, 186; 2 Burr., 882; 7 T. R., 381; 5 East, 316; 10 East, 393, 526; 2 Campb., 466; 3 Binn., 448; 5 Binn., 525; 7 Cr., 358; 1 Marsh., 281, *n.*

ASSUMPSIT for freight of the ship Romeo, from Petersburgh in Russia, to Princetown in Mass.; tried at the N. Y. Circuit, Apr. 12, 1824, before Edwards, *Circuit J.*

The declaration stated that the plaintiff, the owner of the ship, received goods on board at St. Petersburgh, consigned to the defendant at N. Y.; but the ship was forced, by the violence of winds and tempests, to put into Princetown, on her voyage to N. Y., where the defendant elected to receive the goods, and did receive them and releases the plaintiff from his obligation to transport them to N. Y. It contained counts adapted both to full and *pro rata* freight.

505*] *At the trial, the plaintiff proved the shipment of the goods on certain freight, mentioned in the bill of lading, to be paid by the defendant on delivery of the goods at N. Y.; that on her voyage, the vessel put into Princetown, for the cause alleged, where the defendant accepted the goods; and the only question at the trial was, whether the acceptance was made under such circumstances as would legally subject the defendant to the payment of freight.

On this point the proof was, that the defendant, on learning that the ship had put into Princetown in distress, dispatched Laban Gardner (who was sworn as a witness for the defendant on the trial), as his agent, with full power in relation to the goods. Gardner arrived at Princetown, Dec. 15, 1820. The vessel was lying there, unable to prosecute the voyage in question, without being repaired. She was capable, in his opinion, of being taken to Boston, distant from 12 to 15 leagues, where she might have been repaired in a fortnight, at a moderate expense, so as to have taken on the goods to N. Y. The master refused to repair, or procure other vessels to forward the goods, till he heard from his owner; and refused to deliver the goods unless Gardner would pay full freight. Gardner inquired and found that other vessels could be engaged at Princetown to forward the goods, and informed the master; but he refused to employ them. Things remained in this situation till Jan. 5, ensuing; the master, on repeated requests, refusing to take measures for forwarding the goods, or to deliver them free of freight. About Dec. 21, the master said he had received orders to discharge the crew and did, accordingly, discharge them, between that time and Jan. 1. The harbor became obstructed by ice in about a fortnight after Gardner reached Princetown. Jan. 4, he applied, and repeated his requests to the master, who required time to answer till the next morning, when he told Gardner that he intended to repair the vessel at Princetown. Gardner swore that he believed him insincere in that remark, from the difficulty of making the repairs there; and that, at all events, the repairs *could not then be [***506** made in a reasonable time. The goods were in a perishable condition. The master still refused, for some time, to forward the goods. An agreement was made that they should be delivered to the agent, on his order upon his principal for freight, according to the tenor of the bill of lading. Afterwards they were delivered unconditionally, and Gardner received and forwarded them to N. Y., in vessels of his own procuring.

The defendant also offered to prove that the money necessarily expended in freight from Princetown to N. Y. exceeded the whole stipulated freight from Petersburgh to N. Y. This evidence was overruled.

The judge charged, that if a vessel, laden with goods on freight, meets with a disaster in the course of her voyage, and puts into an intermediate port—and the owner of the goods receives them there, he becomes liable to pay a *pro rata* freight, and that the defendant was liable in this case to pay *pro rata* freight, unless he could show an express and positive agreement, on the part of the master, to waive and discharge all claim to freight. That the law necessarily implied an agreement to pay freight, from the act of receiving the goods; and this, notwithstanding the ability of the master to repair in a reasonable time, or send on the goods in other vessels, and his refusal, on request, to do either. That the remedy of the owner of the goods would be to abandon the goods, and bring his action for damages against the master or owner of the vessel; and in every case, under any circumstances, the owner of the goods becomes liable at all events, by the act of accepting them alone, at the port of distress, to pay a *pro rata* freight, unless he can show an express and positive agreement to the contrary. He left it to the jury to say, whether the proof established such an agreement.

Verdict for the plaintiff for $2,526.67 damages.

NOTE.—*Freight* pro rata itineris—*Acceptance by owners at intermediate port.* See Robinson v. Marine Ins. Co., 2 Johns., 323, *note.*

The defendant excepted to the above opinion and charge; and a motion, founded on the bill of exceptions, was now made, in his behalf, for a new trial.

Mr. *G. Griffin*, for defendant. A *pro rata* freight is due only where the acceptance of the
507*] goods is voluntary. It *must be purely a matter of election with the owner; in order to which there must be volition. The doctrine of *pro rata* freight is of modern origin. The general rule is, that, to entitle to freight, the goods must be delivered at the port of destination. The charter-party never provides for freight short of this. There must then be such an acceptance as lays the foundation of a new promise. The action for *pro rata* freight is always *assumpsit*. These views will be found fully supported by the cases. *Luke* v. *Lyde*, 2 Burr., 885; S. C., 1 W. Bl., 190; *Cook* v. *Jennings*, 7 T. R., 377,381; *Mulloy* v. *Backer*, 5 East, 316; *Liddard* v. *Lopes*, 10 *Id.*, 526; *Armroyd* v. *Un. Ins. Co.*, 3 Binn., 437, 447, per Yeates, *J.*; *Mar. Ins. Co. of N. Y.* v. *Un. Ins. Co.*, 9 Johns., 186; *Callender* v. *Ins. Co. of N. A.*, 5 Binn., 525; *Case* v. *Balt. Ins. Co.*, 7 Cr., 358; *Hurtin* v. *Un. Ins. Co.*, 1 Cond. Marsh., 281 *a*, *note; Robinson* v. *Mar. Ins. Co.*, 2 Johns., 323.

The action on the new contract is an equitable one. It rests on the ground of benefit to the owner or consignee of the goods; 3 Chit. Com. Law, 414; and if the judge was right in holding us liable, it does not follow that we are not to be allowed the expense incurred, in transporting the goods from Princetown to N. Y. This should be deducted from, or set off against, the plaintiff's claim. *Coffin* v. *Storer*, 5 Mass., 252.

If the master refused to do what was in his power to forward the goods, he broke his charter-party, and has lost all right to recover upon it. Freight, then, should be denied on this ground; or, at least, equitably reduced. The engagement to the freighter has not been fulfilled. On every principle of equity, here should be at least a deduction. *Hunter* v. *Princep*, 10 East, 394, per Ld. Ellenborough, *Ch. J.; Portland Bank* v. *Stubbs*, 6 Mass., 422; *Osgood* v. *Groning*, 2 Campb., 466. The last case shows that it should have been left to the jury to say, whether the master might reasonably have been required to go on with the voyage. And see Lawes' Charter-Parties, 160.

508*] **Mr. J. Duer*, contra. The questions submitted upon the judge's charge do not arise out of the case contained in the bill of exceptions. True they apply to the charge, which was also out of the case. When the judge says that an acceptance, under any circumstances, will render the defendant liable, he lays down an abstract proposition, which we are not bound to defend. It is enough for us that the defendant is liable, under the circumstances of this case. The court will not grant a new trial on a case, when they see it must result in a verdict against the defendant, at least, as large as the present one. The complaint lies, in truth, on the side of the plaintiff. He was entitled to full freight. The master offered to repair, and proceed with the cargo in the Romeo. To this the owner of the goods refused to accede. It was his own fault that full freight was not earned. The authorities are clear, that we have a right to full freight under such circumstances. We agree that the refusal of the master to repair or proceed in other vessels, gave a right to the agent to demand the goods, if he had done so immediately. Instead of doing so, he continued a negotiation on the subject for several days; and the master finally offered to repair and proceed with the goods while the negotiation was pending. We agree that an immediate demand of the goods would have freed the shipper from freight. It was in consequence of the offer to repair, and a suspicion of its insincerity, that the goods were finally demanded and delivered. Such is the defendant's own testimony. The jury have tried the question, whether the master intended to deliver the goods free of freight. That question was properly submitted to them.

The event on which *pro rata* freight is claimed, is not provided for in the contract between the parties. There may not, therefore, be any positive claim for it on an abandonment of the voyage at an intermediate port; yet there is a demand in justice, if the abandonment be not the fault of the master or ship owner; and the act of acceptance by the owner of the goods works a legal claim. The extent of this claim is not according to the benefit he may receive,
*but the expense incurred in the trans- [***509**
portation so far. It is too much to say that there must not only be an acceptance, but a right freely to elect whether to accept or not. One consequence of this doctrine would be, that though the master can neither repair nor send on the goods by another vessel, yet an acceptance shall not entitle to freight. The contrary is clearly settled, and yet the shipper has no election. In such a case, if the goods be demanded and delivered, a right to entire freight arises. I admit that some of the cases cited do countenance the idea, that there must be a freedom to elect; that the acceptance must be voluntary and unconstrained; that is to say, the master must not coerce an acceptance by a refusal to do all he reasonably can towards forwarding the goods. But the rule, as considered and laid down in Abb. Ship., 336, Story ed., pt. 3, ch. 7, sec. 2, fully accords with the charge of the judge. This book says, if the master be unable or decline to forward the goods, yet an acceptance will bind to pay freight, *pro rata itineris peracti*. It will be seen there that the ancient authorities do not proceed on the ground of a new contract, but that freight was due by the maritime law, by force of the acceptance. This is the ground on which *Luke* v. *Lyde*, 2 Burr., 886, was decided. That case went on *Lutwidge* v. *Grey*, Abb. Ship., Story ed., 340, which was grounded on the acceptance; and the cases in this court have gone on the same principle. 1 Johns. Cas., 383; 2 Cai., 21; *Robinson* v. *Mar Ins Co.*, 2 Johns., 322.

It has been long settled, that expenses or other circumstances in the subsequent disposition of the goods, cannot vary the amount of the recovery. The rule on this head is laid down in the case last cited.

Mr. Griffin, in reply. At least, the judge should have submitted, in terms, to the jury, whether the final offer of the master to repair was sincere and at all to be relied upon.

I have before given several judicial interpretations of *Luke* v. *Lyde*, and I will now give two more: *Post* v. **Robertson*, 1 Johns., [***510**

24, and *Bradhurst* v. *Col. Ins. Co.*, 9 Johns., 19, 20.

I admit that commentators, and Abbott among the number, have differed from the courts. The only collision, however, is in commentators. There is none in the adjudged cases.

Curia, per SUTHERLAND, *J.* This court has repeatedly held, that freight *pro rata itineris* is due, where a ship, in consequence of the perils of the sea, without any fault of the master, goes into a port short of her destination, and is unable to prosecute the voyage; and the goods are received by the owner at such intermediate port. (2 Cai., 21; 1 Johns., 27; 2 Johns., 323, 336; 9 Johns., 19, 20, 186.) This principle has been adopted from the decisions of the English courts, commencing with *Luke* v. *Lyde*, 2 Burr., 882, and continued, without any essential conflict or contrariety, down to the present time. (7 T. R., 381; 5 East, 316; 10 East, 393, 526; 2 Campb., 466; 3 Binn., 448; 5 *Id.*, 525; 7 Cr., 358; 1 Marsh., 281, *note.*)

This general principle is not disputed by the defendant's counsel. On the other hand, it is conceded, that where the master refuses to repair his ship and send on the goods, or to procure other vessels for the purpose, and the owner of the goods then receives them, that this is not such an acceptance of the goods, as will entitle the ship owner to a *pro rata* freight. It is not a voluntary acceptance. He does not elect to receive his goods at the intermediate port, and sell them there, or become his own carrier to the port of destination. He does not assent to the termination of the voyage at the intermediate port; but it having been terminated there against his will, by the refusal of the master to send on his goods to the port of destination, he does not, by receiving them under such circumstances, in judgment of law, promise to pay the freight to the intermediate port.

The judge, in his charge to the jury, entirely excluded the question, whether the acceptance **511***] of the goods was*voluntary or not; and instructed them that the fact of receiving the goods, under any circumstances, rendered the owner liable for a *pro rata* freight; unless he could show an express and positive agreement of the master, at the time of the delivery of the goods, to waive and discharge all claim to the freight. In this I think he erred. The cases already cited, particularly those in 9 Johns., show that, in order to raise an implied *assumpsit* in such cases, the acceptance must be voluntary. No other rule would be consonant with justice or equity.

But the master did finally declare his election to repair his ship and send on the goods and they were agreed to be received by the defendant's agent, after such declaration had been made to him. This was at first upon the express condition of his giving an order on the defendant for the freight, but finally they were delivered and received without any such condition. These circumstances are claimed to be sufficient to sustain the verdict; and it is said, admitting the judge's charge to be incorrect, as it goes beyond the facts, a new trial should not, for that reason, be granted. Under the circumstances of the case, the agent might well have supposed that there was no *bona fide* intention to repair. He swears that such was his opinion; and that the goods were finally delivered unconditionally; that is (as I understand him), without any order having been given for the freight.

I think the judge should have left it to the jury to determine whether the master did intend to repair the vessel, and complete the voyage, and whether the acceptance of the goods by the agent of the defendant was voluntary or not.

New trial granted.

Cited in—7 Cow., 584; 5 Den., 176; 15 Barb., 53; 2 Bos., 204; 8 Wall., 161; 2 McLean., 430; 3 Wood & M., 444.

---

*THE PEOPLE *v.* WALBRIDGE. [*512

Contents of Indictment of Attorney, Under Statute, for Buying a Note—Act of Buying is the Offense—Statute, Constitutional.

An indictment against an attorney &c., upon the statute, sess. 41, ch. 259, sec. 1, for buying a note, need not allege that he bought the note with intent to prosecute, &c.; nor that the note has been prosecuted, nor need it show when it became due, its amount, or other circumstance, from which an intent to prosecute is to be inferred.

The act of buying is the offense, unless it comes within the proviso of the statute; which it lies with the defendant to show.

The statute is constitutional.

The indictment upon it may conclude, contrary to the form of the statute, in the singular. It need not be contrary to the form of the statute.

The omission, in reciting the title, of the word "the," after "the practice of," will not vitiate the indictment.

AT the Rensselaer Oyer and Terminer, in Nov., 1824, an indictment was found against the defendant; the first count of which charged, that, Apr. 20, 1824, he did buy a certain promissory note, of and from one J. B. S., the holder and proprietor of the note, which was made and signed by one W. M. and dated Apr. 14, 1824, by which note W. M. promised to pay one A. V. A. the sum of $125.50, at the Bank of Lansingburgh, in 90 days from the date; that the note was indorsed by A. V. A., whereby it became and was the property of J. B. S. till the purchase by the defendant, for a good and valuable consideration; the defendant, at the time he so purchased, being an attorney and counselor of the Supreme Court of Judicature of the State of N. Y., and of the Court of C. P. of the County of Rensselaer: and that he did not buy or receive the note in payment for any estate real or personal, or for any service actually rendered, or for any debt antecedently contracted, or for any purpose of remittance, without any intent to violate or evade the Act, &c., entitled "An Act to Prevent Abuses in the Practice of Law, and to Regulate Costs in Certain Cases," passed Apr. 21, 1818; to the evil, &c., and against the form of the statute in such case made and provided, and against, &c.

2d count. That the defendant, Nov. 1, 1824, did buy of and from one P. B., and become interested in buying of and from P. B., a certain other promissory note, made and signed by W. M., by which W. M. promised to pay to P. B., or bearer, the sum of $42.60, the defendant at the time he so bought and purchased the last mentioned note, being and still being an attorney and counselor of the Supreme Court of Judicature of the people of the State of N. Y; and that he did not buy or re-

ceive the same note in payment of any estate
513*] *real or personal, or for any service actually rendered, or for any debt before that time contracted, or for any purpose of remittance, to the evil, &c., and against the form of the statute, &c. (as in the first count).

3d count. That the defendant, Nov. 1, 1824, knowingly, willfully and corruptly became and was interested in buying a certain promissory note, made by one W. M. for the sum of $125.50, payable to one A. V. A.; and also one other promissory note, made by W. M., payable to one P. B. or bearer; and also one other promissory note, made by W. M. to one E. G. for the sum of $31.20; also one other promissory note, made by W. M., payable to one C. F., for a sum of money to the jurors unknown; the defendant, at the time of the purchase of each and every of these notes, and at the time he became so interested in the purchase thereof, being and still being an attorney and counselor of the Supreme Court of Judicature of the people of the State of N. Y.; and that he did not become interested in the purchase of either of these notes, by way of payment for any estate real or personal, or for any services rendered before the purchase of these notes respectively, or for any purpose of remittance, without any intent to evade or violate the Act, &c. (as in the first count).

At the Oyer and Terminer of the same county, in June, 1825, the defendant demurred generally to this indictment; and after argument, that court held the indictment sufficient; and rendered judgment against the defendant. They, however, advised the district attorney to have the questions arising on the indictment submitted to the Supreme Court for their decision; and in case this court should agree with the Oyer and Terminer, that the defendant have liberty to plead not guilty.

Pursuant to this advice, the cause was argued and decided here.

Mr. Walbridge, in person. The indictment is defective both in form and substance. 1. In form. It misrecites the title of the Statute, sess. 41, ch. 259, upon which it is founded. The word "the" is omitted after the words
514*] "practice *of." This is a material and fatal variance, (2 Hawk. P. C., ch. 25, sec. 101, 104; 2 Hal. P. C., 172; Bac. Abr., Indictment, H; 1 Doug. 97, per Ld. Mansfield; 1 Ld. Raym., 382; 2 Ld. Raym., 1038, 1039; 1 Esp., 98; 1 Saund., 135, *n.* 3; 6 T. R., 776.) A misrecital of the title is equally fatal, as if it were of the body of a statute. The title is a name given by the maker; and though it be not necessary to set it forth, if this be attempted, it must be done correctly. (Esp. Pen. Act., 101, 7.)

Again; there are two statutes prohibiting the same thing; the Statute of 1813, sess. 36, ch. 48, sec. 7, and the Statute of Apr. 21, 1818, mentioned in the indictment. Yet the indictment concludes against a single statute. It should have concluded *contra formam statutorum.* (3 Bac. Abr., Indictment, H, p. 114; 2 Hawk. P. C. 252; Esp. Pen. Act., 114.)

In substance. The indictment does not set forth the offense which the statute was made to prohibit. It should aver that the notes were purchased for collection or prosecution. An indictment upon a penal statute must state all the circumstances which enter into the definition of the offense. And all penal statutes must be construed most favorable to the defendant. (1 Hal. P. C., 170, 517; 2 *Id.*, 170, 172; Dy., 304; 1 Chit. Pl., 357.) The mere act of buying a note is not an offense against the statute. (1 Cow., 458; 3 Cow., 252.) It does not appear that the notes were even due when they were bought; and as to the note in the first count, it appears on the face of the indictment, not to have been due. The presumption is, that every man will meet his engagements: and it is impossible even to infer from the indictment that the notes were purchased for the purpose of prosecution. They were never prosecuted. Buying a note comes within the proviso of the 1st section, that a promissory note may be received in payment for estate, real or personal. What is money but personal estate? The note mentioned in the second count is less than $50. It could not be sued in a court of record with a view to *costs. So as to three of the [***515**
notes in the third count. All three of these are set forth without date or time of payment, and an additional one without amount. This count is bad for uncertainty.

The abuses in the practice of the law, intended to be prevented by the statute, were buying and prosecuting choses in action, and making bills of costs. The mere buying a note, is no part of the practice of the law.

The statute is unconstitutional, if the construction contended for on the other side be correct. Every class of citizens has equal natural rights, which the Legislature cannot take away more from one class than another. To say that one shall not purchase a chose in action, because he is an attorney, is depriving him of a right which every citizen has an equal claim to; and which the Legislature cannot take from him without his consent. They would have a right to prohibit the same thing to a merchant or mechanic, because he is a merchant or mechanic. They might, on the same principle, forbid the farmer to sell his wheat, for fear that he might loan his money at usury, or purchase rum and get drunk with it.

Mr. J. Pierson, Dist-Atty, contra. As to the form. The variance complained of is immaterial. If it do not alter the sense, it will not vitiate. (1 Chit. Cr. L., 280, and the authorities there cited.) Besides, the recital may be rejected as surplusage. The counts all concluding contrary to the form of the statute, it was not necessary to recite the title at all. (*Id.*, 281.) The second count does not recite the title. The objection not applying to this, though it be good as to the other counts, will not, therefore, support the demurrer, which is general to all the counts. If any count is good, judgment must be against the defendant.

The two statutes referred to on the other side are distinct and wholly unconnected. But the conclusion would be good, if the indictment were grounded on two statutes. It is never necessary to conclude an indictment as being contrary to the form of statutes, in the plural. (1 Chit. *Cr. L., 240; Cro. Eliz., [***516**
750; 1 Saund., 135, *note* 3; 2 Saund., 377, *note* 12; Cro. Jac., 187.)

As to substance. The Act of 1818 does not, either expressly or impliedly, require that the note should be bought for collection or prosecution, or that it must be prosecuted. To require either, would be inconsistent with the object which the Legislature had in view. The construction contended for by the defendant, would render the statute nugatory. It would not go beyond the Act of 1813. This court, whenever they have spoken of these Acts, have recognized a difference, though they say the Acts are *in pari materia*. (3 Cow., 261; 1 Cow., 452.) It is evident that the Legislature esteemed the first Act ineffectual, on account of its requiring an intent to prosecute to be shown. The difficulty of doing this, from the various modes of evasion resorted to, led the Legislature to make the mere act of purchasing a chose in action the offense. They, in this manner, strike at the root of the evil. If this construction be correct, it is immaterial when the notice were dated, what their amount, or when due.

As to the objection for unconstitutionality: The Legislature have the same right to impose restrictions upon attorneys in the practice of law, that they have to regulate inns and taverns, or the inspection of provisions. It is optional with the attorney, whether he will or will not practice under such restrictions. (*b*)

The Court held the indictment to be good both in form and substance. They said the intent with which an attorney or counselor buys a note, need not be alleged in the indictment; nor need it be averred that a prosecution has been commenced on it. The act of buying con-
517*] stitutes *the offense; (*c*) and on this being shown, it lies with the defendant to make out that he is within the proviso of the statute. The date, amount, time when due, &c., with other circumstance going to the question of intent, are, therefore, immaterial. We think the Legislature intended to forbid the purchase of notes, &c., by attorneys or counselors, in all cases, except those coming within the language or spirit of the proviso.

(*b*) I remember that Mr. Cook, of Saratoga, appeared in this court, at the August Term, next after the passage of the Act of 1818, and moved to have his name stricken from the rolls of the court, as attorney and counselor; which the court ordered to be done.

(*c*) The intent of the Legislature, as rendered by the court, if it require manifestation by anything out of the plain language of the statute, is confirmed by a comparison of this statute, with one copied from it in relation to justices and constables. The two Acts are almost *verbatim* the same (*mutatis mutandis*), with the addition of the distinguishing words in the letter, "for the purpose of commencing any action thereon." They run thus:

Stat. sess. 41, ch. 259, sec. 1.	Stat. sess. 43, ch. 159, sec. 1.
"That no attorney or counselor at law of any court of record in this State, shall, directly or indirectly, buy, or be in any way or manner interested in buying any bond, bill, promissory note, bill of exchange, book debt, or other chose in action; nor shall any such attorney or counselor, by himself, or by or in the name of any other person, either before or after suit brought, lend or advance," &c. (provision against procuring debts for collection by loan).	"That no justice of the peace, or constable, shall, directly or indirectly, buy or be interested in buying, any bond, bill or promissory note, bill of exchange, book debt, or other chose in action, for the purpose of commencing any action thereon; nor shall any justice or constable, by himself, or by or in the name of any other person or persons, either before or after suit brought, either lend or advance," &c. (provision against procuring debts for collection, by loan)

Everybody will see that the passage of the last Act is a direct legislative construction of the first, as to the question of purpose or intent in buying the note, &c.; and that this construction accords with that given by the Supreme Court in the principal case.

We have no doubt the Act is constitutional; nor are the exceptions to the indictment, in point of form, well taken.

S. C.—3 Wend., 120.

Cited in—3 Wend., 127; 2 Keyes, 116; 3 Abb. App. Dec., 160; 9 Barb., 301; 33 Barb., 578; 21 How. Pr., 175; 5 Park., 207.

---

*EX PARTE JENNINGS. [*518

*A Transfer of Land, Bounded on Margin of a River above Tide-water, Carries the Land to the Center of the Stream, Subject to the Public Easement—Navigable River, is where the Tide Ebbs and Flows—Practice—Statute—*Mandamus.

A patent or grant of land by the State, bounded on the margin of a river above tide-water, carries the land to the grantee *usque filum aquæ.*

Otherwise, where it is bounded on a navigable river.

A navigable river, in the common law sense of the term, is only where the tide ebbs and flows.

A patent or grant of land was bounded on the margin of the Chitteningo Creek; held, that it carried the land to the grantee, *usque filum aquæ.*

The water of the Chitteningo Creek was diverted from a mill and other hydraulic works on that creek; the right to erect the works being claimed under a patent or grant from the State, bounded on the margin of the creek; held, that the Appraisers appointed pursuant to the Act, sess. 48, ch. 275, sec. 1, were bound to appraise the damages to the owners of the works, they having a right to erect them, and a right to the use of the waters: that this was a case within the Statute, sess. 40, ch. 262, sec. 3.

The Appraisers having refused to act, on the ground that the property of the creek was in the State; and that, therefore, they had no jurisdiction; held, that a *mandamus* should issue commanding them to appraise.

The court granted a peremptory *mandamus*, on the first motion, the case being argued on both sides: and the court understanding that the Appraisers were willing to abide by the decision on the facts as they then stood; but afterwards, on suggestion that the appraisers wished to bring error, they changed the rule into one for an alternative *mandamus*; so that the facts might be put on record by a return.

Citation—Act, sess. 40, ch. 262.

BEFORE, and at the time of the erection of the Erie Canal, the relator was in possession, and claimed to be the owner in fee of various hydraulic works, standing on the margin of the Chittenango Creek, near the rapids, in the Town of Sullivan, in the County of Onondaga. He had, before the erection of the canal, purchased the land on which the works stood, bordering on the creek, with about 200 acres of adjoining land. The works consisted of a flouring mill, two saw-mills, one carding-machine, and one clothier's works, which he claimed to be worth about $10,000; and which were dependent for their operation on the waters of the Chitteningo Creek. Being so possessed, about five years ago, this creek, with its main tributary branches, the Cowassalon and Butternut, above the relator's works, were

NOTE.—*Boundaries—Lands bounded by Rivers.*

Where lands are bounded by a stream or river not navigable, or above tide-water, the owner holds the land under the water to the center of the stream, subject only to the public easement to use the stream as a highway. Case v. Haight, 3 Wend., 632; Canal Commissioners v. People, 5 Wend., 423; Canal Appraisers v. People, 17 Wend., 571; Child v. Starr, 4 Hill, 369; Demeyer v. Legg, 18 Barb., 14; Commissioners, &c., v. Kempshall, 26 Wend., 409; Seneca Nation v. Knight, 23 N. Y., 498; Palmer v. Mulligan,

taken into the Erie Canal for a feeder. Limestone Creek, which also formed a junction with the Chitteningo, above the relator's works, was likewise taken into the canal as a feeder in the fall of the year 1825. All the principal streams which formed the Chitteningo Creek, where the relator's works are situated, are now made use of as feeders to the Erie Canal. This
519*]canal *was erected by the State, which, since thus converting the waters of the Chitteningo to the purposes of the canal, has used the surplus water either for its own use for the benefit of the salt works at Salina, or disposed of it to individuals for the purpose of hydraulic works, they paying an annual revenue to the State for its use. By these operations, the relators works have become nearly useless for the want of water.

About four years ago he applied to the Canal Commissioners, and requested them to appraise his damages arising from thus diverting the water from his mills, pursuant to the Statute, sess. 40, ch. 262, sec. 3, 4 Laws, 302 *b*; and sess. 44, ch. 240, sec. 1, 5 Laws, 248 *c*, but they neglected to make the appraisal. In the summer of 1825, after the passing of the Act, sess. 48, ch. 275, sec. 1, 7 Laws, p. 398 *a*, constituting a new Board of Appraisers, he made his application to them for the same purpose, which he repeated several times last winter, giving them notice in writing. This Board consisted of Henry Seymour, David Woods and Joseph D. Selden, Esqs.

July 10, last, he laid before them his claim for damages, but they absolutely declined and refused to make any appraisal, or to act upon the subject, or allow him any compensation whatever.

On the relator's affidavit showing these facts, *Mr. S. L. Edwards* moved for a *mandamus* commanding the Appraisers to proceed and make an appraisal in the premises.

Mr. S. Beardsley, contra, read an affidavit of Mr. Henry Seymour, one of the Canal Commissioners, and a member of the Board of Appraisal to whom Jennings had submitted his claim for damages, stating that the Appraisers, against whom this motion was made, in their consultations upon Jenning's application, all agreed as he understood, and now believes, that, in point of fact, the State had not parted with the land upon which the Chitteningo passes, at the place claimed by Jennings; but had bounded purchases of and on the margin of the stream; so that, as he believes (and he
520*] *believes the other Appraisers were satisfied of the fact being so), the State was still the owner of the land covered by the waters of the stream; and had not parted with it or contracted to part with it, to any person whatever; or authorized the use of the water of the stream for hydraulic purposes at the place in question.

A similar application was made by N. P. Randall, in behalf of Eglestone, who claimed about $5,000 for damages from the same cause mentioned above in Jennings's case. The only difference was, that Eglestone had taken possession of the premises in question on his part, under a contract for a conveyance in fee, but which was not yet executed.

Both motions were heard together.

Messrs. Edwards and *Randall*, in support of the motions. The Appraisers refuse to act, alleging that they have no jurisdiction. This objection is partly technical, as founded on the construction of their powers under the Act; but, mainly, because they claim the premises in question as the property of the State.

1. Suppose the bed of the creek never to have been granted by the State; can they divert the water from land owned by an individual, extending only to the margin? We contend not. The rule of law is *aqua currit, et debet currere.* Water flows in its natural course, and should always be permitted to run there; so that all through whose land it passes may have the privilege of using it; but not so as to injure another. Ang. Water-courses, 5; *Merritt* v. *Parker, Id.*, App., 134. The right to the use of water flowing by a man's land belongs to the owner, of common right. Co. Litt., 261 *a; Mayor of Hull* v. *Barnes*, Cowp., 102. A man possessing land on the banks of a river has a right to the flow of the water in its natural stream, without alteration or diminution. *Bealy* v. *Shaw*, 6 East, 208, per Graham, B. at *N. P.*, whose doctrine was recognized and affirmed on motion for a new trial.

*Though Jennings does not own [***521**
lands on both sides of the stream, his right is perfect, to have the water flow by and along the side of his land. Ang. Water-courses, 29; Co. Litt., 261 *a;* Cowp., 102.

But a grant bounded on the margin of a fresh water creek, or river, carries the land to the center of the stream. It is well settled that fresh rivers, of what kind soever, do, of common right, belong to the owners of the adjacent soil. Ang. Water-courses, 15; *Palmer* v. *Mulligan*, 3 Cai., 319; Dav. Rep., 152, 155, 157; 12 Mod., 510; 17 Johns., 195; 2 Conn., 481; 20 Johns., 99; 4 Burr., 2162. Where one owns the soil under the water of a running stream, the right to the water-course extends not to the fluid itself; but only to the advantage of its impetus. (Ang., Water-courses, 37, 39.) Where a creek not navigable, and which is beyond the ebb and flow of the tide, forms a boundary, the line must be run in the center. *Jackson* v. *Louw*, 12 Johns., 252, per Yates, *J.*

We concede that the soil of the sea and the soil where the tide ebbs and flows, between high and low water mark, belong to the public. (Co. Litt., 61 *a;* 2 Bl. Com., 262.)

---

3 Cai., 307; Luce v. Carley, 24 Wend., 451; People v. Canal Appraisers, 13 Wend., 355; People v. Law, 34 Barb., 494; Dunham v. Williams, 36 Barb., 136; Kingsland v. Chittenden, 6 Lans., 15; Mott v. Mott, 68 N. Y., 246; Hatch v. Dwight, 17 Mass., 289; Ingraham v. Wilkinson, 4 Pick., 268; Lunt v. Holland, 14 Mass., 149; State v. Gilmanton, 9 N. H., 461; Camden v. Creel, 4 W. Va., 365; Arnold v. Elmore, 16 Wis., 509; Newton v. Eddy, 23 Vt., 319; Brown v. Chadbourne, 31 Me., 9; Thomas v. Hatch, 3 Sumn., 170; Rix v. Johnson, 5 N. H., 520; Kimball v. Schoff, 4 N. H., 190; Arnold v. Mundy, 6 N. J. L., 1; Bradford v. Cressey, 45 Me., 9; Newhall v. Ireson, 13 Gray, 262; R. R. Co. v. Schurmeir, 7 Wall., 272, 287. See, also, 3 Kent Com., pp. 427-432, and authorities there cited.

Where, from the conveyance, it clearly appears the intention was to exclude the stream, the above rule does not apply. Child v. Starr, 4 Hill, 369; Kingman v. Sparrow, 12 Barb., 201; Yates v. Van De Bogert, 56 N. Y., 526; Bradford v. Cressey, 45 Me., 9; Dunlap v. Stetson, 4 Mason, 349.

Nor does the rule apply to lands bounded by navigable streams. Canal Commissioners v. People, 5 Wend., 423; Middletown v. Sage, 8 Conn., 221; Cuson v. Blaze, 2 Binn., 475; Shrunk v. Schuylkill Nav. Co., 22 Miss., 71.

Private rights are not to be impaired by the State unless a compensation is provided. Ang. Water-courses, 53, 54; Gro., bk. 8, ch. 14, sec. 7; Puf., bk. 8, ch. 5, sec. 7; 1 Bl. Com., 141; 2 Johns. Ch., 162. If no compensation be provided, an action lies for the injury. (Ang., Water-courses, 65, 66, and cases cited; *Id.*, 53, 54, and cases cited.)

Mr. S. Beardsley, contra. The Appraisers suppose they had no jurisdiction of the matter in relation to which they were called upon to act. The Act of April 15, 1817, prescribes their power, and lays down the principles of appraisal. (4 L. N.Y., 302 *b*, sec. 3.) The Canal Commissioners are authorized, by this section, to take possession of "any lands, waters and streams," necessary for the prosecution of the canal; and in case these are not granted to the State, there is to be a just and equitable ap-
522*] praisal of the *loss and damage, if any, over and above the benefit and advantage to the respective owners and proprietors, or parties interested in the premises so required. And whether any damages are awarded or not, they are to describe the premises appropriated. The Act of April 7, 1819, sec. 3, 5 L. N. Y., 123 *a*, extends the same principles to other parts of the canals. The subsequent Acts do not alter the principle. The only change made, is in the Board of Appraisal. The 2d section of the last Act, April, 20, 1825, L. N.Y., 398 *a*, gives an appeal from the Board of Appraisers to the Canal Commissioners, whose decision shall be final.

The Appraisers cannot act unless it be in relation to such "lands, waters or streams," as may be given or granted to the people. And these must be such as some person may own, or in which they have an interest. Besides, they must by property, the fee simple of which may vest in the State. For, on appraisal and payment, such is declared to be the consequence.

Water does not admit of ownership. The interest in it is merely usufructuary. It belongs to the first occupant only while he holds possession of it. (2 Bl. Com., 14, 18.) The fee simple cannot be vested in the State. No description can be made of it.

Eglestone had no legal interest, but merely a contract for a deed; and though Jennings purchased and has a deed, it does not appear of whom he made his purchase. A clear title should be made out—such an one as will be worth something to the State.

I am directed to insist tnat the Chittenango is a public stream; that it is public property in every sense of the word; and the State has title to the lands upon which it passes, the patents being bounded upon the margin of the stream and not at its center.

Rivers are of three kinds: 1. Such as are wholly and absolutely private property. 2. Such as are private property, subject to the servitude of the public interest by a passage upon them. The distinguishing test between these two is, whether they are susceptible or
523] not of use for a *common passage. 3. Rivers where the tide ebbs and flows, which are called arms of the sea. (*People* v. *Platt*, 17 Johns., 211; *Hooker* v. *Cumming*, 20 Johns., 90; 4 Burr., 2164, per Ld. Mansfield.)

In the second kind, the public have the right of way; and where the river is not granted in terms, it should not be holden to pass. A boundary upon the margin excludes it. The use of these large streams are important to the State in various ways, and it never was the intention* to part with the right of appropriating them to the use of the public. Individuals enjoy the benefit of them at sufferance from the State.

This is a question of great importance, not only to individual owners and the State, but to the Canal Commissioners. Probably more than $100,000 on the lines of the canals are involved in its issue. If the Canal Commissioners pay out money, on appraisals where there is no jurisdiction, the Act is void; and they are amenable to the State. They are, therefore, bound, in duty to themselves, in a doubtful case, to avoid appraisals; and especially to avoid payment till the decision of this court can be had, which they are very willing to follow. Mr. Seymour, at whose request I now raise these questions, is anxious fully to indemnify these suffering individuals, if he is warranted in doing so; and will most cheerfully follow the directions of this court.

I am not directed to raise the question here, as to the constitutional power of the Legislature, to proceed in this manner: first to take private property, and then to appoint their own agents, dependent upon themselves, to make the appraisal. But I have certainly very serious doubts, whether the decision of *Judge* Patterson, in *Van Horne's Lessee* v. *Dorrance*, 2 Dall., 313, &c., that they are bound to do this through the medium of the ordinary tribunals of the State, is not according to the law of the case. Should this court think the Board itself unconstitutional, of course they will not interfere and compel an appraisal by *mandamus*.

Besides, the Appraisers have a discretion. They are to exercise their judgment whether any damages are due, *over and above [*524 the benefit which the individual derives from the canal. They may have proceeded on this ground. If so, this court certainly will not control or coerce them by *mandamus*. (19 Johns., 262; 12 Johns., 415; 2 Cow., 444.)

Mr. Randall, in reply. It is true, on the authorities cited, that this court will not interfere by *mandamus* where the inferior tribunal has a discretion, and has acted on that discretion. Here is an utter refusal to act at all; and moreover, the ground is stated on which that refusal is founded. This is the very case, of all others, in which the court should interfere, a case where there is no other legal remedy. Such is the language of the cases cited to this point. The Appraisers have been pressed to act again and again. They have uniformly refused. The Legislature have been applied to. They refused to act, on the ground that the case is a proper one for appraisal.

It is true that running water, as such, is not strictly the subject of property. But if we have no property in it, neither have the State. The property in water depends on the ownership of the soil through or by which it flows. Though there cannot be a grant of water *eo nomine*, the right to use it may be granted, in fee, or for any lesser time. The Act should be liberally construed in favor of individual right. If there be no provision for indemnity, the Commissioners are wrong-doers, and are liable to an action. It is not to be supposed that the State will take the property of any individual without providing the means of paying him for it.

It is enough that the applicants are in possession of the premises in question. The Appraisers must satisfy themselves of the extent of their interest, pay them for it, and it then passes to the State, whatever it is. What we complain of is, that they refuse to pass upon the subject—claiming the whole for the State.

It is certainly due to Mr. Seymour to say that he is not only willing but anxious to allow these applicants an indemnity, provided he can feel himself warranted in doing so. **525*]** *We do not know the views of the other gentlemen who compose the Board ; but we presume they are also anxious that justice should be done ; and that it is delayed only by an apprehended want of authority.

Curia. By the 3d section of "An Act respecting Navigable Communications Between the Great Western and Northern Lakes and the Atlantic Ocean," sess. 40, ch. 262, the Canal Commissioners are authorized to take possession of and use any "lands, waters and streams," necessary for the prosecution of the improvements intended by the Act ; and, by the same section, the Commissioners of Appraisal are "to make a just and equitable estimate and appraisal of the loss and damage, if any, over and above the benefit and advantage to the respective owners and proprietors, or parties interested in the premises so required, &c., by and in consequence of making and constructing any of the works aforesaid." It is admitted that the principles of appraisal have not been changed by any subsequent Act.

In this, and the subsequent Act, there is ample provision, we think, for allowing compensation for all damages to private property occasioned by the Canal Commissioners in the prosecution of their duties, whether such damage be direct or consequential. Waters and streams, in which the relators claim an interest, are taken for the use of the canal It is a case within the very words of the Act. If not so, if it were a question of construction, there can be no doubt that such construction should be most liberal in favor of private right. Individual property cannot be taken ; or, which is the same thing, individual rights impaired, for the benefit of the public, without just compensation. Such is the language of the common law, and of the Constitution. It would be derogating from the justice of the Legislature, to suppose they would stop short of providing for compensation in such a case.

Whatever interest the claimant of damages may have, he is to be paid for ; and the State then succeeds to his right. The State becomes a purchaser. True, the same section which **526*]** *provides for the appraisal, &c., says this acquisition shall be in fee simple; but this may well be, though the individual claimant may have only a limited interest, a particular estate, for instance ; or a right merely equitable, the reversion or legal estate residing elsewhere. If so, when the whole shall be paid for, the whole will vest in the State. The question as to the extent and value of interest, is one for the Appraisers, and respects the amount of damages and the persons to whom they are to be paid. We see no more difficulty in describing and entering in a book the various interests which different persons may have in the flow of water, whether immediate, reversionary, legal or equitable, than in designating the like interests in land. It cannot be allowed, because the estate is less than the fee, or because it is merely incidental to, or issuing out of land, that, therefore, the owner should be devested of his right without compensation. The right to the flow of water over land, is commensurate with the interest in the land. It many times constitutes the main value of the property ; and is, accordingly, made the subject of compensation and acquisition by the very terms of the statute. A conventional transfer of such a right, by grant, would, no doubt, be valid.

There can be no doubt that a *mandamus* is the proper remedy. This is not the case of error in the act of appraisal; but the Commissioners have refused to make any appraisal whatever. This is not denied; and a *mandamus* is asked for, commanding the Appraisers to proceed, and value the interests of the relators at what they are worth.

So much as to the preliminary objections. These were considered by the counsel, and are, indeed, of minor consequence, compared with the question of right; which is put by the Appraisers on the construction to be given to the State grant of the lands bordering on the Chittenango. The objection is contained in the affidavits of Mr. Seymour, "that, in point of fact, the State had not parted with the land upon which the Chittenango passes, at the places claimed, but had bounded purchases of land on the margin of the stream; so that, as he believes (and he believes *the other Appraisers **[*527** were satisfied of the fact being so), the State was still the owner of the land covered by the waters of the stream, and had not parted with it, or contracted to part with it to any person whatever; or authorized the use of the water for hydraulic purposes at the places in question."

If the construction set up by the Commissioners be the true one; if the State owns the land covered by the water, it is clear that, though the relators may be entitled to the use of the water flowing by and touching upon them for all ordinary purposes, yet they cannot build mills upon and raise the water of the stream. They are trespassers; and the State may claim not only the water, but the mills themselves, so far as they encroach upon the stream.

We do not, however, entertain a doubt that the Appraisers have misapprehended the construction of the State grants. It is not pretended that the Chittenango is a navigable creek or river, where the tide ebbs and flows. Such is notoriously not the fact. The decisions upon the construction of grants, bordering on streams, are numerous in the reports, not only of this, but of other States, and of England; and, so far as they proceed upon the common law, they are uniform. The cases have generally arisen upon disputes concerning the rights of fishery; and though relating to rivers of the first magnitude, where the public have an acknowledged right of passage for rafts, boats, &c., yet the owners of land on the margin, above tide-water, have been allowed the several and exclusive right of fishery to the center of the stream opposite their respective farms; and where their land lies on both sides, they have been allowed the same right in the whole river, so far as their farms extend.

It is not necessary to go into the various cases on this subject. They were mostly cited upon the argument. They proceed upon the principle that the owner of the land on the margin, owns the bed over which the river passes; and though it be nominally and in terms bounded on the margin, it extends, by construction of law, to the center of the stream. The public **528***] right is one of passage, *and nothing more; as in a common highway. It is called by the cases an easement; and the proprietor of the adjoining land has a right to use the land and water of the river in any way not inconsistent with this easement. If he make any erection rendering the passage of boats, &c., inconvenient or unsafe, he is guilty of a nuisance; and this is the only restriction which the law imposes upon him. It follows, that neither the State nor any individual have a right to divert the stream, or render it less useful or valuable to the owner of the soil. If the State had intended to retain the property in the stream, they should have inserted an express reservation or exception in their grants.

An opposite rule prevails in the construction of grants bounded on the margin of navigable rivers. By the term "navigable river," the law does not mean such as is navigable in common parlance. The smallest creek may be so to a certain extent, as well as the largest river, without being legally a navigable stream. The term has in law a technical meaning, and applies to all streams, rivers or arms of the sea, where the tide ebbs and flows. A public grant, bounded on the margin of such waters, extends by construction no further than high water mark, and leaves, as to the rest, an absolute proprietary interest in the public. Above the flow of the tide, the river becomes private, either absolutely so, or subject to the public right of way, accordingly as it is a small or a large stream.

In this case, we decide that the grant, as set forth by Mr. Seymour, carried the land to the middle of the creek; and that, therefore, the interest is out of the State. We think the relators have shown an interest which entitles them to an appraisal; and it is for the Appraisers to determine its extent, on the hearing before them.

Rule for a peremptory mandamus.

The above arguments and decision were at August Term last.

The following rule was entered in the case of *Eglestone:*

529*] *On reading and filing the affidavit of Darius Eglestone, showing that he is in possession of a lot of land and mill, situated on the Chittenango Creek, in the Town of Sullivan; that the water has been diverted from the said creek for the use of the Erie Canal; that he has made application to Henry Seymour, David Woods and Joseph D. Selden, to estimate and appraise the damages which the said Darius has sustained on occasion of the diversion of the said creek; and that the said Appraisers refuse to make any appraisal or estimate of said damages; and on reading and filing the affidavit of Henry Seymour, explaining the reasons why the said Appraisers refuse to appraise and estimate said damages; on motion of *Mr. N. P. Randall*, and the same being argued by him on behalf of the relator, and by *Mr. Beardsley*, on behalf of the said Appraisers; and it appearing to the court that the said Darius has an interest in the premises, which entitles him to an appraisement of damages, if any have been in fact sustained; it is, therefore, ordered, that a *mandamus* issue, to be directed to the said Henry Seymour, David Woods and Joseph D. Selden, commanding them to proceed to appraise and estimate the damages of the said Darius Eglestone, on occasion of the taking of the waters of the said creek for the use of the Erie Canal, over and above the benefit and advantage to the said Darius, by and in consequence of making and constructing the said canal.

A similar rule was entered in the cause *ex rel. Jennings.*

During the last vacation, on the application of *Mr. Beardsley*, in behalf of the Canal Appraisers, the *Chief Justice* granted an order to stay proceedings in the cause, in order that there might be a reargument; and that, at least, the court might be moved to vacate the rule for a peremptory *mandamus*, and to grant one for an alternative *mandamus* only, so as to bring the question more fully and solemnly before them on the return of the Appraisers.

A motion was now made accordingly.

Mr. Talcott, Atty-Gen., for the motion. So far as the merits of the question are concerned, there is but *one ground on which a [***530** *mandamus* can be claimed, that is, that these relators had such an interest in the water diverted as to be damnified. With deference, it would seem to me that the relators are precluded from taking that ground by the fact that the Appraisers did consider and decide upon the claim. They went into the merits; and held that the grant of the State being bounded on the margin of the creek, would not carry its bed to the original grantees; that, therefore, the relators, could have no interest. Besides, as to Eglestone, he pretends, no legal interest. The relators should have taken their remedy by appeal.

That a party may convey to the margin of a stream, without conveying *ad filum aquæ*, is settled by the case of *Jackson* v. *Halstead*, 5 Cow., 216. If this may be so, the relators are bound to show clearly and particularly, why it was not so in their case. They should set forth the grants, in order that it may be seen whether their claim is justified in the full extent to which it is preferred. We insist that the boundary stopped at the margin. We can do no more, and this is all that should be required of us. We cannot show the deeds. It is not competent for the relators to infer from the words which we use, that the grant extends beyond the margin. Omitting to produce their title, every inference should be made against them.

What Eglestone's contract is, does not fully appear. It is evidently but an executory contract, and passes no legal title. It may have been forfeited; and all equitable title gone.

Messrs. Randall and *Edwards*, contra. This

is the first time we have heard that the Appraisers have made any adjudication. It was not pretended on the former argument. We state in our affidavits that the Appraisers had refused to act; and the contrary is not pretended by the affidavit of Mr. Seymour. So far from this, we understand him as ingenuously admitting that the appraisers had refused to adjudicate. We asked a *mandamus*
531*] compelling them to *make a judicial decision, from which we might appeal, if it should not be satisfactory. This was granted, and is now sought to be set aside or qualified, without any new facts being shown.

The relators are in possession. This is, *prima facie*, evidence of title. It gives them the right to an appraisement according to their interest. The statute is broad in its terms, and extends to all persons who are injured. The decision of the court at the last term, went upon the boundary, as set up by Seymour himself. They held that a boundary on the margin carried the grantee to the center of the river. *Jackson* v. *Halstead*, cited by the Attorney-General, has no more application to the point before the court, than any other case which he might have cited. The question was, whether the words "including the same" (*i. e.* the river), used in a grant, would pass the bed of the river, or only a right of fishery. Clearly the words would not pass the soil. Neither the case, the counsel, nor the court, lisped a word as to the operation of a grant bounded on a river. Not an authority was cited to this point. It turned entirely on the construction of the words used in describing the subject-matter. Because the question now before the court might have arisen, does it follow that the well settled doctrine of the common law is to be overturned? A doctrine to which we before cited many authorities, and against which not one common law authority has been or can be found. We say common law authority, because we except the cases in Pa. They reject the common law, which this court is not authorized to do. We now add other authorities to the point, that where one owns the land on a river above tide-water, he owns the river itself on his side, *ad filum aquæ*. *Ld. Fitzwalter's* case, 1 Mod., 105; *Carter* v. *Murcot*, 4 Burr., 2162; *Rex* v. *Smith*, Doug., 444; 2 Roll. Abr., 170, pl. 14; 15 Johns., 454, per Platt, *J.; Hayes' Ex'r* v. *Bowman*, 1 Rand. (Va.), 417; *Claremont* v. *Carlton*, 2 N. H., 369. A water course does not depend on prescription, but is *ex jure naturæ*. (3 Bulst., 340; 1 Wils., 174.)
532*] *Where grants are made, like those upon this creek, for 12 and 20 miles along the stream, to deprive the grantees of the water, would be a fraud upon the subject. The original purchases and settlements were made, and a consideration paid to the State, on the faith of the various benefits to be derived from using the waters of this stream. High prices have been given by subsequent purchasers with a view to the same privileges. These constitute the main value of the land. If there was an intention in the State to reserve the stream, an express reservation or exception should have been inserted; or the intention in some other way made known to the purchaser. He takes under boundaries terminating at the creek or the margin of the creek. The meaning of the parties is the same. It is that the grantee should have the benefit of the stream. Wherever his grant touches the water, the common law gives him a right to the stream, subject in some cases to a right of passage; but not so in this case. The Chittenango is an inconsiderable creek, hardly navigable for small boats at the place in question. The State might as well claim every insignificant stream within its borders, on the ground of some equivocal words in the grant. The doctrine of Hargrave, cited on the former argument, is the law of this State. It has been recognized by repeated decisions of our courts. If the grant of a party touches a stream above tide-water, he owns of common right to the center.

It is idle now to talk of our having no right. The Appraisers do not place themselves on a defect in our title. They set up a claim in the State. This is the open and avowed ground, under the oath of Mr. Seymour. They do not mean to allow any one damages for subverting these valuable mills and mill privileges. Why did they not enter into an inquiry as to the title? If it is not in the relators, it is in some other person or persons, and damages are due somewhere. No. This valuable property has been converted to the use of the State. The State derives a revenue from rent of the surplus waters to about $1,000 *per annum;* and yet the true owners are set at defiance. The *Appraisers would have had no diffi- [***533**
culty, if the title be not in us, in finding it to be in somebody whom it is their duty to pay. We need not produce our deeds here. Title is a question before them. We are in possession. If that possession has been rendered valueless to us for only three days, instead of more than that number of years, as is the fact, we have sustained some damages for which we are entitled to an appraisement.

But suppose all authority is to be overturned; and that we are to be restrained to the margin, the nominal boundary, according to the terms of the grant as set up by the Appraisers; still we touch the stream; and if the State own the bed, they have no right on that ground to divert the water. It takes its course from nature; and though it runs over the land of another, he has no right to divert it. This was abundantly shown by authorities cited on the former argument. It is a new refinement, to say that a grant bounded on the margin of the creek does not touch the creek.

Mr Talcott, in reply. I shall never appear before this court or any other, to advocate a doctrine which would operate as a fraud on purchasers. When the State desire this, they must seek some other instrument. But I feel bound to resist all claims upon the public not founded in right. I admit that, whether the relators show a right to the land under the water or not, they are entitled to some compensation, provided they make out a right in themselves to the land adjoining the water. The State has no more right to divert the water than an individual; and if these relators own the land under the water, then clearly they are entitled to full damages. The question is, how they are to show their right? If the inquiry had been before a jury, they must have established their claim by a proper deduction of title, or other proof of their interest. And if this be a case in which all that we can require of the parties is, to make their own affidavits, and they omit to set forth their boundaries; is it not to be inferred that had they been set **534*]** *forth, they would have excluded the stream? Is not every presumption to be against them? If an exception or reservation be necessary to exclude the stream, is not this to be presumed? If there may be any case in which they would fail of a right to the center of the stream, is it not to be presumed? If the grants were produced there might be an exception. If the proof here produced is to be sufficient—no matter what the boundary—everyone bounded on a stream, whether there be an exception or not, will obtain damages.

I said the Appraisers have made a decision, and am answered that there was no adjudication. What is there lacking to a complete adjudication? An application was made to the Appraisers; and on what was heard, they decided against the claim. The affidavits of the relators complain that they refused and did not appraise. And they ought not, if the decision be correct. They refused to appraise, because they adjudged that the relators had no right. If there was error in this, the remedy is not by *mandamus*. It is said the refusal to act, if it be so considered, is owing to a mistake of the law. The court will not, I trust, dispose of so important a question by granting a peremptory *mandamus*. They will rather award an alternative *mandamus*, in order that all the facts may be brought before them upon the return, and that the State may have its writ of error. At present they are deprived of this privilege, the facts not appearing on the record.

But if there be no error, then, of course, they will not grant an alternative *mandamus*. The error should be shown positively. On the case made out, the court will presume that the parties dare not swear that their land extended to the center.

When the case of *Jackson* v. *Halstead* is compared with others, it will be found there is no material difference between them. The doctrine of Hargrave, that the owner of the bank owns to the center of the stream, in all rivers where the tide does not ebb and flow, has been too long settled and too often recognized, to be disputed by any one making the least preten- **535*]** sions to legal knowledge. I do *not deny that doctrine. I am insisting that there may be exceptions to that rule. I do this on the authority of *Jackson* v. *Halstead*. There is no need of a positive exception or reservation, if the grantee is limited to a particular boundary on the shore. This stops him short of the center. It may or may not be, that these relators are bounded on the center. If they are, let them be required to show the fact.

It is said the State cannot divert the water, without allowing damages, if the titles of the relators touch the river. I have admitted this; but the same answer applies. Let them show their right particularly. If they do not reach the stream, they have no right to the value of the water. If the boundary stops at the margin, they have no right to the water or the use of the water.

Sutherland, *J.*, intimated when the Attorney-General first moved, that there could be no objection to change the peremptory *mandamus* into an alternative one, if this alone was requested. The court, at the last term, understood the counsel for the Appraisers as saying explicitly, that nothing further was desired than the opinion of the court on the case, as it then stood; which would be acquiesced in by the Appraisers. Otherwise, the course would have been to grant an alternative *mandamus*.

After the argument was closed, and the court had taken several days for advisement,

Savage, *Ch. J.*, remarked that the main question made at the last term related to the extent of the boundary. The court were then of the opinion that it carried the land to the center of the stream. Nothing which had fallen from the Attorney-General on the reargument had changed their opinion upon this point. Objections, that a *mandamus* will not lie, and that the relators do not make out their case, are now started; but we adhere to the opinion that the case is one to which the remedy by *mandamus* is applicable; and that the case is sufficiently made out in evidence. We understand the Appraisers refused to act, because *they thought the bed of the Chit- **[*536** tenango belonged to the State; that they, therefore, had no jurisdiction, private property not being invaded. We hold otherwise; that private property has been invaded; that they have jurisdiction; and should go on and appraise. To what particular individuals the property may belong, is a question for them to decide.

It is, however, suggested, that the question is an important one, on account of the amount of the property involved in it; and that it should be put in such a shape as to be reviewed on error, should the State desire this. We think the suggestion perfectly right; and with a view to that object, we direct the former rule and subsequent proceedings to be vacated, and that an alternative *mandamus* issue. This will enable the Appraisers to put the facts on record by a return, if they shall be so advised; and the judgment to be rendered on that return may be reviewed.

Rule accordingly.(a)

Cited in—3 Wend., 635; 5 Wend., 448, 454 and 460; 13 Wend., 368, 371; 17 Wend., 613; 20 Wend., 152; 5 Den., 604, *n.*; 1 Paige, 448; 5 Paige, 143; 9 Paige, 551; 33 N. Y., 468, 477; 35 N. Y., 458; 72 N. Y., 216; 16 Hun, 383; 2 Barb., 417; 9 Barb., 360; 13 Barb., 441; 14 Barb., 219, 517; 18 Barb., 285; 30 Barb., 15; 34 Barb., 501, 520, 592; 48 Barb., 666; 22 How. Pr., 115, 134; Edm., 551; Olcott, 22; 105 Mass., 355; 10 Minn., 102; 20 Wis., 432; 22 Am. Dec., 474 (5 W. H., 520); 33 Am. Dec., 271 (8 Parker, 9); 46 Am. Dec., 572 (26 Me., 384); 12 Am. Rep., 165 (51 N. H., 504); 40 Am. Rep., 29 (5 Lea, 204); 44 Am. Rep., 398, 401 (92 N. Y., 463); 38 Am. Rep., 409 (83 N. Y., 185).

(a) The Treatise of Sir Matthew Hale, *De jure Maris*, has been so often recognized in this country and in England, that it has become the text book, from which, when properly understood, there seems to be no appeal either by sovereign or subject, upon any question relating to their respective rights, either in the sea, arms of the sea, or private streams of water. *Vide* Palmer v. Mulligan, 3 Cai., 307; *Id.*, 315, per Thompson, *J.*; *Id.*, 318, per Kent, *Ch. J.*; People v. Platt, 17 Johns., 195, 209, 210; Hooker v. Cummings, 20 Johns., 90, 99–101; Adams v. Pease, 2 Conn. N. S., 481, 483, 484; Arnold v. Mundy, 1 Halst., 1, 74; Claremont v. Carlton, 2 N. H., 369, 371; Haye's Exr. v. Bowman, 1 Rand., 417, 420. In England, even on rights of prerogative, the courts scan his words with as much care as if they had been found in Magna Charta; and the meaning once ascertained, they do not trouble themselves to search any further. *Vide* King v. Ld. Yarborough, 3 Barnw. & Cr., 91. They almost justify, in respect to his writings, the extravagant encomium which Mr. Wirt has passed upon

him as a judge: that, "with a mind beaming the effulgence of noon-day, he sat on the bench like a descended god!" 2 Burr. Tr., by Rob., 67. His work is so often quoted, his doctrines are so full, his distinctions so clear, and his illustrations so striking and apposite, that they seem to deserve an insertion in our books, somewhat more at length than they are to be found in the quotations of counsel or judges; especially as there is, I believe, no late edition of the work; and, to many of the profession, it is not, therefore, readily accessible. It was first pub-
537*] lished by the learned Fra. Hargrave *among various other titles, and is usually cited as Harg. Law Tracts. The only title material to our purpose, "*De jure maris et brachiorum ejusdem*," is the first part of a manuscript treatise in three parts, by *Ld. Ch.J.* Hale; and is, therefore, sometimes cited as Hale *de jure*, &c. This first part is divided into seven chapters of about 44 small octavo pages in the whole. The course I propose in this note, is to give the mere text of 4 chapters in this first part, *verbatim*, generally omitting the author's quotations; which are mostly of MSS, or of old treatises, entries and reports; all of which are, *quoad hoc*, superseded by the high authority of Hale. Instead of these, I will insert such late authorities, especially American, as have passed upon the very position laid down by him.

PARS PRIMA.

De jure Maris et Brachiorum ejusdem.

CAP. I.

Concerning the interest of fresh rivers.

Fresh rivers, of what kind soever, do, of common right, belong to the owners of the soil adjacent; so that the owners of the one side have, of common right, the propriety of the soil; and consequently the right of fishing, *usque filum aquæ*; and the owners of the other side, the right of soil or ownership, and fishing unto the *filum aquæ* on their side. And if a man be owner of the land of both sides, in common presumption, he is owner of the whole river; and hath the right of fishing according to the extent of his land in length. With this agrees the common experience. Palmer v. Mulligan, &c., and other cases cited above at the beginning of this note.

But special usage may alter that common presumption; for one man may have the river, and others the soil adjacent; or one man may have the river and soil thereof, and another the free or several fishing in that river.

If a fresh river, between the lands of two lords or owners, do insensibly gain on one side, or the other side, it is held that the propriety continues as before in the river. [What shall be deemed insensible gain. The King v. Ld. Yarborough, cited *ante*, in this note.] But if it be done sensibly and suddenly, then the ownership of the soil remains according to the former bounds. As if the river running between the lands of A and B, leaves his course, and sensibly makes his channel entirely in the lands of A; the whole river belongs to A. *Aqua cedit solo.* And so it is, though if the alteration be by insensible degrees, but there be other known boundaries, as stakes or extent of land. 22 Ass., pl. 93. And though the book make a question, whether it hold the same law in the case of the sea or the arms of it; yet certainly the law will be all one, as we shall have occasion to show in the ensuing discourse.

But yet special custom may alter the case in great rivers. For instance the River of Severn, which is a wild river; yet, by the common custom used below Gloucester Bridge, it is the common boundary of the manors of either side, what course soever the river takes; viz.: the *filum aquæ* is the common mark or boundary; though it borrow great quanti-
538*] ties of *land, sometimes of the one side, sometimes of the other; and gives them to the opposite shore.

Though fresh rivers are, in point of propriety, as before, *prima facie*, of a private interest; yet, as well fresh rivers as salt, or such as flow and reflow, may be under these two servitudes, or affected by them, viz.: one of prerogative belonging to the King, and another of public interest, or belonging to the people in general.

Of these in the ensuing chapters.

CAP. II.

Of the right of prerogative in private or fresh rivers.

The King, by an ancient right of prerogatives, hath had a certain interest in many fresh rivers, even where the sea doth not flow or reflow, as well as in salt or arms of the sea; and those are these which follow:

1st. A right of franchise or privilege, that no man may set up a common ferry for all passengers, without a prescription time out of mind, or a charter from the King. He (the owner) may make a ferry for his own use or the use of his family; but not for the common use of all the King's subjects passing that way; because it doth, in consequent, tend to a common charge; and is become a thing of public interest and use, and every man for his passage pays a toll, which is a common charge, and every ferry ought to be under a public regulation; viz.: that it give attendance at due times, keep a boat in due order, and take but reasonable toll; for if he (the ferryman) fail in these he is finable. And hence it is, that if a common bridge be broken, whereby there is no passage, but by a boat or ferry; it hath been anciently practiced in the Exchequer, to compel that ferryman, that ferries over people for profit, without a charter from the King or a lawful prescription, to account for the benefit above his reasonable pains and charge.

And this that is said in reference to a fresh or private river, holds place much more in a public river or arm of the sea: and therefore, it need not be repeated when we come to that subject.

2d. An interest, as I may call it, of pleasure or recreation. [Inapplicable to the U. S.; and obsolete in England, as Hale says.]

3d. An interest of Jurisdiction, viz.: in reference to common nuisances in or by rivers; as where the sewers were not kept, which gave rise to the commission of sewers, as well for fresh rivers as for salt.

And another part of the King's jurisdiction in reformation of nuisances is, to reform and punish nuisances in all rivers, whether fresh or salt, that are a common passage, not only for ships and greater vessels, but also for smaller, as barges or boats; to reform the obstructions or annoyances that are therein to such common passage; for, as the common highways on the land are for the common land passage, so these kind of rivers, whether fresh or salt, that bear boats or barges, are highways by water; and as the highways by land are ca[lle]d *altæ viæ regiæ*, so these public rivers for public passage are called *fluvii regales*, and *haut streames le Roy*; not in reference to the propriety of the river, but to the public use; all things of public safety and convenience being in a special manner under the King's *care, supervision and protection. [*539
And, therefore, the report in Sir John Davyes, of the piscary of Ban, mistakes the reason of those books, that call these *streames le Roy*, as if they were so called in respect to propriety, as 19 Ass., 6; Dy., 11. For they are called so because they are of public use, and under the King's special care and protection, whether the soil be his or not.

And this leads me to the third chapter.

CAP. III.

Concerning public streams.

There be some streams or rivers that are private, not only in propriety or ownership; but also in use, as little streams and rivers that are not a common passage for the King's people. Again; there be other rivers, as well fresh as salt, that are of common or p[u]blic use, for carriage of boats and lighters. And these whether they are fresh or salt, whether they flow and reflow or not, are *prima facie publici juris*, common highways for man or goods, or both, from one inland town to another. Thus the rivers of Wey, of Severn, of Thames and divers others, as well above the bridges and ports as below; as well above the flowings of the sea as below, and as well where they have come to be of private propriety, as in what part they are of the King's propriety, are public rivers *juris publici*. And, therefore, all nuisances and impediments of passages of boats and vessels, though in the private soil of any person, may be punished by indictments, and removed; and this was the reason of the Statute of Magna Charta, cap. 23.

Omnes kidelli deponantur per Thamifam et Medwayam, et per totam Angliam nisi per costeram maris.

These kind of nuisances were such as hindered or obstructed the passage of boats, as wears, piles, choaking up the passage with filth, diverting of the water by cuts or trenches, decay of the banks, or the like.

And they were reformed.

Sometimes by indictments or presentments in the Leets, Sessions of the Peace, Oyer and Terminer, or before justices of Assize.

Oftentimes in the King's Bench; as Hil., 50, E. 3; B. R. Rot., 23, for nuisances in the River Trent; H. 23, E. 3, B. R. Rot., 61, in the River Ouse; H. 21, E. 1, in the River Severn; Tr., 28 E. 3, Rot., 29, in the

River Leigh; and generally in all other rivers within the bodies of countries, which had common passage of boats or barges, whether the water were fresh or salt; the King's or a subject's.

Sometimes by special commission, as for the River of Leigh.

And sometimes by the parties that were prejudiced by such nuisance, without any process of law.

But if any person at his own charge, makes his own private stream to be passable for boats or barges, either by making of locks or cuts, or drawing together other streams; and hereby that river, which was his own in point of propriety become now capable of carriage of vessels; yet this seems not to make it *juris publici;* and he may pull it down again, or apply it to his own private use. For it is not hereby made to be *juris publici*, unless it were done at a common charge, or by a public authority; or 540*] that by long *continuance of time it hath been freely devoted to a public use. And so it seems also to be, if he that makes such a new river or passage doth it by way of recompence or compensation for some other public stream that he hath stopped for his own conveniency; as in the case of the Abbott of St. Austens, Canterbury, mentioned in the Register. So likewise, if he purchaseth the King's Charter to take a reasonable toll for the passage of the King's subjects, and puts it in use; these seem to be devoting, and, as it were, consecrating of it to the common use. As he that by an *ad quod damnum*, and license thereupon obtained, changeth a way, and sets out another in his own land; this new way is thereupon become *juris publici* as well as a way by prescription. For no man can take a settled or constant toll even in his own private land, for a common passage, without the King's license.

CAP. IV.

Concerning the King's interest in salt waters, the sea and its arms, and the soil thereof; and first, of the right of fishing there.

Thus much concerning fresh waters or inland rivers, which, though they empty themselves mediately into the sea, are not called arms of the sea, either in respect of the distance or smallness of them.

We come now to consider the sea and its arms: and first, concerning the sea itself.

The sea is that which lies within the body of a county or without. That arm or branch of the sea, which lies within the *fauces terræ*, where a man may reasonably discern between shore and shore, is, or at least, may be within the body of a county; and, therefore, within the jurisdiction of the sheriff or coroner.

The part of the sea which lies not within the body of a county, is called the main sea or ocean.

The narrow sea, adjoining to the coast of England, is part of the waste and *demesnes* and dominions of the King of England, whether it lie within the body of any county or not.

The King's right of propriety or ownership in the sea and soil thereof, is evinced principally in these things that follow.

1st. The right of fishing in this sea, and the creeks and arms thereof, is originally lodged in the Crown, as the right of depasturing is originally lodged in the owner of the waste whereof he is lord, or as the right of fishing belongs to him that is the owner of a private or inland river.

But though the King is the owner of this great waste, and as a consequent of his propriety, hath the primary right of fishing in the sea and the creeks and arms thereof; yet the common people of England have regularly a liberty of fishing in the sea or creeks or arms thereof, as a public common of piscary; and may not, without injury to their right, be restrained of it; unless in such places, creeks or navigable rivers, where either the King or some particular subject, hath gained a propriety exclusive of that common liberty.

2d. The next evidence of the King's right and propriety in the sea, and the arms thereof, is his right of propriety to

541*] *The shore; and,

The *Maritima Incrementa.*

(1) The shore is that ground that is between the ordinary high water and low water mark. This doth *prima facie* and of common right belong to the King, both in the shore of the sea, and the shore of the arms of the sea.

And herein there shall be these things examinable.

1st. What shall be said the shore, or *littus marus.*

2d. What shall be said an arm or creek of the sea.

3d. What evidence there is of the King's propriety thereof.

1. For the first of these; it is certain, that that which the sea overflows, either at high spring tides, or at extraordinary tides, comes not, as to this purpose, under the denomination of *littus maris;* and, consequently, the King's title is not of that large extent; but only to land that is usually overflowed at ordinary tides. That, therefore, I call the shore, that is between the common high water and low water mark.

2. For the second; that is called an arm of the sea where the sea flows and reflows; and so far only as the sea flows and reflows; so that the River Thames, above Kingston, and the River of Severn, above Tewkesbury, &c., though there they are public rivers, yet are not arms of the sea. But it seems that although the water be fresh at high water, yet the denomination of an arm of the sea continues, if it flow and reflow as in Thames above the bridge. Doug., 444.

3. For the third; it is admitted that *de jure communi* between the high water and low water mark doth, *prima facie*, belong to the King. 5 Rep., 107; Constable's case; Dy., 326. Although it is true, that such shore may be, and commonly is parcel of the manor adjacent, and so may be belonging to a subject, as shall be shown, yet, *prima facie*, it is the King's.

And as the shore of the sea doth, *prima facie*, belong to the King, viz.: between the ordinary high water and low water mark, so the shore of an arm of the sea between the high water and low water mark, belongs, *prima facie*, to the King, though it may also belong to a subject, as shall be shown in the next chapter. [He mentions here two cases of a number of houses claimed by or in right of the King; in which it was adjudged that the claim was good because they were built between high and low water mark, where the tide flowed and reflowed—the one case arising upon the River Tyne, the other upon the Thames.]

And this shall suffice for the King's right in the shore of the sea, or rivers that are arms of the sea, viz.: the land lying between the high water and the low water mark at ordinary tide.

(2) The King hath a title to *maralima incrementa*, or increase of land by the sea; and this is of three kinds, viz.: L Increase *per projectionem vel alluvionem.* 2. Increase *per relictionem vel desertionem.* 3. *Per insulæ productionem.*

1. The increase *per alluvionem* is, when the sea, by casting up sand and earth, doth by degrees increase the land, and shut itself out further than the ancient bounds went; and this is usual. The reason why this belongs to the Crown is, because in truth the soil, where there is now dry land, *was [*542 formerly part of the very *fundus maris;* and, consequently, belonged to the King. But indeed if such alluvion be so insensible, that it cannot be by any means found that the sea was there, *idem est non esse et non apparere;* the land thus increased belongs, as a perquisite, to the owner of the land adjacent.

2. The increase *per relictionem*, or recess of the sea. This doth, *de jure communi*, belong to the King; for, as the sea is parcel of the waste or *demesne;* so, of necessity, the land that lies under it; and, therefore, it belongs to the King when left by the sea; and so also it regularly holds in lands deserted by a river, that is an arm of the sea or a creek of the sea, *prima facie*, especially if the creek or river be part of a port.

Car. primi, upon an information against Oldsworth and others, for that which is now called Sutton Marsh, that 300 acres of land was *relictum per mare*, and that the defendants had intruded into it; the defendants pleaded specially, and entitled themselves by prescription to the lands project by the sea; and upon a demurrer adjudged against them. That 1st. By the prescription or title made to lands project, which is *jus alluvionis*, no answer is given to the title of information for lands relict, for these were of several natures. 2. It was held that it lies not in prescription to claim lands relict *per mare;* for so if the channel between us and France should dry up, a man might prescribe for it, which is unreasonable; for

Nihil prescribitur nisi quod possidetur.

But this hath found some exceptions, besides these that follow in the ensuing chapter.

If a subject hath had, by prescription, the property of a certain tract, or creek, or navigable river, or arm of the sea, even while it is covered with water, by certain known metes or extent; this, though it should be relicted, the subject will have the propriety in the soil relicted. For he had it before, though covered with water; and although the sea is a fluid, yet the *terra* or *solum subjectum* is fixed; and by force of a clear and evident usage, a subject may have the propriety of a private river; though the acquest of the former be more difficult, and requires a very good evidence to make it out, as shall be said in the ensuing chapter.

If a subject hath land adjoining the sea, and the violence of the sea swallow it up, but so that yet there be reasonable marks to continue the notice of it; or though the marks be defaced; yet if by situation and extent of quantity, and bounding upon the firm land, the same can be known, though the sea leave this land again, or it be by art or industry regained, the subject doth not lose his propriety; and accordingly it was held by Cooke and Foster, M, 7. Jac. C. B., though the inundation continue forty years.

If the mark remain or continue, or extent can reasonably be certain, the case is clear.

3. The third sort of maritime increase are islands arising *de novo* in the King's seas, or the King's arms thereof. These upon the same account and reason, *prima facie*, and of common right belong to the King; for they are part of that soil of the sea that belonged before in point of propriety to the King; for when islands *de novo* arise, it is either by the recess or sinking of the water, or else by the exaggeration of sand and slubb, which, in process 543*] *of time, grow firm land environed with water; and thus some places have arisen, and their original recorded, as about Ravensend, in Yorkshire.

And thus much of the King's right of propriety which he hath in the sea; and also, *prima facie*, and in common presumption, in the ports and creeks and arms of the sea.

Mr. Butler, in his *note* (205) to Co. Litt., 261 *a*, considers Ld. Hale as having exhausted the subject upon which he treats; and had this great man followed out his doctrine of private rivers, with its various consequences and illustrations, as fully as he has done his doctrines of the sea and its arms, very little would have been left for our courts to do in filling up the outline. As his positions are, however, more general in respect to the former, while at the same time they are of more extensive application, they have been oftener the subject of discussion in our courts, and would seem to call for further notice.

The general policy and excellence of his doctrines have been the most fully and ably vindicated in Conn. and N. Y. "A more perfect system of regulations on this subject," says *Ch. J.* Swift, 2 Conn. N. S., 483, "could not be devised. It secures common rights, as far as the public interest requires, and furnishes a proper line of demarcation between them and private rights." This doctrine, says Hosmer, J., "promotes the grand ends of civil society by pursuing that wise and orderly maxim of assigning to everything capable of ownership a legal and determinate owner." These remarks are followed up and vindicated by Spencer, late *Ch.* J., in Hooker v. Cummings, 20 Johns., 101.

The general distinctions deemed of so much excellence and importance by these learned judges, and which, at this day, no lawyer will hazard his reputation by controverting, are that rivers not navigable, that is, fresh rivers, of what kind soever, do, of common right, belong to the owners of the soil adjacent, to the extent of their land in length. But that rivers where the tide ebbs and flows belong, of common right, to the State. That this ownership of the citizen is of the whole river, viz.: the soil and the water of the river; except that in his river, where boats, rafts, &c., may be floated to market, the public have a right of way or easement. In a special manner, where the subject claims under a grant from the State, bounded by a river not navigable, this grant extends *usque filum aquæ*; as was held in Hayes' Exr. v. Bowman, 1 Rand., 420, per *Cur.*; Claremont v. Carlton, 2 N. H., 369, S. P.; and Lunt v. Holland, 14 Mass., 149. This was also admitted by the Atty-Gen., it will be recollected, in arguing the principal case, *ante*, 534.

The only question that can generally arise between the citizen and the State, as to the ownership of rivers above the tide, is whether the former be owner of the soil adjacent, within the meaning of Hale.

As to this question, there is certainly no technical or particular mode of expression in the grant necessary to make him so. In the case of the River Banne, Dav., 152, it is said, in every river not navigable, "the terre-tenants on each side have an interest of common right;" and so is the abbreviation of that case in 2 Roll. Abr., 170, pl. 14, which was edited by Hale. By Holt, 12 Mod., 510: "If a river run contiguously between the land of two persons, each of them is, of common right, owner of that part of the river which is *next his [*544 land." By Ld. Mansfield, in Carter v. Murcot, 4 Burr., 2164: "In rivers not navigable, the proprietors of the land have the right of fishery on their respective sides; and it generally extends *ad filum medium aquæ*."

The proposition for the citizen to establish, then, is that he is the owner, terre-tenant or proprietor of the soil adjacent to the river above the tide; and then, of common right, he owns the river.

1. *Owner, terre-tenant or proprietor.* No doubt this may be either in fee or of any particular estate of an equitable or legal estate; and the ownership of the river shall be co-extensive in estate as well as territory. This was held in the principal case, *ante*, 518.

2. *Of the adjacent soil.* Adjacent (in Lat. *adjacens ab adjaceo*) is defined, lying close, bordering upon. The Lat. verb means, to lie contiguous, or border upon, to abut, adjoin. Thus an assize stated by Hale, *De Jur. Mar.*, ch. 1, is "*quia dicunt, quod omnes, qui tenent terras abuttantes super aquam illam, in ea piscantur pro voluntate sua usque filum aquæ*," &c. This was of the Idell, a fresh water stream; and upon this there is no difference in the cases. All agree that where a man's land abuts upon or adjoins to any river above tide-water, he owns the river to the center of the stream. As long ago as 1805, in Palmer v. Mulligan, it appearing that the defendant owned the shore of the Hudson as low down as Stillwater, this being above tide-water, Thompson, *J.*, and Kent, *Ch. J.*, applied to his case the doctrine of Ld. Hale, that his ownership extended to the center of that great river; and the latter then hinted at what is now established, that if the State will bound a grantee upon a river not navigable, he shall hold to the center, unless there be an exception of the river in the grant. (*Vide* 3 Cai., 319.) In Adams v. Pease, 2 Conn. N. S., 481, the plaintiff owned a large farm bounded east on Connecticut River, above the flowing of the tide, but where it was large, and passable with flat-bottomed boats of from 5 to 30 tons burthen; and sometimes vessels built above had been floated down; yet held that the boundary, in terms, on the river, carried the plaintiff's ownership of the river to its center. The rule is there laid down by Swift, *Ch. J.*, that the adjoining proprietors have this right. The doctrine of this case was approved in its full extent by the Supreme Court of this State, in Hooper v. Cummings, 20 Johns., 91, where it was applied to Salmon River, which empties into Lake Ontario. Spencer, *Ch. J.*, who delivered the opinion of the court, says: "If the soil on both sides be owned by an individual, he has the sole and exclusive right; but if there be different proprietors on each side, they own their respective sides, *ad filum medium aquæ*." And the court approved what Kent, *Ch. J.*, said, in Palmer v. Mulligan, touching the Hudson being private property as low down as Stillwater. They also show that the cases which hold the contrary in Pa. are founded on a repudiation of the common law. (*Vide*, also, 17 Johns., 209, 210, &c.) In Arnold v. Mundy, 1 Halst. N. J., 1, the plaintiff's land ran to or was bounded on a river where the tide did ebb and flow, and he and those under whom he claimed had staked off and planted a bed of oysters, some of which the defendant took away; for which the action was brought. At the trial the defendant's counsel moved for a nonsuit; and the judge in giving his opinion remarked (*Id.*, p. 10) "that a grant of land to a subject or citizen, bounded upon a fresh water stream or *river, where the tide neither ebbs nor flows, [*545 extends to the middle of the channel of such river; but that a grant bounded upon a navigable river, or other water, where the tide does ebb and flow, extends to the edge of the water only, that is to say, to high water mark, when the tide is high, and to low water mark when the tide is low; but it extends no farther;" and he nonsuited the plaintiff upon this distinction. On a motion to set aside the nonsuit, the Supreme Court, after a very learned argument, confirmed the distinction; and refused to set aside the nonsuit. The reporter, in his marginal note, has set down this as one resolution of the court: "A grant of land bounded upon a fresh water stream or river, where the tide neither ebbs nor flows, extends *ad filum aquæ*; but a grant bounded upon a navigable river extends to the edge of the water only." In Claremont v. Carlton, 2 N. H., 369, lot No. 46 was admitted, at the trial, to be bounded south on Sugar

River, above tide-water; and an island lying on the north side of the river was held to pass by the grant, which was by the Government of N. H. The river and island were held to pass upon the principles adopted by Ld. Hale, whose doctrine is recited at length and approved by the court. In Hayes' Exr. v. Bowman, 1 Rand., 417, the words of the grant were, "lying on the west side of South River, and bounded by the same." This was where the tide did not flow. The court say, "where the Commonwealth, having title to lands lying on both sides of a water-course not navigable, grants the lands lying on one side thereof, and bounded thereby, it is universally admitted that such grant carries with it the title to a moiety of the water-course. There can be no reason assigned why this rule, so just in relation to grants by the Commonwealth, should not equally apply to conveyances by individuals." And they held that a moiety of the bed of the stream passed. In the case of King v. King, 7 Mass., 496, it appeared that Benjamin King was seised of two tracts of land, opposite to each other, on the east and west sides of Sheepscut River, and adjoining thereto, conveyed to him by boundary lines, which included a part of the river where it passed over falls and formed a site for mills. And it was held that even this specific boundary could have no effect in excluding the remainder of the river. The court say, "Benjamin King was entitled to two tracts of land, situate on the east and west sides of Sheepscut River, described and conveyed to him by boundary lines which include a part of the river; and, of course, by the legal operation of his title, the falls and bed of the river, with all permanent water privileges, wherever the river flowed between the tracts of land conveyed, or covering any part thereof." *Id.*, 498. King having died so seised, his heirs made partition by deeds, the import of which was an assignment of two parcels on the western side to his son Moses; and of that on the eastern side to his son Peter. The court say, "the legal operation of this partition and assignment is, that the falls and bed of the river, and the water privileges were alike divided and assigned, as parcel of the two tracts; which, after the partition, were to be considered as separated, so far as they lie opposite to each other upon the river, by a central line, or the thread of the river, as it is sometimes expressed." This was evidently decided as will be
546*] seen by *the conclusion of the sentence, on the authority of Hale's doctrine, though he is not formally cited. In Jackson v. Louw, 12 Johns., 252, the line ran south to the Plattekill, above tide-water, thence up the same, to the southwest corner of a lot this day conveyed to the said Abraham Louw, Jr. The court say (p. 255), "the terms 'up the same,' necessarily imply that it is to follow the creek, according to its windings and turnings; and that must be in the middle or center of it. The rule is well settled, that when a creek, not navigable, and which is beyond the ebb and flow of the tide, forms a boundary, the line must be so run." In Lunt v. Holland, 14 Mass., 149, the plaintiff derived title from a grant of the Commonwealth, thus: "A certain tract of land lying in the township numbered one, in the County of Cumberland, which was surveyed and laid out in Apr., 1789, by Samuel Titcomb, and is bounded as follows, to wit: beginning at a hemlock tree, standing by the south side of the River Androscoggin, thence south, &c., to another hemlock tree also standing by said river, thence southeastwardly, and bounding by said river to the first mentioned bound," &c. The plaintiff claimed an island of 30 acres, the river running each side of it, lying between the two hemlock trees, and nearest the shore of the plaintiff's grant. One question was, whether, as Titcomb's survey included the island, it did not pass to the plaintiff for that reason, the survey being referred to by the grant; and the court held that it did. But another question directly raised and passed upon was, whether the boundary by the two hemlock trees, one mentioned as standing on the south side of the river, and the other as standing by the river, would not, in construction of law, extend into the center of the stream on the side of the island farthest from the line running between the two trees. Fessenden, for the defendant, upon this point, contended that the island was excluded by visible and known monuments. "Bounding by the river," must intend that edge of the river on which the hemlock trees stood; or those trees could not be any part of the boundary. The judge, at the trial, charged that "land granted as bounded by a river, is held to extend to the thread or channel of the river; and as here were two channels, it might well be presumed the intent of the parties to the conveyance, that the grant was intended to extend to that channel which would include the island." The court, in delivering their opinion at bar, say, "land granted as bounded by a river extends to the thread of the river, unless from prior grants on the other side of the river, such a construction is negatived; and in this case, the channel on the farthest side of the island may well be considered as intended by the description in this grant." This case was very strong for the State. The line along the river was limited nominally to two trees on the same side of the stream. One of these trees might not have touched the river at all. Yet upon the principles of Hale, these marks are departed from, the river itself adopted as the boundary; and the line extended over, and made to exclude an island lying on the side of the river nearest to it. We have before seen that this very point was adjudged in Claremont v. Carlton, 2 N. H., 369, upon a boundary which was in terms "on the river." But there were no definite monuments to restrain and bind it down to the margin of the stream. Lunt v. Holland decides that a line running between two trees, one standing *by the side of, and the [*547
other by the river, is a bounding or abutting on the river; that the grantee is, therefore, an adjacent owner, and his land extends, of common right *usque filum aquæ*. In Harramond v. M'Glaughon, Tayl., 196, it appears that a somewhat similar question arose in the Superior Court of Law of N. C., in 1798. About 50 years before, the State had granted to the defendant, by patent, a tract of land, beginning at a hickory, standing not far from a river; and running thence down the river a certain course and distance; but the course ran obliquely from the river, leaving between it and the river a triangular piece of land. The State claimed this triangle, and in 1787, granted it by patent to the plaintiff, who brought ejectment. The court held that the river was the boundary of the first grant; and decided against the claim of the State. They say, "when a deed, patent or grant, describes a boundary from a certain point down a river, creek, or the like, mentioning also course and distance; should the latter be found not to agree with the course of the river, creek, &c., it ought to be disregarded, and the river considered the true boundary." The expressions used to designate the boundaries and extent of grants upon the Mississippi are, *tant d'arpents de face*, or *tant d'arpents face au fleuve*, or *tant d'arpents face sur le fleuve*; and these expressions, when thus unqualified, have, without a single exception, been considered as giving the grantee a boundary on the river. (5 Hall Law Jour., 120.) Did the common, instead of the civil law apply to the Mississippi, no doubt such grants would give title to its bed *usque filum aquæ*. As to a boundary on the margin of a creek or river, as stated of that in the principal case (*ante*, 518), it seems to be the very dividing line between the water and the land, the line touching both. It is synonymous with shore, which Parsons, *Ch. J.*, says, in Storer v. Freeman, 6 Mass., 439, when applied to the sea, "must be understood to mean the margin of the sea in its usual and ordinary state. Thus, when the tide is out, low water mark is the margin of the sea; and when the sea is full, the margin is high water mark." In analogy, to the margin of the sea, it would seem that the margin of a fresh water river or creek must be the ordinary water mark. "The shores of a river border on the water's edge." 5 Wh., 385. And then it would be more than splitting hairs: it would be splitting mathematical lines, to separate the boundary from the river. According to this definition, the relators were literary and mathematically adjacent owners within Hale's doctrine. In Storer v. Freeman, *Id.*, 438, one boundary was to the shore of the neck; thence by the shore of the neck; another was to a heap of stones at the shore of the neck, at W. E.'s corner, so called, thence by the shore, &c. This was where the tide ebbs and flows; and Parsons, *Ch. J.*, seems to take it for granted, that such boundaries, if upon a stream above tide-water, would have carried the ownership, *usque filum aquæ*, as being a boundary on the water. He accordingly goes on to draw a distinction between the two cases. He says, "by the common law of England, which our ancestors brought with them, claiming it as their birthright, the owner of the land bounded on a fresh water river, owned the land to the center of the channel of the river, as of common right; but, if his land was bounded on the *sea, or an arm of [*548
the sea, where the tide ebbed and flowed, he could not, by such boundary, hold any land below the ordinary low water mark, for all the land below belonged, of common right, to the King."

Thus explore the books of the common law, wherever that law prevails: And in no case as between sovereign and subject, except the principal one, has it ever been questioned, that where a grant, either actually or constructively, goes to the water's edge, the grantee is the owner to the center of the river, if it be above tide-water. Lastly, he is the owner.

Of common right. It will be remembered that this phrase continually occurs in Hale, and in the decisions which follow him. It is an important, an emphatic part of the proposition with which we set out; and has been defined, in its general sense, by the greatest writer in law; and by one very little his inferior, as to the particular sense in which it is used by Hale. First, I quote from Ld. Coke, who explains its use by Littleton. Co. Litt., 142 *a*. "'*De common droit*,' of common right; that is, by the common law; so called, because the common law is the best and most common birthright that the subject hath, for the safeguard and defense, not only of his goods, lands and revenues, but of his wife and children, his body, fame and life also. So as the meaning of Littleton in this particular case is, that the lord may *distreine* for his rent of common right, that is, by the common law, without any particular reservation or provision of the party. And it is to be observed that the common law of England sometimes is called right, sometimes common right, and sometimes *communis justitia*. Littleton, in this, his treatise, nameth *common droit* sixe times." Thus, within the sense given by Ld. Coke, the party whose grant bounds him by any words on a river, or its margin above tide-water, owns of course, without any express provision in the grant *usque filum aquæ*. The right is incident and annexed by law to his grant, the same as a right of distress to a rent service of which Ld. Coke is speaking. In the notes to Co. Litt. by Hargrave & Butler, the latter (*note* 205 to p. 201 *a*), speaking of Hale *De Jur Mar*., says: "That where, in inquiries of this kind, it is said that a person is entitled to the right, or property in question, by common right, but that it may belong to another, it is intended to say, that the right of property in question is, by the common law, annexed to the particular capacity of the party, or to some property of which he is the owner; yet that it is not so inseparably or inalienably annexed to this capacity of ownership, but that the party may transfer it to another."

Thus, where one owns the shore of the river above tide, by grant from the State; the common law (common right) annexes to his capacity as owner, the right of soil in the river *usque filum aquæ*. And it has often been said by our courts, that the only way in which this right of soil in the river can be withheld from the subject, is by a reservation express or implied. This doctrine, as I before remarked (*ante*, 544), was hinted by the sagacious Kent, the *Chief Justice* of the Supreme Court, in Palmer v. Mulligan, 3 Cai., 319. And it was afterwards directly advanced by the court in Claremont v. Carlton, 2 N. H., 371, 372. It is there said this exception may be by the acts of the parties, or an express provision in their conveyances. So in Hayes' 549*]Exr. v. Bowman, 1 Rand., 420, cited *ante*, *545, the court say: "If it be the wish of the grantor not to convey the bed of the stream, or of any part thereof, it is easy for him to exclude it, by the use of words proper for that purpose. In the absence of such words, the moiety of the bed of the stream passes by such conveyance." So in the principal case (*ante*, 528), the Supreme Court lay down the same doctrine. And all the various expressions running through the books and cases, such as of common right, by operation of law, or by construction of law, mean the same thing: that the law carries the owner of the bank to the center, unless otherwise expressed; and then *expressum facit cessare tacitum*. An exception may sometimes be implied, as where the river, or an island in the river, was previously granted. 14 Mass., 151. Thus, in Hatch v. Dwight, 17 Mass., 289, E., in 1807, mortgaged a strip of land including mills, and running a considerable distance along the river; but in 1810, having sold a small piece of the mortgaged premises, for a hide-mill and lime-vats, he obtained a grant, or rather release from the mortgagee, for a nominal consideration; of what he (E.) had sold: described thus; beginning at the end of a dam; running up the river two rods, and so round, to the bank of the river. The mortgagee afterwards having foreclosed, one question was, whether the grant or release gave a right to the center of the river; and it appeared that if it was to have this effect, it would destroy the value of the mortgagee's mill privileges. For this, and other reasons, it was held that it should not extend beyond the bank. The various reasons assigned by the court were, that the grant or release was limited to the bank: that there were no general words showing that a right to keep up a dam was intended to pass; that the consideration was nominal; and it was not to be inferred that the mortgagee intended to release everything valuable in the mortgaged premises, for which she had given a large consideration. The court considered the release, under all the circumstances, as being no more than a mere exception in the mortgage. There were various and special circumstances in the case, which led the court to infer that the parties intended to limit the release or grant to the bank. And in conclusion they say: "Without doubt, by our law, the owner of land extending to the bank of the river, will own to the middle of the river, if it be not navigable, and so public property. But the owner may sell the land without the privilege of the stream, as he will, if he bounds his grant by the bank." They continue, "the description in the release very clearly excludes any part of the stream; and, as before observed, there are no general words of more extensive signification." This case was between individuals, and must, undoubtedly, be referred to its peculiar circumstances. The court admit that an owner to the bank of a river owns the river; but immediately say that he may bound his grant by the bank, and the stream will not pass. This must evidently mean a bounding by reservation, or plain exclusion express or implied. Otherwise the expression would be inconsistent in itself, and incompatible with all principle and all the cases. It is plain that the naked circumstance of bounding a grant on, to or by a bank, cannot exclude the stream, any more than bounding on the margin of the stream itself; and this the court admit; for certainly, owning "to a bank," is no more than owning on or by a bank. It is further evident that this case *does [*550 not rest on the particular words of release, from the circumstance that the reporter has not mentioned in his marginal note or index, any point as being settled or countenanced by this branch of the case. He doubtless looked upon it as a case entirely *sui generis*, in this respect; and as depending on numerous circumstance which might never again conspire. Indeed, it is not readily perceivable how the case can, in this branch of it, ever be a guide for any other. Another singular circumstance is, that the court should rely on Storer v. Freeman, 6 Mass., 435, for the only general doctrine which they appear to lay down. The question presented by that case was, as to the extent of a grant bounded upon the sea shore. In the case of a river not navigable, every possible intendment is in favor of the grant going to the center; whereas, in case of the sea, the intendment is directly otherwise. Jackson v. Halsted, 5 Cow., 216, was also a question between individuals. It was conceded that the Delaware was private property; but, as remarked by the learned counsel for the relators in the principal case (*ante*, 531), the question was not raised as to the constructive extent of the grant. Probably it could not arise. Palmer, the common source of title, owned the whole river; and in his grant, so far as it related to the river, had used words which would convey a mere right of fishery, and nothing more. It would have been subverting the express intention of the parties, to have allow the usual constructive operation to the grant. It was the same thing in respect to the river as if the grantor had retained both shores, and granted in terms a mere fishery within the water. Had the grantor stopped at the words which bounded the grantee upon the river, beyond all doubt the soil would have passed *usque filum aquæ*; 12 Johns., 252; 1 Rand., 417; 2 Conn. N. S., 481; Tayl., 196; and so would the island, had it lain on the grantee's side of the stream. 2 N. H., 369; 14 Mass., 140. It was not thought worth while, even to inquire which side of the river the island lay. The decision turned wholly on the legal effect of granting a river by its name.

I am sensible that I owe the profession an apology for the length of this dicussion, and its verbal and minute criticisms. But the amount involved is neither verbal nor minute. It is stated by the counsel of the Appraisers (*ante*, 523), to be $100,000, on the line of the canals alone. Take the whole State with its immense inland waters, and it gives an aggregate of millions. Probably there is hardly a patent in the State which gr s the bed of a stream by name. I am informed that our patents have generally selected these streams as the best and most convenient limits for their grants, and are abutted or bounded upon them by different words; leaving it to the common law to say what portion of the stream passes, accordingly as the boundary may be above or below tide-water. Our considerable rivers and creeks are covered with hydraulic machinery, and other establishments, depending for their value and their existence on the doctrine that these patents carry the ownership of the grantees to the thread of the stream What more usual description of parcels than a line running to a given point on a creek or river; and then along the same as it winds and turns, for many miles? It is speaking within bounds, to say that, 551*] *adopting the construction contended for by the Appraisers, would subvert individual claims to millions of property, the private ownership in which, has never before been doubted. The prerogatives of the State, set up by the Appraisers, are not limited by a criticism upon the word "margin" as in the case of the Chittenango. They claim as public property, every stream above tide-water where a raft or a small boat can be navigated, unless that stream has been granted in terms by the State. They claim not merely a right of passage or highway for the people: that is conceded by the common law; but a right of soil in the State. Several instances of this kind have occurred.

Ex-parte GEO. TIBBITS—October Term, 1826.

In this case it appeared that a valuable water fall of 12 feet in the middle sprout of the Mohawk, which falls into the Hudson between Van Schaick and Greene islands, had been destroyed by a dam erected for the use of the canals. That the tide never ebbs and flows at the fall. This fall was granted, in terms, as so much land conveyed with water, May 5, 1792, by Stephen Van Rensselaer to Jacobus Van Schoonhoven; and had come by *mesne* conveyances to the relator; there being an actual individual seisin of the fall *eo nomine* for upwards of 30 years. It is well known that the land on both sides of the fall was granted away at a very early period by the Stat , which had not afterwards asserted the least claim.

The Appraisers refused to allow the relator any damages, on the sole ground that the land under water belonged to the State.

The Supreme Court granted an alternative *mandamus*, in this case, against the Appraisers, at the time they decided Jennings' case.

Mr. J. P. *Cushman*, for the relator.

The following case came under the review of the Supreme Court, on appeal from an appraisal by the Canal Commissioners. It related to a valuable landing or depot for lumber on the River Hudson, which was inundated and destroyed by the colossal dam at Fort Edward:

Ex-parte WALTER and CHARLES ROGERS—Utica, August Term, 1825.

The affidavit of one of the owners stated, that 21 acres at Deadman's Point, above the dam, and lying adjacent to the Hudson River, had for many years before the erection of the dam, been used as a landing ground for lumber, yielding an average income to the two proprietors (to whom it had been devised by their ancestor) of about $400 annually. That it had been rendered nearly useless as a landing, from the time when the Canal Commissioners commenced the dam at Fort Edward, for a feeder to the Northern Canal, in the summer of 1821; and when the dam was completed in the summer of 1822, the landing was inundated, and the buildings removed. That the Canal Commissioners, Messrs. Young and Seymour, had appraised the damages in Mar., 1825, at only $630. And they informed the deponent, "that they estimated the land inundated, for the purpose of tillage, without reference to its value as a landing ground, at $30 per acre." That the value of the land 552*] consisted almost entirely *of its advantages as a lumber yead, which were destroyed by the dam. It appeared that a copy of this affidavit and notice of the appeal had been served on Mr. Young, who did not controvert the truth of the affidavit.

On motion to set aside this appraisal, the single point stated (and it was stated and discussed in writing) was, that the Commissioners should have allowed the value of the premises destroyed as a landing. It was argued that this was its value to the owners; this would have fixed the price in market, which would obviously have been about $6,000, instead of $630. The latter was but little more than the income for a single year. The motion was not opposed by the Commissioners; but the court, as was their course on all appeals from these appraisals, took the papers, examined the question, and set aside the appraisal—deciding that it should have been according to the value as a landing ground.

I was afterwards informed by Mr. Young, that he had acted, in awarding such small damages, on the principle that the soil of the Hudson at the place in question, though far above tide-water, belonged to the State.

With deference, this was evidently adopting a new rule, unknown to the common law. It was not only adopting a new rule; but it was carrying that rule, in its application, one step further than it ever can be carried. Admitting the more despotic rule of the civil law: "*Flumina autem omnia, et portus, publica sunt; ideoque jus piscandi omnibus commune est in portu fluminibusque;*" *Just. Lib.* 2, tit. 1, sec. 2; the conclusion drawn by the Canal Commissioners, would, by no means, follow. The common law, so applied, would authorize them, in the prosecution of their splendid works, to cut up or inundate the valuable lumber yards at Troy, Albany or N. Y., and then to pay, instead of their value as lying on a public stream, the price which they would fetch in market, as wheat fields, meadows, &c., according to their agricultural value. Their value arises from their local situation and advantages, their worth in market, and the revenues derivable from them are to be taken into the account. The Schuylkill Navigation Co. v. Thoburn, 7 Serg. & R., 411; 1 Domat, 431; Of the Restitution of Fruits, 1-3. The State is bound to make restitution upon the same principle as an individual, who should commit the injury. 1 Bl. Com., 141, 142. This is so even in more despotic countries; 2 *Montesq. L'Esp. de Lois*, ch. 15; and the maxim, *sic utere tuo ut alienum non lœdas*, applies with equal force to both. I do not, therefore, think that the decision of the Supreme Court, necessarily involved the question, whether the civil or common law should prevail. I do not believe they stopped to inquire whether the Hudson was a public or private river at the place in question. Such a point was not presented by the affidavit. This did not state whether the place was above or below tide-water; nor was the point raised in argument. It is evident, therefore, that the court held the result to be the same, upon both the civil and common law.

On the case coming before the present Appraisers, the question whether the Hudson, at the landing, was private property, was again raised, as will be seen by the case which they drew up, with a copy of which I have been favored. It is in these words:

*In the matter of CHARLES & WALTER [*553 ROGERS.

"They claim title to a tract of land lying within the bounds of the Kayaderosseras patent, which was granted on the 2d Nov., 1708; bounded as follows: 'thence easterly or northerly to the third falls on Albany River' (Baker's Falls on the Hudson; 1 Johns., 156), 'about 20 miles, more or less; thence along the said river, down southerly, to the northeasterly bounds of Saratoga,' &c.

About 21 acres of that tract lie on the west margin of the Hudson River, and about one half a mile above the dam at Fort Edward. A part of the tract, before the dam was built, was used as a place on which to deposit lumber, for the purpose of rafting and floating it down the river; and which produced an annual revenue to the claimants, as they allege, of $400 or $500; but which, since that dam was built, is rendered totally useless for that purpose; the dam having destroyed the navigation of the river to that place, and covered the land with water about 27 feet deep.

The place in question is about 40 miles above tide-water, and much farther above where the water becomes fresh. There is no natural and continued navigation up the river to the land which is the subject of this claim.

Apr. 15, 1771, 62 years after the grant of the Kayaderosseras patent, the British Government made a grant to Henry Stilson, the subject of which is described as follows: 'All that certain tract of land, ground and soil, under and covered with the water of Hudson's River, in the County of Albany, within our Province of N. Y.; beginning on the west bank of the said river, at the division line between lot No. 7 and lot No. 8, in the 19th allotment of the Kayaderosseras patent; and runs thence into the river; east 3 chains, then parellel to the said bank of the said river, at 3 chains distance, south 13 degrees east, 1 chain and 60 links, and south 30 degrees east, 5 chains and 60 links, then west 3 chains and 65 links to the bank of the river; and then along the said bank, as the same doth wind and turn, northward to the place of beginning, containing 2 acres; together with all and singular, the benefits, liberties, privileges, waters, water-courses, mills, mill dams, easements, emoluments, tenements and hereditaments whatsoever,' &c. Book of Military Patents, No. 2, pp. 379, 590.

The questions are, 1. Are the claimants entitled to

the value of this land, according to its increased value by means of the use and unobstructed navigation of the river, as it was before the dam was built; or are they only entitled to its value for agricultural purposes?

2. Are the claimants entitled to pay for their fishery, which has been destroyed by the dam?"

Now, there is no doubt, upon the cases before cited, that the boundary "to the falls, and thence along the river down southerly," &c., to which the 21 acres in question extend, will, *per se*, carry the right of soil in the claimants to the thread of the Hudson. 2 Johns., 252, 255; 14 Mass., 149; 2 Conn. N. S., 481; 2 N. H., 369. Of course, the exclusive right of fishing goes to the same extent. 20 Johns., 90.

The only argument against this construction is the little two acre military patent to Stilson. Now, had this been granted before the Kayaderosseras patent issued, and had it been a part of the identical
554*] bed of the river covered *by the 21 acres, it must be admitted that, within what the court say in Lunt v. Holland, 14 Mass., 151, it would have operated as an exception from the Kayaderosseras patent, *pro tanto*. But clearly not, being as it is, subsequent to the issuing of the Kayaderosseras patent. The very point was adjudged in Harramond v. M'Glaughon, Tayl., 196. This little river patent lies 8 or 10 miles below the 21 acres. It was a void grant. The very two acres had before passed by the great patent of Kayaderosseras; and so far from being an argument of cotemporaneous construction, this little thing could not have sustained itself upon its own ground, had it been attacked in season by the patentees of the Kayaderosseras.

It will be seen, by the above sketches, that the Board of Canal Appraisal, and the regular and ordinary tribunals of the country, have, in their respective adjudications upon the right annexed to riparian ownership, begun at different points. The former, in effect, have begun at the civil law; the latter at the common law. And even when both have assumed the civil law as the starting point, they have diverged to directly opposite conclusions. The rules which the former have deemed it their duty to adopt, are most unfavorable to the rights of private property. Those by which our court of justice have been gnided, are more favorable, because dictated by the benign spirit of the common law. If the former be right, a large sum of individual suffering and ruin must be the consequence. With the utmost deference to that very able and respectable Board, we must be permitted to doubt the soundness of their legal positions, when we see them overruled by the decisions of the high superintending jurisdictions of our country; and especially when we see those decisions so plainly supported by the sainted doctrines of a Hale, a Holt and a Mansfield.

[END OF OCTOBER TERM, 1826.]

CASE,

BEFORE WOODWORTH, *J.*,

IN VACATION AFTER OCTOBER TERM, 1826.

EX PARTE VERMILYEA ET AL.

Practice—Certiorari *Removes the Record Only—In Criminal Cases Bill of Exceptions, Inapplicable—Admissibility and Legal Effect of Testimony Examined, by Superior Court, Only on Report or Case Stated—Challenge of Juror—Demurrer.*

A *certiorari* removes the record only.

In criminal cases, doubts upon the admission or legal effect of testimony, cannot be brought before a superior court by *certiorari*, or writ of error.

A bill of exceptions is inapplicable to a criminal cause; and in such causes the admissibility, or legal effect of testimony, can be examined in a superior court, only on a report or case agreed upon; the presumption being, that where there is reasonable ground for doubt, the judgment will be suspended till the opinion of the superior court be known.

But a challenge for principal cause, forms a part of the record; and to review this, a *certiorari* will lie in a criminal cause; and a writ of error in a civil cause.

Otherwise of a challenge to the favor.

A challenge for principal cause may be demurred to, or issue may be taken upon it.

Where the facts are admitted and referred to the court, this is, in substance, a demurrer; and should be entered on the record as such.

If a juror have expressed an opinion against the party, though from his knowledge of the cause, and not from any favor or ill will; yet this is a principal cause of challenge.

So, it seems, if his opinion be grounded on the information of those who are acquainted with the facts. Otherwise, where his opinion is grounded on mere rumor.

Citations—3 Bac. Abr., 766; 1 Chit. Cr. L., 548; Skin., 101; Hut., 24; 35 Charles, II.; 2 St. Tr., 435, 450, 451; 14 Car., 2; Stat. Westm., 2, ch. 31; 1 Keb., 324, 3 Burr., 1847; 3 Wood. Lec., 347, *n.* (*i.*); 4 Barn. & Ald., 470; 7 Hen., VI., fol. 25; Hawk., B. 2, ch. 43, sec. 28; Co. Litt., 155 *b*; 1 Johns., 316; 8 Johns., 445; 1 Cow., 432; 1 Marsh., 370, 419; Keling, 15.

ON application to *Mr. Justice* Woodworth, in behalf of *Vermilyea et al.* for the allowance of a *certiorari*, to remove into the Supreme Court the record of their conviction, from the Court of Oyer and Terminer of the City and County of N. Y., His Honor, deeming the question of too much importance to be disposed of without giving the counsel for the people an opportunity to be heard, directed notice to be given to the District Attorney of the City and County of N. Y. Notice having been given accordingly, the questions presented were argued before the judge at his chambers, in Albany, on the 22d and 23d of Dec., 1826, by,

Messrs. A. Spencer and *B. F. Butler*, for the application, and

Mr. Talcott, Atty-Gen., contra.

His Honor afterwards discussed the questions at large, and gave his opinion as follows:

WOODWORTH, *J.* The defendants were convicted at a Court of Oyer and Terminer, held in the City of N. Y., *of a conspiracy [*556 to defraud certain incorporated companies and individuals, of their goods, chattels and effects. Application is now made for the allowance of a *certiorari*, to remove the record and proceedings in the Supreme Court, for the purpose of reviewing the decision of the court below, on a challenge taken to some of the jurors; and also on the ground of a fatal variance between the proof offered at the trial, and the charges contained in the indictment. As to the latter, I will merely observe, that a *certiorari* removes the record only; and as the evidence produced on the trial forms no part of the record, the writ would be a nugatory process. In criminal cases, where questions of law arise at the trial, either as to the admission of testimony, or its legal effect when admitted, if doubts are entertained, the facts are brought before this court in the form of a report, or case agreed on. If the objections afford reasonable ground for doubt, the presumption is that judgment will be suspended until the opinion of the superior court be known. As far as I know, questions of this description have always been submitted to the Supreme Court in that manner. The experience of half a century has not called for any legislative provision to vary this course of practice; nor am I aware that complaints have ever been made, that the exercise of this discretion has been rigorous as respects the accused. On the contrary, it will be found that the cases from inferior tribunals, which have been reviewed, furnish no inconsiderable evidence of the solicitude and tenderness of our courts, in allowing even to the greatest culprits the benefit of every legal objection.

If, however, in any given case, the inferior court should erroneously refuse to interfere, it would afford no ground for a *certiorari*; because the remedy does not apply to, or reach the error sought to be corrected.

If a bill of exceptions would lie in a criminal case, the difficulty would be removed; but it is well settled that it does not.

With respect to the admission of the jurors, I will confine my observations to the case of *Andrew S. Norwood.* *From the affida- [*557 vits and certificates of the clerk, it appears that Mr. Norwood was challenged for the principal cause; and the decision of the challenge referred to the court, without any objection on the part of the District Attorney. The specific ground of the challenge was not, in the first instance, stated. The juror testified that he had heard all the evidence given on the former trial, having been present at it; that he had made up his opinion perfectly, on the evidence, that the defendants were all guilty; and had frequently expressed his opinion to that effect. Upon being inquired of by the District Attorney, he stated that he felt no bias or partiality against any of the defendants; that if the testimony given on this trial should appear as it did on the former, he should certainly find the defendants all guilty; and added, that he thought he felt competent to give a verdict according to his oath, and the evidence as it should appear.

The court decided that the juror stood indifferent, and that the challenge was not true. He was accordingly sworn and sat on the trial.

On this evidence, two questions arise: First. Whether the challenge forms a part of the reccord, so as to be the subject of removal by *certiorari*. Second. Whether the exception to the juror was well taken.

The first question depends on this; do the facts constitute a principal cause of challenge? This arises when there is a manifest presumption of partiality. In that case it excludes the juror; but a challenge to the favor, where the partiality is not apparent, must be left to the discretion of triers. The facts relied on generally consist of slight circumstances, respecting which the law has not laid down any certain rule. In such cases the judgment of the triers is conclusive. The question arising on such a challenge is altogether extrinsic of the record. Evidence may be reviewed in a superior court by demurrer, or bill of exceptions, but neither applies to evidence in support of a challenge for favor.

The next inquiry is, whether a principal cause of challenge may become parcel of the **558***] record, and under what *circumstances. If it cannot in any case, it is unnecessary to consider the objection taken to the juror.

It is laid down in 3 Bac. Abr., 766, that "if a challenge be taken, and the other side demur, and it be debated, and the judge overrules it, it is entered upon the original record; and if at *Nisi Prius*, it appears upon the *postea* what the judge hath done; but if the judge overruled the challenge upon debate, without a demurrer, then it is proper for a bill of exceptions." Chitty, 1st vol. Cr. L., 548, recognizes the same doctrine. He refers to Skinn., 101, and Hut., 24. Chitty also says, at the same page, that if a demurrer be resolved on, either to the array or to the polls, there is no occasion for those circumstances which must attend a demurrer to a plea, such as the signature of counsel; but it is good as soon as agreed on at the bar, and the prothonotaries ought of right to enter it on the record. These authorities suppose a principal cause of challenge, and establish the proposition, that where the facts alleged as cause of challenge are not disputed, the question is decided summarily by the court. On the argument before me, the Atty-Gen. conceded the law to be, that if the challenge was good for principal cause, and the other party demurred, it became parcel of the record, and might be removed. He contended, however, that this was not a challenge of that description; that the facts made out a challenge for favor; and that the judge was substituted in the place of triers by consent of parties; and, consequently, that the question was to be viewed in the same manner as if it had been actually decided by the latter.

If it should turn out that the defendants have not established a principal cause of challenge, the argument is well founded. The real difficulty, if any exists, is, in ascertaining whether the public prosecutor is to be considered as having demurred to the challenge. The proceedings in this stage, were somewhat informal. The more regular course would have been, to have stated, in the first instance, the facts relied on for cause. The prosecutor would then probably have elected to plead or demur. It seems, however, that the juror was challenged without *specifying the cause, and the ques- [***559** tion referred to the court. What was referred to the court? The juror was examined; there was no dispute about facts. When that happens in the case of a principal challenge, as well as in that for favor, triers are appointed. The court were called upon to pronounce the law—to decide whether the facts made out a principal cause of challenge; or, in other words, whether they were sufficient to exclude the juror. I admit, if the facts were only proper to be submitted to triers, in support of a challenge for favor, the defendants are concluded by the decision of the judge; but if, *per se*, they formed a principal cause, they may avail themselves of it as such. A demurrer is an admission of the fact, submitting the law arising on that fact to the court. On a demurrer to a challenge, no strict technical form seems to be required. Have not both parties conceded that the testimony of the juror was true, and have they not called on the court to declare the law arising on that testimony? Will it be denied that this is, in substance, a demurrer; or will it be gravely contended, because the party may not have said in terms, he demurred to the challenge, but submitted to the court whether it was sufficient, in point of law, that, therefore, a substantial difference exists between the two cases—that the one shall be entered on the record, and shall be subject to review, while the other is final and conclusive? I cannot persuade myself that the rights of any party are held by such a tenure, and particularly in a criminal case, where there is no remedy by bill of exceptions. I am, therefore, of opinion that the judge having been called upon to decide whether the challenge was valid in law, it is, in substance, the same as if the party had demurred in express terms. If viewed in the light of a demurrer, it becomes parcel of the record, and is liable to be removed by *certiorari*. That the counsel for the defendants considered the decision on the challenge as subject to the revision of a superior tribunal; and did all that was deemed necessary to secure that right, is apparent from the fact alleged in the affidavit of Mr. Hoyt, who says that the defendants' counsel requested *the court to take [***560** down the testimony as to the competency of the jurors, in order to give the parties the benefit of reviewing the decision; and that the presiding judge, upon such request, read over the notes of evidence, and corrected the same in some particulars, on the suggestion of the defendants' counsel.

It is, however, contended that this case falls

within that part of the doctrine laid down by Chitty and Bacon, where it is said that if the challenge is overruled without demurrer, on being debated, the objection may afterwards be made the subject of a bill of exceptions; and as no bill was taken, the decision could not be brought before the Supreme Court, unless by consent. It seems to me this rule does not apply in criminal cases. Whether the counsel demurs to the challenge, or merely argues that it is not good in law, creates no material distinction. If the distinction was ever entertained in the English courts, it must have been founded on a belief that a bill of exceptions would lie. But if it be a conceded point that no bill of exceptions will lie, I think it goes far to show that the rule laid down is not applicable to criminal, but civil cases. I have traced the doctrine to its source, by examining the cases cited by Chitty. They are to be found in Skinn., 101, and Hut., 24. The case from Skinner was decided 35 Charles II., between the King and the City of Worcester. It was an information in the nature of a *quo warranto*. The case states that the counsel for the City of Worcester came with their bill of exceptions; they challenged the array, because the *venire* was returned as by both the coroners; when, in truth, but one of them returned it. They likewise challenged the polls, for want of freehold, which was overruled. No question was raised, whether a bill of exceptions would lie. Saunders, *Ch. J.*, said, if the judge overruled the challenge upon debate, without a demurrer, then 'tis proper for a bill of exceptions. There are several answers to this case. It was not strictly a criminal proceeding. Informations at the common law, partook of the nature of a civil remedy, and, in modern times, are considered as a **561***] civil remedy only. It must, I *apprehend, have been so considered by the court; otherwise, a bill of exceptions would not have been suggested. This is evident from the fact that prior to the 35th of Charles II., the judges in England had expressed an opinion on this point.

In the case of *Sir Henry Vane*, reported in Keling, 15, and 2 St. Tri., 435, 450, 451; 14 Car. 2, a construction is given to the statute; and it was held, by all the judges, that the Statute of Westm. 2, ch. 31, which gives the bill of exceptions, extends only to civil causes, and not to criminal. Keling states that the court agreed the words of the statute are plain as to this point. So also, 1 Keb., 324, where the same case is reported, the judges observe, a bill of exceptions is not within the statute, or ever heard of, the statute not extending to any indictment. This case having been decided before the case in Skinner, it is manifest the court had no reference to criminal proceedings, when speaking of a bill of exceptions, as applicable to a challenge, disposed of without demurrer. As a civil remedy, it may undoubtedly be pursued, if there is no demurrer to the challenge in form; but even then, in a civil case, its necessity may well be questioned, as will presently be shown. The case then leaves the principle untouched, that where the judge decides the law on a principal challenge, whether arising on demurrer, or by a submission of the question, an entry is made on the record, which may be reviewed.

The decision in Skinner, upon which Chitty and Bacon rest, is an authority to prove there is a remedy, where a good cause of challenge is overruled. It is an admission of this principle. The public prosecutor cannot be compelled to demur. Shall his refusal or admission deprive the accused of a right? Can the right depend on such a contingency? I think not. In accordance with this view of the subject, it seems to me the cause of *Hesketh* v. *Braddock*, 3 Burr., 1847, decided on a writ of error, proceeded. The record states that the defendant challenged the array, to which the plaintiff demurred; the challenge was disallowed. The defendant then, *ore tenus*, in open *court, challenged [***562** the polls, because the jurors were citizens and freemen of the City of Chester. The challenge was disallowed; and thereupon the issue was tried and a verdict found for the plaintiff. The Court of K. B. considered the validity of the challenge, and passed upon it, as parcel of the record. There was no suggestion by the court or counsel, that the challenge to the polls was improperly brought up. The challenge to the polls was not demurred to, but it was disallowed. On what principle did it become part of the record? Manifestly because the decision of the court upon it was substantially the same, as if a demurrer had been filed in form.

In 3 Wood. Lec., 347, *n. i*, the form of the record in the case from Burrows is given. The challenge to the polls is thus entered: "And hereupon the said S. B. *ore tenus*, in open court, challengeth the polls, because, he says that the jurors are citizens and freemen of the City of Chester, which said challenge by the court here is disallowed." Professor Woodeson then states that the challenge *ore tenus* was omitted in the first engrossment of the record; that the defendant alleged diminution, and that it was then inserted by rule. This case sanctions the doctrine contended for by the defendants' counsel, that the challenge may be removed as parcel of the record, provided it was a principal cause of challenge.

The only remaining question is, whether the facts stated by the juror constituted a principal cause of challenge.

It will not be denied that every man, whether in a civil or criminal case, is entitled to an impartial jury. Though our Constitution merely preserves the trial by jury inviolate forever, and does not, in express terms, guarantee an impartial jury, yet, *ex vi termini*, it is embraced in its provisions—as much so, as that the judges shall be impartial men. The same general principle is adopted by the English law. The only question is, as to the application of that principle. Can a juror be impartial or indifferent to the question, who, from a knowledge of the facts, confesses that he has made up his mind that the accused are guilty? It is a fallacy to suppose such a man stands impartial, merely *because he has no malice or ill will [***563** against the defendant. This doctrine, however, has been strenuously urged; and cases have been cited, to show that the law is so understood in England.

In the case of the *King* v. *Emonds*, 4 Barn. & Ald., 470, *Ch. J.* Abbott observes, that expressions used by a juryman are not a cause of challenge, unless they are to be referred to something of personal ill will towards the party challenging. He relies on the doctrine laid

down in the Year Books, 7 Hen. VI., fol. 25, where Babington, *J.*, says, "if the juror has said he will pass with the one party, for the knowledge that he has of the matter, and of the truth, he is indifferent; but if he has said so for any affection of the party, he is favorable." Hawkins, B. 2, ch. 43, sec. 28, is also referred to. He observes, "that it hath been allowed a good cause of challenge, that the juror hath declared his opinion beforehand, that the party is guilty, or will be hanged, or the like." Hawkins adds, "yet it hath been adjudged that if it shall appear that the juror made such declaration from his knowledge of the cause, and not out of any ill will to the party, it is no cause of challenge." The opining of the Court of K. B., in Barn. & Ald., rests on these ancient authorities; it does not profess to consider the soundness of the doctrine advanced. Now, admitting the law had been so applied at an early day, when the prisoner did not profess even the right of producing testimony, I apprehend that after the lapse of centuries, when the rights of parties are better understood, and have been more accurately defined, it would not be presumption to inquire whether the common law, relating to the right of challenge, had not, in this instance, been misapplied; or whether it was consistent with the law as laid down by Ld. Coke, who says, "the rule of law is, that the juror must stand indifferent as he stands unsworn." (Co. Litt., 155 *b*.) It seems to be admitted in some of the old cases, that an opinion formed and expressed is good cause of challenge. Upon what is this founded? On the supposition that it creates a
564*] bias. All experience goes to prove *the infirmity of human nature is such that we cannot at pleasure get rid of preconceived opinions. The question is not how great is the bias, but does any exist? The least is sufficient to exclude. Can the source from whence it is derived be material? As to the accused, it is the same thing, whether the bias proceeds from a preconceived opinion, or malice and ill will. Be it either, he is equally affected. Why then superadd the necessity of proving malice or ill will? Without it the parties do not contend on equal ground; by requiring it to be proved, in order to exclude the juror, it only shows the disparity to be greater. If the question were entirely novel, I should think our courts would incline to take a different view of it. But it has occurred here, and has been well considered. The Supreme Court decided, in the case of *Blake* v. *Millspaugh*, 1 Johns., 316, it was good cause of challenge to a juror, that he had previously given his opinion on the question in controversy between the parties. The case of *Durell* v. *Mosher*, 8 Johns., 445, is not contradictory. There, the juror said, if the reports of the neighbors were correct, the defendant was wrong, and the plaintiff was right. No definite opinion was expressed or formed. The court so adjudged; and observed that the declaration was hypothetical. It is no more than saying, if the defendant has done an illegal act, let him answer for it; which is no evidence of partiality. In the case of *Pringle* v. *Huse*, 1 Cow., 432, a juror was challenged for having expressed an opinion against the plaintiff. It was held that this was a principal cause of challenge, and should be tried by the court; and that the juror challenged might be called as a witness. In the case of *Coleman* v. *Hagerman*, 5 City H. Rec., 63, the same principle was adopted by the Supreme Court. The late *Ch. J.* Spencer has furnished me with a manuscript opinion of his, in that cause. It was an action for an assault and battery of an aggravated character. The verdict was for $4,000 damages. The grounds of the motion were, that Graham, one of the jury, had made use of language, indicating an opinion that the defendant ought to be exemplarily punished. *It [***565**
appeared that Graham was wholly unacquainted with the parties until after the trial; and that the opinions expressed by him were founded on newspaper publications. He swore that he had no bias against, or partiality for, either of the parties, and personally knew nothing of the assault and battery complained of; yet the court unanimously awarded a new trial, on the ground that Graham did not stand indifferent, in consequence of the opinions he had expressed. In the manuscript opinion referred to, the late *Chief Justice* stated the principles adopted by him, on the then recent trial of Van Alstyne, for the murder of Huddlestone. It was thus: if a person had formed or expressed an opinion for or against the prisoner, on a knowledge of any of the facts attending the murder, or from information of those acquainted with the facts, he considered it good cause of challenge; but if the opinions of the jurors were formed on mere rumors and report, he decided that such opinions did not disqualify the jurors; and, as I understood, the opinion delivered on that solemn occasion met the decided approbation of the Supreme Court.

The principle upon which these cases were decided, is that an opinion formed and expressed by a juror, is of itself evidence that he does not stand indifferent between the parties. I do not perceive how the case before me can be distinguished. On the trial of Fries for treason, before *Judge* Iredell, on an application for a new trial, one question was as to the competency of a juror who had expressed himself in strong terms as to the prisoner's guilt. That learned judge put the question on this ground: that when a predetermined opinion is formed, from whatever motives, it creates an improper bias, extremely difficult to get rid of; and may influence an honest man unwarily to give a wrong verdict: that he becomes less able to discriminate facts. The reasoning of *Ch. J.* Marshall, on the trial of Col. Burr, Vol. I., pp. 370, 419, is directly in point. He has shown, in the most satisfactory manner, that a juror who has given his opinion cannot be considered *impartial; that the natural tendency [***566**
of preconceived opinions in a juror is to obstruct the impartial administration of justice. He asks, why a distant relative, or he who has prejudices, cannot serve on a jury? Because he is presumed to have a bias. He may declare that, notwithstanding, he is determined to listen to the evidence and be governed by it; but the law will not trust him. The *Chief Justice* observes: "Is there less reason to suspect him who has prejudged the case, and deliberately formed and delivered an opinion upon it? The law suspects, and not without reason, that he will listen with more favor to that testimony which confirms, than to that which would

change his opinion. It is not to be expected that he will weigh evidence or argument, as fairly as a man whose judgment is not made up in the case." These enlightened views place the question upon the true ground—not whether the juror feels resentment or ill will, but whether for any cause he has a bias on his mind that may disqualify him from deciding with strict impartiality I entirely concur in the reasoning of that case, as containing a luminous exposition of the ground upon which the rule is founded.

The result of my opinion is, that enough has been shown to render the decision in the court below questionable, that the challenge forms a part of the record, and that the defendants are entitled to the allowance of a *certiorari.*

Certiorari *granted.*

Cited in—4 Wend., 238; 14 Wend., 132; 17 Wend., 469; 21 Wend., 545; 25 Wend., 169; 1 Den., 305; 4 Den., 33; 80 N. Y., 493; 20 Barb., 281; 1 Park., 285; 3 Park., 344; 4 Park., 117, 135; 6 Park., 662; Edm., 90; 2 Sum., 106; 21 Am. Dec., 129, 133; 36 Am. Dec., 516 (3 Scam., 76); 47 Am. Dec., 230.

CASES

ARGUED AND DETERMINED

IN THE

SUPREME COURT

OF THE

STATE OF NEW YORK,

IN

FEBRUARY TERM, 1827, IN THE FIFTY-FIRST YEAR OF OUR INDEPENDENCE.

MYERS *v.* FOSTER.

Canal Commisioners Have no Right to Levy a Toll upon Passengers, under Statute—Construction of Penal Statute.

The Canal Commissioners have no right to levy a toll upon passengers on the Erie and Champlain canals, within the Statute, sess. 43, ch. 202, sec. 17, 20.

But the Act was amended and extended to persons, by the Statute of Apr.12,1827. *Vide note a* at the end of this case.

A penal statute is not to be extended by an equitable construction.

ON ERROR from the C. P. of Schenectady Co., where the cause came by appeal from the Justice's Court of the City of Schenectady. Myers, a collector on the Erie Canal, sued Foster for $25, the penalty given by the 17th section of the Act for the Maintenance and Protection of the Erie and Champlain Canals, sess.43, ch. 202. This section requires that every boatman, or person having charge of property moving on the canal, shall give to the collector, &c., a just account or bill of lading, &c., signed by the person, &c., conveying such property, &c., containing a statement of the weight of all property on which toll is charged by the ton, &c., and the number and feet of other articles, &c., a statement of the place from which the property is brought, and where the same is intended to be landed, &c.; and on default in any of these particulars, that the boatman, &c., shall forfeit and pay the penalty of $25. The 20th section authorizes the Canal Commissioners to establish the rates of toll to be paid on all articles conveyed, &c., and to erect toll-houses and weighing scales. The 23d section gives an action for all penalties to the collector, &c.

Foster, the defendant, being master of a freight boat, cleared from Albany; with prop-
568] erty and four passengers, *having paid toll for the property, as established under the 20th section. He afterwards took in one and a half passengers at West Troy; and at Schenectady offered to clear the passengers, with 3½ more passengers taken on board at the latter place (making in all, the number of 8), to a place about 5 miles above the city, which was done, the defendant furnishing a bill of lading accordingly. 6½ of the passengers were discovered by agents (whom the plaintiff had employed to watch), continuing their passage on the boat about ten miles above Schenectady; and it was for the falsity of the bill of lading, in this respect, that the action was brought.

On these facts being proved in the C. P. the plaintiff rested; and the defendant moved for a nonsuit, on the ground that no toll could be assessed on passengers, by the Canal Commissioners—passengers not being property, to which alone the Act extended; and that no assessment on passengers was proved.

The plaintiff then offered in evidence, an establishment of toll, on passengers over 12 years of age by number, and under that age by weight to be estimated at 75 lbs. each, signed by Stephen Van Rensselaer, Samuel Young, Henry Seymour and Wm. C. Bouck, the Canal Commissioners, who claimed in making the assessment, to Act under the 20th section.

This evidence was rejected by the C. P., who nonsuited the plaintiff. He excepted, and brought error to this court on the bill of exceptions.

Mr. N. F. Beck, for the plaintiff in error, conceded that passengers were not mentioned specifically by the Act as a subject of toll; but he contended that the intent and object of the Legislature was to levy a compensation upon every person, as well as upon all property transported upon the canal. Though persons are not within the terms, they are certainly within the reason and equity of the Act. The transportation of passengers occasions the same injury to the canal and works the same benefit and profit to individuals as the transportation of property.

Mr. A. C. Paige*, contra, was stopped [*569**
by the court.

SAVAGE, *Ch. J.* The only question seems to be, whether passengers are property. No mention is made of persons, and there is not a word in the Act from which we can infer that the Legislature intended to make them the subject of toll. The law will not extend a penal statute by equitable construction.

SUTHERLAND, *J.* It is impossible that this law could contemplate passengers as the subject of toll. There is nothing, either in the sense of the words used or in the context, to warrant the construction contended for. It would be extending a penal statute beyond what was ever heard or thought of before.

WOODWORTH, *J.* The judgment must be affirmed. This is a plain *casus omissus* in the Act. The equitable construction contended for would be most extravagant; and is tolerated by no rule. It would be a total departure from the obvious meaning of the Legislature.

Judgment affirmed.(a)

Cited in—5 Hill, 541; 17 Barb., 339; 1 *Blatchf.*, 156.

(a) By the Act passed Apr. 12, 1827, amendatory to the one in question, the right is given to tax persons as well as property, passing on the canal.

ROOT *v.* KING ET AL.

Practice—Right of Counsel to be Heard—Of Judge to Correct Charge.

Counsel have a right to be heard on settling a case before a judge.

A judge has a right to correct his charge as presented by a case, even though the parties may have agreed upon it.

THE defendants having made a case upon which to move for a new trial, and the plaintiff having proposed amendments, in which he did not object to the charge of the circuit judge as set forth in the case made, both the draft of the case and amendments were sent to the judge by the defendant for the purpose of being settled. The judge proceeded to settle the case accordingly. He struck out the charge as inserted by the defendant, and substituted one according to his own notes and recollec-
570] tion; and *made corrections in the facts of the case, without regarding the time and place at which the defendant's attorney had noticed the case for settlement; and without either party being present. The judge certified to this court that it was his practice to settle cases without the counsel of the parties being present, and that he substituted a new charge in this case, because the one inserted by the defendants was unnecessarily prolix, and materialy incorrect.

A motion was now made to refer the case to the judge for review.

Messrs. J. Blunt and *J. Duer*, for the plaintiff.

Messrs. J. Sudam and *E. Williams*, contra.

SAVAGE, *Ch. J.* Whatever course the parties may take in fixing on a judge's charge, to be inserted in a case, it is the right of the judge to see that it is correct. Neither the parties nor their counsel have a right, at their pleasure, to make out such a charge as will appear absurd or ridiculous. All they can require is, that the opinions expressed to the jury be substantially presented. But we think the judge erred in deciding that counsel should not be heard before him in relation to settling the case; and on this ground the motion must be granted.

SUTHERLAND, *J.* The charge is always subject to the correction of the judge, though the parties may agree upon it.

WOODWORTH, *J.* The correction may be made at any time; and we would even stop an argument on the certificate of the circuit judge that his charge had been perverted. His charge need not be inserted *in hæc verba.* The material parts alone are necessary. He should put into the case the substance of his opinions as expressed upon the law and the fact.

Motion granted.

Cited in—39 N. Y., 88; 14 Abb. Pr., 50.

*IN THE MATTER OF APPLICATION OF [*571 THE MAYOR, &c., OF THE CITY OF NEW YORK, Relative to Extending and Opening THIRD STREET.

Action—Supreme Court Acts as Commissioners of Estimate and Assessment under Statute—Report, Irrevocable after Confirmation.

After confirmation of the Commissioners of Estimate and Assessment, under the Statute, 1 R. L., 413, sec. 178, there being no irregularity or surprise, the court will not open the matter, so that the merits may be considered, as to the wrongful assessment of an individual, even with the consent of the Corporation.

The Supreme Court act, under the Statute, as commissioners, not as a court; and a report once regularly confirmed is irrevocable, unless all the parties in interest consent.

Citations—2 R. L., 413; 20 Johns., 272, 273; 7 Johns., 546, 547.

THE report of the Commissioners of Estimate and Assessment, in this matter, was confirmed at the last August Term without opposition, owing to certain papers sent by Mr. Simmons to oppose not arriving in season. Since that time, Simmons complaining to the Corporation that his property had been assessed too high, they resolved that if the Supreme Court should be of opinion that the assesment could be waived by the assent of the Corporation, without impairing the validity of the proceedings, the counsel of the Corporation should waive the assessment, so as to permit Simmons to be heard at this term.

Mr. P. W. Radcliff, for Simmons, now moved that he be heard; and he cited *Matter of Dover St.*, 1 Cow., 74.

Mr. M. Ulshœffer, contra, said the confirmation was conclusive and could not be recalled; and he cited 20 Johns., 269; 7 *Id.*, 541; 6 *Id.*, 1; 11 East, 194; 7 *Id.*, 307; 1 Cai., 510; 2 Dall., 409; 6 Johns. Ch., 49; 2 R. L., 414; Act of Apr. 20, 1818, sess. 41, ch. 210; Sess. 42, ch. 202, sec. 1.

He said the proceedings can now be reviewed only on *certiorari*, upon the allegation that they do not conform to the Statute. (20 Johns., 430; 1 Johns. Ch., 18; 7 Wh., 218; 4 Johns. Ch., 352.)

The Matter of Dover St., cited against us from 1 Cow., was before confirmation.

Mr. Radcliff, in reply, urged the hardship of the rule laid down by some of the cases, which often subjected individuals to great losses; and relied on the consent of the Corporation.

SAVAGE, *Ch. J.* The hardship of these corporation cases is a very common topic of remark when their proceedings *come be-[*572 fore us; but we have no power to give relief. The remedy lies with the Legislature. We act as commissioners under a statute, declaring what we have once done to be conclusive. (2 R. L., 413.) Vested rights are acquired by third persons in virtue of what we do; and the plain import of the statute and the cases cited is, that the report, being once confirmed, becomes irrevocable, unless it be voluntarily waived by all parties concerned. We do not act as a court in these matters, but as commissioners appointed by the Legislature; and such proceedings have been very aptly compared by the cases, to those of a commissioner or Court of C. P., under the Insolvent Act. (20 Johns., 272, 273; 7 Johns., 546, 547.) The consent of the Corporation is nothing, unless it be accompanied with that of all the parties in interest. The Corporation must collect the money assessed, and pay it over according to the statute. The case of *Dover St.* is pressed upon us; but that was before confirmation, and was a case of surprise. If not, the former cases were against it; and we would take it back.

SUTHERLAND, *J.* In this case, the court have acted on the merits. It is not a case of irregularity, surprise or default.

Per totam curiam.

Motion denied.

Cited in—1 Wend., 323; 20 Wend., 620; 7 Hill, 18; 2 Den., 326; 39 N. Y., 88; 6 Trans. App., 123; 17 Barb., 232; 71 Ind., 21; 32 Am. Dec., 608.

THE PEOPLE v. SCHUYLER.

Felony to Take Goods of Another when Eloping with his Wife, though at her Solicitation.

It is felony for a man who elopes with another's wife, to take his goods, though with the consent, and at the solicitation of the wife.

Citations—Stat. Westm. 13, Ed. I., ch. 34; Russ on Crimes, 26, 27; Dalton's County Justice, ch. 157, p. 504; 1 Hal. P. C., 514.

THE defendant was imprisoned for, and convicted of grand larceny in stealing the goods of L., at the Oyer and Terminer for Schoharie Co., Oct. 23, 1826. The cause came here on a *certiorari*, accompanied with a case.

The evidence in the court below was, that the prisoner eloped with L.'s wife in the night, carrying away with him certain household furniture or goods of L. secretly and unknown to L. The prisoner and L.'s wife having agreed to elope with an intention that she should live 573*] with him *as his wife; she told him of her intention to take the furniture. He at first declined to take anything beside her wearing apparel, and said he would have nothing to do with the goods; but at her request, she saying the goods were her own, he assisted in placing them in a wagon when they started; and also assisted in carrying some of them out of the house. They afterwards lived together as man and wife in the State of N. J. The goods were taken with the intention of converting them to the use of the prisoner and L.'s wife; were under their joint control while they lived together; and afterwards, up to the time of the trial, under the control of the wife at her father's.

Mr. H. Hamilton, for the prisoner, said this taking was clearly no felony in the wife and, therefore, could not be so in the prisoner. This is so laid down by Hale; and he is pretty uniformly followed by every subsequent writer on criminal law. 1 Hal. P. C., 514; 1 Hawk., B. 1, ch. 33, sec. 19; 2 East Cr. L., 558, sec. 8; 2 Chit. C. L., 935; *Harrison's* case, 1 Leach Cr. Cas., 47; Dunl. N. Y., Justice, 285; Com. Dig., Justices, O, 6; Show., 52, Shower, *arg.*; 1 Russ. Crimes, 26, 27; 2 *Id.*, 1130. The wife is treated by these authorities, as having an interest in the goods; and it will be seen by them that the Statute Westm. 2, ch. 34 was deemed necessary to make the taking of goods with the wife against her will, felony.

Mr. Talcott, Atty-Gen., contra. Hale is the foundation of the doctrine contended for, and the other writers profess to do no more than follow him. He relies on 13 Ass., 6, which relates to a prosecution on the Statute Westm. 2, ch. 34, for stealing wife and goods. It could never be, that the mere fact of taking the wife with the goods, should mitigate the taking of the latter to a trespass. The crime is aggravated. The statute was evidently intended of those cases only, which were not felony at the common law. It referred to the taking of the wife and goods, and made both a single felony, which might be *charged as such; [*574 and then the statute was referred to in the indictment. Stealing the goods was felony at the common law. The statute created a new felony of which the ravishment was an ingredient. (2 Inst., 434.) This will also be seen by referring to the book cited by Coke and Hale. The place is a note to 13 Ass., 5, instead of being 6, as it is usually cited. Br. Corone, pl. 77, gives the same authority at length; but neither he nor Coke draw any inference from it against the taking of the goods being in itself a felony. *Harrison's* case, 1 Leach, 47, was where the wife had the exclusive possession of the goods by the consent of the husband.

But a note to Hale gives the doctrine of Dalton on this subject, which is in point for the prosecution; and Russell on Crimes, 27, cited on the other side, follows Dalton, and pronounces his opinion a good one.

Curia, per SAVAGE, *Ch. J.* The prisoner took the goods secretly, and no doubt with an intention to convert them to his own use; but this was done by the consent and at the solicitation of the wife, who had agred to elope and live with him in adultery. This is urged as reducing the offense to a trespass. So far as the question depends upon authority, we are left to the conflicting opinions of commentators, without any adjudged case in point. The Statute of Westm. 13, ed. 1, ch. 34, is relied on, which enacts thus: "and of women carried away with the goods of their husbands the King shall have the suit for the goods so taken away." This may mean an abduction with the consent or against the will of the wife. If it be the latter, it strikes one as singular that such a circumstance should reduce an act, which would otherwise be a felony at the common law, to a mere trespass; and that a statute should be necessary to restore it to its proper rank in the scale of crime. It is certainly more consistent with our present ideas on this subject to suppose the statute an affirmance of the common law. Hale and other writers do not assert, with any degree of confidence, that the consent of the wife that the adulterer with whom *she elopes should take the hus- [*575 band's goods, will reduce the crime to a trespass. Hale puts the case by a *semble*, and is followed by some others. The idea may have grown out of a supposed interest which the wife has in her husband's goods; for it is said in some books, he endows her at the marriage with all his worldly goods. (Russ., Crimes, 26, 27.) But I believe it is now universally received as law that she can exercise no control over his goods except as his agent, and not in her own right. The husband may sell the goods or give them away, or bequeath them. Her interest is no more than that of a child. In both cases it is a mere expectancy; and in most cases, the delivery to a stranger by either would protect him from a prosecution for felony. He has reason to presume the consent of the parent or husband, and acts in good faith. On this principle, he would be a mere trespasser, though consent should happen to be wanting. We are happy to find that this is so upon authority. In Dalton's Country Justice, ch. 157, p. 504, Nelson's ed., it is said, "so if a man takes another man's wife, with her husband's goods, against the husband's will, this also is a felony." And again, "if a married woman shall deliver to her adulterer her husband's goods this is a felony in the adulterer." In a note to 1 Hal. P.C., 514, the reason mentioned is, that "in such case no consent of the husband can be presumed." Russell approves of this doctrine, and the reason on which it is founded. (Russ., Crimes, 27.) Here the adulterer did more than merely receive stolen goods from the wife. He assisted in stealing them, carrying some of them out of the house. He had no reason to presume the husband's consent to such a taking, and is plainly guilty of felony.

The court sentenced the prisoner to 3 years imprisonment in the State Prison at the City of N. Y., at hard labor.

Rule accordingly.

Cited in—43 N. Y., 511.

576*] *WILCOX v. HOWLAND.

Supplemental Affidavits for Motion—Service of Copies—Time for.

Copies of supplemental affidavits for a motion, must be served the same length of time before the day mentioned in the notice of motion, as is necessary for the service of copies of the principal affidavits.

An excuse for not obtaining affidavits for a motion, till it is too late for noticing the motion for the first day of term, will warrant a notice for a subsequent day in term, but not a short notice.

MR. N. P. TALLMADGE moved, in behalf of the defendant, for a rule to enter a suggestion on the record, entitling him to judgment for treble costs, on a verdict in his favor. The motion was founded on several affidavits, copies of which, with a notice of the motion, had been served on the plaintiff's attorney more than four days previous to the day for which the motion was noticed. This was the first day of term. Afterwards, and but two days before term, the copy of a supplemental affidavit was served on the plaintiff's attorney with notice that it would be read as an additional ground for the motion; and the affidavit of serving the supplemental affidavit stated an excuse for not making an earlier service.

Mr. T. J. Oakley, contra, objected that the supplemental affidavit could not be read.

Curia. The supplemental affidavit cannot be received. The excuse would have warranted a notice of the motion for a subsequent day in term, but not a short notice. Copies of all supplemental affidavits must be served the same length of time before the day for which the motion is noticed as is necessary for the service of the copies of the principal affidavits. The defendant's counsel may withdraw his papers and renew the motion at the next term.

Papers withdrawn.

Cited in—6 Wend., 494; 2 Den., 78; 22 Am. Dec., 542.

*HOOKER v. ROGERS. [*577

Refusal of Court to Put off Trial for Proper Cause—Contents of Affidavit of Absence of Witnesses.

A circuit judge should put off a cause, on the usual affidavit of the defendant, of the absence of a material witness, &c., at the first circuit, for which the trial is noticed, unless there be suspicion that the application for that purpose is intended merely for delay.

The affidavit need not state when the witnesses were subpœnaed, unless this be made ground of objection.

It is, in general, no answer to the application that the defendant should have offered to take the depositions of sick or absent witnessess.

If the judge refuse to put off the trial for proper cause, the verdict will be set aside, though the defendant appear and contest the suit.

CASE for publishing a libel. At the last Washington Circuit, Nov. 14, the defendant moved to put off this cause, on his affidavit that J. L. Thurman was a material witness for him, without whose testimony he could not safely proceed to trial, as he was advised by counsel and verily believed; that Nov. 11, he went to the house of Thurman for the purpose of subpœnaing him, but found him confined to his bed by sickness, and unable to attend court. The affidavit stated the same thing as to the materiality of two other witnesses whom it stated to have been subpœnaed generally, without showing when; that neither had come to the court; and that the defendant expected to be able to procure the attendance of the witnesses at the next circuit.

The judge held this affidavit insufficient and refused to put off the cause, stating that the defendant should have offered the plaintiff to take the testimony of the absent witnesses before some competent person. He gave time to obtain their depositions, which was not done, and Thurman died before the defendant reached his house for that purpose. The defendant appeared at the circuit by counsel and contested the cause; and a verdict passed for the plaintiff.

A motion was now made in behalf of the defendant to set aside the verdict, and for a new trial, on the above grounds.

Messrs. B. F. Butler and *D. Russell,* for the motion, cited *Ogden* v. *Payne,* 5 Cow., 15.

Messrs. S. Stevens and *H. Buell,* contra.

Curia. The affidavit was clearly sufficient; this being the first time the cause was noticed for trial. It now appears that Thurman being since dead cannot be had as a *witness; [*578 but that is no answer. Had it been known to the defendant in season, he might have supplied his place by other testimony. It does not appear when the other witnesses were subpœnaed; but the judge did not put his refusal on that ground. If he had done so, the defect in the affidavit (if it is to be deemed one), might have been supplied, and the service of the subpœna shown to have been in due season. Substituting an examination of the witnesses on interrogatories, for their personal attendance, might prejudice the defendant's rights. He was entitled, in strictness, to their personal attendance. We are not aware that this practice of making the want of an offer to examine witnesses on interrogatories the ground of refusal to put off a trial has ever been allowed, unless perhaps, in the case of transient or seafaring witnesses. The usual affidavit is enough on the first notice of trial, unless circumstances of suspicion appear in some way, inducing a belief that the application is intended merely for delay; and so we have held, not only in the case cited, but many others. We do not hesitate to say, that had either of us been holding this circuit, we should have deemed it our duty to put off the cause on this affidavit.

Motion granted.

Cited in—7 Cow., 385; 2 Wend., 384; 8 Wend., 70; 6 Hun, 75; 3 How. Pr., 50; 51 How. Pr., 356; 3 Abb. N. S., 296; 6 Rob., 512; 7 Rob., 27; 37 Supr., 427.

JACKSON, ex dem. COATES, v. GAUGER.

Ejectment—Contents of Affidavit on Moving for View.

The affidavit, on moving for a view, in ejectment, should show, not only that boundaries are in question, but the particular circumstances which render a view necessary to the understanding of the cause by the jury; so that the court may judge whether the view be necessary.

Cit ti s—1 R. L., 332, sec. 21; Col. Cas., 46; 4 Cow., 396. a on

MR. S. A. FOOT, for the defendant, moved for a view, and read an affidavit of the defendant's attorney, that on the trial of this cause, an intricate question of boundaries would be inquired into; and the cause could not be tried by a jury understandingly without a view.

Mr. J. L. Wendell, contra, cited 4 Cow., 397.

579*] *WOODWORTH, *J.* The affidavit is insufficient. By the Statute, 1 R. L., 332, sec. 21, we may order a view when it shall appear proper and necessary. Several decisions have limited these views in ejectment to cases where boundaries are in question. (Col. Cas., 46; 4 Cow., 396.) But this alone is not enough. Particular circumstances should be stated, in order that we may judge for ourselves, whether the view be necessary to a full understanding of the cause. The defendant here states merely his own conclusions.

SAVAGE, *Ch. J.* In most cases, the evidence may be made quite as plain to a jury, in respect to boundaries, through proper surveys and diagrams, accompanied with the evidence of surveyors, and even more so, than by a view. We ought, therefore, to see that it is clearly necessary, before we subject parties to the delay and expense of this proceeding. The opinion of the party or his attorney is not sufficient,

Per totam curiam.

Motion denied.

THE PEOPLE, ex rel. JENNINGS,
v.
SEYMOUR, WOODS AND SELDEN.

THE SAME, ex rel. EGLESTON, v. THE SAME.

Owners of Land on Stream, where Tide does not Ebb and Flow, Own the bed of the Stream to the Center—Mandamus.

The owners of land adjoining a stream of water where the tide does not ebb and flow, own also the bed of the stream *usque filum aquæ*.

Peremptory *mandamus* granted on motion; the return to an alternative *mandamus* being insufficient.

TO the writs of alternative *mandamus* granted in these causes on motions reported, *ante*, 518, 520–536, the defendants now made separate returns—Seymour, that after inquiry, the Appraisers came to the conclusion that the State had not parted with the land upon which the Chittenango Creek passes at the places claimed, &c., as set forth in his affidavit, and for the reasons stated by that affidavit, as mentioned in the report above referred to; Woods, that he had ever been of opinion that the claim of the relators to damages was legal and equitable; and that he was ready and willing to appraise; and Selden, that he had a *claim for [***580** damages depending in some measure on the same principle with the claims in question in these causes; and had, therefore, declined to appraise; not deeming it prudent, under the circumstances, to act, until the other appraisers should agree, or the question should be otherwise settled. That the creek at the place in question is an inconsiderable fresh water stream far above tide-water, and in no sense of the term navigable. That since the decision of this court, he was ready to appraise.

On filing these returns,

Mr. S. L. Edwards, for Jennings, and,

Mr. N. P. Randall, for Egleston, moved for writs of peremptory *mandamus*.

Curia. These causes were before us at the terms of August and October last. We granted writs of peremptory *mandamus* at August Term; but at October Term changed the rule in each cause into one for an alternative *mandamus* upon a suggestion that the Appraisers wished to make special returns, and bring writs of error, should the decision here be against them. The facts which we have already twice passed upon, are not denied or questioned by the returns. We accordingly adjudge them insufficient, and grant writs of peremptory *mandamus*.

Rule accordingly.

Cit d in—34 Barb., 520; 22 How. Pr., 134; 20 Wis., 432. e

JACKSON, ex dem. HART, v. SMITH.

Ejectment—Writ of Error by Plaintiff Stays Attachment—Costs.

A writ of error by a plaintiff in ejectment stays an attachment against his lessor, for non-payment of costs.

IN ejectment. The verdict and judgment being for the defendant, he caused the costs to be taxed, and regularly demanded of the lessor of the plaintiff, Jan. 9 last; but they were not paid. Feb. 6 thereafter, the plaintiff sued out and filed with the clerk of this court his writ of error; and put in bail in error.

*A motion was now made, in behalf [***581** of the defendant, for an attachment against the lessor of the plaintiff, for not paying the costs.

This was opposed, on the ground that error had been brought.

Mr. G. B. Throop, for the motion.

Mr. J. T. B. Van Vechten, contra.

Curia. A writ of error stays execution, if brought before it is executed. It has the same

NOTE.—*Boundaries—Lands bounded by rivers.* See *Ex parte* Jennings, *ante*, 518 *note*.

effect upon an attachment against the lessor of the plaintiff, which is in nature of an execution. The motion for the attachment must be denied, without costs.

Motion denied.

EX PARTE WALLIS.

Practice—Attachment.

An attachment, for not performing an award on the submission being made a rule of court, cannot go till the rule be served and performance demanded.

MR. D. B. TALLMADGE moved to make the submission to arbitrators between the relator and Holly a rule of court; and for an attachment for not performing the award, which was in favor of the relator. Performance had been demanded.

Mr. G. F. Tallman, contra.

Curia. Take your motion to make the submission a rule of court. The application for an attachment is premature. That writ is founded on the idea that there has been a contempt of court in disobeying the rule. The party must, therefore, be served with the rule as in other cases, and obedience demanded; and then if it be not obeyed, an attachment goes on showing these facts by affidavit.

Rule accordingly.

S. C.—7 Cow., 522.

582*] *SANDS v. M'CLELAN.

Judgment Against Party Demurring—Leave to Withdraw Demurrer and Plead—Costs.

On judgment against a party demurring, with leave to withdraw the demurrer and plead, on payment of costs, he must seek the opposite attorney and tender him the costs; or offer to pay on their being taxed; and this is a condition precedent to pleading.

ON demurrer to the plaintiffs declaration, this court gave judgment for the plaintiff, with leave to the defendant to withdraw his demurrer and plead, on payment of costs. The plaintiff not demanding the costs, or causing them to be taxed, the defendant filed a plea, and entered a rule to reply, which not being done, he entered a default.

Mr. S. Sherwood moved to set the default aside.

Mr. E. Cowen, contra.

Curia. The payment of costs was a condition precedent to the act of pleading. The defendant should have sought the plaintiff's attorney, and tendered the costs, or demanded a taxation, offering to pay on their being taxed.

Motion granted.

Cited in—3 Hun, 702; 1 Bos., 594.

WHEELER v. RAYMOND.

Practice—Stay of Proceedings.

Proceedings will be stayed against special bail, pending a writ of error brought by the principal.

JUDGMENT was for the plaintiff, who proceeded to fix the special bail of the defendant, and brought a suit against them on their recognizance. The defendant then brought error, putting in bail in error. And now,

Mr. Jas. Edwards, for the defendant, moved to stay all proceedings against the bail, till the writ of error should be determined; and cited Dunl. Pr., 1139; Tidd, 471; 5 Taunt., 264.

Mr. D. B. Tallmadge, contra.

Curia. Take your motion, on paying the costs of the suit against the bail.

Motion granted.

Cited in—16 Abb. Pr., 227.

*LEWIS AND LEWIS [*583
v.
BALL, late Sheriff of ORANGE.

Practice—Motion to Issue Further Execution—Notice—Sureties Not Liable Beyond Penalty of Bond.

The motion to issue further execution upon a judgment obtained against a sheriff and his sureties, on a bond given for the faithful execution of his office under the Statute, 1 R. L., 421, sec. 6, should be on notice to the sheriff and his sureties.

The sureties are not liable beyond the amount of the penalty of the bond.

THE defendant as Sheriff of Orange, had been sued with his sureties; and a judgment obtained in favor of the people, for the penalty of the bond given for the faithful execution of his office, pursuant to the Act concerning Sheriffs, &c., 1 R. L., 418, secs. 2, 6. The suit on the bond was not prosecuted by the present plaintiffs; but by another, on application and leave granted pursuant to the 6th section of the Act. An affidavit was now produced, showing that Lewis and Lewis had obtained a judgment for $106.87, against Ball as Sheriff, for a default within the terms of the bond; and issued an execution for a part of that judgment; which still remained unsatisfied.

Mr J. A. Collier, for the plaintiffs in this suit, now moved for a rule, that such sum be levied on the judgment, in favor of the people as should be sufficient to satisfy the judgment in favor of the Lewises; and that an *alias fi. fa.* issue for that purpose.

But notice of this motion had not been given to the sheriff of his sureties.

Curia. The plaintiffs show enough to entitle them to the rule applied for, in the first instance, but this may be answered by the sheriff and his sureties. It may be that there has been already levied, by execution against them, the full amount of the penalty. Notice of the application should be given, in these cases, to the sheriff and his sureties. They may be able to reduce the amount claimed, or show matter which would defeat the application altogether.

Motion denied.

*COLE v. PERRY. [*584

Statute—Directory—Violation—Motion to Set Aside Verdict.

The Statute relative to Balloting for Jurors, sess. 49, ch. 309, sec. 4, is merely directory; and though it

NOTE.—*Principal and surety—Construction of Contract.*

The contract of suretyship is strictly construed. See Walsh v. Baillie, 10 Johns., 180, *note.*

be violated, this is no ground for moving to set aside the verdict, unless the irregularity be objected to at the time, or there be some abuse or injury to the party moving.

MR. J. L. VIELE, for the defendant, moved that the verdict rendered for the plaintiff in this cause at the last Rensselaer Circuit, be set aside, on the ground of irregularity in drawing the petit jurors. He produced a certificate of the circuit clerk, stating that the names of the jurors summoned and impaneled at the circuit, were written on several and distinct pieces of paper, being all, as near as might be, of equal size; and put into boxes open at the top by an orifice of about five inches in diameter, from which they were drawn to compose the several juries. That they were not rolled or folded together. The counsel also produced an affidavit, showing that the names of the jurors were easily and distinctly visible to the person drawing. That the course was to draw the ballots from one box, and put them into another, till the drawing was through. He cited the Statute, sess. 49, ch. 309, sec. 4.

Mr. H. P. Hunt, contra, read an affidavit of the deputy-clerk of the circuit who drew the jury, denying all abuse, and stating distinctly that he did not see the names till after they were drawn, and that no objection was made to the manner of drawing. He also read an affidavit of the plaintiff's attorney, showing that no objection was made by the defendant to the manner of drawing in this cause. He cited 1 Dunl. Pr., 675; 6 Taunt., 460; 5 Cow., 269; 1 *Id.*, 221; 2 *Id.*, 589; 3 *Id.*, 355; 3 Johns., 252.

Curia. The statute relied upon is merely directory to the officer drawing the ballots. We have often holden this in relation to statutes of a similiar character. No abuse or injury to the defendant being pretended, and no objection made at the time, the mistake of the officer is not a ground for setting aside the proceedings.

Motion denied.

Cited in—7 Wend., 422; 40 How. Pr., 433; 7 Abb. N. C., 369; 54 Mo., 160; 43 Am. Rep., 545 (59 Md., 123).

585*] *EX PARTE ALVORD ET AL.

Contents of Appeal Bond,

An appeal bond must recite the amount of the judgment before the justice.

If not, the C. P. should dismiss the appeal for want of Jurisdiction.

Citations—Stat. sess., 47, ch. 238, sec. 36.

A JUDGMENT having been rendered by a justice of Livingston Co., against Alvord and others, in favor of Sherwood, they appealed to the Livingston C. P.; but the condition of the appeal bond did not recite the amount of the judgment before the justice; nor did the amount appear in any part of the bond. The justice returned the amount of the judgment, and in a supplemental return, stated that no other suit had ever been pending or tried, between the parties before him; or any other judgment rendered before him against Alvord and others in favor of Sherwood.

When the cause was called upon the calendar of the C. P. for trial, the counsel for Sherwood moved that the appeal be dismissed, on the ground that the bond did not sufficiently identify the judgment; and the court granted the motion.

A *mandamus* was now applied for, commanding the C. P. to vacate the rule dismissing the appeal, and proceed with the trial.

Mr. C. H. Bryan, for the relators.

Curia. We think the Legislature intended that the bond should state the judgment below accurately and truly. They have not said so in terms; but one branch of their provisions on the subject is, that the appellant shall pay the judgment below in a certain event. (Stat., sess, 47, ch. 238, sec. 36.) The judgment, therefore, should be stated, with the view to afford as complete a remedy as possible on the face of the instrument. In a suit upon this bond, to recover the amount of the judgment below, matter extrinsic must be averred and proved. The appellant must furnish a bond as perfect as possible for the purpose of a remedy to the appellee, or the C. P. do not acquire jurisdiction. The court were right in dismissing the appeal; and the motion must, therefore, be denied.

Motion denied.

Cited in—7 Cow., 469; 9 Cow., 229; 3 Barb., 608.

---

*JACKSON, ex dem. WOOD ET AL., [*586
v.
WOOD AND HOPKINS.

Consent Rule in Ejectment—Default.

After the consent rule in ejectment, the plaintiff must, before he can enter a default, serve a new or altered declaration.

EJECTMENT. The declaration and notice from the casual ejector were served Oct. 12, 1826; and consent rules exchanged between the attorneys of the parties on the 14th of the same month. Jan. 3, 1827, the plaintiff's attorney, without serving a new declaration, entered the defendants' default for want of a plea. Jan. 1, 1827, the defendants' attorney had sent to the plaintiff's attorney a stipulation to accept the declaration originally served in lieu of a new one, the names of the defendants to be inserted. On this stipulation a plea of not guilty was indorsed; but, this not arriving till after Jan. 3, the plaintiff's attorney refused to receive it on the ground of having previously entered the defendants' default for not pleading. Feb. 6, the defendants' attorney gave notice to the plaintiff's attorney, that common bail had been filed.

A motion was now made, in behalf of the defendants to set aside the default, and all subsequent proceedings, for irregularity; and 1 Dunl. Pr. 381; 2 Johns. Cas., 110; Col. Cas., 120, and 3 Johns., 141, were cited.

Messrs. S. M. Perkins and *H. Stephens*, for the motion.

Mr. D. Wood, contra.

Curia. No new or altered declaration has in this case been served. This is, in strictness, necessary. It has never been waived. The stipulation was not accepted. The default was, therefore, irregular; and the motion must be granted.

Motion granted.

587*] *VARY v. GODFREY.

Certiorari—*Affidavit.*

The affidavit to obtain the allowance of a *certiorari*, may be taken before the attorney who commences the suit.

Citations—12 Johns., 340; Barnes, 60.

ON *certiorari* to a justice's court. The affidavit on which the writ was allowed, was taken before the attorney for the plaintiff in error. On this ground (and another) it was now moved to set it aside as irregular. For the motion was cited, *Taylor* v. *Hatch*, 12 Johns., 340, and *Munro* v. *Baker*, 6 Cow., 396; and against it, 5 Cow., 38; 1 Dunl. Pr., 220; 1 R. L., 140, 396; 2 Cai., 182; L. N. Y., sess. 47, p. 297, sec. 43; 6 Johns., 334; 3 Cow., 345; 2 Johns., 371; 2 Cow., 500; 1 Tidd Pr., 451; Barnes' Notes, 60.

Mr. J. Crocker, for the motion.

Mr. H. Putnam, contra.

Curia. This affidavit does not come within the rule laid down in *Taylor* v. *Hatch*, 12 Johns., 340. That applies only to affidavits made before an attorney in a suit pending; not to those preparatory to the commencement of one. The affidavit is not entitled; and the attorney may or may not be retained at the time when the affidavit is made. The rule is thus qualified by the English cases. *Haward* v. *Nalder*, Barnes, 60. The motion must be denied.

Motion denied.

Cited in—3 How. Pr., 221; 4 How. Pr., 153; 9 How. Pr., 67; 58 How. Pr., 113; 8 Abb. N. C., 242.

588*] *THOMAS, Admr. of HAGERMAN,

v.

VAN NESS ET AL., Heirs and Devisees of VAN NESS.

Proceedings by Mistake Against Heirs and Devisees as Joint Debtors—Amendment.

The plaintiff, by mistake, proceeded against heirs and devisees as joint debtors, within 1 R. L., 521, sec. 13; the process being served on some of the defendants, against whom the plaintiff declared. The defendants served with process, demurred; upon which the parties agreed that judgment should be entered against the plaintiff on demurrer, with leave to amend on payment of the costs, as if the cause had been argued and decided for the defendants on the demurrer: held, that the plaintiff might then bring in the other defendants on *simul cum* process; and declare and proceed against the whole.

THE defendants, were, by mistake, treated by the plaintiff as joint debtors; part being returned by the sheriff as taken, and part not found. He declared against those taken as impleaded with the others. The defendants taken demurred to the declaration specially; and the plaintiff joined in demurrer. This was before *Whitaker* v. *Young*, 2 Cow., 569, was decided. On learning this decision, the attorneys stipulated that judgment should be entered for the defendants on the demurrer, with leave for the plaintiff to amend on payment of costs, as if the cause had been argued and decided in favor of the defendants on the demurrer. This stipulation was filed, and a rule entered according to it; and the costs paid. The plaintiff then issued writs of *capias ad respondendum simul cum;* and brought in the other defendants, the other heirs and devisees. He then amended his declaration accordingly; and offered a copy with notice of the rule to plead to the attorney of the heirs, &c., first brought into court. This he declined receiving, on the ground that the amendment was not warranted by the rule.

This question, among others, between the attorneys was now submitted, by consent, to the court.

Mr. S. Cleveland, for the plaintiff.

Messrs. Hooker and *Radcliff*, for the defendants.

Curia. An order made by this court, in the terms of the stipulation, would, we think, have warranted the amendment by bringing in the defendants not taken, and proceeding against them as the plaintiff has done in this instance. The plaintiff is, therefore, regular.

Papers returned to counsel, with the expression of the above opinion. No rule was entered.

---

*JACKSON, ex dem. RUGBEE ET AL., [*589

v.

STILES, GUBERT, Tenant.

Ejectment—Landlord May Move to Defend.

In ejectment the landlord may move to defend, at the term when the declaration is returnable; especially where the tenant has expressly refused to appear.

EJECTMENT. The declaration was returnable at this term. The tenant held under a demise from Laussat and Bouchaud, and sent them word, on receiving the declaration, that he should not defend; and that if they intended to protect the premises against the claim of the lessors of plaintiff, they must attend to it; for he (the tenant) should not. On these facts,

Mr. S. R. Hobbie moved that the landlords be made defendants; and cited 1 R. L., 443, sec. 29, 30; 1 Cow., 135; 4 Johns., 492; 2 Dunl. Pr., 1022, 1023; 4 Taunt., 820; Adams, Ej., 239, 240 and 361, App., No. 29.

Mr. S. Sherwood, contra, submitted whether the application was not premature; and said that before the landlord could be received to defend alone, judgment should be given against the casual ejector.

Curia. The tenant expressly refused to appear. This was enough. The landlord need not wait till a default is entered against him.

Motion granted.

WITHERWAX v. AVERILL.

Plea—Joinder of.

A plea of *nul tiel record*, to declaration on a judgment in a justice's court, is not triable by the record, but by jury; and may be joined with a plea of payment.

Citation—16 Johns., 233.

THE plaintiff declared on a judgment rendered in a justice's court. The defendant pleaded two pleas: 1. *Nul tiel record;* and 2. Payment.

Mr. J. L. Wendell, for the plaintiff, moved for a rule that the defendant elect which plea he would abide by.

Mr. E. Cowen, contra.

590*] **Curia*. The ground upon which we compel a defendant to elect between a plea of *nul tiel record*, and other pleas, is, that their mode of trial is different; one being by the record, the others by jury. No such consequence follows here from retaining both pleas. The existence of a justice's judgment is not determinable at bar, by the record. It ranks as a specialty. (16 Johns., 233.) And the plea of *nul tiel record*, if it be good and capable of trial, in this case, must be tried by a jury.

Motion denied.

Cited in—1 Wend., 446; 6 Wend., 513; 23 Barb., 318.

JACKSON, ex dem. HILLS, v. TUTTLE.

Amendment—After Bill of Exceptions Signed—Costs.

Declaration in ejectment amended by altering the time of demise, though the cause had been twice noticed for trial; and an objection taken on the trial that the time was laid too early; and a bill of exceptions signed on this point.

Amendment granted, on paying the costs of the motion.

EJECTMENT. The plaintiff's attorney had, by mistake, laid the demise in the declaration Jan. 1, 1822; whereas, the title did not accrue to the lessor of the plaintiff till the 16th of that month. The cause had been once tried, the plaintiff nonsuited, and a new trial granted. On the second trial (Oct., 1826) the defendant objected, for the first time, that the demise was laid before the title accrued, and moved for a nonsuit. The judge overruled the objection, with a view to give the plaintiff a chance to move this court to amend. The defendant excepted, and the judge signed a bill of exceptions upon the point.

Mr. J. A. Spencer now moved to amend the declaration and all subsequent proceedings, by inserting a day of demise subsequent to Jan. 16, 1822. He cited 2 Cow., 515; 4 *Id.*, 124, 394; 5 *Id.*, 265; 18 Johns., 265; Auth. *N. P.*, 180; 7 Cr., 472; 6 Cow., 360.

Mr. G. C. Bronson, contra, said the court had never gone so far as to amend a bill of exceptions; or to amend in any particular which should do away the effect of a bill of exceptions. If, however, an amendment is allowed, it should be on paying the costs of the circuit.

591*] **Curia*. We do not amend the bill of exceptions; but we direct the declaration, and all the other proceedings subsequent, to be amended on payment of the costs of this motion. As to the bill of exceptions, it will probably be rendered unavailing upon this point, by a return of the amended record to the Court of Errors.

Motion granted.

Cited in—22 Am. Dec., 505 (1 Green, 23).

TILLINGHAST v. KING.

Action for Tort—Change of Venue—Affidavit.

To change the venue, in an action for a tort, on the ground that the cause of action arose in a particular county; the affidavit must state, not only that the cause of action arose there, but that it did not arise elsewhere; and this especially of an action for newspaper libel.

Citation—4 Cow., 403.

CASE for a libel, published in the N. Y. American.

Mr. J. Blunt, for the defendant, moved to change the venue from the County of Erie to the City and County of N. Y., on an affidavit that the cause of action, if any, arose in the latter county; but the affidavit did not add, "and not elsewhere out of the City and County of N. Y." On this ground, without proceeding to show that the libel had been dispersed in different counties, and agreeing that unless this was shown, the action being for a tort, the venue must be changed if the affidavit was sufficient.

Mr. Jas. Edwards, contra, objected that it was insufficient, for want of the words, "and not elsewhere, &c."

Curia. We think so. The libel may have been, and probably was, dispersed in many counties. Such a circumstance would bring the case within *Root* v. *King*, 4 Cow., 403, and put the change of venue upon the number of witnesses. The motion must be denied, for the defect in the defendant's papers.

Motion denied.

Limited—1 Hill, 668.

*EX PARTE BENSON. [*592

Appeal Dismissed by C. P. for Want of Jurisdiction—Costs.

Where an appeal is dismissed by the C. P. on motion, upon the ground that they were never possessed of the cause, and had no jurisdiction of it, they should award no costs beyond those of the motion; not the general costs of the cause.

Whether they have power to award the regular costs in the cause, *quære*.

BENSON, the executor of Lawrence, recovered judgment before a justice of the peace of Chenango Co., against John Miller, who appealed to the C. P. The justice's return stated a judgment in the cause of *Benson* v. *Miller*, without the addition of executor; and after the cause was on trial before the jury, the attorney for the plaintiff objected the variance; the appeal bond reciting a judgment in favor of Benson, as executor. The C. P. deemed the variance material, and dismissed the appeal; but refused to award any costs to the appellee, except of the application.

This court were now moved for a *mandamus*, commanding the C. P. to vacate their rule as to costs; and allow the whole costs of the appellee, up to the time of dismissing the appeal.

Mr. J. Foote, for the motion.

It was not opposed; but,

Per Curiam. We think the C. P. were right. The parties were not before them for any purpose except the motion; and they were not bound, even if they had jurisdiction, to award the regular and ordinary costs of the cause. These follow, only where the suit comes into court. Here it never was there. There was a want of jurisdiction as to the cause itself; and when we say the C. P. has jurisdiction of the parties for the purpose of awarding costs, we mean the costs of the motion; the matter alone upon which the court can act.

Motion denied.

Cited in—7 Cow., 469; 9 Cow., 229; 17 Wend., 69; 36 Barb., 249; 2 Wood. & M., 420.
See 4 Wis., 286.

593*] *EX-PARTE MALLARD.

Defective Appeal Bond—Dismissal of Cause Because of—Costs.

Where an appeal cause was noticed for trial several times in the C. P. and was finally dismissed on the motion of the appellee, after the trial had proceeded for some time, upon the ground that the appeal bond was defective; held, that the court ought not, even if they had the power, to have awarded to the appellee any costs beyond those of the motion.

An appeal bond should be conditioned, that if the appeal be not prosecuted with due diligence, the appellant shall pay the costs of the appeal.

ON appeal to the Madison C. P. from a justice's court, by Mallard, against whom the justice had rendered judgment at the suit of Cheesebrough, the cause had been noticed for trial three times. It was once put off at the request of the appellee; and again, on his motion, on payment of costs. On its being brought on for trial upon the third notice, and the jury being impaneled and sworn, the appellee proceeded with his testimony and rested his cause. The appellant then proceeded with his testimony for a considerable time, when the appellee raised an objection that the appeal bond was defective in not providing for the appellant paying the costs of the appeal, if it should not be prosecuted with due diligence. The C. P. dismissed the appeal, with full costs of the cause to the appellee, which were taxed at $57.03, including the costs of the several terms at which the cause had been noticed for trial, except the term at which it was put off by the appellee, on payment of costs.

This court were now moved for a *mandamus*, commanding the C. P. to vacate the rule dismissing the appeal, and proceed in the cause, or, at least, to vacate the rule as to the costs, and allow the costs of the motion only. In support of the present motion, were cited 5 Cow., 34; 4 *Id.*, 61; 5 *Id.*, 34; Laws, sess. 47, p. 295.

Mr. J. Foote, for the motion.

It was not opposed.

Curia. The bond was clearly defective. But, for the reason given in the last case an alternative *mandamus* must go. The practice should be uniform in all these cases; and the present case is a striking illustration of the propriety of the rule just pronounced, aside from the question of jurisdiction. The appellee lay by a long time, being, for aught that appears, fully aware
594*] of the objection *which he finally took, to oust the C. P. of jurisdiction. Great expense was incurred on both sides, in preparing the cause for trial, which he should have prevented by moving the court to dismiss the appeal the very first opportunity. Independent of the question as to the right of the C. P. to award this large sum for the ordinary expenses of the suit; we are prepared to say, that in the exercise of a sound legal discretion, they should not have done so.

Rule for an alternative mandamus.

S. C.—7 Cow., 423.
Distinguished—36 Barb., 249.
Cited in—17 Wend., 69; 8 Abb. Pr., 291; 2 Wood. & M., 420.

JACKSON, ex dem. BRINCKERHOFF,
v.
STILES, MILLER, Tenant.

Contents of Affidavit on Motion that Landlord Defend in Ejectment.

The affidavit on which to move that the landlord defend in ejectment, should show the relation of landlord and tenant. That the tenant claims no interest except as tenant to the landlord, is not sufficient.

EJECTMENT. Motion that J. & T. Spafford be received to defend as landlords, on an affidavit of the defendant's attorney, that Miller, the tenant, "claims no interest in the premises in question, otherwise than as tenant to the Spaffords."

Mr. P. Viele, for the motion.

Mr. S. Ross, contra.

Curia. The affidavit is insufficient. It should show the relation of landlord and tenant. This does not follow from the mere circumstance that the tenant claims no interest except as tenant to the Spaffords.

Motion denied.

Cited in—22 Cal., 205.

*WEBSTER, ET AL., Survivors of WEBSTER, [*595
v.
SCHUYLER.

Voluntary Bill of Particulars.

A bill of particulars voluntarily furnished, on request, without a judge's order, will not, *per se*, operate to enlarge the time for pleading.

THE declaration, containing general counts in *assumpsit*, was served on the agent of the defendant's attorney, Nov. 1, 1826. The defendant's attorney wrote to the plaintiff's attorney, requesting a statement of their demand; which was furnished to the defendant's attorney, 15th of the same November. Dec. 12 following, the 40 days for pleading having expired, the defendant's default for not pleading was entered. The defendant's attorney served pleas on the agent of the plaintiffs' attorney on the next day, Dec. 13. He disregarded the pleas, and proceeded to execute a writ of inquiry. The defendant made an affidavit of merits. On these facts,

A motion was now made to set aside the default, and all subsequent proceedings for irregularity, on the ground that the bill of particulars demanded and furnished, though voluntary, had effect to enlarge the time for pleading, the same as if it had been obtained under a judge's order. If not, then the motion was put on the ground of merits.

Mr. W. Talmage, for the defendant.

Mr. M. H. Webster, for the plaintiffs.

Curia. A voluntary bill of particulars, will not, without a stipulation to that effect, enlarge the time to plead. The plaintiffs were, therefore, regular. But, as there is an affidavit of merits, let the default be set aside, on payment of costs.

Rule accordingly.

596*] *EX PARTE FERGUSON.

Attorney—Demand on, for Money Collected must be made.

Money collected by an attorney for his client, must be demanded before the client can move for an attachment for its non-payment.

AN attorney of this court had collected money for the relators by suit, which he had not paid over. On an affidavit of these facts, a motion was now made for a rule that the attorney pay over the money, or show cause why an attachment should not issue against him. But the affidavit did not show that a demand of the money had been made of the attorney.

Mr. L. Hoyt, for the motion.

It was not opposed. But,

Per Curiam. The money should first have been demanded. The motion must, for that reason, be denied.

Motion denied.

Commented on—5 Hill, 398.
Cited in—4 How. Pr., 242; 2 Co. R., 116; 5 Kan., 67; 40 Am. Dec., 361; 39 Am. Rep., 730 (93 Pa., 121).

CAMPBELL *v.* PALMER.

Discharge should be Pleaded before Judgment.

Though a defendant be discharged under the Insolvent Act, if he have time to plead the discharge, but omit to do so, an *exoneretur* will not, after judgment, be ordered in favor of his special bail, on account of the discharge.

They must surrender in the ordinary way.

Citations—18 Johns., 54; 9 Johns., 392; 1 Cow., 427.

MOTION, in behalf of Norton, the special bail of the defendant, Palmer, that an *exoneretur* be entered on the bailpiece. Apr. 4, 1826, Palmer was discharged under the Insolvent Act to abolish imprisonment for debt in certain cases. He omitted to plead his discharge, or avail himself of it in any way. The cause was tried on its merits in Aug. last, a verdict found for the plaintiff, and judgment perfected in October Term thereafter. No suit had been brought against the bail.

Mr. S. A. Foot, for the motion, cited 4 Johns., 409; 14 East, 599; 1 Cai., 9, 11; 2 Johns. Cas., 403; 1 Burr., 244; 2 Johns., 101; 1 Dunl. Pr., 209; 1 Cow., 165; *Id.*, 42; 5 *Id.*, 289.

597*] **Mr. B. F. Butler*, contra, cited 18 Johns., 54; 9 *Id.*, 392; 1 Cow., 427.

Curia. Post v. *Riley*, 18 Johns., 54, and *Mech. Bank* v. *Hazard*, 9 *Id.*, 392, are in point against the application. The discharge should have been pleaded, being long before judgment. This not being done, the defendant cannot avail himself of it, and the bail are concluded. They must discharge themselves in the ordinary way, by surrender. *Franklin* v. *Thurber*, 1 Cow., 427.

Motion denied.

Cited in—21 How. Pr., 146.

JACKSON, ex dem. EVEREST ET AL.,
v.
STILES, SOPER, Tenant.

Title to Declaration in Ejectment.

The title to a declaration in ejectment is mere form, and good, though of a term after its service. So, though it be without any title at all.

Citations—Adams on Eject., 185.

EJECTMENT. Motion (among other things) to set aside the declaration, on the ground that it was entitled of February Term, 1827, the term at which it was returnable. It was served on the tenant, with the notice from the casual ejector, Feb. 15, 1827, several days before the term commenced.

Mr. H. Bleecker, for the motion.

Mr. W. Swetland, contra, cited 1 Chit. Pl., 265; Dunl. Pr., 998, 999; Adams, Ej., 185.

Curia. The motion must be denied. The entitling of a declaration in ejectment is a mere matter of form; and it is good without any title at all. (Adams, Ej., 185.)

Motion denied.

---

*THE PEOPLE, ex rel. FRY, [*598
v.
THE JUDGES OF THE COURT OF COMMON PLEAS OF THE COUNTY OF DELAWARE.

Justice Court Judgment—Set-Off.

A judgment obtained by attachment in a justice's court, without the defendant appearing there, cannot be set off, on motion, against a judgment in a court of record.

Citation—Stat., sess. 47, ch. 238, sec. 25, p. 291.

AN alternative *mandamus* was granted in this cause, commanding the defendants to vacate a rule, allowing the set-off of a judgment obtained before a justice of the peace on an attachment, against the relator, in favor of Mann, to meet a judgment obtained in the C. P. of Delaware, in favor of the relator, against Mann. The judgment before the justice was obtained June 13, 1825, the defendant not appearing to contest it. In the Court of C. P., affidavits were produced in behalf of the relator, to show that nothing was due to Mann from the relator; but that if the former had any claim, it was in favor of him and another jointly.

On a return of the affidavits showing these facts,

Mr. S. Sherwood, for the relator, moved for a peremptory *mandamus.*

Mr. S. R. Hobbie, contra.

Curia. The motion must be granted. By the Statute, sess. 47, ch. 238, sec. 25, p. 291, a judgment rendered upon attachment, without being contested, is but *prima facie* evidence of a debt. It is impeachable in an action upon it. The court may as well set off a bond or note on motion.

Peremptory mandamus *granted.*

Cited in—4 Hill, 561; 4 How. Pr., 172; 40 Am. Dec., 297.

---

*THE PHŒNIX FIRE INSURANCE [*599
COMPANY
v.
MOWATT.

Discharge of Special Bail.

Special bail will not be discharged, because their principal is imprisoned on conviction for a crime, unless it be for life, or for a long term in another State.

Citations—1 Johns. Cas., 28; 18 Johns., 335.

THE defendant having put in special bail to this action, was afterwards convicted of a conspiracy, and sentenced to the N. Y. Penitentiary for the term of two years.

Mr. S. M. Hopkins, now moved that an *exoneretur* be entered on the bail piece.

Mr. S. A. Foot, contra.

Curia. We have not relieved special bail in this way, by reason of their principal being in prison, unless for life, or for a long term of years in another State. (1 Johns. Cas., 28; 18 Johns., 35.) A temporary imprisonment, for any cause, might as well be urged, as the ground now taken. Bail take the risk of such an event. Time, perhaps, may be given to surrender, where they are pressed with a suit; but to grant an *exoneretur* at once, for every imprisonment, would render the security worthless.

Motion denied.

Cited in—13 How. Pr., 514; 20 How. Pr., 20; 4 Abb. Pr., 251; 12 Abb. Pr., 84.

VAN SCHAICK
v.
TROTTER AND DUNN, Impleaded with DOUGLASS.

Action against Several—Defense by one—Default against Another—Damages—Costs.

In an action against several, if one pleads to issue, and another suffers judgment by default, damages must be assessed against both at the same time, by the jury who try the issue.

The plaintiff cannot carry the cause down to trial, till a judgment by default is entered against the one who omits to plead.

Where a plaintiff inadvertently takes a judgment by default, without filing common bail, or causing the defendant's appearance to be entered, the court will allow either to be done on payment of costs; and if the omission be occasioned by the defendant's fault, then without costs.

Citations—17 Johns., 270; 1 Cai., 512; 2 Cow., 43.

A *capias ad respondendum* was issued and delivered to the sheriff, against the defendants, Oct. 28, 1826, returnable the same day. The suit was to recover the amount of certain promissory notes given by the defendants jointly. The plaintiff required no bail; and the sheriff drew the indorsement of an appearance on the back of the *capias;* and saw Trotter and **600***] Dunn, on the *return day, who promised to indorse their appearance; but this was not done. The sheriff returned the *capias cepi corpora*, as to Trotter and Dunn, the two defendants taken, and *non est inventus* as to the other; and on the Monday following, informed the plaintiff's attorneys that he had served the process on two of the defendants; but the other was not found.

Trotter and Douglass retained an attorney, who gave notice of retainer. The plaintiff declared; and Jan. 8, last, the defendant, Trotter, pleaded the general issue to two counts; and demurred generally to two others; the declaration containing four counts. Dunn did not plead; and his default, for want of a plea, was entered Jan. 22, last. The plaintiff took an inquest upon the issue, and assessed contingent damages on the demurrer at the Albany Circuit, Feb. 6, 1827, on a venire *tam quam;* and the damages were found and assessed by the jury against Trotter only. The plaintiff then, at this term, entered the judgment by default, and noticed the assessment of damages against Dunn, before the clerk. No appearance was yet entered, or common bail filed for Dunn.

Mr. L. Gardenier, moved to set aside the default against Dunn, and the inquest against Trotter, for irregularity. He cited 7 Johns., 270; 1 Dunl. Pr., 569, 570; 3 Saund., 300 *a*; Tidd Pr., 671; Tidd App., 164; 6 Johns., 325; 11 Co., 5; 1 Lill. Ent., 137; 2 Bos. & P., 163; 1 Archb. Pr., 9; 1 Sell. Pr., 11; Rich. Pr., C. P., 11; Rich. Pr. K. B., 225.

Mr. J. King, contra, cited 1 Dunl. Pr., 569, 570; 3 Saund., 300 *a;* Tidd Pr., 671; 3 Johns., 153; 2 Cow., 43.

Curia. The inquest was irregular; and must be set aside with costs. Where there is an issue as to one defendant, and a default as to another, the damages should be assessed against both defendants by a jury at the circuit, on a venire *tam quam.* The note was against all the defendants; they were all sued; and the plaintiff could not *carry down the issue for [***601** trial as to both, till he had obtained judgment by default against Dunn. (17 Johns., 270.) The cause would then have been in a state for trying the issue as to one, and assessing the damages against both. The course taken here might, and probably would, result in a different amount of damages against different defendants, on the same joint contract.

We deny the motion to set aside the default, and any of the subsequent proceedings, except the inquest. The plaintiff proceeded in good faith, having every reason to suppose that an appearance was indorsed upon the process. If this had been done, and the clerk had inadvertently omitted to enter it, we, of course, should have allowed it to be done *nunc pro tunc.* (1 Cai., 512.) It is also much a matter of course to allow common bail to be filed, where it is omitted by the plaintiff through mistake or inadvertence. (2 Cow., 43.) Here the plaintiff was misled, and that, too, in some degree, by the act of the defendants themselves. They promised the sheriff to indorse their appearance, but omitted to do so. The plaintiff may now enter their appearance, or file common bail *nunc pro tunc*, without costs.

This saves the proceedings in their present situation, except as to the inquest. The issue and default both stand, upon which the plaintiff can go regularly down to the next circuit, and try his issue joined with Trotter, and assess damages against Dunn simultaneously.

Rule accordingly.

Cited in—19 Hun, 574, 575; 4 Abb. Pr., 251; 2 Bos., 676; 50 Am. Dec., 499 (2 Green, 55).

GOULD AND BANKS *v.* BRUCE, Sheriff, &c.

Action for Escape—Plea of Voluntary Return Before Suit—Affidavit.

A plea or notice of voluntary return before suit, in an action of escape against a sheriff, is within the Statute, 1 R. L., 426, sec. 23, and must be supported by the defendant's affidavit that the escape was without his consent, privity, &c.

Citation—1 R. L., 426, sec. 23.

CROSS motions. The defendant moved for judgment as in case of nonsuit; and the plaintiffs, to strike out the notice given by the defendant with his plea. The cause being at **602***] *issue, was noticed, but not tried, at the last Niagara Circuit. It was an action of debt for the escape of one Chapin from the custody of the defendant, as sheriff, on a *ca. sa.* Plea, the general issue, and notice of voluntary return before suit. This notice was not accompanied with an affidavit. The plaintiffs noticed the cause for trial without discovering that the omission was material, and offered that as the excuse for not trying, deeming it necessary to move to strike out the notice.

Mr. A. Samson, for the plaintiffs, cited 1 R. L., 426; 16 Johns., 312.

Mr. T. H. Chapin, contra.

Curia. The Statute, 1 R. L., 426, sec. 23, is, that a plea or notice of retaking on fresh suit, shall not be received, unless the defendant make and file an affidavit that the escape was without his knowledge, privity, &c. It is denied that these words extend to the plea or notice of a voluntary return.

We think the latter is within the equity of the statute, which is remedial, and intended to prevent the officer's connivance at escapes.

We, therefore, deny the motion, for judgment as in case of nonsuit, on payment of costs. We grant the motion to strike out the notice—the defendant to be at liberty to retain it, however, on filing the proper affidavit, and paying costs.

Rule accordingly.

CAYWARD v. DOOLITTLE ET AL.

Writ of Replevin—When Voidable.

A writ of replevin, tested at one term, and returnable at the next term but one (an entire term intervening), is voidable.

Semb. it may be amended, but not unless the defect appear to have arisen from mistake, and all suspicion be removed that the long return day was a trick to postpone the trial.

Citation—1 Cow. 38.

MOTION, in behalf of the defendant, to set aside the writ of replevin issued in this **603***] cause, on the ground that it was *tested Aug. 19, 1826, and returnable on the first day of the present term (one entire term intervening).

Mr. D. O. Bell, for the motion.

Messrs. Whiting and *Butler*, contra.

Curia. The writ is clearly voidable at least. Goods cannot be arrested in this way, and the trial of the right postponed to any future time the party pleases. The writ might, perhaps, be amended, if we were satisfied that it was a mistake. (1 Cow., 38.) But how it happened is not shown. It might have been a trick to get possession of the goods, and postpone the trial by a long return day. The affidavits do not entirely remove the suspicion, that this proceeding was rather for the purpose of obtaining the vantage ground, in a negotiation about the property, which had been taken on attachment, than with the *bona fide* intention to try any question of right. The defendants show that the property was taken in Sept. last; and one of the defendants was not summoned till on the eve of this term. There should be a strong excuse, to warrant an amendment under these circumstances.

Motion granted, with costs.

EX PARTE SCHROEDER.

Practice—Foreign Creditor Cannot Proceed here Under Statute against Debtor Residing Abroad.

A foreign creditor cannot proceed here under the Absent and Absconding Debtor Act, 1 R. L., 157, against a debtor residing abroad; the debt not being contracted within this State.

Citations—2 Cai., 318; 6 Johns., ch. 186; 5 Cow., 293.

J. T. IRVING, first judge of the C. P. in the City and County of N. Y., on the application of Hans Harms, granted an attachment against Schroeder, as an absent debtor, within the Statute, 1 R. L., 157. Harms, the creditor, at the time of suing out the attachment, was a citizen of Hamburg—not a resident of the State of N. Y., nor domiciled here, nor in the U. S.; but was transiently in N. Y. Schroeder, the debtor, was then, and continues to be, a permanent resident of *Charles- [***604** ton, S. C., never resided in the State of N. Y., and was esteemed solvent, and in good credit as a merchant. The property attached was merchandise, which arrived at the City of N. Y. in a vessel bound for Charleston, which put into N. Y. by reason of stress of weather.

The attachment was granted early in Feb., 1827. But on the above facts being shown by affidavit, *Judge* Irving ordered cause to be shown before him on the 19th, why the attachment should not be superseded. Cause being shown accordingly, he, on the next day, delivered his opinion as follows:

IRVING, *J.* The 1st section of the Statute for Relief against Absconding and Absent Debtors, 1 R. L., 157, declares that any person, being indebted within this State, who shall secretly depart, or be concealed, &c., may be proceeded against under the Act. The 8th section provides for the appointment of trustees, and the sections which follow to the 17th, prescribe their conduct and duties. The 17th section states how they shall make distribution, and the 18th, who shall be considered creditors, and entitled to share in the debtor's property. The 19th also relates to the creditors—the necessity of their notifying the trustees of their demands, and the consequences of their neglect.

Then comes the 20th section, which appears to be in continuation of the 18th and 19th. It is, "that any creditor out of this State, shall be deemed a creditor within this Act; and his attorney, on producing a letter of attorney duly authenticated, &c., may proceed, and act in the same manner, under this Act, as if the creditor himself was present."

Does this relate to his being entitled to claim a share in the distribution, after trustees are appointed? And is it restricted to this, or is a foreign creditor authorized to proceed against the property of a foreign debtor? If so, will not the provision conflict with the 1st section of the Act, which states that the debtor shall be indebted within *this State? And [***605** with the 23d, which provides that the property of every foreign debtor who resides out of this State, and is indebted within it, shall be liable to be attached, sold, &c., in like manner as the estates of debtors within this State?

The 1st section provides for the attaching of the property of a debtor who resides in this

State, is indebted within it, and absconds. The 23d sections provides for the attaching of the property of a debtor who resides without this State, but is indebted within it. Both would appear to contemplate that debts only of this description could be the foundation of an attachment under this Act.

The decision in 6 Johns. Ch., 185, was in the case of a debtor who resided in this State, and absconding from it; his creditor residing abroad. The case in 5 Cow., 293, was that of a debtor who fled from England, concealed himself here to avoid arrest, and was pursued by his creditor.

The reason given by the Supreme Court in the case of *Fitzgerald*, for not allowing a foreign creditor to attach here the property of his foreign debtor, is very strong; and I do not think I would be justified in going farther than the Supreme Court has authorized in 5 Cow., which is the case of a foreign debtor, who fled from his creditor, came within our jurisdiction, and concealed himself here, to avoid being made to account.

Under such circumstances, as the Supreme Court is in session, I shall leave the parties to make application for a *supersedeas* or relief to them; and, in the meantime, order all proceedings to be stayed.

A motion for a *supersedeas* was accordingly made to this court.

Mr. S. Stevens, for the motion.

Mr. J. Anthon, contra.

Curia. We think *J*. Irving was right in holding that Schroeder was not indebted within this State. Unless this be so, the case is not 606*] embraced by the provisions *of the statute in question. We cannot presume that the debt upon which Harms proceeded was contracted in this State. For aught that appears, the debtor was never within our jurisdiction. Could even a resident creditor proceed by attachment here upon a contract made abroad?

Fitzgerald's case, 2 Cai., 318, is exactly in point; and has not been overruled or questioned, except so far as it denies the right of a foreign creditor to proceed under the Act in any case. *Robbins* v. *Cooper*, 6 Johns. Ch., 186, was the case of a foreign creditor proceeding against a debtor resident in this State; and in *Caldwell's* case, 5 Cow., 293, the foreign debtor had fled to this State, and was concealed here; and, according to our recollection, there was satisfactory evidence of his being domiciled here.(a)

Supersedeas *granted*.

Cited in—23 N. Y., 180; 3 Abb. App. Dec., 238; 2 Barb., 438; 3 How. Pr., 209; 12 How. Pr., 349.

(a) The court, I am sure, considered the debtor domiciled in this State, under the circumstances of that case. I reported the case, merely in reference to the right of a foreign creditor, independent of the question where his debtor is domiciled.

THE UTICA INSURANCE COMPANY
v.
SCOTT.

Pleading and Practice—Amendment Allowed After Judgment in Supreme Court—Costs—Conditions.

Plea amended after replication, demurrer, joinder in demurrer, judgment in Supreme Court for defendant, on the ground that the replication was bad and plea good; writ of error to the Court of Errors and reversal, because plea was bad. But this was on paying the costs of both courts.

The Supreme Court considered the case the same as if the plea had been overruled in that court on the demurrer.

That court will allow a plea, holden bad on the demurrer to the replication, to be amended; though the plea set up an unconscionable defense.

But they will not allow a new plea to be added, setting up a new defense which is unconscionable.

ASSUMPSIT against the defendant, as indorser of a promissory note to the plaintiffs. The defendant pleaded a special plea, to which the plaintiffs replied; and the defendant demurred to the replication, and the plaintiffs joined in demurrer. The Supreme Court gave judgment for the defendant, on the ground that the replication was defective, and held the plea good. This was in May Term, 1821. (See 19 Johns., 1, S. C.) On error to the Court for the Correction of Errors, December session, 1826, the judgment of the Supreme Court was reversed, on the ground that the plea was defective for want of precision or other imperfection (as the *defendant stated in his affidavit). The[*607 record being remitted to this court, a motion was now made by the defendant to amend his plea. The affidavit of the counsel for the plaintiff stated that he heard the opinions delivered in the Court of Errors, and understood the reversal to be on the ground that the replication was good; not on the ground that the plea was bad.

Mr. A. Van Vechten, for the motion, cited 2 Johns., 233; 3 *Id.*, 257; 10 *Id.*, 26; 2 Dunl. Pr., 1139; 5 Taunt., 264.

Mr. Talcott, Atty-Gen., contra, cited 1 Johns. Cas., 246; 1 Cow., 37; 18 Johns., 310; 1 Burr., 54, 322; 18 Johns., 30; Tidd Pr., 657, 660; 9 Johns., 78; 3 *Id.*, 148, 181; 2 Johns. Cas., 284; 3 *Id.*, 140, 141, 300, 301; 1 East, 135, 391; 2 Bos. & P., 482; 3 Bos. & P., 11, 12; 19 Johns., 1; 2 Bl., 1073; 4 Johns. Ch., 332; 4 T. R. 228, 468; 1 Burr., 402; 2 Str., 1002; Tidd Pr., 818; 1 Bos. & P., 339; 2 Burr., 936.

Curia. Allowing this amendment is a matter of discretion. It is objected that the application comes too late: the proceedings being no longer in paper, as it is expressed in England. This might formerly have been an objection; but it is not so at this day, when a much greater latitude than formerly prevails in favor of amendments. It will be seen by consulting the authorities, that courts have, of late, not confined themselves strictly to cases where proceedings may be said to be in paper; but they have been guided by the question whether substantial justice requires the amendment, at whatever stage of the proceedings it may be moved.

The motion is to amend generally. This is objected to; because the defendant may add a new plea, and set up a technical usury in discounting the note—an unconscionable defense undoubtedly—and what we shall not allow. Again; it is said the original defense is unconscionable; which was a plea that the note in question was discounted contrary to the Restraining Act; and the case is likened to the principle which denies a new trial in a hard action; *where the court, in the exer- [*608 cise of their discretion, will sometimes refuse a party the second chance of success, who has failed to recover on the first trial. We agree that we will not allow a new defense which is unconscionable; but we are not aware that the principle can be extended to this case. The plea is to be regarded now as if it had been overruled in this court upon the demurrer, and on the ground that it was so defectively drawn, as not to present the defense which it aimed at. This is much a matter of course; nor has it been denied merely because the particular plea sought to set up an unconscionable defense, provided it was a valid one. The defendant ought not to suffer from the delay, under the circumstances of this case. The plea was holden good in this court, but overruled on error against him. There is, to be sure, some dispute of this; but the defendant so understands it. The dispute probably arises from the manner in which the opinions of the Court for the Correction of Errors are delivered. From the great number of that body, and the different grounds often taken by members in deciding a cause, such difficulties are not unusual. Nor is it very material, as we allow only an amendment of the particular plea, to which we think the party has a right; and which must be done on payment of all costs of the demurrer, of this motion, and of the cause in the Court for the Correction of Errors.

Rule accordingly.

Cited in—3 Wend., 586; 6 Hill, 226; 22 Barb., 164; 7 How. Pr., 235; 17 How. Pr., 292; 22 How. Pr., 230; 44 How. Pr., 318; 13 Abb. Pr., 269; 14 Kan., 406; 19 Am. Rep., 99 (14 Kan., 398).

BUTTERFIELD *v.* COOPER.

Practice—Special Bail—Notice of.

The plaintiff is not bound to know that special bail is in, unless the defendant give regular notice thereof, and may, therefore, though special bail be in, issue a *ca. sa.*, without first having issued a *fi. fa.* if there be no notice of bail given.

MOTION to set aside a *ca. sa.* against the defendant, on the ground that no *fi. fa.* had first been issued, the defendant having put in special bail. But the balance of proof upon the affidavits, was, that no regular notice of special bail had been given to the plaintiff's attorney.

Messrs. E. Fowler and *J. H. Bronson*, for the motion.

609*] **Mr. G. C. Sherman*, contra.

Curia. The plaintiff was not bound to know that special bail was in, without regular notice of bail. The motion must be denied.

Motion denied.

Cited in—10 Wend., 671; 11 Wend., 33.

WELLS *v.* HATCH.

Motion for Rule—Notice.

A motion for such rule as a party is entitled to, upon the ground that a copy of the case is not served upon him, according to the practice of the Supreme Court, must be noticed and brought on as a non-enumerated motion.

Citations—16 Johns., 2; 5 Cow., 22.

THE plaintiff having made a case in this cause, upon which to move for a new trial, a motion was made in his behalf, to bring on the argument upon its order on the calendar; but,

An affidavit of the defendant's attorney was read on the other side, stating that Feb. 28, when it was too late to notice the cause for argument, no copy of the case settled by the circuit judge had been served on him. And a motion was made in his behalf, grounded on this affidavit (he having also served notice of argument), that a new trial be denied. And for him was cited *Honay* v. *Chesterman*, 5 Cow., 22. Contra, was cited *Delamater* v. *Smith*, 16 Johns., 2.

Mr. W. Hay, for the defendant.

Mr. I. W. Paddock, for the plaintiff.

Curia. Delamater v. *Smith*, 16 Johns., 2, lays down the rule of practice, when it is intended to move to strike the case from the calendar, so as to prevent its being argued. Notice must, in such case, be given as for a non-enumerated motion. In *Honay* v. *Chesterman*, 5 Cow., 22, the motion was that a new trial be denied, on the ground that the party making the case had not served a copy in due season, and the opposite party had noticed it for argument. We granted the motion, on the cause being moved upon the calendar, without our attention being called to the inconvenience of thus mingling motions of an *enumerated and non- [***610** enumerated character together, and the surprise which such a practice may many times produce to the party making the case. We think the practice should be uniform in these motions which relate to the calendar, and that where a copy of the case is not served according to the practice of this court, the application to deny the motion sought by the case, or for such rule as the party is entitled to by the neglect, shall come on upon a regular notice, as for a non-enumerated motion.

Rule accordingly.

Cited in—4 Wend., 197.

EX PARTE DREW.

Action of Trespass in Justice Court—Plea of Title—Subsequent Action for Same Trespass in C. P.—Time of—Plea must be Same.

Where the defendant in a justice's court, pleads title to an action of trespass *quare clausum fregit*, he is bound to abide by his plea, on the same action being brought in the C. P. though the action in the C. P. be not commenced at or before the term of the C. P. next after the plea is interposed in the justice's court.

MYERS sued Drew in a justice's court, for trespass *quare clausum fregit*, alleged to have been committed in Rensselaer Co. Drew justified by a plea of title, June 4, 1825, and entered into a recognizance, such as is required by the 9th section of the Fifty Dollar Act, sess. 47, p. 283. In May, 1826, a *capias ad respondendum* was served on Drew, at the suit of Myers, issued out of the Rensselaer C. P., two terms of that court having intervened between the time of pleading, &c., before the justice, and the issuing of the *capias*. Myers declared for the same trespass as the one in question before the justice; Drew put in special bail, and pleaded the general issue, which the C. P. on motion, ordered to be stricken out, with costs.

Mr. J. Van Vleck, for Drew, now moved for a *mandamus*, commanding the C. P. to vacate the rule to strike out, &c., and receive the plea. He said the only question was, whether the plaintiff could hold the defendant to his plea of title, in an action not brought till after the term next following the interposition of the plea in the justice's court; and contended that he could not. He said the C. P. held, that by not commencing his action by the next term of the C. P. the plaintiff merely lost his right to 611*] compel the defendant *to put in special bail, or forfeit his recognizance; but that he was, notwithstanding, compelled to put in his plea of title.

The Court held that the C. P. had decided correctly, and denied the motion.

Motion denied.

BROMAGHAM v. CLAPP ET AL.

Practice— Writ of Error—Does not, per se, *Stay Execution.*

A writ of error from a judgment in partition, does not stay execution, *per se*; but bail in error is necessary.

Citations—1 R. L., 512, secs. 12, 143.

IN PARTITION. The defendants brought a writ of error from this court, but did not put in bail. There was also a defect in the writ of error; but the court for the Correction of Errors allowed it to be amended, and retained the cause. Before the amendment was allowed, the plaintiff issued two writs of *fi. fa.*, one against Clapp, and one against "owners unknown," for different portions of the costs in partition.

Mr. Jas. Edwards, Mr. S. A. Foot same side, now moved to set aside the executions as irregular.

Mr. J. V. N. Yates, contra.

Curia. By the Statute, 1 R. L., 512, sec. 12, "error may be brought within the same time, and under the like restrictions and regulations, as in other cases." This undoubtedly refers to the restrictions and regulations in the previous Act "concerning Writs of Error," &c., 1 R. L., 143. Independent of that Act, there is no restriction on the subject. The writ is one of right, and issues of course, in all actions, real, personal and mixed. That Act requires two things on bringing error from this court—the certificate of counsel, and bail. The former is not necessary on error from the C. P. to this court; and had this writ been, from a judgment in partition, rendered in the C. P., there would be nothing (not even the certificate), to satisfy 612*] the words quoted from the statute *of partition, except bail. Bail is given in ejectment and dower. Doubtless, one reason is, because costs follow, always in the former, and often in the latter. The same principle exists in partition. The reason why bail is not generally required on error from judgments in real actions, is, that the demandant does not recover costs. The principle of requiring bail, therefore, concurs with the words of the statute.

But the point is new in practice, and the party proceeded in good faith. Let the executions, therefore, be set aside, on payment of costs, and putting in and perfecting bail in error.

Rule accordingly.

Cited in—22 Wend., 588.

EXECUTORS OF PROUTY v. McDOUGALL.

Assumpsit *by Executors in Supreme Court—Recovery Less than* $50*—Costs—Referees' Fees.*

In *assumpsit* by executors, brought in the Supreme Court, and referred, they recovered less than $50. Held, that they should not recover costs.

Held, also, that being executors, they were not liable to pay costs.

Held, also, that they were bound to pay the referees' fees within the Statute, 1 R. L., 517, which imposes this upon the prevailing party.

Citations—4 Cow., 396; Stat. 1818, sess. 41, ch. 94, p. 80; 1 R. L., 343, 517; 2 Johns. Cas., 209; 6 Johns., 379; 4 Cow., 396.

IN *assumpsit* on promises made to the testator, the plaintiffs recovered before statute referees $28.70. The suit was commenced in 1820. The accounts of both parties exceeded $400.

The questions were submitted by consent: 1. Whether the plaintiffs were entitled to costs. 2. If not, whether they should pay costs to the defendant. 3. Whether the plaintiffs or defendant were bound to pay the referees' fees.

Mr. S. W. Jones, for the plaintiffs.

Mr. N. F. Beck, for the defendant.

Curia. The suit being in this court, the plaintiffs are not entitled to costs. Had it been in the Common Pleas, the rule would have been otherwise, because the accounts of both parties exceeded $400. (4 Cow., 396.)

Nor is the question affected by the 5th section of the Statute of 1818, sess. 41, ch. 94, p. 80. This provides that in any action which may be brought in a justice's court, the plaintiff, suing in a court of record, shall not recover *costs, unless he recovers damages to [*613 more than $50. That section says nothing of the defendant's costs.

The next question is, whether the defendant shall have costs. This depends on the 2d and 4th sections of the Statute concerning costs, 1 R. L., 343. The 2d section denies costs to the defendant, where the plaintiff sues as executor or administrator in right of the testator or intestate, though he fail to recover anything. The 4th section declares that the plaintiff not recovering in the Supreme Court more than $50, shall pay costs. But the latter section has never been construed to apply to executors or administrators. The same provisions run through various revisals of our laws; but the cases have been uniform in protecting personal representatives against costs; and that, too, even since they might sue before justices. (2 Johns. Cas., 209; 6 Johns., 379.) The rule laid down in *Hamlin* v. *Hart*, 4 Cow., 396, applies only to parties suing in their own right.

Another question is: who shall pay the referees' fees? By the Statute, 1 R. L., 517, they are to be paid by the prevailing party; that is to say, the one in whose favor the report is made. The plaintiffs are here the prevailing party. They are to pay the referees, though the fees cannot, as in ordinary cases, be allowed to them in taxation against the defendant.

Rule accordingly.

HEPBURN *v.* HOAG AND HEPBURN. (*a*)

Set-off—Not Allowed against Uncertain Damages—Statute.

A set-off is not allowable against uncertain damages; *e. g.*, in debt for the penalty in articles of agreement, by which the defendants covenanted to maintain the plaintiff, &c., and provide him with proper medicine and attendance.

Damages due upon such an agreement cannot be set off; and where damages are not, in their nature, capable of set-off, they cannot be met by a set-off, in an action for them.

The difference in the phraseology of the Act of 1813, 1 R. L., 515, sec. 1, in the last revision of the laws, from former Acts, has not extended the right of set-off; but the present statute should be construed as were the former statutes on that subject.

Citations—2 Johns., 155; 5 Johns., 105; Mont. Set-off, 18, 19; 3 Johns., 351; 4 Johns., 292; 1 R. L., 575, sec. 1; 3 Johns. Ch., 351; 4 Cow., 57.

DEBT on the penalty of articles of agreement, tried at the Columbia Circuit, in Sept., 1824, before Betts, late *Circuit J.*

614*] *By the articles, the defendants agreed (*inter alia*) to pay $500, and maintain and support the plaintiff, his mother and sister, in sickness and health, in all necessary and comfortable meat, drink, washing, lodging, wearing apparel, medicine and medical attendance; and in all other convenient and comfortable respects, which their circumstances and situations might require. To these things they bound themselves in the penalty of $2,000. One of the breaches assigned was, that the defendants had not maintained and supported the plaintiff; and on this breach alone was evidence offered at the trial.

The defendants offered in evidence a set-off, under a notice, for that purpose, of money paid for the plaintiff, amounting to $1,172.89, before the commencement of the suit. This was objected to, and overruled as inadmissible, by the judge; but he received the evidence of the amount paid, and allowed the jury to certify the balance due to the defendants, over and above the $500 mentioned in the articles, with a view to have the question settled by this court. They assessed the plaintiff's damages at a specific sum, and certified the balance due to the defendants accordingly.

Mr. E. Williams, for the defendants, moved for a new trial. He cited 1 R. L., 515; 3 Johns. Cas., 360, *note a; Id.*, 573; Willes, 261; 2 Burr., 820.

Mr. C. Bushnell, contra, cited 4 Cow., 57, 498; 2 Johns., 155; 5 *Id.*, 105; Mont. Set-off, 18, 19; Dunl. Pr., 476, 478-500; 3 Johns. Ch., 351; 354, 357, 358; *Id.*, 473, 475; 4 *Id.*, 292, and cases cited; 1 R. L., 515; 1 K. & R., 347, sec. 1; 2 Cow., 173, per Woodworth, *J.*

Curia, per WOODWORTH, *J.* It seems to me this is clearly a case of unliquidated damages. The question is, not simply, what is the value of boarding and lodging by the week or otherwise, or how much should be charged by a physician for defined and specific services; or what is a reasonable sum for a certain quantity of medicine; but it involves this inquiry: **615***] what shall be considered as *necessary and comfortable support and apparel? It must be suited to the circumstances of the plaintiff, and depends on a fair and reasonable construction of the covenant. On this point, a jury would be obliged to exercise a sound discretion; and perhaps different jurors would form different opinions. How then can it be said the damages are certain? Again; medicine and medical attendance are to be provided in sickness. Suppose the parties disagree as to the medicine and medical attendance required; and the plaintiff considers himself warranted, under the covenant, to procure other and more frequent medical attendance than the defendants are willing to afford; would not the jury be called on, in assessing the damages, to pass on this question? And if it appeared that reasonable attendance and medicine, according to the degree or severity of the sickness, had not been furnished, to allow the plaintiff damages for whatever additional expense he had necessarily incurred in this respect? This view of the subject does, in my opinion, place the plaintiff's claim among the cases where uncertain damages are sought to be recovered; and consequently it could not be set off. If it could not be set off by the plaintiff in an action against him by the defendants, it is well settled that the defendants are not entitled to the benefit of it as a set-off. The law on this point is laid down in several cases. (2 Johns., 155; 5 *Id.*, 105; Mont. Set-Off, 18, 19; 3 Johns., 351; 4 *Id.*, 292.)

But it is contended that the Statute, 1 R. L., 515, sec. 1, has extended the doctrine of set-off, by the insertion of the words, "or have demands arising on contract or credits against each other." I think it is evident the Legislature did not intend to change the law, so as to give a party the benefit of uncertain damages by way of set-off. If they did, why does the same section provide that if the suit be brought on a bond or other contract, for the recovery of a penalty for the non-payment of money only, and such bond be given in evidence by the plaintiff or defendant, the sum *bona fide* due, and not the penalty, shall be deemed to be the debt? Such a bond or contract, unless for the payment *of money only, cannot [***616** be given in evidence. If the former part of the section was intended to extend the doctrine of set-off, it may be presumed the Legislature would have allowed a bond conditioned for the performance of covenants, to be given in evidence, equally as if for the payment of money.

The question of set-off has frequently arisen since the passing of the Statute of 1813; and I apprehend that, in no case, have the courts of law or equity given that statute a construction variant from what obtained previous to the last revision of the laws. In the case of *Duncan* v. *Lyon*, 3 Johns. Ch., 351, *Chancellor* Kent examined the question elaborately; and decided that a breach assigning the non-performance of a covenant, in not furnishing timber and provisions, was a demand at law in the nature of redress for a wrong or injury committed, and not for a debt due; that it rested entirely in uncertain and unliquidated damages. This case was several years after the Act of 1813; and is an authority to show that no alteration had been made in the doctrine of set-off by that Act. The decision of the judge at the circuit on this point was correct; but he erred in allowing the balance claimed by the defendants, to be certified in their favor. In this very case (4 Cow., 57) we decided that the certificate was a nullity.

(*a*) *Vide* 4 Cow., 57 S. C.

As to the hardship of this particular case, the answer is, we do not possess the power of applying the remedy. The statute is remedial, and embraces certain cases only. Until the Legislature interfere, and alter the law, a defense like that relied on by the defendants, cannot be available by way of set-off. The motion for a new trial must be denied.

New trial denied.

Cited in—28 Wend., 411; Wend., 112; 13 Wend., 157, 15 Wend., 58; 2 Edw., 75; 16 Hun, 359; 51 How. Pr.; 195; 54 How. Pr., 485; 9 Bos., 188; 2 Rob., 672; 50 Am. Dec., 362 (6 Ga., 509).

617*]*JACKSON, ex dem. TEN EYCK ET UX., *v.* RICHARDS.

1. *Deeds — Delivery and Acceptance Essential to Validity — Fact of Non-Acceptance Must be Proved by Disinterested Witnesses — 2. Disclaimer— What Necessary to Validity of—May be by Deed or* in Pais—*Written Disclaimer Need Not be Acknowledged, Proved or Recorded —Adverse Possession of One of Several Lots.*

It is essential to the validity of a deed, that it should be delivered and accepted.

But the fact of non-acceptance cannot be shown by the written declaration of the grantee; especially where third persons are interested in maintaining or defeating the deed. It must be proved, like any other fact, by disinterested witnesses under oath.

It is essential to a valid disclaimer, that the case be such that the estate or thing disclaimed would pass or vest, but for the disclaimer; unless it be made an express condition of the grant, that the grantee shall elect.

This proposition illustrated by the cases.

A disclaimer may be by record, and sometimes by deed or *in pais.*

Where a conveyance of land is drawn and sealed, but not delivered, it is void; and not a case for disclaimer on the part of the grantee.

A written disclaimer, therefore, in such case, being put on that ground, not affecting the title to lands in any way, is not an instrument which can be acknowledged, or proved, and recorded, within the Registry Act, 1 R. L., 369.

Where a large tract of land is divided into lots, the possession of one lot adversely will not create a constructive adverse possession of other parts of the tract.

Citations—Act 112, Apr., 1813; 1 R. L., 369, sec. 5; 1 Johns. Cas., 114; 12 Johns., 422; 20 Johns., 187; Vin. Abr., Disagreement, a, pl., 2, 4, 5; Vin. Abr., Disclaimer, C, pl. 1, 2, 3, 4, 5; Vin. Abr., Waiver, B, pl. 3; 1 Inst., 23; Cruise Dig., tit. 32; Deed, sec. 1; 3 Co., 25, 26, 27; 1 Cow., 276; Jac. L. D., tit. Waiver and Disclaimer.

EJECTMENT for a part of land called tract H, Massena, St. Lawrence Co.; tried at the circuit in that county, Feb. 9, 1826, before Walworth, *Circuit J.*

At the trial, the plaintiffs having deduced a regular title to one undivided half of the premises in question, to Ann, wife of Ten Eyck, who are the lessors of the plaintiff, by descent from Ann's, the wife's father, M. Vischer, who died in 1793, rested.

The defendant, to show title out of the plaintiff, gave in evidence a conveyance of the premises in question (among other land) from Ann, while sole, and her co-heir, Sebastian Vischer, to their mother, Lydia Vischer, in fee, dated Mar. 13, 1800. This proof was by an exemplified copy of the conveyance from the Secretary's office.

In answer to this, the plaintiff's counsel read in evidence an instrument dated Oct. 12, 1824, which was attached to the conveyance from Ann and Sebastian Vischer, and executed by their mother; by which she certified that the conveyance from Ann and Sebastian Vischer was never executed and delivered to her, or agreed to be executed and delivered to her, by the grantors, or either of them; and that she never had seen, or had the possession of it, or done any act signifying her assent to take the estate conveyed by it. And she thereby declared her dissent; and that the conveyance was, as to her, her heirs, &c., inoperative and void; and that the land conveyed by it was vested in Ann and Sebastian Vischer. This instrument was acknowledged the 12th, and recorded in the Secretary's office Oct. 14, 1824, in the usual form of acknowledging and recording deeds of land. It was read without *proof of its execution, otherwise than [*618 by the acknowledgment and recording.

The admission of this deed was objected to by the defendant's counsel, on the ground that it was not an instrument proper to be acknowledged and recorded, and was inoperative as a deed; but it was received by the judge, by consent, subject to the opinion of this court.

Verdict for the plaintiff, subject to the opinion of this court.

The judge also decided a point of adverse possession, which was not discussed on the argument, but which will be found mentioned at the close of the opinion of the court.

Mr. J. V. Henry, for the plaintiff. The exemplification of the conveyance from the Secretary's office was mere *prima facie* evidence, liable to be opposed by the disclaimer, or dissent of the grantee. An exemplification of the disclaimer was admissible. Every deed, conveyance, or writing concerning real estate, may be proved and recorded; and then becomes evidence of itself. The grantee had a right to dissent, and the writing is evidence of the fact that she did dissent. He cited 4 Johns., 161; 1 Johns. Cas., 114, 116; Shep. Touch., 58, 68; 8 Vin., 487, 488, Disagreement, A, pl. 2, 10; *Id.*, 489, pl. 18; *Id.*, 490, pl. 23; Moore, 300; 4 Cruise, 529, tit. 32, Deed, ch. 22, sec. 1; 22 Vin., 529, Waiver, A, pl. 4.

Mr. P. S. Parker, contra, cited 10 Johns., 456; 6 *Id.*, 149; 20 Johns., 187; 3 Co. Rep., 26; 4 Cruise, 367, tit. Deed; 2 Co. Rep., 60, 61.

He strenuously contended, that the paper set up as a disclaimer, was a mere memorandum; and could not be received as testimony, any more than a written statement from a stranger; stranger; that Lydia Vischer was a competent witness, and should have been sworn.

Curia, per SUTHERLAND, *J.* The material question in this case is, as to the admissibility and effect of what is called the disclaimer of Lydia Vischer, of *Oct. 12, 1824. This [*619 instrument was duly acknowledged before a competent officer, and recorded in the office of the Secretary of State, Oct. 14, 1824. It was produced and read upon the trial, without further proof, as an instrument entitled to be recorded under the Act of Apr. 12, 1813, entitled "An Act concerning Deeds," 1 R. L., 369, sec. 5. It was objected to on the part of the defendant, 1. As not coming within that Act, and, therefore, not duly proved; and 2d. That admitting it to be technically within this

fore, it is considered that the said plaintiff do recover," &c. And in February Term, 1825, the damages of the plaintiff were asssessed on a *venire tam quam* at $96.64, on the first two counts, for which the court rendered judgment with costs.

At the trial the plaintiff proved the note, warranty, death of Stroud intestate, and that no letters of administration of his estate had been taken out, as mentioned in the declaration. The defendants offered to show that he left real and personal estate sufficient to satisfy the note; but the evidence was rejected by the court, and the defendants excepted.

Mr. G. C. Bronson, for the plaintiffs in error. The first two counts are bad in substance (the second especially so), in not averring an attempt to collect of Stroud, his heirs or devisees. The pleas demurred to were good. The court also rejected proper evidence. The attempt to collect was a condition precedent; and Stroud's death was no excuse. If he had made no will, appointed no executor, and no letters of administration were taken out, still there was a remedy against the heir, or some one as executor *de son tort*. The plaintiff might also have applied to the surrogate, and himself taken out letters, and retained for his debt.

If the attempt to collect be a condition precedent, nothing will excuse its omission; not even the act of God. (19 Johns., 71, 72; 6 T. R., 210, 320, 710; 2 H. Bl., 574–582 and *notes;* 1 *Id.*, 254; 3 Mass., 443; 7 T. R., 377; 1 Johns., 267.) The act of the defendants below could alone furnish such an excuse as would maintain the action. Though a defendant, sued for not doing an act, may excuse himself in many cases, yet the only excuse for not performing a condition precedent, which is to give a right of action, must arise from the act of the party sued. Beside, here was, in fact, very great delay and negligence.

626*] **Mr. J. A. Spencer*, contra. The death and intestacy of Stroud were a sufficient excuse for not attempting to collect the note by a legal proceeding. The warranty was, that the note should be paid, if not collected in the ordinary course of legal proceedings. This became impossible by Stroud's dying intestate, and no letters of administration being taken out. That Stroud should be where he could be sued when the note fell due, was a condition precedent to be performed by Taylor and Otis, before Bullen was obliged to prosecute. He was under no obligation to prosecute any one as executor *de son tort*, or any supposed heir or devisee. A proceeding against these must have been very hazardous and uncertain. It was not offered to be shown that any such persons resided within the jurisdiction of any court in this State, and no such facts were alleged in the pleas. If the prosecution be a condition precedent, it may certainly be excused, short of any act of ours; and this is agreed by the cases. (19 Johns., 71, 72.)

He referred to 2 Cow., 786, and the cases there cited, as to the construction of contracts.

Curia, per SAVAGE, *Ch. J.* The question is, whether the plaintiff below was not bound to prosecute those who were in possession of Stroud's property, and endeavor to collect the money by suit at law.

It is admitted that the plaintiff below was bound to sue Stroud, or show a legal excuse for omitting to do so. And it is contended that the death of Stroud intestate, and no administration granted, constitute a legal excuse.

The pleas state that Stroud left property enough, subject to the payment of his debts, and that the plaintiff below never took any legal measures to collect the money.

The guaranty supposes that a resort to legal measures might become necessary, and the defendants below engage to pay costs on any suits legally commenced. My construction of the guaranty is, that Bullen was to take the trouble of the collection, and Taylor and Otis the responsibility.

*It seems to be conceded by the dec- [***627** claration, that if Stroud had left executors, or administrators had been appointed, the plaintiff must have sued them before he could resort to his guaranty.

But if there is property enough, the law points out sufficient remedies. The plaintiff was surely bound to pursue such legal remedies as he was entitled to, before he could prosecute the defendants. Suppose Stroud had not died, but had gone to some other place, without this State, and had left property sufficient to pay the debt; must not the holder of the note use the remedy applicable to such a state of facts? The contract is not that Stroud shall remain and be served with a *capias* in an action of *assumpsit;* but any suit legally commenced, was contemplated. If there was property, as is represented by the pleas, some suit or proceeding might have been instituted. Here was a condition precedent; that condition was not confined to a prosecution of Stroud himself. Had it been so, then indeed the plaintiff would possibly have been excused, as that was rendered impossible by the act of God, the death of Stroud. Even this, however, may be doubted. In *Moakley* v. *Riggs*, 19 Johns., 69, Spencer, *Ch. J.*, says, "though the act of God, or the act of the law which renders the performance of an act stipulated to be done, unlawful, may excuse a party from a strict compliance with his contract as matter of defense, it may well be doubted whether an engagement by one to perform an act on the previous performance of another act by the other, can be enforced without showing the previous act done, or that its performance was dispensed with, or prevented by him who was to perform the subsequent act." This is in accordance with the settled law in relation to conditions precedent. In *Wood* v. *Worsley*, 2 H.Bl., 574, which was an action on a policy against fire, the condition was to produce a certificate of the minister and church-wardens, of certain facts. The certificate was not procured, though other evidence of the facts was; and that the minister, &c., refused, without cause, to give the certificate. The C. P. held this tantamount to a production of the certificate. But the judgment *was reversed in the K. B. (7 [***628** T. R., 710), that court holding the production of the certificate, a condition precedent, and that it was immaterial that the minister wrongfully refused. In *Routledge* v. *Burrell*, 1 H. Bl., 258, the court upon a similar point, said the matter was too clear to admit of a doubt. In *Campbell* v. *French*, 6 T. R., 200, a bond was conditioned to pay certain bills of exchange, if returned from India, protested for non-payment. The bills were returned protested for non-acceptance, and the court held the obligors discharged, the condition not being performed, though it might have been. So here, a suit or suits, at law, might have been prosecuted, and the money collected, as is inferable from the pleas. The plaintiff has not made any effort to collect the money; and, in my judgment, his suit on the guaranty was premature. The judgment of the Common Pleas must be reversed.

Judgment reversed.

Cited in—11 Wend., 105; 12 Wend., 460, 590; 13 Wend., 200, 544; 21 Wend., 257; 40 N. Y., 188; 7 Barb., 618; 14 Barb., 80; 23 Barb., 631; 38 Barb., 108; 6 Duer, 303; 3 Bos., 543; 10 Bos., 213; 4 E. D. S., 476; 4 McLean, 584, 585; 39 Mich., 713; 33 Am. Rep., 448 (39 Mich., 710).

JANSEN AND HARDENBURGH *v.* BALL.

Declaration on Deed with Profert and Oyer—Loss of Deed—Amendment of Declaration may be Allowed—Covenant Purporting to Assign Judgment, which Does not Exist—Action for Breach of Covenant Lies—Proof of Breach—Measures of Damages.

Whether a declaration on a deed, with profert and oyer, can be supported by showing a deed lost after declaration filed, and not produced at the trial, *quære.*

The lost deed may be received in evidence at the trial, and if there be no surprise, and the execution of the deed is not contested, the plaintiff may afterwards amend his declaration so as to make it conform to the case.

An instrument purporting to be an assignment of a judgment, when in truth there is no judgment, and by which instrument the party covenants that the judgment, as described, is due and unpaid, will subject him to an action for a breach of covenant.

The fact that there was no such judgment, if it be described as one in the Supreme Court, may be shown by a witness who has examined the dockets and transcripts of dockets in any one of the clerk's offices of that court, and failed to find the docket of the judgment described.

The measure of damages in an action on such a covenant, is the value of the property owned by the judgment debtor, and which might have been taken in execution intermediate the time of assignment and the commencement of the suit, with interest from the time when the money might have been raised by a sale.

The Supreme Court, on a motion for a new trial, will look into the evidence, and see whether, according to this rule, the damages are too high; and if so, they will grant a new trial, unless, within a time to be fixed by them, the plaintiff remit so much as shall reduce them to the true sum.

Citations—Shep. Touch., 73, 74; 4 East, 585; 4 Cow., 124; 3 T. R., 151; 3 Taunt., 81.

COVENANT, tried at the Ulster Circuit, Apr., 1825.

The action was upon an instrument in these words and figures:

629*] *"SUPREME COURT.

AMZEY L. BALL v. ABRAHAM VAN KUREN. } May 20th, 1819.

Bond pen.,	$345 82
Condition,	172 91
Pltff's costs,	9 36
Deft's do.,	68

I do hereby assign, transfer and set over, for a valuable consideration, unto Joseph Jansen and Abraham I. Hardenburgh all my right, title and interest in and to the judgment as above stated, together with sheriff's fees; amounting in all to $198.84; and warrant that all the above sum remains due and unpaid. Witness my hand and seal, this 3d Sept., 1819. AMZI L. BALL (L. S.)."

The declaration alleged that, at the above date, Van Kuren had sufficient property to satisfy the demand, but that no judgment had been entered. The declaration made profert of the deed, and oyer was prayed and given. Plea, *non est factum.*

On the trial, it appeared that the instrument declared on had been lost after issue joined, and could not be found upon diligent search. It was satisfactorily proved that the oyer was a true copy of the original, which had been executed by the defendant. A witness testified that he had examined the docket of judgments in the clerk's office of this court in the City of N. Y., and the transcripts there from the clerk's offices of this court in Albany and Utica; and found no judgment in favor of the defendant. Proof of the deed, without its production, was objected to; and also the proof of search in the clerk's office—the former as being inadmissible under the profert and oyer, and the latter as incompetent, to show that there was no judgment. The objections were overruled.

Proof was then given of the amount of the defendant's property, which was lost, as a means of paying the supposed judgment, in order to fix the measure of damages. This evidence is sufficiently stated in the opinion of the court.

The judge charged that the measure of damages was the amount of property belonging to Van Kuren, which could *have been [*630 taken under an execution; that the property in his possession at the time of the assignment which had been sold under another execution, did not belong to him, and should not be included in the estimate of damages; that the plaintiffs were entitled to recover the fair value of the property that Van Kuren owned, from the time of the assignment until the commencement of the suit, with interest from the time the money might have been collected. Verdict for the plaintiff for $283.33.

A motion was now made for a new trial.

Mr. G. F. Tallman, for the defendant. Proof of the loss and contents of the instrument declared on was inadmissible. (2 Str., 1186; 1 Phil. Ev., 403; 4 East, 585; 4 Cow., 124.) The evidence of examining the docket and transcripts was incompetent. The docket itself, or an exemplified copy, should have been produced. No breach of the covenant was proved. The verdict was also against evidence in the amount of damages.

Mr. C. H. Ruggles, contra, cited Shep. Touch., 73; 1 Phil. Ev., 157.

Curia, per WOODWORTH, *J.* As to the non-production of the assignment, the rule seems to be, that the plaintiff may state the loss specially, and omit the making of a profert; but here the deed was lost subsequently to the declaring. The plaintiff could not, at the time, declare specially. After a profert is made, the deed is supposed to remain in court; and, if denied, is kept there until it be determined. (Shep. Touch., 73, 74.) The case of *Smith* v.

Woodward, 4 East, 585, decides that where a plaintiff declared on bond with a profert, on *non est factum* pleaded, secondary evidence by means of a copy, and showing that the defendant had taken away the original, and, before action brought, said he had burnt it, was not sufficient to sustain the declaration. The question there decided is not analogous. It is true, Ld. Ellenborough remarks, that if the bond were lost or destroyed after having declared on it, the plaintiff might move to put off
631*] the *trial, and amend. I incline to think it not necessary, for the purpose of justice, nor required by any adjudged case, that a party should incur such delay and expense, when it manifestly appears there has been no surprise; and the due execution of the instrument has not been made a question at the trial. Under these circumstances, I am of opinion that the plaintiff be permitted to amend his declaration, by adapting it to the case, which gets rid of the technical objection. Amendments, which subserve the justice of the case, are frequently made after verdict. They are always addressed to the discretion of the court. It is, perhaps, safer to take this course than to lay down a general rule, that where a deed is lost after issue joined, it shall be competent to give secondary evidence. (4 Cow., 124; 3 T.R., 151; 3 Taunt., 81; *vide ante*, 365.)

The evidence entitled the plaintiffs to recover, and I think the charge of the judge was correct.

The only remaining question is, whether the verdict was not against the weight of evidence, as to the amount of damages.

It appeared that Van Kuren had in his possession (and which was reputed to be his property) a mare, valued at $35; a wagon, $50; a colt, $60; a cow and heifer, $30; and a pong and harness, $30. Van Kuren testified that the wagon was left with him by his father-in-law; that he used, and afterwards sold it. He did not say who was the owner. The jury, in the absence of further proof, were justified in considering him the owner. The weight of evidence was, that the colt had not been sold until after the assignment. The cow, heifer, pong and harness had been sold under another execution, and left in Van Kuren's possession by the purchaser. The cow was subsequently redeemed.

The highest valuation of the property that might have been levied on was $145. The cow, being exempt from execution, is not included. From Mar. 3, 1820 (allowing 6 months to collect the money), to Sept. 3, 1824, supposing that to be the time when the suit was commenced,
632*] *the amount is $45.67, making in the whole, $190.67. It seems to me this evidence did not authorize a verdict for a greater amount. As the damages are susceptible of calculation with considerable accuracy, I am not inclined to subject the parties to the expense of a new trial, if the plaintiff consent to remit a portion of the damages.

My opinion is that a new trial be granted, with costs to abide the event of the suit, unless the plaintiff shall, within 20 days, remit $92.66, parcel of the damages recovered.

Rule accordingly.

Cited in—61 N. Y., 226; 4 T. & C., 76; 33 Wis., 627.

JACKSON, ex dem. BRADT ET AL., v. WHITBECK.

Possession of One Tenant in Common for 40 Years—Presumption of Ouster, Action by Cotenants, Barred—Verdict Subject to Opinion of Court—Adverse Possession.

After an exclusive and uninterrupted possession, by one tenant in common of land, for nearly 40 years, without any account with his co-tenants, a jury are authorized to presume an ouster: and an action of ejectment by his co-tenants, is barred.

The court, on a verdict subject to their opinion upon a case, may draw the same inferences as, in their opinion, a jury would be warranted in drawing from the facts in the case.

Whether a possession, claiming title, under a parol gift of land from the owner, is such an adverse possession as will bar an ejectment, *quære.*

Citations—Cowp., 217; 1 Cai., 84; 13 Johns., 120.

EJECTMENT, for 70 acres, in Greenbush, Rensselaer Co.; tried at the circuit in that county, July, 1824, before Betts, late *Circuit J.*

A verdict was taken for the plaintiff, subject to the opinion of this court on the following facts:

The lessors of the plaintiff are the children and heirs at law of Bernardus Bradt, and claimed the premises in question as such. The defendant claimed under Hendrick Bradt, who was also a son of Bernardus. Bernardus Bradt moved from the premises in question to the Town of Hoosick, in Rensselaer Co., about the period of the Treaty of Peace in 1783, leaving his son, Hendrick, in possession; who, from that period, until his death, about a year before the trial, occupied them, either in person or by his tenants, claiming them as his own. Bernardus, the father, died about forty years before the trial. Hendrick always openly asserted his title to the premises. He said that his father had given them to him; that he directed him to get a deed drawn, and he would sign it; but *he was young, and did [***633** not look abroad, and neglected to do it. When the farmers' turnpike was laid through the farm Hendrick claimed the damages done to the farm as his own. His father and sisters lived in Hoosick, between 30 and 40 miles from the premises, ever after the father removed there in 1783; and the witnesses never heard the title of Hendrick questioned, or of any claim to the premises on the part of his brothers and sisters, or of any other person, until suits or proceedings in partition were instituted about 15 years before the trial. But by whom those proceedings were instituted, or in what manner they were terminated, was not stated in the case.

Mr. A. Van Vechten, for the plaintiff.

Mr. J. V. Henry, contra, cited Cowp., 217; 1 Cai., 84; Adams, Ej., 55.

Curia, per SUTHERLAND, *J.* Without determining whether a claim of title under a parol gift, is sufficient to lay the foundation of an adverse possession (*vide* 13 Johns., 120), it appears to me, that, admitting the premises in question to have descended to the children of Bernardus Bradt, as tenants in common, the evidence in the case warrants the presumption of an actual ouster of his co-tenants by Hendrick. Here has been an exclusive possession, under claim of title, for forty years, without any assertion of right, or claim to any portion of the profits of the premises on the part of his co-tenants, although they all resided in the same county, within 40 miles of the premises. In *Doe* v. *Prosser*, Cowp., 217, it was held that 36 years sole and uninterrupted possession, by one tenant in common, without any account to, or claim by, his companion, was a sufficient ground for a jury to presume an actual ouster of the co-tenant. Ld. Mansfield says, "the possession of one tenant in common, *eo nomine*, as tenant in common, can never bar his companions; because such possession is not adverse to his right, but in support of their common title; and by paying him his share, he acknowledges him to be tenant. Nor is a **634***] refusal to pay, *without denying his title, sufficient. But if, upon demand by the co-tenant, of his moiety, the other refuses to pay, and denies his title, saying he claims the whole, and will not pay, and continues in possession; such possession is adverse, and ouster enough." "In this case," he continues, "no evidence, whatsoever, appears of any account demanded, or of any payment of rents and profits, or of any claim by the lessors of the plaintiff, or of any acknowledgment of a title in them, or in those under whom they would now set up a right. I am, therefore, clearly of opinion that an undisturbed and quiet possession, for such a length of time, is sufficient ground for a jury to presume an actual ouster." Aston, *J.*, says, "in this case, there has been a sole and quiet possession for 40 years, by one tenant in common only, without any demand or claim of any account by the other, and without any payment to him during that time. What is adverse possession or ouster, if the uninterrupted receipts of the rents and profits, without any account for near forty years, is not?" Willes and Ashurst, *JJ.*, expressed the same opinion. That case was, in no respect, a stronger one for the defendant, than the one at bar.

So in *Van Dyck* v. *Van Beuren*, 1 Cai., 84, the same doctrine was held—that a sole possession under claim of right for 40 years, by one tenant in common, amounts to an ouster; not that the jury might presume it from this fact, but that the law raises the presumption; and the jury were not at liberty to resist it. Whether it be a presumption of fact, to be found by the jury, as was held in *Doe* v. *Prosser*, or a presumption of law to be drawn by the court, as was said in *Van Dyck* v. *Van Beuren*, is not material in this case; for the verdict being subject to the opinion of the court, we are substituted for the jury, and have the right to draw the same conclusions from the testimony, which the jury, in the opinion of the court, would have been authorized to draw.

We are, therefore, of opinion that the defendant is entitled to judgment.

Judgment for the defendant.

Cited in—9 Cow., 252; 1 Barb. Ch., 541, n.; 16 Hun, 92; 19 Hun, 274; 28 Mich., 312, 324; 43 Am. Dec., 293 (25 Me., 434).

635*] *LUCAS

v.

THE JEFFERSON INSURANCE COMPANY in the City of New York.

Insurance—Construction of Clause for Ratable Payment—Several Policies Containing this Clause—Each Liable for Portion Mentioned in this Clause—No Contribution Between Them—Contra *where All or Part of the Policies are Without this Clause.*

Construction of the clause in a policy of insurance against loss by fire, providing for only a ratable payment, in case of other policies on the same subject.

Where there are several policies containing this clause, they are all and each liable to pay the ratable portion mentioned in the clause, though it happen that some have paid more than their share, and even enough to cover the whole loss; and this, whether they had knowledge of all the policies at the time or not.

There is no contribution between policies containing this clause.

Where, however, there are several policies, and one only contains this clause, and the others pay to the extent of their subscriptions, which is more than their ratable share, this will be a defense *pro tanto*, in an action against the underwriters on the policy containing that clause; and if the policies, without the clause, have paid enough to cover the loss, it is a complete defense for the others, for they are liable to contribute to the underwriters who have paid.

And so where all the policies are without this clause.

If underwriters, sued on a policy containing this clause, seek to defend themselves on the ground that other policies, without it, have paid the whole loss, or more than their ratable share; it lies with them to show, affirmatively, the other policies without the clause. This is matter of defense, and the absence of the clause in the other policies will not be intended.

Where there are several policies on the same subject, without this clause, it is double insurance; they are all deemed but one policy, the insured can recover but one indemnity, and contribution prevails between the insurers.

Citations—1 Bl., 416; 1 Marsh. Ins., ch. 4, sec. 4, p 116; or Condy's ed., p. 146.

ASSUMPSIT on a policy of insurance; tried at the N. Y. Circuit, July 13, 1826, before Edwards, *Circuit J.*, when the following facts appeared:

The defendants, by a policy dated Aug. 23, 1824, insured the plaintiff against loss by fire to the amount of $4,000, on certain cotton and woolen machinery, at Mechanic Ville, Saratoga Co. The Chatham and Ætna Fire Ins. Cos. also insured the plaintiff on the same property—the former to $5,500, the latter $6,000. A loss had been sustained by fire. The evidence on the part of the plaintiff, made the amount about $20,000; and that on the part of the defendants, between $9,000 and $10,000. The policy underwritten by the defendants contained the following clause: "In case of any other insurance upon the property hereby insured, whether prior or subsequent to the date of this policy, the insured shall not, in case of loss or damage, be entitled to demand or recover on this policy, any greater portion of the loss or damage sustained, than the amount insured shall bear to the whole amount insured on the said property." The Chatham and Ætna Companies had each paid the amount of their insurance, deducting one sixth, making together $9,583.34. These were voluntary payments without suit, by arrangement between the parties.

The judge charged the jury, that in ascertaining the amount to be recovered, they were not to take into consideration *the pay- [***636** ments made to the plaintiffs by other insurance Companies, provided those Companies were aware of the existence of all the policies on the

property at the time they paid the plaintiff for his loss, and made the settlement solely with the view of discharging the claim of the plaintiff against themselves. And that if the value of the property insured, and the amount of the loss by fire, were equal to all the sums insured by the different underwriters, the verdict, if the jury should think the plaintiff entitled to recover, ought to be for the face of the policy, with interest. But if the value of the property insured and the loss by fire were less than the aggregate amount of the sums insured by the different underwriters, the verdict ought to be only for such a proportion of the loss or damage sustained by the plaintiff, as the amount insured by the defendants bore to the whole amount insured.

To this charge the defendants excepted ; the judge sealed a bill of exceptions, on which the defendants now moved for a new trial.

Mr. J. Platt, for the defendants. The clause as to other insurances differs from the clause relating to those in marine policies. By this, the loss must be distributed among all, in proportion to the sum insured by each. If, therefore, the whole loss was paid by the other offices, the judge should have charged for the defendants, leaving the other companies to seek contribution. No act done by the other companies could deprive the defendants of a right to have the loss apportioned among all. It does not appear that their policies contain any clause providing for the case of double insurance. The object of insurance is indemnity ; and if the plaintiff was fully paid, this purpose was answered. The plaintiff can claim nothing farther against any underwriter. He cited 1 Marsh. Ins., 1 ; *Id.*, ch. 15, p. 529, 1 Am. ed ; *Id.*, 115, 119, 598, 602 ; 2 Burr., 1198 ; 1 Bl., 276 ; *Id.*, 416 ; Beawes, 242.

Mr. G. Griffin, contra. Contribution generally exists only where there is a joint liability, as in case of several sureties or partners. It is the same in the law of insurance. (Marsh. Ins., 637*] *148.) But if an individual pays my debt, without request, he cannot call on me to refund. The error of the other side lies in considering this a case of double insurance. It is not so. The language of the policy precludes the idea of joint liability. The authorities relied on by the other side relate to marine policies, which are signed by different underwriters till they are filled up, the names being often on the same instrument. This, unexplained, creates a joint obligation, and several suits upon a single policy will be consolidated. The payment by the other companies must be considered, in reference to this suit, as merely gratuitous, and cannot make the defendants liable to contribute. (2 Com. Cont., 151.) If we have received too much of them, their remedy is against us, if they paid by mistake. If wittingly, they must abide the loss. (4 Johns., 240.) We ask no more than indemnity. The contract is to pay a ratable indemnity. If the other policies did not contain the clause as to double insurance, it lay with the defendants to show this. The presumption is that they were all alike. All containing the same provision, how can either of these underwriters avoid their express agreement to pay, by setting up a pretense that they are liable to contribution. This is superseded by the clause in question.

Curia, per WOODWORTH, *J.* No objection was raised on the argument as to the finding of the jury, nor can this be questioned on a bill of exceptions. It was contended that the charge of the judge was erroneous, on the ground that the defendants were entitled to the benefit of the payments made by the other companies ; and that, inasmuch as the whole of the loss sustained had been already paid, the defendants were entitled to a verdict. It is well settled, that upon a double insurance, though the insured is not entitled to two satisfactions, yet in the first action he may recover the whole sum insured, leaving the defendant to recover a ratable satisfaction from the other insurers. (1 Bl., 416.) In such cases, the two policies are considered as making but one insurance. They *are good to the extent of the value of *[638 the effects put in risk. The insured may sue the underwriters on both policies, but he can only recover the real amount of his loss, to which all the underwriters shall contribute in proportion to their several subscriptions. (Marsh. Ins., B. 1, ch. 4, sec 4, p. 116, or Condy ed., p. 146.)

In the case before us, it is said that the clause in the policy, as to prior and subsequent insurances, differs essentially from the like clause in marine policies. I have looked at some of the printed forms of policies against fire in the books, but have not discovered any such clause. There is no direct evidence to show that the policies made by the Chatham and Ætna offices were similar to this. Whether they are or not, the parties in this action must be governed by the contract they have made. That is express. Suppose the plaintiff had not received anything from the other offices, could he recover the whole amount of the defendant's subscription, provided his loss was equal to that amount ? In a policy, not containing the clause referred to, the plaintiff would be entitled to recover the sum insured, leaving the defendants to seek contribution from other insurers. Here there is a stipulation against that course, in very explicit language : "The insured shall not, in case of loss or damage, be entitled to demand or recover on this policy any greater portion of the loss or damage sustained than the amount insured bears to the whole amount insured on the property." The defendants did not intend to be liable for the whole of their subscription in the first instance, and then seek indemnity by way of contribution. If, notwithstanding this clause, the defendants should voluntarily pay the whole amount of their subscription, towards the plaintiff's loss, I do not perceive on what ground they could claim contribution. The answer to such a claim would be, that they paid in their own wrong ; and *volenti non fit injuria*. If there is redress, it must be against the party who received more than he was entitled to demand. The principle of contribution can only be enforced where the party paying was under a legal obligation to pay. If the policies of the Chatham and Ætna Companies are similiar to *this, the de- *[639 fendants have no concern with the amount paid by them. In that case, they acted for themselves, and if they have paid more than the plaintiff could by law recover, it was done voluntarily. In the present case, the amount of the plaintiff's loss is controverted. He claims much more than the defendant is willing to admit. The weight of evidence on this point may be as contended for by the defendants, but still it is a disputable fact. The Chatham and Ætna offices may have chosen to pay on the exhibition of the plaintiff's proof, in preference to a protracted litigation. They may have erroneously considered the damages much greater than they really were. They acted voluntarily, and for themselves. This was submitted to the jury, and they have passed upón it. The act of settling for themselves raises a presumption that the different policies were alike, and that no claim for contribution was contemplated as against each other.

On the supposition that the policies of the Chatham and Ætna Companies did not contain the clause in question, the plaintiff might recover the amount of their subscriptions, if necessary to satisfy his loss; and in such case, I apprehend, it would be competent for the defendants to show the plaintiff had received satisfaction. As indemnity can only be claimed, there is no right of action after it is obtained. If the policies of the Chatham and Ætna offices were such as to entitle the plaintiff to recover of them all their subscription, if requisite to pay his loss, then their right to contribution against the defendants would be undoubted. The clause in the defendants' policy would not affect that question, but would apply when they should be prosecuted by the plaintiff, so as to protect them against his claim beyond a ratable proportion of the loss. If the loss has been already recovered and paid, the claim for a ratable proportion is necessarily extinguished. The Chatham and Ætna offices incurred no risk in making payment, provided the clause is not in their policies, because it is conceded by the defendants that the loss was, at least, equal to those payments. On this principle the defendants are **640***] liable to contribute a portion *to those Companies. If the amount received was to be taken into consideration on the trial, the duty of the jury would have been to ascertain the whole amount of loss, and if it exceeded the sums paid, then, after deducting the payment, to find a verdict against the defendants for the balance, provided it did not exceed the proportion of the whole loss, which, according to the contract, the defendants ought to bear; and if the amount of the loss remaining unsatisfied was less than such ratable share of the whole loss, then the verdict should have been for such balance. In the action for contribution an adjustment would be made between the parties on these principles. In the view thus taken I think that part of the judge's charge incorrect which directed the jury not to take into consideration the payments made to the plaintiff by the other Insurance Companies, provided those Companies were aware of the existence of all the policies on the property at the time, and made the settlement solely with a view of discharging the plaintiff's claim against themselves. If the Chatham and Ætna Companies were liable to the amount of their subscriptions, which I apprehend they were, unless protected by a clause like that in the defendant's policy, their knowledge of other policies was immaterial. Whether they had knowledge or not, the plaintiff was entitled to recover against them; and, if so, they had a remedy over against the other insurers. Neither can the fact that they settled to discharge the claim solely against themselves defeat such remedy over, if it appears they have not paid more than the loss sustained. Suppose those Companies had settled under a belief that their proportion of the loss would be equal to the amount paid, and, therefore, did not, at the time, contemplate a recovery against others for a portion of it. This would not invalidate their right to claim contribution, when it is shown that they had paid more than their relative proportion. In this point of view the charge was calculated to produce a result unfavorable to the defendants. The verdict was for the plaintiff; for how much does not appear; probably for the whole sum insured. A new trial should be granted, if the *Chatham and Ætna [***641** Companies were legally bound to pay what the plaintiff received. But if those policies were like the one in question, the defendants can derive no benefit from the payments made. They should be put out of view on this trial; and, if so, that part of the charge on which I have commented was incorrect as respects the plaintiff. The defendants have no cause to complain. It was allowing them the benefit of the payments, if the jury were satisfied of certain facts submitted to them; whereas they should have been instructed not to regard the payments, if the policies subscribed by those Companies bound them only to pay, in the first instance, a ratable proportion of the loss.

The question then is, what was the form of the Chatham and Ætna policies? Neither party has adduced any express testimony to this fact. On whom devolved the necessity of showing what those policies contained? Certainly not the plaintiff. His case was made out without this. He claims of the defendants the proportion they are bound to pay under their policy for the whole loss. They contend it has been paid by other Companies. But to make that defense available it must be shown, either that the Companies paid in fact a sum of money which was received in full satisfaction of all the insurances, or that the amount paid by them was in pursuance of a policy which authorized such payment. The first is not pretended. As to the second, the court is left to conjecture. It is a fact on which the defense rests. There is not sufficient ground for presumption that those policies did not contain the clause in question. The defendant's policy contains it. Some of the forms in the books do not. We cannot assume the fact that the policy differed from the one in this case. I think it may rather be presumed they are alike. The settlement made between the plaintiff and the Companies strengthens the presumption. They each deducted one sixth. They certainly had no right to make that deduction, if the loss exceeded the sums insured by them. The plaintiff claimed considerably more.* It is not probable the plaintiff would have consented to a deduction of one sixth, if the policies *were so drawn as to allow [***642** him to recover the whole sum insured. Be this, however, as it may, I think the defendants ought to have shown the other policies were different, in order to avail themselves of the payments. The remainder of the charge is correct. If the loss was equal to all the sums insured, the plaintiff was entitled to the face of the policy. If less, to a proportion only. Whether the jury have found too much or too little, is not before us. The motion for a new trial must be denied.

New trial denied.

Cited in—5 Hill, 301; 18 Wis., 239.

THE PEOPLE ex rel. INGERSOLL v. GAREY.

Legislature Cannot Directly or Indirectly Shorten Constitutional Term of Justice—Territorial Jurisdiction may be Changed—Erection of New Counties—Justices are Town Officers with County Powers.

The Legislature have no power to shorten the constitutional term of office of a justice of the peace.

This cannot be done indirectly, by the erection or division of counties.

Where a town is transferred from one county to another, or a new county made out of several towns, the justices of these towns continue to hold their offices, as justices of the town or towns in the new counties.

The Legislature have power to enlarge or contract the territorial jurisdiction of justices of the peace.

The office of justice of the peace is, under the new Constitution and the Statute which it adopts, sess. 41, ch. 60, sec. 2, a town office, though it has county powers.

The appointment of more than four justices in a town would be void.

Citations—Act, sess. 41, ch. 60, sec. 2; March 27, 1818; 1 Cow., 550.

ON demurrer to the replication. On information in nature of a *quo warranto*, against Garey, calling upon him to show by what warrant he acted as a justice of the peace of the County of Orleans, he pleaded the Statute to Erect a New County from Part of the County of Genesee, by the name of Orleans, passed Nov. 12, 1824, sess. 47, ch. 266, providing that all that part of the County of Genesee comprising the towns of Gaines, Barre, Murray, Clarendon, Ridgeway, Yates and Oak Orchard, in the County of Genesee, should, from and after Jan. 1, 1826, be a separate and distinct county, by the name of Orleans; and that it should be the duty of the supervisors and judges of Orleans to meet on the 3d Monday of May, 1826, and nominate justices for that county, proceeding in the same manner as in other cases; and that the former justices in that county should hold until the new appointments; that by another statute passed Apr. 15, 1825, sess. 48, ch. **643***] 181, it was provided that the *County of Orleans should be a distinct county from the time of the last mentioned Act, instead of the time mentioned in the first; and that the Town of Shelby, in Genesee Co., should be annexed to Orleans; and that the time of appointing justices should be on the 3d Wednesday in May, 1825. That the judges and supervisors met on the last mentioned day, and nominated the defendant, a justice of the peace of Shelby, who took the oath of office; and acted as justice of the peace for the new county, during the time mentioned in the information. Replication, that the Town of Shelby, on and before the 3d Tuesday of Feb. 1823, was a town of Genesee Co., when the judges and supervisors of Genesee Co. nominated two justices for that town; but disagreeing as to the other nominations, the judges nominating the relator, he with a fourth justice were selected by the Governor as justices of Shelby. That the commission of the peace for Genesee was filled. That the four justices for Shelby were, Feb. 27, 1823, duly sworn; and took upon themselves the office, and entered upon its duties, Shelby being then a town of Genesee Co.; and so continued till after the supposed appointment of the defendant; that they are now such justices of Shelby, and still continue to exercise their offices in that town.

General demurrer and joinder.

Mr. T. J. Oakley, in support of the demurrer. The Legislature had power to erect the new county, and separate Shelby from Genesee Co., and make it a part of Orleans. By the separation, the duties and powers of the former justices ceased. They could not be exercised out of the county for which they were appointed. They could not act as members of the General Sessions in Orleans, or do other county duties. Can their offices be retained in part? The locality as to appointment was intended merely as a measure of expediency, to limit their number; not to confer powers on them as town officers. Their powers are generally co-extensive with the county; and when their town is taken from the county for which they were appointed, *those powers cease [***644** from non-residence in that county; and cannot exist in the new one, unless continued by the Legislature. The constitutional tenure for four years is dependent on the county remaining entire, and the justices continuing in their town, as a part of it. Again; the appointment of the new justices is valid, even if the old ones are to continue in office. The Legislature may increase the number of justices in any town or county. Every person is deemed to assent to an Act of the Legislature.

Mr. Talcott, Atty-Gen., contra. We rely on the case *Ex parte M'Collum*, 1 Cow., 550, as conclusive. The justices have a right to hold their offices four years, unless sooner removed in the manner pointed out by the Constitution. The assent of no one is to be presumed to an unconstitutional statute. The only inquiry is, whether the Legislature have power to put the relator in such a situation that he cannot hold his office, before his constitutional term has expired. This point is directly decided in the case cited. If the Legislature may increase the number of justices, they have not attempted to do so. The Act contemplates the old number of four. The annexation of an old town to a new county is not analogous to the removal of a justice from his former residence. This is voluntary. He incapacitates himself. The Legislature could give no power to the judges and supervisors of Orleans, beyond supplying vacancies among the old justices as they should arise. So far, and no farther was this act constitutional. Probably this alone was intended.

Mr. J. V. Henry, in reply. *Ex parte M'Collum*

NOTE.—*Constitutional term of office—Power of Legislature to affect by legislation.* In connection with above case of People v. Garey, see same case as reported in 9 Cow., 640. Compare People v. Morrell, 21 Wend., 563, 582.

The Legislature may extend or limit the territorial jurisdiction of judicial officers. *Ex parte* McCollum, 1 Cow., 550.

decides no more than that the old justices may be transferred by statute with their town to another county. The provision in the Constitution that these officers shall not be removed except in a certain way, does not deprive the Legislature of the power to erect new counties and alter old ones. If that remains, the incidental right of officering those counties is essential. **645***] If the Legislature, as is admitted *in *M'Collum's* case, can contract or enlarge the jurisdiction of justices in the exercise of that right; does it not follow, that they may take it away? But if the Act cannot otherwise have effect, the court will construe it as creating an additional number of justices.

Curia, per SUTHERLAND, *J.* It is contended, by the counsel for the defendant: 1. That by the separation of the Town of Shelby from the County of Genesee, and its annexation to the County of Orleans, the duties and powers of the justices of the peace of that town ceased, and could not be exercised out of the county in and for which they were appointed; and 2. Admitting that the old justices still retained their powers, that the appointment of the defendant was valid, the Legislature having power to increase the number of justices in any town or county.

The power of the Legislature to increase the number of justices in any town or county is conceded. But it is contended, and we think with entire success, that there is nothing in the Acts creating and organizing the County of Orleans from which the slightest inference can be drawn that such was their intention in this case. The number of justices to be appointed in any town being limited to four, by a general law of the State (sess. 41, ch. 60, sec. 2), every presumption is against the intention of the Legislature, to vary that law in relation to a particular town or county. The reason for a departure from the general regulation, must appear on the face of the Act, or the intention be otherwise clearly expressed, in order to operate as a modification or partial repeal of it. But here such intention is clearly negatived by an express provision, that the (then) present justices of the peace in the new county shall hold their offices until the new appointments are made. (Sec. 14.) After they are made, then, so far as depends upon the provisions and operation of this Act, the former justices must cease to hold their offices.

The question then resolves itself into the inquiry, whether it was within the constitutional **646***] power of the Legislature, *under the circumstances of this case, to dismiss the old justices from office, and to direct the election of new ones, two years of the term for which they were elected still remaining. It is supposed to be very clear, that the justices in the towns which were erected into the County of Orleans, ceased to be justices of the County of Genesee, to which those towns belonged at the time of their election. Residence within the county is indispensable to the jurisdiction of this class of magistrates; and the Legislature, possessing the power of erecting new counties, from parts of counties already organized, necessarily have the right of separating one or more towns from the county to which they were originally attached, and as a consequence, of depriving the magistrates residing in those towns of the jurisdiction which they originally possessed over the territory from which they have been separated.

The power of the Legislature to erect new counties has been exercised from the foundation of the government, and is expressly recognized in the 7th section of the 1st article of the Amended Constitution. The justices of such towns must, therefore, become magistrates of the new county to which they are attached, or lose their offices entirely.

The mode of appointment to, and the tenure of, their offices, is particularly specified in the 7th section of the 4th article of the Constitution. It is there declared, "that every person appointed a justice of the peace, shall hold his office for four years, unless removed by the county court, for causes particularly assigned by the judges of the said court." It was the intention of the framers of the Constitution to make this important class of judicial officers entirely independent during the period for which they were chosen. No authority was conferred upon the Legislature of interfering with them under any circumstances. They were made amenable for misconduct, not to the Legislature, but to the judges of the county court, a co-ordinate branch of the domestic tribunal, from which they received their appointment. All direct control on the part of the Legislature, being thus carefully guarded against, *in relation to these officers, it *[**647** would be strange, indeed, if the power of removing them from office at pleasure, should be found to belong to the Legislature, as incident to their acknowledged power, of dividing old and erecting new counties. Every presumption is against it; and in expounding that part of the Constitution, and those laws which are applicable to the subject, that rule of construction should be adopted which is least favorable to such a pretension.

It is contended that justices of the peace are strictly county officers, and that when separated from the county for which they were chosen, their powers must cease in that county, on account of their non-residence, and cannot exist in the new county to which they are attached, because they were not elected or chosen for that county. If, by county officers, be meant officers who possess some powers coextensive with the county, it is conceded that justices of the peace are such. But according to that definition, the supervisors and constables of the different towns are county officers also: and would, by the same argument, lose their offices whenever the towns to which they belonged were set off to a different county. The most important duties of the supervisors of each town are as members of the Board of Supervisors, and relate to the county generally, and not to their respective towns. They settle and allow all accounts chargeable against the county, and determine what sum ought to be raised for defraying the public and contingent charges of the county. They determine each town's proportion of the county charges; and direct such sums to be raised, and issue their warrants to the different collectors for that purpose. They audit and allow the accounts of the County Treasurer, and it is to them that the bond for the faithful performance of his duties is given. They receive conveyances of land for the use of the county; they superintend the county court house and jail, and direct such repairs as may be necessary.

A constable also, has the same right to execute process in every town in the county, as **648***] in that in which he was *chosen, and where he resides. In this respect, his territorial jurisdiction is co-extensive with that of the sheriff. Yet it is conceded that supervisors and constables are town officers. The territorial extent of jurisdiction, then, is not a decisive test, to determine whether a particular office is a town or county office.

Nor does it depend upon the mode of appointment. Many considerations may render it expedient to confer the power of appointing local officers upon bodies of men not to be affected by the exercise of those powers; and by adverting to the debates in the convention upon that part of the Amended Constitution which provides for the appointment of justices of the peace, it will be perceived, that the power of appointment was not conferred upon the supervisors and judges of the county court, because justices were considered county officers. The principal objection made to the election of these magistrates by the different towns was, that deriving their offices from those among whom their powers were principally to be exercised, it was apprehended that they would not be exercised with impartiality and firmness. It was conceded that the inhabitants of the different towns were principally interested in the character and qualifications of the magistrates of their town; that they were essentially local magistrates, and that if it were not for the reason which has been adverted to, their selection ought to be left to the different towns. They are, undoubtedly, in the exercise of the largest and most important part of their duties, practically and substantially local officers. The respective towns have a deep interest in the character and qualifications of their own justices, and very little in those of the justices of any other town.

I am also inclined to think, that by the Act of Mar. 27, 1818, sess. 41 ch. 60, justices of the peace must reside in the towns for which they were appointed. The 2d section of that Act provides, "that it shall not be lawful to appoint any more than four justices of the peace in any town in this State." The object of the Legislature was not merely to prescribe a rule **649***] by which the aggregate *number of justices of each county should be limited. If it had been, a different phraseology would have been adopted. They would have said, at once, that no more justices shall be appointed in any county than at the rate of four for each town therein. This would have left it in the discretion of the appointing power to apportion them among the towns, in such manner as they might deem expedient. Have they that discretion under this law? Can they locate all the justices in the county in one town? It cannot, I apprehend, admit of a question, that such appointments would be absolutely void, except as to the four first named. And why would they be void? Not because the law declares that it shall not be lawful to appoint all the justices for the county in one town; but because it enacts that no more than four shall be appointed in any town. Whether the excess be great or small is not material. Whatever it is, is a violation of the Act, and void *pro tanto*. If there is any discretion upon this subject left to the appointing power, it is an unlimited discretion. The certificate of the supervisors and judges, which, by the Act of Apr. 12, 1822, is directed to be filed in the county clerk's office, must, I apprehend, specify the town for which the respective individuals are appointed. Under the old Constitution, when justices were appointed by the Council of Appointment, their commissions, undoubtedly, subsequent to the Act of 1818, specified the town for which they were appointed.

The object of the Act was, not only to limit the aggregate number of justices, but to secure a proper distribution of them among the different towns. Four were supposed to be equal to the wants of the largest town; and it was left to the discretion of the appointing power, whether they would appoint that number or less, where the circumstances of the town did not require so many.

If all the justices of one town should remove into the adjoining town, I apprehend their offices would be vacated. They would cease to be justices in the town for which they were appointed. If it is unlawful to appoint more than four justices for any one town, it would seem to follow, *that no one town can [***650** lawfully have more than four justices.

The article of the Constitution, prescribing this mode of appointing these officers, recognizes the existing law limiting their number, and speaking of them as justices to be appointed in the different towns.

Although, therefore, their criminal and civil jurisdiction, for many purposes, is co-extensive with the county, yet the Constitution and laws recognize them as attached to particular towns; and the practical exercise of their powers is confined almost exclusively to the towns in which they reside. When, therefore, the circumstance of a town being separated from the county to which it formerly belonged, renders it necessary to determine, whether the magistrates of the towns can retain their offices, in the new county to which their town is attached, I think we may consider them as substantially town officers, and as retaining their authority during the period prescribed by the Constitution, in whatever county the Legislature may be pleased to place their town.

The Constitution says they shall hold their offices for four years. The law of 1818 says, according to what is deemed its just construction, that they shall hold them only in the town for which they were appointed. It would seem necessarily to follow, that they become magistrates of whatever county their towns are attached to. In the case of *M'Collum*, 1 Cow., 550, it was held that the Legislature had power to enlarge or contract the territorial jurisdiction of justices of the peace. In that case, the County of Wayne had been erected from parts of Ontario and Seneca Cos.; and the question before the court was, whether the magistrates in the towns of which the county was composed, who were chosen while those towns belonged to the Counties of Ontario and Seneca, became justices of the peace in the new County of Wayne. The only distinction between that case and this, is, that there the Act organizing the County of Wayne, declares "that every person who shall have been appointed a justice of the peace, in and for the Counties of Ontario 651*] *and Seneca, and who shall now reside within the County of Wayne, shall, by virtue of this Act, be and remain a justice of the peace, in and for the County of Wayne, for the same time, and with the same powers and authority, in the town in which he shall reside within the County of Wayne, as he would have had in the Counties of Ontario and Seneca, if this Act had not been passed."

In the case now before the court, the election of new justices is directed, and that the old justices shall hold their offices until the new appointments are made. But it is conceived that these different provisions do not essentially vary the two cases. It is not in the power of the Legislature either to extend or shorten the duration of this office. They may enlarge or diminish the territory over which its powers are to be exercised. But the office itself exists independently of and above them.

In the case at bar, all the towns composing the new county were taken from the County of Genesee; so that the justices of those towns, if they retain their offices, acquire no additional territorial jurisdiction; nor do they become the magistrates of a people who had no voice in their election. The objection, therefore, which was urged with some plausibility in the Wayne Co. case, that magistrates were imposed upon the county, in whose election a portion of the county had no voice, does not apply here. But if it did, the decisive answer is this: that it is a condition imposed by the Constitution itself, and not by the Legislature, upon every new county, that the justices of the peace, in the towns of which it is composed, shall retain their jurisdiction, until the constitutional period of their offices shall expire. The power of the Legislature to erect new counties is subject to this limitation. It must be exercised in subordination to the imperative provision of that instrument, that justices of the peace shall hold their offices for four years, unless removed for misconduct.

Before the amendment of our Constitution, justices of the peace were appointed by and held their offices during the pleasure of the 652*]Council of Appointment. The effect *of transferring a town from one county to another, upon the magistrates of that town, never was drawn into discussion, at that time; because, from the tenure of the offices, and the character of the appointing power, there were no obstacles or objections to its exercise at any time. The fact, therefore, probably is, that new appointments were made, whenever new counties were created. And the offices being held at the pleasure of the appointing power, the exercise of that power could never be impeached by the party removed or superseded. There being no constitutional obstacle to the exercise of the appointing power, it is conceived, also, that it may have been competent for the Legislature to require that power to be exerted, whenever so important a change took place in the organization of the State, as that which was produced by the erection of a new county.

We are sensible of the difficulties which surround this question, and it is probable many may exist which have not been anticipated and answered by the court. But it seems to us there can be no mistake in the opinion which we have expressed, that it is not in the power of the Legislature to shorten the constitutional term of a justice of the peace; that the office must endure, unless vacated by the act of the incumbent, for four years; and that the only difficulty is in determining the territorial limits within which it is to be exercised. For the reasons which have been assigned, we think it must be the county in which the officer is placed under the new organization.

Judgment for the plaintiffs.

Affirmed—9 Cow., 640.

Cited in—5 Wend., 234; 9 Wend., 323; 11 Wend., 134; 21 Wend., 582; 2 Den., 292; 66 N. Y., 607; 53 Barb., 356; 37 How. Pr., 187; 2 Sandf., 368; 50 Mo., 356; 21 Am. Dec., 216.

---

*HALL [*653
v.
DAGGET AND KENSETT.

Trover—Cannot be Maintained without Right of Possession—Where Agent has an Interest in Goods Placed in His Hands, Under a Contract to be Sold, Principal has no Right to Demand Possession—Contract not Usurious.

D. and K. agreed with H. that the former should carry on the business of preserving fresh provisions; and in consideration of the use of $600 advanced by H., made him their only agent for selling the provisions in the City of N. Y., for 10 years; agreed that he should be allowed 20 *per cent.* on all sales; and one third of the net proceeds, after deducting the *per cent.* to apply on the amount advanced, till it should be liquidated; H. to furnish a repository at his own cost, and be responsible for his sales.

Held, that D. and K. had no right to demand the goods delivered to H. under this contract; he having an interest in them, and a right to detain and sell them pursuant to the contract.

Held, also, that the contract was not usurious.

Citations—7 T. R., 9; 1 Campb., 410; 1 M. & S., 148; 2 Bos. & P., 438; 4 T. R., 353; 2 Burr., 891.

ON ERROR from the C. P. of the City and County of N. Y.

The action in the court below was trover by Daggett and Kensett against Hall, for certain cases and boxes of provisions preserved fresh. The plaintiffs produced, on the trial, an agreement between themselves and the defendant below, dated Apr. 15, 1822, by which they agreed to carry on the business of preserving fresh provisions, which they warranted to keep sweet and good for any voyage or climate; and agreed, in consideration of the use of $600, received of Hall, that Hall should be the only agent for selling the provisions in the City of N. Y., for 10 years, and should be allowed 20 *per cent.* on all sales made by him, or through his agency in that city, or any other place where it might be advisable to go for the sale; and that he should be entitled to one third of the net proceeds of sales, after deducting the 20 *per cent.* to apply on the amount advanced by him until it should be liquidated. Hall agreed to furnish a suitable repository for the sale, at his own cost and expense, and be responsible for all sales made by him. Wherever he might go for the sale, it should be at his own expense.

The plaintiffs below proved that the defendant had received provisions under this contract, from the plaintiffs, to the value of $6,762.30, and had returned to the value of $1,184.17, and paid the plaintiffs $4,194.22. This was between Jan. 12, 1822, and Aug. 2, 1824, and proof was also given of the delivery of other provisions; all in pursuance of the contract. On the last of Dec., 1824, Kensett went to Hall's store in N. Y., and demanded all the provisions so delivered which were then unsold; and forbid Hall making any more sales; asked Hall to render his account; and offered that if he had any demand, or any storage, he (K.) would pay.
654*] Hall *then produced the contract, and asked Kensett if he intended to comply with it? This was repeated about the middle of Jan., when Hall offered to render his account, but said he would consult his attorney first.

The plaintiffs resting on this proof, the defendant moved for a nonsuit, which was overruled; and the judge charged that the plaintiffs had a right to demand the goods, on paying the defendant's lien, if any, whose duty it was to assert his lien, and render his account. If he had not done so, he had waived it. Whether it was asserted, and what the value of the remaining goods was, he left to the jury, who found for the plaintiffs $500 damages, on which judgment was rendered with costs. A bill of exceptions was taken to the opinion and charge of the court.

Mr. J. Platt, for the plaintiff in error, contended that the defendant below had a special property in the goods under the contract, with the right of possession. He was entitled to retain for his advances. The contract being in full force, and the defendant in the act of performing it, there was no conversion. He cited 7 T. R., 9, 387, 394, per Lawrence, *J.*; 2 Selw., *N. P.*, 1265; 2 Bos. & P., 438.

Mr. S. P. Staples, contra. If the defendant below had any lien, he should have put himself upon it. (1 Campb., 410, *n.*; 1 Maule & S., 147.) Not doing this, he waived it. But he had none. An offer was made to pay his demand, but no account was rendered. It is a mistake to say he had any interest in the provisions. His interest was in the contract. But suppose he had an interest in the goods, it was merely as agent or factor; and on payment or tender of his lien, he was bound to give up the goods. A factor, even on *del credere*, can do no less. An action on the case could have been only for not selling the provisions according to contract. If trover will not lie, we are remediless.

Besides, the contract was usurious and void.

655*] **Curia*, per SAVAGE, *Ch. J.* The law is well settled, that the action of trover cannot be maintained, without the right of possession. The right of property alone is not enough. (7 T. R., 9.) This principle is not controverted; but it is contended that the plaintiffs below, having the right of property, became entitled also to the right of possession, by the demand of an account, and an offer to pay any lien which the defendant had; and further, that the defendant not having asserted any lien when the demand was made, such lien, if any existed, was waived. And it has been decided, that if one having a lien upon goods, when they are demanded of him, claims to retain them upon a different ground, making no mention of the lien, trover may be maintained against him, without evidence of any tender having been made of the amount of his lien. (1 Campb., 410; 1 Maule & S., 148.)

The defendant in this case asserted no lien, except such as he was entitled to under his contract with the plaintiffs. The property in question had gone into his possession under that contract. If it was valid, and he had a right to retain the property and make sale of it, he was then entitled to 20 *per cent.* for commissions, and one third of the residue, to apply towards his advance of $600.

The rights of the parties seem to me to be different from those of principal and factor generally. As between the latter, no doubt the principal may demand his goods, on tendering to the factor the amount of his lien for advances and expenses. As to commissions, there can be none, I apprehend, when there is no sale. But when parties choose to make a special contract, their rights must be determined by it. According to this contract, the defendant below advances money, as may be inferred, to purchase the raw material. The plaintiffs below are to manufacture it, and the defendant is to sell the manufactured article, and the 20 *per cent.* commissions pay him for the use of his money, for his trouble in making sales, and for guarantying those sales. If the plaintiffs below have it in their power to recover the property delivered to the defendant, they virtually abrogate their own agreement. They *take away from the defendant the ad- [*656 vantages resulting to him from the business; and trifle with their contract. The case of *Bromley* v. *Coxwell*, 2 Bos. & P., 438, is an authority to show that trover does not lie for goods delivered under a special contract, unless that contract is violated by the defendant. There the plaintiff sent some prints to the defendant in India to be sold. They were not sold, because the price was too high. The plaintiff brought trover; but the court held that the conduct of the defendant (who had left the prints with another person for sale) did not amount to a conversion.

There is no pretense that the defendant below violated the contract. He was, therefore, lawfully in possession; and all the plaintiffs below had a right to ask of him, was the proceeds of sales, after deducting his commissions, and one third of the residue.

It is contended, however, on the part of the plaintiffs below, that the contract was usurious. There was a loan of $600, it may be inferred; though from the phraseology of the contract, it might equally be inferred that there was a previous indebtedness to that amount. But I am willing to consider the advance of $600, as made at the date of the contract. The parties were then about to begin a new business, the success of which was doubtful. The defendant was to incur a considerable expense on his part, preparatory to the sale of the goods in question; and it was by no means certain that the commissions would amount to 7 *per cent.* upon the money loaned, to say nothing of the interest of the money expended by him in furnishing a suitable repository, and of his personal services in making sale of the provisions.

How can it be said that there was reserved an interest of any per centage at all? The defendant was to receive his principal from the proceeds of the sales. Suppose the articles had not found a ready market, but had remained on hand; could the defendant have recovered of the plaintiffs either principal or interest? The whole contract seems to me to show the commencement of a new adventure—a speculation in which these parties were separately 657*] interested; and each was liable *to loss, or, perhaps, might make large profits. If, indeed, the transaction was merely colorable, and intended to cover a loan reserving more than 7 *per cent.*, the form of the contract would not shield the lender. Thus, if the lender, besides interest, is to have a certain portion of the profits of a trade which exceeds legal interest, and is not liable to losses, it is usurious. (4 T. R., 353.) But if money is loaned, and the lender is to have part of the profits, and is subject to loss, it is not usurious. (2 Burr., 891.) The case under consideration is not within these authorities. The lender here does not receive his interest, and profits beside; nor is his principal otherwise at risk, than as it may depend on the solvency of the borrowers, or their compliance with their contract. But it is also distinguishable in another important particular—the lender in this case renders personal services, and incurs other expenses in carrying on the business; and after all this, his compensation depends upon an untried experiment in this new branch of business.

It seems to me, then, that this contract is above all suspicion of usury; that the defendant was lawfully in possession of the goods in question, according to the terms of the contract; and was entitled to hold them, by the provisions of the contract, for sale; and that the plaintiffs had no claim for the goods themselves, but only for the proceeds, after deducting the defendant's commissions, and one third towards payment of the demand due to him. Of course trover would not lie. The judgment below must be reversed.

Judgment reversed.

Cited in—22 Barb., 124; 59 Barb., 658; 7 Bos., 166; 101 Ill., 529.

658*] *OVERSEERS OF THE TOWN OF HAMILTON

v.

OVERSEERS OF THE TOWN OF EATON.

Pauper—Indenture Binding Infant Pauper by One Overseer, Voidable Only—Settlement.

An indenture binding an infant pauper executed by only one Overseer of the Poor of a town, though with the assent of two justices, and the binding be to another Overseer, &c., of the same town, is defective, but is not void. It is voidable only, and if there be a complete service under it, the servant thereby gains a settlement.

Citations—1 R. L., 136; Burr. Sett. Cas. No. 28, p. 91; 13 Johns., 245; 5 Cow., 527, S. P.; 5 W. & M. Ch., 21; Burr. Sett. Cas., 199.

ON *certiorari* to the General Sessions of the Peace of the County of Madison.

Two justices made an order to remove one Elizabeth Watson from the Town of Hamilton to the Town of Eaton, in Madison Co.; and she was removed accordingly. On appeal by the Overseers of Eaton to the General Sessions of Madison that court quashed the order; whence the Overseers of Hamilton brought a *certiorari* to this court. The facts on which the decision of the sessions was founded are stated in the opinion of this court.

Mr. I. Foote, for the plaintiffs in error, cited 1 R. L., 270, sec. 2; *Id.*, 136, secs. 4, 5; *Id.*, 138; 5 Cow., 367; 8 T. R., 379; 4 T. R., 769, 790; 3 T. R., 380; Reeve Dom. Rel., 341, and cases cited; 1 Bl. Com., 452, 453; 1 Salk., 68.

Mr. P. Gridley, contra, cited 1 R. L., 279; 5 Cow., 527; 13 Johns., 245; 5 Cow., 363.

Curia, per WOODWORTH, *J.* The pauper was bound an apprentice to Fuller, one of the Overseers of the Poor of the Town of Hamilton, and served the full term. Maynard, the other Overseer of that town, executed the indenture. Two justices were present and approved. Fuller never executed it. It was left in the possession of Maynard, who testified that it was regular, but could not be found on search. The parol evidence was admissible, but the binding was defective; the Act, 1 R. L., 136, declaring that the Overseers of the Poor, with the consent of any two justices, may bind out any child who is chargeable.

The binding, however, was not absolutely void, but voidable by the parties. It has had its effect between *them. Neither party [*659 has chosen to take advantage of the defect, and it cannot be done by a third person. The town has had the benefit of the service, and cannot object. (Burr. Set. Cas., No. 28, p. 91.) The same principle is recognized in *Hudson* v. *Taghkanac*, 13 Johns., 245. There the mother bound the child, her husband being alive; and it was held that the town could not take advantage of the defect. *Owasco* v. *Oswegatchie*, 5 Cow., 527, S. P.

The cases in which it has been held that a settlement could not be gained under an indenture not stamped, were decided on the words of the Statute, 5 W. & M., ch. 21, which says the indenture shall not be given in evidence, or available in any court. (Burr. Set. Cas., 199.) The order of the General Sessions must be affirmed.

Order affirmed.

HOMAN *v.* LISWELL.

Execution Renewed is not an Original—Action will not Lie Against Constable for not Serving—Renewal by Constable—Computation of Time.

An action will not lie against a constable for not serving an original execution, after it has been renewed by the plaintiff.

If it is renewed on the constable's responsibility, and on good consideration, the action, if any will lie, should be *assumpsit*, not case for neglect in omitting to serve or return it.

An execution renewed ceases to be an original.

If an execution be renewed on the constable's responsibility, before it has run out, such engagement of the constable is *nudum pactum*, and void.

Where computation of time in a statute is to be from the date, or from an act done, the day of the date, or act, is exclusive.

Where an execution was dated the 7th of March, and returnable within 30 days from the date; held, that it would not expire till after the 6th of April, and that the constable holding it, had the whole of that day in which to execute and return it.

Citations—Act, sess. 47, ch. 238, sec. 14, p. 287, 288; 2 Cow., 518, 605.

ON ERROR from the C. P. of the County of Schenectady.

Mr. A. C. Page, for the plaintiff in error, cited 2 Cow., 518, 605 and 612, *note;* 1 Serg. & R., 411, per Tilghman, *Ch. J.;* 1 Com. Cont., 8-10, 58, 59; Statute of 1824, sess. 47, ch. 238, sec. 17, p. 289.

Mr. M. T. Reynolds, contra.

The facts are stated in the opinion of the court, which was delivered by,

660*] *SUTHERLAND, *J.* Liswell sued Homan before a justice, and declared against him in case for not returning an execution, which had been delivered to Homan as a constable, in favor of Liswell against Dudley and Temple. Liswell recovered, before the justice, the amount of the execution. Homan appealed to the C. P., where Liswell again recovers, and Homan brings his writ of error.

The execution bore date Mar. 7, 1825; and Apr. 6, following it was renewed by direction and with the assent of Liswell's agent, with a full knowledge of the time when it issued and of all the circumstances of the case.

This was a perfect defense to the action. No action can be sustained for not returning an execution which the plaintiff himself has directed and permitted to be renewed. After it was renewed no return could be made upon it as an original execution; and after the plaintiff has assented to an act which rendered a return impossible, he cannot have an action for not making such return. But it appeared that the agent of the plaintiff consented to the renewal, upon the express condition that Homan, the constable, would be responsible. The language used was, that it was renewed upon his responsibility, to which Homan assented. The action should have been *assumpsit* upon this promise, if it was valid. Clearly no other action could be maintained.

But we are also of opinion that there was no legal consideration for the promise. The execution was returnable in thirty days from the date, pursuant to the Act of 1824, sess. 47, ch. 238, sec. 14, pp. 287, 288. According to the principles of construction established by this court as applicable both to statutes and notices, the constable had the whole Apr. 6, to serve and return the execution. In *Ex parte Dean*, 2 Cow., 605, it was held that where the computation of time in a statute is to be from an act done, the first day should be excluded. That was on a statute prescribing the time within which an appeal should be brought from a justice's court. It was held that the day on which 661*] the judgment was rendered *should be excluded. The same principle was adopted in relation to the Redemption Act. (2 Cow., 518.) If the execution, then, had not run out, and the constable had not become fixed, his promise was without consideration. It was a naked promise, by parol, to pay the debt of a third person. There is nothing in the case to show that the execution might not have been served. The judgment must be reversed.

Judgment reversed.

Cited in—7 Wend., 238; 25 Wend., 697; 2 Hill, 356; 3 Den., 16; 69 N. Y., 550; 28 Barb., 286; 11 How. Pr., 195; 6 Abb., N. S., 99; 1 Sheld., 168; 4 Leg. Obs., 149; 3 McLean, 288; 10 Mich., 496; 50 Am. Dec., 252 (19 Conn., 376).

THE PEOPLE *v.* WHALEY.

Practice—Justice Court — Discontinuance—Extortion by Justice—Indictment Sustained.

Where a defendant appeared before a justice, on a summons returnable at 10 A. M., and waited till about 12 o'clock, when the justice told him, he (the justice) must tax the plaintiff with the costs, upon which the defendant departed; but the justice afterwards adjourned the cause to another day; and gave judgment as upon the summons, with $3 or $4 costs; and the defendant afterwards paid to the justice the amount of the note on which the suit was brought; and the justice demanded the costs; which the defendant refused to pay in full; but paid the justice 12½ cents; held, that this was extortion in the justice, for which he might be indicted and punished criminally.

Held, also, that the motives of the justice, as whether corrupt, or whether he acted through a mistake of the law, were a proper question for the jury.

Held, that he had a right to receive the money on the note, as the agent of the plaintiff; but the extortion lay in receiving the 12½ cents under pretense of the judgment.

Extortion is the taking of money by any officer by color of his office, either where none at all is due, or not so much due, or when it is not yet due.

When a cause is discontinued before a justice, by the laches of a plaintiff, the justice has no jurisdiction; and if he proceeds in it, his proceedings are *coram non judice*, and void.

Extortion may be laid generally, in an indictment, by color of office.

Citations—1 Hawk., B. 68, sec. 1.

THE defendant was indicted, at the General Sessions of Oneida Co., for extortion as a justice of the peace.

The 1st count of the indictment stated that Butler appeared before the defendant, a justice of Oneida, at the suit of Grant, on the return day of a summons, Feb. 7, 1826, at 10 A. M.; that the suit was discontinued by the non-appearance of the plaintiff. And that Mar. 7, the defendant, by color of his office, extorted from Butler, $25, under pretense that the suit had been adjourned Feb. 7, to another day, when judgment was entered against Butler. The 2d count was more general. Without setting out the proceedings, it charged the defendant with extortion, by color of his office, under pretense that a judgment had been entered before him.

On a plea of not guilty, it was proved at the trial, that Butler appeared Feb. 7, between 11 and *12 A. M., on the summons as set [*662 forth in the indictment; that the plaintiff did not appear. That, just before, or after 12 o'clock, the defendant told Butler he must tax the plaintiff with the costs. But after Butler left the defendant, he adjourned the cause to Feb. 10. In the afternoon of the 7th, Butler again saw the justice, conversed with him about the note on which the suit was instituted, and ascertained the balance, for which Butler offered to confess judgment. But the defendant said nothing to him about any adjournment. On the 10th the defendant entered judgment against Butler, not only for the note, but $3 or $4 costs of previous summonses, fees of constable and witnesses. Butler afterwards paid the defendant the amount of the note, and 12½ cents; the defendant at the same time demanding the $3 or $4 costs.

The court charged the jury, that if they believed that Grant was nonsuited by the justice, or that the cause was discontinued before him, the subsequent proceedings were *coram non judice*, and void for want of jurisdiction; and the receipt of any money from Butler, as fees upon a judgment, would be extortion, if they believed the defendant acted through corrupt motives. That if such were his motives, the judgment would not protect him; that it was for the jury to determine whether these facts were so or not. But that if they believed the defendant acted without corrupt or dishonest motives, supposing that he had a right to proceed as he had done, it would be their duty to acquit him. That if his error was one of judgment merely, they should acquit.

The counsel for the defendant, considering the charge incorrect, suggested this, and the sessions made a case for the opinion of this court, which was attached to the indictment.

Mr. S. Beardsley, for the defendant, *Mr. G. C. Bronson*, same side, now insisted that the judgment before the defendant was valid, either by the confession of Butler or as rendered on the trial of a cause regularly adjourned. At most, **663***] *it was merely erroneous. (8 Johns., 391; 11 *Id.*, 407; 12 *Id.*, 217.) The court erred in leaving it to the jury, to say whether there was a nonsuit or discontinuance. No nonsuit is charged in the first count of the indictment; and no evidence was given, which, in its nature, would prove a nonsuit. The jury were bound, therefore, not to regard it. (5 Cow., 246.) A judgment could be rendered, only by entering it in writing. (Burr. Set. Cas., 322.) The mere declaration of the justice, that he would tax the plaintiff with the costs, was not a judgment. The question whether the cause was discontinued by the lapse of time, and absence of the plaintiff, should have been left to the jury.

The indictment is defective, in omitting to charge, that the money paid by Butler was not due in fact. (4 Bl. Com., 141; 2 Ch. Cr. L., 295, *note p;* Co Litt., 368 *b;* 1 Hawk. P. C., 316.) Besides, it is not extortion, unless received by the defendant, as fees for his own use. The payment was voluntary, and was due to Grant, excepting the 12½ cents, which were due to the justice, for entering the judgment.

Mr. H. Denio, Dist. Atty, and *Mr. Talcott*, Atty-Gen., contra, cited 9 Johns., 140; 1 Hawk. P. C., 316; 14 Vin. Abr., 363, pl. 8; 7 East, 218.

Curia, per SAVAGE, *Ch. J.* An objection is taken to the indictment, that the defendant is not charged with taking the money, as fees, or to his own use. It was not necessary to lay the offense in that manner; it is sufficient that he extorted it by color of his office. Extortion signifies, in an enlarged sense, any oppression under color of right. In a stricter sense, it signifies the taking of money by any officer, by color of his office; either, where none at all is due, or not so much due, or when it is not yet due. (1 Hawk., B. 68, sec. 1.) And the cases cited by the defendant's counsel, do not show any necessity for the averment insisted on.

The other questions relate to the correctness of the charge. I think it sound. The word **664***] "nonsuit" was probably *used as synonymous with "discontinuance;" and though, perhaps, not technically correct, it could not mislead the jury. If the cause had become discontinued by the laches of the plaintiff, then the justice had no jurisdiction; and as well the adjournment as the subsequent proceedings, were void. If void, then the defendant received from Butler one shilling, by color of his office, which was not due. The amount of the note was due; and, as the agent of Grant, the payee, the defendant had a right to receive it. The justice was authorized to enter judgment on the note, by confession; and we might presume it to have been so entered, were it not positively proved that it was entered as upon trial, and not upon confession.

The questions of fact and intent, were fairly submitted to the jury. It was their province to judge of both, and of the credibility of the witnesses. The jury have found, by the verdict, that the cause before the defendant had become discontinued before he entered the adjournment; and that he received and demanded the money by color of his office, and with the corrupt intent charged in the indictment. These facts being proved, the offense was complete. We are not now to inquire whether the verdict is such as we might have found. We are not here to decide the fact, but the law. There was no error in the charge, and I am of opinion that the proceedings of the court below are not questionable in any view.

Cited in—30 How. Pr., 145; 3 Blatchf., 323; 36 N. J. L., 127.

---

*MILLER *v.* PLUMB. [*665

Fixtures Pass to Vendee, though for Purposes of Trade or Manufacture—Contra as Between Landlord and Tenant—Practice.

As between vendor and vendee of land, all fixtures pass to the latter, though they were erected by the vendor for the purposes of trade or manufactures.

The rule is the same as between heir and executor.

But it is otherwise as between tenant and landlord or reversioner, and as between tenant for life and remainder-man.

In the C. P. a record, immediately after the issue (of June Term, 1825), continued the cause by a general continuance to October Term then next; and then said, "therefore, let there come a jury, &c., at December Term next;" and then said, "at which day, &c., come the parties, &c., and the jurors, &c., also come, who, to speak the truth, &c." Held, that this referred the appearance of the parties, and jury; and the rendition of the verdict, to December Term, and that there was no error, therefore, in the record. But that, at most, it was a mere miscontinuance, which was cured by the Statute of Amendments and Jeofails.

Citations—3 Johns., 183; Bull. *N.* P., 34; 2 Johns., 30; 3 East, 38; 7 Bac., 258; Easter, 22 Geo. III.; 1 H. Bl., 259, *n.*

ON ERROR from the C. P. of Monroe Co.

Plumb brought trover in the court below against Miller, for certain materials appertaining to a building for manufacturing ashes, viz.: 2 potash kettles, 2 five-pail kettles, 2 troughs, 5 leaches and 500 feet of boards. It appeared, at the trial, that while Plumb owned the ashery, the materials in question belonged to it. The two potash kettles were set in an arch of mason work with a chimney. The arches were set upon a platform, but not fastened to the building. The troughs were sunk in the ground, so that the upper part was nearly even with the top. The boards were for an upper floor in the building. Two small kettles were not set in any way, but stood in the building, and were necessary for use. In this state of things, the plaintiff below, Mar. 3, 1824, articled to convey the premises on which the ashery stood, to the defendant below, Apr. 15 following, if the consideration money was paid; by which day it was paid, and the defendant took possession. Feb. 11, 1825, Plumb conveyed the premises to Miller, by deed of common warranty, without any reservation. Miller then demised the ashery; the lessee took possession, and used the kettles until the building was burnt down; and afterwards paid for the use.

The court below charged that the plaintiff, Plumb, was entitled to recover; and a verdict and judgment was rendered for him accordingly. The defendant below excepted to the charge.

Immediately after issue on the record, which was of June Term, 1825, the cause was continued thus: "And hereupon the proceedings thereof are continued, &c., until the 1st Monday of October next (the next term). Therefore,
666*] *let there come a jury thereof, &c., on the 1st Monday of December next, &c. (the next term), at which day, &c., come the parties, &c., and the jurors, &c., also come, who, to speak the truth, &c." (setting forth the verdict).

Mr. J. Boughton, for the plaintiff in error, contended that the fixtures passed by the conveyance, and cited Bull. *N. P.*, 34; 2 Bl. Com., 428; Toll. L. Ex., 197, 198, and cases cited; 3 East, 51; 3 Atk., 13; 20 Johns., 32; 7 Mass., 432; 13 Johns., 404, 406.

Mr. R. Beach, contra, insisted that there was no formal error in the record; but if otherwise, the defect was cured by the Statute of Amendments and Jeofails. (3 Johns., 183; 7 *Id.*, 467; 5 *Id.*, 89; 1 Cow., 189.)

That the fixtures did not pass, he cited 6 Johns., 5; 3 Atk., 13.

Curia, per WOODWORTH, *J.* The first objection is to the form of the record.

A continuance is entered from June to October Term; and then an award of *venire* to December Term then next; at which day came the parties; and the jurors also came. This is sufficiently plain, and must be understood, that the parties and jurors appeared at December Term. Although, under the statute, the continuance might have been awarded from June to Dec., without any award of *venire*, the present entry is substantially the same; and, at most, is only a miscontinuance, which is cured by the Statute of Jeofails. (3 Johns., 183.)

The more important question is, whether the potash kettles, being affixed to the freehold, passed with the land. If they did, the court below erred; and the judgment must be reversed, unless the case falls within some of the qualifications or exceptions to the general rule. That rule appears to be well established, whatever is affixed to the freehold becomes part of it, and cannot be removed. Exceptions have been admitted between landlord and tenant; between tenant for life or in tail and the reversioner; yet the rule still holds between heir
667*] and *executor. (Bull. *N. P.*, 34.) In *Holmes* v. *Tremper*, 20 Johns., 30, *Ch. J.* Spencer says, "when a farm is sold without any reservation, the same rule would apply, as to the right of the vendor to remove fixtures, as exists between the heir and executor."

Ld. Ellenborough, in the case *Elwes* v. *Maw*, 3 East, 38, lays down the law relative to fixtures as arising between three classes of persons: 1. Between heir and executor. 2. Between the executors of tenant for life or in tail and the remainder-man, or reversioner. 3. Between landlord and tenant; and observes that, "in the first case, the rule obtains with the most rigor in favor of the inheritance, and against the right to disannex therefrom, and to consider as a personal chattel, anything which has been affixed thereto." In the latter cases, the reasons for relaxing the rule are obvious, upon motives of public policy. The tenant is thereby encouraged to make improvements, and the interest of trade promoted, while the landlord or reversioner has no cause to complain, inasmuch as the farm is restored to him in the same state as when he parted with it. A different rule would effectually check all improvements by the tenant, where it is known that, at the end of the term, they are to be surrendered to the landlord, or the reversioner of tenant for life. But the case between heir and executor, and vendor and vendee, is widely different. The ancestor or vendor has the absolute control not only of the land, but of the improvements. The heir and executor are both representatives of the ancestor; the vendor has an election to sell or not to sell the inheritance.

If he does elect to sell, he knows that, by law, the fixtures pass; and there is no good reason why that law should interpose in his behalf, and protect him against the loss of improvements which he has deliberately chosen to part with. It is for reasons of this kind, I apprehend, the old rule of law seems still to hold. In 7 Bac., 258, this is expressly recognized. The author observes, that although in an action of trover by an executor against an heir, for a cider-mill, tried at Worcester, before *Ld. Ch. B.* Comyns, His *Lordship was of opin- [***668**
ion that it was personal estate, and directed the jury to find for the executor; yet Ld. Mansfield has observed, that that case, in all probability, turned upon a custom; and that where no circumstances of that kind arise, the rule still holds on favor of the heir, seems fully established by the decision of the Court of K. B., in *Lawton* v. *Lawton*, Easter, 22 Geo. III. The title of the case referred to seems to be *Lawton* v. *Salmon*, and is to be found in 1 H. Bl., 259, *note a.* As reported, I do not find that Ld. Mansfield, in giving this opinion of the court, says that the case before Comyns, *Ch. B.*, turned upon a custom. Yet the whole scope of the opinion is clearly against it. He recognizes the relaxation of the old rule as confined to cases between landlord and tenant, and tenant for life and remainder-man; where, for the benefit of trade, and as an encouragement to lay out money in improving the estate, there has been a departure from the old rule, which is no injury to the remainder-man, because he takes the estate in the same condition, as if the thing in question had never been raised. He adds: "I cannot find that, between heir and executor there has been any relaxation of this sort, except in the case of the cider-mill, which is not printed at large." It was a *Nisi Prius* decision, and evidently considered as not controlling the general law.

From this review, it appears to me that the

case of vendor and vendee rests on the same ground as that of heir and executor; and that the fixtures in such cases are not considered as personal property. I incline to think the evidence of conversion was sufficient; and that the plaintiff was entitled to recover for some articles not annexed to the freehold; but as damages were recovered for the whole, which cannot now be severed, the judgment in the court below must be reversed, and a *venire de novo* awarded by the C. P. of Monroe.

Judgment reversed.

Cited in—7 Cow., 321; 20 Wend., 639; 3 Edw., 247; 1 N.Y., 570; 18 N. Y., 31; 20 N. Y., 349; 3 Keyes, 352; 4 Abb. App. Dec., 59; 1 Trans. App., 358; 7 Barb., 267; 11 Barb., 57; 37 How. Pr., 392; 5 Abb. N. S., 48; 1 E. D. S., 612; 37 Am. Dec., 214, 215 (12 N. H., 205); 44 Am. Dec., 355 (17 Vt., 533); 41 Am. Rep., 255 (58 Cal., 126).

669*] *M'FARLAND v. SMITH.

Letter Promising to Pay Debts of Another After One Year, Provided Arrangements should be made with Creditors—Means all Creditors—Assumpsit by One not Maintainable unless on Special Agreement to Wait.

S. wrote a letter in Salem, addressed to C. of Salem, stating that he (S.) had told R., his brother, that if he (R.) could make an arrangement with his creditors there (Salem), he would be responsible for payment in one year.

M. was one of the creditors, and on the letter being shown to him, he waited one year, and then demanded his debt of S.; and brought an action on the promise contained in the letter. R. had other creditors at Salem, with whom no arrangements had been made. Held, that the promise in the letter was upon the condition that an arrangement should be made with all the creditors at Salem; and the action would not, therefore, lie.

Held, also, that if it referred to an arrangement with a single creditor, yet M. must prove a binding agreement not to sue upon the original debt within the year; and that there was nothing in the fact that he knew of the letter, and actually waited a year, which would authorize a jury to infer such an arrangement.

ASSUMPSIT, tried at the Washington Circuit, Dec. 14, 1825, before Walworth, *Circuit J.*

The action was founded on the following letter written by the defendant: "April 15th, 1824. John Crary, Esq., Dear Sir, I have told Richard that if he can make an arrangement with his creditors here, that I will be responsible for the payment of the same in one year from this date; and as I have not time to make the arrangement now, you may give them that assurance if referred to." (Signed) Ezra Smith. It appeared at the trial, that the defendant had written this letter, which was delivered to Mr. Crary; that Richard, named in the letter, was Richard W. Smith, a brother of the defendant. Richard owed the plaintiff on a note of $91.17, then due. A few days after the letter was received by Mr. Crary, he showed it to the plaintiff, on his inquiring whether the defendant had given any assurance that Richard's debts should be paid. Other creditors of Richard also called on Mr. Crary; and some of them left their demands with him. The plaintiff, when he called, asked Mr. Crary if the letter would legally bind the defendant to pay Richard's debts, and Mr. C. answered that it would. In June, 1825, the attorney for the plaintiff gave the defendant notice of the debt due on the note, and demanded payment, which the defendant refused.

On these facts, the plaintiff rested. The defendant moved for a nonsuit, which was overruled.

The defendant then proved the existence of other demands against Richard, at Salem, where the letter was written, on which no agreements had been made to delay payment.

The objections taken to the plaintiff's recovery were, among others, that the defendant's letter was intended *of an arrangement [*670 with Richard's creditors generally; and that if an arrangement with any particular creditor was intended, yet that none had been shown with the plaintiff.

The judge overruled the first objection, and left it to the jury to say, whether the plaintiff had agreed to delay the collection of his debt, on the faith of the letter, for one year. The defendant excepted to the decision and charge. The jury found for the plaintiff.

Other particulars will be found stated in the opinion of the court.

On the bill of exceptions,

Mr. S. Stevens, for the defendant, now moved for a new trial.

Mr. J. Willard, contra.

Curia, per SUTHERLAND, *J.* I think the judge erred in the construction of the letter, or agreement of the defendant, which is the foundation of this action. He charged the jury that the true construction of that agreement was, if any one of the creditors of Richard W. Smith would agree to wait and, in pursuance thereof, did wait for the payment of his debt one year, he, the defendant, promised to pay the debt. Now it appears to me, from the terms of the letter, that the defendant contemplated an arrangement with the creditors of his brother at Salem, generally. He uses the plural noun, without adding the qualifying terms, "or any of them," and the very nature and object of the undertaking seems to imply an expectation and understanding, on the part of the defendant, that the creditors generally should assent to it. The motive of the defendant must have been, either to prevent his brother's property (if he had any) from being sacrificed by his creditors, or to save him from arrest or imprisonment. Neither of these objects would be accomplished by the assent of a single creditor to the propositiou. It appears from the testimony of Mr. Crary, that Richard W. Smith, the brother of the defendant, had just been admitted an attorney of this court; that the defendant had purchased a *library for [*671 him, and was desirous of having him remove from Salem to Whitehall, for the purpose of establishing himself in business at that place. And it is to be inferred from the evidence, that the defendant apprehended that the creditors of his brother would not permit him to leave Salem, unless they had some security for their demands; or if they did, that he could not prosecute his profession, with any prospect of success, with these debts impending over him.

The intention of the defendant, therefore, as derived from the terms of his letter, is strongly corroborated by all the circumstances in the case. Admitting the letter to contain a binding promise on the part of the defendant to pay the debts of his brother, in one year, it is upon the condition that his brother can make an arrangement with all his creditors at Salem for a year's indulgence.

Having instructed the jury as to the legal import of the contract, he further charged them, "that if they were satisfied from the testimony, that the plaintiff had agreed to wait and delay payment of his debt, so that he had no right to sue Richard for his debt for one year, then they must find for the plaintiff."

If the judge was right in the construction which he put upon the contract, then the legal proposition embraced in the succeeding part of the charge was undoubtedly correct, as an abstract proposition. But the objection to it is, that there is not a particle of evidence in the case, that the plaintiff ever did make any agreement with the defendant or his brother Richard, or any one in their behalf, to suspend the collection of his debt against Richard for a single hour. All the evidence on this point is contained in the testimony of Mr. Crary. He states that the plaintiff called on him, and asked him if the defendant had given any assurance that R. W. Smith's debts would be paid. That the witness then showed the letter as containing the assurance which had been given by him. That the plaintiff showed the witness a note against R. W. Smith. That no other agreement, whatever, was made between witness and the plaintiff, that the plaintiff should wait on R. W. Smith for his pay, than
672*] *what might be inferred from the transaction stated. The plaintiff asked the witness if the letter would legally bind the defendant to pay the debts of R. W. Smith, and the witness answered in the affirmative. He requested the witness to keep the letter, and appeared to be satisfied.

There is nothing in this that amounts to an agreement of any sort. The plaintiff might, the next day, have put his demand in suit, without the violation of any legal or moral obligation on his part. The charge of the judge was calculated to mislead the jury. They had a right to infer from it, that in the opinion of the judge, the evidence in the case warranted the conclusion that the plaintiff had made such an agreement, or that the fact of abstaining from suing was equivalent to an agreement not to sue.

It was clearly proved that there were other creditors of Richard besides the plaintiff, by some of whom he was sued. On these grounds, we are of opinion that the verdict ought to be set aside, and a new trial granted.

We have not thought it necessary to express any opinion upon the other points raised in the case, because, according to our construction of the defendant's letter, it was, at most, a promise to pay the debts of Richard upon a certain condition, which the case shows conclusively never was complied with on the part of his creditors. Whether the defendant would have been bound to pay, if that condition had been complied with, is of no importance to determine.

New trial granted.

*FLOWER ET AL. [*673
v.
THE ÆTNA FIRE INSURANCE COMPANY OF THE CITY OF NEW YORK.

1. On Charge of Specific Fraud, against a Party in Civil Action, His Character not Generally in Issue. 2. Description of Property Insured in Policy is Warranty that it is as Described.

In general, where a party is charged with a specific fraud in a civil action, his character is not in issue, The evidence of fraud cannot be repelled, therefore, by pr[illegible]i[illegible]g his general good character for integrity.

The case of Ruan v. Perry, 3 Cai., 120, was an exception to this rule, being a charge of gross depravity and fraud upon circumstances merely.

The description of the property insured in a policy against loss by fire, is a warranty that the property is as described; and if untrue in substance, the policy is void, though the misdescription arise from mistake: and there be no fraud.

Thus, where a policy of this kind described the subject insured, as the stock in trade of the insured, contained in a two story frame house filled in with brick, No. 152 Chatham St.; the house No. 152 being a frame house not filled in with brick; held, that the policy was void.

Citations—3 Cai., 120; 2 Bos. & P., 532, *n. a*; 4 Mass. 337; 1 Marsh. Ins., 335, 339, 347; 2 Cai., 48; 20 Johns., 198; Phil. Ins., 125; 8 Johns., 237, 319; 2 H. Bl., 574; 3 Burr., 1909.

ASSUMPSIT, on a policy of insurance against fire; tried at the N. Y. Circuit, July 6, 1826, before Edwards, *Circuit J.*

The plaintiffs, at the trial, proved a policy executed by the defendants, on the stock in trade of the plaintiffs, consisting of, &c., contained in a two story frame house, filled in with brick, situate at No. 152 Chatham St., in the City of N. Y. It appeared that the house No. 152 Chatham St. was burned, with the plaintiffs' stock in trade; but that the house was a wooden building, with hollow walls, and not filled in with brick. That one of the conditions attached to the policy was, that if any person insuring any building or goods at the Ætna office, should describe the same otherwise than as they really were, so that the same might be insured at less than the rate of premium specified in the printed proposals of the Company, such insurance should be void and of no effect. Evidence was given at the trial on the question, whether the plaintiffs had been guilty of fraud in procuring an over valuation of the goods destroyed; and among other evidence, the judge allowed proof on the part of the plaintiffs, of their good character for integrity. This was objected to, and made one point of exception by the defendants.

The defendants insisted that the description of the goods, as being in a house filled in with brick, was a warranty which must be strictly complied with. The judge so considered it; but he received evidence to show that the wrong description was either a mistake of the plaintiffs, or of the agent of the defendants; and charged the jury that if the plaintiffs made no representation of the character of the property *insured, but the agent of the Com- **[*674** pany took it upon himself to describe it, the plaintiffs were not bound to answer for the error. That if the plaintiffs did made the descrption, but not fraudulently, for the purpose of getting insurance at a reduced rate, but through mistake, still they were entitled to recover.

The defendants' counsel excepted to the decisions and charge of the judge.

Verdict for the plaintiffs for $3,042.80.

On the bill of exceptions,

Mr. Talcott, Atty-Gen., for the defendants, now moved for a new trial. He insisted that the judge erred in admitting evidence of the plaintiffs' character. (4 Esp., 50; Bull. *N. P.*, 296.)

The description of the premises in the policy was conclusive in a court of law. It amounted to an express warranty; and being written, controlled the printed clauses. The description was material to the risk. (Phil. Ins., 125; Whart. Dig., 321, pl. 36; *Id.*, 329, pl. 118; 14 Mass., 106; 1 Dall., 164.) A representation amounts to a warranty, if it appear to have been so intended by the parties. (2 Cai., 48; 2 Binn., 371, 372; 4 Mass., 337, 340; 3 Dow, 262.)

The warranty being falsified, it was not material whether it was the result of fraud or mistake. In neither view could the plaintiffs recover. (3 Dow, 255.)

Messrs. G. C. Bronson and *H. Maxwell*, contra. It is well settled in this court, that good character may be given in evidence in answer to a charge of fraud. (3 Cai., 120.)

The surveyors of the insurance company generally describe the subject of insurance. If this be their business, the plaintiffs should not suffer for the inaccuracy.

The description is mere matter of representation, and not a warranty. The authorities cited on the other side are of marine insurance, and do not apply. That description of insurance forms an exception in this respect. The present case must rest on general principles; and 675*] *clearly, upon that foundation, this mere representation cannot be considered a warranty. Marine polices are a peculiar class of contracts; and their meaning was settled by judicial decisions. (1 Burr., 347.) These policies are generally effected on the representation of the assured (3 Burr., 1909); and many times the subject is at too great distance to undergo the examination of the underwriter. If the clause in question is to be tested by ordinary rules, it is clearly no warranty. (1 Johns., 96; 4 *Id.*, 421; 20 *Id.*, 196.) The proposals show the meaning of the parties. They are, substantially, that misdescription shall not vitiate, unless it be fraudulent. Whether the description was intended as a warranty, was a question of intention, as in other cases of representation.

Curia, per SAVAGE, *Ch. J.* As to the evidence of character, it was said by this court, in *Ruan* v. *Perry*, 3 Cai., 120, "that in actions of tort, and especially charging a defendant with gross depravity and fraud, upon circumstances merely, evidence of uniform integrity and good character, is oftentimes the only testimony which a defendant can oppose to suspicious circumstances." The rule in England is this: "that in a direct prosecution for a crime, such evidence is admissible; but when the prosecution is not directly for the crime, but for the penalty, it is not." *Atty-Gen.* v. *Bowman*, 2 Bos. & P., 532, *note a.* That was an information against the defendant for keeping false weights, and for attempting to corrupt an officer. Eyre, *Ch. B.*, said: "I cannot admit this evidence in a civil suit." If such evidence is admissible here, it will be proper in every case where unfair practices are alleged. A specific fraud is charged, that must be met upon its own merits, unless supported only by circumstances; as in the case of *Ruan* v. *Perry*, where a naval officer was charged with gross fraud and collusion with a foreign officer, upon slight circumstances. If such evidence is proper, then a person may screen himself from the punishment due to fraudulent conduct, till his character becomes bad. Such a rule of evidence would be extremely dangerous. Every *man must be answerable for every im- [*676 proper act; and the character of every transaction must be ascertained by its own circumstances, and not by the character of the parties.

I think it very immaterial as regards this action, whether the error in description arose from design or mistake. The question is, did this description amount to a warranty that the property answered the description? The judge at the circuit so considered it; and it was admitted on the argument, that if the principles of marine insurance are applicable to fire insurance, it is a warranty. In the case of *Stetson* v. *Mass. Mutual Fire Ins. Co.*, 4 Mass., 337, Sewall, *J.*, lays down the law thus: "The estimate of the risk undertaken by an insurer must, generally, depend upon the description of it made by the insured or his agent. A mistake or omission in his representation of the risk, whether willful or accidental, if material to the risk insured, avoids the contract." For this he cites 1 Marsh. Ins., 335, 339. That writer states that a warranty being in the nature of a condition precedent, must be fulfilled by the insured, before performance can be enforced against the insurer; and whether the thing warranted was material or not, whether the breach of it proceeded from fraud, negligence, misinformation, or any other cause, the consequence is the same. (1 Marsh., 347.)

In relation to the sale of personal property, it is held that a bill of parcels is not a warranty that the goods are what they are represented to be. (2 Cai., 48, and other cases down to 20 Johns., 198.) But in relation to policies of insurance, it is held that a description of a vessel is a warranty. For instance, the description of a vessel as Swedish is a warranty of her national character. (Phil. Ins., 125, and cases cited; 8 Johns., 237, 319.) Several cases in 2 H. Bl., 574, &c., show that the conditions attached to the policy are to be considered parcel of the instrument.

No cases have been produced, to show that a description of property insured by a policy against fire, is to be *construed differ- [*677 ently from a description in a marine policy. I can perceive no reason why there should be a difference. "Insurance," says Ld. Mansfield, "is a contract upon speculation." (3 Burr., 1909.) "The special facts upon which the contingent chance is to be computed, lie most commonly in the knowledge of the insured only; the underwriter trusts to his representation," &c. He says the insured need not state what the insurer knows, but the keeping back the true state of the property is a fraud.

In this case, the plaintiffs ought to have known the true state and condition of their house, and have truly represented it. Not having done so, they fail in their action. The property burned is not the property insured.

This is not a case in which equities should be considered. It is a sort of gambling, a speculating upon chances; and the parties must be held strictly and literally to their contract.

I think the judge misdirected the jury, and that a new trial should be granted.

New trial granted.

S. C.—7 Wend., 270.
Opposed—1 Md., 295.
Denied—27 Am. Rep., 196 (28 Kan., 756).
Cited in—7 Wend., 274; 12 Wend., 460; 16 Wend., 654; 5 Hill, 193; 5 N. Y., 480; 7 N. Y., 372; 2 Barb., 151; 10 Barb., 290; 22 Barb., 537; 1 Hall, 418; 2 Hall, 638; 1 Sand., 555; 8 How. (U. S.), 248; 65 Mo., 243; 40 Am. Dec., 348; 26 Am. Rep., 63 (57 Ind. 381); 40 Am. Rep., 9 (4 Lea., 233); 41 Am. Rep., 119 (56 Iowa, 571); 42 Am. Rep., 196 (28 Kan., 756).

JACKSON, ex. dem. HASBROUCK,
v.
VERMILYEA.

Possession of Small Tract Under Lease, with Claim of Title to Whole, Constitutes Adverse Possession of Whole—Conveyance of Land held Adversely, Void—Constructive Possession—Reservation of Mill-site—Includes What—Not an Easement.

A lease of a small tract of land, *e. g.*, 63 acres, and actual possession by the lessee, of a part, with a claim of title to the whole, constitutes an adverse possession of the whole.

And while it is so possessed, a conveyance, by any one except the adverse possessor, to another, of a part of the land so possessed, though it also include an adjoining parcel not so possessed, and the grantee enter upon the latter parcel, claiming to the whole extent of his conveyance, will not constitute the grantee, a constructive, or actual possessor, beyond the parcel on which he enters.

If one have constructive possession by color of title, and occupying a part, another cannot acquire a constructive possession to the same extent, in the same manner; but though the latter enter on part, with color of title to the whole, and claim the whole, his possession will be confined in extent, to the part which he actually occupies.

An exception of a mill-site, in a grant or lease, operates as an exception of the soil of the mill-site; and so much land as is necessary for the mill-pond, and for erecting and carrying on the business of a mill.

It is not the reservation of a mere easement; but of the soil itself; and the grantor or lessor, or his assigns, may enter upon and locate under the exception, even after the grantee, or lessee, has conveyed, or assigned, or mortgaged his interest to another.

Citation—1 Cow., 286.

EJECTMENT for 25 acres of land, including a grist-mill in Middletown, Delaware Co; **678***] tried at the circuit in that *county, Sept. 1, 1823, before Nelson, *Circuit J.*; when a verdict was taken for the plaintiff, subject to the opinion of this court, on a case.

Messrs. Ruggles and *Hasbrouck*, for the plaintiff, cited 16 Johns., 184; 4 *Id.*, 81; 10 Johns., 435.

Messrs. Sherwood and *Parker*, contra, cited 2 Cow., 283; Runn. Ej., 113; 1 Wils., 220; Bull. *N. P.*, 110.

The facts are stated in the opinion of the court, which was delivered by,

WOODWORTH, *J* The plaintiff claimed title as the assignee of a mortgage, executed by Noah Ellis to Phillip Sickler, dated Oct. 5, 1811.

The premises described contained 25 acres, and included part of a grist-mill in possession of the defendant. It appeared that Ellis was in possession of the premises at the date of the mortgage, by virtue of a lease from Gen. Armstrong to him, and continued in possession for several years thereafter, when he surrendered to the mortgagee.

The defendant disclaimed having possession of any part of the 25 acres, excepting the mill and mill-site. He read, in evidence, a lease from Armstrong to Andrew Sickler, dated Oct. 10, 1818, for the mill and mill-site, and 25 acres of land, being the premises in question, which lease was assigned to the defendant. A lease from Armstrong to Ellis, dated May 1, 1802, was given in evidence by the plaintiff. It was admitted to have lately come from the hands of Armstrong. The signatures were erased and the seals torn off. A corner of the lease with part of the description of the premises were also torn off.

By the case, the lease was to be produced on the argument; it has not been delivered to me. I am, therefore, unable to say whether it contained any reservation of part of the premises. This fact is, then, to be ascertained by the testimony of Ellis, which was not objected to. He says the lease was in his possession when the mortgage was given; that the corner was torn off accidentally; that the seals remained on as long as he held it. The description of the *premises included a part of the mill. [***679** Ellis also testified that he did not know that the defendant had ever been in the actual occupation of any part of the premises, excepting the mill and pond. He could not say from recollection, but he believed the lease contained an exception of mill-sites, from the circumstance of his obtaining permission from Armstrong to build the mill; and from knowing that mill-sites were excepted in all his leases. The witness never claimed the mill-site under his lease. On this state of facts, I think we are to consider, that, in the lease to Ellis, the mill-site was excepted. I presume by inspection of the lease, it cannot be determined whether excepted or not. This, however, is not expressly stated. I apprehend that neither party would be disposed to rest on parol testimony, as to the contents, unless the lease had been defaced, or a part of it destroyed.

On this statement, the plaintiff made out a title to recover the 25 acres, excepting so much as was comprehended within the mill-site reserved, provided the defendant was in possession of the land not included in the mill-site. He admitted he had possession of a part (the mill and mill-site), not exceeding two acres. The plaintiff offered no testimony as to the extent of the defendant's actual occupancy; but contends that, as Armstrong conveyed to the person under whom the defendant derives title, the whole 25 acres, the defendant is to be considered as the possessor to that extent.

It appears that the premises are woodland. There are no improvements. The right of Ellis passed to the plaintiff by virtue of the mortgage. The land had never been actually occupied; but it will be recollected that the lease to Ellis contained 63 acres, of which the 25 acres mortgaged were parcel; that Ellis actually occupied a part of the 63 acres, and claimed title to the whole; so that, although the 25 acres were unimproved, he had a good adverse possession to the whole, on the ground of occupancy of a part, and a lease including the 63 acres. The conveyance obtained from Armstrong in 1818, although it includes the 25 acres, conferred no title to anything but the mill-site; **680*]** *neither can it operate so as to transfer to the defendant a constructive possesssion of the 25 acres, in consequence of his having possession of the small parcel comprising the mill-site.

I think the defendant must be considered as claiming title to the 25 acres, having accepted an assignment of the lease which comprised them.

Color of title under a deed, and occupancy of a part, is sufficient proof to constitute an adverse possession to a single lot. (1 Cow., 286.) This principle applies only to cases where there is no actual occupancy under a different claim. Thus, if A takes a lease or conveyance for a lot of 63 acres, and improves a part, his possession is valid for the whole lot; not on the ground of having title, which draws the possession after it, until an actual adverse possession commences; but on the ground of a claim of title to the whole, and a possession of part, which constitutes a good adverse possession. When a valid possession is acquired in the latter mode, it cannot be defeated by a subsequent entry on the same lot, making an improvement of a part, and obtaining title to the whole. The effect of such subsequent entry would be, to give the person so entering a possession of the part actually occupied and improved, but no further. A constructive possession to the unimproved part of the lot, would remain in him who made the first entry under claim of title, and improved a part. Apply this principle to the present case. The possession under Ellis, of the 25 acres, was not impaired by the assignment of the lease of 1818, to the defendant, and occupation of the mill by him. It appears that Ellis never claimed the mill-site. The consequence is, that the defendant was not in possession of the 25 acres, except that part thereof which constituted the mill-site; and for that portion the plaintiff is not entitled to recover.

Neither can he recover that part which is covered by a part of the mill and the pond, supposed to contain not more than 2 acres; because Armstrong, having reserved mill-sites in his lease to Ellis, afterwards granted the same by a conveyance under which the de- **681*]** fendant claims. And although *there is no specific description of the quantity of land reserved, it must be intended to include so much as might reasonably be required for the purpose of erecting and carrying on the business of a mill. The defendant has located and entered upon a small parcel for that purpose; which the facts in the case do not enable me to say was unreasonable or too extensive. It is contended that the reservation was merely an easement or privilege; but this is evidently a mistake. A mill-site is reserved, which is a reservation of so much land as may be necessary for the purpose of erecting and working a mill. The plaintiff has not shown how much land the defendant actually occupies as a mill-site. The defendant admits the quantity of two acres. Under his grant, he must be considered as having located this parcel, as appurtenant and necessary to the mill. There is nothing in the case to show that this was too extensive. It is not material, whether the location was made before or after the execution of the mortgage; for if the mill-site was reserved, no right to it was acquired by the mortgage; and the defendant might actually enter on, and locate the premises, as well after as before.

I am, therefore, of opinion that, as to the mill-site on which the mill was erected, the defendant has shown title; and as to the 25 acres of woodland, the defendant was not, in judgment of law, the possessor. Consequently, the defendant is entitled to judgment.

Judgment for the defendant.

Limited and distinguished—59 N. Y., 50.

Cited in—9 Cow., 282; 11 Wend., 37; 18 Wend., 84; 21 Wend., 294; 23 Wend., 321; H. & D., 20; 9 N. Y., 329; 8 Barb., 263; 33 Barb., 391; 54 Barb., 28; 1 Abb., N. S., 299; 1 Rob., 271; 2 Leg. Obs., 368 (37 Wis., 604); 25 Am. Dec., 234 (10 Me., 224); 37 Am. Dec., 191 (12 N. H., 9).

---

*WINCHELL [*682
v.
LATHAM, Executor of PORTER.

New Trial—Not Granted, because Verdict is Against Weight of Evidence—Examination of Witnesses—Promissory Note—Consideration—A Party Cannot go to the Jury on two Contradictory and Irreconcilable Grounds.

Where the testimony before a jury is contradictory, and the character and credit of witnesses are in question, a new trial will not be granted on the ground that the verdict is against the weight of evidence.

Where a witness is introduced by a party, and is interrogated as to a particular fact, and the opposite party, on cross-examination, asks him, generally, if he ever communicated that fact to any one, and to whom, and he answers that he communicated it to the party calling him; this does not entitle the party calling him to pursue the inquiry as to his own reply, and other conversation with the witness at the time of the communication.

Otherwise, if the witness be asked, on cross-examination, specifically, whether he made the communication to the party calling him.

It seems that a note given by a devisor, in his lifetime, to secure a devisee in a will, against the alteration or revocation of the will, is without consideration and void.

Where the maker, the defendant, sought to impeach a note, by showing the want of a valuable consideration; and the plaintiff answered by proving a pecuniary consideration; and the defendant replied by evidence of the plaintiff's declarations, that the consideration was not pecuniary, but the note was given upon a special agreement between the parties; held, that it should not be left to the jury, to say whether the note was not sustained by the consideration stated in the plaintiff's declarations, as proved by the defendant.

A plaintiff cannot go to a jury upon two distinct and inconsistent propositions proved by himself, or established by his own proof, in connection with his declarations as proved by the defendant.

Citations—1 Johns., 139; 3 Johns., 506; 7 Johns., 341; 2 W. Bl., 1249.

ASSUMPSIT, tried at the Oneida Circuit, Apr., 1826, before Williams, *Circuit J.*

The action was on three promissory notes, dated respectively Jan. 21, Apr. 21, and Nov. 13, 1823, the last for $2,100.20, made by the testator and payable to the plaintiff.

NOTE.—*New trial—Conflict of evidence—Verdict against weight of evidence—Newly discovered evidence.* See Wilkie v. Roosevelt, 3 Johns. Cas., 208, *note*; Halsey v. Watson, 1 Cai., 24, *note*; Mercer v. Sayre, 7 Johns., 306, *note*.

After the plaintiff had proved the handwriting of the testator to the several notes, the parties went into evidence touching the consideration of the large one, which, with the points arising upon it, and the other matters material to the questions decided, will be found stated in the opinion of the court.

The jury found for the plaintiff, with $2,-468.44 damages.

A motion was now made, in behalf of the defendant, for a new trial.

Messrs. W. H. Maynard and *T. J. Oakley*, for the motion, cited 1 Johns., 139; 3 *Id.*, 506; 7 *Id.*, 341; 4 *Id.*, 235; 3 *Id.*, 199; 13 *Id.*, 379; 4 Dall., 111, 130.

Messrs. S. Beardsley and *G. C. Bronson*, contra.

Curia, per SUTHERLAND, *J.* The only matter in controversy between the parties, is the note of Nov. 13, 1823, for $2,100.20, which purports to have been signed by Oliver Porter, the testator of the defendant. There seems to be no doubt of the genuineness of the signature. But it is contended by the defendant, **683***] either that *it was obtained from Porter by imposition, when he was in a state of intoxication, or that he supposed it to be a small note, probably for twenty-one dollars and twenty cents; and that the word "hundred" was fraudulently inserted by the plaintiff, either before or after it was signed; or if signed with a knowledge of its contents, that it was given without any legal consideration. The body of the note is in the handwriting of the plaintiff.

The real nature of this transaction is involved in great doubt and mystery; and I have seldom had occasion to examine a case, in which I found it so difficult to arrive at a satisfactory conclusion. The witnesses were very numerous, and their testimony extremely contradictory; and the verdict of the jury must have been very essentially influenced by the general character and appearance of the witnesses, and their manner of testifying. Some of them were directly impeached; others were shown to have given various and contradictory accounts of the same transaction; others stood in different degrees of relationship, or connection with the parties; and may have been supposed, by the jury, to have testified under the influence of strong prepossessions.

In truth, the case is characterized by all the circumstances which render it peculiarly proper for the determination of a jury; and, without intending to express any opinion as to the weight or preponderance of evidence, we have no hesitation in saying that the verdict is not so clearly and unquestionably against it, as to justify us in setting it aside on that ground.

The motion for a new trial must, therefore, be denied, unless the judge erred in the admission or rejection of evidence, or in his charge to the jury.

It does not appear, from the case, that any exception was taken upon the trial, to any decision of the judge, or to any opinion expressed by him in his charge to the jury. We should be justified, therefore, in refusing to entertain any question in relation to either. But it is not within the recollection of the court, that this objection was taken upon the argument. In a case of so much importance, therefore, *we will presume that exceptions were, [***684** in fact, taken, and that the formal statement of them was unintentionally omitted in drawing the case.

The first exception relates to the testimony of Simon Hyde. He was a witness for the defendant; and, in his direct examination, stated, that in Nov. or Dec., 1823, Winchell showed him a note, upon the back of which was written Oliver Porter's note, for $2,100 and some cents, which he believes to be the note in question. Winchell was then on his way to Connecticut, and the witness asked him how he came by such a note against Porter? Winchell replied that he had some money which he did not wish to carry with him to Conn., and he had left it with Porter, because he knew it would be safe, and that he would not use it.

Upon his cross-examination, he was asked by the plaintiff's counsel, if he had ever told anybody that he had seen such a note, or that the plaintiff had such a note, and if he had, when and whom? The witness answered, that the first person to whom he mentioned it was Porter, the testator; that it was after Winchell's return from Conn.; but how long he could not tell. The counsel for the defendant then asked the witness what Porter said about the large note when he gave him the information? This question was objected to by the plaintiff's counsel, on the ground that the defendant could not give in evidence the declarations of Porter in his own favor; and the objection was sustained, and the question excluded by the judge. The decision of the judge was undoubtedly correct. The witness was not asked whether he had ever informed Porter that he had seen the note. But the question was general, if he had informed anybody, and whom. He was the defendant's witness; and it is not to be supposed that the plaintiff knew what his answer would be. The question was not, therefore, put with the view or expectation of bringing home to Porter knowledge of the existence of the note; but for the purpose, probably, of testing the accuracy of the witness, by compelling him to name the individuals to whom he had communicated the *fact, if any; [***685** so that they might be called to corroborate or impeach him. The disclosure, therefore, came out accidentally; and did not lay the foundation for a course of inquiry which the defendant had not a right to pursue upon the direct examination. Occurrences of this sort are not only common, but inevitable in almost every trial. It is impossible to anticipate what the answer of a witness will be, to a general question, until his answer is given. If it is of a nature which would have been inadmissible upon a direct and specific inquiry, the course is, not to permit the inquiry to be pursued, and the evidence to be repelled by other testimony, but to exclude the answer from the consideration of the jury, so far as it was improper to have been given. There is no danger of a jury being misled or prejudiced by such circumstance. The presiding judge will explain to them why they are to disregard the evidence; and that no inference is to be drawn from it against the opposite party, because he is precluded from pursuing the inquiry, and explaining it. If the plaintiff's counsel had asked specifically, whether the witness ever communicated the information in relation to the note to Porter, what Porter said on that occasion would probably have been competent evidence, for the inquiry could have been made with no other view than to raise the presumption of his admission of the genuineness and validity of the note; and that presumption the opposite party, of course, ought to be permitted to repel. The question would be considered as embracing, not only the information communicated by the witness to Porter, but Porter's answer also; and the answer would then be evidence against the plaintiff, having been called for by him. But there would be no safety in putting a general question to a witness upon his cross-examination, if his answer might be the means of rendering the declaration of the opposite party evidence in his own favor, without being called for by his antagonist.

The remaining objections are to the charge of the judge.

686*] *The first exception is unfounded in fact. It is, that the judged erred in not charging the jury, when required so to do, that if the note of $2,100.20, was given as a security for the will made by Porter, the testator, in favor of the plaintiff, it was not given on a good legal consideration; and that, therefore, the plaintiff could not recover upon it. The defendant submitted that proposition in writing to the judge, and requested him so to charge the jury. And he did expressly charge them, that the legal proposition, so submitted by the defendant, and which he repeated to the jury, was well founded in law; and that it was for the jury to decide whether it was or was not applicable to the state of facts in the cause. That is, if they believed, from the evidence, that the note in question was given by Porter to the defendant, as a security or guaranty against Porter's canceling or altering his will, by which he had devised his farm to the plaintiff, then the plaintiff could not recover on that note—the consideration being one which would not support such a promise. The charge, on this point, is unexceptionable.

The next point taken, is, "that the judge erred in charging the jury that the plaintiff could recover, if the note was given for any other consideration than the one the plaintiff had attempted to prove."

The course taken upon the trial was this: the plaintiff first proved the execution of the note, and that he had worked for Porter for about a year, at $1 per day, and had paid and advanced several small sums of money for him. He then rested; and the defendant proceeded to impeach the note, by proving the declarations of the plaintiff, about the time when the note was given, which went to show that he then claimed only a small sum as due from Porter. 2. By showing, that from Porter's circumstances in life, and means of living, and habits of business and industry, it was extremely improbable that he could have contracted so large a debt. That the productions of his farm were nearly, if not quite, sufficient to support his family; and that he studiously avoided contracting debts; and that his representatives found no money among his effects **687***] after *his death. 3. By proving the declarations and admissions of the plaintiff, that the note was given for the security of the will, as he expressed it. To these declarations, several witnesses testified—Noah Clark, Israel Phelps, Jesse Carpenter, Solomon Stockwell and Robert Eells.

The defendant then rested, and the plaintiff called witnesses to prove that this note had been recognized and admitted by Porter. That it was composed of several smaller notes—one of $500, one of $450, and several others, the amounts of which were not recollected by the witness; and $450 in cash, and a book account, &c. That he repeatedly declared that he owed the plaintiff money, and offered his farm for sale, and demanded $2,000 down; and then told the plaintiff, he being present, that if he sold his farm he would pay him. On other occasions, he declared he owed the plaintiff a great deal of money, as much as his farm was worth; and that he could not pay him without selling his farm.

Thus, the effort on the part of the plaintiff was to sustain the note, by proving an actual pecuniary consideration for it, either by express proof of that fact or by implication, from the acknowledgment and recognition of the note by Porter. He did not pretend that it was given for any other consideration; and all the evidence on his part was intended to repel and rebut the evidence given on the part of the defendant, the object of which was to show, either that the note was fraudulently obtained, or altered by the plaintiff; or if not, that it was given as a guaranty against the change of Porter's will. All the evidence as to the latter point consisted in the proof of the plaintiff's declarations and admissions. The plaintiff, of course, gave no evidence in support of that allegation.

Upon this state of the evidence, after the counsel for the defendant had submitted the written legal proposition to the judge, which has already been stated, the plaintiff's counsel also submitted a proposition, upon which they asked the judge to instruct the jury. It was, "that if, from the facts in the case, the jury believed that the plaintiff, having the will of Porter in his favor, was apprehensive that *Porter might will the farm to some [***688** one else; and was, therefore, about to leave him; and that Porter, to induce him to remain with him, and labor for him while he lived, gave him the note in question; and that the plaintiff faithfully performed that agreement on his part; that it was a sufficient legal consideration for the note; and if they believed that the note rested wholly upon this consideration, or upon this, coupled with a pecuniary consideration, as to a part of the amount, that the note in either case was founded upon a sufficient legal consideration." In relation to this proposition, the judge remarked to the jury, that it was substantially correct; and that they were to consider whether the note had been given upon a full and valuable consideration, either for money due, or money and services rendered, or to be rendered, by the plaintiff for Porter, or on the consideration stated in the proposition, submitted by the plaintiff's counsel, which was supported, the judge observed, by the evidence to be drawn from the confessions of the plaintiff, compared with other evidence. And if they should be of opinion, from the evidence, that either of the considerations alluded to was the consideration of the note, and that the plaintiff had performed what he had undertaken on his part, and that no fraud or imposition had been practiced by the plaintiff in obtaining the note, then it was supported by a sufficient legal consideration, and the plaintiff would be entitled to their verdict.

It appears to me that this charge was calculated to mislead the jury. There was not a particle of evidence that the note was given upon the consideration mentioned in the plaintiff's proposition, to wit: that Porter, having made his will in Winchell's favor, and Winchell being apprehensive he would change it, was about to leave him; and that Porter then, to induce him to remain and work for him as long as he lived, gave him the note in question. It will be perceived that the previous will had nothing to do with the consideration supposed. And all that relates to it might be expunged without affecting the legal character of the proposition. It is neither more nor less than this: that if Winchell agreed to live with, work **689***] for, and *take care of Porter during his life, and in consideration thereof, Porter gave him the note for $2,100, and Winchell performed his part of the agreement, there was a good consideration for the note. Now there was not a particle of evidence of any such agreement or contract. The confessions or declarations of Winchell, as proved, were, that the note was given to secure the will, or for fear Porter would alter his will, and cheat him out of his property and earnings.

But the judge also charged the jury that this consideration was supported by the evidence to be drawn from the confessions of the plaintiff, as proved on the part of the defendant; thus making the plaintiff's own confessions and declarations evidence to support a consideration, totally different from that which he had endeavored, during the whole course of the trial, to prove was the true consideration; and which he had produced witnesses to support by their oaths. If the consideration for this note was not entirely pecuniary, then Benjamin Shattuck, the principal witness for the plaintiff, was guilty of the most gross and deliberate perjury, and must have been suborned by the plaintiff himself. Can a party be permitted to go to a jury upon two distinct and entirely contradictory and irreconcilable grounds? Suppose the plaintiff had first proved that the note was given upon a pecuniary consideration; but apprehensive, from the evidence given by the opposite party, that his witnesses would not be credited, had then called another lot of witnesses, who testified that it was given upon the contract or agreement which has been supposed: in the first place, would he have been permitted to do it? And if he had been, should the jury have been instructed, that either of the considerations proved, would support the note? Ought they not rather to have been charged, that the witnesses effectually destroyed each other; and that neither were entitled to credit? That the plaintiff, by taking two contradictory grounds, had deprived himself of the benefits of both? Can the declarations of the plaintiff himself, when proved by the defendant, be more available to the plaintiff than the **690***] same facts *would be, if the plaintiff himself had established them by competent evidence? If the plaintiff had acquiesced in the evidence given by the defendant, as to the consideration of the note, and had reposed himself upon it as a legal consideration, there would have been no objection to it. But instead of that, he denies that that was the consideration, and produces a multitude of witnesses to establish another and entirely different one. He maintains, and he labors by his evidence to prove, that the declarations which he is shown to have made as to the considerations, were false; and yet the jury are instructed that if they believe those declarations, the plaintiff is entitled to recover.

Under these circumstances, the case appears to me to bear a strong analogy in principle to that class of cases in which it has been held, that, where the consideration is set forth in a written contract, evidence to show that a greater or different consideration was intended, is inadmissible. (1 Johns., 139; 3 Johns., 506; 7 Johns., 341; 2 W. Bl., 1249.) That rule, it is true, is founded on the established doctrine, that a written contract cannot be contradicted or varied by parol. But so far as that doctrine has any foundation in moral principle, independent of considerations of public policy, it is this: that a party shall be concluded by his own solemn declarations, and shall not be permitted to prove that what he has once declared in writing was the sole consideration was not so. With how much more force does the principle apply to a case, where that declaration is made by the oaths of moral and responsible beings, in the presence of God and man, swearing by the procurement, and at the instigation of the party himself; and where the contradictory evidence consists of his own declarations and confessions? To permit those declarations under such circumstances to be used in this way, appears to me to be subversive of all morals.

In this respect, therefore, we think the judge erred, and that a new trial must be granted.

New trial granted.

Cited in—24 Wend., 352; 5 Barb., 457; 11 Barb., 384; 37 Barb., 529; 39 Barb., 96; 6 Duer, 125.

---

*COLES *v.* CARTER. [*691

Assault and Battery—Evidence of Former Recovery Inadmissible Under General Issue.

A former recovery is not admissible evidence under the general issue, in an action of trespass; *e. g.*, an action of assault and battery.

Whether it is otherwise in an action on the case, or *assumpsit*, *quære*.

Citations—3 Cow., 120; 4 Cow., 559; 3 Burr., 1353; 1 Chit. Pl., 472, 475, 496; 10 Johns., 111, 246; 12 Johns., 455; 14 Johns., 511.

ASSAULT and battery, tried at the N. Y. Circuit, Oct. 13, 1825, before Edwards, *Circuit J.*

The plea was not guilty, with notice of *son assault demesne*, and *molliter manus imposuit*, in defense of the defendant's possession.

After proof had been given at the trial, touching the assault, the defendant offered in evidence the record of a former recovery by him for an assault and battery, in an action in the

C. P. of N. Y., by the defendant against the plaintiff, and one Clason, in which the very question now in controversy was tried. The record was objected to as not between the same parties, and because it was not pleaded in this action. The judge, however, received it. The weight of evidence was decidedly in favor of the identity of the question in the two actions of assault and battery, and that the points of trial were the same in both suits; but the judge left this (among other questions of fact) to the jury, who found for the plaintiff.

A motion was now made in behalf of the defendant, for a new trial, on the ground, among others, that the jury should have found for the defendant, upon the evidence of the former recovery.

Mr. J. Anthon, for the motion, relied on *Gardner* v. *Buckbee*, 3 Cow., 120, and *Burt* v. *Sternburgh*, 4 Cow., 559, as conclusive upon this point.

Mr. G. S. Raymond, contra, denied the application of those cases. He said, the first was in *assumpsit*, where special pleading is almost entirely dispensed with, and in the latter no question of pleading was raised. The rule is different in trespass, and *assumpsit*. In trespass, it is well settled that a former recovery must always be pleaded. (3 Burr., 1353.)

Curia, per SAVAGE, *Ch. J.* In the cases of *Gardner* v. *Buckbee*, 3 Cow., 120, and *Burt* v. **692***] *Sternburgh*, 4 *Cow., 559, the rule was recognized as sound law, which was very deliberately settled by the twelve judges in the *Duchess of Kingston's* case; that the judgment of a court of concurrent jurisdiction, directly upon the point in issue, is, as a plea, a bar, or, as evidence, conclusive between the same parties, upon the same matter directly in question in another court.

If the jury, in this case, by their verdict, intended to negative the fact of the transaction being the same, it is certainly a verdict against evidence. But if the record was improperly admitted, and that testimony be stricken from the case, then the verdict is sustained by the evidence.

The important question, therefore, is, whether the evidence was admissible under the general issue, for it is not embraced by the notice. The defendant's counsel contends that this point has been settled in the two cases referred to; but, in the latter case, the point could not arise; and though it was raised in the first, yet Woodworth, *J.*, who gave the opinion of the court, expressly declined deciding it. But if it had been decided in that case, the decision would not govern this. That was *assumpsit*; this is trespass. In *Bird* v. *Randall*, 3 Burr., 1353, Ld. Mansfield took a distinction between actions on the case, and actions for torts. He says, a former recovery, release, or satisfaction, cannot be given in evidence in actions for torts, but must be pleaded. But an action on the case is founded on the mere justice and conscience of the plaintiff's case, and is in the nature of a bill in equity and, in effect, is so; and therefore, in such a former recovery, &c., need not be pleaded, but may be given in evidence. Chitty adopts the same distinction. (1 Chit. Pl., 472, 475, 496.)

This court has often decided, in actions on contract, that a former recovery must be pleaded. In *Fowler* v. *Hait*, 10 Johns., 111, the court say: "The defendant, having omitted to plead or give notice of the former trial and judgment, was precluded from giving evidence of it at the trial." So, also, in *Dexter* v. *Hazen*, 10 Johns., 246, and in *Brown* v. *Wilde*, 12 Johns., 455. These were all actions *on the case; [***693** the first two on contract, the last for fraud. They were also in a justice's court, where, at least, as great latitude in pleading is permitted, as in the higher courts. In *Lyon* v. *Tallmadge*, 14 Johns., 511, on an appeal from chancery, Spencer, *J.*, says, "the decree in the former cause, to have been available, should have been pleaded, or relied on in the answer as a bar.

From all these cases, it seems to be settled, that evidence of a former recovery cannot be admitted under the general issue, at least, in trespass. I am of opinion, therefore, that the motion for a new trial be denied.

New trial denied.

Cited in—2 Hill, 481; 50 Barb., 111.

JOHNSON *v.* BRIDGE.

Set-Off—Must be Against Plaintiff of Record.

A set-off cannot be made of a debt or demand against any one, other than the plaintiff on the record.

Thus, where the plaintiff purchased a negotiable promissory note of the payee, after the note was due; and the payee was indebted at the time of the purchase to the maker; in an action by the holder against the maker, held, that the demand of the latter could not be set off against the holder; and that it was not in any view, a defense to the action.

Citation—5 Cow., 231.

ASSUMPSIT; tried at the Madison Circuit, Mar., 1826, before Williams, *Circuit J.*; when a verdict was found for the plaintiff.

Certain exceptions were taken to the decision of the judge, who sealed a bill of exceptions, on which,

Mr. J. A. Spencer now moved for a new trial. He cited 5 Johns., 118; 5 Cow., 376.

Mr. P. Gridley, contra, cited 16 Johns., 226; 19 *Id.*, 49, 52.

The facts, with the points decided, are stated in the opinion of the court, which was delivered by,

WOODWORTH, *J.* The plaintiff declared on a promissory note, dated Mar. 12, 1823, payable June 1, 1824, to Shelden Smith or bearer. The defendant gave notice of a set-off of a note, made by Smith to J. A. Spencer, or bearer, payable on demand; and dated July 12, 1825. Also a judgment obtained by the defendant against Smith, in June, 1825.

*The plaintiff proved that he pur- [***694** chased the note; and July 25, 1825, called on the defendant, demanded payment, and stated that he had purchased the note on the Saturday preceding. The defendant said he would settle or pay it. Shortly after, the defendant called at the plaintiff's house, said he had failed to obtain money, as he expected, and wished the plaintiff not to prosecute.

The defendant offered to prove his note and

the judgment as a defense. The judge rejected the evidence, on the ground that the defendant had not set up such claim at the time the plaintiff made a demand of payment, but had promised to pay or settle. The defendant excepted, and a verdict was found for the plaintiff.

The promise, in this case, to pay, was without consideration, as the plaintiff had previously purchased the note; and the defendant did nothing to induce the plaintiff to purchase.

On a different ground, however, I think the evidence inadmissible. In the case of *Wheeler* v. *Raymond*, 5 Cow., 231, the doctrine of set-off, when relied on against the plaintiff on the record, was fully considered. It was there held that the Act has reference to persons dealing together, and having demands against each other; that, in such cases, a set-off is allowed; but that where the plaintiff on the record is a stranger to the set-off, and the demand not against him, the set-off was not within the provisions of the Act, which declares, that if the plaintiff is overpaid, the jury shall find a verdict for the defendant, and certify how much the plaintiff is indebted more than the sum demanded; and that the defendant shall have judgment and execution for the balance. If this be a sound construction of the Act, it follows that the set-off is allowable only in those cases where, if it exceeds the plaintiff's demand, the defendant may compel the plaintiff to pay the excess.

It will not be pretended that this plaintiff was liable to judgment and execution, had the defendant's set-off exceeded his note. It is true, the plaintiff took the note, subject to the equity which existed between the payee and **695***] maker. *But it must always be understood as inseparable from that principle, that the equity, or defense relied on, is such as may be used consistently with the established forms of proceeding in a court of law. They cannot be made to yield to the particular hardship, if any, of a given case. A set-off is only available, in consequence of the statute, and in the manner there pointed out. When a defendant cannot place his defense within its provisions, he can derive no benefit from it. In the case of negotiable paper, a defendant who has a *bona fide* set-off may sustain an injury; but it is for the Legislature to extend the remedy. This construction of the Act does not impair any defense, not depending on the question of set-off. If the defendant had paid the note in fact, or shown it was not valid in its origin, or otherwise discharged, before transfer, and after due, no difficulty would lie in his way. But that is not the case. The ground of defense is a set-off, which would be unobjectionable in an action in the name of the payee; but it is not valid against the plaintiff, who sues in the character of indorser, or bearer. The motion for a new trial must be denied.

New trial denied.

Affirmed—5 Wend., 342.

Cited in—9 Cow., 299; 7 Wend., 226; 4 Hill, 197; 4 N. Y., 527; 23 How. Pr., 296; 5 Mason, 213, 217; 25 Am. Dec., 54 (10 Conn., 30); 26 Am. Dec., 708 (6 N. H., 469).

See 11 Wend., 504.

TOWNSEND & TOWNSEND
v.
CARMAN, Impleaded with RING.

Debt on Judgment Against Two Joint Debtors—One not Arrested.

Debt lies on a judgment against two joint debtors, though one was not arrested, and did not appear in the original action.

In debt on such a judgment, it is sufficient, in answer to a plea of the one who was not taken in the original action, that the debt for which that action was brought, was the sole debt of the other defendant, to prove the sole admission of the former, that the debt was joint.

As to the one who was taken, *semb.* the record is conclusive that the debt was joint.

Whether it is conclusive against both, *quære.*

Citations—2 Johns., 87; 16 Johns., 66; 6 Johns., 98; 1 R. L., 521, sec. 13.

DEBT on judgment, tried at the Albany Circuit, Sept. 6, 1826, before Duer, *Circuit J.*

The judgment declared on, was in favor of the plaintiffs against Ring, as impleaded with Carman, the latter not being brought into court or appearing. This appeared upon the *record in the original action. And [***696** now Carman pleaded those facts to this action; and also that the promises, &c., for the non-performance of which, the judgment in that action was rendered, were the promises of Ring solely—and not the joint promises of both the defendants. Replication, taking issue on their being the sole promises of Ring, and not the joint promises of the defendants.

At the trial, the judge held that the only material question was upon this issue; and he overruled the counsel for the defendants, who insisted that the record in the former cause was inadmissible as evidence; and that no action could be maintained upon the judgment, its operation being limited by statute. The judge also decided that the jury need not pass upon the first branch of the plea.

The plaintiffs, therefore, had a verdict, on proving by (Carman's admissions, which were objected to as evidence) that the original promises were joint. The defendants excepted; and now on the bill of exceptions,

Mr. J. L. Wendell, for the defendants, moved for a new trial.

Mr. P. S. Parker, contra.

Curia, per SUTHERLAND, *J.* It is admitted, on the face of the pleadings, that the judgment was obtained in the manner stated in the plea. The judge, at *Nisi Prius*, therefore, decided correctly in saying, that the only inquiry was, whether there was a partnership between Ring and Carman, when the original debt was contracted. That was the only issue joined; and it was the duty of the judge to try it, whatever might be his opinion of its materiality. The evidence given by Cameron and by Wheeler was offered for the purpose of proving a partnership, from the confessions and admissions of Carman himself, and not for the purpose of establishing an original individual liability on his part. The objection to its admission under the pleadings was properly overruled.

The general objection, that an action of debt cannot be maintained on such a judgment, is

disposed of by the cases of *Dando* v. *Doll*, 2 Johns., 87; *Bank of Columbia* v. *Newcomb*, 6
697*] *Johns., 98, and *Taylor* v. *Pettibone*, 16 Johns., 66; in all of which the point was presented, and clearly and distinctly passed upon by the court. The Statute, 1 R. L., 521, sec. 13, declares that the plaintiff shall have his judgment and execution against such of the defendants as were brought into court, and against the other joint debtors named in the process, in the same manner as if they had all been taken and brought into court, by virtue of such process; and the only restriction imposed by the Act upon the effect of the judgment and execution is, "that it shall not be lawful to issue or execute any such execution, against the body, or against any lands or goods, the sole property of any person not brought into court." There is nothing in the Act restraining the plaintiff from bringing an action of debt upon such judgment, against all the defendants, nor from using the judgment as evidence of the indebtedness of all. If an action can be sustained upon such judgment, it must be against all. The judgment is to be entered in the usual form; and so far as depends upon the Act, is to be followed by the usual consequences, with the restrictions particularly specified. The judgment is, *prima facie*, evidence of a debt against the party not brought into court. (16 Johns., 66.) How far, or in what respect, he may be permitted again to enter into the merits of the original action, and show that he ought not to have been charged, it was not thought necessary in the previous cases, nor is it in this, to determine. The defendant here, was allowed the benefit of the only defense which he claimed; that the original debt was contracted by Ring solely, and not by Ring and himself jointly. But he failed, in the opinion of the jury, in establishing that fact; and we see no ground for disturbing the verdict. The motion for a new trial must be denied.

New trial denied.

Affirmed—6 Wend., 206.
Cited in—14 Wend., 223; 23 Wend., 295; 4 Den., 58; 4 N. Y., 538; 2 Sandf., 17; 1 Duer., 23; 4 Rob., 242; 8 Leg. Obs., 125; 47 Am. Dec., 240.

698*] *FARNSWORTH v. GROOT.

Erie and Champlain Canals—Packet Boats not to be Detained by Freight Boats.

In passing on the Erie and Champlain Canals freight boats are bound to afford every facility for the passage of packet boats, as well through the locks, as elsewhere on the canal. And where a freight boat, passing west on the Erie Canal was waiting for the emptying of a lock, when a packet boat overtook her, held that the packet boat should pass first.

On request, the master of the freight boat refusing to consent to this, the master of the packet may use all necessary means to obtain the preference due to him, short of a breach of the peace; as by pulling back the freight boat, and forcing his own forward; for which no action of trespass will lie, no unnecessary damage to the freight boat being done.

If the freight boat be detained or injured through the obstinate resistance of the master, to the exercise of the right of preference of the packet; this is the fault of the former, for which, he cannot recover damages, against the master of the latter.

Citations—Act, April 13, 1820 (sess. 43, ch. 202, secs. 4, 10.

ON ERROR from the Schenectady C. P. Groot sued Farnsworth in a justice's court, in trespass, for obstructing the former in passing a lock on the Erie Canal, and recovered $5. On appeal to the Schenectady C. P., Groot recovered $15.

In the latter court, it was proved at the trial, that Groot had arrived at the lock before Farnsworth, both passing west. It was regularly Groot's turn to pass the lock, which was not more than a quarter empty when Farnsworth arrived. Groot commanded a freight boat, and Farnsworth a packet boat. Farnsworth, on coming up, asked permission of Groot to pass first, which Groot refused. Farnsworth then demanded it as a right. On being refused, he ordered his hands to push back Groot's boat, which (on seeing the packet boat approaching) the latter had hauled up into the jaws of the lock. The boats were thus both wedged into the lock. Farnsworth's hands attempted to push back Groot's boat, but it was held fast by his hands. This was substantially the case, as made out by Groot, the plaintiff below. According to the defendant's witnesses, he (the defendant below) gave no orders to interfere with Groot's boat, but it was some of the passengers who pushed the boat. After about half an hour's detention, the defendant below ordered his boat back, and the plaintiff below passed first.

The court below denied a motion for a nonsuit, at the close of the plaintiff's testimony; and after the defendant had closed his case, decided that his matters of defense were insufficient, and so instructed the jury, who found for the plaintiff below.

*The defendant below excepted; and [*699 the cause came here on the record and bill of exceptions.

Messrs. Beck and *Linn*, for the plaintiff in error.

Mr. M. T. Reynolds, contra.

Curia, per SAVAGE, *Ch. J.* It is important, first, to ascertain the relative rights of the parties. By the 4th section of the Act for the Maintenance and Protection of the Erie and Champlain Canals, and the works connected therewith, passed Apr. 13, 1820, sess. 43, ch. 202, it is, among other things, enacted that, "if there shall be more boats, or other floating things, than one below, and one above any lock, at the same time, within the distance aforesaid (100 yards), such boats and other floating things shall go up and come down through such lock by turns as aforesaid, until they shall have passed the same; in order that one lock full of water may serve two boats or other floating things." By the 10th section (p. 186), it is enacted "that, in all cases in which a boat, intended and used chiefly for the carriage of persons and their baggage, shall overtake any boat, or other floating thing, not intended or used chiefly for such purpose, it shall be the duty of the boatman, or person having charge of the latter, to give the former every practicable facility for passing; and, whenever it shall become necessary for that purpose, to stop, until such boat for the carriage of passengers shall have fully passed." And a penalty of $10 is imposed for a violation of this duty.

It was evidently the intention of the Legis-

lature that packet boats should not be detained by freight boats, as it was known that the packets would move faster than the freight boats; and, in the language of the Act, every facility was intended to be afforded them. But the right of passing when both are in motion might be of little use, if the packets must be detained at every lock until all the freight boats there have passed before it. The fair construction of the Act, undoubtedly, is, that the packets shall have a preference on any part
700*] of the canal; and to be of *any use, this right must exist at the locks as well as on any other part of the canal.

In my judgment, therefore, the defendant below had the right of entering the lock first, and the plaintiff below was the aggressor in attempting to obstruct the exercise of that right. Did the defendant, then, do more than he lawfully might, in endeavoring to enforce his rights? No breach of the peace is pretended. No injury to the boat was done. The plaintiff below was detained, and so was the defendant; but the detention was occasioned by the fault and misconduct of the plaintiff himself. What right, under this view of the subject, has the plaintiff below to complain? The defendant below was the injured party. The plaintiff below was indeed liable to a penalty; but that could not prevent the defendant below from using proper means to propel his boat, and to remove the obstruction caused by the plaintiff below. Suppose, in any part of the canal, the defendant below had overtaken the plaintiff below; and the latter had refused to permit the former to pass; and had placed his boat across the canal; would not the defendant below have been justified in attempting to remove the obstruction, without injury or breach of the peace? This, I presume, will not be denied. The defendant below has done no more. I think, therefore, the court below erred in refusing to instruct the jury that the plaintiff was not entitled to recover, and the judgment should be reversed.

Judgment reversed.

701*] *GRAVES ET AL.
v.
MERRY AND GILBERT.

Partnership—Dissolution of—General Notice Sufficient, Except as to Those who have had Dealings with Firm—Authority of One Partner to Sign Notes in Firm Name, Implied from Circumstances.

General notice in the Gazette of the dissolution of a partnership is sufficient, as to all persons who have had no previous dealings with the firm.

But as to those with whom the firm has dealt, such constructive notice is not enough. Actual notice must be shown; otherwise, as to these, the act of one of the former firm in the partnership name, will bind all the former partners.

An authority to one partner, to sign notes in the partnership name, for debts of the firm, may be implied from circumstances.

From what circumstances such authority may be inferred.

Ci i s—2 Johns., 304; Peake *N. P.*, 254; 6 Johns., 144. tat on

ASSUMPSIT on a promissory note; tried at the Oneida Circuit, Oct., 1825, before Williams, *Circuit J.*, when the following facts appeared.

The defendants executed a promissory note, Mar. 19, 1824, dated that day, and payable to the plaintiffs, by the style of Graves, Griffin & Co., for $537, on which was indorsed a payment. Dec. 3, 1823, Griffin, one of the plaintiffs, signed a note, of that date, Graves, Griffin & Co., payable to the order of John Johnson & Sons, of the City of N. Y., for $472.65; and Oct. 11, 1824, it was indorsed by them to the defendants, without recourse. The plaintiffs, Graves, Griffin & Hickox, had been partners in trade at Paris, in Oneida Co.; but, by agreement in writing, dated and executed Apr. 1, 1823, dissolved their partnership. On the same day, a notice of dissolution signed with their names at length, was published in the Utica Gazette, printed in the County of Oneida, and put up at several places in the neighborhood of their residence. The notice stated that the business would be continued by Graves & Griffin, under a firm of that title; and they immediately after carried on business accordingly, at the place of the old firm. The plaintiffs did no business afterwards as partners. The defendants had knowledge of the dissolution, before the note was given to Johnson & Sons.

In Oct., 1824, the note to Johnson & Sons was shown to Hickox, who said it was an honest debt against the firm; but they could not avow it, as they could not then pay their old debts; that they must have the amount due from the defendants, to pay their bank debt; and the defendants ought not to have bought the note. After this, Graves said the plaintiffs intended to sue the defendants so quick that they could not set off the Johnson note. Three notes had been signed Graves, Griffin & Hickox, *in the handwriting of Graves, in [***702**
Oct. and Nov., 1823.

The defendants relied on the note to Johnson & Sons as a set-off; and a verdict was taken for the plaintiffs, subject to the question whether it was admissible.

Mr. C. P. Kirkland, for the plaintiffs. One partner cannot bind another in any case after dissolution, even by giving a note for a previous debt of the firm. (The cases cited in 2 Johns. Dig., new ed., 169, 170.) The cases there cited also show, that the notice of dissolution in this case was sufficient.

Mr. H. R. Storrs, contra. Admitting the dissolution and notice to have been perfect, there is evidence in the case of an implied authority to each member of the firm, still to execute partnership notes for the old debts of the firm. (3 Esp., 6; 1 *Id.*, 61; 1 Camph., 485; 1 Johns. Cas., 110; 2 Stark., 290; 5 B. & A., 447; 2 Johns., 307; 1 Cai., 184.)

But we stand in the place of the payees, Johnson & Sons. With them the plaintiffs had dealings before their dissolution. Johnson & Sons, therefore, were not affected by a constructive notice in the newspaper. As to them, the plaintiffs continued partners till actual notice was given. None is proved to have been given at any time.

Curia, per WOODWORTH, *J.* The question to be decided, is, whether the note signed by Joel Griffin, in the copartnership name, to Johnson & Sons, was obligatory on all the plaintiffs.

In the notice of set-off, it is stated that the

defendants would, on the trial, give in evidence, that Dec. 3, 1823, certain persons, under the name of John Johnson & Sons, were partners in the City of N. Y., and that the plaintiffs on that day, at N. Y., made a promissory note, the handwriting of one of them being thereto subscribed; and thereby promised to pay John Johnson & Sons, or order, one day after date, $472.65, with interest, which was indorsed to the defendants Oct. 11, 1824.

703*] *At the trial, a note of this description was given in evidence without objection. The case states that the defendants proved that the signature of the note was in the handwriting of Joel Griffin; and that it was indorsed to the defendants by the payees. From this statement I infer that the payees composed a firm in the City of N. Y.

If the note was valid against all the plaintiffs, when in the hands of Johnson & Sons, the defendants are entitled to the benefit, for they acquired the right of the payees. Whether the defendants had knowledge or not, of the dissolution, at and before the giving of the note, is perfectly immaterial. The contract in favor of Johnson was negotiable. Whether prosecuted in their names, or that of an indorsee, does not affect the question of liability.

A further inquiry is, was the note of Dec. 3, 1823, given for a debt contracted at that time, or previous to the dissolution of the partnership? This is a material fact. There is nothing expressly stated in the case on this point. If the cause had been submitted to the jury, one question would have been, whether the evidence warranted the inference, that the note was given for a debt contracted during the existence of the partnership? On the finding of this fact, would in part depend the question, whether the notice of dissolution was published in such a manner as to affect Johnson & Sons with notice? As the verdict is subject to the opinion of the court, we may draw the same conclusion from the facts proved that the jury might have done.

I incline to think that, during the acknowledged existence of the partnership, the plaintiffs became debtors to Johnson & Sons. I infer this from the fact proven, that the plaintiffs did no business of any kind; as partners, after their dissolution in Apr., 1823; that Hickox admitted it as a joint debt against the firm, and spoke of it as an old debt; and the remarks of Graves, who does not seem to question their being indebted; but rather that the defendants could not avail themselves of a set-off. I should certainly understand the witness, who said the **704***] plaintiffs did *no business as partners after the dissolution, as affirming that no new copartnership debt was contracted As then, it is evident, from all the testimony, that the plaintiffs were debtors, at some time, to Johnson & Sons, it is necessarily referred to a period prior to the dissolution, in Apr., 1823.

If, then, the facts are established, that the payees of the note were merchants residing in N. Y., that the plaintiffs, while partners, became indebted to them, and afterwards one of the firm gave a note for the debt in the copartnership name, the question of law arises, whether Johnson & Sons had notice of the dissolution when the note was executed. No other notice as to the payees is pretended, except the publication in Utica.

The rule seems to be, that notice in the newspapers, of a dissolution of a partnership, is sufficient notice to all persons who have had no previous dealings with the firm. This doctrine was recognized as reasonable and just, in *Lansing* v. *Gaine & Ten Eyck*, 2 Johns., 304. It has received repeated sanction in the English courts. The case of *Graham* v. *Hope*, Peak. *N. P.* Cas., 254, is directly in point. The defendants had been in partnership when the plaintiffs sold them goods. Afterwards the partnership was dissolved, and notice given in the London Gazette; and after this notice, the plaintiffs sold and delivered the goods for which the action was brought. Ld. Kenyon held that the Gazette was not, of itself, sufficient notice to the plaintiffs. He laid it down as a general rule, that it was incumbent on persons dissolving a partnership, to send notice of such dissolution to all the persons with whom they had dealings in partnership. In *Ketchum* v. *Clarke*, 6 Johns., 144, this question was considered. *Mr. Justice* Van Ness, in giving the opinion of the court, observed, that it had not been settled by any decision in this court, when a partnership is to be dissolved, so as not to bind the copartnership by a new contract. He thought, we ought at least to go so far as to say, that public notice must be given in a newspaper of the city or county where the partnership business was carried on; *that public no- [***705** tice in some reasonable manner must be given; and that would conclude all persons who have had no previous dealings with the firm; but as to persons in the habit of dealing with the firm, public notice was not sufficient by the English law. The necessity and justice of these rules, in that case, received the sanction of this court. It follows that Johnson & Sons, having dealt with the plaintiffs previous to the notice of the dissolution, cannot be affected by it. Although the giving of the note was a new contract, yet, until notice of dissolution was given to Johnson & Sons, such partner was competent to bind the firm, to all persons not chargeable with notice of such dissolution.

Independent, however, of this ground, I think it may be inferred that Joel Griffin acted with the knowledge and assent of the former partners. It is not necessary to prove assent expressly. It may be inferred from circumstances. Perhaps a jury, had this question been submitted to them, might have considered the evidence not satisfactory. I cannot say, that had they found a verdict either way I should be disposed to set it aside. That, however, is a question not before us; we are called on to decide this fact. Upon mature deliberation, I am satisfied that neither Hickox nor Graves, intended to draw in question the authority to give the note. Hickox's admission is express. When he says it was an honest debt against the firm, it must refer to the note, for that was then presented to him. It was an admission that the firm were holden. There is no direct admission by Graves. He does not put this objection on the want of authority, but on other ground. If there was no authority, the presumption is, it would have been suggested, because that disposed of the question at once. Instead of doing so, he puts his objections on ground altogether untenable—the commencement of a suit by the plaintiff so quick as to defeat a set-off. This was said after the note was indorsed to the defendants. No matter how soon the plaintiffs prosecuted, they could not, by that act, gain any advantage. The right to a set-off was valid, provided the plaintiffs were liable on the note. **706***] *From the facts, I think the court are warranted in presuming the assent of Graves. The defendants are entitled to judgment for $7.54, being the excess of their note over the plaintiff's demands.

Judgment for the defendants.

Cited in—8 Wend., 424; 17 Wend., 528; 22 Wend., 193; 12 N. Y., 287; 69 N. Y., 575 (25 Am. Rep., 248); 24 Hun, 262; 2 Barb., 553; 12 Barb., 54; 5 Bos., 12; 2 McLean, 461; 57 Ill., 219.

JACKSON, ex dem. ERWIN ET AL., v. MOORE.

Conveyance of Land—Quantity Yields to Boundaries—What is most Material and Certain Prevails Over that which is Less so—Extrinsic Evidence Inadmissible—How far Tenants in Common are Affected by Acts of Co-tenants in 'Locating Lands under Deed—Presumption of Grant—When Allowed—Trusts—How Evidenced.

In the description of parcels in a conveyance of land by boundaries, or number of the lot, or other certain designation, the quantity being mentioned in addition, without an express covenant that the land contains that quantity, the whole is considered as mere description; and quantity being the least certain part, must yield to boundaries, or the number of the lot, or other more certain description.

Effect should be given to every part of the description, if practicable. But if the thing to be granted, appear clearly from any part of the description, and other circumstances are mentioned, not applicable, the grant will not be defeated; but the false or mistaken part will be rejected.

What is most material and most certain, shall prevail over that which is less material and less certain. Thus, course and distance shall yield to natural and ascertained objects, as a river, a stream, a spring, or a marked tree.

Thus, where a conveyance was, of "two tracts or parcels of land, lying, &c., being township No. 3, &c., also township No. 4, &c., to be 6 miles square; and containing 23,040 acres each, and no more," &c., though these tracts were in fact 6 by 8 miles in size; held that the whole 6 by 8 miles passed.

Such a description is not ambiguous in a legal sense, so as to be a subject of elucidation from extrinsic evidence.

The acts of a portion of the grantees, tenants in common, in locating land under a deed, will not affect the co-tenants, unless it appear that they sanctioned these acts in some way.

And the court will not, in such a case, presume a grant, for the purpose of quieting ancient possessions.

A grant of land will never be presumed from lapse of time, unless it be so great as to create the belief that it was actually made; or unless the facts and circumstances in the case show that the party to whom it is presumed to have been made, was legally, or equitably entitled to it.

A trust in lands (except a resulting trust) must be manifested in writing; but it may be declared either before or after the conveyance to the trustee.

To make out a resulting trust, by the payment of the consideration money by one, the deed being taken in the name of another, the money must be paid at or before the execution of the deed.

One may, by the same conveyance, take an undivided portion of the land to himself in his own right; and be a trustee for other portions in the same land; and afterwards he may buy in, and take a conveyance to himself from any or all of his *cestui que trust*; in which case he ceases to be a trustee, and becomes the absolute owner of the share or shares so purchased in by him.

Note (*a*) to this case, contains the English doctrine of parcels.

Citations—1 Cai., 493; 2 Johns., 37; 15 Johns., 471; 5 Mass., 355; 13 Vin. Abr., pl. 24; Cro. Car., 447, 473; 7 Johns., 217, 238; 18 Johns., 81; 4 Mass., 146; 5 East. 41; 1 Cow., 612; 5 Cow., 74, 371; 6 Wh., 582; 7 Wh., 10; 4 Johns., 140; 9 Johns., 100; 11 Johns., 123; 17 Johns., 29; 3 Johns. Cas., 109; 10 Johns., 377; 1 Cowp., 102; Bull. *N.* P., 74; 3 T. R., 157-159; Phil. Ev., 455, 129, *n.* (*a*); 1 R. L., 54; 2 Ves., 696; 5 Johns. Ch., 12, 19; 2 Johns., Ch., 405, 409; 2 Atk., 71; 16 Johns., 197; 3 Johns., 216.

EJECTMENT; tried at the Steuben Circuit, Jan. 13, 1824, before Throop, *Circuit J.*, when the following facts appeared:

The lessors of the plaintiff claimed as the children and grandchildren and heirs at law of Arthur Erwin, who died in June, 1791, intestate, leaving ten children, five of whom are lessors. The seven remaining lessors are the children of his daughter, Sarah Mulhollon; she left eight *children, one of whom is not [***707** a lessor. The extent of the plaintiff's claim was five tenths and seven eighths of another tenth of the interest of their ancestor in the premises in question. But it was conceded that the right of all the lessors, except the children of Sarah Mulhollon, were barred by the Statute of Limitations; so that the recovery of the plaintiff, if he should be entitled to recover at all, could only be for seven eighths of one tenth of the interest of which Arthur Erwin died seised, in the premises in question. The premises were designated as lot No. 4, in the Gore, east of township 3, 5th range (as surveyed by Augustus Porter), in the Town of Canisteo, in the County of Steuben, containing 162 acres. It was admitted, at the trial, that the defendant was in possession of that lot when the action was commenced. When that was, did not appear in the case, but the demise was laid May 2, 1816.

Both parties derived their title from Oliver Phelps. The conveyance under which the plaintiff claimed bore date Sept. 17, 1790, and was from Oliver Phelps to Arthur Erwin, Solomon Bennet, Joel Thomas and Uriah Stephens. It purported to convey to them, their heirs and assigns, "two tracts or parcels of land, lying and being in the district of Erwin, County of Ontario, and State of N. Y., being township number three in the 5th range; also number four in the 6th range; to be six miles square, and containing twenty-three thousand and forty acres each, and no more; and known by the name of the old Canisteo Castle." The consideration expressed in the deed was £2,666 13*s.* 4*d.* This conveyance was confirmed by Nathaniel Gorham (who was a joint proprietor with Phelps of the large tract called Phelps and Gorham's purchase, of which these townships were a part), by his deed of Feb. 1, 1792.

This tract was surveyed and run into townships by Augustus Porter and Frederick Saxton, for Phelps and Gorham, in 1789. The corners of the townships were marked, though the lines were not run so as to test the contents with accuracy.

*The original agreement for the Er- [***708** win purchase was made Aug. 18, 1789, be-

NOTE.—1. *Real property—Deed—Construction of—Natural objects control distances, &c.* 2. *Resulting trust.*

1. *As a general rule of construction, what is most material and certain controls that which is less so; courses and distances* yield to visible and ascertained objects. See Doe v. Thompson, 5 Cow., 371, *note.*

2. *Resulting trust.* See Jackson v. Matsdorf, 11 Johns., 91, *note.*

tween Oliver Phelps of the one part and Solomon Bennet and Elisha Brown of the other. It was before the tract was run into townships by Porter; and the numbers of the towns were not specified. It was for two townships, each town to be six miles north and south and five miles and a half east and west, lying in the County of Ontario, &c.; to be located in such a manner as to take in part or all of the old Canisteo Flat, and not to derange the adjacent towns.

The history of this purchase appeared from the testimony of Uriah Stephens, Jr., to be this: In the early part of 1789 a number of persons came into the western part of this State to buy land. In order to purchase cheaper and on better terms they formed a Company, consisting of twelve persons, and Solomon Bennet and Elisha Brown, two of the associates, were selected to go to Oliver Phelps and make a purchase for the Company. In pursuance of such authority they went and entered into the contract of Aug. 18, 1789. The purchase was approved of by the Company, and soon after Arthur Erwin, Solomon Bennet and Joel Thomas were deputed by the Company to go to Canandaigua, where Phelps resided, to complete the purchase. They accordingly went, and took a deed for township 3, 5th range, and township 3, 6th range. Uriah Stephens was made a party to the deed by the request of Phelps, and afterwards signed the notes which were given for the consideration money. It was soon discovered that the Canisteo Flats, which the Company wished to purchase, were not covered by these lots, but were covered by township 3, 5th range, and township 4, 6th range. Erwin, Bennet, Thomas and Stephens accordingly went to Canandaigua in Sept., 1790, to get a deed for those townships, and to deliver up the former one. Phelps agreed to give them a new deed, provided they would consent to strike ½ mile by 6 from each township, so as to make them 5½ by 6 miles. As considerable improvements had been made on township 3, 5th range, it was agreed that, in-
709*] stead of taking ½ mile from that *township, one mile in width should be taken from township 4, 6th range, so as to leave township 3 six miles square, and township 4 five miles by six. In pursuance of this arrangement, the deed of Sept. 17, 1790, was executed by Phelps to Erwin, Bennet, Thomas and Stephens, for the two entire townships; and they, on the same day, reconveyed to him one mile by six off the west side of township 4, 6th range.

Before these representatives of the Company went to Canandaigua to consummate the previous contract, and soon after that contract was made, to wit: Oct. 18, 1789, they entered into a covenant with their eight associates, that they should have eight twelfths of the two townships purchased of Phelps. The eight associates covenanted to pay to them eight twelfths of the consideration paid for the land, and also the same proportion of the costs and expense of procuring it; to be paid in three equal installments, May 1, 1790, 1791 and 1792. The four covenanted to execute a good deed to the eight associates for their shares, whenever they gave security for the payment of their proportion of the price and expenses.

The title to these two townships having been thus vested in the four, and they having given their associates legal evidence of their rights and interests, immediate measures were taken to survey and divide the townships into lots, and to distribute them among the partners.

Accordingly, Sept. 25, 1790, Arthur Erwin entered into a written agreement with the Company, to survey the townships into lots, for the consideration of £95. He staked out all the lots in township 4, and part of township 3, before his death, in June, 1791; but the lines were not closed. Sept. 20, 1791, the associates, by an instrument in writing, appointed Solomon Bennet, John Jamison and Uriah Stephens, Jr., a committee to assize and proportion the lots, and superintend the surveying thereof. This instrument was signed by seven of the original associates, and by Joseph Erwin, the son of Arthur, who professed to be the administrator of his father's estate, and to represent the family in the partition *and division of these townships. [***710**
Previously to that time, however, it had been discovered by Phelps and Gorham that there had been a mistake in the survey of these townships; and that instead of being six miles square, they were about six by eight miles. Phelps, in Aug., 1791, sent Augustus Porter, who had made the original survey, to correct the mistake. He cut off from the east side of township 3 12,099 acres, and from the north side of township 4 9,406 acres, which reduced them to the size originally intended. Porter, at that time, found upon township 3 Solomon Bennet, one of the twelve proprietors, who resided there, had made considerable improvements, and was then engaged in erecting mills upon his property. Porter stayed at Bennet's house, who was fully acquainted with the object of his coming; and he and others who were interested in the two townships accompanied and assisted Porter in making the survey.

The committee appointed by the Company Sept. 20, 1791, of whom Solomon Bennet was one, in Oct. following, after Porter had cut off the gores from these lots, employed one John Dunham, a surveyor, to complete the survey and subdivision of the township. The directions given to him by the committee were to close the lines in township 3, which had already been staked out, and to run out the remainder of the six miles square into other lots, to be in all 48 lots. In this number were included two, one for Hadley and one for Elisha Brown, in the place of two which, upon a former draft or division, had fallen to their shares, and which, upon Porter's survey, proved to be within the gore, and beyond the six miles. The directions to Dunham, in relation to the 4th township, were to run it into twelve lots of equal size, the whole being six miles north and south, and five miles east and west.

Those townships were accordingly divided, conformably to these directions, the proprietors conceding that they had no right to the gores run off by Porter. No claim was ever made to any portion of the land included in the gores, by any of the persons interested in those 711*] townships *from 1791 to the commencement of this suit in 1816. The survey and division thus made, was carried into effect by an agreement in writing, signed by several of the proprietors, and by Joseph Erwin, who declared himself to be the agent of the Erwin family, and professed to act for them. But no other member of the family was present, or participated in any of these proceedings. Nor was there any evidence of Joseph's authority to act for them, except what was derived from his own declarations, and their long acquiescence. Conveyances were executed by all the surviving associates, in conformity to the corrected survey of Porter; and all their acts and proceedings have practically admitted its correctness.

After the survey of Porter, the proprietors, Phelps and Gorham, treated and disposed of the lands within the gores in the same manner as they did the other parts of their purchase. Nov. 18, 1790, they sold and conveyed to Robert Morris the greater portion of their purchase, including the gores. Morris, Apr. 11. 1792. conveyed to Charles Williamson; who, Dec. 16, 1793, conveyed the premises in question to John Moore, the defendant. The residue of the tract was conveyed by Williamson to Sir William Pultney, Dec. 13, 1800; and from him, through several descents and devises, it has passed to the trustees of Sir John L. Johnstone's will, who are now the proprietors of what is undisposed of. Robert Troup, Esq., is their agent, in the management of this immense tract.

Arthur Erwin, Aug. 23, 1790, purchased from Christian Kress, one of the original associates, his share of the two townships: which Kress, on that day, conveyed to him by a quitclaim deed.

Verdict for the plaintiff, subject to the opinion of the court on a case, with liberty to either party to turn it into a special verdict or bill of exceptions.

Mr. E. Griffin, for the plaintiff, briefly opened the case, and stated the grounds on which the plaintiff relied. He said he had found no case 712*] where the description in the deed *was precisely like that in the conveyance of Sept. 7, 1790; but there are several cases substantially analogous; and he thought the court would find it settled upon authority, that the entire townships, mentioned in the deed, passed to the grantees, without regard to their quantity. (Cro. Eliz., 113; 2 Johns., 37; 15 Johns., 471.) He said the words, to be six miles, &c., are mere words of computation or description; and if there be a contradiction in the description, the part which is the most certain should be received. If the length of line is to control, from what part is the excess to be cut off? How is it to be located? The words are equivalent to giving lot No. 3, &c., in such a range, going round the tract by lines, boundaries and fixed monuments. Six miles, to such a monument, which is eight miles, carries us to the monument. Phelps' cutting off the excess shows that he understood the extent of the conveyance perfectly. Nothing has been done by the lessors of the plaintiff, to prevent their claiming according to the full extent of the grant to their ancestor. All the cases of binding location contrary to a grant, are where the parties have agreed and acquiesced for a long time. (7 Johns., 238.)

Mr. Platt, same side, said he should rely also on the following authorities: Cro. Car., 7; 14 Vin., 80, pl. 21, 24; Bac. Law. Tr., 106; 18 Johns., 81; 2 Mass. R., 380.

Messrs. C. G. Troup and *J. Emott*, contra. The words of the deed of 1790, do not embrace the whole of the township of eight by six miles. Both the language of the deed, and all the acts of the associates, show that towns of six miles only were intended. The towns passed by the deed; but were to be limited to six miles square. The words "to be" are strong to show the intent. The future tense is used, indicating some further act of location or restriction, should it become necessary. The words are not being so much, as in the leading authority relied on. (2 Johns., 37.) Probably neither party knew precisely what the contents were. The main view was to the Canisteo Flats. Neither party acted particularly in reference to quantity. A grant is but the declaration of the owner's will to transfer *what he has to another. (Hob., [*713 229.) There is no technical force in words describing parcels; though it is otherwise as to the quantity of interest. (Cowp., 9; 7 Johns., 217; 18 Johns., 81; *Id.*, 107.)

The intention of the parties should govern. (Cowp., 600; 1 Burr., 282; 3 Atk., 136; Willes, 332.) Here it is plain. The sale was by count; and when the grantees get their count, the deed is satisfied. We rely on the words "to be," as peculiarly expressive of intention. They meant, if the towns should turn out to be more than six miles square, they should be reduced to six miles. The words are restrictive. (Shep. Touch., 88; 1 Co., 154 *b;* Hob., 275; *Id.*, 175; 1 Wood, Convey., 355, Pow., *note;* 18 Johns., 110; 2 Cai., 327; 5 Johns., 345.) There is no difficulty in the location. The words of the description are answered, if the towns are reduced to six miles square in any way. When this is once done, it is final. *Id certum est quod certum reddi potest.* (Shep. Touch., 250; 10 Co., 64; Hob., 174; Perk., sec. 73; Bac. Max., Rule 23; 3 Bac. Abr., by Gwill, 391, tit. Grants, H; 1 Leon., 30; *Id.*, 254; 1 Roll. Abr., 725; 14 Mass., 149; 17 *Id.*, 211, 212; 3 Johns., 387.) A location by a part of the grantees is enough; and binds the others. A location by one of several grantees will bind, where the grant is to be located by the election of the grantees. (Co. Litt., 145 *a.*) This need not be done by the name of location. Any words or acts amounting to it are sufficient. (1 Roll. Abr., 725; Wing. Max., p. 21, Max., 15.) If the grantee die before the location is made, the grant is void. (Co. Litt., 145 *a;* 2 Co., 36 *a;* 1 Leon., 253; Hob., 174; 13 Johns., 212.) It may be void as to one, but good as to others. (Shep. Touch., 81; 4 Cruise Dig., 313, sec. 1, pl. 8.) In this view, if a location was necessary, the property never vested in Erwin at all.

The cases cited against us, are cases of intention; and cannot be wrested to pervert the meaning of the parties. (9 Johns., 267.) They go on the ground that the words of quantity in the deed, were intended as mere words of description or estimation. Not so in this case. To call them *so, would be doing vio- [*714 lence to the intention of the parties, and the very words they use, which should be taken together. (Bac. Max., Rule 25, p. 105; 1 Cai., 493; 16 Johns., 172.) If it be doubtful whether the words are those of description or restraint, they should be deemed the latter; for the law will not imply that words of erroneous description would be used. (Bac. Max., p. 76, Rule 13; 8 East, 104; 5 *Id.*, 51, 78, 81.)

Nor let it be said that the words are to be taken most strongly against the grantor. This rule is never resorted to, even in a deed poll, till every other rule of construction fails. (Bac. Max., Rule 3.) Here several deeds passed between the parties, in relation to the same subject matter, or at least having the same object in view, viz.: towns six miles square. They are explicit on this head; and not only show the intention of the parties, but for that purpose are to be regarded as one deed, as a single transaction. (1 Wood. Conv. by Powell, 355, *note;* 1 Johns., Cas., 91; 15 Johns., 458.) Not only the quantity is given, but we virtually have the length of line which is to fix the quantity.

But suppose the description in the deed to Erwin and others, to be equivocal. It is an ancient deed (3 Johns., 205; *Id.*, 296), and the usage under it will control as to location. That the cotemporaneous exposition of the parties shall, in such a case, be evidence, is a well settled rule. (3 Atk., 576, 577; 16 Johns., 23; *Id.*, 24; 13 Johns., 346, 347; 3 Johns., 8, 269; 2 Cai., 198; 1 Cai., 363; 1 Cow., 621.) The heirs of Erwin may be considered as adopting the prior acts of the others, and making them their own, by their long continued recognition and acquiescence. (4 Bart. Conv., 379; Pal.. Agency, 249.)

Even if the location of the parties was erroneous at the time, the court will not, at this day, disturb the possession. (9 Johns., 100; 17 *Id.*, 29; 11 *Id.*, 123; 7 *Id.*, 238.) Indeed, the court will presume a conveyance, in order to quiet that possesion. (6 Binn., 416; 10 Johns., 380, 381.)

715*] *Again; if Erwin, the grantee, had any title to the gore, he held as a trustee with others (3 Ves., 696; 12 *Id.*, 74; 5 Johns. Ch., 12, 18), and on his death, the title survived to the co-trustees. Thus, the legal title passed from his heirs by his death. (2 Cow., 229; 1 R. L., 54, sec. 7.) Nor is this a case where the court will presume a conveyance to the heirs from the co-trustees. They will sometimes do so, as between trustee and *cestui que trust.* (2 T. R., 684; 8 *Id.*, 122; 2 Johns. Cas., 321, 325.) But this is only under special circumstances, as where the equity is plain. (7 T. R., 50; 11 East, 483; 7 T. R., 2, 3; 4 *Id.*, 683; 8 East, 263, 266, 267.) Courts of law never interfere in this way, where the equity is doubtful (1 T. R., 737; 2 Johns. Cas., 325; 4 Johns. Ch., 310; 5 *Id.*, 184); or when there are facts to rebut the presumption of a conveyance. (2 Johns., 226.)

Here is, at least, a resulting trust, that may be proved by parol. (3 Johns., 221; 11 *Id.*, 96; 13 *Id.*, 63; 16 *Id.*, 197; 1 Johns. Ch., 582; 2 *Id.*, 405.) This resulting trust may exist, whether there be one or more purchasers. The money advanced by the ostensible purchasers was, by arrangement and agreement in writing, for the use of themselves and others. They acted as agents for the 12 associates, and the trust resulted to the whole. (1 Atk., 59, No. 414; 2 Ves. & B., 388; 2 Johns. Ch., 410.)

Lastly, the claim of the plaintiff is barred by the Statute of Limitations.

Mr. J. Platt, in reply. There cannot be a doubt, upon the various cases decided by this court, that the whole of the two townships passed to the four grantees, whether those townships were more or less. On this point, we have referred to the leading cases; nor need we do more. They are in point to the principles of construction for which we contend. If the deed be not good for the whole, it is void for uncertainty. No human being can tell where the six miles should be taken. If there was a mistake, a court of equity alone is competent to relieve. The townships had been surveyed, and their boundaries known and *fixed, and re- [***716** ferred to in the grant. The grantor was bound to know the quantity, at his peril. The acts of survey, grant and location were all his own. The deed locates itself.

We deny that here was a trust, within the meaning of the statute which saves the doctrine of joint tenancy. That means a declared or technical trust; not one existing merely in the minds of the parties. Here was no trust which could ever be enforced as such, either at law, or in equity. If it is relied on as a resulting trust, that may be, and is, in this case, repelled by parol evidence. (2 Johns. Ch., 405; 5 Johns. Ch., 1; 16 Johns., 197.)

At any rate, here was no trust as to the one twelfth, which was to be allotted absolutely to Erwin, or the other one twelfth which he purchased of Kress. In these portions Erwin had both the equitable and legal estate.

Curia, per SUTHERLAND, *J.* The plaintiff, if he can recover at all, is entitled, under the demise from the Mulhollons, the grandchildren of Arthur Erwin, to seven eighths of one tenth of two twelfths of the premises in question. Upon the same principle, he is entitled to that proportion of the residue of the 22,000 acres included in the gores. The case, therefore, is important, not only in principle, but in the extent of property which may be affected by its decision; and deserves, as it has received, the most deliberate consideration of the court.

The first question which arises is, as to the construction of the deed of Sept. 17, 1790.

It will be recollected that the terms of that deed in its descriptive part, are, "two tracts or parcels of land, situate in the district of Erwin, in the County of Ontario, being township No. 3, in the 5th range, also No. 4, in the 6th range, to be six miles square, and containing 23,040 acres each, and no more. If, instead of this verb "to be," the phraseology had been "being" six miles square, and containing 23,040 acres each, there is no question that the whole lots would have passed, whatever might have been their size and contents. (1 Cai., 493; 2 Johns., 37.) A lot *may be as precisely and [***717** definitely described by its number as by metes and bounds. A large portion of the land in the western district of this State is held under conveyances containing no other description or designation of the premises intended to be conveyed than the number of the lot; and it is perfectly settled, that when a piece of land is conveyed by metes and bounds, or any other certain description, all included within those bounds, or that description, will pass, whether it be more or less than the quantity stated in the deed. And when the quantity is mentioned, in addition to a description of the boundaries, or other certain designation of the land, without an express covenant that it contains that quantity, the whole is considered as mere description. The quantity being the least certain part of the description, must yield to the boundaries or number, if they do not agree. *Jackson* v. *Barringer*, 15 Johns., 471; *Powell* v. *Clark*, 5 Mass., 355. If a man lease to another the meadows in D. and S., containing 10 acres, and they, in truth, contain 20, all shall pass. (13 Vin. Abr., 79, pl. 24.)

In construing deeds, effect is to be given to every part of the description, if practicable; but if the thing intended to be granted appears clearly and satisfactorily from any part of the description, and other circumstances of description are mentioned which are not applicable to that thing, the grant will not be defeated; but those circumstances will be rejected, as false or mistaken. Cro. Car., 447, 473; *Jackson* v. *Clark*, 7 Johns., 217; *Jackson* v. *Loomis*, 18 Johns., 81; 4 Mass., 146; 5 East, 41.

What is most material and most certain in a description, shall prevail over that which is less material and less certain. Thus, course and distance shall yield to natural and ascertained objects; as a river, a stream, a spring, or a marked tree. (1 Cow., 612; 5 Cow., 371; 6 Wh., 582; 7 Wh., 10.)

To apply these principles to the case before us: It is contended by the defendant, that the **718***] words, "to be" six miles *square, "and containing 23,040 acres and no more," are words of restriction, and that they limit the grant to the size and quantity expressed. It is not pretended that they amount to a covenant. They are in the descriptive part of the deed, and form a portion of the only sentence which attempts to designate or describe the premises intended to be conveyed. The whole clause is, undoubtedly, to be considered as matter of description merely.

The parties to this deed, unquestionably, intended that it should operate as a complete and perfect conveyance. No subsequent survey was contemplated by them, as necessary to the location of the grant. The lots had previously been surveyed, and their corners marked by Porter. It is not an executory contract, but the consummation of an executory agreement, made in Aug., 1789; and by adverting to that contract, we shall perceive how the verb "to be" came to be used in the conveyance, instead of the participle "being." That contract was made in Aug., 1789, before the townships were run out. It was for two townships of land, to be so located, as to embrace the Canisteo Flats; and to be six miles north and south, and five and a half miles east and west. When the deed came to be drawn, the contract was undoubtedly referred to, as containing the stipulations between the parties: and the conveyancer adopted the phraseology of the executory agreement, without adverting to the fact that a survey had subsequently been made, and the towns run out, and their corners marked, and their size thereby ascertained. The acts of the grantees and their associates show that they considered the conveyance as perfect, and that no subsequent survey was to be made, nor anything else to be done on the part of the grantor. They immediately proceeded to locate their deed, and to subdivide the townships among the proprietors. The acts of Phelps also show that he entertained the same opinion, for as soon as he ascertained that the townships were more than six miles square, he had the excess run off, without any application to or consultation with his grantees. The original parties and their grantees, have proceeded throughout *upon the ad- [***719** mission that their rights were definitely settled by the deed; and that the only question was as to its construction. No future or prospective sense is, therefore, to be attached to the words "to be." Everything was complete and executed. The whole descriptive part of the deed was intended to designate a present subject of conveyance. To put a different construction upon it, would be inconsistent with the very nature of the transaction, and the manifest intention of the parties.

The words, "township No. 3, in the fifth range," constituted, of themselves, a perfect description, and designated the subject of the conveyance, beyond all doubt or ambiguity. If no other terms of description had been used, there would have been no difficulty in locating the grant, nor any doubt that the whole township would have passed. The subsequent part of the description, "being, or to be, 6 miles square," &c., is inconsistent and irreconcilable with that which preceded it. The one or the other must, therefore, be rejected. We have seen that that must be retained which is most certain and most material, and that the number of the township is, of itself, a perfect description. If the number of the township be rejected, there is no description left. It is a tract of land in the district of Erwin and County of Ontario, six miles square, and containing 23,040 acres; but in what part of the district or county, there is no means of ascertaining. The grant would, therefore, be void for the want of a sufficient designation of the subject. But suppose those terms to be retained and to operate by way of restriction or limitation; how are the six miles square to be located? From which part of the lot is the excess to be taken? From the north, the east, the west or the south side? The truth is, that no location could be made under the deed upon that construction, and it would have been void for uncertainty. Upon what principle did Phelps ascertain that the excess was to be taken from the east side of township 3, and the north side of township 4? Could he have recovered those portions of the townships from the proprietors, if they had been in possession, in an action of *ejectment? Unquestion-[***720** ably not. The rule of construction, contended for by the defendant, would lead to all these difficulties, and would be subversive of the whole grant.

The size and contents of the townships must, therefore, be considered as false or mistaken circumstances of description, and must yield to the precise and certain designation of the range and number of the townships.

We are, accordingly, of opinion that the whole of township No. 3, as originally surveyed by Porter, including the premises in question, passed by the deed from Phelps, of Sept. 7, 1790.(*a*)

(*a*) The English authorities upon this point do not vary from the American. The doctrine of parcels

721*] *The deed is not ambiguous, in a legal sense, so as to be subject to explanation or elucidation from extrinsic evidence.

The next inquiry is, whether the lessors of the plaintiff are concluded by a practical location of their deed, or an acquiescence in the corrected survey of Porter. It will be well recollected that Arthur Erwin died in June, 1791; that the gores were not run off by Porter, until the month of Aug. in that year; and that no practical location was made, as to that town-
722*] ship, by a survey and division *among the associates, until October following. Sarah, the daughter of Arthur Erwin, and the mother of his grandchildren who are lessors, was at that time a *feme covert*. She was married in 1777, and died in 1809. Her husband, Mulhollon, survived her, and died in 1815. There has, therefore, been no participation or acquiescence, on the part of the lessors or their ancestors, in the locations made, by which they are concluded. The cases upon the subject of location by the acts of the parties, and from long acquiesence, have, therefore, no application. (4 Johns., 140; 7 Johns., 238; 9 Johns., 100; 11 Johns., 123; 17 Johns., 29.)

The acts and declarations of Joseph Erwin,
723*] cannot affect *the lessors. There is no evidence that he was the authorized agent and representative of any portion of the Erwin family. He must be considered, therefore, as speaking and acting for himself alone. That the lessors have accepted their portion of the townships, as ascertained by the division made upon Dunham's survey in 1792, is highly probable, though it does not appear from the case. It does appear from the testimony of Thomas M'Burney and Dugald Cameron that other members of the family have paid the taxes upon their undivided portions of the Erwin share; but even that fact is not proved in relation to the Mulhollons.

It is not a case in which a grant will be presumed, for the sake of quieting ancient possessions. It is the ordinary case, of a legal title on one side, and an adverse possession short of twenty years on the other, unsupported by any admission or recognition of right derived from the acts or declarations of the lessor of the plaintiff, or those under whom they claim. In *Jackson* v. *Lunn*, 3 Johns. Cas., 109, a deed from the original patentees to Sir Peter Warren was presumed, under the following circumstances: The patent was granted in 1735, and the tract immediately surveyed and laid out into lots. In 1736, Sir Peter Warren asserted his claim to the whole tract, and took possession of it, by executing eleven leases, for different lots, to different persons, for lives, with a reservation of rent, and by putting the lessees into possession of the demised premises. In 1737 and 1742, he paid the quit-rents on the whole tract, and died in possession in 1752, by which the descent was cast upon his heirs. In the year 1767, these heirs leased two other lots, reserving rent; and at the commencement of the Revolutionary War, there were about 100 settlers on the land, all of whom acknowledged the title of the heirs. The defendant came into possession about 35 years after the first entry by Sir Peter Warren; and the court remark, that it is necessarily to be inferred, from the case, that he entered in subordination to his claim; as it is stated that that claim was not disputed and, consequently, was admitted by all the *settlers, until many years after [*724
the entry of the defendant. The defendant showed no title, but relied upon his possession, and the title which was shown in the original patentees, and which he contended, upon the evidence in the case, had never been conveyed to Sir Peter Warren. It was held, however, that, from the facts in the case, a deed from the original patentees to Sir Peter Warren was to be presumed. In *Jackson* v. *M'Call*, 10 Johns., 377, the question was as to the division line between two lots. The lots had been held and occupied, according to the line set up by the defendant, for 41 years. The occupants on both sides, and especially the ancestors of the lessor of the plaintiff, and the lessor himself, by building a stone wall on that line, had recognized it as the true line; and the court held that it ought not to be disturbed. The lessor of the plaintiff professed to hold his lot as patented to one Provost. No patent was produced or proved; but an order of the Colonial Council in favor of Provost, dated Feb. 8, 1764, directing a survey, and a sworn copy of a survey made by the Surveyor-General in pursuance of that order, were produced and proved. A subsequent patent was proved, which was bounded on the Provost patent. The court thought the evidence warranted the presumption that the ancestor of the lessor of the plaintiff was in possession as early as 1776, under a claim of title; and upon his death the descent was cast upon the lessor, who retained the possession at the time of the trial, in 1812. Upon this state of facts, the court remark, "we are then to conclude that the father purchased the Provost title at an early day; and from the fact of the order of the Council and the original survey by the government in 1764; and the recognition of it in the patent to M'Kenzie, in 1765, and the continual and undisturbed possession by the family of the lessor (for 36 years), a patent to Provost, and a deed from him to the elder M'Donald, might even have been presumed, for the sake of quieting the possession."

The distinction between these cases and the one at bar, is too apparent to require illustration.

*A grant of land will never be pre- [*725
sumed, unless the lapse of time is so great as to create the belief that it was actually made; or unless the facts and circumstances in the case show that the party to whom it is presumed to have been made, was legally or equi-

was very fully considered by several of the ancient, and some of the modern English books. These were fully referred to on the argument of the principal case, by the counsel for the defendant. Most of the ancient authorities were gone over in Stukely v. Butler, Hob., 168; and both ancient and modern are summed up and illustrated by Preston, in his Essay on Abstracts of English Titles, Vol. III., 205-210, 2d Lond. ed. This work combines authority with the present opinions and practice of English conveyancers.

The following cases will best explain the numerous difficulties and nice distinctions in which this subject is involved: Doddington's case, 2 Rep., 32; Prest. Shep. Touch., 244, 246; Doe v. Greathed, 8 East, 91; Ognel's case, 4 Rep., 48; Stukely v. Butler, Hob., 170; Goodtitle v. Paul, 2 Burr., 1089.

tably entitled to it. (1 Cowp., 102; Bull. *N.P.*, 74; 3 T. R., 157-159; Phil. Ev., 121, *et seq.*; and 129, *note a.*) None of those circumstances exist in this case.

If the whole townships passed by the conveyance of September, 1790, as we hold they did, then there certainly was no legal obligation on the part of the grantees to reconvey any part. Nor were they equitably bound to do it. If the township had contained less than was supposed, they would have had no claim on the grantor for the deficiency. The parties took their chance as to the size and contents of the townships; and neither was legally or equitably responsible for the result.

Those of the proprietors who have recognized the title of Phelps to the gores, would probably be concluded by such recognition. But the lessors of the plaintiff cannot be affected by their acts.

The only remaining inquiry is, whether Arthur Erwin had a legal interest in the two townships, to any extent, which descended to his heirs. The defendant contends that Erwin, Bennet, Thomas and Stephens, to whom the conveyance was made by Phelps, were trustees for the 12 associates; that they, therefore, held those townships as joint tenants, within the exception in the 6th section of the Act "Regulating Descents," &c., 1 R. L., 54; and that upon the death of Erwin, the legal title survived to his co-trustees.

The trust is not declared on the face of the deed. It is an absolute conveyance, in fee, to the four grantees. It is necessary, therefore, to resort to the instrument by which the trust is declared or proved, in order to ascertain its nature and extent. A trust (other than a resulting trust) must be manifested or proved by writing; though it may be created by parol.
726*] And the declaration of trust need *not be made at the time of the purchase. It may be subsequently, or, as I apprehend, in contemplation or anticipation of it. (2 Ves., 696; 5 Johns. Ch., 12.)

The trust, in this case, is proved by the covenant or agreement of the 18th of October, 1789, between the four grantees of the one part, and their eight associates of the other. This was after the contract for the purchase was made with Phelps; but before the deed was executed. The grantees covenanted to convey to their associates eight twelfths of the purchase, upon their paying eight twelfths of the consideration money and costs; and the associates covenanted to make those payments in three annual installments. Whether this is to be considered a declaration of trust, or only a resale, it is not material to inquire; for if it be admitted to be the former, it proves a trust only as to eight twelfths; leaving the grantees seised in their own right as tenants in common as to the residue. Holding the legal estate of the eight twelfths, subject to the equitable interest of their *cestuis que trust*, no legal objection is perceived to their being joint tenants, so far as their legal estate was affected by the trust; and tenants in common as to the residue. The covenant of the eight associates or *cestuis que trust*, bound them to pay their portion of the consideration in three annual installments. There is no evidence that any portion of this money was paid, before or at the time of the purchase or deed from Phelps. In order to raise a resulting trust, strict proof is required; and the payment of the money at the time of the purchase, is indispensable. A subsequent payment would not raise the trust. (2 Johns. Ch., 409; 5 *Id.*, 19; 2 Atk., 71.) There is, therefore, no ground for contending that there was a resulting trust, in this case, which might be proved by parol.

Kress, one of the *cestuis que trust*, conveyed his one twelfth to Erwin. Thus he had both the legal and equitable estate in two twelfths. For these he had paid his money; and even if the deed had been taken in the name of another, upon a consideration paid by him, the trust would have resulted to him. (2 Johns. Ch., 405; 16 Johns., 197; 3 Johns., 216.)

*As to the two twelfths then, there [***727** could have been no survivorship. Suppose the eight *cestuis que trust* had conveyed all their interest to the four grantees; would not the effect have been, to have extinguished the outstanding equity, and to have left them seised, as they would have been, if it had never been created; that is, as tenants in common, the share of each to descend to his heirs?

Without deeming it material to determine whether the statute applies to any other than pure trusts, declared on the face of the deed, such as trusts to executors to sell or to trustees to sell for the benefit of creditors, we are clearly of opinion that there was no survivorship as to the two twelfths which belonged to Arthur Erwin, and that the legal title to these descended to his heirs.

The plaintiff is, therefore, entitled to recover seven eighths of one tenth of two twelfths of the premises in question, upon the demise of the children of Sarah Mulhollon. She was married in 1777, before the death of her father; she was covert until 1809, and her husband survived until 1815. The ten years after her death, allowed for the children to bring their action, had not expired when this suit was commenced. They are, therefore, not barred, within the case of *Jackson* v. *Johnson*, 5 Cow., 74.

Judgment for the plaintiff pro tanto.

Reversed—4 Wend., 58.
Criticised—14 N. Y., 150.
Courses and distances yield to monuments. Cited in—56 N. Y., 531; 3 Barb., 357; 22 How. (U. S.), 19; 34 N. J. L., 405; 36 Am. Dec., 451 (3 Ala., 18).
Resulting trust. Cited in—1 Wend., 658; Hoffm., 93; 6 Barb., 106; 9 Barb., 602; 11 Barb., 407.
Grant when presumed from lapse of time. Cited in—18 Barb., 22; 26 Barb., 408; 3 Wood. & M., 549.
Also cited in—26 Wend., 556; 11 Barb., 188; 43 N. J. L., 394; 23 Minn., 64; 54 Mo., 477.

---

*HUNTER [***728**
v.
LE CONTE AND ELLIS.

Landlord and Tenant—Tender of Rent—Where made—If Prior to Distress, the Distress is Tortious—Subsequent Tender—Replevin—Pleading—Costs—Affidavit.

Though a tender of rent is good on the land, yet a personal tender is also good off the land.

A personal tender before distress, makes it tortious; and such tender afterwards, and before impounding, makes the detainer unlawful; but tender, after impounding, makes neither the one nor the other unlawful.

In replevin, a plea of tender, to an avowry or cognizance, need not say *tout temps prist*; nor make a profert of the money in court.

A tender of rent takes away a right to distrain, till a subsequent demand and refusal.

But a tender does not take away the right to sue for the rent as for a debt. It only saves interest and costs.

A tender of rent makes a distress wrongful though the tender be not made till after the rent day.

But if costs have been incurred by the landlord, as if he have drawn a warrant of distress, or, in the City of N. Y., made and filed the necessary affidavit, these costs must also be tendered, or the distress will be lawful.

The affidavit of rent due, in the City of N. Y., required by the Statute, sess. 38, ch. 153, to be made and filed, before distress, is, *prima facie*, sufficient, though the *jurat* be subscribed simply with the name of the officer before whom it is taken, without the addition of his title of office.

Citations—Co. Litt., 201 *b*, 211 *a*; 8 Co., 292; Woodfall, 315; 8 Johns., 476, 477; Cro. Eliz., 48; 2 Chit. Pl., 633, 498; 3 Wils., 74; 1 Salk., 583; 1 Ld. Raym., 639; 1 R. L., 435.

ON ERROR from the C. P. of N. Y. The action in the court below was replevin, by Hunter against Le Conte and Ellis, for goods taken in the City of N. Y. Le Conte avowed, and Ellis, as his bailiff, made cognizance of the taking of the goods Feb. 20, 1824, as a distress for $62.50 rent, due Feb. 1, 1824, on a demise of premises in the city. Pleas, 1. That the defendant, L., did not file an affidavit of rent being due, under the Statute, sess. 38, ch. 153; 3 L. N. Y., 156 *c*; and 2. That before distress made, viz.: Feb. 16, 1824, the plaintiff tendered the $62.50, which was refused; and no demand afterwards made of the money. Replication to the 1st plea, that an affidavit was filed; and to the 2d, that after rent due, and before tender, the defendant, L., was put to the expense of a distress warrant and filing the affidavit, which the plaintiff refused to pay, concluding the last with a verification. Issue on the 1st, and demurrer and joinder on the last replication.

The court below decided the demurrer against the plaintiff, on the ground that his plea was defective in not averring that the tender was on the land. On the trial of the issue of fact, the defendants showed an affidavit, duly filed Feb. 14, 1824, in the clerk's office of the City of N. Y., the *jurat* whereof was signed H. Abell, without any addition. This was objected to as inadmissible on that ground. It was received, however, as competent, and the plaintiff excepted.

729*] **Mr. W. Mulock*, for the plaintiff in error:

Though a tender on the land would have been sufficient (Co. Litt., 202 *a*; 7 Rep., 370; Co. Litt., 105 *a*; Hob, 208; Roll. Abr., 427), a personal tender is equally so. (8 Johns., 370; 2 Chit., 681.) A tender, after the rent falls due, and at any time before impounding, is good. (17 Vin. Abr., 592, Rent.)

The landlord could not distrain for the costs of the distress warrant and affidavit. The Statute, 1 R. L., 435, sec. 5, allows no charges incurred before distress made. Besides, as to the warrant, it was unnecessary. The landlord might have distrained in person. The statute, requiring the affidavit, makes no provision that it shall be paid for. We were not liable in any shape for either of these charges.

The objection on the bill of exceptions, is also sufficient ground for reversal. (Stat., sess. 38, ch. 153; 3 Cai., 128.) The tenant, by his default, making a distress warrant and affidavit necessary, should be holden to pay for it.

Mr. J. R. Hedley, contra:

If the plea of a personal tender of rent, not saying on the land, be good, yet it should aver that the tenant was always ready, and still is ready; and he should bring the money into court. (Story, Pl., 422; Willes, 632; 2 Wils., 74.)

The signature, "H. Abell," to the *jurat* was sufficient. His office might have been shown, by extrinsic evidence, thus making out a compliance with the statute.

Mr. Mulock said *tout temps prist* cannot be a necessary averment. The action is not to collect the debt. That is not in question; but whether the distress was rightful or wrongful. The tender made it wrongful. (2 Chit. Pl., 633, 498.)

Curia, per SAVAGE, *Ch. J.* 1. As to the demurrer. The defendants, no doubt, have a right to show that the plaintiff's plea is defective in substance. The objection taken by the judge was, that the tender should have been *on the land. Another exception is [*730 now taken, to wit: that the plaintiff did not say he was always ready after the tender, and bring the money into court.

There are authorities which say, that when rent is payable on a particular day, it must be demanded on the land; and also that a tender on the land is good and prevents a forfeiture. (Co. Litt., 201 *b*, 211 *a*.) But Hargrave, in a note on this subject, states that a tender "to the lessor himself, either upon, or out of the land, is good." In *The Six Carpenters'* case, 8 Co., 292, it is said, "tender upon the land, before the distress, makes the distress tortious; tender after the distress and before the impounding, makes the detainer, and not the taking, wrongful; tender after impounding, makes neither the one nor the other wrongful; for then it comes too late." The same doctrine is found in other books. In Woodf., 315, it is said a distress must not be made after tender of payment. These authorities say, that tender on the land is good even when the landlord comes to distrain, but it does not follow that it is not also good off the land. I cannot see how the place of a tender, after a default by the tenant, can be material. If the rent is tendered in any place, to the landlord, he can ask nothing more; and a distress becomes not only unnecessary, but vexatious. In *Slingerland* v. *Morse*, 8 Johns., 476, 477, the court say, "the general rule is, that if no place be appointed for the payment, or performance, a tender to the person is good; and this, too, in cases in which a personal tender was not required, as of rent issuing out of land." *Cropp* v. *Hambleton*, Cro. E., 48, is a direct authority, that tender of the land is good.

The next objection to the plea is, that there should have been an averment of *tout temps prist*. This objection is well answered by the plaintiff's counsel. The question is, not as to the debt which is tendered, but as to the regularity of the distress. Suppose the money were brought into court, what effect could that have on the cause? The question here is, whether the defendants were not trespassers? The precedents referred to in Chitty, 2 Chit. Pl., 633 *498 shows that, in replevin, no such [*731 averment is necessary, though in covenant it is. And the reason I apprehend to be, that a tender takes away the right to distrain, till a subsequent demand and refusal. But a tender does not take away a right to prosecute on the covenant. It only prevents the recovery of interest and costs. In *French* v. *Watson*, 2 Wils., 74, no tender was pleaded ; but only a readiness to pay, which the court say is not issuable. In *Horn* v. *Lewin*, 1 Salk., 583; S. C., 1 Ld. Raym., 639, it was determined that a profert of the money was not necessary in replevin, and in that case the money was brought into court and accepted ; but all was held superfluous, because the question was, whether the distress was rightful. In my judgment, therefore, the plea is good.

I can see no fault in the replication, in point of form. It protests the tender, which, as to this cause, admits it ; because it is not denied.

But other matter is set up, which it is supposed avoids the tender, to wit: that costs had been incurred which should have been paid.

From the cases cited, it seems that a tender of the rent before an actual distress, renders the distress unlawful, but the case of costs incurred is not attended to. It is highly reasonable that costs should be paid, when they have been properly and fairly incurred. The rent was due Feb. 1. The affidavit was filed on the 14th, the tender on the 16th, the distress was on the 20th. Before the tender, a warrant had been made to a bailiff. Our statute directs the retaining of the charges in case of sale. (1 R. L., 435.) A fair construction of the Act, I think, must entitle the party distraining to his lawful costs at any time, after they have been incurred. It seems to me, therefore, that the replication is good, both in form and substance.

If I am right in my conclusion, the judgment of the court below, upon the demurrer, must be affirmed.

2. The only remaining question, is that arising on the bill of exceptions. By the Act al-
732*] ready referred to, no landlord *shall distrain the goods of his tenant in the City of N. Y., unless he, or his agent, shall "make an affidavit before a justice of the peace, or other magistrate in the said city and county, authorized by law to administer oaths," &c. It does not appear by the affidavit, that H. Abell was a magistrate authorized to administer oaths ; nor was the fact proved or offered to be proved or disproved in the court below.

It is fairly inferable that the fact of his being a justice was conceded. But it was contended that his official character should appear affirmatively. We think that the fact of Mr. Abell's taking an affidavit, and of the clerk's receiving and filing it, were, *prima facie*, sufficient ; and threw on the other side the burden of proving the want of authority. The judgment must, therefore, be affirmed.

Judgment affirmed.

Cited in—26 Wend., 556; 5 Den., 453; 11 N. Y., 91; 21 N. Y., 347; 9 Hun, 339; 25 How. Pr., 465; 60 Ill., 478.

THE MIDDLE DISTRICT BANK
v.
DEYO, late Sheriff of ULSTER.

Action for Several Escapes—Pleading—Defenses—After Extinguishment of Right of Action, there can be no Revivor.

Under a declaration for several escapes, the defendant may plead a voluntary return, &c., to the escapes set forth ; and may, on issue thereon, excuse any and all escapes which the plaintiff proves at the trial, by showing a subsequent voluntary return, &c.

If the plaintiff wishes to confine the defense to any escape or escapes, in particular, he should new assign.

The day of the escape or escapes, laid in the declaration, is not material, unless made so by a novel assignment.

Where a plaintiff declares for several escapes, on different days, from a *ca. sa.* upon different judgments, but at the trial proves only one judgment, he is entitled to recover upon only one count.

The usual averment in the plea, of a voluntary return or recaption, to an action for an escape, that the prisoner continued in custody intermediate the return or recaption and the suit, is immaterial; and no proof of it need be given under an issue upon the plea. Griffiths v. Eyles, 1 Bos. & P., 413, and Chambers v. Jones, 11 East, 405, contra, overruled.

It is a good defense to an action for a negligent escape, that the prisoner was taken on fresh pursuit, or voluntarily returned, before suit brought ; and was in custody at the time of suit brought, without an allegation, that he continued in custody intermediate the recaption or return, and the time of suit brought.

A recaption on fresh pursuit, or voluntary return of a prisoner before suit brought, *per se*, purges an escape ; and a subsequent escape will not revive the right of action for a former one.

A right of action once extinguished is gone forever, and cannot be revived or continued by any subsequent, distinct, and independent act.

Modo et forma puts in issue matter of substance, only.

Citations—1 Bos. & P., 413; 11 East, 406, 488 ; 2 Bac. Abr., 529, tit. Execution ; 1 Vent., 217 ; 24 Car., 2 ; 10 Vin., 118, pl. 43 ; 1 Lutw., 382 ; 3 Keb., 55 ; W. Jones, 144 ; Cro. Jac., 657 ; 1 Com., 554 ; 1 Str., 423 ; 5 Went., 228, 241; Lit. Ent., 152 ; 2 T. R., 126 ; 2 Johns. Cas., 208; 2 Johns., 433; 4 Johns., 47 ; 6 Johns., 123; 7 Johns., 177; 10 Johns., 549, 563; 16 Johns., 307; 1 Ld. Raym., 39.

DEBT for the escape of one Lawrence, from the defendant's custody on a *ca. sa.*, at the suit of the plaintiff, upon *a judgment [***733** for $652.17 ; tried at the Ulster Circuit, Apr. 19, 1826, before Betts, late *Circuit J.*

The declaration contained three counts, substantially alike, except that the escapes were stated on different days. The defendant pleaded : 1. *Nil debit*, with notice of special matter. 2. In answer to the first count, a return before suit brought ; and that the defendant, after that escape and return, safely kept the prisoner in his custody, until he went out of office, and then delivered him over to his successor. Replication, that the defendant did not keep and detain the prisoner in his custody, in manner and form, &c. The 3d and 4th pleas to the 2d and 3d counts, and the replications, were similar. There was also a 5th plea to the whole declaration, alleging that the judgments, executions, commitments and escapes, stated in the several counts, were one and the same ; and a return before suit brought. Replication, that the escapes were different, and not one and the same.

At the trial, the plaintiffs proved that Lawrence was arrested upon the *ca. sa.* Sept. 13, 1825 ; that he was seen off the limits five several times prior to Jan. 1, 1826 ; and had returned before that day. The action was commenced Jan. 2, 1826 ; on which day, it was admitted, that the defendant, in due form of law, assigned the prisoner to his successor. It appeared that the prisoner was on the limits when the *capias ad respondendum*, in this cause, was delivered to the coroner.

The plaintiffs offered to prove that Lawrence had given bail for the limits, and deposited $800 as security ; and that this suit was defended at his expense. The judge rejected the evidence, but charged the jury, that as it was alleged by the defendant that the prisoner continued in his custody after voluntary return, if the plaintiffs had satisfactorily proved that after the escapes stated in the 1st and 2d counts, and the voluntary return of the prisoner, he had again made other escapes, the plaintiffs were entitled to a verdict. The jury found a verdict for the plaintiffs on each of the issues.

734*] **Mr. *Talcott*, Atty-Gen., for the defendant, now moved for a new trial, on the ground that the charge of the judge was incorrect, and that the defendant was entitled to a verdict upon the evidence. He said the plaintiff was not entitled to recover on the first two counts. There was but one judgment upon which the prisoner was committed.

The allegation, that the defendant detained the prisoner, till he was turned over to his successor, was unnecessary. The return was an answer to the escape, and if the plaintiffs relied on a subsequent escape, they should have new assigned. The defendant is bound to answer no escapes beside those contained in the declaration. No subsequent escape could revive a right of action on the first. This was purged by the return; and if the plaintiffs had intended to avail themselves of the second, they should have brought their action for that. The cases and precedents are numerous that a recaption on fresh suit, or a voluntary return, are a defense, *per se*, without adding that the prisoner was detained. (7 Johns., 177; 4 *Id.*, 47; 10 *Id.*, 578; 6 *Id.*, 123; 16 *Id.*, 313; 2 Johns. Cas., 208; Com., 554; Cro. Eliz., 439; Latch, 200; Noy, 93; Godb., 177, 433; Browne Ent., 159; 5 Instr. Cler., 123; 2 T. R., 126; 1 Str., 423; 6 Cow., 65.)

He examined *Chambers* v. *Jones*, 11 East, 406, and contended that it is not law, and not supported by the authorities there relied upon. But if law in England, it is not so here. The sheriff is, with us, bound to let the defendant to bail upon the limits, which sometimes cover a whole city. This is not so in England. It is impossible for him here to know and plead all the escapes of a prisoner to an action for one. Such a doctrine would subject him to the payment of every *ca. sa.* upon which his prisoners are committed.

The allegation of detention, being wholly immaterial, is not put in issue. *Modo et forma* extends only to substance.

Mr. C. H. Ruggles, contra, relied on *Chambers* v. *Jones*, 11 East, 406, as in point for the

735*]plaintiff. He also cited *5 Wentw., 228, 229, 242; 2 Johns. Cas., 208; 6 Johns., 123; 10 *Id.*, 561; 2 *Id.*, 433; *Griffiths* v. *Eyles*, 1 Bos. & P., 413, 418, per Eyre, *Ch. J.*

Curia, per WOODWORTH, *J.* It is very clear that the plaintiffs are not entitled to recover upon more than one count. There was only one judgment on which the prisoner was committed.

The important inquiry is, whether all the facts stated in the plea were material. If they were, the plaintiffs ought to recover. But if the defense was complete on proving a voluntary return before suit brought, and that the prisoner was in custody when the action was commenced, the verdict ought have been for the defendant.

The decision of this question will depend on the inquiry, whether the allegation that the defendant detained the prisoner in custody upon the voluntary return, until he was handed over to the new sheriff, was or was not material. If immaterial, then it was not put in issue by the replication (*modo et forma* only putting in issue matter of substance) and, consequently, need not be proved.

On the argument of this cause, great reliance was placed upon the cases of *Griffiths* v. *Eyles*, 1 Bos. & P., 413, and *Chambers* v. *Jones*, 11 East, 406. If these cases were correctly decided, I admit that the law, as understood in England, is in favor of the plaintiffs.

With great deference for the learned opinions of the judges who then presided, I cannot yield my assent to the doctrine there advanced, believing it to be repugnant to the principles of the common law, and the weight of authority deducible from the decisions of their learned predecessors. Before I consider the two cases referred to, I will examine the doctrine as laid down in other authorities. The 2 Bac. Abr., 529, tit. Execution, lays down the rule, that if a prisoner in execution escape, without the assent of the sheriff, and he make fresh pursuit, and retake him before any action brought, it shall excuse the sheriff; and that a voluntary return of the prisoner, before action, is equal to a retaking on fresh pursuit. The proposition *is not qualified, and seems [*736 to be a full answer to the escape. There is no suggestion that a continuance in custody until suit brought enters at all into the nature of the defense; and from the reason of the thing, if the plaintiffs relied upon a subsequent escape, they should have new assigned. The defendant is not bound to do more than give an answer to the escapes in the declaration. This he has done by excusing as many as are there alleged. If the first escape is purged, how can a subsequent one revive the right of action? There is a complete defense to the action for the first escape, by the voluntary return. It is against established principles, to say that a right of action, once extinguished, can be restored by a subsequent disconnected and independent act. The day laid in the declaration is immaterial. Proof of an escape on a different day is admissible. How, then, can the plaintiffs, on these pleadings, raise the objection, that the escape in issue between the parties is the first escape, and that the defendant's plea must have reference to that? I think it may equally well apply to the last escape; and then, by the plaintiff's own showing, the prisoner returned and remained in custody until he was assigned. If the day alleged be not material, the defendant cannot be precluded from applying his plea to such escape as he thinks proper. In that case, he may answer to the last escape proved, that the prisoner returned. This latitude is given to the defendant under the pleadings; which the plaintiffs might have restricted in their replication, by alleging in certain the identical escape on which they relied, and thereby confining the plea of the defendant to such escape. I do not intend, however, to rest my opinion on that ground; but on the sufficiency of a return before action commenced, and that the prisoner was, at that time, in custody.

In Sir *Ralph Bovy's* case, 1 Vent., 217; 24

Car. 2, the action was debt for a voluntary escape. The defendant, protesting that he did not let him voluntarily escape, pleaded, that he took him upon fresh pursuit. The plaintiff demurred, because he did not traverse the voluntary escape; and resolved for the defendant; **737***] for it is not necessary *for the plaintiff to allege it in his declaration. It must be alleged in the replication. This case is approved in 10 Vin., 118, pl. 43, and 1 Lutw., 382; S. C., 3 Keb., 55. Here there was no averment, that after the retaking, the prisoner was kept in custody until suit brought; nor was it suggested by the court or counsel. So, also, in *Harvey* v. *Reynel*, W. Jones., 144, Car. 2, the declaration alleged an escape at D. in the County of H. The defendant confessed that the prisoner was committed in the County of S. and escaped; and that the defendant made fresh pursuit, and retook him before suit, and that he was in his custody; and demanded judgment. It was resolved on demurrer, that although the plaintiff alleged the escape at D., and the defendant confessed it at S., in another county, this was good, without a traverse of the escape at D.; for when a man is at large, it is an escape in every county. In *Whiting* v. *Reynel*, Cro. Jac., 657, the plea was, that the defendant had retaken the prisoner, and yet hath him. No objection was taken to the plea, on the ground that it did not allege a continuance in custody after recaption. There might have been ten escapes and recaptions after the first; and yet, after the tenth, the prisoner was in lawful custody, which supported the averment in the plea. In *Chambers* v. *Jones*, 11 East, 408, Ld. Ellenborough, after laying down the proposition that the plea must allege a continued detention to the time of action, refers, among others, to the case of *Whiting* v. *Reynel*, to support his doctrine. I apprehend it does not. So far from it, the detention averred, is an existing one when the action was commenced; which would be equally true, whether one or two escapes and returns had taken place between that time and the recaption or return, on the first escape made by the prisoner. The plea neither affirms nor denies a continued detention; and, manifestly, because, at that day, it was not deemed material. The case of *Chambers* v. *Gambier*, Com., 554, was also cited. There, in debt for an escape, the defendant pleaded, that, before action brought, the prisoner returned, and was in execution, for the damages on the judgment. On demurrer, **738***] *judgment was given for the defendant, on the ground that this was equal to a retaking on fresh pursuit. If a continued detention was necessary to be averred, it seems to me judgment should have been given for the plaintiff. This form of pleading is in accordance with the principle laid down, that a voluntary return excuses the sheriff; but it cannot be so, if the defendant is bound to show the continuance of the detention. He is not protected by proving a recaption or return, if the law be as contended for by the plaintiffs. The averment, then, that the prisoner was in custody when the suit was commenced, must be made; and that is all that is necessary after setting out the recaption or return. A detention at the time is indispensable, for unless the fact be so, the sheriff is clearly liable. In an *Anonymous* case, 1 Str., 423, it was held that if a man escapes and returns, and afterwards commits a second escape, he cannot be taken up for the first escape, it being purged by the return. Ld. Ellenborough considered the case of *Meriton* v. *Briggs*, 1 Ld. Raym., 39, as an unequivocal case, to prove that a recaption was no protection to the sheriff, nor any answer to the action, unless there was a subsequent detention to the time of the action. The case was this: the defendant pleaded a recaption on fresh pursuit merely; the plaintiff replied, *de injuria sua propria, absque hoc quod* he retook, &c., upon fresh pursuit, *et adhuc detinet.* The defendant demurred, for that the plaintiff had traversed matter not alleged in the plea, viz.: *quod adhuc detinet;* and contended that if the defendant had suffered the prisoner to escape a month after the recaption, yet the plaintiff should be bound by the recaption for the old escape, and should have a new action for the new escape, which Holt, *Ch. J.*, denied; for both are but one escape. Judgment for the plaintiff. If I understand this case, the point before the court was a distinct question from the one before us. It was this: does a plea of recaption or voluntary return imply that the prisoner was in custody at the time of action; for it will be seen that the only part of the traverse that relates to the detention, is as to *et adhuc detinet;* *that is to say, whether [***739** he was then a prisoner; not that, at no time since the recaption, had he ceased to be a prisoner. Viewed in this light, it corresponds with all the cases I have referred to. The language of Holt, therefore, so far as it attempts to lay down law not applicable to the point then in issue, must be regarded as an *obiter dictum*, and is directly opposed to the case in Strange.

It is true, that in some of the books of precedents, the form of the plea is that of a continued detention to the time of action. Such are the pleas in 5 Went., 228, 241, and Lilt. Ent., 152. Indeed, the form of the plea in modern times, I apprehend, generally contains that allegation. But, as far as I know, it has been the sense of the profession, that the plea was supported, if the prisoner was actually in custody when the suit was commenced, provided the sheriff had not suffered a voluntary escape; and that the fact of the prisoner having escaped several times previously, and returned, did not invalidate the allegation of having remained a true prisoner. If the retaking, or return, purges the escape, it is the same as if no escape had taken place.

I have not been able to discover any adjudged cases previous to *Griffiths* v. *Eyles*, and *Chambers* v. *Jones*, that support the doctrine contended for by the plaintiffs, or seem to sanction it, except the case containing the dictum of Ld. Holt, which has been noticed. In *Chambers* v. *Jones*, it appears to me, the court principally rely on forms of pleas to be found in the books.

That the law was understood in England to be as I have attempted to show, is very evident from the case of *Bonafous* v. *Walker*, 2 T. R., 126. The first count was for a voluntary escape; the second for a negligent escape. Pleas, 1. *Nil debet.* 2. As to the second count, recaption on fresh pursuit; and that the defendant had and detained the prisoner in execution for the damages. 3. As to the second count, that the prisoner returned; and, continually, after return, that the prisoner had been detained in execution. Replication, that the defendant did not diligently pursue the prisoner in order to **740***] retake him; and as to the *third plea, that the prisoner was not continually after his return, detained in the defendant's custody in execution. Here the last issue was substantially the same as in the case under consideration. At the trial before Buller, *J.*, it appeared that the prisoner was out of the rules of the prison on three several days. On the defendant's hearing that the prisoner had escaped, he was put into close custody, before action brought. The defendant made two objections: 1. That the plaintiff ought to have brought the action as administratrix, because the judgment was obtained in that character. 2. That the plaintiff could not give a negligent escape in evidence under the first count. The judge overruled, both objections; and a verdict passed for the plaintiff. On motion for a new trial, Erskine, *arguendo*, contended that, as the defendant could not plead a recaption to the first count for a voluntary escape, the plaintiff could not give in evidence a negligent escape under that count; and, therefore, it must be considered as if there was but one count for a negligent escape, in which case the defendant was entitled to a verdict. He insisted that the number of escapes could not vary the question, as the prisoner was in safe custody before the commencement of the action. It appears, then, that this question was distinctly presented; it was not contradicted by the opposing counsel, nor denied by the court. On the contrary, they must have considered it sound; otherwise, there was no necessity for granting a new trial on the ground stated. Buller, *J.*, observes that, at the trial, the law was mistaken by both parties, and by himself; the plaintiff contending that it was a voluntary escape, which was denied by the defendant—both of them going on the mistaken idea that a voluntary escape was material to be proved on the first issue. The court, therefore, interposed, and granted a new trial, with liberty to amend the pleadings. As the case stood, three escapes were proved. The defense was considered complete as to the second count; but inasmuch as the plaintiff had proved another negligent escape, which he might do under the first count, to which there was no plea of re- **741***] caption or voluntary return, *he was, under the pleadings, entitled to a verdict. But if the doctrine contended for be correct, the plaintiff had falsified the plea in a material part, by showing that the prisoner had not been, continually, after the return, detained in execution. Three escapes were proved; so that without reference to the first count, the plaintiff made out a right to recover on the second. It cannot be imagined that at that day, 1787, the Court of King's Bench considered the doctrine now advanced, as law; and especially, that if such had been the law, it should escape the notice of Buller, *J.*, who is not only admitted to have been among the ablest lawyers, but ranked among the most skillful special pleaders of his time.

The case of *Griffiths* v. *Eyles*, 1 Bos. & P., 413, is the first case I have met with that seems to be at variance with the law, as understood in *Bonafous* v. *Walker*. When the case in Bos. & P. was decided (1799) Buller was a justice of the Common Pleas, having resigned his seat in the King's Bench; but he was not a party to the decision of *Griffiths* v. *Eyles*, Apr. 30, 1799, having been absent from the 20th of April, to the end of the term (May 6th), from indisposition. Heath, *J.*, was also absent; so that the law as there laid down was by two judges only. I make this remark, as somewhat impairing the weight of that case, inasmuch as there is no reason to believe that *Judge* Buller had changed his opinion since the case of *Bonafous* v. *Walker;* or that, had he been present, he would have concurred in the decision in *Griffiths* v *Eyles*. In this last case, the action was debt for an escape. The defendant pleaded a negligent escape and voluntary return, since which the prisoner had been safely kept. The replication admitted the escape and return, but alleged the prisoner had not been safely kept since that time, having again escaped, which was a different escape from that alleged in the plea. The defendant, in his rejoinder, traversed the allegation that the prisoner had not been safely kept; and then pleaded to the latter part of the replication, a negligent escape, voluntary return, and safe keeping since, in the same manner as in the plea. The *court [***742** held the latter part of the rejoinder bad on special demurrer. Eyre, *Ch. J.*, considered that the common form of replication stopped at the allegation that the prisoner had not been kept in custody since the first voluntary return; and that the latter part of the replication, in that case, was only an amplification of the denial that the defendant had kept the prisoner in safe custody. He observes, "the defendant, by his plea, excuses an escape, upon the ground of the prisoner having returned, and remained in custody ever since. Now, put the case that the prisoner had made two or three escapes, and had returned as many times; the defendant was bound to state them all, in order to establish the averment, that the prisoner had been kept in safe custody ever since."

If this case is to be followed, our decision should be for the plaintiffs; but I consider it a departure from the principles recognized in *Bonafous* v. *Walker*, which seem to be founded on the established doctrine, that a voluntary return or recaption on fresh pursuit, are, *per se*, a sufficient answer to an action for an escape; and being, of themselves, sufficient, it follows that the further allegation, that the prisoner has ever since continued in custody, is immaterial. If it be material, then, indeed, the defendant would, in order to protect himself, be bound at his peril, to set out all the escapes if there were more than one; and give an answer to each, although the plaintiff had declared for only one escape in his declaration. The peculiar hardship of such a doctrine is not more manifest to my mind than this anomaly in the law, that a defendant is bound to answer more than is charged; to protect himself by plea against causes of action which the plaintiff may, but has not alleged. Nor is it less difficult to support this doctrine, by putting it on the ground that the first escape, although purged, may be revived, and continue a good cause of action, by reason of subsequent escapes, with which there is no necessary connection. Eyre, *Ch. J.*, places the reason of this doctrine on the ground that the sheriff knows, or is bound to know, the state of his prison; and whether there has been **743***] one escape or ten escapes. *However that may be in England, where the sheriff may or may not allow the rules of the prison, and where these rules, when allowed, are not analogous to the limits prescribed by statute for our prisons; it may be observed, that here, the allowance of the limits is imperative on the sheriff upon giving security. Those limits are extensive; so that it cannot be presumed that the sheriff is able to state the number of escapes committed by a prisoner. Therefore, to apply the principle here, and say that the sheriff shall state all the escapes, would be, in most cases, the same thing as to say he should be liable for the debt, where several escapes had been committed, although, in each case, the prisoner had voluntarily returned. If the sheriff had discovered that his prisoner had escaped ten times, and returned, he would plead those returns, but the plaintiff who proved the eleventh escape would recover; because, as to that, the defendant being ignorant that it had been made, had no means of protecting himself. Besides the unreasonableness of the doctrine, and unsupported, as I think it is, by the weight of authority even in the English courts, it is apparent that there is no necessity to adopt it for the purposes of justice.

If the prisoner is in custody when the suit is commenced, that is an answer to every claim on the ground of a subsequent escape. Why subject the sheriff for escapes which have been previously committed, and are necessarily purged by the fact that the prisoner is in actual custody when the suit is commenced?

If the plaintiffs relied on a subsequent escape, they should have new assigned, for the defendant is not bound to do more than give an answer to the escape or escapes in the declaration, which is done by excusing as many as are there alleged. In *Chambers* v. *Jones*, Ld. Ellenborough admits that a new assignment would be necessary, if it be not necessary to state a detention down to the period when the suit is commenced. The Court of King's Bench held that the new assignment was unnecessary, deciding that it was essential to state a detention; and show that it either continued when the action was commenced, or that something **744***] *had intervened to put a legal termination to it; and as the evidence negatived such a detention in that case, the verdict was right. I have endeavored to show that the cases and precedents relied on by the court, do not go the length of supporting that opinion.

I will, in the next place, briefly examine some of the decisions in our own courts, which go fully to support the view I have taken. And here I must observe that I have never known an action even hazarded, for a negligent escape, after the prisoner had actually returned into custody. The question now raised appears to me novel; and but for the cases of *Griffiths* v. *Eyles* and *Chambers* v. *Jones*, it may well be doubted whether an experiment like the present would have been made.

In the case of *Dole* v. *Moulton*, 2 Johns. Cas., 208, the action was on the bond given to the sheriff. The plea averred the return before action, and that the prisoner continued in custody after the return. No question was raised as to a subsequent escape. The court held that the return of the prisoner saved the condition of the bond, and was a competent defense on the part of the sheriff.

In *Currie & Whitney* v. *Henry*, 2 Johns., 433, one plea alleged an escape and voluntary return, and that the prisoner continued in custody, until afterwards he was discharged out of prison by the Court of Common Pleas of the County of Rensselaer, pursuant to the Act for the Relief of Debtors, &c. The plaintiff demurred specially, and contended that the plea was double. The court held the plea good. Spencer, *J.*, observed, "the defendant could not have pleaded the involuntary escape and return before action brought, without also alleging that the prisoner was, at the time of the plea pleaded, in his custody. This is manifest from all the precedents." This case was cited by the plaintiffs' counsel; but is an authority against the doctrine they contend for. It accords with the view I have taken, viz.: that the plea must show a recaption or return, and that the prisoner is in custody; not that he has continued in custody from the time of return to the time of action. The court understood the precedents to *require that, and no [***745** more. It has been shown that so are the pleas in all the old cases, and in several of those cited by Ld. Ellenborough. This court, in *Currie* v. *Henry*, did not understand that such a plea implied a continued detention from the time of voluntary return, as the Court of King's Bench in the last case did. And therein consisted a difference of opinion on a material point.

In *Tillman* v. *Lansing*, 4 Johns., 47, the court lay down the law in an unqualified manner: "It is not to be denied, that fresh suit and recaption is a good defense against a negligent escape; and a voluntary return, before suit brought, will also purge an escape of this description." So, also, in *Peters* v. *Henry*, 6 Johns., 123, the court say, "a voluntary return before action purges the escape." (7 Johns., 177, and 10 Johns., 549, 563, S. P.) In the case of *Richmond* v. *Tallmadge*, 16 Johns., 307, in error, this question seems to have been put at rest. The *Chancellor*, in delivering the opinion of the court, says, "the case is then reduced to this point: whether, to an action of escape, a plea of a voluntary return by the prisoner within the limits before suit brought, and that plea certified by the jury to be true in point of fact, be not a valid defense? Under the decisions of this court, there can be no doubt of the validity of such a defense."

It follows as a necessary consequence, if this is a valid defense (accompanied with the fact which is always understood as connected with it, the prisoner being in custody at the time of suit brought), that the plea, in this case, was perfect, without averring a continued intermediate detention; and although averred, it is surplusage, and immaterial. Taking an issue upon that part, makes an immaterial issue, and requires no proof by the defendant, to sustain it; neither can it avail the plaintiff, to prove it untrue. A subsequent escape was a distinct cause of action, not connected with the first escape, and no ground for reviving after it had been purged by a voluntary return.

On these grounds, without inquiring whether

the defendant might not protect himself un-
746*] der the notice, I am *of opinion that the defendant has answered the escapes set not in the declaration, by showing a return of the prisoner, and that he was in custody at the time the suit was commenced.

There must be a new trial, with costs to abide the event of the suit.

New trial granted.

Cited in—9 Cow., 92; 63 Barb., 203; 4 How. Pr., 298.

REES v. OVERBAUGH.

Deed—Seals Torn Off by Mistake, by Third Person Having it in Custody as Agent of Both Parties—Covenant Lies.

Where the seals of an agreement were torn off by one with whom it had been left for safe keeping by both parties, held, that this did not destroy the deed; but an action of covenant would still lie upon it.

A stranger tearing off the seal will not vitiate a deed.

Citations—6 East, 309; 4 T. R., 329, 330, 338, 339; 3 T. R., 150, 151, 153, *n.*; 11 Co., 27; 5 Co., 119; Dy., 59, *a*, *n.*; Dy., 112 *a*; 2 Str., 1186; 1 Ves., 387, 389; 1 Gall., 69; 5 Cow., 368; Palm., 403.

COVENANT, tried at the Montgomery Circuit, Dec., 1824, before Walworth, *Circuit J.*

The action was for money claimed by the plaintiff, to be due from the defendant to him, on sealed articles of agreement, dated Feb. 8, 1808, executed by the parties, and left with one Jackson, for safe keeping. The plaintiff afterwards authorized Jackson to receive $2,500 (the whole debt being $3,000) of the money due on the agreement, and pass it to the plaintiff's credit on account. Jackson received money at different times; and on a cast, when the last payment was made to him, he thought the sum due on the agreement was fully paid; and, on that supposition, tore the seals off the agreement. These facts being proved at the trial, various evidence was given upon the question, whether the whole was in fact paid, as supposed by Jackson; and whether the seals were torn from the agreement upon a mistaken supposition, &c.

The defendant's counsel objected to reading the agreement, on the ground that the seals had been torn off, by which its force was utterly destroyed. The judge overruled the objection, received the agreement as evidence, and submitted the questions of fact to the jury, who found for the plaintiff $431.75.

Mr. J. J. Danforth now moved for a new trial, on the ground, among others, that the
747*] instrument in question became *void, by the destruction of the seals in the manner proved. He cited to this point 1 Gall., 69; Shep. Touch., 69; Dy., 112; 11 Rep., 27; Perk., 135, 136; 2 Bl. Com., 308; 5 Cow., 368.

Mr. M. T. Reynolds, contra, cited 2 Roll. Abr., 29, U, pl. 5; Moore, 35, pl. 116; 1 Roll., 40; 5 Rep., 119*b*; Dy., 59; Cro. Eliz., 120; Palm., 403; 6 East, 309, 311; 4 T. R., 339, per Bull., *J.*; 3 T. R., 151, 153, *note c.*

Curia, per SUTHERLAND, *J.* The questions of facts were properly submitted to the jury. They have found that the defendant has not paid to the plaintiff the amount, which by his covenant he was bound to pay; and that the seals were torn from the agreement, by Jackson, under the mistaken supposition that the defendant had paid to him, upon that agreement, $200, June 1, 1808, when, in truth, that payment was made by the plaintiff, and not by the defendant; and had been credited by Jackson to the defendant, by mistake. We assume, therefore, that the sum found by the jury is justly due to the plaintiff, upon the contract; and the question, then, is, whether his right of action is gone, in consequence of the seals having been torn off under such circumstances.

It was a mutual agreement, signed by both parties. Rees covenanted to sell a farm to Overbaugh, and Overbaugh covenanted to pay him for it. There was no counterpart; and the agreement itself, instead of being retained by either party, was left in the hands of Jackson, as he expresses it, for the benefit of both parties. He did not hold it, therefore, exclusively as the agent of the plaintiff; nor had he any authority to receive the whole consideration money. His right to receive any portion of it did not result from the fact of his having the possession of the contract; for that he received as the agent of both parties, for safe keeping only. But Rees, the plaintiff, authorized him to receive $2,500, and pass it to his credit. That, then, was the extent of his authority; and he had no power to cancel the contract, or to interfere, in any other way, *with the [*748 plaintiff's right to recover the remaining balance of $500.

In tearing the seals from the agreement, therefore, he did not act as the authorized agent of the plaintiff, but as a stranger.

The ancient doctrine, that an alteration, or spoliation of a deed, by a stranger, or by accident or mistake, without the privity or consent of the party interested, destroys it, has been materially modified, if not substantially exploded, by modern decisions. *Henfree* v. *Bromley*, 6 East, 309; *Master* v. *Miller*, 4 T. R., 339, per Buller, *J.*; 3 T. R., 151, 153, *note.*

The second resolution in *Piggot's* case, 11 Co., 27, is, "that when any deed is altered, in a point material, by the plaintiff himself, or by any stranger, without the privity of the obligee, be it by interlineation, addition, erasing, or by drawing a pen through a line or through the midst of any material word, the deed thereby becomes void."

In *Whelpdale's* case, 5 Co., 119, it is said, "that in all cases where the bond was once the deed of the defendant, and afterwards, before the action brought, becomes no deed, either by rasure or addition, or other alteration of the deed, or by breaking off the seal, the defendant may safely plead *non est factum;* for, without question, at the time of the plea, which is in the present tense, it was not his deed." And the case of one *Hawood* is there mentioned, in which, in an action of debt on bond, he has pleaded *non est factum*, and before the day of appearance of the inquest (or trial) by the negligence of the clerk, in whose custody it was, rats did eat the label by which the seal was fixed, the justices charged the jury, that if they should find that it was the deed of the defendant at the time of plea pleaded, they should give a special verdict; which was done, and the plaintiff recovered. (Dy., 59 *a*, S. C., and *note*; *Id.*, 112 *a*.)

Mr. Justice Buller, in *Master* v. *Miller*, 4 T. R., 338, 339, considers this doctrine as having owed its origin very much to the technical forms of pleading, applicable to deeds alone. **749*]** *The plaintiff, in such cases, must make a profert of the deed under seal; and the deed or profert produced must agree with that stated in the declaration, or the plaintiff must fail. A profert of a deed without a seal, will not support the allegation of a deed with a seal. But he remarks, that it is not universally true that a deed is destroyed by an alteration, or by tearing off the seal. In Palm., 403, a deed which had erasures in it, and from which the seal was torn, was held good, it appearing that the seal was torn off by a little boy. So in any case where the seal is torn off by accident after plea pleaded. And in these days, he continues, I think, even if the seal were torn off before the action brought, there would be no difficulty in framing a declaration which would obviate every doubt upon that point, by stating the truth of the case. It was not settled in England, that a deed which had been lost or destroyed by time or accident, could be pleaded, according to the truth of the case, without profert, until the case of *Read* v. *Brookman*, 3 T. R., 151; and Gross, *J.*, dissented from that decision. *Vide Soresby* v. *Sparrow*, 2 Str., 1186; *Whitfield* v. *Faugset*, 1 Ves.. 387, 389; *Totty* v. *Nesbitt*, and *Matison* v. *Atkinson*, 3 T. R., 153, *note c.*

Ld. Kenyon, in *Read* v. *Brookman*, says, that which was supposed to be the old law, was founded on a mistake; and that the law of the country has, in this respect, in modern times, been better adapted to general convenience.

If a deed may be rendered available to a party, notwithstanding its total destruction, upon what principle can he be deprived of the benefit of it, when it has suffered a partial injury, either from accident, or the act of a stranger, over which he had no control? Ld. Kenyon, in *Master* v. *Miller*, 4 T. R., 329, 330, seems to admit, that an alteration in a deed, by accident, would not destroy it.

In *Henfree* v. *Bromlee*, 6 East, 309, Ld. Ellenborough expresses a decided opinion upon this point. The question there was, whether an award was void, in consequence of an alteration made by the umpire in the amount **750*]** *awarded, after he signed the award, and delivered it to his attorney, for the purpose of being delivered to the parties. The alteration consisted in running his pen through the £57, the amount originally awarded, and inserting the sum of £66, leaving the £57, however, still legible. It was contended by Erskine and Pooley, that the alteration in the award vitiated it altogether; and they referred to the second resolution in *Piggot's* case, 11 Co., 27, in support of their argument. But Ld. Ellenborough, for the whole court, said: "I consider the alteration of the award, by the umpire, after his authority was at end, the same as if it had been made by a stranger, a mere spoliator; and I still read it with the eyes of the law, as if it were an award for £57, such as it originally was. If the alteration had been made by a person who was interested in the award, I should have felt myself pressed by the objection; but I can no more consider this as avoiding the instrument, than if it had been obliterated or canceled by accident."

In *Cutts* v. *U. S.*, 1 Gall., 69, it was held that a deed is not avoided by the seal being torn off fraudulently, or innocently, by the obligor; but may be declared on as a subsisting deed. *Judge* Story has there collected and reviewed all the cases upon this subject; but it was not necessary for him to decide what would be the effect of an alteration in a deed by a stranger; and he, therefore, expressed no opinion upon that point.

The case of *Williams* v. *Orary*, 5 Cow., 368, is in no respect analogous to this. There the bond was canceled by the defendant himself, in obedience to the express directions of his testatrix, the plaintiff having complied with the condition upon which the executor was directed by the will to cancel it. We held, that the executor could not afterwards avail himself of that bond, by way of set-off against a demand of the plaintiff; and with a view to that state of facts, we remarked, that "after canceling the bond, the defendant cannot avail himself of it, by way of set-off, at law. If it was surrendered through *mistake, or **[*751** misapprehension of his rights, the defendant's remedy must be sought in a different way."

We are, therefore, of opinion that the motion for a new trial be denied.

New trial denied.

Cited in—8 Cow., 73; 2 Barb. Ch., 133; 58 N. Y., 321; 5 Lans., 369; 3 Barb., 408; 24 Hun, 393; 50 Ind., 506; 18 Am. Dec., 429; 47 Am. Dec., 302.

JACKSON, ex dem. WILLIAMS and WASHBURN,

v.

MILLER.

Evidence—Book Purporting to Contain Proceedings of Commissioners of Forfeitures as—Certificate of Commissioners not Evidence of Title—Conveyance should be Produced—In Ejectment, Prior Possession Prima Facie *Evidence of Title—Adverse Possession—Parol Declarations Inadmissible to Prove Title.*

A book purporting to contain the proceedings of the Commissioners of Forfeitures, but not proved ever to have been in their possession, though found in the clerk's office in 1806, and having lain 17 years there, is not admissible in evidence to show a sale by the Commissioners; nor will a conveyance be presumed, where such a book is shown to be genuine, unless the requisites of the statute, creating the Commissioners and defining their duty, appear to have been complied with by the purchaser; and the certificate state that a conveyance was given.

The certificate of the Commissioner is not evidence of title; and a conveyance should be produced or its absence accounted for, and secondary evidence given.

A prior possession is, *prima facie*, evidence of title in an action of ejectment; but where a recovery by ejectment is had against a prior possessor, he cannot set up his possession as the foundation of a recovery in a cross ejectment, unless it was of sufficient length to be evidence of title; as where it was for 20 years and more.

Where A's tenant from year to year takes a lease from B, the act is void, and cannot work an adverse possession against A.

Parol declarations are inadmissible to prove or disprove title, or a disclaimer of title to lands.

Citations—Act, May 12, 1784, 1 Greenl., 127, 132, 139; 2 Greenl., 200; 11 Johns., 456; 1 Cai., 89; 3 Mass., 399; 10 Mass., 105; 1 Johns., 326; 1 R. L., 443; 1 K. & R., 145; 1 Phil. Ev., 126; 6 Johns., 22; 7 Johns., 186; 5 Cow., 74.

EJECTMENT for lot No. 14, in Jessup's little patent, Warren Co., tried at the Warren Circuit, July 11, 1823, before Walworth, *Circuit J.*

The lessors of the plaintiff claimed title to the premises on several grounds; and, among others, under an alleged sale made by the Commissioners of Forfeitures, to the ancestor of Williams, one of the lessors; also on the ground of a prior possession in Washburn, the other lessor, against whom the defendant had some time before recovered the premises in question, in an action of ejectment, which was defended by Williams.

A verdict was taken for the plaintiff, subject to the opinion of this court.

The facts, so far as they are material to the points decided, are stated in the opinion of the court.

Mr. J. L. Viele, for the plaintiff, cited 1 Greenl. ed. L. N. Y., 139; 1 Phil. Ev., 123, 302, 306, 312; 4 Dall., 415; 1 Cai., 89; 4 T. R., 642; Bull. *N. P.*, 110; 11 Johns., 456; 3 Mass., 399; 10 *Id.*, 105; 13 Johns., 118; 1 R. L., 128, 129, secs. 1, 2; 1 Shep. Touch., 256; *Id.*, 253; 3 Johns., 386; 6 *Id.*, 265; 4 *Id.*, 211; 10 Johns., 377; Cowp., 102.

752*] **Mr. W. Hay*, contra, cited 1 R. L., 443; Statute of 1784, 1 Greenl. ed. L. N. Y., 135, 138, secs. 15, 20; Statute of 1788, 2 *Id.*, 200; 1 K. & R., 145; 1 Burr., 119; 7 Johns., 157; 6 *Id.*, 21; 1 R. L., 128, secs. 1, 2; 8 Johns., 107; 1 Johns., 322; 2 *Id.*, 445.

Curia, per SAVAGE, *Ch. J.* The first question arising in the cause is, as to the admissibility of the book from the clerk's office, purporting to be the return of the Commissioners of Forfeitures. By an Act passed May 12, 1784, 1 Greenl., 127, Commissioners of Forfeitures were to be appointed, whose duty it was to sell all lands confiscated and forfeited to the people of this State, and to give good and sufficient deeds to the purchasers. By the 26th section (*Id.*, 139), the Commissioners were to make an abstract of all sales made by them; to contain the names of the purchasers, the description of the estates by them sold, the sums for which the same were sold, the dates of the respective conveyances, and the names of those to whom they were supposed to belong before the forfeiture. At the end of every three months, such abstracts were to be filed in the office of the clerk of the county where the lands lay. And the clerks were to record such abstracts in a book or books to be provided for that purpose.

The book produced at the trial is certainly no compliance with the statute. In the first place, there is no evidence that it was ever in the possession of the Commissioners of Forfeitures or came from them. It bears no date. It has no signature, and there is no evidence that it was in the clerk's office prior to 1806, eighteen years after the functions of the Commissioners had ceased. (2 *Id.*, 200.) By whom it was deposited, does not appear. It was not considered by the clerk a genuine official return in compliance with the statute, or it would have been recorded by him in a book. The only certainty about it is, that it was in the handwriting of the purchaser. In my judgment, it is not entitled to any weight, and ought not to have been received as evidence. The circuit judge received it on the ground, that being found in the clerk's office, he would presume it the book of records of the returns of the *Commissioner, made by the county clerk, in pursuance of the Act. [*753 The fact of its having been 17 years in the clerk's office can give it no validity. The clerk would probably have permitted any other manuscript to have been deposited in his office for safe keeping.

But suppose we are to consider this book as the official return of the Commissioners, and to have been made within three months after the sale. By the Act, one third of the purchase money was to be paid down, and the residue at a future day (1 Greenl., 132); and if the purchaser failed in the final payment, he forfeited the first payment; and the Commissioner was to resell the land. (*Ib.*) The fact, therefore, that Gen. Williams, the ancestor of one of the lessors, became the purchaser (and made the first payment, though even that does not appear), cannot complete his title. He may, notwithstanding, never have received a deed. And if such a certificate is to be received as evidence of title, a purchaser who paid one third, but never completed his purchase, may, notwithstanding, obtain the property. The presumption is, that the Commissioner certified all that was true in favor of the purchaser, particularly as he drew the certificate himself; and because, if a conveyance had been given, it was his duty so to certify. In *Jackson* v. *Woolsey*, 11 Johns., 456, the court say: "It is correct here to presume the Commissioners did their duty." So here the Commissioner would have certified a conveyance, if one had been given. It was his duty to give one, upon a certain contingency. Whether that ever happened, we know not; but the silence of the certificate raises a presumption against it. In *Van Dyck* v. *Van Beuren*, 1 Cai., 89, there were facts to found a presumption upon; the provision in the will, that the daughters might purchase; the fact that Hyletje, one of the daughters, took possession at an early day, and that possession continued down to the time of trial. The case of *Gray* v. *Gardner*, 3 Mass., 399, merely proves that after a possession under an administrator's sale, the previous requisites as to notice, &c., will be presumed to have been regular. So in *Coleman* v. *Anderson*, 10 Mass., 105, the same presumption was allowed in support of a collector's sale, after 30 years.

*In my opinion, the presumption of [*754 law is, that no conveyance ever was given.

But suppose it to be otherwise, and that a conveyance is to be presumed; then it should have been produced, or its non-production should be accounted for, in order to lay a foundation for secondary proof. Or are we also to presume its loss, or destruction? The statute does not make the Commissioner's certificate evidence of title. From the very nature of the instrument, it could afford no sort of evidence, unless there was a certificate that a conveyance had been given. It seems to me, therefore, the plaintiff totally failed in making out a paper title to the premises in question.

But the plaintiff claims to recover upon a prior possession. Such a possession is, *prima facie*, sufficient to authorize a recovery in certain cases—as where no title is shown other than possession; and the law proceeds upon the ground that he who first had possession, had the better right; but when the defendant has obtained possession by virtue of a judgment in ejectment, the presumption then is changed; and a prior possession, in such case, is of no avail, unless it be such an one as is evidence of title; for instance, an adverse possession of 20 years and upwards. The points in relation to the possession are, that, 38 or 39 years before the trial, one Buttolph made a clearing on the lot, not knowing who was the owner; but Andrew Hall, then, or soon after, produced his power of attorney from the defendant, and cut timber and exercised acts of ownership. Thirty-four years previous to the trial, Buttolph, doubting Hall's authority, sent his son to Dutchess Co. to purchase from Miller, the defendant. About 28 or 29 years before the trial, Buttolph sold his possession to Washburn, one of the lessors. Thirty-one years before the trial, Washburn had purchased of Hall, who was tenant to the defendant. This tenancy was, according to the case of *Jackson* v. *Bryan*, 1 Johns., 326, a tenancy from year to year. It is there decided, that a holding by permission of the landlord, for an indefinite period, is to be construed a tenancy **755***] from year to year, though there *be no reservation of rent; the right to sue for use and occupation being equivalent to such reservation.

Washburn, who purchased from Hall, became the tenant of Miller. He became invested with the rights and liabilities of Hall. Four years afterwards, or 27 years before the trial, Washburn took an agreement for a lease from Williams. If this be considered an attornment, it is void, and would authorize an action of ejectment, without notice to quit; but I apprehend it would not amount to an adverse possession against Miller. In *Jackson* v. *Johnson*, 5 Cow., 74, a person who took possession, under an agreement to purchase, was considered a tenant; but it was held that the tenancy was put an end to by a subsequent purchase from a stranger; and that after such purchase, the possession of the former tenant became adverse, because the act of the tenant was an assertion of title in himself. The conduct of Washburn, however, had a tendency to transfer the possession from Miller, the landlord under whom he entered, to a stranger. This is what was intended to be prohibited by the statute; and such attornments are declared to be void. (1 R. L., 443; 1 K. & R., 145).

But suppose the agreement with Williams was the commencement of an adverse possession; it had not the necessary length of time to ripen into a right, before the commencement of Miller's action of ejectment, which was in Jan., 1814. The first negotiation with Williams was 27 years before the trial. That was in 1796: of course, but 18 years had elapsed.

Adverse possession for less than 20 years, will not afford ground to presume a grant. It is partly upon this presumption, that a title by adverse possession rests for its efficacy. (1 Phil. Ev., 26, and cases cited.)

Having come to the conclusion, that the plaintiff cannot recover upon the strength of his own title, it seems unnecessary to examine that of the defendant; but as the whole case has been examined, I will merely state my opinion upon it, without giving reasons at length. The defendant, being one of the patentees, must still be deemed the owner, unless *devested of his title by his own act, [***756** or the operation of law upon the acts of others. I have already endeavored to show that there was no adverse possession when he asserted his claim in 1814. His declarations have been shown, disclaiming title. It is singular that he should do so, at the time when he had possession by his tenant, Hall; and when two called upon him for the same purpose that he should disclaim to one and assert title to the other. If evidence of this kind was admissible, it is clear, that neither the defendant nor the plaintiff had title, for Williams disclaimed about the same time (1796), though if the latter ever had title, he must have procured it before 1788, when the powers of the Commissioners ceased. But it was settled in *Jackson* v. *Shearman*, 6 Johns., 22, that parol declarations are inadmissible to prove or disprove title. So in *Jackson* v. *Vosburgh*, 7 Johns., 186, it was held that parol evidence of a disclaimer of title is inadmissible. This principle has been frequently recognized since; and is not to be disputed. All that part of the evidence is improper, and can have no influence on the question of title. The defendant's title, therefore, is perfect; for, after such a length of time, under a separate possession, with claim of title to the whole lot, it being known 40 years ago as the Miller lot, a partition would be presumed.

In my opinion the defendant is entitled to judgment.

Judgment for the defendant.

Affirmed—6 Wend., 228.
Cited in 4 Wend., 482; 34 N. Y., 303; 26 Wis., 328.

---

*PACKARD *v.* GETMAN. [*757

Trover against Master of Canal Boat—What Constitutes Sufficient Delivery to Master—Proof of Conversion—Practice.

What will constitute a delivery of goods to the master of a canal boat, so as to make him accountable in trover.

If it be a sufficient delivery, according to the usages of business, to leave them on the dock by or near the boat; yet this must be accompanied with express notice to the master.

Either case or trover may be brought against a carrier, for the non-delivery of goods; but in the latter action, a conversion must be proved.

Citation—1 Cow., 320.

TROVER for a box of dry goods; tried at the circuit, and a verdict found for the plaintiff for $249.71.

Mr. L. Ford, for the defendant, moved for a new trial.

Mr. J. W. Cady, contra.

The facts are stated in the opinion of the court, which was delivered by,

WOODWORTH, *J.* This is an action of trover, to recover the value of a box of dry goods, alleged to have delivered to the defendant as master of a canal boat, to be transported from the City of Albany to Charlestown, in Montgomery Co.

Two questions arise:

1. Has the plaintiff proved a delivery to the defendant ?

2. If he has, is there sufficient evidence of a conversion ?

It appeared that before any goods were put on board, the plaintiff requested the defendant to receive a quantity of merchandise ; that he consented, and Nov. 20, 1824, gave a receipt for 30*s*. in full, for transporting the plaintiff's goods, described as four boxes of dry goods, and other articles. The bill of lading, dated Nov. 24, in the handwriting of the plaintiff, and subscribed by the defendant, states four boxes of dry goods. On the evening of Nov. 20, the plaintiff came on board, the defendant inquired what dry goods he had, and he replied four boxes. He then made out the bill of lading, and delivered it to the defendant. It also appeared that no more than four boxes of dry goods were actually received on board; and after being so received, on the evening of Nov. 20, the plaintiff came and inquired for his goods. He was informed of their reception, went into the room where they were, and returned, saying it was all right. The defend-
758*] ant delivered the four *boxes according to his contract. On the part of the plaintiff, it appeared that five boxes of dry goods had been deposited on the dock, near the defendant's boat, in the evening of Nov. 20. A man in the boat said the defendant was not on board, and the boxes were left lying on the dock. A person from the boat came and assisted in unloading two of the four boxes brought by one of the cartmen. It also appeared, that it was customary for masters of canal boats to receive, on the dock, goods they were to transport. That the fifth box was brought in the evening, and placed on the dock where a boat lay. That some person on board said it was the defendant's boat, and that more goods of the plaintiff were coming on board.

Admitting that, according to the usual custom and understanding of parties, a delivery on the dock, near a boat, is a good delivery so as to charge the carrier, it must always be accompanied with express notice ; otherwise, he is not answerable. Has that been done in the present case ? So far from it, it appears to me that, in every stage of this transaction, the defendant was informed there were four boxes only. So the plaintiff declared to the defendant ; such is the language of the receipt for the freight, and so is the invoice. From all this, the defendant was warranted in taking on board four boxes of dry goods, and ought not be chargeable for not taking on board the fifth box, although it might have been left on the dock. From the evidence, I think the defendant might well presume a fifth box was not intended for his boat. But whether it was or not, there was a failure on the part of the plaintiff to give the defendant information. The plaintiff was probably ignorant that there were more than four boxes. That is his misfortune ; not a ground to charge the defendant, who appears to have acted with good faith ; and could not know, from the instructions he had received, that any more than four boxes belonged to the plaintiff. The defendant not having received the fifth box on board, it may, by mistake, have been put on board another boat, or, perhaps, stolen ; but there is no presumption that the defendant ever converted *it. [***759**
All the facts in the case negative that presumption. I am, therefore, of opinion, on the first point, that the plaintiff has not proved sufficient to make a delivery of the goods ; and that on this ground the verdict is against evidence.

As to the second question, if it be conceded that the delivery, such as it was, made the defendant answerable, it is necessary to prove a conversion. The plaintiff might have brought a special action on the case, against the carrier, and have avoided this question. He has brought trover, which will also lie ; but then he is bound to show that the defendant converted the goods. A demand and refusal, is *prima facie* evidence of a conversion ; but the defendant may give evidence to negative the presumption. *Lockwood* v. *Bull*, 1 Cow., 330. I think it is plain the defendant never had actual possession of the goods. His witnesses swear that all the goods on board were delivered, and it is fairly to be inferred he had no knowledge of any more than four boxes. There is nothing on which to found a presumption that he clandestinely secreted, or in any way disposed of the fifth box. On the contrary, if lost to the plaintiff, it was without the defendant's knowledge or interference. On these facts, it ought to have been submitted to the jury, whether they were satisfied that the defendant had converted to his own use the goods in question. The verdict must be set aside, and a new trial granted, with costs to abide the event.

New trial granted.

Cited in—4 Wend., 615; 39 N. Y., 36; 6 Trans. App., 313; 3 Barb., 390; 5 Abb. N. S., 348; 4 Rob., 498; 1 Daly, 495; 2 Abb. U. S., 51; 21 Ind., 57.

---

*OVERSEERS OF THE TOWN OF OTSEGO [***760**

v.

OVERSEERS OF THE TOWN OF SMITHFIELD.

Practice—Appeal to Sessions from Order of Removal of Pauper—Order not Evidence of Facts Contained—Settlement of Wife of Man who has None in this State.

On appeal to the sessions from an order of removal of a pauper, the order is no evidence of the facts it contains ; but the respondents are bound to begin *de novo*, and make out their case independent of the other.

A woman, having a settlement, marries a man who has none in this State ; she retains her maiden settlement ; and, with her children, may be removed to it, if her husband fail to provide for her.

Citations—3 Johns., 26 ; Act, sess. 33, ch. 109, sec. 4 ; 1 R. L., 310 ; 2 R. L., 556 ; 3 Burn's Justice, 375-380, 11th ed.; 1 Str., 544 ; Burr. Sett. Cas., 153 ; Foley's Poor Laws, 249 ; 1 Bl.Com., 363 ; 5 East, 113 ; 16 Johns., 186 ; 3 Conn. N. S., 602.

ON *certiorari* to the General Sessions of the Peace of the County of Madison.

Two justices made an order of removal of Maria Chadwick and her children, from the Town of Smithfield, in the County of Madison, to the Town of Otsego, in the County of Otsego. On appeal in behalf of Otsego to the General Sessions of Madison, it was insisted in behalf of Otsego, that the Overseers of Smithfield were bound to begin *de novo*, and sustain the order by evidence; but the court decided that the order of removal should be received as, *prima facie*, evidence of the facts contained in it; and that it was incumbent on the appellants to impeach it.

Proof was accordingly introduced under this decision; by which it appeared that one Elisha Chadwick, having a settlement in Conn., but not in this State, married Maria, the pauper, who had a settlement in the Town of Otsego. They went to the Town of Smithfield in 1816, and resided there till the wife, with the children of the marriage, were removed to Otsego in 1823. For about four weeks before the removal, they had no house; and the wife and children lived on the charity of the neighbors. Chadwick was intemperate, and provided but badly for his family.

The sessions affirmed the order.

Mr. S. Starkweather, for the plaintiffs in error, insisted that the respondents should have been required to begin *de novo*, and support the order.

But on the merits, he said, the sessions also erred. The removal of the wife and children was not warrantable. The law will not tolerate the dispersion of families in this way. The husband had not voluntarily separated from, and ceased to provide for his family. (16 Johns., 186.)

761*] *Mr. J. A. Spencer*, contra, cited 13 East, 311; 3 Johns., 28; 5 East, 114; 16 Johns., 186; 1 Str., 683; *Id.*, 544.

Curia, per SAVAGE, *Ch. J.* On the hearing before the sessions, it was decided that the order of the justices was, *prima facie*, evidence of the facts it contained, and that it was incumbent on the appellants to impeach it.

The practice was so settled in cases of bastardy, in *Sweet* v. *Overseers of Clinton*, 3 Johns., 26, decided in February Term, 1808. The Legislature, in 1810, sess. 33, ch. 109, sec. 4, enacted, that in appeals, as well under the Act concerning Bastards, as under that relating to the settlement of the poor, the Court of Sessions should begin *de novo;* and the respondents were required to substantiate the order, before the appellant should be called on to impeach it. In the revision of 1813, the same provision is found in the Act concerning Bastards, 1 R. L., 310; but nothing is said as to proceedings under the Act concerning the Poor. By the Act repealing the Acts previous to the revised laws, all Acts and parts of Acts, which come within the purview or operation of any of the Acts called the Revised Acts, are repealed. (2 R. L., 556.) No provision on this subject is found among the Revised Acts; and as the Statute of 1810 is not repealed by its title, but only so much as comes within the purview and operation of the Revised Acts, it remains in force. Perhaps the Legislature thought the full re-enactment of that Statute unnecessary. The decision in *Sweet* v. *Clinton* related to a case of bastardy. It may have been thought, that regulating the practice in that case, was a sufficient expression of the legislative will, on the subject of appeals from orders of removal; and as there is a close analogy in the proceedings in both cases, it would be incongruous to establish a different practice for them. This was so considered in the case of *Knox* v. *Bern*, decided last term. The judges of the sessions, therefore, erred in considering the order as conclusive, until impeached.

On the main question, I think the court below was right. In 3 Burns' Justice, 375–380, 11th ed., the doctrine of *settlement by mar- **[*762**
riage is discussed with ability; and all the cases he found, when that work was published, are collected. It is well settled, that in case a woman having a settlement, marries a man who has also a settlement, her settlement follows the husband's; but that a woman marrying a husband who has no settlement, does not lose her maiden settlement. Whether it is so suspended during coverture, that she cannot be removed to it, has been much agitated; and the cases do not all agree. When the wife survives the husband, then, without dispute, her former settlement is revived. In several cases, it was adjudged that marriage does not put the woman in a worse condition than she was in before. But in *Stretford* v. *Norton*, it was held that the settlement of the wife was suspended during coverture. The same thing was held in *Shadwell* v. *St. John's Wapping.* This case was alluded to in the catch reported by Burrow:

> "A woman, having a settlement,
> Married a man with none;
> The question was, he being dead,
> If that she had was gone.
> Quoth Sir John Pratt, her settlement
> Suspended did remain,
> Living the husband; but him dead,
> It doth revive again."

This case was overruled by that of *St. John's Wapping* v. *St. Botolphs' Bishopsgate.* In that case, the wife was sent to her former settlement; the husband being absent on board a man-of-war. The *Chief Justice* stated these propositions: 1. That she had once a settlement at St. Botolphs. 2. That settlement continues till she gains a new one. 3. That she had never gained a new one. The separation of husband and wife, when they are living together, is the only objection to this doctrine. In *St. Michael* v. *Nunny*, 1 Str., 544, it was held, that if the husband was in the parish when the order was made, it would be vicious; and the court would not presume he was absent. In a subsequent case, the court said they would not suppose *it to be wrong un- **[*763**
less it appeared so. (Burr. Sett. Cas., 153.) In the case of *Dunsford* v. *Willsborough Green*, Foley Poor Laws, 249, it was held that sending a woman away from her husband was no divorce, for the husband, having no settlement, might come to his wife as well at one place as another. Blackstone understands the rule to be, that the wife's settlement is suspended during coverture, if the husband remains in England, and is able to maintain her; but in his absence, or after his death, or, perhaps, during his inability, she may be removed to her old settlement. (1 Bl. Com., 363.) In a later case, *The King* v. *Eltham*, 5 East, 113, the wife was removed to her former settlement, with the consent of the husband and wife. In the case of *Sherburn* v. *Norwich*, 16 Johns., 186, the general doctrine is recognized. *Mr. Justice* Platt, who gave the opinion of the court, says the fact of the husband's inability was not proved (the contrary was proved in that case); but if

it had been, it would be with great reluctance he would consent that a wife should be removed from her husband, merely because he was unable to maintain her. This was the individual opinion of that learned judge; but not the opinion of the court, as that question was not raised. Opposed to this, stands the opinion of the *Chief Justice* of the Supreme Court of Conn., in *Newtown* v. *Stratford*, 3 Conn. N. S., 602. The correct principle, he says, is, "that the wife's maiden settlement remains, having never been determined; but only, as it were, suspended during the time that she continued under the power and protection of the husband; and was maintained and supported by him." Until a new settlement is acquired, he says, there is not even a temporary suspension of this right, nor of the enjoyment of it, if the necessities of the *feme covert* imperiously require it. The separation of husband and wife, upon this principle, he adds, will always be voluntary, or arising from the coercion of his utter inability to support her.

I hope I duly appreciate rights of marriage to the individuals concerned, and to society. But I can see neither reason, propriety or humanity in compelling one *town to sup- [*764 port paupers, having a settlement in another, merely to accomodate a vagabond, intemperate husband, as in this case, with the society of the wife and children, whom he has, by his misconduct, reduced to pauperism; thus enabling him, perhaps, to add to the number of paupers, and the burdens of the town into which he has happened to stray. It is enough that Smithfield is compelled to support one idle, useless member of society, casually thrown upon them, and they ought not to be further aggrieved by supporting those who have a settlement elsewhere within the State.

But there is no evidence, in this case, of the maiden settlement, except the order of the justices. That order was received as evidence of the facts it contained. In that particular, the court below erred, and the order of the sessions must be quashed.

Order of Sessions quashed.

INDEX TO NOTES

TO THIS EDITION.

COWEN, VOLUMES 3-6.

GENERAL INDEX

TO

COWEN, VOLUMES 3-6, CONTAINED IN THIS BOOK.

N. B.—Black-faced figures indicate the page of this book on which the volume paging referred to is found.

COURTS.

COVENANT.

CRIMINAL LAW.

DAMAGES.

DEBT.

DECEIT.

DEED.

DISSEISIN.

DOWER.

EJECTMENT.

ELISORS.

EQUITY.

ERROR.

ESCAPE.

ESTOPPEL.

EVIDENCE.

(1) GENERALLY.

(2) DOCUMENTARY.

(3) ADMISSIONS AND DECLARATIONS.

EXECUTION.

EXECUTORS AND ADMINISTRATORS.

FACTOR.

HUSBAND AND WIFE.

Wife's equity cannot be disposed of by husband without first making suitable provision for her.
Udall v. Kenney, 3 Cow. 590, 234

When equity resorted to by husband or his assignee for value to enable him to get possession of wife's property, court will first make suitable provision for her. *Idem.* 234

Where father, by deed of trust, made settlement in favor of infant daughter, who married during infancy, and with her husband assigned such property to one with knowledge of trust on bill brought by wife against husband and assignee, assignment held null and void so far as respected wife's equity, and assignee directed to pay dividends to wife during her infancy. *Idem.* 234

IMPRISONMENT.

Act to Relieve Debtors from Imprisonment includes those imprisoned on judgments for wrongs.
People v. Justices of N. Y. Marine Court, 3 Cow. 366, 157

Feme covert may be imprisoned on *ca. sa.* with or without her husband.
M'Kinstry v. Davis, 3 Cow. 339, 147

INDEMNITY.

Obligor of bond of indemnity against costs and expenses of certain act, liable for costs of defending groundless suit; also for costs incurred by another and recovered of obligee.
Trustees of Newburgh v. Galatian, 4 Cow. 340, 406

Bond of indemnity against act palpably illegal is void; otherwise if act *prima facie* legal.
Idem. 406

Bonds of indemnity not governed by rules governing covenants for quiet enjoyment, which latter are not broken until lawful suit and eviction.
Idem. 406

Bond given on decretal order to pay over part of estate to trustee for legatees, held to be for indemnity of executors and not to extend to *cestuis que trust*, and on trustee not complying with order of court, executors, not being damnified, could not maintain action against sureties thereon.
Elmendorf v. Lansing, 5 Cow. 468, 721

Surety for deputy sheriff became surety for sheriff on sheriff's agreeing to indemnify him against being surety for deputy. Subsequently, with sheriff's knowledge, he defended suits against sheriff for deputy's misconduct. Held, under the circumstances, he was entitled to recover of sheriff expenses of such suits.
Hale v. Andrus, 6 Cow. 225, 889

A bond by creditor to indemnify his debtor against the debt, operates as a release of the debt, unless bond is discharged as by payment of the penalty.
Clark v. Bush, 3 Cow. 151, 83

INDICTMENT.

After cause once discontinued, justice has no jurisdiction and it is extortion for him to demand of defendant costs for entering up judgment thereafter, for which extortion he may be indicted and punished criminally.
People v. Whaley, 6 Cow. 661, 1042

Contents of indictment of attorney, under statute for buying a note.
People v. Walbridge, 6 Cow. 512, 989

The act of buying the note is the offense.
Idem. 989

Omissions of immaterial words in. *Idem.* 989

Indictment lies for maliciously killing cow of another. Acts injurious to private persons which tend to excite violent resentment, and produce disturbance of peace, are indictable.
People v. Smith, 5 Cow. 258, 646

INFANTS.

Statute for Protection of Infants does not protect others joined with them.
Shooke v. Phillips, 5 Cow. 440, 712

Where plaintiff appears for infant heirs by nominal guardian, they will be let in to defend at any time before judgment finally executed.
Van Deusen v. Brower, 6 Cow. 50, 829

How nominal guardian appointed on failure of infants to appear in non-bailable action. See *Idem.* 829

Infant not liable to breach of contract of marriage.
Hunt v. Peake, 5 Cow. 475, 724

INJUNCTION.

Injunction not granted to secure claim to statute privileges if right be doubtful.
Steamboat Co. v. Livingston, 3 Cow. 713, 275

INQUIRY.

Where sheriff erred upon execution of writ of inquiry, inquisition set aside.
Jackson v. Rathbone, 3 Cow. 296, 129

In debt on bond where verdict is for plaintiff, but no assignment of breaches and assessment of damages by jury, this may be done on writ of inquiry.
Rogers v. Coleman, 3 Cow. 62, 52

INSOLVENCY.

See DISCHARGE, ATTACHMENT, &c.

INSURANCE.

See MARINE INSURANCE.

Where one was appointed agent, with power to make contracts providing the office would on receipt of premium recognize the rate and be otherwise satisfied with the risk, and premises insured were destroyed after contract by agent, but before ratification by company; held, the premium being according to the established rate, that the company was liable.
Perkins v. Wash. Ins. Co. of N. Y., 4 Cow. 645, 516

A mere warrant of survey given by an Insurance Co. does not authorize the surveyor to do any act binding upon it. *Idem.* 516

Description of property by insured in policy is a warranty that it is as described and a misdescription arising from mistake will avoid it.
Fowler v. Ætna Fire Ins. Co., 6 Cow. 673, 1046

INTEREST.

On affirmance in error of plaintiff's judgment in trover, he is entitled to interest from time of judgment below and also double costs.
Bissell v. Hopkins, 4 Cow. 53, 307

Interest not allowed on unliquidated account for work and labor.
Reid v. Rens. Glass Factory, 3 Cow. 393, 166
Aff'd Rens. Glass Factory v. Reid, 5 Cow. 587, 763

Officer of company allowed interest on advances made to company necessary to keep it in operation, up to time his account demanded.
Reid v. Rens. Glass Factory, 3 Cow. 393, 166
Rens. Glass Factory v. Reid, 5 Cow. 587, 763

Where one accepts position of agent without stated salary, he can only recover on *quantum meruit*; and so interest is not allowed.
Reid v. Rens. Glass Factory, 3 Cow. 393, 166
Rens. Glass Factory v. Reid, 5 Cow. 587, 763

Rule for casting interest on bond, payable in installments, on which partial payments have been made.
Williams v. Houghtaling, 3 Cow. 86, 60

Contract to pay interest generally, means at legal rate.
Archibald v. Thomas, 3 Cow. 284 126

Interest recoverable by plaintiff in trover on value of goods from time of conversion.
Bissell v. Hopkins, 4 Cow. 53, 307

On unliquidated account for goods sold and work done, not allowed unless on express agreement therefor.
Van Beuren v. Van Gaasbeck, 4 Cow. 496, 463

Account running for thirty years not allowed to be credited as payment from time to time, as it accrued, on bond of equal age bearing interest, but can only be set off to its amount at the end.
Idem. 463

Interest runs on arrears of taxes due from county to State, after thirty days from time account current is made up and rendered to Comptroller pursuant to statute.
People v. County of N.Y., 5 Cow. 331, 673

Interest not allowed on unliquidated account for goods sold on no stated term of credit.
Tucker v. Ives, 6 Cow. 189, 878

Interest generally allowed on cash advances by one to another, though resting in mutual, current,

TROVER.

TRUST AND TRUSTEES.

TURNPIKE COMPANIES.

UNDUE INFLUENCE.

USURY.

VARIANCE.

WATER-COURSES.

WILLS.

WITNESS.

Lightning Source UK Ltd.
Milton Keynes UK
UKHW010347120219
337137UK00004B/155/P

9 780260 063144